THE OFFICIAL GUI[DE]
AMERICAN HISTORI[C]

D0599028

Rated "Outstanding" by Morgan Rand
Winner of Benjamin Franklin Award
Best Travel Guide
Winner of Travel Publishing News
Best Travel Reference
Winner of Benjamin Franklin Award
Best Directory

Comments from print media:

". . . helps you find the very best hideaways (many of the book's listings appear in the National Register of Historic Places)." — **Country Living**

"I love your book!" — **Lydia Moss, Travel Editor, McCall's**

"Delightful, succinct, detailed and well-organized. Easy to follow style . . ." — **Don Wudtke, Los Angeles Times**

"This is one of the best guidebooks of its kind. It's easy to use, accurate and the thumbnail sketches give the readers enough description to choose among the more than 1,000 properties detailed . . ." — **Dallas Morning News**

". . . thoughtfully organized and look-ups are hassle-free . . . well-researched and accurate . . . put together by people who know the field. There is no other publication available that covers this particular segment of the bed & breakfast industry - a segment that has been gaining popularity among travelers by leaps and bounds. The information included is valuable and well thought out." — **Morgan Directory Reviews**

"This guide has become the favorite choice of travelers and specializes only in professionally operated inns and B&Bs rather than homestays (lodgings in spare bedrooms)." — **Laguna Magazine**

"This is the best bed & breakfast book out. It outshines them all!" — **Maggie Balitas, Rodale Book Clubs**

Comments from innkeepers:

"Your book is wonderful. I have been reading it as one does a novel." — Olallieberry Inn, Cambria, Calif.

"We want to tell you how much we love your book. We have it out for guests to use. They love it, each featured inn stands out so well. Thank you for the privilege of being in your book." — Fairhaven Inn, Bath, Maine.

"What a wonderful book! We love it and have been very pleased with the guests who have made reservations using your book." — Vermont innkeeper

"We have had fantastic response. Thanks!" — Liberty Rose Colonial B&B, Williamsburg, Va.

"We've been with you for years and we are doing wonderfully through your books. We get a lot of business from it." — Homestead Inn, New Milford, Conn.

"We get many good leads from you throughout the year. Anything that we can do to support, we'll be glad to. Thanks for a great publication." — A Grand Inn-Sunset Hill House, Sugar Hill, N.H.

"Your guide has high praises from guests who use it." — The Inn on South Street, Kennebunkport, Maine.

"Thank you for all the time and work you put into this guidebook. We have had many guests find our inn because of you." — Kaleidoscope Inn, Nipomo, Calif.

＊〜＊〜＊〜＊〜

To Ethan

＊〜＊〜＊〜＊〜

THE OFFICIAL GUIDE
—— TO ——
AMERICAN HISTORIC I N N S

BED & BREAKFASTS AND COUNTRY INNS

EIGHTH EDITION

BY DEBORAH EDWARDS SAKACH

Published By

AMERICAN HISTORIC INNS INCORPORATED

PO Box 669
Dana Point
California
92629-0669
www.iLoveInns.com
E-mail:comments@bnbinns.com

FRONT COVER (CLOCKWISE FROM TOP LEFT):

La Residence Country Inn, Napa, Calif.
Photo by David Livingston

Litchfield Plantation, Island, S.C.
Photo by Louise Parsons

Gaige House Inn, Glen Ellen, Calif.
Photo by Richard Jung

Two Meeting Street Inn, Charleston, S.C.
Photo by American Historic Inns, Inc.

BACK COVER (FROM TOP):

The Castle Inn Riverside "The Historic Campbell Castle," Wichita, Kan.

Victoria-On-Main B&B, Whitewater, Wis.
Photo by Peter Hlavacek

Rose Inn, Ithaca, N.Y.
Photo by Andy Olenick

Grand Victorian B&B Inn, Bellaire, Mich.
Photo by Don Rutt

Castle Hill Inn & Resort, Newport, R.I.

COVER DESIGN:
David Sakach

PRODUCTION MANAGER:
Andy Prizer

ASSISTANT EDITORS:
Tiffany Crosswy, Joshua Prizer, Patricia Purvis, Stephen Sakach, Shirley Swagerty

OPERATIONS MANAGER:
Sandy Imre

DATABASE ASSISTANT:
Molly Thomson

PROGRAMMING AND CARTOGRAPHY:
Chris Morton

DIGITAL SCANNING:
Kevin Curtis, Travis Ross

Publisher's Cataloging in Publication Data
Sakach, Deborah Edwards
American Historic Inns, Inc.
The Official Guide to American Historic Inns

1. Bed & Breakfast Accommodations - United States, Directories, Guide Books.
2. Travel - Bed & Breakfast Inns, Directories, Guide Books.
3. Bed & Breakfast Accommodations - Historic Inns, Directories, Guide Books.
4. Hotel Accommodations - Bed & Breakfast Inns, Directories, Guide Books.
5. Hotel Accommodations - United States, Directories, Guide Books.
I. Title. II. Author. III Bed & Breakfast, The Official Guide to American Historic Inns

ISBN: 1-888050-09-8
Softcover
Printed in the United States of America.
10 9 8 7 6 5 4 3 2 1

Contents

How To Use This Book

Welcome! You hold in your hands the most comprehensive collection of our nation's best historic bed & breakfast and country inns. Most were built in the 17th, 18th or 19th centuries, but a few inns from the early 20th century have been included. The National Register of Historic Places requires that buildings be constructed prior to 1950 in order to gain historic standing, and we follow this guideline as well.

When you stay at a historic inn, not only do you enjoy a unique getaway, you also promote and support the preservation of our nation's architectural and cultural heritage. Most of these homes are owned privately and have been restored with the private funds of individual families. They are maintained and improved by revenues collected from bed & breakfast guests.

With a few exceptions, we have omitted homestays. These are B&Bs with only one or two rooms, often operated casually or as a hobby.

Accommodations

Among the listings, you'll find B&Bs and country inns in converted schoolhouses, lighthouses, 18th-century farmhouses, Queen Anne Victorians, adobe lodges and a variety of other unique places, both new and old.

The majority of inns included in this book were built in the 17th, 18th, 19th or early 20th centuries. We have stated the date each building was constructed at the beginning of each description. Many of the inns are steeped in the traditions of Colonial America, the Victorian Era, The Civil War, Spanish colonization or the Old West. Many are listed in the National Register of Historic Places.

A Variety of Inns

A **Country Inn** generally serves both breakfast and dinner and may have a restaurant associated with it. Many have been in operation for years, some since the 18th century as you will note in our "Inns of Interest" section. Although primarily found on the East Coast, a few country inns are in other regions of the nation.

A **Bed & Breakfast** facility's primary focus is lodging. It can have from three to 20 rooms or more. The innkeepers often live on the premises. Breakfast usually is the only meal served and can be a full-course, gourmet breakfast or a simple buffet. B&B owners often pride themselves on their culinary skills.

As with country inns, many B&Bs specialize in providing historic, romantic or gracious atmospheres with amenities such as canopied beds, fireplaces, spa tubs, afternoon tea in the library and scenic views.

Some give great attention to recapturing a specific historic period, such as the Victorian or Colonial eras. Many display antiques and other furnishings from family collections.

A **Homestay** is a room available in a private home. It may be an elegant stone mansion in the best part of town or a charming country farm. Homestays have one to three guest rooms. Because homestays are often operated as a hobby-type business and open and close frequently, only a very few such properties are included in this publication.

A Note About Innkeepers

Your innkeepers are a tremendous resource. Most knowledgeable innkeepers enjoy sharing regional attractions, local folklore, area history, and pointing out favorite restaurants and other special features of their areas. Unlike hotel and motel operators, innkeepers often bring much of themselves into creating an experience for you to long remember. Many have personally renovated historic buildings, saving them from deterioration and often, the bulldozer. Others have infused their inns with a unique style and personality to enliven your experience with a warm and inviting environment.

Area Codes

Although we have made every effort to update area codes throughout the book, new ones appear from time to time. The phone companies provide recordings for several months after a change, but beyond that point, it can be difficult to reach an inn or B&B. Although they are listed by state or province, the new codes were added only in certain sections of the state or province. For example, the new 620 area code in Kansas applies only to certain areas in southern Kansas.

The following list includes the most recent area code changes that were available at press time.

State/Province	Old Code	New Code	Effective Date of Change
Alabama	334	251	6/18/01
Arizona	520	928	6/23/01
Arkansas	501	479	1/19/02
California	310	424	TBD
California	818	747	TBD
Florida	561	772	TBD
Florida	904	386	2/15/01
Florida	941	239	3/11/02
Indiana	219	260	12/11/01
Indiana	219	574	12/11/01
Iowa	319	563	3/25/01
Kansas	316	620	2/3/01
Louisiana	504	985	2/12/01
Michigan	517	989	4/7/01
Michigan	616	269	7/13/02
Michigan	810	586	9/22/01
New Mexico	505	575	3/3/02
New York	716	585	11/15/01
Utah	801	385	3/30/02
Virginia	540	276	9/1/01

How to Use This Book

Note: We try to keep the use of codes to a minimum, but they help create a more comprehensive listing for each of the inns and B&Bs. We encourage you to read this entire section, as it will help plan a getaway that is just right for you.

Baths

Not all bed & breakfasts and country inns provide a private bath for each guest room. We have included the number of rooms and the number of private baths in each facility. The code "PB," indicates how many guest rooms include a private bath. If you must have a private bath, make sure the room reserved for you provides this facility. If a listing indicates that there are suites available, assume that a suite includes a private bath. Most cottages also include a private bath, sometimes more than one, but be sure to inquire with the innkeeper about facilities in these units.

Beds

K, Q, D, T indicates King, Queen, Double or Twin beds available at the inn.

Children

Many innkeepers go out of their way to provide a wonderful atmosphere for families. In fact, more and more inns are catering to families.

However, this is always a sensitive subject. We do not list whether children are allowed at inns or B&Bs in this guide because it is illegal in several states to discriminate against persons of any age. Occasionally innkeepers do "discourage" children as guests. Some innkeepers consider their inn a place for romance or solitude, and often do not think younger guests fit into this scheme. Also, many inns are filled with fine antiques and collectibles, so it may be an inappropriate place for very small children. Some innkeepers discourage children simply because they are not set up to accommodate the needs of a family. If you plan to bring your children, always ask your innkeeper if children are welcome, and if so, at what age.

Meals

Continental breakfast: Coffee, juice and toast or pastry.

Continental-plus breakfast: A continental breakfast plus a variety of breads, cheeses and fruit.

Full breakfast: Coffee, juice, breads, fruit and an entree.

Full gourmet breakfast: May be a four-course candlelight offering or especially creative cuisine.

Vegetarian breakfast: Entrees can cater to special vegetarian diets and are created without meat.

Country breakfast: Hearty country fare may include fresh farm eggs gathered on the premises or sausages and cheeses made in the area.

Gourmet lunch: Specially creative sandwiches, soups or other items not normally found in a lunch box.

Gourmet dinner: May include several courses and finer cuisine, usually featuring local produce, fish, fowl, etc. prepared with creative flair.

Teas: Usually served in the late afternoon with cookies, crackers or other in-between-meal offerings.

Meal Plans

AP: American Plan. All three meals may be included in the price of the room. Check to see if the rate quoted is for two people (double occupancy) or per person (single occupancy).

MAP: Modified American Plan. Breakfast and dinner may be included in the price of the room.

EP: European Plan. No meals are included. We have listed only a few historic hotels that operate on an EP plan.

Always find out what meals, if any, are included in the rates. Not every establishment in this guidebook provides breakfast, although most do. Please do not assume meals are included in the rates featured in the book. Occasionally, an innkeeper has indicated *MAP* and *AP* when she or he actually means that both programs are available and you must specify in which program you are interested.

Payments

MC: MasterCard
VISA
DS: Discover
AX: American Express
DC: Diner's Club
CB: Carte Blanche
TC: Traveler's Cheques
PC: Personal Checks

Pets Allowed

Under some listings, you will note that pets are allowed. Despite this, it is always wise to inform the innkeeper that you have a pet. Some innkeepers charge a fee for pets or only allow certain types and sizes of animals. The innkeeper also may have set aside a specific room for guests with pets, so if this room is booked, you may not be able to bring your pet along this trip.

Rates

Rates are usually listed in ranges, i.e., $45-105. The LOWEST rate is almost always available during off-peak periods and may only apply to the least expensive room. Rates are always subject to change and are not guaranteed. You should always confirm the rates when making the reservations. Rates for Canadian listings usually are listed in Canadian dollars. Rates are quoted for double occupancy.

Breakfast and other meals MAY or MAY NOT be included in the rates.

Minimum stays

Many inns require a two-night minimum stay on weekends. A three-night stay often is required during holiday periods or special events.

Cancellations

Cancellation policies are individual for each bed & breakfast. It is not unusual to see 7- to 14-day cancellation periods or more. Please verify the inn's policy when making your reservation.

Rooms

Under some listings, you will note that suites are available. We typically assume that suites include a private bath.

Additionally, under some listings, you will note a reference to cottages. A cottage may be a rustic cabin tucked in the woods, a seaside cottage or a private apartment-style accommodation.

Fireplaces

When fireplaces are mentioned in the listing they may be in guest rooms or in common areas and are abbreviated as "F.P." A few have fireplaces that are non-working because of city lodging requirements. Please verify this if you are looking forward to an evening in front of a crackling fire.

Historic Interest

Many of the inns included have listed items of historic interest nearby that guests can visit. To help you plan your trip, most of the inns also have included the distance to the sites of significant historic interest.

Smoking

The majority of country inns and B&Bs, especially those located in historic buildings, prohibit smoking; therefore, if you are a smoker, we advise you to call and specifically check with each inn to see if and how they accommodate smokers.

State maps

The state maps have been designed to help travelers find an inn's location quickly and easily. Each city shown on the maps contains one or more inns. As you browse through the guide, you will notice coordinates next to each city name, i.e. "C3." The coordinates designate the location of inns on the state map.

Media coverage

Some inns have provided us with copies of magazine or newspaper articles written by travel writers about their establishments and we have indicated that in the listing. Articles written about the inns may be available either from the source as a reprint, through libraries or from the inn itself. Also, TV coverage, catalogue and movie appearances are included.

Comments from guests

Over the years, we have collected reams of guest comments about thousands of inns. Our files are filled with these documented comments. At the end of some descriptions, we have included a guest comment received about that inn.

Descriptions

This book contains descriptions of more than 2,300 inns, and each establishment was reviewed carefully prior to being approved for this guide. Many inns and B&Bs were turned away from this guide because they did not meet our standards. We also do not allow innkeepers to write their own descriptions. Our descriptions are created from visits to the inns, interviews with innkeepers and from a bulk of other information, including ratings, guest comments and articles from top magazines and newspapers.

Inspections

Each year we travel across the country visiting inns. Since 1981, we have had a happy, informal team of inn travelers and prospective innkeepers who report to us about new bed & breakfast discoveries and repeat visits to favorite inns.

Although our staff usually sees hundreds of inns each year, inspecting inns is not the major focus of our travels. We visit as many as possible, photograph them and meet the innkeepers. Some inns are grand mansions filled with classic, museum-quality antiques. Others are rustic, such as reassembled log cabins or renovated barns or stables. We have enjoyed them all and cherish our memories of each establishment, pristine or rustic.

Only rarely have we come across a truly disappointing inn, poorly kept or poorly managed. This type of business usually does not survive because an inn's success depends upon repeat guests and enthusiastic word-of-mouth referrals from satisfied guests. We do not promote these types of establishments.

Traveler or tourist

Travel is an adventure into the unknown, full of surprises and rewards. A seasoned "traveler" learns that even after elaborate preparations and careful planning, travel provides the new and unexpected. The traveler learns to live with uncertainty and considers it part of the adventure.

To the "tourist," whether "accidental" or otherwise, new experiences are disconcerting. Tourists want no surprises. They expect things to be exactly as they had envisioned them. To tourists we recommend staying in a hotel or motel chain where the same formula is followed from one locale to another.

We have found that inngoers are travelers at heart. They relish the differences found at these unique bed & breakfasts and country inns. This is the magic that makes traveling from inn to inn the delightful experience it is.

What if the inn is full?

Ask the innkeeper for recommendations. They may know of an inn that has recently opened or one nearby but off the beaten path. Call the local Chamber of Commerce in the town you hope to visit. They may also know of inns that have recently opened. Please let us know of any new discoveries you make.

We want to hear from you!

We've always enjoyed hearing from our readers and have carefully cataloged all letters and recommendations. If you wish to participate in evaluating your inn experiences, use the Inn Evaluation Form in the back of this book. You might want to make copies of this form prior to departing on your journey.

We hope you will enjoy this book so much that you will want to keep an extra copy or two on hand to offer to friends and family. Many readers have called to purchase our books for hostess gifts, birthday presents, or for seasonal celebrations. It's a great way to introduce your friends to America's enchanting country inns and bed & breakfasts.

Visit us online!

Would you like more information about the inns listed in this book? For color photos, links to the inns' web sites and more, search our web site at **www.iLoveInns.com**. You'll find thousands of inns from the United States and Canada. We think you'll agree it's *"the only online bed & breakfast guide you will ever need.™"*

How to Read an Inn Listing

Anytown ❶ G6

An American Historic Inn
❷ 123 S Main St
Anytown, VT 12345-6789
(123)555-1212 (800)555-1212 Fax:(123)555-1234
❸ E-mail: americaninn@mail.com
Web: www.americaninn.com

❹ **Circa 1897.** Every inch of this breathtaking inn offers something special. The interior is decorated to the hilt with lovely furnishings, plants, beautiful rugs and warm, inviting tones. Rooms include four-poster and canopy beds combined with the modern amenities such as fireplaces, wet bars and stocked refrigerators. Enjoy a complimentary full breakfast at the inn's gourmet restaurant. The chef offers everything from a light breakfast of fresh fruit, cereal and a bagel to heartier treats such as pecan peach pancakes and Belgium waffles served with fresh fruit and crisp bacon.

❺

❻ **Historic Interest:** Indian Burial Grounds (15 miles), Fort Morgan (30 miles).

❼ Innkeeper(s): Andrew & Chaya Jordan. ❽$125-195. ❾MC VISA AX DS PC TC. ❿TAC10. ⓫13 rooms with PB, 4 with FP, 1 suite and 1 conference room. ⓬ Breakfast and afternoon tea included in rates. MAP. ⓭Types of meals: full breakfast, gourmet breakfast and early coffee/tea. Dinner, picnic lunch, gourmet lunch, banquet service, catering service and room service available. Restaurant on premises. ⓮Beds: KQTC. ⓯Phone, turndown service, ceiling fan, TV and VCR in room. Air conditioning. Fax, copier and bicycles on premises. Handicap access. Antiques, fishing, parks, shopping, theater and watersports nearby.

⓰ Pets allowed: With prior approval, $50 deposit.

⓱ Publicity: *Beaufort, Southern Living, Country Inns, Carolina Style, US Air, Town & Country.*

⓲ *"A dream come true!"*

① Map coordinates
Easily locate an inn on the state map using these coordinates.

② Inn address
Mailing or street address and all phone numbers for the inn.

③ E-mail and web address
Many inns have included their e-mail and web addresses. Use the e-mail address to contact innkeepers regarding reservations or other questions. Often, additional information, including color photographs, can be found on the inn's web site.

④ Description of inn
Descriptions of inns are written by experienced travel writers based on visits to inns, interviews and information collected from inns.

⑤ Drawing of inn
Many listings include artistic renderings.

⑥ Historic interest
Indicates items of special historic significance near the inn's location.

⑦ Innkeepers
The name of the innkeeper(s).

⑧ Rates
Rates are quoted for double occupancy. The rate range includes off-season rates and is subject to change.

⑨ Payment types accepted
MC-MasterCard, VISA, DS-Discover, AX-American Express, DC-Diner's Club, CB-Carte Blanche, TC-Traveler's Check, PC-Personal Check.

⑩ Travel agent commission
Indicates the percentage an inn has agreed to offer a travel agent. Example: TAC10=10%

⑪ Rooms
Number and types of rooms available. PB-Private Bath FP-Fireplace

⑫ Included meals
Types of meals included in the rates. Also may list any meal plans offered by the inn. AP-American Plan, MAP-Modified American Plan, EP-European Plan

⑬ Available meals
This section lists the types of meals that the inn offers. These meals may or may not be included in the rates.

⑭ Beds
King, Queen, Double, Twin

⑮ Amenities and activities
Information included here describes other amenities or services available at the inn. Nearby activities also are included.

⑯ Pets allowed
Indicates the inn's policy on pets.

⑰ Publicity
Newspapers, magazines and other publications which have featured articles about the inn.

⑱ Guest comments
Comments about the inn from guests.

Alabama

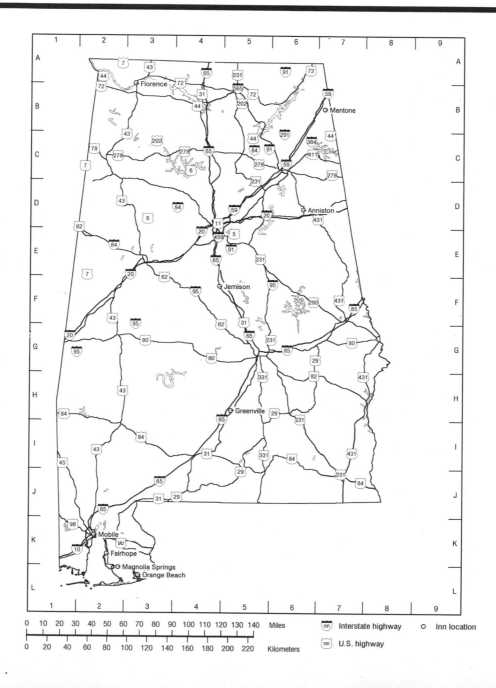

	Miles
0 10 20 30 40 50 60 70 80 90 100 110 120 130 140	
0 20 40 60 80 100 120 140 160 180 200 220	Kilometers

Interstate highway ○ Inn location

U.S. highway

Anniston D6

The Victoria, A Country Inn & Restaurant

1604 Quintard Ave, PO Box 2213
Anniston, AL 36202-2213
(256)236-0503 (800)260-8781 Fax:(256)236-1138
E-mail: thevic@mindspring.com

Circa 1887. This Victorian estate, an Alabama landmark, occupies almost an entire square block on Quintard Avenue, Anniston's major thoroughfare. The first floor of the main house has four din-

ing rooms, a piano lounge and a glass-enclosed veranda. The guest rooms in the house are furnished with antiques, while those in the hotel feature reproduction pieces. Covered walkways, verandas and gazebos flow among the massive hardwoods, gardens, courtyard and pool.

Innkeeper(s): Beth & Fain Casey, Jean Ann Oglesby. $79-319. MC, VISA, AX, DC, DS, TC. TAC10. 60 rooms with PB, 4 with FP, 1 cottage and 4 conference rooms. Breakfast included in rates. Types of meals: Full bkfst and room service. EP. Beds: KQD. Cable TV and phone in room. Air conditioning. VCR, fax, copier, swimming and fine dining on premises. Handicap access. Weddings, small meetings, family reunions and seminars hosted. Amusement parks, antiquing, live theater, parks and shopping nearby.

Publicity: *Southern Living, New York Times, Anniston Star, Birmingham Post Herald, Decatur Daily, Birmingham News and Good Housekeeping.*

Fairhope K2

Bay Breeze Guest House

742 S Mobile St
Fairhope, AL 36533
(866)928-8976 Fax:(251)929-2389

Circa 1938. A white shell driveway leads to this gracious home, located on three acres of landscaped gardens of camellias and azaleas on Mobile Bay. A wide sandy beach and 462-foot private pier gives guests an unparalleled experience. The

pier is popular for waterside picnics, naps, fishing, sunbathing and an occasional barbecue. Furnished with family heirlooms and period antiques, the rooms also offer stained glass, Oriental rugs and quilts. Guests are treat-

ed to bountiful breakfasts in view of pelicans in flight or diving into the bay. Southern hospitality is extended in a variety of ways throughout your stay.

Innkeeper(s): Bill & Becky Jones. $115-145. MC, VISA, AX, DS, PC, TC. 5 rooms with PB and 4 suites. Breakfast included in rates. Types of meals: Full bkfst. Beds: Q. Cable TV and ceiling fan in room. Air conditioning. VCR, fax, copier, swimming and bicycles on premises. Antiquing, fishing, golf, parks, shopping and water sports nearby.

Church Street Inn B&B

51 S Church St
Fairhope, AL 36532-2343
(866)928-8976 (866)928-8976 Fax:(251)929-2389

Circa 1921. Guests at Church Street choose from three bedchambers, each decorated with family antiques and heirlooms. The home, listed in the National Register, contains many origi-

nal features, including a clawfoot tub in the Ashley Anne room. Breakfasts offer self-serve deluxe continental. Fairhope, a small town on Mobile Bay, offers a quaint downtown area with galleries, boutiques, antique shops and restaurants.

Innkeeper(s): Marisha Chavers. $100. MC, VISA, AX, DS, PC, TC. 3 rooms with PB. Breakfast included in rates. Types of meals: Cont plus. Beds: KQ. Cable TV and ceiling fan in room. Air conditioning. Antiquing, fishing, golf, parks, shopping and water sports nearby.

Florence B3

Limestone Manor B&B

601 North Wood Ave
Florence, AL 35630
(256)765-0314 (888)709-6700 Fax:(256)765-9920
E-mail: info@limestonemanor.com

Circa 1915. Florence's mayor once owned this historic home, which is fashioned out of Alabama limestone. Among his notable guests were Humphrey Bogart, Thomas Edison and

Henry Ford. Each has a guest room named in his honor. The rooms are decorated with antiques, and two include a decorative fireplace. Mornings begin with a candle-lit breakfast. Fresh fruit is garnished with mint from the inn's garden. From there, a

savory egg dish is accompanied by a grits soufflé, sausage and homemade baked goods. The National Register home is located in the Wood Avenue Historic district, surrounded by gracious homes and just down the road from the University of North Alabama. The town of Florence boasts more than 400 properties listed in the National Register.

Historic Interest: Helen Keller's birthplace (5 miles), W.C.Handy birthplace (1 mile)..

Innkeeper(s): Bud & Lois Ellison. $83-110. MC, VISA, AX, PC, TC. TAC10. 3 rooms with PB and 2 suites. Breakfast included in rates. Types of meals: Full bkfst, veg bkfst and early coffee/tea. Beds: Q. Cable TV and ceiling fan in room. Central air. VCR, fax, copier, library, video library and courtesy refrigerator on premises. Antiquing, art galleries, bicycling, canoeing/kayaking, fishing, golf, hiking, live theater, museums, parks, shopping, sporting events and water sports nearby.

Publicity: *Southern Living and Alabama Public Television-innkeeper's kitchen.*

Greenville H4

The Martin House B&B

212 E Commerce St
Greenville, AL 36037-2212
(334)382-2011 (877)627-8465 Fax:(334)382-0728
E-mail: themartinhouse@greenlynk.com
Web: www.martinbb.com

Circa 1853. Experience old-fashioned Southern hospitality at this unique home in the historic city of Greenville. Built from an original 1853 cottage, a Queen Anne addition was added in 1895 during the Victorian era. Furnished with antiques and family pieces, the atmosphere of another time is sustained in nine accent fireplaces, a formal sitting room, cozy sunroom, and wraparound porch with wicker furniture and lush plants.

Guest rooms include private baths, and special features such as a pencil-post bed, clawfoot tub or private balcony. Guests can enjoy breakfast or snacks in the tea room, formal dining room or outdoors on the deck or porch. There are many unique shops to visit nearby, as well as churches, homes and cemeteries dating back to the early 1800s.

Historic Interest: Churches, cemeteries.

Innkeeper(s): Jo Weitman. $75-85. MC, VISA, AX, DS, PC, TC. TAC10. 4 rooms with PB and 1 conference room. Types of meals: Full bkfst, veg bkfst, early coffee/tea, gourmet lunch, picnic lunch, afternoon tea, snacks/refreshments and gourmet dinner. Beds: KQT. Cable TV, phone, turndown service, ceiling fan and VCR in room. Central air. Fax and copier on premises. Weddings, small meetings, family reunions and seminars hosted. Antiquing, art galleries, beaches, bicycling, fishing, golf, museums, parks and shopping nearby.

Jemison   F4

The Jemison Inn Bed & Breakfast and Gardens

212 Hwy 191
Jemison, AL 35085
(205)688-2055
E-mail: theinn@scott.net
Web: www.bbonline.com/al/jemison

Circa 1920. Shaded by tall oak trees, this gabled brick home features fountains and flowers in the gardens created by the innkeeper, a certified Master Gardener. Relax on antique white wicker on the arched, wraparound porch. Inside, the inn is filled with heirloom-quality Victorian furnishings, Roseville and Waterford crystal,and marble-top tables. Vintage holiday decorations and collections of old musical instruments are creatively displayed. Enjoy flexible accommodations, and afternoon refreshments. A swimming pool is an inviting activity in the summer.

Innkeeper(s): Nancy Rogers. $85-152. MC, VISA, AX, DC, CB, DS, PC, TC. 3 rooms with PB. Breakfast and snacks/refreshments included in rates. Types of meals: Full bkfst and picnic lunch. Beds: KQ. Cable TV, VCR and one whirlpool tub in room. Swimming on premises.

Publicity: *Southern Living, Birmingham News, Prime Time and Birmingham Post-Herald.*

Magnolia Springs   L2

Magnolia Springs

14469 Oak St
Magnolia Springs, AL 36555
(251)965-7321 (800)965-7321 Fax:(251)965-3035
E-mail: msbbdw@gulftel.com
Web: www.magnoliasprings.com

Circa 1897. A canopy of ancient oak trees line the streets leading to the Magnolia Springs bed & breakfast. Softly framed by more oaks, and in springtime, pink azaleas, the National Register inn with its dormers and spacious wraparound porch offers an inviting welcome. Warm hospitality enfolds guests in the Great Room with its pine walls and ceilings and heart pine floors, as well as the greeting from the innkeeper. Curly pine woodwork is found throughout

the home, which was originally an area hotel. Guest rooms are appointed with a variety of carefully chosen antiques. Breakfast favorites often include pecan-topped French toast, bacon, grits, fresh fruit with cream dressing and blueberry muffins. Guests may also request a special breakfast to accommodate dietary needs. The innkeepers will recommend some memorable adventures, or simply stroll to Magnolia River and enjoy the area.

Historic Interest: Fairhope (15 miles), Fort Morgan (30 miles).

Innkeeper(s): David Worthington. $97-144. MC, VISA, AX, DS, PC, TC. 5 rooms, 4 with PB and 1 suite. Breakfast, afternoon tea and snacks/refreshments included in rates. Types of meals: Full bkfst and early coffee/tea. Beds: KQDT. Cable TV, phone, turndown service and ceiling fan in room. Central air. Fax and copier on premises. Weddings, small meetings and family reunions hosted. Amusement parks, antiquing, art galleries, beaches, canoeing/kayaking, fishing, golf, hiking, museums, parks, shopping and water sports nearby.

Publicity: *Southern Living, Fox 10 Mobile and HGTV-Bob Vila's Restore America.*

Mentone   B7

Mentone Inn

Hwy 117, PO Box 290
Mentone, AL 35984
(205)634-4836 (800)455-7470

Circa 1927. Located at the top of Lookout Mountain amidst forests and meadows of wild flowers Mentone Inn offers a refreshing stop for those in search of the cool breezes and natural air conditioning of the mountains. This lodge has been welcoming travelers since 1927. Here antique treasures mingle with modern-day conveniences and favorite places are the fireplace in the main lounge and the gracious porch. Sequoyah Caverns, Little River Canyon and DeSoto Falls are moments away.

Innkeeper(s): Ms. Sherri Brown. $85-115. MC, VISA, PC, TC. 12 rooms with PB. Types of meals: Full bkfst and early coffee/tea. Beds: QT. TV, ceiling fan and central heat in room. Central air. VCR and porch on premises. Small meetings, family reunions and seminars hosted. Antiquing, canoeing/kayaking, golf, hiking, horseback riding, parks, downhill skiing and water sports nearby.

Publicity: *Birmingham News, Weekend Getaways Magazine, Montgomery Advertiser and Nashville Traveler.*

Mobile   K2

Towle House

1104 Montauk Ave
Mobile, AL 36604
(334)432-6440 (800)938-6953 Fax:(334)433-4381
E-mail: jfvereen@aol.com

Circa 1874. Originally a boy's boarding school, this home is composed of three smaller houses. The Italianate wooden architecture features a friendly porch with handsome gingerbread trim. Breakfast is a gourmet affair and may include items such as shirred eggs atop a bed of mushrooms in sherry and butter on a Holland rusk. Freshly baked cinnamon rolls are served after the main course.

Innkeeper(s): Felix & Carolyn Vereen. $80-95. MC, VISA, PC, TC. TAC10. 3 rooms with PB. Breakfast included in rates. Types of meals: Gourmet bkfst and early coffee/tea. Beds: Q. Cable TV, phone, turndown service and ceiling fan in room. Air conditioning. Fax, copier and library on premises. Weddings, small meetings and family reunions hosted. Antiquing, golf, live theater, parks, shopping and sporting events nearby.

Publicity: *Mobile Register.*

"Your hospitality has surpassed our highest expectations."

Orange Beach   *L3*

The Original Romar House

23500 Perdido Beach Blvd
Orange Beach, AL 36561-3007
(334)974-1625 (800)487-6627 Fax:(334)974-1163
E-mail: original@gulftel.com
Web: www.bbonline.com/al/romarhouse/

Circa 1924. From the deck of the Purple Parrot Bar, guests at this seaside inn can enjoy a cocktail and a view of the Gulf of Mexico. Each of the guest rooms is named and themed after a

local festival and decorated with authentic Art Deco furnishings. Stained and beveled glass windows add to the romantic atmosphere. A full Southern breakfast is served each morning, and in the evening, wine and cheese is served in the Purple Parrot Bar.

Innkeeper(s): Darrell Finley. $79-139. MC, VISA, AX, PC. 6 rooms with PB, 1 suite, 1 cottage and 1 conference room. Breakfast included in rates. Types of meals: Full bkfst. Beds: Q. Turndown service and ceiling fan in room. Air conditioning. VCR, spa, swimming, bicycles and library on premises. Weddings, small meetings and family reunions hosted. Amusement parks, antiquing, fishing, golf, night clubs, seafood restaurants, parks, shopping and water sports nearby.

Alaska

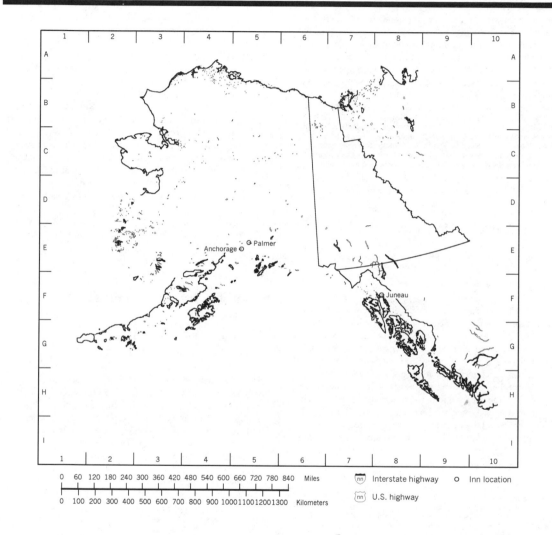

| | | 0 | 60 | 120 | 180 | 240 | 300 | 360 | 420 | 480 | 540 | 600 | 660 | 720 | 780 | 840 | Miles |

| | | 0 | 100 | 200 | 300 | 400 | 500 | 600 | 700 | 800 | 900 | 1000 | 1100 | 1200 | 1300 | Kilometers |

Anchorage ⊙ ⊙ Palmer

⊙ Juneau

⬡ Interstate highway   ⊙ Inn location

⬡ U.S. highway

Anchorage E5

Alaska Private Lodgings

PO Box 200047
Anchorage, AK 99520
(907)258-1717 Fax:(907)258-6613
E-mail: ahi@alaskabandb.com
Web: www.alaskabandb.com

Circa 1900. Alaska Private Lodgings, operated by Mercy Dennis, is a reservation service for private homes. Among the many listed in Anchorage is a charming suite in one of the oldest buildings in town. Additional accommodations are available in apartments. Homes are located in Homer, Kenai, Talkeetna, Alyeska, Seward, Valdez, Wasilla, Willow, Denali and Seldovia. Mercy is knowledgeable about tours, sightseeing trips and discount car rentals.

Innkeeper(s): Mercy Dennis. $50-125. MC, VISA, AX, PC, TC. 300 rooms, 200 with PB, 50 suites, 25 cottages and 25 cabins. Breakfast included in rates. Types of meals: Gourmet bkfst, cont plus and cont. Beds: KQDT. Cable TV, phone, ceiling fan, VCR and fireplace in room. Spa, sauna and bicycles on premises. Russian, Swedish, French and Spanish spoken. Art galleries, bicycling, canoeing/kayaking, fishing, hiking, museums, parks, shopping, downhill skiing, cross-country skiing, sporting events and tennis nearby.

"We had a really great time during our eight days in Alaska. We enjoyed all four of our hosts, who were all outstanding in different ways. Thanks for your arrangements."

The Oscar Gill House

1344 W 10th Ave
Anchorage, AK 99501-3245
(907)279-1344 Fax:(907)279-1344
E-mail: oscargill@gci.net
Web: www.oscargill.com

Circa 1913. This clapboard, Craftsman-style home was built in Knik, Alaska, but later disassembled and moved to Anchorage in 1916. The home is the city's oldest, and the innkeepers have kept the decor simple and comfortable, with antiques here and there, as well as vintage furnishings from the '30s and '40s. Down comforters and bathrooms stocked with toiletries are a few of the special touches guests will find. Breakfasts are served up in the cheery dining room, which features panoramic photos of Anchorage and the home in its original location. Innkeeper Susan Lutz prepares a variety of entrees for the morning meal, including items such as sourdough French toast or Mexican egg casseroles accompanied by freshly ground coffee, a selection of teas and homemade hot chocolate.

Historic Interest: Anchorage Historical & Fine Arts Museum and Oscar Anderson House Museum are among the nearby historic sites.

Innkeeper(s): Mark & Susan Lutz. $65-110. MC, VISA, AX, PC. TAC10. 3 rooms, 1 with PB and 1 conference room. Breakfast included in rates. Types of meals: Full bkfst, veg bkfst and early coffee/tea. Beds: QDT. Cable TV, phone, turndown service, fireplace, hot tub, robes and body shop products in room. Fax and bicycles on premises. Weddings, small meetings, family reunions and seminars hosted. A little French spoken. Antiquing, art galleries, bicycling, canoeing/kayaking, fishing, brew pubs, restaurants, live theater, museums, parks, shopping, cross-country skiing and sporting events nearby.

Juneau F7

Alaska's Capital Inn

113 W Fifth St
Juneau, AK 99801
(907)586-6507 (888)588-6507 Fax:(907)586-6508
E-mail: innkeeper@alaskacapitalinn.com
Web: www.alaskacapitalinn.com

Circa 1906. This American Four Square-style home was built of old growth Douglas Fir by gold rush pioneer John Olds. Olds was one of the first miners in the Juneau area after word got out about the discovery of gold, and he became the mayor. The inn is furnished in period antique pieces and newer Stickly pieces. A gourmet breakfast is served on china and with silver and it incorporates local seafood specialties. A lucky guest might awake to a treat like a smoked salmon omelet or a crab quiche. The inn has five guest bedrooms and two suites. It is within the downtown historic district, next door to a park with a 100-year-old lilac tree, and it has mountain views. The inn has a yard with room for croquet and secluded areas to swing in the hammock. Its rear porch is a perfect place to eat breakfast or just relax. Guests may request a pick up at the airport or ferry terminal in the inn's vintage Cadillac limousine.

Innkeeper(s): Linda Wendeborn & Mark Thorson. $99-199. MC, VISA, PC. TAC10. 5 rooms with PB, 2 with FP and 2 suites. Breakfast included in rates. Types of meals: Full bkfst, country bkfst, cont plus, cont, early coffee/tea and afternoon tea. Beds: KQT. Cable TV, phone, turndown service, VCR, fireplace, hair dryers, irons and robes in room. Fax, spa and bicycles on premises. Small meetings hosted. Art galleries, beaches, bicycling, canoeing/kayaking, fishing, hiking, tram ride, wildlife viewing, live theater, museums, parks, shopping, downhill skiing and cross-country skiing nearby.

Publicity: HGTV "If walls could talk"

Silverbow Inn & Restaurant

120 2nd St
Juneau, AK 99801-1215
(907)586-4146 (800)586-4146 Fax:(907)586-4242
E-mail: silverbo@alaska.net
Web: www.silverbowinn.com

Circa 1914. For more than 100 years, Alaska's oldest operating bakery has been located here. The innkeepers, an architect and urban planner, have brought the building to life with a luxurious lobby and romantic restaurant. The inn offers B&B and European-style pension rooms. Freshly made bagels, breads and pastries are served at breakfast. Within two blocks are the state capitol, convention center, waterfront and shopping district.

Innkeeper(s): Jill Ramiel/Ken Alper. $78-135. MC, VISA, DS. TAC10. 6 rooms with PB and 2 conference rooms. Breakfast, afternoon tea and snacks/refreshments included in rates. Types of meals: Cont and early coffee/tea. Beds: QT. Cable TV, phone and VCR in room. Fax, copier, library, social hour with wine and cheese and bakery on premises. Weddings, small meetings, family reunions and seminars hosted. Antiquing, fishing, live theater, parks, shopping, downhill skiing and cross-country skiing nearby.

Publicity: Travel & Leisure, Destinos and Frommers Choice 2000.

Palmer   *E5*

Colony Inn
325 E Elmwood
Palmer, AK 99645-6622
(907)745-3330 Fax:(907)746-3330

Circa 1935. Historic buildings are few and far between in Alaska, and this inn is one of them. The structure was built to house teachers and nurses in the days when President  Roosevelt was sending settlers to Alaska to establish farms. When innkeeper Janet Kincaid purchased it, the inn had been empty for some time. She restored the place, including the wood walls, which now create a cozy ambiance in the common areas. The 12 guest rooms are nicely appointed, and 10 include a whirlpool tub. Meals are not included, but the inn's restaurant offers breakfast and lunch. The inn is listed in the National Register.

Innkeeper(s): Janet Kincaid. $80. MC, VISA, AX, DS, PC, TC. TAC10. 12 rooms with PB. Types of meals: Full bkfst and lunch. Beds: QDT. Cable TV and phone in room. Handicap access. Weddings, small meetings and family reunions hosted. Antiquing, fishing, golf, parks, shopping, downhill skiing, cross-country skiing and tennis nearby.

"Love the antiques and history."

Arizona

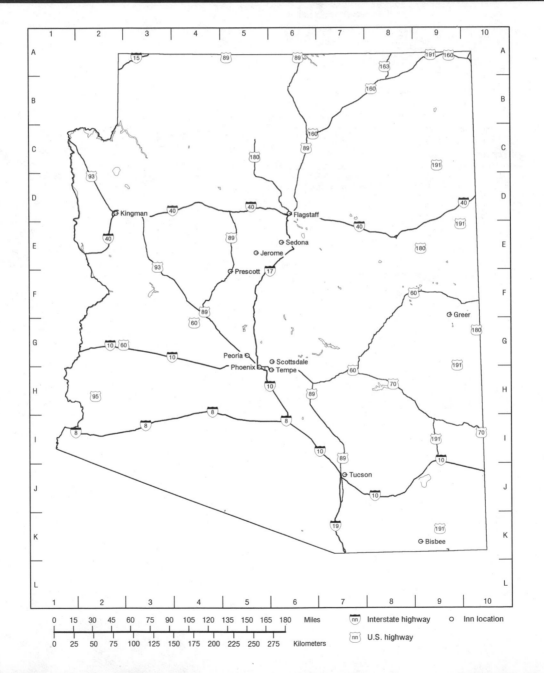

Bisbee K9

Bisbee Grand Hotel, A B&B Inn

61 Main Street, Box 825
Bisbee, AZ 85603
(520)432-5900 (800)421-1909
E-mail: bisbeegrandhotel@msn.com
Web: www.bisbeegrandhotel.com

Circa 1906. This National Register treasure is a stunning example of an elegant turn-of-the-century hotel. The hotel originally served as a stop for mining executives, and it was restored back to its Old West glory in the 1980s. Each of the rooms is decorated with Victorian furnishings and wall coverings. The suites offer special items such as clawfoot tubs, an antique Chinese wedding bed, a fountain or four-poster bed. Try the Old Western Suite with an authentic covered wagon modified to fit a queen-size bed. The Grand Western Salon boasts the back bar fixture from the Pony Saloon in Tombstone. After a full breakfast, enjoy a day touring the Bisbee area, which includes mine tours, museums, shops, antiquing and a host of outdoor activities.

Historic Interest: Located in downtown historic Bisbee, features 110-year-old back bar fixture.

Innkeeper(s): Bill Thomas. $75-150. MC, VISA, AX, DS. TAC10. 8 rooms and 7 suites. Breakfast included in rates. Types of meals: Full bkfst.

Flagstaff D6

Birch Tree Inn

824 W Birch Ave
Flagstaff, AZ 86001-4420
(928)774-1042 (888)774-1042 Fax:(928)774-8462
E-mail: info@birchtreeinn.com
Web: www.birchtreeinn.com

Circa 1917. Situated in a cool Ponderosa Pine forest, this pristine white bungalow with blue shutters and trim is surrounded by an inviting wraparound veranda supported with Corinthian columns. The inn's guest rooms represent a variety of styles. A full breakfast and afternoon refreshments are served. Nearby are hiking trails and ski runs. Historic downtown Flagstaff is within walking distance for shops, restaurants and entertainment. The Grand Canyon and Sedona are each an hour's drive away.

Innkeeper(s): Donna & Rodger Pettinger, Sandy & Ed Znetko. $59-119. MC, VISA, AX, TC. TAC10. 5 rooms, 3 with PB. Breakfast included in rates. Types of meals: Full bkfst and early coffee/tea. Beds: KQT. Air conditioning. Fax, copier, spa and pool table on premises. Antiquing, fishing, live entertainment nearby, live theater, parks, shopping, downhill skiing, cross-country skiing and sporting events nearby.

Publicity: *Arizona Daily Sun, Arizona Republic, San Francisco Chronicle, New York Times, Phoenix Gazette and Orange County Register.*

"Charming hosts and wonderful food-like visiting old friends."

Comfi Cottages

1612 N Aztec St
Flagstaff, AZ 86001-1106
(928)774-0731 (888)774-0731 Fax:(928)773-7286
E-mail: pat@comficottages.com
Web: www.comficottages.com

Circa 1920. Each of the six cottages has been thoughtfully decorated and features a variety of styles. One cottage is decorated in a Southwestern motif, while the others feature antiques and English-Country decor. Five cottages include fireplaces, and all include kitchens stocked with full equipment and all staples. They also have the added luxury of a washer and dryer. Sleds and bicycles are available for guest use, as well as picnic tables, a barbecue grill and picnic baskets. The Grand Canyon and national parks are close by, and the cottages are in the perfect location to enjoy all Flagstaff has to offer.

Historic Interest: The cottages are located near the many activities available in historic downtown Flagstaff. Several Indian ruins are within 50 miles of the cottages.

Innkeeper(s): Ed & Pat Wiebe. $110-250. MC, VISA, DS, PC. TAC10. 6 cottages. Breakfast and snacks/refreshments included in rates. Types of meals: Full bkfst. Beds: KQDT. Cable TV, phone, ceiling fan and VCR in room. Bicycles, sleds, BBQ and picnic tables on premises. Handicap access. Small meetings, family reunions and seminars hosted. French spoken. Antiquing, fishing, golf, hiking, indian ruins, live theater, parks, shopping, downhill skiing, cross-country skiing, sporting events, tennis and water sports nearby.

Publicity: *Arizona Republic, Arizona Daily Sun, Washington Post and Phoenix Magazine.*

"A delightful stay; and the view of the San Francisco Peaks was gorgeous."

Inn at 410 B&B

410 N Leroux St
Flagstaff, AZ 86001-4502
(928)774-0088 (800)774-2008 Fax:(928)774-6354
E-mail: info@inn410.com
Web: www.inn410.com

Circa 1894. This inn, once the stately family residence of a wealthy banker, businessman and cattle rancher, has been frequented over the years by travelers interested in exploring the Grand Canyon. Today, guests enjoy hospitality, outstanding cuisine and a wonderful home base from which to enjoy Northern Arizona. Each of the guest rooms is individually decorated in a unique style. Eight of the guest rooms include a fireplace, and some offer an oversized Jacuzzi tub. Award-winning recipes are featured during the gourmet breakfasts, and afternoon cookies and tea are served in the dining room. A two-block walk takes guests to shops, galleries and restaurants in historic downtown Flagstaff. Sedona, Native American sites, the Grand Canyon and the San Francisco Peaks are nearby.

Historic Interest: Riordan Mansion State Park and Lowell Observatory both are located in Flagstaff. Wupatki National Monument (Anasazi Indian Ruins) is 35 miles away. Hopi and Navajo Indian Reservations are within 45 to 100 miles away. Walnut Canyon National Monument (Sinaqua Indian ruins) is seven miles away.

Innkeeper(s): Howard & Sally Krueger. $135-190. MC, VISA, PC, TC.

TAC10. 9 rooms with PB, 8 with FP and 4 suites. Breakfast and snacks/refreshments included in rates. Types of meals: Gourmet bkfst. Beds: KQT. Ceiling fan, coffee, tea and three with Jacuzzi tubs in room. Air conditioning. Library on premises. Antiquing, hiking, museums, observatory, live theater, parks, shopping, downhill skiing and cross-country skiing nearby.

Publicity: *Westways, Arizona Daily Sun, Mountain Living, Mountain Morning, PBS TV, Women's World, Lands End Corporate Catalog, Arizona Highways, Old House Journal, Phoenix Magazine and Sunset.*

Lynn's Inn

614 W Santa Fe Ave
Flagstaff, AZ 86001-5323
(520)226-1488 (800)530-9947 Fax:(520)226-1488
E-mail: info@lynnsinn.com
Web: www.lynnsinn.com

Circa 1905. Built in 1905 from locally quarried stone, this Victorian, homestead-style house is surrounded by tall green trees, creating peaceful privacy in each room. In the winter, snow-covered trees and rooftops create a winter wonderland.

Within walking distance from Downtown Main Street Historic District, the two-story sandstone home is centrally located in Flagstaff, about an hour's drive from the Grand Canyon. An elegant full breakfast prepared by hosts Bob and Linda Gray, who pride themselves on their gourmet selections, awaits each guest in the dining room. Each of the guest rooms are individually named and decorated, as with the entire house, in 1700s to 1900s eclectic.

Historic Interest: Riordan Mansion (4 miles), Lowell Observatory (1 mile).
Innkeeper(s): Bob & Linda Gray. $99-109. MC, VISA, AX, DC, CB, DS, PC, TC. TAC10. 3 rooms with PB and 1 suite. Breakfast and snacks/refreshments included in rates. Types of meals: Gourmet bkfst, veg bkfst and early coffee/tea. Beds: KQT. Franklin Room with feather bed in room. Fax and library on premises. Family reunions hosted. Antiquing, art galleries, bicycling, canoeing/kayaking, fishing, golf, hiking, horseback riding, Grand Canyon, live theater, museums, parks, shopping, downhill skiing, cross-country skiing, sporting events, tennis and water sports nearby.

Publicity: *Arizona Highways.*

Greer   F9

White Mountain Lodge

PO Box 143
Greer, AZ 85927-0143
(520)735-7568 (888)493-7568 Fax:(520)735-7498
E-mail: bast@cybertrails.com

Circa 1892. This 19th-century lodge affords views of Greer meadow and the Little Colorado River. The guest rooms are individually decorated in a Southwestern or country style. The common rooms are decorated with period antiques, Southwestern art and Mission-style furnishings. The Lodge's living room is an ideal place to relax with its stone fireplace. While dining on the hearty

breakfasts, guests not only are treated to entrees that range from traditional country fare to the more gourmet, they also enjoy a view from the picture window. The cookie jar is always filled with homemade goodies and hot drinks are available

throughout the day. The inn is near excellent hiking trails.

Innkeeper(s): Charles & Mary Bast. $95-145. MC, VISA, AX, DC, DS, PC, TC. 7 rooms with PB, 4 with FP, 6 cabins and 1 conference room. Breakfast and snacks/refreshments included in rates. Types of meals: Gourmet bkfst, country bkfst, veg bkfst, early coffee/tea and picnic lunch. Beds: KQD. TV, ceiling fan, VCR and two rooms with whirlpool tubs in room. Fax, copier and spa on premises. Small meetings and family reunions hosted. Antiquing, art galleries, fishing, golf, hiking, museums, shopping, downhill skiing and cross-country skiing nearby.

Pets allowed: One small pet per unit. Must not be left unattended in room.
Publicity: *Independent & Arizona Republic, Arizona Foothills, Vista Magazine, KOY Radio and Channel 3.*

Jerome   E5

Ghost City Inn

541 N Main St
Jerome, AZ 86331
(520)634-4678 Fax:(520)639-2144
E-mail: reservations@ghostcityinn.com
Web: www.ghostcityinn.com

Circa 1898. Porches and verandas stretch across the front of this inn, overlooking the town, Verde Valley and the red rocks of Sedona. Originally built as a boarding house for mining company employees, the old hotel has been refurbished by the innkeepers. (Dave is an architect.) Many guest rooms are furnished with Victorian antiques. In the morning, an abundant selection of breakfast items are offered, in addition to a main course such as strawberry cream cheese stuffed, caramelized French toast topped with whipped cream and more strawberries or a green chili tortilla strata with sour cream and salsa. There is an outdoor Jacuzzi for soaking and enjoying starlit nights, or you can enjoy the shops, restaurants and galleries of the historic landmark town of Jerome.

Innkeeper(s): David & Stacy Phillips. $85-100. PC. 6 rooms, 2 with PB and 1 conference room. Breakfast and afternoon tea included in rates. Types of meals: Full bkfst, early coffee/tea and snacks/refreshments. Beds: QD. TV and ceiling fan in room. Air conditioning. Spa and library on premises. Antiquing, art galleries, fishing, golf, hiking, horseback riding, scenic train ride, museums and shopping nearby.

Jerome Grand Hotel

PO Box H, 200 Hill St
Jerome, AZ 86331
(928)634-8200 (888)817-6788 Fax:(928)639-0299
E-mail: hotel@wildapache.net
Web: www.jeromegrandhotel.net

Circa 1926. Originally the United Verde Hospital, this five-story Spanish Mission building made of poured-in-place, reinforced concrete is one of the highest structures in Verde Valley, promising spectacular scenic views. The inn is a A National Historic Landmark Hotel. Restoration has preserved all of the exterior, while most of the interior remains original. Phones in the guest bedrooms and suites are serviced by an antique switchboard. The lobby offers round-the-clock hospitality, and the gift shop also is open 24 hours. A restaurant and lounge provide indoor and outside seating.

Historic Interest: Jerome State Historic Park (1 mile), Town of Clarkdale (4 miles), Indian Ruins (6-30 miles).
Innkeeper(s): Larry & LaWanda Altherr. $85-195. MC, VISA, AX, DS, TC. TAC10. 22 rooms, 19 with PB and 3 suites. Types of meals: Early coffee/tea. Beds: QT. TV, phone, ceiling fan and VCR in room. Central air. Weddings, small meetings and family reunions hosted. Antiquing, art galleries, golf, hiking, museums, parks and shopping nearby.

Kingman D3

Hotel Brunswick

315 E Andy Devine Ave
Kingman, AZ 86401
(520)718-1800 Fax:(520)718-1801
E-mail: rsvp@hotel-brunswick.com
Web: www.hotel-brunswick.com

Circa 1909. Built at the turn of the 20th century, the Hotel Brunswick was, for awhile, the tallest building in three counties. The hotel was built to accommodate the many railroad passengers who traveled through Kingman. Later in the century, the hotel fell into disrepair until the current owners purchased the property, restoring the historic charm. Each of the guest rooms has been appointed individually. Rooms range from the spacious honeymoon suite to the cozy, economical Cowboy and Cowgirl rooms. In addition to the accommodations, the hotel includes a European-style café, Mulligan's Bar, and a full-service business center. Your hosts can arrange a massage service or create a honeymoon package with flowers and champagne. Kingman, a stop along the famed Route 66, maintains many historic buildings and sites.

Historic Interest: Historic Kingman, downtown.

$25-110. MC, VISA, AX, DC, DS, TC. TAC10. 24 rooms, 7 with PB and 8 suites. Breakfast included in rates. Types of meals: Cont plus, early coffee/tea and gourmet dinner. AP. Beds: QDT. Cable TV, phone and VCR in room. Air conditioning. Fax and copier on premises. Handicap access. Weddings, small meetings, family reunions and seminars hosted. French and German spoken. Antiquing, canoeing/kayaking, fishing, golf, hiking, horseback riding, ghost towns, museums, parks, shopping and water sports nearby.

Pets allowed: $10 charge.

Publicity: *Kingman Daily Miner, Standard News, Arizona Holidays and TV 77.*

Peoria G5

Old Town B&B

8276 W Monroe St
Peoria, AZ 85345
(623)412-7797 Fax:(623)412-7797
E-mail: vicki_hunt@breadnet.middlebury.edu
Web: www.oldtownbb.com

Circa 1947. This red brick home sits on half an acre of gardens, secluded gazebo and fountains. Its three rooms are the Victorian Rose Room, which is decorated in roses and wicker, the Americana Room, which is adorned with quilts and Americana antiques, and the Country Cottage Room with private bath and clawfoot tub in-room. Enjoy breakfast delicacies such as muffins, juice, omelets, bacon or sausage and baked tomatoes in the breakfast room, dining room or gazebo. The inn is three miles from Catlin Court, a haven for antiquers, and it's near the Peoria Sports Complex, which holds two of the nation's largest baseball spring training camps. The area also offers fishing and boating at Lake Pleasant Regional Park and hiking and picnicking at White Tank Mountain Park.

Innkeeper(s): Vicki & Tom Hunt. $75-95. MC, VISA, AX, DS, PC. TAC5. 3 rooms. Breakfast included in rates. Types of meals: Full bkfst and early coffee/tea. Beds: Q. Turndown service and ceiling fan in room. Central air. VCR, fax and copier on premises. Weddings and small meetings hosted. Antiquing, fishing, golf, shopping, sporting events and water sports nearby.

Phoenix H5

Maricopa Manor

15 W Pasadena Ave
Phoenix, AZ 85013
(602)274-6302 (800)292-6403 Fax:(602)266-3904
E-mail: res@maricopamanor.com

Circa 1928. The secluded Maricopa Manor stands amid palm trees on an acre of land. The Spanish-style house features four graceful columns in the entry hall, an elegant living room with a marble mantel and a music room. The spacious suites are decorated with satins, lace, antiques and leather-bound books. Guests may relax on the deck, on the patio, by the pool or in the gazebo spa.

Historic Interest: Arizona Biltmore Resort (2 miles), Heard Museum (3 miles), Pueblo Grand Indian Ruins and Museum.

Innkeeper(s): Jeff Vadheim. $89-219. MC, VISA, AX, DS, PC, TC. TAC10. 7 suites, 4 with FP. Breakfast included in rates. Types of meals: Cont plus. Beds: KQ. Cable TV, phone, ceiling fan and VCR in room. Air conditioning. Fax, copier, spa, swimming, library and off-street parking on premises. Handicap access. Amusement parks, antiquing, golf, restaurants, live theater, parks, shopping, sporting events, tennis and water sports nearby.

Publicity: *Arizona Business Journal, Country Inns, AAA Westways, San Francisco Chronicle, Focus and Sombrero.*

"I've stayed 200+ nights at B&Bs around the world, yet have never before experienced the warmth and sincere friendliness of Maricopa Manor."

Prescott E5

The Cottages at Prescott Country Inn

503 S Montezuma St
Prescott, AZ 86303-4225
(520)445-7991

Circa 1940. Flowerbeds surround the renovated cottages of this 1940s tourist park. Each cottage is handsomely decorated with English country, French country or Early American decor with fluffy quilts and designer sheets. Breakfast is brought to your room. The streets of historic Prescott are three blocks from the inn, and a few blocks south is a ponderosa pine forest.

Innkeeper(s): Morris "Mo" & Sue Faulkner. $49-129. MC, VISA, AX, DS. 12 rooms, 2 with PB and 10 cottages. Types of meals: Cont plus. Beds: KQ. Phone in room. Front decks and parking on premises. Fishing, hiking, swimming, boating and tennis nearby.

Publicity: *Courier and Country Register News.*

"Our room was absolutely charming. The most refreshing, revitalizing days of our trip."

Prescott Pines Inn

901 White Spar Rd
Prescott, AZ 86303-7231
(520)445-7270 (800)541-5374 Fax:(520)778-3665
E-mail: info@prescottpinesinn.com
Web: www.prescottpinesinn.com

Circa 1934. A white picket fence beckons guests to the veranda of this comfortably elegant country Victorian inn, originally the Haymore Dairy. There are masses of fragrant pink roses, lavenders and delphiniums, and stately ponderosa pines that tower above the inn's three renovated guesthouses, which were once shelter for farm hands. A three-bedroom, two-bath on-site

chalet that sleeps up to ten guests is perfect for a family or group. Seven of the eleven rooms are equipped with kitchenettes and three have fireplaces. The acre of grounds includes a garden fountain and romantic tree swing. A full breakfast is offered at an additional charge.

Innkeeper(s): Harry & Debbie Allen. $65-269. MC, VISA. 11 rooms with PB, 3 with FP. Types of meals: Full bkfst and early coffee/tea. EP. Beds: KQ. Cable TV, phone and ceiling fan in room. Air conditioning. Fax and copier on premises. Small meetings and family reunions hosted. Antiquing, hiking, live theater, parks and shopping nearby.

Publicity: *Sunset, Arizona Republic News* and *Arizona Highways.*

"The ONLY place to stay in Prescott! Tremendous attention to detail."

Scottsdale G6

Arizona Trails

PO Box 18998
Scottsdale, AZ 85269
(480)837-4284 (888)799-4284 Fax:(480)816-4224
E-mail: aztrails@arizonatrails.com

Circa 1940. Many of Arizona's B&Bs, inns and hotels that this reservation service represents are historic or depict Southwestern style. Some are situated on or near historic sites including the Cochise stronghold, Tombstone, the OK Corral, Grand Canyon, Indian cliff dwellings and archaeological sites. Listings include a restored adobe Victorian inn, an authentic stagecoach stop where a mercantile store was converted to a bed & breakfast and the renowned Fred Harvey Historic Hotel, frequented by celebrities from the early days of Hollywood. Exclusive getaway locations feature desert or mountain settings with panoramic views. Accommodations range from one guest bedroom to 80, with seasonal rates. Breakfasts vary from continental fare to regional recipes. A travel consultant will assist in planning custom itineraries and packages.

Innkeeper(s): Roxanne Boryczki. $85-495. MC, VISA, AX, DS, PC, TC. Breakfast, picnic lunch, afternoon tea and snacks/refreshments included in rates. Types of meals: Gourmet bkfst, country bkfst, veg bkfst, cont plus, cont and early coffee/tea. MAP, AP, EP. Beds: KQDT. Cable TV, phone, turndown service, ceiling fan and VCR in room. Central air. Fax, spa, swimming, sauna, stables, bicycles, tennis, library and pet boarding on premises. Handicap access. Weddings, small meetings, family reunions and seminars hosted. Antiquing, art galleries, bicycling, fishing, golf, hiking, horseback riding, museums, parks, shopping, downhill skiing, cross-country skiing, sporting events, tennis and wineries nearby.

Sedona E6

Briar Patch Inn

3190 N Hwy 89A
Sedona, AZ 86336-9602
(520)282-2342 (888)809-3030 Fax:(520)282-2399
E-mail: briarpatch@sedona.net
Web: www.briarpatchinn.com

Circa 1943. Getting in touch with nature should come easy at this cluster of cottages on 9 acres found along the lush banks of Oak Creek and located three miles north of the town of Sedona. Fireplaces, shaded patios and privacy help guests relax along with massages offered in your own cottage. Each cottage is different in size, layout and unique decor, which includes

Arizona Indian and Mexican art. Healthy breakfasts can be enjoyed by the fireplace in the lounge, on a tray in the cottages or creekside. Throughout the year, small workshops in painting, Navajo weaving, Indian arts and other self-enrichment classes are given.

Innkeeper(s): Rob Olson. $159-295. MC, VISA, PC, TC. TAC10. 17 cabins. Breakfast, afternoon tea and snacks/refreshments included in rates. Types of meals: Full bkfst. Beds: KQT. Ceiling fan in room. Air conditioning. Fax, copier, swimming, library and BBQ area on premises. Weddings, small meetings, family reunions and seminars hosted. Antiquing, fishing, golf, hiking, shopping, downhill skiing, cross-country skiing and tennis nearby.

Publicity: *Sedona Magazine.*

Tempe H6

Mi Casa Su Casa Reservation Service

PO Box 950
Tempe, AZ 85280-0950
(480)990-0682 (800)456-0682 Fax:(480)990-3390
E-mail: micasa@primenet.com
Web: www.azres.com

Mi Casa Su Casa, "My House (is) Your House," is a highly respected reservation service. Established in 1981 with listings throughout Arizona, the selection has grown to include New Mexico, Nevada, Utah, California, Mexico and Spain. A wide variety of hand-picked bed and breakfasts, ranches, cottages, villas, and even furnished apartments provide delightful accommodations that meet short- or long-term needs. Choose an historic Southwest adobe hacienda, a posh planetarium or an elegant inn. The personal attention and knowledgeable assistance ensures a pleasant stay.

$50-350. MC, VISA, AX, DC, DS, TC. Breakfast included in rates. Types of meals: Gourmet bkfst, cont plus, cont, early coffee/tea and snacks/refreshments. Beds: KQDT. TV, phone, ceiling fan and fireplace in room. Central air. VCR, fax, copier, spa, swimming, bicycles, tennis, library and pet boarding on premises. Handicap access. Weddings, small meetings, family reunions and seminars hosted. Amusement parks, antiquing, art galleries, beaches, bicycling, fishing, golf, hiking, horseback riding, live theater, museums, downhill skiing, cross-country skiing, sporting events, tennis, water sports and wineries nearby.

Publicity: *Daily News, Arizona Republic, Washington Post, Boston Globe, Minneapolis Tribune, Sacramento Bee* and *Rocky Mountain News.*

Tucson J7

Casa Alegre B&B

316 E Speedway Blvd
Tucson, AZ 85705-7429
(520)628-1800 (800)628-5654 Fax:(520)792-1880
E-mail: alegre123@aol.com
Web: www.casaalegreinn.com

Circa 1915. Innkeeper Phyllis Florek decorated the interior of this Craftsman-style home with artifacts reflecting the history of Tucson, including Native American pieces and antique mining tools. Wake to the aroma of fresh coffee and join other guests as you enjoy fresh muffins, fruit and other breakfast treats, such as  succulent cheese pancakes with raspberry preserves. The Arizona sitting room opens onto serene gardens, a pool and a Jacuzzi. An abundance of shopping and sightseeing is found nearby.

Historic Interest: The innkeeper serves on the board of directors of the West University Historic District and is full of information about historic sites and the history of the area.

Innkeeper(s): Phyllis Florek. $70-135. MC, VISA, DS, PC, TC. TAC10. 7 rooms with PB, 1 with FP and 1 conference room. Breakfast included in rates. Types of meals: Gourmet bkfst. Beds: KQ. TV and ceiling fan in room. VCR, fax, spa and swimming on premises. Weddings, small meetings and family reunions hosted. Antiquing, restaurants, live theater, parks, shopping and sporting events nearby.

Publicity: *Arizona Daily Star, Travel Holiday and Arizona Times.*

"An oasis of comfort in Central Tucson."

Catalina Park Inn

309 E 1st St
Tucson, AZ 85705-7821
(520)792-4541 (800)792-4885
E-mail: info@catalinaparkinn.com
Web: www.catalinaparkinn.com

Circa 1927. Classical music sets the mood as guests linger in front of a roaring fireplace at this inn, located in Tucson's West University Historic District. The main house offers a spacious

room with mountain views and two rooms with private porches that overlook Catalina Park. Colorful rooms are furnished with antiques and other unique pieces. A bounty of patterned linens, down pillows and comforters dress the beds. The inn is just a few blocks from the University of Arizona and the eclectic shops and restaurants that line Fourth Avenue.

Historic Interest: The San Javier Mission is 10 miles away as is a national park. Closer attractions include the El Presidio and Barrio Historic Districts only a mile away, and the Arizona Historical Society Museum, which is only five blocks from the inn.

Innkeeper(s): Paul Richard & Mark Hall. $114-144. MC, VISA, AX, DS, TC. TAC10. 6 rooms with PB. Breakfast and afternoon tea included in rates. Types of meals: Gourmet bkfst and early coffee/tea. Beds: Q. Cable TV, phone, robes, hair dryers and iron and ironing board in room. Air conditioning. Fax on premises. Antiquing, live theater, parks and sporting events nearby.

Publicity: *Dateline Downtown, Arizona Daily Star, Arizona Illustrated, Tucson Weekly, Tucson Guide Quarterly, Reno Air Approach Magazine. and Arizona Illustrated.*

"Our stay here in your beautiful home was wonderful and your hospitality was unsurpassed. Can't wait to return."

Copper Bell B&B

25 N Westmoreland Ave
Tucson, AZ 85745-2966
(520)629-9229 Fax:(520)629-9229

Circa 1907. Uniquely constructed of lava stone, this home includes an old copper bell brought from a German church. Stained-glass windows, quilts and antiques decorate the rooms. Some guest rooms are in a separate guest house, which also offers a honeymoon suite. Breakfast features items such as German bread, waffles, egg dishes and fresh-squeezed orange juice from the orange tree in the garden.

Innkeeper(s): Gertrude Eich. $79-95. PC, TC. 6 rooms, 4 with PB and 1 suite. Breakfast included in rates. Types of meals: Full bkfst, early coffee/tea and afternoon tea. EP. Beds: QD. Cable TV and ceiling fan in room. Fax and copier on premises. Weddings and family reunions hosted. German and French spoken. Antiquing, golf, parks, shopping and tennis nearby.

The El Presidio B&B Inn

297 N Main Ave
Tucson, AZ 85701-8219
(520)623-6151 (800)349-6151
Web: www.bbonline.com/az/elpresidio

Circa 1886. The cobblestone courtyards, fountains, and lush gardens surrounding El Presidio are filled with an old-world Southwestern ambiance. The inn is comprised of a Victorian-Territorial adobe built around a traditional zaguan, or large central hall, plus separate suites in the former carriage house and gate house. Innkeeper Patti Toci conducted a 10-year, award-

winning restoration of this inn. Rooms are immaculate, romantic and richly appointed. Gourmet breakfasts are served in a dining room that overlooks the courtyard. Beverages are served throughout the day. This inn was voted the "Best B&B in Tucson" for 1995-96 and the "Best B&B in Southern Arizona" for 1998. Restaurants and museums are nearby.

Innkeeper(s): Patti Toci. $95-125. TAC10. 3 suites, 1 with FP and 1 conference room. Breakfast included in rates. Beds: Q. Restaurants, museums, live theater and shopping nearby.

Publicity: *Gourmet, Travel & Leisure, Glamour, Tucson Home & Garden, Arizona Highways and Innsider.*

"Thank you again for providing such a completely perfect, pampering, relaxing, delicious, gorgeous vacation 'home' for us."

Elysian Grove Market Bed

400 W Simpson St
Tucson, AZ 85701-2283
(520)628-1522
Web: www.bbonline.com/az/elysiangrove

Circa 1920. Originally built as a corner market, this adobe home has been transformed with charm. It is located next to the downtown arts district, in an Historic Barrio. Wood floors, 14-foot ceilings, skylights and wood-burning fireplaces are accented by folk art and antique furnishings from the Southwest and Mexico. Guest bedrooms boast tribal rugs and comfortable vintage beds. Two rooms have French doors that open onto the garden of cactus, flowers and fountains, and two others have been converted from what were the wine cellars. Mexican tile and pull chain toilets add to the ambiance in the bathrooms. The fully equipped kitchen was once the meat locker. Music is played during a tasty breakfast that includes pan dulce (a pastry), cheese, fresh fruit and beverages.

Historic Interest: Ancient Indian ruins, cliff dwellings, Arizona Sonoran Desert Museum, 18th-century mission.

Innkeeper(s): Deborah Lachapelle. $85. 4 rooms. Breakfast included in rates. Types of meals: Cont plus. Fully equipped kitchen and fireplaces on premises. Weddings hosted. Bicycling, golf, hiking and shopping nearby.

Hacienda del Sol Guest Ranch Resort

5601 N Hacienda del Sol
Tucson, AZ 85718-5129
(520)299-1501 (800)728-6514 Fax:(520)299-5554
E-mail: hdelsol@azstarnet.com
Web: www.haciendadelsol.com

Circa 1929. What began as a finishing school for girls became a hot spot for Hollywood royalty. In its earlier days as an exclusive resort, Hacienda del Sol hosted the likes of Clark Gable,

Katharine Hepburn and Spencer Tracy. Located in the Catalina foothills with panoramic views of mountains, city lights and spectacular Arizona sunrises and sunsets. The lush grounds have a front courtyard with a fountain. Rooms are decorated to look like a Spanish hacienda with Southwestern accents. Or stay in one of the three private casitas. There is a pool and a tennis court, and horseback riding is available year-round. An award-winning restaurant on the premises features regional cuisine. On Sunday a special brunch is available.

$75-345. MC, VISA, AX, PC, TC. TAC10. 30 rooms with PB, 7 with FP, 5 suites, 3 cottages and 2 conference rooms. Breakfast included in rates. Types of meals: Cont and gourmet dinner. Beds: KQ. Cable TV and phone in room. Air conditioning. Fax, copier, spa, swimming, stables, tennis and library on premises. Weddings, small meetings, family reunions and seminars hosted. Antiquing, golf, hiking, 60 miles to Mexican border, parks, shopping and sporting events nearby.

Publicity: *New York Times, Travel and Leisure, Esquire, Gourmet, Bon Appetit, National Geographic Traveler, Chicago Magazine and Wine Spectator.*

La Posada Del Valle

1640 N Campbell Ave
Tucson, AZ 85719-4313
(520)795-3840 (888)404-7113 Fax:(520)795-3840
E-mail: laposadabandbinn@hotmail.com

Circa 1929. This Southwestern adobe has 18-inch-thick walls, which wraparound to form a courtyard. Ornamental orange trees and lush gardens surround the secluded property. All the

rooms have private entrances and open to the patio or overlook the courtyard and fountain. Furnishings include antiques and period pieces from the '20s and '30s. Breakfasts are served in a dining room that offers a

view of the Catalina Mountains. The University of Arizona, University Medical Center, shops, dining and more all are within walking distance.

Innkeeper(s): Karin Dennen. $75-149. MC, VISA, PC, TC. TAC7. 5 rooms with PB and 1 cottage. Breakfast included in rates. Types of meals: Gourmet bkfst. Beds: KQT. Cable TV in room. Air conditioning. VCR, fax, library, off street parking and fireplace in living room on premises. Weddings, small meetings and family reunions hosted. German spoken. Antiquing, live theater, parks, shopping, downhill skiing and sporting events nearby.

Publicity: *Gourmet, Los Angeles Times, USA Today, Travel & Leisure, Channel 4 Television and Sunset.*

The Peppertrees B&B Inn

724 E University Blvd
Tucson, AZ 85719-5045
(520)622-7167 (800)348-5763
E-mail: pepperinn@gci-net.com
Web: www.peppertreesinn.com

Circa 1905. Inside this historic home, you will find English antiques inherited from the innkeeper's family. There is a patio filled with flowers and a fountain. Each of two newly built

Southwestern-style guest houses features two bedrooms, two bathrooms, a kitchen, laundry and a private patio. Blue-corn pecan pancakes and Scottish shortbread are house specialties. Peppertrees is within walking distance to the University

of Arizona, shops, theaters, museums and restaurants.

Innkeeper(s): Marjorie G. Martin. $88-185. MC, VISA, DS, PC, TC. 3 rooms with PB, 1 cottage and 2 guest houses. Breakfast included in rates. Types of meals: Gourmet bkfst. EP. Beds: KQT. TV, phone, ceiling fan and microwaves in room. Air conditioning. Weddings, small meetings and family reunions hosted. Hiking, live theater, museums, shopping and sporting events nearby.

Publicity: *Tucson Guide, Travel Age West, Country, Tucson Homes & Gardens, Sunset, Tucson Lifestyle, Arizona Highways and Arizona Business Magazine.*

"We have not yet stopped telling our friends what a wonderful experience we shared at your lovely home."

The Royal Elizabeth Bed & Breakfast Inn

204 S Scott Ave
Tucson, AZ 85701
(520)670-9022 (877)670-9022 Fax:(520)629-9710
E-mail: inn@royalelizabeth.com

Circa 1878. Listed in the National Register, this adobe mansion was built with a Victorian design. Imparting a casual elegance, the inn's original trim and millwork are enhanced by modern renovations. Refreshments in the parlor are enjoyed throughout the day. Some of the spacious guest bedrooms can be made into adjoining suites. They feature fine linens, period antiques, Jacuzzi tubs, dish network TV, VCR and a refrigerator concealing armoire. Gourmet breakfast is served in the grand dining hall. A pool and spa offer refreshment. Historic downtown has much to offer only a few blocks away.

Historic Interest: St. Augustine Cathedral (1 block), San Xavier Mission (6 miles), Presidio/Barrio (4 blocks).

Innkeeper(s): Jack Nance & Robert Ogburn. $90-180. MC, VISA, AX, DS, PC, TC. 6 rooms with PB and 4 suites. Breakfast, afternoon tea and snacks/refreshments included in rates. Types of meals: Gourmet bkfst, veg bkfst and early coffee/tea. Beds: QD. Cable TV, phone, ceiling fan and VCR in room. Central air. Fax, copier, spa, swimming and library on premises. Small meetings, family reunions and seminars hosted. Some Spanish spoken. Antiquing, art galleries, bicycling, golf, hiking, horseback riding, live theater, museums, parks, shopping, sporting events, tennis and wineries nearby.

Publicity: *HGTV.*

Arkansas

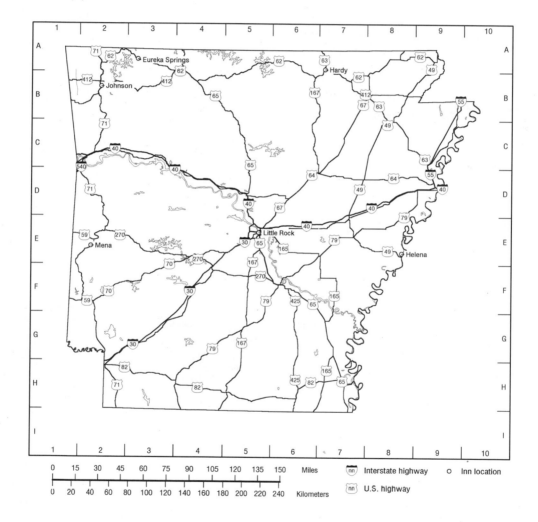

0   15   30   45   60   75   90   105   120   135   150   Miles

0   20   40   60   80   100   120   140   160   180   200   220   240   Kilometers

(nn) Interstate highway   o   Inn location

(nn) U.S. highway

Eureka Springs   A3

11 Singleton House B&B

11 Singleton St
Eureka Springs, AR 72632-3026
(501)253-9111 (800)833-3394
E-mail: info@singletonhouse.com

Circa 1895. This pink Queen Anne Victorian is highlighted
with bird-shaped exterior brackets. Guest rooms are whimsically decorated with an eclectic collection of folk art and antique
family treasures. Some rooms offer two beds.
Breakfast is served on the balcony
overlooking colorful wildflower
gardens, lily-filled goldfish pond
and scenic wooded view. Created
by a local artist, the garden features a unique birdhouse collection
and winding stone paths. Guests

may stroll one block down a wooded footpath to shops and
restaurants, ride the trolley through town or enjoy a horse and
carriage ride through the historic district.

Innkeeper(s): Barbara Gavron. $65-125. MC, VISA, AX, DS, PC, TC. TAC10.
4 rooms with PB, 1 suite and 1 cottage. Breakfast and afternoon tea included in rates. Types of meals: Full bkfst, veg bkfst and early coffee/tea. Beds:
QDT. Cable TV and most with ceiling fans in room. Air conditioning. Fax,
copier and library on premises. Family reunions hosted. Some Spanish spoken. Antiquing, Passion Play, dinner train and music shows nearby.
Publicity: *Arkansas Gazette, The Houston Post and The Wichita Eagle-Beacon.*

*"All the many little surprises were so much fun. We enjoyed the quiet-
ness of sitting on the porch and walking through your garden."*

1881 Crescent Cottage Inn

211 Spring St
Eureka Springs, AR 72632-3153
(501)253-6022 (800)223-3246 Fax:(501)253-6234
E-mail: raphael@ipa.net

Circa 1881. This Victorian inn was home to the first governor
of Arkansas after the Civil War. Two long verandas overlook a
breathtaking valley and two mountain ranges. The home is
graced by a beautiful tower, spindlework and coffered ceilings.
A huge arch joins the dining and living rooms, which, like the
rest of the inn, are filled with
antiques. All of the guest rooms feature Jacuzzi tubs, and two have a
fireplace. The inn is situated on the
quiet, residential street at the beginning of the historic loop. A five-
minute walk into town takes guests
past limestone cliffs, tall maple
trees, gardens and refreshing springs. Try a ride on a horse carriage or on the steam engine train that departs nearby.

Historic Interest: Excluding a few new areas, the entire town of Eureka
Springs is a National Historic District and filled with beautiful homes, buildings and shops to explore. The Crescent Cottage is listed in the National
Register and designated as a state and city landmark.
Innkeeper(s): Ray & Elise Dilfield. $99-145. MC, VISA, DS, PC, TC. TAC10.
4 rooms with PB, 2 with FP and 1 suite. Breakfast included in rates. Types
of meals: Full bkfst and early coffee/tea. Beds: Q. Cable TV, ceiling fan, VCR
and two with private Jacuzzi in room. Air conditioning. Fax and copier on
premises. Weddings and family reunions hosted. Amusement parks,
antiquing, fishing, golf, hiking, boating, live theater, parks, shopping, sporting
events, tennis and water sports nearby.
Publicity: *Country Home, Country Inn, Ft.Lauderdale News, Minneapolis
Tribune, "Victorian Express" and "America's Painted Ladies".*

1884 Bridgeford House B&B

263 Spring St
Eureka Springs, AR 72632-3154
(501)253-7853 (888)567-2422 Fax:(501)253-5497
E-mail: henry@bridgefordhouse.com

Circa 1884. Victorian charm abounds at this Queen Anne-
Eastlake-style home, located in the heart of the historic district.
The Southern hospitality begins upon arrival as guests are treated
to homemade pecan pralines. Fresh
flowers add extra romance to rooms
that include a variety of amenities.
Several rooms include double
jacuzzis, a fireplace and decks.
Gourmet breakfasts are served on antique
china and silver. The bed & breakfast is just a
few blocks from gift boutiques, antique shops,
spas, restaurants and much more. The innkeepers offer discount-
ed rates for those who wish to enjoy a spa treatment.

Historic Interest: Pea Ridge National Park (30 min.), War Eagle Mill &
Cavern (30 min.), North Arkansas Railway (1 block).
Innkeeper(s): Henry & Linda Thornton. $95-200. MC, VISA, AX, DS. 5 rooms
with PB. Breakfast included in rates. Types of meals: Full bkfst, early
coffee/tea, snacks/refreshments and room service. Beds: KQ. Cable TV and
fans in room. Air conditioning. VCR on premises. Weddings, small meetings,
family reunions and seminars hosted. Antiquing, fishing, golf, live theater,
shopping and water sports nearby.
Publicity: *Times Echo Flashlight, Arkansas National Tour Guide and
Country Almanac.*

"You have created an enchanting respite for weary people."

5 Ojo Inn B&B

5 Ojo St
Eureka Springs, AR 72632-3220
(501)253-6734 (800)656-6734 Fax:(501)253-8831
E-mail: romance@5ojo.com
Web: www.5ojo.com

Circa 1900. Guests at 5 Ojo choose between four restored
buildings ranging in vintage from an 1891 Victorian to a 1940s
cottage. Rooms are decorated with antiques but include modern amenities such as refrigerators and coffee makers. Several
rooms include whirlpool tubs and
fireplaces. The Carriage House
Cottage and the Anniversary Suite
are ideal places for honeymooners
or those celebrating a special
occasion. Among its romantic
amenities, the Anniversary Suite
includes a private porch with a swing. Gourmet breakfasts are
served in the Sweet House's dining room, but private dining
can be arranged. Eureka Springs with its 63-65 springs, has
been a sought after spa town for more than a century.

Innkeeper(s): Paula Kirby Adkins. $72-139. MC, VISA, AX, DS, PC, TC.
TAC10. 10 rooms with PB, 6 with FP, 2 suites and 1 cottage. Breakfast
included in rates. Types of meals: Gourmet bkfst. Beds: QT. Cable TV, ceiling
fan and whirlpool tubs in room. Air conditioning. VCR, fax, spa and library on
premises. Weddings, small meetings and family reunions hosted. Antiquing,
art galleries, fishing, golf, massage therapy, Victorian village, live theater,
parks, shopping, sporting events and water sports nearby.
Publicity: *Arkansas Democrat Gazette, Southern Living and Country Inns.*

The Arbour Glen B&B & Guesthouse

7 Lema St
Eureka Springs, AR 72632-3217
(501)253-9010 (800)515-4536
E-mail: arbglen@ipa.net

Circa 1879. One might say romance is in the air at Arbour
Glen. Guest rooms are decorated in Victorian style with

antiques, handmade quilts, luxurious linens and fresh flowers, which create a warm, intimate atmosphere. Some rooms also have double Jacuzzi tubs. There are wraparound verandas to enjoy, and from the porch swing, guests can take in a view of woods and the town's historic district. Gourmet breakfasts are served on the veranda on tables set with china and silver.
Innkeeper(s): The Roses. $95-135. MC, VISA, AX, DS, PC, TC. TAC10. 5 rooms with PB, 3 with FP, 2 suites and 1 cottage. Breakfast included in rates. Types of meals: Full bkfst. Beds: Q. Cable TV, ceiling fan and VCR in room. Air conditioning. Weddings and family reunions hosted. Antiquing, fishing, golf, live theater, parks, shopping, sporting events and water sports nearby.
Publicity: *Country Heart and Traditional Country Christmas.*

Arsenic & Old Lace B&B Inn

60 Hillside Ave
Eureka Springs, AR 72632-3133
(501)253-5454 (800)243-5223 Fax:(501)253-2246
E-mail: ArsenicOldLaceBB@aol.com

Circa 1992. This bed & breakfast is a meticulous reproduction of Queen Anne Victorian style, and it offers five guest rooms decorated with antique Victorian furnishings. Popular with

honeymooners, the guest rooms offer whirlpool tubs, balconies and fireplaces. The inn's gardens complement its attractive exterior, which includes a wraparound veranda and stone wall. Its location in the historic district makes it an excellent starting point for a sightseeing stroll or shopping.
Innkeeper(s): Debbie & Jens Hansen. $140-195. MC, VISA, DS, TC. 5 rooms with PB, 5 with FP. Breakfast and snacks/refreshments included in rates. Types of meals: Gourmet bkfst. Beds: KQ. Cable TV, ceiling fan, VCR, private patios, robes and five with Jacuzzi in room. Air conditioning. Video library on premises. Weddings, small meetings and family reunions hosted. Antiquing, fishing, golf, music festivals, car festivals, Passion Play, live theater, parks, shopping, tennis and water sports nearby.
Publicity: *Gail Greco's Romance of Country Inns, Houston Chronicle, Oklahoma Living. and KLSM-TV.*
"It was well worth the 1,000 miles we traveled to share your home for a short while...thanks for a four-star vacation."

Cliff Cottage Inn - Luxury B&B Suites & Cottages

Heart of Historic Downtown
Eureka Springs, AR 72632
(479)253-7409 (800)799-7409
E-mail: cliffctg@aol.com
Web: www.cliffcottage.com

Circa 1880. In the heart of historic downtown, this Painted Lady Eastlake Victorian is listed in the National Register. Accommodations also are available in a Victorian replica called The Place Next Door. Guest suites feature a mini refrigerator stocked with champagne and beverages, a double Jacuzzi and private decks. There are two historic cottages with hot tubs and champagne or white wine; breakfast delivery is optional. Picnic lunches and sunset dinner cruises are offered aboard a 24-foot pontoon boat, which explores the area's romantic coves. Enjoy golf and tennis privileges at Holiday Island, only five miles away. The inn is the recipient of the "Garden of the Season" award.
Innkeeper(s): Sandra CH Smith. $155-195. MC, VISA, PC. TAC10. 6 rooms, 4

suites and 2 cottages. Types of meals: Gourmet bkfst, early coffee/tea, gourmet lunch and picnic lunch. Beds: KQ. Cable TV, ceiling fan, VCR, fire-places and Jacuzzi's in room. Air conditioning. Library and art gallery on premises. Weddings, small meetings, family reunions and seminars hosted. French, Spanish and German spoken. Amusement parks, antiquing, fishing, golf, live theater, parks, shopping, tennis and water sports nearby. Pets allowed: small dogs only, $30 charge.
Publicity: *Arkansas Democrat Gazette, Country Inns, Modern Bride and Southern Living.*

The Heartstone Inn & Cottages

35 King's Hwy
Eureka Springs, AR 72632-3534
(501)253-8916 (800)494-4921 Fax:(501)253-5361
E-mail: heartinn@ipa.net
Web: www.heartstoneinn.com

Circa 1903. A white picket fence leads to this spacious Victorian inn and its pink and cobalt blue wraparound porch filled with potted geraniums and Boston ferns. Located on the Eureka Springs historic loop the inn offers English country

antiques, private entrances and pretty linens. Private Jacuzzis, refrigerators and VCRs are available. Pamper yourself in the inn's massage therapy studio. Walk to shops, restaurants and galleries or hop on the trolley to enjoy all the pleasures of the town. Golf privileges at a private club are extended to guests. The New York Times praised the inn's cuisine as the "Best Breakfast in the Ozarks."
Historic Interest: Pea Ridge Civil War Battle Ground (20 miles), War Eagle Mill (20 miles).
Innkeeper(s): Rick & Cheri Rojek. $75-139. MC, VISA, AX, DS, PC, TC. TAC10. 12 rooms with PB, 2 with FP, 3 suites and 2 cottages. Breakfast and snacks/refreshments included in rates. Types of meals: Gourmet bkfst. Beds: KQ. Cable TV, ceiling fan, VCR, fireplace and Jacuzzi in room. Air conditioning. Fax, copier, spa, massage therapy and gift shop on premises. Weddings and family reunions hosted. Amusement parks, antiquing, art galleries, bicycling, canoeing/kayaking, fishing, golf, hiking, horseback riding, restaurants, live theater, parks and shopping nearby.
Publicity: *Innsider, Arkansas Times, New York Times, Arkansas Gazette, Southern Living, Country Home, Country Inns and USA Today.*
"Extraordinary! Best breakfasts anywhere!"

Ridgeway House B&B

28 Ridgeway Ave
Eureka Springs, AR 72632-3025
(501)253-6618 (877)501-2501
E-mail: rheureka@ipa.net
Web: www.ridgewayhouse.com

Circa 1908. Declared a stress-free environment, this renovated two-story, white Colonial Revival in the historic district has four columns, original woodwork and a spiral staircase going

between the first- and second-floor verandas. Tastefully decorated guest bedrooms and suites are furnished with antiques and offer access to a veranda or deck overlooking the Ozark Mountains. Some boast a Jacuzzi, parlor, kitchen, cable TV and VCR. Keith's breakfasts are so satisfying, lunch won't be needed. An afternoon dessert is also prepared, and hot and cold beverages always are available.
Innkeeper(s): Keith & Gayla Hubbard. $99-159. MC, VISA, DS, PC, TC. 5 rooms with PB, 1 with FP and 2 suites. Breakfast, afternoon tea and snacks/refreshments included in rates. Types of meals: Gourmet bkfst and early coffee/tea. Beds: KQ. Cable TV, ceiling fan and VCR in room. Central

air. Fax, copier and library on premises. Small meetings hosted. Antiquing, art galleries, beaches, bicycling, canoeing/kayaking, fishing, golf, hiking, horseback riding, live theater, museums and shopping nearby.
Publicity: *Tour of Homes.*

"True southern hospitality at its best."

The Piedmont House B&B

165 Spring St
Eureka Springs, AR 72632-3151
(501)253-9258 (800)253-9258
E-mail: piedmont@ipa.net
Web: www.eureka-usa.com/piedmont

Circa 1880. An original guest book from the inn's days as a tourist home is a cherished item here. The Piedmont offers the best views of Christ of the Ozarks and is listed in the National Register. The guest rooms are decorated with antiques and include private exits that lead to the two stories of wraparound verandas where swings and rockers await. For guests booking a two-night, weekend stay, the innkeepers offer a complimentary moonlight dinner on Friday nights. Private parking.
Historic Interest: In National Register.
Innkeeper(s): Kathy & Vince DiMayo. $79-135. MC, VISA, AX. 10 rooms, 9 with PB and 1 suite. Types of meals: Full bkfst and early coffee/tea. Beds: KQ. Ceiling fan and antique furnishings in room. Air conditioning. Refreshments available on premises. Weddings, small meetings, family reunions and seminars hosted. Amusement parks, antiquing, lakes, caves, live theater and shopping nearby.
Publicity: *Arkansas Times, USA Today, Tulsa People and Edmond Monthly.*
"Wonderful atmosphere and your personalities are exactly in sync with the surroundings."

Sleepy Hollow Inn

92 S Main
Eureka Springs, AR 72632
(501)253-5561 Fax:(501)253-9837
E-mail: sleepyhollowbnb@aol.com
Web: hometown.aol.com/sleepyhollowbnb/page/index.html
Circa 1904. Ideal for honeymooners or those in search of privacy, this three-story Victorian cottage with gingerbread trim provides a romantic retreat. Fine attention to detail has been given to the inn's elegant decor. Guest bedrooms and a luxuri-

ous main suite encompass all of the second floor, and a third-story guest bedroom boasts a view of impressive limestone cliffs. For the ultimate in intimacy and seclusion, the entire cottage is available to one or two couples at a time, offering the freedom to relax and make this a vacation home away from home. Soak in the antique clawfoot tub or snuggle up on the porch swing. Fresh-baked pastries and other treats await in the spacious kitchen. Red bud trees give shade to the peaceful garden setting across the street from a historical museum. Chilled champagne and wedding packages are available.
Historic Interest: Table Rock Lake (5 miles), Beaver Lake and White River in the Ozark Mountains.
Innkeeper(s): Jan. $129. MC, VISA, DS, PC. 2 rooms and 1 suite. Types of meals: Cont; early coffee/tea and snacks/refreshments. Beds: QD. Cable TV, phone, ceiling fan and VCR in room. Air conditioning. Private parking on premises. Antiquing, fishing, golf, vintage train rides, live theater, museums, parks, shopping and water sports nearby.
Publicity: *Bestfares.com Magazine.*

"Truly a delightful experience. The love and care going into this journey back in time is impressive."

Hardy   A7

The Olde Stonehouse B&B Inn

511 Main St
Hardy, AR 72542-9034
(870)856-2983 (800)514-2983 Fax:(870)856-4036
E-mail: oldestonehouse@centurytel.net
Web: www.hardy-stonehouse.com

Circa 1928. The stone fireplace gracing the comfortable living room of this former banker's home is set with fossils and unusual stones, including an Arkansas diamond. Lace table-cloths, china and silver make breakfast a special occasion. Each

room is decorated to keep the authentic feel of the Roaring '20s. The bedrooms have antiques and ceiling fans. Aunt Jenny's room boasts a clawfoot tub and a white iron bed, while Aunt Bette's room is filled with Victorian-era furniture.
Spring River is only one block away and offers canoeing, boating and fishing. Old Hardy Town caters to antique and craft lovers. The innkeepers offer "Secret Suites," located in a nearby historic home. These romantic suites offer plenty of amenities, including a Jacuzzi for two. Breakfasts in a basket are delivered to the door each morning. The home is listed in the National Register. Murder-mystery weekends, romance packages, golf, canoeing and fly-fishing are available.
Historic Interest: Olde Hardy Town 19th-Century commercial buildings (2 blocks), Old Court House and Jail (2 blocks), Railroad Station/Museum at Mammoth Springs (18 miles), vintage car museum.
Innkeeper(s): Peggy Volland. $79-135. MC, VISA, AX, DS, PC, TC. TAC10. 6 rooms with PB and 2 suites. Breakfast and snacks/refreshments included in rates. Types of meals: Full bkfst, early coffee/tea and picnic lunch. Beds: QD. Ceiling fan in room. Air conditioning. VCR, fax, copier, library, guest refrigerator, coffee service and phones on premises. Small meetings hosted. Antiquing, fishing, museums, fly fishing with guide available, murder mystery weekends, live theater, parks, shopping and water sports nearby.
Publicity: *Memphis Commercial Appeal, Jonesboro Sun, Vacations, Southern Living, Arkansas at Home, Democrat Gazette and Midwest Living.*
"For many years we had heard about 'Southern Hospitality' but never thought it could be this good. It was the best!"

Helena   E8

Edwardian Inn

317 S Biscoe
Helena, AR 72342
(870)338-9155 Fax:(870)338-4215

Circa 1904. In his book Life on the Mississippi, Mark Twain wrote, "Helena occupies one of the prettiest situations on the river." William Short, cotton broker and speculator, agreed and built his stately home here. The Edwardian Inn boasts a large rotunda and two verandas wrapping around both sides of the house. Inside are wood carpets and floor designs imported from Germany that are composed of 36

pieces of different woods arranged in octagon shapes. Polished-oak paneling and woodwork are set off with a Victorian-era decor.
Innkeeper(s): John Crow. $70-100. MC, VISA, AX, DC, CB, DS, PC, TC. TAC10. 12 rooms with PB, 3 suites and 1 conference room. Breakfast included in rates. Types of meals: Full bkfst, early coffee/tea and snacks/refreshments. Beds: KQD. Cable TV, phone and ceiling fan in room. Air conditioning. VCR, fax, copier and library on premises. Handicap access. Weddings, small meetings, family reunions and seminars hosted. Antiquing,

fishing, golf, live theater, parks and shopping nearby.
Publicity: *Arkansas Times, Dallas Morning News, Southern Living, Country Inns* and *USA.*

"The Edwardian Inn envelopes you with wonderful feelings, smells and thoughts of the Victorian era."

Johnson   B2

Johnson House B&B

5371 S 48th St, PO Box 431
Johnson, AR 72741-0431
(501)756-1095

Circa 1882. This elegant country home on the rolling hillside was built with handmade bricks and offers authentic Ozark hospitality. Gracefully restored and filled with wonderful antiques, the inn's peaceful ambiance enhances a pleasant stay. Relax fireside in the front parlor that boasts an intricately painted ceiling. Large guest bedrooms reflect an old-fashioned

charm and comfort. The window-filled dining room is perfect for lingering over a mouth-watering breakfast. Stroll the gardens, browse the Smokehouse Antique Shop, play a game of horseshoes or croquet. Enjoy an Arkansas sunset from the upstairs veranda.

Innkeeper(s): Mary K. Carothers. $105. Types of meals: Full bkfst and picnic lunch. Turndown service & ceiling fan in room. Air conditioning. VCR, croquet, horseshoes & shuffle on premises. Weddings, small meetings, family reunions and seminars hosted. Antiquing, live theater, shopping & sporting events nearby.

Little Rock   E5

The Empress of Little Rock

2120 Louisiana St
Little Rock, AR 72206-1522
(501)374-7966 (877)374-7966 Fax:(501)375-4537
E-mail: hostess@theEmpress.com
Web: www.theEmpress.com

Circa 1888. Day lilies, peonies and iris accent the old-fashioned gardens of this elaborate, three-story Queen Anne Victorian. A grand center hall opens to a double staircase, lit by

a stained-glass skylight. The 7,500 square feet include a secret card room at the top of the tower. The Hornibrook Room features a magnificent Renaissance Revival bedroom set with a high canopy. The Tower Room mini-suite has a king-size Austrian bed. The two-course gourmet breakfast is served in the dining room "before the Queen" by candlelight.

Historic Interest: At one time it was the first women's college in the state. Arkansas territorial restoration, old state house, state capitol, Villa Marre, MacArthur's birthplace (1-2 miles), Toltec Indian Mounds (5 miles).
Innkeeper(s): Sharon Welch-Blair & Robert Blair. $125-195. MC, VISA, AX, PC. TAC10. 5 rooms with PB, 3 with FP, 3 suites and 1 conference room. Breakfast and snacks/refreshments included in rates. Types of meals: Gourmet bkfst, veg bkfst, cont, early coffee/tea and picnic lunch. Beds: KQT. Cable TV, phone, turndown service, ceiling fan, luxury robes, complimentary liquors and antique fireplace with gas logs in room. Central air. VCR, fax, copier and library on premises. Weddings, small meetings and family reunions hosted. Antiquing, art galleries, bicycling, fishing, golf, hiking, horseback riding, tours, high tea, bridal brunches, portraits, live theater, museums, parks, shopping, sporting events, tennis and water sports nearby.
Publicity: *National Geographic Traveler, Nation's Business, Victorian Home, Victorian Decorator & Life Styles, Southern Living* and *Home and Garden Television.*

"Staying at the Empress of Little Rock was a 'dream come true!' We've read about and admired it for years. It was definitely a trip to a more gracious time—one that we should all try to implement more in our daily lives."

Rosemont Luxury Bed & Breakfast

515 W 15th St
Little Rock, AR 72202
(501)374-7456 Fax:(501)374-2111
E-mail: rosemontbb@aol.com
Web: www.rosemontoflittlerock.com

Circa 1880. Downtown in the Governor's Mansion Historic District, this two-story Italianate with rose-toned roof and exterior was built by a gentleman farmer as an in town estate. The Victorian decor is comfortable, with well-placed period antiques and lace curtains. Relax in the parlor and borrow books, audio tapes and videos from the library. A self-serve guest fridge and pantry with microwave are stocked with refreshments, snacks and beverages. The business center offers anytime access to modern technology. Choose from spacious guest bedrooms featuring Mission and Eastlake furnishings, four-poster and iron feather beds. Some have a fireplace and Jacuzzi or clawfoot tub. A suite boasts an enclosed porch. Breakfast

may include blueberry pancakes with maple-flavored bacon served in the formal dining room or on a tray brought to the room. Enjoy a private retreat on the front porch with wicker rockers and a swing.

Historic Interest: Old State House (1/2 mile), MacArthur Park Military Museum (1/2 mile).
Innkeeper(s): Susan Payne Maddox. $85-115. MC, VISA, AX, PC, TC. TAC10. 5 rooms with PB, 2 with FP. Breakfast and snacks/refreshments included in rates. Types of meals: Gourmet bkfst, veg bkfst and early coffee/tea. Beds: KQ. Cable TV, phone, ceiling fan, VCR, data ports, fireplace, luxurious robes, hair dryer and iron & ironing board in room. Central air. Fax, copier, library, old-fashioned front porch with swing, rockers and wicker chairs and secluded garden on premises. Weddings, small meetings, family reunions and seminars hosted. Antiquing, art galleries, golf, live theater, museums, parks, shopping and sporting events nearby.

Mena   E2

Willowbrook

1047 Polk 42
Mena, AR 71953
(501)783-8683 (800)305-9240 Fax:(419)781-9908
E-mail: macmahon@arknasas.net
Web: www.greatstays.com/sear1007.html

Circa 1910. Snuggled in the foothills of Ouachita Mountains sits this stone cottage with ivy-covered gates, a bay window, gabled roof and sculptured chimney. The perfect blend of Victorian and English country cottage decor is enhanced by knotty pine walls, an original fireplace in the living room and assorted collections showcased in the dining area. The guest bedrooms are private hideaways, one with a jetted tub. The Rose Room boasts a triple corner window with a view of the hillside and stream. Ten acres of landscaped flower gardens, woods, a waterfall and brook offer a peaceful stay. Relax in the sunroom or in the hot tub on the patio.

Historic Interest: Wilhelmina Inn and Mountain Park (14 miles), Lake Ouachita (80 miles).
Innkeeper(s): Carolyn & Dr. Tom MacMahon. $95. TAC5. 2 rooms, 1 with PB. Types of meals: Cont. Beds: Q. Phone, ceiling fan, VCR, fireplace & jet tub in bath in room. Air conditioning. Spa on premises. Antiquing, bicycling, canoeing/kayaking, fishing, golf, hiking, live theater, parks, shopping & tennis nearby.

California

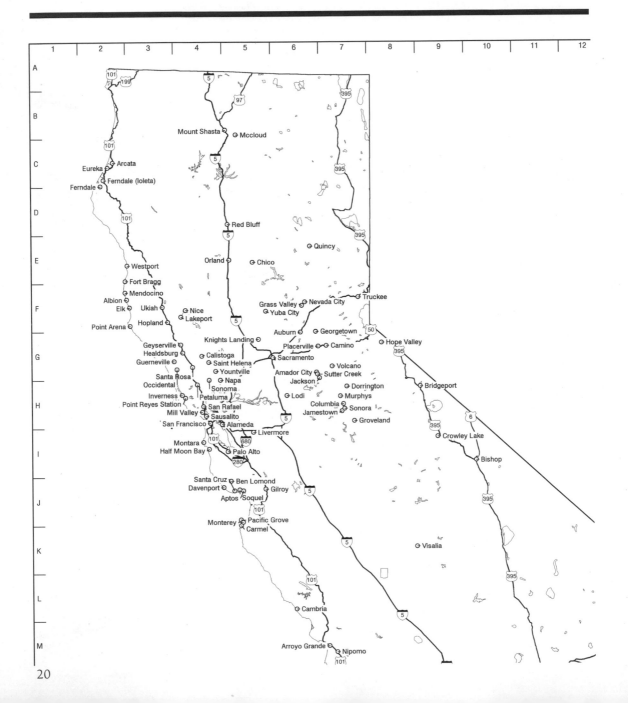

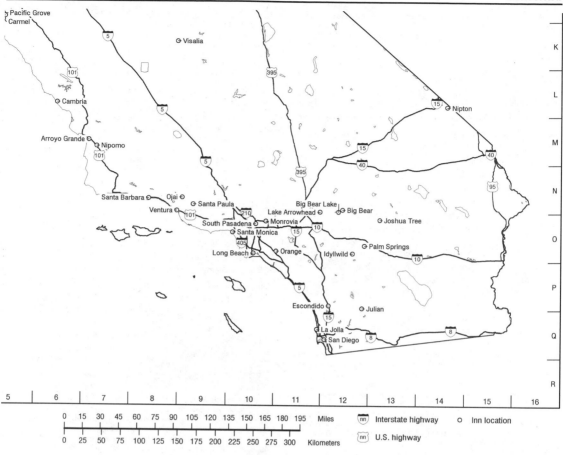

| | 5 | 6 | 7 | 8 | 9 | 10 | 11 | 12 | 13 | 14 | 15 | 16 |

| 0 15 30 45 60 75 90 105 120 135 150 165 180 195 Miles |
| 0 25 50 75 100 125 150 175 200 225 250 275 300 Kilometers |

[nn] Interstate highway   o   Inn location
{nn} U.S. highway

Alameda   H4

Garratt Mansion

900 Union St
Alameda, CA 94501-4143
(510)521-4779 Fax:(510)521-6796
E-mail: garrattm@pacbell.net
Web: www.garrattmansion.com

Circa 1893. This handsome, 27-room Colonial Revival mansion
was built for industrialist W.T. Garratt. It features walnut and
oak paneling, crystal windows and ornate-manteled fireplaces.
The staircase rises three stories with hundreds of gleaming
Jacobean turned balusters. A set of stained-glass windows encircles a bay at the stairwell landing. The elegance of the mansion
is matched by the warmth of its proprietress, Betty Gladden.

Historic Interest: Unique architecture in neighborhood.

Innkeeper(s): Royce & Betty Gladden. $95-175. MC, VISA, AX, DC, PC, TC.
TAC10. 8 rooms, 6 with PB, 1 with FP, 2 suites and 1 conference room.
Breakfast and snacks/refreshments included in rates. Types of meals: Full
bkfst and early coffee/tea. Beds: QDT. TV, phone and ceiling fan in room.
VCR, fax and library on premises. Weddings and small meetings hosted.
Antiquing, live theater, parks, sporting events and water sports nearby.

Publicity: *Alameda Times Star, Denver Post, Contra Costa Times and New
York Times.*

*"I can't wait to return as I found an exception to the saying, 'there's
no place like home.'"*

Albion   F2

Fensalden Inn

33810 Navarro Ridge Rd
Albion, CA 95410-0099
(707)937-4042 (800)959-3850
E-mail: info@fensalden.com
Web: www.fensalden.com

Circa 1860. Originally a stagecoach station, Fensalden looks
out over the Pacific Ocean as it has for more than 100 years.
The Tavern Room has witnessed many a rowdy scene, and if
you look closely you can see bullet holes in the original redwood ceiling. The inn provides
20 acres for walks, whale-watching, viewing deer and bicycling.
Relax with wine and hors d'oeuvres in the evening.

Innkeeper(s): Lyn Hamby. $125-225.
MC, VISA. TAC10. 8 rooms with PB, 8

21

with FP, 3 suites, 1 cottage and 2 conference rooms. Breakfast included in rates. Types of meals: Full bkfst. Beds: Q. The Bungalow is a cottage with a Jacuzzi tub in room. Handicap access. Weddings, small meetings, family reunions and seminars hosted. Antiquing, fishing, live theater, parks, shopping and water sports nearby.

Publicity: *Sunset, Focus, Peninsula and Country Inns.*

"Closest feeling to heaven on Earth."

Amador City　　　　　　　　　G7

Mine House Inn

PO Box 245
Amador City, CA 95601-0245
(209)267-5900 (800)646-3473
E-mail: minehse@cdepot.net
Web: www.minehouseinn.com

Circa 1870. Mine House Inn was headquarters for one of the most profitable gold mines in the mother lode of 1853, known as the Keystone Mine. Each room in this inn is named for its original function. All are furnished with authentic 19th-century antiques. Rooms include the Vault, Bookkeeping, Directors, Mill Grinding and Assay rooms. Over $24 million of gold was processed into gold bars in the Retort Room. The acre of land surrounding the inn is shaded by 200-year-old oaks and pines. Just steps away is the historic downtown of Amador City with shops and fine restaurants. Within easy driving distance are the towns of Volcano and Columbia.

Historic Interest: Abandoned gold mines, Keystone mine and ruins are across the highway. Knight Foundry in Sutter Creek is two miles away. It is the last operational water-powered foundry in U.S.

Innkeeper(s): Allen & Rose Mendy. $95-245. MC, VISA, AX, DS. 13 rooms, 6 with PB and 5 suites. Breakfast included in rates. Types of meals: Full bkfst and gourmet dinner. Beds: KQ. Some rooms have fireplaces and suites are in adjacent 1930s guest house and have Jacuzzi tubs for two in room. Air conditioning. Swimming, outdoor spa in enclosed gazebo and inn limousine for wine country tours on premises. Family reunions hosted. Antiquing, fishing, live theater, shopping, downhill skiing, cross-country skiing, water sports and wineries nearby.

Publicity: *Fun Times, LA Times and HGTV restore America.*

"We enjoyed the nostalgia and the decor and the challenge of trying to crack the safe."

Aptos　　　　　　　　　　　J5

Historic Sand Rock Farm

6901 Freedom Blvd
Aptos, CA 95003
(831)688-8005 Fax:(831)688-8025
E-mail: staff@sandrockfarm.com
Web: www.sandrockfarm.com

Circa 1890. Cradled in the foothills, this Arts and Crafts country estate sits on 10 acres of spectacular gardens, fountains and woodland. Built as one of the region's first wineries, the ivy-covered ruins are located near the giant saw that milled the redwood trees onsite for the home's frame and finished woodwork. Lovingly restored with hand-printed wallpaper, vintage lighting and antique furnishings, this bed & breakfast offers gracious hospitality. The well-appointed guest bedrooms and suites feature down comforters for comfort and Internet connections for convenience. Indulge your senses with the culinary talent of renown chef Lynn Sheehan. Lounge on the deck under a moss-covered heritage oak or on the rose garden hammock.

Historic Interest: Roaring Camp Railroad (3 miles), Historical School House (1 mile).

Innkeeper(s): Kristin Sheehan; Chef Proprietor Lynn Sheehan. $155-225. MC, VISA, AX, PC, TC. 5 rooms with PB and 3 suites. Breakfast included in rates. Types of meals: Gourmet bkfst, cont plus, early coffee/tea, gourmet lunch, picnic lunch, afternoon tea, snacks/refreshments, gourmet dinner and room service. Beds: KQT. Cable TV, phone, turndown service, VCR, down comforters, Jacuzzi tubs, antiques and sitting areas in room. Fax, spa, library and world-class chef on premises. Weddings, small meetings, family reunions and seminars hosted. French spoken. Amusement parks, antiquing, art galleries, beaches, bicycling, canoeing/kayaking, fishing, golf, hiking, horseback riding, specialty fruit, Herb and Mushroom growers, Monterey Bay Aquarium, spa/massage, fine dining, live theater, museums, parks, shopping, tennis, water sports and wineries nearby.

Publicity: *San Francisco Downtown, Home and Garden, Metro Santa Cruz, New York Times, Travel and Leisure, San Francisco Chronicle, Los Angeles Times, Via Magazine, Travel Holiday Magazine, Metro San Jose and Santa Cruz Sentinel.*

Mangels House

570 Aptos Creek Rd
Aptos, CA 95003
(831)688-7982
E-mail: mangels@cruzio.com
Web: www.innaccess.com/mangels

Circa 1886. Claus Mangels made his fortune in sugar beets and built this house in the style of a Southern mansion. The

inn, with its encircling veranda, stands on four acres of lawns and orchards. It is bounded by the Forest of Nisene Marks, 10,000 acres of redwood trees, creeks and trails. Monterey Bay is three-quarters of a mile away.

Historic Interest: Santa Cruz Mission (6 miles).

Innkeeper(s): Jacqueline Fisher. $135-175. MC, VISA. 6 rooms with PB, 1 with FP and 1 conference room. Breakfast included in rates. Types of meals: Full bkfst and early coffee/tea. Beds: KQT. Refrigerator and phone available on premises. Small meetings, family reunions and seminars hosted. Antiquing, golf, whale watching, elephant seals, live theater, water sports and wineries nearby.

Publicity: *Inn Serv and Innviews.*

"Compliments on the lovely atmosphere. We look forward to sharing our discovery with friends and returning with them."

Arcata　　　　　　　　　　　C2

Hotel Arcata

708 9th St
Arcata, CA 95521-6206
(707)826-0217 (800)344-1221 Fax:(707)826-1737
E-mail: info@hotelarcata.com

Circa 1915. This historic landmark hotel is a fine example of Beaux Arts-style architecture. Several rooms overlook Arcata's downtown plaza, which is just outside the front door. A variety of rooms are available, each decorated in turn-of-the-century style. All rooms include pedestal sinks and clawfoot tubs. The hotel offers a full-service, renown Japanese restaurant, offering excellent cuisine, and there are many other fine restaurants within walking distance. Guests also enjoy free use of a nearby full-scale health club. The starting point of Arcata's architectural homes tour is within walking distance of the hotel.

Innkeeper(s): Virgil Moorehead. $115-125. MC, VISA, AX, DC, CB, DS, TC. 31 rooms with PB, 7 suites and 1 conference room. Breakfast included in rates. Types of meals: Cont, lunch, dinner and room service. Beds: KQT. Cable TV and phone in room. Fax, copier and free health club privileges on premises. Handicap access. Weddings, small meetings, family reunions and seminars hosted. State parks, beaches, redwoods, rivers, theater nearby, parks and shopping nearby.

Arroyo Grande   M7

House of Another Tyme B&B

227 Le Point St
Arroyo Grande, CA 93420
(805)489-6313

Circa 1916. An old tree swing sways gently in the breeze in the garden of this grey and white shingled home. A Koi pond, gazebo and a variety of finches add to the garden's interest.

There's a stone fireplace and French doors in the living room. Guest rooms feature antiques and comfortable beds. The house is one block from antique shops and restaurants, and nearby is San Luis Obispo and Santa Maria with live theatre. Ask the innkeepers to help you find the swinging bridge.

Innkeeper(s): Jack & Judy. $100. MC, VISA, DS. 3 rooms with PB. Breakfast and afternoon tea included in rates. Types of meals: Country bkfst and early coffee/tea. Beds: Q. Antiquing, art galleries, beaches, fishing, golf, hiking, horseback riding, live theater, museums, parks, shopping and wineries nearby.

Auburn   G6

Powers Mansion Inn

164 Cleveland Ave
Auburn, CA 95603-4801
(530)885-1166 Fax:(530)885-1386
E-mail: powerinn@westsierra.net

Circa 1898. This elegant Victorian mansion was built by Harold Power with the proceeds from his gold mine. Many prominent people, including engineer Herbert Hoover, visited here. The parlor and the second floor halls contain notes and memorabilia concerning its history. The luxury of the inn is typified by the honeymoon suite, which has a heart-shaped whirlpool tub and a fireplace at the foot of the brass bed.

Innkeeper(s): Arno & Jean Lejnieks. $89-169. MC, VISA, AX. TAC10. 13 rooms with PB, 2 with FP and 1 conference room. Types of meals: Full bkfst. Beds: Q. TV in room.

Publicity: *Sierra Heritage Magazine.*

"The rooms are so relaxing and the breakfast is fantastic."

Ben Lomond   J5

Chateau Des Fleurs

7995 Highway 9
Ben Lomond, CA 95005-9715
(408)336-8943 (800)291-9966
E-mail: laura@chateaudesfleurs.com
Web: www.chateaudesfleurs.com

Circa 1879. Once the home of the Bartlett pear family, this house offers gables, porches and gardens. The Rose Room has an antique clawfoot tub. A private deck is part of the Orchid

Room, which features wicker furnishings and orchid watercolors. Breakfast is in the formal dining room and includes entrees such as cheese blintzes and egg dishes. In the early evening wine and hors d'oeuvres are served in the Gallery.

Innkeeper(s): Lee & Laura Jonas. $110-145. MC, VISA, DS, PC, TC. 3 rooms with PB, 2 with FP and 1 suite. Breakfast included in rates. Types of meals: Full bkfst and early coffee/tea. Beds: KQ. Ceiling fan in room. Air conditioning. VCR, fax and copier on premises. Handicap access. Weddings, small meetings, family reunions and seminars hosted. German spoken. Amusement parks, antiquing, fishing, golf, live theater, parks, shopping, sporting events, tennis and water sports nearby.

Fairview Manor

245 Fairview Ave
Ben Lomond, CA 95005-9347
(831)336-3355 (800)553-8840
E-mail: fairviewbandb@aol.com

Circa 1924. The Santa Cruz Mountains serve as a backdrop at Fairview Manor, set on more than two acres of woods and lush grounds. The tranquil, parklike setting includes little paths that wind through the grounds and you'll find lily ponds and the San Lorenzo River. The home rests on the former site of the Ben Lomond Hotel, which was destroyed by fire in 1906. A prominent San Francisco attorney chose this spot to build his summer home, and the manor  stayed in the family until the 1980s when the current innkeepers purchased it. The cozy guest rooms are decorated with antiques. The innkeepers serve a full, country breakfast in a dining room that overlooks the river. Restaurants and the beach are just minutes away.

Innkeeper(s): Nancy Glasson. $119-129. MC, VISA. 5 rooms with PB and 1 conference room. Breakfast and snacks/refreshments included in rates. Types of meals: Full bkfst. Beds: KQ. Sitting area in room. Refrigerator-complimentary drinks on premises. Handicap access. Weddings, small meetings, family reunions and seminars hosted. Antiquing, fishing, parks, shopping and water sports nearby.

Big Bear   N12

Gold Mountain Manor Historic B&B

1117 Anita, PO Box 2027
Big Bear, CA 92314
(909)585-6997 (800)509-2604 Fax:(909)585-0327
E-mail: info@goldmountainmanor.com
Web: www.goldmountainmanor.com

Circa 1928. This spectacular log mansion was once a hideaway for the rich and famous. Eight fireplaces provide a roaring fire in each room in fall and winter. The Lucky Baldwin Room offers a hearth made from stones gathered in the famous Lucky Baldwin mine nearby. In the Clark Gable room is the fireplace Gable and Carole Lombard enjoyed on their honeymoon.

Gourmet country breakfasts and afternoon hors d'oeuvres are served. In addition to the guest rooms, there are home rentals.

Historic Interest: Small Historic Museum in Big Bear City (1 mile) and gold mining.

Innkeeper(s): Trish & Jim Gordon. $125-225. MC, VISA, DS. TAC10. 7 rooms with PB, 7 with FP, 2 suites and 1 conference room. Afternoon tea and snacks/refreshments included in rates. Types of meals: Gourmet bkfst and early coffee/tea. Beds: Q. Ceiling fan and jacuzzi in suites in room. VCR, fax, spa, bicycles, library and pool table on premises. Weddings, small meetings, family reunions and seminars hosted. Spanish spoken. Fishing, hiking/forest, parks, downhill skiing, cross-country skiing, sporting events and water sports nearby.

Publicity: *Best Places to Kiss, Fifty Most Romantic Places and Kenny G holiday album cover.*

"A majestic experience! In this magnificent house, history comes alive!"

Big Bear Lake N12

Knickerbocker Mansion Country Inn

869 Knickerbocker Rd
Big Bear Lake, CA 92315
(909)878-9190 (877)423-1180 Fax:(909)878-4248
E-mail: knickmail@aol.com
Web: www.knickerbockermansion.com

Circa 1920. The inn is one of the few vertically designed log structures in the United States. The inn was built of local lumber by Bill Knickerbocker, the first dam keeper of Big Bear. The inn includes two historic buildings set on two-and-a-half wooded acres, backing to a national

forest. Although, the inn offers a secluded setting, the village of Big Bear Lake is within walking distance. The village offers shopping, restaurants, fishing, hiking, mountain biking and excellent downhill skiing.

Innkeeper(s): Stanley Miller & Thomas Bicanic. $110-280. MC, VISA, AX, DS. TAC10. 9 rooms with PB, 2 suites and 1 conference room. Types of meals: Full bkfst, early coffee/tea and snacks/refreshments. Beds: KQ. TV, phone and VCR in room. Weddings, small meetings, family reunions and seminars hosted. Antiquing, bicycling, fishing, hiking, live theater, shopping, downhill skiing and cross-country skiing nearby.

Publicity: *Los Angeles Magazine and Yellow Brick Road.*

"Best breakfast I ever had in a setting of rustic elegance, a quiet atmosphere and personal attention from the innkeepers. The moment you arrive you will realize the Knickerbocker is a very special place."

Bishop I9

The Matlick House

1313 Rpwan Ln
Bishop, CA 93514-1937
(760)873-3133 (800)898-3133
E-mail: matlickb@gte.net
Web: www.thesierraweb.com/lodging/matlickhouse

Circa 1906. This gray and white home with a double veranda was built by Alan Matlick, one of the area's pioneers. The spacious parlor features an antique recliner, original cherry-wood fireplace and quilted settee in the Lenna room. Guests will enjoy the home's views of both the Sierra Nevadas and the White Mountains. A hearty American breakfast with eggs, bacon and homemade biscuits is served in the dining room. The Eastern Sierras provide a wealth of activities, year-round catch-and-release fly fishing is within 20 minutes from the home.

Historic Interest: Laws Museum is only three miles away. For an entertaining day trip, try Bodie Ghost Town, which is about 90 miles from the inn.

Innkeeper(s): Ray & Barbara Showalter. $65-85. MC, VISA, AX, DS, TC. TAC10. 5 rooms with PB. Breakfast included in rates. Types of meals: Full bkfst, country bkfst, early coffee/tea, lunch and snacks/refreshments. Beds: QT. Phone and ceiling fan in room. Air conditioning. VCR and fax on premises. Weddings, small meetings, family reunions and seminars hosted. Antiquing, art galleries, bicycling, fishing, golf, hiking, horseback riding, museums, parks, downhill skiing and cross-country skiing nearby.

Pets allowed: Small pet in downstairs bedroom only.

Publicity: *Inyo Register and Sunset.*

"Like sleeping on a nice pink cloud after our Rock Creek Horse drive."

Bridgeport H9

The Cain House

340 Main St
Bridgeport, CA 93517
(760)932-7040 (800)433-2246 Fax:(760)932-7419
E-mail: cainhouse@qnet.com

Circa 1920. The grandeur of the Eastern Sierra Mountains is the perfect setting for evening refreshments as the sun sets, turning the sky into a fiery, purple canvas. The innkeeper's

experiences while traveling around the world have influenced The Cain House's decor to give the inn a European elegance with a casual western atmosphere. Travelers can take a short drive to the ghost town of Bodie where 10,000 people once lived in this gold-mining community. Outdoor enthusiasts can find an abundance of activity at Lake Tahoe, which is an hour-and-a-half away.

Innkeeper(s): Chris & Marachal Gohlich. $90-135. MC, VISA, AX, DS, PC, TC. TAC10. 7 rooms with PB. Breakfast and snacks/refreshments included in rates. Types of meals: Full bkfst and early coffee/tea. Beds: KQ. Cable TV and phone in room. Air conditioning. Fax and copier on premises. Family reunions hosted. Fishing, parks, cross-country skiing, tennis and water sports nearby.

Publicity: *Los Angeles Times.*

Calistoga G4

Bear Flag Inn

2653 Foothill Blvd
Calistoga, CA 94515-1221
(707)942-5534 (800)670-2860 Fax:(707)942-8761

Circa 1900. The home's location boasts some interesting California history. The Bear Flag rebels were a group of American settlers who planned a takeover of California when it was under Mexican rule. Although, it was actually a declaration of war by the United States that eventually landed California in American hands, the state flag still resembles the flag created by these early rebels. As legend has it, the man who created one of the bear flags did so on this property. The inn rests on what was the homestead of John and Lovina Cyrus. Another interesting item is that Mrs. Cyrus was a member of the infamous Donner Party.

Innkeeper(s): Marge & Dennis McNay. $150-200. MC, VISA, DS, PC, TC. TAC5. 5 rooms with PB. Breakfast and snacks/refreshments included in rates. Types of meals: Full bkfst and early coffee/tea. Beds: Q. Cable TV, ceiling fan and VCR in room. Air conditioning. Fax, copier, spa and swimming pool on premises. Weddings and family reunions hosted. Antiquing, golf, hiking, parks, shopping, tennis and wineries nearby.

Pets allowed: With prior approval.

Publicity: *Sunset and Chronical.*

Calistoga Wayside Inn

1523 Foothill Blvd
Calistoga, CA 94515-1619
(707)942-0645 (800)845-3632 Fax:(707)942-4169
Web: www.calistogawaysideinn.com

Circa 1928. Lavish landscaping surrounds this mission-style inn. Enjoy the soothing sounds of fountains and a waterfall which cascades into a picturesque pond. Comfortable guest bedrooms continue the theme, decorated with garden motifs. Down comforters, robes and special soaps are a few of the thoughtful amenities. A full country breakfast is the perfect start to a day touring the popular Napa Valley. Enjoy wine and hors d'ouerves in the afternoon, and port and chocolates may be a bedtime treat. Walk to the famed spas, or the innkeepers can help plan wine-tasting tours and glider or hot-air balloon rides.

Innkeeper(s): Diane Byrne. $140-165. MC, VISA, AX, DS, PC, TC. TAC10. 3 rooms with PB. Breakfast included in rates. Types of meals: Full bkfst and early coffee/tea. Beds: KQ. Ceiling fan in room. Air conditioning. Fax and library on premises. Small meetings and family reunions hosted. Antiquing, spas, wineries, mud baths, glider planes, balloon rides, parks and shopping nearby.

"This was my first stay at a B&B and now, certainly the first of many."

The Elms B&B Inn

1300 Cedar St
Calistoga, CA 94515-1608
(707)942-9476 (888)399-ELMS Fax:(707)942-9479
E-mail: info@theelms.com
Web: www.theelms.com

Circa 1871. In the National Register of Historic Places, this white three-story Victorian has a French-style mansard roof and is located on a quiet street close to the main part of town. Romantic, antique-filled rooms have extras such as bathrobes, coffeemakers and chocolates. Down comforters, feather beds, fireplaces and whirlpools are featured. In the afternoon, wine and cheese are served.

Innkeeper(s): Alicia Sylvia. $135-245. MC, VISA, DS, PC, TC. TAC10. 7 rooms with PB, 6 with FP. Breakfast and snacks/refreshments included in rates. Types of meals: Gourmet bkfst. Beds: KQ. Cable TV, ceiling fan, VCR, most with hot tub and fireplace in room. Air conditioning. Hot tub and wine and cheese in the afternoon on premises. Handicap access. Weddings, small meetings and family reunions hosted. Spanish spoken. Antiquing, art galleries, canoeing/kayaking, golf, hiking, horseback riding, spas, museums, parks, shopping and wineries nearby.

Pets allowed: Dogs allowed only in rooms with prigvate entrances, call for further restrictions.

Fannys

1206 Spring St
Calistoga, CA 94515-1637
(707)942-9491 Fax:(707)942-4810
E-mail: deanna.higgins@att.net
Web: www.fannysnapavalley.com

Circa 1915. In a shingled Craftsman-cottage style, painted forest green and red, this inn offers an inviting shaded porch with swing, rockers and spots for dining. Inside, comfortable interiors include over-stuffed chairs, a fireplace, library and upstairs guest rooms with plank floors and window seats. The innkeeper, a former restaurateur, provides a full breakfast and knowledgeable touring suggestions.

Innkeeper(s): Deanna Higgins. $95-145. PC, TC. 2 rooms with PB. Breakfast included in rates. Types of meals: Full bkfst and country bkfst. Beds: Q. Ceiling fan in room. Air conditioning. Fax and library on premises. Weddings hosted. Antiquing, golf, winery tours & tasting, parks and shopping nearby.

Foothill House

3037 Foothill Blvd
Calistoga, CA 94515-1225
(707)942-6933 (800)942-6933 Fax:(707)942-5692
E-mail: gusgus@aol.com
Web: www.foothillhouse.com

Circa 1892. This country farmhouse overlooks the western foothills of Mount St. Helena. Graceful old California oaks and pockets of flowers greet guests. Each room features country antiques, a four-poster bed, a fireplace and a small refrigerator.

Breakfast is served in the sun room or is delivered personally to your room in a basket. Three rooms offer private Jacuzzi tubs.

Historic Interest: Old Faithful Geyser (1 mile), Petrified Forest (3 miles).

Innkeeper(s): Doris & Gus Beckert. $175-325. MC, VISA, AX, DS, PC, TC. TAC10. 4 suites, 4 with FP. Breakfast and snacks/refreshments included in rates. Types of meals: Gourmet bkfst and early coffee/tea. Beds: KQT. Cable TV, phone, turndown service, ceiling fan, VCR, robes, bottled water, coffee and tea in room. Air conditioning. Fax, copier and library on premises. Weddings, small meetings and family reunions hosted. Amusement parks, antiquing, fishing, wineries, balloon rides, glider port, health spas, parks, shopping and water sports nearby.

Publicity: *Sunset Magazine, San Francisco Examiner, Herald Examiner and Baltimore Sun.*

"Gourmet treats served in front of an open fire. Hospitality never for a moment flagged."

Scarlett's Country Inn

3918 Silverado Trl
Calistoga, CA 94515-9611
(707)942-6669 Fax:(707)942-6669
E-mail: scarletts@aol.com
Web: members.aol.com/scarletts

Circa 1900. Formerly a winter campground of the Wappo Indians, the property now includes a restored farmhouse. There are green lawns and country vistas of woodland and vineyards. Each room has a private entrance. Breakfast is often served beneath the apple trees or poolside.

Historic Interest: Old Bale Mill (2 miles), Beringer and Charles Krug Wineries (4 miles), Schramsberg Champagne Cellars (2 miles), Sharpstein Museum (4 miles), graveyard in Boothe State Park (2 miles).

Innkeeper(s): Scarlett Dwyer. $135-205. PC. TAC10. 3 rooms with PB, 1 with FP, 2 suites and 1 cottage. Breakfast and afternoon tea included in rates. Types of meals: Gourmet bkfst, early coffee/tea and room service. Beds: Q. TV, phone and turndown service in room. Air conditioning. Fax, copier and swimming on premises. Small meetings and family reunions hosted. Spanish spoken. Antiquing, fishing, ballooning, gliders, winetasting, parks, shopping and water sports nearby.

Publicity: *Daily News.*

"Wonderful, peaceful, serene."

Scott Courtyard

1443 2nd St
Calistoga, CA 94515-1419
(707)942-0948 (800)942-1515 Fax:(707)942-5102

Circa 1940. Reminiscent of a Mediterranean villa, this delightfully different inn is located in Napa Valley. Three two-room suites are available in the main house. The romantic ground-level Rose Suite has a private entrance and large sitting room

with fireplace. Next door, the adjoining Burgundy Suite is perfect for groups traveling together. The second-floor Palisades Suite boasts a four-poster bed and small balcony overlooking the pool. A full breakfast is served in the dining room, deck or garden with fresh-brewed coffee from a local roastery. Enjoy evening wine and cheese, and cold drinks all day. Explore the grounds' extensive gardens as well as fruit and nut trees including pear, peach, apple, olive and walnut. Local shops, wineries, spas and restaurants are a block away.

Innkeeper(s): Derek & Robin Werrett. $160-195. MC, VISA, AX, DS, PC. TAC10. 3 suites. Types of meals: Full bkfst. Beds: Q. Central heating, refrigerator, iron hair dryer, dressing gown and some with TV in room. Central air. Fax, copier, spa, swimming, library and internet connection on premises.
Publicity: *Sunset Magazine.*

Trailside Inn

4201 Silverado Trl
Calistoga, CA 94515-9605
(707)942-4106 Fax:(707)942-4702
E-mail: h.gray@.att.net
Web: www.trailsideinn.com

Circa 1932. This secluded valley farmhouse overlooks Three Palms Vineyard and the distant Sterling Winery. Each accommodation is a tastefully decorated suite with its own porch, private entrance, small kitchen, private bath and fireplace. Furnished with country antiques and old quilts, two suites have an extra bedroom to accommodate a family of four. House specialties are banana and blueberry breads, freshly baked and brought to your room. Complimentary wine and mineral water also are offered.

Historic Interest: Robert Louis Stevenson State Park (3 miles), Beringer Winery (4 miles), Calistoga (3 miles).
Innkeeper(s): Lani Gray. $165-185. MC, VISA, AX, DS. TAC10. 3 suites, 3 with FP. Breakfast included in rates. Types of meals: Cont plus. Beds: QDT. Complimentary wine in room. Swimming on premises.
Publicity: *San Francisco Examiner and Wine Country Review.*

"If Dorothy and Toto were to click their heals together they would end up at the Trailside Inn."

Cambria L6

Olallieberry Inn

2476 Main St
Cambria, CA 93428-3406
(888)927-3222 Fax:(805)927-0202
E-mail: olallieinn@olallieberry.com
Web: www.olallieberry.com

Circa 1873. This restored Greek Revival home features rooms decorated with fabrics and wall coverings and furnished with period antiques. Six of the guest rooms feature fireplaces.

Butterfly and herb gardens and a 118-year-old redwood grace the front yard. The cheery gathering room boasts a view of the Santa Rosa Creek. Full breakfast with fresh breads, fruits and a special entree start off the day, and wine and hors d'oeuvres are served in the afternoon. The inn is within walking distance to restaurants and shops.

Historic Interest: Hearst Castle is six miles from the inn.
Innkeeper(s): Marilyn & Larry Draper. $105-200. MC, VISA, AX, PC, TC. TAC10. 9 rooms with PB, 6 with FP and 1 suite. Breakfast and snacks/refreshments included in rates. Types of meals: Gourmet bkfst and early coffee/tea. Beds: KQ. Fireplace six rooms in room. Fax on premises. Handicap access. Weddings, small meetings, family reunions and seminars hosted. Antiquing, fishing, Hearst Castle, shopping, water sports and wineries nearby.
Publicity: *Los Angeles Times and Elmer Dills Radio Show.*

"Our retreat turned into relaxation, romance and pure Victorian delight."

The Squibb House

4063 Burton Dr
Cambria, CA 93428-3001
(805)927-9600 Fax:(805)927-9606

Circa 1877. A picket fence and large garden surround this Victorian inn with its Italianate and Gothic Revival architecture. Guests may relax in the main parlor, stroll the gardens or sit and rock on the porch. The home was built by a Civil War veteran and young school teacher. The downstairs once was used as a classroom while an addition was being made in the town's school. Each guest room has a fire stove.

Historic Interest: Hearst Castle is six miles away, and further attractions include the San Luis Obispo Mission and San Miguel Mission, both about 35 miles from the home.
Innkeeper(s): Lynn. $95-175. MC, VISA, PC, TC. TAC10. 5 rooms with PB, 5 with FP. Breakfast included in rates. Types of meals: Cont plus and cont. Beds: Q. Retail shop in historic 1885 carpentry shop on premises. Weddings and small meetings hosted. Antiquing, fishing, golf, Hearst Castle, wine tasting, galleries, parks and shopping nearby.
Publicity: *Cambrian.*

Camino G7

The Camino Hotel-Seven Mile House

4103 Carson Rd, PO Box 1197
Camino, CA 95709-1197
(530)644-7740 (800)200-7740 Fax:(530)647-1416
E-mail: inquire@caminohotel.com

Circa 1888. Once a barracks for the area's loggers, this inn now caters to visitors in the state's famed gold country. Just east of Placerville, historic Camino is on the Old Carson Wagon Trail in Apple Hill. Nine guest rooms are available, including the E.J. Barrett Room, a favorite with honeymooners. Other rooms feature names such as Pony Express, Stage Stop and Wagon Train. The family-oriented inn welcomes children, and a local

park offers a handy site for their recreational needs. Popular area activities include apple picking, antiquing, hot air ballooning, white-water rafting, hiking and wine tasting. The inn also offers a Self-Indulgence Package, on-site wine tasting and an in-house masseuse.

Innkeeper(s): Paula Nobert. $65-95. MC, VISA, AX, DS, TAC15. 9 rooms, 3 with PB and 1 conference room. Breakfast and snacks/refreshments included in rates. Types of meals: Full bkfst, early coffee/tea and picnic lunch. AP. Beds: QDT. Turndown service and coolers in room. Wine tasting room and two massage therapists on premises. Weddings, small meetings, family reunions and seminars hosted. Antiquing, fishing, wine tasting, white-water rafting, hot air ballooning, live theater, parks, shopping, downhill skiing, cross-country skiing and water sports nearby.

Publicity: *Better Homes & Gardens, Sunset and Sierra Heritage.*

Capitola-by-the-Sea   J5

Inn at Depot Hill

250 Monterey Ave
Capitola-by-the-Sea, CA 95010-3358
(831)462-3376 (800)572-2632 Fax:(831)462-3697
E-mail: lodging@innatdepothill.com
Web: www.innatdepothill.com

Circa 1901. Once a railroad depot, this inn offers rooms with themes to represent different parts of the world: a chic auberge in St. Tropez, a romantic French hideaway in Paris, an Italian coastal villa, a summer home on the coast of Holland and a traditional English garden room, to name a few. Most rooms have garden patios with hot tubs. The rooms have many amenities, including a fireplace, white marble bathrooms and featherbeds. Guests are greeted with fresh flowers in their room. Gourmet breakfast, tea, wine, hors d' oeuvres and dessert are offered daily.

Innkeeper(s): Tom Cole. $190-355. MC, VISA, AX, DS, TC. TAC10. 12 rooms with PB, 12 with FP, 4 suites and 1 conference room. Breakfast and snacks/refreshments included in rates. Beds: KQT. Cable TV, phone, turndown service and VCR in room. Fax and spa on premises. Handicap access. Small meetings, family reunions and seminars hosted. Amusement parks, antiquing, fishing, golf, live theater, parks, shopping and water sports nearby.

Publicity: *Country Inn, Santa Cruz Sentinel, McCalls, Choices & Vacation, San Jose Mercury News, Fresno & Sacramento Bee, San Francisco Focus, American Airline Flight, SF Examiner and Sunset Magazine.*

"The highlight of our honeymoon. Five stars in our book!"

Carmel   J5

Happy Landing Inn

PO Box 2619
Carmel, CA 93921-2619
(831)624-7917

Circa 1926. Built as a family retreat, this early Comstock-design inn has evolved into one of Carmel's most romantic places to stay. The Hansel-and-Gretel look is accentuated with a central garden and gazebo, pond and flagstone paths. There are cathedral ceilings and the rooms are filled with antiques. Breakfast is brought to your room.

Innkeeper(s): Robert Ballard and Dick Stewart. $95-185. MC, VISA, PC, TC. 7 rooms with PB, 3 with FP and 2 suites. Breakfast included in rates. Types of meals: Cont plus. Beds: KQD. Handicap access. Restaurants and beach and shopping nearby.

Publicity: *San Francisco Chronicle.*

"Just what the doctor ordered!"

Sandpiper Inn-by-the-Sea

2408 Bay View Ave
Carmel, CA 93923-9118
(831)624-6433 (800)633-6433 Fax:(831)624-5964
E-mail: sandpiper-inn@redshift.com

Circa 1929. Only a half block from miles of pristine coastline, this early California-style inn is set in a quiet residential neighborhood of million-dollar estates. There are 17 guest rooms, all

individually decorated in English and French antiques. Several offer fireplaces or ocean views. For a more intimate stay, guests can request one of the three cottage rooms. With its beautifully furnished interiors, the inn has been a favorite getaway spot for a host of famous people. An expanded continental buffet breakfast is served in the dining room. In the afternoon, guests are invited to enjoy tea or a glass of imported Amontillado sherry.

Innkeeper(s): John Henion & Audie Housman. $95-285. MC, VISA, AX, DS, PC, TC. TAC10. 17 rooms with PB, 3 with FP. Breakfast and afternoon tea included in rates. Types of meals: Cont plus and early coffee/tea. Beds: KQ. 6 with ocean view in room. Fax and 3 cottage rooms on premises. Antiquing, golf, live theater, parks, shopping, tennis and water sports nearby.

The Stonehouse Inn

PO Box 2939
Carmel, CA 93921
(831)624-4569 (800)748-6618

Circa 1906. This quaint Carmel country house boasts a stone exterior, made from beach rocks collected and hand shaped by local Indians at the turn of the century. The original owner, "Nana" Foster, was hostess to notable artists and writers from the San Francisco area, including Sinclair Lewis, Jack London and Lotta Crabtree. The romantic Jack London room features a dramatic gabled ceiling, a brass bed and a stunning view of the

ocean. Conveniently located, the inn is a short walk from Carmel Beach and two blocks from the village.

Innkeeper(s): Terri Navailles. $165-214. MC, VISA, AX, DS. 6 rooms. Breakfast included in rates. Types of meals: Full bkfst. Beds: KQDT. Weddings and family reunions hosted. Fishing, live theater, parks, shopping and water sports nearby.

Publicity: *Travel & Leisure and Country Living.*

"First time stay at a B&B — GREAT!"

Vagabond's House Inn

PO Box 2747, Dolores & 4th
Carmel, CA 93921-2747
(831)624-7738 (800)262-1262 Fax:(831)626-1243
E-mail: innkeeper@vagabondshouseinn.com
Web: www.vagabondshouseinn.com

Circa 1940. Shaded by the intertwined branches of two California live oaks, the stone-paved courtyard of the Vagabond's House sets the tone of this romantic retreat. The inn is comprised of a cluster of white stucco cottages built into a slope. Some include kitchens, but all feature a fireplace and an antique clock. In the morning, continental breakfast is delivered to you near the camellias or in the privacy of your room.

Historic Interest: Carmel Mission (2 miles), Robinson Jeffers' Tor House (1 mile).
Innkeeper(s): Dawn Dull. $115-205. MC, VISA, AX, PC, TC. TAC10. 11 rooms with PB, 9 with FP. Types of meals: Cont plus. Beds: KQD. Cable TV and phone in room. Fax and copier on premises. Weddings hosted. Spanish and Korean spoken. Antiquing, fishing, live theater, parks and shopping nearby.
Pets allowed: $20 per night - pet policy.
Publicity: *Diversion and Cat Fancy.*

"Charming & excellent accommodations and service. Very much in keeping with the character and ambiance of Carmel's historic setting."

Chico   E5

The Esplanade B&B
620 The Esplanade
Chico, CA 95926
(530)345-8084
E-mail: esplanade@now2000.com
Web: www.now2000.com/esplanade

Circa 1915. Appreciate the charm of a bygone era and the comfort of modern amenities at this remodeled Craftsman bungalow. Across the street from the landmark Bidwell Mansion, the inn is just a short walk to the park, Chico Museum, Chico State University or downtown. Guest bedrooms offer a variety of accommodations, all with fluffy down pillows. Each morning in the formal dining room a hearty breakfast is served. Enjoy an evening glass of wine served in the parlor or relax on the garden patio.
Innkeeper(s): Lois I. Kloss & George Fish. $75-95. MC, VISA, DS, TC. 5 rooms with PB. Breakfast, afternoon tea and snacks/refreshments included in rates. Types of meals: Full bkfst, early coffee/tea and room service. Beds: QD. Cable TV in room. Air conditioning. Weddings, small meetings, family reunions and seminars hosted. Antiquing, fishing, hospitals, live theater, parks, shopping, downhill skiing, cross-country skiing, sporting events and water sports nearby.

Pets allowed: with a deposit.

Columbia   H7

Columbia City Hotel & Restaurant
22768 Main St
Columbia, CA 95310
(209)532-1479 (800)532-1479 Fax:(209)532-7027
E-mail: inof@cityhotel.com

Circa 1856. Built in 1856 during the height of the Gold Rush Era, this two-story Victorian was known as the "What Cheer House." Now a state historical site, it has been authentically

restored by the State of California, and the state owns the hotel's antique furniture and fixtures. The hotel was listed in Sunset Magazine's February 2000 issue as one of the 24 best bed & breakfasts. No televisions or telephones intrude on the historic ambiance of the hotel's 10 guest rooms. Indoor plumbing is the only historical compromise. Each room has a half-bath, and showers are down the hall. The beautifully restored restaurant offers fine selections of French cuisine. The hotel hosts family reunions, meetings, and weddings. Inquire about the Getaway Lodging, Dinner and Theatre Package for two.
Innkeeper(s): Tom Bender. $105-125. MC, VISA, DS, PC, TC. TAC10. 10 rooms and 1 conference room. Breakfast included in rates. Types of meals: Cont plus, early coffee/tea and gourmet dinner. Beds: QDT. Central air. Weddings, small meetings, family reunions and seminars hosted. Antiquing, bicycling, fishing, golf, hiking, horseback riding, live theater, museums, parks, shopping, downhill skiing, cross-country skiing, tennis, water sports and wineries nearby.

Fallon Hotel
11175 Washington St
Columbia, CA 95310-1870
(209)532-1479 (800)532-1479 Fax:(208)532-7027
E-mail: info@cityhotel.com

Circa 1857. The Fallon Hotel, restored and operated by the State of California Parks and Recreation Department, still boasts the main-floor theater where productions are featured year-round. Original furnishings from the hotel's Gold-Rush days have been repaired, polished and reupholstered, including a fine Turkish loveseat in the parlor. Bradbury & Bradbury redesigned the nine wallpaper patterns featured. The best rooms are upstairs with balconies overlooking the town's four blocks of saloons, cash stores, an ice cream parlor, blacksmith shop and the stage coach that periodically rambles through town.
Innkeeper(s): Tom Bender. $60-125. MC, VISA, AX, DS, PC, TC. TAC10. 14 rooms, 1 with PB and 1 suite. Breakfast included in rates. Types of meals: Cont plus. Beds: DT. Handicap access. Antiquing, fishing, wine tasting, live theater, downhill skiing and water sports nearby.
Publicity: *Home & Garden, Innsider, Motorland and Sunset.*

"Excellent service."

Crowley Lake   I9

Rainbow Tarns B&B at Crowley Lake
HC 79 Box 55C
Crowley Lake, CA 93546-9702
(760)935-4556 (888)588-6269
E-mail: info@rainbowtarns.com
Web: www.rainbowtarns.com

Circa 1920. Just south of Mammoth Lakes, at an altitude of 7,000 feet, you'll find this secluded retreat amid three acres of ponds, open meadows and the High Sierra Mountains. Country-style here includes luxury touches, such as a double Jacuzzi tub, queen-size bed, down pillows, comforters and a skylight for stargazing. In the '50s, ponds on the property served as a "U-Catch-Em." Folks rented fishing poles and paid 10 cents an inch for the fish  they caught. Nearby Crowley Lake is still one of the best trout-fishing areas in California. Romantic country weddings are popular here. Guests are free to simply relax in the peaceful setting, but hiking, horseback riding and skiing all are available in the area. In the afternoons, guests are treated to snacks and wine.
Innkeeper(s): Brock & Diane Thoman. $90-140. PC. 3 rooms with PB. Breakfast included in rates. Types of meals: Full bkfst and early coffee/tea. Beds: QD. Handicap access.
Publicity: *Mammoth-Sierra, Bishop Vacation Planner, Eastern Sierra Fishing Guide, Sunset and Scenic 395.*

Davenport   J4

New Davenport B&B
31 Davenport Ave
Davenport, CA 95017
(831)425-1818 (800)870-1817 Fax:(831)423-1160
E-mail: inn@swanton.com

Circa 1906. Captain John Davenport came here to harvest the gray whales that pass close to shore during migration. The oldest building remaining originally was used as a public bath. It

later became a bar, restaurant and dance hall before conversion into a private home. Completely renovated, it now houses four of the inn's rooms. In addition to breakfast, guests also enjoy two complimentary drinks at the bar in the inn's restaurant.

Historic Interest: The Wilder Ranch State Park is five miles away. Davenport Jail, Giovvini Cheesehouse, Old Davenport Pier and the St. Vincent DePaul Catholic Church, built in 1902, are nearby.

Innkeeper(s): Bruce & Marcia McDougal. $99-155. MC, VISA, AX. 12 rooms with PB. Breakfast included in rates. Types of meals: Full bkfst, lunch and dinner. Beds: KQ.

Publicity: *Monterey Life, Travel & Leisure, Sacramento Bee and Peninsula Time Tribune.*

"*The warmth of the rooms, the people who work here and the ocean keeps us coming back year after year.*"

Dorrington

The Dorrington Hotel & Restaurant

3431 Hwy 4, PO Box 4307
Dorrington, CA 95223
(209)795-5800

Circa 1852. This historic hotel was built by Dorrington's town founders as a hotel and restaurant for those traveling through the area on stagecoach. More than a century later, guests still arrive for that purpose. Guest rooms are decorated in country style with antiques and brass beds topped with handmade quilts. A separate accommodation, "Cabin Sweet Cabin" offers a kitchenette, stone fireplace and whirlpool tub and may be rented apart from the bed and breakfast. The innkeepers want  their guests to have a relaxing stay, free from the modern world, so there are no televisions or phones in guest rooms. Continental fare in the mornings, and Northern Italian cuisine nightly in the restaurant. According to legend, the ghost of the hotel's former mistress sometimes walks the hallways.

Innkeeper(s): Bonnie Saville. $85-125. MC, VISA, DS, PC, TC. 5 rooms. Breakfast included in rates. Types of meals: Cont and early coffee/tea. Beds: Q. Weddings and small meetings hosted. Antiquing, fishing, live theater, parks, shopping, downhill skiing, cross-country skiing and water sports nearby.

Publicity: *Robert Conrads Series "Search and Rescue"*

"*The Dorrington has always existed in the dreams of all those out there that love romance.*"

Elk   F3

Elk Cove Inn

6300 S Hwy One
Elk, CA 95432
(707)877-3321 (800)275-2967 Fax:(707)877-1808
E-mail: elkcove@mcn.org
Web: www.elkcoveinn.com

Circa 1882. This mansard-style Victorian home was built as a guest house for lumber baron L. E. White. Operated as a full-service country inn for more than 35 years, Elk Cove Inn com-

mands a majestic view from atop a scenic bluff. There are four cabins and four new ocean-front luxury suites with large windows, fireplaces, spa tubs and balconies. There is also a new hot tub with a view of the ocean. Most rooms have a fireplace and an ocean view. Antiques, hand-embroidered linens and down comforters add to the amenities. Below the inn is an expansive driftwood-strewn beach. Gourmet breakfasts are served in the ocean-view dining room. Guests can enjoy cocktails, beer or wine in the ocean-front bar. Coffee makers with fresh ground coffee, teas, cider and hot chocolate are available in the rooms.

Historic Interest: Fort Ross original Russian settlement (1 hour away).

Innkeeper(s): Elaine Bryant. $128-328. MC, VISA, AX, DS, PC, TC. TAC10. 15 rooms with PB, 15 with FP, 4 suites and 4 cottages. Breakfast included in rates. Types of meals: Gourmet bkfst and early coffee/tea. Beds: KQ. VCR, fax, copier and library on premises. Handicap access. Small meetings and family reunions hosted. Spanish and Italian spoken. Art galleries, canoeing/kayaking, fishing, golf, hiking, horseback riding, whale watching, Skunk Train, bird watching, botanical garden, live theater, parks, shopping, tennis and water sports nearby.

Publicity: *National Geographic and Sunset.*

"*Quiet, peaceful, romantic, spiritual. This room, the inn, and the food are all what the doctor ordered.*"

The Harbor House Inn

5600 S Hwy 1
Elk, CA 95432
(707)877-3203 (800)720-7474 Fax:(707)877-3452
E-mail: harborhs@mcn.org
Web: www.theharborhouseinn.com

Circa 1916. The Harbor House Inn rests on a cliff overlooking Greenwood Cove and the Pacific Ocean. Built by a lumber company for executives visiting from the East, the inn is constructed entirely of redwood. Most of the antique-filled guest rooms include a fireplace, and some have decks. Guests are treated to both a full breakfast as well as an award winner four-course dinner. A path winds through the inn's gardens down to a private beach below.

Innkeeper(s): Elle Haynes. $225-450. MC, VISA, AX, PC, TC. 10 rooms with PB, 9 with FP, 4 cottages and 1 conference room. Breakfast and dinner included in rates. Types of meals: Gourmet bkfst. MAP. Beds: KQ. Fax and copier on premises. Weddings and seminars hosted. Antiquing, art galleries, beaches, bicycling, canoeing/kayaking, fishing, golf, hiking, horseback riding, live theater, museums, parks, shopping and wineries nearby.

Publicity: *Travel & Leisure, Sunset, Departures and Wine Spectator-Award of Excellence.*

"*The Harbor House has become the most luxurious Inn along this seaside coast.*"

Sandpiper House Inn

5520 S Hwy 1
Elk, CA 95432
(707)877-3587 (800)894-9016
Web: www.sandpiperhouse.com

Circa 1916. A garden path leads Sandpiper guests to a garden sitting area overlooking the California coast. The path continues onward to a private beach. The historic home was built by a local lumber company. The living room and dining room have virgin redwood paneling. Guest quarters are appointed to look like rooms in an English country home. Canopied beds, Oriental rugs and polished wood floors create a romantic ambiance. Rooms offer either ocean or countryside views, and four have a fireplace. Gourmet breakfasts are served on tables set with lace and fresh flowers. In-house massages also are available.

Innkeeper(s): Claire & Richard Melrose. $145-225. MC, VISA, AX, DS, PC, TC. 5 rooms with PB, 4 with FP and 2 suites. Breakfast and afternoon tea included in rates. Types of meals: Gourmet bkfst and early coffee/tea. MAP. Beds: KQ. In-house massage therapy on premises. Fishing, live theater, parks, shopping, water sports and wineries nearby.

Escondido P12

Zosa Gardens B&B
9381 W Lilac Rd
Escondido, CA 92026-4508
(760)723-9093 (800)711-8361 Fax:(760)723-3460
E-mail: zosamd@aol.com
Web: www.zosagardens.com

Circa 1940. Escondido, located in northern San Diego County, is the setting for this Spanish Hacienda. The home rests on 22 well-landscaped acres atop a bluff in the Monserate Mountains. Rooms bear flowery themes. Angel-lovers should try the Angel Room. The Master Suite includes a fireplace. In the evenings, gourmet tidbits are served with a selection of local wines. Billiards, hiking trails, a tennis court and massages are available. Golf courses, restaurants and other sites are just minutes away.

Innkeeper(s): Noli & Nena Zosa. $145-250. MC, VISA, AX, DC, CB, DS, PC, TC. TAC10. 15 rooms, 12 with PB, 3 with FP, 3 suites and 2 cabins. Breakfast and snacks/refreshments included in rates. Types of meals: Gourmet bkfst. Beds: KQ. Jacuzzi in room. Air conditioning. VCR, fax, copier, spa, swimming and tennis on premises. Handicap access. Weddings, small meetings, family reunions and seminars hosted. Spanish, Filipino, English and Italian spoken. Amusement parks, antiquing, fishing, golf, Buddhist Monastery, wineries, hot air balloons, live theater, parks, shopping, sporting events, tennis and water sports nearby.

Publicity: *On The Town Getaways.*

Eureka C2

A Weaver's Inn
1440 B St
Eureka, CA 95501-2215
(707)443-8119 (800)992-8119 Fax:(707)443-7923
E-mail: info@aweaversinn.com
Web: www.aweaversinn.com

Circa 1883. The stately Queen Anne Colonial Revival house features a spacious fenced garden, parlor and gracious dining room. All four guest rooms are furnished with down com-

forters, fresh flowers from the garden and are decorated to reflect the genteel elegance of the Victorian era. The Pamela Suite has a sitting room and fireplace, while the Marcia Room includes a two-person soaking tub in its private bath. The full breakfast often features home-grown treats from the garden.

Historic Interest: Redwood Forests (30 miles).

Innkeeper(s): Robin Montgomery, Bill De Mello & Lea L. Montgomery. $80-140. MC, VISA, AX, DC, DS. TAC10. 4 rooms, 3 with PB, 2 with FP and 1 suite. Breakfast included in rates. Types of meals: Gourmet bkfst. Beds: KQDT.

"It's a charming inn, warm ambiance and very gracious hosts!"

Abigail's 'Elegant Victorian Mansion' B&B Lodging
1406 C St
Eureka, CA 95501-1765
(707)444-3144 Fax:(707)442-3295
E-mail: info@eureka-california.com
Web: www.eureka-california.com

Circa 1888. One of Eureka's leading lumber barons built this picturesque home, a National Historic Landmark, from 1,000-year-old virgin redwood. Original wallpapers, wool carpets and antique light fixtures create a wonderfully authentic Victorian

ambiance. A tuxedoed butler and your hosts, decked in period attire, greet guests upon arrival. Croquet fields and Victorian gardens surround the inn. The hosts provide complimentary "horseless" carriage rides. The beds in the well-appointed guest quarters are topped with custom-made mattresses. There is a video library of vintage silent films. The inn has been host to many historic personalities, including actresses Lillie Langtry and Sarah Bernhardt, and many senators and representatives. The Pacific Ocean, beaches and the Giant Redwoods are only a few minutes away.

Historic Interest: Historic Fort Humboldt State Park, Redwood parks, Clark Historic Museum, Maritime Museum, historic "Old Town" (all within walking distance).

Innkeeper(s): Doug & Lily Vieyra. $85-215. MC, VISA. TAC10. 4 rooms, 2 with PB, 1 suite and 1 conference room. Breakfast, afternoon tea and snacks/refreshments included in rates. Types of meals: Full bkfst and early coffee/tea. EP. Beds: Q. Phone, turndown service, chocolate truffles and B&B guidebooks in room. Air conditioning. VCR, fax, copier, sauna, bicycles, library, croquet field, antique automobiles and horseless carriages on premises. Small meetings and seminars hosted. French, Dutch and German and English spoken. Antiquing, beaches, horseback riding, carriage rides, bay cruise, sailing, Giant Redwoods, live theater, tennis and water sports nearby.

Publicity: *New York Times, San Francisco Chronicle, Boston Globe, LA Times, Wall Street Journal, Outbreak and Jay Leno.*

The Carter House Victorians
301 L St
Eureka, CA 95501
(707)444-8062 (800)404-1390 Fax:(707)444-8067
E-mail: reserve@carterhouse.com
Web: www.carterhouse.com

Circa 1884. Superior hospitality is offered in these historic district inns sitting in Victorian Eureka. Perched alongside Humboldt Bay, the views are appealing. Luxurious guest bedrooms and suites feature fireplaces, antique furnishings and spas. Mornings begin with highly acclaimed breakfasts. Renown for regional, seasonal cuisine, the inn uses many ingredients grown in the garden or by local purveyors. Restaurant 301 boasts a coveted international Wine Spectator Grand Award, maintaining in its cellars an extensive selection of the world's finest vintages.

Historic Interest: Redwood forests, historic architecture, wildlife/bird sanctuary, Victorian Sawmill (all within 10 miles).

Innkeeper(s): Mark & Christi Carter. $95-495. MC, VISA, AX, DC, CB, DS, PC, TC. TAC10. 31 rooms with PB, 15 with FP, 15 suites, 1 cottage and 2 conference rooms. Breakfast and afternoon tea included in rates. Types of meals: Gourmet bkfst, cont plus, cont, early coffee/tea, snacks/refreshments, gourmet dinner and room service. MAP, AP, EP. Beds: KQDT. Cable TV, phone, turndown service and VCR in room. Air conditioning. Fax, copier and spa on premises. Handicap access. Small meetings, family reunions and seminars hosted. Italian, Spanish and French spoken. Antiquing, fishing, live theater, parks, shopping, sporting events and water sports nearby.

Publicity: *Sunset, U.S. News & World Report, Country Home, Country Living, Bon Appetit, San Francisco Focus, Northwest Palate, Gourmet, Art Culinare, San Francisco Chronicle, Wine Spectator, New York Times Magazine and Organic Gardening.*

Cornelius Daly Inn

1125 H St
Eureka, CA 95501-1844
(707)445-3638 (800)321-9656 Fax:(707)444-3636
E-mail: innkeeper@dalyinn.com
Web: www.dalyinn.com

Circa 1905. This 6,000-square-foot Colonial Revival mansion is located in the historic section of Eureka. The inn's gracious atmosphere includes four wood-burning fireplace and a third floor ballroom. Enjoy the romantic French bedroom suite with

dressing table, armoire and bedstead in Annie Murphey's Room. It offers a fireplace and a view over the Victorian garden and fish pond. Miss Martha's Room features Dutch, bleached-pine antiques and was once the nursery.
Breakfast is served fireside in the inn's formal dining room or in the breakfast parlor or garden patio. In the evenings, wine and cheese are served.

Historic Interest: The Carson Mansion, historic Old Town, Fort Humboldt and a Victorian sawmill are among the nearby historic attractions.

Innkeeper(s): Sue & Gene Clinesmith. $85-150. MC, VISA, AX, DS, PC, TC. TAC10. 5 rooms, 3 with PB, 1 with FP and 2 suites. Breakfast and snacks/refreshments included in rates. Types of meals: Gourmet bkfst and early coffee/tea. Beds: QT. Turndown service and antiques in room. VCR, fax, copier and library on premises. Weddings, small meetings, family reunions and seminars hosted. Antiquing, fishing, redwood park, ocean, live theater and shopping nearby.

"A genuine delight."

Old Town B&B Inn

1521 3rd St
Eureka, CA 95501-0710
(707)443-5235 (888)508-5235 Fax:(707)442-4390
E-mail: oldtownbandb@aol.com
Web: www.oldtownbnb.com

Circa 1871. This early Victorian was built in the Greek Revival style as the original family home of lumber baron William Carson. It was constructed of virgin redwood and Douglas fir and moved three blocks to its current location in 1905. Called a "Humboldt County jewel" by the local visitors' and convention bureau, the inn is the original bed & breakfast of the area and was opened in 1983. Spacious guest rooms offer heirloom quilts, antiques, and TV/VCRs. (There's a large movie collection to peruse.) In the morning, a variety of gourmet breakfasts are served under the light of oil lamps and beside a flickering fireplace.

Innkeeper(s): Steve & Karen Albright. $75-130. MC, VISA, DC, DS, PC, TC. 6 rooms with PB, 1 with FP. Breakfast included in rates. Types of meals: Gourmet bkfst, early coffee/tea and afternoon tea. Beds: KQT. TV, phone, VCR and much more in room. Family reunions hosted. Antiquing, beaches, bicycling, fishing, hiking, eco-tours, Redwood State National, live theater, museums, parks, sporting events and water sports nearby.

Publicity: *Times-Standard, Country, San Francisco Chronicle, Sunset, San Francisco Examiner and L.A.Times.*

"From the moment we opened the door, we knew we had chosen a special place to stay."

Ferndale   C2

Gingerbread Mansion Inn

PO Box 40, 400 Berding St
Ferndale, CA 95536-1380
(707)786-4000 (800)952-4136 Fax:(707)786-4381
E-mail: innkeeper@gingerbread-mansion.com
Web: gingerbread-mansion.com

Circa 1899. Built for Dr. H.J. Ring, the Gingerbread Mansion is now the most photographed of Northern California's inns. Near Eureka, it is in the fairy-tale Victorian village of Ferndale (a National Historical Landmark). Gingerbread Mansion is a unique combination of Queen Anne and Eastlake styles with

elaborate gingerbread trim. Inside are spacious and elegant rooms including two suites with "his" and "her" clawfoot bathtubs. The Empire Suite is said to be the most opulent accommodation in Northern California. Another memorable choice would be "The Veneto", an imaginative experience where guests stay within a piece of artwork. Extensive formal English gardens beautifully surround the mansion and it is a stroll away to Victorian shops, galleries and restaurants. A Wilderness park and bird sanctuary are a half mile away.

Historic Interest: Victorian shops and galleries along Main Street, The Ferndale Museum, wilderness park and bird sanctuary (one-half mile).

Innkeeper(s): Ken Torbert. $150-385. MC, VISA, AX, PC, TC. TAC10. 11 rooms with PB, 5 with FP and 5 suites. Breakfast and afternoon tea included in rates. Types of meals: Full bkfst and early coffee/tea. Beds: KQT. Turndown service in room. Library and gardens on premises. Small meetings and family reunions hosted. Antiquing, fishing, hiking, live theater, parks and shopping nearby.

Publicity: *San Francisco Focus, Sunset, Travel Holiday, Country Inns, Los Angeles Times, Sunset, , Outbreak (Warner Bros.), PBS (Inn Country USA) and HGTV-Restore America.*

"Absolutely the most charming, friendly and delightful place we have ever stayed."

Shaw House B&B Inn

PO Box 1369
Ferndale, CA 95536-1369
(707)786-9958 (800)557-7429 Fax:(707)786-9958
E-mail: stay@shawhouse.com

Circa 1854. The owners of Ferndale's most historic structure note that the Shaw House was opened to the public in 1860 (six years after its construction) "to serve man and beast". A carpenter Gothic house with gables, bays and balconies it is set back on an acre of garden. An old buckeye tree frames the front gate, and in the back, a secluded deck overlooks a creek. Nestled under the wallpapered gables are several guest rooms filled with antiques and fresh flowers.

Historic Interest: Listed in the National Register.

Innkeeper(s): Jan Culbert. $85-185. MC, VISA. 8 rooms with PB. Breakfast and afternoon tea included in rates. Types of meals: Full bkfst and cont. Beds: QD. Antiquing, fishing and live theater nearby.

Publicity: *Travel & Leisure and New York Times.*

"Lovely place and lovely people—Willard Scott."

Ferndale (Loleta)   C2

Southport Landing

444 Phelan Rd
Ferndale (Loleta), CA 95551
(707)733-5915
E-mail: southprt@northcoast.com

Circa 1898. Situated on more than two acres, this early Colonial Revival with its wraparound front porch offers spectacular views of the hills and Humboldt Bay National Wildlife Refuge. Besides the inn's traditional country manor atmosphere with its period antiques, guests will enjoy the uninterrupted silence and the bounty of wildlife. There are five individually decorated guest rooms all with dramatic views of the hillside or the bay. A third-floor game room features a pool table, ping-pong, darts and cards. The country breakfasts include items such as local sausage, homemade muffins and fresh pastry. Snacks are provided in the evening. Hiking, bird-watching, bicycling and kayaking available locally.

Historic Interest: Redwood forests, Arcata Marsh, Somoa Dunes, Lost Coast are located nearby.

Innkeeper(s): Kathy Major, owners-Barbara Groom, Kathy Stecke, Kurt Kovacs. $110-135. MC, VISA. TAC10. 5 rooms, 4 with PB. Breakfast included in rates. Types of meals: Full bkfst, country bkfst, early coffee/tea and afternoon tea. Beds: Q. Turndown service in room. VCR, fax and library on premises. Handicap access. Weddings, small meetings and family reunions hosted. Antiquing, art galleries, beaches, bicycling, canoeing/kayaking, fishing, golf, hiking, bird watching, beachcombing, live theater, museums, parks, shopping and wineries nearby.

"Our greatest B&B experience!"

Fort Bragg   E2

Avalon House

561 Stewart St
Fort Bragg, CA 95437-3226
(707)964-5555 (800)964-5556 Fax:(707)964-5555
E-mail: anne@theavalonhouse.com
Web: www.theavalonhouse.com

Circa 1905. This redwood California Craftsman house was extensively remodeled in 1988 and furnished with a mixture of antiques and willow furniture. Some rooms feature fireplaces,

whirlpool tubs, or ocean views and decks. The inn is in a quiet residential area, three blocks from the Pacific Ocean, one block west of Hwy. 1, and two blocks from the Skunk Train depot.

Innkeeper(s): Anne Sorrells. $85-155. MC, VISA, AX, DS, PC, TC. TAC10. 6 rooms with PB, 4 with FP. Breakfast included in rates. Types of meals: Full bkfst and early coffee/tea. Beds: QD. Weddings, small meetings and family reunions hosted. Antiquing, fishing, whale watching, Skunk Train, live theater, parks, shopping and water sports nearby.

Publicity: *Advocate News.*

"Elegant, private and extremely comfortable. We will never stay in a motel again."

Country Inn

632 N Main St
Fort Bragg, CA 95437-3220
(707)964-3737 (800)831-5327
E-mail: cntryinn@mcn.org
Web: www.beourguests.com

Circa 1893. The Union Lumber Company once owned this two-story townhouse built of native redwood. It features rooms with slanted and peaked ceilings, and several rooms have fireplaces. Camellia trees, flower boxes, and a picket fence accent the landscaping, while two blocks away a railroad carries visitors on excursions through the redwoods.

Innkeeper(s): Cynthia & Bruce Knauss. $60-139. MC, VISA, AX. 8 rooms with PB. Breakfast included in rates. Types of meals: Full bkfst. Beds: KQ. Handicap access. Antiquing, beaches, bicycling, fishing, hiking, horseback riding, Skunk Train, live theater, parks and shopping nearby.

Publicity: *The Santa Rosa Press Democrat.*

"Each room is so charming, how do you choose one?."

Glass Beach B&B

726 N Main St
Fort Bragg, CA 95437-3017
(707)964-6774
E-mail: glassbeachinn@hotmail.com
Web: www.glassbeachinn.com

Circa 1920. Each of the guest rooms at this Craftsman-style home is decorated in a different theme and named to reflect the decor. The Malaysian and Oriental Jade rooms reflect Asian artistry, while the Forget-Me-Not and Victorian Rose rooms are bright, feminine rooms with walls decked in floral prints. Antiques are found throughout the home and the back cottage, which includes three of the inn's nine guest rooms. The inn also offers a hot tub for guest use. Breakfasts are served in the inn's dining room, but guests are free to take a tray and enjoy the meal in the privacy of their own room.

Innkeeper(s): Nancy & Richard. $100-160. MC, VISA, DS, TC. 9 rooms with PB, 4 with FP and 1 suite. Breakfast included in rates. Types of meals: Full bkfst and afternoon tea. Beds: Q. Cable TV in room. Handicap access. Family reunions hosted. Antiquing, fishing, live theater, parks, shopping and water sports nearby.

Grey Whale Inn

615 N Main St
Fort Bragg, CA 95437-3240
(707)964-0640 (800)382-7244 Fax:(707)964-4408
E-mail: stay@greywhaleinn.com

Circa 1915. As the name implies, whales can be seen from many of the inn's vantage points during the creatures' migration season along the West Coast. The stately four-story redwood inn features airy and spacious guest rooms with neighborhood ocean views. Some rooms include a fireplace, whirlpool tub for two or private deck. Near the heart of downtown Fort Bragg, it's an easy walk to the Skunk Train, shops, galleries, a microbrewery and restaurants. There is also a fire-

side lounge, TV/VCR room and a recreation area with pool table.

Historic Interest: The Georgia Pacific Logging Museum and the Guest House Museum are two blocks away, while the Kelley House Museum and Ford House are a 10-mile drive.

Innkeeper(s): Michael Dawson. $100-200. MC, VISA, AX, PC, TC. TAC10. 14 rooms with PB, 4 with FP and 2 conference rooms. Breakfast included in rates. Types of meals: Full bkfst. Beds: KQDT. Cable TV, phone and coffee maker in room. VCR, fax, copier and library on premises. Handicap access. Weddings, small meetings, family reunions and seminars hosted. German and Spanish spoken. Antiquing, fishing, whale watching, golf, hiking, bicycling, microbrewery, live theater, parks and shopping nearby.

Publicity: *Inn Times, San Francisco Examiner, Travel, Fort Bragg Advocate News, Mendocino Beacon, Los Angeles Times, Sunset and Contra Costa Times.*

"We are going to return each year until we have tried each room. Sunrise room is excellent in the morning or evening."

Old Stewart House Inn

511 Stewart St
Fort Bragg, CA 95437-3226
(707)961-0775 (800)287-8392
E-mail: galli@mcn.org

Circa 1876. This is the oldest house in Fort Bragg and was built for the founding partner of the town mill. The Victorian theme is enhanced by rooms that may feature amenities such as a fireplace or spa, as well as period furnishings. Within a three-block area of the inn are the Skunk Train Depot, restaurants and beaches. Nearby are ocean cliffs, stands of redwood, waterfalls and botanical gardens.

Innkeeper(s): Darrell Galli. $85-145. MC, VISA, DS. TAC10. 6 rooms with PB, 2 with FP and 2 cabins. Breakfast and snacks/refreshments included in rates. Types of meals: Full bkfst. Beds: Q. Spa and library on premises. Handicap access. Weddings, small meetings and family reunions hosted. Italian spoken. Antiquing, fishing, golf, live theater, parks, shopping, tennis and water sports nearby.

Pets allowed: in cabins, on approval.

The Weller House Inn

524 Stewart St
Fort Bragg, CA 95437
(707)964-4415 (877)8WE-LLER Fax:(707)964-4198
E-mail: innkeeper@wellerhouse.com
Web: www.wellerhouse.com

Circa 1886. In the National Register, this three-story Italianate Victorian offers dormers, bay windows, a porch and an unusual historic water tower. Breakfast is provided in the redwood paneled ballroom on the top floor and includes baked goods, asparagus quiche or a variety of other dishes created by your Swedish hostess. Guest rooms are decorated in the theme of a different country and include some furnishings original to the house as well as hand-painted tiles,  fireplaces and stained glass. From the water tower, guests enjoy expansive ocean views and often spot whales. The innkeepers are musicians, Ted plays the trombone and Eva plays the bassoon. Ask for directions to MacKerricher State Park, which juts into the ocean and allows close up views of harbor seals or the locals' favorite, Glass Beach.

Historic Interest: Guest House Museum (1/4 mile), Mendocino Village (6 miles).
Innkeeper(s): Eva & Ted Kidwell. $95-175. MC, VISA, AX, DC, DS, PC, TC. TAC10. 8 rooms with PB, 2 with FP and 1 conference room. Breakfast and snacks/refreshments included in rates. Types of meals: Gourmet bkfst and early coffee/tea. Beds: KQT. Phone in room. Fax, spa and library on premises. Weddings, small meetings, family reunions and seminars hosted. Antiquing, art galleries, beaches, bicycling, canoeing/kayaking, fishing, golf, hiking, horseback riding, live theater, museums, parks, shopping and wineries nearby.

Georgetown   G6

American River Inn

PO Box 43, Gold Country
Georgetown, CA 95634-0043
(530)333-4499 (800)245-6566 Fax:(530)333-9253
E-mail: ari@pcweb.net
Web: www.americanriverinn.com

Circa 1853. Just a few miles from where gold was discovered in Coloma stands this completely restored miners' boarding house. Mining cars dating back to the original Woodside Mine Camp are visible. The lode still runs under the inn. Swimmers will enjoy a spring-fed pool on the property. There is also a Jacuzzi,  croquet field, putting green and complimentary mountain bikes. In the evenings, guests are treated to complimentary wines and hors d'oeuvres. Georgetown was a designated site for the California sesquicentennial celebration.

Innkeeper(s): Maria & Will. $85-115. MC, VISA, AX, DS. TAC10. 25 rooms, 14 with PB, 3 with FP and 1 conference room. Types of meals: Gourmet bkfst. Beds: KQ. Fax, copier and spa on premises. Handicap access. Fishing and hiking nearby.

Publicity: *Los Angeles Times, Sunset, Gourmet, Westways and 50 Romantic Getaways.*

"Our home away from home. We fell in love here in all its beauty and will be back for our fourth visit in April, another honeymoon for six days."

Geyserville   G4

Hope-Merrill House & Hope Bosworth House

21253 Geyserville Ave
Geyserville, CA 95441-9637
(707)857-3356 (800)825-4233 Fax:(707)857-4673
E-mail: moreinfo@hope-inns.com

Circa 1870. The Hope-Merrill House is a classic example of the Eastlake Stick style that was so popular during Victorian times. Built entirely from redwood, the house features original wainscoting and silk-screened wallcoverings. A swimming pool, vineyard and gazebo are favorite spots for guests to relax. The Hope-Bosworth House, on the same street, was built in 1904 in the Queen Anne style by an early Geyserville pioneer who lived in the home until the 1960s. The front picket fence is covered with roses. Period details include oak woodwork, sliding doors, polished fir floors and antique light fixtures.

Innkeeper(s): Cosette & Ron Scheiber. $122-218. MC, VISA, AX, DS, PC, TC. TAC10. 12 rooms with PB, 5 with FP and 1 suite. Breakfast included in rates. Types of meals: Gourmet bkfst, early coffee/tea and picnic lunch. Beds: Q. Ceiling fan in room. Fax, copier, coffee, tea and hot chocolate available 24 hours a day on premises. Weddings, small meetings and family reunions hosted. Antiquing, redwoods, parks, shopping, water sports and wineries nearby.

Publicity: *New York Times, San Francisco Chronicle, San Diego Union, Country Homes, Sunset, Sacramento Union, Los Angeles Times and Bay Area Back Roads.*

Gilroy   J5

Country Rose Inn - B&B

PO Box 2500
Gilroy, CA 95021
(408)842-0441 Fax:(408)842-6646
E-mail: countryrosebnb@earthlink.net
Web: www.countryrose-b-n-b.com

Circa 1920. Amid five acres, and set between Morgan Hill and
Gilroy, a half-hour's drive south of San Jose, is the aptly named
Country Rose Inn. A roomy Dutch Colonial manor, this inn
was once a farmhouse on a
chicken ranch. Every room features a rose theme, including
wallpaper and quilted bedspreads. Each window offers a
relaxing view of grazing horses,
fertile fields, or the tranquil
grounds, which boast magnificent 100-year-old oak trees. The
inn is 20 minutes north of the San Juan Bautista Mission.

Historic Interest: San Juan Bautista Mission.

Innkeeper(s): Rose Hernandez. $149-239. MC, VISA, DC, DS, PC, TC.
TAC10. 5 rooms with PB, 1 with FP, 1 suite and 2 conference rooms. Types
of meals: Full bkfst and early coffee/tea. Beds: KQDT. Turndown service in
room. Air conditioning. Fax and library on premises. Weddings, small meetings and seminars hosted. Spanish spoken. Antiquing, golf, Bonfante Gardens
Theme Park, Monterey Peninsula, Henry W. Coe State Park, live theater,
parks, shopping and wineries nearby.

*"The quiet, serene country setting made our anniversary very special.
Rose is a delightful, gracious hostess and cook."*

The 1890 Chesbro House

7541 Church St
Gilroy, CA 95020
(408)842-3750
E-mail: chesbro@gilroy.com
Web: www.chesbro.gilroy.com

Circa 1890. A visit to this Eastlake Victorian provides a taste of
the gracious past. The home was built in the heart of the historic district for the current owner's great-grandfather, a pioneer
physician whose descendants of four generations have since
lived here. The all-redwood Painted Lady boasts rooftop iron
cresting, ornate ceiling medallions, original woodwork and period fixtures. Have tea in the antique-filled front parlor, or relax
in the Arts and Crafts-style sitting room. Guest bedrooms feature heirlooms and furnishings of wicker, brass, walnut and
marble. A wholesome and hearty breakfast may include Big Sur
omelette, turkey sausage and home-baked fig muffins. A century-old trumpet vine adorns the front porch, while a variety of
old fruit trees shade the garden.

Historic Interest: San Juan Bautista (9 miles), Monterey/Carmel (45 miles).

Innkeeper(s): Dick & Elizabeth Barratt. $110-125. MC, VISA, DS, PC. 2
rooms, 1 with PB. Breakfast included in rates. Types of meals: Gourmet
bkfst, veg bkfst, early coffee/tea and afternoon tea. Beds: KQ. Cable TV,
phone, ceiling fan and VCR in room. Spanish, French and Arabic spoken.
Amusement parks, antiquing, beaches, bicycling, fishing, golf, hiking, live
theater, museums, parks, shopping and wineries nearby.

Publicity: *Gilroy Business Focus and Ripon College (WI) Magazine.*

Glen Ellen   G4

Gaige House Inn

13540 Arnold Dr
Glen Ellen, CA 95442-9305
(707)935-0237 (800)935-0237 Fax:(707)935-6411
E-mail: gaige@sprynet.com
Web: www.gaige.com

Circa 1890. This wine country inn, offers 15 individually decorated guest rooms and suites with Southeast Asian and West
Indian influences. The most opulent of the rooms, the Gaige
Suite, includes an enormous Jacuzzi tub. The lush grounds feature gardens and a creek meanders through the property. Guests
enjoy use of a heated swimming pool and spa. Sonoma Valley's
many wineries are near the inn. Restaurants are within walking
distance. The innkeepers offer a taste of local wines each evening.

Innkeeper(s): Ken Burnet & Greg Nemrow. $170-395. MC, VISA, AX, DS,
TC. TAC10. 15 rooms with PB, 15 with FP. Breakfast and snacks/refresh-
ments included in rates. Types of meals: Gourmet bkfst and early coffee/tea.
Beds: KQ. Cable TV, phone, ceiling fan and CD players in room. Air conditioning. Fax, copier, spa, swimming and library on premises. Small meetings,
family reunions and seminars hosted. French and Spanish spoken. Antiquing,
golf, parks, shopping and tennis nearby.

Publicity: *Travel & Leisure, Sunset, Sacramento Bee, San Francisco
Examiner. and Bay Area Back Roads.*

Grass Valley   F6

Swan-Levine House

328 S Church St
Grass Valley, CA 95945-6709
(530)272-1873

Circa 1897. Originally built by a local mine owner, this Queen
Anne Victorian was converted into a hospital by Dr. John Jones,
and it served the area as a medical center until 1968.
Innkeepers/artists Howard and Margaret Levine renovated the
house including a printmaking studio and guesthouse. The old
surgery is now a guest room with rose-painted walls and octagonal white floor tiles and provides a grand view from the wicker-furnished turret.

Innkeeper(s): Howard & Peggy Levine. $75-100. MC, VISA. 4 rooms with
PB, 1 with FP and 1 suite. Types of meals: Full bkfst. Beds: KQT. Fireplace
in suite in room.

Publicity: *Country Living Magazine.*

*"You made us feel at home. An atmosphere of open-hearted friend-
ship is rather rare these days."*

Groveland   H7

The Groveland Hotel

18767 Main St, PO Box 481
Groveland, CA 95321-0481
(209)962-4000 (800)273-3314 Fax:(209)962-6674
E-mail: peggy@groveland.com

Circa 1849. Located 23 miles from Yosemite National Park, the
1992 restoration features both an 1849 adobe building with
18-inch-thick walls constructed during the Gold Rush and a
1914 building erected to house workers for the Hetch Hetchy
Dam. Both feature two-story balconies. There is a Victorian
parlor, a gourmet restaurant and a Western saloon. Guest

rooms feature European antiques, down comforters, some featherbeds, in-room coffee, phones with data ports, and hair dryers. The feeling is one of casual elegance.

Innkeeper(s): Peggy A. & Grover C. Mosley. $135-210. MC, VISA, AX, DC, CB, DS, PC, TC. TAC10. 17 rooms with PB, 3 with FP, 3 suites and 1 conference room. Breakfast included in rates. Types of meals: Cont plus, early coffee/tea, picnic lunch and room service. Beds: QT. Phone, ceiling fan and hair dryers in room. Air conditioning. VCR, fax, copier and library on premises. Handicap access. Weddings, small meetings, family reunions and seminars hosted. Antiquing, fishing, golf, parks, shopping, downhill skiing, cross-country skiing, tennis and water sports nearby.

Pets Allowed.

Publicity: *Sonora Union Democrat, Los Angeles Times, Peninsula, Sunset (February 2001-Wests Best Inns), Stockton Record, Country Inns Magazine (Top 10 inns in U.S.). & Wine Spectator Award of Excellence for our wine list.*

Guerneville   G3

Fern Grove Cottages

16650 River Rd
Guerneville, CA 95446-9678
(707)869-8105 Fax:(707)869-1615
E-mail: innkeepers@ferngrove.com

Circa 1926. Clustered in a village-like atmosphere and surrounded by redwoods, these craftsman cottages have romantic fireplaces, private entrances, and are individually decorated. The cottages were built in the 1920s and served as little vacation houses for San Francisco families visiting the Russian River. Some units have a kitchen, some have double whirlpool tubs and other cottages are suitable for families. Guests enjoy use of the swimming pool. The cottages are just a few blocks from shops and restaurants, as well as a swimming beach by the river. A state park and winery tour are within three miles of the cottages.

Innkeeper(s): Anne & Simon Lowings. $69-199. MC, VISA, AX, DS, PC, TC. TAC10. 21 cottages with PB, 11 with FP and 1 conference room. Breakfast included in rates. Types of meals: Cont. Beds: Q. Cable TV in room. Swimming and library on premises. Small meetings, family reunions and seminars hosted. Antiquing, beaches, canoeing/kayaking, fishing, golf, Armstrong Redwater State Park, parks, shopping, tennis, water sports and wineries nearby.

Pets allowed: One per cottage, on leash, clean animals only. $15 charge.

Ridenhour Ranch

12850 River Rd
Guerneville, CA 95446-9276
(707)887-1033 (888)877-4466 Fax:(707)869-2967
E-mail: ridenhourinn@earthlink.net
Web: www.ridenhourranchhouseinn.com

Circa 1906. Located on a hill overlooking the Russian River, this ranch house is shaded by redwoods, oaks and laurels. There are eight guest rooms including two cottages overlooking the informal gardens. Guests can relax in the hot tub below the majestic oak trees. The Korbel Champagne cellars are nearby, and it's a five-minute walk to the river. Wineries, vineyards, the ocean and California's famous redwoods all are nearby.

Innkeeper(s): Chris Bell & Meilani Naranjo. $105-185. MC, VISA, AX, PC, TC. TAC10. 8 rooms with PB, 1 with FP and 1 suite. Breakfast and snacks/refreshments included in rates. Types of meals: Gourmet bkfst and early coffee/tea. Beds: KQ. Cable TV and ceiling fan in room. Antiquing, fishing, golf, live theater, parks, shopping and water sports nearby.

Publicity: *Los Angeles Times, Orange County Register and Los Altos Town Crier.*

"Your hospitality and food will ensure our return!"

Santa Nella House

12130 Highway 116
Guerneville, CA 95446-9480
(707)869-9488 (800)440-9031 Fax:(707)869-0355
E-mail: santanella@earthlink.net
Web: www.santanellahouse.com

Circa 1870. This Victorian farmhouse was the residence of the builder of the Santa Nella Winery. It was also the site of one of the first sawmills in the area and served as a stagecoach stop. An enchanting trail winds down to the Russian River, and in the summer the bridge across it leads to the Korbel Winery. High ceilings, antiques, a browsing library and a woodstove in the parlor set the stage for a relaxing stay.

Historic Interest: Armstrong Woods (4 miles), Korbel Champagne Cellars (one mile), Russian River (1/2 mile).

Innkeeper(s): Kristine Tellefsen & Francis Ranney. $120-130. MC, VISA. 4 rooms with PB, 4 with FP. Breakfast and snacks/refreshments included in rates. Types of meals: Full bkfst. Beds: QT. Phone and ceiling fan in room. VCR and spa on premises. Small meetings, family reunions and seminars hosted. Beaches, fishing, horseback riding, Pacific Coast, Redwoods, Russian River and water sports nearby.

"It is rare to find a home as warm and gracious as its owners."

Half Moon Bay   I4

Mill Rose Inn

615 Mill St
Half Moon Bay, CA 94019-1726
(650)726-7673 (800)900-7673
E-mail: info@millroseinn.com
Web: www.millroseinn.com

Circa 1903. This Victorian country inn is part of the original Miramontes land grant and played an important part in local coastal history. English country gardens bloom year-round under the magical hand of innkeeper and landscape designer Terry Baldwin. Canopy beds, clawfoot tubs, hand-painted fireplaces and an inside garden spa create an opulent setting in which to relax.

Innkeeper(s): Eve & Terry Baldwin. $190-360. MC, VISA, DC, DS. TAC10. 6 rooms with PB, 5 with FP and 1 conference room. Types of meals: Full bkfst. Beds: KQ. Spa on premises.

Publicity: *New York Times, LA Times, Dallas Morning News and Sunset Magazine.*

"One of the loveliest retreats this side of the Cotswolds. - San Diego Union."

Old Thyme Inn

779 Main St
Half Moon Bay, CA 94019-1924
(650)726-1616 (800)720-4277 Fax:(650)726-6394
E-mail: innkeeper@oldthymeinn.com
Web: www.oldthymeinn.com

Circa 1898. Enjoy the tranquility of this "Princess Anne" Victorian inn located on the historic Main Street of Old Town, Half Moon Bay. Its lush, aromatic English flower and herb gar-

den with a bubbling fountain provides a perfect backdrop for casual conversations or romantic tete-a-tetes. Just 28 miles from San Francisco and less than half an hour from San Jose and the Silicon Valley, the inn is within walking distance of a crescent-shaped beach, art galleries, shops and fine dining. Furnished in antiques and adorned with the innkeeper's art collection, it offers seven newly decorated guest rooms, each with a queen bed and hypoallergenic featherbed and down comforter. Two rooms have both Jacuzzis and fireplaces. Savor the inn's tantalizing full breakfast before a day of relaxing or sightseeing.

Historic Interest: San Francisco is just 25 miles away, Filoli Gardens nearby.

Innkeeper(s): Rick & Kathy Ellis. $130-290. MC, VISA, AX, DS, PC, TC. 7 rooms with PB, 3 with FP. Breakfast included in rates. Types of meals: Full bkfst. Beds: Q. TV, VCR, some with Jacuzzi tubs and fireplaces in room. Fax on premises. Small meetings and family reunions hosted. French spoken. Antiquing, fishing, golf, live theater, parks, shopping and water sports nearby.

Publicity: *California Weekends, Los Angeles, San Mateo Times, San Jose Mercury News, Herb Companion and San Francisco Examiner.*

Zaballa House

324 Main St
Half Moon Bay, CA 94019-1724
(650)726-9123 Fax:(650)726-3921
E-mail: zaballa@coastside.net
Web: zaballahouse.com

Circa 1858. The Zaballa House is the oldest building still standing in Half Moon Bay. The inn features an elegant reception room, a breakfast nook and a parlor with comfortable Victorian-style chairs. Guest rooms have such amenities as 10-foot ceilings, vaulted ceilings, fireplaces, clawfoot tubs and garden views. Some rooms have double-size whirlpool tubs. They have private entrances and kitchenettes.

Historic Interest: Historical walking tour of Half Moon Bay.

Innkeeper(s): Maryann Fox, Marian Greer, Susanne Ball & Janie Gandolfi. $109-275. MC, VISA, AX, DS, PC, TC. TAC10. 21 rooms, 12 with PB, 17 with FP, 4 suites and 1 conference room. Breakfast and snacks/refreshments included in rates. Types of meals: Full bkfst. Beds: Q. Cable TV, phone and ceiling fan in room. Fax and copier on premises. Small meetings, family reunions and seminars hosted. Antiquing, fishing, flower market, live theater, parks, shopping and water sports nearby.

Pets allowed: Must be clean, confined to bedroom during meals, $10 extra.

Publicity: *Half Moon Bay Review, San Francisco Examiner and Los Angeles Times.*

"The hospitality extended to us made us feel very welcome."

Healdsburg   G4

Calderwood Inn

25 West Grant St
Healdsburg, CA 95448-4804
(707)431-1110 (800)600-5444
E-mail: calderwd@aol.com
Web: www.calderwoodinn.com

Circa 1902. This romantic Queen Anne Victorian is surrounded by lush acres of redwoods, cedars and cypress trees. Each of the six rooms has been decorated with elegant, yet comfort-

able antiques. Two rooms offer clawfoot tubs, while others include amenities such as fireplaces and whirlpool tubs. Window seats, down comforters and four-poster beds are some of the romantic touches guests might find in their rooms. Fresh seasonal fruit and baked goods accompany the morning entree. Appetizers, wine and port are served in the evenings.

Historic Interest: Luther Burbank Home & Gardens, Sonoma County Museum are some of the area's historic sites.

Innkeeper(s): Jennifer & Paul Zawodny. $145-225. PC, TC. 6 rooms with PB and 1 conference room. Breakfast included in rates. Types of meals: Full bkfst, early coffee/tea and snacks/refreshments. Beds: KQ. Antiquing, fishing, hiking, gift shop, 65+ Sonoma County wineries within 5-10 minutes, live theater and water sports nearby.

George Alexander House

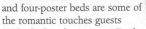

423 Matheson St
Healdsburg, CA 95448-4207
(707)433-1358 (800)310-1358 Fax:(707)433-1367
E-mail: info@georgealexanderhouse.com
Web: www.georgealexanderhouse.com

Circa 1905. Embellished with ornamental details and quatrefoil windows, this Queen Anne Victorian has an eclectic charm. The inn is surrounded by Sonoma's award-winning vineyards, and guests will enjoy complimentary wine upon arrival. Two adjoining parlors with a wood-burning fireplace have comfortable sitting areas to sip a glass of sherry. Antique beds and furnishings tastefully enhance the guest bedrooms and suite, while down comforters, plush towels and robes add comfort. Choose from two fireplaces, a double Jacuzzi or a clawfoot tub, a sitting room area and a private entrance leading to a deck overlooking a garden and fountains. Fresh fruit, pastries or muffins, lemon ricotta pancakes, breakfast bread pudding, eggs Florentine and bacon are some of the morning delights served in the formal dining room.

Innkeeper(s): Mel & Holly Schatz. $130-235. MC, VISA, PC, TC. 4 rooms with PB, 2 with FP. Breakfast and snacks/refreshments included in rates. Types of meals: Gourmet bkfst, veg bkfst and early coffee/tea. Beds: KQ. Ceiling fan, hot tub and fireplace in room. Central air. Fax, copier and sauna on premises. Weddings, small meetings, family reunions and seminars hosted. Antiquing, art galleries, bicycling, canoeing/kayaking, fishing, hiking, museums, parks, shopping and wineries nearby.

Grape Leaf Inn

539 Johnson St
Healdsburg, CA 95448-3907
(707)433-8140 Fax:(707)433-3140
E-mail: grapeleafinn@home.com
Web: www.grapeleafinn.com

Circa 1900. This magnificently restored Queen Anne home was built in what was considered the "Nob Hill" of Healdsburg. It was typical of a turn-of-the-century, dream house. It is situated

near the Russian River and the town center. Twenty-five skylights provide an abundance of sunlight, fresh air, and stained glass. Ten guest rooms offer whirlpool tubs and showers for two. The innkeepers make the most of their wine country location, hosting a wine tasting each evening with a display of at least five Sonoma County wines. Each guest room is named for a wine variety, such as Zinfandel or Merlot. The inn is just a few blocks from many of Healdsburg's fine restaurants and shops.

Innkeeper(s): Richard & Kae Rosenberg. $125-250. MC, VISA, PC, TC. TAC10. 10 rooms with PB. Breakfast and snacks/refreshments included in rates. Types of meals: Full bkfst. Beds: KQ. 5 rooms have whirlpool tub/showers for two in room. Air conditioning. Antiquing, fishing, over 70 wineries close by, shopping and water sports nearby.

Publicity: *Sonoma County Guide and Historic Homes of Healdsburg.*

"It was our first time at a real one and we were delighted with our lovely accommodations, delicious breakfasts and most of all you graciousness in trying to please your guests. Thank you for making our 38th anniversary a very special one that we will always remember."

Haydon Street Inn

321 Haydon St
Healdsburg, CA 95448-4411
(707)433-5228 (800)528-3703 Fax:(707)433-6637
E-mail: innkeeper@haydon.com
Web: www.haydon.com

Circa 1912. Architectural buffs will have fun naming the several architectural styles found in the Haydon House. It has the curving porch and general shape of a Queen Anne Victorian, the expansive areas of siding and unadorned columns of the Neo-Classic style, and the exposed roof rafters of the Craftsman. The decor is elegant and romantic, with antiques. The Turret

Room includes a clawfoot tub and a fireplace. Two rooms are located in the inn's Victorian Cottage, and both have whirlpool tubs. The Pine Room offers a pencil post bed with a Battenburg lace canopy, while the Victorian Room includes fine antiques and a Ralph Lauren wicker bed.

Innkeeper(s): Dick & Pat Bertapelle. $110-250. MC, VISA, DS, PC, TC. TAC10. 8 rooms with PB, 1 with FP. Breakfast, afternoon tea and snacks/refreshments included in rates. Types of meals: Gourmet bkfst and early coffee/tea. Beds: QD. TV, ceiling fan and double whirlpool tubs (two rooms) in room. Air conditioning. VCR and fax on premises. Family reunions and seminars hosted. Antiquing, fishing, biking, wine tasting, parks, shopping and water sports nearby.

Publicity: *Los Angeles and San Francisco.*

"Adjectives like class, warmth, beauty, thoughtfulness with the right amount of privacy, attention to details relating to comfort, all come to mind. Thank you for the care and elegance."

Healdsburg Inn on The Plaza

110 Matheson St, PO Box 1196
Healdsburg, CA 95448-4108
(707)433-6991 (800)431-8663 Fax:(707)433-9513
E-mail: innpressions@earthlink.net
Web: www.healdsburginn.com

Circa 1900. A former Wells Fargo building, the inn is a renovated brick gingerbread overlooking the plaza in historic downtown Healdsburg. Ornate bay windows, embossed wood paneling and broad, paneled stairs present a welcome entrance. There are fireplaces and the halls are filled with sunlight from vaulted, glass skylights. A

solarium is the setting for breakfast and evening wine and hors d'oeuvres. A large covered balcony extends along the entire rear of the building. Shops on the premises sell gifts, toys, quilts and fabric. An antique shop and art gallery can be found there, as well. The surrounding area is full of things to do, including wineries and wine-tasting rooms.

Innkeeper(s): Genny Jenkins & LeRoy Steck. $255-295. MC, VISA. 10 rooms with PB, 9 with FP and 1 conference room. Breakfast and snacks/refreshments included in rates. Types of meals: Gourmet bkfst and early coffee/tea. Beds: KQT. Cable TV, phone, ceiling fan and VCR in room. Air conditioning. Fax, copier and wine tasting on premises. Small meetings, family reunions and seminars hosted. Antiquing, fishing, wineries, balloon, canoe, historic walking tour, parks, shopping and water sports nearby.

Publicity: *Healdsburg Tribune, Los Angeles Daily News and New York Times.*

"The first-thing-in-the-morning juice and coffee was much appreciated."

Madrona Manor, Wine Country Inn & Restaurant

1001 Westside Road
Healdsburg, CA 95448-0818
(707)433-4231 (800)258-4003 Fax:(707)433-0703
E-mail: madronaman@aol.com
Web: www.madronamanor.com

Circa 1881. This handsome estate consists of five historic structures including the Mansion, Schoolhouse and a Gothic-style Carriage House. Embellished with turrets, bay windows, porches and a mansard roof, the stately inn is surrounded by eight acres of manicured lawns, terraced flower and vegetable gardens and wooded areas. Elegant antique furnishings are offered. The inn's noteworthy four-star restaurant offers California cuisine featuring fresh local ingredients served in romantic dining rooms.

Historic Interest: Luther Burbank home (15 miles), Simi Winery (3 miles).

Innkeeper(s): Joe & Maria Hadley. $185-395. MC, VISA, PC, TC. TAC10. 17 rooms with PB, 5 suites and 2 conference rooms. Breakfast included in rates. Types of meals: Gourmet bkfst and dinner. Beds: KQ. Phone in room. Air conditioning. Fax and data port on premises. Handicap access. Weddings, small meetings, family reunions and seminars hosted. Antiquing, bicycling, fishing, parks, shopping, sporting events, water sports and wineries nearby.

Pets allowed: In select buildings.

Publicity: *Travel & Leisure, Conde Naste, Gourmet, Woman's Day Home Decorating Ideas, US News, Diversions, Money, Good Housekeeping. and Great Country Inns of America.*

"Our fourth visit and better every time."

Raford House

10630 Wohler Rd
Healdsburg, CA 95448-9418
(707)887-9573 (800)887-9503 Fax:(707)887-9597

Circa 1880. Situated on more than four acres of rose gardens and fruit trees, this classic Victorian country estate originally was built as a summer home and ranch house in the 1880s. Just 70 miles north of San Francisco, Raford House is nestled in the heart of the Sonoma County wine country, minutes away from award-winning wineries and many fine restaurants. Located close to the Russian River, between Healdsburg and the beautiful Northern California coast, the area has scenic country roads and rugged coastlines.

Innkeeper(s): Carole & Jack Vore. $120-190. MC, VISA, AX, DS. TAC10. 6 rooms with PB. Breakfast and snacks/refreshments included in rates. Types of meals: Full bkfst and early coffee/tea. Beds: Q. Fax on premises. Antiquing, fishing, live theater, parks, shopping and water sports nearby.

Publicity: Los Angeles Times, Travel & Leisure, Country and Wine Spectator Magazine.

"Truly a 'serendipity' experience! Wonderful, welcoming ambiance, great food, lovely hosts. I am 'renewed'."

Hope Valley   G8

Sorensen's Resort

14255 Hwy 88
Hope Valley, CA 96120
(530)694-2203 (800)423-9949
E-mail: sorensensresort@yahoo.com
Web: www.sorensensresort.com

Circa 1876. Where Danish sheepherders settled in this 7,000-foot-high mountain valley, the Sorensen family built a cluster of fishing cabins. Thus began a century-old tradition of valley hospitality. The focal point of Sorensen's is a "stave" cabin — a reproduction of a 13th-century Nordic house. Now developed as a Nordic ski resort, a portion of the Mormon-Emigrant Trail and Pony Express Route pass near the inn's 165 acres. In the summer, river rafting, fishing, pony express re-rides and llama treks are popular Sierra pastimes. Lake Tahoe lies 20 miles to the north. Breakfast is included in the rates for bed & breakfast units only. All other cabins are equipped with kitchens.

Historic Interest: Alpine County Museum (12 miles), Old Indian Trade Ports, Emigrant Road.

Innkeeper(s): John & Patty Brissenden. $80-450. MC, VISA, AX, DS, PC, TC. TAC10. 33 rooms, 31 with PB, 23 with FP, 28 cottages and 2 conference rooms. Types of meals: Full bkfst, cont plus, early coffee/tea, lunch, picnic lunch, snacks/refreshments and gourmet dinner. Beds: QD. Copier, sauna, library, e-mail hook-up, complimentary, wine and tea and cocoa on premises. Handicap access. Weddings and family reunions hosted. Spanish spoken. Antiquing, fishing, parks, downhill skiing, cross-country skiing and water sports nearby.

Publicity: Sunset, San Francisco Chronicle, Los Angeles Times, Motorland, Outside, New York Times and Travel & Leisure.

"In one night's stay, I felt more comfortable, relaxed, and welcome than any vacation my 47 years have allowed. Thank you for the happiness you have given my children."

Hopland   F3

Thatcher Inn

13401 S Hwy 101
Hopland, CA 95449
(707)744-1890 (800)266-1891 Fax:(707)744-1219
E-mail: info@thatcherinn.com

Circa 1890. Elegant Victorian furnishings fill the rooms at this late Victorian manor, which has been restored to its original state. The guest rooms are appointed with floral, Victorian-era wallcoverings and decorated with antiques. The Fireside Library with its rich, wood bookshelves, marble fireplace and highback chairs is an inviting place to enjoy a good book, and there are more than 4,000 volumes to enjoy. A full, country breakfast is served each morning. Special pris fixe dinners are available for bed & breakfast guests anytime by advance reservation. Guests also enjoy full

bar service featuring Mendocino wines and fine liquors. Plus, the inn is able to host tour special functions, holiday parties and rehearsal dinners, diligently prepared by chefs Don and Marlena Sacca. The innkeepers can help guests plan visits to local wineries, as well as other interesting local attractions.

Innkeeper(s): Don & Marlena Sacca. $115-175. MC, VISA, AX. TAC10. 20 rooms with PB, 2 suites and 1 conference room. Breakfast included in rates. Types of meals: Gourmet bkfst and early coffee/tea. Beds: KQT. Phone, ceiling fan, hair dryers and bath robes in room. Air conditioning. VCR, fax, copier, swimming and library on premises. Small meetings, family reunions and seminars hosted. Antiquing, fishing, wine tasting, golf, parks and water sports nearby.

Publicity: Sunset.

"We appreciate your attention to details and efforts which made our visit so pleasant."

Idyllwild   O12

The Pine Cove Inn

23481 Hwy 243
Idyllwild, CA 92549
(909)659-5033 (888)659-5033 Fax:(909)659-5034
E-mail: pinecoveinn@aol.com

Circa 1935. These rustic, A-frame cottages offer a variety of amenities in a natural, mountain setting. Refrigerators and microwaves have been placed in each unit, several of which include a wood-burning fireplace. One unit has a full kitchen. A full breakfast is served in a separate lodge which dates back to 1935. The village of Idyllwild is three miles down the road, and the surrounding country offers a variety of activities.

Innkeeper(s): Thom Canning & Bart Skinner. $80-110. MC, VISA, AX, DS. TAC10. 10 rooms with PB, 4 with FP, 4 suites and 1 conference room. Breakfast included in rates. Types of meals: Full bkfst and country bkfst. Beds: QT. Microwave and some with fireplace in room. VCR and fax on premises. Weddings, small meetings, family reunions and seminars hosted. Spanish spoken. Antiquing, art galleries, bicycling, fishing, hiking, horseback riding, hiking, mountain hiking and shopping nearby.

Inverness   H4

Ten Inverness Way

10 Inverness Way, PO Box 63
Inverness, CA 94937-0063
(415)669-1648 Fax:(415)669-7403
E-mail: inn@teninvernessway.com
Web: www.teninvernessway.com

Circa 1904. Shingled in redwood, this handsome bed & breakfast features a stone fireplace, a sunny library with many good books, and close access to a wonderful hiking area. After an afternoon of hiking, guests can enjoy a soak in the garden hot tub. Inverness is located on Tomales Bay, offering close access to nearby beaches at Point Reyes National Seashore. The Golden Gate Bridge is 45 minutes from the inn.

Innkeeper(s): Teri Mowery. $125-187. MC, VISA, PC, TC. 5 rooms with PB. Breakfast and afternoon tea included in rates. Types of meals: Full bkfst and early coffee/tea. Beds: Q. Fax, spa and library on premises. Antiquing, fishing, parks and water sports nearby.

Publicity: Los Angeles Times, New York Times, Travel & Leisure, Sunset and Gourmet.

"Everything we could have wanted for our comfort was anticipated by our hosts. Great hot tub. Lovely rooms and common areas."

Jackson   **G6**

Gate House Inn

1330 Jackson Gate Rd
Jackson, CA 95642-9539
(209)223-3500 (800)841-1072 Fax:(209)223-1299
E-mail: info@gatehouseinn.com
Web: www.gatehouseinn.com

Circa 1902. This striking Victorian inn is listed in the National Register of Historic Places. Set on a hillside amid lovely gardens, the inn is within walking distance of a state historic park

and several notable eateries. The inn's country setting, comfortable porches and swimming pool offer many opportunities for relaxation. Accommodations include three rooms, a suite and a romantic cottage with a gas log fireplace and whirlpool tub. All of the guest rooms feature queen beds and elegant furnishings. Nearby are several lakes, wineries and golf courses.

Historic Interest: Chaw Se' Indian State Park (8 miles), Kennedy Wheels State Park (one-half mile), Setters Fort/Mill (25 miles).

Innkeeper(s): Mark & Donna Macola. $110-185. MC, VISA, AX, DS. TAC10. 6 rooms with PB, 3 with FP, 1 suite and 2 cottages. Breakfast included in rates. Types of meals: Full bkfst, early coffee/tea and afternoon tea. Beds: Q. Ceiling fan in room. Air conditioning. Fax, copier and swimming on premises. Weddings, small meetings and family reunions hosted. Antiquing, fishing, casino, live theater, parks, shopping, downhill skiing, cross-country skiing and water sports nearby.

"Most gracious, warm hospitality."

Wedgewood Inn

11941 Narcissus Rd
Jackson, CA 95642-9600
(209)296-4300 (800)933-4393 Fax:(209)296-4301
E-mail: vic@wedgewoodinn.com

Circa 1987. Located in the heart of Sierra gold country on a secluded, five acres, this Victorian replica is crammed full of sentimental family heirlooms and antiques. Each room has been designed with careful attention to

detail. A baby grand piano rests in the parlor. The carriage house is a separate cottage with its own private entrance. It boasts four generations of family heirlooms, a carved canopy bed, a wood-burning stove and a two-person Jacuzzi tub. The innkeepers' 1921 Model-T, "Henry," is located in its own special showroom. Gourmet breakfasts are served on bone china and include specialties such as cheese-filled blintzes, fruit and baked goods. Breakfast is available in selected guest rooms by request. There is a gift shop on the premises.

Innkeeper(s): Vic & Jeannine Beltz. $125-185. MC, VISA, AX, DS, PC, TC. TAC10. 6 rooms with PB and 1 suite. Breakfast included in rates. Types of meals: Gourmet bkfst, early coffee/tea and snacks/refreshments. Beds: Q. Turndown service, ceiling fan and Jacuzzi in room. Air conditioning. Fax, copier, croquet, hammocks and horseshoes on premises. Antiquing, fishing, golf, live theater, shopping, downhill skiing and cross-country skiing nearby. Publicity: *San Francisco Chronicle, Contra Costa Times, Stockton Record, Country Magazine and Victorian Magazine.*

Windrose Inn

1407 Jackson Gate Rd
Jackson, CA 95642-9575
(209)223-3650 (888)568-5250 Fax:(209)223-3793
E-mail: windrose@volcano.net
Web: www.windroseinn.com

Circa 1897. This Victorian farmhouse overlooking Jackson Creek was built in the Mother Lode Country just North of Jackson, a town that had two of the most productive gold mines a century ago. The inn

has a large wraparound porch and gardens with sitting areas, a gazebo, a pond, a creek with a footbridge and a bench on the bank. There's a hammock for two slung between walnut trees. Guestrooms are elegantly appointed with items such as a mahogany sleigh bed, clawfoot bathtubs, fireplaces and a champagne bubble bath spa tub for two. Choose whether you want your breakfast served in the solarium dining room or outside overlooking the pond or rose garden. The inn's gourmet breakfasts offers eggs, meats, scones or croissants, potatoes or pancakes. Activities include visiting gold rush sites like Colombia, a fully restored gold mining town an hour from the inn. You may also go hiking or biking, enjoy river and lake sports, take tours of the mines or visit museums, wineries or antique stores.

Innkeeper(s): Paula & Bruce Stanbridge. $100-185. MC, VISA, AX. TAC10. 4 rooms, 2 with FP and 1 suite. Breakfast and snacks/refreshments included in rates. Types of meals: Gourmet bkfst, veg bkfst, early coffee/tea and picnic lunch. AP. Beds: Q. Turndown service, ceiling fan and fireplace in room. Air conditioning. Fax, copier and pond and creek on premises. Weddings, small meetings, family reunions and seminars hosted. Antiquing, art galleries, bicycling, canoeing/kayaking, fishing, golf, hiking, live theater, museums, parks, shopping, downhill skiing, cross-country skiing and wineries nearby. Publicity: *Amador Ledger Dispatch.*

Jamestown   **H7**

1859 Historic National Hotel, A Country Inn

18183 Main St, PO Box 502
Jamestown, CA 95327
(209)984-3446 (800)894-3446 Fax:(209)984-5620
E-mail: info@national-hotel.com
Web: www.national-hotel.com

Circa 1859. Located between Yosemite National Park and Lake Tahoe, this is one of the 10 oldest continuously operating hotels in California. In the Gold Country, the inn maintains its original redwood bar where thousands of dollars in gold dust were once spent. Electricity and plumbing were added for the first time when the inn was restored. Original furnishings, Gold Rush period antiques, as well as brass beds, lace curtains and quilts are among the guest room appointments. A soaking room is an additional amenity, although all rooms have their own private baths. A bountiful continental breakfast is complimentary. Be sure and arrange for romantic dining at the inn's

gourmet restaurant, considered to be one of the finest in the Mother Lode. Order a favorite liquor or espresso from the saloon or try the area's wine tasting. Favorite diversions include gold panning, live theatre and antiquing.

Historic Interest: Railtown 1897 State Historic Park, located in Jamestown, is a few blocks from the hotel.

Innkeeper(s): Stephen Willey. $90-130. MC, VISA, AX, DC, CB, DS, PC, TC. TAC10. 9 rooms with PB and 1 conference room. Breakfast included in rates. Types of meals: Cont plus, early coffee/tea, gourmet lunch, picnic lunch, snacks/refreshments and gourmet dinner. Beds: QT. Cable TV in room. Air conditioning. VCR and fax on premises. Weddings, small meetings, family reunions and seminars hosted. Spanish spoken. Antiquing, fishing, live theater, parks, downhill skiing, cross-country skiing and water sports nearby.

Pets allowed: By arrangement - credit card or cash deposit required.

Publicity: *Bon Appetit, California Magazine, Focus, San Francisco Magazine, Gourmet and Sunset.*

Jamestown Hotel

18153 Main St, PO Box 539
Jamestown, CA 95327-9748
(209)984-3902 (800)205-4901 Fax:(209)984-4149
E-mail: info@jamestownhotel.com
Web: www.jamestownhotel.com

Circa 1858. Originally constructed as a boarding house this gold rush inn has undergone a variety of occupations-hospital, bus depot and bordello. Sarah Bernhardt, Calamity Jane, Jenny Lind and Diamond Lil all have something in common-each has a namesake room at the Jamestown Hotel, honoring the gold rush era's powerful women. The rooms boast antique furnishings and feature a selection of amenities such as sitting areas,  clawfoot tubs, pull chain toilets and whirlpool tubs. A balcony stretches across the front of the inn affording overviews of the town. There's a cocktail lounge, and the inn's Cafe On the Patio serves burgers, prime rib, lamb and salmon, wine and desert.

Innkeeper(s): Annette & Norbert Mede. $80-145. MC, VISA, AX, DC, DS, PC, TC. TAC10. 11 rooms with PB, 5 suites and 1 conference room. Breakfast included in rates. Types of meals: Cont plus, early coffee/tea, lunch, picnic lunch, snacks/refreshments and dinner. Beds: KQD. Ceiling fan and some whirlpool tubs in room. Central air. VCR, fax, copier, library and cocktail lounge on premises. Handicap access. Weddings, small meetings, family reunions and seminars hosted. Antiquing, art galleries, canoeing/kayaking, fishing, golf, hiking, horseback riding, live theater, museums, parks, shopping, downhill skiing, cross-country skiing, tennis, water sports and wineries nearby.

Publicity: *Country Inns and Gourmet.*

The Palm Hotel B&B

10382 Willow St
Jamestown, CA 95327-9761
(209)984-3429 (888)551-1852 Fax:(209)984-4929
E-mail: innkeeper@palmhotel.com

Circa 1890. Enjoy Gold Country at this Victorian, which was home to Albert and Amelia Hoyt, publishers of the Mother Lode Magnet. In the 1890s, the home served as a boarding house. Today, it offers eight guest rooms with lacy curtains, fresh flowers, clawfoot tubs, marble showers and robes. A full breakfast is served each morning along with The Palm's special blend of coffee. The inn is located two-and-a-half hours from San Francisco and about an hour from Yosemite Valley, and it is within walking distance of Main Street, boutiques, galleries, restaurants and Railtown State Park.

Innkeeper(s): Rick & Sandy Allen. $95-155. MC, VISA, AX, TC. TAC10. 8 rooms with PB. Breakfast included in rates. Types of meals: Full bkfst. Beds: KQD. Cable TV in room. Central air. Fax and copier on premises. Handicap access. Small meetings and family reunions hosted. Antiquing, fishing, golf, Railtown State Park, Yosemite and Calaveras Big Trees, live theater, parks, shopping and water sports nearby.

Publicity: *Avalon Bay News, San Jose Mercury News, Sacramento Bee, Modesto Bee, San Francisco Chronicle, Sonora Union Democrat, Central Valley Chronicles on KVIE TV and Central Sierra Bank 1999 calendar.*

"The simple elegance of our room and ambiance of the Palm in general was a balm for our souls."

Joshua Tree O13

Joshua Tree Inn

61259 29 Palms Hwy, PO Box 340
Joshua Tree, CA 92252-0340
(760)366-1188 (800)366-1444 Fax:(760)366-3805
E-mail: inn@joshuatreeinn.com

Circa 1940. The hacienda-style inn was once a '50s motel. It now offers country-style rooms with a choice of one or two beds. Antiques add to the decor. Two and three-bedroom off-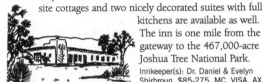site cottages and two nicely decorated suites with full kitchens are available as well. The inn is one mile from the gateway to the 467,000-acre Joshua Tree National Park.

Innkeeper(s): Dr. Daniel & Evelyn Shirbroun. $85-275. MC, VISA, AX, DC, CB, DS, TC. TAC10. 10 rooms with PB, 2 suites and 1 conference room. Types of meals: Cont, early coffee/tea and afternoon tea. MAP. Beds: KQDT. Cable TV, phone and ceiling fan in room. Air conditioning. VCR, fax, copier and swimming on premises. Weddings, small meetings, family reunions and seminars hosted. Antiquing, golf, Joshua Tree National Park, live theater, parks, shopping and tennis nearby.

Pets allowed: In designated rooms.

Publicity: *Los Angeles Times and Press Enterprise.*

"Quiet, clean and charming."

Spin and Margies Desert Hide-A-Way

PO Box 1092
Joshua Tree, CA 92252
(760)366-9124 Fax:(760)366-2954
E-mail: mindela@earthlink.net

Circa 1940. Escape to this Hacienda-style inn situated on three acres of desert landscape featuring palms, pines, native trees and succulents and a small pond. Three well-designed suites are arranged around an interior courtyard with cactus, yuccas and a soothing fountain. Blending an eclectic mix of Southwest, Mexican and modern furnishings and decor, the private suites include sitting rooms, kitchens and patios in some. Each offers everything needed to make coffee, tea, cereal, waffles or pancakes for breakfast and even margaritas to enjoy while watching the sunsets.

Historic Interest: Keys Ranch-Joshua Tree National Park (10 miles), The Integretron (20 miles), Old Town-Yucca Valley (8 miles), The Oasis of Mara-29 Palms (8 miles).

Innkeeper(s): Drew Reese/Mindy Kaufman. $75-125. MC, VISA, PC, TC. 3 suites, 2 with FP. Types of meals: Early coffee/tea. Beds: Q. TV, phone, ceiling fan, VCR, fireplace, tape system and full kitchen with breakfast items available in room. Goats, pond, bocce ball court, horseshoes and swamp coolers on premises. Weddings, small meetings and family reunions hosted. Antiquing, art galleries, bicycling, hiking, horseback riding, live theater, museums, parks and shopping nearby.

Julian P12

Butterfield B&B

2284 Sunset Dr
Julian, CA 92036
(760)765-2179 (800)379-4262 Fax:(760)765-1229
E-mail: butterfield@abac.com
Web: butterfieldbandb.com

Circa 1935. On an ivy-covered hillside surrounded by oaks and pines, the Butterfield is a peaceful haven of hospitality and country comfort. Overlooking the countryside, several of the charming guest bedrooms feature fireplaces and fluffy featherbeds. A delicious gourmet breakfast is served in the gazebo during summer or by a warm fire in cooler months. The parlor is a delightful place to enjoy hot beverages and afternoon treats. Whether it is scheduling an in-room massage, or arranging a horse-drawn carriage, the innkeepers are always happy to oblige.

Innkeeper(s): Ed & Dawn Glass. $125-175. MC, VISA, AX, PC. TAC10. 5 rooms with FP and 1 cottage. Breakfast and snacks/refreshments included in rates. Types of meals: Gourmet bkfst and early coffee/tea. AP. Beds: QD. Cable TV and ceiling fan in room. Air conditioning. Library on premises. Antiquing, fishing, golf, live theater, parks and shopping nearby.

Publicity: *South Coast and Travel Agent.*

Julian Gold Rush Hotel

2032 Main St, PO Box 1856
Julian, CA 92036-1856
(760)765-0201 (800)734-5854

Circa 1897. The dream of a former slave and his wife lives today in this sole surviving hotel in Southern California's "Mother Lode of Gold Mining." This Victorian charmer is listed in the National Register of Historic Places and is a designated State of California Point of Historic Interest (#SDI-09). Guests enjoy the feeling of a visit to Grandma's and a tradition of genteel hospitality.

Historic Interest: Entire townsite is a State Historic Landmark.

Innkeeper(s): Steve & Gig Ballinger. $82-190. MC, VISA, AX, PC, TC. TAC10. 15 rooms with PB, 2 with FP, 1 suite, 2 cottages and 1 conference room. Breakfast and afternoon tea included in rates. Types of meals: Full bkfst. Beds: QDT. Weddings, small meetings and seminars hosted. Antiquing, fishing, live theater and parks nearby.

Publicity: *San Diego Union and PSA.*

"Any thoughts you have about the 20th century will leave you when you walk into the lobby of this grand hotel— Westways Magazine."

Knights Landing G5

Snowball Mansion Inn

42485 Front St, PO Box 118
Knights Landing, CA 95645
(530)735-1122 Fax:(530)735-1122
E-mail: cherylfuhring@yahoo.com
Web: www.snowballmansion.com

Circa 1877. One of the area's pioneer estate houses, this impressive home was built by John Wells for his bride who was the daughter of William Knight, town founder. Recently renovated, the inn is decorated with period American Victorian antiques and Bradbury & Bradbury wallpapers. Two of the elegant guest bedrooms feature fireplaces. Enjoy a gourmet breakfast before exploring the seven-and-a-half acres situated on the Sacramento River. A private lake offers the pleasures of a dock and paddleboat.

Historic Interest: Gold Country (1 hour), Napa (1 hour), Marys Chapel (10 miles), Gibson Mansion (15 miles), Sacramento (25 miles).

Innkeeper(s): James & Cheryl Fuhring. $145-195. MC, VISA, AX, DS. TAC10. 3 rooms with PB, 2 with FP. Breakfast and snacks/refreshments included in rates. Types of meals: Gourmet bkfst, country bkfst, veg bkfst and early coffee/tea. AP. Beds: KQ. Fireplace in room. Central air. Fax, copier and library on premises. Weddings, small meetings, family reunions and seminars hosted. Antiquing, art galleries, fishing, golf, hiking, live theater, museums, parks, shopping, sporting events, water sports and wineries nearby.

Publicity: *Sacramento Magazine.*

La Jolla Q11

The Bed & Breakfast Inn at La Jolla

7753 Draper Ave
La Jolla, CA 92037
(858)456-2066 (800)582-2466 Fax:(858)456-1510
E-mail: bedbreakfast@innlajolla.com
Web: www.innlajolla.com

Circa 1913. This historic gem truly is a treasure, surrounded by the coastal beauty of La Jolla. The home was designed for George Kautz and was built by Irving Gill in his Cubist style. John Philip Sousa and his family lived in the house for several years during the 1920s. The guest rooms and suites offer beautiful furnishings and romantic décor. The Holiday room includes a massive four-poster, canopy bed, hardwood floors topped with antique Oriental rugs and a fireplace. Other rooms include amenities such as clawfoot tubs and fireplaces; some rooms offer ocean and sunset views. The gourmet breakfasts are a treat, rivaled only by the setting. Guests partake of their morning meal either in the dining room by candlelight or in the high garden. Californians have long enjoyed the splendor of La Jolla, a charming village with a spectacular coastline. Guests can walk to the many unique shops or take a stroll along the beach and enjoy an unforgettable sunset. A short drive out of La Jolla will take guests to the myriad of sites in San Diego. After a day exploring the area, guests return to the inn and enjoy a sampling of wine and cheese.

Historic Interest: Bishop's School (next door), Old Town (5 miles), Balboa Park (5 miles).

Innkeeper(s): Ron Shanks. $139-379. MC, VISA, AX, DS, PC, TC. TAC10. 15 rooms with PB, 4 with FP, 2 suites and 1 conference room. Breakfast and snacks/refreshments included in rates. Types of meals: Early coffee/tea and picnic lunch. Beds: KQT. Cable TV, phone, turndown service and some with VCR and ceiling fans in room. Central air. VCR, fax, bicycles, library, picnic lunches, beach chairs, towels and tennis rackets on premises. Weddings, small meetings, family reunions and seminars hosted. Spanish spoken. Amusement parks, antiquing, art galleries, beaches, bicycling, canoeing/kayaking, fishing, golf, hiking, live theater, museums, parks, shopping, sporting events, tennis and water sports nearby.

Publicity: *New York Times, Los Angeles Times, Glamour, Country Inns, Travel & Leisure. and ABC.*

La Jolla Inn

1110 Prospect St
La Jolla, CA 92037-4533
(858)454-0133 (800)433-1609 Fax:(858)454-2056

Circa 1946. Although this is a newer property, built in 1946, the hotel is located within walking distance to many wonderful shops, restaurants and sites in beautiful La Jolla, an upscale suburb of San Diego. Guests enjoy stunning ocean views from some rooms. The decor is done in a modern and pleasing hotel style. Made-to-order continental breakfasts are served on the sun deck, which faces the Pacific and La Jolla Cove. San Diego is just minutes away, but guests can easily spend a whole day enjoying this seaside village.

Innkeeper(s): Tony Torbati. $150-400. MC, VISA, AX, DC, CB, DS, TC. TAC10. 22 rooms with PB and 2 suites. Breakfast and afternoon tea included in rates. Types of meals: Cont. Beds: KQT. Cable TV and phone in room. Air conditioning. Fax, copier, bicycles, library and sun deck on premises. Weddings, small meetings, family reunions and seminars hosted. Spanish, German, Russian and Arabic spoken. Amusement parks, fishing, golf, live theater, parks, shopping, sporting events, tennis and water sports nearby.

Publicity: *Diversions and Coastal Living.*

Lake Arrowhead   N12

Bracken Fern Manor

815 Arrowhead Villas Rd, PO Box 1006
Lake Arrowhead, CA 92352-1006
(909)337-8557 Fax:(909)337-3323
E-mail: bfm@dreamsoft.com
Web: www.brackenfernmanor.com

Circa 1929. Opened during the height of the '20s as Lake Arrowhead's first membership resort, this country inn provided refuge to Silver Screen heroines, the wealthy and the prominent. Old letters from the Gibson Girls found in the attic bespoke of elegant parties, dapper gentlemen, the Depression, Prohibition and homesick hearts. Each room is furnished with antiques collected from a lifetime of international travel. There is also a game parlor, wine tasting cellar, library, art gallery and garden Jacuzzi and sauna. Wine is offered in the afternoon. The Crestline Historical Society has its own museum and curator and a map of historical sites you can visit.

Historic Interest: Lake Arrowhead's first private membership resort with electricity, opened in 1929 by Bugsy Segal.

Innkeeper(s): Cheryl Weaver. $80-225. MC, VISA, TC. 10 rooms, 9 with PB and 3 suites. Breakfast included in rates. Types of meals: Full bkfst and early coffee/tea. Beds: KQDT. VCR, jacuzzi, art gallery and garden & wine cellar on premises. Weddings, small meetings, family reunions and seminars hosted. Antiquing, fishing, live theater, shopping, downhill skiing, cross-country skiing and water sports nearby.

Publicity: *Mountain Shopper & Historic B&B, The Press Enterprise, Sun and Lava.*

"My husband brought me here for my 25th birthday and it was everything I hoped it would be - peaceful, romantic and so relaxing .... Thank you for the wonderful memories I will hold close to my heart always."

Lake Tahoe/Soda Springs   F7

Royal Gorge's Rainbow Lodge

9411 Hillside Dr PO Box 1100
Lake Tahoe/Soda Springs, CA 95728
(530)426-3871 (800)500-3871 Fax:(530)426-9221
E-mail: info@royalgorge.com

Circa 1928. Located in the Sierras by a bend of the Yuba River, this old mountain lodge is a nostalgic, picturesque getaway spot. The lodge was built using local granite and hand-hewn timber. A mountain decor permeates the 32 guest rooms. There are two dining rooms, featuring fine Californian and French cuisine. The Engadine Cafe offers breakfast, lunch, dinner and Sunday brunch. The cocktail lounge, which offers a bar menu

throughout the day and into the evening, is decorated with a variety of photographs documenting the area's history. Chairs and tables have been set up for those who wish to relax and enjoy the river view. The lodge is adjacent to the Royal Gorge Ski Area, which is the largest cross-country ski area in North America. Summer activities include hiking, mountain biking and fishing.

Historic Interest: Donner Party Museum.

Innkeeper(s): Alan Davis. $145-165. MC, VISA, TC. 32 rooms, 10 with PB, 2 suites and 1 conference room. Breakfast included in rates. Types of meals: Full bkfst, country bkfst, veg bkfst, early coffee/tea, gourmet lunch, picnic lunch, snacks/refreshments and gourmet dinner. Beds: QDT. Fax and library on premises. Small meetings hosted. Antiquing, beaches, bicycling, canoeing/kayaking, fishing, golf, hiking, museums, parks, downhill skiing, cross-country skiing, water sports and wineries nearby.

Publicity: *Sunset and Sacramento News.*

Lakeport   F4

Forbestown B&B Inn

825 N Forbes St
Lakeport, CA 95453-4337
(707)263-7858 Fax:(707)263-7878
E-mail: forbestowninn@zapcom.net
Web: www.innaccess.com/fti

Circa 1863. Beckoned by an inviting front porch, this early California farmhouse-style inn is located just a few blocks from downtown Lakeport and Clear Lake. Appealing guest bed-rooms are tastefully decorated and furnished with oak antiques. A delicious breakfast is served by a vintage window wall in the dining room or in the secluded garden. Enjoy a refreshing swim in the pool as one of the day's pleasant activities.

Innkeeper(s): Wally & Pat Kelley. $85-120. MC, VISA, AX, DC, DS, PC, TC. TAC10. 4 rooms with PB. Types of meals: Full bkfst, early coffee/tea and snacks/refreshments. Beds: KQ. Ceiling fan in room. Air conditioning. VCR, fax, swimming, library, wood stove and internet access on premises. Weddings, small meetings, family reunions and seminars hosted. Antiquing, bicycling, fishing, golf, hiking, festivals, local events, birding, parks, shopping, water sports and wineries nearby.

Publicity: *Sunset.*

Thompson House

3315 Lakeshore Blvd
Lakeport, CA 95453
(707)263-4905 Fax:(707)263-6276
E-mail: thompsonhouse@pacific.net
Web: www.thompsonhouse.net

Circa 1895. This Spanish stucco home's interior is decorated in an English Tudor style. Located on two acres, the home's grounds include lawns, a gazebo and space for 300-400 people for garden weddings and parties. Owners of Anthony's Restaurant nearby, the innkeepers offer kitchen dinners for 40 twice a month at the inn and a 30% discount at Anthony's is also offered on Thursday and Sunday. A 1,400-square-foot suite is the only accommodation offered. It's comprised of a bed-room with a romantically draped four-poster bed, a private bath, and a living room with ceiling fan, fireplace and a wall of bookcases. Porcelain dolls, crafted by the innkeeper, are displayed. A popular breakfast item is puff pastry filled with home-canned fruits, home-baked muffins and fruit compote. The grounds feature croquet, badminton and a horseshoe pit. Berries are grown on the property and there's a grape arbor, roses, azaleas, rhododendrons and fruit and nut trees.

Innkeeper(s): Jan & Bill Thompson. $125. MC, VISA, AX, DS, PC, TC. 1 suites, 1 with FP. Breakfast included in rates. Types of meals: Cont plus and early coffee/tea. Beds: Q. Cable TV, turndown service, ceiling fan, VCR and fireplace in room. Air conditioning. Fax, copier and library on premises. Weddings, small meetings, family reunions and seminars hosted. Antiquing, art galleries, beaches, bicycling, canoeing/kayaking, fishing, golf, hiking, horseback riding, water slides, live theater, museums, parks, shopping, tennis, water sports and wineries nearby.

Publicity: *Lake County Record Bee.*

Livermore   I5

The Queen Anne Cottage on 8th

2516 Eighth Street
Livermore, CA 94550
(925)606-7140 Fax:(925)373-1737
E-mail: info@queenanneon8th.com
Web: www.queenanneon8th.com

Circa 1875. Offering a memorable pairing of romance and luxury, the Cottage Rose, a pioneer cottage, is adjacent to the main house, a Queen Anne Victorian. Loving restoration has retained both historical integrity and original architectural detail. Antiques and collectibles add a warm, personal touch. Gorgeous guest bedrooms provide the utmost comfort with down duvets, hand-ironed cotton sheets, bathrobes and hair dryers. Some boast canopy beds, a large whirlpool tub, marble shower and private balcony entrance overlooking gardens. Vintage china enhances a resplendent breakfast in the dining room. A rock spa and secluded waterfall is a blissful haven.

Historic Interest: Wente Vineyare & Winery (1.5 miles), The Carnegy Hall Museum (1/2 mile), Ravenswood (1 mile).

Innkeeper(s): Melanie & Terry Wetton. $135-250. MC, VISA, AX, DC, DS, PC, TC. TAC10. 3 rooms with PB, 1 with FP, 2 suites and 1 cottage. Breakfast, afternoon tea and snacks/refreshments included in rates. Types of meals: Gourmet bkfst, early coffee/tea and room service. Beds: QT. Cable TV, phone, turndown service, ceiling fan, VCR, fireplace, hair dryers and bath robes in room. Central air. Fax, library, hot tub, gazebo and double person hammock on premises. Weddings and small meetings hosted. Amusement parks, antiquing, art galleries, bicycling, canoeing/kayaking, fishing, golf, hiking, horseback riding, Alameda County Fairgrounds, BART, museums, parks, shopping, sporting events, tennis, water sports and wineries nearby.

Lodi   H6

Wine & Roses Country Inn

2505 W Turner Rd
Lodi, CA 95242-4643
(209)334-6988 Fax:(209)334-6570

Circa 1902. This historic inn has attracted guests such as Margaret Thatcher and Martha Stewart, who were attracted by the inn's excellent reputation for food, lodging and service. Rooms in the historic house are furnished with antiques and country pieces, and there are 40 new cottage rooms opening in the spring. These will be tucked among the gardens and around the inn's ancient canopy of trees. They will feature beamed ceilings and old-fashioned built-ins as well as modern amenities such as spa-tubs, fireplaces, garden views and veran-

das. Business travelers will enjoy the rooms with large desks and modem connections and the room service. The restaurant offers excellent dining in its beautiful garden setting, and in summer a special treat is to sit under the graceful shade of the inn's trees while having lunch. A winery building on the property is host to the county's wine industry, and there is a new banquet facility. The inn enjoys popularity with honeymooners, tourists and business people, and its location five miles off I-5 makes it an ideal midway stop between Los Angeles and San Francisco.

Innkeeper(s): Del & Sherri Smith. $99-145. MC, VISA, AX, CB, DS. 10 rooms with PB, 4 suites and 1 conference room. Breakfast included in rates. Types of meals: Gourmet bkfst, early coffee/tea, picnic lunch, snacks/refreshments, gourmet dinner and room service. Beds: Q. Phone and ceiling fan in room. Air conditioning. Fax and copier on premises. Handicap access. Weddings, small meetings, family reunions and seminars hosted. Antiquing, fishing, live theater, shopping, sporting events and water sports nearby.

Publicity: *Los Angeles, Business Tribune and Country Inns.*

"*Hospitality here exceeds Southern hospitality. I feel as if I am somewhere in time.*"

Long Beach   O10

Kennebec Corner B&B

2305 E 2nd St
Long Beach, CA 90803-5126
(562)439-2705 (877)227-4060 Fax:(562)439-2705
E-mail: kennebec@earthlink.net
Web: bbhost.com/kennebeccorner

Circa 1912. This California Craftsman-style home offers a large four-room suite with a sitting room, office, fireplace, bathroom with a double sunken tub and a bedroom with a one-of-a-kind,

four-poster king-size bed. There is an outdoor spa available in the home's courtyard. The innkeepers deliver the morning paper and a tray with coffee or tea to your door an hour prior to breakfast. On weekdays, a healthy California or continental breakfast is served, and on weekends, guests enjoy a full, gourmet meal. The home is located in Bluff Park, a local historic district two blocks from the beach.

Innkeeper(s): Michael & Marty Gunhus. $125-150. MC, VISA, AX, PC, TC. TAC20. 1 suites. Breakfast included in rates. Types of meals: Gourmet bkfst, cont plus, early coffee/tea and picnic lunch. Beds: K. Cable TV, phone and VCR in room. Fax, spa, bicycles and library on premises. Antiquing, fishing, live theater, parks, shopping, sporting events and water sports nearby.

Lord Mayor's B&B Inn

435 Cedar Ave
Long Beach, CA 90802-2245
(562)436-0324 Fax:(562)436-0324
E-mail: innkeepers@lordmayors.com
Web: www.lordmayors.com

Circa 1904. This collection of carefully restored homes includes the Main House where the city's first mayor lived. Granite pillars flank the veranda of this historical landmark with a golden oak wood interior. The Eastlake Room boasts a

family heirlooom fainting couch. Hand-carved Austrian twin beds accent Margarita's Room. The Hawaiian Room has a small clawfoot tub. A four-poster bed and Dutch wardrobe adorn Beppe's Room. The Apple and Cinnamon Houses are suitable for families or large groups. The Garden House, a studio that was originally part of the horse barn, provides tranquil privacy. Breakfast is a tasty assortment of home-baked treats and a hot entree. Enjoy the city garden, or walk to the nearby convention center, restaurants and beach.

Historic Interest: Queen Mary (three-fourth mile), Port of Long Beach (half mile).

Innkeeper(s): Laura & Reuben Brasser. $85-140. MC, VISA, AX, DC, CB, DS, PC, TC. TAC10. 12 rooms, 10 with PB, 1 cottage and 1 conference room. Breakfast and snacks/refreshments included in rates. Types of meals: Full bkfst and early coffee/tea. Beds: QDT. VCR, fax and library on premises. Weddings, small meetings, family reunions and seminars hosted. Danish and Dutch spoken. Antiquing, art galleries, beaches, bicycling, golf, Aquarium of Pacific, Gateway to Catalina, Island and Carnival Cruise Line terminal, live theater, museums and parks nearby.

Publicity: *KCET Magazine, Daily News Los Angeles, Press Telegram and Yellow Brick Road.*

"Your hospitality and beautiful room were respites for the spirit and body after our long trip."

The Turret House Victorian B&B

556 Chestnut Ave
Long Beach, CA 90802-2213
(562)983-9812 (888)488-7738 Fax:(562)437-4082
E-mail: innkeepers@turrethouse.com
Web: www.turrethouse.com

Circa 1906. This Queen Anne Victorian does, of course, display a turret as one of its delightful architectural features. The home, located in a Long Beach historic district, remained in the same family until it was purchased by the current owners. The decor is elegant and romantic. Fine linens top the beds and the wallpapers and furnishings are all coordinated with similar prints and colors. Each room has a clawfoot tub, and bubble bath is provided for a relaxing soak. The breakfasts are an imaginative gourmet treat. Guests might partake of a menu with a granola parfait, followed by cranberry scones and spinach parasol pie. There are two Victorian parlors to enjoy, and a proper afternoon tea is served with succulent treats such as a mocha cheesecake or rich peanut butter pie. Long Beach offers plenty of shops and restaurants, and the city is well situated for those enjoying the many attractions in Southern California.

Historic Interest: Queen Mary (half mile), Civil War Drum Barracks (7 miles), waterfront amusement park.

Innkeeper(s): Nina & Lee Agee. $100-150. MC, VISA, AX, DS, PC, TC. TAC10. 5 rooms with PB. Breakfast and afternoon tea included in rates. Types of meals: Gourmet bkfst and early coffee/tea. AP. Beds: KQT. Turndown service, ceiling fan, table and chairs and balcony in room. Air conditioning. VCR, fax and piano on premises. Weddings, small meetings, family reunions and seminars hosted. Amusement parks, antiquing, art galleries, beaches, bicycling, canoeing/kayaking, fishing, golf, hiking, horseback riding, aquarium, Queen Mary, live theater, museums, parks, shopping, sporting events, tennis, water sports and wineries nearby.

Publicity: *Press Telegram, L.A. Daily News, L. A. Times, Long Beach Press Telegram, Signal Hill News and Local cable station.*

McCloud Hotel B&B

408 Main St, PO Box 730
McCloud, CA 96057-0730
(530)964-2822 (800)964-2823 Fax:(530)964-2844
E-mail: mchotel@snowcrest.net
Web: www.mccloudhotel.com

Circa 1915. In a quiet town with no stop lights or fast food restaurants, this grand hotel offers privacy and hospitality. With meticulous detail, the hotel has been restored and richly decorated. A nostalgic journey begins in the wood-paneled lobby with its splendid staircase and adjacent great room featuring comfy overstuffed furniture, a cozy fireplace and antique piano. The luxurious oversized guest bedrooms and suites boast canopied or four-poster beds, antique trunk tables, magnificent balcony views and fluffy robes. A leisurely gourmet breakfast is served at intimate English tables for two, or groups of four and six. The must-have recipes are in a cookbook for sale in the gift shop. New releases and classic movies are shown each evening in the DVD viewing room with large screen digital TV. The ample grounds are a glorious infusion of garden rooms, perennials, vine arbors and evergreens. Nearby, McCloud's registered historic district features mill houses and a general store in the heart of Shasta Cascade.

Historic Interest: Mount Shasta (5 miles).

Innkeeper(s): Marilyn & Lee Ogden. $79-177. MC, VISA, AX, DS, TC. TAC10. 17 rooms with PB, 4 suites and 1 conference room. Breakfast and afternoon tea included in rates. Types of meals: Gourmet bkfst, veg bkfst, early coffee/tea, picnic lunch, snacks/refreshments and room service. Beds: QT. Ceiling fan and fireplace in room. Air conditioning. Fax, copier, library, gift shop and DVD viewing room on premises. Handicap access. Weddings, small meetings, family reunions and seminars hosted. Antiquing, bicycling, fishing, golf, hiking, dinner train, museums, parks, shopping, downhill skiing, crosscountry skiing and water sports nearby.

Publicity: *Sunset, Miami Herald, Best Places., ESPN Fishing and PBS California Gold.*

McCloud River Inn

325 Lawndale Ct
McCloud, CA 96057-1560
(530)964-2130 (800)261-7831 Fax:(530)964-2730
E-mail: mort@snowcrest.net
Web: www.riverinn.com

Circa 1900. Nestled within the beauty of Shasta National Forest rests this country Victorian. Five serene acres of lawns and woodland create a peaceful setting at this home, on the National Register of Historic Places. The interior has been painstakingly restored, and each of the five guest rooms has its own individual charm. Breakfasts are a treat, and a typical menu might include a savory Greek quiche, homemade pastries and a selection of fresh fruits. Shops and historic sites are within walking distance, and it's a 15-minute drive to Mt. Shasta Ski Park.

Innkeeper(s): Ron & Marina Mort. $75-145. MC, VISA, AX, DS, PC, TC. TAC10. 5 rooms with PB and 2 suites. Breakfast included in rates. Types of meals: Full bkfst. Beds: QDT. Some with Jacuzzi tub in room. Air conditioning. Fax, copier and gift shop on premises. Small meetings hosted. Antiquing, bicycling, fishing, golf, hiking, train excursions, parks, shopping, downhill skiing, cross-country skiing and water sports nearby.

Publicity: *Sunset, Berkeley Guide, Siskiyou County Railroad Gazette, Siskiyou County Scene and Miami Herald.*

Mendocino F2

Agate Cove Inn

11201 Lansing, PO Box 1150
Mendocino, CA 95460-1150
(707)937-0551 (800)527-3111
E-mail: agate@mcn.org
Web: www.agatecove.com

Circa 1860. Perched on a blufftop above the Pacific Ocean, Agate Cove Inn offers splendid ocean views in a two-acre setting of gardens and 100-year-old cypress trees. Most rooms boast stunning ocean views or garden vistas and have fireplaces and decks. Select from a Jacuzzi tub, showers for two or deep-soaking tub. Down comforters and feather beds invite snuggling in the king or queen beds. TVs, VCRs and CD players as well as daily morning newspapers are additional amenities. Guests enjoy a full country breakfast with freshly baked muffins or the innkeeper's award-winning bread. Eggs Benedict, omelets, frittatas and other entrees are served along with baked apples, poached pears and homemade applesauce as accompaniments. The Farmhouse breakfast room offers a spectacular ocean view. Fine dining, hiking, art walks and other activities may be arranged with the help of the inn's knowledgeable staff.

Innkeeper(s): Dennis & Nancy Freeze. $119-269. MC, VISA. 10 rooms with PB, 9 with FP. Types of meals: Full bkfst. Beds: KQ. Cable TV, VCR, fireplace, ocean view, feather bed, down comforter, hair dryer, Sherry, newspaper delivery, HBO and some with Jacuzzi in room. Fax, cottages, internet connection, concierge service, refrigerator, CD library, video library and paperback book exchange on premises.

Publicity: *Travel & Leisure, San Francisco Magazine, San Francisco Examine, Glamour, Sacramento Bee, Travel Holiday, Wine Spectator, Country Inns, Inns & Retreats Newsletter and St. Louis Post Dispatch.*

"Warmest hospitality, charming rooms, best breakfast and view in Mendocino."

Brewery Gulch Inn

9401 Coast Hwy One N
Mendocino, CA 95460-9767
(707)937-4752 (800)578-4454 Fax:(707)937-1279
E-mail: info@brewerygulchinn.com
Web: www.brewerygulchinn.com

Circa 1864. Ten acres of bliss are found at this new Craftsman-style Shake inn, built with eco-salvaged, old virgin redwood timbers from Big River. Sitting next to the original historic farmhouse on a scenic hillside, Arts and Crafts furnishings and ocean views create an eye-pleasing decor. The romantic guest bedrooms boast fireplaces, private decks, soundproofing, and pampering touches including terry robes and CD players. Mouth-watering breakfast al fresco on the common deck is prepared with organic ingredients by a trained chef. Relax in the fireplaced Great Room with afternoon wine and hors d'oeuvres.

Innkeeper(s): Glenn Lutge. $150-285. MC, VISA, AX, PC, TC. TAC10. 10 rooms with PB, 10 with FP. Breakfast and snacks/refreshments included in rates. Types of meals: Gourmet bkfst, early coffee/tea and picnic lunch. Beds: KQT. Cable TV, phone, turndown service, VCR and fireplace in room. Fax, copier, library and gift shop on premises. Handicap access. Weddings hosted. Antiquing, art galleries, beaches, bicycling, canoeing/kayaking, fishing, golf, hiking, horseback riding, Skunk steam engine train, live theater, museums, parks, shopping, tennis, water sports and wineries nearby.

Publicity: *Coastal Living, Food & Wine, Sunset Magazine, San Francisco Chronicle and KGO Radio.*

Glendeven Inn

PO Box 914
Mendocino, CA 95456
(707)937-0083 (800)822-4536
E-mail: innkeeper@glendeven.com
Web: www.glendeven.com

Circa 1867. Lumber merchant Isaiah Stevens built this farmhouse on a two-acre headland meadow with the bay of Little River in the distance. Gray clapboard siding and high-pitched roof lines reflect the architecture of Stevens' native Maine. The Stevenscroft annex has four rooms, each with its own fireplace, views of the bay and breakfast in your room. The Carriage House suite offers two fireplaces, a king-size bed and a private balcony.

Innkeeper(s): Sharon & Higgins. $110-240. MC, VISA, AX, DS. 10 rooms with PB. Breakfast included in rates. Types of meals: Full bkfst. Beds: KQ.

Publicity: *USA Today, San Francisco Examiner and Santa Rosa Press Democrat.*

"We just returned from our stay at your beautiful inn and had to let you know how wonderful and very special we felt for the two days we we were there."

The Inn at Schoolhouse Creek

N Hwy 1, PO Box 1637
Mendocino, CA 95460
(707)937-5525 (800)731-5525 Fax:(707)937-2012
E-mail: innkeeper@schoolhousecreek.com
Web: www.schoolhousecreek.com

Circa 1860. The Inn at School House Creek offers private cottages and rooms on its eight acres of rose gardens, forests and meadows. (The inn's gardens have been featured in several magazines.) Many cottages include views of the ocean and all offer a fireplace. Located three miles from Mendocino, the inn was a motor court in the '30s. Private beach access to Buckhorn Cove allows guests to enjoy whale watching, sea lions and the crashing waves of the Pacific. Organize your day to include a picnic lunch (available by advance notice) to enjoy at a secluded waterfall in the redwoods. Then take a sunset soak in the inn's ocean view hot tub. The next morning's breakfast may include Fruit Basket Breakfast Pudding with whipped cream, eggs, fruit and a variety of freshly baked muffins and breads, jams and juices.

Innkeeper(s): Al & Penny Greenwood. $115-255. MC, VISA, AX, DS, PC, TC. TAC10. 15 rooms with PB, 15 with FP, 2 suites and 9 cottages. Breakfast included in rates. Types of meals: Full bkfst, early coffee/tea and picnic lunch. MAP. Beds: KQD. Cable TV, phone, VCR, some with whirlpools, kitchens and refrigerators and microwaves in room. Fax, spa and evening hors d'oeuvres on premises. Weddings, small meetings, family reunions and seminars hosted. Fishing, golf, hiking, live theater, parks, shopping, tennis and water sports nearby.

Pets allowed: In designated units, extra fee.

John Dougherty House

571 Ukiah St
Mendocino, CA 95460
(707)937-5266 (800)486-2104
E-mail: jdhbmw@mcn.org
Web: www.jdhouse.com

Circa 1867. Early American furnishings and country-style stenciling provide the decor at this welcoming inn. Four rooms have outstanding water views, including the Captain's Room. The

water tower room has an 18-foot ceiling and wood-burning stove. The inn's grounds sparkle with an array of beautiful flowers. The inn has been featured on the cover of Country Homes. New jet tubs in room.

Historic Interest: Located in Mendocino Historic Village.

Innkeeper(s): David & Marion Wells. $95-205. MC, VISA, DS, PC, TC. TAC10. 8 rooms with PB, 7 with FP, 2 suites, 1 cottage and 2 cabins. Breakfast included in rates. Types of meals: Gourmet bkfst and early coffee/tea. Beds: KQ. Cable TV in room. Antiques on premises. Antiquing, fishing, golf, live theater, parks, shopping, tennis and water sports nearby.

Publicity: *Mendocino Beacon, Country Home, Los Angeles Times (Travel Section August 2001) and San Francisco Times/Tribune.*

"A treasure chest of charm, beauty and views."

Joshua Grindle Inn

PO Box 647
Mendocino, CA 95460-0647
(707)937-4143 (800)474-6353
E-mail: stay@joshgrin.com
Web: www.joshgrin.com

Circa 1879. The town banker, Joshua Grindle, built this New England-style home on two acres. The decor is light and airy, with Early American antiques, clocks and quilts. In addition

to lodging in the house, there are rooms in the water tower and in an adjacent cottage. Six of the guest rooms have fireplaces. Some have views over the town to the ocean.

Innkeeper(s): Charles & Cindy Reinhart. $130-245. MC, VISA, TC. 10 rooms with PB, 6 with FP. Breakfast and

snacks/refreshments included in rates. Types of meals: Gourmet bkfst. Beds: KQT. Fishing, live theater, parks and shopping nearby.

Publicity: *Peninsula, Copley News Service, Orange Coast Magazine, San Francisco Magazine, Sacramento Magazine, AT&T Commercial and San Francisco News.*

"We are basking in the memories of our stay. We loved every moment."

The Larkin Cottage

44950 Larkin Rd
Mendocino, CA 95460
(707)937-2567 Fax:(707)937-4714
E-mail: stay@larkincottage.com
Web: www.larkincottage.com

Circa 1940. If you're searching for a touch of romance, a stay at this cozy, one-bedroom cottage might be just the place. In addition to the bedroom, the cottage includes a living room, kitchen and a private deck. Antiques, lacy curtains, and a fireplace add to the romance of the cottage's interior, and the garden setting provides quiet and privacy. Although breakfast isn't provided, the owners stock the cottage with plenty of goodies, including coffee, tea, fruit juice, bagels, pastries, fresh fruit, cookies, cheese, crackers and even wine and sherry. The cottage is just one mile out of Mendocino, and close to the beach, as well.

Innkeeper(s): Bob & Diann Gerbo. $135-150. MC, VISA, PC. 1 cottages.

Snacks/refreshments included in rates. Types of meals: Cont plus and early coffee/tea. Beds: Q. Cable TV, phone, VCR, full kitchen and fireplace in room. Fax, copier and bicycles on premises. Antiquing, art galleries, beaches, bicycling, canoeing/kayaking, fishing, golf, hiking, horseback riding, live theater, parks, shopping, tennis and wineries nearby.

MacCallum House Inn

45020 Albion St
Mendocino, CA 95460
(707)937-0289 (800)609-0492 Fax:(707)937-2243
E-mail: machouse@mcn.org

Circa 1882. Built by William H. Kelley for his newly wed daughter, Daisy MacCallum, the MacCallum House Inn is a splendid example of New England architecture in the Victorian village of Mendocino. Besides the main house, accommodations include the barn, carriage house, greenhouse, gazebo and water tower rooms.

Innkeeper(s): Melanie & Joe Reding. $100-190. MC, VISA, DS. 19 rooms with PB. Types of meals: Cont. Beds: KQT. Handicap access.

Publicity: *California Visitors Review.*

Mendocino Village Inn

44860 Main St
Mendocino, CA 95460
(707)937-0246 (800)882-7029 Fax:(707)937-1549
E-mail: lodging@mendocinoinn.com
Web: www.mendocinoinn.com

Circa 1882. Originally the home of physician Dr. William McCornack, this graceful Victorian has been beautifully restored. One of the architectural gems of Mendocino, the inn has a variety of rooms with Victorian, country and early Californian decor. The ocean and the pleasures of the North Coast lie just beyond the house's white picket fence. Enjoy two-course breakfasts and afternoon refreshments.

Historic Interest: Historic museums in town.

Innkeeper(s): Jessica Rock. $65-185. MC, VISA, PC, TC. 12 rooms, 10 with PB, 8 with FP. Breakfast, afternoon tea and snacks/refreshments included in rates. Types of meals: Gourmet bkfst, veg bkfst and early coffee/tea. Beds: KQD. Fireplace and Jacuzzi (in three rooms) in room. Spa, sauna, gift shop and professional massage on premises. Handicap access. Weddings, small meetings and family reunions hosted. Antiquing, art galleries, beaches, bicycling, canoeing/kayaking, fishing, golf, hiking, horseback riding, whale watching, mushroom hunting, live theater, museums, parks, shopping, tennis, water sports and wineries nearby.

Publicity: *Wine Country Review.*

"A house with good spirit and great people."

Packard House

PO Box 1065
Mendocino, CA 95460
(707)937-2677 Fax:(707)937-1323
E-mail: info@packardhouse.com

Circa 1878. One of four landmark homes on Executive Row, this Carpenter's Gothic Victorian was built for the town chemist. The original watertower is listed in the National Register. Elegantly furnished with an eclectic blend of old and new, antiques and custom-made pieces dwell easily with an extensive collection of fine art. Luxurious items like fine linens, soft robes, slippers and Spanish sherry add to the enchantment of the gorgeous guest bedrooms. Anticipate the pleasure of two-person jet tubs, fireplaces, VCRs and CD players, as well as colorful garden or ocean views. Mouth-watering breakfasts are served in the dining room, as are wine and appetizers in the afternoon.

Innkeeper(s): Maria & Dan Levin. $125-205. MC, VISA, DS, PC, TC. TAC10. 5 rooms with PB, 5 with FP and 1 suite. Breakfast and snacks/refreshments included in rates. Types of meals: Gourmet bkfst and early coffee/tea. Beds: KQ. Cable TV, phone, VCR and fireplace in room. Fax, spa, library and gift shop on premises. Portuguese spoken. Antiquing, art galleries, beaches, bicycling, canoeing/kayaking, fishing, golf, hiking, horseback riding, live theater, museums, parks, shopping, tennis, water sports and wineries nearby.

Sea Rock B&B Inn

11101 Lansing St
Mendocino, CA 95460
(707)937-0926 (800)906-0926
E-mail: searock@mcn.org
Web: www.searock.com

Circa 1930. Enjoy sea breezes and ocean vistas at this inn, which rests on a bluff looking out to the Pacific. Most of the accommodations include a wood-burning Franklin fireplace and featherbed. Four guest rooms are available in the Stratton House, and each affords a spectacular ocean view. There are six cottages on the grounds, most offering a sea view. The innkeepers also offer deluxe accommodations in four special suites. Each has an ocean view, wood-burning fireplace, private entrance and a deck, whirlpool or ocean view tub. The grounds, which now feature gardens, were the site of an 1870s brewery. The inn is less than half a mile from Mendocino.

Innkeeper(s): Susie & Andy Plocher. $139-269. MC, VISA, AX, DS, PC, TC. 14 rooms with PB, 14 with FP, 8 suites and 6 cottages. Breakfast included in rates. Types of meals: Cont plus. Beds: KQ. Cable TV, phone and VCR in room. Antiquing, fishing, golf, live theater, parks, shopping, tennis and water sports nearby.

Publicity: *California Visitors Review and Sunset Magazine.*

The Stanford Inn By The Sea

PO Box 487
Mendocino, CA 95460-0487
(707)937-5615 (800)331-8884 Fax:(707)937-0305
E-mail: info@stanfordinn.com

Circa 1856. Tucked against a forested hillside, the Stanford Inn, a new building, affords every guest a view of the ocean. Its 10 acres include an expansive lawn studded with flower gardens that slope down to a duck pond and redwood barn where the inn's llamas and horses graze. Each room has a four-poster bed, a wood-burning fireplace and watercolors and paintings by local artists. A '30s cottage is  on the premises and there is a turn-of-the-century homestead. Complimentary Mendocino wines are offered.

Historic Interest: Mendocino Village (immediately adjacent).

Innkeeper(s): Joan & Jeff Stanford. $215-325. MC, VISA, AX, DC, CB, DS. TAC10. 33 rooms with PB, 26 with FP, 3 suites and 1 conference room. Breakfast and afternoon tea included in rates. Beds: KQT. Spa and sauna on premises. Handicap access. Live theater and water sports nearby. Pets Allowed.

Publicity: *Oakland Tribune, Brides and Contra Costa Times.*

"As working parents with young children, our weekends away are so terribly few in number, that every one must be precious. Thanks to you, our weekend in Mendocino was the finest of all."

Whitegate Inn

499 Howard St
Mendocino, CA 95460
(707)937-4892 (800)531-7282 Fax:(707)937-1131
E-mail: staff@whitegateinn.com
Web: www.whitegateinn.com

Circa 1883. When it was first built, the local newspaper called Whitegate Inn "one of the most elegant and best appointed residences in town." Its bay windows, steep gabled roof, redwood siding and fish-scale shingles are stunning examples of Victorian architecture. The house's original wallpaper and candelabras adorn the double parlors. There, an antique 1827 piano, at one time part of Alexander Graham Bell's  collection, and inlaid pocket doors take you back to a more gracious time. French and Victorian antique furnishings and fresh flowers add to the inn's elegant hospitality and old world charm. The gourmet breakfasts are artfully presented in the inn's sunlit dining room. The inn is just a block from the ocean, galleries, restaurants and the center of town.

Historic Interest: Mendocino Headlands State Park surrounds the village, which was once the property of the original lumber mill.

Innkeeper(s): Carol & George Bechtloff. $149-289. MC, VISA, AX, DC, DS, PC, TC. TAC10. 6 rooms with PB, 6 with FP, 1 suite, 1 cottage and 1 conference room. Breakfast and snacks/refreshments included in rates. Types of meals: Full bkfst and early coffee/tea. Beds: KQT. Cable TV and phone in room. Fax, copier and welcome basket and evening sherry on premises. Weddings, small meetings, family reunions and seminars hosted. Italian and Spanish spoken. Antiquing, fishing, golf, horseback riding, whale watching, live theater, parks, shopping, tennis and water sports nearby.

Publicity: *Innsider, Country Inns, Country Home, Glamour, Santa Rosa Press Democrat, San Francisco Chronicle, Bon Appetit, Victoria Magazine, Sunset and San Francisco Examiner.*

Mill Valley   H4

Mountain Home Inn

810 Panoramic Hwy
Mill Valley, CA 94941-1765
(415)381-9000 Fax:(415)381-3615

Circa 1912. At one time the only way to get to Mountain Home was by taking the train up Mount Tamalpais. With 22 trestles and 281 curves, it was called "the crookedest railroad in the world." Now accessible by auto, the trip still provides a spectacular view of San Francisco Bay. Each guest room has a view of the mountain, valley or bay.

Innkeeper(s): Josh Sperry. $159-289. MC, VISA, AX, PC, TC. TAC10. 10 rooms with PB, 5 with FP and 1 conference room. Breakfast included in rates. Types of meals: Full bkfst, lunch and gourmet dinner. Beds: KQ. Phone in room. Fax and copier on premises. Weddings, small meetings and family reunions hosted. Parks and shopping nearby.

Publicity: *San Francisco Examiner and California.*

"A luxurious retreat. Echoes the grand style and rustic feeling of national park lodges — Ben Davidson, Travel & Leisure."

Monrovia
O10

Chez Noel

210 W Colorado Blvd
Monrovia, CA 91016
(626)256-6622 (877)256-6622
E-mail: cheznoel@earthlink.net

Circa 1886. It's rare to find 19th-century homes in the Los
Angeles area, so Chez Noel is a rare find. The Eastlake Victorian
was built by a Civil War captain. The home is decorated in an
eclectic style and features artwork created by the innkeepers.
Healthy, gourmet breakfasts include items such as whole-grain
French toast, homemade muffins and fresh fruit. Chez Noel is
located in Old Town Monrovia. Pasadena is five minutes away,
and most popular local attractions are less than 40 minutes
from the inn, including Disneyland and Knott's Berry Farm.

Innkeeper(s): Scott & Cammie Noel. $100-140. MC, VISA, PC. 3 rooms with
PB. Breakfast included in rates. Types of meals: Gourmet bkfst, early
coffee/tea, picnic lunch and snacks/refreshments. Beds: KQT. Air conditioning. VCR, fax, bicycles and library on premises. Amusement parks, antiquing,
golf, old town Monrovia, Pasadena nearby,
Disneyland 30 minutes, live theater, parks, shopping, downhill skiing and
sporting events nearby.

Montara
I4

The Goose & Turrets B&B

835 George St, PO Box 937
Montara, CA 94037-0937
(650)728-5451 Fax:(650)728-0141
E-mail: rhmgt@montara.com
Web: goose.montara.com

Circa 1908. Now a haven focusing on comfort and hospitality,
this classic bed & breakfast once served as Montara's first post
office, the town hall, and a country club for Spanish-American

War veterans. Large living
and dining room areas
are filled with art and collectibles. Sleep soundly
in one of the tranquil
guest bedrooms then
linger over a leisurely
four-course breakfast. Stimulating conversation comes easy during afternoon tea. There are plenty of quiet spots including a
swing and a hammock, to enjoy the fountains, orchard, rose,
herb and vegetable gardens.

Historic Interest: The historic district of Half Moon Bay is eight miles away.
Pescadero and a historic mansion and gardens are about 15 miles away.

Innkeeper(s): Raymond & Emily Hoche-Mong. $125-180. MC, VISA, AX, DC,
DS, PC, TC. TAC10. 5 rooms with PB, 3 with FP. Breakfast and afternoon
tea included in rates. Beds: KQDT. Library, bocce ball court and piano on
premises. French spoken. Antiquing, bicycling, fishing, golf, hiking, horseback
riding, nature reserves, whale watching, aero sightseeing, birding, parks and
water sports nearby.

Publicity: *San Diego Union, Tri-Valley, Los Angeles Times, Pilot Getaways,
AOPA Magazine, San Jose Mercury News, Half Moon Bay Review,
Peninsula Times Tribune, San Mateo Times, Contra Costa Times and The
Wall Street Journal.*

*"You have truly made an art of breakfast and tea-time conversation.
We will be back."*

Monterey
J5

The Jabberwock

598 Laine St
Monterey, CA 93940-1312
(831)372-4777 (888)428-7253 Fax:(831)655-2946
E-mail: innkeeper@jabberwockinn.com
Web: www.jabberwockinn.com

Circa 1911. Set in a half-acre of gardens, this Craftsman-style
inn provides a fabulous view of Monterey Bay with its famous
barking seals. When you're ready to settle in for the evening,

you'll find huge Victorian beds
complete with lace-edged sheets
and goose-down comforters. Two
rooms include Jacuzzi tubs. In the
late afternoon, hors d'oeuvres and
aperitifs are served on an enclosed
sun porch. After dinner, guests are
tucked into bed with homemade
chocolate chip cookies and milk. To help guests avoid long
lines, the innkeepers have tickets available for the popular and
nearby Monterey Bay Aquarium.

Historic Interest: Historic adobes and Cannery Row are within walking distance of The Jabberwock.

Innkeeper(s): Joan & John Kiliany. $115-235. MC, VISA. 7 rooms, 5 with
PB, 3 with FP. Types of meals: Gourmet bkfst and early coffee/tea. Beds: KQ.
Two with Jacuzzi in room. Fax and copier on premises. Weddings, small
meetings and family reunions hosted. Antiquing, fishing, restaurants, live theater, parks, shopping and water sports nearby.

Publicity: *Sunset, Travel & Leisure, Sacramento Bee, San Francisco
Examiner, Los Angeles Times, Country Inns, San Francisco Chronicle,
Diablo. and Elmer Dill's KABC-Los Angeles TV.*

*"Words are not enough to describe the ease and tranquility of the
atmosphere of the home, rooms, owners and staff at the Jabberwock."*

Mount Shasta
B5

Mount Shasta Ranch B&B

1008 W.A. Barr Rd
Mount Shasta, CA 96067-9465
(530)926-3870 Fax:(530)926-6882
E-mail: alpinere@snowcrest.net
Web: www.stayinshasta.com

Circa 1923. This large two-story ranch house offers a full view
of Mt. Shasta from its 60-foot-long redwood porch.
Spaciousness abounds from the 1,500-square-foot living room
with a massive rock fireplace to the large suites with private
bathrooms that include large tubs and roomy showers. A full
country breakfast may offer cream cheese-stuffed French toast
or fresh, wild blackberry crepes. Just minutes away, Lake
Siskiyou boasts superb fishing, sailing, swimming, and 18 hole
golf course with public tennis courts.

Historic Interest: Built in 1923 by HD "Curley" Brown as a thoroughbred
horse ranch.

Innkeeper(s): Bill & Mary Larsen. $55-115. MC, VISA, AX, DS, PC, TC. 9
rooms, 4 with PB, 1 cottage and 1 conference room. Breakfast included in
rates. Types of meals: Full bkfst, early coffee/tea and afternoon tea. Beds: Q.
Cable TV and ceiling fan in room. Air conditioning. VCR, fax, copier and
library on premises. Small meetings, family reunions and seminars hosted.
Antiquing, fishing, parks, shopping, downhill skiing, cross-country skiing and
water sports nearby.

Pets Allowed.

Murphys H7

Dunbar House, 1880

271 Jones St
Murphys, CA 95247-1375
(209)728-2897 (800)692-6006 Fax:(209)728-1451
E-mail: innkeep@dunbarhouse.com
Web: www.dunbarhouse.com

Circa 1880. A picket fence frames this Italianate home, built by Willis Dunbar for his bride. The porch, lined with rocking chairs, is the perfect place to take in the scenery of century-old gardens decorated by fountains, birdhouses and swings. A collection of antiques, family heirlooms and comfortable furnishings fill the interior. The two-room garden suite includes a bed dressed with fine linens and a down comforter and a two-person Jacuzzi spa. Guests can enjoy the morning fare in the dining room, garden or opt for breakfast in their room.

Historic Interest: Columbia State Park (10 miles), Big Trees State Park (14 miles).

Innkeeper(s): Bob & Barbara Costa. $155-215. MC, VISA, AX, PC, TC. TAC10. 5 rooms with PB, 5 with FP and 2 suites. Breakfast and afternoon tea included in rates. Types of meals: Gourmet bkfst, early coffee/tea and room service. Beds: KQ. Cable TV, phone, turndown service, ceiling fan and VCR in room. Air conditioning. Fax, copier and library on premises. Antiquing, fishing, live theater, parks, shopping, downhill skiing, cross-country skiing and water sports nearby.

Publicity: *San Francisco Chronicle, Los Angeles Times, Gourmet, Victorian Homes, Country Inns, Travel & Leisure.* and *Search & Rescue.*

"Your beautiful gardens and gracious hospitality combine for a super bed & breakfast."

Trade Carriage House

230 Big Trees Rd
Murphys, CA 95247
(209)728-3404 (800)800-3408 Fax:(209)728-2527
E-mail: sales@realtyworld-murphys.com
Web: www.realtyworld-murphys.com

Circa 1930. A white picket fence surrounds the Trade Carriage House, originally built in Stockton and later moved to Murphys. There are two bedrooms, both furnished with antiques and wicker pieces. A sunroom overlooks a private deck. Three doors down is a second vacation home, Tree Top House, that boasts a deck overlooking the treetops. This home has two bedrooms and two baths, a pine vaulted ceiling and, like the Trade Carriage House, is within two blocks of historical Main Street, with shops, restaurants and local wineries. Nearby are the gold rush towns of Columbia and Sonora. Main Street Lodge is a third vacation house situated across the street from Murphys' famous donkeys, Cass and Clarissa attached. Murphys is located between Lake Tahoe and Yosemite.

Innkeeper(s): Cynthia Trade. $95-150. PC, TC. TAC10. 3 cottages. Beds: QD. Cable TV and phone in room. Air conditioning. One apartment on premises. Antiquing, fishing, golf, major area for wineries, live theater, parks, shopping, downhill skiing, cross-country skiing, tennis and water sports nearby.

Napa H4

Beazley House

1910 1st St
Napa, CA 94559-2351
(707)257-1649 (800)559-1649 Fax:(707)257-1518
E-mail: innkeeper@beazleyhouse.com
Web: www.beazleyhouse.com

Circa 1902. Nestled in green lawns and gardens, this graceful shingled mansion is frosted with white trim on its bays

and balustrades. Stained-glass windows and polished-wood floors set the atmosphere in the parlor. There are six rooms in the main house, and the carriage house features five more, many with fireplaces and whirlpool tubs. The venerable Beazley House was Napa's first bed & breakfast inn.

Historic Interest: Bale Gristmill at Napa Bothe State Park, Beringer Vineyards, Chas Krug Winery, Old Town Napa.

Innkeeper(s): Carol Beazley, Jim Beazley, Veronica Becerra, Lorna T. $125-295. MC, VISA, AX, PC. 11 rooms with PB. Breakfast included in rates. Types of meals: Full bkfst. Phone, ceiling fan and fireplaces in room. Central air. Fax and library on premises. Handicap access. Amusement parks, antiquing, art galleries, bicycling, fishing, golf, hiking, horseback riding, museums, parks, shopping, tennis and wineries nearby.

Publicity: *Los Angeles Times, USA Today, Sacramento Bee, Yellow Brick Road and Emergo.*

"There's a sense of peace & tranquility that hovers over this house, sprinkling magical dream dust & kindness."

Belle Epoque

1386 Calistoga Ave
Napa, CA 94559-2552
(707)257-2161 (800)238-8070 Fax:(707)226-6314
E-mail: innkeeper@labelleepoque.com
Web: labelleepoque.com

Circa 1893. This Queen Anne Victorian has a wine cellar and tasting room where guests can casually sip Napa Valley wines. The inn, which is one of the most unique architectural structures found in the wine country, is located in the heart of Napa's Calistoga Historic District. Beautiful original stained-glass windows include a window from an old church. Six guest

rooms offer a whirlpool tub. A selection of fine restaurants and shops are within easy walking distance, as well as the riverfront, art museums and the Wine Train Depot.

Innkeeper(s): Georgia Jump. $170-325. MC, VISA, AX, DS, PC, TC. TAC10. 9 rooms with PB, 3 with FP, 3 suites and 1 conference room. Breakfast and snacks/refreshments included in rates. Types of meals: Gourmet bkfst and early coffee/tea. Beds: KQT. Cable TV, phone, ceiling fan, VCR and whirlpools in room. Air conditioning. Fax, copier and spa on premises. Weddings, small meetings, family reunions and seminars hosted. Amusement parks, antiquing, golf, live theater, parks, shopping, sporting events and tennis nearby.

"At first I was a bit leery, how can a B&B get consistent rave reviews? After staying here two nights, I am now a believer!"

The Candlelight Inn

1045 Easum Dr
Napa, CA 94558-5524
(707)257-3717 Fax:(707)257-3762
E-mail: mail@candlelightinn.com
Web: www.candlelightinn.com

Circa 1929. Located on a park-like acre with gardens, this elegant English Tudor-style house is situated beneath redwood groves and towering trees that shade the banks of Napa Creek. Each suite features a two-person marble fireplace and two-person marble Jacuzzi inside the room, and the Candlelight Suite boasts a canopy bed and private sauna. The inn's breakfast room has French doors and windows overlooking the garden. Breakfast is served by candlelight.

Innkeeper(s): Johanna & Wolfgang Brox. $135-295. MC, VISA, AX, DS. 10

rooms with PB, 6 with FP and 6 suites. Breakfast included in rates. Types of meals: Gourmet bkfst. Beds: Q. Cable TV, phone and jacuzzi's in room. Air conditioning. Fax, copier, swimming and wine and hors d'oeuvres on premises. Small meetings and family reunions hosted. German and French spoken. Antiquing, golf, winetasting, restaurants, parks, shopping and wineries nearby.

"We still haven't stopped talking about the great food, wonderful accommodations and gracious hospitality."

Cedar Gables Inn

486 Coombs St
Napa, CA 94559-3343
(707)224-7969 (800)309-7969 Fax:(707)224-4838
E-mail: info@cedargablesinn.com
Web: www.cedargablesinn.com

Circa 1892. This gracious country manor was designed by English architect Ernest Coxhead, who patterned the home after designs prevalent during Shakespeare's time. The innkeep-

ers received an award of merit for their restoration efforts and it's clearly deserved. Guests ascend winding staircases to reach their posh rooms decorated in rich colors and filled with antiques. Each room features its own color scheme and unique touches. The Churchill Chamber, the original master bedroom, is adorned in grays, tans and black and boasts ornate furnishings, a wood-burning fireplace and a two-person whirlpool tub. Four guest rooms include gas fireplaces, and others feature clawfoot, whirlpool or Jacuzzi tubs. A complete breakfast is served either in the dining room or in the bright sun room, a perfect start to a full day exploring Napa Valley.

Historic Interest: Aside from the area's bounty of historic wineries, museums and Old Grist Mill are some of the historic sites.

Innkeeper(s): Craig & Margaret Snasdell. $169-319. MC, VISA, AX, DS. TAC10. 9 rooms with PB, 4 with FP and 1 suite. Breakfast included in rates. Types of meals: Full bkfst. Beds: Q.

Publicity: *California Visitor's Review.*

"Charming and elegant, yet strikingly cozy. This place tops the list in atmosphere and hospitality."

Churchill Manor

485 Brown St
Napa, CA 94559-3349
(707)253-7733 Fax:(707)253-8836

Circa 1889. Listed in the National Register of Historic Places, each room of this stately Napa Valley manor is individually deco-rated with fine European antiques. Six rooms have fireplaces, four have two-person showers and five have two-person vintage bath-

tubs. Priceless artifacts have been preserved, such as the original bath and fireplace tiles in Edward's Room and Rose's Room trimmed with 24-karat gold. Guests are treated to delicious breakfasts and freshly baked cookies and refreshments in the afternoons. In the evening, there is a complimentary two-hour wine and cheese reception. The breakfast buffet offers an abundant selection of fresh fruits, fresh-baked croissants and muffins, gourmet omelets and French toast made-to-order as each guest arrives. The innkeepers add Victorian

flavor by keeping complimentary tandem bicycles and a croquet set on hand for their guests. The Napa Wine Train and historic downtown Napa are within walking distance.

Historic Interest: Churchill Manor, which is listed in the National Register, is located in the National Register Historic District of Old Town Napa.

Innkeeper(s): Joanna Guidotti & Brian Jensen. $135-235. MC, VISA, AX, DS, PC, TC. TAC10. 10 rooms with PB, 6 with FP and 3 conference rooms. Breakfast included in rates. Beds: KQ. Phone in room. Air conditioning. VCR, fax, copier, bicycles, library, grand piano and croquet on premises. Handicap access. Weddings, small meetings, family reunions and seminars hosted. Spanish spoken. Amusement parks, antiquing, fishing, wineries, mud baths, galleries, live theater, parks, shopping and water sports nearby.

Publicity: *Napa County Record, Food & Beverage Journal, ABC-KGO TV and San Francisco Bay Guardian.*

"Retaining the ambiance of the 1890s yet providing comfort for the 1990s."

Hennessey House-Napa's 1889 Queen Anne Victorian B&B

1727 Main St
Napa, CA 94559-1844
(707)226-3774 Fax:(707)226-2975
E-mail: inn@hennesseyhouse.com
Web: www.hennesseyhouse.com

Circa 1889. Colorful gardens surround this gracious Victorian, once home to Dr. Edwin Hennessey, a Napa County physician and former mayor. Pristinely renovated, the inn features stained-glass windows and a curving wraparound porch. A handsome hand-painted, stamped-tin ceiling graces the dining

room. The inn's romantic rooms are fur-nished in antiques and some offer fireplaces, feather beds and spa tubs. The bathrooms all feature marble floors and antique brass fixtures. There is a sauna and a garden foun-tain. The innkeepers serve gourmet breakfasts with specialties such as blueberry-stuffed French toast and Eggs Florentine. Tea and cookies are offered at 3 p.m., and later in the evening, wine and cheese is served. Walk to inviting restaurants and shops. Nearby are the world-famous Napa Valley wineries. The innkeepers will be happy to make recommendations or reserva-tions for wineries, the area's spas and mud baths, hot air bal-loons, the Wine Train, horseback riding, cycling and hiking.

Historic Interest: Historic Old Town Napa.

Innkeeper(s): Gilda & Alex Feit. $105-295. MC, VISA, AX, DC, DS, PC. TAC10. 10 rooms with PB, 6 with FP. Breakfast included in rates. Types of meals: Full bkfst. Beds: KQT. Phone, ceiling fan, some with Jacuzzi and some with fireplace in room. Air conditioning. Fax and sauna on premises. Weddings, small meetings, family reunions and seminars hosted. Antiquing, wine train packages and shopping nearby.

Publicity: *AM-PM Magazine.*

"A great place to relax in Napa!"

Inn on Randolph

411 Randolph St
Napa, CA 94559-3374
(707)257-2886 (800)670-6886 Fax:(707)257-8756
E-mail: randolph@i-cafe.net
Web: www.innonrandolph.com

Circa 1860. Located in Napa's historic district, this shuttered Gothic Revival is a city landmark and one of the oldest homes in the valley. Common rooms feature antique Victorian furnishings, hardwood floors and a sweeping spindled staircase. A hand-painted flower mural, white wicker and sleigh bed are just a few of the romantic touches featured in the five guest rooms located in the original house. Besides privacy, the Randolph and Laurel cottages each offer two separate, but adjoining rooms decorated in antiques, fireplaces and whirlpool tubs for two. The Arbor Cottage overlooks a semi-private stone patio and is complete with a fireplace, kitchenette, two-person walk-in shower and whirlpool tub for two. Breakfast begins with freshly ground coffee, tea and juice, followed by a hot entree such as peach and strawberry French toast or Mexican quiche served with fresh salsa. Wine tasting, shopping, bicycling and golf are nearby.

Innkeeper(s): Deborah Coffee. $144-289. MC, VISA, AX, DS. TAC10. 10 rooms with PB, 7 with FP. Breakfast and snacks/refreshments included in rates. Types of meals: Full bkfst and early coffee/tea. Beds: KQT. Phone, turn-down service, ceiling fan, robes, cottages have TV, VCR and CD player and 8 with whirlpool tubs in room. Fax and library on premises. Antiquing, golf, live theater, parks and shopping nearby.

"You reinforced our reason for staying in lovely bed & breakfasts."

La Residence Country Inn

4066 Saint Helena Hwy
Napa, CA 94558-1635
(707)253-0337 Fax:(707)253-0382
Web: www.laresidence.com

Circa 1870. This inn offers luxurious accommodations for those exploring the enchanting Napa Valley wine country. The uniquely decorated rooms in the French-style farmhouse or Gothic Revival Mansion are spacious and well-appointed, with fine antiques and designer fabrics. Many rooms also feature fireplaces, patios or balconies. Guests will be impressed with the lovely gardens and pool area at the inn, not to mention the discreet but attentive service. Be sure to inquire about excursions into the winery-rich valley.

Innkeeper(s): David Jackson, Craig Claussen. $195-350. MC, VISA, AX, DC, DS, PC, TC. TAC10. 20 rooms with PB, 16 with FP, 5 suites and 1 conference room. Breakfast and snacks/refreshments included in rates. Types of meals: Full bkfst, early coffee/tea and room service. Beds: Q. Phone in room. Air conditioning. Fax, copier, spa, swimming and child care on premises. Handicap access. Weddings, small meetings, family reunions and seminars hosted. Spanish spoken. Antiquing, fishing, golf, wineries, ballooning, biking, glider riding, live theater, parks, shopping and tennis nearby.

Publicity: *Travel & Leisure.*

Napa Inn

1137 Warren St
Napa, CA 94559-2302
(707)257-1444 (800)435-1144
E-mail: info@napainn.com
Web: www.napainn.com

Circa 1899. Two Victorian homes comprise this inn. The oldest, built in 1877, is listed in the National Register; the other, built in 1899, is a stately Queen Anne. Located in historic downtown Napa on a tranquil tree-lined street, many world-class wineries are minutes away. Most of the guest bedrooms and suites feature whirlpool tubs and fireplaces. Each morning enjoy a full gourmet breakfast. The gardens are an eye-pleasing adventure. Dessert and liqueur on the patio and in front of the fireplace is the perfect way to spend an evening.

Innkeeper(s): Brooke & Jim Boyer. $140-300. MC, VISA, AX, DS, PC, TC. TAC10. 14 rooms with PB, 12 with FP. Breakfast and snacks/refreshments included in rates. Types of meals: Full bkfst. Beds: KQ. Phone, seven with spa and most with TV/VCR in room. Air conditioning. VCR on premises. Weddings, small meetings and family reunions hosted. Antiquing, golf, horse-back riding, hot air balloon rides, limousine wine tours, Napa Valley Wine Train, parks and shopping nearby.
Publicity: *San Francisco Examiner.*

"Best night's sleep this side of the Atlantic Ocean! Thank you for your warm welcome and delicious breakfast."

Old World Inn

1301 Jefferson St
Napa, CA 94559-2412
(707)257-0112 (800)966-6624 Fax:(707)257-0118
E-mail: theworldinn@aol.com

Circa 1906. The decor in this exquisite bed & breakfast is second to none. In 1981, Macy's sought out the inn to showcase a new line of fabrics inspired by Scandinavian artist Carl Larrson. Each romantic room is adorned in bright, welcoming colors and includes special features such as canopy beds and clawfoot tubs. The Garden Room boasts three skylights, and the Anne Room is a must for honeymoons and romantic retreats. The walls and ceilings are painted in a warm peach and blue, bows are stenciled around the perimeter of the room. A decorated canopy starts at the ceiling in  the center of the bed and falls downward producing a curtain-like effect. A buffet breakfast is served each morning and a delicious afternoon tea and wine and cheese social will curb your appetite until dinner. After sampling one of Napa's gourmet eateries, return to the inn where a selection of desserts await you.

Innkeeper(s): Sam Van Hoeve. $145-250. MC, VISA, AX, DS, PC, TC. TAC10. 10 rooms with PB, 6 with FP, 1 suite and 1 cottage. Breakfast, afternoon tea and snacks/refreshments included in rates. Types of meals: Gourmet bkfst and early coffee/tea. Beds: KQT. Cable TV, phone, ceiling fan and VCR in room. Air conditioning. Fax and spa on premises. French and Dutch spoken. Antiquing, fishing, golf, live theater, parks, shopping, sporting events and tennis nearby.

Publicity: *Napa Valley Traveller.*

"Excellent is an understatement. We'll return."

Stahlecker House B&B Country Inn & Garden

1042 Easum Dr
Napa, CA 94558-5525
(707)257-1588 (800)799-1588 Fax:(707)224-7429
E-mail: stahlbnh@aol.com
Web: www.stahleckerhouse.com

Circa 1949. This country inn is situated on the banks of tree-lined Napa Creek. The acre and a half of grounds feature rose and orchard gardens, fountains and manicured lawns. Guests often relax on the sun deck. There is an antique refrigerator stocked with soft drinks and lemonade. Full, gourmet breakfasts are served by candlelight in the glass-wrapped dining room that overlooks the gardens. In the evenings, coffee, tea and freshly made chocolate chip cookies are served. The Napa

Wine Train station is five minutes away. Wineries, restaurants, antique shops, bike paths and hiking all are nearby.

Innkeeper(s): Ron & Ethel Stahlecker. $148-268. MC, VISA, AX, DS, TC. TAC5. 4 rooms with PB, 4 with FP and 1 suite. Breakfast and snacks/refreshments included in rates. Types of meals: Gourmet bkfst and afternoon tea. Beds: QT. TV, phone, turndown service and Couple Spa/Couple Shower in room. Air conditioning. Library and croquet on premises. Antiquing, fishing, golf, hiking, hot air balloons, live theater, parks, shopping, tennis and wineries nearby.

Publicity: *Brides Magazine and Napa Valley Traveler.*

"Friendly hosts and beautiful gardens."

Nevada City   F6

Deer Creek Inn

116 Nevada St
Nevada City, CA 95959
(530)265-0363 (800)655-0363 Fax:(530)265-0980
E-mail: deercreek@gv.net

Circa 1860. A prominent local citizen who served as postmaster, as well as holding several other important city and county posts built this Queen Anne Victorian. The inn boasts many original features, including an abundance of stained glass, which frames many of the windows. Guest rooms and common

areas are decorated with period antiques. Beds are topped with down comforters, and some rooms include a canopy bed or clawfoot tub. Each room is named for one of the women who have owned the house throughout the years. Breakfasts, served on a veranda overlooking Deer Creek, include several courses, beginning with a fruit dish such as poached pears in apricot nectar. This is followed by an egg dish, perhaps a mushroom and spinach strata accompanied by honey maple sausage and potatoes. Finally, guests are treated to a special entrée. One delectable example is orange pecan French toast topped with hot orange-maple syrup. During California's gold rush, hundreds of pounds of gold were discovered in Deer Creek, which runs behind the inn's one-acre property. This local gold rush was the catalyst that created Nevada City, a quaint historic town that offers shops, walking tours, carriage rides, art galleries and museums. Two state parks represent the area's mining history, and there are plenty of outdoor activities, as well.

Historic Interest: Deer Creek, Empire State Mine (3 miles), longest covered bridge at Bridgeport (9 miles), restored Colfax Narrow Gauge Railroad (3 miles).
Innkeeper(s): Chuck & Elaine Matroni. $105-160. MC, VISA, AX, PC, TC. TAC10. 5 rooms with PB and 1 conference room. Breakfast and snacks/refreshments included in rates. Types of meals: Full bkfst and early coffee/tea. Beds: KQ. Ceiling fan and roman tub in room. Central air. VCR and fax on premises. Family reunions hosted. Antiquing, art galleries, beaches, bicycling, canoeing/kayaking, fishing, golf, hiking, horseback riding, live theater, museums, parks, shopping, cross-country skiing, tennis, water sports and wineries nearby.

Emma Nevada House

528 E Broad St
Nevada City, CA 95959-2213
(530)265-4415 (800)916-3662 Fax:(530)265-4416
E-mail: mail@emmanevadahouse.com
Web: www.emmanevadahouse.com

Circa 1856. The childhood home of 19th-century opera star Emma Nevada now serves as an attractive Queen Anne Victorian inn. English roses line the white picket fence in front, and the forest-like back garden has a small stream with benches. The Empress' Chamber is the most romantic room with ivory Italian linens atop a French antique bed, a bay window and a massive French armoire. Some rooms have whirlpool baths and TV. Guests enjoy relaxing in the hexagonal sunroom and on the inn's wraparound porches. Empire Mine State Historic Park is nearby.

Historic Interest: Malakoff Diggins (20 miles), Nevada City Historical District (3 blocks).
Innkeeper(s): Laura DuPee. $110-165. MC, VISA, AX, DC, PC, TC. TAC10. 6 rooms with PB, 2 with FP. Breakfast and afternoon tea included in rates. Types of meals: Full bkfst and early coffee/tea. Beds: Q. Clawfoot and Jacuzzi tubs in room. Air conditioning. Fax and library on premises. Weddings and small meetings hosted. Antiquing, fishing, live theater, parks, shopping, downhill skiing and water sports nearby.

Publicity: *Country Inns, Gold Rush Scene, Sacramento Focus, The Union, Los Angeles Times, San Jose Mercury News, Sacramento Bee and Karen Browns.*

"A delightful experience: such airiness and hospitality in the midst of so much history. We were fascinated by the detail and the faithfulness of the restoration. This house is a quiet solace for city-weary travelers. There's a grace here."

Grandmere's Inn

449 Broad St
Nevada City, CA 95959-2430
(530)265-4660
E-mail: grandmeresinn@oro.net
Web: grandmeresinn.com

Circa 1856. Aaron Sargent, U.S. Congressman, senator and author of the women's suffrage bill, was the first owner of this white Colonial Revival house. He and his wife often received Susan B. Anthony here. Shaker pine furnishings and white wooden shutters predominate the spacious interior design. Lavish creature comforts include six pillows on the four-poster beds. Huge country breakfasts may include onion-caraway quiche, cornbread and the inn's trademark, Grandmere's French Toast. A half acre of terraced gardens cascade behind the inn.
$125-190. MC, VISA, AX, PC, TC. TAC10. 6 rooms with PB. Types of meals: Full bkfst. Beds: Q. Weddings hosted. Antiquing, fishing, restaurants, live theater and shopping nearby.

Publicity: *Country Living, Gourmet, Sierra Heritage and New York Times.*

The Parsonage B&B

427 Broad St
Nevada City, CA 95959-2407
(530)265-9478 Fax:(530)265-8147

Circa 1865. Guests in search of California history would do well to stop in Nevada City and at the Parsonage. The Gold Rush town is a registered National Monument, and the home is one of the older homes in the state, dating to the 1860s. Innkeeper Deborah Dane's family has been in California since Gold Rush days, and the home features many heirlooms. Although used to house Methodist ministers for 80 years, the home was in a quite ungodly state by the time Deborah found it. She painstakingly restored the gem and filled it with beautiful antiques and delightful, elegant decor. Special furnishings, knickknacks and artwork are located throughout, including an amazing carved mahogany bed the Dane family brought along the Oregon Trail. In addition to her flair for restoration and decorating, Deborah is a dietitian and Cordon Bleu graduate, so be prepared for a gourmet breakfast that's as healthy as it is delicious.

Innkeeper(s): Deborah Dane. $75-140. MC, VISA, PC, TC. TAC10. 6 rooms with PB, 1 with FP, 1 cottage and 1 conference room. Breakfast included in rates. Types of meals: Full bkfst, cont plus and early coffee/tea. Beds: QT. Cable TV and ceiling fan in room. Air conditioning. Fax, copier and library on premises. Weddings, small meetings, family reunions and seminars hosted. Antiquing, fishing, golf, live theater, shopping, downhill skiing, cross-country skiing and water sports nearby.

Publicity: *Country Inns.*

Nice   F4

Featherbed Railroad Company B&B

2870 Lakeshore Blvd, PO Box 4016
Nice, CA 95464
(707)274-4434 (800)966-6322
E-mail: rooms@featherbedrailroad.com
Web: www.featherbedrailroad.com

Circa 1940. Located on five acres on Clear Lake, this unusual inn features guest rooms in nine luxuriously renovated, painted and papered cabooses. Each has its own featherbed and private bath, most have Jacuzzi tubs for two. The Southern Pacific cabooses have a bay window alcove, while those from the Santa Fe feature small cupolas.

Innkeeper(s): Lorraine Bassignani. $102-180. MC, VISA, AX, DS. 9 rooms with PB. Breakfast included in rates. Types of meals: Full bkfst. Beds: QDT. Cable TV and VCR in room. Spa on premises.

Publicity: *Santa Rosa Press Democrat, Fairfield Daily Republic, London Times, Travel & Leisure and Bay Area Back Roads.*

Nipomo   M7

The Kaleidoscope Inn

130 E Dana St
Nipomo, CA 93444
(805)929-5444 Fax:(805)929-5440
E-mail: kaleidoscopeinn@hotmail.com
Web: www.kaleidoscopeinn.com

Circa 1887. The sunlight that streams through the stained-glass windows of this charming Victorian creates a kaleidoscope effect and thus the name. The inn is surrounded by one acre of gardens. Each romantic guest room is decorated with

antiques, and the library offers a fireplace. The parlor includes an 1886 Steinway upright piano. Fresh flowers add a special touch. Breakfast is served either in the dining room or in the gardens. L.A. Times readers voted the inn as one of the best lodging spots for under $100 per night.

Historic Interest: Lived in by the founding family of Nipomo, the Dana Family.

Innkeeper(s): Edward & Carol De Leon. $95-110. MC, VISA. 3 rooms with PB and 1 conference room. Breakfast included in rates. Types of meals: Gourmet bkfst and early coffee/tea. Beds: KQ. Turndown service and ceiling fan in room. VCR and library on premises. Weddings, small meetings and family reunions hosted. Antiquing, fishing, golf, live theater, parks, shopping and water sports nearby.

Publicity: *71 Places To Stay Under $100.00, Santa Maria Times, Los Angeles Times and Country.*

"Beautiful room, chocolates, fresh flowers, peaceful night's rest, great breakfast."

Nipton   L14

Hotel Nipton

HC 1, BOX 357, 107355 Nipton Rd
Nipton, CA 92364-9735
(760)856-2335
E-mail: hotel@nipton.com

Circa 1904. This Southwestern-style adobe hotel with its wide verandas once housed gold miners and Clara Bow, wife of movie star Rex Bell. It is decorated in period furnishings and

historic photos of the area. A 1920s rock and cactus garden blooms, and an outdoor spa provides the perfect setting for watching a flaming sunset over Ivanpah Valley, the New York Mountains and Castle Peaks. Later, a magnificent star-studded sky appears undimmed by city lights.

Historic Interest: Gold mining town started in 1885.

Innkeeper(s): Gerald & Roxanne Freeman. $60. MC, VISA, DS. TAC7. 4 rooms. Breakfast included in rates. Types of meals: Cont and early coffee/tea. Beds: DT. Air conditioning. Fax, library and Jacuzzi on premises. Weddings, small meetings, family reunions and seminars hosted. Amusement parks, fishing, golf, golf and stables, live theater, parks, shopping, sporting events and water sports nearby.

Publicity: *Los Angeles Times, New York Times, National Geographic Traveler, Town & Country, U.S. News & World Report. and Breakdown.*

"Warm, friendly, unpretentious, genuine. The hotel's historical significance is well-researched and verified."

Occidental   G3

The Inn at Occidental of Sonoma County

3657 Church St
Occidental, CA 95465
(707)874-1047 (800)522-6324 Fax:(707)874-1078
E-mail: innkeeper@innatoccidental.com
Web: www.innatoccidental.com

Circa 1877. Stenciled walls, shiny woodwork and a gracious collection of American and European antiques create the warm, idyllic environment at this 19th-century Victorian. All the guest rooms offer fireplaces, eleven offer spa tubs and most overlook the garden. There are plenty of places to relax, from a wicker-filled veranda to a manicured English courtyard with a fountain as its centerpiece. The innkeepers serve gourmet country breakfasts, afternoon refreshments and in the evenings, local wines. The inn offers convenient access to the many wineries of Sonoma county. Point Reyes National Seashore, Bodega Bay and the redwoods are other attractions.

Innkeeper(s): Jack, Bill & Jean Bullard. $195-320. MC, VISA, AX, DS, PC, TC. TAC10. 16 rooms with PB, 16 with FP and 1 conference room. Breakfast and afternoon tea included in rates. Types of meals: Full bkfst and early coffee/tea. Beds: KQT. Cable TV, phone and 11 with spa tub for two in room. Fax, copier and evening wine on premises. Handicap access. Weddings, small meetings, family reunions and seminars hosted. Limited French and limited Spanish spoken. Antiquing, bicycling, fishing, hiking, live theater, parks, shopping, sporting events, water sports and wineries nearby.

Publicity: *Wine Spectator, Country Inns, Traveler, Sunset, National Geographic Traveler, Andrew Harper's Hideaway Report and Romantic Inns of America.*

Ojai N9

The Moon's Nest Inn

210 E Matilija St
Ojai, CA 93023-2722
(805)646-6635 Fax:(805)646-5665
Web: www.moonsnestinn.com

Circa 1874. Built in 1874, The Moon's Nest Inn is the oldest building in the small town of Ojai (OH hi). The city's first school house and community center, the structure was later used as a residence and then an inn. Three years ago the new owners renovated the inn, adding heating and air conditioning, private baths and balconies. They enclosed the gardens and pond with walls and vines to accent the property and the magnificent old oak trees, creating an oasis within the convenient small town location. The Ojai Valley is often referred to as Shangri-La. This may be because the area was used as the location for the original film by that name, or because the valley is surrounded by millions of acres of the Los Padres National Forest. The region offers seashores, lake shores, mountains, hiking trails and streams.

Historic Interest: Buenaventura Mission (15 miles).

Innkeeper(s): Rich & Joan Assenberg. $95-145. MC, VISA, AX, DC, DS, PC, TC. 7 rooms, 5 with PB and 1 conference room. Breakfast and snacks/refreshments included in rates. Types of meals: Gourmet bkfst, veg bkfst and early coffee/tea. Beds: QDT. Central air. VCR, fax, library, modem hook-up and afternoon wine on premises. Weddings, small meetings, family reunions and seminars hosted. Antiquing, art galleries, bicycling, canoeing/kayaking, fishing, golf, hiking, live theater, museums, parks, shopping, tennis and wineries nearby.

Pets allowed: Non-chewers, housebroken, no barkers.

The Theodore Woolsey House

1484 E Ojai Ave
Ojai, CA 93023-9623
(805)646-9779
Web: www.theodorewoolseyhouse.com

Circa 1887. This historical landmark appears as a Connecticut farmhouse in the middle of sunny California. The house is full of antiques and hand-woven rugs. The living room boasts a custom-made walnut piano. All the bedrooms are decorated with nostalgic period lace curtains and original furniture. To give your stay a romantic twist, add some extras such as flowers and champagne or breakfast in bed. All guests will enjoy an expanded continental breakfast of fresh fruits, coffee cakes, flavored yogurt, cereals and freshly-squeezed juices.

Innkeeper(s): Ana Cross. $85-150. 5 rooms, 6 with PB, 3 with FP and 1 cottage. Types of meals: Cont plus. Beds: QD.

Orange O11

Old Towne Inn

274 N Glassell St
Orange, CA 92866
(714)628-1818 (888)592-6606 Fax:(714)628-1820

Circa 1910. A charming 1910 Sears Craftsman home, the Old Towne Inn sits in the midst of the historic district of the city of Orange, just minutes from Disneyland. Its large front porch, original leaded windows and fixtures, and its two cozy living rooms appointed with antiques bespeak a time when Orange County was full of adventuresome pioneers, who lived in the midst of orange groves. The three guest bedrooms have hand-painted murals and offer elegant touches such as fresh flowers. Each morning guests may breakfast on such fare as fresh fruit with honey-orange-yogurt topping, fresh juice, stuffed French toast with cinnamon, apple and cream cheese, turkey maple sausage and eggs Benedict. The innkeepers happily accommodate dietary requirements upon request. Complimentary evening beverages are a great way to end a day of visiting the many theme parks, museums or antique shops just minutes away.

Innkeeper(s): Tim & Kathy Reynolds. $115-135. MC, VISA, PC, TC. TAC10. 3 rooms with PB. Breakfast included in rates. Types of meals: Gourmet bkfst, early coffee/tea and snacks/refreshments. Beds: Q. Turndown service and one with Cable TV in room. Central air. Fax on premises. Weddings, small meetings, family reunions and seminars hosted. Amusement parks, antiquing, art galleries, beaches, fishing, golf, hiking, horseback riding, live theater, museums, parks, shopping and sporting events nearby.

Orland E5

Inn at Shallow Creek Farm

4712 County Rd DD
Orland, CA 95963
(530)865-4093 (800)865-4093
E-mail: inn-farm@orland.net

Circa 1900. This vine-covered farmhouse was once the center of a well-known orchard and sheep ranch. The old barn, adjacent to the farmhouse, was a livery stop. The citrus orchard, now restored, blooms with 165 trees. Apples, pears, peaches, apricots, persimmons, walnuts, figs, and pomegranates are also grown here. Guests can meander about and examine the Polish crested chickens, silver guinea fowl, Muscovy ducks, and African geese. The old caretaker's house is now a four-room guest cottage. Hundreds of narcissus grow along the creek that flows through the property.

Innkeeper(s): Mary & Kurt Glaeseman. $60-85. MC, VISA, PC. TAC10. 4 rooms, 2 with PB and 1 suite. Breakfast included in rates. Types of meals: Full bkfst and early coffee/tea. Beds: QT. Phone and ceiling fan in room. Air conditioning. Library on premises. French, German and Spanish spoken. Antiquing, fishing, birding and parks nearby.

Publicity: *Adventure Road, Orland Press Register, San Francisco Focus, Chico Enterprise Record and Minneapolis Star.*

"Now that we've discovered your country oasis, we hope to return as soon as possible."

Pacific Grove   J5

Centrella B&B Inn

612 Central Ave
Pacific Grove, CA 93950-2611
(408)372-3372 (800)433-4732 Fax:(408)372-2036
E-mail: concierge@innsbythesea.com
Web: www.centrellainn.com

Circa 1889. Pacific Grove was founded as a Methodist resort in
1875, and this home, built just after the town's incorporation,
was billed by a local newspaper as, "the largest, most com-
modious and pleasantly located boarding house in the Grove."

Many a guest is still sure to agree. The
rooms are well-appointed in a comfortable, Victorian style. Six guest
rooms include fireplaces. The
Garden Room has a private
entrance, fireplace, wet bar,
Jacuzzi tub and a canopy bed
topped with designer linens.

Freshly baked croissants or pastries and made-to-order waffles
are common fare at the inn's continental buffet breakfast. The
inn is within walking distance of the Monterey Bay Aquarium,
the beach and many Pacific Grove shops.

Innkeeper(s): John Haveles. $109-239. MC, VISA, AX, DS, PC, TC. TAC10.
26 rooms with PB, 6 with FP, 2 suites and 5 cottages. Breakfast, afternoon
tea and snacks/refreshments included in rates. Types of meals: Cont plus.
Beds: KQT. Phone in room. VCR, fax, copier and TVs upon request on
premises. Antiquing, golf, parks and water sports nearby.

Publicity: *Country Inns, New York Times and San Francisco Examiner.*

*"I was ecstatic at the charm that the Centrella has been offering trav-
elers for years and hopefully hundreds of years to come. The bed—
perfect! I am forever enthralled by the old beauty and will remember
this forever!"*

Gatehouse Inn

225 Central Ave
Pacific Grove, CA 93950-3017
(831)649-8436 (800)753-1881 Fax:(831)648-8044
E-mail: lew@redshift.com

Circa 1884. This Italianate Victorian seaside inn is just a block
from the Monterey Bay. The inn is decorated with Victorian and
20th-century antiques and touches of Art Deco. Guest rooms
feature fireplaces, clawfoot tubs and down comforters. Some rooms have ocean views.
The dining room boasts opulent
Bradbury & Bradbury Victorian wallpapers as do some of the guest
rooms. Afternoon hors d'oeuvres,
wine and tea are served. The
refrigerator is stocked for snacking.

$125-195. MC, VISA, AX, DS, PC, TC. TAC10. 9 rooms with PB, 5 with FP.
Breakfast, afternoon tea and snacks/refreshments included in rates. Beds:
KQT. Phone and turndown service in room. Fax and copier on premises.
Weddings and family reunions hosted. Antiquing, fishing, live theater, parks,
shopping and water sports nearby.

Publicity: *San Francisco Chronicle, Monterey Herald, Time, Newsweek,
Inland Empire and Bon Appetit.*

"Thank you for spoiling us."

Gosby House Inn

643 Lighthouse Ave,
Pacific Grove, CA 93950-2643
(831)375-1287 (800)527-8828 Fax:(831)655-9621
E-mail: info@foursisters.com
Web: www.foursisters.com

Circa 1887. Built as an upscale Victorian inn for those visiting
the old Methodist retreat, this sunny yellow mansion features
an abundance of gables, turrets and bays. During renovation
the innkeeper slept in all the rooms to determine
just what antiques were needed and how the
beds should be situated. Eleven of the
romantic rooms include fireplaces and
many offer canopy beds. The Carriage
House rooms include fireplaces, decks
and spa tubs. Gosby House, which has
been open to guests for more than a
century, is in the National Register. Gosby House is one of the
Four Sisters Inns. The Monterey Bay Aquarium is nearby.

Innkeeper(s): Kalena Mittelman. $95-170. MC, VISA, AX, TC. TAC10. 22
rooms, 20 with PB, 11 with FP. Breakfast and afternoon tea included in
rates. Types of meals: Gourmet bkfst and early coffee/tea. Beds: KQD. Phone,
turndown service, bath robes and newspaper in room. Fax, copier and bicycles on premises. Handicap access. Antiquing, aquarium, 17-mile drive and
shopping nearby.

Publicity: *San Francisco Chronicle, Oregonian, Los Angeles Times and Travel
& Leisure.*

Grand View Inn

557 Ocean View Blvd
Pacific Grove, CA 93950-2653
(831)372-4341
Web: www.pginns.com

Circa 1910. Overlooking Lover's Point beach on the edge of
Monterey Bay, this site was chosen by noted marine biologist
Dr. Julia Platt to build this Edwardian-style home. As the first
mayor of Pacific Grove, she was also one of those responsible
for preserving the landmark beach and park for future generations. All of the 10 guest rooms offer unsurpassed ocean views
and are elegantly appointed with authentic and reproduction
antiques. Guests will delight in strolling the gardens surrounding the inn or venturing outdoors to walk along the seashore. A
full breakfast and afternoon tea are served in the ocean-view
dining room.

Historic Interest: The world-famous 17-Mile Drive along the ocean to Pebble
Beach and Carmel, Cannery Row and Monterey Bay made famous by John
Steinbeck. Old Fisherman's Wharf is also located nearby.

Innkeeper(s): Susan & Ed Flatley. $175-295. MC, VISA, TC. TAC10. 10
rooms with PB. Breakfast and afternoon tea included in rates. Types of
meals: Full bkfst and early coffee/tea. Beds: Q. Turndown service in room.
Fireplace on premises. Handicap access. Antiquing, fishing, golf, live theater,
parks, shopping, tennis and water sports nearby.

Green Gables Inn

104 5th St
Pacific Grove, CA 93950-2903
(831)375-2095 (800)722-1774 Fax:(831)375-5437
E-mail: info@foursisters.com
Web: www.foursisters.com

Circa 1888. This half-timbered Queen Anne Victorian appears
as a fantasy of gables overlooking spectacular Monterey Bay.
The parlor has stained-glass panels framing the fireplace and

bay windows looking out to the sea. A favorite focal point is an antique carousel horse. Most of the guest rooms have panoramic views of the ocean, fireplaces, gleaming woodwork, soft quilts and teddy bears, and four rooms have spa tubs. Across the street is the Monterey Bay paved oceanfront cycling path. (Mountain bikes may be borrowed from the inn.) Green Gables is one of the Four Sisters Inns.

Innkeeper(s): Lucia Root. $155-260. MC, VISA, AX, TC. 11 rooms, 7 with PB, 7 with FP and 1 suite. Breakfast and afternoon tea included in rates. Types of meals: Gourmet bkfst. Beds: KQD. TV, phone, turndown service, terry robes and newspaper in room. Fax, copier, bicycles and afternoon wine and hors d'oeuvres on premises. Handicap access. Antiquing, aquarium, live theater and shopping nearby.

Publicity: *Travel & Leisure and Country Living.*

Inn at 213 Seventeen Mile Dr

213 Seventeen Mile Dr
Pacific Grove, CA 93950-2400
(831)642-9514 Fax:(831)642-9546
E-mail: innkeeper@innat17.com
Web: www.innat17.com

Circa 1925. The only challenging part of a visit to this 1920s craftsman-style house is figuring out where the deep blue sea ends and clear skies begin. Located in the heart of the Monterey Peninsula, this two-story, three-building inn offers sea or garden views from the main house, while you will find rustic ambiance, surrounded by oak and redwood trees, in the cottage and redwood chalet rooms. Relax in the spa beneath the tall trees in the gardens, which are often visited by deer and monarch butterflies, or enjoy a glass of champagne while observing Koi in the fountain ponds. Or, spend time in the wood-paneled dining, sitting and reading rooms while enjoying complimentary hors d'oeuvres and planning a day full of activities.

Historic Interest: Monterey Adobes and First Capitol Building (2 miles), Cannery Row & Steinbeck Country (1 mile), Early Lighthouse-Point Pinos (1/2 mile), Carmel Mission (5 miles).

Innkeeper(s): Tony, Glynis Greening, Sally Goss. $108-240. MC, VISA, AX, PC, TC. TAC10. 14 rooms with PB and 1 cottage. Breakfast and snacks/refreshments included in rates. Types of meals: Gourmet bkfst and veg bkfst. Beds: KQ. Cable TV and phone in room. VCR, fax, copier, spa and library on premises. Handicap access. Weddings, small meetings, family reunions and seminars hosted. Antiquing, art galleries, beaches, bicycling, canoeing/kayaking, fishing, golf, hiking, Monterey Bay Aquarium, The Monarch Butterfly Sanctuary, live theater, museums, parks, shopping, sporting events, tennis, water sports and wineries nearby.

Seven Gables Inn

555 Ocean View Blvd
Pacific Grove, CA 93950-2653
(831)372-4341
Web: www.pginns.com

Circa 1886. At the turn of the century, Lucie Chase, a wealthy widow and civic leader from the East Coast, embellished this Victorian with gables and verandas, taking full advantage of its spectacular setting on Monterey Bay. All guest rooms feature wonderful ocean views, and there are elegant antiques, intricate Persian carpets, chandeliers and beveled-glass armoires throughout. A full breakfast and afternoon tea are served in a dining room that features wraparound ocean views. Sea otters,

harbor seals and whales often can be seen from the inn.

Innkeeper(s): The Flatley Family. $175-385. MC, VISA, TC. TAC10. 14 rooms with PB. Breakfast and afternoon tea included in rates. Types of meals: Full bkfst, early coffee/tea and picnic lunch. Beds: Q. Turndown service and some with fireplace in room. Antiquing, fishing, golf, live theater, parks, shopping, tennis and water sports nearby.

Publicity: *Travel & Leisure and Country Inns.*

"Our stay was everything your brochure said it would be, and more."

Palm Springs 012

Casa Cody Country Inn

175 S Cahuilla Rd
Palm Springs, CA 92262-6331
(760)320-9346 (800)231-2639 Fax:(760)325-8610
E-mail: casacody@aol.com

Circa 1920. Casa Cody, built by a relative of Wild Bill Cody and situated in the heart of Palm Springs, is the town's oldest continuously operating inn. The San Jacinto Mountains provide a scenic background for the tree-shaded spa, the pink and purple bougainvillea and the blue

waters of the inn's two swimming pools. Each suite has a small kitchen and features terra cotta and turquoise Southwestern decor. Several have wood-burning fireplaces. There are Mexican pavers, French doors and private patios. The area offers many activities, including museums, a heritage center, boutiques, a botanical garden, horseback riding and golf.

Historic Interest: Village Heritage Center, Village Theater and numerous historic estates within blocks; Mooten Botanic Gardens and Indian Canyons within minutes.

Innkeeper(s): Elissa Goforth. $89-349. MC, VISA, AX, DC, CB, DS, PC, TC. TAC10. 23 rooms, 24 with PB, 10 with FP, 8 suites and 2 cottages. Breakfast included in rates. Types of meals: Cont plus. Beds: KQT. Cable TV, phone and ceiling fan in room. Air conditioning. Fax, copier, spa and swimming on premises. Weddings, small meetings, family reunions and seminars hosted. French, Dutch and limited German & Spanish spoken. Antiquing, hiking, horseback riding, tennis, golf, ballooning, polo and live theater nearby.

Pets Allowed.

Publicity: *New York Times, Washington Post, Los Angeles Times, San Diego Union Tribune, Seattle Times, Portland Oregonian, Los Angeles, San Diego Magazine, Pacific Northwest Magazine, Sunset, Westways and Alaska Airlines Magazine.*

"Outstanding ambiance, friendly relaxed atmosphere."

Estrella Inn

415 South Belardo Road
Palm Springs, CA 92262
(760)320-4117 (800)237-3687 Fax:(760)323-3303
E-mail: info@estrella.com
Web: www.estrella.com

Circa 1938. "Estrella" means star, and this secluded resort is legendary for the famous movie stars who stayed here during Hollywood's glamour days. Built in Mexican casita-style, the personal attention to service treats everyone like a star. Impressive accommodations include guest bedrooms, studios, suites and villas, each offering luxury and comfort. A continental breakfast is a daily treat. The lush grounds with cascading fountains, palm and fruit trees, and colorful flowers are a panoramic oasis. Awesome views of Mt. San Jacinto are blissfully absorbed while relaxing at one of the pools or spas.

Innkeeper(s): Paul Birchall. $79-385. MC, VISA, AX, DC, CB, TC. TAC10. 67 rooms with PB, 14 with FP, 11 suites and 14 cottages. Breakfast included in rates. Types of meals: Cont. Beds: KQ. Cable TV, phone and fireplace in room. Central air. Fax, copier, spa, swimming, pet boarding and free parking on premises. Weddings, small meetings, family reunions and seminars hosted. Art galleries, bicycling, golf, hiking, Aerial Tramway, Indian Canyons, Village Fest on Thursdays, live theater, museums, parks, shopping and tennis nearby.

Pets allowed: Max 2 dogs weighing no more than 40 pounds per dog. $20 fee.

Orchid Tree Inn

261 S Belardo Rd
Palm Springs, CA 92262-6329
(760)325-2791 (800)733-3435 Fax:(760)325-3855
E-mail: info@orchidtree.com
Web: www.orchidtree.com

Circa 1915. Nineteen buildings comprise this desert retreat offering a variety of Mediterranean, ranch, and modern designs representing more than 50 years of Palm Springs architecture.

Said to be the oldest continuously operating lodging establishment in Palm Springs, the inn's mature, lush gardens meander throughout the three acres of property and offer excellent mountain views. Each accommodation has its own decorating style including Mission Oak, Prairie, ranch oak, lodge pole pine, Mexican folk and wicker. Restored in 1999, some units feature private whirlpools and fireplaces. A deluxe continental breakfast is offered.

Innkeeper(s): Robert Weithorn & Karen Prince-Weithorn. $70-395. MC, VISA, AX, DS, TC. TAC10. 40 rooms with PB, 7 with FP, 8 suites, 1 cottage, 8 cabins, 1 guest house and 1 conference room. Types of meals: Cont plus, early coffee/tea and room service. Beds: KQDT. Cable TV, phone, turndown service, one suite with private steam room, some rooms with hot tub/spa, refrigerators, microwave ovens and most with full kitchens in room. Central air. VCR, fax, copier, spa, swimming, bicycles, tennis, library, data ports, shuffleboard and on premises. Weddings, small meetings, family reunions and seminars hosted. Spanish spoken. Amusement parks, antiquing, art galleries, bicycling, fishing, golf, hiking, horseback riding, aerial tramway, Joshua Tree National Park, live theater, museums, shopping, cross-country skiing and tennis nearby.

Villa Royale Inn

1620 Indian Tr
Palm Springs, CA 92264
(760)327-2314 (800)245-2314 Fax:(760)322-3794
E-mail: info@villaroyale.com
Web: www.villaroyale.com

Circa 1940. Rich European decor and furnishings create the ambiance of a secluded Mediterranean inn at this Palm Springs retreat. Rooms are charming and romantic, decorated with European antiques. Some rooms have wooden beams and tile

floors. In many rooms, French doors lead out to a private patio. The suites and rooms are secluded on more than three acres. Paths meander through the gardens. There are two pools and a spa on the premises. Europa, the inn's acclaimed restaurant, serves Mediterranean/continental specialties for dinner.

Innkeeper(s): Amy Aquino. $99-325. MC, VISA, AX, DC, DS, TC. TAC10. 31 rooms with PB, 17 with FP and 11 suites. Breakfast included in rates. Types of meals: Full bkfst, gourmet dinner and room service. Beds: KQT. Cable TV,

phone, thick terry cloth robes and some with kitchens in room. Air conditioning. Fax, spa, swimming, private patio and spa on premises. Weddings, small meetings and family reunions hosted. Antiquing, golf, hiking, horseback riding, water parks, live theater, parks, shopping and tennis nearby.

The Willows Historic Palm Springs Inn

412 W Tahquitz Canyon Way
Palm Springs, CA 92262
(760)320-0771 (800)966-9597 Fax:(760)320-0780
E-mail: innkeeper@thewillowspalmsprings.com
Web: www.thewillowspalmsprings.com

Circa 1927. This beautiful Italianate Mediterranean estate was once the abode of Marion Davies, mistress of William Randolf Hearst. Carole Lombard and Clark Gable stayed here as part of "the world's longest honeymoon," and Albert Einstein was also

a guest. The building's architecture includes the construction of a second shell inside the exterior to provide a natural cooling effect with the air pocket created. Mahogany beams, hardwood floors, a grand piano and a carved fireplace accentuate the Great Hall. It's difficult to choose a

room, but for your first trip you might try the Rock Room with a shower flowing onto a protruding piece of San Jacinto Mountain and a double tub built into a rock. The Marion Davies Room offers fine antiques, a balcony with view, and a fireplace. Its bath has a stone floor, silver chandelier, chaise lounge and double tub as well as a shower with a private garden view. The arches of the inn's veranda are set off with long drapes and there are frescoed ceilings and views out over the pool. Guests enjoy wine and hors d'oeuvres in the evening, sometimes with live music, and in the morning, a full gourmet breakfast is served within view of a hillside waterfall. Cross the street to Le Vallauris, an excellent French restaurant, or walk to several historical sites.

Historic Interest: Desert Museum (1 block), Historic Adobe & Museum (3 blocks), Palm Springs Aerial Tran (5 miles).

$295-550. MC, VISA, AX, DC, CB, DS, PC, TC. TAC10. 8 rooms with PB, 4 with FP and 1 conference room. Breakfast and snacks/refreshments included in rates. Types of meals: Gourmet bkfst, early coffee/tea and room service. MAP. Beds: KQ. Cable TV, phone, turndown service and VCR in room. Central air. Fax, copier, spa and swimming on premises. Weddings, small meetings and family reunions hosted. Spanish spoken. Antiquing, bicycling, golf, hiking, horseback riding, live theater, museums, parks, shopping and tennis nearby.

Publicity: *Travel & Leisure, Los Angeles, Avenues, Westways Departures, Chicago Tribune, Los Angeles Times, Country Inns, Gourmet, Instyle* and *New York Times.*

Palo Alto   I5

The Victorian on Lytton

555 Lytton Ave
Palo Alto, CA 94301-1538
(650)322-8555 Fax:(650)322-7141
E-mail: victorianonlytton@aol.com

Circa 1896. This Queen Anne home was built for Hannah Clapp, a descendant of Massachusetts Bay colonist Roger Clapp. The house has been graciously restored, and each guest room features its own sitting area. Most rooms boast a canopy or four-poster bed. Stanford University is within walking distance.

Innkeeper(s): Susan & Maxwell Hall. $183-250. MC, VISA, AX. 10 rooms with PB, 1 with FP. Breakfast and snacks/refreshments included in rates.

Types of meals: Cont plus and early coffee/tea. EP. Beds: KQ. Cable TV, phone and modem line in room. Air conditioning. Fax and computer modem jacks on premises. Handicap access. Antiquing, parks, shopping and sporting events nearby.

Publicity: *USA Today.*

"A beautiful inn! My favorite."

Petaluma   H4

Cavanagh Inn

10 Keller St
Petaluma, CA 94952-2939
(707)765-4657 (888)765-4658 Fax:(707)769-0466
E-mail: info@cavanaghinn.com

Circa 1902. Embrace turn-of-the-century California at this picturesque Georgian Revival manor. The garden is filled with beautiful flowers, plants and fruit trees. Mouth-watering breakfasts

are served each morning in the formal dining room. The innkeepers also serve wine at 5:30 p.m. The parlor and library, which boasts heart-of-redwood paneled walls, is an ideal place to relax. Cavanagh Inn is located at the edge of Petaluma's historic district, and close to shops and the riverfront. Petaluma is 32 miles north of the Golden Gate.

Innkeeper(s): Ray & Jeanne Farris. $100-145. MC, VISA, AX, PC. TAC10. 7 rooms, 5 with PB and 1 conference room. Breakfast included in rates. Types of meals: Gourmet bkfst. Beds: KQDT. VCR, fax and library on premises. Small meetings, family reunions and seminars hosted. Spanish spoken. Antiquing, live theater, parks, shopping and wineries nearby.

Publicity: *Argus-Courier, Arizona Daily Star, Travel Today, L.A. Times and Readers Digest New Choices.*

"This is our first B&B. . .sort of like learning to drive with a Rolls-Royce!"

Placerville   G6

Chichester-McKee House B&B

800 Spring St
Placerville, CA 95667-4424
(530)626-1882 (800)831-4008
E-mail: info@innlover.com
Web: www.innlover.com

Circa 1892. This fanciful Victorian home, with all its gables, gingerbread and fretwork draws the breath of many a passerby. The house is full of places to explore and admire, including the

parlor, library and conservatory. Guest rooms are filled with family treasures and antiques, and the home features fireplaces and stained glass. Breakfast at the inn includes freshly baked goods and delicious entrees. Evening refreshments are a treat, and the special blends of morning coffee will wake your spirit. Ask the innkeepers about the discovery of a gold mine beneath the dining room floor and for advice on adventures in the Placerville and Sierra Foothills area.

Historic Interest: Marshall State Historic Gold Discovery Park, Gold Bug Park Mine, Apple Hill.

Innkeeper(s): Doreen & Bill Thornhill. $95-130. MC, VISA, AX, DS, PC, TC. TAC10. 4 rooms. Breakfast and snacks/refreshments included in rates. Types of meals: Gourmet bkfst and early coffee/tea. Beds: QT. VCR and library on premises. Small meetings and family reunions hosted. Antiquing, fishing, wineries, live theater, parks, shopping, cross-country skiing and water sports nearby.

Publicity: *Hi Sierra, Mountain Democrat, Sierra Heritage and Crosscut.*

Point Arena   F3

Coast Guard House Historic Inn

695 Arena Cove
Point Arena, CA 95468
(707)882-2442 Fax:(707)882-3233
E-mail: coast@mcn.org
Web: www.coastguardhouse.com

Circa 1901. This National Register, Cape Cod-style home was built by the Lifesaving Service and later was used by the U.S. Coast Guard. A collection of photographs and memorabilia also is displayed. Guest rooms are decorated in arts and crafts and all afford ocean or canyon views. The Boathouse, a replica of the ground's original boathouse, is a romantic cabin with a woodburning stove, private patio and spa with an ocean view. The Point Arena Lighthouse and Museum, as well as many shops and restaurants are just a few miles away.

Historic Interest: Built in 1901 by Life Saving Service.

Innkeeper(s): Mia & Kevin Gallagher. $125-245. MC, VISA, DC. 7 rooms. Breakfast included in rates. Types of meals: Full bkfst.

Point Reyes Station   H4

Holly Tree Inn

3 Silverhills Rd, PO Box 642
Point Reyes Station, CA 94956-0642
(415)663-1554 Fax:(415)663-8566

Circa 1939. Innkeepers Diane and Tom Balogh have created an environment to please any guest at their elegant bed & breakfast inn. Located on 19 acres adjoining the Point Reyes National Seashore, the inn is ideal for families. The Vision Cottage is a perfect place for parents and children. The cottage includes two bedrooms, each with a queen-size pine bed dressed with handmade quilts and down comforters. Extra futons are available for children, and there's a wood-burning fireplace and a kitchen. For honeymooners or those seeking solitude, the innkeepers offer Sea Star Cottage, a romantic hamlet for two. The cottage sits at the end of a 75-foot dock on Tomales Bay. Both cottages are several miles from the main inn, but guests also can opt for four, well-appointed rooms in the main inn or the Cottage in the Woods.

Innkeeper(s): Diane & Tom Balogh. $120-250. MC, VISA, PC, TC. TAC10. 4 rooms with PB, 4 with FP and 3 cottages. Breakfast included in rates. Types of meals: Full bkfst, early coffee/tea and afternoon tea. Beds: KQ. Fax, spa and library on premises. Small meetings and seminars hosted. Limited Spanish and limited French spoken. Antiquing, fishing, Pt. Reyes National Seashore, live theater, parks, shopping and water sports nearby.

Publicity: *Country Homes and Gourmet.*

Quincy   E6

The Feather Bed

542 Jackson St PO Box 3200
Quincy, CA 95971-9412
(530)283-0102 (800)696-8624
E-mail: info@featherbed-inn.com
Web: www.featherbed-inn.com

Circa 1893. Englishman Edward Huskinson built this Queen Anne house shortly after he began his mining and real estate ventures. Ask for the secluded cottage with its own deck and claw-foot tub. Other rooms in the main house overlook downtown Quincy or the mountains. Check out a bicycle to explore the countryside.

Historic Interest: County Historic Designation.

Innkeeper(s): Bob & Jan Janowski. $90-150. MC, VISA, AX, DC, DS, PC, TC. TAC10. 7 rooms with PB, 4 with FP, 1 suite and 2 cottages. Breakfast and snacks/refreshments included in rates. Types of meals: Gourmet bkfst and early coffee/tea. Beds: QT. TV, phone, ceiling fan and radio in room. Air conditioning. VCR, fax, copier, bicycles and library on premises. Handicap access. Antiquing, fishing, theater, parks, shopping, cross-country skiing and water sports nearby.

Publicity: *Parade, Focus, Reno Gazette, Bay Area Back Roads, San Francisco Chronicle, Country Accents and Sunset.*

"After living and traveling in Europe where innkeepers are famous, we have found The Feather Bed to be one of the most charming in the U.S. and Europe!"

Red Bluff   D5

Faulkner House

1029 Jefferson St
Red Bluff, CA 96080-2725
(530)529-0520 (800)549-6171
E-mail: faulknerbb@snowcrest.net
Web: www.snowcrest.net/faulknerbb

Circa 1890. This Queen Anne Victorian stands on a quiet, tree-lined street in the Victorian town of Red Bluff. Furnished in antiques, the house has original stained-glass windows, ornate molding, and eight-foot pocket doors separating the front and back parlors. The Tower Room is a cozy spot or choose the Rose Room with its brocade fainting couch and queen bed.

Historic Interest: Ide Adobe (1 mile), Kelly Griggs Museum (one-half mile).

Innkeeper(s): Harvey & Mary Klingler. $75-100. MC, VISA, AX. 4 rooms with PB. Breakfast included in rates. Types of meals: Full bkfst. Beds: QD. Antiquing, fishing, parks and cross-country skiing nearby.

Publicity: *Red Bluff Daily News.*

"Enjoyed our stay at your beautiful home."

Sacramento   G6

Amber House

1315 22nd St
Sacramento, CA 95816-5717
(916)444-8085 (800)755-6526 Fax:(916)552-6529
E-mail: innkeeper@amberhouse.com

Circa 1905. These three historic homes on the city's Historic Preservation Register are in a neighborhood of fine historic homes eight blocks from the capitol. Each room is named for a famous poet, artist or composer and features stained glass, English antiques, and amenities such as bath robes and fresh flowers. Ask about the Van Gogh Room

where you can soak in the heart-shaped Jacuzzi tub-for-two or enjoy one of the rooms with marble baths and Jacuzzi tubs in either the adjacent 1913 Mediterranean mansion or the 1895 Colonial Revival. A gourmet breakfast can be served in your room or in the dining room at a time you request.

Historic Interest: California State Capitol, State Railroad Museum, Crocker Art Museum, Governor's Mansion, Old Sacramento State Historic Park (all within 8 to 22 blocks).

$139-269. MC, VISA, AX, DC, CB, DS, PC, TC. TAC10. 14 rooms with PB, 3 with FP and 1 conference room. Breakfast included in rates. Types of meals: Gourmet bkfst and early coffee/tea. Beds: KQ. Cable TV, phone, turn-down service, VCR, hair dryers and irons and boards in room. Air conditioning. Fax, bicycles and library on premises. Weddings, small meetings and seminars hosted. Antiquing, fishing, live theater, parks, shopping, downhill skiing, cross-country skiing and water sports nearby.

Publicity: *Travel & Leisure and Village Crier.*

"Your cordial hospitality, the relaxing atmosphere and delicious breakfast made our brief business/pleasure trip so much more enjoyable."

Inn At Parkside

2116-6th St
Sacramento, CA 95818
(916)658-1818 (800)995-7275 Fax:(916)658-1809
E-mail: gmcgreal@2xtreme.net

Circa 1936. This home was built for the North American ambassador from Nationalist China, and he lived here for 40 years. The architecture is Mediterranean, and in the spirit of its former owner, the exterior is decorated by several different flags. The interior is elegant and somewhat eclectic, with a mix of antiques and Art Deco stylings, including murals on the hallway wall, in a guest room and in the ballroom. A stained-glass ceiling in one room is another unique item. Two suites offer double Jacuzzi tubs, and three rooms include a fireplace. The inn's location affords close access to many attractions in Sacramento, including the convention center and Capitol. The innkeepers specialize in serving low-fat, gourmet vegetarian breakfasts. The inn's conference room and ballroom are popular for groups and special events.

Innkeeper(s): Georgia McGreal & Weldon Reeves. $90-250. MC, VISA, AX, PC, TC. TAC10. 7 rooms with PB, 3 with FP, 1 suite and 1 conference room. Breakfast included in rates. Types of meals: Gourmet bkfst, cont plus and early coffee/tea. Beds: KQ. Cable TV, phone, ceiling fan and VCR in room. Air conditioning. Fax, copier, spa and library on premises. Handicap access. Weddings, small meetings and family reunions hosted. Amusement parks, antiquing, fishing, golf, old Sac, American & Sacramento Rivers, live theater, parks, sporting events, tennis and water sports nearby.

Publicity: *LA Times, San Francisco Chronicle, CABBI Journal, IBBEX Newsletter and SOCA Journal.*

Saint Helena   G4

Ambrose Bierce House

1515 Main St
Saint Helena, CA 94574-1851
(707)963-3003 Fax:(707)993-9367
E-mail: ambrose@napanet.net
Web: www.ambrosebiercehouse.com

Circa 1872. A white iron archway welcomes guests to this three-story Victorian, once home to short story writer Ambrose Bierce. (Gregory Peck visited the house and starred as Bierce in

the movie Old Gringo.) Guest rooms offer high ceilings, antiques, fine linens, fresh flowers and high beds. Rooms offer special features such as Jacuzzi tubs, a fireplace or canopy bed. Enjoy evening wine or early morning coffee from the balcony while admiring the massive redwood providing the shade, or listen to the classical music that plays softly in the parlor. At breakfast, expect entrees such as eggs Benedict or Belgian waffles as well as freshly baked croissants. Champagne is offered each morning. John is a hobby winemaker (200 cases a year) and Lisa is famous for her award-winning landscaping and flowerbeds. Galleries, shops and restaurants are a stroll away in historic downtown.

Innkeeper(s): John & Lisa Wild-Runnells. $199-269. MC, VISA, PC, TC. TAC10. 3 rooms with PB, 1 with FP and 1 suite. Breakfast and snacks/refreshments included in rates. Types of meals: Gourmet bkfst and early coffee/tea. Beds: Q. Cable TV and VCR in room. Central air. Fax, copier, spa, coffee maker and refrigerator on premises. Antiquing, art galleries, bicycling, canoeing/kayaking, fishing, golf, hiking, horseback riding, museums, parks, shopping, tennis and wineries nearby.

Ink House

1575 Saint Helena Hwy
Saint Helena, CA 94574-9775
(707)963-3890
E-mail: inkhousebb@aol.com

Circa 1884. Theron H. Ink, owner of thousands of acres in Marin, Napa and Sonoma counties, was an investor in livestock, wineries and mining. He built his Italianate Victorian with a glass-walled observatory on top, and from this room, visitors can enjoy 360-degree views of the Napa Valley and surrounding vineyards. Listed in the National Register, the Ink House is an elegant, spacious retreat of a time gone by.

Innkeeper(s): Diane DeFilipi. $110-215. MC, VISA, PC, TC. TAC10. 7 rooms, 5 with PB. Breakfast included in rates. Types of meals: Gourmet bkfst. Beds: Q. Air conditioning. VCR, bicycles, library, pool table, observatory, picnic table, historic barn and gardens on premises. Weddings and family reunions hosted. Italian spoken. Antiquing, fishing, golf, spas, horseback riding, hot air balloon rides, parks, shopping, tennis and water sports nearby.

Publicity: *Newsweek, Time, Forbes, Los Angeles Times, Wine Spectator and CBS.*

"Your hospitality made us feel so much at home. This is a place and a time we will long remember."

San Diego   Q12

A Victorian Heritage Park Inn

2470 Heritage Park Row
San Diego, CA 92110-2803
(619)299-6832 (800)995-2470 Fax:(619)299-9465
E-mail: innkeeper@heritageparkinn.com
Web: www.heritageparkinn.com

Circa 1889. Situated on a seven-acre Victorian park in the heart of Old Town, this inn is two of seven preserved classic structures. The main house offers a variety of beautifully appointed guest rooms, decked in traditional Victorian furnishings and decor. The opulent Manor Suite includes two bedrooms, a Jacuzzi tub and sitting room. Several rooms offer ocean views, and guest also can see the nightly fireworks show at nearby Sea World. A collection of classic movies is available, and a different movie is shown each night in the inn's parlor.

Guests are treated to a light afternoon tea, and breakfast is served on fine china on candlelit tables. The home is within walking distance to the many sites, shops and restaurants in the historic Old Town.

Innkeeper(s): Nancy & Charles Helsper. $125-250. MC, VISA, TC. TAC10. 12 rooms with PB, 1 suite and 1 conference room. Breakfast and afternoon tea included in rates. Types of meals: Gourmet bkfst and early coffee/tea. MAP. Beds: KQT. Phone and turndown service in room. Air conditioning. VCR, fax and copier on premises. Small meetings and seminars hosted. Antiquing, fishing, San Diego Zoo, Tijuana, live theater, parks, shopping, sporting events and water sports nearby.

Publicity: *Los Angeles Herald Examiner, Innsider, Los Angeles Times, Orange County Register, San Diego Union, In-Flight, Glamour and Country Inns.*

"A beautiful step back in time. Peaceful and gracious."

Carole's Bed & Breakfast Inn

3227 Grimm Ave
San Diego, CA 92104
(619)280-5258 (800)975-5521

Circa 1904. This delightful Craftsman-style home stands on nearly an acre of land in North Park, just minutes from San Diego's historic area and tourist attractions. Paneled walls, beamed ceilings and hardwood floors with Oriental carpets create warmth, beauty and period ambiance. The inn offers eight guest bedrooms, two garden studios, a one-bedroom house and a two-bedroom apartment. Before heading out for the many nearby historical sites and attractions, guests are served a generous continental breakfast that includes items such as baked French toast or freshly baked bread, fruit in season, juice and hot beverages. The San Diego Zoo, Balboa Park, Mission Bay Park, San Diego Harbor, Old Town San Diego, the Scripps Aquamuseum and the Wild Animal Park are just a few of the nearby attractions.

Historic Interest: Balboa Park, (1/2 mile), Old Town (4 miles), Star of India Ship (2 miles), Gas lamp (2 miles).

Innkeeper(s): Carole Dugdale/Michael O'Brien. $89-189. MC, VISA, AX, DS, TC. TAC10. 8 rooms, 3 with PB and 1 cottage. Breakfast included in rates. Types of meals: Veg bkfst, cont plus and early coffee/tea. Beds: KQ. Cable TV, phone and ceiling fan in room. Pool, some with A/C and there is a one-bedroom house and a two-bedroom apartment on premises. Family reunions hosted. Spanish spoken. Antiquing, art galleries, beaches, bicycling, golf, hiking, museums, parks, shopping and tennis nearby.

Keating House

2331 Second Ave
San Diego, CA 92101-1505
(619)239-8585 (800)995-8644 Fax:(619)239-5774
E-mail: inn@keatinghouse.com
Web: www.keatinghouse.com

Circa 1888. This Queen Anne Victorian built during San Diego's boom years stands on the once prominent Banker's Hill, half a mile from the ocean and half a mile from Balboa Park. It is surrounded by other Victorian and Craftsman homes of yesteryear. The exterior boasts ornate shingle wall panels, gables, turrets and a porch with turned spindles. Inside are 12-foot ceilings and four fireplaces. The grounds have lush tropical gardens that include orchids, roses, cacti, jasmine, jacaranda and banana trees. A fountain, patio and outdoor seating area add to the charm. The owners of Keating House have restored several homes and placed them all in the city's historic register, and one that is in the National Register. The inn offers nine guest bedrooms, including one cottage with two bedrooms.

Breakfast is served in the light, airy dining room.

Historic Interest: Balboa Park (1/4 miles).

Innkeeper(s): Ben Baltic, Doug Scott. $85-125. MC, VISA, AX. TAC5. 9 rooms with PB, 1 with FP, 1 suite and 1 cottage. Breakfast and snacks/refreshments included in rates. Types of meals: Gourmet bkfst, veg bkfst and early coffee/tea. Beds: QDT. Ceiling fan in room. Central air. Fax and copier on premises. Weddings and family reunions hosted. Spanish and French spoken. Amusement parks, antiquing, art galleries, beaches, bicycling, fishing, golf, hiking, live theater, museums, parks, shopping and wineries nearby.

San Francisco   H4

Andrews Hotel

624 Post St
San Francisco, CA 94109-8222
(415)563-6877 (800)926-3739 Fax:(415)928-6919
E-mail: res@andrewshotel.com

Circa 1906. This historic hotel originally was constructed in 1905 as a Turkish bath. After being damaged by earthquake, the Andrews was rebuilt in 1906 and transformed into a hotel.

Today it offers 48 guest rooms; each decorated in a pleasant, modern style. High ceilings and bay windows are a reminder of the hotel's turn-of-the-century construction. In the mornings, guests will find continental breakfast fare just outside their door. In the afternoons, a complimentary glass of wine is available to guests at the hotel's restaurant and bar, Fino's. The Andrews Hotel is located two blocks west of Union Square.

Innkeeper(s): Barbara, Yvonne. $105-175. MC, VISA, AX, DC, TC. TAC10. 48 rooms with PB and 5 suites. Breakfast included in rates. Types of meals: Cont, early coffee/tea, afternoon tea, gourmet dinner and room service. Beds: KQDT. Cable TV, phone and 10 rooms with ceiling fans and refrigerators in room. Fax, copier, child care and restaurant and bar on premises. Weddings hosted. Spanish and French spoken. Antiquing, golf, live theater, parks, sporting events and tennis nearby.

Archbishop's Mansion

1000 Fulton St (at Steiner)
San Francisco, CA 94117-1608
(415)563-7872 (800)543-5820 Fax:(415)885-3193

Circa 1904. This French Empire-style manor was built for the Archbishop of San Francisco. It is designated as a San Francisco historic landmark. The grand stairway features redwood paneling, Corinthian columns and a stained-glass dome. The parlor has a hand-painted ceiling. Each of the guest rooms is named for an opera. Rooms have antiques, Victorian window treatments and embroidered linens. Continental breakfast is served in the dining room, and guests also are treated to a complimentary wine and cheese reception each night.

Innkeeper(s): Jennifer Huggins. $165-425. MC, VISA, AX, DC. TAC10. 15 rooms with PB, 11 with FP and 5 suites. Breakfast included in rates. Types of meals: Cont. Beds: KQ. Cable TV, phone, turndown service and VCR in room. Fax and copier on premises. Weddings and small meetings hosted. Parks nearby.

Publicity: *Travel-Holiday, Travel & Leisure.* and *Country Inns.*

"The ultimate, romantic honeymoon spot."

Carol's Cow Hollow Inn

2821 Steiner St
San Francisco, CA 94123
(415)775-8295 (800)400-8295 Fax:(415)775-8296
E-mail: forbestowninn@zapcom.net
Web: www.innaccess.com/fti

Circa 1907. An old wisteria, roses and hydrangeas sit under walnut trees in front of this Edwardian inn built during the Civil War. Sharing a rich local history, the church rectory aross the street was once a stage coach stop and hotel. Ask about Anna Makin, an interesting resident many years ago. There is a comfortable feeling of being in a quiet and peaceful home. Guest bedrooms and suites, one with a fireplace, are decorated in subtle palates pleasing to both male and female. Fresh flowers or live plants also add a nice touch. Breakfast might feature fruit compote with lime yogurt dressing; an omelet with cheese, mushrooms, asparagus, ham; fresh baked pumpkin muffins or nut breads and beverages. Relax in the hammock for two amid a secluded garden with a pool and an ivy-covered arch with old mission bell.

Historic Interest: Lakeport Museum nearby.

Innkeeper(s): Carol Blumenfeld, Alexander Sachal. $100-250. MC, VISA, AX, DC, DS, PC, TC. TAC10. 3 rooms, 2 with PB, 1 with FP and 1 suite. Breakfast, afternoon tea and snacks/refreshments included in rates. Types of meals: Full bkfst, veg bkfst and early coffee/tea. Beds: Q. Cable TV, phone, VCR and fireplace in room. Fax and copier on premises. Weddings, small meetings, family reunions and seminars hosted. French, Spanish, Russian and German spoken. Antiquing, art galleries, beaches, bicycling, canoeing/kayaking, fishing, golf, hiking, horseback riding, concerts at Konocti, live theater, museums, parks, shopping, tennis, water sports and wineries nearby.

Publicity: *Sunset Magazine* and *Bay Area Backroads.*

The Chateau Tivoli

1057 Steiner St
San Francisco, CA 94115-4620
(415)776-5462 (800)228-1647 Fax:(415)776-0505
E-mail: mail@chateautivoli.com
Web: www.chateautivoli.com

Circa 1892. Built for lumber magnate Daniel Jackson, this 10,000-square-foot mansion is painted in 22 colors with highlights of glimmering gold leaf accentuating its turrets and towers. It has been named "The Greatest Painted Lady in the World" by Elizabeth Pomada and Michael Larson, authors of the Painted Ladies series. Antiques and art from the estates of Cornelius Vanderbilt, Charles de Gaulle and J. Paul Getty are featured throughout. Canopy beds, marble baths, fireplaces and balconies recall San Francisco's Golden Age of Opulence. Chateau Tivoli holds the California Heritage Council's 1989 award for best restoration of a Victorian house in California. During the week, guests are served continental-plus fare. On weekends, a champagne brunch is served. Complimentary wine and cheese is offered in the evening. All rooms offer dataports with computer-dedicated lines for guests.

Innkeeper(s): Geraldine & Stephen Shohet. $99-250. MC, VISA, AX. TAC10. 9 rooms, 7 with PB, 2 with FP. Breakfast included in rates. Types of meals: Cont plus and snacks/refreshments. Beds: KQD. Fax, copier and e-mail access on premises. Victoriana and jazz nearby.

Publicity: *Bay City Guide, Elle Decor, Northern California Jewish Bulletin* and *Country Inns.*

"The romance and charm has made Chateau Tivoli the place to stay whenever we are in San Francisco."

Golden Gate Hotel

775 Bush St
San Francisco, CA 94108-3402
(415)392-3702 (800)835-1118 Fax:(415)392-6202
E-mail: inof@goldengatehotle.com

Circa 1913. News travels far when there's a bargain. Half of the guests visiting this four-story Edwardian hotel at the foot of Nob Hill are from abroad. Great bay windows on each floor provide many of the rooms with gracious spaces at humble prices. An original bird cage elevator kept in working order floats between floors. Antiques, fresh flowers, and afternoon tea further add to the atmosphere. Union Square is two-and-a-half blocks from the hotel.

Innkeeper(s): John & Renate Kenaston. $85-130. MC, VISA, AX, DC, TC. TAC10. 25 rooms, 14 with PB. Breakfast and afternoon tea included in rates. Types of meals: Cont. Cable TV and phone in room. Fax on premises. French, German and Spanish spoken. Antiquing, restaurants and live theater nearby.

Publicity: *Toronto Globe & Mail, Los Angeles Times, Melbourne Sun (Australia) and Sunday Oregonian.*

"Stayed here by chance, will return by choice!"

Inn San Francisco

943 Van Ness Ave
San Francisco, CA 94110-2613
(415)641-0188 (800)359-0913 Fax:(415)641-1701
E-mail: innkeeper@innsf.com
Web: www.innsf.com

Circa 1872. Built on one of San Francisco's earliest "Mansion Rows," this 21-room Italianate Victorian is located near the civic and convention centers, close to Mission Dolores.

Antiques, marble fireplaces and Oriental rugs decorate the opulent grand double parlors. Most rooms have featherbeds, Victorian wallcoverings and desks, while deluxe rooms offer private spas, fireplaces or bay windows. There is a rooftop deck with a 360-degree view of San Francisco. Complimentary beverages are always available. The inn is close to the opera, symphony, theaters, Mission Dolores, gift and jewelry centers and antique shopping.

Innkeeper(s): Marty Neely & Connie Wu. $95-265. MC, VISA, AX, DC, CB, DS, PC, TC. TAC10. 21 rooms, 19 with PB, 3 with FP, 3 suites and 1 cottage. Breakfast included in rates. Types of meals: Full bkfst and afternoon tea. Beds: QD. TV, phone, one suite with redwood hot tub, flowers and truffles in room. Fax, garden, rooftop view sundeck and parlor on premises.

Publicity: *Insider, Sunset Magazine, San Francisco Chronicle and American Airlines Magazine.*

"Breakfast; marvelous. The best B&B we've visited.. We were made to feel like family."

The No Name Victorian B&B

847 Fillmore St
San Francisco, CA 94117-1703
(415)899-0060 Fax:(415)899-9923
E-mail: reservations@bbsf.com
Web: www.bbsf.com/noname.html

Circa 1890. Located in the historic district of Alamo Square, this Victorian sits close to the Civic Center, Opera House, Davies Symphony Hall and Union Square. An 1830s wedding bed from mainland China adorns the honeymoon room. The other rooms are tastefully decorated in antiques and antique reproductions. There's a family accommodation with a private entrance, full kitchen and a crib.

Innkeeper(s): Richard & Susan Kreibich. $79-135. MC, VISA, AX, PC, TC. 5 rooms, 3 with PB, 4 with FP and 1 suite. Breakfast included in rates. Types of meals: Full bkfst and early coffee/tea. Beds: QT. Spa on premises. Weddings and family reunions hosted. Opera, symphony, ballet, live theater, parks, shopping and sporting events nearby.

Petite Auberge

863 Bush St
San Francisco, CA 94108-3312
(415)928-6000 (800)365-3004 Fax:(415)775-5717
E-mail: info@foursisters.com
Web: www.foursisters.com

Circa 1917. This five-story hotel features an ornate baroque design with curved bay windows. Now transformed to a French country inn, there are antiques, fresh flowers and country accessories. Most rooms also have working fireplaces. It's a short walk to the Powell Street cable car. In the evenings, wine and hors d'oeuvres are served. Petite Auberge is one of the Four Sisters Inns.

Innkeeper(s): Lou Rosenberger. $145-245. MC, VISA, AX, TC. TAC10. 26 rooms with PB, 17 with FP and 1 suite. Breakfast and afternoon tea included in rates. Types of meals: Gourmet bkfst and early coffee/tea. Beds: KQ. Phone, turndown service, terry robes and valet parking in room. Fax and copier on premises. Handicap access. Antiquing, historic sites, museums, cable, live theater, parks, shopping and sporting events nearby.

Publicity: *Travel & Leisure, Oregonian, Los Angeles Times and Brides.*

"Breakfast was great, and even better in bed!"

Stanyan Park Hotel

750 Stanyan St
San Francisco, CA 94117-2725
(415)751-1000 Fax:(415)668-5454
E-mail: info@stanyanpark.com

Circa 1904. In the National Register of Historic Places, many of the guest rooms of this restored Victorian inn overlook Golden Gate Park. Rooms are decorated in period decor and the turret

suites and bay suites are good choices for special occasions or for longer stays. All the suites include kitchens, dining rooms and parlors. Guests enjoy an expanded continental breakfast and evening tea service. Museums, horseback riding and biking are available in the park, as well as the Japanese Tea Garden.

Innkeeper(s): John Brocklehurst. $125-325. MC, VISA, AX, DC, CB, DS, TC. TAC10. 36 rooms with PB and 6 suites. Types of meals: Cont plus. Beds: QT. Cable TV, phone and suites have kitchens in room. Fax, copier and bicycles on premises. Handicap access. Live theater, parks, shopping and sporting events nearby.

Publicity: *Metropolitan Home, New York Times and Sunset Magazine.*

Victorian Inn on The Park

301 Lyon St
San Francisco, CA 94117-2108
(415)931-1830 (800)435-1967 Fax:(415)931-1830
E-mail: vicinn@aol.com
Web: www.victorianinnonthepark.com

Circa 1897. This grand three-story Queen Anne inn, built by William Curlett, has an open belvedere turret with a teahouse roof and Victorian railings. Silk-screened wallpapers, created especially for the inn, are accentuated by intri-

cate mahogany and redwood paneling. The opulent Belvedere Suite features French doors opening to a Roman tub for two. Overlooking Golden Gate Park, the inn is 10 minutes from downtown.

Innkeeper(s): Lisa & William Benau. $159-199. MC, VISA, AX, DC, CB, DS, PC, TC. TAC10. 12 rooms with PB, 3 with FP and 2 suites. Breakfast included in rates. Types of meals: Cont plus and early coffee/tea. Beds: QT. Phone and balcony in room. Fax, library, child care and refrigerator on premises. Small meetings and family reunions hosted. Russian and Spanish spoken. Antiquing, museums, live theater, parks and sporting events nearby.

Publicity: *New York Times Sunday Travel, Innsider, Country Inns, Good Housekeeping, Good Morning America, Country Inns USA, Great Country Inns of America., PBS Country Inn Series and Traveling Inn Style.*

"The excitement you have about your building comes from the care you have taken in restoring and maintaining your historic structure."

White Swan Inn

845 Bush St
San Francisco, CA 94108-3300
(831)775-1755 (800)999-9570 Fax:(415)775-5717
E-mail: info@foursisters.com
Web: www.foursisters.com

Circa 1915. This four-story inn is near Union Square and the Powell Street cable car. Beveled-glass doors open to a reception

area with granite floors, an antique carousel horse and English artwork. Bay windows and a rear deck contribute to the feeling of an English garden inn. The guest rooms are decorated with bold English wallpapers and prints. All rooms have fireplaces. Turndown service and complimentary newspapers are included, and in the evenings, wine and hors d'oeuvres are served. White Swan is a Four Sisters Inns.

Innkeeper(s): Lou Rosenberger. $180-275. MC, VISA, AX, TC. TAC10. 26 rooms with PB, 26 with FP, 3 suites and 1 conference room. Breakfast and afternoon tea included in rates. Types of meals: Gourmet bkfst and early coffee/tea. Beds: KQT. Phone, turndown service, terry robes and newspaper in room. Fax and copier on premises. Small meetings hosted. Antiquing, museums, live theater, parks, shopping and sporting events nearby.

Publicity: *Travel & Leisure, Victoria and Wine Spectator.*

"Wonderfully accommodating. Absolutely perfect."

San Rafael

Casa Soldavini

531 C St
San Rafael, CA 94901-3809
(415)454-3140

Circa 1932. The first Italian settlers in San Rafael built this home. Their grandchildren now own it and proudly hang pictures of their family. Grandfather Joseph, a wine maker, planned and planted what are now the lush gardens surrounding the home. The many Italian antiques throughout the house complement the Italian-style decor. A homemade breakfast is included, and snacks and beverages are served throughout the day.

Innkeeper(s): Linda Soldavini Cassidy. $85-125. TAC10. 3 rooms. Breakfast included in rates. Types of meals: Cont plus.

Santa Barbara N8

The Bayberry Inn

111 W Valerio St
Santa Barbara, CA 93101-2927
(805)569-3398
E-mail: bayberryinn@aol.com
Web: www.bayberryinnsantabarbara.com

Circa 1894. A quiet neighborhood near downtown is the setting for this inn, a designated Historic Structure of Merit. The extensive grounds provide pleasant spots to relax. The guest bedrooms are all named after berries, some feature fireplaces, canopy beds, antique clawfoot tubs and private decks. Linger over a wonderful gourmet breakfast on the garden deck before embarking on delightful adventures. Later in the day, enjoy fresh flowers, hot beverages and a homemade dessert.

Innkeeper(s): Jill & Kenneth Freeland. $100-180. MC, VISA, AX, DS. 8 rooms with PB, 4 with FP. Breakfast, afternoon tea and snacks/refreshments included in rates. Types of meals: Full bkfst and early coffee/tea. Beds: Q. TV in room. Antiquing, fishing, golf, hiking, horseback riding, live theater, parks, shopping, sporting events, tennis and water sports nearby.

Pets allowed: Upon innkeeper/owner approval.

Publicity: *Santa Barbara News Press and Sighting.*

Blue Dolphin Inn

420 W Montecito St
Santa Barbara, CA 93101-3879
(805)965-2333 (877)722-3657 Fax:(805)962-4907
E-mail: BDolphinn@aol.com
Web: www.sbbluedolphininn.com

Circa 1920. It's a short walk to the beach and harbor from this Victorian inn, which offers accommodations in the main house and adjacent carriage house. Guest rooms are decorated in period style with antiques. Brass beds, tapestry pillows, and fluffy comforters add a romantic touch. Several rooms include fireplaces, Jacuzzi tubs or private balconies.

Historic Interest: The Trussel Winchester Adobe and Fernald House.

Innkeeper(s): Pete Chiarenza, Edward Skolak. $125-245. MC, VISA, AX, PC, TC. TAC10. 9 rooms, 7 with PB and 2 suites. Breakfast, afternoon tea and snacks/refreshments included in rates. Types of meals: Gourmet bkfst and veg bkfst. Beds: KQT. Cable TV, phone and VCR in room. Air conditioning. Fax, copier and library on premises. Small meetings and family reunions hosted. French and Spanish spoken. Antiquing, art galleries, beaches, bicycling, golf, hiking, horseback riding, roller skating, live theater, museums, parks, water sports and wineries nearby.

Publicity: *Los Angeles Times.*

Cheshire Cat Inn & Spa

36 W Valerio St
Santa Barbara, CA 93101-2524
(805)569-1610 Fax:(805)682-1876
E-mail: cheshire@cheshirecat.com
Web: www.cheshirecat.com

Circa 1894. This elegant inn features three Queen Anne Victorians, a Coach House and three cottages surrounded by fountains, gazebos and lush flower gardens. The guest bedrooms and suites are furnished with English antiques, Laura Ashley fabrics and wallpapers or oak floors, pine furniture and down comforters. Some boast fireplaces, Jacuzzi tubs, private balconies, VCRs and refrigerators. Wedgewood china set in the formal dining room or brick patio enhances a delicious breakfast. Local wine and hors d'oeuvres are served in the evening. Spa facilities offer massage and body treatments.

Historic Interest: Santa Barbara Beautiful Award.

Innkeeper(s): Christine Dunstan. $150-375. MC, VISA, PC, TC. 21 rooms with PB, 7 suites and 1 conference room. Breakfast included in rates. Types of meals: Full bkfst and room service. Beds: KQT. Cable TV, phone and ceiling fan in room. Spa facilities on premises. Small meetings, family reunions and seminars hosted. Amusement parks, antiquing, fishing, live theater, shopping, sporting events and water sports nearby.

Publicity: *Two on the Town, KABC, Los Angeles Times, Santa Barbara, American In Flight and Elmer Dills Recommends.*

"Romantic and quaint."

Glenborough Inn

1327 Bath St
Santa Barbara, CA 93101-3630
(805)966-0589 (800)962-0589 Fax:(805)564-8610
E-mail: info@glenborough.com
Web: www.glenboroughinn.com

Circa 1885. The Victorian and California Craftsman-style homes that comprise the Glenborough are located in the theatre and arts district. Antiques, rich wood trim and elegant fireplace suites with canopy beds are offered. Some rooms also have mini refrigerators or whirlpools tubs. There's always plenty of hospitality and an invitation to try the secluded garden hot tub. Homemade breakfasts, served in the privacy of your room, have been written up in Bon Appetit and Chocolatier. Bedtime cookies and beverages are served, as well. It's a three-block walk to restaurants, shops and the shuttle to the beach.

Historic Interest: Walking distance to historic downtown Santa Barbara, Mission Santa Barbara (1 1/4 mile).

Innkeeper(s): Marlies Marburg. $110-325. MC, VISA, AX, DC, CB, PC, TC. TAC10. 18 rooms with PB, 12 with FP and 6 cottages. Breakfast included in rates. Types of meals: Full bkfst and cont. Beds: KQD. TV, phone, ceiling fan, coffee maker, robes, A/C (some rooms) and mini-fridge (some rooms) in room. Fax and spa on premises. Spanish spoken. Antiquing, fishing, live theater, parks, shopping, sporting events and water sports nearby.

Publicity: *Houston Post, Los Angeles Times and Pasadena Choice.*

"Only gracious service is offered at the Glenborough Inn."

The Old Yacht Club Inn

431 Corona Del Mar
Santa Barbara, CA 93103-3601
(805)962-1277 (800)676-1676 Fax:(805)962-3989
E-mail: info@oldyachtclubinn.com
Web: www.oldyachtclubinn.com

Circa 1912. One block from famous East Beach, this California Craftsman house was the home of the Santa Barbara Yacht Club during the Roaring '20s. It was opened as Santa Barbara's first B&B and has become renowned for its gourmet food and superb hospitality.

Innkeeper(s): Eilene Bruce. $110-220. MC, VISA, AX, DS, PC, TC. 12 rooms with PB and 1 conference room. Breakfast included in rates. Types of meals: Gourmet bkfst, early coffee/tea and gourmet dinner. Beds: KQ. TV and phone in room. Fax, copier, bicycles, wine social and beach chairs and beach towels on premises. Small meetings and seminars hosted. Antiquing, fishing, live theater, shopping, sporting events and water sports nearby.

Publicity: *Los Angeles, Valley, Bon Appetit and Gourmet.*

"One of Santa Barbara's better-kept culinary secrets."

Olive House Inn

1604 Olive St
Santa Barbara, CA 93101-1115
(805)962-4902 (800)786-6422 Fax:(805)962-9983
E-mail: olivehse@aol.com

Circa 1904. The Craftsman-style home is located a short walk from Santa Barbara's Mission and downtown. The living room is decorated with bay windows, redwood paneling and a fireplace. Guests can enjoy city and ocean views, private decks and hot tubs. In the afternoon, tea and cookies are offered and in the evening, wine, cheese and sherry are presented.

Historic Interest: Santa Barbara Mission, a museum of natural history, Santa Barbara Historical Museum and The Arlington Theatre are all within walking distance.

Innkeeper(s): Ellen Schaub. $125-195. MC, VISA, AX, DS. 6 rooms with PB, 1 with FP. Breakfast included in rates. Types of meals: Gourmet bkfst, early coffee/tea and snacks/refreshments. Beds: KQ. TV, phone, cable TV (one room), one fireplace and two hot tubs in room. Fax on premises. Small meetings, family reunions and seminars hosted. Antiquing, live theater, parks, shopping and sporting events nearby.

"Thank you for providing not only a lovely place to stay but a very warm and inviting atmosphere."

The Parsonage

1600 Olive Street
Santa Barbara, CA 93101-1115
(805)962-9336 (800)775-0352

Circa 1892. Built for the parson of the Trinity Episcopal Church, The Parsonage is one of Santa Barbara's most notable and romantic Queen Anne Victorians. Each room is elegantly decorated in fine antiques and furnishings distinctive to the period. Located in a quiet neighborhood a few minutes from the Pacific Ocean and the historic Santa Barbara Mission, the inn offers ocean and mountain views. Within walking distance are the Mission, shops, theater and restaurants.

Innkeeper(s): Tony R Navarro. $95-295. MC, VISA, AX, DC, DS. 6 rooms with PB, 2 with FP and 1 suite. Breakfast and snacks/refreshments included in rates. Types of meals: Full bkfst. Beds: KQ. Fax, wine and hors d' oeuvres, homemade baked goods, fresh fruit and coffee and tea on premises. Antiquing, fishing, live theater and water sports nearby.

Publicity: *Los Angeles Times, Epicurean Review, Country Inns B&B and The California Getaway Guide.*

"Bravo! You have created a beautiful treasure here in Santa Barbara."

Prufrock's Garden Inn By The Beach

600 Linden Ave
Santa Barbara, CA 93101
(805)566-9696 (877)837-6257 Fax:(805)566-9404
E-mail: innkeepers@prufrocks.com
Web: www.prufrocks.com

Circa 1904. Tucked between a mountain wilderness, flower fields and an ocean, this inn is located one block from State Beach Park and 10 minutes from the City Center. Santa Barbara Independent named it a "Most Romantic Getaway," and the LA. Times voted it a "Readers' Favorite." Other recognitions include being pictured in Land's End catalog and a"Community Beautiful" award. Explore Salt Marsh Park and waterfront bluffs, or visit specialty shops and cafes. The inn is close to an Amtrak station. A quote from The Love Song of J. Alfred Prufrock, by TS Eliot is lived out at this inn: "Time for you and time for me, before the taking of a toast and tea."

Historic Interest: The Old Mission and historic county courthouse are about 12 minutes away in Santa Barbara. Other nearby historic attractions include adobes and a state historic park.

Innkeeper(s): Judy & Jim Halvorsen. $119-249. MC, VISA, DS. 7 rooms, 5 with PB. Breakfast, afternoon tea & snacks/refreshments included in rates. Types of meals: Full bkfst, cont & early coffee/tea. Beds: Q. Turndown service, sitting area and daybeds in room. VCR, bicycles and gardens on premises. Small meetings, family reunions and seminars hosted. Antiquing, beaches, bicycling, fishing, hiking, tide pools, live theater, parks, shopping, sporting events and wineries nearby.

Publicity: *Santa Barbara Independent's "Most Romantic Getaway"; Carpinteria's "Community Beautification" award; pictured in Land's End catalog and LA Times "Reader's favorite."*

Secret Garden Inn and Cottages

1908 Bath St
Santa Barbara, CA 93101-2813
(805)687-2300 (800)676-1622 Fax:(805)687-4576
E-mail: garden@secretgarden.com
Web: www.secretgarden.com

Circa 1908. The main house and adjacent cottages surround the gardens and are decorated in American and English-Country style. The Hummingbird is a large cottage guest room with a queen-size white iron bed and a private deck with a hot tub for your exclusive use. The two suites have private outdoor hot tubs. Wine and light hors d'oeuvres are served in the late afternoon, and hot apple cider is served each evening.

Innkeeper(s): Dominique Hannaux. $121-231. MC, VISA, AX, PC, TC. TAC10. 11 rooms with PB, 1 with FP, 3 suites and 4 cottages. Breakfast, afternoon tea and snacks/refreshments included in rates. Types of meals: Full bkfst and early coffee/tea. Beds: KQ. TV in room. Fax and copier on premises. Small meetings, family reunions and seminars hosted. Antiquing, fishing, live theater, shopping and water sports nearby.

Publicity: *Los Angeles Times, Santa Barbara and Independant.*

"A romantic little getaway retreat that neither of us will be able to forget. It was far from what we expected to find."

Simpson House Inn

121 E Arrellaga
Santa Barbara, CA 93101
(805)963-7067 (800)676-1280 Fax:(805)564-4811
E-mail: reservations@simpsonhouseinn.com
Web: www.simpsonhouseinn.com

Circa 1874. The Simpson House is currently the only bed and breakfast in North America holding a Five Diamond award from AAA. If you were one of the Simpson family's first visitors, you would have arrived in Santa Barbara by stagecoach or by ship. The railroad was not completed for another 14 years. A stately Italianate Victorian house, the inn, a historic landmark, is situated on an acre of English gardens hidden behind a 20-foot-tall eugenia hedge. In the evenings, guests are treated to a sampling of local wines, as well as a lavish Mediterranean hors d'oeuvre buffet. The evening turndown service includes delectable chocolate truffles. The innkeepers can arrange for in-room European spa treatments, and guests can workout at a nearby private health club. Guests also receive complimentary passes for the Santa Barbara trolley.

Historic Interest: Santa Barbara Mission, Presidio, El Paseo all within 1 mile.

Innkeeper(s): Linda & Glyn Davies, Dixie Adair Budke(GM). $215-550. MC, VISA, AX, DS. TAC10. 14 rooms with PB, 8 with FP, 5 suites and 1 conference room. Breakfast, afternoon tea and snacks/refreshments included in rates. Beds: KQ. Fax, copier, bicycles and evening mediterranean hors d'oeuvres buffet and local wine tasting on premises. Handicap access. Antiquing, fishing, live theater and water sports nearby.

Publicity: *Country Inns, Santa Barbara, LA Magazine, Avenues, Sunset, San Diego Magazine, USA Today and Los Angles Times.*

"Perfectly restored and impeccably furnished. Your hospitality is warm and heartfelt and the food is delectable. Whoever said that 'the journey is better than the destination' couldn't have known about the Simpson House."

Tiffany Country House

1323 De La Vina St
Santa Barbara, CA 93101-3120
(805)963-2283
E-mail: uphamhotel@verizon.net
Web: www.tiffanycountryhouse.com

Circa 1898. This Victorian house features a steep front gable and balcony accentuating the entrance. Colonial diamond-paned bay windows and a front veranda welcome guests to an antique-filled inn. The Honeymoon Suite is a favorite with its secluded garden entrance, garden window seat, Jacuzzi tub and fireplace. The Penthouse occupies the entire third floor and includes a living room with a fireplace, a terrace offering mountain views and a Jacuzzi tub. Other rooms are just as interesting, with antique furniture, cozy atmosphere and comfortable beds. Fine restaurants and shops are within walking distance.

Innkeeper(s): Jan Martin Winn. $145-350. MC, VISA, AX, DC. TAC10. 7 rooms with PB, 5 with FP. Types of meals: Full bkfst. Beds: Q. Phone and Jacuzzi tub in three rooms in room.

"We have stayed at a number of B&Bs, but this is the best. We especially liked the wonderful breakfasts on the porch overlooking the garden."

The Upham Hotel & Garden Cottages

1404 De La Vina St
Santa Barbara, CA 93101-3027
(805)962-0058 (800)727-0876 Fax:(805)963-2825
E-mail: upham.hotel@verizon.net
Web: www.uphamhotel.com

Circa 1871. Antiques and period furnishings decorate each of the inn's guest rooms and suites. The inn is the oldest continuously operating hostelry in Southern California. Situated on an acre of gardens in the center of downtown, it's within easy walking distance of restaurants, shops, art galleries and museums. The staff is happy to assist guests in discovering Santa Barbara's varied attractions. Garden cottage units feature porches or secluded patios and several have gas fireplaces.

Innkeeper(s): Jan Martin Winn. $160-425. MC, VISA, AX. TAC10. 50 rooms with PB, 8 with FP, 4 suites, 3 cottages and 3 conference rooms. Breakfast included in rates. Types of meals: Cont plus, early coffee/tea and snacks/refreshments. Beds: KQ. Cable TV, phone and ceiling fan in room. Fax and copier on premises. Small meetings, family reunions and seminars hosted. Antiquing, golf, live theater, parks, shopping and water sports nearby.

Publicity: *Los Angeles Times, Santa Barbara, Westways, Santa Barbara News-Press and Avenues.*

"Your hotel is truly a charm. Between the cozy gardens and the exquisitely comfortable appointments, The Upham is charm itself."

Santa Cruz   J5

Babbling Brook B&B Inn

1025 Laurel St
Santa Cruz, CA 95060-4237
(831)427-2437 (800)866-1131 Fax:(831)427-2457
E-mail: lodging@babblingbrookinn.com

Circa 1909. This inn was built on the foundations of an 1870 tannery and a 1790 grist mill. Secluded, yet within the city, the inn features a cascading waterfall, historic waterwheel and mean-

...dering creek on one acre of gardens and redwoods. Country French decor, cozy fireplaces, and deep-soaking whirlpool tubs are luxurious amenities of the Babbling Brook. In the evenings, complimentary wine and cheese are served.

$140-250. MC, VISA, AX, DS, PC, TC. TAC10. 13 rooms with PB, 13 with FP and 1 conference room. Breakfast and snacks/refreshments included in rates. Types of meals: Full bkfst and early coffee/tea. Beds: KQT. Cable TV and phone in room. Fax and spa on premises. Handicap access. Weddings hosted. Amusement parks, antiquing, fishing, golf, live theater, parks, shopping, sporting events, water sports and wineries nearby.

Publicity: *Country Inns, Yellow Brick Road, Times-Press-Recorder, Reno Air Magazine and Romantic Homes Magazine.*

"We were impressed with the genuine warmth of the inn. The best breakfast we've had outside our own home!"

Chateau Victorian

118 1st St
Santa Cruz, CA 95060-5402
(831)458-9458

Circa 1885. This Victorian is within a block of the waterfront and offers seven guest rooms. The romantic Bay Side Room is a favorite of guests, as it offers a marble fireplace and a clawfoot tub with an overhead shower. Breakfasts, including a variety of tempting fruits and pastries, can be enjoyed on the patio, dining room or on the secluded side deck.
After a day of exploring Santa Cruz and its surroundings, evening refreshments are a perfect touch. The inn is within walking distance to downtown, the wharf, a variety of restaurants, the Boardwalk Amusement Park and the beach.

Innkeeper(s): Alice June. $120-150. MC, VISA, PC. 7 rooms with PB, 7 with FP. Breakfast included in rates. Types of meals: Cont plus. Beds: Q. Small meetings hosted. Amusement parks, antiquing, fishing, live theater, parks, shopping and water sports nearby.

Publicity: *Times Tribune, Santa Cruz Sentinel and Good Times.*

"Certainly enjoyed our most recent stay and have appreciated all of our visits."

Cliff Crest Bed & Breakfast Inn

407 Cliff St
Santa Cruz, CA 95060-5009
(831)427-2609 (831)252-1057 Fax:(831)427-2710
E-mail: info@cliffcrestbedandbreakfast.com

Circa 1887. Warmth, friendliness and comfort characterize this elegantly restored Queen Anne Victorian home. An octagonal solarium, tall stained-glass windows, and a belvedere overlook Monterey Bay and the Santa Cruz Mountains. The mood is airy and romantic. The spacious gardens were designed by John McLaren, landscape architect for Golden Gate Park. Antiques and fresh flowers fill the rooms, once home to William Jeter, lieutenant governor of California.

Innkeeper(s): Constantin Gehriger, Adriana Gehriger Gil. $95-275. MC, VISA, AX, DS, PC, TC. TAC10. 5 rooms with PB, 2 with FP. Breakfast and snacks/refreshments included in rates. Types of meals: Full bkfst and early coffee/tea. Beds: KQ. TV and phone in room. Fax on premises. Amusement parks, antiquing, fishing, live theater, parks, shop-

ping and water sports nearby.

Publicity: *Contra Costa Times and Los Angeles Times.*

"Delightful place, excellent food and comfortable bed."

Pleasure Point Inn

23665 E Cliff Dr
Santa Cruz, CA 95062-5543
(831)469-6161 (877)557-2567
E-mail: inquiries@pleasurepointinn.com
Web: www.pleasurepointinn.com

Circa 1942. Located in front of the popular Pleasure Point Surfing Beach, this oceanfront estate was completely remodeled recently. The modern Mediterranean-style architecture and design has an upscale appearance. Guest bedrooms all feature gas fireplaces, custom furniture, private patios and entrances. Some offer heated floor tiles and Jacuzzi tubs. Enjoy the sights and sounds of the sea from the large roof top deck overlooking Monterey Bay. Chaise lounges encourage soaking up the sun by day. A heater gas lamp placed near the outdoor dining tables provides warmth for cool evenings. Gaze at the stars while relaxing in the big hot tub. Capitola Village, only two miles away, offers shopping, dining, a sandy beach and nightly entertainment. Cruises can be arranged at the local yacht harbor.

Innkeeper(s): Claire & Tom. Call for rates. MC, VISA, PC, TC. 4 rooms with PB. Breakfast and snacks/refreshments included in rates. Types of meals: Cont plus. Beds: KQ. TV, phone, fireplace and some with Jacuzzi tubs in room. Small meetings, family reunions and seminars hosted. Amusement parks, antiquing, shopping and sporting events nearby.

Santa Monica   O10

Channel Road Inn

219 W Channel Rd
Santa Monica, CA 90402-1105
(310)459-1920 Fax:(310)454-9920
Web: www.channelroadinn.com

Circa 1910. This shingle-clad building is a variation of the Colonial Revival Period, one of the few remaining in Los Angeles. The abandoned home was saved from the city's wrecking crew by owner Susan Zolla, with the encouragement of the local historical society. The rooms feature canopy beds, fine linens, custom mattresses and private porches. Chile Cheese Puffs served with salsa are a popular breakfast speciality. The Pacific Ocean is one block away, and guests often enjoy borrowing the inn's bicycles to pedal along the 30-mile coastal bike path. In the evening, the inn's spectacular cliffside spa is popular.

Innkeeper(s): Heather Suskin. $165-350. MC, VISA, AX, PC, TC. TAC10. 13 rooms with PB, 2 with FP and 1 suite. Breakfast, afternoon tea and snacks/refreshments included in rates. Types of meals: Full bkfst and early coffee/tea. Beds: KQT. Cable TV, phone, ceiling fan and VCR in room. Fax, copier, spa and bicycles on premises. Handicap access. Antiquing, fishing, beach, bike path, Paul Getty Museum, live theater, parks, shopping, sporting events and water sports nearby.

Publicity: *New York Times, Los Angeles, Brides and Country Inns.*

"One of the most romantic hotels in Los Angeles."

Santa Paula   N9

Fern Oaks Inn

1025 Ojai Rd
Santa Paula, CA 93060-1250
(805)525-7747 Fax:(805)933-5001
E-mail: info@fernoaksinn.com
Web: www.fernoaksinn.com

Circa 1929. Paladian windows are the remarkable architectural features of this gracious Spanish Revival home with its beautiful setting of rose gardens, citrus and fruit trees and a swimming pool. There is a handsome solarium, and the inn is appointed in Oriental rugs, hardwood floors and antiques. Guest room decor includes choices such as a four-poster or canopy bed. Breakfast is especially inviting with its antique dining room and gourmet dishes that include Scottish Eggs or Paine Perdu, created by innkeeper Anthony. The innkeepers can arrange vintage train rides and make suggestions for excursions to beaches, stables and Ojai festivals.

Historic Interest: Union Oil Company Building (1890), George Washington Faulkner House, First National Bank, Odd Fellows Building, Ebell Clubhouse, Limoneria Company Building, Santa Clara Elementayr School, Southern Pacific Milling Company, Souther Pacific Railroad Depot, Farmers and Merchants Bank, Santa Paula Airport.

Innkeeper(s): Anthony & Marcia Landau. $95-150. PC, TC. 4 rooms with PB, 1 with FP, 1 suite and 1 conference room. Breakfast and afternoon tea included in rates. Types of meals: Gourmet bkfst. Beds: Q. Ceiling fan and fireplace in room. Central air. VCR, fax, copier, swimming and library on premises. Weddings, small meetings and family reunions hosted. Amusement parks, antiquing, art galleries, beaches, bicycling, canoeing/kayaking, fishing, golf, hiking, horseback riding, antique airplanes (Santa Paula Airport), live theater, museums, parks, shopping, tennis, water sports and wineries nearby.

Publicity: *Pilot Getaways Magazine, Dove Magazine, Ventura County Star, Business Digest and The Camarillo Daily News.*

Santa Rosa   G4

The Gables Inn

4257 Petaluma Hill Rd
Santa Rosa, CA 95404-9796
(707)585-7777 (800)422-5376 Fax:(707)584-5634
E-mail: innkeeper@thegablesinn.com
Web: www.thegablesinn.com

Circa 1877. Fifteen gables accentuate this striking Gothic Revival house with a French influence. Situated on three-and-a-half acres in the center of Sonoma Wine Country, the inn has 12-foot ceilings, a winding staircase with ornately carved balustrades and three marble fireplaces. The Brookside Suite overlooks Taylor Creek and is decorated in an Edwardian theme. Other rooms feature views of the sequoias, meadows and the barn. The surrounding Sonoma Wine Country offers more than 150 wineries and vineyards, as well as the Pacific coast and California Redwoods Park.

Innkeeper(s): Michael & Judy Ogne. $175-250. MC, VISA, AX, DS. TAC10. 8 rooms with PB, 4 with FP, 1 suite and 1 cottage. Breakfast and afternoon tea included in rates. Types of meals: Gourmet bkfst and early coffee/tea. Beds: KQT. Handicap access. 200+ wineries and redwood forest nearby.

Publicity: *Press Democrat, Victorian Homes Magazine and Los Angeles Times.*

"You all have a warmth about you that makes it home here."

Pygmalion House B&B Inn

331 Orange St
Santa Rosa, CA 95401-6226
(707)526-3407 Fax:(707)526-3407

Circa 1880. This historic Victorian, which has been restored to its 19th-century grandeur, is just a few blocks from Santa Rosa's Old Town, "Railroad Square" and many antique shops, cafes, coffeehouses and restaurants. The home is filled with a unique mix of antiques, many of which belonged to famed, Gypsy Rose Lee. Each of the Victorian guest rooms

includes a bath with a clawfoot tub. Five different varieties of coffee are blended each morning for the breakfast service, which includes homemade entrees, freshly baked breads and fresh fruit.

Innkeeper(s): Caroline Berry. $99-119. MC, VISA, PC, TC. 6 rooms with PB. Breakfast included in rates. Cable TV in room. Air conditioning. Fax, copier, library and mall on premises. Antiquing, fishing, golf, live theater, parks, shopping and wineries nearby.

Sausalito   H4

Gables Inn Sausalito

62 Princess St
Sausalito, CA 94965
(415)289-1100 (800)966-1554 Fax:(415)339-0536
E-mail: gablesinns@aol.com
Web: www.gablesinnsausalito.com

Circa 1869. An 1869 Pioneer-style inn with Gothic revival elements, the Gables Inn Sausalito is just five minutes north of the Golden Gate Bridge and sits 200 yards from the water with a view of the San Francisco Bay. Ferry service to San Francisco is a three-minute walk, and guests also may walk to more than 200 shops, art galleries and gourmet restaurants. The inn has nine guest bedrooms and seven suites, some of which have amenities such as fireplaces, oversized spa tubs and balconies with water views. The honeymoon suite overlooks the bay. A continental plus breakfast is served each morning and includes cereal, fresh juice, pastries, fruit and cheese. In the afternoons and evenings, wine, soft drinks, cheese and fruit are served. Muir Woods National Park is 30 minutes from the inn, and the Napa Valley Wine country is an hour's drive.

Innkeeper(s): Abraham & Patricia Chador. $155-300. MC, VISA, AX, DC, CB, DS. TAC10. 9 rooms with PB, 8 with FP, 7 suites and 1 conference room. Breakfast and snacks/refreshments included in rates. Types of meals: Veg bkfst, cont plus and early coffee/tea. Beds: KQ. Cable TV, phone and VCR in room. Fax, copier and library on premises. Handicap access. Weddings and family reunions hosted. Antiquing, art galleries, beaches, bicycling, canoeing/kayaking, fishing, golf, hiking, horseback riding, live theater, museums, parks, shopping, tennis, water sports and wineries nearby.

Sequoia National Park   K9

Plantation B&B

33038 Sierra Hwy 198
Sequoia National Park, CA 93244-1700
(559)597-2555 (800)240-1466 Fax:(559)597-2551
E-mail: relax@plantationbnb.com
Web: www.plantationbnb.com

Circa 1908. The history of orange production is deeply entwined in the roots of California, and this home is located on what once was an orange plantation. The original 1908 house burned in the 1960s, but the current home was built on its foundation. In keeping with the home's plantation past, the innkeepers decorated the bed and breakfast with a "Gone With the Wind" theme. The comfortable, country guest rooms sport names such as the Scarlett O'Hara, the Belle Watling, and of course, the Rhett Butler. A hot tub is located in the orchard, and there also is a heated swimming pool.

Innkeeper(s): Scott & Marie Munger. $89-199. MC, VISA, AX, DC, DS, PC, TC. TAC10. 8 rooms, 6 with PB, 2 with FP and 2 suites. Breakfast and snacks/refreshments included in rates. Types of meals: Gourmet bkfst and early coffee/tea. Beds: KQDT. Cable TV, ceiling fan and VCR in room. Air conditioning. Fax, spa and swimming on premises. Small meetings and family reunions hosted. Antiquing, fishing, golf, parks, shopping, cross-country skiing, sporting events and water sports nearby.

Publicity: *Exeter Sun, Kaweah Commonwealth, Los Angeles Times, Fresno Bee and Visalia Delta Times.*

"Scarlett O'Hara would be proud to live on this lovely plantation."

Sonoma   H4

Brick House Bungalows

313 1st St E
Sonoma, CA 95476
(707)996-8091 Fax:(707)996-7301
E-mail: info@brickhousebungalows.com
Web: www.brickhousebungalows.com

Circa 1907. The main two-story house is reminiscent of the Italian stone farmhouses of the builder's homeland. Four classic California bungalows were added later. Features include fully equipped kitchens, fireplaces and private patios. Fine linens,

vibrant fabrics, distressed leather couches, antique Kilim pillows and carpets enhance a luxurious stay in wine country. Relax in a big hammock or sip complimentary wine by the fireplace. Set amidst lush gardens and a secluded central court-

yard with a fountain, this tranquil compound provides the perfect getaway. In-room massage and spa services are available.

Historic Interest: Mission SF de Solano, Old West sites, Bear Flag Monument.

Innkeeper(s): BJ Clarke, Joe Gough. $125-275. MC, VISA, AX, PC. TAC5. 5 cottages. Breakfast included in rates. Types of meals: Cont plus and early coffee/tea. Beds: KQ. Cable TV, phone, ceiling fan, VCR and fireplace in room. Fax and copier on premises. Family reunions hosted. Amusement parks, antiquing, art galleries, bicycling, golf, hiking, horseback riding, hot air balloons, museums, parks, shopping, tennis and wineries nearby.

Hidden Oak Inn

214 E Napa St
Sonoma, CA 95476-6721
(707)996-9863
E-mail: vep@sonic.net
Web: www.hiddenoakinn.com

Circa 1914. This shingled California craftsman bungalow, now painstakingly restored features a vine-covered gabled roof and front porch with stone pillars. Located a block from the historic Sonoma Plaza, the inn offers spacious rooms furnished with antiques and wicker. Tasty breakfasts are served, and there is a

therapeutic hot tub on the premises. The innkeepers maintain a small fleet of complimentary bicycles for touring the area's award-winning wineries, and they also provide local health club passes for their guests.

Innkeeper(s): Valerie & Don Patterson. $145-225. MC, VISA, AX, DS. 3 rooms with PB. Breakfast and afternoon tea included in rates. Types of meals: Cont plus and early coffee/tea. Beds: KQ. Bicycles on premises. Small meetings and family reunions hosted. Antiquing, golf, horseback riding, parks, shopping, sporting events and wineries nearby.

"The room was delightful and breakfast was excellent."

Sonoma Hotel

110 W Spain St
Sonoma, CA 95476-5696
(707)996-2996 (800)468-6016 Fax:(707)996-7014
E-mail: sonomahotel@aol.com
Web: www.sonomahotel.com

Circa 1879. Located on the renowned Sonoma Plaza, this historic inn was recently remodeled. French-country furnishings and antiques fill the lobby. Guest rooms also are decorated with French-country furnishings. Maya Angelou wrote "Gather Together in My Name" while staying here. Wine service is offered to guests between 5 p.m. and 6 p.m., and in the

morning, a continental breakfast is served. Restaurants, antique stores, spas, and museums are within steps of the inn and a short walk away from the tree-lined plaza are several wineries.

Historic Interest: Mission San Francisco Solano, Bear Flag Revolt, Casa Grande Indian Servants Quarters (all within walking distance).

Innkeeper(s): Timothy Farfan & Craig Miller. $110-245. MC, VISA, AX, DC, TC. TAC5. 16 rooms with PB. Breakfast included in rates. Types of meals: Cont, early coffee/tea and dinner. Beds: QDT. Fax and copier on premises. Weddings and family reunions hosted. Antiquing, spas, shops and wineries nearby.

Publicity: *Press Democrat, California Getaway Guide, Americana and House Beautiful.*

"Great food and service! I was so pleased to see such a warm and lovable place."

Trojan Horse Inn

19455 Sonoma Hwy
Sonoma, CA 95476-6416
(707)996-2430 (800)899-1925 Fax:(707)996-9185
E-mail: trojaninn@aol.com

Circa 1887. This Victorian home rests on one acre on the banks of Sonoma Creek. Recently restored, the pristine interior offers antiques and a romantic country decor. The Bridal Veil Room has a canopied bed, wood-burning stove and windows overlooking a

magnolia tree, while a private Jacuzzi tub is a popular feature in the Grape Arbor Room. Bicycles, an additional outdoor Jacuzzi, flower gardens and grand old bay and spruce trees add to the experience.

Innkeeper(s): Joe & Sandy Miccio. $155-185. MC, VISA, AX. TAC10. 6 rooms with PB, 1 with FP and 1 conference room. Types of meals: Full bkfst and early coffee/tea. Beds: Q. Ceiling fan in room. Air conditioning. Spa and bicycles on premises. Handicap access. Small meetings and family reunions hosted. Antiquing, live theater and shopping nearby.

Publicity: *Contra Costa Times, Mobil Travel Guide and Sonoma Index Tribune.*

"We came for one night and stayed for four."

Victorian Garden Inn

316 E Napa St
Sonoma, CA 95476-6723
(707)996-5339 (800)543-5339 Fax:(707)996-1689
E-mail: Vgardeninn@aol.com
Web: www.victoriangardeninn.com

Circa 1870. Authentic Victorian gardens cover more than an acre of grounds surrounding this Greek Revival farmhouse. Pathways wind around to secret gardens, and guests can walk to world-famous wineries and historical sites. All rooms are decorated with the romantic flair of the innkeeper, an interior designer. Ask to stay in the renovated water tower. Enjoy a therapeutic spa in the gardens.

Historic Interest: Northernmost mission in California chain; home of General M.G. Vallejo; historic Sonoma Plaza, site of 1846 "Bear Flag Rebellion" (establishment of California Republic); Sonoma Barracks - all within 4 blocks.

Innkeeper(s): Donna Lewis. $129-229. MC, VISA, AX, DC, PC, TC. TAC10. 4 rooms, 3 with PB, 2 with FP, 1 suite and 1 conference room. Breakfast included in rates. Types of meals: Veg bkfst, cont plus, early coffee/tea, snacks/refreshments and room service. Beds: QDT. Phone, ceiling fan and some with fireplaces in room. Air conditioning. Spa, swimming, sauna, library and beautiful gardens on premises. Antiquing, therapeutic spa, beautiful gardens, restaurants, live theater and wineries nearby.

Publicity: *Denver Post and Los Angeles Times.*

"I'll be back! So romantic, this place is for lovers! What a perfect spot for a honeymoon! Great! Wonderful! Fabulous! We could not have asked for anything more."

Sonora   H7

Barretta Gardens Inn Bed & Breakfast

700 Barretta St
Sonora, CA 95370-5131
(209)532-6039 (800)206-3333 Fax:(209)532-8257
E-mail: barrettagardens@hotmail.com
Web: www.barrettagardens.com

Circa 1900. Three porches offer views over an acre of lawns and gardens and terraced hillside to Sonora. Living room with fireplace and two parlors are gathering places for guests. Request the Odette Suite and you'll enjoy an original chandelier, 10-foot ceiling, floor-to-ceiling mirror, a 10-foot-high armoire and a Victorian queen bed as well as a whirlpool tub and a solarium/sitting room. The Isabelle room has a whirlpool tub, stained glass and a wall of windows for sunset views.

Breakfast is served under the chandelier in the dining room or on the breakfast porch. Pecan-apple puffed pancakes with sausage are a favorite entree, and there are gratins, crepes and fresh french pastries. Walk to shops and restaurants or drive to Jamestown to try the steam train or Columbia State Park. Yosemite National Park is an hour away.

Innkeeper(s): Bruno & Sally Trial. $95-235. MC, VISA, AX, PC, TC. TAC5. 5 rooms with PB and 2 suites. Breakfast and snacks/refreshments included in rates. Types of meals: Gourmet bkfst, country bkfst and veg bkfst. Beds: KQ. Cable TV and VCR in room. Central air. Fax on premises. Weddings, small meetings and family reunions hosted. French spoken. Antiquing, bicycling, fishing, golf, hiking, horseback riding, live theater, parks, shopping, downhill skiing, cross-country skiing, tennis, water sports and wineries nearby.

Publicity: *Los Angeles Times, Modesto Bee and Travel Channel.*

Soquel   J5

Blue Spruce Inn

2815 S Main St
Soquel, CA 95073-2412
(831)464-1137 (800)559-1137 Fax:(831)475-0608
E-mail: innkeeper@bluespruce.com

Circa 1875. The Blue Spruce is located four miles south of Santa Cruz and one mile from Capitola Beach and the Monterey Bay Marine Sanctuary. Spa tubs, fireplaces and colorful gardens add to the pleasure of this renovated farmhouse. The Seascape is a

favorite room with a private entrance and a bow-shaped Jacuzzi tub for two. The Carriage House offers skylights above the bed, a king-size featherbed and an in-room Jacuzzi. Plush robes and private baths are features and in the morning, hearty gourmet breakfasts, the inn's specialty, are served. Afterwards enjoy a ride along the beach or a hike through the redwoods.

Historic Interest: Redwood Forests (5 miles), Santa Cruz Mission (4 miles), Carmel-by-the-Sea (30 miles), Monterey (20 miles).

Innkeeper(s): Victoria & Thomas Jechart. $125-215. MC, VISA, AX, PC, TC. TAC10. 6 rooms with PB, 5 with FP. Breakfast included in rates. Types of meals: Full bkfst and early coffee/tea. Beds: KQ. Cable TV, phone, turndown service, four with Jacuzzi tubs, five with deck or patio and private entrance in room. Spanish spoken. Antiquing, beaches, golf, parks, shopping and wineries nearby.

Publicity: *L.A. Weekly, Aptos Post, San Francisco Examiner and Village View.*

"You offer such graciousness to your guests and a true sense of welcome."

South Pasadena   O10

The Artists' Inn B&B

1038 Magnolia St
South Pasadena, CA 91030-2518
(626)799-5668 (888)799-5668 Fax:(626)799-3678
E-mail: artistsinn@artistsinns.com
Web: www.artistsinns.com

Circa 1895. A poultry farm once surrounded this turn-of-the-century home. Today, the streets are lined with trees and a variety of beautiful homes. Interior designer Janet Marangi restored the historic ambiance of the cheery, yellow home and cottage, filling them with antiques and original artwork. Each of the guest rooms captures a different artistic style. Soft, soothing colors enrich the Impressionist room, which includes a clawfoot tub and antique brass bed. The 18th Century English room is filled with pieces by Gainsborough, Reynolds and Constable and includes a romantic canopied bed. Fireplaces and Jacuzzis are offered in the inn's five newest cottage suites. There are plenty of helpful amenities, including hair dryers, toiletries and desks in each room. The innkeeper creates a breakfast menu with freshly made breads, homemade granola, fruit and a special entree. The home is just a few blocks from South Pasadena's many shops, boutiques, cafes and restaurants.

Historic Interest: The historic Mission West district is a short distance from the inn. The Norton Simon Museum of Art, Old Town Pasadena, Mission San Gabriel and the Huntington Library are other nearby historic attractions.

Innkeeper(s): Janet Marangi. $115-205. MC, VISA, AX, PC, TC. 9 rooms with PB and 4 suites. Breakfast and afternoon tea included in rates. Types of meals: Gourmet bkfst, cont, early coffee/tea and picnic lunch. Beds: KQDT. Ceiling fan, fresh flowers, TV, Jacuzzi's and fireplace in room. Air conditioning. Fax and library on premises. Weddings, small meetings and family reunions hosted. Amusement parks, antiquing, live theater, parks, shopping and sporting events nearby.

Publicity: *Pasadena Star News, San Marino Tribune, Stanford, Pasadena Weekly, South Pasadena Review, Recommended by Elmer Dills, Travel & Leisure, New York Times and West Ways.*

Sutter Creek   G6

Eureka Street Inn

55 Eureka St
Sutter Creek, CA 95685
(209)267-5500 (800)399-2389 Fax:(209)267-1164
E-mail: innkeepers@eurekastreetinn.com

Circa 1914. This Craftsman-style bungalow located in the heart
of the gold country boasts the best porch in town. Antiques and
art decorate the inn including a large collection of Bauer pottery.
Leaded- and stained-glass windows, rosewood cabinets and redwood beams, wainscoting and a handsome staircase are architectural features. The Aurora Room offers a view of the foothills
from your draped and king-size bed. Up to a three-course
gourmet breakfast is offered with items such as puff pancakes,
shirred eggs, poached pears and creme biscuits. Nearby are
Amador County wineries and there are gold mine sites and
many scenic areas to explore for hiking, fishing and picnicking.
Historic Interest: Knight Foundry (100 feet), heart of California Gold Country,
Kentucky and Sutter mines.
Innkeeper(s): Chuck & Sandy Anderson. $100-135. MC, VISA, DS, PC, TC. 4
rooms with PB, 4 with FP. Breakfast and snacks/refreshments included in
rates. Types of meals: Gourmet bkfst, country bkfst, veg bkfst, early coffee/tea
and room service. Beds: KQ. Fireplace in room. Air conditioning. Fax and
library on premises. Antiquing, art galleries, bicycling, canoeing/kayaking,
fishing, golf, hiking, horseback riding, live theater, museums, parks, shopping, downhill skiing, cross-country skiing, water sports and wineries nearby.
Publicity: *Santa Cruz Sentinel and Amador County Ledger.*

Foxes In Sutter Creek

77 Main St, PO Box 159
Sutter Creek, CA 95685
(209)267-5882 (800)987-3344 Fax:(209)267-0712
E-mail: foxes@cdepot.net
Web: www.foxesinn.com

Circa 1857. Known for its elegant furnishings, this Greek
Revival home offers luxurious accommodations and amenities.
Canopy beds and armoires are found in the guest bedrooms

and suites. Most feature old-fashioned tubs with showers and fireplaces, some boast a built-in music
system, library or sitting area. The
Fox Den and the Hideaway also
boast a private entry. Choose breakfast from a menu. Cooked-to-order
and presented on a silver service, it
will be delivered to the room when desired. For a change of
scenery, arrange to be served in the gazebo.
Innkeeper(s): Bob & Annie Elliott. $140-215. MC, VISA, AX, DS, PC, TC.
TAC10. 7 rooms with PB, 5 with FP. Types of meals: Full bkfst. Beds: Q.
Cable TV and VCR in room.
Publicity: *San Francisco Focus, Sunset, Bon Appetite and Travel & Leisure.*
"Foxes is without a doubt the most charming B&B anywhere."

Grey Gables B&B Inn

161 Hanford St, PO Box 1687
Sutter Creek, CA 95685-1687
(209)267-1039 (800)473-9422 Fax:(209)267-0998
E-mail: reservations@greygables.com
Web: www.greygables.com

Circa 1897. The innkeepers of this Victorian home offer poetic
accommodations both in the delightful decor and by the names
of their guest rooms. The Keats, Bronte and Tennyson rooms

afford garden views, while
the Byron and Browning
rooms include clawfoot
tubs. The Victorian Suite,
which encompasses the
top floor, affords views of
the garden, as well as a
historic churchyard. All of the guest rooms boast fireplaces. Stroll
down brick pathways through the terraced garden or relax in the
parlor. A proper English tea is served with cakes and scones. Hors
d'oeuvres and libations are served in the evenings.
Historic Interest: Property was once owned by Patrick Riordan, Archbishop of
San Francisco.
Innkeeper(s): Roger & Susan Garlick. $150-210. MC, VISA, DS, PC, TC.
TAC10. 8 rooms with PB, 8 with FP. Breakfast and afternoon tea included in
rates. Types of meals: Gourmet bkfst and early coffee/tea. Beds: KQT. Ceiling
fan in room. Air conditioning. Fax and copier on premises. Handicap access.
Antiquing, fishing, live theater, parks, shopping, downhill skiing, cross-coun-
try skiing, water sports and wineries nearby.

The Hanford House B&B Inn

61 Hanford St Hwy 49
Sutter Creek, CA 95685
(209)267-0747 (800)871-5839 Fax:(209)267-1825
E-mail: bobkat@hanfordhouse.com
Web: www.hanfordhouse.com

Circa 1929. Hanford House is located on the quiet main street
of Sutter Creek, a Gold Rush town. The ivy-covered, brick inn
features spacious, romantic guest rooms, five with a fireplace.
The Gold Country Escape includes a Jacuzzi tub, canopy bed,
sitting area and a private deck. Guests can enjoy breakfast in
their room or in the inn's cheerful breakfast room. Guests can
relax in the front of a fire in the Hanford Room, which doubles
as facilities for conferences, retreats, weddings and social
events. Wineries, antique shops and historic sites are nearby.
Innkeeper(s): Bob & Karen Tierno. $99-225. MC, VISA, AX, DS, PC, TC.
TAC10. 9 rooms with PB, 8 with FP, 3 suites and 1 conference room.
Breakfast, afternoon tea and snacks/refreshments included in rates. Types of
meals: Gourmet bkfst and early coffee/tea. Beds: KQ. Cable TV, phone and
ceiling fan in room. Air conditioning. VCR and fax on premises. Handicap
access. Weddings, small meetings, family reunions and seminars hosted.
Antiquing, fishing, golf, skiing, Gold Rush historic sites, 25 wineries, live theater and water sports nearby.
Publicity: *Best Places to Kiss.*

Sutter Creek Inn

PO Box 385
Sutter Creek, CA 95685-0385
(209)267-5606 Fax:(209)267-9287
E-mail: info@suttercreekinn.com
Web: www.suttercreekinn.com

Circa 1859. Nestled among fruit trees, many of the guest
rooms open onto latticed enclaves or trellised grapevines.
Columbine and lilacs are part of the lawn and garden's charm.
As depicted in Thomas Kinkade's painting of the inn called
"The Village Inn", guests can relax in chaise lounges or in the
hammocks. Many rooms offer private patios, fireplace, swinging
beds and tubs for two. Country breakfasts are served family
style in the dining room. The
area offers a variety of activities,
including wineries, golfing, gold
panning and historical sites.
Massage and handwriting analy-
sis is available by appointment.

Innkeeper(s): Jane Way. $82-185. MC,

VISA. 17 rooms with PB. Breakfast included in rates. Types of meals: Full bkfst. Beds: QDT. Antiquing, fishing, wineries, live theater, cross-country skiing and water sports nearby.

Publicity: *Fun Times, Motorland and Country Inns.*

Truckee   F7

Bocks 10064 House

10064 SE River St
Truckee, CA 96161-0307
(530)582-1923

Circa 1991. Designed and built as a perfect replica of a Victorian home, this bed & breakfast offers contemporary comfort in a vintage setting. One of the guest bedrooms features an antique soaking tub. Greeted downstairs in the morning with fresh fruit, juice, coffee and tea, guests enjoy a made-to-order breakfast prepared of eggs Benedict, French toast, an omelet or banana pancakes. Located on the Truckee River, downtown is an easy walk. There is a local activity for every season. Ten ski resorts are only 15 minutes away, and seven golf courses are nearby. Lake Tahoe is slightly further, and Reno, twice that distance.

Innkeeper(s): Kent & Monica Bocks. $100-120. PC, TC. 3 rooms with PB. Breakfast included in rates. Types of meals: Gourmet bkfst. Beds: QD. Fax on premises. Antiquing, art galleries, beaches, bicycling, canoeing/kayaking, fishing, golf, hiking, horseback riding, museums, parks, shopping, downhill skiing, cross-country skiing, tennis and water sports nearby.

Hania's Bed & Breakfast

10098 High St
Truckee, CA 96161
(530)582-5775 (888)600-3735 Fax:(530)587-4424
E-mail: truckeerealty@hotmail.com

Circa 1884. Situated above historic downtown Truckee, this white farmhouse Victorian framed by a white picket fence offers visitors a panoramic view of mountains and the town. A hot tub, especially inviting during sunsets and on starry nights, is popular with guests. Inside, the interiors are decorated in a Southwestern decor and offer a touch of European elegance. Guest rooms feature log furnishings. Breakfast specialties include eggs a la Hania, Polish-style potato pancakes and crepes with cinnamon apple served in the dining area. In the afternoon, complimentary wine is offered from a rustic bar in front of the wood stove. Restaurants are just downhill, and factory stores as well as the old jail are nearby.

Historic Interest: Historic downtown Truckee.

Innkeeper(s): Hania Davidson. $125-135. MC, VISA, AX, PC, TC. TAC10. 4 rooms with PB. Breakfast and snacks/refreshments included in rates. Types of meals: Gourmet bkfst, veg bkfst and early coffee/tea. Beds: Q. Cable TV, phone and VCR in room. Spa, library and refrigerator with refreshments on premises. Handicap access. Weddings, small meetings and family reunions hosted. Polish and German Russian spoken. Antiquing, art galleries, beaches, bicycling, canoeing/kayaking, fishing, golf, hiking, horseback riding, museums, parks, shopping, downhill skiing, cross-country skiing, tennis and water sports nearby.

Publicity: *San Francisco Chronicle and Reno Gazette Journal.*

Richardson House

10154 High St
Truckee, CA 96161-0110
(530)587-5388 (888)229-0365 Fax:(530)587-0927
Web: www.richardsonhouse.com

Circa 1887. Guests enjoy views of the rugged Sierra Nevadas and the charm of a historic Old West town while at Richardson House. The historic Victorian bears the name of the prominent

lumber baron who built it, Warren Richardson. Each guest room is individually appointed with timely antiques and accessories and the elegant touch of fresh flowers, fine linens, feather beds and down comforters. Some rooms offer views of the Sierra Mountains, while others have views of gardens. The gingerbread-adorned gazebo is the highlight of the Victorian gardens, a perfect setting for a memorable wedding. Inside, the parlor is set up for relaxation with a player piano, television, VCR and stereo. The innkeepers also provide a well-stocked, 24-hour refreshment center. Freshly baked cookies are another treat.

Innkeeper(s): Patty Zwers. $100-175. MC, VISA, AX, DS, PC, TC. TAC15. 8 rooms, 6 with PB. Breakfast included in rates. Types of meals: Gourmet bkfst and early coffee/tea. Beds: KQDT. Air conditioning. VCR, fax, copier, morning paper and books and videos on premises. Handicap access. Weddings, small meetings and family reunions hosted. Fishing, golf, hiking, parks, shopping, downhill skiing, cross-country skiing and water sports nearby.

The Truckee Hotel

10007 Bridge St
Truckee, CA 96161-0211
(530)587-4444 (800)659-6921 Fax:(530)587-1599
E-mail: thetruckeehotel@sierra.net
Web: www.truckeehotel.com

Circa 1873. As guests enter the historic Truckee Hotel they are suddenly transported back to the Victorian era, and one can almost imagine the days when the hotel served as a stagecoach stop. Eventually, the hotel became home to railroad workers who were building the Transcontinental Railroad. By the turn of the 20th century, the hotel once again served vacationers to the Truckee area. The interior boasts a rich, authentic Victorian decor. In guest rooms, antiques, canopy beds and clawfoot tubs add to the historic romance. Weekend guests enjoy afternoon tea service, and the hotel has a restaurant and bar that serve lunch and dinner daily, as well as Sunday brunch. There is also a gift boutique and cigar shop on the premises. The area offers many places to go, including Donner Lake and the historic Emigrant Trail. More than one dozen ski areas are 25 miles away.

Innkeeper(s): Jenelle Potvin. $50-135. MC, VISA, AX, TC. 37 rooms, 8 with PB. Breakfast included in rates. Types of meals: Cont plus. Beds: KQDT. VCR and fax on premises. Weddings, small meetings, family reunions and seminars hosted. Antiquing, fishing, golf, parks, shopping, downhill skiing, cross-country skiing, tennis and water sports nearby.

Ukiah   F3

Vichy Hot Springs Resort & Inn

2605 Vichy Springs Rd
Ukiah, CA 95482-3507
(707)462-9515 Fax:(707)462-9516
E-mail: vichy@vichysprings.com
Web: www.vichysprings.com

Circa 1854. This famous spa, now a California State Historical Landmark (#980), once attracted guests Jack London, Mark Twain, Robert Louis Stevenson, Ulysses Grant and Teddy Roosevelt. Nineteen rooms and eight cottages comprise the property. Some of the cottages are historic and some are new. The 1860s naturally warm and carbonated mineral baths remain unchanged. A hot soaking pool and historic, Olympic-size pool await your arrival. A magical waterfall is a 30-minute walk along a year-round stream.

Historic Interest: Sun House Museum California Historic Landmark (4 miles west), Tallest trees in the world-Montgomery Woods (18 miles west, Redwoods).

Innkeeper(s): Gilbert & Marjorie Ashoff. $110-245. MC, VISA, AX, DC, CB, DS, PC, TC. TAC10. 27 rooms with PB, 8 with FP, 8 cottages and 1 conference room. Breakfast included in rates. Types of meals: Full bkfst. Beds: QT. Phone in room. Air conditioning. Fax, copier, spa, swimming, massages and facials on premises. Handicap access. Family reunions and seminars hosted. Spanish spoken. Antiquing, fishing, redwood parks, live theater, museums, parks, water sports and wineries nearby.

Publicity: Sunset, Sacramento Bee, San Jose Mercury News, Gulliver (Japan), Oregonian, Contra Costa Times, New York Times, San Francisco Chronicle, San Francisco Examiner, Adventure West, Gulliver (Italy). and Bay Area Back Roads (TV).

Ventura   N8

Bella Maggiore Inn

67 S California St
Ventura, CA 93001-2801
(805)652-0277

Circa 1925. Albert C. Martin, the architect of the former Grauman's Chinese Theater, designed and built this Spanish Colonial Revival-style hotel. Located three blocks from the beach, it is noted for its richly-carved caste-stone entrance and frieze. An Italian chandelier and a grand piano dominate the parlor. Rooms surround a courtyard with a fountain. Miles of coastal bike paths are nearby, as well as restaurants and antique shops.

Innkeeper(s): Thomas Wood. $75-175. MC, VISA, AX, DC, DS. TAC10. 24 rooms with PB, 6 with FP and 1 conference room. Types of meals: Full bkfst. Beds: KQD. Some with spa tubs in room. Fax and copier on premises. Handicap access.

Publicity: Ventura County & Coast Reporter and Sunset.

"Very friendly and attentive without being overly attentive."

La Mer European B&B

411 Poli St
Ventura, CA 93001-2614
(805)643-3600 Fax:(805)653-7329
E-mail: LaMerBB@aol.com
Web: www.lamerbnb.com

Circa 1890. This three-story Cape Cod Victorian overlooks the heart of historic San Buenaventura and the spectacular California coastline. Each room is decorated to capture the feeling of a specific European country. French, German, Austrian, Norwegian and English-style accommodations are available. Gisela, your hostess, is a native of Siegerland,

Germany. Midweek specials include romantic candlelight dinners, therapeutic massages and a mineral spa in the country. Horse-drawn antique carriage rides and island cruises are also available.

Historic Interest: The old Mission, Archaeological Dig County Museum and many historical homes, within one-half block.

Innkeeper(s): Gisela & Mike Baida. $95-185. MC, VISA, AX. TAC10. 5 rooms, 1 with FP. Breakfast included in rates. Types of meals: Full bkfst. Beds: KQ. TV, ceiling fan and historic radio in room. Fax on premises. Antiquing, fishing, golf, parks, tennis and water sports nearby.

Publicity: Los Angeles Times, California Bride, Los Angeles Magazine, Westways, The Tribune, Daily News. and Los Angeles Channel 7 news.

"Where to begin? The exquisite surroundings, the scrumptious meals, the warm feeling from your generous hospitality! What an unforgettable weekend in your heavenly home."

Visalia   K8

Spalding House

631 N Encina St
Visalia, CA 93291-3603
(559)739-7877 Fax:(559)625-0902
E-mail: spaldinghouse@mediaone.net
Web: www.thespaldinghouse.com

Circa 1901. This Colonial Revival home, built by a wealthy lumberman, has been restored and decorated with antiques and reproductions. The elegant interior includes polished wood

floors topped with Oriental rugs and rich wallcoverings. The music room features a 1923 Steinway player grand piano. The library, which boasts some of the home's rich woodwork, includes shelves filled with books.

Breakfasts include fresh fruit, yogurt, muffins and entrees such as a cheese blintz, apple crepe or French toast. The home is near downtown Visalia, as well as Sequoia National Park.

Innkeeper(s): Wayne & Peggy Davidson. $85. MC, VISA, AX, DS, PC. TAC10. 3 suites. Breakfast included in rates. Types of meals: Gourmet bkfst. AP. Beds: QD. Ceiling fan in room. Air conditioning. Fax, copier and library on premises. Antiquing, fishing, golf, Sequoia National Park, live theater, parks, shopping, downhill skiing, cross-country skiing, tennis and water sports nearby.

Volcano   G7

St. George Hotel

16104 Main Street
Volcano, CA 95689-0009
(209)296-4458 Fax:(209)296-4457
E-mail: stgeorge@stgeorgehotel.com
Web: www.stgeorgehotel.com

Circa 1862. Listed in the National Register, this handsome three-story hotel was the most prominent of the Gold Country hotels. Carefully renovated, it features a double-tiered wrap-around porch, and there is a full service restaurant, bar and banquet/parlor. It is situated on an acre of lawns that afford croquet, horseshoes and volleyball. Volcano is a Mother Lode town that has been untouched by supermarkets and modern motels and remains much as it was during the Gold Rush, except that the population has dwindled from 5,000 to 100 today. Modified American Plan (breakfast and dinner) is available. Guests enjoy walking to the local swimming hole or fishing.

Innkeeper(s): Mark & Tracey Berkner. $65-110. MC, VISA, DS, PC, TC. 20 rooms, 15 with PB and 1 conference room. Breakfast included in rates. Types of meals: Cont. MAP. Beds: QDT. All original in room. Fax, copier, deck, horseshoes, fire pit, croquet, volleyball and baby sitting on premises. Weddings, small meetings, family reunions and seminars hosted. Antiquing, fishing, golf, swimming, mountain lakes, live theater, parks, shopping, downhill skiing, cross-country skiing, tennis and water sports nearby.

"Quiet, peace, yummy breakfasts and outrageous dinners. C. B., San Francisco."

Westport   E3

DeHaven Valley Farm

39247 N Highway 1
Westport, CA 95488-8712
(707)961-1660 (877)334-2836 Fax:(707)961-1677
E-mail: info@dehaven-valley-farm.com
Web: www.dehaven-valley-farm.com

Circa 1875. This farmhouse was built by Alexander Gordon, a prosperous sawmill owner and cattle rancher. A double-tiered porch wraps around the front and side of the house and

extends across the wing, offering vistas of the ocean and the inn's 20 acres of meadows, woodland and coastal hills. A hillside hot tub provides a panoramic view of the valley. Guest rooms are in the main house and in cottages. The DeHaven Cottage features cabbage rose prints, a Franklin stove and a king-size bed. Dinner is served when at least six make reservations. There are farm animals, picnic areas, walking trails and a secluded beach.

Innkeeper(s): Christa Stapp. $89-144. MC, VISA, AX, DS, PC. TAC10. 8 rooms, 6 with PB, 5 with FP, 2 suites and 3 cottages. Breakfast included in rates. Types of meals: Full bkfst and gourmet dinner. Beds: KQT. Phone and one room with wet bar in room. VCR, spa, walking trails, picnic areas, decks, balcony with ocean view and farm animals on premises. Weddings, small meetings, family reunions and seminars hosted. German spoken. Antiquing, art galleries, beaches, bicycling, canoeing/kayaking, fishing, hiking, horseback riding, live theater, parks, shopping, tennis, water sports and wineries nearby.

Publicity: *Forbes, Sacramento Magazine, San Francisco Focus and Bay Area Backroads.*

"We've talked about it so much that convoys of Southern California folks might be heading your way this very minute!"

Howard Creek Ranch

40501 N Hwy One, PO Box 121
Westport, CA 95488
(707)964-6725 Fax:(707)964-1603
E-mail: lostcst@mcn.org
Web: www.howardcreekranch.com

Circa 1871. First settled as a land grant of thousands of acres, Howard Creek Ranch is now a 40-acre farm with sweeping views of the Pacific Ocean, sandy beaches and rolling mountains. A 75-foot bridge spans a creek that flows past barns and outbuildings to the beach 200 yards away. The farmhouse is surrounded by green lawns, an award-winning flower garden, and grazing cows, horses and llama. This rustic rural location

offers antiques, a hot tub, sauna and heated pool. A traditional ranch breakfast is served each morning.

Innkeeper(s): Charles & Sally Grigg. $75-160. MC, VISA, AX, PC, TC. 11 rooms, 10 with PB, 5 with FP, 3 suites and 3 cabins.

Breakfast included in rates. Types of meals: Gourmet bkfst. Beds: KQD. Ceiling fan in room. Fax, spa, swimming, sauna, library and massages on premises. German, Spanish, Dutch and Italian spoken. Antiquing, art galleries, beaches, bicycling, canoeing/kayaking, fishing, hiking, horseback riding, farm animals, live theater, museums, shopping and wineries nearby.

Pets allowed: By prior arrangement.

Publicity: *California, Country, Vacations, Forbes, Sunset and Diablo.*

"This is one of the most romantic places on the planet."

Yountville   G4

Maison Fleurie

6529 Yount St
Yountville, CA 94599-1278
(707)944-2056 (800)788-0369 Fax:(707)944-9342
E-mail: info@foursisters.com
Web: www.foursisters.com

Circa 1894. Vines cover the two-foot thick brick walls of the Bakery, the Carriage House and the Main House of this French country inn. One of the Four Sisters Inns, it is reminiscent of a bucolic setting in Provence. Rooms are decorated in a warm, romantic style, some with vineyard and garden views. Rooms in the Old Bakery have fireplaces. A pool and outdoor hot tub are available and you may borrow bicycles for wandering the countryside. In the evenings, wine and hors d'oeuvres are served. Yountville, just north of Napa, offers close access to the multitude of wineries and vineyards in the valley.

Innkeeper(s): Jessica Anderegg. $115-275. MC, VISA, AX, TC. 13 rooms with PB, 7 with FP. Breakfast and afternoon tea included in rates. Types of meals: Gourmet bkfst. Beds: KQD. Phone, turndown service, terry robes and newspaper in room. Fax, bicycles, outdoor pool and hot tub on premises. Handicap access. Weddings hosted. Antiquing and wineries nearby.

"Peaceful surroundings, friendly staff."

Yuba City   F5

Harkey House B&B

212 C St
Yuba City, CA 95991-5014
(530)674-1942 Fax:(530)674-1840

Circa 1875. An essence of romance fills this Victorian Gothic house set in a historic neighborhood. Every inch of the home has been given a special touch, from the knickknacks and photos in the sitting room to the quilts and furnishings in the guest quarters. The Harkey Suite features a poster bed with a down comforter and extras such as an adjoining library room and a gas stove. Full breakfasts of muffins, fresh fruit, juice and freshly ground coffee are served in a glass-paned dining room or on the patio.

Historic Interest: Located in the oldest part of Yuba City.

Innkeeper(s): Bob & Lee Jones. $85-160. MC, VISA, AX, DS, PC, TC. TAC10. 4 rooms with PB, 2 with FP, 1 suite and 1 conference room. Breakfast included in rates. Types of meals: Full bkfst and early coffee/tea. Beds: Q. Cable TV, phone, turndown service and ceiling fan in room. Air conditioning. VCR, spa and library on premises. Weddings, small meetings and family reunions hosted. Antiquing, fishing, live theater, parks, shopping and water sports nearby.

Publicity: *Country Magazine.*

"This place is simply marvelous...the most comfortable bed in travel."

Colorado

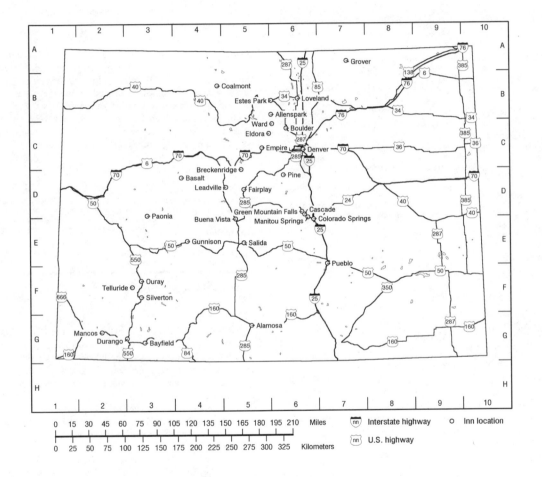

Alamosa G5

Cottonwood Inn & Gallery: A B&B Inn

123 San Juan Ave
Alamosa, CO 81101-2547
(719)589-3882 (800)955-2623 Fax:(719)589-6437
E-mail: relax@cottonwoodinn.com
Web: www.cottonwoodinn.com.

Circa 1912. This refurbished Colorado bungalow is filled with antiques and paintings by local artists. Blue-corn blueberry pancakes, banana crepes with Mexican chocolate are the inn's specialties. A favorite day trip is riding the Cumbres-Toltec Scenic Railroad over the La Magna Pass, site of an Indiana Jones movie. The inn offers five rooms, four suites and a carriage house.

Innkeeper(s): Deb and Kevin Donaldson. $56-125. MC, VISA, AX, DS, PC, TC. TAC10. 6 rooms with PB and 4 suites. Breakfast and afternoon tea included in rates. Types of meals: Gourmet bkfst, veg bkfst and gourmet dinner. Beds: KQD. Cable TV and phone in room. Fax, library, child care and courtyard hot tub on premises. Small meetings, family reunions and seminars hosted. Spanish spoken. Antiquing, art galleries, bicycling, fishing, golf, hiking, horseback riding, live theater, museums, parks, shopping, cross-country skiing, sporting events and tennis nearby.

Pets allowed: In two suites with guests present.

Publicity: *Colorado Expressions, Rocky Mountain News, Country Inns, Denver Post, Milwaukee Journal, Channel 4 Denver and Colorado Get Away.*

"Your place is so inviting and with the front porch and birds singing, our visit was so peaceful and relaxing."

Allenspark B6

Allenspark Lodge

PO Box 247, 184 Main St
Allenspark, CO 80510-0247
(303)747-2552 Fax:(303)747-2552

Circa 1933. Since its opening in the 1930s, this lodge has welcomed visitors with a combination of beautiful scenery and hospitality. The lodge was constructed out of Ponderosa pine, and its rustic interior still maintains exposed log walls and a fireplace of native stone. Rooms are comfortable and each has its own unique atmosphere. Three rooms include antique clawfoot tubs. There is plenty to do in the area, no matter the season.

Skiing, snowshoeing, hiking, backpacking, horseback riding and birdwatching are among the options.

Innkeeper(s): Bill & Juanita Martin. $65-135. MC, VISA, AX, DS, PC, TC. TAC10. 14 rooms, 7 with PB, 1 with FP and 1 conference room. Breakfast included in rates. Types of meals: Full bkfst. Beds: QDT. Ceiling fan in room. Fax, spa, library, espresso coffee bar and snack bar on premises. Weddings, small meetings, family reunions and seminars hosted. Antiquing, fishing, golf, horseback riding, extensive hiking, cross-country trails, live theater, parks, shopping, downhill skiing, cross-country skiing, tennis and water sports nearby.

Publicity: *New England Hiking Holidays, Travelers Magazine, Mobile Travel Guide and Sunset Magazine.*

Basalt D4

Shenandoah Inn

600 Frying Pan Rd
Basalt, CO 81621
(970)927-4991 (800)804-5520 Fax:(970)927-4990
E-mail: shenando@sopris.net

Circa 1897. On the banks of the Frying Pan River, the Shenandoah Inn has been restored into a peaceful country inn. The innkeepers completed an amazing restoration of the house, which was very dilapidated when they discovered the property. In addition to restoring the 1960-era main house, they brought back to life a century-old log cabin. Innkeepers Bob and Terri Ziets can tell an array of fascinating stories about the former occupants, as well as their own exhaustive work. The idyllic setting includes decks for relaxing and a riverside hot tub. On a

chilly day, enjoy a hot drink in front of the 16-foot rock fireplace in the living room. Rooms are decorated with antiques, and beds are topped with down quilts. The historic cabin is especially well suited to honeymooners in search of privacy, or families, as it sleeps up to five guests. Breakfasts are a treat. Peach-stuffed French toast is a possibility, accompanied by gourmet coffee and a fruit appetizer. Everything is homemade, from the freshly baked breads to the preserves and apple butter.

Innkeeper(s): Bob & Terri Ziets. $95-175. MC, VISA, AX, PC, TC. TAC10. 4 rooms with PB and 1 cabin. Breakfast included in rates. Types of meals: Full bkfst and early coffee/tea. Beds: KQT. Turndown service, robes, fresh flowers and candy in room. VCR, fax, spa and library on premises. Weddings, small meetings and family reunions hosted. French and Spanish spoken. Antiquing, fishing, golf, horseback, kayak, rafting, live theater, parks, shopping, downhill skiing, cross-country skiing, tennis and water sports nearby.

Publicity: *Denver Post, Aspen Times, Valley Journal, Health, Roaring Fork Sunday and Washington Observer.*

Bayfield G3

Wit's End Guest Ranch

254 Country Rd 500
Bayfield, CO 81122
(970)884-4113 (800)236-9483 Fax:(970)884-3261
E-mail: witsend@bwn.net
Web: www.witsendranch.com

Circa 1870. When the owners of this Adirondack-style guest ranch bill their place as "luxury at the edge of the wilderness," it isn't just a snappy slogan, it's true. If a half million acres of wilderness and stunning views of snow capped mountain peaks don't entice you, the historic lodge's interior should. Picture polished exposed beams and wood-paneled or log walls, a mix of Victorian and country French furnishings and just enough antlers to create that rustic, lodge atmosphere. Each guest room includes a stone fireplace. There is also an assortment of cabins to consider, some more than a century old. The cabins include a living room, stone fireplace,

kitchen and a private porch or deck. There is a full-service, fine-dining restaurant and a tavern often hosting live musical groups from nearby Durango. Now an Orvis endorsed fly-fishing lodge, the inn offers fly fishing in ponds, rivers and lakes. The San Juan River is rated third in the nation for fine fly fishing. (Fly-tying clinics and instruction are offered and there's a fly-fishing lodge.) Other activities include hay rides, mountain biking, dog sled rides, snowshoeing, sleigh rides and watersports. Horseback and trail riding, of course, are a major part of the fun. The ranch offers a full children's program with many interesting activities. As is typical of dude ranches, rates are quoted for weekly visits.

Innkeeper(s): Jim Custer. $5417-5826. MC, VISA, AX, DS, PC, TC. TAC10. 4 rooms and 34 cabins. Breakfast, snacks/refreshments and dinner included in rates. Types of meals: Gourmet bkfst, cont plus, gourmet lunch and room service. AP. Beds: Q. Phone, turndown service, VCR and luxury furniture and decor in room. Fax, copier, spa, swimming, stables, bicycles, tennis, library, full children's program, riding and tours on premises. Weddings, small meetings, family reunions and seminars hosted. Spanish, French, Italian and German spoken. Antiquing, snowmobiling, jeep tours, fly fishing program, retail shop, boutique, live theater, parks, shopping, downhill skiing, cross-country skiing, sporting events and water sports nearby.

Publicity: *Jeopardy, Wheel of Fortune, Quicksilver, Family Feud, Country Inns, Country Living, Learning Channel, Homes & Garden, Great Country Inns & Network and Prize of Wheel of Fortune.*

Boulder C6

Briar Rose B&B

2151 Arapahoe Ave
Boulder, CO 80302-6601
(303)442-3007 Fax:(303)786-8440
E-mail: brbbx@aol.com

Circa 1896. Known locally as the McConnell House, this English-style brick house is situated in a neighborhood origi-

nally comprised of bankers, attorneys, miners and carpenters. The inn recently was selected as "Best Bed and Breakfast Inn" in Boulder County by the readers of the Boulder Weekly. Fresh flowers, handmade feather comforters and turndown service

with chocolates are among the inn's offerings.

Historic Interest: Historic Boulder offers walking tours of the town, including tours of four historic districts and a cemetery.

Innkeeper(s): Bob & Margaret Weisenbach. $119-189. MC, VISA, AX, DC, PC, TC. TAC10. 9 rooms with PB, 2 with FP. Breakfast and afternoon tea included in rates. Types of meals: Cont plus and early coffee/tea. Beds: QDT. TV, phone, turndown service, ceiling fan and modem attach in room. Air conditioning. Fax and copier on premises. Weddings, small meetings and family reunions hosted. Spanish and American Sign Language spoken. Antiquing, fishing, many summer festivals, hiking, biking, live theater, parks, shopping, downhill skiing, cross-country skiing and sporting events nearby.

Publicity: *Inn Country USA.*

The Inn on Mapleton Hill

1001 Spruce St
Boulder, CO 80302-4028
(303)449-6528 (800)276-6528 Fax:(303)415-0470
E-mail: maphillinn@aol.com
Web: www.innonmapletonhill.com

Circa 1899. Located two blocks from the downtown Pearl Street Mall, in a quiet residential neighborhood is this century-old Edwardian red brick home in Boulder's Mapleton Hill

Historic District. The home was first occupied by Emma Clark, a widowed dressmaker who took in boarders. Today its seven guest bedrooms are decorated with period antiques and reproductions that include four-poster beds, clawfoot tubs, rockers, wicker chairs, Victorian writing desks, lace curtains and antique art. Guests are served breakfast in the "great room" with its marble and wood fireplace. The morning breakfast includes a hot entree, such as orange-flavored French toast or an egg dish, as well as homemade granola, home-baked breads, fruit salad in season, cereals and yogurt. Refreshments also are available in the late afternoon. The inn is located on the edge of the Rockies near hiking, walking and biking trails, national parks, waterfalls and other natural wonders.

Innkeeper(s): Judi & Ray Schultze. $88-167. MC, VISA, AX, TC. TAC5. 7 rooms, 4 with PB, 2 with FP and 1 suite. Breakfast included in rates. Types of meals: Full bkfst, early coffee/tea, afternoon tea and snacks/refreshments. Beds: QD. Phone and ceiling fan in room. Air conditioning. Fax, copier and library on premises. Small meetings hosted. Amusement parks, antiquing, art galleries, bicycling, canoeing/kayaking, fishing, golf, hiking, horseback riding, live theater, museums, parks, shopping, downhill skiing, cross-country skiing, sporting events, tennis and water sports nearby.

Breckenridge D5

Bed & Breakfasts on North Main Street

303 N Main St
Breckenridge, CO 80424
(970)453-2975 (800)795-2975
E-mail: bnb@imageline.com

Circa 1880. Within the Breckenridge National Historic District, the Williams House and exceptionally private Victorian Cottage have been meticulously restored to offer visitors period antiques in a romantic setting. The main house has two parlors with manteled fireplaces. Ask for the deluxe room and enjoy

mountain views, fireplace, large whirlpool and TV. The cottage offers three rooms, a fireplace, private parlor, kitchenette, double shower, whirlpool for two, TV, VCR and stereo. Or consid-

er a room in the new post and beam country-style "Barn Above the River" with fireplaces, double showers and decks with mountain and river views. Complimentary afternoon refreshments are served each day. A candlelight breakfast, often morning burritos with stir-fried potatoes, is served in the dining room. The inn was featured on the Travel Channel's Romantic Inns of America series and Home and Garden Television, "If Walls Could Talk".

Innkeeper(s): Fred Kinat & Diane Jaynes. $79-365. MC, VISA, AX, PC. TAC10. 11 rooms with PB, 6 with FP and 1 cottage. Breakfast included in rates. Types of meals: Full bkfst and early coffee/tea. Beds: KQT. Cable TV, phone, ceiling fan and VCR in room. Spa on premises. Antiquing, bicycling, fishing, golf, hiking, snowmobiling, ice skating, music festivals, bike/rollerblade path, hiking, historic tours, live theater, shopping, downhill skiing, cross-country skiing, tennis and water sports nearby.

Publicity: *Denver Post, Rocky Mountain News, Summit Daily News and Los Angeles Times.*

Buena Vista E5

Trout City Berth & Breakfast

East Highway 24/285
Buena Vista, CO 80908
(719)495-0348

Circa 1880. Restored in 1987, this unique inn provides an opportunity to sleep in an elegantly decorated Victorian Pullman car or in the driver's caboose. Located on 40 scenic acres in the San Isabel National Forest, the inn has the 1880 reconstructed depot on its historic narrow-gauge railway site. Depot rooms, dining room and game room/gift shop all are decorated in Victorian style. A wildlife area, mountain trails and trout stream pass through the property. The surrounding region boasts some of the world's best fishing, whitewater rafting, mountain climbing, rock hounding and trail riding, shopping and summer theater.

Innkeeper(s): Juel & Irene Kjeldsen. $50-70. MC, VISA, AX, TC. TAC10. 4 rooms with PB and 1 conference room. Breakfast included in rates. Types of meals: Full bkfst. Beds: DT. VCR, movies and hiking on premises. Weddings and family reunions hosted. Antiquing, bicycling, fishing, live theater, parks, shopping and water sports nearby.

Cascade D6

Eastholme In The Rockies

PO Box 98, 4445 Haggerman Ave
Cascade, CO 80809
(719)684-9901 (800)672-9901
E-mail: eastholm@rmi.net

Circa 1885. Although Cascade is only six miles from Colorado Springs, guests will feel as though they are staying in a secluded mountain getaway at this Victorian inn, in the National Register. An affluent New Yorker built the historic hotel, which accommodates the many guests traveling the Ute Pass. The most recent innkeeper, Terry Thompson, redecorated the inn, added double Jacuzzi tubs and fireplaces in the two cottages and a gazebo for  small weddings. The decor is Victorian, but rooms are uncluttered and airy. Several rooms are furnished with antiques original to the hotel. Three different homemade breads and entrees such as frittatas with herbed potatoes are served during breakfast service.

Innkeeper(s): Terry Thompson. $75-150. MC, VISA, AX, DS, PC, TC. TAC10. 8 rooms, 6 with PB, 2 with FP, 2 suites, 2 cottages and 1 conference room. Breakfast and snacks/refreshments included in rates. Types of meals: Gourmet bkfst, veg bkfst and early coffee/tea. Beds: QDT. Cable TV, ceiling fan, VCR, guest kitchen on second floor and cottages with Jacuzzi tubs in room. Outdoor hot tub on premises. Weddings, small meetings, family reunions and seminars hosted. Antiquing, art galleries, bicycling, canoeing/kayaking, fishing, golf, hiking, horseback riding, climbing, rafting, live theater, museums, parks, shopping, downhill skiing, cross-country skiing, sporting events, tennis, water sports and wineries nearby.

Chipita Park D6

Chipita Lodge B&B

9090 Chipita Park Rd
Chipita Park, CO 80809
(719)684-8454 Fax:(719)684-8234

Circa 1927. Overlooking Chipita Lake and at the base of Pikes Peak, this native stone and log lodge features a hot tub and gazebo with views of mountains on its two-acre knoll-top location. Formerly the local post office and general store, the lodge boasts rooms with fresh Western decor as well as rooms with Native American influences. A three-course breakfast is served with country-style entrees. Evening and afternoon refreshments are offered before the large stone fireplace in the handsome gathering room or on the deck overlooking the lake. The Garden of the Gods, Manitou Springs and Cripple Creek are nearby.

Innkeeper(s): Kevin & Martha Henry. $88-126. MC, VISA, AX, PC, TC. TAC10. 3 rooms with PB and 1 conference room. Breakfast and snacks/refreshments included in rates. Types of meals: Gourmet bkfst and country bkfst. Beds: Q. Turndown service and ceiling fan in room. Fax, copier and spa on premises. Weddings and small meetings hosted. Amusement parks, antiquing, art galleries, fishing, golf, hiking, horseback riding, live theater, museums, parks, shopping, cross-country skiing, sporting events and wineries nearby.

Publicity: *Denver Post.*

Coalmont B4

Shamrock Ranch

4363 Rd 11
Coalmont, CO 80430
(970)723-8413

Circa 1934. At an elevation of 8,800 feet and below the crest of the Continental Divide, the ranch is adjacent to thousands of acres of wilderness in the Routt National Forest. Overlooking the secluded cattle country of North Park, Colo., the lodge is built of native spruce logs and provides comfortable accommodations for 10 guests. The innkeeper likes to provide a personalized touch and secluded atmosphere for your family or small group and offers both a full breakfast and gourmet dinners included in nightly rates. Guests may enjoy outstanding fly-fishing and a variety of hiking trails.

Innkeeper(s): Cindy Wilson. $200. 2 suites. Breakfast and dinner included in rates. Types of meals: Full bkfst. VCR, fly fishing and wildlife on premises. Small meetings and family reunions hosted.

Colorado Springs E6

Cheyenne Canon Inn

2030 W Cheyenne Blvd
Colorado Springs, CO 80906
(719)633-0625 (800)633-0625 Fax:(800)633-8826
E-mail: info@cheyennecanoninn.com
Web: cheyennecanoninn.com

Circa 1921. This massive, 10,000-square foot mansion features Arts and Crafts-style architecture. The manor was built as an upscale casino and bordello. During its heyday, the famous guests included the Marx Brothers and Lon Chaney. The casino room now serves as the location for the inn's nightly wine and cheese hour. The room has more than 100 panes of glass

affording views of Cheyenne Canon and Cheyenne Mountain. The guest rooms and adjacent honeymoon cottage are decorated with treasures and antiques from around the world. There is a greenhouse spa on the second floor and complimentary beverages and fruit always are available. Modem outlets, TVs and in-room phones are among the amenities for business travelers. Downtown Colorado Springs is minutes away, and hiking trails and waterfalls are across the street.

Historic Interest: Cripple Creek is an hour's drive from the inn, and closer attractions include cliff dwellings, Old Colorado City and the Broadmoor Hotel.

Innkeeper(s): Keith Hampton. $95-200. MC, VISA, AX, DS, TC. TAC10. 10 rooms with PB, 4 with FP, 3 suites, 1 cottage and 2 conference rooms. Types of meals: Full bkfst, early coffee/tea, snacks/refreshments and gourmet dinner. Beds: KQ. Cable TV, phone, turndown service, ceiling fan and hair dryers in room. Air conditioning. Fax, library and day spa on premises. Weddings, small meetings and seminars hosted. Antiquing, fishing, golf, hiking, gambling, live theater, parks, shopping and sporting events nearby.

Publicity: *Denver Post, Colorado Source, Beacon, National Geographic Traveler and Country Inns.*

"It truly was 'home away from home.' You have made it so welcoming and warm. Needless to say our breakfasts at home will never come close to the Cheyenne Canon Inn!."

Crescent Lily Inn

6 Boulder Cresecent St
Colorado Springs, CO 80903-3320
(719)442-2331 (800)869-2721 Fax:(719)442-6947
E-mail: info@crescentlilyinn.com

Circa 1898. This Queen Anne Victorian-style home was built by Major Robert Waugh, who was the oldest Civil War veteran in Colorado at the time of his death in 1929. The inn has been magnificently restored and now is a beautiful representation of the best of that era's architecture, woodworking and attention to detail. The entry has eight beveled-glass windows, the interior has intricate tiger-eye oak woodwork and the parlor boasts a Van Briggle tiled fireplace. The three-story inn has a multi-gabled roof with fish-scale shingles, a balcony that overlooks a nearby park and a wraparound porch with Tuscan columns and dentil detailing. The inn offers five guest bedrooms and one suite, all of which have at least one luxury amenity like a jetted tub, gas-log fireplace, attached sitting room or balcony. The inn's gourmet breakfast includes pastries or muffins, whole-grain cereals, seasonal fruit and a hot entrée. After a great breakfast guests can travel eight miles to Pike's Peak and five miles to the Garden of the Gods. Or, they can enjoy walking and biking trails, shops, restaurants, historic districts and museums — all within walking distance of the inn.

Historic Interest: Pikes Peak (8 miles), Garden of the Gods (5 miles).

Innkeeper(s): Lin Moeller, Mark Medicus. $95-130. MC, VISA, AX, DS, PC, TC. TAC8. 5 rooms with PB, 3 with FP, 1 suite and 1 conference room. Breakfast included in rates. Types of meals: Gourmet bkfst, veg bkfst and snacks/refreshments. Beds: KQ. Cable TV, phone and fireplace in room. Central air. VCR, fax, copier, library and gift shop on premises. Weddings, small meetings and seminars hosted. Antiquing, art galleries, bicycling, canoeing/kayaking, fishing, golf, hiking, horseback riding, live theater, museums, parks, shopping, downhill skiing, cross-country skiing, sporting events, tennis and wineries nearby.

Publicity: *Denver Post.*

Holden House-1902 B&B Inn

1102 W Pikes Peak Ave
Colorado Springs, CO 80904-4347
(719)471-3980 (888)565-3980 Fax:(719)471-4740
E-mail: mail@holdenhouse.com
Web: www.holdenhouse.com

Circa 1902. Built by the widow of a prosperous rancher and businessman, this Victorian inn has rooms named after the many Colorado towns in which the Holdens owned mining

interests. The main house, adjacent carriage house and Victorian house next door include the Cripple Creek, Aspen, Silverton, Goldfield and Independence suites. The inn's suites boast fireplaces and oversized tubs for two. Guests can relax in the living room with fireplace, front parlor with TV, or veranda with mountain views. There are friendly cats in residence.

Historic Interest: Miramont Castle, McAllister House, Glen Eyrie Castle, The Pioneer's Museum, the Broadmoor Hotel & Carriage House Museum, Cliff Dwellings Museum, Pikes Peak, and Garden of the Gods Park are among the area's many historic attractions.

Innkeeper(s): Sallie & Welling Clark. $135-145. MC, VISA, AX, DC, CB, DS, TC. TAC10. 5 suites, 5 with FP. Breakfast included in rates. Types of meals: Full bkfst, early coffee/tea and afternoon tea. Beds: Q. Phone, turndown service, ceiling fan, tubs for two, fireplaces and modem hookups in room. Air conditioning. VCR, fax and copier on premises. Seminars hosted. Antiquing, fishing, hiking, biking, horseback riding, live theater, parks, shopping and sporting events nearby.

Publicity: *Denver Post, Victorian Homes, Pikes Peak Journal, Glamour, Country Inns, Vacations, Rocky Mountain News, Cats. and KKTV.*

"Your love of this house and nostalgia makes a very delightful experience."

Room at the Inn A Victorian Bed & Breakfast

618 N Nevada Ave
Colorado Springs, CO 80903-1006
(719)442-1896 (800)579-4621 Fax:(719)442-6802
E-mail: roomatinn@pcisys.net
Web: www.roomattheinn.com

Circa 1896. A Colorado pioneer built this Queen Anne Victorian, a delightful mix of turret, gables and gingerbread trim. While restoring their century-old Victorian, the innkeepers discovered several hand-painted murals had once decorated the interior. Original fireplace mantels and a collection of antiques add to the nostalgic ambiance. Fresh flowers, turndown service and a bountiful breakfast are just a few of the amenities. Several rooms include a fireplace or double whirlpool tub.

Innkeeper(s): Dorian & Linda Ciolek. $99-160. MC, VISA, AX, DS, PC, TC. TAC10. 8 rooms with PB, 4 with FP and 2 suites. Breakfast, afternoon tea and snacks/refreshments included in rates. Types of meals: Full bkfst, cont and early coffee/tea. Beds: Q. Phone, turndown service, clocks and whirlpool tubs in room. Air conditioning. VCR, fax, copier and spa on premises. Handicap access. Small meetings, family reunions and seminars hosted. Antiquing, fishing, museums, Fine Arts center, live theater, parks, shopping and sporting events nearby.

Publicity: *Denver Post and Colorado Springs Gazette-Telegraph.*

Denver C6

Capitol Hill Mansion Bed & Breakfast

1207 Pennsylvania St
Denver, CO 80203-2504
(303)839-5221 (800)839-9329 Fax:(303)839-9046
E-mail: info@capitolhillmansion.com
Web: www.capitolhillmansion.com

Circa 1891. Although only open a few years, owners Bill and Wendy Pearson have mastered the art of innkeeping at this beautiful 1891 ruby sandstone mansion. Choose from eight antique-appointed guest rooms, all with private baths, some with a whirlpool tub for two, a fireplace or balcony. Each of the guest rooms is uniquely decorated. The Gold Banner Suite features a brass bed, fireplace and cozy sitting area. The Pasqueflower Room on the third  floor boasts a six-foot, round whirlpool tub located in the turret of the mansion. Enjoy a full breakfast each morning and Colorado wine in the evening. Experience the Victorian luxury of yesterday in present-day Denver.

Historic Interest: The Capitol Hill Mansion is one block from the Molly Brown Home and only four blocks from the Governor's Mansion. Guests can walk to several other historic homes, including the Grant-Humphreys Mansion.

Innkeeper(s): Bill & Wendy Pearson. $85-175. MC, VISA, AX, DC, DS, TC. TAC10. 8 rooms with PB, 2 with FP and 3 suites. Breakfast included in rates. Types of meals: Full bkfst. Beds: KQT. Cable TV, phone, whirlpool tubs and fireplaces in room. Air conditioning. Fax, copier and CD player on premises. Handicap access. Weddings, small meetings and family reunions hosted. Spanish spoken. Amusement parks, antiquing, fishing, golf, live theater, parks, shopping, downhill skiing, cross-country skiing, sporting events, tennis and water sports nearby.

Publicity: *Yellow Brick Road, Life on Capitol Hill, Journal Constitution, Denver Post, Rocky Mountain News, Westword and Citysearch.com.*

Castle Marne - A Historic Urban Inn

1572 Race St
Denver, CO 80206-1308
(303)331-0621 (800)926-2763 Fax:(303)331-0623
E-mail: jim@castlemarne.com
Web: www.castlemarne.com

Circa 1889. This 6,000-square-foot fantasy was designed by William Lang and is on the National Register. It is constructed of hand-hewn rhyolite stone. Inside, polished oak, cherry and black ash woodwork enhance  the ornate fireplaces, period antiques and opulent Victorian decor. For special occasions ask for the Presidential Suite with its tower sitting room, king-size tester bed, whirlpool tub in the solarium and private balcony.

Historic Interest: Downtown Historic District (7 minutes), State Capitol (2 minutes), Byers-Evans Museum (5 minutes), Molly Brown House Museum (3 minutes), State Historical Society (4 minutes), Four Mile House (20 minutes).

Innkeeper(s): The Peiker Family. $95-245. MC, VISA, AX, DC, CB, DS. TAC10. 9 rooms with PB, 2 suites and 1 conference room. Breakfast and afternoon tea included in rates. Types of meals: Full bkfst and gourmet dinner. Beds: KQDT. Hot tubs for two (two rooms) and private balconies (three rooms) in room. Fax and copier on premises. Antiquing, fishing, live theater, downhill skiing, cross-country skiing and water sports nearby.

Publicity: *Denver Post, Innsider, Rocky Mountain News, Los Angeles Times, New York Times, Denver Business Journal, Country Inns, Brides and U.S. Air.*

"The beauty, service, friendliness, delicious breakfasts - everything was so extraordinary! We'll be back many times."

Haus Berlin B&B

1651 Emerson St
Denver, CO 80218-1411
(303)837-9527 (800)659-0253 Fax:(303)837-9527
E-mail: haus.berlin@worldnet.att.net
Web: www.hausberlinbandb.com

Circa 1892. This brick Victorian townhouse is a delightful place from which to enjoy Denver. The inn is listed in the National Register of Historic Places and located in a neighborhood filled with charming architecture. The cozy guest rooms are well-appointed and feature beds dressed in fine linens and topped with down comforters. The suite is the most luxurious, and it offers a view of downtown Denver, which is a 10-minute walk from Haus Berlin. The breakfast menu varies, one morning it might be eggs Benedict, the next day could bring a traditional European breakfast with freshly baked rolls, scones with lemon curd and imported hams and cheeses.

Innkeeper(s): Christiana & Dennis Brown. $100-140. MC, VISA, AX, PC, TC. TAC10. 4 rooms with PB and 1 suite. Breakfast included in rates. Types of meals: Gourmet bkfst and early coffee/tea. Beds: KQ. Cable TV, phone, ceiling fan, fresh flowers and hair dryers in room. Air conditioning. VCR and fax on premises. German spoken. Amusement parks, antiquing, fishing, golf, live theater, parks, shopping, downhill skiing, cross-country skiing, sporting events, tennis and water sports nearby.

Publicity: *Denver Post and Life on Capital Hill.*

Queen Anne Bed & Breakfast Inn

2147-2151 Tremont Pl
Denver, CO 80205-3132
(303)296-6666 (800)432-4667 Fax:(303)296-2151
E-mail: travel@queenannebnb.com
Web: www.queenannebnb.com

Circa 1879. Recipient of the Outstanding Achievement Award by the Association of American Historic Inns, this Queen Anne Victorian was designed by Colorado's most famous architect, Frank Edbrooke. Furnishings, chamber music and art add to the Victorian experience. In an area of meticulously restored homes and flower gardens, the inn is two blocks from the center of the central business district.

Historic Interest: Molly Brown House (7 blocks), State Capitol (5 blocks), Brown Palace Hotel (4 blocks), Buffalo Bill Cody grave (20 miles).

Innkeeper(s): The King Family. $75-175. MC, VISA, AX, DC, DS. TAC10. 14 rooms with PB, 2 with FP and 4 suites. Breakfast included in rates. Types of meals: Full bkfst and early coffee/tea. Beds: KQDT. Cable TV, phone and ceiling fan in room. Central air. VCR, fax, copier, bicycles and library on premises. Weddings and seminars hosted. Some French and Spanish spoken. Amusement parks, antiquing, art galleries, bicycling, golf, hiking, horseback riding, live theater, museums, parks, shopping, downhill skiing, cross-country skiing, sporting events and tennis nearby.

Publicity: *New York Times, USA Today, Travel Holiday, New Woman, Bon Appetit and Conde Nast Traveler.*

"A real dream, a real home away from home."

Durango   G3

Gable House Bed & Breakfast

805 E 5th Ave
Durango, CO 81301-5358
(970)247-4982
E-mail: ghbb@frontier.net
Web: creativelinks.com/gablehouse

Circa 1892. In a picturesque, quiet neighborhood, within walking distance of the downtown historic district, nostalgia awaits at this elegant Queen Anne Victorian home listed in the national-

al and state historic registers. Once inside the private hedge with iron gate, a relaxing journey unfolds. The parlor is perfect for learning about the area from hostess Heather. Antique-filled guest bedrooms and suite are spacious yet intimate, boasting private entrances. A deliciously prepared breakfast is highlighted with elegant table settings of Blue Willow china and vintage silver. The balconies or lawn chairs offer a restful view of the manicured grounds and flower beds.

Historic Interest: Mesa Verde, DGO Silverton Train.

Innkeeper(s): Heather Bryson. $95-150. MC, VISA, PC, TC. TAC10. 4 rooms, 1 with PB, 1 suite and 1 conference room. Breakfast included in rates. Types of meals: Gourmet bkfst, veg bkfst, early coffee/tea and afternoon tea. Beds: QDT. Turndown service in room. VCR, bicycles and library on premises. Weddings, small meetings, family reunions and seminars hosted. Antiquing, art galleries, bicycling, canoeing/kayaking, fishing, golf, hiking, horseback riding, live theater, museums, parks, shopping, downhill skiing, cross-country skiing, sporting events and water sports nearby.

Publicity: *Victorian Home, Durango Magazine and Dallas Morning News.*

Leland House B&B Suites

721 East Second Ave
Durango, CO 81301-5403
(970)385-1920 (800)664-1920 Fax:(970)385-1967
E-mail: stay@leland-house.com

Circa 1927. The rooms in this Craftsman-style brick building are named after historic figures associated with this former apartment house and Durango's early industrial growth. The decor features unique cowboy and period antiques designed for both comfort and fun. In addition to

regular rooms with queen-size beds, the suites also include queen sofa beds or fold-outs for those traveling with a child, friends or family. Gourmet breakfasts include inn specialties

of homemade granola, cranberry scones and a variety of entrees like Southwest burritos and multi-grain waffles. Located in the historic district downtown, guests can take walking tours or enjoy specialty shops, restaurants, galleries and museums nearby.

Innkeeper(s): Kirk & Diane Komick. $109-320. MC, VISA, AX, DC, CB, DS, PC, TC. TAC10. 10 rooms with PB, 6 with FP, 6 suites and 1 conference room. Breakfast and snacks/refreshments included in rates. Types of meals: Gourmet bkfst, veg bkfst, early coffee/tea and afternoon tea. Beds: Q. Cable TV, phone and ceiling fan in room. Air conditioning. VCR, fax and copier on premises. Weddings, small meetings and family reunions hosted. Antiquing, art galleries, bicycling, canoeing/kayaking, fishing, golf, hiking, live theater, museums, parks, shopping, downhill skiing, cross-country skiing, tennis and water sports nearby.

"It is great! Charming and warm, friendly staff and superb food. Marvelous historic photo collection."

The Rochester Hotel

721 East Second Ave
Durango, CO 81301-5403
(970)385-1920 (800)664-1920 Fax:(970)385-1967
E-mail: stay@rochesterhotel.com
Web: www.rochesterhotel.com

Circa 1892. This Federal-style inn's decor is inspired by many Western movies filmed in and around the town. The building is an authentically restored late-Victorian hotel with the charm and

luxury of the Old West, completely furnished in antiques from the period. The inn is situated on a beautifully landscaped setting that features a flower-filled courtyard, and is located just one block from historic Main Avenue downtown. The inn is close to all major attractions, museums, galleries, shops, restaurants, and outdoor activities.

Historic Interest: Listed in National Register of Historic Places.

Innkeeper(s): Kirk & Diane Komick. $139-209. MC, VISA, AX, DS, PC, TC. TAC10. 15 rooms with PB, 2 suites and 2 conference rooms. Breakfast included in rates. Types of meals: Gourmet bkfst, picnic lunch and afternoon tea. Beds: KQ. Cable TV, phone and ceiling fan in room. Air conditioning. VCR, fax and copier on premises. Handicap access. Weddings, small meetings, family reunions and seminars hosted. Spanish spoken. Antiquing, fishing, Mesa Verde National Park, live theater, parks, shopping, downhill skiing, cross-country skiing and water sports nearby.

Pets allowed: Small pets, prior permission needed.

Publicity: *Conde Naste Traveler, Denver Post and National Geo Adventure.*

"In a word — exceptional! Far exceeded expectations in every way."

Strater Hotel

699 Main Ave
Durango, CO 81301-5423
(970)247-4431 (800)247-4431 Fax:(970)259-2208
E-mail: res@strater.com
Web: www.strater.com

Circa 1877. This ornate, Victorian hotel is an impressive site, built with red brick and adorned in white trim. The hotel is stunning, inside and out, with rooms boasting fine furnishings and Old West Victorian decor. A stay at this inn is truly a step back in time. The hotel was built just a few years after Durango's founding during the Gold Rush days. For more than a century, guests have enjoyed hospitality at the Strater. The Diamond Belle Saloon, an Old West bar, is a wonderful place to relax and enjoy a drink. The waitresses and bartenders are decked out in authentic costumes. The hotel's Victorian restaurant serves fine cuisine in a picturesque setting with stained glass and ornate, carved walls. Guests can enjoy turn-of-the-century plays at the hotel's Diamond Circle Theatre. The hotel is located two blocks from the narrow gauge railroad depot.

Innkeeper(s): Rod Barker. $69-250. MC, VISA, AX, DC, CB, DS, PC, TC. TAC10. 93 rooms with PB and 6 conference rooms. Types of meals: Dinner and room service. AP. Beds: KQT. Cable TV, phone and turndown service in room. Air conditioning. VCR, fax and copier on premises. Handicap access. Weddings, small meetings, family reunions and seminars hosted. Limited French and limited Spanish spoken. Antiquing, bicycling, fishing, live theater, parks, shopping, downhill skiing, cross-country skiing, sporting events and water sports nearby.

Publicity: *Art, Antiques and Collectibles. and Romantic Inns of America.*

Durango (Hesperus) G3

Blue Lake Ranch

16919 Hwy 140
Durango (Hesperus), CO 81326
(970)385-4537 Fax:(970)385-4088
E-mail: bluelake@frontier.net
Web: www.bluelakeranch.com

Circa 1910. Built in 1910 by Swedish immigrants, this beautiful Victorian farmhouse has become a luxurious country inn and estate on 200 acres that include spectacular flower gardens, wildlife and splendid views. The inn is filled with comforts such as down quilts, vases of fresh flowers and family antiques. The property is designated as a wildlife refuge and there is a cabin overlooking trout-filled Blue Lake, and a cottage on the river. Uninterrupted mountain views add to the appeal. Enjoy a European/Southwest buffet breakfast. Named by American Historic Inns as one of the 10 most Romantic Inns, 2001.

Innkeeper(s): David Alford & Shirley Isgar. $95-325. PC, TC. TAC10. 16 rooms with PB, 13 with FP, 2 suites, 2 cottages, 1 cabin, 5 guest houses and 1 conference room. Breakfast and afternoon tea included in rates. Types of meals: Gourmet bkfst. Beds: K. Phone, turndown service, VCR and some with kitchen in room. Fax, child care, gardens, seasonal hot tub, lake, river and fishing on premises. Handicap access. Weddings, small meetings, family reunions and seminars hosted. Antiquing, bicycling, fishing, golf, hiking, mountain climbing, river rafting, Mesa Verde National Park, Durango Silverton Train, live theater, parks, shopping, downhill skiing, cross-country skiing, sporting events, tennis and water sports nearby.

Publicity: *Town & Country, Conde Nast Traveler, National Geographic Traveler, Sunset, Country Living, Metropolitan Home and USA Today.*

"We have been visiting the Ranch for the last 15 years and each stay gets better. The setting is ideal and the staff incredible — so beautiful and relaxing."

Eldora C6

Goldminer Hotel

601 Klondyke Ave
Eldora, CO 80466-9542
(303)258-7770 (800)422-4629 Fax:(303)258-3850

Circa 1897. This turn-of-the-century National Register hotel is a highlight in the Eldora National Historic District. Suites and rooms are decorated with period antiques. The inn provides packages that include guided jeep, horseback, hiking and fishing tours in the summer and back-country ski tours in the winter.

Historic Interest: The surrounding historic district offers many interesting homes and sites. The Goldminer Hotel was dedicated as a Boulder County landmark in 1996.

Innkeeper(s): Scott Bruntjen. $89-229. MC, VISA, AX, DS, TC. 7 rooms, 5 with PB, 1 with FP, 1 suite, 1 cottage and 1 conference room. Breakfast included in rates. Types of meals: Full bkfst and early coffee/tea. Beds: KD. TV in room. VCR, fax, copier, spa, library and cross country skis on premises. Weddings, small meetings, family reunions and seminars hosted. Antiquing, fishing, parks, shopping, downhill skiing, cross-country skiing and sporting events nearby.

Pets allowed: Cottage only.

Publicity: *Daily Camera and Mountain Ear.*

Empire C5

The Peck House

PO Box 428
Empire, CO 80438-0428
(303)569-9870 Fax:(303)569-2743
E-mail: info@thepeckhouse.com
Web: www.thepeckhouse.com

Circa 1862. Built as a residence for gold mine owner James Peck, this is the oldest hotel still in operation in Colorado. Many pieces of original furniture brought here by ox cart remain in the  inn, including a red antique fainting couch and walnut headboards. Rooms such as Mountain View provide magnificent views of the eastern slope of the Rockies, and a panoramic view of Empire Valley can be seen from the old front porch.

Historic Interest: The Hamill House Museum, Georgetown Loop Narrow Guage Railroad, Hotel de Paris Museum, Silver Plume National Historic District.

Innkeeper(s): Gary & Sally St. Clair. $50-100. MC, VISA, AX, DC, CB, DS, PC, TC. TAC10. 11 rooms, 9 with PB and 1 suite. Breakfast included in rates. Types of meals: Cont and gourmet dinner. Beds: QDT. Fax, spa and library on premises. Small meetings and seminars hosted. French spoken. Antiquing, art galleries, bicycling, fishing, hiking, horseback riding, museums, parks, shopping, downhill skiing, cross-country skiing and tennis nearby.

Publicity: *American West, Rocky Mountain News, Denver Post and Colorado Homes.*

Estes Park B6

Anniversary Inn

1060 Mary's Lake Rd
Estes Park, CO 80517
(970)586-6200
E-mail: thebert@gte.net

Circa 1890. High in the Colorado Rockies, at 7,600 feet, this authentic log home is surrounded by spectacular views. There are two acres with a pond and river nearby. An exposed-log living room is dominated by a massive mossrock fireplace. The guest rooms boast stenciled walls and other country accents. The full breakfasts are served on a glass-enclosed wraparound porch. The  inn specializes in honeymoons and anniversaries and features a honeymoon cottage.

$100-175. MC, VISA, AX, DS. TAC10. 4 rooms with PB, 1 with FP and 1 cottage. Breakfast and snacks/refreshments included in rates. Types of meals: Gourmet bkfst. Beds: Q. TV, refrigerator and fireplace in room. VCR and library on premises. Weddings and family reunions hosted. Antiquing, art galleries, fishing, golf, hiking, horseback riding, backpacking, snowshoeing, Rocky Mountain National Park, shopping and cross-country skiing nearby.

Publicity: *Denver Post, Columbus Dispatch and Rocky Mountain News.*

"The splendor and majesty of the Rockies is matched only by the warmth and hospitality you showed us during our stay."

The Baldpate Inn

PO Box 4445
Estes Park, CO 80517-4445
(970)586-6151
E-mail: baldpatein@aol.com
Web: www.baldpateinn.com

Circa 1917. This National Register inn is nestled on the side of Twin Sisters Mountain, adjacent to Rocky Mountain National Park. The front porch affords a spectacular view. Guest rooms and private cabins feature country decor with quilts and down comforters. The lobby and library are ideal places to relax, each with a massive native stone fireplace. The inn also boasts a unique collection of more than 15,000 keys and a notable photo collection. Three-course breakfasts are served, as well as lunch and dinner in the inn's dining room. With such an inspiring setting for the inn, outdoor weddings are often held here.

Innkeeper(s): Lois & MacKenzie Smith, Jen & Pete Macakanja. $95-150. MC, VISA, DS, PC, TC. TAC7. 12 rooms, 2 with PB, 3 cottages and 1 conference room. Breakfast and snacks/refreshments included in rates. Types of meals: Gourmet bkfst, early coffee/tea and picnic lunch. Beds: KQDT. VCR and library on premises. Weddings, small meetings and seminars hosted. Fishing, Rocky Mountain National Park, parks, shopping and water sports nearby.

Publicity: *Rocky Mountain News, Country Living. and Discovery Channel.*

"This place unlocked my heart."

Black Dog Inn

PO Box 4659, 650 S Saint Vrain Ave
Estes Park, CO 80517-4659
(970)586-0374
E-mail: blkdoginn@aol.com

Circa 1910. Imagine relaxing in a private romantic whirlpool enjoying a warm fire while surrounded by views of the majestic Rocky Mountains. Travelers are sure to enjoy this romantic getaway and mountain retreat. All rooms have private baths with

marble showers, and three rooms include Jacuzzi tubs and fireplaces. Tasteful family antiques decorate each room. The innkeepers invite guests to enjoy the many seasons of the Rockies.

Historic Interest: Stanley Hotel (one-half mile), Historical Museum (one-quarter mile), Enos Mills Cabin (8 miles), McGregor Ranch Museum (3 miles).

Innkeeper(s): Norm & Dee Pritchard. $85-150. MC, VISA. TAC10. 4 rooms with PB, 3 with FP and 3 suites. Breakfast and snacks/refreshments included in rates. Types of meals: Gourmet bkfst and early coffee/tea. Beds: Q. Ceiling fan and tubs for two in room. VCR, library and 100+ movies on premises. Weddings, small meetings and seminars hosted. Antiquing, fishing, golf, hiking, horseback riding, boating, snowshoeing, river rafting, fly fishing, white water rafting, rock climbing, backpacking, Rocky Mt. National Park, shopping and cross-country skiing nearby.

Publicity: *Rocky Mountain News, Denver Post and Country Inns.*

"The peace and tranquility are so refreshing."

Eagle Cliff Bed & Breakfast

2383 State Highway 66
Estes Park, CO 80517-8343
(970)586-5425 (800)414-0922 Fax:(970)571-0132
E-mail: nancye1938@hotmail.com

Circa 1949. Within walking distance of Rocky Mountain National Park among Ponderosa Pines stands Eagle Cliff House, a mountain home built in 1949. The innkeepers are hiking

consultants, and provide excellent advice to outdoor enthusiasts who stay at the inn. The Southwestern décor and warm woods create a relaxing atmosphere. The inn includes two bedrooms and one cottage (perfect for honeymooners) furnished in Victorian manner except for the jetted tub, kitchenette and deck facing the mountains. Breakfast, served in the breakfast nook, includes items like fruit compote, homemade biscuits, scrambled eggs, bacon, sausage, juice, coffee and tea. A full cookie jar is ever ready for happy, hungry guests. Hiking, golf, tennis, swimming, horseback riding, cross-country skiing and snow shoeing are available in season.

Historic Interest: Rocky Mountain National Park.

Innkeeper(s): Nancy & Michael Conrin. $125-150. MC, VISA, PC, TC. TAC10. 3 rooms, 2 with PB and 1 cottage. Breakfast and snacks/refreshments included in rates. Types of meals: Gourmet bkfst, country bkfst, veg bkfst and early coffee/tea. Beds: Q. Cable TV, phone and VCR in room. Spa and library on premises. Art galleries, fishing, golf, hiking, horseback riding, parks, shopping, cross-country skiing and tennis nearby.

Pets allowed: Outdoors.

Eagle Manor-A Bed and Breakfast Place

441 Chiquita Lane
Estes Park, CO 80517-1013
(970)586-8482 (888)603-3578 Fax:(970)586-1748
E-mail: mike@eaglemanor.com
Web: www.eaglemanor.com

Circa 1917. Elk and deer often roam across the grounds that surround Eagle Manor. The historic home boasts Rocky Mountain views. Frank Bond, a local pioneer built the home. There are four guest rooms, and all guests enjoy amenities such as an indoor swimming pool, sauna, and outdoor hot tub. Enjoy a game of billiards in the manor's great room, which is warmed by a fireplace. The stunning wilderness around Estes Park includes a host of activities, including rock climbing, hiking, whitewater rafting, horseback riding and a variety of festivals and seasonal events.

Historic Interest: Stanley Hotel (1/4 mile), Baldpate Inn (8 miles).

Innkeeper(s): Mike Smith. $125-145. MC, VISA, AX, DS, PC, TC. TAC7. 4 rooms, 3 with PB and 1 suite. Breakfast and snacks/refreshments included in rates. Types of meals: Full bkfst, veg bkfst and early coffee/tea. Beds: QT. Cable TV, phone and VCR in room. Fax, copier, spa, swimming, library, billiard table and basketball half court on premises. Weddings, small meetings, family reunions and seminars hosted. Antiquing, art galleries, bicycling, canoeing/kayaking, fishing, golf, hiking, horseback riding, live theater, museums, parks, shopping, downhill skiing, cross-country skiing, sporting events, tennis and wineries nearby.

Romantic RiverSong B&B

1765 Lower Broadview Rd, PO Box 1910
Estes Park, CO 80517-8221
(970)586-4666 Fax:(970)577-0699
E-mail: riversng@frii.com
Web: www.romanticriversong.com

Circa 1930. This Craftsman-style country inn sits on a private wildlife habitat of 27 acres adjacent to Rocky Mountain National Park. Each of the enchanting guest bedrooms, appropriately named after nine local wildflowers, exudes a romantic charm. They all feature fireplaces; large antique, jetted, sunken or whirlpool tubs; and unique showers such as a rock wall waterfall and a rooftop shower for two. Stargaze through skylights, and enjoy spectacular views from private decks. Start the day with RiverSong coffee or Mexican hot chocolate. A generous breakfast includes a fruit starter, a savory, potato or sweet main entree, and perhaps grits with sour cream peach muffins. Outdoors, the breath-taking scenery is enhanced by extensive varieties of birds, trout streams and deer. Close by are some of the nation's best hiking and snowshoeing trails. RiverSong's forte is offering fantastic wedding packages.

Historic Interest: Old Man Mountain, Historic Stanley Hotel, McGregor Ranch.
Innkeeper(s): Gary & Sue Mansfield. $150-295. MC, VISA, DS, PC. TAC10. 9 rooms with PB, 9 with FP, 6 suites and 2 cottages. Breakfast and afternoon tea included in rates. Types of meals: Country bkfst, veg bkfst, early coffee/tea, picnic lunch and dinner. Beds: Q. Turndown service, ceiling fan, fireplace, radiant heated floors, skylights and libraries in room. Spa, library, ponds, mountain stream, hiking trails and tree swings on premises. Handicap access. Weddings and seminars hosted. Antiquing, art galleries, bicycling, canoeing/kayaking, fishing, golf, hiking, horseback riding, Rocky Mountain national Park, museums, parks, shopping and cross-country skiing nearby.
Publicity: *America's Romantic Inns, Denver Post, Rocky Mountain News, Trail Gazette, Colorado Springs Telegraph, Frontier Airline In-flight Magazine, Channel 7 Denver, Colorado and Great Country Inns.*

Fairplay   D5

Hand Hotel Bed & Breakfast
531 Front St
Fairplay, CO 80440-1059
(719)836-3595 Fax:(719)836-1799
E-mail: info@handhotel.com
Web: www.handhotel.com

Circa 1932. Choose from rooms such as Trapper, Outlaw, Silverheels and Mattie Silk in this Western lodge. Rooms reflect the characters that originally inhabited Fairplay. Ask for China Mary, for instance, and you'll enjoy Oriental furnishings. Grandma Hand's room features quilts on the beds. Overlooking the Middle Fork of the South Platte River, the inn offers views you'll long remember. A sun room and a lobby with fireplace are popular, but almost everyone enjoys the upstairs deck to take in spectacular vistas of the 14,000-foot Rocky Mountain peaks. Stroll a block away to the South Park City Museum.

Innkeeper(s): Dale & Kathy Fitting. $60. MC, VISA, AX, DC, CB, DS, PC, TC. TAC10. 11 rooms with PB and 1 conference room. Breakfast included in rates. Types of meals: Cont plus and cont. Beds: QDT. Fax and copier on premises. Weddings, small meetings and family reunions hosted. Antiquing, art galleries, bicycling, canoeing/kayaking, hiking, horseback riding, fly fishing, museums, parks, shopping, downhill skiing and cross-country skiing nearby.
Pets allowed: well behaved.

Green Mountain Falls   D6

Outlook Lodge B&B
6975 Howard St, PO Box 586
Green Mountain Falls, CO 80819
(719)684-2303 (877)684-7800
E-mail: goofy7@worldnet.att.net

Circa 1889. Outlook Lodge was originally the parsonage for the historic Little Church in the Wildwood. Located at the 7,800-foot altitude above the secluded mountain village of Green Lake at the foot of Pikes Peak, the inn is within 10 miles of Colorado Springs and Manitou Springs. Hand-carved balustrades surround a veranda that frames the alpine village view, and many original parsonage furnishings are inside. Antiques and quilts decorate the lodge rooms and two-room

suites. Hearty mountain breakfasts are offered, which include eggs to order, pancakes and freshly baked breads. Ride the cog railroad, fish the trout streams, hike or ice skate in winter on Green Mountain Falls Lake by the gazebo.

Innkeeper(s): Pat & Diane Drayton. $85-115. MC, VISA, AX, DS. TAC10. 5 rooms with PB. Breakfast included in rates. Types of meals: Full bkfst and early coffee/tea. Beds: Q. Spa on premises. Weddings, small meetings, family reunions and seminars hosted. Hiking and Pikes Peak nearby.
Publicity: *Denver Post and Colorado Springs Gazette.*

"Found by chance, will return with purpose."

Grover   A7

West Pawnee Ranch B&B
29451 Country Road 130
Grover, CO 80729
(970)895-2482 Fax:(970)895-2482
E-mail: wprbb@juno.com
Web: www.bbonline.com/co/pawnee/

Circa 1914. On a peaceful prairie near the Pawnee National Grassland, this working ranch makes dream adventures come true. Ride horseback while participating in daily activities like moving cattle, checking water wells and fences. Go for a gallop across the plains or visit Michener's "Rattlesnake Buttes." Retire to a comfortable guest bedroom, suite or The Prairie House, featuring a moss rock fireplace or soaking tub and views of the Chalk Bluffs or Rocky Mountains. There is a children's toy room with books and games. A hearty rancher's breakfast may include To Die For Sticky Buns, and WPR Frittata. Enjoy hiking and bird watching, or gaze from the patio at an amazing sunset.

Historic Interest: Pawnee Buttes (30 miles).
Innkeeper(s): Paul & Louanne Timm. $60-100. MC, VISA, PC, TC. 3 rooms, 1 with PB, 1 with FP, 1 suite and 1 guest house. Breakfast and snacks/refreshments included in rates. Types of meals: Country bkfst, veg bkfst, lunch, picnic lunch and dinner. Beds: KQ. TV, phone, ceiling fan, VCR and fireplace in room. Air conditioning. Fax, copier, stables, gift shop, horseback riding and bird watching on premises. Small meetings hosted. Antiquing, art galleries, bicycling, golf, hiking, horseback riding, live theater, museums, parks and shopping nearby.
Publicity: *Denver Rocky Mountain News.*

Gunnison   E4

Mary Lawrence Inn
601 N Taylor St
Gunnison, CO 81230-2241
(970)641-3343 Fax:(970)641-6719
E-mail: marylinn@gunnison.com

Circa 1885. A local entrepreneur and saloon owner built this Italianate home in the late 19th century, but the innkeepers named their home in honor of Mary Lawrence, a later resident. Lawrence, a teacher and administrator for the local schools, used the building as a boarding house. The innkeepers have created an inviting interior with touches such as patchwork

quilts, antique furnishings and stenciled walls. A variety of treats are served each morning for breakfast, and the cookie jar is kept full. The inn offers convenient access to the area's bounty of outdoor activities.

Historic Interest: In the hills near Gunnison are several mining ghost towns. A local museum is open during the summer months. Self-guided tours of the historic buildings are available. The Crested Butte historic district is 30 miles away.

Innkeeper(s): Janette McKinny. $69-135. MC, VISA, AX. TAC10. 7 rooms with PB and 2 suites. Breakfast included in rates. Types of meals: Gourmet bkfst and early coffee/tea. Beds: KQT. Fax, copier, library and hot tub on premises. Family reunions hosted. Fishing, live theater, parks, shopping, downhill skiing, cross-country skiing and water sports nearby.

Publicity: *Rocky Mountain News, Denver Post and Gunnison Country.*

"You two are so gracious to make our stay a bit of 'heaven' in the snow."

The Ranch House B&B

233 County Road 48
Gunnison, CO 81230
(970)642-0210 Fax:(970)642-0211
E-mail: ranchhoou@ranchhousebnb.com

Circa 1875. Originally a hand-hewn log cabin, this 1875 ranch/Victorian inn provides guests comfort in the midst of glorious views. At the entrance to beautiful Ohio Creek Valley and 25 miles from Crested Butte Historic District, the inn offers three guest bedrooms that accommodate children. Hearty and

lite breakfasts are offered each morning. The hearty country breakfasts of egg dishes, bacon/sausage, hash browns, homemade baked goods and fresh fruit is perfect for the guest who intends to go hiking, biking, rafting, fishing, climbing, horseback riding, hunting, skiing, wrangling, snowmobiling or snowshoeing. An afternoon snack awaits hungry guests each afternoon in the ranch house dining room. End your evening by watching the stars as you soak in the hot tub or sit around the fire pit.

Innkeeper(s): Steve & Tammy Shelafo. $75-100. MC, VISA, AX, PC, TC. 3 rooms, 2 with PB. Breakfast and snacks/refreshments included in rates. Types of meals: Country bkfst and early coffee/tea. AP. Beds: QD. TV and VCR in room. Fax, copier, spa, bicycles, satellite TV and picnic area on premises. Antiquing, art galleries, bicycling, canoeing/kayaking, fishing, golf, hiking, horseback riding, museums, parks, shopping, downhill skiing, cross-country skiing and water sports nearby.

Pets allowed: dogs only.

Leadville   D5

The Apple Blossom Inn Victorian B&B

120 W 4th St
Leadville, CO 80461-3630
(719)486-2141 (800)982-9279 Fax:(719)486-0994
E-mail: applebb@amigo.net

Circa 1879. Featuring comfort and hospitality, this elegant Victorian home sits on downtown's historic Millionaire's Row. The living room features an antique fireplace, perfect for relaxing with friends. Spacious guest bedrooms are furnished with feather beds and terry cloth robes and boast stained glass windows and fireplaces. Escape from city life to this quiet location, perfect for enjoying the area's many outdoor activities.

Innkeeper(s): Elizabeth Lang. $79-149. MC, VISA, AX, DC, DS, PC, TC. 5 rooms with PB, 2 with FP and 2 suites. Breakfast and afternoon tea included in rates. Types of meals: Gourmet bkfst and early coffee/tea. MAP. Beds: KQDT. Weddings, small meetings and family reunions hosted. Antiquing, fishing, golf, hiking, live the-

ater, parks, shopping, downhill skiing, cross-country skiing, tennis and water sports nearby.

Publicity: *Rocky Mountain News and Denver Post.*

"We have stayed at other bed & breakfasts, but the Apple Blossom Inn really felt like home."

Historic Delaware Hotel

700 Harrison Ave
Leadville, CO 80461-3562
(719)486-1418 (800)748-2004 Fax:(719)486-2214
E-mail: desk@delawarehotel.com
Web: www.delawarehotel.com

Circa 1886. Often referred to as the Crown Jewel of Leadville, this hotel has served as an architectural cornerstone of the town's National Historic District. The interior has an elegant

Victorian lobby, which includes period antiques, crystal chandeliers, brass fixtures and oak paneling that reflects Leadville's Boom Days. Adding to the atmosphere are lace curtains and quilts in the guest rooms.

Innkeeper(s): Gail Dunning & Kit Williams. $70-125. MC, VISA, AX, DC, DS. 36 rooms with PB, 4 suites and 1 conference room. Types of meals: Cont. Beds: KQDT. Fax and copier on premises. Antiquing, fishing, museums, downhill skiing and cross-country skiing nearby.

Publicity: *Denver Post, Rocky Mountain News and Sunday Summit Daily News.*

The Ice Palace Inn Bed & Breakfast

813 Spruce St
Leadville, CO 80461-3555
(719)486-8272 (800)754-2840 Fax:(719)486-0345
E-mail: icepalace@bwn.net
Web: icepalaceinn.com

Circa 1899. Innkeeper Kami Kolakowski was born in this historic Colorado town, and it was her dream to one day return and run a bed & breakfast. Now with husband Giles, she has created a restful retreat out of this turn-of-the-century home built with lumber from the famed Leadville Ice Palace. Giles and Kami have filled the home with antiques and pieces of history from the Ice Palace and the town. Guests are treated to a mouth-watering gourmet breakfast with treats such as stuffed French toast or German apple pancakes. After a day enjoying Leadville, come back and enjoy a soak in the hot tub.

Historic Interest: The Baby Doe Tabor Museum, National Mining Hall of Fame, Tabor Opera House and Healy House are among Leadville's historic attractions, and all are near the Ice Palace Inn.

Innkeeper(s): Giles & Kami Kolakowski. $89-149. MC, VISA, AX, DC, DS, PC, TC. TAC10. 5 rooms with PB, 7 with FP. Breakfast, afternoon tea and snacks/refreshments included in rates. Types of meals: Gourmet bkfst, early coffee/tea and room service. Beds: KQDT. TV, turndown service, ceiling fan and VCR in room. Spa, library and hot tub on premises. Weddings, small meetings, family reunions and seminars hosted. Antiquing, fishing, live theater, parks, shopping, downhill skiing, cross-country skiing and water sports nearby.

Publicity: *Herald Democrat, The Denver Post and The Great Divide.*

The Leadville Country Inn

127 E 8th St
Leadville, CO 80461-3507
(719)486-2354 (800)748-2354 Fax:(719)486-0300

Circa 1892. Colorado's spectacular scenery follows along the route of the Silver Kings into Leadville at a height of 10,200 feet. Staying in this restored Victorian adds more magic to your experience. Built by a mining executive, this Queen Anne offers a romantic turret and many original features. There is a hot tub in the garden. The inn is often selected for anniversaries and is a popular retreat for couples.

Innkeeper(s): Maureen & Gretchen Scanlon. $68-160. MC, VISA, AX, DS. 9 rooms with PB. Breakfast included in rates. Types of meals: Gourmet bkfst, early coffee/tea and snacks/refreshments. Ceiling fan and some rooms with TV in room. VCR and spa on premises. Weddings, small meetings, family reunions and seminars hosted. Antiquing, fishing, hiking, shopping, downhill skiing and cross-country skiing nearby.

Publicity: *Rocky Mountain News, Herald Democrat and Country Travels.*

"This Inn has more charm than a love story written for entertainment."

Loveland   B6

The Lovelander B&B Inn

217 W 4th St
Loveland, CO 80537-5524
(970)699-0798 (800)459-6694 Fax:(970)699-0797
E-mail: love@ezlink.com

Circa 1902. Prepare to be pampered at the Lovelander. Fresh flowers, whirlpool tubs and bubble bath are just a few of the idyllic touches. Guest rooms are appointed in an uncluttered and romantic Victorian style. Four rooms include either a fireplace or whirlpool tub. Enjoy the gentle sounds of a waterfall in the garden or sit back and relax on the wraparound porch. If weather permits, specialties such as pumpkin apple waffles topped with caramel pecan sauce can be enjoyed on the veranda or in the garden. The inn's memorable cuisine has been featured on the TV shows "Inn Country USA" and "Inn Country Chefs." In addition to the more romantic amenities, there is a fax and copier available, a concierge and tour planning service, and conference facilities, which are located across the street.

Innkeeper(s): Lauren & Gary Smith. $102-150. MC, VISA, AX, DS, PC, TC. TAC10. 11 rooms with PB, 1 with FP and 1 conference room. Breakfast included in rates. Types of meals: Gourmet bkfst, early coffee/tea and picnic lunch. Beds: KQDT. Phone and turndown service in room. Air conditioning. Fax and copier on premises. Weddings, small meetings, family reunions and seminars hosted. Antiquing, parks, shopping and cross-country skiing nearby.

Wild Lane Bed & Breakfast Inn

5445 Wild Ln
Loveland, CO 80538-9241
(970)669-0303 (800)204-3320
E-mail: wildlane@info2000.net
Web: www.wildlane.com

Circa 1905. Regally situated on a hilltop in the Rocky Mountain area, this luxurious mansion has been owned by the Wild family for more than a century. Proudly given the Historic Structure Award by the State Historical Society and the Colorado Centennial Farm Status, the inn features numerous heirlooms and antiques. Several common rooms offer a casually elegant ambiance. The gorgeous guest bedrooms are each named after a specific colored rose, and are very spacious, some boasting a walk-in closet and sitting area. Each morning a full-course culinary masterpiece with an herbal emphasis is served in the formal dining room or cheery sun porch. Explore the enchanting gardens, gift and gallery shop, or escape on the three-mile nature trail.

Innkeeper(s): Steven Lanette Wild. $90-150. MC, VISA, AX, DS, PC. 5 rooms with PB. Breakfast included in rates. Types of meals: Gourmet bkfst and early coffee/tea. Beds: KQD. Phone and ceiling fan in room. Central air. Fax, copier, sauna, gift shop and four-mile nature trail on premises. Weddings, small meetings, family reunions and seminars hosted. Antiquing, art galleries, bicycling, canoeing/kayaking, fishing, golf, hiking, horseback riding, live theater, museums, parks, shopping, cross-country skiing, sporting events, tennis and wineries nearby.

Publicity: *Victoria Magazine and Herb Companion Magazine.*

Mancos   G2

Bauer House

100 Bauer Ave
Mancos, CO 81328
(970)533-9707 (800)733-9707 Fax:(970)533-7022
E-mail: bauerhse@fone.net

Circa 1890. George Bauer, Mancos' town founder, built this three-story, brick and stone Victorian. Several of the prominent family's possessions are on display, as well as old town newspapers, pictures and bank ledgers. The five guest rooms feature classic decor with antiques.
A penthouse offers a kitchen with a bar. All of the guest quarters boast mountain views. There are porches and patios to relax on, and the innkeeper has

added a putting green, croquet lawn and a place for bocce ball, as well as an antique shop. Bobbi Black tries a new, creative menu for each day. Breakfast treats include her signature eggs Benedict, stuffed pancakes, homemade waffles or stratas accompanied by fresh fruit, muffins and breads. The Mancos area offers many activities, including stagecoach rides in addition to golfing, hiking and whitewater rafting. The inn is seven miles from the entrance to Mesa Verde National Park.

Innkeeper(s): Bobbi Black. $75-125. MC, VISA, PC, TC. TAC10. 5 rooms with PB. Breakfast, afternoon tea and snacks/refreshments included in rates. Types of meals: Gourmet bkfst, early coffee/tea and picnic lunch. Beds: QT. Turndown service, ceiling fan and penthouse has kitchenette in room. VCR, fax, copier and computer E-Mail on premises. Weddings, small meetings, family reunions and seminars hosted. Antiquing, fishing, golf, live theater, parks, shopping, downhill skiing, cross-country skiing, sporting events, tennis and water sports nearby.

Publicity: *"Colorado Homes & Life Styles", "Four Corners Style", Denver Post and Durango Herald.*

"Bobbi went out of her way to make our visit to Mancos more enjoyable. She is an excellent ambassador for the Mancos Valley and quite an interesting person to know. The Bauer House should be recommended as the place to stay, to anyone visiting the area."

Manitou Springs   E6

Blue Skies B&B

402 Manitou Ave
Manitou Springs, CO 80829
(719)685-3899 (800)398-7949 Fax:(719)685-3099
E-mail: sally@blueskiesbb.com
Web: www.blueskiesbb.com

Circa 1873. Located on a secluded two-acre estate in the foothills of Pike's Peak, this cluster of three new buildings with board-and-batten siding perfectly matches the Gothic Revival architecture of the original Briarhurst Carriage House, the adjacent red stone mansion that is now a five-star restaurant. Spacious suites with sitting rooms and gas fireplaces are furnished and decorated with Sally's creative artistry. Appreciate the modern conveniences and upscale amenities as well as the private and semi-private entrances, tiled showers, bathtubs or Jacuzzis. A complete, hot breakfast is brought to each suite every morning, or opt to eat on one of the covered porches or shaded garden courtyard. The lawns and flower gardens reside well with willows and cottonwoods. Stargaze from the hot tub gazebo that boasts 21 jets as stress becomes an unknown word.

Historic Interest: Ancient Hearths in Garden of Gods (1/2 mile), Miramont Castle (1 mile), Pioneer Museum (4 miles).

Innkeeper(s): Sally Thurston and Mike Dutcher. $135-235. MC, VISA, AX, DS, TC. TAC7. 10 suites, 5 with FP. Breakfast and snacks/refreshments included in rates. Types of meals: Full bkfst and room service. AP. Beds: KQT. Cable TV, phone, ceiling fan, VCR and fireplace in room. Central air. Fax, copier, spa and gift shop on premises. Handicap access. Family reunions hosted. Antiquing, art galleries, bicycling, canoeing/kayaking, golf, hiking, horseback riding, Pikes Peak Cog Railway, Garden of Gods, Cave of the Winds, Manitou Cliff Dwellings, live theater, museums, parks, shopping, cross-country skiing, water sports and wineries nearby.

Publicity: *Denver Post.*

Gray's Avenue Hotel

711 Manitou Ave
Manitou Springs, CO 80829-1809
(719)685-1277 (800)294-1277 Fax:(719)685-1847
E-mail: mackeson1@aol.com

Circa 1886. This 1886 Queen Anne shingled Victorian inn is in the Manitou Springs Historic Preservation District, which is listed in the National Register of Historic Places. It was one of Manitou Spring's original hotels. The four guest rooms and three suites are comfortably appointed — from the cozy Bird Room with its bay window to the Orange Suite, which has three rooms, each with a double bed. Start off your day with a

 hearty breakfast, including courses like waffles with fresh strawberries and whipped cream, bacon, fresh fruit, coffee and tea. Then relax on the large front porch, stroll through the town with its shops and restaurants or put on your hiking boots to explore the incredible natural wonderland. Within walking or driving distance is the Cog Railroad, Pikes Peak, the Cave of the Winds, cliff dwellings, the Air Force Academy, the Commonwheel Artist Co-op and a number of museums and art galleries. Hikers will enjoy Mueller State Park, Waldo Canyon, Intemann and Barr Trails, Garden of the Gods and more. Airport pickup and return can usually be arranged.

Historic Interest: Garden of the Gods (1/2 miles), Cripple Creek (40 miles).

Innkeeper(s): Tom & Lee Gray. $65-85. MC, VISA, AX, DS, PC. TAC10. 7 rooms with PB, 3 suites and 1 conference room. Breakfast and snacks/refreshments included in rates. Types of meals: Full bkfst and early coffee/tea. Beds: KQDT. TV in room. VCR, fax, copier, spa and library on premises. Small meetings and family reunions hosted. Antiquing, art galleries, bicycling, fishing, golf, hiking, horseback riding, live theater, museums, parks, shopping, sporting events, tennis and wineries nearby.

Red Crags B&B Inn

302 El Paso Blvd
Manitou Springs, CO 80829-2308
(719)685-1920 (800)721-2248 Fax:(719)685-1073
E-mail: info@redcrags.com
Web: www.redcrags.com

Circa 1880. Well-known in this part of Colorado, this unique, four-story Victorian mansion sits on a bluff with a combination of views that includes Pikes Peak, Manitou Valley, Garden of  the Gods and the city of Colorado Springs. There are antiques throughout the house. The formal dining room features a rare cherrywood Eastlake fireplace. Two of the suites include double whirlpool tubs. Outside, guests can walk through beautifully landscaped gardens or enjoy a private picnic area with a barbecue pit and a spectacular view. Wine is served in the evenings.

Innkeeper(s): Howard & Lynda Lerner. $85-185. MC, VISA, AX, DS, PC, TC. TAC10. 8 rooms with PB, 8 with FP and 5 suites. Breakfast, afternoon tea and snacks/refreshments included in rates. Types of meals: Full bkfst and early coffee/tea. Beds: K. Two jetted tubs for two, clock, feather beds and phones in room. Fax, copier, spa and TV available upon request on premises. Weddings, small meetings, family reunions and seminars hosted. Antiquing, fishing, golf, Pikes Peak, Olympic Training Center, live theater, parks, shopping, cross-country skiing, sporting events and tennis nearby.

Publicity: *Rocky Mountain News, Bridal Guide, Denver Post, Los Angeles Times, Springs Woman and Colorado Springs Gazette.*

"What a beautiful, historical and well-preserved home - exceptional hospitality and comfort. What wonderful people! Highly recommended."

Rockledge Country Inn

328 El Paso Blvd
Manitou Springs, CO 80829-2319
(719)685-4515 (888)685-4515 Fax:(719)685-1031
E-mail: rockinn@webcom.com
Web: www.rockledgeinn.com

Circa 1912. Built originally for a wealthy entrepreneur, legend has it that in 1922 a prominent Texas oilman was so taken by the inn's stonework, that he bought the 20-room estate as well as the quarry from which the  stone had come. Each of the four spacious luxury suites are distinctively decorated with contemporary furnishings and Civil War-era antiques and boast feather beds and sitting rooms. Visitors are invited to enjoy Colorado wines or cocktails in the evening in front of the copperwork fireplace or on the stone patio with a view of Pikes Peak. The inn is minutes from the downtown historic district.

Historic Interest: Minutes from Colorado Springs, Colorado College, U.S. Air Force Academy, and the many attractions of Manitou Springs.

Innkeeper(s): Hartman & Nancy Smith. $170-295. MC, VISA, AX, DS. TAC10. 4 suites, 4 with FP and 1 conference room. Breakfast, afternoon tea and snacks/refreshments included in rates. Types of meals: Full bkfst. EP. Beds: K. Cable TV, phone and turndown service in room. Fax, copier, library, computer station and exercise room on premises. Weddings, small meetings, family reunions and seminars hosted. Amusement parks, antiquing, fishing, parks, shopping and sporting events nearby.

Publicity: *The Gazette and named "Colorado's Most Romantic B&B" by the Denver Post.*

Two Sisters Inn-A Bed and Breakfast

10 Otoe Pl
Manitou Springs, CO 80829-2014
(719)685-9684 (800)274-7466
Web: www.twosisinn.com

Circa 1919. Voted the most romantic place in Pikes Peak, this Victorian inn was originally built by two sisters as the Sunburst boarding house. Now celebrating its 12th anniversary, the inn continues to be a favorite. A honeymoon cottage in the back garden, a beautiful stained-glass  door, hardwood floors, a stone fireplace in the parlor and a library are among the special features. A three-course breakfast (a winner of a national innkeeper breakfast contest) features inspired mouth-watering dishes. Nestled at the base of Pikes Peak, it is one block from the center of the historic district and close to mineral springs, art galleries, shops, restaurants and the beginning of the historic Manitou Springs Walking Tour. The Garden of the Gods and the Cog Railway are one mile away while the Cave of the Winds and Cliff Dwellings are within a quarter of a mile. Guests come back to the inn for the fine cuisine and the camaraderie with the caring innkeepers.

Historic Interest: Pikes Peak, Garden of the Gods, Pikes Peak Cog Railway.
Innkeeper(s): Wendy Goldstein & Sharon Smith. $69-125. MC, VISA, DS. TAC10. 5 rooms, 4 with PB. Breakfast included in rates. Types of meals: Gourmet bkfst. Beds: D. Antiquing, bicycling, hiking and shopping nearby.
Publicity: *Rocky Mountain News, Gazette Telegraph, The Denver Post* and *Country Inns.*

"The welcome is so sincere you'll want to return again and again."

Victoria's Keep

202 Ruxton Ave
Manitou Springs, CO 80829
(719)685-5354 (800)905-5337 Fax:(719)685-5913
E-mail: info@victoriaskeep.com

Circa 1892. A stream passes by the wraparound front porch of this Queen Anne Victorian. Stained glass windows and a turret complete the picture. The home is furnished in period antiques, and there are coordinated wallpapers. Every room has a fireplace of its own as well as queen beds. Most have whirlpool tubs for two and feather beds. Afternoon dessert is offered, and in the morning a gourmet breakfast is served.
Innkeeper(s): Gerry & Donna Anderson. $85-180. MC, VISA, AX, DS, TC. 6 rooms with PB, 6 with FP. Four rooms with jetted tubs for two in room. VCR, spa and library on premises. Walking distance to shops and restaurants nearby.

Ouray   F3

Christmas House B&B Inn

310 Main
Ouray, CO 81427
(970)325-4992 (888)325-9627 Fax:(970)325-4992
E-mail: xmasbb@rmi.net

Circa 1889. Peace and goodwill abound at this delightful romantic Victorian lodge surrounded by the San Juan Range of the Rocky Mountains. The tiny town, population 700, is nine blocks long and six blocks wide. It sits at the northern end of the portion of Highway 550 known as "The Million Dollar Highway" because of its spectacular views. The inn has five deluxe suites, each with a double whirlpool tub and awesome views. Four have fireplaces and private entrances. Guests can enjoy the Dickensesque English Ivy suite with its antique Victorian bed and breathtaking mountain view. Or they may choose the Mistletoe (perfect for honeymooners and other lovers) with its fireplace and pink half canopy bed. Breakfast is a celebration of menus with names like "Joy To the World," "Up on the Housetop" and "Feliz Navidad." Happy, hungry guests will enjoy entrees like maple/rosemary grilled ham, crepes, waffles, omelets and juices.

Historic Interest: Ouray National Historic District, Wright Opera House (1 block), Beaumont Hotel (3 blocks), Red Mountain Mining District (10 miles), Otto Mears Monument (3 miles), Silverton Narrow Guage Train (25 miles), Mesa Verde National Park (95 miles), Black Canyon National Park (40 miles).
Innkeeper(s): George Allyson Crosby. $88-165. MC, VISA, TC. TAC3. 5 suites, 4 with FP. Breakfast and snacks/refreshments included in rates. Types of meals: Gourmet bkfst, veg bkfst, early coffee/tea and gourmet dinner. Beds: QT. Cable TV, phone, turndown service, ceiling fan, VCR, fireplace, private Jacuzzis for two, private entrances, private & shared saunas for two, robes and dryers in room. Air conditioning. Fax, copier, sauna, library, gift shop, video/CD library, telescope, local menus, ice and iron/board on premises. Antiquing, art galleries, bicycling, canoeing/kayaking, fishing, golf, hiking, horseback riding, jeep tours and rentals, mine tours, ballooning, mountain biking, ice climbing, sledding, snowmobiling, snowshoeing, ice skating, live theater, museums, parks, shopping, downhill skiing, cross-country skiing, tennis, water sports and wineries nearby.
Publicity: *Westwind, West Life* and *KJYE.*

St. Elmo Hotel

426 Main St, PO Box 667
Ouray, CO 81427-0667
(970)325-4951 Fax:(970)325-0348
E-mail: steh@rmi.net
Web: www.stelmohotel.com

Circa 1898. The inn was built by Kitty Heit, with views of the amphitheater, Twin Peaks and Mt. Abrams, and it has operated as a hotel for most of its life. Rosewood sofas and chairs covered in red and green velvet, and a piano furnish the parlor. The Bon Ton Restaurant occupies the stone-walled basement, and it's only a short walk to the hot springs.

Historic Interest: The Town of Ouray is a National Historical District.
Innkeeper(s): Dan & Sandy Lingenfelter. $85-135. MC, VISA, AX, DS. TAC10. 9 rooms with PB and 2 suites. Breakfast included in rates. Beds: KQ. Spa and sauna on premises. Antiquing, fishing, downhill skiing, cross-country skiing and water sports nearby.
Publicity: *Colorado Homes & Lifestyles.*

"So full of character and so homely, it is truly delightful. The scenery in this area is breathtaking."

Paonia   D3

The Bross Hotel B&B

312 Onarga, PO Box 85
Paonia, CO 81428
(970)527-6776 Fax:(970)527-7737
E-mail: brosshotel@paonia.com
Web: www.paonia-inn.com

Circa 1906. A group of artisans, carpenters and craftspeople restored this turn-of-the-century western hotel to its original splendor with front porch and balcony. Wood floors and trim, dormer windows and exposed brick walls all add to the Victorian decor. For pleasure, relax in the sitting area or library/TV/game room. A conference room and communications center is perfect for business. Guest bedrooms feature antiques and handmade quilts. Some can be adjoined into suites. Breakfast is an adventure in seasonal culinary delights that cover the antique back bar in the dining room. Explore the many activities Gunnison National Park offers. Visit Black Canyon, Grand Mesa, West Elk and Ragged Wilderness areas.

Historic Interest: Marble mines (40 miles), Redstone (45 miles), Aspen (80 miles).

Innkeeper(s): Linda Lentz, Susan Steinhardt. $90. MC, VISA, DC, PC, TC. 10 rooms with PB and 1 conference room. Breakfast and snacks/refreshments included in rates. Types of meals: Full bkfst. Beds: KQDT. Phone and ceiling fan in room. VCR, fax, spa and library on premises. Small meetings, family reunions and seminars hosted. German, Italian and French spoken. Antiquing, art galleries, bicycling, canoeing/kayaking, fishing, golf, hiking, horseback riding, concerts, festivals, museums, parks, shopping, cross-country skiing and wineries nearby.

Pets allowed: well-behaved dogs, extra cleaning fee.

Publicity: *Denver Post.*

Pine   D6

Meadow Creek B&B Inn

13438 Hwy 285
Pine, CO 80470
(303)838-4167 (303)838-0360 Fax:(303)838-0360
E-mail: info@meadowcreekbb.com
Web: www.meadowcreekbb.com

Circa 1929. This marvelous stone structure, shrouded by pines and aspens, was built as a summer home for Italian Prince Balthasar Gialma Odescalchi, a descendant of rulers of the Holy Roman Empire. Enjoy views of the surrounding mountains as you breath in Colorado's cool, clean air. The

lush 35-acre grounds include the main house, barns, a smoke house and a cabin. Grandma's Attic, a secluded loft bedroom, offers a sitting area and views at tree-top level. The Colorado Sun Suite offers the modern amenities of a bar, microwave, coffee pot and refrigerator, combined with the romantic amenities of a private sitting room and a Jacuzzi underneath a skylight, perfect for stargazing. Some rooms boast fireplaces, and all guests are pampered with stocked cookie jars and refreshments available throughout the day. A luscious full breakfast with unique entrees, home-baked breads and other treats is served each morning.

Historic Interest: The main house and surrounding structures are listed in the Colorado Historical Register. Meadow Creek is just 45 minutes out of Denver, which offers many historic attractions.

Innkeeper(s): Loren & Ivan Fuentes. $110-205. MC, VISA, AX. 7 rooms with PB and 3 suites. Breakfast and snacks/refreshments included in rates. Types of meals: Full bkfst and early coffee/tea. Beds: KQ. Jacuzzis in room. Weddings, small meetings, family reunions and seminars hosted. Antiquing, bicycling, fishing, golf, hiking, horseback riding, shopping and cross-country skiing nearby.

Pueblo   E7

Abriendo Inn

300 W Abriendo Ave
Pueblo, CO 81004-1814
(719)544-2703 Fax:(719)542-6544
E-mail: info@abriendoinn.com
Web: www.abriendoinn.com

Circa 1906. Upon entering this inn, it becomes apparent why it was chosen "Pueblo's Best Weekend Getaway" and "Best Bed and Breakfast Inn for the Colorado Front Range." Special details include curved stained-glass windows, a spiral staircase and parquet floors. Comfortably elegant guest bedrooms feature canopy or brass beds, heart-shaped double whirlpool tubs, cable TV, VCR, microwave and small refrigerator. A typical breakfast served at flexible times, might include a fruit cup, tomato-basil frittata, nectarine

kuchen, cheddar toast, Dutch crumb muffin and beverages. A 24-hour complimentary snack/refreshment center is an added convenience. Enjoy the one acre of park-like grounds and a wraparound porch lined with wicker rockers and chairs for a relaxing change of pace.

Historic Interest: Historic Union Avenue District (within 4 blocks), where Bat Masterson walked the streets & site of "Old Monarch," the Hanging Tree.

Innkeeper(s): Kerrelyn Trent. $74-130. MC, VISA, AX, DC, PC, TC. TAC10. 10 rooms, 9 with PB and 1 suite. Types of meals: Gourmet bkfst, veg bkfst, cont plus, cont, early coffee/tea and snacks/refreshments. Beds: KQ. Cable TV, phone, ceiling fan, VCR and whirlpool tub for two in room. Air conditioning. Fax, copier and gift shop on premises. Family reunions hosted. Antiquing, art galleries, beaches, bicycling, canoeing/kayaking, fishing, golf, hiking, horseback riding, live theater, museums, parks, shopping, cross-country skiing, sporting events, tennis and water sports nearby.

Publicity: *Pueblo Chieftain, Rocky Mountain News, Denver Post, Colorado Springs Gazette, Sunset Magazine and Boulder Daily Camera.*

"This is a great place with the friendliest people. I've been to a lot of B&Bs this one is top drawer."

The Baxter Inn

325 W 15th St
Pueblo, CO 81003
(719)542-7002 Fax:(719)583-1560
E-mail: baxtrinn@rmi.net

Circa 1893. The Victorian era lives on at this historic inn, listed in the National Register. Fine furnishings and period antiques decorate the rooms. Intricately carved fireplace mantels and a grand main staircase add to the period ambiance. Guest rooms have been designed with romance in mind; some include a whirlpool tub for two. The Charles Kretschmer Room, named to honor the home's builder, includes a fireplace, damask wallcoverings, a four-poster bed and a bath with a whirlpool tub set among stained glass. The inn is named for the home's most notable resident, a pioneer businessman, rancher and politician. A three-course, gourmet breakfast is served each morning, beginning with a special "wake-up" course that is set up on a sideboard outside the guest rooms. The final two courses, a fresh fruit dish and a savory egg dish, are served in the formal dining room.

Historic Interest: Rosemount Museum, El Pueblo Museum, Union Avenue, Riverwalk of Pueblo.

Innkeeper(s): Dave & Lois Jones. $85-125. MC, VISA, AX, DC, PC, TC. TAC10. 5 rooms with PB, 1 with FP, 1 suite and 1 conference room. Breakfast included in rates. Types of meals: Gourmet bkfst, veg bkfst, early coffee/tea, picnic lunch, afternoon tea and snacks/refreshments. Beds: Q. Cable TV, phone, turndown service and robes in room. Central air. Fax, copier, library and music room baby grand piano on premises. Weddings, small meetings, family reunions and seminars hosted. Antiquing, art galleries, bicycling, canoeing/kayaking, golf, hiking, horseback riding, museums, parks, cross-country skiing, tennis and water sports nearby.

Publicity: *Sunset Magazine, Denver Post, Pueblo Chieftain and Images.*

Salida E5

River Run Inn

8495 Co Rd 160
Salida, CO 81201
(719)539-3818 (800)385-6925 Fax:(801)659-1878
E-mail: riverrun@amigo.net

Circa 1895. This gracious brick home, a National Register building, is located on the banks of the Arkansas River, three miles from town. It was once the poor farm, for folks down on their luck who were willing to work in exchange for food and lodging. The house has been renovated to reflect a country-eclectic style and has seven guest rooms, most enhanced by mountain views. The location is ideal for anglers, rafters, hikers,

bikers and skiers. A 13-bed, third floor is great for groups. A full country breakfast, afternoon cookies and refreshments, and evening brandy and sherry are offered daily.

Historic Interest: Downtown Salida, CO. (3 miles).

Innkeeper(s): Virginia Nemmers. $70-160. MC, VISA, AX, PC, TC. TAC10. 8 rooms, 4 with PB and 1 conference room. Breakfast and snacks/refreshments included in rates. Types of meals: Gourmet bkfst, veg bkfst, early coffee/tea, picnic lunch and dinner. EP. Beds: KQT. VCR, library, fishing and lawn games on premises. Weddings, small meetings, family reunions and seminars hosted. Antiquing, art galleries, bicycling, canoeing/kayaking, fishing, golf, hiking, horseback riding, snowshoeing, live theater, museums, parks, shopping, downhill skiing, cross-country skiing, tennis, water sports and wineries nearby.

Publicity: *Men's Journal, Denver Post, Colorado Springs Gazette., CBS Denver, The Travel Channel and MSNBC.com.*

"So glad we found a B&B with such character and a great owner as well."

Thomas House

307 E 1st St
Salida, CO 81201-2801
(719)539-7104 (888)228-1410
E-mail: office@thomashouse.com
Web: www.thomashouse.com

Circa 1888. This home was built as a boarding house to help accommodate the thousands of railroad workers and travelers who passed through Salida. Today, the home still serves as a restful place for weary travelers drawn to the Colorado wilderness. The inn is decorated with antiques, collectibles and contemporary furnishings. Each guest room is named for a mountain. The Mt.

Princeton suite includes a bedroom, private bath with an antique clawfoot tub and a separate sitting area. The innkeepers keep reading materials on hand, and there is an outdoor hot tub as well. Breakfasts are continental, yet hearty, with a variety of freshly baked breads and muffins, yogurt, granola, cheese and fruit.

Innkeeper(s): Tammy & Steve Office. $66-120. MC, VISA, AX, DS, PC, TC. TAC10. 6 rooms with PB, 1 suite and 1 cottage. Breakfast included in rates. Types of meals: Cont and early coffee/tea. Beds: KQT. Ceiling fan and kitchenette in suite in room. Spa, library and shared kitchen on premises. Small meetings and family reunions hosted. Antiquing, fishing, art galleries, live theater, parks, shopping, downhill skiing, cross-country skiing and water sports nearby.

Silverton F3

Grand Imperial Hotel

1219 Greene St
Silverton, CO 81433
(970)387-5527 (800)341-3340
E-mail: grandimperial@frontier.com
Web: www.silverton.org/grandimperial

Circa 1882. Enter an old-time era at this Victorian hotel, centrally located in a famous picturesque mountain town. Relax on the third floor in the large sunroom, furnished with antique wicker. Tastefully decorated guest bedrooms with 14-foot-high ceilings, pretty wallpaper, lace and antiques offer comfort and spectacular views of the San Juan Mountains. Downstairs, a restaurant serves delectable food, and live ragtime music is enjoyed. In the famous 100-year-old bar, renowned Sheriff Bat Masterson's bullet hole remains. Catering is available for private parties and weddings.

Innkeeper(s): George & Debby Foster. $69-150. MC, VISA, DS, TC. 40 rooms with PB and 1 conference room. Types of meals: Picnic lunch, snacks/refreshments and gourmet dinner. Beds: KQD. Cable TV, phone, ceiling fan and just peace & quiet in room. Weddings, small meetings, family reunions and seminars hosted. Antiquing, fishing, hiking, horseback riding, snowmobiling, ice skating, ice climbing, snowshoeing, jeeping, four-wheeling, live theater, shopping, downhill skiing and cross-country skiing nearby.

The Wyman Hotel & Inn

1371 Greene St
Silverton, CO 81433
(970)387-5372 (800)609-7845 Fax:(970)387-5745
E-mail: thewyman@frontier.net
Web: www.thewyman.com

Circa 1902. A stately building renown for its ballroom in the early 1900s, The Wyman is listed in the National Register of Historic Places. Now a modern luxury bed & breakfast, it boasts a smoke-free environment. There are two common rooms to enjoy with access to a large video library. The Breakfast Room is where highly acclaimed gourmet breakfasts are served with the sweet sounds of Mozart. Sunnyside Souffle with roasted potatoes is one of the mouth-watering entrees that may accompany the homemade breads and muffins, fresh fruit, juice and Costa Rican coffee. The antique-filled guest bedrooms are well-appointed with comfort aplenty and spectacular views. The romantic suites are elegant with whirlpool baths made for two. Mountain bikes are available to rent for a closer look at the majestic San Juan Mountains.

Historic Interest: Durango and Silverton Narrow Gauge Railroad, Mesa Verde National Park and Anasazi ruins.

Innkeeper(s): Lorraine & Tom Lewis. $95-195. MC, VISA, AX, DS, TC. TAC10. 18 rooms, 14 with PB and 4 suites. Breakfast and afternoon tea included in rates. Types of meals: Gourmet bkfst, early coffee/tea and picnic lunch. Beds: KQ. TV, phone, ceiling fan, VCR and whirlpool tubs in room. Fax, copier, library and videos on premises. Weddings, small meetings and family reunions hosted. Fishing, hiking, horseback riding, folk and music festival, mountain biking, jeeping to ghost towns, snowshoeing, sledding, live theater, parks, shopping, downhill skiing and cross-country skiing nearby.

Publicity: *The Denver Post, The New York Times, Albuquerque Journal, The Gazette, Douglas County News-Press, The Salt Lake Tribune, Austin American Statesman and The Travel Channel.*

Telluride F3

New Sheridan Hotel

231 W Colorado Ave, PO Box 980
Telluride, CO 81435-0980
(970)728-4351 (800)200-1891 Fax:(970)728-5024
E-mail: info@newsheridan.com
Web: www.newsheridan.com

Circa 1895. This charming hotel reflects the Victorian ambiance of a historic mining town. The building was redecorated recently to its former glory and is the only remaining original Victorian hotel and bar in Telluride. Much of the bar's interior is original, including a cherrywood back bar with carved lions imported from Austria. The adjoining Sheridan Opera House hosted such stars as Sarah Bernhardt, Lillian Gish and William Jennings Bryan. Guests can relax in their cozy guests rooms or in the library or parlor. Fluffy terry robes, in-room ceiling fans, a fitness room and rooftop hot tubs await to pamper you. The hotel is a two-block walk from ski lifts and gondola.

Historic Interest: All the sites of charming, historic Telluride are within 10 blocks of the hotel.

Innkeeper(s): Ray Farnsworth. $90-400. MC, VISA, AX, TC. TAC10. 32 rooms, 24 with PB and 6 suites. Breakfast included in rates. Types of meals: Full bkfst and gourmet dinner. Beds: KQ. Phone in room. Fax, copier

and computer on premises. Handicap access. Small meetings, family reunions and seminars hosted. Antiquing, fishing, concerts. Horseback riding, live theater, parks, shopping, downhill skiing, cross-country skiing and water sports nearby.

Publicity: *Rocky Mountain News, San Francisco Examiner, Inn Style, Ski, Bon Appetit, Sunset and Arizona Republic.*

Ward C6

Gold Lake Mountain Resort & Spa

3371 Gold Lake Rd
Ward, CO 80481-9602
(303)459-3544 (800)450-3544 Fax:(303)459-9080
E-mail: goldlake@goldlake.com
Web: www.goldlake.com

Circa 1922. Surrounded by National Forest and overlooking the Continental Divide, this resort was originally a summer camp for girls. Romantic cabins, suites and a guesthouse are all tastefully furnished with period antiques and local art. Plush down comforters and gas stoves add extra comfort. A variety of pampering spa treatments are offered. The inn's gourmet candlelight dining features highly acclaimed, hearty "Mountain Spa Cuisine" with wild game, fish or vegetarian options. There are more than 95 acres to explore with hiking trails and fly fishing. A favorite spot is soaking in the hot pools overlooking Gold Lake. Canoes, kayaks and row boats are available.

Historic Interest: Enos Mills Cabin, founder of Rocky Mtn. National Park (30 miles), Nederland Mining Museum (15 miles), St. Malos Chapel, site of Pope visit nearby.

Innkeeper(s): Jill Fleming. $145-515. MC, VISA, PC. 18 cottages, 18 with FP, 8 suites, 1 guest house and 1 conference room. Breakfast and afternoon tea included in rates. Types of meals: Cont plus, lunch and gourmet dinner. Ceiling fan in room. Fax, spa, sauna and stables on premises. Weddings and small meetings hosted. Bicycling, canoeing/kayaking, fishing, hiking, horseback riding, boating, spa services and downhill skiing nearby.

Connecticut

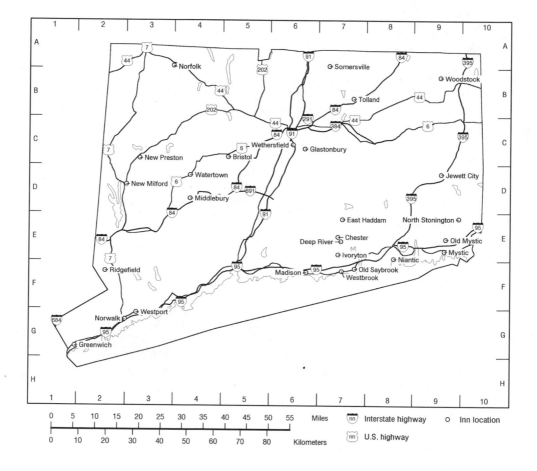

0   5 10 15 20 25 30 35 40 45 50 55   Miles

0   10   20   30   40   50   60   70   80   Kilometers

(nn) Interstate highway   o Inn location

(nn) U.S. highway

Bristol   C5

Chimney Crest Manor

5 Founders Dr
Bristol, CT 06010-5209
(860)582-4219 Fax:(860)584-5903
E-mail: chimnycrst@aol.com

Circa 1930. This 32-room Tudor mansion possesses an unusual castle-like arcade and a 45-foot living room with a stone fireplace at each end. Many of the rooms are embellished with oak paneling  and ornate plaster ceilings. One suite includes a thermo spa. The inn is located in the historically registered Federal Hill District, an area of large colonial homes.

Historic Interest: American Clock and Watch Museum (3 blocks), New England Carousel Museum (one-half mile).

Innkeeper(s): Dante & Cynthia Cimadamore. $95-165. MC, VISA, AX, TC. TAC10. 5 rooms with PB, 1 with FP, 3 suites and 1 conference room. Breakfast included in rates. Types of meals: Full bkfst and early coffee/tea. Beds: KQ. Cable TV, turndown service, ceiling fan, fireplace and spa or view in room. Air conditioning. VCR and fax on premises. Weddings, small meetings, family reunions and seminars hosted. Amusement parks, antiquing, golf, museums, parks, downhill skiing, cross-country skiing and tennis nearby.

Publicity: *PM Magazine and Record-Journal.*

"Great getaway — unbelievable structure. They are just not made like this mansion anymore."

Chester   F7

The Inn at Chester

318 W Main St
Chester, CT 06412-1026
(860)526-9541 (800)949-7829 Fax:(860)526-4387
E-mail: innkeeper@innatchester.com
Web: www.innatchester.com

Circa 1778. More than 200 years ago, Jeremiah Parmelee built a clapboard farmhouse along a winding road named the Killingworth Turnpike. The Parmelee Homestead stands as a reflection of the past and is an inspiration for the Inn at Chester. Each of the rooms is individually appointed with Eldred Wheeler Reproductions. The Lincoln Suite has a sitting room with a fireplace. Enjoy lively conversation or live music while imbibing your favorite drink at the inn's tavern, Dunk's Landing. Outside Dunk's Landing, a 30-foot fireplace soars into the rafters. Fine dining is offered in the inn's post-and-beam restaurant.

Innkeeper(s): Leonard Lieberman. $105-215. MC, VISA, AX. TAC10. 42 rooms with PB, 2 with FP, 1 suite and 3 conference rooms. Breakfast included in rates. Types of meals: Cont plus, lunch and gourmet dinner. Beds: KQDT. Cable TV and phone in room. Air conditioning. VCR, fax, copier, sauna, bicycles, tennis and library on premises. Handicap access. Weddings, small meetings, family reunions and seminars hosted. Antiquing, fishing, golf, live theater, parks, shopping, downhill skiing, cross-country skiing and water sports nearby.

Pets Allowed.

Publicity: *New Haven Register, Hartford Courant, Pictorial Gazette, Discover Connecticut, New York Times, Connecticut Magazine. and Food Network.*

Deep River   E7

Riverwind

209 Main St
Deep River, CT 06417-2022
(860)526-2014
E-mail: innkeeper@riverwindinn.com
Web: www.riverwindinn.com

Circa 1790. Chosen "most romantic inn in Connecticut" by Discerning Traveler Newsletter, this inn features numerous common areas for socializing or privacy. A happy, informal country decor includes antiques from Barbara's Virginia home. There are fireplaces everywhere, including a 12-foot cooking fireplace in the keeping room.

Innkeeper(s): Barbara Barlow & Bob Bucknall. $95-175. MC, VISA. 8 rooms with PB. Breakfast included in rates. Types of meals: Full bkfst. Beds: QD. Weddings hosted. Antiquing, hiking trails and live theater nearby.

Publicity: *Hartford Courant, Country Living, Country Inns, Country Decorating, New York, Travel & Leisure, New York Times, Boston Globe and Los Angeles Times.*

"Warm, hospitality, a quiet homey atmosphere, comfortable bed, well thought-out and delightful appointments, delicious light hot biscuits — a great find!"

East Haddam   E7

Bishopsgate Inn

7 Norwich Rd
East Haddam, CT 06423-0290
(860)873-1677 Fax:(860)873-3898
E-mail: ctkagel@bishopsgate.com

Circa 1818. This Colonial house is furnished with period antiques, and each floor of the inn has a sitting area where guests often relax with a good book. Four of the guest rooms include a fireplace and the suite has a sauna. The innkeepers serve a hearty  breakfast, and for an additional charge, they can prepare picnic lunches. Although secluded on two acres, the inn is a short walk to the Goodspeed Opera House and shopping.

Innkeeper(s): Kagel Family. $100-150. MC, VISA, PC. 6 rooms with PB, 4 with FP and 1 suite. Breakfast and afternoon tea included in rates. Types of meals: Full bkfst and early coffee/tea. MAP. Beds: KQD. Sauna in room. Air conditioning. Small meetings and family reunions hosted. Antiquing, fishing, live theater, parks, shopping, downhill skiing, cross-country skiing and water sports nearby.

Publicity: *Boston Globe, Discerning Traveler, Adventure Road and Manhattan Cooperator.*

". . . Attention to detail, ambiance and amenities . . . Bishopsgate is truly outstanding."

Glastonbury   C6

Butternut Farm

1654 Main St
Glastonbury, CT 06033-2962
(860)633-7197 Fax:(860)659-1758

Circa 1720. This Colonial house sits on two acres of landscaped grounds amid trees and herb gardens. Prize-winning goats, pigeons, chickens, ducks, and pigs are housed in the old barn on the property. Eighteenth-century Connecticut antiques are placed throughout the inn, enhancing the natural beauty of the pumpkin-pine floors and eight brick fireplaces.

Innkeeper(s): Don Reid. $85-105. AX, PC, TC. 4 rooms with PB, 3 with FP and 2 suites. Breakfast included in rates. Types of meals: Full bkfst. Beds: DT. Phone and VCR in room. Air conditioning. Fax on premises. Family reunions hosted. Antiquing, fishing, live theater, parks, shopping, downhill skiing, cross-country skiing and sporting events nearby.

Publicity: *New York Times, House Beautiful, Yankee and Antiques.*

Greenwich   G1

Cos Cob Inn

50 River Rd
Greenwich, CT 06807
(203)661-5845 (877)549-4063 Fax:(203)661-2054
E-mail: innkeeper@coscobinn.com
Web: www.coscobinn.com

Circa 1870. Located in the Cos Cob section of Greenwich, this three-story, Federal-style inn offers 14 individually decorated guest rooms. Each elegant bed chamber is special. The Wedding Room is spacious, and with its bay window, working gas fireplace, Jacuzzi bath and four-poster bed, a perfect choice for a romantic getaway. Suites include sitting areas and Jacuzzis. For business travelers, the innkeepers have provided data ports and voice mail

in each guest room. Many rooms offer a river view. Restaurants, museums, shops and outdoor activities are all nearby.

Innkeeper(s): Rick & Cindy Kral. $59-249. MC, VISA, AX, DC. 14 rooms with PB, 1 with FP and 5 suites. Breakfast and snacks/refreshments included in rates. Types of meals: Cont. Beds: KQ. Cable TV, phone, ceiling fan, VCR, hair dryer, irons & ironing boards and refrigerator in room. Air conditioning. Fax and copier on premises. Small meetings and family reunions hosted. Antiquing, fishing, golf, live theater, parks, shopping and tennis nearby.

Stanton House Inn

76 Maple Ave
Greenwich, CT 06830-5698
(203)869-2110

Circa 1900. It took 150 years for one of the Saketts to finally build on the land given them in 1717. The manor they built was remodeled on a grand scale at the turn-of-the-century under architect Sanford White. In the '40s, the house became a tourist home and received visitors for many years. Renovated recently, it now offers spacious rooms decorated in a traditional, country inn style.

Innkeeper(s): Tog & Doreen Pearson. $65-135. MC, VISA, AX, DS, TC. TAC10. 24 rooms with PB, 6 with FP and 2 suites. Breakfast included in rates. Types of meals: Cont. Beds: KQDT. Cable TV, phone and suites with two-person whirlpool tub in room. Air conditioning. Fax, copier, swimming and valet on premises. Weddings, small meetings and family reunions hosted. French and Spanish spoken. Antiquing, live theater, parks and shopping nearby.

Publicity: *Foster's Business Review.*

"For a day, or a month or more, this is a special place."

Ivoryton   E7

The Copper Beech Inn

46 Main St
Ivoryton, CT 06442-1004
(860)767-0330 (888)809-2056
Web: www.copperbeechinn.com

Circa 1887. The Copper Beech Inn was once the home of ivory importer A.W. Comstock, one of the early owners of the Comstock Cheney Company, which produced ivory combs and keyboards. The village took its name from the ivory trade centered here. An enormous copper beech tree shades the property. Each room in the renovated Carriage House boasts a whirlpool bath and French doors opening onto a deck. The

wine list and French-country cuisine at the inn's restaurant have received numerous accolades.

Historic Interest: Connecticut River Museum (4 miles), Goodspeed Opera House (15 miles), Ivoryton Playhouse (one-half mile), Mystic Seaport (25 miles).

Innkeeper(s): Eldon & Sally Senner. $123-202. MC, VISA, AX, DC, CB, PC, TC. 13 rooms with PB and 1 conference room. Breakfast included in rates. Types of meals: Cont plus and gourmet dinner. Beds: KQDT. Cable TV in room. Air conditioning. Library on premises. Handicap access. Weddings, small meetings and seminars hosted. Limited Spanish and Portuguese spoken. Antiquing, fishing, live theater, parks, shopping and water sports nearby.

Publicity: *Los Angeles Times, Bon Appetit, Connecticut, Travel & Leisure and Discerning Traveler.*

"The grounds are beautiful ... just breathtaking ... accommodations are wonderful."

Jewett City   D9

Homespun Farm Bed and Breakfast

306 Preston Rd
Jewett City, CT 06351
(860)376-5178 (888)889-6673 Fax:(860)376-5587
E-mail: relax@homespunfarm.com
Web: www.homespunfarm.com

Circa 1740. The Brewster family, whose great-great grandfather arrived on the Mayflower, owned this Colonial farmhouse for 250 years. Now the Bauers have lovingly renovated the home, which is listed in the National Register. Furnished with antiques and period reproductions, the inn's tasteful decor is accented with an artistic hand-stenciled wood floor and wall border. A sitting room overlooks the golf course and offers gorgeous sunset views. Charming guest bedrooms are well suited for romance, families or business. Luxury abounds with plush robes, candles, aromatherapy personal products, fresh flowers and fine linens on the handmade white oak and pencil post beds. Farm-fresh eggs are part of a scrumptious candlelight breakfast served in the Keeping Room. The extensive grounds, a Certified National Wildlife Federation Backyard Habitat, feature a koi pond, kitchen garden, orchard, grape arbor and flower gardens that welcome birds and butterflies.

Historic Interest: Hempstead house (25 miles), Fort Griwold battlefield (25 miles), Mystic Seaport (17 miles), Leffingwell House (14 m miles), USS Nautilus (23 miles), Prudence Crandall House (25 miles).

Innkeeper(s): Kate & Ron Bauer. $95-140. MC, VISA, DS, TC. 2 rooms with

PB, 1 with FP and 1 suite. Breakfast and snacks/refreshments included in rates. Types of meals: Full bkfst, country bkfst, veg bkfst, cont plus and early coffee/tea. Beds: QT. Cable TV, VCR and fireplace in room. Air conditioning. Fax, library, child care and gift shop on premises. Small meetings and family reunions hosted. Amusement parks, antiquing, art galleries, bicycling, canoeing/kayaking, fishing, golf, hiking, horseback riding, Foxwood casino, live theater, museums, parks, shopping, sporting events and wineries nearby.

Pets allowed: Must check with Innkeeper first. Only one pet in B&B at a time allowed.

Publicity: *The New London Day.*

Madison   F6

Madison Beach Hotel

PO Box 546, 94 W Wharf Rd
Madison, CT 06443-0546
(203)245-1404 Fax:(203)245-0410

Circa 1800. Since most of Connecticut's shoreline is privately owned, the Madison Beach Hotel is one of the few waterfront lodgings available. It originally was constructed as a stagecoach

stop and later became a popular vacation spot for those who stayed for a month at a time with maids and chauffeurs. Art Carney is said to have driven a Madison Beach Hotel bus here when his brother was the manager. Rooms are furnished in a variety of antiques and wallpapers. Many rooms have splendid views of the lawn and the Long Island Sound from private porches.

Innkeeper(s): Mollie Cardner. $80-225. MC, VISA, AX, DC, DS, TC. 35 rooms with PB, 6 suites and 1 conference room. Breakfast included in rates. Types of meals: Cont plus, cont, early coffee/tea, lunch, picnic lunch, dinner and room service. Beds: QT. Cable TV and phone in room. Air conditioning. Fax and copier on premises. Handicap access. Weddings, small meetings, family reunions and seminars hosted. Antiquing, fishing, live theater, shopping, sporting events and water sports nearby.

Publicity: *New England Travel.*

"The accommodations were wonderful and the service was truly exceptional."

Tidewater Inn

949 Boston Post Rd
Madison, CT 06443-3236
(203)245-8457
E-mail: tidewaterinn@aol.com

Circa 1880. Long ago, this 19th-century home was no doubt a welcome site to travelers needing a rest after a bumpy stagecoach ride. Although its days as a stagecoach stop have long since past, the inn is still a welcoming place for those needing a romantic getaway. The rooms are elegantly appointed with items such as four-poster or canopy beds, Oriental rugs and fine furnishings. The inn's sitting area is a cozy place to relax, with its fireplace and exposed beams. The one-and-a-half-acre grounds include an English garden. The inn is within walking distance to many of Madison's sites, and beaches are just a mile away.

Innkeeper(s): Jean Foy & Rich Evans. $80-185. MC, VISA, AX, PC, TC. 9 rooms with PB, 2 with FP. Breakfast included in rates. Types of meals: Full bkfst, cont and early coffee/tea. Beds: KQDT. Cable TV and one with Jacuzzi in room. Air conditioning. Antiquing, fishing, live theater, parks, shopping and water sports nearby.

Publicity: *New York Times, New Yorker and New Britain Herald.*

Middlebury   D4

Tucker Hill Inn

96 Tucker Hill Rd
Middlebury, CT 06762-2511
(203)758-8334 Fax:(203)598-0652
E-mail: tuckerhill2@yahoo.com

Circa 1923. There's a cut-out heart in the gate that opens to this handsome three-story estate framed by an old stone wall.

The spacious Colonial-style house is shaded by tall trees. Guests enjoy a parlor with fireplace and an inviting formal dining room. Guest rooms are furnished with a flourish of English country or romantic Victorian decor.

Innkeeper(s): Susan & Richard Cebelenski. $95-145. MC, VISA, AX, PC, TC. TAC10. 4 rooms, 2 with PB. Breakfast included in rates. Types of meals: Full bkfst, early coffee/tea and afternoon tea. Beds: QT. Cable TV, ceiling fan and VCR in room. Air conditioning. Fax on premises. Small meetings and family reunions hosted. Amusement parks, antiquing, golf, lake, live theater, parks, shopping, cross-country skiing and tennis nearby.

Publicity: *Star, Waterbury American Republican and Voices.*

"Thanks for a special visit. Your kindness never went unnoticed."

Mystic   E9

Harbour Inne & Cottage

15 Edgemont St
Mystic, CT 06355-2853
(860)572-9253
E-mail: harbourinne@earthlink.net

Circa 1898. Known as Charley's Place after its innkeeper, this New England inn located on the Mystic River is comfortably decorated with cedar paneling and hardwood floors throughout. A large stone fireplace and piano are featured in the common room. There is a gazebo, six-person hot tub, picnic area and boat dock on the grounds. The inn is minutes from the Olde Mystic Village, Factory Outlet Stores and casinos.

Innkeeper(s): Charles Lecouras, Jr. $55-250. TC. TAC10. 6 rooms with PB, 1 with FP and 1 cottage. Types of meals: Cont. Beds: D. Cable TV in room. Air conditioning. Spa, picnic area, gazebo and boat dock on premises. Weddings, small meetings and family reunions hosted. Greek spoken. Antiquing, fishing, golf, nautilus submarine, aquarium, casino, live theater, museums, parks, shopping, tennis and water sports nearby.

Six Broadway Inn

6 Broadway Ave
Mystic, CT 06378-1250
(860)536-6010 (888)446-9784 Fax:(860)536-5956
E-mail: geraldasullivan@cs.com
Web: www.visitmystic.com/sixbroadway

Circa 1854. One of Mystic's founding families built this pre-Civil War Victorian home, which is now part of the town's historic home tour. The interior is filled with period antiques and Victorian décor, a perfect complement to its impeccable restoration in 1997. The guest rooms include antique bedroom sets from Belgium and France, and beds are topped with fine, luxury linens. For breakfast, guests enjoy freshly baked oversized muffins, fruit salad, croissants, cereals and yogurts with gourmet coffees and teas. The inn is located in the center of downtown Mystic, close to shops, galleries, restaurants and the railroad depot.

Historic Interest: Mystic Seaport museum (2 blocks), G. Palmer House (4 miles), Denison Homestead Museum (2 miles).

Innkeeper(s): Jerry Sullivan. $90-245. MC, VISA, AX, DC, DS, PC, TC. 5 rooms with PB. Breakfast and snacks/refreshments included in rates. Types of meals: Cont plus, early coffee/tea and afternoon tea. Beds: Q. Turndown service, some with modem hook-up, data ports and cable TV in room. Air conditioning. Fax, copier and storage for bicycles and kayaks on premises. Weddings, small meetings and family reunions hosted. Antiquing, art galleries, beaches, bicycling, canoeing/kayaking, fishing, golf, hiking, live theater, museums, parks, shopping and wineries nearby.

Publicity: *New London Day, HGTV and Sixty minutes II.*

New Milford   D3

Homestead Inn

5 Elm St
New Milford, CT 06776-2995
(860)354-4080
Web: www.homesteadct.com

Circa 1853. Built by the first of three generations of John Prime Treadwells, the inn was established 80 years later.

Victorian architecture includes high ceilings, spacious rooms and large verandas. There is a small motel adjacent to the inn.

Innkeeper(s): Rolf & Peggy Hammer. $102-134. MC, VISA, AX, DC, DS. TAC10. 14 rooms with PB. Types of meals: Cont plus. Beds: KQDT. Cable TV and phone in room. Air conditioning.

Publicity: *Litchfield County Times, ABC Home Show and Food & Wine.*

"One of the homiest inns in the U.S.A. with most hospitable hosts. A rare bargain to boot."

New Preston   C3

Boulders Inn

East Shore Rd, Rt 45
New Preston, CT 06777
(860)868-0541 (800)55B-OULDE Fax:(860)868-1925
E-mail: boulders@bouldersinn.com

Circa 1895. Views of Lake Waramaug and its wooded shores can be seen from the living room and most of the guest rooms and cottages of this country inn. The terrace is open in the summer for cocktails, dinner and sunsets over the lake. Antique furnishings, a basement game room, and a beach house with a hanging wicker swing are all part of Boulders Inn. There is a private beach with boats, and bicycles are available.

Innkeeper(s): Kees & Ulla Adema. $225-395. MC, VISA, AX, PC, TC. TAC10. 17 rooms with PB, 11 with FP, 2 suites, 8 cottages and 1 conference room. Breakfast, afternoon tea and dinner included in rates. Types of meals: Gourmet bkfst, early coffee/tea and room service. MAP. Beds: KQ. TV, phone, turndown service and ceiling fan in room. Air conditioning. VCR, fax, copier, swimming, bicycles and library on premises. Handicap access. Weddings, small meetings, family reunions and seminars hosted. Dutch, German, French and Spanish spoken. Antiquing, fishing, golf, live theater, parks, shopping, downhill skiing, cross-country skiing, tennis and water sports nearby.

Publicity: *New York Times, Travel & Leisure and Country Inns.*

Niantic   E8

Inn at Harbor Hill Marina

60 Grand St
Niantic, CT 06357
(860)739-0331 Fax:(860)691-3078
E-mail: info@innharborhill.com
Web: www.innharborhill.com

Circa 1890. Arise each morning to panoramic views of the Niantic River harbor at this traditional, late-19th century inn. Travel by boat or car to neighboring cities and enjoy the finest culture New England has to offer. This three-story, harbor-front inn offers rooms filled with antiques and seaside décor. Some have balconies. Experience true adventure at sea on a chartered fishing trip, or spend the day in town shopping or relaxing on the beach, all within walking distance. During the summer, guests can listen to outdoor concerts in the park while overlooking Long Island Sound. Whatever the day has in store, guests can start each morning the right way with a fresh, continental breakfast on the wraparound porch overlooking the marina.

Historic Interest: Florence Griswold Museum (7 miles), Mystic Aquarium (15 miles), Olde Mystic Village (15 miles), Mystic Seaport (15 miles).

Innkeeper(s): Andrea Bunnell. $90-195. MC, VISA, AX, PC, TC. TAC10. 9 rooms, 8 with PB, 1 suite and 1 conference room. Breakfast and snacks/refreshments included in rates. Types of meals: Cont plus. Beds: QT. Cable TV and ceiling fan in room. Air conditioning. Fax and copier on premises. Weddings, small meetings and family reunions hosted. Italian, French and Spanish spoken. Antiquing, art galleries, beaches, canoeing/kayaking, fishing, golf, live theater, museums, parks, shopping, water sports and wineries nearby.

Norfolk   A3

Blackberry River Inn

538 Greenwoods Road W
Norfolk, CT 06058
(860)542-5100 Fax:(860)542-1763
E-mail: blackberry.river.inn@snet.net
Web: www.blackberryriverinn.com

Circa 1763. In the National Register, the Colonial buildings that comprise the inn are situated on 27 acres. A library with cherry paneling, three parlors and a breakfast room are offered for guests' relaxation. Guest rooms are furnished with antiques and a Laura Ashley decor. Guests can choose from rooms in the main house with a fireplace or suites with a fireplace or Jacuzzi. The Cottage includes a fireplace and Jacuzzi. A full country breakfast is included.

Innkeeper(s): Jose Lucas. $75-215. MC, VISA, AX, PC. 18 rooms with PB and 1 cottage. Breakfast and afternoon tea included in rates. Types of meals: Full bkfst. Cable TV in room. Air conditioning. Swimming, library, hiking and fishing on premises. Weddings hosted. Antiquing, canoeing/kayaking, golf, horseback riding, sleigh rides, hay rides, auto racing, music festivals, shopping, downhill skiing, cross-country skiing and tennis nearby.

Manor House

69 Maple Ave
Norfolk, CT 06058-0447
(860)542-5690 Fax:(860)542-5690
E-mail: innkeeper@manorhouse-norfolk.com
Web: www.manorhouse-norfolk.com

Circa 1898. Charles Spofford, designer of London's subway, built this home with many gables, exquisite cherry paneling and grand staircase. There are Moorish arches and Tiffany win-

dows. Guests can enjoy hot-mulled cider after a sleigh ride, hay ride, or horse and carriage drive along the country lanes nearby. The inn was named by "Discerning Traveler" as Connecticut's most romantic hideaway.

Historic Interest: Norfolk is a historic community with many historic homes; the Yale Chamber Music Festival is held at one such historic estate. Litchfield County has many museums and historic homes to tour.
Innkeeper(s): Hank & Diane Tremblay. $125-250. MC, VISA, AX, DS, PC, TC. TAC10. 9 rooms with PB, 4 with FP, 1 suite and 1 conference room. Breakfast and afternoon tea included in rates. Types of meals: Gourmet bkfst, early coffee/tea and room service. Beds: KQDT. Ceiling fan and three with double whirlpools in room. Fax and library on premises. Weddings, small meetings, family reunions and seminars hosted. French spoken. Antiquing, fishing, live theater, parks, shopping, downhill skiing, cross-country skiing, sporting events and water sports nearby.
Publicity: *Good Housekeeper, Gourmet, Boston Globe, Philadelphia Inquirer, Innsider, Rhode Island Monthly, Gourmet, National Geographic Traveler and New York Times.*

"Queen Victoria, eat your heart out."

North Stonington E9

Antiques & Accommodations

32 Main St
North Stonington, CT 06359-1709
(860)535-1736 (800)554-7829 Fax:(800)535-2613
Web: www.visitmystic.com/antiques

Circa 1861. Set amongst the backdrop of an acre of herb, edible flower, perennial and cutting gardens, this Victorian treasure offers a romantic location for a weekend getaway. Rooms filled with antiques boast four-poster canopy beds and fresh flowers surrounded by a soft, pleasing

decor. Honeymooners or couples celebrating an anniversary are presented with special amenities such as balloons, champagne and heart-shaped waffles for breakfast. Candlelit breakfasts include unique items such as edible flowers along with the delicious entrees. Historic Mystic Seaport and Foxwood's Casino are just minutes from the inn.

Historic Interest: Historic Mystic and Stonington Village are eight miles from the inn, Newport is a 38-mile drive.
Innkeeper(s): Ann & Tom Gray. $110-229. MC, VISA. 5 rooms with PB and 2 suites. Breakfast included in rates. Types of meals: Full bkfst and gourmet dinner. Beds: Q. Cable TV and VCR in room. Air conditioning. Antiquing and fishing nearby.
Publicity: *Country Inns, Woman's Day, New London Day, Connecticut Magazine and Connecticut Public Radio.*

"I loved the great attention to detail and authenticity. A lovely labor of love."

Norwalk G2

Silvermine Tavern

194 Perry Ave
Norwalk, CT 06850-1123
(203)847-4558 Fax:(203)847-9171
E-mail: silvtavfcw@aol.com
Web: www.silverminetavern.com

Circa 1790. The Silvermine consists of the Old Mill, the Country Store, the Coach House and the Tavern itself. Primitive

paintings and furnishings, as well as family heirlooms, decorate the inn. Guest rooms and dining rooms overlook the Old Mill, the waterfall and swans gliding across the millpond. Some guest rooms offer items such as canopy bed or private decks. In the summer, guests can dine al fresco and gaze at the mill pond.

Historic Interest: Lockwood Matthews Mansion (10 miles).
Innkeeper(s): Frank Whitman, Jr. $110-145. MC, VISA, AX, DC, CB, PC, TC. TAC10. 10 rooms with PB and 1 suite. Breakfast included in rates. Types of meals: Cont, lunch and dinner. Beds: QDT. Some canopied beds in room. Air conditioning. VCR, fax and copier on premises. Weddings, small meetings, family reunions and seminars hosted. Antiquing, fishing, parks and shopping nearby.

Old Mystic E9

The Old Mystic Inn

52 Main St, Box 733
Old Mystic, CT 06372-0733
(860)572-9422
E-mail: omysticinn@aol.com
Web: visitmystic.com/oldmysticinn

Circa 1784. Charles Vincent ran the Old Mystic Bookstore from this house for 35 years. Although it once housed 20,000 old books and maps, it has been renovated to a bed & breakfast inn. The old maps and drawings hung around the stairwell have been preserved. There are wide board floors and stone fireplaces in all the rooms. Furnishings include replica Colonial period pieces.

Innkeeper(s): Michael Cardillo. $125-185. MC, VISA, AX, PC, TC. TAC10. 8 rooms with PB, 5 with FP. Breakfast and snacks/refreshments included in rates. Types of meals: Full bkfst, country bkfst and early coffee/tea. Beds: Q. Two with whirlpool tubs in room. Air conditioning. Gazebo and Saturday evenings complimentary wine and cheese is served on premises. Weddings, small meetings, family reunions and seminars hosted. Antiquing, parks and water sports nearby.
Publicity: *New Jersey Monthly and New London Day.*

"A real delight and the breakfast was sumptuous!"

Red Brook Inn

PO Box 237
Old Mystic, CT 06372-0237
(860)572-0349
E-mail: redbrookin@aol.com
Web: www.redbrookinn.com

Circa 1740. If there was no other reason to visit Mystic, a charming town brimming with activities, the Red Brook Inn would be reason enough. The Crary Homestead features three unique rooms with working fireplaces, while the Haley Tavern offers seven guest rooms, some with canopy beds and fireplaces. Two have whirlpool tubs. Innkeeper Ruth Keyes has beautiful antiques decorating her inn. Guests are sure to enjoy her wonderful country breakfasts. A special winter dinner takes three days to complete and she prepares it over an open hearth. In addition to a full breakfast, afternoon and evening

beverages are provided. The aquarium, Mystic Seaport Museum, a cider mill, casinos and many shops are only minutes away.

Historic Interest: Mystic Seaport Museum.

Innkeeper(s): Ruth Keyes. $129-189. MC, VISA, AX, DS, PC, TC. 10 rooms with PB, 7 with FP and 3 conference rooms. Breakfast included in rates. Types of meals: Full bkfst. Beds: QDT. VCR, tennis, library, terrace and parlors on premises. Small meetings, family reunions and seminars hosted. Amusement parks, antiquing, fishing, casino, live theater, museums, parks, shopping, sporting events and water sports nearby.

Publicity: *Westerly Sun, Travel & Leisure, Yankee, New York, Country Decorating, Philadelphia Inquirer, National Geographic Traveler and Discerning Traveler.*

"The staff is wonderful. You made us feel at home. Thank you for your hospitality."

Old Saybrook   F7

Deacon Timothy Pratt Bed & Breakfast Inn

325 Main St
Old Saybrook, CT 06475
(860)395-1229 Fax:(860)395-4748
E-mail: shelley.nobile@snet.net

Circa 1746. Built prior to the Revolutionary War, this slate blue house is an outstanding example of center chimney Colonial-style architecture. Listed in the National Register, the inn's original features include six working fireplaces, hand-hewn beams, wide board floors, a beehive oven and built-in cupboard. Four-poster and canopy beds, Oriental rugs and period furnishings accentuate the New England atmosphere. Fireplaces and Jacuzzi tubs invite romance and relaxation. On weekends a multi-course, candlelight breakfast is served in the elegant dining room. Enjoy homemade muffins or scones, fresh fruit and entrees such  as heart-shaped blueberry pancakes or eggs Benedict. Among the variety of local historic house museums to visit, the William Hart house is across the street. The area offers many shopping and dining opportunities as well as galleries to explore. Beaches, a state park and river cruises also are available.

Innkeeper(s): Shelley Nobile. $100-225. MC, VISA, AX, PC, TC. 6 rooms with PB, 4 with FP, 3 suites and 1 conference room. Breakfast, afternoon tea and snacks/refreshments included in rates. Types of meals: Full bkfst, veg bkfst and cont plus. Beds: QDT. Cable TV, phone, turndown service, Four with fireplaces, four with Jacuzzi tubs, twin roll-away bed, cot and twin roll-away available, comfortable sitting areas, working fireplaces, phones and modem lines in room. Air conditioning. Fax, library, guest refrigerator with complimentary soft drinks, tea, cookies, sherry and massage therapy on premises. Weddings, small meetings, family reunions and seminars hosted. Antiquing, art galleries, beaches, bicycling, canoeing/kayaking, fishing, golf, hiking, horseback riding, casinos, spas, playhouses, factory outlet malls, live theater, museums, parks, shopping, downhill skiing, cross-country skiing, sporting events, tennis and wineries nearby.

Plymouth Village   A2

Shelton House B&B

663 Main St (Rt 6)
Plymouth Village, CT 06782
(860)283-4616 Fax:(860)283-4616
E-mail: sheltonhbb@prodigy.net

Circa 1825. This home's most famous resident was a carriage maker whose wares were sold as far away as Chicago. The Greek Revival is listed in the National Register and was a stop

on the town's bicentennial homes tour. Antiques and reproductions decorate the interior. Beds are topped with fine quality linens and soft, fluffy comforters. There are  three tranquil acres of grounds, shaded by trees. After breakfast, guests can take a trip to historic Litchfield, which is just 12 miles down the road. Antique shops, restaurants, skiing and other activities are all nearby.

Innkeeper(s): Pat & Bill Doherty. $75-95. PC, TC. 4 rooms, 2 with PB. Breakfast and afternoon tea included in rates. Types of meals: Full bkfst. Beds: QDT. Robes, window fans and alarm clocks in room. Air conditioning. Fax, pineapple fountain and perrenial gardens on premises. Amusement parks, antiquing, fishing, golf, soaring center, live theater, museums, parks, shopping and cross-country skiing nearby.

"Accommodations were excellent. Breakfast was great. I was pampered and I loved it."

Ridgefield   F2

West Lane Inn

22 West Ln
Ridgefield, CT 06877-4914
(203)438-7323 Fax:(203)438-7325
E-mail: westlaneinn@aol.com
Web: www.westlaneinn.com

Circa 1849. This National Register Victorian mansion on two acres features an enormous front veranda filled with black wrought iron chairs and tables overlooking a manicured lawn. A polished oak staircase rises to a third-floor landing and lounge. Chandeliers, wall sconces and floral wallpapers help to establish an intimate atmosphere. Although the rooms do not have antiques, they feature amenities such as heated towel racks, extra-thick towels, air conditioning, remote control cable TVs, VCRs and desks.

Innkeeper(s): Maureen Mayer & Deborah Prieger. $110-175. MC, VISA, AX, DC, DS. 17 rooms with PB, 2 with FP. Breakfast included in rates. Types of meals: Cont and room service. Beds: Q. TV, phone, ceiling fan and VCR in room. Air conditioning. Small meetings hosted. Antiquing, fishing, live theater, shopping and cross-country skiing nearby.

Publicity: *Stanford-Advocate, Greenwich Times and Home & Away Connecticut.*

"Thank you for the hospitality you showed us. The rooms are comfortable and quiet. I haven't slept this soundly in weeks."

Riverton

Old Riverton Inn

436 E River Rd
Riverton, CT 06065
(860)379-8678 (800)378-1796 Fax:(860)379-1006
E-mail: mark.telford@snet.net
Web: rivertoninn.com

Circa 1796. Originally a stagecoach stop between Hartford and Albany and now listed in the National Register of Historic Places, this Colonial inn sits on an acre in a quaint village setting overlooking the Farmington River. The enclosed Grindstone Terrace, named after the floor made of quarried grindstone from Nova Scotia, features a raised fireplace and white wrought iron furniture. Decorated in early-American style, one of the guest bedrooms boasts a fireplace. A country breakfast is served in the dining room, and the Hobby Horse Bar with Vermont flagstone floors has saddles on kegs for bar stools.

Historic Interest: Hitchcock Museum, Stone Museum, Village of Riverton.

Innkeeper(s): Mark & Pauline Telford. $85-195. MC, VISA, AX, DC, DS, TC. TAC10. 12 rooms, 11 with PB, 1 with FP, 1 suite and 1 conference room. Breakfast included in rates. Types of meals: Full bkfst, country bkfst, lunch and dinner. Beds: KQDT. Cable TV, phone and fireplace in room. Air conditioning. Fax, copier and library on premises. Weddings, small meetings, family reunions and seminars hosted. Antiquing, beaches, bicycling, canoeing/kayaking, fishing, golf, hiking, horseback riding, museums, parks, shopping, cross-country skiing and wineries nearby.

Pets allowed: limited rooms, prior approval only.

Somersville   B7

The Old Mill Inn B&B

63 Maple St
Somersville, CT 06072
(860)763-1473

Circa 1860. Giant maples and landscaped grounds create a private, peaceful ambiance at this Greek Revival home, secluded along the banks of the Scantic River. There is a hammock set up for those hoping for a nap among the trees, or perhaps you'd prefer a trip up the river on the inn's canoe. The grounds also are decorated with a gazebo. Rooms feature romantic decor, with comforters, fine linens and furnishings such as a brass bed or a wicker loveseat. In the evenings, hors d'oeuvres and beverages are served in the fireplaced parlor. One of your innkeepers is an accomplished chef and professional cake decorator, so guests should expect something wonderful during the gourmet breakfast service. The innkeepers provide bicycles for those who wish to tour the area, and there is a spa on premises. The inn is often the site of weddings, parties and family reunions.

Innkeeper(s): Jim & Stephanie D'Amour. $85-95. PC, TC. 5 rooms. Types of meals: Gourmet bkfst and early coffee/tea. Beds: KD. Sun deck in room. Spa and bicycles on premises. Weddings and family reunions hosted. Antiquing, fishing, museums, Basketball Hall of Fame, golfing, horseback riding and shopping nearby.

"We loved staying here! You are both delightful. P.S. We slept like a log."

Tolland   B7

Old Babcock Tavern

484 Mile Hill Rd (route 31)
Tolland, CT 06084-3606
(860)875-1239
E-mail: babcockbb@juno.com

Circa 1720. This 18th-century post-and-beam home is listed in the National Register. The innkeepers have decorated their historic gem in a warm, inviting style with Early American furnishings, and they are happy to share their vast knowledge of restoration upon request. Rich wood panels and polished floors add to the interior's charm. Breakfasts are served by candlelight to the pleasant sounds of classical music. The innkeepers offer a morning feast with juice, coffee, tea, freshly baked muffins, herbed potatoes, eggs, turkey ham, fruit and homemade apple pie. The inn is close to many attractions, including an herb farm, historic jail, Old Sturbridge village and plenty of antique shops.

Innkeeper(s): Barb & Stu Danforth. $70-85. PC, TC. 3 rooms with PB, 1 with FP and 1 suite. Breakfast included in rates. Types of meals: Gourmet bkfst and early coffee/tea. Beds: D. Window Fans in room. Antiquing, fishing, herb Farms, live theater, parks, shopping and sporting events nearby.

Tolland Inn

63 Tolland Green, PO Box 717
Tolland, CT 06084-0717
(860)872-0800 (877)465-0800 Fax:(860)870-7958
E-mail: tollinn@ntplx.net

Circa 1790. This late 18th-century Colonial offers seven guest rooms, three with sitting rooms. A first-floor room and two second-floor suites offer both a hot tub and fireplace. All rooms have private baths, air conditioning and phones. The inn is decorated in antiques and hand-built furniture throughout. Susan was raised in Nantucket and is a third-generation innkeeper, while Stephen is a designer and builder of fine furniture. Guests are invited to enjoy breakfast and afternoon tea, fireside in cool weather. The inn is convenient to UCONN, Old Sturbridge Village, Brimfield Antique Shows, Caprilands.

Innkeeper(s): Susan & Stephen Beeching. $95-179. MC, VISA, AX, DC, CB, DS, PC, TC. TAC10. 7 rooms with PB, 4 with FP, 3 suites and 1 conference room. Breakfast and afternoon tea included in rates. Types of meals: Gourmet bkfst and early coffee/tea. Beds: KQDT. Phone in room. VCR, fax, spa and library on premises. Small meetings, family reunions and seminars hosted. Antiquing, fishing, live theater, parks, shopping, cross-country skiing and sporting events nearby.

Publicity: *Journal Inquirer, Hartford Courant and Tolland County Times.*

Watertown   D4

Addington's B&B

1002 Middlebury Rd
Watertown, CT 06795-3025
(860)274-2647 (877)250-9711

Circa 1840. Addington's is a beautifully preserved Italianate home, once part of a 19th-century dairy farm. Guests can relax on the porch swing or take in the view from the widow's walk. The interior is decorated in country style accented by quilts, dolls and collectibles, many of which are made by the innkeeper and available for purchase. One guest room includes a Jacuzzi tub. The B&B is close to a multitude of antique shops, as well as outdoor activities.

Historic Interest: Litchfield Country (5 miles), antique shops.

Innkeeper(s): Jan Lynn & Eric Addington. $90-145. MC, VISA, PC, TC. 4 rooms, 2 with PB. Breakfast and snacks/refreshments included in rates. Types of meals: Full bkfst, veg bkfst, cont plus, cont and early coffee/tea. Beds: KQ. Cable TV and VCR in room. Library on premises. Amusement parks, antiquing, art galleries, beaches, canoeing/kayaking, fishing, golf, hiking, horseback riding, museums, parks, shopping, downhill skiing, cross-country skiing, sporting events, tennis and water sports nearby.

Westbrook   F7

Talcott House

161 Seaside Ave
Westbrook, CT 06498
(860)399-5020

Circa 1890. This restored Newport-style Georgian manor offers an ideal location on Long Island Sound. From the expansive lawn, guests can enjoy the view as the sun sets over the Sound.

The home is less than a mile from Pilots Point Marina. The suites all face the oceanfront; one boasts a private veranda. The inn is listed on the local historic register. The Mystic Seaport, Gillette Castle, Essex Village and the Essex Steam Train are among the area's attractions.

Innkeeper(s): Barbara Slusser. $125-175. MC, VISA, AX, PC, TC. 4 rooms with PB. Breakfast included in rates. Types of meals: Gourmet bkfst, cont plus and early coffee/tea. Beds: QD. Ceiling fan in room. VCR, swimming, piano and refrigerator on premises. Handicap access. Weddings, small meetings and family reunions hosted. Antiquing, art galleries, beaches, bicycling, canoeing/kayaking, fishing, hiking, live theater, parks, shopping, tennis, water sports and wineries nearby.

Welcome Inn

433 Essex Rd
Westbrook, CT 06498-1504
(860)399-2500 Fax:(860)399-1840
E-mail: r.bambino@snet.net

Circa 1895. This handsome Victorian farmhouse is located on a half acre of grounds with tall trees, mature plantings and flowerbeds. A descendant of one of the town's founding fathers built the home, which features antiques and family heirlooms. A full breakfast is prepared and often features fresh vegetables and regional fruits from neighboring orchards. Westbrook, on the Connecticut coastline, offers appealing historic homes and museums. Popular activities include outlet shopping, the Essex Steam Train, river cruises, local theatre and the Goodspeed Opera House. There are more than 400 antique dealers in the surrounding area. In winter, a popular activity is bundling up for a romantic carriage ride complete with sleigh bells and white horses.

Innkeeper(s): Helen Spence. $79-149. MC, VISA, AX, PC, TC. TAC5. 4 rooms with PB. Breakfast and snacks/refreshments included in rates. Types of meals: Gourmet bkfst, country bkfst, veg bkfst, cont plus, cont, early coffee/tea and gourmet dinner. Beds: QD. Cable TV, ceiling fan, split of wine & candies and masseuse upon request made in advance in room. Air conditioning. Fax, copier and library on premises. Weddings, small meetings, family reunions and seminars hosted. Antiquing, art galleries, beaches, bicycling, canoeing/kayaking, fishing, golf, hiking, live theater, museums, parks, shopping, tennis, water sports and wineries nearby.

Westport   G3

The Inn at National Hall

2 Post Rd W
Westport, CT 06880-4203
(203)221-1351 (800)628-4255 Fax:(203)221-0276
E-mail: info@innatnationalhall.com
Web: www.innatnationalhall.com

Circa 1873. This exquisite inn is consistently named as one of the nation's best, and it is quite deserving of its four-star and five-diamond rating. The inn is situated on the Saugatuck River and guests can meander by the water on the boardwalk. The renovation of this National Register gem cost upwards of $15 million, and the result is evident. Rooms are masterfully appointed with the finest fabrics and furnishings. The Acorn Room is a stunning example. Walls are painted a deep red hue, and guests slumber atop a massive canopy bed enveloped in luxurious yellow fabrics. The conference room is filled with regal touches. Guests can enjoy a European-style continental breakfast in the Drawing Room. There are ample amenities, valet and room service. Gourmet dinners can be enjoyed at the inn's restaurant. Westport's posh boutiques, art galleries and antique shops are a stone's throw away.

Innkeeper(s): Gary Bedell. $225-700. MC, VISA, AX, DC, TC. TAC10. 16 rooms with PB, 1 with FP, 8 suites and 1 conference room. Breakfast included in rates. Types of meals: Cont plus, early coffee/tea and gourmet dinner. Beds: KQT. Cable TV, phone, turndown service and VCR in room. Air conditioning. Fax and copier on premises. Weddings, small meetings, family reunions and seminars hosted. Antiquing, beaches, live theater, parks, shopping and tennis nearby.

Publicity: *Architectural Digest and Country Inns.*

Wethersfield   C6

Chester Bulkley House B&B

184 Main St
Wethersfield, CT 06109-2340
(860)563-4236 Fax:(860)257-8266
E-mail: chesterbulkley@aol.com

Circa 1830. Offering the best of both worlds, this renovated Greek Revival structure is ideally located in the historic village of Old Weathersfield with its quaint sites, museums and shops, yet the inn also boasts a 10-minute drive to downtown Hartford with ballet, Broadway shows, opera and the symphony. Hand-carved woodwork, wide pine floors, working fireplaces and period pieces enhance the comfortable ambiance. Cut flowers, pillow chocolates and other thoughtful treats ensure a pleasant and gracious stay for business or leisure.

Innkeeper(s): Tom Aufiero. $90-105. MC, VISA, AX, DS, TC. 5 rooms, 3 with PB and 1 suite. Breakfast included in rates. Types of meals: Full bkfst, early coffee/tea, afternoon tea and room service. Beds: KQDT. Ceiling fan in room. Air conditioning. Fax on premises. Weddings, small meetings, family reunions and seminars hosted. Antiquing, fishing, live theater, parks, shopping, downhill skiing and sporting events nearby.

Woodstock   B9

Elias Child House B&B

50 Perrin Rd
Woodstock, CT 06281
(860)974-9836 (877)974-9836
E-mail: tfelice@compuserve.com
Web: www.eliaschildhouse.com

Circa 1700. Nine fireplaces warm this heritage three-story colonial home, referred to as "the mansion house" by early settlers. There are two historic cooking hearths, including a beehive oven. Original floors, twelve-over-twelve windows and paneling remain. A bountiful breakfast is served fireside in the dining room and a screened porch and a patio provide nesting spots for reading and relaxing. The inn's grounds are spacious and offer a pool and hammocks. Woodland walks on the 47 acres and antiquing are popular activities.

Innkeeper(s): Anthony Felice, Jr. & MaryBeth Gorke-Felice. $85-135. MC, VISA, AX, DS, PC, TC. TAC10. 3 rooms with PB and 1 suite. Breakfast included in rates. Types of meals: Full bkfst and early coffee/tea. Beds: QDT. Turndown service and fireplace in room. Air conditioning. VCR, fax, copier, swimming, bicycles, hearth-cooking demonstrations and cross-country skiing on premises. Small meetings and family reunions hosted.

Pets allowed: Small dogs with cage.

Publicity: *Time Out New York, Best Fares Magazine, Distinction, Wine Gazette and Car & Driver Magazine.*

"Comfortable rooms and delightful country ambiance."

Delaware

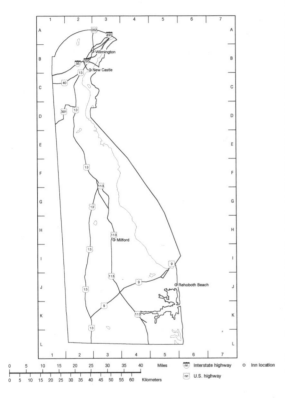

	1	2	3	4	5	6	7	
A								A
B								B
C								C
D								D
E								E
F								F
G								G
H								H
I								I
J								J
K								K
L	1	2	3	4	5	6	7	L

0 5 10 15 20 25 30 35 40 Miles   [nn] Interstate highway   o Inn location
0 5 10 15 20 25 30 35 40 45 50 55 60 Kilometers   [nn] U.S. highway

Milford   H3

Causey Mansion Bed & Breakfast

2 Causey Ave
Milford, DE 19963-1936
(302)422-0979

Circa 1763. Originally a Georgian-style home, this stately inn was renovated in 1849 to a Greek Revival mansion. It is on the National Register of Historic Places, and was the home of two governors, one from the 18th century and one from the 19th century. Two of the original slave quarters are still on the three-acre property near the beaches of Delaware Bay and the Atlantic Ocean. The inn itself has a large porch and a solarium, and sits on a meticulously landscaped yard. It offers five guest bedrooms. A hearty breakfast is served each morning. Guests may then explore the beautiful natural and historic surround-

ings. Swimming, tennis and golf, fishing, boating and antiquing are available nearby. Or guests may prefer to relax with a book in the library or stroll through the formal boxwood gardens.
Historic Interest: John Dilkinson Mansion (25 miles), Ross Mansion (25 miles).
Innkeeper(s): Kenneth & Frances Novak. $85. MC, VISA, PC, TC. 5 rooms, 4 with PB and 1 suite. Breakfast and snacks/refreshments included in rates. Types of meals: Full bkfst and early coffee/tea. Beds: QDT. Air conditioning. VCR and library on premises. Weddings and small meetings hosted. Antiquing, beaches, canoeing/kayaking, fishing, golf, live theater, museums, shopping and tennis nearby.

The Towers B&B

101 NW Front St
Milford, DE 19963-1022
(302)422-3814 (800)366-3814
E-mail: mispillion@ezol.com
Web: www.mispillion.com

Circa 1783. Once a simple colonial house, this ornate Steamboat Gothic fantasy features every imaginable Victorian architectural detail, all added in 1891. There are 10 distinct styles of gingerbread as well as towers, turrets, gables, porches and bays. Inside, chestnut and cherry wood-work, window seats and stained-glass windows are complemented with  American and French antiques. The back garden boasts a gazebo porch and swimming pool. Ask for the splendid Tower Room or Rapunzel Suite.
Historic Interest: Historic districts in Milford, town of Lewes, Dickinson Plantation, historic city of Dover.
Innkeeper(s): Daniel & Rhonda Bond. $95-135. MC, VISA, AX. TAC15. 6 rooms with PB and 2 suites. Breakfast included in rates. Beds: QD. Ceiling fan in room. Air conditioning. Swimming on premises. Russian spoken. Antiquing, fishing, live theater, parks, shopping and water sports nearby.
Publicity: *Washington Post, Baltimore Sun, Washingtonian and Mid-Atlantic Country.*

"I felt as if I were inside a beautiful Victorian Christmas card, surrounded by all the things Christmas should be."

New Castle   B2

Armitage Inn

2 The Strand
New Castle, DE 19720-4826
(302)328-6618 Fax:(302)324-1163
E-mail: armitageinn@earthlink.net
Web: www.armitageinn.com

Circa 1732. The major portion of this historic home was constructed in the early 1730s, but the back wing may have been constructed in the 17th century. For centuries, the Armitage

has been a place of elegance, and its current state as a country inn is no exception. Deluxe bed linens, fluffy towels, canopy beds and whirlpool tubs are just a few of the romantic amenities guests might find in their quarters. Gourmet coffee and teas accompany the breakfasts of fruit, cereal, yogurt, homemade baked goods and a special entree.

Innkeeper(s): Stephen Marks. $110-185. MC, VISA, AX, DS. TAC10. 5 rooms with PB, 3 with FP. Breakfast included in rates. Types of meals: Gourmet bkfst. Beds: KQ. Cable TV, phone, ceiling fan, whirlpool bath in two rooms and hair dryer in room. Air conditioning. Fax and copier on premises. Amusement parks, antiquing, fishing, riverwalk, Battery Park, summer concerts, live theater, parks, shopping and tennis nearby.

"I could not have dreamed of a lovelier place to wake up on Christmas morning."

William Penn Guest House

206 Delaware St
New Castle, DE 19720-4816
(302)328-7736 Fax:(302)328-0403

Circa 1682. William Penn slept here. In fact, his host Arnoldus de LaGrange witnessed the ceremony in which Penn gained possession of the Three Lower Colonies. Mrs. Burwell, who lived next door to the historic house, "gained possession" of the house one day about 44 years ago while her husband was away. After recovering from his wife's surprise purchase, Mr. Burwell rolled up his sleeves and began restoring the house. Guests may stay in the very room slept in by Penn.

Innkeeper(s): Irma & Richard Burwell. $70-89. MC, VISA, PC, TC. 4 rooms, 1 with PB. Types of meals: Cont. Beds: KDT. Phone in room. Museums nearby.

Publicity: *Asbury Press.*

"An enjoyable stay, as usual. We'll return in the spring."

Rehoboth Beach   J5

Lord Hamilton Seaside Inn B&B

20 Brooklyn Ave
Rehoboth Beach, DE 19971
(302)227-6960 (877)227-6960
E-mail: innkeeper@lordhamilton.com
Web: www.lordhamilton.com

Circa 1871. Encounter endless ocean views at this vintage Victorian inn, situated less than half a block from the beach. Antique furnishings blend well with English country decor, creating a comfortable charm. The parlor, with a wood stove, is perfect for playing games, watching a video or finding a book from the reading library. A generous amount of windows encourage seaside gazing and lots of light in some of the well-appointed guest bedrooms. Breakfast is a satisfying assortment of delicious foods served in the pretty Sunroom. Relax in the wicker rockers on the wraparound porch, enjoy the flower gardens, or head for the water.

Historic Interest: Anna Hazzard House (.2 miles), Rehoboth Art League Complex (1 mile), Cannonball House (.5 miles), Fisher Martin House (5 miles), Shipcarpenter's Square (5 miles), Zwaandael Museum (5 miles), Cape Henlopen State Park Grounds (1 mile).

Innkeeper(s): Grady Thompson. $95-225. MC, VISA, PC, TC. 6 rooms with PB and 2 suites. Breakfast included in rates. Types of meals: Veg bkfst and cont plus. Beds: KQ. Ceiling fan, canopy beds and antique furnishings in room. Air conditioning. VCR, library, beach chairs, towels, coolers available for guests and wraparound porch w/ocean views on premises. Small meetings

and family reunions hosted. German and French spoken. Antiquing, art galleries, beaches, bicycling, fishing, golf, hiking, Cape May-Lewes ferry, Rehoboth outlets, Cape Henlopen State Park, Delaware National Seashore, museums, parks, shopping, tennis, water sports and wineries nearby.

Publicity: *Coast Press, The Cape Gazette, Coastal Living and Sandra Soule's Mid Atlantic B&B Inn Review.*

Wilmington   B3

Darley Manor Inn

3701 Philadelphia Pike
Wilmington, DE 19703-3413
(302)792-2127 (800)824-4703 Fax:(302)798-6143
E-mail: darley@darinn.com

Circa 1790. Charles Dickens once stayed in this 18th-century Colonial manor, and one of the guest rooms bears his name. Tasteful rooms are furnished with period antiques and reproductions. One of the suites includes porch railings from the "White House" in Richmond, Va., while two suites boast working fireplaces. A leisurely, full breakfast is served in the dining room with a selection of entrees. Darley Manor is close to many restaurants, shops and Brandywine Valley attractions.

Historic Interest: The Longwood Gardens, Old New Castle, Brandywine River Museum and historic Philadelphia are all within 30 minutes from the inn.

Innkeeper(s): Ray & Judith Hester. $95-139. MC, VISA, AX, DC, DS, TC. TAC10. 6 rooms with PB, 3 with FP and 4 suites. Breakfast, afternoon tea and snacks/refreshments included in rates. Types of meals: Full bkfst, cont plus and early coffee/tea. Beds: Q. Cable TV, phone, turndown service, ceiling fan, VCR and suites with refrigerator in room. Air conditioning. Fax, garden Jacuzzi in season and business center on premises. Antiquing, live theater, parks, shopping and sporting events nearby.

Publicity: *Wilmington News Journal.*

"Comfort cannot be beat and hospitality is tops. It is truly a world apart."

White House Bed & Breakfast

2311 Newport Gap Pike (The Cedars)
Wilmington, DE 19808
(302)999-1495 Fax:(302)994-3914

Circa 1902. Previously called the Spring Hill Estate, this Colonial Revival home is embellished with elegant Victorian furnishings and accents. The innkeepers are proud of the personal attention given to make each stay a cherished one. A spacious living room boasts cozy sitting areas, movie entertainment and a fireplace. Large guest bedrooms feature antique brass or canopy beds with quilts or comforters and Oriental carpets on hardwood floors. Wicker, lace, crystal, soft music and a fresh rose create a setting on the terrace for an entree of banana pancakes, Belgian waffles or an omelette. Dinners can be arranged with advance notice. Three-and-a-half acres of appealing landscaping include trees, plants, a gazebo and lily pond with frogs and fish. The grounds are perfect for weddings or other special occasions.

Historic Interest: Longwood Gardens (12 miles), Winterthor Museum (7 miles), Hagley Museum (4 miles), Brandywine River Museum (14 miles).

Innkeeper(s): Eric & Sandra Semke. $98. MC, VISA, TC. 4 rooms. Breakfast and snacks/refreshments included in rates. Types of meals: Gourmet bkfst, country bkfst, veg bkfst, early coffee/tea and afternoon tea. Beds: QD. Turndown service and ceiling fan in room. Air conditioning. VCR, fax and spa on premises. Weddings, small meetings and family reunions hosted. Antiquing, art galleries, beaches, canoeing/kayaking, fishing, golf, hiking, horseback riding, museums, parks, shopping, sporting events, tennis and wineries nearby.

"My extended family and I wish to thank you for the excellent service and exquisite meal you provided to us."

Florida

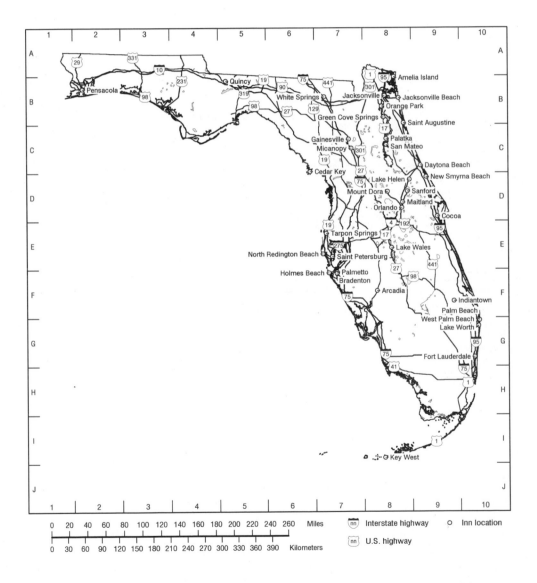

0 20 40 60 80 100 120 140 160 180 200 220 240 260 Miles

0 30 60 90 120 150 180 210 240 270 300 330 360 390 Kilometers

nn Interstate highway   ○ Inn location

nn U.S. highway

Amelia Island   B8

1857 Florida House Inn

PO Box 688, 22 S 3rd St
Amelia Island, FL 32034-4207
(904)261-3300 (800)258-3301
E-mail: innkeepers@floridahouseinn.com
Web: www.floridahouseinn.com

Circa 1857. Located in the heart of a 50-block historic
National Register area, the Florida House Inn is thought to be
the oldest continuously operating tourist hotel in Florida.
Recently renovated, the inn features a small pub, guest parlor,
library and a New Orleans-style courtyard in which guests may
enjoy the shade of 200-year-old oaks. Rooms are decorated
with country pine and oak antiques, cheerful handmade rugs
and quilts, and 10 rooms offer fireplaces and Jacuzzi tubs. The
Carnegies, Rockefellers and Ulysses S. Grant have been guests.
Innkeeper(s): Bob & Karen Warner. $79-189. MC, VISA, AX, DS. TAC10. 15
rooms with PB, 10 with FP, 1 suite and 1 conference room. Breakfast included in rates. Types of meals: Full bkfst, early coffee/tea, lunch, picnic lunch
and dinner. Beds: KQT. Cable TV, phone, ceiling fan and 10 Jacuzzi tubs in
room. Air conditioning. Fax and copier on premises. Handicap access. Small
meetings, family reunions and seminars hosted. Antiquing, fishing, live theater and sporting events nearby.
Publicity: *Amelia Now, Tampa Tribune, Miami Herald, Toronto Star, Country
Living, Ft. Lauderdale Sun Sentinel, Country Inns, Consumer Report and
Money Magazine.*

Addison House

614 Ash St
Amelia Island, FL 32034-3933
(904)277-1604 (800)943-1604 Fax:(904)277-8124
E-mail: addisonhouse@net-magic.net
Web: www.addisonhousebb.com

Circa 1876. Located in the historic district, this 19th-century
Victorian offers guests a comfortable romantic retreat to relax
and enjoy the cool ocean breezes. Elegant furnishings highlight
the five spacious guest rooms in the main house. The Garden
House and Coulter Cottage surrounding the courtyard feature

rooms with whirlpools and private porches.
Guests will enjoy the inn's fountains and well-manicured secret
gardens. A full breakfast and
afternoon snack is offered in the
dining room or porches. Located
minutes from the ocean, golf, sailing, fishing and hiking.

Innkeeper(s): John, Donna & Jennifer Gibson. $109-189. MC, VISA, AX, PC.
TAC10. 14 rooms with PB and 1 conference room. Breakfast included in
rates. Types of meals: Full bkfst. Beds: KQT. Cable TV, phone, ceiling fan and
VCR in room. Air conditioning. Fax on premises. Handicap access. Weddings,
small meetings and family reunions hosted. Antiquing, fishing, golf, live theater, parks, shopping, tennis and water sports nearby.

"You have personified the Southern experience."

Amelia Island Williams House

103 S 9th St
Amelia Island, FL 32034-3616
(904)277-2328 (800)414-9257 Fax:(904)321-1325
E-mail: topinn@aol.com
Web: www.williamshouse.com

Circa 1856. It's not this grand Antebellum mansion's first
owner, but its second for whom the house is named. Marcellus
Williams and his wife, a great-great-granddaughter of the King

of Spain, are its most esteemed residents. Among their many
influential guests, the two once hosted Jefferson Davis, and,
ironically, the first owners used part of the home for the
Underground Railroad. It will be hard for guests to believe that
the home was anything but opulent. The innkeepers painstakingly restored the home and the result is fabulous. Antiques
from nine different countries decorate the home. The guest
rooms are romantic; the gourmet breakfast served on the finest
china; and the lush, fragrant grounds are shaded by a 500-year-
old oak tree. The innkeepers also have restored the historic
home next door, which was used as an infirmary during the
Civil War. Four of the guest rooms are housed here, complete
with clawfoot or Jacuzzi tubs.
Innkeeper(s): Dick Flitz & Chris Carter. $150-235. MC, VISA, PC. TAC10. 8
rooms with PB, 5 with FP and 2 suites. Breakfast and afternoon tea included
in rates. Types of meals: Gourmet bkfst. Beds: K. Cable TV, phone, turndown
service, ceiling fan, VCR and daily maid service in room. Air conditioning.
Fax, copier, bicycles and video Library on premises. Handicap access. Family
reunions hosted. Antiquing, fishing, golf, zoo, live theater, parks, shopping,
sporting events, tennis and water sports nearby.
Publicity: *Country Inns, Southern Living, Southern Accents, Victoria,
Veranda, Palm Beach Life, National Geographic Traveler., CNN International
Travel and Inn Country USA.*

Bailey House

28 S 7th St
Amelia Island, FL 32034-3960
(904)261-5390 (800)251-5390 Fax:(904)321-0103
E-mail: bailey@bellsouth.net
Web: www.bailey-house.com

Circa 1895. This elegant Queen Anne Victorian was a wedding
present that steamship agent Effingham W. Bailey gave to his
bride. He shocked the locals by spending the enormous sum of

$10,000 to build the house with all its tow-
ers, turrets, gables and verandas. The parlor and dining room open to a fireplace in a reception hall with the
inscription "Hearth Hall -
Welcome All." A spirit of hospitality has reigned in this home from
its beginning.

Historic Interest: The historic seaport is within walking distance, Fort
Clinch (2 miles).
Innkeeper(s): Tom & Jenny Bishop. $129-189. MC, VISA, AX, DS, PC.
TAC10. 10 rooms with PB, 7 with FP. Breakfast included in rates. Types of
meals: Full bkfst and early coffee/tea. AP. Beds: KQT. Cable TV, phone and
ceiling fan in room. Air conditioning. Fax, copier and bicycles on premises.
Small meetings hosted. Antiquing, fishing, golf, history museum, live theater,
parks, shopping, sporting events, tennis and water sports nearby.
Publicity: *Victorian Homes, Innsider, Southern Living, Victorian Homes,
Saint Petersburg Times, Jacksonville., Travel Network and Romantic Inns.*

The Fairbanks House

227 S 7th St
Amelia Island, FL 32034
(904)277-0500 (888)891-9939 Fax:(904)277-3103
E-mail: email@fairbankshouse.com
Web: www.fairbankshouse.com

Circa 1885. The living and dining room fireplace tiles of this
Italianate-style mansion bring to life scenes from Shakespeare's
works and "Aesop's Fables." Other features include polished
hardwood floors, intricately carved moldings and eight other
fireplaces that grace spacious rooms. Each of the guest rooms is
furnished with a four-poster or canopied king, queen or twin

bed, Jacuzzi and clawfoot tubs or showers. Guests can step outside to enjoy an inviting courtyard, swimming pool and gardens bursting with roses, palms and magnolias. The Fairbanks was named one of the "Top 10 Luxury Inns In America" by Country Inns Magazine. The inn is a smoke-free property, which includes the grounds.

Innkeeper(s): Bill & Theresa Hamilton. $175-275. MC, VISA, AX, DS. TAC10. 12 rooms with PB, 9 with FP, 3 suites and 3 cottages. Breakfast included in rates. Types of meals: Gourmet bkfst. Beds: KQT. Cable TV, phone, ceiling fan, hair dryer and ironing board in room. Air conditioning. Bicycles, beach towels, beach chairs, swimming pool and social hour on premises. Antiquing, beaches, fishing, golf, restaurants, live theater, parks, shopping, sporting events, tennis and water sports nearby.

Publicity: *Country Inns, Veranda, Southern Living, Amelia Now, Islander, Florida Living, New York Times and Mother's Day.*

Hoyt House B&B

804 Atlantic Ave
Amelia Island, FL 32034-3629
(904)277-4300 (800)432-2085 Fax:(904)277-9626
E-mail: reservations1@hoythouse.com
Web: www.hoythouse.com

Circa 1905. Built by banker Fred Hoyt for his family, this Victorian home is a centerpiece in the Historic District of Fernandina Beach. Offering gracious hospitality with the elegance of a bygone era, enjoy great books, Southern iced tea, wine and hors d'oeuvres fireside in the common rooms. Large guest bedrooms are comfortable with pleasant amenities. Savor a delightful breakfast while conversing with newfound friends. Walk among the gardens with ancient oaks and magnolias, relax in the gazebo or porch swings. Follow the road leading directly to the Atlantic Ocean. Bikes and beach gear are available. A daily Sunset Social with fun, food and beverages is not to be missed. Ask about the inn's vacation packages.

Innkeeper(s): Gayl Blount. $129-169. MC, VISA, AX, DS, TC. TAC10. 10 rooms with PB, 2 with FP and 1 conference room. Breakfast and snacks/refreshments included in rates. Types of meals: Full bkfst and picnic lunch. Beds: KQ. TV, phone, hair dryers and first floor rooms with ceiling fans in room. Air conditioning. VCR, fax, copier, modem, bicycles, beach gear and complimentary evening wine and beer on premises. Handicap access. Weddings, small meetings, family reunions and seminars hosted. Antiquing, fishing, golf, live theater, parks, shopping, sporting events, tennis and water sports nearby.

Pets allowed: small, with kennel.

Publicity: *The Washington Times, PBS, Southern Living, Intimate Destinations and Jacksonville Times-Union.*

Walnford Inn

102 S 7th St
Amelia Island, FL 32034-3923
(904)277-4941 (800)277-6660 Fax:(904)277-4646
E-mail: info@walnford.com
Web: www.walnford.com

Circa 1904. Two Victorian homes comprise the inn, situated behind a handsome white picket fence and one block from downtown Centre Street. A library and several porches are favorite guest respites. Guest rooms include features such as whirlpool tubs, private balconies, antique bedsteads and Oriental carpets. The innkeepers offer bicycles and can arrange for special activities such as a carriage ride through the historic district or horseback riding on the beach.

Innkeeper(s): Rob & Chris. $89-179. MC, VISA, AX, DS, PC, TC. TAC10. 10 rooms. Breakfast included in rates. Types of meals: Full bkfst and afternoon tea. Beds: KQD. Cable TV, phone and ceiling fan in room. Air conditioning. Fax and copier on premises. Handicap access. Weddings, small meetings and family reunions hosted. Antiquing, fishing, golf, live theater, parks, tennis and water sports nearby.

Arcadia   F8

Historic Parker House

427 W Hickory St
Arcadia, FL 34266-3703
(863)494-2499 (800)969-2499
E-mail: parkerhouse@desoto.net

Circa 1895. Period antiques, including a wonderful clock collection, grace the interior of this turn-of-the-century home, which was built by a local cattle baron. Along with two charming rooms and a bright, "yellow" suite, innkeepers Shelly and Bob Baumann added the spacious Blue Room, which offers a white iron and brass bed and clawfoot bathtub. An expanded continental breakfast with pastries, fresh fruits, cereals, muffins and a variety of beverages is offered each morning, and afternoon teas can be prepared on request.

Historic Interest: The home, which is listed in the National Register, is within walking distance of historic downtown Arcadia with more than 350 buildings also listed on the register.

Innkeeper(s): Bob & Shelly Baumann. $69-85. MC, VISA, AX, TC. TAC10. 4 rooms, 2 with PB, 2 with FP and 1 conference room. Breakfast and afternoon tea included in rates. Types of meals: Cont plus, early coffee/tea and room service. Beds: QDT. Cable TV, phone and ceiling fan in room. Air conditioning. Small meetings and family reunions hosted. Antiquing, fishing, historical sites, parks, shopping and water sports nearby.

Publicity: *Tampa Tribune, Desoto Sun Herald, Florida Travel & Life, Miami Herald (Palm Beach Edition) and WINK-TV News.*

"Everything was first class and very comfortable."

Bradenton   E7

Betts House Bed & Breakfast

1523 1st Ave W
Bradenton, FL 34205-6801
(941)747-3607 Fax:(941)747-3607
E-mail: betts@TIZART.com

Circa 1913. Stroll to Memorial Pier for water views and restaurants from this two-story, American, four-square style home. The owner is an artist and many of her original works are highlighted in the two guest rooms. The Northwest Room features a king bed and direct access to the porch. Breakfast menus include bagels or croissants stuffed with chopped eggs and capers, served with fruit, cheese, cereal and sometimes custard breakfast pies. Walk to Twin Dolphin Marina and restaurant.

Innkeeper(s): Churchill Mallison. $60-65. MC, VISA, PC, TC. TAC10. 2 rooms. Breakfast included in rates. Types of meals: Cont plus and early coffee/tea. Beds: KDT. Cable TV and ceiling fan in room. Central air. Fax, wrap-around porch and garden on premises. Antiquing, art galleries, beaches, bicycling, canoeing/kayaking, fishing, golf, hiking, horseback riding, live theater, museums, parks, shopping, sporting events, tennis and water sports nearby.

Publicity: *Southern Living.*

Cedar Key C6

Island Hotel

2nd & B St
Cedar Key, FL 32625
(352)543-5111 (800)432-4640
E-mail: info@islandhotel-cedarkey.com
Web: www.islandhotel-cedarkey.com

Circa 1859. The history of Island Hotel begins at about the same time as the history of Cedar Key. Constructed from seashell tabby with oak supports, the hotel and its walls have

withstood wind and weather for a century and a half. Owners and innkeepers Dawn and Tony Cousins have worked to restore the home's traditional charm. Some rooms boast views of the Gulf or Back Bayou. All rooms include access to the inn's balcony, an ideal spot for relaxation. A casual, gourmet seafood restaurant is located on the premises, promising a delightful array of local catch, and Neptune Bar, also at the inn, is open to guests and locals.

Historic Interest: 1859 building has original murals dating from 1915 and 1948.

Innkeeper(s): Dawn & Tony Cousins. $75-125. MC, VISA, DS, TC. 13 rooms with PB. Breakfast included in rates. Types of meals: Gourmet bkfst. Beds: QD. Air conditioning. Weddings, small meetings, family reunions and seminars hosted. Antiquing, fishing, parks, sporting events and water sports nearby.

Cocoa D9

Indian River House

3113 Indian River Dr
Cocoa, FL 32922-6501
(321)631-5660 Fax:(321)631-5268
E-mail: suzanne@indianriverhouse.com
Web: www.indianriverhouse.com

Circa 1900. Built at the turn of the 20th century, this historic home offers four comfortable guest rooms. The home is casually decorated, and a few antiques have been placed among the furnishings. The home is located along the Intracoastal Waterway, and guests only have to walk a few feet to reach the inn's dock where they can fish or just enjoy the scenery. Breakfasts include items such as freshly baked biscuits, fresh fruit, eggs Benedict or perhaps French toast. The home offers close access to many attractions,

including the sites of Orlando, the Daytona Speedway, National Seashore and Wildlife Refuge, fishing, kayaking and biking. Space shuttle launches can be seen from the front porch.

Historic Interest: Historic Cocoa Village (3 miles).

$95. MC, VISA, AX, PC, TC. 4 rooms with PB, 2 with FP. Breakfast and snacks/refreshments included in rates. Types of meals: Full bkfst and veg bkfst. AP. Beds: KQ. Central air. VCR, fax, copier, bicycles and library on premises. Antiquing, art galleries, beaches, bicycling, fishing, horseback riding, kayaking, live theater, museums, parks, shopping, tennis and water sports nearby.

Daytona Beach C9

Coquina Inn B&B

544 S Palmetto Ave
Daytona Beach, FL 32114-4924
(386)254-4969 (800)805-7533
E-mail: coquinabnb@aol.com
Web: www.coquinainndaytonabeach.com

Circa 1912. Located in the Daytona Beach Historic District, this handsome house boasts an exterior of coquina rock blended from shells, arched windows, and a picket porch on the second floor. The Jasmine Room is accentuated with a seven-foot canopy bed draped in a delicate netting. French leather chairs, a fireplace and a Victorian tub are featured. The Hibiscus Room is decorated with an iron canopy bed, wicker settee chair and coffee table and includes a French door that lead to a private balcony.

Historic Interest: Sugar Mill Gardens (5 miles), Gamble House (8 miles), Tomoka State Park & Museum (14 miles).

Innkeeper(s): Ann Christoffersen & Dennis Haight. $80-110. MC, VISA, AX, DS. 4 rooms with PB, 1 with FP. Breakfast included in rates. Types of meals: Gourmet bkfst. Beds: QD. TV and ceiling fan in room. Air conditioning. Bicycles on premises. Antiquing, fishing, live theater, shopping, sporting events and water sports nearby.

Publicity: *Country Inns, Florida Sports, Sun Sentinel, Southern Living and Miami Herald.*

"Better than chocolate. A little bit of heaven on earth."

The Villa

801 N Peninsula Dr
Daytona Beach, FL 32118-3724
(904)248-2020 Fax:(904)248-2020

Circa 1926. This Spanish Revival manor is listed in the National Register of Historic Places and is located within walking distance of the beach. The acre-and-a-half grounds are tropical, highlighted by soaring palm trees. The interior boasts many original elements, as well as stenciled ceilings and artwork. Rooms, with names such as the Queen Isabella and Christopher Columbus, honor the state's history of Spanish exploration. Within an hour of Daytona Beach, guests can reach Orlando, St. Augustine and

Cape Canaveral or stay and explore Daytona, which offers plenty of shopping and restaurants, as well as the ocean.

Innkeeper(s): Jim Camp. $100-250. MC, VISA, AX, TC. 4 rooms with PB. Breakfast included in rates. Types of meals: Cont plus and early coffee/tea. AP. Beds: KQ. Cable TV and ceiling fan in room. Air conditioning. VCR, fax, copier, spa and swimming on premises. Weddings, small meetings and family reunions hosted. Antiquing, fishing, golf, live theater, parks, shopping, sporting events, tennis and water sports nearby.

Fort Lauderdale — G10

Caribbean Quarters B&B

3012 Granada St
Fort Lauderdale, FL 33304
(954)523-3226 (888)414-3226 Fax:(954)523-7541
E-mail: cqbandb@aol.com
Web: www.caribbeanquarters.com

Circa 1939. With its unique South Florida architectural style, this three-story home built in 1939 features a plantation-like wooden veranda with a series of louvered doors that open onto the interior. Lush tropical plants and flowers surround the house. Decor throughout is Caribbean with a hint of the 1930s. Guest rooms and suites come in various sizes, with white gauzy mosquito netting hanging over beds covered in tropical floral spreads. Rattan or white wicker tables, chairs and sofas furnish the sitting areas of the suites. Innkeeper Bernd Metz is a professional cook who oversees the continental breakfast-usually fruit, croissants, bagels with smoked salmon, capers, cream cheese and fresh baked bread. Situated in the older part of Fort Lauderdale, the house is only half a block from the beach and half a block from the water taxi on the inland waterway.

Historic Interest: Bonnet House (1 mile).

Innkeeper(s): Bernd Metz. $75-220. MC, VISA, AX, DS, TC. TAC10. 15 rooms, 12 with PB and 3 suites. Breakfast included in rates. Types of meals: Gourmet bkfst, country bkfst, cont plus and room service. Beds: KQDT. Cable TV, phone, ceiling fan and VCR in room. Air conditioning. Fax, spa, bicycles, library, sundeck and breakfast bar on premises. Weddings, small meetings and family reunions hosted. German spoken. Antiquing, art galleries, beaches, bicycling, fishing, golf, hiking, live theater, museums, parks, shopping, tennis and water sports nearby.

Gainesville — C7

Magnolia Plantation

309 SE 7th St
Gainesville, FL 32601-6831
(352)375-6653 Fax:(352)338-0303
E-mail: info@magnoliabnb.com

Circa 1885. This restored French Second Empire Victorian is in the National Register. Magnolia trees surround the house. Five guest rooms are filled with family heirlooms. All bathrooms feature clawfoot tubs and candles. There are also private historic cottages available with Jacuzzis. Guests may enjoy the gardens, reflecting pond with waterfalls and gazebo. Bicycles are also available. Evening wine and snacks are included. The inn is two miles from the University of Florida.

Innkeeper(s): Joe & Cindy Montalto. $90-160. MC, VISA, AX. TAC10. 5 rooms with PB, 5 with FP and 3 cottages. Breakfast and afternoon tea included in rates. Types of meals: Full bkfst. AP. Beds: Q. TV, turndown service and ceiling fan in room. Air conditioning. VCR, fax, bicycles and library on premises. Antiquing, live theater, parks, shopping and sporting events nearby.

Publicity: *Florida Living Magazine. and Inn Country USA.*

"This has been a charming, once-in-a-lifetime experience."

Green Cove Springs — B8

River Park Inn

103 S Magnolia Ave
Green Cove Springs, FL 32043-4100
(904)284-2994 (888)417-0363
E-mail: pat@riverparkinn.com
Web: www.riverparkinn.com

Circa 1887. Experience small-town charm while staying at this frame, vernacular-style inn located in the city's waterfront district. It was originally built for those partaking of the medicinal warm mineral springs which still flow, supplying the chemical-free community pool. The overflow then feeds a gentle stream  winding through the park before emptying into the mighty St. John's River. The decor befits the 1800s era with period antiques and tasteful furnishings. Comfortable guest bedrooms offer modern conveniences for business and pleasure. Savor a wholesome breakfast before taking a self-guided historic walking tour. A porch swing and double rocker invite relaxation on the two verandas. Ask about special packages available such as golf, day spa, kayaking and basket weaving.

$65-100. MC, VISA, AX, DS, PC, TC. 5 rooms with PB. Breakfast and snacks/refreshments included in rates. Types of meals: Full bkfst. Beds: QDT. Cable TV, phone, ceiling fan, hair dryers and irons in room. Air conditioning. VCR, fax, copier, spa and bicycles on premises. Bicycling, canoeing/kayaking, fishing, golf, hiking, museums, parks, water sports and wineries nearby.

Holmes Beach — F7

Harrington House Beachfront B&B Inn

5626 Gulf Dr N
Holmes Beach, FL 34217-1666
(941)778-5444 (888)828-5566 Fax:(941)778-0527
E-mail: harhousebb@mail.pcsonline.com
Web: www.harringtonhouse.com

Circa 1925. A mere 40 feet from the water, this gracious home, set among pine trees and palms, is comprised of a main house and two beach houses. Constructed of 14-inch-thick coquina blocks, the house features a living room with a 20-foot-high beamed ceiling, fireplace, '20s wallpaper and French doors. Many of the guest rooms have four-poster beds, antique wicker furnishings and French doors opening onto a deck that overlooks the swimming pool and Gulf of Mexico. Some offer Jacuzzi-type tubs and fireplaces. Kayaks are available for dolphin watching.

Innkeeper(s): Jo & Frank Davis. $129-249. MC, VISA. TAC10. 16 rooms with PB. Breakfast included in rates. Types of meals: Full bkfst. Beds: KQDT. TV, phone, ceiling fan and VCR in room. Air conditioning. Handicap access. Weddings, small meetings, family reunions and seminars hosted. Amusement parks, antiquing, fishing, live theater, shopping, sporting events and water sports nearby.

Publicity: *Southern Living, Sarasota Herald Tribune, Island Sun, Palm Beach Post, Tampa Tribune, Glamour, Atlantic Monthly and Travel Holiday.*

"Elegant house and hospitality."

Indiantown   F9

Seminole Country Inn

PO Box 1818-15885 SW Warfield Blvd
Indiantown, FL 34956
(561)597-3777 (888)394-3777 Fax:(561)597-2883
E-mail: seminole@treco.net

Circa 1926. Selected as one of the top 20 inns in Florida by
the St. Petersburg Times, this historic inn is located halfway
between Palm Beach and Lake Okeechobee in a citrus and cattle ranch area. Wallis Simpson was once a guest here because
the Duchess was the niece of the inn's builder, a banker and
railroad man. A winding
staircase that leads to
an upstairs sitting room
highlights an inviting
lobby. Guest rooms are

filled with antiques and period decor. A restaurant is in the
inn's dining room, an impressive site to behold with tall
Palladium windows and 20-inch-thick walls. The menu features
a wide variety of Southern favorites mingled with a bit of nouveau cuisine and is acclaimed for its fine offerings. An assortment of interesting events and tours are available such as traditional Thanksgiving and Christmas dinners, trail rides, barbecues and swamp tours.

Innkeeper(s): Sheri Hubbard & Jonnie Flewelling. $65-125. MC, VISA, AX,
DS, TC. 22 rooms with PB and 2 conference rooms. Breakfast included in
rates. Types of meals: Cont, lunch, picnic lunch and gourmet dinner. Beds:
KQD. Cable TV, phone and king rooms with robes in room. Air conditioning.
VCR, fax, copier, swimming, bicycles and native border gardens on premises.
Small meetings hosted. Antiquing, bicycling, fishing, golf, hiking, horseback
riding, eco tours, bird watching, live theater, parks, shopping, tennis and
water sports nearby.

Publicity: *St. Petersburg Times and The Sun Sentinel.*

Jacksonville   B8

House on Cherry St

1844 Cherry St
Jacksonville, FL 32205-8702
(904)384-1999 Fax:(904)384-5013
E-mail: houseoncherry@compuserve.com

Circa 1909. Seasonal blooms fill the pots that line the circular
entry stairs to this Federal-style house on tree-lined Cherry
Street. It was moved in two pieces to its present site on St.
Johns River in the historic Riverside area. Traditionally decorated rooms include antiques, collections of hand-carved decoy
ducks and old clocks that chime and tick. Most rooms overlook the river. A canoe and kayak are available for guest use.
Your host is a guidance counselor and tennis official.

Innkeeper(s): Carol Anderson. $85-115. MC, VISA, AX, PC, TC. TAC10. 4
suites. Breakfast and snacks/refreshments included in rates. Types of meals:
Cont. Beds: QT. Cable TV, phone, ceiling fan, some refrigerators and flowers
in room. Air conditioning. VCR, fax, copier, fishing, canoeing and kayaking on
premises. Small meetings, family reunions and seminars hosted. Antiquing,
live theater, parks, shopping, sporting events and water sports nearby.

Publicity: *Southern Living, Florida Wayfarer, Tampa Tribune and New
York Times.*

Jacksonville Beach   B8

Fig Tree Inn

185 4th Ave S
Jacksonville Beach, FL 32250
(904)246-8855 (877)217-9830 Fax:(904)543-1085
E-mail: egghouse@mediaone.net

Circa 1915. Whether staying here for a romantic getaway or to
cheer for your favorite football team, this cedar shake inn with
Victorian accents offers a relaxing atmosphere. The acclaimed
front porch has been considered one of the area's best, with a
swing, rocking chairs and ocean breeze. Games, books and
magazines as well as a video library are found in the parlor.
Themed guest bedrooms feature a handmade willow and
canopy beds, Jacuzzi and clawfoot tubs. The inn's namesake in
the backyard produces enough fruit to make fig walnut pancakes, as well as fig jelly and preserves served with scones. A
light meal is served on weekdays, a full breakfast is enjoyed on
the weekends. The kitchen is available to use at any time.

Historic Interest: Saint Augustine (20 miles).

Innkeeper(s): Dawn & Kevin Eggleston. $75-200. MC, VISA, AX, DC, DS, TC.
5 rooms with PB and 1 suite. Breakfast, afternoon tea and snacks/refresh-
ments included in rates. Types of meals: Gourmet bkfst, country bkfst, veg
bkfst, cont plus, cont, early coffee/tea, picnic lunch and room service. Beds:
QT. Cable TV, phone, ceiling fan, VCR, hot tub, hair dryer and iron & ironing
boards in room. Fax, copier, bicycles, library and hot tub on premises.
Weddings, small meetings, family reunions and seminars hosted. Amusement
parks, antiquing, art galleries, beaches, bicycling, canoeing/kayaking, fishing,
golf, hiking, horseback riding, live theater, museums, parks, shopping, sporting events, tennis and water sports nearby.

Key West   I8

Andrews Inn

0 Whalton Ln
Key West, FL 33040
(305)294-7730 (888)263-7393 Fax:(305)294-0021
E-mail: kwandrews@aol.com
Web: www.andrewsinn.com

Circa 1920. You may never run with the bulls in Pamplona or
hunt rhinoceros in the wilds of Africa, but at this Key West inn,
you won't be far from the spirit of Hemingway. The famed
author's estate adjoins the property of the historic Andrews
Inn, separated only by a fence. Aside from this claim to fame,
the inn is within easy walking distance of Duval Street, shops
and restaurants. The grounds are lush with tropical plants and
there's a swimming pool, as well. Continental-plus breakfasts
include a variety of goodies, but champagne adds an extra
touch of elegance to the morning meal. Breakfast and cocktails
are not included at the cottages.

Historic Interest: Hemingway Estate, Lighhouse Museum (1 block).

Innkeeper(s): Sally Garratt. $115-359. MC, VISA, AX, DS, TC. TAC10. 6
rooms with PB and 2 cottages. Breakfast and snacks/refreshments included
in rates. Types of meals: Cont plus. Beds: KQ. Cable TV, phone and ceiling
fan in room. Air conditioning. Swimming on premises. Weddings, small meetings and family reunions hosted. Spanish spoken. Antiquing, art galleries,
beaches, bicycling, canoeing/kayaking, fishing, golf, live theater, museums,
parks, shopping, tennis and water sports nearby.

Blue Parrot Inn

916 Elizabeth St
Key West, FL 33040-6406
(305)296-0033 (800)231-2473
E-mail: bluparotin@aol.com
Web: www.blueparrotinn.com

Circa 1884. This Bahamian-style inn is decorated in a pleasing, tropical style and all the rooms are air conditioned. The grounds are lush and peaceful. Continental-plus breakfasts of fresh fruit, bagels, muffins and quiche are served poolside. There is plenty of space around the pool to relax and tan. The inn is located in a historic neighborhood and is near shops and restaurants. The ocean is just a few blocks away. Kittens are in residence.

Innkeeper(s): Larry Rhinard & Frank Yaccino. $79-209. MC, VISA, AX, DC, CB, DS, TC. TAC10. 10 rooms with PB. Breakfast included in rates. Types of meals: Cont. Beds: KQD. Cable TV, phone, ceiling fan and air conditioning in room. Fax, copier, swimming and bicycles on premises. Handicap access. Weddings, small meetings and family reunions hosted. Antiquing, fishing, live theater, parks, shopping and water sports nearby.

Center Court-Historic Inn & Cottages

915 Center St
Key West, FL 33040
(305)296-9292 (800)797-8787 Fax:(305)294-4104
E-mail: centerct@aol.com
Web: www.centercourtkw.com

Circa 1873. The main house at Center Court was built by a ship's captain around 1873. Three circa 1880 cottages also are located on the property, and all four buildings are listed in the National Register. In all, guests can choose from four rooms in the main guest house and 14 private cottages. The decor is contemporary with a tropical flair. The cottages include a full or efficiency kitchen, and most have private decks or verandas and spas; one has a private pool. Several cottages can accommodate four to six guests. There are two pools, several Jacuzzis and an exercise area for guest use.

Innkeeper(s): Naomi R. Van Steelandt. $98-368. MC, VISA, AX, DS, PC, TC. TAC10. 6 rooms with PB and 11 cottages. Types of meals: Cont plus. Beds: KQD. TV, phone, ceiling fan, hair dryer and exercise pavilion in room. Air conditioning. VCR, fax, copier, spa, exercise pavilion and swimming pool on premises. Weddings, small meetings and family reunions hosted. Antiquing, fishing, golf, one half block off famous Duval Street, live theater, parks, shopping and water sports nearby.

Pets allowed: In cottages, $10 pet fee per night.

Publicity: *Town & Country and Florida Keys.*

Cuban Club Suites

1108 Duval St
Key West, FL 33040
(305)296-0465 (800)432-4849 Fax:(305)293-7669
E-mail: info@keywestcubanclub.com
Web: www.keywestcubanclub.com

Circa 1900. Built in old Key West style and located on Duval Street just three blocks from the water, this Victorian inn is within walking distance to many of the island's attractions. Cuban cigar makers founded the site and used it as a meeting place to play games and dance. It was built with 50 cents or a dollar from each man's paycheck. Today the inn has panoramic views of Key West from its wide porches filled with authentic antique Cuban

rockers. The inn has 12 guest bedrooms, including eight roomy suites, which have cathedral ceilings and tiled baths. Many of the guest bedrooms have French doors that open to wraparound balconies, overlooking historic Duval Street.

Historic Interest: Hemingway House (3 blocks), Lighthouse Museum (3 blocks).
Innkeeper(s): Jennifer Cleaver. $159-299. MC, VISA, AX. TAC10. 12 rooms and 8 suites. Beds: KQ. Cable TV, phone, ceiling fan, washer and dryer in room. Central air. Museum on premises. Family reunions hosted. Antiquing, art galleries, beaches, bicycling, canoeing/kayaking, fishing, golf, live theater, museums, parks, shopping, tennis, water sports and wineries nearby.

Pets allowed: Most suites, small dogs only $200 refundable pet deposit.

The Curry Mansion Inn

511 Caroline St
Key West, FL 33040-6604
(305)294-5349 (800)253-3466 Fax:(305)294-4093
E-mail: frontdesk@currymansion.com
Web: www.currymansion.com

Circa 1892. This three-story white Victorian was billed as the most elaborate home on Caroline Street when it was built in 1867 by Florida's first millionaire. The inn still contains original features such as bookcases, chandeliers and fireplaces, as well as an abundance of antiques. The innkeepers use the inn to display some of their beautiful collectibles, including a family Limoges service for 120. Guests enjoy Key West's mild weather while enjoying a European-style breakfast. Piano music serenades guests at a nightly "cocktail" party with hors d'oeuvres and a full open bar.

Innkeeper(s): Albert & Edith Amsterdam. $140-275. MC, VISA, AX, DC, CB, DS, PC, TC. 28 rooms with PB and 10 suites. Breakfast and snacks/refreshments included in rates. Types of meals: Gourmet bkfst. Beds: KQ. Cable TV, phone and ceiling fan in room. Air conditioning. VCR, fax, copier, spa, swimming, bicycles and library on premises. Handicap access. Weddings, small meetings, family reunions and seminars hosted. Antiquing, fishing, swimming, boating, live theater, shopping and water sports nearby.

Pets allowed: under 20 pounds.

Publicity: *Mariner Outboards SLAM, New York Times, Southern Living and Colonial Homes.*

"Everything was so tastefully tended to. We truly felt like 'Royalty'. We certainly will not consider returning to Key West unless we are able to book accommodations at the Curry Mansion."

Cypress House

601 Caroline St
Key West, FL 33040-6674
(305)294-6969 (800)525-2488 Fax:(305)296-1174
E-mail: cypresskw@aol.com
Web: www.cypresshousekw.com

Circa 1888. There's much to see and do in popular Key West, and Cypress House is an ideal place for those visiting the area. The National Register inn was built by one of Key West's first settlers, and it still maintains many original features. Guest rooms are airy and spacious, decorated in a variety of styles. A continental breakfast with muffins, bagels, fresh fruit and more is served daily. A cocktail hour also is included in the rates. The inn is just a block from Duval Street, which offers shops, galleries, eateries and plenty of nightlife.

Innkeeper(s): Dave Taylor. $99-300. MC, VISA, AX, DS, TC. TAC10. 14 rooms, 8 with PB and 1 suite. Breakfast included in rates. Types of meals: Cont plus. Beds: KQD. Cable TV, phone, ceiling fan and refrigerator in room.

Air conditioning. Swimming on premises. Weddings, small meetings, family reunions and seminars hosted. Antiquing, fishing, live theater, parks, shopping and water sports nearby.

Douglas House

419 Amelia St
Key West, FL 33040-3120
(305)294-5269 (800)833-0372 Fax:(305)292-7665
E-mail: doughous4u@aol.com
Web: www.douglashouse.com

Circa 1896. This 19th-century Victorian was built during Key West's heyday of cigar production. Rooms are decorated in a contemporary tropical style. Suites with kitchens are available. The grounds include two swimming pools and a Jacuzzi. The home is three blocks from the ocean and beaches, and located right off popular Duval Street.

Innkeeper(s): Robert Marrero. $88-228. MC, VISA, AX. TAC10. 16 rooms. Breakfast and afternoon tea included in rates. Types of meals: Cont plus, cont and early coffee/tea. Beds: KQD. Cable TV, phone and ceiling fan in room. Air conditioning. Fax, copier, spa and swimming on premises. Weddings hosted. Antiquing, fishing, golf, live theater, parks, shopping, tennis and water sports nearby.

Pets Allowed.

Duval House

815 Duval St
Key West, FL 33040-7405
(305)294-1666 (800)223-8825 Fax:(305)292-1701
E-mail: duvalhs@attglobal.net
Web: www.duvalhousekeywest.com

Circa 1880. Seven historic houses, painted in island pastel shades, surround a lush tropical garden and a pool. Located on an estate in the heart of the historic Old Town, guests relish the

cozy spaces to relax such as the hammock for two, gazebo, sun decks and private balconies. The inn's white picket fences and plentiful porches are bordered by tropical trees, flowers and vines. A continental-plus breakfast is served from the pool house. Rooms have wicker and antique furniture, Victorian armoires and Bahamian fans.

Historic Interest: Hemingway House (1 block).

Innkeeper(s): Sarah Goldstein. $110-325. MC, VISA, AX, DC, DS, TC. TAC10. 25 rooms with PB and 4 suites. Breakfast included in rates. Beds: KQ. Cable TV and phone in room. Air conditioning. Swimming on premises. Antiquing, spa, historic touring, shopping and water sports nearby.

Publicity: *Palm Beach Post, Orlando Sentinel, Brides, Vacations, Honeymoon, St. Petersburg Times and Sun Sentinel.*

"You certainly will see us again."

Eden House

1015 Fleming St
Key West, FL 33040-6962
(305)296-6868 (800)533-5397 Fax:(305)294-1221
E-mail: mike@edenhouse.com

Circa 1924. This Art Deco hotel was once a hot spot for writers, intellectuals and European travelers. Innkeeper Mike Eden improved the home, adding a 10-person Jacuzzi, decks, gazebos, an elevated sun deck, waterfalls and hammocks. Ceiling fans and wicker furniture complete the tropical atmosphere found in each room. The home was the site for the

Goldie Hawn movie, "Criss Cross." Guests are served cold refreshments upon arrival, and there is a complimentary happy hour. Caribe Soul is the inn's restaurant, offering Caribbean cuisine with specialities such as stir-fried cabbage, sweet potatoes, collard greens and crab cakes. Poolside breakfasts, although not included in the room price, offer cinnamon coffee and a variety of entrees. Smoking allowed outside only.

Innkeeper(s): Mike Eden. $55-275. MC, VISA, AX, TC. 42 rooms, 26 with PB and 6 suites. EP. Beds: QDT. Ceiling fan in room. Air conditioning. Fax, swimming, bicycles and jacuzzi on premises. Fishing, shopping and water sports nearby.

Publicity: *Chicago Tribune, Woman's Day, Southern Living and Miami Herald.*

The Garden House

329 Elizabeth St
Key West, FL 33040-6804
(305)296-5368 (800)695-6453 Fax:(305)292-1140
E-mail: keywestgarden@aol.com
Web: www.keywestgardenhouse.com

Circa 1850. Located in a quiet neighborhood in the heart of Old Town, the country's largest wooden historic district, this tropical conch house is a romantic treasure. Surrounded by palms, Royal Poinciana trees and fragrant gardens of frangipani, relaxation comes easy at this personable inn. The cheerful guest bedrooms offer comfortable amenities. Breakfast is a culinary adventure to enjoy on the front porch or sun deck. Lee is known for his homemade Southern grits, sometimes with fresh pink shrimp. Jeff's fresh-baked key lime pie is always a refreshing treat. The courtyard features a gentle waterfall flowing into a lagoon-like pool with spa. Many getaway packages are available.

Historic Interest: Ernest Hemingway House (1 mile), John James Audubon House (1/2 mile).

Innkeeper(s): Lee Phelan & Joe Wells. $80-175. MC, VISA, AX, DS, TC. TAC10. 10 rooms, 8 with PB. Breakfast included in rates. Types of meals: Veg bkfst and cont plus. Beds: KQD. Cable TV, phone and ceiling fan in room. Air conditioning. Fax, copier, spa, swimming and bicycles on premises. Weddings, small meetings and family reunions hosted. Antiquing, art galleries, beaches, bicycling, canoeing/kayaking, fishing, golf, live theater, museums, parks, tennis and water sports nearby.

Pets allowed: Small pets allowed in one room only.

Heron House

512 Simonton St
Key West, FL 33040-6832
(800)294-1644 Fax:(305)294-5692
E-mail: heronkyw@aol.com
Web: www.heronhouse.com

Circa 1856. Orchid gardens in a rain forest-style landscape is an inviting aspect of Heron House, one of the oldest homes remaining in Key West. With its Conch architecture, the inn showcases many beautiful features, including hand-crafted

wood walls, marble baths, stained-glass transoms and Chicago brick patios. Rated four diamonds by AAA, there are many other amenities such as private decks and balconies and French doors. Suites with wet bars and sitting areas also are available.

Duval Street is one block away, and guests can walk to restaurants and beaches or rent a bicycle or motor scooter.
Innkeeper(s): Fred Geibelt. $119-369. MC, VISA, AX, DC, CB. 23 rooms. Breakfast included in rates. Types of meals: Cont plus. Beds: KQD. Phone in room.
Publicity: *Sun Sentinel.*

Island City House

411 William St
Key West, FL 33040-6857
(305)294-5702 (800)634-8230 Fax:(305)294-1289
E-mail: islcity@flakeysol.com
Web: www.islandcityhouse.com

Circa 1889. The oldest operating guest house in Key West, the Island City House was built for a wealthy Charleston merchant who later converted it to a small hotel, anticipating the arrival of the railroad in 1912. Restored by two active preservationists, Island City House and Arch House provide suites in beautifully restored environs with turn-of-the-century decor. Private porches and ceiling fans are historical amenities that remain. The Cigar House is a cypress wood building with spacious suites in an elegant island decor with rattan and wicker. Many of its accommodations offer porches with hammocks overlooking the pool.
Innkeeper(s): Stanley & Janet Corneal. $115-315. MC, VISA, AX, DC, CB, DS, PC, TC. TAC10. 24 suites. Breakfast included in rates. Types of meals: Cont plus. Beds: KQD. Cable TV, phone and ceiling fan in room. Air conditioning. VCR, fax, copier, swimming and bicycles on premises. Antiquing, fishing, golf, live theater, parks, shopping, tennis and water sports nearby.
Publicity: *Palm Beach Daily News, London Times, Miami Herald and Palm Beach Post.*

"We enjoyed relaxing on our hammock on the veranda of the Cigar House. We'll be back."

Key West Harbor Inn

219 Elizabeth St
Key West, FL 33040
(305)296-2978 (800)608-6569 Fax:(305)294-5858
E-mail: kwharborinn@yahoo.com
Web: www.keywestharborinn.com

Circa 1850. This elegant three-story mansion is surrounded by ornate Victorian homes in Old Town Key West. It's steps away from Historic Key West Seaport's boardwalk and two blocks from Duval Street. Built in a different location in 1850 by a local physician, the mansion was bought by two women who moved the inn in 1950 to its current location so that the home would face the harbor with its beautiful sunsets. The inn's many guest bedrooms include touches like four poster beds, French doors leading to verandas and views of the tropical gardens or the harbor. The home, the Pool House and the Carriage House are surrounded by a walled tropical garden, which adds an air of wild seclusion. Guests enjoy the swimming pool and Jacuzzi and all kinds of local water sports, including snorkeling in the only living reef in North America, treasure hunting, deep sea fishing, sea kayaking, jet skiing, dolphin watching and touring the beautiful local sights.
Innkeeper(s): Steve & Alexis. $100-350. MC, VISA, AX, DS, PC. TAC15. 6 rooms with PB. Breakfast and snacks/refreshments included in rates. Types of meals: Cont plus. Beds: KQ. Cable TV, phone, ceiling fan, hair dryers and some with full wet bars with sink in room. Air conditioning. Spa and swimming on premises. Canoeing/kayaking, fishing, snorkeling, jet skis, dolphin eco-tours and water sports nearby.

Old Town Resorts

504 & 506 South Street
Key West, FL 33040
(305)296-6577 (800)354-4455 Fax:(305)294-8272
E-mail: lamerdewey@aol.com
Web: www.oldtownresorts.com

Circa 1900. La Mer Hotel and Dewey House are the only oceanfront bed & breakfasts in Key West. The Dewey House is the original home of philosopher and educator John Dewey. Both restored Victorians are located in historic Old Town on famous Duval Street, and both have high ceilings, private balconies, verandas and views of the ocean and the tropical gardens on site. The Dewey House has Jacuzzi tubs and French doors. Guests of both inns may use the swimming pool located at the Dewey House. The inns serve a scrumptious continental breakfast with fresh breads, coffee cakes, croissants and English muffins in the oceanfront gathering place. In the afternoon, guests enjoy complimentary tea and crumpets, fruits and cheeses. Guests always make it a point to be back in time to enjoy the beautiful sunset and balmy evening breezes.
Historic Interest: Historic old town.
Innkeeper(s): Matthew & Carrie Babich. $150-330. MC, VISA, AX, TC. TAC10. 19 rooms, 16 with PB and 3 suites. Breakfast and afternoon tea included in rates. Types of meals: Cont. Beds: KQD. Cable TV, phone, turndown service, ceiling fan, robes, hair dryer, iron and ironing board in room. Air conditioning. Fax, copier, spa, swimming and library on premises. Weddings and small meetings hosted. German and Spanish spoken. Art galleries, beaches, bicycling, fishing, golf, live theater, museums, parks, shopping and tennis nearby.

The Popular House, Key West B&B

415 William St
Key West, FL 33040-6853
(305)296-7274 (800)438-6155 Fax:(305)293-0306
E-mail: relax@keywestbandb.com
Web: www.keywestbandb.com

Circa 1890. This pink and white Victorian sits elegantly behind a white picket fence. It was constructed by shipbuilders with sturdy heart-pine walls and 13-foot ceilings. With two stories of porches, the inn is located in the center of the Historic District.

Innkeeper(s): Jody Carlson. $59-285. MC, VISA, AX, DC, DS, PC, TC. TAC10. 8 rooms, 4 with PB and 1 suite. Breakfast included in rates. Types of meals: Cont plus and early coffee/tea. Beds: KQDT. Ceiling fan in room. Air conditioning. Fax, copier, spa, swimming, sauna, bicycles, library and specimen garden on premises. Weddings, small meetings, family reunions and seminars hosted. Antiquing, fishing, historic tours, museums, live theater, shopping and water sports nearby.
Publicity: *Palm Beach Life, South Florida, Food Arts, London House & Gardens, Conde Naste Traveler and New York Times.*

"The essence of charming."

Seascape

420 Olivia St
Key West, FL 33040-7411
(305)296-7776 (800)765-6438 Fax:(305)296-6283
E-mail: info@seascapetropicalinn.com
Web: www.seascapetropicalinn.com

Circa 1889. This inviting restored two-story clapboard inn with blue shutters offers privacy among the hustle and bustle of Key West's Old Town. It features tropical gardens, a heated pool/spa and sundecks. Seascape is located a few blocks from the Atlantic Ocean and the Gulf of Mexico and is walking distance to restaurants and shops. There are 11 accommodations including bed & breakfast rooms, studio apartments and a two-bedroom cottage. Guest rooms feature white wicker and tropical furnishings as well as a unique collection of local art. Breakfast is served under the shade of the sapodilla tree on a private courtyard. Guests may join the hosts for the complimentary wine hour in season. The inn was featured on the front page of the New York Times travel section and has received several excellent recommendations by travel writers.

Innkeeper(s): Tom & Nancy Coward. $79-269. MC, VISA, AX, DS. 6 rooms with PB and 4 cottages. Breakfast included in rates. Types of meals: Cont. Beds: KQT. Fishing, live theater and water sports nearby.

Publicity: *New York Times, San Francisco Chronicle and Florida Keys Magazine.*

Simonton Court

320 Simonton St
Key West, FL 33040-6869
(305)294-6386 (800)944-2687 Fax:(305)293-8446
E-mail: simontoncourt@aol.com
Web: www.simontoncourt.com

Circa 1870. Just three blocks from the Gulf of Mexico and a stroll from famous Duval Street on Key West Island is Simonton Court. This secluded two-acre estate with rustling palm trees and fragrant tropical flowers is one of the most romantic properties on the island. There are secluded pools and hot tubs for guests to enjoy. The estate boasts 26 guest rooms ranging from individual cottages with kitchenettes to restored historic buildings. Enjoy a poolside breakfast, and then walk or bike through town. Or charter a boat and go fishing, diving or sailing.

Innkeeper(s): Terry Sullivan. $125-495. 26 rooms. Cable TV, phone, ceiling fan and VCR in room. Air conditioning. Lushly landscaped gardens on premises. Weddings, small meetings and seminars hosted. Antiquing, live theater and shopping nearby.

Treetop Inn Historic B&B

806 Truman Ave
Key West, FL 33040-6426
(305)293-0712 (800)926-0712 Fax:(305)294-3668
E-mail: treetopinn@flakeysol.com
Web: www.treetopinn.com

Circa 1898. Treetop Inn, a Florida plantation-style home, was built at the beginning of the 20th century by a prominent cigar maker. The picturesque home is listed in the National Register. The exterior grounds are surrounded by a picket fence and the lush grounds include a small swimming pool. The three guest rooms are comfortable and decorated in a light, airy style. Wicker furnishings and some antique pieces add to the historic ambiance. Guests can walk to shops, beaches, restaurants and other Key West offerings.

Historic Interest: Old Town Key West.

Innkeeper(s): Sue & Fred Leake. $98-178. MC, VISA. TAC10. 3 rooms with PB. Breakfast included in rates. Types of meals: Cont. Beds: K. Cable TV, phone and ceiling fan in room. Air conditioning. Swimming on premises. Antiquing, art galleries, beaches, bicycling, canoeing/kayaking, fishing, golf, live theater, museums, parks, shopping, tennis and water sports nearby.

Publicity: *Travel Holiday Magazine.*

Westwinds

914 Eaton St
Key West, FL 33040-6923
(305)296-4440 (800)788-4150 Fax:(305)293-0931
E-mail: frontdesk@westwindskeywest.com
Web: www.westwindskeywest.com

Circa 1921. The verdant flora that surrounds this historic inn will make guests feel as though they have left the city and entered a tropical paradise. However, Westwinds is located in the historic seaport district of Old Town Key West, and shops, restaurants and galleries are just steps away. Wicker and bright floral prints decorate the guest rooms. The grounds include a pool and a waterfall.

Innkeeper(s): Robin Chippas. $70-170. MC, VISA, DS, TC. TAC10. 26 rooms, 22 with PB and 4 suites. Breakfast included in rates. Types of meals: Cont plus. Beds: KQDT. Phone and ceiling fan in room. Air conditioning. Fax, copier and swimming on premises. Weddings, small meetings, family reunions and seminars hosted. Antiquing, fishing, golf, live theater, shopping and tennis nearby.

Whispers-Gideon Lowe House

409 William St
Key West, FL 33040-6853
(305)294-5969 (800)856-7444 Fax:(305)294-5141
E-mail: bbwhispers@aol.com
Web: www.whispersbb.com

Circa 1845. Tropical elegance awaits each guest at this mid 19th-century, three-story Greek Revival home, listed in the National Register of Historic Places. Ample verandas and shuttered windows reveal the local Bahamian influence, while tall white walls and ceilings fans cool the antique Victorian-decorated rooms, which offer a romantic touch of canopies and lace. Lounge in the tropical garden, complete with a pond for fish and a pool and hot tub for guests. Welcome each bright and glorious day in Key West with croissants dipped in egg nog and spiced rum, fresh fruit and a special lemon dill omelet wrapped around honey maple ham, cheese and sautéed asparagus. Other amenities include use of a private beach and health club nearby.

Innkeeper(s): John & Bonita Marburg. $99-175. MC, VISA, AX, DS, TC. TAC10. 7 rooms with PB. Breakfast included in rates. Types of meals: Gourmet bkfst and veg bkfst. Beds: KQ. Cable TV and ceiling fan in room. Air conditioning. Fax, spa, swimming and bicycles on premises. Spanish spoken. Antiquing, art galleries, beaches, bicycling, canoeing/kayaking, fishing, golf, hiking, live theater, museums, parks, shopping, tennis and water sports nearby.

Pets allowed: Call first.

Publicity: *National Geographic Traveler.*

Lake Helen   D8

Clauser's B&B

201 E Kicklighter Rd
Lake Helen, FL 32744-3514
(386)228-0310 (800)220-0310 Fax:(386)228-2337
E-mail: clauserinn@totcon.com
Web: www.clauserinn.com

Circa 1890. This three-story, turn-of-the-century vernacular Victorian inn is surrounded by a variety of trees in a quiet, country setting. The inn is listed in the national, state and local historic registers, and offers eight guest rooms, all with private bath. Each room features a different type of country decor, such as Americana, English and prairie. Guests enjoy hot tubbing in the Victorian gaze-bo or relaxing on the inn's porches, which feature rockers, a swing and cozy wicker furniture. Borrow a bike to take a closer look at the historic district. Stetson University, fine dining and several state parks are nearby.

Innkeeper(s): Tom & Marge Clauser. $95-140. MC, VISA, AX, DS, PC, TC. TAC10. 8 rooms with PB, 1 with FP. Breakfast and snacks/refreshments included in rates. Types of meals: Full bkfst and early coffee/tea. Beds: KQ. Phone, ceiling fan and private screened porch in room. Air conditioning. VCR, fax, copier, spa, bicycles, library and nature trail through forest on premises. Handicap access. Small meetings, family reunions and seminars hosted. Amusement parks, antiquing, fishing, atlantic beaches, live theater, parks, sporting events and water sports nearby.

Lake Wales   E8

Chalet Suzanne Country Inn & Restaurant

3800 Chalet Suzanne Dr
Lake Wales, FL 33859-7763
(863)676-6011 (800)433-6011 Fax:(863)676-1814
E-mail: info@chaletsuzanne.com
Web: www.chaletsuzanne.com

Circa 1924. Situated on 70 acres adjacent to Lake Suzanne, this country inn's architecture includes gabled roofs, balconies, spires and steeples. The superb restaurant has a glowing reputation and offers a six-course candlelight dinner. Places of inter-

est on the property include the Swiss Room, Wine Dungeon, Gift Boutique, Autograph Garden, Chapel Antiques, Ceramic Salon, Airstrip and the Soup Cannery. The inn has been transformed into a village of cottages and miniature chateaux, one connected to the other seemingly with no particular order.

Historic Interest: This wonderful inn is located in a National Historic District.

Innkeeper(s): Vita Hinshaw & Family. $169-229. MC, VISA, AX, DC, CB, DS, PC, TC. TAC10. 30 rooms with PB. Breakfast included in rates. Types of meals: Full bkfst, lunch, gourmet dinner and room service. Beds: KDT. Cable TV, phone and ceiling fan in room. Air conditioning. VCR, fax, copier, swimming and library on premises. Handicap access. Weddings, small meetings, family reunions and seminars hosted. German spoken. Amusement parks, antiquing, fishing, golf, live theater, parks, shopping, sporting events, tennis and water sports nearby.

Publicity: *National Geographic Traveler, Southern Living, Country Inns, Uncle Ben's 1992 award. and Country Inn Cooking.*

"I now know why everyone always says, 'Wow!' when they come up from dinner. Please don't change a thing."

Lake Worth   G10

Mango Inn

128 N Lakeside Dr
Lake Worth, FL 33460
(561)533-6900 (888)626-4619 Fax:(561)533-6992
E-mail: info@mangoinn.com
Web: www.mangoinn.com

Circa 1915. After a stay at Mango Inn, you'll want to take the decorator back to your own home and redo everything inside and out. Inside the historic home are eight unique guest rooms, each

with luxurious and imaginative décor. From the Seagrape Room with its verdant walls and a bed that includes a picket fence headboard trailed with ivy to the romantic Rose Room with a gingham comforter and rose-covered walls. The poolside cottage is a private retreat with a four-poster bed and French doors that lead out to a private patio. For a longer stay, try the picturesque Little House, a 1,200-square-foot cottage with two bedrooms, two bathrooms, a living room, dining room, full kitchen and laundry facilities. Breakfast treats might include the inn's signature mango-cashew muffins, and the meal is served either by the fireplace in the dining room or on a veranda that looks out to the pool. The innkeepers offer a variety of special packages to add an extra touch of elegance and romance to your stay. The shops of Palm Beach are just a few miles away, and Lake Worth offers plenty of antique shops.

Historic Interest: Jupiter Lighthouse (20 miles).

Innkeeper(s): Erin & Bo Allen. $70-225. MC, VISA, AX, DS, PC. TAC10. 8 rooms with PB and 1 cottage. Breakfast included in rates. Types of meals: Gourmet bkfst, early coffee/tea and picnic lunch. Beds: Q. Cable TV, phone, ceiling fan and VCR in room. Central air. Fax, swimming and bicycles on premises. Weddings and family reunions hosted. Antiquing, art galleries, beaches, bicycling, canoeing/kayaking, fishing, golf, horseback riding, live theater, museums, parks, shopping, sporting events, tennis and water sports nearby.

Sabal Palm House B&B Inn

109 N Golfview Rd
Lake Worth, FL 33460
(561)582-1090 (888)722-2572 Fax:(561)582-0933
E-mail: mrbsph@aol.com
Web: www.sabalpalmhouse.com

Circa 1936. Located across from the Intracostal Waterway and just minutes from white, sandy Atlantic beaches, this two-story, 1936 Key West Colonial-style home welcomes each guest with its tall ceilings, covered balconies, antique furniture and fine art. Surrounded by palm trees, bushes and white picket fences, guests will feel embraced in the sunny climate and romantic, European-tropical courtyard. Each detail in the recently renovated home was carefully preserved, from the oakwood floors to the tropical elegance of its original architecture and décor. With ample activities to fill both day and night in the surrounding area, the comfort of coming home to freshly cut flowers and a turned-down bed each night soothes the weariest of travelers and allows them to truly relax and enjoy their stay in one of Florida's most intriguing cities. Sabal Palm House is the only four-diamond inn located between Miami and Orlando.

Innkeeper(s): Michael & Lorraine Breece. $75-180. MC, VISA, AX, DS, TC. TAC10. 7 rooms with PB & 1 suite. Breakfast and afternoon tea included in rates. Types of meals: Gourmet bkfst, veg bkfst & early coffee/tea. Beds: KQT. Phone, turndown service, ceiling fan, two with Jacuzzi tubs, wine & appetizer in room. Central air. Fax, copier, bicycles and evening appetizers with wine and beer on premises. Family reunions hosted. Amusement parks, antiquing, art galleries, beaches, bicycling, canoeing/kayaking, fishing, golf and horseback riding nearby.

Publicity: *Palm Beach Post, Sun Sentinel, Miami Herald and New York Post.*

Maitland   D8

Thurston House

851 Lake Ave
Maitland, FL 32751-6306
(407)539-1911 (800)843-2721 Fax:(407)539-0365
E-mail: thurstonbb@aol.com
Web: www.thurstonhouse.com

Circa 1885. Just minutes from busy Orlando and the many attractions found nearby, this classic Queen Anne Victorian inn boasts a lakefront, countryside setting. Two of the inn's screened porches provide views of Lake Eulalia. Two parlors provide additional relaxing spots, and many guests like to stroll the grounds, which feature fruit trees and several bountiful gardens.

Innkeeper(s): Carole Ballard. $140-160. MC, VISA, AX. TAC10. 4 rooms with PB. Breakfast and snacks/refreshments included in rates. Types of meals: Full bkfst, cont plus and early coffee/tea. Beds: Q. Phone and ceiling fan in room. Air conditioning. VCR, fax, copier and library on premises. Antiquing, fishing, live theater, parks, shopping and sporting events nearby.

Publicity: *New York Times, US Air, Fort Lauderdale Sun Sentinel, Orlando Sentinel, Florida Living, Country Almanac, Palm Beach Post and WESH-TV - Channel 2 News.*

"Gracious hosts. What a jewel of a place. We couldn't have enjoyed ourselves more!"

Micanopy   C7

Herlong Mansion

402 NE Cholokka Blvd
Micanopy, FL 32667
(352)466-3322 (800)437-5664 Fax:(352)466-3322
E-mail: info@herlong.com
Web: www.herlong.com

Circa 1845. This mid-Victorian mansion features four two-story, carved-wood Roman Corinthian columns on its veranda. The mansion is surrounded by a garden with statuesque old

oak and pecan trees. Herlong Mansion features leaded-glass windows, mahogany inlaid oak floors, 12-foot ceilings and floor-to-ceiling windows in the dining room. Guest rooms with Jacuzzi tubs are available. All rooms are furnished with antiques.

Historic Interest: St. Augustine is about one and one-half hours from the mansion. The Marjorie Kinnan Rawlings Home is eight miles away. Micanopy is the oldest inland town in Florida, and has been the site for several movies.

Innkeeper(s): Julia & Lon Boggs. $89-189. MC, VISA, PC, TC. TAC10. 11 rooms with PB, 4 suites, 2 cottages and 1 conference room. Breakfast and snacks/refreshments included in rates. Types of meals: Gourmet bkfst, veg bkfst and early coffee/tea. Beds: KQDT. Cable TV, phone, turndown service, ceiling fan and some with VCR/TV in room. Central air. VCR, fax, bicycles and library on premises. Handicap access. Weddings, small meetings, family reunions and seminars hosted. Antiquing, art galleries, bicycling, canoeing/kayaking, fishing, golf, hiking, horseback riding, Marjorie Kennan Rawlings House, museums, parks, shopping and sporting events nearby.

Pets allowed: Cottage only.

Publicity: *Country Inns, Travel & Leisure, National Geographic Traveler, Southern Living, Florida Living and Florida Trend.*

Mount Dora   D8

The Emerald Hill Inn

27751 Lake Jem Rd
Mount Dora, FL 32757-9304
(352)383-2777 (800)366-9387

Circa 1941. This inn is secluded on two wooded acres that overlook Lake Victoria. The home has been the site of weddings, anniversary celebrations and a few proposals. Guest rooms are decorated in English country style. Each room is named after a gemstone, and some of the furnishings include

antiques. Mount Dora offers antique shops and restaurants, Ocala National Forest is nearby. The many sites of Orlando are less than an hour away.

Innkeeper(s): Colleen McGinley & Ron Oimoen. $99-149. MC, VISA, DS. TAC10. 4 rooms with PB, 1 suite and 1 conference room. Breakfast included in rates. Types of meals: Gourmet bkfst and early coffee/tea. Beds: KQT. Turndown service, ceiling fan and SAT TV in room. Air conditioning. Fax, stereo, CD and refrigerator on premises. Weddings, small meetings, family reunions and seminars hosted. Amusement parks, antiquing, fishing, golf, live theater, parks, shopping and water sports nearby.

Publicity: *Florida Living, Entertainment Express, Lake Sentinel Newspaper and Palm Beach Post.*

"Just what we were looking for, someplace quiet and peaceful. A great view."

Mount Dora Historic Inn

221 E 4th Ave
Mount Dora, FL 32757
(352)735-1212 (800)927-6344 Fax:(352)735-9743
E-mail: info@mountdorahistoricinn.com
Web: www.mountdorahistoricinn.com

Circa 1886. This century-old Victorian is on half an acre in quaint Mount Dora. Just a quarter of a mile from

the water and 25 minutes from Orlando, the inn offers four guest bedrooms. Early risers may enjoy coffee and tea. The full six-course gourmet breakfast includes fruit, a breakfast casserole and homemade bread. Afternoon tea also is served. Guests are encouraged to enjoy all the local area has to offer: nature walks, antique and craft stores, gourmet restaurants and horse-drawn carriage rides.

Historic Interest: Historic district of Mt. Dora (1 1/2 block).

Innkeeper(s): Lindsay & Nancy Richards. $85-125. MC, VISA, AX, DS, PC, TC. TAC10. 4 rooms with PB. Breakfast, afternoon tea and snacks/refreshments included in rates. Types of meals: Gourmet bkfst, veg bkfst, early coffee/tea and room service. Beds: KQ. Phone, turndown service and ceiling fan in room. Central air. Fax and copier on premises. Amusement parks, antiquing, art galleries, bicycling, canoeing/kayaking, fishing, golf, hiking, horseback riding, live theater, museums, parks, shopping, tennis, water sports and wineries nearby.

New Smyrna Beach   D9

Little River Inn B&B

532 N Riverside Dr
New Smyrna Beach, FL 32168-6741
(888)424-0102
E-mail: little-river-inn@juno.com
Web: www.little-river-inn.com

Circa 1883. Located on two acres of brick pathways, gardens and oak trees, this historic Inn offers wide, wraparound verandas and a cozy second floor porch. Guests enjoy views of scenic Indian River Lagoon and a variety of birds and wildlife that take refuge in the nature preserve. Spacious rooms are appointed

pleasantly and each has a special theme. Gourmet breakfasts are served in the dining room with colorful views of the gardens and grounds, which include fountains, a tennis court and a hammock. Nearby, New Smyrna Beach offers antique shops, galleries, marinas and "the world's safest bathing beach."

Innkeeper(s): Doug & Joyce MacLean. $89-159. MC, VISA, AX, DS, PC, TC. 6 rooms, 4 with PB and 1 conference room. Breakfast and snacks/refreshments included in rates. Types of meals: Gourmet bkfst, early coffee/tea and picnic lunch. Beds: KQ. Phone, ceiling fan, fireplace six rooms and portable TV on request in room. Air conditioning. VCR, fax, copier, spa, bicycles and tennis on premises. Handicap access. Weddings, small meetings, family reunions and seminars hosted. Amusement parks, antiquing, fishing, parks, shopping and water sports nearby.

"Our retreat turned into relaxation, romance and pure Victorian delight."

North Redington Beach   E7

Park Circle B&B

7 Park Circle
North Redington Beach, FL 33708
(727)394-8608 (866)440-7275 Fax:(727)397-9368
E-mail: parkcirclebb@aol.com
Web: www.parkcircle.com

Circa 1938. Enter the private courtyard and lush landscaping to find seven Mediterranean-style bungalows with jewel-toned windows. This secluded vintage resort, once for the rich and famous, now offers ideal romantic getaways and family outings. Fully restored, hardwood floors and antiques instill a rich history, while microwaves, central heat and air conditioning provide modern relief. Each bungalow is furnished with everything needed for a pleasant stay, including fresh flowers. An expanded continental breakfast featuring family recipes is served at the Manor House. Relax on screened porches with swings or enjoy hammocks on the brick patios surrounded by tropical gardens.

Innkeeper(s): Margaret Bourgeois. $125-225. MC, VISA, AX, DC, CB, DS, PC, TC. TAC10. 17 rooms and 7 guest houses. Breakfast and snacks/refreshments included in rates. Types of meals: Cont plus. Beds: KQT. Cable TV, phone, ceiling fan, private screened porches and brick patios in room. Central air. Tennis on premises. Weddings and family reunions hosted. Amusement parks, antiquing, art galleries, beaches, bicycling, canoeing/kayaking, fishing, golf, hiking, live theater, museums, parks, shopping, sporting events, tennis and water sports nearby.

Orange Park   B8

The Club Continental Suites

2143 Astor St
Orange Park, FL 32073-5624
(904)264-6070 (800)877-6070 Fax:(904)264-4044

Circa 1923. This waterfront estate was constructed for the Palmolive family and overlooks the St. Johns River. The architecture is Italian Renaissance with stucco and clay tile roof. Formal grounds include gardens with fountains, giant oaks and an elegant courtyard. Riverfront views are enjoyed. There are seven tennis courts, a marina and the pre-Civil War River House Pub, as well as the Club Continental Restaurant, a dinner club. A complimentary breakfast is served daily. Lunch is served Tuesday through Friday; brunch is available on Sunday.

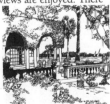

Innkeeper(s): Caleb Massee & Karrie Stevens. $75-160. MC, VISA, AX, DC, PC, TC. TAC10. 22 rooms with PB, 2 with FP, 4 suites and 2 conference rooms. Breakfast included in rates. Types of meals: Cont, gourmet lunch and dinner. Beds: KQ. Cable TV and phone in room. Air conditioning. Fax, copier, swimming, tennis, dinner, gourmet lunches Tuesday-Friday and Sunday

brunch on premises. Weddings, small meetings, family reunions and seminars hosted. Antiquing, fishing, live theater, parks, shopping and sporting events nearby.

Pets allowed: In two rooms only.

Publicity: *Miami Herald, Sun Sentinel and Tampa Tribune.*

"Superb dining with spectacular grounds."

Orlando   D8

The Courtyard at Lake Lucerne

211 N Lucerne Circle E
Orlando, FL 32801-3721
(407)648-5188 (800)444-5289 Fax:(407)246-1368
E-mail: info@orlandohistoricinn.com
Web: www.orlandohistoricinn.com

Circa 1885. This award-winning inn, precisely restored with attention to historical detail, consists of four different architectural styles. The Norment-Parry House is Orlando's oldest home.

The Wellborn, an Art-Deco Modern Building, offers one-bedroom suites with kitchenettes. The I.W. Phillips is an antebellum-style manor where breakfast is served in a large reception room with a wide veranda overlooking the courtyard fountains and lush gardens. The Grand Victorian Dr. Phillips House is listed in the National Register of Historic Places. For an enchanting treat, ask for the Turret Room.

Innkeeper(s): Charles Meiner. $89-225. MC, VISA, AX, DC. 30 rooms with PB and 1 conference room. Breakfast included in rates. Types of meals: Cont plus. Beds: KQD. Cable TV and phone in room. Air conditioning. Copier on premises. Weddings, small meetings and family reunions hosted. Amusement parks, antiquing, fishing, live theater, shopping, sporting events and water sports nearby.

Publicity: *Florida Historic Homes, Miami Herald, Southern Living and Country Victorian.*

"Best-kept secret in Orlando."

Meadow Marsh Bed & Breakfast

940 Tildenville School Rd
Orlando, FL 34787
(407)656-2064 (888)656-2064
E-mail: cavelle5@aol.com
Web: www.meadowmarsh.net

Circa 1877. Meadow Marsh is located on 12 tranquil acres just 14 miles west of downtown Orlando. One of the town's original settlers and "Citrus Kings" built the Victorian manor, which is highlighted by verandas on the first and second stories.

Current owners, John and Cavelle Pawlack, had the home placed in the National Register while adding many pleasant amenities to their historic home. Whirlpool tubs as well as gas fired or electric fireplaces are in

three of the five rooms. A three-course breakfast is served promptly at 8:30 a.m. in the glassed sunporch. Snacks are always available on the buffet for Meadow Marsh guests. Providing the feeling of the countryside of Old Florida, the inn is near all Central Florida's attractions.

Innkeeper(s): Cavelle & John Pawlack. $119-229. MC, VISA, TC. TAC10. 5 rooms with PB, 1 with FP, 2 suites and 1 cottage. Breakfast included in rates.

Types of meals: Lunch, picnic lunch and dinner. Beds: QD. Ceiling fan in room. Air conditioning. VCR, fax, copier, library and piano on premises. Amusement parks, antiquing, live theater, parks, sporting events and water sports nearby.

"What a beautiful home with such warm, gracious Southern hospitality."

Things Worth Remembering

1475 Kempton Chase Parkway
Orlando, FL 32818
(407)291-2127 Fax:(407)291-7725
E-mail: bandborlando@aol.com
Web: www.bedandbreakfast.com/bbc/p602893.asp

Circa 1900. The architectural style of this home is a combination contemporary Victorian farmhouse that overlooks a small lake, woods and flower gardens. Filled with antique furnishings, it is a showcase for an extensive collection of movie memorabilia, Broadway costumes and autographs. Guest bedrooms display artifacts relating to the theme of each decor, including the romantic Titanic, sophisticated Hollywood, whimsical Oz, outer space Sci, or artistic Music room. Generous amenities offer privacy and comfort. Enjoy a buffet breakfast served on the patio or in the dining room. Take a refreshing swim in the pool before visiting the local attractions.

Innkeeper(s): James & Lindsey. $90-200. MC, VISA, AX, TC. TAC15. 4 rooms with PB, 1 suite and 1 conference room. Breakfast and snacks/refreshments included in rates. Types of meals: Veg bkfst, cont plus and early coffee/tea. Beds: Q. Cable TV, phone, ceiling fan and VCR in room. Central air. Fax, copier, spa and library on premises. Handicap access. Small meetings and family reunions hosted. Amusement parks, antiquing, art galleries, beaches, bicycling, canoeing/kayaking, fishing, golf, hiking, horseback riding, live theater, museums, parks, shopping, sporting events, tennis, water sports and wineries nearby.

Pets allowed: Must make reservations for kennel or if the pet is small, reserve room set aside for pet owners.

Palatka   C8

Azalea House

220 Madison St
Palatka, FL 32177-3531
(386)325-4547
E-mail: azaleahouse@gbso.net

Circa 1878. Located within the Palatka Historic District, this beautifully embellished Queen Anne Victorian is painted a cheerful yellow with complementing green shutters. Bay windows, gables and verandas have discrete touches of royal blue, gold, white and aqua on the gingerbread trim, a true "Painted Lady." There are oak, magnolia and palm trees and an 85-year-old, grafted camellia tree with both pink and white blossoms. Double parlors are furnished with period antiques including an arched, floor-to-ceiling mirror. A three-story heart and curly pine staircase leads to the guest rooms. Breakfast is served on fine china in the formal dining room. Two blocks away is the mile-wide north flowing St. John's River. An unaltered golf course designed by Donald Ross in 1925 is nearby, as well as the Ravine State Botanical Garden. It's 25 minutes to Cresent Beach.

Innkeeper(s): Doug & Jill de Leeuw. $75-135. MC, VISA, AX, TC. 6 rooms, 4 with PB. Breakfast and snacks/refreshments included in rates. Types of meals: Full bkfst, cont plus and early coffee/tea. Beds: Q. Phone, turndown service, ceiling fan and alarm clocks in room. Air conditioning. Spa, swimming and porch swings on premises. Weddings and small meetings hosted. Antiquing, fishing, golf, live theater, parks, shopping and water sports nearby.

Publicity: *American Treasures.*

Palm Beach   G10

Palm Beach Historic Inn

365 S County Rd
Palm Beach, FL 33480-4449
(561)832-4009 Fax:(561)832-6255
E-mail: innkeeper@palmbeachhistoricinn.com
Web: www.palmbeachhistoricinn.com

Circa 1923. Visitors are welcomed into a lobby with the look of an elegant European parlor. Intimate, comfortable, meticulously clean accommodations with every modern convenience await each guest. Besides choice lodging, travelers will enjoy being just one block from the beach. Also a few short steps away are a

variety of entertainment options, gift and antique shopping, spectacular dining experiences, and tours of legendary mansions and art galleries. Recreational activities range from horseback riding, tennis and golf to snorkeling, scuba diving or fishing. Ask the concierge for advice in exploring this tropical paradise.

Historic Interest: Flagler Museum is more than a mile away. World-famous Worth Ave., known for its 1920s Mizner architecture, is within walking distance, two blocks from the inn. Even closer is the historic Town Hall, located right across the street.

Innkeeper(s): Sean & Jody Herbert. $85-325. MC, VISA, AX, DC, DS, TC. TAC10. 9 rooms with PB and 4 suites. Breakfast included in rates. Types of meals: Cont. Beds: KQD. Cable TV, phone and built in hair dryers in room. Air conditioning. VCR, fax, copier and library on premises. Family reunions hosted. Fishing, live theater, parks, shopping, sporting events and water sports nearby.

Publicity: *PB Today and PB Society.*

Palmetto   F7

The Palmetto House B&B

1102 Riverside Dr
Palmetto, FL 34221
(941)723-1236 (800)658-4167 Fax:(941)723-1507
E-mail: info@thepalmettohouse.com
Web: www.thepalmettohouse.com

Circa 1912. This gracious historic manor, along with its three cottages, is situated directly on the Manatee River with views of moss-draped oaks and waterfront sunsets. Overlooking the Regatta Pointe Marina, the inn's acre of gardens include hibiscus, sabal palms, plumbago and Royal Palms. In the National Register, the home has been newly renovated. Guest rooms offer Victorian or Arts and Crafts furnishings and decor and most rooms have Jacuzzi tubs, walk-in-showers as well as a plethora of amenities. Breakfast is served in the dining room or on the inviting sunroom, but beforehand be sure to enjoy early morning coffee along the river or on the courtyard. The Ringling Museum, Anna Maria Island, Marie Selby Botanical Gardens and the Mote Aquarium are area attractions.

Innkeeper(s): Bob & Linda Gehring. $100-160. MC, VISA, PC. TAC10. 8 rooms with PB, 2 suites and 3 cottages. Breakfast, afternoon tea and snacks/refreshments included in rates. Types of meals: Full bkfst and early coffee/tea. Beds: KQ. Cable TV, phone, turndown service, ceiling fan and VCR in room. Central air. Fax, copier, spa, swimming and library on premises. Weddings, small meetings, family reunions and seminars hosted. Amusement parks, antiquing, art galleries, beaches, bicycling, canoeing/kayaking, fishing, golf, Anna Maria Island, DeSoto National Memorial, Ringling Museum, Mote Aquarium, Marie Selby Botanical Gardens, live theater, museums, parks, shopping, sporting events, tennis, water sports and wineries nearby.

Publicity: *Bradenton Herald and Sarasota Herald Tribune.*

Pensacola   B2

Noble Manor

110 W Strong St
Pensacola, FL 32501-3140
(850)434-9544
E-mail: nmanor@bellsouth.net

Circa 1905. This two-story home offers Tudor Revival-style
architecture. It is set on lavish grounds planted with camellias,
azaleas and roses. The inn is decorated with traditional furnishings, antiques and fine art prints, and guests will enjoy a dramatic central staircase and handsome fireplaces. Breakfast is
served in the dining room. A front porch and a gazebo with a
hot tub are among guests' favorite spots. Pensacola's North Hill
Historic District is a historic preservation area. Nearby are Civil
War forts and a restored 1800s area.

Historic Interest: Civil war forts (3 miles).

Innkeeper(s): John & Carol Briscoe. $65-100. MC, VISA, AX, PC, TC. TAC10.
4 rooms with PB, 3 with FP and 1 conference room. Breakfast and
snacks/refreshments included in rates. Types of meals: Cont plus and early cof-
fee/tea. Beds: KQ. Cable TV and ceiling fan in room. Central air. Spa, swimming and library on premises. Weddings and small meetings hosted. Antiquing,
art galleries, beaches, live theater, museums, parks and sporting events nearby.

Pets allowed: Small dogs.

Springhil Guesthouse

903 N Spring St
Pensacola, FL 32501
(850)438-6887 (800)475-1956 Fax:(850)438-9075
E-mail: guesthouse@pcola.gulf.net

Circa 1900. Traditional comfort and antiques augment this
spacious yet intimate Queen Anne Victorian. Generous and
creative hospitality is the home's hallmark. The Turret Suite
boasts two hand-crafted fireplaces, a guest bedroom with sitting area, parlor, full kitchen and dining area. The Bay Suite features a parlor with a fireplace, a dining area and a butler's
pantry kitchen. It can sleep up to four people. Both of the well-
decorated suites offer privacy and a romantic ambiance. Books,
games and videos are available. Breakfast is provided at
Hopkins House, a local landmark and family restaurant. Relax
on the front porch or enjoy the landscaped grounds with a
New Orleans-style patio area.

Historic Interest: Pensacola Historic Village.

Innkeeper(s): Don & Wanda laird. $79-149. PC, TC. TAC10. 2 suites, 2 with
FP. Breakfast included in rates. Types of meals: Country bkfst, cont plus and
early coffee/tea. Beds: Q. Cable TV, phone, ceiling fan, VCR and fireplace in
room. Central air. Fax and copier on premises. Weddings hosted. Amusement
parks, antiquing, art galleries, beaches, canoeing/kayaking, fishing, golf, hiking, live theater, museums, parks, tennis and water sports nearby.

Quincy   B5

Allison House Inn

215 N Madison St
Quincy, FL 32351
(850)875-2511 (888)904-2511 Fax:(850)875-2511
E-mail: innkeeper@tds.net

Circa 1843. Crepe myrtle, azaleas, camellias and roses dot the
acre of grounds that welcomes guests to the Allison House. A
local historic landmark located in the 36-block historic district,
the inn is in a Georgian, English-country style with shutters and

an entrance portico. It was built for General Allison, who became
Governor of Florida. There are two parlors, and all the rooms are
appointed with English antiques. Homemade biscotti is always
available for snacking and for breakfast, English muffins and
freshly baked breads are offered. Walk around the district and
spot the 51 historic homes and buildings. Nearby dining opportunities include the historic Nicholson Farmhouse Restaurant.

Innkeeper(s): Stuart & Eileen Johnson. $75-120. MC, VISA, DS, PC, TC.
TAC10. 6 rooms with PB. Breakfast and snacks/refreshments included in
rates. Types of meals: Full bkfst and cont plus. AP. Beds: KQD. Cable TV,
phone, ceiling fan, individual air conditioning controls and hair dryers in
room. Fax and bicycles on premises. Handicap access. Family reunions hosted. Antiquing, art galleries, bicycling, golf, horseback riding, live theater,
sporting events and tennis nearby.

Pets Allowed.

McFarlin House B&B Inn

305 E King St
Quincy, FL 32351
(850)875-2526 (877)370-4701 Fax:(850)627-4703
E-mail: inquiries@mcfarlinhouse.com
Web: mcfarlinhouse.com

Circa 1895. Tobacco farmer John McFarlin built this Queen
Anne Victorian, notable for its left-handed turret and grand,
wraparound porch. The home, which is listed in the National
Register, boasts original woodwork, hand-carved mantels, Italian
tile work and stained glass. Romantic guest rooms are decorated

with Victorian furnishings, and each
is unique. The Southern Grace
includes a fireplace and whirlpool
tub for two. In the King's View,
the double whirlpool tub is set
in front of bay windows. The
Pink Magnolia Room is located
in the home's turret. The Ribbons and Roses Room includes a
six-foot-long clawfoot tub, a fireplace and a canopy bed draped
in netting. Breakfast begins with two different baked goods, followed by a main course, perhaps an omelet or quiche. McFarlin
House is located in a Quincy historic district, just a short drive
from Florida's capital city, Tallahassee.

Historic Interest: B&B within 30 block historic district.

Innkeeper(s): Richard & Tina Fauble. $75-175. MC, VISA, AX, DC, DS, PC,
TC. 9 rooms with PB. Breakfast and snacks/refreshments included in rates.
Types of meals: Full bkfst. Beds: KQD. Cable TV, phone, ceiling fan and VCR
in room. Central air. Fax and spa on premises. Weddings, small meetings,
family reunions and seminars hosted. Antiquing, art galleries, fishing, golf,
museums and sporting events nearby.

Saint Augustine   B8

Agustin Inn

29 Cuna St
Saint Augustine, FL 32084-3681
(904)823-9559 (800)248-7846 Fax:(904)824-8685
E-mail: www.agustin@aug.com
Web: www.agustininn.com

Circa 1903. Situated in the historic walking district of our
nation's oldest city, this Victorian inn captures the ambiance of
old downtown St. Augustine. Innkeepers Robert and Sherri
Brackett, members of Historic Inns of St. Augustine and
Superior Small Lodging, have furnished the home in comfortable elegance. The twelve guest bedrooms boast mahogany or

canopy beds and oval Jacuzzi tubs. Some of the bedrooms have private entrances and terraces where early coffee or tea and evening wine and hors d'oeuvres can be enjoyed while overlooking the fragrant courtyards. Sherri's full homemade breakfasts are satisfying and may feature Belgian waffles with fried apples and bananas, delicious omelets, and home fries with buttermilk biscuits. Venturing out on the cobblestone streets offers a variety of activities and historical sites.

Innkeeper(s): Robert & Sherri Brackett. $89-175. MC, VISA, AX, DS, PC, TC. 12 rooms with PB. Breakfast and snacks/refreshments included in rates. Types of meals: Full bkfst and early coffee/tea. Beds: Q. Ceiling fan and Jacuzzi tubs in room. Central air. Fax and copier on premises. Handicap access. Antiquing, art galleries, beaches, fishing, golf, museums, parks and shopping nearby.

Alexander Homestead B&B

14 Sevilla St
Saint Augustine, FL 32084-3529
(904)826-4147 (888)292-4147 Fax:(904)823-9503
E-mail: bonnie@aug.com
Web: www.alexanderhomestead.com

Circa 1888. Green pastel hues dotted with white create a fanciful, tropical look at this Victorian bed & breakfast. Polished wood floors, colorful rugs and a mix of antiques and family pieces set the stage for a nostalgic getaway. Oversized tubs, lace, scented sachets and fresh flowers are just a few treats awaiting guests. The plentiful breakfasts are served in the elegant dining room. In the evening, guests also may enjoy a cordial in the Victorian parlor. The inn is located in St. Augustine's downtown historic area, so there is plenty of nearby activity.

Historic Interest: Fort Castillo de San Marco (1/2 mile), Lightner Museum (1/2 mile), Oldest Wooden Schoolhouse in US (1/2 mile), Fountain of Youth (1 mile), World Golf Hall of Fame (9 miles).

Innkeeper(s): Bonnie Alexander. $115-175. MC, VISA, AX, DS, PC, TC. TAC10. 4 rooms with PB, 3 with FP. Breakfast and afternoon tea included in rates. Types of meals: Country bkfst, early coffee/tea, picnic lunch, snacks/refreshments and room service. Beds: QT. Cable TV and one with whirlpool Jacuzzi tub in room. Central air. Fax and bicycles on premises. Weddings and family reunions hosted. Antiquing, art galleries, beaches, bicycling, canoeing/kayaking, fishing, golf, live theater, museums, parks, shopping, tennis and water sports nearby.

Publicity: US Air, Florida Living, Palm Beach Post, Orlando Sentinal and WPEC TV 12 West Palm Beach.

"We want to thank you for the 'oasis' we found in your home. Everything was perfection. We feel the love that you extend to your guests."

Bayfront Westcott House

146 Avenida Menendez
Saint Augustine, FL 32084-5049
(800)513-9814 Fax:(904)824-1502
E-mail: westcott@aug.com
Web: www.westcotthouse.com

Circa 1890. Dr. John Westcott, a man notable for his part in building the St. John Railroad and linking the Intracoastal Waterway from St. John's River to Miami, built this stunning vernacular Victorian. The elegant inn overlooks Matanzas bay, affording guests an enchanting view both inside and out. The interior is filled with Victorian furnishings, from marble-topped tables to white iron beds. The inn is located in St. Augustine's

historic district, and plenty of historic sites, restaurants and shops are within walking distance.

Innkeeper(s): Janice & Robert Graubard. $95-250. MC, VISA, AX, DS. 9 rooms with PB, 4 with FP. Breakfast included in rates. Types of meals: Full bkfst. Beds: KQ. Cable TV, turndown service, ceiling fan, three with Jacuzzi, six with bay views and phones in room. Air conditioning. Antiquing, fishing, golf, marina and shopping nearby.

Publicity: *Country Homes and AAA Magazine.*

Carriage Way B&B

70 Cuna St
Saint Augustine, FL 32084-3684
(904)829-2467 (800)908-9832 Fax:(904)826-1461
E-mail: bjohnson@aug.com
Web: www.carriageway.com

Circa 1883. A two-story veranda dominates the facade of this Victorian. Painted creamy white with blue trim, the house is located in the heart of the historic district. It's within a three-block walk to restaurants and shops and the Intracoastal Waterway. Guest rooms reflect the charm of a light Victorian touch, with brass canopy and four-poster beds. Many furnishings have been in the house for 60 years. The "Cottage"offers two guest rooms, a comfortable living/dining room and a kitchenette. A full gourmet breakfast is provided in the morning.

Innkeeper(s): Bill Johnson & son, Larry. $89-175. MC, VISA, AX, DS, TC. 11 rooms with PB, 1 with FP. Breakfast and snacks/refreshments included in rates. Types of meals: Full bkfst, early coffee/tea and picnic lunch. Beds: KQD. Phone and ceiling fan in room. Air conditioning. Fax, copier and bicycles on premises. Weddings, small meetings and family reunions hosted. Amusement parks, antiquing, fishing, live theater, parks, shopping, sporting events and water sports nearby.

Publicity: *Miami Herald, Florida Times Union, Palm Beach Post and Sunday Oklahoman.*

Casa De La Paz Bayfront B&B

22 Avenida Menendez
Saint Augustine, FL 32084-3644
(904)829-2915 (800)929-2915
E-mail: innkeeper@cascadelapaz.com
Web: www.casadelapaz.com

Circa 1915. Overlooking Matanzas Bay, Casa de la Paz was built after the devastating 1914 fire leveled much of the old city. An ornate stucco Mediterranean Revival house, it features clay barrel tile roofing, bracketed eaves, verandas and a lush walled courtyard. The home is listed in the National Register of Historic Places. Guest rooms offer ceiling fans, central air, hardwood floors, antiques, a decanter of sherry, chocolates and complimentary snacks.

Historic Interest: Fountain of Youth, Castillo de San Marcos, Lightner Museum, Flagler College (walking distance).

Innkeeper(s): Sherri & Marshall Crews. $120-240. MC, VISA, AX, DS, PC, TC. 7 rooms with PB, 3 with FP. Breakfast included in rates. Types of meals: Full bkfst and early coffee/tea. Beds: KQ. Cable TV, phone and ceiling fan in room. Air conditioning. Antiquing, fishing, live theater, parks, shopping, sporting events and water sports nearby.

Publicity: *Innsider, US Air Magazine, Southern Living. and PBS.*

"We will always recommend your beautifully restored, elegant home."

Casa De Solana, B&B Inn

21 Aviles St
Saint Augustine, FL 32084-4441
(904)824-3555 (888)796-0980 Fax:(904)824-3316
E-mail: info@cascadesolana.com
Web: www.casadesolana.com

Circa 1763. Spanish military leader Don Manuel Solana built
this home in the early European settlement, and Spanish
records show that a Solana child was the first European child

born in America. The thick
coquina-shell walls (limestone
formed of broken shells and
corals cemented together), high
ceilings with dark, hand-hewn
beams and polished hand-pegged
floors are part of the distinctive
flavor of this period. Five Minorican fireplaces are in the house.
A Southern breakfast is served in an elegant dining room.

Innkeeper(s): Joe Finnegan. $125-225. MC, VISA, AX, DS, PC. TAC10. 8
rooms with PB and 2 suites. Breakfast included in rates. Types of meals: Full
bkfst. AP. Beds: KQD. Cable TV, phone, most with fireplace, whirlpool tubs
and balconies in room. Air conditioning. Amusement parks, antiquing, fishing, golf, live theater, parks, shopping, tennis and water sports nearby.

Publicity: *Times Union, House Beautiful, Palm Beach Post, Innsider, North
Florida Living, Jacksonville Today and PM Magazine.*

Castle Garden B&B

15 Shenandoah St
Saint Augustine, FL 32084-2817
(904)829-3839
E-mail: castleg@aug.com
Web: www.castlegarden.com

Circa 1860. This newly-restored Moorish Revival-style inn was
the carriage house to Warden Castle. Among the seven guest
rooms are three bridal rooms with in-room Jacuzzi tubs and
sunken bedrooms with cathedral
ceilings. The innkeepers offer
packages including carriage rides,
picnic lunches, gift baskets and
other enticing possibilities.
Guests enjoy a homemade full,
country breakfast each morning.

Historic Interest: Castle Warden next door, Fort Mantanza's (200 yards to
south), Alligator Farm, Saint Augustine Lighthouse (nearby).

Innkeeper(s): Bruce & Brian Kloeckner. $65-179. MC, VISA, AX, DS. TAC10.
7 rooms with PB and 3 suites. Breakfast included in rates. Types of meals:
Full bkfst, early coffee/tea and picnic lunch. Beds: KQT. Ceiling fan and some
with TV in room. Air conditioning. Common sitting room with cable on
premises. Antiquing, fishing, golf, ballooning nearby, live theater, shopping,
tennis and water sports nearby.

Cedar House Inn Victorian B&B

79 Cedar St
Saint Augustine, FL 32084-4311
(904)829-0079 (800)233-2746 Fax:(904)825-0916
E-mail: info@cedarhouseinn.com
Web: www.cedarhouseinn.com

Circa 1893. A player piano entertains guests in the parlor of
this restored Victorian, which offers plenty of relaxing possibilities. Enjoy refreshments on the veranda or simply curl up with a
good book in the library. Innkeepers Russ and Nina Thomas
have preserved the home's luxurious heart-of-pine floors and

10-foot ceilings. They highlighted
this architectural treasure with
period furnishings and reproductions. Guests rooms are decked
in Victorian decor and boast
either clawfoot or Jacuzzi tubs.
The innkeepers also offer an outdoor
Jacuzzi spa. Elegant breakfasts are served either in the dining
room or on the veranda. Guests may borrow bicycles perfect for
exploring historic Saint Augustine or nearby beaches.

Innkeeper(s): Russ & Nina Thomas. $119-215. MC, VISA, AX, DS, PC, TC.
TAC10. 6 rooms with PB, 3 with FP, 1 suite and 1 conference room.
Breakfast and snacks/refreshments included in rates. Types of meals: Gourmet
bkfst, early coffee/tea, picnic lunch and dinner. Beds: Q. Ceiling fan in room.
Air conditioning. Fax, spa and bicycles on premises. Weddings, small meetings, family reunions and seminars hosted. Antiquing, fishing, historic sites
and museums, live theater, parks, shopping and water sports nearby.

Publicity: *Palm Beach Times,Palm Beach Post, Southern Living and New
York Times.*

*"What a special 'home' to spend our honeymoon! Everything was
terrific! We feel this is our place now and will be regular guests here!
Thank you!"*

Inn on Charlotte Street

52 Charlotte St
Saint Augustine, FL 32084-3647
(904)829-3819 Fax:(904)810-2134
E-mail: innoncharlotte@webtv.net
Web: www.innoncharlotte.com

Circa 1914. Majestic palms accentuate the exterior of this brick
home, adorned by a sweeping second-story veranda. The inn is
located among many historic gems within Saint Augustine's historic district. Innkeeper Vanessa Noel
has been an innkeeper for more than
30 years, hosting guests in Maine and
New Hampshire. Now she has
brought her considerable talents to
Saint Augustine, a perfect vacation
spot for history buffs. Noel has decorated the inn with antiques, over-
stuffed sofas and wicker. Some rooms include a Jacuzzi tub, fireplace or private veranda. The inn is within walking distance to
many shops and restaurants, as well as the Castillo de San
Marcos. Golf, sailing and fishing are other popular local activities.

Historic Interest: Castillo De San Marcos, Cathedral, Bridge of Lions, all
within a three minute walk.

Innkeeper(s): Vanessa Noel. $85-165. MC, VISA, AX, PC, TC. TAC10. 6 rooms
with PB, 2 with FP and 1 suite. Breakfast and afternoon tea included in rates.
Types of meals: Full bkfst, country bkfst, veg bkfst and early coffee/tea. Beds:
KQ. Cable TV, ceiling fan and VCR in room. Central air. Fax, copier and library
on premises. Weddings, small meetings, family reunions and seminars hosted.
Antiquing, art galleries, beaches, bicycling, canoeing/kayaking, fishing, golf, hiking, oldest city in the U.S, live theater, museums, parks, shopping, sporting
events, tennis, water sports and wineries nearby.

Publicity: *Southern Living.*

Kenwood Inn

38 Marine St
Saint Augustine, FL 32084-4439
(904)824-2116 (800)824-8151 Fax:(904)824-1689
Web: www.oldcity.com/kenwood

Circa 1865. Originally built as a summer home, the Kenwood
Inn has taken in guests for more than 100 years. Early records
show that it was advertised as a private boarding house as early

as 1886. Rooms are decorated in periods ranging from the simple Shaker décor to more formal colonial and Victorian styles.

Historic Interest: Lightner Museum, Oldest House Museum, Bridge of Lions (walking distance).

Innkeeper(s): Mark & Kerrianne Constant. $110-200. MC, VISA, DS, PC, TC. 14 rooms with PB and 4 suites. Breakfast included in rates. Types of meals: Cont. Beds: KQD. TV and ceiling fan in room. Air conditioning. Fax and swimming on premises. Antiquing, fishing, live theater, shopping and water sports nearby.

Publicity: *Palm Beach Post, Florida Living, Southern Living and Seabreeze.*

"It's one of my favorite spots for a few days of relaxation and recuperation."

Old City House Inn & Restaurant

115 Cordova St
Saint Augustine, FL 32084-4413
(904)826-0113 Fax:(904)826-3294
E-mail: oldcityhousebb@aol.com

Circa 1873. Saint Augustine is a treasure bed of history, and this inn is strategically located in the center. A red-tile roof covers this former stable, and a veranda and courtyard add to the Spanish atmosphere. Guest rooms offer four-poster, hand-carved beds and some feature Jacuzzi tubs. Inn guests are privy to the expansive gourmet breakfasts, but can join others for lunch and

dinner in the restaurant. Appetizers include baked brie and Alligator Fritters. For lunch, unique salads, fresh fish and chicken create the menu, while dinner choices include gourmet standards such as Filet Mignon or a more unusual Thai coconut milk beef curry with sesame rice.

Historic Interest: Castillo de San Marcos (one-fourth miles), Ripley's Believe It or Not Museum (one-half mile), Lightner Museum (across street).

Innkeeper(s): James & Ilse Philcox. $85-175. MC, VISA, AX, DC, CB, DS. 7 rooms with PB. Breakfast included in rates. Types of meals: Full bkfst, early coffee/tea and gourmet dinner. Beds: Q. Cable TV, ceiling fan, four-poster hand-carved beds and some with Jacuzzi's in room. Air conditioning. VCR, fax, copier and bicycles on premises. Handicap access. Antiquing, fishing, live theater, shopping and water sports nearby.

Publicity: *Florida Times Union, Florida Trend and Ft. Lauderdale Sun Sentinal.*

St. Francis Inn

279 Saint George St
Saint Augustine, FL 32084-5031
(904)824-6068 (800)824-6062 Fax:(904)810-5525
E-mail: innceasd@aug.com
Web: www.stfrancisinn.com

Circa 1791. Long noted for its hospitality, the St. Francis Inn is nearly the oldest house in town. A classic example of Old World architecture, it was built by Gaspar Garcia, who

received a Spanish grant to the plot of land. Coquina was the main building material. A buffet breakfast is served. Some rooms have whirlpool tubs and fireplaces. The city of Saint Augustine was founded in 1565.

Historic Interest: The nation's oldest house (free admission for guests at the St. Francis Inn), Saint Augustine Antigua.

Innkeeper(s): Joe Finnegan. $79-189. MC, VISA, AX, PC. TAC10. 14 rooms with PB, 8 with FP, 4 suites, 1 cottage and 2 conference rooms. Breakfast included in rates. Types of meals: Full bkfst. Beds: KQDT. Cable TV, phone, ceiling fan and whirlpool tubs in room. Air conditioning. Fax, copier, swimming, bicycles and whirlpool tubs on premises. Weddings, small meetings, family reunions and seminars hosted. American Sign Language spoken. Antiquing, fishing, parks, shopping, sporting events and water sports nearby.

Publicity: *Orlando Sentinel.*

"We have stayed at many nice hotels but nothing like this. We are really enjoying it."

Victorian House B&B

11 Cadiz St
Saint Augustine, FL 32084-4431
(904)824-5214 (877)703-0432
E-mail: kjc50@aol.com

Circa 1897. Enjoy the historic ambiance of Saint Augustine at this turn-of-the-century Victorian, decorated to reflect the grandeur of that genteel era. Stenciling highlights the walls, and the innkeepers have filled the guest rooms with canopy beds and period furnishings complementing the heart of pine floors. A full breakfast includes homemade granola, fresh fruit, a hot entree and a variety of freshly made breads.

Innkeeper(s): Ken & Marcia Cerotzke. $89-170. MC, VISA, AX, DS. TAC10. 8 rooms with PB and 4 suites. Breakfast included in rates. Types of meals: Full bkfst. Beds: KQDT. Ceiling fan and refrigerator (one room) in room. Air conditioning. Antiquing, fine restaurants, live theater, parks and shopping nearby.

Whale's Tale

54 Charlotte St
Saint Augustine, FL 32084-3647
(904)829-5901 (888)989-4253
E-mail: whale@oldcity.com
Web: www.WhalesTaleBandB.com

Circa 1910. Whale's Tale is within one or two blocks from the Bay Front, Castillo de San Marcos, Plaza de Constitution, St. George Street and within a mile of dozens of historic sites, including the Fountain of Youth, Victorian Village The Fort and Mission de Nombre de Dias. The Lightener Museum is three blocks away. The home itself is historic, built in the early 20th century. Gardens and two tall palm trees mark the front of the house, and there's a porch off all the rooms. The décor includes lacy curtains, turn-of-the-century antiques and patchwork quilts. A full breakfast is served each morning and the innkeepers have a repertoire of 14 different breakfasts, such as Whale's Tale quiche on a hashbrown potato crust and apple-peach smoothies. The innkeepers are happy to help guests find a special restaurant or plan daily activities. Parking on the premises and a dozen restaurants are nearby.

Historic Interest: Fountain of Youth (1 miles), Gonzalez-Alvarez House (1 block), St. Augustine Lighthouse (2 miles), Ponce de Leon Hotel (3 blocks), Bridge of Lions (1 block), Tolomato Cemetery (3 blocks), Cathedral of St. Augustine (1 1/2 blocks), Flagler College (1 1/2 blocks).

Innkeeper(s): Betty & Denis Cunningham. $89-149. MC, VISA, DS, TC. TAC10. 7 rooms with PB. Breakfast included in rates. Types of meals: Full bkfst and veg bkfst. Beds: Q. Ceiling fan in room. Central air. Weddings, small meetings, family reunions and seminars hosted. Antiquing, art galleries, beaches, bicycling, canoeing/kayaking, fishing, golf, hiking, horseback riding, live theater, museums, parks, shopping, sporting events, tennis, water sports and wineries nearby.

"The perfect setting for celebrating our first wedding anniversary. We have told all our friends about your beautiful establishment. Thanks for such a wonderful place."

Saint Petersburg E7

Bay Gables Bed & Breakfast and Garden

340 Rowland Ct NE
Saint Petersburg, FL 33701
(727)822-8855 (800)822-8803 Fax:(727)824-7223
E-mail: baygables@aol.com
Web: www.baygables.com

Circa 1901. Located in the heart of downtown, this historic Key West-style Victorian is filled with a delightful combination of period antiques and modern amenities. Each guest bedroom and suite offers generous amenities for comfort. The Yorkshire and Oxford Suites also feature a sitting room daybed and kitchenette. The spacious Camelot Suite boasts a whirlpool tub. Breakfast can be enjoyed in the Devonshire Suite, gazebo or on the wide wraparound porches. Weddings are popularly held in the garden. Walk to the waterfront parks, pier, shops, restaurants and museums.

Historic Interest: Ft. DeSoto (20 miles).
Innkeeper(s): Terri Hockensmith. $99-150. MC, VISA, AX, DS. TAC10. 10 rooms with PB. Breakfast and snacks/refreshments included in rates. Types of meals: Cont plus, cont and early coffee/tea. Beds: KQDT. Cable TV, phone, ceiling fan and hair dryers in room. Air conditioning. Fax and copier on premises. Handicap access. Weddings hosted. Antiquing, art galleries, beaches, bicycling, fishing, golf, live theater, museums, parks, shopping, sporting events, tennis and water sports nearby.

Bayboro House B&B on Old Tampa Bay

1719 Beach Dr SE
Saint Petersburg, FL 33701-5917
(877)823-4955 Fax:(877)823-4955
E-mail: bayboro@tampabay.rr.com
Web: www.bayborohousebandb.com

Circa 1907. Victorian decor and beautiful antique furnishings fill the Bayboro House, a charming turn-of-the-century manor. The veranda is set up for relaxation with a variety of rockers, swings, wicker chairs and chaise lounges. Breakfasts, served in the formal dining room, feature what every Florida breakfast should, freshly squeezed juices and in-season fruits. Before heading out to one of Saint Petersburg's many restaurants, relax and sip a glass of wine in the parlor.

Historic Interest: The Bayboro House is only minutes from six museums and downtown Saint Petersburg.
Innkeeper(s): Sandy & Dave Kelly. $125-249. MC, VISA, AX, DC, DS, PC, TC. 5 rooms with PB and 2 suites. Breakfast included in rates. Types of meals: Cont plus. Beds: KQ. Ceiling fan and VCR in room. Air conditioning. Fax, spa and swimming on premises. Amusement parks, antiquing, fishing, live theater, parks, shopping, sporting events and water sports nearby.
Publicity: *Miami Herald, Sun Sentinel.* and *Home Shopping CBS.*

"It was well worth the price, a long weekend that I'll never forget. It was everything that you advertised it to be and so much more. Thanks so much."

Inn at the Bay Bed and Breakfast

126 4th Ave NE
Saint Petersburg, FL 33701
(727)822-1700 (888)873-2122 Fax:(727)896-7412
E-mail: info@innatthebay.com
Web: www.innatthebay.com

Circa 1910. Conveniently located on Tampa Bay, this newly renovated inn is near many of the state's popular attractions. The plush guest bedrooms and suites, themed in regional motifs, showcase Florida. Allergy-free feather beds and whirlpool tubs soothe and rejuvenate. Hospitality is abundant in the provision of thoughtful amenities like fluffy robes, lighted makeup mirrors, cable TV and Internet access. After a delicious breakfast, enjoy reading the daily newspaper in the garden gazebo.

Innkeeper(s): Dennis & Jewly Youschak. $89-240. MC, VISA, AX. TAC10. 12 rooms with PB and 1 conference room. Breakfast included in rates. Types of meals: Full bkfst and early coffee/tea. Beds: KQ. Cable TV, phone, turndown service, ceiling fan, VCR and one with fireplace in room. Central air. Fax and copier on premises. Handicap access. Weddings, small meetings, family reunions and seminars hosted. Amusement parks, antiquing, art galleries, beaches, canoeing/kayaking, fishing, golf, hiking, horseback riding, live theater, museums, parks, shopping, sporting events and water sports nearby.

Lee Manor Inn

342 3rd Ave N
Saint Petersburg, FL 33701-3821
(727)894-3248 (866)219-7260 Fax:(727)895-8759
E-mail: leemanorinn@yahoo.com
Web: www.leemanorinn.com

Circa 1937. Located in downtown Saint Petersburg, the attractions of the city are literally at your doorstep at this charming 1930s Victorian Inn. Spend the day wandering world class museums, strolling along the waterfront pier at beautiful Tampa Bay, or take in the local theater. The warm, sunny weather is perfect for enjoying outdoor activities such as golf, fishing, bicycling and water sports. Start the day with a continental breakfast featuring a variety of breads and cereals, waffles or delicious raisin toast. The vintage hotel rooms are furnished with antiques and private baths and have updated amenities such as coffee makers and small refrigerators. This oasis in the city provides a relaxing alternative for both the business and leisure traveler.

Innkeeper(s): Dave & Susie Anderson. $69-149. MC, VISA, AX, DS. TAC10. 21 rooms with PB and 2 suites. Breakfast included in rates. Types of meals: Cont and snacks/refreshments. Beds: QDT. Cable TV and phone in room. Air conditioning. Fax on premises. Weddings, small meetings and family reunions hosted. Antiquing, art galleries, beaches, bicycling, fishing, golf, live theater, museums, parks, shopping, sporting events, tennis and water sports nearby.
Publicity: *Oldsmobile (A Swedish film).*

Mansion House B&B

105 5th Ave NE
Saint Petersburg, FL 33701
(727)821-9331 (800)274-7520 Fax:(727)821-6906
E-mail: mansion1@ix.netcom.com
Web: www.mansionbandb.com

Circa 1901. The first mayor of St. Petersburg once lived here, and the inn is so named in the English tradition that states the home of a mayor shall be known as the mansion house. The home's architecture is Arts and Crafts in style, and has been completely restored, winning awards for beautification and enhancement. The Pembroke Room, in the inn's carriage house, is especially remarkable. Wicker pieces and hand-painted furnishings by Artist Marva Simpson, exposed beams painted a rich teal green, and trails of flowers and ivy decorating the lace-covered windows create the ambiance of an English seaside cottage. The Edinburgh Room is another beauty with its canopy bed topped with luxurious coverings. Guests can walk from the home to a natural harbor, restaurants, popular local parks and the beach. Busch Gardens, museums, an arboretum and a botanical garden are other nearby attractions.

Historic Interest: First open air Post Office.
Innkeeper(s): Robert & Rose Marie Ray. $145-220. MC, VISA, AX, DS, PC, TC. TAC10. 12 rooms with PB and 4 conference rooms. Breakfast and

snacks/refreshments included in rates. Types of meals: Gourmet bkfst, veg bkfst, early coffee/tea, picnic lunch and afternoon tea. Beds: KQT. Cable TV, phone and ceiling fan in room. Central air. VCR, fax, copier, bicycles, library, swimming pool and courtyard/garden on premises. Weddings, small meetings, family reunions and seminars hosted. French and Portuguese spoken. Amusement parks, antiquing, art galleries, beaches, bicycling, canoeing/kayaking, fishing, golf, hiking, horseback riding, eco-nature tours, live theater, museums, parks, shopping, sporting events, tennis and water sports nearby.

Sunset Bay Inn

635 Bay St, NE
Saint Petersburg, FL 33701
(727)896-6701 (800)794-5133 Fax:(727)898-5311
E-mail: wrbcom@aol.com
Web: www.sunsetbayinn.com

Circa 1911. After restoring this historically designated Georgian Colonial Revival, the inn is now a safe and healthy place, with luxurious traditional decor. A sunroom with large screen TV and comfy furniture boasts the original Cuban red tile floor. Read by the fireplace in the salmon-painted living room. Beverages and baked goods always are available in the butler's pantry. Romantic guest bedrooms feature a variety of amenities to pamper and please including robes, wine, whirlpool tubs, VCRs and CD players. Breakfast is enjoyed in the elegant green dining room or outside on the veranda. A lush courtyard separates the main house from the carriage house in an intimate setting.

Innkeeper(s): Bob & Martha Bruce. $130-270. MC, VISA, AX, DC, DS, PC, TC. TAC10. 8 rooms, 6 with PB, 2 suites and 1 conference room. Breakfast and snacks/refreshments included in rates. Types of meals: Full bkfst, early coffee/tea and picnic lunch. AP. Beds: KQT. Cable TV, phone, turndown service, ceiling fan, VCR, hair dryers, iron and ironing board and plush robes in room. Central air. Fax, copier, bicycles, library and gift shop on premises. Weddings, small meetings, family reunions and seminars hosted. Antiquing, art galleries, beaches, bicycling, fishing, golf, hiking, live theater, museums, parks, shopping, sporting events, tennis, water sports and wineries nearby. Pets allowed: must call for approval.

Publicity: *Southern Living, Florida Magazine, Tampa Tribune, Palm Beach Post, Fort Lauderdale-Sun Sentinel, St. Petersburg Times, The Black Stallion, Budweiser beer commercial, CBS and 48 Hours.*

San Mateo   C8

Ferncourt B&B

150 Central Ave
San Mateo, FL 32187-0758
(386)329-9755
E-mail: ferncourt@gbso.net

Circa 1889. This Victorian "painted lady," is one of the few remaining relics from San Mateo's heyday in the early 1900s. Teddy Roosevelt once visited the elegant home. The current owners have restored the Victorian atmosphere with rooms decorated with bright, floral prints and gracious furnishings. Awake to the smells of brewing coffee and the sound of a rooster crowing before settling down to a full gourmet  breakfast. Historic Saint Augustine is a quick, 25-mile drive.

Innkeeper(s): Jack & Dee Morgan. $65-85. MC, VISA, PC, TC. 6 rooms, 5 with PB. Breakfast included in rates. Types of meals: Gourmet bkfst and early coffee/tea. Beds: KQD. Ceiling fan in room. Air conditioning. Bicycles and library on premises. Handicap access. Small meetings and family reunions hosted. Antiquing, fishing, golf, live theater, parks and shopping nearby.

"First class operation! A beautiful house with an impressive history and restoration. Great company and fine food."

Sanford   D8

The Higgins House

420 S Oak Ave
Sanford, FL 32771-1826
(407)324-9238 (800)584-0014 Fax:(407)324-5060
E-mail: reservations@higginshouse.com

Circa 1894. This inviting blue Queen Anne-style home features cross gables with patterned wood shingles, bay windows and a charming round window on the second floor. Pine floors, paddle fans and a piano in the parlor, which guests are encouraged to play, create Victorian ambiance. The second-story balcony affords views not only of a charming park and Sanford's oldest church, but of Space Shuttle launches from nearby Cape Canaveral. The Queen Anne room looks out over a Victorian box garden, while the Wicker Room features a bay window sitting area. The Country Victorian room boasts a 19th-century brass bed. Guests also can opt to stay  in Cochran's Cottage, which features two bedrooms and baths, a living room, kitchen and porch. Nature lovers will enjoy close access to Blue Spring State Park, Ocala National Forest, Lake Monroe and the Cape Canaveral National Seashore. And of course, Walt Disney World, Sea World and Universal Studios aren't far away.

Historic Interest: Historic downtown Sanford offers a variety of early Cracker and Victorian architecture and many book stores, antique shops, cafes and art galleries. Twenty-two buildings in the district are listed in the National Register.

Innkeeper(s): Walter & Roberta Padgett. $110-165. MC, VISA, AX, DS, PC, TC. TAC10. 3 rooms and 1 cottage. Breakfast and snacks/refreshments included in rates. Types of meals: Cont plus, early coffee/tea and picnic lunch. Beds: QD. Turndown service and ceiling fan in room. Air conditioning. VCR, spa and bicycles on premises. Small meetings and seminars hosted. Antiquing, fishing, parks, shopping and water sports nearby.

Publicity: *Southern Living, Sanford Herald, Connecticut Traveler, LifeTimes, Orlando Sentinel, Southern Accents, Country Inns and Florida Living.*

"The Higgins House is warm and friendly, filled with such pleasant sounds, and if you love beauty and nature, you're certain to enjoy the grounds."

Tarpon Springs   E7

Spring Bayou Inn

32 W Tarpon Ave
Tarpon Springs, FL 34689-3432
(727)938-9333

Circa 1905. This large Victorian house is surrounded by a wraparound veranda and a balcony. Inside, glowing curly pine paneling adorns the staircase and fireplace. The parlor offers a baby grand piano. Stroll to the nearby bayou surrounded by high green banks and huge oak trees, a block from the inn. The sponge docks, made famous by Greek sponge divers, are within walking distance, as well, or you can browse the antique shops, choose from a variety of restaurants or take in a cultural event.

Innkeeper(s): Sharon Birk, Linda & John Hall. $80-125. 5 rooms with PB. Types of meals: Gourmet bkfst. Beds: KQD. Baby grand piano and wraparound porch on premises. Antiquing and shopping nearby.

Publicity: *Florida Home & Garden Magazine, Sunshine Magazine, Miami Today and Palm Beach Post.*

"Lots to do in the area, and the decor was very nice."

West Palm Beach   G10

Casa de Rosa

520 27th St
West Palm Beach, FL 33407
(561)833-1920 (888)665-8666 Fax:(561)835-3566
E-mail: casaderosa@aol.com
Web: www.casaderosa.com

Circa 1928. This historic Florida house has recently been fully restored including its extensive gardens, offering guests a private enclave while visiting West Palm Beach. Freshly decorated guest spaces include the inviting parlor, a brand new kitchen and the dining room. (If you can pull yourself away from the joys of the garden, pool and arched verandas covered with rose vines.) Two gazebos, a cottage garden, rock garden and rose garden offer additional inspiration. Four guest rooms provide a selection of size and décor.

Historic Interest: El Cid (1 mile), Flamingo Park (1 mile), Grandview Heights (1 mile).

Innkeeper(s): John & Diane Bates. $225. MC, VISA, AX, DS, TC. 4 rooms with PB and 1 cottage. Breakfast included in rates. Types of meals: Gourmet bkfst, snacks/refreshments and room service. Beds: KQ. Cable TV, phone, ceiling fan and fireplace in room. Central air. Fax, copier, swimming, library, daily room service, wine, soft drinks, juices, ice tea and lemonade anytime on premises. Antiquing, art galleries, beaches, bicycling, canoeing/kayaking, fishing, golf, horseback riding, live theater, museums, parks, shopping, tennis and water sports nearby.

Pets Allowed.

Tropical Gardens Bed and Breakfast

419 32nd St
West Palm Beach, FL 33407
(561)848-4064 (800)736-4064 Fax:(561)848-2422
E-mail: tropgard@bellsouth.net
Web: www.tropicalgardensbandb.com

Circa 1937. A relaxed and colorful atmosphere is found at these historic Key West-style accommodations located in a secluded, tropical setting only minutes from beaches, city life and the airport. Guest bedrooms and cottages with cypress ceilings, crown molding, French doors and wicker furniture are comfortable retreats. An expanded continental buffet breakfast with fresh-squeezed Florida orange juice starts the day's adventures. Lounge by the pool, or enjoy the lush native foliage in the quiet courtyard. Bicycles are available.

Innkeeper(s): Jean Deschesnes & Lillian Tamayo. $65-125. MC, VISA, AX, DS, PC, TC. 4 rooms, 2 with PB and 2 cottages. Breakfast included in rates. Types of meals: Cont plus. Beds: QT. Cable TV, phone, turndown service, ceiling fan, VCR, fireplace and pool in room. Central air. Fax, copier, swimming, tennis, library and pool on premises. Small meetings, family reunions and seminars hosted. Spanish spoken. Antiquing, art galleries, beaches, bicycling, canoeing/kayaking, fishing, golf, hiking, live theater, museums, parks, shopping, tennis and water sports nearby.

White Springs   B7

White Springs Bed and Breakfast Inn

PO Box 403
White Springs, FL 32096
(386)397-1665 (888)412-1665 Fax:(386)397-1665
E-mail: kgavronsky@aol.com

Circa 1905. Formerly known as the Kendrick-Lindsey House in the historic district near the Suwannee River, this Vernacular inn is listed in the National Register. Recently restored with modern conveniences, a Victorian ambiance remains with original woodwork and staircase, heart of pine floors, stained-glass window, tin roof, four fireplace mantels and two clawfoot tubs. The parlor is perfect for watching movies, listening to a CD or playing the piano. The suites and guest bedrooms are furnished in an assortment of English Country Cottage, French Country and Victorian decor. A delicious full breakfast is served on fine china in the formal dining room. Enjoy the landscaped grounds with a rose garden and shade trees.

Innkeeper(s): Kerry & Jake Gavronsky. $65-85. MC, VISA, PC, TC. TAC10. 4 rooms, 2 with FP. Breakfast and snacks/refreshments included in rates. Types of meals: Gourmet bkfst. Beds: QDT. Cable TV, turndown service, ceiling fan and fireplace in room. Air conditioning. Fax, copier, library, gift shop, refrigerator upstairs for guest convenience, flexible breakfast time and check-in times and VCR and movie tapes available on premises. Antiquing, bicycling, canoeing/kayaking, fishing, golf, hiking, horseback riding, white water rafting, walking tour of homes, museums, parks and shopping nearby.

Georgia

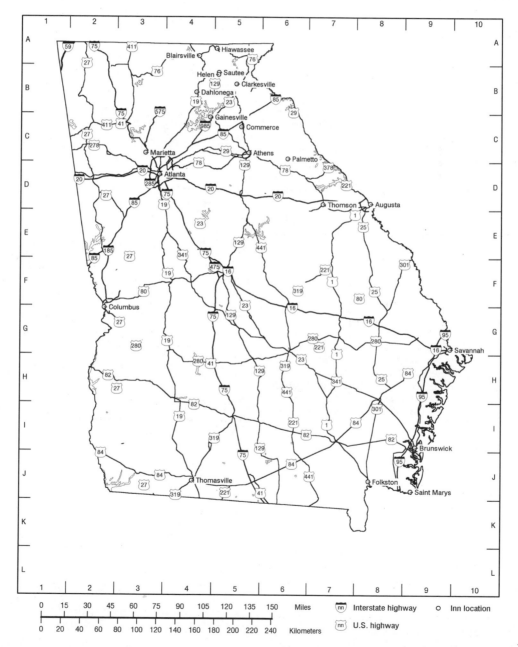

	Miles										Interstate highway	o Inn location
0	15	30	45	60	75	90	105	120	135	150		
0	20	40	60	80	100	120	140	160	180	200	220	240			

Miles

Interstate highway   o Inn location

U.S. highway

Kilometers

Athens   C5

The Nicholson House

6295 Jefferson Rd
Athens, GA 30607-1714
(706)353-2200
E-mail: 1820@nicholsonhouseinn.com
Web: www.nicholsonhouseinn.com

Circa 1820. For a distinctive stay in this classic city, this
Antebellum inn depicts the splendor of the Old South. Built in
Colonial Revival style, the meticulously renovated home boasts an
historic elegance that is accented with Civil War artifacts, antiques
from the early 19th century and limited-edition prints. Two parlors and an extensive library are delightful common areas to
enjoy. Evening sherry is offered. Spacious guest bedrooms and
suites provide private luxury. Morning brings a healthy and hearty
breakfast of fresh fruit, a hot entree, warm breads, cereal,
Southern pecan coffee and juice served in the formal dining
room. Relax in a rocking chair on the veranda or stroll among the
six wooded acres with natural springs, towering trees, colorful
flowers and plants. Downtown is just five miles away where the
state's Antebellum Trail begins, and there are many museums.
Historic Interest: Inn was a stagecoach stop on "Old Federal Road" for most
of the 1800s.
Innkeeper(s): Celeste & Harry Neely. $99-109. MC, VISA, AX, DS. 6 rooms
with PB and 3 suites. Breakfast included in rates. Types of meals: Full bkfst.
Beds: KQ. Cable TV and phone in room. Air conditioning.

Atlanta   D3

Ansley Inn

253 15th St NE
Atlanta, GA 30309-3512
(404)872-9000 (800)446-5416 Fax:(404)892-2318
E-mail: ansleyinn@mindspring.com

Circa 1907. This handsome English Tudor-style house was the
original home of George Muse of Muse Department Stores. Its
location on one acre in a neighborhood of stately homes is near
Peachtree and Piedmont. Guest rooms offer four-poster beds and
Jacuzzi tubs, and some have fireplaces and ceiling fans. A full,
Southern breakfast is served and includes eggs, potatoes, bacon,
homemade biscuits and fresh fruit. Guests can walk to the Atlanta
Botanical Gardens, Symphony Hall and High Museum of Art.
Innkeeper(s): Curt Levy & Morris Levy. $99-199. MC, VISA, AX. TAC10. 22
rooms with PB, 3 with FP and 1 conference room. Breakfast and
snacks/refreshments included in rates. Types of meals: Full bkfst. Beds: QD.
Cable TV and phone in room. Fax, copier, jacuzzi tubs, hair dryers, ironing
boards and makeup mirrors on premises. Amusement parks, antiquing, golf,
live theater, museums, parks, shopping, sporting events and tennis nearby.
Publicity: *Country Inns and Atlantic Business Chronicle.*

Gaslight Inn B&B

1001 St Charles Ave NE
Atlanta, GA 30306-4221
(404)875-1001 Fax:(404)876-1001
E-mail: innkeeper@gaslightinn.com
Web: www.gaslightinn.com

Circa 1913. Flickering gas lanterns outside, original gas lighting inside and six working fireplaces add to the unique quality
of this inn. Beautifully appointed guest rooms offer individual
decor. The Ivy Cottage is a romantic bungalow with a living
room and kitchen. The regal English Suite boasts a four-poster
bed covered in rich blue hues and a private deck. The Rose

Room features a fireplace and four-
poster bed covered with lace.
Located in the Virginia Highlands
neighborhood, the inn is approximately five minutes from downtown and is served by Atlanta's
public transportation system.

Innkeeper(s): Jim Moss. $95-195. MC, VISA, AX, DC, DS, PC, TC. TAC10. 7
rooms with PB, 3 with FP, 3 suites, 2 cottages and 1 conference room.
Breakfast included in rates. Types of meals: Cont plus and early coffee/tea.
Beds: KQ. Cable TV, phone, ceiling fan and VCR in room. Air conditioning.
Fax, copier, spa, sauna and library on premises. Handicap access. Weddings,
small meetings, family reunions and seminars hosted. Amusement parks,
antiquing, live theater, parks, shopping and sporting events nearby.
Publicity: *Vacations Magazine,, CNN Travel Guide Show, Discover Channel,
CBS's 48 hours and Travel Channel.*

"Best B&B I've ever stayed in."

King-Keith House B&B

889 Edgewood Ave NE
Atlanta, GA 30307
(404)688-7330 (800)728-3879 Fax:(404)584-8408
E-mail: kingkeith@mindspring.com
Web: www.kingkeith.com

Circa 1890. This beautifully restored and preserved Queen Anne
Victorian features many wonderful elements, including a whimsical chimney that vividly declares "1890," the year the home was
built. Inside, the hardwood floors and intricate woodwork glisten. Walls are painted in deep, rich
hues and antiques fill the rooms.
Marble-topped tables and delicate
love seats decorate the parlor. Each
guest room is special, and beds are
topped with luxury linens. One
room is lit by a colorful stained-
glass window, another features a Victorian dollhouse. The opulent home is located in an Atlanta historic district listed in the
National Register. It's just two blocks from the subway station.

Innkeeper(s): Jan & Windell Keith. $90-175. MC, VISA, AX, DS, PC, TC.
TAC10. 3 rooms with PB, 1 suite and 1 cottage. Breakfast included in rates.
Types of meals: Gourmet bkfst and early coffee/tea. Beds: KQDT. Cable TV,
phone, ceiling fan, hair dryer and cottage with Jacuzzi and fireplace in room.
Air conditioning. Weddings, small meetings, family reunions and seminars
hosted. Antiquing, golf, restaurants, live theater, parks, shopping, sporting
events and tennis nearby.

Augusta   D8

The Partridge Inn

2110 Walton Way
Augusta, GA 30904-6905
(706)737-8888 (800)476-6888 Fax:(706)731-0826
E-mail: info@partridgeinn.com
Web: www.partridgeinn.com

Circa 1879. The original structure of this inn was built prior to
the Civil War, and it was Morris Partridge who purchased the
house in the 1890s and transformed it into an inn. By 1929, the
inn had blossomed into a 129-room hostelry with a quarter-mile
of porches and balconies. Throughout its history, the inn has
hosted prominent personali-
ties, such as senators, actors
and even a president. For
those on an extended stay,
some rooms offer small

kitchens. Guests enjoy use of an on-site swimming pool as well as a nearby health spa. There are plenty of dining options here. The Bar & Grill is a popular spot for lunch or an informal dinner, and often is host to jazz ensembles. The inn's Dining Room is the place for a romantic, gourmet meal, and the Veranda offers a variety of light fare. Visit their web site for golf and vacation packages.

Innkeeper(s): David Jones. $99-150. MC, VISA, AX, DC, DS. TAC10. 155 rooms with PB, 43 suites and 7 conference rooms. Types of meals: Lunch and room service. AP. Beds: KQD. Cable TV, phone and coffee makers in room. Air conditioning. Fax, copier, swimming pool and two-line phone on premises. Handicap access. Weddings, small meetings, family reunions and seminars hosted. Amusement parks, antiquing, Paine College, Augusta Tech, parks, shopping and sporting events nearby.

Queen Anne Inn

406 Greene St
Augusta, GA 30901
(706)723-0045 (877)460-0045 Fax:(706)826-7920
E-mail: william.mundell@worldnet.att.net

Circa 1890. This inviting three-story inn, filled with marble-topped antiques, stained glass windows and working fireplaces offers a special family suite in its handsome turret. Shaded by tall trees, the inn's veranda is a favorite spot for relaxing after returning from the Savannah River Walk, which starts three blocks away. Rooms are furnished with antique beds such as a Second Empire, an ornate Eastlake and a high-backed sleigh bed. The parlors offer fringed Victorian pieces, Oriental carpets and original paintings. Breakfast is continental, or you can walk down the tree-shaded street to a local cafe, which provides Queen Anne guests a full hot breakfast. Evening in-suite dining is available by selecting room service dinners from quality restaurants working with the inn. The family tower suite offers parents with children a chance to enjoy an elegant inn, yet have quiet quarters for themselves and their young children in a special section of the inn. Best of all, your well-traveled schoolteacher/innkeepers can arrange baby-sitting services for families. A shuttle service is offered as well.

Innkeeper(s): Val & Bill Mundell. $69-99. 7 rooms with PB. VCR, fax, bicycles, library, parking and Jacuzzi on premises. Antiquing, bicycling, canoeing/kayaking, golf, hiking, museums and shopping nearby.
Publicity: *Applause.*

"Thank you so much for taking such good care of my husband on his first trip to Augusta."

Blairsville   A4

Misty Mountain Inn & Cottages

4376 Misty Mountain Ln
Blairsville, GA 30512-5604
(706)745-4786 (888)647-8966 Fax:(706)781-1002
E-mail: mistyinn@whitelion.net
Web: www.jwww.com/misty

Circa 1890. This Victorian farmhouse is situated on a four-acre compound and also features six mountain-side cottages located in the woods surrounding the inn. There are four spacious guest rooms in the main house, all appointed with private baths and fireplaces. All are decorated in country antiques with hand-crafted accessories, quilts and green plants. Two cottages boast antique beds and Jacuzzi tubs. The lofted bedroom cottages can comfortably sleep more than two people,

while offering separate bedrooms, living rooms and eat-in kitchens. Flea markets, festivals, antique shops and arts and crafts are located nearby.

Historic Interest: Close to Lake Winfield Scott, Lake Nottely, Lake Chatuge, Young Harris College, Georgia Mountain Fair, Vogel State Park and the Appalachian Trail.

$65-90. MC, VISA, AX, TC. TAC10. 4 rooms with PB, 10 with FP and 6 cottages. Types of meals: Full bkfst, cont plus and early coffee/tea. Beds: QT. Ceiling fan and fireplace & private balcony in room. Air conditioning. Fax and copier on premises. Handicap access. Weddings, small meetings and family reunions hosted. Antiquing, fishing, golf, parks, shopping and water sports nearby.
Pets allowed: in cottages.

Brunswick   I9

Brunswick Manor

825 Egmont St
Brunswick, GA 31520-7825
(912)265-6889

Circa 1866. Nestled in the heart of historic Old Town Brunswick, this Victorian inn features the original carved-oak staircase, high ceilings and Victorian mantels with beveled mirrors, antiques and period reproductions. Guests may relax on the rockers or wicker swing on the columned veranda and enjoy the moss-draped oaks and tall palm trees. A stroll through the gardens leads to the greenhouse, fish pond, fountain, patio and arbor-covered hot tub. The inn boasts a Country Inns/Waverly Fabrics award-winning room. Captained day charters are available. A full, complimentary breakfast is offered each morning and afternoon tea is always a treat.

Historic Interest: Fort Frederica, Coastal Historic Museum, Jekyll Island Historic District.

Innkeeper(s): Claudia & Harry Tzucanow. $65-90. MC, VISA, PC, TC. 7 rooms with PB and 3 suites. Breakfast and afternoon tea included in rates. Types of meals: Gourmet bkfst, picnic lunch and gourmet dinner. Beds: QT. TV and phone in room. Antiquing, fishing, golf, live theater, tennis and water sports nearby.
Publicity: *Southern Homes, Bon Appetit and Country Inns.*

"Your great charm and warm hospitality is your legacy. We've never stayed in such a room and house full of such treasures before. We'd say one of the best B&Bs in the country!"

McKinnon House B&B

1001 Egmont St
Brunswick, GA 31520-7554
(912)261-9100 (866)261-9100

Circa 1902. This 1902 Victorian built by lumber magnate L.T. McKinnon, a local naval stores/lumber baron, was once featured in the movie Conrack. Just 10 miles from Fort Frederica, 12 miles from Fort King George, and 10 miles from Christ Church and St. Simon's Light House, the inn is formally landscaped with a Victorian garden on the side. It has 17 Corinthian columns made of Georgia cypress on the exterior and Georgia marble front steps that lead to double front doors with stained glass. Its nine working fireplaces have intricately carved mantelpieces. The home is filled with family heirlooms and antiques from Charleston and New Orleans. Fresh flowers and candles add to the ambiance. Sleep in one of three guest rooms and arise to a breakfast including treats like fresh fruit, gourmet coffee, a hot entrée, side meats and homemade rolls, muffins or biscuits.

Historic Interest: Fort Frederica (10 miles), Fort King George (12 miles), Christ Church (10 miles), St. Simons Light House (10 miles), Jekyll Island State Park with historic homes and clubhouse.

Innkeeper(s): Jo Miller. $100-125. PC. TAC10. 3 rooms with PB, 3 with FP. Breakfast and snacks/refreshments included in rates. Types of meals: Full bkfst. Beds: KDT. Fireplace in room. Central air. VCR on premises. Weddings and family reunions hosted. Antiquing, art galleries, beaches, bicycling, canoeing/kayaking, fishing, golf, hiking, live theater, museums, parks, shopping, tennis and water sports nearby.

Publicity: *Conrack.*

Clarkesville   B5

Glen-Ella Springs Hotel

1789 Bear Gap Rd
Clarkesville, GA 30523
(706)754-7295
E-mail: inof@glenella.com

Circa 1875. This renovated hotel just south of the new Tallulah Gorge State Park is an outstanding example of early 19th- and 20th-century inns that dotted the Georgia countryside. The luxury of private baths and a plethora of porches have been added. A great stone fireplace is the focal point of the parlor, decorated in bright chintzes. Local hand-crafted pieces and antiques furnish the guest rooms. Two suites feature stone fireplaces. Bordered by Panther Creek, the property includes a swimming pool, 17 acres of meadows, flower and herb gardens and original mineral springs. The dining room features gourmet breakfast and dinner by reservation.

Historic Interest: Listed in the National Register of Historic Places.

Innkeeper(s): Barrie & Bobby Aycock. $125-195. MC, VISA, AX. 16 rooms with PB, 2 with FP and 1 conference room. Types of meals: Gourmet bkfst and dinner. EP. Beds: KQT. Fax, copier and swimming on premises. Handicap access.

Publicity: *Atlanta, Georgia Journal and Country Inns.*

"Quality is much talked about and too seldom found. With you folks it's a given."

Columbus   G2

Gates House Bed & Breakfast

737 Broadway
Columbus, GA 31901-2920
(706)322-7321 (800)891-3187 Fax:(706)323-3086
E-mail: info@gateshouse.com
Web: www.gateshouse.com

Circa 1880. Experience Southern hospitality at this two-story Colonial Revival home located in the middle of the historic district. The elegance of the Victorian period is reflected in the decor and antique furnishings. Oriental carpets and opulent window treatments enhance the ambiance. The parlor has an added French influence and displays extensive collections including bronzes. Vintage puppets from Thailand, books, magazines and games are available in the library. A honeymoon suite features a canopy bed, candles, Jacuzzi tub and fireplace. French toast made out of homemade sourdough or brown sugar-cinnamon pecan bread rounds off a bountiful breakfast served in the formal dining room or enjoyed on the wicker-filled front porch.

Innkeeper(s): Carolyn & Tom Gates. $95-135. MC, VISA, AX, PC, TC. TAC10. 33 rooms. Breakfast and snacks/refreshments included in rates. Types of meals: Gourmet bkfst, veg bkfst, early coffee/tea, gourmet lunch, afternoon tea, gourmet dinner and room service. Beds: KQT. Cable TV, phone, turndown service, ceiling fan and VCR in room. Central air. Fax, copier, spa and library on premises. Weddings, small meetings and seminars hosted. Amusement parks, antiquing, art galleries, bicycling, fishing, golf, live theater, museums, parks, shopping, sporting events and tennis nearby.

Commerce   C5

Harber House Inn

2280 N Broad St
Commerce, GA 30529
(706)335-9388 (877)226-9886
E-mail: rrichard@nbank.net
Web: www.jacksoncountyga.com

Circa 1896. Harber House includes both Victorian and Greek Revival architecture, and it is named for the Harber family who owned the historic home for half a century. A wraparound porch adds a Victorian element to the gabled roof and stately columns that flank the front entrance. Soaring 12-foot ceilings and floated-glass windows grace the interior. The three tastefully appointed guest rooms with shared baths include antique beds. Breakfasts are a highlight of a stay at Harber House, and guests partake of a meal that might include homemade strawberry muffins with strawberry butter, gingerbread pancakes, cheese grits, frittatas or the innkeeper's special "ham-it-up" casserole. Outlet stores, antique shops, flea markets, golfing, the Peach State Speedway and Lake Lanier all are nearby.

Innkeeper(s): Rose & Art Richard. $60-70. MC, VISA, AX, PC. 3 rooms. Breakfast included in rates. Types of meals: Gourmet bkfst. Beds: D. Ceiling fan in room. Central air. VCR on premises. Weddings, small meetings, family reunions and seminars hosted. Antiquing, fishing, golf, museums, parks, shopping, sporting events and wineries nearby.

Cumberland Island   J9

Greyfield Inn

Cumberland Island
Cumberland Island, GA 30339
(904)261-6408 Fax:(904)321-0666
E-mail: seashore@net-magic.net

Circa 1900. The Thomas Carnegies built this four-story home on the barrier island of Cumberland Island. Guests seeking seclusion have the advantage of 1,300 private acres on an island most of which has been designated as a National Seashore. Only 300 persons a day are allowed to visit, a stipulation of the National Park Service. The mansion affords elegant dining opportunities and picnics are available. There's an honor bar in the old gun room, and guests enjoy mingling fireside in the living and dining room or out on the swing on the tree shaded porch. Expansive views of the Intracoastal Waterway may be seen from the inn's balcony. All guest rooms are furnished in family antiques and traditional pieces including four-poster beds, high boys and lounge chairs. Enjoy one of the inn's bicycles and tour the island to view wild horses, deer, an occasional bobcat, armadillos and a variety of birds. Hiking in the marshes, beach combing and clam digging are favored activities. Plan on making phone calls before arriving on the island since only a radio phone is available.

Innkeeper(s): Zachary Zoul. $290-450. MC, VISA, DS, PC, TC. 17 rooms, 9 with PB, 5 suites and 2 cottages. Breakfast, picnic lunch, afternoon tea, snacks/refreshments and dinner included in rates. Types of meals: Gourmet bkfst and early coffee/tea. AP. Beds: KQDT. Turndown service and ceiling fan in room. Central air. Fax, copier, swimming, bicycles and library on premises. Weddings, small meetings, family reunions and seminars hosted. Beaches, bicycling, canoeing/kayaking, fishing, hiking, museums, parks and water sports nearby.

Publicity: *Southern Living.*

Dahlonega   B4

The Royal Guard Inn
65 Park St S
Dahlonega, GA 30533-1232
(706)864-1713 (877)659-0739
E-mail: royalguardbnb@yahoo.com

Circa 1938. Shaded by tall magnolias, a large wraparound veranda surrounds this Cape Cod-style house, located a one block from the town square. Guest rooms are furnished in contemporary style with plantation shutters. Afternoon tea or wine and cheese is offered. A delicious full breakfast is served and includes a variety of dishes including egg casseroles, French toast, waffles, pancakes, fresh fruit and a number of side dishes.
Innkeeper(s): Suzanne & Steve. $95-110. MC, VISA, PC. 4 rooms with PB. Breakfast included in rates. Types of meals: Gourmet bkfst. Beds: Q. Air conditioning. Library on premises. Antiquing, canoeing/kayaking, fishing, golf, hiking, horseback riding, gold mining/panning, tubing, live theater, parks, shopping, tennis and water sports nearby.

Folkston   J8

Inn at Folkston
509 W Main St
Folkston, GA 31537
(912)496-6256 (888)509-6246 Fax:(912)496-6256
E-mail: info@innatfolkston.com
Web: www.innatfolkston.com

Circa 1920. A prominent Folkston citizen built this historic home to enjoy the nearby beauty and natural setting of Okefenokee Swamp. The historic Arts and Crafts home has been restored to its former glory, the heart-of-pine floors, woodwork and wainscoting all are original to the home. Each of the guest rooms has been decorated artfully in its own special style. Two rooms include a fireplace, and one offers a double whirlpool tub. Breakfasts include gourmet entrees such as an artichoke and feta souffle or perhaps blueberry French toast accompanied with fresh seasonal fruit and homemade muffins and breads. The area's most popular attraction, Okefenokee Swamp, is home to an abundance of plant life, as well as American alligators and more than 200 species of birds. Folkston also offers a historic train depot and train viewing platform, shops and restaurants.
Historic Interest: Okefenokee Swamp (10 miles), Cumberland Island/Amelia Island, Jekyll Island (30-35 miles).
Innkeeper(s): Genna & Roger Wangsness. $95-150. MC, VISA, AX, DC, CB, DS, PC, TC. TAC10. 4 rooms with PB, 2 with FP and 1 suite. Breakfast and snacks/refreshments included in rates. Types of meals: Gourmet bkfst, veg bkfst, early coffee/tea, picnic lunch, afternoon tea and room service. Beds: KQ. Phone, turndown service, ceiling fan and fireplace in room. Central air. VCR, fax, copier, library, gift shop, hot tub and sun deck on premises. Handicap access. Small meetings and family reunions hosted. Antiquing, art galleries, beaches, bicycling, canoeing/kayaking, fishing, golf, hiking, horseback riding, train watching, skeet shooting, live theater, museums, parks, shopping, tennis and water sports nearby.
Publicity: *Waters Edge, Southern Living, Atlanta Journal/Constitution, N.G. Traveler and Trembling Waters video.*

Gainesville   C4

Dunlap House
635 Green St N W
Gainesville, GA 30501-3319
(770)536-0200 (800)276-2935 Fax:(770)503-7857
E-mail: dunlaphouse@mindspring.com

Circa 1910. Located on Gainesville's historic Green Street, this inn offers 9 uniquely decorated guest rooms, all featuring period furnishings. Custom-built king or queen beds and remote-controlled cable TV are found in all of the rooms, several of which have romantic fireplaces. Guests may help themselves to coffee, tea and light refreshments in the inn's common area. Breakfast may be enjoyed in guests' rooms or on the picturesque veranda, with its comfortable wicker furniture. Road Atlanta, Mall of Georgia, Lake Lanier, Brenau University, Riverside Academy and the Quinlan Art Center are nearby.
Innkeeper(s): David & Karen Peters. $85-155. MC, VISA, AX, TC. 9 rooms with PB, 2 with FP. Breakfast and snacks/refreshments included in rates. Types of meals: Full bkfst and early coffee/tea. Beds: KQ. Cable TV, phone, laptop computer and phone hook-up in room. Air conditioning. Copier on premises. Handicap access. Weddings, small meetings and family reunions hosted. Antiquing, fishing, golf, Road Atlanta Racing, Lake Lanier, live theater, parks, shopping and water sports nearby.
Publicity: *Southern Living, Atlanta Journal Constitution, Country Inns and North Georgia Journal.*

Helen   B5

Black Forest Bed & Breakfast
8902 N Main St
Helen, GA 30545
(706)878-3995 Fax:(706)878-7013
E-mail: blackforestbb@aol.com
Web: www.blackforest-bb.com

Circa 1940. Experience Alpine lodging at this elegant Cape Cod-style home and chalet-style cabins at the foot of the Blue Ridge Mountains. The location is convenient to easily enjoy the area's Bavarian cultural activities whether by foot or in the electric car shuttle. Gather in the den or warming room with homemade cookies and a hot beverage. Many of the quaint guest bedrooms and suites feature fireplaces and Jacuzzis. Indulge in satisfying European breakfast cuisine served in the Dutch breakfast room or outdoors beside a 20-foot waterfall and koi pond. Spend relaxing moments on a swing in the gazebo.
Innkeeper(s): Art & Lou Ann Connor. $135-275. MC, VISA, AX, DC, DS, PC, TC. 12 rooms, 2 with PB, 10 with FP, 5 suites and 5 cabins. Breakfast and snacks/refreshments included in rates. Types of meals: Full bkfst, country bkfst, veg bkfst and early coffee/tea. Beds: KQ. Cable TV, ceiling fan, VCR, fireplace and large custom built waterfalls in room. Air conditioning. Fax, copier and gift shop on premises. Handicap access. Weddings, small meetings, family reunions and seminars hosted. Amusement parks, antiquing, art galleries, bicycling, canoeing/kayaking, fishing, golf, hiking, horseback riding, live theater, museums, parks, shopping, downhill skiing, tennis, water sports and wineries nearby.
Publicity: *Helen Information Channel.*

Hiawassee   A5

Enota Bed & Breakfast, Cabin, Retreat, Conference, Lodge
1000 Hwy 180
Hiawassee, GA 30546
(706)896-9966 (800)990-8869 Fax:(706)896-4737
E-mail: enota@enota.com
Web: www.enota.com

Circa 1940. Sitting in a lush valley surrounded by the Appalachian Mountains in the Chattahoochee National Forest, the Enota experience awaits. Amidst spectacular waterfalls, streams and trout ponds, there are a variety of accommodations. Fully equipped cabins in a rustic charm offer casual comfort and privacy. A continental breakfast is provided in the lodge or guests may opt (additional cost) for a country breakfast, which boasts eggs, home fries, biscuits, waffles and salmon cakes. The bunkhouses are great for family reunions or retreats. Campgrounds have landscaped RV sites with full hook-ups. Tent sites also are available. The more adventurous stay in tipis and yomes. Conference facilities, with a commercial kitchen, are perfect for meetings and seminars. Swimming, hiking, volleyball, ping pong, horseshoes, in-ground trampolines, playgrounds, and an enclosed basketball court are among the many activities to enjoy.

Innkeeper(s): Kent Milliken. $20-165. MC, VISA, PC, TC. 16 rooms, 13 with PB, 10 with FP, 10 cabins and 1 conference room. Breakfast included in rates. Types of meals: Gourmet bkfst, country bkfst, veg bkfst, cont plus, early coffee/tea, lunch, picnic lunch, snacks/refreshments and gourmet dinner. Beds: QDT. TV, VCR, fully equipped kitchens in every cabin, linens, towels, dishes and cookware furnished in room. Fax, copier, spa, swimming, bicycles, library, pony rides, fishing, trout ponds, waterfalls, streams, playground, sandbox, basketball, hiking, wading, volleyball, in-ground trampolines, outdoor kitchen, tipi village, yomes and tent and RV sites with full hook-ups on premises. Handicap access. Weddings, small meetings, family reunions and seminars hosted. Antiquing, art galleries, beaches, bicycling, canoeing/kayaking, fishing, golf, hiking, horseback riding, Lake Chatuge, live theater, parks, shopping, tennis, water sports and wineries nearby.

Pets allowed: $15 per day in cabins with $25-50 deposit required.

Little St. Simons Island   I9

The Lodge on Little St. Simons Island

PO Box 21078
Little St. Simons Island, GA 31522-0578
(912)638-7472 (888)733-5774 Fax:(912)634-1811
E-mail: lssi@mindspring.com
Web: www.littlestsimonsisland.com

Circa 1917. Deer roam freely and birds soar over 10,000 acres of pristine forests, fresh water ponds, isolated beaches and marshland. There are more than 220 species of birds, and guests can enjoy horseback riding on
miles of private trails. There are
seven miles of isolated beach to
enjoy, as well as boating, canoeing, fishing, birdwatching, swimming and naturalist programs.
All activities are included in the
rates. To ensure solitude and privacy, the innkeepers allow only 30 overnight guests at a time. Full-Island rates, ranging from $5,000 to $6,500 are available. The inn is accessible only by boat. Breakfast, lunch and dinner, served family style, are included in the rates. The Lodge also offers extras such as barge cruises, oyster roasts, beach picnics and crab boils.

Historic Interest: Fort Frederica National Monumet (neighboring Island), Fort George (13 miles), Jekyll Island Club and historic district homes of turn-of-the-century millionaires (Jekyll Island).

Innkeeper(s): Maureen Ahern. $375-950. MC, VISA, AX, DS, PC. TAC10. 13 rooms with PB, 2 suites and 3 conference rooms. Breakfast, picnic lunch and dinner included in rates. AP. Beds: KQT. Ceiling fan, suites with fireplace and coffee maker in room. Air conditioning. Fax, copier, swimming, stables, bicycles, boats, interpretive guides, fishing and fishing gear and kayaks on premises. Weddings, small meetings, family reunions and seminars hosted. Publicity: *Forbes, Conde Nast, Meeting Destinations, Gourmet, Today Show, Great Country Inns, Southern Living, Coastal Living, Andrew Harper's Hideaway Report, Atlanta Good Morning and CNN Travel.*

"The staff is unequaled anywhere."

Marietta   C3

Sixty Polk Street, A B&B

60 Polk St
Marietta, GA 30064-2349
(770)419-1688 (800)845-7266 Fax:(770)590-7959
E-mail: JMertes@aol.com

Circa 1872. This French Regency Victorian has been completely restored. Period antiques decorate the rooms. Guests are encouraged to enjoy the library or relax in the parlor. Afternoon treats are served in the dining room, and guests are treated to a hearty Southern breakfast. Marietta offers an abundance of antique stores, restaurants and museums, as well as a delightful town square. The inn is just 30 minutes from Atlanta.

Historic Interest: Sixty Polk Street is within walking distance of the Marietta Square and Northwest Marietta Historic District. Kennesaw Mountain National Battlefield and Confederate and national cemeteries also are found in the area.

Innkeeper(s): Joe & Glenda Mertes. $95-175. MC, VISA. 4 rooms with PB, 1 with FP and 1 suite. Breakfast included in rates. Types of meals: Full bkfst. Beds: KQ. Antiquing, golf and live theater nearby.

Publicity: *North Georgian Journal and Victorian Homes Magazine.*

"Better than dreamed of."

Whitlock Inn

57 Whitlock Ave
Marietta, GA 30064-2343
(770)428-1495 Fax:(770)919-9620
E-mail: alexis@whitlockinn.com

Circa 1900. This cherished Victorian has been restored and is located in a National Register Historic District, one block
from the Marietta Square.
Amenities even the Ritz doesn't
provide are in every room, and
you can rock on the front verandas. An afternoon snack also is
served. There is a ballroom
grandly suitable for weddings
and business meetings.

Historic Interest: Kennesaw Mountain Battlefield & Civil War National Park (3 miles), numerous historic homes, several from Civil War era (within 6 blocks).

Innkeeper(s): Alexis Edwards. $125-145. MC, VISA, AX, DS. TAC10. 5 rooms with PB and 3 conference rooms. Breakfast included in rates. Types of meals: Cont plus. Beds: KQT. Cable TV, phone and ceiling fan in room. Air conditioning. Fax and copier on premises. Weddings, small meetings, family reunions and seminars hosted. Amusement parks, antiquing, live theater, parks, shopping and sporting events nearby.

Publicity: *Marietta Daily Journal.*

"This is the most beautiful inn in Georgia and I've seen nearly all of them."

Palmetto   C6

Serenbe Bed & Breakfast

10950 Hutcheson Ferry Rd
Palmetto, GA 30268-2233
(770)463-2610 Fax:(770)463-4472
E-mail: steve@serenbe.com
Web: www.serenbe.com

Circa 1905. Enjoy a truly unique experience at this 350-acre farm in rural Georgia. Choose from a variety of accommodations, such as a lake house with large, screened porch or a converted 1930s horse barn. Over 100 farm animals provide an interactive experience for children, from feeding goats and holding rabbits, to gathering eggs and visiting with cows, pigs and horses. Families can enjoy a hayride or roast marshmallows over a campfire. Activities for all ages include canoeing, fishing, a hot tub under the stars or a picnic on a granite rock near a waterfall. Rates include a full country breakfast, afternoon southern tea and·sweets at bedtime. Just south of Atlanta, many city attractions also are conveniently available.

Historic Interest: Warm Springs (45 miles).

Innkeeper(s): Steve & Marie Nygren. $140-175. PC, TC. 1996 rooms, 8 with PB, 1 cabin and 1 conference room. Breakfast and afternoon tea included in rates. Types of meals: Country bkfst. Beds: KQDT. Ceiling fan in room. Central air. VCR, fax, copier, spa, swimming, bicycles, library and child care on premises. Handicap access. Weddings, small meetings, family reunions and seminars hosted. Amusement parks, antiquing, art galleries, bicycling, canoeing/kayaking, fishing, golf, hiking, horseback riding and parks nearby.

Publicity: *Country Inns Magazine, I Do Magazine and HGTV.*

Rabun Gap   A5

Sylvan Falls Mill

Box 548, Taylors Chapel Rd
Rabun Gap, GA 30568
(706)746-7138
E-mail: linda3010@aol.com
Web: www.sylvanfallsmill.com

Circa 1840. The Sylvan Falls Mill Site has been the location of a working gristmill for more than 150 years. The mill was constructed in 1840 from wormy chestnutwood. The original waterwheel was replaced in 1946 by a steel waterwheel from Tennessee. The mill is still powered  by the waterfall that cascades over one side of the property that overlooks picturesque Wolffork Valley. The property has been a home since then, offering four unique guest rooms with private baths.

Refreshments are served at check-in and a full, gourmet breakfast is served in the morning. Outdoor activities are the highlight of the inn. Guests will delight in hiking the Bartram Trail or rafting down the Chattooga River.

Innkeeper(s): Michael & Linda Johnson. $95. MC, VISA, PC, TC. 4 rooms with PB. Breakfast and snacks/refreshments included in rates. Types of meals: Gourmet bkfst and early coffee/tea. Beds: QD. Ceiling fan in room. Library on premises. Weddings, small meetings and family reunions hosted. Antiquing, fishing, golf, hiking, foliage, parks, shopping, downhill skiing and water sports nearby.

Pets Allowed.

Publicity: *Country Inns, Mountain Review and The Atlanta Journal-Constitution.*

Saint Marys   J9

Spencer House Inn B&B

200 Osborne Street
Saint Marys, GA 31558-8361
(912)882-1872 (888)834-1817 Fax:(912)882-9427
E-mail: info@spencerhouseinn.com
Web: www.spencerhouseinn.com

Circa 1872. A white picket fence surrounds this Victorian era house, painted a pleasant pink with white trim on the wide two-level veranda. The Inn is in the St. Marys' Historic District and is on the National Register. Heart-pine floors, original

moldings and high ceilings are features of the rooms. Carefully selected reproductions, fine antiques, coordinated fabrics and rugs have been combined to create a sunny, fresh decor. There are four-poster beds and clawfoot soaking tubs. Breakfast is buffet style with peaches and cream, bread pudding or frittatas as specialties. The Inn is one block to the ferry to Georgia's largest barrier island, Cumberland Island, with 17 miles of white sand beaches, live oak forests, salt marshes and wild horses. Okefenokee National Wildlife Refuge is 45 minutes away.

Innkeeper(s): Mary & Mike Neff. $80-145. MC, VISA, AX, DS, PC, TC. 14 rooms with PB and 1 suite. Breakfast included in rates. Types of meals: Full bkfst, early coffee/tea and picnic lunch. Beds: KQDT. Cable TV, phone, ceiling fan and HBO in room. Air conditioning. Fax, library and elevator on premises. Weddings, small meetings, family reunions and seminars hosted. Antiquing, fishing, golf, Cumberland Island National Seashore, Okefenokee Swamp, Kings Bay Submarine Base, new waterfront park, shopping and sporting events nearby.

Publicity: *Seabreeze and Water's Edge Magazine.*

"I don't see how it could be improved!"

Sautee   B5

The Stovall House

1526 Hwy 255 N
Sautee, GA 30571
(706)878-3355
E-mail: info@stovallhouse.com

Circa 1837. This house, built by Moses Harshaw and restored in 1983 by Ham Schwartz, has received two state awards for its restoration. The handsome farmhouse has an extensive wraparound porch providing vistas of 26 acres of cow pastures and mountains. High ceilings, polished walnut woodwork and decorative stenciling provide a pleasant backdrop for the inn's collection of  antiques. Victorian bathroom fixtures include pull-chain toilets and pedestal sinks. The inn has its own restaurant.

Historic Interest: Sautee Nacoochee Arts and Community Center (1 mile), Museum of Indian and local history, Stovall Covered Bridge (1 mile).

Innkeeper(s): Ham Schwartz. $84-92. MC, VISA, AX, PC, TC. 5 rooms with PB. Breakfast included in rates. Types of meals: Cont and dinner. Beds: KQDT. Ceiling fan in room. Air conditioning. Library on premises. Weddings, small meetings and family reunions hosted. Amusement parks, antiquing, fishing, live theater, parks, shopping and water sports nearby.

Publicity: *Atlanta Journal. and GPTV - Historic Inns of Georgia.*

"Great to be home again. Very nostalgic and hospitable."

Savannah   G9

Broughton Street Bed & Breakfast

511 E Broughton St
Savannah, GA 31401-3501
(912)232-6633 Fax:(912)447-8980
E-mail: savbnb@aol.com

Circa 1883. This historic Victorian townhouse offers five guest rooms. Each is decorated with Victorian furnishings, antiques and contemporary artwork. One room includes a Jacuzzi tub and a fireplace. In the afternoons, the innkeepers serve hors

d'oeuvres to their guests. Breakfasts feature such items as quiche, homemade Amish bread and fresh fruit.

Innkeeper(s): Miranda Taylor. $125-250. MC, VISA, AX. TAC10. 3 rooms, 2 with PB and 1 cottage. Breakfast, afternoon tea and snacks/refreshments included in rates. Types of meals: Full bkfst. Beds: KQ. Cable TV, phone, turndown service, ceiling fan and VCR in room. Air conditioning. Fax, copier and library on premises. Weddings hosted. Antiquing, fishing, golf, live theater, parks, shopping, sporting events, tennis and water sports nearby.

"Our stay was so romantic, we're rejuvenated and ready to take on the world!"

East Bay Inn

225 E Bay St
Savannah, GA 31401-1203
(912)238-1225 (800)500-1225 Fax:(912)232-2709
E-mail: innkeeper@eastbayinn.com
Web: www.bedandbreakfastsofsavannah.com

Circa 1852. This historic establishment, once a cotton warehouse, is now richly restored with hardwood floors and antique furnishings. Private, refined accommodations are only steps away from the busy waterfront, cobblestones and River Street activities. The well-appointed guest bedrooms boast four-poster rice beds. Each morning, breakfast is served in the quaint cafe. A wine and cheese reception is enjoyed in the parlor in the evening. Ask about the romantic and golf packages available.

Innkeeper(s): Ronnie Jones. $149-189. MC, VISA, AX, DC, DS. TAC10. 28 rooms with PB. Breakfast included in rates. Types of meals: Cont plus. Beds: Q. Cable TV, phone, turndown service and some with desk in room. Air conditioning. Weddings, small meetings, family reunions and seminars hosted. Art galleries, beaches, bicycling, canoeing/kayaking, fishing, golf, hiking, museums, parks, shopping and water sports nearby.

Pets allowed: weight, additional fee.

Eliza Thompson House

5 W Jones St
Savannah, GA 31401-4503
(912)236-3620 (800)348-9378 Fax:(912)238-1920
E-mail: innkeeper@elizathompsonhouse.com
Web: www.bedandbreakfastsofsavannah.com

Circa 1847. Spared General Sherman's wrath during the Civil War, this elegantly restored Federalist-style mansion built by Eliza Thompson is one of Savannah's oldest operating inns. Set on a brick-paved street in the heart of the historic district, this architectural landmark built around a magnificent courtyard consists of 25 spacious guest rooms, all featuring gleaming heart-pine floors and period antiques. Many of the rooms offer fireplaces. Richly brewed coffee, freshly baked croissants, pastries and homemade muffins along with fresh seasonal fruits and cereals are offered each morning. Guests can explore the historic downtown just a few minutes away by foot.

Innkeeper(s): Jean Bearden. $149-250. MC, VISA, AX, TC. TAC10. 25 rooms with PB, 12 with FP. Breakfast, afternoon tea and snacks/refreshments included in rates. Types of meals: Full bkfst and early coffee/tea. Beds: KQD. Cable TV, phone and turndown service in room. Fax on premises. Weddings, small meetings and seminars hosted. Antiquing, fishing, golf, live theater, parks and shopping nearby.

The Granite Steps

126 E Gaston St
Savannah, GA 31401
(912)233-5380 Fax:(912)236-3116
E-mail: info@granitesteps.com
Web: www.granitesteps.com

Circa 1881. This glorious inn is the very picture of grand elegance with a whisper of scandalous intrigue. This rich, complex atmosphere is surely what made the producers of the movie "Midnight in the Garden of Good and Evil" choose the inn as the backdrop for two of its scenes. Named for its magnificent granite double curved entry steps, the Italianate mansion is located in the historical district of Savannah on Forsyth Park. Its garden has raised flowerbeds, a wall fountain and paved walkways. Its two guest bedrooms and five suites, all with fireplaces, are exquisitely decorated and have high ceilings, large windows, wood floors and Oriental rugs. Period details like ornate window treatments, original hardwood and marble floors, marble fireplaces, crystal chandeliers, elaborate moldings and bay windows will delight the connoisseur of Victorian décor and craftsmanship. Unforgettable breakfasts include courses such as fresh fruit, homemade coffee cake, English muffins, Savannah crabcakes and poached eggs on a bed of shrimp and, which will delight the most discriminating gourmet palate.

Historic Interest: Located in Savannah Historic District.

Innkeeper(s): Donna Sparks/Mary Strickler. $275-500. MC, VISA, AX, DS, PC, TC. TAC10. 7 rooms with PB, 7 with FP, 5 suites and 1 conference room. Breakfast, afternoon tea and snacks/refreshments included in rates. Types of meals: Gourmet bkfst, cont plus, early coffee/tea and room service. Beds: KQ. Cable TV, phone, turndown service and VCR in room. Central air. Fax, copier, spa and library on premises. Handicap access. Weddings, small meetings, family reunions and seminars hosted. Antiquing, art galleries, beaches, bicycling, canoeing/kayaking, fishing, golf, hiking, horseback riding, live theater, museums, parks, shopping, tennis and water sports nearby.

Publicity: Savannah Magazine, Atlanta Journal, USA Today and Midnight in the Garden of Good and Evil.

Joan's on Jones

17 W Jones St
Savannah, GA 31401-4503
(912)234-3863 (888)989-9806 Fax:(912)234-1455

Circa 1883. This Victorian townhouse offers two suites in the heart of the Savannah National Historic Landmark District. The Jones Street Suite and offers antiques, fireplaces, pine floors and a sitting room separated by Victorian pocket doors, a great accommodation for families or two couples traveling together. It also offers a stocked refrigerator (breakfast makings, wine, fruit, etc.) The inn's other suite offers a kitchen, fireplace and original brick walls. Both have private entrances, TV, cable and off-street parking. Walk one block to Sherman's Headquarters, Pulaski Square and St. John's. The innkeepers are former restaurateurs and will be happy to share their favorite restaurant recommendations in Savannah and as far away as Europe, since they travel there extensively.

Innkeeper(s): Joan & Gary Levy. $145-160. PC, TC. 2 suites, 2 with FP. Breakfast included in rates. Types of meals: Cont. Beds: Q. Cable TV and phone in room. Central air. Fax and copier on premises. Antiquing, art galleries, beaches, bicycling, canoeing/kayaking, fishing, golf, hiking, horseback riding, live theater, museums, parks, shopping, tennis and water sports nearby.

Pets allowed: Dogs only in Garden Suite $50 fee.

Magnolia Place Inn

503 Whitaker St
Savannah, GA 31401-4830
(912)236-7674 (800)238-7674
E-mail: info@magnoliaplaceinn.com

Circa 1878. This southern Victorian features a two-story, ornately styled veranda that stretches across the entire facade of the house, providing views of Forsyth Park Square. It was built for a descendant of the Declaration of Independence signer Thomas W. Hayward. Romantic four-poster or canopy beds are complemented by antiques and fireplaces. Some rooms have a whirlpool tub. Turn down service is provided.

Innkeeper(s): Rob & Jane Sales. $145-270. MC, VISA, AX. 13 rooms with PB, 11 with FP and 2 suites. Types of meals: Full bkfst and cont plus. Beds: KQ. Wine and tea service every afternoon on premises.
Publicity: *Esquire and New York Magazine.*

"Absolutely quintessential Southern excess."

Planters Inn

29 Abercorn Street
Savannah, GA 31401
(912)232-5678 (800)554-1187 Fax:(800)232-8893
E-mail: planinn@aol.com
Web: www.plantersinnsavannah.com

Circa 1913. Opening onto historic Reynolds Square, this elegant award-winning inn is a boutique-style property with a rich background. Offering intimacy with deluxe service, lavish attention is paid to details. Using the finest fabrics and Baker furnishings, some guest bedrooms boast fireplaces, refrigerators and balconies as well as four-poster rice beds. Overlook the park and bustling Riverfront from the penthouse hospitality suite where continental breakfast is served. An evening wine hour is enjoyed in the impressive lobby. Dinner room service is available from the Olde Pink House next door. Nightly chocolates and turndown service are added delights.

Historic Interest: River Street (1 block), City Market (3 blocks), Cotton Exchange (1 block), historic homes and museums (walking distance).
Innkeeper(s): Natalie A. Miller. $115-185. MC, VISA, AX, DC, TC. TAC10. 60 rooms with PB and 1 conference room. Breakfast included in rates. Types of meals: Cont plus and room service. Beds: QT. TV, phone, turndown service, some with fireplace, refrigerator and balconies in room. Central air. Fax, copier and child care on premises. Handicap access. Weddings, small meetings and family reunions hosted. Antiquing, art galleries, beaches, bicycling, canoeing/kayaking, fishing, golf, fitness center and spa, live theater, museums, parks, shopping and water sports nearby.

RSVP Savannah B&B Reservation Service

611 E 56th St
Savannah, GA 31405
(912)232-7787 (800)729-7787 Fax:(912)353-8060

Circa 1848. This is a reservation service that offers several historic accommodations for travelers, including more than 30 inns and guest houses. One phone call offers you these special accommodations in Savannah's Historic District, Tybee Island, Brunswick Georgia, Charleston and Beaufort, South Carolina. All accommodations have been personally inspected by the staff and all provide free parking and refreshments in the afternoon.

Innkeeper(s): Sonja Lazzaro. Call for rates. MC, VISA, AX, PC. 250 rooms with PB. Breakfast and afternoon tea included in rates. Types of meals: Full bkfst, cont plus, cont, early coffee/tea and snacks/refreshments. Beds: KQDT. Cable TV, phone, VCR, many with fireplace and some will accept small pets in room. Central air. Fax and pet boarding on premises. Handicap access. Art galleries, museums and shopping nearby.
Pets allowed: In some Inns.

The President's Quarters Inn and Guesthouse

225 E President St
Savannah, GA 31401-3806
(912)233-1600 (888)592-1812 Fax:(912)238-0849
E-mail: info@presidentsquarters.com
Web: www.presidentsquarters.com

Circa 1855. In the heart of Savannah's Historic District, The President's Quarters is comprised of Federal-style townhouses constructed by the W.W. Gordon estate. In 1870 Robert E. Lee paid a call here. Nineteen presidents are thought to have visited Savannah and the rooms at the inn today offer suitable accommodations for such dignitaries. Antique period furnishings, working fireplaces, four-poster rice beds, canopy or carved beds are featured, and the suites boast additional amenities such as balconies, hand-painted ceilings and loft bedrooms. Special services include fruit, afternoon hors d'oeuvres, nightly turndown service with cordials and local sweets and 24-hour concierge service. Breakfast is served in your room or in the courtyard. River Street is three blocks away.

Innkeeper(s): Stacy Stephens/ Hank Smalling. $137-250. MC, VISA, DC, DS, PC, TC. TAC10. 19 rooms with PB, 19 with FP and 8 suites. Types of meals: Full bkfst and snacks/refreshments. Beds: KQD. Turndown service in room. Fax, copier, telephones with data ports and elevator on premises. Handicap access.
Publicity: *Country Inns, Southern Homes, London Herald, Working Women and Travel Holiday.*

"President's Quarters was truly a home away from home." - Karl Malden

Sarah's Garden

402 E Gaston St
Savannah, GA 31419
(912)234-7716 (877)545-5425 Fax:(912)236-8297
E-mail: sjrreed@aol.com
Web: www.sarahsgarden.com

Circa 1888. Anticipation builds while walking up the front steps, through the front doors of this massive Victorian home situated on a scenic street in the historic district. A mosaic tiled floor, almost 120 years old, has been preserved. The floor pattern has been replicated on the hand-painted walls. The grand stairway and natural woodwork are kept in pristine condition. There are several parlors and 12 fireplaces throughout the inn and in each of the guest bedrooms. Hand-painted stenciling highlights the Rose, Camellia, Magnolia and Dahlia Suite. Encounter antique four-poster, canopy, carved mahogany and rice beds. The Garden of Good and The Garden of Evil suites offer complimentary wine, a kitchen, living room and private entrances. Relax on one of the porches, the bricked courtyard and, of course, in Sarah's garden.

Innkeeper(s): Jane & Rocky Reed. Call for rates. MC, VISA, AX, PC, TC. 6 rooms, 3 with PB, 6 with FP, 3 suites and 1 conference room. Breakfast and afternoon tea included in rates. Types of meals: Full bkfst and country bkfst. Beds: KQ. Cable TV, phone, ceiling fan and fireplace in room. Central air. Swimming on premises. Weddings, small meetings and family reunions hosted. Antiquing, art galleries, beaches, bicycling, canoeing/kayaking, fishing, golf, horseback riding, live theater, museums, parks, shopping, tennis and water sports nearby.

William Kehoe House

123 Habersham St
Savannah, GA 31401-3820
(912)232-1020 (800)820-1020 Fax:(912)231-0208
E-mail: classmanagement@aol.com
Web: www.williamkehoehouse.com

Circa 1892. A wealthy Irish businessman built this Renaissance Revival manor. The interior has been impeccably restored and decorated in Victorian style with antiques, reproductions and original artwork. In honor of the original owner, the individually decorated guest rooms are named for a county

in Ireland. Each day begins with a gourmet, Southern-style breakfast. Fresh fruit, freshly squeezed orange juice and home-baked breads accompany such entrees as eggs Savannah, bacon, grits and potatoes. The staff is always happy to assist guests and can direct you to fine restaurants, shops and attractions in the Savannah area. This inn has received both a four-diamond rating from AAA and four stars from Mobil.

Innkeeper(s): Martha Geiger. $205-345. MC, VISA, AX. TAC10. 15 rooms with PB, 2 suites and 2 conference rooms. Breakfast and snacks/refreshments included in rates. Types of meals: Gourmet bkfst, early coffee/tea and afternoon tea. Beds: KQT. Cable TV, phone, turndown service and ceiling fan in room. Air conditioning. Fax and copier on premises. Handicap access. Small meetings hosted. Antiquing, fishing, live theater, parks, shopping and water sports nearby.
Publicity: *Hideaway, Atlanta Homes & Lifestyles, Discerning Traveler and Romantic Inns of America.*

Thomasville   J4

Melhana, the Grand Plantation

301 Showboat Ln
Thomasville, GA 31792
(229)226-2290 (888)920-3030 Fax:(229)226-4585
E-mail: info@melhana.com
Web: www.melhana.com

Circa 1820. More than 50 acres surround the historic Melhana Plantation comprised of 30 buildings including the manor, The Hibernia Cottage and a village. There are 30 buildings, all in the National Register. Traditional décor includes furnishings and amenities such as king- and queen-size four-poster beds, desks, paintings, puffy down comforters and handmade duvets. Some accommodations offer marble Jacuzzis and veranda entrances. Most include views of expansive green lawns, the Avenue of Magnolias, camellia gardens, the sunken garden or the plantation's pasture land. The inn's elegantly appointed restaurant has received acclaims from prestigious critics for its Southern cuisine, enhanced by herbs garnered from private kitchen gardens. To fully enjoy the plantation, consider arranging for horseback riding, quail hunting or a carriage ride, but be sure to allow time to linger on the veranda or to enjoy the indoor swimming pool, theater and fitness center.

$250-650. MC, VISA, AX, DS, PC, TC. TAC10. 38 rooms with PB, 7 with FP, 14 suites, 2 cottages and 4 conference rooms. Afternoon tea included in rates. Types of meals: Full bkfst, early coffee/tea, gourmet lunch, picnic lunch, snacks/refreshments, gourmet dinner and room service. Beds: KQ. Cable TV, phone, turndown service, VCR on request and terry cloth bath robes in room. Central air. VCR, fax, copier, spa, stables, tennis, library, carriage rides, aromatherapy massages, indoor heated pool and fitness center on premises. Weddings, small meetings and seminars hosted. Amusement parks, antiquing, art galleries, beaches, bicycling, fishing, golf, horseback riding, live theater, museums, parks, shopping, sporting events, tennis and water sports nearby.

Thomson   D7

1810 West Inn

254 N Seymour Dr
Thomson, GA 30824-7209
(706)595-3156 (800)515-1810
E-mail: dm1810westinn@aol.com
Web: www.1810westinn.com

Circa 1810. The new owners desire this historic 15-acre farm, only 30 minutes from Augusta, to reflect the romance of the past while offering modern comforts and embracing the future. Accommodations include the plantation farmhouse and several adjoining tenant houses, moved here and restored. Many guest bedrooms and suites offer cozy fireplaces. A hearty country breakfast is made with farm fresh eggs and may include hot baked biscuits and fresh fruit. Enjoy the new heated

pool with overflowing hot tub and a jogging trail. A horse pasture is perfect for equestrians. Peacocks mingle on the picturesque grounds, dotted with magnolias and lush gardens. The inn specializes in memorable weddings and receptions.

Historic Interest: Nearby Wrightsborough, one of Georgia's first communities, includes the historic Rock House, which was built in 1785. Other historic attractions in the area include the site of a Quaker settlement and part of the Bartram Trail.

Innkeeper(s): David Moore. $85-200. MC, VISA, AX, PC, TC. 10 rooms with PB and 3 suites. Types of meals: Full bkfst. Spa and heated pool on premises. Hiking, boating and shopping nearby.

Four Chimneys B&B

2316 Wire Rd SE
Thomson, GA 30824-7326
(706)597-0220

Circa 1800. The architecture of the Four Chimneys is referred to as Plantation Plain and was built by Quakers. All the wood in the house is heart pine, including floors, walls and ceilings. Four-poster beds and working fireplaces tastefully accentuate the home's authentic simplicity. The innkeeper is a master gardener with a specialty in herb gardens, and there are herb and heirloom flower gardens scattered about the three acres of grounds. The back

yard is a certified wildlife habitat. Fresh herbs often enhance entrees presented at breakfast, and the innkeepers serve seasonally, peaches, blueberries or strawberries with cream. Although many visitors to the inn find it difficult to venture past the wide front veranda with its enticing rockers and porch swing, the area offers antiquing, equestrian events, golf and fox hunting. November's "Blessings of the Hounds" is the start of the hunting season, which continues through March. Nearby Augusta hosts the Master's golf tournament each April.

Innkeeper(s): Maggie & Ralph Zieger. $45-75. MC, VISA, PC, TC. 3 rooms, 2 with PB, 3 with FP and 1 suite. Breakfast included in rates. Types of meals: Full bkfst, picnic lunch and afternoon tea. Beds: QD. TV and ceiling fan in room. Central air. VCR and library on premises. German spoken. Antiquing, art galleries, fishing, golf, historic sites, live theater, museums, parks, shopping and sporting events nearby.
Publicity: *The McDuffie Progess and Southern Living Magazine.*

Hawaii

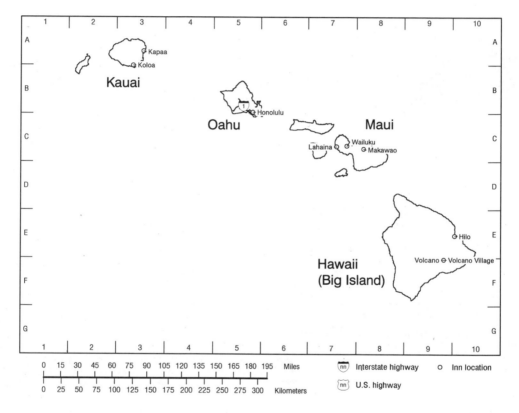

Miles: 0 15 30 45 60 75 90 105 120 135 150 165 180 195

Kilometers: 0 25 50 75 100 125 150 175 200 225 250 275 300

Interstate highway | Inn location
U.S. highway

Hawaii (Big Island)

Hilo   E10

Maureen's Bed & Breakfast

1896 Kalanianaole Ave
Hilo, HI 96720-4918
(808)935-9018 (800)935-9018 Fax:(808)961-5596
E-mail: maurbnb@hilo.net
Web: www.maureenbnb.com

Circa 1932. Known to locals as the Saiki Mansion, named after its original owner, this fully restored home has a baronial ambiance that befits an Aloha experience. The rich blend of redwood and cedar line the 30-foot vaulted living room ceiling, walls, double staircases and wraparound balcony. The Japanese Tea Room is elegant in cherry wood. Antique furnishings made of koa (a precious wood native to Hawaii) as well as mahogany and oak add to the luxury of silk paintings and tapestries. The guest bedrooms boast mountain views of Mauna Kea or the relaxing sounds of ocean surf. A satisfying breakfast includes island specialties with macadamia nuts, tropical fruits and Kona coffee. The koi ponds or botanical gardens with fragrant flowers and colorful plants can be enjoyed from the front and rear lanais. Across the street, a beach park offers swimming.

Historic Interest: Lyman Museum-Tsunami Museum.

Innkeeper(s): Maureen Goto. $50-100. TC. TAC10. 5 rooms with PB. Breakfast included in rates. Types of meals: Gourmet bkfst and veg bkfst. Beds: KQDT. Ceiling fan in room. VCR, fax and library on premises.

Antiquing, art galleries, beaches, bicycling, canoeing/kayaking, fishing, golf, hiking, horseback riding, museums, parks, shopping, tennis, water sports and wineries nearby.

Pets Allowed.

Shipman House Bed & Breakfast Inn

131 Kaiulani St
Hilo, HI 96720-2529
(808)934-8002 (800)627-8447 Fax:(808)934-8002
E-mail: bighouse@bigisland.com
Web: www.hilo-hawaii.com

Circa 1899. Locals know Shipman House as "The Castle," no doubt because of both its size and grandeur. The manor, a mix of Italianate and Queen Anne styles, is listed on both the state and national historic registers. The home's former mistress,

Mary Shipman, not only was the granddaughter of a Hawaiian chiefess, but a friend of Queen Lili'uokalani. Jack London and his wife once stayed here for a month as guests of the Shipmans. The grounds still feature many of

the plants, palms and flowers nurtured by the Shipmans. Inside, the innkeeper has decorated the home with a mix of antiques and traditional furnishings, many pieces are original to the house. There is a cottage available as well, secluded by trees and foliage. A lavish, continental-plus breakfast buffet is served on the home's lanai, offering such items as homemade granola, local fruit (and there are 20 different varieties of fruit trees on the property), freshly baked breads, homemade passionfruit butter, and pancakes, waffles or French toast. With advance notic.

Historic Interest: Historic Hilo (2 blocks), Lyman House (1/4 mile).
Innkeeper(s): Barbara & Gary Andersen. $145-200. MC, VISA, AX, PC, TC. TAC10. 5 rooms with PB and 1 cottage. Breakfast and snacks/refreshments included in rates. Types of meals: Veg bkfst, cont plus and early coffee/tea. Beds: QT. Ceiling fan, fresh flowers, maps and robes in room. Fax, copier, library, botanical garden and views on premises. Antiquing, beaches, bicycling, canoeing/kayaking, fishing, golf, hiking, volcano; observatories, live theater, museums, parks, shopping, downhill skiing, sporting events and wineries nearby.
Publicity: *New York Times, Los Angeles Times, Boston Globe, Honolulu Advertiser, Sunset Magazine, Victorian Homes, Wings Magazine, Travel & Leisure, Island Magazine, Hawaii Magazine, PBC documentary on non-resort vacations on Hawaii Island and HGTV.*

Volcano   *F9*

Aloha Junction Bed & Breakfast

19-4037 Post Office Ln, PO Box 91
Volcano, HI 96785
(808)967-7289 (888)967-7286 Fax:(808)967-7289
E-mail: relax@aloha.net
Web: www.bbvolcano.com

Circa 1927. Sugar mill managers from the Hamakua Coast originally stayed at this plantation retreat home for their vacations. Situated on a little more than an acre of mountain rain forest, the lush surroundings melt away any stress. The rooms are comfortable and large, boasting 10-foot ceilings. A typical tropical breakfast may include a fresh papaya boat filled with bananas and coconut, made-to-order free-range eggs and signature macadamia nut pancakes. Hawaii Volcanoes National Park is less than a mile away. Be sure to visit Green Sand and Black Sand Beaches.

Innkeeper(s): Robert & Susan Hughes. $75-125. MC, VISA, TC. TAC10. 4 rooms, 3 with PB. Breakfast included in rates. Types of meals: Full bkfst, veg bkfst and early coffee/tea. Beds: KQDT. Cable TV in room. VCR, fax, copier, spa, 52" TV and Hawaiian books & music on premises. Antiquing, art galleries, beaches, bicycling, canoeing/kayaking, fishing, golf, hiking, horseback riding, thermal hot ponds, green sand beach, black sand beach, live theater, museums, parks, shopping, tennis and wineries nearby.

Hale Ohia Cottages

PO Box 758
Volcano, HI 96785-0758
(808)967-7986 (800)455-3803 Fax:(808)967-8610
E-mail: information@haleohia.com
Web: www.haleohia.com

Circa 1930. These country cottages, nestled in the quaint Volcano Village area, are surrounded by Hawaiian gardens and lush forest. You can stroll the serene property on paths made of lava rock and enjoy the many orchids and native plants. The gardens are some of the finest in Volcano. Volcano National Park is only one mile from the cottage.

Historic Interest: The home is a historic estate, built by locals, and preserving Hawaii's heritage. Volcano Village itself has more than 150 historic homes or buildings. The historic town of Hilo is 23 miles away.

Innkeeper(s): Michael Tuttle. $95-150. MC, VISA. TAC10. 8 rooms with PB, 4 with FP, 4 suites, 4 cottages and 1 guest house. Breakfast included in rates. Types of meals: Cont plus and cont. Beds: QDT. VCR, fax, copier, spa and sauna on premises. Handicap access. Weddings, small meetings, family reunions and seminars hosted. Antiquing, art galleries, beaches, bicycling, canoeing/kayaking, fishing, golf, hiking, horseback riding, live theater, museums, parks, shopping, tennis, water sports and wineries nearby.
Publicity: *National Geographic Traveler, New York Times, Hawaii Bride, Pacific Connection and Travel & Leisure.*

"The hospitality and accommodations couldn't have been better. A beautiful cottage in a peaceful, tropical garden."

Kilauea Lodge

PO Box 116
Volcano, HI 96785-0116
(808)967-7366 Fax:(808)967-7367
E-mail: stay@kilauealodge.com
Web: www.kilauealodge.com

Circa 1938. Guests are pampered at this gorgeous tropical paradise, only a mile from the entrance to Volcanoes National Park. Fluffy towels, towel warmers, robes, cozy, comfortable beds and rich decor create a feeling of warmth and romance in each of the guest rooms. Fresh flowers and original art add to

the majesty of the lodge. The wonderful, gourmet meals are served in front of the lodge's historic

Fireplace of Friendship, which is decked with all sorts of artifacts. The innkeepers offer truly memorable meals, praised by such publications as Bon Appetit and Gourmet Magazine. The inn has an interesting history. Built as a YMCA, it later was used during World War II as offices and a military bivouac.

Historic Interest: Historical Hilo Town is 26 miles away and the Volcano Art Center and the original Volcano House, built in the 1890s, are only two miles away.

Innkeeper(s): Lorna & Albert Jeyte. $125-155. MC, VISA, PC, TC. 14 rooms with PB, 8 with FP, 3 cottages and 1 conference room. Breakfast included in rates. Types of meals: Full bkfst, country bkfst, dinner and room service. Beds: KQT. Heaters and heated towel warmers in room. VCR, fax, copier, spa, library and gazebo on premises. Handicap access. Weddings, small meetings, family reunions and seminars hosted. German and Spanish spoken. Antiquing, art galleries, beaches, bicycling, golf, hiking, horseback riding, volcano viewing, live theater, museums, parks, shopping and wineries nearby.

Publicity: *National Geographic Traveler, Bon Appetit, Pacific Business News and Conde Nast.*

"Your rooms were outstanding both for cleanliness and decor. As to the dinner we had, it was superb, and as far as I'm concerned the best four-course dinner I have ever eaten."

Ma'ukele Lodge

194145 Kolani Honua Loop
Volcano, HI 96785
(808)507-7421 (888)507-7421 Fax:(808)985-7421
E-mail: volcanobb@hotmail.com
Web: www.volcano-bb.com

Circa 1949. Expect to be enchanted at this eclectic inn that was designated a Biosphere Preserve and World Heritage Site by the United Nations. In the Kilauea rain forest, high on the

slopes of Mauna Loa, the lush foliage of giant native ferns and towering trees entice singing birds and awestruck guests. A blend of Hawaiian, Mideastern and Balinese decor accents the intimate, tropical ambiance. The fireplace in the open-beamed living room offers warmth on a misty winter evening A full breakfast of exotic fruits, hot entree, fresh-baked bread and locally grown coffee is served in the dining room with a view out the bay window. Explore the national park, only minutes away.

Historic Interest: Volcanoes National Park (1.5 miles).

$95. MC, VISA, AX, PC, TC. TAC10. 3 rooms with PB, 2 with FP. Breakfast included in rates. Types of meals: Gourmet bkfst, country bkfst, veg bkfst, lunch, picnic lunch and gourmet dinner. Beds: Q. Phone and turndown service in room. Fax, copier, bicycles and library on premises. Weddings, small meetings, family reunions and seminars hosted. Antiquing, beaches, bicycling, canoeing/kayaking, fishing, golf, hiking, horseback riding, live theater, museums, parks, shopping, water sports and wineries nearby.

Volcano Village   F9

The Chalet Kilauea Collection

Box 998, Wright Rd
Volcano Village, HI 96785
(808)967-7786 (800)937-7786 Fax:(808)967-8660
E-mail: h.haan@volcano-hawaii.com
Web: www.volcano-hawaii.com

Circa 1945. This collection of lodging accommodations includes deluxe boutique inns, modest lodges, and spacious vacation homes. There are five inns and lodges and six vacation homes. The main inn, the Inn at Volcano, has six rooms, each with a special theme. The rooms sport names such as the Out of Africa, Treehouse or Oriental Jade. The Bridal and Treehouse suites include Jacuzzi tubs. Inn guests are treated to

a three-course, gourmet breakfast served by candle-light, as well as afternoon tea. There's an outdoor Jacuzzi for stargazing.

Innkeeper(s): Lisha & Brian Crawford. $49-399. MC, VISA, AX, DC, DS, PC. TAC10. 40 rooms and 1 conference room. Breakfast included in rates. Types of meals: Gourmet bkfst, veg bkfst, cont plus, cont, early coffee/tea and afternoon tea. Beds: KQT. Cable TV, phone, turndown service and VCR in room. Fax, copier, spa and library on premises. Weddings, small meetings, family reunions and seminars hosted. French, Dutch and German spoken. Antiquing, art galleries, beaches, bicycling, canoeing/kayaking, fishing, golf, hiking, horseback riding, lava viewing, live theater, museums, shopping, sporting events, tennis, water sports and wineries nearby.

Publicity: *PBS.*

"Your attention to detail is what makes Chalet Kilauea special to all who stay here. Everything from the mints on the bed to the tea service set you apart from other establishments. Thank you for the enjoyable and relaxing atmosphere."

Kauai

Kapaa   A3

Lani-Keha Bed & Breakfast

848 Kamalu Rd
Kapaa, HI 96746
(808)822-1605 (800)821-4898 Fax:(808)822-2429
E-mail: lanikeha@hawaiian.net
Web: www.lanikeha.com

Circa 1948. Against the backdrop of mountains and island beauty, solitude surrounds this plantation home built in the the sugar cane heyday. Sprawling on a three-acre estate of lawns and fruit trees, the tropical decor features rattan furnishings. Pleasant guest bedrooms offer leisurely comfort, with thoughtful fruit baskets. The casual atmosphere extends to the kitchen where breakfast fixings are provided for self-preparation and is open to use for other meals, too. Bicycles are available. Grove Farm Homestead and Kauai Museum are must-see places to visit.

Historic Interest: Many Heiaus (ancient temple ruins) (nearby), Kauai Museum (nearby).

Innkeeper(s): Karena Biber & Criss Kidder. $65. PC, TC. TAC10. 3 rooms with PB. Breakfast included in rates. Beds: KT. Cable TV, ceiling fan and VCR in room. Fax, bicycles, library, BBQ and full kitchen use on premises. Art galleries, beaches, bicycling, canoeing/kayaking, fishing, golf, hiking, horseback riding, live theater, museums, parks, shopping, sporting events, tennis and water sports nearby.

Rosewood

872 Kamalu Rd
Kapaa, HI 96746-9701
(808)822-5216 Fax:(808)822-5478
E-mail: rosewood@aloha.net
Web: www.rosewoodkauai.com

Circa 1900. For a truly Polynesian experience, guests can stay at this inn's rustic Thatched Cottage, which appears as a dream from "Robinson Crusoe." The cottage includes sleeping, living and dining areas as well as a small kitchen. There is also a Victorian Cottage with a kitchen, two bedrooms, dining area and laundry facilities. Inside the turn-of-the-century, plantation-style house, there are two guest rooms featuring country decor. For those on a budget, the innkeepers also offer accommodations in the Bunkhouse. Guests in the main house or cottages are treated to breakfasts of tropical fruits, homemade granola with macadamia nuts, Kona coffee and entrees such as Hawaiian sweet bread served as French toast. The acre grounds are lush with flowers, tropical plants, a variety of fruit trees and ponds with waterfalls.

Innkeeper(s): Norbert & Rosemary Smith. $40-125. PC, TC. TAC10. 7 rooms, 4 with PB and 2 cottages. Types of meals: Cont plus. Beds: K. Ceiling fan and some with breakfast included in room. VCR, fax, copier, child care and internet access on premises. Weddings and family reunions hosted. Fishing and water sports nearby.

Koloa B3

Poipu Inn & Kauai Inn

2720 Hoonani Rd
Koloa, HI 96756
(808)742-0100 (800)808-2330 Fax:(808)742-1794
E-mail: poipu@aloha.net
Web: www.poipu.net

Circa 1933. This restored plantation house preserves the character of old Kauai, while providing for every modern convenience. The handcrafted wood interiors and old-fashioned lanais provide the perfect backdrop for the ornate white Victorian wicker, carousel horses, pine antiques and tropical color accents. Most of the rooms feature whirlpool tubs. Local art and handcrafts abound as one of the innkeepers is an avid collector and artist.

The beach is one block away, and the innkeepers can help guests arrange every detail of their stay, including helicopter tours, short-term health spa memberships and dinner reservations.
Historic Interest: Menehuene fish ponds (1/8 mile), Koloa landing (500 ft).
Innkeeper(s): Richard & Marylou. $89-149. MC, VISA, AX, DS. TAC10. 48 rooms, 46 with PB and 2 suites. Breakfast included in rates. Types of meals: Cont plus and early coffee/tea. Beds: KQDT. Cable TV, phone and ceiling fan in room. Fax and swimming on premises. Weddings and family reunions hosted. French and German spoken. Art galleries, beaches, bicycling, canoeing/kayaking, fishing, golf, hiking, horseback riding, museums, parks, shopping, tennis and water sports nearby.
Publicity: *Travel & Leisure, Smart Money, Country Inns and Travel-Holiday.*

"Thank you for sharing your home as well as yourself with us. I'll never forget this place; it's the best B&B we've stayed at."

Poipu Plantation Resort

1792 Pee Rd
Koloa, HI 96756-9535
(808)742-6757 (800)634-0263 Fax:(808)742-8681
E-mail: plantation@poipubeach.com
Web: www.poipubeach.com

Circa 1938. Across the road from the ocean, this historic plantation house is located on one acre. In addition to guest rooms in the house there are nine cottage-style condominium units. (The cottages offer one and two bedrooms.) All accommodations feature a pleasant tropical decor, and have wood floors and some with vaulted ceilings. There's a laundromat, hot tub and barbecue on the grounds. An island breakfast is served in view of the water from the inn's lanai. Walk a block or two to Brenneck's or Poipu Beach Park where there are many scenic coves and beaches. The innkeepers will help you arrange helicopter tours, boating or snorkeling activities, and the area offers an abundance of great spots for hiking, surfing, swimming and horseback riding.
Innkeeper(s): Chris Moore. $90-160. MC, VISA, PC, TC. TAC10. 12 rooms, 3 with PB and 9 cottages. Beds: Q. TV, phone, ceiling fan and cottages with VCR in room. Air conditioning. Fax, copier, spa, child care, BBQ and beach supplies on premises. Weddings, small meetings, family reunions and seminars hosted. Fishing, hiking, horseback riding and shopping nearby.

Koloa-Poipu B3

Old Koloa House Bed & Breakfast

3327 Waikomo Road
Koloa-Poipu, HI 96756
(808)742-2099
E-mail: oldkoloahouse@webtv.net
Web: www.oldkoloahouse.com

Circa 1928. Originally, this bungalow-style home was built on McBryde Sugar Plantation for one of the managers. It was later moved to this neighborhood, popularly known for its local walking tour. Lovingly renovated, the style of decor is reminiscent of old Kauai. The Aloha spirit is evident in the fresh flowers and welcome basket. Tropical tranquility and grace are reflected in the appealing guest bedrooms. Each has a private entrance that leads onto a lanai, the perfect place to enjoy a Hawaiian-style continental breakfast. The lush grounds are surrounded by colorful native plants and flowers, which fill the air with a sweetness.
Historic Interest: Old Koloa Town and Sugar Mill, St. Rafael Church.
Innkeeper(s): Bob and Linda Keane. $78. MC, VISA, AX, PC, TC. TAC10. 3 rooms, 2 with PB. Breakfast included in rates. Types of meals: Cont. Beds: QD. Cable TV, phone and ceiling fan in room. Antiquing, beaches, canoeing/kayaking, museums, shopping, tennis and water sports nearby.
Publicity: *Garden Island Newspaper.*

Maui

Haiku C8

Haikuleana Country Inn

555 Haiku Rd
Haiku, Maui, HI 96708-5884
(808)575-2890 Fax:(808)575-9177
E-mail: blumblum@earthlink.net
Web: www.haikuleana.com

Circa 1860. A true plantation house, the Haikuleana sits in the midst of pineapple fields and Norfolk pine trees. With high ceilings and a tropical decor, the inn has been licensed since 1989

and boasts all of the flavor of Hawaiian country life. The porch looks out over exotic gardens. Beaches and waterfalls are nearby.
Historic Interest: Baldwin Estate (1/4 mile).
Innkeeper(s): Ralph H. & Jeanne Elizabeth Blum. $100-150. PC, TC. TAC10. 3 rooms with PB and 1 guest house. Breakfast and snacks/refreshments included in rates. Types of meals: Gourmet bkfst, veg bkfst and early coffee/tea. Beds: KQT. TV, phone and ceiling fan in room. VCR, fax, copier, spa, library and fully stocked guest refrigerator on premises. Weddings, small meetings, family reunions and seminars hosted. Russian, French, Italian, German and Spanish spoken. Antiquing, art galleries, beaches, bicycling, fishing, golf, hiking, horseback riding, live theater, parks, shopping and water sports nearby.
Publicity: *Honolulu Advertiser, Maui News, Los Angeles Times and Portland Oregonian.*

"Great, great, extra great! Maui is paradise thanks to your daily guidance, directions and helpful hints."

Lahaina C7

Garden Gate B&B

67 Kaniau Rd
Lahaina, HI 96761
(808)661-8800 (800)939-3217 Fax:(808)661-0209

Circa 1949. Just a block from the ocean and a mile from old Lahaina town (a whaling village of yesteryear and the erstwhile royal capital of Hawaii) stands this glorious 10,050-square-foot inn. Guests walk across a bridge over a stream to the tropical oasis that surrounds the inn. Hibiscus, plumeria and birds of paradise fill the garden, which has many sitting areas where guests may listen to bird calls and breathe in the fragrance of the tropical flowers. The four guest bedrooms, two with private decks and ocean views, are designed with comfort in mind. The inn serves a continental breakfast of guava juice, tropical fruit, Kona coffee and fresh pastries. After this invigorating breakfast, guests may walk three minutes to Wahikuli Wayside Park, 10 minutes to Lahaina harbor and 20 minutes to the beaches of Kaanapali. Those wanting to stay close to the inn's paradise garden oasis enjoy a sandy swimming beach 300 yards long, just minutes from the inn.

Innkeeper(s): Bill & Jaime Mosley. $69-115. MC, VISA, AX, DS, PC, TC. TAC10. 4 rooms with PB and 1 cottage. Breakfast included in rates. Types of meals: Cont plus and cont. Beds: KQDT. Cable TV, phone, ceiling fan and VCR in room. Air conditioning. Fax, copier and bicycles on premises. Weddings, small meetings and family reunions hosted. Art galleries, beaches, bicycling, canoeing/kayaking, fishing, golf, hiking, horseback riding, live theater, museums, parks, shopping, tennis and water sports nearby.

Lahaina Inn

127 Lahainaluna Rd
Lahaina, Maui, HI 96761-1502
(808)661-0577 (800)669-3444 Fax:(808)667-9480
E-mail: inntown@lahainainn.com
Web: www.lahainainn.com

Circa 1938. In the center of Old Lahaina Town, this elegant inn is filled with Victorian antiques and inviting decor. Each guest room or spacious parlor suite boasts balconies with exciting views of the harbor or mountains. Romantic antique beds, lamps and Oriental rugs add warmth and luxury to the rooms. There are both ceiling fans and air conditioning. An antique sideboard outside the guest rooms is stocked each morning with steaming Kona coffee, tea, juice, croissants and muffins. The inn has been featured in many articles and newspapers and was named to the list of "Top Ten Romantic Inns" by American Historic Inns.

Historic Interest: A walking tour of this charming Hawaiian town includes such sites as the Baldwin House, Government Market, a courthouse, fort and canal. The Hauola Stone, a stop of the tour, was believed to have been used by Hawaiians as a healing place.

Innkeeper(s): Melinda A Mower. $99-169. MC, VISA, AX, DC, PC, TC. TAC10. 9 rooms and 3 suites. Breakfast included in rates. Types of meals: Cont and early coffee/tea. Beds: KQDT. Phone and ceiling fan in room. Air conditioning. Fax, copier and internet access on premises. Antiquing, beaches, golf, harbor activities, shopping and tennis nearby.

Publicity: *Tour & Travel News, Hawaii Magazine, Honolulu, Pacific Business News, Glamour* and *Travel & Leisure.*

"Outstanding lodging and service. Ahhh! Paradise. Fantastic. Excellent. Exquisite."

Makawao C8

Banyan Tree House

3265 Baldwin Ave
Makawao, HI 96768-9629
(808)572-9021 Fax:(808)573-5072
E-mail: info@banyantreehouse.com
Web: www.banyantreehouse.com

Circa 1926. Banyan Tree is comprised of three rooms in a Hawaiian plantation-style house and four cottages. Ethel Smith Baldwin, a prominent local citizen who served as secretary of the Red Cross and founded a flourishing artist organization, was the most well-known inhabitant of this house. The home was built by the Maui Agricultural Company, of which Baldwin's husband was president. The lush setting includes two acres of gardens, with tree swings and hammocks. Guests in the main house enjoy a full restaurant kitchen. Three of the cottages include kitchenettes. The largest cottage has a full kitchen, spacious living room, fireplace, formal dining room and a lanai with a view of the ocean. It is popular for groups, families and workshops. Tropical Hawaii is the decorating theme throughout the rooms and cottages. Beach activities, galleries, shops and restaurants all are nearby.

Innkeeper(s): Suzy Papanilcokas. $75-225. TAC10. 7 rooms with PB, 1 with FP, 4 cottages, 1 guest house and 1 conference room. Beds: QDT. Cable TV, phone and VCR in room. Fax, copier, library, child care, swimming pool and spa on premises. Small meetings, family reunions and seminars hosted. Antiquing, art galleries, beaches, bicycling, canoeing/kayaking, fishing, golf, hiking, horseback riding, live theater, museums, parks, shopping, water sports and wineries nearby.

Hale Ho'okipa Inn

32 Pakani Pl
Makawao, HI 96768-9073
(808)572-6698 (877)572-6698 Fax:(808)573-2580
E-mail: mauibnb@maui.net
Web: www.maui.net/~mauibnb

Circa 1924. Historic Maui is at its best at this Craftsman-style plantation home. Architectural details include shingle-clad walls, multiple gables, decorative eaves, wood floors and high ceilings. The common areas and guest bedrooms feature local art and Hawaiian and Oriental decor. Antique furnishings of clawfoot tubs and a brass bed enhance the warm ambiance. Savor the island's fresh fruit and juice. Local-made jellies top fresh-baked breads. Incredible views of Haleakala, the central valley and mountains to the west are seen from  lanais. The hillside grounds are a breathtaking blend of fragrant tropical fruit, Cook Island pine trees and colorful flowers. The Kipa Cottage will be available for rental summer of 2002.

Historic Interest: Historic town of Makawao (walking distance).

Innkeeper(s): Cherie Attix. $85-155. MC, VISA, PC, TC. TAC10. 5 rooms, 4 with PB and 1 cottage. Breakfast and afternoon tea included in rates. Types of meals: Cont plus and early coffee/tea. Beds: QD. Cable TV in room. VCR, fax and library on premises. Weddings, small meetings, family reunions and seminars hosted. Spanish spoken. Antiquing, art galleries, beaches, bicycling, fishing, golf, hiking, horseback riding, live theater, parks, shopping, tennis, water sports and wineries nearby.

Publicity: *Seattle Times* and *Maui News.*

Paia   C8

Kuau Cove Plantation B&B

2 Wa'a Pl
Paia, Maui, HI 96779
(808)579-8988 Fax:(808)579-8710
E-mail: kuaubnb@maui.net
Web: www.maui.net/~kuaubnb/

Circa 1939. This historic plantation-style home is just 50 yards from the pristine waters of Maui. The interior is light and airy, decorated in island style with period wicker and rattan furnishings. The home was built in the 1930s and once housed the doctor who served the Paia Sugar Plantation. There are two rooms in the main house, and the innkeepers offer two studio apartments. The apartments include a kitchenette, and guests can even get a peak of the ocean from the lanai of the Ocean Studio. The innkeepers offer beach chairs, boogie boards and coolers to their guests. Surfing and windsurfing is available at Ho'okipa Beach, just a mile away. Golfing is nearby as well, and there are plenty of places to enjoy a memorable bike ride, including a trip to the Haleakala Crater.
Innkeeper(s): Russell & Jane Mori. $85-95. MC, VISA, DS, PC. TAC10. 4 rooms, 2 with PB and 2 suites. Breakfast included in rates. Types of meals: Cont plus. Beds: Q. TV, phone, ceiling fan and VCR in room. Fax and library on premises. Weddings, small meetings, family reunions and seminars hosted. Antiquing, art galleries, beaches, canoeing/kayaking, fishing, golf, hiking, horseback riding, live theater, parks, shopping and water sports nearby.
Publicity: *San Francisco Chronicle.*

Wailuku   C7

Old Wailuku Inn

2199 Kahookele St
Wailuku, HI 96793
(808)244-5897 (800)305-4899 Fax:(808)242-9600
E-mail: mauibandb@aol.com
Web: www.mauiinn.com

Circa 1924. Not everything wonderful in Hawaii is located along its impressive shoreline. A case in point is this restored plantation-style home located in Wailuku's historic district and away from the crowded tourist spots. Wailuku is where the people of Maui live and offers shopping, dining and cultural events. The home maintains many original features, including floors made of eucalyptus and a unique elliptical shower. The innkeepers, both of whom are born-and-raised islanders, have been in the hotel and restaurant businesses for more than 30 years, and their expertise is evident. The décor is imaginative and romantic with an eclectic mix of styles that all seem to fit together perfectly. The Hawaiian influence is predominant; each guest room is named after a flower. The Ilima Room is done in a creamy shade of yellow. The bed is topped with a quilt featuring its namesake flower, and the room also includes a spacious whirlpool tub. Several guest rooms afford mountain views. The half-acre grounds are decorated with palms, and guests can enjoy the setting on the inn's wicker-filled porch. The innkeepers serve breakfast on the enclosed porch with a view of Mt. Haleakala, and the menu might include the following: a fresh papaya filled with mango and garnished with strawberries, a Portuguese version of the beignet, and a spinach, tofu and mushroom tart. The inn's central location offers close access to most Maui attractions, including Kahului Airport. The innkeepers offer many amenities for business travelers, including modem jacks, phones with voice mail and fax service.
Historic Interest: Bailey House (1/2 mile), Alexander House (half a mile), courthouse (2 blocks), Union church (1 block(, Historic Wailuku Town(half a mile), Halekii and Piihana Kalani Heiau (1 mile).

Innkeeper(s): Janice & Thomas Fairbanks. $120-180. MC, VISA, AX, DC, CB, DS, PC, TC. TAC10. 7 rooms with PB. Breakfast & snacks/refreshments included in rates. Types of meals: Gourmet bkfst. Beds: KQT. Cable TV, phone, turndown service, ceiling fan & VCR in room. Central air. Fax, copier & library on premises. Weddings & family reunions hosted. German and Spanish spoken. Antiquing, art galleries, beaches, bicycling, canoeing/kayaking, fishing, golf, hiking, horseback riding, live theater, museums, parks, shopping, sporting events, tennis, water sports and wineries nearby.
Publicity: *New York Times, L.A. Times, Sunset Magazine & Best places to kiss.*

Oahu

Honolulu   B5

Be Back Hawaii All Islands Reservation Service

3429 Kanaina Ave
Honolulu, HI 96815
(808)732-6618 (877)4BE-BACK Fax:(808)732-6618
E-mail: beback@lava.net
Web: www.bebackhawaii.com

Circa 1900. Explore the Hawaiian Islands with the help of a personal vacation planner and stay at some of the finest bed & breakfasts each island has to offer, with accommodations ranging from a comfortable guest house to the native adventure of a tree house. Perhaps listening to the waves crash along the warm shore from a beach cottage, or enjoying the privacy of a secluded vacation home depicts the ideal relaxing location. Whatever the taste, guests can experience one or all of the islands with the expertise of Hawaii's knowledgeable Brigitte Baccus, personal travel consultant and Hawaii specialist, who will set up "Island Exploring" stays or offer assistance in choosing the perfect Inn or bed & breakfast to spend an entire vacation. With more than 20 years of experience, Be Back Hawaii offers the magnificence of the islands that everyday tourists so often miss and helps guests discover a new view of the Hawaiian Islands.
Innkeeper(s): Brigitte Baccus. $50-250. Types of meals: Cont plus.

The Manoa Valley Inn

2001 Vancouver Dr
Honolulu, HI 96822-2451
(808)947-6019 Fax:(808)946-6168
E-mail: manoavalleyinn@aloha.net
Web: www.aloha.net/~wery/

Circa 1915. This exquisite home offers the best of two worlds, a beautiful, country home that is also surrounded by a tropical paradise. Each restored room features lavish decor with ornate beds, ceiling fans and period furniture. Little amenities such as the his and her robes create a romantic touch. Breakfasts with kona coffee, juices, fresh fruits and baked goods are served. The inn's common rooms offer unique touches such as a nickelodeon and antique Victrola. The Manoa Valley is a perfect location to enjoy Hawaii and is only blocks away from the University of Hawaii.
Historic Interest: The Honolulu Art Academy, founded by an early missionary, features a unique architectural mix of Polynesian design and missionary style. The Iolani Place was built by King David Kalakaua and was the home of Hawaiian royalty until the demise of the monarchy in 1893.
Innkeeper(s): Theresa Wery. $99-190. MC, VISA, TC. TAC10. 8 rooms, 3 with PB, 1 suite & 1 cottage. Breakfast included in rates. Types of meals: Cont. Beds: KQD. TV, phone, ceiling fan & daily maid service in room. Fax, copier, billiard room, Port wine on coffee table in living room & upstairs sitting room & iron on premises. Weddings & small meetings hosted.
Museums & art museums nearby.
Publicity: *Travel Age, Travel Holiday, Travel & Leisure and LA Style.*

"A wonderful place!! Stepping back to a time of luxury!"

Idaho

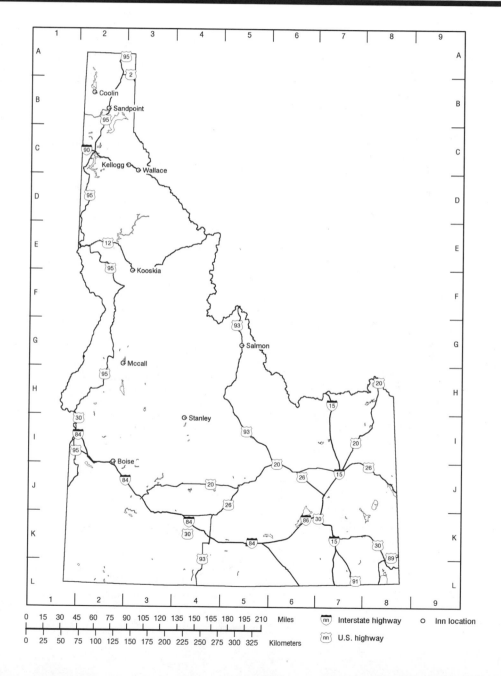

0   15 30 45 60 75 90 105 120 135 150 165 180 195 210   Miles

0   25 50 75 100 125 150 175 200 225 250 275 300 325   Kilometers

(nn) Interstate highway   ○ Inn location

(nn) U.S. highway

Boise

I2

Idaho Heritage Inn

109 W Idaho St
Boise, ID 83702-6122
(208)342-8066 Fax:(208)343-2325
Web: www.idheritageinn.com

Circa 1904. This Colonial Revival home, set back on a tree-lined street near downtown, was once the home of Senator Frank Church and is in the National Register. Because of its location in the historic Warm Springs district, geothermal water

is used for heating and bathing. Period furnishings and wall coverings are found throughout. Bicycles are available for enjoying the nearby greenbelt, which winds along the Boise River.

Innkeeper(s): Phyllis Lupher. $65-105. MC, VISA, AX, DS, PC, TC. TAC10. 6 rooms with PB, 3 suites and 1 cottage. Breakfast included in rates. Types of meals: Gourmet bkfst and early coffee/tea. Beds: Q. TV and phone in room. Air conditioning. VCR, fax and bicycles on premises. Small meetings and seminars hosted. Antiquing, fishing, golf, parks, shopping, downhill skiing, cross-country skiing, sporting events, tennis and water sports nearby.

Publicity: *Idaho Statesman, Denver Post, San Antonio Sun and NY Times.*

"Thanks so much for the hospitality and warmth."

J.J. Shaw House B&B

1411 W Franklin St
Boise, ID 83702
(208)344-8899 (877)344-8899 Fax:(208)344-6677
E-mail: jjshaw@earthlink.net

Circa 1907. J.J. Shaw House, a graciously restored Queen Anne Victorian, was named for its builder, a lumber baron and one of the founding fathers of Boise. Tastefully decorated rooms include antiques and special touches, such as the trail of ivy that adorns the ceiling of Shaw's Retreat. Gertrude's Chamber includes a four-poster bed and a rose-colored, antique clawfoot tub encircled by a curtain of lace. In other rooms, guests might enjoy a jetted tub or a view of the local mountains. Breakfasts with fresh strawberries, stuffed French toast with blueberry syrup and Canadian bacon provide an excellent start to your days in Boise. Hyde Park and the Capitol building are within walking distance. Bogus Basin Ski Resort is just 16 miles from the home.

Historic Interest: Built in 1907 by Lumber Baron John James Shaw, a Boise founding father.

Innkeeper(s): Junia Stephens. $79-109. MC, VISA, AX, DS, PC, TC. 5 rooms with PB, 1 suite and 1 conference room. Breakfast and snacks/refreshments included in rates. Types of meals: Gourmet bkfst. Beds: KQT. Phone, ceiling fan and jetted tub in room. Air conditioning. Fax and library on premises. Weddings, small meetings, family reunions and seminars hosted. Antiquing, art galleries, bicycling, canoeing/kayaking, fishing, golf, hiking, horseback riding, live theater, museums, parks, shopping, downhill skiing, cross-country skiing, sporting events, tennis, water sports and wineries nearby.

Publicity: *Idaho Statesman, Touched by an Angel, Idaho Statesman News and Channel 7 "Eye on Idaho."*

Coeur d' Alene

C2

Gregory's McFarland House

601 E Foster Ave
Coeur d'Alene, ID 83814
(208)667-1232 (800)335-1232

Circa 1905. This yellow and white three-story historic home, shaded by tall trees, offers a wraparound porch with swaying swing, a deck and summerhouse, overlooking green lawns and gardens. English chintz, Oriental rugs and antiques are found

throughout. A three-course gourmet breakfast is offered in the glass conservatory, next to the scenic deck. The inn has a resident minister and professional photographer, so it is popular for weddings and for

renewing marriage vows. Water skiing, fishing, bird watching, skiing and digging for garnets are favorite activities. Coeur d'Alene Lake, within walking distance, is considered one of the most beautiful lakes in the world. Spokane is 30 minutes away and the international airport 45 minutes.

Innkeeper(s): Winifred, Carol & Stephen Gregory. $90-175. MC, VISA, DS, PC, TC. 5 rooms with PB, 4 suites and 1 conference room. Breakfast included in rates. Types of meals: Gourmet bkfst. Beds: KQ. Turndown service, ceiling fan and bath robes in room. Air conditioning. VCR and central air conditioning on premises. Weddings, small meetings, family reunions and seminars hosted. Amusement parks, antiquing, fishing, golf, live theater, parks, shopping, downhill skiing, cross-country skiing, sporting events, tennis and water sports nearby.

Kingston 5 Ranch B&B

PO Box 2229
Coeur d' Alene, ID 83816
(208)682-4862 (800)254-1852 Fax:(208)682-9445
E-mail: info@k5ranch.com
Web: www.k5ranch.com

Circa 1930. With the Coeur d'Alene Mountains as its backdrop, this red roofed farmhouse has been renovated with French door and wraparound decks to make the most of its sweeping mountain views and pastoral setting. Innkeepers Walt and Pat Gentry have graced the guest rooms with lace, down comforters, cozy chairs and romantic touches such as four-poster beds. The suites offer outdoor spas on private decks with mountain views, fireplaces, and baths with whirlpool tubs. The innkeep-

er is a recipient of several national awards for her recipes. Specialties include Kingston Benedict and stuffed French Toast topped with fresh huckleberry sauce along with freshly baked, prize winning lemon huckleberry muffins. Enjoy activities such as touring two historic gold mines, the Kellogg Gondola, boating or dinner cruises on Lake Coeur d'Alene, skiing, hiking, fishing, bird watching and driving excursions where you may encounter elk, deer, eagles and other wildlife. Often guests find the greatest pleasure to be watching the horses grazing in the pasture or volunteering to pick fresh strawberries, raspberries or loganberries to top an evening desert of vanilla ice cream.

Historic Interest: The Historic Cataldo Mansion, the oldest building in Idaho, is just five minutes away. Wallace, a town listed on the historic register, is 20 minutes from the farmhouse.

Innkeeper(s): Walter & Pat Gentry. $125-190. MC, VISA, TC. TAC10. 2 suites, 2 with FP. Breakfast included in rates. Types of meals: Full bkfst and early coffee/tea. Beds: Q. Digital clocks, fireplaces, Jacuzzi tub and central heat in room. Air conditioning. VCR, fax, copier, spa, stables, bicycles and kennel one mile off site on premises. Small meetings hosted. Amusement parks, antiquing, fishing, horseback riding, canoeing, mountain biking, live theater, parks, shopping, downhill skiing, cross-country skiing and water sports nearby.

Publicity: *A Destination Resort.*

The Roosevelt Inn

105 E Wallace Ave
Coeur d' Alene, ID 83814-2947
(208)765-5200 (800)290-3358 Fax:(208)664-4142
E-mail: info@therooseveltinn.com
Web: www.therooseveltinn.com

Circa 1905. This turn-of-the-century, red brick home was named for President Roosevelt and is the oldest schoolhouse in town. Roosevelt translates to Rosefield in Dutch, and the innkeepers have created a rosy theme for the inn. The Bell Tower Suite and the Honeymoon Suite are the favorite room requests, but all rooms offer Victorian antiques and some have lake views. Coeur d' Alene has been recognized by National Geographic Magazine as one of the five most beautiful lakes in the world. The area offers the world's longest floating boardwalk and Tubb's Hill Nature Park. A variety of shops and restaurants are within a five minute stroll from the inn. The natural surroundings offer mountain biking, boating, skiing and hiking.

Innkeeper(s): John & Tina Hough. $80-249. MC, VISA, AX, DS. TAC10. 15 rooms, 12 with PB, 3 with FP, 6 suites and 2 conference rooms. Breakfast and snacks/refreshments included in rates. Types of meals: Gourmet bkfst, veg bkfst, early coffee/tea and afternoon tea. Beds: Q. Cable TV and turn-down service in room. Central air. VCR, fax, copier, spa, sauna, library, rose greeting in room and exercise room on premises. Handicap access. Weddings, small meetings, family reunions and seminars hosted. Amusement parks, antiquing, art galleries, beaches, bicycling, canoeing/kayaking, fishing, golf, hiking, horseback riding, live theater, museums, parks, shopping, downhill skiing, cross-country skiing, sporting events, tennis, water sports and wineries nearby.

Pets allowed: house pets only in two rooms, $25 deposit.

Coolin   B2

Old Northern Inn

PO Box 177, 220 Bayview
Coolin, ID 83821-0177
(208)443-2426 Fax:(208)443-3856

Circa 1890. This historic inn was built to serve guests riding the Great Northern rail line. Today, travelers come to enjoy trout-filled Priest Lake and all its offerings. The inn is located on the lake shore, and guests enjoy use of a small marina and private beach. There is also a volleyball court, but guests are welcome to simply sit and relax on the spacious deck. The natural surroundings are full of wildlife, and it's not unusual to see deer, caribou and even a moose. The hotel itself is a two-story log and shingle structure, quite at home among the tall cedars. The interior is warm and inviting. There is a common area with a stone fireplace and country furnishings, as well as a view of mountains and the lake. Rooms are decorated with turn-of-the-century antiques, and the suites include a small sitting room.

Huckleberry pancakes have been a staple at the inn's breakfast table since the 19th century. In the afternoons, wine, cheese and fruit are served.

$90-140. MC, VISA, PC, TC. TAC10. 6 rooms with PB and 2 suites. Breakfast included in rates. Types of meals: Full bkfst and early coffee/tea. Beds: Q. Fax, copier and swimming on premises. Handicap access. Small meetings and family reunions hosted. Antiquing, fishing, golf, shopping, tennis and water sports nearby.

Publicity: *Seattle Times.*

Kellogg   C2

Mansion on the Hill B&B

105 S Division St, PO Box 456
Kellogg, ID 83837
(208)786-4455 (877)943-4455 Fax:(208)786-0157
E-mail: stay@mansionbnb.com
Web: www.mansionbnb.com

Circa 1944. Classic elegance comes to life at first glance of this Federal home and cottages. Country French decor accents each spacious, bright room, creating an atmosphere of home away from home. Experience ultimate privacy in either of the two cottages on the outskirts of the main house, or enjoy the comfort of a suite in the Mansion. Celebrate each morning with fresh fruit and juice, quiche, herbed potatoes, muffins, scones, coffee and tea. Only one hour away from Spokane, Wash., this B&B is found in historic Silver Valley. Numerous outdoor activities include the Hiawatha Trail and gondola rides on Silver Mountain for summer concerts and skiing.

Historic Interest: The Cataldo Mission (12 miles), Wallace historic mining town (10 miles), Lookout Mountain (25 miles).

Innkeeper(s): Dana Musick & Giovanni Pizzato. $115-150. MC, VISA, AX, DS, PC, TC. 4 rooms, 2 suites and 2 cottages. Breakfast, afternoon tea and snacks/refreshments included in rates. Types of meals: Gourmet bkfst, veg bkfst and early coffee/tea. AP. Beds: KQT. Central air. Small meetings and seminars hosted. Italian, French and Spanish spoken. Amusement parks, antiquing, bicycling, canoeing/kayaking, fishing, golf, hiking, live theater, museums, parks, shopping, downhill skiing, cross-country skiing and water sports nearby.

Kooskia   E3

Three Rivers Resort

Hwy 12 in Lowell, Idaho
Kooskia, ID 83539-9500
(208)926-4430 Fax:(208)926-7526

Circa 1927. Once a meeting ground for the Nez Perce Indians, the campground and rustic hand-hewn log cabins overlook the Lochsa river. Each of the 15 cabins is decorated in western antiques and feature ceiling fans and outdoor barbeques. Old #1 Log Cabin, a former ranger's cabin, offers a Jacuzzi, VCR, full breakfast and champagne. Set on 200 wooded acres, Three Rivers Resort boasts a heated swimming pool, three Jacuzzis, a gift shop and small grocery store. There is an on-site restaurant, and Lochsa Louie's Bar serves cocktails every night. Whitewater rafting, fish and game licenses are available.

Innkeeper(s): Mike & Marie Smith. $77. MC, VISA, AX, DC, CB, DS, PC, TC. TAC15. 1 rooms. Types of meals: Full bkfst. Beds: Q. VCR in room. Fax, copier, spa and stables on premises. Weddings, small meetings and family reunions hosted. Spanish/Chinese spoken. Antiquing, fishing, raft trips and water sports nearby.

Pets Allowed.

Publicity: *Grizzly Bear, Wolf Recovery Wilderness Specials and Lewis & Clark (Ken Burns).*

McCall G2

Northwest Passage

201 Rio Vista, PO Box 4208
McCall, ID 83638-8208
(208)634-5349 (800)597-6658 Fax:(208)634-4977
E-mail: nwpass@ctcweb.net

Circa 1938. This mountain country inn rests on five acres and offers six guest rooms, two of them suites. Guests enjoy the inn's two sitting rooms, fireplace and full breakfasts. The inn is

furnished in country decor and provides easy access to a myriad of recreational opportunities found in the area. Payette Lake is just a short distance from the inn, and the Brundage Mountain Ski Area and Ponderosa State Park are nearby.

Historic Interest: Inn built in 1938 to house the cast of the movie "Northwest Passage".

Innkeeper(s): Steve & Barbara Schott. $70-100. MC, VISA, AX. 6 rooms with PB, 1 with FP, 2 suites and 1 conference room. Breakfast included in rates. Types of meals: Full bkfst. VCR, fax, television and horse corrals on premises. Weddings, small meetings, family reunions and seminars hosted. Antiquing, fishing, live theater, shopping, downhill skiing and cross-country skiing nearby.

Salmon G5

Greyhouse Inn B&B

1115 Hwy 93 South
Salmon, ID 83467
(208)756-3968 (800)348-8097
E-mail: osgoodd@salmoninternet.com
Web: www.greyhouseinn.com

Circa 1894. The scenery at Greyhouse is nothing short of wondrous. In the winter, when mountains are capped in white and the evergreens are shrouded in snow, this Victorian appears as a safe haven from the chilly weather. In the summer, the rocky peaks are a contrast to the whimsical house, which looks like something out of an Old West town. The historic home is known around town as the old maternity hospital, but there is nothing medicinal about it now. The rooms are Victorian in style with antique furnishings. The parlor features deep red walls and floral overstuffed sofas and a dressmaker's model garbed in a brown Victorian gown. Outdoor

enthusiasts will find no shortage of activities, from facing the rapids in nearby Salmon River to fishing to horseback riding. The town of Salmon is just 12 miles away.

Innkeeper(s): David & Sharon Osgood. $60-90. MC, VISA, AX, DS, PC, TC. TAC10. 7 rooms, 5 with PB, 1 cottage and 2 cabins. Breakfast included in rates. Types of meals: Full bkfst, country bkfst, veg bkfst, picnic lunch and dinner. Beds: KQDT. Ceiling fan and VCR in room. Bicycles, library and carriage house and two log cabin rooms on premises. Weddings, small meetings and family reunions hosted. Antiquing, bicycling, canoeing/kayaking, fishing, golf, hiking, horseback riding, float trips, hot springs, mountain biking, live theater, museums, parks, shopping, downhill skiing and cross-country skiing nearby.

Pets allowed: Kept in crate or tied outside.

"To come around the corner and find the Greyhouse, as we did, restores my faith! Such a miracle. We had a magical evening here, and we plan to return to stay for a few days. Thanks so much for your kindness and hospitality. We love Idaho!"

Sandpoint B2

The Coit House B&B

502 N Fourth Avenue
Sandpoint, ID 83864-1513
(208)265-4035 (866)265-COIT Fax:(208)265-5558

Circa 1907. Period, Victorian furnishings, polished wood floors, fine woodwork and a wraparound porch are some of the charming elements at this bed & breakfast. There are four guest rooms, each decorated with unique antiques. Two rooms include clawfoot tubs. Breakfast features a changing menu: Homemade breads, French toast, and savory quiches are among the possibilities.

The inn is located near the Schweitzer Mountain Resort, walking distance to downtown Sandpoint and is less than 50 miles from Coeur d'Alene.

Innkeeper(s): Tod & Karin Wehse. $70-100. MC, VISA, PC, TC. 4 rooms with PB and 1 suite. Breakfast included in rates. Types of meals: Full bkfst and early coffee/tea. Beds: Q. Cable TV, phone and suite with kitchen in room. Air conditioning. Fax on premises. Weddings and family reunions hosted. Amusement parks, antiquing, art galleries, beaches, bicycling, canoeing/kayaking, fishing, golf, hiking, horseback riding, parks, shopping, downhill skiing, cross-country skiing, tennis, water sports and wineries nearby.

"The antiques are exquisite, your home is beautiful, we look forward to our next visit."

Stanley I4

Idaho Rocky Mountain Ranch

HC 64 Box 9934
Stanley, ID 83278-9602
(208)774-3544 Fax:(208)774-3477
E-mail: idrocky@ruralnetwork.net
Web: www.idahorocky.com

Circa 1930. This thousand-acre ranch is situated at the 6,600-foot level in the Sawtooth Valley. The lodge dining room and spacious front porch overlook the Salmon River, which runs through the property, and beyond to the spectacular ragged ridges of the Sawtooth Mountains. Near the edge of the river, the inn has a swimming pool completely fed by a natural

hot springs. Charming accommodations in lodgepole pine cabins feature handmade log, hickory and cane furniture and fieldstone fireplaces. The lodge is listed in the National Register of Historic Places.

Historic Interest: Ghost towns of Vienna, Boulder, Bonanza and Custer (within 50 miles), Stanley Historical Museum (10 miles), Yankee Fork Dredge/Museum (30 miles), Sun Valley Ski Museum (50 miles).

Innkeeper(s): Bill Leavell & Sandra Beckwith. $152-255. MC, VISA, PC, TC.

21 rooms with PB, 17 with FP and 9 cottages. Breakfast and dinner included in rates. Types of meals: Full bkfst and picnic lunch. MAP. Beds: QT. Fax, copier, swimming, stables, bicycles, library, fishing pond and hiking trails on premises. Spanish spoken. Bicycling, fishing, hiking, horseback riding, whitewater rafting, rock climbing, parks and water sports nearby.

Publicity: *Washington Post, National Geographic Traveler, Sunset, New York Times. and CNN.*

"We had such a great time! The kids loved it! Can't you adopt us so we can stay longer?."

Wallace   C3

The Beale House

107 Cedar St
Wallace, ID 83873-2115
(208)752-7151 (888)752-7151

Circa 1904. This attractive, three-story Colonial Revival home is listed in the National Register, as is the town of Wallace. Original parquet wood floor, antiques and memorabilia combine to lend an authentic aura of the past. Each of the five guest rooms offers a unique feature, such as a fireplace, balcony

or wall of windows. The innkeepers are well versed in their home's history, and guests are welcome to look over a photographic record of the house and its former owners. A backyard hot tub provides views of the mountains and creek, while the large front porch invites slowing down with its swing and rocking chairs. Guests can enjoy birdwatching on the property. Recreational activities abound in the vicinity, famous for its silver mines. There are also museums nearby.

Historic Interest: Town of Wallace, Cataldo Mission, Route of the Hiawatha biking trail.

Innkeeper(s): Jim & Linda See. $105-175. PC, TC. TAC10. 5 rooms, 1 with FP and 1 suite. Breakfast included in rates. Types of meals: Full bkfst. Beds: QDT. Turndown service in room. VCR, spa and library on premises. Weddings hosted. Antiquing, bicycling, fishing, golf, hiking, bird watching, live theater, museums, parks, shopping, downhill skiing, cross-country skiing and water sports nearby.

Publicity: *Shoshone News Press, Spokesman Review, Silver Valley Voice, Off the Beaten Path/ Guide to Unique Places, Northern Rockies:Best Places Guide to the Outdoors and Americas Most Charming Towns and Villages.*

Illinois

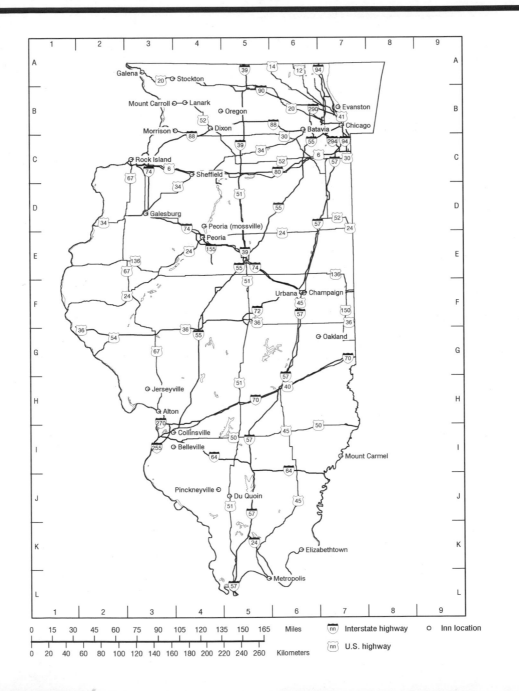

	Miles
0 15 30 45 60 75 90 105 120 135 150 165	Miles
0 20 40 60 80 100 120 140 160 180 200 220 240 260	Kilometers

Interstate highway   ○ Inn location

U.S. highway

Alton H3

Beall Mansion, An Elegant B&B

407 East 12th St
Alton, IL 62002-7230
(618)474-9100 (866)843-2325 Fax:(618)474-9090
E-mail: bepampered@beallmansion.com
Web: www.beallmansion.com

Circa 1903. An eclectic blend of Neoclassic, Georgian and Greek Revival styles, this mansion was designed by renown architect, Lucas Pfeiffenberger. The original woodwork, eleven-and-a-half-foot ceilings, leaded-glass windows, pocket doors and crystal chandeliers reflect and embrace a luxury befitting that era. The ambiance is further enhanced by imported bronze and marble statuary, handwoven Oriental and Persian rugs and Chinese artwork. Choose an exquisite guest bedroom, distinct in size and decor, complete with private bath that includes a whirlpool for two or clawfoot tub, imported marble floor and chandelier.

Innkeeper(s): Jim & Sandy Belote. $90-189. MC, VISA, AX, DS, PC, TC. TAC10. 5 rooms with PB, 2 with FP, 1 suite and 2 conference rooms. Types of meals: Gourmet bkfst, veg bkfst, cont plus, cont, early coffee/tea and room service. AP, EP. Beds: KD. Cable TV, phone, turndown service, ceiling fan, fireplace, whirlpool, iron and ironing board, homemade lavender bath salts and radiator heat in room. Central air. Fax, copier, veranda, hammock, badminton, horseshoes and croquet on premises. Weddings, small meetings, family reunions and seminars hosted. Amusement parks, antiquing, art galleries, bicycling, canoeing/kayaking, fishing, golf, hiking, horseback riding, live theater, museums, parks, shopping, sporting events, tennis, water sports and wineries nearby.

Batavia B6

Villa Batavia

1430 S Batavia Ave
Batavia, IL 60510-3003
(630)406-8182

Circa 1844. This historic home is a mix of Greek Revival and Italianate styles. The manor is set on seven acres, which include a meadow, a Christmas tree farm and a quaint path that winds its way down to the Fox River. There are two guest rooms and a three-room suite at this intimate bed & breakfast, each decorated in Victorian style. The Caroline Room includes an impressive four-poster bed with a lace canopy. Gourmet breakfasts are served on a table set with china and sterling silver. The home is close to a variety of outdoor activities, as well as antique shops and riverboat casinos.

Innkeeper(s): Dick Palmer & Fran Steiner. $90-150. MC, VISA, DS, PC. 3 rooms with PB, 2 with FP and 1 suite. Breakfast included in rates. Types of meals: Gourmet bkfst and early coffee/tea. Beds: Q. Cable TV and phone in room. Air conditioning. Weddings, small meetings, family reunions and seminars hosted. Limited French and German spoken. Amusement parks, antiquing, fishing, golf, Cougars baseball, parks, shopping, cross-country skiing, sporting events and tennis nearby.

Publicity: *Chicago Tribune and Midwest Living.*

Belleville I3

Swans Court B&B

421 Court St
Belleville, IL 62220-1201
(618)233-0779 (800)840-1058 Fax:(618)277-3150
E-mail: mdixon@isbe.accessus.net

Circa 1883. This home, designated by the Department of the Interior as a certified historic structure, was once home to David Baer, known as the "mule king of the world." Baer sold more than 10,000 mules each year to British troops in World War I and to American troops in World War II. The home is furnished almost entirely in antiques. Innkeeper Monty Dixon searched high and low to fill her B&B with authentic pieces, creating a nostalgic ambiance.  The library offers a selection of books, games and puzzles for guests to enjoy. The home is located in a historic neighborhood, within walking distance to shops and restaurants. Belleville is convenient to St. Louis, and there are casinos, historic sites, a racetrack and a state park nearby.

Innkeeper(s): Ms. Monty Dixon. $65-90. MC, VISA, AX, DS, PC, TC. TAC10. 4 rooms, 2 with PB, 2 with FP. Breakfast and snacks/refreshments included in rates. Types of meals: Full bkfst. Beds: QD. Phone, ceiling fan and folding tables upon request in room. Air conditioning. VCR and library on premises. Handicap access. Weddings, small meetings, family reunions and seminars hosted. Spanish spoken. Antiquing, golf, live theater, shopping, sporting events and tennis nearby.

Publicity: *St. Louis Magazine.*

"We feel like we have made a new friend. We appreciated all of the nice little touches, such as the fresh flowers."

Victory Inn

712 S Jackson St
Belleville, IL 62220-2672
(618)277-1538 (888)277-8586 Fax:(618)277-1576
E-mail: jo@victoryinn.com
Web: www.victoryinn.com

Circa 1877. Carefully chosen period reproductions and decor create the Victorian ambiance at Victory Inn, a historic home just minutes from downtown Belleville. Two rooms share a bath, but can be combined as a suite. Two rooms include a Jacuzzi tub.  Breakfasts include several different types of homemade breads and fresh fruit. Belleville offers shops, restaurants and two historic house museums. St. Louis is a short drive away.

Innkeeper(s): Jo & Tom Brannon. $60-115. MC, VISA, AX, PC, TC. TAC10. 2 rooms with PB and 1 suite. Breakfast included in rates. Types of meals: Cont plus and early coffee/tea. Beds: Q. Phone, turndown service and two whirlpool's in room. Air conditioning. VCR and fax on premises. Antiquing, fishing, golf, live theater, parks, shopping and sporting events nearby.

Publicity: *St. Louis Magazine, Metro East Gazette and Show Me St. Louis.*

Champaign F6

Golds B&B

2065 County Road 525 E
Champaign, IL 61822-9521
(217)586-4345
E-mail: reg@prairienet.org

Circa 1874. Visitors to the University of Illinois area may enjoy a restful experience at this inn, west of town in a peaceful farmhouse setting. Antique country furniture collected by the innkeepers over the past 25 years is showcased in the inn and is beautifully offset by early American stenciling on its walls. Seasonal items from the garden are sometimes used as breakfast fare.

Innkeeper(s): Rita & Bob Gold. $45-50. PC, TC. TAC10. 3 rooms, 1 with PB. Breakfast included in rates. Types of meals: Cont plus and early coffee/tea. Beds: QT. Air conditioning. VCR on premises. Antiquing, fishing, live theater, parks and shopping nearby.

Chicago B7

Windy City B&B Inn

607 W Deming Pl
Chicago, IL 60614
(773)248-7091 (877)897-7091 Fax:(773)529-4183
E-mail: stay@chicago-inn.com
Web: www.chicago-inn.com

Circa 1886. Built as a Victorian mansion, it is now an eclectic urban inn proudly reflecting its namesake city. Chicago memorabilia and art are featured in the decor. The guest bedrooms and coach house apartments continue the regional theme, each named after a well-known local author. Relish the luxury of whirlpool tubs, fireplaces, and plush robes. The common rooms offer wonderful places to relax, read, or play the piano. Enjoy refreshments in the colorful courtyard garden with ivy-covered brick walls.

Innkeeper(s): Mary & Andy Shaw. $115-325. MC, VISA, AX, DC, CB, DS, PC, TC. TAC10. 7 rooms, 4 with PB, 3 with FP, 3 suites and 1 conference room. Breakfast and snacks/refreshments included in rates. Types of meals: Cont plus and early coffee/tea. Beds: KQ. Cable TV, phone, ceiling fan, VCR and fireplace in room. Central air. Fax, copier, spa and library on premises. Weddings, small meetings, family reunions and seminars hosted. Spanish spoken. Antiquing, art galleries, beaches, bicycling, fishing, golf, hiking, live theater, museums, parks, shopping and sporting events nearby.

Publicity: *Time Magazine.*

Wooded Isle Suites

5750 S Stony Island Ave
Chicago, IL 60637-2049
(773)288-6305 (800)290-6844 Fax:(773)288-8972
E-mail: reserve@woodedisle.com
Web: www.woodedisle.com

Circa 1914. Although neither bed & breakfast nor country inn, this collection of two- and three-room apartment suites serves as a convenient, relaxing alternative to hotel travel. The suites are located in Chicago's Hyde Park area and are convenient to the many museums, shops, restaurants and attractions in the downtown area and Lake Michigan. The early 20th-century complex originally served as housing for employees of the Illinois Central Railroad Hospital. Each suite includes a long list of practical amenities, such as a kitchen stocked with pots, pans, dishes, coffee makers, coffee, tea bags and more. The decor is a pleasant, contemporary style.

Innkeeper(s): Charlie Havens & Sara Pitcher. $135-189. MC, VISA, AX, DS, PC. TAC10. 13 suites. Beds: Q. Cable TV, phone, ceiling fan, microwave, stove and answering machine in room. Air conditioning. Laundry facility on premises. Fishing, museums, antique bookstores, live theater, parks, sporting events and water sports nearby.

"We have all had very positive experiences at Wooded Isle. Everyone has been pleasant and tuned in to our joy."

Collinsville I3

Maggie's B&B

2102 N Keebler Ave
Collinsville, IL 62234-4713
(618)344-8283
E-mail: maggies-b-n-b@charter-il.com

Circa 1900. A rustic two-acre wooded area surrounds this friendly Victorian inn, once a boarding house. Rooms with 14-foot ceilings are furnished with exquisite antiques and art objects collected on worldwide travels. Downtown St. Louis, the Gateway Arch  and the Mississippi riverfront are just 10 minutes away.

Historic Interest: Cahokia Indian Mounds (3 miles), Gateway Arch (15 miles).

Innkeeper(s): Maggie Leyda. $45-100. PC, TC. 5 rooms, 3 with PB, 2 with FP and 1 conference room. Breakfast included in rates. Types of meals: Full bkfst and early coffee/tea. Beds: QDT. Cable TV, turndown service, ceiling fan and VCR in room. Air conditioning. Spa and library on premises. Handicap access. Weddings, small meetings and family reunions hosted. Amusement parks, antiquing, fishing, live theater, parks, shopping and sporting events nearby.

Publicity: *USA Today, Cooking Light, Collinsville Herald Journal, Innsider, Belleville News, Democrat, Saint Louis Homes & Gardens, Edwardsville Intelligences and St. Louis Business Journal.*

"We enjoyed a delightful stay. You've thought of everything. What fun!"

Dixon B4

Crawford House Inn

204 E Third St
Dixon, IL 61021
(815)288-3351
E-mail: crwfordinn@cin.net

Circa 1869. In 1869, Joseph Crawford, who counted Abraham Lincoln among his friends, built the Italianate Victorian style house that now bears his name. His descendants maintained the family home until the 1950s when it was converted into a nursing facility and then lawyer offices. Enjoying life today as a B&B, Crawford House offers its guests a glimpse into small-town America. Three guest rooms have either king- or queen-size feather beds; bathrooms are shared. Breakfasts are served in the dining room and are presented with white linens, china and stemware. Gourmet breakfasts include juice, coffee, an egg entree, fresh baked goods and seasonal fruits. Dixon has just been named "Petunia Capital of the United States," and its  streets are lined with colorful beds of the blooms all summer long. At the center of five state parks, the area is popular for cycling. Scenic country roads and paths offer opportunities for walking and horseback riding, as well. Visits can be made to the Ronald Reagan boyhood home, the John Deere Historical Site or local antique stores. Rock River is two blocks away for boating, fishing and canoeing, and across the street is the historical courthouse square where summertime concerts are popular in the evenings. Cross-country skiing and snowmobiling are available during the winter months.

Historic Interest: Ronald Reagan boyhood home, War Memorial Arch.
Innkeeper(s): Lyn Miliano. $65-85. MC, VISA, DS, PC, TC. TAC5. 3 rooms, 1 with FP. Breakfast included in rates. Types of meals: Gourmet bkfst. Beds: KQ. Cable TV, ceiling fan and VCR in room. Air conditioning. Library on premises. Small meetings hosted. Antiquing, bicycling, canoeing/kayaking, fishing, golf, hiking, horseback riding, live theater, museums, parks, shopping, tennis and water sports nearby.

Du Quoin   J5

Francie's Inn On-Line

104 S Line St
Du Quoin, IL 62832-2344
(618)542-6686 (877)877-2657
E-mail: cathy@franciesinnonline.com
Web: www.franciesinnonline.com

Circa 1908. This solid three-story home on three acres served as an orphanage for 39 years. The inside is decorated with a Victorian flair, and the rooms feature extravagant touches such as puffy comforters, as well as writing desks and lounge chairs. The Ciara room has a brass and iron bed, while the Desiree room boasts a view of the front and side grounds. The Van Arsdale Suite has a four-poster bed, antique wardrobe and claw-foot tub, and a first-floor room, The Willow, offers a king bed and sofa sleeper. Breakfasts are served on the balcony, back deck or in the Tea Room, which seats 30 and is an ideal location for a wedding reception or business function. There's a wide veranda that stretches across the front and rear of the inn. Southern Illinois University and Shawnee National Forest is nearby.
Innkeeper(s): Cathy & Benny Trowbridge. $60-85. MC, VISA, AX, DS, PC. 6 rooms with PB. Types of meals: Full bkfst. Beds: KQT. TV and phone in room. Shopping nearby.

Elizabethtown   K6

River Rose Inn B&B

1 Main St PO Box 78
Elizabethtown, IL 62931-0078
(618)287-8811 Fax:(208)330-8715
E-mail: riverose@shawneelink.com

Circa 1914. Large, shade trees veil the front of this Greek Gothic home, nestled along the banks of the Ohio River. From the grand front entrance, guests look out to polished woodwork and a staircase leading to shelves of books. Rooms are cheerful and nostalgic, decorated with antiques. Each guest room offers something special. One has a four-poster bed, another offers a fireplace. The Scarlet Room has its own balcony and whirlpool tub, and the Rose Room has a private patio with a swing. The Magnolia Cottage is ideal for honeymooners and includes a whirlpool tub for two, fireplace and a deck that overlooks the river. Breakfasts are served in the dining room where guests can enjoy the water views.

Innkeeper(s): Don & Elisabeth Phillips. $68-99. MC, VISA, PC, TC. 5 rooms with PB, 2 with FP and 1 cottage. Breakfast included in rates. Types of meals: Gourmet bkfst and early coffee/tea. Beds: QT. Cable TV, ceiling fan, VCR and Three whirlpool tubs in room. Air conditioning. Fax, copier, spa, swimming and library on premises. French and German spoken. Amusement parks, antiquing, fishing, golf, hiking, biking, parks, shopping and water sports nearby.
Publicity: *Chicago Tribune and Midwest Living.*

Evanston   B7

The Homestead

1625 Hinman Ave
Evanston, IL 60201-6021
(847)475-3300 Fax:(847)570-8100
E-mail: office@thehomestead.net
Web: www.thehomestead.net

Circa 1927. This hotel, the only lodging in Evanston's Lakeshore Historic District, was built by a local architect. The Colonial structure is very much unchanged from its beginnings in the 1920s. Several rooms offer views of Lake Michigan, which is just two blocks away. Northwestern University also is just a two-block walk from the hotel. The inn harbors the nationally renowned restaurant, Trio, acclaimed for its contemporary cuisine.

Innkeeper(s): David Reynolds. $120-140. MC, VISA, AX, DC, DS, PC, TC. 35 rooms, 15 suites and 1 conference room. Breakfast included in rates. Types of meals: Cont and gourmet dinner. Beds: QDT. Cable TV in room. Air conditioning. Fax, copier and library on premises. Small meetings and seminars hosted. Live theater, parks, sporting events, tennis and water sports nearby.

Margarita European Inn

1566 Oak Ave
Evanston, IL 60201-4298
(847)869-2273 Fax:(847)869-2353

Circa 1927. This stately inn, once the proper home to young area working women, has a proud tradition in the city's history. The Georgian architecture is complemented by an impressive interior, featuring arched French doors, vintage period molding and a large parlor with floor-to-ceiling windows. Near the lakefront and Northwestern University, it also boasts, a library, large-screen TV room and VaPenisero, a restaurant serving regional Italian specialties. Guests often enjoy renting a bike and exploring the area's many attractions, including 24 nearby art galleries.
Innkeeper(s): Barbara & Tim Gorham. $75-145. MC, VISA, AX, DC, TC. 41 rooms, 21 with PB and 1 conference room. Breakfast included in rates. Types of meals: Cont and early coffee/tea. Beds: KQDT. Phone and ceiling fan in room. Air conditioning. Weddings, small meetings, family reunions and seminars hosted. Antiquing, live theater, shopping and sporting events nearby.

Galena   A3

Captain Harris Guest House & Honeymoon Cottage

713 S Bench St
Galena, IL 61036-2501
(815)777-4713 (800)996-4799 Fax:(815)777-4723
E-mail: inquiry@captainharris.com
Web: www.captainharris.com

Circa 1836. One of the area's oldest homes, it was built in the vernacular style and has retained its historical character. Leaded-glass windows made and installed by Frank Lloyd

Wright's partner enhances the appeal. Original artwork graces the walls, residing with elegant furnishings of antiques, family heirlooms and historic artifacts. A large suite with fireplace boasts a two-person whirlpool, private entrance and front porch. Guest bedrooms with hardwood floors and Oriental rugs are well decorated with wallpaper, tapestry bedding, Battenburg lace and window treatments. A secluded honeymoon cottage offers VCR, fridge, coffeemaker and front porch. Enjoy a hearty homemade breakfast prepared daily.

Historic Interest: Grants Home, Washburne House.

Innkeeper(s): Judy Dixon/Ed Schmit. $80-190. MC, VISA, DS. 5 rooms, 3 with PB, 1 suite and 1 cottage. Breakfast and afternoon tea included in rates. Types of meals: Gourmet bkfst and early coffee/tea. Beds: Q. Cable TV, ceiling fan, some with fireplace, refrigerator, coffee maker, hot tub and VCR in room. Central air. Library on premises. Greek and Danish spoken. Antiquing, art galleries, bicycling, fishing, golf, hiking, horseback riding, live theater, museums, parks, shopping, downhill skiing, cross-country skiing and wineries nearby.

Farmers' Guest House

334 Spring St
Galena, IL 61036-2128
(815)777-3456 Fax:(815)777-3514
E-mail: farmersgh@galenalink.net
Web: www.farmersguesthouse.com

Circa 1867. This two-story brick Italianate building was built as a bakery and served as a store and hotel, as well. Rows of arched, multi-paned windows add charm to the exterior. The rooms are decorated with antiques, lace curtains and floral wallpapers. The accommodations include seven rooms with queen-size beds, one room with a double bed, and two, two-room king Master Suites. There's a bar, featured in the movie "Field of Dreams." A hot tub is offered in the backyard. The inn also has a cabin in the woods available for rent.

Innkeeper(s): Kathie, Jess Farlow. $99-165. MC, VISA, AX, DS, PC. 10 rooms with PB. Breakfast included in rates. Types of meals: Cont plus. Beds: KQD. Cable TV in room. Air conditioning. Fax, hot tub and evening wine and cheese hour on premises. Small meetings, family reunions and seminars hosted. Antiquing, golf, horseback riding, hot air ballooning, live theater, parks, shopping, downhill skiing and cross-country skiing nearby.

Publicity: *Better Homes & Gardens, Country Discoveries and Field of Dreams.*

"Neat old place, fantastic breakfasts."

Park Avenue Guest House

208 Park Ave
Galena, IL 61036-2306
(815)777-1075
E-mail: parkave@galenalink.com

Circa 1893. A short walk from Grant Park sits this attractive Queen Anne Victorian with turret and wraparound porch. Gardens and a gazebo add to this peaceful neighborhood charm, as does the original woodwork throughout. The Helen Room features a gas fireplace, TV, tub and shower, while Miriam Room's brass bed highlights a cheerful floral decor and a fireplace. The Anna Suite also has a fireplace and boasts a comfortable sitting room in the inn's turret area and the Lucille Room is tastefully furnished in mauve, gray and white tones. The Inn has a permant display of

165 house Dickens Village. The holiday decorations, including twelve Christmas trees, are not to be missed.

Innkeeper(s): Sharon Fallbacher. $95-135. MC, VISA, DS, PC, TC. 4 rooms with PB, 3 with FP and 1 suite. Snacks/refreshments included in rates. Types of meals: Full bkfst and early coffee/tea. Beds: QT. Cable TV and ceiling fan in room. Air conditioning. VCR on premises. Weddings, small meetings and family reunions hosted. Antiquing, fishing, casino, riverboat, live theater, shopping, downhill skiing and cross-country skiing nearby.

Publicity: *Gail Greco Romance of Country Inns, Daily Herald, Country Inns, Chicago Tribune, Better Homes & Gardens and Gourmet.*

Galesburg   D3

Seacord House

624 N Cherry St
Galesburg, IL 61401-2731
(309)342-4107
E-mail: paarentj@galesburg.net

Circa 1891. A former county sheriff and businessman built this Eastlake-style Victorian, which is located in the town's historic district. The home was named for its builder, Wilkens Seacord, a prominent local man whose family is mentioned in Carl Sandburg's autobiography. In keeping with the house's

historical prominence, the innkeepers have tried to maintain its turn-of-the-century charm. Victorian wallpapers, lacy curtains and a collection of family antiques grace the guest rooms and living areas. The bedrooms, however, feature the modern amenity of waterbeds. For those celebrating romantic occasions, the innkeepers provide heart-shaped muffins along with regular morning fare.

Historic Interest: Built in 1894, house has natural woodwork on first floor and working pocket doors.

Innkeeper(s): Gwen and Lyle. $50. MC, VISA, DS. 3 rooms. Breakfast included in rates. Types of meals: Cont plus. Fax on premises.

Jerseyville   H3

The Homeridge B&B

1470 N State St
Jerseyville, IL 62052-1127
(618)498-3442
E-mail: innkeeper@homeridge.com

Circa 1867. This red brick Italianate Victorian features ornate white trim, a stately front veranda and a cupola where guests often take in views of sunsets and the surrounding 18 acres. The home was constructed by Cornelius Fisher, just after the Civil War. In 1891, it was purchased by Senator Theodore Chapman and remained in his family until the 1960s. The innkeepers have filled the 14-room

manor with traditional and Victorian furnishings, enhancing the high ceilings and ornate woodwork typical of the era. Guests are invited to take a relaxing dip in the inn's swimming pool or relax with a refreshment on the veranda.

Innkeeper(s): Sue & Howard Landon. $95. MC, VISA, AX, PC, TC. 4 rooms with PB. Breakfast included in rates. Types of meals: Full bkfst, early coffee/tea and afternoon tea. Beds: KQDT. Ceiling fan in room. Air conditioning. VCR, fax, copier, swimming, bicycles and library on premises. Weddings, small meetings, family reunions and seminars hosted. Amusement parks, antiquing, fishing, live theater, parks, shopping, cross-country skiing, sporting events and water sports nearby.

Publicity: *Chicago Sun Times, Midwest Living Magazine, Midwest Living Magazine and St. Louis Post Dispatch.*

"A most beautiful, entertaining, snow-filled few days."

Lanark   B4

Standish House

540 W Carroll St
Lanark, IL 61046-1017
(815)493-2307 (800)468-2307
E-mail: standish@zeroinc.net

Circa 1882. Four generations of Standishes are associated with this Queen Anne Victorian house. The current owner is Norman Standish, descendant of Captain Myles Standish. Furnishings include English antiques from the

17th and 18th centuries and canopy beds. The second Saturday of November each year the innkeepers recreate the First Thanksgiving and they sponsor a series of lectures on early American history and Myles Standish for school groups. A full breakfast is served by candlelight in the formal dining room.
Historic Interest: First two Blackhawk Indiana War Battlefields (nearby), historic Galena and lead mines (nearby), restored river boat gambling (near Mississippi River).

Innkeeper(s): Ingrid Standish. $60-70. MC, VISA. 5 rooms, 1 with PB. Breakfast included in rates. Types of meals: Full bkfst. Beds: Q. A living museum of Early American history and the pilgrims on premises. Antiquing, fishing, live theater, downhill skiing, cross-country skiing and water sports nearby.

Publicity: *Northwestern Illinois Dispatch, Country, Midwest Living, Daily Telegraph, Daily Leader and Taste of Homes.*

"Absolutely beautiful! Immaculate, enjoyable, comfortable, very refreshing."

Metropolis   L5

Isle of View B&B

205 Metropolis St
Metropolis, IL 62960-2213
(618)524-5838 (800)566-7491
E-mail: kimoff@hcis.net
Web: www.bbonline.com/il/isleofview

Circa 1889. Metropolis, billed as the "home of Superman," is not a bustling concrete city, but a quaint, country town tucked along the Ohio River. The Isle of View, a stunning Italianate manor, is just a short walk from shops, restaurants and the Players Riverboat Casino. All the guest rooms are appointed in Victorian design with antiques. The Master Suite was originally the home's library and includes a unique coal-burning fireplace, canopy bed and two-person whirlpool tub.
Innkeeper(s): Kim & Gerald Offenburger. $65-125. MC, VISA, AX, DC, CB, DS, TC. 5 rooms with PB.

Breakfast included in rates. Types of meals: Gourmet bkfst and early coffee/tea. Beds: KQD. Cable TV, phone and ceiling fan in room. Air conditioning. Small meetings and family reunions hosted. Antiquing, fishing, riverboat casino, live theater, parks, shopping and water sports nearby.

Pets allowed: please ask.

"You may never want to leave."

Morrison   B4

Hillendale B&B

600 W Lincolnway
Morrison, IL 61270-2058
(815)772-3454 Fax:(815)772-7023
E-mail: hillend@clinton.net
Web: www.hillend.com

Circa 1891. Guests at Hillendale don't simply spend the night in the quaint town of Morrison, Ill., they spend the night in France, Italy, Hawaii or Africa. Each of the guests rooms in this Tudor manor reflects a different theme from around the world. Travelers and innkeepers Barb and Mike Winandy cleverly decorated each of the guest quarters. The Kimarrin room reflects Mayan culture with photographs of antiquities. The Outback, a private cottage, boasts a fireplace and whirlpool spa for two along with Australian decor. The Failte room includes a rococo Victorian antique highback bed, fireplace and Irish-themed decor. And these are just a few of the possibilities. Barb creates wonderful breakfasts full of muffins, breads and special entrees. Stroll the two-acre grounds and you will encounter a three-tier water pond, which sits in front of a teahouse, built by the original owner after a trip to Japan. One of the tiers houses Japanese Koi and another a water garden. The area has riverboat gambling and plenty of outdoor activities.

Innkeeper(s): Barb & Mike Winandy. $65-170. MC, VISA, AX, DS, TC. TAC10. 10 rooms with PB. Breakfast included in rates. Types of meals: Full bkfst. Beds: KQT. Cable TV, phone, ceiling fan, VCR and selected amenities in select rooms only in room. Air conditioning. Fax, copier, pool table and fitness room on premises. Small meetings hosted. Antiquing, fishing, gambling, live theater, parks and cross-country skiing nearby.

Publicity: *New York Times, Sterling Gazette, Whiteside News Sentinel, Midwest Living, Home & Away and Moline Dispatch.*

"We've never been any place else that made us feel so catered to and comfortable. Thank you for allowing us to stay in your beautiful home. We feel very privileged."

Mount Carmel   I7

Living Legacy Homestead

3759 N 900 Blvd
Mount Carmel, IL 62863
(618)298-2476
E-mail: llfarm@wworld.com

Circa 1870. This turn-of-the-century German homestead stands on 10 hilltop acres with a panoramic view of the local area. The eight farm buildings are full of artifacts and equipment that reflect their original functions. These include the shop and garage, smokehouse, scale shed, machine shed, hen house, corncrib and feed house, and of course, the outhouse. The barn hayloft, constructed using wooden pegs, is available for large group functions. The property was bought in 1902 by second-generation German immigrants. Their daughter, innkeeper Edna Schmidt Anderson, was born at the Farmstead and returned home following her parents' deaths. Accommodations include the Heritage Room in the farmhouse, the detached Summer Cottage and some rustic bunk house rooms with tractor themes: Ford, Oliver, John Deere and Case. Guests enjoy a full country breakfast in the 1860 Log Room, a part of the original log cabin, which has exposed interior log walls. Lunch, dinner, picnics, snacks and refreshments are available upon request. Guests may choose to study nature, reflect quietly or go on hikes, picnics and other outdoor activities. An amphitheater made of barn beams offers an exquisite view of the sunset. The inn is located near the Beall Woods State Park and Historic New Harmony, Ind. Guests may tour the grounds by themselves or with a guide.

Innkeeper(s): Edna Schmidt Anderson. $30-70. PC, TC. 4 rooms, 2 with PB, 1 cottage and 1 conference room. Breakfast included in rates. Types of meals: Full bkfst, early coffee/tea, lunch, picnic lunch, snacks/refreshments and dinner. Beds: DT. Ceiling fan in room. Air conditioning. Library, Treasures Gift Shop in attic loft and nature walks on premises. Handicap access. Small meetings, family reunions and seminars hosted. Antiquing, fishing, historic village and parks nearby.

The Poor Farm B&B

11216 N 1550 Blvd
Mount Carmel, IL 62863-9803
(618)262-4663 (800)646-3276 Fax:(618)236-4618
E-mail: poorfarm@midwest.net

Circa 1915. This uniquely named inn served as a home for the homeless for more than a century. Today, the stately Federal-style structure hosts travelers and visitors to historic Southeastern Illinois, offering a "gracious glimpse of yesteryear." An antique player piano and a selection of 4,600 in-room movies are available for guests' enjoyment. There are bicycles for those wishing to explore the grounds. The Poor Farm B&B sits adjacent to a recreational park with a well-stocked lake and is within walking distance of an 18-hole golf course and driving range. Riverboat gambling is 45 minutes away in Evansville, Ind.

Historic Interest: Historic New Harmony, Indiana (40 Minutes), Amish Communities (45 minutes).

Innkeeper(s): Liz & John Stelzer. $45-85. MC, VISA, AX, DS, PC, TC. TAC10. 5 rooms with PB, 2 with FP, 2 suites and 2 conference rooms. Breakfast included in rates. Types of meals: Full bkfst, early coffee/tea, lunch, afternoon tea, snacks/refreshments and dinner. Beds: QDT. Phone, turndown service, ceiling fan and VCR in room. Air conditioning. Fax, copier, bicycles and library on premises. Handicap access. Weddings, small meetings, family reunions and seminars hosted. Amusement parks, antiquing, fishing, live theater, parks, shopping, cross-country skiing, sporting events and water sports nearby.

Pets allowed: None inside-outside enclosure.

Mount Carroll   B4

Prairie Path Guest House

1002 N Lowden Rd
Mount Carroll, IL 61053-9476
(815)244-3462
Web: www.bbonline.com/il/prairiepath/

Circa 1876. Thirty-five acres of woods and fields surround this historic Victorian country home. If warm hospitality and natural beauty seem appealing, then this is the right place. Comfortable guest bedrooms feature hand stenciling, patchwork quilts, marble-top dressers, antiques and even

Grandma's feather bed. Homemade jellies and jams accompany a hearty breakfast. Gaze at the deer, wild birds and other wildlife from the upstairs veranda's porch swing.

Innkeeper(s): Delos (Buster) & Fern Stadel. $80. MC, VISA, PC. 3 rooms, 1 with PB. Breakfast and snacks/refreshments included in rates. Types of meals: Country bkfst, early coffee/tea and afternoon tea. Beds: Q. Cable TV, ceiling fan and VCR in room. Central air. Library and gift shop on premises. Antiquing, bicycling, fishing, golf, hiking, horseback riding, live theater, parks, shopping, downhill skiing and cross-country skiing nearby.

Publicity: *Chicago Tribune, Dallas Morning News, Quad City Times* and *Wisconsin State Journal.*

Oakland   G6

Inn on The Square

3 Montgomery
Oakland, IL 61943
(217)346-2289 Fax:(217)346-2005
E-mail: innonsq@advant.net

Circa 1878. This inn features hand-carved beams and braided rugs on wide pine flooring. The Tea Room has oak tables, fresh flowers and a hand-laid brick fireplace. Guests may wander in the forest behind the inn or relax in the library with a book or jigsaw puzzle. Guest rooms have oak poster beds and handmade quilts. The Pine Room boasts an heirloom bed with a carved headboard. In addition to guest rooms,

the inn houses shops selling ladies apparel, gifts and antiques. The Amish communities of Arthur and Arcola are 14 miles away.

Innkeeper(s): Linda & Gary Miller. $55-65. MC, VISA, PC, TC. 3 rooms with PB, 1 with FP and 1 conference room. Breakfast included in rates. Types of meals: Full bkfst, early coffee/tea, lunch and picnic lunch. Beds: D. TV, ceiling fan and homemade cookies in room. Air conditioning. VCR and library on premises. Weddings, small meetings, family reunions and seminars hosted. Antiquing, golf, Amish Community, forest preserve, Lincoln sites, boating, live theater, parks, shopping, sporting events, tennis and water sports nearby.

Publicity: *Amish Country News, PM, Midwest Living* and *Country Living.*

Oregon   B4

Patchwork Inn

122 N 3rd St
Oregon, IL 61061
(815)732-4113 Fax:(815)732-6557
E-mail: patchworkinn@essex1.com

Circa 1845. Would you like to sleep where Abraham Lincoln once stayed? This historic inn actually can boast of Mr. Lincoln having "slept here." The Patchwork Inn is the sort you can imagine as providing a speaking platform as well from its two-level veranda across the front facade. Guest rooms feature access to the veranda, and there are high-ceilings and beds with handmade quilts, the theme of the inn. Guests are pampered at breakfast with a choice of service in your room, the parlor, sun room or on the front porch. A walk away is the river, dam and tree-lined streets filled with historic houses. Guests often enjoy canoeing on Rock River, picnicking in one of the three state parks or visiting Ronald Reagan's homestead in Dixon.

Historic Interest: Black Hawk Statue-1 mile, John Deere Historic Site-6 miles, Ronald Regan boyhood home-15 miles.

Innkeeper(s): Michael & Jean McNamara & Ron Bry. $75-115. MC, VISA,

DS, TC. 10 rooms with PB and 1 conference room. Breakfast and snacks/refreshments included in rates. Types of meals: Cont. Beds: DT. Cable TV, phone and two rooms have whirlpools in room. Air conditioning. Fax, copier, library and whirlpool tubs in two guest rooms on premises. Family reunions and seminars hosted. Antiquing, art galleries, bicycling, canoeing/kayaking, fishing, golf, hiking, horseback riding, live theater, museums, parks, shopping and cross-country skiing nearby.

Peoria D4

Randolph Terrace Historic Bed & Breakfast

201 W Columbia Ter
Peoria, IL 61606
(309)688-7858 (877)264-8266 Fax:(309)688-7858
E-mail: rthbb@horizon222.net
Web: www.rthbb.com

Circa 1914. Built for a prominent local civic leader, this elegant Georgian Revival home has been recently restored with leaded-glass windows and hardwood floors. The common areas include a living room, east room, sun room and library. Appointed with European antiques, the luxurious guest bedrooms and suites offer spacious comfort. Robes and hair dryers are thoughtful amenities. A candlelight breakfast is served on china and crystal with a romantic flair. Flower gardens and greenery surround a brick patio.
Historic Interest: Grand View Drive (4 miles).
Innkeeper(s): Kia Vega, Mercedes Vega. $95-145. MC, VISA, AX, PC, TC. 4 rooms with PB, 1 suite and 1 conference room. Breakfast, afternoon tea and snacks/refreshments included in rates. Types of meals: Full bkfst, veg bkfst and cont. Beds: Q. Turndown service and suite has desk in room. Central air. VCR, fax, copier and library on premises. Small meetings, family reunions and seminars hosted. Spanish spoken. Antiquing, art galleries, bicycling, fishing, golf, hiking, live theater, museums, parks, shopping, sporting events, tennis and water sports nearby.

Peoria (Mossville) D4

Old Church House Inn

1416 E Mossville Rd
Peoria (Mossville), IL 61552
(309)579-2300
E-mail: churchhouse@prodigy.net

Circa 1869. Discover this restored Colonial to be a true sanctuary. The inn once served as a country church but now promises hospitality and relaxation. Each guest bedroom offers a unique feature, such as an antique carved bedstead, featherbeds, handmade quilts and lacy curtains. A cup of tea and fresh-baked cookies can be enjoyed by a warm fire or among the garden's colorful assortment of flowers. Chocolates are a pleasant treat at turndown in the evening.

Innkeeper(s): Dean & Holly Ramseyer. $75-115. MC, VISA, DS. 2 rooms, 1 with PB. Breakfast included in rates. Types of meals: Cont plus, early coffee/tea, picnic lunch and room service. Beds: Q. Turndown service in room. Air conditioning. Weddings and small meetings hosted. Antiquing, fishing, bike trail, live theater, shopping, cross-country skiing, sporting events and water sports nearby.
Publicity: *Chillicothe Bulletin, Journal Star, Country Inns and The Chicago Tribune.*

"Your hospitality, thoughtfulness, the cleanliness, beauty, I should just say everything was the best."

Pinckneyville J4

Oxbow B&B

3967 State Rt 13/127
Pinckneyville, IL 62274
(618)357-9839 (800)929-6888
E-mail: oxbowbb@midwest.net
Web: www.bbonline.com/il/oxbow/

Circa 1929. Several of the guest rooms at this unique brick veneer farmhouse feature beds designed and built by innkeeper Al Doughty, who among his other trades has been a rural veterinarian, Civil War historian and coal miner. His wife, innkeeper Peggy Doughty, raises prize Arabian horses, some of which have gone on to reach Top Ten Championships. Each of the antique-filled guest rooms features names from the Civil War. The Shiloh room boasts a seven-foot headboard, marble-top dresser and quaint wash stand with a pitcher and mirror, while the Pilot Knob room features a four-poster, canopy bed made from aged barn timbers. There's is a large parking area at the B&B.
Historic Interest: Oxbow B&B is near several historic sites, including Fort Kaskaskia, St. Mary River Covered Bridge, Charter Oak Schoolhouse, Pierre Menard Home, The Old Slave House and Fort De Chartes. The Perry County Historical Jail is only one mile from the home.
Innkeeper(s): Al & Peggy Doughty. $50-65. MC, VISA. 5 rooms with PB and 1 suite. Breakfast included in rates. Types of meals: Full bkfst. Beds: Q. Spa, swimming, library, exercise equipment and pool table on premises. Antiquing, fishing and water sports nearby.

Rock Island C3

Victorian Inn

702 20th St
Rock Island, IL 61201-2638
(309)788-7068 (800)728-7068 Fax:(309)788-7086
E-mail: dparker@victorianinnbandb.com

Circa 1876. Built as a wedding present for the daughter of a Rock Island liquor baron, the inn's striking features include illuminated stained-glass tower windows. Other examples of  the Victorian decor are the living room's beveled-plate-glass French doors and the dining room's Flemish Oak ceiling beams and paneling, crowned by turn-of-the-century tapestries. Standing within sight of three other buildings listed in the National Register, the inn's wooded grounds are home to many songbirds from the area. A glassed-in Florida porch is perfect for relaxing during any season and a patio table in the gardens is a great place to enjoy a glass of pink lemonade on warm evenings.
Innkeeper(s): David & Barbara Parker. $75-150. MC, VISA, AX, PC, TC. 5 rooms with PB, 2 with FP. Breakfast included in rates. Types of meals: Gourmet bkfst, early coffee/tea, afternoon tea and snacks/refreshments. Beds: KQDT. Ceiling fan in room. Air conditioning. Fax, copier and library on premises. Small meetings, family reunions and seminars hosted. Antiquing, fishing, live theater, parks, cross-country skiing, sporting events and water sports nearby.

Sheffield C4

Chestnut Street Inn

301 E Chestnut St
Sheffield, IL 61361
(815)454-2419 (800)537-1304
E-mail: gail@chestnut-inn.com
Web: www.chestnut-inn.com

Circa 1854. Originally built in Italianate style, this mid-19th-century reborn Colonial Revival is the dream-come-true for innkeeper Gail Bruntjen. She spent more than 15 years searching for just the right country home to open a bed & breakfast. With its gracious architectural character and well-organized

interior spaces, the Chestnut Street Inn fit the bill. Classic French doors open to a wide foyer with gleaming chandeliers and a floating spindle staircase.

Sophisticated chintz fabrics and authentic antiques highlight each room. The four guest rooms offer down comforters, four-poster beds and private baths. Guests will be delighted by the gourmet selections offered every morning such as broccoli mushroom quiche, homemade breads and fresh fruit, all exquisitely presented by candlelight on fine China and crystal. Afternoon tea and evening snacks are served in the public rooms. Antiquing, shops ,bicycling, hiking, golf and fishing are located nearby.

Innkeeper(s): Gail Bruntjen. $75-175. MC, VISA, AX, DS, PC, TC. TAC10. 4 rooms with PB, 1 with FP, 1 suite and 1 conference room. Breakfast, afternoon tea and snacks/refreshments included in rates. Types of meals: Full bkfst and early coffee/tea. Beds: KQT. Cable TV, turndown service and VCR in room. Air conditioning. Library on premises. Weddings and small meetings hosted. Antiquing, bicycling, fishing, golf, parks and shopping nearby.

Publicity: *The Illinois Review and Illinois Country Living.*

"Without a doubt, the best B&B I've ever been to."

Stockton A3

Hammond House B&B

323 N Main St
Stockton, IL 61085-1115
(815)947-2032
E-mail: haas@blkhawk.net
Web: www.hammondhouse.com

Circa 1900. Merwin Hammond built this Colonial Revival mansion for his bride who requested the finest and largest home in the area. Recently renovated, this inn features the orig-inal open staircase and ornate second-story skylight. A big screen TV and video selection invites movie viewing in the great room. The color-themed guest suites have a contemporary Victorian decor. A bottle of wine, chocolates and a welcome basket are sure to pamper and appeal. Breakfast may be enjoyed on the double deck showcasing wisteria vines. Listen to the songbirds while relaxing on the pillared front porch wicker furniture.

Innkeeper(s): LaVonneda & Spencer Haas. $55-150. MC, VISA, DS, PC, TC. 5 rooms with PB and 3 suites. Breakfast and snacks/refreshments included in rates. Types of meals: Cont plus and early coffee/tea. Beds: QT. Cable TV, ceiling fan and VCR in room. Central air. Fax, copier, library and gift shop on premises. Small meetings and family reunions hosted. Antiquing, art galleries, bicycling, canoeing/kayaking, fishing, golf, hiking, horseback riding, live theater, museums, parks, shopping, downhill skiing, cross-country skiing, tennis, water sports and wineries nearby.

Urbana F6

Lindley House

312 W Green St
Urbana, IL 61801-3222
(217)384-4800
E-mail: lindley@shout.net
Web: www.lindley.cc

Circa 1895. Designed by architect Rudolph Zachariah Gill from the University of Illinois for Dr. Austin Lindley, a prominent physician, this classic Queen Anne Victorian displays many of the whimsical architectural details popular during this era. The facade features imposing gables, an octagonal turret and a curved porch. Gleaming parquet floors in the four public rooms, a magnificent oak gingerbread staircase, beveled- and stained-glass windows are all part of the interior Victorian detailing. All second-floor queen guest rooms are decorated in antiques, while the spacious third-floor king suite offers a sitting area and private bath. There is also a two bedroom carriage house. Fresh fruit, homemade breads, a by-request hot dish and Columbian coffee are offered in the morning. Lindley House is located close to restaurants, parks, sports activities and the University of Illinois.

Innkeeper(s): Carolyn Baxley. $75-150. MC, VISA, PC, TC. 5 rooms, 2 with PB, 1 suite and 1 cottage. Breakfast included in rates. Types of meals: Cont plus. Beds: KQDT. Cable TV, ceiling fan and VCR in room. Air conditioning. Internet Access and phone on premises. Weddings, small meetings and family reunions hosted.

Indiana

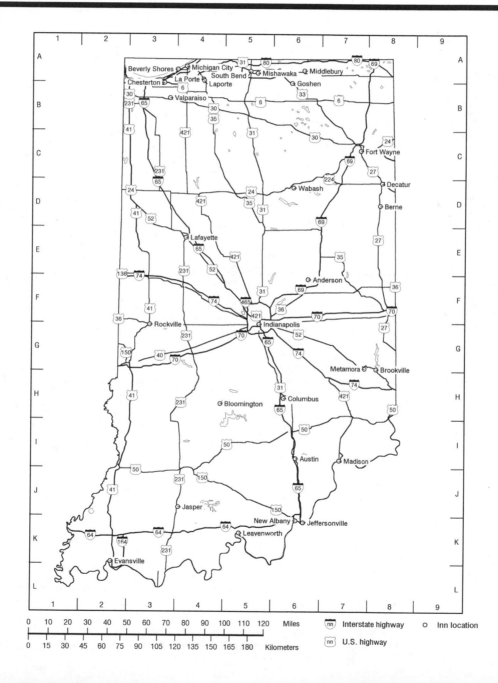

0 10 20 30 40 50 60 70 80 90 100 110 120 Miles

0 15 30 45 60 75 90 105 120 135 150 165 180 Kilometers

nn Interstate highway   o Inn location

nn U.S. highway

Anderson   F6

Plum Retreat B&B

926 Historic W Eighth St
Anderson, IN 46016
(765)649-7586 Fax:(765)649-9928

Circa 1892. This Queen Anne Victorian, so named because of
its light purple hue, is surrounded by a wrought-iron fence,
roses and foliage. The front doors, fashioned out of a rich

 wood, feature an intricate glass pat-
tern. The veranda offers wicker fur-
nishings so guests can enjoy the
scenery and relax. The three guest
rooms include antiques such as a
high-back walnut bed. The home was
built by the vice president of a local
loan association, and at one time the
grounds included a racetrack. Antique shops, museums, horse
racing and wilderness areas are nearby.

$70-120. PC. 3 rooms, 1 with PB, 1 with FP, 1 suite and 2 conference rooms.
Breakfast, afternoon tea and snacks/refreshments included in rates. Types of
meals: Full bkfst and early coffee/tea. Beds: QD. Central air. VCR and library on
premises. Weddings, small meetings, family reunions and seminars hosted.
Antiquing, golf, live theater, parks, shopping, sporting events and tennis nearby.
Publicity: *Indianapolis Woman.*

*"This house was a life long dream of my wife, we both fell in love
with it. We appreciate you letting us have this most wonderful experience in your home."*

Austin   I6

Carousel Inn B&B

190 N High St
Austin, IN 47102-1634
(812)794-2990 (877)323-3334 Fax:(812)794-2991

Circa 1937. A quaint Midwestern town is the backdrop for this
one-and-a-half-story inn that offers laid-back leisure and modern
business conveniences. Enjoy fresh-baked cookies in the main
sitting area with a fireplace. A refrigerator is in the upstairs sitting room. Antiques furnish some of the guest bedrooms, the
master suite features a two-person whirlpool tub. Savor a homemade sit-down breakfast while soft music pleasantly accents the
meal. Snacks and beverages are offered in the evenings. Relax on
the deck or large front porch overlooking the koi pond.

Historic Interest: Lanier Mansion (20 miles).

Innkeeper(s): Bob & Marti Lawyer. $80-100. MC, VISA, DS, TC. 3 rooms with
PB. Breakfast and snacks/refreshments included in rates. Types of meals:
Gourmet bkfst and early coffee/tea. Beds: QD. Cable TV, phone, turndown service, ceiling fan and double whirlpool tub in room. Central air. Fax, hot tub
and gift shop on premises. Beaches, fishing, golf, hiking and shopping nearby.

Berne   D8

Schug House Inn

706 W Main St
Berne, IN 46711-1328
(219)589-2303
E-mail: schughousebnb@onlyinternet.net

Circa 1907. This Queen Anne home was built in 1907 by
Emanuel Wanner. It was constructed for the Schug family, who
occupied the home for 25 years, and whom the innkeepers chose

the name of their inn. Victorian features decorate the home,
including inlaid floors, pocket doors and a wraparound porch.
Guest rooms boast walnut, cherry and oak furnishings. Fruit,
cheeses and pastries are served on antique china each morning in
the dining room. Horse-drawn carriages from the nearby Old
Order Amish community often pass on the street outside.

Innkeeper(s): John Minch. $35-40. MC, VISA. 9 rooms with PB and 1 con-
ference room. Breakfast included in rates. Types of meals: Cont. Beds: KQDT.

Beverly Shores   A4

Dunes Shore Inn

33 Lakeshore County Rd
Beverly Shores, IN 46301-0807
(219)879-9029

Circa 1940. The Dunes Shore Inn started out as a summer
hotel catering to Lithuanian folk, who were fond of the area
because of its resemblance to the Baltic Sea region. It later
became a boarding house for national park employees of the
Indiana Dunes National Lakeshore. A concrete-block and frame
building, the inn is located one block from Lake Michigan. Its
pleasant interior features an eclectic collection of furnishings.
Guests gather in one of the upstairs lounges or around a
Swedish masonry stove in the knotty-pine lounge. The
innkeepers have an apartment available May to October, which
includes a private bath and kitchen.

Innkeeper(s): Rosemary & Fred Braun. $60-88. PC, TC. 10 rooms. Breakfast
included in rates. Types of meals: Cont plus and early coffee/tea. Beds: DT.
Ceiling fan in room. VCR, library, guest refrigerator, screen house and picnic
tables on premises. Small meetings, family reunions and seminars hosted.
German spoken. Amusement parks, antiquing, fishing, golf, live theater,
parks, shopping, downhill skiing, cross-country skiing, sporting events, tennis
and water sports nearby.
Publicity: *Milwaukee Journal, Chicago Sun-Times and Travel Holiday.*

Bloomington   H4

Grant Street Inn

310 N Grant St
Bloomington, IN 47408-3736
(812)334-2353 (800)328-4350 Fax:(812)331-8673
E-mail: gsi@grantstinn.com
Web: www.grantstinn.com

Circa 1883. Built originally before the turn of the century by
William P. Rogers, dean of the Indiana University Law School,
for his bride Belle, the home served as both a private home and
student residence until 1990. It was moved to its present location at 7th and Grant Street in the historic district and restored
to its original elegance of hardwood flooring, crown moldings
and raised porches. There are 24 individually decorated rooms,
all featuring antique-style furnishings. All of the rooms offer private baths, TV and phones. Some of the rooms feature fireplaces and separate entrances. Suites offer the romance of
Jacuzzi tubs and fireplaces. Guests can enjoy a leisurely full
breakfast in the breakfast room. The inn is located within walking distance of Indiana's largest antique mall and cultural
events at Indiana University.

Historic Interest: The inn is a short drive to Lake Monroe, Brown County and
McCormick's Creek State Park.

Innkeeper(s): Bob Bohler. $99-169. MC, VISA, AX, DS, PC. TAC10. 24
rooms with PB, 14 with FP and 2 suites. Breakfast included in rates. Types
of meals: Full bkfst. Beds: KQT. Cable TV and phone in room. Air conditioning. Fax and copier on premises. Handicap access. Antiquing, fishing, golf,
live theater, parks, shopping, sporting events, tennis and water sports nearby.

Brookville G8

The Hermitage Bed and Breakfast

650 East 8th St
Brookville, IN 47012
(765)647-5182 (877)407-9198
E-mail: hermitage@cnz.com

Circa 1835. J. Ottis Adams and T.C. Steele, two renown Indiana artists, set up their home and art studios on this large estate that spans 6.5 acres. The Hoosier Group painted here in the heart of the scenic Whitewater River Valley for several years. Join Martha for a tour of this 19-room house, and then converse over refreshments in the living room or studios. A library features a wood-burning fireplace, antique books and magazines. A 112-foot-long veranda with vintage furniture and a hammock overlooks the picturesque grounds. The adjacent Town Park and nearby lake offer many outdoor activities. Visit the historic region of Metamora, a Canal town and South Central area's covered bridge communities.

Historic Interest: Old Brick Church, Franklin County Seminary/Museum, Little Cedar Grove Baptist Church.

Innkeeper(s): Martha Shea. $75. PC. 6 rooms with PB and 1 conference room. Breakfast and snacks/refreshments included in rates. Types of meals: Gourmet bkfst, country bkfst, cont plus, cont, early coffee/tea and dinner. Beds: KDT. Turndown service and ceiling fan in room. Air conditioning. VCR, bicycles and library on premises. Weddings, small meetings, family reunions and seminars hosted. Antiquing, beaches, bicycling, canoeing/kayaking, fishing, golf, hiking, horseback riding, Historic Canal Town, Metamora, parks, shopping, downhill skiing, sporting events, tennis, water sports and wineries nearby.

Publicity: *Outdoor Indiana.*

Chesterton B3

The Gray Goose

350 Indian Boundary Rd
Chesterton, IN 46304-1511
(219)926-5781 (800)521-5127 Fax:(219)926-4845
E-mail: graygoose@niia.net
Web: www.graygooseinn.com

Circa 1939. Situated on 100 wooded acres, just under one hour from Chicago, this English country inn overlooks a private lake. Guests can see Canadian geese and ducks on the lake and sur-

rounding area. Rooms are decorated in 18th-century English, Shaker and French-country styles. Some of the rooms feature fireplaces, Jacuzzi and poster beds. Complimentary snacks, soft drinks, coffee and tea are available throughout the day. Strains of Mozart or Handel add to the ambiance.

Historic Interest: The Dunes State and National Lakeshore is less than three miles from the inn.

Innkeeper(s): Tim Wilk & Chuck Ramsey. $90-185. MC, VISA, AX, DS, PC, TC. TAC10. 8 rooms with PB, 3 with FP, 3 suites and 1 conference room. Breakfast, afternoon tea and snacks/refreshments included in rates. Types of meals: Gourmet bkfst and early coffee/tea. Beds: KQ. TV, phone, ceiling fan, VCR and one room with fireplace and Jacuzzi in room. Air conditioning. Fax, copier, library, snack/service bar, large screened gazebo and gift shop on premises. Weddings, small meetings, family reunions and seminars hosted. Antiquing, fishing, golf, live theater, parks, shopping, downhill skiing, cross-country skiing, sporting events, tennis and water sports nearby.

Publicity: *Insider, Post-Tribune, Glamour, Country Inns, Midwest Living, Indianapolis Star and Indianapolis Woman.*

"Extremely gracious! A repeat stay for us because it is such a wonderful place to stay."

Columbus H6

The Columbus Inn

445 5th St
Columbus, IN 47201-6206
(812)378-4289 Fax:(812)378-4289

Circa 1895. Dances, basketball games and poultry shows once convened in the auditorium of the old Columbus City Hall during its years as the focal point of town. The original terra-cotta floors, enormous brass chandeliers and hand-carved oak woodwork now welcome overnight guests. Lavishly decorated rooms feature reproduction antiques such as cherry sleigh beds. Twelve-foot-high windows and 21-foot ceilings grace the Charles Sparrell Suite with its separate sleeping level.

Historic Interest: In the National Register.

$90. MC, VISA, AX, DC, CB, DS, PC, TC. 34 rooms with PB, 5 suites and 3 conference rooms. Breakfast included in rates. Types of meals: Gourmet bkfst, early coffee/tea, afternoon tea and gourmet dinner. Beds: QD. Cable TV and phone in room. Air conditioning. VCR, fax and copier on premises. Handicap access. Weddings, small meetings, family reunions and seminars hosted. Amusement parks, antiquing, fishing, live theater, parks, shopping, downhill skiing, sporting events and water sports nearby.

Publicity: *Chicago Sun-Times, Country Inns, Home & Away, Cincinnati Enquirer, Glamour, Innsider and InnReview.*

"A delicious and beautifully served breakfast was the crowning glory of our stay."

Decatur D8

Cragwood Inn B&B

303 N 2nd St
Decatur, IN 46733-1329
(219)728-2000
E-mail: cragwood@adamswells.com

Circa 1900. This Queen Anne Victorian with four porches, gingerbread frosting, a turret and a graceful bay facade was built by a Decatur banker. Finely carved oak is magnificently displayed in the paneled ceilings, staircase and pillars of the parlor. Ornate tin ceilings, beveled leaded-glass windows and a crystal chandelier are among other highlights. Twin wicker beds in the Garden Room looks out through a Palladian window. Two other rooms have their own fireplace.

Innkeeper(s): George & Nancy Craig. $60-65. MC, VISA, PC, TC. 4 rooms, 2 with PB, 2 with FP. Breakfast and snacks/refreshments included in rates. Types of meals: Full bkfst and early coffee/tea. Beds: QDT. Air conditioning. VCR, library and beautiful flower gardens on premises. Antiquing and parks nearby.

Publicity: *Inside Chicago, Great Lakes Getaway and Christmas Victorian Craft.*

"Your wonderful hospitality, beautiful home and company made my trip that much more enjoyable."

Evansville K2

Starkey Inn

214 SE First St
Evansville, IN 47713
(812)425-7264 (800)580-0305 Fax:(812)425-7333
E-mail: webmaster@starkeyinn.com
Web: www.starkeyinn.com

Circa 1850. A prominent attorney built this Greek Revival mansion for his bride who longed for a fashionable city home typical to those in the South. The current owner, also an attorney, has made extensive renovations to ensure modern comfort while retaining its original integrity. Two of the children's names are still found etched on an upstairs window. Tastefully decorated guest bedrooms boast antique furnishings including four-poster and sleigh beds. Using recipes from a well-worn cookbook, host Veda serves favorites like cheese strata, French toast with peaches, lemon yogurt muffins and quick quiche. Choose to eat in the dining room, kitchen, or even breakfast in bed. Only a block from the Ohio River, it is a short walk to the historic city's main street shops and restaurants.

Innkeeper(s): Veda & Walt Taylor. $85-185. MC, VISA, AX. 5 rooms, 3 with PB, 3 with FP and 1 suite. Breakfast included in rates. Types of meals: Full bkfst, early coffee/tea and room service. Beds: KQD. Phone in room. Central air. VCR, fax, copier and library on premises. Weddings, small meetings, family reunions and seminars hosted. Antiquing, art galleries, bicycling, fishing, golf, live theater, museums, parks, shopping, downhill skiing, sporting events, tennis and water sports nearby.

Fort Wayne C7

The Carole Lombard House B&B

704 Rockhill St
Fort Wayne, IN 46802-5918
(219)426-9896 (888)426-9896

Circa 1895. Jane Alice Peters, a.k.a. Carole Lombard, spent her first six years in this turn-of-the-century home located in Ft. Wayne's historic West-Central neighborhood. The innkeepers named two guest rooms in honor of Lombard and her second husband, Clark Gable. Each of these rooms features memorabilia from the Gable-Lombard romance. A video library with a collection of classic movies is available, including many of Lombard's films. The innkeepers provide information for a self-guided architectural tour of the historic area.

Historic Interest: On Oct. 6, 1908, Jane Alice Peters was born in the handsome house at the foot of Rockhill Street. The world knew her as Carole Lombard.
Innkeeper(s): Bev Fiandt. $75-85. MC, VISA, DS, PC, TC. TAC5. 4 rooms with PB. Breakfast included in rates. Types of meals: Full bkfst and early coffee/tea. Beds: KQDT. Cable TV and phone in room. Air conditioning. VCR and bicycles on premises. Small meetings hosted. Antiquing, live theater, parks and sporting events nearby.

Publicity: *Playboy and Michigan Living.*

"The elegance and ambience are most appreciated."

Goshen B6

Prairie Manor B&B

66398 US Hwy 33
Goshen, IN 46526-9482
(219)642-4761 Fax:(219)642-4762
E-mail: jetson@npcc.net

Circa 1925. Local craftsman created this elegant English-style country manor home. The home's original features have remained unchanged, including the original window seats, arched doorways and a winding staircase. The inn's 12 acres include a swimming pool and play area for children. Breakfasts include items such as crepes filled with fresh strawberries and bananas

topped with a yogurt-whipped cream sauce or baked eggs with fresh herbs and three cheeses. Homemade breads, such as raspberry cream cheese coffeecake, also are served.

Historic Interest: Goshen Historic District (5 miles), Bonneyville Mill (15 miles).
Innkeeper(s): Jean & Hesston Lauver. $65-95. MC, VISA, DS, PC, TC. 3 rooms with PB, 1 suite and 2 conference rooms. Breakfast and snacks/refreshments included in rates. Types of meals: Full bkfst, veg bkfst and early coffee/tea. Beds: QT. Cable TV and ceiling fan in room. Air conditioning. Fax, swimming, stables and library on premises. Weddings, small meetings, family reunions and seminars hosted. Antiquing, art galleries, bicycling, canoeing/kayaking, fishing, golf, hiking, live theater, museums, parks, shopping, cross-country skiing, sporting events and tennis nearby.
Pets allowed: only in barn.

Indianapolis G5

Speedway B&B

1829 Cunningham Dr
Indianapolis, IN 46224-5338
(317)487-6531 (800)975-3412 Fax:(317)481-1825
E-mail: speedwaybb@msn.com

Circa 1906. This two-story white columned inn reflects a plantation-style architecture. The inn is situated on an acre of lawn and trees. The bed & breakfast has a homey decor that includes a wood-paneled common room and elegantly furnished guest rooms. Breakfast includes items such as homemade coffee cake and Danish or sausage and egg casserole. Nearby attractions include President Harrison's home, the Hall of Fame Museum and the largest city park in the nation, Eagle Creek Park.

Innkeeper(s): Pauline Grothe. $65-135. PC, TC. 5 rooms with PB. Breakfast included in rates. Types of meals: Full bkfst. Beds: KQD. Cable TV and phone in room. Air conditioning. VCR, fax and bicycles on premises. Weddings, small meetings, family reunions and seminars hosted. Antiquing, fishing, golf, live theater, parks, shopping, cross-country skiing, sporting events, tennis and water sports nearby.

"It is people like you who have given B&Bs such a good reputation."

Jasper J4

Powers Inn B&B

325 W 6th St
Jasper, IN 47546-2719
(812)482-3018

Circa 1880. This B&B's location was meant for hospitality. A local attorney built this Second Empire Victorian on this spot, but it once was the site of a local log cabin inn. The innkeepers painstakingly restored their Victorian, which included rebuild-

ing the foundation. They managed to save many original elements along the way. The rooms are elegant, decorated with antiques and reproductions. Antique dressers house the bathroom sinks, and one bathroom includes an original clawfoot tub.

Innkeeper(s): Alice & Larry "Joe" Garland. $60. MC, VISA, PC. 3 rooms with PB. Breakfast included in rates. Types of meals: Full bkfst. Beds: DT. Air conditioning. VCR on premises. Amusement parks, antiquing, fishing, golf, live theater, parks, shopping, downhill skiing, tennis and water sports nearby.
Publicity: *Chicago Tribune and Dubois County Daily Herald.*

"Warm, cozy and very friendly!"

Jeffersonville   K6

1877 House Country Inn

2408 Utica-Sellersburg Rd
Jeffersonville, IN 47130
(812)285-1877 (888)284-1877
E-mail: house1877@peoplepc.com

Circa 1877. Sugar maples shade the lawn of this inn, located on more than two acres. There are two guest rooms and a cottage available on the property. The renovated farmhouse is decorated with country pieces and memorabilia collected for several years by the innkeepers. German pancakes, savory bread pudding and poppyseed bread are favorites served at the inn that also have been included in the food section of the local paper.

Innkeeper(s): Steve & Carol Stenbro. $75-125. PC, TC. 2 rooms with PB, 2 with FP and 1 cottage. Breakfast, afternoon tea and snacks/refreshments included in rates. Types of meals: Gourmet bkfst. Beds: QD. Cable TV, ceiling fan and cottage with Jacuzzi in room. Air conditioning. VCR, fax, library, child care and outside eight-person hot tub on premises. Small meetings hosted. Amusement parks, antiquing, fishing, golf, live theater, parks, shopping, downhill skiing, sporting events and tennis nearby.

Publicity: *Courier Journal and Tribune.*

The Old Bridge Inn

131 W Chestnut St
Jeffersonville, IN 47130
(812)284-3580 Fax:(812)284-3561
E-mail: innbridge@aol.com

Circa 1840. A Georgian Colonial in Jeffersonville's historic districts, the Old Bridge Inn is within walking distance of the Ohio River and has a delightful garden that is a mix of perennials and herbs. It offers three guest bedrooms, and a daily multi-course breakfast that includes tasty items such as fruit, muffins, granola or muesli, a breakfast casserole or Belgian waffles. Complimentary beverages are available throughout the day. Guests may venture out to nearby attractions like the falls of the Ohio State Park, the Howard Steamboat Museum and Churchill Downs.

Historic Interest: Falls of the Ohio State Park (1 miles), Howard Steamboat Museum (1 mile), Churchill Downs (10 miles).

Innkeeper(s): Linda Williams. $60-115. MC, VISA, AX, DS, PC, TC. TAC10. 3 rooms with PB, 1 with FP, 1 suite and 1 conference room. Breakfast included in rates. Types of meals: Full bkfst, early coffee/tea, gourmet lunch, picnic lunch, afternoon tea and gourmet dinner. Beds: QD. TV and fireplace in room. Central air. VCR, fax, copier, library, pet boarding and gift shop on premises. Weddings, small meetings, family reunions and seminars hosted. Amusement parks, antiquing, art galleries, fishing, golf, hiking, live theater, museums, parks, shopping, downhill skiing, sporting events, tennis, water sports and wineries nearby.

Pets allowed: Must be house broken, in pet carrier or leashed.

La Porte   A4

Hidden Pond B&B

5342 N US Hwy 35
La Porte, IN 46350-8279
(219)879-8200 Fax:(219)879-1770
E-mail: edberent@adsnet.com
Web: www.bbonline.com/in/hiddenpond/

Circa 1918. Ten wooded acres with wetlands, pond and meadows surround this country house and its hot tub, heated pool and gazebo. Each guest room offers picturesque views and country decor. An egg entree, breakfast meat and pastries are provided at breakfast. Your hosts will advise you on nearby excursions and activities such as the Blue Chip Casino, La Porte antique shops and the Indiana Dunes along the shores of Lake Michigan. Or you can try your hand at angling for one of the pond's inhabitants and simply enjoying nature. Chicago is 60 miles away.

Innkeeper(s): Sue & Ed Berent. $89-159. MC, VISA, PC, TC. 4 rooms, 3 with PB and 1 conference room. Breakfast and snacks/refreshments included in rates. Types of meals: Gourmet bkfst, veg bkfst, early coffee/tea, gourmet lunch and gourmet dinner. Beds: KT. Ceiling fan in room. Air conditioning. Fax, copier, spa and library on premises. Small meetings, family reunions and seminars hosted. Amusement parks, antiquing, art galleries, beaches, bicycling, fishing, golf, hiking, horseback riding, live theater, museums, parks, shopping, sporting events, tennis, water sports and wineries nearby.

Pets allowed: we will consider.

Publicity: *South Bend Trib, La Porte Herald Argus, Michigan City Dispatch and Gary Post Tribune.*

Lafayette   E4

Historic Loeb House Inn

708 Cincinnati St
Lafayette, IN 47901
(765)420-7737 Fax:(765)420-7805
Web: www.qlink.com/loebinn

Circa 1882. This pristine brick Italianate manor was once the home of a prominent Lafayette family, but was later turned into apartments. In 1996, it was painstakingly restored to its former glory. The home boasts crown molding and ceiling medallions, gleaming woodwork and intricate wood floors. Fine Victorian antiques and appointments decorate the inn. Three guest rooms include a fireplace, and the private baths include either a whirlpool or clawfoot tub. Guests are pampered in Victorian style with a full breakfast, afternoon tea and turndown service. The home is located in Lafayette's Centennial historic district and is close to many local sites, including Purdue University.

Innkeeper(s): Jan Alford & Dick Nagel. $85-175. MC, VISA, AX, PC, TC. TAC10. 5 rooms with PB, 3 with FP, 1 suite and 1 conference room. Breakfast, afternoon tea and snacks/refreshments included in rates. Types of meals: Full bkfst and early coffee/tea. Beds: D. Cable TV, phone, turndown service and ceiling fan in room. Air conditioning. Fax, copier, pantry stocked with snacks and beverages and ice machine on premises. Weddings, small meetings and seminars hosted. Amusement parks, antiquing, golf, festivals, live theater, parks, shopping, sporting events, tennis and water sports nearby.

Publicity: *Purdue Magazine and Lafayette Journal & Courier.*

Leavenworth   K5

The Leavenworth Inn

930 West State Road 62
Leavenworth, IN 47137
(812)739-2120 (888)739-2120 Fax:(812)739-2012
E-mail: leavenworthinn@aol.com
Web: www.leavenworthinn.com

Circa 1800. Gardens highlight the exterior of The Leavenworth Inn, and the six-acre grounds afford views of the Ohio River. The inn was once part of Forest Grove Farm, and guests would visit the farmhouse to enjoy fresh milk, homegrown vegetables and wine produced on the grounds. Today, guests can relax and enjoy the Ohio River view from the Inn's gazebo, curl up with a book in front of the fireplace in the library or select a classic movie and pop it into the VCR. The grounds are perfect

for a game of croquet or horse-shoes, and guests can borrow bicycles from the innkeepers and take a tour of the town. Leavenworth offers craft shops, galleries and antique shops. Other unique attractions include trips to Wyandotte Cave, Marengo Cave, Squire Boone Caverns or Cave Country Canoes.

Historic Interest: Lincoln Boyhood Memorial (45 miles), Corydon Capitol State Historic Site (15 miles).

Innkeeper(s): Bert Collins. $74-99. MC, VISA, AX, DS, TC. 11 rooms with PB, 1 with FP, 1 suite and 1 conference room. Breakfast included in rates. Types of meals: Full bkfst. Beds: KQT. Cable TV, phone and VCR in room. Central air. Fax, bicycles, tennis, library and internet access on premises. Weddings, small meetings, family reunions and seminars hosted. Amusement parks, antiquing, bicycling, canoeing/kayaking, fishing, golf, hiking, horseback riding, live theater, museums, parks, shopping, downhill skiing, sporting events, tennis, water sports and wineries nearby.

Madison I7

Schussler House B&B

514 Jefferson St
Madison, IN 47250
(812)273-2068 (800)392-1931
E-mail: schussler@voyager.net

Circa 1849. This Federal-style home was built by a local doctor who used it as both house and office. The three guest rooms include antiques and reproductions. The innkeepers pamper guests with a delectable full breakfast, served by candlelight. Madison, a picturesque Ohio River town surrounded by rolling hills, has more than 100 blocks listed in the National Register and designated a National Trust Historic District. The B&B is within walking distance to many shops and sites, and the river is just five blocks away.

Innkeeper(s): Judy & Bill Gilbert. $110-170. MC, VISA, DS, PC, TC. TAC10. 3 rooms with PB. Breakfast and snacks/refreshments included in rates. Types of meals: Full bkfst and early coffee/tea. Beds: QT. Turndown service in room. Air conditioning. Refrigerator on premises. Small meetings and family reunions hosted. Antiquing, fishing, golf, parks, shopping and tennis nearby.

Publicity: *Update, Cincinnati Magazine, The Downtowner and Midwest Living.*

"Five star all the way!"

Metamora G7

The Thorpe House Country Inn

19049 Clayborne St, PO Box 36
Metamora, IN 47030
(765)647-5425 (888)427-7932
E-mail: thorpe_house@hotmail.com

Circa 1840. The steam engine still brings passenger cars and the gristmill still grinds cornmeal in historic Metamora. The Thorpe House is located one block from the canal. Rooms feature original pine and poplar floors, antiques, stenciling and country accessories. Enjoy a hearty breakfast selected from the inn's restaurant menu. (Popular items include homemade biscuits, egg dishes and sourdough pecan rolls.) Walk through the village to explore more than 100 shops.

Historic Interest: Indian mounds, historic Brookville, Laurel, and "village of spires" Oldenburg are within 10 minutes. Historic Connersville and Batesville are within one-half hour.

Innkeeper(s): Mike & Jean Owens. $70-125. MC, VISA, AX, DS, PC, TC. TAC10. 5 rooms with PB and 1 suite. Breakfast and snacks/refreshments included in rates. Types of meals: Full bkfst, early coffee/tea, lunch and picnic lunch. Beds: KDT. Air conditioning. Gift shops/pottery studio on premises. Small meetings and family reunions hosted. Amusement parks, antiquing, fishing, golf, parks, shopping, tennis and water sports nearby.

Pets allowed: by prior arrangement.

Publicity: *Cincinnati Enquirer, Chicago Sun-Times and Midwest Living.*

"Thanks to all of you for your kindness and hospitality during our stay."

Michigan City A4

Brickstone B&B

215 W 6th St
Michigan City, IN 46360
(219)878-1819
E-mail: shoover20@home.com
Web: members.home.net/shoover20/

Circa 1880. Originally the parsonage of the First Congregational Church, the Brickstone offers a Great Room with fireplace and a wicker-filled screened porch. There are four guest rooms, each decorated in a style reflecting one of the four seasons. All feature fresh flowers and double or single Jacuzzi tubs. A breakfast buffet is provided in the morning and afterward you can walk or take a bicycle to the marina, beach or zoo. Guests often enjoy walking across to the Light House Mall Outlet Center.

Innkeeper(s): Jim & Sidney Hoover. $80-140. MC, VISA, PC. 4 rooms with PB. Breakfast included in rates. Types of meals: Gourmet bkfst and early coffee/tea. Beds: QT. Ceiling fan in room. VCR, fax and library on premises. Weddings hosted. Antiquing, fishing, golf, live theater, parks, shopping and water sports nearby.

Pets allowed: House trained.

Creekwood Inn

Route 20/35
Michigan City, IN 46360
(219)872-8357 (800)400-1981 Fax:(219)872-6986
E-mail: creekwd@adsnet.com
Web: www.creekwoodinn.com

Circa 1930. The exterior of Creekwood Inn conjures up images of a charming English country estate, perhaps the home of a young viscount and his bride. The 33-acre grounds include English gardens and the shade of towering trees. The interior rooms have been decorated in traditional style. Three guest rooms include a fireplace; others include a private terrace. In-room refrigerators and modem hook-ups are among the thoughtful modern amenities. On Friday and Saturday nights, gourmet dinners, prepared by a local chef, are available. The inn is just an hour's drive from Chicago. Outlet malls, golfing, wineries, orchards and the attractions of Lake Michigan all are nearby.

Innkeeper(s): Mary Ellen Hatton/Peggie Wall. $130-190. MC, VISA, AX, DC, PC, TC. TAC10. 12 rooms with PB, 3 with FP, 1 suite and 2 conference rooms. Breakfast included in rates. Types of meals: Full bkfst, veg bkfst, cont and early coffee/tea. Beds: KQ. TV and phone in room. Central air. VCR, fax, copier, spa and bicycles on premises. Handicap access. Weddings, small meetings, family reunions and seminars hosted. Antiquing, art galleries, beaches, bicycling, fishing, golf, hiking, horseback riding, live theater, museums, parks, shopping, cross-country skiing, sporting events, tennis, water sports and wineries nearby.

Publicity: *Chicago Tribune, Midwest Living and Crane Chicago Business.*

The Hutchinson Mansion Inn

220 W 10th St
Michigan City, IN 46360-3516
(219)879-1700

Circa 1875. Built by a lumber baron in 1875, this grand, red-brick mansion features examples of Queen Anne, Classic Revival and Italianate design. The mansion boasts 11 stained-glass panels and the front parlor still has its original plaster friezes, ceiling medallion and a marble fireplace. The dining room's oak-paneled walls include a secret panel. The library is stocked with interesting books and games, and classical compositions and Victorian parlor music are piped in. The second floor offers a host of places perfect for relaxation, including a small game room, mini library and a sun porch. Rooms are filled with antiques and unusual pieces such as the Tower Suite's octagonal/post Gothic-style bed. The carriage house suites include a sitting room, refrigerator and either a whirlpool or large, soaking tub.

Historic Interest: The mansion is nestled in Michigan City's historic district and a short distance from other gracious homes. The Barker Mansion, a house museum, is only three blocks away. A lighthouse museum is less than a mile from the inn. Bailly Homestead and Chellberg Farm, a turn-of-the-century Swedish farm, are 15 minutes away.

Innkeeper(s): Mary DuVal. $85-140. MC, VISA, AX. 10 rooms, 5 with PB and 5 suites. Breakfast included in rates. Beds: QD. Antiquing, fishing, golf, National Lakeshore, stables, shopping, hiking, live theater, museums and cross-country skiing nearby.

Publicity: *Midwest Living, Midwest Motorist, Heritage Country, Indianapolis Star, Michigan Living, South Bend Tribune and Chicago Tribune.*

"Beautiful, romantic inn, exceptional hospitality, your breakfasts were fabulous."

Middlebury   A6

Patchwork Quilt Country Inn

11748 CR 2
Middlebury, IN 46540
(219)825-2417 Fax:(219)825-5172
E-mail: rgminn@aol.com
Web: www.patchworkquiltinn.com

Circa 1800. Located in the heart of Indiana's Amish country, this inn offers comfortable lodging and fine food. Some of the recipes are regionally famous, such as the award-winning Buttermilk Pecan Chicken. All guest rooms feature handsome quilts and country decor, and The Loft treats visitors to a whirlpool tub and kitchenette. Ask about the three-hour guided tour of the surrounding Amish area. The alcohol- and smoke-free inn also is host to a quilt and gift shop.

Innkeeper(s): Ray & Rosetta Miller. $70-110. MC, VISA, PC, TC. TAC10. 15 rooms with PB, 2 suites and 2 conference rooms. Breakfast included in rates. Types of meals: Full bkfst, early coffee/tea, lunch, snacks/refreshments and gourmet dinner. Beds: KQT. Cable TV, have TV and no cable in room. Air conditioning. VCR, fax and copier on premises. Handicap access. Weddings, small meetings, family reunions and seminars hosted. Antiquing, fishing, golf, amish buggy rides & tours, live theater, parks, shopping, downhill skiing, cross-country skiing and sporting events nearby.

Tiffany Powell's Bed & Breakfast

523 South Main St
Middlebury, IN 46540-9004
(219)825-5951 Fax:(219)825-2992
E-mail: tiff@npcc.net
Web: www.tiffanypowells.com

Circa 1914. The porch of this B&B is a favorite spot for guests to sit and watch Amish buggies pass by, especially on Saturday nights. The inn features leaded and beveled glass and original oak floors and woodwork. Guest rooms reflect a fresh country decor with bright handmade quilts sewn by Judy's grandmother. Known locally and acknowledged nationally on the Oprah show for her hospitality, the innkeeper offers a full breakfast. Amish Sausage Casserole is a speciality of the house and is served in the dining room. Shipshewana is seven minutes away, and Amish markets and craft shops are nearby.

Innkeeper(s): Judy Powell. $89. PC, TC. 5 rooms, 3 with PB, 1 with FP. Afternoon tea and snacks/refreshments included in rates. Types of meals: Cont plus and early coffee/tea. Beds: QDT. Cable TV, turndown service and ceiling fan in room. Air conditioning. VCR and bicycles on premises. Small meetings and seminars hosted. Antiquing, fishing, golf, live theater, parks, shopping, cross-country skiing, sporting events, tennis and water sports nearby.

Publicity: *South Bend Tribune, Goshen News. and Oprah.*

Mishawaka   A5

The Beiger Mansion Inn

317 Lincoln Way E
Mishawaka, IN 46544-2012
(219)256-0365 (800)437-0131 Fax:(219)259-2622
E-mail: beiger@michiana.org
Web: business.michiana.org/beiger/

Circa 1903. This Neoclassical limestone mansion was built to satisfy Susie Beiger's wish to copy a friend's Newport, R.I., estate. Palatial rooms that were once a gathering place for local society now welcome guests who seek gracious accommodations. On the premises is a restaurant with a full bar and a pub. Notre Dame, St. Mary's and Indiana University in South Bend are nearby.

Innkeeper(s): Ron Montandon & Dennis Slade. $95-125. MC, VISA, AX, DC, CB, DS, PC, TC. TAC10. 6 rooms with PB and 1 suite. Breakfast included in rates. Types of meals: Full bkfst and gourmet dinner. Beds: Q. Cable TV and phone in room. Air conditioning. VCR, fax and copier on premises. Weddings, small meetings, family reunions and seminars hosted. Antiquing, fishing, golf, live theater, parks, sporting events and tennis nearby.

Publicity: *Tribune.*

"Can't wait until we return to Mishawaka to stay with you again!"

New Albany   K6

Honeymoon Mansion B&B & Wedding Chapel

1014 E Main St
New Albany, IN 47150-5843
(812)945-0312 (800)759-7270
E-mail: wdshoneymoon@earthlink.net

Circa 1850. The innkeepers at Honeymoon Mansion can provide guests with the flowers, wedding chapel and honeymoon suite. All you need to bring is a bride or groom. An ordained minister is on the premises and guests can marry or renew their vows in the inn's Victorian wedding chapel. However, one need not be a newlywed to enjoy this bed & breakfast. Canopy beds, stained-glass windows and heart-shaped rugs are a few of the romantic touches. Several suites include marble Jacuzzis flanked on four sides with eight-foot-high marble columns, creating a dramatic and elegant effect. The home itself, a pre-Civil War Italianate-style home listed in the state and national historic registers, boasts many fine period features. Gingerbread trim, intricate molding and a grand staircase add to the Victorian ambiance. Guests are treated to an all-you-can-eat country breakfast with items such as homemade breads, biscuits and gravy, eggs, sausage and potatoes.

Innkeeper(s): Bill & Donna Stepp. $90-170. MC, VISA, PC, TC. TAC10. 6 suites, 1 with FP and 2 conference rooms. Breakfast included in rates. Types of meals: Full bkfst. Beds: Q. Cable TV, ceiling fan and VCR in room. Air conditioning. Handicap access. Weddings, small meetings, family reunions and seminars hosted. Amusement parks, antiquing, fishing, three state parks, three caves, Culbertson Mansion, riverboat casino, live theater, parks, shopping, downhill skiing, cross-country skiing, sporting events and water sports nearby.
Publicity: *Courier-Journal, Evening News, Tribune.* and *WHAS TV.*

Rockville   G3

Owl Nest B&B

303 Howard Ave
Rockville, IN 47872
(765)569-1803

Circa 1889. High ceilings, walnut woodwork, a stately staircase and an original chandelier are charming features of this lovely Queen Anne home just three blocks from Historic Rockville Town Square in Parke County, Ind., the "covered bridge capital of the world." The inn has a wraparound porch, and a 100-foot tulip tree shades the yard. The guest bedrooms are decorated

with everything from vintage clothes to teddy bears to quilts. After a breakfast at the inn, guests pay visit the 32 historic covered bridges nearby or go to parks, museums, golf courses, art galleries and antique shops.

Innkeeper(s): Richard & Tulie Ann Jadzak. $95-105. PC, TC. 4 rooms. Breakfast, afternoon tea and snacks/refreshments included in rates. Types of meals: Gourmet bkfst and early coffee/tea. Beds: QT. Turndown service and ceiling fan in room. Air conditioning. Bicycles, outdoor swing and chairs on premises. Small meetings and family reunions hosted. Antiquing, fishing, golf, live theater, parks, shopping, tennis and water sports nearby.

Suits Us B&B

514 N College St
Rockville, IN 47872-1511
(765)569-5660 (888)478-4878
E-mail: liannaw@wico.net

Circa 1883. Sixty miles west of Indianapolis is this stately Colonial Revival inn, where Woodrow Wilson, Annie Oakley and James Witcomb Riley were once guests of the Strause Family. The inn offers video library and bicycles. There are 32 covered bridges to visit in the small, surrounding county. Turkey Run State Park is nearby. The Ernie Pyle State Historic Site, Raccoon State Recreation Area and four golf courses are within easy driving distance.
Historic Interest: There are 32 covered bridges in the area.

Innkeeper(s): Andy & Lianna Willhite. $60-150. TC. 4 rooms with PB and 1 suite. Breakfast included in rates. Types of meals: Full bkfst and early coffee/tea. Beds: KQD. Cable TV, ceiling fan and VCR in room. Air conditioning. Bicycles and movie library on premises. Antiquing, fishing, golf, parks, shopping and water sports nearby.
Publicity: *Touring America and Traces Historic Magazine.*

South Bend   A5

English Rose Inn

116 S Taylor St
South Bend, IN 46601
(219)289-2114 Fax:(219)287-1311
E-mail: info@englishroseinn.com
Web: www.englishroseinn.com

Circa 1892. A stunning Queen Anne Victorian, the English Rose is indeed adorned in a fanciful light pink hue. A prominent local doctor built the turn-of-the-20th-century home. The innkeeper has filled the inn with antiques and period-style decorations. The inviting guest rooms include quilt-topped beds with coordinating linens and special touches, such as a delicate tea set. Guests can enjoy the multi-course breakfast in the privacy of their room. The inn is close to Notre Dame, as well as historic sites such as Tippecanoe Place and the Copshalom Home.
Historic Interest: Tippecanoe Place, Copshalom Home.

Innkeeper(s): Barry & Susan Kessler. $75-155. MC, VISA, PC, TC. 5 rooms with PB. Breakfast and snacks/refreshments included in rates. Types of meals: Full bkfst. Beds: QDT. Cable TV in room. Central air. VCR, fax and library on premises. Small meetings, family reunions and seminars hosted. Sign spoken. Antiquing, art galleries, canoeing/kayaking, fishing, golf, hiking, live theater, museums, parks, shopping, sporting events, tennis and wineries nearby.

Oliver Inn

630 W Washington St
South Bend, IN 46601-1444
(219)232-4545 (888)697-4466 Fax:(219)288-9788
E-mail: oliver@michiana.org
Web: www.oliverinn.com

Circa 1886. This stately Queen Anne Victorian sits amid 30 towering maples and was once home to Josephine Oliver Ford, daughter of James Oliver, of chilled plow fame. Located in South Bend's historic district, this inn offers a comfortable library and nine inviting guest rooms, some

with built-in fireplaces or double Jacuzzis. The inn is within walking distance of downtown and is next door to the Tippecanoe Restaurant near the Studebaker Mansion.

Innkeeper(s): Richard & Venera Monahan. $95-165. MC, VISA, AX, DS, PC, TC. TAC10. 9 rooms, 7 with PB, 2 with FP, 3 suites and 1 conference room. Breakfast and snacks/refreshments included in rates. Types of meals: Full bkfst and early coffee/tea. Beds: KQ. Cable TV, phone, ceiling fan and several with double whirlpool tubs in room. Air conditioning. Fax and baby Grand with computer disk system on premises. Weddings, small meetings, family reunions and seminars hosted. Antiquing, canoeing/kayaking, fishing, fine dining, Amish country and Notre Dame, live theater, museums, parks, shopping, cross-country skiing, sporting events and water sports nearby.

Valparaiso   B3

The Inn at Aberdeen

3158 South SR 2
Valparaiso, IN 46385
(219)465-3753 Fax:(219)465-9227
E-mail: inn@innataberdeen.com

Circa 1890. An old stone wall borders this inn, once a dairy farm, horse farm and then hunting lodge. Recently renovated and expanded, this Victorian farmhouse is on more than an acre. An elegant getaway, there's a solarium, library, dining room and parlor for relaxing. The inn offers traditional Queen Anne furnishings in the guest rooms. The Timberlake Suites include fireplaces, two-person Jacuzzi tubs and balconies. The Aberdeen Suite includes a living room and fireplace, while the Alloway Suite offers a living room, kitchenette and a balcony. A conference center on the property is popu-  lar for executive meetings and special events, and there is a picturesque gazebo overlooking the inn's beautifully landscaped lawns and English gardens. Golf packages and mystery weekends have received enthusiastic response from guests. There is a golf course, spa and microbrewery adjacent to the inn.

Innkeeper(s): Bill Simon. $97-169. MC, VISA, AX, DC, CB, DS, TC. 11 suites, 10 with FP and 1 conference room. Breakfast and snacks/refreshments included in rates. Types of meals: Gourmet bkfst and early coffee/tea. Beds: KQ. Cable TV, phone, ceiling fan and VCR in room. Air conditioning. Fax, copier, swimming, bicycles, tennis, library, snack bar and gazebo on premises. Handicap access. Weddings, small meetings, family reunions and seminars hosted. Antiquing, fishing, golf, live theater, parks, shopping, downhill skiing, cross-country skiing, sporting events, tennis and water sports nearby.

Publicity: *Midwest Living, Chicago Magazine, Chicago Tribune and Country Inns.*

"Every time we have the good fortune to spend an evening here, it is like a perfect fairy tale, transforming us into King and Queen."

Wabash   D6

Lamp-Post Inn B&B

261 W Hill St
Wabash, IN 46992
(219)563-3094
E-mail: lamppostbb@comteck.com

Circa 1896. Built in Romanesque style, this home features many original features, including handsome oak woodwork. The home is comfortably decorated and includes antiques. The Pink Room, which has a private bath, also has a turret window and four-poster bed. One of the shared bathrooms has a clawfoot tub. Belgian waffles, topped with fruit, are a specialty of the house.

Innkeeper(s): Janet L. Conner. $50-70. MC, VISA, PC, TC. 4 rooms, 1 with PB. Breakfast included in rates. Types of meals: Full bkfst and early coffee/tea. Beds: QDT. Cable TV, phone, turndown service and ceiling fan in room. Air conditioning. VCR and piano on premises. Small meetings hosted. Antiquing, fishing, golf, live theater, parks, shopping, sporting events, tennis and water sports nearby.

Iowa

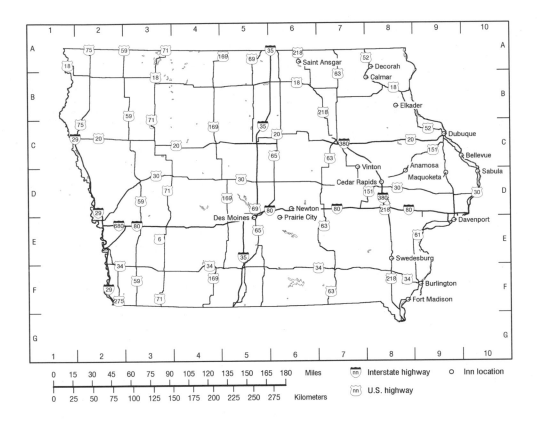

Map legend:
- (nn) Interstate highway
- (nn) U.S. highway
- O Inn location

Miles: 0 15 30 45 60 75 90 105 120 135 150 165 180

Kilometers: 0 25 50 75 100 125 150 175 200 225 250 275

Map labels: Saint Ansgar, Decorah, Calmar, Elkader, Dubuque, Bellevue, Sabula, Vinton, Anamosa, Maquoketa, Cedar Rapids, Newton, Prairie City, Des Moines, Swedesburg, Davenport, Burlington, Fort Madison

Anamosa   D8

The Shaw House

509 S Oak St
Anamosa, IA 52205-1537
(319)462-4485
E-mail: mckeanfamily@msn.com

Circa 1872. Framed by enormous old oak trees, this three-story Italianate mansion was built in the style of a Maine sea captain's house. Bordered by sweeping lawns and situated on a hillside on 45 acres, the inn provides views of graceful pasture-land from the front porch swing and the tower. Polished oak, walnut and pine floors highlight the carved woodwork and antique furnishings. Guests can enjoy a short walk to downtown.

Innkeeper(s): Constance & Andy McKean. $70-90. 4 rooms, 2 with PB, 1 with FP, 1 suite and 1 conference room. Breakfast included in rates. Types of meals: Full bkfst, early coffee/tea and snacks/refreshments. Beds: QDT. TV and phone in room. Air conditioning. Child care on premises. Weddings, small meetings, family reunions and seminars hosted. Antiquing, canoeing/kayaking, fishing, live theater, shopping, downhill skiing, cross-country skiing and sporting events nearby.

Publicity: *Cedar Rapids Gazette* and *Anamosa Journal-Eureka.*

"The views were fantastic as was the hospitality."

Bellevue C9

Mont Rest

300 Spring St
Bellevue, IA 52031-1125
(319)872-4220 (800)872-4220 Fax:(319)872-5094
E-mail: innkeeper@montrest.com
Web: www.montrest.com

Circa 1893. Mont Rest was built by Seth Lewellyn Baker, developer of the Chicago suburb of Glen Ellyn. A compulsive gambler, he played high-stakes poker in the turret. Within three years he lost his home. Because the architecture is an unusual mix of styles, the owners and the Iowa Historical Society labeled it Gothic Steamboat Revival. A clearly Victorian atmosphere prevails inside. Guests will find homemade cookies most everywhere in the house.

Innkeeper(s): Christine Snyder. $69-175. MC, VISA, PC, TC. 11 rooms with PB and 2 conference rooms. Breakfast and snacks/refreshments included in rates. Types of meals: Gourmet bkfst, early coffee/tea, picnic lunch, afternoon tea, gourmet dinner and room service. Beds: KD. Cable TV, phone, turndown service, ceiling fan and most with Jacuzzi in room. Air conditioning. VCR, fax, copier, spa, sauna, bicycles and child care on premises. Weddings, small meetings, family reunions and seminars hosted. Antiquing, fishing, live theater, parks, shopping, downhill skiing, cross-country skiing, sporting events and water sports nearby.

Publicity: *Quad City Times, The Register, Mature Outlook and Ladies Home Journal.*

Bentonsport F8

Mason House Inn of Bentonsport

21982 Hawk Dr
Bentonsport, IA 52565
(319)592-3133 (800)592-3133
E-mail: mhibprt@netins.net

Circa 1846. A Murphy-style copper bathtub folds down out of the wall at this unusual inn built by Mormon craftsmen, who stayed in Bentonsport for one year on their trek to Utah. More than half of the furniture is original to the home, including a nine-foot walnut head-board and a nine-foot mirror. This is the only operating pre-Civil War steamboat inn in Iowa. Guests can imagine the days  when steamboats made their way up and down the Des Moines River, while taking in the scenery. A full breakfast is served, but if guests crave a mid-day snack, each room is equipped with its own stocked cookie jar.

Innkeeper(s): Chuck & Joy Hanson. $64-84. MC, VISA, PC, TC. TAC10. 8 rooms with PB and 1 conference room. Breakfast included in rates. Types of meals: Full bkfst, early coffee/tea and lunch. Beds: KQD. Filled cookie jar and fireplace in room. Air conditioning. Handicap access. Weddings, small meetings, family reunions and seminars hosted. Antiquing, shopping and cross-country skiing nearby.

Publicity: *Des Moines Register, Decatur Herald & Review, AAA Home & Away and Country Magazine.*

"The attention to detail was fantastic, food was wonderful and the setting was fascinating."

Burlington F9

Mississippi Manor

809 N 4th St
Burlington, IA 52601-5008
(319)753-2218
Web: www.mississippimanor.com

Circa 1877. Located just four blocks from the Mississippi River in the National Landmark District, this Victorian Italianate manor house was built by a lumber baron who incorporated European craftsmanship into the fine architectural detailing.  Inside, the inn is elegantly decorated and includes four guest rooms with private baths. Two spacious suites offer wood burning fireplaces. A continental breakfast is included in the rates. The inn is close to downtown and the Mississippi River.

Innkeeper(s): Linda Clark. $75-125. MC, VISA, PC. TAC10. 4 rooms with PB, 2 with FP. Breakfast included in rates. Types of meals: Cont plus. Beds: QT. Cable TV, phone and ceiling fan in room. Air conditioning. VCR on premises. Weddings, small meetings, family reunions and seminars hosted. Antiquing, fishing, golf, magnificent park system and arboretum, parks, shopping, tennis and water sports nearby.

Publicity: *Hawkeye.*

Schramm House B&B

616 Columbia St
Burlington, IA 52601
(800)683-7117 Fax:(319)754-0373
E-mail: visit@schramm.com

Circa 1866. "Colossal" would be an excellent word to describe this Queen Anne Victorian. The home is an impressive site in this Burlington historic district. The exterior is brick on the first story with clapboard on the second, and a third-story tower is one of the architectural highlights. Inside, the parquet floors and woodwork have been restored to their 19th-century grandeur. The home was built just after the Civil War by a local department store owner. Additions were made in the 1880s. Eventually, the home was converted into apartments, so the innkeepers took on quite a task refurbishing the place back to its original state. The Victorian is decorated with the innkeepers collection of antiques. One particularly appealing guest room includes an exposed brick wall and tin ceiling. Breakfast might begin with a baked pear topped with toasted almonds and a raspberry sauce. From there, freshly baked muffins arrive, followed by an entree, perhaps a frittata or French toast. All courses are served with fine china and crystal. The home is just six  blocks from the Mississippi, and don't pass up a walk down the historic Snake Alley.

Innkeeper(s): Sandy & Bruce Morrison. $85-125. MC, VISA, AX, DC, DS, PC, TC. TAC10. 4 rooms with PB. Breakfast included in rates. Types of meals: Full bkfst and early coffee/tea. Beds: Q. Turndown service, ceiling fan, robes and hair dryers in room. VCR, fax and library on premises. Weddings and small meetings hosted. Antiquing, fishing, golf, parks, shopping and tennis nearby.

Publicity: *Hawk Eye.*

Calmar B8

Calmar Guesthouse

103 W North St
Calmar, IA 52132-7605
(563)562-3851
E-mail: lbkruse@salamander.com

Circa 1890. This beautifully restored Victorian home was built by John B. Kay, a lawyer and poet. Stained-glass windows, carved moldings, an oak-and-walnut staircase and gleaming woodwork highlight the gracious interior. A grandfather clock ticks in the living room. In the foyer, a friendship yellow rose is incorporated into the stained-glass window pane. Breakfast is served in the formal dining room. The Laura Ingalls Wilder Museum is nearby in Burr Oak. The Bily Brothers Clock Museum, Smallest Church, Luther College and Norwegian Museum are located nearby.

Historic Interest: The Norwegian Museum is 10 minutes away. The Smallest Church, Bily Brothers Clocks Museum and Luther College are nearby.

Innkeeper(s): Lucille Kruse. $59-65. MC, VISA, PC, TC. Breakfast included in rates. Types of meals: Full bkfst and early coffee/tea. Beds: Q. Cable TV in room. Air conditioning. VCR, bicycles and library on premises. Small meetings hosted. Antiquing, fishing, live theater, parks, shopping, downhill skiing, cross-country skiing, sporting events and water sports nearby.

Publicity: *Iowa Farmer Today, Calmar Courier, Minneapolis Star-Tribune, Home and Away* and *Iowan*.

"What a delight it was to stay here. No one could have made our stay more welcome or enjoyable."

Cedar Rapids D8

Belmont Hill Victorian B&B

1525 Cherokee Dr NW
Cedar Rapids, IA 52405
(319)366-1343
E-mail: belmonthil@aol.com
Web: www.belmonthill.com

Circa 1882. Built by Cedar Rapids brickyard owner, Philip Wolff, both buildings here were constructed with three courses of brick, resulting in 14-inch-thick walls. The gracious Italianate architecture along with a secluded location at the edge of a woodland, creates a magical setting. English gardens surround the old criss-cross wooden doors to the pristinely renovated Carriage House. The Belmont Suite, located in the upper floor, offers a walnut bed handcrafted in the Amanas along with antiques and luxurious linens. Breakfast is provided in the dining room of the Main House.

Innkeeper(s): Ken and Shelley Sullens. $99-152. MC, VISA, PC. 3 rooms with PB and 1 suite. Breakfast included in rates. Types of meals: Gourmet bkfst, cont plus, early coffee/tea, afternoon tea and snacks/refreshments. Beds: KQ. TV, turndown service and VCR in room. Air conditioning. Perennial gardens on premises. Handicap access. Small meetings hosted. Antiquing, fishing, golf, live theater, parks, shopping, sporting events, tennis and water sports nearby.

Publicity: *Cedar Rapids Gazette* and *KGAN News*.

"What a place and what a setting."

Davenport E9

Fulton's Landing Guest House

1206 E River Dr
Davenport, IA 52803-5742
(563)322-4069 Fax:(563)322-8186
Web: www.fultonslanding.com

Circa 1871. Enjoy views of the Mississippi River from the porches of this stone, Italianate home, which is listed in the National Register. The guest rooms are decorated with antiques, including ceiling fans. After enjoying the morning meal, guests have a variety of activities to choose. Riverboat gambling, shopping and downtown Davenport all are nearby.

Innkeeper(s): Pat & Bill Schmidt. $60-125. MC, VISA, AX. 5 rooms with PB and 1 suite. Breakfast included in rates. Types of meals: Gourmet bkfst. Beds: Q. Cable TV, phone and ceiling fan in room. Air conditioning. Fax, copier and bicycles on premises. Antiquing, fishing, live theater, parks, shopping, cross-country skiing, sporting events and water sports nearby.

"I have never felt more pampered and cared for staying away from home."

Decorah A8

Elmhurst Cottage

3618 - 258th Ave
Decorah, IA 52101
(319)735-5310 (888)413-5600
E-mail: elmcottage@aol.com

Circa 1885. Located on 80 acres, this family cottage and B&B, provides simple accommodations in a peaceful farm setting. Outdoor activities such as volleyball, horseshoes, tetherball and badminton are available on the property. Area attractions include the Laura Ingalls-Wilder Museum, Norwegian-American Museum, local caves and Amish community tours and shops. Additional rental options are available, including suite, two bedroom apartment and cottage.

Innkeeper(s): Bobbi Underbakke. $34-90. MC, VISA, DS, PC. 9 rooms. Breakfast included in rates. Types of meals: Full bkfst, country bkfst, lunch, picnic lunch, afternoon tea, snacks/refreshments, dinner and room service. Beds: KQDT. TV, VCR, alarm clock and wall clock in room. Air conditioning. Handicap access. Weddings, small meetings, family reunions and seminars hosted. Antiquing, canoeing/kayaking, fishing, golf, live theater, parks, shopping, downhill skiing, sporting events and water sports nearby.

Pets allowed: deposit required, restricted areas.

Des Moines D5

Butler House on Grand

4507 Grand Ave
Des Moines, IA 50312
(515)255-4096
E-mail: Clark@butlerhouseongrand.com
Web: www.butlerhouseongrand.com

Circa 1923. Constructed entirely from steel and concrete with an all-brick veneer, this American Tudor home has withstood change of ownership and renovations. This bed & breakfast proudly showcases the work of area designers and artists throughout its tasteful decor. Both floors offer a common area with refrigerator and snack bar. Some of the suites and guest bedrooms feature spa tubs, fireplaces and VCRs. A fruit starter is served first, then breads, an egg dish and bacon or sausages for a full breakfast. Prairie flowers and other indigenous plants grace the landscaped grounds.

Historic Interest: Salisbury House (1/2 mile).

Innkeeper(s): Clark Smith & Lauren Kernan Smith. $90-160. MC, VISA, AX, DS, PC. 7 rooms. Breakfast and snacks/refreshments included in rates. Types of meals: Gourmet bkfst, veg bkfst and early coffee/tea. Beds: QD. Cable TV, phone, turndown service, VCR, two suites with spa tubs, four with ceiling fans, two with fireplaces and four with VCR in room. Air conditioning. Fax, copier, library, refrigerator, snack bar and hot tub on premises. Small meetings and family reunions hosted. Amusement parks, antiquing, art galleries, bicycling, fishing, golf, hiking, horseback riding, live theater, museums, parks, shopping, tennis and wineries nearby.

Publicity: *Des Moines Register, Better Homes & Gardens, Intro Magazine and BH&G TV.*

Dubuque C9

The Mandolin Inn

199 Loras Blvd
Dubuque, IA 52001-4857
(563)556-0069 (800)524-7996 Fax:(563)556-0587
E-mail: innkeeper@mandolininn.com
Web: www.mandolininn.com

Circa 1908. This handicapped accessible three-story brick Edwardian with Queen Anne wraparound veranda boasts a mosaic-tiled porch floor. Inside are in-laid mahogany and rosewood floors, bay windows and a turret that starts in the parlor and ascends to the second-floor Holly Marie Room, decorated in a wedding motif. This room features a seven-piece French  Walnut bedroom suite and a crystal chandelier. A gourmet breakfast is served in the dining room with a fantasy forest mural from the turn-of-the-century. There is an herb garden outside the kitchen. A church is across the street, and riverboat gambling is 12 blocks away.

Innkeeper(s): Amy Boynton. $85-150. MC, VISA, AX, DS, PC, TC. 8 rooms, 6 with PB and 2 conference rooms. Breakfast included in rates. Types of meals: Gourmet bkfst and early coffee/tea. Beds: KQ. Cable TV in room. Central air. Fax on premises. Weddings, small meetings, family reunions and seminars hosted. Antiquing, live theater, parks, shopping, downhill skiing, cross-country skiing, sporting events and water sports nearby.

"From the moment we entered the Mandolin, we felt at home. I know we'll be back."

The Richards House

1492 Locust St
Dubuque, IA 52001-4714
(563)557-1492

Circa 1883. Owner David Stuart estimates that it will take several years to remove the concrete-based brown paint applied by a bridge painter in the '60s to cover the 7,000-square-foot, Stick-style Victorian house. The interior, however, only needed a tad of polish. The varnished cherry and bird's-eye

maple woodwork is set aglow under electrified gaslights. Ninety stained-glass windows, eight pocket doors with stained glass and a magnificent entryway reward those who pass through.

Historic Interest: Five historic districts are in Dubuque.

Innkeeper(s): Michelle A. Delaney. $45-105. MC, VISA, AX, DC, CB, DS, TC. 7 rooms, 4 with PB, 4 with FP, 1 suite and 1 conference room. Breakfast included in rates. Types of meals: Full bkfst, early coffee/tea, afternoon tea and snacks/refreshments. Beds: Q. Cable TV, phone, VCR and vCR in room. Fax on premises. Weddings, small meetings and family reunions hosted. Antiquing, fishing, live theater, parks, shopping, downhill skiing, cross-country skiing and water sports nearby.

Pets Allowed.

Publicity: *Collectors Journal and Telegraph Herald.*

"Although the guide at the door had warned us that the interior was incredible, we were still flabbergasted when we stepped into the foyer of this house."

Elkader B8

Elkader Bed & Breakfast

401 1st St NW
Elkader, IA 52043
(563)245-1500 (800)944-4860
E-mail: bduwe@alpinecon.net

Circa 1892. In a quiet historical neighborhood, this Queen Anne Victorian home sits proudly on a corner. Appreciate the original stained-glass windows, incredible woodwork and pristine yellow pine floors. The large wraparound porch is ideal for relaxing and gazing at the garden. Air-conditioned guest bedrooms and suites feature cable TV, bathrobes and ice water. A continental breakfast is served weekdays. Enjoy a full, home-cooked meal on the weekends. Relax by the fireplace with a good book, stroll downtown and explore the two riverwalks, or take a boat cruise on the Mississippi River.

Historic Interest: Nine National Register Historic sites in walking distance.

Innkeeper(s): Barb Duwe. $55-80. MC, VISA, AX, DS, PC, TC. 5 rooms, 3 with PB and 2 suites. Breakfast and snacks/refreshments included in rates. Types of meals: Full bkfst and cont. Beds: Q. Cable TV, phone, ceiling fan and suites with coffeemaker in room. Central air. VCR on premises. Weddings, small meetings and family reunions hosted. Antiquing, bicycling, canoeing/kayaking, fishing and parks nearby.

Fort Madison F8

Kingsley Inn

707 Avenue H (Hwy 61)
Fort Madison, IA 52627
(319)372-7074 (800)441-2327 Fax:(319)372-7096
E-mail: kingsley@interl.net
Web: www.kingsleyinn.com

Circa 1858. Overlooking the Mississippi River, this century-old inn is located in downtown Fort Madison. Though furnished with antiques, all 14 rooms offer modern amenities and private baths (some with whirlpools) as well as river views. A two-bedroom, two-bath suite also is available. There is a restaurant, Alphas on the Riverfront, and a gift shop on the premises.

Historic Interest: A museum and historic fort are nearby. Historic Nauvoo, Ill., known as the "Williamsburg of the Midwest," is only 11 miles from the inn.

Innkeeper(s): Alida Willis. $75-135. MC, VISA, AX, DC, DS. TAC10. 14 rooms with PB, 1 suite and 1 conference room. Breakfast included in rates. Types of meals: Full bkfst and cont plus. Beds: KQD. Cable TV and phone in room. Air conditioning. VCR, fax, elevator and off-street parking on premises. Handicap access. Weddings, small meetings, family reunions and seminars hosted. Antiquing, fishing, casino, historic sites including Nauvoo, IL and shopping nearby.

Publicity: *Midwest Living.*

Maquoketa   D9

Squiers Manor B&B

418 W Pleasant St
Maquoketa, IA 52060-2847
(319)652-6961
E-mail: innkeeper@squiersmanor.com
Web: www.squiersmanor.com

Circa 1882. Innkeepers Virl and Kathy Banowetz are ace antique dealers, who along with owning one of the Midwest's largest antique shops, have refurbished this elegant, Queen Anne Victorian. The inn is furnished with period antiques that are beyond compare. Guest rooms boast museum-quality pieces such as a Victorian brass bed with lace curtain wings and inlaid mother-of-pearl or an antique mahogany bed with carved birds and flowers. Six guest rooms include whirlpool tubs, and one includes a unique Swiss shower. The innkeepers restored the home's original woodwork, shuttered-windows, fireplaces, gas and electric chandeliers and stained- and engraved-glass windows back to their former glory. They also recently renovated the mansion's attic ballroom into two luxurious suites. The Loft, which is made up of three levels, features pine and wicker furnishings, a sitting room and gas-burning wood stove. On the second level, there is a large Jacuzzi, on the third, an antique queen-size bed. The huge Ballroom Suite boasts 24-foot ceilings, oak and pine antiques, gas-burning wood stove and a Jacuzzi snuggled beside a dormer window. Suite guests enjoy breakfast delivered to their rooms. Other guests feast on an array of mouth-watering treats, such as home-baked breads, seafood quiche and fresh fruits. Evening desserts are served by candlelight.

Historic Interest: The area has 70 sites listed in the National Register.

Innkeeper(s): Virl & Kathy Banowetz. $80-195. MC, VISA, AX, DS. 8 rooms with PB and 3 suites. Breakfast included in rates. Types of meals: Gourmet bkfst. Beds: KQT. Small meetings hosted. Antiquing, fishing, parks, shopping, downhill skiing, cross-country skiing and water sports nearby.

Publicity: *Des Moines Register Datebook and Daily Herald.*

"We couldn't have asked for a more perfect place to spend our honeymoon. The service was excellent and so was the food! It was an exciting experience that we will never forget!"

Newton   D6

La Corsette Maison Inn

629 1st Ave E
Newton, IA 50208-3305
(641)792-6833

Circa 1909. This unusual Mission-style building has an arts-and-crafts interior. All the woodwork is of quarter-sawn oak, and the dining room furniture was designed by Limbert. Stained and beveled glass is found throughout. French bed-chambers feature reproduction and antique furnishings. One

of the suites includes a fireplace and double whirlpool tub. The inn's restaurant has received four-and-one-half stars from the Des Moines Register's Grumpy Gourmet. The mansion also has three working wood-burning fireplaces.

Historic Interest: Jasper County Courthouse (7 blocks), Saint Stevens Episcopal Church (3 blocks).

Innkeeper(s): Kay Owen. $75-190. MC, VISA, AX. TAC10. 7 rooms with PB, 3 with FP and 2 suites. Breakfast included in rates. Types of meals: Full bkfst, picnic lunch and gourmet dinner. AP. Beds: KQD. Fax on premises. Antiquing, fishing, downhill skiing and cross-country skiing nearby.

Pets allowed: by prior arrangements.

Publicity: *Cedar Rapids Gazette, American Airlines, Innsider, Midwest Living, AAA Home and Away, Des Moines Register, Bon Appetit, Conde Nast Traveler and Chicago Sun Times.*

"We shall return. You and your house are an inspiration."

Prairie City   E6

The Country Connection B&B

9737 West 93rd St S
Prairie City, IA 50579
(515)994-2023

Circa 1910. This sixth generation Four Square home is on three acres in a friendly working farm community. Much of the home's original walnut woodwork remains, and there are many original furnishings, as well. Grandma's Room has a walnut wardrobe and is accessorized with antique linens, a pair of high button shoes, a sleigh and handmade dolls. Coming to this homestay is very much as if you were staying at Grandma's house, complete with cookie jar, home-canned fruit, home-baked breads, sour-

dough pancakes and turkey or sausage and many other delicious foods. In honor of your adulthood, Grandma pulls out beautiful pieces of antique china and lights candles for you at breakfast. Children of all ages are welcome. (Ask Grandpa about making some home made ice cream before you go to bed.) There's a train room in the house or enjoy the lawn swing. Nearby are the Neal Smith National Wildlife Refuge, Lake Red Rock, Pella Tulip Time, Trainland USA and many antique stores.

Historic Interest: Pella (15 miles), Historic Valley Junction (25 miles), Newton Museum.

Innkeeper(s): Jim & Alice Foreman. $50-65. MC, VISA, PC, TC. 2 rooms. Breakfast and snacks/refreshments included in rates. Types of meals: Country bkfst. AP. Beds: Q. TV and ceiling fan in room. Central air. VCR and library on premises. Amusement parks, antiquing, art galleries, bicycling, hiking, Neal Smith National Wildlife Refuge, live theater, museums, parks, shopping, sporting events, tennis and water sports nearby.

Sabula D10

Castle B&B

616 River St
Sabula, IA 52070
(319)687-2714

Circa 1898. This home's location offers views of the Mississippi River from its location along the riverbank. Built more than a century ago, the home has a cream, brick exterior. Guests enjoy the carved staircase and views of the river from their rooms. Take your early morning coffee out to the screened in wrap-around porch. A full breakfast with eggs or waffles is served.
Historic Interest: Potters Mill (20 miles), Pulpord Opera House Antique Mall (3 miles), Crystal Cave (20 miles).

Innkeeper(s): Joan W. Thompson. $50-70. PC, TC. 3 rooms. Breakfast included in rates. Types of meals: Full bkfst, country bkfst, early coffee/tea and snacks/refreshments. Beds: KQ. Cable TV, phone and VCR in room. Air conditioning. Weddings, small meetings, family reunions and seminars hosted. Antiquing, bicycling, fishing, hiking, horseback riding, parks, shopping, downhill skiing and cross-country skiing nearby.

Pets Allowed.

Publicity: *The Iowan Magazine.*

Saint Ansgar A6

Blue Belle Inn B&B

PO Box 205, 513 W 4th St
Saint Ansgar, IA 50472-0205
(641)713-3113 (877)713-3113
E-mail: sherrie@bluebelleinn.com
Web: www.bluebelleinn.com

Circa 1896. This home was purchased from a Knoxville, Tenn., mail-order house. It's difficult to believe that stunning features, such as a tin ceiling, stained-glass windows, intricate woodwork and pocket doors could have come via the mail, but these original items are still here for guests to admire. Rooms are named after books special to the innkeeper. Four of the rooms include a whirlpool tub for two, and the Never Neverland room has a clawfoot tub. Other rooms  offer a skylight, fireplace or perhaps a white iron bed. During the Christmas season, every room has its own decorated tree. The innkeeper hosts a variety of themed luncheons, dinners and events, such as the April in Paris cooking workshop, Mother's Day brunches, the "Some Enchanted Evening" dinner, Murder Mysteries, Ladies nights, Writer's Retreats, quilting seminars and horse-drawn sleigh rides.

Innkeeper(s): Sherrie Hansen. $70-150. MC, VISA, AX, DS, PC, TC. TAC10. 6 rooms, 5 with PB, 2 with FP, 2 suites and 2 conference rooms. Breakfast included in rates. Types of meals: Gourmet bkfst, cont plus, cont, early coffee/tea, gourmet lunch, afternoon tea, snacks/refreshments, gourmet dinner and room service. Beds: KQT. TV, VCR and jacuzzi for two in room. Air conditioning. Fax, library, kitchenette, Internet access, piano, treadmill and movies on premises. Weddings, small meetings, family reunions and seminars hosted. German spoken. Antiquing, canoeing/kayaking, fishing, golf, hunting, parks, shopping and water sports nearby.

Publicity: *Minneapolis Star Tribune, Post-Bulletin, Midwest Living, Country, AAA Home & Away, Des Moines Register, Country Home, Iowan Magazine and American Patchwork and Quilting.*

Swedesburg E8

Carlson House Bed & Breakfast

105 Park Ave
Swedesburg, IA 52652
(319)254-2451 (888)841-7199 Fax:(319)254-8809

Circa 1918. A large front veranda highlights the exterior of this National Register home, an excellent example of American Four Square design. Guests can choose from among three guest rooms, one of which includes a whirlpool tub. There's also a hot tub for all guests to use on the inn's deck. As the name Swedesburg suggests the country village is awash in Swedish heritage. The innkeepers provide Scandinavian specialties, such as Swedish pancakes with lingonberries during the morning meal. After breakfast, guests can enjoy a trek through the town's historic Swedish district.

Innkeeper(s): Ned & Ruth Ratekin. $60. PC, TC. 3 rooms with PB. Types of meals: Gourmet bkfst, veg bkfst, early coffee/tea and snacks/refreshments. Beds: QT. TV, phone, turndown service and VCR in room. Central air. Fax, copier and spa on premises. Family reunions hosted. Antiquing, museums, parks and shopping nearby.

Vinton C7

Lion & The Lamb B&B

913 2nd Ave
Vinton, IA 52349-1729
(319)472-5086 (888)390-5262 Fax:(319)472-5086
E-mail: lionlamb@lionlamb.com
Web: www.lionlamb.com

Circa 1892. This Queen Anne Victorian, a true "Painted Lady," boasts a stunning exterior with intricate chimneys, gingerbread trim, gables and turrets. The home still maintains its original pocket doors and parquet flooring, and antiques add to the nostalgic flavor. One room boasts a 150-year-old bedroom set. Breakfasts, as any meal in such fine a house should, are served on china. Succulent French toast topped with powdered sugar and a rich strawberry sauce is a specialty. In the evenings, desserts are served.

Innkeeper(s): Richard & Rachel Waterbury. $75-105. MC, VISA, AX, DS, PC, TC. TAC10. 5 rooms, 2 with PB, 2 with FP. Breakfast included in rates. Types of meals: Full bkfst and early coffee/tea. Beds: KQ. TV and ceiling fan in room. Air conditioning. VCR, fax and bicycles on premises. Weddings, small meetings, family reunions and seminars hosted. Antiquing, fishing, golf, live theater, parks, shopping, cross-country skiing, tennis and water sports nearby.

Publicity: *Cedar Valley Times, Waterloo Courier, Cedar Rapids Gazette. and KWWL-Channel 7 Neighborhood News.*

"It is a magical place!"

Kansas

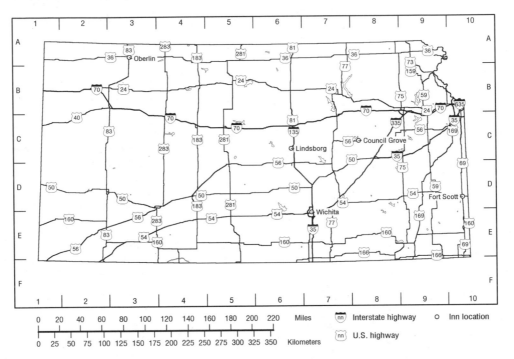

| Miles | 0 20 40 60 80 100 120 140 160 180 200 220 | Interstate highway | Inn location |
| Kilometers | 0 25 50 75 100 125 150 175 200 225 250 275 300 325 350 | U.S. highway | |

Baxter Springs   E10

Little Brick Inn

1101 Military Ave
Baxter Springs, KS 66713
(316)856-5646 (877)223-3466 Fax:(316)856-5646
E-mail: cafeontheroute@yahoo.com

Circa 1860. Fashioned entirely of brick, this historic building
conjures up images of the Old West. In fact, this inn once served
as the Baxter Bank building and was robbed by Jesse James in
1876. The restored inn includes its original hardwood floors and
transoms above the doors. Rooms are decorated with antiques.
There is a kitchen available for guest use. Guests are treated to a
full, country breakfast in an upstairs dining room. Lunch and
dinner also are available in the inn's restaurant. The inn rests on
historic Route 66, which offers many interesting attractions along
its path. Baxter Springs is Kansas' first cow town.
Historic Interest: Ft. Blair, Quantrail's Raid, 1st cowtown in KS.
Innkeeper(s): Richard & Amy Sanell. $40-100. MC, VISA, AX, DS, PC, TC.

TAC10. 7 rooms with PB, 3 suites and 2 conference rooms. Breakfast included
in rates. Types of meals: Full bkfst, country bkfst and early coffee/tea. AP. Beds:
KQD. Cable TV, ceiling fan, microwave, tea and popcorn in room. Central air.
Library on premises. Weddings, small meetings, family reunions and seminars
hosted. Antiquing, canoeing/kayaking, fishing, golf and shopping nearby.
Pets Allowed.
Publicity: *Joplin Globe and KC Star.*

Council Grove   C8

The Cottage House Hotel

25 N Neosho St
Council Grove, KS 66846-1633
(316)767-6828 (800)727-7903

Circa 1898. The inn is located in Council Grove, the rendezvous
point on the Santa Fe Trail. The building grew from a boarding
house to an elegant home before it became the hotel of a local
banker. The home's original section dates to 1872, and the home
was built in stages until 1898. Listed in the National Register of
Historic Places, the inn has been completely renovated and is a

beautiful example of Victorian architecture in a prairie town. There is a honeymoon cottage on the premises, as well.

Historic Interest: National Register.

Innkeeper(s): Connie Essington. $60-140. MC, VISA, AX, DC, DS. 26 rooms with PB, 1 cottage and 2 conference rooms. Types of meals: Cont. Beds: KQD. Whirlpool tubs in room. Spa and sauna on premises. Handicap access. Fishing, golf and riverwalk nearby.

Publicity: *Manhattan Mercury, Gazette, Globe & Mail, Kansas City Star, Wichita Eagle, Midwest Living* and *Kansas Magazine.*

"A walk back into Kansas history; preserved charm and friendliness."

Fort Scott   D10

Lyons' Victorian Mansion Bed & Breakfast and Spa

742 S National Ave
Fort Scott, KS 66701-1319
(316)223-3644 (800)784-8378
E-mail: bedandbreakfast@lyonsmansion.com
Web: www.lyonsmansion.com

Circa 1876. For a business trip, vacation or romantic getaway, this landmark Victorian mansion is a luxurious choice. This gracious home has parlors to gather in, and Paradise, a full service spa. Spacious guest bedrooms offer refined comfort and modern technology with candles, refreshment centers and dedicated computer lines. The suites feature oversized jetted whirlpools that are made to look like antique clawfoot tubs. Enjoy a hearty breakfast in the grand  dining room, unless a breakfast basket delivered to the door is preferred. The grounds are showcased by a gazebo, fish ponds, picnic areas and an enclosed star-lit hot tub. Ask about the creative specialty packages offered.

Innkeeper(s): Pat Lyons. $89-150. MC, VISA, AX, DS. 7 rooms, 3 with PB and 4 suites. Breakfast included in rates. Types of meals: Full bkfst. Three suites with whirlpool in room.

Lindsborg   C6

Smoky Valley Bed & Breakfast

130 N Second St
Lindsborg, KS 67456-2212
(785)227-4460 (800)532-4407
E-mail: smokyvalleybnb@ks-usa.net
Web: www.kbba.com

Circa 1880. The oldest residence in the community, this red brick Georgian-style home offers a taste of Sweden in its decor and hospitality. The original fireplace is showcased in the living room. Antiques accent the cultural theme in each of the corner guest bedrooms, with Swedish pottery, crystal, woodcarvings and linens. Blue and yellow themes, wicker and Vikings continue the heritage pride. Breakfast is a blend of American and Swedish food that always includes traditional rye bread, sweet bread, King Oscar and Gevalia coffees, as well as standard favorites and dishes like pancakes with lingonberries. The extensive gardens offer a glider and swing or table with chairs to fully absorb the flowers, trees and plants.

Historic Interest: Sandzen Art Gallery (2 blocks), Bethany College (2

blocks) Old Mill Museum (5 blocks).

Innkeeper(s): JoAn Hamilton. $55-90. MC, VISA, DS, TC. 3 rooms with PB, 1 with FP and 1 suite. Breakfast and snacks/refreshments included in rates. Types of meals: Gourmet bkfst, veg bkfst, cont plus, cont and early coffee/tea. Beds: KQT. Turndown service, fireplace and sitting room in room. Air conditioning. VCR, fax, spa, bicycles, glider, yard swing, hammock and off-street parking on premises. Weddings, small meetings, family reunions and seminars hosted. Antiquing, art galleries, bicycling, fishing, golf, hiking, live theater, museums, parks, shopping and tennis nearby.

Publicity: *Lindsborg News Record.*

Swedish Country Inn

112 W Lincoln St
Lindsborg, KS 67456-2319
(785)227-2985 (800)231-0266

Circa 1904. Founded in the 1860s by Swedish immigrants, the town of Lindsborg is still known as "Little Sweden," maintaining its heritage through a variety of cultural events, festivals, galleries, shops and restaurants. The Swedish Country Inn adds to the town's ethnic flavor. All the furnishings have been imported from Sweden. Bright, airy rooms feature pine furnishings, handmade quilts and hand-painted cupboards. A Swedish-style buffet breakfast is served each morning, with items such as meatballs, lingonberries, herring, knackebread, fruit, cheese, cold meats and fresh baked goods. The Christmas season is an especially festive time to visit this inn and picturesque small town.

Innkeeper(s): Becky Anderson. $55-101. MC, VISA, AX, DS, PC, TC. 19 rooms with PB and 2 suites. Breakfast, afternoon tea and snacks/refreshments included in rates. Types of meals: Gourmet bkfst and early coffee/tea. Beds: QD. Cable TV, phone and sauna in room. Air conditioning. Sauna and bicycles on premises. Weddings, small meetings, family reunions and seminars hosted. Antiquing, parks and shopping nearby.

Publicity: *Midwest Living.*

Oberlin   A3

The Landmark Inn at The Historic Bank of Oberlin

189 S Penn
Oberlin, KS 67749
(785)475-2340 (888)639-0003
E-mail: landmarkinn@juno.com

Circa 1886. In 1886, this inn served as the Bank of Oberlin, one of the town's most impressive architectural sites. The bank lasted only a few years, though, and went through a number of uses, from county courthouse to the telephone company. Today, it serves as both inn and a historic landmark, a reminder of the past with rooms decorated Victorian style with antiques. One room includes a fireplace; another has a whirlpool tub. In addition to the inviting rooms, there is a restaurant serving dinner specialties  such as buttermilk pecan chicken and roasted beef with simmered mushrooms. The inn is listed in the National Register.

Innkeeper(s): Gary Anderson. $69-109. MC, VISA, AX, DS, PC, TC. 7 rooms with PB, 1 with FP, 1 suite and 2 conference rooms. Breakfast included in rates. Types of meals: Gourmet bkfst, early coffee/tea, gourmet lunch, afternoon tea, snacks/refreshments, gourmet dinner and room service. Beds: QD. Cable TV, phone, ceiling fan and VCR in room. Air conditioning. Fax, sauna, bicycles and library on premises. Handicap access. Weddings, small meetings, family reunions and seminars hosted. Antiquing, golf, parks, shopping and tennis nearby.

Publicity: *Kansas Magazine, Dining out in Kansas, Wichita Eagle-Beacon, Salina Journal, Hays Daily News, 2001 Bed & Breakfast Calendar, KSN TV-Wichita, KS, High Plains Public TV and Kansas Public TV Taste of Kansas.*

Topeka B9

Brickyard Barn Inn

4020 NW 25th St
Topeka, KS 66618
(785)235-0057 Fax:(785)234-0924
E-mail: umoo2me@cjnetworks.com
Web: www.cjnetworks.com/~umoo2me

Circa 1927. Designed by novice architectural students at Kansas State University, this bed & breakfast was built for use as a dairy barn. Each of the guest rooms is comfortable and casually furnished with antiques. Modem hookups are available for the business traveler. Breakfast specialties include Brickyard Barn Inn Swiss Quiche Pie and a fresh fruit salad topped with raspberry sauce. The inn is 10 miles from the state capitol building. Other nearby points of interest include casinos and the historic Menninger site.

Historic Interest: Topeka Capital Bldg (10 miles), Menninger Site (10 miles), Civil War battle sites (30 miles).

Innkeeper(s): Scott & Truanna Nickel. $65-95. MC, VISA, PC. TAC10. 3 rooms with PB and 2 conference rooms. Breakfast and snacks/refreshments included in rates. Types of meals: Gourmet bkfst, veg bkfst, early coffee/tea, gourmet lunch, picnic lunch, gourmet dinner and room service. Beds: Q. Ceiling fan in room. Central air. VCR, fax, swimming and reception facility on premises. Weddings, small meetings, family reunions and seminars hosted. Amusement parks, antiquing, art galleries, fishing, golf, hiking, horseback riding, casinos, live theater, museums, parks, shopping, sporting events, tennis, water sports and wineries nearby.

Publicity: *Midwest Living, Country, Kansas City Home and Garden, Kansas and Local commercials.*

Wichita E7

Castle Inn Riverside

1155 N River Blvd
Wichita, KS 67203
(316)263-9300
E-mail: lcastle@gte.net
Web: www.castleinnriverside.com

Circa 1886. This luxurious inn is a stunning example of Richardsonian Romanesque architecture. The home includes 14 guest rooms, each individually appointed. Twelve of the guest rooms include a fireplace, and six include a double whirlpool tub. Guests are pampered with a full breakfast, and later in the day, with a selection of wine, cheeses, light hors d'oeuvres, gourmet coffees and teas and homemade desserts. A liquor cabinet also is available in the evening for night caps or after-dinner drinks. The inn offers  many amenities for its business travelers, including rooms equipped with TVs, VCRs, telephones and dataports. The inn is just a few minutes from downtown Wichita.

Historic Interest: The area offers several historic attractions, including nearby Old Town, a Native American center and several museums.

Innkeeper(s): Terry & Paula Lowry. $125-275. MC, VISA, DC, CB, DS, PC, TC. TAC10. 14 rooms with PB, 12 with FP, 1 suite and 1 conference room. Breakfast included in rates. Types of meals: Gourmet bkfst and

snacks/refreshments. Beds: KQ. TV, phone and VCR in room. Air conditioning. Fax and copier on premises. Handicap access. Weddings, small meetings, family reunions and seminars hosted. Antiquing, fishing, live theater, parks, shopping, sporting events and water sports nearby.

Publicity: *Country Inns, Midwest Living, Travel Holiday, Runners World, The Wichita Business Journal and PBS.*

Inn at the Park

3751 E Douglas Ave
Wichita, KS 67218-1002
(316)652-0500 (800)258-1951 Fax:(316)652-0525
E-mail: iap@innatthepark.com
Web: www.innatthepark.com

Circa 1910. This popular three-story brick mansion offers many special touches, including unique furnishings in each of its 12 guest rooms, three of which are suites. Most of the rooms feature fireplaces. The inn's convenient location makes it ideal for business travelers or those interested in exploring Wichita. The inn's parkside setting provides additional opportunities for relaxation or recreation. Close to shops, restaurants, Old Town, Exploration Place and museums.

Innkeeper(s): Judy Hess and/or Jan Lightner. $89-164. MC, VISA, AX, DS. 12 rooms with PB, 8 with FP, 3 suites and 1 conference room. Breakfast included in rates. Types of meals: Cont plus and early coffee/tea. Beds: KQ. Cable TV, phone, turndown service and VCR in room. Air conditioning. Fax, copier and spa on premises. Antiquing, adjacent to conference facility, live theater and shopping nearby.

Publicity: *Wichita Business Journal.*

"This is truly a distinctive hotel. Your attention to detail is surpassed only by your devotion to excellent service."

Little River House B&B

6137 Fairfield Rd.
Wichita, KS 67204
(316)838-3127
E-mail: coupmk@aol.com

Circa 1920. In a quiet neighborhood on the Little Arkansas River, this restored bungalow-style home is surrounded by flower beds. A living room and two dining areas offer plenty of places to relax in. Furnished in a classic style with antiques and Oriental rugs, a guest bedroom features a four-poster bed. The fully equipped kitchen is stocked with fresh breakfast foods and ingredients. Enjoy snacks and beverages as well as stuffed cookie and candy jars. Relax on the intimate front porch, or view the scenic woods from the back patio. Birding, walking and jogging are popular activities, or explore the local area on one of the bikes available.

Historic Interest: American Fan Museum (20 min.), New York Paramount Theatre (10 min.)

Innkeeper(s): Michael & Karen Coup. $125-149. MC, VISA, PC. 2 rooms, 1 with PB and 1 guest house. Breakfast and snacks/refreshments included in rates. Types of meals: Gourmet bkfst, full bkfst, country bkfst, veg bkfst, dinner, early coffee/tea and snacks/refreshments. Beds: KQ. Cable TV, phone, VCR, refrigerator, and stereo in room. Air conditioning. Fax, copier, laundry facilities, library, VCR, fully furnished kitchen dishwasher, fans, and free crib/high chair on premises. Handicap access. Weddings hosted. Antiquing, live theater, parks, shopping, sporting events, Wichita State University, Newman University, virgin prairies, art galleries, golf, hiking, bicycling, tennis and museums nearby.

Kentucky

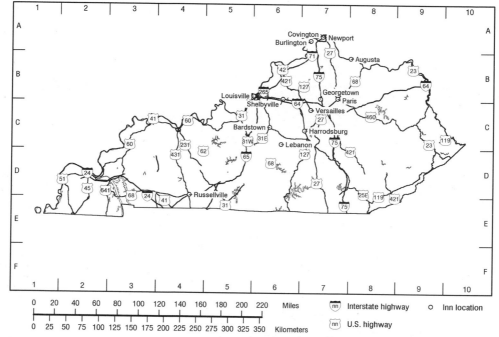

		Miles		Interstate highway	○ Inn location
0 20 40 60 80 100 120 140 160 180 200 220			(nn)		
0 25 50 75 100 125 150 175 200 225 250 275 300 325 350		Kilometers	(nn)	U.S. highway	

Augusta   B8

Doniphan Home

302 E 4th St
Augusta, KY 41002-1120
(606)756-2409

Circa 1825. This brick Georgian-style house, with porch and white shutters, was built around a core constructed of logs in the late 18th century. There are 16-inch-thick walls.

Antiques are featured in the wallpapered guest rooms. An antique dish collection and handsome sideboard add to the warmth of the bed & breakfast's decor. Full breakfasts are served in the formal dining room, which features a chandelier and polished walnut woodwork. An old ferry boat still plies the river.

Innkeeper(s): Ruth & George Cummins. $80. TC. 3 rooms, 1 with FP and 1 suite. Breakfast and snacks/refreshments included in rates. Types of meals: Gourmet bkfst. Beds: KD. Cable TV and phone in room. Air conditioning. VCR and library on premises. Antiquing, fishing, scenic riverwalk, parks and shopping nearby.
Publicity: *Country Home* and *Southern Living.*

"Everywhere I look I see the beauty in this home and in this town. Augusta is forever in my heart."

Bardstown   C6

A RoseMark Haven

714 N Third St
Bardstown, KY 40004
(502)348-8218
E-mail: arosemarkhaven@aol.com
Web: www.arosemarkhaven.com

Circa 1830. This antebellum mansion is listed in the National Register of Historic Places. The inn features elegantly carved woodwork, stained glass, yellow popular and ash floors, a grand entrance foyer and spiral staircase. There is a lookout on top of the house. The inn is furnished with antiques.

Innkeeper(s): Rosemary & Ches Mark Southard. $110-150. MC, VISA, AX. 7 rooms with PB, 7 with FP. Types of meals: Gourmet bkfst. Beds: K.
Publicity: *Kentucky Travel Guide.*

171

Arbor Rose B&B

209 E Stephen Foster Ave
Bardstown, KY 40004-1513
(502)349-0014 (888)828-3330 Fax:(502)349-0014
E-mail: arborrose@bardstown.com

Circa 1820. This late Victorian style home in the National Register, is located in the historic district a block and a half from Courthouse Square. Some of the rooms offer fireplaces, all have cable TV and VCRs. (The inn's fireplaces were made by Alexander Moore, the master craftsman of "My Old Kentucky Home.") Full gourmet country breakfasts are served, often on the outdoor terrace in view of the gardens, Koi pond and fountain. Smoking is not permitted.

Historic Interest: My Old Kentucky Home (1/4 mile), Wickland Mansion (1/4 mile).

Innkeeper(s): Judy & Derrick Melzer. $99-139. MC, VISA, AX, DS, PC, TC. TAC10. 5 rooms with PB, 4 with FP and 1 conference room. Breakfast and snacks/refreshments included in rates. Types of meals: Gourmet bkfst and early coffee/tea. Beds: KQT. Cable TV, phone, ceiling fan, VCR and fireplace in room. Central air. Fax, copier, hot tub/spa and gift shop on premises. Small meetings hosted. Antiquing, art galleries, golf, hiking, horseback riding, distilleries, Civil War Monastery, live theater, museums, parks, shopping and tennis nearby.

Publicity: *Kentucky's Best B&B 2001.*

"The food was delicious, our room very attractive and cozy."

Jailer's Inn

111 W Stephen Foster Ave
Bardstown, KY 40004-1415
(502)348-5551 (800)948-5551 Fax:(502)349-1837
E-mail: cpaul@jailersinn.com
Web: www.jailersinn.com

Circa 1819. As the innkeepers say, guests can come and "do time" at this inn, which was used as a jail as late as 1987. However, today, accommodations are bit less restrictive. Each

of the elegant guest rooms is individually appointed. From the Victorian Room to the Garden Room, each captures a different theme. Two guest rooms include a double Jacuzzi tub. Only one guest room resembles a jail cell, it contains two bunks, as well as the

more luxurious addition of a waterbed. In the summer, the full breakfasts are served in a courtyard. The inn is located in the heart of historic Bardstown.

Historic Interest: Tours of "My Old Kentucky Home," conducted by guides in antebellum costumes, are a popular attraction. Lincoln's birthplace and boyhood home and the oldest cathedral west of Alleghany are nearby, as is the Getz Museum of Whiskey History.

Innkeeper(s): Paul McCoy. $70-125. MC, VISA, AX, DS, PC, TC. TAC10. 6 rooms with PB. Breakfast included in rates. Types of meals: Full bkfst and early coffee/tea. Beds: KQD. Cable TV, turndown service and ceiling fan in room. Air conditioning. VCR on premises. Weddings, small meetings and family reunions hosted. Antiquing, live theater, parks and shopping nearby.

Publicity: *Vacations, New Choices, Kentucky Standard, USA Weekend, New York Times, Cincinnati Enquire, Honeymoon Magazine, Country Inns, Southern Living, Courier Journal Newspaper., Nashville's Crossroads and Jeopardy.*

"Wonderful experience! A very special B&B."

Old Talbott Tavern

107 W Stephen Foster Ave, PO Box 365
Bardstown, KY 40004-0036
(502)348-3494 (800)482-8376 Fax:(502)348-3404

Circa 1779. Old Talbott Tavern is the oldest continuously operating "western" stagecoach inn in America. The stone building is filled with antiques, and there are murals painted by King Philippe of France and his entourage. If you look closely, you'll find bullet holes left by Jesse James. There are five guest rooms, including two suites. In addition to the unusual Kentucky Bourbon Bar and gift shop, the inn's full service restaurant offers five dining/meeting rooms, popular for group bookings as well as business and special occasion dining.

Innkeeper(s): The Kelley Family. $70-125. MC, VISA. 5 rooms with PB. EP.

Burlington   A7

Burlington's Willis Graves B&B

5825 Jefferson St
Burlington, KY 41005
(606)689-5096 (888)226-5096
E-mail: inn@burligrave.com
Web: www.burligrave.com

Circa 1830. Located next to the county fair grounds on an acre and a half of lawn and garden, is this brick Federal home. Once hidden behind aluminum siding, the home is now filled with antiques and is in the National Register. Handsome mantels, antique art and old floorboards add to the inn's authenticity. Nearby are shops and restaurants, or you can drive to the Covington riverfront area.

Innkeeper(s): Nancy & Bob Swartzal. $75-135. MC, VISA, DS, PC, TC. 3 rooms with PB and 1 suite. Breakfast included in rates. Types of meals: Full bkfst and early coffee/tea. Beds: QD. Cable TV, phone, turndown service and VCR in room. Air conditioning. Antiquing, fishing, golf, horseback riding, restaurants, parks, shopping and downhill skiing nearby.

Publicity: *The Courier-Journal, Kentucky Monthly Magazine and Cincinnati Magazine.*

"Lovely retreat and absolutely beautiful breakfasts. Lima, Oh."

Covington   A7

Amos Shinkle Townhouse

215 Garrard St
Covington, KY 41011-1715
(859)431-2118 (800)972-7012 Fax:(859)491-4551

Circa 1854. This restored mansion has won several preservation awards. It features a Greco-Italianate facade with a cast-iron filigree porch. Inside there are lavish crown moldings and Italianate mantels on the fireplaces. Sixteen-foot ceilings and Rococo Revival chandeliers add to the formal elegance. Guest rooms boast four-poster or massive Victorian-style beds and period furnishings. Here, Southern hospitality is at its finest.

Historic Interest: National Register.

Innkeeper(s): Don Nash & Bernie Moorman. $95-165. MC, VISA, AX, DC, DS, PC, TC. TAC10. 7 rooms with PB, 1 with FP and 1 conference room. Breakfast included in rates. Types of meals: Full bkfst. Beds: QD. TV and phone in room. Air conditioning. Fax and copier on premises.

Publicity: *Everybody's News, Plain Dealer,*

New York Times, Country Inn, Washington Post, Southern Living, ComAir
Wing Tips and National Geographic Traveler.

"It's like coming home to family and friends."

Georgetown B7

Pineapple Inn

645 S Broadway St
Georgetown, KY 40324-1135
(502)868-5453

Circa 1876. White gingerbread trim decorates the yellow
Victorian Pineapple Inn, highlighting its gables, large front
porch, dentil trim and bay window. In the Kentucky Historic
Register and the Bluegrass historic list, the house provides a
cheerful welcome to guests visiting Kentucky's antique center.
Polished antiques throughout, a country French dining room
and handsome wallcoverings make the interiors pristine and
inviting. A full Kentucky breakfast is served.

Innkeeper(s): Muriel & Les. $65-95. MC, VISA. 4 rooms with PB. Breakfast
included in rates. Types of meals: Full bkfst and gourmet dinner. Beds: QD.
Antiquing and fishing nearby.

Publicity: Country Extra.

"Your hospitality was wonderful. The food was fantastic."

Harrodsburg C7

Bauer Haus

362 N College
Harrodsburg, KY 40330-1116
(859)734-6289 (877)734-6289
E-mail: bauerhaus@kycom.net

Circa 1880. This Queen Anne Victorian, sans gingerbread, features a wicker-filled front porch, complete with swing. In the
National Register, it was built on one of the first outlots in

Harrodsburg. The town is the
state's oldest settlement, established in 1774. Inside the parlor,
archways adorn the mantel and
date back to the early 19th century. The spacious guest bedrooms are furnished with
antiques in a traditional decor.
Coffee or tea is served to each room before the breakfast seating. Lower-fat dishes and fresh fruit accompany low-fat, made-
from-scratch breakfast cakes or muffins. Adjacent to the main
house is the new carriage house, with deluxe accommodations
featuring a fireplace, whirlpool tub, TV/VCR and small kitchen.

Innkeeper(s): Dick & Marian Bauer. $70-125. MC, VISA, AX, DS, PC, TC. 4
rooms, 2 with PB, 3 with FP. Breakfast and snacks/refreshments included in
rates. Types of meals: Full bkfst and early coffee/tea. Beds: QDT. Air conditioning. VCR on premises. Small meetings, family reunions and seminars hosted.
Antiquing, fishing, golf, historic sites, live theater and water sports nearby.

Lebanon C6

Myrtledene B&B

370 N Spalding Ave
Lebanon, KY 40033-1557
(502)692-2223 (800)391-1721
E-mail: info@myrtledene.com

Circa 1833. Once a Confederate general's headquarters at one
point during the Civil War, this pink brick inn, located at a bend
in the road, has greeted visitors entering Lebanon for more than
150 years. When General John Hunt Morgan returned in 1863
to destroy the town, the white flag hoisted to signal a truce was
flown at Myrtledene. A country breakfast usually features ham
and biscuits as well as the
innkeepers' specialty, peaches and
cream French toast.

Historic Interest: Headquarters of confederate General John Hunt Morgan. Morgan
rode his mare up to front hall stairs.

Innkeeper(s): James F. Spragens. $85.
MC, VISA, PC, TC. TAC10. 4 rooms, 2
with PB, 1 with FP and 1 conference room. Breakfast included in rates.
Types of meals: Gourmet bkfst, early coffee/tea and afternoon tea. Beds: DT.
Turndown service, Makers Mark bourbon and bourbon chocolates in room. Air
conditioning. VCR and library on premises. Weddings, small meetings, family
reunions and seminars hosted. Antiquing, fishing, live theater, parks, shopping and water sports nearby.

Publicity: Lebanon Enterprise, Louisville Courier-Journal, Lebanon/Marion
County Kentucky. and Sunnyside.

*"Our night in the Cabbage Rose Room was an experience of another
time, another culture. Your skill in preparing and presenting breakfast was equally elegant! We'll be back!"*

Louisville B6

Aleksander House

1213 S First St
Louisville, KY 40203
(502)637-4985 Fax:(502)635-1398
E-mail: alekhouse@aol.com
Web: www.aleksanderhouse.com

Circa 1882. French impressionist paintings, French Toile wall
coverings in the dining room, gas light fixtures, 12-foot ceilings, fireplaces and walnut woodwork create the pleasant decor
of this three-story Italianate Victorian. Ask for Katharine's

Room on the third floor and enjoy a
four-poster bed, writing desk and settee.
Pecan waffles served with glazed peaches and cream or eggs Benedict are popular breakfast entrees. Mystery weekend
packages are offered on occasion. The
inn is listed in the National Register.

Historic Interest: Churchill Down (1-2 miles),
Filson Club (3 blocks), Conrad-Caldwell House
(6 blocks).

Innkeeper(s): Nancy Hinchliff. $85-169. MC, VISA, AX, DS, PC, TC. TAC10.
5 rooms, 3 with PB, 5 with FP, 1 suite and 1 conference room. Breakfast
and snacks/refreshments included in rates. Types of meals: Gourmet bkfst,
country bkfst, cont plus, cont and early coffee/tea. Beds: KQDT. TV, phone,
ceiling fan, VCR, terry cloth robes, irons and hair dryers in room. Central air.
Fax, library and video library on premises. Weddings, small meetings, family
reunions and seminars hosted. Spanish spoken. Amusement parks, antiquing,
art galleries, bicycling, golf, hiking, horseback riding, live theater, museums,
parks, shopping, sporting events, tennis, water sports and wineries nearby.

Pets allowed: depends on size and behavior.

Publicity: *Country Inns, Louisville Magazine, Today's Woman Magazine, The Courier-Journal and Channel 11-WGN.*

Central Park B&B

1353 S Fourth St
Louisville, KY 40208-2349
(502)638-1505 (877)922-1505 Fax:(502)638-1525
E-mail: centralpar@win.net

Circa 1884. This three-story Second Empire Victorian is listed in the National Register, and it is located in the heart of "Old Louisville," amid America's largest collection of Victorian homes. Enjoy the fine craftsmanship of the home's many amenities, including the reverse-painted glass ceiling of the front porch and the polished woodwork and stained glass. Among its 18 rooms are seven guest rooms, all with private baths and two with whirlpool tubs. There are 11 fireplaces, some with carved mantels and decorative tile. The Carriage House suite has a full kitchen. Antiques are found throughout. The University of Louisville and Spalding University is within easy walking distance. Across the street is Central Park.

Innkeeper(s): Mary & Joseph White. $89-169. MC, VISA, AX, PC, TC. 7 rooms with PB and 3 suites. Breakfast and snacks/refreshments included in rates. Types of meals: Full bkfst and early coffee/tea. Beds: KQ. Cable TV, phone, turndown service, hair dryers and computer port in room. Air conditioning. Weddings, small meetings, family reunions and seminars hosted. Spanish spoken. spoken. Antiquing, fine dining, live theater, shopping and sporting events nearby.

Columbine Inn

1707 S Third St
Louisville, KY 40208-1917
(502)635-5000 (800)635-5010
E-mail: BBColumbin@aol.com

Circa 1896. This 1896 Greek revival inn is the former the estate of a mahogany king of Louisville. It is located in historical old Louisville amid the largest collection of Victorian homes in America. Victorian craftsmanship is evident throughout the inn — from the rare Honduran mahogany in the dining room to the fireplace with rose marble to the intricately carved dining chairs. Sunshine shining through the stained-glass windows and doors creates prisms of light all over the inn. The eight working gas fireplaces and original hardwood floors set a wonderful mood throughout the inn and the five guest bedrooms. Lucky indeed are the guests who partake of Anne's full gourmet breakfast, which includes such specialties as his Chocolate Heart Waffle with Raspberry Sauce or Fresh Basil Pesto Omelet or Egg in the Blossom with Bacon. Upon request, authentic Tuscan cuisine will be served for dinner. Complimentary evening snacks are the perfect end to a pampered day.

Historic Interest: Edison House (3 miles), Locust Grove (15 miles), Farmington (6 miles).

Innkeeper(s): Anne Eppinger. $85-120. MC, VISA, AX, TC. 5 rooms with PB, 4 with FP. Breakfast and snacks/refreshments included in rates. Types of meals: Gourmet bkfst, veg bkfst and gourmet dinner. AP. Beds: QT. Cable TV, phone, ceiling fan and VCR in room. Central air. Small meetings, family reunions and seminars hosted. Italian and French spoken. Amusement parks, antiquing, art galleries, bicycling, golf, horseback riding, live theater, museums, parks, shopping, tennis and wineries nearby.

Publicity: *Courier Journal.*

Gallery House Bed & Breakfast

1386 South Sixth Street
Louisville, KY 40208
(502)635-2550 Fax:(502)635-6204
E-mail: galleryhse@aol.com

Circa 1997. This modern Victorian is situated in the Historic Preservation District of Old Louisville. Blending in well, it is a constant surprise that Gallery House is not old or renovated but newly built to replace what had completely burned to the ground. The interior is filled with original artwork, favorite books and comfortable furnishings. A parlor fireplace is a welcome spot, or visit the art studio on the third floor. The themed guest bedrooms are filled with thoughtful items to make each stay a splendid experience. A daily newspaper and hot coffee or tea awaits the early riser, before partaking of breakfast, a sumptuous delight. Overlook Central Park from the second floor balcony, or relax in the pocket garden by the fish pond. Enjoy evening snacks placed on an antique sugar chest outside the Rose Room.

Historic Interest: Conrad-Caldwell House (across the street).

Innkeeper(s): Leah Stewart & Gordon Moffett. $80-85. MC, VISA, AX, DS. 3 rooms with PB. Breakfast and snacks/refreshments included in rates. Types of meals: Gourmet bkfst, veg bkfst and early coffee/tea. Beds: Q. Cable TV, phone, ceiling fan and original art in room. Central air. Amusement parks, antiquing, art galleries, golf, live theater, museums, parks, shopping, sporting events and tennis nearby.

Inn at The Park

1332 S 4th St
Louisville, KY 40208-2314
(502)637-6930 (800)700-7275 Fax:(502)637-2796
E-mail: info@innatpark.com
Web: www.innatpark.com

Circa 1886. An impressive sweeping staircase is one of many highlights at this handsome Richardsonian Romanesque inn, in the historic district of Old Louisville. Guests also will appreciate the hardwood floors, 14-foot ceilings and stone balconies on the second and third floors. The seven guest rooms offer a variety of amenities and a view of Central Park.

Innkeeper(s): John & Sandra Mullins. $89-179. MC, VISA, AX, DC, DS, PC, TC. TAC10. 7 rooms with PB, 5 with FP and 3 suites. Breakfast included in rates. Types of meals: Full bkfst and early coffee/tea. Beds: KQ. Cable TV, phone and ceiling fan in room. Air conditioning. VCR and fax on premises. German spoken. Amusement parks, antiquing, churchill Downs, live theater, parks, shopping and sporting events nearby.

Publicity: *Country Inns, Ohio Magazine and Kentucky Monthly.*

Inn at Woodhaven

401 S Hubbard Ln
Louisville, KY 40207-4074
(502)895-1011 (888)895-1011
E-mail: info@innatwoodhaven.com
Web: www.innatwoodhaven.com

Circa 1853. This Gothic Revival, painted in a cheerful shade of yellow, is still much the same as it was in the 1850s, when it served as the home on a prominent local farm. The rooms still feature the outstanding carved woodwork, crisscross window designs, winding staircases, decorative mantels and hardwood floors. Guest quarters are tastefully appointed with antiques, suitable for their 12-foot, nine-inch tall ceilings.

Complimentary coffee and tea stations are provided in each room. There are several common areas in the Main House, and guests also take advantage of the inn's porches. Rose Cottage is octagon shaped and features a 25-foot vaulted ceiling, a king bed, fireplace, sitting area, double whirlpool, steam shower and wraparound porch. The National Register home is close to all of Louisville's attractions.

Innkeeper(s): Marsha Burton. $75-225. MC, VISA, AX, DS. 8 rooms with PB, 3 with FP, 2 suites and 1 cottage. Breakfast included in rates. Types of meals: Gourmet bkfst, picnic lunch and gourmet dinner. Beds: KQDT. Cable TV, phone, ceiling fan, coffee, tea and hot chocolate facility in room. Air conditioning. Fax, copier, library and three rooms with double whirlpools on premises. Handicap access. Weddings, small meetings, family reunions and seminars hosted. Amusement parks, antiquing, golf, live theater, parks, shopping, sporting events, tennis and water sports nearby.

Publicity: *Courier Journal, New York Times, WAVE and WHAS.*

Pinecrest Cottage and Gardens - A Bed and Breakfast

2806 Newburg Rd
Louisville, KY 40205
(502)454-3800 Fax:(502)452-9791
E-mail: pinecrestbb@prodigy.net
Web: www.bbonline.com/ky/pinecrest

Circa 1775. On more than six landscaped acres including century-old trees, three ponds and a dozen perennial flower beds stands the Pinecrest Cottage, a 1,400-square-foot, five-room guesthouse with one bedroom. Guests are afforded full privacy, and may even cook their own breakfast with food provided in the fully stocked kitchen. Summer visitors enjoy tennis and swimming on the grounds. Fall visitors enjoy the colors of autumn, and winter visitors see the landscape blanketed with snow. Nearby attractions include Churchill Downs and Derby museum, Louisville Slugger Museum, the Louisville Zoo, and various restaurants and antique shops.

Historic Interest: Farmington (2 miles), Locust Grove (8 miles).

Innkeeper(s): Nancy Morris. $95-145. MC, VISA, AX, PC, TC. 1 rooms with PB, 1 with FP. Breakfast and snacks/refreshments included in rates. Types of meals: Cont plus. Beds: K. Cable TV, phone, VCR and fireplace in room. Central air. Fax, copier, swimming and tennis on premises. Amusement parks nearby.

Publicity: *Courier Journal.*

Tucker House Bed & Breakfast

2406 Tucker Station Rd
Louisville, KY 40299
(502)297-8007 Fax:(502)896-68915
E-mail: tuckerhouse1840@aol.com

Circa 1840. A state landmark, this meticulously restored brick, Federal-style farmhouse is listed in the National Register. The ambiance of early country living is enhanced by original poplar floors and trim, seeded-glass windows, solid brick walls and seven fireplaces. The parlor holds two historical book collections. Distinctive guest chambers feature thick robes, big towels and soft linens. Freshly brewed coffee and other refreshments are available in the common room that leads to a relaxing deck. A hearty breakfast is served on antique china in the formal dining room or on Kentucky Bybee pottery in the cheery gathering room. Five acres of spectacular surroundings include formal gardens, woods, a spring-fed lake and a swimming pool.

Historic Interest: Blackacre Nature Preserve.

Innkeeper(s): Devona & Steve Porter. $95-115. MC, VISA, AX, PC, TC. 4 rooms with PB and 2 conference rooms. Breakfast and snacks/refreshments included in rates. Types of meals: Country bkfst, veg bkfst and early coffee/tea. Beds: QD. TV and VCR in room. Central air. Fax, copier, swimming, stables, library, lake and woods on premises. Weddings, small meetings, family reunions and seminars hosted. Amusement parks, antiquing, art galleries, bicycling, fishing, golf, hiking, horseback riding, live theater, museums, parks, shopping and sporting events nearby.

Publicity: *Louisville Courier-Journal and Today's Woman.*

Newport   A7

Cincinnati's Weller Haus B&B

319 Poplar St
Newport, KY 41073-1108
(859)431-6829 (800)431-4287 Fax:(859)431-4332
E-mail: innkeepers@wellerhaus.com
Web: www.wellerhaus.com

Circa 1880. Set in Taylor Daughter's Historic District and five minutes from downtown Cincinnati, this inn consists of two historic homes. The inn has received awards for preservation, and special features include original woodwork and doors. Secluded gardens are inviting, and there is a wrought iron fence setting off the property. A full breakfast is served by candlelight. Rooms offer antiques, and suites feature double Jacuzzi tubs. A sky-lit great room has cathedral ceilings, and an ivy-covered gathering kitchen is open for snacks and drinks. Guests enjoy walking to the Newport Aquarium and the Riverboat Row Restaurants as well as downtown Cincinnati stadiums. Other attractions include live theater and water sports. Business travelers are provided modem telephones and desks, and a copy machine and fax are on the premises. Private space is available for small meetings. Breakfast can accommodate business schedules.

Innkeeper(s): Valerie & David Brown. $89-168. MC, VISA, AX, DC, DS, PC, TC. TAC10. 5 rooms with PB and 4 suites. Breakfast included in rates. Types of meals: Full bkfst and early coffee/tea. Beds: QDT. Cable TV, phone, ceiling fan and suites with Jacuzzi for two in room. Air conditioning. Small meetings and seminars hosted. Amusement parks, antiquing, fishing, live theater, museums, shopping, sporting events and water sports nearby.

Publicity: *Downtowner, Bellevue Community News, Cincinnati Enquirer and Country Inns.*

"You made B&B believers out of us."

Paris   B7

Rosedale B&B

1917 Cypress St
Paris, KY 40361-1220
(859)987-1845 (800)644-1862 Fax:(859)988-9876

Circa 1862. This brick Italianate bed & breakfast, once the home of Civil War General John Croxton and his family, rests on three park-like acres. Guests can select a book and read in the mahogany paneled library and relax on the screened-in porch, in rockers on the front porch, or on one of the garden benches. Paris is in the heart of Kentucky horse country, and the Kentucky Horse Park and Keeneland Race Courses are nearby. Rupp Arena

and the University of Kentucky are a short drive.

Historic Interest: Hopewell Museum, Kentucky Garden Club Headquarters, Cane Ridge Shrine, Keeneland Race Course, Rupp Arena, the Kentucky Horse Park and many historic homes are nearby.

Innkeeper(s): John Gerard. $90. MC, VISA, PC, TC. 3 rooms with PB. Breakfast included in rates. Types of meals: Full bkfst and early coffee/tea. Beds: QT. Ceiling fan in room. Air conditioning. Library and TV/VCR on premises. Small meetings, family reunions and seminars hosted. Antiquing, fishing, horse farms, museums, Keeneland Race Course, live theater, parks, shopping and sporting events nearby.

Publicity: *Lexington Herald Leader. and Lexington and Louisville.*

"Your hospitality has been lovely and your home is a fine example of tradition and comfort."

Russellville   D4

The Log House

2139 Franklin Rd
Russellville, KY 42276-9410
(270)726-8483 Fax:(270)726-4610
E-mail: hossom@logantele.com

Circa 1976. This ideal log cabin retreat was built from hand-hewn logs from old cabins and barns in the area. Rooms are full of quilts, early American furnishings and folk art from around the world. The log walls and hardwood floors create an unparalleled atmosphere of country warmth. An impressive kitchen is decorated with a working fireplace and brick floor. The innkeepers create hand-woven garments and hand-spun items in an adjacent studio. Nashville and Opry Mills are about an hour's drive, and the local area boasts a number of antique shops. Mammoth Cave is also a popular excursion.

Innkeeper(s): Mike & Sam Hossom. $85. MC, VISA, DS, PC. 4 rooms with PB, 2 with FP. Breakfast included in rates. Types of meals: Gourmet bkfst. Beds: QDT. Air conditioning. VCR, fax, copier, spa, swimming, library and pool on premises. Amusement parks, antiquing, fishing, live theater, parks, shopping, sporting events and water sports nearby.

Publicity: *Courier Journal, Nashville Tennessean, WHAS, Louisville; WBKO and Bowling Green.*

Shelbyville   B6

The Wallace House

613 Washington St
Shelbyville, KY 40065-1131
(502)633-2006
E-mail: elaurent@iglou.com

Circa 1804. This Federal-style house, midway between Louisville and Frankfort, is listed in the National Register of Historic Places. Its four well-appointed guest suites all feature breakfast rooms.

Historic Interest: Kentucky Horse Park (50 miles), Shakertown (50 miles), Churchill Downs Derby Museum (30 miles).

Innkeeper(s): Evelyn Laurent. $65-85. MC, VISA, AX. 4 suites. Types of meals: Cont plus. Beds: Q. Cable TV in room. Air conditioning. Antiquing, fishing, live theater and shopping nearby.

Versailles   C7

1823 Historic Rose Hill Inn

233 Rose Hill
Versailles, KY 40383-1223
(859)873-5957 (800)307-0460
E-mail: innkeepers@rosehillinn.com
Web: www.rosehillinn.com

Circa 1823. This Victorian mansion, in the National Register, was occupied at different times by both Confederate and Union troops during the Civil War. Near Lexington, the home maintains many elegant features, including original stained-glass windows, 14-foot ceilings and hardwood floors fashioned from timber on the property. The decor is comfortable, yet elegant. Two guest baths include double Jacuzzis. Guests enjoy relaxing in the library, the parlor, or on the porch swing on the veranda. The home's summer kitchen is now a private cottage with a kitchen, two bedrooms and a Jacuzzi. The Cottage and Auntie's Apartment are perfect for those traveling with children or for guests with well-behaved dogs. The innkeepers offer a hearty, full breakfast with specialties such as Mexican eggs, or Banana-filled French toast in the dining room. In summer it's often served on the veranda overlooking the water gardens, lawns and trees where cardinals fly about. Walk to the historic districts, antique shops restaurants and a museum. Additional attractions include Shaker Village, scenic drives past bucolic horse farms, Keeneland Race Track and a wildlife sanctuary.

Innkeeper(s): Sharon Amberg & Bonnie James. $99-149. MC, VISA, AX, DS, TC. TAC10. 4 rooms with PB, 1 suite and 1 cottage. Breakfast included in rates. Types of meals: Full bkfst and early coffee/tea. Beds: KQDT. TV, phone, turndown service and ceiling fan in room. Library and A/C on premises. Small meetings and family reunions hosted. Antiquing, fishing, golf, horse farm tours, Kentucky Horse Park, Shaker Village, Keeneland, parks, shopping and sporting events nearby.

Pets allowed: In cottage with prior approval.

Louisiana

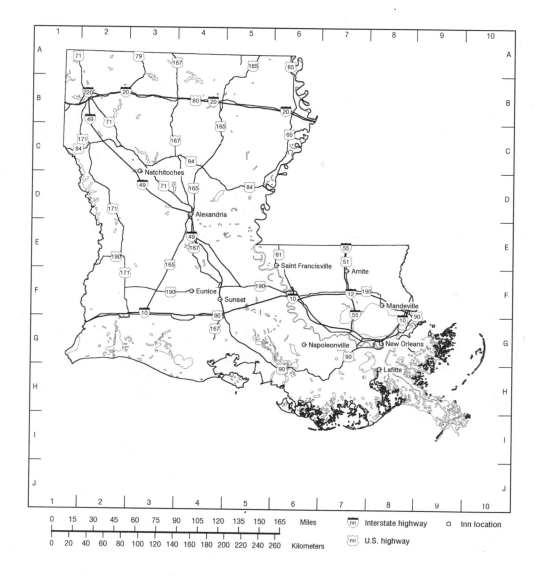

0 15 30 45 60 75 90 105 120 135 150 165   Miles

0 20 40 60 80 100 120 140 160 180 200 220 240 260   Kilometers

(nn) Interstate highway   ○ Inn location

(nn) U.S. highway

Alexandria   D4

Inglewood Plantation

6379 Old Baton Rouge Hwy
Alexandria, LA 71302
(318)487-8340 (888)575-6288 Fax:(318)448-0441
E-mail: susan@inglewoodplantation.com

Circa 1836. Family-owned for generations, this 3,500-acre working farm is one of the few in the area to survive the Civil War. Secluded in a grove of majestic oaks and pecan trees, accommodations include two cottages: Matt's Cabin (originally a sharecropper's home) and the 1850s Schoolhouse. The entire plantation house, in a National Register Historic District, can be leased for a two-night minimum. Enjoy homemade banana or wheat bread topped with hand-harvested mayhaw jelly, cereals, fresh fruit and beverages. Lawn games, tennis courts, swimming pool, ping pong, jungle gym, swings and porches with rocking chairs offer pleasurable activities for all ages.

Historic Interest: Loyd Hall Plantation (10 miles), Kent House Plantation (5 miles), Saxon Guild Studio.

Innkeeper(s): Susan & Georgia. $125-150. MC, VISA, AX, TC. 2 cottages. Breakfast included in rates. Types of meals: Cont. Beds: KQT. TV, phone, ceiling fan, VCR, fireplace, fresh garden bouquets and bathrobes in room. Central air. Fax, swimming, stables, tennis, library, front porch rocking chairs, RV parking, croquet, tree swings, jungle gym and 1500 acre nature preserve on premises. Weddings and family reunions hosted. French and Japanese spoken. Amusement parks, antiquing, art galleries, fishing, golf, spa, cajun dancing, live theater, museums, parks, shopping and water sports nearby.

Publicity: *Southern Living Magazine, Chef John Folse B&B Cookbook, Elle and PBS Chef John Folse's Cooking series.*

Amite   F7

Elliott House

801 N Duncan Ave
Amite, LA 70422-2222
(985)748-8553 (800)747-8553
E-mail: elliotthouse@i-55.com

Circa 1880. Innkeeper Flora Elliott Landwehr's grandfather, a State Court of Appeals judge, built this Neoclassical home. Flora and husband Joseph painstakingly restored the inheritance, which had deteriorated and was shrouded in overgrown brush. Now, the old pine floors shine and rooms feature Victorian antiques. Two bedchambers have a fireplace. In the mornings, homemade granola, fresh fruit and Louisiana coffee accompany entrees such as eggs

Benedict. Guests can spend the day relaxing at the inn and enjoying the five acres. The area offers plenty of outdoor activities, and New Orleans is an hour away.

Innkeeper(s): Joseph and Flora Landwehr. $75-125. MC, VISA, AX, PC, TC. TAC10. 4 rooms, 3 with PB, 2 with FP, 1 suite and 1 conference room. Breakfast included in rates. Types of meals: Gourmet bkfst, early coffee/tea and snacks/refreshments. Beds: KD. Ceiling fan in room. Air conditioning. Library and refreshments on arrival included in rates on premises. Small meetings, family reunions and seminars hosted. Antiquing, golf, historic sites, wildlife parks, swamp tours, parks, shopping and water sports nearby.

Publicity: *Times Picayune, Hammond Star, Country Roads Magazine, Hot Beignets and Warm Boudoirs. and PBS.*

"What you are doing and the type of people you are, give folks a memory, not just a place to stay."

Eunice   F4

Seale Guesthouse

123 Seale Lane
Eunice, LA 70535
(337)457-3753 Fax:(337)457-3753
Web: www.angelfire.com/la2/guesthouse

Circa 1890. A variety of historic accommodations are offered at these Victorian lodgings. The Bridal Cottage was the home of the town's first postmaster. The conference center was originally an old grocery store once robbed by Bonnie and Clyde. Encounter fresh flowers and antiques in the comfortable guest bedrooms. A deluxe continental breakfast is served weekdays, expanded to a full Southern meal on weekends. Enjoy handmade cypress rockers and swings on the wraparound porch and explore some of the 68 acres that incudes a fish pond and towering pines.

Historic Interest: Liberty Center-a restored Vaudville Theater.

Innkeeper(s): Mark Seale. $75. VISA, PC, TC. TAC15. 6 rooms with PB, 2 suites, 3 cottages and 1 conference room. Breakfast included in rates. Types of meals: Cont plus, cont and early coffee/tea. Beds: Q. TV, phone, ceiling fan, VCR and hot tub in room. Central air. Fax on premises. Handicap access. Weddings, small meetings, family reunions and seminars hosted. French spoken. Antiquing, art galleries, canoeing/kayaking, fishing, golf, Cajun Culture National Park, live theater, museums, parks and shopping nearby.

Pets Allowed.

Publicity: *Houston Life,Best Places to Stay and Boston Globe.*

Lafitte   H8

Victoria Inn

4707 Jean Lafitte Blvd
Lafitte, LA 70067
(504)689-4757 (800)689-4797 Fax:(504)689-3399
E-mail: info@victoriainn.com
Web: www.victoriainn.com

Circa 1878. Located on the site of the Mulligan Plantation, this inn consists of three West Indies-style homes on more than six acres of landscaped gardens. The grounds include an

antique rose garden, a parterre herb garden and an iris pond. A private pier and swimming pool extend out into the lake, which was once the field of this Louisiana sugar plantation. All of the rooms are uniquely furnished and the galleries offer a place to relax and enjoy the tropical breezes. Swamp tours, fishing charters, hiking or canoeing in the National Park are available.

Innkeeper(s): Roy & Dale Ross. $85-165. MC, VISA, AX, DS, TC. TAC10. 14 rooms with PB, 7 suites and 1 conference room. Breakfast included in rates. Types of meals: Gourmet bkfst, veg bkfst, cont plus, cont, early coffee/tea, afternoon tea and snacks/refreshments. Beds: QDT. Cable TV, phone, ceiling fan, VCR and fireplace in room. Central air. Fax, copier, spa, swimming, stables, library and gift shop on premises. Handicap access. Weddings, small meetings, family reunions and seminars hosted. Amusement parks, antiquing, art galleries, beaches, bicycling, canoeing/kayaking, fishing, golf, hiking, live theater, museums, parks, shopping, sporting events, tennis and water sports nearby.

Publicity: *Times Picayune, Shreveport Times, San Francisco Examiner, Lonely Planet and Discovery.*

"You contributed greatly to the fine memories of our 35th wedding anniversary."

Mandeville F8

Cozy Corner Guest House

736 Lafayette St
Mandeville, LA 70448
(504)626-9189

Circa 1889. Sections of this historic house date back more than a century. The guesthouse includes two comfortable bedrooms, each with a private bath and eclectic furnishings. Upon arrival, guests are treated to refreshments, and in the mornings, an English-style breakfast is served. The home is five blocks from Mandeville Lake, and 30 minutes from downtown New Orleans. Borrow a bicycle from the innkeepers and enjoy the 31-mile bike path that runs through the area.

Innkeeper(s): Barbara & Chris Clark. $85-95. MC, VISA, PC, TC. 2 rooms with PB. Breakfast included in rates. Types of meals: Full bkfst, country bkfst, veg bkfst, cont, afternoon tea and snacks/refreshments. Beds: KQ. Cable TV, phone and ceiling fan in room. Central air. VCR, swimming and bicycles on premises. Antiquing, beaches, bicycling, canoeing/kayaking, fishing, golf, hiking, live theater, shopping and wineries nearby.

"Your warm home and generous hospitality makes us eager to return."

Napoleonville G6

Madewood Plantation House

4250 Highway 308
Napoleonville, LA 70390-8737
(985)369-7151 (800)375-7151 Fax:(985)369-9848
E-mail: madewoodpl@aol.com
Web: www.madewood.com

Circa 1846. Six massive ionic columns support the central portico of this striking Greek Revival mansion, a National Historic Landmark. Framed by live oaks and ancient magnolias, Madewood, on 20 acres, across from Bayou Lafourche. It was

designed by Henry Howard, a noted architect from Cork, Ireland. There are elegant double parlors, a ballroom, library, music room and dining room where regional specialties are served by candlelight.

Historic Interest: Swamp tours, other plantations (one-half hour).
Innkeeper(s): Keith Marshall. $225-285. MC, VISA, AX, DS. 8 rooms with PB, 1 with FP, 2 suites and 1 conference room. Breakfast and dinner included in rates. Types of meals: Full bkfst. MAP. Beds: QDT. Copier on premises.
Publicity: Travel & Leisure, Travel Holiday, Los Angeles Times, Country Home, Country Inns (1 of 12 best inns in 1993) and Top 54 inns in US National Geographic Traveler 1999.

"We have stayed in many hotels, other plantations and English manor houses, and Madewood has surpassed them all in charm, hospitality and food."

Natchitoches C3

Judge Porter House B & B

321 2nd St
Natchitoches, LA 71457-4373
(318)352-9206 (800)441-8343
E-mail: judgeporter@judgeporterhouse.com
Web: www.judgeporterhouse.com

Circa 1912. Delightful treats and elegant treasures ensure a pleasant stay at this impressive home in the National Historic Landmark District. A Queen Anne influence in the wraparound

two-story gallery blends with Colonial Revival architecture reflected in the huge columns on brick pillars. Almost half of the 33 windows are more than eight feet tall. High ceilings, heart pine floors and five fireplaces showcase exquisite mid 19th-century antiques and European cut crystal chandeliers. Two comfortable parlors provide books, newspapers, magazines, videos and refreshments. The quiet guest bedrooms and private guest house offer mahogany and rosewood tester and four-poster beds, silk brocade drapes, tapestry chairs and most every luxurious amenity desired. The multi-course candlelight breakfast in the formal dining room is truly a feast for the senses.

Historic Interest: Kate Chopin Home/Bayou Fok Museum, Cane River National Heritage Area, St. Augustine Catholic Church, Birarwood-Caroline Dormon Nature Preserve, Fort St. Jean Baptiste State Commemorative Area, Natchitoches Parish Old Courthouse State Museum, St. Denis Walk of Fame, Rebel State Commemorative Area, Kisatchie National Forest.

Innkeeper(s): Tod Working. $105-135. MC, VISA, AX, PC, TC. 5 rooms, 4 with PB and 1 guest house. Breakfast and snacks/refreshments included in rates. Types of meals: Gourmet bkfst, veg bkfst and early coffee/tea. Beds: Q. Cable TV, phone, ceiling fan, VCR, fireplace, robes, complimentary wine, soft drinks, coffee/tea, chocolates and snacks in room. Central air. Library and Two parlors on premises. Small meetings and family reunions hosted. Antiquing, art galleries, bicycling, canoeing/kayaking, fishing, golf, hiking, horseback riding, Fish Hatechery Aquarium, Bayou Pierre Gator Park and Show, live theater, museums, parks and tennis nearby.

Publicity: Southern Living, Southern Lady and Gourmet.

Levy House Bed & Breakfast

358 Jefferson St
Natchitoches, LA 71457-4382
(318)352-0662 (800)840-0662
E-mail: judy@levyeasthouse.com
Web: www.levyeasthouse.com

Circa 1838. In the heart of Natchitoches National Historic Landmark district stands the Levy-East House, a Greek Revival home built in 1838 by Trizzini and Soldini. The house, with its gabled roof, brick chimneys and iron lace of the same design that was used in the old New Orleans Mint, was sold (along with two slaves) at an auction in 1840 for $3,700. Both the home and the antique furnishings were restored in 1994, and many pieces of the antique furniture have been in the home for more than 100 years. A century-old Magnolia tree flourishes in the side yard, and the ravine on the south side was originally called "Bayou a Mule" because traders once tied their mules to trees on the banks of the ravine. The four guest rooms are decorated with antiques like grand Romanesque Revival beds and Louisiana armoires. Window dressings in the parlor are replicas of those hanging at the historic Rosedown Plantation in St. Francisville. Guests enjoy a gourmet breakfast including such dishes as French toast topped with strawberries, bananas and warm maple syrup. The inn was featured on PBS's "A Taste of Louisiana" and in Southern Living Magazine.

Innkeeper(s): Judy and Avery East. $125-200. MC, VISA, AX, PC, TC. TAC10. 4 rooms with PB. Breakfast included in rates. Types of meals: Gourmet bkfst and early coffee/tea. Beds: Q. Cable TV, phone, turndown service, ceiling fan, VCR and whirlpool baths in room. Central air. Fax and copier on premises. Antiquing, art galleries, fishing, golf, hiking, museums, shopping and tennis nearby.

Publicity: Southern Living, Southern Lady Magazine and PBS.

Queen Anne B&B

125 Pine St
Natchitoches, LA 71457
(318)352-0989 (888)685-1585 Fax:(318)352-9500
E-mail: 1howell@cp-tel.net
Web: www.queenannebandb.com

Circa 1905. The city's Historic Landmark District is where to find this almost 100-year-old, two-story Victorian inn, listed in the National Register. It was built by a Civil War veteran and has been recently restored, retaining its character and integrity. American ingenuity and French sophistication are combined to create a comfortable elegance. There is a guest refrigerator and a movie selection for in-room VCRs. Some guest bedrooms feature clawfoot and whirlpool tubs. A multi-course breakfast includes hearty regional dishes. Stroll the generous grounds and swing in the arbor before taking an easy walk downtown.

Innkeeper(s): Catherine Howell. $95-150. MC, VISA, AX, DS, PC, TC. 5 rooms with PB. Breakfast included in rates. Types of meals: Gourmet bkfst, veg bkfst, early coffee/tea and snacks/refreshments. Beds: KQD. Cable TV, phone, ceiling fan, VCR, complimentary wine, bottled water, soft drinks and light snacks in room. Central air. Refrigerator and movie selection on premises. Family reunions hosted. Antiquing, fishing, golf, Riverboat tours, city trolley tours, live theater, museums, parks, shopping, sporting events and tennis nearby.

New Orleans   G8

1890 St. Charles Guest House

1748 Prytania St
New Orleans, LA 70130-5261
(504)529-2952 Fax:(504)522-6340
E-mail: dhilton111@aol.com
Web: stcharlesguesthouse.com

Circa 1850. Savor the eclectic essence of vintage New Orleans while staying at one of the area's oldest small hotels that was originally an old maritime boarding house. Sitting in the picturesque Lower Garden District near the French Quarter, this late Victorian is low tech with a quaint ambiance. Shelves lined with books are found throughout the rooms. Filled with antiques, the assortment of guest bedrooms meet a variety of needs. Enjoy a continental breakfast and afternoon beverages. Among banana trees, a secluded patio and pool area offer relaxation. The knowledgeable staff are helpful with local recommendations.

Innkeeper(s): Joanne & Dennis Hilton. $35-150. AX. 38 rooms, 26 with PB. Breakfast included in rates. Types of meals: Cont and snacks/refreshments. Beds: QDT. Ceiling fan and fireplace in room. Air conditioning. Fax, swimming and library on premises. Family reunions hosted. Spanish spoken. Amusement parks, antiquing, art galleries and bicycling nearby.

Publicity: *Chicago-Sun Times, Daily News, Huntsville Times, Doctor's Review, Gambit, Travel Holiday, American Flyer, Good Housekeeping, Toronto Star and Washington Post.*

"You had an intuitive understanding of how a group like ours should experience New Orleans."

A Creole House Hotel

1013 Saint Ann St
New Orleans, LA 70116-3012
(504)524-8076 (800)535-7858 Fax:(504)581-3277
E-mail: ach5555@aol.com

Circa 1830. The many sites of the French Quarter surround this historic hotel located in the Center of the French Quarter. Guests can walk to fine restaurants and boutiques, and Bourbon Street is just two blocks away.

Innkeeper(s): Brent Kovach. $49-189. MC, VISA, AX, DS, TC. TAC10. 29 rooms. Breakfast included in rates. Types of meals: Cont. Beds: KQDT. Phone in room. Air conditioning. Fax and copier on premises. Antiquing, fishing, golf, live theater, parks and sporting events nearby.

Auld's Sweetolive B&B

2460 N Rampart St
New Orleans, LA 70117
(504)947-4332
E-mail: s2auld@aol.com
Web: www.sweetolive.com

Circa 1800. Get away from it all in New Orleans in an early 19th-century Creole bungalow that is a 10-minute walk from the French Quarter. Built before the Civil War, this inn was possibly a bordello. It's located near the birthplace of Jelly Roll Morton, the self-proclaimed "inventor of jazz." The inn's five guest bedrooms have been hand-painted and decorated by co-owner Stuart Auld. The bedrooms have individual tree motifs: Cypress, Oak, Palmetto, Magnolia and Sweetolive. A complimentary breakfast of locally baked French pastries, a house blend of café au lait, juices, fresh fruit and exotic teas and jellies is served in the sunroom or in the garden. Porch hammocks are on a "first come first snooze" basis.

Historic Interest: French Quarter, St. Roch Cemetery.

Innkeeper(s): Stuart Auld. $99-150. MC, VISA, AX, DS, PC, TC. 5 rooms with PB. Types of meals: Cont plus, early coffee/tea, afternoon tea and snacks/refreshments. Beds: QD. Turndown service and ceiling fan in room. Air conditioning. VCR, bicycles, library and grand piano on premises. Amusement parks, antiquing, art galleries, beaches, bicycling, canoeing/kayaking, fishing, golf, hiking, horseback riding, live theater, museums, parks, shopping, sporting events, tennis and water sports nearby.

Bonne Chance B&B

621 Opelousas Ave
New Orleans, LA 70114
(504)367-0798 Fax:(504)368-4643
E-mail: watsondolores@aol.com
Web: www.bonne-chance.com

Circa 1890. This recently renovated two-story Eastlake pale pink Victorian with gentle lavender and green trim boasts four balconies and a porch with fretwork and columns. Antique furnishings and Oriental rugs are found throughout, and fully furnished apartments with kitchens are available. A secluded courtyard with fountain and gardens are in the rear of the inn. A free five-minute ferry boat ride takes you to the French Quarter.

Innkeeper(s): Dolores Watson. $85-175. MC, VISA, AX. TAC10. 3 suites. Breakfast included in rates. Types of meals: Cont plus. Beds: Q. Cable TV, phone, ceiling fan and three apartments with fully equipped kitchens in room. Air conditioning. VCR, fax, copier and library on premises. French spoken. Amusement parks, antiquing, fishing, golf, French Quarter, live theater, parks, shopping, sporting events and tennis nearby.

Publicity: *New Orleans.*

Bougainvillea House

841 Bourbon St
New Orleans, LA 70116-3106
(504)525-3983 Fax:(504)283-7777
E-mail: patkahn@aol.com

Circa 1822. Originally built by a plantation owner, and located directly in the French Quarter, this French Townhouse served as a hospital during the Civil War. The Riverboat Suite faces the courtyard and has French doors that open onto a balcony. It offers a living room and full kitchen. The inn is furnished with

Victorian antiques and traditional pieces. The courtyard and patio are behind private locked gates. Bourbon Street is one block away, while Royal Street and its restaurants and museums is two blocks away. Guests can walk to Antoines for dinner.

Innkeeper(s): Flo Cairo. $90-250. VISA, AX. TAC10. 3 suites. Beds: KQD. Cable TV, phone and ceiling fan in room. Air conditioning. Fax on premises. Antiquing, golf, live theater, parks, shopping and sporting events nearby.

"We love your home and always enjoy our visits here so much!"

Chateau du Louisiane

1216 Louisiana Ave
New Orleans, LA 70115
(504)269-2600 (800)734-0137 Fax:(504)269-2603
E-mail: chateau@accesscom.net
Web: www.chateaulouisiane.com

Circa 1885. Built in Greek Revival style, Chateau du Louisiane is located on the edge of New Orleans' famous Garden District. The home, along with the myriad of other historic homes and buildings, is listed in the National Register of Historic Places. Period furnishings decorate the guest rooms, suites and common areas. Each guest room is named after someone famous in Louisiana history, such as Louis Armstrong. The chateau is one mile from the French Quarter, and the St. Charles streetcar stops just three blocks away.

Historic Interest: In Garden District, French Quarter (1 mile), St. Charles Streetcar (3 blocks).

Innkeeper(s): Penny Toohey. $79-159. MC, VISA, AX, DS, TC. TAC10. 5 rooms with PB, 2 suites and 2 conference rooms. Breakfast and snacks/refreshments included in rates. Types of meals: Cont plus and early coffee/tea. Cable TV, phone and ceiling fan in room. Central air. Fax, copier, bicycles and library on premises. Weddings, small meetings, family reunions and seminars hosted. Antiquing, art galleries, bicycling, fishing, golf, live theater, museums, parks, shopping, sporting events, tennis and water sports nearby.

Columns Hotel

3811 Saint Charles Ave
New Orleans, LA 70115-4638
(504)899-9308 (800)445-9308 Fax:(504)899-8170

Circa 1883. The Columns was built by Simon Hernsheim, a tobacco merchant, who was the wealthiest philanthropist in New Orleans. The two-story columned gallery and portico provide a grand entrance into this restored mansion. The estate was selected by Paramount Studios for the site of the movie "Pretty Baby," with Brooke Shields. The hotel is in the National Register of Historic Places. Jazz performances are scheduled Tuesday, Wednesday and during the Sunday champagne brunch.

Historic Interest: Garden District (one-half mile), aquarium (two miles), zoo (one-half mile), universities (one-half mile), French Quarter (two miles on streetcar).

Innkeeper(s): Claire & Jacques Creppel. $90-200. MC, VISA, AX. 20 rooms with PB, 3 suites and 1 conference room. Breakfast included in rates. Types of meals: Cont.

Pets Allowed.

Publicity: *Good Housekeeping, New York Times, Vogue, Good Morning America, Elle, Forbes FYI, Travel Holiday and Conde Nast.*

"...like experiencing life of the Old South, maybe more like living in a museum. We came to New Orleans to learn about New Orleans, and we did... at The Columns."

Cornstalk Hotel

915 Royal St
New Orleans, LA 70116-2701
(504)523-1515 Fax:(504)522-5558

Circa 1816. This home belonged to Judge Francois Xavier-Martin, the author of the first history of Louisiana and Louisiana's first State Supreme Court Chief Justice. Andrew Jackson stayed here and another guest,  Harriet Beecher Stowe, wrote Uncle Tom's Cabin after viewing the nearby slave markets. The Civil War followed the widely read publication. Surrounding the inn is a 160-year-old wrought-iron cornstalk fence. Stained-glass windows, Oriental rugs, fireplaces and antiques grace the property. Breakfast and the morning newspaper can be served in your room or set up on the balcony, porch or patio.

Innkeeper(s): Debi & David Spencer. $75-185. MC, VISA, AX. 14 rooms with PB. Beds: KQDT.

Publicity: *London Sunday Times.*

Essem's House New Orleans 1st B&B

3660 Gentilly Blvd
New Orleans, LA 70122-4910
(504)947-3401 Fax:(504)838-0140
E-mail: nobba@bellsouth.net
Web: www.neworleansbandb.com

Circa 1930. A grassy lawn sets off this two-story brick Mediterranean-style house located on a tree-lined street. There's a steep gabled roof and red tile. A solarium and parlor with fireplace are inviting spots. The innkeeper has offered bed and breakfast to New Orleans visitors for more than 20 years. Art Deco and traditional decor is featured in the guest rooms and there are some antiques.

Innkeeper(s): Sarah-Margaret Brown. $75-95. MC, VISA, AX, DS, TC. 5 rooms, 2 with PB, 1 suite and 1 cottage. Breakfast included in rates. Types of meals: Cont plus. Beds: KQDT. Ceiling fan in room. Air conditioning. VCR, fax and guest Common Room on premises. Family reunions hosted. Amusement parks, antiquing, fishing, golf, live theater, parks, shopping, sporting events and tennis nearby.

Pets allowed: With restrictions.

Fairchild House

1518 Prytania St
New Orleans, LA 70130-4416
(504)524-0154 (800)256-8096 Fax:(504)568-0063
E-mail: info@fairchildhouse.com
Web: www.fairchildhouse.com

Circa 1841. Situated in the oak-lined Lower Garden District of New Orleans, this Greek Revival home was built by architect L.H. Pilie. The house and its guest houses maintain a Victorian ambiance with elegantly appointed guest rooms. Wine and cheese is served upon guests' arrival. Afternoon tea can be served upon request. The bed & breakfast, which is on the Mardi Gras parade route, is 17 blocks from the French Quarter and eight blocks from the convention center. Streetcars are just one block away, as are many local attractions, including paddleboat cruises, Canal Place and Riverwalk shopping, an aquarium, zoo, the Charles Avenue mansions and Tulane and Loyola universities.

Innkeeper(s): Rita Olmo & Beatriz Aprigliano-Ziegler. $75-165. MC, VISA, AX, TC. TAC10. 20 rooms with PB and 3 suites. Breakfast included in ra... Types of meals: Cont plus. Beds: KQDT. Phone and voice mail in room. A...

conditioning. Fax and copier on premises. Weddings and family reunions hosted. Antiquing, restaurants and shopping nearby.

"Accommodations were great; staff was great...Hope to see y'all soon!"

The Frenchmen Hotel

417 Frenchmen
New Orleans, LA 70116-2003
(504)948-2166 (800)831-1781 Fax:(504)948-2258
E-mail: fm5678@aol.com

Circa 1897. The Mississippi River is just a few blocks away from this historic hotel, located in New Orleans' famed French Quarter. The trolley stops less than a block away, whisking you to museums, shops, gourmet restaurants and many unique attractions. The elegant guest rooms boast period furnishings, and each room has been individually decorated. The inn's lush courtyard includes a pool and Jacuzzi. A concierge service is available around the clock, and the staff can help you plan tours and other activities.

Innkeeper(s): Brent Kovach. $59-175. MC, VISA, AX, DS, TC. TAC10. 28 rooms. Breakfast included in rates. Types of meals: Cont. Beds: QD. Cable TV, phone and ceiling fan in room. Air conditioning. Fax, copier, swimming and jacuzzi on premises. Antiquing, fishing, golf, live theater, parks, shopping and sporting events nearby.

Grand Victorian

2727 St. Charles Ave
New Orleans, LA 70130
(504)895-1104 (800)977-0008 Fax:(504)896-8688
E-mail: brabe2727@aol.com
Web: www.gvbb.com

Circa 1893. Thomas Sully, a celebrated New Orleans architect, built this Queen Anne Victorian located at the edge of the Garden District. Gables, porches, balconies, bay windows, dormers, flower boxes and a wraparound porch have all been carefully renovated. Furnishings are antique to complement the inn's original millwork, pine floors and beautiful staircase. Guest rooms feature romantic old beds and armoires and there are suites with Jacuzzis and private balconies. The innkeeper is a native of New Orleans and is enthusiastic about all that it offers. She will be glad to help you plan your stay as well as suggest tours to nearby plantations within an hour's drive. The inn is located on the streetcar route.

Innkeeper(s): Bonnie Rabe. $150-300. MC, VISA, AX, DS, TC. TAC10. 8 rooms, 6 with PB and 2 suites. Breakfast and snacks/refreshments included in rates. Types of meals: Cont plus and early coffee/tea. Beds: KQD. Cable TV, phone and ceiling fan in room. Central air. Fax on premises. Handicap access. Weddings, small meetings and family reunions hosted. Amusement parks, antiquing, art galleries, beaches, fishing, golf, live theater, museums, parks, shopping and sporting events nearby.

Publicity: Travel, Channel-Mardi Gras 2001, Times Picayune, Southern Living, Detroit Free Press and Local Mayorial Press Conference.

H Whitney House on the toric Esplanade

Esplanade Ave
Orleans, LA 70116-1706
8-9448 (877)944-9448 Fax:(504)949-7939
hwhitneyhouse@home.com
.hhwhitney.com

The Civil War had barely ended when builders n this elegant Italianate mansion. More than a sts step into a home that maintains much of its

original charm. The intricate molding and plasterwork are of the highest quality. Common rooms with Victorian furnishings and appointments complement the architectural work. Some of the notable antiques include an early 20th-century player piano. The Bride's Room is perfectly decorated for those with romance in mind with its lace-draped canopy bed. This room can be combined with the Solarium or Groom's rooms to form a spacious suite. The Solarium and the Honeymoon Suite both include a private bath and a fireplace. HH Whitney House is located in New Orleans Esplanade Ridge historic district, and the French Quarter is a half-mile walk from the home.

Innkeeper(s): Glen Miller/ Randy Saizan. $75-225. MC, VISA, AX, DS, PC, TC. TAC10. 5 rooms, 2 with PB, 5 with FP and 1 suite. Snacks/refreshments included in rates. Types of meals: Cont and early coffee/tea. Beds: QD. Cable TV, phone, turndown service, ceiling fan, safes, bathrobes and in room. Central air. VCR, fax and spa on premises. Weddings, small meetings and family reunions hosted. Amusement parks, antiquing, art galleries, bicycling, canoeing/kayaking, fishing, golf, horseback riding, French Quarter, live theater, museums, parks, shopping, sporting events and tennis nearby.

The House on Bayou Road

2275 Bayou Rd
New Orleans, LA 70119-2666
(504)945-0992 (800)882-2968 Fax:(504)945-0993
E-mail: hobr@aol.com
Web: www.housonbayouroad.com

Circa 1798. Romantic guest rooms, gourmet cuisine and two-acre grounds dotted with ponds, herb and flower gardens await guests at this Creole Plantation home. The home was built as the main house to an indigo plantation just prior to the turn of the 19th century. The lush surroundings are a distraction from

city life, yet this restful inn is just a few blocks from the French Quarter. The guest quarters are appointed with fine linens and elegant furnishings. Breakfast is a don't-miss, three-course event. The innkeeper is co-director of a New Orleans cooking school. Guests with a flair for the gourmet might consider signing up for the school's popular Grand or Mini classes, which include tuition and lodging.

Innkeeper(s): Cynthia Reeves. $125-295. MC, VISA, AX, TC. TAC10. 8 rooms with PB, 2 with FP, 3 suites and 2 cottages. Breakfast included in rates. Types of meals: Gourmet bkfst. Beds: KQT. Cable TV, phone, turndown service, ceiling fan and mini Bars in room. Air conditioning. VCR, fax, copier, spa and swimming on premises. Weddings and small meetings hosted. Spanish and French spoken. Antiquing, fishing, live theater and parks nearby.

Publicity: Southern Living and Travel & Leisure.

"Once again our stay was delightful. I can't imagine coming to New Orleans without staying here."

Lafitte Guest House

1003 Bourbon St
New Orleans, LA 70116-2707
(504)581-2678 (800)331-7971 Fax:(504)581-2677
E-mail: lafitte@travelbase.com
Web: www.lafitteguesthouse.com

Circa 1849. This elegant French manor house has been meticulously restored. The house is filled with fine antiques and paintings collected from around the world. Located in the heart of the

French Quarter, the inn is near world-famous restaurants, museums, antique shops and rows of Creole and Spanish cottages. Between 5:30 p.m. and 7 p.m., there is a wine and cheese social hour.

Historic Interest: Historic New Orleans Collection, Keyes House, Beauregard House, Gallier House (few blocks away), famous Jackson Square and Saint Louis Cathedral (4 blocks), French Market (3 blocks).

Innkeeper(s): Edward G. Dore & Andrew J. Crocchiolo. $129-219. MC, VISA, AX, DC, DS, TC. 14 rooms with PB, 7 with FP and 2 suites. Breakfast included in rates. Types of meals: Cont plus. Beds: KQ. TV, phone and ceiling fan in room. Air conditioning. Fax and copier on premises. Amusement parks, antiquing, fishing, live theater, parks, shopping, sporting events and water sports nearby.

Publicity: *Glamour, Antique Monthly, McCall's, Dixie and Country Living.*

"This old building offers the finest lodgings we have found in the city — McCall's Magazine."

Lamothe House

621 Esplanade Ave
New Orleans, LA 70116-2018
(504)947-1161 (800)367-5858 Fax:(504)943-6536
E-mail: lam5675842@aol.com

Circa 1830. A carriageway that formerly cut through the center of many French Quarter buildings was enclosed at the Lamothe House in 1866, and it is now the foyer. Splendid Victorian furnishings enhance moldings, high ceilings and hand-turned mahogany stairway railings. Gilded opulence goes unchecked in the Mallard and Lafayette suites. Registration takes place in the second-story salon above the courtyard.

Historic Interest: National Register.

Innkeeper(s): Carol Chauppette. $59-250. MC, VISA, AX, PC, TC. TAC10. 20 rooms with PB, 1 with FP, 9 suites, 2 cottages and 1 conference room. Breakfast included in rates. Types of meals: Cont plus and afternoon tea. Beds: QDT. Cable TV, phone, turndown service and ceiling fan in room. Air conditioning. VCR, fax, copier, child care, free parking, swimming pool and Jacuzzi on premises. Weddings, small meetings and family reunions hosted. Amusement parks, antiquing, fishing, French Quarter, live theater, parks, shopping and sporting events nearby.

Publicity: *Southern Living (Cover), Los Angeles Times, Houston Post and Travel & Leisure.*

Macarty Park Guest House

3820 Burgundy St
New Orleans, LA 70117
(504)943-4994 (800)521-2790
E-mail: macpar@aol.com
Web: www.macartypark.com

Circa 1899. Relax on the porch swing of this romantic turn-of-the-century home. The parlor is inviting with a beautifully polished carved mantelpiece, balloon curtains and appealing antiques. Guest rooms are tastefully furnished with antiques and reproductions in an elegant uncluttered traditional style and some offer four-poster beds. In addition to the guest rooms, cottages and condos are available. The inn's tropical setting can be enjoyed next to the heated in-ground pool or from the spacious hot tub.

$59-225. MC, VISA, AX, DS, TC. TAC10. 8 rooms with PB, 3 with FP, 1 suite and 2 cottages. Breakfast included in rates. Types of meals: Cont plus. Beds: KQDT. Cable TV and phone in room. Air conditioning. Fax, spa and swimming on premises. Small meetings, family reunions and seminars hosted. French spoken. Antiquing, French Quarter, live theater, shopping, sporting events and tennis nearby.

New Orleans Bed & Breakfast Accommodations

PO Box 8163
New Orleans, LA 70182
(504)838-0071 (888)240-0070 Fax:(504)838-0140
E-mail: nobba@bellsouth.net
Web: www.neworleansbandb.com

Circa 1883. For more than 20 years this reservation service has successfully matched guests and hosts. It specializes in providing personalized service for someone traveling solo on business, a couple wanting a romantic getaway, a family vacation or a group retreat. There are many historic bed & breakfasts and guest houses offering local flavor, including a home built by a bootlegger and an 1883 Italianate Mansion designed by architect Henry Howard. Some listings are available for short or longer stays, as well as city apartments with daily and weekly rates.

$75-350. MC, VISA, AX, DS, TC. 150 rooms. Types of meals: Cont plus and cont. Beds: KQDT. Cable TV, phone and ceiling fan in room. Central air. Weddings and family reunions hosted. Amusement parks, antiquing, art galleries, beaches, bicycling, fishing, golf, live theater, museums, parks, shopping and sporting events nearby.

Pets allowed: some smaller pets.

Nine-O-Five Royal Hotel

905 Royal St
New Orleans, LA 70116
(504)523-0219
E-mail: info@905royalhotel.com
Web: www.905royalhotel.com

Circa 1800. This European-style hotel is in New Orleans's French Quarter. It offers eight guest rooms and three suites around a private courtyard and three suites that have balconies overlooking Royal Street where horse-drawn carriages regularly pass by. Each guest room and suite has its own kitchenette. The hotel is in the heart of the French Quarter, world-renowned restaurants and historic sites including Bourbon Street.

$125-250. MC, VISA, PC, TC. TAC10. 8 rooms with PB and 3 suites. Beds: KQD. Cable TV, phone, private maid service and front balconies in room. Central air. Antiquing, art galleries, Convention Center, parks, shopping and sporting events nearby.

Publicity: *My Name is Nobody, Drowning Pool and Believe it or Not.*

Olde Victorian Inn

914 N Rampart St
New Orleans, LA 70116
(504)522-2446 (800)725-2446 Fax:(504)522-8646
E-mail: oldeinn@aol.com
Web: www.oldevictorianinn.com

Circa 1841. Experience the romantic 1840s at this two-story Victorian Inn in the heart of the New Orleans Historic French Quarter. Enjoy tea in the lush tropical courtyard or inside, surrounded by floor to ceiling windows, antiques and plenty of lace and ruffles. Gourmet breakfast awaits each guest to help start off an adventurous day down the front door steps to Rampart Street. Large beds and private baths invite each guest to sleep in and relax before and after enjoying some of the best nightlife in America. Embrace America's past both in town and in the inn, which was one of the first French Quarter homes owned by a freed slave following the Civil War.

Historic Interest: Congo Square, Voo Doo Temple.

Innkeeper(s): Keith & Andre West-Harrison. $135-250. MC, VISA, AX, DC, CB, PC, TC. TAC10. 6 rooms with PB, 4 with FP and 1 conference room. Breakfast and afternoon tea included in rates. Types of meals: Gourmet bkfst, veg bkfst and early coffee/tea. Beds: D. Ceiling fan and clawfoot tub and shower in room. Central air. VCR, fax and copier on premises. Weddings, small meetings, family reunions and seminars hosted. German spoken. Amusement parks, antiquing, art galleries, live theater, museums, parks, shopping and sporting events nearby.

Publicity: *Courier and Australian Travel Channel.*

Park View Guest House

7004 St Charles Avenue
New Orleans, LA 70118
(504)861-7564 (888)533-0746 Fax:(504)861-1225
E-mail: pmarigny@aol.com

Circa 1884. A visit to this European-style Grand Victorian guest house listed in the National Register, is a splendid experience. An old-world elegance is enhanced by hardwood floors and 12-foot high ceilings. Decorated with antiques and modern furnishings, many of the well-appointed guest bedrooms feature balconies overlooking Audubon Park or St. Charles Avenue. A breathtaking view is enjoyed each morning in the Audubon Dining Room, where a continental breakfast is served. Conveniently located uptown, just step outside for a trolley ride to the French Quarter, Riverbend shopping or many other local attractions.

Historic Interest: Garden District (2 miles).

Innkeeper(s): Joann Bird. $119-359. MC, VISA, AX, DC, DS, TC. TAC10. 22 rooms, 15 with PB. Breakfast included in rates. Types of meals: Cont plus and early coffee/tea. Beds: KQD. Cable TV, phone and ceiling fan in room. Air conditioning. Fax, copier and child care on premises. Weddings and family reunions hosted. Amusement parks, antiquing, art galleries, bicycling, fishing, golf, horseback riding, museums, parks, shopping, sporting events and tennis nearby.

Rathbone Inn

1227 Esplanade Ave
New Orleans, LA 70116-1975
(504)947-2100 (800)947-2101 Fax:(504)947-7454
E-mail: rathboneinn@aol.com
Web: www.rathboneinn.com

Circa 1850. Built prior to the Civil War, Rathbone Inn appears just as a genteel New Orleans mansion should. Two stories, accentuated with stately columns, wrought-iron fencing, and delicate exterior trim create a perfect historic ambiance. Guests are just blocks from the French Quarter and famed Bourbon Street. The innkeepers can help arrange unique tours of the city. Guests are pampered with wine and cheese upon arrival, and each morning, a continental breakfast buffet is provided. There is a courtyard complete with a hot tub, a perfect place to relax after touring the Quarter. Rooms include helpful amenities such as dataports and coffeemakers. Some rooms have balconies, and others include a kitchenette.

Historic Interest: French Quarter, Preservation Hall (1 mile) Plantations (10-20 miles).

Innkeeper(s): Chayim & Tina. $59-300. MC, VISA, AX, DC, DS. TAC10. 13 suites. Breakfast, afternoon tea and snacks/refreshments included in rates. Types of meals: Veg bkfst, cont plus and early coffee/tea. Beds: KQ. Cable TV, phone and ceiling fan in room. Air conditioning. VCR, fax, copier and spa on premises. Weddings hosted. German spoken. Amusement parks, antiquing, art galleries, bicycling, golf, hiking, horseback riding, French Quarter, Bourbon Street, live theater, museums, parks and shopping nearby.

Pets Allowed.

St Vincent Guest House

1507 Magazine St
New Orleans, LA 70130-4723
(504)566-1515 Fax:(504)566-1518
E-mail: peterschreiber@compuserve.com
Web: www.stvincentsguesthouse.com

Circa 1861. Built in 1861, this three-story Victorian-Colonial guest house is a recognized historic landmark within walking distance of New Orleans' French Quarter. Tall white pillars invite guests to enter through the doors and step into the traditional décor of wicker and pastels, followed by a stroll down wraparound, tiered balconies. Located in lower Garden District, guests can absorb rich Louisiana history in Coliseum Square or live it up in the New Orleans night life. Following a full Southern breakfast, spend a soothing day by the pool in the courtyard or with your friends in the tea room. With the variety of festivities that New Orleans has to offer, this guest house provides an optimum location for travelers seeking a comfortable place to stay in a city that is alive.

Historic Interest: French Quarter (1.5 miles), Garden District.

Innkeeper(s): Sally Leonard Schreiber, Peter Schreiber. $59-89. MC, VISA, AX, DC, DS, PC, TC. TAC10. 76 rooms, 74 with PB and 2 suites. Breakfast included in rates. Types of meals: Full bkfst. Beds: KQDT. TV, phone and ceiling fan in room. Air conditioning. Fax and swimming on premises. Handicap access. Weddings, small meetings and family reunions hosted. Amusement parks, antiquing, art galleries, bicycling, canoeing/kayaking, fishing, golf, horseback riding, live theater, museums, parks, shopping, sporting events and tennis nearby.

Pets Allowed.

St. Peter Guest House Hotel

1005 Saint Peter St
New Orleans, LA 70116-3014
(504)524-9232 (800)535-7815 Fax:(504)523-5198
E-mail: sptlj678z@aol.com

Circa 1800. The St. Peter House, which is ideally situated in the middle of the French Quarter, offers a delightful glance at New Orleans French heritage and 18th-century charm. From the lush courtyards to the gracious balconies, guests will enjoy the view of the busy quarter. Rooms are individually appointed, some with period antiques.

Innkeeper(s): Brent Kovach. $59-225. MC, VISA, AX, DS, PC, TC. TAC10. 28 rooms with PB and 11 suites. Breakfast included in rates. Types of meals: Cont plus. Beds: KQDT. Cable TV, phone and ceiling fan in room. Air conditioning. Fax on premises. Amusement parks, antiquing, fishing, live theater, parks and shopping nearby.

Sun & Moon Bed & Breakfast

1037 N Rampart St
New Orleans, LA 70116-2405
(504)529-4652 (800)638-9169 Fax:(504)529-4652
E-mail: sunmoon4@bellsouth.net
Web: www.sunandmoonbnb.com

Circa 1819. Built in the early part of the 19th century, Sun & Moon offers a historic experience just blocks from Bourbon Street and many French Quarter attractions. The Sun Suite has a private balcony, and the Moon Suite has a private deck. The Jazz Gallery is an excellent spot for a longer stay. It includes a bedroom, kitchen, living room with a sofa bed and a bathroom with a hand-painted clawfoot tub. In the mornings, guests are served a continental New Orleans-style breakfast with freshly brewed chicory coffee and pastries. Innkeeper Glinda Mantle is a New Orleans native and can point you to jazz clubs, restaurants and the best local attractions.

Historic Interest: St. Louis Cemeteries, Jackson Square, St. Louis Cathedral, Cafe du Monde.

Innkeeper(s): Glinda Mantle. $85-115. MC, VISA, AX, TC. 4 rooms with PB. Types of meals: Cont. Beds: KQ. TV, ceiling fan and refrigerator in room. Air conditioning. Fax and garden with classic fountain on premises. Antiquing, art galleries, live theater, museums, parks and shopping nearby.

Sun Oak Guest House

2020 Burgundy St
New Orleans, LA 70116-1606
(504)945-0322 Fax:(504)945-0322
E-mail: sunoaknola@home.com
Web: http://members.home.net/sunoaknola

Circa 1836. This historic home was restored to its former glory as an early 19th-century manor by innkeeper Eugene Cizek. Cizek heads the preservation program at Tulane University and has won awards for historic preservation. His expertise has turned a dilapidated home into a beautiful showplace. Rooms feature a variety of French, Creole, Acadian and mid-French Louisiana antiques, Oriental rugs, ceiling fans, fine fabrics and beautiful light fixtures. Behind the home lie lush, landscaped patios, gardens and the Sun Oak tree.

Historic Interest: The edge of the French Quarter is five minutes from the historic Sun Oak, and the inn itself is located in a local and national historic district.

Innkeeper(s): Eugene D. Cizek & Lloyd L. Sensat, Jr. $100-200. PC, TC. TAC10. 2 rooms with PB. Breakfast included in rates. Types of meals: Cont. Beds: D. Phone and ceiling fan in room. Air conditioning. Library on premises. Weddings, small meetings, family reunions and seminars hosted. Some Spanish spoken. Amusement parks, antiquing, fishing, golf, cafes, restaurants, night clubs, live theater, parks, shopping, sporting events, tennis and water sports nearby.

Publicity: *Traditional Home, New Orleans Elegance and Decadence, Classic New Orleans, Colonial Homes, Better Homes & Gardens, Journal and This Old House.*

"From A-Z we loved our visit to Sun Oak. The house is so warm and charming."

Saint Francisville   E6

Butler Greenwood Plantation

8345 US Highway 61
Saint Francisville, LA 70775-6671
(225)635-6312 Fax:(225)635-6370
E-mail: butlergree@aol.com
Web: www.butlergreenwood.com

Circa 1795. Still owned and occupied by the original family, this beautiful English-country-style 1796 plantation offers more than 50 acres with hundreds of graceful ancient live oaks and blooming gardens on the landscaped grounds. Accommodations are in a variety of cottages offering privacy and seclusion. Each cottage offers a unique experience such as the Treehouse, which features a king cypress four-poster bed, three-level deck and fireplace. The 1796 Old Kitchen cottage boasts skylights, the plantation's original well and a double Jacuzzi. On the National Register, the home offers a daily tour narrated by one of the plantation's family members. The formal Victorian parlor in the house is filled with original antiques and high Victorian decor. Each accommodation has its own kitchen, but the innkeeper, a historian and author, (her books are available in the gift shop) also provides a continental breakfast.

Innkeeper(s): Anne Butler. $125. AX, PC, TC. TAC10. 7 cottages. Breakfast included in rates. Types of meals: Cont plus. Beds: KQD. Cable TV, phone, ceiling fan, kitchen, fireplaces, Jacuzzi's and BBQ in room. Central air. Swimming on premises. Small meetings, family reunions and seminars hosted. Antiquing, bicycling, fishing, golf, hiking, horseback riding, museums, parks, shopping, water sports and wineries nearby.

Pets allowed: well behaved, quiet, non-destructive.

Green Springs Inn & Cottages

7463 Tunica Trace
Saint Francisville, LA 70775-5716
(225)635-4232 (800)457-4978 Fax:(225)635-3355
E-mail: madeline@greenspringsinn.com
Web: www.greenspringsinn.com

Circa 1990. Although this replica of a bluffland cottage, in the Feliciana style, was constructed just several years ago, its historic roots run deep. The inn rests on 150 acres that were owned by the innkeeper's family for 200 years, and on the grounds is a 2,000-year-old Indian mound. The inn's name comes from a natural spring found in a glen on the property, and Big Bayou Sara Creek is on the  property borders. Visitors can choose from three guest rooms, decorated in an attractive blend of antique and contemporary furnishings or six cottages with king or queen beds, Jacuzzi tubs and fireplaces. A full plantation breakfast is served.

Innkeeper(s): Madeline Nevill. $95-195. MC, VISA, AX. 10 rooms with PB, 1 suite and 6 cottages. Breakfast included in rates. Types of meals: Full bkfst and early coffee/tea. Beds: KQT. Cable TV and ceiling fan in room. Air conditioning. VCR on premises. Antiquing, bicycling, fishing, golf, hiking, Civil War battlefield, Mississippi River ferry, shopping and sporting events nearby.

Publicity: *Houston Chronicle, Saint Francisville Democrat, Star Telegram, Country Roads, Advocate, Southern Living, Country Magazine and Gourmet Magazine.*

"The most picturesque setting in Louisiana."

St. Francisville Inn

5720 Commerce St, PO Box 1369
Saint Francisville, LA 70775-1369
(225)635-6502 (800)488-6502 Fax:(225)635-6421
E-mail: staff@wolfsinn.com
Web: www.stfrancisvilleinn.com

Circa 1880. Formerly known as the Wolf-Schlesinger House, this one-acre estate in the historic district features Victorian Gothic architecture and 100-year-old oak trees draped with moss. Antiques and reproductions blend with a touch of country decor for a pleasant appeal. Relaxation comes easy in the parlor and den. Guest bedrooms connect to the main house by wide covered porches in the front and back. They all open onto a New Orleans-style courtyard. One room boasts an oversized Jacuzzi. A breakfast buffet includes an assortment of egg dishes, breads and muffins, grits, blintz, fruit and sausage. Enjoy a swim in the pool. Ask about special packages available.

Innkeeper(s): Patrick & Laurie Walsh. $75-90. MC, VISA, AX, DC, DS, PC, TC. TAC10. 10 rooms with PB and 1 conference room. Breakfast included in rates. Types of meals: Gourmet bkfst and afternoon tea. Beds: KQD. Cable TV, phone and ceiling fan in room. Air conditioning. Fax, copier, swimming and gift shop on premises. Small meetings, family reunions and seminars hosted. Amusement parks, antiquing, art galleries, bicycling, golf, hiking, horseback riding, museums, parks, shopping, sporting events, water sports and wineries nearby.

Maine

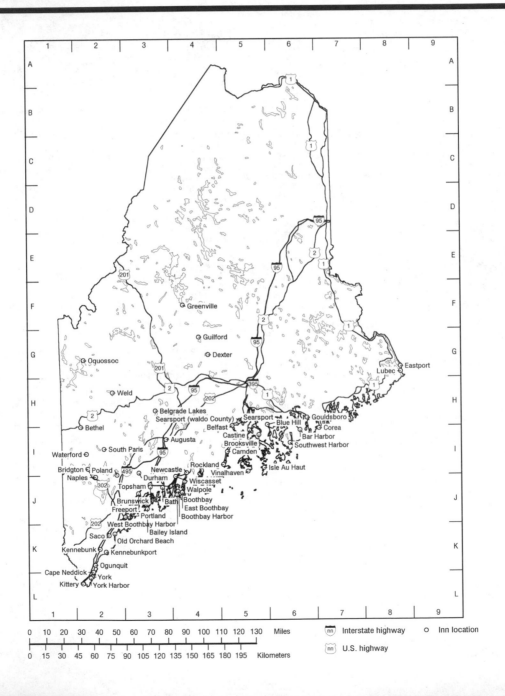

1	2	3	4	5	6	7	8	9

Greenville

Guilford

Dexter

Oquossoc

Eastport
Lubec

Weld

Belgrade Lakes
Searsport (waldo County)   Searsport   Gouldsboro
Belfast   Blue Hill   Corea
Bethel   Castine   Bar Harbor
Brooksville   Southwest Harbor
Waterford   South Paris   Augusta   Camden
Bridgton   Poland   Rockland   Isle Au Haut
Naples   Newcastle   Vinalhaven
Durham   Wiscasset
Topsham   Walpole
Brunswick   Bath   Boothbay
Freeport   East Boothbay
Portland   Boothbay Harbor
West Boothbay Harbor
Saco   Bailey Island
Old Orchard Beach
Kennebunk   Kennebunkport
Ogunquit
Cape Neddick   York
Kittery   York Harbor

| 0 | 10 | 20 | 30 | 40 | 50 | 60 | 70 | 80 | 90 | 100 | 110 | 120 | 130 | Miles |

| 0 | 15 | 30 | 45 | 60 | 75 | 90 | 105 | 120 | 135 | 150 | 165 | 180 | 195 | Kilometers |

Interstate highway   Inn location

U.S. highway

Acadia Schoodic H8

Acadia Oceanside Meadows Inn

PO Box 90, Rt 195, Prospect Harbor Rd
Acadia Schoodic, ME 04669
(207)963-5557 Fax:(207)963-5928
E-mail: oceaninn@oceaninn.com
Web: www.oceaninn.com

Circa 1860. Dunes, a sandy beach, a salt marsh, ponds, tidal pools, bald eagles and 200 acres of forest and meadows surround this oceanfront classic New England home. The inn is comprised of two houses originally built as inns by sea captain George Allen. Enjoy a sunset stroll and a starlit sky, then cuddle up to sounds of the crashing waves and a roaring fire in your room. Art from local artists are featured throughout, and the décor includes country furnishings and an occasional carved mahogany chest or table. Breakfast offerings feature freshly baked treats (strawberry-rhubarb bread is a favorite) and an entrée such as cheese-filled crepes garnished with edible flowers from the inn's organic garden. The innkeepers have had careers in geology, marine biology and geography and offer a wealth of information to help you enjoy the area. They have created Oceanside Meadows Innstitute in a converted barn on the grounds for cultural and educational events. Hike the grounds, bird watch, visit the nearby lighthouse or take your camera in case you spot a moose.

Historic Interest: Acadia National Park, Gouldsboro Historical Society Museum, Prospect Harbor Lighthouse, Grindstone Neck, Black House, Ellsworth; Ruggles House, Columbia Falls (all within 30 miles), Abby Museum, Bar Harbor, FDR's summer cottage, Campobello Island (within 60 miles).
Innkeeper(s): Ben Walker & Sonja Sundaram. $90-155. MC, VISA, AX, DC, CB, PC, TC. 14 rooms, 12 with PB, 2 suites and 1 conference room. Breakfast and afternoon tea included in rates. Types of meals: Gourmet bkfst, veg bkfst and early coffee/tea. Beds: KQT. Phone, ceiling fan, table fans, fresh flowers, quilts, wingback chairs, rocking chairs and bedtime stories in room. Fax, swimming, library, refrigerator, coffeemaker, stereo, croquet, horseshoes, gardens and art gallery on premises. Weddings, small meetings, family reunions and seminars hosted. Antiquing, art galleries, beaches, bicycling, canoeing/kayaking, fishing, golf, hiking, live theater, museums, parks, shopping and water sports nearby.
Pets allowed: well behaved.

"This is our best bed and breakfast experience. Hope to return soon."

Augusta I3

Maple Hill Farm B&B Inn

RR 1 Box 1145, Outlet Rd
Augusta, ME 04347
(207)622-2708 (800)622-2708 Fax:(207)622-0655
E-mail: stay@maplebb.com
Web: www.maplebb.com

Circa 1906. Visitors to Maine's capitol city have the option of staying at this nearby inn, a peaceful farm setting adjacent to a 600-acre state wildlife management area that is available for canoeing, fishing, hiking and hunting. This Victorian Shingle-style inn was once a stagecoach stop and dairy farm. Four rooms include large double whirlpool tubs and fireplaces. The inn, with its 130-acre grounds, easily accommodates conferences, parties and receptions. Guests are welcome to visit the many farm animals. Cobbossee Lake is a five-minute drive from the inn. The

center portion of Hallowell is listed as a National Historic District and offers antique shops and restaurants.
Historic Interest: State capitol building, state museum, archives, & Fort Western (5 miles).
Innkeeper(s): Scott Cowger & Vince Hannan. $65-175. MC, VISA, AX, DC, CB, DS, PC, TC. TAC10. 8 rooms with PB, 5 with FP, 1 suite and 1 conference room. Breakfast and afternoon tea included in rates. Types of meals: Full bkfst, early coffee/tea and snacks/refreshments. Beds: KQD. TV, phone, VCR, 3 with private decks and 4 with large whirlpool tubs in room. Handicap access. Weddings, small meetings, family reunions and seminars hosted. Antiquing, live theater, shopping, cross-country skiing and water sports nearby.
Publicity: *Family Fun, An Explorer's Guide to Maine, The Forecaster, Portland Press Herald, Kennebec Journal* and *Maine Times.*

"You add many thoughtful touches to your service that set your B&B apart from others, and really make a difference. Best of Maine, hands down!" (Maine Times)

Bailey Island J3

Captain York House B&B

Rt 24, PO Box 298
Bailey Island, ME 04003
(207)833-6224
E-mail: athorn7286@aol.com
Web: www.iwws.com/captainyork

Circa 1906. Bailey Island is the quaint fisherman's village of stories, poems and movies. Guests cross the world's only cribstone bridge to reach the island, where beautiful sunsets and dinners of fresh Maine lobster are the norm. This shingled, turn-of-the-cen-

tury, Mansard-style B&B was the home of a famous Maine sea captain, Charles York. Now a homestay-style bed & breakfast, the innkeepers have restored the home to its former glory, filling it with many antiques. Guests at Captain York's enjoy water views from all the guest rooms. Wild Maine blueberries often find a significant place on the breakfast menu.
Innkeeper(s): Alan & Jean Thornton. $70-110. MC, VISA, PC, TC. TAC10. 5 rooms with PB. Breakfast included in rates. Types of meals: Full bkfst. Beds: QT. VCR on premises. Weddings, small meetings, family reunions and seminars hosted. Antiquing, P. McMilan Museum, Maine Maritime Museum, live theater, parks, shopping, sporting events and water sports nearby.
Publicity: *Tri-Town News* and *Palm Beach Post.*

"Bailey Island turned out to be the hidden treasure of our trip and we hope to return for your great hospitality again."

Bar Harbor I6

The Atlantean Inn

11 Atlantic Ave
Bar Harbor, ME 04609
(207)288-5703 (800)722-6671 Fax:(207)288-0452
E-mail: waysideinn@acadia.net
Web: www.wayside-inn.com

Circa 1903. Experience a taste of the opulent Victorian era at this English Tudor-style bed & breakfast, located in historic downtown. Original watercolors and oil paintings, antique fixtures and furnishings all are placed with care in eye-pleasing and comfortable arrangements. Hospitality is generous, with guest bedrooms and suites offering room service, a video library and answering machines. Some feature working fireplaces and Jacuzzis. Several suites accommodate families with ease. Lobster quiche and blueberry muffins are two breakfast treats using delicious regional ingredients. Enjoy the perennial gardens, and relax under the shade of a maple tree.

Innkeeper(s): Mary Zeiher. $135-250. MC, VISA, AX, DS, PC, TC. TAC10. 8 suites, 5 with FP and 1 conference room. Breakfast and snacks/refreshments included in rates. Types of meals: Full bkfst and early coffee/tea. Beds: KQDT. Cable TV, phone, VCR and fireplace in room. Air conditioning. Fax and copier on premises. Weddings, small meetings and seminars hosted. Antiquing, art galleries, beaches, bicycling, canoeing/kayaking, fishing, golf, hiking, horseback riding, whale watching, live theater, museums, parks, shopping and water sports nearby.

Atlantic Oakes By-the-Sea

119 Eden Street
Bar Harbor, ME 04609
(207)288-5801 (800)336-2463 Fax:(207)288-8402
E-mail: oakes@barharbor.com
Web: www.barharbor.com

Circa 1913. Formerly the estate of Sir Harry Oakes, this 12-acre property has both a charming bed & breakfast inn and a motel complex that totals 153 guest bedrooms, including 150 ocean-view rooms with balconies. "The Willows," a 1913 colonial mansion has 10 guest bedrooms and is the structure closest to Frenchman's Bay. A continental breakfast is served each morning. The estate is a 20-minute walk from Bar Harbor's business and shopping district and a short drive to Acadia National Park's Visitor's Center.

Historic Interest: Acadia National Park.

Innkeeper(s): (Sonny) Bernard Cough, Jimmy Cough. $152-268. MC, VISA, AX, TC. TAC10. 153 rooms with PB and 6 conference rooms. Types of meals: Full bkfst, early coffee/tea and picnic lunch. Beds: KQD. Cable TV and phone in room. Air conditioning. Fax, copier, spa, swimming and tennis on premises. Handicap access. Weddings, small meetings, family reunions and seminars hosted. Antiquing, art galleries, beaches, bicycling, canoeing/kayaking, fishing, golf, hiking, breweries, live theater, museums, parks, shopping, cross-country skiing and tennis nearby.

Balance Rock Inn on The Ocean

21 Albert Meadow
Bar Harbor, ME 04609-1701
(207)288-2610 (800)753-0494 Fax:(207)288-5534
E-mail: barhbrinns@aol.com
Web: www.barharborvacations.com

Circa 1903. Built for a Scottish railroad tycoon, the Shingle-style structure was designed by a prestigious Boston architectural firm often used by wealthy summer residents of Bar Harbor. The inn is set on a secluded tree-covered property with views of the islands and Frenchman's Bay. Bar Harbor is two short blocks away. Off the back veranda, overlooking the pool, and past nearly an acre of sweeping lawns is the Historic Shore Path that winds its way around the waterfront.

Innkeeper(s): Mike & Nancy Cloud. $135-575. MC, VISA, AX, DS, PC, TC. TAC10. 20 rooms with PB, 12 with FP and 3 suites. Breakfast included in rates. Types of meals: Full bkfst, early coffee/tea and afternoon tea. Beds: KQ. Cable TV, phone and turndown service in room. Air conditioning. VCR, fax, swimming, many rooms with porches and gym on premises. Weddings hosted. Antiquing, Acadia National Park, ocean activities, live theater, parks and water sports nearby.

Pets Allowed.

Bar Harbor Hotel-Bluenose Inn

90 Eden Street (Rte 3)
Bar Harbor, ME 04609
(207)288-3348 (800)445-4077
E-mail: jreeves@bhinn.com

Circa 1883. Sitting on top of a granite-terraced hillside with spectacular views of Frenchman Bay, this modern inn and hotel is luxury and elegance. Queen Anne-style furnishings further

enhance the ambiance. Classically appointed guest bedrooms and suites offer gracious service and privacy. Some boast fireplaces and balconies with panoramic ocean views. Award-winning Rose Garden Restaurant serves breakfast and dinner. The culinary team includes an executive chef trained at the Ritz Carlton in Chicago. Enjoy the gorgeous Great Room, heated indoor and outdoor pools, Jacuzzi and fitness center.

Innkeeper(s): Wil Gaines. $75-339. MC, AX, DC, DS, PC, TC. 97 rooms with PB, 46 with FP, 21 suites and 1 conference room. Types of meals: Full bkfst, early coffee/tea, gourmet dinner and room service. MAP, EP. Beds: KQD. Cable TV, phone, turndown service, fireplace and irons and ironing boards in room. Air conditioning. VCR, fax, copier, swimming, Jacuzzi and gift shop on premises. Handicap access. Weddings, small meetings, family reunions and seminars hosted. Antiquing, art galleries, beaches, bicycling, canoeing/kayaking, fishing, golf, hiking, Acadia National Park, live theater, museums, parks and shopping nearby.

Publicity: Boston Globe and Portland Press Herald.

Bar Harbor Inn

Newport Drive
Bar Harbor, ME 04609-0007
(207)288-3351 (800)248-3351 Fax:(207)288-5296
E-mail: bhinn@acadia.net

Circa 1887. Once known as the Oasis Club, this historic waterfront inn was the first social club on Mt. Desert Island. A Bar Harbor landmark, it survived the 1947 fire that destroyed many of the town's famous hotels. Overlooking Frenchman Bay, in summer the yellow umbrellas of the inn's Terrace Grille-Cafe dot the lawns in view of the fishing vessels and windjammers that frequent the harbor. The inn's private pier is home to a four-masted schooner, Margaret Todd, and day sails are offered. Choose between completely refurbished rooms in the historic main inn, the Oceanfront Lodge or Newport Building.

Innkeeper(s): David J. Witham. $75-395. MC, VISA, AX, DC, DS, PC, TC. TAC5. 153 rooms with PB and 1 conference room. Breakfast included in rates. Types of meals: Cont plus, early coffee/tea, lunch, dinner and room service. Beds: KQD. Cable TV, phone, turndown service, VCR and some with safes in room. Air conditioning. Fax, copier, swimming, gift shop and Jacuzzi on premises. Handicap access. Weddings, small meetings, family reunions and seminars hosted. French and German spoken. Antiquing, fishing, golf, shopping and water sports nearby.

Pets allowed: Limited number of designated rooms.

Publicity: New York Times, Boston Globe and Chicago Tribune.

Bar Harbor Tides B&B

119 West St
Bar Harbor, ME 04609-1430
(207)288-4968
E-mail: info@barharbortides.com

Circa 1887. Sweeping views of Frenchman Bay are seen from this exquisite Greek Revival inn, listed in the National Register of Historic Places. Gracious and personalized hospitality is offered in an intimate atmosphere. Luxurious suites boast elegant formal parlors and fireplaces. Enjoy a delicious gourmet breakfast before embarking on the day's activities. The Tides is  conveniently located on the water, two blocks from downtown Bar Harbor, and minutes away from Acadia National Park.

Historic Interest: Acadia National Park, the first national park established east of the Mississippi River, is nearby and includes the Abbe Museum, with its vast collection of Native American artifacts. The Islesford Museum on Little Cranberry Island offers many maritime exhibits. The Bar Harbor Historical Museum provides documents and photographs from Bar Harbor's heyday as grand resort for the country's wealthiest citizens.

Innkeeper(s): Ray & Loretta Harris. $195-375. MC, VISA, AX. 4 rooms with PB, 3 with FP and 3 suites. Breakfast included in rates. Types of meals: Full bkfst. AP. Beds: KQ. Cable TV, phone and 3 suites with fireplace in room. Antiquing, live theater, parks, shopping, cross-country skiing and water sports nearby.

Black Friar Inn

10 Summer St
Bar Harbor, ME 04609-1424
(207)288-5091 Fax:(207)288-4197
E-mail: blackfriar@acadia.net

Circa 1900. When this three-story house was renovated in 1981, the owners added mantels, hand-crafted woodwork and windows gleaned from old Bar Harbor mansions that had been torn down. Victorian and country furnishings are accentuated with fresh flowers and soft carpets. Breakfast is presented in the greenhouse, a room that boasts cypress paneling and embossed tin recycled from an old country church.

Historic Interest: Acadia National Park, the second most popular park in the U.S. (nearby).
Innkeeper(s): Perry & Sharon Risley & Falke. $65-150. MC, VISA, DS, PC, TC. 7 rooms with PB, 1 with FP and 1 suite. Breakfast and afternoon tea included in rates. Types of meals: Gourmet bkfst. Beds: KQ. Ceiling fan in room. Air conditioning. VCR on premises. Antiquing, fishing, concerts, art fairs, museums, live theater, parks, shopping, cross-country skiing and water sports nearby.

"A great place and great innkeepers!"

Castlemaine Inn

39 Holland Ave
Bar Harbor, ME 04609-1433
(207)288-4563 (800)338-4563 Fax:(207)288-4525

Circa 1886. This Queen Anne charmer was once the summer home to the Austro-Hungarian ambassador to the United States. Rooms are decorated in a light, comfortable Victorian style. Five guest rooms include a whirlpool tub and most include a private balcony or deck and a fireplace. In the mornings, a generous breakfast buffet is presented, with freshly baked scones, muffins, breads and coffee cake, as well as bagels, cream cheese, fresh fruit, cereals and a variety of beverages.

Innkeeper(s): Terence O'Connell & Norah O'Brien. $50-195. MC, VISA, PC, TC. 15 rooms with PB, 11 with FP and 5 suites. Breakfast included in rates. Types of meals: Cont plus. Beds: KQ. Cable TV and VCR in room. Air conditioning. Fax and copier on premises. Antiquing, fishing, golf, live theater, parks, shopping, tennis and water sports nearby.
Publicity: *Country Inns.*

"This year we celebrate our tenth anniversary in our relationship with Castlemaine."

Cleftstone Manor

92 Eden St
Bar Harbor, ME 04609-1123
(207)288-8086 (888)288-4951 Fax:(207)288-2089
E-mail: innkeeper@cleftstone.com
Web: www.cleftstone.com

Circa 1880. Listed in the National Register, this historic Victorian mansion was one of the area's first summer cottages. Sitting on a terraced hillside with gardens on two sides, this inn has offered warm hospitality for more than 50 years. Enjoy games, puzzles and books or converse by the fire. In the after-

noon, beverages are served with fresh-baked cookies. The spacious guest bedrooms and suites are traditionally decorated and elegantly furnished with antiques. Some feature fireplaces, balconies and beamed ceilings. Three hot entrees are served each morning with baked goods and fresh fruit. Choices may include rolled herb souffle, cinnamon raisin French toast and pancakes with bacon or sausage.

Innkeeper(s): Steve & Kelly Hellmann. $70-200. MC, VISA, DS. 16 rooms with PB, 5 with FP, 2 suites and 1 conference room. Breakfast, afternoon tea and snacks/refreshments included in rates. Types of meals: Gourmet bkfst, country bkfst and early coffee/tea. Beds: KQD. Cable TV, phone, ceiling fan and fireplace in room. Air conditioning. Fax and library on premises. Small meetings hosted. Antiquing, beaches, bicycling, canoeing/kayaking, fishing, golf, hiking, parks and shopping nearby.
Pets Allowed.

Coach Stop Inn

PO Box 266 Rt 3
Bar Harbor, ME 04609
(207)288-9886 Fax:(207)288-4241
E-mail: info@coachstopinn.com
Web: www.coachstopinn.com

Circa 1804. Built during Thomas Jefferson's presidency, this two-story, shingled building was previously known as "Halfway Tavern" and served the community as a stagecoach stop and tavern. Each of the five guest rooms offers a fireplace, sitting room, private porch or brick patio and a private bath. A full country breakfast and afternoon refreshment are served each day, featuring specialties such as Colonial bread pudding, blueberry corn pancakes and stuffed French toast with sauteed apples harvested from ancient apple trees on the property. Just two miles from the entrance to Acadia National Park, there are miles of carriage roads and hiking tails to explore, as well as canoeing, sailing, whale-watching or antiquing.

Historic Interest: Joshua Chamberlain House (100 miles), Fort Knox in Prospect Maine (30 miles), Bass Harbor Lighthouse (10 miles), Colonel Black Mansion (10 miles).
Innkeeper(s): Kathy Combs. $59-135. MC, VISA, AX, PC, TC. 5 rooms with PB, 2 with FP. Breakfast and snacks/refreshments included in rates. Types of meals: Gourmet bkfst, country bkfst and early coffee/tea. Beds: Q. Ceiling fan in room. Air conditioning. Amusement parks, antiquing, art galleries, beaches, bicycling, canoeing/kayaking, fishing, golf, hiking and cross-country skiing nearby.

Graycote Inn

40 Holland Ave
Bar Harbor, ME 04609-1432
(207)288-3044 Fax:(207)288-2719
E-mail: history@graycoteinn.com
Web: www.graycoteinn.com

Circa 1881. Hospitality is generous at this Victorian inn, originally built for the first rector of St. Saviour's Episcopal Church. Sitting beside the living room fireplace or on the veranda is a relaxing way to enjoy afternoon refreshments. Find a tray of hot beverages placed near guest bedrooms every morning, before savoring a gourmet breakfast on the enclosed porch. Hammocks beckon nappers, and the lawn is ready for croquet. Free off-street parking makes it easy to explore opportunities for

hiking, birdwatching, biking, photography, and other local activities. The innkeepers are happy to make recommendations.

Historic Interest: Acadia National Park is less than two miles from the inn. Innkeeper(s): Pat & Roger Samuel. $70-165. MC, VISA, DS, PC, TC. 12 rooms with PB, 3 with FP. Breakfast included in rates. Types of meals: Full bkfst. Beds: KQ. Ceiling fans in some rooms and some with air conditioning in room. Small meetings and seminars hosted. Antiquing, golf, music, theatre, Acadia National Park, walk to excellent restaurants, concerts, live theater, parks, shopping, cross-country skiing and water sports nearby.

Publicity: *Country Inns and Washington Post and Victorian Decorating & Lifestyles.*

Hatfield B&B

20 Roberts Ave
Bar Harbor, ME 04609-1820
(207)288-9655
E-mail: hatfield@hatfieldinn.com

Circa 1895. Located a short stroll from the waterfront in Bar Harbor, this country Victorian inn offers a pleasant and welcoming atmosphere. St. Saviors Church, boasting original stained glass Tiffany windows, is a block from the inn. Each of the six guest rooms have private baths and names as individual as their décor: Uncle Frank, John Wayne, Knotsberry, Norma Jean, Corner and Eldorado. Awaken each day to the aroma of fresh coffee and a hearty hot entrée in addition to fresh fruit, juice and fresh home-baked muffins and breads. Sip afternoon iced tea on the porch or enjoy the view from the third floor sun deck as you plan your next day's activities. Mt. Desert Island, home to Acadia National park, boasts scenic vistas, hiking, biking, swimming, whale watching and sailing. During the winter the surrounding area offers cross-country skiing, snowshoeing, hiking, snowmobiling, ice-skating and ice fishing.

Historic Interest: St. Saviors Church (1 block), Rockefeller Gardens, Criterion Theatre.
Innkeeper(s): Sandy & Jeff Miller. $55-120. MC, VISA, DS, TC. 6 rooms with PB. Breakfast and afternoon tea included in rates. Types of meals: Country bkfst, early coffee/tea and picnic lunch. Beds: Q. Ceiling fan in room. Air conditioning. Family reunions hosted. Antiquing, art galleries, beaches, bicycling, canoeing/kayaking, fishing, golf, hiking, ocean, mountains, micro-breweries, live theater, museums, parks, shopping, cross-country skiing, sporting events, tennis and water sports nearby.

Publicity: *Discovery Channel.*

"Excellent in every way. Thanks for the fine food, accommodations and company."

Hearthside Bed & Breakfast

7 High St
Bar Harbor, ME 04609-1816
(207)288-4533
E-mail: bnbinns@hearthsideinn.com
Web: www.hearthsideinn.com

Circa 1907. Originally built for a doctor, this three-story shingled house sits on a quiet street in town. Guests enjoy four working fireplaces and a porch. Three rooms include a whirlpool bath. The parlor includes a library and fireplace. Acadia National Park is five minutes away.

Innkeeper(s): Susan & Barry Schwartz. $95-145. MC, VISA, DS, PC, TC. 9 rooms with PB, 3 with FP. Breakfast and afternoon tea included in rates. Types of meals: Full bkfst. Beds: Q. Ceiling fan and whirlpool baths in room. Air conditioning. Bicycling, canoeing/kayaking, golf, hiking, cross-country skiing and water sports nearby.

Publicity: *Philadelphia Jewish Exponent.*

"I have only one word to describe this place, 'Wow!' My wife and I are astonished at the splendor, the warmth of your care and the beauty of the surroundings."

Holbrook House

74 Mount Desert St
Bar Harbor, ME 04609-1323
(207)288-4970
E-mail: info@holbrookhouse.com
Web: www.holbrookhouse.com

Circa 1876. A local landmark of hospitality for more than 100 years, this Victorian inn is in an ideal New England setting and location. An ambiance of nostalgic elegance is enhanced by antiques, chintz and flowers. The enchanting guest bedrooms with comfy bathrobes showcase a clawfoot tub, four-poster and lace-covered canopy bed. The two cottages with welcoming window boxes feature private patios with hammocks and sitting rooms. Savor a wonderful breakfast served in the cheery sunroom. Afternoon tea and refreshments are enjoyed on the spacious front porch.

Historic Interest: Located one mile from Acadia National Park.
Innkeeper(s): Phil & Lesley DiVirgilio. $125-155. MC, VISA. 10 rooms with PB and 2 suites. Types of meals: Full bkfst. Beds: QDT.
Publicity: *The Discerning Traveler.*

"When I selected Holbrook House all my dreams of finding the perfect inn came true."

Holland Inn

35 Holland Ave
Bar Harbor, ME 04609-1433
(207)288-4804
E-mail: info@hollandinn.com
Web: www.hollandinn.com

Circa 1895. The fresh sea air surrounds this fully-restored, 1895 Federal-style bed & breakfast. Reflecting its humble beginnings as a New England farmhouse, the hosts and 20-year Mount Desert Island residents, Evin and Tom Hulbert, have paid every attention to detail in the renovation of the old house. Each room is tastefully decorated in country shaker, resembling the ambiance of the old Quaker farms. A full breakfast can be savored while overlooking the town on the sunny porch, or perhaps warm up with  a cup of coffee and a good book by the fire in the study. Lush gardens surround the grounds and many activities are within walking distance, including Acadia National Park and the many restaurants and shops near historic Bar Harbor.

Innkeeper(s): Evin & Tom Hulbert. $55-145. MC, VISA, PC. 5 rooms with PB. Breakfast included in rates. Types of meals: Gourmet bkfst. Beds: Q. Cable TV and ceiling fan in room. Library on premises. Small meetings and family reunions hosted. Antiquing, art galleries, beaches, bicycling, canoeing/kayaking, fishing, golf, hiking, horseback riding, Acadia National Park, live theater, museums, parks, shopping, cross-country skiing, tennis and water sports nearby.

The Kedge

112 West St
Bar Harbor, ME 04609-1429
(207)288-5180 (800)597-8306

Circa 1870. Originally, this bed & breakfast was located at the edge of the harbor and served as a social club for gentlemen. In the 1880s, it was moved to its current location on West Street. The home rests on a portion of the street that is listed in the National Register of Historic Places. The interior is Victorian in style, and flowered wallpapers brighten the rooms. One room has a whirlpool tub. The veranda is filled with hunter green wicker furnishings for those who wish to relax. For breakfast, innkeeper Margaret Roberts serves items such as baked peaches with Maine blueberries followed by gingerbread pancakes topped with marmalade syrup.

$60-170. MC, VISA, AX, PC, TC. 3 rooms with PB, 2 with FP. Breakfast included in rates. Types of meals: Full bkfst and early coffee/tea. Beds: KQ. Cable TV in room. Family reunions hosted. Antiquing, golf, museums, oceanarium, concerts, movies, ocean activities, Acadia National Park, live theater, parks, shopping, cross-country skiing, tennis and water sports nearby.

Ledgelawn Inn

66 Mount Desert St
Bar Harbor, ME 04609-1324
(207)288-4596 (800)274-5334 Fax:(207)288-9968
E-mail: barhbrinns@aol.com
Web: www.barharborvacations.com

Circa 1904. Gables, a mansard roof, red clapboard, bays, columns and verandas characterize this three-story summer mansion located on an acre estate in the Historic Corridor. This elegant country inn offers lodging in the original house or the newly constructed Carriage House, made to look as if built at the same time. A grand wood staircase leads from a common area to upstairs guest bedrooms, many with whirlpool tubs. Some feature four-poster beds, saunas and working fireplaces. Relax in the lounge, or by the pool. The town and waterfront are within walking distance.

Innkeeper(s): Nancy Cloud & Mike Miles. $65-250. MC, VISA, AX, DS, PC, TC. TAC10. 33 rooms with PB, 12 with FP and 1 suite. Breakfast included in rates. Types of meals: Cont, early coffee/tea and afternoon tea. Beds: KQD. Cable TV, phone and turndown service in room. Fax, swimming and child care on premises. Family reunions hosted. Antiquing, Acadia National Park, live theater, parks and water sports nearby.
Pets Allowed.
Publicity: *New York Times.*

"A lovely place to relax and enjoy oneself. The area is unsurpassed in beauty and the people friendly."

Manor House Inn

106 West St
Bar Harbor, ME 04609-1856
(207)288-3759 (800)437-0088 Fax:(207)288-2974
E-mail: manor@acadia.net
Web: www.barharbormanorhouse.com

Circa 1887. Colonel James Foster built this 22-room Victorian mansion, now in the National Register. It is an example of the tradition of gracious summer living for which Bar Harbor was and is famous. In addition to the main house, there are several charming cottages situated in the extensive gardens on the property.

Innkeeper(s): Mac Noyes. $65-225. MC, VISA, DS. TAC10. 17 rooms with PB, 11 with FP and 7 suites. Breakfast and afternoon tea included in rates. Types of meals: Full bkfst and early coffee/tea. Beds: KQT. TV, ceiling fan and fireplaces some rooms in room. Fax and copier on premises. Weddings, small meetings, family reunions and seminars hosted. Antiquing, fishing, national park, parks, shopping and water sports nearby.
Publicity: *Country Folks Art Magazine and Discerning Traveler.*

"Wonderful honeymoon spot! Wonderful inn, elegant, delicious breakfasts, terrific innkeepers. We loved it all! It's our fourth time here and it's wonderful as always."

The Maples Inn

16 Roberts Ave
Bar Harbor, ME 04609-1820
(207)288-3443 Fax:(207)288-0356
E-mail: info@maplesinn.com
Web: www.maplesinn.com

Circa 1903. This Victorian "summer cottage" once served wealthy summer visitors to Mt. Desert Island. Located on an attractive residential street, away from Bar Harbor traffic, it has been tastefully restored and filled with Victorian furnishings.

 The inn is within walking distance of shops, boutiques and restaurants. Acadia National Park is five minutes away. Hiking, kayaking and cycling are among the nearby activities.

Innkeeper(s): Tom & Sue Palumbo. $65-160. MC, VISA, DS, PC, TC. 6 rooms with PB, 1 with FP and 1 suite. Breakfast and afternoon tea included in rates. Types of meals: Gourmet bkfst and early coffee/tea. Beds: Q. Air conditioning. Fax and library on premises. Weddings, small meetings, family reunions and seminars hosted. Antiquing, fishing, live theater, parks, shopping, cross-country skiing, sporting events and water sports nearby.
Publicity: *San Diego Tribune, New York Times, Gourmet, Bon Appetit and Los Angeles Times.*

"What a wonderful place this is. Warm, comfortable, friendly, terrific breakfasts, great tips for adventure around the island. I could go on and on."

Mira Monte Inn & Suites

69 Mount Desert St
Bar Harbor, ME 04609-1327
(207)288-4263 (800)553-5109 Fax:(207)288-3115
E-mail: mburns@miramonte.com
Web: www.miramonte.com

Circa 1864. A gracious 18-room Victorian mansion, the Mira Monte has been newly renovated in the style of early Bar Harbor. It features period furnishings, pleasant common rooms, a library and wraparound porches. Situated on estate grounds, there are sweeping lawns, paved terraces and many gardens. The inn was one of the earliest of Bar Harbor's famous summer cottages. The two-room suites each feature canopy beds, two-person whirlpools, a parlor with a sleeper sofa, fireplace and kitchenette unit. The two-bedroom suite includes a full kitchen, dining area and parlor. The suites boast private decks with views of the gardens.

Historic Interest: Acadia National Park is nearby. Many estates are still visible by water tours around the island.

Innkeeper(s): Marian Burns. $155-265. MC, VISA, AX, DC, DS, TC. TAC10. 16 rooms with PB, 14 with FP and 3 suites. Breakfast and afternoon tea included in rates. Types of meals: Full bkfst and early coffee/tea. Beds: KQT. Cable TV, phone and VCR in room. Air conditioning. Fax, library and data ports and internet access on premises. Handicap access. Small meetings hosted. Antiquing, fishing, Acadia National Park, live theater, parks and shopping nearby.
Publicity: *Los Angeles Times.*

"On our third year at your wonderful inn in beautiful Bar Harbor. I think I enjoy it more each year. A perfect place to stay in a perfect environment."

Primrose Inn

73 Mount Desert St
Bar Harbor, ME 04609-1327
(207)288-4031 (877)846-3424
E-mail: relax@primroseinn.com
Web: www.primroseinn.com

Circa 1878. One of the last remaining grand residences of its time, this impressive Stick-Style Victorian is situated in downtown's Historic Corridor. The inn offers spacious guest bedrooms furnished with antiques and period reproductions, plush carpeting and floral wallpaper. Many feature whirlpool tubs, gas fireplaces, private balconies or French doors leading onto the wraparound porches. A hearty breakfast and afternoon tea are served daily. Private off-street parking is available. For longer visits or for families, stay in the inn's self-catering apartments.
Innkeeper(s): Pamela & Bryan. $75-175. MC, VISA, DS, TC. 15 rooms with PB, 4 with FP and 4 suites. Breakfast and afternoon tea included in rates. Types of meals: Full bkfst. Beds: QT. Cable TV, phone, ceiling fan, VCR and fireplace in room. Central air. Fax and library on premises. Antiquing, art galleries, beaches, bicycling, canoeing/kayaking, fishing, golf, hiking, Acadia National Park, whale/puffin watch, live theater, museums, parks and shopping nearby.
Pets allowed: One pet unit.

Stratford House Inn

45 Mount Desert St
Bar Harbor, ME 04609-1748
(207)288-5189
E-mail: inkeeper@downeast.net
Web: www.stratfordinn.com

Circa 1900. Lewis Roberts, Boston publisher of Louisa Mae Alcott's "Little Women" constructed a 10-bedroom cottage for his guests. It was modeled on Shakespeare's birthplace in an

English Tudor style with Jacobean period furnishings and motifs throughout. The rooms are all furnished with antiques such as four-poster mahogany and brass bow-bottom beds. The entrance and dining room are paneled in ornate black oak.
Innkeeper(s): Barbara & Norman Moulton.
$75-150. MC, VISA. 10 rooms, 8 with PB. Types of meals: Cont. Beds: KQD.

"Marvelous visit. Love this house. Great hospitality."

Town Motel & Moseley Cottage Inn

12 Atlantic Ave
Bar Harbor, ME 04609-1704
(207)288-5548 (800)458-8644 Fax:(207)288-9406
Web: www.mainesunshine.com/townmotl

Circa 1894. Although the innkeepers do offer simple, comfortable accommodations in their nine-room motel, they also offer a more historic experience in a late 19th-century Queen Anne Victorian. Bar Harbor has been a popular vacation spot for well over a century. This spacious house was built as a "cottage" for a wealthy family who spent their summers on Maine's scenic coast. The rooms are decorated with period furnishings, Oriental rugs, lacy curtains and flowery wallpapers. Each of eight rooms in the historic home has been decorated individually. Guests at the historic inn are treated to a full breakfast. Guests can walk to many attractions, and

everything, from the harbor to Acadia National Park, is nearby.
Innkeeper(s): The Paluga Family. $105-175. MC, VISA, AX, DS, PC, TC. TAC10. 18 rooms with PB, 4 with FP. Breakfast included in rates. Types of meals: Full bkfst and early coffee/tea. Beds: QDT. Cable TV and ceiling fan in room. Air conditioning. VCR, fax and copier on premises. Small meetings and family reunions hosted. Antiquing, fishing, golf, live theater, parks, shopping, tennis and water sports nearby.

Bath   J3

Benjamin F. Packard House

45 Pearl St
Bath, ME 04530-2746
(207)443-6069 (800)516-4578
E-mail: packardhouse@aol.com
Web: www.mainecoast.com/packardhouse/

Circa 1790. Shipbuilder Benjamin F. Packard purchased this handsome home in 1870. The inn reflects the Victorian influence so prominent in Bath's busiest shipbuilding years. The Packard family, who lived in the house for five genera-

tions, left many family mementos. Period furnishings, authentic colors and shipbuilding memorabilia all reflect Bath's romantic past. The mighty Kennebec River is just a block away. A full breakfast is served daily.
Historic Interest: The inn is situated in a historic district, and nearby historic Front Street offers many antique stores and other commercial business in historic buildings. Maine Maritime Museum, 10-acre site on original shipyard (1 mile), Front Street (one-half mile); forts and lighthouses at Mouth of Kennebec River (12 miles south).
Innkeeper(s): Taylor & Stephen Kluckowski. $80-100. MC, VISA, AX, DC, DS, PC, TC. 3 rooms with PB and 1 suite. Breakfast included in rates. Types of meals: Full bkfst. Beds: KQT. Library on premises. Antiquing, golf, live theater, parks, shopping and water sports nearby.
Publicity: *Coastal Journal, Times Record and Maine Sunday Telegram.*

"Thanks for being wonderful hosts."

The Donnell House Inn B&B

251 High St
Bath, ME 04530
(207)443-5324 (888)595-1664
E-mail: donlhseinn@clinic.net
Web: www.mainelodging.com

Circa 1860. From the cupola atop the roof of this Italianate home, guests may enjoy a moonlit view of the Kennebec River. The inn's exterior is elegantly painted in gray with white on the

columns and trim. Inside are hardwood floors and antiques, set against cheerful wall colors and white woodwork. There are two front parlors, one a sunny yellow and white, and the other with marble fireplace, Oriental rug and a rose-patterned wallpaper. Guest bedrooms offer four-poster beds, and some have fireplaces. One room boasts a Roman tub. A three-course breakfast is served on Blue Willow china in the formal dining room.
Historic Interest: Maine Maritime Museum (1/10 of a mile).
Innkeeper(s): Kenneth & Rachel Parlin. $100-225. MC, VISA, DS, PC, TC. 4 rooms with PB, 2 with FP and 1 suite. Breakfast and afternoon tea included in rates. Types of meals: Full bkfst, cont plus and early coffee/tea. Beds: Q. Cable TV and one with a fireplace and Roman tub whirlpool in room. Air conditioning. Piano room and background stereo music on premises. Antiquing, art galleries, beaches, bicycling, canoeing/kayaking, fishing, golf, hiking,

maine Maritime Museum, boat landing, live theater, museums, parks, shopping, cross-country skiing and tennis nearby.

"Your beautiful home offered the space and energy we all needed."

Fairhaven Inn

118 N Bath Rd
Bath, ME 04530
(207)443-4391 (888)443-4391 Fax:(207)443-6412
E-mail: fairhvn@gwi.net
Web: www.mainecoast.com/fairhaveninn

Circa 1790. With its view of the Kennebec River, this site was so attractive that Pembleton Edgecomb built his Colonial house where a log cabin had previously stood. His descendants occupied it for the next 125 years. Antiques and country furniture fill the inn. Meadows and lawns, and woods of hemlock, birch and pine cover the inn's 16 acres.

Innkeeper(s): Susie & Dave Reed. $70-130. MC, VISA, DS, PC, TC. TAC10. 8 rooms, 6 with PB, 1 suite and 1 cottage. Breakfast included in rates. Types of meals: Gourmet bkfst and early coffee/tea. Beds: KQT. VCR, fax and library on premises. Small meetings, family reunions and seminars hosted. Antiquing, art galleries, beaches, bicycling, canoeing/kayaking, fishing, golf, hiking, live theater, museums, parks, shopping, cross-country skiing, sporting events, tennis and water sports nearby.

Publicity: *The State and Coastal Journal.*

"The Fairhaven is now marked in our book with a red star, definitely a place to remember and visit again."

The Galen C. Moses House

1009 Washington St
Bath, ME 04530-2759
(207)442-8771 (888)442-8771 Fax:(207)443-0808
E-mail: stay@galenmoses.com
Web: www.galenmoses.com

Circa 1874. This Victorian mansion is filled with beautiful architectural items, including stained-glass windows, wood-carved and marble fireplaces and a grand staircase. The innkeepers have filled the library, a study, morning room and the parlor with antiques. A corner fireplace warms the dining room, which overlooks the lawns and gardens. Tea is presented in the formal drawing room.

Historic Interest: Maine Maritime Museum, Fort Popham, weekly historic house tours, Bath Iron Works (boat launchings).

Innkeeper(s): James Haught, Larry Kieft. $109-149. MC, VISA, AX, DS, PC, TC. TAC5. 4 rooms with PB. Breakfast and afternoon tea included in rates. Types of meals: Gourmet bkfst and cont. Beds: QDT. Turndown service in room. Air conditioning. VCR and library on premises. Family reunions and seminars hosted. Antiquing, beaches, fishing, boats, live theater, parks, shopping, cross-country skiing and water sports nearby.

Publicity: *Philadelphia and Back Roads USA.*

"For our first try at B&B lodgings, we've probably started at the top, and nothing else will ever measure up to this. Wonderful food, wonderful home, grounds and wonderful hosts!"

Kennebec Inn

1024 Washington St
Bath, ME 04530
(207)443-5202 (800)822-9393 Fax:(207)443-1411
E-mail: innkeeper@kennebecinn.com
Web: www.kennebecinn.com

Circa 1860. This elegant Italianate brick mansion on a stretch of the Kennebec River just a block from the ocean, is a classic example of the sea captains' homes in the historic city of Bath. The captain who built this fine home brought the bricks from England aboard his ship, Halcyon, and hired renowned architect Francis

Fasseett to design the home. The mansion has parquet floors and crystal chandeliers. It stands on two acres in mid-coast Maine, an area few outsiders know is delightfully temperate in the summer (the daily average is 70 degrees), yet averages 60 to 90 inches of snow in the winter. The seven comfortable guest bedrooms feature charming anachronisms like hooked rugs and Jacuzzi tubs, antique beds and televisions. A full homemade breakfast is served from the butler's pantry each morning. The meal includes homemade bread (possibly Anadama bread) and coffee cake or fruit crisps served with two entrees like eggs Florentine, pancakes with blueberry sauce, pumpkin Belgian waffles with scrambled eggs, spinach strata and scrambled eggs or the inn's signature French toast recipe that is similar to warm upside down cake. After a hearty breakfast, guests may go outside to enjoy kayaking, canoeing, boating, fishing, camping, hiking, bicycling, golfing, playing tennis or whale and puffin watching. Or they can take an architectural walking tour of Bath, stroll country lanes that wind through meadows past the shipyards and historic homes or visit lighthouses on the river and the ocean. Local Popham Beach, a white sand beach, was chosen as the location for the movie "Message in a Bottle," starring Kevin Costner and Paul Newman.

Historic Interest: Maine Maritime Museum (2 miles), Joshua L. Chamberlain Museum (8 miles), Popham Fort (14 miles).

Innkeeper(s): Blanche & Ron Lutz. $90-175. MC, AX, DC, DS, PC, TC. TAC10. 7 rooms with PB. Breakfast included in rates. Types of meals: Full bkfst. Beds: KQ. Cable TV, phone, down comforters and pillows, some with Jacuzzi and fireplace in room. Air conditioning. VCR, fax, copier and library on premises. Small meetings, family reunions and seminars hosted. Antiquing, art galleries, beaches, bicycling, canoeing/kayaking, fishing, golf, hiking, horseback riding, live theater, museums, parks, shopping, cross country skiing, tennis and water sports nearby.

Publicity: *Colonial Homes.*

Riverside Bed & Breakfast

1115 Washington Street
Bath, ME 04530
(207)386-0445 (800)705-0367 Fax:(207)442-9588
E-mail: stay@riversidebedandbreakfast.com
Web: www.riversidebedandbreakfast.com

Circa 1850. A resplendent reflection of a bygone era, this three-story Italianate mansion has been lovingly renovated with historical preservation and extraordinary elegance. The professionally designed interior resonates Victorian grandeur and French Provincial grace. The spacious double parlor and library feature marble fireplaces, a grand piano, Persian rugs, crystal chandeliers, an impressive antique book collection and intimate seating areas. Comfortable luxury highlights the guest bedrooms and suites, each with a library. Enjoy a delicious breakfast overlooking the Kennebec River in the formal dining room, and Five o'clock Tea with an assortment of sweets and savories.

Historic Interest: Popham Beach.

Innkeeper(s): Marianna Boas. $89-129. MC, VISA, AX, PC, TC. TAC20. 6 rooms, 4 with PB, 1 with FP, 2 suites and 1 conference room. Breakfast and afternoon tea included in rates. Types of meals: Gourmet bkfst, country bkfst, veg bkfst, cont plus, cont, early coffee/tea, picnic lunch and room service. AP. Beds: K. Cable TV, phone, turndown service, VCR and fireplace in room. Fax, copier and library on premises. Weddings, small meetings, family reunions and seminars hosted. French, German, Dutch, Hungarian, Czech, Polish, Russian, Italian and Spanish spoken. Amusement parks, antiquing, art galleries, beaches, bicycling, canoeing/kayaking, fishing, golf, hiking, horseback riding, live theater, museums, parks, shopping, downhill skiing, cross-country skiing, sporting events, tennis and water sports nearby.

Pets Allowed.

Publicity: *Times-Record and Victorian Homes Magazine.*

Belfast H5

The Alden House Bed & Breakfast

63 Church St
Belfast, ME 04915-6208
(207)338-2151 (877)337-8151 Fax:(207)338-2151
E-mail: info@thealdenhouse.com
Web: www.thealdenhouse.com

Circa 1840. This pre-Civil War, pristinely restored Greek Revival manor was built for prominent Belfast citizen Hiram Alden. Alden was editor of the local paper, town postmaster and vice-president of American Telegraph. The interior still boasts grand features, such as marble fireplace mantels, tin ceilings and a hand-carved curved staircase. Early risers enjoy the view from the front porch as they sip a cup of freshly ground coffee. Breakfast begins with juice, fresh fruit and muffins, followed by a special entree. During raspberry season, guests are treated to fresh berries from the inn's grounds.

Innkeeper(s): Bruce & Susan Madara. $88-125. MC, VISA, DS. TAC10. 7 rooms, 5 with PB, 1 with FP. Breakfast and afternoon tea included in rates. Types of meals: Full bkfst and early coffee/tea. EP. Beds: QDT. Natural body care products, hair dryers and robes in room. VCR, fax and library on premises. Weddings, small meetings and family reunions hosted. Antiquing, fishing, golf, live theater, parks, shopping, downhill skiing, cross-country skiing, tennis and water sports nearby.
Publicity: *Bangor Daily Mews* and *Waldo Independent*.

Bay Meadows Inn, The Country Inn by the Sea

192 Northport Ave
Belfast, ME 04915-6011
(207)338-5715 (800)335-2370
E-mail: bbmi@baymeadowsinn.com
Web: www.baymeadowsinn.com

Circa 1890. A shingled waterfront estate overlooking Penobscot Bay sits on eight acres of flowering meadows and woods. The Victorian decor is enhanced by high ceilings and ornate wood trim. In the midst of a diverse collection of antiques, paintings and Persian rugs, hospitality and comfort are in abundance. Families and pets are welcome, and children will enjoy the play room and jungle gym. Many of the spacious guest bedrooms offer private entrances with decks boasting gorgeous ocean views. The highly acclaimed gourmet country breakfast may include a lobster omelette, or scrambled eggs with smoked salmon, among other delights. The inn's own beach is only a short walk away on grassy paths.

Innkeeper(s): John & Patty Lebowitz. $65-165. MC, VISA, AX, DS, PC, TC. TAC10. 20 rooms with PB, 1 with FP. Breakfast included in rates. Types of meals: Gourmet bkfst and country bkfst. Beds: KQ. Cable TV, phone, ceiling fan and fireplace in room. Air-conditioning. VCR, fax and copier on premises. Weddings, small meetings, family reunions and seminars hosted. Antiquing, art galleries, beaches, bicycling, canoeing/kayaking, fishing, golf, hiking, live theater, museums, parks, shopping, downhill skiing, cross-country skiing, tennis and water sports nearby.
Pets allowed: Dogs only. May not be left in rooms unattended unless crated and quiet.

Belhaven Inn

14 John St
Belfast, ME 04915-6650
(207)338-5435
E-mail: stay@belhaveninn.com
Web: www.belhaveninn.com

Circa 1851. This 16-room 1851 Federal Victorian stands on an acre in the heart of Belfast, a historic harbor community with roots in shipbuilding. Mullioned windows, pumpkin pine floors and carved mantels are some of the many period features of the inn. A circular staircase leads to the four guest bedrooms, each appointed with period pieces. A three-course country breakfast is served daily on the side porch, weather permitting. It includes items such as fruit cup with yogurt or granola, freshly baked muffins, hot breads and a hot entrée of either eggs, pancakes, crepes or sausage. Locally grown berries and produce are used in season. After breakfast relax on the porch or head into Belfast to explore the many art galleries and shops. Take a ride on the vintage Belfast and Moosehead Train or arrange for a boat to explore the islands in the Penobscot Bay or take a drive and explore the nearby lighthouses.

Innkeeper(s): Anne & Paul Bartels. $65-105. MC, VISA, PC, TC. 5 rooms, 3 with PB and 1 suite. Breakfast and snacks/refreshments included in rates. Types of meals: Country bkfst and early coffee/tea. Beds: KQDT. Turndown service in room. VCR, tennis, library, badmitton and volleyball on premises. Family reunions hosted. Antiquing, art galleries, beaches, bicycling, canoeing/kayaking, fishing, golf, hiking, horseback riding, live theater, museums, parks, shopping, cross-country skiing, tennis and wineries nearby.
Pets allowed: Efficiency suite only.

Londonderry Inn

133 Belmont Ave (Rt 3)
Belfast, ME 04915
(207)338-2763 (877)529-9566 Fax:(207)338-6303
E-mail: info@londonderry-inn.com
Web: www.londonderry-inn.com

Circa 1803. Built in 1803, this Maine farmhouse provides elegant comfort and spacious common areas to enjoy a vacation with the whole family. Wake up each morning to an old-fashioned, three-course "farmer's breakfast" featuring such gourmet touches as homemade blueberry pancakes and muffins, which can be enjoyed on the screened farmer's porch, outside patio, sun porch or next to the fireplace in the country kitchen. Children will enjoy playing in the large backyard or watching a movie in the room from the inn's extensive video selection of over 200 films. Discover the peaceful woodlands surrounding the inn, complete with a berry garden and farm pond, while catching a glimpse of wildlife such as deer along the way. With such historic sites as Fort Knox within driving distance, guests will find many other discoveries in the surrounding area.

Historic Interest: Penobscot Maine Museum (8 miles), Historic Fort Knox.
Innkeeper(s): Fletcher & Marsha Oakes. $100-145. MC, VISA, AX, DS, PC, TC. 5 rooms with PB, 1 with FP. Breakfast and snacks/refreshments included in rates. Types of meals: Full bkfst, country bkfst, early coffee/tea and afternoon tea. Beds: KQDT. Cable TV, phone and VCR in room. Air conditioning. Fax, library and backyard patio on premises. Weddings, small meetings, family reunions and seminars hosted. Antiquing, art galleries, bicycling, canoeing/kayaking, fishing, golf, hiking, horseback riding, lighthouses, live theater, museums, parks, shopping, downhill skiing and water sports nearby.

The Thomas Pitcher House B&B

19 Franklin St
Belfast, ME 04915-6518
(207)338-6454 (888)338-6454
E-mail: tpitcher@acadia.net
Web: www.thomaspitcherhouse.com

Circa 1873. This richly appointed home was considered state-of-the-art back in 1873, for it was one of only a few homes offering central heat and hot or cold running water. Today, innkeepers have added plenty of modern amenities, but kept the ambiance of the Victorian era. Some vanities include original walnut and marble, while another bathroom includes tin ceilings and a step-down bath. Some rooms have cozy reading areas. Guests enjoy a full breakfast each morning with menus that feature specialties such as Maine blueberry buttermilk pancakes or a French toast puff made with homemade raisin bread.

Historic Interest: A short walk from the Thomas Pitcher House will take you into the center of historic Belfast, which includes a variety of shops and galleries and the harbor. Walking tours through historic tree-lined streets are available and nearby Seasport offers plenty of antiquing. The Penobscot Marine Museum is 10 miles away, Fort Knox and Montpelier are easy day trips, as is the Owl's Head Transportation Museum.

Innkeeper(s): Fran & Ron Kresge. $85-105. MC, VISA, DS, PC, TC. TAC10. 4 rooms with PB. Breakfast included in rates. Types of meals: Gourmet bkfst and early coffee/tea. Beds: QDT. Clocks, portable fans and reading bays/areas in room. VCR, library, porch with rockers and deck with wicker furniture on premises. German and limited French spoken. Antiquing, fishing, museums, historic sites, lighthouses, live theater, parks, shopping, downhill skiing, cross-country skiing and water sports nearby.

Publicity: *Boston Herald, Jackson Clarion-Ledger, Toronto Sunday Sun, Bride's, Knoxville News-Sentinel, Saturday Evening Post, Allentown Morning Call, Waldo Independent and Victorian Homes.*

"A home away from home."

Belgrade Lakes   H3

Wings Hill Inn

PO Box 386
Belgrade Lakes, ME 04918-0386
(207)495-2400 (866)495-2400
E-mail: wingshillinn@earthlink.net
Web: wingshillinn.com

Circa 1800. In a picturesque lakefront village setting, this post and beam farmhouse is an ideal romantic getaway. Relaxation comes easy by the fireplace in the Great Room or the extensive screened wraparound porch overlooking Long Pond. The guest bedrooms boast a comfortable elegance. Hospitality is abundant, as experienced in the optional breakfast basket delivered to the door, or join others in the dining area. Hiking, fishing, boating and golf are only steps away. Other popular New England sites and activities are an easy drive away.

Innkeeper(s): Christopher & Tracey Anderson. $95-140. MC, VISA, DS. 8 rooms with PB. Breakfast and afternoon tea included in rates. Types of meals: Full bkfst and early coffee/tea. Antiquing, fishing, golf, hiking, shopping, downhill skiing, cross-country skiing, sporting events and water sports nearby.

Bethel   I2

Chapman Inn

PO Box 1067
Bethel, ME 04217-1067
(207)824-2657 (877)359-1498
E-mail: chapman@nxi.com

Circa 1865. As one of the town's oldest buildings, this Federal-style inn has been a store, a tavern and a boarding house known as "The Howard." It was the home of William Rogers Chapman, composer, conductor and founder of the Rubenstein Club and the Metropolitan Musical Society, in addition to the Maine Music Festival. The inn is a convenient place to begin a walking tour of Bethel's historic district.

Innkeeper(s): Sandra & Fred. $25-105. MC, VISA, AX, DS, PC, TC. 10 rooms with PB and 2 suites. Breakfast included

in rates. Types of meals: Full bkfst, early coffee/tea and afternoon tea. TV and phone in room. Air conditioning. VCR, fax and sauna on premises. Weddings, small meetings, family reunions and seminars hosted. Antiquing, fishing, golf, live theater, parks, shopping, downhill skiing, cross-country skiing, tennis and water sports nearby.

Pets Allowed.

L'Auberge Country Inn

Mill Hill Rd, PO Box 21
Bethel, ME 04217-0021
(207)824-2774 (800)760-2774 Fax:(207)824-0806
E-mail: laubergeinn@ctel.net
Web: www.laubergecountryinn.com

Circa 1870. In the foothills of the White Mountains, surrounded by five acres of gardens and woods, this former carriage house was converted to a guest house in the 1920s. Among its seven guest rooms are two spacious suites. The Theater Suite offers a four-poster queen bed and dressing room. The Family Suite can accommodate up to six guests. Mount Abrahms and Sunday River ski areas are just minutes away.

Innkeeper(s): Alexandra & Adam Adler. $65-135. MC, VISA, AX, DS. 6 rooms, 2 suites and 1 conference room. Breakfast included in rates. Types of meals: Full bkfst, early coffee/tea and gourmet dinner. VCR and child care on premises. Weddings, small meetings, family reunions and seminars hosted. Antiquing, shopping, downhill skiing and cross-country skiing nearby.

Sudbury Inn

Lower Main St
Bethel, ME 04217
(207)824-2174 (800)395-7837 Fax:(207)824-2329
E-mail: sudbury2@thesudburyinn.com
Web: www.thesudburyinn.com

Circa 1873. After a day of skiing at one of the many local ski areas, guests will enjoy the warmth and comfort that this late 19th-century Colonial inn has to offer. There are 10 spacious guest rooms and six suites, some geared to accommodate families. Although visitors may appreciate the inn's original architectural details such as its coffered ceilings and wraparound porch, the inn is most famous for its restaurant and pub that occupies the entire first floor. The menu offers a selection of fresh seafood, steaks and pasta and

features an extensive wine list. After dinner, guests can retire to the Suds Pub where they can enjoy late-night dancing, a wide variety of draft beer or an after-supper snack. Located in the foothills of the White Mountains, the inn is close to hiking trails, golf and wildlife.

Historic Interest: The Appalachian Trail and Sunday River are located nearby.

Innkeeper(s): Bill & Nancy White. $69-169. MC, VISA, AX, TC. 17 rooms with PB and 7 suites. Breakfast included in rates. Types of meals: Full bkfst, cont plus, cont, early coffee/tea and dinner. Beds: KQDT. Cable TV in room. Fax on premises. Family reunions hosted. Amusement parks, antiquing, fishing, golf, parks, shopping, downhill skiing, cross-country skiing and water sports nearby.

Pets allowed: Limited.

Publicity: *Yankee Traveler and Boston Globe.*

Blue Hill   H5

Auberge Tenney Hill B&B

#1 Mines Rd
Blue Hill, ME 04614
(207)374-5710
E-mail: raguay@midmaine.com

Circa 1869. Built by a sea captain on a coastal mountain, this Victorian inn features interesting architectural details. Discover stacked, two-story bay windows, an arboretum and a common sitting room with French doors opening onto a 30-foot balcony. The decor is a blend of Victorian and Oriental antiques and artwork. After a good night's sleep in one of the guest bedrooms, enjoy fresh fruit, hot croissants with wild blueberry jam, organic granola, quiche Lorraine and wild blueberry waffles with Maine maple syrup. Take time for tea with the host in the afternoon, and learn more about the local region. This resort village is in the center of the Acadia-Downeast area, close to the national park and Bar Harbor.
Historic Interest: Jonathan Fisher historic house/museum (1/10 mile), Holt House (1/2 mile).
Innkeeper(s): Richard & Marjorie. $55-95. MC, VISA, TC. 5 rooms, 3 with PB. Breakfast, afternoon tea and snacks/refreshments included in rates. Types of meals: Gourmet bkfst, veg bkfst and early coffee/tea. Beds: QD. Cable TV in room. Fax and library on premises. Weddings hosted. French and Spanish spoken. Amusement parks, antiquing, art galleries, beaches, bicycling, canoeing/kayaking, fishing, golf, hiking, horseback riding, Acadia Park, Bar Harbor, Castine, Deer Isle, Isle au Haut, Stonington, live theater, museums, parks, shopping, downhill skiing, cross-country skiing, sporting events, tennis, water sports and wineries nearby.
Publicity: *Weekly & Business Monthly.*

The Blue Hill Inn

Union St, Rt 177
Blue Hill, ME 04614-0403
(207)374-2844 (800)826-7415 Fax:(207)374-2829
E-mail: bluehillinn@hotmail.com
Web: www.bluehillinn.com

Circa 1830. Sitting on an acre in the heart of the historic town center, this Federalist-style inn has operated continuously for more than 160 years. Near Blue Hill Bay, it is distinguished by its shuttered windows, clapboards, brick ends and five chimneys. The wide pumpkin-pine floors are accented by antique period furnishings. Enjoy reading or socializing in two common rooms. Some of the romantic guest bedrooms feature comfortable sitting areas and fireplaces. The Cape House is a luxury suite. Breakfast includes a choice of entrees. Afternoon tea with refreshments as well as evening drinks with hors d'oeuvres are served in the garden or parlor. Ask about the seasonal Wine Dinners prepared by visiting chefs.
Historic Interest: Located close to Acadia National Park and the Maine coast.
Innkeeper(s): Mary & Don Hartley. $148-260. MC, VISA, TC. TAC10. 11 rooms with PB, 4 with FP. Breakfast included in rates. Types of meals: Gourmet bkfst, early coffee/tea, gourmet dinner and room service. MAP. Beds: KQDT. Fax, one luxury suite-cottage, hors d'oeuvres and gourmet wine dinners on premises. Handicap access. Family reunions hosted. Antiquing, fishing, golf, boating, kayaking, parks and cross-country skiing nearby.
Publicity: *Washington Post and Country Inn Cooking with Gail Greco-Second Series.*

Boothbay   J4

Hodgdon Island Inn

PO Box 492, Barter Island Rd
Boothbay, ME 04571
(207)633-7474 Fax:(207)633-0571
Web: www.hodgdonislandinn.com

Circa 1810. This early 19th-century Victorian still boasts many original features, including molding and windows. Antiques and wicker furnishings decorate the guest rooms. There is a heated swimming pool available to summer guests. The historic inn is minutes from downtown Boothbay Harbor.
Innkeeper(s): Peter Wilson & Peter Moran. $105-135. MC, VISA, DS, PC, TC. 8 rooms with PB. Breakfast included in rates. Types of meals: Gourmet bkfst and early coffee/tea. Beds: KQ. Ceiling fan, water views and some with fireplaces in room. VCR, swimming and library on premises. Antiquing, art galleries, bicycling, canoeing/kayaking, fishing, golf, hiking, lobster bake on island cruise, museums, parks, shopping, cross-country skiing and water sports nearby.

Kenniston Hill Inn

Rt 27, PO Box 125
Boothbay, ME 04537-0125
(207)633-2159 (800)992-2915 Fax:(207)633-2159
E-mail: innkeeper@maine.com

Circa 1786. The elegant clapboard home is the oldest inn at Boothbay Harbor and was occupied by the Kenniston family for more than a century. Five of the antique-filled bedrooms have fireplaces. After a walk through the gardens or  woods, warm up in the parlor next to the elegant, open-hearthed fireplace. Boothbay Harbor offers something for everybody, including whale-watching excursions and dinner theaters.
Innkeeper(s): Jim & Gerry Botti. $85-125. MC, VISA, AX, DS, PC, TC. TAC10. 10 rooms with PB, 5 with FP. Breakfast and afternoon tea included in rates. Types of meals: Country bkfst and early coffee/tea. Beds: KQDT. Ceiling fan in room. VCR, fax and copier on premises. Weddings and family reunions hosted. Antiquing, art galleries, beaches, bicycling, canoeing/kayaking, fishing, golf, hiking, live theater, museums, parks, shopping and tennis nearby.
Publicity: *Boothbay Register.*

"England may be the home of the original bed & breakfast, but Kenniston Hill Inn is where it has been perfected!"

Boothbay Harbor   J4

1830 Admiral's Quarters Inn

71 Commercial St
Boothbay Harbor, ME 04538-1827
(207)633-2474 (800)644-1878 Fax:(207)633-5904
E-mail: loon@admiralsquartersinn.com
Web: www.admiralsquartersinn.com

Circa 1830. Set on a rise looking out to the ocean, this renovated sea captain's home commands a view of the harbor and its activities. Guest bedrooms are decorated with white wicker,  antiques and quilts that enhance the ambiance. They all feature fireplaces and decks or patios with entrances. Savor a homemade breakfast served on the porch or in the glass solarium, complete with wood-burning stove, overlooking manicured lawns and the water beyond. Afternoon refreshments can be enjoyed in front of the fireplace or while watching the lobster boats glide by. Boat excursions and restaurants are within walking distance.

Historic Interest: Maine Maritime Museum, St. Patricks Roman Catholic Church (35 minutes).
Innkeeper(s): Les & Deb Hallstrom. $85-195. MC, VISA, DS, PC, TC. 6 rooms with PB, 6 with FP and 4 suites. Breakfast, afternoon tea and snacks/refreshments included in rates. Types of meals: Full bkfst, country bkfst, veg bkfst and early coffee/tea. Beds: KQT. Cable TV, phone, ceiling fan, toiletries and all with fireplaces in room. Air conditioning. Fax, copier, library and glider swing on premises. Weddings, small meetings, family reunions and seminars hosted. Antiquing, art galleries, beaches, canoeing/kayaking, fishing, golf, hiking, horseback riding, boat trips, pottery shops, live theater, museums, parks, shopping, downhill skiing, cross-country skiing, sporting events, tennis and water sports nearby.
Publicity: *Franklin Business Review, Down East Magazine and Yankee Traveler.*

"If you're looking to put down stakes in the heart of Boothbay Harbor, the Admiral's Quarters Inn provides an eagle's eye view on land and at sea." —Yankee Traveler

Anchor Watch Bed & Breakfast

9 Eames Rd
Boothbay Harbor, ME 04538-1882
(207)633-7565
E-mail: diane@lincoln.midcoast.com
Web: www.anchorwatch.com

Circa 1920. Listen to the lapping of the waves and the call of seabirds, smell the salt air and gaze out on the harbor from this Colonial inn on the waterfront in Boothbay Harbor. The inn has a private pier for swimming or fishing, a butterfly/azalea garden and a patio on the rocks. The comfortably appointed inn is decorated with quilts and stenciling. Its five guest rooms are each named for a Monhegan ferryboat from years gone by. Breakfast fare includes items like baked orange French toast, sausage and popovers with strawberry jam — all served in the sunny breakfast nook overlooking the sea. Walk to shops, restaurants, clambakes and boat trips. The innkeepers' Balmy Day Cruises include harbor tours, all-day excursions to Monhegan Island and sailing trips.
Innkeeper(s): Diane Campbell & Kathy Campbell-Reed. $80-150. MC, VISA, DS, PC, TC. TAC10. 5 rooms with PB and 1 conference room. Breakfast included in rates. Types of meals: Full bkfst. Beds: KQ. Antiquing, art galleries, beaches, canoeing/kayaking, fishing, golf, hiking, museums, parks, shopping, cross-country skiing and tennis nearby.

Five Gables Inn

PO Box 335 Murray Hill Rd
Boothbay Harbor, ME 04544
(207)633-4551 (800)451-5048
E-mail: info@fivegablesinn.com
Web: www.fivegablesinn.com

Circa 1896. One could hardly conjure up a more perfect setting than this Maine inn's location, just yards from Linekin Bay with wooded hills as a backdrop. For more than a century, guests have come here to enjoy the Maine summer. The porch offers a hammock and rockers, as well as a pleasing view. Guest rooms offer bay views, and five include a fireplace. Breakfasts offer a wide assortment of items, a menu might include puffed apple pancakes, grilled tomatoes, ham, freshly baked scones, fruit and homemade granola. The inn is open from mid-May to October.
Innkeeper(s): Mike & De Kennedy. $120-185. MC, VISA, TC. TAC10. 16 rooms with PB, 5 with FP. Breakfast and afternoon tea included in rates.

Types of meals: Gourmet bkfst and early coffee/tea. Beds: KQT. Phone in room. Library on premises. Antiquing, fishing, golf, whale watching, windjammers, live theater, parks, shopping, tennis and water sports nearby.
Publicity: *Calendar, Atlanta Journal-Constitution, Down East Magazine and Yankee Traveler.*

Greenleaf Inn at Boothbay Harbor

65 Commercial St
Boothbay Harbor, ME 04538
(207)633-7346 (888)950-7724 Fax:(207)633-2642
E-mail: info@greenleafinn.com

Circa 1850. For well over a century, guests have stopped at Greenleaf Inn. The guest rooms are decorated in a cozy, New England-country style. The suites have the added luxury of a harbor view. In the mornings, the innkeeper provides a variety of breakfast items, including a special daily entrée. Guests can enjoy the meal in the cheerful country dining room or on the front porch where a view of the harbor may be enjoyed. Boothbay offers a variety of festivals throughout the year, as well as plenty of outdoor activities.
Innkeeper(s): Jeff Teel. $105-155. MC, VISA, AX, DS, PC, TC. 5 rooms with PB, 4 with FP, 1 suite and 1 conference room. Breakfast and snacks/refreshments included in rates. Types of meals: Full bkfst and early coffee/tea. Beds: QDT. Cable TV, phone, ceiling fan, VCR and fireplace in room. Fax, copier, bicycles, library and gift shop on premises. Weddings, small meetings, family reunions and seminars hosted. Antiquing, art galleries, beaches, bicycling, canoeing/kayaking, fishing, golf, hiking, live theater, museums, parks, shopping and tennis nearby.

The Harborage Inn on the Edge of the Bay

75 Townsend Ave
Boothbay Harbor, ME 04538
(207)633-4640 (800)565-3742
E-mail: info@harborageinn.com
Web: www.harborageinn.com

Circa 1872. A family-run business for three generations, this Victorian is the oldest original inn in the harbor. Completely restored, it is decorated throughout with Laura Ashley fabrics and designs. The warm ambiance and country atmosphere reflect the local coastal area. Guest bedrooms and suites are romantic retreats featuring Colonial furnishings, antique stenciling and private entrances. Some offer bay views. The meticulous waterfront grounds with colorful flower boxes offer eye-pleasing scenes from the wraparound porches. Visit historical Fort William Henry, only 15 miles away. There are several local museums and sites, including the Maine Maritime Museum and Boothbay Railway Village.
Historic Interest: Maine Maritime Museum (30 miles), Boothbay Railway Village (10 miles), Fort William Henry (15 miles), Lincoln County Jail Museum (20 miles).
Innkeeper(s): The Chapman & Wallace Family's. $65-160. MC, VISA, PC, TC. TAC10. 9 rooms, 5 with PB and 4 suites. Breakfast included in rates. Types of meals: Cont plus. Beds: KQD. Cable TV, phone and wraparound porches with scenic views in room. Swimming and private waterfront lawn with seating on premises. Weddings, small meetings, family reunions and seminars hosted. Antiquing, art galleries, beaches, bicycling, canoeing/kayaking, fishing, golf, hiking, horseback riding, deep sea fishing, aquarium, botanical gardens, nature preserves, lighthouses, sailboat rentals, festivals, live theater, museums, parks, shopping, cross-country skiing, tennis and water sports nearby.

Harbour Towne Inn on The Waterfront

71 Townsend Ave
Boothbay Harbor, ME 04538-1158
(207)633-4300 (800)722-4240 Fax:(207)633-2442
E-mail: gtme@gwi.net
Web: www.harbourtowneinn.com

Circa 1880. This Victorian inn's well-known trademark boasts that it is "the Finest B&B on the Waterfront." The inn's 12 rooms offer outside decks, and the Penthouse has an outstanding view of the harbor from its private deck. Breakfast is served  in the inn's Sunroom, and guests also may relax in the parlor, which has a miniature antique library and a beautiful antique fireplace. A conference area is available for meetings. The inn's meticulous grounds include flower gardens and well-kept shrubs and trees. A wonderful new addition is a dock and float for sunning, sketches/painting, reading or hopping aboard a canoe, kayak or small boat. It's an easy walk to the village and its art galleries, restaurants, shops and boat trips. Special off-season packages are available. Ft. William Henry and the Fisherman's Memorial are nearby.
Historic Interest: Boothbay Region Historical Building (3 blocks), lighthouses (5 to 50 minutes).
Innkeeper(s): George Thomas & family. $79-299. MC, VISA, AX, DS, PC, TC. TAC10. 12 rooms with PB and 1 conference room. Breakfast included in rates. Types of meals: Cont. Beds: KQDT. Cable TV and phone in room. Air conditioning. Fax, copier and outside decks and new waterfront dock on premises. Handicap access. Weddings, small meetings, family reunions and seminars hosted. Antiquing, fishing, boating, live theater, parks, shopping, downhill skiing, cross-country skiing and water sports nearby.

Bridgton   I2

Bridgton House Bed & Breakfast

2 Main St
Bridgton, ME 04009-1130
(207)647-8175

Circa 1900. Guests have been enjoying Maine vacations from this spot since 1815. The original structure was destroyed by fire in 1900 and what remained was restored and rebuilt. The five guest rooms include a mix of traditional and Victorian furnishings and country décor. Guests are treated to a full, country breakfast with fresh juices and fruit, homemade breads and a daily entrée. Outdoor activities include boating, swimming and fishing at local lakes, skiing and hunting for antiques.
Historic Interest: Narimissic, Scribners Mills, Conway Train Station.
Innkeeper(s): William and Christina Berghoff. $95. PC. 5 rooms, 3 with PB. Breakfast included in rates. Types of meals: Country bkfst. Ceiling fan in room. VCR and library on premises. Family reunions hosted. Antiquing, canoeing/kayaking, fishing, golf, hiking, horseback riding, shopping and water sports nearby.

Brooksville   I5

Oakland House Seaside Resort

435 Herrick Rd
Brooksville, ME 04617
(207)359-8521 (800)359-7352 Fax:(207)359-9865
E-mail: jim@oaklandhouse.com
Web: www.oaklandhouse.com

Circa 1907. This oceanfront historic inn boasts 50 acres and a half-mile of private oceanfront and panoramic views. It is one of the few remaining original coastal Maine resorts. Guests enjoy a sandy lake beach and an ocean beach as well as mossy woodland hiking trails. Your host, a fourth-generation innkeeper, is a descendant of John Billings, who received the property's original land grant from King George of England in 1767. The land has remained in the family since then. In 1889, the old homestead (named Oakland House) was opened to guests who arrived at the ocean landing via steamship. Through the years the resort has grown and now includes 15 cottages as well as Shore Oaks Seaside Inn. The historic homestead now houses the Oakland House restaurant, a fine dining establishment, offering five-course dinners. Built in 1907 as a private summer home, Shore Oaks is an excellent example of Arts and Crafts style. Ten guest rooms are appointed with period furnishings and fine linens. The living room is an inviting gathering place with a weathered stone fireplace and vintage furnishings. Outside, an extraordinary panoramic view of lighthouse, island and setting sun entices guests to unwind on porch rockers and soak up the experience. Full breakfasts for Shore Oaks guests are served in the dining room. The cottages, with one to five bedrooms, are situated along the shore or tucked among the trees. Most offer living rooms with wood burning fireplaces and kitchenettes or full kitchens. (The cottages rent by the week in season MAP.) There is a dining room specifically for families with children.
Historic Interest: The Brooksville area was a trading post of the Puritans of Plymouth in the early 1600s and was taken by the French in 1635, then captured by the Dutch and later abandoned. Fort George was the largest fort built by the British during the Revolutionary War. In the waters off nearby Castine, America suffered its greatest naval disaster until Pearl Harbor.
Innkeeper(s): Jim & Sally Littlefield. $95-295. MC, VISA, PC, TC. TAC10. 10 rooms, 7 with PB, 2 with FP, 15 cottages and 2 conference rooms. Breakfast and dinner included in rates. Types of meals: Full bkfst and picnic lunch. MAP. Beds: KQDT. VCR, fax, copier, swimming, library, row boats and recreation room on premises. Weddings hosted. Antiquing, fishing, concerts, musical events, boating, whale watching, parks, shopping, cross-country skiing and water sports nearby.
Publicity: *US Air "Attache", Redbook, Yankee Magazine's Travel Guide to New England, Downeast Magazine's Tasting the Cottage Life and Maine Public Broadcasting's "Home; A Place Apart"*

"We have dreamt of visiting Maine for quite some time. Our visit here at Shore Oaks and the beautiful countryside surpassed our dreams. We will be back to enjoy it again."

Brunswick   J3

Brunswick B&B

165 Park Row
Brunswick, ME 04011-2000
(207)729-4914 (800)299-4914 Fax:(207)725-0990
E-mail: inn@brunswickbnb.com
Web: www.brunswickbnb.com

Circa 1849. The Brunswick, a Greek Revival-style home, overlooks the town green. Guests often relax in one of the two front parlors, with their inviting fireplaces. Summertime guests enjoy the wraparound front porch. Rooms are filled with antiques, collectibles and quilts. In the years that the bed & breakfast served as a family home for law professor Daniel Stanwood, the home was host to an array of famed personalities, including Edna St. Vincent Millay, Thornton Wilder and Admiral Richard Byrd. Ice skating in the "mall" across the street is a popular winter activity. Freeport, only a 10-minute drive, is perfect for shoppers, and several state parks are nearby. Bowdoin College is a short walk away from the inn.
Innkeeper(s): Mercie & Steve Normand. $95-150. MC, VISA, AX, PC, TC. 8

rooms with PB, 3 suites and 1 cottage. Breakfast included in rates. Types of meals: Full bkfst and early coffee/tea. Beds: KQD. TV in suites, terry robes, hair dryers and iron/ironing board in room. Air conditioning. Fax, copier, library and kitchenette available 24 hours on premises. Weddings, small meetings and family reunions hosted. American Sign spoken. Antiquing, fishing, golf, museums, live theater, parks, shopping and sporting events nearby. Publicity: *Times Record, Coastal Journal and Atlanta Journal.*

"Good bed, great shower, fine breakfast (nice mix of substance and sweets and excellent java) and of course convivial hosts."

Camden   I5

The Belmont Inn

6 Belmont Ave
Camden, ME 04843-2029
(207)236-8053 (800)238-8053 Fax:(207)236-9872
E-mail: info@thebelmontinn.com
Web: www.thebelmontinn.com

Circa 1890. The crisp sea air, coupled with the sweet aroma of fresh flowers will soothe your senses while relaxing on the gazebo-wraparound porch of this late 19th-century Edwardian home

located two blocks from downtown shops and the harbor. Once inside, brilliant light fills each crevice of the house through its 99 windows, accenting the tastefully decorated interior of antiques and romantic classics. Start each day with a multi-course feast including fresh fruits and beverages, homemade muffins, and indulgences such as French toast, pancakes or Belgium waffles. Experience the many attractions of the downtown area and retreat to the serene neighborhood of The Belmont for coffee and cookies straight from the oven. In the evening, you'll want to be sure to dine at the inn's award-winning restaurant, the Marquis, which offers innovative American cuisine with fine wine offerings, in beautifully appointed dining rooms.

Innkeeper(s): Scott Marquis & Rebecca Brown. $95-225. MC, VISA, AX, PC, TC. 6 rooms with PB, 3 with FP, 3 suites and 1 guest house. Breakfast and afternoon tea included in rates. Types of meals: Country bkfst. Beds: KQDT. Phone, robes, three with gas fireplaces, three suites have full kitchens, separate living and sleeping areas and cable TV in room. Air conditioning. Fax, cable TV and in room massage therapist available on premises. Antiquing, art galleries, bicycling, canoeing/kayaking, fishing, golf, hiking, horseback riding, live theater, museums, parks, shopping, downhill skiing, cross-country skiing and tennis nearby.

The Camden Windward House B&B

6 High St
Camden, ME 04843-1611
(207)236-9656 (877)492-9656 Fax:(207)230-0433
E-mail: bnb@windwardhouse.com
Web: www.windwardhouse.com

Circa 1854. Each guest room at this Greek Revival home has been individually decorated and features names such as the Carriage Room, Trisha Romance Room, Brass Room, or Silver Birch Suite. Expansive views of Mt. Battie may be seen from its namesake room. It offers a private balcony, skylights, cathedral

ceilings, sitting area with fireplace, an extra large TV and a Jacuzzi and separate shower. All rooms include antiques and romantic amenities such as candles and fine linens. The innkeepers further pamper guests with a

hearty breakfast featuring a variety of juices, freshly ground coffee and teas and a choice of items such as featherbed eggs, pancakes, French toast or Belgian waffles topped with fresh Maine blueberries. After the morning meal, guests are sure to enjoy a day exploring Camden, noted as the village where "the mountains meet the sea." The inn is open year-round.

Innkeeper(s): Del & Charlotte Lawrence. $99-240. MC, VISA, AX, PC, TC. 8 rooms with PB, 5 with FP. Breakfast and afternoon tea included in rates. Types of meals: Gourmet bkfst and early coffee/tea. Beds: KQ. TV, ceiling fan, two with Jacuzzi whirlpool tubs, two with antique claw foot soaking tubs, phones with dataport, individual air conditioning, some with private balcony or deck and some with VCRs and/or separate sitting rooms in room. Fax, copier and library on premises. Small meetings hosted. Antiquing, fishing, windjammer cruises, hiking, live theater, parks, shopping, downhill skiing, cross-country skiing and water sports nearby.

Castleview By The Sea

59 High St
Camden, ME 04843-1733
(207)236-2344 (800)272-8439
Web: www.castleviewinn.com

Circa 1856. This classic American cape house is the only B&B located on the waterside of the ocean view section of Camden's flowered historic district. Guest rooms feature wide pine floors,

beamed ceilings, stained glass and balconies. The inn reflects the owner's world-wide travel in its eclectic decorating. Guests can literally enjoy views of the ocean right from their bed. Rooms offer cable TV and air conditioning.

Innkeeper(s): Bill Butler. $139-195. PC. TAC10. 3 rooms with PB. Breakfast included in rates. Types of meals: Full bkfst and cont plus. Beds: KQ. Cable TV and ceiling fan in room. Air conditioning. VCR and library on premises. Family reunions hosted. Antiquing, fishing, live theater, museums, parks, shopping, downhill skiing, cross-country skiing, tennis and water sports nearby.

"Wonderful food, wonderful view, wonderful host."

Lord Camden Inn

24 Main St
Camden, ME 04843-1704
(207)236-4325 (800)336-4325 Fax:(207)236-7141
E-mail: lordcam@midcoast.com

Circa 1893. Lord Camden Inn, housed in a century-old brick building, offers the gentle warmth of a seaside inn with all the comforts and services of a modern downtown hotel. Located in the midst of Camden's fine shops and restaurants, the bustling waterfront and beautiful parks, Lord Camden Inn offers splendid views of the harbor, Camden Hill and the village. Amenities include private baths, cable TV, air conditioning, phones and elevator services.

Historic Interest: Conway House (1 mile), Fort Knox (45 minutes), Children Chapel (1-1/2 miles), Owls Head Museum Montpelier (8 miles), Lime Kilns Rockport Harbor.

Innkeeper(s): Stuart & Marianne Smith. $88-208. MC, VISA, PC. TAC10. 31 rooms with PB, 4 suites and 1 conference room. Breakfast included in rates. Types of meals: Cont plus and early coffee/tea. Beds: KQD. Phone, some desks and refrigerators in room. Fax, copier and valet service available in high season on premises. Weddings, small meetings, family reunions and seminars hosted. Antiquing, fishing, sailing, fine dining, bicycle rentals, kayaking, hiking, live theater, parks, shopping, downhill skiing, cross-country skiing and water sports nearby.

Publicity: *Portland Magazine and Thinner.*

Swan House B&B

49 Mountain St
Camden, ME 04843-1635
(207)236-8275 (800)207-8275 Fax:(207)236-0906
E-mail: hikeinn@swanhouse.com
Web: www.swanhouse.com

Circa 1870. Nestled on just under an acre of wooded grounds at the foot of Mt. Battie, this Victorian is a welcoming site inside and out. Antique-filled guest rooms are comfortable, each named for a different variety of swan. Four of the rooms offer private entrances. The Lohengrin Suite is a spacious room with its own  sitting area, while the Trumpeter Room offers a private deck. Hearty breakfasts include country-style fare, fruit, homemade granola and special pastry of the day. The village of Camden and the surrounding area offer plenty of activities, and the innkeepers are happy to point guests in an interesting direction.
Innkeeper(s): Lyn & Ken Kohl. $100-150. MC, VISA, PC, TC. 6 rooms with PB and 1 suite. Breakfast included in rates. Types of meals: Full bkfst, early coffee/tea and afternoon tea. Beds: QD. Phone in room. Fax, gazebo and mountain hiking trails on premises. Small meetings and family reunions hosted. Antiquing, fishing, mountain hiking trails, live theater, parks, shopping, downhill skiing, cross-country skiing and water sports nearby.

"We loved our stay at the Swan House and our breakfast there was by far the most excellent breakfast we have ever had."

Cape Neddick — K2

Cape Neddick House

1300 Rt 1, PO Box 70
Cape Neddick, ME 03902-0070
(207)363-2500 Fax:(207)363-4499
E-mail: capeneddickhouse@aol.com
Web: www.capeneddickhouse.com

Circa 1885. Rest assured, as the scent of fresh-baked blueberry poppyseed scones and ham and sticky buns drifts up upward, an alarm clock is not needed at this renovated Victorian farmhouse. Begin the day's breakfast feast with fresh flowers and settings of china and crystal in the dining room. For a more casual meal on the deck, overlook the 10 acres of gardens and woods. In winter, a fun treat is to gather by the Glenwood as Dianne has mastered the lost art of cooking with a real woodstove. Sustained for the day's adventures, explore York, Kittery and Ogunquit. The Diana Card Folk Gallery, a few steps away, is in what was the post office, run for 75 years by the Goodwins. The ocean, beaches, historic sites, Nubble Lighthouse and the Marginal Way are all just minutes away.
Innkeeper(s): Dianne Goodwin. $95-150. PC, TC. 5 rooms with PB, 1 with FP and 1 suite. Breakfast included in rates. Types of meals: Gourmet bkfst, early coffee/tea and gourmet dinner. Beds: QD. Air conditioning. VCR, fax and library on premises. Small meetings, family reunions and seminars hosted. Amusement parks, antiquing, fishing, live theater, parks, shopping, cross-country skiing and water sports nearby.
Publicity: *WFBS From Hartford and CT.*

"A wonderful vacation from all. Breakfast was super."

Castine — I5

The Castine Harbor Lodge

PO Box 215
Castine, ME 04421-0215
(207)326-4335
E-mail: chl@acadia.net
Web: www.castinemaine.com

Circa 1893. Relax on the expansive harbor-side verandas of this Edwardian mansion and soak up the ocean views while you enjoy the sounds of waves crashing on the shore. Guest quarters boast ocean views, and the innkeepers also offer a waterfront cottage. The delicious, homemade breakfasts are a treat. A variety of outdoor activities and antique shopping are available nearby.
Historic Interest: Castine, which has been claimed as the property of four countries, is home to the Maine Maritime Academy. The academy includes old British barracks and the school keeps a training ship anchored at the town dock.
Innkeeper(s): Paul & Sara Brouillard. $75-195. MC, VISA, DC, DS, PC, TC. 16 rooms, 10 with PB and 1 cottage. Breakfast included in rates. Types of meals: Cont plus. Beds: KQDT. Swimming and library on premises. Weddings, small meetings and family reunions hosted. Antiquing, fishing, golf, parks and tennis nearby.
Pets allowed: Well-behaved, leash $10 charge.
Publicity: *Conde Nast Travel, Yankee and Boats & Harbors.*

Corea — I7

The Black Duck Inn on Corea Harbor

PO Box 39 Crowley Island Rd
Corea, ME 04624-0039
(207)963-2689 (877)963-2689 Fax:(207)963-7495
E-mail: bduck@acadia.net
Web: www.blackduck.com

Circa 1890. Two of the guest rooms at this turn-of-the-century farmhouse boast harbor views, while another offers a wooded scene out its windows. The innkeepers have decorated the home in an eclectic mix of old and new with antiques and contemporary pieces. There are two waterfront cottages for those who prefer more privacy. The full, gourmet breakfasts include specialties, such as "eggs Black Duck" or items such as orange glazed French toast, blintzes or perhaps eggs Benedict.
Innkeeper(s): Barry Canner & Bob Travers. $100-175. MC, VISA, DS, PC, TC. TAC10. 6 rooms, 4 with PB, 2 suites, 2 cottages and 1 conference room. Breakfast included in rates. Types of meals: Gourmet bkfst and early coffee/tea. Beds: QDT. VCR, fax, copier and library on premises. Small meetings, family reunions and seminars hosted. Danish spoken. Antiquing, art galleries, beaches, bicycling, canoeing/kayaking, fishing, golf, hiking, live theater, parks, shopping, cross-country skiing and wineries nearby.
Publicity: *Boston Globe and Miami Herald.*

"Never could we have known how warmly received we would all four feel and how really restored we would be by the end of the week."

Damariscotta Mills — I4

Mill Pond Inn

50 Main St
Damariscotta Mills, ME 04555
(207)563-8014

Circa 1780. The one acre of grounds surrounding this 18th-century home are packed with scenery. A pond with a waterfall flows into the adjacent Damariscotta Lake and trees offer plenty of shade. Rooms are decorated in a whimsical country style and they have pond views and fresh flowers. Breakfasts are served in a room that overlooks the pond and grounds.

Innkeeper Bobby Whear is a registered Maine guide, and the innkeepers offer private fishing trips. Complimentary canoeing and biking are available.

Innkeeper(s): Bobby & Sherry Whear. $95. 6 rooms with PB, 3 with FP and 1 suite. Breakfast and afternoon tea included in rates. Types of meals: Full bkfst and early coffee/tea. Beds: KQT. VCR, bicycles, private fishing trips available with Registered Maine Guide and canoes on premises. Weddings, small meetings, family reunions and seminars hosted. Antiquing, fishing, bird watching, live theater, parks, shopping, downhill skiing, cross-country skiing, sporting events and water sports nearby.

Dexter G4

Brewster Inn of Dexter, Maine

37 Zions Hill Rd
Dexter, ME 04930-1122
(207)924-3130 Fax:(207)924-9768
E-mail: brewster@nconline.net
Web: www.bbonline.com/me/brewsterinn

Circa 1934. Located on two acres with rose and perennial gardens, this handsome Colonial Revival-style house was built by architect John Calvin Stevens for Governor Ralph

Brewster. It is in the National Register. Some guest rooms offer fireplaces, window seats, original tile bathrooms and views of the gardens. One has a whirlpool tub for two. Furnishings include antiques and reproductions. A breakfast buffet includes hot entrees such as quiche, gingerbread pancakes or stuffed apples.

Innkeeper(s): Ivy & Michael Brooks. $59-100. MC, VISA, DS, PC, TC. TAC10. 10 rooms with PB, 2 with FP and 2 suites. Breakfast and snacks/refreshments included in rates. Types of meals: Full bkfst, early coffee/tea, gourmet lunch, picnic lunch and dinner. MAP. Beds: KQDT. Cable TV, phone and books in room. Air conditioning. VCR, fax, copier, tennis and library on premises. Handicap access. Weddings, small meetings, family reunions and seminars hosted. Antiquing, fishing, golf, parks, shopping, cross-country skiing, tennis and water sports nearby.
Publicity: *Bangor Daily News, People and Places & Plants.*

Durham I3

The Bagley House

1290 Royalsborough Rd
Durham, ME 04222-5225
(207)865-6566 (800)765-1772 Fax:(207)353-5878
E-mail: bglyhse@aol.com
Web: www.bagleyhouse.com

Circa 1772. Six acres of fields and woods surround the Bagley House. Once an inn, a store and a schoolhouse, it is the oldest house in town. Guest rooms are decorated with colonial furnishings and hand-sewn quilts. For breakfast, guests gather in the country kitchen in front of a huge brick fireplace and beehive oven.

Historic Interest: Bowdoin College, Maritime Museum and Old Sea Captain Homes.
Innkeeper(s): Suzanne O'Connor & Susan Backhouse. $75-160. MC, VISA, AX, DC, DS, PC, TC. TAC10. 8 rooms

with PB, 4 with FP and 1 conference room. Breakfast and afternoon tea included in rates. Types of meals: Full bkfst, early coffee/tea, picnic lunch and snacks/refreshments. Beds: KQDT. Fax and blueberry picking on premises. Small meetings and family reunions hosted. Antiquing, live theater, shopping, downhill skiing, cross-country skiing and sporting events nearby.
Publicity: *Los Angeles Times, New England Getaways, Lewiston Sun,*

Springfield Register and 2001 Yankee Magazine-Editors Pick.
"I had the good fortune to stumble on the Bagley House. The rooms are well-appointed and the innkeepers are charming."

East Boothbay J4

Ocean Point Inn

Shore Rd
East Boothbay, ME 04544-0409
(207)633-4200 (800)552-5554
E-mail: opi@oceanpointinn.com
Web: www.oceanpointinn.com

Circa 1898. Ocean Point Inn is comprised of a white clapboard main house, lodge, cottages, apartments and motel units located on three oceanfront acres. There are gardens and a lovely road along the bay where guests watch lobstermen, seals

and passing windjammers. Four lighthouses may be viewed among the nearby islands. Boothbay Harbor is six miles away, but right at hand is the town pier and

the inn's restaurant with a view of the ocean. In addition to lobster dishes and crab cakes, the specialty of the house is fresh Maine salmon poached in Court Boullion served with dill sauce. Select from a wide choice of activities such as swimming, fishing and hiking, or simply settle into the Adirondack chairs and watch the soothing sea. Guests can rent motor boats or kayaks in Boothbay Harbor.

Innkeeper(s): Beth & Dave Dudley. $125-189. MC, VISA, AX, DS, TC. TAC10. 61 rooms with PB, 3 with FP, 10 suites and 7 cottages. Types of meals: Full bkfst and dinner. EP. Beds: KQDT. Cable TV, phone, mini-refrigerators and most with air conditioning in room. Swimming, outdoor heated pool and hot tub on premises. Family reunions hosted. Antiquing, fishing, golf, live theater, parks, shopping, tennis and water sports nearby.

Eastport G8

The Milliken House B&B

29 Washington St
Eastport, ME 04631
(207)853-2955 (888)507-9370

Circa 1846. This inn is filled with beautiful furnishings and knickknacks, much of which belonged to the home's first owner, Benjamin Milliken. Ornately carved, marble-topped pieces and period decor take guests back in time to the Victorian era. Milliken maintained a wharf on Eastport's waterfront from which he serviced the tall trading ships that used the harbor as a port of entry to the United States. An afternoon glass of port or sherry and chocolate turn-down service are among the amenities. Breakfasts are a gourmet treat, served in the dining room with its carved, antique furnishings.

Historic Interest: The waterfront historic district is just two blocks away as is the Barracks Historical Museum.
$65. MC, VISA, PC, TC. 6 rooms. Types of meals: Full bkfst.
"A lovely trip back in history to a more gracious time."

Todd House

Todd's Head
Eastport, ME 04631
(207)853-2328

Circa 1775. Todd House is a typical full-Cape-style house with a huge center chimney. In 1801, Eastern Lodge No. 7 of the

Masonic Order was chartered here. It became temporary barracks when Todd's Head was fortified. Guests may use barbecue facilities overlooking Passamaquoddy Bay. Children and well-behaved pets are welcome.

Innkeeper(s): Ruth McInnis. $50-90. MC, VISA. 6 rooms, 2 with PB, 3 with FP and 2 suites. Breakfast included in rates. Types of meals: Cont plus. Beds: QDT. Handicap access. Fishing and live theater nearby.
Pets Allowed.
Publicity: *Portland Press Herald.*

"Your house and hospitality were real memory makers of our vacation."

Weston House

26 Boynton St
Eastport, ME 04631-1305
(207)853-2907 (800)853-2907 Fax:(207)853-0981
E-mail: westonhouse@prexar.com

Circa 1810. Jonathan Weston, an 1802 Harvard graduate, built this Federal-style house on a hill overlooking Passamaquoddy Bay. James Audubon stayed here as a guest of the Westons while awaiting passage to Labrador in 1833. Each

guest room is furnished with antiques and Oriental rugs. The Weston and Audubon rooms boast views of the bay and gardens. Breakfast menus vary, including such delectables as heavenly pancakes with hot apricot syrup or freshly baked muffins and coddled eggs. Seasonal brunches are served on weekends and holidays. The area is full of outdoor activities, including whale watching. Nearby Saint Andrews-by-the-Sea offers plenty of shops and restaurants.

Historic Interest: Nearby historic attractions include Campobello Island, where Franklin D. Roosevelt spent his summers. King's Landing, a restored Loyalist settlement dating back to 1780, is two hours away.
Innkeeper(s): Jett & John Peterson. $65-80. PC, TC. 4 rooms, 2 with PB. Breakfast and afternoon tea included in rates. Types of meals: Gourmet bkfst and picnic lunch. Beds: KQD. Weddings, small meetings and family reunions hosted. Fishing, whale watching, nature, live theater, shopping and tennis nearby.
Publicity: *Down East, Los Angeles Times, Boston Globe, Boston Magazine and New York Times.*

"All parts of ourselves have been nourished."

Freeport J3

Captain Briggs House B&B

8 Maple Ave
Freeport, ME 04032-1315
(207)865-1868 (888)217-2477 Fax:(207)865-6083
E-mail: briggsbb@suscom-maine.net

Circa 1853. This mid-19th-century home's most notable resident was John A. Briggs, a shipbuilder whose ancestors arrived in America via the Mayflower. There are six comfortable guest rooms, all with private baths. A full breakfast prepares guests for a day of outlet shopping in Freeport. The famous L.L. Bean factory store and about a hundred more outlets are just minutes away. Harbor cruises, fish-

ing, seal watching, hiking and just enjoying the scenery in this coastal town are other options.
Historic Interest: Jameson Tavern (1/10 mile).
Innkeeper(s): Celia & Rob Elberfeld.
$85-130. MC, VISA, AX, DS, PC, TC. 6

rooms with PB. Breakfast, afternoon tea and snacks/refreshments included in rates. Types of meals: Gourmet bkfst. Beds: KQDT. Air conditioning. VCR, fax and copier on premises. Family reunions hosted. Amusement parks, antiquing, art galleries, beaches, bicycling, canoeing/kayaking, fishing, golf, hiking, LL Bean Outlets, seal watching, harbor cruises, live theater, museums, parks, shopping, cross-country skiing and water sports nearby.
Publicity: *New York Times.*

Country at Heart B&B

37 Bow St
Freeport, ME 04032-1519
(207)865-0512 (877)877-9444 Fax:(207)865-0777
E-mail: info@countryatheart-freeport.com
Web: www.countryatheart-freeport.com

Circa 1870. Enjoy New England Americana at this comfortable Victorian inn. True to its name, a country charm highlights the casual atmosphere where relaxation is easy to come by. Meet new friends in the living room, or watch the world go by on the front porch. The guest bedrooms feature handmade crafts, sten-

ciled borders and an accompanying themed decor. Breakfast is a culinary delight in the dining room. Quietly sitting at the base of a hill next to a quaint village park, the inn is within walking distance of the area's outlet shops, specialty stores and restaurants.

Innkeeper(s): Shawn & Dina. $70-150. MC, VISA, AX, PC, TC. 3 rooms with PB and 1 suite. Breakfast included in rates. Types of meals: Full bkfst and early coffee/tea. Beds: QD. Ceiling fan in room. Air conditioning. VCR, fax and copier on premises. Amusement parks, antiquing, art galleries, beaches, bicycling, canoeing/kayaking, fishing, golf, hiking, horseback riding, live theater, museums, parks, shopping, cross-country skiing, sporting events, tennis and water sports nearby.

"Thank you for your genuine hospitality! Wonderful breakfast, too!"

Harraseeket Inn

162 Main St
Freeport, ME 04032-1311
(207)865-9377 (800)342-6423 Fax:(207)865-1684
E-mail: harraseeke@aol.com
Web: www.stayfreeport.com

Circa 1889. The tavern and drawing room of this inn are decorated in the Federal style. Guest rooms are furnished with antiques and half-canopied beds. Some have whirlpools and fireplaces. The inn features two restaurants and offers a buffet breakfast. The L.L. Bean store is just two blocks away, with 130 outlet stores such as Ralph Lauren and Anne Klein nearby.
Innkeeper(s): Gray Family. $140-325. MC, VISA, AX, DC, DS. TAC10. 93 rooms with PB, 16 with FP, 3 suites and 5 conference rooms. Breakfast and afternoon tea included in rates. Types of meals: Gourmet bkfst, lunch, dinner and room service. EP. Beds: KQD. Fax, copier, swimming, wood fired oven & grill, exercise equipment and indoor pool on premises. Handicap access. Antiquing, fishing, live theater and cross-country skiing nearby.

Maple Hill B&B

18 Maple Ave
Freeport, ME 04032-1315
(207)865-3730 (800)867-0478 Fax:(207)865-6727
E-mail: mplhll@aol.com
Web: www.maplehill.net

Circa 1831. Maple Hill is comprised of a Greek Revival farmhouse and attached barn located on two tree-shaded acres of lawns and gardens. Furnished with antiques, the inn is in an amazing location two blocks from L. L. Bean. A family suite is

offered (the innkeepers have raised six children and enjoy hosting families). Queen-size guest rooms are also available, and a romantic atmosphere is provided at the inn with its fireplace, candlelight, flowers and music. Hearty breakfasts are served in the morning, featuring fruit compotes, French toast, waffles, blueberry muffins or biscuits.

Innkeeper(s): Lloyd & Susie Lawrence. $97-166. MC, VISA, AX, DS, PC, TC. 3 rooms with PB, 1 suite and 1 conference room. Types of meals: Full bkfst, country bkfst, veg bkfst, early coffee/tea, afternoon tea and snacks/refreshments. Beds: KQT. Cable TV and VCR in room. Air conditioning. Fax, copier, bicycles, library and child care available on premises. Weddings, small meetings, family reunions and seminars hosted. Antiquing, art galleries, beaches, bicycling, canoeing/kayaking, fishing, golf, hiking, horseback riding, live theater, museums, parks, shopping, cross-country skiing, sporting events, tennis and water sports nearby.

Pets Allowed.

Publicity: *McCalls.*

Gouldsboro   H6

Sunset House

Rt 186, HCR 60
Gouldsboro, ME 04607
(207)963-7156 (800)233-7156 Fax:(207)963-5859
E-mail: lodging@sunsethousebnb.com

Circa 1898. This coastal country farm inn is situated near Acadia National Park. Naturalists can observe rare birds and other wildlife in an unspoiled setting. Seven spacious bedrooms are spread over three floors. Four of the bedrooms have ocean views; a fifth overlooks a freshwater pond behind the house. During winter, guests can ice skate on the pond, while in summer it is used for swim-  ming. The innkeepers have a resident cat and poodle, and they also raise goats. Guests enjoy a full country breakfast cooked by Carl, who has been an executive chef for more than 20 years.

Innkeeper(s): Kathy & Carl Johnson. $79-99. MC, VISA, AX, DS, PC, TC. 7 rooms, 4 with PB. Breakfast included in rates. Types of meals: Gourmet bkfst, veg bkfst and early coffee/tea. Beds: KQDT. Turndown service in room. VCR, fax, copier and swimming on premises. Family reunions hosted. German spoken. Antiquing, art galleries, bicycling, canoeing/kayaking, fishing, golf, parks, shopping, cross-country skiing, tennis and wineries nearby.

Greenville   F4

Blair Hill Inn

1 Lily Bay Rd
Greenville, ME 04441
(207)695-0224 Fax:(207)695-4324
E-mail: blairhill@moosehead.net
Web: www.blairhill.com

Circa 1891. An impressive Queen Anne Victorian, this 15-acre estate is breathtaking. Majestically situated on a tranquil hill, guarded by cannons and a high stone wall, there are spectacular panoramic views of Moosehead Lake, its islands and the surrounding mountains. Luxurious pleasures abound throughout the elegant inn with seven fireplaces, a 90-foot veranda, outdoor Jacuzzi, exercise room, massage therapy, art gallery and concierge. The plush guest bedrooms are filled with unexpected surprises. Encounter feather beds and fine linens, soft robes,

aromatherapy candles and personal products, fresh flowers and bottled water. Breakfast is a gastronomical masterpiece with delicious creations to devour. On-site seasonal activities include croquet, badminton, bocce ball, a catch and release trout pond, snowshoeing and hiking.

Historic Interest: Historic steamship Katahdin (1 mile).

Innkeeper(s): Dan & Ruth McLaughlin. $195-300. MC, VISA, DS, PC, TC. 8 rooms with PB, 4 with FP and 1 conference room. Breakfast and snacks/refreshments included in rates. Types of meals: Gourmet bkfst and early coffee/tea. Beds: KQ. Turndown service, CD players, plush terry robes, feather beds, down comforters and pillows, 312 count linens, all natural bath and body products produced locally especially for the Blair Hill Inn, candles, fresh flowers and hair dryers in room. VCR, fax, copier, spa, library, spa towels and guest refridgerator with spring water and juices, hiking trails, snowshoeing, massage therapy, catch and release trout pond, Adirondack chairs, extensive gardens and wildflower fields and woodlands on premises. Weddings, small meetings and family reunions hosted. Antiquing, art galleries, beaches, bicycling, canoeing/kayaking, fishing, golf, hiking, horseback riding, Moose safari, snowshoeing, dog sledding, sea plane tours, white water rafting, parks, shopping, downhill skiing, cross-country skiing, tennis and water sports nearby.

Publicity: *Boston Globe, Down East Magazine, Yankee Magazine-2000 Editor's Pick, ESPN, NESN, Maine PBS and The Wild Web Show.*

Guilford   G4

The Trebor Inn

11 Golda Ct
Guilford, ME 04443
(207)876-4070

Circa 1830. Seven guest rooms are available at this stately, turreted Victorian inn, which overlooks Guilford from high on a hill along the Moosehead Trail. Those who enjoy hunting bear, deer, partridge and pheasant should inquire about the inn's special rates for hunters. Meals are served family-style, and dinners are available on request. The family-oriented inn also accommodates business meetings, family reunions and weddings. Within five minutes of the inn, visitors will find basketball courts, a nine-hole golf course and tennis courts. Peaks-Kenny State Park and Sebec Lake are nearby.

Innkeeper(s): Larraine Vernal. $50-65. MC, VISA, AX, PC, TC. 7 rooms, 2 with PB. Breakfast included in rates. Types of meals: Full bkfst, early coffee/tea and dinner. Beds: DT. VCR on premises. Weddings, small meetings, family reunions and seminars hosted. Antiquing, fishing, golf, hunting, snowmobiling, parks, shopping, downhill skiing, cross-country skiing, tennis and water sports nearby.

Isle Au Haut   I5

The Keeper's House

PO Box 26
Isle Au Haut, ME 04645-0026
(207)367-2261
Web: www.keepershouse.com

Circa 1907. Designed and built by the U.S. Lighthouse Service, the handsome 48-foot-high Robinson Point Light guided vessels into this once-bustling island fishing village. Guests arrive on the mailboat. Innkeeper Judi Burke, whose father was a keeper at the Highland Lighthouse on Cape Cod, provides picnic lunches so guests may explore the scenic island trails. Dinner is served in the keeper's dining room. The lighthouse is adjacent to the most remote section of Acadia National Park. It's not uncommon to hear the cry of an osprey, see deer approach the inn, or watch seals and porpoises cavorting off the

point. Guest rooms are comfortable and serene, with stunning views of the island's ragged shore line, forests and Duck Harbor.

Historic Interest: Acadia National Park, adjacent 18th-century one-room school house, church & town hall (1-mile walk away).
Innkeeper(s): Jeff & Judi Burke. $294-335. PC, TC. 5 rooms and 1 cottage. Breakfast, picnic lunch and dinner included in rates. Types of meals: Gourmet bkfst and early coffee/tea. Beds: D. Wood stove in room. Swimming, bicycles and library on premises. Weddings, small meetings, family reunions and seminars hosted. Spanish spoken. Parks and shopping nearby.
Publicity: *New York Times, USA Today, Los Angeles Times, Ladies Home Journal, Christian Science Monitor, Down East, New York Woman, Philadelphia Inquirer, McCalls, Country, Men's Journal, Travel & Leisure, Gourmet, House Beautiful, PBS, CBS and CNN.*

"Simply one of the unique places on Earth."

Kennebunk   K2

The Kennebunk Inn

45 Main St
Kennebunk, ME 04043-1888
(207)985-3351 Fax:(207)985-8865
E-mail: info@thekennebunkinn.com

Circa 1799. Built at the turn of the 19th century, Kennebunk Inn has been serving guests since the 1920s. The rooms and suites feature a variety of decor; guests might discover a clawfoot tub or four-poster bed. Games and a selection of books are available for guests, as well as televisions. For a special treat, make dinner reservations at the inn's restaurant, which serves a seasonally changing menu with fresh local seafood and produce. Guests can choose from filet mignon wrapped in puff pastry and topped with Brie cheese or perhaps pan-seared scallops and basil ravioli with a pink peppercorn and white wine cream sauce. Portland Press heralded the inn's restaurant with four stars.

Innkeeper(s): Kristen & John Martin. $55-155. MC, VISA, AX, DS, PC, TC. TAC10. 27 rooms with PB, 1 with FP, 5 suites and 1 conference room. Breakfast included in rates. Types of meals: Cont plus, cont, early coffee/tea and dinner. MAP. Beds: KQDT. Cable TV, phone and VCR in room. Air conditioning. Fax, copier, library, pet boarding and on-line access on premises. Handicap access. Weddings, small meetings, family reunions and seminars hosted. French spoken. Amusement parks, antiquing, fishing, golf, live theater, parks, shopping, cross-country skiing, sporting events, tennis and water sports nearby.
Pets allowed: One dog per room.
Publicity: *Down East Magazine.*

Kennebunk Beach   K2

The Ocean View

171 Beach Ave
Kennebunk Beach, ME 04043-2524
(207)967-2750
E-mail: arena@theoceanview.com
Web: www.theoceanview.com

Circa 1900. This brightly painted Victorian is literally just steps to the beach. Nine oceanfront guest rooms are located either in the turn-of-the-century Victorian or in the Ocean View Too, a wing of the main house with four suites. Hand-painted furniture and colorful fabrics decorate the whimsical, eclectic guest rooms. Breakfast is served in an oceanfront breakfast room. Specialties, which are served on colorful china, include baked pears with yogurt, honey and slivered almonds, followed by Belgian waffles topped with seasonal fresh fruit and a dollop creme fraiche. Suite guests also can opt to enjoy breakfast in bed. The village of Kennebunkport is just one mile away.

Historic Interest: National Register Historic Walk.
Innkeeper(s): Carole & Bob Arena. $140-325. MC, VISA, AX, DS, TC. 9 rooms with PB and 5 suites. Breakfast and snacks/refreshments included in rates. Types of meals: Gourmet bkfst, early coffee/tea and afternoon tea. Beds: KQT. TV, phone, ceiling fan, VCR, luxurious robes, fresh flowers, mini refrigerator, iron/ironing board, hair dryer, clock radio and CD player in room. Fax, library, fireplaced living room and TV room on premises. French spoken. Antiquing, beaches, fishing, ocean, live theater, parks, shopping, sporting events and water sports nearby.
Publicity: *New York Times, Boston, Boston Magazine, Entree and Elegance.*

Kennebunkport   K2

1802 House

15 Locke Street
Kennebunkport, ME 04046-1646
(207)967-5632 (800)932-5632 Fax:(207)967-0780
E-mail: inquiry@1802inn.com
Web: www.1802inn.com

Circa 1802. The rolling fairways of Cape Arundel Golf Course, old shade trees and secluded gardens create the perfect setting for this historic 19th-century farmhouse. Located along the gentle shores of the Kennebunk River, the inn is accentuated by personal service and attention to detail. Romantic guest bedrooms offer four-poster canopy beds, two-person whirlpool tubs and fireplaces. The luxurious three-room Sebago Suite tucked into a private wing is a favorite choice. Homemade specialties and regional delights are part of a gourmet breakfast served in the sunlit dining room. Popular Dock Square is within walking distance for browsing in boutiques and art galleries. Golf packages are available.

Historic Interest: Nott House (1/2 mile).
Innkeeper(s): Edric & Mary Ellen Mason. $149-369. MC, VISA, AX, DS, PC. 6 rooms with PB and 1 suite. Breakfast included in rates. Types of meals: Gourmet bkfst and early coffee/tea. Beds: Q. Cable TV, turndown service, VCR, most with fireplace and some with double whirlpool in room. Air conditioning. Fax and gift shop on premises. Weddings hosted. Antiquing, art galleries, beaches, bicycling, canoeing/kayaking, fishing, golf, hiking, horseback riding, live theater, museums, parks, shopping, cross-country skiing, sporting events, tennis, water sports and wineries nearby.

Captain Fairfield Inn

8 Pleasant St
Kennebunkport, ME 04046-2690
(207)967-4454 (800)322-1928 Fax:(207)967-8537
E-mail: jrw@captainfairfield.com
Web: www.captainfairfield.com

Circa 1813. This romantic country inn is located in the heart of Kennebunkport, a seaport resort. A handsome, shuttered sea captain's mansion, Captain Fairfield Inn overlooks the scenic Kennebunkport River Green. Shaded by tall trees, and in the National Register, it offers an enticing and gracious spot for celebrating anniversaries and honeymoons. Guest rooms are spacious, all with sitting areas, and boast period furnishings such as four-poster and canopy beds as well as fireplaces and views of the gar-dens or the neighborhood's historic homes. Down comforters and bouquets of fresh garden flowers are additional amenities. Ask for the Library Suite for a special occasion and you'll enjoy a whirlpool tub for two. Breakfast is a lavish four-course affair and is served next to an open-hearth fireplace in the gathering room or in view of the inn's gardens. Guests enjoy the location's access to the ocean and beaches, boutique shops, art galleries and restaurants. Carriage rides and theater and spa packages are offered.

Activities include kayaking, cycling, fishing, whale watching and sailing. Other options include touring the Brick Store Museum, the Rachel Carson Preserve and the Seashore Trolley Museum.

Innkeeper(s): Janet & Rick Wolf. $110-275. MC, VISA, AX, DC, DS. 9 rooms with PB, 4 with FP. Types of meals: Gourmet bkfst, early coffee/tea, afternoon tea and snacks/refreshments. Beds: QT. Phone, bottled water, hair dryers, iron/ironing board and some with fireplace in room. Air conditioning. Piano, guest refrigerator, ice machine, maps, menus and concierge service on premises. Antiquing, fishing, golf, live theater, shopping and cross-country skiing nearby.

"It couldn't have been nicer...Your breakfasts were delicious and your hospitality unequaled...all in all a wonderful experience."

Captain Jefferds Inn

PO Box 691, 5 Pearl St
Kennebunkport, ME 04046-0691
(207)967-2311 (800)839-6844 Fax:(207)967-0721
E-mail: captjeff@captainjefferdsinn.com
Web: www.captainjefferdsinn.com

Circa 1804. This Federal-style home was given as a wedding gift from a father to his daughter and new son-in-law. It was constructed the same year Thomas Jefferson was re-elected to the

presidency. Each guest room is different. Several offer two-person whirlpools, eight have a fireplace. Canopy, four-poster and sleigh beds are among the furnishings. In the afternoons, tea is served in the garden room. The breakfasts feature gourmet fare and are served by candlelight. The inn is located in a local historic district, just minutes from shops and restaurants.

Innkeeper(s): Pat & Dick Bartholomew. $145-295. MC, VISA, AX, PC, TC. TAC10. 16 rooms with PB, 8 with FP and 5 suites. Breakfast and afternoon tea included in rates. Types of meals: Gourmet bkfst, cont and early coffee/tea. Beds: KQDT. Air conditioning. VCR, fax and library on premises. Weddings, small meetings and family reunions hosted. Antiquing, fishing, golf, whale watching, parks, shopping, downhill skiing, cross-country skiing and water sports nearby.

Pets allowed: Dogs with prior approval.

The Captain Lord Mansion

Corner Pleasant & Green, PO Box 800
Kennebunkport, ME 04046
(207)967-3141 Fax:(207)967-3172
E-mail: innkeeper@captainlord.com
Web: www.captainlord.com

Circa 1812. In the National Register, the Captain Lord Mansion was built during the War of 1812 and is one of the finest examples of Federal architecture on the coast of Maine. The home rests at the edge of the village green within view of the Kennebunk River and within walking distance of the town's many historic sites. The romantically appointed guest rooms include roomy four-poster beds, gas fireplaces and heated marble and tile floors in the bathrooms. Some rooms include a double Jacuzzi tub. Guests are further pampered with fresh flowers, a full breakfast and afternoon treats.

Innkeeper(s): Bev Davis & Rick Litchfield. $125-399. MC, VISA, DS. TAC7. 16 rooms with PB, 16 with FP and 2 conference rooms. Breakfast included in rates. Types of meals: Full bkfst, early coffee/tea and afternoon tea. Beds: KQ. Phone in room. Air conditioning. Fax, copier and library on premises. Small meetings, family reunions and seminars hosted. Antiquing, fishing, live theater, shopping and cross-country skiing nearby.

Publicity: *Andrew Harper's Hideaway Report, Colonial Homes, Yankee* and *New England Getaways.*

"A showcase of elegant architecture. Meticulously clean and splendidly appointed. It's a shame to have to leave."

English Meadows Inn

141 Port Rd
Kennebunkport, ME 04043
(207)967-5766 (800)272-0698 Fax:(207)967-3868

Circa 1860. For more than 100 years this Victorian farmhouse has warmly welcomed travelers, and has been lovingly maintained to stay in pristine condition. Peaceful surroundings include at least two acres of manicured lawns, flowers, trees and antique lilacs. The main house offers comfortable guest bedrooms furnished with antiques and lace curtains. The carriage house boasts a cozy fireplace in the

large common room. A guest house has a screened porch amidst the trees. A hearty breakfast may include fresh fruit, Honey Nut Crunch French toast, sausage and egg casserole. Dock Square is just a short walk for shopping or restaurants, and there are many historic sites and nearby beaches.

Historic Interest: Walkers Pointe, President Bush's summer residence (1.5 miles).

Innkeeper(s): Kathy & Peter Smith. $90-165. MC, VISA, AX, PC, TC. 12 rooms, 8 with PB, 1 suite and 1 cottage. Breakfast and snacks/refreshments included in rates. Types of meals: Full bkfst, country bkfst, early coffee/tea, afternoon tea and room service. Beds: KQDT. Some with AC in room. Library on premises. Small meetings and family reunions hosted. Amusement parks, antiquing, art galleries, beaches, bicycling, canoeing/kayaking, fishing, golf, hiking, horseback riding, live theater, museums, parks, shopping, cross-country skiing, tennis and water sports nearby.

"Thanks for the memories! You have a warm Yankee hospitality here!"

The Inn on South Street B&B

PO Box 478A
Kennebunkport, ME 04046-1778
(207)967-5151 (800)963-5151
E-mail: innkeeper@innonsouthst.com
Web: www.innonsouthst.com

Circa 1806. This early 19th-century Greek Revival manor is within walking distance of Kennebunkport's many shops, restaurants and the ocean. A unique "Good Morning" staircase will be one of the first items guests will notice upon entering the inn. Richly appointed rooms are full of beautiful furnishings, lovely window dressings and pine plank floors. Guests will enjoy such amenities as telephones, fireplaces and fresh flowers in the guest rooms. Breakfasts are a treat, served up in the second-floor country kitchen with views of the river and ocean

or, if weather permits, in the garden. The morning meal features special dishes with herbs from the inn's herb garden.

Historic Interest: Kennebunkport boasts many two- and three-story wooden Federal-style dwellings, which date back to the early 19th century. Cape Arundel, one mile away, features the work of John Calvin Stevens, a noted 19th-century architect. Among the roomy summer cottages he created was the home of former President Bush.

Innkeeper(s): Jacques & Eva Downs. $105-250. MC, VISA. 3 rooms with PB, 2 with FP and 1 suite. Breakfast and afternoon tea included in rates. Types of meals: Gourmet bkfst and early coffee/tea. Beds: QT. Phone in room.

German, Spanish and Russian spoken. Antiquing, fishing, live theater, parks and water sports nearby.

Publicity: *Los Angeles Times, Summertime, Country Inns and Down East.*

"Superb hospitality. We were delighted by the atmosphere and your thoughtfulness."

Kennebunkport Inn

One Dock Sq
Kennebunkport, ME 04046
(207)967-2621 (800)248-2621 Fax:(207)967-3705
E-mail: stay@kennebunkportinn.com
Web: www.kennebunkportinn.com

Circa 1899. Intimate charm, excellent service and tasteful luxury are distinctively found at this elegant Victorian mansion. Choose from a variety of well-appointed guest bedrooms; some

feature sitting areas and fireplaces. Dining and lodging packages are available which include breakfast and/or dinner served in the dining rooms or al fresco on the patio. There is ample private parking, convenient for a pleasant walk to the historic harbor and shops of Dock Square. Or enjoy a refreshing swim in the outdoor pool. In the evening, the hotel's Victorian Pub offers live entertainment.

Historic Interest: Nott House.

Innkeeper(s): Debra Lennon & Tom Nill. $89-299. MC, VISA, AX, PC, TC. TAC10. 34 rooms with PB, 3 with FP, 5 suites and 2 conference rooms. Types of meals: Full bkfst, country bkfst, picnic lunch and gourmet dinner. MAP. Beds: KQDT. Cable TV and phone in room. Air conditioning. Fax, copier, swimming, bicycles, library, gift shop, wonderful restaurant serving regional cuisine, lively piano bar, outdoor garden patio serving dinner and outdoor pool and deck on premises. Weddings, small meetings, family reunions and seminars hosted. Antiquing, art galleries, beaches, bicycling, fishing, golf, hiking, horseback riding, live theater, museums, shopping, tennis and water sports nearby.

Publicity: *Getaways for Gourmets and Coast Guide.*

"From check-in to check-out, from breakfast through dinner, we were treated like royalty."

Lake Brook Bed & Breakfast

57 Western Ave, Lower Village
Kennebunkport, ME 04046
(207)967-4069
E-mail: carolyn@lakebrookbb.com

Circa 1900. This pleasant old farmhouse is situated on a tidal brook. Comfortable rockers offer an inviting rest on the wrap-

around porch where you can enjoy the inn's flower gardens that trail down to the marsh and brook. Gourmet breakfasts are served. Walk to Kennebunkport's Dock Square and lower village to visit fine galleries, shops and restaurants.

Historic Interest: The Brick Store Museum and other historical sites are nearby.

Innkeeper(s): Carolyn A. McAdams. $95-130. MC, VISA, PC, TC. TAC10. 4 rooms, 3 with PB and 1 suite. Breakfast included in rates. Types of meals: Gourmet bkfst. Beds: QD. Ceiling fan in room. Spanish spoken. Amusement parks, antiquing, fishing, golf, live theater, parks, shopping, cross-country skiing, tennis and water sports nearby.

"Truly wonderful atmosphere."

Maine Stay Inn & Cottages

PO Box 500A
Kennebunkport, ME 04046-6174
(207)967-2117 (800)950-2117 Fax:(207)967-8757
E-mail: innkeeper@mainestayinn.com
Web: www.mainestayinn.com

Circa 1860. In the National Register, this is a square-block Italianate contoured in a low hip-roof design. Later additions reflecting the Queen Anne period include a suspended spiral

staircase, crystal windows, ornately carved mantels and moldings, bay windows and porches. A sea captain built the handsome cupola that became a favorite spot for making taffy. In the '20s, the cupola was a place from which to spot offshore rumrunners. Guests enjoy afternoon tea with stories of the Maine Stay's heritage. Two suites and one room in the main building and six of the cottage rooms have working fireplaces.

Innkeeper(s): Carol & Lindsay Copeland. $105-250. MC, VISA, AX, PC, TC. 17 rooms with PB, 9 with FP, 4 suites and 10 cottages. Breakfast and afternoon tea included in rates. Types of meals: Full bkfst and early coffee/tea. Beds: KQDT. Cable TV, VCR and six with whirlpool tubs in room. Air conditioning. Fax and copier on premises. Antiquing, fishing, golf, whale watching, live theater, shopping, cross-country skiing and water sports nearby.

Publicity: *Boston Globe, New York Post, Washington Times, Discerning Traveler, Montreal Gazette, Innsider, Tourist News, Down East, Staten Island Advance, Birmingham News, Delaware County Times and Family Travel Times.*

"We have traveled the East Coast from Martha's Vineyard to Bar Harbor, and this is the only place we know we must return to."

Old Fort Inn

Old Fort Ave, PO Box M 1
Kennebunkport, ME 04046-1688
(207)967-5353 (800)828-3678 Fax:(207)967-4547
E-mail: info@oldfortinn.com
Web: www.oldfortinn.com

Circa 1880. The Old Fort Inn is a luxurious country inn located in a secluded setting, minutes away from Kennebunkport's shops, art galleries and beaches. The inn's gracious interiors feature antiques, canopy and four-poster beds. Some rooms have a whirlpool tub and fireplace. There is an antique shop, a tennis court and a fresh-water pool on the property. The ocean is just a block away.

Historic Interest: Trolly Car Museum, Brick Store Museum, historic homes and landmarks.

Innkeeper(s): Sheila & David Aldrich. $95-325. MC, VISA, AX, DS, PC, TC. TAC10. 16 rooms with PB and 1 conference room. Breakfast included in rates. Types of meals: Full bkfst. Beds: KQD. Cable TV, phone, Jacuzzis and some whirlpool tubs in room. Air conditioning. Fax, copier, swimming and tennis on premises. Small meetings hosted. Antiquing, fishing, live theater, parks and shopping nearby.

Publicity: *Country Inns and Down East Magazine.*

"My husband and I have been spending the last two weeks in August at the Old Fort Inn for years. It combines for us a rich variety of what we feel a relaxing vacation should be."

Kittery L2

Enchanted Nights B&B

29 Wentworth St
Kittery, ME 03904-1720
(207)439-1489
Web: www.enchanted-nights-bandb.com

Circa 1890. The innkeepers bill this unique inn as a "Victorian fantasy for the romantic at heart." Each of the guest rooms is unique, from the spacious rooms with double whirlpool tubs and fireplaces to the cozy turret room.

A whimsical combination of country French and Victorian decor permeates the interior. Wrought-iron beds and hand-painted furnishings add to the ambiance. Breakfasts, often with a vegetarian theme, are served with gourmet coffee in the morning room on antique floral china.

Historic Interest: There are museums, forts, churches, historic homes and buildings all within five miles in Portsmouth, NH and Kittery, Stranbery Banke Museum.

Innkeeper(s): Nancy Bogenberger & Peter Lamandia. $52-275. MC, VISA, AX, DC, CB, DS, PC, TC. TAC6. 8 rooms with PB, 2 with FP and 2 conference rooms. Breakfast included in rates. Types of meals: Gourmet bkfst, veg bkfst, cont plus, cont and early coffee/tea. Beds: KQDT. Cable TV, ceiling fan, VCR, microwave and 3 with whirlpools and 2 also have fireplaces in room. Air conditioning. Refrigerator on premises. Handicap access. Weddings, small meetings, family reunions and seminars hosted. Antiquing, art galleries, beaches, bicycling, canoeing/kayaking, golf, hiking, horseback riding, outlet shopping, historic homes, whale watching, harbor cruises, live theater, museums, parks, shopping, sporting events, tennis, water sports and wineries nearby. Pets Allowed.

"The atmosphere was great. Your breakfast was elegant. The breakfast room made us feel we had gone back in time. All in all it was a very enjoyable stay."

The Inn at Portsmouth Harbor

6 Water St
Kittery, ME 03904
(207)439-4040 Fax:(207)438-9286
E-mail: info@innatportsmouth.com
Web: www.innatportsmouth.com

Circa 1879. Built during the Victorian era, this historic brick home features ornate exterior trim and a sweeping veranda. The five guest rooms are decorated with English antiques, and some rooms include a harbor view. A full breakfast is served in a dining room illuminated by firelight. The town offers antique shops, boutiques and more than 80 restaurants to enjoy.

Innkeeper(s): Kim & Terry O'Mahoney. $135-175. MC, VISA, PC, TC. 5 rooms with PB. Breakfast included in rates. Types of meals: Gourmet bkfst and early coffee/tea. Beds: KQ. Cable TV, phone and ceiling fan in room. Air conditioning. Library on premises. Weddings, small meetings, family reunions and seminars hosted. Antiquing, art galleries, beaches, bicycling, canoeing/kayaking, fishing, golf, hiking, horseback riding, live theater, museums, parks and shopping nearby. Publicity: *Charlotte Observer.*

Lubec G8

Peacock House

27 Summer St
Lubec, ME 04652-1134
(207)733-2403

Circa 1860. Built by a sea captain from Bedford, England, the inn is nestled in the country's most northeastern town. Six generations of the Peacock family have lived here, hosting some prominent people. Guests included Margaret Chase Smith, several governors, Donald McMillen (Arctic explorer), Sen. Edmund Muskie and members of the Roosevelt family and their staff. The house originally was constructed as a Victorian with later updates making it more of a mixture of Federal and Greek Revival architectural styles. The Bay of Fundy is two blocks away. The Peacock House is a three-diamond rated B&B.

Historic Interest: The island home of Franklin Delano Roosevelt is a nearby historic attraction.

Innkeeper(s): Debra Norris & Veda Childs. $60-80. MC, VISA. 5 rooms with PB and 3 suites. Breakfast and afternoon tea included in rates. Types of meals: Full bkfst. Beds: KQT. Fax on premises. Handicap access. Antiquing nearby. Publicity: *Quoddy Tides and Downeast Coastal Press.*

"A perfect B&B — great beds, fantastic breakfast and a hospitable family."

Naples J2

Augustus Bove House

Corner Rts 302 & 114, RR 1 Box 501
Naples, ME 04055
(207)693-6365
E-mail: augbovehouse@pivot.net
Web: www.maineguide.com/naples/augustus

Circa 1830. A long front lawn nestles up against the stone foundation and veranda of this house, once known as the Hotel Naples, one of the area's summer hotels in the 1800s. In the 1920s, the inn was host to a number of prominent guests, including Enrico Caruso, Joseph P. Kennedy and Howard Hughes. The guest rooms are decorated in a Colonial style and modestly furnished with antiques. Many rooms provide a view of Long Lake. A fancy country breakfast is provided.

Innkeeper(s): David & Arlene Stetson. $59-175. MC, VISA, AX, DS, PC, TC. TAC10. 11 rooms, 7 with PB and 1 suite. Breakfast and afternoon tea included in rates. Types of meals: Full bkfst and early coffee/tea. Beds: KQT. Cable TV and phone in room. Air conditioning. VCR, fax and spa on premises. Weddings, small meetings and family reunions hosted. Antiquing, fishing, live theater, parks, shopping, downhill skiing, cross-country skiing and water sports nearby. Pets Allowed.

Publicity: *Brighton Times, Yankee Magazine and Quality Travel Value Award.*

"Beautiful place, rooms, and people."

Lamb's Mill Inn

RR 1, Box 676, Lambs Mill Rd
Naples, ME 04055
(207)693-6253
E-mail: lambsmil@pivot.net
Web: www.lambsmillinn.com

Circa 1800. This cheery, yellow farmhouse offers six guest rooms, each filled with comfortable furnishings. Guests are pampered with down comforters, a hot tub and 20 peaceful acres of woods, fields and perennial gardens. Fresh vegetable frittata with items picked from the garden and raspberry Belgian waffles are among the breakfast entrees. Evening snacks are served

as well. The home is close to cross-country and alpine skiing, golf, tennis, parasailing, shopping, restaurants and antiquing.

Innkeeper(s): Laurel Tinkham & Sandy Long. $80-125. MC, VISA, AX, PC. TAC10. 6 rooms with PB. Breakfast, afternoon tea and snacks/refreshments included in rates. Types of meals: Gourmet bkfst, veg bkfst and early coffee/tea. Beds: KQD. Cable TV, turndown service and VCR in room. Air conditioning.

Spa, bicycles, library, outside stone barbeque pit and horseback riding on premises. Weddings, small meetings and family reunions hosted. Amusement parks, antiquing, art galleries, beaches, bicycling, canoeing/kayaking, fishing, golf, hiking, horseback riding, live theater, museums, parks, shopping, downhill skiing, cross-country skiing, tennis, water sports and wineries nearby.

"We really enjoyed our week in your lovely home."

Newcastle J4

The Harbor View Inn at Newcastle

34 Main St
Newcastle, ME 04553
(207)563-2900 Fax:(207)563-2900
E-mail: joe@theharborview.com
Web: www.theharborview.com

Circa 1841. The Harbor View Inn is a recently restored New England cape situated on a rise overlooking the villages of Newcastle and Damariscotta and just down the River Road from Boothbay Harbor, 20 minutes away. Two of the three guest rooms have their own private deck and fireplace. Innkeeper Joe McEntee was the chef and manager of several Philadelphia restaurants before he purchased the inn. Multicourse gourmet breakfasts are served including orange juice, a fresh fruit plate, scrambled eggs, ham, roasted potatoes, broiled tomatoes, homemade ginger-peach muffins, coffee and tea. On sunny mornings have your breakfast served on the spacious deck that provides views of the harbor. Shops, art galleries, restaurants and antique dealers are a short walk away and you can drive to Pemaquid to photograph the lighthouse and fort or visit New Harbor for lobsters or cruises to Monhegan Island.
Innkeeper(s): Joe McEntee. $120-160. MC, VISA. 3 rooms with PB. Breakfast included in rates. Types of meals: Gourmet bkfst. Beds: KQT. Cable TV, phone and ceiling fan in room. Fax and copier on premises. Antiquing, art galleries, beaches, canoeing/kayaking, fishing, golf, hiking, lighthouses, museums, parks, shopping, cross-country skiing and tennis nearby.

Ogunquit K2

Hartwell House Inn & Conference Center

312 Shore Rd, PO Box 1937
Ogunquit, ME 03907-0393
(207)646-7210 (800)235-8883
E-mail: info@hartwellhouseinn.com
Web: www.hartwellhouseinn.com

Circa 1921. Hartwell House offers suites and guest rooms furnished with distinctive early American and English antiques. Many rooms are available with French doors opening to private balconies overlooking sculpted flower gardens. Guests are treated to both a full, gourmet breakfast and afternoon tea. Seasonal dining packages are available. Restaurants, beaches, hiking and outlet shopping is nearby.
Innkeeper(s): Daryl McGann & Jana Dedek. $100-200. MC, VISA, AX, DS, TC. 16 rooms with PB, 3 suites and 4 conference rooms. Types of meals: Gourmet bkfst and afternoon tea. Beds: KQ. Air conditioning. Fax on premises. Weddings hosted. Antiquing, fishing, restaurants, outlet and boutique shopping, beaches, live theater, parks, shopping, cross-country skiing, sporting events and water sports nearby.
Publicity: *Insider.*

"This engaging country inn will be reserved for my special clients."

Morning Dove B&B

13 Bourne Ln, PO Box 1940
Ogunquit, ME 03907-1940
(207)646-3891
E-mail: info@themorningdove
Web: www.themorningdove.com

Circa 1865. Surrounded by country gardens and a pond, this Victorian farmhouse was built by one of the area's first families. The inn offers delightful accommodations all year. In the warmer months, breakfast is served on the spacious porch, and in the fireplaced gathering room during winter. Expect to partake of hot and cold beverages, fruit, yogurt, cereals, as well as entrees such as stuffed French toast and omelettes. The ideal location is perfect for strolling the Marginal Way, a gorgeous one-mile walk along rugged ocean cliffs. Equally close is Perkins Cove, sandy beaches and the Ogunquit Playhouse.
Historic Interest: Ogunquit Library (1/4 mile).
Innkeeper(s): Jane & Fred Garland. $75-150. MC, VISA, PC, TC. 7 rooms, 5 with PB. Breakfast included in rates. Types of meals: Full bkfst. Beds: KQD. Television in two rooms and one with private deck in room. Air conditioning. Amusement parks, antiquing, art galleries, beaches, bicycling, fishing, horseback riding, live theater, museums, shopping and tennis nearby.

Rockmere Lodge

150 Stearns Rd
Ogunquit, ME 03907
(207)646-2985 Fax:(207)646-6947
E-mail: info@rockmere.com
Web: www.rockmere.com

Circa 1899. Offering an outstanding view of the Atlantic from its site on Marginal Way (the town's oceanside path), this shingle-style Victorian is enhanced by gardens, fountains and a wraparound veranda filled with white wicker. The inn is furnished with period antiques and  Victorian collectibles. Every room except one enjoys an ocean view. Walk to galleries, boutiques and fine restaurants. Ten miles south is Kittery, a center for factory outlets.
Innkeeper(s): Andy Antoniuk & Bob Brown. $100-200. VISA, AX, DS, TC. 8 rooms with PB. Types of meals: Cont plus. Beds: QD. Cable TV in room. VCR, fax and library on premises. Antiquing, fishing, golf, live theater, parks, shopping, cross-country skiing, sporting events and water sports nearby.
Publicity: *York County Coast Star.*

Old Orchard Beach K2

Atlantic Birches Inn

20 Portland Ave Rt 98
Old Orchard Beach, ME 04064-2212
(207)934-5295 (888)934-5295
E-mail: info@atlanticbirches.com
Web: www.atlanticbirches.com

Circa 1903. The front porch of this Shingle-style Victorian and 1920s bungalow are shaded by white birch trees. Badminton and croquet are set up on the lawn. The houses are a place for relaxation and enjoyment, uncluttered, simple havens filled with comfortable furnishings. The guest rooms are decorated with antiques and pastel wallcoverings. Maine's coast offers

an endless amount of activities, from boating to whale watching. It is a five-minute walk to the beach and the pier.
Innkeeper(s): Ray & Kim Deleo. $89-114. MC, VISA, AX, DS, TC. TAC10. 10 rooms with PB. Breakfast included in rates. Types of meals: Cont plus. EP. Beds: KQDT. Ceiling fan in room. Air conditioning. VCR, copier, swimming and library on premises. Small meetings and family reunions hosted. Amusement parks, antiquing, fishing, parks, shopping, sporting events and water sports nearby.

"Your home and family are just delightful! What a treat to stay in such a warm & loving home."

Oquossoc   G2

Oquossoc's Own B&B

Rangeley Ave, PO Box 27
Oquossoc, ME 04964-0027
(207)864-5584

Circa 1903. The recreation-rich mountains of Western Maine are home to this Victorian inn, which offers five guest rooms and easy access to local outdoor attractions. The inn's living

room offers a cozy spot for guests to read or watch TV. Basketball and tennis courts are nearby, and a grocery store and post office are within easy walking distance of the inn. Innkeeper Joanne Conner Koob is well-known in the area for her catering skills. The Saddleback Mountain Ski Area, elevation 4,116 feet, is nearby. Three popular restaurants and the marina cove are within walking distance.
Innkeeper(s): Joanne Conner Koob. $40-70. 5 rooms. Types of meals: Full bkfst, early coffee/tea and picnic lunch. Beds: QDT. VCR on premises. Small meetings and family reunions hosted. Antiquing, snowmobiling, shopping, downhill skiing and cross-country skiing nearby.

Poland   I2

Wolf Cove Inn

5 Jordan Shore Dr
Poland, ME 04274-7111
(207)998-4976 Fax:(207)998-7049
E-mail: wolfcove@exploremaine.com
Web: www.wolfcoveinn.com

Circa 1910. The pristine lakeside setting of this inn calms the spirit of the busiest traveler, and there are more than two acres of grounds with perennial gardens, giant pine trees and an herb garden. The inn offers a variety of rooms, most with lake or garden views, period furnishings and queen or king beds. Request a third-floor room for a fireplace and whirlpool tub. The Calla Lily Suite includes a sitting area as well as a tub overlooking Tripp Lake. The inn's favorite guest space is the flagstone terrace overlooking the water. Breakfast offerings are provided in the glassed-in porch (also a great spot to watch the sunset).
Historic Interest: All Souls Chapel, The Maine Stark building, Paris Hill.
Innkeeper(s): Rose Aikman. $70-250. MC, VISA, AX, PC, TC. TAC10. 10 rooms, 8 with PB. Breakfast and snacks/refreshments included in rates. Types of meals: Full bkfst and early coffee/tea. Beds: KQT. Air conditioning. VCR, fax and swimming on premises. Weddings, small meetings, family reunions and seminars hosted. Antiquing, beaches, bicycling, canoeing/kayaking, golf, hiking, horseback riding, shopping, downhill skiing and cross-country skiing nearby.

Portland   J3

Inn At St John

939 Congress St
Portland, ME 04102-3031
(207)773-6481 (800)636-9127 Fax:(207)756-7629
E-mail: theinn@mainrr.com
Web: www.innatstjohn.com

Circa 1897. Tucked on a city street, this Victorian inn is conveniently located near many Portland sites, including museums, restaurants and shops. The guest rooms feature antiques and traditional furnishings, and hardwood floors are topped with Oriental rugs. Pictures showcasing Portland's railroad history are on display. The inn is European in style, and some rooms have a shared bath. Children are welcome, and those younger than 12 can stay for free.
Innkeeper(s): Paul Hood. $46-186. MC, VISA, DC, CB, DS, PC, TC. TAC15. 37 rooms, 22 with PB. Breakfast included in rates. Types of meals: Cont plus and early coffee/tea. Beds: KQDT. Cable TV, phone and HBO in room. Air conditioning. Fax, copier, bicycle storage and free parking on premises. Amusement parks, antiquing, fishing, golf, historic district, live theater, parks, shopping, cross-country skiing, sporting events, tennis and water sports nearby.
Pets allowed: Not to be left unattended in guest room.
Publicity: *Down East, Portland Press Herald, Houston Chronicle, New York Times and WCSH/Fox/WGME.*

"We were surprised at how much charm there is tucked in to this building."

Rockland   I5

Lakeshore Inn Bed & Breakfast

184 Lakeview Dr (Rt 17)
Rockland, ME 04841-5705
(207)594-4209 Fax:(207)596-6407
E-mail: info@lakeshorebb.com
Web: www.lakeshorebb.com

Circa 1767. Surrounded by a 200-year-old apple orchard, hemlock and pine trees, this recently renovated farmhouse is one of the most historic buildings in the area. Providing pleasant vistas, the inn's green lawns slope down toward the lake. It was built by one of the 23 children of Isaiah Tolman. Each of the guest rooms offer a view

of Lake Chickawaukie, and two have decks. Guests are invited to enjoy the outdoor Jacuzzi hot tub spa or come

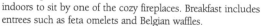

indoors to sit by one of the cozy fireplaces. Breakfast includes entrees such as feta omelets and Belgian waffles.
Innkeeper(s): Joseph McCluskey & Paula Nicols. $135-160. MC, VISA. 4 rooms with PB. Breakfast and snacks/refreshments included in rates. Types of meals: Gourmet bkfst and early coffee/tea. Beds: Q. Phone, fluffy robes, hair dryers, soaps, chocolates and theme baskets are available by prior arrangement in room. Air conditioning. Massage therapist and reflexologist on call by prior arrangement. VCR, fax, copier, Jacuzzi hot tub in it's own little teahouse, library and video tape library on premises. Weddings, small meetings and family reunions hosted. Greek spoken. Antiquing, art galleries, beaches, bicycling, canoeing/kayaking, fishing, golf, hiking, museums, parks, shopping, tennis and water sports nearby.
Publicity: *Bangor Daily News and Boston Ch 5.*

Saco K2

Crown 'n' Anchor Inn

121 North St, PO Box 228
Saco, ME 04072-0228
(207)282-3829 (800)561-8865 Fax:(207)282-7495
E-mail: cna@gwi.net

Circa 1827. This Greek Revival house, listed in the National Register, features both Victorian baroque and colonial antiques. Two rooms include whirlpool tubs. A collection of British coronation memorabilia displayed throughout the inn includes 200 items. Guests gather in the Victorian parlor or the formal library.

The innkeepers, a college librarian and an academic bookseller, lined the shelves with several thousand volumes, including extensive Civil War and British royal family collections and travel, theater and nautical books. Royal Dalton china, crystal and fresh flowers create a festive breakfast setting.

Historic Interest: Kennebunkport, The George Bush Estate, The Victorian Mansion, Portland Head Lighthouse.

Innkeeper(s): John Barclay & Martha Forester. $70-120. MC, VISA, AX, PC, TC. TAC10. 6 rooms with PB, 2 with FP. Breakfast included in rates. Types of meals: Gourmet bkfst, early coffee/tea and afternoon tea. Beds: KQDT. Cable TV and two rooms with whirlpools in room. VCR and library on premises. Weddings, small meetings, family reunions and seminars hosted. Limited French spoken. Amusement parks, antiquing, fishing, live theater, parks, shopping, downhill skiing, cross-country skiing, sporting events and water sports nearby.

Pets allowed: Small or caged.

Publicity: Yankee, Saco, Biddeford, Old Orchard Beach Courier, Country, Portland Press Herald. and HGTV.

"A delightful interlude! A five star B&B."

Searsport H5

Brass Lantern Inn

81 W Main St
Searsport, ME 04974-3501
(207)548-0150 (800)691-0150
E-mail: stay@brasslanternmaine.com
Web: www.brasslanternmaine.com

Circa 1850. This Victorian inn is nestled at the edge of the woods on a rise overlooking Penobscot Bay. Showcased throughout the inn are many collectibles, antiques and family heirlooms, as well as artifacts from innkeeper Maggie Zieg's

home in England and two-year stay in Ethiopia. Enjoy breakfast by candlelight in the dining room with its ornate tin ceiling, where you'll feast on Maine blueberry pancakes and other sumptuous treats. Centrally located between Camden and Bar Harbor, Searsport is known as the antique capital of Maine. There are many local attractions, including the Penobscot Marine Museum, fine shops and restaurants, as well as a public boat facility.

Historic Interest: Fort Knox (8 miles).

Innkeeper(s): Maggie & Dick Zieg. $85-105. MC, VISA, DS, PC, TC. TAC5. 5 rooms with PB. Breakfast included in rates. Types of meals: Full bkfst and early coffee/tea. Beds: QDT. VCR, library and piano on premises. Small meetings and family reunions hosted. Antiquing, fishing, live theater, parks, shopping and cross-country skiing nearby.

Publicity: Country Living, Republication Journal, Travel Today, Down East,

Saturday Evening Post and AAA Car & Travel.

"We had a wonderful stay here at your lovely home. Your warmth, friendliness and kindness is unmatched at any other inn we have been to. Your personal touches show how much you care and strive to please. Every detail for your guests' personal comfort...Your meals are incredible!! We have been spoiled-and we loved it. THank you so very much."

Homeport Inn

RR 1 Box 647
Searsport, ME 04974-9728
(207)548-2259 (800)742-5814 Fax:(978)443-6682
E-mail: hportinn@acadia.net
Web: www.bnbcity.com/inns/20015

Circa 1861. Captain John Nickels built this home on Penobscot Bay. On top of the two-story historic landmark is a widow's walk. A scalloped picket fence frames the property.

Fine antiques, black marble fireplaces, a collection of grandfather clocks and elaborate ceiling medallions add to the atmosphere. Landscaped grounds sweep out to the ocean's edge. Some rooms have an ocean view. There are Victorian cottages available for weekly rental.

Historic Interest: Fort Knox, Owl's Head Lighthouse, historical architecture homes.

Innkeeper(s): Dr. & Mrs. F. George Johnson. $55-90. MC, VISA, AX, DS, PC, TC. 10 rooms, 7 with PB. Breakfast included in rates. Types of meals: Full bkfst. Beds: KQD. TV in room. Library on premises. Weddings, small meetings and family reunions hosted. Antiquing, art galleries, beaches, canoeing/kayaking, golf, hiking, live theater, museums, parks, shopping, cross-country skiing and tennis nearby.

Publicity: Yankee and Down East.

"Your breakfast is something we will never forget."

Searsport (Waldo County) H5

1794 Watchtide... by the Sea

190 W Main St, US Rt 1
Searsport (Waldo County), ME 04974-3514
(207)548-6575 (800)698-6575 Fax:(207)548-0938
E-mail: stay@watchtide.com
Web: www.watchtide.com

Circa 1794. Watch the tides and ships while enjoying a bountiful four-course breakfast overlooking the bay from the sun porch of this historic inn, in the National Register of Historic Places. Once owned by General Henry Knox, first Secretary of War, the inn also was host to several wives of Presidents including Eleanor Roosevelt who visited frequently. There are three seaside acres of lawns and gardens, as well as a bird sanctuary and spectacular views of Penobscot Bay. The rooms offer king-size beds and one has a two-person Jacuzzi. There's an antique/gift shop adjacent to the inn which offers special guest discounts. (The area is known for its excellent antiquing.) Walk to the beach at Moosepoint State Park for swimming, or enjoy the area's lighthouses, sea sports, theater, or golf, boating and fishing. The Penobscot Marine Museum is nearby. Conveniently located between Rockland and Bar Harbor,

Watchtide affords easy day trips to everything from Pemiquid Point to Schoodic Point.

Historic Interest: Penobscot Marine Museum, Acadia National Park (nearby). Innkeeper(s): Nancy-Linn Nellis & Jack Elliott. $95-175. MC, VISA, DS, PC, TC. TAC10. 5 rooms with PB. Breakfast and snacks/refreshments included in rates. Types of meals: Full bkfst and early coffee/tea. Beds: KQT. Turndown service, robes, hair dryers, clock-radios, sound therapy units, Nan's Crans and Vermont Sweet Water in room. Library, guest lounge with large screen TV, game table, piano, picnic tables, horseshoes, croquet, 60' year-round sun porch and sitting room with fireplace on premises. Limited French spoken. Antiquing, fishing, golf, lighthouses, concerts, whale watching, Acadia National Park, rail and sail trips, live theater, museums, parks, shopping, sporting events and water sports nearby.
Publicity: *Boston Globe, Green Bay Press Gazette, Maine-an Explorer's Guide, City Line News, Deseret News, Asbury Park Press, Yankee Magazine Editor's Choice 2001, Berkshire Eagle and Patriot Ledger.*

South Paris 12

King's Hill Inn

56 King Hill Rd
South Paris, ME 04281
(207)744-0204 (877)391-5464 Fax:(207)744-0204
E-mail: kingsinn@megalink.net
Web: members.aol.com/kingsinn56/inn.htm

Circa 1780. Best known for being the birthplace of Horatio King, Postmaster General under Presidents Buchanan and Lincoln, this historic country farmhouse with post and beam barn is a Victorian inn furnished with antiques. Peaceful and tranquil settings, most guest bedrooms and suites offer gas log or wood stoves, as well as outstanding views of mountains, gardens and the pasture. Some feature decks, and Suite No. 1 boasts a 200-year-old rope bed, a bidet and Jacuzzi. Breakfast is served in the dining room and refreshments are available at any time.
Historic Interest: Paris Hill (2-3 miles), mining of gems (10 miles). Innkeeper(s): Janice & Glenn Davis. $65-135. MC, VISA, AX, DS, PC, TC. TAC5. 6 rooms with PB, 4 with FP. Breakfast and snacks/refreshments included in rates. Types of meals: Gourmet bkfst, early coffee/tea and afternoon tea. Beds: KQDT. Ceiling fan and fireplace in room. Fax, copier, library, garden, walking trails and mountain views on premises. Handicap access. Weddings, small meetings, family reunions and seminars hosted. Antiquing, art galleries, bicycling, canoeing/kayaking, fishing, golf, hiking, horseback riding, live theater, museums, parks, shopping, downhill skiing, cross-country skiing and water sports nearby.
Publicity: *Sun Journal.*

Southwest Harbor 16

Inn at Southwest

371 Main St, PO Box 593
Southwest Harbor, ME 04679-0593
(207)244-3835 Fax:(207)244-9879
E-mail: innatsw@acadia.net
Web: www.innatsouthwest.com

Circa 1884. Peaceful harbor views are abundant from this three-story Victorian bed and breakfast centrally located in an idyllic New England town. The new owners have lovingly restored its original grandeur while renovating with modern comforts. Each of the well-appointed guest bedrooms and suites are named after the state's historic lighthouses. They boast antique furnishings, fine linens and towels, and most have gas log fireplaces. Hospitality and service are highly evident in the savory gourmet breakfast served in the dining room or wraparound porch. Specialties such as crab potato bake and eggs Florentine complement the many regional dishes that include famous Maine blue-

berries. Coffee and tea are always available, and guests enjoy warm cookies every afternoon. Majestic Acadia National Park and Bar Harbor are among the many local sights to explore.
Innkeeper(s): Andrea Potapovs and Sandy Johnson. $70-160. MC, VISA, DS, PC. 7 rooms with PB, 3 with FP and 2 suites. Breakfast and afternoon tea included in rates. Types of meals: Gourmet bkfst and early coffee/tea. Beds: KQD. Ceiling fan, down comforters and fireplace in room. Fax, copier and library on premises. Family reunions hosted. Antiquing, bicycling, canoeing/kayaking, fishing, golf, hiking, horseback riding, Acadia National Park (5 minutes), museums, parks, shopping and tennis nearby.
Publicity: *Yankee Travel Guide.*

"How could any place that serves dessert for breakfast be bad?."

The Island House

121 Clark Point Rd
Southwest Harbor, ME 04679
(207)244-5180
E-mail: islandab@acadia.net

Circa 1850. The first guests arrived at Deacon Clark's door as early as 1832. When steamboat service from Boston began in the 1850s, the Island House became a popular summer hotel. Among the guests was Ralph Waldo Emerson. In 1912, the hotel was taken down and rebuilt as two separate homes using much of the wood-work from the original building.
Innkeeper(s): Ann and Charles Bradford. $70-145. PC, TC. 4 rooms with PB and 1 guest house. Breakfast included in rates. Types of meals: Full bkfst and early coffee/tea. Beds: KQDT. TV and refrigerator in Carriage House in room. VCR, library, Cable TV, CD player, telephone and guest house with private bath on premises. Small meetings, family reunions and seminars hosted. Antiquing, art galleries, beaches, bicycling, canoeing/kayaking, fishing, golf, hiking, horseback riding, live theater, museums, parks, shopping, cross-country skiing, tennis and water sports nearby.

"Island House is a delight from the moment one enters the door! We loved the thoughtful extras. You've made our vacation very special!"

Penury Hall Bed & Breakfast

374 Main St
Southwest Harbor, ME 04679-4245
(207)244-7102 Fax:(207)244-5651
E-mail: tstrong@penuryhall.com
Web: www.penuryhall.com

Circa 1830. Located by Acadia National Park on Mount Desert Island in Southwest Harbor is a Victorian home that originated in 1830 when the first part of the house was built. Little by little, the house was added to. Eventually, the three homes had been combined into this one rambling structure, a common occurrence in New England in the 1800s. Today the asymmetrical roofline reveals that history. The seven garden areas have perennial and annual flowers as well as vegetables and herbs. The home is decorated with fine art, antiques and memorabilia that reflects the innkeepers' interests in gardening, music and sailing. At Penury Hall, every effort is made to make guests feel at home. Guests may store food items in the fridge, wash clothes in the laundry room and play games or listen to music in the library. Retire in one of the three guest rooms, then awake to a gourmet breakfast that offers such courses as eggs Benedict, "Penurious Omelets" or cinnamon-raisin French toast. Then take out the inn's canoe to explore nearby lakes or else rent mountain bikes and carracks next door and head out for bike trails. Or, enjoy sauntering through the antique shops or the 14 local museums. End the day by relaxing in the sauna.

Innkeeper(s): Toby & Gretchen Strong. $75-95. MC, VISA, PC, TC. 3 rooms with PB. Breakfast included in rates. Types of meals: Full bkfst and early coffee/tea. Beds: QDT. Fax, sauna and library on premises. Antiquing, art galleries, beaches, bicycling, canoeing/kayaking, golf, hiking, live theater, museums, parks, shopping, cross-country skiing and water sports nearby.

St. George I4

Craignair Inn

5 Third St
St. George, ME 04860
(207)594-7644 (800)320-9997 Fax:(207)596-7124
E-mail: innkeeper@craignair.com

Circa 1930. Craignair originally was built to house stonecutters working in nearby granite quarries. Overlooking the docks of the Clark Island Quarry, where granite schooners once were loaded,  this roomy, three-story inn is tastefully decorated with local antiques. A bountiful continental breakfast is served in the inn's dining room which offers scenic ocean and coastline views. **Historic Interest:** General Knox (Washington's Secretary of War) Mansion, called Montpelier (8 miles).
Innkeeper(s): Steve & Neva Joseph. $83-120. MC, VISA, DS, PC, TC. TAC10. 21 rooms, 12 with PB. Breakfast included in rates. Types of meals: Cont plus and gourmet dinner. Beds: KQDT. Phone in room. Fax and copier on premises. Weddings, small meetings, family reunions and seminars hosted. Antiquing, fishing, live theater, parks, shopping, downhill skiing, cross-country skiing and water sports nearby.
Pets allowed: With prior approval.
Publicity: Boston Globe, Free Press and Tribune.

"A coastal oasis of fine food and outstanding service with colonial maritime ambiance!"

Topsham J3

Black Lantern B&B

6 Pleasant St
Topsham, ME 04086
(207)725-4165 (888)306-4165 Fax:(207)725-2489
E-mail: blacklantern@clinic.net
Web: www.blacklanternbandb.com

Circa 1810. Rev. Amos Wheeler, minister at Bowdoin College, once owned this welcoming Federal-style home, with its shuttered, many-paned windows, large lawn and shade trees. It is in the National Register of Historic Places. Plaid sofas next to a fireplace invite guests to relax, and there are cozy corners for conversation, games and quilting. Guest rooms feature country curtains, quilts and hardwood floors. A popular breakfast dish, often served fireside in the dining room, is puff pancakes with fresh fruit, omelets and bacon. (In summer, the porch is the breakfast spot.) Fresh rhubarb crisp is offered for desert. Take advantage of the inn's complimentary bicycles and helmets and hop on the bike trail that runs alongside the inn. Summer theater is offered at Bowdoin College, a mile away. Popham Beach and Freeport are nearby.
Innkeeper(s): Judy & Tom Connelie. $70-85. MC, VISA, AX, DS, PC, TC. 3 rooms with PB. Breakfast included in rates. Types of meals: Full bkfst, veg bkfst and early coffee/tea. Beds: KQT. Fax, copier and bicycles on premises. Antiquing, art galleries, beaches, bicycling, canoeing/kayaking, fishing, golf, live theater, museums and shopping nearby.

Vinalhaven I5

Fox Island Inn

PO Box 451
Vinalhaven, ME 04863-0451
(207)863-2122

Circa 1880. Discover island life during your stay at this country farmhouse-style inn where you are warmly welcomed to flea markets, church suppers and art shows featuring local artists. You can prepare a picnic in the guest kitchen before your day of exploring the coastal island of Vinalhaven, a fishing village nestled around picturesque Carver's Harbor. During the unstressed days, you'll have time to jog, pick berries, write, read or just sit on a rock and contemplate the sea. You'll need to take a ferry from Rockland across scenic Penobscot Bay through islands surrounding Vinalhaven.
Innkeeper(s): Gail Reinertsen. $45-105. 5 rooms. Breakfast included in rates. Types of meals: Cont plus and early coffee/tea. Bicycles and spring-fed granite quarries on premises. Family reunions hosted.

Payne Homestead at the Moses Webster House

Atlantic Ave
Vinalhaven, ME 04863
(207)863-9963 (888)863-9963 Fax:(207)863-2295
E-mail: payne@foxislands.net

Circa 1873. Situated on an island, a half-mile from the ferry, this handsome Second Empire French Victorian is at the edge of town. Enjoy a game room, reading nooks and a parlor. The Coral Room boasts a view of Indian Creek, while shadows of Carver's Pond may be seen through the windows of Mama's Room. A favorite selection is the Moses Webster Room that features a marble mantel, tin ceiling and a bay window looking out at the town. Breakfast usually offers fresh fruit platters and either egg dishes or pancakes. Restaurants and Lane Island Nature Conservancy are close. Take scenic walks past private fishing boats, ponds and shoreline, all part of the hideaway quality noted by National Geographic in "America's Best Kept Secrets.".
Innkeeper(s): Lee & Donna Payne. $90-145. PC, TC. 5 rooms. Breakfast included in rates. Types of meals: Full bkfst and early coffee/tea. VCR, fax and copier on premises. Weddings and family reunions hosted. Antiquing, bicycling, canoeing/kayaking and parks nearby.
Publicity: National Geographic's "Best kept secrets".

"Our first stay in a B&B contributed greatly to the perfection of our honeymoon."

Walpole J4

Brannon-Bunker Inn

349 S St Rt 129
Walpole, ME 04573
(207)563-5941 (800)563-9225
E-mail: brbnkinn@lincoln.midcoast.com

Circa 1820. This Cape-style house has been a home to many generations of Maine residents, one of whom was captain of a ship that sailed to the Arctic. During the '20s, the barn served as a dance hall. Later, it was converted into comfortable guest rooms. Victorian and American antiques are featured, and there are collections of WWI military memorabilia.

Innkeeper(s): Joe & Jeanne Hovance. $70-80. MC, VISA, AX, DC, CB, DS, PC, TC. TAC10. 7 rooms, 5 with PB and 1 suite. Breakfast included in rates. Types of meals: Cont plus. Beds: QDT. TV in room. VCR, library and child care on premises. Handicap access. Weddings, small meetings, family reunions and seminars hosted. Antiquing, art galleries, beaches, bicycling, canoeing/kayaking, fishing, golf, hiking, horseback riding, museums, parks, shopping, tennis and water sports nearby.
Publicity: *Times-Beacon Newspaper.*

"Wonderful beds, your gracious hospitality and the very best muffins anywhere made our stay a memorable one."

Waterford   I2

Kedarburn Inn
Rt 35 Box 61
Waterford, ME 04088
(207)583-6182 Fax:(207)583-6424
E-mail: kedarburn@cybertours.com

Circa 1858. The innkeepers of this Victorian establishment invite guests to try a taste of olde English hospitality and cuisine at their inn, nestled in the foothills of the White Mountains in Western Maine. Located in a historic village, the inn sits beside

the flowing Kedar Brook, which runs to the shores of Lake Keoka. Each of the spacious rooms is decorated with handmade quilts and dried flowers. Explore the inn's shop and you'll discover a variety of quilts and crafts, all made by innkeeper Margaret Gibson. Ask about special quilting weekends. With prior reservation, the innkeepers will prepare an English afternoon tea.
Innkeeper(s): Margaret & Derek Gibson. $71-125. MC, VISA, AX, DS, PC, TC. 7 rooms, 5 with PB and 1 suite. Breakfast included in rates. Types of meals: Full bkfst, early coffee/tea, afternoon tea and snacks/refreshments. Beds: KQDT. Air conditioning. VCR and fax on premises. Weddings, small meetings, family reunions and seminars hosted. Antiquing, fishing, live theater, shopping, downhill skiing, cross-country skiing and water sports nearby.
Publicity: *Maine Times.*

Weld   H2

Kawanhee Inn Lakeside Lodge
Rt 142 Webb Lk
Weld, ME 04285
(207)585-2000
E-mail: maineinn@somtel.com

Circa 1929. This rustic lodge offers outstanding views of Webb Lake and the surrounding mountains (Tumbledown, Big Jackson, Mt. Blue and Bald Mt.). In cool weather, guests gather around the massive fieldstone fireplace. Cabins and lodge rooms are available, and if you reserve ahead you may be able to stay in one at the water's edge. Gold panning on the Swift River, enjoying the sandy beach, moose watching, viewing Angel Falls and Smalls Falls and hiking are favorite activities. The inn was chosen as the Editor's Pick in Yankee Magazine.
Innkeeper(s): Martha Strunk & Sturges Butler. $85-165. MC, VISA. TAC15. 9 rooms, 5 with PB, 1 suite and 12 cabins. Types of meals: Cont and early coffee/tea. EP. Beds: QDT. Canoe and Kayak rentals on premises. Weddings, small meetings, family reunions and seminars hosted. Antiquing, beaches, fishing, hiking, gold panning, fall foliage, parks, shopping and tennis nearby. Pets allowed: Some cabins, not the Inn.
Publicity: *1997 & 1998 Editor Pick Yankee Magazine Travel Guide.*

"It was just great, relaxed and fun!"

West Boothbay Harbor   J4

Lawnmeer Inn
PO Box 505
West Boothbay Harbor, ME 04575-0505
(800)633-7645
E-mail: cooncat@lawnmeerinn.com
Web: www.lawnmeerinn.com

Circa 1899. This pleasant inn sits by the shoreline, providing a picturesque oceanfront setting. Located on a small, wooded island, it is accessed by a lift bridge. Rooms are clean and homey and there is a private honeymoon cottage in the Smoke House. The dining room is waterside and serves continental cuisine with an emphasis on seafood. Boothbay Harbor is two miles away.
Innkeeper(s): Lee & Jim Metzger. $95-195. MC, VISA. TAC10. 32 rooms with PB, 1 suite and 1 cottage. Types of meals: Full bkfst, early coffee/tea and gourmet dinner. Beds: KQD. Weddings, small meetings and family reunions hosted. Antiquing, fishing, live theater, shopping and water sports nearby. Pets allowed: Small pets in some rooms.
Publicity: *Los Angeles Times and Getaways for Gourmets.*

"Your hospitality was warm and gracious and the food delectable."

Wiscasset   J4

Snow Squall B&B
5 Bradford Rd
Wiscasset, ME 04578
(207)882-6892 (800)775-7245 Fax:(207)882-6832
E-mail: snowsquall@maine.com
Web: www.snowsquallinn.com

Circa 1848. A quarter mile from the water on Route 1 in mid-coast Maine stands this Colonial inn. Stone walkways cross the beautifully landscaped two-and-a-half acres set in the town of Wiscasset, known as "the prettiest village in Maine." The four

main house guest bedrooms and two Carriage House suites are all named after clipper ships and are all decorated in Down East tradition. Guests enjoy a full breakfast in the dining room at individual tables. The menu includes cereal, juice, fresh fruit and one of the inn's specialty hot entrees such as Sausage Strata, baked French toast with blueberries or Baked Eggs Supreme. After this hearty meal guests may explore the natural beauty of the area, which is renowned for its rugged coastline, estuaries, peninsulas and islands. Other options include sea kayaking, sailing, fishing, bicycling, hiking or a whale/puffin cruise from Boothbay Harbor or Pemaquid. In the evening, relax in the den or watch videos that will help plan your next day's adventure.
Innkeeper(s): Anne & Steve Kornacki. $95-220. MC, VISA, AX, DS, PC, TC. 6 rooms with PB, 2 with FP and 2 suites. Breakfast included in rates. Types of meals: Full bkfst. Beds: KQT. Ceiling fan and fireplace in room. Air conditioning. VCR, fax, copier and library on premises. Seminars hosted. Antiquing, art galleries, beaches, bicycling, canoeing/kayaking, fishing, hiking, museums, parks, shopping and water sports nearby.

The Squire Tarbox Inn

Box 1181 Westport Island
Wiscasset, ME 04578-3501
(207)882-7693 Fax:(207)882-7107
E-mail: squiretarbox@prexar.com
Web: squiretarboxinn.com

Circa 1763. Meadows, stone walls and woods surround this country inn. Squire Tarbox built this rambling farmhouse around a building originally constructed in 1763. Today, the

rooms are warm and comfortable in the inn and in the remodeled hayloft. The innkeepers raise Nubian goats, all photogenic, that have become part of the entertainment (milking and goat cheese). A house-party atmosphere pervades the inn. Beaches, harbors and lobster shacks are some of the nearby visitor hot spots.

Historic Interest: Maritime Museum, old forts, lighthouses, sea captain's homes, abundant antique shops, fishing museums, windjammers, beaches, lobster shacks, etc. (30 minutes). World's finest Music Box Museum.

Innkeeper(s): Bill & Karen Mitman. $95-195. MC, VISA, AX, DS, PC, TC. TAC10. 11 rooms with PB, 4 with FP. Breakfast included in rates. Types of meals: Full bkfst, early coffee/tea, afternoon tea and gourmet dinner. Beds: KQDT. Air conditioning. Bicycles, library, row boat and farm animals on premises. Antiquing, fishing, beaches, lobster shacks, museums, harbors, live theater, parks and shopping nearby.

Publicity: *Washington Post, New York Times, Yankee, Bon Appetit, USA Today and Public.*

"Your hospitality was warm, friendly, well-managed and quite genuine. That's a rarity, and it's just the kind we feel best with."

York L2

Dockside Guest Quarters

PO Box 205
York, ME 03909-0205
(207)363-2868 (800)270-1977 Fax:(207)363-1977
E-mail: info@docksidegq.com
Web: www.docksidegq.com

Circa 1900. This small resort provides a panoramic view of the Atlantic Ocean and harbor activities. Guest rooms are located in the classic, large New England home, which is the Maine House, and modern multi-unit

buildings. Most rooms have private balconies or porches with unobstructed views of the water. Some rooms have fireplaces. The on-premise restaurant is bi-level with floor to ceiling windows, affording each table a view of the harbor. Child-care services are available.

Historic Interest: The York Historic District offers several interesting sites.
Innkeeper(s): Lusty Family. $85-215. MC, VISA, DS, PC. TAC10. 25 rooms, 2 with FP, 6 suites and 1 conference room. Types of meals: Cont plus, early coffee/tea, lunch and afternoon tea. Beds: KQDT. Cable TV in room. Fax, bicycles, library and child care on premises. Amusement parks, antiquing, fishing, live theater, parks, shopping, cross-country skiing and water sports nearby.

Publicity: *Portland Press Herald, Boston Globe and Yankee Travel Guide.*

"We've been back many years. It's a paradise for us, the scenery, location, maintenance, living quarters."

York Harbor L2

Canterbury House

432 York Street
York Harbor, ME 03911
(207)363-3505 (888)385-3505 Fax:(207)363-6178
E-mail: cntrbryhse@aol.com
Web: www.canterburybandb.com

Circa 1910. This Colonial inn stands on a sheltered cove with a sandy beach in the otherwise rocky and rugged village of York Harbor. Canterbury House has seven large guest bedrooms and a suite appointed with period furniture and fine art. Breakfast is a choice of hot beverages, fruit, freshly baked muffins and other breads, a hot entrée and hot cereal upon request. After breakfast, guests may stay on the grounds and enjoy the spectacular ocean views. Or they may stroll through the city or go beachcombing, hiking, kayaking or exploring lighthouses. Afternoon tea is served on the front porch that overlooks the harbor. Guests may walk to restaurants and antique stores or drive to landmarks and historic sites. The inn is 10 miles north of historic Portsmouth, N.H..

Historic Interest: York Village Historical District (1 mile).
Innkeeper(s): Michael Cirucci, Michael Glennon. $65-115. MC, VISA, AX. 8 rooms, 3 with PB, 1 suite and 1 conference room. Breakfast and afternoon tea included in rates. Types of meals: Full bkfst, veg bkfst and early coffee/tea. Beds: KQDT. Ceiling fan in room. Air conditioning. Fax on premises. Weddings, small meetings, family reunions and seminars hosted. Amusement parks, antiquing, art galleries, beaches, bicycling, canoeing/kayaking, fishing, golf, hiking, horseback riding, live theater, museums, parks, shopping and water sports nearby.

York Harbor Inn

PO Box 573, Rt 1A
York Harbor, ME 03911-0573
(207)363-5119 (800)343-3869 Fax:(207)363-7151
E-mail: info@yorkharborinn.com
Web: www.yorkharborinn.com

Circa 1800. Experience a relaxing coastal getaway or business retreat at this luxurious oceanfront inn, located in the historical district with period estates listed in the National Register.

Gathering rooms include the Cabin room, originally a sail loft from the 1600s, showcasing a massive field-stone fireplace. Many of the large guest bedrooms and suites feature fireplaces, Jacuzzi tubs, heated tile bathroom floors, decks and seascapes.

Taste award-winning gourmet dining overlooking the Atlantic, or enjoy a pub menu and entertainment in the English Wine Cellar Pub. A gift shop and outdoor hot tub offer pleasant indulgences.

Historic Interest: Old York Historical Society Museum buildings (1.5 miles), Strawberry Banke Colonial Village Museum (6 miles).

Innkeeper(s): Garry Dominguez. $99-319. MC, VISA, AX, PC, TC. 47 rooms with PB, 18 with FP, 10 suites and 7 conference rooms. Breakfast included in rates. Types of meals: Cont plus, early coffee/tea, lunch, gourmet dinner and room service. MAP. Beds: KQD. Cable TV, phone, many with fireplaces, Jacuzzi spa tubs, 19 with ocean views and/or decks and iron/ironing board in room. Air conditioning. VCR, fax, copier, hot tub, restaurant and pub on premises. Weddings, small meetings, family reunions and seminars hosted. Antiquing, art galleries, beaches, bicycling, canoeing/kayaking, fishing, golf, horseback riding, Kittery Outlet shopping, seaside drives, area lighthouses, whale watching, island and river boat tours, deep sea fishing Historic house tours, holiday festivals, seasonal dinner theatre, live theater, museums, parks, shopping, cross-country skiing and water sports nearby.

Publicity: *New York Times, Down East, Food & Wine, The Learning Channel, Ladies Home Journal., The Travel Channel's "Great Country Inns of America." and Travel Channel-"Great Country Inns"*

"It's hard to decide where to stay when you're paging through a book of country inns. This time we chose well."

Maryland

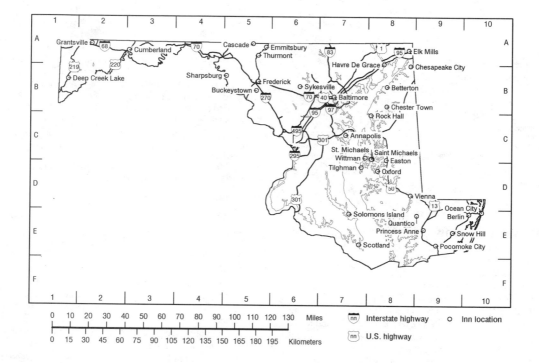

Grantsville ⊙—🛡68 Cumberland ⚬ 🛡70 Cascade ⚬ Emmitsburg ⚬
🛡219 🛡220 Sharpsburg ⚬ Thurmont ⚬ 🛡83 🛡1 🛡95 Elk Mills ⚬
Deep Creek Lake ⚬ Frederick ⚬ Sykesville ⚬ Havre De Grace ⚬ Chesapeake City ⚬
Buckeystown ⚬ 🛡270 🛡70 🛡40 Baltimore ⚬ Betterton ⚬
🛡95 🛡97 Chester Town ⚬
🛡495 Rock Hall ⚬
🛡301 Annapolis ⚬
🛡295 St. Michaels ⚬ Saint Michaels ⚬
Wittman ⚬ Easton ⚬
Tilghman ⚬ Oxford ⚬
🛡50 Vienna ⚬
🛡301 🛡13 Ocean City ⚬
Solomons Island ⚬ Berlin ⚬
Quantico ⚬ Snow Hill ⚬
Princess Anne ⚬
Scotland ⚬ Pocomoke City ⚬

0 10 20 30 40 50 60 70 80 90 100 110 120 130	Miles	🛡 nn Interstate highway ⚬ Inn location
0 15 30 45 60 75 90 105 120 135 150 165 180 195	Kilometers	🛡 nn U.S. highway

Annapolis
C7

The Annapolis Inn

144 Prince George St
Annapolis, MD 21401
(410)295-5200 Fax:(410)295-5201
E-mail: info@annapolisinn.com
Web: www.annapolisinn.com

Circa 1762. A classic example of Georgian and Greek architecture, this landmark townhouse sits in the center of the Historic District. Six men who signed the Declaration of Independence stayed here, and countless slaves were smuggled through the cellar's Underground Railroad tunnel. The spacious foyer features dark walnut and pine plank floors, rare in this region. Original ornate gilded rosette moldings still crown the living and dining rooms, highlighting the imported Austrian crystal chandeliers and marble fireplaces. Oriental rugs, paintings, sculptures, tapestries and antiques furnish the inn with luxury and elegance. Guest bedrooms are sure to pamper with chocolates, fresh flowers, hot air-jet whirlpool tubs, robes and slippers, heated marble floors and towel warmers. The third-floor sundeck, Koi pond, garden and patio offer tranquil privacy.

Innkeeper(s): Joseph Lespier/Alexander DeVivo. $250-475. MC, VISA, AX, PC, TC. TAC10. 3 rooms with PB, 2 with FP, 1 suite and 1 conference room. Breakfast, afternoon tea and snacks/refreshments included in rates. Types of meals: Gourmet bkfst, early coffee/tea and picnic lunch. Beds: K. Turndown service, fireplace, heated air-jet whirlpool tubs, heated marble floors in baths, heated towel warmers, robes, slippers, fresh flowers and chocolates in room. Central air. Fax and copier on premises. Small meetings, family reunions and seminars hosted. Spanish and Italian spoken. Antiquing, art galleries, beaches, bicycling, canoeing/kayaking, fishing, golf, live theater, museums, parks, shopping, sporting events and water sports nearby.

The Barn on Howard's Cove

500 Wilson Rd
Annapolis, MD 21401-1052
(410)266-6840 Fax:(410)266-7293
E-mail: gdgutsche5@aol.com
Web: www.bnbweb.com/howards-cove.html

Circa 1850. This renovated 1850 horse barn is located just outside Annapolis on a cove of the Severn River. The six-and-a-half-acre grounds create a restful environment. The two guest rooms, which are decorated with antiques and handmade quilts, offer water and garden views. There is also a small kitchen area between the two guest rooms for preparing snacks and coffee. A

private balcony adjoins one guest room. The innkeepers, a U.S. Naval Academy professor and an artist also keep a unique Noah's Ark collection on display. The innkeepers have canoes and kayaks on the premises for guests.

Historic Interest: U.S. Naval Academy, the Paca House, Saint Johns College.
Innkeeper(s): Graham & Libbie Gutsche. $125. PC, TC. TAC10. 2 rooms with PB and 1 conference room. Breakfast included in rates. Types of meals: Gourmet bkfst. Beds: Q. Cable TV, ceiling fan and VCR in room. Central air. Fax, copier, swimming, canoe and dock on premises. Family reunions hosted. Antiquing, art galleries, beaches, bicycling, canoeing/kayaking, fishing, golf, hiking, live theater, museums, parks, shopping, sporting events, tennis and water sports nearby.

Publicity: *Baltimore Sun, New York Times, Mid-Atlantic Country, Christian American, Washington Post* and *Annapolis Capital "Home of the Week"*

"Thank you so much for your gracious hospitality and for making our wedding night special."

Chez Amis B&B

85 East St
Annapolis, MD 21401-1729
(410)263-6631 (888)224-6455
E-mail: stay@chezamis.com
Web: www.chezamis.com

Circa 1854. This historic bed & breakfast once served as a local grocery store, and the guest rooms were once the living quarters of the former store owner. Guest rooms are decorated with brass beds and antique quilts. The innkeepers can provide champagne or perhaps a heart-shaped cake for guests celebrating a special occasion. Guests can walk to the capitol and the U.S. Naval Academy, as well as shops, restaurants and the harbor. Innkeepers Don and Mickie Deline have interesting former careers. Don, a former army lawyer, was the head lawyer for the Senate Armed Services Committee. Mickie was a tour guide in Washington, D.C., for nearly a decade and is equally full of knowledge about Annapolis.

Innkeeper(s): Don & Mickie Deline. $115-140. MC, VISA, PC, TC. TAC10. 4 rooms with PB. Breakfast included in rates. Types of meals: Gourmet bkfst. Beds: KQT. Cable TV in room. Air conditioning. VCR, fax and copier on premises. Weddings, small meetings, family reunions and seminars hosted. Antiquing, fishing, sailing, live theater, parks, shopping, sporting events and water sports nearby.

Publicity: *Baltimore Sun, Tate County Democrat, Washington Post, Chesapeake Home and Channel 9 News.*

Flag House Inn Bed & Breakfast

26 Randall St
Annapolis, MD 21401-1720
(410)280-2721 (800)437-4825 Fax:(410)280-0133
E-mail: info@flaghouseinn.com
Web: www.flaghouseinn.com

Circa 1878. Reflecting its name, the state or national flag of each guest is hung outside this inn, located in the center of the National Historic District. Originally two Victorian townhouses, the traditional decor blends Oriental and nautical motifs with antiques and reproductions. The spacious guest library is a welcome spot to enjoy fireside reading of local area guides and related books and magazines. Comfortable seating, good lighting and privacy are appealing amenities of the guest bedrooms. Fruit, cereals, fresh-baked breads, pastries and hot entrees are prepared for a satisfying breakfast in the dining room. The full-length front porch offers swings and teak benches to linger in. Coveted off-street parking is available on-site, and the many attractions of this bayside Colonial town are an easy walk.

Historic Interest: Washington, DC (25 miles), Baltimore (30 miles), St. Michaels (40 miles).

Innkeeper(s): Charlotte & Bill Schmickle. $95-225. MC, VISA, AX, PC, TC. TAC10. 5 rooms with PB, 1 suite and 1 conference room. Breakfast included in rates. Types of meals: Full bkfst. Beds: KT. Cable TV and ceiling fan in room. Central air. Fax, copier, library, front porch with swings and off-street parking on premises. Small meetings and seminars hosted. Amusement parks, antiquing, art galleries, beaches, canoeing/kayaking, fishing, golf, historic homes and public buildings, sailing, boat tours, Naval museum and model shop gallery, historic waling tours, live theater, museums, parks, shopping, sporting events and water sports nearby.

Georgian House B&B

170 Duke of Gloucester St
Annapolis, MD 21401-2517
(410)263-5618 (800)557-2068
E-mail: georgian@erols.com
Web: www.georgianhouse.com

Circa 1747. Walk to all the city's historic locations from this elegant old red brick Georgian home, once the meeting place of the Forensic Society with three of its members signers of the Declaration of Independence.

Dark green shutters grace the exterior, and there are six fireplaces and original pine floors inside. Period furniture, reproductions and original art furnish the guest rooms. Listen to soft piano music while you enjoy a sumptuous breakfast complete with hot entree, fresh seasonal fruit and home-baked muffins or rolls. Relax at the end of the day on the brick patio surrounded by gardens.

Innkeeper(s): Sandy & Hank Mayer. $130-180. MC, VISA, AX, PC, TC. TAC10. 4 rooms with PB, 1 with FP and 1 suite. Breakfast included in rates. Types of meals: Gourmet bkfst and early coffee/tea. Beds: Q. Phone, ceiling fan and VCR in room. Air conditioning. Copier on premises. Antiquing, fishing, golf, live theater, parks, shopping, sporting events, tennis and water sports nearby.

Publicity: *National Geographic Traveler and Chesapeake Life.*

Gibson's Lodgings

110 Prince George St
Annapolis, MD 21401-1704
(410)268-5555
E-mail: gibsonslodging@starpower.net

Circa 1774. This Georgian house in the heart of the Annapolis Historic District was built on the site of the Old Courthouse, circa 1680. Two historic houses make up the

inn, and there was a new house built in 1988. All the rooms, old and new, are furnished with antiques. Only a few yards away is the City Dock Harbor and within two blocks is the Naval Academy visitor's gate.

Historic Interest: U.S. Naval Academy, Chesapeake Bay.

Innkeeper(s): Bev Snyder & John Lauer. $89-269. MC, VISA, AX, TC. 21 rooms, 17 with PB, 6 suites and 1 conference room. Breakfast included in rates. Types of meals: Cont. Beds: QDT. Air conditioning. Parking on premises. Handicap access. Small meetings and seminars hosted. Antiquing, fishing, live theater, parks, shopping, sporting events and water sports nearby.

Publicity: *Mid-Atlantic Country and New York.*

"We had a delightful stay! We enjoyed the proximity to the waterfront, the fun atmosphere and the friendly people."

Baltimore   B7

Abacrombie Badger B&B

58 W Biddle St
Baltimore, MD 21201-5534
(410)244-7227 (888)922-3437 Fax:(410)244-8415
E-mail: info@badger-inn.com
Web: www.badger-inn.com

Circa 1890. This five-story row house was once the home to Colonel Biddle of the Union Army. The home includes a dozen guest rooms with English appointments. Guests can relax in the first-floor parlor and enjoy dinner at La Tesso Tana, also located in the inn. The Meyerhoff Symphony Hall is across the street from the B&B, which is located in Baltimore's cultural center. Antique shops and an opera house are just a few blocks away, as is the streetcar line, which will take guests to the convention center, stadiums and other attractions.

Historic Interest: Basilica of the Assumption 1st Catholic Cathedral in US (half mile).

Innkeeper(s): Paul Bragaw. $115-155. MC, VISA, AX, DC, DS, PC, TC. TAC8. 12 rooms with PB. Breakfast included in rates. Types of meals: Cont plus. Beds: Q. Cable TV and phone in room. Central air. Fax, copier, library and parking off street on premises. French, German and Dutch spoken. Antiquing, art galleries, canoeing/kayaking, golf, live theater, museums, parks, shopping and sporting events nearby.

Hopkins Inn

3403 St Paul St
Baltimore, MD 21218
(410)235-8600 (800)537-8483 Fax:(410)235-7051

Circa 1920. Major renovations have turned this inn with Spanish Revival architecture into uptown elegance. Victorian decor and antique furnishings reside with original artwork in tasteful luxury. A meeting room and a conference room are available for business or pleasure. The inviting guest bedrooms have a cozy ambiance. Start the day with a continental breakfast. Centrally located across from John Hopkins University on renown Homewood Campus, it is close to all the attractions this area has to offer.

Historic Interest: Homewood House (2 blocks), Historic Mt. Vernon (2 miles), Inner Harbor (4 miles).

$89-159. MC, VISA, AX, DC, CB, DS, TC. TAC10. 25 rooms with PB, 5 suites and 2 conference rooms. Breakfast included in rates. Types of meals: Cont plus. Beds: QT. Cable TV and phone in room. Air conditioning. Fax, copier and modem hook-up on premises. Small meetings hosted. Antiquing, art galleries, live theater, museums, parks, shopping, sporting events and tennis nearby.

Inn at 2920

2920 Elliott St
Baltimore, MD 21224
(410)342-4450 (877)774-2920 Fax:(410)342-6436
E-mail: reservations@theinnat2920.com
Web: www.theinnat2920.com

Circa 1920. Decorated with an eclectic contemporary style, this large, old-fashioned Rowhouse features original details like exposed brick, a copper ceiling and wood staircase. The inn sits in Canton, a premier waterfront neighborhood located downtown. Each well-appointed guest bedroom provides an assortment of comforts including a Jacuzzi, fine linens, hypoallergenic bedding and Kingsdown mattress. Tall ceilings, large windows, sleigh and wrought iron canopy beds accent a spacious ambiance. Sensitive to the needs of the business traveler, corporate packages are available, offering high-tech assistance. Chef David uses mostly farm fresh, organic ingredients to make delicious and well-presented breakfasts. He maintains an herb and vegetable garden in the dining room bay window. Exciting city life is within walking distance.

Innkeeper(s): David & Debbie Schwartz. $140-215. MC, VISA, AX, DS, TC. TAC10. 4 rooms with PB. Breakfast and snacks/refreshments included in rates. Types of meals: Gourmet bkfst and veg bkfst. Beds: KQ. Cable TV, turndown service, ceiling fan, VCR, corporate package includes high-speed and wireless internet access and mobile phone for the duration of stay in room. Central air. Fax and copier on premises. Small meetings hosted. Antiquing, art galleries, fishing, Camden yards, Ravens stadium, inner harbor, Baltimore convention center, live theater, museums, parks, shopping and sporting events nearby.

Mr. Mole B&B

1601 Bolton St
Baltimore, MD 21217-4317
(410)728-1179 Fax:(410)728-3379
E-mail: info@mrmolebb.com

Circa 1869. Set on a quiet, upscale street in the historic Bolton Hill neighborhood, this restored brick town house, named after the fastidious character in The Wind in the Willows, is a combination of whimsical romantic ambiance and old Baltimore society. Throughout the house, 18th- and 19th-century antiques

enhance wainscoting, painted draped ivy and 14-foot ceilings. Each guest room and suite features a different theme. The Garden Suite, blooming with sunny floral prints and plaid, offers a bright, third-floor sun room, sitting room and a spacious private bath. The Explorer Suite features sophisticated leopard-print fabrics and a zebra-skin rug. This inn received

Mobil's four-star rating from '95-'99. It is located six blocks from the Meyerhoff Symphony Hall, the Lyric Opera House, the Metro and the beginning of Baltimore's Antique Row.

Historic Interest: On historic Bolton Hill. Located close to Johns Hopkins University and the University of Baltimore. Downtown Baltimore, the Inner Harbor and Fells Point are five minutes away by car, Metro or trolley.

Innkeeper(s): Paul Bragaw & Collin Clarke. $119-175. MC, VISA, AX, DC, DS, PC, TC. TAC8. 5 rooms with PB, 4 with FP and 2 suites. Breakfast included in rates. Types of meals: Cont plus. Beds: Q. Phone and turndown service in room. Air conditioning. Fax and library on premises. Antiquing, golf, live theater, parks, shopping and sporting events nearby.

Publicity: Baltimore Magazine, Maryland Magazine, Travel Holiday, Mid-Atlantic, Washingtonian, New York Times and National Geographic.

Berlin   E10

Merry Sherwood Plantation

8909 Worcester Hwy
Berlin, MD 21811-3016
(410)641-2112 (800)660-0358 Fax:(410)641-9528
E-mail: info@merrysherwood.com
Web: www.merrysherwood.com

Circa 1859. This magnificent pre-Civil War mansion is a tribute to Southern plantation architecture. The inn features antique period furniture, hand-woven, Victorian era rugs and a square grand piano. The ballroom, now a parlor for guests, boasts twin fireplaces and pier mirrors. (Ask to see the hidden

cupboards behind the fireside bookcases in the library.) Nineteen acres of grounds are beautifully landscaped and feature azaleas, boxwoods and 125 varieties of trees.

Innkeeper(s): Kirk Burbage. $125-175. MC, VISA. 8 rooms, 6 with PB, 4 with FP and 1 suite. Breakfast included in rates. Types of meals: Gourmet bkfst, afternoon tea and gourmet dinner. Beds: QD. Air conditioning. Weddings, small meetings, family reunions and seminars hosted. Amusement parks, antiquing, fishing, shopping and water sports nearby.

Publicity: Washington Post, Baltimore Sun and Southern Living.

"Pure elegance and privacy at its finest."

Betterton   B8

Lantern Inn

115 Ericsson Ave, PO Box 29
Betterton, MD 21610-9746
(410)348-5809 (800)499-7265 Fax:(410)348-2323
E-mail: lanterninn@dmv.com

Circa 1904. Framed by a picket fence and a wide two-story front porch, this four-story country inn is located one block from the nettle-free public beach on Chesapeake Bay. Comfortable rooms are furnished with antiques and hand-made quilts. The surrounding area is well-known for its wildlife preserves. Antique shops and restaurants are nearby. Kent County offers plenty of cycling possibilities, and there are detailed maps available at the inn for trips that start at the inn and go for 10 to 90 miles. Tennis courts are two blocks away.

Historic Interest: Historic Chestertown (12 miles), Chesapeake Bay (1 block).

Innkeeper(s): Ray & Sandi Sparks. $75-90. MC, VISA, AX. 14 rooms, 4 with PB. Breakfast included in rates. Types of meals: Cont plus. Beds: KQDT. VCR on premises. Antiquing, fishing, horseback riding and sporting clays nearby.

Publicity: Richland Times-Dispatch, North Carolina Outdoorsman, Washingtonian and Mid-Atlantic Country.

Buckeystown   B5

Catoctin Inn and Conference Center

3613 Buckeystown Pike
Buckeystown, MD 21717
(301)874-5555 (800)730-5550 Fax:(301)874-2026
E-mail: catoctin@fred.net
Web: www.catoctininn.com

Circa 1780. The inn's four acres of dogwood, magnolias, maples and sweeping lawns overlook the village and the Catoctin Mountains range. Some special features of the inn include a fine-dining restaurant serving breakfast and dinner and a handsome wraparound veranda. A Victorian carriage house marks the site for weddings, showers and receptions for up to

200 guests. Fifteen of the guest rooms include a fireplace and a whirlpool tub. Nearby villages to visit include Harper's Ferry, Antietam and New Market. Buckeystown's Monocacy River provides canoeing and fishing.

Innkeeper(s): Terry & Sarah MacGillivray. $85-150. MC, VISA, AX, DS, PC. 20 rooms with PB, 15 with FP, 8 suites, 3 cottages and 3 conference rooms. Breakfast included in rates. Types of meals: Full bkfst and afternoon tea. Beds: KQ. Cable TV, phone, turndown service and VCR in room. Air conditioning. Weddings, small meetings, family reunions and seminars hosted. Antiquing, fishing, hiking, biking, Appalachian Trail, Harper's Ferry, Sugarloaf Mountain, swimming, boating, Civil War history nearby, live theater, shopping, downhill skiing, cross-country skiing and sporting events nearby.

The Inn at Buckeystown

3521 Buckeystown Pike
Buckeystown, MD 21717
(301)874-5755 (800)272-1190 Fax:(301)831-1355
E-mail: info@innatbuckeystown.com
Web: www.innatbuckeystown.com

Circa 1897. Gables, bay windows and a wraparound porch are features of this grand Victorian mansion located on two-and-a-half acres of lawns and gardens (and an ancient cemetery). The inn features a polished staircase, antiques and elegantly decorated guest rooms. Ask for the Deja Vu Suite, which boasts a working fireplace and oak decor. A gourmet dinner is served by request. High tea and monthly murder mysteries are also offered. The inn also hosts weddings, rehearsals and retreats. The village of Buckeystown is in the National Register.
Historic Interest: Frederick, Barbara Fritchie and Francis Scott Key grave sites (4 miles), National Battle of the Monocacy Civil War Battlefield Park (3 miles), Camp David (15 miles).
Innkeeper(s): Janet Wells. $80-225. MC, VISA, AX, DS, PC, TC. TAC10. 8 rooms, 5 with PB. Breakfast and snacks/refreshments included in rates. Types of meals: Gourmet bkfst, country bkfst, veg bkfst, early coffee/tea and dinner. MAP. Beds: QD. Cable TV in room. Air conditioning. VCR, fax and tea room on premises. Weddings, small meetings, family reunions and seminars hosted. Antiquing, art galleries, bicycling, canoeing/kayaking, fishing, golf, live theater, museums, parks, shopping, downhill skiing, sporting events and wineries nearby.
Publicity: *Mid-Atlantic, Innsider, The Washingtonian, Washington Post and Baltimore Sun.*

"This was one of the best bed and breakfast experiences we have ever had."

Cascade   A5

Bluebird on the Mountain

14700 Eyler Ave
Cascade, MD 21719-1938
(301)241-4161 (800)362-9526

Circa 1900. In the mountain village of Cascade, this gracious shuttered Georgian manor is situated on two acres of trees and wildflowers. Three suites have double whirlpool tubs. There is an outdoor hot tub as well. The Rose Garden Room and Mt. Magnolia suites have fireplaces and porches overlooking the back garden. The inn is appointed with antiques, lace and white linens, and white wicker. On Sundays, a full breakfast is served. Cascade is located in between Frederick, Md., and Gettysburg, Pa.

Innkeeper(s): Eda Smith-Eley. $105-130. MC, VISA, PC. TAC10. 5 rooms with PB, 2 with FP and 2 suites. Breakfast included in rates. Types of meals: Full bkfst, cont plus, early coffee/tea and room service. Beds: KQT. Cable TV, turndown service, ceiling fan and VCR in room. Air conditioning. Spa on premises. Small meetings, family

reunions and seminars hosted. Antiquing, fishing, hiking, live theater, parks, shopping, downhill skiing, sporting events and water sports nearby.
Publicity: *Warm Welcomes, Baltimore Sun, Frederick News and Washington Post.*

"A wonderful balance of luxury and at-home comfort."

Chesapeake City   B8

Blue Max

300 Bohemia Ave, PO Box 30
Chesapeake City, MD 21915-1244
(410)885-2781 (877)725-8362 Fax:(410)885-2809
E-mail: innkeeper@bluemaxinn.com
Web: www.bluemaxinn.com

Circa 1854. Known as "the house with generous porches," this is one of the town's largest residences, built with Georgian architecture by the owner of the sawmill. This elegant inn has working fireplaces and a parlor with a grand player piano. Elaborate upscale amenities in the romantic suites and guest bedrooms include robes, flowers, chocolates and luxurious linens. Whirlpool tubs, a private balcony and second-floor verandas are also featured. Mouth-watering dishes like peaches and kiwi

with amaretto cream sauce, apple crisp pancakes and country bacon, and eggs Benedict souffle are enjoyed in the fireside dining room or in the solarium overlooking gardens and a fish pond. A waterfall and gazebo highlight lush landscaping.
Innkeeper(s): Wayne & Wendy Mercer. $90-185. MC, VISA, AX, DC, DS, PC, TC. 8 rooms with PB and 1 suite. Breakfast and afternoon tea included in rates. Types of meals: Gourmet bkfst, cont plus, cont, early coffee/tea and snacks/refreshments. Beds: KQ. Cable TV, phone, ceiling fan and VCR in room. Air conditioning. Fax, copier, bicycles and library on premises. Handicap access. Small meetings, family reunions and seminars hosted. Antiquing, art galleries, bicycling, canoeing/kayaking, fishing, golf, hiking, horseback riding, museums, parks, shopping, tennis and water sports nearby.

Inn at The Canal

104 Bohemia Ave
Chesapeake City, MD 21915-1218
(410)885-5995 Fax:(410)885-3585

Circa 1870. A favorite activity here is watching the parade of boats and ships from the waterfront porch. The Inn at the Canal was built by the Brady family, who owned the tugboats that operated on the canal. Rooms are furnished in antiques and quilts, set off by original hand-painted and elaborately designed ceilings. Guests enjoy European soaking tubs. The historic canal town offers a fine collection of restaurants and shops.

Innkeeper(s): Mary & Al Ioppolo. $85-175. MC, VISA, AX, DC, CB, DS, PC, TC. TAC10. 7 rooms with PB, 1 suite and 1 conference room. Breakfast and snacks/refreshments included in rates. Types of meals: Full bkfst and early coffee/tea. Beds: KQD. Cable TV and phone in room. Air conditioning. Fax on premises. Small meetings hosted. Antiquing, fishing, golf, horseback riding, live theater, parks, shopping, sporting events, tennis and water sports nearby.

Chestertown   B8

Great Oak Manor

10568 Cliff Rd
Chestertown, MD 21620-4115
(410)778-5943 (800)504-3098 Fax:(410)778-5943
E-mail: innkeeper@greatoak.com
Web: www.greatoak.com

Circa 1938. This elegant Georgian mansion anchors vast lawns
at the end of a long driveway. Situated directly on the
Chesapeake Bay, it is a serene and picturesque country estate. A
library with fireplace, den and formal parlors are available to

guests. With its grand circular
stairway, bayside gazebo, private
beach and nearby marina, the
Manor is a remarkable setting
for events such as weddings
and reunions. Chestertown is
eight miles away.

Innkeeper(s): Don & Dianne Cantor. $124-235. MC, VISA, PC, TC. TAC10.
11 rooms with PB, 5 with FP, 1 suite and 2 conference rooms. Breakfast
included in rates. Types of meals: Full bkfst and early coffee/tea. Beds: KT.
Phone, some VCRs and refrigerator (in suite) in room. Air conditioning. VCR,
fax, copier, bicycles, library and computer ready-two rooms on premises.
Weddings, small meetings, family reunions and seminars hosted. Antiquing,
canoeing/kayaking, fishing, golf, Historic Washington College, live theater,
shopping and tennis nearby.
Publicity: *Philadelphia, Diversions, Road Best Traveled, Washingtonian, Country
Inns, Southern Living, New Choices, Chesapeake Life and Time Magazine.*

*"The charming setting, professional service and personal warmth
we experienced at Great Oak will long be a pleasant memory.
Thanks for everything!"*

The Inn at Mitchell House

8796 Maryland Pkwy
Chestertown, MD 21620-4209
(410)778-6500
E-mail: innatmitch@friend.ly.net
Web: www.chestertown.com/mitchell/

Circa 1743. This pristine 18th-century manor house sits as
a jewel on 12 acres overlooking Stoneybrook Pond. The
guest rooms and the inn's several parlors are preserved and
appointed in an authentic Colonial mood, heightened by
handsome polished wide-board floors. Eastern Neck Island

National Wildlife Refuge, Chesapeake
Farms, St. Michaels, Annapolis and
nearby Chestertown are all delightful
to explore. The Inn at Mitchell
House is a popular setting for
romantic weddings and small
corporate meetings.

Innkeeper(s): Tracy & Jim Stone. $95-120. MC, VISA, PC, TC. 6 rooms, 5
with PB, 4 with FP. Breakfast included in rates. Types of meals: Full bkfst
and early coffee/tea. Beds: KQ. Turndown service in room. Air conditioning.
VCR on premises. Weddings, small meetings, family reunions and seminars
hosted. Antiquing, fishing, live theater, shopping, sporting events and water
sports nearby.
Publicity: *Washingtonian, New York Magazine, Glamour, Philadelphia
Inquirer, Baltimore Sun, Kent County News, Ten Best Inns in the Country,
New York Times, Washington Post and National Geographic Traveler.*

Cumberland   A3

The Inn at Walnut Bottom

120 Greene St
Cumberland, MD 21502-2934
(301)777-0003 (800)286-9718 Fax:(301)777-8288
E-mail: iwb@iwbinfo.com
Web: www.iwbinfo.com

Circa 1820. Two historic homes comprise the Inn at Walnut
Bottom: the 1820 Federal-style Cowden House and the 1890
Queen Anne Victorian-style Dent House, both located on
Cumberland's oldest street.

Antiques and reproduction furnishings decorate the parlors,
guest rooms and family suites.
Each morning a delicious full
breakfast is served and in the afternoon, tasty refreshments. Enjoy a
stroll to the historic district and restaurants or ask to borrow one
of the inn's bicycles for exploring the C&O Canal Towpath.
Innkeeper(s): Grant M. Irvin & Kirsten O. Hansen. $87-200. MC, VISA, AX,
DS, PC, TC. 12 rooms, 8 with PB and 2 suites. Breakfast included in rates.
Types of meals: Full bkfst, cont and early coffee/tea. MAP. Beds: KQDT. Cable
TV, phone, ceiling fan and hair dryers in room. Air conditioning. Fax, copier,
bicycles and 2 family suites on premises. Small meetings, family reunions
and seminars hosted. Danish, German and French spoken. Bicycling, fishing,
scenic train ride, Frank Lloyd Wrights Falling Water, live theater, parks, down-
hill skiing and cross-country skiing nearby.
Publicity: *Washington Post, Mid-Atlantic Country, Southern Living and
Baltimore Magazine.*

Deep Creek Lake   C8

Haley Farm B&B and Retreat Center

16766 Garrett Hwy
Deep Creek Lake, MD 21550-4036
(301)387-9050 (888)231-FARM Fax:(301)387-9050
E-mail: kam@haleyfarm.com
Web: www.haleyfarm.com

Circa 1920. This farmhouse is surrounded by 65 acres of rolling
hills and farmland in the mountains of Western Maryland.
Inside, the innkeepers have added many elegant touches, transforming the home into a gracious retreat with Chinese carpets,
tapestries and European furnishings. There are three luxury
suites, which include a heart-shaped Jacuzzi, king-size bed,
kitchenette and sitting room with a fireplace. In addition, there
are four smaller suites and four deluxe rooms. Croquet and badminton are set up on the grounds. Other popular activities are
fishing in the trout pond, soaking in the hot tub, stretching out
in the hammock or taking a picnic to the gazebo. The innkeepers
offer special romantic packages with flowers and champagne,
massages and even horseback riding. A variety of retreats and
workshops are offered with subjects ranging from conflict resolu-
tion and negotiating strategies to yoga. The farm is three hours
from Washington, D.C., and minutes from Deep Creek Lake, five
state parks and the WISP ski and golf resort.
Innkeeper(s): Fred & Tammy. $130-210. MC, VISA, AX, DS, PC, TC. 11
rooms with PB, 7 with FP and 7 suites. Breakfast included in rates. Types of
meals: Full bkfst. Beds: KQ. Ceiling fan in room. Air conditioning. VCR, spa,
bicycles, library and trout pond on premises. Weddings, small meetings, family reunions and seminars hosted. German, limited French and limited
Spanish spoken. Antiquing, fishing, white water rafting, parks, shopping,
downhill skiing, cross-country skiing and water sports nearby.
"A beautiful setting for a quiet, romantic escape."

Easton   C8

The Bishop's House Bed & Breakfast

214 Goldsborough St
Easton, MD 21601
(410)820-7290 (800)223-7290 Fax:(410)820-7290
E-mail: bishopshouse@skipjack.bluecrab.org

Circa 1880. The innkeepers of this in-town Victorian lovingly restored it in 1988. The three-and-a-half-story clapboard and gabled roof home includes three spacious first-floor rooms with 14-foot-high ceilings and generously sized second- and third-floor guest rooms. With its period-style fur-

nishings, working fireplaces and whirlpool tubs, the inn offers its guests both romance and the ambiance of the Victorian era. An appetizing full break-fast is served every morning. Located in Easton's Historic District, it is within three blocks of boutiques, antique shops, restaurants and historic sites. The inn provides off-street parking and secured overnight storage for bicycles.

Historic Interest: Within 10 miles of historic Oxford and St. Michaels.

Innkeeper(s): John & Diane Ippolito. $110-120. PC, TC. TAC10. 5 rooms with PB. Breakfast included in rates. Types of meals: Early coffee/tea. Fireplaces on premises.

Chaffinch House B&B

132 S Harrison St
Easton, MD 21601-2928
(410)822-5074 (800)861-5074
E-mail: innkeeper@chaffinchhouse.com
Web: www.chaffinchhouse.com

Circa 1893. Chaffinch House is an outstanding example of the whimsy in Victorian architecture. The exterior boasts gables, a turret, bays, a keyhole window and a wrap around front porch. Inside, there are more than 60 windows, each a different size. The home is appointed with period furnishings. Guest rooms include the Wedding Room suite, with a four-poster rice bed, bathroom, sitting room and a screened-in porch. Easton, called one of the best small towns in America, is about an hour-and-a-half drive from Washington, D.C., and minutes from St. Michaels and Oxford. Fine restaurants, museums, boutique shops, antique stores and art galleries are within walking distance of the inn.

Innkeeper(s): Laura Brandt. $100-135. MC, VISA, PC, TC. TAC10. 6 rooms with PB and 1 suite. Types of meals: Gourmet bkfst and early coffee/tea. Beds: KQ. Ceiling fan in room. Central air. Small meetings and family reunions hosted. Antiquing, art galleries, bicycling, canoeing/kayaking, fishing, golf, hiking, horseback riding, live theater, museums, parks, shopping, tennis and water sports nearby.

Publicity: *Mid-Atlantic Magazine, Washington Post and Silent Fall-opening scene.*

The John S. McDaniel House B&B

14 N Aurora St
Easton, MD 21601-3617
(410)822-3704 (877)822-5702
E-mail: jsmcdanielhouse@netscape.net

Circa 1840. A wide veranda wraps around this three-story Queen Anne Victorian, complete with octagonal tower and dormers. Located in the historic district, considered to be the

"Colonial Capital of the Eastern Shore," it's within walking distance to the classic Avalon Theater, Academy of Art, many good restaurants and unique shops.

Innkeeper(s): Mary Lou & Fran Karwacki. $115-165. MC, VISA, AX, PC, TC. 6 rooms with PB and 1 suite. Types of meals: Full bkfst. Beds: KQDT. Cable TV, ceiling fan and VCR in room. Central air. Gift certificates available and off-street parking on premises. Antiquing, fishing, parks, shopping and water sports nearby.

Elk Mills   A8

Elk Forge Bed & Breakfast Inn, Spa, and Retreat

807 Elk Mills Rd
Elk Mills, MD 21921
(410)392-9007 (877)ELK-FORG Fax:(410)392-2954
E-mail: reservations@elkforge.com
Web: www.elkforge.com

Circa 1760. Rich in history and gorgeous surroundings, this Colonial manor house with Victorian elegance offers warm hospitality and maximum comfort. This five-and-a-half-acre estate features a variety of common areas. Some are perfect for intimate weddings, family reunions or business meetings. Appealing guest bedrooms and suites boast numerous amenities for a pleasurable stay. A well-prepared breakfast may include fresh fruit, Belgian waffles, an egg dish and daily organic selections. Create memorable moments playing badminton or croquet, walking in the woods or strolling the gardens before afternoon tea. Plan tri-state excursions from a hammock or lawn swing. Browse through the quaint gift shop, and enjoy an evening reception with sumptuous desserts. Be pampered with a Swedish massage or other spa services.

Historic Interest: Winethur (20 miles), Hagley Museum, Rockwood Museum Brandywine River Museum.

Innkeeper(s): Harry & LeAnn Lenderman. $89-185. MC, VISA, AX, DS, PC, TC. 12 rooms with PB, 5 with FP, 5 suites and 2 conference rooms. Breakfast, afternoon tea and snacks/refreshments included in rates. Types of meals: Gourmet bkfst, veg bkfst, early coffee/tea and picnic lunch. Beds: Q. Cable TV, phone, turndown service, VCR, hot tub, fireplace, ironing board and iron in room. Central air. Fax, copier, library, hot tub and gift shop on premises. Handicap access. Weddings, small meetings, family reunions and seminars hosted. Antiquing, bicycling, fishing, golf, hiking, horseback riding, Longwood Gardens, Lancaster, Penn., museums, parks, shopping, sporting events and tennis nearby.

Publicity: *News Journal.*

Emmitsbury   A5

The Gallery Suites

304 E Main St
Emmitsbury, MD 21727
(301)447-1666
E-mail: lindaposte@aol.com

Circa 1912. This collection of suites is so named because the two suites are located on the second story of a building that once housed an art gallery. Innkeeper Linda Postelle is an artist and her work is featured throughout the suites, including murals on doors and walls. Antiques fill the whimsically decorated rooms. The suites are located in a historic building and were once used as apartments, so the rooms have been completely renovated and restored. Linda delivers breakfast to your door. The Main Street Grill, a local eatery, also is on the premises.

Innkeeper(s): Linda Postelle. $100-135. MC, VISA, PC, TC. 2 suites.

Breakfast included in rates. Types of meals: Gourmet bkfst, cont plus, cont and early coffee/tea. Beds: Q. Cable TV, phone and ceiling fan in room. Air conditioning. Restaurant on premises. Antiquing, golf, parks, downhill skiing and sporting events nearby.

Publicity: *Frederick Gazette.*

Frederick   B5

McCleery's Flat

121 E Patrick St
Frederick, MD 21701-5677
(301)620-2433 (800)774-7926

Circa 1876. Indulge in quiet European elegance at this French second empire-style townhouse. Located in the the heart of downtown on historic Antique Row, the decor blends period antiques and reproductions. Well-appointed guest bedrooms and suites offer a variety of delightful features. Choose from a whirlpool or soaking tub, private balcony or covered outdoor sitting area, and a touch of whimsy, Victorian or historical furnishings. Beds include canopy, sleigh, poster, cast-iron and wicker. Creative international recipes collected by the innkeepers are served for breakfast. The landscaped grounds and courtyard offer areas to relax and listen to the soft-flowing fountains and gaze at the colorful flowers.

Historic Interest: Antietam, Gettysburg (within 35 miles).

Innkeeper(s): Jutta & George Terrell. $100-135. MC, VISA, AX, DC, CB, PC, TC. 5 rooms, 3 with PB and 2 suites. Breakfast and snacks/refreshments included in rates. Types of meals: Gourmet bkfst, veg bkfst and early coffee/tea. Beds: KQD. Ceiling fan in room. Air conditioning. VCR and library on premises. Weddings, small meetings and family reunions hosted. German spoken. Antiquing, art galleries, bicycling, canoeing/kayaking, fishing, golf, hiking, live theater, museums, parks, shopping, downhill skiing, sporting events, tennis and wineries nearby.

Middle Plantation Inn

9549 Liberty Rd
Frederick, MD 21701-3246
(301)898-7128
E-mail: bandb@mpinn.com

Circa 1810. The innkeepers at this unique Colonial log house worked around the original 1810 structure to create their inn, which offers four guest rooms. The house still includes the authentic, early 19th-century hardwood floors, the stone and log frame and wood beams. These original features give the inn a cozy, rustic feel. Guest rooms are decorated with quilts, stenciling and country furnishings, including a lace-covered canopy bed. Guests are welcome to relax in the Keeping Room, which offers comfortable furnishings, stained-glass windows, skylights and a huge, stone fireplace. The 26-acre grounds include a garden and a brook. The home is located just a few miles to the east of Frederick.

Innkeeper(s): Shirley & Dwight Mullican. $90-110. MC, VISA, PC, TC. TAC10. 4 rooms with PB. Breakfast included in rates. Types of meals: Cont plus. Beds: QD. Cable TV, phone, ceiling fan and alarm clock in room. Air conditioning. Walking trail on premises. Antiquing, fishing, historic area, museums, parks and shopping nearby.

Publicity: *Baltimore Magazine, Frommer's and Innsider.*

"Inn was furnished elegantly with authentic antiques. Blueberry muffins were a heavenly delight that melted in my mouth."

Spring Bank, A B&B Inn

7945 Worman's Mill Rd
Frederick, MD 21701
(301)694-0440 (800)400-4667
E-mail: rcomp1880@aol.com
Web: www.bbonline.com/md/springbank

Circa 1880. Both Gothic Revival and Italianate architectural details are featured in this National Register brick Victorian. High ceilings accommodate 10-foot arched windows. The original interior shutters remain. The parlor has a marbleized slate fireplace, and there is original hand-stenciling and a plaster fresco in the Billiards Room. Victorian furnishings and Oriental rugs have been collected from the family's antique shop. Black birch, pine, maple and poplar trees dot the inn's 10 acres.

Historic Interest: Barbara Fritchie House, Roger Brooke Taney House, National Museum of Civil War Medicine, Civil War Battlefields: Monocacy (5 miles), Gettysburg (30 miles), Antietam (23 miles).

Innkeeper(s): Beverley & Ray Compton. $105-120. MC, VISA, AX, DS. TAC10. 5 rooms, 1 with PB. Breakfast included in rates. Types of meals: Cont plus. Beds: D. Air conditioning. VCR, fax, copier, bicycles and library on premises. Antiquing, bicycling, canoeing/kayaking, fishing, golf, hiking, live theater, museums, parks, shopping, downhill skiing, tennis and wineries nearby.

Publicity: *Weekend Magazine, HGTV Christmas Across America 2000 hosted by Willard Scott and WRC-Washington.*

Tyler-Spite House

112 W Church St
Frederick, MD 21701-5411
(301)831-4455

Circa 1814. The Tyler-Spite House was home to Dr. John Tyler, the country's first opthamologist. Tyler built his home almost overnight and hoped its construction would prevent the extension of a local street. Thus, Tyler's home also bears the nickname, "Spite" house. Inside, elaborate woodwork, 14-foot ceilings with raised paneling and eight working fireplaces with marble mantels, create an elegant, inviting atmosphere. A winding staircase, lit by an Austrian crystal chandelier, leads guests up to the five, well-appointed bedchambers decorated with Oriental rugs and antiques. Multi-course breakfasts are served in the formal dining room or on the patios in warm weather. High tea is served each afternoon. For an extra charge, the innkeepers offer romantic carriage rides through the park and historic district.

Historic Interest: The Brunswick R.R. Museum, in nearby Brunswick, offers a look at the history of the railroad in the United States. Mount Olivet Cemetery in Frederick is the final resting place of such esteemed Americans as Francis Scott Key and Barbara Fritchie. Fritchie, who angrily confronted General Stonewall Jackson in 1862, was memorialized in a poem.

Innkeeper(s): Bill & Andrea Myer. $150-250. MC, VISA, AX. TAC10. 3 suites. Types of meals: Full bkfst, afternoon tea and gourmet dinner. Beds: KQD. Antiquing, fishing, golf and tennis nearby.

Publicity: *Potomac.*

Grantsville   A2

Walnut Ridge Bed & Breakfast

92 Main St, PO Box 368
Grantsville, MD 21536
(301)895-4248 (888)419-2568
E-mail: walnutridge@usa.net
Web: www.walnutridge.net

Circa 1864. A grove of walnut trees and a wood-fired hot tub next to a vegetable garden are the unique offerings of this historic farmhouse B&B. The living room is decorated with Amish items and there are country pieces throughout. The accommodations offered include a family suite with full kitchen. The inn's cabin in the woods has its own clawfoot tub, stone fireplace, deck and queen bed. The innkeeper's husband is a local Mennonite minister.

Innkeeper(s): Tim & Candace Fetterly. $80-150. MC, VISA, PC, TC. TAC10. 4 rooms with PB, 4 with FP, 1 suite and 1 cabin. Breakfast included in rates. Types of meals: Full bkfst, country bkfst and early coffee/tea. AP. Beds: Q. Cable TV, phone, ceiling fan, VCR and fireplace in room. Air conditioning. Fax, spa, library and gift shop on premises. Family reunions hosted. Antiquing, bicycling, canoeing/kayaking, fishing, golf, hiking, horseback riding, museums, parks, shopping, downhill skiing, cross-country skiing, sporting events, tennis, water sports and wineries nearby.

Pets allowed: in suite and cabin.

Publicity: *Washington Post and Lancaster Farming.*

"Best nights' sleep I've had this summer."

Havre De Grace A8

La Cle D'Or Guesthouse

226 N Union Ave
Havre De Grace, MD 21078-2907
(410)939-6562 (888)HUG-GUEST Fax:(410)939-1833
Web: www.lacledorguesthouse.com

Circa 1868. Johns Hopkins' family built this Second Empire Victorian-style home located in the canal town's historic district. The decor is reminiscent of eclectic post-Civil War. The parlor

features a domed recessed alcove, bay window and fireplace. Strauss crystal chandeliers, Ronald Redding wallpapers and local artworks are found throughout the inn. Eastlake furnishings and reproductions fill exquisite guest bedrooms. An all-you-can-eat breakfast includes traditional fare served in the formal dining room. Stroll the brick-walled secret garden with wrought iron gates, relax on the flagstone terrace, or enjoy the outdoor spa.

Historic Interest: Steppinstone Museum & Susquehanna State Park (5 miles), Concord Point Lighthouse (1 mile).

Innkeeper(s): Ron Browning. $110-135. MC, VISA, PC, TC. TAC10. 3 rooms, 2 with PB. Breakfast and snacks/refreshments included in rates. Types of meals: Full bkfst, veg bkfst, early coffee/tea and room service. Beds: QD. Cable TV, turndown service, VCR and hair dryer in room. Central air. Fax, copier, library, pet boarding, hot tub and snack bar/refrigerator on premises. Weddings, small meetings, family reunions and seminars hosted. Spanish and French spoken. Antiquing, art galleries, bicycling, canoeing/kayaking, fishing, golf, hiking, seafood restaurants, live theater, museums, parks, shopping, sporting events, tennis, water sports and wineries nearby.

Pets allowed: Downstairs or outside only.

Publicity: *Country Extra Magazine.*

Spencer Silver Mansion

200 S Union Ave
Havre De Grace, MD 21078-3224
(410)939-1097 (800)780-1485
E-mail: spencersilver@erols.com

Circa 1896. This elegant granite Victorian mansion is graced with bays, gables, balconies, a turret and a gazebo veranda. The Victorian decor, with antiques and Oriental rugs, complements the house's carved-oak woodwork, fireplace mantels and par-

quet floors. The Concord Point Lighthouse (oldest continuously operated lighthouse in America) is only a walk away. In addition to the four rooms in the main house, a romantic carriage house suite is available, featuring an in-room fireplace, TV, whirlpool bath and kitchenette.

Historic Interest: Fort McHenry (45 minutes), Concord Point Lighthouse (1 minute).

Innkeeper(s): Carol Nemeth. $70-140. MC, VISA, AX, DS, PC, TC. TAC10. 5 rooms, 3 with PB, 1 with FP and 1 cottage. Breakfast included in rates. Types of meals: Full bkfst and early coffee/tea. Beds: QDT. Cable TV, phone and turndown service in room. Air conditioning. Weddings, small meetings and family reunions hosted. Antiquing, fishing, museums, restaurants, parks, shopping and water sports nearby.

Pets allowed: In Carriage House only.

Publicity: *Mid-Atlantic Country and Maryland.*

"A fabulous find. Beautiful house, excellent hostess. I've stayed at a lot of B&Bs, but this house is the best."

Vandiver Inn, Kent & Murphy Homes

301 S Union Ave
Havre De Grace, MD 21078-3201
(410)939-5200 (800)245-1655 Fax:(410)939-5202
E-mail: innkeeper@vandiverinn.com

Circa 1886. Three acres surround this three-story National Historic Register mansion. A chandelier lights the entrance. Some of the rooms offer gas fireplaces and clawfoot tubs, and all are furnished with Victorian antiques. For instance, a king-size Victorian bed, original to the house, is one of the features of the Millard E. Tydings Room, also offering a decorative fireplace and sitting area. The innkeeper creates breakfasts of freshly baked scones or muffins and Victorian eggs Benedict with tarragon-flavored hollandaise sauce. Spend some time in the back garden where a summer gazebo is supported by 12 cedar tree trunks. The innkeeper comes from an extensive hospitality background, and her experience is appreciated for weddings and corporate retreats.

Historic Interest: Concord Point light house, Stepping Stone Museum.

Innkeeper(s): Suzanne Mottek. $68-185. MC, VISA, AX, DS, PC, TC. TAC25. 9 rooms with PB, 2 with FP, 3 suites and 3 conference rooms. Breakfast included in rates. Types of meals: Gourmet bkfst, veg bkfst, cont plus, early coffee/tea, picnic lunch and dinner. Beds: KQDT. Cable TV and phone in room. Central air. Fax and bicycles on premises. Handicap access. Weddings, small meetings and family reunions hosted. Antiquing, art galleries, bicycling, canoeing/kayaking, fishing, golf, hiking, horseback riding, live theater, museums, parks, shopping, tennis, water sports and wineries nearby.

Ocean City E10

An Inn on the Ocean

1001 Atlantic Avenue
Ocean City, MD 21842
(410)289-8894 (877)226-6223 Fax:(410)289-8215
E-mail: innonoc@aol.com
Web: www.InnOnTheOcean.com

Circa 1920. From the wraparound porch of this inn, guests can watch birds soar and ocean waters crash upon the shore.. The Inn includes six elegant guest rooms, each individually decorated with rich fabrics and designer linens. The Hunt and Tapestry rooms each boast an ocean view. The Oceana Suite includes a private balcony that looks out to the sea. The

Veranda Room has its own oceanfront porch. Most rooms include a Jacuzzi tub. The gourmet breakfasts include home-made breads, fruit and special egg dishes, such as a frittata. The Inn is oceanfront, so guests need only walk a few steps to enjoy the beach and nearby Boardwalk. Golfing, outlet stores, fishing, water sports, antique shops and harness racing are other local attractions.

Historic Interest: Snow Hill(15 miles), Berlin (10 miles).

Innkeeper(s): The Barrett's. $125-290. MC, VISA, AX, DS, TC. 6 rooms with PB and 1 conference room. Breakfast and snacks/refreshments included in rates. Types of meals: Full bkfst, early coffee/tea and gourmet dinner. Beds: KQ. Cable TV, ceiling fan, VCR, jacuzzi and bathrobes in room. Air conditioning. Fax, copier, bicycles, beach chairs and umbrellas on premises. Weddings, small meetings, family reunions and seminars hosted. Amusement parks, antiquing, art galleries, beaches, bicycling, canoeing/kayaking, fishing, golf, hiking, horseback riding, live theater, museums, parks, shopping, sporting events, tennis and water sports nearby.

Oxford   D8

The Robert Morris Inn

314 N Morris St, PO Box 70
Oxford, MD 21654
(410)226-5111 Fax:(410)226-5744
E-mail: bestcrabcakes@webtv.net
Web: www.robertmorrisinn.com

Circa 1710. Once the home of Robert Morris Sr., a representative of an English trading company, the house was constructed by ship carpenters with wooden-pegged paneling, ship's nails and hand-hewn beams. Bricks brought to Oxford as ballast in trading ships were used to build the fireplaces. Robert Morris Jr., a partner in a Philadelphia law firm, used his entire savings to help finance the Continental Army. He signed the Declaration of Independence, Articles of Confederation and United States Constitution. James A. Michener, author of "Chesapeake," rated the inn's crab cakes as his favorite.

Historic Interest: Talbot Historic Society (15 minutes), Chesapeake Maritime Museum (25 minutes).

Innkeeper(s): Jay Gibson. $110-280. MC, VISA, AX, PC. TAC10. 35 rooms with PB and 1 conference room. EP. Beds: KQDT. Air conditioning. Fax, copier, library and 2 efficiencies on premises. Handicap access. Small meetings and seminars hosted. Antiquing, fishing, live theater, parks and shopping nearby.

Publicity: *Southern Accents, The Evening Sun, Maryland, Mid-Atlantic Country, Bon Appetite and Select Registry.*

"Impressed! Unbelievable!"

Pocomoke City   E9

Littletons Bed & Breakfast

407 2nd St
Pocomoke City, MD 21851-1417
(410)957-1645 Fax:(410)957-1936

Circa 1860. Recently awarded its place in the National Register of Historic Places, this classic Second Empire-style home was built by two prominent merchants. Completely renovated in 1994, guests will take pleasure in the warmth and hospitality offered by innkeepers Walter and Pamela Eskiewicz. Upon arrival, guests are treated to a refreshing beverage. All rooms are decorated in a combination of antiques and tra-

ditional furnishings. An accomplished gourmet cook, Pamela prides herself on her unique breakfast specialties such as Gingerbread Pancakes with Currant Pear Maple Syrup, Chocolate Walnut Butter Bread, potato pancakes with sausage and Carmella's Omelet. Pocomoke River, creeks and tributaries are located nearby.

Historic Interest: Located close to the View Trail 100 that offers a unique cycling experience through the Worcester County countryside and historic district. Within walking distance to the wild and scenic Pocomoke River that offers canoeists, kayakers and fishermen 73 miles of uninterrupted natural splendor.

Innkeeper(s): Walter & Pam Eskiewicz. $75-125. MC, VISA, AX, DS, PC. 4 rooms, 3 with PB. Breakfast included in rates. Types of meals: Gourmet bkfst. Beds: QDT. Ceiling fan and ice & beverage with glasses in room. Air conditioning. Fax, bicycles and library on premises. Small meetings hosted. Amusement parks, antiquing, fishing, golf, parks, shopping, sporting events, tennis and water sports nearby.

Publicity: *The Daily Times.*

"Very pretty and cozy atmosphere. It was so nice to feel safe over the night. The accommodations were as comfortable as being at home. Thanks for good conversation!"

Princess Anne   E9

Waterloo Country Inn

28822 Mount Vernon Rd
Princess Anne, MD 21853
(410)651-0883 Fax:(410)651-5592
E-mail: innkeeper@waterloocountryinn.com
Web: www.waterloocountryinn.com

Circa 1750. In the midst of 300 acres of land encircled by small cottages, brick walkways, century-old trees and flower beds, lies this pre-Revolutionary Georgian brick plantation house, beautifully restored and furnished with Swiss antiques. Listed in the National Register of Historical Places, the Waterloo Country Inn is situated on a tidal pond that is a habitat for wildlife and birds. Owners Theresa and Erwin Kraemer, natives to Switzerland, have brought "a taste of Europe to Maryland," according to a Maryland newspaper, with its elegant décor and European flair in dining. Enjoy the crisp Eastern Shore air while canoeing, bicycling, relaxing at the pool or strolling along Monie Creek. Ride the ferry to nearby antique shops and golf courses.

Innkeeper(s): Erwin & Theresa Kraemer. $105-245. MC, VISA, AX, DS, PC, TC. TAC5. 6 rooms with PB, 5 with FP and 2 suites. Breakfast and snacks/refreshments included in rates. Types of meals: Gourmet bkfst. Beds: KQT. Cable TV, phone, VCR, suites with Jacuzzi, fireplace, coffeemaker, bathrobes and clock radio in room. Central air. Fax, copier, swimming, bicycles, library and canoes on premises. Handicap access. Weddings, family reunions and seminars hosted. German, French and Italian spoken. Antiquing, beaches, bicycling, canoeing/kayaking, fishing, golf, hiking, horseback riding, Famous wild ponies on Assateague Island, Chesapeake Bay Island cruises, museums, parks and water sports nearby.

Pets allowed: one room only.

Publicity: *Gourmet Magazine, Baltimore Sun, Chesapeake Life Magazine and Daily Times.*

"What a find! We have traveled all over the world and this is really special."

Quantico E9

Whitehaven B&B

23844 River St #48
Quantico, MD 21856-2506
(410)873-3320 (888)205-5921 Fax:(410)873-2162
E-mail: whavnbb@dmv.com
Web: www.whitehaven.com

Circa 1850. Two historic properties comprise this bed & breakfast. The Charles Leatherbury House, which dates to 1886, includes two guest rooms, decorated in country Victorian style. The two rooms share a bath, perfect for couples traveling together. Book both rooms and you'll enjoy the utmost of privacy in a historic setting. The Otis Lloyd House, constructed prior to the Civil War, includes three guest rooms, each with a private bath. Guests at both houses enjoy a full breakfast, including farm-fresh eggs and homemade baked goods. The village of Whitehaven, originally chartered in 1685, includes 22 buildings listed in the National Register.
Historic Interest: Pemberton Hall (12 miles).

Innkeeper(s): Maryen, Carlton & Mark Herrett. $75-100. MC, VISA, AX, DS, PC, TC. 5 rooms, 3 with PB. Breakfast and snacks/refreshments included in rates. Types of meals: Full bkfst, veg bkfst and early coffee/tea. Beds: KQ. VCR, fax, copier, library and refrigerator on premises. Weddings and family reunions hosted. Antiquing, art galleries, beaches, bicycling, canoeing/kayaking, fishing, golf, museums, parks and water sports nearby.

Rock Hall C8

Huntingfield Manor B&B

4928 Eastern Neck Rd
Rock Hall, MD 21661
(410)639-7779 (800)720-8788 Fax:(410)639-2924
E-mail: manorlord@juno.com
Web: www.huntingfield.com

Circa 1850. This 1,365-foot-long, telescope-type Colonial farmhouse is a working farm that dates back to the middle 1600s. In the 1850s, the property was called "The Prevention of Inconvenience." Today, the inn sites on 67 secluded pastoral acres that include seven perennial gardens and six acres of grass. The inn is near the shores of Chesapeake Bay and the Chester and Sassafras rivers. Those larger bodies of water and the many creeks are excellent places to fish, crab, and enjoy all manner of water sports. The Eastern Neck Wildlife Refuge has seven miles of trails for the hiker and bird watcher. Guests also may drive through the country and visit old churches and other historic buildings. Eating a wide variety of seafood is almost a requirement of the serious guests, who can easily get their fill of seafood like crabs, oysters, clams and rockfish. Nearly every week there is a church supper or fish fry nearby. The inn offers six guest bedrooms, including one suite and a fully appointed cottage. The continental breakfast is a scrumptious variety of fresh breads and fruits in season.

Innkeeper(s): George & Bernie Starkey. $100-150. MC, VISA, AX, PC. TAC10. 6 rooms, 4 with PB, 1 suite and 1 cottage. Breakfast and afternoon tea included in rates. Types of meals: Cont plus. Beds: KT. Turndown service in room. Air conditioning. Fax, copier, swimming, bicycles, library and pet boarding on premises. Weddings, small meetings, family reunions and seminars hosted. Antiquing, art galleries, beaches, bicycling, canoeing/kayaking, fishing, golf, horseback riding, museums, parks and shopping nearby.
Pets allowed: Cottage only.

Moonlight Bay Marina & Inn

6002 Lawton Ave
Rock Hall, MD 21661-1369
(410)639-2660 Fax:(410)639-7739

Circa 1850. Moonlight Bay offers an ideal setting, right at the edge of the Chesapeake Bay. The pre-Civil War home includes a veranda lined with wicker furnishings and a swing, and the grounds boast a gazebo. Five rooms are located in the main inn, and several offer outstanding bay views. The West Wing includes five bay-front rooms, all with a whirlpool bath. Guests are pampered in Victorian style with a  full breakfast and afternoon tea. Guests can rent boats, fish, golf or take a nature walk at one of two local wildlife preserves. Other local attractions include auctions and antique shops.

Innkeeper(s): Robert & Dorothy Santangelo. $116-152. MC, VISA, DS, PC, TC. TAC10. 10 rooms with PB and 2 conference rooms. Breakfast and afternoon tea included in rates. Types of meals: Full bkfst and early coffee/tea. Beds: KQT. Ceiling fan and whirlpool tub in room. Air conditioning. VCR, fax and bicycles on premises. Handicap access. Weddings, small meetings, family reunions and seminars hosted. Antiquing, fishing, golf, live theater, shopping and tennis nearby.
Publicity: *Washingtonian* and *Washington Post.*

Saint Michaels C8

Kemp House Inn

412 Talbot St, PO Box 638
Saint Michaels, MD 21663-0638
(410)745-2243
E-mail: info@kemphouseinn.com
Web: www.kemphouseinn.com

Circa 1807. This two-story Georgian house was built by Colonel Joseph Kemp, a shipwright and one of the town forefathers. The inn is appointed in period furnishings accentuated by candlelight. Guest rooms include patchwork quilts, a collection of four-poster rope beds and old-fashioned nightshirts. There are several working fireplaces. Robert E. Lee is said to have been a guest.
Historic Interest: Listed in the National Register.

Innkeeper(s): Diane M. & Steve Cooper. $90-120. MC, VISA, DS. 8 rooms with PB, 4 with FP and 1 cottage. Breakfast included in rates. Types of meals: Cont and early coffee/tea. Beds: QDT. Air conditioning. Antiquing, fishing, shopping and water sports nearby.
Pets allowed: in cottage only.
Publicity: *Gourmet* and *Philadelphia.*

"It was wonderful. We've stayed in many B&Bs, and this was one of the nicest!"

Parsonage Inn

210 N Talbot St
Saint Michaels, MD 21663-2102
(410)745-5519 (800)394-5519
E-mail: parsinn@dmv.com
Web: www.parsonage-inn.com

Circa 1883. A striking Victorian steeple rises next to the wide bay of this brick residence, once the home of Henry Clay Dodson, state senator, pharmacist and brickyard owner. The

house features brick detail in a variety of patterns and inlays, perhaps a design statement for brick customers.

Porches are decorated with filigree and spindled columns. Laura Ashley linens, late Victorian furnishings, fireplaces and decks add to the creature comforts. Six bikes await guests who wish to ride to Tilghman Island or to the ferry that goes to Oxford. Gourmet breakfast is served in the dining room.

Historic Interest: Maritime Museum & Historic Boats (2 blocks), Town of Oxford (10 miles), Town of Easton (9 miles).

Innkeeper(s): Marcie Stalter. $100-195. MC, VISA, PC, TC. TAC10. 8 rooms with PB, 3 with FP. Breakfast included in rates. Types of meals: Gourmet bkfst. Beds: KQD. Ceiling fan and TV (two rooms) in room. Air conditioning. Bicycles on premises. Handicap access. Small meetings and family reunions hosted. Antiquing, fishing, Chesapeake Bay Maritime Museum, shopping and water sports nearby.

Publicity: *Philadelphia Inquirer Sunday Travel, Wilmington and Delaware News Journal.*

"Striking, extensively renovated."

Wades Point Inn on The Bay

PO Box 7, Wades Point Rd, McDaniel
Saint Michaels, MD 21663
(410)745-2500 (888)923-3466

Circa 1819. This waterfront organic farm is located on 120 acres and was named for Zachary Wade, who received the land grant in 1657. Thomas Kemp, a notable ship builder, built the house in 1819. The Kemp families' burial grounds are adjacent to the inn's mile-long walking trail. The trail passes the farm's crops and cultivated flowers and ponds. Deer, rabbit, fox, raccoons, bald eagles, blue heron, swans and osprey are often seen. There is a fishing pier. All  rooms afford a water view. Rooms are available in the historic main house and in an adjoining building with balconies and screened porches overlooking the Chesapeake Bay.

Innkeeper(s): The Feiler Family. $115-230. MC, VISA. 24 rooms, 17 with PB, 1 suite and 1 conference room. Breakfast included in rates. Beds: QDT.

Publicity: *Maryland Magazine, Travel & Leisure, Chesapeake Bay Magazine, Washingtonian and Mid-Atlantic Country.*

Scotland   E7

St. Michael's Manor B&B

50200 St Michael's Manor Way
Scotland, MD 20687-3107
(301)872-4025 Fax:(301)872-4025
E-mail: stmichaelsman@olg.com

Circa 1805. Twice featured on the Maryland House and Garden Tour, St. Michael's Manor is located on Long Neck Creek, a half-mile from Chesapeake Bay. The original hand-crafted woodwork provides a handsome backdrop for the inn's antique collection. A three-acre vineyard and swimming pool are on the property.

Historic Interest: Saint Mary's City, Sotterly Mansions, Old Mill & Country Store, Solomon's Island and Calvert Marine Museum, US Air Museum, Civil War Museum and Point Lookout State Park.

Innkeeper(s): Joe & Nancy Dick. $55-

85. PC, TC. 4 rooms. Breakfast included in rates. Types of meals: Gourmet bkfst, cont plus and early coffee/tea. Beds: QDT. Phone in room. Air conditioning. Fax, copier, swimming, bicycles, rowboat, canoe and paddleboat on premises. Weddings, small meetings, family reunions and seminars hosted. Antiquing, fishing, golf, crabbing, boats, live theater, parks, shopping, cross-country skiing, sporting events, tennis and water sports nearby.

Publicity: *Washington Post.*

"Your B&B was so warm, cozy and comfortable."

Sharpsburg   B5

The Inn at Antietam

220 E Main St, PO Box 119
Sharpsburg, MD 21782-0119
(301)432-6601 (877)835-6011
E-mail: innatantietam@juno.com
Web: www.innatantietam.com

Circa 1908. Eight acres of meadows surround this gracious Victorian framed by English walnut trees. A columned veranda provides a view of the countryside, the town with its old stone churches and the Antietam Battlefield. Gleaming floors accentuate romantically designed Victorian guest rooms, all with sitting rooms. The Smokehouse Suite offers a wide brick fireplace, a sleeping loft, refrigerator,  wet bar and television. The entire third floor comprises the Penthouse Suite, which features skylights, an enclosed balcony with views of the Blue Ridge Mountains and a spiral staircase that leads to a library. A solarium, library, parlor, patio and wide wraparound porches are gathering places.

Innkeeper(s): Bob LeBlanc & Charles Van Metre. $110-175. MC, VISA, AX. 5 suites, 1 with FP. Types of meals: Full bkfst. EP. Beds: Q. Parks nearby.

Publicity: *Country Inns.*

"A romantic setting and a most enjoyable experience."

Snow Hill   E9

Chanceford Hall B&B

209 W Federal St
Snow Hill, MD 21863-1159
(410)632-2900 Fax:(410)632-2479
E-mail: chancefordhall@chancefordhall.com
Web: www.chancefordhall.com

Circa 1759. Chanceford Hall is a gracious Greek Revival manor house. The inn is a National Historic Landmark that sits on an acre of landscaped grounds along the Pocomoke River. The gardens include one of the oldest black walnut trees in the state. Handsome architectural details are found throughout and include gleaming wide-plank floors and 10-foot-high ceilings. The inn has 10 working fireplaces and an inviting outdoor lap pool. The four large guest rooms-Chanceford, Chadwick, Cliveden and Conway-are decorated in antiques and include four-poster, queen-size beds. Elegantly served breakfasts include such fare as multi-grain pancakes, French toast, omelettes, fruit crisp, Italian strata and fresh scones.

Historic Interest: Furnace Town (5 miles), Julia Purnel Museum (1/2 mile).

Innkeeper(s): Alice Kesterson & Randy Ifft. $120-150. MC, VISA, TC. 4 rooms with PB, 3 with FP and 1 conference room. Breakfast and snacks/refreshments included in rates. Types of meals: Gourmet bkfst and veg bkfst. Beds: Q. Three with wood-burning fireplaces and sitting areas in room.

Central air. Fax, copier, swimming, bicycles and library on premises. Weddings, small meetings, family reunions and seminars hosted. Amusement parks, antiquing, art galleries, beaches, bicycling, canoeing/kayaking, fishing, golf, hiking, museums, parks, shopping and water sports nearby.

Publicity: *Washington Post, Daily Times, Washingtonian Magazine, Southern Living, Chesapeake Life Magazine, Baltimore Sun and WBOC-CBS affiliate.*

River House Inn

201 E Market St
Snow Hill, MD 21863-2000
(410)632-2722 Fax:(410)632-2866
E-mail: innkeeper@riverhouseinn.com
Web: www.riverhouseinn.com

Circa 1860. This picturesque Gothic Revival house rests on the banks of the Pocomoke River and boasts its own dock. Its two acres roll down to the river over long tree-studded lawns.

Lawn furniture and a hammock add to the invitation to relax as do the inn's porches. Some guest rooms feature faux marble fireplaces. The 17th-century village of Snow Hill boasts old brick sidewalks and historic homes. Canoes can be rented two doors from the inn.

Innkeeper(s): Larry & Susanne Knudsen. $140-220. MC, VISA, AX, DS, TC. TAC10. 10 rooms with PB, 8 with FP, 4 suites and 2 cottages. Breakfast and snacks/refreshments included in rates. Types of meals: Full bkfst and early coffee/tea. Beds: KQT. Ceiling fan in room. Air conditioning. VCR, fax, copier, bicycles, library and child care on premises. Handicap access. Weddings, small meetings and family reunions hosted. Amusement parks, antiquing, fishing, boating, canoeing, beaches, historic sites, shopping and water sports nearby.
Pets allowed: dogs welcome.

Publicity: *Newsday, Daily Times, Washington Times, Washingtonian, Washington Post, Los Angeles Times, Baltimore Sun and Southern Living.*

Solomons Island   E7

Solomons Victorian Inn

125 Charles Street
Solomons Island, MD 20688-0759
(410)326-4811 Fax:(410)326-0133
E-mail: info@solomonsvictorianinn.com
Web: www.solomonsvictorianinn.com

Circa 1906. The Davis family, renowned for their shipbuilding talents, constructed this elegant Queen Anne Victorian at the turn of the century. Each of the inn's elegant common rooms and bedchambers boasts special touches such as antiques,

Oriental rugs and lacy curtains. The inn's suites include whirlpool tubs. The home affords views of Solomons Harbor and its entrance into the picturesque Chesapeake Bay. Guests are treated to an expansive breakfast in a dining room, which overlooks the harbor.

Historic Interest: Historic Saint Mary's City is a half hour from the inn, while Washington, D.C., is just an hour away.

Innkeeper(s): Richard & Helen Bauer. $90-175. MC, VISA, AX, PC. 8 rooms with PB and 3 suites. Breakfast and snacks/refreshments included in rates. Types of meals: Full bkfst and early coffee/tea. Beds: KQ. Whirlpool tub in suite in room. Air conditioning. Fax and library on premises. Small meetings hosted. Antiquing, fishing, live theater, parks, shopping and water sports nearby.

"Instead of guests at a place of lodging, you made us feel like welcome friends in your home."

St. Michaels   C8

Barrett's Bed & Breakfast

204 N Talbot St
St. Michaels, MD 21663
(410)745-3322 Fax:(410)745-3888
E-mail: jwbarrett@yahoo.com
Web: www.barrettbb.com

Circa 1860. Located on Chesapeake Bay's eastern shore, this Colonial-style inn is perfect for a restful getaway or a romantic honeymoon. Furnished with antiques, the guest bedrooms boast fireplaces, handmade quilts, fresh flowers, candles, outside entrances and some feature double Jacuzzi tubs. A gourmet breakfast in the Tea Room may include bacon, egg and cheese souffle with fresh breads and jam, cereal and fruit. The rose garden is a pleasant diversion, or sit on the patio or shaded porch with wicker furniture. Ask about the many specialty packages offered that pamper and please.

Historic Interest: Chesapeake Bay Maritime Museum (1/4 mile).

$120-250. MC, VISA, AX, DS, PC, TC. TAC5. 7 rooms with PB, 7 with FP. Breakfast included in rates. Types of meals: Gourmet bkfst, early coffee/tea, afternoon tea and snacks/refreshments. Beds: Q. Cable TV, fireplace and double Jacuzzi tub in room. Central air. Fax, copier, spa and gift shop on premises. Family reunions hosted. Antiquing, art galleries, bicycling, canoeing/kayaking, fishing, golf, museums, parks and shopping nearby.

Sykesville   B6

Inn at Norwood

7514 Norwood Ave
Sykesville, MD 21784
(410)549-7868
E-mail: kelly@innatnorwood.com

Circa 1906. Romance is the trademark of this Colonial Revival home that sits in the center of Sykesville, a quaint town on the National Register of Historic Places. The front porch and cozy parlor are both perfects spots for relaxation. The guest bedrooms and suite are tastefully decorated to reflect the four seasons. They boast two-person Jacuzzi and clawfoot tubs, canopy and poster beds and some fireplaces. A three-course breakfast features homemade baked goods such as cinnamon applesauce cake, a house specialty, fresh fruit, bacon or apple sausage and an entree. A refreshment bar with snacks and beverages is always available. Stroll the landscaped grounds with a deck and tranquil pond.

Historic Interest: Town of Sykesville is in the National Register of Historic places, Gettysburg, PA (50 miles), Harpers Ferry, WV (50 miles).

Innkeeper(s): Kelly & Steve Crum. $90-150. MC, VISA, PC, TC. 4 rooms with PB, 2 with FP and 2 suites. Breakfast, afternoon tea and snacks/refreshments included in rates. Types of meals: Gourmet bkfst. Beds: Q. Cable TV, ceiling fan, VCR, fireplace and hot tub in room. Central air. Bicycles, library and hot tub on premises. Weddings, small meetings, family reunions and seminars hosted. Antiquing, bicycling, fishing, golf, hiking, live theater, museums and parks nearby.

Publicity: *Baltimore Sun and Carroll County Times.*

Thurmont
A5

Cozy Country Inn

103 Frederick Rd
Thurmont, MD 21788-1813
(301)271-4301 Fax:(301)271-4301
E-mail: cozyville@aol.com
Web: www.cozyvillage.com

Circa 1929. This Country Victorian-style inn has evolved into a unique destination point for travelers throughout the years. The six-acre village includes the inn, a restaurant with

seating capacity for 700 and a craft and antique village. Still operated by the founding family, the Cozy features lodging that pleases a variety of travelers. Many of the rooms are themed after past presidents. Memorabilia from nearby Camp David, past presidents and political dignitaries are displayed throughout.

Innkeeper(s): Jerry & Becky Freeze. $47-150. MC, VISA, AX, DS, TC. 21 rooms with PB, 5 with FP, 4 suites, 5 cottages and 5 conference rooms. Breakfast included in rates. Types of meals: Full bkfst, cont, lunch, picnic lunch, gourmet dinner and room service. EP. Beds: KQD. Cable TV, phone, VCR, Jacuzzi, robes, wet bars, hair dryers and towel warmers in room. Air conditioning. Fax and copier on premises. Handicap access. Weddings, small meetings, family reunions and seminars hosted. Antiquing, fishing, village of shops, presidential golf course, parks, downhill skiing, cross-country skiing and tennis nearby.

Tilghman
D7

Black Walnut Point Inn

Black Walnut Rd, PO Box 308
Tilghman, MD 21671
(410)886-2452 Fax:(410)886-2053
E-mail: mward@intercom.net
Web: www.tilghmanisland.com/blackwalnut

Circa 1843. Located on 57 beautiful acres set aside as a wildlife sanctuary, this handsome Colonial Revival manor commands waterfront views from its private peninsula location. Charter fishing and island river cruises can be arranged by the innkeepers. From its bayside hammock to its nature walk, swimming pool and tennis court, the inn provides an amazingly private getaway. Accommodations are in the main house as well as the Riverside Cottage. The Cove Cottage has its own kitchen and screened porch facing the river.

Innkeeper(s): Tom & Brenda Ward. $120-175. MC, VISA, PC, TC. 7 rooms with PB, 2 cottages and 1 conference room. Breakfast included in rates. Types of meals: Cont plus and early coffee/tea. Beds: Q. Air conditioning. Fax, copier, spa, swimming, tennis and library on premises. Small meetings, family reunions and seminars hosted. Antiquing, fishing, parks, shopping and water sports nearby.

Chesapeake Wood Duck Inn

Gibsontown Rd, PO Box 202
Tilghman, MD 21671
(410)886-2070 (800)956-2070 Fax:(413)677-7256
E-mail: woodduck@bluecrab.org
Web: www.woodduckinn.com

Circa 1890. This Tilghman Island Victorian overlooks Dogwood Harbor and a fleet of old wooden sailing vessels still used for oystering. A favorite breakfast is Jeff's fresh banana bread French toast with peaches and cinnamon cream and grilled smoked turkey sausage, served with fine china and fresh flowers in the formal dining room or the wicker-filled porch overlooking the water. Borrow bicycles or fishing gear or have the innkeepers arrange sunset sailing. The island is linked to the peninsula by a drawbridge.

Innkeeper(s): Kimberly, Jeffrey Bushey. $139-219. MC, VISA, PC. TAC10. 7 rooms. Breakfast included in rates. Types of meals: Gourmet bkfst and dinner. Beds: QD. Ceiling fan in room. Air conditioning. VCR and fax on premises. Small meetings, family reunions and seminars hosted. Spanish spoken. Antiquing, bicycling, canoeing/kayaking, fishing, golf, horseback riding, museums, parks, shopping and water sports nearby.

Vienna
D8

Tavern House

111 Water St, PO Box 98
Vienna, MD 21869-0098
(410)376-3347
E-mail: oldgod@shore.intercom.net

Circa 1730. Enjoy a wonderful view of the Nanticoke River and marshes while staying at this restored Colonial tavern. Authenticated colors and stark white lime, sand and hair plaster accent the carved details of the woodwork. The inn boasts six fireplaces including the cooking hearth in the cellar. More than a meal, the mouth-watering specialty breakfasts are a social affair. Explore the Eastern Shore from this excellent base. Visit interesting small towns, Blackwater Wildlife Refuge, the bay and the marshes of Dorchester.

Innkeeper(s): Harvey & Elise Altergott. $70-75. PC, TC. 4 rooms, 3 with PB, 2 with FP. Types of meals: Full bkfst. Ceiling fan in room. Air conditioning. Bicycling, canoeing/kayaking, fishing and bird watching nearby.

"Delightful and invigorating and as serene as the tide."

Wingate
E8

Wingate Manor Bed & Breakfast

2335 Wingate Bishops Head Rd
Wingate, MD 21675-2010
(410)397-8717 (888)397-8717
E-mail: bbwingate@aol.com

Circa 1897. Located near Blackwater National Wildlife Refuge, this waterfront Victorian was home to Phillip Wingate, a distinguished author and former vice-president of Du Pont. The Bay Room offers a panoramic view of the bay, one of the inn's ponds, Honga River and Lower Hooper's Island. Hearty breakfasts are served to fuel the adventurous cyclists, bird watchers and boaters who frequent the inn. At the boat ramp you can rent canoes, windsurfers, a hydro-bike and other water toys. Should you bring your own boat, you may enjoy another offering, a secluded cottage on the Choptank River with two acres of waterfront and a private dock.

Innkeeper(s): Leslie & Scott McCoy. $80-120. MC, VISA, AX, PC. 6 rooms, 1 with PB. Breakfast included in rates. Types of meals: Gourmet bkfst and gourmet dinner. Beds: KQDT. Phone and ceiling fan in room. Air conditioning. Bicycles, boats and bistro picnic lunches and bag lunches available on premises. Family reunions hosted. Antiquing, fishing, golf, birding, bicycling, live theater, parks, shopping and water sports nearby.

Pets allowed: no cats.

Publicity: *Washington Post and Baltimore Sun.*

Wittman

The Inn at Christmas Farm

8873 Tilghman island Rd
Wittman, MD 21676-1330
(410)745-5312 (800)987-8436 Fax:(410)745-5618
E-mail: xmasfarm@goeaston.net
Web: www.innatchristmasfarm.com

Circa 1800. Set on the water's edge at Cummings Creek, the Inn at Christmas Farm offers a combination of wildlife, farm animals and six exquisitely restored suites. The kitchen, dining room and two suites make up the main house originally built around 1800. One guest room, the Brother's Palmer's Still suite, is named for a still that had been concealed in a false ceiling during prohibition. The adjacent Christmas Cottage features a private entrance, fireplace and two-person Jacuzzi. Each suite in the St. James Chapel includes a fireplace, refrigerator and wet bar in the sitting room and deck or patio that overlooks the pond. A farm breakfast is served in the enclosed sun porch of the farm house overlooking the inn's "toy farm" that features horses, sheep, chickens and peacocks.

Innkeeper(s): Bea & David Lee. $179-195. MC, VISA, PC, TC. TAC10. 6 rooms with PB, 5 suites and 1 cottage. Breakfast included in rates. Types of meals: Full bkfst. Beds: K. Ceiling fan in room. Air conditioning. Fax and swimming on premises. Weddings, small meetings, family reunions and seminars hosted. Antiquing, bicycling, canoeing/kayaking, fishing, golf, sailing, live theater, museums, parks, shopping, tennis and water sports nearby.

Massachusetts

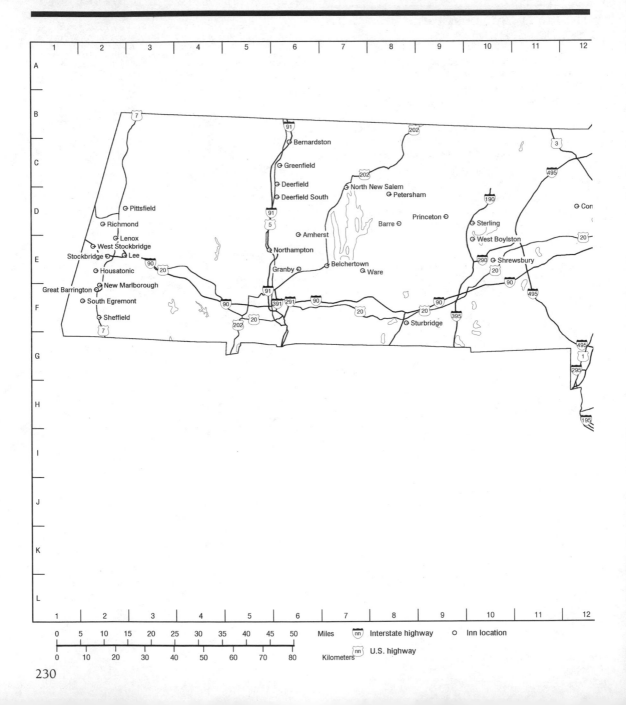

Miles

Kilometers

Interstate highway

U.S. highway

Inn location

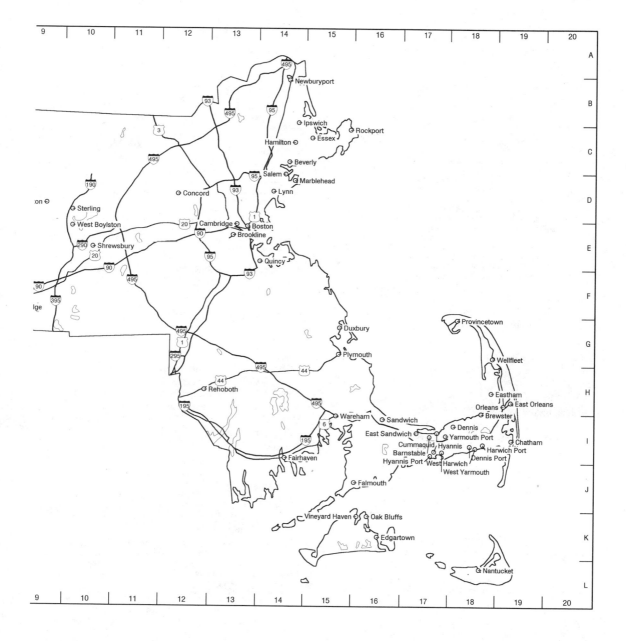

Amherst D6

Allen House Victorian Inn

599 Main St
Amherst, MA 01002-2409
(413)253-5000
E-mail: allenhouse@webtv.net
Web: www.allenhouse.com

Circa 1886. This stick-style Queen Anne is much like a Victorian museum with guest rooms that feature period reproduction wallpapers, pedestal sinks, carved golden oak and brass beds, painted wooden floors and plenty of antiques.

Among its many other treasures include Eastlake fireplace mantels. Unforgettable breakfasts include specialties such as eggs Benedict or French toast stuffed with rich cream cheese. Afternoon tea is a treat, and the inn offers plenty of examples of poetry from Emily Dickinson, whose home is just across the street from the inn.

Historic Interest: Aside from the Dickinson home, the area offers many museums and the inn is within walking distance of Amherst College, Hampshire College and the University of Massachusetts. Emily Dickinson Homestead (less than one-fourth mile), historic Deerfield (15 miles north), Norman Rockwell Museum and Tanglewood (less that 1 hour away).

Innkeeper(s): Alan & Amanda Zieminski. $75-175. PC, TC. 7 rooms with PB. Breakfast, afternoon tea and snacks/refreshments included in rates. Types of meals: Full bkfst and early coffee/tea. Beds: QDT. Phone, ceiling fan and down comforters & pillows in room. Air conditioning. Fax, copier and library on premises. Small meetings and seminars hosted. Amusement parks, antiquing, fishing, golf, live theater, parks, shopping, downhill skiing, cross-country skiing, sporting events, tennis and water sports nearby.
Publicity: *New York Times, Boston Magazine, Bon Appetit, Yankee Travel and Victorian Homes.*

"Our room and adjoining bath were spotlessly clean, charming, and quiet, with good lighting. Our meals were delicious and appetizing, and the casual, family-like atmosphere encouraged discussions among the guests."

Black Walnut Inn

1184 N Pleasant St
Amherst, MA 01002-1328
(413)549-5649
E-mail: bwalnut@mediaone.net
Web: www.blackwalnutinn.com

Circa 1745. This stately brick Federal-style inn is just three miles from Emily Dickinson's home and nine miles from the Smith College Museum of Art, which houses works by Picasso, Degas, Monet and Winslow. The inn sits on one and a half acres and is shaded by black walnut trees. Guests who stay there in October can have their fill of free walnuts. The yard is manicured and country flower gardens surround the home. The seven guest bedrooms are all soundproofed to accommodate children. Furnishings include antiques and period reproductions. Guests are served a continental plus breakfast that includes hot fruit pies and muffins, fresh squeezed orange juice and a choice of four different hot entrees. The inn has been featured in the New York Times; it received the 2000 Historical Preservation Award; and it won The Maine Yankee Editor's Pick Award.

Innkeeper(s): Dan Burbine. $115-180. AX, PC, TC. 7 rooms with PB. Breakfast and snacks/refreshments included in rates. Types of meals: Gourmet bkfst, veg bkfst, cont plus, cont, early coffee/tea and afternoon tea. Beds: KQT.

Cable TV, phone, VCR and some with desk in room. Central air. Fax and outdoor fireplace on premises. Small meetings and family reunions hosted. Antiquing, art galleries, beaches, bicycling, canoeing/kayaking, fishing, golf, hiking, museums, parks, shopping, sporting events and tennis nearby.
Publicity: *New York Times.*

Barnstable I17

Beechwood Inn

2839 Main St, Rt 6A
Barnstable, MA 02630-1017
(508)362-6618 (800)609-6618 Fax:(508)362-0298
E-mail: info@beechwoodinn.com
Web: www.beechwoodinn.com

Circa 1853. Beechwood is a beautifully restored Queen Anne Victorian offering period furnishings, some rooms with fireplaces or ocean views. Its warmth and elegance make it a favorite hideaway for couples looking for a peaceful and romantic return to the Victorian era. The inn is named for rare old beech trees that shade the veranda.

Historic Interest: Plymouth Rock (30 minutes), Kennedy Compound and JFK Monument (10 minutes), Oldest library in USA (walking distance).

Innkeeper(s): Debbie & Ken Traugot. $95-180. MC, VISA, AX, DS, PC, TC. TAC10. 6 rooms with PB, 3 with FP. Breakfast and afternoon tea included in rates. Types of meals: Full bkfst and early coffee/tea. Beds: KQD. Fans, wine glasses and corkscrew in room. Air conditioning. Fax, copier and bicycles on premises. Weddings, small meetings and family reunions hosted. French spoken. Antiquing, fishing, historic sites, whale watching, bird watching, horseback riding, live theater, parks, shopping, sporting events and water sports nearby.
Publicity: *National Trust Calendar, New England Weekends, Rhode Island Monthly, Cape Cod Life, Boston Magazine and Yankee Magazine.*

"Your inn is pristine in every detail. We concluded that the innkeepers, who are most hospitable, are the best part of Beechwood."

Cape Cod's Lamb and Lion

2504 Main St, Rt 6A, PO Box 511
Barnstable, MA 02630
(508)362-6823 (800)909-6923 Fax:(508)362-0227
E-mail: info@lambandlion.com
Web: www.lambandlion.com

Circa 1740. This rambling collection of Cape-style buildings sits on four acres overlooking the Old King's highway. Newly decorated, the inn offers a feeling of casual elegance. The Innkeeper's Pride is a romantic suite with sunken tub, fireplace, kitchenette and a deck overlooking a garden and woods. The Barn-stable is

one of the original buildings and now offers three sleeping areas, a living and dining area and French doors to a private patio. A large central courtyard houses a generous sized heated pool and hot tub spa.

Innkeeper(s): Alice Pitcher. $95-250. MC, VISA, PC, TC. TAC10. 10 rooms with PB, 7 with FP, 1 cottage and 1 conference room. Breakfast included in rates. Types of meals: Cont plus. Beds: KQDT. Cable TV, phone, VCR and fireplace in room. Air conditioning. Fax, copier, spa and swimming on premises. Weddings, small meetings, family reunions and seminars hosted. Antiquing, art galleries, beaches, bicycling, canoeing/kayaking, fishing, golf, hiking, horseback riding, live theater, museums, parks, shopping, cross-country skiing, sporting events, tennis, water sports and wineries nearby.
Pets allowed: Must be groomed prior to arrival. Must be leashed in common area.

Honeysuckle Hill B&B

591 Old Kings Hwy, Rt 6A
Barnstable, MA 02668
(508)362-8418 (866)444-5522 Fax:(508)362-8386
E-mail: stay@honeysucklehill.com

Circa 1810. This Queen Anne Victorian, which is listed in the National Register, is set on a picturesque acre with gardens. The interior is decorated with antiques and white wicker furnishings. The hearty breakfasts include items such as Captain's

Eggs, homemade granola, fresh fruit and cranberry-orange muffins. Nearby are the dunes of Sandy Neck Beach. Hyannis is 10 minutes away.

Historic Interest: Plimouth Plantation, Hyannisport, Sandwich Village, Plymouth Rock and Mayflower II.

Innkeeper(s): Bill & Mary Kilburn. $100-210. MC, VISA, AX, DS, PC, TC. 5 rooms, 4 with PB and 1 suite. Breakfast and snacks/refreshments included in rates. Types of meals: Gourmet bkfst and early coffee/tea. Beds: QD. Ceiling fan, feather beds, fresh flowers and terry cloth robes in room. Air conditioning. VCR, fax, copier, library, beach towels, chairs and umbrellas, guest refrigerator, fish pond, porch and gardens on premises. Antiquing, art galleries, beaches, bicycling, canoeing/kayaking, fishing, golf, hiking, beach, ferries, whale watching, live theater, museums, parks, shopping, tennis and wineries nearby.

Publicity: *Atlanta Constitution, Saint Louis Journal, Prime Time, Cape Cod Travel Guide, Cape Cod Life and Secondhome.*

"The charm, beauty, service and warmth shown to guests are impressive, but the food overwhelms. Breakfasts were divine!—Judy Kaplan, St. Louis Journal."

Barnstable, Cape Cod   I17

Ashley Manor Inn

3660 Olde Kings Hwy PO Box 856
Barnstable, Cape Cod, MA 02630
(508)362-8044 (888)535-2246
E-mail: stay@ashleymanor.net
Web: www.ashleymanor.net

Circa 1699. This manor house has lived through a succession of expansions, the first addition built in 1750. The final effect is wonderful and mysterious. The inn, thought to be a hiding place for Tories during the Revolutionary War, features a huge open-hearth fireplace with bee-

hive oven and a secret passageway connecting the upstairs and downstairs suites. The inn is reminiscent of a gracious English country house and is filled with Oriental rugs and antiques. All but one of the guest rooms boasts fireplaces, and four have large whirlpool baths. Two acres of manicured lawns include a regulation-size tennis court. Nature-lovers will enjoy the landscape, dotted with cherry and apple trees. The romantic gazebo is the perfect location to view the fountain garden. A full gourmet breakfast is served on the brick terrace or fireside in the formal dining room.

Historic Interest: Nantucket and Martha's Vineyard, Chatham, the National Seashore and Provincetown on the Cape.

Innkeeper(s): Kathy Callahan. $140-200. MC, VISA, AX, DS, PC, TC. TAC10. 6 rooms with PB, 5 with FP and 4 suites. Breakfast included in rates. Types of meals: Gourmet bkfst. Beds: KQ. Four with whirlpool baths, flowers, chocolates, beverages and coffee in room. Air conditioning. VCR, fax, tennis and library on premises. Small meetings, family reunions and seminars hosted. French spoken. Antiquing, art galleries, beaches, bicycling,

canoeing/kayaking, fishing, golf, hiking, horseback riding, historic sites, live theater, museums, parks, shopping, tennis, water sports and wineries nearby.

Publicity: *Chicago Tribune, Boston Globe, Bon Appetit, Tennis, New York Times, Pittsburgh Press, Gourmet, GBH and Newsday.*

"This is absolutely perfect! So many very special, lovely touches."

Barre   D8

Stevens Farm B&B

Old Coldbrook Rd
Barre, MA 01005
(978)355-2227 Fax:(978)355-2234

Circa 1789. Guests enjoy an old-fashioned country experience at Stevens Farm. The 18th-century farmhouse has been in the innkeepers' family for nine generations since 1789. Guests can

take tours of the 350-acre working farm, enjoy a swimming pool or just relax and enjoy the view from the gazebo. During the winter months,

guests can cross-country ski on the property or ice skate on the pond. Colorful, handmade Afghans and comfortable antiques decorate the bedchambers. The parlor features Victorian furnishings, an upright piano and a tin ceiling. The innkeeper once worked as a cook and professional baker and prepares the savory full breakfasts. Dinner, featuring items such as Yankee pot roast, homemade bread and cranberry walnut pie, can be arranged.

Historic Interest: Quark Walker slave grave, first all girls school, Sturbridge Village, Rocking Stone Park.

Innkeeper(s): Richard & Irene Stevens. $75-95. MC, VISA, AX, DC, DS, PC, TC. 5 rooms, 1 with PB and 1 conference room. Breakfast and afternoon tea included in rates. Types of meals: Full bkfst, cont plus, cont, early coffee/tea, picnic lunch, snacks/refreshments and room service. AP. Beds: D. Window fans in room. Weddings, small meetings, family reunions and seminars hosted. Antiquing, art galleries, bicycling, canoeing/kayaking, fishing, golf, hiking, horseback riding, live theater, museums, shopping, downhill skiing, cross-country skiing, tennis and wineries nearby.

Belchertown   E7

Ingate Farms B&B

60 Lamson Ave-S. Amherst Line
Belchertown, MA 01007-9710
(413)253-0440 (888)464-2832 Fax:(413)253-0440

Circa 1740. This Cape-style home was built as a bobbin factory, and eventually it was moved and reassembled at its current location on a 400-acre equestrian center. The interior is homey, with an emphasis on early American decor. Guests can relax on the enclosed porch, which is filled with comfortable furnishings. From the porch, guests can watch horses and enjoy the countryside. The grounds offer an Olympic-size swimming pool, hiking trails, and

guests can rent a boat and fish at nearby Quabbin Reservoir. Amherst and Hampshire colleges are nearby, as well as the University of Massachusetts at Amherst.

Innkeeper(s): Virginia Kier & Bill McCormick. $60-90. MC, VISA, AX, DS, PC, TC. 5 rooms, 3 with PB. Breakfast and afternoon tea included in rates. Types of meals: Cont plus and early coffee/tea. Beds: KQT. TV, phone, ceiling fan and ice Water in room. Air conditioning. VCR, fax, copier, swimming, stables, library, pressing/irons, hair dryers, riding and hiking trails, riding lessons and riding summer day camp for children ages 6-14 weekly or daily basis on premises. Family reunions hosted. Amusement parks, antiquing, fishing, golf, live theater, parks, shopping, downhill skiing, cross-country skiing, sporting events & tennis nearby.

"I've felt so at home here this week and also charmed by the calm and loveliness of this place."

Bernardston   C6

Falls River Inn

PO Box 762
Bernardston, MA 01337-9532
(413)648-9904 Fax:(413)648-0538
E-mail: flsrivin@javanet.com
Web: www.fallsriverinn.com

Circa 1905. Guests have been welcomed to this site since the late 18th century. The first inn burned down in the 1800s, and the current Federal-style Victorian inn was built in its place. Guests will find various styles of antiques in their comfortable, country rooms, five of which include a  fireplace. During the week, a continental breakfast is served, and on weekends, guests are treated to a full breakfast. The inn's restaurant is open Wednesday through Sunday, and features everything from chicken pot pie to pepper shrimp served on a bed of angel hair pasta and surrounded by an orange cream sauce. Don't forget to try the restaurant's signature "Vampire Chasers."

Innkeeper(s): Kerber Family. $70-170. MC, VISA, AX, DS. TAC10. 11 rooms with PB, 5 with FP. Breakfast included in rates. Types of meals: Country bkfst, lunch and dinner. Beds: KQDT. Ceiling fan in room. Air conditioning. Weddings, small meetings, family reunions and seminars hosted. Antiquing, bicycling, fishing, golf, hiking, live theater, parks, shopping, cross-country skiing, sporting events, tennis and water sports nearby.

Publicity: *Snow Country Magazine, America's Favorite and Franklin County Magazine.*

"The food was excellent, the rooms charming and clean, the whole atmosphere so relaxing."

Beverly   C14

Bunny's B&B

17 Kernwood Hgts
Beverly, MA 01915
(978)922-2392 Fax:(978)922-2392
E-mail: bbnb17@juno.com

Circa 1940. This Dutch Colonial inn is located on a scenic route along the state's northeastern coast. One room features a decorative fireplace and a handmade Oriental rug. Breakfasts in the formal dining room always feature homemade muffins and the innkeepers will make every effort to meet special dietary needs if notified in advance.

Innkeeper(s): Bunny & Joe Stacey. $75-150. PC, TC. 3 rooms, 1 with PB. Breakfast included in rates. Types of meals: Cont plus. Beds: QDT. Weddings, small meetings, family reunions and seminars hosted. Antiquing, historic sites, live theater, parks and shopping nearby.

Boston   E13

Host Homes of Boston

PO Box 117-Waban Branch
Boston, MA 02468-0001
(617)244-1308 (800)600-1308 Fax:(617)244-5156
E-mail: info@hosthomesofboston.com
Web: www.hosthomesofboston.com

Circa 1864. One of the many fine homes available through this reservation service includes a stately townhouse on Commonwealth Avenue in Boston's chic Back Bay, less than one block away from the Boston Common and a short walk to Copley Square. Host Homes offers a variety of vacation possibilities throughout the Boston area and its suburbs.

Historic Interest: Boston and its surrounding areas are full of historic sites. Each of the accommodations is near something unique.

Innkeeper(s): Marcia Whittington. $80-175. MC, VISA, AX, PC. 75 rooms. Breakfast included in rates. Types of meals: Cont plus. Beds: KT. Varies in room. Varies on premises. Antiquing, historic sites, whale watching, live theater, museums, shopping and sporting events nearby.

Publicity: *The Sunday Times, USA Today, What's Doing in Boston, BBC Holiday and Marie Claire.*

"Very special. I have never stayed at such an excellent, elegant B&B. Our hosts were delightful, the place, magnificent!"

Oasis Guest House

22 Edgerly Rd
Boston, MA 02115-3007
(617)267-2262 Fax:(617)267-1920
E-mail: oasisgh@tiac.net
Web: www.oasisgh.com

Circa 1885. Located in the Back Bay area of Boston, this historic row house offers an excellent location from which to enjoy the city. More than one half of the guest rooms include a private bath, and all are comfortably furnished with antiques and contemporary pieces. The home still maintains some of its Victorian features, including a grand fireplace in one of the common areas. Continental fare is available in the mornings.

Innkeeper(s): Joe Haley. $80-135. MC, VISA, AX. TAC10. 16 rooms, 10 with PB. Breakfast included in rates. Types of meals: Cont. Beds: QDT. Cable TV and phone in room. Air conditioning. Fax and copier on premises. Antiquing, live theater, museums, parks, shopping and sporting events nearby.

Brewster   H18

The Beechcroft Inn

1360 Main St
Brewster, MA 02631-1724
(508)896-9534 (877)233-2446
E-mail: info@beechcroftinn.com
Web: www.beechcroftinn.com

Circa 1828. Hospitality has been a tradition for more than 140 years at this delightful Greek Revival inn, which before that time was a church meeting house in idyllic Cape Cod. Special attention is given to personal touches that pamper and please.

 English antiques furnish the tastefully decorated guest bedrooms. Some boast a sitting area, private deck and offer a variety of views including the extensive gardens, famous beech tree and bay. A full breakfast is served on site in The Brewster Teapot, an authentic English tearoom. Complimentary evening wines and sherries are served in the living room. A croquet lawn is a new addition, and bicycles are available for local exploring.

Innkeeper(s): Jan & Paul Campbell. $115-165. MC, VISA, AX, DS. TAC10. 10 rooms with PB. Breakfast included in rates. Types of meals: Full bkfst, early coffee/tea, lunch and afternoon tea. Beds: KQDT. VCR and bicycles on premises. Weddings, small meetings, family reunions and seminars hosted. Antiquing, fishing, golf, live theater, parks, shopping and water sports nearby.

Candleberry Inn

1882 Main St
Brewster, MA 02631-1827
(508)896-3300 (800)573-4769 Fax:(508)896-4016
E-mail: candle@cape.com
Web: www.candleberryinn.com

Circa 1750. The two-acre grounds of this 250-year-old inn feature gardens complete with lawn swings. Wainscoting is dominant in the guest rooms, which feature Oriental rugs on top of pine-planked floors.

Antiques and family heirlooms decorate the inn. Three rooms include working fireplaces and one has a Jacuzzi. A full, gourmet breakfast is served in the dining room, which is also the inn's oldest room. The beach is less than a mile away, and Brewster offers many shops and restaurants.

Innkeeper(s): Gini & David Donnelly. $90-205. MC, VISA, AX, DS, PC, TC. 9 rooms with PB, 3 with FP and 2 suites. Breakfast included in rates. Types of meals: Gourmet bkfst. Beds: KQDT. Robes and hair dryers in room. Air conditioning. Fax and copier on premises. Family reunions hosted. Antiquing, fishing, golf, bike and nature trails, live theater, parks, shopping, tennis and water sports nearby.

Publicity: *Brewster Oracle and New York Times.*

"Wonderful, relaxing time, don't want to leave."

Old Manse Inn

1861 Main St PO Box 745
Brewster, MA 02631-0745
(508)896-3149 Fax:(508)896-1546
E-mail: oldmanse@cape.com
Web: www.oldmanseinn.com

Circa 1800. Built by sea Captain Winslow Lewis Knowles at the turn of the 19th century, this Federal-style bed and breakfast is run today by third-generation innkeepers and restaurateurs of the Old Manse, David and Susanne Plum. Graduates of the Culinary Institute of America, the Plums delight in creating tantalizing breakfast feasts for each of their guests and operate a restaurant out of the 50-seat dining area in the

evenings. Recently renovated, each of the eight guest rooms houses a pleasant combination of antique period pieces with complimentary new furnishings and a private bath. The Old Manse lies in the heart of Cape Cod's historic district and is considered by locals to be one of the town's proudest landmarks.

Innkeeper(s): David & Suzanne Plum. $105-125. MC, VISA, AX, DS. 8 rooms with PB. Types of meals: Full bkfst and gourmet dinner. Beds: QDT. Cable TV, phone and ceiling fan in room. Air conditioning. Weddings, small meetings and family reunions hosted. Antiquing, fishing, live theater and shopping nearby.

Publicity: *Travel & Leisure, Boston Herald and Boston Globe.*

"Our stays at the Old Manse Inn have always been delightful. The innkeepers are gracious, the decor charming and the dining room has a character all its own."

Old Sea Pines Inn

2553 Main St, PO Box 1026
Brewster, MA 02631-1959
(508)896-6114 Fax:(508)896-7387
E-mail: innkeeper@oldseapinesinn.com
Web: www.oldseapinesinn.com

Circa 1900. Formerly the Sea Pines School of Charm and Personality for Young Women, this turn-of-the-century mansion sits on three-and-one-half acres of trees and lawns. Recently renovated, the inn displays elegant wallpapers and a grand sweeping stairway. On Sunday

evenings, mid June through mid September, enjoy a dinner show in conjunction with Cape Cod Repertory Theatre. Beaches and bike paths are nearby, as are village shops and restaurants.

Historic Interest: Local Historic Registry.

Innkeeper(s): Michele & Stephen Rowan. $75-150. MC, VISA, AX, DC, DS. 24 rooms, 16 with PB, 2 with FP, 2 suites and 2 conference rooms. Breakfast and snacks/refreshments included in rates. Types of meals: Full bkfst, early coffee/tea, afternoon tea and room service. Beds: QDT. Cable TV in room. Air conditioning. Handicap access. Weddings, small meetings, family reunions and seminars hosted. Antiquing, fishing, dinner theatre in summer, live theater, shopping and water sports nearby.

Publicity: *New York Times, Cape Cod Oracle, For Women First, Home Office, Entrepreneur, Boston Magazine, Redbook, Travel & Leisure and Better Homes & Gardens-British Edition.*

"The loving care applied by Steve, Michele and staff is deeply appreciated."

Poore House Inn

2311 Main St
Brewster, MA 02631-1813
(508)896-0004 (800)233-6662

Circa 1837. Once home to Brewster's poor, this historic Greek Revival inn now offers comfortable quarters to inn visitors. Rooms are furnished with antiques and other eclectic stylings.

Guests will find shops, beaches and outstanding eateries within easy walking distance. Roland C. Nickerson State Park is in the immediate vicinity. Hiking and bike trails are nearby.

Innkeeper(s): Ken & Cherie Anderson. Call for rates. Family reunions hosted. Antiquing, beaches, live theater and shopping nearby.

"Thank you for super food, pristine surroundings and warm friendship."

Brookline   E13

Anthony's Town House

1085 Beacon St
Brookline, MA 02446
(617)566-3972 Fax:(617)232-1085
E-mail: info@anthonystownhouse.com
Web: www.anthonystownhouse.com

Circa 1890. Family-operated for more than 55 years, this authentically restored Brownstone town house is listed in the National Register. Centrally located, it is easily accessible from Logan Airport, which is six miles away, and close to the subway, buses and trains. Delightful guest bedrooms offer French Roccoco, Venetian and Victorian furnishings and decor.

Discover a variety of amenities that will enhance a pleasant stay. Visit the many famous sites of nearby Boston, known for its Freedom Trail walking tour. Enjoy activities from major league sports to acclaimed museums and everything in between.
Innkeeper(s): Viola & Barbara Anthony. $68-110. PC. TAC10. 14 rooms. Beds: QDT. Cable TV and clock in room. Air conditioning. VCR, fax and copier on premises. Antiquing, art galleries, beaches, bicycling, golf, live theater, museums, parks, shopping, sporting events and tennis nearby.

The Bertram Inn

92 Sewall Ave
Brookline, MA 02446-5327
(617)566-2234 (800)295-3822 Fax:(617)277-1887
E-mail: bertraminn@msn.com

Circa 1907. Antiques and authenticity are the rule at this turn-of-the-century Gothic Revival inn, found on a peaceful, tree-lined street two miles from central Boston. The Bertram Inn features old-English stylings and Victorian decor. Guests can enjoy

breakfast or afternoon tea by the fire in the common room or, if weather permits, on the front porch overlooking the garden. Boston College, Boston University, Fenway Park and the F.L. Olmstead National Historic Site all are nearby. Shops and

restaurants are within walking distance, and the Boston area's many attractions are nearby. Parking is included in the rates.
Historic Interest: Faneuil Hall and the Freedom Trail (10 minutes).
Innkeeper(s): Bryan Austin. $99-239. MC, VISA, AX, DC, DS, TC. TAC10. 14 rooms with PB, 2 with FP and 4 suites. Breakfast included in rates. Types of meals: Cont plus and afternoon tea. Beds: KQDT. Cable TV, phone and hair dryer in room. Air conditioning. Fax on premises. Spanish spoken. Sporting events nearby.
Pets Allowed.

"The Bertram Inn is a gem, and you may be sure I will highly recommend it to anyone coming this way. So pleased to have discovered you!"

Cambridge   E13

A Cambridge House B&B Inn

2218 Massachusetts Ave
Cambridge, MA 02140-1836
(617)491-6300 (800)232-9989 Fax:(617)868-2848
E-mail: innach@aol.com
Web: www.acambridgehouse.com

Circa 1892. Listed in the National Register, A Cambridge House has been restored to its turn-of-the-century elegance. A remarkable carved cherry fireplace dominates the den, and most rooms have four-poster canopy beds and fireplaces. The library is often the setting for mulled cider, hors d'oeuvres or tea served fireside on brisk afternoons. Parking is available and the subway is two blocks away.
Historic Interest: National Register.
Innkeeper(s): Ellen Riley. $109-275. MC, VISA, AX, DC, DS, PC, TC. TAC10. 15 rooms with PB, 11 with FP. Breakfast included in rates. Types of meals: Full bkfst. Beds: KQDT. Cable TV, phone and voice mail in room. Air conditioning. Fax and copier on premises. Italian & Portuguese spoken. Antiquing, live theater, parks, shopping and sporting events nearby.

Publicity: *Glamour, Los Angeles Times, Entrepreneur, Working Woman* and *Oprah Winfrey* show.

"I'm afraid you spoiled us quite badly! Your home is elegant, charming and comfortable. Breakfasts were delicious and beautifully served."

Harding House

288 Harvard St
Cambridge, MA 02139
(617)876-2888 Fax:(617)497-0953
E-mail: harding@irvinghouse.com

Circa 1867. Located in the mid-Cambridge area, this historic Victorian is within walking distance to Harvard Square, and guests can hop on the Red Line and head into Boston. The

guest rooms feature a comfortable decor and amenities include fax service and in-room hair dryers. A continental buffet is set up in the breakfast room. The owners also operate Irving House at Harvard.
Innkeeper(s): Rachael Solem. $79-290. MC, VISA, AX, DC, PC, TC. TAC10. 14 rooms with PB. Breakfast included in rates. Types of meals: Cont plus. Beds: QT. TV and phone in room. Air conditioning. Fax and limited parking on premises. Antiquing, historic tours, restaurants, shopping and sporting events nearby.

Irving House at Harvard

24 Irving Street
Cambridge, MA 02138-3007
(617)547-4600 (877)547-4600 Fax:(617)576-2814
E-mail: reserve@irvinghouse.com
Web: www.irvinghouse.com

Circa 1893. Irving House is located in a historic, turn-of-the-century Colonial Revival and has been receiving guests since the 1940s. The simple, comfortable rooms feature a modern hotel decor, and more than half include a private bath. In the mornings, a continental buffet with fruit, pastries and cereals is set up for guests to enjoy. Harvard Square is just minutes away, and guests can walk to the Red Line stop that goes into Boston.
Innkeeper(s): Patsy Yike. $75-200. MC, VISA, AX, DS, TC. TAC10. 44 rooms, 27 with PB and 1 conference room. Breakfast included in rates. Types of meals: Cont plus. Beds: QDT. Phone and TV in some rooms in room. Air conditioning. Fax and library on premises. Handicap access. Antiquing, bookstores, history, live theater, shopping and sporting events nearby.

The Mary Prentiss Inn

6 Prentiss St
Cambridge, MA 02140-2212
(617)661-2929 Fax:(617)661-5989
E-mail: njfandetti@aol.com
Web: www.maryprentissinn.com

Circa 1843. Only a half-mile from Harvard Square, this restored Greek Revival Inn features ionic fluted columns and Doric trim. During summer months, guests are treated to breakfast under umbrella-covered tables on the outdoor deck, while wintertime guests enjoy their morning fare in front of a roaring fire in the parlor room. Several of the unique guest rooms feature kitchenettes, three suites include a working fireplace. The inn was the winner of the Massachusetts Historic Commission Preservation Award.
Historic Interest: Cambridge offers no shortage of activities, including the Cambridge Common where George Washington took command of the Continental Army, and the church where he and wife, Martha, worshipped. Historic battlefields and Walden Pond are only a short drive away.
Innkeeper(s): Jennifer & Nicholas Fandetti. $99-229. MC, VISA, AX, PC, TC. TAC10. 20 rooms with PB, 3 with FP and 5 suites. Breakfast and afternoon tea included in rates. Types of meals: Full bkfst. Beds: QT. Cable TV, phone and ceiling fan in room. Air conditioning. Fax on premises. Handicap access. Weddings and family reunions hosted. Antiquing, golf, live theater, parks, shopping, sporting events, tennis and water sports nearby.
Publicity: *Cambridge Chronicle, Travel & Leisure, Discerning Traveler* and *Cambridge Current.*

"We thank you for the special privilege of staying at such a magnificent inn. We had a wonderful time, and you helped to make it so."

Prospect Place

112 Prospect St
Cambridge, MA 02139-2503
(617)864-7500 (800)769-5303 Fax:(617)576-1159
E-mail: prospectb-b@juno.com
Web: www.prospectpl.com

Circa 1866. This 5,000-square-foot Italianate Victorian was owned by the same family for more than 100 years (until 1994). Located in the heart of Cambridge, the inn is within walking distance of Harvard University, MIT and the Boston Freedom Train Trolley Tours. The inn, including its three guest bedrooms, has a Victorian décor that makes the most of an eclectic collection of antiques, including two grand pianos in the parlor. Period details are evident throughout the charming inn, from classic archways to cut-glass windows and extraordinary marble fireplaces. The delightful breakfast is served in the Victorian dining room and includes a variety of freshly baked breads, pastries, scones and muffins, a fresh-fruit bowl, juices and eggs to order. Afternoon tea is available upon request. After breakfast, guests can head out on foot or grab the subway or bus, which are just a few minutes' walk from the inn, and explore the area's rich history. Metropolitan Boston is just across the river from the inn.

Historic Interest: Boston Freedom Trail.
Innkeeper(s): Eric Huenneke. $85-160. MC, VISA, TC. 3 rooms, 1 with PB. Types of meals: Gourmet bkfst. Beds: KDT. Phone in room. Central air. Fax on premises. Antiquing, art galleries, beaches, live theater, museums, parks, shopping and sporting events nearby.

Cape Cod, Harwich Port   118

Augustus Snow House

528 Main St
Cape Cod, Harwich Port, MA 02646-1842
(508)430-0528 (800)320-0528 Fax:(508)432-6638
E-mail: info@augustussnow.com
Web: www.augustussnow.com

Circa 1901. This gracious, Queen Anne Victorian is a turn-of-the-century gem, complete with a wide, wraparound veranda, gabled windows and a distinctive turret. Victorian wallpapers, stained glass and rich woodwork complement the interior, which is appropriately decorated in period style. Each of the romantic

guest quarters offers something special. One room has a canopy bed and all rooms have fireplaces, while another includes a relaxing clawfoot tub. Three rooms have Jacuzzi tubs. The beds are dressed in fine linens. As is the Victorian way, afternoon refreshments are served each day. The breakfasts include delectables, such as banana chip muffins, baked pears in raspberry cream sauce or, possibly, baked French toast with layers of homemade cinnamon bread, bacon and cheese.

Innkeeper(s): Joyce & Steve Roth. $105-225. MC, VISA, AX, DS, PC, TC. 5 rooms with PB, 5 with FP. Breakfast included in rates. Types of meals: Gourmet bkfst and early coffee/tea. Beds: KQ. Cable TV, phone, ceiling fan and fireplace in room. Air conditioning. Fax and copier on premises. Weddings, small meetings and family reunions hosted. Antiquing, fishing, golf, private beach, restaurants, bike trails, bicycle rentals, parks, shopping and water sports nearby.

Chatham   119

The Bradford Inn of Chatham

26 Cross Street
Chatham, MA 02633
(508)945-1030 (800)562-4667 Fax:(508)945-9652
E-mail: bradford@bradfordinn.com
Web: www.bradfordinn.com

Circa 1860. A village-like atmosphere is found at the Bradford Inn, created by its variety of buildings, including some newer additions constructed to blend in with the historic surroundings. There are two acres of gardens and winding pathways. Guest rooms are decorated in Colonial style. Several offer four-poster beds, fireplaces, whirlpool tubs, private balconies or terraces, and there are suites with separate parlors. Hardwood floors, some antiques, handsome draperies and bed covers enhance the decor. A heated outdoor pool is popular. Chatham, a Cape Cod town, offers shops, restaurants and galleries.

Innkeeper(s): Sharon Loeffler. $105-425. MC, VISA, DS, TC. TAC10. 38 rooms with PB. Breakfast included in rates. Types of meals: Cont and snacks/refreshments. EP. Beds: KQ. Cable TV, phone and VCR in room. Air conditioning. Fax, copier and swimming on premises. Handicap access. Small meetings and seminars hosted. Antiquing, fishing, golf, beaches, live theater, shopping, tennis and water sports nearby.

Captain's House Inn

369-377 Old Harbor Rd
Chatham, MA 02633
(508)945-0127 (800)315-0728 Fax:(508)945-0866
E-mail: info@captainshouseinn.com
Web: www.captainshouseinn.com

Circa 1839. A white picket fence opens to an inviting estate on two manicured acres of English gardens and perfect lawns. Romantic accommodations offer lavishly decorated rooms with amenities such as four-poster canopy beds, fireplaces, and Jacuzzis located in one of the inn's historic buildings: the Carriage House, the Captain's Cottage, the Mansion or the magically transformed Stables. A favorite choice is the Lydia Harding Suite in the former stables. It offers two rooms with French doors opening to a balcony, two fireplaces, a lavish bath and several sitting areas. Afternoon tea and a deluxe gourmet breakfast is served in the dining room with views to the fountain and gardens. The innkeepers, one a native of Britain, also own a 16th-century coaching inn near Oxford and enjoy sharing their experiences and knowledge of both areas with their guests. Specially prepared picnics are available along with beach chairs, towels and coolers, and there are bicycles to borrow. Be sure to take advantage of the innkeepers excellent concierge services to maximize your experience while on the Cape.

Historic Interest: Atwood House (1 mile), Chatham Lighthouse (2 miles).
Innkeeper(s): Dave & Jan McMaster. $185-400. MC, VISA, AX, DS, PC, TC. TAC10. 16 rooms with PB, 15 with FP and 4 suites. Breakfast, afternoon tea and snacks/refreshments included in rates. Types of meals: Gourmet bkfst, veg bkfst, early coffee/tea and room service. Beds: KQ. Cable TV, phone, turndown service, ceiling fan, VCR and fireplace in room. Air conditioning. Fax, copier, spa, bicycles, library and gift shop on premises. Handicap access. Family reunions hosted. Antiquing, art galleries, beaches, bicycling, canoeing/kayaking, fishing, golf, hiking, horseback riding, whale watching, live theater, museums, parks, shopping, tennis, water sports and wineries nearby.
Publicity: *Providence Journal, Cape Cod Life, Cape Cod Travel Guide, Country Inns, Toronto Sun, Cosmopolitan, Elle, Featured on Best Inns of New England on Cable TV Network, HGTV and Food TV.*

Carriage House Inn

407 Old Harbor Rd
Chatham, MA 02633-2322
(508)945-4688 (800)355-8868 Fax:(508)945-8909
E-mail: carriageh@capecod.net

Circa 1890. This graceful Cape inn offers a tasteful traditional decor with antiques and family pieces. Pristine rooms offer a light and airy ambiance. The carriage house rooms each include a fireplace and an entrance to an outside sitting area.

Breakfast items such as fresh fruit, juices, pancakes, French toast, eggs Benedict and quiche can be enjoyed either in the dining room or on the sun porch. Guests can walk to Chatham's Main Street and its shops and galleries, or just relax and enjoy the grounds, which include flower-filled gardens and shaded sitting areas. Beach towels are furnished for trips to the shore, just a quarter mile away.

Historic Interest: Cape Cod National Seashore (20 minutes).
Innkeeper(s): Patty & Dennis O'Neill. $105-195. MC, VISA, AX, DS, PC, TC. TAC10. 6 rooms with PB, 3 with FP. Breakfast and snacks/refreshments included in rates. Types of meals: Full bkfst and early coffee/tea. Beds: Q. Ceiling fan in room. Air conditioning. Antiquing, fishing, hiking, live theater, parks, shopping and water sports nearby.

"This might well have been our best B&B experience ever. It was the hosts who made it so memorable."

Chatham Wayside Inn

512 Main St PO Box 685
Chatham, MA 02633-2239
(508)945-5550 (800)391-5734 Fax:(508)945-3407
E-mail: info@waysideinn.com
Web: www.waysideinn.com

Circa 1860. For well over a century, guests have been staying at this historic inn, which served originally as a stagecoach stop. The inn's Main Street address offers an ideal location for enjoying the Cape Cod village of Chatham. The individually appointed guest rooms are designed in a romantic mix of Colonial and English country styles. A dozen rooms include a fireplace. Canopy and four-poster beds, as well as whirlpool tubs, are some of the romantic offerings. There is a veranda lined with wicker chairs, and the inn also offers an outdoor heated swimming pool. The inn has a full-service restaurant, and the menu is filled with traditional New England fare, including fresh local seafood.

Innkeeper(s): Shane Coughlin. $95-365. MC, VISA, DS, TC. TAC10. 56 rooms with PB. Types of meals: Gourmet bkfst, lunch and dinner. EP. Beds: KQ. Cable TV, phone and VCR in room. Air conditioning. Fax, copier and swimming on premises. Handicap access. Weddings, family reunions and seminars hosted. Antiquing, fishing, golf, beaches, live theater, parks, shopping and tennis nearby.

The Cranberry Inn of Chatham

359 Main St
Chatham, MA 02633-2425
(508)945-9232 (800)332-4667 Fax:(508)945-3769
E-mail: info@cranberryinn.com
Web: www.cranberryinn.com

Circa 1830. Continuously operating for over 150 years, this inn originally was called the Traveler's Lodge, then the Monomoyic after a local Indian tribe. An un-harvested cranberry bog adjacent to the property inspired the current name.

Recently restored, the inn is located in the heart of the historic district. It's within walking distance of the lighthouse, beaches, shops and restaurants. Guest rooms feature four-poster beds, wide-planked floors and coordinated fabrics. Antique and reproduction furnishings throughout.

Innkeeper(s): Kay & Bill DeFord. $110-270. MC, VISA, PC, TC. TAC5. 18 rooms with PB, 8 with FP and 2 suites. Breakfast and afternoon tea included in rates. Types of meals: Gourmet bkfst. Beds: QDT. Private balconies and wet bars and fireplaces in some rooms in room. Fully licensed tavern on premises. Antiquing, art galleries, bicycling, fishing, golf, live theater, parks and sporting events nearby.
Publicity: *Country Inns, Cape Cod Life and Cape Cod Travel Guide.*

Cyrus Kent House

63 Cross St
Chatham, MA 02633-2207
(508)945-9104 (800)338-5368 Fax:(508)945-9104
E-mail: cyrus@cape.com
Web: www.capecodtravel.com/cyruskent

Circa 1877. A former sea captain's home, the Cyrus Kent House was built in the Greek Revival style. The award-winning restoration retained many original features such as wide pine floorboards, ceiling rosettes, and marble fireplaces. Although furnished with antiques and reproductions, all modern amenities are available. Most bedrooms have four-poster beds. Suites feature sitting rooms with fireplaces. Chatham's historic district is a short stroll away.

Innkeeper(s): Steve & Sandra Goldman. $95-290. MC, VISA, AX. 10 rooms with PB. Breakfast and afternoon tea included in rates. Types of meals: Cont plus and early coffee/tea. Beds: QD. Cable TV and phone in room. Fax on premises. Weddings, small meetings, family reunions and seminars hosted. Antiquing, beaches, fishing, shopping and water sports nearby.
Publicity: *Country Inns.*

Moorings

326 Main St
Chatham, MA 02633-2428
(508)945-0848 (800)320-0848 Fax:(508)945-1477
E-mail: moorings@capecod.net

Circa 1864. This Italianate mansion with a Tuscan porch in the old village district of Chatham was once owned by Admiral Charles H. Rockwell, USN. In summer, the garden at the entrance is a riot of flowers with blooms climbing up the structure of the gazebo. The manicured lawn is visited by rabbits, which munch on the flowers. Fifteen guest bedrooms, some with fireplaces, are a perfect retreat from today's hectic world. Breakfast is served in the gazebo, and consists of delicious courses such as freshly ground coffee or a hot beverage with pancakes, breakfast puddings, orange or cranberry juice, fruit cup or plate, and a hot entrée for instance, zucchini/cheese strata, ham and baked apple. Guests may eat their fill and then borrow some of the inns many bikes and tour the historic town and the glorious oceanfront, or they may simply take a short walk to the beach.

$80-165. MC, VISA, AX, DS, PC, TC. 15 rooms with PB, 5 with FP, 3 suites and 1 cottage. Breakfast included in rates. Types of meals: Gourmet bkfst. Beds: KQDT. Cable TV, phone, ceiling fan and VCR in room. Central air. Fax and bicycles on premises. Family reunions hosted. Antiquing, art galleries, beaches, bicycling, canoeing/kayaking, fishing, golf, horseback riding, whale watching, live theater, museums, parks, shopping, sporting events and tennis nearby.

Moses Nickerson House

364 Old Harbor Rd
Chatham, MA 02633-2374
(508)945-5859 (800)628-6972 Fax:(508)945-7087
E-mail: tmnhi@mediaone.net
Web: www.capecodtravel.com/mosesnickersonhouse

Circa 1839. This historic, rambling sea captain's house, built
in 1839, features wide pine floors, many fireplaces and colorful gardens. Unforgettably charming, the inn is decorated with
antique furnishings and Oriental rugs, retaining the character
of by-gone days. Each of the
rooms offers its own distinctive
decor. Breakfast is served in a
glass-enclosed dining area that
radiates morning sunlight. The
inn provides an ambiance of
simple elegance.

Innkeeper(s): Linda & George Watts. $99-199. MC, VISA, AX, DS, PC, TC. 7
rooms with PB, 3 with FP. Breakfast included in rates. Types of meals: Full
bkfst. Beds: KQ. Cable TV, phone, ceiling fan and fireplace in room. Air conditioning. VCR, library, hair dryer, beach towels and beach chairs on premises. Family reunions and seminars hosted. Antiquing, beaches, fishing, golf,
whale watching, National Seashore, seal tours, live theater and tennis nearby.
Publicity: Cape Cod Life and The Discerning Traveler.

"The attention to detail in unsurpassed."

Port Fortune Inn

201 Main St
Chatham, MA 02633-2423
(508)945-0792 (800)750-0792
E-mail: porfor@capecod.net

Circa 1910. The fronts of these charming Cape Cod buildings
are decorated with colorful flowers and plants. The interior of
each of the inn's two historic buildings is elegant and inviting
with traditional furnishings, and most of the guest
rooms are decorated with four-poster beds. The
breakfast room and some of the guest
rooms have ocean views. The
grounds include perennial gardens
and a patio set up with furniture
for those who wish to relax and
catch a few sea breezes. The inn is featured on the walking tour
through the historic Old Village, which is Chatham's oldest
neighborhood. Port Fortune Inn is a short walk away from
beaches and the historic Chatham Lighthouse.

Innkeeper(s): Mike & Renee Kahl. $100-200. MC, VISA, AX. 13 rooms with
PB. Breakfast included in rates. Types of meals: Cont plus and early
coffee/tea. Beds: Q. Phone and some with TV in room. Air conditioning. Fax,
copier, library and beach towels and chairs on premises. Amusement parks,
antiquing, fishing, golf, whale watching, live theater, parks, shopping, tennis
and water sports nearby.

"Excellent. The entire experience was wonderful as usual."

Concord   D12

Colonel Roger Brown House

1694 Main St
Concord, MA 01742-2831
(978)369-4580 (800)292-1369 Fax:(978)369-1305
E-mail: innkeeper@colrogerbrown.com

Circa 1775. This house was the home of Minuteman Roger
Brown, who fought the British at the Old North Bridge. The frame
for this center-chimney Colonial was being raised on April 19,

1775, the day the battle took place.
Some parts of the house were built
as early as 1708. Among the
many nearby historic sites are Thoreau's
Walden Pond, the Concord
Museum, the Alcott House, Old
North Bridge, Lexington, the
National Heritage Museum, Lowell Mills and much more.

Historic Interest: Thoreau's Walden Pond, Concord Museum, Alcott House,
Wayside, Old Manse, Old North Bridge (all 3 miles), Lexington, National Heritage
Museum (11 miles), Lowell Mills and national historic district (15 miles).
Innkeeper(s): Lauri Berlied. $85-165. MC, VISA, AX, PC, TC. TAC5. 5 rooms
with PB and 2 suites. Breakfast and afternoon tea included in rates. Types of
meals: Cont plus. Beds: QDT. Cable TV, phone, color TV and refrigerator upon
request in room. Air conditioning. Fax, copier, library and data port on premises. Family reunions and seminars hosted. Antiquing, fishing, live theater,
parks, shopping, downhill skiing, cross-country skiing and water sports nearby.
Publicity: Middlesex News, Concord Journal and Washingtonian.

*"The Colonel Roger Brown House makes coming to Concord even
more of a treat! Many thanks for your warm hospitality."*

Hawthorne Inn

462 Lexington Rd
Concord, MA 01742-3729
(978)369-5610 Fax:(978)287-4949
E-mail: hawthorneinn@concordmass.com
Web: www.concordmass.com

Circa 1870. Share the joy of history, literature, poetry and artwork at this intimate New England bed & breakfast. For 25 years,
the inn's ambiance has imparted the spirit of writers and philos-
phers such as the Alcotts, Emerson, Hawthorne and Thoreau,
who once owned and walked the
grounds. Antique furnishings, weav-
ings, hardwood floors, a welcoming
fireplace and stained-glass windows
all exude a wonderful warmth and
gentility. Enjoy afternoon tea on a
rustic garden bench in the shade of

aged trees and colorful plants. The area offers woods to explore,
rivers to canoe, a quaint village with museums, infamous Sleepy
Hollow Cemetary, and untold treasures.

Historic Interest: Old North Bridge and Walden Pond are just a few minutes away.
Innkeeper(s): Marilyn Mudry & Gregory Burch. $175-275. MC, VISA, AX,
DS, PC, TC. TAC10. 7 rooms with PB. Breakfast and afternoon tea included
in rates. Types of meals: Cont plus. Beds: QDT. Phone in room. Air conditioning. Fax, library and piano on premises. Weddings, small meetings and family
reunions hosted. Antiquing, fishing, authors homes, parks, shopping and
cross-country skiing nearby.
Publicity: Yankee, New York Times, Los Angeles Times, Le Monde, Early
American Life, Evening and National Geographic Traveler.

*"Surely there couldn't be a better or more valuable location for a
comfortable, old-fashioned country inn."*

Cummaquid   I17

The Acworth Inn

4352 Old Kings Hwy, PO Box 256
Cummaquid, MA 02637
(508)362-3330 (800)362-6363
E-mail: host@acworthinn.com

Circa 1860. This inn, located on the Olde Kings Highway on the
north side of Cape Cod, offers a strategic midway point for those
exploring the area. The historic Cape-style farmhouse features five
guest rooms, including a luxury suite. Hand-painted, restored fur-

niture adds charm to the inn's interior. Guests select from the Cummaquid, Chatham, Yarmouth Port, Barnstable and Orleans rooms, all named for Cape Cod villages. Visitors will find the shore just a half-mile from the inn.

Historic Interest: Sturgis Library (2 miles away in Barnstable), Old Colonial Courthouse. Route 6A is part of America's largest historic district.
Innkeeper(s): Joan Tognacci. $95-185. MC, VISA, AX, DS, PC, TC. 5 rooms with PB, 2 with FP. Breakfast included in rates. Types of meals: Full bkfst and afternoon tea. Beds: QT. Newspaper on premises. German spoken. Antiquing, fishing, live theater, museums, parks, shopping and water sports nearby.
Publicity: *Boston, Connecticut and Cape Cod Life.*

"Great accommodations, food, tour guiding, local flavor, etc...We will be back."

Deerfield   C6

Deerfield Inn

81 Old Main St
Deerfield, MA 01342-0305
(413)774-5587 (800)926-3865 Fax:(413)775-7221
E-mail: information@deerfieldinn.com
Web: www.deerfieldinn.com

Circa 1884. The village of Deerfield was settled in 1670. Farmers in the area still unearth bones and ax and arrow heads from French/Indian massacre of 1704. Now, 50 beautifully restored 18th- and 19th-century homes line the mile-long main street, considered by many to be the loveliest street in New England. Fourteen of these houses are museums of Pioneer Valley decorative arts and are open year-round to the public. The Memorial Hall Museum, open from May to November, is the oldest museum in New England and full of local  antiquities. The inn is situated at the center of this peaceful village, and for those who wish to truly experience New England's past, this is the place. The village has been designated a National Historic Landmark.

Innkeeper(s): Jane & Karl Sabo. $188-255. MC, VISA, AX. 23 rooms with PB and 1 conference room. Breakfast and afternoon tea included in rates. Types of meals: Full bkfst, lunch and dinner. Beds: KQT. TV in room. Fax and copier on premises. Handicap access. Antiquing, fishing, live theater and cross-country skiing nearby.
Publicity: *Travel Today, Colonial Homes, Country Living, Country Inns B&B, Yankee and Romantic Homes.*

"We've stayed at many New England inns, but the Deerfield Inn ranks among the best."

Deerfield South   C6

Deerfield's Yellow Gabled House

111 N Main St
Deerfield South, MA 01373-1026
(413)665-4922

Circa 1800. Huge maple trees shade the yard of this historic house, four miles from historic Deerfield and one mile from Route 91. Decorated with antiques, the bed chambers feature coordinating bedspreads and window treatments. One suite includes a sitting room, and canopy beds are another romantic touch. Breakfasts include items such as three-cheese stuffed

French toast, an apple puff or fresh fruit topped with a yogurt-cheese sauce. The home is near historic Deerfield, and guests can walk to restaurants. The battle of Bloody Brook Massacre in 1675 occurred at this site, now landscaped with perennial English gardens. Yankee Candle is only one-half mile away and Historic Deerfield is only three miles away.

Innkeeper(s): Edna Julia Stahelek. $75-125. 3 rooms, 1 with PB. Breakfast included in rates. Types of meals: Gourmet bkfst and early coffee/tea. Beds: QT. Cable TV, phone and ceiling fan in room. Air conditioning. VCR on premises. Small meetings and family reunions hosted. Antiquing, bicycling, fishing, restaurants, live theater, shopping, downhill skiing, cross-country skiing and sporting events nearby.
Publicity: *Recorder, Boston Globe and Springfield Republican.*

"We are still speaking of that wonderful weekend and our good fortune in finding you."

Dennis   I18

Isaiah Hall B&B Inn

152 Whig St, PO Box 1007
Dennis, MA 02638
(508)385-9928 (800)736-0160 Fax:(508)385-5879
E-mail: info@isaiahhallinn.com
Web: www.isaiahhallinn.com

Circa 1857. Adjacent to the Cape's oldest cranberry bog is this Greek Revival farmhouse built by Isaiah Hall, a cooper. His grandfather was the first cultivator of cranberries in America and Isaiah designed and patented the original barrel for shipping cranberries. In 1948, Dorothy Gripp, an artist, established the inn. Many examples of her artwork remain. The inn  is located in the heart of the Cape and within walking distance to beaches, Dennis village and the Cape Playhouse.

Historic Interest: Cape Playhouse (one-third mile), Old Kings Highway (one-third mile), Old Salt Works (2 miles).
Innkeeper(s): Dick & Marie Brophy. $111-188. MC, VISA, AX, DS, TC. TAC10. 9 rooms, 10 with PB, 1 with FP and 1 suite. Breakfast included in rates. Types of meals: Cont plus and early coffee/tea. Beds: KQDT. Cable TV and phone in room. Air conditioning. Fax on premises. Antiquing, fishing, golf, whale watching, bike paths, live theater, parks, shopping and water sports nearby.
Publicity: *Cape Cod Life, New York Times, Golf and National Geographic Traveler.*

"Your place is so lovely and relaxing."

Scargo Manor Bed & Breakfast

909 Main St, Rt 6A
Dennis, MA 02638-1405
(508)385-5534 (800)595-0034 Fax:(508)385-9791
E-mail: scargomanor@mediaone.net
Web: www.scargomanor.com

Circa 1895. A sea captain built Scargo Manor, just before the turn of the 19th century. The six guest rooms and two suites of this Cape Cod inn are decorated with New England-style furnishings, such as canopy or four-poster beds. The suites include a separate sitting area. All rooms include amenities such as mini refrigerators, irons and ironing boards and hairdryers. The innkeepers provide homemade breads and freshly brewed coffee for early risers. Later, a gourmet breakfast is served, with items such as eggs Benedict or stuffed French toast. The innkeepers can supply guests with kayaks, a canoe or a small sailboat. Lawn games, such as croquet and badminton are available, as well.

Innkeeper(s): Rich & Lin Foa. $90-195. MC, VISA, AX, DC, DS, PC, TC. 6 rooms with PB, 1 with FP and 2 suites. Breakfast and snacks/refreshments included in rates. Types of meals: Gourmet bkfst and early coffee/tea. Beds: KQT. Cable TV, iron, ironing board, hair dryer and fireplace in room. Air conditioning. Fax, swimming, bicycles, kayaks, canoe, small sailboat and lawn games on premises. Weddings, small meetings, family reunions and seminars hosted. Italian and French spoken. Antiquing, art galleries, beaches, bicycling, canoeing/kayaking, fishing, golf, hiking, live theater, museums, parks, shopping, tennis and water sports nearby.

Dennis Port   I18

By The Sea Guests Bed & Breakfast & Suites

57 Chase Ave
Dennis Port, MA 02639-2627
(508)398-8685 (800)447-9202 Fax:(508)398-0334
E-mail: bythesea@capecod.net
Web: www.bytheseaguests.com

Circa 1890. Guests can pass their time lounging on the private beach that adjoins this historic, oceanfront inn. A huge wrap-around porch is a favorite spot to enjoy views of Nantucket Sound. The porch is also the location where breakfast is served. The interior is decorated with a mix of traditional and New England country furnishings and appointments. Some rooms offer an ocean view. Several rooms can accommodate more than two guests. Two rooms include relaxing, soaking tubs. The current innkeepers are the second generation to welcome guests to this seaside home.
$78-165. MC, VISA, AX, DC, CB, TC. 12 rooms with PB and 5 suites. Breakfast and snacks/refreshments included in rates. Types of meals: Cont plus, early coffee/tea and afternoon tea. Beds: QDT. Cable TV and ceiling fan in room. Fax, copier and swimming on premises. Greek, French and German spoken. Antiquing, art galleries, beaches, bicycling, canoeing/kayaking, fishing, golf, hiking, horseback riding, live theater, museums, parks, shopping, tennis, water sports and wineries nearby.

Rose Petal B&B

152 Sea St PO Box 974
Dennisport, MA 02639-2404
(508)398-8470
E-mail: info@rosepetalofdennis.com
Web: www.rosepetalofdennis.com

Circa 1872. Surrounded by a white picket fence and picturesque gardens, the Rose Petal is situated in the heart of Cape Cod. The Greek Revival-style home was built for Almond Wixon, who was a Mayflower descendant and member of a prominent seafaring family. His homestead has been completely restored and offers guest rooms with spacious private baths. Home-baked pastries highlight a

full breakfast served in the dining room. Walk through the historic neighborhood past century-old homes to Nantucket Sound's sandy beaches.
Historic Interest: JFK Museum, family compound (10 miles).
Innkeeper(s): Gayle & Dan Kelly. $79-115. MC, VISA, AX. 3 rooms with PB. Breakfast included in rates. Types of meals: Gourmet bkfst and early coffee/tea. Beds: QT. Air conditioning. Family reunions hosted. Some French spoken. Antiquing, fishing, whale watching, live theater, parks, shopping and water sports nearby.

"Perfect. Every detail was appreciated."

Duxbury   G15

The Winsor House Inn

390 Washington St
Duxbury, MA 02332-4552
(781)934-0991 Fax:(781)934-5955

Circa 1803. A visit to this inn is much like a visit back in time to Colonial days. The early 19th-century home was built by a prominent sea captain and merchant, Nathaniel Winsor, as a wedding gift for his daughter, Nancy. With an eye for the authen-

tic, the innkeepers have restored parts of the inn to look much the way it might have when the young bride and groom took up residence. Rooms are decorated with Colonial furnishings, canopied beds and fresh flowers. Guests may enjoy a drink or a casual dinner at the inn's English-style pub. For a romantic dinner, try the inn's Dining Room, which serves everything from roasted venison with a juniper berry and mushroom crust to herb-seared salmon with plum tomato saffron vinaigrette.
Historic Interest: Plimoth Plantation, Mayflower and Plymouth Rock, 15 minutes away. Twenty miles to Cape Cod.
Innkeeper(s): David and Patricia O'Connell. $140-210. MC, VISA, AX, DS, PC, TC. 4 rooms with PB and 2 suites. Breakfast included in rates. Types of meals: Full bkfst, picnic lunch and dinner. Beds: QT. Fax and copier on premises. Small meetings and family reunions hosted. Antiquing, fishing, Plymouth, shopping, cross-country skiing and water sports nearby.
Publicity: *Colonial Homes.*

East Orleans   H19

The Nauset House Inn

143 Beach Rd, PO Box 774
East Orleans, MA 02643
(508)255-2195 Fax:(508)240-6276
E-mail: info@nausethouseinn.com

Circa 1810. Located a 1/2 mile from Nauset Beach, this inn is a renovated farmhouse set on three acres, which include an old apple orchard. A Victorian conservatory was purchased from a Connecticut estate and reassembled here, then filled with wicker furnishings, Cape flowers and stained glass. Hand-stenciling, handmade quilts, antiques and more bouquets of flowers decorate the rooms. The breakfast room features a fireplace, brick floor and beamed ceiling.

Breakfast includes treats such as ginger pancakes or waffles with fresh strawberries. Wine and cranberry juice are served in the evenings.
Innkeeper(s): Al & Diane Johnson, John & Cindy Vessella. $75-150. MC, VISA, DS, PC, TC. 14 rooms, 8 with PB and 1 cottage. Breakfast and snacks/refreshments included in rates. Types of meals: Full bkfst, early coffee/tea and afternoon tea. Beds: KQDT. Terry robes for shared bath guests in room. Antiquing, fishing, biking, tennis, ocean, golf, live theater, parks, shopping, sporting events and water sports nearby.
Publicity: *Country Living, Glamour, West Hartford News and Travel & Leisure.*

"The inn provided a quiet, serene, comforting atmosphere."

The Parsonage Inn

202 Main St, PO Box 1501
East Orleans, MA 02643
(508)255-8217 (888)422-8217 Fax:(508)255-8216
E-mail: innkeeper@parsonageinn.com

Circa 1770. Originally a parsonage, this Cape-style home is now a romantic inn nestled in the village of East Orleans and only a mile and a half from Nauset Beach. Rooms are decorated with antiques, quilts, Laura Ashley fabrics and stenciling, and they include the original pine floors  and low ceilings. Freshly baked breakfasts are served either in the dining room or on the brick patio. The innkeepers keep a selection of menus from local restaurants on hand and serve appetizers and refreshments each evening while guest peruse their dining choices. The Parsonage is the perfect location to enjoy nature, with the national seashore, Nickerson State Park and whale-watching opportunities available to guests.

Historic Interest: Cape Cod offers plenty of historic homes and sites.
Innkeeper(s): Ian & Elizabeth Browne. $120-145. MC, VISA, AX. 8 rooms with PB and 2 suites. Breakfast included in rates. Beds: QDT. TV, phone and ceiling fan in room. Air conditioning. Fax, refrigerator in parlor and piano on premises. Antiquing, restaurants, live theater, shopping and water sports nearby.
Publicity: Conde Nast Traveler and Bon Appetit.

"Your hospitality was as wonderful as your home. Your home was as beautiful as Cape Cod. Thank you!"

Ship's Knees Inn

186 Beach Rd, PO Box 756
East Orleans, MA 02643
(508)255-1312 Fax:(508)240-1351
E-mail: capecodtravel.com/shipskneesinn
Web: capecodtravel.com/shipskneesinn

Circa 1820. This 180-year-old restored sea captain's home is a three-minute walk to the ocean. Rooms are decorated in a nautical style with antiques. Several rooms feature authentic ship's knees, hand-painted trunks, old clipper ship models and four-poster beds. Some  rooms boast ocean views, and the Master Suite has a working fireplace. The inn offers swimming and tennis facilities on the grounds. About three miles away, the innkeepers also offer three rooms, a bedroom efficiency apartment and two heated cottages on the Town Cove. Head into town, or spend the day basking in the beauty of Nauset Beach with its picturesque sand dunes.

Innkeeper(s): Pat & Tom Como. $55-140. MC, VISA. TAC10. 19 rooms, 9 with PB, 1 with FP. Breakfast included in rates. Types of meals: Cont. Beds: KQDT. Weddings, small meetings and family reunions hosted. Amusement parks, antiquing, fishing, live theater, parks, shopping and water sports nearby.
Publicity: Boston Globe.

"Warm, homey and very friendly atmosphere. Very impressed with the beamed ceilings."

East Sandwich
I17

Wingscorton Farm Inn

Rt 6A, Olde Kings Hwy
East Sandwich, MA 02537
(508)888-0534

Circa 1763. Wingscorton is a working farm on 13 acres of lawns, gardens and orchards. It adjoins a short walk to a private ocean beach. This Cape Cod manse, built by a Quaker family, is a historical landmark on what once was known as the King's Highway, the oldest historical district in the United States. All the rooms are furnished with antiques and working fireplaces (one with a secret compartment where runaway slaves hid). Breakfast features fresh produce with eggs, meats and vegetables from the farm's livestock and gardens. Pets and children welcome.

Innkeeper(s): Sheila Weyers & Richard Loring. $125-175. MC, VISA, AX, PC, TC. TAC10. 7 rooms, 7 with FP, 4 suites and 2 cottages. Breakfast included in rates. Types of meals: Gourmet bkfst. Beds: QDT. TV in room. Swimming, library, child care and private beach on premises. Weddings, small meetings and family reunions and seminars hosted. Antiquing, fishing, live theater, parks, shopping, downhill skiing, cross-country skiing, sporting events and water sports nearby. Pets Allowed.
Publicity: US Air and Travel & Leisure.

"Absolutely wonderful. We will always remember the wonderful time."

Eastham
H18

Over Look Inn, Cape Cod

3085 County Rd, PO Box 771
Eastham, MA 02642-0771
(508)255-1886 Fax:(508)240-0345
E-mail: stay@overlookinn.com

Circa 1869. Schooner Captain Barnabus Chipman built this three-story home for his wife. In 1920 it opened as an inn and was frequented by author and naturalist Henry Beston as he wrote "The Outermost House." Located on three acres of grounds, the inn is furnished with Victorian antiques.

Historic Interest: Coast Guard Beach (1 mile), Nauset Lighthouse (2 miles), Cape Cod National Seashore Museum (one-fourth mile).
Innkeeper(s): Don & Pam Andersen. $95-195. MC, VISA, AX, DC, CB, DS. TAC10. 14 rooms with PB. Breakfast and afternoon tea included in rates. Types of meals: Full bkfst. Beds: QDT. Antiquing, fishing, biking, live theater, parks and water sports nearby.
Publicity: Conde Nast Traveler, Victorian Homes, New York Times, Cape Code Life and Outside.

"A delightful experience."—Max Nichols, Oklahoma City Journal Record

Penny House Inn

4885 County Rd, PO Box 238
Eastham, MA 02651
(508)255-6632 (800)554-1751 Fax:(508)255-4893
E-mail: pennyhouse@aol.com
Web: pennyhouseinn.com

Circa 1690. In the early 1980s, this former 17th-century sea captain's home was carefully restored and renovated into a memorable country inn. Retaining its Colonial heritage, the great room and dining room feature 200-year-old ceiling beams and traditional wide-plank floors. Choose among an assortment of amenities in some of the guest rooms, including fireplaces, whirlpool tubs, plush robes, VCRs, refrigerators and coffeemakers. Enjoy a hearty country breakfast each morning. Afternoon tea with fresh baked goods are served in the sunroom. Secluded on two picturesque acres, the inn is conveniently located near beaches, fishing, boating, bike trails, whale watching and Audubon Sanctuary.

Innkeeper(s): Margaret & Rebecca Keith. $150-285. MC, VISA, AX, DS, PC, TC. TAC10. 12 rooms with PB, 4 with FP, 2 suites and 1 conference room. Breakfast and afternoon tea included in rates. Types of meals: Full bkfst and early coffee/tea. Beds: KQT. Phone, hairdryers. some with fireplace, cable TV, VCR, Coffeemakers, refrigerator, whirlpool tubs and plush robes in room. Air conditioning. VCR, fax and copier on premises. Weddings, small meetings, family reunions and seminars hosted. Antiquing, bicycling, fishing, hiking, boating, health club, restaurants, live theater, parks, shopping and tennis nearby.

Publicity: *Cape Cod Life and Cape Codder.*

"Enjoyed my stay tremendously. My mouth waters thinking of your delicious breakfast."

Edgartown   K16

Chadwick Inn

67 Winter St
Edgartown, MA 02539
(508)627-4435 Fax:(508)627-5656
Web: www.chadwickinn.com

Circa 1840. The winding staircase in this Greek Revival house was crafted by the carpenter who built the Edgartown Old Whaling Church tower. You may wish to stay in the original house, or newer Manor House with its high ceilings, fireplaces and balconies, or in the

Garden Wing. Numerous shops and galleries are just down the block.

$99-399. MC, VISA. 24 rooms with PB, 12 with FP, 5 suites and 1 conference room. Types of meals: Cont. Beds: KQT. TV and phone in room. Fax and copier on premises. Antiquing, bicycling, fishing, golf and water sports nearby.

Publicity: *Cape Cod Life.*

"Wonderful hospitality. I hated to leave, it's such a comfortable, caring inn."

Charlotte Inn

27 S Summer St
Edgartown, MA 02539
(508)627-4751

Circa 1864. Shaded by linden and chestnut trees and just minutes from the historic town center, this white clapboard merchant's house is a combination of old-world charm and modern-day elegance. To maintain

its historic character, the inn remains purposely behind the times. The inn features 19th-century American and English art, Oriental rugs and crystal chandeliers. Richly paneled

mahogany walls, antique fixtures, standing clocks and converted gas lamps add to the inn's natural romantic ambiance. Guest rooms are accented with late 19th-century English antiques, down comforters and four-poster beds. The inn's restaurant features a combination of continental cooking with traditional New England ingredients from the fields, streams and sea.

Innkeeper(s): Gery & Paula Conover. $250-850. 23 rooms and 2 suites. Breakfast included in rates. Types of meals: Cont. Cable TV and phone in room. Air conditioning.

Colonial Inn of Martha's Vineyard

38 N Water St, PO Box 68
Edgartown, MA 02539-0068
(508)627-4711 (800)627-4701 Fax:(508)627-5904
E-mail: info@colonialinnmvy.com
Web: www.colonialinnmvy.com

Circa 1911. This impressive Colonial structure has served as an inn since opening its doors in 1911. Somerset Maugham and Howard Hughes were among the regulars at the inn. Guests at Colonial Inn can sit back and relax on a porch lined with rockers as they gaze at the harbor and enjoy refreshing sea breezes. Flowers, an atrium and courtyards decorate the grounds. The inn has a full-service restaurant, a hair salon, spa facility, art gallery and several boutiques on the premises. Some guest rooms boast harbor views, and all are decorated in an elegant country style. The inn is located in the heart of the town's historic district.

Innkeeper(s): CJ Rivard. $115-400. MC, VISA, AX, TC. TAC10. 43 rooms with PB, 5 suites and 2 conference rooms. Breakfast included in rates. Types of meals: Cont and dinner. Beds: QD. Cable TV, phone, VCRs, some with refrigerators and central heat in room. Air conditioning. Fax and library on premises. Handicap access. Small meetings and seminars hosted. Portuguese and Spanish spoken. Antiquing, art galleries, bicycling, fishing, golf, concerts, swimming, live theater, parks, shopping, tennis and water sports nearby.

Publicity: *Glamour, Vineyard Gazette and Mitsubishi commercials.*

Edgartown Inn

56 N Water
Edgartown, MA 02539
(508)627-4794

Circa 1798. The Edgartown Inn originally was built as a home for whaling Captain Thomas Worth. (Fort Worth, Texas, was named for his son.) The house was converted to an inn around 1820, when Daniel Webster was a guest. Nathaniel Hawthorne stayed here while writing much of his "Twice Told Tales." He proposed to the innkeeper's daughter Eliza Gibbs (who turned him down). Later, John Kennedy stayed at the inn as a young senator.

Innkeeper(s): Earle Radford. $100-220. 20 rooms, 16 with PB. Beds: KQD. Antiquing, fishing, live theater and water sports nearby.

Publicity: *Vineyard Gazette.*

The Kelley House

23 Kelly Street
Edgartown, MA 02539-0037
(508)627-7900 (800)225-6005 Fax:(508)627-8142
Web: www.kelley-house.com

Circa 1742. Located in the heart of both downtown Edgartown and the historic district, this is one of the island's oldest inns. Over the years, four additional buildings have been added, all maintaining the inn's colonial style. It has recently been extensively restored and refurbished. Rooms include many modern amenities, such as television, radio and iron with ironing board. There is a swimming pool. Private parking is another plus. The inn is open from May through October.

Innkeeper(s): Marica Helliwell. $185-800. MC, VISA, AX. TAC10. 53 rooms. Breakfast included in rates. Types of meals: Cont. EP. TV and irons and ironing boards in room. Air conditioning. Swimming and private parking on premises. "News from America" pub on site nearby.

Publicity: *Boston Globe and Boston Magazine.*

Essex
C15

George Fuller House

148 Main St, Rt 133
Essex, MA 01929-1304
(978)768-7766 (800)477-0148 Fax:(978)768-6178

Circa 1830. This three-story, Federal-style home is situated on a lawn that reaches to the salt marsh adjoining the Essex River. Original Indian shutters and Queen Anne baseboards remain. Guest accommodations boast Boston rockers, canopy beds and fireplaces. Belgian waffles and praline French toast are a house specialty. Many of the town's 50 antique shops are within walking distance of the inn.

Innkeeper(s): Kathy, Ryan & Michael. $115-225. MC, VISA, AX, DS, PC. TAC10. 7 rooms with PB, 5 with FP. Breakfast and afternoon tea included in rates. Types of meals: Full bkfst. Beds: KQDT. Cable TV and phone in room. Air conditioning. Fax on premises. Family reunions hosted. Antiquing, fishing, live theater, shopping, cross-country skiing and water sports nearby.
Publicity: *Gloucester Times, Yankee Traveler, Discerning Traveler, Internet and Cape Ann.*

"Thank you for the wonderful time we had at your place. We give you a 5-star rating!"

Fairhaven
I14

Fairhaven Harborside Inn & Spa

One Main St
Fairhaven, MA 02719-2907
(508)990-7760 (888)575-STAY Fax:(508)990-7722
E-mail: fhi@mediaone.net
Web: www.fairhavenharborsideinn.com

Circa 1912. As its name suggests, this red brick Colonial inn sits right on the waterfront. The Grand Foyer highlights a regal staircase with an Oriental carpet runner. The Bradford Sitting Room, named after world-renowned artist William Bradford who originally had his studio on this site, is ideal for chatting by the fire or watching TV. Period furniture including brass and four-poster wooden beds accent the spacious guest bedrooms that feature tasteful quilts and elegant wallpapers. A changing breakfast of the day is offered in addition to a continental breakfast served in the banquet-size formal dining room or glass-enclosed wraparound porch/function room where the views of the harbor are spectacular. Enjoy two acres of landscaped grounds. Plans are to add a Spa with Jacuzzi, sauna and pool.

Historic Interest: Whaling Museum (1.5 miles), Unitarian Church and Town Hall Fort Phoenix (waling distance).
Innkeeper(s): Sandra & Stephen Ledogar. $85-145. MC, VISA, AX, DC, CB, DS, PC, TC. 6 rooms, 5 with PB and 1 suite. Breakfast included in rates. Types of meals: Gourmet bkfst and afternoon tea. Beds: Q. Ceiling fan and hair dryer in room. Fax, copier, swimming, sauna, tennis and gift shop on premises. Antiquing, art galleries, beaches, bicycling, canoeing/kayaking, fishing, golf, hiking, horseback riding, live theater, museums, parks, shopping, tennis, water sports and wineries nearby.

Falmouth
J16

Copper Beech

105 Locust St
Falmouth, MA 02540
(508)540-5588 (877)540-5588

Circa 1800. This 200-year-old, 20,000-square-foot Queen Anne Shingle-style inn stands a scant mile from the ocean in Falmouth's historic district. First built in 1800 by housewright Thatcher Lewis, the inn was altered in 1881 by architect Frank Hill Smith.

It was one of his first Shingle-style buildings. A majestic old Copper Beech tree stands in the side yard. The inn is listed in the National Register and features original wood floors, fancy brickwork in the fireplaces and Queen Anne windows with the original glass panes. It has six guest bedrooms and one suite, most with fireplaces and all decorated with antiques and collectibles and stocked with fluffy robes and fresh flowers. Some of the bedsteads have been in the home for a century. Guests are invited to use the kitchen for lunch and snacks, and an afternoon tea is offered. A full gourmet breakfast is served beside the fireplace in the elegant dining room. Breakfast fare includes such items as fresh fruit in raspberry sauce, apple strudel, vanilla cream French toast with bacon and juices. Horseshoes, croquet and bocci-ball are available on the manicured grounds. Bicycles are available for guests' use on the shining Sea Bike Path just steps from the inn. Beach towels and sand chairs are provided for those headed to the beach. Guests may take the ferry to Martha's Vineyard or Nantucket, visit Provincetown and go whale watching or just explore the beaches of the Cape Cod National Seashore.

Innkeeper(s): The Walsh Family. $85-165. MC, VISA, AX, DS, TC. 6 rooms with PB and 1 suite. Breakfast included in rates. Types of meals: Gourmet bkfst. Beds: QD. Cable TV, VCR, robes and fresh flowers in room. Central air. Bicycles, beach towels and sand chairs on premises. Small meetings and family reunions hosted. Antiquing, art galleries, beaches, bicycling, canoeing/kayaking, fishing, golf, hiking, horseback riding, live theater, museums, parks, shopping, tennis, water sports and wineries nearby.
Publicity: *Cape Cod Life.*

The Inn at One Main Street

1 Main St
Falmouth, MA 02540-2652
(508)540-7469 (888)281-6246
E-mail: innat1main@aol.com

Circa 1892. In the historic district, where the road to Woods Hole begins, is this shingled Victorian with two-story turret, an open front porch and gardens framed by a white picket fence. It first became a tourist house back in the '50s. Cape Cod cranberry pecan waffles and gingerbread pancakes with whipped cream are favorite specialties. Within walking distance, you'll

find the Shining Sea Bike Path, beaches, summer theater, tennis, ferry shuttle and bus station. The innkeepers are available to offer their expertise on the area.

Innkeeper(s): Ilona & Bill Geise. $80-150. MC, VISA, AX, DS, PC, TC. 6 rooms with PB. Breakfast included in rates. Types of meals: Full bkfst. Beds: QT. Ceiling fan in room. Air conditioning. Antiquing, bike path, ferries to islands, Woods Hole Oceanographic Institute, live theater, shopping and water sports nearby.

"The art of hospitality in a delightful atmosphere, well worth traveling 3,000 miles for."

La Maison Cappellari at Mostly Hall

27 Main St
Falmouth, MA 02540-2652
(508)548-3786 (800)682-0565 Fax:(508)457-1572
E-mail: mostlyhall@aol.com

Circa 1849. In the historic district off Falmouth Village green, a secluded Italianate Villa listed in the National Register sits on more than an acre of park-like gardens and landscaped grounds.

Built for a sea captain's bride, Mostly Hall was aptly named after the home's spacious central hallways. All of the guest bedrooms feature canopy beds, mural paintings, idyllic sitting areas and hand-painted furniture. In the fireplaced living room or on the veranda, feast on a delicious breakfast that may include seafood, European cheeses, pastries and fruit. Bicycles are available to explore the area, take the ferry to Martha's Vineyard or enjoy the many sites and activities of Cape Cod.

Historic Interest: The birthplace of Kathryn Lee Bates, author of "America the Beautiful," is across the street. Plymouth and Plimoth Plantation is 35 miles, and the Kennedy Museum and Monument in Hyannisport is 23 miles.
Innkeeper(s): Christina & Bogdan Simcic. $185-225. MC, VISA, AX, DS, PC, TC. 6 rooms with PB. Breakfast and afternoon tea included in rates. Types of meals: Gourmet bkfst and early coffee/tea. Beds: Q. Ceiling fan and two comfortable reading chairs in room. Central air. VCR, fax, bicycles, library and gazebo on premises. German spoken. Antiquing, art galleries, beaches, bicycling, golf, Martha's Vineyard ferries, restaurants, island ferries, nature trails, live theater, shopping and tennis nearby.
Publicity: *Bon Appetit, Boston Globe, Yankee Magazine "Editor's Pick." and Discovery "Seekers of Lost Treasure"*

"Of all the inns we stayed at during our trip, we enjoyed Mostly Hall the most. Imagine, Southern hospitality on Cape Cod!"

Village Green Inn

40 Main St
Falmouth, MA 02540-2667
(508)548-5621 (800)237-1119 Fax:(508)457-5051
E-mail: vgi40@aol.com
Web: www.villagegreeninn.com

Circa 1804. The inn, listed in the National Register, originally was built in the Federal style for Braddock Dimmick, son of Revolutionary War General Joseph Dimmick. Later, "cranberry king" John Crocker moved the house onto a granite slab foundation, remodeling it in the Victorian style. There are inlaid floors, large porches and gingerbread trim.

Historic Interest: Plimoth Plantation and Heritage Plantation are nearby.
Innkeeper(s): Diane & Don Crosby.
$90-225. MC, VISA, AX, TC. TAC10. 5 rooms with PB, 2 with FP and 1 suite. Breakfast and afternoon tea included in rates. Types of meals: Full bkfst, early coffee/tea and snacks/refreshments. Beds: Q. Cable TV, phone, ceiling fan and hair dryers in room. Air conditioning. Bicycles on premises. Small meetings and family reunions hosted. Antiquing, fishing, golf, whale watching, live theater, parks, shopping and water sports nearby.
Publicity: *Country Inns, Cape Cod Life, Yankee, London Observer, Escape and New York Magazine.*

"Tasteful, comfortable and the quintessential New England flavor ... You have turned us on to the B&B style of travel and we now have a standard to measure our future choices by."

Wildflower Inn

167 Palmer Ave
Falmouth, MA 02540-2861
(508)548-9524 (800)294-5459 Fax:(508)548-9524
E-mail: wldflr167@aol.com
Web: www.wildflower-inn.com

Circa 1898. This three-story Victorian combines modern amenities with the inn's original architectural character. Gleaming wood floors throughout are topped by Oriental rugs and period antiques. All second-floor and third-floor guest rooms are uniquely decorated for romance and comfort. For a

more intimate stay, the inn offers its Loft-Cottage that boasts a private entrance, porch, a full kitchen and a spiral staircase leading to a romantic loft bedroom. Breakfast includes edible flowers and features stuffed lemon

pancakes, blueberry country flower muffins and pansy butter. The inn is a short walk to the Village Green, restaurants and the shuttle to island ferries.
Innkeeper(s): Phil & Donna Stone. $95-225. MC, VISA, AX, TC. TAC10. 6 rooms with PB, 1 suite and 1 cottage. Breakfast, afternoon tea and snacks/refreshments included in rates. Types of meals: Gourmet bkfst and early coffee/tea. Beds: QT. Ceiling fan and whirlpool in room. Air conditioning. VCR, fax, copier and bicycles on premises. Antiquing, fishing, golf, ferry to Martha's Vineyard, live theater, shopping, tennis and water sports nearby.
Publicity: *Cape Cod Times, Cape Cod Travel Guide, Romantic Homes Magazine, Honeymoon Magazine, Yankee-Blue Ribbon and PBS.*

Woods Hole Passage B&B Inn

186 Woods Hole Rd
Falmouth, MA 02540-1670
(508)548-9575 (800)790-8976 Fax:(508)540-4771
E-mail: inn@woodsholepassage.com

Circa 1880. This Cape Cod-style carriage house was moved more than 50 years ago to its present site, surrounded by trees and wild berry bushes. The home's common area provides a spacious, comfortable setting, while guest quarters feature country decor. Breakfasts often are served on the patio, which overlooks the

one-and-a-half-acre grounds or in the garden. Items such as homemade breads, fresh fruit and quiche are among the fare. It's just a short walk through the woods to the beach. A bike path, Martha's Vineyard, an aquarium, shopping and restaurants are just a few of the nearby attractions.
Innkeeper(s): Deb Pruitt. $85-165. MC, VISA, AX, DC, DS, PC, TC. TAC10. 5 rooms with PB. Breakfast and afternoon tea included in rates. Types of meals: Gourmet bkfst and early coffee/tea. Beds: Q. Ceiling fan and sitting area in room. Air conditioning. Fax, copier, tennis and library on premises. Small meetings, family reunions and seminars hosted. Antiquing, fishing, golf, live theater, parks, shopping and water sports nearby.

Falmouth Heights　　　　　J16

Grafton Inn

261 Grand Ave S
Falmouth Heights, MA 02540-3784
(508)540-8688 (800)642-4069 Fax:(508)540-1861
E-mail: alamkid@aol.com
Web: www.graftoninn.com

Circa 1870. If you want to enjoy grand ocean views while staying at an inn in Cape Cod, this is the place. Oceanfront and within walking distance to the ferries, the inn is an ideal place to hop on board a ferry and spend a day on Nantucket Island or Martha's Vineyard and return that evening to relax and watch the moon over the ocean from your bedroom window. Snacks of wine and cheese are served in the afternoon. The inn is often seen on television and ESPN because of its unique loca-

tion at the final leg of the Falmouth Road Race.

Historic Interest: Plimoth Plantation (30 miles), Heritage Plantation (15 miles), Bourne Farm (6 miles).

Innkeeper(s): Liz & Rudy Cvitan. $110-235. MC, VISA, AX, TC. 11 rooms with PB. Breakfast included in rates. Beds: KQD. Cable TV, ceiling fan, bathrobes and makeup mirrors in room. Air conditioning. Fax, swimming, library and sand chairs on premises. Small meetings hosted. Antiquing, fishing, live theater, parks, shopping and water sports nearby.

Publicity: *Enterprise, At Your Leisure, Cape Cod Life, Cape Cod Times and Cape Cod Travel Guide.*

"*You have certainly created a lovely inn for those of us who wish to escape the city and relax in luxury.*"

Granby E6

An Old Indian Trail Bed & Breakfast

664 Amherst Road
Granby, MA 01033
(413)467-3528
E-mail: reispd@mediaone.net
Web: bbonline.com/ma/oit

Circa 1944. This impressive Colonial stone home and cottages are located in a quaint rural setting at the base of the Holyoke Mountain Range. The bed & breakfast offers the best of both worlds with its Amherst location and its proximity to the nearby Five College area of New England. A comfortable blend of contemporary country decor is interspersed with fine artwork throughout the inn. Plenty of good books are found in the living room for relaxed reading. The guest bedrooms, suites and cottages are bright and cheery, some with cozy fireplaces. A wonderful breakfast is served in the dining room of the main house or can be happily delivered. Choose the delicious special of the day from a menu that offers hot and cold selections.

Historic Interest: Emily Dickinson House (5 miles), Skinner Museum (3 miles).
Innkeeper(s): Peter & Dolores Reis. $85-135. MC, VISA, AX, DC, DS, PC, TC. TAC10. 3 rooms with PB, 1 suite and 2 cottages. Breakfast included in rates. Types of meals: Full bkfst. Beds: QD. Cable TV, ceiling fan, VCR and some with fireplace in room. Fax and copier on premises. Small meetings and family reunions hosted. Amusement parks, antiquing, art galleries, bicycling, fishing, golf, hiking, horseback riding, Six Flags, Big E Grounds, Mullin Center, live theater, museums, parks, shopping, cross-country skiing, sporting events and tennis nearby.

Great Barrington F2

Baldwin Hill Farm B&B

121 Baldwin Hill Rd N/S
Great Barrington, MA 01230-9061
(413)528-4092 (888)528-4092 Fax:(413)528-6365
E-mail: rpburds@aol.com
Web: www.baldwinhillfarm.com

Circa 1840. Several barns, dating back to the mid-18th century are still to be found on this 450-acre farm. The main house, a Victorian-style, New England farmstead, features a screened-in front porch where guests can enjoy the spectacular scenery of hills, fields, valleys, mountains, gardens and orchards. As the home has been in the family since 1912, the four guest rooms include many family antiques. Homemade country breakfasts are served in the formal dining room. The inn is 20 minutes or less from many attractions, including museums, golf courses, ski areas, Tanglewood and antique shops.

Innkeeper(s): Richard & Priscilla Burdsall. $89-130. MC, VISA, AX, PC, TC. TAC10. 4 rooms, 2 with PB and 2 conference rooms. Breakfast and afternoon tea included in rates. Types of meals: Full bkfst. Beds: KQD. Fans and clocks in room. Air conditioning. VCR, copier, swimming, stables, library and refrigerator on premises. Weddings, small meetings and family reunions hosted. Antiquing, fishing, historical and cultural attractions, biking, hiking, camping, live theater, parks, shopping, downhill skiing, cross-country skiing, sporting events and water sports nearby.

"*We enjoyed your home immensely - from the wonderful views to your beautiful perennial flower beds to your sumptuous breakfasts.*"

Windflower Inn

684 S Egremont Rd
Great Barrington, MA 01230-1932
(413)528-2720 (800)992-1993 Fax:(413)528-5147
E-mail: wndflowr@windflowerinn.com
Web: www.windflowerinn.com

Circa 1870. Situated on 10 tranquil acres in the Berkshire Mountains, this Federal-style country inn was built for gracious living. The informal blend of antiques and comfortable decor make the public rooms perfect spots to gather for a board game, play the piano or read a good book in front of a crackling fire. Making new friends and sharing great conversations are regular occurrences at the Windflower. Several of the spacious guest bedrooms feature working fireplaces. An organic garden provides fresh vegetables, herbs and berries that enhance a delicious breakfast including homemade pastries and breads. The four seasons offer beautiful scenery and a changing variety of activities. Guests can enjoy the private swimming pool bordered with perennials after playing golf across the street at the Egremont Country Club, or head to the local resorts for a day of skiing.

Historic Interest: Chesterwood, the home of Daniel Chester French, Herman Melville's home and the site of Shay's Rebellion are all nearby.
Innkeeper(s): Barbara & Gerald Liebert, Claudia & John Ryan. $100-200. AX, PC, TC. 13 rooms with PB, 6 with FP. Breakfast and afternoon tea included in rates. Types of meals: Full bkfst and early coffee/tea. MAP. Beds: KQT. Air conditioning. Fax, copier, swimming and library on premises. Weddings, small meetings, family reunions and seminars hosted. Antiquing, bicycling, fishing, golf, Tanglewood, live theater, parks, shopping, downhill skiing and cross-country skiing nearby.

Publicity: *Los Angeles Times, Boulevard, Redbook, Country Inns, Countryside, Road Best Traveled and Discerning Traveler.*

"*Every creative comfort imaginable, great for heart, soul and stomach.*"

Greenfield C6

The Brandt House

29 Highland Ave
Greenfield, MA 01301-3605
(413)774-3329 (800)235-3329 Fax:(413)772-2908
E-mail: info@brandthouse.com

Circa 1890. Three-and-a-half-acre lawns surround this impressive three-story Colonial Revival house, situated hilltop. The library and poolroom are popular for lounging, but the favorite gathering areas are the sunroom and the covered north porch. Ask for the aqua and white room with the fireplace, but all the rooms are pleasing. A full breakfast often includes homemade scones and is sometimes available on the slate patio in view of the

expansive lawns and beautiful gardens. A full-time staff provides for guest needs. There is a clay tennis court and nature trails, and in winter, lighted ice skating at a nearby pond. Historic Deerfield and Yankee Candle Company are within five minutes.
Historic Interest: Poet's Seat Tower & Historic Homes (walking distance), Shelburne Falls & the Bridge of Flowers (15 minutes).
Innkeeper(s): Full time staff. $105-205. MC, VISA, AX, DS, TC. TAC10. 9 rooms, 7 with PB, 2 with FP, 1 suite and 1 conference room. Breakfast included in rates. Types of meals: Full bkfst, cont plus and early coffee/tea. Beds: KQT. Cable TV, phone, ceiling fan, refrigerators, fireplaces in two rooms and microwave in room. Air conditioning. VCR, fax, copier, tennis and library on premises. Weddings, small meetings, family reunions and seminars hosted. Antiquing, fishing, Old Deerfield, Lunt Silver, live theater, parks, shopping, downhill skiing, cross-country skiing, sporting events and water sports nearby.
Pets allowed: Call for approval.

Hamilton C14

Miles River Country Inn

823 Bay Rd, Box 149
Hamilton, MA 01936
(978)468-7206 Fax:(978)468-3999
E-mail: milesriver@mediaone.net
Web: www.milesriver.com

Circa 1789. This rambling colonial inn sits on more than 30 acres of magnificent curving lawns bordered by trees and ten gardens that lead to the Miles River. There are meadows, woodlands and

wetlands available for exploring. The river flows through the property, which is a haven for a wide variety of wildlife. There are a cottage and apartment that each sleep up to six people. The guest rooms include four with fireplaces. (There are 12 fireplaces altogether.) Family heirloom antiques and original art compliment the interior.
Historic Interest: Ipswich, which features the nation's largest collection of homes built prior to 1800, is one of the area's many historic attractions. Salem, home to the House of Seven Gables, is another interesting destination.
Innkeeper(s): Gretel & Peter Clark. $95-210. MC, VISA, AX, PC, TC. 8 rooms, 6 with PB, 4 with FP, 1 suite and 2 conference rooms. Breakfast included in rates. Types of meals: Full bkfst, early coffee/tea and afternoon tea. Beds: QDT. Fans and most with clocks in room. Air conditioning. VCR, fax, copier, library, walking trails, gardens and Caretaker Cottage and one housekeeping apartment on premises. Small meetings, family reunions and seminars hosted. Spanish and French spoken. Antiquing, fishing, world class horse events, live theater, parks, cross-country skiing and water sports nearby.
Publicity: *Boston Globe, Beverly Times, Rhode Island Monthly, Boston and Yankee Magazines, Local cable TV and Salem Evening News.*

Harwich Port I18

Harbor Breeze of Cape Cod

326 Lower County Rd
Harwich Port, MA 02646-1625
(508)432-0337 (800)455-0247 Fax:(508)432-1276
E-mail: harborbreeze@yahoo.com
Web: www.harborbreezeinn.com
Circa 1945. Ideally located across the street from picturesque Allens Harbor, this inn is a classic Cape Cod home best enjoyed by couples and families for its casual, friendly atmosphere. A rambling connection of cedar shake additions nestled in an attractive pine setting, surrounds a garden courtyard to form a guest wing. Flowered walkways lead to the private entrances of guest bedrooms furnished in wicker, wood and country florals. Enjoy ocean

breezes while at restful sitting areas and the swimming pool. It is a short walk to Brooks Road Beach on Nantucket Sound.
Innkeeper(s): Mary & Michael Geragosian. $99-200. MC, VISA, AX, DS, PC, TC. TAC10. 10 rooms with PB, 1 with FP. Breakfast included in rates. Types of meals: Cont plus and early coffee/tea. Beds: KQT. Cable TV and some air conditioning and ceiling fans in room. Swimming on premises. Family reunions hosted. Antiquing, fishing, golf, whale watching, live theater, parks, shopping, tennis and water sports nearby.

Housatonic E2

Christine's Bed-Breakfast

325 N Plain Rd
Housatonic, MA 01236-9741
(413)274-6149 (800)536-1186 Fax:(413)274-6296
E-mail: innkeepers@christinesinn.com
Web: www.christinesinn.com

Circa 1780. Centrally located between Stockbridge and Great Barrington in the middle of the Berkshires, this country cottage farmhouse has sat at the foothill of Tom Ball Mountain for more than 200 years. Large, open beams, slant ceilings and wide pine floors reflect its original character. Check-in is at the back parlor, once a small barn. High poster and canopy beds highlight the Colonial-style guest bedrooms. A suite features a fireplace and private terrace. Enjoy breakfast crepes with strawberries or baked French toast with peaches and cream in the garden dining room. Afternoon tea is served on the screened-in porch.
Historic Interest: Chesterwood (2.5 miles), Housatonic dates back to the early 1800s.
Innkeeper(s): Christine Kelsey. $85-190. MC, VISA, PC, TC. 4 rooms with PB, 1 with FP and 1 suite. Breakfast, afternoon tea and dinner included in rates. Types of meals: Full bkfst, country bkfst, veg bkfst and room service. Beds: QT. Cable TV, phone, turndown service, ceiling fan, VCR and fireplace in room. Air conditioning. Fax, copier and library on premises. Seminars hosted. Antiquing, art galleries, bicycling, canoeing/kayaking, fishing, golf, hiking, horseback riding, live theater, museums, parks, shopping, downhill skiing, cross-country skiing, sporting events and tennis nearby.

Hyannis I17

The Inn on Sea Street & Golf Course

358 Sea St
Hyannis, MA 02601-4509
(508)775-8030 Fax:(508)771-0878
E-mail: info@innonseastreet.com
Web: www.innonseastreet.com
Circa 1849. This white Victorian inn is comprised of two homes, both are listed in the town's register of historic buildings. Guest rooms are decorated with four-poster canopy beds. Its charm includes Colonial portraits, Persian carpets and a grand curved staircase. Breakfast is served on the sun porch or elegant dining room on tables set with sterling silver, china, crystal and fresh flowers from the garden. A log book in the living  room is open for guests to rate local restaurants and get opinions before going out on the town.
Historic Interest: Kennedy Library & Compound is less than one mile from the home.
Innkeeper(s): Fred LaSelva. $85-150. MC, VISA, AX, DS. TAC10. 9 rooms, 7 with PB and 1 cottage. Breakfast included in rates. Types of meals: Full bkfst. Beds: QDT. Cable TV, phone, umbrellas, floor fans and clocks in room. Air conditioning. Small meetings and family reunions hosted. Antiquing, fishing, golf, live theater, shopping and water sports nearby.
Publicity: *Journal.*
"A lot of people really don't know how much they are missing, until they visit you."

Hyannis Port　　　I17

The Simmons Homestead Inn

288 Scudder Ave
Hyannis Port, MA 02647
(508)778-4999 (800)637-1649 Fax:(508)790-1342
E-mail: simmonshomestead@aol.com
Web: www.simmonshomesteadinn.com

Circa 1805. This former sea captain's home features period decor and includes huge needlepoint displays and lifelike

ceramic and papier-mache animals that give the inn a country feel. Some rooms boast canopy beds, and each is individually decorated. Traditional full breakfasts are served in the formal dining room. Evening wine helps guests relax after a day of touring the Cape. There is a billiard room on the premises and an outdoor hot tub.

Innkeeper(s): Bill Putman. $120-330. MC, VISA, AX, DS, PC, TC. TAC10. 14 rooms with PB, 2 with FP and 2 suites. Breakfast included in rates. Types of meals: Full bkfst and early coffee/tea. Beds: KQT. Ceiling fan in room. VCR, fax, copier, bicycles, library, pet boarding, child care, billiard room and modem hook-up on premises. Weddings, small meetings and family reunions hosted. Antiquing, fishing, golf, live theater, parks, shopping, tennis and water sports nearby.

Pets Allowed.

Publicity: *Bon Appetit, Cape Code Life and Yankee.*

"I want to say that part of what makes Cape Cod special for us is the inn. It embodies much of what is wonderful at the Cape. By Sunday, I was completely rested, relaxed, renewed, and restored."

Ipswich　　　B14

Ipswich Bed & Breakfast

2 East St
Ipswich, MA 01938

Circa 1863. Stroll on walkways throughout this almost-one-acre estate that is accented by terraced perennial gardens. The Victorian home with Italianate detail was built by a Civil War veteran who became a general merchant. Accommodations include guest bedrooms in the main house and the restored Carriage House, which offers more privacy. The innkeepers will work with food restrictions and preferences. A wholesome breakfast is served in the formal dining room, on the garden deck, in the kitchen with the cook or brought to the room. A tranquil ambiance is imparted during a visit here.

Call for rates. 4 rooms with PB and 1 guest house. Types of meals: Full bkfst.

Town Hill Bed & Breakfast

16 N Main St
Ipswich, MA 01938-2218
(978)356-8000 (800)457-7799 Fax:(978)356-8000
E-mail: reserve@townhill.com
Web: www.townhill.com

Circa 1845. Colorful perennial gardens surround this elegant yet family friendly 1845 Greek Revival inn located in the historical district of Ipswich. Nearby residences were built prior to the 1700s. Appointed with antiques, the inn offers 11 guest rooms — two suites, nine rooms with private baths and two with shared baths. Enjoy breakfasting on hot entrees like sausage and eggs or French toast, as well as lighter fare like cereal and juices

before walking in to see the quaint shops in town.

Innkeeper(s): Chere & Bob Statho. $90-165. MC, VISA, AX. TAC10. 11 rooms, 9 with PB and 2 suites. Breakfast included in rates. Types of meals: Full bkfst and country bkfst. Beds: KQDT. Air conditioning. Family reunions hosted. Antiquing, art galleries, beaches, bicycling, canoeing/kayaking, golf, hiking, live theater, museums, parks and shopping nearby.

Lee　　　E2

Applegate

279 W Park St
Lee, MA 01238-1718
(413)243-4451 (800)691-9012
E-mail: lenandgloria@applegateinn.com
Web: www.applegateinn.com

Circa 1920. This romantic bed & breakfast is an ideal accommodation for those visiting the Berkshires. Well-dressed, four-poster beds rest atop polished wood floors. Gracious furnishings, Oriental rugs and soft lighting add to the ambiance. Most guest rooms offer fireplaces and whirlpool tubs, and several offer views of woods or gardens. Fresh flowers, brandy and Godiva chocolates are just a few extras that await guests. In the early evening, wine and cheese is served. Breakfasts are served by candlelight, with crystal stemware and antique china. The innkeepers offer several special getaway packages, such as a wine-tasting and dinner weekends. Golf and tennis facilities are located across the street.

Historic Interest: Norman Rockwell Museum is nearby.

Innkeeper(s): Len & Gloria Friedman. $95-295. MC, VISA, PC, TC. 8 rooms with PB, 6 with FP and 1 cottage. Breakfast included in rates. Types of meals: Full bkfst. Beds: KQD. Steam shower, whirlpool tubs, flowers and brandy and chocolates in room. Air conditioning. VCR, fax, copier, swimming, bicycles, library, CD player, baby grand piano and screened porch overlooking gardens on premises. Weddings, small meetings, family reunions and seminars hosted. Antiquing, Norman Rockwell museum, Tanglewood concerts, Jacobs Pillow, live theater, parks, shopping, downhill skiing, cross-country skiing and water sports nearby.

Publicity: *Country Inns and Sep/Oct 95.*

Devonfield

85 Stockbridge Rd
Lee, MA 01238-9308
(413)243-3298 (800)664-0880 Fax:(413)243-1360

Circa 1800. The original section of this Federal inn was built by a Revolutionary War soldier. Guest rooms are spacious with charming furniture and patterned wallcoverings. Three of the rooms feature fireplaces. The one-bedroom cottage has both a fireplace and an efficiency kitchen. Guests are treated to a full breakfast. One need not wander far from the grounds to find

something to do. The innkeepers offer a tennis court, swimming pool and bicycles for guests, and a nine-hole golf course is just across the way. Inside, guests can relax in the living room with its fireplace and library or in the television room. The area is full of boutiques, antique shops and galleries to explore, as well as hiking, fishing and skiing. Tanglewood, summer home of the Boston Symphony, is close by.

Historic Interest: Among the many historic sites offered in this part of Massachusetts are the Norman Rockwell Museum and the Hancock Shaker Village. There's no shortage of historic homes to visit.

Innkeeper(s): Jim & Pam Loring. $90-275. MC, VISA, AX, DS, PC, TC. TAC10. 10 rooms with PB, 4 with FP, 4 suites and 1 cottage. Beds: KQT. Cable some rooms in room. Air conditioning. Fax, copier, swimming, bicycles, tennis and library on premises.

Publicity: *Discerning Traveler and New York Magazine.*

"A special thank you for your warm and kind hospitality. We feel as though this is our home away from home."

The Parsonage on The Green B&B

20 Park Pl
Lee, MA 01238-1618
(413)243-4364 Fax:(413)243-2372
E-mail: parsonage@berkshire.net
Web: www.bbhost.com/parsonageonthegreen

Circa 1851. As the former parsonage to the first Congregational Church (known as having the highest wooden steeple in the country), this white colonial inn is tucked behind a white picket fence on a quiet side of the village com-

mon. The boughs of an old apple tree shade a pleasant wicker-filled side veranda. Family heirlooms, 18th-century American antiques and Oriental rugs are set against polished maple and oak hardwood floors. An elegant afternoon tea is served graciously from the teacart in the parlor and includes freshly made sweets such as Victorian lace cookies and scones. Homemade breads accompany a full breakfast served on fine china in the candle-lit dining room. Walk to restaurants, galleries and shops. Stockbridge and Lenox are nearby, as is outlet shopping. One mile from exit 2 of Mass. Pike.

Innkeeper(s): Barbara & Don Mahony. $70-175. PC, TC. 4 rooms with PB. Breakfast and afternoon tea included in rates. Types of meals: Full bkfst and early coffee/tea. Beds: QD. Turndown service, ceiling fan, robes and hand-dipped chocolates in room. Air conditioning. VCR, bicycles, library, piano and newspapers on premises. Antiquing, bicycling, fishing, golf, hiking, swimming in Laurel Lake, live theater, parks, shopping, downhill skiing, cross-country skiing, sporting events, tennis and water sports nearby.
Publicity: *Berkshire Eagle.*

"Our dream came true, the perfect romantic getaway."

Lenox   E2

Arbor Rose B&B

8 Yale Hill, Box 114
Lenox, MA 01262
(413)298-4744 (877)298-4744 Fax:(413)298-4235
E-mail: innkeeper@arborrose.com
Web: www.arborrose.com

Circa 1810. This New England farmhouse overlooks an 1800s mill, pond and gardens with the mountains as a backdrop. During the winter months, guests often relax in front of the wood stove in the inn's cozy front parlor. Four-poster beds, antiques and rural-themed paint-

ings decorate the rooms. The inn's 19th-century mill now houses guests. The mill was one of five in the vicinity and was still in operation as late as the 1930s. The Berkshire Theatre, open for the summer season, is across the street. The Norman Rockwell Museum, Tanglewood Music Festival, ski areas and antique, outlet and specialty shops are all within a seven-mile radius.

Historic Interest: Mission House, the first mission set up for the Stockbridge Indians, and the historic Main Street of Stockbridge are among the nearby historic sites.
Innkeeper(s): Christina Alsop. $95-175. MC, VISA, PC, TC. TAC10. 6 rooms

with PB. Breakfast included in rates. Types of meals: Full bkfst, country bkfst, cont plus, cont and early coffee/tea. Beds: KQT. Cable TV, ceiling fan and TVs in some rooms in room. Air conditioning. VCR and library on premises. Family reunions hosted. Antiquing, art galleries, bicycling, canoeing/kayaking, fishing, golf, hiking, horseback riding, music festival, Tanglewood, live theater, museums, parks, shopping, downhill skiing, cross-country skiing and tennis nearby.
Publicity: *Yankee Traveler.*

"If houses really do exude the spirit of events and feelings stored from their history, it explains why a visitor feels warmth and joy from the first turn up the driveway."

Birchwood Inn

7 Hubbard St, Box 2020
Lenox, MA 01240-4604
(413)637-2600 (800)524-1646 Fax:(413)637-4604
E-mail: innkeeper@birchwood-inn.com
Web: www.birchwood-inn.com

Circa 1767. This inn, which is the only privately owned Lenox building listed on the National Register, is situated on a hilltop and overlooks the village. The gardens and lawns are surrounded by old New England stone

fences. Guests can enjoy the wood-burning fireplaces and large library. Full country breakfasts include items such as Rise and Shine Souffl'e, waffles and home-baked muffins.

Historic Interest: Edith Wharton's home is two miles away, while Herman Melville's home is three miles from the inn. The Norman Rockwell Museum is about four miles away.
Innkeeper(s): Ellen Gutman Chenaux. $75-260. MC, VISA, AX, DS, PC, TC. 12 rooms, 10 with PB, 5 with FP and 1 conference room. Breakfast and afternoon tea included in rates. Types of meals: Full bkfst and early coffee/tea. Beds: KQDT. Cable TV, phone and ceiling fan in room. Air conditioning. VCR, fax, copier and library on premises. Weddings, small meetings, family reunions and seminars hosted. Antiquing, fishing, golf, Tanglewood, live theater, parks, shopping, downhill skiing, cross-country skiing and water sports nearby.
Publicity: *Country Inns and Country Living.*

"Inn-credible! Inn-viting! Inn-spiring! Inn-comparable! Our ultimate getaway. Wonderful ambiance, great food and the finest hosts we ever met. We have been going to the Birchwood Inn for more than 15 years and each time we enjoy it even more."

Brook Farm Inn

15 Hawthorne St
Lenox, MA 01240-2404
(413)637-3013 (800)285-7638 Fax:(413)637-4751
E-mail: innkeeper@brookfarm.com
Web: www.brookfarm.com

Circa 1870. Brook Farm Inn is named after the original Brook Farm, a literary commune that sought to combine thinker and worker through a society of intelligent, cultivated members. In keeping with that theme, this gracious Victorian inn offers poetry and story telling and has a large volume poetry library. Canopy beds, Mozart and a swimming pool tend to the spirit.

Historic Interest: Home of Edith Wharton (the Mount), home of Herman Melville (Arrowhead), home of Daniel Chester French, Lincoln Memorial (Chesterwood).
Innkeeper(s): Linda & Phil Halpern. $95-215. MC, VISA. 12 rooms with PB, 6 with FP. Breakfast and afternoon tea included in rates. Types of meals: Full bkfst and early coffee/tea. Beds: KQT. Phone, ceiling fan, fluffy towels and toiletries in room. Air conditioning. Fax, copier, swimming, butler's pantry, round-the-clock coffee and tea on premises. Family reunions hosted. Antiquing, fishing, Tanglewood, live theater, parks, shopping, downhill skiing, cross-country skiing, sporting events and water sports nearby.
Publicity: *Berkshire Eagle, Country Inns, Travel & Leisure and Boston Globe.*

"We've been traveling all our lives and never have we felt more at home."

Cornell Inn

203 Main St
Lenox, MA 01240-2384
(413)637-0562 (800)637-0562 Fax:(413)637-0927
E-mail: info@cornellinn.com
Web: www.cornellinn.com

Circa 1880. Located one-and-a-half miles from Tanglewood, this welcoming inn has a 70-year history. Originally, the Main House was a guest house and the adjacent Carriage house was a speakeasy. The MacDonald House was the former home of a Civil War veteran and U.S. Representative. The decor of each building, respectively, is Victorian, country primitive and Colonial. Many of the guest bedrooms feature fireplaces, whirlpool tubs, mini-bars and decks. The suites offer a fully equipped kitchen. Breakfast can be enjoyed overlooking the waterfall and Koi pond. Every evening a private full-service pub opens. Experience classic hospitality just minutes from New England's sites and activities.

Innkeeper(s): Billie & Doug McLaughlin. $100-300. MC, VISA, AX, DC, CB, DS, PC, TC. 30 rooms with PB, 18 with FP. Breakfast included in rates. Types of meals: Cont plus. Beds: KQDT. Cable TV and phone in room. Air conditioning. Spa and sauna on premises. Bicycling, golf, hiking, cultural activities, downhill skiing and cross-country skiing nearby.

"The MacDonald House, built in 1777, was the former home of U.S. Representative and Civil War veteran Edward MacDonald."

The Gables Inn

81 Walker St, Rt 183
Lenox, MA 01240-2719
(413)637-3416 (800)382-9401

Circa 1885. At one time, this was the home of Pulitzer Prize-winning novelist, Edith Wharton. The Queen Anne-style Berkshire cottage features a handsome eight-sided library and Mrs. Wharton's own four-poster bed. An unusual indoor swimming pool with spa is available in warm weather.

Innkeeper(s): Mary & Frank Newton. $90-250. MC, VISA, DS, PC, TC. 17 rooms with PB, 15 with FP and 4 suites. Breakfast included in rates. Beds: Q. Cable TV and VCR in room. Air conditioning. Fax, swimming and tennis on premises. Family reunions hosted. Antiquing, fishing, live theater, parks, shopping, downhill skiing, cross-country skiing, sporting events and water sports nearby.

Publicity: *P.M. Magazine and New York Times.*

"You made us feel like old friends and that good feeling enhanced our pleasure. In essence, it was the best part of our trip."

Garden Gables Inn

135 Main Street, PO Box 52
Lenox, MA 01240-0052
(413)637-0193 Fax:(413)637-4554
E-mail: innkeeper@lenoxinn.com
Web: lenoxinn.com

Circa 1780. Several distinctive gables adorn this home set on five wooded acres. Deer occasionally wander into the garden to help themselves to fallen apples. Breakfast is served in the dining room, which overlooks tall maples, flower gardens and fruit trees. The swimming pool was the first built in the county and

is still the longest. Guests will find many special amenities including in-room phones, fireplaces and whirlpool tubs. There is a Baby Grand Piano in the living room.

Innkeeper(s): Mario & Lynn Mekinda. $80-275. MC, VISA, AX, DS, PC, TC. 18 rooms with PB, 8 with FP, 2 suites and 4 cottages. Breakfast and afternoon tea included in rates. Types of meals: Full bkfst and early coffee/tea. Beds: KQT. Cable TV, phone, hair dryers and canopy beds in room. Air conditioning. VCR, fax and summer swimming on premises. Weddings, small meetings, family reunions and seminars hosted. French and German spoken. Antiquing, Tanglewood Music Festival, live theater, parks, shopping, downhill skiing, cross-country skiing and water sports nearby.

Publicity: *National Geographic Traveler, Berkshire Eagle, Los Angeles Times, Long Island News and Yankee Magazine.*

"Charming and thoughtful hospitality. You restored a portion of my sanity and I'm very grateful—Miami Herald."

The Kemble Inn

2 Kemble St
Lenox, MA 01240-2813
(413)637-4113 (800)353-4113
Web: www.kembleinn.com

Circa 1881. Named for a famous 19th-century actress, Fanny Kemble, this three-story Georgian-style inn boasts an incredible view of the mountains in the Berkshires. The inn's 14 elegant guest rooms are named for American authors, including Nathaniel Hawthorne, Henry Wadsworth Longfellow, Herman Melville, Mark Twain and Edith Wharton. The impressive Fanny Kemble Room, which features mountain views, includes two fireplaces, a Jacuzzi tub and a king-size, four-poster bed. The inn is within minutes of five major ski areas, and Tanglewood is less than two miles away.

Historic Interest: Norman Rockwell Museum, Edith Wharton Restoration.

Innkeeper(s): J. Richard & Linda Reardon. $105-305. MC, VISA, DS, TC. 14 rooms with PB, 6 with FP. Types of meals: Cont. Cable TV and phone in room. Air conditioning. Refrigerator for guest use on premises. Handicap access. Antiquing, fishing, cultural attractions, parks, shopping, downhill skiing, cross-country skiing and water sports nearby.

Publicity: *Country Inns.*

"Kemble Inn was a showcase B&B - just what we had hoped for."

Lilac Inn

PO Box 2294, 33 Main St
Lenox, MA 01240-5294
(413)637-2172 Fax:(413)637-2172
E-mail: aliceatlilacinn@msn.com
Web: www.thelilacinn.com

Circa 1836. Aptly named for a flower, this Italian Revival inn features guest rooms that appear much like a garden. Flowery prints, wicker and antique furnishings and views of Lilac Park from the two porches enhance this cheerful atmosphere. Guests are treated to afternoon refreshments, with a proper mix of savory and sweet tidbits. Breakfasts are bountiful and delicious, yet surprisingly healthy with low-fat, vegetarian versions of treats such as banana nut bread, French toast and vegetable quiche. The library is stocked with books, and the living room, which has a fireplace, is a good place to curl up and relax. The innkeeper also offers a one-bedroom apartment with a kitchen.

Innkeeper(s): Alice Maleski. $100-225. PC. 6 rooms with PB, 1 with FP. Breakfast and afternoon tea included in rates. Types of meals: Gourmet bkfst and early coffee/tea. Beds: KQT. Turndown service and ceiling fan in room. VCR, fax, copier and library on premises. Handicap access. Weddings, small meetings, family reunions and seminars hosted. French and Lithuanian spoken. Antiquing, fishing, golf, outlet shops, live theater, parks, shopping, downhill skiing, cross-country skiing and water sports nearby.

"We are really looking forward to shamelessly overindulging in your breakfasts, and being carried away by the music, the time and the place."

Rookwood Inn

11 Old Stockbridge Rd, PO Box 1717
Lenox, MA 01240-1717
(413)637-9750 (800)223-9750
E-mail: stay@rookwoodinn.com
Web: www.rookwoodinn.com

Circa 1885. This turn-of-the-century Queen Anne Victorian inn offers 20 elegant guest rooms, including suites. Among the amenities in the air-conditioned guest rooms are antiques and fireplaces. The public rooms and halls are decorated with the innkeepers' collection of antique handbags and Wallace Nutting prints. The day begins with a bountiful heart-healthy breakfast. The beautiful Berkshires are  famous for cultural and recreational opportunities, and guests can walk to shops and restaurants. Tanglewood is one mile away.
Innkeeper(s): Amy Lindner-Lesser. $85-300. MC, VISA, AX, DC, DS, PC, TC. TAC10. 20 rooms with PB, 8 with FP, 3 suites and 2 conference rooms. Breakfast and snacks/refreshments included in rates. Types of meals: Full bkfst. Beds: KQT. Phone and some with television in room. Air conditioning. Weddings, small meetings, family reunions and seminars hosted. Antiquing, fishing, golf, live theater, parks, shopping, downhill skiing, cross-country skiing, tennis and water sports nearby.
Publicity: *New York Times, Boston Globe, London Times, New York Magazine and Philadelphia Magazine.*

"Of all the inns I've visited, Rookwood, by far, was the most comfortable, with personable, friendly and obliging innkeepers, excellent breakfasts and cozy atmosphere."

Seven Hills Country Inn & Restaurant

40 Plunkett St
Lenox, MA 01240-2795
(413)637-0060 (800)869-6518 Fax:(413)637-3651
E-mail: 7hills@berkshire.net
Web: www.sevenhillsinn.com

Circa 1911. Descendants of those who sailed on the Mayflower built this rambling, Tudor-style mansion. The inn's 27 acres of terraced lawns and stunning gardens often serve as the site for weddings, receptions and meetings. The grounds include two tennis courts and a swimming pool. Guest rooms are elegantly appointed with antiques, and the mansion still maintains its hand-carved fireplaces and leaded glass windows. In addition to the original elements, some rooms contain the modern amenities of a jet tub, fireplace and kitchenette. The inn's chef, whose cuisine has been featured in Gourmet magazine, prepares creative, continental specialties. Seven Hills offers close access to many attractions in the Berkshires.
Innkeeper(s): Patricia & Jim Eder. $85-325. MC, VISA, AX, DC, CB, DS, PC, TC. TAC10. 58 rooms with PB, 11 with FP, 3 suites and 4 conference rooms. Breakfast included in rates. Types of meals: Full bkfst, cont plus and dinner. MAP, EP. Beds: KQD. Cable TV and phone in room. Air conditioning. VCR, fax, copier, swimming, tennis and library on premises. Handicap access. Spanish and French spoken. Antiquing, fishing, live theater, museums, parks, shopping, downhill skiing, cross-country skiing and water sports nearby.
Pets allowed: Sometimes.
Publicity: *Gourmet and Entrepreneur.*

Summer Hill Farm

950 East St
Lenox, MA 01240-2205
(413)442-2059 (800)442-2059 Fax:(413)448-6106
E-mail: innkeeper@summerhillfarm.com
Web: www.summerhillfarm.com

Circa 1796. Situated on a scenic 19 acres, this Colonial home was once part of a 300-acre farm deeded to the Steven family just after the French & Indian War. Several rooms include fireplaces or brass beds. The Loft and Mountain View rooms both offer superb views. The Cottage, an old  hay barn, includes a bedroom as well as sitting, dining and cooking areas. Fresh fruit, homemade granola, and home-baked bread accompany the morning's special breakfast entree. After a hearty breakfast, guests should have no trouble finding something to do. Arts and sports activities are nearby, as are museums, Hancock Shaker Village, antique shops, Tanglewood, theatres and many other cultural attractions. The innkeepers also have a three-bedroom, two-bath farmhouse on the property. The farmhouse is self-contained and can be rented by the week or month.
Historic Interest: Herman Melville's "Arrowhead" (1 mile), Edith Wharton's "The Mount" (6 miles).
Innkeeper(s): Sonya & Michael Wessel. $90-220. MC, VISA, AX, PC, TC. TAC10. 7 rooms with PB, 3 with FP and 2 cottages. Breakfast included in rates. Types of meals: Full bkfst. Beds: KQDT. Cable TV, refrigerator (two rooms) and ceiling fan (one room) in room. Air conditioning. VCR on premises. Family reunions hosted. Amusement parks, antiquing, art galleries, beaches, bicycling, canoeing/kayaking, fishing, golf, hiking, horseback riding, live theater, museums, parks, shopping, downhill skiing, cross-country skiing, tennis, water sports and wineries nearby.

"You and your home are wonderfully charming."

The Village Inn

16 Church St
Lenox, MA 01240
(413)637-0020 (800)253-0917 Fax:(413)637-9756
E-mail: villinn@vgernet.net
Web: www.villageinn-lenox.com

Circa 1771. Four years after the Whitlocks built this Federal-style house, they converted it and two adjoining buildings for lodging. Since 1775, it has operated as an inn. Now, there are luxurious amenities, including rooms with four-poster canopy beds, fireplaces, VCRs and Jacuzzi tubs. Stenciled walls, Oriental rugs, maple floors and country antiques and reproductions furnish the inn. Rates include a continental-plus breakfast that is served midweek in winter and spring and a full breakfast served in summer, fall and weekends throughout the year. Be sure to try afternoon tea and enjoy the freshly baked scones served with real clotted cream. Candlelight dinners featuring regional American cuisine are available summer and fall and on weekends throughout the year.
Historic Interest: The Mount (1 mile), Arrowhead (3 miles), Hancock Shaker Village (5 miles), Grandma Moses museum (20 miles), Clark Art Institute (10 miles), Tanglewood (1 mile).
Innkeeper(s): Clifford Rudisill & Ray Wilson. $55-265. MC, VISA, AX, DC, CB, DS, TC. TAC10. 32 rooms with PB, 6 with FP, 1 suite and 2 conference rooms. Breakfast included in rates. Types of meals: Gourmet bkfst, cont plus, afternoon tea and gourmet dinner. EP. Beds: KQDT. Phone, VCR, hair dryers, magnifying mirror, satellite TV, complimentary VCR library, voice mail, A/C in summer and many rooms with Jacuzzi tubs in room. Fax, library and cookies available throughout the day and evening on premises. Handicap access. Weddings, small meetings, family reunions and seminars hosted. Spanish, French, German and Italian spoken. Antiquing, art galleries, beaches, bicycling, fishing, golf, hiking, canoeing, Tanglewood summer music festival, live

theater, museums, parks, shopping, downhill skiing, cross-country skiing, sporting events, tennis, water sports and wineries nearby.
Publicity: *The London Independent.*

"Kathy and I stayed at your beautiful inn in early October. It was the highlight of our trip to New England."

Whistler's Inn

5 Greenwood St
Lenox, MA 01240-2029
(413)637-0975 (866)637-0975 Fax:(413)637-2190
E-mail: rmears3246@aol.com
Web: www.whistlersinnlenox.com

Circa 1820. Whistler's Inn is an English Tudor Manor surrounded by seven acres of woodlands and gardens. Inside, elegance is abundant. In the impressive Louis XVI music room, you'll find a Steinway piano, chandeliers and gilt palace furniture. There is an English

library with chintz-covered sofas, paintings and etchings, hundreds of volumes of books and a fireplace of black marble.
Here, guests have sherry or tea and perhaps engage in conversation with their well-traveled hosts, both authors. A baronial dining room features Baroque candelabrums, chinoiserie and a huge marble and limestone fireplace.
Innkeeper(s): Richard & Joan Mears. $80-275. MC, VISA, AX, DS, PC, TC. TAC10. 14 rooms with PB, 2 with FP and 3 conference rooms. Breakfast included in rates. Types of meals: Full bkfst and afternoon tea. Beds: KQDT. Cable TV in room. Air conditioning. Fax, copier and library on premises. Small meetings, family reunions and seminars hosted. Antiquing, art museums, live theater, parks, shopping, downhill skiing, cross-country skiing and water sports nearby.
Publicity: *Berkshire Book and Best Places to Stay in New England.*

Lynn   D14

Diamond District Inn

142 Ocean St
Lynn, MA 01902-2007
(781)599-4470 (800)666-3076 Fax:(781)595-2200
E-mail: diamonddistrict@msn.com
Web: www.diamonddistrictinn.com

Circa 1911. This Georgian house was built for shoe manufacturer P.J. Harney-Lynn. Many of the original fixtures remain, and the inn is suitably furnished with Oriental rugs and antiques. The parlor features a collection of antique musical instruments. There are several views of the ocean from the house, but the veranda is

the most popular spot for sea gazing. There is a heated outdoor spa for guest rooms and two romantic suites feature fireplaces, whirlpool tubs, ocean view and deck. Candlelight

breakfast is served in the dining room or on the porch. Fresh fruits, homemade breads and hot coffee, tea or cider start off the meal, followed by a special entree. The beach is just steps away, and guests can walk to the promenade and restaurants.
Historic Interest: The Lynn Museum, Mary Baker Eddy home, the founder of Christian Science, Grand Army of the Republic meeting hall and museum are within walking distance. Located eight miles north of Boston.
Innkeeper(s): Sandra & Jerry Caron. $135-265. MC, VISA, AX, DC, CB, DS, PC, TC. 11 rooms with PB, 2 suites and 1 conference room. Breakfast included in rates. Types of meals: Full bkfst. Beds: KQDT. Cable TV, phone

and ceiling fan in room. Air conditioning. Fax, copier, spa and voice mail and modem on premises. Antiquing, fishing, North Shore & Salem, cross-country skiing and water sports nearby.
Publicity: *Sunday Post and Fox TV - Pets Show.*

"The room was spectacular and breakfast was served beautifully. Bed and breakfast were both outstanding! Thanks so much for your hospitality."

Marblehead   D14

A Nesting Place B&B

16 Village St
Marblehead, MA 01945-2213
(781)631-6655
E-mail: louisehir@aol.com
Web: www.anestingplace.com

Circa 1890. Tastefully furnished, this bright and cheerful home is embellished with colorful hand-painted furniture and a touch of whimsy. Homemade breakfasts may include seasonal fruits, fresh baked goods, bread pudding, apple crisp and french toast. Relax in the outdoor hot tub or on the deck. Ask about arranging personalized spa services. The renowned sailing harbor is within an easy walk, as are beaches, restaurants, shops, parks and historic sites. Boston airport and Cape Ann are only 30 minutes away.
Innkeeper(s): Louise Hirshberg. $65-80. MC, VISA, PC, TC. 2 rooms. Breakfast included in rates. Types of meals: Cont plus, early coffee/tea and afternoon tea. Beds: KQT. VCR and spa on premises. Antiquing, fishing, historic sites, live theater, parks, shopping, cross-country skiing, sporting events and water sports nearby.

Brimblecomb Hill

33 Mechanic St
Marblehead, MA 01945-3448
(781)631-3172
E-mail: garnould@gis.net
Web: www.brimblecomb.com

Circa 1721. This gracious pre-Revolutionary War Colonial home is a fun place to soak in New England's history and charm. The home was host to a variety tradesmen including a cooper and a wigmaker, not to mention a friend of Benjamin Franklin. The bed & breakfast is only about 20 miles from Boston and the town of Marblehead offers many fine galleries, shops and restaurants, and of course, Marblehead Harbor.

Historic Interest: Marblehead was incorporated in 1649 and features an array of historic buildings and churches. Some of the highlights include the town's Old North Church, Abbot Hall. A walking tour can be arranged. The American Navy began in Marblehead's historic harbor, and the original painting "Spirit of '76," hangs in the town hall.
Innkeeper(s): Gene Arnould. $75-95. MC, VISA. 3 rooms, 1 with PB. Breakfast included in rates. Types of meals: Cont plus and cont. Beds: QD. Air conditioning. Antiquing, fishing, live theater and water sports nearby.

"Thank you for such wonderful hospitality. We really enjoyed our stay & loved the B&B atmosphere! We will definitely plan a trip back!"

Harbor Light Inn

58 Washington
Marblehead, MA 01945
(781)631-2186 Fax:(781)631-2216
E-mail: hli@shore.net

Circa 1729. This early 18th-century inn is an elegant New England retreat. Oriental rugs, refined furnishings, fine paintings and items such as four-poster beds create a warm, invit-

ing character. A dozen of the guest rooms include a fireplace, and some offer sunken Jacuzzi tubs. For three years, Vacations magazine ranked the inn as one of the nation's most romantic. The inn is located within walking distance of shops and restaurants, as well as Marblehead Harbor.

Innkeeper(s): Peter & Suzanne Conway. $125-295. MC, VISA, AX, PC, TC. TAC10. 22 rooms with PB, 12 with FP, 2 suites, 1 cabin and 1 conference room. Breakfast included in rates. Types of meals: Cont. Beds: KQT. Cable TV, phone, VCR and Jacuzzis in room. Air conditioning. Fax, copier and swimming on premises. Weddings, small meetings, family reunions and seminars hosted.
Publicity: *Vacations*.

Harborside House B&B

23 Gregory St
Marblehead, MA 01945-3241
(781)631-1032
E-mail: stay@harborsidehouse.com
Web: www.harborsidehouse.com

Circa 1840. Enjoy the Colonial charm of this home, which overlooks Marblehead Harbor on Boston's historic North Shore. Rooms are decorated with antiques and period wallpaper. A third-story sundeck offers excellent views. A generous continental breakfast of home-baked breads, muffins and fresh fruit is served each morning in the well-decorated dining room or on the open porch.

The village of Marblehead provides many shops and restaurants. Boston and Logan airport are 30 minutes away.

Historic Interest: Lee Mansion (1768), King Hooper Mansion (1745) and St. Michael's Church (1714).

Innkeeper(s): Susan Livingston. $70-90. PC, TC. TAC10. 2 rooms. Breakfast, afternoon tea and snacks/refreshments included in rates. Types of meals: Cont plus. Beds: DT. Bathrobes in room. Bicycles on premises. Antiquing, parks, shopping and water sports nearby.
Publicity: *Marblehead Reporter*.

"Harborside Inn is restful, charming, with a beautiful view of the water. I wish we didn't have to leave."

Pheasant Hill Inn

71 Bubier Rd
Marblehead, MA 01945-3630
(781)639-4799 Fax:(781)639-4799
E-mail: information@pheasanthill.com

Circa 1917. Stay in an authentic, shingled-style home with original woodwork, hardwood floors and built-in cabinets. Early antiques and painted furniture decorate the rooms, and some offer hand-painted ceilings with puffy white clouds. The artist innkeeper also has painted murals around the inn. A favorite accommodation is the spacious Garden Suite. It offers polished hardwood floors, a marbleized fireplace, handsome desk and plaid easy chairs. There's a door to the deck for views to the water. Homemade scones are a favorite breakfast item. An acre of lawns and gardens invite strolls and include a massive cluster of pink and red rhododendrons. The Spirit of '76 painting may be viewed within a half mile. Salem is five miles from the inn where whale watching and harbor/dinner cruises can be arranged. Boston is 18 miles away.

Historic Interest: Marblehead Harbor (1 mile), Salem Museums (5 miles), Boston (18 miles).
Innkeeper(s): Nancy & Bill Coolidge. $100-175. MC, VISA, AX, PC, TC. 3 suites. Breakfast and afternoon tea included in rates. Types of meals: Cont plus and early coffee/tea. Beds: KQT. Cable TV, phone, decks and fireplace in room. Air conditioning. Fax, copier, library, lawn games, crockett bocc, gardens, fountain and outdside seating on premises. Antiquing, art galleries, beaches, bicycling, fishing, golf, whale watching, harbor cruise, live theater, museums, parks, shopping and tennis nearby.

Martha's Vineyard   K16

Martha's Place

114 Main
Martha's Vineyard, MA 02568
(508)693-0253
E-mail: info@marthasplace.com
Web: www.marthasplace.com

Circa 1840. Pink roses surround this beautifully decorated inn offering a romantic setting in an elegant Greek Revival-style home. Polished wood floors, Oriental rugs, antiques, chandeliers and meticulously detailed decor provides a nestling place after a day of playing tennis on nearby clay courts, sailing, cycling the island or poking around nearby shops. Ask for the suite for special water view, velvet half-canopy bed and a sitting room separated by French doors. Floor-to-ceiling windows light the dining room where breakfast is served with crystal and silver. You may enjoy it brought to your room upon prior arrangement, as well. The inn is directly across from Owen Park Beach overlooking Vineyard Haven Harbor. The ferry is only a block away.

Innkeeper(s): Martin & Richard. $100-395. MC, VISA, PC. 6 rooms with PB, 3 with FP, 1 suite and 1 conference room. Types of meals: Cont plus. Beds: QD. Phone in room. Air conditioning. Bicycles on premises. Weddings and family reunions hosted. Antiquing, art galleries, beaches, bicycling, canoeing/kayaking, fishing, golf, hiking, horseback riding, live theater, museums, parks, shopping, tennis and water sports nearby.
Publicity: *Boston Magazine, Frommer's Cape Cod, Out & About Magazine, Boston Sunday Herald, Our World Magazine, Cape Cod Travel Guide, Maisons Cote'Quest Magazine.* and AMC television.

Thorncroft Inn

460 Main St, PO Box 1022
Martha's Vineyard, MA 02568-1022
(508)693-3333 (800)332-1236 Fax:(508)693-5419
E-mail: innkeeper@thorncroft.com
Web: www.thorncroft.com

Circa 1918. The Thorncroft Estate is a classic craftsman bungalow with a dominant roof and neo-colonial details. It was built by Chicago grain merchant John Herbert Ware as the guest house of a large oceanfront estate. Most guest rooms include working fireplaces and canopied beds. Some also boast two-person whirlpool tubs or private 300-gallon hot tubs. The inn is situated in three buildings on three-and-one-half acres of lawns and woodlands. In its naturally romantic setting,

the Thorncroft provides the perfect ambiance for honeymooners, anniversaries and special couples' getaways. Full breakfasts and afternoon teas are served in the dining rooms, but guests can opt for a continental breakfast served in their room.

Innkeeper(s): Karl & Lynn Buder. $225-475. MC, VISA, AX, DC, CB, DS. TAC10. 14 rooms with PB, 10 with FP and 1 cottage. Breakfast and afternoon tea included in rates. Types of meals: Full bkfst and room service. Beds: KQD. TV in room. Fax and copier on premises. Antiquing, fishing, live theater and water sports nearby.

Publicity: *Cape Cod Life, Travel & Leisure, Wheel of Fortune, Hollywood Squares and Travel Channel-Great Country Inns.*

"It's the type of place where we find ourselves falling in love all over again."

Nantucket L18

Century House

10 Cliff Rd
Nantucket, MA 02554-3640
(508)228-0530
E-mail: centurybnb@aol.com
Web: www.centuryhouse.com

Circa 1833. Captain Calder built this Federal-style house and supplemented his income by taking in guests when the whaling industry slowed down. According to late historian Edouard Stackpole, the house is the oldest continually operating guesthouse on the island. It is surrounded by other large homes on a knoll in the historic district. Museums, beaches and restaurants are a short walk away. The inn's motto for about the last 100 years has been, "An inn of distinction on an island of charm." Cottages are also available.

Innkeeper(s): Husband & wife, Gerry Connick & Jean E Heron. $95-295. 14 rooms with PB. Breakfast included in rates. Types of meals: Cont plus. Beds: KQD.
Publicity: *Palm Beach Daily News, Boston Globe, Spur Magazine and Figaro.*

"Gerry's breakfast is outrageously great!"

Cobblestone Inn

5 Ash St
Nantucket, MA 02554-3515
(508)228-1987 Fax:(508)228-6698
E-mail: cobble@nantucket.net

Circa 1725. Two blocks from Steamboat Wharf and located on a cobbled side street, the Cobblestone Inn boasts four fireplaces, wide floorboards, curved-corner support posts from the frame of a ship and a quiet outside sitting area. Guest rooms have period decorations and canopy or four-poster queen size beds. A third-floor suite offers a good view of the boats sailing in the harbor. A continental breakfast is provided.

Innkeeper(s): Robin Hammer-Yankow & Keith Yankow. $75-290. MC, VISA. 6 rooms with PB. Breakfast included in rates. Types of meals: Cont. TV and phone in room. Central air. Guest pantry with refrigerator and ice maker and microwave on premises. Antiquing, beaches, fishing, live theater and water sports nearby.
Publicity: *Yankee and Woman's Day.*

"Your warmth and hospitality made our stay all the more pleasureful!"

Corner House

49 Center St, PO Box 1828
Nantucket, MA 02554-1828
(508)228-1530
E-mail: info@cornerhousenantucket.com
Web: www.cornerhousenantucket.com

Circa 1790. The Corner House is a charming 18th-century village inn. Architectural details such as the original pine floors, paneling and fireplaces have been preserved. A screened porch overlooks the English perennial garden, where guests often take afternoon tea. All of the romantically appointed bedchambers feature canopy or four-poster beds. Three rooms are adorned with non-working fireplaces, some have refrigerators.

Innkeeper(s): John & Sandy Knox-Johnston. $65-235. MC, VISA, AX, TC. 15 rooms with PB and 2 suites. Breakfast and afternoon tea included in rates. Types of meals: Cont plus. AP. Beds: QDT. Cable TV in room. Air condition-

ing. Fax, library, beach towels, bike rack and concierge services on premises. Limited French and German spoken. Antiquing, fishing, golf, art galleries, whaling museum, sportfishing, live theater, tennis and water sports nearby.
Publicity: *Detroit Free Press, Atlanta Journal, Newsday, Gourmet, Elle Decor, Travel & Leisure and Yankee Magazine.*

"Thank you so much for the care, atmosphere, cleanliness and peace you provided for us this week."

House of The Seven Gables

32 Cliff Rd
Nantucket, MA 02554-3644
(508)228-4706
E-mail: walton@nantucket.net
Web: www.houseofthesevengables.com

Circa 1880. Originally the annex of the Sea Cliff Inn, one of the island's oldest hotels, this three-story Queen Anne Victorian inn offers 10 guest rooms. Beaches, bike rentals, museums, restaurants, shops and tennis courts are all found nearby. The guest rooms are furnished with king or queen beds and period antiques. Breakfast is served each morning in the guest rooms and often include homemade coffee cake, muffins or Portuguese rolls.

Innkeeper(s): Sue Walton. $100-300.
MC, VISA, AX. 10 rooms, 8 with PB. Breakfast included in rates. Types of meals: Cont. Beds: KQ. Antiquing, fishing, live theater, shopping and water sports nearby.

"You have a beautiful home and one that makes everyone feel relaxed and at home."

Jared Coffin House

29 Broad St
Nantucket, MA 02554-3502
(508)228-2400

Circa 1845. Jared Coffin was one of the island's most successful ship owners and the first to build a three-story mansion. The house's brick walls and slate roof resisted the Great Fire of 1846  and, in 1847, it was purchased by the Nantucket Steamship Company for use as a hotel. Additions were made and a century later, the Nantucket Historical Trust purchased and restored the house. Today, the inn consists of five historic houses and a 1964 building. The oldest is the Swain House.

Innkeeper(s): John J. Cowden, Jr. $125-375. MC, VISA, AX, DC, DS. TAC10. 60 rooms with PB and 3 conference rooms. Beds: QDT. Fax, copier, serving breakfast, lunch and dinner and two restaurants on premises.
Publicity: *Coast & Country.*

"The dining was superb, the atmosphere was gracious and the rooms were charming and spotless."

Pineapple Inn

10 Hussey St
Nantucket, MA 02554-3612
(508)228-9992 Fax:(508)325-6051
E-mail: info@pineappleinn.com
Web: www.pineappleinn.com

Circa 1838. Built for a prominent whaling ship captain, this classic colonial has been restored and refurnished to inspire the gracious and elegant standard of a time in history that most of us only read about in books. Reproduction and authentic 19th-century antiques, artwork and Oriental rugs are featured throughout the inn. Luxurious goose down comforters and Ralph Lauren linens top beautiful handmade, four-poster canopy beds in most of the 12 guest rooms. The innkeepers, seasoned restaurateurs, offer guests a delightful combination of steaming cappuccinos, freshly squeezed orange juice, hot or cold cereals, a fresh fruit plate and a selection of pastries served restaurant-style in the formal dining room or on the bricked garden patio.

Innkeeper(s): Caroline & Bob Taylor. $145-325. MC, VISA, AX, PC, TC. 12 rooms with PB, 3 with FP and 1 conference room. Breakfast included in rates. Types of meals: Cont plus, cont and early coffee/tea. Beds: KQ. Cable TV and phone in room. Air conditioning. Fax and copier on premises. Weddings, small meetings, family reunions and seminars hosted. Antiquing, fishing, golf, historic homes, whaling museum, live theater, shopping, tennis and water sports nearby.

"Our time here was more than just a lovely room. The patio breakfast was heavenly... and you always took time to chat and make us feel welcome. The essence of elegance—the most modern comforts and the charm of an old whaling Captain's house."

Sherburne Inn

10 Gay St
Nantucket, MA 02554-3650
(508)228-4425 (888)577-4425 Fax:(508)228-8114
E-mail: sherinn@nantucket.net
Web: www.sherburneinn.com

Circa 1835. This Greek Revival inn with Nantucket wood shingles once was home to the Atlantic Silk Company. On a quiet side street in the core historic district, it became an elegant guest house in 1872 and still retains its 19th-century charm while offering fine decor, furnishings and plush linens. Two parlors, both with fireplaces, are available for guests wishing to read, relax or watch TV. Continental plus breakfasts may be enjoyed in front of the fireplace, in the flower garden, or on the deck. The inn offers easy access to Nantucket's fine restaurants and shops and the beach is just 500 feet away. The Steamship Authority dock is also nearby.

Innkeeper(s): Dale & Susan Hamilton. $85-295. MC, VISA, AX, DS, PC, TC. 8 rooms with PB, 1 with FP. Breakfast included in rates. Types of meals: Cont plus, early coffee/tea, afternoon tea and snacks/refreshments. Beds: KQ. Cable TV, phone, ceiling fan, VCR, fireplace, imported French & English wallcoverings, Oriental rugs and original artwork in room. Central air. Fax, copier, library, outside ceck, flower garden with tables and chairs and bike rack on premises. Small meetings and family reunions hosted. German spoken. Antiquing, art galleries, beaches, bicycling, canoeing/kayaking, fishing, golf, hiking, Nantucket Whaling Museum, cranberry bogs, bike paths, 83 miles of beaches, world-class boat basin, sailing, restaurants, live theater, museums, parks, shopping, tennis, water sports and wineries nearby.
Publicity: *New York Times, Town and Country and Travel and Leisure.*

Stumble Inne

109 Orange Street
Nantucket, MA 02554-3947
(508)228-4482 (800)649-4482 Fax:(508)228-4752
E-mail: romance@nantucket.net

Circa 1820. This Nantucket Island bed and breakfast is appointed with fine antiques and period reproductions. The tastefully furnished rooms feature wide pine floors, antique beds and oriental carpets. At the back of the inn's hydrangea-filled gardens, there is a two-bedroom cottage that can accommodate up to four people. The cottage also includes a bathroom, kitchen, living room and a private deck. The inn was voted "Best Nantucket B&B" by Cape Cod Magazine for several years including 1997-2000.
Historic Interest: Nantucket Historical Association Exhibits (one-half mile).
Innkeeper(s): Jeanne & George Todor. $75-280. MC, VISA, AX, TC. 6 rooms

with PB and 1 suite. Breakfast included in rates. Types of meals: Cont plus and early coffee/tea. Beds: Q. Cable TV, ceiling fan, VCR and refrigerator in room. Air conditioning. Fax on premises. Small meetings, family reunions and seminars hosted. Antiquing, fishing, restaurants, live theater, shopping and water sports nearby.
Publicity: *Innsider.*

"A relaxing, comfortable week with gracious hosts. Thanks for your Southern hospitality in the Northeast."

The Woodbox Inn

29 Fair St
Nantucket, MA 02554-3798
(508)228-0587
E-mail: woodbox@nantucket.net
Web: www.woodboxinn.com

Circa 1709. In the heart of the historic district, the Woodbox Inn was built in 1709 by Captain George Bunker. Guest rooms are decorated with antiques and reproductions and some have canopy beds. The six suites offer
sitting rooms and fireplaces. Walk to Main Street and enjoy fine boutiques and art galleries. Other activities include biking, tennis, golf, whale watching and sandy beaches for sunning. The inn's award-winning gourmet dining room features
an early American atmosphere with low-beamed ceilings and pine-paneled walls. (Meals are not included in room rates.).

Innkeeper(s): Dexter Tutein. $185-319. PC, TC. 9 rooms with PB, 6 with FP and 6 suites. Types of meals: Full bkfst. Beds: KQDT. Weddings, small meetings and family reunions hosted. French, German and Spanish spoken. Antiquing, fishing, live theater, parks, shopping, tennis and water sports nearby.
Publicity: *Wharton Alumni, Cape Cod Life, Boston Magazine, Wine Spectator., James Beard Foundation and Phantom Gourmet.*

New Marlborough   E2

Old Inn on The Green

Rt 57
New Marlborough, MA 01230
(413)229-3131 (800)286-3139 Fax:(413)229-8236
E-mail: brad@oldinn.com
Web: www.oldinn.com

Circa 1760. This former stagecoach stop, tavern, store and post office offers guest rooms in two locations. Gedney Farm, on 300 acres, is a short walk away from the main house. It accommodates the guest suites in two enormous Normandy-style barns, where Percheron stallions and Jersey cattle were once housed. The elegant country decor is warmed by hardwood floors, handhewn beams and granite fireplaces. There are tiled whirlpool tubs in some of the rooms. The dining room offers colonial elegance in candle-lit rooms. "Superb" is the most frequently stated complement about the inn's fine dining experience.

Innkeeper(s): Leslie Miller & Brad Wagstaff. $175-350. MC, VISA, AX, PC, TC. TAC10. 26 rooms with PB, 17 with FP, 2 suites and 3 conference rooms. Breakfast included in rates. Types of meals: Cont plus, early coffee/tea and gourmet dinner. Beds: KQT. Phone, turndown service, ceiling fan, 11 with A/C and 11 with whirlpools in room. Fax, swimming, library and pool on premises. Weddings, small meetings and family reunions hosted. Antiquing, fishing, golf, hiking, boating, spa, facials and massage, live theater, parks, shopping, downhill skiing and cross-country skiing nearby.
Publicity: *NYTm Country Inn, Country Living, Wine Spectator, Boston Globe, Atlantic Monthly and Travel Channel.*

Newburyport B14

Clark Currier Inn

45 Green St
Newburyport, MA 01950-2646
(978)465-8363
E-mail: drn1947@mediaone.net

Circa 1803. Once the home of shipbuilder Thomas March Clark, this three-story Federal-style inn provides gracious accommodations to visitors in the Northeast Massachusetts

area. Visitors will enjoy the inn's details added by Samuel McEntire, one of the nation's most celebrated home builders and woodcarvers. Breakfast is served in the dining room or garden room, with an afternoon tea offered in the garden room. The inn's grounds also boast a picturesque garden and gazebo. Parker River National Wildlife Refuge and Maudslay State Park are nearby, as well as Plum Island beaches.

Historic Interest: The Cushing House Museum, Firehouse Center, Custom House Museum and Market Square are within walking distance. Lowell's Boat Shop, a museum across the river, houses the Amesbury dory and highlights more than 200 years of boat building.

Innkeeper(s): Bob Nolan. $95-165. MC, VISA, AX, DS. 8 rooms with PB. Breakfast and afternoon tea included in rates. Types of meals: Cont plus. Beds: QDT. Phone in room. Air conditioning. Sherry and fruit are available in the library on premises. Amusement parks, antiquing, fishing, many acclaimed and varied restaurants and shops, live theater, parks, shopping, cross-country skiing and water sports nearby.

"We had a lovely stay in your B&B! We appreciated your hospitality!"

Windsor House

38 Federal St
Newburyport, MA 01950-2820
(978)462-3778 (888)873-5296 Fax:(978)465-3443
E-mail: windsorinn@earthlink.net
Web: www.bbhost.com/windsorhouse

Circa 1786. This brick Federal-style mansion was designed as a combination home and ship's chandlery (an outfitter and broker for cargo). The Merchant Suite was once the sales room and features a 14-foot ceiling with hand-hewn, beveled beams. The Bridal Suite was once the master suite. The newest suite, England's Rose, is a tribute to Princess Diana. The English innkeepers serve a hearty English-country breakfast and an English tea in the afternoon.

Historic Interest: William Lloyd Garrison birthplace (across the street), Newburyport Custom's House and Caleb Cushing House (walking distance).

Innkeeper(s): Judith & John Harris. $125-155. MC, VISA, AX, DS, PC, TC. TAC10. 4 rooms with PB. Breakfast and afternoon tea included in rates. Types of meals: Full bkfst. Beds: KQD. TV, phone, ceiling fan, fans/alarm clocks and tea and coffee facilities in rooms in room. Air conditioning. VCR, fax and copier on premises. Small meetings and seminars hosted. Antiquing, fishing, golf, bird watching, wildlife refuge, live theater, parks, shopping, cross-country skiing, tennis and water sports nearby.

Pets allowed: Special arrangement.

Publicity: *New York Times, Boston Globe, Boston Herald Sunday* and *Le Monde.*

"You will find what you look for and be met by the unexpected too. A good time!"

North New Salem D7

Bullard Farm B&B

89 Elm St
North New Salem, MA 01355-9502
(978)544-6959 Fax:(978)544-6959

Circa 1793. This inn's four guest rooms are found in a farmhouse containing six working fireplaces. The farm has been in the family of the innkeeper's mother since 1864, and guests

are welcome to hike the inn's grounds, observing its history as a lumber mill and tannery. The inn features many original pieces used in its coun-

try-style decor. Full breakfasts may include banana sour cream coffee cake. Winter visitors may enjoy a sleigh ride or cross-country skiing on the inn's 300 acres. Quabbin Reservoir is a one-mile drive from the inn.

Innkeeper(s): Janet F. Kraft. $75-100. MC, VISA, PC. 4 rooms, 2 with FP and 2 conference rooms. Breakfast included in rates. Types of meals: Full bkfst. Beds: QDT. Phone in room. Air conditioning. VCR and fax on premises. Small meetings, family reunions and seminars hosted. Antiquing, fishing, hiking, swimming, shopping, downhill skiing, cross-country skiing and sporting events nearby.

Publicity: *Boston Globe* and *Worcester Telegram.*

Northampton E5

Lupine House

185 North Main St
Northampton, MA 01060
(413)586-9766 (800)890-9766

Circa 1872. This Colonial offers a comfortable setting for those enjoying a New England getaway. Rooms are simply furnished with antiques adding to the ambiance. Continental-plus fare is served in the mornings, including homemade granola, fresh fruit, cereals, breads and muffins. The B&B is a short drive

from downtown Northampton and many area schools, including Amherst, Smith, Hampshire and Mount Holyoke colleges and the University of Massachusetts.

Historic Interest: Old Deerfield is just a few minutes drive away.

Innkeeper(s): Evelyn & Gil Billings. $75-85.

MC, VISA, DS, PC, TC. 3 rooms with PB. Breakfast included in rates. Types of meals: Cont plus and early coffee/tea. Beds: QDT. Turndown service in room. Air conditioning. Library on premises. Antiquing, fishing, golf, biking, museums, live theater, parks, shopping, cross-country skiing, sporting events and tennis nearby.

Publicity: *Daily Hampshire Gazette.*

"You certainly provide 'the extra mile' of hospitality and service. Thank you."

Oak Bluffs K16

Nashua House

30 Kennebec Ave, PO Box 2221
Oak Bluffs, MA 02557-0803
(508)693-0043
E-mail: calebcaldwellmv@hotmail.com
Web: www.nashuahouse.com

Circa 1865. Built as a Victorian rooming house in 1865, this recently renovated landmark is a gem for the budget-minded

traveler. Its central location is perfect for exploring Martha's Vineyard. The 15 bright and airy guest bedrooms are delightfully decorated and furnished in true cottage style. Several bedrooms have balcony access and glorious ocean views. Enjoy a 10 percent discount when dining at Zapotec, the island's only Mexican food restaurant. In addition to the abundance of seaside-related activities, there is much to see and do. Innkeeper Caleb Caldwell says, "On Martha's Vineyard, every acre has significant history.".
Historic Interest: On Martha's Vineyard.
Innkeeper(s): Caleb Caldwell, Chris Blake. $49-109. MC, VISA, AX, PC, TC. TAC10. 15 rooms. Beds: DT. VCR on premises. Amusement parks, antiquing, art galleries, beaches, bicycling, canoeing/kayaking, fishing, golf, hiking, horseback riding, live theater, museums, parks, shopping, tennis, water sports and wineries nearby.
Publicity: *The Boston Sunday Globe and Newsday.*

The Oak House

PO Box 299AA Seaview Ave
Oak Bluffs, MA 02557
(508)693-4187

Circa 1872. Massachusetts Gov. William Claflin purchased this gingerbread cottage because of its fine location and splendid view of the ocean. He imported oak timbers and employed ship's carpenters to carve oak ceilings, wall panels and interior pillars. A servants' wing, an additional floor, and a wide veranda were added, all for the purpose of entertaining important Massachusetts leaders. As a bed & breakfast, the Oak House maintains the grand style with authentic Victorian furnishings and refined hospitality.
Innkeeper(s): Betsi Convery-Luce. $130-220. MC, VISA, AX, DS. 10 rooms with PB. Breakfast included in rates. Types of meals: Cont plus and afternoon tea. Beds: KQ. TV and phone in room.
Publicity: *Vineyard Gazette.*

"I feel like a guest in a friend's home."

Pequot Hotel

19 Pequot Avenue
Oak Bluffs, MA 02557
(508)693-5087 (800)847-8704 Fax:(508)696-9413
E-mail: vacation@pequothotel.com
Web: www.pequothotel.com

Circa 1900. The straight-back wooden rockers, typical of those that traditionally grace the verandas of Martha's Vineyard, bid a warm welcome to this classic Victorian gingerbread inn. Furnished with a contemporary charm, the ambiance of the island is highlighted in decorative accents. The comfortable guest bedrooms are especially suitable for families traveling together. Surrounded by colorful flowers and plants, the garden patio is a delightful setting for a buffet-style continental breakfast and afternoon tea and pastries. Ask about the sailing and dinner packages that are offered.
Historic Interest: Flying Horses Carousel (1/2 mile).
Innkeeper(s): Isabelle Morley. $65-175. MC, VISA, AX, DS, TC. TAC10. 29 rooms, 27 with PB, 1 with FP, 1 suite, 1 cottage and 1 conference room. Breakfast and afternoon tea included in rates. Types of meals: Cont. Beds: KQDT. Cable TV, ceiling fan and fireplace in room. Air conditioning. VCR and fax on premises. Weddings, small meetings, family reunions and seminars hosted. Antiquing, art galleries, beaches, bicycling, canoeing/kayaking, fishing, golf, museums, parks, shopping and water sports nearby.

Orleans H19

The Farmhouse at Nauset Beach

163 Beach Rd
Orleans, MA 02653-2732
(508)255-6654

Circa 1870. Feel the intimacy of Orleans and capture the flavor of Cape Cod at this quiet country inn resting in a seashore setting. Rooms in this Greek Revival-style inn are comfortably furnished to depict their 19th-century past. Some rooms offer ocean views, and one includes a decorated fireplace. Nauset Beach  is a short walk away. To make your stay complete, your itinerary can include charter fishing, antiquing, shopping, exploring quiet country lanes or a day at the beach. The inn offers gift certificates and is open year-round.
Innkeeper(s): Dorothy Standish. $52-110. MC, VISA, TC. 8 rooms with PB, 1 with FP. Breakfast included in rates. Types of meals: Cont plus. Beds: KQD. Ceiling fan in some rooms in room. Bike rack on premises. Family reunions hosted. Antiquing, fishing, horseback riding, windsurfing, bike trails, live theater, shopping and water sports nearby.

Orleans Waterfront Inn

Rt 6A on Town Cove, PO Box 188
Orleans, MA 02653
(508)255-2222 Fax:(508)255-6722
E-mail: info@orleansinn.com
Web: www.orleansinn.com

Circa 1875. Recently refurbished, this Sea Captain Mansion, which was built by a descendant of the Mayflower Pilgrims, features a waterfront setting and a Victorian decor. The lobby showcases an original stone fireplace, vintage dolls and a grandfather clock. Expect gracious service that begins with a welcome box of fine chocolates. Quiet guest bedrooms boast custom furnishings and floral quilts. Enjoy a continental breakfast in bed or in the Snow Dining Room. A kitchenette with toaster oven, refrigerator and microwave is available for guest use. Casual fare can be found on-site at O'Hagan's Irish Pub. Relax on the deck with a cold beverage and watch the boats sail by.
Historic Interest: Old Cove burying ground (3 miles), Pilgrim Monument (20 miles).
Innkeeper(s): Ed & Laurie Maas and children. $75-250. MC, VISA, AX, DC, DS, PC, TC. TAC10. 11 rooms with PB, 3 suites and 1 conference room. Breakfast, afternoon tea and snacks/refreshments included in rates. Types of meals: Cont plus, cont, early coffee/tea, gourmet lunch, picnic lunch, gourmet dinner and room service. EP. Beds: KQT. Cable TV and phone in room. Air conditioning. VCR, fax, copier, library and pet boarding on premises. Antiquing, art galleries, beaches, bicycling, canoeing/kayaking, fishing, golf, hiking, horseback riding, live theater, museums, parks, shopping, sporting events, tennis, water sports and wineries nearby. Pets Allowed.
Publicity: *Cape Codder, Cape Cod Life, Cape Cod Times & Albany Times Union.*

Petersham D8

The Inn at Clamber Hill

111 N Main St
Petersham, MA 01366-9501
(978)724-8800 (888)374-0007 Fax:(978)724-8829
E-mail: clamber@tiac.net
Web: www.clamberhill.com

Circa 1927. A statuesque 1927 European country estate, the Inn at Clamber Hill sits in the midst of a peaceful, secluded

33-acre wooded estate just minutes from Quabbin Reservoir. Located in the North Central Massachusetts forests, which are known for their dramatic seasonal color changes, the inn is a haven for "leaf peepers." Furnished with antiques and Oriental carpets, the inn boasts two suites with private baths and sitting rooms with fireplaces as well as three other accommodations. Breakfast is a gourmet's delight and includes items like fresh fruit, homemade cinnamon rolls, muffins, waffles with fresh strawberries, peach-stuffed French toast and wild blueberry pancakes. Dinner and high tea are available by arrangement. Enjoy strolling through the woods and gardens on the estate or leave the estate to go golfing, swimming, biking, hiking, horseback riding or bird watching. Cross-country skiing and snowshoeing are available in the winter months. Harvard University's forestry research center and Fisher Museum are just three miles from the inn at the 3000-acre Harvard Forest.

Historic Interest: Quabbin Reservoir (2 miles), Daniel Shays Highway (1 mile). Innkeeper(s): Mark & Deni Ellis. $108-185. MC, VISA, AX, PC, TC. 5 rooms, 3 with PB, 4 with FP, 2 suites and 1 conference room. Breakfast and snacks/refreshments included in rates. Types of meals: Veg bkfst, cont plus, early coffee/tea and afternoon tea. Beds: QT. Fireplace in room. Air conditioning. VCR, fax, copier, library, parlor and terraces and gardens on premises. Weddings, small meetings, family reunions and seminars hosted. German and French spoken. Antiquing, art galleries, beaches, bicycling, canoeing/kayaking, fishing, golf, hiking, horseback riding, live theater, museums, parks, shopping, downhill skiing, cross-country skiing and water sports nearby.
Pets allowed: $15 per night, owners are responsible.

Winterwood at Petersham

19 N Main St
Petersham, MA 01366-9500
(978)724-8885
E-mail: winterwoodatpetersham@juno.com
Web: www.winterwoodinn.com

Circa 1842. The town of Petersham is often referred to as a museum of Greek Revival architecture. One of the grand hous-

es facing the common is Winterwood. It boasts fireplaces in almost every room. Private dining is available for groups of up to 70 people. The inn is listed in the National Register.
Innkeeper(s): Jean & Robert Day. $119.
MC, VISA, AX, DS. TAC10. 6 rooms with PB, 5 with FP and 1 conference room. Types of meals: Cont plus. Beds: QT. Weddings, small meetings, family reunions and seminars hosted. Antiquing, hiking, downhill skiing and cross-country skiing nearby.
Publicity: *Boston Globe* and *Yankee Magazine.*

"Between your physical facilities and Jean's cooking, our return to normal has been made even more difficult. Your hospitality was just a fantastic extra to our total experience."

Pittsfield   D2

Olde White Horse Inn

378 South St
Pittsfield, MA 01201-6804
(413)442-2512
E-mail: whorsein@bcn.net

Circa 1902. Innkeeping runs in the family at the White Horse, which features an elegant Colonial exterior set on an acre of manicured lawn. The current innkeeper's grandparents also were innkeepers, and two rooms are named in honor of them. The Colonial theme continues into the home and to its eight

guest rooms, decorated with antiques and beds topped with cozy comforters. The innkeepers' daughters also pitch in and help run the inn; the oldest prepares the breakfasts. The morning meal includes such items as quiche, pancakes, homemade muffins or breads and fresh fruit.
Innkeeper(s): Joe & Linda Kalisz. $95-180. MC, VISA, AX, DC, CB, DS, TC. 8 rooms with PB. Breakfast included in rates. Types of meals: Full bkfst, early coffee/tea and snacks/refreshments. Beds: QD. TV, phone and turndown service in room. Air conditioning. Fax and copier on premises. Weddings, small meetings and family reunions hosted. Antiquing, fishing, live theater, parks, shopping, downhill skiing, cross-country skiing, sporting events and water sports nearby.

Plymouth   G15

Foxglove Cottage

101 Sandwich Rd
Plymouth, MA 02360-2503
(800)479-4746
E-mail: tranquility@foxglove-cottage.com
Web: www.foxglove-cottage.com

Circa 1820. Follow tree-lined Sandwich Road, the original Colonial highway to Boston, as it meanders to Foxglove Cottage, a pink 1820 Cape-style house. There are 40 acres of meadow, woodland, and a lawn with rhododendron and parts of an old stone fence. Horses graze in a pasture shared by red fox, deer, coyote and other wildlife. Wideboard floors, Victorian antiques, six working fireplaces and coordinating fabrics and wallpapers create a warm, welcoming environment. Ask for the Rose Room for a handsomely decorated retreat with a four-poster canopy bed or the Canopy Room for a king-size bed. Baked French toast with blueberries or a sausage, egg and cheese casserole are popular breakfast items. Plimoth Plantation is nearby, and guests can also go whale watching.
Innkeeper(s): Mr. & Mrs. Charles K. Cowan. $95-115. PC, TC. TAC10. 3 rooms with PB, 3 with FP. Breakfast included in rates. Types of meals: Full bkfst. Beds: KQT. Air conditioning. VCR, fax and copier on premises. Antiquing, fishing, whale watching and Plimoth Plantation nearby, live theater, parks, shopping and water sports nearby.

"A very charming place."

Princeton   D9

Fernside Inn

PO Box 303, 162 Mountain Rd
Princeton, MA 01541-0303
(978)464-2741 (800)545-2741 Fax:(978)464-2065
E-mail: innkeeper@fernsideinn.com
Web: www.fernsideinn.com

Circa 1835. Originally built by Capt. Benjamin Harrington, this elegant Federal mansion was transformed in 1870 into a tavern and boarding house for Harvard professors and students. In 1890, the home changed owners and served as a vacation house for working women for more than 100 years. In 1994, the Morrisons transformed it once again and meticulously restored it. Situated on the eastern slope of Mount Wachusett, the inn is nestled on 15 acres with breathtaking sunrise views. Designed for entertaining, there are eight cozy fireplaces, numerous sitting rooms and a variety of porches. The common rooms as well as the guest rooms are elegantly decorated with antiques, peri-

od reproductions, and Oriental rugs. A home-cooked breakfast includes fresh fruit, pastries and a variety of entrees.

Innkeeper(s): Jocelyn & Richard Morrison. $120-165. MC, VISA, AX, DS, TC. TAC10. 6 rooms with PB, 4 with FP, 2 suites and 1 conference room. Breakfast included in rates. Types of meals: Gourmet bkfst and early coffee/tea. Beds: QT. Phone and turndown service in room. Fax, copier and refreshments served on premises. Handicap access. Small meetings and seminars hosted. Antiquing, golf, parks, shopping, downhill skiing, cross-country skiing and tennis nearby.

"You cannot help but feel at ease the moment you walk into the inn."

Provincetown   G18

Bradford Carver House

70 Bradford St
Provincetown, MA 02657-1363
(508)487-4966 (800)826-9083 Fax:(508)487-7213
E-mail: bradcarver@capecod.net
Web: www.bradfordcarver.com

Circa 1800. One block from Cape Cod Bay, this mid-1800s Victorian inn is painted Federal blue with a white picket fence, roses, gladioli and azaleas, creating a welcoming invitation. Inside, there's always a bowl of fruit and in summer, fresh cut flowers. The innkeeper's collections of Hummels, chandeliers and candelabras (Bill confesses to being a candelabra fanatic) are found throughout the parlor and guest rooms. Antiques such as a Victorian sofa and French settee furnish the living room with its handsome fireplace. The five rooms all offer large beds, phones with voicemail and data ports, VCRs and many other amenities. A 900-piece video library is cataloged, categorized and color coded for guests. Enjoy a complimentary continental breakfast in the parlor or on one of the patios and plan your day's activities. Located in the heart of historic Provincetown, it is located just one block from Commercial Street with its many unique shops, restaurants and stores. Try booking a boating excursion or visit Pilgrims' First Landing Park and Museum.

Innkeeper(s): Bill & Jose. $49-179. MC, VISA, AX, DS, TC. TAC10. 5 rooms with PB, 2 with FP. Types of meals: Cont. Beds: KQ. Cable TV, phone, ceiling fan and VCR in room. Air conditioning. Antiquing, art galleries, beaches, bicycling, canoeing/kayaking, fishing, hiking, museums, parks, shopping, tennis and wineries nearby.

Christopher's By The Bay

8 Johnson St
Provincetown, MA 02657
(508)487-9263 (877)487-9263 Fax:(508)487-9263
E-mail: christophers.bythebay@verizon.net
Web: www.christophersbythebay.com

Circa 1860. Overlooking the harbor, this three-story Victorian inn sits quietly on a side street in the heart of town. The fireplace in the front room is the perfect catalyst for relaxation. The guest bedrooms and suite, named after famous artists, have so much to offer. Some feature bay windows, wide plank hardwood floors, a fireplace and stunning views. Choose from an extensive video library for in-room use. Wake up to a delicious breakfast served in the sunny dining room. The garden is a delight, as is exploring the local sites just around the corner.

Historic Interest: First landing of Pilgrims.

Innkeeper(s): Ash Calder & Jason Real. $50-170. MC, VISA, AX. TAC10. 10 rooms, 5 with PB, 1 with FP and a suite. Breakfast included in rates. Types of meals: Cont and early coffee/tea. Beds: QD. Cable TV, phone, ceiling fan and VCR in room. Air conditioning. Fax on premises. Weddings, small meetings, family reunions and seminars hosted. German, Spanish, Italian and French spoken. Antiquing, art galleries, beaches, bicycling, canoeing/kayaking, fishing, golf, hiking, horseback riding, live theater, museums, parks, shopping, tennis, water sports and wineries nearby.

Crowne Pointe Historic Inn

82 Bradford St
Provincetown, MA 02657
(508)487-6767 (877)216-9631 Fax:(508)487-5554
E-mail: welcome@crownepointe.com
Web: www.crownepointe.com

Circa 1800. A prominent sea captain built this historic inn, which has been restored to its 19th-century glory. The home's stunning Victorian architecture includes a two-story wrap-around porch and a turret. The interior maintains the original wainscoting and pine floors, and the historic ambiance is enhanced by period antiques. Guests enjoy a variety of amenities, as all rooms include helpful items such as refrigerators, coffee makers, data ports, and private phones with voice

mail. Rooms also include private access to the inn's two-story porch. Guests can book rooms with a fireplace or whirlpool tub or perhaps a private deck. The Deluxe Suites include a king-size, four-poster bed, fireplace and a private balcony overlooking the garden. The hot breakfasts feature fresh fruit, yogurt and breads, as well as a hot, homemade dish.

Innkeeper(s): David Sanford, Tom Walter. $95-350. MC, VISA, AX, DS, TC. TAC10. 40 rooms with PB, 25 with FP, 3 suites and 2 conference rooms. Breakfast and afternoon tea included in rates. Types of meals: Gourmet bkfst, snacks/refreshments and room service. Beds: KQ. Cable TV, phone, turndown service, ceiling fan and VCR in room. Air conditioning. Fax, copier, spa, library and heated in-ground pool on premises. Weddings, small meetings, family reunions and seminars hosted. Polish & English spoken. Antiquing, art galleries, beaches, bicycling, canoeing/kayaking, fishing, golf, hiking, horseback riding, live theater, museums, parks, shopping, tennis, water sports & wineries nearby. Publicity: *Our World Magazine and Chronicle.*

Gifford House

11 Carver St
Provincetown, MA 02657-2111
(508)487-0688 (800)434-0130

Circa 1858. Enjoy splendid views of Cape Cod Bay and Long Point or the dunes and Pilgrim Monument from some of the rooms in this former stagecoach stop. The 15,000-square-foot Greek Revival hotel once hosted Ulysses S. Grant, Theodore Roosevelt and William Taft. Guests are provided with a continental breakfast, and the inn restaurant offers seafood and pasta dishes. There is a bar and dance club on the premises. Pilgrim monument is a quarter mile away.

Innkeeper(s): James Foss. $48-200. MC, VISA, AX, TC. 25 rooms, 23 with PB and 2 suites. Breakfast included in rates. Types of meals: Cont plus. Beds: QD. Window fans in room. Lounge on premises. Antiquing, art galleries, beaches, bicycling, canoeing/kayaking, fishing, hiking, horseback riding, live theater, museums, parks, shopping, tennis, water sports and wineries nearby.

John Randall House

140 Bradford St
Provincetown, MA 02657-1435
(508)487-3533 (800)573-6700 Fax:(508)487-3533
E-mail: johnrandallhouse@aol.com
Web: www.johnrandallhouse.com

Circa 1900. Once the home of Provincetown's family doctor, the historic home boasts many original features, including its fine woodwork. Antiques decorate the 12 guest rooms, four of which include a private bathroom. Each room is decorated in its own special style. Guests can relax on the enclosed porch or on the deck. The inn is within walking distance to shops, galleries and restaurants.

Historic Interest: Pilgrim Monument (1/4 mile).

Innkeeper(s): Richard Brunson/Tim Richmond. $65-150. MC, VISA, AX, DS, TC. TAC10. 12 rooms, 4 with PB. Breakfast and afternoon tea included in rates. Types of meals: Cont plus. Beds: QDT. Cable TV, ceiling fan, VCR and small refrigerator in room. Air conditioning. Fax, copier and library on premises. Handicap access. Weddings and family reunions hosted. Antiquing, art galleries, beaches, bicycling, canoeing/kayaking, fishing, golf, hiking, horseback riding, live theater, museums, shopping and wineries nearby.

Land's End Inn

22 Commercial St
Provincetown, MA 02657-1910
(508)487-0706 (800)276-7088

Circa 1904. Built originally as a summer bungalow for Charles Higgins, a Boston merchant, Lands End commands a panoramic view of Provincetown and Cape Cod Bay. It still houses part

of the Higgins' collection of Oriental wood carvings and stained glass. While David Schoolman was the inn's owner, he enhanced it by decorating with an eclectic array of wonderful antiques. Amid luxuriant gardens, the inn successfully retains an air of quiet and relaxation.

Innkeeper(s): Ron Morgan. $87-285. MC, VISA, PC, TC. 16 rooms with PB. Breakfast included in rates. Types of meals: Cont and early coffee/tea. Beds: QD. Ceiling fan in room. Refrigerator in breakfast room and view of Cape Cod Bay on premises. Weddings, small meetings, family reunions and seminars hosted. Antiquing, fishing, live theater, parks, shopping and water sports nearby.

Publicity: *Travel Magazine, Cape Cod Review and Cape Cod Life.*

Revere Guest House Inc

14 Court St
Provincetown, MA 02657-2114
(508)487-2292 (800)487-2292
E-mail: info@reverehouse.com
Web: www.reverehouse.com

Circa 1830. This restored Captain's home on Court Street was built in 1830 when Provincetown (where the Pilgrims landed in 1620) was still a thriving fishing port. It was awarded the 1998 Preservation Award by the Provincetown Historical Commission. The inn is surrounded by gardens and a picket fence, and it has nine guest rooms — two with private bath and six with shared baths. Enjoy a continental breakfast before walking to the beach or biking across paths in the sand dunes. Or bike on into town — the slow traffic in town is also excellent for biking.

Innkeeper(s): Gary Palochko. $40-165. MC, VISA, AX, DS, PC, TC. TAC10. 9 rooms, 2 with PB. Breakfast included in rates. Types of meals: Cont. Beds: QD. Cable TV and VCR in room. Air conditioning. Antiquing, art galleries, beaches, bicycling, fishing, hiking, horseback riding, live theater, museums, parks, shopping and water sports nearby.

Watership Inn

7 Winthrop St
Provincetown, MA 02657-2116
(508)487-0094 (800)330-9413
E-mail: watership@capecod.net

Circa 1820. This stately manor was built as a home port for a Provincetown sea captain. During the past 10 years, it has been renovated and the original beamed ceilings and polished plank floors provide a background for the inn's antiques and simple

decor. Guests enjoy the inn's sun decks and large yard, which offers volleyball and croquet sets.

Historic Interest: Landing site of the Pilgrims, The Provincetown Heritage Museum, Pilgrim Monument and Museum (within walking distance).

Innkeeper(s): Richard Conley. $40-205.

MC, VISA, AX, DS. 15 rooms with PB. Breakfast included in rates. Types of meals: Cont plus. Beds: QDT. Cable TV in room. Antiquing, beaches, whale watching, museums and parks nearby.

Publicity: *Boston "In."*

"We found your hospitality and charming inn perfect for our brief yet wonderful escape from Boston."

Quincy E13

Quincy Adams Bed & Breakfast

24 Whitney Rd
Quincy, MA 02169
(617)479-6215 Fax:(617)479-1065
E-mail: marylee@quincyadamsbandb.com
Web: www.quincyadamsbandb.com

Circa 1906. An elegant Victorian shingle-style home offers traditional New England hospitality. Ideally located in a quiet, historic area close to shops and the beach, it boasts easy access to Boston's variety of attractions. The lounge is a perfect gathering place to plan the day or to relax. The large guest bedrooms feature four-poster, canopy and spindle beds. Other lavish delights include a clawfoot tub, marble-topped dresser, fireplace, window seats and velvet chaise lounge. Hospitality is prominent, and especially evidenced in the hearty breakfasts served.

Historic Interest: Boston Common, Faneuil Hall, Boston's Freedom Trail (7 miles); Fenway Park, USS Constitution, Bunker Hill Monument (9 miles); John Adams and John Quincy Adams Home, summer White House (1/4 mile).

Innkeeper(s): Mary Lee & Ken Caldwell. $80-100. MC, VISA, AX, PC, TC. TAC10. 3 rooms with PB, 1 with FP. Types of meals: Full bkfst and early coffee/tea. Beds: QDT. Ceiling fan and fireplace in room. VCR and fax on premises. Antiquing, art galleries, beaches, live theater, museums, parks, shopping and sporting events nearby.

Rehoboth H12

Gilbert's Tree Farm B&B

30 Spring St
Rehoboth, MA 02769-2408
(508)252-6416
E-mail: glbrtsbb@aol.com
Web: members.aol.com/glbrtsbb

Circa 1835. This country farmhouse sits on 17 acres of woodland that includes an award-winning tree farm. Cross-country skiing, hiking, and horse-cart rides are found right outside the door. If they choose to, guests can even help with the farm chores, caring for horses and gardening. A swimming pool is open during summer. Three antique-filled bedrooms share a second-floor sitting room. There are two first-floor rooms with a working fireplace and private bath. The nearby town of Rehoboth is 350 years old.

Historic Interest: Battleship Massachusetts (8 miles), Museum of Lizzie Borden artifacts (8 miles), Carpenter Museum (4 miles), Plimoth Plantation (1 hour), Newport mansions (45 minutes).

Innkeeper(s): Jeanne Gilbert. $65-85. PC, TC. TAC10. 5 rooms. Breakfast,

afternoon tea and snacks/refreshments included in rates. Types of meals: Full bkfst and early coffee/tea. Beds: KDT. Two with fireplace in room. VCR, copier, swimming, stables, bicycles, library and horse boarding only on premises. Antiquing, fishing, live theater, parks, shopping, cross-country skiing, sporting events and water sports nearby.
Publicity: *Attleboro Sun Chronicle, Country, Somerset Spectator, Country Gazette and Pawtucket Times.*

"This place has become my second home. Thank you for the family atmosphere of relaxation, fun, spontaneity and natural surroundings."

Perryville Inn

157 Perryville Rd (Providence, RI)
Rehoboth, MA 02769-1922
(508)252-9239 (800)439-9239 Fax:(508)252-9054
E-mail: pvinn@hotmail.com
Web: www.perryvilleinn.com

Circa 1820. The Perryville Inn was a dairy farm for more than 140 years. During that time, in 1897, the original two-story colonial was remodeled into a handsome three-story Victorian, now

in the National Register. (The house was raised and an additional floor added underneath.) The pasture is now a public golf course, but the icehouse remains. There are old stone walls, a mill pond, trout stream and wooded paths. Inside the inn, cozy rooms are decorated with comfortable antiques.
Innkeeper(s): Tom & Betsy Charnecki. $75-105. MC, VISA, AX, DS, PC, TC. 4 rooms with PB, 1 suite and 1 conference room. Breakfast included in rates. Types of meals: Cont plus. Beds: KQDT. Phone and high speed data ports in room. Air conditioning. Bicycles on premises. Antiquing, fishing and cross-country skiing nearby.
Publicity: *Providence Journal.*

"The family voted the Perryville the best place we stayed on our entire trip, without hesitation!"

Richmond   D2

Inn At Richmond

802 State Rd
Richmond, MA 01254
(413)698-2566 (888)968-4748 Fax:(413)698-2100
E-mail: innkeeper@innatrichmond.com
Web: www.innatrichmond.com

Circa 1775. The inn at Richmond was built just a year prior to the Revolutionary War. The property was part of a land grant from King George. The inn has been restored impeccably, and each room has been decorated individually with Waverly and Schumacher fabrics and appointments. Furnishings include a mix of antiques and reproductions, and five of the accommodations include a fireplace. The suites are especially luxurious, and the Federal Suite includes a clawfoot tub. Three private, one-bedroom cottages are available; each is decorated with antiques, reproductions and family heirlooms. In addition to the beautiful surroundings, which include views of the rolling Berkshire Hills, guests are pampered with a gourmet breakfast. The menu changes daily, but always includes Berkshire granola, fruit yogurt, muffins or special pastries and a selection of fresh, seasonal fruits. Entrees range from lemon, poppyseed pancakes with fresh raspberries from the inn's garden to a savory spinach, tomato and Brie tart with a cracked black pepper crust. After this luscious meal, there's much for guests to do in the Richmond area. Skiing, the Appalachian Trail, Tanglewood, museums, auctions

and Hancock Shaker Village are among the many attractions.
Historic Interest: Hancock Shaker Village (2 1/2 m iles), Naumkeag (12 miles), Red Lion Inn (11 miles), Chesterwood (9 miles), The Mount (10 miles).
Innkeeper(s): Jerri & Dan Buehler. $110-295. MC, VISA, AX, PC, TC. TAC10. 10 rooms, 4 with PB, 5 with FP, 3 suites and 3 cottages. Breakfast and snacks/refreshments included in rates. Types of meals: Gourmet bkfst. Beds: KQ. Cable TV, phone and cottage and suite have VCR in room. Air conditioning. VCR, fax, stables and library on premises. Weddings, small meetings and family reunions hosted. Antiquing, art galleries, bicycling, canoeing/kayaking, fishing, golf, hiking, horseback riding, modern dance, live theater, museums, parks, shopping, downhill skiing, cross-country skiing, tennis and water sports nearby.
Publicity: *New York Magazine.*

Rockport   C15

Emerson Inn By The Sea

Phillips Ave
Rockport, MA 01966
(798)546-6321 (800)964-5550 Fax:(798)546-7043
E-mail: info@emersoninnbythesea.com
Web: www.emersoninnbythesea.com

Circa 1840. This Greek Revival inn's namesake, Ralph Waldo Emerson, once called the place, "thy proper summer home." As it is the oldest continuously operated inn on Cape Ann, decades of travelers agree with his senti-

ment. The guest rooms are comfortable, yet tastefully furnished, and some boast ocean views. The grounds include a heated, saltwater swimming pool as well as a sauna and whirlpool. Breakfast is included in the rates. Guests also can enjoy dinner at the inn's dining room, an area added to the 19th-century inn in 1912.
Innkeeper(s): Bruce & Michele Coates. $95-325. MC, VISA, AX, DC, DS, TC. TAC10. 35 rooms with PB, 3 suites and 3 conference rooms. Types of meals: Full bkfst, cont plus, cont, early coffee/tea and gourmet dinner. EP. Beds: KQDT. Phone in room. Air conditioning. VCR, fax, copier, spa, swimming and sauna on premises. Weddings, small meetings, family reunions and seminars hosted. Antiquing, fishing, whale watches, live theater, parks and water sports nearby.
Publicity: *TV 40 Springfield.*

"We were very impressed with every aspect of the Emerson Inn."

The Inn on Cove Hill

37 Mount Pleasant St
Rockport, MA 01966-1727
(978)546-2701 (888)546-2701 Fax:(978)546-1095

Circa 1771. Pirate gold found at Gully Point paid for this Federal-style house. A white picket fence and granite walkway welcome guests. Inside, an exquisitely crafted spiral staircase, random-width, pumpkin-pine floors and hand-forged hinges display the original artisan's handiwork. Furnishings include family

heirlooms, four-poster canopy beds, and paintings by area artists. Muffin Du Jour is baked fresh each day by Betsy. Bicycles can be rented, and you can enjoy whale watching, fishing the local waters, or simply exploring the antique shops and village streets.
Historic Interest: For historic sites, Gloucester is just five miles away, offering tours of Beauport, a historic 1907 home and the Hammond Castle Museum.
Innkeeper(s): Betsy Eck. $55-140. MC, VISA, PC, TC. 8 rooms, 6 with PB. Breakfast included in rates. Types of meals: Cont and early coffee/tea. Beds: QDT. Air conditioning. Antiquing, fishing, live theater and parks nearby.

Linden Tree Inn

26 King St
Rockport, MA 01966-1444
(978)546-2494 (800)865-2122 Fax:(978)546-3297
E-mail: ltree@shore.net

Circa 1870. The breakfasts at this Victorian-style inn keep guests coming back year after year. Guests feast on homebaked treats such as pumpkin chocolate chip bread, blueberry cake or Sunday favorites, lemon nut bread and sour cream chocolate chip coffee cake. Each of the bedchambers features individual decor, and the innkeepers offer a formal living room and sun room for relaxation. The cupola affords a view of Mill Pond and Sandy Bay.

Historic Interest: Motif No. 1 is less than one mile from the home, and Boston is about 40 miles away.

Innkeeper(s): Dawn & Jon Cunningham. $75-130. MC, VISA, PC, TC. TAC5. 17 rooms, 12 with PB and 4 cottages. Breakfast included in rates. Types of meals: Cont plus. Beds: KQDT. TV and some with air conditioning in room. Fax and copier on premises. Amusement parks, antiquing, art galleries, beaches, bicycling, fishing, golf, hiking, live theater, museums, parks, shopping, tennis and water sports nearby.

Publicity: *Boston Magazine.*

"Great coffee! Love that apple walnut bread. Thank you for making this home."

Seacrest Manor

99 Marmion Way
Rockport, MA 01966-1927
(978)546-2211
Web: www.seacrestmanor.com

Circa 1911. After more than two decades of serving guests, the innkeepers at this estate inn have achieved "ace" status, welcoming travelers with well-polished hospitality. Their inn was once summer home to a prominent Boston restaurateur and looks out to the sea. The two-and-a-half acres include gardens

to stroll through, and inside there is a well-stocked library. Fresh flowers are placed in each guest room, and some rooms are further enhanced with decorative fireplaces. Various types of berry pancakes, Irish oatmeal topped with dates, corn fritters and French toast are just a few of the items that might be found on the morning table. The inn is located across the street from the nine-acre John Kieran Nature Reserve. This is a non-smoking inn.

Innkeeper(s): Leighton Saville & Dwight MacCormack, Jr. $120-170. PC, TC. 8 rooms, 6 with PB. Breakfast and afternoon tea included in rates. Types of meals: Gourmet bkfst and early coffee/tea. Beds: KQDT. Cable TV and turndown service in room. Bicycles, library and prize winning gardens on premises. French spoken. Antiquing, fishing, tours, whale watching, bicycling, sailing, music festival, art galleries, live theater, parks, shopping and water sports nearby.

Publicity: *Yankee and Art and Antiques.*

"We'll always have many fond memories."

Tuck Inn B&B

17 High St
Rockport, MA 01966-1644
(978)546-7260 (800)789-7260
E-mail: tuckinn@shore.net
Web: www.thetuckinn.com

Circa 1790. Two recent renovations have served to make this charming Colonial inn all the more enticing. Period antiques and paintings by local artists are featured throughout the spacious inn. A favorite gathering spot is the living room with its

fireplace, wide pine floors, tasteful furnishings and a piano available for guest use. Buffet breakfasts feature homemade breads, muffins, cakes and scones, granola accompanied by fresh fruit and yogurt. Guests may take a dip in the swimming pool or at local beaches. Located on a quiet secondary street within easy walking distance to many art galleries, restaurants and shops of Bearskin Neck. A nearby train station offers convenient access to Boston.

Historic Interest: The inn is 10 minutes from Gloucester. Other historic towns, such as Salem, Boston, Lexington and Concord, are within an hour's drive of the inn.

Innkeeper(s): Liz & Scott Wood. $69-149. MC, VISA, PC, TC. 11 rooms with PB and 1 suite. Breakfast included in rates. Types of meals: Cont plus and early coffee/tea. Beds: KQDT. Cable TV, all private baths and no smoking in room. Air conditioning. VCR, swimming, bicycles and library on premises. Antiquing, fishing, live theater, parks, shopping, cross-country skiing, sporting events and water sports nearby.

Publicity: *Fall River Herald News, North Shore News, Cape Ann Weekly and San Francisco Chronicle.*

"Wonderful people, lovely scenery, and great food, all good for the soul! Your hospitality and service was wonderful and we look forward to returning very soon!"

Yankee Clipper Inn

PO Box 2399
Rockport, MA 01966-3399
(978)546-3407 (800)545-3699 Fax:(508)546-9730
Web: www.yankeeclipperinn.com

Circa 1840. Sweeping views of the ocean and the rocky shoreline are eye-pleasers at this white clapboard, Art Deco oceanfront mansion and quarter deck. Polished mahogany woodwork and fireplaces reside with fine antiques imparting an old-fashioned, elegant ambiance. Sitting on one-and-a-half acres of breathtaking beauty, every guest bedroom overlooks an expansive vista. Some feature canopy beds and balconies. Enjoy the heated salt-water pool and New England hospitality.

Historic Interest: Town of Salem - House of Seven Gables, etc. (one-half hour), Concord, Lexington - Revolutionary War sites (one hour). Rockport and Gloucester founded in 1600s.

Innkeeper(s): Randy & Cathy Marks. $120-289. MC, VISA, AX, DS, PC, TC. TAC10. 16 rooms with PB and 1 conference room. Breakfast included in rates. Types of meals: Gourmet bkfst, cont plus, gourmet dinner and room service. MAP. Beds: KQDT. TV, phone, cable TV, VCRs some rooms, hair dryers and jet tubs in room. Air conditioning. VCR, fax, copier, swimming and library on premises. Weddings, small meetings, family reunions and seminars hosted. German spoken. Antiquing, fishing, whale watching, live theater, parks, shopping and water sports nearby.

Publicity: *Gloucester Daily Times, Los Angeles Times, North Shore Life, Country Living, Discerning Traveler, Country Inns, Travel Holidays, Great Country Inns TV Show. and Channel 5 Chronicle.*

"The rooms were comfortable, the views breathtaking from most rooms, and the breakfasts delicious, with prompt and courteous service."

Salem   D14

Amelia Payson House

16 Winter St
Salem, MA 01970-3807
(978)744-8304
E-mail: bbamelia@aol.com
Web: www.ameliapaysonhouse.com

Circa 1845. This elegantly restored two-story house features four white columns and is a prime example of Greek Revival architecture. Period antiques and wallpapers decorate the guest rooms and the formal dining room. Located in the heart of the Salem Historic District, it is a short walk to shops, museums, Pickering Wharf and waterfront restaurants. Train service to Boston is four blocks away. This is a non-smoking establishment.

Historic Interest: House of Seven Gables (2 blocks), Peabody Museum (1 block), Witch Museum (1 block), Maritime Historic Site (2 blocks).
Innkeeper(s): Ada & Donald Roberts. $95-150. MC, VISA, AX. 4 rooms with PB. Breakfast included in rates. Types of meals: Cont plus. Beds: QT. Antiquing and water sports nearby.

"Your hospitality has been a part of my wonderful experience."

Coach House Inn

284 Lafayette St
Salem, MA 01970-5462
(978)744-4092 (800)688-8689 Fax:(978)745-8031
E-mail: coachhse@star.net
Web: www.coachhousesalem.com

Circa 1879. Captain Augustus Emmerton, one of the last Salem natives to earn his living from maritime commerce, built this stately home. Emmerton's house is an imposing example of Second Empire architecture and situated just two blocks from the harbor in a Salem historic district. Guest rooms are cheerful and romantic, furnished with antiques, four-poster beds and Oriental rugs. The House of Seven Gables and the Salem Witch Museum are nearby. Boston is just a short drive away.
$95-155. MC, VISA, AX, DS. 11 rooms, 9 with PB, 7 with FP. Breakfast included in rates. Types of meals: Cont. Beds: QT.
Publicity: *The North Shore and Gourmet.*

Inn on Washington Square

51 Washington Sq
Salem, MA 01970
(978)741-4997 Fax:(978)741-3874

Circa 1850. Overlooking the other historical homes surrounding Salem Commons, this Greek Revival house has many original details including wood mouldings and windows. Offering privacy for romance and relaxation, deluxe guest bedrooms feature four-poster or canopy beds, candles, Jacuzzi tubs, a video library for in-room VCRs, and one with a fireplace. A breakfast basket of baked goods is delivered to the door. Hot beverages can be made in the personal coffeemakers, or freshly brewed coffee is available in the inn's main sitting area. Perennial gardens and a small koi pond grace the grounds.
Innkeeper(s): Ellen & David Dixey. Call for rates. 3 rooms with PB, 1 with FP. Beds: KQ. Cable TV in room. Air conditioning.

The Salem Inn

7 Summer St
Salem, MA 01970-3315
(978)741-0680 (800)446-2995 Fax:(978)744-8924
E-mail: salem.inn@verizon.net
Web: www.saleminnma.com

Circa 1834. Located in the heart of one of America's oldest cities, the inn's 41 individually decorated guest rooms feature an array of amenities such as antiques, Jacuzzi baths, fireplaces and canopy beds. Comfortable and spacious one-bedroom family suites with kitchenettes, are available. A complimentary continental breakfast is offered. Nearby are fine restaurants, shops, museums, Pickering Wharf and whale watching boats for cruises.

Historic Interest: Located 18 miles from Boston, the inn is the perfect base to explore nearby Concord and Lexington, as well as the coastal towns of Rockport and Gloucester. Historic Salem is home to the Salem Witch Museum, the Peabody Essex Museum, the House of Seven Gables, Salem Maritime National Historic Site, Pickering Wharf and whale watching cruises.
Innkeeper(s): Richard & Diane Pabich. $129-290. MC, VISA, AX, DC, DS, TC. TAC10. 41 rooms with PB, 18 with FP and 11 suites. Breakfast included in rates. Types of meals: Cont. Beds: KQT. Cable TV and phone in room. Air conditioning. Fax on premises. Antiquing, fishing, live theater, parks, shopping, sporting events and water sports nearby.
Pets Allowed.
Publicity: *New York Times, Boston Sunday Globe and Country Living Magazine.*

Suzannah Flint House

98 Essex St
Salem, MA 01970-5225
(978)744-5281 (800)893-9973
E-mail: sfhouse@go.com
Web: www.salemweb.com/biz/suzannahflint

Circa 1808. Adjacent to Salem Common and the historic district, this fine example of a Federal-style home is completely restored both inside and out. Antiques, Oriental rugs and original hardwood floors add to the inn's natural charm. The inn's original 1808 fireplaces, featured in each room, although not operating,

add to the inn's architectural character. Muffins, croissants, bagels and fresh fruit are the morning fare. The home is one block from the visitor's center and close to the Maritime Historic Site, Peabody Essex Museum, the Salem Witch Museum, House of Seven Gables and whale-watching cruises. Guests can walk to the train and head out for a day exploring Boston.
Innkeeper(s): Scott Eklind. $90-130. MC, VISA, AX, DS, PC, TC. 3 rooms with PB. Breakfast included in rates. Types of meals: Cont plus. Beds: Q. Cable TV, VCR and writing tables in room. Air conditioning. Antiquing, fishing, golf, museums and historic sites, live theater, parks, shopping, sporting events and tennis nearby.
Publicity: *Washington Post.*

Sandwich   I16

Inn At Sandwich Center

118 Tupper Rd
Sandwich, MA 02563-1828
(508)888-6958 (800)249-6949 Fax:(508)888-2746
E-mail: info@innatsandwich.com
Web: www.innatsandwich.com

Circa 1750. In the National Register, this 18th Century Federal home has many original features including a keeping room with a beehive oven. There are hardwood floors and period antiques throughout, and the guest rooms are spacious, some with fireplaces and four-poster beds. Air conditioning is available in summer. Breakfast is served in the keeping room on the inn's handmade table. Across the street is the Sandwich Glass

Museum and guests can also walk to antique and gift shops as well as historic attractions such as the Gristmill and Hoxie House. Heritage Plantation with 76 acres of rhododendrons is also within walking distance. Sandwich is Cape Cod's most historic town, founded in 1637.
Innkeeper(s): Joe & Louise Trapp. $85-135. MC, AX, PC, TC. 5 rooms with

PB, 3 with FP. Breakfast included in rates. Types of meals: Gourmet bkfst. MAP. Beds: KQT. Clock and chocolates in room. Small meetings and family reunions hosted. French, Italian and some Spanish spoken. Antiquing, fishing, golf, museums in village, live theater, parks, shopping, tennis and water sports nearby.
Publicity: *The Sandwich Broadsider.*

"A warm inviting inn where you are "at home"."

The Summer House

158 Main St
Sandwich, MA 02563-2232
(508)888-4991 (800)241-3609
E-mail: sumhouse@earthlink.net
Web: www.summerhousesandwich.com

Circa 1835. The Summer House is a handsome Greek Revival in a setting of historic homes and public buildings. (Hiram Dillaway, one of the owners, was a famous mold maker for the

Boston & Sandwich Glass Company.) The house is fully restored and decorated with antiques and hand-stitched quilts. Four of the guest rooms have fireplaces. The breakfast room and parlor have black marble fireplaces.
The sunporch overlooks an old-fashioned perennial garden, antique rose bushes, and a 70-year-old rhododendron hedge. The inn is open year-round.

Historic Interest: Sandwich Glass Museum (1 block), Thornton Burgess Museum (1 block), Heritage Plantation Museum (1 mile).
Innkeeper(s): Erik Suby & Phyllis Burg. $65-110. MC, VISA, AX, DS, PC, TC. 5 rooms with PB, 4 with FP. Breakfast and afternoon tea included in rates. Types of meals: Gourmet bkfst and early coffee/tea. Beds: KQT. Window fan in room. Library, lawn & gardens and sunroom on premises. Weddings, small meetings and family reunions hosted. Antiquing, fishing, live theater, parks, shopping, cross-country skiing and water sports nearby.
Publicity: *Country Living, Boston and Cape Cod Times.*

"An absolutely gorgeous house and a super breakfast. I wish I could've stayed longer! Came for one night, stayed for three! Marvelous welcome."

Sheffield   F2

B&B at Howden Farm

303 Rannapo Road
Sheffield, MA 01257
(413)229-8481 Fax:(413)229-0443
E-mail: bhowden@rnetworx.com
Web: www.howdenfarm.com

Circa 1830. Follow a quiet country road to this recently renovated home reflecting Greek Revival architecture. This working farm spans 250 acres, including 40 acres of crops that include pumpkins, sweet corn, blueberries and raspberries. Decorated and furnished with antiques, this intimate bed & breakfast offers romantic accommodations. Linger over a hearty breakfast before embarking on the day's adventures. This picturesque mountain area provides many opportunities for activities ranging from photography to skiing.

Historic Interest: Colonial Ashley House (1 mile), Stockbridge Estates (15 miles), The Mount (20 miles).
Innkeeper(s): Bruce Howden, David Prouty. $89-119. MC, VISA, PC. 3 rooms. Breakfast included in rates. Types of meals: Full bkfst. Beds: QDT. Cable TV in room. Air conditioning. Antiquing, art galleries, bicycling, canoeing/kayaking, fishing, golf, hiking, live theater, museums, parks, downhill skiing and cross-country skiing nearby.

Birch Hill Bed & Breakfast

254 S Undermountain Rd
Sheffield, MA 01257-9639
(413)229-2143 (800)359-3969 Fax:(413)229-3405
E-mail: info@birchhillbb.com
Web: birchhillbb.com

Circa 1780. A slice of history is felt at this Colonial home that was built during the American Revolution. Graciously situated on 20 scenic acres in the Berkshires, it is adjacent to the Appalachian Trail. The Chestnut Room has a fantastic view and

invites gathering to play the piano or games in front of the fire, listening to a CD or watching TV. Guest bedrooms and suites offer total relaxation. Some feature sitting areas and fireplaces. Creative, mouthwatering breakfasts begin a day of serendipity. Swim in the pool, try croquet and kayak or canoe in the lake across the street. Bicycles are available to explore the local area.

Historic Interest: Shay's Rebellion site (5 miles), Hancock Shaker Village, Norman Rockwell Museum and the Colonial Ashley House are all nearby.
Innkeeper(s): Wendy & Michael Advocate. $110-215. MC, VISA, PC, TC. 7 rooms, 5 with PB, 3 with FP, 2 suites and 1 conference room. Breakfast and afternoon tea included in rates. Types of meals: Gourmet bkfst, veg bkfst and early coffee/tea. Beds: KDT. Fireplace in room. Air conditioning. Fax, copier, swimming, bicycles and library on premises. Small meetings, family reunions and seminars hosted. Amusement parks, antiquing, art galleries, beaches, bicycling, canoeing/kayaking, fishing, golf, hiking, horseback riding, live theater, museums, parks, shopping, downhill skiing, cross-country skiing, tennis and water sports nearby.
Pets allowed: Most dog breeds, stay with owner at all times.

"My experience at your B&B was among the most pleasant I've ever experienced, from the moment I walked in to hear classical music. It was all divine. I can't wait to come back!"

Staveleigh House

59 Main St
Sheffield, MA 01257-9701
(413)229-2129

Circa 1821. The Reverend Bradford, minister of Old Parish Congregational Church, the oldest church in the Berkshires, built this home for his family. Afternoon tea is served and the inn is especially favored for its elegant brunch and gracious hos-

pitality. Located next to the town green, the house is in a historic district in the midst of several fine antique shops. It is also near Tanglewood, skiing and all Berkshire attractions.

Innkeeper(s): Ali A. Winston. $100-150. MC, VISA, AX, PC, TC. 7 rooms, 2 with PB. Breakfast and afternoon tea included in rates. Types of meals: Full bkfst and early coffee/tea. Beds: KQDT. Turndown service and ceiling fan in room. Air conditioning. Handicap access. Weddings, small meetings, family reunions and seminars hosted. Antiquing, fishing, art galleries, live theater, parks, shopping, downhill skiing, cross-country skiing and water sports nearby.
Publicity: *Los Angeles Times, Boston Globe and House and Garden Magazine.*

"The hospitality at Staveleigh House is deeper and more thoughtful than any you will find elsewhere."

Shrewsbury E10

Sumner House

5 Church Rd
Shrewsbury, MA 01545-1836
(508)845-6446 Fax:(508)846-6446
E-mail: info@sumnerhouse.com
Web: www.sumnerhouse.com

Circa 1797. Commissioned by Reverend Joseph Sumner, this sprawling Colonial home sits on two acres of shaded lawns and perennial gardens. Listed in the National Register, the inn's pristine character has been retained
for all these years. A letter from
George Washington to Artemus
Ward was found in the home's
safe. Furnished with family heirlooms, the array of common
rooms includes a study, great
room with fireplace, parlor, living

room, sunroom boasting a TV and an antique tool collection. Sunny guest bedrooms feature wide plank and splatter-painted floors. The Ward Room boasts a deep soaker tub. Expect signature breakfast dishes like Sumner Egg Casserole, blueberry, raspberry or apple pancakes or cheese strata to round off the meal.
Innkeeper(s): Bill & Ellen Glascock. $85-100. MC, VISA, PC, TC. 5 rooms, 3 with PB. Breakfast and snacks/refreshments included in rates. Types of meals: Full bkfst, veg bkfst, cont plus, cont and early coffee/tea. Beds: KDT. Turndown service, fireplace. some with modem hook-up, TV and VCR in room. Air conditioning. VCR, fax, copier, library, upstairs sitting room with coffee and soda on premises. Weddings, small meetings, family reunions and seminars hosted. Antiquing, art galleries, bicycling, canoeing/kayaking, fishing, golf, museums, parks, shopping, downhill skiing, sporting events, tennis, water sports and wineries nearby.
Pets allowed: Use of spare bedroom in private quarters.

South Egremont F2

Egremont Inn

Old Sheffield Rd
South Egremont, MA 01258
(413)528-2111 (800)859-1780 Fax:(413)528-3284
E-mail: egremontinn@taconic.net

Circa 1780. This three-story inn, listed in the National Register of Historic Places, was once a stagecoach stop. Guest rooms are furnished with country antiques. Dinner is available
Wednesday through Sunday in
the elegant dining room, and
there is also a tavern. Five fireplaces adorn the common
rooms. A wraparound porch,

tennis courts and a swimming
pool are on the premises.
Historic Interest: Minutes from the site of Shays Rebellion, formerly a mustering-in location and hospital during the Revolutionary War.
Innkeeper(s): Karen & Steven Waller. $90-175. MC, VISA, AX, DS, PC, TC. TAC10. 20 rooms with PB, 2 suites and 3 conference rooms. Breakfast included in rates. Types of meals: Full bkfst, cont plus and dinner. MAP. Beds: KQDT. Phone in room. Air conditioning. VCR, swimming and tennis on premises. Weddings, small meetings, family reunions and seminars hosted. Antiquing, fishing, hiking, live theater, parks, shopping, downhill skiing and cross-country skiing nearby.

"All the beauty of the Berkshires without the hassle, the quintessential country inn."

Weathervane Inn

Rt 23, Main St
South Egremont, MA 01258
(413)528-9580 (800)528-9580 Fax:(413)528-1713
E-mail: innkeeper@weathervaneinn.com

Circa 1785. The original post-and-beam New England farmhouse with its beehive oven was added on to throughout its history. It has been restored to combine today's modern amenities with the charm of the inn's historic past. The inn's historic architectural features include broad plank floors, tree trunk supports and granite columns. A full breakfast is offered every morning.
Historic Interest: Norman Rockwell Museum, Berkshire Museum, The Clark Museum and Hoosac Railroad Tunnel built during the Civil War are all nearby.
Innkeeper(s): Maxine & Jeffrey Lome. $115-245. MC, VISA, AX. TAC10. 8 rooms with PB and 2 suites. Breakfast included in rates. Types of meals: Full bkfst. Beds: KQD. Limited Handicap Access on premises. Antiquing, fishing, golf, live theater, downhill skiing, cross-country skiing and water sports nearby. Publicity: *New York Times, Berkshire Eagle, Boston Herald, Newsday and Daily News.*

Sterling D10

Sterling Orchards B&B

60 Kendall Hill Rd
Sterling, MA 01564-1515
(978)422-6595

Circa 1740. The orchards planted in 1920 by Robert Smiley's father provide a suitable setting to frame the 250-year-old farmhouse that has been thoroughly renovated. Original Indian shutters are still in place. A hiding place in the 12-square-foot center chimney, originally built by settlers, can still be found. The largest guest room (20x30) served as the town ballroom at the 1881 centennial.
Innkeeper(s): Bob & Sue Smiley. $65. 2 rooms with PB. Types of meals: Full bkfst and early coffee/tea. Beds: QT. Phone, turndown service and ceiling fan in room. VCR on premises. Amusement parks, antiquing, live theater, shopping, downhill skiing, cross-country skiing and sporting events nearby. Publicity: *Boston Globe and Worcester Telegram.*

"It's like stepping back in time with every modern convenience."

Stockbridge E2

Historic Merrell Inn

1565 Pleasant St, Rt 102
Stockbridge, MA 01260
(413)243-1794 (800)243-1794 Fax:(413)243-2669
E-mail: info@merrell-inn.com
Web: www.merrell-inn.com

Circa 1794. This elegant stagecoach inn was carefully preserved under supervision of the Society for the Preservation of New England Antiquities. Architectural drawings of Merrell Inn have been preserved by the Library of Congress. Eight fireplaces in
the inn include two with original
beehive and warming ovens. An
antique circular birdcage bar serves
as a check-in desk. Comfortable
rooms feature canopy and four-
poster beds with Hepplewhite and
Sheraton-style antiques. The

Riverview Suite is tucked on the back wing of the building and has a private porch which overlooks the Housatonic River.
Historic Interest: Hancock Shaker Village and the Norman Rockwell Museum are all nearby.
Innkeeper(s): George Crockett. $90-245. MC, VISA. 10 rooms with PB, 4

with FP. Breakfast included in rates. Types of meals: Full bkfst. Beds: KQT. Phone and fireplaces (some rooms) in room. Air conditioning. Fax on premises. Family reunions and seminars hosted. Antiquing, fishing, hiking, Tanglewood Music Festival, Norman Rockwell Museum, live theater, parks, shopping and cross-country skiing nearby.

Publicity: *Americana, Country Living, New York Times, Boston Globe, Country Accents, Travel Holiday and USA Today.*

"We couldn't have chosen a more delightful place to stay in the Berkshires. Everything was wonderful. We especially loved the grounds and the gazebo by the river."

The Inn at Stockbridge

PO Box 618
Stockbridge, MA 01262-0618
(413)298-3337 (888)466-7865 Fax:(413)298-3406
E-mail: innkeeper@stockbridgeinn.com
Web: www.stockbridgeinn.com

Circa 1906. Twelve secluded acres surround this white-pillared Georgian-style mansion, restored to a delightful bed & breakfast. A comfortable elegance is enhanced by antiques and a tasteful decor. Soft music, warm fires and good books are found in the library, living room and TV game room. The formal dining room is the perfect setting for a candlelight breakfast that includes culinary delights such as lemon cottage cheese pancakes. Spacious guest bedrooms offer charm and style for every taste. Some feature a porch with sweeping views of the meadow, or a deck overlooking the reflecting pond.
Canopied four-poster beds, fireplaces, skylights and whirlpools instill a touch of romance and luxury. For an afternoon repose, enjoy varieties of wine and cheese. Visit the nearby Norman Rockwell Museum and attend concerts at Tanglewood.

Innkeeper(s): Alice & Len Schiller. $130-310. MC, VISA, AX, DS, PC, TC. TAC10. 16 rooms with PB, 9 with FP, 8 suites and 1 conference room. Breakfast and snacks/refreshments included in rates. Types of meals: Gourmet bkfst and early coffee/tea. Beds: KQT. Cable TV, phone, ceiling fan and VCR in room. Air conditioning. Fax, copier, swimming and library on premises. Handicap access. Antiquing, art galleries, bicycling, canoeing/kayaking, fishing, golf, hiking, horseback riding, live theater, museums, parks, shopping, downhill skiing, cross-country skiing and tennis nearby.
Publicity: *Vogue, New York, New York Daily News, Country Inns Northeast, Arts & Antiques and Travel channel.*

"Classy & comfortable."

The Red Lion Inn

Main St
Stockbridge, MA 01262
(413)298-5545 Fax:(413)298-5130
E-mail: reservations@redlioninn.com
Web: www.redlioninn.com

Circa 1773. The venerable white clapboard Red Lion Inn has operated as a tavern and inn since its inception. The originator, Silas Pepoon, is said to have hosted a rally to protest the use of British goods. This meeting led to the approval of a document said to have been the first Declaration of Independence. A vital part of the area's history, the inn is onr of the last of the 18th-century Berkshire hotels still in operation. The collection of fine antique furnishings, colonial pewter and Staffordshire china found in the inn's parlor was gathered in the late 19th century by proprietor Mrs. Charles Plumb. The inn is part of the Norman Rockwell "Stockbridge Main Street at Christmas" painting. Traditional decor extends to the comfortable guest rooms and some have four-

poster and canopy beds, fireplaces, antique vanities and desks. The inn is home to three restaurants. Rocking on the long front porch is a favored activity, and one wonders if former visitors such as presidents Cleveland, McKinley, Theodore Roosevelt, Coolidge and Franklin Roosevelt enjoyed the privilege. Contemporary New England cuisine is the specialty of the inn's restaurants.

Innkeeper(s): Brooks Bradbury. Call for rates. MC, VISA, AX, DC, CB, DS, PC, TC. TAC10. 109 rooms, 95 with PB, 26 suites, 7 cottages and 3 conference rooms. Types of meals: Full bkfst, cont plus, cont, early coffee/tea, lunch, picnic lunch, gourmet dinner and room service. EP. Beds: KQDT. Cable TV, phone and turndown service in room. VCR, fax, copier, swimming and library on premises. Handicap access. Weddings, small meetings, family reunions and seminars hosted. Antiquing, fishing, golf, live theater, shopping, downhill skiing, cross-country skiing and tennis nearby.
Publicity: *Country Folk Art, The Age and USA Today.*

"My family and I travel quite a bit and your facility and employees top them all."

Roeder House B&B

Rt 183
Stockbridge, MA 01262
(413)298-4015 Fax:(413)298-3413
E-mail: innkeeper@roederhouse.com
Web: www.roederhouse.com

Circa 1856. Shaded by tall trees, this Federal country house sits on a knoll overlooking four acres of private grounds with perennial beds, green lawns, an in-ground pool and a period carriage barn. Decorated in an American cottage style, the guest bedrooms feature four-poster canopy beds and upcountry antiques. A library and
living room each offer a fireplace for cool weather. And in summer, a plentiful hot breakfast is enjoyed on the screened porch. The inn is close to Rockwell Museum, Stockbridge Center and minutes to all Berkshire attractions.

Innkeeper(s): Diane & Vernon Reuss. $145-320. MC, VISA, AX, DS, PC, TC. TAC10. 7 rooms with PB. Breakfast included in rates. Types of meals: Full bkfst and early coffee/tea. Beds: QT. Ceiling fan in room. Air conditioning. VCR, fax, copier and swimming on premises. Small meetings and family reunions hosted. Antiquing, upscale outlets, shopping, downhill skiing and cross-country skiing nearby.

"A wonderful experience, please adopt me."

Seasons on Main B&B

47 Main St
Stockbridge, MA 01262
(413)298-5419 Fax:(413)298-0092

Circa 1862. Seasons on Main was built during the Civil War. The historic Greek Revival home includes a sweeping veranda where guests can relax on wicker chairs and loveseats. The interior is Victorian in style, and two of the rooms include a fireplace. Breakfasts include items such as fresh fruit, muffins or coffeecake and entrees such as baked French toast strata. The inn offers close access to Tanglewood, the Norman Rockwell Museum, Berkshire Botanical Gardens, Edith Wharton's home, hiking, skiing and biking.

$135-250. MC, VISA, AX, DS, PC, TC. TAC5. 4 rooms with PB, 2 with FP. Breakfast and snacks/refreshments included in rates. Types of meals: Full bkfst. Beds: KQD. Cable TV, turndown service, ceiling fan and VCR in room. Air conditioning. Fax on premises. Antiquing, art galleries, bicycling, fishing, golf, hiking, live theater, museums, parks, shopping, downhill skiing, cross-country skiing and tennis nearby.

Sturbridge   F8

Commonwealth Cottage

11 Summit Ave
Sturbridge, MA 01566-1225
(508)347-7708
E-mail: ccbb@meganet.net

Circa 1873. This 16-room Queen Anne Victorian house, on an acre near the Quinebaug River, is just a few minutes from Old Sturbridge Village. Both the dining room and parlor have fireplaces. The Baroque theme of the Sal Raciti room makes it one of the guest favorites and it features a queen mahogany bed. Breakfast may be offered on the gazebo porch or in the formal dining room. It includes a variety of homemade specialties, such as freshly baked breads and cakes.

Historic Interest: Old Sturbridge Village is approximately 1-1/2 miles away.
Innkeeper(s): Robert & Wiebke Gilbert. $95-145. PC, TC. 3 rooms with PB. Types of meals: Full bkfst, early coffee/tea and snacks/refreshments. Beds: QDT. Ceiling fan in room. Library on premises. Weddings and family reunions hosted. German spoken. Antiquing, fishing, museum, live theater, parks, shopping and water sports nearby.
Publicity: *Long Island Newsday, Villager, WGGB in Springfield MA and Pax TV-Boston.*

"Your home is so warm and welcoming we feel as though we've stepped back in time. Our stay here has helped to make the wedding experience extra special!"

Publick House Historic Inn & Country Motor Lodge

PO Box 187, On The Common Rte 131
Sturbridge, MA 01566-0187
(800)PUB-LICK Fax:(508)347-5073
E-mail: info@publickhouse.com
Web: www.publickhouse.com

Circa 1771. This property includes four lodging facilities, two restaurants, 12 meeting rooms and 60 acres of countryside. Many special events take place throughout the year, including a New England Lobster Bake, a Beer and Wine Maker's Dinner, Harvest Weekend and Yankee Winter Weekends. All the rooms in the main building are decorated with period furnishings.

Innkeeper(s): Albert Cournoyer. $75-160. MC, VISA, AX, DC, CB, PC, TC. TAC10. 126 rooms with PB and 6 suites. Types of meals: Gourmet bkfst, cont plus, cont, early coffee/tea, gourmet lunch, picnic lunch, afternoon tea, snacks/refreshments and gourmet dinner. Beds: KQDT. Cable TV, phone and TVs available on request in room. Air conditioning. Fax and swimming on premises. Handicap access. Weddings, small meetings, family reunions and seminars hosted. Spanish and French spoken. Antiquing, fishing, live theater, parks, shopping, cross-country skiing and sporting events nearby.

Sturbridge Country Inn

PO Box 60, 530 Main St
Sturbridge, MA 01566-0060
(508)347-5503 Fax:(508)347-5319
E-mail: info@sturbridgecountryinn.com
Web: www.sturbridgecountryinn.com

Circa 1840. Shaded by an old silver maple, this classic Greek Revival house boasts a two-story columned entrance. The

attached carriage house now serves as the lobby and displays the original post-and-beam construction and exposed rafters. All guest rooms have individual fireplaces and whirlpool tubs. They are appointed gracefully in reproduction colonial furnishings, including queen-size, four-posters. A patio and gazebo are favorite summertime retreats.

Innkeeper(s): Patricia Affenito. $59-179. MC, VISA, AX, DS, PC, TC. TAC10. 9 rooms with PB, 9 with FP, 1 suite and 1 conference room. Breakfast included in rates. Types of meals: Cont, early coffee/tea and room service. Beds: KQ. Cable TV, phone, ceiling fan and VCR in room. Air conditioning. Fax, copier, spa, swimming, restaurant and luxury suites on premises. Weddings, small meetings, family reunions and seminars hosted. Spanish spoken. Antiquing, fishing, old Sturbridge Village, live theater, parks, shopping, downhill skiing, cross-country skiing and water sports nearby.
Publicity: *Southbridge Evening News and Worcester Telegram & Gazette.*

"Best lodging I've ever seen."

Vineyard Haven   K16

The Crocker House Inn

12 Crocker Ave, PO Box 1658
Vineyard Haven, MA 02568
(508)693-1151 (800)772-0206 Fax:(508)693-1123
E-mail: crockerinn@aol.com
Web: www.crockerhouseinn.com

Circa 1900. Enjoy all that Martha's Vineyard has to offer at this historic inn, which has close access to beaches, restaurants, galleries, museums, shops and a winery. Guest rooms offer amenities such as fireplaces, Jacuzzi's, water views or private porches. The front porch is lined with rockers, a perfect spot for relaxation with a splendid harbor view. The innkeepers provide a continental breakfast to get guests started before heading out and enjoying the island. The inn is within walking distance to the ferry service.
Innkeeper(s): Jeff & Jynell Kristal. $115-365. MC, VISA, AX, TC. 8 rooms, 7 with PB, 2 with FP and 1 suite. Breakfast and snacks/refreshments included in rates. Types of meals: Cont plus. Beds: KQDT. Cable TV, phone and suite with hot tub/spa in room. Air conditioning. Fax on premises. Small meetings and family reunions hosted. Antiquing, art galleries, beaches, bicycling, canoeing/kayaking, fishing, golf, hiking, horseback riding, live theater, parks, shopping, tennis and wineries nearby.

Hanover House

28 Edgartown Rd
Vineyard Haven, MA 02568
(508)693-1066 (800)339-1066 Fax:(508)696-6099
E-mail: tomrichardson@aol.com
Web: www.hanoverhouseinn.com

Circa 1906. Located within walking distance from the ferry on the Island of Martha's Vineyard, this 1906 Victorian sits on a beautifully landscaped half-acre in the quaint, unhurried town of Vineyard Haven. Its 12 bedrooms and three suites are decorated in antiques and reproductions. Many rooms have private entrances that open onto a sundeck. Each of the three suites in the separate carriage house has a private deck or patio; two have kitchenettes. A continental-plus breakfast including our new "on demand" coffee machine and homemade baked goods is served on the sun porch. Within walking distance are bike paths, shopping, restaurants, theater, sailing, windsurfing, fishing and swimming. Horseback riding, tennis and golf are nearby. Guests always enjoy exploring the beauty of the island with its dramatic cliffs, sandy beaches and century-old stone fences that crisscross rolling green meadows.

Innkeeper(s): Tom Richardson/Teri Cook. $148-305. MC, VISA, AX, DS. TAC10. 12 rooms with PB, 1 with FP, 3 suites and 1 conference room. Breakfast included in rates. Types of meals: Cont plus. Beds: KQD. Cable TV, ceiling fan and one with fireplace in room. Air conditioning. Fax and copier on premises. Antiquing, art galleries, beaches, bicycling, canoeing/kayaking, fishing, golf, hiking, horseback riding, live theater, museums, parks, shopping, tennis, water sports and wineries nearby.

Publicity: *New York Times.*

Ware E7

The Wildwood Inn

121 Church St
Ware, MA 01082-1203
(413)967-7798 (800)860-8098
E-mail: freelanc@massed.net

Circa 1880. This yellow Victorian has a wraparound porch and a beveled-glass front door. American primitive antiques include a collection of New England cradles and heirloom quilts, a sad-

dlemaker's bench and a spinning wheel. The inn's two acres are dotted with maple, chestnut and apple trees. Through the woods, you'll find a river.

Historic Interest: Old Sturbridge Village (15 miles), Old Deerfield (30 miles), Amherst College (15 miles).

Innkeeper(s): Fraidell Fenster & Richard Watson. $60-100. MC, VISA, AX, DC, DS, PC, TC. TAC10. 9 rooms, 7 with PB, 1 suite and 2 conference rooms. Breakfast and afternoon tea included in rates. Types of meals: Full bkfst and early coffee/tea. Beds: KQDT. Turndown service in room. Air conditioning. Library and canoe on premises. Handicap access. Weddings, small meetings, family reunions and seminars hosted. Amusement parks, antiquing, fishing, hiking, kayaking, great restaurants, live theater, parks, shopping, downhill skiing, cross-country skiing and sporting events nearby.

Publicity: *Boston Globe, National Geographic Traveler, Country and Worcester Telegram & Gazette.*

"Excellent accommodations, not only in rooms, but in the kind and thoughtful way you treat your guests. We'll be back!"

Wareham I15

Mulberry B&B

257 High St
Wareham, MA 02571-1407
(508)295-0684 (866)295-0684
E-mail: mulberry257@aol.com

Circa 1847. This former blacksmith's house is in the historic district of town and has been featured on the local garden club house tour. Frances, a former school teacher, has decorated the

guest rooms in a country style with antiques. A deck, shaded by a tall mulberry tree, looks out to the back garden.

Historic Interest: Plymouth (18 miles), New Bedford Whaling Capitol (17 miles), Provincetown/Eastham, where Pilgrims first landed (70 miles).

Innkeeper(s): Frances Murphy. $55-75. MC, VISA, AX, DS, PC, TC. TAC10. 3 rooms. Breakfast included in rates. Types of meals: Full bkfst and afternoon tea. Beds: KDT. TV and turndown service in room. Air conditioning. VCR on premises. Antiquing, fishing, whale watching, live theater, parks, shopping, cross-country skiing, sporting events and water sports nearby.

Publicity: *Brockton Enterprise and Wareham Courier.*

"Our room was pleasant and I loved the cranberry satin sheets."

Wellfleet G18

Blue Gateways

252 Main St
Wellfleet, MA 02667-7437
(508)349-7530 Fax:(508)349-2511
E-mail: info@bluegateways.com
Web: www.bluegateways.com

Circa 1712. Built by Squire Higgins in 1712 when George I was on the throne of England and Louis XIV was King of France, this Georgian inn is listed in the National Register. The house always has been a residence, but at times it also has served as a dry and fancy goods store, a pin and needle shop, a dressmaker's shop and a tearoom. Its three bedrooms are appointed with family antiques. The private back yard has two ornamental fish ponds. A daily continental breakfast includes delights like juices, fruit, yogurt, specialty homemade granola and fresh to-die-for baked goods. Guest may go beach combing, biking, boating, golfing, hiking, swimming or whale watching. Or they may visit art galleries, museums, wineries or theaters. The inn was featured as Editor's Pick in the 1999 Yankee Magazine's Travel Guide to New England, and it was termed "elegant" in the Cape Cod Travel Guide.

Innkeeper(s): Richard & Bonnie Robicheau. $100-125. MC, VISA, DS, PC, TC. 3 rooms with PB. Breakfast and snacks/refreshments included in rates. Types of meals: Cont plus. Beds: KQ. Air conditioning. VCR and fax on premises. Small meetings and family reunions hosted. Antiquing, art galleries, beaches, bicycling, canoeing/kayaking, fishing, golf, hiking, horseback riding, Audubon and National seashore, live theater, museums, parks, shopping, tennis, water sports and wineries nearby.

The Inn at Duck Creeke

70 Main St, PO Box 364
Wellfleet, MA 02667-0364
(508)349-9333 Fax:(508)349-0234
E-mail: duckinn@capecod.net
Web: www.capecod.net/duckinn

Circa 1815. The five-acre site of this sea captain's house features both a salt-water marsh and a duck pond. The Saltworks house and the main house are appointed in an old-fashioned style with antiques, and the rooms are comfortable and cozy. Some have views of the nearby salt marsh or the pond.

The inn is favored for its two restaurants; Sweet Seasons and the Tavern Room. The latter is popular for its jazz performances.

Historic Interest: Marconi Station (first wireless Trans Atlantic radio transmission). Wellfleet Historical Museum.

Innkeeper(s): Bob Morrill & Judy Pihl. $50-100. MC, VISA, AX, PC, TC. 25 rooms, 17 with PB and 1 conference room. Breakfast included in rates. Types of meals: Cont plus and dinner. Beds: QDT. Air conditioning in some rooms in room. Weddings, small meetings, family reunions and seminars hosted. Antiquing, fishing, national seashore, Audubon Sanctuary, bike trail, live theater, parks, shopping and water sports nearby.

Publicity: *Italian Vogue, Travel & Leisure, Cape Cod Life, Providence Journal, New York Times, Provincetown and Conde Nast Traveler.*

"Duck Creeke will always be our favorite stay!"

West Boylston D10

The Rose Cottage

24 Worcester St, Rte 12 and 140
West Boylston, MA 01583-1413
(508)835-4034 Fax:(508)835-4034

Circa 1850. This landmark Gothic Revival with its classic gabled roof and gingerbread dormers overlooks Wachusett

Reservoir. Elegant antique furnishings complement the white marble fireplaces, gaslight hanging lamps, lavender glass doorknobs, wide-board floors and floor-to-ceiling windows. The delightful guest bedrooms feature vintage quilts, white iron, brass, Art Deco or spool beds, ceiling fans and fluffy towels. At breakfast, guests will find delicious signature entrees and regional specialties. The carriage house loft is now a secluded, fully equipped apartment with a skylight cathedral ceiling, and is available by the month.

Innkeeper(s): Michael & Loretta Kittredge. $90. PC, TC. 5 rooms and 1 conference room. Breakfast included in rates. Types of meals: Gourmet bkfst and early coffee/tea. Beds: DT. At additional cost ($20), an extra twin bed can be put in some rooms and some with private bath in room. Golf and tennis nearby.
Publicity: *The Evening Gazette, Item Worcester Telegram and Landmark/Banner.*

"Your concern, your caring, your friendliness made me feel at home!"

West Harwich   I18

Cape Cod Claddagh Inn

77 West Main St
West Harwich, MA 02671-0667
(508)432-9628 (800)356-9628 Fax:(508)432-6039
E-mail: claddagh@capecod.net
Web: www.capecodcladdaghinn.com

Circa 1880. The owner of Chase and Sanborn coffee built this historic inn, and its original use was as a parsonage. Rumor has it that friendly ghosts may inhabit the home. The interior is a whimsical mix of Victorian, Colonial and even a little Caribbean. Guest rooms include stately poster beds and traditional furnishings. As the name of the inn suggests, there is an Irish influence at work here, as well. This is ever apparent in the Claddagh Pub, where guests can enjoy a hearty, gourmet dinner, rich desserts or a fine selection of spirits.

Historic Interest: 1890 Baptist Church.
Innkeeper(s): Eileen & Jack Connell. $95-175. MC, VISA, AX, PC. TAC10. 12 rooms with PB and 1 conference room. Breakfast included in rates. Types of meals: Full bkfst, country bkfst, veg bkfst, early coffee/tea, gourmet lunch, afternoon tea, snacks/refreshments and gourmet dinner. Beds: KQT. Cable TV, phone, ceiling fan and VCR in room. Central air. Fax and swimming on premises. Weddings, small meetings, family reunions and seminars hosted. Amusement parks, antiquing, art galleries, beaches, bicycling, canoeing/kayaking, fishing, golf, hiking, horseback riding, live theater, museums, parks, shopping, sporting events, tennis, water sports and wineries nearby.
Pets allowed: Call first.

West Stockbridge   E2

Card Lake Inn

PO Box 38
West Stockbridge, MA 01266-0038
(413)232-0272 Fax:(413)232-0294
E-mail: innkeeper@cardlakeinn.com

Circa 1880. Located in the center of town, this Colonial Revival inn features a popular local restaurant on the premises. Norman Rockwell is said to have frequented its tavern. Stroll around historic West Stockbridge then enjoy the inn's deck cafe with its flower boxes and view of the sculpture garden of an art gallery across the street. Original lighting, hardwood floors and antiques are features of the inn. Chesterwood and Tanglewood are within easy driving distance.

Historic Interest: The Norman Rockwell Museum is approximately 2 miles away.
Innkeeper(s): Ed & Lisa Robbins. $100-150. MC, VISA, AX, DS. 8 rooms.

Breakfast included in rates. Types of meals: Cont and early coffee/tea. Beds: KQ. Ceiling fan in room. Air conditioning. VCR on premises. Weddings, small meetings, family reunions and seminars hosted. Amusement parks, antiquing, shopping and sporting events nearby.

Williamsville Inn

Rt 41
West Stockbridge, MA 01266
(413)274-6118 Fax:(413)274-3539
E-mail: williamsville@taconic.net
Web: www.williamsvilleinn.com

Circa 1797. At the foot of Tom Ball Mountain is this Federal-style inn, formerly the Tom Ball farm. Some guest rooms feature fireplaces or wood stoves. The inn's grounds sport gardens, a swimming pool, tennis court, and a sculpture garden May-October. Guests often enjoy relaxing in a swing that hangs from an ancient elm. Chesterwood, Mission House, The Norman Rockwell Museum and Tanglewood are within easy driving distance.

Innkeeper(s): Gail & Kathleen Ryan. $130-195. MC, VISA, AX, PC, TC. TAC10. 16 rooms with PB, 2 with FP, 1 suite and 1 conference room. Breakfast included in rates. Types of meals: Full bkfst, early coffee/tea and picnic lunch. Beds: KQDT. Air conditioning. Fax, copier, swimming and tennis on premises. Weddings, small meetings, family reunions and seminars hosted. Antiquing, fishing, golf, live theater, parks, shopping, downhill skiing and cross-country skiing nearby.
Pets allowed: By special arrangement, subject to availability.
Publicity: *Boston Globe, Bon Appetit, Genre, Ladies Home Journal and Travel & Leisure.*

West Yarmouth   I17

Inn at Lewis Bay

59 Maine Ave
West Yarmouth, MA 02673
(508)771-3433 (800)962-6679
E-mail: innatlewisbay@mediaone.net
Web: www.innatlewisbay.com

Circa 1920. This bed & breakfast is located on Cape Cod's south shore overlooking Lewis Bay, and just a block from the beach. Whale watching, golfing, bicycling and restaurants are just minutes away, as well as ferries to the islands. Guests can relax in the fireplaced sitting room or enjoy the stars and water views in the backyard.

Innkeeper(s): Rick & Liz Latshaw. $108-128. MC, VISA, AX, PC, TC. TAC10. 6 rooms with PB. Breakfast and afternoon tea included in rates. Types of meals: Cont plus and early coffee/tea. Beds: QD. VCR and library on premises. Antiquing, fishing, whale watching, bicycling, live theater, parks, shopping and water sports nearby.

"An experience I am anxious to repeat."

Yarmouth Port   I17

Colonial House Inn

Rt 6A, 277 Main St
Yarmouth Port, MA 02675
(508)362-4348 (800)999-3416 Fax:(508)362-8034
E-mail: inof@colonialhousecapecod.com

Circa 1730. Although the original structure was built in pre-revolutionary times, a third floor was later added and another section was shipped in from Nantucket. The innkeepers renovated the carriage house, creating 10 new rooms. Dining areas include the

Colonial Room with hand-stenciled walls and a fireplace, and the Common Room, a recent glass-enclosed addition with a view of the veranda and town green. A traditional Thanksgiving dinner is served every year, and guests may enjoy other specialties, including murder-mystery, Las Vegas and wine-tasting weekends.

Innkeeper(s): Malcolm Perna. $80-120. MC, VISA, AX, DS, PC, TC. TAC10. 21 rooms with PB, 3 with FP, 2 suites and 3 conference rooms. Breakfast and dinner included in rates. Types of meals: Cont plus, cont and lunch. MAP, AP, EP. Beds: KQDT. Phone, ceiling fan, VCR, TV and canopy beds in room. Air conditioning. Fax, copier, spa, swimming, sauna and library on premises. Handicap access. Weddings, small meetings, family reunions and seminars hosted. French, Spanish and Italian spoken. Antiquing, fishing, golf, live theater, parks, shopping, cross-country skiing, sporting events, tennis and water sports nearby.

Pets allowed: Certain rooms.

Publicity: *Country Living, New York Daily News, New York Times, Yankee, Cape Cod Life, Boston Globe, Newsday.* and *Chronicle (Peter Mehegan).*

"The nicest place I've ever stayed."

Liberty Hill Inn

77 Main St, Rt 6A
Yarmouth Port, MA 02675
(508)362-3976 (800)821-3977
E-mail: libertyh@capecod.net
Web: www.libertyhillinn.com

Circa 1825. Just back from historic Old King's Highway, in a seaside village, this country inn is a restored Greek Revival mansion built by shipwrights. It is located on the site of the original Liberty Pole dating from Revolutionary times. A roman-

tic decor includes fine antiques and original architectural features, enhancing the tall windows and high ceilings. Guests can request rooms with a fireplace and whirlpool tub in a restored historic barn. Stroll past the inn's lawns for a brief walk to antique shops, restaurants and an old-fashioned ice cream parlor.

Historic Interest: Two historic restorations from the 18th century are within a half mile. Maritime history is celebrated each May with tours of historic buildings.

Innkeeper(s): Ann & John Cartwright. $90-190. MC, VISA, AX, PC, TC. TAC10. 9 rooms with PB. Types of meals: Gourmet bkfst and afternoon tea. Beds: KQT. Cable TV and honeymoon rooms with whirlpools in room. Air conditioning. Fax, copier and guest refrigerator on premises. Small meetings and seminars hosted. Antiquing, fishing, golf, whale watching, historic restorations, auctions, live theater, parks, shopping, tennis and water sports nearby.

Publicity: *Cape Cod Life* and *Colonial Homes.*

"Immaculate and incredibly clean. Plenty of information for one and all. Thank you for a delightful stay."

Olde Captain's Inn on The Cape

101·Main St Rt 6A
Yarmouth Port, MA 02675-1709
(508)362-4496 (888)407-7161
E-mail: general@oldecaptainsinn.com
Web: www.oldecaptainsinn.com

Circa 1812. Located in the historic district and on Captain's Mile, this house is in the National Register. It is decorated in a traditional style, with coordinated wallpapers and carpets, and there are two suites that include kitchens and living rooms. Apple trees, blackberries and raspberries grow on the acre of

grounds and often contribute to the breakfast menus. There is a summer veranda overlooking the property. Good restaurants are within walking distance.

Historic Interest: Plymouth Rock and Plantation (30 miles).

Innkeeper(s): Sven Tilly. $60-120. 3 rooms, 1 with PB and 2 suites. Breakfast included in rates. Types of meals: Cont plus. Beds: QD. Cable TV in room. Antiquing, fishing, live theater, shopping, sporting events and water sports nearby.

One Centre Street Inn

1 Center St
Yarmouth Port, MA 02675-1342
(508)362-8910 (888)407-1653 Fax:(508)362-0195
E-mail: spottydog@capecod.net
Web: www.onecentrestreetinn.com

Circa 1824. Originally a church parsonage in the 1800s, this Greek Revival-style inn is listed in the National Register. Just one mile from Cape Cod Bay, the inn has an understated elegance that enhances the comfort and conveniences offered,

including fresh flowers and imported chocolates. After a restful night's sleep, indulge in fresh-baked scones, homemade granola, fruit and perhaps orange French toast with strawberry-Grand

Marnier sauce or the signature dish, eggs karina, served in the formal dining room or screened porch. Take a bike ride into town or a short stroll to the long boardwalk at Gray's Beach.

Innkeeper(s): Karen Iannello. $105-145. MC, VISA, DS, PC, TC. TAC10. 6 rooms, 5 with PB, 1 with FP. Breakfast included in rates. Types of meals: Gourmet bkfst. Beds: QDT. Some with cable TV in room. Bicycles on premises. Small meetings and family reunions hosted. Antiquing, fishing, live theater, parks, shopping and water sports nearby.

Wedgewood Inn

83 Main St
Yarmouth Port, MA 02675-1709
(508)362-5157 Fax:(508)362-5851
E-mail: info@wedgewood-inn.com
Web: www.wedgewood-inn.com

Circa 1812. This three-story Greek Revival home was built for a maritime attorney and was the first architecturally designed home in town. A built-in hallway clock is written up in the town's local history. Wide-board floors, pencil-post beds,

antiques, fireplaces and private porches create a romantic ambiance. Three deluxe suites are available in a restored barn. Each suite includes a fireplace and private deck. Afternoon tea is served.

Innkeeper(s): Milt & Gerrie Graham. $135-205. MC, VISA, AX, PC, TC. TAC10. 9 rooms with PB, 7 with FP and 5 suites. Breakfast and afternoon tea included in rates. Types of meals: Full bkfst and early coffee/tea. Beds: KQ. TV and private porches in room. Air conditioning. Fax on premises. Small meetings and seminars hosted. Antiquing, fishing, whale watching, bird watching, nature and bike trails, live theater, shopping and water sports nearby.

Publicity: *Cape Cod Life, Fine Life of America (Japanese), Colonial Home, London Telegraph* and *Homes Across America.*

"Fabulous — wonderful little getaway. We'll be back. Great romantic getaway."

Michigan

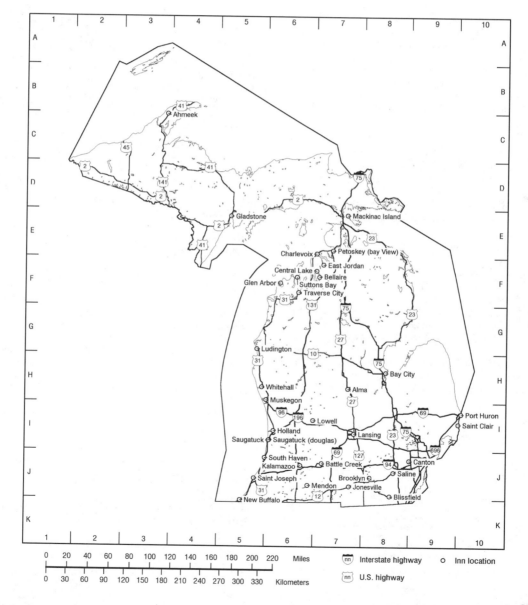

- Ahmeek — 41
- 45
- 2
- 141
- 2
- Gladstone — 41
- 2
- Mackinac Island — 75
- 23
- Charlevoix — Petoskey (bay View)
- East Jordan
- Central Lake — Bellaire
- Glen Arbor — Suttons Bay
- Traverse City
- 31
- 131
- 75
- 23
- Ludington
- 31
- 10
- 27
- 75
- Bay City
- Whitehall — Alma
- Muskegon — 27
- 96 — 196 — Lowell — 69 — Port Huron
- Holland — Lansing — 75 — Saint Clair
- Saugatuck — Saugatuck (douglas) — 23
- South Haven — 69 — 696
- Kalamazoo — Battle Creek — 127 — Canton
- Saint Joseph — Brooklyn — 94 — Saline
- Mendon — Jonesville
- 31 — 12 — Blissfield
- New Buffalo

| 0 | 20 | 40 | 60 | 80 | 100 | 120 | 140 | 160 | 180 | 200 | 220 | Miles |

| 0 | 30 | 60 | 90 | 120 | 150 | 180 | 210 | 240 | 270 | 300 | 330 | Kilometers |

nn Interstate highway   o Inn location

nn U.S. highway

Ahmeek C3

Sand Hills Lighthouse Inn

5 Mile Point Road
Ahmeek, MI 49901
(906)337-1744
E-mail: frabotta@up.net
Web: www.sandhillslighthouseinn.com

Circa 1917. Located on 35 acres on the Keweenaw Peninsula, including 3,000 feet of private Lake Superior shoreline, this yellow-brick lighthouse was constructed around a seven-story, steel-beam core. Inside the massive structure are carved oak railings on the staircase, plaster medallions around all the light fixtures and antique Victorian furnishings throughout. The parlor offers a fireplace and walls that are covered in floor-to-ceiling oak wainscoting. For a special anniversary ask for the lavish King Room. It features 96 yards of purple velvet in a crown canopy that flows around the bed, and there is a fireplace and scenic water views. The inn is open year-round, and from mid-May to mid-August lighthouse guests enjoy the unique experience of both sunrise and sunset views over the water. Gourmet breakfasts are served, including melt-in-your-mouth English scones.

Innkeeper(s): William H. Frabotta. $125-185. PC, TC. 8 rooms with PB, 1 with FP and 1 suite. Breakfast included in rates. Types of meals: Gourmet bkfst, early coffee/tea and snacks/refreshments. Beds: KQ. Whirlpool (two rooms) in room. Air conditioning. Copier, swimming, library and grand piano on premises. Weddings and small meetings hosted. Antiquing, fishing, golf, live theater, parks, shopping, cross-country skiing, sporting events and water sports nearby.

Alma H7

Saravilla

633 N State St
Alma, MI 48801-1640
(989)463-4078
E-mail: Ljdarrow@saravilla.com
Web: www.saravilla.com

Circa 1894. This 11,000-square-foot Dutch Colonial home with its Queen Anne influences was built as a magnificent wedding gift for lumber baron Ammi W. Wright's only surviving child, Sara. Wright spared no expense building this mansion for his daughter, and the innkeepers have spared nothing in restoring the home to its former prominence. The foyer and dining room boast imported English oak woodwork. The foyer's hand-painted canvas wallcoverings and the ballroom's embossed wallpaper come from France. The home still features original leaded-glass windows, built-in bookcases, window seats and light fixtures. In 1993, the innkeepers added a sunroom with a hot tub that overlooks a formal garden. The full, formal breakfast includes such treats as homemade granola, freshly made coffeecakes, breads, muffins and a mix of entrees.

Historic Interest: Alma is within three hours of almost every portion of Michigan's lower peninsula and plenty of historic sites.

Innkeeper(s): Linda and Jon Darrow. $85-140. MC, VISA, DS, PC, TC. TAC10. 7 rooms with PB. Types of meals: Full bkfst and room service. Beds: KQT. One with whirlpool tub and three with wood-burning fireplace in room. Complimentary beverages and snacks available on premises. Antiquing, fishing, canoeing, live theater and cross-country skiing nearby.

Publicity: *Morning Sun, Saginaw News and Sault Sunday.*

"I suggest we stay longer next time. We are looking forward to that visit."

Battle Creek J7

Greencrest Manor

6174 Halbert Rd E
Battle Creek, MI 49017-9449
(616)962-8633 Fax:(616)962-7254

Circa 1934. Once used as monestary, this 13,000-square-foot French Normandy mansion rests on 20 acres. Extensive gardens are lush with apple orchards, tiered gardens, herb gardens, reflecting pools, Japanese maples and cherry trees. It is in the National Register as a rare example of Norman-style architecture in the United States. The inn's inviting drawing room boasts egg-and-dart molding, sofas and drapes in an English cabbage-rose print and floor-to-ceiling French windows. The dining room has a white marble fireplace, Parisian chandelier and Oriental carpet. Ask for the VIP Suite for a king bed, white marble fireplace and double whirlpool showers.

Innkeeper(s): Tom & Kathy VanDaff. $95-235. MC, VISA, AX, DC, PC, TC. 8 rooms, 6 with PB, 1 with FP, 6 suites and 3 conference rooms. Breakfast included in rates. Types of meals: Cont. Beds: KQD. Cable TV, phone and ceiling fan in room. Air conditioning. Fax, copier, library and porch with snacks and beverages on premises. Weddings and small meetings hosted. Antiquing, golf, parks, shopping, cross-country skiing and tennis nearby.

Publicity: *Country Inns and Lifestyles.*

"I've been in Normandy many times, I've never seen anything like your "French Chateau"."

Bay City H8

Keswick Manor

1800 Center Ave
Bay City, MI 48708
(989)893-6598
E-mail: keswickmanor@aol.com
Web: www.keswickmanor.com

Circa 1898. Built in the last years of the 19th century, Keswick Manor is an impressive Georgian-style home located in the center of Bay City's historic district. An iron fence surrounds the front grounds, lending an impressive air to this stately manor, which is part of the town's historic heritage tour. The guest rooms and common areas are English in style, a tribute to trips abroad made by the innkeepers. Guests will find much to do in Bay City, including hunting for antiques in the state's largest antique center. Other local attractions include river cruises along the Saginaw, historic sites and tours.

Innkeeper(s): Tom & Deb Pietrzak. $89-189. MC, VISA. 4 rooms, 1 with FP and 2 suites. Breakfast and snacks/refreshments included in rates. Types of meals: Cont plus. Beds: Q. Cable TV, turndown service and fireplace in room. Central air. Spa and library on premises. Weddings, small meetings, family reunions and seminars hosted. Antiquing, art galleries, beaches, bicycling, canoeing/kayaking, fishing, golf, live theater, museums, parks, shopping, downhill skiing, cross-country skiing, tennis and water sports nearby.

Publicity: *Bay City Times and Detroit Free Press.*

Bellaire F7

Bellaire Bed & Breakfast

212 Park St
Bellaire, MI 49615-9595
(231)533-6077 (800)545-0780

Circa 1879. Maple trees line the drive to this American Gothic home. Relax on the porch swing, or enjoy the warmth of a crack-

ling fire in the English-style library. The fresh, family-style continental-plus breakfast is a treat. A nearby park offers swimming, tennis, basketball, shuffleboard and a playground. Browse through the downtown shops or hunt for antiques. Guests can take in 18 rounds at "The Legend" at Shanty Creek golf course, and in winter, enjoy skiing.

Innkeeper(s): David Schulz & Jim Walker. $70-100. MC, VISA, DS. 5 rooms, 3 with PB. Types of meals: Cont plus and afternoon tea. Beds: QD.

Grand Victorian B&B Inn

402 N Bridge St
Bellaire, MI 49615-9591
(231)533-6111 (800)336-3860 Fax:(231)533-4214
E-mail: innkeeper@grandvictorian.com
Web: www.grandvictorian.com

Circa 1895. Featured in Country Inns and Midwest Living magazines, this Queen Anne Victorian mansion boasts three original fireplaces, hand-carved mantels, intricate fretwork and numerous architectural details. Relax with a glass of wine before the fire in the formal front parlor, or listen to music while playing cards and games in the back parlor. Guest bedrooms offer an eclectic mix of antique furnishings including Victorian Revival, Eastlake and French Provincial. Soak in an 1890s clawfoot tub, or enjoy the park view from a private balcony. Be

pampered with a satisfying breakfast and an innkeepers' reception in the evening. The gazebo is a perfect spot to while away the day, or take advantage of the area's many nearby activities.

Innkeeper(s): Amy Savage & Curtis Sherwood. $100-130. MC, VISA, AX, DS. 5 rooms with PB. Breakfast and afternoon tea included in rates. Types of meals: Full bkfst, early coffee/tea and picnic lunch. Beds: QD. Air conditioning. Weddings, small meetings, family reunions and seminars hosted. Antiquing, fishing, fine dining restaurants, shopping, downhill skiing, cross-country skiing and water sports nearby.
Publicity: *Midwest Living, Country Inns and Featured on Nabisco Crackers/Cookies Boxes Promotion.*

"*We certainly enjoyed our visit to the Grand Victorian. It has been our pleasure to stay in B&Bs in several countries, but never one more beautiful and almost never with such genial hosts.*"

Blissfield J8

Hiram D. Ellis Inn

415 W Adrian St US Hwy 223
Blissfield, MI 49228-1001
(517)486-3155
E-mail: ellisinn@cass.net
Web: www.blissfield.net

Circa 1883. This red brick Italianate house is in a village setting directly across from the 1851 Hathaway House, an elegant historic restaurant. Rooms at the Hiram D. Ellis Inn feature handsome antique bedsteads, armoires and floral wallpapers. Breakfast is served in the inn's common room, and the innkeeper receives rave reviews on her peach and apple dishes. (There are apple and peach trees on the property.) Bicycles are available for riding around town, or you can walk to the train station and board the murder-mystery dinner train that runs on weekends.

Innkeeper(s): Christine Webster & Frank Seely. $80-100. MC, VISA, AX, PC,

TC. TAC10. 4 rooms with PB. Breakfast included in rates. Types of meals: Full bkfst, cont plus and early coffee/tea. Beds: QD. Cable TV and phone in room. Air conditioning. Bicycles on premises. Small meetings, family reunions and seminars hosted. Antiquing, fishing, golf, live theater, parks, shopping and cross-country skiing nearby.
Pets allowed: small pets only.
Publicity: *Ann Arbor News and Michigan Living.*

"*I have now experienced what it is truly like to have been treated like a queen.*"

Brooklyn J8

Dewey Lake Manor

11811 Laird Rd
Brooklyn, MI 49230-9035
(517)467-7122
E-mail: deweylk@frontiernet.net
Web: www.getaway2smi.com/dewey

Circa 1868. This Italianate house overlooks Dewey Lake and is situated on 18 acres in the Irish Hills. The house is furnished in a country Victorian style with antiques. An enclosed porch is a favorite spot to relax and take in the views of the lake while having breakfast. Favorite pastimes include lakeside bonfires in the summertime and ice skating or cross-country skiing in the winter. Canoe and paddleboats are available to guests.

Historic Interest: The Great Saulk Trail (2 miles from U.S. 12), Walker Tavern, a stagecoach stop on the trail (2 miles), Saint Joseph Catholic Shrine (5 miles).
Innkeeper(s): Barb & Joe Phillips. $72-130. MC, VISA, AX. TAC10. 5 rooms with PB, 5 with FP and 1 conference room. Breakfast included in rates. Types of meals: Full bkfst, early coffee/tea, picnic lunch and snacks/refreshments. Beds: QT. Cable TV, phone, ceiling fan, one with Jacuzzi and two with VCR in room. Air conditioning. VCR in sitting room and baby grand piano on premises. Weddings, small meetings and family reunions hosted. Antiquing, fishing, golf, live theater, shopping, cross-country skiing, sporting events and water sports nearby.
Publicity: *Ann Arbor News.*

"*I came back and brought my friends. It was wonderful.*"

Canton J9

Willow Brook Inn

44255 Warren Rd
Canton, MI 48187-2147
(734)454-0019 (888)454-1919
E-mail: wbibnb@earthlink.net
Web: www.willowbrookinn.com

Circa 1929. Willow Brook winds its way through the backyard of this aptly named inn, situated on a lush, wooded acre. Innkeepers Bernadette and Michael Van Lenten filled their home with oak and pine country antiques and beds covered with soft quilts. They also added special toys and keepsakes from their own childhood to add a homey touch. After a peaceful rest, guests are invited to partake in the morning meal either in the "Teddy Bear" dining room, in the privacy of their rooms or on the deck. Breakfasts consist of luscious treats such as homemade breads, scones topped with devon cream and a choice of entree.
Historic Interest: The Henry Ford Museum and historic Greenfield Village are just 20 minutes away.
Innkeeper(s): Bernadette & Michael Van Lenten. $95-125. MC, VISA, AX. TAC10. 3 suites. Breakfast and snacks/refreshments included in rates. Types of meals: Gourmet bkfst, early coffee/tea, picnic lunch, afternoon tea and dinner. Beds: KQDT. Phone, turndown service, ceiling fan and VCR in room. Air conditioning. Fax, copier, bicycles and pet boarding on premises. Small meet-

ings hosted. French spoken. Antiquing, Henry Ford Museum, zoo, live theater, parks, shopping, cross-country skiing, sporting events and water sports nearby. Pets allowed: Not permitted in bedrooms.
Publicity: *Canton Observer, Canton Eagle, Detroit News and Local PBS station.*

"We've stayed in B&Bs in Europe, Australia and New Zealand, and we put yours at the top of the list for luxury, friendly care and delicious food (especially the scones). We're glad we found you. Thanks."

Central Lake F7

Bridgewalk B&B

2287 S Main, PO Box 399
Central Lake, MI 49622-0399
(231)544-8122

Circa 1895. Secluded on a wooded acre, this three-story Victorian is accessible by crossing a foot bridge over a stream. Guest rooms are simply decorated with Victorian touches, floral prints and fresh flowers. The Garden Suite includes a clawfoot

tub. Much of the home's Victorian elements have been restored, including pocket doors and the polished woodwork. Breakfasts begin with such items as a cold fruit soup, freshly baked muffins or scones accompanied with homemade jams and butters. A main dish, perhaps apple-sausage blossoms, tops off the meal.

Innkeeper(s): Janet & Tom Meteer. $85-95. MC, VISA, PC, TC. TAC10. 5 rooms with PB and 1 suite. Breakfast included in rates. Types of meals: Full bkfst and early coffee/tea. Beds: KQT. Ceiling fan in room. Small meetings hosted. Antiquing, fishing, golf, gourmet restaurants, parks, shopping, downhill skiing and cross-country skiing nearby.

Charlevoix E7

Bridge Street Inn

113 Michigan Ave
Charlevoix, MI 49720-1819
(231)547-6606 Fax:(231)547-1812
E-mail: vmckown@voyager.net
Web: www.bridgestreetinn-chx.com

Circa 1895. This three-story Colonial Revival structure recalls the bygone era when Charlevoix was home to many grand hotels. Originally a guest "cottage" of one of those large hotels, this inn boasts seven gracious guest rooms,

many of which are available with private bath. The rooms sport antique furnishings, floral rugs and wooden floors and some offer views of the surrounding lakes. Guests are within walking distance of Lake Michigan's beaches, Round Lake's harbor and Lake Charlevoix's boating and fishing. Be sure to inquire in advance about the inn's many discounts and special rate for small groups.

Innkeeper(s): Vera & John McKown. $83-145. MC, VISA, PC, TC. TAC10. 7 rooms, 6 with PB. Breakfast included in rates. Types of meals: Full bkfst. Beds: QT. Ceiling fan in room. VCR and fax on premises. Family reunions hosted. German spoken. Antiquing, fishing, live theater, parks, shopping, downhill skiing, cross-country skiing, sporting events and water sports nearby.

The Inn at Grey Gables

306 Belvedere Ave
Charlevoix, MI 49720-1413
(616)547-2251 (800)280-4667 Fax:(616)547-1944

Circa 1887. Guests at this attractive two-story inn are just a short walk from a public beach. Visitors have their choice of seven

rooms, including two suites. The Pine Suite features a kitchen and private entrance, perfect for honeymooners or for those enjoying a longer-than-usual stay. All of the rooms offer private baths and most have queen beds. Guests may opt to relax and enjoy the beautiful surroundings or take advantage of the many recreational activities available in the Charlevoix area, including Fisherman's Island State Park.

Innkeeper(s): Gary & Kay Anderson. $110-135. MC, VISA, PC, TC. 7 rooms, 5 with PB and 2 suites. Breakfast included in rates. Types of meals: Full bkfst. Beds: KQT. Ceiling fan in room. Small meetings and family reunions hosted. Antiquing, fishing, parks, shopping, downhill skiing, cross-country skiing and water sports nearby.
Publicity: *USA Today.*

East Jordan F7

Easterly Inn

209 Easterly, PO Box 366
East Jordan, MI 49727-0366
(231)536-3434

Circa 1906. A wraparound porch embellishes this three-story Victorian home. Period wall coverings and handsome antiques furnish the rooms. The library offers a cozy fireplace for guest's relaxation. Accommodations include the Turret Room, which features a tall, carved walnut and burl queen bed, and the Romantic Lace Room, with Victorian rose prints and a queen canopy bed. Breakfast is served in the formal semi-circular dining room. The inn is two blocks from Lake Charlevoix and the harbor. Fine dining is available nearby at Tapawingo.

Innkeeper(s): Joan Martin. $60-85. MC, VISA, PC. 4 rooms with PB. Breakfast included in rates. Types of meals: Full bkfst. Beds: QD. Ceiling fan in room. Small meetings hosted. Antiquing, fishing, golf, fine dining, parks, shopping and water sports nearby.

"A wonderful inn, full of history and romance. Thank you for sharing yourself with us."

Georgetown H9

The Grey Havens

96 Seguinland Rd
Georgetown, MI 04548-0308
(207)371-2616
E-mail: inn@greyhavens.com
Web: www.greyhavens.com

Circa 1906. For more than two decades, Haley and Bill Eberhart have welcomed guests to this handsome shingle-style hotel on Georgetown Island. From the wraparound porch and most of the

rooms, guests may view the harbor, islands, lighthouses and the open ocean. The lounge features a huge rock fireplace and a 12-foot-tall window. Furnishings are antique. Ask for one of the four turret rooms for a 180-degree ocean view. Reid State Park,

Bath, the Maine Maritime Museum and Freeport are nearby.
Innkeeper(s): Bill & Haley Eberhart. $75-220. MC, VISA, PC, TC. 13 rooms with PB and 1 suite. Breakfast included in rates. Types of meals: Cont plus, early coffee/tea and snacks/refreshments. Beds: KQD. Fax, copier, bicycles, library, guest canoes, "fully rockered" porch, great coffee and small "honor bar on premises. Weddings, small meetings, family reunions and seminars hosted. Antiquing, art galleries, beaches, bicycling, canoeing/kayaking, fishing, golf, hiking, Audubon Bird Sanctuary, Nature Conservancy, fishing village, live theater, museums, parks and shopping nearby.
Publicity: *Victoria, Travel & Leisure, House Beautiful, Yankee Magazine, Coastal Living and Down East.*

"We keep coming back. This place is wonderful."

Gladstone
E5

Kipling House Bed & Breakfast

1716 N Lake Shore Dr
Gladstone, MI 49837-2751
(906)428-1120 (877)905-ROOM Fax:(906)428-4696
E-mail: info@kiplinghouse.com

Circa 1897. Stay here and learn why this historical Four Square house is named after Rudyard Kipling. Relax on the front porch rockers or by the fire in the parlor. Choose a guest bedroom with a whimsical or elegant decor. The cottage features a sleeping loft and a free-standing fireplace. Gourmet Chef Ralph takes great pride in presenting a splendid candlelight breakfast in the dining room, as well as a tasty dessert in the evenings. The grounds offer a gazebo, deck perennial and water garden. Bikes are available to explore the local Upper Peninsula area. Enjoy nearby Hiawatha National Forest boasting almost one million acres, or visit a restored mining village at Fayette State Park.
Innkeeper(s): Ann & Ralph Miller. $75-150. PC. 6 rooms, 2 with PB, 2 suites and 1 cottage. Breakfast and snacks/refreshments included in rates. Types of meals: Gourmet bkfst, early coffee/tea and afternoon tea. Beds: KQD. Cable TV, turndown service, ceiling fan and VCR in room. Air conditioning. Fax, copier, bicycles and library on premises. Weddings, small meetings, family reunions and seminars hosted. Antiquing, art galleries, beaches, bicycling, canoeing/kayaking, fishing, golf, hiking, museums, parks, shopping, downhill skiing, cross-country skiing and water sports nearby.

Glen Arbor
F6

White Gull Inn

5926 SW Manitou Tr
Glen Arbor, MI 49636-9702
(231)334-4486 Fax:(231)334-3546
E-mail: gullinglen@aol.com
Web: www.whitegullinnbb.com

Circa 1900. One of Michigan's most scenic areas is home to the White Gull Inn. With the Sleeping Bear Dunes and alluring Glen Lake just minutes away, visitors will find no shortage of sightseeing or recreational activities during a stay here. The inn's farmhouse setting, country decor and five comfortable guest rooms offer a relaxing haven no matter what the season. Lake Michigan is a block away, and guests also will enjoy the area's fine dining and shopping opportunities.

Innkeeper(s): Bill & Dotti Thompson. $75-85. MC, VISA, AX, DS, PC. 5 rooms, 1 with FP. Breakfast included in rates. Types of meals: Cont plus. Beds: QDT. Cable TV in room. Air conditioning. Fax on premises. Weddings and family reunions hosted. Antiquing, fishing, golf, parks, shopping, downhill skiing, cross-country skiing, tennis and water sports nearby.

Holland
I6

Inn at Old Orchard Road

1422 S Shore Dr
Holland, MI 49423
(616)335-2525

Circa 1906. One of the first houses built on the south shore of Lake Macatawa, this turn-of-the-century Dutch farmhouse offers gorgeous lake and sunset views. Recently renovated, it is furnished with antiques. Private guest bedrooms boast a comfortable coziness. The home-cooked breakfast is always appreciated. Relax on the outdoor patio or front porch. The lush, tree-studded grounds are accented by many flowers and a vegetable garden.
Historic Interest: Big Red Lighthouse (2 1/2 mile), Cappon House & Museum (4 mile).
Innkeeper(s): Elizabeth DeWaard. $90-95. PC, TC. 3 rooms with PB. Breakfast included in rates. Types of meals: Gourmet bkfst and early coffee/tea. Beds: Q. Cable TV and ceiling fan in room. Central air. Antiquing, art galleries, beaches, bicycling, fishing, golf, hiking, live theater, museums, parks, shopping, cross-country skiing, tennis and wineries nearby.

Jonesville
J7

Horse & Carriage B&B

7020 Brown Rd
Jonesville, MI 49250-9720
(517)849-2732 Fax:(517)849-2732
E-mail: horsecarriagebb@yahoo.com

Circa 1898. Enjoy a peaceful old-fashioned day on the farm. Milk a cow, snuggle shetland sheep, gather eggs and cuddle baby chicks. In the winter, families are treated to a horse-drawn sleigh ride at this 18th-century home, which is surrounded by a 700-acre cattle farm. In the warmer months, horse-drawn carriage rides pass down an old country lane past Buck Lake. The innkeeper's family has lived on the property for more than 150 years. The home itself was built as a one-room schoolhouse. A mix of cottage and Mission furnishings decorate the interior. The Rainbow Room, a perfect place for children, offers twin beds and a playroom. Guests are treated to hearty breakfasts made with farm-fresh eggs, fresh fruits and vegetables served on the porch or fireside.
Innkeeper(s): Keith Brown & family. $85-100. PC. 3 rooms, 1 with PB. Breakfast and snacks/refreshments included in rates. Types of meals: Gourmet bkfst, cont plus, cont and early coffee/tea. Beds: KQT. Phone in room. Air conditioning. Fax, copier, milk a cow, pet lambs, gather eggs and horse/carriage rides on premises. Small meetings and family reunions hosted. Portuguese spoken. Antiquing, fishing, Jackson Space Center, Speedway, Country Fair, live theater, parks, shopping, cross-country skiing, sporting events and water sports nearby.
Publicity: *Detroit Free Press, The Toledo Blade, Hillsdale Daily News and MSU Alumni.*

Munro House B&B

202 Maumee St
Jonesville, MI 49250-1247
(517)849-9292 (800)320-3792 Fax:(517)849-7685
E-mail: stay@munrohouse.com
Web: www.munrohouse.com

Circa 1834. This spectacular Greek Revival mansion located in south central Michigan is within 90 minutes of Detroit, Toledo, Fort Wayne and Lansing. Ten fireplaces and two Franklin stoves are found in the rooms. Munro House was built by George C. Munro, a Civil War brigadier general. Hillsdale County's first brick house also served as a safe

haven for slaves on the Underground Railroad. Many guests enjoy selecting a book or a movie to spend a quiet evening in front of the fireplace in their room. Five guest rooms include a fireplace, and two rooms have a whirlpool tub. Breakfast is enjoyed before an open-hearth fireplace. Hillsdale College is just five miles away.

Historic Interest: Grosvenor House (1 mile).
Innkeeper(s): Mike & Lori Venturini. $99-199. MC, VISA, AX, DS. TAC10. 7 rooms with PB, 5 with FP. Breakfast and snacks/refreshments included in rates. Types of meals: Full bkfst and country bkfst. AP. Beds: Q. Cable TV, phone, ceiling fan, VCR and fireplace in room. Air conditioning. Fax, copier, library, video library and homemade cookies on premises. Weddings, small meetings and family reunions hosted. Antiquing, golf, horseback riding, live theater and museums nearby.

"Your home is a wonderful port for the weary traveler. I love it here. The rooms are great and the hospitality unsurpassed."

Kalamazoo J6

Hall House

106 Thompson St
Kalamazoo, MI 49006-4537
(616)343-2500 (888)761-2525 Fax:(616)343-1374
E-mail: thefoxes@hallhouse.com
Web: www.hallhouse.com

Circa 1923. In a National Historic District, this Georgian Colonial Revival-style house was constructed by builder H.L. Vander Horst as his private residence. Special features include polished mahogany woodwork and marble stairs. The living room boasts a domed ceiling, while the Library Room is graced with a hand-painted mural. Other special features of the house

include an early intercom system. The inn is located on the edge of Kalamazoo College campus. Western Michigan University and downtown are a few minutes away.

Innkeeper(s): Scott & Terri Fox. $79-145. MC, VISA, AX, PC, TC. 6 rooms with PB, 2 with FP and 2 suites. Breakfast included in rates. Types of meals: Full bkfst and cont plus. Beds: KQDT. Cable TV, phone, VCR and one Jacuzzi in room. Air conditioning. Antiquing, golf, live theater and shopping nearby.
Publicity: *Canton Observer and Encore.*

"A step into the grace, charm and elegance of the 19th century but with all the amenities of the 21st century right at hand."

Lansing I7

Ask Me House

1027 Seymour Ave
Lansing, MI 48906-4836
(517)484-3127 (800)275-6341 Fax:(517)484-4193
E-mail: mekiener@aol.com
Web: www.askmehouse.com

Circa 1911. This early 20th-century home still includes its original hardwood floors and pocket doors. A hand-painted mural was added to the dining room in the 1940s. Guests can enjoy the unique art during the breakfasts, which are served on antique Limoges china and Depression glass. The home is near a variety of museums, theaters, a historical village and Michigan State University.

Innkeeper(s): Mary Elaine Kiener & Alex Kruzel. $65. MC, VISA, PC, TC. TAC10. 2 rooms. Breakfast included in rates. Types of meals: Gourmet bkfst and

early coffee/tea. Beds: DT. Ceiling fan in room. VCR and fax on premises. Weddings and small meetings hosted. Polish spoken. Antiquing, live theater, parks and sporting events nearby.

Lowell I6

McGee Homestead B&B

2534 Alden Nash NE
Lowell, MI 49331
(616)897-8142
E-mail: mcgeebb@iserv.net
Web: www.iserv.net/~mcgeebb

Circa 1880. Just 18 miles from Grand Rapids, travelers will find the McGee Homestead B&B, an Italianate farmhouse with four antique-filled guest rooms. Surrounded by orchards, it is one of the largest farmhouses in the area. Breakfasts feature the inn's own fresh eggs. Guests may golf at a nearby course or

enjoy our hot tub on the screen porch. Lowell is home to Michigan's largest antique mall, and historic covered bridges are found in the sur-

rounding countryside. Travelers who remain on the farm may relax in a hammock or visit a barn full of petting animals.

Innkeeper(s): Bill & Ardie Barber. $55-75. MC, VISA, AX, DS, PC, TC. 4 rooms with PB and 1 conference room. Breakfast and snacks/refreshments included in rates. Types of meals: Full bkfst and early coffee/tea. Beds: KDT. TV and ceiling fan in room. Air conditioning. VCR and library on premises. Small meetings hosted. Antiquing, fishing, parks, shopping, downhill skiing and cross-country skiing nearby.

Ludington G5

The Inn at Ludington

701 E Ludington Ave
Ludington, MI 49431-2224
(231)845-7055 (800)845-9170
Web: www.inn-ludington.com

Circa 1890. This Queen Anne Victorian was built during the heyday of Ludington's lumber era by a local pharmacist and doctor. The innkeepers stress relaxation at the inn despite its elegant exterior with its three-story turret. The rooms are filled with comfortable, vintage furnishings. Guests can snuggle up with a book in front of a warming fireplace or enjoy a soak in a clawfoot tub. A hearty, buffet-style breakfast is served each morning. The innkeepers take great pride in their cuisine and are always happy to share some of their award-winning recipes with guests. After a day of beachcombing, antiquing, cross-country skiing or perhaps a bike ride, guests return

to the inn to find a chocolate atop their pillow. Don't forget to ask about the innkeepers' murder-mystery weekends.

Innkeeper(s): Diane & David Nemitz. $80-100. MC, VISA, AX, DS, PC, TC. TAC10. 6 rooms with PB, 2 with FP and 1 suite. Types of meals: Full bkfst and early coffee/tea. Beds: KQD. Cable TV, turn-down service and ceiling fan in room. Air conditioning. Fax, copier and library on premises. Weddings, small meetings and seminars hosted. Amusement parks, antiquing, fishing, live theater, parks, shopping, downhill skiing, cross-country skiing and water sports nearby.
Publicity: *Ludington Daily News, Detroit Free Press, Chicago Tribune, Country Accents and Michigan Living.*

"Loved the room and everything else about the house."

Lamplighter B&B

602 E Ludington Ave
Ludington, MI 49431-2223
(231)843-9792 (800)301-9792 Fax:(231)845-6070
E-mail: catsup@aol.com

Circa 1895. This Queen Anne home offers convenient access to Lake Michigan's beaches, the Badger car ferry to Wisconsin and Ludington State Park. A collection of European antiques, original paintings and lithographs decorate the inn. The home's centerpiece, a golden oak curved staircase, leads guests up to their rooms. Two rooms feature whirlpool tubs, one a fireplace. The innkeepers have created a mix of hospitality and convenience that draws both vacationers and business travelers. A full, gourmet breakfast is served each morning. The innkeepers are fluent in German.

Innkeeper(s): Judy & Heinz Bertram. $115-145. MC, VISA, AX, DS, PC, TC. TAC10. 5 rooms with PB, 1 with FP. Breakfast included in rates. Types of meals: Gourmet bkfst and early coffee/tea. Beds: Q. Cable TV, phone, turndown service and two with Jacuzzi in room. Air conditioning. VCR, fax, copier and gazebo and terrace on premises. Amusement parks, antiquing, fishing, golf, parks, shopping, cross-country skiing, tennis and water sports nearby.

"For my husband's first bed and breakfast experience, it couldn't have been better."

Schoenberger House

409 E Ludington Ave
Ludington, MI 49431
(231)843-4435

Circa 1903. The carved white columns of this elegant brick Greek Revival mansion rise two stories to a beautifully designed pediment. A wide balcony with balustrades overlooks the front garden. Inside, a variety of finely crafted woodwork is highlighted throughout the mansion starting with the white oak entrance hall. There's a black walnut library, a cherry living room, American sycamore dining room and mahogany music room. Original chandeliers and five fireplaces are complemented with antique and reproduction furnishings and contemporary art. An abundant, expanded continental breakfast is served. Ludington and this part of the Lake Michigan shoreline offer beautiful uncrowded beaches.

Historic Interest: Mason County Courthouse (1 block), Big Sable Point Lighthouse (8.5 miles), White Pine Village (3 miles).

Innkeeper(s): Marlene Schoenberger. $135-215. MC, VISA, AX, PC, TC. 5 rooms with PB and 1 suite. Breakfast included in rates. Types of meals: Cont plus and early coffee/tea. Beds: KQD. Fax, copier and library on premises. Small meetings and seminars hosted. Antiquing, beaches, bicycling, canoeing/kayaking, fishing, golf, hiking, horseback riding, live theater, parks, shopping and cross-country skiing nearby.

Publicity: *The Saginaw News, Grand Rapids Press, Ann Arbor News, Rockford Independent Flint Journal and Kalamazoo Gazette.*

Mackinac Island   E7

Cloghaun

PO Box 1540
Mackinac Island, MI 49757-0203
(906)847-3885 (888)442-5929
E-mail: cloghaun@aol.com

Circa 1884. Pronounced "Clah han," the inn's name is Gaelic for "stoney ground" in reference to Mackinac Island's beaches. Built spacious enough to house Thomas and Bridgett Donnelly's large Irish family, this handsome Victorian home is owned and operated by their great grandson James Bond.

The inn's gracious exterior boasts a front porch and upper balcony where guests enjoy watching the horse-drawn carriages pass by. Guest rooms are furnished in period antiques. Kelton Library is a welcoming retreat for reading or watching videos. Afternoon tea is served. The inn's location on Market Street affords easy access to parks, restaurants, ferries and shops.

Innkeeper(s): Marti & Paul Carey. $100-165. PC. 11 rooms, 9 with PB. Breakfast included in rates. Types of meals: Cont plus. Beds: KQD. VCR and library on premises. Weddings, small meetings, family reunions and seminars hosted. Restaurants and ferry lines, parks and shopping nearby.

Publicity: *Country Inns, Michigan Living and Country Discoveries.*

Haan's 1830 Inn

PO Box 123
Mackinac Island, MI 49757-0123
(906)847-6244
E-mail: gringo@imaxx.net

Circa 1830. The clip-clopping of horses is still heard from the front porches of this inn as carriages and wagons transport visitors around the island. In the Michigan Register of Historic Places, Haan's 1830 Inn is the oldest Greek Revival-style home in the Northwest Territory. It is behind a picket fence and just across the street from Haldimand Bay. Victorian and early American antiques include a writing desk used by Colonel Preston, an officer at Fort Mackinac at the turn of the century and a 12-foot breakfast table formerly used by Amish farmers when they harvested each other's crops. The inn is open from May to October.

Historic Interest: Original British Fort Mackinac, Indian dormitory, Dr. Beaumont Memorial (discoverer of human digestion), John Jacob Astor Fur Trading Warehouse.

Innkeeper(s): Nicholas & Nancy Haan. $95-175. 8 rooms and 2 suites. Breakfast included in rates. Types of meals: Cont plus. Beds: QD. Antiquing, fishing and shopping nearby.

Publicity: *Detroit Free Press, Chicago Tribune, Innsider, Chicago Sun-Times and Good Housekeeping.*

"The ambiance, service and everything else was just what we needed."

Mendon   J6

The Mendon Country Inn

PO Box 98
Mendon, MI 49072-9502
(616)496-8132 (800)304-3366 Fax:(616)496-8403
E-mail: vasame@aol.com
Web: www.rivercountry.com

Circa 1873. This two-story stagecoach inn was constructed with St. Joseph River clay bricks fired on the property. There are eight-foot windows, high ceilings and a walnut staircase. Country antiques are accentuated with woven rugs, collectibles and bright quilts. There are nine antique-filled guest rooms and nine suites which include a fireplace and Jacuzzi tub. Depending on the season, guests may also borrow a tandem bike or

arrange for a canoe trip. Special events are featured throughout the year. The inn's Golden Getaway package includes lodging, a dinner for two and special activity, which might be golfing, a river canoe trip, skiing or perhaps a relaxing massage. A rural Amish community and Shipshewana are nearby.

Historic Interest: National Register.
Innkeeper(s): Geff & Cheryl Clarke. $69-159. MC, VISA, AX, DS, PC, TC. TAC10. 18 rooms with PB, 14 with FP, 9 suites, 2 cottages and 1 conference room. Breakfast included in rates. Types of meals: Full bkfst and early coffee/tea. Beds: QD. TV, ceiling fan and most rooms with fireplaces in room. Air conditioning. Fax, sauna, bicycles, library and canoeing on premises. Handicap access. Family reunions and seminars hosted. Antiquing, fishing, canoeing, shopping, downhill skiing and cross-country skiing nearby.
Publicity: *Insider, Country Home, Country Magazine and Midwest Living.*

"A great experience. Good food and great hosts. Thank you."

Muskegon   H6

Port City Victorian Inn

1259 Lakeshore Dr
Muskegon, MI 49441-1659
(231)759-0205 (800)274-3574 Fax:(616)759-0205
E-mail: pcvicinn@gte.net
Web: www.portcityinn.com

Circa 1877. Lumber baron and industrialist Alexander Rodgers, Sr. built this Queen Anne-style home. Among its impressive features are the grand entryway with a natural oak staircase and paneling, carved posts and spindles. The curved,

leaded-glass windows in the inn's parlor offer a view of Muskegon Lake. Beveled-glass doors enclose the natural wood fireplace in the sitting room. High ceilings, intricate molding, polished oak floors and antiques further enhance the charm of this house. Guest rooms offer views of the lake, as well as double whirlpool tubs. A full breakfast is served either on the sun porch or in the dining room, or guests can enjoy the meal in the privacy of their room.

Innkeeper(s): Barbara Schossau. $80-150. MC, VISA, AX, DC, CB, DS, PC, TC. TAC10. 6 rooms with PB & 3 suites. Breakfast included in rates. Types of meals: Full bkfst & room service. AP. Beds: Q. Cable TV, phone, turndown service, ceiling fan & double whirlpool tubs in room. Air conditioning. VCR, fax, copier, bicycles and second floor sun deck on premises. Weddings, small meetings, family reunions and seminars hosted. Amusement parks, antiquing, golf, Lake Michigan, Muskegon Lake, cruise ship: Port City Princess, parks & water sports nearby.
Publicity: *Muskegon Chronicle, Michigan Living, PASS and local TV Channel 40.*

"The inn offers only comfort, good food and total peace of mind."

New Buffalo   K5

Sans Souci Euro Inn

19265 S Lakeside Rd
New Buffalo, MI 49117-9276
(616)756-3141 Fax:(616)756-5511
E-mail: sans-souci@worldnet.att.net

Circa 1940. Fifty acres of wildflower meadows and tall pine trees surround Lake Sans Souci (French for "without a care"). The inn's European decor is a crisp contemporary style featuring king-size beds. Rather than simply rooms, honeymoon suites, family homes and fisherman's cottages are available. For a family or two couples, for example, the Dutch House offers two bedrooms, a whirlpool, sunken den and kitchen. Outdoor weddings, reunions and meetings are popular here. Chicago is 70 miles away.
Innkeeper(s): The Siewert Family. $140-210. MC, VISA, AX, DS, PC, TC. 9

rooms with PB, 2 suites, 2 cottages and 2 guest houses. Beds: K. Whirlpools and fireplaces on premises.

"A little piece of heaven."

Petoskey (Bay View)   E7

Terrace Inn

1549 Glendale
Petoskey (Bay View), MI 49770
(231)347-2410 (800)530-9898 Fax:(231)347-2407
E-mail: info@theterraceinn.com
Web: www.theterraceinn.com

Circa 1911. This Victorian inn is located on what began as a Chautauqua summer resort, surrounded by more than 400 Victorian cottages. Terrace Inn was built in 1911, and most of its furnishings are original to the property. Guests will enjoy stunning views of Lake Michigan and Little Traverse Bay, and

they can enjoy the shore at the private Bay View beach. In keeping with the surrounding homes, the guest rooms are decorated in a romantic-country cottage style. To take guests back in time, there are no televisions or telephones in the rooms. This historic resort town offers many attractions, from swimming and watersports to hiking to summer theater. During the summer season, the inn's restaurant (open all year) and outdoor veranda are great spots for dinner.

Historic Interest: Mackinaw Island (30 miles).
Innkeeper(s): Tom & Denise Erhart. $49-107. MC, VISA, AX, PC, TC. TAC5. 43 rooms with PB, 1 suite & 2 conference rooms. Breakfast included in rates. Types of meals: Cont plus, snacks/refreshments & dinner. Beds: QDT. 10 have A/C & suite with hot tub in room. VCR, fax, copier, bicycles, tennis, library, beach & cross-country skiing on premises. Weddings, small meetings & family reunions hosted. Antiquing, art galleries, beaches, bicycling, canoeing/kayaking, fishing, golf, hiking, horseback riding, Chautauqua, live theater, museums, parks, shopping, downhill skiing, cross-country skiing, tennis, water sports & wineries nearby.
Publicity: *Oakland Press & Observer Eccentric, Midwest Living, Michigan Magazine and Detroit News.*

Port Huron   I10

Davidson House Bed & Breakfast

1707 Military St
Port Huron, MI 48060-5934
(810)987-3922
Web: www.davidsonhouse.com

Circa 1888. Across the street from the St. Clair River in the tranquil Military Street Home District, sits this grand Queen Anne Victorian, steeped in history and listed in the National Register. A stately home with high ceilings, fancy plasterwork, rich woodwork, stain-jeweled and leaded glass, it boasts seven fireplaces. The parlor and sitting room are finished in butternut. A large, open oak staircase is showcased in the reception hall. Private guest bedrooms offer quilted poster beds, clawfoot tubs and bubble bath. One boasts a double Jacuzzi and balcony overlooking flower gardens and the river. Brown sugar baked bacon and stuffed blueberry French toast are typical favorites served in

a setting of vintage lace and linens, accented with candles and flowers.
Historic Interest: Fort Gratiot Lighthouse (2 miles).
Innkeeper(s): Mark & Odette LaPrairie. $100-150. PC, TC. 4 rooms with PB, 2 with FP. Breakfast and afternoon tea included in rates. Types of meals: Full

bkfst, country bkfst, veg bkfst and early coffee/tea. Beds: QD. Cable TV and fireplace in room. Air conditioning. VCR and library on premises. Weddings and small meetings hosted. Antiquing, beaches, fishing, golf, museums, parks, shopping and water sports nearby.

Victorian Inn

1229 7th St
Port Huron, MI 48060-5303
(810)984-1437
E-mail: marv-sue@victorianinn-mi.com

Circa 1896. This finely renovated Queen Anne Victorian house has both an inn and restaurant. Gleaming carved-oak woodwork, leaded-glass windows and fireplaces in almost every room reflect the home's gracious air. Authentic wallpapers and draperies provide a background for carefully selected antiques. At the three-star, AAA-rated Pierpont's Pub & Wine Cellar, Victorian-inspired menus include such entrees as rack-o-lamb, filets, fish and seafood, all served on antique china.

Innkeeper(s): Marv Burke. $100-150. MC, VISA, AX, DC, CB, DS, PC, TC. 4 rooms, 2 with PB, 2 with FP and 1 suite. Breakfast included in rates. Beds: QDT. Pub on premises. Weddings and small meetings hosted. Antiquing, fishing, live theater, parks, shopping, cross-country skiing and water sports nearby.

Publicity: *Detroit News, Detroit Free Press, Heritage, Crains Business Magazine, Good Afternoon Detroit and HGTV-Bob Villa's Restore America.*

"In all of my trips, business or pleasure, I have never experienced such a warm and courteous staff."

Saint Clair   I10

William Hopkins Manor

613 N Riverside Ave
Saint Clair, MI 48079-5417
(810)329-0188 Fax:(810)329-6239

Circa 1876. This three-story Second Empire Victorian, encompasses 10,000 square feet and comes complete with tower, slate mansard roof, dormers, porches and an elaborate wrought iron fence. Its riverfront location across the street from the St. Clair River affords the pastime of watching freighters and barges pass by. Guest rooms feature reproductions and antiques, and some rooms have fireplaces. A billiard room and two parlors are available for relaxing. Breakfast is served family style in the dining room. The Historic St. Clair Inn, a five-minute walk away, offers an interesting dining option.

Innkeeper(s): Sharon Llewellyn/Terry Mazzarese. $80-100. MC, VISA, PC. 5 rooms, 1 with PB, 1 with FP. Breakfast included in rates. Types of meals: Full bkfst, veg bkfst and early coffee/tea. Beds: QD. Air conditioning. CD players on premises. Small meetings, family reunions and seminars hosted. Antiquing, art galleries, beaches, canoeing/kayaking, fishing, golf, horseback riding, live theater, museums, parks, shopping and water sports nearby.

Publicity: *Southern Sunrise, Midwest Living, The Voice, Between the Lines and Detroit Free Press.*

Saint Joseph   J5

South Cliff Inn B&B

1900 Lakeshore Dr
Saint Joseph, MI 49085-1668
(616)983-4881 Fax:(616)983-7391

Circa 1915. Overlooking Lake Michigan is this charming English cottage, which features seven luxurious guest rooms. One of the most popular is the teal-toned Sunset Suite, with its

panoramic lake view and custom marble tub. Many guests enjoy relaxing in front of the inn's living room fireplace, or on one of two decks that provide vistas of the lake. St. Joseph, a popular getaway for Chicago and Detroit residents, offers many opportunities for visitors. Guests may walk to the beach or downtown for shopping and dining. Several state parks are within easy driving distance.

Innkeeper(s): Bill Swisher. $85-195. 1 suites. Cable TV, phone and ceiling fan in room. Air conditioning. VCR on premises. Amusement parks, antiquing, live theater, shopping, cross-country skiing and sporting events nearby.

Saline   J8

The Homestead B&B

9279 Macon Rd
Saline, MI 48176-9305
(734)429-9625

Circa 1851. The Homestead is a two-story brick farmhouse situated on 50 acres of fields, woods and river. The house has 15-inch-thick walls and is furnished with Victorian antiques and family heirlooms. This was a favorite camping spot for Native Americans while they salted their fish, and many arrowheads have been found on the farm. Activities include long walks through meadows of wildflowers and cross-country skiing in season. It is 40 minutes from Detroit and Toledo and 10 minutes from Ann Arbor.

Innkeeper(s): Shirley Grossman. $70-75. MC, VISA, AX, DS, PC, TC. 5 rooms and 1 conference room. Breakfast and snacks/refreshments included in rates. Types of meals: Full bkfst and early coffee/tea. Beds: DT. TV in room. Air conditioning. VCR on premises. Small meetings, family reunions and seminars hosted. Antiquing, parks, shopping, cross-country skiing and sporting events nearby.

Publicity: *Ann Arbor News, Country Focus and Saline Reporter.*

"We're spoiled now and wouldn't want to stay elsewhere! No motel offers deer at dusk and dawn!"

Saugatuck   I6

Bayside Inn

618 Water St Box 186
Saugatuck, MI 49453
(616)857-4321 Fax:(616)857-1870
E-mail: info@baysideinn.net
Web: www.baysideinn.net

Circa 1926. Located on the edge of the Kalamazoo River and across from the nature observation tower, this downtown inn was once a boathouse. The common room now has a fireplace and view of the water. Each guest room has its own deck. The inn is near several restaurants, shops and beaches. Fishing for salmon, perch and trout is popular.

Innkeeper(s): Kathy Wilson. $85-250. MC, VISA, AX, DS. 10 rooms with PB, 4 with FP, 4 suites and 1 conference room. Breakfast included in rates. Types of meals: Cont plus. Beds: KQ. Cable TV, phone and VCR in room. Air conditioning. Fax, copier and spa on premises. Weddings, small meetings, family reunions and seminars hosted. Antiquing, fishing, live theater, shopping, cross-country skiing and water sports nearby.

"Our stay was wonderful, more pleasant than anticipated, we were so pleased. As for breakfast, it gets our A 1 rating."

Ivy Inn

421 Water
Saugatuck, MI 49453
(616)857-4643
Web: www.ivy-inn.com

Circa 1890. Relaxation begins when stepping onto the porch with an enticing swing. Originally a boarding house, it is now more than 100 years old and renovated for pleasurable getaways. An inviting common room with fireplace features an extensive library. Gorgeous views of the Kalamazoo River or Village Park are seen from the well-decorated guest bedrooms. Hard-boiled eggs, sausage, cheese, muffins, cobbler, cereal and fruit are typical of the deluxe continental breakfast offered daily. A breakfast basket can be prepared for the room or for a picnic outdoors. Encounter friendly people and unique shops in the quaint village.

Innkeeper(s): Linda Brooks/Kay VanHorn. $90-120. MC, VISA, DS, PC, TC. 6 rooms with PB. Breakfast included in rates. Types of meals: Cont plus. Cable TV and ceiling fan in room. Air conditioning. Library on premises. Weddings, small meetings, family reunions and seminars hosted. Antiquing, art galleries, beaches, bicycling, canoeing/kayaking, fishing, golf, hiking, horseback riding, live theater, parks, shopping, cross-country skiing, tennis, water sports and wineries nearby.

J. Paules' Fenn Inn

2254 S 58th St
Saugatuck, MI 49408
(616)561-2836 Fax:(616)561-2836
E-mail: jpaules@accn.org

Circa 1900. This traditional bed and breakfast is peacefully situated in the countryside. Choose from a variety of impressive guest bedrooms, some with sun decks. There is a two-bedroom suite that is perfect for families. Starting with a gourmet breakfast, the hospitality continues throughout the day. Hot beverages, baked goods and fruit are available in the main dining room. Popcorn is offered as the perfect companion while watching a video. There is an exercise room, and children and pets are welcome to roam the grounds or play on the swings.

Innkeeper(s): Paulette Clouse & Ewald Males. $80-130. MC, VISA, DS, PC. TAC10. 4 rooms, 1 with PB and 1 suite. Breakfast, afternoon tea and snacks/refreshments included in rates. Types of meals: Gourmet bkfst, veg bkfst and early coffee/tea. AP. Beds: KQDT. Ceiling fan in room. Air conditioning. VCR, fax, copier, spa, bicycles and library on premises. Amusement parks, antiquing, art galleries, beaches, bicycling, fishing, golf, hiking, horseback riding, live theater, museums, parks, shopping, downhill skiing, cross-country skiing, tennis, water sports and wineries nearby.

Pets allowed: $10 fee per pet per day.

"Your house is gorgeous and we really enjoyed spending time with you."

The Kirby House

PO Box 1174
Saugatuck, MI 46453
(800)521-6473
E-mail: kirbyinn@aol.com
Web: www.kirbyhouse.com

Circa 1890. This impressive Queen Anne Victorian manor is surrounded by woods and adorned with a veranda that wraps around three sides. Kirby House has five fireplaces, an in-ground heated pool and a hot tub. The home is a registered state historic site. Breakfast is a truly memorable affair, each day

starts off with a lavish entree accompanied by a special blend of granola, fresh fruit and an assortment of breads, muffins and coffee cakes. Some of the delectable dishes include

French toast stuffed with bananas and pecans with a frittata Lorraine and smoked salmon hash.

Innkeeper(s): Raymond Riker & Jim Gowran. $100-175. MC, VISA, AX, DS. 8 rooms, 6 with PB. Types of meals: Full bkfst. Beds: QDT. Spa and bicycles on premises.

Publicity: *Michigan Today Magazine and Lansing State Journal.*

Maplewood Hotel

428 Butler St, PO Box 1059
Saugatuck, MI 49453-1059
(616)857-1771
E-mail: info@maplewoodhotel.com
Web: www.maplewoodhotel.com

Circa 1860. Maplewood Hotel stands on the quiet village green in the center of Saugatuck. Built during Michigan's lumber era, the elegant three-story Greek Revival hotel boasts four massive wooden pillars, each 25 feet high. The interiors include crystal chandeliers, period furniture and well-appointed lounge areas.

Innkeeper(s): Catherine Simon. $120-240. MC, VISA, AX, DS. 15 rooms with PB and 1 conference room. Types of meals: Cont. Beds: KQ. TV and phone in room. Outdoor pool on premises.

"Staying at the Maplewood provided the pleasure of listening to classical music on the player grand piano. It was so easy vacationing...steps from boutiques, art galleries and antique shops."

Newnham Suncatcher Inn

PO Box 1106
Saugatuck, MI 49453-1106
(616)857-4249 (800)587-4249
Web: www.suncatcherinn.com

Circa 1902. Just minutes from Lake Michigan, this 1902 Victorian inn with a wraparound porch, hardwood floor and country antiques, offers seven guest rooms and a double-suite cottage. Guests are offered a full breakfast from 9:30 to 10:30 a.m., including such fare as apple puff pancakes, stratas,

peach French toast, cold strawberry soup and chocolate chip coffeecake. The nearby lake offers numerous outdoor activities, such as swimming, fishing and boating.

Innkeeper(s): Barb Wishon & Nancy Parker. $65-125. MC, VISA, DS, PC. 7 rooms, 5 with PB, 3 with FP, 1 suite and 2 cottages. Breakfast included in rates. Types of meals: Gourmet bkfst and veg bkfst. Beds: QDT. Cable TV, ceiling fan and VCR in room. Air conditioning. Copier, spa and swimming on premises. Family reunions hosted. Antiquing, art galleries, beaches, bicycling, canoeing/kayaking, fishing, golf, hiking, horseback riding, live theater, museums, parks, shopping, cross-country skiing, sporting events, tennis, water sports and wineries nearby.

"A hot tub and a swim before bed, then waking up to the smell of coffee and breakfast...we can't imagine anything better."

The Park House Inn

888 Holland St
Saugatuck, MI 49453-9607
(616)857-4535 (800)321-4535 Fax:(616)857-1065
E-mail: info@parkhouseinn.com
Web: www.parkhouseinn.com

Circa 1857. This Greek Revival-style home is the oldest residence in Saugatuck and was constructed for the first mayor. Susan B. Anthony was a guest here for two weeks in the 1870s, and the local Women's Christian Temperance League was established in the parlor. A country theme pervades the inn, with antiques, old woodwork and pine floors. A cottage with a

hot tub and a river-front guest house are also available.

Historic Interest: Listed in the National Register.

Innkeeper(s): Sallie & John Cwik. $65-235. MC, VISA, AX, DS, PC, TC. TAC10. 9 rooms with PB, 6 with FP, 3 suites, 4 cottages and 1 conference room. Breakfast included in rates. Types of meals: Full bkfst, veg bkfst, early coffee/tea, gourmet lunch, picnic lunch, snacks/refreshments, gourmet dinner and room service. Beds: KQDT. Cable TV in room. Air conditioning. VCR, fax, copier, tennis, library and child care on premises. Handicap access. Weddings, small meetings, family reunions and seminars hosted. Antiquing, art galleries, beaches, bicycling, canoeing/kayaking, fishing, golf, hiking, live theater, museums, parks, shopping, cross-country skiing, water sports and wineries nearby.

Publicity: *Detroit News, Insider, Gazette, South Bend Tribune and NBC.*

"Thanks again for your kindness and hospitality during our weekend."

Twin Gables Inn

PO Box 1150, 900 Lake St
Saugatuck, MI 49453-1150
(616)857-4346 (800)231-2185
E-mail: relax@twingablesinn.com
Web: www.twingablesinn.com

Circa 1865. Twin Gables, a state historic site, overlooks Kalamazoo Lake. The interior features comfortable guest rooms, furnished with antiques. Some rooms include a fireplace. After a day of cross-country skiing, golfing or just exploring the area, enjoy a soak in the indoor hot tub. There is also a heated outdoor pool. This inn is the only remaining original mill left in the area, a reminder of the busy lumbering days of Saugatuck's past. Among its other uses, the home has served as a brewery icehouse, a tannery and a boat building factory. The inn is within walking distance to the many shops in Saugatuck and is a good base for those hoping to take in the variety of outdoor activities.

Historic Interest: Saugatuck has its own historical museum and a retired Victorian cruiseliner is docked nearby. Guided tours are available.

Innkeeper(s): Bob Lawrence & Susan Schwaderer. $75-150. MC, VISA, AX, DS. 14 rooms with PB and 3 cottages. Breakfast included in rates. Types of meals: Full bkfst. Beds: KQDT. Air conditioning. VCR, fax, spa, swimming and bicycles on premises. Handicap access. Weddings, small meetings, family reunions and seminars hosted. Antiquing, beaches, fishing, golf, live theater, parks, shopping, cross-country skiing, tennis, water sports and wineries nearby.

Saugatuck (Douglas)   I6

Sherwood Forest B&B

938 Center St
Saugatuck (Douglas), MI 49453
(616)857-1246 (800)838-1246 Fax:(616)857-1996
E-mail: sf@sherwoodforestbandb.com
Web: www.sherwoodforestbandb.com

Circa 1902. As the name suggests, this gracious Victorian is surrounded by woods. A large wraparound porch, gables, and leaded-glass windows add to the appeal. There are hardwood floors and each guest room features antiques, wing chairs and queen-size beds. Two suites offer a Jacuzzi and fireplace. Another room boasts a gas fireplace and a unique hand-painted mural that transforms the room into a canopied tree-top loft. A breakfast of delicious coffees or teas and homemade treats can be enjoyed either in the dining room or on the porch. The outdoor heated pool features a hand-painted mural of a sunken Greek ship embedded in a coral reef and surrounded by schools of fish. The eastern shore of Lake Michigan is only a half block away.

Innkeeper(s): Keith & Sue Charak. $95-175. MC, VISA, DS, PC. TAC10. 5 rooms with PB, 3 with FP, 2 suites, 1 cottage and 1 conference room. Breakfast included in rates. Types of meals: Gourmet bkfst, veg bkfst, early coffee/tea and gourmet dinner. Beds: Q. Ceiling fan and wet bars in room. Central air. VCR, fax, swimming and bicycles on premises. Weddings and family reunions hosted. Antiquing, art galleries, beaches, bicycling, canoeing/kayaking, fishing, golf, hiking, horseback riding, boat charters, live theater, museums, parks, shopping, cross-country skiing, sporting events, tennis and water sports nearby.

Publicity: *Commercial Record, Chicago SunTimes, New York Times, Detroit Free Press, Sun-Time, Grand Rapids Press and Michigan Living.*

"We enjoyed our weekend in the forest, the atmosphere was perfect, and your suggestions on where to eat and how to get around was very appreciated. Thanks for remembering our anniversary."

South Haven   J5

Sand Castle Inn

203 Dyckman Ave
South Haven, MI 49090
(616)639-1110 Fax:(616)637-1050
E-mail: innkeeper@thesandcasinn.com
Web: www.thesandcastleinn.com

Circa 1898. Two towers, several balconies and a wraparound porch are features of this unique Queen Anne Victorian Its romantic location half way between the Black River walkway and Lake Michigan offers an pleasant waterside strolls and close proximity to the beach. The inn is also across from Stanley Johnson Park. Request one of the three round guest rooms in the towers; all offer fireplaces and private balconies. The Tower Suite boasts splendid views as well. The decor is in a classic cottage design. Breakfast features a gourmet entree such as wild rice quiche, creamy breakfast lasagna, or an egg casserole and includes fresh fruit and baked goods. The inn was built as part of a resort and during recent renovation, old love letters now on display, were found in the walls. Enjoy the white wicker swing on the porch underneath the soft breeze of ceiling fans. Evening snacks are served at 6 p.m. and bedtime cookies at 8.

Innkeeper(s): Mary Jane & Charles Kindred. $95-225. MC, VISA, AX, DS, PC. 9 rooms with PB, 6 with FP and 3 suites. Breakfast included in rates. Types of meals: Gourmet bkfst, early coffee/tea and snacks/refreshments. Beds: K. Cable TV, ceiling fan and VCR in room. Central air. Fax on premises. Handicap access. Weddings hosted. Antiquing, art galleries, beaches, bicycling, canoeing/kayaking, fishing, golf, hiking, horseback riding, live theater, museums, parks, shopping, downhill skiing, cross-country skiing, sporting events, tennis, water sports and wineries nearby.

The Seymour House

1248 Blue Star Hwy
South Haven, MI 49090-9696
(616)227-3918 Fax:(616)227-3010
E-mail: seymour@cybersol.com
Web: www.seymourhouse.com

Circa 1862. Less than half a mile from the shores of Lake Michigan, this pre-Civil War, Italianate-style home rests upon 11 acres of grounds, complete with nature trails. The Austrian Room, popular with honeymooners, includes a double Jacuzzi tub. Poached pears with raspberry sauce, buttermilk blueberry pancakes and locally made sausages are a few of the items that might appear on the breakfast menu. The inn is midway between Saugatuck and South Haven, which offer plenty of activities. Beaches, Kal-Haven Trail, shopping, horseback riding and winery tours are among the fun destination choices.

Innkeeper(s): Friedl Scimo. $85-145. MC, VISA, PC, TC. TAC10. 5

rooms with PB, 2 with FP and 1 cabin. Breakfast and afternoon tea included in rates. Types of meals: Gourmet bkfst and early coffee/tea. Beds: KQD. TV, ceiling fan, VCR and two with jacuzzi in room. Air conditioning. Fax, copier, swimming and library on premises. Antiquing, fishing, golf, live theater, parks, shopping, downhill skiing, cross-country skiing and water sports nearby.
Publicity: *Country and Michigan Living.*

"As one who comes from the land that invented B&Bs, I hope to say that this is a truly superb example."

Yelton Manor Bed & Breakfast

140 N Shore Dr
South Haven, MI 49090-1135
(616)637-5220
E-mail: elaine@yeltonmanor.com
Web: www.yeltonmanor.com

Circa 1872. Sunsets over Lake Michigan, award-winning gardens and gourmet breakfasts are just a sampling of what guests will partake of at this restored Victorian. There are 11 guest rooms from which to choose, each named for a flower. The anniversary and honeymoon suites offer lakeside views. Most rooms include a Jacuzzi tub. Each of the guest rooms includes a TV and VCR, and there is a large video library to peruse. Bountiful breakfasts include items such as blueberry pancakes or a homemade egg strata with salsa. Yelton Manor guests also enjoy evening hors d'oeuvres, and don't forget to sample one of the inn's signature chocolate chip cookies. During the Christmas season, a tree is placed in every room, and more than 15,000 lights decorate the inn. The innkeepers also offer six additional rooms in the Manor Guest House, a Victorian home built in 1993. Those staying at the guest house enjoy a continental breakfast delivered to their room door.

Innkeeper(s): Elaine Herbert & Robert Kripaitis. $95-270. MC, VISA, AX. 17 rooms with PB, 7 with FP and 1 conference room. Types of meals: Full bkfst. Beds: KQ. Cable TV, phone, VCR, gardens, books and music in room. Library on premises.
Publicity: *Great Lakes Getaway, Adventure Roads, Chicago Tribune, New York Times, Hour Detroit, Chicago Sun Times and Country Living.*

"The Yelton Manor is a lovely place to unwind and enjoy the special amenities provided by the very friendly staff. We appreciate all your hard work and will definitely plan to be back! Thank You!"

Suttons Bay   F6

Korner Kottage B&B

503 N St Josephs Ave, PO Box 174
Suttons Bay, MI 49682-0174
(231)271-2711 Fax:(231)271-2712
E-mail: info@kornerkottage.com
Web: www.kornerkottage.com

Circa 1920. The lake stone screened porch of this restored vintage home reflects an idyllic quaintness. Located in a Nordic village on Leelanau Peninsula, it is within view of the bay and downtown. Relax in an inviting living room. Cheery guest bedrooms are clean and crisp with ironed bed linens. Enjoy a hearty breakfast in the dining room before taking a short walk to the public beach or unique shops.
Innkeeper(s): Sharon Sutterfield. $90-135. PC, TC. 3 rooms with PB. Types of meals: Full bkfst. Beds: KQ. Cable TV and refrigerator in room. Air conditioning. Antiquing, art galleries, beaches, golf, casinos, dining, marina, National Parks, live theater and shopping nearby.
Publicity: *The Detroit News.*

"Thank you very much for making our stay here in your home a very pleasant experience."

Traverse City   F6

Historic Victoriana 1898

622 Washington St
Traverse City, MI 49686-2646
(231)929-1009
E-mail: rscherme@traverse.net
Web: www.historicvictoriana.org

Circa 1898. Egbert Ferris, a partner in the European Horse Hotel, built this Victorian manor and carriage house. Later the bell tower from the old Central School was moved onto the property and now serves as a Greek Revival gazebo. The house sits on manicured grounds with mature trees. It has three parlors and authentic Victorian touches like fretwork, etched glass and stained glass, which give the interior a charming ambiance. The three guest bedrooms and suite are appointed with antiques and family heirlooms. The inn's breakfast specialty is Belgian waffles with homemade cherry sauce, served by candlelight. Antique shops, fishing museums and University Center are all nearby. Guests also may enjoy water sports, downhill and cross-country skiing.

Innkeeper(s): Flo & Bob Schermerhorn. $65-95. PC. TAC10. 3 rooms with PB, 1 with FP and 1 suite. Breakfast and afternoon tea included in rates. Types of meals: Gourmet bkfst and early coffee/tea. Beds: QD. TV and turn-down service in room. Air conditioning. VCR, fax and library on premises. Antiquing, fishing museums and University Center, live theater, parks, shopping, downhill skiing, cross-country skiing and water sports nearby.
Publicity: *Michigan Living, Minneapolis Star-Tribune, Midwest Living and Oakland Press.*

"In all our B&B experiences, no one can compare with the Victoriana 1898. You're 100% in every category!"

Whitehall   H5

White Swan Inn

303 S Mears Ave
Whitehall, MI 49461-1323
(231)894-5169 (888)948-7926 Fax:(231)894-5169
E-mail: info@whiteswaninn.com
Web: www.whiteswaninn.com

Circa 1884. Maple trees shade this sturdy Queen Anne home, a block from White Lake. A screened porch filled with white wicker and an upstairs coffee room are leisurely retreats. Parquet floors in the dining room, antique furnishings and chandeliers add to the comfortable decor. Chicken and broccoli quiche is a favorite breakfast recipe. Cross the street for summer theater or walk to shops and restaurants nearby.
Historic Interest: White River Light Station (5 miles), Hackley-Hume Historic Homes (20 miles), Little Sable Lighthouse (20 miles), Owasippe Scout Reservation (5 miles).
Innkeeper(s): Cathy & Ron Russell. $85-135. MC, VISA, AX, DS, PC, TC. TAC10. 4 rooms with PB. Breakfast and snacks/refreshments included in rates. Types of meals: Full bkfst and early coffee/tea. Beds: KQDT. Cable TV, ceiling fan, VCR and one suite with whirlpool tub in room. Air conditioning. Fax, copier, gift shop and beverage center on premises. Small meetings and family reunions hosted. Amusement parks, antiquing, art galleries, beaches, bicycling, canoeing/kayaking, fishing, golf, hiking, thoroughbred racing, seasonal festivals, live theater, museums, parks, cross-country skiing, sporting events, tennis and water sports nearby.
Publicity: *White Lake Beacon, Muskegon Chronicle, Michigan Travel Ideas and Cookbook-Inn Time for Breakfast.*

"What a great place to gather with old friends and relive past fun times and create new ones."

Minnesota

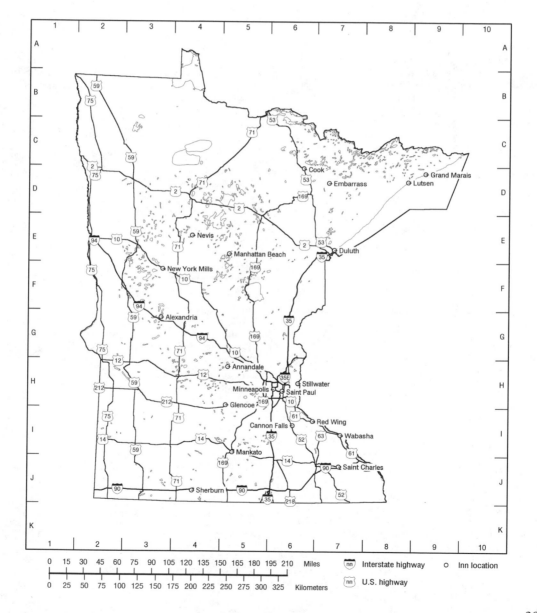

	Miles		Interstate highway	○	Inn location
0 15 30 45 60 75 90 105 120 135 150 165 180 195 210					
0 25 50 75 100 125 150 175 200 225 250 275 300 325	Kilometers		U.S. highway		

Alexandria G3

Cedar Rose Inn

422 7th Ave W
Alexandria, MN 56308
(320)762-8430 (888)203-5333 Fax:(320)762-8044
E-mail: cedarose@gctel.com
Web: www.echopress.com/cedarose

Circa 1903. Diamond-paned windows, gables, a wraparound porch with a swing for two and stained glass enhance the exterior of this handsome three-story Tudor Revival home in the National Register. Located in what was once referred to as the  "Silk Stocking District," the home was built by the town's mayor. Arched doorways, Tiffany chandeliers, a glorious open staircase, maple floors and oak woodwork set the atmosphere. There's a library, a formal dining room and a parlor with fireplace and window seat. Request the Noah P. Ward room and enjoy the king-size bed and double whirlpool with mood lights for a special celebration. Wake to the aroma of freshly baked caramel rolls, scones or cinnamon buns. Entrees of sausage and quiche are favorites. In the evening, enjoy watching the sunset over Lake Winona. Reserve a mountain bike ahead of time with the innkeeper, or enjoy a day of lake activities, shopping, antiquing or horseback riding.

Innkeeper(s): Aggie & Florian Ledermann. $75-135. MC, VISA, PC. 4 rooms with PB. Breakfast and snacks/refreshments included in rates. Types of meals: Full bkfst, early coffee/tea and room service. Beds: KQ. Air conditioning. Bicycles and library on premises. Weddings, small meetings and family reunions hosted. Antiquing, bicycling, fishing, golf, hiking, live theater, parks, shopping, downhill skiing, cross-country skiing, tennis and water sports nearby.

"The Cedar Rose Inn was more than we imagined it would be. We felt like royalty in your beautiful dining room."

Annandale H5

Thayer's Historic Bed n' Breakfast

PO Box 246 Hwy 55 60 West Elm St
Annandale, MN 55302
(320)274-8222 (800)944-6595 Fax:(320)274-5051
E-mail: thayers@hotmail.com
Web: www.thayers.net

Circa 1895. Gus Thayer, the town constable, school bus driver, thresher and mill operator, originally built this old railroad-style hotel to accommodate weary road and rail travelers. At that time, the inn epitomized the unique turn-of-the-century gaiety of dining, dancing, singing and sleeping all under one roof. Although there have been many changes throughout its 100 years, innkeeper, and psychic, Sharon Gammell, has restored the home to its original intended purpose. Richly appointed rooms feature authentic period furnishings, four-poster beds and hot tubs. On scheduled weekends Thayers offers packages such as "Mystery Dinners to Die For." All visitors will enjoy a gourmet breakfast with specialties such as raspberry cheese blintzes served on smoked bacon and hand-dipped chocolate covered strawberries. A cocktail lounge features 38 varieties of Scotch and a wide selection of beers. The home is listed on the National Register of Historic Places.

Innkeeper(s): Sharon Gammell. $99-225. MC, VISA, AX, DS, PC, TC. TAC10. 11 rooms with PB, 1 with FP and 1 conference room. Breakfast included in rates. Types of meals: Gourmet bkfst, cont plus, cont, early coffee/tea, gourmet lunch, picnic lunch, afternoon tea, snacks/refreshments and gourmet dinner. Beds: QDT. Cable TV and VCR in room. Air conditioning. Fax, copier, spa, sauna and liquor lounge and dining on weekends on premises. Weddings, small meetings, family reunions and seminars hosted. Amusement parks, antiquing, fishing, live theater, parks, shopping, downhill skiing, cross-country skiing and water sports nearby.

Pets allowed: prior approval necessary.

Cannon Falls I6

Quill & Quilt

615 Hoffman St W
Cannon Falls, MN 55009-1923
(507)263-5507 (800)488-3849
E-mail: info@quillandquilt.com
Web: www.quillandquilt.com

Circa 1897. This three-story, gabled Colonial Revival house has six bay windows and several porches and decks. The inn features a well-stocked library, a front parlor with a fireplace, and handsomely decorated guest rooms. A favorite is the room with a double whirlpool tub, two bay windows, a king-size oak canopy bed and private sitting area..

Innkeeper(s): Jean Schulte. $75-160. MC, VISA. 4 rooms with PB and 1 suite. Breakfast included in rates. Types of meals: Full bkfst and cont. AP. Beds: KQ. TV in room. Antiquing, bicycling, downhill skiing, cross-country skiing and water sports nearby.

Publicity: *Minneapolis Tribune and Country Quilts.*

"What a pleasure to find the charm and hospitality of an English country home while on holiday in the United States."

Cook D6

Ludlow's Island Lodge

8166 Ludlow Dr
Cook, MN 55723
(218)666-5407 (877)583-5697 Fax:(218)666-2488
E-mail: info@ludlowsresort.com
Web: www.ludlowsresort.com

Circa 1939. A collection of 18 rustic cabins is nestled on two shores of the lake and a private island. They range in style and size and are from one to five bedrooms. All have fireplaces, kitchens and outdoor decks. All cabins have multiple baths and are equipped with tubs and showers. This resort is very private with many activities on the property that are free of charge including tennis, racquetball, canoeing and sailboating. A 24-hour convenience grocery store is also on premises. Children may enjoy watching movies that are shown every evening in the lodge, and there are daily activities that focus on the surrounding environment.

Innkeeper(s): Mark & Sally Ludlow. $200-400. MC, VISA, AX, DS, PC. TAC10. 56 rooms. Types of meals: Dinner. Beds: KQDT. Cable TV, ceiling fan, VCR and kitchen in room. Fax, copier, swimming, sauna, tennis, library, child care, fishing, sailing, canoeing and racquetball on premises. Weddings, small meetings, family reunions and seminars hosted. Golf and shopping nearby.

Publicity: *Midwest Living, USA Today, Parents, Country Inns, Minnesota Monthly, Architecture Minnesota. Outside Magazine. and Family Circle.*

Duluth E7

A Charles Weiss Inn- A Return to Victorian Duluth

1615 E Superior St
Duluth, MN 55812-1642
(218)724-7016 (800)525-5243
E-mail: dglee@uslink.net
Web: www.duluth.com/acw

Circa 1895. In summer, flower gardens frame this large three-story turn-of-the-century home. Inside, gleaming wood paneling, carved woodwork, handsome tiled or marble fireplaces and a beamed ceiling in the parlor are among the inn's historic features. Rooms are furnished with antiques and have features such as a fireplace, whirlpool tub or bay window. White oak, bird's-eye maple and cherry are among the fine woods selected by the home's builder, A. Charles Weiss, original publisher of the Duluth Herald. Located in the historic district, guests enjoy viewing a variety of historic homes as they walk three blocks to the boardwalk along Lake Superior and on to Canal Park and the downtown area for shopping and restaurants.

Innkeeper(s): Dave & Peg Lee. $95-145. MC, VISA, DS. 5 rooms with PB, 2 with FP and 1 suite. Breakfast included in rates. Types of meals: Full bkfst and early coffee/tea. Beds: QD. One with hot tub and five with A/C in room. VCR, spa and library on premises. Antiquing, art galleries, beaches, bicycling, canoeing/kayaking, fishing, golf, hiking, horseback riding, live theater, museums, parks, shopping, downhill skiing, cross-country skiing, sporting events, tennis and water sports nearby.

A.G. Thomson House

2617 E Third St
Duluth, MN 55812
(218)724-3464 (877)807-8077 Fax:(218)724-5177
E-mail: thomsonhouse@duluth.com
Web: www.thomsonhouse.com

Circa 1909. A Dutch Colonial Revival with a delightful history of prominent owners, this inn was recently renovated to maximize comfort and style. Each guest bedroom has its own distinct personality. Choose from a variety of decor: classic elegance, Southwest, Northwoods or French Country. A double whirlpool bath or deep clawfoot tub, private sunporch or deck, gas fireplace and CD player add a touch of romance. A continental breakfast basket can be delivered to the room, or a full breakfast can be enjoyed in the sunny dining room. Entrees may include orange-spiced French toast or wild rice quiche. The quiet one-and-a-half-acre property overlooks Lake Superior. A well-manicured lawn accented with perennial beds, scotch pines and spruce trees resides peacefully with wildflowers and sumac.

Innkeeper(s): Bill & Becky Brakken. $119-219. MC, VISA, AX, DS, PC, TC. TAC10. 6 rooms with PB, 5 with FP. Breakfast and snacks/refreshments included in rates. Types of meals: Gourmet bkfst, cont plus and early coffee/tea. Beds: KQ. Ceiling fan and fireplace in room. Air conditioning. Fax, library and gift shop on premises. Weddings, small meetings, family reunions and seminars hosted. French spoken. Antiquing, art galleries, beaches, bicycling, canoeing/kayaking, fishing, golf, hiking, live theater, museums, parks, shopping, downhill skiing, cross-country skiing, sporting events, tennis and water sports nearby.

Publicity: Duluth News-Tribune, Duluth TV Channel 3, 6 and 10.

The Cotton Mansion

2309 East 1st St
Duluth, MN 55812
(218)724-6405 (800)228-1997 Fax:(218)728-0952
E-mail: cottonmansion@msn.com
Web: www.cottonmansion.com

Circa 1908. Four blocks from Lake Superior in the historic East Side, this 16,000-square-foot, three-story Italian Renaissance mansion was once the home of Joseph Bell Cotton, John D. Rockefeller's attorney. Its grand entrance, beautiful solarium, library and elegant parlor with carved alabaster fireplace and beamed ceiling offer a refined experience. Generous guest bedrooms and suites are distinctive, romantic retreats. Some feature fireplaces, whirlpools, overstuffed lounge chairs and sofas, Oriental rugs and antique furnishings. A candlelight breakfast is served on fine china, crystal and silver in the exquisite dining room. Eggs Benedict and stuffed French toast are among the mouth-watering creations. Wine and cheese are enjoyed in the evening. This gracious setting is perfect for small weddings or other romantic occasions and corporate gatherings.

Historic Interest: Historic Congdon Estate.
Innkeeper(s): Ken & Kimberly Aparicio. $125-245. MC, VISA, AX, DS, PC, TC. TAC10. 7 rooms with PB, 4 with FP and 6 suites. Types of meals: Full bkfst and early coffee/tea. Beds: Q. Library on premises. Family reunions hosted. Antiquing, bicycling, canoeing/kayaking, fishing, golf, hiking, horseback riding, live theater, museums, parks, shopping, downhill skiing, cross-country skiing, tennis and water sports nearby.
Publicity: HGTV's The Good Life.

The Firelight Inn on Oregon Creek

2211 East Third St
Duluth, MN 55812
(218)724-0272 (888)724-0273 Fax:(218)724-0304
E-mail: firelightinn@duluth.com
Web: www.duluth.com/firelightinn

Circa 1910. This three-story red brick mansion boasts twelve fireplaces built of a variety of materials including marble, granite and copper. A massive glassed-in porch overlooks the inn's creek, which flows to Lake Superior a few blocks away. In addition to a gas fireplace, five suites offer a Jacuzzi tub and a brass, canopy or four-poster bed. The inn features beautifully preserved woodwork, a carved staircase and polished wood floors. There's a baby grand piano in the living room. Breakfast is brought to your room, and it is usually eaten fireside. Specialties include dishes such as stuffed strawberry French toast, bacon, fruit and lemon pecan bread.

Historic Interest: Gooseberry Falls (40 miles), Split Rock Lighthouse (55 miles).
Innkeeper(s): Jim & Joy Fischer. $135-235. MC, VISA, AX, DS, PC. 6 rooms with PB, 6 with FP. Breakfast and snacks/refreshments included in rates. Types of meals: Full bkfst, early coffee/tea and picnic lunch. Beds: KQ. Cable TV, ceiling fan and VCR in room. Fax and copier on premises. Weddings, small meetings, family reunions and seminars hosted. Antiquing, art galleries, beaches, bicycling, canoeing/kayaking, fishing, golf, hiking, museums, parks, shopping, downhill skiing, cross-country skiing and sporting events nearby.
Publicity: Minneapolis Star Tribune, Duluth Area Women Magazine and MSP Magazine.

Manor On The Creek Inn/Bed & Breakfast

2215 E 2nd St
Duluth, MN 55812-1864
(218)728-3189 (800)428-3189 Fax:(218)724-6227
E-mail: manor@cpinternet.com
Web: www.manoronthecreek.com

Circa 1907. Set on two wooded, park-like acres along Oregon Creek yet in the heart of the historic East End, this exquisite

mansion is Duluth's third largest home. Built by architects Bray and Nystrom, who were originally influenced by Louis Sullivan and Frank Lloyd Wright, the home boasts finely crafted woodwork, a grand great hall, a unique parlor ceiling and a Tiffany fireplace in the dining room. Decorated with traditional furnishings appropriate to the period and the manor, the living room entices guests to relax. There are eight accommodations including the two-bedroom Carriage House. Most feature fireplaces and ceiling fans. There are five suites, three with double whirlpool tubs. Common rooms include a sunroom, billiards room and a conference room. A full breakfast is served and dinner and picnic lunches may be reserved ahead. Enjoy cultural events, concert and sports packages and a wide range of activities such as antiquing, fishing and shopping.

Innkeeper(s): Chris & Tom Kell. $99-229. MC, VISA, DS, PC, TC. TAC10. 8 rooms with PB, 6 with FP, 5 suites and 1 conference room. Breakfast and afternoon tea included in rates. Types of meals: Full bkfst, cont plus, early coffee/tea, picnic lunch, snacks/refreshments, dinner and room service. MAP. Beds: KQD. Phone and ceiling fan in room. Air conditioning. VCR, fax, bicycles, Carriage House with 2 bedrooms, private bath, kithcen and living room, special event dining, internet access available and on premises. Weddings, small meetings, family reunions and seminars hosted. Antiquing, fishing, golf, hiking, symphony, live theater, parks, shopping, downhill skiing, cross-country skiing, sporting events, tennis and water sports nearby.

Publicity: *MN Monthly, Rochester Press, St. Paul Pioneer Press and Duluth News-Tribune.*

Olcott House Bed & Breakfast

2316 E 1st St
Duluth, MN 55812-1807
(218)728-1339 (800)715-1339
E-mail: olcott@pressenter.com
Web: olcotthouse.com

Circa 1904. Georgian Colonial architecture surrounded by brick and wrought iron creates an antebellum ambiance at this home and carriage house in the historic East End Mansion District. Soaring pillars, bay windows, beamed ceilings, hardwood floors, a grand center staircase and 11 fireplaces add a regal elegance to the stately inn. The multi-room suites and carriage house offer spacious grandeur with antique Victorian furnishings, four-poster and canopy beds, clawfoot or whirlpool tubs, fireplaces, private porches, CD players and other pleasures to enjoy. More than a meal, breakfast is a delicious luxury with candlelit table settings of silver, crystal, fine china and fresh flowers. Lake Superior and North Shore attractions are minutes away.

Historic Interest: Glenshaw Mansion (10 blocks), Depot Museum (3 miles).

Innkeeper(s): Don & Barb Trueman. $125-185. MC, VISA, DS, PC, TC. TAC10. 6 suites, 6 with FP. Breakfast and snacks/refreshments included in rates. Types of meals: Gourmet bkfst, cont and early coffee/tea. Beds: QT. Phone, VCR, fireplace and one with hot tub in room. Air conditioning. Library and gift shop on premises. Antiquing, art galleries, beaches, bicycling, canoeing/kayaking, fishing, golf, hiking, horseback riding, live theater, museums, parks, shopping, downhill skiing, cross-country skiing, sporting events, tennis and water sports nearby.

Publicity: *HGTV-"If Walls Could Talk"*

Embarrass   D7

Finnish Heritage Homestead

4776 Waisanen Rd
Embarrass, MN 55732-8347
(218)984-3318 (800)863-6545
E-mail: finnbnb@rangenet.com

Circa 1901. This secluded turn-of-the-century, Finnish-American log house offers outdoor recreation and family-style full breakfasts to visitors, who receive many personal touches, such as bathrobes and slipper socks. The warmth of hand hewn logs, handmade rugs and quilts and family heirlooms create a welcoming interior, especially when combined with the unique nature views and an occasional  evening howling of the wolves. Guests also enjoy the inn's relaxing Finnish sauna and playing badminton, boccie ball, croquet and horseshoes on the spacious grounds. There are flower and berry gardens, and a gazebo and gift shop are on the premises. Be sure to inquire about the availability of picnic lunches to take along on excursions to nearby historic and mining sites.

Innkeeper(s): Elaine Braginton & Buzz Schultz. $79-105. MC, VISA. 3 rooms and 1 suite. Breakfast included in rates. Types of meals: Full bkfst and early coffee/tea. Beds: QT. Turndown service and ceiling fan in room. VCR, gazebo, horseshoe, badminton and wood fired sauna on premises. Weddings and family reunions hosted. Antiquing, fishing, international Wolf Center, historic tours, snowmobiling, parks, shopping and downhill skiing nearby.

Glencoe   H5

Glencoe Castle B&B

831 13th St E
Glencoe, MN 55336-1503
(320)864-3043 (800)517-3334
E-mail: becky@glencoecastle.com

Circa 1895. Glencoe Castle was built as a wedding promise to lure a bride from New York to Minnesota. She would move to Glencoe only if her husband built her a castle. This grand manor did the trick, with its carved woodwork, stained glass and ornate wood floors. The third floor originally was built as a ballroom. The home is decorated with antiques, Oriental and country pieces. Guests are treated to a lavish candlelight breakfast with such items as baked eggs in cream and Havarti cheese, Canadian bacon, blueberry French toast, homemade bread, pastries and fresh fruit. In the evenings, tea and dessert are served. There is a Victorian gift shop on the premises. For an extra charge, guests can arrange small meetings, parties, group teas, dinner or teas for two. The teas range from a light breakfast tea to the more extravagant Victorian High Tea. Murder-Mystery events also can be arranged.

Innkeeper(s): Becky & Rick Schoeneck. $85-175. MC, VISA, AX, DS, PC. 4 rooms, 1 with PB, 1 with FP. Breakfast and snacks/refreshments included in rates. Types of meals: Gourmet bkfst, afternoon tea and gourmet dinner. Beds: KD. Air conditioning. VCR on premises. Weddings and small meetings hosted. Amusement parks, antiquing, fishing, live theater, parks, shopping, downhill skiing, cross-country skiing and sporting events nearby.

Grand Marais D9

Snuggle Inn Bed & Breakfast

8 Seventh Ave W, PO Box 915
Grand Marais, MN 55604-0915
(218)387-2847 (800)823-3174 Fax:(218)387-2847
E-mail: info@snuggleinnbb.com
Web: www.snuggleinnbb.com

Circa 1913. Original clapboard siding on the exterior and restored hardwood floors inside reflect the history of this Colonial Four Square inn. The decor is casual, highlighted by local art, prints and paintings. Common areas provide welcome gathering spots to relax or converse in a warm and cozy atmosphere. In the dining room, indulge in a changing breakfast menu that may include lemon souffle pancakes with fresh raspberry syrup, apple sausage and fruit with a homemade sauce. The inn's award-winning, made-from-scratch pumpkin-apple streusel muffins are enjoyed every day. Open year-round and located near the Gunflint Trail only one-half block from the harbor, there is ample opportunity to enjoy watching the sun rise over the water.

Historic Interest: Grand Portage Nat'l Monument/fur trading post (33 miles).

Innkeeper(s): Tim Nauta & Greg Spanton. $70-100. MC, VISA, AX, DC, CB, DS, PC, TC. TAC10. 4 rooms with PB. Breakfast and snacks/refreshments included in rates. Types of meals: Gourmet bkfst, veg bkfst and picnic lunch. Beds: QD. Fresh flowers, lake/harbor views, local art works and books by local authors in room. VCR, fax and large harbor view deck on premises. Family reunions and seminars hosted. Antiquing, art galleries, beaches, bicycling, canoeing/kayaking, fishing, golf, hiking, live theater, museums, parks, shopping, downhill skiing, cross-country skiing, tennis and water sports nearby.

Lutsen D8

Cascade Lodge

3719 W Hwy 61
Lutsen, MN 55612
(218)387-1112 (800)322-9543 Fax:(218)387-1113
E-mail: cascade@cascadelodgemn.com

Circa 1939. Cascade River State Park surrounds these accommodations that span 11 acres on Lake Superior. Choose from a variety of lodgings including a house with spa, motel, or private log cabins, at this distinctly family-oriented inn that features a playground, game room and restaurant with a children's menu. Recreation facilities are abundant with ping pong, pool table, video arcade games, volleyball, and table games. Explore and enjoy the area by renting mountain or ten-speed bikes; canoes, paddles and life preserves; cross-country skis, boots and poles; snowshoes; and even backpacks.

Historic Interest: Grand Portage National Monument (45 miles), Split Rock Lighthouse (60 miles).

Innkeeper(s): Gene & Laurene Glader. $36-205. MC, VISA, AX, DS, PC, TC. TAC10. 27 rooms with PB, 10 with FP, 1 suite, 11 cabins, 1 guest house and 1 conference room. Types of meals: Full bkfst, early coffee/tea, lunch, picnic lunch and dinner. Beds: QDT. TV, phone, VCR, fireplace and whirlpool baths in room. Fax, copier, spa, sauna, bicycles and gift shop on premises. Weddings, small meetings and family reunions hosted. Antiquing, art galleries, bicycling, canoeing/kayaking, fishing, golf, hiking, horseback riding, alpine slide and gondola ride, museums, parks, shopping, downhill skiing, cross-country skiing and tennis nearby.

Lindgren's B&B on Lake Superior

5552 County Rd 35
Lutsen, MN 55612
(218)663-7450
E-mail: info@lindgrenbb.com

Circa 1926. Get away from it all at this romantic 1920s Northwoods Rustic Lodge Log home, sitting on Lake Superior's walkable shoreline. Located a half-mile off Scenic Highway 61 on the lake's Circle Tour, this secluded hideaway with spacious manicured grounds features a baby grand piano, wildlife decor, massive stone fireplaces, whirlpool and Finnish sauna. The comfortable accommodations make it difficult to leave. A hearty continental-plus breakfast is served. Enjoy the natural beauty from the sunrise over the lake to a

moonlit view of deer. Relax to the sounds of gentle waves, birds in song and breezes stirring the trees. Swing by the water's edge in a love seat, nap in a hammock or play horseshoes.

Innkeeper(s): Shirley Lindgren. $105-150. MC, VISA, PC. TAC10. 4 rooms with PB, 1 with FP. Breakfast included in rates. Types of meals: Cont plus, early coffee/tea, picnic lunch and snacks/refreshments. Beds: KDT. One room with two-person whirlpool in room. VCR, library and CD player on premises. Antiquing, bicycling, canoeing/kayaking, fishing, golf, hiking, horseback riding, fall colors, snowmobiling, state parks, live theater, shopping, downhill skiing, cross-country skiing, tennis and water sports nearby.

Publicity: *Country, Brainerd Daily Dispatch, Duluth News-Tribune, Tempo, Midwest Living, Minnesota Monthly, Lake Superior and Minneapolis-St. Paul.*

Manhattan Beach E5

Manhattan Beach Lodge

39051 County Road 66
Manhattan Beach, MN 56442
(218)692-3381 (800)399-4360
E-mail: info@mblodge.com
Web: mblodge.com

Circa 1929. Experience the beauty and tradition of the great Northwoods at this 1920s lodge. Inside, the lodge is wonderfully rustic, with an original stone fireplace, handmade log furniture and hand-crafted quilts. Each guest room features a king- or queen-size log bed and private bath, and suites include fireplaces, refrigerators and microwaves. All the rooms overlook Big Trout Lake, and provide stunning views of the sunset. A continental breakfast is included Monday through Saturday, and an acclaimed full-service restaurant offers delectable specialties such as cranberry-almond chicken, roast duck, or parmesan-crusted walleyed pike. Outside, the old northern forests and Whitefish Chain of Lakes provide year-round activities from boating on the lake or bicycling the Paul Bunyan Trail, to snowmobiling and cross-country skiing.

Innkeeper(s): Mary & John Zesbaugh. $69-199. MC, VISA, AX, DS, PC, TC. TAC10. 18 rooms with PB, 6 suites and 2 conference rooms. Breakfast included in rates. Types of meals: Cont, early coffee/tea, lunch, snacks/refreshments and dinner. EP. Beds: KQ. Cable TV, phone, ceiling fan and handmade log furniture in room. Air conditioning. VCR, fax, copier, spa, swimming, sauna, lakeshore, boat docking and boat rental on premises. Handicap access. Weddings, small meetings, family reunions and seminars hosted. Amusement parks, antiquing, beaches, bicycling, canoeing/kayaking, fishing, golf, hiking, horseback riding, snowshoeing, live theater, parks, shopping, cross-country skiing, tennis and water sports nearby.

Publicity: *Midwest Living, Lake Country Journal, Minnesota Monthly, Travel, Current Catalog and Home & Away Magazine.*

Mankato   I5

Butler House Bed and Breakfast

704 S Broad St
Mankato, MN 56001-3820
(507)387-5055
E-mail: butler1@mnic.net
Web: www.butlerhouse.com

Circa 1905. Beamed ceilings and hand-painted murals grace the interior of this turn-of-the-century home. Fireplaces and window seats create the elegant feel of an English country manor. The main hall features a Steinway grand piano. Rooms are furnished with canopy beds and down comforters.

One boasts its own fireplace, and one has a private Jacuzzi. A three-course gourmet breakfast is served in the formal dining room. On weekdays, a deluxe continental breakfast is served. The surrounding area provides many activities, including downhill and cross-country skiing, cycling, golf, antique shopping and college theater.

Innkeeper(s): Ron & Sharry Tschida. $79-129. MC, VISA. 5 rooms, 3 with PB, 1 with FP. Types of meals: Full bkfst. Jacuzzi (one room) and fireplace (one room) in room. Bicycles on premises. Weddings hosted. Antiquing, bicycling, golf, live theater, downhill skiing and cross-country skiing nearby.

Minneapolis   H6

Nan's B&B

2304 Fremont Ave S
Minneapolis, MN 55405-2645
(612)377-5118
E-mail: zosel@mn.mcad.edu

Circa 1895. Guests at Nan's enjoy close access to downtown Minneapolis, including the Guthrie Theatre, shopping and restaurants. The Lake of the Isles with its scenic walking paths is just four blocks away, and a bus stop is just down the street. The late Victorian home is furnished with antiques and decorated in a country Victorian style. The innkeepers are happy to help guests plan their day-to-day activities.

Innkeeper(s): Nan & Jim Zosel. $60-70. MC, VISA, AX, DC, PC, TC. 3 rooms. Breakfast included in rates. Types of meals: Full bkfst. Beds: QD. Air conditioning. Antiquing, fishing, lakes, walking, biking, live theater, shopping, cross-country skiing and water sports nearby.

"I had a wonderful stay in Minneapolis, mostly due to the comfort and tranquility of Nan's B&B."

Nevis   E4

The Park Street Inn

106 Park St
Nevis, MN 56467-9704
(218)652-4500 (800)797-1778
E-mail: psi@eot.com
Web: www.parkstreetinn.com

Circa 1912. This late Victorian home was built by one of Minnesota's many Norwegian immigrants, a prominent businessman. He picked an ideal spot for the home, which over-

looks Lake Belle Taine and sits across from a town park. The suite includes an all-season porch and a double whirlpool tub. The Grotto Room, a new addition, offers an oversize whirlpool and a waterfall. Oak lamposts light the foyer, and the front parlor is highlighted by a Mission oak fireplace. Homemade fare such as waffles, pancakes, savory meats, egg dishes and French toast are served during the inn's daily country breakfast. Bicyclists will appreciate the close access to the Heartland Bike Trail, just half a block away.

Innkeeper(s): Irene & Len Hall. $75-125. MC, VISA, PC, TC. TAC10. 4 rooms with PB and 1 suite. Breakfast included in rates. Types of meals: Full bkfst, early coffee/tea and picnic lunch. MAP. Beds: KQD. VCR, spa, bicycles and library on premises. Weddings, small meetings and family reunions hosted. Amusement parks, antiquing, fishing, golf, parks, shopping, cross-country skiing and water sports nearby.

Pets allowed: By arrangement only.

"Our favorite respite in the Heartland, where the pace is slow, hospitality is great and food is wonderful."

New York Mills   F3

Whistle Stop Inn B&B

RR 1 Box 85
New York Mills, MN 56567-9704
(218)385-2223 (800)328-6315
E-mail: whistlestop@wcta.net

Circa 1903. A choo-choo theme permeates the atmosphere at this signature Victorian home. Antiques and railroad memorabilia decorate guest rooms with names such as Great Northern or Burlington Northern. The Northern Pacific room includes a bath with a clawfoot tub. For something unusual, try a night in the beautifully restored 19th-century Pullman dining car. It is paneled in mahogany and features floral carpeting as well as a

double whirlpool, TV, VCR and refrigerator. A caboose offers a queen-size Murphy bed, whirlpool, TV, VCR and refrigerator. A second Pullman car with the same amenities has just been added and it features a gas-burning fireplace.

Innkeeper(s): Roger & Jann Lee. $65-135. MC, VISA, AX, DS, PC. TAC10. 5 rooms with PB, 1 suite and 1 conference room. Breakfast included in rates. Types of meals: Full bkfst, cont, early coffee/tea and microwave in room. Beds: QD. Cable TV, phone, ceiling fan and microwave in room. Bicycles on premises. Weddings, small meetings, family reunions and seminars hosted. Antiquing, fishing, golf, snowmobiling trails & cultural center, parks, shopping, cross-country skiing and tennis nearby.

Publicity: USA Weekend, Minneapolis Tribune, Fargo Forum, ABC-Fargo, WDAY, Fargo, Channel 14 and Fergus Falls.

Red Wing   I6

Golden Lantern Inn

721 East Ave
Red Wing, MN 55066-3435
(651)388-3315 (888)288-3315 Fax:(651)385-8509
E-mail: info@goldenlantern.com
Web: www.goldenlantern.com

Circa 1932. Follow the cobblestone path into the luxury of this Tudor revival manor, built in 1932 by the president of Red Wing Shoe Company. Within its 6,000 square feet lie five guest rooms and spacious common areas to relax with friends. Grab a book from the library to read on the stone porch, or take a break in the living room in front of the marble fireplace. Adjourn to a wooden bench beside the stone fireplace on the private patio, or unwind in the hot tub after an exciting day in Red Wing's historic district. Travel up the winding staircase to a room complete with canopy bed, soothing whirlpool bath and cozy fireplace to cap off a night of small-town fun near the Mississippi Bluffs.

Innkeeper(s): Rhonda & Timothy McKim. $95-199. MC, VISA, AX, DS, PC. TAC10. 5 rooms with PB, 4 with FP, 3 suites and 2 conference rooms. Breakfast and snacks/refreshments included in rates. Types of meals: Full bkfst, early coffee/tea and room service. Beds: KQD. Cable TV and ceiling fan in room. Central air. VCR, fax, copier, spa, bicycles, library and outdoor patio with fireplace and hot tub on premises. Weddings, small meetings, family reunions and seminars hosted. Amusement parks, antiquing, art galleries, beaches, bicycling, canoeing/kayaking, fishing, golf, hiking, horseback riding, casino, live theater, museums, parks, shopping, downhill skiing, cross-country skiing, sporting events, tennis and water sports nearby.

Moondance Inn

1105 W 4th St
Red Wing, MN 55066-2423
(651)388-8145 (866)388-8145 Fax:(651)388-9655
E-mail: moondance@redwing.net
Web: www.moondanceinn.com

Circa 1874. Experience exquisite surroundings at this magnificent Italianate home sitting on two city lots in the historic district. Listed in the National Register, the inn has exterior walls made of thick limestone block, and massive butternut and oak pieces for beams, walls and window sills. A grand staircase, gilded stenciled ceiling, Steuben and Tiffany chandeliers, and a huge living room imparts a European influence. The great room showcases a Red Wing tile and oak fireplace. Each of the spacious guest bedrooms and the Garden Suite features a two-person whirlpool tub and antique furnishings. Luxurious fabrics include gold satin, red silk, brocade, damask and tapestry. A full breakfast buffet is offered on weekends, a hearty meal is served during the week. Appetizers are available mid-afternoon. Retreat to private gardens and a terraced hillside or relax on the front porch.

Historic Interest: Downtown Redwing (5 blocks).

Innkeeper(s): Mikel Waulk & Chris Brown Mahoney. $110-189. MC, VISA, AX. 5 rooms with PB and 1 conference room. Breakfast and snacks/refreshments included in rates. Types of meals: Gourmet bkfst, veg bkfst, early coffee/tea, gourmet lunch and gourmet dinner. Beds: KQ. Hot tub and two-person whirlpools in room. Central air. VCR, fax, copier, library and porch on premises. Weddings, small meetings, family reunions and seminars hosted. Amusement parks, antiquing, art galleries, bicycling, canoeing/kayaking, fishing, golf, hiking, live theater, museums, parks, shopping, downhill skiing, cross-country skiing, sporting events, tennis and water sports nearby.

Publicity: *Minnesota Monthly, Saint Paul, Pioneer Press, Applause Magazine and Wisconsin Public Radio.*

Saint Charles J7

Victorian Lace Inn B&B and Tea Room

1512 Whitewater Ave
Saint Charles, MN 55972-1234
(507)932-4496
E-mail: viclaceskv@prodigy.net
Web: www.bluffcountry.com

Circa 1869. This newly restored brick Victorian features a pleasant front porch where guests often linger to watch an occasional Amish buggy pass by. Lace curtains and antique furnishings are features of the guest rooms.

Innkeeper(s): Sharon Vreeman. $75-85. MC, VISA, AX, PC, TC. 4 rooms. Breakfast included in rates. Types of meals: Gourmet bkfst, early coffee/tea, gourmet lunch, afternoon tea and gourmet dinner. Beds: QD. Clock in room. Air conditioning. Library on premises. Weddings, small meetings, family reunions and seminars hosted. Antiquing, fishing, golf, live theater, parks, shopping, cross-country skiing, tennis and water sports nearby.

"They have thought of everything."

Saint Paul H6

Covington Inn Bed and Breakfast

Pier #1 Harriet Island B3
Saint Paul, MN 55107
(651)292-1411
E-mail: towboat@mninter.net
Web: www.covingtoninn.com

Circa 1946. Buoyed by the Mississippi River, this romantic towboat is moored against a backdrop of the downtown skyline. Now a floating B&B, this authentic line boat was the prototype for modern-era towboats. Trimmed stem to stern in brass, bronze and mahogany, the authentic nautical theme is elegant. The comfortable salon, lit with clerestory windows, offers tables with a view, fireside couches and a library of historic books. Private staterooms feature built-in cabinets, antique fixtures and vintage art. The galley provides a breakfast blend of gourmet and hearty regional fare like wild rice French toast with fresh strawberries, organic maple syrup and bacon or sausage. Enjoy a quiet getaway or explore the active city life.

Historic Interest: Fort Snelling (6 miles).

Innkeeper(s): Ann Holt & Tom Welna. $140-235. MC, VISA, DS, PC. 4 rooms, 2 with PB, 2 suites and 1 conference room. Breakfast included in rates. Types of meals: Full bkfst. Beds: QD. Fireplace and decks in room. Air conditioning. Library on premises. Weddings, small meetings, family reunions and seminars hosted. French spoken. Antiquing, bicycling, live theater, museums, parks and sporting events nearby.

Sherburn J4

Four Columns Inn

668 140th St
Sherburn, MN 56171-9732
(507)764-8861

Circa 1884. This Greek Revival home rests on a 320-acre working farm, with 10 acres of flowers, trees and lawns surrounded by wrought iron and wood fences. The five guest rooms are decorated with antiques. Rooms are further adorned with wicker, Handel lamp, stained-glass windows and decorative fireplaces. Guests can take a look at the greenhouse filled

with flowers or use the redwood hot tub. For those celebrating a special occasion, try the Bridal Suite, which offers a rooftop deck with a view of the peaceful countryside. Hearty breakfasts are served in the formal dining room. There are music rooms with a player piano, phonographs, an antique pump organ and a jukebox. The inn is located two miles north of I-90 in between Chicago and the Black Hills. The inn also is close to Iowa's Lake Okoboji. Ask about the romantic getaway package.

Historic Interest: Lake Okoboji.

Innkeeper(s): Norman & Pennie Kittleson. $70-80. PC, TC. TAC10. 5 rooms with PB. Breakfast included in rates. Types of meals: Gourmet bkfst. Beds: KQD. Phone, ceiling fan, balcony, widows walk and musical instruments in room. Air conditioning. Gazebo and deck on premises. Weddings, small meetings and family reunions hosted. Amusement parks, antiquing, fishing, Queen Excursion Boat, live theater, parks, shopping, downhill skiing, cross-country skiing and water sports nearby.

Publicity: *Sentinel-Fairmont, Country Extra, Federated Rural Electric Connections Magazine and Fairmont Cable TV (Focus on Fairmont).*

"I think I'm in heaven. This has been so enjoyable."

Stillwater   H6

Ann Bean Mansion
319 W Pine St
Stillwater, MN 55082-4933
(651)430-0355 Fax:(651)351-2152

Circa 1878. This butter-colored, four-story Victorian beauty is just six blocks from the St. Croix River. It is the oldest surviving lumber baron mansion in Stillwater. Purchased in 1880 by lumber baron Jacob Bean, the mansion was the site of his daughter Ann's elaborate wedding, and then was given to her.

It remained in the family until 1957. The inn has two towers with views of the river and the valley. The Victorian design includes items such as carved oak fireplace mantels and shutters that fold into 18-inch walls. Candle and lamplight, mirrors and flickering fireplaces reflect off the gleaming rich woodwork throughout the structure. The inn's five guest bedrooms all have fireplaces and double whirlpool baths. The 18-inch walls lend privacy and give a cozy ambiance to the rooms. The Tower Room is furnished in antique wicker and has a view of the St. Croix River. Ann and Albert's room is a 400-square-foot room with a large bay window and a hand-carved oak bedroom set. Jacob's Room offers an original marble shower, and Cynthia's room boasts a cherry mantel. Breakfast is served on linens with china next to a cozy fireplace. The meal includes four courses of such gourmet delights as poached pears with vanilla custard, homemade caramel rolls, eggs Florentine and homemade sherbet. Or guests may request a gourmet continental breakfast in bed and enjoy fresh pastries and breads and piping hot coffee or tea in the privacy of their own rooms.

Historic Interest: For Snelling (10 miles).

Innkeeper(s): Kari Stimac, John Wubbels. $99-199. MC, VISA, AX, DS, PC, TC. 5 rooms. Breakfast and snacks/refreshments included in rates. Types of meals: Gourmet bkfst and early coffee/tea. Beds: QD. Ceiling fan in room. Central air. Fax and library on premises. Weddings, small meetings, family reunions and seminars hosted. Antiquing, art galleries, bicycling, canoeing/kayaking, fishing, golf, hiking, live theater, parks, shopping, downhill skiing, cross-country skiing, water sports and wineries nearby.

Publicity: *Holiday Travel Magazine.*

Aurora Staples Inn
303 N 4th St
Stillwater, MN 55082
(651)351-1187 Fax:(651)430-9755
E-mail: info@aurorastaplesinn.com
Web: www.aurorastaplesinn.com

Circa 1892. This Queen Anne Victorian in Stillwater was built in 1892 by a Civil War veteran. It has an attached porch and garden swing and a formal garden with a fountain. Its five guest rooms

offer a variety of amenities such as fireplaces and double whirlpool bathtubs. Breakfasts include fresh fruit, orange juice, muffins, baked eggs, sausage and toast. Enjoy the delightful grounds or drive through the scenic St. Croix River Valley.

Historic Interest: Minnesota territorial prison (1 mile), Warden House Museum (1 mile), Historic Courthouse (1 mile).

Innkeeper(s): Jenny Roesler. $129-179. MC, VISA, AX, PC, TC. 5 rooms with PB, 3 with FP. Breakfast included in rates. Types of meals: Full bkfst. Beds: KQD. Air conditioning. Library on premises. Weddings, small meetings, family reunions and seminars hosted. Antiquing, art galleries, beaches, bicycling, canoeing/kayaking, fishing, golf, hiking, horseback riding, train rides, trolley rides, live theater, museums, parks, shopping, downhill skiing, cross-country skiing, tennis, water sports and wineries nearby.

Cover Park Manor
15330 58th St N
Stillwater, MN 55082-6508
(651)430-9292 (877)430-9292 Fax:(651)430-0034
E-mail: coverpark@coverpark.com
Web: www.coverpark.com

Circa 1850. Cover Park, a historic Victorian home, rests adjacent to its namesake park on an acre of grounds. Two guest rooms offer a view of the park and the St. Croix River. Each room includes a fireplace and a whirlpool tub. Amenities

include items such as refrigerators, stereos and TVs. In addition to the whirlpool and fireplace, Adell's Suite includes a king-size white iron bed, a sitting room and a private porch. Breakfasts include fresh fruit, one-half-dozen varieties of freshly baked pastries and special entrees. The manor is one mile from historic Stillwater's main street.

Innkeeper(s): Chuck & Judy Dougherty. $95-179. MC, VISA, AX, DC, DS, PC, TC. TAC10. 4 rooms with PB, 4 with FP and 2 suites. Breakfast and snacks/refreshments included in rates. Types of meals: Gourmet bkfst, early coffee/tea, picnic lunch, afternoon tea and room service. Beds: KQ. Cable TV and phone in room. Air conditioning. Fax and copier on premises. Handicap access. Small meetings and seminars hosted. Amusement parks, antiquing, fishing, golf, live theater, parks, shopping, downhill skiing, cross-country skiing, sporting events, tennis and water sports nearby.

Publicity: *Pioneer Press, Star Tribune, Country Magazine and Courier.*

Elephant Walk
801 Pine St W
Stillwater, MN 55082-5685
(651)430-0359 (888)430-0359 Fax:(651)351-9080
E-mail: info@elephantwalkbb.com
Web: www.elephantwalkbb.com

Circa 1886. Innkeeper Rita Graybill has filled her unusually named bed & breakfast with items she collected during 20 years in the diplomatic corp. Each room is named for a different place in the world, such as the Rangoon Room or Cadiz Garden Suite. The suite includes a rooftop garden, fireplace and whirlpool tub. For breakfast, homemade scones and tropical fruit accompany a special entree. Guests will enjoy strolling the streets of  Stillwater, Minnesota's oldest town, which features many restored Victorian homes. Elephant Walk is a 35-minute drive from the Twin Cities.

Innkeeper(s): Rita Graybill. $129-269. MC, VISA, DS, PC, TC. 4 rooms with PB, 4 with FP and 1 suite. Breakfast and snacks/refreshments included in rates. Types of meals: Gourmet bkfst and early coffee/tea. Beds: Q. Ceiling fan, fireplaces and four with double whirlpools in room. Air conditioning. Fax and copier on premises. Small meetings hosted. Thai and Spanish spoken. Antiquing, fishing, golf, mall of America - 30 minutes, live theater, parks, shopping, downhill skiing, cross-country skiing and tennis nearby.

Publicity: *Midwest Living, Discover, Minneapolis St. Paul Magazine, City Pages-2000 and Channel WCCO.*

"You made our visit at the Elephant Walk incredibly delightful. Thank you for sharing your world with us."

James A. Mulvey Residence Inn

622 W Churchill
Stillwater, MN 55082
(651)430-8008 (800)820-8008
E-mail: truettldem@aol.com
Web: www.jamesmulveyinn.com

Circa 1878. A charming river town is home to this Italianate-style inn, just a short distance from the Twin Cities, but far from the metro area in atmosphere. Visitors select from seven guest rooms, many decorated Victorian style. The three suites have Southwest, Art Deco or Country French themes, and there are double Jacuzzi tubs and fireplaces. The inn, just nine blocks from the St. Croix River, is a popular stop for couples celebrating anniversaries.
Guests enjoy early coffee or tea service that precedes the full breakfasts. A handsome great room in the vine-covered Carriage House invites relaxation. Antiquing, fishing and skiing are nearby, and there are many picnic spots in the area.

Innkeeper(s): Truett & Jill Lawson. $99-209. MC, VISA, PC, TC. 7 rooms with PB, 7 with FP and 3 suites. Breakfast and afternoon tea included in rates. Types of meals: Gourmet bkfst and early coffee/tea. Beds: QD. Seven double whirlpool Jacuzzi tubs in room. Air conditioning. Bicycles on premises. Small meetings and family reunions hosted. Antiquing, fishing, 30 minutes from Mall of America, live theater, parks, shopping, downhill skiing, cross-country skiing and water sports nearby.

Publicity: *Cover of Christian B&B Directory and Bungalow Magazine.*

Wabasha   17

The Anderson House

333 Main St, PO Box 270
Wabasha, MN 55981-0262
(651)565-4524 (800)535-5467
E-mail: info@theandersonhouse.com
Web: theandersonhouse.com

Circa 1856. Said to be Minnesota's oldest continuously operating hotel, the inn has been filled with high-back beds, marble-topped dressers and antiques. A filled cookie jar sits at the front desk, and guests can choose an actual kitty (complete with cat food and litter box) to spend the night in their rooms. Breakfast is extra, but the giant cinnamon rolls and omelets with red flannel hash are worth it. Fireplaces and Jacuzzi tubs are available, and there's no charge for the warming brick if your feet are cold. Ask about the romantic weekend packages. The inn is adding a 20-unit lodge with mini-suites overlooking the new French Quarter, which has outdoor courtyard seating for more than 400 people.

$50-145. MC, VISA, AX, DS, PC, TC. TAC10. 51 rooms with PB. Beds: QD. TV in room. Fax and copier on premises. Weddings, small meetings and seminars hosted. Fishing, golf, house boat rental, snowmobiling, eagle watching, downhill skiing and cross-country skiing nearby.

Publicity: *The Wall Street Journal, Newsweek., ABC World News Tonight, CBS Evening News, NBC News, People Magazine, Ford Times, Readers Digest, Ladies Home Journal, Insight Magazine, Country Living, Diversion, Omni, Sojurn, The Star, National Enquirer, Continental Air Lines Magazine, Signature Magazine, United Press International, Associated Press and Eye on LA.*

The Lofts of Wabasha

PO Box 185
Wabasha, MN 55981
(651)565-4561 (800)482-8188
E-mail: sandy@eaglesontheriver.com
Web: www.eaglesontheriver.com

Circa 1900. So successful with Eagles on the River B&B, Sandy has renovated these buildings in the historic downtown district. These private, upscale suites impart a cozy romantic ambiance. Artsy River Loft offers a deck overlooking the Mississippi River. Odd Fellow Loft is quaint with antique furnishings. Two of the Grumpy Old Men Lofts have sofa sleepers, ideal for families. Each suite features a fireplace, whirlpool, living/dining area and kitchenette. Breakfast is extra and can be brought to the door by local restaurants. Movie and pizza delivery is also available.

Historic Interest: The Lofts, downtown historical district.

Innkeeper(s): Dewey & Sandy Lexvold. $149-189. MC, VISA, AX, DS. TAC10. 6 suites. Types of meals: Full bkfst, country bkfst, dinner and room service. Beds: Q. Cable TV, VCR, fireplace, whirlpool and kitchenette in room. Air conditioning. Amusement parks, antiquing, beaches, bicycling, canoeing/kayaking, fishing, golf, hiking, horseback riding, birding, eagle watching, live theater, museums, parks, shopping, downhill skiing, cross-country skiing, tennis and water sports nearby.

Publicity: *Minneapolis Star Tribune, Rochester Post Bulletin, Detroit Free Press and Country Living.*

Mississippi

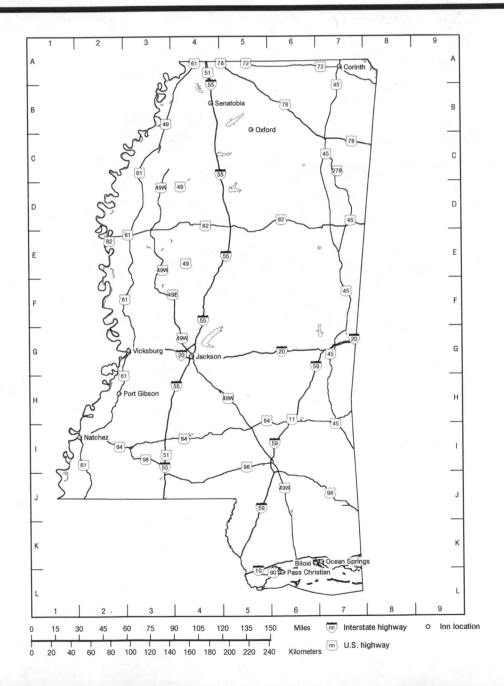

Biloxi K6

Old Santini House B&B

964 Beach Blvd
Biloxi, MS 39530-3740
(228)436-4078 (800)686-1146 Fax:(228)392-9193
E-mail: jad39530@cs.com

Circa 1837. This pre-Civil War home is named not for its first resident, but for the residents that lived there for the longest time. The Santini family lived in this historic home for more

than a century. Each room is decorated with a different theme. One room features a Western motif, one is African in style and the third is decorated with an Oriental flair. In addition to the guest rooms in the main house, the innkeepers also offer a private honeymoon cottage with a Jacuzzi tub, wet bar and king-size bed. A full, Southern-style breakfast is served in the formal dining room on a table set with fine china, sterling silver and crystal. Among the nearby attractions is Jefferson Davis' home, Beauvoir. Charter boats, sunset cruises, walking tours, a lighthouse, NASA and outlet shops are other options.

Historic Interest: Biloxi Lighthouse (4 blocks), Jeff Davis' last home (5 miles).
Innkeeper(s): James A & Patricia S Dunay. $60-175. MC, VISA, AX, DS, TC. TAC5. 4 rooms, 3 with PB, 1 with FP, 1 cottage and 1 conference room. Breakfast and afternoon tea included in rates. Types of meals: Full bkfst and early coffee/tea. Beds: KD. Cable TV, phone and turndown service in room. Air conditioning. Spa, bicycles and BBQ grills and picnic area on premises. Weddings, small meetings and family reunions hosted. Amusement parks, antiquing, art galleries, beaches, bicycling, canoeing/kayaking, fishing, golf, live theater, museums, parks, shopping, sporting events and water sports nearby.

Corinth A7

Bed & Breakfast at Robbins Nest

1523 E Shiloh Rd
Corinth, MS 38834-3632
(662)286-3109 Fax:(662)286-0018
E-mail: twhyte@tsixroads.com

Circa 1869. Remodeled over the years, this gracious Colonial home still maintains its Southern charm. It is conveniently located near the historic downtown area of this Civil War city.

Featured in films, on television and in articles and books, it is listed in "Oldest Homes of Mississippi." Enjoy a full Southern-style breakfast and evening refreshments.

Historic Interest: Shiloh National Military Park (20 miles).
Innkeeper(s): Anne & Tony Whyte. $85-100. MC, VISA, PC, TC. 3 rooms with PB and 1 suite. Breakfast and snacks/refreshments included in rates. Types of meals: Gourmet bkfst. Beds: QDT. Cable TV, phone, turndown service and ceiling fan in room. Air conditioning. VCR on premises. Weddings and small meetings hosted. Antiquing, fishing, golf, live theater, parks, shopping, tennis and water sports nearby.

"We felt like we were visiting a favorite cousin."

The Generals' Quarters B&B Inn

924 Fillmore St
Corinth, MS 38834-4125
(662)286-3325 Fax:(662)287-8188

Circa 1872. History buffs will enjoy this inn, located 22 miles from Shiloh National Military Park and in the historic district of Corinth, a Civil War village. Visitors to this Queen Anne

Victorian, with its quiet, tree-lined lot, enjoy a full breakfast and grounds decorated with a pond and flowers. Five guest rooms and four suites are available. Fort Robinette and Corinth National Cemetery are nearby. The inn is within walking distance to shops, museums, historic sites, restaurants and more.

Innkeeper(s): Charlotte Brandt & Luke Doehner. $75-120. MC, VISA, DS, TC. 10 rooms with PB, 5 with FP, 4 suites & 1 conference room. Breakfast included in rates. Types of meals: Gourmet bkfst, early coffee/tea & picnic lunch. Beds: KQDT. Cable TV, phone, turndown service, ceiling fan & VCR in room. Air conditioning. Fax, bicycles & private dining on premises. Handicap access. Weddings, small meetings, family reunions and seminars hosted. Antiquing, bicycling, fishing, hiking, historical tours, live theater, parks, shopping and water sports nearby.

"Ranks with the best, five stars. You have thought of many comforts."

Jackson G4

Fairview Inn

734 Fairview St
Jackson, MS 39202-1624
(601)948-3429 (888)948-1908 Fax:(601)948-1203
E-mail: fairview@fairviewinn.com
Web: www.fairviewinn.com

Circa 1908. Elegant and romantic canopied beds are among the enticements at this magnificent Colonial Revival mansion. Designed by an associate of Frank Lloyd Wright, the home boasts unforgettable polished hardwood floors, a beautiful marble floor, fine furnishings and tasteful decor. The innkeepers, Carol and William Simmons, pamper guests with a plentiful cook-to-order breakfast and fresh flowers and have hosted many a wedding reception and party. Underneath the shade of ancient oaks and graceful magnolia trees, an inviting deck offers a quiet space to reflect or enjoy conversation. History buffs will appreciate William's knowledge of Mississippi's past. There are

helpful business amenities here, including in-room dataports. The inn has been hailed for its hospitality and cuisine by Country Inns magazine and the James Beard Foundation.

Historic Interest: The home, one of few of its kind remaining in Jackson, is listed in the National Register. The Old Capitol Museum is just over a mile from Fairview. Historic Manship House is only half a mile, and an art museum and agriculture and forestry museum are two miles away.
Innkeeper(s): Carol & William Simmons. $115-290. MC, VISA, AX, DS, PC, TC. TAC10. 18 rooms with PB and 4 conference rooms. Breakfast included in rates. Types of meals: Gourmet bkfst, cont, early coffee/tea, gourmet lunch, snacks/refreshments and gourmet dinner. EP. Beds: KQ. Cable TV, phone and turndown service in room. Air conditioning. VCR, fax, copier, library, voice mail and dataports on premises. Handicap access. Weddings, small meetings, family reunions and seminars hosted. French spoken. Antiquing, live theater, parks, shopping, sporting events and tennis nearby.
Publicity: *Country Inns, Travel & Leisure, Southern Living. & ETV Documentary.*

"Fairview Inn is southern hospitality at its best — Travel and Leisure."

Natchez I2

The Briars Inn & Garden

PO Box 1245
Natchez, MS 39121-1245
(601)446-9654 (800)634-1818 Fax:(601)445-6037
E-mail: thebriarsinn@bkbank.com
Web: www.thebriarsinn.com

Circa 1814. Set on 19 wooded and landscaped acres overlooking the Mississippi River, the Briars is most noted for having

been the family home of Varina Howell where she married Jefferson Davis in 1845. One can only imagine the romance evoked from the simple ceremony in the parlor in front of the carved wood Adam-style mantel. Everything about this elegant and sophisticated Southern Planter-style home brings to life glorious traditions of the Old South, from the 48-foot drawing room with its twin staircases, five Palladian arches and gallery to the lush gardens with more than 1,000 azaleas and camellias. The current owners are interior designers, which is evident in their fine use of fabrics, wall coverings, tastefully appointed guest rooms decorated in period antiques, Oriental rugs and selected art. A gourmet breakfast is served each morning.

Innkeeper(s): R E Canon-Newton Wilds. $160-360. MC, VISA, AX, PC, TC. TAC10. 16 rooms with PB, 6 with FP, 3 suites, 1 cottage and 1 conference room. Breakfast included in rates. Types of meals: Gourmet bkfst and early coffee/tea. Beds: KQT. Cable TV, phone, turndown service and ceiling fan in room. Central air. Fax, copier and swimming on premises. Handicap access. Family reunions hosted. Antiquing, bicycling, fishing, golf, hiking, museums, parks, shopping, tennis and wineries nearby.

"We so enjoyed the splendor of your beautiful gardens. Breakfast was superb and the service outstanding! Thanks!"

Governor Holmes House

207 S Wall St
Natchez, MS 39120-3427
(601)442-2366 (888)442-0166
E-mail: mmcates@earthlink.net

Circa 1794. One of the oldest residences in historic downtown, this 18th century, two-story brick home is listed in the National Register. Named after its earliest owner and the state's first governor, the inn is a short walk from many antebellum homes, restaurants, shops and the bluffs overlooking the Mississippi River. The spacious suites boast private entrances and are furnished in antiques and family heirlooms that date to The War Between the States. Enjoy morning coffee and afternoon refreshments in the courtyard. A hearty breakfast is served at nearby Dunlieth Plantation Carriage House restaurant.

Historic Interest: Stanton Hall, Rosalia, Longwood.
Innkeeper(s): Michael & Eugenie Cates. $115. MC, VISA, PC, TC. TAC10. 2 rooms with PB. Breakfast and snacks/refreshments included in rates. Types of meals: Gourmet bkfst, veg bkfst and early coffee/tea. Beds: Q. Cable TV in room. Air conditioning. Antiquing, fishing, golf, hiking, live theater, shopping, tennis and wineries nearby.

Linden

1 Linden Pl
Natchez, MS 39120-4077
(601)445-5472 (800)254-6336 Fax:(601)442-7548

Circa 1800. Mrs. Jane Gustine-Connor purchased this elegant white Federal plantation home in 1849, and it has remained in her family for six generations. Nestled on seven wooded acres, the inn boasts one of the finest collections of Federal antique furnishings in the South. The stately dining room contains an original Hepplewhite banquet table, set with many pieces of family coin silver and heirloom china. Three Havell editions of John James Audubon's bird prints are displayed on the walls.

Throughout the years, the inn has served as a respite for famous Mississippi statesmen, including the wife of Senator Percy Quinn. Each of the seven guest rooms features canopy beds and authentic Federal antiques. A full Southern breakfast is included in the rates. The Linden is on the Spring and Fall Pilgrimages.

Historic Interest: The inn is in the National Register.
Innkeeper(s): Jeanette Feltus. $95-125. PC, TC. TAC10. 7 rooms with PB. Breakfast included in rates. Types of meals: Gourmet bkfst and early coffee/tea. Beds: KQDT. Ceiling fan in room. Air conditioning. Fax, copier, library and TV on back gallery on premises. Handicap access. Antiquing, fishing, golf, live theater, parks, shopping, tennis and water sports nearby.

Magnolia Hill Plantation B & B

16 Wild Turkey Rd
Natchez, MS 39120-9772
(601)445-2392 (877)642-2392 Fax:(601)442-5782
E-mail: mwheelis@aol.com
Web: www.magnoliahillplantation.com

Circa 1834. Enter the gates of the 60-acre Magnolia Hill Plantation and leave the present behind. The estate has five authentically restored buildings that provide guest accommodations, including a schoolhouse, a kitchen building, doctor's office, carriage house and dairy house. Thirty acres of green lawns include a nine-hole golf course and there are woodlands, fishing ponds and hillsides for secluded picnics. (By prior arrangement, guests may head out with a plantation-packed picnic lunch.). There is hunting in season and fishing. Although most guests are reluctant to leave the grounds, the plantation is convenient to historical downtown Natchez. Many historic homes are 10 miles away, and Vicksburg is 60 miles from the plantation. Guests feast on a hearty southern breakfast in the dining room of the main house. Wedding receptions and family reunions are popular here.

Historic Interest: Natchez Trace (15 miles), Vicksburg (60 miles), Antebellum homes (10 miles).
Innkeeper(s): Michael Wheelis/ Pam White. $125-150. MC, VISA, AX, PC, TC. TAC10. 5 rooms, 4 with FP, 1 suite and 3 cottages. Breakfast included in rates. Types of meals: Full bkfst, country bkfst, early coffee/tea, lunch, picnic lunch, snacks/refreshments, gourmet dinner and room service. Beds: QDT. TV, phone, turndown service, ceiling fan & VCR in room. Central air. Fax, copier, swimming, bicycles, pet boarding, 9 hole golf course w/golf carts & 2 large fishing ponds on premises. Handicap access. Weddings, small meetings, family reunions & seminars hosted. French spoken. Antiquing, bicycling, fishing, golf, hiking, horseback riding, live theater, parks, shopping, tennis, water sports & wineries nearby.

Monmouth Plantation

36 Melrose Ave
Natchez, MS 39120-4005
(601)442-5852 (800)828-4531 Fax:(604)446-7762
E-mail: luxury@monmouthplantation.com
Web: www.monmouthplantation.com

Circa 1818. Monmouth was the home of General Quitman who became acting Governor of Mexico, Governor of Mississippi, and a U.S. Congressman. In the National Historic Landmark, the inn features antique four-poster and canopy beds, turndown service and an evening cocktail hour. Guests Jefferson Davis and Henry Clay enjoyed the same acres of gardens, pond and walking paths available today. Elegant, five-course Southern dinners are served in the beautifully appointed dining room and parlors.

Innkeeper(s): Ron & Lani Riches. $155-375. MC, VISA, AX, DC, CB, DS, PC, TC. 31 rooms with PB, 18 with FP, 16 suites, 6 cottages and 1 conference room. Breakfast included in rates. Types of meals: Full bkfst, early coffee/tea and dinner. Beds: KQDT. Cable TV and turndown service in room. Air conditioning. Fax and copier on premises. Weddings, small meetings, family reunions and seminars hosted. French and German spoken. Antiquing and shopping nearby.

"The best historical inn we have stayed at anywhere."

Myrtle Corner

600 State St
Natchez, MS 39120
(601)445-5999 (877)508-6800 Fax:(604)446-5150
E-mail: myrtlecorner@bkbank.com
Web: www.myrtlecorner.com

Circa 1897. The exterior of Myrtle Corner appears as a fanciful confection of light pink with snow-white trim along the streets of historic downtown Natchez. Antiques and reproductions decorate the interior. The Magnolia Suite includes two bedrooms, a gas log fireplace and bathroom with a Jacuzzi tub. A carved mahogany, four-poster bed graces the Myrtle Room. The Cypress and Raintree rooms include a clawfoot tub. Guests are greeted with a bottle of wine, and each morning, a full breakfast is served at the innkeepers' plantation home with traditional Southern items such as biscuits and grits and gourmet treats such as eggs Benedict or pecan waffles.

Historic Interest: Antebellum Mansions, churches, museums.
Innkeeper(s): Layne Taylor/Don Vesterse. $100-160. MC, VISA, AX, DS, PC, TC. TAC10. 4 rooms, 3 with PB, 2 with FP and 1 suite. Breakfast included in rates. Types of meals: Full bkfst and country bkfst. Beds: KQT. Cable TV, ceiling fan, VCR and private balconies in room. Central air. Courtyard on premises. Antiquing, art galleries, bicycling, fishing, golf, historic walking tours, live theater, museums, parks, shopping and water sports nearby.
Publicity: *WYES TV-12 New Orleans.*

Oakland Plantation

1124 Lower Woodville Rd
Natchez, MS 39120-8132
(601)445-5101 (800)824-0355 Fax:(601)442-5182

Circa 1785. Andrew Jackson courted his future wife, Rachel Robards, at this gracious 18th-century home. This working cattle plantation includes fishing ponds, a tennis court and canoeing. Rooms are filled with antiques, and the innkeepers provide guests with a tour of the main home and plantation. They also will arrange tours of Natchez.

Historic Interest: The historic mansions of Natchez are all within 10 miles of the inn.
Innkeeper(s): Jean & Andy Peabody. $90-100. MC, VISA, AX, TC. TAC10. 3 rooms, 2 with PB, 3 with FP and 1 conference room. Breakfast included in rates. Types of meals: Full bkfst. AP. Beds: KT. Air conditioning. Tennis on premises. Small meetings hosted. Antiquing, fishing, golf, touring Natchez Mansions, live theater, parks and water sports nearby.
Publicity: *Southern Living and Country Inns.*

"Best kept secret in Natchez! Just great!"

Ocean Springs K7

Shadowlawn B&B

112 A Shearwater Dr
Ocean Springs, MS 39564
(228)875-6945 Fax:(228)875-6595
E-mail: shadowos@ametro.net

Circa 1907. A canopy of trees shades the long drive that leads up to Shadowlawn. The home rests on the edge of the Mississippi Sound. Innkeeper Nancy Wilson's grandparents once owned this turn-of-the-century home. A screened-in porch

affords a view of the grounds and water and offers a great place to relax. Antiques and traditional furnishings decorate the home's interior. The full breakfasts often include Southern items such as grits and homemade biscuits.

Innkeeper(s): Bill & Nancy Wilson. $100-125. MC, VISA, PC, TC. TAC10. 4 rooms with PB. Breakfast and afternoon tea included in rates. Types of meals: Full bkfst and early coffee/tea. Beds: Q. Cable TV, ceiling fan and VCR in room. Air conditioning. Fax, copier and library on premises. Weddings, small meetings, family reunions and seminars hosted. Antiquing, fishing, golf, gambling casinos, live theater, parks, shopping, sporting events, tennis and water sports nearby.
Publicity: *Coast Magazine, Sun Herald, Mississippi Press Register and Lonely Planet.*

Oxford B5

Oliver-Britt House

512 Van Buren Ave
Oxford, MS 38655-3838
(662)234-8043
E-mail: eoliver@ebicom.net

Circa 1905. White columns and a picturesque veranda highlight the exterior of this Greek Revival inn shaded by trees. English country comfort is the emphasis in the interior, which includes a collection of antiques. On weekends, guests are treated to a Southern-style breakfast with all the trimmings.
Innkeeper(s): Glynn Oliver & Mary Ann Britt. $55-85. MC, VISA, AX, DS, TC. TAC10. 5 rooms with PB. Types of meals: Early coffee/tea. Beds: KQ. Cable TV and ceiling fan in room. Air conditioning. Weekends we serve a full breakfast on premises. Weddings, small meetings, family reunions and seminars hosted. Antiquing, parks, shopping and sporting events nearby.
Pets Allowed.

Pass Christian L6

Inn At The Pass

125 E Scenic Dr
Pass Christian, MS 39571-4415
(228)452-0333 (800)217-2588 Fax:(228)452-0449
E-mail: innatpas@aol.com
Web: www.innatthepass.com

Circa 1885. Listed in the National Register, this Victorian is adorned by a veranda where guests can relax and catch a tranquil breeze wafting off the Mississippi Gulf Coast. Five of the rooms are located in the main house, but there is also a secluded cottage out back. The décor is Victorian in style, but the rooms include modern amenities. On the weekends, a full, Southern-style breakfast is served. A beach resort town for more than a century, Pass Christian and its surrounding area offers a variety of activities, including water sports, fishing and casinos.

Historic Interest: Beauvoir (Jefferson Davis' home).
Innkeeper(s): Phyllis Hines & Mimi Smith. $85-125. MC, VISA, AX, DS. TAC10. 5 rooms with PB, 3 with FP and 1 cottage. Breakfast included in rates. Types of meals: Full bkfst, veg bkfst, cont plus and early coffee/tea. Beds: QDT. Cable TV, phone, ceiling fan and VCR in room. Central air. Fax, copier and bicycles on premises. Weddings hosted. Antiquing, art galleries, beaches, fishing, golf and water sports nearby.

Port Gibson H2

Oak Square Bed & Breakfast

1207 Church St
Port Gibson, MS 39150-2609
(601)437-4350 (800)729-0240 Fax:(601)437-5768
E-mail: kajunmade@aol.com

Circa 1850. Six 22-foot-tall fluted Corinthian columns support the front gallery of this 30-room Greek Revival plantation. The owners furnished the mansion with 18th- and 19th-century Mississippi heirloom antiques and the guest rooms offer beautiful canopy beds. The parlor holds a carved rosewood Victorian suite, original family documents and a collection of Civil War memorabilia. A hearty southern breakfast is served. Enormous oaks and magnolia trees grace the grounds.

Historic Interest: Listed in the National Register.
Innkeeper(s): Ms. William D. Lum. $95-135. MC, VISA, AX, DS, PC, TC. TAC10. 10 rooms with PB. Breakfast included in rates. Types of meals: Full bkfst. Beds: QT. Cable TV and phone in room. Air conditioning. VCR and fax on premises. State park, Civil War battlefields and museums nearby.
Publicity: *Quad-City Times and Dallas Morning News.*

Senatobia   B4

Spahn House B&B

401 College St
Senatobia, MS 38668-2128
(612)562-9853 (800)400-9853 Fax:(612)562-8160
E-mail: spahn@gmi.net
Web: www.spahnhouse.com

Circa 1904. Originally built by a cotton and cattle baron, this 5,000-square-foot Neoclassical house sits on two acres and is listed in the National Register. Professionally decorated, it fea-

tures fine antiques and luxuriously furnished rooms with elegant bed linens and Jacuzzi tubs. Separate from the main house, a brand new bridal suite offers a large Jacuzzi bath, a king bed and a kitchen. Private

candlelight dinners are available by advance request. Breakfasts feature gourmet cuisine as the inn also manages a full-time catering business. (Guests sometimes are invited to sample food in the kitchen before it makes its way to local parties and events.) Memphis is 30 minutes north.
Historic Interest: Elvis Presley's Graceland, Sun Studio, Clarksdale's Delta Blues Museum.
Innkeeper(s): Daughn & Joe Spahn. $65-225. MC, VISA, AX, DS, PC, TC. TAC10. 5 rooms with PB and 1 suite. Breakfast included in rates. Types of meals: Full bkfst. Beds: KQ. Cable TV, phone, ceiling fan and abundant toiletries in room. Air conditioning. VCR, fax, library and full catering staff/floral supply on premises. Weddings, small meetings, family reunions and seminars hosted. Limited French, German and Spanish spoken. Amusement parks, antiquing, fishing, hiking, wetlands, live theater, parks, shopping, sporting events and water sports nearby.
Publicity: *South Florida Magazine, Mississippi Magazine, B&B Management Magazine, ABC and PBS.*
"*I hope everyone gets to experience that type of Southern hospitality just once in their lifetime.*"

Vicksburg   G3

Anchuca

1010 First East St
Vicksburg, MS 39183
(601)661-0111 (888)686-0111 Fax:(601)661-0111

Circa 1832. This early Greek Revival mansion rises resplendently above the brick-paved streets of Vicksburg. It houses magnificent period antiques and artifacts. Confederate President Jefferson Davis once addressed the townspeople from the balcony while his brother was living in the home after the Civil War. The turn-of-the-century guest cottage has been trans-

formed into an enchanting hideaway and rooms in the mansion are appointed with formal decor and four-poster beds. A swimming pool and Jacuzzi are modern amenities.
Historic Interest: Vicksburg National Military Park (5 minutes), Old Courthouse Museum (2 blocks), Cairo Museum (one-half mile).
Innkeeper(s): Thomas Pharr & Christopher Brinkley. $95-150. MC, VISA, AX, DS, PC, TC. 7 rooms with PB, 4 with FP. Breakfast included in rates. Types of meals: Gourmet bkfst, country bkfst, veg bkfst, cont plus, cont, early coffee/tea, gourmet lunch, picnic lunch, afternoon tea, snacks/refreshments, gourmet dinner and room service. Beds: KQT. Cable TV and turndown service in room. Central air. Fax, spa, swimming and library on premises. Weddings, small meetings, family reunions and seminars hosted. Antiquing, fishing, golf, National Military Park, museums, parks, shopping, sporting events and tennis nearby.
Publicity: *Times Herald, Southern Living, Innsider and Country Inns.*
"*The 'Southern Hospitality' will not be forgotten. The best Southern breakfast in town.*"

Cedar Grove Mansion Inn

2200 Oak St
Vicksburg, MS 39180-4008
(601)636-1000 (800)862-1300 Fax:(601)634-6126
E-mail: info@cedargroveinn.com

Circa 1840. It's easy to relive "Gone With the Wind" at this grand antebellum estate built by John Klein as a wedding present for his bride. Visitors sip mint juleps and watch gas chandeliers flicker in the finely appointed parlors. Many rooms contain their original furnishings. Although Cedar Grove survived the Civil War, a Union cannonball is still lodged in the parlor wall. There is a magnificent view of the Mississippi from the terrace and front gallery. Four acres of gardens include fountains and gazebos. There is a bar, and the inn's restaurant opens each evening at 6 p.m, except on Mondays.
Historic Interest: National Military Park (5 miles) and museums.
$100-190. MC, VISA, AX, DS, TC. TAC10. 30 rooms with PB, 6 with FP, 11 suites, 8 cottages and 4 conference rooms. Breakfast and afternoon tea included in rates. Types of meals: Full bkfst, gourmet dinner and room service. Beds: KQDT. Cable TV, phone and turndown service in room. Air conditioning. Fax, copier, swimming, bicycles, tennis and library on premises. Handicap access. Weddings, small meetings and family reunions hosted. Amusement parks, antiquing, fishing, casino river boat gaming, live theater, parks, shopping and water sports nearby.
Publicity: *Vicksburg Post, Southern Living, Victorian Homes, Country Inns. and Miss Firecracker.*
"*Love at first sight would be the best way to describe my feelings for your home and the staff.*"

Floweree Cottage

2309 Pearl St
Vicksburg, MS 39180-4013
(601)638-2704 (800)262-6315 Fax:(601)636-0052

Circa 1873. "Cottage" is an unassuming way to describe this majestic estate adorned by ornate, Post Bellum plaster work, which was created by Bavarian immigrants. The home is named for Charles Conway-Floweree, the youngest colonel in the Confederate Army and a leader in Pickett's charge at Gettysburg. The innkeeper is an architect, and his restoration efforts have recreated the grand era of this Italianate manor, which is listed in the National Register as well as the Historic American Building Survey. The lush grounds include a swimming pool and greenhouse, and the area offers many outdoor activities.
Historic Interest: Historic homes and a historic garden district are within walking distance of the home and a military park is five miles away.
Innkeeper(s): Skippy & Gayle Tuminello. $85-130. MC, VISA, DS, PC. TAC10. 8 rooms with PB, 7 with FP and 2 suites. Breakfast included in rates. Types of meals: Full bkfst and cont plus. Beds: KQT. Cable TV, phone and ceiling fan in room. Air conditioning. VCR, swimming, golf and gift shop on premises. Small meetings hosted. Amusement parks, antiquing, fishing, live theater, parks, shopping and water sports nearby.
Publicity: *1,001 Ideas and Southern Living.*

Missouri

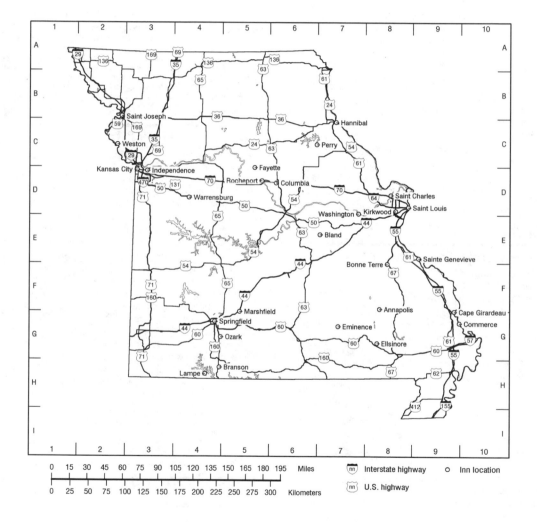

0 15 30 45 60 75 90 105 120 135 150 165 180 195 Miles

0   25 50 75 100 125 150 175 200 225 250 275 300 Kilometers

Interstate highway   Inn location

U.S. highway

Annapolis   F8

Rachel's B&B

202 West Second
Annapolis, MO 63620
(573)598-4656 (888)245-7771 Fax:(573)598-3439
E-mail: info@rachelsbb.com
Web: www.rachelsbb.com

Circa 1920. Formerly the Bolch Mansion, now this renovated Arts and Craft-style B&B is named after the innkeepers' youngest daughter. Annapolis' oldest home, with original glass doorknobs, woodwork, built-in book cases and country elegance, sits on one acre surrounded by mountains and hills. Perfect for a remote romantic getaway, enjoy two-person Jacuzzis, bath salts, robes, fireplace, soft music, romantic in-room videos and private decks. Some rooms are specifically family friendly. In the common room an antique rocking horse is available. There is a large video selection. Enjoy the landscaped grounds with garden pond, goldfish and waterfall, then relax in the outdoor hot tub.

Historic Interest: Ft. Davidson Civil War Musuem (20 miles), Ursaline Girls Academy (20 miles), Antique shops.

Innkeeper(s): Joe & Sharon Cluck. $55-125. MC, VISA, AX, DS, PC. 7 rooms with PB, 1 with FP, 4 suites, 1 cottage and 1 conference room. Breakfast and snacks/refreshments included in rates. Types of meals: Gourmet bkfst, country bkfst, veg bkfst, early coffee/tea and gourmet dinner. Beds: KQDT. Cable TV, phone, ceiling fan, VCR, fireplace, hot tub, snuggly robes and in room. Central air. Fax, copier, spa, library, video library, private entrances, large veranda sitting area and evening dining on premises. Handicap access. Weddings, small meetings, family reunions and seminars hosted. Antiquing, art galleries, beaches, bicycling, canoeing/kayaking, fishing, golf, hiking, horseback riding, museums, parks and water sports nearby.

Publicity: *Journal Banner, Mountain Echo News and Mustang Club.*

Bland   E7

Caverly Farm & Orchard B&B

100 Cedar Ridge Rd
Bland, MO 65014
(573)646-3732 Fax:(573)646-5274

Circa 1850. Built prior to the Civil War, this farmhouse has been renovated completely. The innkeepers preserved many original features, and to keep the home authentic, they used original as accents within the home. Guest rooms are decorated in Colonial style and include family antiques. Take a stroll around the inn's 50-plus acres, and you'll find woods, a pond, a variety of birds and perhaps a deer or two. Breakfasts include items such as farm-fresh cheesy eggs with chives, Canadian bacon, fresh fruit and homemade breads served with homemade preserves and jams.

The home is within an hour's drive of antique shops, craft stores, farm auctions, wineries and the state capital, Jefferson City. Hermann, a historic town about 45 miles away, is an interesting place to visit, especially during its famous Oktoberfest.

Historic Interest: State Capital (43 miles), Wineries, Several 1850-1900 stone farmhouses.

Innkeeper(s): David & Nancy Caverly. $55-60. PC, TC. 3 rooms with PB. Breakfast included in rates. Types of meals: Full bkfst, country bkfst, veg bkfst and early coffee/tea. Beds: QDT. Ceiling fan in room. Central air. VCR and library on premises. Antiquing, canoeing/kayaking, fishing, golf, hiking, shopping and wineries nearby.

Publicity: *Southern Living, St. Louis Post Dispatch and High Performance People.*

Bonne Terre   F8

Victorian Veranda

207 E School St
Bonne Terre, MO 63628
(573)358-1134 (800)343-1134
E-mail: victoriaveranda@ldd.net

Circa 1868. A veranda encircles this blue and white Queen Anne and there are finely crafted decorative details such as porch columns and dentil work. Furnishings in the dining room are country-style enhanced by light floral wallpaper, fine wood paneling and woodwork around the doors, all painted white. Egg casseroles, potatoes and coffee cakes are served here. There are eight state parks in the area and Cherokee Landing offers canoe trips along the river.

Innkeeper(s): Galen & Karen Forney. $70-110. MC, VISA, PC, TC. TAC5. 4 rooms with PB, 1 with FP and 1 suite. Breakfast, afternoon tea and snacks/refreshments included in rates. Types of meals: Gourmet bkfst, early coffee/tea, picnic lunch, gourmet dinner and room service. Beds: Q. Phone and ceiling fan in room. Air conditioning. VCR on premises. Weddings, small meetings and family reunions hosted. Antiquing, fishing, golf, scuba diving/cave, live theater, parks, shopping, sporting events, tennis and water sports nearby.

Branson   H4

Branson Hotel B&B Inn

214 W Main St
Branson, MO 65616-2724
(417)335-6104 (800)933-0651
E-mail: info@bransonhotelbb.com
Web: www.bransonhotelbb.com

Circa 1903. A picket fence frames the Branson Hotel, a Four Square style Victorian and a Branson Historic Landmark. Adirondack chairs fill the fieldstone veranda and the front balcony, affording guests the pleasure of visiting and enjoying the view. As Branson's oldest commercial structure, important gatherings here played a significant part in the history of Branson, and the novel "Shepherd of the

Hills" was written here. A harvest table in the glass-enclosed dining room is laden with hearty gourmet breakfast offerings including bacon quiche, cinnamon spiced pears and broiled grapefruit.

Historic Interest: Lake Taneycomo and historic downtown Branson.

Innkeeper(s): Randy & Cynthia Parker. $75-105. MC, VISA, AX, TC. TAC10. 7 rooms with PB. Breakfast, afternoon tea and snacks/refreshments included in rates. Types of meals: Early coffee/tea. Beds: KQ. Cable TV, phone, turn-down service, ceiling fan and robes in room. Central air. Guest refrigerator on premises. Family reunions hosted. Antiquing, art galleries, bicycling, canoeing/kayaking, fishing, golf, hiking, horseback riding, live theater, parks, shopping, water sports and wineries nearby.

Publicity: *Southern living, Midwest Living, Glamour and Automobile Magazine.*

Cape Girardeau   G9

Bellevue B&B

312 Bellevue St
Cape Girardeau, MO 63701-7233
(573)335-3302 (800)768-6822 Fax:(573)332-7752
E-mail: bellevuebb@compuserve.com

Circa 1891. Within three blocks of Mississippi River front Park, this Queen Anne Victorian with gables and bay windows is in the local historic register. The house is painted deep

hunter green with taupe and cranberry trim, emphasizing the historic craftsmanship of its gables, bay windows, balustrades, cornices and stained glass windows. A glider and two wicker rocking chairs sit on the front porch. Inside, the original woodwork remains as well as several sets of original pocket doors and fireplaces. Ask for the Parkridge Room where a six-foot high antique headboard is the focal point or for the Shea Lorraine or Dearborn rooms, both with large whirlpool tubs. There's a fireplace on the patio for evening get-togethers. SEMO University is nearby.

Innkeeper(s): Marsha Toll. $70-105. MC, VISA, AX, DS, PC, TC. TAC10. 4 rooms with PB. Breakfast included in rates. Types of meals: Full bkfst. AP. Beds: Q. Cable TV, ceiling fan, whirlpool and phones in some rooms in room. Air conditioning. Weddings, small meetings and family reunions hosted.

Columbia   D6

University Avenue B&B

1315 University Ave
Columbia, MO 65201
(573)499-1920 (800)499-1920
E-mail: universityavenue@cs.com
Web: www.universityavenuebnb.com

Circa 1920. Just minutes from the University of Missouri campus, this bed & breakfast provides an excellent location from which to enjoy many nearby attractions. It's just a 15-minute drive into Jefferson City, the state capitol. Stephens College, University of Missouri, restaurants and shops in Columbia's downtown area also are nearby. The historic home is filled with antiques. Guest rooms include beds topped with quilts. Some guest baths include amenities such as a jetted or clawfoot tub. In addition to the four guest rooms, the innkeepers also can provide a meeting room for up to 40 people. Business amenities include in-room desks and modem ports. Breakfast at University Avenue begins with homemade muffins and fresh fruit, followed by an entrée such as caramel French toast.

Historic Interest: Capitol building of Missouri (3 miles).

Innkeeper(s): Willa Adelstein, Susan Schabilion. $80-90. MC, VISA, AX, DS, PC, TC. 4 rooms with PB and 1 conference room. Breakfast, afternoon tea and snacks/refreshments included in rates. Types of meals: Gourmet bkfst, veg bkfst and early coffee/tea. Beds: KQT. TV, phone, ceiling fan and one with hot tub and two with VCR in room. Central air. VCR, fax and bicycles on premises. Weddings, small meetings, family reunions and seminars hosted. Antiquing, art galleries, bicycling, golf, hiking, live theater, museums, parks, shopping, sporting events and wineries nearby.

Commerce   G10

Anderson House

River Rd
Commerce, MO 63742
(573)264-4123 (800)705-1317
E-mail: jsteel5591@aol.com

Circa 1845. A wealthy businessman built and entertained many guests and social galas at this Antebellum guest house made out of Hawthorn handmade brick. Cradled by trees, it proudly sits on a bluff overlooking the lazy Mississippi River.

The inn has been restored and decorated with antiques and furnishings reflecting its historical beginnings. Appreciate the generous hospitality and slower-paced appeal of the region.

Innkeeper(s): Susan Steel. $80-120. MC, VISA, AX, DC, DS, PC, TC. 3 rooms, 1 with PB. Breakfast and snacks/refreshments included in rates. Types of meals: Gourmet bkfst, country bkfst, early coffee/tea and gourmet dinner. Beds: KQD. Ceiling fan in room. Air conditioning. Fax, copier, pet boarding and shrimp market on premises. Small meetings hosted. Antiquing, art galleries, bicycling, fishing, golf, hiking, live theater, museums, parks, shopping, sporting events and wineries nearby.

Pets Allowed.

Ellsinore   G8

Alcorn Corner B&B

HCR 3 Box 247
Ellsinore, MO 63937
(573)322-5297

Circa 1904. Surrounded by 20 acres, this simple Victorian farmhouse is the kind of bed & breakfast guests will enjoy sharing with their children. There are farm animals, and the innkeeper, a former teacher, is like a grandma to families. Early American furnishings are found in the two guest rooms, and a family-style breakfast with three menu choices is offered.

Innkeeper(s): Virgie Alcorn Evans. $35-50. TC. 2 rooms. Beds: DT. Turndown service in room. VCR and library on premises. Family reunions hosted. Antiquing, museums, parks and shopping nearby.

Eminence   G7

Old Blue House B&B

301 S Main St
Eminence, MO 65466-0117
(573)226-3498 (800)474-9695
E-mail: oldbluehouseb-b@webtv.net

Circa 1800. This old two-story frame house once was home to a beauty shop, grocery store and pharmacy. There are antiques throughout and framed prints, much of which is for sale. The garden is shaded by maple and magnolia trees and there are peonies, lilacs and roses. Breakfast is continental plus. However, if you'd like a country breakfast with sausage, gravy, scrambled eggs and homemade biscuits there is an extra charge. Eminence is located in the Ozark National Scenic Riverway.

Innkeeper(s): Wanda L. Pummill. $60-85. MC, VISA, AX, DS, PC, TC. TAC10. 3 rooms with PB. Breakfast and snacks/refreshments included in rates. Types of meals: Full bkfst, cont plus and early coffee/tea. Beds: D. Cable TV and ceiling fan in room. Air conditioning. Antiquing, fishing, golf, cross-country trail rides, parks, shopping and water sports nearby.

Publicity: *St. Louis Post Dispatch, Midwest Living and B&B Guest House and Inns of Missouri.*

Fayette   D5

Bedford House B&B

308 S Main St
Fayette, MO 65248
(660)248-2204
E-mail: gkoelker@coin.org
Web: www.bedfordhousebandb.com

Circa 1850. Feel like royalty at this B&B, built in the Federal style. Hardwood floors with inlays, and hand-carved doors and mantels are enhanced by antiques and traditional furnishings. A spacious guest bedroom and suite offer an intimate ambiance. A full breakfast is highlighted by silverplate and crystal. The large tree-shaded grounds with day lillies offer a tranquil setting. There are three historic districts within walking distance.

Historic Interest: Boone's Lick State Historic site (12 miles).

Innkeeper(s): Georgette & Rod Koelker. $45-60. PC, TC. 2 rooms, 1 with PB and 1 suite. Breakfast and snacks/refreshments included in rates. Types of meals: Full bkfst, veg bkfst, early coffee/tea and dinner. Beds: QD. Ceiling fan in room. Central air. VCR and library on premises. Weddings, small meetings, family reunions and seminars hosted. Antiquing, art galleries, bicycling, fishing, hiking, farmers market, Morrison Observatory, swimming pool, live theater, museums, parks, sporting events and tennis nearby.

Hannibal   C7

Garth Woodside Mansion

11069 New London Rd
Hannibal, MO 63401-9644
(573)221-2789 (888)427-8409
E-mail: innkeeper@garthmansion.com
Web: www.garthmansion.com

Circa 1871. This lovingly restored Italian Renaissance Victorian mansion is set on 39 acres of flower gardens, rolling meadows, ponds and woodland. Relax in the many original Victorian antiques that fill the parlors, dining room, sitting room and library. Guests enjoy sitting down and playing the gleaming 1869 Steinway square grand piano or stretching out on the spacious front porch. Sip lemonade on the second floor balcony or read that Mark Twain novel you've saved for  your trip to Hannibal. An unusual flying staircase with no visible means of support rises to three stories. Best of all is the Samuel Clemens Room where Mark Twain slept. All guest rooms offer feather beds and old-fashioned nightshirts, antiques and air conditioning. Afternoon snacks are served with tea or a cold drink when you check in and in the morning, full country breakfasts are offered.

Historic Interest: Mark Twain Boyhood Home (3 miles), a rare inland lighthouse lit by the President (3 miles).

Innkeeper(s): Julie & John Rolsen. $93-195. MC, VISA. 8 rooms with PB, 4 with FP. Breakfast and afternoon tea included in rates. Types of meals: Gourmet bkfst and early coffee/tea. Beds: QD. Turndown service, fireplaces and two-person whirlpool tubs in room. Air conditioning. Small meetings hosted. Amusement parks, antiquing, fishing, live theater and parks nearby.

Publicity: *Inn Country USA, Country Inns, Chicago Sun-Times, Glamour, Victorian Homes, Midwest Living, Insider, Country Living, Conde Nast Traveler and Bon Appetit.*

"So beautiful and romantic and relaxing, we forgot we were here to work—Jeannie and Bob Ransom, Innsider."

Independence   D3

Serendipity B&B

116 S Pleasant St
Independence, MO 64050
(816)833-4719 (800)203-4299 Fax:(816)833-4719

Circa 1887. This three-story brick home offers guests the ultimate Victorian experience. Antique furnishings and period appointments create an authentic period ambiance. Victorian children's books and toys, antique pictures, china figurines and a collection of antique colored glassware add to the home's charm. Stereoscopes and music boxes are other special touches. A full breakfast is served by candlelight in the formal dining

 room. Outside gardens include arbors, Victorian gazing balls, birdhouses, birdbaths, a hammock, swing and fountain. If time and weather permit, guests may request a ride in an antique car and tour of the house.

Innkeeper(s): Susan & Doug Walter. $30-95. MC, VISA, DS, TC. TAC10. 6 rooms with PB. Types of meals: Full bkfst. Beds: KQD. Air conditioning. VCR, fax and copier on premises. Amusement parks, antiquing, fishing, golf, historic sites, casinos, live theater, parks, shopping, sporting events, tennis and water sports nearby.

Pets allowed: Limited.

"It was so special to spend time with you and to share your lovely home."

Woodstock Inn B&B

1212 W Lexington Ave
Independence, MO 64050-3524
(816)833-2233 (800)276-5202 Fax:(816)461-7226
E-mail: tjustice@independence-missouri.com
Web: www.independence-missouri.com

Circa 1900. This home, originally built as a doll and quilt factory, is in the perfect location for sightseeing in historic Independence. Visit the home of Harry S Truman or the Truman Library and Museum. The Old Jail Museum is another popular attraction. A large country breakfast is served each morning featuring malted Belgian waffles and an additional entree. Independence is less than 30 minutes from Kansas City, where you may spend the day browsing through the shops at Country Club Plaza or Halls' Crown Center.

Innkeeper(s): Todd & Patricia Justice. $75-189. MC, VISA, AX, DS, PC, TC. TAC10. 11 rooms with PB and 2 suites. Breakfast included in rates. Types of meals: Full bkfst and early coffee/tea. Beds: KQD. Cable TV, phone, turndown service, VCR and fireplaces in room. Air conditioning. Fax on premises. Handicap access. Weddings, small meetings, family reunions and seminars hosted. Spanish spoken. Amusement parks, antiquing, art galleries, fishing, golf, live theater, museums, parks, shopping and sporting events nearby.

Publicity: *Country, San Francisco Chronicle, Independence Examiner, Kansas City Star and New York Times.*

"Pleasant, accommodating people, a facility of good character."

Kansas City   D3

The Inn on Crescent Lake

1261 Saint Louis Ave
Kansas City, MO 64024
(816)630-6745 Fax:(816)630-9326
E-mail: info@crescentlake.com
Web: www.crescentlake.com

Circa 1915. Located on 22 acres of lush grounds with woodland and bucolic ponds, this three-story, Georgian-style house is just a half-hour drive from downtown Kansas City and the airport. Spacious suites and guest rooms all have private baths, and guests can choose to have either a whirlpool or clawfoot tub. Try the Train Room or the Treehouse Suite. Both innkeepers graduated from the French Culinary Institute in New York City, and guests are encouraged to book a dinner reservation at the inn's dining room. Try the paddle boats, or borrow a fishing rod and take out the bass boat.

Innkeeper(s): Bruce & Anne Libowitz. $135-275. MC, VISA. 9 rooms with PB and 2 suites. Breakfast included in rates. Types of meals: Full bkfst. Beds: KQT. Cable TV, phone and ceiling fan in room. Air conditioning. Copier on premises. Weddings hosted. Antiquing, fishing, parks and shopping nearby.

Kirkwood   D8

Fissy's Place

500 N Kirkwood Rd
Kirkwood, MO 63122-3914
(314)821-4494

Circa 1939. The innkeeper's past is just about as interesting as the history of this bed & breakfast. A former Miss Missouri, the innkeeper has acted in movies with the likes of Burt Reynolds and Robert Redford, and pictures of many movie stars decorate the home's interior. A trained interior designer, she also shares this talent in the cheer-fully decorated guest rooms. Historic downtown Kirkwood is within walking distance to the home, which also offers close access to St. Louis.

Innkeeper(s): Fay & Randy Sneed. $69-76. MC, VISA, PC, TC. TAC10. 3 rooms with PB and 1 conference room. Breakfast and snacks/refreshments included in rates. Types of meals: Full bkfst, cont plus and early coffee/tea. Beds: QDT. Cable TV, phone, turndown service, ceiling fan and VCR in room. Air conditioning. Copier on premises. Handicap access. Small meetings, family reunions and seminars hosted. Antiquing, many fine restaurants, live theater, parks, shopping and sporting events nearby.

Lampe   H4

Grandpa's Farm B&B

4738 W State Hwy 86
Lampe, MO 65681
(417)779-5106 (800)280-5106
E-mail: keithpat@inter-linc.net
Web: www.grandpasfarmbandb.com

Circa 1891. This limestone farmhouse in the heart of the Ozarks offers guests a chance to experience country life in a relaxed farm setting. Midway between Silver Dollar City and Eureka Springs, Ark., and close to Branson, the inn boasts several lodging options, including a duplex with suites and a honeymoon suite. The innkeepers are known for their substantial country breakfast and say guests enjoy comparing how long the meal lasts before they eat again. Although the inn's 116 acres are not farmed extensively, domesticated farm animals are on the premises.

Innkeeper(s): Keith & Pat Lamb. $65-95. MC, VISA, DS, PC, TC. TAC15. 4 suites. Breakfast included in rates. Types of meals: Full bkfst. Beds: KQ. Ceiling fan in room. Air conditioning. VCR, fax, spa and RCA satellite dish with 32-inch TV screen on premises. Handicap access. Small meetings, family reunions and seminars hosted. Amusement parks, antiquing, fishing, country western shows, Passion Plays in Branson & Eureka Springs, live theater, parks, shopping and water sports nearby.

Marshfield   G5

The Dickey House B&B, Ltd.

331 S Clay St
Marshfield, MO 65706-2114
(417)468-3000 (800)450-7444 Fax:(417)859-2775
E-mail: info@dickeyhouse.com

Circa 1913. This Greek Revival mansion is framed by ancient oak trees and boasts eight massive two-story Ionic columns. Burled woodwork, beveled glass and polished hardwood floors accentuate the gracious rooms. Interior columns soar in the parlor, creating a suitably elegant setting for the innkeeper's outstanding collection of antiques. A queen-size canopy bed, fire-

place and sunporch are featured in the Heritage Room. Some rooms offer amenities such as Jacuzzi tubs and a fireplace. All rooms include cable TV and a VCR. The innkeepers also offer a sun room with a hot tub.

Innkeeper(s): Larry & Michaelene Stevens. $65-145. MC, VISA, AX, DS, PC, TC. TAC10. 7 rooms, 3 with PB and 4 suites. Breakfast included in rates. Types of meals: Gourmet bkfst. Beds: KQD. Cable TV, phone, ceiling fan, VCR and four with double Jacuzzi in room. New sun room with therapeutic hot tub on premises. Handicap access. Weddings, small meetings, family reunions and seminars hosted.

Ozark   G4

BarnAgain Bed & Breakfast

904 W Church St
Ozark, MO 65721
(417)581-2276 (877)462-2276
E-mail: barnbnb@gte.net
Web: bbim.org/barnagain

Circa 1910. Listed in the Ozark Historical Register, this was the area's last dairy farm to bottle and sell white and chocolate milk. Sitting on 40 acres, two converted barns and a Victorian farmhouse restored by Amish craftsmen offer pleasant accommodations. Guest bedrooms are decorated in themes ranging from rustic to romantic. Soft drinks and fresh-baked cookies are placed in each room. The Tulip

Tree Suite features a downstairs sitting room with gas fireplace, upstairs bedroom and bath with footed tub. Peaches and cream-stuffed French toast may be one of the entrees served for breakfast. The swimming pool is open May to September. Sit on the porch swing, hike the trails or play a game of horseshoes. Relax under the stars by the warm fire pit.

Historic Interest: Wilson's Creek National Battlefield (10 miles), Laura Ingalls Wilder Home (40 miles), Shepherd of the Hills Farm (25 miles).

Innkeeper(s): Mark & Susan Bryant. $99-129. MC, VISA, AX, DS, PC, TC. TAC10. 4 rooms, 3 with PB, 1 with FP and 1 suite. Breakfast and snacks/refreshments included in rates. Types of meals: Gourmet bkfst, veg bkfst and room service. Beds: Q. TV, turndown service, ceiling fan, VCR and fireplace in room. Central air. Swimming, bicycles, walking trails, horseshoes and basketball court on premises. Amusement parks, antiquing, art galleries, bicycling, canoeing/kayaking, fishing, golf, hiking, live theater, museums, parks, shopping, tennis, water sports and wineries nearby.

Publicity: *Midwest Living and Springfield News-Leader.*

Perry   C6

Kennedy's Red Barn Inn

22748 Joanna Dr
Perry, MO 63462
(573)565-9612 (866)565-9612 Fax:(775)416-3984
E-mail: redbarn@redbarninn.com
Web: www.redbarninn.com

Circa 1848. Country living is at its best at this old Missouri red barn that has been restored as a delightful home on Mark Twain Lake. Beamed ceilings, an antique staircase, rustic wood floors and lots of room inside and out instill a relaxing ambiance. The main floor includes a gift shop, sitting room, library and dining room where a hearty breakfast is served.

Guest bedrooms feature quilt-covered brass beds, lace curtains, antiques and wicker. A red heart whirlpool tub with bath products enhances a romantic setting. After a workout in the exercise room, an outdoor aroma-scented hot tub feels great.

Historic Interest: Mark Twain birthplace (3 miles).

Innkeeper(s): Jack & Rebecca Kennedy. $50-60. MC, VISA, AX, PC, TC. 3 rooms. Breakfast and snacks/refreshments included in rates. Types of meals: Full bkfst, country bkfst, early coffee/tea and afternoon tea. Beds: QD. Ceiling fan in room. Central air. VCR, fax, copier, spa, bicycles, library and gift shop on premises. Family reunions hosted. Amusement parks, antiquing, art galleries, beaches, bicycling, canoeing/kayaking, fishing, golf, hiking, horseback riding, live theater, museums, parks, shopping, tennis and water sports nearby.

Publicity: *Courier Post and Lake Gazette.*

Rocheport   D5

School House B&B Inn

504 Third Street
Rocheport, MO 65279
(573)698-2022
E-mail: innkeeper@schoolhousebandb.com
Web: www.schoolhousebandb.com

Circa 1914. This three-story brick building was once a schoolhouse. Now luxuriously appointed as a country inn, it features 13-foot-high ceilings, small print wallpapers and a bridal suite with Victorian furnishings and a private spa. Rooms feature names such as The Spelling Bee and The Schoolmarm. The basement houses an antique bookshop, The Bookseller. Nearby is a winery and a trail along the river providing many scenic miles for cyclists and hikers.

Historic Interest: Historic Katy Trail (2 blocks), Missouri River (4 blocks), local museum (4 blocks), Rocheport, has 80 buildings in the National Register.

Innkeeper(s): Vicki Ott & Penny Province. $85-215. MC, VISA, DS. TAC10. 10 rooms with PB, 1 suite and 1 conference room. Breakfast and snacks/refreshments included in rates. Types of meals: Full bkfst, cont plus, cont, early coffee/tea and afternoon tea. Beds: KQDT. Phone and ceiling fan in room. Air conditioning. Library on premises. Small meetings and family reunions hosted. Antiquing, art galleries, fishing, hiking, bicycling, live theater, parks, shopping and sporting events nearby.

Publicity: *Midwest Living, Midwest Motorist, Successful Farming, Hallmark Greeting Cards, Romance of Country Inns, Southern Living, New York Times, Denver Post, St. Louis Post Dispatch and Romantic Homes.*

"We are still talking about our great weekend in Rocheport. Thanks for the hospitality, the beautiful room and delicious breakfasts, they were really great."

Saint Charles   D8

Boone's Lick Trail Inn

1000 South Main St
Saint Charles, MO 63301-3514
(636)947-7000 (888)940-0002
E-mail: innkeeper@booneslick.com

Circa 1840. This Federal-style brick and limestone house, overlooks the wide Missouri River and Katy Trail. Situated in an old river settlement with its brick street and green spaces, the inn is at the start of the Boone's Lick Trail. V'Anne's delicate lemon biscuits, fresh fruit and hot entrees are served amid regional antiques and Paul's working duck decoy collection. Because of its setting and decor, travelers have remarked at how close the inn resembles a European inn.

Historic Interest: Goldenrod Showboat (one-fourth mile), Missouri First State Capitol (one-half mile), Daniel Boone Homestead (25 miles), Gateway Arch (20 minutes), Jefferson Memorial Courthouse.

Innkeeper(s): V'Anne & Paul Mydler. $110-175. MC, VISA, AX, DC, CB, DS, PC, TC. 6 rooms with PB. Breakfast included in rates. Types of meals: Full bkfst and cont plus. Beds: QT. TV and phone in room. Antiquing, golf, historic district, museums, wineries, casino, birding, biking, restaurants, swimming, hiking and shopping nearby.

Publicity: *New York Times, Southern Living, Country Home and Midwest Living.*

Geery's Bed & Breakfast

720 N 5th St
Saint Charles, MO 63301
(636)916-5344 Fax:(636)916-4702
E-mail: pgeeryktj1@aol.com

Circa 1891. The neighborhood where this Four Square Colonial Revival home sits is a registered National Landmark in historic Frenchtowne. A delightful blend of Victorian elegance and Scottish culture creates a warm and inviting atmosphere. Distinctive reproductions and 19th-century antiques furnish the parlors and guest bedrooms. The Lindsay Room features a four-poster bed, double whirlpool, corner fireplace and private porch. A hearty breakfast is well presented on Royal Doulton china with gold silverware. Three sitting porches offer views of the flower and shade gardens.

Historic Interest: First State Capital of Missouri (1/2 mile), Lewis and Clark Center (3/4 mile).

Innkeeper(s): Peter & Mrilyn Geery. $70-125. MC, VISA, AX, DS, PC, TC. TAC10. 3 rooms with PB, 1 with FP and 2 conference rooms. Breakfast included in rates. Types of meals: Gourmet bkfst, veg bkfst, early coffee/tea, picnic lunch and afternoon tea. Beds: KQ. Cable TV, phone, ceiling fan and fireplace in room. Central air. Fax, copier, spa, bicycles, library, gardens and gazebo on premises. Weddings, small meetings and seminars hosted. Amusement parks, antiquing, art galleries, canoeing/kayaking, fishing, golf, hiking, horseback riding, Casino, live theater, museums, parks, shopping, downhill skiing, sporting events, tennis, water sports and wineries nearby.

Publicity: *The Star and St. Louis Post-Dispatch.*

Mueller House

710 N 5th St
Saint Charles, MO 63301
(636)947-1228
E-mail: muellerhouse@juno.com
Web: www.bbhost.com/muellerhouse

Circa 1908. Pristinely restored, this two-and-a-half-story brick home features French architecture and original brass lighting fixtures, pocket doors, transoms and high ceilings. Warm and inviting, the Victorian decor boasts jewel-toned floral wallpaper and window treatments. In the front foyer a grand oak staircase leads to well-appointed guest bedrooms offering wrought iron, four-poster and sleigh beds. Hearty breakfast fare is served in the formal dining room on an antique carved oak table. Relax and watch the world go by on the front porch swing. Hike the Katy Trail or visit wineries, quaint shops and riverfront attractions.

Historic Interest: First state capitol of Missouri (1/4 mile), Daniel Boone Home (30 miles), St. Louis Arch (25 miles).

Innkeeper(s): Ray & Ruth Mueller. $75-110. MC, AX, PC, TC. 3 rooms, 1 with PB. Breakfast and snacks/refreshments included in rates. Types of meals: Gourmet bkfst, veg bkfst and early coffee/tea. Beds: Q. Cable TV, turndown service, ceiling fan and VCR in room. Central air. Fax and copier on premises. Amusement parks, antiquing, art galleries, bicycling, fishing, golf, hiking, live theater, museums, parks, shopping, sporting events, tennis and wineries nearby.

Saint Joseph   C3

Shakespeare Chateau B&B

809 Hall St
Saint Joseph, MO 64501
(816)232-2667 (888)414-4944 Fax:(816)232-0009
E-mail: chateau@ponyexpress.net

Circa 1885. This gabled and turreted confection offers three stories of lavish antique furnishings, carved woodwork and at least 40 original stained-glass windows. The inn is in the Hall Street Historic District, known as "Mansion Hill". All the homes in this area are listed in the National Register. The fireplace in the inn's foyer has boasted a bronze of Shakespeare for more than 100 years and with this as a starting point, the innkeeper has created a Victorian, Shakespearean theme. Two of the inn's room offer whirlpools. A two-course breakfast is served in the romantic dining room.

Innkeeper(s): Kellie. $110-175. MC, VISA, AX, DS, PC, TC. TAC5. 5 rooms with PB, 3 suites and 1 conference room. Breakfast and snacks/refreshments included in rates. Types of meals: Full bkfst, veg bkfst and early coffee/tea. Beds: KQ. Ceiling fan and hot tub in room. Air conditioning. VCR, fax and library on premises. Family reunions hosted. Antiquing, art galleries, bicycling, fishing, golf, live theater, museums, parks, shopping, downhill skiing and tennis nearby.

Publicity: *Midwest Living, Victorian Decorating & Llfestyle Magazine and Kansas City Magazine.*

Saint Louis   D8

Eastlake Inn Bed & Breakfast

703 N Kirkwood Rd
Saint Louis, MO 63122-2719
(314)965-0066 Fax:(314)966-8615
E-mail: info@eastlakeinn.com

Circa 1920. Tall trees shade this colonial-style inn on one acre of grounds. Eastlake antiques are found throughout along with an antique doll collection. Guest rooms include the Garden Room with a queen Eastlake bed and a view of the perennial gardens. The Magnolia Room has a fireplace and a double whirlpool tub. A full breakfast is offered in the dining room under the lights of a chandelier. Dishes include items such as peach French toast, maple sausage, and fruit from the local farmer's market. The inn's two golden retrievers may enjoy a garden tour with you or stroll through the pleasant neighborhood on a walk to Mudd Grove.

Historic Interest: Mudd's Grove (5 blocks).
Innkeeper(s): Lori & Dean Murray. $70-200. MC, VISA, TC. TAC5. 3 rooms, 2 with PB, 1 with FP and 1 suite. Breakfast included in rates. Types of meals: Gourmet bkfst and early coffee/tea. Beds: KQD. Turndown service, ceiling fan and fireplace in room. Central air. VCR, fax and spa on premises. Weddings and family reunions hosted. Amusement parks, antiquing, art galleries, bicycling, fishing, golf, hiking, horseback riding, live theater, museums, parks, shopping, downhill skiing, sporting events, tennis, water sports and wineries nearby.

Lehmann House B&B

10 Benton Pl
Saint Louis, MO 63104-2411
(314)231-6724
E-mail: lehmann.house.bed.breakfast

Circa 1893. This National Register manor's most prominent resident, former U.S. Solicitor General Frederick Lehmann, hosted Presidents Taft, Theodore Roosevelt and Coolidge at this gracious home. Several key turn-of-the-century literary figures also visited the Lehmann family. The inn's formal dining room, complete with oak paneling and a fireplace, is a stunning place to enjoy the formal breakfasts. Antiques and gracious furnishings dot the well-appointed guest rooms. The home is located in St. Louis' oldest historic district, Lafayette Square.

Historic Interest: Presidents Taft, Roosevelt & Coolidge visited Lehmann House.
Innkeeper(s): Marie & Michael Davies. $75-99. MasterCard, Visa, Discover, personal checks and Traveler's Cheques. TAC10. 4 total guest accommodations, 2 with private bath, 2 with fireplaces. Breakfast included in rates. Types of meals: Full bkfst and early coffee/tea. Beds: King, Queen, double and twin.. Ceiling fan in room. Air conditioning. Swimming, tennis and library on premises. Weddings, small meetings, family reunions and seminars hosted. Amusement parks, antiquing, museums, zoos, botanical gardens, live theater, parks, shopping and sporting events nearby.

Publicity: *St. Louis Post Dispatch and KTVI-St. Louis.*

"Wonderful mansion with great future ahead. Thanks for the wonderful hospitality."

Napoleon's Retreat

1815 Lafayette Ave
Saint Louis, MO 63104
(314)772-6979 (800)700-9980 Fax:(314)772-7675
E-mail: info@napoleonsretreat.com

Circa 1880. This three-story, French-style Second Empire Victorian townhouse is located in Lafayette Square, a National Historic District that offers the largest collection of French Second Empire Victorians in the country. Pocket doors, twelve-foot ceilings, pine floors, artworks, collectibles and period antiques are features of the inn. Ask for the green room for beautifully draped windows and an elegant decor. The innkeeper offers Napoleon French Toast, quiche or Belgian waffles along with fruit and other freshly baked breads for breakfast. The inn is a mile and a half from the convention center and close to historic Soulard Market, the Missouri Botanical Gardens, the zoo, St. Louis Cathedral and Fox Theater.

Historic Interest: Jefferson National Expansion Memorial Arch (1-1/2 miles).
Innkeeper(s): Jeff Archuleta/Michael Lance. $85-125. MC, VISA, AX, DC, DS, PC, TC. TAC10. 5 rooms, 4 with PB, 1 with FP and 1 suite. Breakfast and snacks/refreshments in rates. Types of meals: Gourmet bkfst and early coffee/tea. Beds: Q. Cable TV, phone and ceiling fan in room. Central air. Fax and copier on premises. Amusement parks, antiquing, art galleries, fishing, golf, hiking, horseback riding, live theater, museums, parks, shopping, sporting events and wineries nearby.

Publicity: *St. Louis Commerce and Show Me St. Louis.*

The Winter House

3522 Arsenal St
Saint Louis, MO 63118-2004
(314)664-4399
E-mail: kmwinter1@juno.com
Web: www.thewinterhouse.com

Circa 1897. Original brass hardware, three fireplaces and a turret provide ambiance at this turn-of-the-century brick Victorian. Embossed French paneling adds elegance. The suite features a balcony, and the bedroom has a pressed-tin ceiling. The Rose Room is decorated with its namesake flower and a king-size bed. The home is ideally located three miles from the downtown area. Exotic restaurants are within walking distance. Breakfast is served on antique Wedgwood china and includes hand-squeezed orange

juice, gourmet coffees, teas and a full breakfast. With special reservations, guests can enjoy breakfast accompanied by professional piano music.

Historic Interest: Tower Grove Park (one-half block), Missouri Botanical Garden (2 miles).

Innkeeper(s): Kendall Winter. $95-135. MC, VISA, AX, DC, CB, DS, PC, TC. TAC10. 3 rooms, 2 with PB and 1 suite. Breakfast included in rates. Types of meals: Full bkfst. Beds: KQD. Ceiling fan in room. Air conditioning. Live piano music w/breakfast on premises. Antiquing, live theater, museums, parks, shopping and sporting events nearby.

Publicity: *Innsider and St. Louis Post Dispatch.*

"A delightful house with spotless, beautifully appointed rooms, charming hosts. Highly recommended."

Sainte Genevieve   E9

Inn St. Gemme Beauvais

78 N Main St
Sainte Genevieve, MO 63670-1336
(573)883-5744 (800)818-5744 Fax:(573)883-3899
E-mail: buffin@msn.com

Circa 1848. This three-story, Federal-style inn is an impressive site on Ste. Genevieve's Main Street. The town is one of the oldest west of the Mississippi River, and the St. Gemme Beauvais is the oldest operating Missouri bed & breakfast. The rooms are nicely appointed in period style, but there are modern amenities here, too. The Jacuzzi tubs in some guest rooms are one relaxing example. There is an outdoor hot tub, as well. The romantic carriage house includes a king-size bed, double Jacuzzi tub and a fireplace. Guests are pampered with all sorts of cuisine, including full breakfasts served at individual candle-lit tables with a choice of six entrees. Later, tea, drinks, hors d'oeuvres and refreshments are also served.

Innkeeper(s): Janet Joggerst. $89-179. MC, VISA, DS, PC, TC. 9 rooms with PB, 1 with FP, 6 suites and 1 conference room. Breakfast, afternoon tea and snacks/refreshments included in rates. Types of meals: Gourmet bkfst. AP. Beds: KQD. Cable TV and ceiling fan in room. Air conditioning. VCR, fax, copier, spa and bicycles on premises. Weddings, small meetings, family reunions and seminars hosted. Antiquing, golf, historic area, parks and shopping nearby.

Somewhere Inn Time B&B

383 Jefferson St, PO Box 29
Sainte Genevieve, MO 63670
(573)883-9397 (888)883-9397
E-mail: somewhere@brick.net

Circa 1920. Completely restored to offer the delights of yesterday and the comforts of today, this two-story French Colonial is an award-winning home. Guest bedrooms feature whirlpool tubs, and one boasts a fireplace. Gracious hospitality includes a full breakfast, a social hour offering hors d'oeuvres, wine and beverages and a homemade dessert at bedtime. Fountains and flowers grace the grounds. Swim in the in-ground pool or soak in the hot tub. Visit the marina or local winery.

Innkeeper(s): Mary Beth & Jim Ferguson. $85-125. MC, VISA, AX, DS, PC, TC. 4 rooms with PB, 1 with FP, 1 cottage and 1 conference room. Breakfast and snacks/refreshments included in rates. Types of meals: Gourmet bkfst. AP. Beds: QD. Cable TV, ceiling fan, VCR and fireplace in room. Central air. Fax, copier, spa and swimming on premises. Weddings and small meetings hosted. Antiquing, art galleries, fishing, golf, hiking, museums, parks, shopping and wineries nearby.

Publicity: *St. Louis Post-Dispatch.*

The Southern Hotel

146 S 3rd St
Sainte Genevieve, MO 63670-1667
(573)883-3493 (800)275-1412 Fax:(573)883-9612
E-mail: mike@southernhotelbb.com

Circa 1790. Located at the square in historic Sainte Genevieve, the Southern Hotel is a landmark and was known for the providing the best accommodations between Natchez and St. Louis, as well as good food, gambling and pool. Guests now enjoy two parlors, a dining room and a game room on the first floor where a quilt is always underway. Guest rooms offer country Victorian furnishings along with whimsical collectibles. Highlights include a rosewood tester bed, a unique iron bed, several hand-painted headboards and a delicately carved Victorian bed. The clawfoot tubs are hand-painted. Guests also can browse the Summer Kitchen Gift Shop, stroll through the gardens or relax on the long front porch.

Innkeeper(s): Mike & Barbara Hankins. $73-138. MC, VISA, AX, DS, PC, TC. 8 rooms with PB, 4 with FP and 1 conference room. Breakfast included in rates. Types of meals: Gourmet bkfst, veg bkfst and snacks/refreshments. Beds: KQD. Ceiling fan in room. Air conditioning. Fax, copier and bicycles on premises. Small meetings and family reunions hosted. Antiquing, bicycling, fishing, golf, hiking, horseback riding, museums, parks, shopping and wineries nearby.

Publicity: *Midwest Living, Southern Living and Country Inns.*

"I can't imagine ever staying in a motel again! It was so nice to be greeted by someone who expected us. We felt right at home."

Springfield   G4

Virginia Rose B&B

317 E Glenwood St
Springfield, MO 65807-3543
(417)883-0693
E-mail: vrosebb@sisna.com

Circa 1906. Three generations of the Botts family lived in this home before it was sold to the current innkeepers, Virginia and Jackie Buck. The grounds still include the rustic red barn. Comfortable, country rooms are named after Buck family members and feature beds covered with quilts. The innkeepers also offer a two-bedroom suite, the Rambling Rose, which is decorated in a sportsman theme in honor of the nearby Bass Pro. Hearty breakfasts are served in the dining room, and the innkeepers will provide low-fat fare on request.

Historic Interest: Wild Bill Hickok shot Dave Tutt on the public square in Springfield, which is about two miles from the inn. Wilson's Creek National Battlefield is about eight miles away. Other Springfield attractions include Springfield National Cemetery, The Frisco Railroad Museum and the History Museum for Springfield and Greene County.

Innkeeper(s): Jackie & Virginia Buck. $70-120. MC, VISA, AX, DS, PC, TC. TAC10. 4 rooms, 2 with PB and 1 suite. Breakfast included in rates. Types of meals: Full bkfst, early coffee/tea, picnic lunch and snacks/refreshments. Beds: KQT. Phone and turndown service in room. Air conditioning. VCR and fax on premises. Family reunions and seminars hosted. Amusement parks, antiquing, fishing, live theater, parks, shopping, sporting events and water sports nearby.

Publicity: *Auctions & Antiques, Springfield Business Journal, Today's Women Journal and Springfield News-leader.*

"The accommodations are wonderful and the hospitality couldn't be warmer."

Walnut Street Inn

900 E Walnut St
Springfield, MO 65806-2603
(417)864-6346 (800)593-6346 Fax:(417)864-6184
E-mail: stay@walnutstreetinn.com
Web: www.walnutstreetinn.com

Circa 1894. This three-story Queen Anne gabled house has cast-iron Corinthian columns and a veranda. Polished wood floors and antiques are featured throughout. Upstairs you'll find the gathering room with a fireplace. Ask for the McCann guest room with two bay windows, or one of the five rooms with a double Jacuzzi tub. A full breakfast is served, including items such as strawberry-filled French toast.

Historic Interest: Springfield History Museum (3 blocks), Laura Ingalls Wilder Museum (40 minutes), Wilson's Creek National Battlefield (20 minutes), General Sweeney's Civil War Museum (20 minutes).

Innkeeper(s): Gary & Paula Blankenship. $89-169. MC, VISA, AX, DC, DS, PC, TC. TAC10. 14 rooms with PB, 10 with FP and 2 suites. Breakfast included in rates. Types of meals: Gourmet bkfst, early coffee/tea and afternoon tea. Beds: KQD. Cable TV, phone, turndown service, ceiling fan, VCR, beverage bars and modem in room. Air conditioning. Fax and copier on premises. Handicap access. Amusement parks, antiquing, fishing, live theater, parks, shopping, sporting events and water sports nearby.

Publicity: *Southern Living, Women's World, Midwest Living, Victoria, Country Inns, Innsider, Glamour, Midwest Motorist, Missouri, Saint Louis Post, Kansas City Star and USA Today.*

"Rest assured your establishment's qualities are unmatched and through your commitment to excellence you have won a life-long client."

Warrensburg   D4

Camel Crossing Bed & Breakfast

210 E Gay St
Warrensburg, MO 64093-1841
(660)429-2973 Fax:(660)429-2722
E-mail: camelx@iland.net
Web: www.bbim.org/camelx/index.html

Circa 1906. This beautiful big inn has a huge front porch and dormers on the third floor. Birds, squirrels and cottontail rabbits often frequent the meticulously landscaped yard. The inn has four guest bedrooms, two with shared baths. The third-floor suite is an impressive 363 square feet. The Middle Eastern décor reflects the background of the innkeepers themselves, who are former Aramcons, while the exterior is traditional American architecture with beveled and stained glass. It serves a delicious breakfast with courses like fruit, bacon, ham, sausage, eggs, hotcakes and waffles.

Historic Interest: Trueman Home and Museum (50 miles), Steaamboat Arabia (50 miles), Nelson Art Gallery (50 miles).

Innkeeper(s): Joyce & Ed Barnes. $70-90. MC, VISA, AX, DS, PC, TC. 4 rooms, 2 with PB, 1 with FP and 1 suite. Breakfast and snacks/refreshments included in rates. Types of meals: Gourmet bkfst, country bkfst and early coffee/tea. Beds: Q. Cable TV, phone, ceiling fan, VCR and fireplace in room. Air conditioning. Fax and copier on premises. Antiquing, fishing, golf, Amtrak train station (5 blocks), live theater, parks, shopping, sporting events, tennis and wineries nearby.

Cedarcroft Farm/Cottage on the Knoll B&B

431 SE County Rd Y
Warrensburg, MO 64093-8316
(660)747-5728 (800)368-4944
E-mail: itg@cedarcroft.com
Web: www.cedarcroft.com

Circa 1867. Two distinct accommodations comprise this National Register farm with 80 acres of woodlands, meadows and creeks where deer, fox, coyotes and wild turkeys still roam. The 1867 farmhouse was built by John Adams, a Union army veteran, and Sandra's great grandfather. Guests stay in a private, two-bedroom suite. A newly constructed romantic hideaway cottage is secluded on the property and offers a thermal tub, king bed and a fireplace. Bill participates in Civil War reenactments and is happy to demonstrate clothing, weapons and customs of the era. Sandra cares for her four horses and provides the home-baked, full country breakfasts.

Innkeeper(s): Sandra & Bill Wayne. $125-220. MC, VISA, AX, DC, DS, PC, TC. 2 rooms, 1 with PB and 1 suite. Breakfast and snacks/refreshments included in rates. Types of meals: Full bkfst. Beds: KD. Phone, VCR, satellite TV, fireplace and stereo in room. Air conditioning. Antiquing, fishing, hiking, rodeos, bike trails, Civil War re-enactment, state fair, live theater, parks and shopping nearby.

Publicity: *Midwest Motorist, Country America, Entrepreneur, Small Farm Today, Kansas City Star, Daily Star-Journal, Higginsville Advance, KCTV, KMOS, KSHB and CNN.*

"We enjoyed the nostalgia and peacefulness very much. Enjoyed your wonderful hospitality and great food."

Washington   D7

Schwegmann House

438 W Front St
Washington, MO 63090-2103
(636)239-5025 (800)949-2262
E-mail: cathy@schwegmannhouse.com
Web: www.schwegmannhouse.com

Circa 1861. John F. Schwegmann, a native of Germany, built a flour mill on the Missouri riverfront. This stately three-story home was built not only for the miller and his family, but also to provide extra lodging for overnight customers who traveled long hours to the town. Today, weary travelers enjoy the formal gardens and warm atmosphere of this restful home. Patios overlook the river, and the gracious rooms are decorated with antiques and handmade quilts. The new Miller Suite boasts a tub for two and breakfast can be delivered to their door. Guests enjoy full breakfasts complete with house specialties such as German apple pancakes or a three-cheese strata accompanied with homemade breads, meat, juice and fresh fruit. There are 11 wineries nearby, or guests can visit one of the historic districts, many galleries, historic sites, antique shops, excellent restaurants and riverfront park located nearby.

Historic Interest: The home is part of the historic downtown Washington area and full of homes and buildings to admire. Daniel Boone's home is 20 miles away. Old Bethel Church and Anna Belle Chapel are short drives. The house is 10 blocks from the Washington Historical Museum.

Innkeeper(s): Catherine & Bill Nagel. $95-150. MC, VISA, AX, PC, TC. TAC10. 9 rooms with PB and 1 suite. Breakfast and snacks/refreshments included in rates. Types of meals: Gourmet bkfst and early coffee/tea. Beds: QD. Phone and ceiling fan in room. Air conditioning. Small meetings, family reunions and seminars hosted. Antiquing, Missouri River Wine Country and Katy Bike Trail nearby.

Publicity: *St. Louis Post-Dispatch, West County Journal, Midwest Living, Country Inns, Midwest Motorist and Ozark.*

"Like Grandma's house many years ago."

Weston   C2

The Hatchery House

618 Short St
Weston, MO 64098-1228
(816)640-5700 (888)640-4051
E-mail: hatcherybb@earthlink.net
Web: www.hatcherybb.com

Circa 1845. This brick Federal home, built prior to the Civil War, was constructed by one of Weston's mayors. It derives its unusual name from its years serving as a boarding house. It

seems that many young couples started their families in the house, and the townspeople began calling it the "hatchery," because of the hatching of babies. The inn is still family oriented, and there are antique dolls, toys and books for children to enjoy. Breakfasts include fanciful items such as homemade chocolate chip muffins baked in heart-shaped tins. Entrees include specialty items such as French toast almondine. Local wines are served in the early evenings. Weston offers a variety of antique shops, wineries, a brewery, and an orchard. Fort Leavenworth and the Snow Creek Ski Resort are other attractions. Kansas City is an easy drive to the south.

Historic Interest: McCormick's Distillery (1 mile), Pirtle's Winery (2 blocks), The Downtown Weston (1 block).

Innkeeper(s): Bill & Anne Lane. $95-140. MC, VISA, AX, PC, TC. 4 rooms with PB, 4 with FP. Breakfast and afternoon tea included in rates. Types of meals: Gourmet bkfst, veg bkfst, cont plus, early coffee/tea and picnic lunch. Beds: QT. TV, ceiling fan and one with Jacuzzi for two in room. Central air. Handicap access. Weddings and small meetings hosted. Amusement parks, antiquing, art galleries, bicycling, hiking, festivals, orchards, farms, museums, parks, shopping, downhill skiing and wineries nearby.

Montana

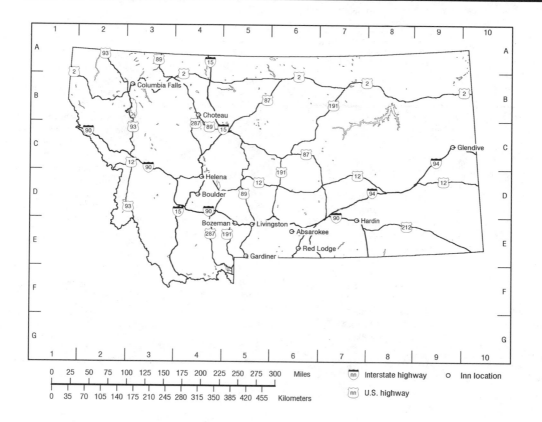

	1	2	3	4	5	6	7	8	9	10

Columbia Falls

Choteau

Helena
Boulder

Glendive

Bozeman · Livingston
Absarokee
Red Lodge
Gardiner
Hardin

| 0 | 25 | 50 | 75 | 100 | 125 | 150 | 175 | 200 | 225 | 250 | 275 | 300 | Miles |
| 0 | 35 | 70 | 105 | 140 | 175 | 210 | 245 | 280 | 315 | 350 | 385 | 420 | 455 | Kilometers |

Interstate highway   o   Inn location

U.S. highway

Absarokee   E6

River Haven Bed & Breakfast

RR 1 Box 2870
Absarokee, MT 59001-9709
(406)328-4138

Circa 1934. True to its name, this waterfront ranch-style home sits peacefully along the Stillwater River, providing a relaxing retreat. The decor is mostly Western with a touch of Southwest and Early American. Betty's original artwork of oil and acrylics grace the walls of this B&B. The spacious guest suite boasts a sitting room and private entrance. It also can be used as two adjoining bedrooms. A satisfying breakfast may include fresh fruit, bacon, eggs and Dutch apple pancake served in the dining room featuring lodge-pole pine furniture. Full-length floor-

to-ceiling dining and living room windows enlarge the impressive views across the river to the Beartooth Mountains. Fly-fish from the redwood deck, go rafting or horseback riding, or play golf. Visit Charmed, Inc., where Shari sells wonderful gifts and treasures to bring home.
Call for rates.

Boulder   E7

Boulder Hot Springs B&B

PO Box 930
Boulder, MT 59632-0930
(406)225-4339 Fax:(406)225-4345
E-mail: bhs@initco.net

Circa 1888. This Spanish-style hotel with its peaked Moorish gables and red roofline is under restoration. In the National Register, the 33 rooms in the east wing, the pool and bath-

house have been renovated. Forty springs are on the inn's 274 acres. There are hotel rooms as well as B&B rooms, which offer antiques and original paintings. A comfortable lobby with wood stove provides a variety of games. Breakfast is generous with omelets and sausage or French toast and pancakes. Enjoy the geothermal baths or hike along Deerlodge National Forest. An abundant wildlife includes bear, deer, fox, antelope and moose. Some guests enjoy exploring the area's radon mines which are nearby. $45-120. MC, VISA, PC. 33 rooms, 15 with PB and 2 conference rooms. Breakfast included in rates. Types of meals: Full bkfst. Beds: DT. Fax, copier, spa, swimming and sauna on premises. Handicap access. Weddings, small meetings, family reunions and seminars hosted. Fishing, shopping and cross-country skiing nearby.

Bozeman   E5

Gallatin Gateway Inn

Hwy 191
Bozeman, MT 59715
(406)763-4672
E-mail: gatewayinn@gallatingatewayinn.com
Web: www.gallatingatewayinn.com

Circa 1927. Just outside of Bozeman, and 75 miles north of Yellowstone National Park, lies one of the grand railroad hotels of the Rocky Mountains West. Stunningly restored, the original hand-hewn beams, palatial windows and mahogany woodwork still grace the common rooms. The inn is located in the heart of Yellowstone Country amid spectacular scenery, hiking and fly-fishing opportunities. The inn has its own casting pond, outdoor swimming pool and outdoor Jacuzzi. The rooms are comfortable and well appointed, and a continental breakfast is served every morning. The inn's historic dining room offers fine dining and more casual fare is found in the Baggage Room Pub.

Innkeeper(s): Pam Butterworth. $70-175. MC, VISA, AX, DS. 34 rooms. Types of meals: Cont and dinner. Beds: KQT. TV, radios, coffee maker and hair dryer in room. Fax, conference facilities, pool (summer only) and hot tub on premises. Bicycling and casting pond nearby.

Publicity: *Travel & Leisure, Conde Naste Traveler, Bon Appetite, Country Living, House & Garden, Diversions, Bon Appetit, Historic Gourmet, Travel Holiday and Adventure West.*

Voss Inn

319 S Willson Ave
Bozeman, MT 59715-4632
(406)587-0982 Fax:(406)585-2964
E-mail: vossinn@bigsky.net

Circa 1883. The Voss Inn is a restored two-story Victorian mansion with a large front porch and a Victorian parlor. Antique furnishings include an upright piano and chandelier. Two of the inn's six rooms include air conditioning. A full breakfast is served, with freshly baked rolls kept in a unique warmer that's built into an ornate 1880s radiator.

Historic Interest: Little Big Horn (Custer battle site, 18 miles), Virginia City and Nevada City (60 miles), Madison Buffalo Jump (30 miles).

Innkeeper(s): Bruce & Frankee Muller. $95-125. MC, VISA, AX, PC, TC. TAC7.

6 rooms with PB. Breakfast and afternoon tea included in rates. Types of meals: Gourmet bkfst and picnic lunch. Beds: KQ. Phone in room. Fax on premises. Weddings, small meetings and family reunions hosted. Spanish and some Dutch spoken. Antiquing, fishing, golf, hunting, hiking, biking, parks, shopping, downhill skiing, cross-country skiing and water sports nearby.

Publicity: *Sunset, Cosmopolitan, Gourmet, Countryside and Country Inns.*

"First class all the way."

Choteau   B4

Styren Guest House

961 20th Rd NW
Choteau, MT 59522
(406)466-2008 (888)848-2008
E-mail: stay@styrenguesthouse.com

Circa 1912. Located in an area known as the Rocky Mountain Front, where the prairie meets the Rockies, this country guest house was built during the days of homesteading. It sits on a five-acre family ranch and farm with a cow calve herd, alfalfa hay and barley grown. There are three bed-rooms and twice that many beds. A kitchen and bath were added after the arrival of plumbing and electricity. Fully equipped, modern appliances include a microwave for cooking ease. A barbecue grill is outside. A second-story deck overlooking surroundings of green trees, a large lawn and flower beds is perfect for watching colorful sunsets.

Historic Interest: Lewis & Clark Interpretive Center (60 miles), Dinosaur digs (5-20 miles), Glacier National Park (90 miles).

Innkeeper(s): Herb & Deanna Styren. $75-95. PC. 3 guest houses. Types of meals: Country bkfst, cont plus and early coffee/tea. Beds: QDT. Cable TV, ceiling fan, VCR and fireplace in room. Pet boarding, gas grill and upper and lower deck on premises. Family reunions hosted. Antiquing, art galleries, bicycling, fishing, hiking, horseback riding, museums, parks, shopping, downhill skiing, cross-country skiing and water sports nearby.

Publicity: *Travel Montana, Teton Co Visitor Guide and Chamber of Commerce.*

Columbia Falls   B3

Bad Rock Country B&B

480 Bad Rock Dr
Columbia Falls, MT 59912-9213
(406)892-2829 (888)892-2829 Fax:(406)892-2930
E-mail: jalper@digisys.net

Circa 1995. These two newly constructed log buildings that are lavish versions of an old settler's home offer a comfortable stay. Hand-hewn square logs with dove-tail corners were fashioned to create the structures, using the original building techniques of Montana settlers 150 years ago. The main house is furnished in Old West antiques, while the log house features handmade lodge-pole furniture. Sundance eggs, Montana Potato Pie and Bad Rock's famous breakfast pastry are just a few of the specialties served. This bed & breakfast is ideally located for visiting Glacier National Park or enjoying the area's many activities.

Innkeeper(s): Jake & Marilyn Thompson. $130-179. MC, VISA, AX, DC, CB, DS, PC, TC. TAC10. 7 rooms with PB, 4 with FP. Breakfast included in rates. Types of meals: Gourmet bkfst. Beds: KQT. Phone, turndown service, ceiling fan and four rooms with fireplaces in room. Air conditioning. VCR, fax, copier and spa on premises. Antiquing, fishing, golf, Glacier National Park, live theater, parks, shopping, downhill skiing, cross-country skiing, tennis and water sports nearby.

Publicity: *Country Inns.*

Gardiner E5

Yellowstone Suites B&B

506 4th St
Gardiner, MT 59030
(406)848-7937 (800)948-7937
E-mail: bandb@gomontana.com
Web: www.wolftracker.com/ys

Circa 1904. This three-story stone Victorian home is located just three blocks from the historic Roosevelt Arch, the original gateway to Yellowstone Park. Seasonal activities for the adventure-minded

include whitewater rafting, fishing, horseback riding, hiking and canoeing in the summer and snowshoeing, snowmobiling and cross-country skiing in the winter. The road from Gardiner to Cooke City travels through the northern range where antelope, bison, elk, deer, big-horn sheep and wolves are commonly seen. At the end of the day, relax in a rocking chair on the inn's spacious, covered veranda, or soak in the hot tub.

Historic Interest: Fort Yellowstone (5 miles).
Innkeeper(s): Vicki LaPlant. $47-98. MC, VISA, AX, PC, TC. 4 rooms, 2 with PB, 1 suite and 1 conference room. Breakfast and snacks/refreshments included in rates. Types of meals: Full bkfst, country bkfst, veg bkfst and picnic lunch. Beds: QT. Cable TV, phone, ceiling fan and VCR in room. Spa, library, landscaped garden and covered porch veranda on premises. Weddings and family reunions hosted. Art galleries, canoeing/kayaking, fishing, hiking, horseback riding, museums, parks, shopping and cross-country skiing nearby.
Publicity: *Sunset Magazine.*

Glendive C9

The Hostetler House B&B

113 N Douglas St
Glendive, MT 59330-1619
(406)377-4505 (800)965-8456 Fax:(406)377-8456
E-mail: hostetler@midrivers.com

Circa 1912. Casual country decor mixed with handmade and heirloom furnishings are highlights at this Prairie School home. The inn features many comforting touches, such as a romantic hot tub and gazebo, enclosed sun porch and sitting room filled with books. The two guest rooms share a bath, and are furnished

by Dea, an interior decorator. The full breakfasts may be enjoyed on Grandma's china in the dining room or on the sun porch. The Yellowstone River is one block from the inn, and downtown shopping is two blocks away. Makoshika State Park, home of numerous fossil finds, is nearby.

Historic Interest: Guests are invited to tour Glendive's historic district on the innkeeper's tandem mountain bike.
Innkeeper(s): Craig & Dea Hostetler. $50. PC, TC. TAC10. 2 rooms. Breakfast included in rates. Types of meals: Gourmet bkfst and early coffee/tea. Beds: DT. Ceiling fan and air conditioning in room. VCR, fax, spa, bicycles, library and secretarial service on premises. Small meetings hosted. German spoken. Antiquing, fishing, fossil and agate hunting, live theater, parks, shopping, cross-country skiing, sporting events and water sports nearby.
Publicity: *Ranger Review/Circle Banner.*

"Warmth and loving care are evident throughout your exquisite home. Your attention to small details is uplifting. Thank you for a restful sojourn."

Hardin E7

Kendrick House Inn, B&B

206 N Custer Ave
Hardin, MT 59034-1917
(406)665-3035

Circa 1915. Originally a boarding house, this bed & breakfast also served as a local hospital and private apartments before falling into disrepair. Innkeepers Steve and Marcie restored this historic gem, transforming it into a Victorian B&B. The elegant decor includes period furnishings, Oriental rugs and chandeliers. Enjoy a vast array of books. Each guest bedroom includes a pedestal sink. A downstairs room has a private bath. Expect a hearty, Montana-style breakfast of fresh fruit, savory meats, made-to-order eggs and French toast. Little Bighorn Battlefield National Monument is nearby.

Innkeeper(s): Steve & Marcianna Smith. $65-85. MC, VISA, PC, TC. TAC10. 5 rooms. Beds: D. Air conditioning. VCR and library on premises.

Helena D4

Appleton Inn B&B

1999 Euclid Avenue
Helena, MT 59601-1908
(406)449-7492 (800)956-1999 Fax:(406)449-1261
E-mail: appleton@ixi.net

Circa 1890. Montana's first resident dentist called this Victorian his home. It remained in his family until the 1970s when it was transformed into apartments. Fortunately, the innkeepers bought and restored the home, bringing back the original beauty. The innkeepers have their own furniture-making company and have created many of the pieces that

decorate the guest rooms. Rooms range from the spacious Master Suite, with its oak, four-poster bed and bath with a clawfoot tub, to the quaint and cozy Attic Playroom. The inn is a convenient place to enjoy the Helena area.

Historic Interest: West Mansion District, Montana Historic Society Museum and the state capitol building all are nearby historic sites.
Innkeeper(s): Tom Woodall & Cheryl Boid. $90-165. MC, VISA, AX, DS, PC, TC. TAC10. 5 rooms with PB and 1 suite. Breakfast included in rates. AP. Beds: Q. Cable TV and phone in room. Air conditioning. VCR, fax and copier on premises. Antiquing, fishing, national forest, live theater, parks, shopping, downhill skiing, cross-country skiing, sporting events and water sports nearby. Pets allowed: Need prior approval.

"Cheryl and Tom have provided a perfect place to call home away from home. The surroundings are delightful - the rooms, the plants, the grounds - and the breakfast very tasty. And they provide lots of helpful information to help you enjoy touring the area. A truly delightful B&B."

The Sanders - Helena's B&B

328 N Ewing St
Helena, MT 59601-4050
(406)442-3309 Fax:(406)443-2361
E-mail: thefolks@sandersbb.com
Web: www.sandersbb.com

Circa 1890. This historic inn is filled with elegantly carved furnishings, paintings and collections that are original to the house. Wilbur Sanders, an attorney and a Montana senator and his wife Harriet, built their home in the heart of Helena. The three-story house features a front and side porch, and balconies and bay windows that provide views of the mountains and downtown Helena. In addition to the rich interior and hospitality, guests are pampered with gourmet breakfasts that might include items such as an orange souffle, sourdough or huckleberry pancakes, French toast with sauteed fruit or savory frittatas. The main dish is accompanied by fresh fruit, juice, freshly ground organically grown coffee and an assortment of homemade muffins, coffee cakes or breads.

Historic Interest: Montana State Historical Museum, Cathedral of St. Helena, Reeders Alley & Capital.

Innkeeper(s): Bobbi Uecker & Rock Ringling. $85-105. MC, VISA, AX, DS, DC, PC, TC. 7 rooms with PB and 2 conference rooms. Breakfast included in rates. Types of meals: Full bkfst, full gourmet bkfst, afternoon tea and early coffee/tea. Beds: Q. Cable TV, phone, fireplace, hair dryer, computer hook-up and turn-down service in room. Air conditioning. VCR, fax, copier library, porch with garden, smoke free, off-street parking, cookies, fruit, sherry and data port on premises. Antiquing, fishing, live theater, museums, parks, Carroll University, state capitol, Governor's mansion, Helena's Cathedral, shopping, downhill skiing, cross-country skiing, sporting events and water sports nearby.

Publicity: National Geographic Traveler, Country Travels, Pacific Northwest, Washington Post, Boston Globe, New York Times.

Livingston   E5

Sixty Three Ranch

PO Box 979
Livingston, MT 59047
(406)222-0570
Web: www.63ranch.com

Circa 1863. Experience the best of Big Sky Country at this working dude ranch, the first in Montana to be declared a National Historic Site. It borders the immense Gallatin National Forest with the majestic Absaroka Mountain Range as an incredible backdrop. Rustic log or frame guest cabins with modern bathrooms are tucked among pine and aspen. The main log lodge is a central gathering place with fireside discussions, a billiards room, two antique pianos and an extensive collection of books. Three hearty daily meals are served family-style in the dining room. Morning and afternoon horseback rides plus a full-day ride are offered with more than 100 miles of breathtaking trails. Fly-fishing in Mission Creek, nature hikes, bird watching, square dancing, cookouts and singalongs, volleyball, horseshoes, ping pong and bumper pool all are popular. Pack trips and off-ranch activities are available.

Innkeeper(s): Bud, Sandra & Jeff Cahill. $1150. 8 cabins. Beds: DT. Horseback riding, fly fishing, volleyball, horseshoes, billiards, ping-pong, bumper pool, gift shop and soda machine on premises.

Red Lodge   E6

The Pollard

2 N Broadway
Red Lodge, MT 59068
(406)446-0001 (800)POLLARD Fax:(406)446-0002
E-mail: pollard@pollardhotel.com
Web: www.pollardhotel.com

Circa 1893. A distinctive architectural landmark, this red brick building is a grand hotel listed in the National Register. Learn of its rich heritage and restorations in the oak-paneled History Room or relax by the fireplace in the gallery with coffered ceilings. Early guests included Calamity Jane, Buffalo Bill Cody and William Jennings Bryan. Stay in an upscale guest bedroom or suite with a balcony, hot tub, steambath or mountain view. Breakfast is made to order in the award-winning dining room. Enjoy the health club's exercise room, sauna, whirlpool and racquetball. After a beautiful ceremony at the Canyon Wedding Chapel, this is the perfect place for a lavish or intimate reception and honeymoon.

Innkeeper(s): Sharon Torcaso. Call for rates. 39 rooms with PB. Breakfast included in rates. Types of meals: Full bkfst. Cable TV, phone, VCR, hair dryers, bathrobes, some with Jacuzzi and balconies in room. Health club, racquetball courts, hot tub and saunas nearby.

Willows Inn

224 S Platt Ave, PO Box 886
Red Lodge, MT 59068-0886
(406)446-3913
E-mail: willowinn@earthlink.net
Web: www.bbhost.com/willowsinn

Circa 1909. Dreams do come true at this three-story Queen Anne Victorian with gingerbread trim and white picket fence. An assortment of common rooms are accented with original wood molding, leaded-glass windows and boast reading nooks, a TV parlor with extensive videos and a living room. Two storybook cottages offer privacy. Antique furnishings and specialty bath products highlight the well-appointed guest bedrooms. Savor a gourmet breakfast and Elven's tasty afternoon refreshments in the cheery wicker-filled dining room. Relax on comfy chairs and enjoy the mountain view from the large front porch that overlooks the colorful flowerbeds and manicured lawn. Stroll down Main Street and stop for lunch or dinner cuisine at Bridge Creek Backcountry Kitchen and Wine Bar.

Innkeeper(s): Elven, Carolyn & Kerry Boggio. $65-120. MC, VISA. 5 rooms, 3 with PB and 2 cottages. Breakfast and snacks/refreshments included in rates. Types of meals: Full bkfst. Beds: KQT. TV and phone in room.

Publicity: The Billings Gazette and Innsider.

"It was heavenly. The bed was comfortable and we loved the decor."

Nebraska

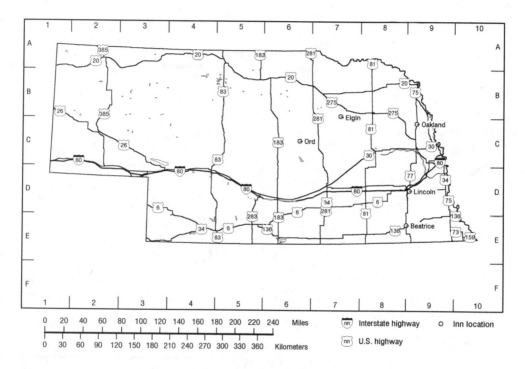

```
        1      2      3      4      5      6      7      8      9     10
A                                                                         A
B                                                                         B
C                                                                         C
D                                                                         D
E                                                                         E
F                                                                         F
        1      2      3      4      5      6      7      8      9     10
```

```
0   20   40   60   80  100  120  140  160  180  200  220  240   Miles
├───┼────┼────┼────┼────┼────┼────┼────┼────┼────┼────┼────┤

0   30   60   90  120  150  180  210  240  270  300  330  360
├───┼────┼────┼────┼────┼────┼────┼────┼────┼────┼────┼────┤   Kilometers
```

[nn] Interstate highway   o Inn location

[nn] U.S. highway

Beatrice   E9

The Carriage House B&B
25478 S 23rd Rd
Beatrice, NE 68310
(402)228-0356 (888)228-0356

Circa 1930. The two-story brick house and accompanying 10 acres are listed in the State Historic Register. A quiet and tranquil ambiance is enhanced by the elegantly furnished period antiques. The Victorian Guest Parlor welcomes relaxation with music and a fireplace. Choose from well-decorated, quaint guest bedrooms like the Garden Room with French doors leading to a private veranda, or the Victorian Suite with antique clawfoot tub, pedestal sink and dressing table. Enjoy a generous breakfast served in the large dining room. Hand-feed the llamas in the 1887 barn, delight in the peaceful gazebo and watch a gorgeous sunset from the wraparound porch.
Innkeeper(s): David & Lorraine Bigley. $60-95. MC, VISA. 7 rooms, 1 with PB and 1 suite. Breakfast and snacks/refreshments included in rates. Types of meals: Gourmet bkfst. Beds: DT. Central air. VCR, stables, pet boarding and private living room on premises. Weddings and family reunions hosted. Fishing, golf, hiking, parks, shopping and tennis nearby. Pets allowed: Outside kennels.

Elgin   B7

Plantation House
401 Plantation St
Elgin, NE 68636-9301
(402)843-2287 Fax:(402)843-2287
E-mail: plantation@gpcom.net

Circa 1916. This historic mansion sits adjacent to Elgin City Park, and guests will marvel at its beauty and size. Once a small Victorian farmhouse, the Plantation House has evolved into a 20-room Greek Revival treasure. Visitors will be treated to a tour and a large family-style breakfast, and may venture to the park to play tennis or horseshoes. The antique-filled guest rooms include the Stained Glass Room, with a queen bed and available twin-bed anteroom, and the Old Master Bedroom, with clawfoot tub and pedestal sink.
Innkeeper(s): Kyle & Deb Warren. $55-75. PC, TC. TAC10. 5 rooms with PB, 1 cottage and 2 conference rooms. Breakfast included in rates. Types of meals: Full bkfst and early coffee/tea. Beds: QT.

Ceiling fan in room. Air conditioning. VCR, fax, copier and library on premises. Weddings, small meetings, family reunions and seminars hosted. Antiquing, fishing, historical parks and sites, parks and shopping nearby.
Publicity: *Omaha World Herald, Norfolk Daily News, Home & Away, Midwest Living and Nebraska Life.*

"Gorgeous house! Relaxing atmosphere. Just like going to Mom's house."

Lincoln   D9

The Atwood House B&B

740 S 17th St
Lincoln, NE 68508-3708
(402)438-4567 (800)884-6554 Fax:(402)477-8314
E-mail: larry@atwoodhouse.com

Circa 1894. Located two blocks from the state capitol, this 7,500-square-foot mansion, in the Neoclassical Georgian Revival style, features four massive columns. Interior columns are repeated throughout such as on the dressing room vanity, on the staircase and on the parlor fireplace. Classically appointed, the parlor and entranceway set an elegant yet inviting tone. Guest suites are large and feature spacious sitting rooms, fireplaces, massive bedsteads and Oriental carpets. The 800-square-foot bridal suite consists of three rooms, and it includes a fireplace, a carved walnut bed and a large whirlpool tub set off by columns. Breakfast is served on bone china with Waterford crystal and sterling flatware.
Innkeeper(s): Ruth & Larry Stoll. $85-179. MC, VISA, AX, DS, PC, TC. 4 suites, 2 with FP and 1 conference room. Breakfast and snacks/refreshments included in rates. Types of meals: Gourmet bkfst and early coffee/tea. Beds: KQ. Cable TV, phone, turndown service, VCR and three with two-person whirlpool in room. Air conditioning. Fax, copier and library on premises. Weddings and small meetings hosted. Antiquing, fishing, golf, live theater, parks, shopping, cross-country skiing, sporting events, tennis and water sports nearby.
Publicity: *Lincoln Journal Star and Channel 8 local.*

"Such a delightful B&B! It is such a nice change in my travels."

The FM Hall House B&B

1039 S 11th St
Lincoln, NE 68508
(402)475-4255 (877)475-4255
E-mail: info@fmhallhouse.com
Web: www.fmhallhouse.com

Circa 1884. The Queen Anne-style FM Hall House began life more than 100 years ago as one of Lincoln's grandest private homes. Its namesake, prominent local attorney Frank M. Hall, bought the house a few years after it was built and used it to display an extensive art collection gathered from his world travels. Following his death, the home was turned into a boarding house and later apartments. Many of the home's unique architectural features were covered up over the years and only recently rediscovered when the present owners decided to convert the house to an inn. They have restored the original stained-glass windows and fine woodwork for guests to enjoy today. The inn offers three suites. The Empire Suite-the original master bedroom-is distinguished by a stained-glass bay window and two decorative fireplaces. A wet bar offers complimentary sodas, juices and snacks.

The Belvedere Suite encompasses the entire third floor. This fully equipped apartment has a modern kitchen, living room with dining area, sitting room, large bedroom and bath, and is highlighted by arched stained-glass windows,

hardwood floors and a view of the neighborhood and State Capitol. The Carriage House Suite has a large Jacuzzi. A typical breakfast consists of fruit parfaits, chocolate croissants, spinach and mushroom frittatas with peppered-slab bacon and herb-roasted Yukon Gold potatoes. Downtown Lincoln, the historic Haymarket District and the University of Nebraska campus are only a short drive away.
Historic Interest: Nebraska State Capitol (1/4 miles), Kennard House (1/4 miles), Germans from Russia Museum (1/4 mile).
Innkeeper(s): Ed & Yana Beranek. $85-175. MC, VISA, AX, DS, PC, TC. 3 suites, 1 with FP. Breakfast included in rates. Types of meals: Gourmet bkfst. Beds: KQ. Cable TV, phone, turndown service and VCR in room. Central air. Library, large porch and landscaped gardens with fish pond on premises. Antiquing, art galleries, bicycling, fishing, golf, live theater, museums, parks, shopping, sporting events, tennis and wineries nearby.
Publicity: *Lincoln Journal Star.*

Oakland   C9

Benson B&B

402 N Oakland Ave
Oakland, NE 68045-1135
(402)685-6051
E-mail: sanderson@genesisnet.net

Circa 1905. This inn is on the second floor of the Benson Building, a sturdy, turreted brick structure built of walls nearly 12 inches thick. Decorated throughout in mauve, blue and cream, the Benson B&B features three comfortable guest rooms, and a restful, small-town atmosphere. Guests often visit the Swedish Heritage Center and a nearby city park. An 18-hole golf course is a five-minute drive away. The bed & breakfast features a small gift shop, as well as a collection of soft drink memorabilia. Be sure to ask about the Troll Stroll.
Innkeeper(s): Stan & Norma Anderson. $53-60. DS, PC, TC. TAC10. 3 rooms. Breakfast and snacks/refreshments included in rates. Types of meals: Full bkfst and early coffee/tea. Beds: QD. Toiletries in room. VCR, spa and library on premises. Antiquing, parks, shopping and sporting events nearby.
Publicity: *World Herald, West Point, Omaha World Herald, KMTV Channel 3, Omaha, KWPN West Point and KWPN Radio.*

Ord   C6

The Shepherds' Inn, Inc.

Rt 3, Box 108A
Ord, NE 68837
(308)728-3306 (800)901-8649
E-mail: ddvshep@cornhusker.net
Web: www.bbonline.com/ne/shepherd

Circa 1917. Innkeeper Don Vancura was born in this house, and his grandparents built the early 20th-century farmhouse. The quaint bed & breakfast offers three guest bedrooms, decorated with antiques that are a mix of family pieces and items innkeeper Doris Vancura selected at local auctions. The country setting is ideal for a quiet, secluded getaway. Adults, as well as children, will especially love this inn, as there is a petting zoo on the grounds featuring goats, sheep, a llama and three miniature donkeys. In the mornings, guests enjoy items such as waffles, French toast or egg dishes and fruits.
Innkeeper(s): Don & Doris Vancura. $55-65. MC, VISA, PC, TC. 3 rooms with PB. Breakfast and snacks/refreshments included in rates. Types of meals: Full bkfst. Beds: Q. Turndown service, ceiling fan and alarm clocks in room. Air conditioning. VCR, spa, gift shop and front porch table and chairs on premises. Small meetings and family reunions hosted. Antiquing, fishing, golf, gift shop, parks, shopping, cross-country skiing, tennis and water sports nearby.
"We drive hours out of our way just to stay here for a reason—it's home and it's wonderful."

Nevada

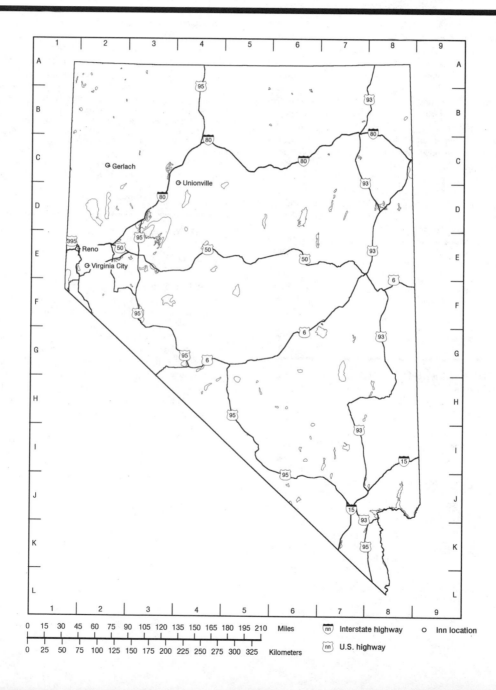

0 15 30 45 60 75 90 105 120 135 150 165 180 195 210 Miles

0 25 50 75 100 125 150 175 200 225 250 275 300 325 Kilometers

| | Interstate highway | ○ Inn location |
| | U.S. highway | |

313

Gerlach   C2

Soldier Meadows Guest Ranch & Lodge

Soldier Meadows Rd
Gerlach, NV 89412
(530)233-4881 Fax:(530)233-1183
E-mail: soldier@hdo.net
Web: www.soldiermeadows.com

Circa 1865. Once known as Fort McGarry, this historic working ranch once housed the troops who were assigned to protect
pioneers traveling the Applegate-Lassen Trail from the Paiute
Indians of the area. The Estill family now runs cattle on the
land. Green meadows and willow trees frame the ranch house
and the bunkhouse. Stone stables erected by the U. S. Army
are still in use, as well as the original Officers' Quarters. There
are two natural hot springs for swimming. Wildlife is abundant
in the area, including wild mustangs, mule deer and antelope.
Guests may opt to work the range with the ranch's cowhands
and enjoy trail riding, hunting, fishing or hiking. Some like to
mine for opals at the adjacent opal mine, while others organize
a camping experience at one of the two sheep camps in the
aspen and mahogany forests of the foothills. For the complete
experience, join the crew in the cookhouse early for breakfast
or later for lunch. A ranch supper is offered in the evening
where, after a day or two, you may find yourself spinning a
yarn of your own about the Old West.
Historic Interest: Applegate-Lassen Trail-7 miles, High Rock Canyon-12 miles.
Innkeeper(s): Mackey & Candi Hedges. $45-125. MC, VISA, PC, TC. TAC10.
10 rooms, 1 suite and 1 conference room. Breakfast, picnic lunch,
snacks/refreshments and dinner included in rates. Types of meals: Full bkfst,
early coffee/tea and lunch. AP. Beds: QT. Natural hot springs and BBQ supper
almost every night on premises. Small meetings and family reunions hosted.
Bicycling, canoeing/kayaking, hiking, horseback riding and historic Pioneer
Trails nearby.
Pets Allowed.

Reno   E1

Bed and Breakfast: South Reno

136 Andrew Ln
Reno, NV 89511-9740
(775)849-0772

Circa 1948. The location of this B&B, is 12 miles from Reno.
There are three acres of landscaped lawns, 40 trees, a pool and
several patios and decks for relaxing and enjoying views of

neighboring ranches and of
Mount Rose and Slide Mountain.
Early American furnishings
include four-poster beds and wing
chairs. Nearby Washoe Lake offers
windsurfing, and it's 20 miles to
good skiing, sledding and snowmobiling areas.

Innkeeper(s): Caroline Walters & Robert McNeill. $75-85. PC, TC. TAC5.
3 rooms, 2 with PB and 1 suite. Breakfast included in rates. Types of
meals: Cont and early coffee/tea. Beds: QT. Cable TV, phone and VCR in
room. Swimming and library on premises. Weddings and seminars hosted.
Amusement parks, antiquing, fishing, casinos, live theater, parks, shopping, downhill skiing, cross-country skiing, sporting events and water
sports nearby.

Unionville   D4

Old Pioneer Garden Country Inn

2805 Unionville Rd
Unionville, NV 89418-8204
(775)538-7585

Circa 1861. Once a bustling silver mining town, Unionville
now has only a handful of citizens, and Old Pioneer Garden
Guest Ranch is just down the road from town.
Accommodations are in a renovated blacksmith's house, a
farmhouse and across the meadow in the Hadley House.
Guests can settle down in front of a fire in the inn's library. A
Swedish-style gazebo rests beside a bubbling stream, and there
are orchards, grape arbors, vegetable gardens, sheep and goats.
A country supper is available. The innkeepers can accommo-
date visiting horses in their barn and corrals.
Innkeeper(s): Mitzi & Lew Jones. $85-95. 12 rooms, 4 with PB, 1 with FP, 1
suite and 1 conference room. Breakfast included in rates. Types of meals:
Gourmet bkfst, early coffee/tea, gourmet lunch, picnic lunch and dinner.
Beds: D. Library and tournament size pool table on premises. Handicap
access. Antiquing and fishing nearby.
Publicity: *Denver Post.*

"An array of charm that warms the heart and delights the soul."

Virginia City   E2

Chollar Mansion

565 S D St
Virginia City, NV 89440
(775)847-9777

Circa 1861. Built in 1861, this National Register home is the
perfect spot to immerse yourself into the mining mystique
when the home served as a mining office. The innkeepers are
knowledgeable about the mine's history and enjoy touring
guests to the 164-square-foot underground vault where the
company's bullion was stored. There's a paymaster's booth
next to the kitchen, a men's and ladies' parlor, a library, and a
formal dining room where breakfast is served (full breakfasts
are provided in the winter and a continental breakfast is
offered at other times of the year). Furnishings include
antiques that highlight the inn's detailed Victorian craftsmanship. A cottage on the property, decorated in country style, is
popular with families who have children. Other accommodations include a suite with a private bath and two rooms that
share a bath between them. Guests enjoy views through Six
Mile Canyon for up to 140-180 miles across to the mountain
ranges on clear days.
Innkeeper(s): Kenneth & Kay Benton. Call for rates.. 4 rooms with PB. Types
of meals: Full bkfst and cont. TV and ceiling fan in room.

New Hampshire

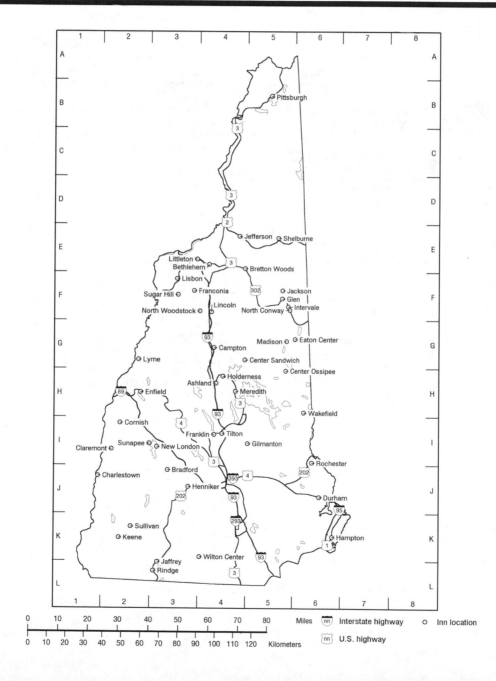

| | Miles | nn Interstate highway | o Inn location |
| | Kilometers | nn U.S. highway | |

Albany
F5

The Darby Field Country Inn & Restaurant

185 Chase Hill Rd
Albany, NH 03818
(603)447-2181 (800)426-4147 Fax:(603)447-5726
E-mail: marc@darbyfield.com
Web: www.darbyfield.com

Circa 1826. This rambling, blue clapboard farmhouse has a huge fieldstone fireplace, stone patio and outstanding views of the Mt. Washington Valley and the Presidential Mountains. For

many years, it was called the Bald Hill Grand View Lodge, but was renamed to honor the first European to climb Mt. Washington, Darby Field. Bed & breakfast rates range from $100 to $250 per couple.

Innkeeper(s): Marc & Maria Donaldson. $100-250. MC, VISA, PC, TC. 11 rooms with PB and 3 suites. Types of meals: Country bkfst and gourmet dinner. Beds: KQT. TV, ceiling fan, VCR and fireplace and Jacuzzi available in room. Air conditioning. Cross-country skiing, horse-drawn sleigh and carriage rides on premises. Weddings, small meetings, family reunions and seminars hosted. Amusement parks, antiquing, live theater, shopping, downhill skiing and cross-country skiing nearby.

Ashland
H4

Anniversary Inn - A Glynn House Inn

59 Highland St, PO Box 719
Ashland, NH 03217-0719
(603)968-3775 (800)637-9599 Fax:(603)968-9415
E-mail: glynnhse@lr.net
Web: glynnhouse.com

Circa 1895. A three-story turret, gables and verandas frosted with Queen Anne gingerbread come together in an appealing mass of Victoriana in the Glynn House. Carved oak woodwork and pocket doors accentuate the foyer. Period furnishings and ornate Oriental wall coverings decorate the parlor. The village of Ashland is located in the "On Golden Pond" (Squam Lake) and the White Mountains area. The inn is about two hours from Boston and one hour from Manchester airport.

Circa 1895

Historic Interest: Shaker Village (20 minutes), Polar Caves (10 minutes).

Innkeeper(s): Jim & Gay Dunlop. $99-199. MC, VISA. 12 rooms with PB, 5 with FP and 5 suites. Breakfast included in rates. Types of meals: Gourmet bkfst and early coffee/tea. Beds: KQT. Cable TV, VCR, fireplace and two person whirlpools in room. Air conditioning. Fax on premises. Weddings, small meetings, family reunions and seminars hosted. Amusement parks, antiquing, fishing, discount stores, parks, shopping, downhill skiing, cross-country skiing, sporting events and water sports nearby.

"Boston was fun, but the Glynn House is the place we'll send our friends."

Bethlehem
E4

Angel of the Mountains

2007 Main St
Bethlehem, NH 03574
(603)869-6493 (888)704-4004 Fax:(603)869-5490
E-mail: info@angelofthemountains.com
Web: www.angelofthemountains.com

Circa 1893. This 1893 Victorian inn with original woodwork, fireplaces and fixtures stands on one acre in

New Hampshire's White Mountains. It's across the street from the oldest continually operated movie theater in the United States and near the Cog railroad, Mt. Washington Hotel and the Robert Frost home. Built as a summer cottage when Bethlehem was the leading resort destination in America, the inn has often been renamed (The Red Gables, The Howard House Annex, The Gables, The Angel), but has always been an elegant peaceful retreat for the work weary. Each of its five guest bedrooms has a view of Mt. Washington. The carriage house is a private cottage near the main house. Guests breakfast on juice, fruit, muffins and an egg dish, all artfully served. Historic walking tours are offered, and guests can also partake of the other local activities in season: snowmobiling, downhill and cross-country skiing, golf, hiking and antiquing. Complimentary afternoon wine and cheese await those who arrive home after a day exploring the area. The town's Mystery Lantern Tour is free of charge for guests of Angel of the Mountains. A number of great packages are available upon request, including the romantic getaway package, the golf package and the Bethlehem Christmas Experience.

Historic Interest: Mt. Washington Hotel (15 miles), Old Man of the Mountain (12 miles), Robert Frost home (10 miles), Oldest continually operated move theater in the USA (across the street).

Innkeeper(s): Sally & Ben Gumm. $95-225. MC, VISA, PC, TC. TAC10. 5 rooms, 3 with PB and 1 suite. Breakfast included in rates. Types of meals: Gourmet bkfst and early coffee/tea. Beds: QT. Cable TV, phone, ceiling fan and VCR in room. Air conditioning. Fax, swimming and afternoon wine and cheese on premises. Weddings, small meetings, family reunions and seminars hosted. Amusement parks, antiquing, beaches, bicycling, canoeing/kayaking, fishing, golf, hiking, horseback riding, live theater, museums, parks, shopping, downhill skiing, cross-country skiing, tennis and water sports nearby.

Pets allowed: Two nights on weekends, three nights on Columbus Day weekend.

Publicity: *New Hampshire Magazine.*

The Mulburn Inn

2370 Main St, Rt 302
Bethlehem, NH 03574
(603)869-3389 (800)457-9440 Fax:(603)869-5633
E-mail: info@mulburninn.com

Circa 1908. This English Tudor mansion was once the summer estate of the Woolworth family. The home was built by notable architect Sylvanius D. Morgan, whose inspired design includes many intricate details. The home's romantic ambiance entices a multitude of visitors, and it is within these idyllic walls that Cary Grant and Barbara Hutton enjoyed their honeymoon. Today, guests also have use of a hot tub.

Historic Interest: Crawford Notch State Park, Franconia Notch State Park, Heritage, Mount Washington.

Innkeeper(s): Christina Ferraro & Alecia Loveless. $85-175. MC, VISA, PC. TAC10. 7 rooms with PB. Breakfast and afternoon tea included in rates. Types of meals: Gourmet bkfst and snacks/refreshments.

Beds: KQ. Air conditioning. VCR, fax, spa and library on premises. Weddings, small meetings, family reunions and seminars hosted. Antiquing, bicycling, canoeing/kayaking, fishing, golf, romantic getaways, live theater, parks, shopping, downhill skiing, cross-country skiing, tennis and water sports nearby.
Publicity: *The Record, Yankee and Boston Globe.*

"You have put a lot of thought, charm, beauty and warmth into the inn. Your breakfasts were oh, so delicious!!"

The Wayside Inn

Rt 302 at Pierce Bridge, 3738 Main Stree
Bethlehem, NH 03574
(603)869-3364 (800)448-9557 Fax:(603)869-5765
E-mail: info@thewaysideinn.com
Web: www.thewaysideinn.com

Circa 1825. The Ammonosuc River flows gently a few yards from this historic inn, which was built in the early 1800s. Additions were added in 1910 and again in the 1950s. The inn originally was the home of John Pierce, nephew of President Franklin Pierce. Of the 26 guest rooms, 14 are located in the inn. These rooms are decorated in traditional New England style with beds topped with quilts. Some rooms include a poster bed. The rest of the rooms have contemporary furnishings. Guests can enjoy the gardens and mountain views or head down to the sandy beach. In the winter, guests can go snowmobiling or cross-country skiing. Breakfast is included in the rates, and Chef Victor Hofmann was named Chef of the Year by the American Culinary Federation in 1994. The Hofmann family has owned and operated the Wayside Inn for more than a decade.
Innkeeper(s): Victor & Kathie Hofmann. $88-112. MC, VISA, AX, DS, TC. 26 rooms with PB. Breakfast included in rates. Types of meals: Full bkfst, early coffee/tea and dinner. MAP, EP. Beds: KQD. Some with TV, refrigerator, whirlpool tub and balconies in room. Air conditioning. Fax, copier, swimming and bocce court on premises. Handicap access. Weddings, small meetings and family reunions hosted. German and French spoken. Amusement parks, antiquing, fishing, golf, live theater, parks, shopping, downhill skiing, cross-country skiing, tennis and water sports nearby.

Bradford   J3

Candlelite Inn

5 Greenhouse Ln
Bradford, NH 03221-3505
(603)938-5571 (888)812-5571
E-mail: candlelite@conknet.com
Web: www.candleliteinn.com

Circa 1897. Nestled on three acres of countryside in the valley of the Lake Sunapee region, this Victorian inn has all of the grace and charm of an era gone by. The inn offers a gazebo porch perfect for sipping lemonade on a summer day. On winter days, keep warm by the parlor's fireplace, while relaxing with a good book. Enjoy a three-course gourmet breakfast, including dessert, in the sun room overlooking the pond. Country roads invite fall strolls, cross-country skiing and snowshoeing.

Historic Interest: Close to the John Hay.
Innkeeper(s): Les & Marilyn Gordon. $90-125. MC, VISA, AX, DS. 6 rooms with PB. Breakfast included in rates. Types of meals: Full bkfst, early coffee/tea and snacks/refreshments. Beds: Q. Antiquing, live theater, shopping, downhill skiing, cross-country skiing and sporting events nearby.
Publicity: *Grapevine, InterTown News, Sunday Monitor, N.H. Business Review, The Bradford Bridge, Antiques & Auction News and Concord Area Buywise.*

Mountain Lake Inn

2871 Rt 114, PO Box 443
Bradford, NH 03221
(603)938-2136 (800)662-6005
E-mail: ahi@mountainlakeinn.com
Web: www.mountainlakeinn.com

Circa 1760. Originally built as an inn, this white colonial house overlooks Lake Massasecum and is situated on 168 acres, including eight acres of lakefront. Four rooms are in the main house, while the remaining accommodations are in the wing. Breakfast is served in the dining room with a different entree each morning as well as fruit and baked goods. The inn's private sandy beach on Lake Massasecum offers sunning, swimming and fishing, but guests often prefer to take out the canoe and rowboat. Ice skating and snowmobiling on the lake is a popular activity in winter, and there's a snowmobile trail through the property that connects the Bradford and Henniker trails. In summer, enjoy the inn's picnic area and barbecue by the beach, or better yet, take a picnic basket to the waterfall 50 yards from the inn. Mount Sunapee and Pat's Peak ski resorts are nearby.

Innkeeper(s): Bob & Tracy Foor. $85. MC, VISA, AX, DS. 10 rooms, 9 with PB and 1 conference room. Types of meals: Full bkfst and country bkfst. Beds: KQDT. Antiquing, canoeing/kayaking, fishing, golf, hiking, snowmobiling, snowshoeing and downhill skiing nearby.
Publicity: *Country Inns, Boston Globe and Star Ledger.*

The Rosewood Country Inn

67 Pleasant View Rd
Bradford, NH 03221-3113
(603)938-5253
E-mail: rosewood@conknet.com
Web: www.rosewoodcountryinn.com

Circa 1850. This three-story country Victorian inn in the Sunapee Region treats its guests to a candlelight and crystal breakfast and elegant accommodations that manage to avoid being stuffy. The inn prides itself on special touches. The innkeepers like to keep things interesting with ideas such as theme weekends and special breakfast fare, including cinnamon apple pancakes with cider sauce. Mount Sunapee Ski Area and Lake Sunapee are less than eight minutes away.
Innkeeper(s): Lesley & Dick Marquis. $119-239. MC, VISA, AX, DC, DS, PC, TC. TAC10. 11 rooms with PB, 6 with FP and 3 conference rooms. Breakfast included in rates. Types of meals: Gourmet bkfst and early coffee/tea. Beds: KQ. Six with Jacuzzi and sherry in room. Fax, swimming, cross-country skiing, hiking, snowshoeing, ice skating and fishing on premises. Handicap access. Weddings, small meetings, family reunions and seminars hosted. French spoken. Antiquing, fishing, live theater, shopping, downhill skiing, cross-country skiing, sporting events and water sports nearby.
Publicity: *Modern Bride, Country Inn, Boston Magazine, Boston Globe, New York Newsday and New York Times.*

Thistle and Shamrock Inn & Restaurant

11 West Main St
Bradford, NH 03221
(603)938-5553 (888)938-5553 Fax:(603)938-5554
E-mail: stay@thistleandshamrock.com
Web: www.thistleandshamrock.com

Circa 1898. The front porch beckons with wicker furniture and hanging flower baskets. Originally a hotel accommodating traveling salesmen to area mill towns, this historic Federal-style inn with wide halls and stairways features quiet comfort. Relax by the fireplace in the large parlor, or read in the well-stocked library. Experience 19th century furnishings and modern conveniences in the guest bedrooms, mini-suites or family suites. Chef Jim's culinary expertise is enjoyed for breakfast in the Roters Dining Room. The cozy Pub Room offers a beverage and hors d'oeuvre menu. Lake and Mount Sunapee are nearby, contributing to the area's many year-round activities.

Innkeeper(s): Jim & Lynn Horigan. $85-140. MC, VISA, AX, DS, PC, TC. TAC10. 10 rooms with PB and 7 suites. Breakfast included in rates. Types of meals: Full bkfst and gourmet dinner. Beds: KQT. Ceiling fan in room. Library on premises. Weddings, small meetings, family reunions and seminars hosted. Antiquing, art galleries, beaches, bicycling, canoeing/kayaking, fishing, golf, hiking, live theater, museums, parks, shopping, downhill skiing, cross-country skiing and water sports nearby.

Publicity: *Soonipi Magazine, Valley News, WMUR-TV, Manchester and Cook's Corner.*

Bretton Woods   E4

Bretton Arms Country Inn

Route 302
Bretton Woods, NH 03575
(603)278-1000 (800)258-0330 Fax:(603)278-8838
E-mail: info@mtwashington.com
Web: www.mtwashington.com

Circa 1896. This magnificent Victorian was once a private home and later served as lodging at the prestigious Mount Washington Resort. The inn eventually closed, but it now has been completely restored and reopened. The guest rooms and suites are appointed in Victorian style. The inn has been designated a National

Historic Landmark. Guests enjoy use of all that the Mount Washington Resort has to offer, including 2,600 scenic acres. There are a dozen tennis courts, two golf courses, swimming pools, cross-country and alpine ski trails and a Jacuzzi and sauna. Sleigh and carriage rides can be arranged, or guests can simply stroll through the beautifully maintained gardens. Guests can enjoy a gourmet dinner in the inn's impressive dining room. Nightly entertainment is provided mid-May through mid-October and late November through early April at the resort's Cave Lounge, an intimate setting reminiscent of an old speakeasy.

Innkeeper(s): Eleanor Imrie. $89-229. MC, VISA, AX, DS, PC, TC. TAC10. 34 rooms with PB and 3 suites. Types of meals: Full bkfst and gourmet dinner. EP. Beds: Q. Cable TV and phone in room. VCR, fax, copier, swimming, sauna, stables, bicycles, tennis, library, child care, downhill skiing and cross country skiing and golf on premises. Handicap access. Weddings, small meetings, family reunions and seminars hosted. Bicycling, fishing, golf, hiking, live theater, parks, shopping, downhill skiing and tennis nearby.

Campton   G4

Colonel Spencer Inn

3 Colonel Spencer Rd
Campton, NH 03223
(603)536-3438
Web: www.colonelspencerinn.com

Circa 1764. This pre-Revolutionary Colonial boasts Indian shutters, gleaming plank floors and a secret hiding place. Joseph Spencer, one of the home's early owners, fought at

Bunker Hill and with General Washington. Within view of the river and the mountains, the inn is now a cozy retreat with warm Colonial decor. A suite with a kitchen is also available.

Innkeeper(s): Carolyn & Alan Hill. $45-65. PC, TC. TAC10. 7 rooms with PB and 1 suite. Breakfast and snacks/refreshments included in rates. Types of meals: Full bkfst. Beds: D. Fans in room. Small meetings and family reunions hosted. Antiquing, fishing, water parks, live theater, parks, shopping, downhill skiing, cross-country skiing, sporting events and water sports nearby.

"You have something very special here, and we very much enjoyed a little piece of it!"

Mountain-Fare Inn

Mad River Rd, PO Box 553
Campton, NH 03223
(603)726-4283
E-mail: mtnfareinn@cyberportal.net
Web: www.mountainfareinn.com

Circa 1830. Located in the White Mountains between Franconia Notch and Squam Lake, this white farmhouse is surrounded by flower gardens in the summer and unparalleled

foliage in the fall. Mountain-Fare is an early 19th-century village inn in an ideal spot from which to enjoy New Hampshire's many offerings. Each season brings with it different activities, from skiing to biking and hiking or simply taking in the beautiful scenery. Skiers will enjoy the inn's lodge atmosphere during the winter, as well as the close access to ski areas. The inn is appointed in a charming New Hampshire style with country-cottage decor. There's a game room with billiards and a soccer field for playing ball. The hearty breakfast is a favorite of returning guests.

Historic Interest: Franconia Notch (Old Man of the Mountain), Squam Lake (Golden Pond), and drive the Scenic Kancamagus Highway.

Innkeeper(s): Susan & Nick Preston. $85-135. MC, VISA. 10 rooms, 8 with PB. Breakfast and afternoon tea included in rates. Types of meals: Full bkfst. MAP, EP. Beds: QDT. VCR, sauna, game room with billiards and soccer field on premises. Weddings, small meetings and family reunions hosted. Antiquing, fishing, hiking, live theater, parks, downhill skiing, cross-country skiing, sporting events and water sports nearby.

Publicity: *Ski, Skiing and Snow Country.*

"Thank you for your unusually caring attitude toward your guests."

Center Ossipee   H5

Hitching Post Village Inn

Grant Hill Rd
Center Ossipee, NH 03814
(603)539-3360 (800)482-POST

Circa 1830. All the rooms of this historic inn are spacious and comfortable and overlook the main street, yard or garden. Two second-story rooms offer views of the white steeple of the First Congregational Church and the ever-changing colors of Ossipee Mountains. The canopy room boasts an antique four-poster queen canopy, while the Rose Room features a vintage dental cabinet filled with antique dolls. Items such as homemade sticky buns, stuffed French toast with apples and walnuts, potato pie or

chocolate chip pancakes are served for breakfast, often by the innkeeper's children donned with hats and aprons. This is one of the few inns in the area that welcome families with children, so there's plenty of thought given to their entertainment. They can play ping pong in the barn, climb Michael's Fort, a two-story playhouse, cross the street for basketball or the ice cream shop, or go down the road to pick apples. Other activities include canoeing, fishing, swimming and skiing.

Innkeeper(s): Michael & Jessica Drakely. $57-67. MC, VISA, AX, DS, PC, TC. 9 rooms, 1 with PB and 1 conference room. Breakfast and afternoon tea included in rates. Types of meals: Country bkfst and early coffee/tea. Beds: KQDT. VCR on premises. Weddings and family reunions hosted. Amusement parks, antiquing, beaches, bicycling, canoeing/kayaking, fishing, golf, hiking, horseback riding, live theater, parks, shopping, downhill skiing, cross-country skiing, tennis, water sports and wineries nearby.

Pets Allowed.

Center Sandwich   G4

Overlook Farm B&B

14 Mountain Rd
Center Sandwich, NH 03227-3557
(603)284-6485
E-mail: b.b.farm@juno.com

Circa 1783. If one were to conjure up an image of a representative New England farmhouse, Overlook Farm might spring to mind. Nestled on 15 rolling acres with mountains as a backdrop, the bed & breakfast offers four comfortable guest rooms with Colonial decor and antiques. Among the historical arti-

facts of this 18th-century house is a wheel for the original well bucket, an old barn and granite walls. Innkeeper Phyllis Olafsen prepares a different, homemade breakfast every day, and also varies the table settings. Squam Lake is nearby, as is Lake Winnipesaukee and the White Mountains.

Innkeeper(s): Phyllis Olafsen. $65-85. PC, TC. 4 rooms, 2 with PB and 1 suite. Breakfast included in rates. Types of meals: Gourmet bkfst and early coffee/tea. Beds: QDT. Turndown service in room. VCR, library, wood stoves and canoe on premises. Family reunions hosted. Amusement parks, antiquing, fishing, golf, hiking in White Mountains, live theater, parks, shopping, tennis and water sports nearby.

"When we look back on our trip, your lovely home and warm hospitality is one of the things we remember the most."

Charlestown   J1

MapleHedge B&B

355 Main St, PO Box 638
Charlestown, NH 03603
(603)826-5237 (800)962-7539 Fax:(603)826-5237
E-mail: debrine@fmis.net
Web: www.maplehedge.com

Circa 1820. This elegantly restored home is set among acres of lawn and 200-year-old maple trees. The bed & breakfast boasts five distinctive bedrooms. The Beale Room is named for the innkeeper's grandparents from Buffalo; her grandma's high button shoes and Larkin products are displayed. The Butterfly Suite

is filled with white wicker and Victorian butterfly trays. The rooms are furnished in antiques and beds are topped with freshly ironed linens. A delectable three-course breakfast is served includes fresh fruit, homemade muffins or scones and a special hot entree. Evening refreshments include California wine with New Hampshire cheese. Guests can go antiquing, attend country auctions or visit historic sites. There are many

outdoor activities, as well. The innkeeper keeps brochures and tourist information on hand and will send them on request.

Historic Interest: Located within the longest National Historic District in the state, Fort Number Four (1 mile), Saint Gauden's National Historic Site (20 minutes), and Dartmouth College (35 minutes).

Innkeeper(s): Joan & Dick DeBrine. $90-105. MC, VISA, PC. TAC10. 5 rooms with PB, 1 suite and 1 conference room. Breakfast and afternoon tea included in rates. Types of meals: Gourmet bkfst, early coffee/tea and snacks/refreshments. Beds: QT. Turndown service in room. Central air. Fax, copier, library and life safety system on premises. Small meetings, family reunions and seminars hosted. Antiquing, fishing, golf, live theater, parks, shopping, downhill skiing, cross-country skiing, sporting events, tennis and water sports nearby.

Publicity: *Country Living, San Mateo Times, San Francisco Chronicle, Union Leader, Newsday, Buffalo News, Country Magazine, BBC and WHTV-"If these walls could talk"*

"The highlight of my two weeks in New England. A breakfast worth jumping out of bed for."

Claremont   I2

Goddard Mansion B&B

25 Hillstead Rd
Claremont, NH 03743-3317
(603)543-0603 (800)736-0603 Fax:(603)543-0001
E-mail: deb@goddardmansion.com
Web: www.goddardmansion.com

Circa 1905. This English-style manor house and adjacent garden tea house is surrounded by seven acres of lawns and gardens. Each of the guest rooms is decorated in a different style.

One features French Country decor, another sports a Victorian look. The living room with its fireplace, window seats and baby grand piano is a perfect place to relax. Homemade breakfasts, made using natural ingredients and fresh produce, include items such as souffles, pancakes, freshly baked muffins and fruit. The hearty breakfasts are served in the wood paneled dining room highlighted by an antique Wurlitzer jukebox.

Innkeeper(s): Debbie Albee. $75-125. MC, VISA, AX, DS, PC, TC. 10 rooms, 3 with PB, 1 suite and 2 conference rooms. Breakfast included in rates. Types of meals: Gourmet bkfst and cont plus. Beds: KQDT. TV, phone, turndown service and some desks in room. Air conditioning. VCR, fax, bicycles, library, child care available and internet connection on premises. Weddings, small meetings, family reunions and seminars hosted. Antiquing, fishing, live theater, parks, shopping, downhill skiing and cross-country skiing nearby.

Publicity: *Eagle Times, Yankee (editors pick), Boston Globe and Manchester Union Leader.*

"A perfect romantic getaway spot."

Cornish

I2

Chase House B&B Inn

Rt 12A, RR 2 Box 909
Cornish, NH 03745
(603)675-5391 (800)401-9455 Fax:(603)675-5010
Web: www.chasehouse.com

Circa 1776. Cornish's first English settler, Dudley Chase, built this Federal house noted for its fine architecture. In 1845, it was moved to accommodate the Sullivan County Railroad. Designated a National Historic Landmark, it was the birthplace

of Salmon Chase, Governor of Ohio, Secretary of the Treasury for President Lincoln and Chief Justice of the Supreme Court. The Chase Manhattan Bank was named after him.

Historic Interest: Saint Gauden's Historic Site (5 minutes), Fort Number Four (30 minutes), American Precision Museum (5 minutes), Dartmouth College (30 minutes).

Innkeeper(s): Barbara Lewis & Ted Doyle. $115-150. MC, VISA. 6 rooms with PB, 1 with FP and 3 suites. Breakfast included in rates. Types of meals: Full bkfst. Beds: KQDT. Antiquing, hiking and canoeing nearby, downhill skiing and cross-country skiing nearby.

Publicity: *Hartford Courant, The Philadelphia Inquirer and USA Today.*

Durham

J6

The Pines Guest House

47 Dover Rd, Rt 108
Durham, NH 03824
(603)868-3361
E-mail: coescorner@aol.com
Web: www.pinesguesthouse.com

Circa 1870. This rambling Victorian manor is surrounded by 15 acres of countryside, including a pond. The home has remained in the same family for five generations, and many of the furnishings are family pieces. The screened-in porches are set up with wicker furniture for those who wish to relax. Three of the guest rooms include a fireplace. Breakfasts are served in a dining room decorated with period furniture. Tables are set with antique china and silver. The University of New Hampshire is a half-mile from the home.

Innkeeper(s): Roger & Mary Margaret Jaques. $75-115. MC, VISA, AX, PC, TC. TAC10. 4 rooms with PB, 3 with FP. Breakfast included in rates. Types of meals: Cont plus and early coffee/tea. Beds: QDT. Cable TV, phone and VCR in room. Air conditioning. Library and screened porch with wicker in season; family room/art gallery for reading on premises. French spoken. Antiquing, fishing, live theater, parks, shopping, cross-country skiing, sporting events and water sports nearby.

"What a beautiful setting with these towering pines."

East Andover

I4

Highland Lake Inn B&B

32 Maple St, PO Box 164
East Andover, NH 03231-0164
(603)735-6426 Fax:(603)735-5355
E-mail: highlandlakeinn@msn.com
Web: www.highlandlakeinn.com

Circa 1767. This early Colonial-Victorian inn overlooks three mountains, and all the rooms have views of either the lake or the mountains. Many guest rooms feature handmade quilts and

some have four-poster beds. Guests may relax with a book from the inn's library in front of the sitting room fireplace or walk the seven-acre grounds and enjoy old apple and maple trees, as well as the shoreline of the lake. Adjacent to a 21-acre nature conservancy, there are scenic trails and a stream to explore. Highland Lake is stocked with bass and also has trout. Fresh fruit salads, hot entrees, and home-made breads are featured at breakfast.

Historic Interest: Two Shaker Villages, old one-room school house.

Innkeeper(s): Steve & Judee Hodges. $85-125. MC, VISA, AX, DS. 10 rooms with PB, 2 with FP. Breakfast and snacks/refreshments included in rates. Types of meals: Gourmet bkfst, country bkfst and early coffee/tea. Beds: KQT. Ceiling fan and fireplace in room. VCR, fax, copier, swimming, library and gift shop on premises. Weddings, small meetings, family reunions and seminars hosted. Antiquing, art galleries, beaches, bicycling, canoeing/kayaking, fishing, golf, hiking, shopping, downhill skiing and cross-country skiing nearby.

Publicity: *Intertown, Neighbors and Valley Business Journal.*

"New Hampshire at its most magical."

Eaton Center

G6

The Inn at Crystal Lake

Rt 153 Eaton Center
Eaton Center, NH 03832
(603)447-2120 (800)343-7336 Fax:(603)447-3599
E-mail: stay@innatcrystellake.com
Web: www.innatcrystallake.com

Circa 1884. Balconies with flower boxes, a veranda and shutters add an inviting warmth to this three-story, yellow and white, Greek Victorian Revival inn. A cheerful dining room is just one of the inn's common rooms. There is a library, parlor and billiards room, as well. An old-fashioned country decor extends throughout the inn. The innkeepers provide a canoe or paddle boat to explore the shoreline of Crystal Lake. In winter, there is ice skating, ice fishing and sleigh rides. Five major ski areas and the National Forest are all nearby, and Conway is six miles away.

Historic Interest: Built in 1884, it was a stagecoach stop and the first post office.

Innkeeper(s): Bobby Barker & Tim Ostendorf. $79-209. MC, VISA, PC, TC. 11 rooms with PB and 1 suite. Breakfast and snacks/refreshments included in rates. Types of meals: Full bkfst, country bkfst and early coffee/tea. Beds: QDT. Cable TV, phone, VCR, fireplace, library and collection of CDs and videos in room. Air conditioning. Library on premises. Weddings, small meetings, family reunions and seminars hosted. Antiquing, art galleries, beaches, bicycling, canoeing/kayaking, fishing, golf, hiking, horseback riding, live theater, museums, parks, shopping, downhill skiing, cross-country skiing, tennis and water sports nearby.

Rockhouse Mountain Farm Inn

PO Box 90
Eaton Center, NH 03832-0090
(603)447-2880

Circa 1900. This handsome old house is framed by maple trees on 450 acres of forests, streams, fields, wildflowers and songbirds. A variety of farm animals provide entertainment for city youngsters of all ages. Three generations of the Edges have operated this inn, and some guests have been coming since 1946, the year it opened. A 250-

year-old barn bulges at times with new-mown hay, and there is a private beach nearby with swimming and boating for the exclusive use of Rockhouse guests.

Innkeeper(s): Johnny & Alana Edge. $68. PC, TC. 15 rooms, 7 with PB, 1 with FP. Breakfast and dinner included in rates. Types of meals: Full bkfst. MAP. Beds: DT. TV in room. Swimming, library and farm animals on premises. Handicap access. Small meetings and family reunions hosted. French spoken. Antiquing, fishing, golf, live theater, parks, shopping, tennis and water sports nearby.

Publicity: *New York Times, Family Circle, Woman's Day, Boston Globe and Country Vacations.*

"We have seen many lovely places, but Rockhouse remains the real high spot, the one to which we most want to return."

Enfield   H2

Mary Keane House

Box 5 Lower Shaker Village, Rt 4 A
Enfield, NH 03748
(603)632-4241 (888)239-2153
E-mail: mary.keane.house@valley.net
Web: www.marykeanehouse.com

Circa 1930. This lakeside Queen Anne Victorian is pristinely restored and painted mauve with gray and white trim. It adjoins a chapel, all encircled with a white picket fence. Views from the porches and balconies include the inn's flower beds, Lake Mascoma and 1,200 acres of woodland and meadow. A handsome drawing room with antiques and fireplace, mahogany paneling,  stained and beveled glass, and a gracious front staircase are featured. Mini frittatas with salsa, rhubarb coffee cake and hot oatmeal scones are among the items offered on the inn's bountiful table. Walk to the Shaker Museum, herb gardens, Shaker Village and the Dana Robes Woodcraftsmen Workshop where Shaker furniture is fashioned.

Innkeeper(s): Sharon & David Carr. $95-155. MC, VISA, AX, DS, TC. TAC10. 5 rooms with PB. Breakfast included in rates. Types of meals: Gourmet bkfst and early coffee/tea. AP. Beds: KQDT. Cable TV in room. VCR, copier, swimming, library, 3 suites and air conditioning on premises. Weddings, small meetings and family reunions hosted. Antiquing, fishing, golf, live theater, shopping, downhill skiing, cross-country skiing, sporting events, tennis and water sports nearby.

Pets allowed: If well-behaved.

Shaker Farm Bed & Breakfast

597 NH Route 4-A
Enfield, NH 03748-9317
(603)632-7664 (800)613-7664 Fax:(603)632-9290
E-mail: shaker.farm@valley.net
Web: www.shakerfarm.com

Circa 1794. Sleep in an authentic 18th-century South Family Shaker Farmhouse on five acres and enjoy the hospitality of an innkeeper who knows all about the Shakers. Charlotte Toms, who, with her husband Hal, owns the inn, writes historical novels, including two Shaker novels. The inn's six large guest bedrooms, some with views of Mascoma Lake and the mountains, are decorated in period antiques and reproductions. Each morning a country breakfast is served, which includes mouth-watering delights - for instance, fruit medley, eggs Benedict, blueberry

muffins, bacon and sausage, French toast, baked apples and home fries. A fruit bowl and snacks are also provided throughout the day. The inn itself is a city, state and national historic site. It is located near the Shaker Museum, the Shaker Cemetery and other historic Shaker sites. Guests can also enjoy outdoor activities including wintertime snowmobiling and cross-country skiing, and summertime swimming, fishing and boating in the Mascoma Lake. A computer is available, should guests need one, or they can step out onto the secluded deck and simply enjoy the view.

Historic Interest: Shaker Museum, Shaker Cemetery, Dartmouth College.

Innkeeper(s): Hal & Charlotte Toms. $75-125. MC, VISA, PC, TC. TAC5. 6 rooms with PB. Breakfast and snacks/refreshments included in rates. Types of meals: Country bkfst and early coffee/tea. Beds: K. Cable TV, ceiling fan and VCR in room. Air conditioning. Fax, copier and library on premises. Small meetings hosted. Antiquing, art galleries, beaches, bicycling, canoeing/kayaking, fishing, golf, hiking, horseback riding, live theater, museums, parks, shopping, downhill skiing, cross-country skiing, sporting events, tennis and water sports nearby.

Franconia   F3

Franconia Inn

1300 Easton Rd
Franconia, NH 03580-4921
(603)823-5542 (800)473-5299 Fax:(603)823-8078
E-mail: info@franconiainn.com
Web: www.franconiainn.com

Circa 1934. Beautifully situated on 117 acres below the White Mountain's famous Franconia Notch, this white clapboard inn is three stories high. An oak-paneled library, parlor, rathskeller lounge and two verandas offer relaxing retreats. The inn's rooms are simply decorated in a pleasing style and there is a special honeymoon suite with private Jacuzzi. Bach, classic wines and an elegant American cuisine are featured  in the inn's unpretentious dining room. There's no shortage of activity here. The inn offers four clay tennis courts, horseback riding, a heated swimming pool, croquet, fishing, cross-country ski trails and glider rides among its outdoor amenities.

Innkeeper(s): Alec Morris. $103-188. MC, VISA, AX. 34 rooms, 29 with PB, 3 with FP, 4 suites, 1 cottage and 1 conference room. Breakfast included in rates. Types of meals: Gourmet bkfst, early coffee/tea, picnic lunch and gourmet dinner. MAP, EP. Beds: KQDT. VCR, copier, spa, swimming, bicycles, tennis, child care, sleighs and ice skating on premises. Weddings, small meetings, family reunions and seminars hosted. Amusement parks, antiquing, fishing, live theater, parks, shopping, downhill skiing, cross-country skiing and sporting events nearby.

Publicity: *Philadelphia Inquirer, Boston Globe, Travel & Leisure and Powder.*

"The piece de resistance of the Franconia Notch is the Franconia Inn—Philadelphia Inquirer."

Franklin   I4

Maria W. Atwood Inn

Rt 3A
Franklin, NH 03235
(603)934-3666
E-mail: info@atwoodinn.com
Web: www.atwoodinn.com

Circa 1830. Candles in the windows welcome guests to this handsome two-and-a-half story brick Federal home, which was built by Joseph Burleigh. Well-landscaped grounds with tall trees and green lawns frame the house. Many original features remain, including interior Indian shutters, old locks, Count Rumford fireplaces and wide-plank wood floors. Recently renovated, the rooms offer country furnishings, quilts, antiques and art. Full breakfasts are served by candlelight in the inn's library. Tilton School, Proctor Academy and New Hampton School are nearby. The Lakes Region provides a wide variety of outdoor recreation. Especially popular is canoeing and kayaking on the Pemigewasset and Merrimack Rivers. Theater, antique shops, boutiques and restaurants are also at hand.

Innkeeper(s): Fred & Sandi Hoffmeister. $80-90. MC, VISA, AX, DC, PC, TC. TAC10. 7 rooms with PB, 4 with FP. Breakfast, afternoon tea and snacks/refreshments included in rates. Types of meals: Full bkfst and early coffee/tea. Beds: QDT. Ceiling fan in room. Air conditioning. Small meetings and family reunions hosted. Antiquing, bicycling, fishing, golf, hiking, snow-mobiling, outlets, boating, live theater, parks, shopping, downhill skiing and cross-country skiing nearby.

Publicity: *Concord, Monitor and Wiers Times.*

"Wouldn't stay anywhere else."

Gilmanton   I5

The Historic Temperance Tavern

PO Box 369
Gilmanton, NH 03237-0369
(603)267-7349 Fax:(603)267-7503

Circa 1793. This historic Colonial inn has been welcoming visitors for more than 200 years, and it acquired its name during a temperance movement in the early 19th century. The inn offers five guest rooms, including one suite, all of which feature private baths and turndown service. The rooms all boast furnishings that reflect an authentic Federal decor. Visitors enjoy the inn's many fireplaces, its common rooms and fine food. Guests often schedule outings to Gunstock Mountain Ski Resort, Loudon Raceway and Shaker Village.

Innkeeper(s): Beverly Nemetz. $75-125. MC, VISA, TC. 6 rooms, 5 with PB, 2 with FP, 1 suite and 1 conference room. Breakfast included in rates. Types of meals: Gourmet bkfst, early coffee/tea, gourmet lunch, picnic lunch and gourmet dinner. MAP. Beds: T. VCR, fax and copier on premises. Weddings, small meetings, family reunions and seminars hosted. Amusement parks, antiquing, fishing, parks, shopping, downhill skiing, cross-country skiing, sporting events and water sports nearby.

Pets allowed: By prior arrangement.

Publicity: *New Hampshire Magazine.*

Glen   F5

Bernerhof Inn

Rt 302, PO Box 240
Glen, NH 03838-0240
(603)383-9132 (800)548-8007 Fax:(603)383-0809
E-mail: stay@bernerhofinn.com
Web: www.bernerhofinn.com

Circa 1880. This historic inn was built in the late 19th century for travelers passing through Crawford Notch. The inn was given its current name in the 1950s by the proprietors, the Zumsteins, who became known for providing fine accommodations, musical entertainment and foods reflecting their Swiss heritage. Today's innkeepers, entering their 25th year, are proud to continue to offer European-influenced cuisine. The Black Bear

Pub serves more casual fare. Guest bedrooms are decorated with antiques and many include two-person Jacuzzi tubs. One features a fireplace. Novice and experienced chefs alike enjoy learning tricks of the trade at Taste of the Mountains Cooking School. Located in the foothills of the White Mountains. There is easy access to a variety of outdoor activities including alpine and summer water slides at Attitash Bear Peak.

Innkeeper(s): Sharon Wroblewski. $79-175. MC, VISA, AX, DS, PC, TC. 9 rooms with PB and 2 suites. Breakfast included in rates. Types of meals: Full bkfst, early coffee/tea, picnic lunch, gourmet dinner and room service. MAP. Beds: KQ. Cable TV, phone, ceiling fan, VCR, most with spa-tub Jacuzzi and one with fireplace in room. Air conditioning. Fax, copier and sauna on premises. Weddings, small meetings and family reunions hosted. Amusement parks, antiquing, bicycling, fishing, golf, hiking, rock climbing, ice climbing, snow shoeing, live theater, parks, shopping, downhill skiing and cross-country skiing nearby.

Publicity: *Yankee Magazine, Boston Globe, Bon Appetit, Good Housekeeping, Skiing, Gault Millau, Country New England Inns and Weekends for Two in New England:50 Romantic Getaways Inn Spots & Special Places in New England.*

"When people want to treat themselves, this is where they come."

Covered Bridge House B&B

Rt 302
Glen, NH 03838
(603)383-9109 (800)232-9109 Fax:(603)383-8089
E-mail: info@coveredbridgehouse.com
Web: www.coveredbridgehouse.com

Circa 1910. The two-acre grounds at this inn boast the only privately owned covered bridge with a gift shop inside. The bridge, which dates to 1850, houses the inn's gift shop. The grounds also include a private beach area that rests along side a river where guests can go swimming or tubing. Guest rooms are decorated in a country Colonial style with quilts, floral comforters and stenciled walls. Breakfasts include fresh fruit, homemade muffins and made-to-order eggs or perhaps French toast.

Innkeeper(s): Dan & Nancy Wanek. $59-109. MC, VISA, AX, DS, PC, TC. 6 rooms, 4 with PB. Breakfast included in rates. Types of meals: Full bkfst and early coffee/tea. Beds: KQT. Ceiling fan in room. Air conditioning. Spa, swimming and in warmer weather breakfast served on the patio on premises. Family reunions hosted. Amusement parks, antiquing, fishing, golf, live theater, parks, shopping, downhill skiing, cross-country skiing, tennis and water sports nearby.

Hampstead   K5

Stillmeadow B&B at Hampstead

545 Main St, PO Box 565
Hampstead, NH 03841
(603)329-8381 Fax:(603)329-0137
E-mail: stillmeadowb@yahoo.com

Circa 1850. The old Ordway home rests on several acres on the Main Street of Hampstead. The Dawn Suite features a brass bed and a sitting area with a trundle bed. Children are welcome in the Tulip Suite, which offers a crib and other amenities. The cookie jar at Stillmeadow is said to always be full. Walk to orchards, hiking and cross-country conservation trails, as well as shops. Sunset Lake and the Robert Frost Farm are nearby. The inn is convenient to Boston, Manchester, Salem, Portsmouth, the seacoast and the mountains.

Innkeeper(s): Lori Offord. $75-100. MC, VISA, AX, DS. 4 rooms with PB. Types of meals: Cont plus. Beds: QD.

Publicity: *Lawrence Eagle Tribune, New Hampshire Profiles, Yankee Magazine and Carriage Town News.*

"No less than monumental."

Hampton K6

The Oceanside Inn

365 Ocean Blvd
Hampton, NH 03842-3633
(603)926-3542 Fax:(603)926-3549
E-mail: oceansid@nh.ultranet.com

Circa 1900. Directly across the street from the ocean and adjacent to the Oceanside Mall, this romantic two-story inn with upper veranda is an adult-oriented, smoke-free establishment. Elegant interiors include a pillared living room/library with fire

place, Oriental rugs, paintings and comfortable sitting areas. The Moses Leavitt Room, a typical guest bedroom, features a canopy bed. Nightly turndown service is offered. Each night, order a light continental, or choice of eggs and occasional specialties from a breakfast menu served fresh the next morning. Chairs and towels are available for taking to the local beaches.

Innkeeper(s): Skip & Debbie Windemiller. $150-195. MC, VISA, AX, DS, TC. TAC5. 9 rooms with PB. Breakfast included in rates. Types of meals: Cont plus. Beds: KQDT. Phone, turndown service and safe in room. Central air. VCR, fax, copier and library on premises. Amusement parks, antiquing, golf, live theater, shopping, tennis and water sports nearby.

Henniker J3

Colby Hill Inn

3 The Oaks, PO Box 779
Henniker, NH 03242-0779
(603)428-3281 (800)531-0330 Fax:(603)428-9218
E-mail: info@colbyhillinn.com
Web: www.colbyhillinn.com

Circa 1797. This 18th-century Colonial and its surrounding five acres is a classic example of an old New England Farm. There are antique barns on the grounds, as well as a restored carriage house. Stroll the grounds and you'll find gardens, a swimming pool and a picturesque gazebo. Antiques fill the guest rooms, each of which is individually appointed in an elegant, traditional style. Four rooms have working fireplaces. Guests and others can enjoy a romantic din

ner by candlelight at the inn's dining room which overlooks the lush perennial gardens.

Innkeeper(s): Cyndi & Mason Cobb. $105-195. MC, VISA, AX, DC, CB, DS, PC, TC. TAC10. 16 rooms with PB, 4 with FP and 1 conference room. Breakfast included in rates. Types of meals: Gourmet bkfst, early coffee/tea, snacks/refreshments, gourmet dinner and room service. Beds: KQDT. Phone and data port in room. Air conditioning. VCR, fax, copier and swimming on premises. Weddings, small meetings, family reunions and seminars hosted. Antiquing, fishing, Canterbury Shaker village, parks, downhill skiing and cross-country skiing nearby.

Holderness H4

The Inn on Golden Pond

Rt 3, PO Box 680
Holderness, NH 03245
(603)968-7269 Fax:(603)968-9226
E-mail: innongp@lr.net
Web: www.innongoldenpond.com

Circa 1879. Framed by meandering stone walls and split-rail fences more than 100 years old, this inn is situated on 50 acres of woodlands. Most rooms overlook picturesque countryside and nearby is Squam Lake, setting for the film "On Golden Pond." An inviting, 60-foot screened porch provides a place to relax during the summer.

Innkeeper(s): Bill & Bonnie Webb. $105-165. MC, VISA, AX, DS, PC, TC. TAC10. 8 rooms with PB, 1 suite and 1 conference room. Breakfast included in rates. Types of meals: Full bkfst, country bkfst and early coffee/tea. Beds: KQT. Turndown service in room. Air conditioning. Fax, library and gift shop on premises. Antiquing, art galleries, beaches, bicycling, canoeing/kayaking, fishing, golf, hiking, horseback riding, live theater, museums, parks, shopping, downhill skiing, cross-country skiing, sporting events, tennis and water sports nearby.

Publicity: *Boston Globe, Baltimore Sun and Los Angeles Times.*

"Another sweet flower added to my bouquet of life."

Manor on Golden Pond

Rt 3 Box T
Holderness, NH 03245
(603)968-3348 (800)545-2141 Fax:(603)968-2116
E-mail: info@manorongoldenpond.com
Web: www.manorongoldenpond.com

Circa 1903. An Englishman and land developer had a boyhood dream of living in a beautiful mansion high on a hill overlooking lakes and mountains. After he discovered these beautiful 13 acres, he brought craftsmen from around the world to build an English-style country mansion. Old world charm is reflected at this manor by marble fireplaces and the hand-carved mahogany lobby.

Innkeeper(s): Brian & Mary Ellen Shields. $165-375. MC, VISA, AX, PC, TC. TAC10. 25 rooms with PB, 13 with FP. Breakfast and afternoon tea included in rates. Types of meals: Gourmet bkfst and gourmet dinner. EP. Beds: DT. Phone and nine with whirlpool tubs in room. Air conditioning. Fax and copier on premises. Hiking, bird watching, downhill skiing and water sports nearby.

Publicity: *The Best of New England "Hideaway Report" August 1999, Connecticut Magazine and Frommer's.*

"Out of a magazine on how the rich decorate but still comfortable and relaxing."

Intervale F5

The Forest - A Country Inn

PO Box 37
Intervale, NH 03845-0037
(603)356-9772 (800)448-3534 Fax:(603)356-5652
E-mail: forest@moose.ncia.net
Web: www.forest-inn.com

Circa 1830. Situated on 25 wooded acres with a stream, this country Victorian bed & breakfast offers easy access to the many attractions of Mt. Washington Valley. Relax while enjoying afternoon refreshments on the screened-in porch or fireside in the living room. Well-decorated guest bedrooms are furnished with antique treasures. The romantic stone cottage rooms offer a private setting and boast four-poster beds and fireplaces. Morning brings the anticipation of fresh fruit, homemade baked goods, and entrees like Apple Pancakes, Spiced Belgian Waffles and Amaretto French Toast. Cross-country skiing, river canoeing and swimming in the pool are fun seasonal activities.

Innkeeper(s): Bill & Lisa Guppy. $70-169. MC, VISA, AX, DS, PC, TC. TAC10. 11 rooms with PB, 5 with FP and 3 cottages. Breakfast and snacks/refreshments included in rates. Types of meals: Full bkfst. Beds: Q. Ceiling fan in room. Fax and swimming on premises. Family reunions and seminars hosted. Amusement parks, antiquing, fishing, live theater, parks, shopping, downhill skiing, cross-country skiing, sporting events and water sports nearby.

Jackson   F5

Carter Notch Inn

Carter Notch Rd, Box 269
Jackson, NH 03846
(603)383-9630 (800)794-9434
E-mail: dunwell@landmarknet.net
Web: www.carternotchinn.com

Circa 1900. This turn-of-the-century home rests on a wooded acre, offering views of the surrounding mountains, Eagle Mt. Golf Course and the Wildcat River. Guest rooms are charming, some have painted wood floors, throw rugs, quilts and wicker or oak furnishings. The innkeepers latest addition is "The Treehouse," which features suites with two-person Jacuzzi tubs, private decks and fireplaces. Breakfast is a treat; be sure to ask for Jim's Grand Marnier French toast. Cross-country ski trails begin right out the front door, as does golfing. Hiking and other outdoor activities abound in the area. After a day touring the area, return to the inn for a relaxing soak in the outdoor hot tub or sit on the wraparound front porch and enjoy the view.

Innkeeper(s): Jim & Lynda Dunwell. $69-179. MC, VISA, AX, DS, PC, TC. TAC10. 7 rooms, 6 with PB and 1 suite. Breakfast and afternoon tea included in rates. Types of meals: Gourmet bkfst and early coffee/tea. Beds: KQD. Air conditioning. VCR, fax, spa, swimming, tennis, golf and fishing on premises. Weddings, small meetings, family reunions and seminars hosted. Antiquing, live theater, parks, downhill skiing, cross-country skiing, tennis and water sports nearby.

The Crowes' Nest

PO Box 427 Thorn Mountain Road
Jackson, NH 03846
(603)383-8913 (800)511-8383 Fax:(603)383-8241
E-mail: tcn@crowesnest.net
Web: www.crowesnest.net

Circa 1922. Each season brings a new adventure to this elegant Colonial inn surrounded by the tranquil beauty of White Mountain National Forest. There is room to roam outdoors as well as inside with spacious areas including the living room in the main house and the lodge's common room. The decor has an international flavor, in keeping with the innkeepers' extensive travels. Many of the guest bedrooms feature a fireplace, private balcony, Jacuzzi and breathtaking views. Breakfast in the dining room is an event to be savored. Poached pears in port

wine, coffee cake made with fresh blueberries from the garden and florentine frittata with fresh herbs are some of the mouth-watering dishes served. Relax on the patio and gardens overlooking the village, and be sure to visit Jackson Falls.

Innkeeper(s): Myles & Christine Crowe. $79-209. MC, VISA, AX, DS, PC, TC. TAC10. 7 rooms with PB, 4 with FP and 2 suites. Breakfast and afternoon tea included in rates. Types of meals: Full bkfst. Beds: KQ. Ceiling fan and fireplace in room. Air conditioning. Fax, library and gift shop on premises. Weddings, small meetings, family reunions and seminars hosted. French spoken. Amusement parks, antiquing, art galleries, bicycling, canoeing/kayaking, fishing, golf, hiking, horseback riding, live theater, museums, parks, shopping, downhill skiing, cross-country skiing, tennis and water sports nearby.

Pets Allowed.

Publicity: *Skeletons in the Closet.*

Dana Place Inn

Rt 16, Pinkham Notch Rd
Jackson, NH 03846
(603)383-6822 (800)537-9276 Fax:(603)383-6022
E-mail: contact@danaplace.com
Web: www.danaplace.com

Circa 1860. The original owners received this Colonial farmhouse as a wedding present. The warm, cozy atmosphere of the inn is surpassed only by the spectacular mountain views. During autumn, the fall leaves explode with color, and guests can enjoy the surroundings while taking a hike or bike ride through the area. The beautiful Ellis River is the perfect place for an afternoon of fly-fishing or a picnic. After a scrumptious country breakfast, winter guests can step out the door and into skis for a day of cross-country skiing.

Historic Interest: Mount Washington Auto Road (5 miles), 1860s Coq. Railroad (30 miles).

Innkeeper(s): The Levine Family. $95-175. MC, VISA, AX, DC, CB, DS, PC, TC. TAC10. 35 rooms with PB. Breakfast and afternoon tea included in rates. Types of meals: Full bkfst, picnic lunch, gourmet dinner and room service. Beds: KQDT. VCR, fax, copier, spa, swimming, tennis, library and hiking on premises. Weddings, small meetings, family reunions and seminars hosted. Amusement parks, antiquing, fishing, golf, White Mountain attractions, live theater, parks, shopping, downhill skiing, cross-country skiing and water sports nearby.

Pets allowed: Exterior rooms.

Publicity: *Travel & Leisure, Inn Spots, Bon Appetit and Country Journal.*

"We had such a delightful time at Dana Place Inn. We will recommend you to everyone."

Nestlenook Farm Resort

Dinsmore Rd
Jackson, NH 03846
(603)383-9443 (800)659-9443 Fax:(603)383-4515
E-mail: inn@luxurymountaingetaways.com
Web: www.nestlenook.com

Circa 1790. Watch the sunset from the romantic gingerbread-trimmed lakeside gazebo complete with fireplace on this pristine 65-acre estate. The 200-year-old Victorian main house and the new addition, Victorian Village, offer a wide choice of accommodations including penthouses and villas. An abundance of activities are provided such as fly fishing on the scenic river that runs alongside the property. Horse-drawn sleigh rides, ice skating and snow shoeing are popular in cold weather, while summer finds

guests lining up for the carriage ride, complete with champagne service. Boating, hiking, biking and enjoying the award-winning gardens are popular, as well. Each guest room has its own two-person Jacuzzi and antique furnishings. In the dining room is a handsome Victorian bird cage housing exotic finches. The resort is smoke-free.

Innkeeper(s): Robert Cyr. $125-679. MC, VISA, DS. TAC10. 21 rooms with PB. Types of meals: Full bkfst and snacks/refreshments. Beds: KQ. Phone in room. Air conditioning. Fax, copier, swimming, bicycles, recreation room with stereo, VCR and surround sound and antique pool table on premises. Antiquing, fishing, hiking, carriage rides, live theater, parks, shopping, downhill skiing, cross-country skiing and water sports nearby.

Publicity: *Country Living, Country Inns, Ski, Friends, Manage Quebec and Discerning Traveler.*

Whitneys' Inn Jackson

Rt 16B, PO Box 822
Jackson, NH 03846
(603)383-8916 (800)677-5737 Fax:(603)383-6886
E-mail: whitneys@ncia.net
Web: whitneysinn.com

Circa 1842. This country inn offers romance, family recreation and a lovely setting at the base of the Black Mountain Ski Area. The inn specializes in recreation, as guests enjoy cookouts, cross-country and downhill skiing, hiking, lawn games, skating, sledding, sleigh rides, swimming and tennis. Popular nearby activities include trying out Jackson's two golf courses and picnicking at Jackson Falls.

Innkeeper(s): Bob Bowman. $74-163. MC, VISA, AX, DC, DS, PC, TC. TAC10. 30 rooms with PB, 3 with FP, 8 suites, 2 cottages and 2 conference rooms. Breakfast and afternoon tea included in rates. Types of meals: Country bkfst, early coffee/tea and lunch. MAP. Beds: KQDT. Cable TV and some with refrigerator in room. Air conditioning. VCR, fax, copier, spa, swimming, tennis, library, child care and heated swimming pool on premises. Weddings, small meetings, family reunions and seminars hosted. Amusement parks, antiquing, art galleries, bicycling, canoeing/kayaking, fishing, golf, hiking, horseback riding, live theater, shopping, downhill skiing, cross-country skiing, tennis and water sports nearby.

Pets allowed: some rooms and cottages.

Publicity: *Bon Appetit, Ladies Home Journal and Ski.*

Jaffrey L3

The Benjamin Prescott Inn

Rt 124 E, 433 Turnpike Rd
Jaffrey, NH 03452
(603)532-6637 (888)950-6637 Fax:(603)532-6637
E-mail: bprescottinn@aol.com
Web: www.benjaminprescottinn.com

Circa 1853. Colonel Prescott arrived on foot in Jaffrey in 1775 with an ax in his hand and a bag of beans on his back. The family built this classic Greek Revival many years later. Now, candles light the windows, seen from the stonewall-lined lane adjacent to the inn. Each room bears the name of a Prescott family member and is furnished with antiques.

Innkeeper(s): Mimi and Lee Atwood. $80-160. MC, VISA, AX, PC, TC. TAC10. 10 rooms with PB and 3 suites. Breakfast included in rates. Types of meals: Full bkfst, country bkfst and early coffee/tea. EP. Beds: KQDT. TV, phone, ceiling fan, toiletries and private label glycerine soaps in room. Fax, copier, library, open cookie jar in winter and tea (on request) on premises. Weddings, small meetings, family reunions and seminars hosted. Antiquing, art galleries, bicycling, canoeing/kayaking, fishing, golf, hiking, horseback riding, national Shrine, lectures, concerts., live theater, museums, parks, shopping, downhill skiing, cross-country skiing, sporting events and water sports nearby.

"The coffee and breakfasts were delicious and the hospitality overwhelming."

Jefferson E4

Applebrook B&B

Rt 115A, PO Box 178
Jefferson, NH 03583-0178
(603)586-7713 (800)545-6504
E-mail: vacation@applebrook.com
Web: www.applebrook.com

Circa 1797. Panoramic views surround this large Victorian farmhouse nestled in the middle of New Hampshire's White Mountains. Guests can awake to the smell of freshly baked muffins made with locally picked berries. A comfortable, fire-lit sitting room boasts stained glass, a goldfish pool and a beautiful view of Mt. Washington. The romantic Nellie's Nook, includes a king-size bed and a balcony with views of the mountains and a two-person spa. Test your golfing skills at the nearby 18-hole championship

course, or spend the day antique hunting. A trout stream and spring-fed rock pool are nearby. Wintertime guests can ice skate or race through the powder at nearby ski resorts or by way of snowmobile, finish off the day with a moonlight toboggan ride. After a full day, guests can enjoy a soak in the hot tub under the stars, where they might see shooting stars or the Northern Lights.

Historic Interest: The area boasts several covered bridges within 10 miles of the bed & breakfast. The Cog Railroad is 15 miles away, while the Jefferson Historical Museum is only one mile from the inn.

Innkeeper(s): Sandra Conley & Martin Kelly. $60-100. MC, VISA, PC, TC. TAC10. 14 rooms, 8 with PB and 1 conference room. Breakfast included in rates. Types of meals: Full bkfst and early coffee/tea. Beds: KQDT. Ceiling fan in room. Spa and library on premises. Weddings, small meetings, family reunions and seminars hosted. Amusement parks, antiquing, fishing, live theater, parks, shopping, downhill skiing, cross-country skiing and water sports nearby.

Pets allowed: Two rooms kept pet-free; $6.00/night per pet-half of which is donated to Lancaster Humane Society.

Publicity: *Outside, PriceCostco Connection, New Hampshire Outdoor Companion and Outdoor.*

"We came for a night and stayed for a week."

Jefferson Inn

RR 1 Box 68 A, Rt 2
Jefferson, NH 03583
(603)586-7998 (800)729-7908 Fax:(603)586-7808
E-mail: jeffinn@ncia.net
Web: www.jeffersoninn.com

Circa 1896. A turret, gables and wraparound verandas characterize this romantic 19th-century Victorian home. Cradled in the White Mountain National Forest, the inn overlooks Jefferson Meadows to Franconia Notch, Mt. Washington and the north-

ern Presidential range. Each of the guest bedrooms and family suites boast a distinctively unique decor and offers privacy. Indulge in a leisurely full breakfast. Swim in the spring-fed pond across the street. During winter, it transforms into an ice skating rink. A horse-drawn wagon and sleigh rides are available. Afternoon beverages and homemade baked goods are served in the afternoon. The Weathervane Summer Theater provides nightly entertainment. Bikng and golf are nearby.

Innkeeper(s): Mark & Cindy Robert and Bette Bovio. $85-175. MC, VISA, AX, DS, PC, TC. 9 rooms with PB and 2 suites. Breakfast, afternoon tea and snacks/refreshments included in rates. Types of meals: Full bkfst and early coffee/tea. EP. Beds: KQDT. Turndown service, suites with TV and refrigerator in room. Fax, copier, board and card games on premises. Handicap access. Weddings, family reunions and seminars hosted. Amusement parks, antiquing, hiking, moose tours, snowmobiling, horse drawn sleigh rides, live theater, parks, downhill skiing and cross-country skiing nearby.

"Marvelous breakfast and a warm, comfortable atmosphere."

Keene   K2

Carriage Barn Guest Room
358 Main St
Keene, NH 03431-4146
(603)357-3812
E-mail: carriagebarn@carriagebarn.com
Web: www.carriagebarn.com

Circa 1870. Any season is the perfect time to visit New England, but if you come in the fall to Keene, you can see the most carved jack-o'lanterns ever assembled in one place—over 17,000 grinning pumpkins lining the streets and holding the current world record. Adding to this great experience is a stay at this renovated 19th-century barn, now a comfortable and homey B&B. All four guest rooms, decorated with antiques found in local shops, have private baths. Games, books and a refrigerator filled with cold drinks are available in the common room. A substantial continental breakfast includes muffins or coffee cake, bread, cereals, yogurt and fruit. If it's not Halloween, there's still plenty to do here. The nearby villages with their covered bridges, lakes and antique shops are postcard perfect. For the active visitor, hiking the popular Mount Monadnock, biking, canoeing, skiing and horseback riding are easily arranged.

Innkeeper(s): Dave & Marilee Rouillard. $75-125. MC, VISA, AX. 4 rooms with PB. Breakfast and snacks/refreshments included in rates. Types of meals: Cont plus. Beds: QT. Central air. VCR on premises. Antiquing, bicycling, canoeing/kayaking, fishing, golf, hiking, horseback riding, live theater, museums, parks, shopping, downhill skiing, cross-country skiing, sporting events and tennis nearby.

Lincoln   F4

Red Sleigh Inn
PO Box 562
Lincoln, NH 03251-0562
(603)745-8517
E-mail: redsleigh@linwoodnet.com

Circa 1900. This 1900 Colonial home in the heart of the White Mountains has seven guest rooms and offers splendid views and easy access to the area's abundant recreation. After breakfasting on innkeeper Loretta's famous blueberry muffins, guests may explore the countryside and enjoy skiing, snowmobiling, golfing, swimming, hiking and biking. Or guests may choose to wander through the town of Lincoln, enjoying its charm and indulging in shopping and dinner theatre.

Innkeeper(s): Bill & Loretta Deppe. $75-110. MC, VISA, TC. 7 rooms, 3 with PB. Breakfast included in rates. Types of meals: Full bkfst. Beds: KQT. VCR on premises. Weddings and family reunions hosted. Amusement parks, antiquing, fishing, live theater, parks, shopping, downhill skiing, cross-country skiing, sporting events and water sports nearby.

Publicity: *Newsday, Ski and Skiing.*

"Your ears must be ringing because we haven't stopped talking about the Red Sleigh Inn and its wonderful, caring owners."

Lisbon   F3

Ammonoosuc Inn
641 Bishop Road
Lisbon, NH 03585
(603)838-6118 (888)546-6118
E-mail: amminn@mail.com
Web: www.amminn.com

Circa 1880. Enjoy panoramic views at this 100-year-old Colonial inn on two acres in the Ammonoosuc

River Valley surrounded by the White Mountains. The inn has early American Décor. Next to a golf course, the inn offers golf packages. In the summer, guests relax on the wicker chairs on the wraparound porch and soak in the scenery. In the winter, they snuggle up to the wood stove in the pub. A continental breakfast is served in the honey-pine beamed dining room. Candlelight dinners with selections such as rack of lamb, salmon and steak are available. Besides golfing, guests can fish for brook trout in the river (Ammonoosuc means "fishing ground"), or they can travel just minutes to the White Mountains National Forest with attractions such as Old Man of the Mountain in Franconia Notch, Flume Gorge and Cannon Mountain Aerial Tramway. Hiking, horseback riding, biking, kayaking, canoeing, tennis, antiquing, theater and concerts are also available nearby. In the winter, there are numerous cross-country ski trails and a nearby major snowmobile trail.

Innkeeper(s): Jeni & Jim Lewis. $60-130. MC, VISA, PC, TC. TAC5. 9 rooms. Breakfast included in rates. Types of meals: Cont plus, afternoon tea and dinner. MAP. Beds: KQDT. VCR, fax, copier and library on premises. Weddings, small meetings, family reunions and seminars hosted. Antiquing, bicycling, canoeing/kayaking, fishing, golf, hiking, horseback riding, live theater, parks, downhill skiing, cross-country skiing and tennis nearby.

Pets allowed: One room, deposit required.

Littleton   E3

Beal House Inn Flying Moose Restaurant
2 W Main St
Littleton, NH 03561-3502
(603)444-2661 Fax:(603)444-6224
E-mail: info@bealhouseinn.com
Web: www.bealhouseinn.com

Circa 1833. Mrs. Beal first opened the doors of this Federal Renaissance farmhouse to lodgers in 1938. The Main Street landmark is centrally located in the White Mountains for year-round enjoyment. Refurbished and elegantly furnished with antiques,

the suites feature four-poster and canopy beds, fireplaces and clawfoot tubs. Relax in luxury with down comforters, bathrobes, coffee makers, CD players and satellite TV. A feta and fresh spinach fritatta with home-baked wheat bread, banana buttermilk pancakes served with local maple syrup, or other delicious recipes may be served for breakfast. Enjoy the pleasant interlude of afternoon tea. The inn's Flying Moose restaurant offers an extensive menu for fine dining.

Historic Interest: Located in the heart of the White Mountains. Littleton Opera House, Robert Frost House (1 mile).

Innkeeper(s): Jose Luis & Catherine Pawelek. $105-205. MC, VISA, AX. 9 rooms with PB, 5 suites and 1 conference room. Breakfast and afternoon tea included in rates. Types of meals: Full bkfst. Beds: KQD. Some with A/C and some with ceiling fans in room. Fax on premises. Small meetings hosted. Antiquing, bicycling, fishing, hiking, horseback riding, sleigh rides, live theater, parks, shopping, downhill skiing, cross-country skiing and water sports nearby.

Publicity: *Country Inns, Glamour, Le Soleil, Star Ledger, Miami Herald and Yankee.*

"These innkeepers know and understand people, their needs and wants. Attention to cleanliness and amenities, from check-in to check-out, is a treasure."

Edencroft Inn

120 North Littleton Rd
Littleton, NH 03261
(603)444-1158 (877)460-7101 Fax:(603)444-5671
E-mail: stay@edendroftinn.com
Web: www.edencroftinn.com

Circa 1886. Originally part of a vast summer estate sitting on a hill outside of this picturesque town in North Country, this turn-of-the-century home on five acres was wonderfully renovated as a bed & breakfast. The cheery foyer bids a warm welcome. Inviting common rooms offer a relaxing retreat. Spacious guest bedrooms, some with fireplaces and spa tubs, instill an elegant, leisurely ambiance with CD players and robes. Indulge in a well-prepared breakfast before embarking on the day's adventures.

Innkeeper(s): Dan & Kathy Hinds. $100-180. MC, VISA, AX, DS, PC, TC. 7 rooms with PB, 4 with FP and 1 suite. Breakfast included in rates. Types of meals: Gourmet bkfst. Beds: KQ. Cable TV, turndown service, ceiling fan, VCR, fireplace and terry robes in room. Air conditioning. Fax, copier, library and gift shop on premises. Amusement parks, antiquing, bicycling, canoeing/kayaking, fishing, golf, hiking, horseback riding, live theater, parks, shopping, downhill skiing and cross-country skiing nearby.

Thayers Inn

111 Main St
Littleton, NH 03561-4014
(603)444-6469 Fax:(800)634-8179
E-mail: don@thayersinn.com
Web: www.thayersinn.com

Circa 1843. Ulysses Grant is said to have spoken from the inn's balcony in 1869. In those days, fresh firewood and candles were delivered to guest rooms each day as well as a personal thunder-jug. The handsome facade features four 30-foot, hand-carved pillars and a cupola with views of the surrounding mountains.

Innkeeper(s): Don & Carolyn Lambert. $60-120. MC, VISA, AX, DC, CB, DS. 41 rooms, 38 with PB and 6 suites. Breakfast included in rates. Types of meals: Lunch and dinner. AP. Beds: KQDT. Fax, copier and Movies on premises. Antiquing, fishing, live theater, downhill skiing, cross-country skiing and water sports nearby.

Publicity: *Business Life, Vacationer, Bon Appetit and Yankee.*

"This Thanksgiving, Russ and I spent a lot of time thinking about the things that are most important to us. It seemed appropriate that we should write to thank you for your warm hospitality as innkeepers."

Lyme   G2

Alden Country Inn

One Market St
Lyme, NH 03768
(603)795-2222 (800)794-2296 Fax:(603)795-9436
E-mail: info@aldencountryinn.com
Web: www.aldencountryinn.com

Circa 1809. This handsome country inn, standing at the village common, first became a stagecoach stop in the 1830s. It has been restored recently and is decorated in a traditional style with antiques. A full breakfast is served, and the inn's restaurant offers New England cookery. Guests staying on Saturday night especially will enjoy the next morning's Sunday brunch, included in the rates. Townsfolk mingle with guests on the porch or in the inn's tavern and restaurant.

Innkeeper(s): Mickey Dowd. $75-145. MC, VISA, AX, DC, DS. 15 rooms with PB, 4 with FP and 2 conference rooms. Breakfast included in rates. Types of meals: Full bkfst, country bkfst, early coffee/tea and dinner. MAP, EP. Beds: KQ. Cable TV, phone and TV upon request in room. Air conditioning. Fax and copier on premises. Weddings, small meetings, family reunions and seminars hosted. Antiquing, art galleries, beaches, bicycling, canoeing/kayaking, fishing, golf, hiking, horseback riding, live theater, museums, shopping, downhill skiing, cross-country skiing, sporting events, tennis and water sports nearby.

Madison   G5

Maple Grove House

21 Maple Grove Rd
Madison, NH 03849
(603)367-8208 (877)367-8208
Web: www.maplegrovehouse.com

Circa 1911. Alongside a quiet country road and across from an apple orchard, this white Victorian farmhouse offers a spacious wraparound porch with views of the White Mountains. A wood burning stove warms the living room, and there is an original guest register from the home's early years. Common rooms include a library and sunny dining room. Polished hardwood floors are highlights of the bedrooms. North Conway outlet shops and restaurants are nearby.

Innkeeper(s): Celia & Don Pray. $85-105. MC, VISA, AX, DS, PC, TC. 6 rooms, 4 with PB and 1 suite. Breakfast and snacks/refreshments included in rates. Types of meals: Full bkfst and early coffee/tea. Beds: QT. Cable TV, ceiling fan, VCR and window fans in room. Library on premises. Small meetings and family reunions hosted. Antiquing, fishing, golf, live theater, parks, shopping, downhill skiing, cross-country skiing and tennis nearby.

Meredith H4

Meredith Inn

2 Waukewan
Meredith, NH 03253
(603)279-0000 Fax:(603)279-4017
E-mail: inn1897@meredithinn.com
Web: www.meredithinn.com

Circa 1897. Located at the northwestern tip of Lake Winnipesaukee at the gateway to the White Mountains, the town of Meredith has the feel of a New England village. The Meredith Inn has a two-story turret and walk-out bay windows. The inn's exterior has three different styles of shingles and clapboard siding and interesting roof angles. Its eight guest bedrooms have fireplaces, whirlpool tubs, luxury linens, and brick fireplaces with recessed mantels of intricate Victorian design. The interior has lots of hard yellow pine trim and doors, etched brass doorknobs and doorplates, and a recessed china cabinet with a leaded-glass door. Breakfast includes such delightful courses as juice, fruits in season with yogurt, hot and cold cereals and a hot entrée of the day like plain or berry pancakes, French toast with pure maple syrup, eggs frittata, omelets and blueberry blintzes. The inn is a mile from the Anna Lee Doll Museum, two miles from the Old Paint Barn and half a mile from the Meredith Historical Society and Farm Museum.

Historic Interest: Anna Lee Doll Museum (1 mile), Old Paint Barn (2 miles), Science Center of NH (5 miles), Meredith Historical Society & Farm Museum (1/2 mile).

Innkeeper(s): Janet Carpenter. $79-159. MC, VISA, DS, PC, TC. TAC10. 8 rooms with PB, 2 with FP. Breakfast included in rates. Types of meals: Gourmet bkfst, country bkfst and veg bkfst. Beds: KQT. Cable TV and phone in room. Fax, copier and library on premises. Handicap access. Weddings and family reunions hosted. Amusement parks, antiquing, art galleries, beaches, bicycling, canoeing/kayaking, fishing, golf, hiking, horseback riding, live theater, museums, parks, shopping, downhill skiing, cross-country skiing, tennis and water sports nearby.

Mount Sunapee I2

Blue Goose Inn

24 Rt 103B, Box 2117
Mount Sunapee, NH 03255
(603)763-5519 (866)763-5519 Fax:(603)763-8720
E-mail: info@bluegooseinn.com
Web: www.bluegooseinn.com

Circa 1900. Under new ownership, this intimate 19th-century farmhouse offers ample opportunity to do as little or as much as desired. Relax by the fireplace with a good book or take advantage of the close location, only 3/10 of a mile, to Mt.  Sunapee resort. Enjoy private baths in each of the guest bedrooms furnished with queen and/or single beds. A hearty New England breakfast starts the day. The inn sits on almost four acres and is on the rail trail used for snowmobiling, cross-country skiing and snowshoeing in winter or used for biking, hiking and walking during the warmer months. Ice skating and sledding are just minutes away, as is the beach.

Innkeeper(s): Robin & Joe. $80. MC, VISA, PC, TC. 4 rooms with PB.

Breakfast included in rates. Types of meals: Full bkfst. Beds: QT. TV in room. VCR, piano and kitchen on premises. Handicap access. Antiquing, fishing, live theater, parks and cross-country skiing nearby.

"Lots of fun and great hospitality."

New London I3

The Inn at Pleasant Lake

125 Pleasant St, PO Box 1030
New London, NH 03257-1030
(603)526-6271 (800)626-4907 Fax:(603)526-4111
E-mail: bmackenz@kear.tds.net
Web: www.innatpleasantlake.com

Circa 1790. In its early days, this inn served as a farmhouse. By the late 1870s, it was serving guests as a summer resort. Its tradition of hospitality continues today with relaxing guest rooms, which offer lake or wood views. The five-acre grounds  face Pleasant Lake, which has a private beach. Guests may enjoy the lake on their own rowboat or canoe, but the innkeepers will lend theirs if requested. Meander over wooded trails or take a stroll around New London. Innkeeper and Culinary Institute of America graduate Brian MacKenzie prepares the inn's five-course, prix fixe dinners.

Innkeeper(s): Linda & Brian MacKenzie. $110-175. MC, VISA, DS, PC, TC. TAC10. 9 rooms with PB, 1 suite and 1 conference room. Breakfast and afternoon tea included in rates. Types of meals: Full bkfst and dinner. Beds: KQD. Three with hot tub in room. Central air. Fax, copier, swimming and exercise room on premises. Weddings, small meetings, family reunions and seminars hosted. Antiquing, bicycling, canoeing/kayaking, fishing, golf, hiking, live theater, museums, parks, shopping, downhill skiing, cross-country skiing and water sports nearby.

Publicity: *Country Inns Magazine and James Beard Dinner.*

"What a perfect setting for our first ever visit to New England."

North Conway F5

1785 Inn & Restaurant

3582 White Mountain Hwy
North Conway, NH 03860-1785
(603)356-9025 (800)421-1785 Fax:(603)356-6081
E-mail: the1785inn@aol.com
Web: www.the1785inn.com

Circa 1785. The main section of this center-chimney house was built by Captain Elijah Dinsmore of the New Hampshire Rangers. He was granted the land for service in the American Revolution. Original hand-hewn beams, corner posts, fireplaces, and a brick oven are still visible and operating. The inn is located at the historical marker popularized by the White Mountain School of Art in the 19th century.

Historic Interest: Mount Washington.

Innkeeper(s): Becky & Charles Mallar. $89-209. MC, VISA, AX, DC, CB, DS, PC, TC. TAC10. 17 rooms, 12 with PB, 1 suite and 1 conference room. Breakfast included in rates. Types of meals: Full bkfst, country bkfst, early coffee/tea, afternoon tea, snacks/refreshments, gourmet dinner and room service. Beds: KQDT. Cable TV, turndown service, ceiling fan and VCR in room.

Air conditioning. Fax, copier, swimming, library, cross-country skiing and nature trails on premises. Weddings, small meetings, family reunions and seminars hosted. French spoken. Amusement parks, antiquing, art galleries, beaches, bicycling, canoeing/kayaking, fishing, golf, hiking, horseback riding, walking, gardens, nature trails, rock climbing, ice climbing, live theater, museums, parks, shopping, downhill skiing, cross-country skiing, tennis and water sports nearby.

Publicity: *Country, Bon Appetit, Travel & Leisure, Ski, Travel Holiday, Connecticut, Better Homes & Gardens and The Wedding Story.*

"Occasionally in our lifetimes is a moment so unexpectedly perfect that we use it as our measure for our unforgettable moments. We just had such an experience at The 1785 Inn."

Buttonwood Inn

Mount Surprise Rd
North Conway, NH 03860
(603)356-2625 (800)258-2625 Fax:(603)356-3140
E-mail: innkeeper@buttonwoodinn.com
Web: www.buttonwoodinn.com

Circa 1820. Sitting on 17 secluded acres of scenic mountain beauty, this New England farmhouse is located two miles from the village. Experience a memorable blend of hospitality and laughter at this delightful inn. The comfortable guest bedrooms feature antiques and Shaker furniture, quilts and stenciling. Award-winning perennial gardens are an eye-pleasing adventure. Swim, hike or cross-country ski, as weather permits. An added treat during the holidays is the highly acclaimed seasonal decor.

Historic Interest: Mount Washington (20 minutes), Cog Railway (40 minutes), Heritage, N.H. (10 minutes).
Innkeeper(s): Claudia & Peter Needham. $95-225. MC, VISA, AX, DS, PC, TC. 10 rooms with PB, 1 with FP, 2 suites and 1 conference room. Breakfast and afternoon tea included in rates. Types of meals: Gourmet bkfst and early coffee/tea. Beds: KQT. Clock and Jacuzzi (one room) and fireplace (one room) in room. Air conditioning. VCR, fax, swimming and hiking on premises. Antiquing, fishing, hiking, live theater, parks, shopping, downhill skiing and cross-country skiing nearby.
Publicity: *Classic American Homes, Boston Globe, Boston Herald and Boston Magazine.*

"The very moment we spotted your lovely inn nestled midway on the mountainside in the moonlight, we knew we had found a winner."

Cabernet Inn

Rt 16, Box 489
North Conway, NH 03860
(603)356-4704 (800)866-4704 Fax:(603)356-5399
E-mail: info@cabernetinn.com
Web: www.cabernetinn.com

Circa 1842. Built prior to the Civil War, this historic home features a deep burgundy exterior highlighted by hunter green shutters and trim. Window boxes filled with flowers add a touch more color. The one-acre grounds are shaded by trees and colored by a variety of flowers. More than half of the guest rooms include a fireplace, and some have double whirlpool tubs. In the afternoons, homemade treats are served, and in the mornings, guests enjoy a full country breakfast with items such as eggs, French toast, pancakes, bacon, sausages and fresh seasonal fruits.

Historic Interest: Mt. Washington Auto Road, Cog Railway (18 miles).
Innkeeper(s): Debbie & Rich Howard. $85-225. MC, VISA, AX, DS, PC, TC. TAC10. 11 rooms with PB, 6 with FP. Breakfast and afternoon tea included in rates. Types of meals: Full bkfst, country bkfst and early coffee/tea. Beds: Q. Ceiling fan and antiques in room. Air conditioning. VCR and fax on premises. Small meetings, family reunions and seminars hosted. Antiquing, art galleries, bicycling, canoeing/kayaking, fishing, golf, hiking, horseback riding, live theater, parks, shopping, downhill skiing and cross-country skiing nearby.

Isaac Merrill House Inn

720 Kearsage Rd
North Conway, NH 03860
(800)328-9041 (800)328-9041 Fax:(603)356-9055
Web: www.isaacmerrillhouse.com

Circa 1773. Built in 1773 as a farm house, this family home opened as a full time inn around 1850. A treasured guest book still at the inn dates from 1875. Now a National Landmark, the inn has been renovated and offers modern amenities such as color television and air conditioning but still retains the colonial tone. Several rooms boast fireplaces, skylights or canopy beds, and there are two family suites. A wide wraparound porch is a favored lounging point, and there are three sitting rooms and a main dining room. Breakfast is served fireside with the signature morning dish, Eggs Benedict, prepared by the inn's chef. Across the street flows a babbling brook, and an old-fashioned swimming hole awaits nearby.
Innkeeper(s): Levine Family. $79-179. MC, VISA, AX, DS, TC. 17 rooms with PB, 5 with FP, 2 suites and 1 conference room. Breakfast included in rates. Types of meals: Gourmet bkfst, early coffee/tea and afternoon tea. Beds: KQDT. Cable TV, phone and ceiling fan in room. Air conditioning. VCR, fax, copier, swimming, library and BBQ grill on premises. Weddings, small meetings, family reunions and seminars hosted. Amusement parks, antiquing, art galleries, beaches, bicycling, canoeing/kayaking, fishing, golf, hiking, horseback riding, live theater, museums, parks, shopping, downhill skiing, cross-country skiing, tennis and water sports nearby.
Pets Allowed.
Publicity: *Standard-Times, Irregular, Fosters Business Review, Granite State News, Boston Globe and Yankee.*

"Although I expected this to be a nice, cozy place, I was not prepared for the royal treatment my family and I received."

Nereledge Inn

River Rd, Off Main St, PO Box 547
North Conway, NH 03860-0547
(603)356-2831 Fax:(603)356-7085

Circa 1787. This big white house is decorated simply in a New England style featuring cozy English eiderdowns and rocking chairs in many of the guest rooms. Wood stoves warm the breakfast room and the sitting room. There is an English-style pub room with a fireplace, darts and backgammon. For breakfast you may be served apple pie with ice cream as a dessert after the main course. Innkeeper Valerie Halpin grew up in Burnley, England. The area is bursting with activity for those who wish to bask in the outdoors. The river, a perfect place to enjoy swimming, canoeing and fishing, is within walking distance, as are shopping and restaurants in the village. The area boasts wonderful rock and ice climbing. Nereledge Inn is a non-smoking inn. Families and small groups are welcome.

Historic Interest: Dartmouth College is two- and-one-half hours away.
Innkeeper(s): Valerie & Suzanne. $59-159. MC, VISA, AX, DS, PC, TC. TAC10. 11 rooms, 5 with PB and 1 suite. Breakfast included in rates. Types of meals: Full bkfst. Beds: QDT. Antiquing, fishing, climbing, hiking, live the-

ater, downhill skiing and cross-country skiing nearby.
Publicity: *White Mountain Region Newspaper, Outside* and *Men's Journal.*

"Our home away from home."

Old Red Inn & Cottages

PO Box 467
North Conway, NH 03860-0467
(603)356-2642 (800)338-1356 Fax:(603)356-6626
E-mail: oldredin@nxi.com

Circa 1810. Guests can opt to stay in an early 19th-century home or in one of a collection of cottages at this country inn. The rooms are decorated with handmade quilts and stenciling dots the walls. Several rooms include four-poster or canopy beds. Two-bedroom cottages both feature a screened porch. A hearty, country meal accompanied by freshly baked breads, muffins and homemade preserves starts off the day. The inn is near many of the town's shops, restaurants and outlets.
Innkeeper(s): Dick & Terry Potochniak. $98-178. MC, VISA, AX, DS. 17 rooms, 15 with PB, 1 suite and 10 cottages. Breakfast included in rates. Types of meals: Full bkfst and early coffee/tea. Beds: QDT. Cable TV in room. Air conditioning. Fax, copier and swimming on premises. Weddings, small meetings, family reunions and seminars hosted. Amusement parks, antiquing, fishing, golf, live theater, parks, shopping, downhill skiing, cross-country skiing, sporting events, tennis and water sports nearby.

Victorian Harvest Inn

28 Locust Ln, Box 1763
North Conway, NH 03860
(603)356-3548 (800)642-0749 Fax:(603)356-8430
E-mail: help@victorianharvestinn.com
Web: www.victorianharvestinn.com

Circa 1853. Each guest room at this Victorian inn offers a mountain view, and some have fireplaces. Perched atop a hill in the Mt. Washington Valley, the inn features country Victorian furnishings highlighted by quilts. The Windsor Room offers a fireplace and double Jacuzzi, as well as a king-size bed, while the

Victoria Station Room boasts its own carousel horse, and the Nook & Cranny Room includes a view of the entire Moat Range. Cotswold Hideaway features a skylight and gas fireplace. Guests can relax by the pool, lounge in the library while listening to Beethoven, Vivaldi and Bach or hike around the Puddin Pond conservation trail. The grounds include a foot bridge, gardens and the pool. Dutch pannekuchen, Belgian waffles, frittatas or cornmeal and currant pancakes are served at breakfast.
Innkeeper(s): David & Judy Wooster. $90-220. MC, VISA, TC. 8 rooms with PB. Breakfast and afternoon tea included in rates. Types of meals: Gourmet bkfst. Phone if requested in room. Air conditioning. VCR, fax, copier, swimming and library on premises. Family reunions hosted. Antiquing, canoeing/kayaking, golf, hiking, horseback riding, tubing, outlet shopping, live theater, parks, shopping, downhill skiing, cross-country skiing and water sports nearby.

North Woodstock   F4

Wilderness Inn B&B

Rfd 1, Box 69, Rts 3 & 112
North Woodstock, NH 03262-9710
(603)745-3890 (800)200-9453
E-mail: wildernessinn@juno.com
Web: www.thewildernessinn.com

Circa 1912. Surrounded by the White Mountain National Forest, this charming shingled home offers a picturesque getaway

for every season. Guest rooms, all with private baths, are furnished with antiques and Oriental rugs. The innkeepers also offer family suites and a private cottage with a fireplace, Jacuzzi and a view of Lost River. Breakfast is a delightful affair with choices ranging from fresh muffins to brie cheese omelets, French toast topped with homemade apple syrup, crepes or specialty pancakes. For the children, the innkeepers create teddy bear pancakes or French toast. If you wish, afternoon tea also is served.
Innkeeper(s): Michael & Rosanna Yarnell. $65-150. MC, VISA, AX, PC, TC. 7 rooms with PB and 1 cottage. Breakfast included in rates. Types of meals: Gourmet bkfst. MAP. Beds: QDT. TV in room.

"The stay at your inn, attempting and completing the 3D jig-jaw puzzle, combined with those unforgettable breakfasts, and your combined friendliness, makes the Wilderness Inn a place for special memories."

Pittsburgh   B5

The Glen

First Connecticut Lake, 77 The Glen Rd
Pittsburgh, NH 03592
(603)538-6500 (800)445-GLEN Fax:(603)538-7121

Circa 1900. This lakeside mountain lodge is located on the 45th parallel, midway between the equator and the North Pole. More than 160 acres surround the lodge, offering a bounty of activities. Guests can fish in a lake stocked with trout and salmon, or they can fish at the river, which offers rainbow and brown trout. The surrounding area also provides opportunities for hunters. Birdwatchers can enjoy gazing at dozens of different species. The Glen provides stunning views of the mountains and First Connecticut Lake, as

well as the vast expanse of forestland. The interior of the lodge features natural wood paneling and hardwood floors; rooms are decorated in a comfortable lodge style. In addition to the lodge rooms and suite, there are 10 cabins. Breakfast, lunch and dinner are included in the rates. The hosts have been welcoming guests for nearly 40 years.
Innkeeper(s): Betty Falton. Call for rates. 6 rooms with PB, 1 suite and 10 cabins. Beds: QDT. Fishing on lake nearby.

Tall Timber Lodge

231 Beach Road
Pittsburgh, NH 03592
(603)538-6651 (800)835-6343 Fax:(603)538-6582
E-mail: relax@talltimber.com
Web: www.talltimber.com

Circa 1946. Explore the North Woods on Back Lake at this relaxed resort that offers deluxe accommodations, including a rustic lodge with air-conditioned guest bedrooms, lakeshore log cabins and luxury cottages. For delicious, economical meals, the Rainbow Grille is a highly acclaimed restaurant in the main lodge. Natural panoramic beauty is unparalleled in this wilderness region, anda a variety of activities are available. Experience mountain biking, fishing, canoeing, hiking, kayaking, moose watching and loon listening.
Historic Interest: History of Indian Stream Republic Marker (3 miles), Indian Chief "Metallak" grave site, (10 miles), 45th Parallel Marker (8 miles).
Innkeeper(s): The Caron Family. $50-295. MC, VISA, DS, PC, TC. 26 rooms, 2

with PB, 9 with FP, 2 suites, 4 cottages and 12 cabins. Types of meals: Country bkfst, picnic lunch and gourmet dinner. MAP. Beds: QDT. Cable TV, phone, ceiling fan and VCR in room. Air conditioning. Fax, copier, swimming, bicycles and library on premises. Weddings and family reunions hosted. Bicycling, canoeing/kayaking, fishing, golf, hiking, moose watching & snowmobiling nearby.

Pets allowed: $10 a day.

Publicity: *Yankee Magazine, Boston Globe, Boston Magazine, Field & Stream and North America's Greatest Fishing Lodges.*

Rindge   L3

Cathedral House B&B

63 Cathedral Entrance
Rindge, NH 03461
(603)899-6790

Circa 1850. This pre-Civil War, Colonial-style farmhouse is surrounded by 450 acres with meadows, a fishing pond, nature trails and scenic vistas. The five, comfortable bedrooms have been decorated in Colonial style,  with artwork and fresh flowers in season. Rooms offer views of mountains and Emerson Pond. A hearty country breakfast is served. The bed & breakfast is located on the grounds of the Cathedral of the Pines, a non-denominational place of worship, which offers solitude in natural surroundings. The grounds originally were selected by a young pilot and his wife as a location for their home upon his return from World War II. The pilot was killed in the line of duty, and his parents created the Cathedral of the Pines in his memory and others who served. The site has been recognized by the U.S. Congress as a national memorial.

Innkeeper(s): Donald & Shirley Mahoney. $45-125. MC, VISA, PC. 5 rooms. Breakfast included in rates. Types of meals: Full bkfst. Beds: QDT. Library on premises. Antiquing, fishing, live theater, parks, shopping, downhill skiing, cross-country skiing, sporting events and water sports nearby.

Publicity: *New York Times, Hartford Courant and Yankee.*

"Thank you for making our wedding day such a success and for making our family feel so welcome."

Woodbound Inn

62 Woodbound Rd
Rindge, NH 03461
(603)532-8341 (800)688-7770 Fax:(603)532-8341
E-mail: woodbound@aol.com
Web: www.woodbound.com

Circa 1819. Vacationers have enjoyed the Woodbound Inn since its opening as a year-round resort in 1892. The main inn actually was built in 1819, and this portion offers 19 guest rooms, all appointed with classic-style furnishings. The innkeepers offer more modern accommodations in the Edgewood Building, and there are eleven cabins available. The one- and two-bedroom cabins rest along the shore of Lake Contoocook. The inn's 162 acres include a private beach, fishing, hiking, nature trails, tennis courts, a volleyball court, a game room and a golf course. There is a full service restaurant, a cocktail lounge and banquet facilities on premises. If for some reason one would want to venture away from the inn, the region is full of activities, including ski areas, more golf courses and Mount Monadnock.

Innkeeper(s): Kohlmorgen Family. $89-139. MC, VISA, AX, PC. TAC10. 45 rooms, 40 with PB, 11 cabins and 5 conference rooms. Breakfast included in rates. Types of meals: Full bkfst, lunch and dinner. EP. Beds: QDT. Phone and cabins are lakefront with fireplaces in room. Air conditioning. VCR, copier, swimming, tennis and library on premises. Handicap access. Weddings, small meetings, family reunions and seminars hosted. Amusement parks, antiquing, fishing, live theater, parks, shopping, downhill skiing, cross-country skiing and water sports nearby.

Pets allowed: In cabins only.

Rochester   I6

The Agnes Pease House

1 May Street
Rochester, NH 03867
(603)332-5509 Fax:(603)332-7276
E-mail: msclemons@ttlc.net
Web: www.agnespeasehouse.com

Circa 1930. The interior of this restored Victorian is eclectic — a mix of antique furnishings and modern pieces. Each room has its own special touch. The Sun Room is especially cheerful, encapsulated by two walls of leaded windows. It also features a bed topped with a hand-made quilt. The Lilac Room includes a king-size iron and wicker bed. This spacious room can be combined with the cozy Bay Room to form a suite, perfect for those traveling together. In addition to providing a hearty, full breakfast, the innkeepers provide plenty of helpful amenities, such as a modern jack and fax service for business clients. As well, ingoers enjoy privileges at a local health club.

Innkeeper(s): Paul Bear Ross & M. Susan Clemons. $55-160. MC, VISA, AX. 5 rooms, 3 with PB and 1 suite. Breakfast included in rates. Types of meals: Gourmet bkfst, veg bkfst and early coffee/tea. Beds: KQ. Cable TV, phone and VCR in room. Central air. Fax, copier and library on premises. Amusement parks, antiquing, art galleries, beaches, fishing, golf, hiking, live theater, museums, parks, shopping, downhill skiing, cross-country skiing, sporting events, tennis and water sports nearby.

Publicity: *Channel 12.*

Shelburne   E5

Wildberry Inn B&B

592 State Rt 2
Shelburne, NH 03581
(603)466-5049
E-mail: rec@ncia.net
Web: www.northernwhitemountains.com/wildberry

Circa 1877. This colonial salt-box home is located on seven acres in the White Mountains National Forest with the Appalachian Trail passing through part of the property. Rooms are decorated in a fresh country style with quilts and Priscilla curtains. There's a separate suite in the "barn" with fireplace, upstairs bedroom and a downstairs living room with views of the pond, waterfall and garden from its many windows. In winter, snowshoeing, cross-country skiing and snowmobiling are popular activities. In  summer and fall, guests enjoy canoeing and fishing or simply hiking along the property to enjoy the golden oaks, birches, and red and orange maple foliage. Breakfast usually features freshly picked berries in season, homemade breads and dishes to accommodate a lavish pouring of local maple syrup.

Historic Interest: Northern New Hampshire Heritage Park (8 miles).

Innkeeper(s): Bob & Jackie Corrigan. $75-125. MC, PC, TC. TAC10. 3 rooms with PB, 1 with FP & 1 cottage. Breakfast and afternoon tea included in rates. Types of meals: Gourmet bkfst and country bkfst. Beds: QDT. TV & VCR in room. Air conditioning. Swimming on premises. Weddings & family reunions hosted. Antiquing, bicycling, canoeing/kayaking, fishing, golf, hiking, gourmet dining, snowmobiling, parks, shopping, downhill skiing & cross-country skiing nearby.

Publicity: The Berlin Daily Sun.

Snowville   G5

Snowvillage Inn

Stewart Rd, PO Box 68
Snowville, NH 03832
(603)447-2818 (800)447-4345 Fax:(603)447-5268
E-mail: kevin@snowvillageinn.com

Circa 1915. Peacefully sitting on a secluded hillside with panoramic views of the entire Presidential mountain range, this Victorian inn is a wonderful blend of Apine flair and New England charm. In the Main House, built by author Frank Simonds, enjoy many common rooms to gather in, there are books to read by the fireplace, or watch a gorgeous sunset on the front porch. Each of the comfortable guest bedrooms in the Chimney House and Carriage House are named after a writer, in honor of the inn's heritage. Discover more breathtaking vistas, fireplaces and antique furnishings. Renown for its elegant country dining, breakfast is a satisfying culinary delight. Explore the award-winning gardens and nature trails.

Historic Interest: Remnick Farm Museum (15 miles), Portsmouth NH (55 miles), Strawberry Banke Museum, Sherburn House, Goodwin Mansion, Shapiro House.

Innkeeper(s): Kevin, Caitlin & Maggie Flynn. $99-249. MC, VISA, AX, DC, DS, PC, TC. TAC7. 18 rooms with PB, 4 with FP. Breakfast included in rates. Types of meals: Gourmet bkfst and gourmet dinner. MAP. Beds: KQD. Phone and fireplace in room. Fax, copier, library and Cross-country skiing and showshoeing on premises. Weddings, small meetings, family reunions and seminars hosted. Bulgarian and Polish spoken. Antiquing, art galleries, bicycling, canoeing/kayaking, fishing, golf, hiking, horseback riding, live theater, museums, downhill skiing, cross-country skiing and water sports nearby.

Publicity: Yankee Magazine, Wine Spectator, Boston Glove and WMUR New Hampshire.

Sugar Hill   F3

A Grand Inn-Sunset Hill House

231 Sunset Hill Rd
Sugar Hill, NH 03585
(603)823-5522 (800)786-4455 Fax:(603)823-5738
E-mail: innkeeper@sunsethillhouse.com
Web: www.sunsethillhouse.com

Circa 1882. This Second Empire luxury inn has views of five mountain ranges. Three parlors, all with cozy fireplaces, are favorite gathering spots. Afternoon tea is served here. The inn's lush grounds offer many opportunities for recreation or relaxing, and guests often enjoy special events here, such as the Fields of Lupine Festival. The Cannon Mountain Ski Area and Franconia Notch State Park are nearby, and there is 30 kilometers of cross-country ski trails at the inn. Be sure to inquire about golf and ski packages. In the fall, a Thanksgiving package allows guests to help decorate the inn for the holidays as well as enjoy Thanksgiving dinner together. NH Magazine just named A Grand Inn — Sunset Hill House the "Very Best in NH for a Spectacular Meal."

Historic Interest: Robert Frost Cottage (1 mile), site of first ski school (one-half mile), Sugar Hill Historic Museum (one-half mile).

Innkeeper(s): Lon, Nancy, Mary Pearl & Adeline Henderson. $100-350. MC, VISA, AX, DS, PC, TC. TAC10. 28 rooms with PB and 1 conference room. Breakfast included in rates. Types of meals: Full bkfst, early coffee/tea, picnic lunch, snacks/refreshments and dinner. MAP. Beds: KQDT. Suites with fireplaces and/or whirlpools and ceiling fans (many rooms) in room. Fax and tavern on premises. Weddings, small meetings, family reunions and seminars hosted. Antiquing, fishing, golf course, live theater, parks, shopping, downhill skiing, cross-country skiing and water sports nearby.

Publicity: Yankee, Courier, Caledonia Record, Boston Globe, Portsmouth Herald, Manchester Union Leader, Journal Enquirer, Sunday Telegraph, Boston Herald and New Hampshire Magazine.

"I have visited numerous inns and innkeepers in my 10 years as a travel writer, but have to admit that few have impressed me as much as yours and you did."

Sullivan   K2

The Post and Beam B&B

18 Centre St
Sullivan, NH 03445
(603)847-3330 (888)376-6262 Fax:(603)847-3306
E-mail: postandbeam@monad.net
Web: www.postandbeambb.com

Circa 1797. Situated on a hill above Otter Brook and the Sullivan countryside, this late 18th-century, Colonial post-and-beam farmhouse was home to the Union Store and first town telephone company. Today, the  inn's rustic hand-hewn exposed beams are a prominent architectural feature of the main living room. The guest rooms feature fireplaces, wide pine floors and antiques collected throughout the area. Guests also can enjoy the hot tub in the outdoor gazebo. A family-style, three-course New England breakfast is served in the dining room each morning.

Historic Interest: The Monadnock region offers kayaking, fishing, horseback riding, downhill and cross country skiing. There are nearby covered bridges and nine state parks are a short drive away. Nearby Keene and Peterborough offers 30 local craft and gift shops.

Innkeeper(s): Darcy Bacall & Priscilla Hardy. $75-115. MC, VISA, AX, DS, PC, TC. 7 rooms, 2 with PB, 5 with FP. Breakfast and afternoon tea included in rates. Types of meals: Full bkfst, cont and early coffee/tea. Beds: KQ. VCR, fax, copier, spa, library, deck/gazebo, kayaks, data port and refrigerator on premises. Handicap access. Family reunions and seminars hosted. French spoken. Antiquing, fishing, golf, live theater, parks, shopping, downhill skiing, cross-country skiing, sporting events and water sports nearby.

Publicity: Keene Shopper and Sunday Sentinel.

"Warm, cozy, beautiful B&B run by special people! Thanks for taking such good care of us! We'll be back."

Sunapee   I2

Dexter's Inn

258 Stagecoach Rd
Sunapee, NH 03782
(603)763-5571 (800)232-5571
E-mail: dexters@tds.net
Web: www.bbhost.com/dextersinn

Circa 1801. Proud of continuing its 50-year history of quality innkeeping, this Federalist-style inn was recently renovated. Tastefully furnished with a blend of antiques and country collectibles, it reflects the nostalgic essence of New England. The library is perfect for sipping a hot beverage while reading a good book by the fireplace; or play games and meet new friends in the family room. Choose one of the guest bedrooms in the main inn or annex, or stay in the Holly House Cottage-a home away from home. A generous country breakfast, regaled for its eggs Benedict and French toast, is served in the dining room. Enjoy the scenic beauty of the gardens, lake and the surrounding mountains from the large screened porch, play a game of tennis or soak up the sun after a swim in the pool.

Innkeeper(s): Holly & Michael Durfor. $115-165. MC, VISA, DS, PC. TAC10. 19 rooms, 17 with PB, 1 cottage and 2 conference rooms. Breakfast included in rates. Types of meals: Full bkfst, country bkfst and early coffee/tea. EP. Beds: KQDT. Air conditioning. VCR, fax, swimming, tennis and library on premises. Weddings, small meetings, family reunions and seminars hosted. Antiquing, art galleries, beaches, bicycling, canoeing/kayaking, fishing, golf, hiking, horseback riding, live theater, museums, parks, shopping, tennis and water sports nearby.

Pets allowed: In annex only, $10/day-damages.

"Just like being at home."

Tilton   I4

Tilton Manor

40 Chestnut St
Tilton, NH 03276-5546
(603)286-3457 Fax:(603)286-3308
E-mail: tiltonmanor@usa.com

Circa 1862. This turn-of-the-century Folk Victorian inn is just two blocks from downtown Tilton. The inn's comfortable guest rooms are furnished with antiques and sport handmade afghans. Guests are treated to a hearty country breakfast. Visitors enjoy relaxing in the sitting room, where they can play games, read or watch TV after a busy day exploring the historic area. Gunstock and Lake Winnipesaukee are nearby, and the Daniel Webster Birthplace and Shaker Village are within easy driving distance. Shoppers will enjoy Tilton's latest addition-an outlet center.

Historic Interest: Historic Concord is just 15 minutes from the manor.

Innkeeper(s): Peggy & Al. $80. MC, VISA, AX, TC. 4 rooms, 2 with PB, 1 with FP and 1 suite. Breakfast included in rates. Types of meals: Gourmet bkfst. Beds: KDT. Some televisions in room. VCR, fax, copier and child care on premises. Weddings, small meetings and family reunions hosted. Antiquing, beaches, canoeing/kayaking, fishing, golf, hiking, horseback riding, outlet mall, parks, shopping, downhill skiing, cross-country skiing, tennis and water sports nearby.

Pets allowed: Small pets with responsible owners.

Wakefield   H6

Wakefield Inn

2723 Wakefield Rd
Wakefield, NH 03872-4374
(603)522-8272 (800)245-0841

Circa 1804. Early travelers pulled up to the front door of the Wakefield Inn by stagecoach, and while they disembarked, their luggage was handed up to the second floor. It was brought in through the door, which is still visible over the porch roof. A spiral staircase, ruffled curtains, wallpapers and a wraparound porch all create the romantic ambiance of days gone by. In the living room, an original three-sided fireplace casts a warm glow on guests as it did more than 190 years ago.

Historic Interest: New Hampshire Farm Museum, Museum of Childhood.

Innkeeper(s): Harry & Lou Sisson. $70-85. MC, VISA, PC, TC. 7 rooms with PB. Breakfast included in rates. Types of meals: Full bkfst and early coffee/tea. Beds: QDT. Ceiling fan in room. VCR on premises. Antiquing, fishing, golf, shopping and cross-country skiing nearby.

"Comfortable accommodations, excellent food and exquisite decor highlighted by your quilts."

Wilmot   I3

Take it For Granite Farm B&B

PO Box 53
Wilmot, NH 03287
(603)526-6376 (877)864-1496 Fax:(801)409-2058
E-mail: heim@kear.tds.net
Web: www.granitebb.com

Circa 1840. Secluded on 10 acres of lush grounds in the Lake Sunapee region, this New England Farmhouse with expanded Cape offers outstanding mountain views. Common areas include two public sitting rooms and a library. Two of the spacious guest bedrooms feature fireplaces. A pine-paneled studio with vaulted ceilings and kitchenette is attached to the barn with a 100-foot walkway to the house. Choose from a selection of newspapers to read with a deluxe continental breakfast. Games, videos and recreational equipment are available.

Historic Interest: Augustus St. Gaudens home (40 miles), Dartmouth College (38 miles).

Innkeeper(s): Craig & Lindy Heim. $85-125. MC, VISA, AX, PC, TC. 4 rooms with PB, 2 with FP and 1 suite. Breakfast included in rates. Types of meals: Cont plus. Beds: KQ. Some with air conditioning, cable TV, fireplace, modem hook-up, reading lamps, refrigerator, telephone, television and VCR in room. Fax, bicycles, library and desk on premises. Weddings and family reunions hosted. Antiquing, art galleries, beaches, bicycling, canoeing/kayaking, fishing, golf, hiking, live theater, museums, parks, shopping, downhill skiing, cross-country skiing, tennis and water sports nearby.

Wilton Center   K4

Stepping Stones B&B

Bennington Battle Tr
Wilton Center, NH 03086
(603)654-9048 (888)654-9048

Circa 1790. Decks and terraces overlook the enormous gardens of this Greek Revival house, listed in the local historic register. Guest rooms feature white-washed pine, cherry or Shaker-style country pieces accented with botanical prints, handwoven throws, rugs, pillows and fresh flowers. Breakfast is served in the solar garden room. Poached eggs on asparagus with hollandaise sauce, blueberry Belgian waffles and jumbo apple muffins with streusel topping are guests' favorite breakfast choices. The innkeeper is both a garden designer and weaver, and there is a handweaving studio on the premises. The inn is an Editor's Pick in Yankee Magazine.

Innkeeper(s): D. Ann Carlsmith. $65-70. PC, TC. 3 rooms with PB. Breakfast included in rates. Types of meals: Full bkfst, early coffee/tea and afternoon tea. Beds: QDT. Library on premises. Weddings and family reunions hosted. Antiquing, hiking, handweaving studio on premises, chamber music, live theater, parks, downhill skiing and cross-country skiing nearby.

Pets allowed: If well-behaved.

Publicity: *Yankee Magazine.*

"A very relaxing and beautiful getaway. The color and fragrance of the gardens is stunning."

New Jersey

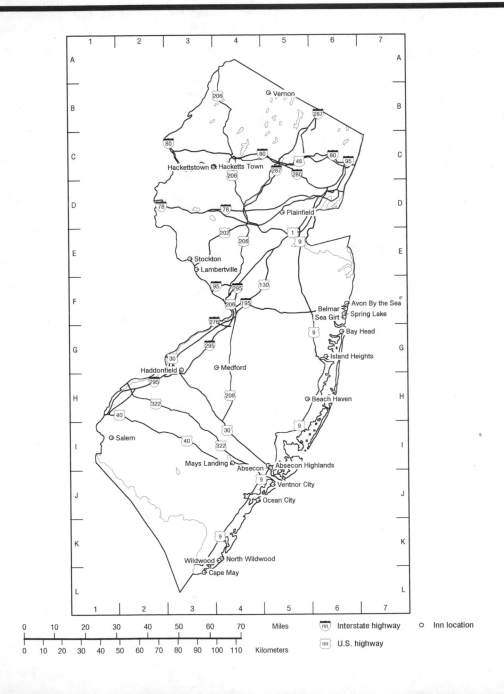

Absecon I5

Dr. Jonathan Pitney House

57 North Shore Rd
Absecon, NJ 08201
(609)569-1799 (888)774-8639 Fax:(609)569-9224
E-mail: drpitney@pitneyhouse.com
Web: www.pitneyhouse.com

Circa 1799. A picket fence surrounds this recently renovated Italianate and Colonial inn. It was the home of Dr. Pitney, considered the Father of Atlantic City. Some of the inn's rooms feature Colonial decor, while others are in a Victorian motif. There are clawfoot tubs, whirlpools, ceiling fans and fireplaces. Breakfast is offered gourmet-style and features an entree, freshly baked breads and cakes. Nearby is Atlantic City, Smithville, a winery, beaches, boardwalk, the convention center and a bird sanctuary.

Innkeeper(s): Don Kelly & Vonnie Clark. $100-250. MC, VISA, PC, TC. TAC10. 10 rooms with PB, 10 with FP and 4 suites. Breakfast and afternoon tea included in rates. Types of meals: Gourmet bkfst and early coffee/tea. Beds: QD. Cable TV, ceiling fan and VCR in room. Air conditioning. Fax and library on premises. Handicap access. Weddings and small meetings hosted. Antiquing, fishing, golf, casinos, parks, shopping, sporting events, tennis and water sports nearby.

Absecon Highlands I5

White Manor Inn

739 S 2nd Ave
Absecon Highlands, NJ 08201-9542
(609)748-3996 Fax:(609)652-0073
E-mail: whitemanor@netzero.net

Circa 1932. This quiet country inn was built by the innkeeper's father and includes unique touches throughout, many created by innkeeper Howard Bensel himself, who became a master craftsman from his father's teachings and renovated the home extensively. Beautiful flowers and plants adorn both the lush grounds and the interior of the home. Everything is comfortable and cozy at this charming B&B, a relaxing contrast to the glitz of nearby Atlantic City.

Historic Interest: A short drive will take guests to a number of historic sites, including the Towne of Smithville, Atlantic City Boardwalk, Renault Winery, Wharton State Forest, the Somers Mansion, and Margate, home of Lucy the Elephant, a National Historic Landmark.

Innkeeper(s): Anna Mae & Howard R. Bensel Jr. $65-105. PC, TC. 7 rooms, 5 with PB, 1 suite and 1 conference room. Breakfast and snacks/refreshments included in rates. Types of meals: Cont plus, cont and early coffee/tea. Beds: QDT. Ceiling fan in room. Air conditioning. Small meetings, family reunions and seminars hosted. Amusement parks, antiquing, fishing, golf, bird watching, casinos, live theater, parks, shopping, sporting events and water sports nearby.

"We felt more like relatives than total strangers. By far the most clean inn that I have seen — spotless!"

Avon By The Sea F6

Atlantic View Inn

20 Woodland Ave
Avon By The Sea, NJ 07717-1435
(732)774-8505 Fax:(732)869-0187
E-mail: nita@monmouth.com
Web: www.atlanticviewinn.com

Circa 1900. This inn offers splendid ocean views. In fact, guests often are treated to their morning meal on the open porch, which overlooks the sea. The turn-of-the-century home includes many Victorian features, including high ceilings and delicate, carved mantels. Guest quarters are decorated in a romantic, English country style. Three rooms offer a fireplace and many boast ocean views. For a special occasion ask for the room with the whirlpool tub for two and private balcony overlooking the ocean. The inn often serves as a romantic getaway for honeymooners and for intimate weddings, and is perfect for reunions, retreats and corporate events.

Innkeeper(s): Nita & Pete Rose. $90-275. MC, VISA, AX, DS, TC. TAC10. 13 rooms, 11 with PB, 3 with FP and 2 suites. Breakfast and afternoon tea included in rates. Types of meals: Gourmet bkfst and early coffee/tea. Beds: KQDT. Ceiling fan in room. Air conditioning. Fax, swimming and includes beach badges on premises. Weddings, small meetings, family reunions and seminars hosted. Amusement parks, antiquing, fishing, two race tracks, Garden Street Arts Center, live theater, parks, shopping and water sports nearby.

Publicity: *Bergen Record.*

"Your place is quaint and beautiful. The food is delicious."

Bay Head G6

Bentley Inn

694 Main Ave
Bay Head, NJ 08742-5346
(732)892-9589 (866)423-6853 Fax:(732)701-0030
E-mail: bentleyinn@home.com
Web: www.bentleyinn.com

Circa 1886. Built in the 19th century, this Queen Anne-style Victorian mansion sits only three houses from the Atlantic in a picturesque seaside town. The many common areas include a library and spacious living room with comfortable furnishings and a warm fireplace. Thoughtful amenities ensure a pleasant stay in relaxed ease. Read the morning paper after choosing a delicious breakfast served in the sunlit solarium or dining room. Ocean and bay views are distinctly appreci-

ated from the first- and second-story covered porches. All that is needed for fun at the beach is provided. The local area also offers many water sports, birding and biking.

Innkeeper(s): Janet & Glenn Kithcart. $120-300. MC, VISA, AX, DS. TAC10. 19 rooms and 3 suites. Breakfast included in rates. Types of meals: Full bkfst. AP. Beds: QDT. TV, phone, VCR and hair dryers in room. Air conditioning. Beach badges, chairs, umbrellas, towels, adult bicycles, film library and metal detectors on premises. Amusement parks, antiquing, fishing, golf, parks, shopping, tennis and water sports nearby.

Beach Haven H5

Amber Street Inn

118 Amber St
Beach Haven, NJ 08008-1744
(609)492-1611
E-mail: inn118@aol.com

Circa 1885. Located on Long Beach Island, just six miles off the New Jersey Coast, this historic inn was one of Beach Haven's earliest homes. The Victorian rests within the town's historic district across from Bicentennial Park. Rooms are decorated in an eclectic Victorian style with refurbished antiques. Breakfasts are continental-plus and served buffet style with fresh fruit, granola, muffins, homemade tea breads and, perhaps, baked eggs. The beach is a short walk away, and the innkeepers provide beach passes and chairs.

Innkeeper(s): Joan & Michael Fitzsimmons. $125-225. PC, TC. 6 rooms with PB and 1 suite. Breakfast included in rates. Types of meals: Cont plus, early coffee/tea and snacks/refreshments. Beds: KQ. Phone and ceiling fan in room. Air conditioning. Fax, bicycles, library, English garden and porch rockers on premises. Weddings and small meetings hosted. Spanish spoken. Antiquing, beaches, fishing, golf, live theater, parks, shopping, tennis and water sports nearby.

Publicity: Gannett Travel.

Belmar F6

The Inn at The Shore Bed & Breakfast

301 4th Ave
Belmar, NJ 07719-2104
(732)681-3762 Fax:(732)280-1914
E-mail: tomvolker@aol.com

Circa 1880. This child friendly country Victorian actually is near two different shores. Both the ocean and Silver Lake are within easy walking distance of the inn. From the inn's wrap-

around porch, guests can view swans on the lake. The innkeepers decorated their Victorian home in period style. The inn's patio is set up for barbecues.

Innkeeper(s): Rosemary & Tom Volker. $110-195. MC, VISA, AX, PC, TC. TAC10. 10 rooms, 4 with PB and 1 conference room. Breakfast included in rates. Types of meals: Full bkfst. Cable TV, phone, modem, whirlpool tubs and fireplaces in room. Air conditioning. VCR, bicycles, aquarium, patio with gas grill, guest pantry w/refrigerator and microwave on premises. Weddings, small meetings, family reunions and seminars hosted. Amusement parks, antiquing, fishing, live theater, parks, shopping, sporting events and water sports nearby.

"You both have created a warm, cozy and comfortable refuge for us weary travelers."

Cape May L3

The Abbey Bed & Breakfast

34 Gurney at Columbia Ave
Cape May, NJ 08204
(609)884-4506 Fax:(609)884-2379
E-mail: theabbey@bellatlantic.net
Web: www.abbeybedandbreakfast.com

Circa 1869. This historic inn consists of two buildings, one a Gothic Revival villa with a 60-foot tower, Gothic arched windows and shaded verandas. Furnishings include floor-to-ceiling mirrors, ornate gas chandeliers, marble-topped dressers and beds of carved walnut, wrought iron and brass. The cottage

adjacent to the villa is a classic Second Empire-style cottage with a mansard roof. A full breakfast is served in the dining room in spring and fall and on the veranda in the summer. Late afternoon refreshments and tea are served each day at 5 p.m. The beautiful inn is featured in the town's Grand Christmas Tour, and public tours and tea are offered three times a week in season.

Innkeeper(s): Jay & Marianne Schatz. $100-295. MC, VISA, DS, TC. 14 rooms with PB, 2 suites and 2 conference rooms. Breakfast and afternoon tea included in rates. Types of meals: Full bkfst. AP. Beds: KQD. Ceiling fan, some air conditioning, small refrigerator and desks and antiques in room. Beach chairs and on and off site parking on premises. Small meetings and seminars hosted. Antiquing, art galleries, beaches, bicycling, canoeing/kayaking, fishing, hiking, horseback riding, birding, live theater, museums, parks, shopping, tennis and wineries nearby.

Publicity: Richmond Times-Dispatch, New York Times, Glamour, Philadelphia Inquirer, National Geographic Traveler. Smithsonian and Victorian Homes Magazine.

"Staying with you folks really makes the difference between a 'nice' vacation and a great one!"

Abigail Adams B&B By The Sea

12 Jackson St
Cape May, NJ 08204-1418
(609)884-1371 (888)827-4354
E-mail: info@abigailadamsinn.com
Web: www.abigailadamsinn.com

Circa 1888. This charming Victorian is only 100 feet from the beach which affords refreshing sea breezes and ocean views. There

is a free-standing circular staircase, as well as original fireplaces and woodwork throughout. The decor is highlighted with flowered chintz and antiques, and the dining room is hand-stenciled. A full breakfast features the inn's homemade baked sweets.

Historic Interest: One of the "Seven Sisters of Cape May" built by Stephen Decatur Button.

Innkeeper(s): Kate Emerson. $85-195. MC, VISA, AX, TC. 6 rooms, 4 with PB. Breakfast included in rates. Types of meals: Full bkfst and afternoon tea. Beds: QD. Phone and ceiling fan in room. Air conditioning. Amusement parks, antiquing, fishing, live theater and water sports nearby.

"What a wonderful time. Comfortable & homey."

Albert Stevens Inn

127 Myrtle Ave
Cape May, NJ 08204-1237
(609)884-4717 (800)890-2287 Fax:(609)884-8320
E-mail: albertstevensinn@hotmail.com
Web: www.beachcomber.com/Capemay/Bbs/stevens.html

Circa 1898. Dr. Albert Stevens built this Queen Anne Free Classic house for his home and office. Carved woodwork and Victorian antiques enhance the delightful architectural details. The floating staircase and tower lead to spacious air-conditioned guest bedrooms. Enjoy a complete breakfast as well as afternoon tea and refreshments. Relax in the comfortably heated sunroom, or on the inviting veranda. The outside hot tub offers to soothe and rejuvenate. Free on-site parking is convenient for shopping, restaurants and the beach a short walk away. Beach towels and chairs are gladly provided.

Innkeeper(s): Jim & Lenanne Labrusciano. $90-200. MC, VISA. 10 rooms, 7 with PB and 3 suites. Breakfast and afternoon tea included in rates. Types of meals: Full bkfst. Beds: KQD. TV and ceiling fan in room. Air conditioning. Hot tub and on site parking on premises. Weddings, small meetings, family reunions and seminars hosted. Amusement parks, antiquing, beaches, bicycling, fishing, bird watching, live theater, shopping and water sports nearby.

Publicity: *The Jersey Shore, Mid-Atlantic Country, Atlantic City Press, Cape May Star and Wave, The Herald, Washington Post, The New York Times, Philadelphia Inquirer, and NBC News.*

Angel of The Sea

5 Trenton Ave
Cape May, NJ 08204-2735
(609)884-3369 (800)848-3369 Fax:(609)884-3331
Web: www.angelofthesea.com

Circa 1850. This recently renovated Victorian mansion features a mansard roof, a tower and views of the ocean from almost every room. A double-tiered, ocean-front veranda stretches

across the house. Each room is uniquely furnished and some boast handsome antique beds. Afternoon tea is offered as well as wine and cheese. Complimentary bicycles, beach tags, chairs, umbrellas and towels are available.

Innkeeper(s): Greg & Lorie Whissell. $95-285. MC, VISA, AX, PC. TAC10. 27 rooms with PB. Breakfast and afternoon tea included in rates. Types of meals: Gourmet bkfst and early coffee/tea. Beds: KQD. Cable TV and turndown service in room. Air conditioning. Bicycles and wine and cheese which are included in rates are on premises. Weddings and family reunions hosted. Art galleries, beaches, bicycling, canoeing/kayaking, fishing, golf, hiking, horseback riding, live theater, museums, shopping, tennis, water sports and wineries nearby.

Publicity: *Victoria, Mid Atlantic Country, Philadelphia Magazine and New Jersey Monthly.*

"We've travelled bed and breakfasts for years and this is by far the best."

Barnard-Good House

238 Perry St
Cape May, NJ 08204-1447
(609)884-5381

Circa 1865. The Barnard-Good House is a Second Empire Victorian with a mansard roof and original shingles. A wraparound veranda adds to the charm of this lavender, blue and tan cottage along with the original picket fence and a concrete-formed

flower garden. The inn was selected by New Jersey Magazine as the No. 1 spot for breakfast in New Jersey, and breakfasts are a special, four-course, gourmet feast.

Innkeeper(s): Nan & Tom Hawkins. $100-175. MC, VISA, PC. 5 rooms with PB and 2 suites. Breakfast included in rates. Types of meals: Gourmet bkfst. Beds: KQ. Ceiling fan and alarm clocks in room. Air conditioning. Antiquing, fishing, live theater, parks, shopping and water sports nearby.

Publicity: *New York Times, New Jersey Monthly, McCalls and Philadelphia Inquirer.*

"Even the cozy bed can't hold you down when the smell of Nan's breakfast makes its way upstairs."

Bedford Inn

805 Stockton Ave
Cape May, NJ 08204-2446
(609)884-4158 Fax:(609)884-6320
E-mail: info@bedfordinn.com
Web: www.bedfordinn.com

Circa 1880. The Bedford, decked in gingerbread trim with verandas on both of its two stories, has welcomed guests since

its creation in the 19th century. Electrified gaslights, period wallcoverings and rich, Victorian furnishings create an air of nostalgia. The inn is close to many of Cape May's shops and restaurants, as well as the beach, which is just half a block away. Guests are pampered with breakfasts of quiche, gourmet egg dishes, French toast and freshly baked breads.

Innkeeper(s): Cindy & James Schmucker. $90-235. MC, VISA, AX, DS, PC, TC. TAC10. 11 rooms with PB and 3 suites. Breakfast and afternoon tea included in rates. Types of meals: Gourmet bkfst. Beds: KQDT. Cable TV, ceiling fan and VCR in room. Air conditioning. Library, refrigerator and free limited driveway parking on premises. Antiquing, fishing, house tours, trolley tours, restaurants, beach, live theater, parks and water sports nearby.

Buttonwood Manor

115 Broadway
Cape May, NJ 08204-1264
(609)884-4070
E-mail: ring@dandy.net
Web: www.buttonwoodmanorbb.com

Circa 1908. While most of us enjoy the usual silverware, plates and towels, Lizzie H. Richardson received this stately Colonial Revival manor as her wedding gift. The interior includes four guest rooms, decorated with turn-of-the-century furnishings. A multi-course, gourmet breakfast is served each morning. Guests enjoy items such as baked fruit, egg puffs, and buttermilk biscuits. The inn is located slightly away from the hustle and bustle of downtown Cape May, yet close enough to walk to shops, restaurants and other attractions.

Historic Interest: HIstoric Cold Spring Village (2 miles), Phusic Estate (1 mile), Cape May Point lighthouse (1 1/2 miles).

Innkeeper(s): Diane & Roger Ring. $100-175. MC, VISA, PC. 6 rooms, 4 with PB. Breakfast and afternoon tea included in rates. Types of meals: Gourmet bkfst, veg bkfst and early coffee/tea. Beds: KQT. Cable TV and ceiling fan in room. Air conditioning. Library on premises. Antiquing, art galleries, beaches, bicycling, canoeing/kayaking, fishing, golf, hiking, birding, live theater, museums, parks, shopping, tennis and water sports nearby.

Captain Mey's B&B Inn

202 Ocean St
Cape May, NJ 08204-2322
(609)884-7793 (800)981-3702
E-mail: captainmeys@netscape.net
Web: www.captainmeys.com

Circa 1890. Named after Dutch explorer Capt. Cornelius J. Mey, who named the area, the inn displays its Dutch heritage with table-top Persian rugs, Delft china and imported Dutch lace curtains. The dining room features chestnut and oak Eastlake paneling and a fireplace. Two guest rooms have dou-

ble whirlpool tubs. Some guest rooms include both a queen and a single bed. A hearty breakfast is served by candlelight or on the wraparound veranda in the summertime. The ferry and lighthouse are nearby.

Historic Interest: Cold Spring Village and the Cape May Lighthouse are five minutes away. Lewes, Del., is one hour by ferry.

Innkeeper(s): George & Kathleen Blinn. $85-225. MC, VISA, AX, PC, TC. TAC10. 7 rooms with PB and 1 suite. Breakfast and afternoon tea included in rates. Types of meals: Full bkfst. Beds: QT. Ceiling fan and some with two-person whirlpool tubs and TV in room. Air conditioning. Small meetings and family reunions hosted. Amusement parks, antiquing, fishing, bicycling, bird watching, lighthouse, ferry, live theater, parks, shopping and water sports nearby.

Publicity: *Americana, Country Living, New Jersey Monthly, WKYW News (CBS) Philadelphia, WNJN (N.J. Network News Trenton), New Jersey Country Roads Magazine and Traveller.*

"The innkeepers pamper you so much you wish you could stay forever."

The Carroll Villa B&B

19 Jackson St
Cape May, NJ 08204-1417
(609)884-9619 Fax:(609)884-0264
E-mail: cvres@eticomm.net
Web: www.carrollvilla.com

Circa 1882. This Victorian hotel is located one-half block from the ocean on the oldest street in the historic district of Cape May. Breakfast at the Villa is a memorable event, featuring dishes acclaimed by the New York Times and Frommer's. Homemade fruit breads, Italian omelets and Crab Eggs Benedict are a few specialties. Meals are served in the Mad Batter Restaurant on a European veranda, a secluded garden terrace or in the sky-lit Victorian dining room. The restaurant serves breakfast, lunch, dinner and cocktails daily. The decor of this inn is decidedly Victorian with period antiques and wallpapers.

Innkeeper(s): Mark Kulkowitz & Pamela Ann Huber. $75-180. MC, VISA, AX, DS, PC. TAC10. 22 rooms with PB and 2 conference rooms. Breakfast included in rates. Types of meals: Full bkfst, lunch and dinner. Beds: QD. TV, phone, ceiling fan and VCR in room. Air conditioning. Fax and copier on premises. Weddings, small meetings, family reunions and seminars hosted. Amusement parks, antiquing, fishing, live theater, parks and shopping nearby.

Publicity: *Atlantic City Press, Asbury Press, Frommer's, New York Times and Washington Post.*

"Mr. Kulkowitz is a superb host. He strives to accommodate the diverse needs of guests."

The Chalfonte Hotel

301 Howard St, PO Box 475
Cape May, NJ 08204-0475
(609)884-8409 Fax:(609)884-4588
E-mail: chalfontnj@aol.com
Web: www.chalfonte.com

Circa 1876. This 108-room hotel was built by Civil War hero Colonel Henry Sawyer. The hotel features wraparound porches, simply appointed rooms with marble-topped dressers and other original antiques. The fare in the Magnolia Room is Southern-style with fresh fish daily and vegetarian options. Children of all

ages are welcome, and there is a supervised children's dining room for guests aged six and under. Much of the hotel's restoration and preservation is accomplished by dedicated volunteers and architectural students who have adopted the hotel as their own. Painting workshops, Elderhostel educational programs, weekly events and entertainment, group retreats, weddings and family reunions are offered.

Historic Interest: Cold Springs Village (4 miles).

Innkeeper(s): Anne LeDuc & Judy Bartella. $110-265. MC, VISA, AX, DS, PC, TC. TAC10. 70 rooms, 10 with PB, 2 cottages and 2 conference rooms. Breakfast and dinner included in rates. Types of meals: Full bkfst and early coffee/tea. MAP. Beds: KQDT. TV and ceiling fan in room. VCR, fax and copier on premises. Weddings, small meetings, family reunions and seminars hosted. Amusement parks, antiquing, fishing, golf, nature trails, whale watching, birding, live theater, parks, shopping, sporting events, tennis and water sports nearby.

Publicity: *Dallas Morning News, Washington Post, Travel & Leisure, Washingtonian, Philadelphia Inquirer, New York Times, Country Inns, Richmond Times, Mid-Atlantic Country, Star and Wave, Virginian Pilot & Ledger-Star, USA Today, Los Angeles Times, National Public Radio, South Jersey Weddings., PBS Channel 12, Discovery Channel and Maryland Public TV.*

"We love the relaxed and genteel atmosphere, the feeling of having stepped into another time is delightful."

Fairthorne B&B

111 Ocean St
Cape May, NJ 08204-2319
(609)884-8791 (800)438-8742 Fax:(609)898-6129
E-mail: fairthornebnb@aol.com
Web: www.fairthorne.com

Circa 1892. Antiques abound in this three-story Colonial Revival. Lace curtains and a light color scheme complete the charming decor. There is a new, yet historic addition to the B&B. The innkeepers now offer guest quarters (with fireplaces) in The Fairthorne Cottage, a restored 1880s building adjacent to the inn. The signature breakfasts include special daily entrees along with an assortment of home-baked breads and muffins. A light afternoon tea also is served  with refreshments. The proximity to the beach will be much appreciated by guests, and the innkeepers offer the use of beach towels, bicycles and sand chairs. The nearby historic district is full of fun shops and restaurants.

Innkeeper(s): Diane & Ed Hutchinson. $170-250. MC, VISA, AX, DS, TC. 8 rooms with PB and 1 suite. Breakfast and afternoon tea included in rates. Types of meals: Full bkfst and early coffee/tea. Beds: KQ. Ceiling fan in room. Air conditioning. Fax on premises. Antiquing, fishing, historic lighthouse & Victorian architectural tours, live theater, parks, shopping and water sports nearby.

Publicity: *New Jersey Countryside.*

"I feel as if I have come to stay with a dear old friend who has spared no expense to provide me with all that my heart can desire! ... I will savor the memory of your hospitality for years to come. Thanks so much."

Gingerbread House

28 Gurney St
Cape May, NJ 08204
(609)884-0211
E-mail: frede@bellatlantic.net
Web: gingerbreadinn.com

Circa 1869. The Gingerbread is one of eight original Stockton Row Cottages, summer retreats built for families from Philadelphia and Virginia. It is a half-block from the ocean and breezes waft over the wicker-filled porch. The inn is listed in the National Register. It has been meticulously restored and decorated with period antiques and a fine collection of paintings. The inn's woodwork is especially notable, guests enter through handmade teak double doors.

Historic Interest: Historic tours are available.

Innkeeper(s): Fred & Joan Echevarria. $90-260. MC, VISA, PC, TC. 6 rooms, 3 with PB and 1 suite. Breakfast and afternoon tea included in rates. Types of meals: Full bkfst. Beds: QD. Air conditioning. Small meetings and family reunions hosted. Antiquing, fishing, birding. Victorian homes, live theater, parks, shopping and water sports nearby.

Publicity: *Philadelphia Inquirer, New Jersey Monthly and Atlantic City Press Newspaper.*

"The elegance, charm and authenticity of historic Cape May, but more than that, it appeals to us as `home'."

The Duke of Windsor Inn

817 Washington St
Cape May, NJ 08204-1651
(609)884-1355 (800)826-8973
E-mail: innkeeper@dukeofwindsorinn.com
Web: www.dukeofwindsorinn.com

Circa 1896. This Queen Anne Victorian was built by Delaware River boat pilot Harry Hazelhurst and his wife, Florence. They were both six feet tall, so the house was built with large open rooms and doorways, and extra-wide stairs. The inn has a carved, natural oak open staircase with stained-glass windows at top and bottom. Five antique chandeliers grace the dining room. Parking is available on premises.

Historic Interest: National Register.

Innkeeper(s): Patricia Joyce. $95-220. MC, VISA, PC, TC. 10 rooms with PB. Breakfast and afternoon tea included in rates. Types of meals: Full bkfst and early coffee/tea. Beds: QDT. Ceiling fan in room. Air conditioning. Off-street parking, outside hot and cold shower and refrigerator available for guest use on premises. Antiquing, fishing, live theater, parks, shopping and water sports nearby.

Publicity: *Philadelphia Inquirer, Innsider and Mainline Magazine.*

"Breakfast at 9:00 am and tea at 4:00 pm were delicious and relaxing. We can't wait to come back."

The Henry Sawyer Inn

722 Columbia Ave
Cape May, NJ 08204-2332
(609)884-5667 (800)449-5667 Fax:(609)884-9406

Circa 1877. This fully restored, three-story peach Victorian home boasts a gingerbread embellished veranda, brick-colored shutters and brown trim. Inside, the parlor features Victorian antiques, a marble fireplace, polished wood floors, an Oriental rug, formal wallcoverings, a crystal chandelier and fresh flowers. Guest rooms have been decorated with careful attention to a romantic and fresh Victorian theme, as well. One room includes a whirlpool tub, one includes a private porch, and another a fireplace.

Innkeeper(s): Mary & Barbara Morris. $85-225. MC, VISA, AX, DC, DS, PC, TC. TAC5. 5 rooms with PB, 1 with FP and 2 suites. Breakfast and afternoon tea included in rates. Types of meals: Full bkfst and early coffee/tea. Beds: KQT. Cable TV, ceiling fan, one with whirlpool, private porch and small refrigerator in room. Air conditioning. VCR, fax and parking on premises. Weddings, small meetings, family reunions and seminars hosted. Antiquing, fishing, golf, carriage, Victorian trolley, live theater, parks, shopping, tennis and water sports nearby.

Humphrey Hughes House

29 Ocean St
Cape May, NJ 08204-2411
(609)884-4428 (800)582-3634

Circa 1903. Stained-glass windows mark each landing of the staircase, and intricately carved American chestnut columns add to the atmosphere in this 30-room mansion. The land was purchased by the Captain Humphrey Hughes family in the early 1700s. The majestic grandfather clock remains as one of many late-Victorian antiques.

Historic Interest: The inn is listed in National Register.

Innkeeper(s): Lorraine & Terry Schmidt. $140-255. MC, VISA, PC. 7 rooms with PB and 4 suites. Breakfast and afternoon tea included in rates. Beds: KQ. Cable TV and ceiling fan in room. Air conditioning. Antiquing, live the-

ater, shopping and water sports nearby.

Publicity: *New York Times. and AM Philadelphia.*

"Thoroughly enjoyed our stay."

The Inn on Ocean

25 Ocean St
Cape May, NJ 08204-2411
(609)884-7070 (800)304-4477 Fax:(609)884-1384
E-mail: innocean@bellatlantic.net
Web: www.theinnonocean.com

Circa 1880. A strawberry pink roof adorned with a crown of wrought iron is accentuated with bright green, white and yellow accents at this Second Empire Victorian. The interior is done in an elegant Victorian style. The inn boasts the only Victorian billiard room in Cape May.

Innkeeper(s): Jack & Katha Davis. $129-259. MC, VISA, AX, DC, CB, DS, TC. TAC10. 4 rooms with PB, 1 with FP and 1 suite. Breakfast and afternoon tea included in rates. Types of meals: Full bkfst. Beds: KQ. Cable TV, ceiling fan and suite has fireplace in room. Air conditioning. Antiquing, fishing, tennis, golf, live theater, parks, shopping and water sports nearby.

Publicity: *Delta Airlines, United Airlines & Southwest Airlines In-Flight Magazines, Washington Post Sunday Magazine and Long Island Newsday Newspaper.*

"A wonderful and beautiful experience. Great comfort, great breakfast and great hospitality."

John F. Craig House

609 Columbia Ave
Cape May, NJ 08204-2305
(609)884-0100 (877)544-0314 Fax:(609)898-1307
E-mail: fe6119@bellatlantic.net
Web: www.johnfcraig.com

Circa 1866. Upon entering this historic home, guests are transported into opulent surroundings befitting an Edith Wharton novel. Fine woodwork, Oriental rugs, original lighting and reproduction wallcoverings create a lavish, Victorian setting. The cozy rooms are elegant, decorated with antiques, but not so opulent that you dare not touch anything. The third-story rooms are among the most comfortably furnished with country antiques and wicker furnishings, and made still cozier with the sloping ceilings formed by the dormers. Multi-course breakfasts and afternoon teas complete the Victorian experience. A variety of games are available for use, and guests can check out beach towels and beach chairs. The innkeepers are happy to help guests plan activities or make dinner reservations.

Innkeeper(s): Connie & Frank Felicetti. $115-205. MC, VISA, DS, PC, TC. TAC10. 8 rooms, 7 with PB and 1 suite. Breakfast and afternoon tea included in rates. Types of meals: Gourmet bkfst, veg bkfst and early coffee/tea. Beds: KQDT. Ceiling fan in room. Air conditioning. Fax, copier and library on premises. Small meetings, family reunions and seminars hosted. Amusement parks, antiquing, art galleries, beaches, bicycling, canoeing/kayaking, fishing, golf, hiking, horseback riding, live theater, museums, parks, shopping, tennis, water sports and wineries nearby.

John Wesley Inn

30 Gurney St
Cape May, NJ 08204
(609)884-1012

Circa 1869. The innkeepers of this graciously restored Carpenter Gothic home have won awards for their captivating exterior Christmas decorations, and holidays at the inn are a seasonal delight. The interior decor preserves the Victorian era so treasured in this seaside village. Antiques are set in rooms decorated with bright, patterned wallpapers and windows decked in lace. The innkeepers also offer a restored carriage house, featuring the same period decor, but the modern amenity of a stocked kitchen.

Innkeeper(s): John & Rita Tice. $95-180. PC, TC. 6 rooms, 4 with PB, 2 cottages and 1 conference room. Breakfast included in rates. Types of meals: Cont plus. Beds: QD. Phone and ceiling fan in room. Air conditioning. Weddings, small meetings, family reunions and seminars hosted. Amusement parks, antiquing, fishing, live theater, parks, shopping and water sports nearby.

The King's Cottage

9 Perry St
Cape May, NJ 08204-1460
(609)884-0415 (877)258-1876
E-mail: kingscottage@snip.net
Web: www.kingscottage.com

Circa 1878. Enjoy the beautiful ocean views as you relax on antique wicker on the wraparound verandas at this architectural gem, designed by Frank Furness. The railings boast ceramic tiles that were part of a Japanese exhibition from the Philadelphia Centennial of 1876, and a measured drawing is recorded in the Library of Congress. Many of the guest rooms afford ocean views and some offer private verandas. All feature unique period decor and antiques. Breakfasts are served in the formal dining room on tables set with china, crystal and silver.

Historic Interest: The King's Cottage is listed in the National Register and located in Cape May's primary historic district. The Victorian Mall, restored Cape May Lighthouse and Physick Estate Museum are just a few of the nearby historic attractions.

Innkeeper(s): Roseann Baker, Maryrose Wineburg. $95-225. MC, VISA, PC. 9 rooms with PB. Types of meals: Full bkfst and early coffee/tea. Beds: QD. Air conditioning. Private verandah with some accomodations and on-site parking on premises. Weddings, small meetings, family reunions and seminars hosted. Amusement parks, antiquing, fishing, dolphin watching, lighthouse, casinos, live theater, parks, shopping and water sports nearby.

Publicity: *Victorian Affair, Atlantic City Press, Newark Star and Cape May Videos.*

"Thanks so much for your warm and inviting hospitality. I never expected to feel so at home at a bed and breakfast. Your personal touch made this a memorable experience and not just 'a place to stay.' The views and ocean breezes were more than you described. Truly great."

Leith Hall Historic Seashore Inn

22 Ocean St
Cape May, NJ 08204-2412
(609)884-1934
E-mail: stay@leithhall.com
Web: www.leithhall.com

Circa 1884. Most guest rooms and suites of this Second Empire Victorian feature an ocean view. There is a handsome library and parlor, and the opulently decorated bed chambers feature Victorian beds, mahogany tables and multi-patterned wallpapers. The first-floor room has stained-glass French doors. Quiches, crepes and egg entrees are served on antique silver, crystal and Royal Worcester china. An English afternoon tea is offered. Antiquing, live theatre and shopping are available nearby.

Innkeeper(s): Elan & Susan Zingman-Leith. Call for rates. 2 suites. Ocean views from most rooms and suites, fireplaces and whirlpool tubs in room. Air conditioning. Small meetings, family reunions and seminars hosted. Antiquing, fishing, horse carriage rides, birding, tours, whale watching, live theater and shopping nearby.

Mainstay Inn

635 Columbia Ave
Cape May, NJ 08204-2305
(609)884-8690

Circa 1872. This was once the elegant and exclusive Jackson's Clubhouse popular with gamblers. Many of the guest rooms and the grand parlor look much as they did in the 1870s. Fourteen-foot-high ceilings, elaborate chandeliers, a sweeping veranda and a cupola add to the atmosphere. Tom and Sue Carroll received the American Historic Inns award in 1988 for their preservation efforts, and have been making unforgettable memories for guests  for decades. A writer for Conde Nast Traveler once wrote, "architecturally, no inn, anywhere, quite matches the Mainstay."

Historic Interest: Cape May Lighthouse & State Park Museum (2 miles).

Innkeeper(s): Tom & Sue Carroll. $95-295. PC, TC. 16 rooms with PB, 4 with FP and 7 suites. Breakfast and afternoon tea included in rates. Types of meals: Full bkfst, cont plus and early coffee/tea. Beds: KQD. Phone, suites with phones and some with ceiling fans in room. Air conditioning. Library on premises. Handicap access. Small meetings and seminars hosted. Amusement parks, antiquing, fishing, historic attractions, tennis, golf, birding, biking, hiking, live theater, parks, shopping, sporting events and water sports nearby.

Publicity: *Washington Post, Good Housekeeping, New York Times, Conde Nast Traveler, Smithsonian, Americana, Travel & Leisure and National Geographic Traveler.*

"By far the most lavishly and faithfully restored guesthouse...run by two arch-preservationists—Travel & Leisure."

Poor Richard's Inn

17 Jackson St
Cape May, NJ 08204-1417
(609)884-3536
Web: www.poorrichardsinn.com

Circa 1882. The unusual design of this Second-Empire house has been accentuated with five colors of paint. Arched gingerbread porches tie together the distinctive bays of the house's facade. The combination of exterior friezes, balustrades and fretwork has earned the inn an individual listing in the National Register. Some rooms sport an eclectic country Victorian decor with patchwork quilts and pine furniture, while others tend toward a more traditional turn-of-the-century ambiance. An apartment suite is available.

Innkeeper(s): Richard Samuelson. $59-147. MC, VISA. 10 rooms with PB and 1 suite. Breakfast included in rates. Types of meals: Cont plus and early coffee/tea. EP. Beds: QDT. Cable TV in room. Air conditioning. Copier on premises. Small meetings and family reunions hosted. Amusement parks, antiquing, fishing, ocean beach, live theater, parks and water sports nearby.

Publicity: *Washington Post, New York Times, National Geographic Traveler and New Jersey.*

"Hold our spot on the porch. We'll be back before you know it."

The Queen Victoria

102 Ocean St
Cape May, NJ 08204-2320
(609)884-8702
E-mail: qvinn@bellatlantic.net
Web: www.queenvictoria.com

Circa 1881. This nationally acclaimed inn, a block from the ocean and shops in the historic district, is comprised of two beautiful Victorian homes, restored and furnished with antiques. "Victorian Homes" magazine featured 23 color photographs of The Queen Victoria, because of its décor and luxury amenities. Guest

rooms offer handmade quilts, antiques, air conditioning, mini-refrigerators and all have private baths. Some luxury suites include handsome fireplaces and whirlpool tubs. Afternoon tea is enjoyed while rocking on the porch in summer or before a warm fireplace in winter. Breakfast is hearty buffet style and the inn has its own cookbook. The innkeepers keep a fleet of complimentary bicycles available for guests and there are beach chairs and beach towels as well. The inn is open all year with special Christmas festivities and winter packages.

Innkeeper(s): Dane & Joan Wells. $100-300. MC, VISA, PC. 21 rooms with PB and 6 suites. Breakfast and afternoon tea included in rates. Types of meals: Full bkfst and early coffee/tea. Beds: QD. Phones & televisions (some rooms) in room. Air conditioning. Bicycles on premises. Small meetings hosted. Amusement parks, antiquing, beaches, golf, historic tours, parks and water sports nearby.

Publicity: *Philadelphia Inquirer and Travel channel.*

Queen's Hotel

601 Columbia Ave
Cape May, NJ 08204-2305
(609)884-1613
E-mail: qvinn@bellatlantic.net
Web: www.queenshotel.com

Circa 1876. This elegant Victorian hotel is located just a block from the beach in the center of Cape May's historic district. Period decor graces the luxurious guest rooms. The feeling is both romantic and historic. Many of the rooms and suites offer

double whirlpool tubs or glass-enclosed marble showers. Other amenities include hair dryers, TV, heated towel bar, air conditioning, coffee makers and mini refrigerators. Some have private balconies and ocean views. As this is a hotel, meals are not included in the

rates; however, a multitude of restaurants and cafes are within walking distance or you can ask for the continental breakfast basket for a small charge. The hotel's staff includes professional concierge service. Shops are one block away. There are bicycles on the premises to explore the town and scenic water views.

Innkeeper(s): Dane & Joan Wells. $85-275. MC, VISA, PC. 11 rooms with PB, 1 with FP and 1 suite. Beds: QD. Cable TV, phone, ceiling fan, hair dryer, coffeemaker and heated towel bar in room. Air conditioning. Bicycles on premises. Small meetings hosted. Amusement parks, antiquing, bicycling, fishing, golf, historic tours, live theater, parks and water sports nearby.

Publicity: *Philadelphia Inquirer.*

Saltwood House

28 Jackson St
Cape May, NJ 08204-1465
(609)884-6754 (800)830-8232
E-mail: saltwoodhouse@aol.com

Circa 1906. The peach-colored awnings and the Colonial Revival architecture of Saltwood House welcome guests to a Victorian experience in a setting of hand-carved antique oak furniture, Tiffany-style lamps and a collection of Victorian silver plate serving pieces. A favorite room is the Saratoga with a

bay window view overlooking the street, a carved gargoyle oak bedstead, chrysanthemum wallpaper and a Larkin desk. Located one-half block from the beach and in

the middle of Cape May's oldest street with gas lamps, sycamore trees and horse-drawn carriages, there are restaurants, shops and the walking mall on Washington Street to enjoy. Egg casseroles, bacon and fresh fruit are often served at breakfast.

Innkeeper(s): Don Schweikert. $80-295. MC, VISA, AX, PC, TC. 4 rooms, 2 with PB and 2 suites. Breakfast and afternoon tea included in rates. Types of meals: Full bkfst. Beds: KQ. Cable TV, ceiling fan and VCR in room. Air conditioning. Fax, copier and parking on premises. Amusement parks, antiquing, fishing, golf, live theater, tennis and water sports nearby.

Publicity: *Newark Star-Ledger, Philadelphia's Channel and QVC & PBS.*

"We're back. Every stay gets better and better. Thanks so much for your wonderful hospitality. See you again next year."

Summer Cottage Inn

613 Columbia Ave
Cape May, NJ 08204-2305
(609)884-4948
E-mail: sumcot@bellatlantic.net
Web: www.summercottageinn.com

Circa 1867. A cupola tops this Italianate-style inn located on a quiet tree-lined street in the historic district. It's close to the beach (one block) and the Victorian Mall. Period Victorian pieces are featured in the parlor and the veranda is filled with plants and rockers. There's a fireplace in the sitting room and a Baby Grand piano in the parlor.

Innkeeper(s): Linda & Skip Loughlin. Call for rates. MC, VISA, DS. 9 rooms with PB. Breakfast and afternoon tea included in rates. Types of meals: Full bkfst. Beds: Q. Ceiling fan in room. Air conditioning. Antiquing, beaches, fishing, live theater, shopping and water sports nearby.

Publicity: *Star Ledger and Philadelphia Inquirer.*

"Comfortable. Home away from home."

White Dove Cottage

619 Hughes St
Cape May, NJ 08204-2317
(609)884-0613 (800)321-3683
Web: www.whitedovecottage.com

Circa 1866. The beautiful octagonal slate on the Mansard roof of this Second Empire house is just one of the inn's many handsome details. Bright sunny rooms are furnished in American and European antiques, period wallpapers, paintings, prints and handmade quilts.

Suites with fireplaces or Jacuzzi tub are available. Breakfast is served to the soft music of an antique music box and boasts heirloom crystal, fine china and lace. Located on a quiet, gas-lit

street, the inn is two blocks from the beach, restaurants and shops. Ask about mystery weekends and the inn's Honeymoon and Romantic Escape packages.

Innkeeper(s): Frank & Sue Smith. $90-235. TAC10. 4 rooms with PB and 2 suites. Breakfast and afternoon tea included in rates. Types of meals: Gourmet bkfst and early coffee/tea. Beds: KQD. Two suites with fireplace and Jacuzzi in room. Antiquing, fishing, live theater, shopping and water sports nearby.

Publicity: *Bride.*

Woodleigh House

808 Washington St
Cape May, NJ 08204-1652
(609)884-7123 (800)399-7123

Circa 1866. Rocking chairs line the veranda of this 1866 Victorian farmhouse. Its natural cedar siding is highlighted with burgundy and creme trim. Period antiques are featured. The dining room, for instance, boasts a carved antique sideboard from Brussels, an Oriental carpet and an original chandelier. Guest rooms offer romantic, seven-foot-high, carved antique headboards and marble-top dressers. Popular breakfast dishes are Banana Blinni (a French toast made from banana bread) and breakfast casseroles featuring herbs from the garden. Afternoon tea is hot or cold depending upon the season and may feature Heath-nut crunch cookies or other homemade goodies. The innkeepers have developed a secret garden complete with pond and a wisteria arbor to add to the inn's inviting outdoor spaces.
Innkeeper(s): Joe & Joanne Tornambe. $110-185. MC, VISA. 5 rooms with PB and 1 suite. Breakfast and afternoon tea included in rates. Types of meals: Full bkfst. Beds: KQ. TV in room. Air conditioning. Bike rack, off-street parking and beautiful gardens on premises. Antiquing, beaches, fishing, live theater, shopping, tennis and water sports nearby.

"Clean and comfortable, delicious breakfast, charming hosts."

Hackettstown   C3

The Everitt House, A Victorian Bed & Breakfast

200 High Street
Hackettstown, NJ 07840
(908)684-1307 Fax:(908)684-8049
E-mail: everitthouse@email.com
Web: www.everitthouse.com

Circa 1876. Named in honor of its first owner, an influential man and former mayor, this Second Empire Victorian with Mansard roof is located in the town's historic district, only one hour from New York City. The formal living room is the perfect place to plan the day's activities. Guest bedrooms feature sitting areas and a warm and appealing atmosphere. The bountiful morning meal, which may include stuffed pancakes, chocolate croissants and a frittata, can only be overshadowed by the picturesque views from the glass-enclosed breakfast room. Enjoy snacks and beverages available any time. Manicured lawns, colorful flowers, rose and rock gardens all combine to create a park-like setting. The Delaware Water Gap is a 30-minute drive.
Innkeeper(s): Lotis & Russ Markowitz. $115-150. MC, VISA, AX, DS, PC, TC. 4 rooms with PB, 1 suite and 1 conference room. Breakfast included in rates. Types of meals: Gourmet bkfst, early coffee/tea, afternoon tea and snacks/refreshments. Beds: KQD. Cable TV, phone and ceiling fan in room. Air conditioning. Fax and copier on premises. Weddings, small meetings, family reunions and seminars hosted. Antiquing, bicycling, canoeing/kayaking, fishing, golf, hiking, horseback riding, live theater, parks, shopping and wineries nearby.
Publicity: WRNJ Radio.

Haddonfield   G3

Haddonfield Inn

44 West End Ave
Haddonfield, NJ 08033-2616
(856)428-2195 (800)269-0014 Fax:(856)354-1273
E-mail: innkeeper@haddonfieldinn.com
Web: www.haddonfieldinn.com

Circa 1865. This three-story Victorian house, complete with gabled roofs, a turret and veranda, is in the National Trust. Its location is historic Haddonfield, said by Philadelphia Magazine to be the most picturesque village in the Delaware Valley. Handsome heritage homes, fine museums, symphony orchestras, theater and more than 200 shops and restaurants are nearby. Parlors are furnished with antiques and chandeliers, and the guest rooms offer whirlpools and fireplaces, each in the theme of a European country or other culture. Upon arrival, guests are offered snacks and beverages. In the morning, a gourmet breakfast is served before a flickering fireplace in the dining room or on the wraparound veranda overlooking the inn's lawns. For guest convenience, there is an elevator, and the innkeeper provides concierge service. The inn is popular for small meetings and special events. Walk to the train to visit Philadelphia (17 minutes away) and connect to stadiums, the airport and Amtrak.
Innkeeper(s): Nancy & Fred Chorpita. $140-215. MC, VISA, AX, DS, PC, TC. 8 rooms with PB and 1 suite. Breakfast included in rates. Types of meals: Gourmet bkfst and snacks/refreshments. Cable TV and phone in room. Air conditioning. Handicap access. Weddings and family reunions hosted. Golf, swimming, health clubs, parks and tennis nearby.

Pets allowed: Dogs only, subject to restrictions.

Island Heights   G6

Studio of John F. Peto

102 Cedar Ave., PO Box 306
Island Heights, NJ 08732-0306
(732)270-6058

Circa 1889. This Victorian home is listed in the National Register of Historic Places and is of note because it was built by renowned artist John F. Peto. His granddaughter has opened the home for guests. Filled with artifacts, eclectic furnishings, memorabilia and reproductions of his art, the studio is decorated much as it was originally. There is a large screened porch with rocking chairs providing views down the hill to the river. A full breakfast is usually served.
Innkeeper(s): Joy Peto Smiley. $75-95. AX, DS, PC, TC. TAC10. 4 rooms. Breakfast included in rates. Types of meals: Full bkfst. Beds: DT. Cable TV and phone in room. Air conditioning. Bicycles and library on premises. Small meetings and family reunions hosted. Amusement parks, antiquing, fishing, parks, shopping and water sports nearby.
Publicity: Asbury Park Press, House and Gardens Magazine and Observer Entertainer.

"Breakfast is so great-we won't need any lunch."

Lambertville   E3

Chimney Hill Farm Estate & The Ol' Barn Inn

207 Goat Hill Rd
Lambertville, NJ 08530
(609)397-1516 (800)211-4667 Fax:(609)397-9353
E-mail: chbb@erols.com
Web: www.chimneyhillinn.com

Circa 1820. Chimney Hill, in the hills above the riverside town of Lambertville, is a grand display of stonework, designed with both Federal and Greek Revival-style architecture. The inn's sunroom is particularly appealing, with its stone walls, fireplaces and French windows looking out to eight acres of gardens and fields. All eight of the guest rooms in the

estate farmhouse include fireplaces, and some have canopied beds. The Ol' Barn has four suites with fireplaces, Jacuzzis, steam rooms, guest pantries, spiral staircases and loft bedrooms. The innkeepers offer adventure, romance and special

interest packages for their guests, and the inn is also popular for corporate retreats. There are plenty of seasonal activities nearby, from kayaking to skiing. New Hope is the neighboring town and offers many charming restaurants and shops, as well.

Innkeeper(s): Terry Ann & Richard Anderson. $125-299. MC, VISA, AX, PC, TC. TAC10. 12 rooms with PB, 8 with FP and 2 conference rooms. Breakfast and snacks/refreshments included in rates. Types of meals: Full bkfst, cont plus and early coffee/tea. MAP, AP. Beds: KQD. Phone in room. Air conditioning. Copier, library and butler pantry with snacks on premises. Weddings, small meetings, family reunions and seminars hosted. Antiquing, fishing, live theater, parks, shopping, downhill skiing, cross-country skiing, sporting events and water sports nearby.

Publicity: *Country Inns (Cover), Colonial Homes, Country Roads Magazine and New Jersey Network.*

"We would be hard pressed to find a more perfect setting to begin our married life together."

York Street House

42 York St
Lambertville, NJ 08530-2024
(609)397-3007 (888)398-3199 Fax:(609)397-3299
E-mail: yorkstreethouse@hotmail.com
Web: www.yorkstreethouse.com

Circa 1909. Built by early industrialist George Massey as a 25th wedding anniversary present for his wife, the gracious manor house is situated on almost an acre in the heart of the historic district. Common rooms are warmed by Mercer Tile fireplaces and an original Waterford Crystal chandelier. A winding three-story staircase leads to well-appointed guest bedrooms with period furnishings. Looking out on the lawn and sitting porch, breakfast is served in the dining room, showcasing built-in leaded-glass china and large oak servers. Art galleries, bookstores and restaurants are nearby. Enjoy mule-drawn barges and carriage rides. New Hope, Pa., is a short walk across the Delaware River Bridge, with many quaint shops.

Innkeeper(s): Laurie and Mark Weinstein. $100-185. MC, VISA, AX, DS, PC, TC. TAC5. 5 rooms with PB. Breakfast included in rates. Types of meals: Gourmet bkfst, early coffee/tea and picnic lunch. Beds: KQ. Cable TV, ceiling fan and fireplaces in room. Air conditioning. VCR and fax on premises. Small meetings hosted. Antiquing, fishing, live theater, parks and shopping nearby.

Mays Landing   I4

Abbott House

6056 Main St
Mays Landing, NJ 08330-1852
(609)625-4400
E-mail: theabbotthouse@email.msn.com
Web: www.bbianj.com/abbott

Circa 1865. Guests at this Victorian-style mansion can relax on the bluff overlooking the Great Egg Harbor River, read on the second-floor veranda with its intricate fretwork or take afternoon tea in the belvedere (cupola) with spectacular views of historic Mays Landing. The inn is within walking distance to Lake Lenape and its various summer attractions. Each room is individually decorated with antiques, wicker, handmade quilts and other special touches. The Victorian Parlor is a place for

games, reading and conversation. Refreshments can be enjoyed on one of the many porches and verandas.

Innkeeper(s): Linda Maslanko, Cathy Foschia. $89-119. MC, VISA, AX, DS. 3 rooms and 1 suite. Breakfast included in rates. Types of meals: Full bkfst. Turndown service in room. Air conditioning. Small meetings and family reunions hosted. Antiquing and shopping nearby.

Medford   G4

The Iris Inn at Medford

45 S Main St
Medford, NJ 08055-2429
(609)654-7528 Fax:(609)714-0277

Circa 1904. Stained glass, original chandeliers and chestnut woodwork accent this pristine Queen Anne Victorian inn, formerly called the Main Stay. It is located in the heart of the historic village that was featured in National Geographic's "Guide to Small Town Escapes." The common room boasts a warm fireplace. Stay in the romantic Bridal Suite, and in the morning enjoy a savory breakfast offering traditional

favorites at a table for two. Sit by candlelight on the front porch. Stroll through the colorful perennial beds. A drive to the Jersey Shore or Philadelphia takes less than an hour.

Historic Interest: Independence National Historic Park, (15 miles), Historic Courthouse, Prison and Quaker Meeting House in Mount Holly (87 miles), Batsto Village (5 miles), Smithville Mansion (5 miles), Kirby's Mill (3 miles).

Innkeeper(s): Jim & Jennifer Cicalese. $90-125. MC, VISA, AX, PC, TC. 9 rooms with PB and 1 suite. Breakfast and snacks/refreshments included in rates. Types of meals: Full bkfst, veg bkfst, cont plus and early coffee/tea. Beds: QDT. Cable TV and phone in room. Air conditioning. Fax on premises. Weddings, small meetings, family reunions and seminars hosted. Amusement parks, antiquing, art galleries, bicycling, canoeing/kayaking, fishing, golf, hiking, horseback riding, small airport, live theater, museums, parks, shopping, sporting events and tennis nearby.

Publicity: *Courier Post and National Geographic.*

North Wildwood   K4

Candlelight Inn

2310 Central Ave
North Wildwood, NJ 08260-5944
(609)522-6200 (800)992-2632 Fax:(609)522-6125
E-mail: info@candlelight-inn.com
Web: www.candlelight-inn.com

Circa 1905. Candlelight Inn offers ten guest rooms in a restored Queen Anne Victorian. The home is decorated with an assortment of period pieces. Among its antiques are a Victorian sofa dating to 1855 and an 1890 Eastlake piano. Breakfasts begin with a fresh fruit course, followed by homemade breads and a daily entrée, such as waffles, pancakes or a specialty egg dish. Candlelight Inn is about eight miles from the

historic towns of Cape May and Cold Spring Village.

Historic Interest: Cape May (8 miles), Cold Spring Village (7 miles).

Innkeeper(s): Bill & Nancy Moncrief. $125-250. MC, VISA, AX, DS, TC. TAC10. 10 rooms with PB, 2 with FP and 3 suites. Breakfast and afternoon tea included in rates. Types of meals: Full bkfst, early coffee/tea and snacks/refreshments. Beds: KQDT. Cable TV, ceiling fan, fireplace and four with double whirlpool tubs in room. Central air. Fax, copier and hot tub on premises. German spoken. Amusement parks, antiquing, art galleries, beaches, bicycling, fishing, golf, live theater, museums, parks, shopping, tennis and water sports nearby.

Ocean City   J4

Castle By The Sea - A Romantic B&B

701 Ocean Ave
Ocean City, NJ 08226-3728
(609)398-3555 (800)622-4894
E-mail: castle701@aol.com
Web: www.castlebythesea.com

Circa 1900. A block from the beach and boardwalk, this joy-
fully painted four-story Victorian specializes in bountiful
gourmet breakfasts and romantic rooms. Most guest rooms
offer large beds, and you can choose from a variety of comforts
such as a fireplace, Jacuzzi or canopy bed. Rooms are appoint-

ed with lavish wallpapers and offer
embroidered bed linens. Ask for the
Romantic Rose room for an especially gracious room with a four-
poster rice bed, cherry woodwork,
a stained glass window and a fireplace. The inn's veranda is the most

popular place for enjoying the ocean air and early morning coffee or afternoon tea. A sample menu includes pumpkin harvest
muffins, apple cranberry crisp with vanilla cream, fresh asparagus cheese and herb pie and hearty breakfast sausage. Evening
turndown service with bedside chocolates is another treat, and
there are evening snacks as well.

Innkeeper(s): Jack & Renee Krutsick. $109-229. MC, VISA, AX, DS, TC.
TAC10. 9 rooms with PB, 2 with FP. Breakfast, afternoon tea and
snacks/refreshments included in rates. Types of meals: Gourmet bkfst and
early coffee/tea. Beds: QD. Cable TV, turndown service, ceiling fan, VCR,
Jacuzzi and fireplace in room. Air conditioning. Fax, copier and library on
premises. Family reunions hosted. Amusement parks, antiquing, art galleries,
beaches, bicycling, canoeing/kayaking, fishing, golf, live theater, museums,
parks, shopping, tennis and water sports nearby.
Publicity: *Philadelphia Inquirer, Courier-Post and Neward Star Ledger.*

Ebbie Guest & Apartment House

820 E 6th St
Ocean City, NJ 08226-3837
(609)399-4744

Circa 1920. This family owned and operated seashore house
includes both rooms and apartments. There is a two-bedroom
apartment with a living area and kitchen, as well as two studio

apartments. Both of the smaller
apartments include a kitchen.
Guest quarters and common
areas are decorated in a comfortable, relaxed-country style. The
home is a half block from the
beach and boardwalk.

Innkeeper(s): Dave & Liz Warrington. $75-100. TC. 7 rooms, 5 with PB.
Types of meals: Cont. Beds: DT. Cable TV in room. Air conditioning. Large
screen TV on premises. Family reunions hosted. Amusement parks, beaches,
fishing, golf, boardwalk, recreational parks, parks, shopping, sporting events,
tennis and water sports nearby.

Northwood Inn B&B

401 Wesley Ave
Ocean City, NJ 08226-3961
(609)399-6071 Fax:(609)398-5553
E-mail: info@northwoodinn.com
Web: www.northwoodinn.com

Circa 1894. This gracious three-story Queen Anne Victorian
with Colonial Victorian touches has been restored by the
innkeeper, who is a wooden boat builder and custom-home
builder. There are gleaming plank floors, a sweeping staircase, a
billiard room and a stocked library. The two-room Tower Suite
in the turret is a favorite, offering a luxurious bath with a double Jacuzzi tub
and over-sized shower. The
Magnolia Room is another popular choice with its taupe-colored
walls, lace curtains and double
Jacuzzi. There is a rooftop, four-

person spa where guests can relax and enjoy the sunset. The
inn is within walking distance of the beach, boardwalk, shops
and restaurants. The innkeepers offer bicycles and beach tags
to their guests. Availability may be checked on line.
Historic Interest: Cape May (30 miles).
Innkeeper(s): Marj & John Loeper. $80-220. MC, VISA, AX, PC. 8 rooms with
PB and 2 suites. Types of meals: Full bkfst and cont plus. Beds: QT. Suites
with Jacuzzi in room. Air conditioning. VCR, fax, spa and library on premises.
Weddings and small meetings hosted. Amusement parks, antiquing, fishing,
casino/Atlantic City, live theater, parks, shopping and water sports nearby.
Publicity: *Philadelphia Magazine. and NJN Discover New Jersey.*

*"In all our years of staying at B&Bs - still our favorite. Comfortable,
relaxing, wonderful breakfasts, and hosts who couldn't be more welcoming. In season, off season, or whenever a break is needed, we
head for the Northwood to renew!"*

Scarborough Inn

720 Ocean Ave
Ocean City, NJ 08226-3787
(609)399-1558 (800)258-1558 Fax:(609)399-4472
E-mail: cgbruno@earthlink.net
Web: www.scarboroughinn.com

Circa 1895. Savor the vintage charm of this 19th century B&B
that artfully offers modern conveniences. Guest bedrooms are
tastefully decorated, featuring many amenities to make each
stay a pampered one, including signature toiletries and the
morning newspaper. Indulge in
a tempting full breakfast and
afternoon refreshments. The
inn is located in the heart of
the island community's historic
district, featuring off-street
parking. The boardwalk, beach,

recreation park, dining and shopping are only 1.5 blocks away.
Historic Interest: Wheaten Village (1 hour), Cold Spring Village (40 minutes),
Leemings Run Gardens (30 minutes), Atlantic City (20 minutes), Cape May
(30 minutes).
Innkeeper(s): Gus & Carol Bruno. $90-210. MC, VISA, AX, DS, TC. TAC10.
18 rooms with PB and 5 suites. Breakfast included in rates. Types of meals:
Gourmet bkfst, early coffee/tea and afternoon tea. Beds: KQDT. Cable TV,
phone, suites have alarm clocks, morning newspaper, hair dryers and VCR in
room. Air conditioning. VCR, fax, library, parking and beach passes on premises. Small meetings and family reunions hosted. Italian spoken. Amusement
parks, antiquing, beaches, fishing, golf, birding, casinos, cultural and historical
sites, live theater, parks, shopping, sporting events and water sports nearby.
Publicity: *Country Inns Bed & Breakfast, Pittsburgh Press and Delaware
County Daily Times.*

Serendipity B&B

712 E 9th St
Ocean City, NJ 08226-3554
(609)399-1554 (800)842-8544 Fax:(609)399-1527
E-mail: info@serendipitynj.com
Web: www.serendipitynj.com

Circa 1912. The beach and boardwalk are less than half a
block from this renovated Dutch Colonial Inn. Healthy full
breakfasts are served, and the innkeepers offer dinners by reservation, October-April, with a mix
of interesting, vegetarian items. In
the summer, breakfasts are served
on a vine-shaded veranda. The
guest rooms are decorated in pas-
tels with wicker pieces.

Innkeeper(s): Clara & Bill Plowfield. $80-
159. MC, VISA, AX, DS, PC, TC. TAC10.
6 rooms, 4 with PB. Breakfast and snacks/refreshments included in rates.
Types of meals: Full bkfst and dinner. Beds: KQDT. Cable TV, ceiling fan,
VCR, bathrobes and bottled water in room. Air conditioning. Dressing rooms
with showers & beach towels, beach chairs, guest refrigerator, microwave and
video library on premises. Amusement parks, antiquing, fishing, ocean beach
and boardwalk, live theater, parks, shopping and water sports nearby.
Publicity: Philadelphia Inquirer Magazine.

"Serendipity is such a gift. For me it's a little like being adopted dur-
ing vacation time by a caring sister and brother. Your home is a home
away from home. You make it so."

Pemberton Boro   G4

Isaac Hilliard House Bed, Breakfast...and Beyond

31 Hanover St
Pemberton Boro, NJ 08068
(609)894-0756 (800)371-0756

Circa 1750. This 250-year-old Federal-era house is situated on
the edge of the scenic Pine Barrens. The inn offers year-round,
lighted, off-street parking. An entertainment center is provided
in the first-floor parlor. Spacious accommodations include guest
bedrooms and the Isaac Hilliard Suite, featuring a a remote-
controlled fireplace, four-poster canopy bed, dressing room,
mini-fridge, cable TV/VCR with video selection and garden tub.
Enjoy a freshly prepared breakfast in the well-appointed dining
room or quaint side porch. Swim in the private in-ground pool.
Take a short walk to rent canoes on the Rancocas River, hike,
golf or visit an amusement park nearby.

Historic Interest: Trenton, N.J., battlefield and buildings (25 minutes),
Washington Crossing State Park (40 minutes), Ye Olde Lock Up Building (5-
minute walk).
Innkeeper(s): Phyllis Davis & Gene R. O'Brien. $85-155. MC, VISA, AX, DC,
CB, DS, PC, TC. TAC10. 3 rooms with PB and 1 suite. Breakfast included
in rates. Types of meals: Full bkfst and veg bkfst. Beds: Q. Turndown service, ceiling fan, hair dryer and suite has remote-controlled gas fireplace in
room. Air conditioning. Swimming and refrigerator on premises. Weddings
and small meetings hosted. Amusement parks, antiquing, fishing, newly
dedicated Pemberton Rail Trail with visitor center, live theater, parks and
water sports nearby.
Publicity: New Jersey Travel Guide, New Jersey Monthly and Burlington
County Times.

"Every little detail was made so kind and warm. For even a short
time, we both felt as if we traveled abroad. Your home is kept gor-
geous and so tasteful."

Plainfield   D5

Pillars of Plainfield B&B

922 Central Ave
Plainfield, NJ 07060
 (888) PILLARS
E-mail: pillars2@aol.com
Web: www.pillars2.com

Circa 1870. Victorian and Georgian influences are mingled in
the design of this grand historic mansion, which boasts majestic columns and a wraparound porch. An acre of well-manicured grounds and gardens surrounds the home, which is
located in Plainfield's Van Wyck
Historic District. Guest rooms and
suites are appointed with traditional furnishings, and each room has
its own special decor. The roman-
tic Van Wyck Brooks Suite
includes a wood-burning fireplace
and a canopy bed topped with a
down quilt. A wicker table and chairs are tucked into the bay
window alcove of the Clementine Yates room. Another spacious
room includes a full kitchen. Business travelers will appreciate
the private in-room phones with voice mail and the separate
data ports. Swedish home cooking highlights the morning
meal, which is accompanied by freshly ground coffee.
Plainfield, the first inland settlement in New Jersey, offers many
historic attractions, including the Drake House Museum.

Innkeeper(s): Chuck & Tom Hale. $114-225. MC, VISA, AX, PC, TC. TAC10.
7 rooms with PB, 1 with FP. Breakfast and snacks/refreshments included in
rates. Types of meals: Full bkfst, veg bkfst and early coffee/tea. Beds: QT.
Cable TV, phone, turndown service, ceiling fan and VCR in room. Air conditioning. Fax, copier and library on premises. Weddings, small meetings, family reunions and seminars hosted. Some Swedish spoken. Amusement parks,
antiquing, art galleries, beaches, golf, hiking, live theater, museums, parks,
shopping, sporting events and tennis nearby.
Pets allowed: only dogs.

Salem   I1

Brown's Historic Home B&B

41-43 Market St
Salem, NJ 08079
(856)935-8595
E-mail: sprite@iopener.net

Circa 1738. Brown's Historic Home originally was built as a
Colonial house. Around 1845, the house was modernized to
the Victorian era. The inn is furnished with antiques and heirlooms, including a handmade chess
set and quilt. The fireplaces are
made of King of Prussia marble.
The backyard garden features a lily
pond, wildflowers and a waterfall.
There is a ferry nearby offering
transport to Delaware. On
Saturdays, guests can enjoy performances at the Cowtown Rodeo, eight miles away.

Historic Interest: Fort Mott State Park is four miles away.
Innkeeper(s): William & Margaret Brown. $65-150. MC, VISA, AX, TC. 4
rooms, 3 with PB, 1 with FP and 1 suite. Breakfast and snacks/refreshments
included in rates. Types of meals: Full bkfst and country bkfst. Beds: DT. Cable
TV, phone, turndown service and ceiling fan in room. Air conditioning. Small
meetings hosted. Antiquing, bicycling, fishing, golf, hiking, hunting, bird

watching, live theater, museums, parks, shopping and water sports nearby.

Publicity: *Newsday, Mid-Atlantic Country, Early American Life and Today's Sunbeam.*

"Down-home-on-the-farm breakfasts with great hospitality."

Sea Girt   F6

Beacon House

100 & 104 Beacon Blvd
Sea Girt, NJ 08750-1609
(732)449-5835 Fax:(732)282-0974
E-mail: beaconhouse@aol.com
Web: www.beaconhouseinn.com

Circa 1879. Built in classic Victorian style, this recently renovated inn has been a relaxing getaway for more than a century. Splendidly furnished parlors with fireplaces, crystal chandeliers and oak floors are pleasurable places to while away time. The two main houses, a cottage and a carriage house offer the best in casual elegance. Encounter wicker, brass and chintz in the sunny guest bedrooms. Some boast ocean or lake views, fireplaces and Jacuzzi tubs. Morning is a celebration when a memorable gourmet breakfast is served in the candle-lit dining room. Enjoy the colorful landscape from a rocker on one of the wraparound porches, lounge by the swimming pool, or take a bike ride to the popular boardwalk in this quaint seaside community.
Historic Interest: Sea Girt Lighthouse (100 yds.), Allaire Village and State Park (6 miles), Town of Spring Lake (1 block), Sandy Hook and Twin Lights Lighthouses (20 miles).
Innkeeper(s): Candy & Alan Ruiter. $100-295. MC, VISA, AX, DS, PC, TC. 18 rooms, 14 with PB, 2 suites and 2 cottages. Breakfast and snacks/refreshments included in rates. Types of meals: Gourmet bkfst, veg bkfst, cont plus and early coffee/tea. EP. Beds: QDT. Cable TV, ceiling fan and fireplace in room. Central air. VCR, fax, copier, swimming, bicycles, library and gift shop on premises. Weddings, small meetings, family reunions and seminars hosted. Spanish and French spoken. Amusement parks, antiquing, art galleries, beaches, bicycling, canoeing/kayaking, fishing, golf, hiking, live theater, museums, parks, shopping, tennis and water sports nearby.
Publicity: *The Coast Star Newspaper.*

Spring Lake   F6

Ashling Cottage

106 Sussex Ave
Spring Lake, NJ 07762-1248
(732)449-3553 (888)274-5464
E-mail: beautifuldream@compuserve.com
Web: www.ashlingcottage.com

Circa 1877. Surrounded by shady sycamores on a quiet residential street, this three-story Victorian residence features a mansard-and-gambrel roof with hooded gambrel dormers. One of the two porches has a square, pyramid-roofed pavilion, which has been glass-enclosed and screened. Guests  can watch the sun rise over the ocean one block away or set over Spring Lake which is one-half block away. A full breakfast can be enjoyed in the plant- and wicker-filled pavilion.
Historic Interest: Allaire State Park (5 miles).
Innkeeper(s): Joanie & Bill Mahon. $99-375. PC, TC. 10 rooms, 8 with PB. Breakfast and afternoon tea included in rates. Types of meals: Full bkfst and early coffee/tea. Beds: Q. Ceiling fan and clock in room. Air conditioning. VCR, bicycles and library on premises. Weddings, small meetings, family reunions and seminars hosted. Limited German spoken. Amusement parks, antiquing, beaches, fishing, race tracks, boardwalk, live theater, parks, shop-

ping, sporting events and water sports nearby.
Publicity: *New York Times, New Jersey Monthly, Town & Country, Country Living, New York, Harrods of London and Travel & Leisure.*

La Maison Inn

404 Jersey Ave
Spring Lake, NJ 07762-1437
(732)449-0969 (800)276-2088 Fax:(732)449-4860
E-mail: lamaisonnj@aol.com
Web: www.lamaisoninn.com

Circa 1870. A French Victorian with a wide wraparound veranda, this historic inn is located four blocks from the ocean. The French influence is repeated in romantic furnishings such as fluffy duvets, sleigh beds and Louis Philippe pieces. At breakfast,  freshly squeezed juice, espresso or cappuccino complements gourmet entrees and freshly baked goods. A cottage, complete with a kitchen, fireplace, queen bed and clawfooted soaking tub is popular for a secluded getaway.
Innkeeper(s): Julianne Corrigan. $125-325. MC, VISA, AX, DS, PC, TC. 8 rooms with PB, 2 suites and 1 cottage. Breakfast included in rates. Types of meals: Gourmet bkfst and early coffee/tea. Beds: QT. Cable TV and phone in room. Air conditioning. Fax, bicycles, health club passes, nightly hors d'oeuvres, beach passes, beach chairs and outside Teak shower on premises. Weddings, small meetings, family reunions and seminars hosted. Antiquing, fishing, live theater, parks, shopping and water sports nearby.
Publicity: *Country Inns, Innspots & Special Places, Gourmet Magazine, New Jersey Countryside, The Star Ledger and News 12-New Jersey.*

The Normandy Inn

21 Tuttle Ave
Spring Lake, NJ 07762-1533
(732)449-7172 (800)449-1888 Fax:(732)449-1070
E-mail: normandy@bellatlantic.net
Web: www.normandyinn.com

Circa 1888. The house was moved onto the present site around 1910. Normandy Inn combines both Italianate and Queen Anne features, and the gracious home is listed in the National Register. The home rises up four stories with a notable circular window gracing the front exterior. The innkeepers have kept the historic home as authentic as possible. The interior is filled with a remarkable selection of period  pieces, including a stunning, museum quality four-poster bed that graces one of the guest rooms. The Victorian antiques are accentuated by Victorian colors documented and researched by Roger Moss. Lavish country breakfasts are served on little lace-covered tables set with fine china and silver. In the afternoons, homemade treats are accompanied with a selection of teas, coffees and other refreshments. Spring Lake is a gem, an idyllic hamlet of historic homes along the Jersey shore.
Historic Interest: Allaire State Park (5 miles).
Innkeeper(s): The Valori Family. $135-350. MC, VISA, AX, DC, CB, DS, PC, TC. TAC10. 18 rooms with PB, 5 with FP, 1 suite and 2 conference rooms. Breakfast included in rates. Types of meals: Full bkfst, country bkfst, early coffee/tea and afternoon tea. Beds: KQDT. Cable TV, phone and VCR in room. Air conditioning. Fax, copier, bicycles and gift shop on premises. Small meetings and seminars hosted. Antiquing, art galleries, beaches, bicycling, fishing, golf, beach and pool passes 1/2 block away, live theater, parks, shopping and tennis nearby.
Publicity: *Washington Post, Country Roads Magazine, New York Times,*

Country and New Jersey Magazine.

"The cozy and delicious accommodations of your inn were beyond expectations."

Ocean House

102 Sussex Ave
Spring Lake, NJ 07762-1215
(732)449-9090 (888)449-9094 Fax:(732)449-9092

Circa 1876. For more than 100 years the Ocean House has welcomed guests. You can't miss it across from the boardwalk. Pale pink with sage green window shutters, a canopied veranda wraps around the outside. The main interior feature is a grand staircase moved from the 1876 Philadelphia Exposition by the home's first owner. Eleven-foot-high ceilings, plaster moldings and antiques continue the Victorian atmosphere. Breakfast, served in either the dining room that is decorated in floral fabrics or on the outside veranda, consists of fresh baked scones and blueberry muffins, French toast, eggs and fruit. The innkeepers can supply you with a bicycle for a fun afternoon exploring the boardwalk and town, or for a more relaxing time, take one of the inn's beach chairs out on the sand.

Historic Interest: Batso Village, Atlantic City, Allaire Village, Sandy Hook Marine Park.

Innkeeper(s): Dennis and Nancy Kaloostian. $80-325. MC, VISA, AX, PC, TC. 35 rooms with PB, 8 suites and 1 conference room. Breakfast, afternoon tea and snacks/refreshments included in rates. Types of meals: Full bkfst, country bkfst and early coffee/tea. Beds: KQDT. Cable TV, phone and ceiling fan in room. Air conditioning. VCR, fax, copier, swimming, bicycles, tennis and library on premises. Weddings, small meetings, family reunions and seminars hosted. Amusement parks, antiquing, art galleries, beaches, bicycling, canoeing/kayaking, fishing, golf, hiking, horseback riding, live theater, museums, parks, shopping, sporting events, tennis, water sports and wineries nearby.

Sea Crest By The Sea

19 Tuttle Ave
Spring Lake, NJ 07762-1533
(732)449-9031 (800)803-9031 Fax:(732)974-0403
E-mail: capt@seacrestbythesea.com
Web: www.seacrestbythesea.com

Circa 1885. You can hear the surf from most rooms in this Victorian mansion, located an hour from New York city or Philadelphia. Guests will be pampered with Egyptian cotton and Belgian-lace linens, queen-size feather beds, fresh flowers and classical music. Six rooms have Jacuzzis for two and there are eight with fireplaces. Tunes from a player piano announce afternoon tea at 4 p.m.—a good time to make dinner reservations at one of the  area's fine restaurants. In the morning family china, crystal and silver add to the ambiance of a full gourmet breakfast. Bicycles are available and the beach is a half block away.

Innkeeper(s): Barbara & Fred Vogel. $175-305. MC, VISA, AX. TAC10. 11 rooms with PB, 8 with FP and 2 suites. Breakfast and afternoon tea included in rates. Types of meals: Full bkfst. Beds: Q. Phone and 6 with Jacuzzis for two in room. Live theater and water sports nearby.

Publicity: *New York Times, Gourmet, Victoria and Country Inns B&B.*

"This romantic storybook atmosphere is delightful! A visual feast."

Victoria House

214 Monmouth Ave
Spring Lake, NJ 07762-1127
(732)974-1882 (888)249-6252 Fax:(732)974-2132
E-mail: victoriahousebb@monmouth.com
Web: www.victoriahouse.net

Circa 1882. Original stained-glass windows, gingerbread accents and gothic shingles make this historic Queen Anne home built in 1882 a destination in itself. Antique furnishings such as the hand-carved Circassian walnut side-  board and chairs in the dining room add to the elegant period ambiance. The inn has two suites, two deluxe guest bedrooms and four premium guest bedrooms, some with double Jacuzzis or fireplaces. Sit and rock on the wraparound porch during warmer seasons or relax by the parlor fireplace during cooler seasons. A full-served breakfast is created in the kitchen. Enjoy your meal at a table for two in the dining room or out on the veranda overlooking the English Cottage garden. The lake, beach and village are all within walking distance. Victoria House provides free tennis and health club passes and bicycles for biking around nearby Spring Lake.

Innkeeper(s): Louise & Robert Goodall. $135-335. MC, VISA, AX, PC, TC. TAC10. 8 rooms with PB, 4 with FP and 2 suites. Breakfast included in rates. Types of meals: Full bkfst and early coffee/tea. Beds: KQ. Ceiling fan and two with whirlpool/shower in room. Air conditioning. Fax and bicycles on premises. Small meetings and seminars hosted. Antiquing, fishing, live theater, parks, shopping, sporting events and water sports nearby.

"A very charming stay. We enjoyed your hospitality."

White Lilac Inn

414 Central Ave
Spring Lake, NJ 07762-1020
(732)449-0211
E-mail: mari@whitelilac.com
Web: www.whitelilac.com

Circa 1880. The White Lilac looks like a sweeping Southern home with wide wraparound porches decorating its three stories. The first story veranda is lined with wicker rockers and baskets of flowering plants hang from the ceiling, creating an ideal spot for relaxation. Inside, the Victorian decor contains period furnishings, antique clawfoot tub, whirlpool tubs and canopy beds. Four guest rooms include a fireplace. Breakfasts  are served on intimate tables for two in the Garden Room and on the enclosed porch. The ocean is less than five blocks from the inn.

Innkeeper(s): Mari Kennelly. $115-220.
MC, VISA, AX, DS, PC, TC. TAC10. 9 rooms with PB, 4 with FP. Breakfast and snacks/refreshments included in rates. Types of meals: Full bkfst and early coffee/tea. Beds: QT. Cable TV and ceiling fan in room. Air conditioning. Bicycles and library on premises. Small meetings and family reunions hosted. Amusement parks, antiquing, fishing, golf, ocean, live theater, parks, shopping, sporting events, tennis and water sports nearby.

Publicity: *The Star-Ledger, Asbury Park Press and Coast Star.*

Stockton E3

The Stockton Inn

1 Main St, PO Box C
Stockton, NJ 08559-0318
(609)397-1250

Circa 1710. The Stockton Inn, known as Colligan's, has operated as an inn since 1796. It received national prominence when Richard Rogers & Lorenz Hart included reference to it in a song from musical comedy — "There is a small hotel with a wishing well." (The Broadway show was "On Your Toes.") Band leader Paul Whiteman later signed off his radio and television shows announcing he was going to dinner at "Ma Colligan's." Guest rooms are scattered throughout the inn's four buildings and feature fireplaces, balconies or canopy beds. The restaurant serves innovative American/Continental cuisine and there is a full service bar.

Historic Interest: Washington's Crossing State Park (one-half hour drive), Mercer Museum (American Artifacts-Tools) (one-half hour).

Innkeeper(s): Jack Boehlert. $90-170. MC, VISA, AX, DC, DS. 11 rooms with PB, 8 with FP, 8 suites and 1 conference room. Breakfast included in rates. Types of meals: Cont, lunch and gourmet dinner. Beds: QDT. Phone in room. Fishing and live theater nearby.

Publicity: *New York Times, Colonial Homes, New York, New Jersey Monthly, New York Great Escapes.* and WABC-TV.

"My well-traveled parents say this is their favorite restaurant."

Ventnor City J5

Carisbrooke Inn

105 S Little Rock Ave
Ventnor City, NJ 08406-2840
(609)822-6392 Fax:(609)822-9710
E-mail: greatinn@msn.com
Web: www.carisbrookeinn.com

Circa 1918. Only one mile from Atlantic City, this enticing inn feels a world away. The inn was named for a Ventnor City hotel, once the grand centerpiece of this seaside town. Flowering plants and lacy curtains add a romantic touch to the guest rooms. The innkeeper offers a huge breakfast with a mix of healthy and decadent treats. Multi-grain pancakes, banana waffles, cheddar potato pie and a basil-tomato frittata are some of the main dishes, accompanied by freshly baked muffins, bagels and fruit. Favorite enticements for guests are the ocean-view deck and secluded back patio. The beach and boardwalk are within walking distance.

Innkeeper(s): Lori McIntyre. $89-230. MC, VISA, DS, PC. TAC10. 8 rooms with PB and 1 suite. Breakfast and afternoon tea included in rates. Types of meals: Gourmet bkfst and early coffee/tea. Beds: KQD. Cable TV, ceiling fan and fresh flowers in room. Air conditioning. Fax, copier, complimentary tea/coffee/snacks in main parlor; beach tags and towels and chairs (in season) on premises. Weddings, small meetings and family reunions hosted. Amusement parks, antiquing, beaches, bicycling, fishing, golf, casinos, live theater, parks, shopping, tennis and water sports nearby.

"You have a beautiful, elegant inn. My stay here was absolutely wonderful."

Vernon B5

Alpine Haus

217 State Rt 94
Vernon, NJ 07462
(973)209-7080 Fax:(973)209-7090
E-mail: alpinehs@warwick.net
Web: www.alpinehausbb.com

Circa 1887. A private hideaway in the mountains, this former farmhouse is more than 100 years old. The renovated Federal-style inn with Victorian accents offers comfortable guest bedrooms named after mountain flowers with a decor reflecting that theme. Antiques also highlight the inn. The adjacent Carriage House has two suites with four-poster beds, stone fireplace and Jacuzzi. A generous country breakfast is enjoyed in the dining room or a continental breakfast on the second-story covered porch with

majestic views. The family room and formal sitting room with fireplace are wonderful gathering places for games or conversation. Located next to Mountain Creek Ski and Water Park.

Innkeeper(s): Jack & Allison Smith. $110-225. MC, VISA, AX, DC, DS. 10 rooms with PB, 2 with FP and 2 suites. Breakfast included in rates. Types of meals: Full bkfst, country bkfst, veg bkfst and early coffee/tea. Beds: QDT. Cable TV, phone, VCR and two suites with fireplace and Jacuzzi in room. Central air. Fax on premises. Handicap access. Weddings, small meetings and family reunions hosted. Antiquing, art galleries, canoeing/kayaking, fishing, golf, hiking, horseback riding, museums, parks, shopping, downhill skiing, cross-country skiing, water sports and wineries nearby.

Wildwood K4

Pope Cottage Bed & Breakfast

5711 Pacific Ave
Wildwood, NJ 08260-4355
(609)523-9272 Fax:(609)523-2208

Circa 1907. This 1907 Queen Anne home was built as a summer home. It has been in turn: a home, an apartment house, a summer cottage, and now a bed & breakfast. Its elegantly appointed and includes five guest bedrooms. Breakfasts include

two hot entrees and various other treats like baked goods, cereal, fruit, coffee and tea. Located near the beach and boardwalk, its wraparound veranda is a perfect place to get away from everything and enjoy the cool ocean breezes.

Historic Interest: Cape May, N.J. (4 miles).

Innkeeper(s): Kathleen & Denny Davis. $100-150. MC, VISA, TC. TAC10. 5 rooms, 3 with PB. Breakfast included in rates. Types of meals: Full bkfst and early coffee/tea. Beds: QDT. Phone and ceiling fan in room. Air conditioning. Fax on premises. Weddings, small meetings, family reunions and seminars hosted. Amusement parks, antiquing, art galleries, beaches, bicycling, canoeing/kayaking, fishing, golf, hiking, live theater, parks, shopping, tennis, water sports and wineries nearby.

New Mexico

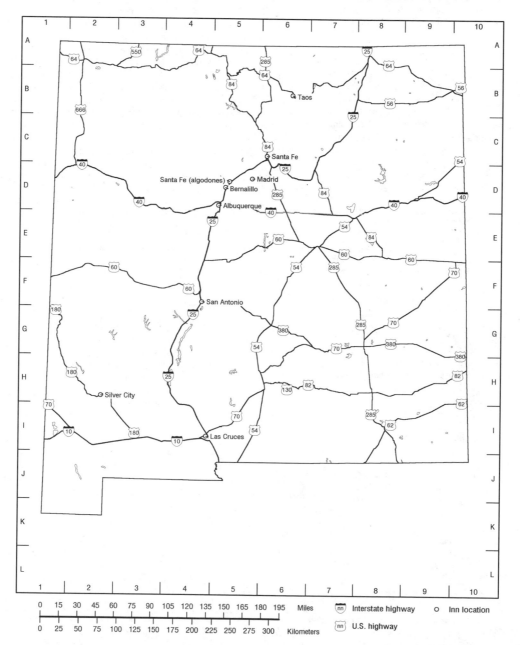

Miles 0 15 30 45 60 75 90 105 120 135 150 165 180 195

Kilometers 0 25 50 75 100 125 150 175 200 225 250 275 300

Interstate highway   Inn location

U.S. highway

Albuquerque   D5

Bottger-Koch Mansion B&B

110 San Felipe NW, Old Town
Albuquerque, NM 87104
(505)243-3639 (800)758-3639 Fax:(505)243-4378
E-mail: bottgerk@aol.com
Web: www.bottger.com

Circa 1912. For Victorian flavor and a superior location close to Old Town Albuquerque, choose the Bottger-Koch Mansion. The pink and white exterior is inviting in the dappled shade from tall trees that shelter the home. The parlor offers a carved

white fireplace, cozy sitting areas, Victorian furnishings, art, Oriental rugs and a chandelier shining from an elaborate ceiling. Polished wood floors, light colors and antiques are found throughout. (Ask for the room

with the canopy bed!) Breakfast is served at several tables in a sun-filled breakfast room. Walk to the New Mexico Museum of Natural History and Science and the Albuquerque Museum or to dozens and dozens of restaurants, galleries and shops in Old Town. A short drive will allow you to visit botanical gardens, the zoo, the Petroglyph National Museum and the University of New Mexico. Santa Fe is an hour away.

Historic Interest: San Felipe de Neri Church (1 1/2 blocks), Petroglyph Park (1-2 miles), historic buildings in the Old Town Square.
Innkeeper(s): Yvonne & Ron Koch. $99-179. MC, VISA, AX, PC, TC. TAC10. 8 rooms with PB and 1 suite. Breakfast, afternoon tea and snacks/refreshments included in rates. Types of meals: Gourmet bkfst. Beds: KQT. Ceiling fan in room. Air conditioning. Fax and copier on premises. Weddings, small meetings & family reunions hosted. Amusement parks, antiquing, fishing, live theater, parks, shopping, downhill skiing, cross-country skiing, sporting events & water sports nearby.
Publicity: *PBS Public Television.*

"Enchanted perfection, the memory of a lifetime. It can't get any better than this."

Brittania & W.E. Mauger Estate B&B

701 Roma Ave NW
Albuquerque, NM 87102-2038
(505)242-8755 (800)719-9189 Fax:(505)842-8835
E-mail: maugerbb@aol.com
Web: www.maugerbb.com

Circa 1897. Now an elegantly restored Victorian, this former boarding house is listed in the National Register. Guest bedrooms offer amenities that include satellite television, refrigerators, a basket with snacks, voice mail and European down comforters on the beds. The inn

is located four blocks from the convention center/business district and Historic Route 66. Old Town is less than one mile away. There are many interesting museums to visit locally, featuring topics from Native American culture to the atomic age.

Historic Interest: Albuquerque is full of unique museums, featuring topics from Native American culture to the atomic age.
Innkeeper(s): Chris Lucas & Rob Thalmann. $89-179. MC, VISA, AX. TAC10. 8 rooms with PB, 2 guest houses and 1 conference room. Breakfast included in rates. Types of meals: Full bkfst and snacks/refreshments. Beds: KQDT. TV, phone, ceiling fan, coffee maker, iron and hair dryer in room. Air conditioning. Small meetings and family reunions hosted. Amusement parks, antiquing, live theater and shopping nearby.

Publicity: *Albuquerque Journal, Phoenix Home and Garden, Albuquerque Monthly, National Geographic Traveler, New Mexico Business Week and Golf Digest.*

"Because of your hospitality, kindness and warmth, we will always compare the quality of our experience by the W.E. Mauger Estate."

Casa Del Granjero & El Rancho Guest House

414 C De Baca Ln NW
Albuquerque, NM 87114-1600
(505)897-4144 (800)701-4144 Fax:(505)897-9788
E-mail: granjero@rt66.com

Circa 1890. Innkeepers Victoria and Butch Farmer, who appropriately named their home Casa del Granjero, or "the farmer's house," have designed their bed & breakfast to reflect Southwestern style with a hint of old Spanish flair. The adobe's guest rooms all include a rustic, kiva fireplace. Cuarto Allegre is the largest suite in the main house, and it includes a canopy bed covered in lace and French doors that open onto a small porch. Cuarto del Rey affords a mountain view and includes Mexican furnishings and handmade quilts. Cuarto de Flores also has quilts, Mexican tile and French doors leading to a private porch. The innkeepers have a hot tub room for guest use in a special garden area. The innkeepers also have restored a historic adobe ranch house across the road. The accommodations here include three suites and a guest room with a double bed. A kitchen, common area and wood-burning stove also are located in this house. A variety of baked goods, New Mexican-style recipes and fresh fruit are served each morning in the dining room or on the portal. Several recipes have been featured in a cookbook.
Innkeeper(s): Victoria Farmer. $79-179. MC, VISA, DS. TAC10. 7 rooms with PB and 5 suites. Breakfast included in rates. Types of meals: Full bkfst, picnic lunch, gourmet dinner and room service. Beds: KQT. Antiquing, fishing, live theater, downhill skiing, cross-country skiing and water sports nearby.
Publicity: *Hidden SW.*

"Wonderful place, wonderful people. Thanks so much."

Hacienda Antigua B&B

6708 Tierra Dr NW
Albuquerque, NM 87107-6025
(505)345-5399 (800)201-2986 Fax:(505)345-3855
E-mail: info@haciendantigua.com
Web: www.haciendantigua.com

Circa 1780. In the more than 200 years since this Spanish Colonial-style hacienda was constructed, the current innkeepers are only the fourth owners. Once a stagecoach stop on the El Camino Real, it also served as a cantina and mercantile store. It was built by Don Pablo Yrisarri, who was sent by the King of Spain to search the area for gold. The home is elegant, yet maintains a rustic, Spanish charm with exposed beams, walls up to 30 inches thick, brick floors and adobe fireplaces. Along with a sitting room and kiva fireplace, the Don Pablo Suite includes a "ducking door" that leads onto the courtyard. Other rooms have clawfoot tubs, antique iron beds or a private patio. The cuisine is notable and one of the inn's recipes appeared in Culinary Trends magazine. Guests might sample a green chile souffle along with bread pudding and fresh fruit. The inn has been featured on the TV series "Great Country Inns."
Innkeeper(s): Mark Brown & Keith Lewis. $109-229. MC, VISA. TAC10. 8 rooms with PB, 7 with FP and 4 suites. Breakfast included in rates. Types of meals: Full bkfst and early coffee/tea. Beds: KQT. Phone and ceiling fan in room. Air conditioning. VCR, fax, spa and swimming on premises. Small meetings, family reunions and seminars hosted. Spanish and Italian spoken. Amusement parks,

antiquing, fishing, golf, hiking, biking, balloon fiesta, live theater, parks, shopping, downhill skiing, cross-country skiing, sporting events and tennis nearby.
Publicity: *Culinary Trends, Cavalcade of Enchantment and Great Country Inns.*

Bernalillo   D5

La Hacienda Grande

21 Baros Ln
Bernalillo, NM 87004
(505)867-1887 (800)353-1887 Fax:(505)771-1436
E-mail: lhg@swcp.com

Circa 1711. The rooms in this historic adobe inn surround a central courtyard. The first European trekked across the grounds as early as 1540. The land was part of a 1711 land grant from Spain, and owned by descendants of the original family until the innkeepers purchased it. The decor is Southwestern, and each bedchamber is filled with beautiful, handcrafted furnishings. One includes an iron high-poster bed and Jacuzzi tub, and others offer a kiva fireplace. Breakfasts are served in a dining room decorated with wood beams and a brick floor.
Innkeeper(s): Gayle & Ray Richmond. $109-139. MC, VISA, AX, DS, TC. 6 rooms with PB, 5 with FP and 1 conference room. Breakfast included in rates. Types of meals: Full bkfst and early coffee/tea. Beds: KQDT. Sitting areas and phone and TV on request in room. Air conditioning. VCR, fax, copier and library on premises. Weddings, small meetings, family reunions and seminars hosted. Spanish spoken. Antiquing, fishing, live theater, parks, shopping, downhill skiing, cross-country skiing, sporting events and water sports nearby.

Las Cruces   I4

T.R.H. Smith Mansion B&B

909 N Alameda Blvd
Las Cruces, NM 88005-2124
(505)525-2525 (800)526-1914 Fax:(505)524-8227
E-mail: smithmansion@zianet.com

Circa 1914. This beautifully preserved Prairie-style mansion, surrounded by park-like grounds and tall pecan and sycamore trees has a somewhat notorious past. The home was designed by Henry Trost and was built by banker/embezzler T.R.H. Smith. The mansion was rumored to have served as a bordello and to have buried treasure somewhere within its walls. Its 5,700 square feet of living area makes it the largest residence in town. The inn offers four well-appointed guest rooms in a variety of styles including Latin American, European, Southwest and Pacific Rim. Guests will enjoy a hearty German-style breakfast of fresh fruit, home-baked breads, imported meats and cheeses along with fresh-ground coffee and teas made from herbs grown on the grounds.
Innkeeper(s): Marlene & Jay Tebo. $63-135. MC, VISA, AX, DS, PC, TC. TAC10. 4 rooms with PB, 1 with FP. Breakfast included in rates. Types of meals: Gourmet bkfst. Beds: KQ. Phone, turndown service, ceiling fan & modem Jacks in room. Air conditioning. VCR, fax, library & pool table on premises. Weddings, small meetings, family reunions and seminars hosted. German spoken. Antiquing, golf, live theater, parks, shopping, sporting events and tennis nearby.
Publicity: *Las Cruces Sun-News, Las Cruces Bulletin, Gateway Magazine and New Mexico Magazine.*

Madrid   D5

Java Junction

2855 State Highway 14 N
Madrid, NM 87010
(505)438-2772 (877)308-8884 Fax:(505)474-8359

Circa 1916. A restored Victorian home in this once-famous railroad and coal mining town is the quaint setting for this delightful inn. Aptly named with its first-floor coffee and gift shop, a

continental breakfast is served from here daily. The second story features a spacious suite with kitchen, private porch and six-foot, clawfoot tub in the bathroom. Nearby, a "fully furnished home" accommodating up to seven also is available.
Innkeeper(s): Linda Dunnill. $59-69. MC, VISA, DS. 1 suites. Breakfast included in rates. Types of meals: Cont. Beds: Q. TV in room. Air conditioning. Art galleries, horseback riding, live theater, museums and shopping nearby.
Pets allowed: Must get approval before registering.
Publicity: *60 minutes.*

San Antonio   F4

Casa Blanca Bed & Breakfast

13 Montoya Street, PO Box 31
San Antonio, NM 87832
(505)835-3027
E-mail: casablancabandb@hotmail.com
Web: www.cb-bb.com/casawebpage.htm

Circa 1880. Constructed with 24-inch-thick double adobe walls, this Victorian farmhouse was the home of Territorial Senator Eutimio Montoya, a well-known politician. It now serves as an intimate bed & breakfast for bird watchers and nature lovers visiting the Bosque del Apache National Wildlife Refuge. Displays of Southwestern Indian and Mexican art, original photography, framed historic documents and antiques highlight the inn. Accommodations in the Crane Room feature a wood-burning stove. The larger Heron Room boasts a whirlpool tub. The Egret Room holds a double and twin bed. A generous continental breakfast includes homemade breads, muffins, coffeecake, fresh fruit, yogurt, cereal, boiled eggs and cheeses. Mountain bikes and a sauna are ready to enjoy.
Innkeeper(s): Phoebe Wood. $60-90. MC, VISA, PC, TC. 3 rooms with PB, 1 with FP. Breakfast included in rates. Types of meals: Cont plus and early coffee/tea. Beds: QDT. Ceiling fan and alarm clocks in room. VCR, sauna, bicycles, library and piano on premises. Bicycling, hiking and bird watching nearby.
Pets Allowed.

Santa Fe   C6

Alexander's Inn

529 E Palace Ave
Santa Fe, NM 87501-2200
(505)986-1431 (888)321-5123 Fax:(505)982-8572
E-mail: alexandinn@aol.com
Web: www.alexanders-inn.com

Circa 1903. Twin gables and a massive front porch are prominent features of this Craftsman-style brick and wood inn. French and American country decor, stained-glass windows and a selection of antiques create a light Victorian touch. The inn also features beautiful gardens of roses and lilacs. The exquisite Southwest adobe casitas are a favorite for families and romantic getaways. Breakfast is often served in the backyard garden. Home-baked treats are offered to guests in the afternoon.
Historic Interest: Puye Cliffs, Bandalier and Pecos National Monument all are within one hour from the inn.
Innkeeper(s): Carolyn Lee. $80-165. MC, VISA, DS, PC, TC. TAC10. 7 rooms with PB, 5 with FP, 1 suite and 3 cottages. Breakfast and afternoon tea included in rates. Types of

meals: Gourmet bkfst, cont plus and early coffee/tea. EP. Beds: KQT. Cable TV, phone and VCR in room. Fax, spa, library and child care on premises. Weddings and family reunions hosted. French spoken. Antiquing, fishing, museums, Pueblos, live theater, parks, shopping, downhill skiing, cross-country skiing and water sports nearby.
Pets allowed: Well behaved.
Publicity: New Mexican, Glamour, Southwest Art and San Diego Union Tribune.

"Thanks to the kindness and thoughtfulness of the staff, our three days in Santa Fe were magical."

Casa De La Cuma B&B

105 Paseo De La Cuma
Santa Fe, NM 87501-1213
(505)983-1717 (888)366-1717 Fax:(505)983-2241
E-mail: info@casacuman.com
Web: www.casacuma.com

Circa 1940. Offering a warm and serene atmosphere, Casa De La Cuma B&B has three unique rooms and a suite decorated with Navajo textiles, original artwork and Southwestern-period furniture. Guests enjoy breakfast on the glassed-in porch or simply relaxing on the shaded patio. During cooler weather, the fireplace in the living room is the gathering spot. The inn features views of the Sangre De Cristo Mountains and is within walking distance of the Plaza.
Historic Interest: The inn is located on the same hill as the original cross which honors Spanish priests killed during the 1680 pueblo revolt.
Innkeeper(s): Dona Fisher. $70-145. MC, VISA, AX, PC, TC. TAC10. 4 rooms. Breakfast and snacks/refreshments included in rates. Types of meals: Cont plus and afternoon tea. Beds: KQT. Cable TV, phone and ceiling fan in room. Antiquing, museums, hiking, rafting, parks and downhill skiing nearby.
Publicity: Denver Post.

Don Gaspar Compound

623 Don Gaspar Ave
Santa Fe, NM 87501-4427
(505)986-8664 (888)986-8664 Fax:(505)986-0696
E-mail: info@dongaspar.com
Web: www.dongaspar.com

Circa 1912. This lush, peaceful hideaway is located within one of Santa Fe's first historic districts. Within the Compounds surrounding adobe walls are brick pathways meandering through beautiful gardens, emerald lawns, trees and a courtyard fountain. The elegant Southwestern decor is an idyllic match for the warmth and romance of the grounds. For those seeking privacy, the innkeepers offer the Main House, a historic Mission-style home perfect for a pair of romantics or a group as large as six. The house has three bedrooms, two bathrooms, a fully equipped kitchen and two wood-burning fireplaces. In addition to the main house, there are three suites in a Territorial-style home with thick walls and polished wood floors. There also are two private casitas, each with a gas-burning fireplace. The Fountain Casita includes a fully equipped kitchen, while the Courtyard Casita offers a double whirlpool tub. All accommodations include a TV, telephone, microwave and refrigerators.
Historic Interest: The inn is a short walk from Santa Fe's historic plaza, as well as several museums.
Innkeeper(s): Shirlee Fasardo. $115-295. MC, VISA, AX, PC, TC. TAC10. 10 rooms, 4 with PB, 3 suites and 1 cottage. Breakfast included in rates. Types of meals: Cont plus. Beds: KQ. Phone and or ceiling fan in room. Air conditioning. Fax, copier, gardens, courtyard, fountain and two casitas on premises. Weddings and family reunions hosted. Antiquing, fishing, art galleries, 200 plus restaurants, live theater, parks, shopping, downhill skiing, cross-country skiing, sporting events and water sports nearby.

"Everything was simply perfect."

Dunshee's

986 Acequia Madre
Santa Fe, NM 87505-2819
(505)982-0988
E-mail: sdunshee@aol.com
Web: www.dunshees.com

Circa 1930. Where better could one experience Santa Fe's rich history than in an authentic adobe casita or a restored adobe home? Innkeeper Susan Dunshee offers accommodations in both. Guests can stay in the adobe home's spacious suite or  rent the casita by the day or week. The casita offers a continental-plus breakfast, two bedrooms, a kitchen, a living room warmed by a rustic, kiva fireplace and a private patio. The antique-filled rooms are decorated in a warm, Santa Fe style, and bedrooms sport a more country look. Guests who opt for the bed & breakfast suite are treated to Southwestern breakfasts with items such as a green chile souffle. The refrigerator at the casita is stocked with treats for the guests' breakfast.
Innkeeper(s): Susan Dunshee. $125. MC, VISA, PC, TC. 3 rooms, 2 with PB, 3 with FP, 1 suite and 1 cottage. Breakfast included in rates. Types of meals: Gourmet bkfst, cont plus and early coffee/tea. Beds: QD. Cable TV, phone, fresh flowers and homemade cookies in room. Library on premises. Weddings, small meetings and family reunions hosted. Antiquing, opera, Indian pueblos, live theater, parks, shopping, downhill skiing and cross-country skiing nearby.

El Farolito B&B Inn

514 Galisteo St
Santa Fe, NM 87501
(505)988-1631 (888)634-8782 Fax:(505)988-4589
E-mail: innkeeper@farolito.com
Web: www.farolito.com

Circa 1900. El Farolito's seven guest rooms and one suite are spread among five adobe buildings, some of which date back to the 1900s. The beamed ceilings, tile or brick floors and kiva fireplaces enhance the Southwestern decor. The bed & breakfast is located within Santa Fe's historic district, and a 10-minute walk will take you to the famous plaza. Other sites, the Capitol building, shops and restaurants are even closer.
Innkeeper(s): Walt Wyss & Wayne Mainus. $140-220. MC, VISA, AX, DS, TC. TAC10. 8 rooms with PB. Breakfast included in rates. Types of meals: Cont plus. EP. Beds: QD. Cable TV and phone in room. Air conditioning. Fax, copier and refrigerators and coffee service in some rooms on premises. Small meetings, family reunions and seminars hosted. Antiquing, fishing, golf, live theater, parks, shopping, downhill skiing, cross-country skiing and sporting events nearby.
Publicity: New Mexican Newspaper, Albuquerque Journal, Romantic Southwest. and Winner of "Best small property of the year" awarded in 1999 by the New Mexico Hotel & Motel Association.

El Paradero

220 W Manhattan Ave
Santa Fe, NM 87501-2622
(505)988-1177
E-mail: info@elparadero.com
Web: www.elparadero.com

Circa 1820. This was originally a two-bedroom Spanish farmhouse that doubled in size to a Territorial style in 1860, was remodeled as a Victorian in 1912, and became a Pueblo Revival in 1920. All styles are present and provide a walk through many years of history.

Historic Interest: Indian Ruins, Pueblos.
Innkeeper(s): Ouida MacGregor & Thomas Allen. $65-145. MC, VISA. TAC10. 14 rooms, 12 with PB, 7 with FP, 2 suites and 1 conference room. Breakfast and afternoon tea included in rates. Types of meals: Gourmet bkfst and early coffee/tea. Beds: QT. Phone, cable TV and refrigerator in suite and fireplaces in room. Air conditioning. Fishing, pueblos, opera, mountains, live theater, shopping and cross-country skiing nearby.
Pets allowed: Only by pre-arrangement and only in certain rooms.
Publicity: *Denver Post, Innsider, Country Inns, Outside, Sunset, New York Times, Los Angeles Times, Travel & Leisure, America West and Travel & Holiday.*

"I'd like to LIVE here."

Four Kachinas Inn

512 Webber St
Santa Fe, NM 87501-4454
(505)982-2550 (888)634-8782 Fax:(505)989-1323
E-mail: info@fourkachinas.com
Web: www.fourkachinas.com

Circa 1910. This inn is built in the Northern New Mexico pitched-tin roof style around a private courtyard. Appealing guest rooms are decorated with Southwestern art and crafts, including Navajo rugs, Kachina dolls and handmade regional furniture. Three bedrooms have individual garden patios, while a fourth offers a view from the second floor. An additional room is located in Digneo cottage, built in 1910. Breakfast is served in a separate adobe building and features home baked goods.

Historic Interest: Santa Fe Plaza (4 1/2 blocks).
Innkeeper(s): Walt Wyss & Wayne Manus. $100-185. MC, VISA, AX, DS, TC. 5 rooms with PB. Breakfast and afternoon tea included in rates. Types of meals: Cont plus. Beds: KQ. Handicap access. Antiquing, art galleries, fishing, live theater, museums, downhill skiing and cross-country skiing nearby.
Publicity: *Rocky Mountain News, New York Times, Travel & Leisure and Denver Post.*

"We found the room to be quiet and comfortable and your hospitality to be very gracious. We also really enjoyed breakfast, especially the yogurt!"

Grant Corner Inn

122 Grant Ave
Santa Fe, NM 87501-2031
(505)983-6678 (800)964-9003 Fax:(505)983-1526
E-mail: gcinn@aol.com

Circa 1905. Judge Robinson and his family lived here for 30 years, and many couples were married in the parlor. A continually romantic setting, the inn is secluded by a garden with willow trees, and there is a white picket fence. Rooms are appointed with antique furnishings and the personal art collections of the innkeeper.

Historic Interest: Bandelier and Pecos National Monuments, Indian Pueblos.
Innkeeper(s): Louise Stewart. $130-225. MC, VISA, AX. TAC10. 10 rooms with PB, 1 with FP. Breakfast included in rates. Types of meals: Gourmet bkfst, gourmet dinner and room service. Beds: KQT. Fax and copier on

premises. Handicap access. Antiquing, fishing, live theater, downhill skiing and cross-country skiing nearby.
Publicity: *New England Bride and Galveston Daily News.*

"The very best of everything — comfort, hospitality, food and T.L.C."

Hacienda Nicholas

320 East Marcy Street
Santa Fe, NM 87501
(505)992-8385 (888)284-3170 Fax:(505)982-8572
E-mail: haciendanicholas@aol.com
Web: www.haciendanicholas.com

Circa 1930. The Southwest meets Provence in this 1930 Adobe Hacienda built around a central garden courtyard full of wisteria, iris, daisies, pansies, geraniums and roses. Heated by an outdoor kiva fireplace on cool days and filled with birdsong on warm days, the courtyard is the perfect place to linger over a breakfast of homemade muffins and quiche or to return for afternoon tea. The high-ceilinged great room is warmed by a huge fireplace and furnished with overstuffed couches. Just blocks from Santa Fe's historic plaza, the inn's seven guest rooms are elegantly furnished in Mexican décor, each with a wrought iron or carved wood four-poster bed.
Historic Interest: Bandalier (20 miles).
Innkeeper(s): Glennon Grush/Carolyn Lee. $95-160. MC, VISA, DS, PC, TC. TAC10. 7 rooms with PB, 3 with FP, 3 suites and 1 conference room. Breakfast and afternoon tea included in rates. Types of meals: Gourmet bkfst, country bkfst and early coffee/tea. EP. Beds: KQ. Cable TV, phone and fireplace in room. Air conditioning. Fax on premises. Handicap access. Small meetings and seminars hosted. French spoken. Antiquing, art galleries, bicycling, canoeing/kayaking, fishing, golf, hiking, horseback riding, live theater, museums, parks, shopping, downhill skiing, cross-country skiing, sporting events, tennis, water sports and wineries nearby.
Pets Allowed.
Publicity: *Travel Holiday.*

Inn of The Turquoise Bear B&B

342 E Buena Vista St
Santa Fe, NM 87505
(505)983-0798 (800)396-4104 Fax:(505)988-4225
E-mail: bluebear@newmexico.com
Web: www.turquoisebear.com

Circa 1880. Tall ponderosa pines shade this rambling Spanish Pueblo Revival adobe, giving it the feeling of being in a mountain setting, although it's only blocks from the plaza. In the National Register, it was the home of poet and essayist Witter Bynner, when it hosted a myriad of celebrities including Edna St. Vincent Millay, Robert Frost, Ansel Adams, Rita Hayworth, Errol Flynn and Georgia O'Keeffe. The walled acre of grounds includes flagstone paths, wild roses, lilacs, rock terraces and stone benches and fountains. In a Southwest decor, there are kiva fireplaces and romantic courtyards. The Shaman room has a king bed, viga beams and a picture window with garden views. Guests are invited to enjoy wine and cheese in the afternoon. Museums, galleries, restaurants and shops are within walking distance. Among its accolades, the inn was the recipient of the Heritage Preservation Award from the city of Santa Fe in 1999, and from the state of New Mexicoin 2000.
Historic Interest: Plaza of Santa Fe (6 blocks), Bandelier National Monument (40 miles).
Innkeeper(s): Robert Frost & Ralph Bolton. $110-315. MC, VISA, AX, DS, PC, TC. TAC10. 11 rooms, 8 with PB, 10 with FP, 1 suite and 1 conference room. Breakfast and snacks/refreshments included in rates. Types of meals: Cont plus. Beds: KQ. Cable TV, phone and VCR in room. Fax, library and child care on premises. Weddings, small meetings, family reunions and seminars hosted. Spanish, French, German and Norwegian spoken. Antiquing, art galleries, bicycling, canoeing/kayaking, fishing, golf, hiking, horseback riding,

opera, live theater, museums, parks, shopping, downhill skiing, cross-country skiing, tennis and wineries nearby.
Pets allowed: small, well-behaved.
Publicity: *Santa Fean, Hidden New Mexico, Our World, New Mexico Magazine. Selected by Sunset Magazine as one of the West's Best Inns, Out Magazine-as one of the 5 best B&B's in the USA and Southern Living.*

"Staying at your inn was a vacation and history lesson we will always remember!"

The Madeleine (formerly The Preston House)

106 Faithway St
Santa Fe, NM 87501
(505)982-3465 (888)877-7622 Fax:(505)982-8572
E-mail: madeleineinn@aol.com
Web: www.madeleineinn.com

Circa 1886. This gracious 19th-century home is the only authentic example of Queen Anne architecture in Santa Fe. This home displays a wonderful Victorian atmosphere with period furnishings, quaint wallpapers and beds covered with down quilts. Afternoon tea is a must, as Carolyn serves up a mouth-watering array of cakes, pies, cookies and tarts. The Madeleine, which is located in downtown Santa Fe, is within walking distance of the Plaza.

Innkeeper(s): George Padilla. $70-165. MC, VISA, DS, PC, TC. TAC10. 8 rooms, 6 with PB, 4 with FP, 2 cottages and 1 conference room. Breakfast and early coffee/tea included in rates. Types of meals: Full bkfst and early coffee/tea. Beds: KQDT. Cable TV, phone and ceiling fan in room. Fax and copier on premises. Weddings, small meetings, family reunions and seminars hosted. Spanish spoken. Antiquing, fishing, live theater, parks, shopping, downhill skiing and cross-country skiing nearby.
Publicity: *Country Inns.*

"We were extremely pleased — glad we found you. We shall return."

Pueblo Bonito

138 W Manhattan Ave
Santa Fe, NM 87501
(505)984-8001 (800)461-4599 Fax:(505)984-3155
E-mail: pueblo@cybermesa.com
Web: www.travelbase.com/destinations/santa-fe/pueblo

Circa 1880. A thick adobe wall surrounds the grounds of this estate, once the home of a circuit judge. An authentic Indian "orno" oven is attached to the house. Red brick pathways, old oak trees and a private hot tub add to the atmosphere. In the late afternoon, guests are treated to complimentary margaritas, wine and afternoon tea fare. The inn was selected as Santa Fe's second best B&B for the year 2000 by The Reporter, the local newspaper.
Innkeeper(s): Amy & Herb Behm. $70-165. MC, VISA, AX, DS, PC. TAC10. 18 rooms with PB, 18 with FP and 7 suites. Breakfast and afternoon tea included in rates. Types of meals: Cont plus and snacks/refreshments. Beds: QD. Cable TV and phone in room. Air conditioning. Fax, copier, spa, complimentary margaritas, wine cheese/crackers and fruit on premises. Handicap access. Fishing, golf, opera, live theater, parks, shopping, downhill skiing and cross-country skiing nearby.
Publicity: *Innsider and Country Inns.*

"You captured that quaint, authentic Santa Fe atmosphere, yet I didn't feel as if I had to sacrifice any modern conveniences."

Spencer House Bed & Breakfast

222 McKenzie St
Santa Fe, NM 87501-1831
(505)988-3024 (800)647-0530 Fax:(505)984-9862
E-mail: jan@spencerhse-santafe.com
Web: www.spencerhse-santafe.com

Circa 1923. Centrally located just four blocks from the historic plaza, this 1923 Mediterranean adobe home delicately combines Hispanic and early 20th-century motifs to create a bright, spacious inn. Antiques, oriental rugs and vivid colors fill the interior, while a serene neighborhood, known as the historic McKenzie corridor residential area, surrounds the exterior. There are plenty of adventures to embark on within walking distance, or some guests may choose to travel further to such historic sites as the Bandelier or Pecos National Monuments, located 40 miles away. Indulge yourself in a gourmet breakfast prepared by your host, who is a former professional chef. Delectables include asparagus omelets with salsa fresca, homemade spicy peach muffins, oatmeal bread toast, granola and cappuccinos to top it off.
Historic Interest: Santa Fe Plaza (1/4 mile),. Bandelier National Monument (40 miles), Pecos National Monument (40 miles).
Innkeeper(s): Jan McConnell & John Pitlak. $99-175. MC, VISA, AX, PC, TC. TAC10. 6 rooms with PB, 3 with FP and 1 suite. Breakfast and snacks/refreshments included in rates. Types of meals: Gourmet bkfst, early coffee/tea and afternoon tea. Beds: QT. Cable TV, phone, ceiling fan and VCR in room. Central air. Antiquing, art galleries, canoeing/kayaking, fishing, golf, hiking, horseback riding, live theater, museums, parks, shopping, downhill skiing and cross-country skiing nearby.

Santa Fe (Algodones)   D5

Hacienda Vargas

PO Box 307
Santa Fe (Algodones), NM 87001-0307
(505)867-9115 (800)261-0006 Fax:(505)867-0640
E-mail: stay@haciendavargas.com
Web: www.haciendavargas.com

Circa 1840. Nestled among the cottonwoods and mesas of the middle Rio Grande Valley, Hacienda Vargas has seen two centuries of Old West history. It once served as a trading post for Native Americans as well as a 19th-century stagecoach stop between Santa Fe and Mesilla. The grounds contain an adobe chapel, courtyard and gardens. The main house features five kiva fireplaces, Southwest antiques, Spanish tile, a library, art gallery and suites with private Jacuzzis.

Historic Interest: Gronado Monument, Indian Ruins (5 miles), Bandelier National Park (40 miles).
Innkeeper(s): Cynthia & Richard Spence. $79-149. MC, VISA, PC, TC. TAC10. 7 rooms with PB, 7 with FP and 4 suites. Breakfast included in rates. Types of meals: Full bkfst. Beds: QT. Ceiling fan and spa in suites in room. Air conditioning. Weddings and family reunions hosted. Spanish and German spoken. Antiquing, fishing, live theater, shopping, downhill skiing, sporting events and water sports nearby.
Publicity: *Albuquerque Journal (Country Inns), Vogue and San Francisco Chronicle.*

"This is the best! Breakfast was the best we've ever had!"

Silver City   H2

Bear Mountain Lodge

2251 Cottage San Road, PO Box 1163
Silver City, NM 88061
(505)538-2538 (877)620-2327 Fax:(505)534-1827
E-mail: innkeeper@bearmountainlodge.com
Web: www.bearmountainlodge.com

Circa 1928. Bordering Gila National Forest, this just-renovated hacienda on 178 acres began as the Rocky Mountain Ranch School, became a country club hotel, a dude ranch, and then a guest house. Donated to the Nature Conservancy, it retains its historic integrity with hand-hewn beams, a distinctive pine staircase, stone fireplaces and hardwood floors, while offering luxurious accommodations. Located in three buildings, spacious guest bedrooms feature hand-crafted Southwestern and Mission-style furnishings and majestic balcony views. Nature in full glory is found here, with abundant plants, birds and wildlife. The lodge naturalist holds conservation workshops and activities.

Historic Interest: Gila Cliff Dwellings (37 miles), Silver City Historic District (3.5 miles).

Innkeeper(s): Maura Gonsior. $95-165. MC, VISA, AX, PC, TC. 11 rooms with PB, 4 suites, 1 cottage and 1 conference room. Breakfast included in rates. Types of meals: Gourmet bkfst, veg bkfst, cont plus, early coffee/tea, picnic lunch, snacks/refreshments and dinner. Beds: KQT. Phone, ceiling fan, private balconies and handcrafted furniture in room. Fax, copier, stables, bicycles, library, nature trails and staff naturalist on premises. Handicap access. Weddings, small meetings, family reunions and seminars hosted. Antiquing, art galleries, bicycling, canoeing/kayaking, fishing, hiking, horseback riding, Archaeological ruins, Gila Cliff Dwellings, Gila National Forest, museums, parks and shopping nearby.

Publicity: *The Nature Conservance Magazine, Albuquerque Journal, Los Angeles Times, Sunset and Las Cruces Sun News.*

Taos   B6

Casa Encantada

416 Liebert St
Taos, NM 87571
(505)758-7477 (800)223-TAOS Fax:(505)737-5085
E-mail: encantada@newmex.com
Web: www.casaencantada.com

Circa 1930. Located only a few blocks from the historic Taos plaza, this historic adobe rests in a quiet neighborhood behind soft adobe walls. Secluded gardens, courtyards and patios add to the serenity. Most guest accommodations include a fireplace, and all have been individually decorated with original local art. Some have kitchenettes. The Santa Fe Suite is popular for anniversaries and special occasions. It includes a living room with fireplace, dressing area, and king bedroom. The Anasazi offers Taos character with a sun room, loft bedroom, living room and gas kiva. The Casita, once the hacienda's chapel, is the most spacious suite and with Southwest style offers two queen bedrooms, two kiva fireplaces, a kitchenette, bath, laundry and a private courtyard. Skiing, shopping, galleries, restaurants and much more are all nearby.

Innkeeper(s): Sharon Nicholson. $100-155. MC, VISA, AX, DS, PC, TC. TAC15. 9 rooms with PB, 6 with FP, 6 suites and 1 conference room. Breakfast included in rates. Types of meals: Gourmet bkfst, cont plus and early coffee/tea. EP. Beds: KQ. Cable TV, ceiling fan and VCR in room. Fax, copier and library on premises. Weddings, small meetings, family reunions and seminars hosted. German, Italian and Spanish spoken. Antiquing, fishing, golf, live theater, parks, shopping, downhill skiing, cross-country skiing, sporting events, tennis and water sports nearby.

Casa Europa Inn & Gallery

HC 68, Box 3 F, 840 Upper Ranchito
Taos, NM 87571-9408
(505)758-9798 (888)758-9798
E-mail: casa-europa@travelbase.com
Web: www.casaeuropanm.com

Circa 1700. Guests will appreciate both the elegance and history at Casa Europa. The home is a 17th-century pueblo-adobe creation with heavy beams, walls three-feet thick and a dining room with a massive kiva fireplace. Freshly baked pastries are served in the afternoons, and during ski season, hors d'oeuvres are provided in the early evening. European antiques fill the rooms, which are decorated in an elegant, Southwestern style. The French Room offers an 1860 bed, kiva fireplace and French doors opening onto the courtyard. Other rooms offer a fireplace, whirlpool tub or private hot tub. The five-room Apartment Suite includes a kitchen-dining room, sitting room with a kiva fireplace, bedroom and a private hot tub. The inn is 1.6 miles from Taos Plaza.

Innkeeper(s): Rudi & Marcia Zwicker. $75-135. MC, VISA, AX, PC, TC. TAC10. 7 rooms with PB, 6 with FP, 2 suites and 2 conference rooms. Breakfast included in rates. Types of meals: Gourmet bkfst, early coffee/tea, afternoon tea and snacks/refreshments. Beds: KQT. Cable TV, phone, turn-down service and ceiling fan in room. Spa and sauna on premises. Small meetings and family reunions hosted. German and Spanish spoken. Antiquing, fishing, live theater, parks, shopping, downhill skiing, cross-country skiing and water sports nearby.

Pets allowed: limited.

Hacienda Del Sol

PO Box 177
Taos, NM 87571-0177
(505)758-0287 Fax:(505)758-5895
E-mail: sunhouse@newmex.com
Web: www.taoshaciendadelsol.com

Circa 1810. Mabel Dodge, patron of the arts, purchased this old hacienda as a hideaway for her Native American husband, Tony Luhan. The spacious adobe sits among huge cottonwoods, blue spruce, and ponderosa pines, with an uninterrupted view of the Taos mountains across 95,000 acres of Native American Indian lands. Among Dodge's famous guests were Georgia  O'Keefe, who painted here, and D. H. Lawrence. The mood is tranquil and on moonlit nights guests can hear Indian drums and the howl of coyotes.

Historic Interest: Taos Pueblo (2 miles), Bandelier National Monument (60 miles), Puye Cliffs (53 miles).

Innkeeper(s): Dennis Sheehan. $95-260. MC, VISA, AX, DS, PC, TC. TAC10. 11 rooms with PB, 10 with FP and 2 suites. Breakfast and snacks/refreshments included in rates. Types of meals: Full bkfst and early coffee/tea. Beds: KQDT. Cassette player in room. Fax, spa and library on premises. Handicap access. Weddings, small meetings, family reunions and seminars hosted. Antiquing, fishing, museums, art galleries, 1500-year-old pueblo, art festivals, cultural programs, Indian ruins, live theater, parks, shopping, downhill skiing, cross-country skiing and water sports nearby.

Publicity: *Cleveland Plain Dealer, Houston Chronicle, Chicago Tribune, Los Angeles Daily News, Denver Post, Globe & Mail, Reunions Magazine, Santa Fe Magazine and Travel Channel.*

"Your warm friendliness and gracious hospitality have made this week an experience we will never forget!"

Inn on La Loma Plaza

PO Box 4159, 315 Ranchitos Rd
Taos, NM 87571
(505)758-1717 (800)530-3040 Fax:(505)751-0155
E-mail: laloma@vacationtaos.com
Web: www.taos-nm.net

Circa 1800. Thick adobe walls, vigas and latillas comprise this restored inn which showcases Pueblo Revival architecture (Santa Fe style). Listed in the national and state registers, this landmark sits on a small hill in the historic district. Two blocks from downtown, an old world setting blends with a Southwest ambiance enhanced by hand-carved wood details, antiques and local art. All guest bedrooms include kitchenettes, patios and exceptional views. Savor a satisfying gourmet breakfast as well as afternoon snacks, beverages, and evening coffee with cookies. The park-like setting features fountains and gardens. Enjoy a children's playground and large outdoor hot tub. Privileges are extended for use of the nearby health club, tennis court and pool. Try white-water rafting or skiing at a local resort.

Innkeeper(s): Jerry & Peggy Davis. $100-300. MC, VISA, AX, DS, PC, TC. TAC10. 7 rooms with PB, 7 with FP, 2 suites and 1 conference room. Breakfast and snacks/refreshments included in rates. Types of meals: Gourmet bkfst and early coffee/tea. Beds: KQ. Cable TV, phone, VCR and FM radios in room. Air conditioning. Fax, library and a poured concrete 6 person hot tub on premises. Weddings, small meetings, family reunions and seminars hosted. Antiquing, fishing, golf, parks, shopping, downhill skiing, cross-country skiing, tennis and water sports nearby.

Publicity: USA Today, Outside, Chicago Tribune, Denver Post, Romantic Getaways, Sunset and Mountain Living.

"Your hospitality while we were there exceeded what we've ever experienced at a B&B."

La Posada De Taos

PO Box 1118
Taos, NM 87571-1118
(505)758-8164 (800)645-4803 Fax:(505)751-4696
E-mail: laposada@laposadadetaos.com
Web: www.laposadadetaos.com

Circa 1907. This secluded adobe is located just a few blocks from the plaza in the Taos historic district. Rooms are decorated in a romantic Southwestern style with antiques, quilts and polished wood or tile floors.

All but one of the guest rooms include a kiva fireplace, and some offer private patios, TV's and telephones. For those in search of solitude, ask about the innkeeper's separate honeymoon house. Guests can walk to galleries, museums, shops and restaurants.

Innkeeper(s): Sandy & Alan Thiese. $90-150. MC, VISA, AX, DC, PC, TC. TAC10. 6 rooms with PB, 5 with FP and 1 conference room. Breakfast and snacks/refreshments included in rates. Types of meals: Full bkfst. Beds: KQ. Some with phone and TV in room. VCR, fax, copier, library and private deck with waterfall on premises. Weddings, small meetings and family reunions hosted. Antiquing, fishing, art galleries, live theater, parks, shopping, downhill skiing, cross-country skiing and water sports nearby.

Publicity: New York Times, Bon Appetit, Country Inns, Glamour and Los Angeles Times.

"We had a wonderful stay in your beautiful B&B. Everything was excellent. I'm giving your name to my travel agent, with the highest recommendation for your B&B."

Orinda B&B

461 Valverde
Taos, NM 87571
(505)758-8581 (800)847-1837
E-mail: orinda@newmex.com

Circa 1935. Current innkeepers Adrian and Sheila Percival are only the fifth owners of this property, which was deeded to its original owners by Abraham Lincoln. The house itself, a traditional adobe with an outstanding view of Taos Mountain, was

built years later, and features Southwestern touches such as kiva fireplaces, original art and turn-of-the century antiques. Sheila serves up a full breakfast such as green chile souffle (a John Wayne favorite), pecan French toast and bottomless cups of the inn's special coffee blend.

Historic Interest: The Kit Carson Home is a 15-minute walk from the bed & breakfast. Taos Pueblo and Martinez Hacienda are within easy driving distance, and the village of Taos offers many historic sites. Art galleries, museums, skiing, hiking, biking, riding, golf and fishing are all located nearby.

Innkeeper(s): Adrian & Sheila Percival. $80-145. MC, VISA, AX, DS, PC, TC. TAC10. 5 rooms with PB, 2 with FP and 1 suite. Breakfast included in rates. Types of meals: Full bkfst. Beds: KQD. One room has two person whirlpool in room. VCR on premises. Weddings and family reunions hosted. Antiquing, fishing, golf, hiking, museums, biking, shopping, downhill skiing and cross-country skiing nearby.

"It really is 'a B&B paradise' with your beautiful surroundings."

The Taos Inn

125 Paseo Del Pueblo Norte
Taos, NM 87571-5901
(505)758-2233 (800)826-7466 Fax:(505)758-5776
E-mail: taosinn@newmex.com
Web: www.taosinn.com

Circa 1880. Voted by National Geographic Traveler as one of "America's 54 Great Inns", The Taos Inn is a historic landmark with sections dating back to the 1600s. The inn's authentic adobe pueblo architecture enhances the inviting wood-burning fireplaces (kivas), vigas and wrought iron. Handsomely decorated rooms include reflections of the area's exotic tri-cultural heritage of Spanish, Anglo and Indian in the hand-loomed Indian bedspreads, antique armoires and Taos furniture. The well reviewed restaurant includes the legendary Adobe Bar. Ancient Taos Pueblo is nearby.

Innkeeper(s): Erik Ranger. $60-225. MC, VISA, AX, DS, TC. TAC10. 36 rooms with PB, 3 suites and 1 conference room. Types of meals: Gourmet bkfst, veg bkfst, cont, early coffee/tea, gourmet lunch, snacks/refreshments and gourmet dinner. Beds: KQDT. Cable TV and phone in room. Air conditioning. VCR, fax, copier, spa, swimming and child care on premises. Handicap access. Weddings, small meetings and family reunions hosted. Art galleries, bicycling, canoeing/kayaking, fishing, golf, hiking, live theater, museums, parks, shopping, downhill skiing, cross-country skiing and wineries nearby.

Publicity: Travel & Leisure, Gourmet, Bon Appetit, National Geographic Traveler and New York Times.

"It is charming, warm, friendly and authentic in decor with a real sense of history."

Touchstone Inn, Spa & Gallery

0110 Mabel Dodge Ln
Taos, NM 87571
(505)758-0192 (800)758-0192 Fax:(505)758-3498
E-mail: touchstone@taosnet.com
Web: www.touchstoneinn.com

Circa 1800. The Touchstone Inn is a quiet, historic adobe estate secluded among tall trees at the edge of Taos Pueblo lands. The grounds have an unobstructed view of Taos Mountain. USA Today calls it "the place to stay in Taos." The inn, connected to a spa and a gallery, features cozy rooms with fireplaces, luxurious textiles, intimate patios and exquisite tiled baths (four of which have Jacuzzi tubs). The inn offers full gourmet vegetarian and continental breakfasts. The common room, called the Leopold, has a library with historical books of the area and novels. Guests are welcome to play the baby grand piano and to browse the gallery's artwork. The spa offers massages, yoga and art classes, facials and therapeutic baths and wraps. Guests enjoy the outdoor hot tub with choice vistas of Taos Mountain. Taos Ski valley is 18 miles to the north.
$95-300. TAC10. 7 rooms with PB, 6 with FP. Types of meals: Gourmet bkfst. Beds: KQD. Cable TV, phone, ceiling fan, VCR, bath robes, hair dryers and four with Jacuzzi in room. Day spa, piano and garden massages on premises. Downhill skiing nearby.
Publicity: *USA Today, Bride's Magazine, Modern Bride, Mountain Living and Getaways.*

The Willows Inn

Box 6560 Ndcbu, 412 Kit Carson Rd
Taos, NM 87571
(505)758-2558 (800)525-8267 Fax:(505)758-5445
E-mail: willows@willows-taos.com
Web: www.willows-taos.com

Circa 1926. This authentic, Southwestern-style adobe was the Taos home to artist E. Martin Hennings, a member of the Taos Society of Artists. Each of the rooms features a unique theme, including Hennings' Studio, which was the artist's workplace. The studio boasts a bed with a seven-foot headboard, high ceilings, a whirlpool tub and private patio. The Santa Fe Room is decked in contemporary, Southwestern style and  has a sitting area. Each of the rooms includes a kiva fireplace. The Conquistador Room reflects old Spanish decor with an antique chest, equipale couch and ropero. The Cowboy and Anasazi rooms include artifacts such as a cowhide rug, handmade quilts, Zuni kachinas and hand-crafted pottery. Breakfasts are highlighted by fresh items right out of the inn's herb and vegetable gardens. Afternoon refreshments are served with lively conversation as guests browse through menus from various Taos eateries.
Historic Interest: The main house, studio and lap pool are listed in the National Registry of Historic Places. Taos Pueblo is less than two miles from the inn, and closer attractions include the Kit Carson Home & Museum, Mabel Dodge Luhan House, and the historic homes of several local artists.
Innkeeper(s): Janet & Doug Camp. $100-155. MC, VISA, AX, DS, PC, TC. TAC10. 5 rooms with PB, 5 with FP and 1 suite. Breakfast and snacks/refreshments included in rates. Types of meals: Gourmet bkfst, early coffee/tea and afternoon tea. Beds: QT. Jacuzzi in the suite, some desks and fans in room. VCR, fax, copier and library on premises. Weddings, small meetings, family reunions and seminars hosted. Spanish spoken. Antiquing, fishing, golf, hiking, archeology studies, live theater, parks, shopping, downhill skiing, cross-country skiing and water sports nearby.
Publicity: *New York Times, Travel Holiday, Taos Magazine, New Mexico Magazine, Sun Herald, Gulfshore Life, Mature Lifestyles and Country Inns.*

New York

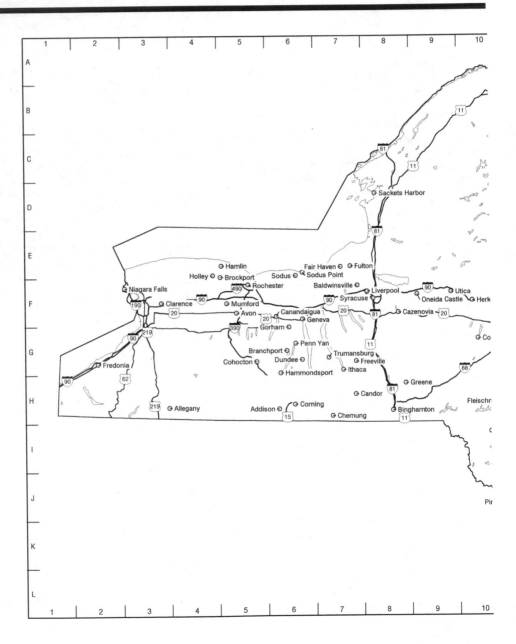

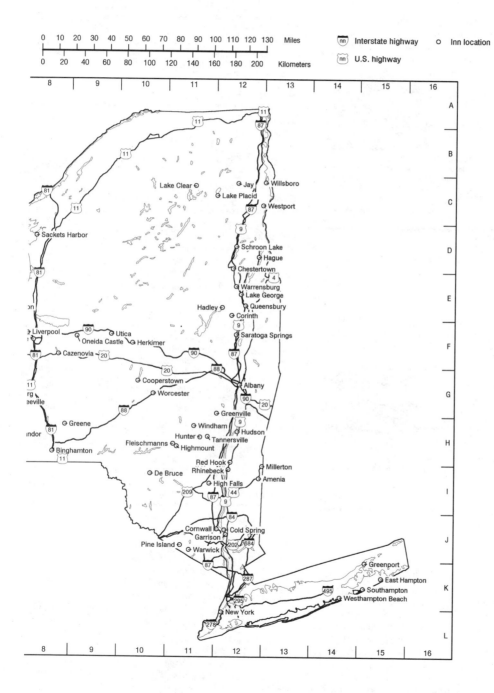

Miles
0 10 20 30 40 50 60 70 80 90 100 110 120 130

Kilometers
0 20 40 60 80 100 120 140 160 180 200

Interstate highway   ○ Inn location
U.S. highway

8   9   10   11   12   13   14   15   16

A

B

Lake Clear ○   ○ Jay   ○ Willsboro
○ Lake Placid
○ Westport   C

○ Sackets Harbor
○ Schroon Lake   D
○ Hague
○ Chestertown
○ Warrensburg
○ Lake George
Hadley ○   ○ Queensbury   E
○ Corinth
○ Liverpool   ○ Utica
Oneida Castle ○   ○ Herkimer
○ Saratoga Springs
○ Cazenovia   F
○ Cooperstown   Albany
○ Worcester
○ Greenville   G
○ Greene   ○ Windham   ○ Hudson
Hunter ○   ○ Tannersville
Fleischmanns ○ ○ Highmount   H
○ Binghamton
Red Hook ○   ○ Millerton
Rhinebeck ○   I
○ De Bruce   ○ High Falls   ○ Amenia
Cornwall ○ ○ Cold Spring
Garrison   J
Pine Island ○   ○ Warwick
○ Greenport
○ East Hampton   K
○ Southampton
○ Westhampton Beach
○ New York

L

8   9   10   11   12   13   14   15   16

359

Addison   H6

Addison Rose B&B

37 Maple St
Addison, NY 14801-1009
(607)359-4650

Circa 1892. Located on a scenic highway south of the Finger Lakes, this Queen Anne Victorian "painted lady" inn is an easy getaway from Corning or Elmira. The inn, which is listed in the National Register, was built by a doctor for his bride and was presented to her on Christmas Eve, their wedding day. The three guest rooms offer authentic Victorian furnishings. Many fine examples of Victorian architecture exist in Addison. Pinnacle State Park is just east of town.

Innkeeper(s): William & Maryann Peters. $95-115. PC, TC. 3 rooms with PB. Breakfast and afternoon tea included in rates. Types of meals: Gourmet bkfst and early coffee/tea. Beds: DT. Ceiling fan and private balcony in room. Air conditioning. Library on premises. Family reunions hosted. Antiquing, fishing, parks, shopping and cross-country skiing nearby.

Albany   G12

Pine Haven B&B

531 Western Ave
Albany, NY 12203-1721
(518)482-1574
E-mail: pinehavenb@aol.com
Web: www.pinehavenbedandbreakfast.com

Circa 1896. This turn-of-the-century Victorian is located in Pine Hills, an Albany historic district. In keeping with this history, the innkeepers have tried to preserve the home's 19th-century charm. The rooms offer old-fashioned comfort with Victorian influences. The Capitol Building and other historic sites are nearby.

Innkeeper(s): Janice Tricarico. $89. MC, VISA, AX, PC, TC. 5 rooms with PB. Breakfast included in rates. Types of meals: Cont plus and early coffee/tea. Beds: QDT. TV and phone in room. Air conditioning. Free off-street parking on premises. Weddings, small meetings, family reunions and seminars hosted. Antiquing, live theater, parks, shopping, cross-country skiing and sporting events nearby.

Allegany   H3

Gallets House B&B

1759 Four Mile Rd
Allegany, NY 14706-9724
(716)373-7493 Fax:(716)806-0384

Circa 1896. Once a summer retreat for Franciscan Friars, this 1896 Victorian inn was built by the current innkeeper's great uncle. Relax on the 100-foot wraparound porch and enjoy the view of the picturesque Alleghany hills. Choose among five guest rooms named after family members: Rose Clara, Mary Elizabeth, Grace Agatha , Regina Barbara and Christina Helen. Larger groups may prefer the Carriage House, which has three bedrooms with queen-size beds, a small kitchen and a spacious living room with a sofa bed. Innkeeper Joan prepares lavish gourmet breakfasts and serves them in the formal dining room

by candlelight. Fruits, homemade breads and biscuits are the prelude to sumptuous hot entrees and Joan's memorable apple cinnamon pancakes. Joan also provides afternoon or evening beverages and freshly baked goods. The inn hosts murder mysteries and tea parties. Ask about their specialty packages.

Innkeeper(s): Joan & Gary Boser. $75-125. MC, VISA, AX. 5 rooms with PB, 1 with FP, 1 guest house and 1 conference room. Breakfast and snacks/refreshments included in rates. Types of meals: Gourmet bkfst, early coffee/tea and afternoon tea. AP. Beds: KQD. Cable TV, phone, ceiling fan and two whirlpool tubs in room. Air conditioning. Fax, copier and spa on premises. Weddings, small meetings and family reunions hosted. Antiquing, art galleries, bicycling, canoeing/kayaking, fishing, golf, hiking, horseback riding, live theater, museums, parks, shopping, downhill skiing, cross-country skiing and sporting events nearby.

Amenia   I12

Troutbeck

Leedsville Rd
Amenia, NY 12501
(845)373-9681 Fax:(845)373-7080
E-mail: innkeeper@troutbeck.com
Web: www.troutbeck.com

Circa 1918. This English country estate on 600 wooded acres enjoyed its heyday in the '20s. The NAACP was conceived here and the literati and liberals of the period, including Teddy Roosevelt, were overnight guests. Weekend room rates, $650 to $1050, include six meals and luxurious accommodations for two. On Sundays, brunch is served. The inn has a fitness center, billiard table, outdoor and indoor pools and tennis courts. During the week the inn is a corporate retreat and has been awarded Executive Retreat of the Year. In July, 1997, Troutbeck was the site of a United Nations Summit meeting. Many weddings are held here each year and a new Great Room/ballroom has been added, which accommodates weddings with up to 250 guests and corporate gatherings for about 70 people.

Innkeeper(s): Jim Flaherty & Garret Corcoran. $650-1050. MC, VISA, AX, DC, PC, TC. TAC5. 42 rooms, 37 with PB, 9 suites with FP, 8 suites and 3 conference rooms. Breakfast, picnic lunch and dinner included in rates. Types of meals: Full bkfst, cont, early coffee/tea and lunch. MAP. Beds: KQDT. Phone, turndown service and some ceiling fans in room. Air conditioning. VCR, fax, copier, swimming, sauna, tennis and library on premises. Weddings, family reunions and seminars hosted. Spanish, Portuguese and Italian spoken. Antiquing, fishing, live theater, parks, shopping, downhill skiing, cross-country skiing and sporting events nearby.

Publicity: *New York Times, Good Housekeeping, New York Magazine, American Express* and *Vogue.*

"This 1920s-style estate makes you wish all life could be this way."

Avon   F5

Avon Inn

55 E Main St
Avon, NY 14414-1438
(716)226-8181 Fax:(716)226-8185

Circa 1820. This Greek Revival mansion, in both the state and national historic registers, has been providing lodging for more than a century. After 1866, the residence was turned into a health center that provided water cures from the local sulphur springs. The guest registry included the likes of Henry Ford, Thomas Edison and Eleanor Roosevelt. Though the inn is no longer a health spa, guests can still relax in the garden with its

towering trees and fountain or on the Grecian-pillared front porch. A full-service restaurant and conference facilities are on the premises.

Historic Interest: 1820 Greek Revival initially the residence of Jonathan H. Gerry, a successful broom corn grower.

Innkeeper(s): Linda Moran. $60-90. MC, VISA, AX, DC, CB, DS, TC. TAC10. 14 rooms with PB. Breakfast included in rates. Types of meals: Cont. Beds: KQD. Phone in room. Air conditioning. Fax and copier on premises. Weddings, small meetings, family reunions and seminars hosted. Amusement parks, antiquing, fishing, golf, museums, parks, shopping, downhill skiing and cross-country skiing nearby.

Baldwinsville F7

Pandora's Getaway

83 Oswego St
Baldwinsville, NY 13027-1130
(315)635-9571 (888)638-8668

Circa 1845. Nestled amid large trees on a hill in a tranquil village setting, this Greek Revival inn is listed in the National Register of Historic Places. Homemade crafts are mingled with antiques and collectibles to decorate the inn. Families with

children are welcomed with a variety of games and toys. Guests enjoy breakfasts of fresh fruit, homemade breads and quiche or a favorite family recipe in the formal dining room. The innkeeper collects depression glassware and uses it in her special table settings. Rockers on the porch afford quiet reading and visiting while listening to the breeze rustle the trees. Located a block from the center of town, the inn provides easy access to all the village offerings, including restaurants, shops, a working river lock of the Barge Canal System and a bakery.

Historic Interest: St. Marie among the Indians (3 miles).

Innkeeper(s): Sandra Wheeler. $65-90. MC, VISA, DC, DS, PC, TC. TAC10. 4 rooms. Breakfast included in rates. Types of meals: Gourmet bkfst and early coffee/tea. Beds: KQD. TV, phone and ceiling fan in room. VCR on premises. Family reunions and seminars hosted. Antiquing, bicycling, fishing, golf, hiking, horseback riding, museums, parks, shopping, cross-country skiing, sporting events, tennis and wineries nearby.

Binghamton H8

Pickle Hill B&B

795 Chenango St
Binghamton, NY 13901-1844
(607)723-0259

Circa 1890. This folksy B&B is a haven for those tired of endless motel nights. Guests feel as if they've stepped into the home of a good friend, and innkeepers Tom Rossi and Leslie Kiersted have made many friends over the last few years. The environment is comfortable country, highlighted by stained-glass windows and rich woodwork. The grounds are equipped for a game of basketball or badminton, and guests are often found gathered around the piano singing old songs.

Innkeeper(s): Tom Rossi & Leslie Kiersted Rossi. $50-60. PC, TC. 3 rooms. Breakfast and snacks/refreshments included in rates. Types of meals: Full bkfst, early coffee/tea and room service. Beds: DT. Radio and tapes in room. VCR, bicycles and piano on premises. Antiquing, fishing, live theater, parks, shopping, downhill skiing, cross-country skiing, sporting events and water sports nearby.

Bloomfield F5

Melody Farm & Teddy Inn

6700 State Rt 5 & 20
Bloomfield, NY 14469
(716)657-4863
E-mail: mldytdybnb@aol.com
Web: www.melodyteddybnb.com

Circa 1820. Relatives of President Taft built this Colonial farmhouse, now restored and a peaceful place to stay while exploring the picturesque and historic Finger Lakes region. The guest bedrooms are decorated in a comfortable country charm. Most feature a fireplace and Jacuzzi for two to inspire romance. The Carriage House, perfect for family retreats, has a full kitchen, dining area, living room and private deck. A hearty breakfast is prepared to please. Enjoy gently swinging in the gazebo loveseat, while planning the day's events.

Innkeeper(s): Patti & Mark. $100-150. MC, VISA, PC, TC. 3 rooms with PB and 1 cottage. Breakfast and snacks/refreshments included in rates. Types of meals: Country bkfst and early coffee/tea. Beds: QT. Ceiling fan, fireplace and two with Jacuzzi in room. Air conditioning. VCR, fax, copier and library on premises. Amusement parks, antiquing, art galleries, beaches, fishing, golf, hiking, horseback riding, live theater, museums, parks, shopping, downhill skiing, cross-country skiing, water sports and wineries nearby.

Branchport G6

Gone With The Wind on Keuka Lake

453 W Lake Rd, Rt 54 A
Branchport, NY 14418
(607)868-4603

Circa 1887. Breezes from Keuka Lake waft up to the front porch where guests often sit with a cup of coffee. The lakeside home, a Victorian, is decorated with an eclectic, uncluttered assortment of reproductions. Each of the bathrooms features unique decor, such as oak, brass or marble. One room includes a fireplace. There's a hot tub in the solarium, and the grounds offer a gazebo by the inn's private beach cove.

Innkeeper(s): Linda & Robert Lewis. $80-130. PC, TC. 10 rooms, 3 with PB, 1 with FP. Breakfast included in rates. Types of meals: Full bkfst. Beds: KQ. Jacuzzi in room. Air conditioning. Fax, spa and swimming on premises. Antiquing, fishing, Curtis Museum, nine wineries, parks, shopping, cross-country skiing, tennis and water sports nearby.

Publicity: *Summer Pleasures, Outdoors, Travel and Wine Times.*

"Thanks once again for a delightful stay. You have a little bit of heaven here."

Brockport E5

The Portico B&B

3741 Lake Rd N
Brockport, NY 14420-1415
(716)637-0220

Circa 1850. Named for its three porches, called porticos, this Greek Revival inn is situated amid blue spruce, maple and sycamore trees in a historic district. Tall columns and a cupola add to its charm. The interior features three fireplaces. Three antique-filled guest rooms are available to visitors, who enjoy a full Victorian breakfast and kettledrum, also known as after-

noon tea. The inn is listed in the National Register, as are several other structures in town. The surrounding area offers many attractions, including the Cobblestone Museum, Darien Lake Amusement Park, George Eastman House and Strasenburgh Planetarium. Several colleges, golf courses and parks are nearby. In winter, sleigh rides also are available nearby.

Innkeeper(s): Anne Klein. $70-80. PC, TC. TAC10. 3 rooms with PB, 3 with FP. Breakfast included in rates. Types of meals: Full bkfst and early coffee/tea. Turndown service in room. VCR on premises. Amusement parks, antiquing, sleigh rides, live theater, shopping, downhill skiing, cross-country skiing and sporting events nearby.

The Victorian B&B

320 S Main St
Brockport, NY 14420-2253
(716)637-7519 Fax:(716)637-7519
E-mail: skehoe@po.brockport.edu
Web: www.victorianbandb.com

Circa 1890. Within walking distance of the historic Erie Canal, this Queen Anne Victorian inn and its sister house are located on Brockport's Main Street. Visitors select from eight second-floor guest rooms, all with phones, private baths and TVs. Victorian furnishings are found throughout the inn. A favorite spot is the solarium, with its three walls of windows and fireplace, perfect for curling up with a book or magazine. Two first-floor sitting areas with fireplaces also provide relaxing havens for guests. Lake Ontario is just 10 miles away, and visitors will find much to explore in Brockport and Rochester.

Brockport is home to the State University of New York.

Innkeeper(s): Sharon Kehoe. $59-98. PC, TC. 8 rooms with PB. Breakfast and afternoon tea included in rates. Types of meals: Full bkfst. Beds: KQDT. Cable TV, phone and Jacuzzi tub in room. Air conditioning. VCR, fax and e-mail access on premises. Small meetings, family reunions and seminars hosted. Antiquing, live theater, shopping, cross-country skiing and sporting events nearby.

"Memories of another time; hospitality of another era."

Canandaigua   F6

Acorn Inn

4508 Rt 64 S, Bristol Ctr
Canandaigua, NY 14424
(716)229-2834 Fax:(716)229-5046
E-mail: acorninn@rochester.rr.com
Web: www.acorninnbb.com

Circa 1795. Guests to this Federal Stagecoach inn can relax before the blazing fire of a large colonial fireplace equipped with antique crane and hanging iron pots. Guest rooms, two with fireplace, are furnished with period antiques, canopy beds, luxury linens and bedding, and each has a comfortable sitting area. Books are provided in each guest room as well as in the libraries. After a day of visiting wineries, skiing, hiking in the Finger Lakes area and dinner at a

local restaurant, guests can enjoy the inn's outdoor Jacuzzi. Beds are turned down each night and chocolates are placed in each room. Complimentary beverages are always available.

Historic Interest: Erie Canal (10 miles), Ganodagan Indian Site, Grauger Homestead, Sonnenberg Gardens.

Innkeeper(s): Joan & Louis Clark. $105-205. MC, VISA, AX, DS, PC, TC. TAC10. 4 rooms with PB, 2 with FP. Breakfast included in rates. Types of meals: Gourmet bkfst and early coffee/tea. Beds: Q. Cable TV, turndown service, VCR, ice machine, down quilt, bathrobe and hair dryer in room. Air conditioning. Fax, copier, spa and library on premises. Weddings, small meetings and family reunions hosted. Antiquing, fishing, live theater, parks, shopping, downhill skiing, cross-country skiing and water sports nearby.

Publicity: *New York and Mid-Atlantic.*

Habersham Country Inn B&B

6124 State Route 5 And 20
Canandaigua, NY 14424-7938
(716)394-1510 (800)240-0644 Fax:(716)396-9271
E-mail: bandb@rochester.rr.com
Web: www.habershaminn.com

Circa 1843. A vast, sweeping front lawn and 11 peaceful acres surround this pre-Civil War home. Guests can relax on the front porch with Muff and Josie, the innkeepers' adorable canine friends, or, when there's a chill in the air, rest near the crackling fireplace of the living room. There are five guest rooms, including a suite with a two-person Jacuzzi. Bristol Ski

Mountain, museums, galleries, Seneca Park Zoo, horse racing, antique shopping and sporting activities are among the local attractions. Tour the many wineries in the fingerlakes region.

Historic Interest: Sonnenberg Gardens (3 1/2 miles), Granger Homestead (3 1/2 miles).

Innkeeper(s): Raymond & Sharon Lesio. $89-175. MC, VISA, AX, PC, TC. TAC10. 5 rooms. Breakfast and snacks/refreshments included in rates. Types of meals: Gourmet bkfst, country bkfst and veg bkfst. Beds: QDT. Cable TV and VCR in room. Central air. Fax on premises. Antiquing, art galleries, beaches, canoeing/kayaking, fishing, golf, hiking, live theater, museums, parks, shopping, downhill skiing, water sports and wineries nearby.

Morgan Samuels B&B Inn

2920 Smith Rd
Canandaigua, NY 14424-9558
(716)394-9232 Fax:(716)394-8044
E-mail: morganbb@aol.com
Web: www.morgansamuelsinn.com

Circa 1812. A luxurious Victorian estate on 46 acres of peaceful countryside, this inn offers elegance and comfort. Fireplaces, floor to ceiling windows, museum-quality furnishings, stained glass, and wide plank floors are delightful features found in both common and private areas. The guest bedrooms boast French doors leading to balconies that overlook landscaped gardens, fountains and a tennis court, or have a private entrance with an ivy-covered archway. Candlelight and soft music accentuate a lavish gourmet breakfast served in the formal dining room, intimate tea room or glass-enclosed stone porch. Afternoon tea and appetizers are welcome treats.

Innkeeper(s): Julie & John Sullivan. $119-275. MC, VISA, DS, PC, TC. TAC10. 6 rooms with PB, 6 with FP, 1 suite and 1 conference room. Breakfast, afternoon tea and snacks/refreshments included in rates. Types of meals: Gourmet bkfst, early coffee/tea and gourmet dinner. Beds: KQ. Turndown service and refrigerator two rooms in room. Air conditioning. VCR, fax, copier, bicycles, tennis, library and child care on premises. Weddings, small meetings, family reunions and seminars hosted. Antiquing, fishing, live theater, parks, shopping, downhill skiing, cross-country skiing, sporting events and water sports nearby.

The Sutherland House B&B Inn

3179 State Route 21 South
Canandaigua, NY 14424-8341
(716)396-0375 (800)396-0375 Fax:(716)396-9281
E-mail: goodnite@frontiernet.net
Web: www.sutherlandhouse.com

Circa 1885. Innkeepers Cor and Diane Van Der Woude refurbished this gracious home, adding more than 40 new windows, but leaving original elements such as a winding cherry staircase and marble fireplaces.

Their restoration effort has created a charming 19th-century atmosphere. Rooms feature elegant, Victorian decor, and some boast two-person whirlpool tubs. Diane serves up a bountiful breakfast each morning. The home is just a mile and a half from Main Street Canandaigua, and wineries, antique shopping and outdoor activities are nearby.

Innkeeper(s): Cor & Diane Van Der Woude. $85-175. MC, VISA, AX, DS, PC. TAC10. 5 rooms with PB, 4 with FP, 1 suite and 1 conference room. Breakfast, afternoon tea and snacks/refreshments included in rates. Types of meals: Country bkfst, veg bkfst and early coffee/tea. Beds: KQT. TV, phone, ceiling fan and VCR in room. Air conditioning. Fax, spa and three double Jacuzzi on premises. Family reunions hosted. Dutch spoken. Antiquing, beaches, bicycling, canoeing/kayaking, fishing, golf, hiking, horseback riding, festivals, live theater, parks, shopping, downhill skiing, cross-country skiing, sporting events, water sports and wineries nearby.

Candor   H7

The Edge of Thyme, A B&B Inn

6 Main St
Candor, NY 13743-1615
(607)659-5155 (800)722-7365 Fax:(607)659-5155
E-mail: innthyme@twcny.rr.com

Circa 1840. Originally the summer home of John D. Rockefeller's secretary, this two-story Georgian-style inn offers gracious accommodations a short drive from Ithaca. The inn sports many interesting features, including an

impressive stairway, marble fireplaces, parquet floors, pergola (arbor) and windowed porch with leaded glass. Guests may relax in front of the inn's fireplace, catch up with reading in its library or watch television in the sitting room. An authentic turn-of-the-century full breakfast is served, and guests also may arrange for special high teas.

Innkeeper(s): Prof. Frank & Eva Mae Musgrave. $75-135. MC, VISA, AX, TC. TAC10. 5 rooms, 3 with PB and 2 suites. Breakfast included in rates. Types of meals: Gourmet bkfst, early coffee/tea and afternoon tea. Beds: KQDT. VCR on premises. Weddings, small meetings, family reunions and seminars hosted. Antiquing, fishing, live theater, parks, shopping, downhill skiing, cross-country skiing and sporting events nearby.

Catskill Mountains   H12

The Inn at Lake Joseph

400 Saint Joseph Rd
Catskill Mountains, NY 12777
(845)791-9506 Fax:(845)794-1948
E-mail: inn@lakejoseph.com
Web: www.lakejoseph.com

Circa 1863. In the Catskill Mountains, just 800 feet from private Lake Joseph is a 135-year-old Queen Anne Victorian Country Estate surrounded by a 2,000-acre wildlife preserve. Steven Crane wrote "The Red Badge of Courage" in a building on the original premises. The inn's 15 guest bedrooms have working fireplaces and whirlpool baths. They are decorated with lacy linens, dried flowers, Persian rugs and attractive period pieces. Common rooms include the billiard room and game room. Aside from the inn, the estate has accommodations in the rustic Carriage House and in the Cottage. Children and pets are welcome in those two buildings.

Most of the Carriage House rooms have kitchens, cathedral ceilings, private sun decks, working fireplaces and whirlpools. "The Cottage" doesn't begin to describe the spacious, elegant,

harmonious structure with a 24-foot cathedral ceiling and exposed wood beams and rafters cut from the surrounding forest. The fieldstone open-hearth fireplace in the living area runs from floor to roof rafters. On the second level is a glassed-in bedroom tower with a view of the forest out each window. The bathroom has a whirlpool bath and doubled-headed shower. A sumptuous breakfast is served on the inn's veranda, which is screened in the summer and fitted with glass in the winter, allowing guests to enjoy the beauty of the landscape during every season. Snacks foods are also provided. Guests may go boating, fishing, hiking or cross-country skiing or enjoy the nearby full service health and fitness club.

Innkeeper(s): Ivan & Ru Weinger. $150-405. MC, VISA, AX, PC, TC. 15 rooms with PB, 14 with FP, 3 suites, 1 cottage, 3 guest houses and 1 conference room. Breakfast and snacks/refreshments included in rates. Types of meals: Gourmet bkfst, country bkfst, veg bkfst, cont, and early coffee/tea. Beds: KQ. Cable TV, phone, ceiling fan, VCR, fireplace & some with full kitchens in room. Air conditioning. Fax, copier, swimming, bicycles, tennis, library, billiard room, game room, fishing, boating, tennis, hiking and cross-country skiing on premises. Handicap access. Weddings, small meetings, family reunions and seminars hosted. Portuguese & Spanish spoken. Antiquing, art galleries, bicycling, canoeing/kayaking, fishing, golf, hiking, horseback riding, live theater, museums, shopping, downhill skiing, cross-country skiing, tennis & wineries nearby.
Pets allowed: Allowed in Carriage House & Cottage Guestrooms.
Publicity: *New York Times* and *New York Magazine.*

"This is a secluded spot where every detail is attended to, making it one of the country's best inns."

Cazenovia   F8

Brae Loch Inn

5 Albany St
Cazenovia, NY 13035-1403
(315)655-3431 Fax:(315)655-4844
E-mail: braeloch1@aol.com
Web: www.cazenovia.com/braeloch

Circa 1805. Hunter green awnings accentuate the attractive architecture of the Brae Loch. Since 1946 the inn has been owned and operated by the same family. A Scottish theme is evident throughout, including in the inn's restaurant. Four of the oldest rooms have fireplaces (non-working). Stickley, Harden and antique furniture add to the old-world atmosphere, and many rooms offer canopy beds. Guest rooms are on the second floor above the restaurant.

Historic Interest: Lorenzo (in village), Chittenango Falls (4 miles).
Innkeeper(s): Jim & Val Barr. $80-140. MC, VISA, AX, TC. 12 rooms with PB and 1 conference room. Breakfast included in rates. Types of meals: Cont and gourmet dinner. Beds: KQDT. Cable TV, phone and three rooms with Jacuzzis in room. Air conditioning. Fax and copier on premises. Weddings, small meetings, family reunions and seminars hosted. Antiquing, fishing, golf, swimming, parks, shopping, downhill skiing, cross-country skiing, sporting events, tennis and water sports nearby.
Publicity: *The Globe and Mail, Traveler Magazine and CNY.*

"Everything was just perfect. The Brae Loch and staff make you feel as if you were at home."

The Brewster Inn

PO Box 507, 6 Ledyard Ave
Cazenovia, NY 13035-0507
(315)655-9232 Fax:(315)655-2130
Web: www.cazenovia.com/brewster

Circa 1890. This large Victorian mansion is located on three acres and offers a terrace and two dining rooms with views of Cazenovia Lake. Originally, the home was constructed by Benjamin Brewster, a partner of John Rockefeller in Standard Oil. Some guest rooms offer fireplaces and Jacuzzi tubs. The inn's renowned restaurant staffs seven chefs preparing gourmet meals with only the freshest ingredients. Dessert souffles are a specialty.
Innkeeper(s): Richard A. Hubbard. $60-225. MC, VISA, DC, CB, DS, PC, TC. 17 rooms with PB, 4 with FP and 1 suite. Breakfast included in rates. Types of meals: Cont plus, early coffee/tea and gourmet dinner. Beds: KQD. Cable TV, phone and ceiling fan in room. Air conditioning. Fax, copier, swimming and child care on premises. Handicap access. Weddings, small meetings, family reunions and seminars hosted. Antiquing, fishing, golf, parks, shopping, downhill skiing, cross-country skiing, sporting events, tennis and water sports nearby.
Publicity: *New York Times, Conde Nast, If Ever I Would See You Again and PBS Travel Series.*

Chemung   H7

Halcyon Place B&B

197 Washington St, PO Box 244
Chemung, NY 14825-0244
(607)529-3544
E-mail: herbtique@aol.com
Web: www.bbonline.com/ny/halcyon

Circa 1820. The innkeepers chose the name "halcyon" because it signifies tranquility and a healing richness. The historic Greek Revival inn and its grounds offer just that to guests, who will appreciate the fine period antiques, paneled doors, six-over-six windows of hand-blown glass and wide plank floors. Three herb garden and screen porch also beckon visitors. Full breakfasts

may include omelets with garden ingredients, raspberry muffins, rum sticky buns or waffles. The inn's three guest rooms feature double beds, and one boasts a romantic fireplace. Fine antiquing and golfing are found nearby. During the summer months, the

innkeepers host a Wednesday afternoon herb series and afternoon tea. Also ask about other special packages. The innkeepers opened an herb and antique shop in their restored barn.
Historic Interest: Sullivan's Monument (6 miles), Mark Twain's study and grave site (12 miles).
Innkeeper(s): Douglas & Yvonne Sloan. $60-95. MC, VISA, PC. 3 rooms, 1 with PB. Breakfast and snacks/refreshments included in rates. Types of meals: Gourmet bkfst. Beds: D. Phone and turndown service in room. Air conditioning. Bicycles on premises. Weddings and small meetings hosted. German spoken. Antiquing, art galleries, bicycling, canoeing/kayaking, fishing, golf, hiking, live theater, museums, parks, cross-country skiing, sporting events and tennis nearby.
Publicity: *Elmira Star Gazette, Chemung Valley Reporter and Evening Star.*

Chestertown   D12

The Chester Inn B&B

6347 Main St
Chestertown, NY 12817
(518)494-4148 Fax:(518)494-7940

Circa 1830. There are 14 acres of meadow surrounding this completely restored early Greek Revival home. Yellow with white trim, there are two front porches, bordered by lilacs, that stretch across the house. Barns, a smoke house and an ancient family cemetery rests on the property. Inside, the inn's grand hall has hand-grained woodwork and mahogany railings. Country Victorian antiques combined with Laura Ashley fabrics, replica wallpapers and down comforters are features. Breakfast specialties such as skillet corn bread and vegetable souffle with pan-fried potatoes are served by candlelight. A block away is the Main Street Ice Cream Parlor & Restaurant and Miss Hester's Emporium Gift Shop owned by the innkeepers.
Innkeeper(s): Bruce & Suzanne Robbins. $89-159. MC, VISA, PC, TC. 4 rooms with PB and 2 suites. Breakfast and afternoon tea included in rates. Types of meals: Full bkfst and early coffee/tea. Beds: QDT. Ceiling fan and one with fireplace in room. Air conditioning. VCR on premises. Weddings and family reunions hosted. Amusement parks, antiquing, fishing, golf, live theater, parks, shopping, downhill skiing, cross-country skiing, sporting events, tennis and water sports nearby.
Publicity: *Adirondack Guide, Glens Falls Post Star, WRGB, Schenectady and New York.*

"We'll shout your praises!"

Friends Lake Inn

963 Friends Lake Rd
Chestertown, NY 12817
(518)494-4751 Fax:(518)494-4616
E-mail: friends@friendslake.com

Circa 1860. Formerly a boardinghouse for tanners who worked in the area, this Mission-style inn now offers its guests elegant accommodations and fine dining. Overlooking Friends Lake, the inn provides easy access to many well-known skiing areas, including Gore Mountain. Guests are welcome to borrow a canoe for a lake outing and use the inn's private beach. Guest rooms are well-appointed and most include four-poster beds. Many have breathtaking lake views or Jacuzzis. Three rooms have a wood-burning fireplace.

An outdoor sauna is a favorite spot after a busy day of recreation. The 32 km Nordic Ski Center is on site with groomed wilderness trails, lessons and rentals. Trails are available for hiking, as well.
Innkeeper(s): Sharon & Greg Taylor. $245-395. MC, VISA, AX, PC, TC. TAC10. 17 rooms with PB. Breakfast and dinner included in rates. Types of meals: Full

bkfst, country bkfst, picnic lunch and room service. MAP. Beds: KQ. Turndown service in room. Air conditioning. VCR, fax, copier, swimming and library on premises. Weddings, small meetings, family reunions and seminars hosted. Amusement parks, antiquing, fishing, live theater, museums, parks, shopping, downhill skiing, cross-country skiing, sporting events and water sports nearby. Publicity: *Country Inns and New York Times.*

"Everyone here is so pleasant, you end up feeling like family!"

Clarence   F3

Asa Ransom House

10529 Main St
Clarence, NY 14031-1684
(716)759-2315 Fax:(716)759-2791
E-mail: innfo@asaransom.com
Web: www.asaransom.com

Circa 1853. Set on spacious lawns, behind a white picket fence, the Asa Ransom House rests on the site of the first grist mill built in Erie County. Silversmith Asa Ransom constructed an inn and grist mill here in response to the Holland Land Company's offering of free land to anyone who would start and operate a tavern. A specialty of the dining room is "Veal Perrott" and "Pistachio Banana Muffins."

Historic Interest: Clarence Center Emporium (5 miles), Amherst Museum, Colony (8 miles), Theodore Roosevelt Inaugural National Historic Site (Wilcox Mansion) (16 miles).

Innkeeper(s): Robert & Abigail Lenz. $95-155. MC, VISA, DS, PC, TC. TAC10. 9 rooms with PB, 7 with FP, 2 suites and 1 conference room. Breakfast included in rates. Types of meals: Full bkfst, early coffee/tea and dinner. MAP, EP. Beds: KQT. Phone, turndown service and old radio tapes in room. Air conditioning. Fax, copier and library on premises. Handicap access. Weddings and small meetings hosted. Antiquing, live theater, parks, shopping and cross-country skiing nearby.
Publicity: *Toronto Star, Buffalo News, Prevention Magazine, Country Living. Country Inns and Inn Country USA.*

"Popular spot keeps getting better."

Cohocton   G5

Villa Serendip Country Victorian B&B

10849 State Route 371N, O Box 304
Cohocton, NY 14826
(716)384-5299 Fax:(716)384-9228
E-mail: inhost@yahoo.com

Circa 1860. Formerly known as the Woodworth Mansion, whose namesake was a direct descendent of one of America's first settlers, this restored Italianate villa still retains its original character. The only additions are modern electricity and plumbing. Two four-story belvederes overlook the hills surrounding Cohocton Valley. Listen to vintage recorded music in the parlor, or play the piano or Victorian pump organ. Some guest bedrooms and suites can be adjoining, and a Jacuzzi or fireplace adds a touch of romance. Mouth-watering recipes like oven-baked French toast, skillet potatoes with rosemary and sausage, scrambled eggs fromage, broiled citrus ambrosia and warm muffins are topped off with juice, teas and coffee. Relax on one of the inn's four porches. Ideally located between Rochester and Corning, it is close to the sites and activities of the Finger Lakes.
Innkeeper(s): Fran Ambroselli. $85-155. MC, VISA, AX, DS, PC, TC. TAC10. 5 rooms with PB, 1 with FP, 2 suites and 1 guest house. Breakfast included in rates. Types of meals: Gourmet bkfst, country bkfst, early coffee/tea, picnic

lunch, afternoon tea, snacks/refreshments and dinner. Beds: KQ. Cable TV, phone, ceiling fan, VCR, fireplace, hot tub and in room. Fax, bicycles, child care and Jacuzzi suite available on premises. Handicap access. Weddings, small meetings, family reunions and seminars hosted. Amusement parks, antiquing, art galleries, beaches, fishing, golf, hiking, horseback riding, Mountain Ski Resort, Swain Ski Resort, Letworth State Park, Stony Brook State Park, Corning Museum of Glass, Keuka Lake, live theater, museums, parks, shopping, downhill skiing, cross-country skiing, water sports and wineries nearby.

Cold Spring   J12

Pig Hill Inn

73 Main St
Cold Spring, NY 10516-3014
(845)265-9247 Fax:(845)265-4614
E-mail: pighillinn@aol.com
Web: www.pighillinn.com

Circa 1808. The antiques at this stately three-story inn can be purchased, and they range from Chippendale to chinoiserie style. Rooms feature formal English and Adirondack decor with special touches such as four-poster or brass beds, painted rockers and, of course, pigs. The lawn features a tri-level garden. The delicious breakfasts can be shared with guests in the Victorian conservatory, dining room or garden, or it may be served in the privacy of your room. The inn is about an hour out of New York City, and the train station is only two blocks away.

Innkeeper(s): Leigh Carmody. $120-170. MC, VISA, AX, TC. 9 rooms, 5 with PB, 6 with FP and 1 conference room. Breakfast included in rates. Types of meals: Full bkfst and lunch. Beds: QDT. Ceiling fans in room. Air conditioning. Weddings, small meetings, family reunions and seminars hosted. Antiquing, fishing, live theater, shopping and sporting events nearby.
Publicity: *National Geographic, Woman's Home Journal, Country Inns and Getaways for Gourmets.*

"Some of our fondest memories of New York were at Pig Hill."

Cooperstown   G10

Cooper Inn

Main & Chestnut Streets
Cooperstown, NY 13326
(607)547-2567 (800)348-6222 Fax:(607)547-1271
E-mail: reservations@cooperinn.com
Web: www.cooperinn.com

Circa 1812. This Federal-style brick house opened as an inn in 1936, although it was built more than a century before that. It has been restored to the elegance of when it was first designed in the early 1800s. Guests can relax in the inn's main parlor. Decorative period woodwork and paintings from the Fenimore Art Museum adorn the main floor. Rooms have been redecorated recently, and the inn is within walking distance to most of Cooperstown's attractions.
Historic Interest: Cooperstown, NY is an historic site.
Innkeeper(s): Steve Walker. $105-280. MC, VISA, AX. TAC10. 20 rooms with PB, 5 suites and 1 conference room. Types of meals: Cont plus and early coffee/tea. Beds: QT. Cable TV and phone in room. Central air. Fax, copier, tennis and library on premises. Weddings, small meetings, family reunions and seminars hosted. Antiquing, art galleries, beaches, bicycling, canoeing/kayaking, fishing, golf, hiking, horseback riding, driving range, live theater, museums, parks, shopping, cross-country skiing, sporting events, tennis and water sports nearby.

The Inn at Cooperstown

16 Chestnut St
Cooperstown, NY 13326-1006
(607)547-5756 Fax:(607)547-8779
E-mail: theinn@telenet.net
Web: www.innatcooperstown.com

Circa 1874. This three-story, Second Empire hotel features a graceful porch filled with wicker furniture and rocking chairs. The inn is located in the center of the Cooperstown National

Historic District. The guest rooms are decorated tastefully and comfortably. A block from Otsego Lake, the inn is within walking distance of most of Cooperstown's attractions.
Historic Interest: Baseball Hall of Fame (2 blocks), The Farmers' Museum & Fenimore Art Museum (1 mile), Glimmerglass Opera (8 miles).

Innkeeper(s): Michael Jerome. $98-275. MC, VISA, AX, DC, DS, PC, TC. TAC10. 17 rooms with PB, 1 suite and 1 conference room. Breakfast included in rates. Types of meals: Cont. Beds: QT. Fax and library on premises. Handicap access. Small meetings hosted. Antiquing, fishing, museum, opera, lake, live theater, parks, shopping, cross-country skiing, sporting events and water sports nearby.

Publicity: *Cleveland Plain Dealer, New York Times, Atlanta Journal, Los Angeles Times, New York Magazine, Conde Nast Traveler, USA Today, Travel & Leisure. and Good Day New York.*

"An unpretentious country inn with 17 rooms, spotless on the inside and stunning on the outside. — Conde Nast Traveler."

Thistlebrook B&B

316 County Hwy 28
Cooperstown, NY 13326
(607)547-6093 (800)596-9305
E-mail: bugonian@aol.com
Web: www.thistlebrook.com

Circa 1866. This sprawling barn with its rustic appearance belies the spacious and elegant rooms awaiting discovery inside. Fluted columns in the living room enhance the inn's original architectural details. Furnishings include American and European pieces, an Egyptian Revival mirror, Oriental rugs and crystal chandeliers. Just up the wide stairway is a library from which the guest rooms are reached. Breakfasts are hearty and may include fresh fruit salad and three-cheese omelets with biscuits and ham. Enjoy valley vistas from the inn's deck. A variety of wildlife such as deer, bullfrogs, wood ducks and an occasional blue heron, gather around the pond.

Innkeeper(s): Paula & Jim Bugonian. $135-165. PC, TC. TAC10. 5 rooms with PB and 2 suites. Breakfast included in rates. Types of meals: Full bkfst and early coffee/tea. Beds: KQ. Ceiling fan in room. Air conditioning. Handicap access. Small meetings and family reunions hosted. Antiquing, fishing, golf, summer opera, live theater, shopping, sporting events, tennis and water sports nearby.

Publicity: *Country Inns, New York Magazine and Home and Garden TV.*

Cooperstown (Sharon Springs) *G10*

Edgefield

Washington St, PO Box 152
Cooperstown (Sharon Springs), NY 13459
(518)284-3339
E-mail: dmwood71@hotmail.com
Web: www.sharonsprings.com/edgefield.htm

Circa 1865. This home has seen many changes. It began as a farmhouse, a wing was added in the 1880s, and by the turn of

the century, sported an elegant Greek Revival facade. Edgefield is one of a collection of nearby homes used as a family compound for summer vacations. The rooms are decorated with traditional furnishings in a formal English-country style. In the English tradition, afternoon tea is presented with cookies and tea sandwiches. Sharon Springs includes many historic sites, and the town is listed in the National Register.
Historic Interest: Near Cooperstown, Glimmerglass Opera and Hyde Hall; Albany (45 miles away).

Innkeeper(s): Daniel Marshall Wood. $110-175. PC, TC. 5 rooms with PB. Types of meals: Gourmet bkfst, early coffee/tea, afternoon tea and snacks/refreshments. Beds: QT. Turndown service and ceiling fan in room. Library, drawing room and veranda on premises. Antiquing, golf, opera, live theater, museums, parks, shopping and water sports nearby.

Publicity: *Colonial Homes Magazine, Philadelphia Inquirer and Boston Globe.*

"Truly what I always imagined the perfect B&B experience to be!"

Corinth *E12*

Agape Farm B&B

4839 Rt 9N
Corinth, NY 12822-1704
(518)654-7777 Fax:(518)654-7777
E-mail: agapefarmbnb@adelphia.net

Circa 1870. Amid 33 acres of fields and woods, this Adirondack farmhouse is home to chickens and horses, as well as guests seeking a refreshing getaway. Visitors have their choice of six guest rooms, all with ceiling fans, phones, private baths and views of the tranquil surroundings. The inn's wraparound porch lures many visitors, who often enjoy a glass of icy lemonade. Homemade breads, jams, jellies and muffins are part of the full breakfast served here, and guests are welcome to pick

berries or gather a ripe tomato from the garden. A trout-filled stream on the grounds flows to the Hudson River, a mile away.
Historic Interest: Built on the site of a hundred year old dairy farm, outbuildings and animals keep this atmosphere alive.

Innkeeper(s): Fred & Sigrid Koch. $79-175. MC, VISA, DS, PC, TC. 6 rooms with PB and 1 conference room. Breakfast and snacks/refreshments included in rates. Types of meals: Gourmet bkfst, country bkfst, veg bkfst and early coffee/tea. Beds: KQDT. Phone and ceiling fan in room. VCR, fax, swimming, child care and downstairs HC room and bath on premises. Handicap access. Weddings, small meetings, family reunions and seminars hosted. Amusement parks, antiquing, art galleries, beaches, bicycling, canoeing/kayaking, fishing, golf, hiking, horseback riding, museums, parks, shopping, downhill skiing, cross-country skiing, sporting events, tennis and water sports nearby.

"Clean and impeccable, we were treated royally."

Corning *H6*

1865 White Birch B&B

69 E 1st St
Corning, NY 14830-2715
(607)962-6355

Circa 1865. This Victorian is a short walk from historic Market Street, the Corning Glass Museum and many restaurants. Guests will appreciate the detailed woodwork, hardwood floors, an impressive winding staircase and many antiques. The rooms are decorated in a cozy, country decor. Home-baked breakfasts provide the perfect start for a day of visiting wineries, antique shops or museums.

Innkeeper(s): Kathy Donahue. $55-85. MC, VISA, AX. 4 rooms, 2 with PB. Breakfast included in rates. Types of meals: Full bkfst. Beds: QT. TV, phone, window fans and comfortable chair in room. Antiquing, fishing, live theater, shopping, cross-country skiing and sporting events nearby.

"This is a beautiful home, decorated to make us feel warm and welcome."

Cornwall J12

Cromwell Manor Inn B&B

174 Angola Rd
Cornwall, NY 12518
(845)534-7136
E-mail: cmi@hvc.rr.com
Web: www.cromwellmanor.com

Circa 1820. Listed in the National Register of Historic Places, this stunning Greek Revival mansion sits on seven lush acres with scenic Hudson Valley views. It is elegantly furnished with period antiques and fine reproductions. The Chimneys Cottage, built in 1764, offers romantic guest bedrooms with a country decor. Savor a bountiful gourmet breakfast before a stroll in the garden. The inn boasts an extensive wine collection and extends afternoon hospitality. After a day of exploring, relax by the fireside or indulge in the Jacuzzi.

Historic Interest: West Point 5 miles, nearby mansions: Roosevelt, Vanderbilt and Boscobel. The Brotherhood Winery, the nation's oldest, is 15 miles. New Windsor Cantonment, Washington's and Knox's headquarters and many others.
Innkeeper(s): Jack & Cynthia Trowell. $135-300. MC, VISA, AX, PC, TC. TAC10. 13 rooms with PB, 7 with FP, 2 suites and 1 conference room. Breakfast included in rates. Types of meals: Gourmet bkfst, early coffee/tea, picnic lunch, afternoon tea and room service. Beds: KQD. Turndown service in room. Air conditioning. VCR and copier on premises. Handicap access. Weddings, small meetings, family reunions and seminars hosted. Antiquing, fishing, Hudson Valley Mansion, outlets, art center, Renaissance Festival, West Point sports, live theater, parks, shopping, downhill skiing, cross-country skiing, sporting events, water sports and wineries nearby.
Publicity: *Orange Life, American Way, Hudson Valley, Monrreal Gazette, Washington Post and Fox.*

De Bruce I10

De Bruce Country Inn on The Willowemoc

De Bruce Rd #982
De Bruce, NY 12758
(845)439-3900

Circa 1917. This inn is located on the banks of the Willowemoc stream, not far from where the first dry fly was cast in the United States. This early 20th-century retreat, with its excellent trout fishing, secluded woodlands, views of the valley and mountains continues to draw visitors today. The inn, situated in the Catskill Forest Preserve, offers wooded trails, wildlife and game, a stocked pond, swimming pool, sauna and whirlpool. Guests enjoy hearty breakfasts and fine dinners on the dining terrace and romantic evenings in the Dry Fly Lounge.

Innkeeper(s): Ron & Marilyn Lusker. $100-250. 13 rooms with PB and 2 suites. Breakfast and dinner included in rates. Types of meals: Full bkfst. MAP. Beds: KQDT. Ceiling fan in room. VCR, fax, copier, spa, swimming, sauna, library, TV in bar and wine cellar on premises. Weddings, small meetings, family reunions and seminars hosted. French, limited German and limited Italian spoken. Antiquing, golf, state park and museums nearby. Pets allowed: at inn owners' discretion.

Dundee G6

The 1819 Red Brick Inn

2081 State Route 230
Dundee, NY 14837-9424
(607)243-8844
E-mail: peacock@eznet.net
Web: www.bbonline.com/ny/redbrick

Circa 1819. This Federal-style inn's impressive exterior, with its 15-inch-thick brick walls, is complemented by its antique-filled interior. Many fine wineries are found in the area. The inn sits on 8 acres, near a mineral springs that in the late 1800s attracted many health-conscious visitors. Keuka Lake and Watkins Glen state parks are within easy driving distance.

Innkeeper(s): Charles & Christine Peacock. $85-105. PC. 5 rooms with PB, 1 with FP. Breakfast included in rates. Types of meals: Full bkfst and early coffee/tea. Beds: D. Antiquing, fishing, golf, parks, shopping, cross-country skiing, sporting events and water sports nearby.

East Hampton K15

J Harper Poor Cottage

181 Main St
East Hampton, NY 11937-2720
(631)324-4081 Fax:(631)329-5931
E-mail: info@jharperpoor.com
Web: www.jharperpoor.com

Circa 1910. Enjoy the luxury of a stately English manor at this elegant inn, located in one of the oldest communities in the United States. A colonial revival staircase leads upstairs to the guest rooms, which offer such unique features as exposed beams, antique wall paneling, fireplaces or clawfoot bathtubs. Rooms facing the front enjoy a view of the picture-perfect town pond and green, and rooms facing the back look over the formal English garden. Relax in the comfortable Great Room, with ample books and reading lamps, and grand piano. A sumptuous breakfast of apple tarts or lemon pancakes can be enjoyed inside or out in the garden. It's just a short walk to unusual shops, galleries, nature trails and some of the finest beaches on the Atlantic Coast.

Innkeeper(s): Gary & Rita Reiswig. $200-600. MC, VISA, AX, DC, PC, TC. 5 rooms with PB, 4 with FP and 2 conference rooms. Breakfast included in rates. Types of meals: Gourmet bkfst, early coffee/tea, picnic lunch, afternoon tea, snacks/refreshments and room service. Beds: KQT. Cable TV, phone, turndown service, ceiling fan and VCR in room. Central air. Fax, spa, sauna and library on premises. Weddings, small meetings, family reunions and seminars hosted. Antiquing, art galleries, beaches, bicycling, canoeing/kayaking, fishing, golf, hiking, horseback riding, live theater, museums, parks, shopping, tennis, water sports and wineries nearby.
Publicity: *Town & Country and Travel & Leisure.*

Maidstone Arms

207 Main St
East Hampton, NY 11937-2723
(516)324-5006 Fax:(516)324-5037
E-mail: maidstay@aol.com

Circa 1860. Situated on the village green, this classic inn has all the characteristics that epitomize this community of winding lanes and sandy white beaches. The inn's restaurant houses a world-class selection of wines in its own climate-controlled underground wine cellar. Nearby activities include whale-watching expeditions and local winery tours.

Historic Interest: The Maidstone Arms is located on Long Island, which offers many historic buildings and sites. New York City is about two hours away.
Innkeeper(s): CokeAnne M. Wilcox. $215-535. MC, VISA, AX. 19 rooms with PB, 4 suites, 3 cottages and 1 conference room. Breakfast included in rates. Types of meals: Full bkfst, cont plus, cont, early coffee/tea, gourmet lunch, picnic lunch, snacks/refreshments, dinner and room service. Beds: KQDT. Cable TV, phone, turndown service and cottages with fireplace in room. Air conditioning. Weddings, small meetings, family reunions and seminars hosted. Antiquing, fishing, live theater and water sports nearby.

Mill House Inn

31 N Main St
East Hampton, NY 11937-2601
(631)324-9766 Fax:(631)324-9793
E-mail: innkeeper@millhouseinn.com
Web: www.millhouseinn.com

Circa 1790. This Colonial house is just opposite the Old Hook Windmill. It is in the center of East Hampton, which has been called "America's most beautiful village." Guest rooms are decorated with a Hamptons' theme in mind, sporting names such as Sail Away or Hampton Holiday. Romantic amenities abound, including fireplaces in six of the guest rooms. Several rooms also have whirlpool tubs. Families are welcome.

Historic Interest: The Village Green, The Liberty Pole, Mulford Farm, Clinton Academy, Osborn-Jackson House, Hook Mill (all within 1 mile).
Innkeeper(s): Sylvia & Gary Muller. $200-450. MC, VISA, AX, DC, CB, DS, PC, TC. 8 rooms with PB, 4 with FP and 1 conference room. Breakfast and snacks/refreshments included in rates. Types of meals: Full bkfst and early coffee/tea. Beds: KQ. Cable TV, phone, ceiling fan, VCR, fireplace, featherbeds and down quilts in room. Air conditioning. Fax, library and gift shop on premises. Handicap access. Small meetings and family reunions hosted. Spanish spoken. Antiquing, art galleries, beaches, bicycling, canoeing/kayaking, fishing, golf, hiking, horseback riding, International film festival, classic horse show, polo, live theater, museums, parks, shopping, tennis, water sports and wineries nearby.
Publicity: New York Magazine, Travel Channel, The New York Times, Newsday, Dan's Papers and The East Hampton.

"Perfect everything, it's hard to leave."

Fair Haven   E7

Black Creek Farm B&B

PO Box 390
Fair Haven, NY 13064-0390
(315)947-5282
E-mail: ksarber@redcreek.net

Circa 1888. Pines and towering birch trees frame this Victorian farmhouse inn, filled with an amazing assortment of authentic antiques. Set on 20 acres, Black Creek Farm is a refreshing escape from big-city life. Guests enjoy relaxing in a hammock on the porch or by taking a stroll along the peaceful back roads. A hearty country breakfast features seasonal fruit raised on the grounds as well as home baked date-nut, banana-nut or pumpkin-raisin bread. A new pond-side guest house is an especially popular accommodation for honeymooners and families, offering

complete privacy. It features a gas fireplace and double shower. Bring your own breakfast makings and enjoy breakfast sitting on the patio or the porch which overlooks the pond, with ducks and geese, bass and perch. Sometimes turkey or deer may be seen in the meadow. There's a peddle boat on the pond in summer. In winter sledding and snowmobiling are popular. The B&B is two miles from Lake Ontario, Fair Haven Beach State Park and minutes away from Sterling Renaissance Festival.

Innkeeper(s): Bob & Kathy Sarber. $60-125. MC, VISA. TAC10. 3 rooms with PB. Types of meals: Full bkfst and early coffee/tea. Beds: Q. Air conditioning. VCR, bicycles, pedal boat, satellite disc and movies available on premises. Family reunions hosted. Fishing, snowmobiling, cross-country skiing and water sports nearby.

Fleischmanns   H11

River Run

Main St, Box 9
Fleischmanns, NY 12430
(845)254-4884
E-mail: riverrun@catskill.net
Web: www.catskill.net/riverrun

Circa 1887. The backyard of this large three-story Victorian gently slopes to the river where the Bushkill and Little Red Kill trout streams meet. Inside, stained-glass windows surround the inn's common areas, shining on the oak-floored dining room and the book-filled parlor. The parlor also includes a fireplace and a piano. Adirondack chairs are situated comfortably on the front porch. Tennis courts, a pool, park, theater and restaurants are within walking distance, as is a country auction held each Saturday night. The inn is two and a half hours out of New York City, 35 minutes west of Woodstock, and accessible by public transportation. Also, the inn was the recipient of the "Catskill Service Award" for best accommodations in the Belleayre Region for 1998,1999 and 2000.

Historic Interest: The Hudson River mansions are all located within one hour of the inn. Bethel, the site of the famed Woodstock concert is within an hour of the inn. Cooperstown is about an hour and a half away.
Innkeeper(s): Ben & Melissa Fenton. $70-125. MC, VISA, AX, PC. TAC10. 8 rooms, 4 with PB and 1 suite. Breakfast and afternoon tea included in rates. Types of meals: Cont plus and early coffee/tea. Beds: KQDT. TV in room. VCR, bicycles, library, refrigerator, two bedroom and two bath suite on premises. Small meetings and family reunions hosted. Antiquing, fishing, golf, hiking, horseback riding, auctions, flea and farmers markets, live theater, parks, shopping, downhill skiing, cross-country skiing, tennis and water sports nearby. Pets allowed: Well behaved, fully trained, over one year old.
Publicity: New York Magazine, Boston Globe, Catskill Mountain News, Kingston Freeman, New York Times, New York Daily News, Philadelphia Inquirer, Inn Country USA and Newsday.

"We are really happy to know of a place that welcomes all of our family."

Fredonia   G2

The White Inn

52 E Main St
Fredonia, NY 14063-1836
(716)672-2103 (888)FRE-DONIA Fax:(716)672-2107
E-mail: res@whiteinn.com
Web: www.whiteinn.com

Circa 1868. This 23-room inn is situated in the center of a historic town. The inn's rooms are pristinely furnished in antiques and reproductions and 11 are spacious suites. Guests as well as

the public may enjoy gourmet meals at the inn, a charter member of the Duncan Hines "Family of Fine Restaurants." In addition to fine dining and catered events, casual fare and cocktails are offered in the lounge or on the 100-foot-long veranda. Nearby the Chautauqua Institution operates during the summer offering a popular selection of lectures and concert performances. Fredonia State College is another avenue to cultural events as well as sporting events. Wineries, golfing, state parks and shops are nearby.

Innkeeper(s): Robert Contiguglia & Kathleen Dennison. $69-179. MC, VISA, AX, DC, DS, PC, TC. TAC10. 23 rooms with PB, 2 with FP, 11 suites and 4 conference rooms. Breakfast included in rates. Types of meals: Full bkfst, lunch and gourmet dinner. EP. Beds: KQD. Cable TV and phone in room. Air conditioning. VCR, fax and copier on premises. Weddings, small meetings, family reunions and seminars hosted. Antiquing, live theater, parks, shopping and cross-country skiing nearby.

Publicity: *Upstate New York Magazine, Country Living, US Air Magazine. and Buffalo News.*

Freeville G7

Bountiful Blessings Bed and Breakfast

147 Lick St
Freeville, NY 13068
(607)898-3370 (877)224-8422 Fax:(607)898-3333
E-mail: tdonlick@mail.odyssey.net
Web: www.geocities.com/bbb_b2000

Circa 1840. The stately maple trees were planted when Scotsman John McKellar built this Victorian home more than 150 years ago. Now carefully restored and decorated with period furnishings, it imparts an elegant atmosphere by mingling modern amenities and old-fashioned charm. Romantic guest bedrooms offer an assortment of amenities including four-poster and sleigh goose down feather beds and pillows, luxury linens, terry robes and sitting areas. The Olde Homer Room boasts a Jacuzzi tub and a view of Owasco Valley. A leisurely candlelight breakfast is served in the dining room with fresh flowers. Enjoy the pond and gardens that embellish the grounds. A large deck and two sitting porches are easy places to sit and daydream. Take a swim in the refreshing pool before exploring the many facets of the Finger Lakes region.

Innkeeper(s): Terry Donlick. $95-165. MC, VISA, PC, TC. TAC10. 5 rooms, 3 with PB, 1 suite and 1 cottage. Breakfast included in rates. Types of meals: Full bkfst, country bkfst and early coffee/tea. Beds: KQDT. TV, phone, ceiling fan and feather beds in room. Air conditioning. Fax, copier, swimming, library, wood stove, genealogical library, large deck, two sitting porches, pond and gardens on premises. Weddings, small meetings, family reunions and seminars hosted. Antiquing, art galleries, bicycling, canoeing/kayaking, golf, hiking, horseback riding, Finger Lakes Wine Trail, live theater, museums, parks, shopping, downhill skiing, cross-country skiing, sporting events, tennis, water sports and wineries nearby.

Fulton E7

Battle Island Inn

2167 State Route 48 N
Fulton, NY 13069-4132
(315)593-3699 Fax:(315)592-5071
E-mail: battleislandinn@usadatanet.net
Web: www.battle-island-inn.com

Circa 1840. Topped with a gothic cupola, this family farmhouse overlooks the Oswego River and a golf course. There are three antique-filled parlors. Guest accommodations are fur-

nished in a variety of styles including Victorian and Renaissance Revival. There are four wooded acres with lawns and gardens. Guests are often found relaxing on one of the inn's four porches and enjoying the views. The Honeymoon suite features a canopy bed, full bath and private Jacuzzi.

Innkeeper(s): Richard & Joyce Rice. $60-125. MC, VISA, AX, DS, PC, TC. 5 rooms with PB and 1 suite. Breakfast included in rates. Types of meals: Gourmet bkfst and early coffee/tea. AP. Beds: QDT. Cable TV, phone and ceiling fan in room. VCR, fax, copier and refrigerator on premises. Handicap access. Small meetings and seminars hosted. Fishing, golf, fort, live theater, parks, shopping, cross-country skiing and water sports nearby.

Publicity: *Lake Effect, Palladium Times, Travel, Journey, Oswego County Business and Valley News.*

"We will certainly never forget our wonderful weeks at Battle Island Inn."

Garrison J12

The Bird & Bottle Inn

Old Albany Post Rd, Rt 9
Garrison, NY 10524
(845)424-3000 Fax:(845)424-3283
E-mail: info@birdbottle.com

Circa 1761. Built as Warren's Tavern, this three-story yellow farmhouse served as a lodging and dining spot on the New York-to-Albany Post Road, now a National Historic Landmark. George Washington, Hamilton, Lafayette and many other historic figures frequently passed by. The inn's eight acres include secluded lawns, a babbling

stream and Hudson Valley woodlands. Timbered ceilings, old paneling and fireplace mantels in the inn's notable restaurant maintain a Revolutionary War-era ambiance. Second-floor guest rooms have canopied or four-poster beds and each is warmed by its own fireplace.

Innkeeper(s): Ira Boyar. $210-240. MC, VISA, AX, DC, PC, TC. 4 rooms with PB, 4 with FP, 1 suite and 1 cottage. Breakfast and dinner included in rates. MAP. Beds: Q. Air conditioning. Fax and copier on premises. Weddings, small meetings, family reunions and seminars hosted. Antiquing, fishing, live theater, parks, shopping and cross-country skiing nearby.

Publicity: *Colonial Homes, Hudson Valley, Spotlight, Travel Channel, The Learning Channel, Conde Nast Traveler Gazette, Country Living, Time Out New York, The News-Times-CT, The New York Times, Kiss Me Goodbye, MTV and Food Network.*

Geneva F6

Geneva On The Lake

1001 Lochland Rd, Rt 14S
Geneva, NY 14456
(315)789-7190 (800)343-6382 Fax:(315)789-0322
E-mail: info@genevaonthelake.com
Web: www.genevaonthelake.com

Circa 1911. This opulent world-class inn is a replica of the Renaissance-era Lancellotti Villa in Frascati, Italy. It is listed in the National Register. Although originally built as a residence, it became a monastery for Capuchin monks. Now it is one of the finest resorts in the U.S. Recently renovated under the direc-

tion of award-winning designer William Schickel, there are 10 two-bedroom suites — some with views of the lake. Here, you may have an experience as fine as Europe can offer, without leaving the states. Some compare it to the Grand Hotel du Cap-Ferrat on the French Riviera. The inn has been awarded four diamonds from AAA for more than a decade. Breakfast is available daily and on Sunday, brunch is served. Dinner is served each evening, and in the summer, lunch is offered on the terrace.

Historic Interest: The Corning Glass Center, where Steuben glass is created by hand, is nearby. The town of Elmira, another close attraction, is the site where "The Adventures of Tom Sawyer" and "Huckleberry Finn," were written by Mark Twain.

Innkeeper(s): William J. Schickel. $138-730. MC, VISA, AX, DS. TAC10. 30 suites, 3 with FP and 3 conference rooms. Breakfast included in rates. Types of meals: Gourmet bkfst, cont, gourmet dinner and room service. Beds: KQDT. TV, phone and turndown service in room. Air conditioning. VCR, fax, copier, swimming, bicycles, sailing, fishing, lawn games and boats on premises. Weddings, small meetings, family reunions and seminars hosted. Antiquing, live theater, parks, shopping, downhill skiing, cross-country skiing, sporting events, water sports and wineries nearby.

Publicity: *Travel & Leisure, Bon Appetit, Country Inns, The New York Times, Bride's, Catholic Register, Pittsford-Brighton Post, New York, Glamour, Gourmet, Washingtonian, Toronto Star, Globe & Mail and Rochester Democrat & Chronicle.*

"The food was superb and the service impeccable."

Gorham G6

The Gorham House

4752 E Swamp Rd
Gorham, NY 14461
(716)526-4402 Fax:(716)526-4402
E-mail: gorham.house@juno.com
Web: gorham-house.freeyellow.com

Circa 1887. The Gorham House serves as a homey, country place to enjoy New York's Finger Lakes region. The five, secluded acres located between Canandaigua and Seneca lakes, include herb gardens, wildflowers and berry bushes. Part of the home dates back to the early 19th century, but it's the architecture of the 1887 expansion that accounts for the inn's Victorian touches. The interior is warm and cozy with comfortable, country furnishings. Some of the pieces are the innkeepers' family heirlooms. There are more than 50 wineries in the area, as well as a bounty of outdoor activities.

Innkeeper(s): Nancy & Al Rebmann. $89-120. PC, TC. 3 rooms, 1 with PB. Breakfast included in rates. Types of meals: Gourmet bkfst and early coffee/tea. Beds: QD. Air conditioning. Library on premises. Family reunions hosted. Antiquing, fishing, live theater, parks, shopping, downhill skiing, cross-country skiing, sporting events and water sports nearby.

Greene H8

Water's Edge Bed & Breakfast

1 Washington St
Greene, NY 13778
(607)656-4891 Fax:(607)656-4892
E-mail: cmhwatersedge@aol.com

Circa 1851. Sitting on the bank of the Chenango River where its first bridge was built, this Italianate Victorian home is conveniently located in a picturesque, quaint village commonly called an Arts and Antique Community. Decorated informally

with country antiques, the original character is enhanced by modern conveniences. The inn features an exercise room, a big screen TV in the parlor, as well as a movie and reading library. After a restful night in one of the comfortable guest bedrooms, enjoy a buffet breakfast with a view, boasting made-to-order eggs. Tourism advice is freely given, gifts and local products are for sale, and a canoe and kayak are available to use.

Historic Interest: Cooperstown (50 miles), Erie Canal (50 miles).

Innkeeper(s): Candace, Rob, Andrew Harrington. $65-85. MC, VISA, AX, DC, CB, DS, PC, TC. 4 rooms with PB. Breakfast and snacks/refreshments included in rates. Types of meals: Gourmet bkfst, country bkfst, veg bkfst and early coffee/tea. Beds: QT. Ceiling fan in room. Central air. Fax and copier on premises. Small meetings, family reunions and seminars hosted. Antiquing, art galleries, bicycling, canoeing/kayaking, fishing, golf, hiking, museums, parks, shopping, downhill skiing, cross-country skiing, sporting events, tennis, water sports and wineries nearby.

Publicity: *Binghamton Press and Norwich Sun.*

Greenport K15

The Bartlett House Inn

503 Front St
Greenport, NY 11944-1519
(631)477-0371
E-mail: bartletthouseinn@aol.com

Circa 1908. A family residence for more than 60 years and then a convent for a nearby church, this large Victorian house became a bed & breakfast in 1982. Features include corinthian columns, stained-glass windows, two fireplaces and a large front porch. Period antiques complement the rich interior. The inn is within walking distance of shops, restaurants, the harbor, wineries, the Shelter Island Ferry and train station.

Innkeeper(s): Michael O'Donoghue. $110-250. MC, VISA, AX, PC, TC. 10 rooms with PB, 1 with FP and 1 conference room. Breakfast included in rates. Types of meals: Cont plus and early coffee/tea. Beds: QDT. Air conditioning. Weddings, small meetings, family reunions and seminars hosted. Antiquing, fishing, maritime museum, outlet shopping, art galleries, golf, fine restaurants, parks, shopping and water sports nearby.

Publicity: *Suffolk Times, Newsday, New York Times and New York Post.*

Greenville G12

Greenville Arms 1889 Inn

Rt 32, South St, PO Box 659
Greenville, NY 12083-0659
(518)966-5219 (888)665-0044 Fax:(518)966-8754
E-mail: info@greenvillearms.com
Web: www.greenvillearms.com

Circa 1889. William Vanderbilt had this graceful Victorian built with Queen Anne gables and cupolas. Seven acres of lush lawns are dotted with gardens, and there is a 50-foot outdoor pool. There are floor-to-ceiling fireplaces, chestnut woodwork, wainscoting and Victorian bead work over the doorways. Painting workshops are held in summer and fall. Dinner is served to inn guests six nights a week.

Innkeeper(s): Eliot & Letitia Dalton. $115-195. MC, VISA, PC, TC. TAC10. 15 rooms, 12 with PB, 1 suite, 2 cottages and 2 conference rooms. Breakfast and afternoon tea included in rates. Types of meals: Full bkfst, early coffee/tea, lunch and gourmet dinner. MAP. Beds: KQDT. Two with double Jacuzzi in room. Air conditioning. VCR, fax, swimming, library and air conditioning on premises. Weddings, small meetings, family reunions and seminars hosted. Amusement parks, antiquing, fishing, hiking, parks and water sports nearby.

Publicity: *Victorian Homes, New York Magazine, Yankee, Sophisticated Traveler, Hudson Valley, Great Country Inns and The Learning Channel.*

"Just a note of appreciation for all your generous hospitality, and wonderful display of attention and affection!"

Hadley   E12

Saratoga Rose Inn & Restaurant

4274 Rockwell St
Hadley, NY 12835-0238
(518)696-2861 (800)942-5025 Fax:(518)696-5319
E-mail: sararose@capital.net
Web: www.saratogarose.com

Circa 1885. This romantic Queen Anne Victorian offers a small, candle-lit restaurant perfect for an evening for two. Breakfast specialties include Grand Marnier French toast and Eggs Anthony. Rooms are decorated in period style. The Queen Anne

Room, decorated in blue, boasts a wood and tile fireplace and a quilt-covered bed. The Carriage House features an iron canopy bed, skylight, TV, fireplace and private deck with a Jacuzzi while the Garden Room offers a pri-

vate sunporch and an outside deck with a Jacuzzi spa. Each of the rooms features something special. Guests can take in the mountain view or relax on the veranda while sipping a cocktail.
Innkeeper(s): Nancy Merlino, Chef Anthony. $145-185. MC, VISA, DS. 6 rooms with PB, 6 with FP. Breakfast included in rates. Types of meals: Gourmet bkfst and gourmet dinner. EP. Beds: KD. Ceiling fan and private Jacuzzi in room. Air conditioning. VCR on premises. Weddings, small meetings, family reunions and seminars hosted. Amusement parks, antiquing, fishing, live theater, parks, shopping, downhill skiing, cross-country skiing and sporting events nearby.
Publicity: *Getaways for Gourmets.*

"A must for the inn traveler."

Hague   D12

Trout House Village Resort

PO Box 510, Lake Shore Dr
Hague, NY 12836-0510
(518)543-6088 (800)368-6088 Fax:(518)543-6124
E-mail: info@trouthouse.com
Web: www.trouthouse.com

Circa 1920. On the shores of beautiful Lake George is this resort inn, offering accommodations in the lodge, authentic log cabins or cottages. Many of the guest rooms in the lodge boast lake views, while the log cabins offer jetted tubs and fireplaces. The guest quarters are furnished

comfortably. The emphasis here is on the abundance of outdoor activities. Outstanding cross-country skiing, downhill skiing and snowmobiling are found nearby. The inn furnishes bicy-

cles, canoes, kayaks, paddle boats, rowboats, sleds, shuffleboard, skis and toboggans. Summertime evenings offer games of capture-the-flag and soccer. Other activities include basketball, horseshoes, ping pong, a putting green and volleyball.
Historic Interest: Fort Ticonderoga (8 miles).

Innkeeper(s): Scott & Alice Patchett. $45-366. MC, VISA, AX, DS, PC, TC. TAC10. 9 rooms, 7 with PB, 15 with FP, 15 cottages and 2 conference rooms. Beds: QDT. Cable TV, phone and VCR in room. Fax, copier, swimming and bicycles on premises. Handicap access. Weddings, small meetings, family reunions and seminars hosted. Amusement parks, antiquing, art galleries, beaches, bicycling, canoeing/kayaking, fishing, golf, hiking, horseback riding, child care, museums, parks, shopping, downhill skiing, cross-country skiing, tennis and water sports nearby.
Pets allowed: During off season.

"My wife and I felt the family warmth at this resort. There wasn't that coldness you get at larger resorts."

Hamlin   E5

Sandy Creek Manor House

1960 Redman Rd
Hamlin, NY 14464-9635
(716)964-7528 (800)594-0400
E-mail: agreatbnb@aol.com
Web: www.sandycreekbnb.com

Circa 1910. Six acres of woods and perennial gardens provide the setting for this English Tudor house. Stained glass, polished woods and Amish quilts add warmth to the home. The innkeep-

ers have placed many thoughtful amenities in each room, such as clock radios, fluffy robes, slippers and baskets of toiletries. Breakfast is served on the open porch in summer. Fisherman's Landing, on the banks of Sandy Creek, is a

stroll away. Bullhead, trout and salmon are popular catches. There is a gift shop, outdoor hot tub and deck on premises. Ask about murder-mystery, sweetheart dinner and spa treatment packages.
Innkeeper(s): Shirley Hollink & James Krempasky. $65-90. MC, VISA, AX, DS, PC, TC. TAC10. 4 rooms, 1 with PB. Breakfast, afternoon tea and snacks/refreshments included in rates. Types of meals: Gourmet bkfst, cont plus, cont and early coffee/tea. Beds: KQDT. Cable TV and VCR in room. Air conditioning. Fishing, player piano and guest refrigerator on premises. Small meetings and family reunions hosted. Antiquing, fishing, farm markets, sky diving, gift shop on premises, parks, shopping, downhill skiing, cross-country skiing, sporting events and water sports nearby.
Pets Allowed.

Publicity: *Democrat & Chronicle, Buffalo News, Rochester Times Union. and It's Time To Take Off.*

"Delightful in every way."

Hammondsport   G6

The Amity Rose Bed & Breakfast

8264 Main St
Hammondsport, NY 14840-9701
(607)569-3402 (800)982-8818
Web: www.amityroseinn.com

Circa 1899. This country Victorian has a two-story veranda and shuttered windows. Sweet Emma's Suite consists of two rooms, one a furnished sitting room. Two rooms offer whirlpool soaking tubs. There is a queen bed, and the decor is floral and stripes. Within walking distance is the village square with a bandstand from which summer concerts are held. There is a nearby trout stream, a track for running or tennis.
Historic Interest: Corning Glass Museum, Winery Museum, Curtiss Museum, Warplane Museum.

Innkeeper(s): Ellen & Frank Laufersweiler. $95-135. PC, TC. 4 rooms with PB, 3 with FP, 1 suite and 1 conference room. Breakfast and afternoon tea included in rates. Types of meals: Full bkfst, country bkfst, veg bkfst and early coffee/tea. Beds: Q. 2 whirlpool Jacuzzi's in room. Air conditioning. Fax, bicycles and tennis on premises. Small meetings and seminars hosted. Antiquing, art galleries, beaches, bicycling, canoeing/kayaking, fishing, golf, hiking, horseback riding, museums, parks, shopping, sporting events, tennis, water sports and wineries nearby.

"How nice, a bathroom big enough to waltz in, well almost!"

J.S. Hubbs B&B

17 Shethar St, PO Box 428
Hammondsport, NY 14840-0428
(607)569-2440

Circa 1840. At the Southern tip of Keuka Lake is the village of Hammondsport, home to this Greek Revival inn, with its charming cupola. The village square and lake are just one-half block from the inn. Because of its
interesting architecture, the inn has
come to be known as the ink bottle house, one of the village's
major landmarks. The inn offers
four guest rooms, including one in
the cupola. Guests enjoy relaxing

in the living room and parlor. Many fine wineries are found in the area, and the Greyton H. Taylor Wine Museum is nearby.
Innkeeper(s): Walter & Linda Carl. Call for rates. 1 suites. Ceiling fan in room. Air conditioning. Small meetings hosted. Antiquing and sporting events nearby.

Herkimer   F10

Bellinger Rose Bed & Breakfast

611 W German St
Herkimer, NY 13350
(315)867-2197
E-mail: bellingerrose@hotmail.com
Web: www.bellingerrose.com

Circa 1865. Originally built in 1865 by the prominent Bellinger family, this recently renovated inn exudes Victorian grace and charm. The exquisite decor and splendid antique fur-nishings invite pleasantries and relaxation. The common rooms include a formal parlor with a perfectly tuned piano, and a sit-ting room offering modern entertainment such as videos or DVD with surround sound. Both areas provide the warmth and ambiance of wood-burning marble fireplaces. In keeping with the name, a romantic theme of roses adorns the two unique guest bedrooms with spacious sitting areas. A full breakfast is served daily in the elegant dining room. The pampering contin-ues with plush robes, a year-round hot tub, and a chair mas-sage that is included with each night's stay.
Historic Interest: Erie Canal (1/2 mile), Cooperstown Hall of Fame (25 miles), General Herkimer Home (8 miles).
Innkeeper(s): Chris & Leon Frost. $85-95. MC, VISA, AX, DS, PC, TC. TAC10. 2 rooms with PB. Breakfast included in rates. Types of meals: Full bkfst. Beds: Q. Cable TV, turndown service and VCR in room. Air conditioning. Spa, bicy-cles, child care and professional massage on premises. Small meetings hosted. Antiquing, art galleries, bicycling, canoeing/kayaking, fishing, golf, hiking, live theater, museums, shopping and cross-country skiing nearby.

High Falls   I11

1797 Depuy Canal House

Route 213 Box 96
High Falls, NY 12440
(845)687-7700

Circa 1870. The proprietors of the nationally acclaimed 1797 Depuy Canal House restaurant also offer overnight accommo-dations at Locktender Cottage across the street — an excellent solution to solve the dilemma of those who sometimes drive

three hours to enjoy chef John
Novi's culinary skills. Located beside
the historic Delaware and Hudson
Canal, there are three guest rooms
(one with a fireplace), and what is
called the Chef's Quarters with its
own whirlpool, kitchenette and laundry. Pick-your-own orchards and veg-

etable farms are nearby. Other activities are winery tours, fish-ing, skiing, taking a Hudson River cruise, riding the Delaware and Ulster Rail Ride or tubing on Esopus Creek.
Historic Interest: FDR's Hyde Park home, Vanderbilt Mansion, Woodstock Art Colony, Delaware and Ulster Rail Ride, Hudson River cruises.
Innkeeper(s): John N Novi. $75-145. MC, VISA, AX. 3 rooms. Beds: QD. Air conditioning. Fishing, hiking, pick your own fruit, vegetable farms, museums, downhill skiing, cross-country skiing and wineries nearby.
Publicity: *Time Magazine, Hudson Valley HJournal and Poughkeepsie Journal.*

"A great home away from home."

Highmount   H11

Gateway Lodge Bed & Breakfast

Rt 28 & Highlands Rd, PO Box 397
Highmount, NY 12441
(845)254-4084
E-mail: gatewayldg@aol.com

Circa 1920. The 1920s-era lodge features a gambrel roof and gingerbread trim done in shades of green. The guest rooms are furnished comfortably with antiques, quilts and country pieces. Breakfasts include a wide assortment of beverages, including coffee, herbal teas and the lodge's signature orange juice. An entrée, such as layers of French toast topped with cinnamon and powdered sugar, is served with breakfast sausage or bacon. The lodge welcomes adults with children all year and has a stay-free/ski-free package for children under 12. The area's many outdoor activities include hiking, fishing, tennis, skiing, horseback riding and much more. Antique shops, gourmet restaurants and flea markets are nearby.
Historic Interest: Hudson Valley Mansions & Estates (40 miles).
Innkeeper(s): Isabella Young. $65-130. PC, TC. 4 rooms with PB and 2 suites. Breakfast and afternoon tea included in rates. Types of meals: Country bkfst. Beds: KQD. Cable TV in room. VCR on premises. Weddings, small meetings and family reunions hosted. Polish spoken. Antiquing, bicycling, canoeing/kayaking, fishing, golf, hiking, parks, shopping, downhill skiing, cross-country skiing and water sports nearby.

Holley   E4

Rosewood B&B

68 Geddes St
Holley, NY 14470-1145
(716)638-6186 Fax:(716)638-7568
E-mail: rosewdbnb@aol.com

Circa 1891. Restoring this splendid Victorian home was a labor of love that resulted in a glorious transformation of comfort and elegance. Double parlors offer a working fireplace and a grand piano. An extensive music and video collection provides listen-ing and viewing entertainment. Pour through the books in the upstairs library that boasts a reading nook. Guest bedrooms fea-ture antique canopy and four-poster featherbeds, a soaking tub surrounded by red marble, vintage linens, Damask wallpaper and stylized painting. Start the day with fresh berry ambrosia, cherry coffee cake, asparagus quiche, herb-roasted potatoes and

beverages. Enjoy the large wraparound porch and the rose and perennial gardens. Browse in the gift shop for antique treasures like lace pillows, linens, silver and jewelry.
Historic Interest: Erie Canal (1/4 mile), Cobblestone Museum (10 miles).
Innkeeper(s): Karen Cook & Roy Nichols. $69-89. MC, VISA, AX, DC, DS. 5 rooms, 2 with PB. Breakfast included in rates. Types of meals: Gourmet bkfst and early coffee/tea. Beds: QT. Ceiling fan in room. Air conditioning. VCR, fax, copier, bicycles, library and gift shop on premises. Amusement parks, antiquing, art galleries, beaches, bicycling, canoeing/kayaking, fishing, golf, hiking, horseback riding, live theater, museums, parks, shopping, water sports and wineries nearby.

Hudson   H12

Hudson City B&B

326 Allen St
Hudson, NY 12534
(518)822-8044 Fax:(518)828-9139
E-mail: hcbb98@aol.com
Web: hudsoncitybnb.com

Circa 1865. The view from the tower, the warmth of the fireplace, the comfort of the canopy beds and the sway of the porch swing become favorite memories of guests who stay at this three-story Second Empire Victorian home. Joshua T. Waterman, railroad baron and mayor of the town in the mid-1800s, built the mansion, and he and his wife watched their 12 children grow up here. Today, guests seek out the same cozy nooks once enjoyed by the original family. In the morning, breakfasts of waffles, pancakes or French toast are served in the dining room before the fireplace. Nearby is The Daughter's of the American Revolution Museum, "Olana," a fireman's museum and many antique shops and galleries.
Historic Interest: DAR Museum, Olana, home of Fredrick Church.
Innkeeper(s): Kenneth Jacobs & John Fraioli. $99-189. MC, VISA, AX, DC, DS, PC. TAC10. 5 rooms, 3 with PB, 2 suites and 1 conference room. Types of meals: Full bkfst, country bkfst, early coffee/tea, afternoon tea and snacks/refreshments. Beds: KQ. Cable TV and ceiling fan in room. Air conditioning. VCR, fax, copier and library on premises. Weddings, small meetings, family reunions and seminars hosted. Antiquing, art galleries, horseback riding, Fireman's Museum, Catskill Game Farm, live theater, museums, shopping, downhill skiing, cross-country skiing, tennis and wineries nearby.

Hunter   H11

Fairlawn Inn

PO Box 182, Main St
Hunter, NY 12442
(518)263-5025 Fax:(518)263-5025

Circa 1902. A three-story turret and a sweeping two-story covered veranda with a gazebo accentuate the exterior of this historic Victorian, which was built by a distinguished New York City businessman. The interior has been restored to its Victorian grandeur and features period-style wallpapers and antiques. The original

woodwork and light fixtures have been preserved, adding to the ambiance. Guest rooms include Victorian reproduction beds, and some include an over-sized clawfoot tub.

Breakfasts feature fresh fruit, homemade breads, a savory egg dish and pancakes or French toast. The Catskill Mountains provide plenty of outdoor activities, as well as outstanding scenery. The Hunter Mountain Ski Area is a half-mile from the inn.
Historic Interest: Olana (30 miles).
Innkeeper(s): Kelly Coughlin. $75-110. MC, VISA, PC, TC. TAC10. 9 rooms

with PB. Breakfast included in rates. Beds: Q. VCR, fax and copier on premises. Weddings, small meetings, family reunions and seminars hosted. Antiquing, bicycling, canoeing/kayaking, fishing, golf, hiking, horseback riding, parks, shopping, downhill skiing, cross-country skiing and tennis nearby.

"This was a wonderful romantic getaway as well as a great chance to meet and make new friends."

Ithaca   G7

Rose Inn

Rt 34N, Box 6576
Ithaca, NY 14851-6576
(607)533-7905 Fax:(607)533-7908
E-mail: info@roseinn.com
Web: www.roseinn.com

Circa 1842. This classic Italianate mansion has long been famous for its circular staircase of Honduran mahogany. It is owned by Sherry Rosemann, a noted interior designer specializing in mid-19th-century architecture and furniture, and her husband Charles, a hotelier from Germany. On 14 landscaped acres with a large formal garden and wedding chapel, it is 10 minutes from Cornell University. The inn has been the recipient of many awards for its lodging and dining, including a four-star rating nine years in a row.
Historic Interest: National Women's Hall of Fame (1 hour), Steuben Glass (1 hour), Cornell University.
Innkeeper(s): Charles & Sherry Rosemann. $125-330. MC, VISA, PC, TC. TAC10. 20 rooms with PB and 2 conference rooms. Breakfast included in rates. Types of meals: Gourmet bkfst, cont, early coffee/tea and gourmet dinner. Beds: KQD. Cable TV, phone, turndown service, ceiling fan, eleven suites have Jacuzzi, seven with fireplace, TV and VCR in room. Air conditioning. VCR, fax, copier and library on premises. Weddings, small meetings, family reunions and seminars hosted. German and Spanish spoken. Antiquing, art galleries, beaches, bicycling, canoeing/kayaking, fishing, golf, hiking, horseback riding, live theater, museums, parks, shopping, downhill skiing, cross-country skiing, sporting events, tennis, water sports and wineries nearby.
Publicity: *New York Times, Toronto Globe and Mail and Inn Country USA.*

"The blending of two outstanding talents, which when combined with your warmth, produce the ultimate experience in being away from home. Like staying with friends in their beautiful home."

Ithaca (Spencer)   G7

A Slice of Home B&B

178 N Main St
Ithaca (Spencer), NY 14883
(607)589-6073
E-mail: slice@lightlink.com

Circa 1850. This Italianate inn's location, approximately equidistant from Ithaca and Watkins Glen, offers a fine vantage point for exploring the Finger Lakes winery region. Although the area is well-known for its scenery, many recreational opportunities also are available. The innkeeper is happy to help guests plan tours and has a special fondness for those traveling by bicycle. The inn offers four guest rooms, and a two-bedroom cottage a hot tub and bicycles for all guests. Guests may relax by taking a stroll on the inn's 10 acres, mountain hiking, biking or having a cookout in the inn's backyard. Guests can begin a cross-country ski excursion right from the back porch.

Innkeeper(s): Bea & Sterling Fulmer. $60-200. MC, VISA. TAC10. 4 rooms with PB and 1 cottage. Types of meals: Full bkfst and early coffee/tea. Beds: KQD. Cable TV in room. Air conditioning. VCR, copier, bicycles, cross-country

skiing, horseshoes, badminton and hot tubs on premises. Weddings, small meetings, family reunions and seminars hosted. Limited German spoken. Antiquing, fishing, swimming, live theater, parks, shopping, downhill skiing, sporting events, water sports and wineries nearby.
Pets Allowed.

Jay   C12

Book and Blanket B&B

Rt 9N, PO Box 164
Jay, NY 12941-0164
(518)946-8323
E-mail: bookinnjay@aol.com

Circa 1860. This Adirondack bed & breakfast served as the town's post office for many years and also as barracks for state troopers. Thankfully, however, it is now a restful bed & breakfast catering to the literary set. Guest rooms are named for authors and there are books in every nook and cranny of the house. Guests may even take a book home with them. Each of the guest rooms is comfortably furnished. The inn is a short walk from the Jay Village Green and the original site of the Historic Jay covered bridge.
Innkeeper(s): Kathy, Fred, Sam & Zoe the Basset Hound. $60-80. AX, PC, TC. 3 rooms, 1 with PB. Breakfast, afternoon tea and snacks/refreshments included in rates. Types of meals: Full bkfst, veg bkfst and early coffee/tea. Beds: QDT. VCR, library, fireplace and whirlpool tub on premises. Family reunions hosted. Antiquing, art galleries, beaches, bicycling, canoeing/kayaking, fishing, golf, hiking, Olympic venues i.e. bobsled, luge, ski jump, ice skating, parks, downhill skiing, cross-country skiing, sporting events, tennis and water sports nearby.

Lake Clear   C11

Hohmeyer's Lodge on Lake Clear

RR1 Box 221
Lake Clear, NY 12945
(518)891-1489 (800)442-2356 Fax:(518)891-5662
E-mail: thelodge@northnet.org
Web: www.lodgeonlakeclear.com

Circa 1886. Surrounded by 25 acres of Adirondack scenery, this German-style lodge with 175 feet of private beachfront is awash in Old World ambiance. The Lodge, run by the same family for more than a century, originally accommodated those traveling along the New York to Montreal rail line. Old tracks still run through the property. The German cuisine served at the inn's restaurant is highly recommended, and knotty pine woodwork and exposed beams add to the dining room's European atmosphere. Guest rooms feature a combination of Adirondack/European style decor with pine floors, Adirondack antiques and custom woodwork. Accommodations are available in the woodland chalet or the Sunwater Guesthaus, as well. The Guesthaus offers two units with lake views, a wood-burning fireplace, kitchen, two bedrooms and a bath with a whirlpool tub. The Lodge, with its location in the St. Regis Wilderness area, provides a multitude of recreational possibilities right at your doorstep. Not far from the Lake Placid Olympic sites, it is also a perfect spot for those enjoying a ski vacation. Lakeside weddings, seminars and reunions are popular here.
Innkeeper(s): Cathy & Ernest Hohmeyer. $89-250. MC, VISA, PC, TC. TAC10. 5 cottages with PB, 4 with FP and 1 conference room. Breakfast included in rates. Types of meals: Gourmet bkfst, cont plus, cont, picnic lunch, afternoon tea, gourmet dinner and room service. Beds: KQDT. Kitchens, fireplaces and jet bathtubs (some rooms) in room. VCR, fax, copier, swimming, child care and boats on premises. Weddings, small meetings, family reunions and seminars hosted. German spoken. Antiquing, canoeing/kayaking, fishing, golf, hiking, live theater, parks, shopping, cross-

country skiing, sporting events and water sports nearby.
Pets allowed: In private chalets only.
Publicity: *Skiing, Birnbaum's, Adirondack Cookbook, Discerning Traveler, National Geographic Traveler and Outside Magazine.*

"Great as it was 20 years ago."

Lake George   E12

Lake George Boathouse B&B

44 Sagamore Rd
Lake George, NY 12814
(518)644-2554 Fax:(518)644-3065
E-mail: stay@boathousebb.com

Circa 1917. When one thinks of a houseboat, the images of Cary Grant and Sophia Loren might arise. Lake George Boathouse offers all of the romance of Grant and Loren without the rustic surroundings. This early 20th-century gem is more manor home than boathouse, located along prestigious Millionaires Row. The home rests at the edge of Lake George, providing panoramic views of the water and the Adirondack Region. There is a veranda filled with wicker furnishings where guests can enjoy the view. Each morning, breakfasts are served in the massive, unique great room, which features exposed beams and fine woodwork. The area offers historic sites, festivals, horse racing and plenty of outdoor activities.
Historic Interest: Blue Mountain Lake Museum (50 miles), Ft William Henry (5 miles), Ft. Ticonderoga and Lake George.
Innkeeper(s): Joe Silipigno/Patti Gramberg. $125-325. MC, VISA, AX. 5 rooms, 4 with PB and 1 suite. Breakfast included in rates. Types of meals: Country bkfst. Beds: KQ. Cable TV, phone, ceiling fan and lake view walk-out porches in room. Fax, copier, spa and swimming on premises. Small meetings and family reunions hosted. Amusement parks, antiquing, art galleries, beaches, bicycling, canoeing/kayaking, fishing, golf, hiking, horseback riding, museums, parks, shopping, downhill skiing, cross-country skiing, tennis and water sports nearby.
Publicity: *Post Star Newspaper, Wall Street Journal and Unique Homes.*

Lake Placid   C11

Interlaken Inn

15 Interlaken Ave
Lake Placid, NY 12946-1142
(518)523-3180 (800)428-4369 Fax:(518)523-0117
E-mail: interlkn@northnet.org
Web: www.innbook.com

Circa 1906. The five-course dinner at this Victorian inn is prepared by innkeeper CIA graduate Kevin Gregg and his talented staff. The high-quality cuisine is rivaled only by the rich decor

of this cozy inn. Walnut paneling covers the dining room walls, which are topped with a tin ceiling. Bedrooms are carefully decorated with wallpapers, fresh flowers and luxurious bed coverings. Spend the afternoon gazing at the mountains and lakes that surround this Adirondack hideaway, or visit the Olympic venues.
Historic Interest: John Brown's grave (4 miles).
Innkeeper(s): Carol & Roy Johnson. $90-180. MC, VISA, AX. 11 rooms with PB and 1 suite. Breakfast included in rates. Types of meals: Full bkfst, early coffee/tea and gourmet dinner. MAP. Beds: KQD. Ceiling fan in room. VCR and fax on premises. Weddings, small meetings and family reunions hosted. Antiquing, fishing, live theater, shopping, downhill skiing, cross-country skiing, sporting events and water sports nearby.
Pets allowed: small, by prior arrangements.
Publicity: *Outside, Country Inns, Wine Trader. and PBS.*

Liverpool   F8

Ancestor's Inn at The Bassett House

215 Sycamore St
Liverpool, NY 13088
(888)866-8591
E-mail: innkeeper@ancestorsinn.com
Web: www.ancestorsinn.com

Circa 1862. Early local residents, George and Hannah Bassett built this Italianate home. The innkeepers call the home Ancestor's Inn because guest rooms are named after a special relative. Valentine's Room includes a double whirlpool tub. A hearty, full breakfast is served each morning. Homemade granola, pastries and breads accompany the daily breakfast entree. In the afternoons, the innkeepers serve refreshments and homemade cookies.
Innkeeper(s): Mary & Dan Weidman. $75-95. MC, VISA, DS, PC, TC. 4 rooms with PB. Breakfast and afternoon tea included in rates. Types of meals: Gourmet bkfst and early coffee/tea. Beds: Q. TV, ceiling fan and VCR in room. Air conditioning. Library, movies available and porch on premises. Weddings hosted. Antiquing, golf, New York State Fair, live theater, parks, shopping, cross-country skiing, sporting events and water sports nearby.

Millerton   I12

Simmons' Way Village Inn

53 Main Street Rt 44E
Millerton, NY 12546
(518)789-6235 Fax:(518)789-6236
E-mail: swvi@taconic.net
Web: www.simmonsway.com

Circa 1854. Enjoy warm American hospitality and a charming European tradition in this 150-year-old Victorian in the Berkshire foothills. Simmon's Way Village Inn is located in the village of Millerton near Poughkeepsie, the birthplace of Eddie Collins. The inn was chosen by American Express/Hertz as the "Quintessential County Inn 1991." Recently, the inn and restaurant were acclaimed by Gannett papers. Its nine guest bedrooms and one suite, some with fireplaces, are decorated with antiques and international collections. An extensive continental breakfast and afternoon tea are included in the tariff. Picnic lunches, dinners, banquets and catering can be arranged through the restaurant on premises. The frequently changing menu includes a variety of fare from seasonal game to pasta to vegetarian and international specialties. Outdoor activities abound, including fishing, hiking, tennis, golf, swimming, boating, cross-country skiing, biking and horseback riding. The inn is near the Baseball Hall of Fame.
Historic Interest: Hudson Valley Historical Sites (25-30 miles).
Innkeeper(s): The Carter Family. $160-190. MC, VISA, AX, DC, CB, DS, PC, TC. TAC10. 9 rooms with PB, 2 with FP and 1 suite. Breakfast and afternoon tea included in rates. Types of meals: Cont plus, early coffee/tea, picnic lunch, snacks/refreshments and gourmet dinner. MAP, EP. Beds: KQDT. Cable TV in room. Central air. VCR, fax, copier and library on premises. Weddings, small meetings, family reunions and seminars hosted. Antiquing, art galleries, bicycling, canoeing/kayaking, fishing, golf, hiking, horseback riding, live theater, museums, parks, shopping, downhill skiing, cross-country skiing, tennis and wineries nearby.

Mumford   F5

Genesee Country Inn

948 George St
Mumford, NY 14511-0340
(716)538-2500 (800)697-8297 Fax:(716)538-4565
E-mail: gbarcklow@aol.com

Circa 1833. This stone mill with two-and-a-half-foot-thick limestone walls served as a plaster mill and later as a hub and wheel factory. Now, it is a country inn set on eight-and-a-half acres with bucolic views of streams, woodlands, ponds and a 16-foot waterfall. Ask for a garden room and enjoy a fireplace and your own balcony overlooking the mill ponds. A full breakfast is served.
Innkeeper(s): Glenda Barcklow. $85-150. MC, VISA, DC, DS. 9 rooms with PB, 3 with FP. Breakfast and afternoon tea included in rates. Types of meals: Full bkfst. Beds: Q. Phone in room. Air conditioning. Fax, copier and fly fishing on premises. Small meetings, family reunions and seminars hosted. Genesee Country Museum, Rochester, Litchworth State Park, Erie Canal, Susan B. Anthony house and museums nearby.
"You may never want to leave."

New York   K12

1871 House

East 60s between Park & Lexington Ave
New York, NY 10021
(212)756-8823 Fax:(212)588-0995
E-mail: infobnbinns@1871house.com
Web: www.1871house.com

Circa 1871. In a tree-lined street on the fashionable Upper East Side, this classic Brownstone offers stylishly elegant accommodations. Old World charm is evident in the decorative ironwork covering the front door, ornate moldings around windows, high ceilings and floors, and ornate marble and wood fireplace mantelpieces. The Cottage was a turn-of-the-century carriage house. Beds of antique iron and brass, a sleigh bed with netting, a Tuscan cottage bed and a cherry sheaf of wheat bed grace the guest bedrooms decorated with lace curtains and country quilts. A pleasant cedar terrace has colorful potted plants, teak furniture and a cafe table and chair set.
Historic Interest: Frick Museum (8 blocks), Museum of Modern Art (9 blocks), Central Park (2.5 blocks).
Innkeeper(s): Lia & Warren Raum. $135-385. MC, VISA, AX, DS. 11 rooms with PB, 6 with FP, 3 suites and 1 cottage. Beds: QDT. Cable TV, phone and fireplace in room. Air conditioning. Antiquing, art galleries, bicycling, canoeing/kayaking, fishing, hiking, horseback riding, live theater, museums, parks and shopping nearby.
Publicity: *Joan Hamburg Show on 710 AM radio in New York.*

Urban Jem Guest House

2005 5th Ave
New York, NY 10035-1804
(212)831-6029 Fax:(212)831-6940
E-mail: JMendel760@aol.com
Web: www.urbanjem.com

Circa 1878. The Urban Jem is located in a historic brownstone in the Mount Morris Park area of Harlem. The guest house includes two studio apartments with private baths and kitchens. The other accommodation includes a two-bedroom suite that can be used as two rooms with a shared bath. Laundry and maid service is available, and guests can prepare their own breakfast in their kitchen or on weekend mornings, opt for a continental breakfast in the parlor. Guests can walk to

Marcus Garvey Memorial Park or browse through shops on 125th Street. The Apollo Theater is just a few blocks away.
Innkeeper(s): Jane. $90-200. MC, VISA, AX, DC, CB, DS, PC, TC. TAC10. 4 rooms, 2 with PB and 1 suite. Breakfast included in rates. Types of meals: Cont and early coffee/tea. Beds: QDT. Cable TV, phone and kitchen in room. Air conditioning. VCR, fax, copier and library on premises. Weddings, small meetings, family reunions and seminars hosted. Cultural museums, historical jazz, live theater, parks and shopping nearby.

Niagara Falls   F3

The Cameo Manor North

3881 Lower River Rd, Rt 18-F
Niagara Falls, NY 14174
(716)745-3034
E-mail: cameoinn@adelphia.net
Web: www.cameoinn.com

Circa 1860. This Colonial Revival inn offers a restful setting ideal for those seeking a peaceful getaway. The inn's three secluded acres add to its romantic setting, as does an interior that features several fireplaces. Visitors select from three suites, which feature private sun rooms, or two guest rooms that share a bath. Popular spots with guests include the library, great room and solarium. Fort Niagara and several state parks are nearby, and the American and Canadian Falls are within easy driving distance of the inn. The inn is actually located about eight miles north of Niagara Falls near the village of Youngstown.
Innkeeper(s): Gregory Fisher. $75-175. 5 rooms. Breakfast included in rates. Types of meals: Full bkfst. Beds: QDT. TV in room. Air conditioning. Amusement parks, antiquing, fishing, live theater, shopping, downhill skiing, cross-country skiing, sporting events and water sports nearby.
Publicity: *Country Folk Art, Esquire, Journey, Seaway Trail, Waterways and Buffalo News.*

"I made the right choice when I selected Cameo."

Manchester House B&B

653 Main St
Niagara Falls, NY 14301-1701
(716)285-5717 (800)489-3009 Fax:(716)282-2144
E-mail: 71210.65@compuserve.com

Circa 1903. This turn-of-the-century home once was used to house doctors' offices. The home, just a mile from the famous falls, and the innkeepers are full of knowledge about their famous local attraction. The home is decorated with comfortable furnishings, family pieces and antiques. Prints and posters depicting scenes of the Niagara Falls area also decorate the home.
Innkeeper(s): Lis & Carl Slenk. $70-100. MC, VISA, TC. TAC10. 3 rooms with PB. Breakfast included in rates. Types of meals: Full bkfst. Beds: KQT. Ceiling fan in room. Air conditioning. VCR and library on premises. Weddings, small meetings, family reunions and seminars hosted. Amusement parks, antiquing, fishing, parks and shopping nearby.

"Thanks for a wonderful stay. All your little extras make for a warm homey feeling. Breakfast knocked our socks off."

The Red Coach Inn

Two Buffalo Avenue
Niagara Falls, NY 14303-1133
(716)282-1459 (800)282-1459 Fax:(716)282-2650
E-mail: info@redcoach.com
Web: www.redcoach.com

Circa 1923. Located 1,500 feet from Niagara Falls, this Old English Tudor inn offers a splendid view of the Rapids from many of its rooms. Furnished with antiques and reproductions suitable to English Country décor most accommodations are

view suites and the majority have wood-burning fireplaces, as well. The Fireside Room is a popular gathering spot for cocktails or an after-dinner drink. Or enjoy the roaring wood fire in the main dining room. The Rapids Room offers a panoramic view of the rapids. A welcoming offering of champagne, fruit and cheese is provided in your room.
Innkeeper(s): Tom Reese. $79-179. MC, VISA, DS. TAC10. 14 rooms with PB, 10 with FP, 12 suites and 1 conference room. Breakfast included in rates. Types of meals: Cont plus, gourmet lunch, gourmet dinner and room service. Beds: KQ. Cable TV, phone, turndown service and VCR in room. Central air. Fax, copier, spa and library on premises. Weddings, small meetings, family reunions and seminars hosted. Bicycling, fishing, golf, hiking, horseback riding, museums, parks, shopping, cross-country skiing, tennis and wineries nearby.
Publicity: *Fortune Magazine, AAA Today, New York Times, Chicago Tribune, Kansas City Star, Toledo Blade and San Diego Union Tribune.*

Oneida Castle   F9

Governors House Bed & Breakfast

50 Seneca Ave
Oneida Castle, NY 13421-2558
(315)363-5643 (800)437-8177 Fax:(315)363-5643
E-mail: dandrews@twcny.rr.com

Circa 1848. Built in the hopes of becoming the first residence for the Governor of New York State, this brick Federal house sits on two acres. The inn's finely crafted architecture includes features such as a mansard roof, elegant cupola and handsome porches. Antiques and canopy beds enhance most of the guest rooms, and there are two parlors, a library and a guest kitchen.

Innkeeper(s): Dawn E. Andrews. $84-195. MC, VISA, AX, DC, CB, DS, PC, TC. TAC15. 5 rooms with PB and 2 suites. Breakfast, afternoon tea and snacks/refreshments included in rates. Types of meals: Gourmet bkfst and early coffee/tea. Beds: KQT. Cable TV, phone and VCR in room. Air conditioning. Bicycles, library and fully stocked guest kitchen with cakes on premises. Handicap access. Weddings, small meetings, family reunions and seminars hosted. Amusement parks, antiquing, fishing, golf, rural driving and walking routes, live theater, parks, shopping, downhill skiing, cross-country skiing, sporting events, tennis and water sports nearby.

Otto   G3

R & R Dude Ranch

8940 Lange Rd
Otto, NY 14766
(716)257-5663 Fax:(716)257-5664
E-mail: alicerf@hotmail.com

Circa 1880. Three hundred acres of trails and breathtaking scenery provide a tranquil setting for this 19th-century farmhouse and log cabin. Horseback riding is a must during a stay here. Each season offers delights to experience, and almost every outdoor activity imaginable awaits the interested enthusiast. Boasting a central location upstate, the ranch is minutes away from Holiday Valley Ski Resort. A trip to Niagara Falls is an easy excursion that shouldn't be missed.
Innkeeper(s): Alice Ferguson. $80-100. MC, VISA, DS, PC. TAC5. 6 rooms, 4 with PB, 2 with FP, 1 suite and 1 cabin. Breakfast included in rates. Types of meals: Gourmet bkfst, country bkfst and veg bkfst. AP. Beds: KQT. TV, phone, ceiling fan, VCR, fireplace and refrigerator in room. Fax, copier, spa, swimming, stables, bicycles, pet boarding, gift shop, Jacuzzi, volleyball, ping pong, badminton, horseback riding, horseshoes, beaches, fishing, tubing, hiking, cross-country skiing, camping, hunting, hay rides, sleigh rides, sled hill and water tubing on premises. Handicap access. Weddings, small meetings, family reunions and seminars hosted. Golf, horseback riding, sailing, parks, shopping, downhill skiing, water sports and wineries nearby.
Pets allowed: Kennel.

Penn Yan G6

Finton's Landing on Keuka Lake

661 E Lake Rd
Penn Yan, NY 14527-9421
(315)536-3146 (9 am - 9 pm)
E-mail: tepperd@eznet.net
Web: home.eznet.net/~tepperd

Circa 1861. A delightful Victorian directly located on Keuka Lake, the inn features relaxing front porch rockers, whimsical period furnishings, painted wall murals and parlor fireplace. The sunny east shore has 165 feet of secluded beach, a restored lakeside gazebo and a two-person hammock. A luscious two-course breakfast is served in the cozy dining room or on the wraparound porch with its views of the lake.

Historic Interest: Located close to the Curtiss Museum of Early Aviation.
Innkeeper(s): Doug & Arianne Tepper. $99-129. MC, VISA, PC. 4 rooms with PB. Breakfast included in rates. Types of meals: Full bkfst. Beds: QDT. Ceiling fan in room. Air conditioning. Antiquing, bicycling, fishing, golf, swimming, parks, shopping, tennis and wineries nearby.

Fox Inn

158 Main St
Penn Yan, NY 14527-1201
(315)536-1100 (800)901-7997
E-mail: cliforr@aol.com

Circa 1820. Experience the pleasant elegance of a fine, historic home at this Greek Revival Inn. Furnished with Empire antiques, the accommodations include a living room with marble fireplace, sun porch, parlor with billiards table and formal rose gardens. Five guest rooms and one two-bedroom suite each have private baths. The gourmet breakfast provides a selection of six different types of pancakes served with fresh blueberries or raspberries and four varieties of French toast. Located near the Windmill Farm Market, the largest farm market in New York, you can spend a casual day shopping or visiting nearby museums or wineries. Or, enjoy more active alternatives such as biking, hiking and picnicking or boating on Keuka Lake.

Innkeeper(s): Cliff & Michele Orr. $89-159. MC, VISA, AX, PC, TC. TAC10. 6 rooms with PB, 1 with FP, 1 suite and 1 conference room. Breakfast included in rates. Types of meals: Gourmet bkfst and early coffee/tea. Beds: QD. Cable TV, phone, turndown service and VCR in room. Library and billiard table on premises. Weddings, small meetings, family reunions and seminars hosted. Amusement parks, antiquing, art galleries, beaches, bicycling, canoeing/kayaking, fishing, golf, hiking, horseback riding, live theater, museums, parks, shopping, downhill skiing, cross-country skiing, tennis, water sports and wineries nearby.
Publicity: *"Top 50 Inns in America Award"-in Inn Times.*

Trimmer House Bed & Breakfast

145 E Main St
Penn Yan, NY 14527-1633
(315)536-8304 (800)968-8735 Fax:(315)536-8304
E-mail: innkeeper@trimmerhouse.com
Web: www.trimmerhouse.com

Circa 1891. Built in 1891, this Queen Anne-style Victorian is complemented by period furnishings, and features such elegant accents as marble and oak floors, ornate ceilings and hand-crafted chandeliers. The guest rooms offer many special options to choose from, including a sleigh bed, vintage clawfoot bathtubs, fireplace or private veranda. Two public parlors, the Library and Music Room, provide cozy areas to relax, read or enjoy a cup of tea. A variety of restaurants, shops and boutiques are within walking distance. Several wineries, craft and farm markets, hik-

ing and bike trails, and public parks are nearby, or guests can pass a quiet afternoon on the front porch swing.
Innkeeper(s): Gary M Smith. $75-185. MC, VISA, PC, TC. 5 rooms with PB, 3 with FP and 1 suite. Breakfast included in rates. Types of meals: Gourmet bkfst. Beds: Q. Cable TV, phone, ceiling fan and VCR in room. Central air. Fax, copier, spa and library on premises. Small meetings and seminars hosted. Antiquing, art galleries, beaches, bicycling, canoeing/kayaking, fishing, golf, hiking, museums, parks, shopping, downhill skiing, cross-country skiing, tennis, water sports and wineries nearby.

Pine Island H11

The Glenwood House B&B

49 Glenwood Rd
Pine Island, NY 10969
(845)258-5066 Fax:(845)258-4226
E-mail: glenwood@warwick.net
Web: www.glenwoodhouse.com

Circa 1855. Built prior to the Civil War, this restored Victorian farmhouse is secluded on more than two picturesque acres in New York's Pochuck Valley. The spacious front veranda is filled with comfortable wicker furnishings, inviting guests to relax and enjoy the country setting. Guest rooms are decorated with a romantic flair. Three rooms include canopied beds. Deluxe cottage suites include a whirlpool tub for two and a fireplace. Seasonal, farm-fresh fruits start off the breakfast service, which might include an entrée such as Texas-style French toast or buttermilk pancakes accompanied by bacon or sausage. The home is close to ski areas, golf courses, wineries, historic home tours and antique stores. The Appalachian Trail, Hudson River and Greenwood Lake are other nearby attractions.

Historic Interest: Goshen Historic Track & Trotter Museum, Historic Warwick Village.
Innkeeper(s): Andrea & Kevin Colman. $110-295. MC, VISA, AX, TC. 5 rooms with PB, 2 with FP, 1 suite, 2 cottages and 1 conference room. Breakfast included in rates. Types of meals: Gourmet bkfst, country bkfst, early coffee/tea, picnic lunch and room service. Beds: KQ. Cable TV, ceiling fan and VCR in room. Air conditioning. Fax, copier and library on premises. Weddings, small meetings, family reunions and seminars hosted. Italian and German spoken. Amusement parks, antiquing, art galleries, beaches, bicycling, canoeing/kayaking, fishing, golf, hiking, horseback riding, live theater, museums, parks, shopping, downhill skiing, cross-country skiing, tennis, water sports and wineries nearby.

Queensbury E12

The Crislip's B&B

693 Ridge Rd
Queensbury, NY 12804-6901
(518)793-6869
E-mail: nedbc@capital.net

Circa 1802. This Federal-style house was built by Quakers and was once owned by the area's first doctor, who used it as a training center for young interns. There's an acre of lawns and annual gardens and a Victorian Italianate veranda overlooks the Green Mountains. The inn is furnished with 18th-century antiques and reproductions, including four-poster canopy beds and highboys. There's a keeping room with a huge fireplace. Historic stone walls flank the property.

Innkeeper(s): Ned & Joyce Crislip.
$55-85. MC, VISA, TC. 3 rooms with PB. Breakfast included in rates. Types of meals: Full bkfst and early coffee/tea. Beds: KD. Air conditioning. Small meetings hosted. Amusement parks, antiquing, fishing, civic center, live theater, parks, shopping, downhill skiing, cross-country skiing, sporting events and water sports nearby.

Red Hook   H12

The Grand Dutchess

7571 Old Post Rd
Red Hook, NY 12571-1403
(845)758-5818 Fax:(845)758-3143
E-mail: grandut@worldnet.att.net

Circa 1874. This Second Empire Victorian was originally built as the Hoffman Inn. It later served as the town school, a speakeasy and then a lonely hearts club. Twin parlors behind etched glass and wood sliding doors feature hardwood floors, antique chandeliers, arched marble fireplaces with massive

 carved mirrors, Oriental rugs and heirloom antiques. Lace curtains decorate the floor-to-ceiling windows. Most of the rooms have queen-sized beds and private baths and are located at the corners of the home to maximize the use of natural light. A full breakfast of homemade breads, a main dish, cereal and fruit is offered. For young guests, the innkeeper will prepare chocolate chip pancakes.
Innkeeper(s): Elizabeth Pagano & Harold Gruber. $95-155. MC, VISA, AX, PC, TC. 6 rooms, 4 with PB, 1 suite and 1 conference room. Breakfast included in rates. Types of meals: Gourmet bkfst, early coffee/tea and snacks/refreshments. Beds: KQDT. Air conditioning. VCR, fax, copier and library on premises. Weddings, small meetings and family reunions hosted. Antiquing, fishing, golf, historic homes, Rhinebeck Aerodrome, live theater, parks, shopping, cross-country skiing and tennis nearby.
Publicity: *Northeast, Gazette Advertiser, Poughkeepsie Journal and "The Eleanor Affair" an award-winning short film.*

"This place is outrageous! We love this place!"

Rhinebeck   I12

Beekman Arms-Delamater Inn

Rt 9
Rhinebeck, NY 12572
(845)876-7080
E-mail: delamaterinn@aol.com
Web: www.delamaterinn.com

Circa 1766. Said to be the oldest landmark inn in America, some walls of the Beekman Arms are two-and three-feet-thick. It has seen a variety of guests-including pioneers, trappers, Indians and Dutch farmers. Among the famous were Aaron Burr, William Jennings Bryan, Horace Greeley, Franklin Roosevelt, Neil Armstrong and Elizabeth Taylor. Like most old taverns and inns, it provided a meeting place for leaders of the day. Mr. LaForge is the 28th innkeeper at Beekman Arms. The Delamater House, an Alexander Jackson Gothic home, was built in 1844 and is in the National Register of Historic Places.
Innkeeper(s): Charles LaForge. $85-150. MC, VISA, AX, DC. 63 rooms with PB, 29 with FP and 1 conference room. Breakfast included in rates. Types of meals: Cont. Beds: KQDT. TV and phone in room. Handicap access.
Publicity: *New York Times.*

"If this is any indication of your general hospitality, it is very easy to see why you have stayed in the business for so long."

Olde Rhinebeck Inn

340 Wurtemburg Rd
Rhinebeck, NY 12572
(845)871-1745
E-mail: innkeeper@rhinebeckinn.com
Web: www.rhinebeckinn.com

Circa 1745. Located on three acres, this is a beautifully maintained early colonial farmhouse. The original buttermilk blue finishes remain and there is original hardware throughout. The innkeeper provides fine linens, antiques, fresh flowers and a breakfast that is served in the historic dining room. Offerings include sweet potato frittata, baked French pear and apple butter maple pecan muffins. There are miniature goats and a bass-stocked pond on the property.
Innkeeper(s): Jonna Paolella. $195-295. MC, VISA, PC, TC. TAC5. 3 rooms with PB. Breakfast included in rates. Types of meals: Full bkfst and afternoon tea. Beds: Q. Cable TV and satellite TV in room. Air conditioning. VCR and fax on premises. Antiquing, golf, parks and shopping nearby.
Publicity: *Country Living.*

Veranda House B&B

6487 Montgomery St
Rhinebeck, NY 12572-1113
(845)876-4133 (877)985-6800 Fax:(845)876-4133
E-mail: visit@verandahous.com
Web: www.verandahouse.com

Circa 1845. For nearly a century, this Federal-style home served as the parsonage for an Episcopal church. The home is located in a Rhinebeck historic district among many notable houses. The home is decorated in a comfortable mix of styles, with a few antiques. If weather permits, breakfasts are served on the terrace, featuring items such as freshly baked pastries or maple walnut coffee cake and a daily entree. The scenic area offers much in the way of activities. Woodstock is a short drive away.
Historic Interest: FDR's home and library, Vanderbilt mansion. Olana, Old Rhinebeck Aerodrome.
Innkeeper(s): Linda & Ward Stanley. $100-150. MC, VISA, AX, PC, TC. 5 rooms with PB. Breakfast included in rates. Types of meals: Gourmet bkfst. Beds: QT. Phone, ceiling fan and clocks in room. Air conditioning. VCR and library on premises. Small meetings, family reunions and seminars hosted. Some German spoken. Antiquing, fishing, golf, hiking, live theater, parks, shopping, downhill skiing, cross-country skiing, tennis and water sports nearby.

"Beautiful rooms, terrific breakfast! We will recommend you highly."

Rochester   F5

"428 Mt. Vernon"

428 Mount Vernon Ave
Rochester, NY 14620-2710
(716)271-0792 (800)836-3159

Circa 1917. Victorian furnishings and decor grace the interior of this stately Irish manor house. Set on two lush acres of shade trees and foliage, this secluded spot is perfect for guests in search of relaxation. Guests can create their morning meals from a varied breakfast menu. The inn is adjacent to Highland Park, great walking park and conservatory.
Innkeeper(s): Philip & Claire Lanzatella. $125. MC, VISA, AX, TC. 7 rooms with PB and 1 conference room. Breakfast included in rates. Types of meals: Gourmet bkfst and early coffee/tea. Beds: QDT. Cable TV, phone, turndown service and ceiling fan in room. Air conditioning. Weddings, small meetings and seminars hosted. Antiquing, Annual Lilac Festival, University of Rochester, Rochester Institute of Technology and Museum, live theater, parks, shopping and cross-country skiing nearby.

"Everything was wonderful, they took care in every detail."

A Bed & Breakfast at Dartmouth House Inn

215 Dartmouth St
Rochester, NY 14607-3202
(716)271-7872
E-mail: stay@DartmouthHouse.com
Web: www.DartmouthHouse.com

Circa 1905. The lavish, four-course breakfasts served daily at this beautiful turn-of-the-century Edwardian home are unforgettable. Innkeeper and award-winning, gourmet cook Ellie Klein starts off the meal with special fresh juice, which is served in the parlor. From this point, guests are seated at the candlelit dining

table to enjoy a series of delectable dishes, such as poached pears, a mouth-watering entree, a light, lemon ice and a rich dessert. And each of the courses is served on a separate pattern of Depression Glass. If the breakfast isn't enough, Ellie and husband, Bill, an electrical engineer, have stocked the individually decorated bathrooms with fluffy towels and bathrobes and guests can soak in inviting clawfoot tubs. Each of the bedchambers boasts antique collectibles and fresh flowers. The inn is located in the prestigious turn-of-the-century Park Avenue Historical and Cultural District. The entire area is an architect's dream. Museums, colleges, Eastman School of Music, Highland Park, restaurants and antique shops are among the many nearby attractions.

Historic Interest: George Eastman's Mansion and International Museum of Photography is a 10-minute walk from the inn. The High Falls Brown's Race Historic Center is two miles, the graves of Susan B. Anthony and Frederick Douglass are two miles away at Mount Hope Cemetery. The Rochester Historical Society is a 10-minute walk.

Innkeeper(s): Elinor & Bill Klein. $125-150. MC, VISA, AX, PC, TC. TAC10. 4 rooms with PB. Breakfast included in rates. Types of meals: Full bkfst and early coffee/tea. Beds: KQT. TV, phone, ceiling fan, VCR, robe, tape deck and lighted makeup mirror in room. Air conditioning. Fax, bicycles and library on premises. Antiquing, George Eastman International Museum of Photography within walking distance, live theater, museums, parks and shopping nearby.

Publicity: Democrat & Chronicle, DAKA, Genesee Country, Seaway Trail, Oneida News, Travelers News, Country Living and The New York Times Travel Section.

"The food was fabulous, the company fascinating, and the personal attention beyond comparison. You made me feel at home instantly."

The Edward Harris House B&B Inn

35 Argyle Street
Rochester, NY 14607
(716)473-9752 (800)419-1213 Fax:(716)473-9752
E-mail: ehhbb@aol.com
Web: www.edwardharrishousebb.com

Circa 1896. Acclaimed as one of the finest early examples of architect Claude Bragdon's work, this Georgian mansion is a restored Landmark home. Its history only enhances the rich warmth, and the immense size reflects a cozy ambiance. Relax in a leather chair in the traditional library. Antiques and collectibles combine well with florals and chintz for a touch of romance. Two guest bedrooms and the Garden Suite boast fireplaces. Four-poster rice beds and hand-painted furniture add to the individual decorating styles. A small kitchen on this floor is for guest use, though not meant for cooking full meals. A six-course candle-light breakfast is served in the formal dining room on crystal and china or on the brick garden patio. The night before, choose a

main entree from a seasonal menu offering seven or eight items. Enjoy afternoon tea on the wicker-filled front porch. A plethora of historic sites, including The George Eastman House and Strong Museum, are within a 15-mile range.

Historic Interest: The George Eastman House (1 mile), The Stone Tolan House (2 miles) Susan B. Anthony House (3 miles), Genesee Country Village & Museum (15 miles), The Stron Museum (2 miles), Roche Public Market (3 miles), Campbell-Whittlesey House (3 miles), lighthouse (6 miles).

Innkeeper(s): Susan Alvarez. $95-130. MC, VISA, PC, TC. TAC10. 5 rooms, 1 with PB, 3 with FP, 2 suites and 1 conference room. Breakfast included in rates. Types of meals: Gourmet bkfst, veg bkfst, cont plus, cont, early coffee/tea, afternoon tea, snacks/refreshments and room service. AP. Beds: KQDT. Cable TV, phone, turndown service, ceiling fan and fireplace in room. Air conditioning. VCR, fax, copier, library, small kitchen on guest room level and gift shop on premises. Weddings, small meetings and seminars hosted. Spanish spoken. Amusement parks, antiquing, art galleries, beaches, bicycling, canoeing/kayaking, fishing, golf, hiking, horseback riding, live theater, museums, parks, shopping, downhill skiing, cross-country skiing, sporting events, tennis, water sports and wineries nearby.

Pets allowed: Please call prior.

Sackets Harbor   D8

George Sacket House Bed and Breakfast

106 South Broad Street, PO Box 337
Sackets Harbor, NY 13685
(315)646-2445 Fax:(315)646-4686
E-mail: gshbb@gisco.net
Web: www.georgesackethouseandb.com

Circa 1839. This recently restored Greek Revival house is rich in history. The grand four-story mansion built in 1839 by George Sacket, son of the founder of the town, sits on welcoming landscaped grounds. The large front porch beckons and begins a delightfully elegant experience. Signed works of art grace the walls, Oriental rugs are underfoot and wonderful stories unfold the history of the original furnishings. There are two spacious guest bedrooms and two luxurious suites, all with private baths; one boasts a whirlpool tub. The Canfield Suite features a fireplace and private porch. Pike's Retreat, on the fourth floor, housed teachers during World War II. It now offers a secluded bedroom with an inviting sleigh bed and a sitting room. Enjoy a full gourmet breakfast on settings of sterling silver and fine china in the formal dining room or in season, on the comfortable back porch. The historic village and nearby waterfront provides something for everyone to explore.

Historic Interest: Sackets Harbor Battlefield (0.5 miles).

Innkeeper(s): Mary Donahue. $90-125. MC, VISA, DS, PC. 4 rooms, 2 with PB and 2 suites. Breakfast included in rates. Types of meals: Gourmet bkfst and early coffee/tea. Beds: KQDT. Cable TV, phone and fireplace in room. Air conditioning. VCR, fax and copier on premises. Weddings, small meetings, family reunions and seminars hosted. Antiquing, art galleries, beaches, bicycling, canoeing/kayaking, fishing, golf, hiking, scuba diving, whitewater rafting, museums, parks, shopping, downhill skiing, cross-country skiing, tennis and water sports nearby.

Saratoga Springs   F12

Adelphi Hotel

365 Broadway
Saratoga Springs, NY 12866-3111
(518)587-4688 (800)860-4086 Fax:(518)587-4688

Circa 1877. This Victorian hotel is one of two hotels still remaining from Saratoga's opulent spa era. A piazza overlooking Broadway features three-story columns topped with Victorian fretwork. Recently refurbished with lavish turn-of-the-century decor, rooms are filled with antique furnishings, opulent draperies and

wall coverings, highlighting the inn's high ceilings and ornate woodwork. A continental breakfast is served buffet-style each morning. There is an inviting swimming pool in the back garden.
Innkeeper(s): Sheila Parkert. $105-400. MC, VISA, AX. TAC5. 39 rooms with PB, 18 suites and 1 conference room. Breakfast included in rates. Types of meals: Cont plus. Beds: QDT. Cable TV, phone and turndown service in room. Air conditioning. Weddings and small meetings hosted. Antiquing, golf, live theater, parks and shopping nearby.
Publicity: *New York Times, Country Inns, Back Roads, Conde Nast and Victorian Homes.*

Apple Tree B&B

49 W High St
Saratoga Springs, NY 12020-1912
(518)885-1113 Fax:(518)885-9758
E-mail: mail@appletreebb.com
Web: www.appletreebb.com

Circa 1878. A pond, waterfall and a garden decorate the entrance to this Second Empire Victorian, which is located in the historic district of Ballston Spa, a village just a few minutes from Saratoga Springs. Guest rooms feature Victorian and

French-country decor, and each has antiques and whirlpool tubs. Guests enjoy fresh fruit, homemade baked goods, a selection of beverages and a daily entree during the breakfast service.
Innkeeper(s): Dolores & Jim Taisey. $85-175. MC, VISA, AX, PC, TC. TAC10. 5

rooms with PB. Breakfast included in rates. Types of meals: Full bkfst and early coffee/tea. Beds: Q. Cable TV, VCR and whirlpool in room. Central air. Small meetings and family reunions hosted. Amusement parks, antiquing, fishing, Saratoga Race Course, live theater, parks, shopping, downhill skiing, cross-country skiing, sporting events and water sports nearby.
Publicity: *Country Folk Art Magazine.*

Chestnut Tree Inn

9 Whitney Pl
Saratoga Springs, NY 12866-4518
(518)587-8681 (888)243-7688

Circa 1870. Linger over breakfast as you sit and enjoy the view from a wicker-filled veranda at this Second Period Empire-style house. The grounds boast what is thought to be the last live chestnut tree in the city. The innkeepers are antique dealers, who operate a local group shop. They have filled the home with turn-of-the-century pieces and have won awards for the preservation of their inn and for having the "best front porch" in Saratoga. The home is within walking distance of the race track, downtown shopping, only a mile from the Saratoga Performing Arts Center and the State Park where guests can enjoy mineral baths.
Historic Interest: The Canfield Casino, a restored local gambling house with a museum on the second floor, is two blocks from the inn. Saratoga Battlefield is about 10 miles away.
Innkeeper(s): Cathleen & Bruce De Luke. $95-165. MC, VISA, PC. 7 rooms with PB. Breakfast included in rates. Types of meals: Cont plus. Beds: QDT. Antiquing, fishing, live theater and water sports nearby.
Publicity: *New York Times.*

The Lombardi Farm B&B

41 Locust Grove Rd
Saratoga Springs, NY 12866-9108
(518)587-2074 Fax:(518)587-2074
E-mail: lombardifarm@msn.com
Web: www.bbinternet.com/lombardi

Circa 1840. A surrey rests in front of this Victorian farmhouse, which is surrounded by 10 acres of scenic countryside. A four-course, gourmet breakfast is served in the farm's Florida Room.

The menu changes daily and items such as breakfast souffles, Belgian waffles, quiche, chocolate crepes and strudels are accompanied by freshly baked muffins, scones or rolls. Guests are invited to take a relaxing dip in the B&Bs indoor hot tub with Jacuzzi. Equestrians will appreciate the home's close access to the Saratoga Thoroughbred Racetrack, Saratoga Harness Track and the National Museum of Polo.
Historic Interest: The Saratoga Battlefield is nearby.
Innkeeper(s): Dr. Vincent & Kathleen Lombardi. $100-175. PC. TAC10. 4 rooms with PB. Breakfast and snacks/refreshments included in rates. Types of meals: Gourmet bkfst and early coffee/tea. Beds: KQDT. Ceiling fan in room. Air conditioning. VCR, fax, copier, spa, bicycles, library, hot tub and jacuzzi on premises. Handicap access. Weddings, small meetings, family reunions and seminars hosted. Antiquing, fishing, golf, performing art centers, museums, Saratoga Battlefield, Saratoga mineral baths with massage, live theater, parks, shopping, cross-country skiing and tennis nearby.
"The stay at Lombardi Farm was a most delightful experience. Your warmth, plus the wonderful food total a perfect 10."

Six Sisters B&B

149 Union Ave
Saratoga Springs, NY 12866-3518
(518)583-1173 Fax:(518)587-2470
E-mail: stay@sixsistersbandb.com
Web: www.sixsistersbandb.com

Circa 1880. The unique architecture of this Victorian home features a large second-story bay window, a tiger oak front door decked with stained glass and a veranda accentuated with rock-

ing chairs. Inside, the marble and hardwoods combine with antiques and Oriental rugs to create an elegant atmosphere. During racing season, guests can rise early and take a short walk to the local race track to watch the horses work out. Upon their return, guests are greeted with the aroma of a delicious, gourmet breakfast. A 10-minute walk to Saratoga Springs' downtown area offers antique shops, boutiques and many restaurants.
Historic Interest: Saratoga Battlefield (15 minutes), Spa State Park (5 minutes), Saratoga Racetrack (across street).
Innkeeper(s): Kate Benton. $85-350. MC, VISA, AX, DS, PC, TC. TAC10. 4 rooms with PB. Breakfast included in rates. Types of meals: Gourmet bkfst and early coffee/tea. Beds: KQ. Cable TV, ceiling fan, three rooms with private balcony and whirlpool in room. Air conditioning. Fax on premises. Amusement parks, antiquing, fishing, spa and mineral baths, museums, live theater, parks, shopping, downhill skiing, cross-country skiing, sporting events and water sports nearby.
Publicity: *Gourmet, Country Inns, Country Folk Art, Country Victorian, McCalls and New York Times.*

Westchester House B&B

102 Lincoln Ave
Saratoga Springs, NY 12866-4536
(518)587-7613 (800)581-7613 Fax:(518)583-9562
E-mail: innkeepers@westchesterhousebandb.com
Web: www.westchesterhousebandb.com

Circa 1885. This gracious Queen Anne Victorian has been welcoming vacationers for more than 100 years. Antiques from four generations of the Melvin family grace the high-ceilinged rooms. Oriental rugs top gleaming wood floors, while antique clocks and lace curtains set a graceful tone. Guests gather on the wraparound porch, in the parlors or gardens for an afternoon refreshment of old-fashioned lemonade. Most attractions are within walking distance.
Historic Interest: Built by master carpenter Almeron King in 1885.

Innkeeper(s): Bob & Stephanie Melvin. $95-325. MC, VISA, AX, PC, TC. TAC10. 7 rooms with PB and 1 conference room. Breakfast and afternoon tea included in rates. Types of meals: Cont plus and early coffee/tea. Beds: KQT. Phone, ceiling fan, data port and voice mail in room. Air conditioning. Fax, copier, library and baby grand piano on premises. Small meetings, family reunions and seminars hosted.

Antiquing, fishing, opera, ballet, horse racing, race track, Saratoga Performing Arts Center, live theater, parks, shopping, cross-country skiing, sporting events and water sports nearby.

Publicity: *Getaways for Gourmets, Albany Times Union, Saratogian, Capital, Country Inns, New York Daily News, WNYT, Newsday* and *Hudson Valley.*

"I adored your B&B and have raved about it to all. One of the most beautiful and welcoming places we've ever visited."

Schroon Lake   D12

Schroon Lake B&B

1525 US Rt 9, PO Box 638
Schroon Lake, NY 12870
(518)532-7042 (800)523-6755
E-mail: info@schroonbb.com

Circa 1922. Sitting on a grassy knoll on two acres, this Victorian farmhouse overlooks the breathtaking Adirondack Mountains. Polished hardwood floors, antiques, Tiffany-style lamps and Oriental rugs create a tastefully elegant inn renovated for comfort and convenience. Guest bedrooms feature a casual sophistication with designer bed linens, terry robes and cozy chairs. Rita takes great pleasure in presenting a bountiful, mouth-watering breakfast that may include zucchini-dill puffed omelettes, apple-walnut French toast with fresh berry fruit sauce or spinach-apple and feta cheese timbales. Savor every bite in the formal dining room or on the porch.

Innkeeper(s): Rita & Bob Skojec. $90-175. MC, VISA, AX, PC, TC. 5 rooms, 3 with PB and 1 suite. Breakfast and snacks/refreshments included in rates. Types of meals: Gourmet bkfst, veg bkfst and early coffee/tea. Ceiling fan in room. Air conditioning. Fax, copier and library on premises. Small meetings, family reunions and seminars hosted. Amusement parks, antiquing, art galleries, beaches, bicycling, canoeing/kayaking, fishing, golf, hiking, horseback riding, live theater, museums, parks, shopping, downhill skiing, cross-country skiing, sporting events, tennis and water sports nearby.

Publicity: *Country Register, New York Newsday Magazine* and *Post Star News.*

"Great food, great atmosphere, comfy bed, heaven on earth!"

Sodus   E6

Maxwell Creek Inn

7563 Lake Rd
Sodus, NY 14551-9309
(315)483-2222 (800)315-2206
E-mail: mcinnbnb@worldnet.att.net

Circa 1846. Located on the shores of Lake Ontario, this historic cobblestone house rests on six acres and is surrounded by a woodland wildlife preserve and apple orchards. On the Seaway Trail near Sodus Bay, the property includes a historic grist mill and is rumored to have been a part of the Underground Railroad. Stroll through the apple orchards to the lake or enjoy the fishing stream, tennis courts and hiking trails. There are kayak and canoes rentals on the premises. Maxwell Creek's spacious accommodations are comprised of five guest rooms in the main house, including a honeymoon suite. The Cobblestone Cottage, a former carriage house, offers two efficiency suites pop-

ular for families and groups.

Guests are treated to a full breakfast served by candlelight in a rustic wood-paneled dining room warmed by a unique fireplace.

Innkeeper(s): Patrick & Belinda McElroy. $85-150. MC, VISA, DS, PC, TC. 7 rooms with PB, 2 suites, 1 cottage and 1 conference room. Breakfast included in rates. Types of meals: Gourmet bkfst. Beds: KQDT. Tennis, library, fishing creek and hiking on premises. Family reunions hosted. Amusement parks, antiquing, canoeing/kayaking, fishing, hiking, fall foliage train rides nearby, snowmobiling, parks, shopping, downhill skiing, cross-country skiing and water sports nearby.

Publicity: *Atlanta Journal* and *Newman Times.*

"The best food I've ever tasted."

Sodus Bay-Wolcott   E7

Bonnie Castle Farm B&B

PO Box 188
Sodus Bay-Wolcott, NY 14590-0188
(315)587-2273 (800)587-4006 Fax:(315)587-4003
E-mail: empgap@zlink.net

Circa 1887. This large, waterfront home is surrounded by expansive lawns and trees, which overlook the east side of Great Sodus Bay, a popular resort at the turn of the century. Accommodations include a suite and large guest rooms with water views. Other

rooms feature wainscoting and cathedral ceilings. A full, gourmet breakfast includes a cereal bar, fresh fruit and juices and an assortment of entrees such as Orange Blossom French toast, sausages, a creamy potato casserole and fresh-baked pastries topped off with teas and Irish creme coffee. Guests can visit many nearby attractions, such as the Renaissance Festival, Erie Canal and Chimney Bluffs State Park.

Historic Interest: Dozens of historic sites await guests at the Bonnie Castle Farm, including the Everson Museum, Susan B. Anthony House, National Women's Hall of Fame, William Phelps General Store Museum, the Sodus Point Maritime Museum, Renaissance Faire and more.

Innkeeper(s): Eric & Georgia Pendleton. $89-165. MC, VISA, AX, DS, PC, TC. TAC10. 8 rooms with PB and 1 suite. Breakfast included in rates. Types of meals: Gourmet bkfst. Beds: KQD. Cable TV, ceiling fan and VCR in room. Air conditioning. Fax, copier, spa and swimming on premises. Small meetings, family reunions and seminars hosted. Antiquing, fishing, live theater, parks, shopping, downhill skiing, cross-country skiing, sporting events and water sports nearby.

"We love Bonnie Castle. You have a magnificent establishment. We are just crazy about your place. Hope to see you soon."

Sodus Point   E6

Carriage House Inn

Corner of Ontario & Wickham
Sodus Point, NY 14555-9608
(315)483-2100 (800)292-2990 Fax:(315)483-2100
E-mail: carrigin@rochester.rr.com
Web: www.carriage-house-inn.com

Circa 1870. This restored Victorian waterfront home sits on four picturesque acres in a residential area of a quaint resort village. Accommodations also include a stone carriage house on the shore of Lake Ontario overlooking a historic lighthouse and efficiencies with kitchenettes in the caretaker's quarters. Enjoy the gentle breeze while relaxing in one of the screened gazebos, or gather in the living room by the fire. The inn offers beach access, and it is an easy walk to restaurants and charter boats.

Historic Interest: The Sodus Point historic lighthouse is adjacent to the inn. Innkeeper(s): The DenDecker's. $75-95. MC, VISA, AX. 10 rooms with PB. Breakfast included in rates. Types of meals: Country bkfst. Beds: KT. Cable TV in room. Refrigerators, gas grills and picnic tables on premises. Amusement parks, antiquing, golf, snowmobiling, charter and stream fishing, boat launch/rentals, shopping, downhill skiing, cross-country skiing and water sports nearby.

Publicity: *Finger Lakes Times, Democrat and Chronicle, Journey, Outdoor, Travel & Leisure, Inn Fisherman, Wayne County Star and WTVH.*

"An outstanding inn, beautifully restored and a delightful waterfront historic setting."

Southampton K15

Evergreen On Pine

89 Pine St
Southampton, NY 11968-4945
(631)283-0564 (877)824-6600
E-mail: rogoski@hotmail.com
Web: www.evergreenonpine.com

Circa 1860. Guests enjoy a short walk to the beach from this two-and-a-half-story cottage, tucked behind an arched hedge and shaded by tall trees. Located in the middle of the village, the bed and breakfast offers guests a front porch and a patio for relaxing. Guest rooms are comfortable and welcoming. Breakfast is continental style and features cereal, muffins and fruit. Nearby Main Street is lined with unique shops and restaurants and a number of antique shops. Visit the area's wineries or glean fresh local produce from the popular fruit and vegetable stands when not strolling the beach.

Innkeeper(s): Peter & Joann Rogoski. $99-325. MC, VISA, AX, DS, PC, TC. TAC10. 5 rooms with PB and 1 suite. Breakfast included in rates. Types of meals: Cont and early coffee/tea. Beds: QD. Cable TV, phone and ceiling fan in room. Air conditioning. Fax and copier on premises. Weddings hosted. Antiquing, art galleries, beaches, bicycling, canoeing/kayaking, fishing, golf, hiking, horseback riding, live theater, museums, parks, shopping and wineries nearby.

Mainstay

579 Hill St
Southampton, NY 11968-5305
(516)283-4375 Fax:(516)287-6240
E-mail: elizmain@hamptons.com

Circa 1870. This Colonial has served as a guest house, country store and now a bed & breakfast with eight guest rooms. Antiques, including iron beds, decorate the bedchambers. One suite includes a clawfoot tub. A decanter of sherry has been placed in each guest room. Several walls feature hand-painted murals. There is a swimming pool for guest use, as well as beach access.

Innkeeper(s): Elizabeth Main. $80-300. MC, VISA, AX, TC. 8 rooms, 5 with PB and 2 suites. Breakfast included in rates. Types of meals: Cont. Beds: KQDT. Ceiling fan in room. Fax on premises. Antiquing, fishing, golf, live theater, parks, shopping, tennis and water sports nearby.

Publicity: *New York Times.*

Stone Ridge I11

Sparrow Hawk Bed & Breakfast

4496 Rte 209
Stone Ridge, NY 12484
(845)687-4492
Web: www.sparrowhawkbandb.com

Circa 1770. Situated on five acres in the picturesque Hudson Valley, this 1770 Registered Brick Colonial with wood shake roof and wide plank floors sits beneath majestic 200-year-old locust trees. Wide hallways lead to the five large air-conditioned guest rooms furnished with special antiques, some with original fireplaces. Behind the old house is the Grand Room, with cathedral windows on three sides and a balcony library full of books, magazines, videos and music for leisurely entertainment. A full gourmet breakfast of freshly baked muffins and special egg dishes with homemade sausage or bacon can be enjoyed on the blue stone patio. The surrounding countryside affords many activities such as hiking, skiing, golf or exploring antique shops, wineries or local artisan's pottery shops.

Innkeeper(s): Howard & Betsy Mont. $100-155. PC, TC. TAC10. 5 rooms, 4 with PB, 1 suite and 1 conference room. Breakfast and afternoon tea included in rates. Types of meals: Gourmet bkfst. Beds: KQDT. Ceiling fan in room. Air conditioning. VCR, fax, copier, bicycles and library on premises. Weddings, small meetings and family reunions hosted. Italian and some spanish spoken. Antiquing, art galleries, bicycling, canoeing/kayaking, fishing, golf, hiking, horseback riding, live theater, parks, shopping, downhill skiing, cross-country skiing, tennis and wineries nearby.

Publicity: *Blue Stone Press, Hudson Valley Magazine and Hudson Valley Guide.*

Syracuse F8

Dickenson House On James

1504 James St
Syracuse, NY 13203-2814
(315)423-4777 (888)423-4777
E-mail: innkeeper@dickensonhouse.com
Web: www.dickensonhouse.com

Circa 1924. As pretty as a picture from a long ago era, this crisp, tidy ornate Tudor home stands on a secluded half acre in an urban neighborhood that is a preservation district. The inn has stained glass, a beautiful beveled mirror foyer, crystal chandeliers, a stone front porch and a porte-cochere. It has four guest bedrooms and a 1300-square-foot loft suite with vaulted ceilings and skylights. All the guest rooms are named for British poets. The literary themed living room includes an old violin, a Victrola, antique cameras, kaleidoscopes and a fireplace. Breakfast is a taste sensation of entrees with fruits juices, coffee, almond scones, fruit parfait, yogurt, granola, and orange/pecan crusted French toast.

Historic Interest: Erie Canal (1 1/2 miles), Salt Museum & French Fort (5 miles). Innkeeper(s): Pam & Ed Kopiel. $99-140. MC, VISA, AX, DS. TAC10. 4 rooms with PB and 1 suite. Breakfast, afternoon tea and snacks/refreshments included in rates. Types of meals: Gourmet bkfst, veg bkfst, cont plus and early coffee/tea. Beds: KQT. Cable TV, phone, ceiling fan and VCR in room. Central air. Fax, copier, library and guest kitchen on premises. Small meetings and family reunions hosted. Amusement parks, antiquing, art galleries, beaches, bicycling, canoeing/kayaking, fishing, golf, hiking, horseback riding, live theater, museums, parks, shopping, downhill skiing, cross-country skiing, sporting events, tennis, water sports and wineries nearby.

Giddings Garden Bed & Breakfast

290 W Seneca Tpke
Syracuse, NY 13207-2639
(315)492-6389 (800)377-3452
E-mail: giddingsb-b@webtv.net
Web: www.giddingsgarden.com

Circa 1810. Formerly Giddings Tavern, this historic federal-style home offers three guest rooms. The Honey Room features a white iron poster bed and a fireplace, as well as a unique private bath with a marble floor and a marble mirrored shower. The Executive Room is decorated in leather and black moiré fabric with mahogany furnishings, or you might prefer the Country Garden Room with a lace canopy and floral décor. All have marble baths, and there are fireplaces. In the morning, try the menu with Baked Apple Flowers and maple syrup, creamed eggs and hollandaise sauce in a filo cup, and strawberry-filled chocolate cups served with Grand Marnier. Afterwards, relax on the old stone patio that overlooks a fishpond or stroll around the inn's gardens.

Innkeeper(s): Pat & Nancy Roberts. $90-150. MC, VISA, AX, DS, TC. TAC5. 3 rooms with PB. Breakfast included in rates. Types of meals: Gourmet bkfst and early coffee/tea. Beds: Q. Cable TV, phone and refrigerator in hall in room. Air conditioning. VCR in rooms. Small meetings hosted. Antiquing, fishing, golf, live theater, parks, shopping, downhill skiing, cross-country skiing, sporting events, tennis and water sports nearby.

Tannersville   H11

The Eggery Inn

County Rd 16
Tannersville, NY 12485
(518)589-5363 (800)785-5364
E-mail: eggeryinn@aol.com
Web: www.eggeryinn.com

Circa 1900. Located on 12 acres in the Catskill Forest Preserve with mountain views and bountiful flower beds, this restored turn-of-the-century home is only a two-and-a-half-hour drive from New York City. A wraparound porch and shutters create a welcoming entrance. Comfortable guest bedrooms feature country furnishings. Breakfasts are served in the formal dining room and may include specialties such as fruit-filled hot cakes and omelets. Ski the nearby slopes of Hunter  Mountain and Ski Windham. Cross-country skiing is within one mile. Enjoy fall colors, Woodstock, and the antique shops of Saugerties, a short drive away. Other attractions are North Lake State Park, hiking trails, cycling and golf. Special dinners for groups may be reserved by prior arrangement.

Innkeeper(s): Julie & Abraham Abramczyk. $95-125. MC, VISA, AX. TAC10. 15 rooms with PB. Breakfast included in rates. Types of meals: Full bkfst. Beds: KQD. Cable TV and phone in room. Air conditioning. Family reunions hosted. Antiquing, bicycling, fishing, golf, hiking, live theater, parks, shopping, downhill skiing, cross-country skiing and tennis nearby.
Publicity: *Kaatskill Life, Newsday, Skiing and AAA Mobil Guide.*

Trumansburg   G7

Gothic Eves Bed & Breakfast

112 E Main St, PO Box 95
Trumansburg, NY 14886-0095
(607)387-6033 (800)387-7712
E-mail: info@gothiceves.com
Web: www.gothiceves.com

Circa 1855. The history of this Carpenter Gothic Revival home includes the locally renown builder Titus Hart, and the Smith Family, descendants of the village founder. Recently renovated by the third and current owners, the decor is entirely Victorian with period antiques and furnishings. A sitting room and parlor are inviting places to read or converse. The comfortable guest bedrooms offer a variety of accommodations and connecting rooms for groups or families traveling together. Breakfast reflects each season's bounty and may include grapefruit topped with grapes, strawberry crepes and stewed Empire apples with walnuts. Boasting a vegetable, fruit, herb and flower cutting garden, as well as swings and a playground, young and old alike will be delighted.

Innkeeper(s): Rose Hilbert & Roman Pausch. $75-140. MC, VISA, PC, TC. 5 rooms with PB. Breakfast included in rates. Types of meals: Gourmet bkfst, veg bkfst, early coffee/tea and picnic lunch. Beds: KQDT. Ceiling fan and down comforters in room. Air conditioning. Library, refrigerator, modem hookup, picnic area and flower cutting garden on premises. Weddings, small meetings and family reunions hosted. German spoken. Antiquing, art galleries, beaches, bicycling, canoeing/kayaking, fishing, golf, hiking, horseback riding, 215-foot waterfall, ice skating, restaurants, live theater, museums, parks, shopping, downhill skiing, cross-country skiing, sporting events, tennis, water sports and wineries nearby.

Utica   F9

Adam Bowman Manor

197 Riverside Dr
Utica, NY 13502-2322
(315)738-0276 Fax:(315)738-0276
E-mail: bargood@msn.com

Circa 1823. The founder of Deerfield, George Weaver, built this graceful brick Federal house for his daughter. It is said to have been a part of the Underground Railroad (there's a secret tunnel) and is in the National Register. Handsomely landscaped grounds include a fountain, a gazebo, tall oaks and borders of perennials. The late Duke and Dutchess of Windsor were guests here and there are rooms named for them.  The Duke's room has French-country furniture, a hand-painted fireplace and a king bed. Enjoy the Drawing Room and library, and in the morning guests are offered a full breakfast in the elegantly appointed dining room.

Innkeeper(s): Marion & Barry Goodwin. $40-75. MC, VISA, PC, TC. TAC10. 4 rooms, 2 with PB, 2 with FP. Breakfast included in rates. Types of meals: Full bkfst, cont plus and cont. Beds: KQD. Air conditioning. VCR, fax and library on premises. Weddings, small meetings and family reunions hosted. Some French and Italian. Some Spanish spoken. Antiquing, golf, live theater, parks, shopping, downhill skiing, cross-country skiing, tennis and water sports nearby.

"Great company, good food and new friends for us."

Warrensburg E12

Country Road Lodge B&B

115 Hickory Hill Rd
Warrensburg, NY 12885-3912
(518)623-2207 Fax:(518)623-4363
E-mail: mail@countryroadlodge.com
Web: www.countryroadlodge.com

Circa 1929. This simple, rustic farmhouse lodge is situated on 35 acres along the Hudson River at the end of a country road. Rooms are clean and comfortable. A full breakfast is provided with homemade breads and muffins. The sitting room reveals panoramic views of the river and Sugarloaf Mountain. Bird watching, hiking and skiing are popular activities. Groups often reserve all four guest rooms.
Historic Interest: French and Indian War battlefields, Fort William Henry, Ticonderoga, and Defiance, Millionaire's Row on Lake George.
Innkeeper(s): Sandi & Steve Parisi. $58-72. PC. TAC10. 4 rooms, 2 with PB. Breakfast included in rates. Types of meals: Full bkfst and early coffee/tea. Beds: QT. Ceiling fan in room. Air conditioning. Amusement parks, antiquing, fishing, live theater, parks, shopping, downhill skiing, cross-country skiing and water sports nearby.
Publicity: North Jersey Herald & News.

"Homey, casual atmosphere. We really had a wonderful time. You're both wonderful hosts and the Lodge is definitely our kind of B&B! We will always feel very special about this place and will always be back."

Warwick J11

Warwick Valley Bed & Breakfast

24 Maple Ave
Warwick, NY 10990-1025
(845)987-7255 Fax:(845)988-5318
E-mail: loretta@warwick.net

Circa 1900. This turn-of-the-century Colonial Revival is located in Warwick's historic district among many of the town's other historic gems. The B&B includes five guest rooms decorated with antiques and country furnishings. Breakfasts are a treat with entrees such as eggs Benedict, apple pancakes or a savory potato, cheese and egg bake. Wineries, antique shops and many outdoor activities are nearby, and innkeeper Loretta Breedveld is happy to point guests in the right direction.
Innkeeper(s): Loretta Breedveld. $100-135. MC, VISA, AX, DS, PC, TC. 5 rooms with PB. Breakfast included in rates. Types of meals: Gourmet bkfst and early coffee/tea. Beds: KQT. TV, phone and sitting area in room. Central air. VCR, fax, copier and bicycles on premises. Family reunions hosted. Amusement parks, antiquing, fishing, golf, wineries, live theater, parks, shopping, downhill skiing, cross-country skiing, sporting events, tennis and water sports nearby.
Publicity: Warwick Advertiser.

Westhampton Beach K14

1880 House Bed & Breakfast

PO Box 648
Westhampton Beach, NY 11978-0648
(516)288-1559 (800)346-3290 Fax:(516)288-7696

Circa 1880. On Westhampton Beach's exclusive Seafield Lane, this country estate includes a pool and tennis court, and it is just a short walk to the ocean. The inn is decorated with Victorian antiques, Shaker benches, and Chinese porcelain, creating a casual, country inn atmosphere.
Innkeeper(s): Elsie Collins. $150-250. MC, VISA, AX. TAC10. 3 suites.

Breakfast included in rates. Types of meals: Full bkfst and afternoon tea. Beds: QD. Weddings, small meetings, family reunions and seminars hosted. Antiquing, live theater and wineries nearby.
Publicity: Mid-Atlantic Getaways and Country Inns.

"From the moment we stepped inside your charming home we felt all the warmth you sent our way which made our stay so comfortable and memorable."

Westport C12

The Victorian Lady

57 S Main St
Westport, NY 12993
(518)962-2345 Fax:(518)962-2345
E-mail: victorianlady@westelcom.com
Web: www.victorianladybb.com

Circa 1856. This Second Empire home features all the delicate elements of a true "Painted Lady," from the vivid color scheme to the Eastlake porch that graces the exterior. Delicate it's not, however, having stood for more than a century. Its interior is decked in period style with antiques from this more gracious era. A proper afternoon tea is served, and breakfasts are served by candlelight. More than an acre of grounds, highlighted by English gardens, surround the home. Lake Champlain is a mere 100 yards from the front door.
Innkeeper(s): Doris & Wayne Deswert. $110-125. PC, TC. 4 rooms with PB. Breakfast and afternoon tea included in rates. Types of meals: Gourmet bkfst and early coffee/tea. Beds: KQT. Ceiling fan in room. VCR, fax, copier and library on premises. Weddings and family reunions hosted. Antiquing, fishing, golf, live theater, parks, shopping, downhill skiing, cross-country skiing, tennis and water sports nearby.
Publicity: Victorian Homes Magazine.

Willsboro C13

Champlain Vistas

183 Lake Shore Rd
Willsboro, NY 12996-3418
(518)963-8029
E-mail: rdehatch@aol.com
Web: www.virtualcities.com

Circa 1860. Incredible views of the Adirondack High Peaks, Lake Champlain and Vermont's Green Mountains are enjoyed at this inn in the state's Northeast region. The original farm buildings are listed in the National Register of Historic Places, and guests are free to explore the complex. Relax and enjoy the view of Lake Champlain from the inn's wraparound porch or perhaps by the stone fireplace in the living room. The area offers many things to do, from visiting historic sites to hiking and biking through the beautiful wilderness. The inn is minutes from the ferry to Vermont.
Historic Interest: Among the nearby historic sites is Fort Ticonderoga, the Lake Champlain Maritime Museum and the Shelburne Museum are nearby in Vermont.

Innkeeper(s): Bob & Barbara Hatch. $75-105. 4 rooms, 2 with PB. Types of meals: Full bkfst. Beds: QDT. VCR and art gallery and fitness equipment on premises. Weddings, small meetings and family reunions hosted. Antiquing, fishing, golf, biking, hiking, shopping, downhill skiing, cross-country skiing and water sports nearby.

"It was a joy to feel ourselves at home in such relaxing and indeed beautiful surroundings. The food and the chatter was a great start to the day."

Windham   H11

Albergo Allegria B&B

Rt 296, PO Box 267
Windham, NY 12496-0267
(518)734-5560 Fax:(518)734-5570
E-mail: mail@albergousa.com
Web: www.albergousa.com

Circa 1892. Two former boarding houses were joined to create this luxurious, Victorian bed & breakfast whose name means "the inn of happiness." Guest quarters, laced with a Victorian theme, are decorated with period wallpapers and antique furnishings. One master suite includes an enormous Jacuzzi tub. There are plenty of relaxing options at Albergo Allegria, including a rustic lounge with a large fireplace and overstuffed couches. Guests also can choose from more than 300 videos in the innkeeper's movie collection. Located just a few feet behind the inn are the Carriage House Suites, each of which includes a double whirlpool tub, gas fire-

place, king-size bed and cathedral ceilings with skylights. The innkeepers came to the area originally to open a deluxe, gourmet restaurant. Their command of cuisine is evident each morning as guests feast on a variety of home-baked muffins and pastries, gourmet omelettes, waffles and other tempting treats. The inn is a registered historic site.
Historic Interest: Blenheim Bridge, the longest covered wooden bridge of its kind in the United States, is about a half hour from the inn, as is Olana Castle.
Innkeeper(s): Leslie & Marianna Leman. $73-299. MC, VISA, TC. TAC10. 21 rooms with PB, 8 with FP and 9 suites. Breakfast included in rates. Types of meals: Gourmet bkfst and afternoon tea. Beds: KQT. Cable TV, phone, ceiling fan and VCR in room. Air conditioning. Fax, copier, bicycles, afternoon tea on Saturdays, 24-hour guest pantry with soft drinks and hot beverages and sweets on premises. Handicap access. Weddings, small meetings and seminars hosted. Italian, African and Croatin spoken. Amusement parks, antiquing, bicycling, fishing, hiking, bird watching, waterfalls, parks, shopping, downhill skiing, cross-country skiing, tennis and water sports nearby.
Publicity: *Yankee.*

Country Suite B&B

Rt 23 W, PO Box 700
Windham, NY 12496-0700
(518)734-4079
E-mail: ctrysuite@aol.com

Circa 1875. This carefully restored country farmhouse in the Catskill Mountains two miles from Ski Windham, offers large lawns and a picturesque gazebo. Five guest rooms, all with private baths and king or queen beds, are available to visitors. The inn's country-style furnishings include antiques and family heirlooms. A full gourmet breakfast is offered. After a busy day of exploring the area's historic sites, boutiques and antique shops or enjoying boating, golfing, tennis and other activities, guests often gather in the inn's comfortable living room to relax.
Historic Interest: 100 year old farmhouse and barn.
Innkeeper(s): Lorraine Seidel. $109-159. MC, VISA, AX. 5 rooms with PB. Breakfast included in rates. Types of meals: Gourmet bkfst. Weddings, small meetings, family reunions and seminars hosted. Antiquing and downhill skiing nearby.

"Country elegance with a distinctly urban flair. A treasure to be discovered over and over again."

Worcester   G10

Charlotte Valley Inn & Antiques

Charlotte Creek Rd
Worcester, NY 12197
(607)397-8164
E-mail: cvinn1832@aol.com
Web: www.charlottevalleyantiques.com

Circa 1832. This elegant, imposing Federal Greek Revival stands on two pastoral acres in this historic hamlet surrounded by a glorious valley. Built as a stagecoach stop, the inn is decorated in period antiques, available for purchase. The five guest bedrooms have antique beds, some with canopies. Guests are served a full country breakfast in the Hepplewhite dining room. The meal includes such items as omelettes, homemade breads, muffins and scones, bacon, sausage, toast and quiches. After breakfast, guests can enjoy the common rooms: the parlor, the Empire Reading Room or the sunroom with the natural flagstone floor and the view of Charlotte Valley. Or they may head out for the local attractions: Hanford Mills Museum, Fenimore Art Museum and the Baseball Hall of Fame.
Historic Interest: Soccer Hall of Fame (15 miles), Hanford Mills Museum (8 miles), Farmer's Musuem (330 miles), Fenimore Art Museum (30 miles), Baseball Hall of Fame (30 miles).
Innkeeper(s): Lawrence & Joanne Kosciusko. $90-125. PC. 5 rooms, 3 with PB. Breakfast and snacks/refreshments included in rates. Types of meals: Full bkfst, country bkfst and early coffee/tea. Beds: DT. VCR and library on premises. Antiquing, art galleries, bicycling, fishing, golf, hiking, horseback riding, live theater, museums, downhill skiing, cross-country skiing, tennis and wineries nearby.

North Carolina

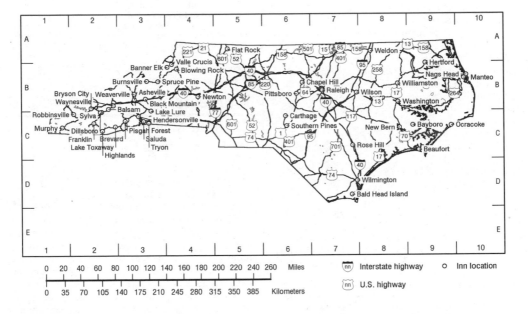

```
0  20  40  60  80  100 120 140 160 180 200 220 240 260   Miles

0   35   70   105  140  175  210  245  280  315  350  385   Kilometers
```

nn Interstate highway   o Inn location

nn U.S. highway

Asheville
B3

1889 WhiteGate Inn & Cottage

173 E Chestnut St
Asheville, NC 28801-2339
(828)253-2553 (800)485-3045 Fax:(828)281-1883
E-mail: innkeeper@whitegate.net
Web: www.whitegate.net

Circa 1889. A white picket fence surrounds this historic home
that prominent businessman Frederick Kent transformed from
Victorian to an English shingle-style structure. Relax in front of
the fire or enjoy the warmth of the solarium. Guest bedrooms
and suites are named to honor American poets and are decorated with antiques and collectibles. The Cottage includes a living room with working fireplace
and full kitchen. A lavish breakfast may include a starter course
of peach halves poached in vanilla
syrup filled with ricotta mousse, a
main course of crab and artichoke
heart egg puff in a white wine and

parsley sauce and a sweet course of chocolate torte in orange
caramel sauce. Afterwards, roam the exotically landscaped yard
with waterfalls, or visit the greenhouse of orchids and tropicals.
Historic Interest: Carl Sandburg house (10 miles), Grove Park Inn (1.5 miles),
Thomas Wolfe house (2 blocks), Biltmore Estate and winery (3 miles).
Innkeeper(s): Frank Salvo & Ralph Coffey. $155-200. MC, VISA, AX, PC.
TAC10. 4 rooms with PB, 3 with FP, 2 suites and 1 cottage. Breakfast
included in rates. Types of meals: Full bkfst, veg bkfst, cont, early coffee/tea
and snacks/refreshments. Beds: Q. Ceiling fan in room. Air conditioning.
VCR, fax and copier on premises. Weddings, small meetings and family
reunions hosted. Antiquing, art galleries, bicycling, canoeing/kayaking, fishing, golf, hiking, horseback riding, live theater, museums, parks, shopping,
downhill skiing, cross-country skiing, tennis and wineries nearby.
Publicity: *Sunset, Bon Appetit, Country Inns and San Francisco Examiner.*

1900 Inn on Montford

296 Montford Ave
Asheville, NC 28801-1660
(828)254-9569 (800)254-9569 Fax:(828)254-9518
E-mail: info@innonmontford.com
Web: www.innonmontford.com

Circa 1900. This National Register home was one of a few
local homes designed by Richard Sharpe Smith, the supervising
architect for the nearby Biltmore Estate. The simple exterior

and pleasing Arts & Crafts style is flanked by a wide veranda for relaxing and enjoying the neighborhood. English and American antiques fill the elegant inn. Well-appointed guest bedrooms feature antique beds and fireplaces. Some

have whirlpool tubs and one boasts a clawfoot tub. A secluded, deluxe five-room whirlpool suite also offers a sitting room and private entrance with balcony. Breakfasts include a special fruit dish such as baked banana souffle, a daily entree and dessert. Spend the day touring historic homes, or hike and raft in nearby wilderness areas.

Innkeeper(s): Ron and Lynn Carlson. $125-295. MC, VISA, AX, DS, PC, TC. TAC10. 5 rooms with PB, 5 with FP and 1 suite. Breakfast included in rates. Types of meals: Gourmet bkfst and early coffee/tea. Beds: KQ. TV, phone and VCR in room. Air conditioning. Fax, copier and library on premises. Weddings, small meetings and seminars hosted. Amusement parks, antiquing, fishing, golf, live theater, parks, shopping, downhill skiing, sporting events, tennis and water sports nearby.

Abbington Green B&B

46 Cumberland Cir
Asheville, NC 28801-1718
(828)251-2454 (800)251-2454 Fax:(828)251-2872

Circa 1908. Innkeeper Valerie Larrea has definitely put her heart and soul into this bed & breakfast. When she discovered the home, located in Asheville's Montfort Historic District, it was desperately in need of a facelift. Through hard work, which included putting in nine bathrooms and replacing the electrical system and all the plumbing, she earned an award for the restoration. The home sports an English decor, and each guest room is named for a park or garden in England. Antiques and reproductions furnish the

home. An inventive breakfast menu is prepared each morning, featuring gourmet tidbits such as homemade pumpkin bread, a warm cherry soup and quiche Florentine with grilled sausage. The home was designed by a supervising architect during the building of the Biltmore Estate, which is nearby and open for tours. The inn also features award-winning gardens. The Blue Ridge Parkway and University of North Carolina also are near.

Innkeeper(s): Valerie, Julie & Gabrielle Larrea. $135-265. MC, VISA, AX, DS, PC, TC. TAC10. 8 rooms with PB, 6 with FP. Breakfast included in rates. Types of meals: Full bkfst. Beds: KQT. Ceiling fan and two and one bedroom suites with whirlpool tubs in room. Air conditioning. VCR, fax, bicycles and library on premises. Antiquing, fishing, golf, white water rafting, live theater, parks, shopping, downhill skiing and tennis nearby.

Publicity: *Asheville Citizen-Times, Summer Magazine, The Plain Dealer, Gazette and Blue Ridge Peak Magazine.*

"Our stay will always be a memorable part of our honeymoon. The breakfasts were outstanding."

Albemarle Inn

86 Edgemont Rd
Asheville, NC 28801-1544
(828)255-0027 (800)621-7435

Circa 1909. Tall Grecian columns mark the majestic entrance to Albemarle. A wide veranda, shaded by mountain pines, welcomes guests. Inside, a carved-oak staircase and massive oak-paneled doors are polished to a high gleam. Guest rooms feature 11-foot ceilings and clawfoot tubs. The Hungarian compos-

er Bela Bartok is said to have written his third concerto for piano while in residence at the inn.

Innkeeper(s): Diana & Tony Morris. $95-160. MasterCard, Visa, Discover, personal checks and Traveler's Cheques. TAC10. 11 total guest accommodations with private bath. Breakfast and snacks/refreshments included in rates. Types of meals: Gourmet bkfst and early coffee/tea. Beds: King, Queen, double and twin. Cable TV, phone and ceiling fan in room. Air conditioning. Swimming on premises. Antiquing, fishing, museum, galleries, horseback riding, tennis, golf, Biltmore Estate, live theater, parks, shopping, sporting events and water sports nearby.

Publicity: *Atlanta Homes, Asheville Citizen-Times, Stages and WLOS TV (ABC).*

"Most outstanding breakfast I've ever had. We were impressed to say the least!"

Applewood Manor Inn

62 Cumberland Cir
Asheville, NC 28801-1718
(828)254-2244 (800)442-2197 Fax:(828)254-0899
E-mail: innkeeper@applewoodmanor.com
Web: www.applewoodmanor.com

Circa 1910. This is a spacious Colonial Revival house furnished comfortably with antiques. Guests can relax in front of the wood-burning fireplace or stroll the inn's two-acre grounds. Accommodations include four guest rooms and a cottage. Cream-cheese omelets, orange French toast, blueberry pancakes or homemade waffles are some of the delectables that appear on the breakfast menu along with fresh fruits, juices and homemade muffins.

Innkeeper(s): Coby & Johan Verhey. $110-125. MC, VISA, PC, TC. TAC10. 4 rooms with PB, 3 with FP and 1 cottage. Breakfast included in rates. Types of meals: Full bkfst and early coffee/tea. Beds: Q. Ceiling fan in room. Air conditioning. Fax, copier and bicycles on premises. Family reunions hosted. French, German and Dutch spoken. Antiquing, Biltmore Estate, live theater, parks and shopping nearby.

Publicity: *Country Inns and Innsider.*

"It goes without saying—the accommodations and breakfasts are outstanding!"

At Cumberland Falls B&B

254 Cumberland Ave
Asheville, NC 28801
(828)253-4085 (888)743-2557 Fax:(828)253-5566

Circa 1903. This Victorian inn stands on nearly an acre in the historic Montford area of Asheville. The grounds have gardens, waterfalls and ponds with koi and lilies. Inside, hardwood floors, Oriental rugs and spacious light-filled rooms with fresh flowers create a serene ambiance perfect for relaxing. The inn has four guest bedrooms and two suites with fireplaces and Jacuzzis. A four-course gourmet breakfast can be served bedside. Guests enjoy delightful offerings like a fresh fruit bowl, pineapple muffins and Belgian waffles with fresh blueberry sauce topped with whipped cream. Home-baked cookies and pastries are available throughout the day. Golfing, biking, horseback riding, hiking and white-water rafting are popular activities. Less rigorous pastimes include touring antique shops, art galleries and wineries. The innkeepers help guests plan day trips to sites like the Thomas Wolfe Memorial.

Historic Interest: Thomas Wolfe Memorial, Vance Memorial, Cherokee Indian Reservation.

Innkeeper(s): Patti & Gary Wiles. $140-210. MC, VISA, AX, DS, PC. 5 rooms with PB, 5 with FP. Breakfast included in rates. Types of meals: Gourmet bkfst, early coffee/tea, afternoon tea, snacks/refreshments and room service. Beds: Q. Cable TV, phone, turndown service, ceiling fan and VCR in room. Central air. Spa on premises. Weddings and family reunions hosted. Antiquing, art galleries, bicycling, canoeing/kayaking, fishing, golf, hiking, horseback riding, Biltmore Estates, white-water rafting, live theater, museums, parks, shopping, tennis and wineries nearby.

Bridle Path Inn

30 Lookout Rd
Asheville, NC 28804
(828)252-0035 Fax:(828)252-0221
E-mail: fjhalton3@aol.com
Web: www.bridlepathinn.com

Circa 1910. Recently renovated, this secluded English-style country inn is surrounded by mountains and offers a quiet setting overlooking the city. Relax in front of the fireplace in the great room. All the guest bedrooms feature small refrigerators stocked with beverages and Wisconsin cheeses and include a porch or private entrance to a veranda. The Lexington Room also boasts a four-poster bed, clawfoot tub and antique shower. Savor a satisfying breakfast in the dining room or on the third-floor veranda with a panoramic view. The nearby Appalachian Trail is full of adventures.

Historic Interest: Biltmore Estate (4 miles), Chimney Rock (19 miles), Smokey Mountains (20 miles).

Innkeeper(s): Fred & Carol Halton. $90-125. MC, VISA, AX, PC, TC. TAC10. 4 rooms with PB. Breakfast included in rates. Types of meals: Gourmet bkfst, veg bkfst and early coffee/tea. Beds: KQT. Cable TV, phone and ceiling fan in room. Air conditioning. Fax and copier on premises. Small meetings and family reunions hosted. Antiquing, art galleries, beaches, bicycling, canoeing/kayaking, fishing, golf, hiking, horseback riding, live theater, museums, parks, shopping, downhill skiing, sporting events, tennis and wineries nearby.

Publicity: *Atlanta Magazine.*

Carolina B&B

177 Cumberland Ave
Asheville, NC 28801-1736
(828)254-3608 (888)254-3608
E-mail: info@carolinabb.com
Web: www.carolinabb.com

Circa 1900. Architect Richard Sharp Smith, whose credits include creating homes for such tycoons as George Vanderbilt, designed this home in Asheville's historic Montford district. Bay windows and porches decorate Carolina's exterior. Inside, rooms feature pine floors, high ceilings and many fireplaces. Guest rooms are furnished with antiques and unique collectibles. The expansive breakfasts include fresh breads, fruits, egg dishes and breakfast meats.

Historic Interest: Historic homes abound in the area, including the famed Biltmore House, Thomas Wolfe home and the Carl Sandburg home.

Innkeeper(s): Sue Birkholz & David Feinstein. $95-175. MC, VISA, DS, PC, TC. TAC10. 6 rooms with PB, 5 with FP and 1 cottage. Breakfast and afternoon tea included in rates. Types of meals: Gourmet bkfst and early coffee/tea. AP. Beds: KQ. Cable TV and ceiling fan in room. Air conditioning. Weddings, small meetings and family reunions hosted. Antiquing, golf, live theater, parks, shopping, downhill skiing and tennis nearby.

Publicity: *Orange County Register, Asheville Citizen-Times, Charlotte and Mid-Atlantic Country.*

"It was like a dream, exactly as we pictured the perfect honeymoon. Excellent host & hostess, very helpful and informative as to local area. Food was wonderful. Rated an A-plus."

Cedar Crest Victorian Inn

674 Biltmore Ave
Asheville, NC 28803-2513
(828)252-1389 (800)252-0310 Fax:(828)253-7667
E-mail: stay@cedarcrestvictorianinn.com
Web: www.cedarcrestvictorianinn.com

Circa 1891. This Queen Anne mansion is one of the largest and most opulent residences surviving Asheville's 1890s boom. A captain's walk, projecting turrets and expansive verandas welcome guests to lavish interior woodwork created by artisans employed by the Vanderbilts. All rooms are furnished in antiques with satin and lace trappings.

Historic Interest: The inn is in the National Register and is three blocks to the Biltmore Estate.

Innkeeper(s): Rita & Bruce Wightman. $140-240. MC, VISA, AX, DC, DS, PC, TC. TAC10. 11 rooms with PB, 5 with FP, 3 suites and 1 cottage. Breakfast and snacks/refreshments included in rates. Types of meals: Full bkfst. Beds: QD. TV, phone, turndown service and ceiling fan in room. Air conditioning. Fax on premises. Antiquing, art galleries, fishing, live theater, parks and shopping nearby.

Publicity: *Travel Holiday, New York Times, New Woman, Southern Living, Good Housekeeping, House Beautiful, Country Inns and National Geographic Traveler.*

"Cedar Crest is a real beauty and will hold a special place in our hearts."

Chestnut Street Inn

176 E Chestnut St
Asheville, NC 28801-2336
(828)285-0705 (800)894-2955
E-mail: innkeeper@chestnutstreetinn.com
Web: www.chestnutstreetinn.com

Circa 1905. This red brick Colonial Revival house in the Chestnut Hill Historic District, features a rotunda-style porch. A front veranda with columns is complete with rockers. Inside are ornate fireplaces, picture rails and high ceilings. Eclectically furnished guest bedrooms offer a variety in decor. Breakfast includes homemade items such as fresh fruit sorbet, scones and blintz souffles. Afternoon tea is available. Dogwoods, maple trees and gardens fill the inn's half acre. Biltmore Estate is a 10-minute drive. Less than one-third mile, downtown Asheville is within walking distance, offering antique shops, art galleries and restaurants.

Innkeeper(s): Beth & Jim Berutich. $130-275. MC, VISA, AX, PC, TC. TAC10. 6 rooms with PB and 2 suites. Breakfast and afternoon tea included in rates. Types of meals: Gourmet bkfst. Beds: KQ. Turndown service and some with fireplaces and whirlpools in room. Air conditioning. Library on premises. Amusement parks, antiquing, fishing, golf, hiking, rafting and Biltmore Estate, parks, shopping, downhill skiing, sporting events, tennis and water sports nearby.

Publicity: *Our State.*

"Spending the weekend in your spotless, charming inn has made an absolutely wonderful impression on us."

Corner Oak Manor

53 Saint Dunstans Rd
Asheville, NC 28803-2620
(828)253-3525 (888)633-3525
E-mail: info@corneroakmanor.com
Web: www.corneroakmanor.com

Circa 1920. Surrounded by oak, maple and pine trees, this English Tudor inn is decorated with many fine oak antiques and handmade items. Innkeeper Karen Spradley has hand-stitched something special for each room, and the house features handmade items by local artisans. Breakfast delights include entrees such as Blueberry Ricotta Pancakes, Four Cheese and Herb Quiche and Orange French Toast. When you aren't enjoying local activities, you can sit on the shady deck, relax in the Jacuzzi, play a few songs on the piano or curl up with a good book.

Historic Interest: Biltmore House and Gardens (one-half mile).
Innkeeper(s): Karen & Andy Spradley. $115-165. MC, VISA, AX, DS, PC, TC. 3 rooms with PB and 1 cottage. Breakfast included in rates. Types of meals: Gourmet bkfst. Beds: Q. Ceiling fan and one cottage with fireplace in room. Air conditioning. Jacuzzi (outdoor) on premises. Family reunions hosted. Antiquing, fishing, live theater, parks and shopping nearby.

"Great food, comfortable bed, quiet, restful atmosphere, you provided it all and we enjoyed it all!"

Dogwood Cottage

40 Canterbury Rd N
Asheville, NC 28801-1560
(828)258-9725
E-mail: dogwoodinn@blueridge.net

Circa 1910. This Carolina mountain home is located a mile-and-a-half from downtown Asheville, on Sunset Mountain. The veranda, filled with white wicker and floral chintz prints, is the focal point of the inn during summer. It affords tree-top views of the Blue Ridge Mountains. Wing chairs and country pieces accent the inn's gleaming hardwood floors. Breakfast is served in the formal dining room or on the covered porch.
Innkeeper(s): Joan & Don Tracy. $110-125. MC, VISA, AX, PC. TAC10. 4 rooms with PB, 3 with FP. Breakfast included in rates. Types of meals: Gourmet bkfst and early coffee/tea. Beds: Q. Ceiling fan in room. Air conditioning. Pet boarding on premises. Handicap access. Weddings and family reunions hosted. Antiquing, fishing, live theater, parks, shopping, downhill skiing, sporting events and water sports nearby.
Pets Allowed.

"Cozy, warm and gracious."

The Lion & The Rose

276 Montford Ave
Asheville, NC 28801-1660
(828)255-7673 (800)546-6988
E-mail: info@lion-rose.com
Web: www.lion-rose.com

Circa 1895. Asheville's Montford Historic District wouldn't be complete without this Queen Anne Georgian, listed in the National Register. Innkeepers Chris & Janis preserve the history of this home with the period decor. The interior is gracious, showcasing the original leaded- and stained-glass windows and

tiger oak wood. A wonderful afternoon tea is served each day, often on the inn's wraparound veranda. Memorable breakfasts are served on English china with silver. Fresh flowers and chocolates welcome guests to their well-appointed rooms.
Innkeeper(s): Chris and Janis Ortwein. $155-255. MC, VISA, AX, DS, TC. 5 rooms with PB and 1 suite. Breakfast and afternoon tea included in rates. Types of meals: Gourmet bkfst. Beds: Q. Cable TV, phone, turndown service, ceiling fan and robes in room. Air conditioning. Small meetings hosted. Antiquing, restaurants, live theater, parks, shopping and water sports nearby.

North Lodge on Oakland

84 Oakland Rd
Asheville, NC 28801-4818
(828)252-6433 (800)282-3602 Fax:(828)252-3034
E-mail: stay@northlodge.com

Circa 1904. This inn was built by an old Asheville family, descendants of the owners of Smith Plantation. It is a three-story lodge that combines native stone work with cedar shingles. There are gables and a portico. Inside, guests enjoy a front parlor, library and French-country dining room. Furnishings include English antiques and Oriental rugs mixed with contemporary pieces. Poached salmon souffle or German apple pancakes are specialties offered at breakfast.

Innkeeper(s): Herb & Lois Marsh. $105-145. MC, VISA, AX, DS, PC, TC. TAC10. 5 rooms with PB. Breakfast and afternoon tea included in rates. Types of meals: Gourmet bkfst. Beds: QDT. Cable TV in room. Air conditioning. Fax on premises. Amusement parks, antiquing, fishing, golf, Biltmore Estate, live theater, parks, shopping, downhill skiing, cross-country skiing, sporting events, tennis and water sports nearby.

"The room was marvelous, breakfasts were delicious, and you certainly were gracious hosts."

The Old Reynolds Mansion

100 Reynolds Hgts
Asheville, NC 28804
(828)254-0496 (800)709-0496
E-mail: innkeeper@oldreynoldsmansion.com

Circa 1855. This handsome, three-story brick antebellum mansion is situated on a four-acre knoll of Reynolds Mountain. Rescued from near ruin by innkeepers Fred and Helen Faber, the home has been restored to its former glory as a gracious Southern manor. Each of the guest quarters reflects a different style from early American to Oriental. Guests can enjoy mountain views from their

own room, by a wood-burning fireplace or on a rocking chair on the inn's wraparound porch. The mansion offers use of a swimming pool set among pine trees.

Historic Interest: Several historic homes, including the Biltmore Estate, Thomas Wolfe home and Carl Sandburg home are a short drive.
Innkeeper(s): Fred, Helen, Lance & Meta Faber. $90-145. MC, VISA, AX, DS, PC, TC. 11 rooms, 9 with PB, 5 with FP, 1 suite and 1 cottage. Breakfast and afternoon tea included in rates. Types of meals: Full bkfst and veg bkfst. Beds: QDT. Ceiling fan in room. Air conditioning. Swimming and library on premises. Amusement parks, antiquing, art galleries, bicycling, canoeing/kayaking, fishing, golf, hiking, horseback riding, live theater, museums, parks, shopping, downhill skiing, tennis and wineries nearby.
Publicity: *Greensboro News & Record and Blue Ridge Country.*

"This was one of the nicest places we have ever stayed. We spent every sundown on the porch waiting for the fox's daily visit."

Richmond Hill Inn

87 Richmond Hill Dr
Asheville, NC 28806-3912
(828)252-7313 (800)545-9238 Fax:(828)252-8726
E-mail: info@richmondhillinn.com
Web: www.richmondhillinn.com

Circa 1889. This renovated Victorian mansion was designed for the Pearson family by James G. Hill, architect of the U.S. Treasury buildings. The elegant estate features a grand entry hall, ballroom, library and 10 master fireplaces with Neoclassical mantels. Guests may choose from accommodations in the luxurious mansion, charming cottages on a croquet court, or the garden rooms amid a striking landscape and facing a waterfall. Gabrielle's Restaurant, which is on the premises, serves gourmet cuisine each evening. The inn is listed in the National Register of Historic Places.

Historic Interest: The Biltmore House and Gardens are 20 minutes away. The Thomas Wolfe Memorial is about 15 minutes from the home, while Carl Sandburg home is an hour away.

Innkeeper(s): Susan Michel. $155-450. MC, VISA, AX, PC, TC. TAC10. 36 rooms with PB, 26 with FP, 3 suites and 3 conference rooms. Breakfast and afternoon tea included in rates. Types of meals: Full bkfst & gourmet dinner. MAP. Beds: KQD. Fax and copier on premises. Handicap access. Croquet court nearby.
Publicity: *Atlanta Journal & Constitution, Southern Living, Victoria, Inn Country USA, Inn Country Chefs, Robb Report and Southern Accents.*

"A great adventure into history. I am moved to tell you how grateful we are that you had the foresight and courage to rescue this wonderful place. The buildings and grounds are elegantly impressive .. and the staff superb! You have created a total experience that fulfills and satisfies."

Wright Inn & Carriage House

235 Pearson Dr
Asheville, NC 28801-1613
(828)251-0789 (800)552-5724 Fax:(828)251-0929
Web: www.wrightinn.com

Circa 1899. Located on a quiet, tree-lined street, this four-story gabled Queen Anne Victorian Mansion is the winner of two restoration awards and its gardens were judged Asheville's best. An inviting wraparound porch with a built-in gazebo, balustrades and columns is a favorite place for morning coffee or evening chats. Guest rooms are furnished with antiques, family heirlooms and lovely linens. Five of the bedrooms feature fireplaces, and one has a balcony. Guests staying in the inn rooms are treated to both afternoon tea, social hour and a breakfast of homemade breads, muffins, granola and tempting entrees. The Celebration Suite is a perfect place for special occasions and includes an entertainment room, two bedrooms, two baths, two fireplaces, a private entrance and a double whirlpool with the same carefully appointed decor evident in the main living area.

Historic Interest: The inn and carriage house are listed in the local and national historic registers. The innkeepers will provide a Sony Walkman and tape for a walking tour of downtown Asheville. The Blue Ridge Parkway, Biltmore House and Smith-McDowell House are only minutes away.

Innkeeper(s): Judi & Bill Ayers. $125-400. MC, VISA, AX, DS, PC, TC. 10 rooms with PB, 3 with FP. Breakfast and afternoon tea included in rates. Types of meals: Gourmet bkfst and early coffee/tea. Beds: KQDT. Cable TV, phone, celebration suite has 5 rooms and both bedrooms have modem access in room.

Central air. Fax, bicycles and library on premises. Small meetings and family reunions hosted. Antiquing, fishing, hiking, live theater, parks, shopping, downhill skiing, cross-country skiing, sporting events and water sports nearby.

Bald Head Island — D7

Theodosia's B&B

2 Keelson Row
Bald Head Island, NC 28461
(910)457-6563 (800)656-1812 Fax:(910)457-6055
E-mail: garrett.albertson@worldnet.att.net
Web: www.theodosias.com

Circa 1817. Although this inn is new, it was built in the grand style of the Victorian era. The home is named after Aaron Burr's daughter, Theodosia, which means, "Gift of God," in Greek. The guest rooms are decorated in an eclectic mix of styles. Guests enjoy views of the ocean, harbor and river from their private porches. The honeymoon suite offers a Jacuzzi tub and beautiful views. Cars are not allowed on the island, but the innkeepers provide guests with golf carts or bicycles, including tandem bikes. The island is a unique place and guests can enjoy a day at the beach or take in the state's oldest lighthouse, which was built in 1817.

Innkeeper(s): Gary & Donna Albertson. $170-275. MC, VISA, DS, PC, TC. TAC5. 13 rooms with PB and 1 suite. Breakfast and snacks/refreshments included in rates. Types of meals: Full bkfst. Beds: KQD. Cable TV and phone in room. Air conditioning. Fax and bicycles on premises. Handicap access. Weddings, small meetings and family reunions hosted. German and Lithuanian spoken. Fishing, golf, parks, tennis and water sports nearby.
Publicity: *The Thomasville Times, Southern Living, Raleigh News and Observer, Charlotte Observer, Money Magazine and Coastal Living.*

Balsam — B2

Balsam Mountain Inn

PO Box 40
Balsam, NC 28707-0040
(828)456-9498 (800)224-9498 Fax:(828)456-9298
E-mail: balsaminn@earthlink.net
Web: www.balsaminn.com

Circa 1905. This inn, just a quarter mile from the famed Blue Ridge Parkway, is surrounded by the majestic Smoky Mountains. The inn was built in the Neoclassical style and overlooks the scenic hamlet of Balsam. The inn is listed in the National Register of Historic Places and is designated a Jackson County Historic Site. It features a mansard roof and wraparound porches with mountain views. A complimentary full breakfast is served daily, and dinner also is available daily.

Innkeeper(s): Merrily Teasley. $115-175. MC, VISA, DS, TC. TAC10. 50 rooms with PB and 8 suites. Breakfast included in rates. Types of meals: Gourmet bkfst, early coffee/tea, picnic lunch and gourmet dinner. Beds: KD. Fax, copier, hiking trails and wildflower walks on premises. Handicap access. Weddings, small meetings, family reunions and seminars hosted. Antiquing, fishing, whitewater rafting, hiking, Blue Ridge Pkwy, parks, shopping and downhill skiing nearby.

"What wonderful memories we have of this beautiful inn."

Banner Elk — B4

1902 Turnpike House

317 Old Turnpike Rd
Banner Elk, NC 28604-7537
(802)898-5611 (888)802-4487 Fax:(802)898-5612
E-mail: info@1902turnpikehouse.com

Circa 1902. This restored farmhouse is located at the foot of Beech Mountain in North Carolina's high country near the Daniel

Boone historic area. It is just minutes from Beech, Sugar and Grandfather mountains. The five spacious guest rooms have down comforters and are appointed with an eclectic blend of antiques and family treasures. Guests may enjoy their first cup of freshly brewed coffee on the covered front porch, or fireside when it's cool, then gather for breakfast around the large farm table set with heirloom china, crystal and turn-of-the-century sterling silver. The breakfast feast begins with home-baked breads and includes such sumptuous courses as chocolate bread pudding in a warm vanilla custard sauce with fresh banana wedges, spicy sausage cheese souffle, yellow and red farm tomatoes, rosemary potatoes and fresh buttermilk biscuits served with local jams and jellies..

Historic Interest: Daniel Boone historic area and battleground (17 miles). Innkeeper(s): Ernie & Becky DuRoss. $75-119. MC, VISA, AX, DS, PC, TC. TAC10. 5 rooms with PB. Breakfast and snacks/refreshments included in rates. Types of meals: Gourmet bkfst and early coffee/tea. Beds: QDT. Cable TV and ceiling fan in room. VCR, fax, spa and guest pantry on premises. Weddings, small meetings and family reunions hosted. Spanish spoken. Antiquing, art galleries, bicycling, canoeing/kayaking, fishing, golf, hiking, horseback riding, live theater, parks, shopping, downhill skiing, cross-country skiing, sporting events, tennis and water sports nearby.

The Banner Elk Inn B&B and Cottages

407 Main St, E
Banner Elk, NC 28604
(828)898-6223
E-mail: info@bannerelkinn.com
Web: www.bannerelkinn.com

Circa 1912. This rose-colored farmhouse was built originally as a church, but later was remodeled by artist Edna Townsend who transformed it into an inn. The home was abandoned eventually and refurbished by current innkeeper Beverly Lait, who decorated it with international flair, filling each room with antiques and

pieces from around the world. Individually decorated rooms feature special items such as an antique brass bed or pewter twin beds, down comforters and bright, airy wallcoverings, lace window dressings and a fabulous new addition room/cottage. For breakfast, Beverly prepares a feast of homemade breads, fresh fruit and mouth-watering entrees such as her sausage and egg casserole and soft cheese pancakes. The inn is a perfect spot to enjoy the natural surroundings of Banner Elk and the Blue Ridge Parkway trails.

Historic Interest: The Mast General Store in Valle Crucis is more than 100 years old.
Innkeeper(s): Beverly Lait. $90-190. MC, VISA. 6 rooms, 5 with PB, 2 suites and 4 cottages. Breakfast and afternoon tea included in rates. Types of meals: Full bkfst, cont and room service. Beds: KQT. Cable TV and phone in room. 2 honeymoon suites on premises. Antiquing, fishing, live theater, downhill skiing and cross-country skiing nearby.
Pets Allowed.
Publicity: *Mountain Getaways, Southern Living, Blue Ridge Country Magazine and Atlanta Magazine.*

"You surely have five-star accommodations with five-star attention."

Bayboro   C9

Bayboro House Hotel

201 Main St
Bayboro, NC 28515
(252)745-7270 (888)BAYBORO
E-mail: bayborohouse@pamilico.net

Circa 1923. Built in the architectural style of a classic Southern plantation house, the inn's large wraparound porch creates a

less intimidating and more relaxing ambiance. Chat by the fire or watch television in the Guest Lounge. Each of the guest bedrooms feature a fireplace, one also boasts a private bath. The home's original kitchen is designated for guest use and is fully equipped. A continental breakfast is served here. The grounds include lawn, shrubs and a rock garden. Visit Tryon Palace, only 16 miles away.

Historic Interest: Tryon Palace (16 miles).
Innkeeper(s): Gus & Janet McDonald. $60. MC, VISA, AX, PC, TC. 4 rooms, 1 with PB, 4 with FP and 1 conference room. Breakfast included in rates. Types of meals: Cont. Beds: QDT. Ceiling fan and fireplace in room. Central air. Fax, copier and library on premises. Small meetings hosted. Spanish spoken. Antiquing, art galleries, bicycling, canoeing/kayaking, fishing, golf, horseback riding, live theater, museums, parks, shopping, tennis and water sports nearby.
Pets Allowed.
Publicity: *As Seen on TV.*

Beaufort   C9

The Cedars Inn

305 Front St
Beaufort, NC 28516-2124
(252)728-7036 Fax:(252)728-1685
Web: www.cedarsinn.com

Circa 1768. The Cedars is comprised of two historic houses, of which, the Main House dates back to 1768. Five of the guest rooms are located in the Main House, and an additional six are located in a restored 1851 house next door. The guest rooms include amenities such as fireplaces, clawfoot tubs, four-poster beds and antiques. All rooms include a private bath, and suites also have a sitting room. The innkeepers also have a honeymoon cottage, which includes a Jacuzzi tub. Both houses include front porches, lined with rocking chairs, on the first and second floors. Hearty breakfasts include such items as banana-walnut pancakes, French toast, croissants, pastries, sausage, bacon, fresh fruit, juices, coffee and tea. The inn has a wine bar featuring a variety of vintages, champagne, beer and non-alcoholic options. The Cedars is located in Beaufort's historic district, and bicycles are available for guests who wish to tour the state's third oldest town.

Historic Interest: The Beaufort Historical Association offers tours of a two-acre complex of historic buildings, including an 1829 jail and a 1796 county courthouse.
Innkeeper(s): Sam & Linda Dark. $95-165. MC, VISA, AX, DS, PC. 11 rooms with PB, 5 with FP, 1 cottage and 1 conference room. Types of meals: Full bkfst. Beds: KQDT. TV in room.
Publicity: *The Washington Post, Greensboro News & Record, Raleigh News & Observer and Chatham News.*

Black Mountain   B3

Red Rocker Country Inn

136 N Dougherty St
Black Mountain, NC 28711-3326
(828)669-5991 (888)669-5991 Fax:(828)669-5560
E-mail: lindbergca@aol.com
Web: www.redrockerinn.com

Circa 1896. Voted as the best B&B in Western North Carolina for 2000 and 2001, an expansive wraparound porch surrounds this three-story country inn located on one acre of pristinely landscaped grounds, 14 miles east of Asheville and the famous Biltmore Estate. Guest rooms such as the Preacher's Room, the

Anniversary Room, Savannah and Elizabeth's Attic are part of the "grandma's place" feel to the inn. Mountain dinners served in the inn's restaurant include Carolina pot roast pie topped with puff pastry with 14 homemade desserts to tempt your sweet tooth nightly.

Innkeeper(s): Craig & Margie Lindberg. $90-155. PC, TC. 17 rooms with PB, 3 with FP. Breakfast, afternoon tea and snacks/refreshments included in rates. Types of meals: Full bkfst, early coffee/tea and dinner. Beds: KQD. Ceiling fan and five with whirlpool tubs in room. Air conditioning. Fax and library on premises. Weddings, small meetings, family reunions and seminars hosted. Antiquing, fishing, golf, live theater, parks, shopping, downhill skiing, tennis and water sports nearby.

Renee Allen House

303 Montreat Rd
Black Mountain, NC 28711-3119
(828)669-1124 (888)393-7829

Circa 1910. Guests at the Renee Allen House choose from a variety of accommodations. There are four bed & breakfast rooms in the main house. The spacious Garden Room includes a canopy bed and a kitchenette. The Captain Tyler Room features a sleigh bed. The innkeepers also offer Eagle Watch, a two-bedroom cabin tucked away in a forested setting. The

cabin sleeps up to six guests and includes a fireplace. For a romantic treat, try the innkeepers' Treehouse. The bedroom ceiling is outfitted with a skylight so guests drift off to sleep under a blanket of starlight. A two-way fireplace warms both the bedroom and living room, and there's a fully equipped kitchen and private deck. The Treehouse sleeps up to four guests. Treehouse and bed & breakfast guests enjoy a full, gourmet breakfast with such treats as French toast stuffed with bananas, nuts and brown sugar, homemade muffins, and fresh fruit. Shops and restaurants are within walking distance, and skiing, golfing and hiking are among the nearby activities.

Innkeeper(s): Sandi Rector/Betty Beahan. $89-125. MC, VISA, PC, TC. TAC10. 6 rooms, 4 with PB, 1 with FP, 1 suite and 1 cabin. Breakfast and snacks/refreshments included in rates. Types of meals: Gourmet bkfst and early coffee/tea. Beds: KQDT. Cable TV and central heat in room. VCR on premises. Small meetings and family reunions hosted. Antiquing, art galleries, bicycling, canoeing/kayaking, fishing, golf, hiking, horseback riding, live theater, museums, parks, shopping, downhill skiing, cross-country skiing, sporting events, tennis and wineries nearby.

Pets allowed: In the mountain cabin only.

Publicity: *Black Mountain News.*

Blowing Rock   B4

The Inn at Ragged Gardens

PO Box 1927, 203 Sunset Dr
Blowing Rock, NC 28605-1927
(828)295-9703 Fax:(828)295-6534
E-mail: innkeeper@ragged-gardens.com
Web: ragged-gardens.com

Circa 1898. Blue Ridge Mountain hospitality and casual elegance are the hallmarks of this inn. The chestnut bark-sided manor with rock columns sits amid an acre of well-tended lawns and gardens. The arts and crafts-style interior features period hardwoods, gran-

ite and hand-forged ironwork. Tastefully furnished guest bedrooms and suites offer hand-pressed linens, European duvets, whirlpool tubs, fireplaces, sitting areas, balconies and patios. The chef creates culinary delights that are enhanced by the inn's organically grown herbs and edible flowers. Breakfast is often enjoyed by the garden.

Innkeeper(s): Lee & Jama Hyett. $170-310. MC, VISA, PC, TC. TAC10. 12 rooms with PB, 12 with FP. Breakfast included in rates. Types of meals: Gourmet bkfst and early coffee/tea. Beds: KQ. Ceiling fan, whirlpools, sitting areas and balconies in room. Air conditioning. Small meetings, family reunions and seminars hosted. Antiquing, fishing, scenic highways, live theater, shopping, downhill skiing and cross-country skiing nearby.

Publicity: *Blue Ridge Country, New York Times* and Member of Select Registry.

"A quiet corner in the heart of the village."

Maple Lodge

152 Sunset Dr
Blowing Rock, NC 28605
(828)295-3331 Fax:(828)295-9986
E-mail: innkeeper@maplelodge.net
Web: www.maplelodge.net

Circa 1943. Guests at this village B&B enjoy a 50-year tradition of innkeeping during their stay. Country antiques and family heirlooms fill the rooms. Lace, handmade quilts and down comforters create a warm, romantic atmosphere in the guest rooms, some of which include canopy beds and fireplaces. The buffet breakfasts are served in the unique Garden Room, which includes a wood-burning stove and stone floor.

Innkeeper(s): Marilyn & David Bateman. $100-180. MC, VISA, AX, PC, TC. TAC10. 11 rooms with PB, 1 suite and 3 conference rooms. Breakfast included in rates. Types of meals: Full bkfst and early coffee/tea. Beds: KQDT. Ceiling fan, some with fireplace and TV in room. Air conditioning. Fax and library on premises. Weddings, small meetings and family reunions hosted. Amusement parks, antiquing, fishing, live theater, parks, shopping, downhill skiing, cross-country skiing, sporting events and water sports nearby.

Brevard   C3

Red House Inn B&B

412 W Probart St
Brevard, NC 28712-3620
(828)884-9349

Circa 1851. Originally built as a trading post, this inn was also the county's first post office and railroad station. It survived the Civil War and years of neglect. Recently renovated, it is furnished with Victorian antiques. The center of town is four blocks away.

Innkeeper(s): Peter & Marilyn Ong. $65-99. MC, VISA, PC, TC. 5 rooms, 4 with PB, 1 with FP, 2 suites and 1 cottage. Breakfast included in rates. Types of meals: Full bkfst and afternoon tea. Beds: QDT. TV and ceiling fan in room. Air conditioning. VCR on premises. Handicap access. Weddings, small meetings and family reunions hosted. Antiquing, fishing, golf, horseback riding, hiking, live theater, parks and tennis nearby.

Publicity: *The Transylvania Times.*

"Lovely place to stay - clean and bright."

Bryson City B2

Charleston Inn

208 Arlington Ave
Bryson City, NC 28713
(828)488-4644 Fax:(828)488-1774
E-mail: staywithus@charlestoninn.com
Web: www.charlestoninn.com

Circa 1926. Framed by a stone wall and shaded by tall trees, Charleston Inn offers rooms in both the original house and the three-story wings, added more recently. Guest rooms feature period reproductions mixed with art and antiques, and each features a stained-glass door created by the innkeepers. There are Jacuzzis, porches set among treetops and a cottage with a fireplace. Hash brown casserole and buttermilk biscuits are favorites at breakfast. The inn's two acres include gardens with a gazebo and a deck with a hot tub overlooking the mountains. Near the southern end of the Blue Ridge Parkway and close to the Great Smoky Mountains National Park, there are opportunities for white-water rafting, hiking, mountain biking and mining for gems.
Innkeeper(s): Scot & Angela. $75-165. MC, VISA, AX, DS, PC, TC. TAC10. 19 rooms with PB and 1 cabin. Breakfast and snacks/refreshments included in rates. Types of meals: Gourmet bkfst and early coffee/tea. Beds: KQ. Ceiling fan and cabin with fireplace in room. Air conditioning. Seven person hot tub on premises. Weddings, small meetings, family reunions and seminars hosted. Amusement parks, antiquing, fishing, golf, parks, shopping, downhill skiing, cross-country skiing, sporting events and water sports nearby.
Publicity: *Southern Living.*

Nantahala Village

9400 Highway 19 W
Bryson City, NC 28713-9129
(828)488-2826 (800)438-1507 Fax:(828)488-9634
E-mail: nvinfo@nvnc.com
Web: www.nvnc.com

Circa 1948. This ridge-top lodge rests on 200 scenic acres in the heart of the Great Smoky Mountains. The lodge, built of fieldstone and wood, houses a wide variety of amenities, including meeting rooms for corporate retreats, gatherings and reunions and a restaurant noted for its traditional Southern cuisine and variety of other dishes. More than 50 additional accommodations offer a choice of private homes, cottages and cabins. The Nantahala River nearby boasts an exciting eight-mile stretch for white-water rafting. Cycling, hiking, fishing and horseback riding are additional pleasures available in the area. Enjoy a scenic train ride on the Great Smoky Mountain Railroad, a Cherokee outdoor theater performance or tubing in Deep Creek, all within a half-hour drive.
Innkeeper(s): John Burton & Jan Letendre. $60-320. MC, VISA, DS, PC, TC. TAC10. Types of meals: Full bkfst, lunch, picnic lunch and gourmet dinner. EP. Beds: KQDT. Cable TV and lake rooms with ceiling fans in room. Air conditioning. VCR, fax, copier, swimming, stables, tennis and fitness room on premises. Handicap access. Weddings, small meetings, family reunions and seminars hosted. Antiquing, bicycling, canoeing/kayaking, fishing, hiking, horseback riding, rafting, scenic train, parks, shopping and water sports nearby.

"A class act, would love to come back and hope to."

Randolph House Country Inn

223 Fryemont Rd, PO Box 816
Bryson City, NC 28713-0816
(828)488-3472 (800)480-3472
Web: www.randolphhouse.com

Circa 1895. Randolph House is a mountain estate tucked among pine trees and dogwoods, near the entrance of Great Smoky Mountain National Park. Antiques, some original to the house, fill this National Register home. Each guest room is appointed in a different color scheme. The house provides an unforgettable experience, not the least of which is the gourmet dining provided on the terrace or in the dining room.
Historic Interest: In the National Register.
Innkeeper(s): Bill & Ruth Randolph Adams. $75-150. MC, VISA, AX, DS, PC, TC. TAC10. 7 rooms, 3 with PB, 4 with FP, 1 cottage and 1 conference room. Breakfast and dinner included in rates. Types of meals: Country bkfst. MAP. Beds: KQD. Air conditioning. Library on premises. Small meetings, family reunions and seminars hosted. Amusement parks, antiquing, bicycling, canoeing/kayaking, fishing, golf, hiking, horseback riding, parks, shopping and tennis nearby.
Publicity: *New York Times and Tourist News.*

"Very enjoyable, great food."

Burnsville B3

The Nuwray Inn

Town Square PO Box 156
Burnsville, NC 28714
(828)682-2329 (800)368-9729 Fax:(828)682-1113
E-mail: nuwrayinn@aol.com

Circa 1833. Surrounded by the scenic Blue Ridge Mountains, this Colonial Revival is the oldest inn continuously operated in the western part of the state. The quaint atmosphere is enhanced by the lobby's large fireplace and the comfortable parlor. The elegant guest bedrooms are decorated with country furnishings. Breakfast choices include an authentic, full English breakfast or traditional Southern regional fare. Relax in the rocking chairs on the first- and second-floor porches while planning  the day's delightful explorations. The changing seasons offer extraordinary beauty and an array of sites, sports and activities.
Historic Interest: Thomas Wolfe Home, Biltmore Estate (Asheville, 45 minutes), Jonesborough, Tennessee (1 hour).
Innkeeper(s): Rosemary & Chuck Chandler. $75-95. MC, VISA, AX, DS, PC. TAC10. 25 rooms, 21 with PB. Breakfast included in rates. Types of meals: Country bkfst, early coffee/tea, afternoon tea and dinner. Beds: KQDT. Cable TV, ceiling fan and antiques in room. Fax on premises. Handicap access. Weddings, small meetings, family reunions and seminars hosted. Antiquing, art galleries, bicycling, canoeing/kayaking, fishing, golf, hiking, horseback riding, Scottish festival, Gemstone festival, arts and crafts fairs, Cherokee casino, live theater, parks, shopping, downhill skiing, tennis and water sports nearby.
Publicity: *Our State, Blue Ridge Mountains Guide, 20/20 and North Carolina Now.*

Wray House B&B

2 South Main St
Burnsville, NC 28714
(828)682-0445 (877)258-8222 Fax:(828)682-3750
E-mail: info@wrayhouse.com
Web: www.wrayhouse.com

Circa 1902. In a quaint small-town setting, this Federal-style inn blends with a Colonial decor to impart a stately elegance. Classic movies, games, books and magazines provide entertainment in the sitting rooms and library. Regal, yet romantic guest bedrooms offer an assortment of luxuries. The Gatehouse offers a private entrance to the courtyard garden, brick floors, beamed ceilings,and a claw-foot tub for two. A satisfying and healthy variety of homemade foods are enjoyed in the breakfast room with a morning paper. The dining room has a separate entrance through a sunroom and can be used for meetings or reserved for a private meal.
Historic Interest: Yancey County Museum (1 mile).

Innkeeper(s): Ron & Julia Thompson. $95-120. MC, VISA, AX, PC, TC. TAC10. 5 rooms with PB, 2 with FP, 1 suite, 1 cottage and 1 conference room. Breakfast, afternoon tea and snacks/refreshments included in rates. Types of meals: Gourmet bkfst, veg bkfst, cont plus, cont and early coffee/tea. Beds: Q. Cable TV and VCR in room. Air conditioning. Fax and copier on premises. Weddings, small meetings, family reunions and seminars hosted. Antiquing, art galleries, canoeing/kayaking, fishing, golf, hiking, horseback riding, live theater, museums, parks, shopping, downhill skiing, cross-country skiing, tennis, water sports and wineries nearby.

Carthage   C6

Lauren's Haven

108 W Barrett St
Carthage, NC 28327
(910)947-2366

Circa 1893. This late 1800s Colonial Revival home celebrates early America with its traditional décor. Also known as The Rose-Hurwitz House, the home received its second story in 1930 and became a bed & breakfast in 1996. The home derives its name from the two families who built and remodeled it — the Roses and the Hurwitzes. Arrangements are delicately crafted for honeymoons and anniversaries, including a private couple's breakfast in the upstairs sun room. Each guest room is tastefully decorated in its own distinct color scheme  and style, complete with a private sitting room and bath. A continental breakfast of muffins, biscuits, poached eggs and seasonal fruit helps start each morning off on the right foot. Just as enjoyable as the house itself are the grounds it rests upon, featuring a small walking garden and fishpond.
Historic Interest: Malcolm Blue Farm (15 miles), Shaw House (10 miles), House-in-the-Horseshoe (17 miles).
Innkeeper(s): Richard & Shaw Oldham. $69. MC, VISA, PC. 3 rooms with PB. Breakfast and snacks/refreshments included in rates. Types of meals: Full bkfst. Beds: QDT. Cable TV and phone in room. Central air. Fax on premises. Small meetings hosted. Antiquing, golf and Asheboro Zoo nearby.
Publicity: *The Pilot.*

Chapel Hill   B6

The Inn at Bingham School

PO Box 267
Chapel Hill, NC 27514-0267
(919)563-5583 (800)566-5583 Fax:(919)563-9826
E-mail: fdeprez@aol.com
Web: www.chapel-hill-inn.com

Circa 1790. This inn served as one of the locations of the famed Bingham School. This particular campus was the site of a liberal arts preparatory school for those aspiring to attend the University at Chapel Hill. The inn is listed as a National Trust property and has garnered awards for its restoration. The property still includes many historic structures including a 1790s log home, an 1801 Federal addition, an 1835 Greek Revival home, the headmaster's office, which was built in 1845, and a  well house, smokehouse and milk house. Original heart of pine floors are found throughout the inn. Guests can opt to stay in the Log Room, located in the log cabin, with a tight-winder

staircase and fireplace. Other possibilities include Rusty's Room with two antique rope beds. The suite offers a bedroom glassed in on three sides. A mix of breakfasts are served, often including pear almond Belgian waffles, quiche or souffles.
Historic Interest: The Orange County Historical Museum is 12 miles from the inn. The Durham Homestead is 20 miles away, and the Horace Williams House and North Carolina Collection Gallery are 10 miles away.
Innkeeper(s): Francois & Christina Deprez. $80-130. MC, VISA, AX, DS, PC, TC. TAC10. 5 rooms with PB, 4 with FP, 1 suite, 1 cottage and 1 conference room. Breakfast and snacks/refreshments included in rates. Types of meals: Gourmet bkfst and early coffee/tea. Beds: QD. Phone, hair dryers and robes in room. Air conditioning. VCR, fax, library, trails and hammocks on premises. Weddings and small meetings hosted. Spanish and French spoken. Antiquing, fishing, live theater, parks, shopping, sporting events and water sports nearby.
Publicity: *Southern Inns, Mebane Enterprise, Burlington Times, Times News and Washington Post.*

Dillsboro   C2

Olde Towne Inn

300 Haywood Rd
Dillsboro, NC 28725-0485
(828)586-3641 (888)528-8840
E-mail: oldetown@gte.net
Web: www.dillsboro-oldetowne.com

Circa 1878. The front porch at the Olde Towne Inn is lined with rockers and benches where guests can enjoy a cool Carolina breeze and view of the town. The home, one of the area's oldest, has been restored and decorated in country style with antiques. A full country breakfast, with items such as homemade muffins, eggs, grits and ham, is served each morning.
Historic Interest: Cherokee Reservation.
Innkeeper(s): Lera Chitwood. $85-125. MC, VISA, AX, DC, CB, DS, PC, TC. 5 rooms, 4 with PB and 1 suite. Breakfast and snacks/refreshments included in rates. Types of meals: Country bkfst. Beds: QDT. Ceiling fan and fireplace in room. Air conditioning. Family reunions hosted. Antiquing, horseback riding, parks and shopping nearby.

Flat Rock   A5

Highland Lake Inn - A Country Retreat

Highland Lake Road
Flat Rock, NC 28731
(828)693-6812 (800)762-1376 Fax:(828)696-8951
E-mail: jgrup@hlinn.com
Web: www.hlinn.com

Circa 1900. A great place for families, this country farm features acres of activities. Besides a visit to the goat barn or watching for the resident peacock, guests may canoe the lake, hike, mountain bike, play volleyball or horseshoes. The inn offers romantic guest bedrooms, some with whirlpool tubs or French doors leading to a porch with rockers. A rustic lodge with cozy rooms and private baths boasts a river rock fireplace in the lobby, and billiards or table tennis in the recreation room. There are several private cabin rooms. Cottages with two to four bedrooms have kitchen facilities and some include a washer, dryer and large outside deck. Fresh organic ingredients from the gardens are used in the restaurant's delicious meals. Explore local Carl Sandburg's home or Flat Rock Playhouse and historic sites in nearby Hendersonville. The Biltmore Estate is 28 miles away.
Innkeeper(s): The Grup Family. $89-215. MC, VISA, AX, DS, PC, TC. TAC10. 52 rooms with PB, 6 with FP, 3 suites, 6 cottages, 10 cabins & 3 conference rooms. Types of meals: Gourmet bkfst, cont plus, cont, gourmet lunch and gourmet dinner. Beds: KQ. Cable TV, phone and ceiling fan in room. Central air. VCR, fax, copier, spa, swimming, bicycles and tennis on premises. Handicap access. Weddings, small meetings, family reunions and seminars hosted. Spanish &

French spoken. Antiquing, art galleries, bicycling, canoeing/kayaking, fishing, golf, hiking, horseback riding, live theater, parks, shopping, tennis & wineries nearby.
Publicity: *Southern Living.*

Franklin   C2

Buttonwood Inn

50 Admiral Dr
Franklin, NC 28734-1981
(828)369-8985 (888)368-8985
E-mail: innkeeperbwbb@msn.com

Circa 1927. Trees surround this two-story batten board house located adjacent to the Franklin Golf Course. Local crafts and handmade family quilts accent the country decor. Wonderful breakfasts are served here—often eggs Benedict, baked peaches and sausage and freshly baked scones with homemade lemon butter. On a sunny morning, enjoy breakfast on the deck and savor the Smoky Mountain vistas. Afterward, you'll be ready for white-water rafting, hiking and fishing.
Innkeeper(s): Liz Oehser. $60-90. MC, VISA, AX, DS. 4 rooms with PB. Breakfast and afternoon tea included in rates. Types of meals: Full bkfst and early coffee/tea. Beds: KDT. Ceiling fan in room. Family reunions hosted. Antiquing, fishing, parks and shopping nearby.

Franklin Terrace

159 Harrison Ave
Franklin, NC 28734-2913
(704)524-7907 (800)633-2431
E-mail: terrace@dnet.net

Circa 1887. This plantation home, built originally to house a school, is listed in the National Register of Historic Places. Each of the guest rooms features period antiques. The innkeepers also offer a cottage that can sleep up to four quite comfortably. Those opting to stay in the historic home are treated to a lavish, breakfast buffet with home-baked muffins, french toast, cereals, juices, fruit, melon, sausages, poached eggs and several different breads. The home is within walking distance to shops, clothing boutiques and a variety of restaurants, but guests are welcome to simply sit and relax on the veranda, which is lined with wicker rocking chairs.
Innkeeper(s): Ed & Helen Henson. $52-69. MC, VISA, AX, DS, PC, TC. TAC10. 9 rooms with PB and 1 cottage. Breakfast included in rates. Types of meals: Full bkfst and early coffee/tea. Beds: KQD. Cable TV and ceiling fan in room. Air conditioning. Small meetings, family reunions and seminars hosted. Fishing, live theater, parks, downhill skiing and water sports nearby.

"We just 'discovered' this wonderful B&B on a trip home from the mountains of North Carolina. The inn offers privacy, porches, unique rooms, comfort, cleanliness and is very pretty."

Hendersonville   C3

Claddagh Inn at Hendersonville

755 N Main St
Hendersonville, NC 28792-5079
(828)697-7778 (800)225-4700 Fax:(828)697-8664
E-mail: innkeepers@claddaghinn.com

Circa 1898. Claddagh has been host for more than 90 years to visitors staying in Hendersonville. The wide, wraparound veranda is filled with rocking chairs, while the library is filled with inviting books. Many of North Carolina's finest craft and antique shops are just two blocks from the inn. Carl Sandburg's house and the Biltmore Estate are nearby, and within a short drive are spectacular sights in the Great Smoky Mountains.

Historic Interest: National Register.
Innkeeper(s): Augie & Gerri Emanuele. $100-150. MC, VISA, AX, DS, PC, TC. TAC10. 14 rooms with PB and 2 suites. Breakfast included in rates. Types of meals: Full bkfst and early coffee/tea. Beds: KQDT. Phone, ceiling fan and TVs in room. Air conditioning. Fax, library, refrigerator and TV on premises. Weddings, small meetings and family reunions hosted. Antiquing, fishing, tennis, golf, live theater, parks, shopping and water sports nearby.
Publicity: *Country Inn, Blue Ridge Country and Southern Living.*

"Excellent food, clean, home-like atmosphere."

Inn on Church Street

201 3rd Ave W
Hendersonville, NC 28739
(828)693-3258 (800)330-3836 Fax:(828)693-7263
E-mail: innonchurch@innspiredinns.com
Web: www.innspiredinns.com

Circa 1920. Restored to its original splendor, this classy yet cozy Craftsman and Art Deco inn sits in the heart of historic downtown, just one block from Main Street. Guests are greeted with fresh-baked cookies around check-in time, and the pleasures continue with a late afternoon social hour and turndown service. Guest bedrooms and suites offer a plethora of decor including folk art, French Country,  Americana, bunnies, golf, Christmas, jungle, horses, birds and teddy bears. The bungalow cottage, perfect for families, features a woodland theme. An upscale breakfast may include almond croissant French toast, Church Street eggs of the day, or spiced pancakes. Relax on the wide, wraparound porch, and enjoy the whimsically decorated gardens.
Historic Interest: Biltmore Estate (25 miles), Carl Sandburg Home (3 miles).
Innkeeper(s): Jessi Eurich. $89-199. MC, VISA, AX, DS, PC, TC. 21 rooms with PB, 2 suites, 1 cottage and 2 conference rooms. Breakfast, afternoon tea and snacks/refreshments included in rates. Types of meals: Gourmet bkfst, veg bkfst, cont plus, early coffee/tea, gourmet lunch and gourmet dinner. Beds: KQ. Cable TV, phone, turndown service, ceiling fan and hot tub in room. Air conditioning. Fax, copier, spa, afternoon social hour and cookies upon check-in on premises. Handicap access. Weddings, small meetings, family reunions and seminars hosted. Antiquing, art galleries, bicycling, canoeing/kayaking, fishing, golf, hiking, horseback riding, live theater, museums, parks, shopping, downhill skiing, sporting events, tennis and wineries nearby.
Publicity: *Our State Magazine, Times News and Asheville Citizen Times.*

Hertford   B9

1812 on The Perquimans B&B Inn

385 Old Neck Road
Hertford, NC 27944-9502
(252)426-1812

Circa 1790. William and Sarah Fletcher were the first residents of this Federal-style plantation home, and the house is still in the family today. The Fletchers were Quakers and the first North Carolina residents to offer to pay the way for workers who wished to return to Africa. The farm rests along the banks of the Perquimans River, and the grounds retain many original outbuildings, including a brick dairy, smokehouse and a 19th-century frame barn. In the National Register of Historic Places, the inn is appropriately appointed with antiques highlighting the restored mantels and woodwork. A lovely, pastoral retreat.
Historic Interest: Federal-style plantation dwelling.
Innkeeper(s): Peter & Nancy Rascoe. $80-85. MC, VISA. 5 rooms. Breakfast included in rates. Types of meals: Full bkfst.

Highlands　　　　　　　C2

Colonial Pines Inn

541 Hickory St
Highlands, NC 28741-8498
(828)526-2060
E-mail: Bnb4info@aol.com

Circa 1937. Secluded on a hillside just half a mile from
Highlands' Main Street, this inn offers relaxing porches that
boast a mountain view. The parlor is another restful option, offer-

ing a TV, fireplace and
piano. Rooms, highlight-
ed by knotty pine, are
decorated with an eclec-
tic mix of antiques. The
guest pantry is always
stocked with refreshments for those who need a little something
in the afternoon. For breakfast, freshly baked breads accompany
items such as a potato/bacon casserole and baked pears topped
with currant sauce. In addition to guest rooms and suites, there
are two cottages available, each with a fireplace and kitchen.

Innkeeper(s): Chris & Donna Alley. $85-150. MC, VISA, PC, TC. 8 rooms, 3
with PB, 3 suites and 2 cabins. Breakfast and afternoon tea included in rates.
Types of meals: Full bkfst. Beds: KQDT. Guest pantry on premises. Antiquing,
fishing, live theater, parks, shopping, downhill skiing and water sports nearby.
Publicity: *Greenville News, Atlanta Journal and Highlander.*

"There was nothing we needed which you did not provide."

Main Street Inn

270 Main St
Highlands, NC 28741-8446
(828)526-2590 (800)213-9142　Fax:(828)787-1142
E-mail: maininn@dnet.net
Web: www.mainstreet-inn.com

Circa 1885. A careful restoration retained the warm character
of this Federal farmhouse built more than 100 years ago.
Cathedral ceilings exposed hand-hewn beams. Original sand-
forged windows were reinstalled as interior windows. Stone fireplaces in the dining room and lobby enhance the mountain
ambiance. Most of the guest bedrooms in the Main House and
the Guest House feature balconies and walk-in showers. Some
offer antique clawfoot tubs and sitting areas. The first-floor
Garden Room boasts a private entrance and patio. Enjoy a hot
country breakfast and afternoon tea. Landscaped grounds
afford impressive photo opportunities as the seasons change.

Innkeeper(s): Farrel & Jan Zehr. $85-185. MC, VISA, AX, PC, TC. TAC10. 19
rooms with PB. Breakfast and afternoon tea included in rates. Types of
meals: Gourmet bkfst and early coffee/tea. Beds: KQDT. Cable TV and phone
in room. Central air. Fax and copier on premises. Weddings, small meetings,
family reunions and seminars hosted. Antiquing, art galleries,
canoeing/kayaking, fishing, golf, hiking, horseback riding, live theater, museums and shopping nearby.

Lake Lure　　　　　　　C3

The Chalet Club

532 Washburn Rd
Lake Lure, NC 28746-0100
(828)625-9315 (800)336-3309　Fax:(828)625-9373
E-mail: bobandanne@chaletclub.com
Web: www.chaletclub.com

Circa 1926. Just 25 miles from Asheville, this compound of
chalets and cottages sits on 300 secluded acres on the eastern
slope of the Blue Ridge Mountains. It's a mile and a half from

Lake Lure. The main chalet has five guest bedrooms and a
main living room. Seven cottages are nearby, some with fireplaces stocked with seasoned wood and balconies with views of
Hickory Nut Gorge and Chimney Rock. The log cabin
Honeymoon Cottage is a favorite for lovers, and Stonehenge 1
and Stonehenge 2 share a pool and are a favorite for reunions.
The inn has earned four Mobil Stars, and it is operated by second and third generation innkeepers. Meals are served in the
main building, but all cottages have refrigerators and coffee
makers. The price includes three meals a day served on the terrace or in the dining room next to the fireplace. A typical dinner consists of delectable courses such as pork loin, sweet
potatoes, green beans, wild rice and blackberry cobbler with ice
cream. Guests also have free use of the club's "On the
Mountain," "Indoor" and "Water Sports" facilities. Guests may
use without charge the club's wet suits, four kayaks, two
canoes and fishing boat. The site also has tennis courts, pools,
seven miles of hiking trails and a recreation house at the lake
that has a pool table and low-impact exercise equipment.

Innkeeper(s): Anne & Bob Washburn. $150-314. MC, VISA, PC, TC. 20 rooms,
17 with PB. Breakfast, picnic lunch, snacks/refreshments and dinner included
in rates. Types of meals: Full bkfst, veg bkfst, early coffee/tea and lunch. AP.
Beds: KQT. Phone, some with fireplaces and decks in room. Central air. VCR,
fax, swimming, tennis, library, canoeing, sea kayaks, waterskiing, shuffleboard
game room and recreation house by lake on premises. Small meetings, family
reunions and seminars hosted. Antiquing, art galleries, bicycling,
canoeing/kayaking, fishing, golf, hiking, horseback riding, Biltmore House and
gardens, Chimney Rock Park, Blue Ridge Parkway, Flat Rock Playhouse, Folk
Art Center, parks, shopping, tennis, water sports and wineries nearby.
Publicity: *Tampa Tribune, Waterski Magazine and Blue Ridge Country Magazine.*

Lake Toxaway　　　　　　　C2

Greystone Inn

Greystone Ln
Lake Toxaway, NC 28747
(828)966-4700 (800)824-5766　Fax:(828)862-5689
E-mail: greystone@citcom.net
Web: www.greystoneinn.com

Circa 1915. Guests the likes of Thomas Edison and John D.
Rockefeller frequented Lake Toxaway for their summer vacations, and the magnificent scenery convinced Savannah heiress
Lucy Armstrong Moltz to build her summer cottage here. Her
magnificent Swiss chalet home now hosts a bounty of guests
hoping to capture the atmosphere of days gone by. Gracious,
elegant rooms feature beautiful antiques and reproductions.
Afternoon tea is served on the wicker-filled sun porch. The
innkeepers host sunset champagne cruises along Lake Toxaway
on a pontoon boat. The inn boasts a restaurant on site which
serves up a variety of breakfast, lunch and dinner specialties. A
championship golf course, tennis, boating, waterskiing and
canoeing are all available.

Historic Interest: Biltmore Estate, George VanderbiltÆs 250-room castle, offers
a vast collection of art and antiques, and is 45 minutes away in Asheville.
Innkeeper(s): Tim & Boo Boo Lovelace. $295-575. MC, VISA. TAC10. 30
rooms with PB and 3 suites. Breakfast, afternoon tea and dinner included in
rates. Types of meals: Full bkfst, picnic lunch and room service. MAP. Beds:
KQD. Cable TV, phone, turndown service, ceiling fan and VCR in room. Air
conditioning. Fax, copier, spa, swimming, sauna, bicycles, tennis, library and
child care on premises. Handicap access. Weddings, small meetings and
family reunions hosted. Antiquing, fishing, golf, live theater, shopping, downhill skiing and water sports nearby.
Publicity: *Country Inns, Southern Living and Southern Accents.*

*"Wonderful! We're already planning our next visit. We haven't felt
this pampered since our last cruise."*

Manteo   B10

White Doe Inn

319 Sir Walter Raleigh St
Manteo, NC 27954-9421
(252)473-9851 (800)473-6091 Fax:(252)473-4708
E-mail: whitedoe@whitedoeinn.com
Web: www.whitedoeinn.com

Circa 1910. For a romantic stay in the Outer Banks, this renovated Queen Anne Victorian on Roanoke Island is enchanting.
Formerly called The Theodore Meekins House and listed in the
National Register, its extraordinary architectural details are frequently photographed. The interior is also an eye-pleaser,
enhanced by comfortable decor and furnishings. Spacious guest
bedrooms are pampering retreats with private garden areas,
bedside fireplaces, two-person whirlpools or an antique clawfoot tub, aromatherapy bath products, fluffy robes, plush
Egyptian cotton linens and towels, CD players and Godiva
chocolates. Southern hospitality excels with a hearty breakfast
garnished with edible flowers and herbs grown on-site, served
in the dining room or on the veranda. Afternoon tea, coffee and
desserts are enjoyed in the library/TV room, and evening sherry
in the parlor. Relax on the wraparound porch with a swing and
rockers or explore the area on a bike.
Historic Interest: Fort Raleigh National Historical Site (3 miles), The
Elizabethan Gardens (3 miles), The Lost colony Outdoor Drama (3 miles), The
NC Maritime Museum on Roanoke Island (3 blocks), Roanoke Island Festiva
Park (4 blocks), NC Aquarium on Roanoke Island (3 miles), Cape Hatteras
National Seashore (5 miles), Wright Brothers National Memorial (15 miles).
Innkeeper(s): Bebe & Bob Woody. $135-230. MC, VISA, AX, PC, TC. TAC10. 8
rooms with PB. Breakfast and afternoon tea included in rates. Types of meals:
Gourmet bkfst, early coffee/tea, picnic lunch and snacks/refreshments. Beds: Q.
Phone, ceiling fan and fireplace in room. Central air. Fax, copier, bicycles, library
and gift shop on premises. Weddings, small meetings, family reunions and seminars hosted. Antiquing, art galleries, beaches, bicycling, canoeing/kayaking, fishing, golf, live theater, museums, parks, shopping, tennis and water sports nearby.

Murphy   C1

Huntington Hall B&B

272 Valley River Ave
Murphy, NC 28906-2829
(828)837-9567 (800)824-6189 Fax:(828)837-2527
E-mail: huntington@grove.net
Web: bed-breakfast-inn.com/

Circa 1881. This two-story country Victorian home was built
by J.H. Dillard, the town mayor and twice a member of the
House of Representatives. Clapboard siding and tall columns
accent the large front porch. An
English country theme is highlighted
throughout. Afternoon refreshments
and evening turndown service are
included. Breakfast is served on the
sun porch. Murder-mystery, summer-
theater, and white-water-rafting packages are available.

Innkeeper(s): Curt & Nancy Harris. $65-125.
MC, VISA, AX, DS, PC, TC. TAC10. 5 rooms with PB. Breakfast included in
rates. Types of meals: Gourmet bkfst and early coffee/tea. MAP. Beds: KQDT.
Cable TV, turndown service and ceiling fan in room. Air conditioning. VCR,
fax, copier and library on premises. Weddings, small meetings, family
reunions and seminars hosted. Antiquing, fishing, live theater, parks, shopping, tennis and water sports nearby.
Publicity: *Atlanta Journal, Petersen's 4-Wheel and New York Times.*

"A bed and breakfast well done."

Nags Head   B10

First Colony Inn

6720 S Va Dare Tr
Nags Head, NC 27959
(252)441-2343 (800)368-9390 Fax:(252)441-9234
E-mail: innkeeper@firstcolonyinn.com
Web: www.firstcolonyinn.com

Circa 1932. This Shingle-style inn features two stories of con-
tinuous verandas on all four sides. It is the last of the original
beach hotels built on the Outer Banks. To save it from destruc-
tion, the Lawrences moved it to family property three miles
south. During the midnight move, townsfolk lined the streets

cheering and clapping to see the preservation of this historic building. First Colony boasts a
pool, croquet court, pri-
vate beach access and
ocean and sound views
from the second and third floors. Furnishings include antiques
and traditional reproductions. There are Jacuzzis, kitchenettes,
an elegant library and a sunny breakfast room.
Historic Interest: Chicamacomico Lifesaving Station (20 miles), Wright Brothers
Memorial (9 miles), the Outer Banks is the "Graveyard of the Atlantic," with
many shipwrecks from the 16th century on. Elizabeth II, replica 16th-century
ship (9 miles), Fort Raleigh, site of first English colony in the New World.
Innkeeper(s): The Lawrences. $80-310. MC, VISA, AX, DS, PC, TC. TAC10. 26
rooms with PB, 6 suites and 1 conference room. Breakfast and afternoon tea
included in rates. Types of meals: Full bkfst, early coffee/tea and room service.
Beds: KQT. Cable TV, phone, VCR, wet bars, kitchenettes, Jacuzzi and hair dryers in room. Air conditioning. Fax, copier, swimming, library, BBQ, beach
chairs, towels, umbrellas and modem ports on premises. Handicap access.
Weddings, small meetings, family reunions and seminars hosted. Beaches, fish-
ing, historic sites, lighthouses, live theater, parks and water sports nearby.
Publicity: *Southern Living, Washington Post, Carolina Style, Greensboro
News & Record, Discerning Traveler, Raleigh News & Observer, High Point
Enterprise, Lexington Dispatch, Portofolio, Coast, Norfolk Virginian, USA
Today, Outer Banks Magazine and Our State Magazine.*

"Great, well done, nothing to change."

New Bern   C8

Aerie Inn Bed & Breakfast

509 Pollock St
New Bern, NC 28562-5611
(252)636-5553 (800)849-5553 Fax:(252)514-2157

Circa 1882. This late Victorian home features an appealing
three-sided bay that adds to its architecture. The innkeepers
offer a choice of three entrees at breakfast. A huge herb and
flower garden on the grounds is
frequented by the cook and
enjoyed by guests. Tryon Palace
with its beautiful kitchen garden
and ornamental garden is a one-
block walk from the inn, and there
are a variety of boutiques, antique
shops and restaurants nearby.

Innkeeper(s): Doug & Donna Bennetts. $89-109. MC, VISA, DS, PC. 7
rooms with PB, 5 with FP. Breakfast included in rates. Types of meals: Full
bkfst and early coffee/tea. Beds: KQT. TV and phone in room. Air conditioning. Fax, herbal/flower garden, player piano and refreshments available on
premises. Antiquing, beaches, golf and museums nearby.

Harmony House Inn

215 Pollock St
New Bern, NC 28560-4942
(252)636-3810 (800)636-3113 Fax:(252)636-3810
E-mail: harmony@cconnect.net
Web: www.harmonyhouseinn.com

Circa 1850. Long ago, this two-story Greek Revival was sawed in half and the west side moved nine feet to accommodate new hallways, additional rooms and a staircase. A wall was then built to divide the house into two sections. The rooms are decorated with antiques, the innkeeper's collection of handmade crafts and other collectibles. Two of the suites includes a heart-shaped Jacuzzi tub. Offshore breezes sway blossoms in the lush garden. Cross the street to an excellent restaurant or take a picnic to the shore.

Innkeeper(s): Ed & Sooki Kirkpatrick. $109-150. MC, VISA, DS, PC, TC. TAC10. 7 rooms, 10 with PB, 10 with FP, 3 suites and 2 conference rooms. Breakfast and snacks/refreshments included in rates. Types of meals: Full bkfst and early coffee/tea. Beds: KQT. Cable TV, phone and ceiling fan in room. Air conditioning. Fax on premises. Weddings, small meetings, family reunions and seminars hosted. Korean spoken. Antiquing, parks, shopping and water sports nearby.
Publicity: *Atlanta Constitution, Raleigh News and Observer and Bon Appetit.*

"We feel nourished even now, six months after our visit to Harmony House."

Newton   B4

The Trott House Inn, Inc

802 N Main Ave
Newton, NC 28658-3148
(828)465-0404 Fax:(828)465-5753
Web: www.trotthouse.com

Circa 1897. Trott House was built originally as a hunting lodge, the section that houses the inn guest rooms was part of a later addition. Room choices include four guest rooms decorated with Victorian accents and a spacious suite. The suite includes an in-room Jacuzzi. For honeymooners, the innkeepers can provide breakfast in the privacy of your bedchamber, as well as providing fresh flowers and champagne. In addition to the gourmet breakfasts, guests are pampered with afternoon refreshments and turndown service.

Innkeeper(s): Anne. $75-110. MC, VISA, PC. 5 rooms with PB and 1 suite. Breakfast and snacks/refreshments included in rates. Types of meals: Gourmet bkfst and early coffee/tea. Beds: KQT. Cable TV, phone and ceiling fan in room. Central air. Fax, copier and spa on premises. Small meetings, family reunions and seminars hosted. Antiquing, art galleries, fishing, golf, live theater, museums and parks nearby.

Ocracoke   C9

The Castle on Silver Lake

PO Box 908
Ocracoke, NC 27960
(252)928-3505 (800)471-8848 Fax:(252)928-3501
E-mail: innkeeper@thecastlebb.com
Web: www.thecastlebb.com

Circa 1948. On North Carolina's famous Outer Banks just yards from Silver Lake and Ocracoke Island's harbor, stands the Castle on Silver Lake. This Colonial American/Williamsburg mansion was built by decoy carvers and boat builders of yesteryear. Cedar shakes and seven cozy dormers with gables make this charming castle a port in anyone's storm. The 9,000-square-foot castle is on two meticulously landscaped acres that

has flowers in bloom nearly all year. A 40-foot jasmine arbor leads to the heated swimming pool, and a Lantana-lined walkway leads to the sundeck on the dock. The castle was built by Sam Jones of Norfolk, Va., over a period of three decades. Jones is a local legend, and he's buried on the island with his horse Ikey D. The inn is in the National Register and the Local Register, and is a State Historic Site. A rental duplex called the Castle Villas was built next to the castle, and this structure is more suitable for children than the bed & breakfast itself. The castle's common rooms include the parlor with large windows that look out over the harbor, and the den with its warm woods. Children enjoy swimming in the pool and fishing from the pier that extends into Silver Lake Harbor. The inn has 20 bikes for guests to use free of charge. The castle has one suite, eight cottages and 10 guest bedrooms. The bathroom in the third-floor Lighthouse Room is a loo with a magnificent view. A country breakfast, afternoon tea and snacks and refreshments are included in the tariff. The breakfast includes delights such as bacon, sausage grilled outdoors, eggs to order, hot biscuits, fruit, cereals, grits or potatoes, juices and hot drinks. The castle is just two blocks from Ocracoke Lighthouse, one of the oldest working lighthouses in America and a short driving distance to Norfolk, Va., and Raleigh, N. C.

Historic Interest: Oracoke lighthouse (2 blocks).

Innkeeper(s): Jim & Mary Ellen Piland, Jenny & David Foss. $109-259. MC, VISA, DS, PC, TC. 10 rooms with PB, 1 suite, 8 cottages and 1 conference room. Breakfast, afternoon tea and snacks/refreshments included in rates. Types of meals: Country bkfst and early coffee/tea. Beds: QT. Cable TV, phone, VCR, fireplace and large decks and porches with water view in room. Central air. Fax, copier, swimming, sauna, bicycles, day spa with masseuse and steamrooms and heated pool on premises. Weddings, small meetings and family reunions hosted. Deaf interpreter spoken. Antiquing, art galleries, beaches, bicycling, canoeing/kayaking, fishing, hiking, offshore fishing, the Castle has docks on the harbor, museums, shopping and water sports nearby.
Publicity: *Metro Magazine.*

Pisgah Forest   C3

Key Falls Inn

151 Everett Rd
Pisgah Forest, NC 28768-8621
(828)884-7559 Fax:(828)885-8342

Circa 1860. The back section of this fascinating Victorian farmhouse was constructed prior to the Civil War and the front section after the war. The meadow in front of the home is reputed to have been a Civil War encampment area. The inn sits on 35 acres near Blue Ridge Parkway and Pisgah National forest with hiking and bike trails and numerous waterfalls. Accommodations include two suites, decorated in Victorian and other antiques and reproductions. In addition to the guest rooms at Key Falls Inn, there is now a guest room with a private entrance at River Bend, which is a historic reproduction home near the inn on five wooded acres overlooking the French Broad River. The spacious guest bedroom has a fireplace and refrigerator. A breakfast basket with fresh baked good and fruit is placed in the room each day. Guests in the farmhouse feast on a full breakfast that includes dishes such as breakfast bacon or sausage with eggs or a hot casserole. Juice, fruit compote, biscuits, sweet rolls, French toast, cereal and bananas are additional offerings. The Key Falls Trail begins at the inn and climbs toward a waterfall. A pond on the property, fed by a cascading stream, has two docks for sunning or fishing for bass or bream. There's also a waterfall on the property. A porch with the requisite rockers boasts a spectacular view of the mountains. The inn is 45 minutes from Biltmore Estate, 15 miles from the Carl Sandburg Home and 35 miles from the Thomas Wolfe Home.

Innkeeper(s): Clark & Patricia Grosvenor & Janet Fogleman. $60-105. MC, VISA, AX, DS, PC, TC. 6 rooms, 4 with PB, 1 with FP and 2 suites. Breakfast and snacks/refreshments included in rates. Types of meals: Full bkfst, country bkfst and early coffee/tea. Beds: KQ. Cable TV, phone, ceiling fan and VCR in room. Central air. Fax and tennis on premises. Family reunions hosted. Antiquing, art galleries, bicycling, canoeing/kayaking, fishing, golf, hiking, horseback riding, Brevard music center, live theater, museums, parks, shopping and tennis nearby.

Pittsboro   B6

The Fearrington House Inn

2000 Fearrington Village Ctr
Pittsboro, NC 27312-8502
(919)542-2121 Fax:(919)542-4202
E-mail: fhouse@fearrington.com
Web: www.fearrington.com

Circa 1927. The Fearrington is an old dairy farm. Several of the original outbuildings, including the silo and barn, have been converted into a village with a potter's shop, bookstore, jewelry shop, and a Southern garden shop. The original homestead houses an award-winning restaurant. The inn itself is of new construction and its rooms overlook pasture land with grazing sheep, as well as a courtyard. Polished pine floors, fresh floral prints and amenity-filled bathrooms are among the inn's offerings.

Innkeeper(s): Richard Delany. $195-385. MC, VISA, AX, PC. TAC10. 33 rooms with PB, 5 with FP, 12 suites and 3 conference rooms. Breakfast and afternoon tea included in rates. Types of meals: Gourmet bkfst, early coffee/tea, lunch, picnic lunch, snacks/refreshments, gourmet dinner and room service. Beds: KQDT. Cable TV, phone, turndown service, VCR and heated towel racks in room. Air conditioning. Fax, copier, spa, swimming, bicycles and tennis on premises. Handicap access. Weddings, small meetings and seminars hosted. German and French spoken. Antiquing, fishing, golf, live theater, parks, shopping, sporting events, tennis and water sports nearby. Publicity: Bon Appetit, Southern Living, Gourmet, Country Inns, Living It Up and North Carolina Homes and Gardens.

"There is an aura of warmth and caring that makes your guests feel like royalty in a regal setting!"

Raleigh   B7

The Oakwood Inn B&B

411 N Bloodworth St
Raleigh, NC 27604-1223
(919)832-9712 (800)267-9712 Fax:(919)836-9263
E-mail: oakwoodbb@aol.com

Circa 1871. Presiding over Raleigh's Oakwood Historic District, this lavender and gray Victorian beauty is in the National Register. A formal parlor is graced by rosewood and burgundy velvet, while guest rooms exude an atmosphere of vintage Victoriana.

Innkeeper(s): Gary & Doris Jurkiewicz. $95-175. MC, VISA, AX, DS. TAC10. 6 rooms with PB, 6 with FP and 1 conference room. Types of meals: Full bkfst. Beds: KQD. Cable TV in room. Fax, copier, afternoon refreshments, complimentary beverage alcove and lighted off-street parking on premises.

Publicity: Business Digest, Connoisseur, Southern Living and The Inside Scoop.
"Resplendent and filled with museum-quality antique furnishings." - Kim Devins, Spectator

The William Thomas House

530 N Blount St
Raleigh, NC 27604
(919)755-9400 (800)653-3466 Fax:(919)755-3966
E-mail: lofton@williamthomashouse.com
Web: www.williamthomashouse.com

Circa 1881. This Victorian home is located in downtown Raleigh, within walking distance of the Governor's mansion and the Capitol building. The interior, which boasts high ceilings, carved molding, hardwood floors, is decorated in an elegant style. Walls are painted in bright, cheerful hues, and the furnishings include antiques. The grounds are decorated with flowers, foliage and shaded by trees, and guests can relax on a porch swing, hammock or rocking chairs. There is ample off-street parking located behind the house. Frances Gray Patton, who wrote the book, "Good Morning, Miss Dove," was born in the home.

Innkeeper(s): Jim & Sarah Lofton. $115-165. MC, VISA, AX, DC, CB, DS, PC, TC. 4 rooms with PB and 1 conference room. Breakfast and snacks/refreshments included in rates. Types of meals: Full bkfst and early coffee/tea. Beds: KQT. Cable TV, phone, turndown service, ceiling fan and VCR in room. Air conditioning. Fax, library and CD stereo player on premises. Weddings, small meetings, family reunions and seminars hosted. Antiquing, golf, live theater, parks, shopping and sporting events nearby. Publicity: News & Observer. and WRAL-TV.

"You have achieved a level of comfort, atmosphere and warmth that most B&Bs strive for."

Robbinsville   C2

Snowbird Mountain Lodge

275 Santeetlah Rd
Robbinsville, NC 28771-9712
(828)479-3433
E-mail: innkeeper@snowbirdlodge.com
Web: www.snowbirdlodge.com

Circa 1940. Panoramic, 40-mile views are one of the many reasons to visit this mountain-top lodge. One innkeeper is a trained chef, and the other a knowledgeable outdoorsman. So guests not only enjoy gourmet meals, but learn where to find the best hiking and nature trails in North Carolina. The lodge is decorated in a rustic style, with an emphasis on comfort. Guest rooms offer handmade quilts, ceiling fans, refrigerators and wood-paneled walls. Each room sports a different variety of wood and some rooms have whirlpool tubs, fireplaces or steam showers. Furnishings have been built by local craftsman using wood native to the area. A favorite place to relax is the 3,000-volume library/main lodge with its huge stone fireplace. Breakfast, lunch and a three-course gourmet dinner is included in the rates. The innkeepers offer many interesting activities, such as a dulcimer clinic, fly-fishing excursions, cooking seminars and nature walks or hikes led by experienced guides.

Innkeeper(s): Karen & Robert Rankin. $175-325. MC, VISA, PC, TC. 25 rooms with PB. Breakfast, picnic lunch and dinner included in rates. Types of meals: Full bkfst and early coffee/tea. AP. Beds: KQDT. Ceiling fan, whirlpool tubs, fireplaces and steam showers available in room. Library on premises. Handicap access. Weddings, small meetings, family reunions and seminars hosted. Bicycling, canoeing/kayaking, fishing, hiking and horseback riding nearby. Publicity: Southern Living, Country Inns, Chicago Suntimes, New York Times, Atlanta Journal, Mens Journal and National Geographic.

Rose Hill   C7

Six Runs Plantation, Inc

2794 Register Sutton Road
Rose Hill, NC 28458
(910)532-4591

Circa 1828. A rice plantation 200 years ago and a hunting pre-serve for 20 years, the rustic lodge of pegged heart pine and juniper logs offers deluxe accommodations. The decor is Colonial, with leather Chippendale and Queen Anne furnish-ings. The large log great room features exposed beams, an open fire, grand piano and satellite TV. There is a fireplace in the lounge, and the formal dining room is spacious and perfect for conferences. The namesake, Six Runs River, weaves through 1,000 acres enhancing the natural habitat of game including quail, ducks and deer. Walking trails, an indoor Jacuzzi, sun porch and decks provide relaxing interludes.
Innkeeper(s): Becky Edwards. $125. 8 rooms, 5 with PB, 1 with FP. Breakfast included in rates. Types of meals: Cont, picnic lunch, snacks/refreshments and gourmet dinner. Canoeing/kayaking, fishing, hiking, bird watching, dirt bike trails, wildflowers, hunting, sporting clays and historic battlefields nearby.
Pets allowed: kennels and guides provided for hunting guests.

Saluda   C3

The Oaks

339 Greenville St
Saluda, NC 28773-9775
(828)749-9613 (800)893-6091
E-mail: oaks@saluda.tds.net
Web: www.theoaksbedandbreakfast.com

Circa 1894. The Oaks is a Victorian bed & breakfast furnished with American and Oriental antiques and original art work.

Guests enjoy the mountain breezes from the wraparound porch and decks, playing croquet in the yard, reading by the fire in the library or chatting in the living room. The Oaks has four bedrooms, each with a private bath, air-conditioning, cable TV and sitting area. Three rooms are furnished with antiques and queen four-poster beds and one room has three single beds. Two suites in a separate guest house are also available. Country break-fasts are served family-style in the dining room.
Innkeeper(s): Crowley & Terry Murphy. $115-175. MC, VISA, AX, DS. TAC10. 4 rooms with PB and 2 suites. Breakfast included in rates. Types of meals: Full bkfst and early coffee/tea. Beds: KQT. Cable TV in room. Air con-ditioning. Weddings and family reunions hosted. Antiquing, fishing, near the Biltmore and shopping nearby.

"Everything about The Oaks was what we wanted it to be, lovely, comfortable, fun and the food delicious."

Southern Pines   C6

Knollwood House

1495 W Connecticut Ave
Southern Pines, NC 28387-3903
(910)692-9390 Fax:(910)692-0609
E-mail: knollwood@pinehurst.net
Web: www.knollwoodhouse.com

Circa 1925. Fairway dreams await golfers at this English-manor-style inn where upstairs sitting rooms overlook the 14th and 15th holes of the beautiful Mid-Pines golf course. The

inn's lawns roll down 100 feet or so to the course, which is a masterpiece by Scottish golf course architect Donald Ross. More than 30 golf courses are within 20 miles. There have been many celebrations under the crystal chandelier and 10-foot ceilings, and the Glenn Miller Orchestra once played on the back lawn.
Innkeeper(s): Dick & Mimi Beatty. $100-170. MC, VISA, PC, TC. TAC10. 6 rooms with PB, 1 with FP and 4 suites. Breakfast included in rates. Types of meals: Gourmet bkfst. Beds: QDT. Turndown service in room. Air condition-ing. VCR, fax, copier, swimming, tennis and library on premises. Weddings, small meetings and family reunions hosted. Antiquing, golf, live theater, parks, shopping and sporting events nearby.

Spruce Pine   B3

Richmond Inn B&B

51 Pine Ave
Spruce Pine, NC 28777-2733
(828)765-6993 Fax:(707)356-4880
E-mail: innkeeper@richmond-inn.com
Web: www.richmond-inn.com

Circa 1939. The scent of freshly baked muffins and steaming coffee serves as a pleasing wake-up call for guests staying at this country mountain home. More than an acre of wooded grounds surround the inn, which overlooks the Toe River valley. Rooms are decorated with family heirlooms and antiques. Several guest rooms include four-poster beds. Crackling flames from the stone fireplace warm the living room, a perfect place to relax. The innkeepers keep a guest refrigerator in the butler's pantry.
Innkeeper(s): Maggie Haskell & Family. $65-125. MC, VISA, DS, TC. 8 rooms with PB, 1 with FP and 2 suites. Breakfast included in rates. Types of meals: Full bkfst and early coffee/tea. Beds: QT. Ceiling fan and Jacuzzi in suite in room. VCR and fax on premises. Small meetings and family reunions hosted. Antiquing, golf, gem mining, crafts, parks, shopping, downhill skiing and cross-country skiing nearby.
Pets Allowed.

Sylva   C2

The Freeze House B&B

71 Sylvan Heights
Sylva, NC 28779-2523
(828)586-8161 Fax:(828)631-0714
E-mail: freezeh@dnet.net

Circa 1917. Two-hundred-year-old oak trees shade this brick cottage, one of the oldest buildings in the village. There's a comfortable porch for enjoying the relaxing views. Guests might enjoy water rafting or taking a train through the Tuckasiegee Valley or the Nantahala Gorge. Guests may break-fast on cheese grits, country sausage and scrambled eggs with sauteed mushrooms and tomatoes on the side.
Innkeeper(s): Patrick & Mary Ellen Montague. $65-150. PC, TC. TAC10. 3 rooms with PB and 2 cottages. Breakfast included in rates. Types of meals: Gourmet bkfst. Beds: D. Cable TV in room. Air conditioning. VCR, fax and library on premises. French and German spoken. Antiquing, art galleries, bicycling, canoeing/kayaking, fishing, hiking, live theater, museums, parks, shopping, tennis and water sports nearby.

Mountain Brook

208 Mountain Brook Rd #19
Sylva, NC 28779-9659
(828)586-4329
E-mail: vacation@mountainbrook.com
Web: www.mountainbrook.com

Circa 1930. Located in the Great Smokies, Mountain Brook consists of 14 cottages on a hillside amid rhododendron, elm, maple and oak trees. The resort's 200-acre terrain is crisscrossed with brooks and waterfalls, contains a trout-stocked pond and nature trail. Two cottages are constructed with logs from the property, while nine are made from native stone. They feature  fireplaces, full kitchens, porch swings and some have Jacuzzi's. Innkeeper(s): Gus, Michele, Maqelle McMahon. $90-140. TC. TAC10. 12. cottages with PB, 12 with FP. Types of meals: Early coffee/tea. Beds: KD. Game room and spa/sauna bungalow on premises. Handicap access. Weddings and family reunions hosted. Amusement parks, antiquing, fishing, golf, casino, Great Smokies National Park, railroad. nature trail, live theater, shopping, downhill skiing, sporting events, tennis and water sports nearby. Publicity: *Brides Magazine, Today and The Hudspeth Report.*

"The cottage was delightfully cozy, and our privacy was not interrupted even once."

Tryon   C3

Foxtrot Inn

PO Box 1561, 210 Fox Trot Lane
Tryon, NC 28782-1561
(828)859-9706 (888)676-8050
E-mail: wim@foxtrotinn.com
Web: www.foxtrotinn.com

Circa 1915. Located on six acres in town, this turn-of-the-century home features mountain views and large guest rooms. There is a private two bedroom guest cottage with its own kitchen and a hanging deck. The rooms are furnished with antiques. The Cherry Room in the main house has a  four-poster, queen-size canopy bed with a sitting area overlooking the inn's swimming pool. The Oak Suite includes a wood-paneled sitting room with cathedral ceiling. A cozy fireplace warms the lobby. Innkeeper(s): Wim Woody. $85-150. PC. 4 rooms with PB, 2 suites and 1 cottage. Breakfast included in rates. Types of meals: Full bkfst. Beds: QDT. Air conditioning. Swimming on premises. Weddings, small meetings, family reunions and seminars hosted. Antiquing, fishing, parks, shopping & water sports nearby. Pets allowed: Pets allowed in cottage by special arrangement.

Pine Crest Inn

85 Pine Crest Ln
Tryon, NC 28782
(828)859-9135 (800)633-3001 Fax:(828)859-9135
E-mail: info@pinecrestinn.com
Web: www.pinecrestinn.com

Circa 1906. Once a favorite of F. Scott Fitzgerald, this inn is nestled in the foothills of the Blue Ridge Mountains. Opened in 1917 by famed equestrian Carter Brown, the inn offers guests romantic fireplaces, gourmet dining and wide verandas that offer casual elegance. The Blue Ridge Parkway and the famous

Biltmore House are a short drive away. Rooms are available in the Main Lodge and cottages. Original buildings include a 200-year-old log cabin, a woodcutter cottage and a stone cottage. Elegant meals are served in a Colonial tavern setting for full breakfasts and gourmet dinners.
Historic Interest: Biltmore House (30 miles), Cowpens Battlefield (30 miles), Chimney Rock (20 miles).
Innkeeper(s): Debby & Barney DuBois. $110-550. MC, VISA, AX, DS. TAC10. 35 rooms with PB, 27 with FP, 17 suites, 5 cottages, 3 cabins, 2 guest houses and 3 conference rooms. Breakfast, afternoon tea and snacks/refreshments included in rates. Types of meals: Gourmet bkfst, early coffee/tea, picnic lunch, gourmet dinner and room service. Beds: KQDT. Cable TV, phone, turndown service, ceiling fan and VCR in room. Central air. Fax, copier, spa, library, child care and gift shop on premises. Weddings, small meetings, family reunions and seminars hosted. Antiquing, art galleries, bicycling, canoeing/kayaking, fishing, golf, hiking, horseback riding, live theater, parks, shopping, tennis, water sports and wineries nearby. Publicity: *Southern Living and Wine Spectator.*

"We felt pampered and at home in your lovely Pine Crest Inn."

Valle Crucis   B4

The Mast Farm Inn

PO Box 704
Valle Crucis, NC 28691-0704
(828)963-5857 (888)963-5857 Fax:(828)963-6404
E-mail: stay@mastfarminn.com
Web: www.mastfarminn.com

Circa 1812. Listed in the National Register of Historic Places, this 18-acre farmstead includes a main house and seven outbuildings, one of them a log cabin built in 1812. The inn features a wrap-around porch with rocking chairs, swings and a view of the mountain valley. Fresh flowers gathered from the garden add fragrance  throughout the inn. Rooms are furnished with antiques, quilts and mountain crafts. In addition to the inn rooms, there are four cottages available, some with kitchens. Before breakfast is served, early morning coffee can be delivered to your room. Organic home-grown vegetables are featured at dinners, included in a contemporary regional cuisine.
Historic Interest: Saint John's Church (2 miles), Mast General Store (1 mile), Maple Spring (on premises).
Innkeeper(s): Wanda Hinshaw & Kay Philipp. $125-250. MC, VISA, AX, DS, TC. 8 rooms with PB and 7 cottages. Breakfast included in rates. Types of meals: Full bkfst and dinner. Beds: KQ. Ceiling fan, cottages with fireplaces, refrigerator and one with full kitchen in room. Air conditioning. Fax on premises. Handicap access. Antiquing, art galleries, bicycling, fishing, golf, hiking, river sports, Blue Ridge Pkwy, Grandfather Mt, live theater, downhill skiing and water sports nearby.
Publicity: *Travel & Leisure, Cooking Light, Blue Ridge Country, Southern Living, New York Times and Our State.*

"We want to live here!"

Washington   B8

Pamlico House

400 E Main St
Washington, NC 27889-5039
(252)946-7184 (800)948-8507 Fax:(252)946-9944
E-mail: pamlicohouse@coastalnet.com
Web: www.pamlicohouse.com

Circa 1906. This gracious Colonial Revival home once served as the rectory for St. Peter's Episcopal Church. A veranda wraps around the house in a graceful curve. Furnished in

Victorian antiques with many family heirlooms. Nearby is the city's quaint waterfront, restaurants, antique shops and art galleries are within walking distance. Washington is on the Historic Albemarle Tour Route and within easy driving distance to the Outer Banks.

Historic Interest: The inn is in the National Register.
Innkeeper(s): George & Jane Fields. $75-95. MC, VISA, AX, DS, PC, TC. TAC10. 4 rooms with PB and 1 conference room. Breakfast included in rates. Types of meals: Gourmet bkfst. Beds: KQT. Cable TV, ceiling fan and VCR in room. Central air. Fax, copier and library on premises. Weddings, family reunions and seminars hosted.
Publicity: *Southern Living.*

Waynesville   B2

Andon House Bed & Breakfast

92 Daisey Ave
Waynesville, NC 28786
(828)452-3089 (800)293-6190 Fax:(828)452-7003
E-mail: info@andonhouse.com

Circa 1902. Designated as one of the town's historic properties, this turn-of-the-century home reflects a traditional style of architecture and interior decor. Large windows, oak floors and tall ceilings are original features that add to the charm of this B&B. The garden room with glass surround invites conversation by the fire or enjoying the impressive landscape and mountain view. A large-screen TV offers further entertainment. Guest bedrooms boast private temperature controls and choices of fireplace, clawfoot or whirlpool tub and private balcony. Partake of a four-course, candlelight breakfast with fresh flowers on the dining room table. Plan the day's excursions on the veranda. The inn is close to downtown and within easy access of many year-round attractions.

Historic Interest: Biltmore Estate (26 miles), County courthouse (1 mile).
Innkeeper(s): Ann & Don Rothermel. $75-125. MC, VISA, AX, DS, PC, TC. TAC15. 4 rooms with PB, 3 with FP and 1 suite. Breakfast and snacks/refreshments included in rates. Types of meals: Full bkfst, veg bkfst and early coffee/tea. Beds: KQT. Cable TV, ceiling fan, fireplace, hot tub and in room. Air conditioning. Fax, copier, hot tub, game tables and mountain views on premises. Family reunions hosted. Amusement parks, antiquing, art galleries, canoeing/kayaking, fishing, golf, hiking, horseback riding, live theater, museums, parks, shopping, downhill skiing, cross-country skiing and tennis nearby.

Grandview Lodge

466 Lickstone Rd
Waynesville, NC 28786
(828)456-5212 (800)255-7826 Fax:(828)452-5432
E-mail: innkeeper@grandviewlodgenc.com

Circa 1890. Grandview Lodge is located on two-and-a-half acres in the Smoky Mountains. The land surrounding the lodge has an apple orchard, rhubarb patch, grape arbor and vegetable garden for the inn's kitchen.

Rooms are available in the main lodge and in a newer addition. The inn's dining room is known throughout the region and Linda, a home economist, has written "Recipes from Grandview Lodge," and its sequel, "More Recipes from Grandview Lodge."

Historic Interest: The Biltmore Estate (45 minutes), Cherokee Indian Reservation (45 minutes).

Innkeeper(s): Stan & Linda Arnold. $110-125. MC, VISA, PC, TC. TAC10. 9 rooms with PB, 3 with FP and 2 suites. Breakfast and dinner included in rates. Types of meals: Full bkfst, early coffee/tea and lunch. MAP. Beds: KQDT. Cable TV, fans and refrigerator in apartments in room. Air conditioning. VCR, fax and library on premises. Weddings, small meetings, family reunions and seminars hosted. Polish, Russian and German spoken. Amusement parks, antiquing, fishing, golf, live theater, parks, shopping, downhill skiing, sporting events and water sports nearby.
Publicity: *Asheville Citizen, Winston-Salem Journal, Raleigh News & Observer and Atlanta Journal & Constitution.*

"It's easy to see why family and friends have been enjoying trips to Grandview."

Herren House

94 East St
Waynesville, NC 28786-3836
(828)452-7837 (800)284-1932
E-mail: herren@brinet.com
Web: www.herrenhouse.com

Circa 1897. Pink and white paint emphasize the Victorian features of this two-story inn with wraparound porch. Inside, the Victorian decor is enhanced with the innkeepers' paintings and

handmade furniture. Soft music and candlelight set the tone for breakfast, which often features the inn's homemade chicken sausage and a baked egg dish along with freshly baked items such as apricot scones. (Saturday evening dinners are available by prior arrangement.)

A garden gazebo is an inviting spot with an overhead fan and piped in music. A block away are galleries, antique shops and restaurants. The Great Smoky Mountains National Park and the Blue Ridge Parkway begin a few minutes from the inn.

Innkeeper(s): Jackie & Frank Blevins. $85-140. MC, VISA, AX, DS, PC, TC. 6 rooms with PB. Breakfast, afternoon tea and snacks/refreshments included in rates. Types of meals: Gourmet bkfst and early coffee/tea. Beds: KQT. Cable TV, ceiling fan and VCR in room. Air conditioning. Fax, copier, library and gourmet dinner served at additional charge Saturday evenings on premises. Handicap access. Small meetings hosted. Antiquing, fishing, golf, live theater, parks, shopping, downhill skiing, cross-country skiing and water sports nearby.

"The two of you have mastered the art of sensory pleasures! Nothing was left unattended."

The Old Stone Inn

109 Dolan Rd
Waynesville, NC 28786-2885
(828)456-3333 (800)432-8499
Web: www.oldstoneinn.com

Circa 1946. Although The Old Stone Inn may be a post-World War II structure, its legacy of innkeeping stretches for more than 50 years. Surrounded by acres of woods and the scenic North Carolina Smokies, the lodge is an ideal location to commune with nature. Exposed-log beams, wooden floors and country furnishings add to the relaxing country atmosphere. Meals are served in the stone and log dining room in front of a crackling fire. The hearty breakfasts prepare guests for a day in the mountains, with treats such as banana nut pancakes, Tennessee sausage pie, fresh fruit and egg dishes. Candle-lit dinners are romantic, with a Southern flair accompanied by freshly baked breads, distinctive appetizers and delectable desserts. The lodge porch is lined with rocking chairs, perfect for relaxing.

Innkeeper(s): Robert & Cindy Zinser. $104-174. MC, VISA, AX, DS, PC. 18 rooms with PB and 4 cottages. Breakfast included in rates. Types of meals: Full bkfst and dinner. Beds: KQD. Cable TV, ceiling fan, VCR (in cottages) and bath robes in room. VCR, library and modem access on premises. Antiquing, art galleries, bicycling, canoeing/kayaking, fishing, golf, hiking, horseback riding, live theater, museums, parks, shopping, downhill skiing, tennis, water sports and wineries nearby.

Publicity: Asheville Citizen Times, Charlotte Observer, National Geographic Traveler, Blue Ridge Country and Southern Living.

"The food was absolutely great and the treatment was top notch."

The Swag Country Inn

2300 Swag Rd
Waynesville, NC 28785-9623
(828)926-0430 Fax:(828)926-2036
E-mail: letters@theswag.com
Web: www.theswag.com

Circa 1795. The Swag is composed of six hand-hewn log buildings, one dating to 1795. They were moved to the site and restored. An old church was reassembled and became the cathedral-ceilinged common room. The fireplace in this room was constructed of fieldstones with no mortar to maintain authenticity. The inn's 250 acres feature a nature trail with five hideaways along the trail, a spring-fed pond, hammocks and thick forests. A two-and-a-half-mile gravel road winds through a heavily wooded hillside to the inn. In the evening, dinner is served on pewter ware at long walnut tables. Listening to folk music and mountain storytelling afterwards is popular. A full list of special events is available each month.

Innkeeper(s): Deener Matthews. $265-580. MC, VISA, AX, DS. 12 rooms with PB, 7 with FP, 3 suites and 1 conference room. Types of meals: Full bkfst, lunch, picnic lunch, snacks/refreshments and dinner. AP. Beds: KQT. Phone in room. VCR, copier, spa and sauna on premises. Handicap access. Small meetings, family reunions and seminars hosted. Antiquing and shopping nearby.

Publicity: The Atlanta Journal, Mid-Atlantic Country, Southern Living, Hideaway Report, Gourmet and Travel & Leisure.

"The Swag gives us both a chance to relax our bodies and revitalize our brains."

Yellow House on Plott Creek Road

89 Oakview Dr
Waynesville, NC 28786-7110
(704)452-0991 (800)563-1236 Fax:(704)452-1140
E-mail: yelhouse@asap-com.com

Circa 1885. This manor, which boasts views of the Blue Ridge Mountains, was built as a summer home to a family from Tampa, Fla. The interior of the home is decidedly French country done in romantic colors. Each room is special, from the Battenburg bedding in the Carolina and S'conset rooms to the four-poster bed and mountain view in the Montecito room. Each of the rooms and suites has a fireplace. The Carriage House, S'conset St. Paul de Vence Suite offer whirlpool tubs. Special amenities, such as bathrobes, fresh flowers, a decanter of port, coffee, hair dryers and toiletries thoughtfully have been placed in each room and suite. Each evening, the innkeepers offer wine and cheese, and in the mornings, a gourmet breakfast is served. Guests are free to enjoy their meal on the veranda or in the privacy of their room.

Innkeeper(s): Sharon & Ron Smith. $125-250. MC, VISA, PC, TC. TAC10. 6 rooms with PB, 6 with FP, 4 suites and 1 cottage. Breakfast and snacks/refreshments included in rates. Types of meals: Gourmet bkfst, early coffee/tea and picnic lunch. Beds: KQT. Phone, turndown service and ceiling fan in room. Air conditioning. Fax, copier and library on premises. Small meetings, family reunions and seminars hosted. Antiquing, fishing, golf, hiking, mountain biking, live theater, parks, shopping, tennis and water sports nearby.

Publicity: Asheville Citizen Times, Mountaineer., WRAL - Raleigh and NC.

"The scenery and quaintness of this community was only surpassed by the gracious surroundings and hospitality here at the Yellow House."

Weaverville   B3

Dry Ridge Inn

26 Brown St
Weaverville, NC 28787-9202
(828)658-3899 (800)839-3899
E-mail: innkeeper@dryridgeinn.com
Web: www.dryridgeinn.com

Circa 1849. This house was built as the parsonage for the Salem Campground, an old religious revival camping area. Because of the high altitude and pleasant weather, it was used as a camp hospital for Confederate soldiers suffering from pneumonia during the Civil War. The area was called Dry Ridge by the Cherokee Indians before the campground was established.

Innkeeper(s): Howard & Kristen Dusenbery. $95-155. MC, VISA, AX, DS, PC, TC. 8 rooms with PB. Types of meals: Full bkfst. Beds: QD. TV and ceiling fan in room. Air conditioning. VCR and outdoor hot tub on premises. Antiquing, art galleries, hiking, Biltmore Estate, fine arts, white water rafting, gift shop, Blue Ridge Parkway outdoor spa and live theater nearby.

Publicity: Asheville Citizen Times and Marshall News Record.

"Best family vacation ever spent."

Inn on Main Street

88 S Main Street
Weaverville, NC 28787
(828)645-4935 (877)873-6074
E-mail: relax@innonmain.com
Web: www.innonmain.com

Circa 1900. Atop a ridge in the breathtaking Blue Ridge Mountains, this 1900 Country Victorian inn has been a retreat from the hustle and bustle of daily life for the past 100 years. Built as a doctor's home and office, the downstairs was used to care for the sick and the upstairs to house paying guests who came to the area for the healthy mountain air. The gardens include rhododendrons, perennials, herbs and vegetables. Its seven comfortably furnished guest rooms are perfect for relaxing after a day of sightseeing, shopping, golfing, hiking, skiing, rafting, trail rides or partaking of local natural hot mineral baths. Breakfasts include such treats as the inn's signature frittata, homemade bread and muffins and yogurt.

Historic Interest: Thomas Wolfe home (6 miles), Vance birthplace (3 miles).
Innkeeper(s): Dan & Nancy Ward. $85-145. MC, VISA, DS, PC, TC. 7 rooms with PB. Breakfast and snacks/refreshments included in rates. Types of meals: Gourmet bkfst, veg bkfst and early coffee/tea. AP. TV, ceiling fan and some with fireplace and whirlpool tub in room. Central air. Fax on premises. Small meetings, family reunions and seminars hosted. Spanish, German and French spoken. Antiquing, art galleries, bicycling, canoeing/kayaking, fishing, golf, hiking, horseback riding, Biltmore Estate, Blue Ridge Parkway, live theater, parks, shopping, downhill skiing, cross-country skiing and wineries nearby.

Weldon   A8

Weldon Place Inn

500 Washington Ave
Weldon, NC 27890-1644
(252)536-4582 (800)831-4470 Fax:(252)536-4708
E-mail: weldonplaceinn@email.com

Circa 1914. Blueberry buckle and strawberry blintzes are a pleasant way to start your morning at this Colonial Revival home. Located in a National Historic District, it is two miles from I-95. Wedding showers and other celebrations are popular

here. There are beveled-glass windows, canopy beds and Italian fireplaces. Most of the inn's antiques are original to the house, including a horse-hair stuffed couch with its original upholstery. Select the Romantic Retreat package and you'll enjoy sweets, other treats, a gift bag, sparkling cider, a whirlpool tub and breakfast in bed.
Innkeeper(s): Bill & Cathy Eleczko. $65-89. MC, VISA, AX, DS, PC, TC. 4 rooms with PB. Breakfast included in rates. Types of meals: Full bkfst. Beds: D. Cable TV and phone in room. Air conditioning. VCR on premises. Weddings and small meetings hosted. Antiquing, fishing, live theater and shopping nearby.

Williamston   B8

Big Mill Bed & Breakfast

1607 Big Mill Rd
Williamston, NC 27892-8032
(252)792-8787
E-mail: bigmill@coastalnet.com
Web: www.bigmill.com

Circa 1918. Originally built as a small arts and crafts frame house, the many renovations conceal its true age. The historic farm outbuildings that include the chicken coop, smokehouse, pack house, tobacco barns and potato house, were built from on-site heart pine and cypress trees that were felled and floated down the streams of this 250-acre woodland estate. The Corncrib guest bedroom is in the pack house that originally housed mules. Each of the guest bedrooms feature climate control, stenciled floors, faux-painted walls, hand-decorated tiles on the wet bar and a private entrance. The suite also boasts a stone fireplace and impressive view. The countryside setting includes a three-acre lake with bridges, fruit orchard, vegetable and flower gardens. Eighty-year-old pecan trees planted by Chloe's parents provide nuts for homemade treats as well as shade for the inn.
Historic Interest: Fort Branch Civil War dirt-mound fort (12 miles), Hope Plantation (15 miles), Historic Edenton (30 miles), Historic Bath (55 miles).
Innkeeper(s): Chloe Tuttle. $55-75. MC, VISA, AX, DS, PC, TC. 3 rooms with PB, 1 with FP, 1 suite, 1 cottage and 1 conference room. Breakfast included in rates. Types of meals: Cont. EP. Beds: QDT. TV, phone, ceiling fan, VCR, private entrances, individual climate control, wet bars with sinks, refrigerators, toaster ovens and coffee pots in room. Air conditioning. Fax, bicycles and lake fishing on premises. Some Spanish spoken. Antiquing, bicycling, canoeing/kayaking, fishing, golf, hiking, horseback riding, horse shows, sporting events and water sports nearby.
Publicity: WRAL-TV.

Wilmington   D7

C.W. Worth House B&B

412 S 3rd St
Wilmington, NC 28401-5102
(910)762-8562 (800)340-8559 Fax:(910)763-2173
E-mail: relax@worthhouse.com
Web: www.worthhouse.com

Circa 1893. This beautifully detailed three-story Queen Anne Victorian boasts two turrets and a wide veranda. From the outside, it gives the appearance of a small castle. The inn was renovated around 1910, and it retains many of the architectural details of the original house, including the paneled front hall. Victorian decor is found throughout the inn, including period antiques. The Rose Suite offers a king four-poster bed, sitting

room and bath with a clawfoot tub and separate shower. Guests are treated to gourmet breakfasts. Freshly baked muffins and entrees such as eggs Florentine, rosemary and goat cheese strata and stuffed French toast are served. A second-story porch overlooks the garden with dogwood, ponds and pecan trees.
Innkeeper(s): Margi & Doug Erickson. $100-150. MC, VISA, AX, DS, PC, TC. TAC10. 7 rooms with PB. Breakfast and snacks/refreshments included in rates. Types of meals: Full bkfst. Beds: KQT. Phone, ceiling fan and one with two-person whirlpool in room. Air conditioning. Modem jack, fax, TV/VCR and copier service available on premises. Small meetings and family reunions hosted. Antiquing, fishing, golf, performing arts, fine dining, museums, parks, shopping, tennis and water sports nearby.

Catherine's Inn

410 S Front St
Wilmington, NC 28401-5012
(910)251-0863 (800)476-0723
E-mail: catherin@wilmington.net

Circa 1883. This Italianate-style home features wrought-iron fences and a Colonial Revival wraparound porch in the front and a two-story screened porch in the back. The 300-foot private garden overlooks a unique

sunken garden and the Cape Fear River. Antiques and reproductions fill the interior, which includes 12-foot ceilings and an heirloom grand piano. Freshly brewed coffee is delivered to each room in the morning, followed by a full breakfast served on family collections of china, crystal and sterling silver in the dining room. Turndown service and complimentary refreshments are some of the other amenities offered by the innkeepers.
Historic Interest: Catherine's Inn is registered as a local, state and national landmark home and is located in the heart of Wilmington's historic district.
Innkeeper(s): Catherine & Walter Ackiss. $85-120. MC, VISA, AX. 5 rooms with PB. Breakfast and afternoon tea included in rates. Types of meals: Gourmet dinner. Beds: KQT. Phone in room. Off-street parking on premises. Antiquing, fishing, live theater and water sports nearby.
Publicity: This Week, Country Inns, Encore, Mid-Atlantic, New York Times, Carolina, Southern Living and Money Magazine.

"This is the best!"

Front Street Inn

215 S Front St
Wilmington, NC 28401-4414
(910)762-6442 (800)336-8184 Fax:(910)762-8991
E-mail: jay@frontstreetinn.com
Web: www.frontstreetinn.com

Circa 1923. The Front Street Inn is in the heart of Wilmington's historic district. The Brick Italianate structure has a European ambiance and is full of American art. There are nine guest bedrooms, including six spacious suites some with Jacuzzis and fireplaces. All have wet-bars, private baths, hardwood floors and private entrances. The second-floor suites open directly onto the balcony. Guests return to the inn for the delicious extensive continental breakfasts, which include healthy items such as fresh bran muffins, whole-grain cereals, hard-boiled eggs, assorted cheeses, smoked salmon, fresh fruit, yogurt and a variety of coffee cakes, breads and biscotti with accompaniments such as jam and local honey. Breakfast is served in the Sol y Sombra Bar and Breakfast Room or in the guest's suite upon request. The inn has an exercise room, bicycles, a wine and beer bar and a game room with a pool table. It is less than a block from Chandler's Wharf, Cape Fear River, half a mile from the USS N.C. Battleship and six miles from Orton Plantation. Guests may stroll along the River Walk, visit St. John's Museum of Art or meander through an extensive residential section of restored homes and delightful gardens.

Historic Interest: USS N.C. Battleship (1/2 mile), Orton Plantation (6 miles). Innkeeper(s): Jay & Stefany Rhodes. $98-180. MC, VISA, AX, DC, CB, DS, PC. 9 rooms with PB. Breakfast included in rates. Types of meals: Veg bkfst, cont plus, early coffee/tea, snacks/refreshments and room service. Beds: KQDT. Cable TV, phone, ceiling fan, VCR, robes, hair dryer, individual heat/AC control and some with Jacuzzi and fireplace in room. Fax, copier, bicycles, CD player, wine & beer bar and game/exercise room on premises. Small meetings, family reunions and seminars hosted. French and Spanish spoken. Amusement parks, antiquing, art galleries, beaches, bicycling, canoeing/kayaking, fishing, golf, horseback riding, river cruises, historic sightseeing, live theater, museums, parks, shopping, sporting events, tennis and water sports nearby.

Graystone Inn

100 S 3rd St
Wilmington, NC 28401-4503
(910)763-2000 (888)763-4773 Fax:(910)763-5555
E-mail: reservations@graystoneinn.com
Web: www.graystoneinn.com

Circa 1906. If you are a connoisseur of inns, you'll be delighted with this stately mansion in the Wilmington Historic District and in the National Register. Recently chosen by American Historic Inns as one of America's Top Ten Romantic Inns, towering columns mark the balconied grand entrance. Its 14,000 square feet of magnificent space includes antique furnishings, art and amenities. A staircase of hand-carved red oak rises three stories. Guests  lounge in the music room, drawing room and library. A conference room and reception area with a fireplace and sitting area are on the third floor, once a grand ballroom. The elegant guest rooms are often chosen for special occasions, especially the 1,300-square-foot Bellevue, which offers a sitting room, king bed, sofa and handsome period antiques.

Innkeeper(s): Paul & Yolanda Bolda. $159-329. MC, VISA, AX, DC, CB, DS, PC, TC. TAC10. 7 rooms with PB, 6 with FP, 2 suites and 1 conference room. Breakfast included in rates. Types of meals: Gourmet bkfst and early coffee/tea. EP. Beds: KQ. TV, phone, turndown service, ceiling fan, four-poster beds (many rooms) and computer jacks in room. Air conditioning. Fax, copier, library, weight training room and PC data ports on premises. Weddings, small meetings and family reunions hosted. Antiquing, fishing, golf, museums, live theater, parks, shopping, sporting events, tennis and water sports nearby.

Publicity: *Country Inns, Movie Rambling Rose, Mary Janes Last Dance and Cats Eye, TV series Young Indiana Jones, Matlock and Dawsons Creek.*

Rosehill Inn Bed & Breakfast

114 S 3rd St
Wilmington, NC 28401-4556
(910)815-0250 (800)815-0250 Fax:(910)815-0350
E-mail: rosehill@rosehill.com
Web: www.rosehill.com

Circa 1848. Architect Henry Bacon Jr., most famous for designing the Lincoln Memorial in Washington, D.C., lived  here in the late 19th century. Located in the largest urban historic district in the country, this Neoclassical Victorian was completely renovated in 1995. The guest rooms are spacious and decorated in period furnishings. Breakfast treats include eggs

Benedict with Cajun Crab Hollandaise and stuffed French toast with orange syrup.

Innkeeper(s): Laurel Jones, Dennis Fietsch. $99-229. MC, VISA, AX, DS, TC. TAC10. 6 rooms with PB. Breakfast included in rates. Types of meals: Gourmet bkfst, cont plus and early coffee/tea. Beds: KQD. Cable TV, phone, VCR, data port and iron and ironing board in room. Fax on premises. Family reunions hosted. Antiquing, fishing, golf, battleship memorial, beaches, live theater, parks, shopping, sporting events, tennis and water sports nearby.

Publicity: *Southern Living, Wilmington Star News, Wilmington Magazine, Washington Post, Insiders Guide to Wilmington, Atlanta Sun, Philadelphia Inquirer and Oprah Winfrey "The Wedding".*

Verandas

202 Nun St
Wilmington, NC 28401-5020
(910)251-2212 Fax:(910)251-8932
E-mail: verandas4@aol.com
Web: www.verandas.com

Circa 1854. It's difficult to believe that this graceful three-story Victorian ever featured shag carpeting and linoleum floors. Hardly a fitting ending for a home that once belonged to a Confederate ship-builder and blockade runner, who burned his shipyard rather than let Union soldiers capture it. Innkeepers Charles Pennington and Dennis Madsen transformed Verandas from an ill-decorated, fire-damaged wreck into an elegant bed & breakfast. The restoration process included two years of painstaking work. For their efforts, they have been awarded a historic preservation award from the Historic Wilmington Foundation. The romantic guest rooms are filled with American, French and English antiques. Most rooms include a fireplace, and the beds are topped with luxurious, hand-ironed linens. Bathrooms now feature oversized tubs and marble floors and vanities. Gourmet coffees and teas accompany the lavish breakfasts, which feature delectable entrees such as a croissant stuffed with smoked salmon and cream cheese and baked in an egg custard. There are many amenities for business travelers, including modem hook-ups, fax service and corporate midweek rates.

Historic Interest: Fort Fisher (15 miles).
Innkeeper(s): Charles Pennington & Dennis Madsen. $135-190. MC, VISA, AX, DS, PC, TC. TAC10. 8 rooms with PB. Breakfast and snacks/refreshments included in rates. Types of meals: Gourmet bkfst and early coffee/tea. Beds: KQ. Cable TV, phone and VCR in room. Central air. Fax on premises. Family reunions hosted. Sign language spoken. Antiquing, art galleries, beaches, bicycling, canoeing/kayaking, fishing, golf, live theater, museums, parks, shopping, tennis and water sports nearby.

"You have done a magnificent job with your property, and you certainly make your guests feel welcome with your food and hospitality."

The Wilmingtonian

101 South Second St
Wilmington, NC 28401
(919)343-1800 (800)525-0909 Fax:(919)251-1149
E-mail: mail@thewilmingtonian.com
Web: www.thewilmingtonian.com

Circa 1841. Unwind and relax at this historic downtown location of five elegant buildings only two blocks from the river in Cape Fear country. The de Rosset House is a luxuriously restored antebellum mansion with aged heart of pine floors. The Dram Tree House, originally a vegetable dye factory, has a rustic Southern ambiance with a Charleston-style courtyard and fish pond. The Maritime Building, once a convent, boasts a nautical theme reflecting this seaport city. The Clarenden, named after a local Earl, is perfect for groups or reunions as some of the suites can interconnect through a conservatory.

The Cinema House, a tribute to the area's active movie industry, offers specially designed suites showcasing themes of a classical movie or star. Most of these romantic lodgings feature private entrances and balconies with rockers overlooking gardens.

Historic Interest: Battleship North Carolina (1/2 mile), Fort Fisher (12 miles). Innkeeper(s): Mike Compton. $110-285. MC, VISA, AX, DC, DS, TC. TAC10. 42 rooms, 7 with FP, 40 suites and 3 conference rooms. Breakfast included in rates. Types of meals: Cont plus, gourmet lunch, snacks/refreshments, gourmet dinner and room service. Beds: KQD. Cable TV, phone, ceiling fan, VCR, microwaves, toasters, hair dryers, irons, ironing boards, fireplace, some with full kitchens and washers/dryers in room. Central air. Fax, copier, library, video tape library, lounge, bar, grill and room/pub on premises. Weddings, small meetings, family reunions and seminars hosted. Amusement parks, antiquing, art galleries, beaches, bicycling, canoeing/kayaking, fishing, golf, live theater, museums, parks, shopping, tennis and water sports nearby.

Wilson   B7

Miss Betty's B&B Inn

600 West Nash St
Wilson, NC 27893-3045
(252)243-4447 (800)258-2058 Fax:(252)243-4447
E-mail: info@missbettysbnb.com

Circa 1858. Located in a gracious setting in the downtown historic district, the inn is comprised of several restored historic homes, chief of which is the two-story National Register Italianate building called the Davis-Whitehead Harris House.

Here there are 12-foot high ceilings, heart-pine and oak floors and wonderful collections of antiques, much of which is for sale. Breakfast is served in the Victorian dining room of the main house, with its walnut antique furniture and clusters of roses on the wallpaper. All the extras, such as lace tablecloths and hearty meals, conjure up the Old South. Smoking is allowed on the outside porches — there are six of them — and the deck. Four golf courses, numerous tennis courts and many fine restaurants are nearby. Wilson is known as the antique capitol of North Carolina.

Historic Interest: The inn is listed in the National Register and located on Nash Street, which once was described as one of the most beautiful streets in the country.

Innkeeper(s): Betty & Fred Spitz. $60-80. MC, VISA, AX, DC, CB, DS, PC, TC. 14 rooms with PB, 11 with FP and 3 suites. Breakfast included in rates. Types of meals: Full bkfst. Beds: KQDT. Cable TV, phone and ceiling fan in room. Air conditioning. Fax and copier on premises. Handicap access. Family reunions hosted. Live theater and sporting events nearby.

Publicity: *Wilson Daily Times-1996, The Philadelphia Enquirer-1999, Southern Living-1997, Mid-Atlantic Country-1995, Our State/NC-1995 and Washington Post-1998.*

"Yours is second to none. Everything was perfect. I can see why you are so highly rated."

Winston-Salem   B5

Augustus T. Zevely Inn

803 S Main St
Winston-Salem, NC 27101-5332
(336)748-9299 (800)928-9299 Fax:(336)721-2211
E-mail: ctheal@dddcompany.com
Web: www.winston-salem-inn.com

Circa 1844. The Zevely Inn is the only lodging in Old Salem. Each of the rooms at this charming pre-Civil War inn have a view of historic Old Salem. Moravian furnishings and fixtures permeate the decor of each of the guest quarters,

some of which boast working fireplaces. The home's architecture is reminiscent of many structures built in Old Salem during the second quarter of the 19th century. The formal dining room and parlor have wood burning fireplaces.

The two-story porch offers visitors a view of the period gardens and a beautiful magnolia tree. A line of Old Salem furniture has been created by Lexington Furniture Industries, and several pieces were created especially for the Zevely Inn.

Historic Interest: Winston-Salem abounds with historic activity. Old Salem, founded in 1766, is a restored, Moravian community. Among the sites are the Historic Bethabara Park, the Piedmont Craftsman, Inc. and Mesda, the nation's only museum dedicated to researching Southern materials and styles. The museum features a variety of furniture, textiles, ceramics and paintings dating back to the 17th century.

Innkeeper(s): Todd Sanders. $80-205. MC, VISA, AX, PC, TC. TAC7. 12 rooms with PB, 3 with FP and 1 suite. Breakfast and snacks/refreshments included in rates. Beds: KQDT. Cable TV, phone and whirlpool tub in room. Air conditioning. Fax and copier on premises. Antiquing, Old Salem Historic District, live theater, shopping and sporting events nearby.

Publicity: *Washington Post Travel, Salem Star, Winston-Salem Journal, Tasteful, Country Living, National Trust for Historic Preservation, Homes and Gardens, Homes Across America, Southern Living. and Home & Gardens Network Show.*

"Colonial charm with modern conveniences, great food. Very nice! Everything was superb."

Colonel Ludlow Inn

434 Summit at W 5th
Winston-Salem, NC 27101
(336)777-1887 (800)301-1887 Fax:(336)777-0518
E-mail: innkeeper@bbinn.com
Web: www.bbinn.com

Circa 1887. Located in a historic urban residential neighborhood, this inn is comprised of two adjacent Victorian homes. Both homes are listed in the National Register and boast such features as wraparound porches, gabled roofs, ornate entrances,

beautiful windows and high ceilings. Guest rooms are decorated with Victorian antiques, and each includes a double whirlpool tub. The innkeepers provide many thoughtful amenities, such as stocked mini-refrigerators, microwaves, coffee makers, stereos, TVs with VCRs and free movies, irons, bathrobes and hair dryers. There is a Nautilus exercise room and a billiards room. Two gourmet restaurants in historic homes are only two blocks away.

Historic Interest: Old Salem, a restored 18th-century German Moravian Village, is one mile away.

Innkeeper(s): Constance Creasman. $89-209. MC, VISA, AX, DC, DS, PC, TC. TAC10. 10 rooms with PB, 5 with FP. Breakfast included in rates. Types of meals: Full bkfst, early coffee/tea, lunch, gourmet dinner and room service. Beds: K. Cable TV, phone, ceiling fan, VCR, towel warmer and hair dryer in room. Air conditioning. Antiquing, live theater, parks, shopping and sporting events nearby.

Publicity: *Winston-Salem Journal, Charlotte Observer, Mid-Atlantic Country, Southern Living, Southern Accents, USA Today and American Way.*

"I have never seen anything like the meticulous and thorough attention to detail. — Dannye Romine, The Charlotte Observer."

North Dakota

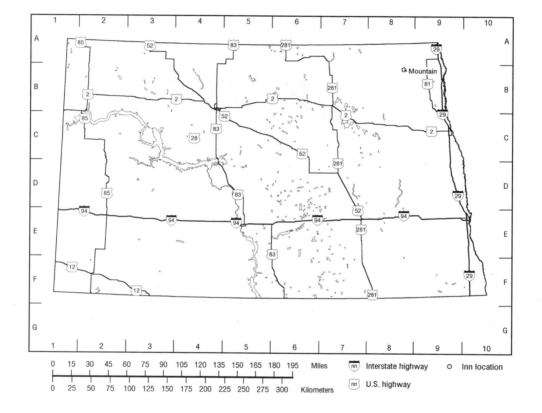

0 15 30 45 60 75 90 105 120 135 150 165 180 195 Miles

0 25 50 75 100 125 150 175 200 225 250 275 300 Kilometers

Interstate highway   o Inn location

U.S. highway

Fessenden C6

Beiseker Mansion

1001 2nd St NE
Fessenden, ND 58438-7409
(701)547-3411

Circa 1899. Situated on nearly a city block, this 15-room Queen Anne Victorian is bordered by an old-fashioned wrought iron fence. Features include a splendid wraparound veranda and two turrets. The original golden oak woodwork is seen in the staircase, fireplace and dining room wainscoting. The turret room, with its king-size sleigh bed and marble-topped dresser, is a favorite choice. A third-floor library, open to guests, contains 3,000 volumes. The house is in the National Register of Historic Places.

Innkeeper(s): Paula & Jerry Tweton. $55-95. MC, VISA. 6 rooms, 2 with PB. Breakfast included in rates. Types of meals: Full bkfst. Cable TV and VCR in room. Air conditioning.

Publicity: *Grand Forks Herald and Fessenden Herald Press.*

"What a beautiful house! The food and atmosphere were lovely."

Luverne D8

Volden Farm

11943 County Rd 26
Luverne, ND 58056
(701)769-2275 Fax:(701)769-2610
E-mail: voldenfarm-bb@broadvu.com

Circa 1926. Perennial gardens and a hedge of lilacs surround this redwood house with its newer addition. A favorite room is the North Room with a lace canopy bed, an old pie safe and a Texas Star quilt made by the host's grandmother. Guests enjoy soaking in the clawfoot tub while looking out over the hills. There are two libraries, a music room and game room. The innkeepers also offer lodging in the Law Office, which dates to 1885 and is a separate little prairie house ideal for families. A stream, bordered by old oaks and formed by a natural spring, meanders through the property. The chickens here lay green and blue eggs. Dinner is available by advanced arrangement. Hiking, birdwatching, snowshoeing and skiing are nearby.

Innkeeper(s): Jim & JoAnne Wold. $60-95. PC. TAC10. 2 rooms and 1 cottage. Breakfast and snacks/refreshments included in rates. Types of meals: Gourmet bkfst, early coffee/tea, picnic lunch and gourmet dinner. Beds: KDT. Bicycles and library on premises. Small meetings and seminars hosted. Limited Russian and limited Norwegian spoken. Antiquing, fishing, hiking, golf, canoeing, snowshoeing, bird watching, downhill skiing and cross-country skiing nearby.

Pets allowed: Outside.

Publicity: *Fargo Forum, Horizons, Grand Forks Herald, Mid-West Living and Getaways.*

"Very pleasant indeed! Jim & JoAnne make you feel good. There's so much to do, and the hospitality is amazing!"

Medora E2

The Rough Riders Hotel B&B

Medora, ND
Medora, ND 58645
(701)623-4444 (800)633-6721 Fax:(701)623-4494
E-mail: medora@medora.com

Circa 1865. This old hotel has the branding marks of Teddy Roosevelt's cattle ranch as well as other brands stamped into the rough-board facade out front. A wooden sidewalk helps to maintain the turn-of-the-century cow-town feeling. Rustic guest rooms are above the restaurant and are furnished with homesteader antiques original to the area. In the summer, an outdoor pageant is held complete with stagecoach and horses. In October, deer hunters are accommodated. The hotel, along with two motels, is managed by the non-profit Theodore Roosevelt Medora Foundation.

Innkeeper(s): Randy Hatzenbuhler. $45-58. MC, VISA, AX, DS. 9 rooms with PB. Breakfast included in rates.

Mountain B8

221 Melsted Place

PO Box 221
Mountain, ND 58262
(701)993-8257 Fax:(701)993-8257
E-mail: 221melpl@polarcomm.com
Web: www.melstedplace.com

Circa 1910. This handsome gabled estate is comprised of unique cast concrete blocks and offers three stories with a wide porch, stained and mullioned windows, and inside, a grand staircase. Elegantly furnished guest accommodations feature antiques. The mansion is popular for tours because of its history and beauty. Candlelight dining, first-class service and many other amenities are making 221 Melsted a popular romantic destination for couples. There's a Victorian spa, and the innkeepers can arrange other activities including a private limousine tour of the countryside, berry picking expedition or an evening playing torch light croquet. The area has Icelandic heritage, and each August, the Deuce Icelandic Festival is held.

Historic Interest: Historic churches nearby.

Innkeeper(s): Lonnette Kelley. $80-120. MC, VISA, DS, PC, TC. TAC10. 4 suites and 1 conference room. Breakfast included in rates. Types of meals: Full bkfst, early coffee/tea and dinner. AP. Beds: KQD. TV, phone, turndown service, ceiling fan and VCR in room. Fax, copier, bicycles, fall torchlight croquette, optional candle-light dinner, all-season spa, fruit juice bar, piano, picnic area, bonfires, flower & vegetable gardens, limousine service and tours on premises. Weddings, small meetings, family reunions and seminars hosted. Antiquing, fishing, golf, live theater, museums, parks, shopping, downhill skiing, cross-country skiing, tennis and water sports nearby.

Ohio

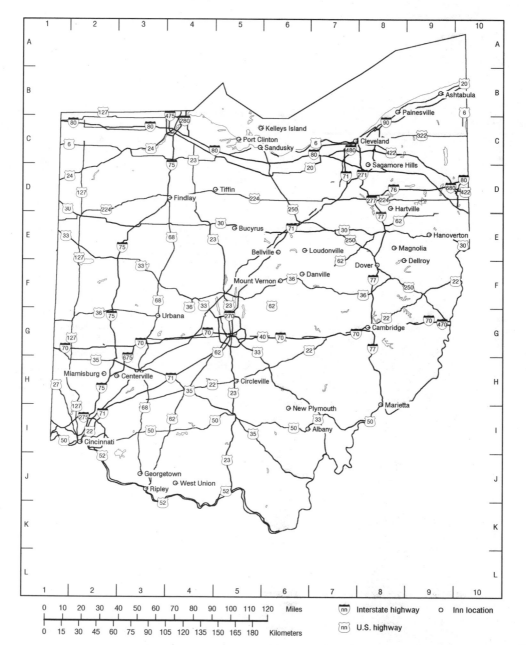

1	2	3	4	5	6	7	8	9	10

Kelleys Island
Port Clinton
Sandusky
Ashtabula
Painesville
Cleveland
Sagamore Hills
Hartville
Hanoverton
Tiffin
Findlay
Bucyrus
Magnolia
Dellroy
Bellville
Loudonville
Dover
Danville
Mount Vernon
Urbana
Cambridge
Miamisburg
Centerville
Circleville
New Plymouth
Marietta
Cincinnati
Albany
Georgetown
West Union
Ripley

0 10 20 30 40 50 60 70 80 90 100 110 120   Miles

0 15 30 45 60 75 90 105 120 135 150 165 180   Kilometers

nn Interstate highway   o Inn location

nn U.S. highway

Albany 17

Albany House

9 Clinton St
Albany, OH 45710
(740)698-6311 (888)212-8163

Circa 1860. Located seven miles from Ohio University in a quaint village setting, this inn is filled with antiques, quilts, Oriental rugs and collectibles. A new addition includes an

indoor pool, fireplace, showers and changing room.
Historic Interest: Adena Mounds, Chillicothe (50 miles), Marietta, first historic town (57 miles).
Innkeeper(s): Sarah & Ted Hutchins. $75-135. PC, TC. 7 rooms with PB and 1 conference room. Breakfast and snacks/refreshments included in rates. Types of meals:
Gourmet bkfst and early coffee/tea. Beds: QDT. Weddings and small meetings hosted. Antiquing, fishing, live theater, parks, shopping and water sports nearby.
Publicity: *Post, A. News, S.E. Ohio Magazine, Midwest and Bike.*

Ashtabula B9

The Gilded Swan B&B

5024 West Ave
Ashtabula, OH 44004
(440)992-1566 (888)345-7926
E-mail: eswanson@suite224.net
Web: www.thegildedswan.com

Circa 1900. Romantic interludes and memorable moments are easily experienced at this lavish Queen Anne Victorian in a Lake Erie harbor town. Painstakingly restored, the B&B is furnished with cherished family heirlooms and antiques. Comfortable guest bedrooms and suites boast welcoming decor, canopy beds, whirlpool tubs, a fireplace and pillow chocolates. In the elegant dining room, a sumptuous breakfast may include raspberry-stuffed French toast and grilled sausage links. Afternoon snacks are also offered. Centrally located, the inn is within easy access to wine country, Cleveland's museums, Pennsylvania's attractions and Amish country.
Innkeeper(s): Elaine Swanson. $75-105. MC, VISA, PC, TC. 4 rooms, 2 with PB, 1 with FP and 2 suites. Breakfast and snacks/refreshments included in rates. Types of meals: Veg bkfst, cont plus & early coffee/tea. Beds: KQ. Cable TV, ceiling fan & fireplace in room. Central air. Spa and library on premises. Amusement parks, antiquing, beaches, canoeing/kayaking, fishing, golf, live theater, museums, parks, shopping, sporting events, water sports and wineries nearby.

Michael Cahill B&B

1106 Walnut Blvd
Ashtabula, OH 44004
(440)964-8449
E-mail: cahillbb@apk.net

Circa 1887. This two-story early Victorian Stick-style home is situated on a bluff overlooking Lake Erie. It was built by Irish immigrants who profited in the 1880s and 1890s as saloon keepers. Walnut Boulevard was then known as "Captain's Row" because of the many ship captains who lived there. The B&B features cherry woodwork, original electric chandeliers and antique and period furnishings. A large wraparound porch allows guests to enjoy Lake Erie breezes. Within easy walking distance is the Marine Museum, Underground Railroad Museum, shopping in restored Bridge Street shops, charter boat fishing and Walnut

Beach. Wineries and many covered bridges are nearby.
Innkeeper(s): Paul & Pat Goode. $60-80. PC, TC. 4 rooms with PB. Breakfast included in rates. Types of meals: Full bkfst. Beds: QD. Air conditioning. Antiquing, golf, covered bridges, live theater, shopping and wineries nearby.
"We enjoyed our stay, we'll be back!"

Peggy's B&B

8721 Munson Hill Road
Ashtabula, OH 44004
(440)969-1996 Fax:(440)964-5767
E-mail: peggy@peggysbedandbreakfast.com
Web: www.peggysbedandbreakfast.com

Circa 1945. Enjoy the privacy of a getaway cottage amid an area of covered bridges, woodlands, wineries, beaches and restaurants. Located an hour east of Cleveland, the cottage sits on the edge of a forest and offers a porch, fireplace, loft bedroom and full kitchen. Decorated with knotty pine, there's a lodge atmosphere with comfortable furnishings, making the cottage feel like your own second home. Breakfasts can be catered according to guest's wishes and picnic lunches and dinners may also be arranged. Recommended restaurants in the surrounding area includes Ferrante's Winery and Ristorante, Seasons Grille and French Farm Market.
Historic Interest: Underground Railroad (6 miles).
Innkeeper(s): Peggy Huggins. $75-125. MC, VISA, PC, TC. TAC10. 1 cottages. Breakfast included in rates. Types of meals: Gourmet bkfst, veg bkfst, early coffee/tea, picnic lunch and dinner. Beds: Q. TV, phone, ceiling fan, VCR and fireplace in room. Air conditioning. Small meetings hosted. Amusement parks, antiquing, art galleries, beaches, bicycling, canoeing/kayaking, fishing, golf, hiking, horseback riding, live theater, museums, parks, shopping, downhill skiing, cross-country skiing, sporting events, tennis, water sports and wineries nearby.
Publicity: *Chamber of Commerce (two areas).*

Bellville E6

Frederick Fitting House, Ltd.

72 Fitting Ave
Bellville, OH 44813-1043
(419)886-2863 Fax:(419)886-2863

Circa 1863. This green and white Italianate Victorian house commands a corner of the town of Bellville. Rooms include the Colonial Room with a queen canopy bed and the Shaker Room with a queen Shaker bed. The Victorian Room includes a queen-
size sleigh bed. Breakfast may be served in the Victorian dining room, garden gazebo or front porch. Guests can relax by a warming fire in the living room and enjoy the variety of books, CDs and movies found in the library. A bike trail, Malabar farms,

Mohican River, skiing and antique shops are nearby.
Innkeeper(s): Barb & Jim Lomax. $75-85. 3 rooms with PB. Breakfast included in rates. Types of meals: Full bkfst, early coffee/tea and snacks/refreshments. Ceiling fan in room. Air conditioning. VCR on premises. Antiquing, shopping, downhill skiing, cross-country skiing and sporting events nearby.

Bucyrus E5

Hide Away B&B

1601 SR 4
Bucyrus, OH 44820-9587
(419)562-3013 (800)570-8233 Fax:(419)562-3003
E-mail: innkeeper@hideawayinn.com
Web: www.hideawayinn.com

Circa 1938. Experience a refreshing getaway while staying at this remarkable inn. Because of the inn's outrageous service, even the business traveler will feel rejuvenated after embarking on a rendezvous with nature here. Exquisite guest suites feature private Jacuzzis, fireplaces and amenities that pamper. Savor a leisurely five-course breakfast. Enjoy fine dining in the restaurant, or ask for an intimate picnic to be arranged. A productive conference room instills a personal quiet and inspires the mind.

Historic Interest: Colonel Crawford battle site, Underground Railroad, Crawford County Courthouse.

Innkeeper(s): Steve & Debbie Miller. $87-287. MC, VISA, DC, DS, PC, TC. TAC10. 11 rooms with PB, 7 with FP, 8 suites, 2 guest houses and 2 conference rooms. Breakfast included in rates. Types of meals: Gourmet bkfst, early coffee/tea, gourmet lunch, picnic lunch, afternoon tea, snacks/refreshments, gourmet dinner and room service. Beds: KQD. TV, phone, turndown service, ceiling fan, VCR, fireplace, satellite TV and Jacuzzi in room. Air conditioning. Fax, copier, swimming, bicycles, library and child care on premises. Weddings, small meetings, family reunions and seminars hosted. Amusement parks, antiquing, bicycling, fishing, golf, hiking, horseback riding, baja boats, live theater, parks, shopping, downhill skiing, sporting events and water sports nearby.

Publicity: *New York Times, Columbus Dispatch, Ohio Country Journal, Akron Beacon Journal, Cleveland Plain Dealer, Travel & Leisure, Neil Zurcker One Tank-Trips-Cleveland, Akron WKBN, Del's Folks and Del's Feasts Cleveland and Cleveland WKYC.*

Cambridge   G8

Colonel Taylor Inn B&B

633 Upland Rd
Cambridge, OH 43725
(740)432-7802 Fax:(740)435-3152
E-mail: coltaylor@peoplepc.com

Circa 1878. The namesake who built this Victorian Painted Lady was a Civil War veteran and congressman. The spacious mansion imparts an intimate ambiance. The Grand Foyer showcases a carved staircase, oak paneling, 11-foot ceilings, hardwood floors and stained-glass windows. A large sitting room boasts a big screen TV and table games. The parlor and library provide quiet places to read or chat. The inns boasts 11 fireplaces, and one of the guest bedrooms even has a fireside whirlpool tub in the bath. Apple French toast, sausage, coffee cake and fresh fruit is one of the delightful breakfasts served daily. The historic downtown district is seven blocks away.

Innkeeper(s): Jim & Patricia Irvin. $105-125. MC, VISA, DS, TC. TAC10. 4 rooms with PB, 4 with FP, 1 suite and 2 conference rooms. Breakfast and afternoon tea included in rates. Types of meals: Gourmet bkfst. Beds: Q. Cable TV, ceiling fan, fireplace and one with bathroom whirlpool tub/fireplace in room. Central air. VCR, library, large screen TV, two parlors, formal dining room and three porches on premises. Weddings, small meetings, family reunions and seminars hosted. Antiquing, art galleries, beaches, bicycling, canoeing/kayaking, fishing, golf, hiking, horseback riding, glass factories, potteries, festivals, concerts, live theater, museums, parks, shopping, cross-country skiing, water sports and wineries nearby.

Morning Glory B&B

5637 Fairdale Dr
Cambridge, OH 43725-9454
(740)439-2499

Circa 1859. This two-story farmhouse set on five acres along the Old National Road is conveniently located between Cambridge and New Concord. The original staircase, constructed of chestnut and walnut, leads to the three guest rooms that offer private baths and ceiling fans. The inn features hardwood floors, antiques and many handmade items, influenced by the Amish, whose enclave is just an hour away. Guests can enjoy a full breakfast in the pantry kitchen by the warmth of the hearth or in the dining room. Shopping, antiques, crafts, museums and parks are located nearby.

Innkeeper(s): Jim & Jane Gibson. $65-75.

MC, VISA, DS, PC, TC. 3 rooms with PB. Breakfast & snacks/refreshments included in rates. Types of meals: Full bkfst & early coffee/tea. Beds: Q. Ceiling fan in room. Air conditioning. Family reunions hosted. Antiquing, golf, "The Wilds" animal preserve, glass factories, live theater, parks, shopping & tennis nearby.

Publicity: *Daily Jeffersonian and Midwest Living.*

"Outstanding, we give it '5 stars.'"

Centerville   H2

Yesterday B&B

39 S Main St
Centerville, OH 45458-2361
(937)433-0785 (800)225-0485

Circa 1882. Take a nostalgic journey to this grand clapboard house in the Centerville historic district outside of Dayton. Furnished with period pieces and unique collectibles, a serene ambiance of gracious living is in abundance. The guest bedrooms offer choices such as an iron or high cherry bed, wicker and a deep clawfooted tub. A hearty breakfast served in the dining room satisfies even the most discriminating tastes.  The parlor is pleasant for conversation, or enjoy the outdoor courtyard and wraparound porch. It is located in the heart of major antique districts and close to the U.S. Air Force Museum and Kings Island theme park.

Innkeeper(s). Judy & Chuck Haun. $75-85. 3 rooms with PB. Types of meals: Full bkfst. Beds: KQT.

Cincinnati   I2

Bed & Breakfast at Phuntsok Dechen Ling

2641 Highland Ave
Cincinnati, OH 45219
(513)961-6455
E-mail: web@buddhistcenter.com
Web: www.buddhistcenter.com

Circa 1885. This inn's classic Victorian architecture features a hypoallergenic-oriented environment utilizing Feng Shui and embracing Tibetan Buddhist traditions. Complimentary slippers are provided for use throughout the inn, which is fully equipped for business-related needs as well as pleasurable comforts. The sitting room boasts a piano, and the office solarium offers high-tech communications. Each of the guest bedrooms reflects the teachings and principles with spiritual iconography, art and antiques. Much attention is paid to amenities which also include Polar Tec robes, filtered air and water, full spectrum lights and triple sheeting. A satisfying, organic breakfast is served in the refectory, an elegant formal dining room with an original hand-carved fireplace. Herbal tea, beverages and snacks are available at any time.

Historic Interest: The Emaculata Church (3 miles), Union Terminal Station by Frank Lloyd Wright (3 miles), Cincinnati Fire Museum (3 miles).

Innkeeper(s): Bob & Leah Moon. $150-275. MC, VISA, AX, DC, CB, DS. 4 rooms with PB, 3 with FP. Breakfast, afternoon tea and snacks/refreshments included in rates. Types of meals: Gourmet bkfst, veg bkfst, cont plus, cont and early coffee/tea. Beds: KQT. Phone and fireplace in room. Central air. Fax, library, Refectory with microwave, stocked guest refrigerator, sitting room with piano, office solarium with high speed web and printer on premises. Small meetings and seminars hosted. Amusement parks, antiquing, art galleries, canoeing/kayaking, fishing, golf, horseback riding, live theater, museums, parks, shopping, sporting events, tennis and water sports nearby.

"Spiritual refuge in an urban environment."

The Victoria Inn of Hyde Park

3567 Shaw Ave
Cincinnati, OH 45208-1415
(513)321-3567 (888)422-4629 Fax:(513)533-2944

Circa 1909. Receiving a Better Homes & Gardens award for outstanding renovation, this home opened in 1990 as Cincinnati's first bed & breakfast. The inn features stained glass, mahogany woodwork and elegant chandeliers. All of the well-appointed guest bedrooms are filled with antiques, feature featherbeds and fluffy robes. The Victorian Suite boasts a sitting room and whirlpool tub. The Country Manor Room includes a screened porch overlooking the swimming pool. Homemade scones, bread and fresh fruit are available for breakfast. Complimentary snacks and beverages are also available. Enjoy a pleasant walk to the shops, galleries and restaurants at Hyde Park Square or a short drive to the formal gardens of Ault Park.

Historic Interest: The Victoria Inn is located in Cincinnati's historic Hyde Park. Hyde Park Square features a variety of architectural styles.

Innkeeper(s): Tom Possert. $99-189. MC, VISA, AX. 4 rooms with PB, 1 suite and 1 conference room. Breakfast included in rates. Types of meals: Cont plus and early coffee/tea. Beds: QD. Phone in room. Air conditioning. Amusement parks, antiquing, live theater, shopping and sporting events nearby.

Publicity: *Vacations, Cincinnati and Ohio Week, New York Times and Cincinnati Business Courier.*

"The suite is a haven of serene peacefulness."

Circleville   H5

Penguin Crossing B&B

3291 Sr 56 W
Circleville, OH 43113-9622
(740)477-6222 (800)736-4846 Fax:(740)420-6060
E-mail: innkeeper@penguin.cc
Web: www.penguin.cc

Circa 1820. This romantic country getaway on 300 acres offers heart-shaped personal Jacuzzis for two, antique appointed rooms, gourmet hot chocolate served fireside, candlelight breakfasts and room amenities such as a wood-burning fire-

place or brass bed. Bright colors and original walnut woodwork add to the decor in this 1820s brick farmhouse, once a stage-coach stop. As the name might suggest, the inn has a collection of penguins on display. In the
evenings, guests enjoy moon-lit walks along the old country lane and in the daytime, exploring the inn's farmland, watching the kittens playing in the barn, or cycling to downtown Circleville, four miles away. Breakfasts include a selection of natural foods, and the innkeeper is happy to cater to special dietary needs.

Historic Interest: Ted Lewis Museum (4 miles), Circleville Pumpkin Show (4 miles), Deer Creek State Park (20 miles).

Innkeeper(s): Ross & Tracey Irvin. $100-225. MC, VISA, AX, DS, PC, TC. 5 rooms with PB, 2 with FP. Breakfast included in rates. Types of meals: Cont and early coffee/tea. Beds: KQDT. Phone and Jacuzzi (four rooms) in room. Air conditioning. VCR and fax on premises. Handicap access. Weddings, small meetings, family reunions and seminars hosted. Antiquing, fishing, live theater, parks, shopping and water sports nearby.

"If I had to describe this home in one word, it would be — enchanting."

Cleveland   C7

Brownstone Inn-Downtown

3649 Prospect Ave
Cleveland, OH 44115
(216)426-1753 Fax:(216)431-0648
E-mail: ryates1@mindspring.com
Web: www.brownstoneinndowntown.com

Circa 1874. A bright blue door welcomes guests at the front of this inn, which is actually located in a historic brownstone in downtown Cleveland. The inn was built just a few years after the Civil War and is listed as a National Landmark Row House and listed in the National Register. Victorian appointments and antiques decorate the inn's interior. The guest rooms range from the opulent Bridal Suite to cozier rooms with double beds. The suite includes a fireplace and private bath. There is a kitchenette, which guests may use to fix that midnight snack.

Historic Interest: Ohio Canal, Millionaire's Row, University Circle.

Innkeeper(s): Mr Robin Yates. $85-105. MC, VISA, AX, DS, PC, TC. TAC15. 5 rooms, 1 with PB, 1 with FP. Breakfast included in rates. Types of meals: Full bkfst and early coffee/tea. Beds: QD. Phone and ceiling fan in room. Central air. Fax on premises. Antiquing, art galleries, beaches, bicycling, fishing, golf, hiking, live theater, museums, parks, shopping and tennis nearby.

Danville   F6

Red Fox Country Inn

26367 Danville Amity Rd, PO Box 717
Danville, OH 43014-0746
(740)599-7369 (877)600-7310
E-mail: sudsimp@aol.com
Web: www.redfoxcountryinn.com

Circa 1830. This inn, located on 15 scenic central Ohio acres, was built originally to house those traveling on the Danville-Amity Wagon Road and later became a farm home. Amish woven rag rugs and country antiques decorate the guest rooms. Some of the furnishings belonged to early owners, and some date to the 18th century. Three rooms include Amish-made oak beds and the fourth an 1880s brass and iron double bed. Breakfasts include fresh pastries, fruits, coffee and a variety of delec-
table entrees. Special dietary needs usually can be accommodated. There are books and games available in the inn's sitting room, and guests also are invited to relax on the front porch. Golfing, canoeing, fishing, horseback riding, hiking, biking, skiing and Mohican State Park are nearby, and the inn is 30 minutes from the largest Amish community in the United States.

Historic Interest: Amish settlements, Malibar Farm, historic Roscoe Village and the National Heisey Glass Museum are less than an hour from the inn.

Innkeeper(s): Sue & Denny Simpkins. $75-85. MC, VISA, AX, DS, PC, TC. TAC10. 4 rooms with PB. Breakfast included in rates. Beds: QD. Air conditioning. Library on premises.

Publicity: *Dealers Automotive, Columbus Dispatch, Mount Vernon News and Cincinnati Enquirer.*

"Our dinner and breakfast were '5 star'. Thank you for the gracious hospitality and special kindness you showed us."

The White Oak Inn

29683 Walhonding Rd, SR 715
Danville, OH 43014
(740)599-6107
E-mail: info@whiteoakinn.com
Web: whiteoakinn.com

Circa 1915. Large oaks and ivy surround the wide front porch of this three-story farmhouse situated on 13 green acres. It is located on the former Indian trail and pioneer road that runs along the Kokosing River, and an Indian mound has been discovered on the property. The inn's woodwork is all original white oak, and guest rooms are furnished in antiques.  Visitors often shop for maple syrup, cheese and handicrafts at nearby Amish farms. Three cozy fireplace rooms provide the perfect setting for romantic evenings.

Historic Interest: Roscoe Village, restored Erie Canal Town (30 minutes).
Innkeeper(s): Yvonne & Ian Martin. $80-140. MC, VISA, AX, DS, PC, TC. TAC10. 10 rooms with PB, 3 with FP and 1 conference room. Breakfast and snacks/refreshments included in rates. Types of meals: Full bkfst, early coffee/tea and gourmet dinner. MAP. Beds: QDT. Phone, ceiling fan, TV jacks and one with whirlpool tub in room. Air conditioning. Library, guest refrigerator and piano on premises. Weddings, small meetings, family reunions and seminars hosted. French spoken. Antiquing, fishing, horseback riding, Amish area/museums, parks, shopping and water sports nearby.
Publicity: *Ladies Home Journal, Columbus Monthly, Cleveland Plain Dealer, Country, Glamour, Columbus Dispatch, Midwest Living.* and PBS - *Country Inn Cooking.*

"The dinner was just fabulous and we enjoyed playing the antique grand piano."

Dellroy — E8

Whispering Pines Bed and Breakfast

1268 Magnolia Rd SW
Dellroy, OH 44620
(330)735-2824 Fax:(330)735-7006
E-mail: info@atwoodlake.com
Web: www.atwoodlake.com

Circa 1880. Blissful memories are made at this Victorian Italianate inn sitting on seven lush acres of rolling hills. Exquisitely furnished with antiques and period pieces, the decor is relaxing and elegant. Romantic guest bedrooms and honeymoon suite offer gorgeous lake views, fluffy robes and CD players to enhance any mood. Some feature wood-burning fireplaces, private balconies and Jacuzzis. Breakfast is such a delight, the frequently requested mouth-watering recipes are now in a cookbook. Each season brings an eye-pleasing adventure to the surrounding area for an ultimate getaway, perfect for any occasion.

Historic Interest: Reeves Museum, Zoar Village, Warther's Museum.
Innkeeper(s): Bill & Linda Horn. $90-195. MC, VISA, AX, DS, PC, TC. TAC5. 5 rooms with PB, 2 with FP. Breakfast, afternoon tea and snacks/refreshments included in rates. Types of meals: Gourmet bkfst, veg bkfst and early coffee/tea. Beds: KQD. Ceiling fan and fireplace in room. Central air. Fax and spa on premises. Weddings hosted. Antiquing, art galleries, beaches, bicycling, canoeing/kayaking, fishing, golf, hiking, horseback riding, live theater, museums, parks, shopping, tennis, water sports and wineries nearby.

Dover — F8

Olde World Bed & Breakfast & Tea Room

2982 State Route 516 NW
Dover, OH 44622-7247
(330)343-1333 (800)447-1273 Fax:(330)364-8022
E-mail: owbb@tusco.net
Web: www.oldeworldbb.com

Circa 1881. The five guest rooms at this red brick Victorian farmhouse have differing themes including Oriental, Parisian, Mediterranean and Alpine. Ask for the Victorian Room, which has a beautiful carved bed and a private bath with clawfoot tub.

The parlor features beautifully preserved woodwork in its pocket doors and fireplace mantel. A chandelier, antique furnishings and floral wallpaper in the dining room add a Victorian  atmosphere to the inn's full breakfast, which often includes Swiss Eggs, rhubarb muffins, cream scones and grilled local whole hog sausage. A favorite activity is retreating to the veranda to munch on warm homemade cookies. "Queen's Tea" is served every Tuesday and Wednesday. The Amish countryside and an abundance of antiquing opportunities are nearby.

Innkeeper(s): Jonna Cronebaugh. $65-110. MC, VISA, DS. 5 rooms with PB, 1 suite and 1 conference room. Breakfast included in rates. Types of meals: Gourmet bkfst, lunch, afternoon tea, snacks/refreshments and dinner. Beds: KQ. Air conditioning. VCR, fax and spa on premises. Family reunions and seminars hosted. Antiquing, fishing, golf, Amish Country historical sites, live theater, shopping, tennis and water sports nearby.
Publicity: *Ohio Magazine, Columbus Dispatch, Canton Repository, Cleveland Plain Dealer, Ohio Pass Magazine* and Wheeling travel show.

Findlay — D4

Rose Gate Cottage Bed & Breakfast

423 Western Ave
Findlay, OH 45840-2447
(419)424-1940 (877)614-4577 Fax:(419)424-1940
E-mail: rosegate@rosegateinn.com
Web: www.rosegateinn.com

Circa 1900. Original hardwood floors, trim and high ceilings accentuate this two-story home of rose-colored stucco. Experience an inviting Victorian atmosphere with warm and friendly innkeepers. The parlor features a piano and offers local restaurant menus to peruse. Antique beds include an oak highback, pine cone posted and four poster, in the wallpapered guest bedrooms. The Garden Villa and the Tea Rose rooms boast whirlpool tubs. Breakfast may include the inn's signature dish, a hot apple puff pancake baked in a ramekin. History is very evident in this quaint midwestern town. Presidents McKinley, Hayes and Harding all have memorial sites within driving distance.

Innkeeper(s): John & Belinda Nesler. $75-95. MC, VISA, AX, DS. TAC10. 4 rooms with PB and 1 conference room. Breakfast included in rates. Types of meals: Gourmet bkfst and cont plus. Beds: QDT. Whirlpool tubs in room. Air conditioning. VCR on premises. Antiquing, art galleries, bicycling and golf nearby.

Georgetown — J3

Bailey House

112 N Water St
Georgetown, OH 45121-1332
(937)378-3087
E-mail: baileyho@bright.net

Circa 1830. The stately columns of this three-story Greek Revival house once greeted Ulysses S. Grant, a frequent visitor during his boyhood when he was sent to buy milk from the Bailey's. A story is told that Grant accidentally overheard that the Bailey boy was leaving West Point. Grant immediately ran through the woods to the home of Congressman Thomas Hamer and petitioned an appointment in Bailey's place which he received, thus launching his military career. The inn has double parlors, pegged oak floors and Federal-style fireplace mantels. Antique washstands, chests and beds are found in the large guest rooms.

Innkeeper(s): Nancy Purdy. $55. PC. TAC10. 4 rooms, 2 with FP. Breakfast included in rates. Types of meals: Full bkfst and early coffee/tea. Beds: QD.

Phone, fireplace (two rooms) and desk (one room) in room. Air conditioning. Library and herb garden on premises. Weddings, small meetings, family reunions and seminars hosted. Antiquing, fishing, golf, private tours of U.S. Grant Home, historic sites, John Ruthven Art Gallery, parks, shopping, tennis and water sports nearby.
Pets Allowed.

"Thank you for your warm hospitality, from the comfortable house to the delicious breakfast."

Hanoverton   E9

The Spread Eagle Tavern & Inn

10150 Plymouth St, PO Box 277
Hanoverton, OH 44423
(330)223-1583 Fax:(330)223-1445
E-mail: jsweat@summitville.com
Web: spreadeagletavern.com

Circa 1837. For nearly two centuries, this three-story brick inn has graced historic Plymouth Street. The interior has been meticulously restored and maintains its early 19th-century ambiance. The restoration effort included repairing brick parts of the inn with bricks that came from an Ohio house more than 30 years older than the inn. Exposed beams, refurbished wood floors and period decor and furnishings adorn the interior. Original fireplaces still showcase color tile. The inn's restaurant offers a variety of dinner specials served in a room with authentic Federal-style decor. Guests might start off with clam chowder or an appetizer of baked Brie, Norwegian smoked salmon or snails in puff pastry followed by a caprese salad with fresh mozzarella, tomatoes and basil. As entree, guests might choose rainbow trout, shrimp scampi or maybe a hearty porterhouse or New York strip steak.
Innkeeper(s): Peter & Jean Johnson. $150-200. MC, VISA, AX, DS. 5 rooms with PB, 4 with FP. Breakfast included in rates. Types of meals: Full bkfst, gourmet lunch and gourmet dinner. Beds: KQDT. Cable TV and phone in room. Air conditioning. Fax and copier on premises. Weddings and small meetings hosted. Antiquing, fishing, golf and parks nearby.
Publicity: *Midwest Living, Colonial Homes* and *Ohio Magazine.*

Hartville   D8

Ivy & Lace

415 S Prospect Ave
Hartville, OH 44632-9401
(330)877-6357
E-mail: suzbnb@juno.com

Circa 1920. Large trees shade the exterior of Ivy & Lace, a historic home built in the Mission and four-square architectural styles, both of which were popular when the property was being constructed. Hartville's blacksmith built this home. Guest rooms feature antique furnishings, including a few pieces from the innkeepers' family. Rates include a full breakfast, and the artfully presented morning specialties include garnishes of

fresh flowers or fresh fruit. Crepes and French toast are among the entrees. Guests can walk from the home to the Town Square with its antique shops. Flea markets, Quail Hollow State Park, Pro Football Hall of Fame and First Ladies Library are popular attractions in the area.
Innkeeper(s): Sue & Paul Tarr. $65-75. AX,

DS, PC. 3 rooms, 1 with PB. Breakfast included in rates. Types of meals: Full bkfst. Beds: QDT. Cable TV, ceiling fan and phones can be arranged in room. Air conditioning. Antiquing, golf, live theater, museums, parks, shopping, cross-country skiing and sporting events nearby.

Kelleys Island   C5

Himmelblau B&B

337 Shannon Way
Kelleys Island, OH 43438
(419)746-2200

Circa 1893. This secluded Queen Anne Victorian on the Eastern Shore of Kellys Island rests on more than eight acres of lake front lawns and cedar groves. Its front yard tree swing and slate blue and white gabled entrance offer an inviting introduction to a pleas-

ant stay. Once the summer home of an Ohio governor, the property was also an early 1900s vineyard. Inside are a screened porch and a second-floor reading corner, which offers expansive Lake Erie views. A favorite activity of guests is to walk along the pristine shoreline at sunrise. The more adventurous enjoy snorkeling around an old shipwreck yards from the shoreline. Watching for white-tail deer after a moonlight swim, sunbathing and stargazing are popular activities, as well.
Innkeeper(s): Marvin Robinson. Call for rates. 3 rooms, 3 with FP. Beds: KQD. Ceiling fan in room. Air conditioning.

House On Huntington Lane

117 Huntington Ln, PO Box 504
Kelleys Island, OH 43438
(419)746-2765 (866)746-2765 Fax:(419)746-2765
E-mail: huntingtonlane@aol.com

Circa 1902. Escape to an island in the middle of Lake Erie, where a recently renovated Queen Anne Vernacular offers old-fashioned charm and modern conveniences like air conditioning. Private baths and televisions are standard amenities for each guest bedroom. A generous continental-plus breakfast is provided. Sit under a shady tree, relax and enjoy the tranquil waterfront or take a bicycle to explore and absorb the slower pace of life.
Innkeeper(s): Patty Hart. $90-110. MC, VISA, PC. 4 rooms with PB and 1 conference room. Breakfast included in rates. Types of meals: Cont plus, early coffee/tea and snacks/refreshments. Beds: QDT. TV and ceiling fan in room. Central air. VCR and bicycles on premises. Weddings and small meetings hosted. Amusement parks, antiquing, beaches, bicycling, canoeing/kayaking, fishing, hiking, parks, shopping, water sports and wineries nearby.

Loudonville   E6

Blackfork Inn

303 N Water St
Loudonville, OH 44842-1273
(419)994-3252
E-mail: bfinn@bright.net
Web: ohiobba.com/blackforkinn.htm

Circa 1865. A Civil War businessman, Philip Black, brought the railroad to town and built the Blackfork. Its well-preserved Second Empire style has earned it a place in the National Register. Noted preservationists have restored the inn with care and it is filled with a collection of Ohio antiques. Located in a scenic Amish area, the three-course breakfasts feature local produce. The innkeepers also offer two large three-room suites in a restored 1847 house, one suite includes a gas fireplace.
Innkeeper(s): Sue & Al Gorisek. $65-125. MC, VISA. 6 rooms with PB and 2 suites. Types of meals: Full bkfst.

Magnolia   E8

Elson Inn

225 North Main St (Rt 183)
Magnolia, OH 44643
(333)866-9242 Fax:(330)866-3398
E-mail: jelson@neo.rr.com
Web: www.elsoninn.com

Circa 1879. Experience small-town America at this brick
Victorian Italianate. This stately home's elegant sense of history
is felt from the 10-foot, leaded-glass double doors to the marble
fireplace. Climb the wooden staircase to the romantic guest
rooms, furnished in antiques and quilts, with spacious ceilings
and private baths. Each day begins with a delicious breakfast featuring specialties such as crème brulee French toast, fresh fruit
and muffins with the inn's own special label jams and jellies. A
shady, wraparound porch provides the perfect place to relax in a
swing or one of the rocking chairs. 1950s bicycles are available
for a leisurely ride through the village established in 1834. There
are ducks to be fed on the pond, and other activities include
fishing, hiking, tennis, golf and fine dining across the street.
Historic Interest: Zoar Village (3 miles), Schoenbrunn Village (12 miles), burial site of William McKinley (12 miles), National football Fall of Fame (12
miles), Elson Mill (next door).
Innkeeper(s): Jo Lane & Gus Elson. $100-120. MC, VISA, DS, PC, TC. 4
rooms with PB and 1 conference room. Breakfast included in rates. Types of
meals: Full bkfst. MAP. Beds: KQD. Central air. VCR, fax, copier, bicycles,
tennis and library on premises. Weddings, small meetings, family reunions
and seminars hosted. Amusement parks, antiquing, art galleries, beaches,
bicycling, canoeing/kayaking, fishing, golf, hiking, National Football Hall of
Fame, National 1st Ladies Library, Amish Settlement, live theater, museums,
parks, shopping, sporting events, tennis and water sports nearby.
Publicity: *Times Reporter, Canton Repository and Free Press News.*

Marietta   H8

The Buckley House

332 Front St
Marietta, OH 45750-2913
(740)373-3080 Fax:(740)373-8000
E-mail: dnicholas@wscc.edu

Circa 1879. Conveniently located in the downtown historic
district, this Southern-style home features impressive views of
Muskingum Park, Lookout Point and Valley Gem, a traditional
river boat on the Mighty
Mississippi. After a peaceful night's
rest in the well-appointed guest
bedrooms, begin a new day with a
delicious breakfast. A New
Orleans-style garden with gazebo
and fish pond grace the grounds
that include a spa. Ponder fond
memories while relaxing on the double porches or decks. The
coveted Pineapple Award for excellence was bestowed on this
inn by the Ohio Bed and Breakfast Association.
Innkeeper(s): Dell & Alf Nicholas. $85-95. MC, VISA, DS, PC, TC. 3 rooms
with PB. Breakfast included in rates. Types of meals: Full bkfst and early cof-
fee/tea. Beds: KDT. Ceiling fan in room. Central air. VCR, fax, spa and library
on premises. Weddings, small meetings, family reunions and seminars hosted. Antiquing, fishing, live theater, parks, shopping and water sports nearby.

Miamisburg   H2

English Manor B&B

505 E Linden Ave
Miamisburg, OH 45342-2850
(937)866-2288 (800)676-9456

Circa 1924. This is a beautiful English Tudor mansion situated
on a tree-lined street of Victorian homes. Well-chosen antiques
combined with the innkeepers' personal heirlooms added to
the inn's polished floors, sparkling leaded-and-stained-glass
windows and shining silver, make this an elegant retreat.
Breakfast is served in the formal dining room. Fine restaurants,
a water park, baseball, air force
museum and theater are close by, as
is The River Corridor bikeway on the
banks of the Great Miami River.
Historic Interest: 10 minutes south of Dayton.
Innkeeper(s): Julie & Larry Chmiel. $79-95.
MC, VISA, AX, DC, CB, DS. 5 rooms and 1
conference room. Breakfast included in rates.
Types of meals: Full bkfst. Phone and turn-
down service in room. Air conditioning. VCR on premises. Weddings, small
meetings, family reunions and seminars hosted. Amusement parks, antiquing,
live theater, shopping and sporting events nearby.

Mount Vernon   F6

The Russell-Cooper House

115 E Gambier St
Mount Vernon, OH 43050-3509
(740)397-8638 Fax:(740)397-3839
E-mail: mdvorak@jdsi.net
Web: www.russell-cooper.com

Circa 1829. Dr. John Russell and his son-in-law, Colonel Cooper,
modeled a simple brick Federal house into a unique Victorian. Its
sister structure is the Wedding Cake House of Kennebunk, Maine.
There is a hand-painted plaster ceiling in the ballroom and a collection of Civil War items and antique medical devices. Woodwork
is of cherry, maple and walnut, and there are etched and stained-
glass windows. Hal Holbrook called
the town "America's Hometown."
Historic Interest: The Russell-Cooper
House is located in historic Mount Vernon,
and the area offers numerous state and
national historic sites.
Innkeeper(s): Tom & Mary Dvorak. $65-
100. MC, VISA, AX, PC, TC. TAC10. 6
rooms with PB and 1 conference room.
Breakfast and snacks/refreshments included in rates. Types of meals:
Gourmet bkfst. Beds: QDT. Cable TV and ceiling fan in room. Air condition-
ing. Fax and copier on premises. Weddings, small meetings, family reunions
and seminars hosted. Antiquing, golf, bike trails, parks and shopping nearby.
Publicity: *Ohio Business, Victorian Homes, Columbus Monthly, Innsider,
Country, Americana, Columbus Dispatch, Ohio, Midwest Living, New York
Times and Washingtonian.*

*"A salute to the preservation of American history and culture. Most
hospitable owners! A romantic memory we will always remember!"*

New Plymouth   I6

Ravenwood Castle

65666 Bethel Rd
New Plymouth, OH 45654-9707
(740)596-2606 (800)477-1541
E-mail: castle@ohiohills.com
Web: www.ravenwoodcastle.com

Circa 1995. Although this is a newer construction, the architect
modeled the inn after a 12th-century, Norman-style castle, offer-

ing a glimpse back at Medieval England. A Great Hall with massive stone fireplace, dramatic rooms and suites with antique stained-glass windows and gas fireplaces make for a unique getaway. The castle, which overlooks Vinton County's Swan township, is surrounded by 50 acres of forest and large rock formations and is reached by a half-mile private road. There is a seasonal tea room and gift shop on the premises.

Historic Interest: The area offers several historic covered bridges, and a scenic railway is nearby.

Innkeeper(s): Jim & Sue Maxwell. $105-275. MC, VISA, DS. 6 rooms with PB, 2 suites and 5 cottages. Breakfast included in rates. Types of meals: Full bkfst, early coffee/tea, picnic lunch, afternoon tea, snacks/refreshments, gourmet dinner and room service. Beds: KQD. Ceiling fan in room. Air conditioning. VCR, fax and copier on premises. Handicap access. Weddings, small meetings, family reunions and seminars hosted. Antiquing, fishing, near caves, waterfalls, shopping and water sports nearby.

Publicity: *Columbus Dispatch, Cincinnati Enquirer, Midwest Living, USA Today, Honeymoon, Ohio Magazine, Milwaukee Journal Sentinel, Copley News Service, PBS-TV* and *"Country Inn Cooking with Gail Greco."*

"The atmosphere is romantic, the food excellent, the hospitality super!"

Painesville   B8

Rider's 1812 Inn

792 Mentor Ave
Painesville, OH 44077-2516
(440)354-8200 Fax:(440)350-9385
E-mail: ridersinn@ncweb.com

Circa 1812. In the days when this inn and tavern served the frontier Western Reserve, it could provide lodging and meals for more than 100 overnight guests. Restored in 1988, the pub features an original fireplace and wavy window panes. Most of the inn's floors are rare, long-needle pine. A passageway in the cellar is said to have been part of the Underground Railroad. An English-style restaurant is also on the premises. Guest rooms are furnished with antiques. Breakfast in bed is the option of choice.

Historic Interest: President Garfield's Home, Shadybrook, Lake County Historical Museum, Harbor Lighthouse.

Innkeeper(s): Elaine Crane & Gary Herman. $75-85. MC, VISA, AX, DS, PC. TAC7. 10 rooms, 9 with PB, 1 suite and 3 conference rooms. Breakfast included in rates. Types of meals: Gourmet bkfst, veg bkfst, early coffee/tea, lunch, picnic lunch, afternoon tea, dinner and room service. AP. Beds: KQDT. Cable TV, phone, turndown service and ceiling fan in room. Central air. Fax, copier, library, pet boarding and child care on premises. Weddings, small meetings, family reunions and seminars hosted. Spanish spoken. Antiquing, art galleries, beaches, fishing, golf, horseback riding, live theater, museums, parks, shopping, cross-country skiing, sporting events, tennis and wineries nearby.

Pets allowed: limited.

Publicity: *Business Review, News-Herald, Midwest Living, Haunted Ohio V, WEWS* and *Channel 5.*

Port Clinton   C5

SunnySide Tower Bed & Breakfast Inn

3612 NW Catawba Rd
Port Clinton, OH 43452-9726
(419)797-9315 (888)831-1263
E-mail: ssidetowr@cros.net
Web: www.sunnysidetower.com

Circa 1879. One of Catawba Island's original landmarks, this classic Victorian farmhouse is the innkeeper's ancestral family home. The hilltop inn and tower with a fourth-story widow's watch sits on 19 acres of wooded nature trails, herb gardens and landscaping. A glacial rock fireplace is showcased in the great room, or relax in the sunroom, a screened porch with wicker furniture. Distinctive country antique guest bedrooms feature comfortable period furnishings. Appetites are awakened

with the aroma of gourmet coffee and teas accompanying a country breakfast. Share a romantic moment in a double hammock, or soak in the hot tub. The area offers easy access to a variety of Lake Erie activities and several state parks.

Historic Interest: Mon Ami Winery, Marblehead Lighthouse, Hayes Memorial.

Innkeeper(s): John Davenport. $69-159. MC, VISA, AX, DS, PC, TC. TAC8. 10 rooms, 4 with PB and 1 conference room. Breakfast included in rates. Types of meals: Country bkfst. Beds: KQD. Ceiling fan in room. Central air. Hot tub and children's play area on premises. Handicap access. Weddings, small meetings, family reunions and seminars hosted. Amusement parks, antiquing, art galleries, beaches, bicycling, canoeing/kayaking, fishing, golf, hiking, basketball courts, baseball/soccer fields, sledding hill, live theater, museums, parks, shopping, tennis, water sports and wineries nearby.

Pets allowed: With prior approval.

Ripley   J3

The Signal House

234 N Front St
Ripley, OH 45167-1015
(937)392-1640 Fax:(937)392-1640
E-mail: signalhouse@webtv.net

Circa 1830. This Greek Italianate home is said to have been used to aid the Underground Railroad. A light in the attic told Rev. John Rankin, a dedicated abolitionist, that it was safe to transport

slaves to freedom. Located within a 55-acre historical district, guests can take a glance back in time, exploring museums and antique shops. Twelve-foot ceilings with ornate plaster-work grace the parlor, and guests can sit on any of three porches anticipating paddlewheelers traversing the Ohio River.

Innkeeper(s): Vic & Betsy Billingsley. $85. MC, VISA, DS, PC, TC. TAC10. 2 rooms. Breakfast included in rates. Types of meals: Full bkfst and early coffee/tea. Beds: Q. Ceiling fan in room. Central air. VCR, fax, copier and library on premises. Small meetings hosted. Antiquing, bicycling, fishing, golf, hiking, canoeing, museums, parks, shopping, tennis, water sports and wineries nearby.

Publicity: *Cincinnati Enquirer, Ohio Columbus Dispatch, Ohio Off the Beaten Path, Cincinnati Magazine, Cincinnati Post, Dayton Daily News, Ohio Magazine, Cleveland Plain Dealer,* Husband's first car in *"Lost in Yonkers", Channel 12* and *WKRC- "One Tank Trip"*

Sagamore Hills   D8

The Inn at Brandywine Falls

8230 Brandywine Rd
Sagamore Hills, OH 44067-2810
(330)467-1812
E-mail: brandywinefallsinn@prodigy.net
Web: www.innatbrandywinefalls.com

Circa 1848. Overlooking Brandywine Falls and situated snuggly on National Parkland, this National Register Greek Revival farmhouse has been meticulously renovated. Antiques made in Ohio are featured in the Greek Revival-style rooms and include sleigh and four-poster beds. Some suites include a double whirlpool tub. The kitchen has been designed to allow guests to chat with the innkeepers while sipping coffee in front of a crackling fireplace and watching breakfast preparations. The Waterfall and hiking trails are just past the gate. Cleveland is a short drive, offering attractions such as the Rock 'n' Roll Hall of Fame and the Cleveland Orchestra.

Innkeeper(s): Katie & George Hoy. $108-295. MC, VISA, DS. 6 rooms with PB, 3 with FP and 3 suites. Breakfast included in rates. Types of meals: Gourmet bkfst. Beds: KDT. Handicap access.

Publicity: *Ohio Magazine, Countryside, Innsider, Western Reserve, Cleveland Plain Dealer, Akron Beacon Journal, Vindicator, Dayton Daily News* and *Michigan Living.*

"The magic of the inn was not forgotten. We will be back to enjoy."

Sandusky   C5

The Red Gables

421 Wayne St
Sandusky, OH 44870-2710
(419)625-1189

Circa 1907. Nestled just blocks from Lake Erie, this beautifully appointed, red-trimmed Tudor home features polished natural woodwork, ornate ceilings and luxurious decor. Costume-maker and innkeeper Jo Ellen Cuthbertson applied her skills as a seamstress to create a light, romantic atmosphere at Red Gables. Guests enjoy a breakfast of fresh muffins and fruit in the enormous great room, which features a huge fireplace and bay window. Red Gables is within walking distance of several island cruise ships and the island ferries. Two nearby nature preserves, wineries and antique shops offer other fun excursions.

Historic Interest: The Red Gables is located in Sandusky's historic Old Plat District. The Follett House Museum is just across the street from the B&B. The Merry-Go-Round Museum is just a few blocks away. Thomas Edison's birthplace and museum is about 10 miles away. Johnson's Island, a Civil War officer's prison camp, is another nearby attraction.
Innkeeper(s): Jo Ellen Cuthbertson. $95-105. MC, VISA. 4 rooms, 2 with PB. Breakfast included in rates. Types of meals: Cont plus. Beds: QDT. Antiquing, fishing, live theater and water sports nearby.
Publicity: *Ohio, Northern Ohio Live, Cuyahoga County Public Library and Ladies' Home Journal.*

Wagner's 1844 Inn

230 E Washington St
Sandusky, OH 44870-2611
(419)626-1726 Fax:(419)626-0002
E-mail: wagnersinn@sanduskyohio.com

Circa 1844. This inn originally was constructed as a log cabin. Additions and renovations were made, and the house evolved into Italianate style accented with brackets under the eaves and black shutters on the second-story windows. A wrought-iron fence frames the house, and there are ornate wrought-iron porch rails. A billiard room and screened-in porch are available to guests. The ferry to Cedar Point and Lake Erie Island is within walking distance.

Innkeeper(s): Barb Wagner. $70-120. MC, VISA, DS. 3 rooms with PB, 2 with FP. Breakfast included in rates. Types of meals: Cont. Beds: Q. Air conditioning. Library and TV on premises. Amusement parks, antiquing, fishing, Lake Erie Islands, golf, parks and shopping nearby.
Pets allowed: Some limitations.
Publicity: *Lorain Journal and Sandusky Register.*
"This B&B rates in our Top 10."

Tiffin   D5

Fort Ball Bed & Breakfast

25 Adams St
Tiffin, OH 44883-2208
(419)447-0776 (888)447-0776 Fax:(419)448-8415
E-mail: ftballbanb@friendlynet.com

Circa 1894. The prominent front turret and wraparound porch are classic details of this Queen Anne Revival house built by John King, builder of the Tiffin Court House and College Hall at Heidelberg College. The innkeepers dedicated more than a year restoring this turn-of-the-century Victorian to its original elegant state. The renovation yielded rich hardwood flooring, wood paneling and many additional architectural details like the elaborate woodwork in the parlor, front entryway and sitting room. Guest rooms are comfortably decorated to accommodate business travelers, families or honeymooners, and offer private and shared baths while some feature whirlpool tubs for two. Breakfast can be enjoyed in the dining room with its elegantly restored woodwork. The inn is within walking distance of the downtown business district, restaurants, antiques, shopping, museums and theater.

Innkeeper(s): Charles & Lenora Livingston. $65-105. MC, VISA, DS, PC, TC. 4 rooms, 2 with PB. Breakfast and snacks/refreshments included in rates. Types of meals: Full bkfst and early coffee/tea. Beds: KQDT. Phone and ceiling fan in room. Air conditioning. VCR, fax and library on premises. Small meetings hosted. Amusement parks, antiquing, golf, historical sites, live theater, parks and tennis nearby.
Publicity: *Advertiser-Tribune.*

Urbana   G3

Northern Plantation B&B

3421 E RR 296
Urbana, OH 43078
(937)652-1782 (800)652-1782

Circa 1913. This Victorian farmhouse, located on 100 acres, is occupied by fourth-generation family members. (Marsha's father was born in the downstairs bedroom in 1914.) The Homestead Library is decorated traditionally and has a handsome fireplace, while the dining room features a dining set and a china cabinet made by the innkeeper's great-grandfather. Most of the guest rooms have canopy beds. A large country breakfast is served. On the property is a fishing pond, corn fields, soybeans and woods with a creek. Nearby are Ohio Caverns and Indian Lake.

Innkeeper(s): Marsha J. Martin. $85-105. MC, VISA, DS. 4 rooms, 1 with PB. Breakfast included in rates. Types of meals: Full bkfst, cont plus and snacks/refreshments. Beds: KD. Air conditioning. VCR and library on premises. Weddings and family reunions hosted. Antiquing, Pratt Castle, parks, shopping and cross-country skiing nearby.

West Union   J4

Murphin Ridge Inn

750 Murphin Ridge Rd
West Union, OH 45693-9734
(937)544-2263 (877)687-7446
E-mail: murphinn@bright.net
Web: www.murphinridgeinn.com

Circa 1810. The inn is contemporary, yet situated on an historic 142-acre woodland farm imparting a tranquil atmosphere. Some of the guest bedrooms feature fireplaces and/or porches. Three new Amish-built log cabins boast two-person showers and double whirlpool tubs. A romantic ambiance is enhanced by three-sided open fireplaces. Meals are served in an 1810 red-brick farmhouse. Visit a neighboring Amish community, Serpent Mound and the Edge of Appalachia Nature Preserve.

Innkeeper(s): Sherry & Darry McKenney. $90-185. 10 rooms with PB and 3 cabins. Breakfast included in rates. Types of meals: Full bkfst, lunch and gourmet dinner. Beds: Q. Antiquing nearby.
Publicity: *Midwest Living, Ohio Magazine, National Geographic Traveler, Cincinnati Enquirer, Midwest Living and Ohio Magazine.*
"Restful, relaxing escape. Outstanding autumn color, trails, hospitality."

Oklahoma

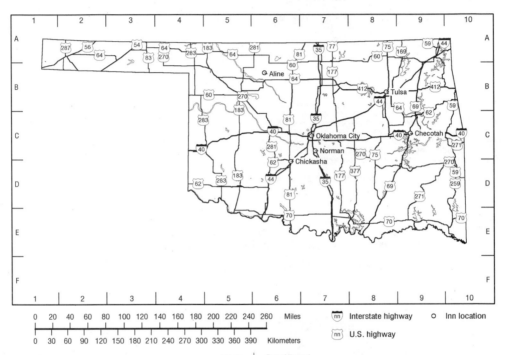

	Miles	
0 20 40 60 80 100 120 140 160 180 200 220 240 260		
0 30 60 90 120 150 180 210 240 270 300 330 360 390	Kilometers	

Interstate highway   ○ Inn location

U.S. highway

Aline B6

Heritage Manor
33 Heritage Road
Aline, OK 73716-9118
(580)463-2563 (800)295-2563
E-mail: heritage@pldi.net

Circa 1903. This inn provides a way to enjoy and experience the ambiance of the turn of the century. Explore and relax in the inn's peaceful gardens and 80-acre wildlife habitat and watch song birds, butterflies, long-haired cattle, donkeys, llamas and ostriches. The inn invites visitors to enjoy its more than 5,000-volume library and more than a 100 channels on Dish TV. Guests can walk the suspension bridge to two roof-top decks and a widow's walk to view the stars and sunsets. There is also an out-door hot tub for soaking. Dine in the parlor, gazebo, courtyard or tree-top-level deck where the choice of time and menu is entirely up to the guest.

Innkeeper(s): A.J. & Carolyn Rexroat. $55-150. PC, TC. 4 rooms, 2 suites and 2 conference rooms. Breakfast and snacks/refreshments included in rates. Types of meals: Full bkfst, early coffee/tea, gourmet lunch, picnic lunch, afternoon tea and gourmet dinner. Beds: QD. Cable TV and phone in room. Air conditioning. VCR, spa and library on premises. Handicap access. Weddings, small meetings, family reunions and seminars hosted. Antiquing, fishing, live theater, parks, shopping, sporting events and water sports nearby.

Pets Allowed.
Publicity: *Country, Enid Morning News, Daily Oklahoman, Cherokee Messenger, Republican, Fairview Republican* and *Discover Oklahoma.*

Checotah C9

Sharpe House
301 NW 2nd St
Checotah, OK 74426-2240
(918)473-2832

Circa 1911. Built on land originally bought from a Creek Indian, this Southern plantation-style inn was a teacherage—the rooming house for single female teachers. It is furnished with heirlooms from the innkeepers' families and hand-crafted accessories. The look of the house is antebellum, but the specialty of the kitchen is Mexican cuisine. Family-style evening meals are available upon request. Checotah is located at the junction of I-40 and U.S. 69. This makes it the ideal base for your day trips of exploration or recreation in Green Country.

Innkeeper(s): Kay Kindt. $35-50. PC, TC. 3 rooms with PB and 1 suite. Breakfast included in rates. Types of meals: Full bkfst, cont plus, cont and early coffee/tea. Beds: D. Cable TV and ceiling fan in room. Air conditioning. Library & child care on premises. Weddings and small meetings hosted. Spanish spoken. Amusement parks, antiquing, fishing, parks, shopping & water sports nearby. Pets Allowed.

Chickasha   D6

Campbell-Richison House B&B

1428 Kansas
Chickasha, OK 73018
(405)222-1754
E-mail: innkeeper@campbellrichison.com
Web: www.campbellrichison.com

Circa 1909. Upon entering this prairie-style home, guests will notice a spacious entryway with a gracious stairway ascending to the second-floor guest rooms. The front parlor is a wonderful spot for relaxing, reading or just soaking up the history of the home. The dining room has a stained-glass window that gives off a kaleidoscope of beautiful colors when the morning sun shines through. A spacious yard encompasses one-quarter of a city block and has large shade trees that can be enjoyed from the wicker-lined porch.
Historic Interest: Grady County Historical Museum (less than a mile), Indian City.
Innkeeper(s): Kami & David Ratcliff. $50-70. 3 rooms with PB. Breakfast included in rates. Types of meals: Full bkfst and early coffee/tea. Beds: KQD. Phone, VCR and sitting area in room. Air conditioning. Small meetings hosted. Antiquing, shopping and sporting events nearby.
Publicity: *OK Today, Chickasha Express, Cache Times Weekly & Chickasha Star.*
"We enjoyed our stay at your lovely B&B! It was just the getaway we needed to unwind from a stressful few weeks. Your hospitality fellowship and food were just wonderful."

Norman   C7

Holmberg House B&B

766 Debarr Ave
Norman, OK 73069-1908
(405)321-6221 (877)621-6221 Fax:(405)321-6221
E-mail: info@holmberghouse.com

Circa 1914. Professor Fredrik Holmberg and his wife Signy built this Craftsman-style home across the street from the University of Oklahoma. Each of the antique-filled rooms has its own individual decor and style. The Blue Danube and Bed & Bath rooms are romantic retreats and both include a two-person whirlpool tub. The Garden Room includes a clawfoot tub. The Sundance Room  is ideal for friends traveling together, as it includes both a queen and twin bed. The parlor and front porch are perfect places to relax with friends, and the lush grounds include a cottage garden. Aside from close access to the university, Holmberg House is within walking distance to more than a dozen restaurants.
Historic Interest: The Oklahoma Museum of Natural History is 6 blocks from the inn. The Cleveland County Historical Society & Lindsey Moor House are about a mile away. Jacobson House, a Native American museum, is 6 blocks away.
Innkeeper(s): Eddie & Bernie Flax. $85-120. MC, VISA, PC, TC. TAC10. 4 rooms with PB. Breakfast included in rates. Types of meals: Gourmet bkfst and early coffee/tea. Beds: QT. Cable TV and ceiling fan in room. Air conditioning. Fax, copier and library on premises. Weddings, small meetings & family reunions hosted. Antiquing, live theater, parks, shopping & sporting events nearby.
Publicity: *Metro Norman, OKZ City Journal Record, Norman Transcript and Country Inns.*
"Your hospitality and the delicious food were just super."

Oklahoma City   C7

The Grandison at Maney Park

1200 N Shartel Ave
Oklahoma City, OK 73103-2402
(405)232-8778 (800)240-4667 Fax:(405)232-5039
E-mail: grandison@juno.com
Web: www.bbonline.com/ok/grandison

Circa 1904. This spacious Victorian has been graciously restored and maintains its original mahogany woodwork, stained glass, brass fixtures and a grand staircase. Several rooms include a Jacuzzi, and all have their own unique decor. The Treehouse Hideaway includes a queen bed that is meant to look like a hammock and walls are painted with a blue sky and stars. The Jacuzzi tub rests beneath a skylight. The home is located north of downtown Oklahoma City in a historic neighborhood listed in the National Register.
Historic Interest: Overholser Mansion (1/2 mile), Heritage Center (1 mile), Harn Homestead (2 miles), Bricktown (2 miles).
Innkeeper(s): Claudia & Bob Wright. $75-150. MC, VISA, AX, DS, PC, TC. TAC10. 9 rooms with PB, 2 suites and 1 conference room. Breakfast and snacks/refreshments included in rates. Types of meals: Full bkfst, cont plus, early coffee/tea and room service. Beds: KQT. TV, phone, ceiling fan, VCR and 7 with Jacuzzi's in room. Air conditioning. Fax, copier, workout room and video library on premises. Handicap access. Weddings, small meetings, family reunions and seminars hosted. Antiquing, live theater, parks and sporting events nearby.
Publicity: *Daily Oklahoman, Oklahoma Pride, Oklahoma Gazette, Discover Oklahoma, Tulsa People Magazine, Travel & Leisure, Country Discoveries Magazine, Discover Oklahoma and Oklahoma Living.*
"Like going home to Grandma's!"

Tulsa   B8

McBirney Mansion B&B

1414 S Galveston Ave
Tulsa, OK 74127-9116
(918)585-3234 Fax:(918)585-9377
Web: www.mcbirneymansion.com

Circa 1927. An oil baron built this immense Tudor mansion, which is listed in the National Register. The home rests on three acres, adjacent to Tulsa River Parks. The countryside, with its spring-fed ponds, was a common gathering spot for local native tribes and early settlers. Washington Irving once camped out on the grounds and later wrote about his experience in "Tour of the Prairies." Winding stone paths lead down to the banks of the Arkansas River, and the grounds are dotted with gardens. The manor's interior is equally impressive. Bedchambers boast fine antiques, some include a marble bath or whirlpool tub. For a romantic getaway, consider the Carriage House  Retreat, a private cottage with a bedroom, sitting room, small kitchen area and a bath with a jetted shower. Guests are treated to a multi-course, gourmet breakfast. The morning meal begins with fresh fruit, perhaps poached pears, strawberry compote or baked apple. The main course might include eggs Benedict, huevos rancheros, a spinach quiche served with cheese grits in a baked tomato and homemade English muffins. McBirney Mansion is close to museums, shops, antique stores, galleries, restaurants and Tulsa's business district and civic center.
Historic Interest: Tall Grass Prairie (80 miles), Council Oak Tree (3 blocks).
Innkeeper(s): Kathy Collins & Renita Shofner. $119-225. MC, VISA, AX, DS, PC, TC. 8 rooms with PB, 1 with FP, 3 suites & 3 conference rooms. Breakfast & snacks/refreshments included in rates. Types of meals: Veg bkfst, cont plus, early coffee/tea & picnic lunch. Beds: KQDT. Cable TV, phone & VCR in room. Central air. Fax, copier & library on premises. Weddings, small meetings, family reunions and seminars hosted. Amusement parks, antiquing, art galleries, bicycling, fishing, golf, hiking, live theater, museums, parks, shopping and tennis nearby.
Publicity: *Southern Living, OK Today, Dallas Morning News and Tulsa People.*

Oregon

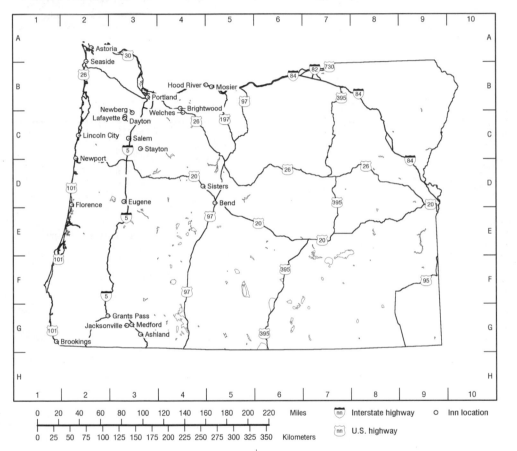

0 20 40 60 80 100 120 140 160 180 200 220 Miles

0 25 50 75 100 125 150 175 200 225 250 275 300 325 350 Kilometers

🔲 Interstate highway   ○ Inn location

🔲 U.S. highway

Ashland   G3

Iris Inn

59 Manzanita St
Ashland, OR 97520-2615
(541)488-2286 (800)460-7650 Fax:(541)488-3709
E-mail: irisinnbb@aol.com

Circa 1905. The Iris Inn is a restored Victorian set on a large
flower-filled yard. It features simple American country antiques.
The upstairs guest rooms have views of the valley and mountains. Evening sips of wine often are taken out on the large
deck overlooking a rose garden. Breakfast boasts an elegant presentation with dishes such as buttermilk scones and eggs
Benedict with smoked salmon.

Innkeeper(s): Vicki & Greg Capp. $80-135. MC, VISA. 5 rooms with PB.
Breakfast included in rates. Types of meals: Full bkfst. Beds: QT. Turndown
service and ceiling fan in room. Air conditioning. Fax on premises. Small meetings and seminars hosted. Antiquing, fishing, golf, live theater, shopping,
downhill skiing, cross-country skiing, sporting events and water sports nearby.
Publicity: *Sunset* and *Oregonian*.

"A favorite place to be pampered since 1982."

Morical House Garden Inn

668 N Main St
Ashland, OR 97520-1710
(541)482-2254 (800)208-0960 Fax:(541)482-1775
E-mail: innkeepers@garden-inn.com
Web: www.garden-inn.com

Circa 1882. Metropolitan luxury is found at this restored
Eastlake Victorian inn with spectacular views of the Cascade

Mountains. The entry and parlor still feature original wide plank, red-fir floors, woodwork and leaded-glass windows. Asian antiques and contemporary furnishings create a

refined ambiance. Some guest bedrooms boast a fireplace and Jacuzzi. Breakfast is served in the dining room or on the extended sun porch overlooking almost two acres of gardens, ponds, waterfalls and a nationally recognized bird sanctuary. Downtown is an easy walk.

Historic Interest: Oregon Shakespeare Festival (1 mile).
Innkeeper(s): Alicia Hwang. $96-200. MC, VISA, AX, DS, PC, TC. TAC10. 8 rooms with PB, 2 with FP. Breakfast and afternoon tea included in rates. Types of meals: Gourmet bkfst, early coffee/tea and snacks/refreshments. Beds: KQT. Phone, whirlpool tubs and three with refrigerator in room. Air conditioning. Fax on premises. Handicap access. Small meetings, family reunions and seminars hosted. Fishing, live theater, shopping, downhill skiing and cross-country skiing nearby.
Publicity: *Pacific Northwest Magazine, Country Inns and Travel & Leisure.*

Pinehurst Inn at Jenny Creek

17250 Hwy 66
Ashland, OR 97520-9406
(541)488-1002
E-mail: boxr@internetcds.com

Circa 1923. In the Southern Oregon cascades, this 1920s former roadhouse over looks scenic mountains and Jenny Creek. The lodge, built from logs harvested on the property, is on the old Applegate Wagon Trail (now Green Springs Highway or Highway

66). Upstairs there are stunning vistas from the sunroom. Guest rooms with antiques and art overlook the mountains or bucolic Jenny Creek. There are wide porches for enjoying the surrounding forest landscape and

the lobby, with its huge stone fireplace, is a welcoming site. The inn's dining room is a local gathering place and offers home cooking served family style in honor of its heritage. A continental breakfast is served. Weddings and other gatherings are popular here. Ashland is a half-hour and Klamath Falls is 39 miles away.

Innkeeper(s): Don & Jean Rowlett. $69-99. MC, VISA. 6 rooms with PB and 2 suites. Breakfast and dinner included in rates. Types of meals: Cont and early coffee/tea. Beds: KQD. Ceiling fan in room. Weddings, small meetings and family reunions hosted. Antiquing, fishing, hiking, live theater, shopping, downhill skiing and cross-country skiing nearby.
Publicity: *Sunset and Travel & Leisure.*

Wolfe Manor Inn

586 B St
Ashland, OR 97520
(541)488-3676 (800)801-3676 Fax:(541)488-4567
E-mail: wolfebandb@aol.com
Web: www.wolfemanor.com

Circa 1910. A glass door with sidelights welcomes guests to this massive Craftsman-style home. A grand parlor/ballroom with original lighting fixtures and fine woodwork is the combination sitting area and dining room. Bedrooms offer views of the mountains or the inn's pleasantly landscaped lawns and gardens. Guests often enjoy relaxing on the inn's porches.

Innkeeper(s): Sybil & Ron Maddox. $89-139. MC, VISA, AX, DC, DS, PC, TC. TAC10. 5 rooms with PB. Breakfast and snacks/refreshments included in rates.

Types of meals: Full bkfst. Beds: QD. Ceiling fan in room. Air conditioning. Fax, copier, library, refrigerator and snack bar on premises. Small meetings and family reunions hosted. Antiquing, fishing, golf, live theater, parks, shopping, downhill skiing, cross-country skiing, sporting events, tennis and water sports nearby.
Publicity: *Getaways Magazine and PNW "Best Places to Stay".*

Astoria   A2

Astoria Inn Bed & Breakfast

3391 Irving Ave
Astoria, OR 97103-2632
(503)325-8153 (800)718-8153

Circa 1890. Perched on the hillside, this stately Victorian inn is just five blocks from the Columbia River and has views of the forest and the river. It offers four guest bedrooms. A country breakfast is served each morning and it includes egg dishes, bacon, sausage or ham, potatoes, fruit and juices. Astoria is rich in historical and natural beauty. It was the first settlement west of the Rockies and was discovered in 1806 by John Jacob Astor. The inn is eight miles from Ft. Clatsop. Guests enjoy watching ships passing in the Columbia River and in the evening, the ships that anchor in the river basin in front of the inn create a wonderland of twinkling lights.

Historic Interest: Fort Clatsop (Lewis & Clark site, 8 miles).
Innkeeper(s): Ms. Mickey Cox. $60-85. MC, VISA, DS, PC, TC. TAC10. 4 rooms with PB. Breakfast and snacks/refreshments included in rates. Types of meals: Full bkfst, country bkfst, veg bkfst and early coffee/tea. Beds: Q. VCR and library on premises. Family reunions hosted. Antiquing, art galleries, beaches, bicycling, canoeing/kayaking, fishing, golf, hiking, horseback riding, museums, shopping, tennis, water sports and wineries nearby.
Publicity: *VIA (AAA) and Los Angeles Times.*

Benjamin Young Inn

3652 Duane St
Astoria, OR 97103-2421
(503)325-6172 (800)201-1286
E-mail: benjamin@benjaminyounginn.com
Web: www.benjaminyounginn.com

Circa 1888. From this Queen Anne Victorian, guests can watch ships and boats travel along the Columbia River. The home is listed in the National Register of Historic Places, and many of its period elements have been preserved and restored. Guest rooms are decorated in a comfortable, eclectic style with antiques, and all offer a river view. The spacious Fireplace Room includes a fireplace, Jacuzzi tub, king-size bed

and a bay window with a river view. It also has an adjoining room with a queen bed and two singles. Shops, museums and restaurants are just a mile and a half away in Astoria.

Innkeeper(s): Carolyn & Ken Hammer. $85-145. MC, VISA, AX, DS, PC, TC. TAC10. 5 rooms with PB, 1 with FP. Breakfast and afternoon tea included in rates. Types of meals: Gourmet bkfst and early coffee/tea. Beds: KQT. Cable TV and one with whirlpool and fireplace in room. Weddings, small meetings, family reunions and seminars hosted. French spoken. Antiquing, fishing, golf, live theater, parks, shopping, tennis and water sports nearby.

"Your home is absolutely gorgeous and the food and ambiance superb — so romantic, so wonderful!"

Franklin Street Station Bed & Breakfast

1140 Franklin Ave
Astoria, OR 97103-4132
(503)325-4314 (800)448-1098 Fax:(801)681-5641
E-mail: franklinstationbb@yahoo.com

Circa 1900. Sit out on the balcony and take in views of the Columbia River and beautiful sunsets from this 1900 Victorian-style inn. Ornate craftsmanship and antique furnishings, right down to the clawfoot bathtubs, transport visitors into the past. The six guest rooms are named Starlight Suite, Sweet Tranquility, the Hide-away,the Magestic, Magnolia Retreat and Enchanted Haven. The full breakfast includes dishes like fruit, waffles and sausage. The Flavel House Museum and Heritage Museum within walking distance, and the Astoria Column and Fort Clatsop are a short drive from the inn.

Innkeeper(s): Sharon Middleton, Rebecca Greenway. $60-135. MC, VISA, AX, DS, PC, TC. 6 rooms, 5 with PB, 1 with FP and 3 suites. Breakfast and snacks/refreshments included in rates. Types of meals: Full bkfst and early coffee/tea. Beds: Q. Cable TV, phone, VCR, claw foot tubs and balconies in room. Weddings, small meetings and family reunions hosted. Antiquing, art galleries, beaches, bicycling, canoeing/kayaking, fishing, golf, hiking, horse-back riding, swimming, live theater, museums, parks and shopping nearby.

Grandview B&B

1574 Grand Ave
Astoria, OR 97103-3733
(503)325-0000 (800)488-3250
E-mail: grandviewbnb@freedom.usa.com
Web: www.pacifier.com/~grndview/

Circa 1896. To fully enjoy its views of the Columbia River, this Victorian house has both a tower and a turret. Antiques and white wicker furnishings contribute to the inn's casual, homey feeling. The Bird Meadow Room is particularly appealing to

bird-lovers with its birdcage, bird books and bird wallpaper. Breakfast, served in the main-floor turret, frequently includes smoked salmon with bagels and cream cheese.

Historic Interest: Flavel House (8 blocks), Heritage Museum (1 block), Firefighters Museum (18 blocks).

Innkeeper(s): Charleen Maxwell. $61-101. MC, VISA, DS. 9 rooms, 7 with PB, 3 with FP and 2 suites. Breakfast and snacks/refreshments included in rates. Types of meals: Full bkfst. Beds: QT. Weddings, small meetings and family reunions hosted. Antiquing, fishing, historic homes tour, old-fashioned trolley, river walk, aqua center, movie complex, forts, live theater, parks, shopping and water sports nearby.

Publicity: *Pacific Northwest Magazine, Northwest Discoveries, Los Angeles Times, Oregonian and Daily Astorian.*

"I have travelled all over the world and for the first time I found in the country of the computers such a romantic house with such poetic rooms at the Grandview Bed & Breakfast." Thanks MD from Paris, France

Bend   D5

The Sather House B&B

7 NW Tumalo Ave
Bend, OR 97701-2634
(541)388-1065 (888)388-1065 Fax:(541)330-0591

Circa 1911. This Craftsman-style home is listed in the local, county and national historic registers. One room includes a clawfoot tub that dates to 1910. Period furnishings are found in the nicely appointed guest rooms, which feature touches of Battenburg and lace. The front porch is lined with wicker for

those who wish to relax and enjoy the surroundings. For break-fast, innkeeper Robbie Giamboi serves items such as apple and banana pancakes topped with her own homemade blackberry, raspberry maple or apple syrup. Guests also enjoy afternoon tea.

Innkeeper(s): Robbie Giamboi. $88-126. MC, VISA, AX, DS, PC, TC. 4 rooms with PB. Breakfast and afternoon tea included in rates. Types of meals: Gourmet bkfst and early coffee/tea. Beds: KQDT. Ceiling fan in room. VCR and library on premises. Small meetings and family reunions hosted. Antiquing, fishing, golf, live theater, parks, shopping, downhill skiing, cross-country skiing, sporting events, tennis and water sports nearby.

Publicity: *Bend Bulletin and Oregonian.*

Brightwood   B4

Brightwood Guesthouse B&B

64725 E Barlow Trail Rd
Brightwood, OR 97011-0189
(503)622-5783 (888)503-5783 Fax:(503)622-5783
E-mail: brightwoodbnb@hotmail.com

Circa 1932. For a private and peaceful romantic getaway, con-sider a trip to this flower-filled cedar cottage, secluded on two acres. The grounds include a creek, Japanese water-garden and waterfall that surround your private deck. A forested hillside ia adjacent to the house. The cottage offers two sleeping areas — a cozy loft and the living room, as well as a kitchen/dining room and amenity-filled bath. The guesthouse is furnished with Oriental artifacts. Cupboards are filled with supplies including coffee, cider, cocoa and tea. A bountiful breakfast is served to you on your deck or at the table and may include Italian scones, brioche, roasted potatoes, fresh fruit plate, amaretto truffle dessert and seared vegetable fritatta's. Special beverages are available for celebrations. Honeymoon, romance and ski packages are offered, as well as a Keepsake Basket Package.

Historic Interest: Oregon Trail, Timberline Lodge.

Innkeeper(s): Jan Estep. $120-135. MC, VISA, AX, PC, TC. TAC10. 1 guest houses. Breakfast included in rates. Types of meals: Gourmet bkfst, veg bkfst and room service. Beds: DT. Phone, turndown service, VCR, kitchenette, kimonos, slippers, bath lotions and hair dryers in room. Fax, copier, bicycles and library on premises. Family reunions hosted. Antiquing, bicycling, canoe-ing/kayaking, fishing, golf, hiking, horseback riding, slug races at Brightwood Tavern (seasonal), live theater, museums, parks, shopping, downhill skiing, cross-country skiing, tennis, water sports and wineries nearby.

Publicity: *Sunset, Mountain Times, Weekend Viaggi, Bridal Resource Guide and Best Places to Kiss in Oregon.*

Brookings   G1

South Coast Inn B&B

516 Redwood St
Brookings, OR 97415-9672
(541)469-5557 (800)525-9273 Fax:(541)469-6615
E-mail: innkeeper@southcoastinn.com

Circa 1917. Enjoy panoramic views of the Pacific Ocean at this Craftsman-style inn designed by renowned San Francisco archi-tect Bernard Maybeck. All rooms are furnished with antiques, ceiling fans, CD player, VCRs and TVs. Two guest rooms afford panoramic views of the coastline and there is a separate cottage. A floor-to-ceiling stone fireplace and beamed ceilings make the parlor a great place to gather with

friends. There are sun decks, a strolling garden, and an indoor hot tub and sauna. The Brookings area offers something for everyone. Outdoor activities include hiking, boating, golfing, digging for clams or simply enjoying a stroll along the spectacular coastline. Concerts, galleries, museums, antiques, specialty shops and fine restaurants all can be found within the area.

Innkeeper(s): Ken Raith & Keith Pepper. $89-129. MC, VISA, AX, DS, PC, TC. TAC10. 4 rooms with PB and 1 cottage. Breakfast included in rates. Types of meals: Gourmet bkfst, cont and early coffee/tea. Beds: KQ. Cable TV, ceiling fan, VCR, hair dryers in baths and 1 with gas fireplace/stove in room. Fax, spa, sauna, library and continental breakfast in cottage on premises. Weddings, small meetings, family reunions and seminars hosted. Antiquing, fishing, live theater, parks, shopping and water sports nearby.

"Thank you for your special brand of magic. What a place!"

Dayton   C3

Wine Country Farm

6855 NE Breyman Orchards Rd
Dayton, OR 97114-7220
(503)864-3446 (800)261-3446 Fax:(503)864-3109
E-mail: winecountryfarm@webtv.net
Web: www.winecountryfarm.com

Circa 1910. Surrounded by vineyards and orchards, Wine Country Farm is an eclectic French house sitting on a hill overlooking the Cascade Mountain Range. Arabian horses are raised here, and five varieties of grapes are grown. Request the master bedroom and you'll enjoy a fireplace. The innkeepers can arrange for a horse-drawn buggy ride and picnic or horseback through the vineyards and forests to other wineries. There are outdoor wedding facilities and a new wine tasting room, where guests can sample wine from the vineyard. Downtown Portland and the Oregon coast are each an hour away.

Innkeeper(s): Joan Davenport. $95-135. MC, VISA, PC. TAC10. 7 rooms with PB, 2 with FP, 1 suite and 1 conference room. Breakfast included in rates. Types of meals: Gourmet bkfst, early coffee/tea and room service. Beds: KQDT. Air conditioning. VCR, fax, copier, stables and library on premises. Weddings, small meetings, family reunions and seminars hosted. Antiquing, fishing, live theater, parks, shopping, downhill skiing, cross-country skiing, sporting events and water sports nearby.

Publicity: *Wine Spectator.*

Eugene   D3

Kjaer's House In Woods

814 Lorane Hwy
Eugene, OR 97405-2321
(541)343-3234 (800)437-4501
E-mail: kajers@pond.net

Circa 1910. This handsome Craftsman house on two landscaped acres was built by a Minnesota lawyer. It was originally accessible by streetcar. Antiques include a square grand piano of rosewood and a collection of antique wedding photos. The house is attractively furnished and surrounded by flower gardens.

Historic Interest: Wayne Moore Historical Park (4 blocks), covered bridges (3 miles). Innkeeper(s): George & Eunice Kjaer. $65-80. PC, TC. TAC10. 2 rooms with PB and 1 conference room. Breakfast included in rates. Types of meals: Gourmet bkfst, cont and early coffee/tea. Beds: Q. VCR and library on premises. Weddings, small meetings, family reunions and seminars hosted. Antiquing, fishing, live theater, parks, shopping and sporting events nearby.

Publicity: *Register Guard and Oregonian.*

"Lovely ambiance and greatest sleep ever. Delicious and beautiful food presentation."

Pookie's B&B on College Hill

2013 Charnelton St
Eugene, OR 97405-2819
(541)343-0383 (800)558-0383 Fax:(541)431-0967
E-mail: pookiesbandb@aol.com
Web: www.pookiesbandblodging.com

Circa 1918. Pookie's is a charming Craftsman house with "yester-year charm." Surrounded by maple and fir trees, the B&B is located in an older, quiet neighborhood. Mahogany and oak antiques decorate the rooms. The innkeeper worked for many years in the area as a concierge and can offer you expert help with excursion planning or business needs.

Historic Interest: Historic downtown (1 1/2 mile). Innkeeper(s): Pookie & Doug Walling. $80-115. PC, TC. 3 rooms, 2 with PB and 1 suite. Breakfast included in rates. Types of meals: Full bkfst, cont plus, cont and early coffee/tea. AP. Beds: KQT. Cable TV, phone and ceiling fan in room. VCR, fax and copier on premises. Antiquing, fishing, baseball stadium, live theater, parks, shopping, sporting events and water sports nearby.

Publicity: *Oregon Wine.*

"I love the attention to detail. The welcoming touches: flowers, the 'convenience basket' of necessary items . . . I'm happy to have discovered your lovely home."

Florence   D2

The Blue Heron Inn

6563 Hwy 126, PO Box 1122
Florence, OR 97439-0055
(541)997-4091 (800)997-7780

Circa 1940. From the porch of this bed & breakfast inn, guests can gaze at rolling, forested hills and watch as riverboats ease their way down the Siuslaw River. Aside from the spectacular view, the inn is located within a few yards of a marina where docking and mooring is available. The ocean, the dunes and historic Florence are just minutes away as well. The Bridal Suite offers king-size bed, sitting area, whirlpool tub and view of the river and grounds.

Fresh, seasonal fare highlights the breakfast menu. Treats such as fresh fruit smoothies, muffins topped with homemade blackberry jam or a smoked salmon and avocado quiche are not uncommon.

Innkeeper(s): Maurice Souza. $65-140. MC, VISA, DS, PC, TC. 5 rooms with PB. Breakfast and afternoon tea included in rates. Types of meals: Full bkfst. Beds: KQT. Ceiling fan and jetted tubs in room. VCR and library on premises. Weddings, small meetings and family reunions hosted. Antiquing, fishing, dune buggies, horseback riding, parks, shopping and water sports nearby.

Publicity: *Best Places to Kiss, Oregon Lodgings Association and KLSR.*

"The entire place was decorated with great taste. Our room was beautiful and relaxing. It made us feel at ease and at peace."

Grants Pass
G2

Lawnridge House

1304 N W Lawnridge Ave
Grants Pass, OR 97526-1218
(541)476-8518
E-mail: lawnhouse@yahoo.com

Circa 1909. This inn, a graceful, gabled clapboard house is shaded by 200-year-old oaks. The home features spacious rooms with comfortable antiques, canopy beds and beamed ceilings. Mini refrigerators, TVs and VCRs are among the amenities. A family suite accommodates up to six people and includes one or two bedrooms, a sitting room and bathroom. The innkeeper serves Northwest regional cuisine for the  full breakfasts. The Rogue River is five minutes away, and the Ashland Shakespearean Festival is a 45-minute drive.

Innkeeper(s): Barbara Head. $70-85. PC, TC. TAC10. 4 rooms with PB and 2 suites. Breakfast included in rates. Types of meals: Full bkfst. Beds: KQ. Air conditioning. Antiquing, fishing, live theater and water sports nearby. Publicity: *Grants Pass Courier, This Week and CBS TV.*

"Thank you for your incredible friendliness, warmth, and energy expended on our behalf! I've never felt so nestled in the lap of luxury - what a pleasure!"

Weasku Inn

5560 Rogue River Hwy
Grants Pass, OR 97527
(541)471-8000 (800)334-4567 Fax:(541)471-7038
E-mail: info@weasku.com
Web: www.weasku.com

Circa 1924. Built as a secluded fishing lodge, this historic inn once hosted the likes of President Herbert Hoover, Zane Grey, Walt Disney, Clark Gable and Carole Lombard. It is said that after Lombard's death, Gable spent several weeks here, lamenting the loss of his beloved wife. A complete restoration took place in the late 1990s, reviving the inn back to its former glory. The log exterior, surrounding by towering trees and 10 fragrant acres, is a welcoming site. Inside, crackling fires from the inn's rock fireplaces warm the common rooms. Vaulted ceilings and exposed log beams add a cozy, rustic touch to the pristine, airy rooms  all decorated in Pacific Northwest style. Many rooms include a whirlpool tub and river rock fireplace, and several offer excellent views of the Rogue River, which runs through the inn's grounds. In addition to the inn rooms, there are riverfront cabins, offering an especially romantic setting. In the evenings, guests are treated to a wine and cheese reception, and in the mornings, a continental breakfast is served. The staff can help plan many activities, including fishing and white-water rafting trips.

Historic Interest: Applegate Trail and Interpretive Center (10 miles), historic downtown (6 miles).

Innkeeper(s): Dayle Sedgmore. $110-295. MC, VISA, AX, DC, CB, DS, TC. TAC10. 21 rooms, 19 with PB, 13 with FP, 3 suites, 12 cabins, 1 guest house and 1 conference room. Breakfast and snacks/refreshments included in rates. Types of meals: Cont plus. MAP. Beds: KQT. Cable TV, phone and ceiling fan in room. Central air. Fax on premises. Handicap access. Weddings, small meetings, family reunions and seminars hosted. Antiquing, canoeing/kayaking, fishing, golf, hiking, jet boat excursions/wildlife park, live theater, museums, parks, shopping, water sports and wineries nearby. Publicity: *Travel & Leisure Magazine, LA Magazine, Sunset and SF Magazine.*

Hood River
B5

Columbia Gorge Hotel

4000 Westcliff Dr
Hood River, OR 97031-9799
(541)386-5566 (800)345-1921 Fax:(541)387-5414
E-mail: reservations@columbiagorgehotel.com
Web: www.columbiagorgehotel.com

Circa 1921. This posh hotel is a gem among gems in the National Register of Historic Places. Idyllic guest quarters offer such ornate furnishings as a hand-carved canopy bed that once graced a French castle. The beautifully landscaped grounds, champagne and caviar social hour, turndown service with rose and chocolates, outdoor river-view dining terrace and a gourmet restaurant are favorite amenities. Last, but not least, are spectacular views of the majestic Columbia River. Guests are treated to the opulent "World Famous Farm Breakfast." The hotel is close to ski areas, golfing and popular windsurfing spots.

Innkeeper(s): Boyd & Halla Graves. $150-275. MC, VISA, AX, DC, CB, DS, TC. TAC10. 39 rooms with PB, 2 with FP and 3 conference rooms. Breakfast included in rates. Types of meals: Full bkfst, early coffee/tea, lunch, picnic lunch, gourmet dinner and room service. Beds: KQD. Cable TV, phone and turndown service in room. VCR, fax and copier on premises. Weddings, small meetings, family reunions and seminars hosted. Spanish, French and Icelandic spoken. Antiquing, fishing, windsurfing, live theater, parks, shopping, downhill skiing, cross-country skiing and water sports nearby. Pets allowed: $25 fee.

Jacksonville
G3

Orth House B&B

105 W Main St, PO Box 1437
Jacksonville, OR 97530
(541)899-8665 (800)700-7301 Fax:(541)899-9146
E-mail: orthbnb@orthbnb.com
Web: www.orthbnb.com

Circa 1880. Surrounded by a white picket fence and a half acre of landscaped grounds, this two-story brick Italianate home, in the National Register, was built during the gold rush in Jacksonville. Collections of teddy bears and pedal cars along with period furnishings decorate the inn. Nearby attractions include the Britt Music Festival, whitewater rafting and superior fishing.

Innkeeper(s): Lee & Marilyn Lewis. $100-250. MC, VISA, PC, TC. TAC10. 4 rooms, 3 with PB and 1 suite. Breakfast included in rates. Types of meals: Full bkfst. Beds: KQT. Ceiling fan in room. Air conditioning. Fax, copier and bicycles on premises. Antiquing, fishing, golf, Britt Music Festival, Ashland Shakespeare Festival, live theater, parks, shopping and downhill skiing nearby. Publicity: *American Profile and Country Discoveries.*

Lafayette   C3

Kelty Estate B&B

675 Third St
Lafayette, OR 97127
(503)864-3740 (800)867-3740

Circa 1872. An early pioneer couple, one a local druggist and
county sheriff and the other, the first woman elected to the
Lafayette School Board, built this home. The grounds are well-
landscaped with gardens, trees and lush plants. Guests can
enjoy the tranquility from the swing on the home's front porch.
There are two guest rooms, decorated in pastels. Furnishings
include period antiques. Breakfasts feature fresh Oregon-grown
items, with specialties such as strawberry-kiwi juice, fresh
strawberries and bananas in a cream sauce, homemade breads
and eggs Benedict accompanied by herbed potatoes. Wineries,
a museum and antiquing are among the nearby attractions.
Innkeeper(s): Ron & JoAnn Ross. $85-95. PC, TC. 2 rooms with PB.
Breakfast and afternoon tea included in rates. Types of meals: Full bkfst and
cont. Beds: Q. VCR and library on premises. Weddings, small meetings, family reunions and seminars hosted. Amusement parks, antiquing, fishing, live
theater, parks, shopping and water sports nearby.

Lincoln City   C2

Coast Inn B&B

4507 SW Coast Ave
Lincoln City, OR 97367
(541)994-7932 Fax:(541)994-7935
E-mail: coastinn@oregoncoastinn.com
Web: www.oregoncoastinn.com

Circa 1939. A short walk from Siletz Bay with its herd of sea
lions, this 4,000-square-foot house is 300 feet from the beach.
Mission-style furnishings in the Great Room provide comfortable
areas. Good books are available from the library. Enjoy the sights
and sounds of the Pacific from a window-wrapped botanical sunroom and deck. Writing journals are placed in each of the guest
bedrooms and suites. The suites offer a choice of luxurious and
romantic amenities including fireplaces, spa robes and soaps, a
private entrance and a vista of ocean or coastal pines. Healthy,
hot breakfasts with fresh Oregon berries and peaches are served
in the dining room, which is accented with vibrant art quilt
decor. Small pets are allowed with prior arrangement.
Innkeeper(s): Rosie Huntemann. $100-150. MC, VISA, PC, TC. TAC10. 4 rooms
with PB, 1 with FP & 2 suites. Breakfast & snacks/refreshments included in rates.
Types of meals: Gourmet bkfst, early coffee/tea, gourmet dinner & room service.
Beds: Q. VCR, fax, copier & library on premises. Weddings, small meetings, family
reunions & seminars hosted. Antiquing, hiking, Oregon Coast Aquarium, factory
outlet shopping, live theater, parks, tennis & water sports nearby.
Pets allowed: With some restrictions, small pets only, must have own pet
bed, must take pets when leaving premises.
Publicity: *Oregonian & L C Newsguard.*

Medford   G3

Under The Greenwood Tree

3045 Bellinger Ln
Medford, OR 97501-9503
(541)776-0000 (800)776-8099
E-mail: grwdtree@internetcds.com
Web: www.greenwoodtree.com

Circa 1862. Pleasurable luxuries and gracious hospitality are
the hallmarks of this romantic country inn. The pre-Victorian
farm with 10 Civil War-era outbuildings sits on 10 idyllic acres
of lawns, gardens, a pond and gazebo. Professionally decorated
guest bedrooms offer amenities such as soft robes, triple sheeting with fine ironed linens, turndown service with chocolate
truffles, fresh flowers and other pampering treats that surpass
expectations. Breakfast changes seasonally, always featuring
Cordon Bleu chef's healthy three-course gourmet dishes made
with just-picked fruit, herbs and farm-fresh eggs. A special signature blend coffee by a local roaster is made with on-site
Artesian spring water. Relax on a hammock in the shade of
300-year-old trees before afternoon tea.
Historic Interest: All National Register Historic Jacksonville (1.5 miles).
Innkeeper(s): Renate Ellam. $125-160. PC, TC. TAC10. 5 rooms with PB
and 1 conference room. Breakfast, afternoon tea and snacks/refreshments
included in rates. Types of meals: Gourmet bkfst, country bkfst, veg bkfst,
early coffee/tea and picnic lunch. Beds: QD. Phone and turndown service in
room. Air conditioning. VCR, stables, bicycles and library on premises.
Weddings, small meetings, family reunions and seminars hosted. German
and French spoken. Antiquing, art galleries, beaches, bicycling,
canoeing/kayaking, fishing, golf, hiking, horseback riding, soccer, live theater,
museums, parks, shopping, downhill skiing, cross-country skiing, sporting
events, tennis, water sports and wineries nearby.
Pets allowed: Will find kennel.
Publicity: *Sunset Magazine and Romantic Homes.*

Mosier   B5

The Mosier House B&B

704 3rd Ave
Mosier, OR 97040
(541)478-3640 Fax:(541)478-3640
E-mail: innkeeper@mosierhouse.com
Web: www.mosierhouse.com

Circa 1896. The Mosier House Bed & Breakfast is a Queen
Anne Victorian located five miles east of Hood River in the
Columbia River Gorge. On the grounds, visitors can still see
remains of cisterns from the old town waterworks. The inn is
listed on the National Register and was featured on the 1999
Historic Homes Calendar: "Historic Attractions of the North
West". One of the owners, an art history major and woodwork-
er by nature, spent 10 years restoring the home to its original
beauty. Today the exterior walls are covered with shiplap and
fishscale, rectangular and diamond-shaped wood shingles. Bay,
diamond, one-over-one and multi-pane windows reflect typical
Queen Anne features. The inn has one guest bedroom with private bath and four bedrooms with shared baths. Guests take
breakfast in the dining parlor overlooking the pond, creek, garden and trees. The inn is just five minutes from Hood River,
which has fine dining, shopping and other activities. Wind
surfing on the Columbia River and snowboarding are available
at nearby Mount Hood.
Historic Interest: Columbia Gorge Scenic Highway.
Innkeeper(s): Cindy Hunter. $77-125. 5 rooms, 1 with PB. Breakfast included
in rates. Types of meals: Gourmet bkfst. Beds: QT. Central air. Fax and gardens
on premises. Weddings, small meetings, family reunions and seminars hosted.
Antiquing, bicycling, canoeing/kayaking, fishing, golf, hiking, horseback riding,
wind surfing, snow boarding, fine dining, parks, shopping, downhill skiing,
cross-country skiing, tennis, water sports and wineries nearby.
Publicity: *Hood River News, The Oregonian, Sunset Magazine., 1999
Historic Homes Calendar and Historic Attractions of the NW.*

Newberg C3

Springbrook Hazelnut Farm

30295 N Hwy 99 W.
Newberg, OR 97132
(503)538-4606 (800)793-8528

Circa 1912. An ancient silver maple tree shades the main house, one of four Craftsman-style buildings on this farm. There are 10 acres of gardens, a pool, tennis court and a 60-acre hazelnut orchard. A blue heron moni-
tors the inn's pond and you may
paddle around in the canoe.
Walking through the orchard to
the adjoining winery is a must, as
is a bicycle ride to other wineries
in the area. Ask for the Carriage
House or the Cottage, and you'll enjoy a pond and garden view.
The inn's cottages have kitchens and private baths.
Historic Interest: Champoeg Park (6 miles).
Innkeeper(s): Charles & Ellen McClure. $95-195. 4 rooms, 2 with PB and 2 cottages. Breakfast included in rates. Types of meals: Full bkfst. Beds: QD. Air conditioning. Orchard, pond and gardens on premises. Small meetings and seminars hosted. Antiquing, wine touring, live theater, shopping and sporting events nearby.
Publicity: *Travel & Leisure, Wine Spectator, Country Living and National Geographic Traveler.*

"An incredible, wonderful refuge! We are beautifully surprised!"

Newport C2

Tyee Lodge Oceanfront B&B

4925 NW Woody Way
Newport, OR 97365
(541)265-8953 (888)553-8933
E-mail: mcconn@teleport.com
Web: www.tyeelodge.com

Circa 1941. Next door to an old manor house, this building was recently renovated into a Northwest-style lodge, and its location on part of the old Bush family estate affords it splendid ocean views. For a special occasion choose any room and you'll enjoy a panoramic view and a gas fireplace. A hearty, healthy Northwest breakfast is served. Take the trail to the beach and explore the tide pools. Touring the lighthouse at Yaquina Head in the summer, whale watching and storm watching in the winter are other favorite activities.
Innkeeper(s): Mark & Cindy McConnell. $100-145. MC, VISA, AX, DS, PC, TC. 5 rooms with PB, 5 with FP. Breakfast included in rates. Types of meals: Gourmet bkfst and early coffee/tea. Beds: Q. Beach trail, complimentary beverage bar and microwave on premises. Spanish, German and French spoken. Antiquing, fishing, golf, tidepools, lighthouse, live theater, parks, shopping and tennis nearby.

Portland B3

Terwilliger Vista B&B

515 SW Westwood Dr
Portland, OR 97201-2791
(503)244-0602 (888)244-0602 Fax:(503)293-8042

Circa 1940. Bay windows accentuate the exterior of this stately Georgian Colonial home. A mix of modern and Art Deco furnishings decorate the interior. The home has an airy, uncluttered feel with its polished floors topped with Oriental rugs

and muted tones. There is a canopy bed and fireplace in the spacious Garden Suite, and the Rose Suite overlooks the Willamette Valley. Other rooms offer garden views, bay windows or wicker furnishings. There is a library, and an area set up with refreshments. The house is located in what will be the Historical Terwilliger Boulevard Preserve.
Innkeeper(s): Dick & Jan Vatert. $85-150. MC, VISA, PC, TC. TAC10. 5 rooms with PB, 1 with FP and 2 suites. Breakfast included in rates. Types of meals: Full bkfst and cont. Beds: KQT. Cable TV in room. Air conditioning. Guest refrigerator, telephone and dataport and fax available on premises. Family reunions hosted. Antiquing, wine country, live theater, parks, shopping and sporting events nearby.

"Like staying in House Beautiful."

Salem C3

A Creekside Inn, The Marquee House

333 Wyatt Ct NE
Salem, OR 97301-4269
(503)391-0837
E-mail: rickiemh@open.org
Web: www.marqueehouse.com

Circa 1938. Each room in this Mt. Vernon Colonial replica of George Washington's house is named after a famous old-time movie. Consider the Auntie Mame room. This gracious view room features a fireplace, fainting couch, costumes, collectibles
and a private bath. The four other
upstairs guest rooms offer
similar themes. There are
regular evening movie
screenings complete with
popcorn in the common
room. The extensive gardens offer guests an opportunity to stroll along historic Mill Creek or enjoy a round of croquet in the spacious backyard, weather permitting. Hazelnut waffles, confetti hash and oatmeal custard are a few of the breakfast specialties. The inn is just two blocks from the Court-Chemeketa Historic District.
Historic Interest: Located close to the state capitol and Willamette University.
Innkeeper(s): Ms. Rickie Hart. $65-95. MC, VISA, DC, DS, PC, TC. TAC10. 5 rooms, 3 with PB, 1 with FP. Breakfast and snacks/refreshments included in rates. Types of meals: Gourmet bkfst and early coffee/tea. Beds: QT. VCR and bicycles on premises. Weddings, small meetings and family reunions hosted. Amusement parks, antiquing, golf, wine country tours, wineries, live theater, parks, shopping and sporting events nearby.
Publicity: *Statesman Journal, The Christian Science Monitor. and Carlton Food Network (United Kingdom).*

"We all agreed that you were the best hostess yet for one of our weekends!"

Seaside A2

10th Avenue Inn Bed & Breakfast

125 10th Ave
Seaside, OR 97138-6241
(503)738-0643 (800)745-2378 Fax:(503)738-0172
E-mail: summerhs@seasurf.com

Circa 1908. Sunlight fills this cozy home, once owned by a circuit court judge. Splendid ocean views are provided through the panoramic windows and guests look out to the Promenade and the coastal mountains range and shoreline. An inviting parlor offers a baby grand piano and a warm fireplace. Guests gather here for evening snacks and to watch the sunsets. The guest rooms are modern and pleasant, and some of the furnishings are antiques. The innkeepers serve a variety of appetizing breakfast entrees and after breakfast, guests can stroll to downtown Seaside or spend the day enjoying the ocean.

Innkeeper(s): Jack & Lesle Palmeri. $89-129. MC, VISA, AX, DS, TC. 3 rooms with PB and 1 suite. Breakfast included in rates. Types of meals: Full bkfst and early coffee/tea. Beds: KDT. Cable TV, one suite with fireplace, sitting room and soaking tub in room. VCR, fax, copier and two vacation rentals on premises. Weddings, small meetings and family reunions hosted. Amusement parks, antiquing, fishing, golf, live theater, parks, shopping, tennis and water sports nearby.

"Very clean, cozy house comfortable beds. Pleasing ocean view, convenient parking."

The Gilbert Inn, B&B

341 Beach Dr
Seaside, OR 97138-5707
(503)738-9770 (800)410-9770 Fax:(503)717-1070
E-mail: gilbertinn@theoregonshore.com
Web: www.gilbertinn.com

Circa 1892. This yellow Victorian with its turret and third-story garret is framed with a white picket fence and gardens of lilies, roses and tulips. There are down quilts, antiques, and fresh country fabrics in the guest rooms. A house specialty is stuffed French toast topped with apricot sauce. The ocean and the historic promenade, which stretches for a mile and a half along the sand, are a block away.

Innkeeper(s): Dick & Carole Rees. $89-125. MC, VISA, AX, DS, PC, TC. 10 rooms with PB, 1 suite and 2 cottages. Breakfast included in rates. Types of meals: Full bkfst and early coffee/tea. Beds: QT. Cable TV and phone in room. Fax and copier on premises. Weddings, small meetings and seminars hosted. Antiquing, art galleries, beaches, bicycling, canoeing/kayaking, fishing, golf, hiking, horseback riding, on the beach volleyball, kite-flying, surfing, beach bikes, sandcastles, live theater, museums, parks, shopping, tennis, water sports and wineries nearby.

Publicity: *The Oregonian, Romantic Homes Magazine* and *"Romantic Getaways"*

Sisters   D4

Conklin's Guest House

69013 Camp Polk Rd
Sisters, OR 97759-9705
(541)549-0123 (800)549-4262 Fax:(541)549-4481
Web: www.conklinsguesthouse.com

Circa 1910. The original portion of this Craftsman-style house was constructed in 1910, with later additions in 1938 and more recent changes in 1992 and 1996. Mountain views and four-and-a-half peaceful acres invite relaxation and romance. There are several ponds on the property stocked with trout for those wanting to try their hand at catch and release fishing. There is also a heated swimming pool. Three guest rooms have clawfoot tubs, and the Suite and Forget-Me-Not rooms offer a pleasing view. For those in a larger group, the inn's Heather room includes a queen bed and two single beds. Sisters' airport is across the street from the home.

Historic Interest: Camp Polk (U.S. Army) established 1865; Camp Polk cemetery remains (5 miles).

Innkeeper(s): Frank & Marie Conklin. $70-150. PC, TC. TAC10. 5 rooms

with PB, 1 with FP and 1 suite. Breakfast and snacks/refreshments included in rates. Types of meals: Gourmet bkfst, country bkfst, veg bkfst and early coffee/tea. Beds: QT. Phone and ceiling fan in room. Central air. Fax, copier and swimming on premises. Handicap access. Weddings, small meetings and family reunions hosted. Spanish spoken. Antiquing, art galleries, bicycling, canoeing/kayaking, fishing, golf, hiking, horseback riding, whitewater rafting, rock climbing, live theater, museums, parks, shopping, downhill skiing, cross-country skiing, tennis and water sports nearby.

Pets allowed: On leash outside.

"A wonderful and romantic time for our wedding anniversary. Thanks so much. Oh - great fishing too."

Stayton   C3

The Inn at Gardner House Bed & Breakfast

633 N 3rd Ave
Stayton, OR 97383-1731
(503)769-6331

Circa 1893. A former Stayton Mayor and business man built this home, which features a wraparound veranda. Accommodations include a suite with a small kitchen and dining room. Each guest room is comfortably furnished with some antiques. The innkeeper prepares creative breakfasts with homemade breads, fresh fruit and entrees.

Innkeeper(s): Dick Jungwirth. $65-75. MC, VISA, AX, DC, CB, DS, PC, TC. 2 rooms with PB and 1 suite. Breakfast included in rates. Types of meals: Gourmet bkfst, picnic lunch and dinner. Beds: QT. Cable TV, phone and VCR in room. Copier and library on premises. Weddings, small meetings and family reunions hosted. Antiquing, fishing, parks, shopping, downhill skiing, cross-country skiing, sporting events and water sports nearby.

Pets Allowed.

Welches   C4

Old Welches Inn B&B

26401 E Welches Rd
Welches, OR 97067-9701
(503)622-3754 Fax:(503)622-5370
E-mail: innmthood@cs.com

Circa 1890. This two-story colonial building, behind a picket fence, was originally the first hotel to be built in the Mt. Hood area. Reconstructed in the '30s, the building now has shutters and French windows. The inn's two acres offer a plethora of flower beds and views of the Salmon River and Hunchback Mountain. Rooms are named for wildflowers and include antiques. If traveling with children or friends try Lilybank, a private cottage which overlooks the first hole of Three Nines. There are two bedrooms, a kitchen and a river rock fireplace.

Innkeeper(s): Judith & Ted Mondun. $96-163. MC, VISA, AX, DS, PC, TC. TAC10. 4 rooms and 1 cottage. Breakfast and snacks/refreshments included in rates. Types of meals: Full bkfst and early coffee/tea. Beds: QD. Turndown service in room. VCR, fax and pet boarding on premises. Weddings, small meetings and family reunions hosted. Antiquing, fishing, golf, parks, shopping, downhill skiing, cross-country skiing, sporting events and tennis nearby.

Pets allowed: House broken, well behaved in cottage only.

Publicity: *Oregonian, Sunset* and *Northwest Best Places.*

Pennsylvania

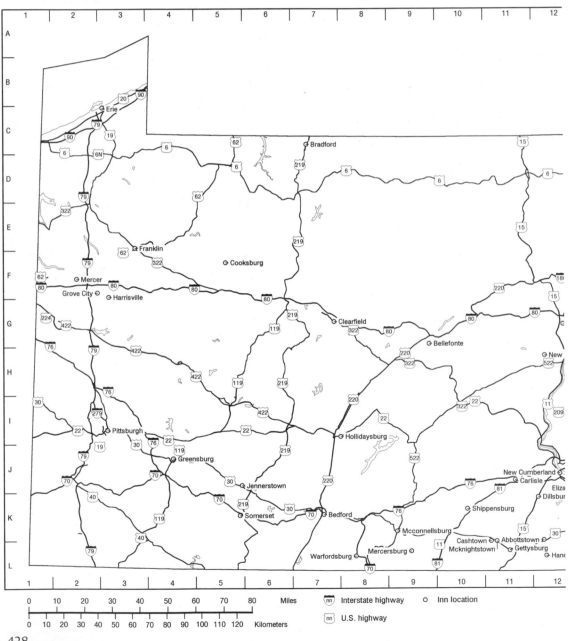

	Miles
0 10 20 30 40 50 60 70 80	
0 10 20 30 40 50 60 70 80 90 100 110 120	Kilometers

Interstate highway   Inn location

U.S. highway

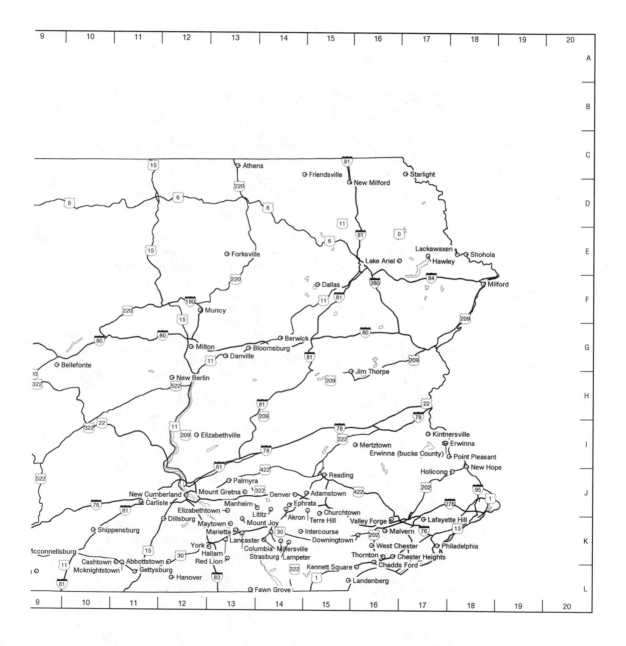

Abbottstown   K12

The Altland House

Rt 30 Center Square
Abbottstown, PA 17301
(717)259-9535
Web: www.altlandhouse.com

Circa 1790. A French mansard roof sits atop this three-story country inn and tavern known for its excellent cuisine and gracious hospitality. Located halfway between York and Gettysburg, it is on an old Conestoga route. The spacious guest rooms offer high ceilings and chestnut woodwork. Whirlpool tubs add plea-  sure to several deluxe rooms. On the third floor, one room offers a sunroom with a deck and hot tub while another includes a comfy sofa, an extra-large whirlpool tub and a kitchenette. The inn's two restaurants present a variety of house specialties. The Underside Restaurant has a more casual atmosphere serving sandwiches as well as entrees, while the Berwick Room Restaurant is noted for more elegant cuisine. A popular Sunday brunch buffet is served from 11:30 a.m. to 2 p.m. Golf and Getaway packages are available, some including wine and dinner.

Innkeeper(s): Mike Haugh. $89-125. MC, VISA, AX, DS, PC, TC. 10 rooms with PB and 2 conference rooms. Breakfast included in rates. Types of meals: Cont plus, cont, lunch, gourmet dinner and room service. Beds: KQ. Cable TV, phone, whirlpool tubs and free HBO in room. Air conditioning. Fax and copier on premises. Weddings and family reunions hosted. Antiquing, fishing, golf, history, history, history, live theater, shopping, downhill skiing and tennis nearby.

Adamstown   J15

Adamstown Inn

62 W Main St
Adamstown, PA 19501
(717)484-0800 (800)594-4808
E-mail: stay@adamstown.com
Web: www.adamstown.com

Circa 1830. This restored Victorian with its 1850s pump organ found in the large parlor and other local antiques, fits right into this community known as one of the antique capitals of America (3,000 antique dealers). Other decorations include family heirlooms, Victorian wallpa-  per, handmade quilts and lace curtains. For outlet mall fans, Adamstown is 10 miles from Reading, which offers a vast assortment of top-quality merchandise.

Historic Interest: The Ephrata Cloister is just seven miles away.

Innkeeper(s): Tom & Wanda Berman. $70-159. MC, VISA, PC, TC. TAC5. 4 rooms with PB and 1 suite. Breakfast, afternoon tea and snacks/refreshments included in rates. Types of meals: Cont plus and early coffee/tea. Beds: KQ. Ceiling fan, fireplace and two with Jacuzzi in room. Air conditioning. Copier and library on premises. Small meetings, family reunions and seminars hosted. Amusement parks, antiquing, fishing, live theater, parks and shopping nearby.

Publicity: *Country Victorian, Lancaster Intelligencer, Reading Eagle, Travel & Leisure, Country Almanac, Lancaster Magazine and Chester County Magazine.*

"Your warm hospitality and lovely home left us with such pleasant memories."

Akron   J14

Bella Vista Bed & Breakfast

1216 Main St
Akron, PA 17501-1635
(717)859-4227 (888)948-9726
E-mail: jshirk@epix.net

Circa 1905. Translated, this historical post Victorian inn's name means "beautiful view," appropriately sitting across from 51 acres of parkland with ponds and trails. A comfortable country coziness is enhanced by antique furnishings. The Family/TV Room boasts a fireplace and large beamed ceiling, the Sitting Room/Parlor is stocked with books and local maps. A full-sized feather bed, queen canopy bed and clawfoot tub are some of the guest bedrooms' highlights. A generous family-style breakfast that may include Lancaster County sausage and peach French toast is enjoyed in the dining room. Venturing beyond the porch swings and rockers, there is much to explore in the surrounding areas.

Historic Interest: Ephrata Cloisters (3 miles), Landis Valley Farm Museum (4 miles).

Innkeeper(s): Sarah & Jeff Shirk. $85-95. MC, VISA, DS, PC, TC. 6 rooms with PB. Breakfast included in rates. Types of meals: Full bkfst, country bkfst, veg bkfst, early coffee/tea and snacks/refreshments. Beds: KQDT. Cable TV in room. Air conditioning. VCR, fax, copier, spa and bicycles on premises. Small meetings and family reunions hosted. Amusement parks, antiquing, bicycling, golf, hiking, live theater, museums, parks, shopping and tennis nearby.

Athens   C13

Failte Inn B&B and Antique Shoppe

RR #2 Box 323 SR 1043
Athens, PA 18810
(570)358-3899 Fax:(570)358-3387
E-mail: thefailteinn@webtv.net

Circa 1925. During its heyday, parties with hundreds of guests where not uncommon at this Gatsby-era estate. The inn's name derives from the innkeepers' Scottish heritage and means welcome in Gaelic. The inn is decorated with a variety of antiques, including some family pieces. One special decoration is an 18th-century quilt designed by the innkeeper's great-great-great-great grand-  mother. The innkeeper also has her father's World War I uniform on display and her mother's wedding dress. Complimentary wine, brandy and other beverages are provided in the inn's pub, which formerly served as a speakeasy during the days of Prohibition. Breakfasts, served either in the formal dining room or on the screened wraparound verandas, include baked goods such as homemade sourdough bread, sticky buns or Amish friendship bread accompanied by homemade jams and jellies. The daily entrée might be cheesy eggs with Canadian bacon or perhaps thick slices of sourdough French toast with Pennsylvania maple syrup. The surrounding area offers lakes, parks and outdoor activities in the Endless Mountains, as well as antique shops, wineries, the Corning Glass Center and New York's Finger Lakes.

Historic Interest: Covered bridge (10 miles), French Azilum (15 miles), PA grand canyon (40 miles), World's End State Park (40 miles), NY wine country, Corning, NY (40 miles), Finger Lakes & Watkins Glen (40 miles).

Innkeeper(s): Jim, Sarah & Jamie True. $65-85. MC, VISA, PC, TC. 5 rooms with PB and 2 suites. Breakfast and snacks/refreshments included in rates. Types of meals: Gourmet bkfst, veg bkfst, cont and early coffee/tea. Beds: KQDT. Cable TV, ceiling fan, one suite with sunken tub, fireplace and wine in room. Air conditioning. VCR, fax, copier, library, huge screened veranda, microwave, web TV and pool table on premises. Weddings, small meetings, family reunions and seminars hosted. Antiquing, bicycling, fishing, golf, hiking, horseback riding, museums, parks, shopping, tennis, water sports and wineries nearby.

Publicity: *Happenings Magazine, Towanda Daily Review, WNEP Home and garden show and PBS special.*

Bedford   K7

Bedford House

203 W Pitt St
Bedford, PA 15522-1237
(814)623-7171
E-mail: bedhouse@bedford.net
Web: www.bedfordcounty.net/bedfordhouse

Circa 1807. Five of the guest rooms in this beautiful 19th-century home feature working, gas-log fireplaces. All rooms contain antiques, reproductions and family heirlooms. The honeymoon guest room offers a king-size bed and whirlpool tub. The guesthouse offers four additional rooms, and a conference room. A full breakfast with seasonal fruits and homemade muffins, breads and entrees is served in the country kitchen. Relax on a porch that overlooks the garden or tour historic Bedford, a pre-Revolutionary War town. The inn is a five-minute walk from the Fort Bedford Museum and Park, shops and restaurants. Old Bedford Village is another popular touring attraction. Shawnee State Park and the Coral Caverns are nearby.

Innkeeper(s): Lyn & Linda Lyon. $80-135. MC, VISA, AX, DS, PC, TC. TAC10. 10 rooms with PB, 5 with FP, 1 suite and 1 guest house. Breakfast included in rates. Types of meals: Full bkfst and early coffee/tea. Beds: KQDT. Cable TV, phone and VCR in room. Air conditioning. Fax on premises. Handicap access. Weddings, small meetings, family reunions and seminars hosted. Antiquing, fishing, old Bedford Village, live theater, parks, shopping, downhill skiing, cross-country skiing and water sports nearby.

Publicity: *Pennsylvania Magazine.*

Bellefonte   G9

Reynolds Mansion B&B

101 W Linn St
Bellefonte, PA 16823-1622
(814)353-8407 (800)899-3929
E-mail: innkeeper@reynoldsmansion.com
Web: www.reynoldsmansion.com

Circa 1885. Bellefonte is a town with many impressive, historic homes, and this exquisite stone mansion is no exception. The home, a combination of late Victorian and Gothic styles, features extraordinary, hand-crafted woodwork and intricately laid wood floors, as well as 10 fireplaces. Five guest rooms include a fireplace and a Jacuzzi tub. All enjoy a romantic atmosphere, heightened by candles, fresh flowers and the poshest of furnishings and decor. There also is a billiards room and library for guests to enjoy. Baked, stuffed French toast served with

bacon or sausage is among the breakfast specialties accompanied by muffins, juices, cereals and a fruit compote created with more than a half dozen different fresh fruits. For an excellent lunch or dinner, the innkeepers suggest the nearby Gamble Mill Tavern, a 200-year-old mill listed in the National Register.

Historic Interest: Penn State University (10 miles).

Innkeeper(s): Joseph & Charlotte Heidt. $95-195. MC, VISA, AX, PC, TC. TAC10. 6 suites, 5 with FP. Breakfast included in rates. Types of meals: Gourmet bkfst, cont plus and early coffee/tea. Beds: KQ. Jacuzzi tubs and Jacuzzi steam shower in room. VCR, fax, copier, library and billiards room on premises. Weddings, small meetings, family reunions and seminars hosted. Antiquing, fishing, golf, victorian architecture, live theater, parks, shopping, downhill skiing, cross-country skiing, sporting events and water sports nearby.

"Your bed & breakfast is such an inspiration to us."

Berwick   G14

Rebecca's Inn

213 W Second St
Berwick, PA 18603-4715
(717)752-3362 (888)506-3260 Fax:(717)752-3362

Circa 1900. The aroma of freshly baked sticky buns and Shoofly Pie (house specialty) from the innkeeper's on-site bakery lends itself to the country atmosphere of this turn-of-the-century Victorian. The inn features a wraparound porch, ebony piano and gazebo. Guests can enjoy breakfast in one of the two dining rooms or, weather permitting, on the wraparound porch. The inn is close to 24 old-fashioned covered bridges, Pocono Ski Resorts, Bloomsburg Fair, antiques and shopping.

Historic Interest: Bloomsburg University, Knoebels Amusement Park.

Innkeeper(s): Timothy B Mason, Nicole Miller. $49-65. MC, VISA, AX, DC, CB, DS, TC. 7 rooms, 2 with PB and 1 conference room. Breakfast included in rates. Types of meals: Full bkfst. Beds: KQDT. Cable TV in room. Air conditioning. VCR on premises. Weddings, small meetings and family reunions hosted. Amusement parks, antiquing, fishing, golf, live theater, parks, shopping, downhill skiing, cross-country skiing, sporting events, tennis and water sports nearby.

"This will always be remembered as one of our best vacations."

Bird-in-Hand   K14

Mill Creek Homestead B&B

2578 Old Philadelphia Pike
Bird-in-Hand, PA 17505-9796
(717)291-6419 (800)771-2578 Fax:(717)291-2171
E-mail: valfone@yahoo.com
Web: www.millcreekhomestead.com

Circa 1790. This 18th-century fieldstone farmhouse is one of the oldest homes in Bird-in-the-Hand. Located in the Pennsylvania Dutch Heartland, the inn is decorated for comfort with Amish influences represented throughout. There are four guest rooms with private baths and fireplaces or stoves. Guests are invited to lounge by the outdoor pool or sit on the porch and watch the horse-drawn buggies go by. A full breakfast is served in the formal dining room, while afternoon refreshments are in

the common rooms. The inn is within walking distance of shops, museums, farmers market, antiques and crafts.

Historic Interest: James Buchannan's Wheatland, Rockford Plantation, Landis Valley Museum, Strasburg Railroad Museum, Americana Museum, Ephrata Cloister, Lancaster Heritage Museum.

Innkeeper(s): Vicki & Frank Alfone. $99-129. MC, VISA, DS, PC, TC. TAC10. 4 rooms with PB. Breakfast, afternoon tea and snacks/refreshments included in rates. Types of meals: Full bkfst and early coffee/tea. Beds: QT. Turndown service and ceiling fan in room. Air conditioning. Swimming and library on premises. Amusement parks, antiquing, fishing, golf, live theater, parks, shopping, tennis and water sports nearby.

Publicity: *Country Inns and Lancaster County Magazine.*

"Thank you for sharing your wonderful home with us. I knew this place would be perfect!"

The Village Inn of Bird-In-Hand

PO Box 253
Bird-In-Hand, PA 17505-0253
(717)293-8369 (800)914-2473 Fax:(717)768-1117
E-mail: lodging@bird-in-hand.com
Web: www.bird-in-hand.com/villageinn

Circa 1734. The history of this property dates back to the 18th century when it served as a hotel for weary guests traveling the Pennsylvania Turnpike. The original inn was destroyed by fire in 1851 and the present, three-story hotel was built in its place. Today, guests will enjoy the inn's historic sense of

ambiance and Victorian decor. Breakfasts are served on the sun porch with its paddle fans and wicker furnishings. Two of the guest rooms feature a large Jacuzzi, and another room boasts a fireplace. Swimming and tennis

facilities are within walking distance of the inn. The inn is adjacent to a farmers' market, country store, bakery, restaurant and several shops and outlets.

Historic Interest: The inn offers a complimentary two-hour tour of the surrounding Amish farm lands, and the Pennsylvania Dutch Convention and Visitors Bureau is only a few miles away.

Innkeeper(s): Rick Meshey. $69-155. MC, VISA, AX, DS, PC, TC. 11 rooms with PB, 1 with FP and 6 suites. Breakfast and snacks/refreshments included in rates. Types of meals: Cont plus. Beds: KQ. Cable TV and phone in room. Air conditioning. Two hour complimentary tour of farm lands on premises. Amusement parks, antiquing, golf, PA Dutch Amish Country, miniature golf, live theater, parks, shopping and tennis nearby.

Publicity: *Country Folk Art.*

"The Village Inn offers the charm and coziness of a B&B with the privacy of a hotel."

Bloomsburg   G13

Magee's Main Street Inn

20 W Main St
Bloomsburg, PA 17815-1703
(570)784-3500 (800)331-9815 Fax:(570)784-5517
E-mail: rusty@magees.com
Web: www.magees.com

Circa 1870. Magee's 43-room downtown inn offers regular rooms and deluxe double rooms with separate living rooms. An expansive breakfast is served, cooked to order in the restaurant, and coffee is available throughout the day. The inn boasts a popular ballroom for wedding receptions and parties of 12 to 200 people. Harry's Grille, an adjoining casual-style restaurant,

serves lunch and dinner in a cozy atmosphere.

Innkeeper(s): The Magee's. $57-93. MC, VISA, AX, DC, CB, DS. 43 rooms with PB and 7 conference rooms. Breakfast included in rates. Types of meals: Full bkfst, lunch and dinner. Beds: KQDT. Cable TV and phone in room. Air conditioning. VCR, fax and copier on premises. Weddings, small meetings, family reunions and seminars hosted. Amusement parks, antiquing, live theater, shopping, cross-country skiing and sporting events nearby.

Bradford   C7

Glendorn, A Lodge in the Country

1032 W Corydon Street
Bradford, PA 16701
(814)362-6511 (800)843-8568 Fax:(814)368-9923
E-mail: glendorn@glendorn.com
Web: www.glendorn.com

Circa 1929. More than 1,200 acres of lakes, woodland trails and rivers are part of the estate surrounding this Adirondack-style log lodge, which is situated on the banks of a musical trout stream. A soaring cathedral, many-paned windows and a massive two-story fireplace grace the spacious gathering room. Its appointments include a grand piano and soft inviting upholstered sofas and easy chairs. Families and friends who gather at the lodge often pay tribute to its wealthy founder, who purposed to provide a place of retreat and bonding for his three-generation family (they nicknamed him Bondieu). Rooms and deluxe private cabins are all beautifully decorated. A wide choice of activities are offered such as hiking, bicycling, canoeing, fishing and picnicking in areas shaded by black cherry, ash, beech, birch and maple trees. Play billiards in the evening or shoot skeet and trap, canoe, cycle or swim in the sunlight. In winter, cross-country ski, ice skate or borrow snowshoes for a winter-wonderland hike. All meals are provided.

Innkeeper(s): Chris Fulvio. $375-675. MC, VISA, AX, PC, TC. TAC10. 15 rooms, 2 with PB, 8 with FP, 2 suites, 6 cabins, 2 guest houses and 1 conference room. Breakfast, picnic lunch, snacks/refreshments and dinner included in rates. Types of meals: Gourmet bkfst, veg bkfst, early coffee/tea, gourmet lunch and room service. AP. Beds: KQT. TV, phone, turndown service, ceiling fan and VCR in room. Fax, copier, swimming, bicycles, tennis and library on premises. Weddings, small meetings, family reunions and seminars hosted. Antiquing and golf nearby.

Pets allowed: In designated cabins.

Publicity: *Departures Magazine, Pittsburgh Post-Gazette, Travel and Leisure, Conde Nast Traveler, Gourmet, Country Inns Magazine and Andrew Harper's Hideaway Report.*

"The variety and creativity displayed in the cooking are remarkable."

Mountain Laurel Inn

136 Jackson Avenue
Bradford, PA 16701
(814)362-8006 Fax:(814)362-4208
E-mail: info@mountainlaurelbradford.com
Web: www.mountainlaurelbradford.com

Circa 1894. Subtly combining Greek and Colonial Revival architecture, this stately inn for adults is an impressive example of hospitality and elegance. Past the grand circular staircase, the living room is perfect for relaxing with complimentary beverages or evening wine. The luxurious guest bedrooms, decorated with charm and sophistication, harbor many special touches to pamper and please. Innkeeper Nora creates extraordinary culinary delights for breakfast, served in a cozy breakfast room or formal dining room. The garden is always in bloom and the landscaped grounds are best appreciated from the comfort of a cushioned wicker rocker on the large pillared front porch. Centrally located in the Allegheny Mountains, there is a variety-of year-round activities.

Innkeeper(s): Nora White. $95-105. MC, VISA, AX, PC. 7 rooms, 2 with PB and 3 suites. Breakfast and snacks/refreshments included in rates. Types of meals: Gourmet bkfst, veg bkfst, early coffee/tea, picnic lunch and afternoon tea. Beds: KQD. Cable TV, phone, turndown service, VCR and fireplace in room. Air conditioning. Fax, copier, bicycles, library, beverage, snack and refrigerator area on premises. Weddings, small meetings, family reunions and seminars hosted. Antiquing, bicycling, canoeing/kayaking, fishing, golf, hiking, Zippo Lighter Museum, Case Knive Museum, live theater, museums, parks, shopping, downhill skiing, cross-country skiing, tennis, water sports and wineries nearby.

Carlisle   *J11*

Jacobs Resting Place

1007 Harrisburg Pike
Carlisle, PA 17013-1616
(717)243-1766 (888)731-1790 Fax:(781)459-6592
E-mail: jacobsrest@pa.net

Circa 1790. Three acres surround this pristine heritage home, located on land purchased from the William Penn Land Grant. The gracious brick Georgian with its white shutters and original floors, doors, woodwork and seven fireplaces offered respite to travelers more than two centuries ago when it was called The Sign of the Green Tree. It is said that George Washington met his army on this site in 1794. You'll enjoy a four-poster rice bed and working fireplace if you request the Chippendale Room, but each room at the inn is steeped in history and decorated in a different period. The Blue and Gray Room combined with the old tavern-keeper's quarters, provides for a family or friends traveling together when they need two bedrooms. Breakfast is served with china, crystal and silver on white linens and may include a crepe dish or stuffed French toast and home-baked breads. Terry is a Civil War historian, a wonderful resource for enjoying the Civil War battlefields and Military History Institute nearby. There is a trout stream on the property as well as a hot tub and pool, or you might enjoy a quarter of a mile walk to the 1800 Indian School.

Historic Interest: Civil war battlefields-30 miles, 1800 indian school- 1/4 mile, Carlisle Barricks- 1/4 mile.

Innkeeper(s): Terry & Marie Hegglin. $60-95. MC, VISA, AX, DS, PC, TC. TAC10. 4 rooms, 2 with PB, 3 with FP, 1 suite and 1 conference room. Breakfast and snacks/refreshments included in rates. Types of meals: Gourmet bkfst. Beds: KQD. TV, phone, turndown service and ceiling fan in room. Central air. VCR, fax, copier, spa, swimming, trout fishing and refrigerator on premises. Small meetings, family reunions and seminars hosted. Amusement parks, antiquing, art galleries, canoeing/kayaking, fishing, golf, hiking, live theater, museums, parks, shopping, downhill skiing, cross-country skiing, sporting events, tennis, water sports and wineries nearby.

Line Limousin Farmhouse B&B

2070 Ritner Hwy
Carlisle, PA 17013-9303
(717)243-1281
E-mail: bline@planetcable.net

Circa 1864. The grandchildren of Bob and Joan are the ninth generation of Lines to enjoy this 200-year-old homestead. A stone and brick exterior accents the farmhouse's graceful style, while inside, family heirlooms attest to the home's longevity. This is a breeding stock farm of 110 acres and the cattle raised here,

Limousin, originate from the Limoges area of France. Giant maples shade the lawn and there are woods and stone fences.

Innkeeper(s): Bob & Joan Line. $65-85. PC, TC. 3 rooms with PB. Breakfast included in rates. Types of meals: Full bkfst. Beds: KQT. Cable TV and phone in room. Air conditioning. VCR and guest refrigerator on premises. Family reunions hosted. Amusement parks, antiquing, fishing, golf, live theater, parks, shopping, cross-country skiing and sporting events nearby.

"Returning to your home each evening was like returning to our own home, that's how comfortable and warm it was."

Pheasant Field B&B

150 Hickorytown Rd
Carlisle, PA 17013-9732
(717)258-0717 (877)258-0717 Fax:(717)258-0717
E-mail: pheasant@pa.net

Circa 1800. Located on 10 acres of central Pennsylvania farmland, this brick, two-story Federal-style farmhouse features wooden shutters and a covered front porch. Rooms include a TV and telephone. An early 19th-century stone barn is on the property, and horse boarding is available. The Appalachian Trail is less than a mile away.

Fly-fishing is popular at Yellow Breeches and Letort Spring. Dickinson College and Carlisle Fairgrounds are other points of interest.

Historic Interest: Gettysburg National Historical Park (32 miles), Molly Pitcher gravesite.

Innkeeper(s): Denise Fegan. $85-120. MC, VISA, AX. 5 rooms with PB. Breakfast included in rates. Types of meals: Full bkfst and early coffee/tea. Beds: KQT. Cable TV and phone in room. Air conditioning. VCR, fax and piano on premises. Weddings, small meetings and family reunions hosted. Amusement parks, antiquing, fishing, live theater, downhill skiing and cross-country skiing nearby.

Publicity: *Outdoor Traveler and Harrisburg Magazine.*

"You have an outstanding, charming and warm house. I felt for the first time as being home."

Carlisle (New Kingstown)   *J11*

Kanaga House B&B Inn

6940 Carlisle Pike (US Rt 11)
Carlisle (New Kingstown), PA 17072
(717)766-8654 Fax:(717)697-3908
E-mail: stay@kanagahouse.com
Web: www.kanagahouse.com

Circa 1775. Stay in this restored 1775 stone house while visiting the area's many tourist attractions such as Gettysburg Civil War Battlefield, Hershey Chocolate World, Lancaster Dutch Country or Harrisburg (the state capital). The well-appointed guest bedrooms offer canopy beds, and one boasts a fireplace. Tree-studded grounds and a large gazebo are perfect for weddings. The first-floor rooms and catering staff also enhance business meetings and retreats. Walk the nearby Appalachian Trail, or fly fish in the Yellow Breeches and Letort Springs.

Innkeeper(s): Mary Jane & Dave Kretzing. $85-125. MC, VISA, AX. 6 rooms with PB, 1 with FP and 1 conference room. Breakfast included in rates. Types of meals: Full bkfst and early coffee/tea. Beds: Q. TV and phone in room. Air conditioning. VCR, copier and gazebo with table and chairs on premises. Weddings, small meetings and seminars hosted. Amusement parks, antiquing, live theater, shopping and downhill skiing nearby.

Cashtown   L11

Cashtown Inn

1325 Old Rt 30, PO Box 103
Cashtown, PA 17310
(717)334-9722 (800)367-1797

Circa 1797. Cashtown Inn's history alone will inspire a visit. The inn was built as a stagecoach stop and has welcomed guests for more than two centuries. It also served as a stop along the Underground Railroad and curiously, also served as a Confederate headquarters prior to the Battle of Gettysburg. The inn's rooms are decorated in country Victorian style with four-poster beds. One room includes a lace canopy bed. In addition to the gourmet breakfasts, which are included in the rates, the inn also serves lunch and includes a renowned restaurant with dinners prepared by a chef. Dinners are served in the rustic bar, which was the inn's original tavern or in the more elegant main dining room. The chef's menus feature starters such as a baked brie in pastry or savory artichoke dip with focaccia bread. From there, guests can partake of homemade soups or salads with freshly prepared dressings. The menu is ever changing, but might include entrees such as pecan-crusted chicken with maple butter sauce or perhaps beef medallions with bourbon walnut sauce. The inn is eight miles from Gettysburg Military Park, and also offers close access to many historic sites, museums, a winery, art galleries and shopping.

Historic Interest: Gettysburg Military Park (8 miles).

Innkeeper(s): Dennis & Eileen Hoover. $76-145. MC, VISA, DS, PC, TC. 7 rooms, 4 with PB and 3 suites. Breakfast included in rates. Types of meals: Gourmet bkfst, early coffee/tea, lunch and dinner. Beds: KQD. Cable TV, ceiling fan and VCR in room. Central air. Fax and copier on premises. Weddings, small meetings, family reunions and seminars hosted. Antiquing, art galleries, golf, hiking, horseback riding, live theater, museums, parks, shopping, downhill skiing, sporting events and wineries nearby.

Publicity: *Philadelphia.*

"We were impressed with your inn, but more importantly with your personal touch toward all your guests...many thanks for your generosity and hospitality."

Chadds Ford   K16

Fairville Inn

506 Kennett Pike
Chadds Ford, PA 19317
(610)388-5900 Fax:(610)388-5902
E-mail: info@fairvilleinn.com
Web: www.fairvilleinn.com

Circa 1826. This old, federal-style country inn offers a fine base to explore the Brandywine Valley—an area known for its stately homes and rural back roads. Guest rooms feature various combinations of cathedral ceilings, fireplaces, king- and queen-size beds (some with canopies). They are found in three different buildings: The Main House, which dates back to 1820, the Springhouse, and the Carriage House. Suites have an additional sitting area and French doors that open onto a private deck. Full breakfasts consist of a hot entree, fruit, fresh-squeezed juice and baked goodies. They also offer an afternoon tea. Nearby activities

include canoeing, biking, golf, art galleries, museums and parks.

Historic Interest: Hagley Museum (4 miles), Brandywine battlefield (4 miles).

Innkeeper(s): Tom & Eleanor Everitt. $150-215. MC, VISA, AX, DS. 15 rooms with PB, 8 with FP and 2 suites. Breakfast and afternoon tea included in rates. Beds: KQT. Cable TV, phone, iron, ironing board and hair dryer in room. Fax, copier and library on premises. Handicap access. Antiquing, art galleries, bicycling, canoeing/kayaking, golf, horseback riding, museums, parks and wineries nearby.

Pennsbury Inn

883 Baltimore Pike
Chadds Ford, PA 19317-9305
(610)388-1435 Fax:(610)388-1436
E-mail: info@pennsburyinn.com
Web: www.pennsburyinn.com

Circa 1714. Listed in the National Register, this country farmhouse with hand-molded Flemish Bond brick facade was built originally with Brandywine Blue Granite rubble stone and later enlarged. Retaining its colonial heritage with slanted doorways, winding wood staircases and huge fireplaces, it boasts modern conveniences. There are elegant public sitting areas such as the living room, music room, library with an impressive book collection and breakfast in the dining room. The comfortable guest bedrooms feature antique feather beds and unique architectural details. The eight-acre estate boasts formal gardens that include a fish pond and reflection pool in a serene woodland setting.

Innkeeper(s): Cheryl. $100-225. MC, VISA, AX, DS, TC. 7 rooms, 6 with PB, 1 suite and 3 conference rooms. Breakfast, afternoon tea and snacks/refreshments included in rates. Types of meals: Full bkfst, country bkfst, veg bkfst, cont plus and early coffee/tea. Beds: KQDT. Cable TV, phone, turndown service and three with decorative fireplaces in room. Central air. VCR, fax, copier and library on premises. Weddings, small meetings and family reunions hosted. Limited French and German spoken. Antiquing, art galleries, bicycling, canoeing/kayaking, golf, hiking, live theater, museums, parks, shopping, sporting events, tennis and wineries nearby.

Chester Heights   K16

Hamanassett B&B

PO Box 366
Chester Heights, PA 19017-0366
(610)459-3000 Fax:(610)459-3000
E-mail: tudorroz@aol.com
Web: www.bbonline.com/pa/hamanassett/

Circa 1856. Located in eastern Brandywine Valley, this Federalist mansion rests on 48 acres of woodlands, gardens and fields dotted with wildflowers. Inside the impressive three-story manor, there is a spacious living room with wood-burning fireplace and a baby grand piano. A billiard room features fireside contemporary and antique games and a pool table. The formal dining room, which looks out to spacious lawns and landmark trees, includes a floor-to-ceiling corner fireplace. Relax in the cozy  solarium with separate sitting areas. Guest bedrooms offer top-of-the-line amenities and TVs, VCRs, fluffy robes and coffee makers. A 10-foot-high Rosewood half-tester queen bed imported from Louisiana is showcased in the Woodlands Room. Refreshments are available in the guest refrigerator.

Historic Interest: Located near many of the Brandywine Valley attractions, including Longwood Gardens, Winterthur, Brandywine Museum (Wyeth), and Nemours. Local dining and historic restaurants are nearby.

Innkeeper(s): Ashley & Glenn Mon. $125-175. TAC15. 6 rooms with PB and 2 suites. Breakfast and afternoon tea included in rates. Types of meals: Full bkfst. Beds: KQ. Fluffy robes in room. Weddings, small meetings and seminars hosted. Antiquing, Brandywine Valley attractions, live theater, shopping and sporting events nearby.

Publicity: *Philadelphia, Back Roads USA, Mid-Atlantic Country, Philadelphia and Its Countryside and awarded best B&B by Main Line Today.*

"For our first try at B&B lodgings, we've probably started at the top, and nothing else will ever measure up to this. Wonderful food, wonderful home, grounds and wonderful hostess!"

Churchtown   J15

Churchtown Inn B&B

2100 Main St, Rt 23
Churchtown, PA 17555-9514
(717)445-7794 (800)637-4446 Fax:(717)445-0962
E-mail: innkeepers@churchtowninn.com
Web: www.churchtowninn.com

Circa 1735. Once known as the Edward Davies Mansion, this handsome stone Federal house with panoramic views was also a tinsmith shop and rectory. It has heard the marching feet of Revolutionary troops and seen the Union Army during the Civil

War. Tastefully furnished with antiques and collectibles, the comfortable guest bedrooms feature canopy, pencil-post and sleigh beds. Breakfast is served in a delightful glass-enclosed garden room with stone floor and rolling farmland vistas. Evening tea and conversation are enjoyed in quaint double parlors or fireside in the den. Ask about dining in an Amish or Mennonite home.

Historic Interest: Located across the street from the Bangor Episcopal Church, the inn is listed in the National Register.

Innkeeper(s): Michael & Diane Franco. $69-145. MC, VISA, DS. 8 rooms with PB and 1 suite. Breakfast included in rates. Types of meals: Full bkfst. Beds: Q. Cable TV in room. Air conditioning. Small meetings, family reunions and seminars hosted. Antiquing, Amish tourist area, ballooning, live theater, parks and shopping nearby.

Publicity: *Bon Appetit, Boston Globe, Intelligencer Journal, Innsider and Chicago Star.*

"Magnificent atmosphere. Outstanding breakfasts. Our favorite B&B."

Clearfield   G7

Christopher Kratzer House

101 E Cherry St
Clearfield, PA 16830-2315
(814)765-5024 (888)252-2632
E-mail: bbaggett@uplink.net

Circa 1840. This inn is the oldest home in town, built by a carpenter and architect who also started Clearfield's first newspaper. The innkeepers keep a book of history about the house and town for interested guests. The interior is a mix of antiques from different eras, many are family pieces. There are collections of art and musical instruments. Two guest rooms afford views of the Susquehanna River. Refreshments and a glass of wine are served in the afternoons. The inn's Bridal Suite Special includes complimentary champagne, fruit and snacks,

and breakfast may be served in the privacy of your room. Small wedding receptions, brunches and parties are hosted at the inn.

Innkeeper(s): Bruce & Ginny Baggett. $65-80. MC, VISA, DS, PC, TC. 4 rooms, 2 with PB. Breakfast, afternoon tea and snacks/refreshments included in rates. Types of meals: Gourmet bkfst and early coffee/tea. Beds: KQT. Cable TV, phone and ceiling fan in room. Air conditioning. Library on premises. Antiquing, fishing, hiking, biking, playground across street, live theater, parks, shopping, cross-country skiing and sporting events nearby.

Publicity: *Local PA newspapers.*

"Past and present joyously intermingle in this place."

Victorian Loft B&B

216 S Front St
Clearfield, PA 16830-2218
(814)765-4805 (800)798-0456 Fax:(814)765-9596
E-mail: pdurant@csrlink.net

Circa 1894. Accommodations at this bed & breakfast are available in either a historic Victorian home on the riverfront or in a private, three-bedroom cabin. The white brick home is dressed with colorful, gingerbread trim, and inside, a grand staircase, stained glass and antique furnishings add to the Victorian charm. The suite is ideal for families as it contains two bedrooms, a living room, dining room, kitchen and a bath with a whirlpool tub. The cabin, Cedarwood Lodge, sleeps six and is located on eight, wooded acres near Parker Dam State Park and Elliot State Park. This is a favorite setting for small groups.

Innkeeper(s): Tim & Peggy Durant. $60-125. MC, VISA, DS, PC, TC. TAC10. 3 rooms, 1 with PB, 2 suites and 1 cottage. Breakfast included in rates. Types of meals: Full bkfst and early coffee/tea. Beds: QD. Phone and VCR in room. Whirlpool on premises. Small meetings and family reunions hosted. Limited Spanish spoken. Antiquing, fishing, live theater, parks, shopping, cross-country skiing, sporting events and water sports nearby.

Pets allowed: By prior arrangement.

Publicity: *Clearfield Progress and Tri-County.*

"A feeling of old-fashioned beauty. The elegance of roses and lace. All wrapped up into a romantic moment."

Columbia   K13

The Columbian

360 Chestnut St
Columbia, PA 17512-1156
(717)684-5869 (800)422-5869
E-mail: inn@columbianinn.com
Web: www.columbianinn.com

Circa 1897. This stately three-story mansion is a fine example of Colonial Revival architecture. Antique beds, a stained-glass window and home-baked breads are among its charms. Guests may relax on the wraparound sun porches.

Historic Interest: The National Watch and Clock Museum (one-half block), The Wrights Ferry Mansion (4 blocks), The Bank Museum (4 blocks).

Innkeeper(s): Chris & Becky Will. $75-125. MC, VISA, PC, TC. 8 rooms with PB, 4 with FP and 2 suites. Breakfast included in rates. Types of meals: Full bkfst. Beds: KQT. Cable TV, ceiling fan and fruit/candy/flowers in room. Air conditioning. Weddings, small meetings and family reunions hosted. Amusement parks, antiquing, art galleries, fishing, Elizabethtown, live theater, museums, parks, shopping, downhill skiing, cross-country skiing, sporting events and water sports nearby.

Publicity: *Philadelphia Inquirer, Lancaster Intelligencer Journal, Columbia News, Washington Post, Potomac and Allentown Morning Call.*

"In a word, extraordinary! Truly a home away from home. First B&B experience but will definitely not be my last."

Cooksburg   F5

Gateway Lodge, Country Inn & Restaurant

Rt 36, Box 125
Cooksburg, PA 16217-0125
(814)744-8017 (800)843-6862 Fax:(814)744-8017
E-mail: info@gatewaylodge.com
Web: www.gatewaylodge.com

Circa 1934. This well-reviewed rustic log lodge was built to accommodate visitors to Cook Forest State Park, a National Natural Landmark. Gateway Lodge borders the park, which offers a multitude of outdoor activities. Guests may opt for cozy rooms in the main lodge, a spacious fireside, whirlpool suite, or a cottage for two to eight people, ideal for families with children. All accommodations are decorated in a comfortable country style. Choose from the European plan (lodging only), Bed & Breakfast (lodging and full breakfast), or Modified American Plan (lodging, seven-course dinner and full breakfast). Inn, suite and BB/MAP cottage guests are offered full access to all the inn's amenities, including afternoon tea. Picnic lunches are available and a wine room with more than 375 varieties of domestic and imported wines is on the premises. Each of the three common rooms, including the library, has a fireplace. Popular for conferences (up to 50 people), there is also a full service restaurant on the premises. The innkeepers offer several different packages, including golf, nature and wellness packages.

Innkeeper(s): Joe & Linda Burney. $90-290. MC, VISA, AX, DS, PC, TC. 32 rooms, 2 with PB, 24 suites, 8 cottages and 1 conference room. Types of meals: Full bkfst, country bkfst, early coffee/tea, lunch, picnic lunch, afternoon tea and gourmet dinner. MAP, EP. Beds: KD. Turndown service, refrigerator and clock radios and Jacuzzi's (in suites only) in room. Air conditioning. Fax, copier, spa, swimming, sauna, library, wine room offering over 375 varieties of domestic and imported wines and exercise room on premises. Handicap access. Weddings, small meetings, family reunions and seminars hosted. Amusement parks, antiquing, fishing, golf, live theater, parks, shopping, cross-country skiing, sporting events, tennis and water sports nearby.
Publicity: *Erie Daily Times, PM Magazine, KDKA Magazine, Sharon Herald, Money Magazine and Innsider Magazine.*

Dallas   F15

Ponda-Rowland B&B Inn and Farm

RR 1 Box 349
Dallas, PA 18612-9604
(570)639-3245 (888)855-9966 Fax:(570)639-5531
E-mail: bbres1@epix.net
Web: www.rowlandfarm.com

Circa 1850. Situated on a 50-acre farm, this historic house overlooks a 30-acre wildlife area with six ponds, often visited by whitetail deer, fox, turkeys, mallard ducks, Canadian geese and, occasionally, blue herons. The home is filled with beautiful American country antiques and collections. There are beamed ceilings and a stone fireplace in the great room.

The scenic setting, hospitable hosts, animals and hearty country breakfast make this a perfect place for a memorable vacation.
Historic Interest: French Azilium, farm museum, covered bridges, Steamtown National Park.

Innkeeper(s): Jeanette & Cliff Rowland. $90-115. MC, VISA, DS, PC, TC. TAC10. 6 rooms with PB, 2 with FP. Breakfast and snacks/refreshments included in rates. Types of meals: Full bkfst and early coffee/tea. Beds: KDT. Ceiling fan in room. Air conditioning. VCR, fax, copier, guest refrigerator and microwave on premises. Antiquing, fishing, horseback riding, Steamtown National Park, live theater, parks, shopping, downhill skiing, cross-country skiing, sporting events and water sports nearby.
Publicity: *Philadelphia Inquirer and Wilkes-Barre Times Leader.*

Danville   G13

The Pine Barn Inn

1 Pine Barn Pl
Danville, PA 17821-1299
(570)275-2071 (800)627-2276 Fax:(570)275-3248
E-mail: innkpr@pinebarninn.com
Web: pinebarninn.com

Circa 1860. The inn is a restored Pennsylvania German barn. Original stone walls and beams accent the restaurant and a large stone fireplace warms the tavern. It is believed to be the first all-electric residence in the state.

Innkeeper(s): Susan Dressler. $50-90. MC, VISA, AX, DC, CB, DS, TC. 102 rooms with PB and 2 conference rooms. Types of meals: Full bkfst. Beds: KQDT.

"For four years we have stayed at the Pine Barn Inn. I thought then, and still think, it is truly the nicest inn I have been in and I've been in many."

Denver   F15

Cocalico Creek B&B

224 S Fourth St
Denver, PA 17517
(717)336-0271 (888)208-7334
E-mail: cocalicocrk@dejazzd.com
Web: www.cocalicocrk.com

Circa 1927. Experience a tranquil pastoral taste of the area's culture and history from this Classic Stone Colonial inn. The interior imparts casual elegance, blending traditional furniture with antiques. The splendid decor is enhanced by detailed wallpaper, lace curtains and Oriental rugs. The charming guest bedrooms, named after local birds that inhabit the area, provide comfort and scenic views. In the dining room, locally made or grown regional fare is highlighted in a four-course candlelight breakfast. Simple pleasures await on the large stenciled porch with wicker furniture. The spacious grounds are inviting to all ages with hillside gardens, ponds, a creek and a play area. Appointments are available for a relaxing in-room massage.

Historic Interest: Ephrata Cloister (5 miles), Landis Valley Museum (10 miles).

Innkeeper(s): Charlene Sweeney. $90-110. MC, VISA, AX, DC, DS, PC, TC. 4 rooms with PB. Breakfast and snacks/refreshments included in rates. Types of meals: Full bkfst, veg bkfst and early coffee/tea. Turndown service in room. Central air. VCR, library and gift shop on premises. Amusement parks, antiquing, art galleries, bicycling, fishing, golf, hiking, horseback riding, live theater, museums, parks, shopping, cross-country skiing, sporting events, tennis and wineries nearby.

Dillsburg   K12

Peter Wolford House

440 Franklin Church Rd
Dillsburg, PA 17019-9766
(717)432-0757 Fax:(717)432-0186

Circa 1797. A Federal farmhouse in the National Register, the Peter Wolford House was constructed of Flemish Bond brick by a prominent grist mill operator. A brick-patterned bank barn, a unique Pennsylvania and Maryland barn style, still stands. There are pine floors and many fireplaces, including a 10-foot-wide, walk-in fireplace used for cooking. Antiques and hand-made quilts fill the guest rooms. Outside on the 10 acres  are meadows, an herb garden and perennial borders accented by a handmade picket fence. State game lands are adjacent to the inn.

Innkeeper(s): Ted & Loretta Pesano. $60-70. PC. 3 rooms, 2 with FP. Breakfast, afternoon tea and snacks/refreshments included in rates. Types of meals: Full bkfst and early coffee/tea. Beds: QD. Air conditioning. Jacuzzi on premises. Small meetings hosted. Amusement parks, antiquing, fishing, golf, downhill skiing and cross-country skiing nearby.

Publicity: *Harrisburg Patriot.*

"Thank you for a splendid getaway."

Downingtown   K16

Glen Isle Farm

130 S Lloyd Ave
Downingtown, PA 19335-2239
(610)269-9100 (800)269-1730 Fax:(610)269-9191

Circa 1730. George Washington was a guest at this 18th-century farmhouse, as well as James Buchanan. Several members of the Continental Congress stayed here while on route to York.  The home is a Revolutionary War site, as well as a stop on the Underground Railroad. Eight wooded acres ensure privacy and a relaxing stay. The farm is within 10 miles of Amish attractions, and a short drive from Valley Forge, Longwood Gardens and antique shops. Philadelphia is 30 miles away.

Historic Interest: Valley Forge (20 miles), Winterthur (25 miles), Underground Railroad site, Revolutionary War site, Longwood Gardens (20 miles), Amish (10 miles).

Innkeeper(s): Tim Babbage & Glenn Baker. $65-80. MC, VISA, DS, PC, TC. TAC10. 4 rooms, 1 with PB. Breakfast and snacks/refreshments included in rates. Types of meals: Gourmet bkfst, cont and early coffee/tea. Beds: KQ. Air conditioning. VCR, fax, copier and library on premises. Weddings, small meetings, family reunions and seminars hosted. Antiquing, art galleries, bicycling, canoeing/kayaking, fishing, golf, hiking and horseback riding nearby.

"Our place to stay when next this way!"

East Berlin (Gettysburg Area)   K12

Bechtel Victorian Mansion B&B Inn

400 W King St
East Berlin (Gettysburg Area), PA 17316
(717)259-7760 (800)579-1108
Web: www.bbonline.com/pa/bechtel/

Circa 1897. The town of East Berlin, near Lancaster and 18 miles east of Gettysburg, was settled by Pennsylvania Germans prior to the American Revolution. William Leas, a wealthy banker, built this many-gabled romantic Queen Anne mansion, now listed in the National Register. The inn is furnished with an abundance of museum-quality antiques and collections. Rooms are decorated in country Victorian style with beautiful quilts and comforters, lace, dolls and teddy bears.

Historic Interest: Gettysburg (18 miles).

Innkeeper(s): Richard & Carol Carlson. $80-150. MC, VISA, AX, DS, PC, TC. TAC10. 7 rooms with PB and 2 suites. Breakfast included in rates. Types of meals: Full bkfst, early coffee/tea and snacks/refreshments. Beds: KQD. Turndown service in room. Air conditioning. VCR on premises. Weddings, small meetings and family reunions hosted. Amusement parks, antiquing, bicycling, fishing, golf, hiking, live theater, museums, shopping, downhill skiing and wineries nearby.

Publicity: *Washington Post and Richmond Times.*

Elizabethtown   J13

West Ridge Guest House

1285 W Ridge Rd
Elizabethtown, PA 17022-9739
(717)367-7783 (877)367-7783 Fax:(717)367-8468
E-mail: wridgeroad@aol.com
Web: www.westridgebandb.com

Circa 1890. Guests at this country home have many choices. They may opt to relax and enjoy the view from the gazebo, or perhaps work out in the inn's exercise room. The hot tub provides yet another soothing possibility. Ask about rooms with whirlpool tubs. The 22-acre grounds also include two fishing ponds. The innkeepers pass out a breakfast menu to their guests, allowing them to choose the time they prefer to eat and a choice of entrees. Along with the traditional fruit, muffins or coffeecake and meats, guests choose items such as omelets, waffles or pancakes.

Innkeeper(s): The Millers. $70-130. MC, VISA, AX, DS. 8 rooms with PB, 5 with FP and 3 suites. Breakfast included in rates. Types of meals: Full bkfst. Beds: KQ. Cable TV, phone, ceiling fan and VCR in room. Spa and air conditioning on premises. Family reunions hosted. Antiquing, fishing, parks and shopping nearby.

Elizabethville   J12

The Inn at Elizabethville

30 W Main St, PO Box 236
Elizabethville, PA 17023
(717)362-3476 Fax:(717)362-1444

Circa 1883. This comfortable, two-story house was owned by a Civil War veteran and founder of a local wagon company. The conference room features an unusual fireplace with cabinets and painted decorations. County auctions, local craft fairs and outdoor activities entice guests. Comfortable living rooms, porches and a sun parlor are available for relaxation.

Innkeeper(s): Heidi Milbrand. $49-65. MC, VISA, PC, TC. 7 rooms with PB and 1 conference room. Breakfast included in rates. Types of meals: Full bkfst. AP. Beds: DT. Ceiling fan in room. Air conditioning. VCR and fax on premises. Weddings, small meetings, family reunions and seminars hosted. Antiquing, fishing, parks, shopping and water sports nearby.

Publicity: *Harrisburg Patriot-News and Upper Dauphin Sentinel.*

Ephrata J14

Doneckers, The Guesthouse, Inns

409 N State St
Ephrata, PA 17522
(717)738-9502 Fax:(717)738-9554
E-mail: mdsimone@doneckers.com

Circa 1777. Jacob Gorgas, a devout member of the Ephrata Cloister and a clock maker, noted for crafting 150 eight-day Gorgas grandfather clocks, built this stately Dutch Colonial-style home. Guests can opt to stay in one of four antique-filled homes. The 1777 House, which includes 12 rooms, features hand-stenciled walls, suites with whirlpool baths, fireplaces, original stone masonry and an antique tiled floor.

The home served as a tavern in the 1800s and an elegant inn in the early 1900s. The Homestead includes four rooms some with fireplaces and amenities such as Jacuzzis, sitting areas and four-poster beds. The Guesthouse features a variety of beautifully decorated rooms each named and themed in honor of local landmarks or significant citizens. The Gerhart House memorializes prominent innkeepers or hotel owners in Ephrata's history. All guests enjoy an expansive breakfast with freshly squeezed juice, fruits, breakfast cheeses and other delicacies. The homes are part of the Donecker Community, which features upscale fashion stores, furniture galleries and a restaurant within walking distance of the 1777 House.

Historic Interest: The Ephrata Cloister, a communal religious society that was instrumental in the Colonial era's development of printing, music and Germanic architecture, is less than a mile away. Wheatland, the home of President James Buchanan, is nearby in Lancaster.

Innkeeper(s): Kelly Snyder & Cori Rife. $65-210. MC, VISA, AX, DC, CB, DS, PC, TC. 40 rooms, 39 with PB and 13 suites. Breakfast included in rates. Types of meals: Cont plus, gourmet lunch and gourmet dinner. Beds: KQDT. Phone and cable music in room. Central air. VCR and fax on premises. Weddings, small meetings, family reunions and seminars hosted. Amusement parks, antiquing, art galleries, golf, live theater, museums, parks, shopping and wineries nearby.

Publicity: *Daily News and Country Inns.*

"A peaceful refuge."

Meadow Valley Farm Guest House

221 Meadow Valley Rd
Ephrata, PA 17522
(717)733-8390 (877)562-4530 Fax:(717)733-9068

Circa 1841. Located in the heart of Lancaster County's beautiful farmland, this 88-acre working farm provides the peaceful relaxation of the rural countryside. Stay in a 150-year-old historic summerhouse that is situated near a quiet pond where swans swim gracefully. Watch the farm dog herd the cows into the barn at milking time, see or help us gather and pack the eggs. Experience life on a real farm! The three guest rooms are furnished in antiques, and while meals are not provided, an antique kitchen is

available for preparing meals or snacks. Historic Lancaster County offers flea markets and antique shops, as well as shopping, museums and fine local dining. Be sure to save time to visit and drive through the many quaint covered bridges in the area.

Historic Interest: Ephrata Cloisters (1 mile).

Innkeeper(s): Walter & Marlene Hurst. $35-45. PC. 3 rooms, 1 with PB. Beds: D. Air conditioning. Bicycles on premises. Antiquing, art galleries, bicycling, fishing, Wild Life Preserve and parks nearby.

Smithton Inn

900 W Main St
Ephrata, PA 17522-1328
(717)733-6094
Web: www.historicsmithtoninn.com

Circa 1763. Henry Miller opened this inn and tavern on a hill overlooking the Ephrata Cloister, a religious society he belonged to, known as Seventh Day Baptists. Several of their medieval-style German buildings are now a museum. This is a warm and welcoming inn with canopy or four-poster beds, candlelight, fireplaces and nightshirts provided for each guest. If you desire, ask for a lavish feather bed to be put

in your room. All rooms boast sitting areas with reading lamps, fresh flowers and the relaxing sounds of chamber music. The grounds include wonderful gardens.

Historic Interest: The Ephrata Cloister Museum is only one block away.

Innkeeper(s): Dorothy Graybill. $75-175. MC, VISA, AX, PC, TC. 8 rooms, 7 with PB, 8 with FP and 1 suite. Breakfast and snacks/refreshments included in rates. Types of meals: Full bkfst. Beds: KQDT. Whirlpools and featherbeds in room. Air conditioning. Flower gardens and candlelight - chamber music on premises. Amusement parks, antiquing, art galleries, golf, hiking, farmland, handcrafts, farmers market, live theater, museums, shopping, tennis and wineries nearby.

Pets allowed: No cats. Dogs, obedience trained, with owners at all times by previous arrangement.

Publicity: *New York, Country Living, Early American Life, Washington Post and Philadelphia Inquirer.*

"After visiting over 50 inns in four countries, Smithton has to be one of the most romantic, picturesque inns in America. I have never seen its equal!"

Erie C3

Spencer House B&B

519 W 6th St
Erie, PA 16507-1128
(814)454-5984 (800)890-7263 Fax:(814)456-5091
E-mail: spencer@erie.net

Circa 1876. This romantic Victorian mansion sits on Millionaire's Row in historic Erie. The original woodwork, 12-foot ceilings and pocket shutters reflect the distinctive quality of yesteryear. Peruse the well-stocked library. Some of the guest bedrooms feature fireplaces and clawfoot tubs. The Tree Top Room offers a floor-to-ceiling canopy bed and reading nook. Enjoy a relaxing rocking chair on the wraparound porch.

$85-149. MC, VISA, AX, DS, PC, TC. 5 rooms with PB. Breakfast included in rates. Types of meals: Full bkfst and early coffee/tea. Beds: Q. Cable TV, phone and ceiling fan in room. Air conditioning. VCR, fax and copier on premises. Weddings, small meetings and family reunions hosted. Amusement parks, antiquing, bicycling, fishing, hiking, live theater, parks, shopping, downhill skiing, cross-country skiing, sporting events and water sports nearby.

Erwinna I17

Golden Pheasant Inn

763 River Rd
Erwinna, PA 18920-9254
(610)294-9595 (800)830-4474 Fax:(610)294-9882
E-mail: barbara@goldenpheasant.com
Web: www.goldenpheasant.com

Circa 1857. The Golden Pheasant is well established as the location of a wonderful, gourmet restaurant, but it is also home to six charming guest rooms decorated by Barbara Faure. Four-poster canopy beds and antiques decorate the rooms, which offer views of the canal and river. The fieldstone inn was
built as a mule-barge stop for travelers heading down the Delaware Canal. The five-acre grounds resemble a French-country estate, and guests can enjoy the lush surroundings in a plant-filled
greenhouse dining room. There are two other dining rooms, including an original fieldstone room with exposed beams and stone walls with decorative copper pots hanging here and there. The restaurant's French cuisine, prepared by chef Michel Faure, is outstanding. One might start off with Michel's special pheasant pate, followed by a savory onion soup baked with three cheeses. A mix of greens dressed in vinaigrette cleanses the palate before one samples roast duck in a luxurious raspberry, ginger and rum sauce or perhaps a sirloin steak flamed in cognac.

Historic Interest: Washington's Crossing (20 miles), Doylestown (10 miles), New Hope (13 miles).

Innkeeper(s): Barbara & Michel Faure. $95-225. MC, VISA, AX, DC, CB, PC, TC. TAC10. 6 rooms with PB, 4 with FP, 1 suite, 1 cottage and 3 conference rooms. Breakfast included in rates. Types of meals: Cont plus, early coffee/tea, picnic lunch, snacks/refreshments, gourmet dinner and room service. EP. Beds: Q. Phone, ceiling fan and jacuzzi tub/fireplaces in room. Air conditioning. Fax, copier, swimming, library and canal path for walking on premises. Small meetings, family reunions and seminars hosted. French and Spanish spoken. Antiquing, art galleries, bicycling, canoeing/kayaking, fishing, golf, hiking, horseback riding, historic Doylestown, New Hope, Washington Crossing, live theater, museums, parks, shopping, cross-country skiing, tennis, water sports and wineries nearby.

Pets allowed: cottage only.

Publicity: *The Philadelphia Inquirer, New York Times, Philadelphia Magazine., Food Network and Fox.*

"A more stunningly romantic spot is hard to imagine. A taste of France on the banks of the Delaware."

Erwinna (Bucks County) I17

Evermay-On-The-Delaware

River Rd, PO Box 60
Erwinna (Bucks County), PA 18920
(610)294-9100 Fax:(610)294-8249
E-mail: moffly@evermay.com
Web: www.evermay.com

Circa 1700. Twenty-five acres of Bucks County at its best — rolling green meadows, lawns, stately maples and the silvery Delaware River, surround this three-story manor. Serving as an inn since 1871, it has hosted such guests as the Barrymore family. Rich walnut wainscoting, a grandfather clock and twin fireplaces warm the parlor, scented by vases of roses or gladio-

lus. Antique-filled guest rooms overlook the river or gardens.

Historic Interest: Washington Crossing State Park, Mercer Museum, Pearl S. Buck House.

Innkeeper(s): Bill & Danielle Moffly. $145-350. MC, VISA, PC, TC. TAC10. 18 rooms with PB, 1 suite, 2 cottages and 2 conference rooms. Breakfast and afternoon tea included in rates. Types of meals: Cont plus, picnic lunch and gourmet dinner. Beds: KQ. Phone and turndown service in room. Air conditioning. VCR, fax, copier and library on premises. Weddings, small meetings and seminars hosted. Antiquing, fishing, live theater, parks, shopping, cross-country skiing, sporting events and water sports nearby.

Publicity: *New York Times, Philadelphia, Travel & Leisure, Food and Wine, Child, Colonial Homes and USAir Magazine.*

"It was pure perfection. Everything from the flowers to the wonderful food."

Fawn Grove L13

Horse Lovers B&B

405 Throne Rd
Fawn Grove, PA 17321
(717)382-4171 Fax:(717)382-4171
E-mail: barb@ixiusa.com
Web: www.horseloversb-b.com

Circa 1840. Guests at this bed & breakfast and stables can enjoy a guided trail ride, take a riding lesson or help with grooming and feeding chores. The 400-acre grounds offer plenty of places to explore. The innkeepers care for a variety of different horse breeds, from Arabians to Belgians. Much of the farmhouse was built in the 1840s, and the home still includes the original plank floor. The home is decorated in country style with antiques. The Victorian Room, ideal for a special occasion, includes a king-size poster bed and a Jacuzzi tub. Breakfasts are served by candlelight and include homemade muffins with fruit from the B&Bs berry patch.

Innkeeper(s): Barb & Dale Torbert. $75-140. PC, TC. 5 rooms. Breakfast, afternoon tea and snacks/refreshments included in rates. Types of meals: Full bkfst, early coffee/tea and room service. Beds: KQDT. Turndown service and ceiling fan in room. Air conditioning. VCR, fax, copier, spa, swimming, stables, bicycles, tennis, library, guided trail rides, wagon rides, exercise room and riding lessons on premises. Weddings, small meetings, family reunions and seminars hosted. Amusement parks, antiquing, fishing, golf, wineries, museums, farm markets, live theater, parks, shopping, downhill skiing, sporting events and tennis nearby.

Forksville E13

Morgan Century Farm B&B

RR 1, Box 1145
Forksville, PA 18616
(570)924-4909 (888)335-1583 Fax:(570)924-4841

Circa 1850. This pre-Civil War farmhouse rests at the edge of a two-lane country road with acres of forests surrounding it. The farmhouse has seen many important uses: as a family home, the village post office, and it was also a stop along the Underground Railroad. The home has remained in the family since its earliest days. Innkeeper Linda Morgan Florentine now opens the family home to guests, offering cozy, comfortable rooms decorated with antiques. There's also a two-story cottage with a wood stove and kitchenette. In the mornings, three-course breakfasts are presented. Fresh seasonal fruits, homemade breads and country entrees make up the fare. In the afternoons, wine and cheese are served. Guests can spend the day relaxing on the 35-acre property or perhaps fishing in the creek. Hiking, golfing and skiing are among the local outdoor activities, and auctions and antique shops abound.

Historic Interest: French Azilum (35 miles), Starrucca Viaduct (40 miles), Nicholson Bridge (35 miles).

Innkeeper(s): Ken & Linda Florentine. $75-95. MC, VISA, PC. 5 rooms, 3 with PB and 1 cottage. Breakfast and afternoon tea included in rates. Types of meals: Full bkfst, country bkfst and early coffee/tea. Beds: DT. Cable TV in room. Central air. Fax, copier, library and gift shop on premises. Weddings and family reunions hosted. Antiquing, art galleries, beaches, bicycling, canoeing/kayaking, fishing, golf, hiking, horseback riding, live theater, museums, parks, shopping, downhill skiing, cross-country skiing and water sports nearby.

Pets allowed: In cottage only $5.00 charge.

Franklin   E3

Quo Vadis B&B

1501 Liberty St
Franklin, PA 16323-1625
(814)432-4208 (800)360-6598

Circa 1867. This three-story brick Queen Anne Victorian has a wraparound porch. Inside are parquet floors, hand-carved woodwork and friezes. The innkeepers' furnishings are family heirlooms that have been collected by four generations and include pieces from the Civil War. Guest rooms are homey with quilts and rocking chairs. The inn's spacious dining room boasts mahogany beams and wainscoting. Breakfast is often an expanded and varied continental. $70-80. MC, VISA, AX, DS, PC, TC. TAC10. 6 rooms with PB. Breakfast

included in rates. Types of meals: Full bkfst. Beds: D. TV, phone, VCR and some with fireplace in room. Air conditioning. Library on premises. Weddings, small meetings, family reunions and seminars hosted. Amusement parks, antiquing, fishing, golf, bike trails, museums, live theater, parks, shopping, cross-country skiing, sporting events, tennis and water sports nearby.

Friendsville   C14

Addison House B&B

RR #1, Box 1586
Friendsville, PA 18818
(570)553-2682
E-mail: info@1811addison.com
Web: www.1811addison.com

Circa 1811. Addison House was built by one of Friendsville's earliest settlers, an Irish immigrant who purchased the vast homestead for just under a dollar an acre. The early 19th-century house is built in Federal style, but its interior includes many Victorian features, from the rich décor to the hand-carved marble fireplaces. A creek rambles through the 260-acre property, and guests will enjoy the secluded, wilderness setting. In the guest rooms, fluffy comforters top antique beds and floral wallcoverings add to the country Victorian

ambiance. Breakfasts begin with items such as fresh berries with cream, followed by a rich entrée. The innkeepers are happy to help guests plan their days. The area offers a multi-

tude of outdoor activities, as well as historic sites, antique shops, covered bridges and much more.

Historic Interest: Steamtown National Historic site (50 miles), Old Mill Village Museum (20 miles), Lackawanna Coal Mine Tour (50 miles), French Azilum Historic site (30 miles), Covered Bridges (30 miles), Pennsylvania Grand Canyon (100 miles), Finger Lakes (50 miles), Salt Springs State Park (10 miles).

Innkeeper(s): Dennis & Gloria McLallen. $65-95. PC. 4 rooms with PB and 1 suite. Breakfast included in rates. Types of meals: Gourmet bkfst, early coffee/tea and afternoon tea. Beds: D. Turndown service, ice water and chocolates in room. Central air. VCR, swimming and library on premises. Weddings and small meetings hosted. Antiquing, art galleries, bicycling, canoeing/kayaking, fishing, golf, hiking, zoo, house tours by appointment., live theater, museums, parks, shopping, cross-country skiing, sporting events and wineries nearby.

Gettysburg   L11

Baladerry Inn at Gettysburg

40 Hospital Rd
Gettysburg, PA 17325
(717)337-1342
E-mail: baladerry@blazenet.net
Web: www.baladerryinn.com

Circa 1812. The quiet and private setting on the edge of the Gettysburg Battlefield, this brick country manor was used as a hospital during the Civil War. Additions were added in 1830 and 1977, and the inn has been completely restored. Guests can snuggle up with a book in their comfortable rooms or in the great room, which includes a fireplace. Some guest rooms include a private patio or a fireplace. The spacious grounds offer

gardens, a gazebo, a tennis court and terraces. Guided tours of the battlefield can be arranged, and guests also can plan a horseback riding excursion on the battlefield.

Historic Interest: Gettysburg Battlefield National Park is just 100 yards from the inn. The area is full of historic sites, including the popular Eisenhower Farm tour.

Innkeeper(s): Caryl O'Gara. $120-175. MC, VISA, AX, DC, CB, DS, PC, TC. TAC10. 8 rooms with PB, 2 with FP and 3 conference rooms. Breakfast included in rates. Types of meals: Full bkfst, early coffee/tea and snacks/refreshments. Beds: KQT. Phone and private patio overlooking grounds in room. Air conditioning. VCR, fax and tennis on premises. Small meetings, family reunions and seminars hosted. Antiquing, fishing, golf, horseback riding, horseback riding on Battlefield, live theater, parks, shopping, downhill skiing, cross-country skiing and sporting events nearby.

Publicity: *Gettysburg Times, Allentown Morning Call, Pennsylvania Magazine and US Air Magazine.*

Baltimore Street B&B

449 Baltimore St
Gettysburg, PA 17325-2623
(717)334-2454 (888)667-8266 Fax:(717)334-6890
E-mail: tannery@cvn.net

Circa 1868. Experience the richness of Civil War history at this three-story Gothic Revival Victorian home, built on the foundation of a home that was here during the Battle of Gettysburg. Union soldiers would stand watch at the front porch, while Confederate soldiers occupied the rear of the house. Hosts Jan and George Newton are Civil War history buffs, who enjoy sharing

their library of more than 700 Civil War books with interested guests. To create the ambiance reminiscent of Civil War history, individually themed rooms feature colors and artwork honoring different battles and moments of America's past. While reflecting on the rich history found in the area, guests can enjoy present-day Gettysburg and the many activities it offers, or watch the sunrise with a hot cup of coffee in a rocking chair on the front porch. A hearty breakfast is served in the dining room.

Historic Interest: Gettysburg battlefields (less than 1 mile).

Innkeeper(s): Jan & George Newton. $100-165. MC, VISA, PC, TC. 7 rooms and 2 suites. Breakfast and snacks/refreshments included in rates. Types of meals: Gourmet bkfst. Beds: KQ. Cable TV in room. Air conditioning. VCR and library on premises. Antiquing, art galleries, bicycling, golf, hiking, horseback riding, live theater, museums, parks, shopping, downhill skiing and wineries nearby.

"We came looking for peace and quiet and found so much more."

The Brafferton Inn

44 York St
Gettysburg, PA 17325-2301
(717)337-3423
E-mail: innkeepers@brafferton.com
Web: www.brafferton.com

Circa 1786. Aside from its notoriety as the first deeded house in what became the town of Gettysburg, The Brafferton bears a bullet shot into the fireplace mantel during the Civil War battle. The rooms are appointed with 18th- and 19th-century antiques that belonged to the owners' ancestors. The dining room boasts a unique mural painted on all four walls depicting the early town of Gettysburg.
Lavish breakfasts are served in the colorful room on tables set with English china, old silver and pineapple-pattern glass gob-

lets. Guest quarters are available in the original house or in the old carriage house across the brick atrium. Carriage house rooms feature stenciling and skylights. The garden area offers a large wooden deck to relax on as guests take in a variety of spring and summer flowers. The National Register inn is near all of Gettysburg's historic attractions, including the Gettysburg National Military Park.

Historic Interest: The inn is listed in the National Register and Gettysburg, site of the Civil War's most infamous battles, offers much history.

Innkeeper(s): Maggie & Bill Ward. $90-160. MC, VISA, AX, DS, PC, TC. TAC10. 11 rooms, 9 with PB and 5 suites. Breakfast included in rates. Types of meals: Full bkfst, early coffee/tea and snacks/refreshments. Beds: QDT. Alarm clocks in room. Air conditioning. Weddings, small meetings and family reunions hosted. Antiquing, fishing, Gettysburg National Park, live theater, parks, shopping, downhill skiing, cross-country skiing and sporting events nearby.

Publicity: *Local newspapers, Early American Life, Country Living and Gettysburg Times.*

Brickhouse Inn

452 Baltimore St
Gettysburg, PA 17325-2623
(717)338-9337 (800)864-3464 Fax:(717)338-9265
E-mail: stay@brickhouseinn.com
Web: www.brickhouseinn.com

Circa 1898. A veranda, dressed in gingerbread trim, decorates the exterior of this red brick Victorian. The interior still maintains its original chestnut woodwork and pocket doors. Family

heirlooms and antiques are featured in the guest rooms. One room offers walls in a deep burgundy hue and a bed topped with a colorful quilt. Another has a black iron bed, fine antiques and a bay window. Breakfast, always featuring homemade items such as shoo-fly pie is

served on the brick patio, which overlooks the lawn. In the afternoons enjoy cookies and lemonade relaxing on our porch rockers. The home is located in Gettysburg's downtown historic district. Gracious accommodations and in-town convenience make the perfect "headquarters" for your stay in Gettysburg.

Innkeeper(s): Craig & Marion Schmitz. $95-150. MC, VISA, AX, DS, PC, TC. TAC10. 10 rooms with PB and 2 suites. Breakfast and snacks/refreshments included in rates. Types of meals: Full bkfst. Beds: QD. Cable TV, ceiling fan and two with fireplace in room. Air conditioning. Fax on premises. Weddings, small meetings, family reunions and seminars hosted. Amusement parks, antiquing, fishing, golf, parks, shopping, downhill skiing, cross-country skiing and tennis nearby.

Publicity: *Washington Post, Washington Flyer, Hanover Sun, Gettysburg Times, Pitttsburgh Post Gazette and WGAL Channel 8-Lancaster.*

The Doubleday Inn

104 Doubleday Ave
Gettysburg, PA 17325-8519
(717)334-9119
E-mail: doubledayinn@blazenet.com

Circa 1929. This Colonial Inn is situated directly on the Gettysburg Battlefield. From its wooded grounds, flower gardens and patios, guests enjoy panoramic views of historic Gettysburg and the National Military Park. The innkeepers have a significant collection of Civil War relics and books on hand, and on selected evenings they feature presentations with battlefield historians. Rooms are furnished with antiques and decorated in English-country style. A full, country-style breakfast is served each morning, and the innkeepers offer a selection of teas in the afternoon.

Historic Interest: Aside from the inn's location on the battlefield, the inn is close to the General Dwight D. Eisenhower Farm.

Innkeeper(s): Ruth Anne & Charles Wilcox. $95-130. MC, VISA, DS. TAC10. 10 rooms, 8 with PB. Breakfast and afternoon tea included in rates. Types of meals: Full bkfst and early coffee/tea. Beds: DT. Weddings, small meetings and family reunions hosted. Amusement parks, antiquing, fishing, battlefield tours, live theater, parks, shopping, downhill skiing, cross-country skiing and sporting events nearby.

Publicity: *Innsider, New York, State College, Washingtonian and Potomac.*

"A beautiful spot on an historic site that we'll long remember."

The Gaslight Inn

33 E Middle St
Gettysburg, PA 17325
(717)337-9100
E-mail: info@thegaslightinn.com
Web: www.thegaslightinn.com

Circa 1872. Gaslights illuminate the brick pathways leading to this 125-year-old Italianate-style, expanded farmhouse. The inn boasts two elegant parlors separated by original pocket doors, a spacious dining room and a first-floor guest room with wheelchair access that opens to a large, brick patio. An open switch-

back staircase leads to the second- and third-floor guest rooms, all individually decorated in traditional and European furnishings. Some of the rooms feature covered decks, whirlpool tubs and steam showers for two. Guests are invited to enjoy a hearty or heart-healthy breakfast and inn-baked cookies and brownies and refreshments in the afternoon. Winter weekend packages are available and carriage rides, private guides and a variety of activities can be arranged with the help of the innkeepers.

Innkeeper(s): Denis & Roberta Sullivan. $100-190. MC, VISA, AX, DS, PC, TC. TAC10. 9 rooms with PB, 6 with FP. Breakfast and snacks/refreshments included in rates. Types of meals: Gourmet bkfst, cont and early coffee/tea. Beds: KQT. Cable TV, phone, ceiling fan and steam baths in room. Air conditioning. VCR, spa and spa facilities on premises. Handicap access. Weddings, small meetings, family reunions and seminars hosted. Antiquing, fishing, golf, historic educational tours and lectures, live theater, parks, shopping, downhill skiing, cross-country skiing, tennis and water sports nearby.

Publicity: *Tyler Texas Times, Hanover Sun, Los Angeles Times, Southern Living and Country Inns.*

Hickory Bridge Farm

96 Hickory Bridge Rd
Gettysburg, PA 17353-9734
(717)642-5261
E-mail: hickory@innbook.com
Web: www.hickorybridgefarm.com

Circa 1750. The oldest part of this farmhouse was constructed of mud bricks and straw on land that once belonged to Charles Carroll, father of a signer of the Declaration of Independence. Inside, there is an attractive stone fireplace for cooking. The farmhouse rooms include whirlpool baths. There are several country cottages in addition to the rooms in the farmhouse, and each includes a fireplace. Fine, country dining is offered in the restored barn on the weekends. The host family members have been innkeepers for more than 25 years.

Historic Interest: Gettysburg (9 miles).

Innkeeper(s): Mary Lynn Martin. $85-145. MC, VISA. 9 rooms, 5 with PB, 4 with FP and 1 conference room. Breakfast included in rates. Types of meals: Full bkfst. Beds: QD. TV and three with whirlpool in room. Antiquing, fishing and downhill skiing nearby.

Publicity: *Hanover Times, The Northern Virginia Gazzette and Taste of Home.*

"Beautifully decorated and great food!"

James Gettys Hotel

27 Chambersburg St
Gettysburg, PA 17325
(717)337-1334 Fax:(717)334-2103
E-mail: info@jamesgettyshotel.com
Web: www.jamesgettyshotel.com

Circa 1803. Listed in the National Register, this newly renovated four-story hotel once served as a tavern through the Battle of Gettysburg and was used as a hospital for soldiers. Outfitted

with cranberry colored awnings and a gold painted entrance, the hotel offers a tea room, nature store and gallery on the street level. From the lobby, a polished chestnut staircase leads to the guest quarters. All accommodations are suites with living rooms appointed with home furnishings, and each has its own kitch-

enette. Breakfasts of home-baked scones and coffee cake are brought to your room.

Historic Interest: Gettysburg NMP/Eisenhower NHS.

Innkeeper(s): Stephanie McSherry. $125-145. MC, VISA, AX, DS, PC, TC. 11 suites. Breakfast included in rates. Types of meals: Cont. Beds: QD. Cable TV, phone and turndown service in room. Air conditioning. VCR and fax on premises. Handicap access. Weddings, small meetings and family reunions hosted. French spoken. Amusement parks, antiquing, art galleries, bicycling, fishing, golf, hiking, horseback riding, museums, parks, shopping, downhill skiing, cross-country skiing, tennis and wineries nearby.

Keystone Inn B&B

231 Hanover St
Gettysburg, PA 17325-1913
(717)337-3888

Circa 1913. Furniture maker Clayton Reaser constructed this three-story brick Victorian with a wide-columned porch hugging the north and west sides. Cut stone graces every door and

window sill, each with a keystone. A chestnut staircase ascends the full three stories, and the interior is decorated with comfortable furnishings, ruffles and lace.

Historic Interest: National Military Park, Eisenhower Farm (1 mile).

Innkeeper(s): Wilmer & Doris Martin. $79-119. MC, VISA. 5 rooms with PB and 1 suite. Breakfast and afternoon tea included in rates. Types of meals: Full bkfst and early coffee/tea. Beds: KQDT. Phone in room. Air conditioning. Library on premises. Family reunions hosted. Amusement parks, antiquing, fishing, Civil War Battlefield, historic sites, live theater, parks, shopping, downhill skiing and cross-country skiing nearby.

Publicity: *Lancaster Sunday News, York Sunday News, Hanover Sun, Allentown Morning Call, Gettysburg Times, Pennsylvania and Los Angeles Times.*

"We slept like lambs. This home has a warmth that is soothing."

Lightner Farmhouse B&B

2350 Baltimore Pike
Gettysburg, PA 17325-7016
(717)337-9508 Fax:(717)337-0754
E-mail: lightner@cvn.net
Web: www.lightnerfarmhouse.com

Circa 1862. Vast green lawns stretch from this brick colonial farmhouse on 19 pastoral acres of historic Gettysburg. A family of deer gathers in the meadow at dusk, perhaps the same scene weary soldiers once watched when the home served as a Civil War field hospital. Recently renovated, the Federal-style home still retains its original random pine floors, and in the gathering room a walk-in fireplace and brick floor. A hearty three-course

breakfast is served in the dining room by firelight. Breathe in the rich history of Adams County with each sway of the rocking chair on the front porch, or while strolling around the flower gardens and new

orchard. Walk on the native trail along White Run Creek, then lounge in the Adirondack chairs on the lawn or catch up on local history with hosts and history buffs Robert and Elaine Smith. Only moments away lie the Gettysburg National Military Park and a wide variety of activities ranging from amusement parks and museums to skiing and shopping.

Historic Interest: Gettysburg National Millitary Park.

Innkeeper(s): Robert & Elaine Smith. $98-145. MC, VISA, PC, TC. 6 rooms with PB, 2 suites and 1 conference room. Breakfast, afternoon tea and snacks/refreshments included in rates. Types of meals: Full bkfst, country bkfst and early coffee/tea. Beds: Q. Turndown service in room. Central air. VCR, fax, copier and library on premises. Family reunions hosted. Amusement parks, antiquing, bicycling, canoeing/kayaking, fishing, golf, hiking, horseback riding, Gettysburg National Park, museums, parks, shopping, downhill skiing and cross-country skiing nearby.

Gordonville (Intercourse)　　　K14

1766 Osceola Mill House

313 Osceola Mill Rd
Gordonville (Intercourse), PA 17529
(717)768-3758 (800)878-7719
E-mail: elalahr@epix.net
Web: www.lancaster-inn.com

Circa 1766. In a quaint historic setting adjacent to a mill and a miller's cottage, this handsome limestone mill house rests on the banks of Pequea Creek. There are deep-set windows and wide pine floors. Guest bedrooms and thekeeping room feature workings fireplaces that add to the warmth and charm. Breakfast fare may  include tasty regional specialties like locally made Pennsylvania Dutch sausage, and Dutch babies, an oven-puffed pancake filled with fresh fruit. Amish neighbors farm the adjacent fields, their horse and buggies enhance the picturesque ambiance.

Innkeeper(s): John & Elaine Lahr. $65-145. MC, VISA, PC, TC. 5 rooms with PB, 4 with FP. Types of meals: Gourmet bkfst. Beds: Q. VCR on premises.

Publicity: *The Journal, Country Living, Washington Times, Gourmet and BBC.*

"We had a thoroughly delightful stay at your inn. Probably the most comfortable overnight stay we've ever had."

Greensburg　　　J4

Huntland Farm B&B

RD 9, Box 21
Greensburg, PA 15601-9232
(724)834-8483　Fax:(724)838-8253

Circa 1848. Porches and flower gardens surround the three-story, columned, brick Georgian manor that presides over the inn's 100 acres. Corner bedrooms are furnished with English antiques. Fallingwater, the Frank Lloyd Wright house, is nearby. Other attractions include Hidden Valley, Ohiopyle water rafting, Bushy Run and Fort Ligonier.

Innkeeper(s): Robert & Elizabeth Weidlein. $75-85. AX, PC, TC. TAC10. 4 rooms, 2 with FP. Breakfast included in rates. Types of meals: Full bkfst. Beds: KQDT. Ceiling fan in room. VCR, fax, copier and library on premises. Small meetings and family reunions hosted. French spoken. Antiquing, live theater, parks and shopping nearby.

Publicity: *Tribune Review.*

Grove City　　　F2

Snow Goose Inn

112 E Main St
Grove City, PA 16127
(724)458-4644 (800)317-4644

Circa 1895. This home was built as a residence for young women attending Grove City College. It was later used as a family home and offices for a local doctor. Eventually, it was trans-

formed into an intimate bed & breakfast, offering four cozy guest rooms. The interior is comfortable, decorated with antiques and touches country with stenciling, collectibles and a few of the signature geese on display. Museums, shops, Amish farms, colleges and several state parks are in the vicinity, offering many activities.

Innkeeper(s): Orvil & Dorothy McMillen. $65. MC, VISA. 4 rooms with PB. Breakfast and snacks/refreshments included in rates. Types of meals: Gourmet bkfst and early coffee/tea. Beds: QD. Air conditioning. VCR on premises. Small meetings and family reunions hosted. Amusement parks, antiquing, fishing, golf, live theater, parks, shopping, downhill skiing, cross-country skiing, sporting events, tennis and water sports nearby.

Publicity: *Allied News.*

"Your thoughtful touches and "homey" atmosphere were a balm to our chaotic lives."

Hallam　　　K13

Stone Mill Inn

305 S Broad St
Hallam, PA 17406
(717)840-9238　Fax:(717)840-9794
E-mail: stonemillinn@blazenet.net
Web: www.stonemillinn.com

Circa 1736. This 8,000-square-foot, 250-year-old inn stands on manicured grounds on 10 acres of land. Just four miles from the water, the early 18th-century inn has deep windowsills, wood beams, original stonework and eight Rumford fireplaces, as well as two walk-in fireplaces. There is a 1736 stone mill on site. The six guest bedrooms are luxuriously appointed. Some have fireplaces, sitting areas and Jacuzzi tubs as well as period pieces like pencil post beds. Breakfast is an event of gourmet delights such as fresh fruit, fresh baked goods, ham and salmon roulades, French toast with fruit glaze and steamed asparagus and French Banana pancakes. After such a hearty meal, guests may strike out to one of many historic sites including York County Colonial Courthouse, General Gates House and Plough Tavern, Central Market and Eastern Market.

Historic Interest: York County Colonial Courthouse (5 miles), General Gates House (5 miles), Plough Tavern (5 miles), Central Market (7 miles), Eastern Market (4 miles).

Innkeeper(s): Ken & Judy Swartz. $90-195. PC, TC. 6 rooms with PB, 5 with FP, 2 suites and 2 conference rooms. Breakfast and afternoon tea included in rates. Types of meals: Gourmet bkfst and early coffee/tea. Beds: KQDT. Turndown service and fireplace in room. Central air. Fax on premises. Weddings, small meetings and seminars hosted. Antiquing, art galleries, bicycling, fishing, golf, hiking, live theater, museums, parks, shopping and wineries nearby.

Hanover　　　L12

The Beechmont B&B Inn

315 Broadway
Hanover, PA 17331-2505
(717)632-3013 (800)553-7009　Fax:(717)632-2769
E-mail: thebeechmont@blazenet.net
Web: www.thebeechmont.com

Circa 1834. Feel welcomed by centuries of charm at this gracious Georgian inn, a witness to the Battle of Hanover, Civil War's first major battle on free soil. A 130-year-old magnolia tree shades the flagstone patio, and wicker furniture invites a lingering rest on the front porch. The romantic Magnolia Suite features a marble fireplace and queen canopy bed. The inn is noted for its sumptuous breakfasts.

Historic Interest: Gettysburg (13 miles).

Innkeeper(s): Kathryn & Thomas White. $85-150. MC, VISA, AX, PC, TC. TAC10. 7 rooms with PB, 3 with FP and 3 suites. Breakfast and snacks/refreshments included in rates. Types of meals: Gourmet bkfst and early coffee/tea. Beds: QD. Cable TV, phone, ceiling fan and fireplace in room. Air conditioning. Fax, copier and library on premises. Weddings, small meetings and family reunions hosted. Antiquing, bicycling, fishing, golf, hiking, horseback riding, live theater, parks, shopping, cross-country skiing, sporting events, water sports and wineries nearby.

Publicity: *Evening Sun and York Daily Record.*

"I had a marvelous time at your charming, lovely inn."

Sheppard Mansion B&B

117 Frederick St
Hanover, PA 17331
(717)633-8075 (877)762-6746 Fax:(717)633-8074
E-mail: reservations@sheppardmansion.com
Web: www.sheppardmansion.com

Circa 1913. Indulge in luxury and elegance at this Neoclassical, greek revival inn. This historic landmark was restored by descendants of the prominent Sheppard family. Decorated with the original antiques and furnishings, mostly Edwardian and some late Victorian, an air of sophistication and hospitality is evident. The spacious public rooms offer amenities that enhance business or pleasure. Appreciate the pampered feeling of fine linens, soaking tubs, marble floors, English toiletries, color TV and PC data ports in the splendid suites. Freshly brewed private blend coffee begins each morning's culinary masterpiece. The formal gardens and English boxwoods reside comfortably with holly, hemlock, copper beech, star and tulip magnolia trees.

Historic Interest: Gettysburg National Park (15 miles).

Innkeeper(s): Kathryn Sheppard, Heather Sheppard, Timothy Bobb. $140-350. MC, VISA, AX, DS, PC. 9 rooms, 5 with PB, 1 with FP, 1 suite and 2 conference rooms. Breakfast and snacks/refreshments included in rates. Types of meals: Gourmet bkfst and early coffee/tea. Beds: QT. Cable TV, phone and VCR in room. Central air. Fax, copier, library and gift shop on premises. Weddings, small meetings and seminars hosted. French, German and Arabic spoken. Amusement parks, antiquing, art galleries, fishing, golf, horseback riding, live theater, museums, parks, shopping, downhill skiing and cross-country skiing nearby.

Publicity: *The Discerning Traveler and Girl Interrupted.*

Harrisville   F3

As Thyme Goes By B&B

214 N Main St, PO Box 493
Harrisville, PA 16038
(724)735-4003 (877)278-4963
E-mail: asthymegoesby@pathway.net

Circa 1846. This country Victorian is furnished with a unique blend of antiques, Art Deco and Oriental decorative arts. The inn features movie memorabilia and guests can spend an evening enjoying old films in the Bogart library or relaxing by the fire in the China Clipper parlor. Guest rooms are decorated with antique beds and offer private baths and air conditioning. A candlelight breakfast is highlighted by the innkeeper's homemade jams. Close to factory outlet shopping, local colleges and historic Volant Mills.

Innkeeper(s): Susan Haas. $60-80. MC, VISA, DS, PC. 3 rooms with PB. Breakfast and snacks/refreshments included in rates. Types of meals: Full bkfst, early coffee/tea and afternoon tea. Beds: KQD. Ceiling fan in room. Air conditioning. VCR and library on premises. Antiquing, fishing, golf, outlet mall, parks, shopping and cross-country skiing nearby.

Publicity: *Allied News and KDKA Pittsburgh.*

"We have been trying for years to make the time to get away for our first B&B experience and you have exceeded all of our expectations for the visit."

Hartsville   K17

Ravenhead Inn

1170 Bristol Road
Hartsville, PA 18974
(215)328-9567 (800)448-3619 Fax:(215)328-9401
E-mail: rvnhdinn@aol.com
Web: www.ravenheadinn.com

Circa 1849. Built for the prominent Darrah family, this grand manor house blends Greek Revival and Victorian styles. Once a stop on the historic underground railroad, it is now a favorite place to visit. Elegant American, English and French antiques are arranged with classic sophistication. The spacious guest bedrooms with trademark high ceilings feature complimentary refreshments kept chilled in refrigerators. A hearty breakfast with an array of regional treats such as Pennsylvania Dutch corn fritters is served in the dining room or on the private patio that boasts a fountain. Encounter tranquil sitting areas and an arbor in the blooming English garden.

Historic Interest: The moland House(1/2 mile), Washington's Crossing (17 miles).

Innkeeper(s): Carol Durborow. $175-190. MC, VISA, AX, PC, TC. TAC10. 4 rooms with PB, 1 with FP. Breakfast and snacks/refreshments included in rates. Types of meals: Country bkfst. Beds: KQT. Cable TV, phone, turndown service and VCR in room. Air conditioning. Fax, copier and gift shop on premises. Small meetings, family reunions and seminars hosted. Antiquing, art galleries, bicycling, golf, hiking, live theater, museums, parks, shopping, water sports and wineries nearby.

Publicity: *Travel/Holiday Magazine, Romantic Homes Magazine, Bucks County Town & Country Magazine, Nouveau Magazine and Cable TV.*

Hawley   E17

The Falls Port Inn & Restaurant

330 Main Ave
Hawley, PA 18428-1330
(570)226-2600

Circa 1902. Constructed by Baron von Eckelberg, this three-story grand brick Victorian is what one would expect to see in a city around the turn of the century. Guests frequent the inn for both the elegance of its rooms and the fine dining in its well-established restaurant that boasts 14-foot-high original windows. Gourmet dinners include Chicken Remi and live lobster. Guest rooms are decorated in antiques, with polished brass fixtures and elegant window treatments. The inn is a favorite for weddings, family reunions and meetings.

Innkeeper(s): Dorothy Fenn. $75-110. MC, VISA, AX, TC. 9 rooms and 1 conference room. Breakfast included in rates. Types of meals: Cont, lunch and gourmet dinner. Beds: QD. Some have cable TV in room. Air conditioning. VCR on premises. Weddings, small meetings, family reunions and seminars hosted. Antiquing, fishing, golf, hiking, movie theater, live theater, parks, shopping, downhill skiing, tennis and water sports nearby.

Pets Allowed.

Settlers Inn at Bingham Park

4 Main Ave
Hawley, PA 18428-1114
(570)226-2993 (800)833-8527 Fax:(570)226-1874
E-mail: settler@ptd.net
Web: www.thesettlersinn.com

Circa 1927. When the Wallenpaupack Creek was dammed up to form the lake, the community hired architect Louis Welch and built this Grand Tudor Revival-style hotel featuring chest-

nut beams, leaded-glass windows and an enormous stone fireplace. The dining room, the main focus of the inn, is decorated with antique prints, hanging plants and chairs that once graced a Philadelphia cathedral.

If you're looking for trout you can try your luck fishing the Lackawaxen River, which runs behind the inn.
Historic Interest: Zane Gray Home & Museum (15 miles), Stourbridge Lion Train (10 miles), Dorflinger Glass Museum (5 miles).
Innkeeper(s): Jeanne & Grant Genzlinger. $85-150. MC, VISA, AX, DS, PC, TC. TAC10. 20 rooms with PB and 3 conference rooms. Breakfast included in rates. Types of meals: Full bkfst, early coffee/tea, lunch, picnic lunch and gourmet dinner. Beds: QD. Cable TV and phone in room. Air conditioning. VCR, fax, copier, tennis and library on premises. Weddings, small meetings, family reunions and seminars hosted. Limited German spoken. Antiquing, fishing, live theater, parks, shopping, downhill skiing, cross-country skiing and water sports nearby.
Publicity: *Philadelphia, New York Newsday, Philadelphia Inquirer, Washington Post and Gail Greco - Country Inn Cooking.*

"Country cozy with food and service fit for royalty."

Holicong   J18

Barley Sheaf Farm

5281 York Rd, Rt 202 Box 10
Holicong, PA 18928
(215)794-5104 Fax:(215)794-5332
E-mail: info@barleysheaf.com
Web: www.barleysheaf.com

Circa 1740. Situated on part of the original William Penn land grant, this beautiful stone house with ebony green shuttered windows and mansard roof is set on 30 acres of farmland. Once owned by noted playwright George Kaufman, it was the gathering place for the Marx Brothers, Lillian Hellman and S.J. Perlman. The bank barn, pond and majestic old trees round out a beautiful setting.
Innkeeper(s): Peter Suess. $105-275. MC, VISA, AX, PC, TC. TAC10. 15 rooms with PB, 6 with FP, 7 suites and 3 conference rooms. Breakfast and afternoon tea included in rates. Types of meals: Full bkfst and early coffee/tea. Beds: KQD. Phone and Jacuzzi's in room. Air conditioning. VCR, fax, copier and swimming on premises. Handicap access. Weddings, small meetings, family reunions and seminars hosted. German and French spoken. Amusement parks, antiquing, fishing, museums, live theater, parks, shopping, downhill skiing, cross-country skiing and water sports nearby.
Publicity: *Country Living, Romantic Inns of America. & CNC Business Channel.*

Hollidaysburg   I7

Hoenstine's B&B

418 N Montgomery St
Hollidaysburg, PA 16648-1432
(814)695-0632 (888)550-9655 Fax:(814)696-7310

Circa 1830. This inn is an antique-lover's dream, as it boasts many pieces of original furniture. Stained-glass windows and the 10-foot-high ceilings add to the atmosphere. Breakfast is

served in the home's formal dining room. The B&B is within walking distance of shops, restaurants and the downtown historic district.
Historic Interest: Horseshoe Curve (10 miles), Portage Railroad National Park (10 miles).

Innkeeper(s): Barbara Hoenstine. $50-80. MC, VISA, PC, TC. TAC10. 4 rooms, 1 with PB. Breakfast included in rates. Types of meals: Full bkfst. Beds: QDT. Cable TV, ceiling fan and VCR in room. Fax, copier and library on premises. Amusement parks, antiquing, fishing, golf, hiking-rails to trails, live theater, parks, shopping, downhill skiing, cross-country skiing, sporting events, tennis and water sports nearby.

"Thank you for a truly calm and quiet week. This was our first B&B experience and it won't be our last."

Intercourse   K14

Intercourse Village B&B Suites

Rt 340-Main Street, Box 340
Intercourse, PA 17534
(717)768-2626 (800)664-0949
E-mail: ivbbs@aol.com
Web: www.amishcountryinns.com

Circa 1909. The Amish country of Pennsylvania abounds in turn-of-the-century, Victorian houses. The Intercourse Village B&B Suites offers four guest rooms in a two-story home that dates to 1909 and eight suites in three, more contemporary buildings to the rear. This B&B caters to couples. The guest rooms in the main house remain true to their Victorian origins: Floral and stripped fabrics and wallpaper cover the walls, while lacy curtains give peeks to the grounds outside; fringed lamps stand to either side of rosewood settees and Oriental carpets cover the hardwood floors. Simpler in decor are the Homestead Suites that feature bright Amish quilts on the beds. Each suite has a fireplace, cable TV, VCR, refrigerator and microwave. Among these suites is the Summer House, which stands alone in its own building and boasts a heart-shaped whirlpool for two. A gourmet three-course breakfast is served by candlelight in the dining room of the main house. Nearby activities include visits to the town's craft, quilt and antique shops or tours through the candle and pretzel factories. You'll find the town of Hershey only an hour away and the Civil War Battlefield site of Gettysburg an hour and a half. Closer to home, you can relax on the white wicker furniture on the front porch and watch the Amish pass by in horse-drawn carriages. This inn has been awarded a four-diamond rating with AAA.
Innkeeper(s): Ruthann Thomas. $119-189. MC, VISA, AX. 8 suites. Breakfast included in rates. Types of meals: Gourmet bkfst. Beds: KQ. Cable TV, phone and VCR in room. Central air. Antiquing, art galleries, golf, live theater and shopping nearby.

Jennerstown   J5

The Olde Stage Coach B&B

1760 Lincoln Hwy
Jennerstown, PA 15547
(814)629-7440
E-mail: carol@oldestagecoachbandb.com
Circa 1752. This renovated two-story Country Victorian farmhouse, located in the Laurel Mountains on historical Lincoln Highway, once served as a stagecoach rest stop. The yellow house has white trim and a wraparound porch overlooking the inn's

acre. The common room features Victorian antiques, and guest rooms offer a fresh country decor. Blueberry French toast is a specialty of the innkeepers as well as home-baked breads and apple pancakes. The immediate area boasts the Mountain Playhouse, three golf courses within three miles, trout streams and lakes, hiking, skiing and outlet shopping — something for all generations. Innkeeper(s): Carol & George Neuhof. $75-85. MC, VISA, PC, TC. 4 rooms with PB. Breakfast and snacks/refreshments included in rates. Types of meals: Full bkfst and early coffee/tea. Beds: QDT. Ceiling fan, chair and table in room. VCR, fax, library and wrap-around porch with swing on premises. Amusement parks, antiquing, fishing, golf, Nascar racing, live theater, parks, shopping, downhill skiing and cross-country skiing nearby.

Jim Thorpe   H15

Arbor Glen

Packer Hill, PO Box 458
Jim Thorpe, PA 18229
(570)325-8566
E-mail: hpmbb@ptd.net

Circa 1850. Relax next to an idyllic stream and pond on the 65 acres where this spacious three-story Victorian farmhouse rests. Sister inn to the Harry Packer Mansion, this estate offers similarly romantic rooms with amenities such as fireplaces, four-poster beds, granite bathrooms and Jacuzzi tubs. . Jim Thorpe is five miles away.

Historic Interest: Jim Thorpe (5 miles), Eckly miners village (15 mile).

Innkeeper(s): Patricia & Robert Handwerk. $195-275. MC, VISA, PC. 4 rooms, 4 with FP, 3 suites, 1 cottage and 1 conference room. Types of meals: Cont plus, early coffee/tea, afternoon tea and snacks/refreshments. AP. Beds: KQ. Cable TV, phone, turndown service, ceiling fan and VCR in room. Air conditioning. Swimming, bicycles and library on premises. Weddings, small meetings, family reunions and seminars hosted. Antiquing, art galleries, beaches, bicycling, canoeing/kayaking, fishing, golf, hiking, horseback riding, live theater, museums, parks, shopping, downhill skiing, cross-country skiing, sporting events, tennis, water sports and wineries nearby.

The Inn at Jim Thorpe

24 Broadway
Jim Thorpe, PA 18229
(570)325-2599 (800)329-2599 Fax:(570)325-9145
E-mail: innjt@ptd.net
Web: www.innjt.com

Circa 1848. This massive New Orleans-style structure, now restored, hosted some colorful 19th-century guests, including Thomas Edison, John D. Rockefeller and Buffalo Bill. All rooms are appointed with Victorian furnishings and have private baths with pedestal sinks and marble floors. The suites include fireplaces and whirlpool tubs. Also on the premises are a Victorian dining Room, Irish pub and a conference center. The inn is situated in the heart of Jim Thorpe, a quaint Victorian town that was known at the turn of the century as the "Switzerland of America." Historic mansion tours, museums and art galleries are nearby, and mountain biking and whitewater rafting are among the outdoor activities.

Historic Interest: Switchboard Railroad, first railroad in U.S. (walking distance), Asa Packer Mansion, Millionaire's Row, Jim Thorpe final resting place (walking distance).

Innkeeper(s): David Drury. $89-279. MC, VISA, AX, DC, DS, TC. TAC10. 34 rooms with PB, 11 suites and 2 conference rooms. Breakfast included in rates. Types of meals: Cont plus, lunch, dinner and room service. MAP. Beds:

KQ. Cable TV, phone and 11 suites with whirlpools and fireplaces in room. Air conditioning. Fax, copier, game room, exercise room and elevator on premises. Handicap access. Weddings, small meetings, family reunions and seminars hosted. Antiquing, art galleries, bicycling, canoeing/kayaking, fishing, golf, hiking, horseback riding, museums, parks, shopping, downhill skiing and wineries nearby.

Publicity: *Philadelphia Inquirer, Pennsylvania Magazine and Allentown Morning Call.*

"We had the opportunity to spend a weekend at your lovely inn. Your staff is extremely friendly, helpful, and courteous. I can't remember when we felt so relaxed, we hope to come back again soon."

Kennett Square   L16

Scarlett House

503 W State St
Kennett Square, PA 19348-3028
(610)444-9592 (800)820-9592
E-mail: do-over@worldnet.att.net
Web: www.virtualcities.com/ons/pa/a/paa2702.html

Circa 1910. This granite American four-square home features an extensive wraparound porch, a front door surrounded by leaded-glass windows and magnificent chestnut woodwork. Beyond the foyer are two downstairs parlors with fireplaces, while a second-floor parlor provides a sunny setting for afternoon tea. Rooms are furnished in romantic Victorian decor with period antiques and Oriental carpets. An elegant gourmet breakfast is served with fine china, silver, crystal and lace linens.

Innkeeper(s): Christina Powell. $89-139. MC, VISA, AX, DS, TC. 4 rooms, 2 with PB, 1 suite and 1 conference room. Breakfast and snacks/refreshments included in rates. Types of meals: Gourmet bkfst. Beds: QD. Ceiling fan in room. Central air. Weddings, small meetings, family reunions and seminars hosted. Longwood Gardens, Brandywine Valley attractions and Amish country nearby.

"Truly an enchanting place."

Kennett Square (Avondale)   L15

B&B at Walnut Hill

541 Chandler's Mill Rd
Kennett Square (Avondale), PA 19311-9625
(610)444-3703
E-mail: millsjt@magpage.com
Web: bbonline.com/pa/walnuthill

Circa 1840. The family who built this pre-Civil War home ran a grist mill on the premises. Innkeepers Sandy and Tom Mills moved into the home as newlyweds. Today, Sandy, a former caterer and Winterthur docent, serves up gourmet breakfasts such as cottage cheese pancakes with blueberry sauce and

homemade teas, lemon butter and currant jam. Her cooking expertise was recognized in Good Housekeeping's Christmas issue. The guest rooms are cozy, welcoming and filled with antiques. One room features a Laura Ashley canopy bed. Another boasts Victorian wicker. The house overlooks horses grazing in a meadow, and a nearby creek is visited by Canadian geese, deer and an occasional fox.

Historic Interest: Winterthur Museum, Brandywine Battlefield, Museum of Natural History, Longwood Gardens, Brandywine River Museum, Hagley Museum, Chaddsford Winery, Barnes Foundation.

Innkeeper(s): Tom & Sandy Mills. $75-100. PC, TC. TAC10. 2 rooms with PB.

Breakfast and snacks/refreshments included in rates. Types of meals: Gourmet bkfst and afternoon tea. Beds: KDT. Cable TV and turndown service in room. Central air. VCR, copier, spa and porch overlooking meadow and stream on premises. Family reunions hosted. Limited Spanish and French spoken. Canoeing/kayaking, golf, horseback riding, hot air balloons and shopping nearby.
Publicity: *Times Record, Suburban Advertiser, Four Seasons of Chester County, Country Inns, Good Housekeeping and Country Magazine.*

Kintnersville   I17

Bucksville House

4501 Durham Rd Rt 412
Kintnersville, PA 18930-1610
(610)847-8948 (888)617-6300 Fax:(610)847-8948

Circa 1795. For over two centuries, Bucksville House served as a stagecoach stop. It also enjoyed use as a tavern and a speakeasy. For nearly two decades, the historic Colonial-Federal home has welcomed guests in the form of a country inn. The five guest rooms have been appointed in a sophisticated style with Colonial and country furnishings. In one room, quilts are

neatly stacked on armoire shelves. A quilt tops the bed and still another decorates a wall. Three rooms include a fireplace. Flowers decorate the exterior, and the grounds include a large deck and a gazebo where guests can enjoy breakfast. A pond and herb garden are other items guests will find while strolling the four-and-a-half-acre grounds. Several friendly, albeit somewhat mischievous, ghosts are said to haunt the inn.

Innkeeper(s): Barb & Joe Szollosi. $125-150. MC, VISA, AX, DS, PC, TC. 5 rooms with PB, 3 with FP and 1 suite. Breakfast and afternoon tea included in rates. Types of meals: Full bkfst. Beds: Q. Air conditioning. VCR, fax, copier, library, pond and water garden on premises. Handicap access. Amusement parks, antiquing, fishing, golf, live theater, parks, shopping, tennis and water sports nearby.

Publicity: *Country Living, Bucks Country Town & Country, Country Decorating, Delaware Today, Lehigh Valley Magazine, Country Inns Magazine, New York Magazine and Country Accents Magazine.*

Lackawaxen   E18

Roebling Inn on The Delaware

Scenic Dr, PO Box 31
Lackawaxen, PA 18435-0031
(570)685-7900 Fax:(570)685-1718
E-mail: roebling@ltis.net
Web: www.roeblinginn.com

Circa 1870. In the National Register of Historic Places, this Greek Revival-style home was once the home of Judge Ridgway, tallyman for the Delaware and Hudson Canal Company. The inn offers country furnishings and antiques. Guest rooms are comfortably furnished and some have fireplaces. There's a cottage, which is popular for families with children. The inn's long front porch is the favorite place to relax, but the sitting room is

inviting as well with its cozy fireplace. Full country breakfasts are provided. Afterward, ask the innkeepers for directions to nearby hidden waterfalls, or walk to the Zane Grey Museum.

Roebling's Delaware Aqueduct is 100 yards downstream from the inn, now the oldest suspension bridge in North America. The scenic Delaware River is fun to explore, and there is a boat launch. Canoe, raft and tube rentals are available nearby. Fishing is a few steps from the inn's front porch or ask about guides for drift boat fishing. In the winter, look for bald eagles or ski at Masthope or Tanglewood. It's a two hour drive from New York City and two-and-a-half hours from Philadelphia.

Innkeeper(s): Don & JoAnn Jahn. $65-130. MC, VISA, AX, DS, TC. 6 rooms, 5 with PB and 1 cottage. Breakfast included in rates. Types of meals: Full bkfst. Beds: QDT. Cable TV and some rooms with fireplace in room. Air conditioning. Fax on premises. Antiquing, fishing, live theater, parks, downhill skiing, cross-country skiing and water sports nearby.

Publicity: *New York Magazine and New York Daily News.*

Lafayette Hill   K17

General Lafayette Inn & Brewery

646 Germantown Pike
Lafayette Hill, PA 19444
(610)941-0600 (800)251-0181 Fax:(610)941-0766
E-mail: ellen.mcglynn@generallafayetteinn.com
Web: www.generallafayetteinn.com

Circa 1732. Steeped in history, this inn was thought to be a headquarters for Generals Smallwood, Hull and Lafayette during the encampment at Barren Hill. Since the Revolutionary War much refurbishing has occurred, adding a unique corner fireplace and one that was made of locally quarried blue marble. The American Colonial inn now houses a microbrewery with upscale dining and live music. Connected by a brick pathway to the restaurant is Lafayette's Retreat, a quiet and secluded Dutch Colonial guest house set amongst tall oak trees. Blending Victorian and Colonial decor, the living room and dining room are comfortable gathering places. Well-appointed guest bedrooms feature gracious comfort. A kitchen stocked with fresh breakfast ingredients offers 24-hour access. Ample grounds, a meditation garden and pond offer relaxing surroundings.

Historic Interest: Center-City Philadelphia and Valley Forge National Historic Park (10 miles).

Innkeeper(s): Michael & Ellen McGlynn. $99-159. MC, VISA, AX, DC. 5 rooms, 3 with PB, 1 suite, 1 guest house and 3 conference rooms. Breakfast and snacks/refreshments included in rates. Types of meals: Cont, early coffee/tea, lunch and gourmet dinner. AP. Beds: KQDT. Cable TV, phone, VCR, iron/ironing board and hair dryer in room. Central air. Meditation garden with pond on premises. Weddings, small meetings, family reunions and seminars hosted. Antiquing, art galleries, bicycling, fishing, hiking, horseback riding, live theater, museums, parks, shopping, downhill skiing, cross-country skiing, sporting events and wineries nearby.

Lake Ariel   E16

Beech Tree Gardens B&B

RR #10 Box 3100
Lake Ariel, PA 18436
(570)226-8677 Fax:(570)226-7461
E-mail: beech@ptd.net

Circa 1876. Sitting on 81 forested acres in the Pocono Mountains, this Victorian inn is just two hours from New York City and Philadelphia. Mahogany woodwork is showcased throughout the parlor. The well-appointed guest bedrooms boast clawfoot tubs, highback marble washstands and pedestal sinks. Breakfast is served in the dining room beneath a ceiling mural adorned with cherubs. Fresh fruit, banana bread, apple dumplings, baked pears and omelets are some of the delicious fare offered. Relax on the wraparound porch's swing and rocking chairs, or enjoy the fountain in the formal garden. Trails offer bird watching and wildlife observation. Walk the lighted paths at night through the woods and sit on the balcony of the Pond House. Steamtown National Historic Park, Lackawanna Coal Mine, Montage Mountain ski area and Dorflinger Glass Museum are within driving distance.

Innkeeper(s): Lynn & Kevin Schultz. $85-115. MC, VISA, TC. TAC10. 3 rooms, 2 with PB and 1 suite. Breakfast and snacks/refreshments included in rates. Types of meals: Full bkfst and veg bkfst. Beds: QD. Air conditioning. Fax, cylinder stove, hiking trails, ponds and snowshoeing on premises. Antiquing, beaches, bicycling, canoeing/kayaking, fishing, golf, hiking, horseback riding, live theater, museums, parks, shopping, downhill skiing, cross-country skiing, sporting events and water sports nearby.

Publicity: *Meet the Chamber-local radio.*

Lampeter   K14

The Australian Walkabout Inn

837 Village Rd, PO Box 294
Lampeter, PA 17537-0294
(717)464-0707 Fax:(717)464-2501

Circa 1925. The inn, situated on beautifully landscaped grounds with an English garden and a lily pond, features a wraparound porch, where guests can watch Amish buggies

pass by. Bedchambers have antique furniture, canopy beds and Pennsylvania Dutch quilts.

Historic Interest: The historic 1719 Hans Herr House is just one mile away.

Innkeeper(s): Jay & Valerie Petersheim. $99-289. MC, VISA, AX, PC, TC. TAC5. 5 suites, 5 with FP and 1 cottage.

Breakfast included in rates. Types of meals: Gourmet bkfst. Beds: KQ. Cable TV and hot tub or whirlpools in room. Air conditioning. VCR, fax and copier on premises. Family reunions hosted. Amusement parks, antiquing, Amish dinner, live theater, parks, shopping and sporting events nearby.

Publicity: *Gourmet, New York Post, Intelligencer Journal and Holiday Travel.*

"The "Walkabout Inn" itself and its surroundings are truly relaxing, romantic and quaint. It's the kind of place that both of us wanted and pictured in our minds, even before we decided to make reservations."

Lancaster   K14

1725 Historic Witmer's Tavern Inn & Museum

2014 Old Philadelphia Pike
Lancaster, PA 17602-3413
(717)299-5305
E-mail: witmerstavern@cs.com
Web: www.witmerstavern.com

Circa 1725. This pre-Revolutionary War inn is the oldest and most complete Pennsylvania inn still lodging travelers in the original building. In the National Register of Historic Places, the

property has been restored to its original, pioneer style with hand-fashioned hardware and "bubbly" glass nine-over-six windows. Guest rooms feature antiques, fresh flowers, quilts and wood-burning fire-

places. Revolutionary and Colonial dignitaries like Washington, Lafayette, Jefferson and Adams were entertained here. The Witmers provisioned hundreds of immigrants as they set up Conestoga Wagon trains headed for western and southern homestead regions. Amish farmland is adjacent to and in the rear of the inn, and a lovely park is located nearby. The innkeeper, native to the area, can provide an abundance of local information. He can also plan extra touches for a special occasion. Guests can make appointments for therapeutic massage. The inn offers Pandora's Antique Shop in the building featuring antique quilts, paintings, prints, furnishings and unique collectibles.

Historic Interest: Hans Herr House, Rockford Plantation, President Buchanan's House, Ephrata Cloister, Amish farms and villages are among the historic sites. Witmer's Heritage Tours provide interesting insight into Lancaster County and national history.

Innkeeper(s): Brant Hartung. $70-110. PC, TC. TAC10. 7 rooms, 2 with PB, 7 with FP. Breakfast included in rates. Types of meals: Cont plus. Beds: D. Seven rooms with wood-burning fireplaces in room. Air conditioning. Small meetings, family reunions and seminars hosted. Amusement parks, antiquing, fishing, golf, nature preserves, auctions, Amish farms and villages, live theater, shopping, sporting events, tennis and water sports nearby.

Publicity: *Stuart News, Pennsylvania, Antique, Travel & Leisure, Mid-Atlantic, Country Living, Early American Life, Colonial Homes and USA Today.*

"Your personal attention and enthusiastic knowledge of the area and Witmer's history made it come alive and gave us the good feelings we came looking for."

The Apple Bin Inn

2835 Willow Street Pike N
Lancaster, PA 17584-9501
(717)464-5881 (800)338-4296 Fax:(717)464-1818
E-mail: bininn@aol.com
Web: www.applebininn.com

Circa 1865. Once the village general store, the Apple Bin Inn has been restored and transformed into a cozy country getaway. The airy rooms are decorated with a mix of country furnishings and Colonial reproductions, creating a cheerful, romantic ambiance. There is also a restored carriage house, an ideal spot for a romantic occasion. The homemade breakfasts include fresh, local ingredients, including fresh fruits. The

innkeepers are both Lancaster County natives and can offer a bounty of information about this popular area. Lancaster County offers many historic sites, antique and craft shops, flea markets and many Amish sites.

Historic Interest: Oldest home in Lancaster County, Hans Herr House (1 mile).

Innkeeper(s): Debbie & Barry Hershey. $95-155. MC, VISA, AX, PC, TC. 4 rooms with PB and 1 guest house. Types of meals: Full bkfst. Beds: QD. Cable TV, phone and ceiling fan in room. Central air. Fax, copier and library on premises. Family reunions hosted. Amusement parks, antiquing, art galleries, beaches, bicycling, canoeing/kayaking, golf, hiking, live theater, museums, parks, shopping, tennis and wineries nearby.

Flowers & Thyme B&B

238 Strasburg Pike
Lancaster, PA 17602-1326
(717)393-1460 Fax:(717)399-1986
E-mail: padutchbnb@aol.com

Circa 1941. This 1941 brick farmhouse overlooks a working farm. Picturesque cottage gardens, as well as an herb garden, were featured in Birds and Blooms Magazine. An Amish carpenter built the home and the present innkeepers grew up here

among the Amish and Mennonite communities. They are knowledgeable about the area and its history. The inn offers antiques and quilts and you can choose from a variety of amenities such as a canopy bed, a Jacuzzi or a fireplace. The Gathering Room hosts the full country breakfast that is served each morning. A few minutes away are outlet stores, farmers markets, antique shops, craft and boutique shops.

Historic Interest: The Central Market in Lancaster is one of the oldest enclosed markets in the country featuring everything from fresh fruits and vegetables to flowers and baked goods. The Hans Herr House, the county's oldest building and second oldest Mennonite meeting house, is four miles from the home. For something unique, try the scenic 45-minute journey through Amish country on America's oldest short line, the Strasburg Railroad.

Innkeeper(s): Don & Ruth Harnish. $85-120. MC, VISA, PC, TC. 3 rooms with PB. Breakfast included in rates. Types of meals: Full bkfst. Beds: Q. Ceiling fan in room. Air conditioning. Library and Jacuzzi in one room on premises. Amusement parks, antiquing, live theater, parks, shopping, sporting events and water sports nearby.

Publicity: *Lancaster newspapers, Allentown Morning Call and Birds & Bloom Magazine.*

Gardens of Eden

1894 Eden Rd
Lancaster, PA 17601-5526
(717)393-5179 Fax:(717)393-7722
E-mail: info@garden-of-eden.com
Web: www.gardens-of-eden.com

Circa 1867. Wildflowers, perennials and wooded trails cover the three-and-a-half-acre grounds surrounding Gardens of Eden. The home, which overlooks the Conestoga River, is an example of late Federal-style architecture with some early Victorian touches. The innkeepers have won awards for their restoration. Their

guest cottage was featured on the cover of a decorating book. The interior, laced with dried flowers, handmade quilts, baskets and country furnishings, has the feel of a garden cottage. This cottage is ideal for families and includes a working fireplace and an efficiency kitchen. Gardens of Eden is within minutes of downtown Lancaster. The innkeepers can arrange for personalized tours of Amish and Mennonite communities and sometimes a dinner in an Amish home.

Innkeeper(s): Marilyn & Bill Ebel. $100-150. MC, VISA. 4 rooms with PB, 1 with FP and 1 cottage. Breakfast included in rates. Types of meals: Full bkfst and afternoon tea. Beds: KQD. Phone and turndown service in room. Air conditioning. VCR, fax, copier, garden tours, canoe and bike maps and storage on premises. Limited French spoken. Amusement parks, antiquing, amish culture, craft shows, live theater, museums and shopping nearby.

The King's Cottage, A B&B Inn

1049 E King St
Lancaster, PA 17602-3231
(717)397-1017 (800)747-8717 Fax:(717)397-3447
E-mail: info@kingscottagebb.com
Web: www.kingscottagebb.com

Circa 1913. This Spanish Mission Revival house features a red-tile roof and stucco walls, common in many stately turn-of-the-century houses in California and New Mexico. Its elegant interiors include a sweeping staircase, a library with marble fireplace,

stained-glass windows and a solarium. The inn is appointed with Oriental rugs and antiques and fine 18th-century English reproductions. Three guest rooms have Jacuzzi/whirlpool tubs and four have fireplaces. The formal dining room provides the location for gourmet morning meals.

Historic Interest: Landis Valley Farm Museum (5 miles), Railroad Museum of Pennsylvania (8 miles), Hans Herr House (5 miles).

Innkeeper(s): Karen Owens. $145-240. MC, VISA, DS. TAC10. 6 rooms with PB, 1 suite and 1 guest house. Breakfast and afternoon tea included in rates. Types of meals: Full bkfst. Beds: KQ. Turndown service and Tv upon request in room. Small meetings and seminars hosted. Amusement parks, antiquing, fishing, golf, outlet shopping, Amish Dinners, quilts, live theater, shopping and sporting events nearby.

Publicity: *Country, USA Weekend, Bon Appetit, Intelligencer Journal, Times, New York Magazine and Forbes.*

"I appreciate your attention to all our needs and look forward to recommending your inn to friends."

Lincoln Haus Inn B&B

1687 Lincoln Hwy E
Lancaster, PA 17602-2609
(717)392-9412
Web: www.800padutch.com/linchaus.html

Circa 1915. A stained-glass entry greets guests as they enter this charming inn, located in the heart of Pennsylvania Dutch country. The home includes five comfortable rooms and two apartments, one a honeymoon suite perfect for romantic getaways and anniversary celebrations. Innkeeper Mary Zook is Amish and happy to provide a rich oral history of the area and Amish community over a hearty breakfast, served Monday through Saturday.

Historic Interest: Wheatland (President Buchanan's home) 5 miles, Lancaster Central Market (4 miles), Amish Country (5-10 miles).

Innkeeper(s): Mary Zook. $63-83. PC, TC. TAC10. 8 rooms with PB and 3 suites. Breakfast included in rates. Types of meals: Full bkfst and country bkfst. Beds: QDT. Ceiling fan in room. Air conditioning. Family reunions hosted. German spoken. Amusement parks, antiquing, art galleries, bicycling, fishing, golf, hiking, live theater, museums, parks, shopping, tennis and wineries nearby.

Publicity: *Keystone Gazette.*

New Life Homestead B&B

1400 E King St, Rt 462
Lancaster, PA 17602-3240
(717)396-8928
E-mail: carolg@newlifebnb.com

Circa 1912. This two-and-a-half story brick home is situated within one mile of Amish Farms, and it's less than two miles from the city of Lancaster. Innkeepers Carol and Bill Giersch, both Mennonites, host evening discussions about the culture and history of Amish and Mennonite people. Carol's homemade breakfasts are made with local produce.

Innkeeper(s): Carol Giersch. $65-85. 3 rooms, 2 with PB and 1 suite. Breakfast included in rates. Types of meals: Full bkfst and snacks/refreshments. Beds: QDT. VCR on premises. Small meetings and family reunions hosted. Amusement parks, antiquing, fishing, live theater, shopping and sporting events nearby.

Publicity: *Keystone Gazette and Pennsylvania Dutch Traveler.*

"Reminded me of my childhood at home."

Landenberg L15

Cornerstone B&B Inn

300 Buttonwood Rd
Landenberg, PA 19350-9398
(610)274-2143 Fax:(610)274-0734
E-mail: corner3000@aol.com
Web: www.belmar.com/cornerstone

Circa 1704. The Cornerstone is a fine 18th-century country manor house filled with antique furnishings. Two fireplaces make the parlor inviting. Wing chairs, fresh flowers and working fireplaces add enjoyment to the guest rooms. Perennial gardens, a water garden and swimming pool with hot tub are additional amenities.

Historic Interest: Brandywine River Museum, Brandywine Battlefield State Park, Franklin Mint, Valley Forge National Historical Park, Longwood Gardens, Winterthur Museum.

Innkeeper(s): Linda Chamberlin & Marty Mulligan. $100-250. MC, VISA, DS, PC, TC. 9 rooms, 5 with FP, 1 suite and 8 cottages. Breakfast included in rates. Types of meals: Full bkfst and early coffee/tea. Beds: KQT. Cable TV in room. Air conditioning. VCR and fax on premises. Small meetings and family reunions hosted. Amusement parks, antiquing, live theater, parks, shopping and sporting events nearby.

Lititz J14

The Alden House

62 E Main St
Lititz, PA 17543-1947
(717)627-3363 (800)584-0753
E-mail: inn@aldenhouse.com
Web: www.aldenhouse.com

Circa 1850. For more than 200 years, breezes have carried the sound of church bells to the stately brick homes lining Main Street. The Alden House is a brick Victorian in the center of this historic district and within walking distance of the Pretzel

House (first in the country) and the chocolate factory. A favorite room is the suite with a loft dressing room and private bath. A full breakfast is served, often carried to one of the inn's three porches.

Innkeeper(s): Tom & Lillian Vazquez. $90-120. MC, VISA, PC, TC. 5 rooms with PB, 1 with FP and 3 suites. Breakfast included in rates. Types of meals: Full bkfst. Beds: Q. Cable TV and ceiling fan in room. Air conditioning. Small meetings hosted. Amusement parks, antiquing, live theater, parks and shopping nearby.

Publicity: *Travel Holiday, Rockland Journal News, Penn Dutch Traveler, Now in Lancaster County and Philadelphia Inquirer.*

"Truly represents what bed & breakfast hospitality is all about. You are special innkeepers. Thanks for caring so much about your guests. It's like being home."

Casual Corners B&B

301 N Broad St
Lititz, PA 17543
(717)626-5299 (800)464-6764
E-mail: ccbb@supernet.com
Web: www.casualcornersbnblititz.com

Circa 1904. This three-story home has a dormer window, shutters and a wide wraparound porch filled with hanging ferns and wicker furnishings. There is a second-floor sitting room for

guests. A country breakfast often includes poached pears and caramel apple French toast. Walk to the Wilbur Chocolate Company or the country's first pretzel bakery.

Historic Interest: PA Amish, Wilbur chocolate factory, oldest pretzel baker in U.S.

Innkeeper(s): Glenn & Ruth Lehman. $70-90. MC, VISA, PC, TC. 4 rooms, 2 with PB and 1 suite. Breakfast included in rates. Types of meals: Full bkfst, country bkfst, veg bkfst and early coffee/tea. Beds: QD. Turndown service and ceiling fan in room. Air conditioning. Amusement parks, antiquing, art galleries, bicycling, golf, hiking, live theater, museums, parks, shopping, tennis and wineries nearby.

Stauffer House B&B

14 Landis Valley Rd
Lititz, PA 17543-8628
(717)627-5663
E-mail: staufferhousebb@supernet.com

Circa 1940. This comfortable Colonial inn sits on a park-like acre in the small town of Lititz in the heart of Amish country. The three guest bedrooms are furnished with family antiques such as a tall pencil-post bed and a ball-post bed. Innkeeper Hagar Scott serves a delightful full breakfast including her wonderful specialties of blueberry French toast, Belgian waffles with fresh fruit and whipped cream or blintzes with sour cream and jam. Tea and coffee are always available in the dining room and home-baked snacks and fruit are offered often, as well. Most guests head out after breakfast to Lancaster, Wheatland (the home of President James Buchanan) or Central Market, which is one of the oldest continual markets in the country, with Amish stands, great food, crafts and flowers. Wilbur Chocolates, located in Lititz, has a chocolate museum and a chocolate factory that flavors the air. After a day of site seeing, guests like to sit and rock on the back porch that overlooks a manicured lawn with flower and vegetable gardens, or play a quiet game of croquet.

Historic Interest: Lancaster (6 miles), Wheatland, home of President James Buchanan, Cloisters in Ephrata (8 miles), Central Market, Rockford.

Innkeeper(s): Hagar Scott. $65. PC, TC. 3 rooms. Breakfast and snacks/refreshments included in rates. Types of meals: Full bkfst. Beds: QDT. Library on premises. Amusement parks, antiquing, art galleries, fishing, golf, hiking, live theater, museums, parks and shopping nearby.

Malvern K16

General Warren Inne

Old Lancaster Hwy
Malvern, PA 19355
(610)296-3637 Fax:(610)296-8084
E-mail: suites@generalwarren.com
Web: www.generalwarren.com

Circa 1745. This 250-year-old inn, once owned by the grandson of William Penn, is surrounded by three wooded acres and is filled with 18th-century charm. The rooms are simple and elegant, featuring chandeliers, painted woodwork, quilts and period

reproductions. Each of the guest rooms offers a special touch. The Presidential Suite features a sitting room with a fireplace, while the William Penn Suite boasts an original cathedral window. Other rooms include four-poster beds and fireplaces. Meals at the General

Warren are a delight in one of the inn's three elegant candle-lit dining rooms. Start with a Caesar salad, prepared tableside or with a stuffed Portabello mushroom. Follow that with Beef Wellington and complete the meal with homemade Grand Marnier ice cream. Summer dishes feature locally grown produce and herbs from the inn's organic gardens. Gourmet magazine rated the inn's restaurant as one of Philadelphia's Top Tables.
Innkeeper(s): Karlie Davies. $120-190. MC, VISA, AX, DC. 8 suites. Breakfast included in rates. Types of meals: Cont, lunch and gourmet dinner. Beds: KQD. Historical sites nearby and live theater nearby.
Publicity: *Colonial Homes and Gourmet Magazine.*

Manheim J14

Penn's Valley Farm & Inn

6182 Metzler Rd
Manheim, PA 17545-8629
(717)898-7386
E-mail: pennsvbandb@cs.com

Circa 1826. This picture-perfect farm was purchased by the Metzler's ancestors in 1770, but it was originally owned by the three Penn brothers. The guest house, built in 1826, features stenciled farm animals painted along the winding stairway that

leads to the bedrooms. An open hearth is in the living room. Breakfast is served in the dining room of the main farmhouse. There also is one room available in the farmhouse. It features a shared bath and a queen bed.

Innkeeper(s): Melvin & Gladys Metzler. $55-65. MC, VISA. 2 rooms and 1 guest house. Types of meals: Full bkfst and cont. Beds: QT. TV in room. Air conditioning. VCR on premises. Amusement parks, antiquing and shopping nearby.

Rose Manor B&B Tea Room and Herbal Gift Shop

124 S Linden St
Manheim, PA 17545-1616
(717)664-4932 (800)666-4932 Fax:(717)664-1611
E-mail: inn@rosemanor.net
Web: www.rosemanor.net

Circa 1905. A local mill owner built this manor house, and it still maintains original light fixtures, woodwork and cabinetry. The grounds are decorated with roses and herb gardens. An herb theme is played out in the guest rooms, which feature names such as the Parsley, Sage, Rosemary and Thyme rooms. The fifth room

is named the Basil, and its spacious quarters encompass the third story and feature the roof's angled ceiling. One room offers a whirlpool and another a

fireplace. The decor is a comfortable Victorian style with some antiques. Afternoon tea is available by prior reservation and there is a gift shop on the premises. The inn's location provides close access to many Pennsylvania Dutch country attractions.
Innkeeper(s): Susan & Anne Jenal. $70-130. MC, VISA, AX, PC. TAC10. 5 rooms, 3 with PB, 1 with FP. Breakfast included in rates. Types of meals: Full bkfst, picnic lunch and afternoon tea. Beds: QDT. Cable TV, ceiling fan and onw with whirlpool in room. Air conditioning. Fax, copier and library on premises. Family reunions hosted. Amusement parks, antiquing, fishing, live theater, parks and shopping nearby.
Publicity: *Harrisburg Patriot, Lancaster County Magazine and Central Pennsylvania Life.*

Marietta K13

The Noble House

113 W Market St
Marietta, PA 17547-1411
(717)426-4389 (888)271-6426 Fax:(717)426-4012
E-mail: info@thenoblehouse.com
Web: www.thenoblehouse.com

Circa 1810. A 12-foot-high ceiling and stenciled front hallway greet guests at this restored Federal-style brick home. Family heirlooms, original art and fresh flowers decorate the home. All three guest rooms offer fireplaces and two have two-person soaking tubs with showers. The first-floor guest room, decorated to look like a 1950s pullman car, has its own private entrance. A full breakfast is served before the fireplace by candlelight. The living room, which has a piano and fireplace, and the garden are popular places to relax.

Historic Interest: Almost half of the buildings in this village have been placed in the National Register. Because of Marietta's close proximity to Gettysburg, two hours from the inn, the city graces its annual tour of historic homes with a Civil War theme.
Innkeeper(s): Elissa & Paul Noble. $115-145. MC, VISA, PC. TAC10. 3 rooms with PB and 1 suite. Breakfast included in rates. Types of meals: Full bkfst. Beds: KQT.
Publicity: *Early American Life, Pennsylvania Dutch Hollydays, Elizabethtown Mount Joy Merchandiser and Lancaster Magazine.*

"Thank you for your hospitality. We felt like royalty, and enjoyed the detail in your beautiful home."

Railroad House Restaurant B&B

280 W Front St
Marietta, PA 17547-1405
(717)426-4141
Web: www.lancnews.com/railroadhouse/

Circa 1820. The Railroad House, a sprawling old hotel, conjures up memories of the days when riding the rail was the way to travel. The house was built as a refuge for weary men who were working along the Susquehanna River. When the railroad finally made its way through Marietta, the rail station's waiting room and ticket office were located in what's now known as the Railroad House. The restored rooms feature antiques, Oriental rugs, Victorian decor and rustic touches such as exposed brick walls. The chefs at the inn's restaurant create a menu of American and continental dishes using spices and produce

from the beautifully restored gardens. The innovative recipes have been featured in Bon Appetit. The innkeepers also host a variety of special events and weekends, including murder mysteries and clambakes serenaded by jazz bands. Carriage rides and special walking tours of Marietta can be arranged.
Historic Interest: Wheatland, the home of President Buchanan, is 15 minutes from the Railroad House. The John Wright and Haldeman mansions are just 10 minutes away, and the Old Town Hall is a few blocks from the inn.
Innkeeper(s): Richard & Donna Chambers. $89-119. MC, VISA, TC. 8 rooms with PB, 1 cottage and 1 conference room. Breakfast included in rates. Types of meals: Gourmet bkfst, early coffee/tea, gourmet lunch, picnic lunch, after-

noon tea, snacks/refreshments and gourmet dinner. Beds: QDT. Air conditioning. Copier, bicycles and gardens and yard games on premises. Weddings, small meetings, family reunions and seminars hosted. Spanish and French spoken. Amusement parks, antiquing, fishing, music box museum, live theater, parks, shopping, downhill skiing, sporting events and water sports nearby.

Maytown K13

Maytown Manor B&B

25 W High St, PO Box 275
Maytown, PA 17550
(717)426-2116 (866)426-2116
E-mail: innkeepers@maytownmanorbandb.com
Web: www.maytownmanorbandb.com

Circa 1880. Known locally as the Hiestand Estate, this Federal-style brick house was recently professionally restored. Traditional and antique furnishings enhance a peaceful ambiance. The parlor

is a delightful gathering place to read by the fire, play the piano, or enjoy conversation. The spacious guest bedrooms are comfortable, with thoughtful amenities for a pleasant stay. Breakfast is a satisfying repast in the formal dining room. An inviting porch swing is perfect for relaxing. The sunlit back patio leads to colorful flower gardens and a manicured lawn. Share the company of innkeepers Jeff and Julie during afternoon tea.

Innkeeper(s): Jeff & Julie Clouser. $80-90. MC, VISA, PC, TC. 3 rooms with PB. Breakfast, afternoon tea and snacks/refreshments included in rates. Types of meals: Full bkfst and early coffee/tea. Beds: QD. Cable TV and ceiling fan in room. Central air. VCR, fax and library on premises. Amusement parks, antiquing, art galleries, golf, hiking, live theater, museums, parks, shopping, downhill skiing, sporting events, tennis and wineries nearby.

Publicity: *Marietta Traveler, Mount Joy/Elizabethtown Merchandiser, Lancaster County Magazine, Donegal Performing Arts Program, Mayfest Program and Millersville Art Auction.*

McConnellsburg K9

The McConnellsburg Inn

131 W Market St
McConnellsburg, PA 17233-1007
(717)485-5495 (866)485-5495 Fax:(717)485-5546
E-mail: Mconburgin@innernet.net
Web: www.innernet.net/mconburgin/

Circa 1903. Located in the historic district, this turn-of-the-century inn was built for a retired Union officer of the Civil War. Guest bedrooms include four-poster canopy beds. Dutch

apple pancakes, savory ham and freshly baked fruit muffins are among the breakfast specialties. Gettysburg, East Broad Top Railroad, Cowans Gap State Park and Buchanan State Forest are nearby, as are Great Cove Golf Course and Whitetail Ski Resort.

Innkeeper(s): Kathryn Beckman. $65-80. MC, VISA, AX, PC, TC. 4 rooms with PB. Breakfast included in rates. Types of meals: Full bkfst and cont. Beds: QD. Cable TV in room. Air conditioning. Small meetings hosted. Antiquing, fishing, golf, nature photography, country auctions, hiking, country auctions, downhill skiing, cross-country skiing and water sports nearby.
Pets allowed: Sometimes.
Publicity: *Pennsylvania.*

McKnightstown L11

Country Escape

275 Old Rt 30, PO Box 195
McKnightstown, PA 17343
(717)338-0611 (800)484-3244 Fax:(717)334-5227
E-mail: merry@innernet.net

Circa 1867. This country Victorian, a brick structure featuring a porch decked in gingerbread trim, rests on the route that Confederate soldiers took on their way to nearby Gettysburg. The home itself was built just a few years after the Civil War. There are

three comfortable guest rooms, decorated in country style. For an extra fee, business travelers can use the inn's typing, copying, faxing or desktop publishing services. All guests can enjoy the outdoor hot tub. There is also a children's play area outside.

A traditional American breakfast is served, with such hearty items as eggs, pancakes, bacon and sausage. The inn offers close access to the famous battlefield, as well as other historic sites.

Innkeeper(s): Merry Bush & Ross Hetrick. $85-125. MC, VISA, AX, DC, DS, PC, TC. TAC10. 3 rooms, 1 with PB and 1 suite. Breakfast and snacks/refreshments included in rates. Types of meals: Full bkfst, country bkfst and veg bkfst. Beds: Q. Air conditioning. VCR, fax, copier, spa, children's play area and gardens on premises. Antiquing, bicycling, golf, horseback riding, crafts, battlefield - Gettysburg, live theater, museums, parks, shopping, downhill skiing and wineries nearby.

Publicity: *Gettysburg Times and Hanover Evening Sun.*

Mercer F2

The John Orr Guest House

320 E Butler St
Mercer, PA 16137
(724)662-0839 (877)849-0839 Fax:(724)662-3883
E-mail: jorrbandb@pathway.net
Web: www.jorrbandb.com

Circa 1905. A prominent local businessman built this turn-of-the-20th-century home, which is constructed in Greek Revival style. The home has been restored, leaving in place the original woodwork and other architectural features. Guest rooms and common areas include period-style furnishings and some antiques. The front porch is set up for those who wish to relax, offering comfortable wicker chairs and a porch swing. The

innkeepers serve a full breakfast with items such as stuffed French toast, Belgian waffles, a hearty egg casserole and scones. Mercer is a quaint Victorian town with many historic homes, fine restaurants and attractions to visit.

Historic Interest: Victorian town with historic homes and county courthouse.
Innkeeper(s): Ann & Jack Hausser. $70-85. MC, VISA, AX, DS, PC, TC. 3 rooms with PB, 2 with FP. Breakfast and snacks/refreshments included in rates. Types of meals: Full bkfst, veg bkfst and early coffee/tea. Beds: QD. Ceiling fan in room. Central air. VCR, fax, copier, CD player, stereo and refrigerator on premises. Small meetings and seminars hosted. Antiquing, bicycling, fishing, golf, lakes, Amish crafts, museums, parks and shopping nearby.

Mercersburg L9

The Mercersburg Inn

405 S Main St
Mercersburg, PA 17236-9517
(717)328-5231 Fax:(717)328-3403
E-mail: sandy@mercersburginn.com
Web: www.mercersburginn.com

Circa 1909. Situated on a hill overlooking the Tuscorora Mountains, the valley and village, this 20,000-square-foot Georgian Revival mansion was built for industrialist Harry Byron. Six massive columns mark the entrance, which opens to a majestic hall featuring chestnut wainscoting and an elegant double stairway and rare scagliola (marbleized) columns. All the rooms are furnished with antiques and reproductions. A local craftsman built the inn's four-poster, canopied king-size beds. Many of the rooms have their own balconies and a few have fireplaces. Thursday through Sunday evening, the inn's chef prepares noteworthy, elegant dinners, which feature an array of seasonal specialties.

Innkeeper(s): Walt & Sandy Filkowski. $135-275. MC, VISA, DS. TAC10. 15 rooms with PB, 3 with FP and 1 conference room. Breakfast included in rates. Types of meals: Gourmet bkfst, picnic lunch and gourmet dinner. Beds: KQT. Phone in room. Air conditioning. VCR and bicycles on premises. Weddings, small meetings, family reunions and seminars hosted. Antiquing, fishing, golf, live theater, shopping, downhill skiing, cross-country skiing and water sports nearby.
Publicity: *Mid-Atlantic Country, Washington Post, The Herald-Mail, Richmond News Leader, Washingtonian, Philadelphia Inquirer and Pittsburgh.*

"Elegance personified! Outstanding ambiance and warm hospitality."

Mertztown I16

Longswamp B&B

1605 State St
Mertztown, PA 19539-8912
(610)682-6197 Fax:(610)682-4854
E-mail: rafer2@msn.com

Circa 1789. Country gentleman Colonel Trexler added a mansard roof to this stately Federal mansion in 1860. Inside is a magnificent walnut staircase and pegged wood floors. As the story goes, the colonel discovered his unmarried daughter having an affair and shot her lover. He escaped hanging, but it was said that after his death his ghost could be seen in the upstairs bedroom watching the road. In 1905, an exorcism was reported to have sent his spirit to a nearby mountaintop.

Innkeeper(s): Elsa Dimick. $83-88. MC, VISA, AX. 10 rooms, 6 with PB, 2 with FP and 2 suites. Breakfast and afternoon tea included in rates. Types of meals: Gourmet bkfst, early coffee/tea, picnic lunch and gourmet dinner. Beds: QT. TV, phone and ceiling fan in room. Air conditioning. VCR and bicycles on premises. Weddings, small meetings, family reunions and seminars hosted. Antiquing, fishing, shopping, cross-country skiing and sporting events nearby.
Publicity: *Washingtonian, Weekend Travel and The Sun.*

"The warm country atmosphere turns strangers into friends."

Milford F18

Black Walnut Inn

179 Firetower Rd
Milford, PA 18337-9802
(570)296-6322 Fax:(570)296-7696
E-mail: stewart@theblackwalnutinn.com
Web: theblackwalnutinn.com

Circa 1897. Situated on 162 wooded acres, it's hard to imagine that this rustic English Tudor-style inn is less than two hours away from Manhattan. The woods, fields and four-acre lake offer guests a variety of on-site activities like picking fresh berries (in season), fishing for bass, horseback riding or mountain biking on endless trails. The grounds also include a petting zoo, a hot tub and paddle boats. The guest rooms are all furnished with brass beds and antique furniture. After a day of activities, guest can relax in front of the historic European fireplace or enjoy a drink while viewing the lake. There is also a game room. Guests begin their day with a hearty breakfast with items such as eggs, hot cakes, French toast, breakfast meats, fresh fruit salads and breads. The inn is often used for weddings, meetings and family reunions. Antique shopping, flea markets, museums, restaurants and canoeing down the Delaware are close by.

Historic Interest: Located near Grey Towers National Historic Landmark, the Applachian Trail and High Point Monument.

Innkeeper(s): Robin & William. $85-175. MC, VISA, AX, DS. 12 rooms, 4 with PB and 1 cabin. Breakfast included in rates. Types of meals: Full bkfst and early coffee/tea. Beds: QD. Cabin with full kitchen, full bathroom and living room with TV/VCR and fireplace in room. VCR, spa, swimming, paddle boats, horseback riding, petting zoo and game room on premises. Weddings, small meetings and family reunions hosted. Spanish spoken. Antiquing, bicycling, canoeing/kayaking, fishing, golf, hiking, boating (row and paddle), antique cars, rafting, lawn games, bird watching, overnight camp-out, museums, shopping, tennis and water sports nearby.

Cliff Park Inn & Golf Course

155 Cliff Park Rd
Milford, PA 18337-9708
(570)296-6491 (800)225-6535 Fax:(570)296-3982
E-mail: info@cliffparkinn.com
Web: www.cliffparkinn.com

Circa 1820. This historic country inn is located on a 600-acre family estate, bordering the Delaware River. It has been in the Buchanan family since 1820. Rooms are spacious with individual climate control, telephone and Victorian-style furnishings. Cliff Park features both a full-service restaurant and golf school. The inn's golf course, established in 1913, is one of the oldest in the United States. Cliff Park's picturesque setting is popular for country weddings and private business conferences. Both B&B or MAP plans are offered.

Historic Interest: Grey Towers National Landmark (2 miles).

Innkeeper(s): Harry W. Buchanan III. $93-160. MC, VISA, AX, DC, CB, DS. 18 rooms with PB and 1 conference room. Breakfast included in rates. Types of meals: Full bkfst, lunch, picnic lunch and dinner. MAP, AP, EP. Beds: KQDT. Fax on premises. Handicap access. Cross-country skiing and water sports nearby.

"Cliff Park Inn is the sort of inn I look for in the English countryside. It has that authentic charm that comes from History."

Laurel Villa Country Inn & Restaurant

Second & E Ann St
Milford, PA 18337
(570)296-9940 Fax:(570)296-7469
E-mail: info@laurelvilla.com
Web: www.laurelvilla.com

Circa 1876. Originally built 125 years ago as an inn and stagecoach stop, the Muhlhauser family has welcomed guests to this traditional Queen Anne for almost 60 years. Set in the picturesque northern Pocono Mountains, Laurel Villa is the second-oldest inn in Victorian Milford. Recently renovated, expect a casual country atmosphere with stylish elegance. The lounge offers fireside relaxation. Enjoy the rocking chairs on the front porch, or venture down a winding path to the side patio. Beyond that, encounter a koi pond and waterfall in an English garden offering benches for lingering. The restaurant, open to the public for lunch and dinner, serves Chef Carl's culinary specialties.

Historic Interest: The Columns (1/2 mile), Grey Towers (1 mile).

Innkeeper(s): Janice Halsted & Carl Muhlhauser. $70-135. MC, VISA, AX, PC, TC. 10 rooms, 9 with PB, 1 with FP, 1 suite and 1 conference room. Breakfast included in rates. Types of meals: Veg bkfst, cont plus, cont and gourmet dinner. Beds: KQD. Cable TV and ceiling fan in room. Air conditioning. Fax, copier, restaurant, bar, lounge, outdoor patio dining, English Gardens w/waterfall and koi pont on premises. Weddings, small meetings, family reunions and seminars hosted. Hungarian and German spoken. Antiquing, art galleries, beaches, bicycling, canoeing/kayaking, fishing, golf, hiking, horseback riding, rafting, water tubing, live theater, museums, parks, shopping, cross-country skiing and tennis nearby.

Publicity: *NJ Herald.*

Millersville   K14

Rock-A-Bye Bed & Breakfast

138 W Frederick St
Millersville, PA 17551-1912
(717)872-5990 (877)872-5990
E-mail: rockabyein@aol.com

Circa 1840. A rocking chair in each room is only the beginning of the charm of this Victorian/Federal inn that sits on a country acre three miles from Lancaster in Amish country. The inn offers four guest bedrooms, including one suite. A family friendly inn, it has a suite complete with a crib and bassinet. There's also a tree house outdoors for youngsters to play in. Breakfast each morning is a delightful offering of items such as juice, cinnamon sticky buns, eggs, potatoes, bacon and apple crisp. Guests of the inn have after-hours access to an antique and collectibles shop on site.

Historic Interest: Lancaster (3 miles).

Innkeeper(s): Ann & Bill Marks. $75-110. MC, VISA, PC. 4 rooms, 3 with PB and 1 suite. Breakfast included in rates. Types of meals: Country bkfst, veg bkfst, early coffee/tea and snacks/refreshments. Beds: KQDT. Cable TV, turndown service, ceiling fan and VCR in room. Air conditioning. Library, balcony and antique shop on premises. Family reunions hosted. Amusement parks, art galleries, bicycling, fishing, golf, hiking, live theater, museums, parks, shopping, cross-country skiing, sporting events, tennis and wineries nearby.

Publicity: *Lancaster Intelligence.*

Milton   G12

Pau-Lyn's Country B&B

RR 3 Box 676
Milton, PA 17847-9506
(570)742-4110
E-mail: paulyns@uplink.net

Circa 1850. This Victorian brick home offers a formal dining room with a fireplace and antique musical instruments. This restful haven offers a porch and patio overlooking the large lawn. Nearby are working farms and dairies, covered bridges, mountains, rivers and valleys.

Innkeeper(s): Paul & Evelyn Landis. $65-75. PC, TC. 7 rooms and 2 suites. Breakfast included in rates. Types of meals: Full bkfst. Beds: QDT. Air conditioning. Large lawn and patio on premises. Amusement parks, antiquing, bicycling, golf, hiking, museum, underground railroad, little league field and shopping nearby.

Mount Gretna   J13

Mount Gretna Inn

16 Kauffman Ave
Mount Gretna, PA 17064
(717)964-3234 (800)277-6602 Fax:(717)964-3641
E-mail: inn@mtgretna.com
Web: www.mtgretna.com

Circa 1921. This original Arts & Crafts-style home is set in the wooded mountains of historic Mt. Gretna, located conveniently close to a unique variety of attractions such as a lake, stream, cross-country skiing and miles of trails for mountain biking and hiking. Each of the inn's seven guest rooms features a sampling of antiques purchased by the innkeeper at local auctions. All rooms offer private baths, while  some feature a private porch, gas fireplace or whirlpool and steam massage shower. Breakfast fare may include baked peaches, egg puff, sausage, homemade coffee cakes and muffins.

Historic Interest: Within 30 minutes of antique shops, famous outlet malls in Reading and Lancaster, Amish Pennsylvania-Dutch Country, Cornwall Furnace, Hershey and the Pennsylvania Renaissance Festival.

Innkeeper(s): Keith & Robin Volker. $105-145. MC, VISA, AX, PC, TC. TAC10. 7 rooms with PB, 6 with FP and 1 conference room. Breakfast included in rates. Types of meals: Full bkfst and early coffee/tea. Beds: KQ. Ceiling fan in room. Air conditioning. Fax, bicycles and cross-country skiing on premises. Weddings, small meetings, family reunions and seminars hosted. Amusement parks, antiquing, fishing, golf, live theater, parks, shopping, cross-country skiing and tennis nearby.

Publicity: *Daily News, Morning Call, Sunday Patriot-News, Bride's Guide, PA Magazine, Baltimore Magazine and Delaware Today.*

"What a wonderful respite from this '90s hustle and bustle world. Quite like visiting an earlier time."

Mount Joy   K13

Cedar Hill Farm

305 Longenecker Rd
Mount Joy, PA 17552-8404
(717)653-4655 Fax:(717)653-9242
E-mail: cedarhill@supernet.com
Web: www.cedarhillfarm.com

Circa 1817. Situated on 51 acres overlooking Chiques Creek, this stone farmhouse boasts a two-tiered front veranda affording pastoral views of the surrounding fields. The host was born in the house and is the third generation to have lived here since the Swarr family first purchased it in 1878. Family heirlooms and antiques include an elaborately carved walnut bedstead, a marble-topped washstand and a "tumbling block" quilt. In the kitchen, a copper kettle, bread paddle and baskets of dried herbs accentuate the walk-in fireplace, where guests often linger over breakfast. Cedar Hill is a working poultry and grain farm.

Innkeeper(s): Russel & Gladys Swarr. $85-105. MC, VISA, AX, DS, PC, TC. 5 rooms with PB. Breakfast included in rates. Types of meals: Cont plus and early coffee/tea. Beds: KQDT. Whirlpool tub in room. Central air. VCR, fax, Internet access, picnic table and meadows and stream on premises. Small meetings and family reunions hosted. Amusement parks, antiquing, fishing, Amish country, live theater, parks, shopping, cross-country skiing, sporting events and water sports nearby.

Publicity: *Women's World, Lancaster Farming, Philadelphia, New York Times, Ladies Home Journal and Lancaster County Heritage.*

"Dorothy can have Kansas, Scarlett can take Tara, Rick can keep Paris — I've stayed at Cedar Hill Farm."

The Victorian Rose

214 Marietta Ave
Mount Joy, PA 17552-3106
(717)492-0050 (888)313-7494
E-mail: victorianrosebb@juno.com

Circa 1896. Central to historical sites like the Gettysburg battlefield, The Victorian Rose in Mount Joy is an elegant but comfortable place from which to explore beautiful Lancaster County. This stately beautiful guest rooms and a number of elegant shared areas including the library and a formal living room. Guests are treated to innkeeper Doris Tyson's home-baked treats for breakfast, and to her homemade candies at other times. Pennsylvania Dutch Country is just 12 miles from the inn.

Historic Interest: Amish country (12 miles), Gettysburg battlefield (50 miles), Hershey Park (15 miles).

Innkeeper(s): Doris L. Tyson. $75-90. MC, VISA, AX, DS. 4 rooms, 3 with PB. Breakfast included in rates. Types of meals: Full bkfst and country bkfst. Beds: Q. TV, ceiling fan and VCR in room. Air conditioning. Library on premises. Amusement parks, antiquing, golf, live theater, museums, shopping and wineries nearby.

Publicity: *Antiques & Auction News and Lancaster Historic Preservation Trust Featured Home 2001 tour.*

Muncy   F12

The Bodine House B&B

307 S Main St
Muncy, PA 17756-1507
(570)546-8949 Fax:(570)546-0607
E-mail: Bodine@pcspower.net

Circa 1805. This Federal-style townhouse, framed by a white picket fence, is in the National Register. Antique and reproduction furnishings highlight the inn's four fireplaces, the parlor, study and library. A favorite guest room features a walnut canopy bed, hand-stenciled and bordered walls, and a framed sampler by the innkeeper's great-great-grandmother. Candlelight breakfasts are served beside the fireplace in a gracious Colonial dining room. Also available is a guest cottage with kitchenette.

Historic Interest: The Pennsdale Quaker Meeting House.

Innkeeper(s): David & Marie Louise Smith. $70-125. MC, VISA, AX, DS, PC, TC. TAC10. 3 rooms with PB, 1 with FP and 1 cottage. Breakfast included in rates. Types of meals: Full bkfst, early coffee/tea and afternoon tea. Beds: QDT. Cable TV and turndown service in room. Air conditioning. VCR, fax, bicycles and library on premises. Small meetings and family reunions hosted. Antiquing, canoeing/kayaking, fishing, parks, shopping, cross-country skiing and sporting events nearby.

Publicity: *Colonial Homes and Philadelphia Inquirer.*

"What an experience, made special by your wonderful hospitality."

New Berlin   H12

The Inn at New Berlin

321 Market St
New Berlin, PA 17855-0390
(570)966-0321 (800)797-2350 Fax:(570)966-9557
E-mail: lodging@newberlin-inn.com
Web: www.innatnewberlin.com

Circa 1906. At this richly appointed Victorian inn, you can relax on the inviting front porch swing or in the step-down living room with its baby grand piano. Carved woodwork and high ceilings accentuate its antique-filled rooms. An herb garden in the patio area supplies seasonings for the acclaimed meals at the inn's restaurant named Gabriel's. Luscious soups, appetizers such as crisp duck won tons with a currant marmalade sauce, and a variety of salads begin a dinner of contemporary American cuisine. Scrumptious desserts such as Amaretto-Bailey's cheesecake and chocolate mousse cake follow dinner. Brunch, available at Gabriel's Restaurant, features unique omelets, fruit crepes, apple streusel French toast and drinks such as raspberry hot chocolate. Gabriel's Gift Collection features Radko collectible mouth-blown hand-painted ornaments and other unique gifts.

Historic Interest: The Slifer House Museum, Packwood House Museum, Mifflinburg Buggy Museum and Bucknell University are only a short drive away.

Innkeeper(s): Nancy & John Showers. $99-169. MC, VISA, AX, DS, PC, TC. TAC10. 7 rooms with PB, 3 with FP, 2 suites and 1 conference room. Breakfast included in rates. Types of meals: Full bkfst, early coffee/tea, lunch and gourmet dinner. Beds: QD. TV and phone upon request in room. Air conditioning. VCR, fax and copier on premises. Weddings, small meetings, family reunions and seminars hosted. Amusement parks, antiquing, fishing, golf, live theater, parks, shopping, sporting events and tennis nearby.

Publicity: *Philadelphia Inquirer, Washington Post, Country Inns Magazine, Wine Spectator Award of Excellence and PBS (Country Inn Cooking with Gail Greco).*

"I left feeling nurtured and relaxed. You've created a very caring, rich lodging as a perfect place for regenerating."

New Cumberland   J12

Farm Fortune

204 Limekiln Rd
New Cumberland, PA 17070-2429
(717)774-2683
E-mail: frmfortune@aol.com
Web: members.aol.com/frmfortune/

Circa 1750. This limestone farmhouse boasts an intriguing history that stretches back to its construction in the mid-18th century. The house may even have been a part of the Underground Railroad. With antiques tastefully placed throughout the home, guests will be reminded of the charming times of years past. The innkeepers invite guests to make themselves at home in the keeping room in front of the huge walk-in fireplace. While relaxing, notice the interesting woodwork that makes this farmhouse so unique. Ski the nearby slopes at Ski Roundtop or relax along the banks of the Yellow Breeches Creek and enjoy some local trout fishing.

Historic Interest: The farmhouse is located within 45 minutes of the historic towns of Gettysburg, Carlisle, York, Harrisburg, Hershey and Lancaster.

Innkeeper(s): Phyllis Combs. $85-185. MC, VISA, AX, DC, CB, DS. TAC10. 4 rooms with PB and 1 cottage. Breakfast included in rates. Types of meals: Full bkfst. Beds: KQDT. Cottage with fireplace and kitchenette in room. Antiquing, fishing, live theater, downhill skiing, cross-country skiing and water sports nearby.

Publicity: *Early American Life, Patriot and Evening News, Pennsylvania Magazine, Carlisle, Sentinal and York Dispatch.*

New Hope   118

Aaron Burr House Inn & Conference Center

80 W Bridge St
New Hope, PA 18938-1303
(215)862-2570 Fax:(215)862-3937
E-mail: stay@new-hope-inn.com
Web: www.new-hope-inn.com

Circa 1870. Aaron Burr hid in this Bucks County house after his infamous duel with Alexander Hamilton. The home also is one of the Wedgwood Collection inns. A Victorian Shingle style, it is in the National Register. Its three stories, including

the spacious parlor, are appointed with antiques and reproductions. Guest rooms offer amenities such as private baths, telephones and TVs, and many have two-person whirlpool tubs and fireplaces. Within walking distance are fine restaurants, shops and art galleries. The

grounds offer two gazebos, stately old trees, a screened-in flagstone patio and a barn perfect for bicycle storage.

Historic Interest: Washington Crossing Historic State Park, Mercer Museums, Bucks County Playhouse, New Hope Steam Train, New Hope Barge Ride, New Hope Ferry, Bowman's Hill Wild Flower Preserve.

Innkeeper(s): Carl Glassman & Nadine Silnutzer. $95-255. MC, VISA, AX, PC, TC. TAC10. 12 rooms with PB, 6 with FP, 6 suites, 1 cottage and 3 conference rooms. Breakfast, afternoon tea and snacks/refreshments included in rates. Types of meals: Cont plus, early coffee/tea and room service. Beds: KQT. Phone, turndown service, ceiling fan and canopy beds in room. Air conditioning. VCR, fax, swimming, tennis and pet boarding on premises. Handicap access. Small meetings, family reunions and seminars hosted. Dutch, French, Spanish and Hebrew spoken. Antiquing, fishing, covered bridge, live theater, parks, shopping, downhill skiing, cross-country skiing, sporting events and water sports nearby.

Publicity: *The Intelligencer Record, Bucks County Courier Times, Time Magazine and CNN Travel Show.*

Centre Bridge Inn

2998 N River Rd
New Hope, PA 18938
(215)862-9139 Fax:(215)862-3244
E-mail: inforequest@centrebridgeinn.com
Web: www.centrebridgeinn.com

Circa 1705. This Williamsburg Colonial inn was rebuilt after a fire in 1959. The original inn was constructed in 1705. Canopy beds, colonial decor, and views of the Delaware River and Canal provide a romantic setting. The inn's dining areas include an outside dining terrace, a glass-enclosed garden dining room or the main dining room with an open-hearth fireplace. Two of the options boast a view of the river. Weddings and corporate gatherings are popular here.

$80-175. MC, VISA, AX. 10 rooms, 7 with PB and 3 suites. Breakfast included in rates. Types of meals: Cont and dinner. Beds: KQD. TV in room. Air conditioning. Fax and copier on premises. Weddings, small meetings and family reunions hosted. Antiquing, fishing, live theater, parks, shopping and water sports nearby.

Logan Inn

10 W Ferry St
New Hope, PA 18938-1312
(215)862-2300 Fax:(215)862-3931
E-mail: loganinnllc@aol.com

Circa 1727. This classic colonial is Bucks County's oldest continuously run inn, and one of the five oldest in the country. Recently renovated, old and new are carefully blended to offer intimate luxury and comfort. Tasteful guest bedrooms are furnished with antiques and period pieces. The tavern's original woodwork, fireplace and restored murals offer a warm and inviting taste of history and late-night menu selections. Choose to dine in the enclosed stained-glass Garden Dining Room, the Colonial Room or alfresco on the tented patio. Experience the area's quaint sites and pleasurable activities. Ask about taking a horse-drawn carriage ride. See our special packages.

Historic Interest: Washington Crossing (3 miles), Bowmans Tower Wildlife Preserve, (3 miles), Mercer Museum (15 miles), Moravian Tile Works (15 miles).

Innkeeper(s): Pam & Carl Asplundh. $110-195. MC, VISA, AX, DC, DS, TC. TAC10. 16 rooms with PB, 2 suites and 1 conference room. Types of meals: Cont, gourmet lunch and gourmet dinner. Beds: KQD. Cable TV and phone in room. Air conditioning. Weddings, small meetings, family reunions and seminars hosted. Amusement parks, antiquing, art galleries, bicycling, canoeing/kayaking, fishing, hiking, horseback riding, live theater, museums, parks, shopping, tennis and wineries nearby.

Publicity: *The Philadelphia Inquirer and The Home News.*

"...the food was PERFECTION and served in a gracious and extremely courteous manner...our intentions had been to explore different restaurants, but there was no reason to explore, we had found what we wanted."

Pineapple Hill

1324 River Rd
New Hope, PA 18938
(215)862-1790 (888)866-8404
E-mail: innkeeper@pineapplehill.com
Web: www.pineapplehill.com

Circa 1790. The pineapple always has been a sign of friendship and hospitality, and guests at Pineapple Hill are sure to experience both. The inn is secluded on six private acres, yet it's just four miles from town. Antique shops, flea markets, auctions and plenty of outdoor activities are all close by. All rooms and suites

include a fireplace, cable TV, phone and private bath. A full breakfast is served at individual tables, afternoon refreshments and evening sherry are also offered. Inside the walls of a stone barn is a tiled swimming pool.

Innkeeper(s): Kathy & Charles. $116-249. MC, VISA, AX, DS, TC. TAC10. 9 rooms with PB, 3 suites and 1 conference room. Breakfast and afternoon tea included in rates. Types of meals: Full bkfst, early coffee/tea and snacks/refreshments. Beds: KQ. Cable TV, phone, living room and private deck in room. Air conditioning. Fax and swimming on premises. Weddings, small meetings, family reunions and seminars hosted. Antiquing, fishing, museums, live theater, parks, shopping and water sports nearby.

"It was a delightful stay in every way. The clicking door latches and the smells of breakfast cooking wafting up to the bedroom were reminiscent of my childhood stays at my grandparents' farmhouse."

New Milford   **D15**

Lynn Lee House Bed & Breakfast

143 Main St
New Milford, PA 18834-2111
(570)465-3505
Web: www.lynn-lee.com

Circa 1868. An ageless warmth and gracious hospitality are found all year at this Second Empire Victorian bed & breakfast, only two and a half hours from Philadelphia and New York City. Wide board pine floors, original full-length windows, antiques and period furnishings enhance the ambiance of a tranquil and refined way of life. Converse around the tiled fireplace in the living room or play a game. Fresh flowers, quilts, down pillows and scented linens appeal to the senses in the guest bedrooms. Enjoy soaking in the seven-foot clawfoot tub. Awake to indulge in breakfast favorites and specialties in the formal dining room or front porch. In the side yard, Adirondack chairs are great for butterfly watching.

Historic Interest: Old Mill Village Museum (3 miles) Lackawanna Coal Mine and Steamtown Historical site (40 miles).

Innkeeper(s): Eleanor & Chuck Lempke. $95-105. PC, TC. TAC10. 4 rooms, 2 with PB. Breakfast, afternoon tea and snacks/refreshments included in rates. Types of meals: Gourmet bkfst and early coffee/tea. Beds: QD. Turndown service and ceiling fan in room. VCR on premises. Small meetings and family reunions hosted. Antiquing, bicycling, canoeing/kayaking, fishing, golf, hiking, parks, shopping, downhill skiing and cross-country skiing nearby.

Publicity: *New York Times, WNEP and Channel 16.*

Palmyra   **J13**

The Hen-Apple B&B

409 S Lingle Ave
Palmyra, PA 17078-9321
(717)838-8282
Web: www.henapplebb.com

Circa 1825. Located at the edge of town, this Georgian farmhouse is surrounded by an acre of lawns and gardens. There are antiques and country pieces throughout. Breakfast is served to guests in the dining room or on the screened veranda. Hershey is two miles away, Lancaster and Gettysburg are nearby.

Innkeeper(s): Flo & Harold Eckert. $55-95. MC, VISA, AX, DS, TC. TAC10. 6 rooms with PB. Breakfast included in rates. Types of meals: Full bkfst and cont. Beds: QDT. Ceiling fan in room. Air conditioning. Amusement parks, antiquing, fishing, live theater, parks, shopping, sporting events and water sports nearby.

Publicity: *Pennsylvania Magazine.*

Philadelphia   **K17**

The Penn's View Hotel

Front & Market Streets
Philadelphia, PA 19106
(215)922-7600 (800)331-7634 Fax:(215)922-7642
Web: www.pennsviewhotel.com

Circa 1828. The original portion of Penn's View Hotel dates to 1828. Today, the elegant hotel includes 40 guest rooms and suites, some of which include a fireplace and whirlpool tub. Ristorante Panorama, the hotel's gourmet restaurant, offers acclaimed Italian cuisine, as well as a wine bar with more than 120 different varieties. The hotel looks out to the Delaware River and is situated within walking distance to many historic sites.

Innkeeper(s): The Sena Family. $120-225. MC, VISA, AX, DC, CB, TC. TAC10. 40 rooms. Breakfast included in rates. Types of meals: Cont plus, lunch and dinner. Beds: KQ. Cable TV and lighted vanity mirror in room. Air conditioning. Fax and copier on premises. Small meetings and family reunions hosted. Spanish and Italian spoken. Antiquing, live theater, parks, shopping, sporting events and tennis nearby.

Publicity: *New York Times.*

Rittenhouse Square B&B

1715 Rittenhouse Square
Philadelphia, PA 19103
(215)546-6500 (877)791-6500 Fax:(215)546-8787
E-mail: hseltzer@rittenhousebb.com
Web: www.rittenhousebb.com

Circa 1911. Experience elegant luxury at this comfortably renovated carriage house, internationally renown for business or pleasure. Impressive art, impeccable decor, lavish furnishings and extraordinary service are the hallmarks of this inn. The guest bedrooms are spectacular, tranquil retreats. Distinctive amenities include CD players, triple sheeting, turndown service, computer workstations, plush robes and marble bathrooms. Enjoy breakfast in The Cafe and early evening wine and snacks in the gorgeous lobby.

Innkeeper(s): Harriet S. Seltzer. $209-259. MC, VISA, AX, PC. 10 rooms with PB, 1 with FP, 2 suites and 1 conference room. Breakfast and snacks/refreshments included in rates. Types of meals: Cont plus and cont. Beds: KQD. Cable TV, phone, turndown service, VCR and fireplace in room. Central air. Fax and copier on premises. Small meetings hosted. Antiquing, art galleries, museums, shopping and sporting events nearby.

Society Hill Hotel

Third & Chestnut Streets
Philadelphia, PA 19106
(215)925-1919 Fax:(215)925-3780
E-mail: sochill3Q1@societyhillhotel.com
Web: www.societyhillhotel.com

Circa 1832. Once temporary housing for longshoremen from all over the world, the Society Hill Hotel, located within two blocks of Independence Hall, housed intellectuals, politicians, patriots and artists before, during and after the Revolutionary War. Today it is Philadelphia's smallest hotel, and it is located in the midst of Independence National Historical Park. The inn has 12 guest bedrooms, six of which are two-room suites. Fresh squeezed juice, coffee or tea and warm rolls are provided for guests each morning, following European tradition. The inn's piano bar and restaurant uses wood, stained glass and plants to create warmth and atmosphere. The specialty of the house is the Philadelphia cheese steak, and the restaurant also offers burgers, omelets and salads. Sunday brunch includes such delicacies as Belgium waffles, eggs Benedict and fresh fruit with brandied cream.

Historic Interest: Independence National Park & Waterfront (2 blocks).

Innkeeper(s): Steve Morris. $88-175. MC, VISA, AX, DC, CB, DS, TC. TAC10. 12 rooms, 6 with PB and 6 suites. Breakfast included in rates. Types of meals: Full bkfst, cont and lunch. Beds: D. Cable TV and phone in room. Central air. Weddings and family reunions hosted. Antiquing, art galleries, bicycling, live theater, museums, parks, shopping and sporting events nearby.

Pets Allowed.

Thomas Bond House

129 S 2nd St
Philadelphia, PA 19106-3039
(215)923-8523 (800)845-2663 Fax:(215)923-8504
E-mail: ctheal@dddcompany.com
Web: www.winston-salem-inn.com/philadelphia

Circa 1769. One way to enjoy the history of Philadelphia is to treat yourself to a stay at this Colonial-period, Georgian-style residence in Independence National Historical Park. White shutters and cornices accentuate the brick exterior, often draped in red, white and blue bunting. A finely executed interi-

or renovation provides a handsome background for the inn's collection of Chippendale reproductions, four-poster beds and drop front desks. Working fireplaces, phones, hair dryers, television and whirlpool tubs provide additional comforts.

Innkeeper(s): Rita McGuire. $95-175. MC, VISA, AX, PC, TC. TAC7. 12 rooms with PB, 2 with FP, 2 suites and 1 conference room. Breakfast included in rates. Types of meals: Full bkfst, cont plus and early coffee/tea. Beds: QDT. Phone and some with whirlpool tubs in room. Air conditioning. Fax, copier, free local calls and evening wine and cheese and freshly baked cookies on premises. Weddings, small meetings, family reunions and seminars hosted. Amusement parks, antiquing, fishing, historic sites, live theater, parks, shopping and sporting events nearby.

Publicity: *Mid-Atlantic Country, Washingtonian, Washington Post, Philadelphia Inquirer, Home & Garden and Boston Globe.*

"Your service was excellent, congenial, made us feel comfortable and welcome."

Pittsburgh   I3

The Priory

614 Pressley St
Pittsburgh, PA 15212-5616
(412)231-3338 Fax:(412)231-4838

Circa 1888. The Priory, now a European-style hotel, was built to provide lodging for Benedictine priests traveling through Pittsburgh. It is adjacent to Pittsburgh's Grand Hall at the

Priory in historic East Allegheny. The inn's design and maze of rooms and corridors give it a distinctly Old World flavor. All rooms are decorated with Victorian furnishings.

Historic Interest: Mexican War Streets Neighborhood, Fort Pitt Blockhouse & Point State Park.

Innkeeper(s): Ed & Mary Ann Graf. $119-155. MC, VISA, AX, DC, DS. 24 rooms with PB, 3 suites and 1 conference room. Breakfast included in rates. Types of meals: Cont plus. Beds: QD. Handicap access.

Publicity: *Pittsburgh Press, US Air, Country Inns, Innsider, Youngstown Vindicator, Travel & Leisure, Gourmet, Mid-Atlantic Country and National Geographic Traveler.*

"Although we had been told that the place was elegant, we were hardly prepared for the richness of detail. We felt as though we were guests in a manor."

Point Pleasant   I18

Tattersall Inn

16 Cafferty Rd, PO Box 569
Point Pleasant, PA 18950
(215)297-8233 (800)297-4988 Fax:(215)297-5093
E-mail: tattersallinn@aol.com
Web: www.tattersallinn.com

Circa 1750. This Bucks County plastered fieldstone house with its 18-inch-thick walls, broad porches and wainscoted entry hall was the home of local mill owners for 150 years.

Today it offers a peaceful place to relax, rebuild and enjoy the bucolic surroundings in Olde Bucks. Breakfast is served in the dining room or brought to your room. The Colonial-style common room features a beamed ceiling and

walk-in fireplace where guests gather for apple cider, cheese and crackers and tea or coffee in the late afternoon.

Historic Interest: Washington Crossing Park (12 miles), William Penn's Pennsbury Manor (25 miles), Valley Forge (40 miles), 11 covered bridges (15 miles).

Innkeeper(s): Donna & Bob Trevorrow. $95-145. MC, VISA, DS. 6 rooms with PB, 2 with FP, 1 suite and 1 conference room. Breakfast and afternoon tea included in rates. Types of meals: Full bkfst. Beds: Q. Air conditioning. Fax, copier, library and refrigerator on premises. Small meetings and family reunions hosted. Antiquing, fishing, live theater, parks, shopping, cross-country skiing and water sports nearby.

Publicity: *Courier Times, Philadelphia, New York Times and WYOU.*

"Thank you for your hospitality and warm welcome. The inn is charming and has a wonderful ambiance."

Reading   J15

Hunter House Bed & Breakfast

118 S Fifth St
Reading, PA 19602-1626
(610)374-6608 Fax:(610)372-7888
E-mail: hunterhous@aol.com

Circa 1846. This inn is a fine example of Greek Revival architecture and features many European touches, such as antique furnishings and elaborate 13-foot ceilings topped with ornate plaster moldings. Guests will find shopping here to be some of the best in the nation, with antique shops and world-famous outlet stores within minutes of the inn. Other attractions include the Hawk Mountain Sanctuary, and the historic Daniel Boone Homestead.

Innkeeper(s): Bill D. Solliday. $95-125. MC, VISA, AX, DS, PC, TC. 4 rooms, 3 with PB and 3 suites. Breakfast, afternoon tea and snacks/refreshments included in rates. Types of meals: Full bkfst. Beds: QT. Cable TV, phone, turndown service and ceiling fan in room. Air conditioning. Fax and copier on premises. Weddings and small meetings hosted. Amusement parks, antiquing, fishing, golf, outlet shopping, live theater, parks, shopping, downhill skiing, sporting events, tennis and water sports nearby.

"The accommodations are lovely, and the hospitality is exceptional."

Red Lion $\qquad$ K13

Red Lion Bed & Breakfast

101 S Franklin St
Red Lion, PA 17356-1903
(717)244-4739 Fax:(717)246-9202
E-mail: staywithus@redlionbandb.com
Web: www.redlionbandb.com

Circa 1930. This three-story brick, Federal-style home makes an unpretentious and quiet base for exploring one of the more popular regions of Pennsylvania. Queen-size beds are found in each of the four corner guest rooms. Bathrooms are shared or half-size, with the exception of the Colonial Room which has a full bath. Guests enjoy snuggling up next to the fireplace in the living room with a book from the well-stocked library or enjoying a cool lemonade on the enclosed sun porch outside patio. Breakfasts are substantial with pancakes, French toast, eggs, muffins, coffee cake and fresh fruit. The town of Red Lion has its share of antique and craft shops, and within an hour's driving distance are vineyards, the Amish country of Lancaster, Hershey and the Gettysburg Battlefield.

Historic Interest: York (10 miles), Gettysburg (40 miles).

Innkeeper(s): George & Danielle Sanders. $65-85. MC, VISA. 4 rooms, 1 with PB and 1 conference room. Breakfast included in rates. Types of meals: Full bkfst and picnic lunch. Beds: Q. TV, ceiling fan and VCR in room. Air conditioning. Library, off street parking and modem hook-up on premises. Small meetings hosted. Amusement parks, antiquing, canoeing/kayaking, fishing, golf, hiking, horseback riding, live theater, parks, water sports and wineries nearby.

Rushland $\qquad$ J17

Cottage at Ross Mill Farm

2464 Walton Rd
Rushland, PA 18956
(215)322-1539 Fax:(215)322-4898
E-mail: rossmill@erols.com
Web: www.rossmillfarm.com

Circa 1600. At the end of a quiet country road is this fieldstone cottage, a 300-year-old historic landmark made of sandstone and shale, with 18-inch-thick walls and hand-cut beams. Sitting next to Little Neshaminy Creek, adjacent to the 35-acre Ross Mill Farm, the Cottage is surrounded by more than 1,000 acres of private nature reserve. The first floor features the Main Room with deep-set windows, a working fireplace, a sun porch and full bath. The kitchen is fully equipped and includes a washer and dryer. A spiral staircase leads to the modest sleeping quarters, two guest bedrooms with exposed beams. Cottage sleeps up to six people (rates are quoted for up to four guests). Visitors will enjoy the scenic beauty and famous sites of Bucks County. Children and pets are welcome.

Historic Interest: Washington's Crossing on the Delaware (5-10 miles), The Thompson Neely Home (5-10 miles), Headquarters Farm (5-10 miles), covered bridges (5-10 miles), Underground Railroad sites (5-10 miles), New Hope (5-10 miles).

Innkeeper(s): Susan Armstrong & Richard Magidson. $100. MC, VISA. 1 cottages. Beds: QDT. TV, ceiling fan, fireplace and cottage with fully equipped kitchen in room. Air conditioning. Fax, pet boarding, gift shop, washer and dryer on premises. Antiquing, art galleries, bicycling, canoeing/kayaking, fishing, golf, hiking, horseback riding, live theater, museums, parks, shopping and wineries nearby.

Pets Allowed.

Publicity: *Philadelphia Inquirer, Trenton Times, The Intelligencer, Currier Times, New York Post, ABC, NBC, CBS, Fox and Animal Planet.*

Shippensburg $\qquad$ K10

Field & Pine B&B

2155 Ritner Hwy
Shippensburg, PA 17257-9756
(717)776-7179
E-mail: fieldpine@aol.com
Web: cvbednbreakfasts.com

Circa 1790. Local limestone was used to build this stone house, located on the main wagon road to Baltimore and Washington. Originally, it was a tavern and weigh station. The house is surrounded by stately pines, and sheep graze on the inn's 80 acres. The bedrooms are hand-stenciled and furnished with quilts and antiques.

Innkeeper(s): Mary Ellen & Allan Williams. $70-80. MC, VISA, PC, TC. TAC10. 3 rooms, 1 with FP and 1 suite. Breakfast and snacks/refreshments included in rates. Types of meals: Gourmet bkfst and early coffee/tea. Beds: QDT. TV and turndown service in room. Air conditioning. VCR on premises. Weddings, small meetings and family reunions hosted. Antiquing, fishing, parks and shopping nearby.

Publicity: *Central Pennsylvania Magazine.*

"Our visit in this lovely country home has been most delightful. The ambiance of antiques and tasteful decorating exemplifies real country living."

Shohola $\qquad$ E18

Pegasus B&B

147 Woodtown Road
Shohola, PA 18458-9721
(570)296-4017 Fax:(570)296-4017
E-mail: pegasus@pikeonline.net
Web: www.pegasus-inn.com

Circa 1910. Pegasus was built as a country inn for travelers to the Pocono Mountains in northeast Pennsylvania. Renovated and expanded, it now offers nine comfortable guest rooms, decorated in a style reminiscent of the early 20th century. Guests relax and enjoy the inn, as well as its wooded acres of nature reserve. A wraparound porch invites guests to linger in view of the surrounding forest, and the inn's living room offers a stone fireplace and comfortable furniture for indoor relaxing. The inn provides close access to the historic landmark town of Milford, PA and the Upper Delaware River National Park, where swimming, rafting and kayaking are available. Fishing, hiking, biking, bird watching and other outdoor activities are in abundance in the area.

Innkeeper(s): John Hunn. $55-100. MC, VISA, AX, DC, PC. 9 rooms, 1 with PB and 1 suite. Breakfast included in rates. Types of meals: Full bkfst, cont plus and early coffee/tea. Beds: KQDT. VCR, fax, copier, library, picnic places, wraparound porch and 3 acres of lawn for casual sports on premises. Weddings, family reunions and seminars hosted. Spanish and Portuguese spoken. Antiquing, canoeing/kayaking, fishing, golf, hiking, horseback riding, birdwatching, rafting, swimming, paintball, museums, parks, shopping and cross-country skiing nearby.

Pets allowed: Welcome.

Somerset K5

Glades Pike Inn

2684 Glades Pike
Somerset, PA 15501-8520
(814)443-4978 (800)762-5942 Fax:(814)443-2562
E-mail: fwmjj@sprynet.com

Circa 1842. This red brick Federal-style inn once served as a stagecoach stop along Glades Pike. The guest rooms feature period Federal décor, and three include a fireplace. In the mornings, country breakfasts are served. The inn's rural setting

includes 200 acres, and the surrounding area and Laurel Mountains offer a variety of outdoor activities. Guests can trek along the Laurel Highlands Hiking Trail, fish or hunt in one of several state game lands, golf at a local course, or ski at nearby Seven Springs, Hidden Valley or Laurel Mountain. Historic forts and Frank Lloyd Wright's famous Fallingwater and Kentock Knob also are nearby.

Historic Interest: Somerset (6 miles), Fort Ligonier (20 miles), Fort Necessary (30 miles).

Innkeeper(s): Janet L Jones. $65-85. MC, VISA, AX, DS, PC, TC. TAC10. 5 rooms with PB, 3 with FP. Breakfast included in rates. Types of meals: Full bkfst, country bkfst, veg bkfst and early coffee/tea. Beds: QD. Cable TV, phone and ceiling fan in room. Air conditioning. Fax, copier and bicycles on premises. Weddings, small meetings, family reunions and seminars hosted. Amusement parks, antiquing, art galleries, beaches, bicycling, canoeing/kayaking, fishing, golf, hiking, horseback riding, live theater, museums, parks, shopping, downhill skiing, cross-country skiing, sporting events, tennis, water sports and wineries nearby.

Pets allowed:.

Quill Haven Country Inn

1519 North Center Ave
Somerset, PA 15501-7001
(814)443-4514 Fax:(814)445-1376
E-mail: quill@quillhaven.com
Web: www.quillhaven.com

Circa 1918. Set on three acres that were once part of a chicken and turkey farm, this historic Arts & Crafts-style home offers guest rooms, each individually appointed. The Bridal Suite includes a four-poster wrought iron bed and sunken tub in the bath. The Country Room includes a decorative pot-bellied stove.

Antiques, reproductions and stained-glass lamps decorate the rooms. Guests are treated to a full breakfast with items such as baked grapefruit or apples, homemade breads and entrees such as stuffed French toast or a specialty

casserole of ham, cheese and potatoes. Guests can spend the day boating or swimming at nearby Youghiogheny Reservoir, take a whitewater-rafting trip, bike or hike through the scenic countryside, ski at one of three ski resorts in the area or shop at antique stores, outlets and flea markets. Frank Lloyd Wright's Fallingwater is another nearby attraction.

Historic Interest: Somerset Historical Center (3 miles), Fallingwater & Kentuck Knob (40 miles).

Innkeeper(s): Carol & Rowland Miller. $85-110. MC, VISA, AX, DS, PC. TAC3. 4 rooms with PB. Breakfast and snacks/refreshments included in rates. Types of meals: Full bkfst and early coffee/tea. Beds: KQ. Cable TV,

turndown service, ceiling fan, VCR and heated mattress pad in room. Air conditioning. Library, outdoor hot tub, common room with fireplace and mini kitchenette on premises. Small meetings and family reunions hosted. Amusement parks, antiquing, bicycling, canoeing/kayaking, fishing, golf, hiking, horseback riding, skiing at Seven Springs and Hidden Valley. Located in the Laurel Highlands, live theater, parks, shopping, downhill skiing, cross-country skiing, tennis, water sports and wineries nearby.

Publicity: *Westsylvania Magazine.*

"What a beautiful memory we will have of our first B&B experience! We've never felt quite so pampered in all our 25 years of marriage."

Starlight C17

The Inn at Starlight Lake

PO Box 27
Starlight, PA 18461-0027
(570)798-2519 (800)248-2519 Fax:(570)798-2672
E-mail: theinn@unforgettable.com

Circa 1909. Acres of woodland and meadow surround the last surviving railroad inn on the New York, Ontario and Western lines. Originally a boarding house, the inn was part of a little village that had its own store, church, blacksmith shop and creamery. Platforms, first erected to accommodate tents for the

summer season, were later replaced by three small cottage buildings that now include a suite with a double whirlpool. A modern three-bedroom house is available for family reunions and conferences. The inn is situated

on the 45-acre, spring-fed Starlight Lake, providing summertime canoeing, swimming, fishing and sailing. (No motorboats are allowed on the lake.) Breakfast is served in the lakeside dining area where dinner is also available.

Innkeeper(s): Jack & Judy McMahon. $135-255. MC, VISA, PC. TAC10. 26 rooms, 20 with PB, 1 with FP, 1 suite, 3 cottages, 1 guest house and 1 conference room. Breakfast and dinner included in rates. Types of meals: Gourmet bkfst, early coffee/tea, gourmet lunch and picnic lunch. MAP. Beds: KQDT. Fax, copier, swimming, bicycles, tennis and library on premises. Weddings, small meetings, family reunions and seminars hosted. Antiquing, fishing, golf, live theater, parks, shopping, downhill skiing, cross-country skiing, tennis and water sports nearby.

Publicity: *New York Times, Philadelphia Inquirer, Newsday, Discerning Traveler and Freeman.*

Strasburg K14

Limestone Inn B&B

33 E Main St
Strasburg, PA 17579-1427
(717)687-8392 (800)278-8392 Fax:(717)687-8366
E-mail: manati@bellatlantic.net

Circa 1786. The Limestone Inn housed the first Chief Burgess and later became the Headmaster's House for Strasburg Academy. It is a handsome five-bay formal Georgian plan. Located in the Strasburg Historic District, the house is on the National Register.

The surrounding scenic Amish farmlands offer sightseeing and antique and craft shopping.

Historic Interest: Lancaster Historic District (5 miles).

Innkeeper(s): Denise & Richard Waller & family. $79-115. MC, VISA, AX, PC, TC. 5 rooms with PB, 1 with FP.

Breakfast and snacks/refreshments included in rates. Types of meals: Gourmet bkfst and early coffee/tea. Beds: KQDT. Central air. Fax, copier and library on premises. Small meetings and family reunions hosted. Spanish spoken. Amusement parks, antiquing, golf, hiking, outlet shopping, live theater, museums, parks, shopping, sporting events, tennis and wineries nearby.

Publicity: Lancaster New Era, Intelligencer Journal, Strasburg Weekly, Washingtonian Magazine, New York Times and Country Magazine.

"A beautiful restoration, great innkeepers and a fantasy location."

Terre Hill   J15

The Artist's Inn & Gallery

117 E Main St
Terre Hill, PA 17581
(717)445-0219 (888)999-4479
E-mail: info@artistinn.com
Web: www.artistinn.com

Circa 1853. Four-course breakfasts and warm and inviting guest rooms are offered at this Federal-style inn. Watch Amish buggies clip clop by from the Victorian veranda and listen to the chimes from the church across the way. Then plan your day with the help of innkeepers Jan and Bruce, avid adventurers who cross-country ski and explore the area's best offerings to share insights with guests. There's an art gallery with works by the resident artist. Guest accommodations are inviting with antiques, hardwood floors and decorative painting, wallpapers and borders. The Rose Room offers a Jacuzzi bath. The Garden Suite offers a whirlpool bath for two, fireplace, king-size featherbed, private balcony and sitting room. Breakfasts feature breads such as scones or muffins, fruit parfaits, crepes or egg dishes and a luscious dessert-perhaps a pie, cake or tart.

Innkeeper(s): Jan & Bruce Garrabrandt. $95-179. MC, VISA, AX, DS, PC. TAC10. 3 rooms with PB, 3 with FP and 2 suites. Breakfast and snacks/refreshments included in rates. Types of meals: Gourmet bkfst, veg bkfst, early coffee/tea and afternoon tea. Beds: KQ. Turndown service, ceiling fan, hair dryers, robes, featherbeds, cd players and clock radios in room. Central air. Library and art gallery on premises. Amusement parks, antiquing, art galleries, bicycling, fishing, golf, hiking, live theater, museums, parks, shopping, cross-country skiing, tennis and wineries nearby.

Thornton   K16

Pace One Restaurant and Country Inn

Thornton Rd & Glen Mills Rd
Thornton, PA 19373
(610)459-3702 Fax:(610)558-0825

Circa 1740. This beautifully renovated stone barn has two-and-a-half-foot-thick walls, hand-hewn wood beams and many small-paned windows. Just in front of the inn was the Gray family home used as a hospital during the Revolutionary War when Washington's army crossed nearby Chadd's Ford.

Innkeeper(s): Ted Pace. $105. MC, VISA, AX, DC, PC, TC. 6 rooms with PB and 3 conference rooms. Breakfast included in rates. Types of meals: Cont plus, lunch, picnic lunch and gourmet dinner. Beds: Q. Phone in room. Air conditioning. Fax and copier on premises. Weddings, small meetings, family reunions and seminars hosted. Antiquing, fishing, live theater, parks, shopping and sporting events nearby.

"Dear Ted & Staff, we loved it here!! The accommodations were great. Thanks for making it a beautiful weekend."

Valley Forge   K16

The Great Valley House of Valley Forge

1475 Swedesford Rd
Valley Forge, PA 19355
(610)644-6759 Fax:(610)644-7019
E-mail: info@greatvalleyhouse.com
Web: www.greatvalleyhouse.com

Circa 1691. This 300-year-old Colonial stone farmhouse sits on four acres just two miles from Valley Forge Park. Boxwoods line the walkway, and ancient trees surround the house. Each of the three antique-filled guest rooms is hand-stenciled and features a canopied or brass bed topped with handmade quilts. Guests enjoy a full breakfast before a 14-foot fireplace in the "summer kitchen," the oldest part of the house. On the grounds are a swimming pool, walking and hiking trails and the home's original smokehouse.

Historic Interest: The grounds have an original keep and tunnel, which were part of the Underground Railroad. Historic Philadelphia, Longwood Gardens and Brandywine River Museum are other nearby attractions. Lancaster Country, famous for its Amish communities, is a popular area to visit.

Innkeeper(s): Pattye Benson. $85-95. MC, VISA, DS, PC, TC. TAC10. 3 rooms with PB. Breakfast included in rates. Types of meals: Gourmet bkfst and early coffee/tea. AP. Beds: QDT. Cable TV, phone and turndown service in room. Air conditioning. Fax, swimming and grand piano on premises. Weddings and small meetings hosted. Spanish and French spoken. Antiquing, fishing, live theater, parks, shopping, cross-country skiing, sporting events and water sports nearby.

Publicity: Main Line Philadelphia, Philadelphia Inquirer, Washington Post, New York Times, Suburban Newspaper. and Travel cable network.

"As a business traveler, Patty's enthusiasm and warm welcome makes you feel just like you're home."

Warfordsburg   L8

Buck Valley Ranch, LLC

1344 Negro Mountain Rd
Warfordsburg, PA 17267-9667
(717)294-3759 (800)294-3759 Fax:(717)294-6413
E-mail: bvranch@nb.net

Circa 1930. Trail riding is a popular activity on the ranch's 64 acres in the Appalachian Mountains of South Central Pennsylvania. State game lands and forests border the ranch. The guest house, decorated in a ranch/cowboy style, is a private farmhouse that can accommodate eight people. Meals are prepared using homegrown vegetables and locally raised meats. Rates also include horseback riding.

Innkeeper(s): Nadine & Leon Fox. $125. MC, VISA, DS, PC, TC. TAC5. 4 rooms. Breakfast, snacks/refreshments and dinner included in rates. Types of meals: Gourmet bkfst, early coffee/tea and gourmet lunch. Beds: DT. Air conditioning. Fax, copier, spa, swimming, sauna and stables on premises. Small meetings, family reunions and seminars hosted. Amusement parks, antiquing, fishing, golf, C&O Canal, steam train rides, trail rides, parks, shopping, downhill skiing, cross-country skiing and water sports nearby.

Publicity: Washington Post, Pittsburgh Press, PA bride, Baltimore Sun and Potomac.

West Chester   K16

1732 Folke Stone Bed and Breakfast

777 Copeland School Road
West Chester, PA 19380
(610)429-0310 (800)884-4666 Fax:(610)918-9228
E-mail: folkbandb@aol.com
Web: www.bbonline.com/pa/folkestone

Circa 1732. A carefully restored William Penn land grant
home, this stone manor house was part of the historical
Underground Railroad. It boasts random-width wood floors
and open beam ceilings. The former winter kitchen is now a
welcoming area with original stone crane fireplace and beehive
oven. A hospitality center offers beverages and snacks. Antiques
and family heirlooms, including a Steinway piano, highlight the
inn. Choose from guest bedrooms featuring a choice of Amish
quilts on brass beds, a Jenny Lind spindle bed set, and French
Provincial furniture with porcelain lamps and Victorian lace.
Enjoy breakfast in the great room, and relaxing moments on
the side porch or the veranda overlooking the pond.

Innkeeper(s): Walter & Marcy Schmoll. $75-100. MC, VISA. 3 rooms with
PB and 1 conference room. Breakfast and snacks/refreshments included in
rates. Types of meals: Gourmet bkfst, veg bkfst and early coffee/tea. AP.
Beds: KQT. Cable TV in room. Central air. VCR, fax, copier and library on
premises. Family reunions and seminars hosted. Antiquing, art galleries,
canoeing/kayaking, golf, hiking, Longwood Gardens, Brandywine River
Museum, Winterthur, live theater, museums, parks, shopping, sporting events
and wineries nearby.

Bankhouse B&B

875 Hillsdale Rd
West Chester, PA 19382-1975
(610)344-7388
E-mail: bankhousebnb@ccis.net

Circa 1765. Built into the bank of a quiet country road, this
18th-century house overlooks a 10-acre horse farm and pond. The
interior is decorated with country antiques, stenciling and folk art.

Guests have a private entrance
and porch. Two bedrooms share a
common sitting room library.
Hearty country breakfasts include
German apple souffle pancakes,
custard French toast and nearly
100 other recipes. West Chester
and the Brandywine Valley attractions are conveniently close.

Historic Interest: Longwood Gardens, the Brandywine River Museum,
Brandywine Battlefield (8 miles).

Innkeeper(s): Diana & Michael Bove. $75-95. TC. 2 rooms and 1 suite.
Breakfast and snacks/refreshments included in rates. Types of meals:
Gourmet bkfst and early coffee/tea. Beds: DT. Phone in room. Central air.
Antiquing, live theater, parks, shopping, cross-country skiing and sporting
events nearby.

Publicity: *Philadelphia Inquirer, Mercury, Bucks County Town & Country
Living, Chester County Living and Washington Post.*

*"Everything was so warm and inviting. One of my favorite places to
keep coming back to."*

Whitewing Farm B&B

370 Valley Rd-RD 6
West Chester, PA 19382
(610)388-2664 Fax:(610)388-3650
E-mail: info@whitewingfarm.com
Web: www.whitewingfarm.com

Circa 1796. Experience the beauty of Discerning Traveler magazine's "1999 Best Romantic Hideaway of Pennsylvania." This
late-1700s English country farmhouse offers spacious luxury
throughout, including the 43 acres it rests upon. The ultimate in
privacy is found in the Gate House where guests can experience
the comfort of a private guest house, complete with a sky light,
fireplace and warm country décor, overlooking a gentle fountain
pond. Visit the farm with the entire family and interact with and
feed the animals. Travel to the Whitewing Farm throughout the
year to experience the majesty of nature as it changes from vivid
greens and blues to autumn reds and oranges, and the often-
white winters. Savor each meal by the fireplace in the dining
room overlooking the green rolling hills and pond.

Historic Interest: Winterthur, Brandywinr battlefield, coverrd bridges,
Brandywine River Museum.

Innkeeper(s): Ed & Wanda DeSeta. $150-259. PC, TC. 10 rooms with PB, 4
with FP, 4 suites and 1 conference room. Breakfast included in rates. Types of
meals: Gourmet bkfst, early coffee/tea and afternoon tea. Beds: KQT. TV and
ceiling fan in room. Central air. Fax, spa, swimming, tennis, library, 10 hole
chip and putt course and fishing on premises. Handicap access. Antiquing, art
galleries, canoeing/kayaking, fishing, golf, hiking, horseback riding, museums,
parks, shopping, sporting events, tennis and wineries nearby.

York   K13

Friendship House B&B

728 E Philadelphia St
York, PA 17403-1609
(717)843-8299
E-mail: friendshiphome@juno.com

Circa 1897. A walk down East Philadelphia Street takes visitors past an unassuming row of 19th-century townhouses. The
Friendship House is a welcoming site with its light blue shutters and pink trim. Innkeepers Becky Detwiler and Karen
Maust have added a shot of Victorian influence to their charming townhouse B&B, decorating with wallcoverings and lacy
curtains. A country feast is prepared some mornings with
choices ranging from quiche to French toast accompanied
with items such as baked apples, smoked sausage and homemade breads. Most items are selected carefully from a nearby
farmer's market. A cozy gathering place is in the living room
with its gas log fireplace.

Innkeeper(s): Becky Detwiler & Karen Maust. $55-65. 3 rooms, 2 with PB
and 1 suite. Breakfast and snacks/refreshments included in rates. Types of
meals: Full bkfst and cont plus. Beds: Q. Air conditioning. VCR on premises.
Antiquing, golf, museums, live theater, parks and shopping nearby.

Rhode Island

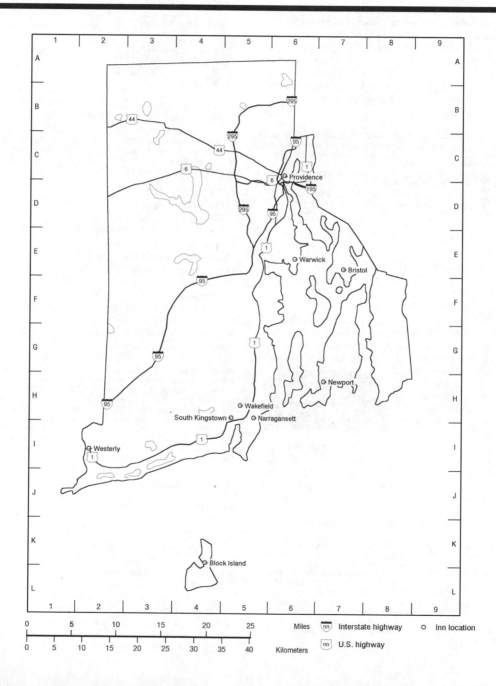

0 5 10 15 20 25 Miles

0 5 10 15 20 25 30 35 40 Kilometers

Interstate highway   U.S. highway   Inn location

Block Island K4

1661 Inn & Hotel Manisses

1 Spring St, PO Box I
Block Island, RI 02807-0001
(401)466-2421 (800)626-4773 Fax:(401)466-3162
E-mail: biresorts@riconnect.com
Web: www.blockisland.com/biresorts

Circa 1875. Seven buildings comprise this island inn and overlook grassy lawns and the ocean. Common rooms and guest rooms are furnished with antiques and art. The luxury rooms in the Nicholas Ball Cottage (a replica of an Episcopal church) offer both Jacuzzis and fireplaces. Dinner is available each night in the summer. Visit the inn's animal farm to watch the antics of the Indian runner ducks, black swans, pygmy goats, llamas and Sicilian donkeys. Flower, vegetable and herb gardens are adjacent to the farm.

Historic Interest: Historic Old Harbor.

Innkeeper(s): Joan & Justin Abrams. $75-370. MC, VISA, PC, TC. TAC10. 60 rooms, 53 with PB and 5 conference rooms. Breakfast included in rates. Types of meals: Gourmet bkfst, cont plus, cont, early coffee/tea, lunch, picnic lunch, snacks/refreshments and gourmet dinner. Beds: KQDT. Child care on premises. Weddings, small meetings, family reunions and seminars hosted. Antiquing, fishing, live theater, shopping and water sports nearby.

Publicity: *Newsday, New England Weekends, The Day, Detroit Free Press, US Air, USA Today, Block Island, New England Travel, Yankee, Gourmet and Bon Apetit.*

Atlantic Inn

PO Box 1788, High St
Block Island, RI 02807-1788
(401)466-5883 (800)224-7422 Fax:(401)466-5678
E-mail: atlanticinn@biri.com
Web: www.atlanticinn.com

Circa 1879. Guests first traveled up the long road to the Atlantic Inn to enjoy its more than two acres of grassy slopes, which overlook the ocean and Old Harbor Village. Today, guests will experience much of the charm that lured vacation-

ers to this island spot during the Victorian era. The inn's 21 guest rooms are individually appointed with antiques and period furnishings. Inn guests enjoy use of two tennis  courts, a formal croquet court, a swing and gym set for children as well as a playhouse, which is a replica of the inn. Take a leisurely stroll around the landscaped grounds and enjoy the gardens, which provide many of the herbs and vegetables used in meals at the inn's gourmet restaurant. President and Mrs. Clinton recently dined here.

Historic Interest: The Block Island Historic District and Old Harbor Village include many historic buildings.

Innkeeper(s): Brad & Anne Marthens. $125-235. MC, VISA, PC, TC. 21 rooms with PB, 1 suite and 1 conference room. Breakfast and afternoon tea included in rates. Types of meals: Cont plus, early coffee/tea and picnic lunch. Beds: QDT. Fax, copier, tennis and child care on premises. Weddings, small meetings, family reunions and seminars hosted. Antiquing, fishing, beaches, biking, live theater, parks, shopping and water sports nearby.

Publicity: *Bon Appetit, Travel and Leisure, New York Times, Baltimore Sun, Newsday, New England Weekends, Detroit Free Press, USA Today, Block Island, New England Travel, Gourmet, Miami Herald, Romantic Weekends, Providence Journal, National Geographic Traveler, and Back Roads of New England.*

The Bellevue House

PO Box 1198, High St
Block Island, RI 02807-1198
(401)466-2912
E-mail: bellevue@riconnect.com
Web: www.blockisland.com/bellevue

Circa 1882. Offering a hilltop perch, meadow-like setting and ocean views, this Colonial Revival farmhouse inn in the Block Island Historic District has served guests for more than a centu-

 ry. A variety of accommodations includes six guest rooms, one with private bath, four suites and two cottages. The Old Harbor Ferry, restaurants and shops are just a five-minute walk from the inn.

Guests may use ferries from New London, Conn., Montauk Point, N.Y., and Point Judith, R.I., to reach the island. Beaches, Block Island National Wildlife Reserve and Rodmans Hollow Nature Area are nearby. Children are welcome.

Innkeeper(s): Neva Flaherty. $65-285. MC, VISA, PC, TC. 6 rooms, 4 suites and 2 cottages. Breakfast included in rates. Types of meals: Cont. Beds: KQD. Library, gas grills and picnic tables on premises. Family reunions hosted. Fishing, parks, shopping and water sports nearby.

Blue Dory Inn

PO Box 488, Dodge St
Block Island, RI 02807-0488
(401)466-5891 (800)992-7290 Fax:(401)466-9910
E-mail: rundezvous@aol.com
Web: www.blockislandinns.com

Circa 1887. This Shingle Victorian inn on Crescent Beach offers many guest rooms with ocean views. The Cottage, The Doll House and The Tea House are separate structures for those desiring more room or privacy. Antiques and Victorian touches are featured throughout. Year-round car ferry service, taking approximately one hour, is found at Point Judith, R.I. The island also may be reached by air on New England Airlines or by charter. Mohegan Bluffs Scenic Natural Area is nearby.

Historic Interest: The Blue Dory is located in the Block Island Historic District, which includes many historic homes dating back 150 years.

Innkeeper(s): Ann Law. $65-225. MC, VISA, AX, DS, PC, TC. TAC10. 12 rooms with PB, 3 suites, 4 cottages and 1 conference room. Breakfast and afternoon tea included in rates. Types of meals: Cont plus and early coffee/tea. Beds: KQDT. Phone, some air conditioning, VCRs and Cable TV in room. VCR, fax, copier, swimming and child care on premises. Weddings, small meetings, family reunions and seminars hosted. Antiquing, beaches, fishing, live theater, parks, shopping and water sports nearby.

Pets allowed: Restricted to certain cottages.

"The Blue Dory is a wonderful place to stay. The room was lovely, the view spectacular and the sound of surf was both restful and tranquil."

Gothic Inn

PO Box 537
Block Island, RI 02807
(401)466-2918 (800)944-8991 Fax:(401)466-5028
E-mail: bennetbirx@cs.com
Web: www.blockisland.com/gothic/

Circa 1860. Built for a sea captain who was a late 18th-century druggist, this Victorian Gothic Inn is now owned by the Wohl family, also pharmacists on this small island. Situated in the center of the historic district, the inn boasts spectacular ocean views of Crescent Beach. Guests can watch pleasure and commercial boats enter and leave Old Harbor. Relax with a deluxe continental breakfast served in the cheery sitting rooms or large porch overlooking the lawn or the sea.

Historic Interest: Lighthouses.

Innkeeper(s): Toube & Bennet Wohl. $65-280. MC, VISA, AX, DS, PC, TC. 13 rooms, 1 with PB and 2 suites. Breakfast included in rates. Types of meals: Cont plus and early coffee/tea. Beds: DT. TV, phone, ceiling fan, VCR and fireplace in room. Handicap access. Small meetings and family reunions hosted. Art galleries, beaches, bicycling, canoeing/kayaking, fishing, hiking, horseback riding, museums, parks, shopping, tennis and water sports nearby.

Rose Farm Inn

Roslyn Rd
Block Island, RI 02807-0895
(401)466-2034 Fax:(401)466-2053
E-mail: rosefarm@riconnect.com
Web: www.blockisland.com/rosefarm

Circa 1897. This romantic inn is comprised of two buildings, the turn-of-the-century farmhouse and the newer Captain Rose House. Canopy beds, sitting areas and whirlpool tubs are among the elegant touches that grace the rooms at the Captain Rose House. Most rooms afford either an ocean or countryside view; and there's always a light sea breeze to be enjoyed from the decks and front porch of the Farm House. A continental-plus buffet is served each morning on the enclosed sun porch, which overlooks the ocean.

Innkeeper(s): Judith B Rose. $124-235. MC, VISA, AX, DS, TC. 19 rooms, 17 with PB. Breakfast and afternoon tea included in rates. Types of meals: Cont plus. Beds: KQDT. Phone in room. VCR, fax, copier and bicycles on premises. Handicap access. Antiquing, fishing, tennis, shopping and water sports nearby.
Publicity: *Block Island and Getaways.*

Sheffield House Bed & Breakfast

PO Box 1387, 351 High St
Block Island, RI 02807
(401)466-2494 (866)466-2494 Fax:(401)466-7745
E-mail: sheffieldhouse@aol.com
Web: www.sheffieldhouse.com

Circa 1888. Step off the ferry and step into a by-gone era at this Queen Anne Victorian, which overlooks the Old Harbor district. Relax on one of the front porch rockers or enjoy the fragrance as you stroll through the private garden. Guest rooms are furnished with antiques and family pieces; each is individually decorated.

Historic Interest: The Old Harbor district is a historic area with plenty of places to explore.

Innkeeper(s): Nancy Sarah. $50-185. MC, VISA, AX, PC, TC. 6 rooms, 4 with PB. Breakfast, afternoon tea and snacks/refreshments included in rates. Types of meals: Full bkfst. Beds: Q. Ceiling fan in room. Weddings and family reunions hosted. Antiquing, beaches, fishing, ocean, nature, restaurants, parks, shopping and water sports nearby.

Bristol   E7

William's Grant Inn

154 High St
Bristol, RI 02809-2123
(401)253-4222 (800)596-4222
E-mail: wmgrantinn@earthlink.net
Web: www.wmgrantinn.com

Circa 1808. This handsome Federal Colonial home was built by Governor William Bradford for his grandson. There are two beehive ovens and seven fireplaces as well as original wide-

board pine floors and paired interior chimneys. Antique furnishings and folk art make the guest rooms inviting. The backyard is an ideal spot for relaxation with its patios, water garden and quaint stone walls.

Historic Interest: The area offers many historic homes, the Blithewold Mansion and Gardens, Coggeshall Farm Museum and several other museums.

Innkeeper(s): Warren & Diane, Matthew & Janet Poehler. $95-110. MC, VISA, AX, DS, PC, TC. TAC10. 5 rooms, 3 with PB, 5 with FP. Breakfast included in rates. Types of meals: Gourmet bkfst and afternoon tea. Beds: QD. Turndown service and ceiling fan in room. Air conditioning. Bicycles and goldfish pond with waterfall on premises. Small meetings hosted. Antiquing, fishing, parks, shopping, sporting events and water sports nearby.

Publicity: *New York Times, Sun Sentinel, Providence Journal & Bristol Phoenix.*

"We felt better than at home with the wonderful treats (the breakfasts were fabulous), the lovely rooms, the inn is full of inspiration and innovation . . ."

Narragansett   H5

The 1900 House B&B

59 Kingstown Rd
Narragansett, RI 02882-3309
(401)789-7971

Circa 1900. For more than a century, Narragansett has been a hot spot for summer vacationers. Guests at the 1900 House enjoy both close access to the town's restaurants and shops as well as a nostalgic look back at the Victorian era. The innkeepers keep a stereoscope, hat boxes filled with antique post cards and other collectibles on hand for guests to discover. You might spot the wedding certificate of the home's original owner. Waffles topped with fresh fruit and cream are typical of the rich treats served at breakfast.

Innkeeper(s): Sandra & Bill Panzeri. $65-105. PC, TC. 3 rooms, 1 with PB. Breakfast included in rates. Types of meals: Gourmet bkfst and early coffee/tea. Beds: D. TV in room. Antiquing, fishing, Foxwoods Casino, bird sanctuary, South County Museum, live theater, parks, shopping, sporting events and water sports nearby.

"Wonderful! So relaxing and lovely, lovely breakfasts."

The Richards

144 Gibson Ave
Narragansett, RI 02882-3949
(401)789-7746

Circa 1884. J.P. Hazard, an influential member of one of the county's most prominent families, built this home, which resembles a English-country stone manor. The rooms are appointed with a beautiful collection of antiques, and each guest room has a fireplace and sitting area. Down comforters, carafes of sherry and candles are among the romantic amenities. After a restful night's sleep, guests are presented with a gourmet breakfast. French toast, made from Portuguese sweet bread, or rich, chocolate pancakes topped with an orange sauce might appear as the daily entree. The home is listed in the National Register of Historic Places.

Innkeeper(s): Nancy & Steven Richards. $95-200. PC, TC. 5 rooms, 4 with PB, 5 with FP and 2 suites. Breakfast included in rates. Types of meals:

Gourmet bkfst. Beds: KQ. Library and guest refrigerator on premises. Antiquing, fishing, golf, live theater, tennis and water sports nearby.

Publicity: *Yankee Traveler, Home, Providence Journal-Bulletin, Narragansett Times and Rhode Island Monthly.*

Newport   H7

1855 Marshall Slocum Guest House

29 Kay St
Newport, RI 02840-2735
(401)841-5120 (800)372-5120 Fax:(401)846-3787
E-mail: info@marshallslocuminn.com
Web: www.marshallslocuminn.com

Circa 1855. Victorian homes line the streets in the Historic Hill District of Newport, where this two-and-a-half-story house is situated on an acre of grounds. Architectural features include shutters, a hip roof with dormer windows and a front porch. The inn is furnished with antiques and contemporary pieces. A favorite breakfast is Fluffy Belgian Waffles served with freshly picked strawberries and mountains of whipped cream. Don't miss the afternoon refreshments, and if you are staying longer than two nights ask about the innkeepers' Lobster Dinner Package. A five- to 10-minute walk will take you to the downtown area and the beach.

Innkeeper(s): Joan & Julie Wilson. $79-195. MC, VISA. TAC10. 5 rooms with PB, 2 with FP. Breakfast and snacks/refreshments included in rates. Types of meals: Gourmet bkfst, early coffee/tea, gourmet lunch, picnic lunch and gourmet dinner. EP. Beds: KQT. Air conditioning. VCR, fax, copier, bicycles and library on premises. Weddings, small meetings, family reunions and seminars hosted. Antiquing, bicycling, fishing, golf, hiking and horseback riding nearby.

Publicity: *Newport Daily News, Providence Journal, Washington Post and LA Times.*

1856 Inn at Shadow Lawn

120 Miantonomi Ave
Newport, RI 02842-5450
(401)847-0902 (800)352-3750 Fax:(401)848-6529
E-mail: randy@shadowlawn.com
Web: www.shadowlawn.com

Circa 1856. This elegant, three-story Stick Victorian inn, listed in the National Register, offers a glimpse of fine living in an earlier age. The innkeepers' attention to detail is evident throughout, with French crystal chandeliers, stained-glass windows and parquet floors in the library as a few of the highlights. Parlors are found on each of the inn's floors. Newport's many attractions, including the Art Museum, sailing and the world famous Newport mansions are just a short drive from the inn.

Historic Interest: Mansions from "Gilded Age" (5 minutes).

Innkeeper(s): Randy & Selma Fabricant. $85-225. MC, VISA, AX, TC. 8 rooms with PB, 8 with FP and 3 conference rooms. Breakfast included in rates. Types of meals: Full bkfst and cont plus. Beds: KQ. Cable TV, phone and VCR in room. Air conditioning. Fax, copier and library on premises. Weddings, small meetings, family reunions and seminars hosted. Antiquing, mansions and sailing nearby.

Publicity: *Newport Daily News, Providence Journal, West Essex Tribune and Mr. Smith.*

"A dream come true! Thanks for everything! We'll be back."

Admiral Fitzroy

389 Thames St
Newport, RI 02840
(401)848-8000
Web: www.admiralfitzroy.com

Circa 1854. In Newport's waterfront district stands this European-style inn. Designed by renowned architect Dudley Newton, the inn was named for Admiral Fitzroy who commanded the HMS Beagle on Charles Darwin's historic voyage that preceded the writing of his famous book. Fitzroy also was famous for developing a barometer. Several examples of working antique barometers are on display in the inn. The inn has 17 attractive hand-painted rooms. A full breakfast is served each morning in the breakfast room. Breakfast fare includes such delights as cheese blintzes, pancakes, bacon, eggs, French toast, scones, cereal and fruits. After breakfast, guests will want to head out on foot to explore the historic waterfront district, which has excellent restaurants, antiquing and harbor activities. Newport boasts more occupied colonial houses than anywhere else in America. It also has the oldest Episcopal church and the first synagogue.

Innkeeper(s): Carol Bamberry. Call for rates.. MC, VISA, AX, DS. TAC10. 17 rooms with PB. Types of meals: Full bkfst and cont. Beds: KQDT. Phone in room. Fax and copier on premises. Antiquing and shopping nearby.

Beech Tree Inn

34 Rhode Island Ave
Newport, RI 02840-2667
(401)847-9794 (800)748-6565 Fax:(401)847-6824
E-mail: beechtreeinn@edgenet.com
Web: www.beechtreeinn.com

Circa 1897. This inn's location in historic Newport offers close access to the famous local mansions, and the turn-of-the-century home is within walking distance of the harbor. Most of the guest rooms include a fireplace. Special furnishings include canopy or poster beds, and suites offer the added amenity of a whirlpool tub. The innkeepers provide a breakfast feast, and guests enjoy made-to-order fare that might include

eggs, pancakes, waffles, omelets, ham, bacon and more. In the winter months, guests are further pampered with homemade clam chowder in the evenings. Snacks, such as freshly baked cookies, are always on hand to curb one's appetite.

Innkeeper(s): Edwin & Kathy Wudyka. $79-275. MC, VISA, AX, DS, TC. TAC10. 5 rooms with PB, 1 suite, 2 guest houses and 1 conference room. Breakfast and afternoon tea included in rates. Types of meals: Full bkfst and early coffee/tea. Beds: KQT. Cable TV, phone, ceiling fan and fireplaces and jacuzzi in room. Air conditioning. Fax and copier on premises. Weddings, small meetings, family reunions and seminars hosted. Polish spoken. Antiquing, fishing, golf, live theater, parks, shopping, downhill skiing, cross-country skiing, sporting events, tennis and water sports nearby.

Black Duck Inn

29 Pelham St
Newport, RI 02840-3018
(401)841-5548 (800)206-5212 Fax:(401)846-4873
E-mail: maryA401@aol.com
Web: www.blackduckinn.com

Circa 1870. This inn derives its name from a ship that smuggled liquor into Newport during the days of Prohibition. The inn is located in the downtown area and within walking distance of the harbor and famed mansions of Newport. In the guest rooms, English country fabrics and coordinating curtains and wallcoverings complete the romantic look. For those celebrating a special occasion, the innkeeper offers rooms with whirlpool tubs and fireplaces. Six of the rooms include a private bath. Two other rooms are joined by a bathroom, creating an ideal family suite. One of the rooms includes a queen bed, the other includes two twin beds. The continental-plus breakfasts include cereals, granola, fresh fruit, croissants, muffins and coffee cake.

Innkeeper(s): Mary A. Rolando. $100-200. MC, VISA, AX, TC. TAC10. 8 rooms, 6 with PB, 2 with FP. Breakfast included in rates. Types of meals: Cont plus. Beds: QT. TV and phone in room. Central air. Fax and copier on premises. Antiquing, art galleries, beaches, bicycling, canoeing/kayaking, fishing, golf, horseback riding, museums, parks, shopping, sporting events, tennis, water sports and wineries nearby.

The Burbank Rose B&B

111 Memorial Blvd W
Newport, RI 02840-3469
(401)849-9457 (888)297-5800
E-mail: burbank@travelbase.com
Web: www.burbankrose.com

Circa 1850. The innkeepers of this cheery, yellow home named their B&B in honor of their ancestor, famed horticulturist Luther Burbank. As a guest, he probably would be taken by the bright, flowery hues that adorn the interior of this Federal-style home. Rooms, some of which afford harbor views, are light and airy with simple decor. The innkeepers serve afternoon refreshments and a substantial breakfast buffet. The home is located in Newport's Historic Hill

district and within walking distance of shops, restaurants and many of the seaside village's popular attractions.

Innkeeper(s): John & Bonnie McNeely. $69-199. AX, PC, TC. TAC10. 3 rooms with PB and 2 suites. Breakfast and afternoon tea included in rates. Types of meals: Full bkfst and early coffee/tea. Beds: QT. Air conditioning. VCR and copier on premises. Antiquing, fishing, sailing, golf, tennis, live theater, shopping and water sports nearby.

Castle Hill Inn & Resort

Ocean Ave
Newport, RI 02840
(401)849-3800 (888)466-1355
E-mail: castlehill@edgenet.net

Circa 1874. A rambling Victorian on 40 oceanfront acres overlooking Narragansett Bay, the Castle Hill Inn was built as a summer home for scientist Alexander Agassiz. A laboratory on the property was a forerunner of the Woods Hole Marine Laboratory. Many original furnishings remain, and there are spectacular views from every room. The inn's luxurious rooms and suites offer spacious whirlpool tubs, fireplaces, fine decor and lavish king beds. Some rooms have French doors that open to sweeping water views. A complimentary gourmet breakfast is offered daily.

On Sundays, eggs Benedict, lobster ravioli and waffles are part of the restaurant's special Jazz Brunch. Dinner specialties include striped bass with clams and Vidalia onions, duck and

grilled lamb. Complimentary afternoon tea is provided. The grounds offer a private beach, lighthouse, walking trails and a cutting garden for the inn's flower arrangements.

Innkeeper(s): Chuck Flanders. $145-600. MC, VISA, AX, DS, TC. 25 rooms with PB. Types of meals: Full bkfst, lunch, afternoon tea and dinner. Beds: KD. Phones with dataports in room. 10 seasonal beach cottages on premises.

Cliffside Inn

2 Seaview Ave
Newport, RI 02840-3627
(401)847-1811 (800)845-1811 Fax:(401)848-5850
E-mail: cliff@wsii.com
Web: www.cliffsideinn.com

Circa 1876. The governor of Maryland, Thomas Swann, built this Newport summer house in the style of a Second Empire Victorian. It features a mansard roof and many bay windows. The rooms are decorated in a Victorian motif. Suites have marble baths, and all rooms have fireplaces. Fourteen rooms have a double whirlpool tub. The Cliff Walk is located one block from the inn.

Innkeeper(s): Stephan Nicolas. $235-510. MC, VISA, AX, DC, DS, PC, TC. TAC10. 16 rooms with PB, 16 with FP, 8 suites and 1 cottage. Breakfast and afternoon tea included in rates. Types of meals: Gourmet bkfst and early coffee/tea. Beds: KQ. Cable TV, phone, turndown service, ceiling fan and VCR in room. Air conditioning. Fax on premises. French spoken. Antiquing, fishing, live theater, shopping and water sports nearby.

Publicity: *Conde Naste, Bostin, New York County Times,Country Inns, Philadelphia, Discerning Traveler, and Good Morning America.*

"...it captures the grandeur of the Victorian age."

Fair Street Guest House

28 Fair St
Newport, RI 02840-3442
(401)849-4046 (888)701-1431 Fax:(401)847-1084
E-mail: milton1084@aol.com
Web: www.fairstreetguesthouse.com

Circa 1880. This 1880 Victorian inn on the National Historic Register is located in Newport Historic District just blocks from the waterfront. It's within blocks of a number of well-known sites, including St. Mary's Church, where Jack and Jacqueline Kennedy were married, Banister's Wharf and Christie's Landing. It has seven guest rooms decorated with furniture from the Victorian era. Breakfast is served in the dining room, on the enclosed porch or in the garden, and offers such dishes as muffins, bagels with cream cheese, cereal and fruit.

Historic Interest: Newport Historic District.

Innkeeper(s): Milton J. Beauregard. $75-150. MC, VISA, AX, DS. TAC10. 7 rooms with PB. Breakfast included in rates. Types of meals: Cont plus and early coffee/tea. Beds: KQDT. Cable TV and ceiling fan in room. Central air. VCR and fax on premises. Small meetings and family reunions hosted. Antiquing, art galleries, beaches, bicycling, canoeing/kayaking, golf, hiking, horseback riding, live theater, museums, parks, shopping, tennis, water sports and wineries nearby.

Francis Malbone House

392 Thames St
Newport, RI 02840-6604
(401)846-0392 (800)846-0392 Fax:(401)848-5956
E-mail: innkeeper@malbone.com

Circa 1760. Newport, during the 18th century, was one of the busiest harbors in the Colonies. A shipping merchant, Colonel Francis Malbone, built the historic portion of this home, which includes nine of the inn's 20 guest rooms. The newer addition was completed in 1996. Fine furnishings fill the rooms, most of which offer a fireplace. Twelve rooms

include a Jacuzzi tub. The inn's location, on the harborfront, is another wonderful feature. The breakfasts, heralded by Bon Appetit, include entrees such as pecan waffles with maple whipped cream or eggs Benedict with a roasted red pepper hollandaise. Guests are sure to be busy exploring Newport with its abundance of historic sites and spectacular mansions.

Innkeeper(s): Will Dewey & Mark & Jasminka Eads. $155-425. MC, VISA, AX. TAC10. 16 rooms with PB, 18 with FP, 4 suites and 6 conference rooms. Breakfast and afternoon tea included in rates. Types of meals: Gourmet bkfst. Beds: KQ. TV, phone and turndown service in room. Air conditioning. Fax on premises. Handicap access. Small meetings hosted. Antiquing, golf, mansion tours, parks, shopping and tennis nearby.

Publicity: *Colonial Homes, Bon Appetit, Country Inns, Gourmet, In-Style and HGTV.*

Jailhouse Inn

13 Marlborough St
Newport, RI 02840-2545
(401)847-4638 (800)427-9444 Fax:(401)849-0605
E-mail: vacation@jailhouse.com
Web: www.jailhouse.com

Circa 1772. Built in 1772, this restored Colonial jail maintains just a touch of jail flavor as a backdrop to comfort and convenience. Prison-striped bed coverings and tin cups and plates for breakfast express the jailhouse motif. Guests can stay in the Cell Block, Maximum Security or Solitary Confinement, each on a separate level of the inn. Nevertheless, because guests pay for their time here, there are luxuries in abundance. A complimentary continental breakfast buffet and afternoon tea service is offered daily.

Historic Interest: The inn is located one block from harbor restaurants and shops.

Innkeeper(s): Susan Mauro. $45-280. MC, VISA, AX, DC, DS, TC. TAC10. 23 rooms with PB and 4 suites. Breakfast and afternoon tea included in rates. Types of meals: Cont and early coffee/tea. Beds: KQ. Cable TV and phone in room. Air conditioning. Fax on premises. Handicap access. Small meetings and family reunions hosted. Antiquing, art galleries, beaches, bicycling, canoeing/kayaking, fishing, golf, hiking, horseback riding, live theater, museums, parks, shopping, tennis, water sports and wineries nearby.

Publicity: *Providence Journal.*

"I found this very relaxing and a great pleasure."

The Melville House

39 Clarke St
Newport, RI 02840-3023
(401)847-0640 Fax:(401)847-0956
E-mail: innkeeper@ids.net
Web: www.melvillehouse.com

Circa 1750. This attractive, National Register two-story Colonial inn once housed aides to General Rochambeau during the American Revolution. Early American furnishings decorate the interior. There is also an unusual collection of old appliances, including a cherry-pitter, mincer and dough maker. A full breakfast includes Portuguese Quiche, Jonnycakes, home-

made bread and berry-stuffed French toast. The inn is a pleasant walk from the waterfront and historic sites.

Historic Interest: Vernon House (across the street).

Innkeeper(s): Christine Leone. $110-165. MC, VISA, AX, DS, PC, TC. TAC10. 7 rooms, 5 with PB, 1 with FP and 1 suite. Breakfast and afternoon tea included in rates. Types of meals: Gourmet bkfst, early coffee/tea and picnic lunch. Beds: KDT. Air conditioning. Fax and bicycles on premises. Small meetings, family reunions and seminars hosted. Antiquing, fishing, live theater, parks, shopping and water sports nearby.

Publicity: *Country Inns, "Lodging Pick" for Newport, Good Housekeeping and New York Post.*

"Comfortable with a quiet elegance."

Old Beach Inn

19 Old Beach Rd
Newport, RI 02840-3237
(401)849-3479 (888)303-5033 Fax:(401)847-1236
E-mail: info@oldbeachinn.com

Circa 1879. Stroll through the backyard at this enchanting Gothic Victorian bed & breakfast and you'll find a garden, lily pond and romantic gazebo. Innkeepers Luke and Cyndi Murray have kept a whimsical, romantic theme running inside and outside. Each of the guest rooms, two of which are located in the carriage house, bears the name of a flower. Delightful decor with bright wall coverings and linens accent the beautiful furnishings. The recently renovated Lily Room has a music theme, while the blue and yellow Forget-Me-Not Room is filled with wicker. Every item in the room is color-coordinated and features special painting and stenciling created by

Cyndi. An expanded continental breakfast is served daily, and on Sundays, the innkeepers offer items such as an egg casserole, quiche or stuffed French toast. The area abounds with shops and restaurants, including a famous eatery managed by Luke.

Historic Interest: Several mansions in the area are open for tours. The Redwood Library is a short walk from the inn, as is the Tennis Hall of Fame. The historic harborfront is a seven-minute stroll.

Innkeeper(s): Luke & Cynthia Murray. $85-195. MC, VISA, AX, DS, PC, TC. 7 rooms with PB, 6 with FP. Breakfast included in rates. Types of meals: Cont plus. Beds: QD. Ceiling fan and one with Jacuzzi in room. Air conditioning. Fax and copier on premises. Weddings, small meetings, family reunions and seminars hosted. Antiquing, fishing, live theater, parks, shopping and water sports nearby.

Publicity: *Canadian Leisure Ways and Seaway Trail.*

"Thanks for your exceptional and stylish innkeeping. We never wanted for one comfort."

On The Point B&B

102 3rd St
Newport, RI 02840-1542
(401)846-8377

Circa 1895. Period antiques fill the rooms of this Shingle Victorian inn, just a block from the bay and within easy walking distance to the town center. The inn's front porch, with its comfortable wicker furniture, is a favorite gathering spot, as is the antique brick patio. A homemade breakfast is featured and special diets are accommodated upon request. Visitors enjoy the convenience of public tennis courts that are just

around the corner from the inn. Be sure to check out the famous Cliff Walk while in town.

Historic Interest: Colony House, Friends (Quaker) Meeting House, White Horse Tavern, Touro Synagogue, U.S. Naval War Collage, Eisenhower House (all within 4 miles).

Innkeeper(s): Sheila & George Perry. $95-150. MC, VISA, AX. TAC10. 4 rooms with PB. Breakfast included in rates. Types of meals: Cont plus. Beds: KQT. TV (non-cable) in room. Air conditioning. Small meetings and family reunions hosted. Antiquing, art galleries, beaches, bicycling, fishing, golf, museums, parks, shopping, sporting events, tennis and water sports nearby.

Queen Anne Inn

16 Clarke St
Newport, RI 02840-3024
(401)846-5676 (888)407-1616 Fax:(401)841-8509
E-mail: queenanne@prodigy.net
Web: www.QueenAnneInnNewport.com

Circa 1900. Located in one of Newport's oldest neighborhoods, this Victorian is just a few blocks from the waterfront and the downtown area. The garden-covered grounds and peaceful residential setting create a pleasing serenity for those in search of relaxation. As it is just steps from the water, the innkeepers chose to decorate the inn in a nautical theme. In addition to the continental breakfast, which features items such as croissants and fresh pastries, afternoon tea is served each day. Museums and the famed mansions of Newport are among the town's attractions.

Historic Interest: Artillery, Touro Synagogue (2 blocks), Museum of Newport History (2 blocks), Fort Adams (5 miles).

Innkeeper(s): Flavia Gardiner. $125-180. MC, VISA, AX, PC, TC. TAC10. 10 rooms, 8 with PB and 1 suite. Breakfast and afternoon tea included in rates. Types of meals: Cont and early coffee/tea. Beds: KQT. Air conditioning. Fax, copier and modem hook-up and parking on premises. Weddings and family reunions hosted. Spanish and Portuguese spoken. Antiquing, art galleries, beaches, bicycling, canoeing/kayaking, golf, hiking, horseback riding, 12 meter sailing and power yachting, live theater, museums, parks, shopping, tennis, water sports and wineries nearby.

The Pilgrim House

123 Spring St
Newport, RI 02840-6805
(401)846-0040 (800)525-8373 Fax:(401)848-0357
E-mail: innkeeper@pilgrimhouseinn.com

Circa 1879. This Victorian inn, located in the heart of Newport, has a rooftop deck with a panoramic view of the harbor. The home is within walking distance of shops, restaurants, the Cliff Walk and the Newport mansions. In the cooler months, the innkeepers serve sherry in the living room, which often is warmed by a crackling fire.

Historic Interest: Touro Synagogue, Trinity Church, Newport Harbor (1 block), Tennis Hall of Fame (3 blocks).

Innkeeper(s): Barry & Debbie Fonseca. $85-230. MC, VISA, PC. TAC10. 10 rooms, 8 with PB and 1 conference room. Breakfast and afternoon tea included in rates. Types of meals: Cont plus. Beds: QDT. Air conditioning. Fax, copier and Big screen TV on premises. Small meetings, family reunions and seminars hosted. Antiquing, fishing, restaurants, live theater, parks and shopping nearby.

Publicity: *The Times.*

"What can I say, it's a perfect hideaway. Great time was had by all."

Reed Rose Cottage

8 Loyola Terrace
Newport, RI 02840
(401)846-8790
E-mail: reedrosecottage@home.com
Web: www.reedrosecottage.com

Circa 1947. Quaint and cozy, this home was built in the style of Cape Cod cottages in a quiet neighborhood. It features an open floor plan with spacious living, dining and kitchen areas. Antiques and wicker furnishings are embellished with a floral decor of cabbage roses. A cheery and comfortable two-bedroom suite overlooks the in-ground swimming pool and perennial gardens. This ocean community offers many water sports and historic sites. Beach towels are provided.

Innkeeper(s): Charron K. Reed. $75-250. MC, VISA. 1 suites. Breakfast included in rates. Types of meals: Cont plus. Beds: QD. Cable TV in room. Central air. Swimming, library, child care and in-ground pool on premises. Weddings, small meetings and family reunions hosted. Amusement parks, antiquing, art galleries, beaches, bicycling, canoeing/kayaking, fishing, golf, hiking, horseback riding, live theater, museums, parks, shopping, downhill skiing, cross-country skiing, sporting events, tennis, water sports and wineries nearby.

Stella Maris Inn

91 Washington
Newport, RI 02840
(401)849-2862

Circa 1861. Made of stone with black walnut woodwork inside, this is a French Victorian with mansard roof and wraparound veranda. The inn's two acres are landscaped with flower beds. Bright yet elegant wall coverings and fabrics set off the antiques, paintings and interior architectural points of interest. In the National Register, the inn is an early Newport mansion that was originally called "Blue Rocks." It later became a convent at which time it was renamed Stella Maris,  "star of the sea." Several of the inn's lavishly appointed rooms offer ocean views, and some have fireplaces.

Innkeeper(s): Dorothy & Ed Madden. $85-225. PC, TC. 9 rooms with PB, 9 with FP and 1 cottage. Breakfast and afternoon tea included in rates. Types of meals: Cont plus and early coffee/tea. Beds: KQDT. Ceiling fan in room. Library and elevator on premises. Small meetings and family reunions hosted. French spoken. Antiquing, fishing, golf, live theater, parks, shopping, tennis and water sports nearby.

"Rejuvenation for the soul!."

Willows of Newport - Romantic Inn & Garden

8-10 Willow St, Historic Point
Newport, RI 02840-1927
(401)846-5486 Fax:(401)849-8215
E-mail: rwakefi368@aol.com
Web: www.thewillowsofnewport.com

Circa 1740. There's little wonder why this inn is known as The Romantic Inn. The spectacular secret garden, with its abundance of foliage, colorful blooms and a heart-shaped fish pond, is a popular stop on Newport's Secret Garden Tour. The inn is a three-time recipient of the Newport Best Garden Award. The French Quarter Queen room and Canopy Room both boast

views of the gardens, and guests awake to the fragrances of the many flowers. The romantic Victorian Wedding Room, decorated in pastel greens and rose, offers a queen canopy bed, hand-painted furniture and a fireplace. The Colonial Wedding Room features lace accents, a hand-crafted king bed and an original 1740s fireplace. A continental breakfast is delivered to your room on bone china with silver services. Innkeeper Pattie Murphy, aside from her gardening and decorating skills, is a native Newporter and is full of information about the city. Ask about the inn's new "Silk & Chandelier" collection.

Historic Interest: The home is listed as National Landmark. Newport is the home of the Touro Synagogue, the oldest Jewish house of worship in North America. The Tennis Hall of Fame and the nation's oldest library, Redwood, are popular attractions. Don't forget to visit the nation's oldest operating tavern, The White Horse Tavern, which first opened in 1687.

Innkeeper(s): Patricia 'Pattie' Murphy. $188-278. PC, TC. TAC10. 5 rooms with PB. Breakfast and snacks/refreshments included in rates. Types of meals: Cont plus. Beds: KQD. Air conditioning. Award-winning secret garden on premises. Antiquing, fishing, mansions, sunset sailing nearby, parks, shopping and water sports nearby.

Publicity: *Bostonia, New Woman, PM Magazine, Wedding Day NE, Travel America, Country Inn and HGTV.*

"We enjoyed our getaway in your inn for its peace, elegance and emphasis on romance."

Yankee Peddler Inn

113 Touro St
Newport, RI 02840-2968
(401)846-1323 (800)427-9444 Fax:(401)849-0426
E-mail: vacation@yankeepeddlerinn.com
Web: www.yankeepeddlerinn.com

Circa 1830. Centrally located in historic downtown Newport, this Greek Revival inn has a stately charm. Antiques, original artwork and fine fabrics lend an elegance to the spacious guest bedrooms. Enjoy a continental breakfast in the common room as well as afternoon pastries and tea service. For a relaxing interlude, the rooftop deck awaits, offering panoramic views of the harbor city.

Historic Interest: Touro Synagogue (across street), Bellevue Avenue (1 block), mansions (1 mile), Fort Adams (3 miles).

Innkeeper(s): Bob Briskin. $45-195. MC, VISA, AX, DS, TC. TAC10. 19 rooms, 17 with PB and 1 conference room. Breakfast and afternoon tea included in rates. Types of meals: Early coffee/tea. Beds: Q. Cable TV and phone in room. Air conditioning. Family reunions hosted. Antiquing, art galleries, beaches, bicycling, canoeing/kayaking, fishing, golf, hiking, horseback riding, live theater, museums, parks, shopping, tennis, water sports and wineries nearby.

"So comfortable! We return four times each year, once per season. The Yankee Peddler is our home in Newport."

Providence   C6

AAA Jacob Hill Inn

PO Box 41326
Providence, RI 02940
(508)336-9165 (888)336-9165 Fax:(508)336-0951
E-mail: host@jacobhill.com
Web: www.inn-providence.com

Circa 1722. This historic Colonial home overlooks 50 acres and is located three miles outside Providence. In the '20s and '30s, it was the Jacob Hill Hunt Club and hosted the

Vanderbilts during hunts and horse shows. Beamed ceilings, wall paintings of horse and hunting scenes and rare Southern long-leaf pine floors create the gracious setting. Guest rooms may include a canopy bed, fireplace or whirlpool tub. Enjoy the inn's in-ground pool or tennis court or take a riding lesson, then relax in the gazebo at sunset. Stuffed French toast with whipped cream and strawberries is often served in the original kitchen area with its large beehive fireplace.

Innkeeper(s): Bill & Eleonora Rezek. $179-299. MC, VISA, AX, DS, TC. 6 rooms with PB, 6 with FP and 3 suites. Breakfast and snacks/refreshments included in rates. Types of meals: Gourmet bkfst and early coffee/tea. Beds: KQDT. Cable TV, phone, turndown service, VCR and whirlpools in room. Air conditioning. Fax, swimming, tennis and library on premises. Handicap access. Small meetings hosted. Polish spoken. Antiquing, fishing, golf, live theater, parks and sporting events nearby.

Edgewood Manor B&B

232 Norwood Ave
Providence, RI 02905
(401)781-0099 (800)882-3285 Fax:(401)467-6311
E-mail: edgemanor@aol.com
Web: www.providence-lodging.com

Circa 1905. This 18-room Greek Revival Colonial mansion is two miles from downtown Providence between Narraganansett Bay and Roger Williams Park and Zoo. Built as a private home in 1905, the structure has served as a convent, an office and a rooming house; now it has been restored as a romantic bed & breakfast. From the hand-carved mantels and hand-painted ceilings in the foyer to the leaded- and stained-glass windows, the mansion harkens back to a bygone elegant era. Each of its eight guest rooms has a Jacuzzi tub and fireplace and is decorated in Victorian and Empire style. Six additional rooms are found in the Newhall House located directly next door. The full breakfast including a hot entrée is served in the dining room or on the patio. The local area offers some of the finest dining in all of New England.

Innkeeper(s): Joy Generali. $99-225. MC, VISA, AX, DC, DS, TC. TAC10. 14 rooms with PB, 2 with FP, 2 suites, 1 cottage, 1 guest house and 3 conference rooms. Breakfast included in rates. Types of meals: Gourmet bkfst. Beds: KQ. TV, turndown service, ceiling fan and VCR in room. Air conditioning. Fax, copier, library and bicycles for rent on premises. Weddings, small meetings, family reunions and seminars hosted. French spoken. Antiquing, art galleries, beaches, bicycling, canoeing/kayaking, fishing, golf, hiking, horseback riding, live theater, museums, parks, shopping, sporting events and wineries nearby.

Pets allowed: in cages.

Old Court B&B

144 Benefit St
Providence, RI 02903-1226
(401)751-2002 Fax:(401)272-4830
E-mail: reserve@oldcourt.com

Circa 1863. Adjacent to the historic Rhode Island Courthouse, this Italianate building originally served as an Episcopal rectory. Indoor shutters, chandeliers hanging from 12-foot ceilings and elaborate Italian marble mantelpieces provide the gracious setting for antique Victorian beds. Some rooms overlook the capitol. Brown University, Rhode Island School of Design and downtown Providence are a short walk away.

Innkeeper(s): Jon Rosenblatt. $115-260. TAC10. 10 rooms with PB.

Breakfast included in rates. Types of meals: Gourmet bkfst. Beds: KQDT. Phone and some refrigerators in room. Air conditioning. Fax and copier on premises. Weddings and small meetings hosted. Antiquing, live theater, parks, shopping and sporting events nearby.

Publicity: *New York Times.*

"My only suggestion is that you do everything in your power not to change it."

State House Inn

43 Jewett St
Providence, RI 02908-4904
(401)351-6111 Fax:(401)351-4261
E-mail: statehouseinn@edgenet.net
Web: www.providence-inn.com

Circa 1889. Shaker and Colonial furniture fill this turn-of-the-century home, located in the midst of a quaint and peaceful Providence neighborhood. The rooms provide amenities that  will please any business traveler and have the country comfort and elegance of days gone by. The common room contains a small library for guest use. A famed historic district, featuring restored homes and buildings, is three blocks away, and the capitol is a five-minute walk.

Innkeeper(s): Frank & Monica Hopton. $89-149. MC, VISA, AX, PC, TC. TAC10. 10 rooms with PB, 2 with FP. Breakfast included in rates. Types of meals: Full bkfst and afternoon tea. EP. Beds: KQ. Cable TV and phone in room. Air conditioning. Fax and copier on premises. Antiquing and parks nearby.

Publicity: *Providence Magazine. and Local Station - Channel 6.*

"Thank you again for the warm, comfortable and very attractive accommodations."

South Kingstown   H5

Admiral Dewey Inn

668 Matunuck Beach Rd
South Kingstown, RI 02879-7053
(401)783-2090 (800)457-2090
E-mail: joaninkp@aol.com
Web: www.admiraldeweyinn.com

Circa 1898. Although the prices have risen a bit since this inn's days as a boarding house (the rate was 50 cents per night), this Stick-style home still offers hospitality and comfort. The National Register inn is within walking distance of Matunuck Beach. Guests can enjoy the sea breeze from the inn's wraparound porch. Period antiques decorate the guest rooms, some of which offer ocean views.

Historic Interest: One half mile to Historic Theatre By The Sea.

Innkeeper(s): Joan Lebel. $100-150. MC, VISA, PC. 10 rooms, 8 with PB. Breakfast included in rates. Types of meals: Cont plus, early coffee/tea and picnic lunch. Beds: QDT. VCR, fax and copier on premises. Weddings, small meetings, family reunions and seminars hosted. Polish spoken. Antiquing, fishing, live theater, parks, shopping and water sports nearby.

Publicity: *Yankee Traveler and Rhode Island Monthly.*

Wakefield   H5

Brookside Manor

380-B Post Rd
Wakefield, RI 02879
(401)788-3527 Fax:(401)788-3530
E-mail: allyson@brooksidemanor.net
Web: www.brooksidemanor.net

Circa 1690. Both architecturally and historically, this Colonial manor house fits in the category of great country homes. Formerly part of a large estate, it has been converted into a luxurious inn. The original one-and-a-half-story, post and beam structure with hearth and chimney still stands. Enjoy public gathering rooms splendidly decorated and furnished with antiques and Oriental rugs. Dramatic guest bedrooms offer an escape to a relaxing yet refined elegance. Homemade sausage, scones, fruit and a frittata are typical af the breakfasts served. Eight acres of professionally landscaped gardens are bordered by brick and stone terraces. A pond and brook add a park-like setting.

Innkeeper(s): Allyson Huskisson & Bob Vitale. $125-250. MC, VISA, AX. 5 rooms with PB, 5 with FP. Breakfast, afternoon tea and snacks/refreshments included in rates. Types of meals: Gourmet bkfst, veg bkfst, early coffee/tea and gourmet dinner. Beds: KQT. Cable TV, phone, turndown service, fireplace and robes in room. Central air. Fax, copier, library, ice machine, complimentary soft drinks and juice on premises. Weddings and family reunions hosted. Italian spoken. Amusement parks, antiquing, art galleries, beaches, canoeing/kayaking, fishing, golf, hiking, horseback riding, live theater, museums, parks, shopping, sporting events, tennis, water sports and wineries nearby.

Publicity: *Italian Travel Magazine, Dove, Harper & Queens and Country Living.*

Larchwood Inn

521 Main St
Wakefield, RI 02879-4003
(401)783-5454 (800)275-5450 Fax:(401)783-1800
E-mail: larchwoodinn@xpos.com
Web: www.xpos.com/larchwoodinn.htm

Circa 1831. The Larchwood Inn and its adjacent sister inn, Holly House, were both constructed in the same era. The two are sprinkled with antiques and are family-run, with 20th-century amenities. Scottish touches are  found throughout the inn and the Tam O'Shanter Tavern. Three dining rooms offer breakfast, lunch and dinner. (Breakfast is an extra charge.) The tavern offers dancing on weekends. Beaches, sailing and deep sea fishing all are nearby.

Innkeeper(s): Francis & Diann Browning. $40-150. MC, VISA, AX, DC, CB, DS. TAC10. 19 rooms, 13 with PB, 3 with FP and 1 conference room. Types of meals: Full bkfst, lunch and dinner. Phone in room. Fax and copier on premises. Weddings, small meetings, family reunions and seminars hosted. Antiquing, live theater, shopping, downhill skiing and cross-country skiing nearby.

Publicity: *Country Inns and Backroads.*

Warwick E6

Fair Street Bed & Breakfast

525 Fair Street
Warwick, RI 02888
(401)781-5158
E-mail: stay@fair-street.com

Circa 1933. In pure New England style, this Dutch Colonial home perfectly depicts the historic charm of the area. Intimate antique-filled rooms exude this old-fashioned elegant charm. Outstanding hospitality and service promise a pleasurable stay. A thoughtful welcome basket of toiletries, bottled water and snacks is placed in each guest bedroom. A complete breakfast is the first delicious event of each day. The fragrant English garden, a profusion of colors, is sure to relax and rejuvenate.

Historic Interest: Historic Providence (6 miles), Pawtuxet Village (1/2 mile).
Innkeeper(s): Eric Gilbert & Richard Laninfa. $100. PC, TC. 2 rooms. Breakfast and snacks/refreshments included in rates. Types of meals: Full bkfst. Beds: QD. Cable TV and ceiling fan in room. Air conditioning. VCR and fax on premises. Italian spoken. Antiquing, art galleries, beaches, bicycling, canoeing/kayaking, fishing, golf, hiking, live theater, museums, parks, shopping, sporting events, tennis, water sports and wineries nearby.

Westerly I2

Kismet B&B

71 High St
Westerly, RI 02891-1812
(401)596-3237
E-mail: kismetbandb@webtv.net
Web: www.kismetbanb.com

Circa 1845. Book on just the right summer night at this inn and you may find yourself listening to summer pops or an old-time band concert from a ring-side seat. This Colonial home boasts a long front veranda lined with rocking chairs and summer furnishings overlooking Wilcox Park. The Victorian home is filled with antiques and a collection of wicker furnishings and is in the National Register of Historic Places. A light breakfast is served and the kitchen is open other times as well to guests during their stay. Shakespeare in the Park and other events are popular at the park or walk to nearby shops, two casinos, galleries, the Granite Theater or the train station. Rhode Island beaches and water activities are close by.

Innkeeper(s): Cindy Slay. Call for rates.. 4 rooms with PB, 1 suite and 1 conference room. Beds: KQD.

Shelter Harbor Inn

10 Wagner Rd
Westerly, RI 02891-4701
(401)322-8883 (800)468-8883 Fax:(401)322-7907

Circa 1810. This farmhouse at the entrance to the community of Shelter Harbor has been renovated and transformed to create a handsome country inn. Rooms, many with fireplaces, are in the main house, the barn and a carriage house. A third-floor deck with a hot tub, overlooks Block Island Sound. The dining room features local seafood and other traditional New England dishes. Nearby are secluded barrier beaches, stone fences and salt ponds.

Innkeeper(s): Jim Dey. $78-156. MC, VISA, AX, DC, CB, DS. 24 rooms with PB and 1 conference room. Breakfast included in rates. Types of meals: Full bkfst, lunch and dinner. Beds: QD. Phone in room. Air conditioning. VCR, spa, croquet court and two paddle tennis courts on premises. Weddings, small meetings and family reunions hosted. Amusement parks, antiquing, beaches, fishing, golf, shopping and tennis nearby.

Publicity: *Rhode Island Monthly and The Day.*

"This inn was, on the whole, wonderful."

South Carolina

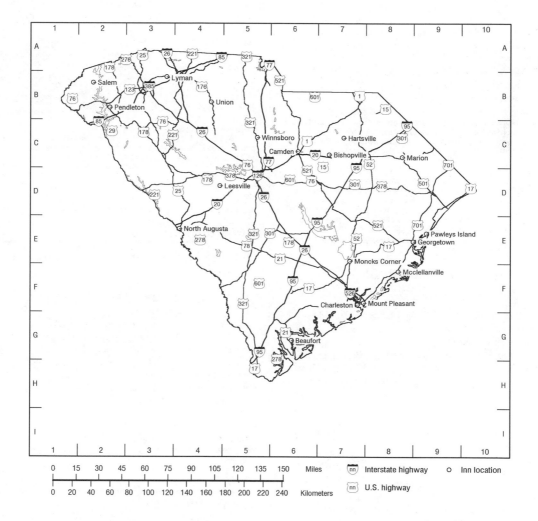

Beaufort   G6

The Beaufort Inn

809 Port Republic St
Beaufort, SC 29901-1257
(843)521-9000 Fax:(843)521-9500
E-mail: bftinn@hargray.com
Web: www.beaufortinn.com

Circa 1897. Every inch of this breathtaking inn offers something special. The interior is decorated to the hilt with lovely furnishings, plants, beautiful rugs and warm, inviting tones. Rooms include four-poster and canopy beds combined with the modern amenities such as fireplaces, wet bars and stocked refrigerators. Enjoy a complimentary full breakfast at the inn's gourmet restaurant. The chef offers everything from a light breakfast of fresh fruit, cereal and a bagel to heartier treats such as pecan peach pancakes and Belgium waffles served with fresh fruit and crisp bacon.

Historic Interest: History buffs can visit Secession House, where the first ordinance for Southern secession was drawn up. Tabby Manse and Old Sheldon Church, burned in both the Revolutionary and Civil wars, still stand today. Penn Center, the first school for freed slaves, is located on St. Helena Island.

Innkeeper(s): Associated Luxury Inns of Beaufort. $145-350. MC, VISA, AX, DS, PC, TC. TAC10. 21 rooms with PB, 9 with FP, 6 suites and 1 conference room. Breakfast included in rates. Types of meals: Gourmet bkfst, early coffee/tea, afternoon tea, gourmet dinner and room service. Beds: KQ. Cable TV, phone, ceiling fan and VCR in room. Air conditioning. Fax and copier on premises. Weddings, small meetings, family reunions and seminars hosted. Antiquing, fishing, live theater, parks, shopping and water sports nearby.
Publicity: *Beaufort, Southern Living, Country Inns, Carolina Style, US Air and Town & Country.*

The Cuthbert House Inn B&B

1203 Bay St
Beaufort, SC 29902-5401
(843)521-1315 (800)327-9275 Fax:(843)521-1314
E-mail: cuthbert@hargray.com
Web: www.cuthberthouseinn.com

Circa 1790. This 18th-century waterfront mansion, listed in the National Register, boasts a veranda overlooking Beaufort Bay. The home was built during Washington's presidency, and General W.T. Sherman was once a guest here. The home has been lovingly restored to its original grandeur. Rich painted walls are highlighted by fine molding. Hardwood floors are topped with Oriental rugs and elegant 19th-century furnishings. The morning meal is served in a breakfast room that overlooks the water. The surrounding area offers plenty of activities in every season, and for those celebrating a new marriage, a honeymoon suite is available.

Historic Interest: Located in the National Landmark district.
Innkeeper(s): Gary & Sharon Groves. $175-265. MC, VISA, AX, DS, PC, TC. TAC10. 7 rooms with PB, 2 suites and 2 conference rooms. Breakfast included in rates. Types of meals: Full bkfst, cont and early coffee/tea. Beds: KQ. Cable TV, phone, mini bar, robes, hair dryers and data port in room. Air conditioning. VCR, fax, bicycles, library, whirlpool, off street parking and beach towels on premises. Weddings, small meetings, family reunions and seminars

hosted. Antiquing, fishing, Parris Island USMC Depot, Ace Basin Tours, National Historic District tours, parks and water sports nearby.
Publicity: *Beaufort Gazette, Atlanta Journal-Constitution, Glamour, Travel & Leisure, Delta Airlines Sky Magazine, Shape Magazine, White Squall and House & Garden Channel.*

TwoSuns Inn Bed & Breakfast

1705 Bay St
Beaufort, SC 29902-5406
(843)522-1122 (800)532-4244 Fax:(843)522-1122
E-mail: twosuns@islc.net
Web: www.twosunsinn.com

Circa 1917. The Keyserling family built this Neoclassical Revival-style home, which was later used by the local board of education as housing for single, female teachers. The home has been completely refurbished, a difficult task, considering the home had been the victim of two fires. The U.S. Department of the Interior noted the renovation with a Historic Building Certification in 1996. Guest rooms boast bay views, and each has its own theme. A gourmet breakfast and "Tea and Toddy Hour" are included in the rates.
Innkeeper(s): Ron & Carrol Kay. $105 and up. MC, VISA, AX, DS, PC, TC. TAC10. 6 rooms with PB. Breakfast and afternoon tea included in rates. Types of meals: Full bkfst. Beds: KQ. TV, phone, ceiling fan and hair dryer in room. Air conditioning. VCR, fax, copier, bicycles and library on premises. Handicap access. Antiquing, fishing, golf, live theater, parks, shopping and tennis nearby.
Publicity: *Beaufort Gazette, Sandlapper, BBC 2 Travel Show December 19 and 1996.*

"One could not wish for a better experience."

Bennetsville   C8

Historic District Inns of Bennettsville

105 Jennings St
Bennetsville, SC 29512
(843)479-2066 (800)248-0128 Fax:(843)479-2393
E-mail: weamia@msn.com
Web: www.historicdistrictinns.com

Circa 1900. Three luxury inns: The Manse, The Ellerbe House and Hugh McColl Inn are situated in the quaint Historic District. All elegantly furnished with antiques, spacious suites offer sitting rooms, fireplaces and kitchens. Comfortable guest bedrooms feature thick comforters, fluffy pillows and plush linens. Continental breakfast is delivered to the room, and lunch is available in the on-site restaurant. This quiet but corporate-savvy town is centrally located to Myrtle Beach, S.C.; Pinehurst, N.C.; renown golf courses; and featured on the South Carolina Cotton Trail.
Innkeeper(s): Mary Altman. $75-125. 12 rooms with PB, 6 suites and 1 cottage. Beds: KQDT.

Bishopville   C7

The Foxfire B&B

416 N Main St
Bishopville, SC 29010-1442
(803)484-5643 (877)304-6335
Web: www.foxfirebedandbreakfast.com

Circa 1922. A cotton broker built this unusual home, tinged with Spanish influences such as its tile roof. The home is fashioned from bricks, and the front exterior is decorated with a wraparound porch with tile floors and ceiling fans. Guests often choose this location to relax, as it's lined with rockers, chairs and a porch swing. The three rooms are comfortable, with pieces

collected from around the world. Children are welcome and the innkeepers have games and swings. For breakfast, the innkeepers serve Swedish coffee, homemade muffins, fresh fruit and special items such as flannel cakes or stuffed French toast.

Innkeeper(s): Harry & Jean Woodmansee. $65-75. PC. 3 rooms, 2 with FP. Breakfast included in rates. Types of meals: Full bkfst, cont and early coffee/tea. Beds: QT. Cable TV and ceiling fan in room. Air conditioning. VCR, bicycles and library on premises. Small meetings hosted. Antiquing, fishing, golf, Darlington raceway, South Carolina Cotton Museum, museums, parks and tennis nearby.

Publicity: *Lee County Observer.*

"True Southern hospitality, we will be back with our family to enjoy your home again."

Camden   C6

Candlelight Inn

1904 Broad St
Camden, SC 29020-2606
(803)424-1057
E-mail: candlelightinncamden@yahoo.com

Circa 1933. Two acres of camellias, azaleas and oak trees surround this Cape Cod-style home. As per the name, the innkeepers keep a candle in each window, welcoming guests to this homey bed & breakfast. The decor is a delightful and tasteful mix of country, with quilts, hand-crafted samplers, poster beds, family antiques and traditional furnishings. Each of the rooms is named for someone significant in the innkeeper's life, and a picture of the special person decorates each room. Guests will enjoy the hearty breakfast, which changes daily. Several of innkeeper Jo Ann Celani's recipes have been featured in a cookbook, and one recipe won a blue ribbon at the Michigan State Fair.

Innkeeper(s): Jo Ann & George Celani. $90-125. MC, VISA, AX, DS, PC, TC. TAC10. 3 rooms, 2 with PB and 1 suite. Breakfast and snacks/refreshments included in rates. Types of meals: Full bkfst and early coffee/tea. Beds: QT. Phone and turndown service in room. Air conditioning. Library on premises. Antiquing, fishing, golf, two steeplechase races, live theater, parks, shopping and tennis nearby.

Publicity: *Chronicle-Independent, Sandlapper and Southern Inns and B&Bs.*

"You have captured the true spirit of a bed & breakfast."

Charleston   F7

1843 Battery Carriage House Inn

20 S Battery St
Charleston, SC 29401-2727
(843)727-3100 (800)775-5575 Fax:(843)727-3130
E-mail: bch@mymailstation.com
Web: www.batterycarriagehouse.com

Circa 1843. Just outside the door of this antebellum house, guests can enjoy the serenity of a Charleston garden. And outside the wrought iron gates lies White Point Gardens, the Battery and Charleston Harbor, enticing guests to romantic moonlight walks and sultry daytime strolls in one of Charleston's most beautiful locations. Guest rooms are in both

the Carriage House and in the ground floor of the Stephen Lathers House, a private residence. Renovations in many rooms have preserved the charm of the past, while increasing amenities, including cable television and steam

baths or Jacuzzis that add to the inn's romantic atmosphere. Silver Tray Continental Breakfast service is provided and evening turndown adds to the pampering, as well. The inn was featured in the filming of "North and South" and the interior rooms have been filmed for "Queen." In the afternoon, visitors often enjoy a glass of wine in the gardens.

Historic Interest: Fort Sumter and Plantations are nearby.

$99-269. MC, VISA, AX, DS, TC. TAC10. 11 rooms with PB. Types of meals: Cont. Beds: QT. Cable TV, phone, turndown service, ceiling fan and some with steam bath showers in room. Air conditioning. Fax on premises. Antiquing, art galleries, beaches, bicycling, fishing, golf, live theater, museums, parks, shopping and water sports nearby.

Publicity: *New York Times, Los Angeles Times and South Carolina Touring.*

A B&B At Unity Alley

4 Unity Alley
Charleston, SC 29401
(843)577-6660 Fax:(843)723-3346
E-mail: Unitybb@aol.com

Circa 1820. Although George Washington never actually slept here, he did keep his horses on the premises while he dined in a restaurant next door. Today, the bed & breakfast is certainly fit for more than a horse. In fact, the innkeepers bill the place as an "antique warehouse." Rooms are pristine and airy with the signature antiques as well as a few modern pieces. The manicured grounds include a small garden filled with orchids. Charleston is known for its outstanding cuisine, and there are many restaurants within walking distance. Guests also can stroll to shops and boutiques or take a walking tour past historic homes. Plantation tours and golf are other nearby attractions just a short drive away.

Innkeeper(s): Rick Schneider, Don Smith. $125-165. MC, VISA, AX, DC, CB, DS, PC, TC. 3 suites. Breakfast included in rates. Types of meals: Gourmet bkfst. Beds: KQ. Cable TV, phone and ceiling fan in room. Central air. Fax, copier and bicycles on premises. Antiquing, art galleries, beaches, bicycling, fishing, golf, live theater, museums, shopping, tennis and water sports nearby. Pets allowed: Small, under 15 lbs.

Ansonborough Inn

21 Hasell St
Charleston, SC 29401-2601
(803)723-1655 (800)522-2073 Fax:(843)577-6888
E-mail: info@ansonboroughinn.com
Web: www.ansonboroughinn.com

Circa 1900. This three-story, all-suite inn in the middle of Charleston's historic district was once a stationer's warehouse that a British admiral won in a poker game. Decorated in period antiques and reproductions, the inn with its 37 spacious suites has exposed heart pine beams, exposed brick walls and a three-story atrium. A delightful continental breakfast is served each morning in the library. It includes such items as fresh raisin bread, Danishes, bagels, fruits and juices. Each afternoon, wine and cheese as well as local delicacies and baked goods are served. The inn is near Waterfront Park, which has a gated entrance, brick walkways and wrought-iron benches. It's also a short distance from the Battery, the open-air Old City Market and a number of historic tours.

Innkeeper(s): Allison Fennell. $109-259. MC, VISA, AX, DS, TC. TAC10. 37 rooms with PB, 2 with FP and 2 conference rooms. Types of meals: Cont plus, early coffee/tea, afternoon tea and snacks/refreshments. Beds: KQT. Cable TV and phone in room. Central air. VCR, fax, copier, modem hook-up and data ports on premises. Handicap access. Weddings, small meetings and seminars hosted. Spanish spoken. Antiquing, art galleries, beaches, bicycling, canoeing/kayaking, fishing, golf, Historic city tours, aquarium, live theater, museums, parks, shopping and sporting events nearby.

Publicity: Southern Living, Travel Host and Seabreeze Magazine.

"Thank you for such charm and hospitality. Elegantly decorated. Warm and friendly staff."

Antebellum B&B at The Thomas Lamboll House

19 King St
Charleston, SC 29401-2734
(803)723-3212 (888)874-0793 Fax:(803)723-5222
E-mail: lamboll@aol.com

Circa 1735. A Colonial South Carolina judge, Thomas Lamboll, was the first resident of this impressive Colonial, located in Charleston's historic district. The home features two

stories of piazzas set up with wicker furnishings, where guests can catch a cool breeze in the afternoon. The rooms are appointed with fine antiques, including Chippendale chairs and an early 19th-century sideboard in the dining room. There are two guest rooms, each with French doors leading to the piazzas, that overlook rooftops and the Charleston Harbor in the distance.

Innkeeper(s): Marie & Emerson Read. $125-175. MC, VISA, DS, PC, TC. 2 rooms with PB, 2 with FP and 1 suite. Breakfast included in rates. Types of meals: Cont. Beds: QT. Cable TV, phone and ceiling fan in room. Air conditioning. Amusement parks, antiquing, fishing, live theater, parks, shopping, sporting events and water sports nearby.

Ashley Inn B&B

201 Ashley Ave
Charleston, SC 29403-5810
(843)723-1848 (800)581-6658 Fax:(843)579-9080
E-mail: ashleyinnbb@aol.com
Web: www.charleston-sc-inns.com

Circa 1832. Pampering guests is the specialty of the house at this bed & breakfast. The rose exterior has green shutters and porches on the first and second stories. Bright, colorful rooms are accented by polished, hardwood floors, beautiful rugs and glorious furnishings and collectibles. Guest rooms boast antique four-poster, pencil-post or canopied rice beds. Breakfasts at Ashley Inn create culinary memories. Savory sausage pie, peaches and cream stuffed waffles with praline sauce or eggs Benedict Ashley are only a few of the

mouth-watering specialties. An afternoon complete with plenty of homemade treats and evening sherry also is served. The innkeepers also provide bicycles for touring scenic Charleston.

Historic Interest: The inn is located in the Charleston historic district, full of interesting sites and shops. Ft. Sumter, The Battery, cabbage row, carriage tours and the market are nearby.

Innkeeper(s): Sally & Bud Allen. $85-250. MC, VISA, AX, DS, PC, TC. TAC10. 6 rooms with PB and 1 suite. Breakfast and afternoon tea included in rates. Types of meals: Full bkfst. Beds: KQDT. Antiquing, fishing, aquarium, live theater and water sports nearby.

Publicity: Charleston Post & Courier, LA Times and Country Inn Cooking.

"A truly pampering experience for both of us!"

Belvedere B&B

40 Rutledge Ave
Charleston, SC 29401-1702
(843)722-0973 (800)816-1664
Web: www.belvedereinn.com

Circa 1900. This Colonial Revival home with its semicircular portico, Ionic columns and four piazzas boasts a beautiful view of Charleston's Colonial Lake. Bright, airy rooms feature high ceilings with fans, polished wood floors, fireplaces, antique furnishings and Oriental rugs. Relax and enjoy the view on the piazzas or in one of the inn's public rooms. Belvedere B&B is close to many wonderful restaurants and shops.

Innkeeper(s): David S. Spell. $150-175. PC, TC. TAC10. 3 rooms with PB. Breakfast included in rates. Types of meals: Cont plus. Beds: Q. Cable TV, ceiling fan and ornamental fireplaces in room. Air conditioning. VCR and refrigerator on premises. Antiquing, fishing, live theater, parks, shopping, sporting events and water sports nearby.

Publicity: Discerning Traveler and Southern Brides.

Cannonboro Inn

184 Ashley Ave
Charleston, SC 29403-5824
(803)723-8572 (800)235-8039 Fax:(803)723-8007
E-mail: cannonboroinn@aol.com
Web: www.charleston-sc-inns.com

Circa 1853. Enjoy a breakfast feast of Cannonboro Inn Eggs Benedict served with warm French puff muffins and local fresh fruit on the columned piazza overlooking the country garden and fountain. Guest rooms feature luxurious furnishings and antique four-poster and canopy beds. After a day in the city on the inn's touring bicycles, return for a scrumptious afternoon tea of home-baked treats and sherry. Cannonboro Inn has been rated as one of the best places to stay in the South.

Historic Interest: The Charleston Museum, Gibbes Museum and Plantations are nearby.

Innkeeper(s): Bud & Sally Allen. $85-250. MC, VISA, AX, DS, PC, TC. TAC10. 5 rooms with PB and 1 suite. Breakfast and afternoon tea included in rates. Types of meals: Full bkfst. Beds: KQD. Cable TV and ceiling fan in room. Air conditioning. Bicycles and free off street parking on premises. Antiquing, fishing, golf, carriage rides, harbor tours, aquarium, live theater, parks, shopping, sporting events, tennis and water sports nearby.

Publicity: Chicago Sun-Times.

"A brochure cannot convey the friendly, warm atmosphere created by Bud & Sally."

Charleston Governor's House

117 Broad St
Charleston, SC 29401-2435
(843)720-2070 (800)720-9812
E-mail: innkeeper@governorshouse.com
Web: www.governorshouse.com

Circa 1760. One of the most classic of Southern cities, Charleston's grace and beauty can be experienced at one of its most historic and gracious inns. At the Charleston Governor's House, civility and romance are a tradition. Declared a National Historic Landmark, the former Governor's Mansion was built in 1760 and was the former home of Edward Rutledge, one of South Carolina's representatives to the First Continental Congress in 1775 and the youngest person to ratify and sign the Declaration of Independence a year later. After his capture and imprisonment by the British, he became governor of South Carolina and lived in this stately home. Today, one of the finest suites in the inn bears his name. Antique Italian chandeliers look down upon a king-size, arched-canopy bed, and a fireplace warms an elegant sitting area. When the weather is fine, a private porch makes a good spot for conversation. Three other beautifully appointed suites also feature fireplaces, canopy beds, marble whirlpools and showers, while four standard rooms have combinations of twelve-foot-high ceilings, canopy beds, sitting areas and porches. Hardwood floors extend throughout the inn. Homemade Charleston muffins and fresh local fruit are presented each morning in the dining room or on the spacious double veranda — also the locations for the inn's Lowcountry afternoon tea and evening sherry. Within walking distance of the inn are the other magnificent homes and gardens of the historic district of Charleston, the Battery and the Old Market.

Innkeeper(s): Karen Shaw. $130-345. PC, TC. 9 rooms with PB, 5 with FP, 4 suites and 2 conference rooms. Breakfast, afternoon tea and snacks/refreshments included in rates. Types of meals: Cont plus, early coffee/tea and room service. Beds: KQ. Cable TV, phone and ceiling fan in room. Central air. Fax, complimentary parking, Lowcountry Afternoon Tea and evening sherry on premises. Small meetings hosted. Antiquing, art galleries, beaches, bicycling, fishing, golf, horseback riding, historic sites, plantations, live theater, museums, parks, shopping, tennis and water sports nearby.
Publicity: *Southern Living, Discerning Traveler and Golf Digest.*

Fulton Lane Inn

202 King Street
Charleston, SC 29401-3109
(843)720-2600 (800)720-2688 Fax:(843)720-2940

Circa 1870. The family of Confederate blockade runner John Rugheimer built this charming brick building after the Civil War ended. Bright cheery decor and fine furnishings highlight the architecture, which includes cathedral ceilings and several fireplaces. The inn affords views of the city skyline, full of historic sites and gracious, Southern buildings. Guest rooms boast canopy beds draped with hand-strung netting and large, whirlpool tubs. The innkeeper includes a refrigerator in each room, and delivers breakfast on a silver tray. Wine and sherry are served in the lobby.

Historic Interest: Fulton Lane Inn is located in Charleston's historic district and the area abounds with historic sites.
Innkeeper(s): Michelle Woodhull. $150-295. MC, VISA, DC. TAC10. 27 rooms with PB, 8 with FP, 4 suites and 2 conference rooms. Breakfast included in rates. Types of meals: Cont and room service. EP. Beds: KQ. Cable TV, phone and turndown service in room. Air conditioning. Fax and child care on premises. Handicap access. Weddings, small meetings, family reunions and seminars hosted. Antiquing, fishing, live theater, parks, shopping and water sports nearby.
Publicity: *Southern Accents.*

Historic Charleston B&B Reservation Service

57 Broad St
Charleston, SC 29401-2901
(843)722-6606 (800)743-3583 Fax:(843)722-9589
E-mail: hcbb@charleston.net

Circa 1795. This bed & breakfast agency provides accommodations throughout Charleston's historic district. Rooms are located in private homes and carriage houses, offering a unique experience into the culture of Charleston. There are more than 50 different options; and guests can choose from accommodations such as two-bedroom cottages or romantic rooms with high-ceilings, fireplaces and family antiques. Some of the lodgings offer continental breakfasts, others might include a full breakfast. A member of the Historic Charleston Bed & Breakfast Reservation Service staff has inspected each of the locations.

$85-300. MC, VISA, PC. 50 rooms, 30 with PB, 6 with FP and 20 cottages. Breakfast included in rates. Types of meals: Full bkfst and cont. Beds: KQDT. TV and phone in room. Air conditioning. Bicycles are available at some locations on premises. Antiquing, fishing, parks, shopping and sporting events nearby.

John Rutledge House Inn

116 Broad St
Charleston, SC 29401
(843)723-7999 (800)476-9741 Fax:(843)720-2615
E-mail: jrh@charminginns.com

Circa 1763. John Rutledge, first governor of South Carolina, Supreme Court Justice, and an author and signer of the Constitution of the United States, wrote first drafts of the document in the stately ballroom of his Charleston home. In 1791 George Washington dined in this same room. Both men would be amazed by the house's recent restoration, which includes three lavish suites with elaborately carved Italian marble fireplaces, personal refrigerators, spas, air conditioning and televisions along with fine antiques and reproductions. Exterior ironwork on the house was designed in the 19th century and features palmetto trees and American eagles to honor Mr. Rutledge's service to the state and country.

Innkeeper(s): Linda Bishop. $185-375. MC, VISA, AX, DC. TAC10. 19 rooms with PB, 8 with FP, 3 suites and 1 conference room. Breakfast and afternoon tea included in rates. Types of meals: Full bkfst, cont plus and room service. EP. Beds: KQD. Cable TV, phone and turndown service in room. Air conditioning. Fax, child care and two carriage houses on premises. Handicap access. Weddings, small meetings, family reunions and seminars hosted. Spanish spoken. Antiquing, fishing, live theater, parks, shopping and water sports nearby.
Publicity: *Innsider, Colonial Homes, New York Times, Southern Living, Southern Accents, Gourmet, Bon Apetit., Deadly Pursuit and NBC.*

"Two hundred years of American history in two nights; first-class accommodations, great staff. John Rutledge should've had it so good!"

King George IV Inn

32 George St, Historic District
Charleston, SC 29401-1416
(843)723-9339 (888)723-1667 Fax:(843)723-7749
E-mail: info@kinggeorgeiv.com
Web: www.kinggeorgeiv.com

Circa 1792. This inn is a four-story Federal-style home with three levels of Charleston porches. All the rooms have decorative fireplaces, high ceilings, original wide-planked hardwood floors and finely crafted original moldings and architectural detail. Peter Freneau, who was a prominent Charleston journalist, merchant, ship owner and Jeffersonian politician, occupied the house for many years. The inn offers a hearty continental breakfast every morning. There is off-street parking available and King Street shopping and restaurants are just a short walk away.

Historic Interest: The inn is located in the United States' largest historic district with more than 3,000 historic homes and mansions.

Innkeeper(s): Debra, Terry. $99-179. MC, VISA, AX, PC, TC. 10 rooms, 8 with PB, 9 with FP and 4 suites. Breakfast included in rates. Types of meals: Cont plus and afternoon tea. Beds: QDT. Phone and television in room. Air conditioning. Fax on premises. Small meetings and family reunions hosted. Antiquing, fishing, aquarium, live theater, parks, shopping, sporting events and water sports nearby.

Kings Courtyard Inn

198 King St
Charleston, SC 29401
(843)723-7000 (800)845-6119 Fax:(843)720-2608
E-mail: kci@charminginns.com

Circa 1853. Having a Greek Revival style with unusual touches of Egyptian detail, this three-story building was designed by architect Francis D. Lee. The inn originally catered to plantation owners, shipping interests and merchant guests. Some of the rooms have fireplaces, canopied beds and views of the two inner courtyards or the garden. The building is one of historic King Street's largest and oldest structures and is at the center of Charleston's historic district.

Historic Interest: The home, which is listed in the National Register, is near all historic Charleston has to offer.

Innkeeper(s): Michelle Woodhull. $99-240. MC, VISA, AX, DC. TAC10. 41 rooms with PB, 13 with FP, 4 suites and 1 conference room. Breakfast included in rates. Types of meals: Full bkfst, cont plus and room service. EP. Beds: KQD. Cable TV, phone, turndown service and morning newspaper in room. Air conditioning. Fax, copier, spa and child care on premises. Handicap access. Weddings, small meetings, family reunions and seminars hosted. Antiquing, fishing, live theater, parks, shopping and water sports nearby.

Publicity: *Southern Living, USA Today, Innsider, Travel Holiday. and Deadly Pursuits.*

The Kitchen House

126 Tradd St
Charleston, SC 29401-2420
(843)577-6362 Fax:(843)965-5615

Circa 1732. This elegant, pre-Revolutionary War house was once the home of Dr. Peter Fayssoux, who served as Surgeon General in the Continental Army during the Revolutionary War. His descendant Bernard Elliot Bee became the Confederate general who bestowed the nickname of "Stonewall" to General Stonewall Jackson. The kitchen building has been restored around its four original fireplaces using antique materials. The inn's patio overlooks a Colonial herb garden, pond and fountain. The pantry and refrigerator are stocked with breakfast items. Juice, cereals, eggs, fresh fruit, specialty teas and coffee are provided for guests. Afternoon sherry awaits guests on arrival and a concierge service is offered.

Historic Interest: Located in the heart of Charleston's historic district, the inn offers close access to many museum homes and antique shopping.

Innkeeper(s): Lois Evans. $150-400. MC, VISA, PC, TC. TAC5. 4 rooms with PB. Breakfast included in rates. Types of meals: Full bkfst. Beds: QT. Cable TV, phone and VCR in room. Air conditioning. Fax, copier, library and concierge Service on premises. Antiquing, fishing, golf, live theater, parks, shopping, sporting events, tennis and water sports nearby.

Publicity: *New York Times and Colonial Homes.*

"By all comparisons, one of the very best."

Lodge Alley Inn

195 E Bay St
Charleston, SC 29401-2193
(843)722-1611 (800)845-1004 Fax:(843)577-7497
E-mail: alleyinn@bellsoiuth.net

Circa 1773. Several 18th-century warehouses, now handsomely restored, surround a courtyard and fountain and comprise the Lodge Alley Inn. Fashioned from the buildings are attractive guest rooms and spacious suites with period reproductions, Oriental rugs, high ceilings and crown moldings. Some offer fireplaces. In the evening, sherry and cookies are served, or you can dine at the inn's restaurant. Walk to galleries and restaurants, Waterfront Park, Rainbow Row, the High Battery or City Market.

Innkeeper(s): David Price. $139-375. MC, VISA, AX. 93 rooms with PB, 59 with FP, 28 suites and 3 conference rooms. Types of meals: Room service. Beds: KQD. Cable TV, phone, turndown service, VCR and personal voice-mail in room. Air conditioning. Fax and copier on premises. Weddings, small meetings, family reunions and seminars hosted. Antiquing, fishing, live theater and shopping nearby.

The Palmer Home B&B

5 East Battery
Charleston, SC 29401
(843)853-1574 (888)723-1574 Fax:(843)723-7983
E-mail: palmerbnb@aol.com
Web: www.palmerhomebb.com

Circa 1849. With its magnificent view of the Charleston Harbour and historic Fort Sumter, this pink and white Italianesque mansion is one of 50 most famous homes in the city. The house features 30 rooms, 15 bedrooms, 10 fireplaces and antiques dating back 200 years. The property includes the main house, carriage house and pool. Little David, the first submarine discharged during the war between the states was invented in this house. Fresh-squeezed orange juice, croissants, bagels and fresh fruit is offered each morning.

Innkeeper(s): Francess Palmer Hogan. $175-300. PC. TAC10. 3 rooms with PB and 1 suite. Breakfast included in rates. Types of meals: Cont. Beds: KQD. Cable TV, phone, ceiling fan and VCR in room. Air conditioning. Fax, swimming and free parking on premises. Weddings and small meetings hosted. Antiquing, fishing, golf, live theater, parks, sporting events, tennis and water sports nearby.

Planters Inn

112 N Market St
Charleston, SC 29401-3118
(843)722-2345 (800)845-7082 Fax:(843)577-2125
E-mail: reservations@plantersinn.com
Web: www.plantersinn.com

Circa 1844. Prepare for a getaway of romance, elegance and history at this opulent, four-diamond-rated inn, located in historic Charleston. Built decades prior to the Civil War, the inn has watched Charleston grow and change. The interior displays the height of Southern elegance and charm. Rooms are decorated with rich wallcoverings, elegant furnishings and four-poster beds topped with the finest of linens. The inn's restaurant, Peninsula Grill, has been named one of the best new restaurants in the country by Esquire magazine, and the dining room serves a hearty breakfast including scrumptious pastries freshly baked in the kitchen and waffles and omelets. Guests, if they choose, may dine al fresco in a landscaped courtyard. Rated "Blue Shield" by Relais & Chateaux and 4 Diamond by AAA, the inn also offers romance and history packages.

Innkeeper(s): Larry Spelts, Jr. $175-300. MC, VISA, AX, DC, DS. TAC10. 62 rooms with PB. Types of meals: Full bkfst. Beds: KQ. Turndown service in room. Air conditioning. Fax and copier on premises. Small meetings hosted. Antiquing, live theater and shopping nearby.

Thirty Six Meeting Street

36 Meeting St
Charleston, SC 29401-2737
(843)722-1034 Fax:(843)723-0068
E-mail: abrandt@awod.com
Web: www.thirtysixmeetingstreet.com

Circa 1740. The gracious craftsmanship of this Georgian Charleston single house offers the best kind of Charleston experience. The historic home has a library, two piazzas with columns and balusters and fine detailing in woodwork and staircase. The drawing room features a fireplace with mahogany fretwork. There's a two-bedroom suite in what was once the old kitchen. It offers two fireplaces, including a 1740 fireplace with finely carved mantel and molding. A mahogany four-poster rice bed and European iron bed are the focal points of the bedrooms. The Pettigrew suite upstairs offers a Thomas Elfe rice bed, a sitting area and a view of the garden of the former Royal Governors House. Kitchenettes are in each suite and a continental breakfast is stocked in each room. There are bicycles to borrow, but walking offers a wealth of experience. Within a block or two is the battery and White Point Gardens, the Nathaniel Russell House Museum and the Calhoun Mansion House Museum. The innkeepers are native Charlestonians.

Historic Interest: Fort Sumter.

Innkeeper(s): Vic & Anne Brandt. $85-160. MC, VISA, DS, PC, TC. 5 rooms, 1 with PB, 2 with FP and 2 suites. Breakfast included in rates. Types of meals: Cont plus. Beds: Q. TV and phone in room. Central air. Fax and copier on premises. Antiquing, art galleries, beaches, bicycling, canoeing/kayaking, fishing, golf, hiking, live theater, museums, parks, shopping, tennis and water sports nearby.

Vendue Inn

19 Vendue Range
Charleston, SC 29401-2129
(843)577-7970 (800)845-7900
E-mail: vendueinnresv@aol.com
Web: www.vendueinn.com

Circa 1864. Created from French Quarter warehouses, Vendue Inn is in the center of Charleston's historic district and a short stroll from the historic harbor and Waterfront Park. The bright lobby features polished pine floors, Oriental rugs, antiques and Low Country art. Fireplaces and marble Jacuzzi tubs with separate showers are offered in the spacious suites. There are four-poster and canopy beds, luxurious bathrooms, French milled soaps, fresh flowers, two-line phones with data ports and many other amenities. The Music Room is the setting for afternoon wine and cheese and evening cordials. Turndown service, a full Southern breakfast buffet and the morning paper are special

features. The inn's Library Restaurant offers American cuisine with a Southern flair. The renovated and expanded Rooftop Terrace is known for its panoramic views. A friendly concierge can arrange carriage rides, historic walking tours and reservations for special events. Walk to fine antique shops, historic neighborhoods, art galleries and the Battery or borrow complimentary bicycles for a ride around town.

Innkeeper(s): Coyne & Linda Edmison. $135-305. MC, VISA, AX, DC, DS, PC, TC. 65 rooms with PB, 26 with FP and 4 conference rooms. Breakfast included in rates. Types of meals: Full bkfst, lunch and dinner. Beds: KQD. Cable TV, turndown service and ceiling fan in room. Air conditioning. VCR, fax and copier on premises. Beaches, golf and live theater nearby.

Publicity: *Southern Living, Bon Appetit, Travel, New York Times and In-Style Magazine.*

Victoria House Inn

208 King St
Charleston, SC 29401
(843)720-2944 (800)933-5464 Fax:(843)720-2930

Circa 1898. Enjoy the gracious decor of the Victorian era while staying at this Romanesque-style inn, located in the heart of Charleston's historic district along King Street's famed Antique

Row. Some rooms boast working fireplaces, while others feature romantic whirlpool baths. Champagne breakfasts are delivered to the bedchambers each morning, and the nightly turndown service includes chocolates on your pillow. Enjoy a glass of sherry before heading out to one of Charleston's many fine restaurants. The Victoria House Inn is close to a variety of antique shops and fashionable boutiques.

Historic Interest: The inn is within walking distance of plenty of historic homes and museums, and walking tours are available.

Innkeeper(s): Michelle Woodhull. $150-270. MC, VISA, DC. TAC10. 18 rooms with PB, 4 with FP, 4 suites and 1 conference room. Breakfast included in rates. Types of meals: Cont plus and room service. EP. Beds: KD. Cable TV, phone and turndown service in room. Air conditioning. Fax, copier and child care on premises. Handicap access. Weddings, small meetings, family reunions and seminars hosted. Antiquing, fishing, live theater, parks, shopping and water sports nearby.

Publicity: *Washington Post and Great Country Inns.*

Villa De La Fontaine B&B

138 Wentworth St
Charleston, SC 29401-1734
(843)577-7709
Web: charleston.cityinformation.com/villa/

Circa 1838. This magnificent Greek Revival manor is among Charleston's finest offerings. The grounds are lush with gardens and manicured lawns, and ionic columns adorn the impressive exterior. The innkeeper is a retired interior designer, and his elegant touch is found throughout the mansion, including many 18th-century antiques. A fully trained chef prepares the gourmet breakfasts, which are served in a solarium with a hand-painted mural and 12-foot windows. The chef's recipe for cornmeal waffles

was featured in a Better Homes & Gardens' cookbook. The inn is located in the heart of Charleston's historic district, three blocks from the market area.

Innkeeper(s): Aubrey Hancock. $125-200. PC, TC. 4 rooms with PB and 1 cottage. Breakfast included in rates. Types of meals: Gourmet bkfst. Beds: KQT. TV in room. Central air. Antiquing, fishing, medical U, live theater, parks, shopping, sporting events and water sports nearby.

Publicity: *New York Times.*

"What a wonderful vacation we had as recipients of your lavish hospitality."

Wentworth Mansion

149 Wentworth St
Charleston, SC 29401
(843)853-1886 (888)466-1886
E-mail: wentworthmansion@aol.com

Circa 1886. This stately Second Empire mansion, designed originally as an opulent private residence for a wealthy cotton merchant, features the architectural details that one would expect to find in a home of this grandeur — hand-carved marble fireplaces, intricately detailed woodwork, Tiffany stained-glass windows and gleaming inlaid wood floors. Guest rooms have been historically restored and boast an elegant combination of antique furnishings and the modern comforts such as oversized whirlpools, most with a separate spacious shower, and working gas fireplaces. A breathtaking view of historic Charleston is accessible via the spiral staircase that leads to the towering cupola. Guests are invited to enjoy a complimentary breakfast buffet, afternoon tea, wine and hors d'oeuvres.

Innkeeper(s): Bob Seidler. $265-695. MC, VISA, AX, DC, DS, PC, TC. TAC10. 21 rooms with PB, 19 with FP, 7 suites and 2 conference rooms. Breakfast and afternoon tea included in rates. Types of meals: Room service. Beds: K. Cable TV, phone and turndown service in room. Air conditioning. Fax, copier and library on premises. Handicap access. Weddings, small meetings and seminars hosted. Antiquing, fishing, golf, live theater, parks, shopping, tennis and water sports nearby.

Georgetown   E8

1790 House B&B Inn

630 Highmarket St
Georgetown, SC 29440-3652
(843)546-4821 (800)890-7432
E-mail: jwiley1212@cs.com
Web: www.1790house.com

Circa 1790. Located in the heart of a historic district, this beautifully restored West Indies Colonial just celebrated its 200th birthday. The spacious rooms feature 11-foot ceilings and seven fireplaces, three in the guest bedrooms. The inn's decor reflects the plantations of a bygone era. Guests can stay in former slave quarters, renovated to include a queen bedroom and sitting area. Each of the romantic rooms features special touches, such as the Rice Planters' Room with its four-poster, canopy bed and window seat. The Dependency Cottage is a perfect honeymoon hideaway with a Jacuzzi tub and a private entrance enhanced with gardens and a patio. The inn is located one hour north of Charleston and 45 minutes south of Myrtle Beach.

Historic Interest: The Prince George Episcopal Church, the first church established in the district, is across the street from the home. The area offers several historic homes, some dating back to the 1740s, including the Kaminski House Museum and Hopsewee Plantation.

Innkeeper(s): John & Patricia Wiley. $95-140. MC, VISA, AX, DS, PC, TC. TAC10. 6 rooms with PB, 1 with FP and 1 cottage. Breakfast and snacks/refreshments included in rates. Types of meals: Gourmet bkfst and picnic lunch. Beds: KQT. Cable TV, phone and ceiling fan in room. Air conditioning. VCR, hammock, ping pong table and board games on premises. Weddings, small meetings and family reunions hosted. Antiquing, fishing, tours, boats, tram, live theater, parks and shopping nearby.

Publicity: *Brides, Georgetown Times, Sun News, Charlotte Observer, Southern Living. USAir, Augusta, Pee Dee and Sandlapper.*

"The 1790 House always amazes me with its beauty. A warm welcome in a lovingly maintained home. Breakfasts were a joy to the palate."

Alexandra's Inn

620 Prince St
Georgetown, SC 29440
(843)527-0233 (888)557-0233 Fax:(843)520-0718

Circa 1890. This stunning Georgian Colonial stands on half an acre in the historic district of Georgetown on the Intracoastal Waterway near Myrtle Beach. Built shortly after the Civil War, it is decorated in a Gone with the Wind style, and all the guest rooms are named after characters in the movie. The grounds are a beautiful mixture of English gardens, brickwork, Magnolia trees and walkways lined with boxwoods. Inside are pine floors and a fireplace in each of the five guest bedrooms, as well as in the two-bedroom carriage house (where children are welcome). Breakfast includes such tasty entrees as fruit, juice, fresh-baked muffins, coffee cake or breads and hot egg puffs, baked French toast, waffles, or pancakes. Georgetown is the "Ghost Capital of the South" and tours of the town may be taken by boat or tram.

Innkeeper(s): Vit & Diane Visbaras. $80-135. MC, VISA, AX, DS, PC, TC. TAC5. 5 rooms with PB, 5 with FP and 1 guest house. Breakfast and snacks/refreshments included in rates. Types of meals: Gourmet bkfst, early coffee/tea and afternoon tea. Beds: KQ. Cable TV, phone, turndown service, ceiling fan and fireplace in room. Central air. Fax, copier and swimming on premises. Weddings hosted. Amusement parks, antiquing, art galleries, beaches, canoeing/kayaking, fishing, golf, live theater, parks, shopping and water sports nearby.

Pets allowed: Small, only in Carriage House.

Du Pre House LLC

921 Prince St
Georgetown, SC 29440-3549
(843)546-0298 (877)519-9499
E-mail: richard.barnett@gte.net
Web: www.duprehouse.com

Circa 1740. The lot upon which this pre-Revolutionary War gem stands was partitioned off in 1734, and the home built six years later. Three guest rooms have fireplaces, and all are decorated with a poster bed. A full breakfast is prepared featuring such items as French toast, specialty egg dishes, fresh fruit and home-baked muffins. For those who love history, Georgetown, South Carolina's third oldest city,

offers more than 60 registered National Historic Landmarks.

Innkeeper(s): Judy & Richard Barnett. $99-125. MC, VISA, AX, PC, TC. TAC10. 5 rooms with PB, 3 with FP. Breakfast, afternoon tea and snacks/refreshments included in rates. Types of meals: Gourmet bkfst, early coffee/tea and picnic lunch. Beds: QT. Turndown service, ceiling fan and bathrobes in room. Air conditioning. Spa, swimming and library on premises. Weddings, small meetings and family reunions hosted. Amusement parks, antiquing, fishing, golf, Myrtle Beach, plantation tours, live theater, parks, shopping and water sports nearby.

Harbor House

15 Cannon St
Georgetown, SC 29440
(843)546-6532 (877)511-0101
E-mail: info@harborhousebb.com
Web: www.harborhousebb.com

Circa 1765. Sitting proudly on the banks of the Sampit River, this impressive three-story Georgian house with distinctive red roof has been a welcoming beacon of hospitality for almost two-and-a-half centuries. Winyah Bay's blue waters and the ocean beyond are easily seen from this immaculately restored B&B. Original Colonial moldings, heart pine floors and eight fireplaces reside with early American antiques, family heirlooms and Oriental rugs. Guest bedrooms include a choice of a four-poster rice, pencil-post or sleigh bed. Served in the formal dining room, a Southern-style  breakfast may include low country shrimp and grits, fresh melon, ham biscuits, sweet potato pancakes with bananas and rum, bacon and baked apples. Enjoy hors d'oeuvres in the parlor or while rocking riverside on the front porch.

Innkeeper(s): Meg Tarbox. $135-155. MC, VISA, PC. TAC10. 4 rooms with PB. Breakfast and snacks/refreshments included in rates. Types of meals: Gourmet bkfst and early coffee/tea. Beds: KQ. Cable TV, phone and fireplace in room. Central air. Bicycles on premises. Amusement parks, antiquing, art galleries, beaches, bicycling, canoeing/kayaking, fishing, golf, museums, parks, shopping and water sports nearby.

Mansfield Plantation B&B Country Inn

1776 Mansfield Rd
Georgetown, SC 29440-6923
(843)546-6961 (800)355-3223 Fax:(843)545-7395
E-mail: mansfield_plantation@prodigy.net
Web: www.bbonline.com/sc/mansfield/

Circa 1800. Listed in the National Register, and featured in Mel Gibson's movie, The Patriot, Mansfield Plantation is a perfect respite for those in search of romance and history in a natural, secluded setting. The large dining room and sitting rooms are furnished with the owner's collections of 19th-century American antiques that include paintings, china, silver, furniture and gilt-framed mirrors. Accommodations include three guesthouses, each decorated in a romantic style and boasting fireplaces, hardwood floors, high ceilings, comfortable furnishings and collectibles. The vast grounds (900 private acres), shaded by moss-draped oaks, provide ideal spots for relaxing. Enjoy azalea and camellia gardens, as well as views of the surrounding marshlands. Guests can relax in hammocks or swings, watch for birds or enjoy a bike ride. Boating on the Black River is another possibility. Guests may bring their own boats or rent canoes or kayaks nearby. Among the plantation's notable historic features are a schoolhouse, kitchen, winnowing house, slave village and chapel, all of which predate the Civil War.

Historic Interest: The Rice Museum and Kaminski House Museum are among the historic sites in downtown Georgtown, which is 3.5 miles from the plantation. Brookgreen Gardens, which features a nationally known sculpture garden, is about a half hour away.

Innkeeper(s): Sally and James Cahalan. $95-135. PC, TC. TAC10. 8 rooms with PB, 8 with FP and 1 conference room. Breakfast included in rates. Types of meals: Full bkfst and gourmet dinner. Beds: KQD. TV and VCR in room. Central air. Fax, bicycles and library on premises. Weddings, small meetings, family reunions and seminars hosted. Antiquing, beaches, golf and live theater nearby.

Pets allowed: In room with prior approval.
Publicity: *Georgetown Times, Charleston News & Courier, Sandlapper, Pee Dee Magazine, Charleston Magazine. and The Patriot.*

"Handsome furnishings, wildlife walks, sports and hunting opportunities galore, and a sumptuous atmosphere all make for a weekend retreat to remember."

Hartsville   C7

Missouri Inn B&B

314 E Home Ave
Hartsville, SC 29550-3716
(843)383-9553 Fax:(843)383-9553
E-mail: stay@missouriinn.com

Circa 1901. It is from the third owners of this Federal-style inn that it derives its name. The home was at that time owned by the innkeepers' grandparents, F.E. and Emily Fitchett, and "Missouri" was the nickname given to Emily by her son-in-law. The entire house, including the five guest rooms, are decorated with antiques, and features wallpaper original to the home. The full breakfasts are hearty and homemade. The home, located in the town historic district, is across the street from Coker College and four blocks from downtown Hartsville.

Innkeeper(s): Kyle & Kenny Segars. $75-85. MC, VISA, AX, PC, TC. 5 rooms with PB, 3 with FP. Breakfast included in rates. Types of meals: Gourmet bkfst, early coffee/tea, lunch, afternoon tea and gourmet dinner. Beds: KQT. Cable TV, phone, ceiling fan, robes, flowers, mints and heated towel racks in room. Air conditioning. VCR, fax, copier and library on premises. Handicap access. Weddings, small meetings, family reunions and seminars hosted. Antiquing, fishing, golf, parks, tennis and water sports nearby.

Leesville   D4

The Able House Inn

244 E Columbia Ave
Leesville, SC 29070-9284
(803)532-2763 Fax:(803)532-2763
E-mail: ablehouse@pbtcomm.net

Circa 1939. This elegant, white brick home was built by a local druggist. Relax in the tastefully decorated living room or lounge on a comfy wicker chair among the large plants in the sunroom. Guest rooms, named after various relatives, boast beautiful amenities such as a canopied bed or window seats. Jennifer's Room opens into a sitting room with a window seat so large, some guests have snuggled down for a restful night's sleep instead of the large, brass and enamel four-poster bed. Innkeepers offer guests snacks/refresh-  ments in the evening and turndown service each night. Wake to freshly ground coffee before taking on the day. During the warmer months, innkeepers offer guests the use of their swimming pool.

Historic Interest: Historic Charleston is three hours from the inn.

Innkeeper(s): Jack & Annabelle Wright. $70-85. MC, VISA, PC, TC. 5 rooms with PB and 1 suite. Breakfast and snacks/refreshments included in rates. Types of meals: Cont plus and early coffee/tea. Beds: QD. Cable TV, phone, turndown service and ceiling fan in room. Air conditioning. VCR, fax, copier and swimming on premises. Weddings, small meetings and family reunions hosted. Antiquing, fishing, golf, live theater, shopping, sporting events, tennis and water sports nearby.

Publicity: *Sandlapper and State Newspaper.*

"Thank you for the warm Southern welcome. Your place is absolutely beautiful, very inviting. The food was extraordinary!"

Lyman   B3

Walnut Lane Inn

110 Ridge Rd
Lyman, SC 29365
(864)949-7230 Fax:(864)949-1633
E-mail: walnutlaneinn@home.com
Web: www.walnutlaneinn.com

Circa 1902. This three-story Greek Revival manor was once
the headquarters for a working cotton plantation. Some of the
home's original furnishings including mantel tops, a bed, and

mirrors are mixed with other
antique pieces in the parlor
and spacious guest rooms.
There's a special suite available for families. Breakfast is
offered in the formal dining
room, which boasts vintage-style wallpapers, wood paneling, a
fireplace and chandelier. A hearty Southern menu is served.
The eight acres that surround the inn include a peach orchard
as well as other fruit trees. Outlet shopping is particularly popular in the area, but there are also galleries, concerts and live
theatre. The innkeepers can help with golf arrangements and
reservations for country club dining.

Historic Interest: Cowpens Battleground (15 miles), Biltmore Estate (50 miles).

Innkeeper(s): David Ades & Hoyt Dottry. $85-105. MC, VISA, AX, DS, PC,
TC. 6 rooms with PB, 1 suite and 1 conference room. Breakfast included in
rates. Types of meals: Full bkfst, early coffee/tea and snacks/refreshments.
Beds: QDT. Cable TV and turndown service in room. Central air. VCR, fax,
copier, library and two-bedroom suite on premises. Weddings, small meetings, family reunions and seminars hosted. Antiquing, art galleries, bicycling,
canoeing/kayaking, fishing, golf, hiking, horseback riding, live theater, museums, parks, shopping and sporting events nearby.

Marion   C8

Montgomery's Grove

408 Harlee St
Marion, SC 29571-3144
(843)423-5220 (877)646-7721

Circa 1893. The stunning rooms of this majestic Eastlake-style
manor are adorned in Victorian tradition with Oriental rugs, polished hardwood floors, chandeliers and gracious furnishings.
High ceilings and fireplaces in each room
complete the elegant look. Guest rooms are
filled with antiques and magazines or
books from the 1890s. Hearty full
breakfasts are served each day, and
candlelight dinner packages can be
arranged. Guests will appreciate this

inn's five acres of century-old trees and gardens. The inn is about
a half-hour drive to famous Myrtle Beach and minutes from I-95.

Historic Interest: Brittons Neck (15 minutes), Camden, S.C., (40 minutes),
Charleston (70 minutes).

Innkeeper(s): Coreen & Richard Roberts. $90-110. 5 rooms, 3 with PB and
1 suite. Breakfast included in rates. Types of meals: Full bkfst, lunch, picnic
lunch, afternoon tea and gourmet dinner. Beds: KQ. Antiquing, fishing, live
theater and water sports nearby.

Publicity: *Pee Dee Magazine, Sandlapper, Marion Star, Palmetto Places TV
and Country Living.*

McClellanville   F8

Laurel Hill Plantation B&B

8913 N Hwy 17
McClellanville, SC 29458-9423
(843)887-3708 (888)887-3708 Fax:(843)887-3878
E-mail: laurelhill@prodigy.net

Circa 1991. The wraparound porches at this reconstructed
1850-style plantation home provide splendid views of salt
marshes, creeks, islands and waterways. The home was
destroyed in 1989 by Hurricane Hugo but has been lovingly

rebuilt in its original Low Country style and
is a nature lover's delight. It is furnished with antiques, primitives
and folk art. Even in the rain, a
favorite spot is rocking on the
porch and taking in the
panoramic water views.

Historic Interest: Historic Charleston is about 30 miles away.

Innkeeper(s): Jackie & Lee Morrison. $125-150. PC, TC. TAC10. 4 rooms
with PB. Breakfast included in rates. Types of meals: Full bkfst, country bkfst
and early coffee/tea. Beds: QD. TV, phone and ceiling fan in room. Central
air. Refreshments available on premises. Antiquing, beaches, canoeing/kayak-
ing, fishing, golf, hiking and horseback riding nearby.

Publicity: *Atlanta Journal, Country Living, Seabreeze, Pee Dee and State.*

Moncks Corner   E7

Rice Hope Plantation Inn

206 Rice Hope Dr
Moncks Corner, SC 29461-9781
(843)761-4832 (800)569-4038 Fax:(843)884-0223
E-mail: ric.edens@mindspring.com
Web: www.ricehope.com

Circa 1840. Resting on 285 secluded acres of natural beauty,
this historic mansion sits among oaks on a bluff overlooking the
Cooper River. A stay here is a visit to yesteryear, where it is said
to be 45 short minutes and three long centuries from downtown Charleston. Formal gardens boast a 200-year-old camellia
and many more varieties of trees and plants, making it a perfect
setting for outdoor weddings or other special occasions. Nearby
attractions include the Trappist Monastery at Mepkin Plantation,
Francis Marion National Forest and Cypress Gardens.

Innkeeper(s): Jamie Edens. $85-165. MC, VISA, AX. 5 rooms with PB and 1
conference room. Breakfast included in rates. Types of meals: Full bkfst, cont
plus, early coffee/tea and lunch. Beds: KQD. Ceiling fan in room. Air conditioning. Weddings, small meetings, family reunions and seminars hosted.
Antiquing and fishing nearby.

Mount Pleasant   F7

Guilds Inn

101 Pitt St
Mount Pleasant, SC 29464-5318
(843)881-0510 (800)331-0510
Web: www.guildsinn.com

Circa 1888. This restored home is located in the heart of Mount
Pleasant's Old Village National Historic District. The inn is six
minutes from historic Charleston and the beaches of Sullivan's
Island and the Isle of Palms. Luxurious amenities include

whirlpool tubs. There also is a doll collection on display. It is located in the famous Shem Creek seafood restaurant district.

Historic Interest: The area is full of historic sites, including Old Village National Register District, Patriots Point Maritime Museum, Boone Hall Plantation, Charles Pinckney Historic Site, Fort Sumter, Fort Moultrie, Magnolia Gardens and the Middleton Plantation and Gardens.

Innkeeper(s): Lou Edens. $85-165. MC, VISA, AX. TAC10. 6 rooms with PB. Types of meals: Cont. Beds: KQT. Cable TV, phone, ceiling fan, VCR and whirlpool tubs in room. Air conditioning.

Publicity: *Travelhost, Charleston News & Courier, Charlotte Observer and Columbia State Paper.*

North Augusta   E3

Rosemary & Lookaway Halls

804 Carolina Ave
North Augusta, SC 29841
(803)278-6222 Fax:(803)278-4877
Web: www.augustainns.com

Circa 1902. These historic homes are gracious examples of Southern elegance and charm. Manicured lawns adorn the exterior of both homes, which appear almost as a vision out of "Gone With the Wind." The Rosemary Hall boasts a spectacular heart-of-pine staircase. The homes stand as living museums, filled to the brim with beautiful furnishings and elegant decor, all highlighted by stained-glass windows, chandeliers and lacy touches. Some guest rooms include Jacuzzis, while others offer verandas. A proper afternoon tea is served each afternoon at Rosemary Hall. The Southern hospitality begins during the morning meal. The opulent gourmet fare might include baked orange-pecan English muffins served with Canadian bacon or, perhaps, a Southern strata with cheese and bacon. The catering menu is even more tasteful, and many weddings, showers and parties are hosted at these inns.

Innkeeper(s): Sandra Croy. $75-195. MC, VISA, AX, DC, CB, DS, TC. TAC10. 23 rooms with PB and 2 conference rooms. Breakfast and snacks/refreshments included in rates. Types of meals: Full bkfst, cont plus and early coffee/tea. Beds: KQDT. Cable TV, phone and turndown service in room. Air conditioning. Fax and copier on premises. Handicap access. Weddings, small meetings, family reunions and seminars hosted. Antiquing, fishing, parks, shopping, sporting events and water sports nearby.

Pawleys Island   E9

Litchfield Plantation

King's River Rd, PO Box 290
Pawleys Island, SC 29585
(843)237-9121 (800)869-1410 Fax:(843)237-1041
E-mail: vacation@litchfieldplantation.com
Web: www.litchfieldplantation.com

Circa 1750. Live oaks line the drive that leads to this antebellum mansion, and in one glance, guests can imagine a time when this 600-acre estate was a prosperous rice plantation. The interior boasts many original features, and although the decor is more modern than it was in 1750, it still maintains charm and elegance. Four-poster and canopy beds, as well as a collection of traditional furnishings, grace the guest rooms, which are located in a variety of lodging options. Guests can stay in a plantation house suite or opt for a room in

the Guest House. There are two- and three-bedroom cottages available, too. The cottages are particularly suited to adult families or couples traveling together and include amenities such as a fireplace, kitchen and washer and dryer. The inn's dining room, located in the Carriage House, is a wonderful place for a romantic dinner. Start off with appetizers such as Terrine al Fresco, followed by a Caesar salad and an entree such as medallions of pork or the Carriage House Grooper. Guests enjoy privileges at the oceanfront Pawleys Island Beach House, and there are tennis courts and a swimming pool on the plantation premises. Many golf courses are nearby. Be sure to ask about the inn's packages.

Innkeeper(s): Karl W Friedrich. $186-620. MC, VISA, AX, DS, TC. TAC10. 38 rooms with PB, 7 with FP, 3 suites, 8 cottages and 3 conference rooms. Breakfast included in rates. Types of meals: Full bkfst and gourmet dinner. Beds: KQT. Cable TV and phone in room. Air conditioning. Fax, copier, swimming, tennis and library on premises. Weddings, small meetings, family reunions and seminars hosted. Amusement parks, antiquing, fishing, golf, oceanfront beach clubhouse, live theater, parks, shopping and water sports nearby.

Publicity: *Tales of the South Carolina Low Country, Golf Week, Augusta Magazine, PeeDee Magazine, Hidden Carolinas and Rice Plantations of Georgetown.*

"*What a wonderful, relaxing place to stay! Your accommodations were excellent-first class.*"

Sea View Inn

414 Myrtle Avenue
Pawleys Island, SC 29585-0210
(843)237-4253 Fax:(843)237-7909
E-mail: seaview@gte.net

Circa 1937. In simple low-country style, this inn rests on Pawley's Island, a narrow barrier island with the ocean on one side and a salt marsh on the other. In summer, you may not need your shoes again till you leave for home. You'll settle in as if this is the family guest house, with comfortable furnishings, wood decks set atop seagrass with ocean front or view rooms. Fruit, sausage, eggs, toast and grits are often served for breakfast. Three meals are included in your room rate, and the main meal is served at 1:15 p.m. Crab divine, red rice with kale, shrimp souffle, mint carrots, poached salmon and Carolina cornbread with scallion butter are samples from the mid-day menu. In the evening, pasta, oyster pie, minestrone soup, fried chicken, poached salmon, marinated shrimp, Cobb Salad or deviled crab may be offered. Dessert features Pecan Pie and Key Lime Pie. All rates are per person. During the summer, reservations are weekly, and the rest of the year there's a two-night minimum. The inn offers wellness, artist and nature weeks and there are half-price children's weeks.

Innkeeper(s): Page Oberlin, Owner. Call for rates. PC, TC. 20 rooms. Beds: DT. Turndown service and ceiling fan in room. Library, umbrellas, beach chairs and outside showers on premises. Beaches, canoeing/kayaking, golf, watercolor workshop, shopping and tennis nearby.

Publicity: *Southern Living and Travel & Leisure.*

Pendleton   B2

Rocky Retreat Bed and Breakfast

1000 Milwee Creek Rd
Pendleton, SC 29670
(864)225-3494
E-mail: jtligon@aol.com
Web: www.bbonline.com/sc/rockyretreat/

Circa 1849. Locally called the Boone-Douthit House for the area's prominent leaders who were previous owners, this classic upcountry plantation house with tin roof has been accurately restored and honored to be in the National Register. Original heart pine floors and wall paneling accent the front hall and parlor. Spacious guest bedrooms with large windows feature eclectic antiques, clawfoot tubs and gas fireplaces. A two-bedroom suite is great for families. Stone-ground grits and sausage strata are regional dishes served with breakfast at an old round table in the dining room. Among the foothills of the Blue Ridge Mountains, farms and woodland views are appreciated from the large front porch, screened side porch and back deck. Enjoy the native flora and fauna while on an exercise trail that circles the grounds.

Innkeeper(s): Jim Ligon. $75-115. MC, VISA, PC, TC. 4 rooms, 2 with PB, 4 with FP and 1 suite. Breakfast and snacks/refreshments included in rates. Types of meals: Full bkfst, country bkfst and early coffee/tea. Beds: QD. Fireplace in room. Central air. Fax, copier, library and guest refrigerator available on premises. Handicap access. Weddings, small meetings and family reunions hosted. Antiquing, art galleries, fishing, golf, hiking, live theater, museums, parks, shopping, sporting events and water sports nearby.

Salem   B2

Sunrise Farm B&B

325 Sunrise Dr
Salem, SC 29676-3444
(864)944-0121 (888)991-0121
E-mail: sfbb@bellsouth.net

Circa 1890. Situated on the remaining part of a 1,000-acre cotton plantation, this country Victorian features large porches with rockers and wicker. Guest rooms are furnished with period antiques, thick comforters, extra pillows and family heirlooms. The "corn crib" cottage is located in the original farm structure used for storing corn. It has a fully equipped kitchen, sitting area and bedroom with tub and shower. The June Rose Garden Cottage includes a river rock fireplace and full kitchen, as well as pastoral and mountain views. The inn offers a full breakfast, snacks and country picnic baskets.

Innkeeper(s): Barbara Laughter. $85-120. MC, VISA, TC. TAC10. 4 rooms with PB and 2 cottages. Breakfast and snacks/refreshments included in rates. Types of meals: Full bkfst, cont plus and picnic lunch. Beds: Q. TV, ceiling fan, VCR and free movies in room. Air conditioning. Llamas, miniature horses, goats, a pot belly pig, cats and dog on premises. Antiquing, fishing, boating, parks, sporting events and water sports nearby.

Pets allowed: With advanced notice.

Publicity: *National Geographic Traveler, Southern Living, Country Extra and Palmetto Places.*

Union   B4

The Inn at Merridun

100 Merridun Pl
Union, SC 29379-2200
(864)427-7052 (888)892-6020 Fax:(864)429-0373
E-mail: info@merridun.com

Circa 1855. Nestled on nine acres of wooded ground, this Greek Revival inn is in a small Southern college town. During spring, see the South in its colorful splendor with blooming azaleas, magnolias and wisteria. Sip an iced drink on the inn's

marble verandas and relive memories of a bygone era. Soft strains of Mozart and Beethoven, as well as the smell of freshly baked cookies and country suppers, fill the air of this antebellum country inn. In addition to a complimentary breakfast, guest will enjoy the inn's dessert selection offered every evening.

Historic Interest: Rose Hill Plantation State Park (8 miles), historic Brattonsville (35 miles).

Innkeeper(s): Peggy Waller & JD, the inn cat. $89-125. MC, VISA, AX, DS, PC, TC. TAC10. 5 rooms with PB and 3 conference rooms. Breakfast included in rates. Types of meals: Gourmet bkfst, early coffee/tea, gourmet lunch, picnic lunch, afternoon tea, gourmet dinner and room service. Beds: KQT. Cable TV, phone, ceiling fan and hair dryers in room. Air conditioning. VCR, fax, copier, library, refrigerator on each floor for guest use, evening dessert and Miss Fannie's Tea Room on premises. Weddings, small meetings, family reunions and seminars hosted. Amusement parks, antiquing, fishing, parks, shopping, sporting events and water sports nearby.

Publicity: *Charlotte Observer, Spartanburg Herald, Southern Living, Atlanta Journal-Constitution, Sandlapper Magazine, SCETV, Prime Time Live, BBC Documentary and Marshall Tucker Band Music Video.*

Winnsboro   C5

Songbird Manor

116 N Zion St
Winnsboro, SC 29180-1140
(803)635-6963 (888)636-7698 Fax:(803)635-6963
E-mail: songbirdmanor@msn.com
Web: www.bbonline.com/sc/songbird

Circa 1912. Influential local businessman Marcus Doty built this home, which features William Morris-style architecture. Doty made sure his home was a showplace from the beveled-glass windows to the molded plaster ceilings with extensive oak and chestnut woodwork. It was also the first home in the county to include indoor plumbing. Three of the guest rooms include the home's original clawfoot or pedestal tubs. All of the guest rooms have a fireplace. The gracious veranda is the location for afternoon refreshments and breakfast in good weather. Although enjoying a lazy day on the inn's swings and rocking chairs is a favorite pastime, you may opt to bicycle through the Winnsboro's historic district or enjoy the area's abundance of outdoor activities, from hunting to fishing to golf.

Innkeeper(s): Susan Yenner. $65-110. MC, VISA, AX, DS, PC. 5 rooms with PB, 5 with FP and 1 suite. Breakfast included in rates. Types of meals: Gourmet bkfst, cont, picnic lunch and dinner. Beds: KQT. Cable TV, phone, turndown service and ceiling fan in room. Air conditioning. VCR, fax, bicycles and library on premises. Weddings, small meetings, family reunions and seminars hosted. Antiquing, fishing, museums, parks and water sports nearby.

Publicity: *Sandlapper and Herald Independent.*

"We had a very restful two-night stay in a beautiful surrounding."

South Dakota

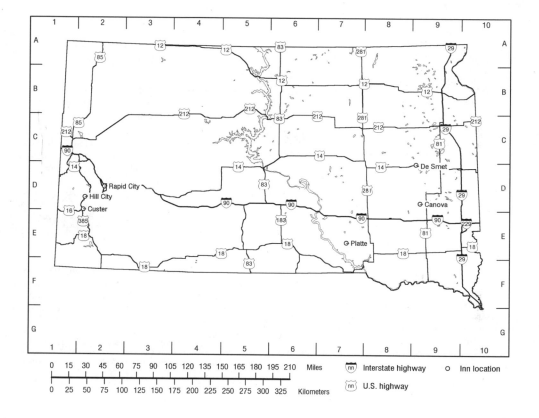

0 15 30 45 60 75 90 105 120 135 150 165 180 195 210   Miles

0   25   50   75   100 125 150 175 200 225 250 275 300 325   Kilometers

⬡ **nn** Interstate highway   ◦ Inn location

⬟ **nn** U.S. highway

Canova   *D9*

B&B at Skoglund Farm

24375 438 Avenue
Canova, SD 57321-9726
(605)247-3445

Circa 1917. This is a working farm on the South Dakota prairie. Peacocks stroll around the farm along with cattle, chickens, emu and other fowl. Guests can enjoy an evening meal

with the family. The innkeepers offer special rates for families with children. The farm's rates are $30 per adult, $25 per teenager and $20 per child. Children age five and younger stay for free.
Innkeeper(s): Alden & Delores Skoglund. $60. PC. TAC10. 4 rooms. Breakfast and dinner included in rates. Types of meals: Full bkfst, early coffee/tea and snacks/refreshments. Beds: QDT. TV in room. VCR and library on premises. Antiquing, fishing, parks, shopping, sporting events and water sports nearby.

Pets allowed: Welcomed.

"Thanks for the down-home hospitality and good food."

Custer   *D2*

Custer Mansion B&B

35 Centennial Dr
Custer, SD 57730-9642
(605)673-3333 (877)519-4948 Fax:(605)673-6696
E-mail: cusmanbb@gwtc.net

Circa 1891. Situated on one and a half acres of gardens and aspens, this two-story Gothic Victorian was built by one of the original Black Hills homesteaders. Architectural features include Eastlake stick trim, seven gables and stained-glass windows. Antiques fill the guest bedrooms and honeymoon or anniversary suites and family suites. Enjoy a hearty breakfast of fresh fruits, home-baked goods, meats, creative egg dishes, pancakes, waffles and French toast before venturing out for a day of activities in the Black Hills. Conveniently located, all area attractions are close by. After a day of sightseeing, relax in the outdoor hot tub. Pastries and hot and cold beverages are always available.
Innkeeper(s): Bob & Patricia Meakim. $76-125. MC, VISA, PC, TC. TAC5. 6 rooms with PB and 2 suites. Breakfast, afternoon tea and snacks/refreshments included in rates. Types of meals: Gourmet bkfst, country bkfst and early coffee/tea. Beds: KQDT. Cable TV, ceiling fan and VCR in room. Fax, spa, library and hot tub on premises. Weddings, small meetings, family reunions and seminars hosted. Antiquing, art galleries, beaches, bicycling, canoeing/kayaking, fishing, golf, hiking, horseback riding, museums, parks, shopping, cross-country skiing, tennis and water sports nearby.

Publicity: *Country Extra Magazine, National Historic Society, Midwest Living Magazine and Classic American Home.*

State Game Lodge

HC 83 Box 74
Custer, SD 57730-9705
(605)255-4541 (800)658-3530 Fax:(605)255-4706

Circa 1921. The State Game Lodge is listed in the National Register of Historic Places. It served as the summer White House for presidents Coolidge and Eisenhower. Although not a bed and breakfast, the lodge boasts a wonderful setting in the

Black Hills. Ask for a room in the historic lodge building. (There are cottages and motel units, as well.) A favorite part of the experience is rocking on the front porch while watching buffalo graze. Breakfast is paid for separately in the dining room, where you may wish to order a pheasant or buffalo entree in the evening.
Innkeeper(s): Pat Azinger. $80-350. MC, VISA, AX, DS. 68 rooms with PB, 3 with FP. Types of meals: Gourmet bkfst, lunch and dinner. EP. Beds: QDT. Fishing and buffalo safari jeep tours nearby.

Publicity: *Bon Appetit, Midwest Living and Sunset.*

"Your staff's cheerfulness and can-do attitude added to a most enjoyable stay."

DeSmet   *D9*

Prairie House Manor B&B

209 Pointsett Ave
DeSmet, SD 57231-9428
(605)854-9131 (800)297-2416 Fax:(605)854-9001
E-mail: phconnie@aol.com

Circa 1894. Laura Ingalls Wilder wrote about the first owner of this house in her novel, "The Long Winter." The homey, country bed & breakfast offers rooms with items such as white iron beds, pedestal sinks and hardwood floors topped with rag rugs. Wilder was a resident of DeSmet, and the town features a church her father helped to build, as well as a schoolhouse where the author once taught. In addition to the six rooms in the main house, the innkeepers also offer a sportsman

facility that is popular in the fall for pheasant hunters. Stay there in the summer to enjoy the great fishing at Lake Thompson, the state's new park. There's a game cleaning shed and freezers. The cottage has its own fully equipped kitchen and is self catering.
Innkeeper(s): Larry & Connie Cheney. $69-89. MC, VISA, PC, TC. 6 rooms with PB. Breakfast included in rates. Types of meals: Full bkfst, cont and early coffee/tea. Beds: KQDT. Cable TV, ceiling fan and VCR in room. Air conditioning. Fax, bicycles, library and one sportsman facility on premises. Antiquing, fishing, golf, Laura Ingalls Wilder-author's museum tours, live theater, parks, shopping, cross-country skiing, tennis and water sports nearby.

Pets allowed: Well-behaved-trained-prearranged.

Publicity: *Plainsman.*

"It was so much fun to stay in the prettiest house on the prairie."

Hill City   *D2*

Pine Rest Cabins

PO Box 377
Hill City, SD 57745-0377
(605)574-2416 (800)333-5306
E-mail: pinerestcabins@aol.com
Web: www.pinerestcabins.com

Circa 1911. Surrounded by Black Hills National Forest, these simple country cabins offer a variety of lodgings. Once located on the site of the Harney Peak Tin mining camp, one cabin is over 100 years old with a handmade stone fireplace and decorative bark walls. Several have knotty pine inside and out, wood floors and a gas fireplace. All the cabins feature kitchenettes and an outside barbecue grill and picnic table. A hot tub and gazebo is a relaxing treat. A sandbox, playground and games provide entertainment for the young at heart. The local setting is perfect for nature and outdoor enthusiasts. It is only a few minutes to historic Mt. Rushmore National Monument.

Historic Interest: Hill City & 1880 Train (1 mile), City of Custer (12 miles), Mt. Rushmore National Monument (9 miles), Crazy Horse Monument (9 miles), Historic Deadwood (46 miles).

Innkeeper(s): Jan & Steve Johnson. $65-250. MC, VISA, DS, PC. 12 cabins, 5 with FP. Beds: KQDT. Cable TV, ceiling fan, fireplace and cabins all have kitchenetts in room. Spa, volleyball, access to National Forest for hiking and kettle-style charcoal grill/picnic table outside each cabin on premises. Antiquing, art galleries, beaches, bicycling, fishing, golf, hiking, horseback riding, canoeing, live theater, museums, parks, shopping, cross-country skiing, tennis and water sports nearby.

Pets allowed: in some cabins with prior approval plus $10 fee per pet per night.

Platte   E7

Grandma's House B&B

721 E 7th St
Platte, SD 57369-2134
(605)337-3589

Circa 1906. This Victorian farmhouse will stir memories of visits to Grandma. The interior is homey, done in a simple country style with antiques. The turn-of-the-century home maintains its original woodwork and a fireplace. The Prairie Queen room features a teal-blue satin bedspread with matching curtains of satin and white lace; an old sewing machine has been transformed into a sink. The Country Blue and Southern Rose rooms share a bath with a clawfoot tub. Breakfast menus feature items such as pancakes or French toast with eggs and bacon. Parks and a swimming pool are nearby, and guests can fish at the Missouri River, which is a 20-minute drive from the home.

Innkeeper(s): Delores & Albert Kuipers. $40-50. PC. 3 rooms, 1 with PB. Breakfast included in rates. Types of meals: Full bkfst and early coffee/tea. Beds: QD. Ceiling fan in room. Air conditioning. VCR on premises. Small meetings and family reunions hosted. Fishing, golf, shopping and water sports nearby.

Rapid City   D2

Abend Haus Cottages & Audrie's B&B

23029 Thunderhead Falls Rd
Rapid City, SD 57702-8524
(605)342-7788
Web: www.audriesbb.com

Circa 1973. Whether guests stay in a historic powerhouse or in private cottages, they're sure to enjoy both the spectacular scenery and the comfortable rooms furnished with European

antiques. The Old Powerhouse dates back to 1910 and was used to generate hydroelectricity. The two suites located in the Abend Haus Cottage both include a private hot tub and feature antique furnishings such as a mahogany sleigh bed. The individual log cottages are other cozy options, also with hot tubs. Guests are provided with a full breakfast, which they can heat and enjoy in the privacy of their own suite or cottage and at their convenience. With all this pampering, one shouldn't forget to mention the seven acres of woods, a creek and mountain views.

Innkeeper(s): Hank & Audry Kuhnhauser. $115-175. PC, TC. 10 rooms with PB, 8 with FP, 4 suites and 6 cottages. Breakfast included in rates. Types of meals: Full bkfst. Beds: KQ. Cable TV, turndown service, ceiling fan and VCR in room. Air conditioning. Bicycles, fishing and hiking on premises. Antiquing, fishing, parks, shopping, downhill skiing, cross-country skiing and water sports nearby.

"I don't want to leave so I'm staying a few days longer! This is a wonderful place."

Carriage House Bed & Breakfast

721 West Blvd
Rapid City, SD 57701-2645
(605)343-6415 (888)343-6415 Fax:(603)925-0061
E-mail: info@carriagehouse-bb.com
Web: www.carriagehouse-bb.com

Circa 1919. Rapid City's first lumber baron built this neo-Colonial manor house. Later it was the home to the Roman Catholic bishops of the Rapid City Diocese, and several archbishops have stayed here. The interior includes Victorian and traditional furnishings and appointments. Each room has been decorated individually. The Sonnet has a heart-shaped whirlpool tub, waterfall shower and a massive Amish oak bed. Other rooms include special touches, such as a four-poster bed, window seat or a Victorian-era fainting couch. Breakfast is hearty with fresh fruit, quiche, potatoes, breakfast meats and homemade baked goods. The home is located in the town's historic district so guests can stroll around the area and enjoy many of Rapid City's historic sites.

Innkeeper(s): Janice & Jay Hrachovec. $115-149. MC, VISA, DS, PC. TAC10. 5 rooms. Breakfast and snacks/refreshments included in rates. Types of meals: Full bkfst, veg bkfst, early coffee/tea and room service. Beds: KQ. Ceiling fan in room. Air conditioning. Fax and copier on premises. Weddings, small meetings and family reunions hosted. Antiquing, art galleries, bicycling, canoeing/kayaking, fishing, golf, hiking, horseback riding, live theater, museums, parks, shopping, downhill skiing, cross-country skiing, tennis and water sports nearby.

Publicity: *Victorian Decorating Ideas-Spring 2001 and Into his Arms.*

Tennessee

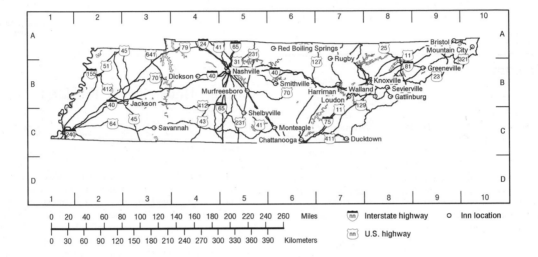

| | 0 | 20 | 40 | 60 | 80 | 100 | 120 | 140 | 160 | 180 | 200 | 220 | 240 | 260 | Miles |
| 0 | 30 | 60 | 90 | 120 | 150 | 180 | 210 | 240 | 270 | 300 | 330 | 360 | 390 | | Kilometers |

Interstate highway   o   Inn location

U.S. highway

Bristol   A9

New Hope B&B

822 Georgia Ave
Bristol, TN 37620-4024
(423)989-3343 (888)989-3343
E-mail: newhope@preferred.com
Web: www.newhopebandb.com

Circa 1892. Abram Reynolds, older brother of R.J. Reynolds, once owned the property that surrounds this inn, and one of the guest rooms is named in his honor. Each of the rooms has been creatively decorated with bright prints and cheerful wallcoverings, emphasizing the high ceilings and wood floors. Clawfoot tubs, transoms over the doors and distinctive woodwork are some of the period elements featured in this late Victorian home. Bristol is known as the birthplace of country music, and the innkeepers pay homage to the history with the whimsically decorated Tennessee Ernie Ford hallway. Ford got his start in Bristol, and pictures, record jackets,

books and wallpaper fashioned from sheet music bedeck the hallway. The home is located in the historic Fairmount area, and a guided walking tour begins at New Hope. Half of the town of Bristol is located in Tennessee and the other half in Virginia.

Innkeeper(s): Tom & Tonda Fluke. $100-225. MC, VISA, AX, PC, TC. TAC10. 4 rooms with PB, 2 with FP. Breakfast and snacks/refreshments included in rates. Types of meals: Full bkfst and early coffee/tea. Beds: KQT. Cable TV, ceiling fan and one with whirlpool tub for two in room. Air conditioning. Library and large game room on premises. Antiquing, fishing, golf, live theater, parks, shopping and downhill skiing nearby.

Publicity: *Tennessee Getaways. Bristol Herald Courier.*

"It was like a second home in such a short time."

Chattanooga   C6

Adams Hilborne Mansion Inn & Restaurant

801 Vine St
Chattanooga, TN 37403-2318
(423)265-5000 Fax:(423)265-5555
E-mail: innjoy@worldnet.att.net
Web: www.innjoy.com

Circa 1889. This former mayor's mansion of Tudor and Romanesque design was presented with the 1997 award for

Excellence in Preservation by the National Trust. The interior of this gracious home boasts 16-foot ceilings and floors patterned from three different woods. The large entrance hall features carved cornices, a coiffured ceiling and a fireplace. Every room offers something special, from Tiffany windows and beveled glass to the mansion's eight fireplaces and luxurious ballroom. The cornerstone of the Fortwood Historic District, Chattanooga's finest historic residential area, the mansion also has received the coveted City Beautiful Award.

Historic Interest: The Chickamauga Battlefields are 15 minutes from the inn and other battle sites, museums and cemeteries are nearby.

Innkeeper(s): Wendy & Dave Adams. $150-295. MC, VISA, AX, TC. TAC10. 11 rooms with PB, 4 with FP and 3 suites. Breakfast included in rates. Types of meals: Full bkfst and gourmet dinner. Beds: KQD. Cable TV, phone, turndown service and VCR in room. Air conditioning. Fax, copier and library on premises. Weddings, small meetings, family reunions and seminars hosted. Amusement parks, antiquing, fishing, live theater, parks, shopping, sporting events and water sports nearby.

Publicity: *Chattanooga News Free, Nashville Tennessean, Southern Accents, National Geographic, Preservation Magazine, Traveler, News Free Press, Blue Ridge Magazine, PBS, CBS and NBC.*

Dickson   B4

East Hills Bed & Breakfast Inn

100 E Hills Ter
Dickson, TN 37055-2102
(615)441-9428 Fax:(615)446-2181
E-mail: jaluther@dickson.net
Web: www.easthills.com

Circa 1948. This traditional Southern home, built by the owner's father, offers 5,000 square feet of gracious common rooms, porches and handsomely decorated guest rooms. The library-den has black and white tiles, book-lined walls, a fireplace and comfortable furniture. There are rocking chairs and swings on the porches. Four acres of lawns and gardens provide privacy for two cottages tucked into a thicket of oaks. Breakfast offerings include favorites such as blueberry pancakes and scrambled eggs or country ham, cheese grits, hot biscuits and potatoes. Walk to nearby Luther Lake or visit Cumberland Furnace or Historic Charlotte.

Historic Interest: Luther Lake, Cumberland Furnace, Historic Franklin church, historic country seat, Charlotte courthouse 1833, Ruskin cave.

Innkeeper(s): John & Anita Luther. $75-125. MC, VISA, AX, DS, PC, TC. TAC10. 4 rooms with PB and 2 cottages. Breakfast, afternoon tea and snacks/refreshments included in rates. Types of meals: Full bkfst and early coffee/tea. Beds: QD. Cable TV, phone, turndown service, ceiling fan and VCR in room. Central air. Fax, bicycles and library on premises. Handicap access. Small meetings, family reunions and seminars hosted. Antiquing, art galleries, bicycling, canoeing/kayaking, fishing, golf, hiking, horseback riding, renaissance Center, museums, parks, shopping, tennis and water sports nearby.

Ducktown   C7

The White House B&B

104 Main St, PO Box 668
Ducktown, TN 37326-0668
(423)496-4166 (800)775-4166 Fax:(423)496-9778
E-mail: mardan@tds.net

Circa 1898. This Queen Anne Victorian boasts a wraparound porch with a swing. Rooms are decorated in traditional style with family antiques. Innkeepers pamper their guests with

Tennessee hospitality, a hearty country breakfast and a mouth-watering sundae bar in the evenings. The innkeepers also help guests plan daily activities, and the area is bursting with possibilities. Hiking, horseback riding, panning for gold and driving tours are only a few choices. The Ocoee River is the perfect place for a river float trip or take on the challenge of roaring rapids. The river was selected as the site of the 1996 Summer Olympic Whitewater Slalom events.

Historic Interest: The Ducktown Mining Museum is a popular local attraction. Fields of the Wood, a biblical theme park, is 20 minutes away and free of charge.

Innkeeper(s): Dan & Mardee Kauffman. $75-79. MC, VISA, DS, PC, TC. TAC10. 3 rooms. Breakfast, afternoon tea and snacks/refreshments included in rates. Types of meals: Gourmet bkfst and early coffee/tea. Beds: QT. Ceiling fan and central heat in room. Central air. VCR, fax and library on premises. Weddings, small meetings and family reunions hosted. Antiquing, fishing, parks, shopping and water sports nearby.

Publicity: *Southern Living.*

"We wanted a relaxing couple of days in the mountains and that's what we got. Thank you."

Gatlinburg   B8

Buckhorn Inn

2140 Tudor Mountain Rd
Gatlinburg, TN 37738-6014
(865)436-4668 Fax:(865)436-5009
E-mail: buckhorninn@msn.com
Web: www.buckhorninn.com

Circa 1938. Set high on a hilltop, Buckhorn is surrounded by more than 25 acres of woodlands and groomed meadows. There are inspiring mountain views and a spring-fed lake on the grounds. Original paintings enhance the antique-filled guest rooms and the cottages and guest houses have wood burning fireplaces, Jacuzzi's and porches.

Innkeeper(s): John & Lee Mellor. $95-250. MC, VISA, DS, PC, TC. 9 rooms with PB, 7 cottages and 2 guest houses. Breakfast included in rates. Types of meals: Gourmet bkfst, early coffee/tea, lunch, picnic lunch, afternoon tea and dinner. Beds: KDT. TV, fireplace, Jacuzzi, coffeemaker and refrigerator in room. Air conditioning. VCR, fax, copier and library on premises. Weddings, small meetings, family reunions and seminars hosted. Amusement parks, antiquing, fishing, Great Smoky Arts & Crafts Community, live theater, parks, shopping, downhill skiing, cross-country skiing, sporting events and water sports nearby.

Publicity: *Atlanta Journal & Constitution, Country, Brides, British Vogue, Birmingham News, New York Times, Travel & Leisure and Travel Holiday.*

Greeneville   B9

Big Spring Inn

315 N Main St
Greeneville, TN 37745-3817
(423)638-2917 Fax:(423)639-4230
Web: www.virtualcities.com/tn/bigspringinn.htm

Circa 1905. This three-story Greek Revival in the historic district of picture-perfect Greeneville sits on two acres that include landscaped gardens and century-old trees. The inn offers the utmost in Southern hospitality and personal attention, including arrangements for pets to board. A veterinarian is available two miles from the inn. After a country breakfast including signature sweet potato waffles, ham and

freshly ground Starbucks coffee, guests may sit in a window seat or out on one of the big porches and enjoy the view. Listed in Fodor's "The South's Best Bed and Breakfasts 1995" and in the Los Angeles Times, the inn has everything a guest needs for retreat and renewal. Fresh flowers, terry cloth robes, coffee waiting outside bedroom door in the mornings and an afternoon snack all add to the indoor delights. Whitewater rafting, hiking, trout fishing, waterfalls, mills, and lovely back roads call to the hardy adventurer.

Innkeeper(s): Marshall & Nancy Ricker. $70-126. MC, VISA, AX, DS. 5 rooms, 4 with PB, 2 with FP and 1 suite. Types of meals: Gourmet bkfst. MAP. Beds: KQD. Cable TV, phone and ceiling fan in room. Central air. Fax on premises.

Publicity: *Kingsport Times News and Winston-Salem Journal.*

"We couldn't have chosen any place more perfect."

Harriman   B7

Bushrod Hall B&B

422 Cumberland St, NE
Harriman, TN 37748
(865)882-8406 (888)880-8406 Fax:(865)882-6056
E-mail: bushrodbb@aol.com

Circa 1892. Bushrod Hall was built as part of a competition to see which town resident could build the most beautiful home, so its original owners spared little expense. Among the home's most notable features are its exquisite restored woodwork and stained glass. Harriman was founded as a utopia for those following the Temperance Movement. Bushrod Hall once served as the Hall of Domestic Science for the American Temperance University. Period-era furnishings add to the historic ambiance. Gourmet breakfast entrees include items such as an egg soufflé or caramel French toast. Guests can take a guided walking tour and see some of the town's historic sites. Antique shops, museums and recreation areas offer other possibilities. Bushrod Hall is located in Harriman's Cornstalk Heights Historic District and is listed in the National Register of Historic Places.

Historic Interest: Ft SW Point (4 miles), Secret City Oak Ridge & Carbide Reactor (20 miles), Museum of Appalachia (30 miles).

Innkeeper(s): Nancy & Bob Ward. $75-95. MC, VISA, AX, PC, TC. 3 rooms with PB. Breakfast and snacks/refreshments included in rates. Types of meals: Gourmet bkfst, veg bkfst and early coffee/tea. Beds: KQ. Ceiling fan in room. Central air. VCR, fax, library and TV on premises. Weddings, small meetings and family reunions hosted. Antiquing, canoeing/kayaking, fishing, golf, hiking and water sports nearby.

Publicity: *Oak Ridge, Knoxville News Sentinel, Ronne Co News, Nashville Tennessean, WVLT and WBIR.*

Jackson   B3

Highland Place B&B

519 N Highland Ave
Jackson, TN 38301-4824
(731)427-1472
E-mail: relax@highlandplace.com
Web: www.highlandplace.com

Circa 1911. Whether traveling for business or pleasure, a stay at this elegant Colonial Revival mansion will relax and inspire. Conveniently located in a quiet downtown historical district, the perfect blend of old and new furnishings provide luxurious comfort and modern convenience. Spacious barely describes the 10-foot-wide hallways, high ceilings, marble fireplace and many exquisite common rooms to gather in and dine together. An audio center enhances the gracious ambiance, and a video library offers further enter-

tainment. The impressive guest bedrooms are well-appointed. Special attention is given to meet personal or corporate needs.

Innkeeper(s): Cindy & Bill Pflaum. $90-140. MC, VISA, AX, PC, TC. TAC10. 4 rooms with PB, 3 with FP and 1 conference room. TV and VCR in room. Library and internet access on premises. Weddings, small meetings, family reunions and seminars hosted. Antiquing, art galleries, live theater, shopping and sporting events nearby.

Knoxville   B8

Maple Grove Inn

8800 Westland Dr
Knoxville, TN 37923-6501
(865)690-9565 (800)645-0713 Fax:(865)690-9385
E-mail: mginn@usit.net
Web: www.maplegroveinn.com

Circa 1805. Enjoy real Southern hospitality in this late 18th-century, 12,000-square-foot, Georgian-style mansion on 16 acres in the foothills of the Great Smoky Mountains. Antiques, hand-carved fireplaces, Oriental rugs, and family heirlooms create a delightful ambiance in this inn that is one of Knoxville's oldest residence. Common rooms include the library, living room, sitting room and sunroom. The inn has eight guest bedrooms including some spacious suites that have Jacuzzis. Gourmet breakfasts prepared by Chef John Luna can be served in the guest's bedroom or in the dining room. Items include such fare as homemade scones with strawberry jam, vegetable quiche with hollandaise sauce, country ham, skillet potatoes and fresh fruit. The gourmet restaurant is open for dinner Thursday through Saturday by reservation.

Historic Interest: James White Fort (10-15 miles), William Blount Mansion (10-15 miles).

Innkeeper(s): Gina Buchanon, Beth Griffis. $125-200. MC, VISA, AX, PC, TC. TAC10. 8 rooms, 6 with PB, 3 with FP, 2 suites and 1 conference room. Breakfast and snacks/refreshments included in rates. Types of meals: Gourmet bkfst, early coffee/tea, lunch and dinner. Beds: QD. Cable TV and phone in room. Air conditioning. VCR, fax, copier, swimming and tennis on premises. Weddings, small meetings and family reunions hosted. Antiquing, art galleries, golf, museums, parks, shopping, sporting events and tennis nearby.

Publicity: *Knoxville News Sentinel and Tennessee Getaways.*

Maplehurst Inn

800 W Hill Ave
Knoxville, TN 37902
(865)523-7773 (800)451-1562
E-mail: mplhrstinn@aol.com

Circa 1917. This townhouse, located in the downtown neighborhood of Maplehurst, is situated on a hill that overlooks the Tennessee River. A parlor with fireplace and piano invites guests to mingle in the evening or to relax quietly with a book. The inn's favorite room is the Penthouse with king bed, cherry furnishings and a sky lit Jacuzzi. The Anniversary Suite offers a double Jacuzzi and canopy bed. A light informal breakfast is served in the Garden Room overlooking the river, while breakfast casseroles, country potatoes, quiches and breads are offered buffet-style in the dining room. Check there for brownies and cookies if you come back in the middle of the day. The inn is within two blocks of the Convention Center and City Hall as well as several fine restaurants. The University of Tennessee and Neyland Stadium are nearby.

Historic Interest: James White Fort (1/2 mile), Mabry-Hazen House (1/2 mile). $69-149. MC, VISA, PC, TC. TAC10. 11 rooms with PB and 2 suites. Breakfast and snacks/refreshments included in rates. Types of meals: Full bkfst, veg bkfst and early coffee/tea. Beds: KD. Cable TV and phone in room. Air conditioning. VCR, fax and spa on premises. Small meetings, family reunions and seminars hosted. Antiquing, art galleries, bicycling, canoeing/kayaking, fishing, golf, hiking, horseback riding, live theater, museums, parks, shopping, downhill skiing, sporting events, tennis, water sports and wineries nearby. Pets Allowed.

Loudon　　　　　　　　**B7**

The Mason Place B&B

600 Commerce St
Loudon, TN 37774-1101
(865)458-3921 Fax:(865)458-6092
E-mail: thempbb@aol.com
Web: www.themasonplace.com

Circa 1865. In the National Register, Mason Place is acclaimed for its award-winning restoration. In the Greek Revival style, the inn has a red slate roof and graceful columns. Three porches overlook three acres of lawns, trees and gardens. Inside, guests are welcomed to a grand entrance hall and tasteful antiques. There are 10 working fireplaces in the mansion's 7,000 square feet. Guests enjoy the Grecian swimming pool, gazebo and wisteria-covered arbor. A favorite honeymoon getaway has been created from the old smoke-house. It features brick walls and

floors, a library loft, feather bed, wood burning Franklin fireplace and a tin bathtub (once featured in the movie Maverick).

Historic Interest: Fort Loudon Park & Museum, The Lost Sea, Sequoyah Museum.

Innkeeper(s): Bob & Donna Siewert. $96-135. PC, TC. 5 rooms with PB, 5 with FP. Breakfast included in rates. Types of meals: Gourmet bkfst, early coffee/tea, picnic lunch and afternoon tea. Beds: Q. Air conditioning. Horseshoe and croquet on premises. Weddings, small meetings and seminars hosted. Amusement parks, antiquing, fishing, white water rafting, parks, shopping, tennis and wineries nearby.

Publicity: *Country Inn, Country Side, Country Travels, Tennessee Cross Roads, Antiquing in Tennessee, Knox-Chattanooga, Oak Ridge and Detroit Magazine.*

"Absolutely wonderful in every way. You are in for a treat! The best getaway ever!"

Monteagle　　　　　　　　**C6**

Adams Edgeworth Inn

Monteagle Assembly
Monteagle, TN 37356
(931)924-4000 Fax:(931)924-3236
E-mail: innjoy@blomand.net
Web: www.relaxinn.com

Circa 1896. Built in 1896 this National Register Victorian inn recently has been refurbished in a country-chintz style. Original paintings, sculptures and country antiques are found throughout. Wide verandas are filled with wicker furnishings and breezy hammocks, and there's an award-winning chef who will prepare delicious candle-lit dinners. You can stroll through the 96-acre Victorian village that surrounds the

inn and enjoy rolling hills, creeks and Victorian cottages. Waterfalls, natural caves and scenic overlooks are along the 150 miles of hiking trails of nearby South Cumberland State Park.

Historic Interest: University of the South, Jack Daniels Distillery, Civil War sites.

Innkeeper(s): Wendy Adams. $100-275. MC, VISA, AX. 12 rooms with PB, 4 with FP, 1 suite and 1 conference room. Breakfast included in rates. Types of meals: Full bkfst and gourmet dinner. MAP, EP. Beds: KQD. Phone, air-conditioning and ceiling fan and TV (some rooms) in room. VCR, fax and copier on premises. Weddings, small meetings, family reunions and seminars hosted. Antiquing, fishing, hiking, caving, historic architecture, live theater, parks, shopping and sporting events nearby.

Publicity: *Country Inns, Chattanooga News Free Press, Tempo, Gourmet, Victorian Homes, Brides, Tennessean, Southern Living, National Geographic, Inn Country, PBS Crossroads, ABC TV, CBS TV and Travel Channel.*

Mountain City　　　　　　**A10**

The Butler House B&B

309 North N Church St
Mountain City, TN 37683-1415
(423)727-4119
E-mail: border3@earthlink.net
Web: www.thebutlerhouse.com

Circa 1870. The peaceful rural setting of the Blue Ridge mountains surrounds this Italianate house listed in the National Register. Decorated with a blend of antiques and reproductions, comfort comes easy. Watch TV or listen to music in one of the parlors. The bright and spacious guest bedrooms with handmade quilts and Victorian furnishings feature private entrances from a large upstairs porch. A delicious breakfast starts the day before exploring

the 15 acres of lawns, flower gardens, meadows and hillside trails. Nearby tourist attractions include Boone, N.C., and Abingdon, Va., only 30 minutes away.

Innkeeper(s): Bill & Joan Trathen. $65-75. MC, VISA, AX, DS, PC, TC. 4 rooms with PB. Breakfast, afternoon tea and snacks/refreshments included in rates. Types of meals: Gourmet bkfst, veg bkfst and early coffee/tea. Beds: QDT. One with modem and one with telephone in room. Air conditioning. VCR, fax, copier and library on premises. Weddings, small meetings, family reunions and seminars hosted. Antiquing, art galleries, bicycling, fishing, golf, hiking, live theater, museums, parks, shopping, tennis and wineries nearby.

Prospect Hill B&B Inn

801 W Main St (Hwy 67)
Mountain City, TN 37683
(423)727-0139 (800)339-5084
E-mail: historic@prospect-hill.com
Web: www.prospect-hill.com

Circa 1889. This three-story shingle-style Victorian manor garners a great deal of attention from passersby with its appealing architecture and commanding hilltop location. Romantic rooms offer tall arched windows, 11-foot ceilings and spectacular views. Fashioned from handmade bricks, it was once home to Major Joseph Wagner, who, like many of his neighbors in far northeastern Tennessee, served on the Union side. The restored home features five guest rooms. A 1910 oak Craftsman dining set complements the oak Stickley furniture (circa 1997) that decorates the living room. Fireplaces, whirlpools and stained glass add luxury to the guest rooms. Prospect Hill boasts views of the Appalachian and Blue Ridge Mountains. From the front window, guests can see three states: Tennessee, Virginia and North Carolina. The inn is within an hour of the Blue Ridge Parkway, Appalachian Trail and Roan and Grandfather mountain, and the Virginia Creeper Trail.

Innkeeper(s): Judy & Robert Hotchkiss. $89-200. MC, VISA, AX, DC, DS, PC, TC. 5 rooms with PB, 5 with FP and 1 conference room. Breakfast included in rates. Types of meals: Full bkfst, cont, early coffee/tea, picnic lunch and snacks/refreshments. Beds: KQ. Cable TV, phone, turndown service, ceiling fan and heat in room. Air conditioning. VCR, fax, copier, library and porch swing on premises. Weddings, small meetings, family reunions and seminars hosted. Antiquing, fishing, golf, mountain trails, bike trails, Eastern Tennessee State University, live theater, parks, shopping, downhill skiing, tennis and water sports nearby.

Publicity: *East Tennessee Marquee Magazine, Appalachian Life Magazine, Tomahawk, Johnson City Press and Old-House Journal.*

"The most wonderful thing I'll always remember about our stay is, by far, the wonderful home we came back to each night."

Murfreesboro   B5

Carriage Lane Inn

411 N Maney Ave
Murfreesboro, TN 37130-2920
(615)890-3630 (800)357-2827 Fax:(615)893-5707
E-mail: sharonpetty@mindspring.com

Circa 1899. Carriage Lane, a century-old home, is situated in a local historic district. The guest rooms include amenities such as fireplaces, whirlpool tubs and featherbeds. In the mornings, guests are served a full breakfast. The inn is just 20 minutes away from Nashville and is close to Civil War battlefields and historic sites.

Historic Interest: Rutherford County Courthouse (1/2 mile), Sam Davis Home (10 miles), Oakland Historic House Museum (1/2 mile), Stones River Battlefield (2 miles).

Innkeeper(s): Sharon & Ted Petty. $105-125. MC, VISA, AX, DS, PC, TC. TAC10. 4 rooms with PB, 1 suite and 5 conference rooms. Breakfast and snacks/refreshments included in rates. Types of meals: Full bkfst and early coffee/tea. Beds: QDT. Cable TV, phone, VCR and fireplace in room. Central air. Fax, library and gift shop on premises. Weddings, small meetings, family reunions and seminars hosted. Antiquing, art galleries, bicycling, fishing, golf, hiking, horseback riding, Civil War battlefield, Grand Old Opry, live theater, museums, parks, shopping, sporting events, tennis, water sports and wineries nearby.

Nashville   B5

Crocker Springs B&B

2382 Crocker Springs Road
Nashville, TN 37072
(615)876-8502 (888)382-9397
E-mail: crockersprings@juno.com

Circa 1880. Once a working farm, the grounds that surround this historic home still include the old barn and outbuildings. Spacious, comfortable guest rooms are decorated with an elegant country style. Todd's Paisley Room includes a masculine paisley comforter atop an antique high-backed oak bed. Stefanie's Quilt Room includes antique furnishings and a feather bed topped with a colorful quilt. The Rose Room, also furnished with antiques, is especially spacious and can accommodate up to four guest, when reserved as a suite. The aroma of freshly brewed coffee wafts throughout the house, a gentle promise to wonderful culinary things to come. The innkeepers prepare a variety of different breakfasts, each ending with a breakfast desert. One guest favorite is a unique tomato pudding that is served along with egg dishes, breakfast meats, orchard-fresh juice and a selection of fruit. Guests can stroll the 58 acres or take the short drive into Nashville where historic homes, Civil War battlefields and the Grand Old Opry await.

Historic Interest: Hermitage, Belle Meade Plantation, Civil War Battlefields.

Innkeeper(s): Jack & Bev Spangler. $110-200. AX, DS, PC, TC. TAC10. 3 rooms with PB, 1 suite and 1 conference room. Breakfast and snacks/refreshments included in rates. Types of meals: Full bkfst, country bkfst, veg bkfst and early coffee/tea. Beds: Q. Ceiling fan in room. Central air. VCR, fax, stables and library on premises. Weddings, small meetings, family reunions and seminars hosted. Antiquing, art galleries, canoeing/kayaking, fishing, golf, hiking, horseback riding, live theater, museums, parks, shopping, sporting events, tennis, water sports and wineries nearby.

Pets allowed: Occasionally by prior arrangement.

Publicity: *Goodlettsville Gazette and Channel 5-Talk of the Town.*

Red Boiling Springs   A6

Armours Hotel

321 E Main St
Red Boiling Springs, TN 37150-2322
(615)699-2180 Fax:(615)699-5111
E-mail: armourshotel@yahoo.com
Web: www.armourshotel.com

Circa 1924. As Tennessee's only remaining mineral bathhouse, this two-story, National Historic Register house is tucked away in the rolling hills of the Cumberland Plateau. Whether resting in one of the 23 antique-furnished guest rooms, listening to the  babbling creek from the second-floor veranda, strolling under covered bridges, or simply enjoying the sunrise in a rocking chair on the porch before breakfast, tranquillity awaits each guest. Spend the afternoon in the gazebo with your favorite book from the library next door, or get in a game of tennis at the park across the street before dinner.

Historic Interest: Al Gore's home.

Innkeeper(s): Joy Pike. $98-120. MC, VISA, AX, PC, TC. TAC10. 22 rooms, 19 with PB and 3 suites. Breakfast and dinner included in rates. Types of meals: Country bkfst and lunch. Beds: KQDT. Bath house (mineral and steam) in room. Air conditioning. VCR, fax, copier, spa and massage room on premises. Weddings, small meetings, family reunions and seminars hosted. Spanish spoken. Antiquing, fishing, golf, hiking, horseback riding, parks, tennis, water sports and wineries nearby.

Publicity: *Southern Living, Tennesseean and Country Crossroads.*

Rugby B7

Newbury House at Historic Rugby

Hwy 52, PO Box 8
Rugby, TN 37733-0008
(423)628-2430 Fax:(423)628-2266
E-mail: rugbytn@highland.net
Web: www.historicrugby.org

Circa 1880. Mansard-roofed Newbury House first lodged visitors traveling to this English village when author and social reformer Thomas Hughes founded Rugby. Filled with authentic Victorian

antiques, the inn includes some furnishings that are original to the colony. There are also several restored cottages on the property, and there is a two-room suite with a queen bed, two twin beds and a private bathroom.

Historic Interest: The inn and entire village are listed in the National Register. There are tours daily.

Innkeeper(s): Historic Rugby. $65-89. MC, VISA, DS, PC, TC. 6 rooms, 4 with PB, 1 suite and 2 cottages. Breakfast included in rates. Types of meals: Full bkfst, early coffee/tea, lunch, picnic lunch and dinner. Beds: QDT. Ceiling fan in room. Air conditioning. Library and veranda on premises. Weddings, small meetings, family reunions and seminars hosted. Antiquing, fishing, hiking, historic village, building tours, parks, shopping and water sports nearby.

Publicity: *New York Times, Americana, USA Weekend, Tennessean, Southern Living, Atlanta Journal-Constitution, Victorian Homes and A&E History Channel.*

"I love the peaceful atmosphere here and the beauty of nature surrounding Rugby."

Savannah C3

White Elephant B&B Inn

200 Church St
Savannah, TN 38372
(731)925-6410
E-mail: stay@whiteelephantbb.com
Web: www.whiteelephantbb.com

Circa 1901. Guests will know they've arrived at the right place when they spot the white elephants on the front lawn of this Queen Anne Victorian. Listed in the National Register as part of the Savannah Historic District, it offers a wraparound veranda, back porch swing and shade from tall sugar maples. The inn is situated on 1.4 acres and the parlors feature rare curved

bay windows. Guest rooms offer antiques and bathrooms with clawfoot tubs. Robes and turndown service are special amenities.

Depression glass and silver service add elegance to the inn's hearty breakfasts. Afternoon refreshments are served, including the innkeeper's award-winning cookies. The White Elephant is the closest bed & breakfast to Shiloh (10

miles away), and historian and innkeeper Ken Hansgen offers guided tours of the battlefield.

Innkeeper(s): Ken & Sharon Hansgen. $100-120. PC, TC. TAC10. 3 rooms with PB. Breakfast and snacks/refreshments included in rates. Types of meals: Full bkfst and room service. Beds: Q. Ceiling fan in room. Central air. VCR, library, central air conditioning, central heat, croquet, radio, CD player, pump organ and fireplace on premises. Weddings and small meetings hosted. Antiquing, beaches, bicycling, fishing, golf, hiking, art gallery, boating, Natchez Trace, scenic Tennessee River (6 blocks), museums, parks, shopping, tennis and water sports nearby.

Publicity: *Nashville Tennessean, Jackson Sun, Birmingham News, Savannah Courier, Memphis Commercial Appeal, Tennessee Magazine, Country Magazine and PBS TV Tennessee Crossroads.*

Sevierville B8

Little Greenbrier Lodge

3685 Lyon Springs Rd
Sevierville, TN 37862-8257
(865)429-2500 (800)277-8100
E-mail: littlegreenbrier@worldnet.att.net
Web: www.littlegreenbrierlodge.com

Circa 1939. The spectacular, forested setting at Little Greenbrier is worth the trip. The rustic lodge is set on five, wooded acres less than a quarter mile from Great Smoky Mountains National Park. Rooms have valley or mountain views and are decorated with Victorian-style furnishings and antiques. The lodge served guests from 1939 until the 1970s when it became a religious retreat. When the innkeepers purchased it in 1993, they tried to preserve some of its early history, including restoring original sinks and the first bathtub ever installed in the valley. A copy of the lodge's original "house rules" is still posted. Within 30 minutes are Dollywood, outlet malls, antiquing, craft stores and plenty of outdoor activities.

Innkeeper(s): Charles & Susan LeBon. $100-125. MC, VISA, DS, PC, TC. TAC10. 9 rooms with PB, 1 cabin and 1 conference room. Breakfast and snacks/refreshments included in rates. Types of meals: Full bkfst and early coffee/tea. Beds: QD. Ceiling fan in room. Air conditioning. VCR, fax and library on premises. Small meetings, family reunions and seminars hosted. Amusement parks, antiquing, fishing, golf, live theater, parks, shopping, downhill skiing, cross-country skiing, sporting events and tennis nearby.

Publicity: *Knoxville News Sentinel, Miami Herald and Detroit Free Press.*

Shelbyville C5

Cinnamon Ridge B&B

799 Whitthorne St
Shelbyville, TN 37160-3501
(931)685-9200 (877)685-9200 Fax:(931)684-0978
Web: www.bbonline.com/tn/cinnamon/

Circa 1927. Tennessee offers many reasons to visit, not the least of which is this hospitable home. The light scent of cinnamon permeates the home, which is decorated with antiques in a mix of Colonial and Traditional styles. Innkeeper Pat Sherrill loves to pamper guests, especially with food. The full breakfasts are accompanied by candlelight and soft, soothing music. Pat serves afternoon teas and has created a few special events, including her Chocolate Lovers' Paradise, where guests enjoy a variety of cocoa-laden delicacies.

Innkeeper(s): Bill & Pat Sherrill. $65-75. MC, VISA, AX, TC. 5 rooms with PB and 1 conference room. Breakfast, afternoon tea and snacks/refreshments included in rates. Types of meals: Full bkfst and early coffee/tea. Beds: KD. Cable TV, phone, ceiling fan and central heat in room. Central air. VCR, fax and bicycles on premises. Weddings, small meetings, family reunions and seminars hosted. Amusement parks, antiquing, fishing, live theater, parks, shopping and water sports nearby.

Smithville B6

The Inn at Evins Mill

1535 Evins Mill Road
Smithville, TN 37166
(615)269-3740 (800)383-2349 Fax:(615)269-3771
E-mail: info@evinsmill.com
Web: www.evinsmill.com

Circa 1939. More than a country inn, this 40-acre secluded retreat includes a main log lodge, three award-winning cottages and a working gristmill. Poplar floors, fieldstone fireplaces and cedar porches invoke a comfortable ambiance for gathering. Resort amenities are offered in a comfortable bed & breakfast style. The Millstone Restaurant provides the perfect mealtime setting. Groups, families, couples and individuals can find team building, personal renewal, romance and rejuvenation. There are rolling hills, creeks and streams, hiking trails, fishing ponds, a ropes course and a swimming hole beneath a cascading waterfall.

Innkeeper(s): Gloria Roberts. $100-220. MC, VISA, DS, PC. TAC10. 14 rooms with PB and 2 conference rooms. Breakfast, picnic lunch, snacks/refreshments and dinner included in rates. Types of meals: Gourmet bkfst, country bkfst, veg bkfst, early coffee/tea and lunch. MAP, AP, EP. Beds: KT. Ceiling fan and private deck in room. Air conditioning. VCR, fax, copier, swimming, library, waterfalls, gristmill, hiking trails, fishing ponds, dart boards, cigars and restaurant on premises. Weddings, small meetings, family reunions and seminars hosted. Antiquing, art galleries, canoeing/kayaking, fishing, golf, hiking, Smithville Fiddler's Jamboree, parks, shopping, water sports and wineries nearby.

Publicity: *Nashville Business Journal, The Review Appeal and Tennessean.*

Walland B8

Blackberry Farm

1471 W Millers Cove Rd
Walland, TN 37886-2649
(865)984-8166 Fax:(865)681-7753
E-mail: info@blackberryfarm.com
Web: www.blackberryfarm.com

Circa 1939. Gracious furnishings, spectacular scenery and gourmet cuisine are three of the reasons why guests return to Blackberry Farm. The 1,100 lush acres offer miles of nature to enjoy, complete with areas perfect for hiking, biking and fly fishing. The front terrace is lined with rocking chairs perfect for relaxing and enjoying the wonderful views. Guests are treated to deluxe breakfasts, lunches and dinners. The innkeepers also keep a pantry stocked  with snacks and beverages. The rooms are exquisitely decorated and furnished with great attention to detail. The original 1870 farmhouse now houses a new spa facility. After a few days of being mercilessly pampered, guests won't want to leave.

Historic Interest: If the bounty of activities available at the inn fails to keep you busy, try visiting Gatlinburg. A 45-minute drive takes guests to this scenic mountain village. Another 40 minutes or so will take guests to Pigeon Forge. The inn backs up onto the Great Smoky Mountains National Park, which includes Cades Cove, a primitive settlement about 30 minutes from the inn.

Innkeeper(s): Kreis & Sandy Beall. $395-895. MC, VISA, AX. TAC8. 43 rooms, 44 with PB. Breakfast, picnic lunch, afternoon tea and dinner included in rates. Types of meals: Full bkfst. Beds: KQDT.

Publicity: *Country Inns, Town & Country, Travel & Leisure, Southern Living, Conde Nast Traveler, Andrew Harper's Hideaway Report, Bon Appetit and Gourmet.*

"Everything was spectacular! A wonderful weekend getaway!"

Texas

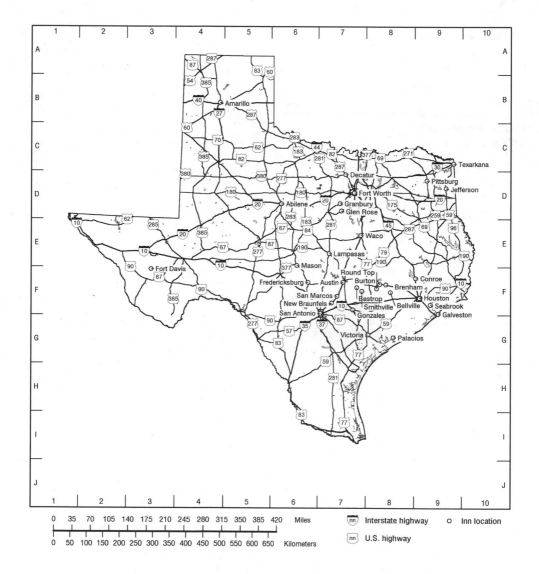

Abilene   D6

BJ's Prairie House B&B

508 Mulberry St
Abilene, TX 79601-4908
(915)675-5855 (800)673-5855 Fax:(915)677-4694
E-mail: bfender@earthlink.net

Circa 1902. This B&B was completely redesigned in 1920, omitting all references to the previous Victorian architecture and transforming into a prairie-style home. The home is filled with

antiques and modern luxuries. Rooms bear the names Love, Joy, Peace and Patience, all clues to the relaxing, hospitable atmosphere. Peace includes a huge clawfoot tub.

Innkeeper(s): Bob & BJ Fender. $75-85. MC, VISA, AX, TC. 4 rooms, 2 with PB. Breakfast included in rates. Types of meals: Full bkfst. Beds: KQDT. Ceiling fan and clocks in room. Central air. VCR on premises. Antiquing, fishing, live theater, parks, shopping, sporting events and water sports nearby.

Amarillo   B4

Parkview House B&B

1311 S Jefferson St
Amarillo, TX 79101-4029
(806)373-9464 Fax:(806)373-3166
E-mail: parkviewbb@aol.com
Web: www.parkviewbb.20m.com

Circa 1908. Ionic columns support the wraparound wicker-furnished front porch of this prairie Victorian. Herb and rose gardens, highlighted by statuary and Victorian gazing ball, surround the property. Antique mahogany, walnut and oak pieces are found throughout. The inn guest rooms feature draped bedsteads and romantic decor. A gourmet, full or continental-plus breakfast is

served in an Andy Warhol-style kitchen or in the formal dining room. Guests may relax and enjoy the fireplaces, either in the kitchen or in the common room. Borrow a bicycle for a tour of the historic neighborhood or enjoy a multitude of area attractions, which include

shopping for antiques along historic Route 66, hiking and horseback riding in Palo Duro Canyon, touring historic homes and museums, seasonal birdwatching or perhaps attending the ballet, opera, symphony or a performance of "Texas," an outdoor musical drama presented nearby. After a day of sightseeing, guests may enjoy a soak in the inn's hot tub under the starry Texas sky.

Historic Interest: Panhandle Plains Museum (15 minutes), Palo Duro State Park (23 miles), Alibates Flint Monument (16 miles).

Innkeeper(s): Carol & Nabil Dia. $65-135. MC, VISA, AX, PC, TC. TAC10. 5 rooms, 3 with PB, 1 suite and 1 cottage. Breakfast included in rates. Types of meals: Gourmet bkfst, cont plus, early coffee/tea and snacks/refreshments. Beds: QD. TV, some ceiling fans, desks and telephones in room. Air conditioning. VCR, fax and bicycles on premises. Weddings and small meetings hosted. Arabic spoken. Amusement parks, antiquing, bicycling, hiking, horseback riding, bird watching, live theater, parks, shopping, tennis and water sports nearby.

Publicity: *Lubbock Avalanche, Amarillo Globe News, Accent West, Sunday Telegraph Review. and Channel 7.*

"You are what give B&Bs such a wonderful reputation. Thanks very much for the wonderful stay! The hospitality was warm and the ambiance incredible."

Austin   F7

Austin's Wildflower Inn B&B

1200 W 22 1/2 St
Austin, TX 78705-5304
(512)477-9639 Fax:(512)474-4188
E-mail: kjackson@io.com
Web: www.austinswildflowerinn.com

Circa 1936. This Colonial-style home fits right into its woodsy street, located in a quiet Austin neighborhood just a few blocks from the University of Texas. Three of the rooms are named for

relatives of innkeeper Kay Jackson, who is related to a former president of the Republic of Texas. Lacy curtains, stenciling, pedestal sinks, quilts and antiques create a homey country atmosphere. One room has a canopy bed, another

includes a four-poster, oak bed. Each morning, a new Wildflower specialty is served at breakfast, along with homemade breads or muffins and fresh fruit. The State Capitol Complex is a few minutes from the home.

Innkeeper(s): Kay Jackson. $94-139. MC, VISA, AX, PC, TC. 3 rooms with PB. Breakfast included in rates. Types of meals: Full bkfst and early coffee/tea. Beds: QD. Ceiling fan and telephones (two rooms) in room. Air conditioning. Fax on premises. Antiquing, fishing, live theater, parks, shopping, sporting events and water sports nearby.

"I was enchanted by your very friendly reception and personal care for my well-being."

Carriage House Inn

1110 West 22 1/2 Street
Austin, TX 78705
(512)472-2333 Fax:(512)476-0218
E-mail: dcarriagehouse@aol.com
Web: www.carriagehouseinn.org

Circa 1930. Downtown is eight minutes from this two-story Colonial inn with carriage house and ranch house accommodations. Antique-filled guest bedrooms and suites feature hardwood floors, lace curtains, wooden beds, fine linens and fresh flowers. Many have private entrances and a porch or deck, and some offer Jacuzzis or soaker tubs. Homemade waffles, biscuits, scones and other delicious favorites are part of the hearty breakfast served on handmade cedar tables or delivered to the suite. The spacious grounds hold pleasant surprises including a gazebo, outdoor swings, a second-floor deck, lily pond with koi and a waterfall. For further relaxation, a massage therapist is recommended.

Historic Interest: Texas State Capital (2 miles), Elizabeth Ney museum (3 miles), Neil Cochran Home (2 blocks), Downtown Austin (1 mile), Caswell House (6 blocks).

Innkeeper(s): Tressie & Jim Damron. $100-175. MC, VISA, AX, DS, TC. 5 rooms with PB and 2 suites. Breakfast included in rates. Types of meals: Gourmet bkfst, veg bkfst and cont. Beds: KQ. Cable TV, phone, turndown service, VCR and hot tub in room. Central air. Fax on premises. Small meetings and family reunions hosted. Antiquing, art galleries, bicycling, canoeing/kayaking, fishing, golf, hiking, LBJ Presidential Library, Texcas History Museum, Music District, Concert Hall, State Capital, Elizabeth Ney Museum, live theater, museums, parks, shopping, sporting events, tennis, water sports and wineries nearby.

Publicity: *Valiente Magazine.*

Governors' Inn

611 W 22nd St
Austin, TX 78705-5115
(512)479-0638 (800)871-8908 Fax:(512)476-4769
E-mail: governorsinn@earthlink.net
Web: www.governorsinnaustin.com

Circa 1897. This Neoclassical Victorian is just a few blocks from the University of Texas campus and three blocks from the State Capitol. Guests can enjoy the view of two acres of trees and foliage from the porches that decorate each story of the inn. The innkeepers have decorated the guest rooms with antiques and named them after former Texas governors. Several of the bathrooms include clawfoot tubs.

Innkeeper(s): Lisa Wiedemann. $59-119. MC, VISA, AX, DC, CB, DS, TC. 10 rooms with PB, 5 with FP and 1 conference room. Breakfast, afternoon tea and snacks/refreshments included in rates. Types of meals: Gourmet bkfst, early coffee/tea and picnic lunch. Beds: KQ. Cable TV, phone, turndown service, ceiling fan, hair dryers and robes in room. Air conditioning. VCR, fax and copier on premises. Handicap access. Weddings, small meetings, family reunions and seminars hosted. Antiquing, fishing, live theater, parks, shopping, sporting events and water sports nearby.

Pets Allowed.

Publicity: *USA Today, Instyle, Austin Chronicle and Romantic Inns of America.*

Healthy Quarters

1215 Parkway
Austin, TX 78703-4132
(512)476-7484 (800)392-6566 Fax:(512)480-9356
E-mail: healthyquarters@webtv.net
Web: www.healthyquarters.com

Circa 1935. This homestay is located near the State Capitol and the University of Texas on the edge of the downtown area. The comfortable accommodations include the Sun Room, which features an arched ceiling, a quilt-topped bed and country décor. The Ivy Room boasts a Jacuzzi shower bathtub, Elizabeth Ashley bed linens and a long series of shuttered windows adorns one wall. The guest refrigerators are stocked with milk, eggs, yogurt, English muffins and organic coffee. Juice, purified water and fresh organic fruit are also provided.

Historic Interest: State Capitol (1/2 mile), French Legation (1.5 miles), LBJ Library (1 mile).

Innkeeper(s): Marilyn Grooms. $65-85. MC, VISA, AX, DS. TAC10. 2 rooms with PB. Breakfast included in rates. Beds: QD. Cable TV, phone, VCR, private entrances and kitchen area in room. Central air. Antiquing, art galleries, bicycling, canoeing/kayaking, golf, hiking, State Capitol, LBJ Library, live theater, museums, parks, shopping and sporting events nearby.

Lazy Oak B&B

211 W Live Oak St
Austin, TX 78704-5114
(512)447-8873 (877)947-8873 Fax:(512)912-1484
E-mail: lazyoakinn@aol.com
Web: www.lazyoakbandb.com

Circa 1911. For a fun getaway, this historic plantation-style farmhouse offers an airy and relaxed ambiance. The mix of eclectic antique furnishings and decor imparts a casual country feel. Luxurious amenities are found in the comfortable guest bedrooms. Arrange for a massage, or soak in the hot tub. Linger over a scrumptious homemade breakfast enjoyed in-room, on the spacious front porch or in the kitchen. Gaze at the fish pond while strolling the landscaped acre. Borrow a bike or take a short walk to the sites and activities of Town Lake and Congress Avenue.

Historic Interest: Capitol Building (1.6 miles).
Innkeeper(s): Renee & Kecin Buck. $89-125. MC, VISA, AX, DC, DS, PC, TC. TAC10. 5 rooms with PB. Breakfast and snacks/refreshments included in rates. Types of meals: Gourmet bkfst, veg bkfst and early coffee/tea. Beds: KQD. Cable TV, phone and ceiling fan in room. Central air. VCR, fax, copier, bicycles, library and hot tub on premises. Small meetings and seminars hosted. Amusement parks, antiquing, art galleries, bicycling, canoeing/kayaking, fishing, golf, hiking, live theater, museums, parks, shopping, sporting events, tennis, water sports and wineries nearby.

Publicity: *Austin Chronicle.*

"The most relaxing and wonderful time. Breakfast was great and the accommodations were the nicest we've stayed in."

Woodburn House B&B

4401 Avenue D
Austin, TX 78751-3714
(512)458-4335 (888)690-9763 Fax:(512)458-4319
E-mail: woodburnhouse@yahoo.com
Web: www.woodburnhouse.com

Circa 1909. This stately home was named for Bettie Hamilton Woodburn, who bought the house in 1920. Hamilton's father was once the provisional governor of Texas and a friend of Abraham Lincoln. The home once was slated for demolition and saved in 1979 when George Boutwell bought the home for $1

 and moved it to its present location. Guests will be taken immediately by the warmth of the home surrounded by old trees. The home is furnished with period antiques. Breakfasts are served formally in the dining room.

Historic Interest: The Elisabeth Ney Sculpture Museum is three blocks from Woodburn House. The bed & breakfast is within a district listed in the National Register and walking tours are offered.

Innkeeper(s): Herb & Sandra Dickson. $90-140. MC, VISA, AX, PC, TC. TAC10. 4 rooms with PB and 1 suite. Breakfast included in rates. Types of meals: Gourmet bkfst and early coffee/tea. Beds: KQT. Phone, ceiling fan, whirlpool for two, double vanity, sitting room with sofa and and TV in suite in room. Air conditioning. VCR, fax and amenities for the deaf on premises. Spanish spoken. Antiquing, fishing, museum, live theater, parks, shopping and sporting events nearby.

"The comfort, the breakfasts and the hospitality were excellent and greatly appreciated."

Bastrop   F7

Pecan Street Inn

1010 Pecan St
Bastrop, TX 78602-3221
(512)321-3315 Fax:(512)321-3880
E-mail: pletsch@bastrop.com
Web: www.pecanstreetinn.com

Circa 1903. Designated as a city landmark and listed in the National Register, this Carpenter Gothic/Queen Anne Victorian home has been meticulously restored. Sitting in a grove of native pecan trees, the inn features elaborate millwork, pocket doors, and long leaf heart of pine floors and American antiques. Games, toys, books and TV/VCR are found in the front and back parlors. Romantic fireplaces are featured in two of the guest bedrooms. Featherbeds, Irish linens and sherry are a few more treats to experience. Signature dishes like Pecan Waffles with Strawberries Grand Marnier are served with other delicious fare on settings of china, crystal and silver in one of the two dining rooms. The massive wraparound porch is pure relaxation with sofas, rockers and swings.

Innkeeper(s): Shawn & Bill Pletsch. $75-95. PC, TC. 6 rooms, 5 with PB, 2 with FP and 1 conference room. Breakfast and snacks/refreshments included in rates. Types of meals: Gourmet bkfst, veg bkfst, cont plus and early coffee/tea. Beds: KQDT. Cable TV, phone, ceiling fan, VCR and fireplace in room. Central air. Bicycles, library and covered parking on premises. Weddings, small meetings, family reunions and seminars hosted. Antiquing, art galleries, bicycling, canoeing/kayaking, fishing, golf, hiking, horseback riding, live theater, museums, parks, shopping and sporting events nearby.

Pets allowed: Must be kenneled in utility room.

Publicity: *Texas Monthly Magazine and Fox Network-Austin.*

Bellville   *F8*

Bluebonnet Inn

214 S Live Oak St
Bellville, TX 77418-2340
(979)865-0027
Web: www.bluebonnet-inn.com

Circa 1906. Use of the downstairs parlor, fenced swimming pool and bottomless cookie jar is encouraged at this Victorian B&B. Porch swings are strategically located on the balcony and front porch. There's a cozy upstairs sitting room for reading, television or conversation. Around 9 a.m. each morning, guests gather in the old family dining room for a full Southern-style breakfast. Innkeepers can provide information on excursions to Blue Bell Creamery, Winedale, Round Top and Festival Hill.
$60-75. 5 rooms. Breakfast included in rates. Types of meals: Full bkfst. Ceiling fan in room. Air conditioning. Weddings, small meetings, family reunions and seminars hosted. Antiquing nearby.

Brenham   *F8*

Ant Street Inn

107 W Commerce St
Brenham, TX 77833-3635
(979)836-7393 (800)481-1951 Fax:(979)836-7595
E-mail: stay@antstreetinn.com

Circa 1899. It seemed a shame to Ant Street's innkeepers to let this historic, Renaissance Revival building go to waste. So, out of what once served as a commercial building, saloon and gambling hall, there is now an elegant inn. From the exterior, it's easy to conjure up images of life in turn-of-the-century Brenham. The  interior also has a nostalgic feel, with rooms decorated in elegant antiques, including a selection of beautifully crafted beds. Exposed brick walls, stained glass and 12-foot ceilings are other special features. In addition to the fine antiques and Oriental rugs, modern amenities include cable TV, data ports and individual climate control. Breakfast is an Epicurean's delight. A typical morning menu might sound something like Canadian bacon, Brie quiche and freshly baked blueberry and peach coffeecake. There is much to see and do in Brenham, but one must make a trek out to the Blue Bell Creameries, for a taste of the famed Blue Bell ice cream.
Innkeeper(s): Tommy & Pam Traylor. $105-235. MC, VISA, AX. TAC10. 14 rooms with PB and 3 conference rooms. Breakfast included in rates. Types of meals: Full bkfst and early coffee/tea. Beds: QD. Cable TV, phone and ceiling fan in room. Air conditioning. Fax and copier on premises. Weddings, small meetings, family reunions and seminars hosted. Antiquing, fishing, live theater, parks and shopping nearby.

"I love your inn and the beautiful furnishings you have brought in."

Mariposa Ranch B&B

8904 Mariposa Ln
Brenham, TX 77833-8906
(979)836-4737 (877)647-4774
E-mail: info@mariposaranch.com

Circa 1870. Several buildings comprise the inn: a Victorian, an 1820 log cabin, a quaint cottage, a farmhouse and a 1836 Greek Revival home. Guests relax on the veranda, stroll through the Live Oaks or explore the ranch's 100 acres of fields and mead-  ows. The inn is furnished with fine antiques. Ask for the Texas Ranger Cabin and enjoy a massive stone fireplace, sofa, clawfoot tub and loft with queen bed. Jennifer's Suite boasts a king canopy bed and two fireplaces. The "Enchanted Evening" package offers champagne, fruit, flowers, candlelight, candy and an optional massage. Guests can select a room with a Jacuzzi for two or a clawfoot tub for additional luxury.
Innkeeper(s): Johnna & Charles Chamberlain. $85-175. MC, VISA, PC, TC. TAC10. 11 rooms with PB, 9 with FP, 3 suites, 3 cottages, 2 cabins and 1 conference room. Breakfast included in rates. Types of meals: Gourmet bkfst, early coffee/tea and gourmet dinner. Beds: KQDT. TV, ceiling fan, VCR and microwaves in room. Air conditioning. Fax, copier and library on premises. Handicap access. Weddings, small meetings, family reunions and seminars hosted. Spanish spoken. Antiquing, fishing, golf, live theater, parks, shopping, tennis and water sports nearby.

Publicity: *Southern Living and Texas Monthly.*

Burton   *F8*

Long Point Inn

3806 FM 390 West
Burton, TX 77835-5584
 (877)979-3171
E-mail: longpointinn@aol.com
Web: www.longpointinn.com

Circa 1978. It might seem unusual to find a Bavarian chalet in Texas, but not when you consider that many German immigrants made the state their home after arriving in America. One of those immigrant families once lived in an 1840s log cabin that has been restored and added to the inn complex. This cabin has a stone fireplace and sleeps six. Although this inn is newer, the innkeepers patterned their dream home in Old World style, including decorating it with treasures picked up during their global travels. The  home rests on a 175-acre working cattle ranch that has been in the family for four generations. So, it's at this Bavarian inn and ranch where guests enjoy the best of Texas with a touch of Europe. Rooms are a little bit Old World and a little bit country. A hearty breakfast is served underneath a German crystal chandelier on a table set with fine china. Guests might partake of a savory egg dish, homemade German sausage, potatoes, freshly baked breads and a fresh fruit compote during their morning meal. The inn is located along FM 390, the only highway in Texas to be designated a historic, scenic highway and is midway between Houston and Austin.
Innkeeper(s): Bill & Jeannine Neinast. $80-130. AX. TAC10. 3 rooms, 2 with PB and 1 cottage. Breakfast and snacks/refreshments included in rates. Types of meals: Gourmet bkfst. Beds: QDT. Phone, ceiling fan and cottage

has fireplace in room. Air conditioning. VCR on premises. German spoken. Antiquing, classical music and Shakespeare, parks and shopping nearby.

Publicity: *Houston Chronicle, Dallas Morning News, Insite, Farm & Ranch Living, Progressive Farmer and Country.*

"The wildflowers, Texas sunshine and the goodness of you two all created a warmth we dearly loved."

Conroe   F9

Heather's Glen . . . A B&B & More

200 E Phillips St
Conroe, TX 77301-2646
(936)441-6611 (800)665-2643 Fax:(936)441-6603
E-mail: heathersbb@aol.com

Circa 1900. This turn-of-the-century mansion still maintains many of its original features, such as heart-of-pine flooring, gracious staircases and antique glass windows. Verandas and covered porches decorate the exterior, creating ideal places to relax. Guest rooms are decorated in a romantic, country flavor. One room has a bed draped with a lacy canopy, and five rooms include double Jacuzzi tubs. Antique shops, an outlet mall and Lake Conroe are nearby, and the home is within an hour of Houston.

Innkeeper(s): Ed & Jamie George. $75-195. MC, VISA, AX, DS, PC, TC. 8 rooms with PB, 3 with FP and 3 conference rooms. Breakfast, afternoon tea and snacks/refreshments included in rates. Types of meals: Gourmet bkfst and early coffee/tea. Beds: QD. Cable TV, phone, turndown service and ceiling fan in room. Air conditioning. Fax and copier on premises. Handicap access. Weddings, small meetings, family reunions and seminars hosted. Limited Spanish spoken. Amusement parks, antiquing, fishing, auctions weekly, live theater, parks, shopping, downhill skiing, sporting events and water sports nearby.

Decatur   D7

Abbercromby Penthouse Suites

103 W Main St
Decatur, TX 76234
(940)627-7005 (888)677-7737
E-mail: txabby@aol.com

Circa 1895. Enter a time of nostalgic fantasy in this Victorian building on historic Town Square. The inn's three, second-story suites are lavish re-creations of a bygone era. Distinctly different in style and theme, they are impressive encounters with old-fashioned pampering, grand luxury or
romantic seclusion. Fully furnished to meet modern needs, thoughtful attention also has been given to providing amenities. Each morning a delicious gourmet continental breakfast is delivered for private dining pleasure. For a delightful splurge, schedule an individual or couple's massage.

Historic Interest: Disney-castle type courthouse more than 100 years old (across the street).

Innkeeper(s): Bob & Margaret Atkinson. $99-135. MC, VISA, AX, DC, DS, PC, TC. TAC15. 3 suites and 1 conference room. Breakfast included in rates. Types of meals: Full bkfst. Beds: KQT. Cable TV, phone, ceiling fan, VCR and fireplace in room. Central air. Fax, copier, spa, pet boarding, three massage therapists on staff and complete wedding packages from harp music to make-up artist on premises. Weddings, small meetings, family reunions and seminars hosted. Spanish spoken. Amusement parks, antiquing, art galleries, hiking, museums and shopping nearby.

Fort Davis   F3

The Veranda Country Inn B&B

PO Box 1238
Fort Davis, TX 79734-1238
 (888)383-2847
E-mail: info@theveranda.com
Web: www.theveranda.com

Circa 1883. A mile above sea level sits this historic inn, which first opened as the Lempert Hotel, a stopping point for travelers on the nearby Overland Trail. An owner later used the building for apartments, but current innkeepers Paul and Kathie Woods returned the home into a place for hospitality. Paul and Kathie have restored their bed & breakfast's high ceilings, wood  floors and beaded wood ceilings back to their original condition. The interior is furnished with antiques and collectibles. All rooms have a private bath, and the separate Carriage House and Garden Cottage are available in addition to the 11 inn rooms. The grounds offer the serene setting of gardens, quiet courtyards and large covered porches with rocking chairs.

Historic Interest: The Fort Davis area is full of historic places to visit, including the Fort Davis Historic Site, an 1854 restored frontier fort. The largest original unpaved portion of the Overland Trail is just a block away, and the Overland Trail Museum is another popular historic attraction. The Neill Doll Museum, which is located in a turn-of-the-century home, features more than 300 antique dolls.

Innkeeper(s): Paul & Kathie Woods. $80-115. MC, VISA, DS. 14 rooms with PB, 4 suites and 2 cottages. Breakfast included in rates. Types of meals: Full bkfst. Beds: KQ. Small meetings hosted. Horseback riding, historic sites, parks and shopping nearby.

Fort Worth   D7

Miss Molly's Bed & Breakfast, Inc

109 1/2 W Exchange Ave
Fort Worth, TX 76106-8508
(817)626-1522 (800)996-6559 Fax:(817)625-2723
E-mail: missmollys@travelbase.com

Circa 1910. An Old West ambiance permeates this hotel, which once was a house of ill repute. Miss Josie's Room, named for the former madame, is decked with elaborate wall and ceiling coverings and carved oak furniture. The Gunslinger Room is filled with pictures of famous and infamous gunfighters. Rodeo memorabilia decorates the Rodeo Room, and twin iron beds and a pot belly stove add  flair to the Cowboy's Room. Telephones and TV sets are the only things missing from the rooms, as the innkeeper hopes to preserve the flavor of the past.

Innkeeper(s): Dawn Street. $125-200. MC, VISA, AX, DC, CB, DS, PC, TC. TAC10. 7 rooms, 1 with PB. Breakfast included in rates. Types of meals: Full bkfst and early coffee/tea. Beds: DT. Ceiling fan in room. Air conditioning. Fax and copier on premises. Small meetings, family reunions and seminars hosted. Amusement parks, antiquing, stockyards National Historic district, live theater, shopping and sporting events nearby.

Publicity: *British Bulldog, Arkansas Gazette, Dallas Morning News, Fort Worth Star-Telegram, Continental Profiles, Fort Worth Gazette and Eyes Of Texas.*

Texas White House B&B

1417 8th Ave
Fort Worth, TX 76104-4111
(817)923-3597 (800)279-6491 Fax:(817)923-0410
E-mail: txwhitehou@aol.com
Web: www.texaswhitehouse.com

Circa 1910. A spacious encircling veranda shaded by an old elm tree, graces the front of this two-story home located within five minutes of downtown, TCU, the zoo and many other area attractions. The inn's parlor and living room with fireplace and gleaming hardwood floors are the most popular spots for relaxing when not lingering on the porch. Guest rooms are equipped with phones and television, and early morning coffee is provided before the inn's full breakfast at a time convenient to your personal schedule. Suites include hot tub, sauna and fireplace. Baked egg casseroles and freshly made breads are served to your room or in the dining room. The owners are Fort Worth experts and keep abreast of cultural attractions and are happy to help with reservations and planning. The inn is popular with business travelers — secretarial services are available, etc. — during the week and appealing to couples on weekends.

Historic Interest: Stockyards National Historic District.

Innkeeper(s): Grover & Jamie McMains. $105-185. MC, VISA, AX, DC, DS, PC, TC. TAC10. 5 rooms with PB and 1 conference room. Breakfast and snacks/refreshments included in rates. Types of meals: Gourmet bkfst, early coffee/tea and room service. AP. Beds: Q. Cable TV, phone, turndown service, ceiling fan and VCR in room. Central air. Fax on premises. Small meetings hosted. Antiquing, art galleries, golf, live theater, museums and parks nearby.

Fredericksburg   *F6*

Alte Welt Gasthof (Old World Inn)

PO Box 628
Fredericksburg, TX 78624
(830)997-0443 (888)991-6749 Fax:(830)997-0040
E-mail: stay@texas-bed-n-breakfast.com
Web: www.texas-bed-n-breakfast.com

Circa 1915. Located on the second floor above a Main Street shop, Alte Welt is in a Basse Block building in the historic district. The entryway opens to an antique-filled foyer. A three-room suite offers a white sofa, silver accents including a silver, tin ceiling, wood floors and an antique iron four-poster bed draped in soft gauze. An armoire with TV and a small refrigerator and microwave add convenience. The innkeeper collects antique, crocheted and embroidered linens for the guest rooms. There is a spacious deck with hot tub adjoining one of the suites. Together, the two suites can accommodate as many as 10 people, so it is popular with families and small groups, who enjoy the freedom of simply going downstairs to Main Street and all its boutiques, shops and restaurants.

Innkeeper(s): Ron & Donna Maddux. $150-165. MC, VISA, AX, DS, PC, TC. 2 suites. Breakfast included in rates. Types of meals: Cont and early coffee/tea. Beds: Q. Cable TV, phone, ceiling fan, microwave, coffee bar and in room. Air conditioning. Small meetings, family reunions and seminars hosted. Antiquing, fishing, golf, museums, hunting, parks, shopping and tennis nearby.

Magnolia House

101 E Hackberry St
Fredericksburg, TX 78624-3915
(830)997-0306 (800)880-4374 Fax:(830)997-0766
E-mail: magnolia@hctc.net

Circa 1923. This Craftsman-style home is listed as a Texas Historic Landmark and was built by Edward Stein, the designer of the Gillespie County Courthouse as well as many other local

buildings. There are porches filled with wicker furnishings for those who wish to relax. Guest rooms are decorated with antiques and reproductions. The Bluebonnet Suite includes a wood-burning fireplace, antique clawfoot tub and a vintage refrigerator in the small kitchen. Southern-style breakfasts are served on tables set with antique china, silver and fresh flowers. The home is located about seven blocks from the main shopping area, which also offers museums, art galleries and wine tasting rooms. The Lyndon Johnson State and National Park are 16 miles away and there are several wineries in the area.

Innkeeper(s): Dee & Dvid Lawford. $95-140. MC, VISA, AX, PC, TC. TAC10. 5 rooms with PB, 2 with FP and 2 suites. Breakfast and snacks/refreshments included in rates. Types of meals: Gourmet bkfst and early coffee/tea. Beds: KQ. Cable TV, ceiling fan and robes in room. Air conditioning. VCR on premises. Small meetings and family reunions hosted. Antiquing, fishing, parks and shopping nearby.

Publicity: *Houston Chronicle.*

Galveston   *F9*

The Inn at 1816 Post Office

1816 Post Office
Galveston, TX 77550
(888)558-9444
E-mail: inn1816@aol.com

Circa 1886. This Victorian inn is a highlight of Galveston's East End Historical District. Each room is decorated in a different style. The Garden Room, so named for its view of the inn's garden, is light and airy with wicker furnishings, a wrought iron bed, stained-glass window, lacy curtains and a cast-iron tub in the bathroom. Other rooms are equally pleasing. The Gain Room features a Jacuzzi tub and china pedestal sink. Antiques and clawfoot tubs, poster beds and family heirlooms are among the surprises you'll find in other rooms. Guests have use of a pool table and TV in the game room, and there are a variety of board games to enjoy. In the afternoons, refreshments are served in the inn's parlor. In the mornings, a gourmet breakfast is served in the dining room; eggs Benedict is a house specialty. There's much to do in Galveston, including viewing historic homes, shopping, visiting the Arts District or enjoying a meal at one of the area's many restaurants. Houston and all of its attractions are a short drive away.

Innkeeper(s): Bettye Hall & Judy Wilkie. $130-195. MC, VISA, AX, DS, PC. 6 rooms with PB. Breakfast and snacks/refreshments included in rates. Types of meals: Gourmet bkfst, veg bkfst and early coffee/tea. Beds: KQ. Ceiling fan in room. Central air. Bicycles, pool table and Jacuzzi's on premises. Amusement parks, antiquing, art galleries, beaches, bicycling, canoeing/kayaking, fishing, golf, horseback riding, live theater, museums, parks, shopping, tennis and water sports nearby.

Glen Rose   *D7*

The Inn on the River

205 SW Barnard St
Glen Rose, TX 76043
(254)897-2929 (800)575-2101 Fax:(254)897-7729
E-mail: inn@innontheriver.com
Web: www.innontheriver.com

Circa 1917. Nestled on the banks of the Paluxy River, the inn boasts beautifully manicured gardens and riverside seating under 300-year-old oaks. A former guest wrote a song about the trees that was later recorded by Elvis Presley. Enchanting decor and furnishings make each room a special place. Each of the 22 guest

rooms is individually decorated with careful attention to detail. The multi-course breakfast is served in the dining room, which overlooks the gardens. Enjoy specialties such as herbed scrambled eggs with cheese-sprinkled grits as you take in the view. A short walk takes you to the historic town square, which includes the stately courthouse and many interesting shops.

Innkeeper(s): Shirley & Ernest Reinke. $129-229. MC, VISA, AX, DS. 22 rooms with PB, 3 suites and 2 conference rooms. Breakfast included in rates. Types of meals: Full bkfst and gourmet dinner. Beds: KQD. Fax on premises. Antiquing, fishing, golf and water sports nearby.

Publicity: *Texas Highway, Dallas Morning News, Chocolatier, American Way, Meeting Manager and Southern Living.*

"What a wonderful place for special memories."

Gonzales   F7

Boothe House

706 Saint George St
Gonzales, TX 78629-3548
(830)672-7509 (877)245-0011
E-mail: aldawn@the-cia.net
Web: www.bbonline.com/tx/boothehouse

Circa 1913. Restoration of this Neoclassical Colonial home has been a labor of love. Great attention was given to the historic preservation of details like paint colors, design and materials used. Even the landscaping was returned to its original beauty with antique roses and a fish pond. The vintage-filled guest bedrooms, two with working fireplaces, adjoin a sitting room that can connect suites. A gourmet, organic breakfast is seasoned with herbs from the garden. The owner makes muffins, cinnamon rolls, scones, crepes, jams, preserves, salsa and granola in addition to various hot entrees. Enjoy swimming in the full-size pool and visiting the many local sites.

Historic Interest: "Come & take it" cannon (1 mile), runaway scrape (8 miles), Sam Houston treaty oak.

Innkeeper(s): Dawn & Al O'Donnell. $95. MC, VISA, AX, PC, TC. TAC5. 3 rooms with PB, 2 with FP and 2 suites. Breakfast and snacks/refreshments included in rates. Types of meals: Gourmet bkfst, early coffee/tea, picnic lunch and gourmet dinner. Beds: QD. Cable TV, fireplace and in room. Central air. Swimming on premises. Antiquing, canoeing/kayaking, fishing, golf, hiking, live theater, museums, parks and shopping nearby.

Pets allowed: Screened by reservation.

Publicity: *Texas Highways and Texmoto.*

The Houston House Bed & Breakfast

621 Saint George St
Gonzales, TX 78629-3545
(830)672-6940 (888)477-0760
E-mail: houstonhouse@gvec.net
Web: www.houstonhouse.com

Circa 1895. Houston House is an exquisite example of Queen Anne Victorian architecture. The exterior boasts a turret and a two-story, wraparound veranda, all beautifully enhanced by gingerbread trim. The interior encompasses more than 6,000 square feet. A prominent cattle baron built the home and his wife hand painted the murals that grace some of the mansion's rooms. Guest rooms all include a fireplace and antique furnishings, some of which date prior to the Civil War. In the mornings, an elegant, gourmet breakfast is served on a table set with fine china and lit by candles. Gonzales is one of the oldest towns in Texas and offers many historic attractions.

Innkeeper(s): Diana & Eugene Smith. Call for rates. MC, VISA, AX, DC, CB, DS, PC, TC. 5 rooms, 4 with PB, 5 with FP and 1 suite. Breakfast included in rates. Types of meals: Gourmet bkfst. Spanish spoken. Antiquing, fishing, golf, museums, parks and shopping nearby.

St. James Inn

723 Saint James St
Gonzales, TX 78629-3411
(830)672-7066 Fax:(830)672-7787
E-mail: email@stjamesinn.com
Web: www.stjamesinn.com

Circa 1914. A premiere bed & breakfast ideally located in the original Old Town Historic District, this three-story home was built by a cattle baron and encompasses 10,000 square feet. A casual elegance is found throughout the inn, featuring the hardwood floors, a tiled solarium and parlor. The cheerfully decorated guest bedrooms and suite with fireplaces and porches encourage relaxation. Feast on a sumptuous four-course gourmet breakfast. Enjoy a fun day in the local rural setting that is often compared to scenic European areas.

Innkeeper(s): Ann & J.R. Covert. Call for rates. MC, VISA, AX, PC, TC. 5 rooms with PB, 5 with FP, 1 suite and 1 conference room. Breakfast and afternoon tea included in rates. Types of meals: Gourmet bkfst and early coffee/tea. Beds: KQ. TV in room. Weddings, small meetings, family reunions and seminars hosted. Antiquing, fishing, golf, walking and driving tours, museums, parks and shopping nearby.

Publicity: *Gonzales Inquirer, Houston Chronicle, Victoria Advocate, Austin American Statesman and San Antonio Express-News.*

"We had a wonderful weekend. It's a marvelous home and your hospitality is superb. We'll be back."

Granbury   D7

Dabney House B&B

106 S Jones St
Granbury, TX 76048-1905
(817)579-1260 (800)566-1260
E-mail: safe-dabney@flash.net
Web: www.flash.net/~safe-dabney

Circa 1907. Built during the Mission Period, this Craftsman-style country manor boasts original hardwood floors, stained-glass windows and some of the original light fixtures. The parlor and dining rooms have large, exposed, wooden beams and the ceilings throughout are 10-feet high. The Dabney Suite has a private entrance into an enclosed sun porch with rattan table and chairs that allow for a private breakfast or a candlelight dinner by advance reservation. The bedroom of this suite is furnished with a four-post tester bed with drapes and an 1800 wardrobe.

Historic Interest: Historic Town Square (one-half mile), Dinosaur Valley State Park (18 miles), Texas Dr. Pepper Plant (45 miles), Elizabeth Crockett (5 miles).

Innkeeper(s): John & Gwen Hurley. $75-110. MC, VISA, AX, PC, TC. TAC10. 4 rooms with PB and 1 suite. Breakfast and snacks/refreshments included in rates. Types of meals: Full bkfst and dinner. Beds: Q. Ceiling fan in room. Air conditioning. VCR, spa, library, hot tub and evening beverage on premises. Small meetings, family reunions and seminars hosted. Antiquing, fishing, live theater, parks, shopping and water sports nearby.

Publicity: *Fort Worth Star Telegram and Dallas Morning News.*

Houston   *F9*

Angel Arbor Bed and Breakfast Inn

848 Heights Blvd
Houston, TX 77007-1507
(713)868-4654 (888)810-0092
E-mail: b-bhoutx@wt.net

Circa 1923. Each of the rooms at Angel Arbor has a heavenly
name, private baths and elegant decor. The Angelique Room
offers a cherry sleigh bed and a garden view. Canopy or poster

beds grace the other rooms and
suites, named Gabriel, Raphael and
Michael. The Georgian-style home is
located in the historic Houston
Heights neighborhood and was built
by a prominent local family. The
innkeeper, a cookbook author, pre-
pares mouthwatering homemade breakfasts each morning. Ask
about the innkeeper's special murder-mystery dinner parties.

Innkeeper(s): Marguerite Swanson. $95-125. MC, VISA, AX, DS, PC, TC.
TAC10. 6 rooms with PB and 1 conference room. Breakfast included in
rates. Types of meals: Gourmet bkfst, early coffee/tea and afternoon tea.
Beds: Q. Cable TV, phone, ceiling fan and VCR in room. Air conditioning. Fax
and video library on premises. Small meetings, family reunions and seminars
hosted. Amusement parks, antiquing, swimming, restaurants, live theater,
museums, parks, shopping and sporting events nearby.

The Lovett Inn

501 Lovett Blvd
Houston, TX 77006-4020
(713)522-5224 (800)779-5224 Fax:(713)528-6708
E-mail: lovettinn@aol.com

Circa 1924. Built by former Houston Mayor and Judge Joseph C.
Hutcheson, this gracious Colonial-style home remained with its
owner until his death in 1973. Located on a tree-lined street in
the center of town, the home has been meticulously restored to
blend its elegant architectural character with today's modern
amenities. Most guest rooms overlook the beautifully landscaped
grounds with its gazebo, pool and spa. Gleaming hardwood floors
and distinctive reproduction period antique furnishings are just a
few of the features that enhance the inn's natural charm. The inn
is available for weddings, receptions, retreats and meetings.

Innkeeper(s): Tom Fricke. $75-175. MC, VISA, AX, DS, TC. TAC10. 8 rooms
with PB, 3 suites and 1 conference room. Breakfast included in rates. Types
of meals: Cont. Beds: KQD. Cable TV, phone, VCR, coffeemakers,
microwaves and refrigerators in room. Air conditioning. Fax, spa, swimming
and library on premises. Weddings, small meetings, family reunions and seminars hosted. Spanish spoken. Amusement parks, antiquing, golf, museum of
Fine Arts, live theater, parks and sporting events nearby.

Pets allowed: In some rooms with prior arrangements.

Publicity: *Houston Chronicle, Dallas Morning News, Texas Monthly, Houston
Business Journal and A Woman of Independent Means.*

Palms on West Main

807 W Main St #1
Houston, TX 77006
(713)522-7987 Fax:(713)522-3150
E-mail: meadeandsmith@pdq.net
Web: www.palmsonwestmain.com

Circa 1914. Centrally located in Houston's historic museum
district, this early 20th-century Dutch Colonial home can be
found in the same neighborhood where Howard Hughes grew
up, possessing unique architecture and mature trees. The inn's

host, Tom Meade, a member of the Greater Houston
Preservation Alliance, has restored many original designs of the
house and enjoys providing ample information on Houston's
history and attractions. Private access to each suite is located
off the "Key West" deck, filled with tropical plants and fountains. Fireplaces and individual design distinguish each room.
With many activities in the Houston area, guests get prepared
each morning with a country breakfast delivered to their room
offering ham frittata, apple cinnamon muffins, fresh fruit, juice
and coffee.

Historic Interest: Historic museum district.

Innkeeper(s): Tom Meade, Rick Smith. $90-150. MC, VISA, AX. 3 suites, 2
with FP and 1 conference room. Breakfast included in rates. Types of meals:
Full bkfst. Beds: KQ. Cable TV, phone, ceiling fan and VCR in room. Air conditioning. Fax and bicycles on premises. Weddings, small meetings and seminars hosted. Amusement parks, antiquing, art galleries, bicycling, golf, live
theater, museums, parks, shopping and sporting events nearby.

Pets allowed: Well behaved.

Patrician B&B Inn

1200 Southmore Blvd
Houston, TX 77004-5826
(713)523-1114 (800)553-5797 Fax:(713)523-0790
E-mail: southmore@ev1.net

Circa 1919. Built in 1919 by attorney George S. King, the
Patrician B&B Inn makes a more intimate choice of accommoda-
tion over Houston's large, impersonal hotels. This three-story,
Colonial Revival mansion, located near the museum district, Rice
University and downtown, caters to both leisure and business

travelers. Antique accents distinguish the guest rooms. Kathleen's
Room features a clawfoot tub, and
Lollie Dee's Room offers a turn-of-
the-century burled walnut bed and
a whirlpool tub. Breakfast, served in
the large dining room or the solarium, usually consists of pear com-

pote, French toast with a generous portion of cream cheese and
marmalade, mandarin orange coffee cake and broccoli cornbread.

$95-140. MC, VISA, AX, DC, CB, DS, TC. TAC10. 5 rooms with PB, 1 suite
and 1 conference room. Breakfast and snacks/refreshments included in rates.
Types of meals: Gourmet bkfst and early coffee/tea. Beds: Q. Cable TV, phone,
ceiling fan and VCR in room. Central air. Fax and copier on premises. Weddings
and small meetings hosted. Amusement parks, antiquing, art galleries, golf, hiking, live theater, museums, parks, sporting events and water sports nearby.

Robin's Nest

4104 Greeley St
Houston, TX 77006-5609
(713)528-5821 (800)622-8343 Fax:(713)521-2154
E-mail: robin@therobin.com
Web: www.therobin.com

Circa 1898. Robin's Nest is the oldest home in Houston's historic Montrose District. A two-story wooden Queen Anne
Victorian, the historic home features original pine hardwoods,
tall windows, high ceilings and a wraparound veranda.
Luxurious fabrics, all custom sewn, warm the interior, which
also boasts wall murals. The home originally was a dairy farm
and now rests on an urban lot surrounded by dozens of rose
bushes and azaleas. Located in the city's museum and arts district, the inn offers close proximity to downtown Houston, theaters and gourmet restaurants. Galveston and Johnson Space
Center are about an hour away.

Historic Interest: The San Jacinto Monument and Armannd Bayou are 30 minutes from the home. Bayou Bend Gardens are 15 minutes away, Theatre District, Port of Houston, Museum and Arts District.

Innkeeper(s): Robin Smith. $89-130. MC, VISA, AX, DS. 4 rooms with PB and 1 conference room. Breakfast included in rates. Types of meals: Full bkfst. Beds: QT. Cable TV, phone, ceiling fan and baths in room. Air conditioning. Weddings, small meetings, family reunions and seminars hosted. Amusement parks, antiquing, fishing, live theater, museums, shopping, sporting events and water sports nearby.

Publicity: *Houston Home and Garden, Houston Business Journal, Woman's Day, Houston Metropolitan, Houston Post, Southern Living, Texas Monthly, Houston Chronicle and Inside Houston.*

"Fanciful and beautiful, comfortable and happy. We saw a whole new side of Houston, thanks to you."

Sara's B&B Inn

941 Heights Blvd
Houston, TX 77008-6911
(713)868-1130 (800)593-1130 Fax:(713)868-3284
E-mail: stay@saras.com

Circa 1898. This mauve and white, gingerbread Victorian is located in the Houston Heights, one of the first planned suburbs in Texas. Book the Tyler Room and climb the stairs that wind up to the cupola. In the Austin Suite in the turret and guests will enjoy a balcony overlooking the street. The rooms and suites are decorated with antiques and collectibles. Downtown Houston is five minutes away, and the inn is a good location to visit the Galleria, the museum district or the Arts and Medical center. The inn is a popular spot for retreats, weddings and business meetings.

Innkeeper(s): Connie & Bob McCreight. $70-200. MC, VISA, AX, DC, CB, DS. 12 rooms with PB and 4 suites. Breakfast included in rates. Types of meals: Full bkfst. Beds: KQDT. Fax on premises. Antiquing and museums nearby.

Publicity: *Houston Chronicle, Texas Homes, Elle, Travellife. and Debra Duncan Show-live.*

Jefferson D9

1st Bed & Breakfast in Texas Pride House

409 Broadway
Jefferson, TX 75657
(800)894-3526 Fax:(903)665-3901
E-mail: jefftx@mind.net
Web: www.jeffersontexas.com

Circa 1889. Mr. Brown, a sawmill owner, built this Victorian house using fine hardwoods, sometimes three layers deep. The windows are nine-feet tall on both the lower level and upstairs.

The rooms include amenities such as fireplaces, balconies, canopy beds and private entrances. Most boast original stained-glass windows, and each room is named after a steamboat that once docked in Jefferson. One room is decorated in crimson reds and features a gigantic clawfoot tub that has received an award from Houston Style Magazine for "best bath in Texas." A wide veranda stretches around two sides of the house.

Innkeeper(s): Carol Abernathy & Christel Frederick. $85-200. MC, VISA, PC, TC. TAC10. 11 rooms with PB, 3 with FP, 1 suite and 1 cottage. Types of meals: Gourmet bkfst & snacks/refreshments. Beds: KQT. Phone, ceiling fan, some fireplaces, internet access for your laptop & TV all but main house in room. Air conditioning. Handicap access. Weddings, small meetings, family reunions and seminars hosted. German spoken. Antiquing, canoeing/kayaking, fishing, steamboat tours, home tours, water skiing, antebellum home tours & live theater nearby.

Publicity: *Woman's Day, Country Home, Texas Highways and Texas Homes.*

"No five star hotel can compare to the hospitality of Pride House."

Falling Leaves Inn

304 E Jefferson St
Jefferson, TX 75657-2020
(903)665-8803

Circa 1855. Not only is Falling Leaves Inn located in Jefferson's historic district, it also has the distinction of being a Texas Historical Landmark and is listed in the National Register. Century-old trees shade the exterior of the Greek Revival home, which was built prior to the Civil War. Antiques and reproductions decorate the four  guest rooms. The innkeepers offer afternoon treats and serve up a full breakfast with items such as Cajun eggs and orange-pecan French toast. Jefferson's downtown area is just a few blocks away.

Innkeeper(s): Lisa & Michael Barry. $100. MC, VISA, DS, PC. 4 rooms with PB. Types of meals: Full bkfst, early coffee/tea and snacks/refreshments. Beds: K. Cable TV in room. Central air. Antiquing, fishing, golf, museums, parks, shopping and water sports nearby.

Lampasas E7

Historic Moses Hughes B&B

RR 2 Box 31
Lampasas, TX 76550-9601
(512)556-5923
E-mail: mhrbb@n-link.com
Web: www.moseshughesranch.com

Circa 1856. Nestled among ancient oaks in the heart of the Texas Hill Country, this native stone ranch house rests on 45 acres that include springs, a creek, wildlife and other natural beauty. The ranch was built by Moses Hughes, the first white settler and founder of Lampasas. He and his  wife decided to stay in the area after her health dramatically improved after visiting the springs. Guests can join the innkeepers on the stone patio or upstairs wooden porch for a taste of Texas Hill Country life.

Historic Interest: Fort Hood, on the road to Colorado Bend State Park and Gorman Falls, Mission San Saba (within an hour), Vanishing Texas River Cruise.

Innkeeper(s): Al & Beverly Solomon. $80-100. MC, VISA, PC, TC. TAC10. 3 rooms with PB. Breakfast included in rates. Types of meals: Gourmet bkfst. Beds: QD. Air conditioning. VCR, library and creek & springs on premises. Antiquing, fishing, hiking, birding, caves, parks and water sports nearby.

Publicity: *Spiegel Catalog, Dallas Morning News, Discover, Texas Highway., Texas Film Commission, CBS and ABC.*

"What a delightful respite! Thank you for sharing your very interesting philosophies and personalities with us at this very special B&B. We hate to leave."

Mason E6

Hasse House and Ranch

1471 Ischar
Mason, TX 76856
(888)414-2773
E-mail: laverne@hctc.net

Circa 1883. Guests may explore the 320-acre Hasse ranch, which is a working ranch where deer, wild turkey, feral hogs, quail and a bounty of wildflowers and bluebonnets are common

sights. After purchasing the land, Henry Hasse and his wife lived in a log cabin on the property before building the sandstone home 23 years later. Three generations of Hasses have lived here, and today it is owned by a great-granddaughter who restored the home in 1980. The house is located in the small German village of Art, Texas, which is located six miles east of Mason. The innkeepers rent the two-bedroom National Register home out to only one group or guest at a time, host free. The home is filled with period furniture and accessories, yet offers the modern convenience of an on-site washer and dryer and a fully stocked kitchen. The ranch grounds include a two-mile nature trail perfect for nature lovers.
Innkeeper(s): Laverne Lee. $100. MC, VISA, PC, TC. 2 rooms with PB. Types of meals: Cont plus. Beds: D. TV, ceiling fan, dishwasher, microwave and etc in room. Air conditioning. Library, washer, dryer, stove, microwave and patio on premises. Handicap access. Weddings, small meetings and family reunions hosted. Antiquing, bicycle routes, 2 mile nature trail on ranch, bird-watching, wildflower viewing, parks, shopping and water sports nearby.
Publicity: San Angelo and Tx Special & "Eyes of Texas"

"We enjoyed every aspect of our stay; the atmosphere, sense of history, rustic setting with a touch of class. We would love to return the same time next year!"

New Braunfels   F7

Gruene Homestead Inn

832 Gruene Rd
New Braunfels, TX 78130
(830)606-0216 (800)238-5534 Fax:(830)625-6390
E-mail: staff@gruenehomesteadinn.com
Web: www.gruenehomesteadinn.com

Circa 1850. The inn is composed of several historic buildings, five that have been moved to a peaceful country setting on eight acres. There are several farmhouses, a cabin, barn and cottage. Rose Cottage, for instance, is an 1800s farm home. It offers the Lady Banks Suite and The Belinda Suite. The inn's accommodations offer a variety of amenities, including Jacuzzi tubs, phones and private porches. The landscaped grounds feature a hot tub and pool and are less than a mile from the Gruene Historical District. In town, the Redbrick Gastehaus is located a half block from Gruene Hall in the Gruene Historic District. Tucked behind a handsome white wrought iron fence there are six guest rooms. The area is noted for its rafting, tubing, fishing, scenic hill country and shopping.
Innkeeper(s): Ed & Billie Miles. $95-162. MC, VISA, DS, PC, TC. TAC6. 23 rooms with PB and 1 conference room. Breakfast included in rates. Types of meals: Cont and early coffee/tea. Beds: KQDT. Cable TV, phone and ceiling fan in room. Central air. Spa and swimming on premises. Weddings, small meetings, family reunions and seminars hosted. Amusement parks, antiquing, canoeing/kayaking, fishing, golf, hiking, museums, parks, shopping, tennis, water sports and wineries nearby.
Publicity: Time Magazine and Texas Highways.

Karbach Haus

487 W San Antonio St
New Braunfels, TX 78130-7901
(830)625-2131 (800)972-5941 Fax:(830)629-1126
E-mail: khausbnb@aol.com
Web: www.karbachhaus.com

Circa 1906. For six decades the Karbach family resided in this turn-of-the-century home, beginning with Dr. Hylmar Karbach and now with innkeepers Kathleen Karbach Kinney and her hus-

band, Ben Jack. The Kinneys have restored the home to its original glory, filling it with family antiques and an eclectic assortment of pieces collected during Ben Jack's 30-year Naval career, which took the pair around the world. Particularly unique pieces include a 19th-century grandfather clock from Germany and many hand-painted porcelain pieces dated and signed by Dr. Karbach's mother. The family is always adding to their homestead. Recent additions include a swimming pool and a whirlpool spa in the gardens. The family also remodeled the carriage house, and the spacious accommodations include Jacuzzi tubs and ceiling fans. The innkeepers serve an expansive, German-style breakfast each morning in the formal dining room or in the sun parlor. The multi-course feast offers specialities of the house such as French toast, waffles or bread pudding.
Historic Interest: The oldest bakery in Texas, Hummel Museum and the Lindheimer Home are nearby. The oldest dance hall in Texas and a historic district are about three miles away, and the historic sites of San Antonio are 28 miles from the inn.
Innkeeper(s): Captain Ben Jack Kinney & Kathleen Kinney. $125-250. MC, VISA, AX, DS. 6 rooms with PB and 2 suites. Breakfast included in rates. Types of meals: Full bkfst. Beds: KQ. Spa and swimming on premises. Antiquing, museums and water sports nearby.
Publicity: Herald-Zeitung, Dallas Morning News, Houston Chronicle and Waco Tribune.

"Many thanks for a very fine stay in your home. You are people of taste and graciousness, and your home reflects both those qualities. We've truly enjoyed being here."

Old Hunter Rd Stagecoach Stop B&B

5541 FM 1102 (Hunter Rd)
New Braunfels, TX 78132
(830)620-9453 (800)201-2912
E-mail: stagecoach@satx.rr.com
Web: www.stagecoachbedandbreakfast.com

Circa 1850. Listed in the National Register, these historic hand-hewn log cabins, along with the main house, were used as a stagecoach stop for 15 years. Filled with Texas antiques, the romantic cabins offer porches, lace and in-season fragrant rose and herb bouquets. Request the LBJ Room and sleep in the former president's grandfather's cedar poster bed. Breakfast is served before the dining room fireplace and may include lemon pancakes with peppered bacon, Belgian waffles, homemade Rose jams and fresh-baked breads. The innkeeper, a landscape designer specializing in xeroscapes, has planted the three acres of gardens with antique roses and other gorgeous plants.
Historic Interest: Texas historic district.
Innkeeper(s): Bettina & Jeff Messinger. $105-180. MC, VISA, AX, PC, TC. TAC10. 5 rooms, 4 with PB. Breakfast included in rates. Types of meals: Gourmet bkfst, country bkfst, veg bkfst and early coffee/tea. Beds: Q. Cable TV, phone, turndown service and ceiling fan in room. Central air. Fax, copier, spa, swimming, bicycles and library on premises. Small meetings, family reunions and seminars hosted. German spoken. Art galleries, beaches, bicycling, canoeing/kayaking, fishing, golf, hiking, horseback riding and museums nearby.

Palacios   G8

Moonlight Bay Bed & Breakfast

506 S Bay Blvd
Palacios, TX 77465-5214
(361)972-2232 (877)461-7070 Fax:(361)972-0463
E-mail: grogers@wcnet.net

Circa 1910. A romantic retreat, or corporate stay will be a delight at this restored Craftsman bungalow home on the waterfront. The library features a collection of music and books, TV and VCR, and showcases the original chandelier and filigree fireplace. During afternoon tea enjoy Gaye's medley of songs from the 1940s on the baby grand piano in the parlor at Moonlight Bay. Wall murals and a bay view accent the Gathering Room at Paper Moon Guest House. Comfortable guest bedrooms offer elegant amenities. A complete breakfast is served on fine china with burgundy linens in the dining room that boasts original leaded-glass cabinet doors. Walk along the sea, or rock on the porch, refreshed by a soothing breeze.

Innkeeper(s): Gaye & Earl Hudson. $95-200. MC, VISA, AX, DC, CB, DS, PC, TC. TAC10. 8 rooms with PB, 1 with FP. Beds: KQD. Cable TV, turn-down service, ceiling fan, VCR, fireplace and piano and music in room. Central air. Fax, spa and library on premises. Handicap access.

Pittsburg   D9

Carson House Inn

302 Mount Pleasant St
Pittsburg, TX 75686-1335
(903)856-2468 (888)302-1878 Fax:(903)856-0709
E-mail: mailus@carsonhouse.com
Web: www.carsonhouse.com

Circa 1878. The city's oldest occupied home, this bed & break-fast with manicured lawns, a Koi pond and patio, also features a highly acclaimed restaurant. The interior was built using more than one mile of curly pine. The milled lumber known for its interesting grain pattern, came from diseased trees, now thought to be extinct. The Carson Room boasts a sleigh bed, sitting area and private entrance. It adjoins the Abernathy Room with a brass bed. The Camp Room offers a relaxing two-person whirlpool tub and two dedicated phone lines to combine business and plea-sure. The private Carson and Barnes Railroad Car, decorated with artifacts, is a fitting tribute to local history. A refrigerator, two-per-son shower and a Jacuzzi just outside make this a perfect retreat. A cooked-to-order breakfast is made when desired.

Innkeeper(s): Eileen & Clark Jesmore. $85-95. MC, VISA, AX, DC, CB, DS. 6 rooms with PB. Breakfast included in rates. Types of meals: Full bkfst, coun-try bkfst, veg bkfst, early coffee/tea, gourmet lunch, picnic lunch, afternoon tea, snacks/refreshments, gourmet dinner and room service. Beds: KQ. TV, phone, VCR, one with Jacuzzi, hair dryers, plush robes, specialty soaps and shampoos in room. Fax, video library and soft beverages on premises. Antiquing, art galleries, bicycling, canoeing/kayaking, fishing, golf, hiking, horseback riding, produce stands, Christmas tree farms, live theater, muse-ums, parks, shopping, tennis and water sports nearby.

Pets allowed: Must place deposit and take responsibility for damages.

Publicity: *Dallas Morning News, Gourmet Magazine, Texas Parks & Wildlife and Romantic America.*

Round Top   F7

Heart of My Heart Ranch B&B

PO Box 106
Round Top, TX 78954-0106
(800)327-1242 Fax:(979)249-3193
E-mail: heart17@cvtv.net
Web: www.heartofmyheartranch.com

Circa 1825. This log frontier home was built by Jared Groce, known as the father of Texas agriculture. Groce planted the state's first cotton, and built the first cotton gin in Texas. Well-appointed rooms feature antiques such as a cannonball or canopy bed. The Lone Star and Brookfield rooms boast fire-places. The Lone Star has a unique staircase that leads up to the second-story Harwood Room. The innkeepers also offer accom-

modations in the charming carriage house, Granny's Cottage, the Victorian Main House and a rustic setting in the 170-year-old log cabin. The cabin boasts a sleeping loft, stone fireplace, clawfoot tub and a complete kitchen. Rockers have been set up on the expansive front porch, perfect for relaxing. The lush grounds offer a swimming pool, Jacuzzi, fruit tree orchard and gardens. A hearty, country breakfast is served each morning, and for an extra charge, the innkeepers will prepare a picnic lunch.

Innkeeper(s): Bill & Frances Harris. $145-250. MC, VISA, AX, DS, PC, TC. 17 rooms. Breakfast included in rates. Types of meals: Full bkfst.

San Antonio   F7

A Beckmann Inn and Carriage House Bed and Breakfast

222 E Guenther Street
San Antonio, TX 78204-1405
(210)229-1449 (800)945-1449 Fax:(210)229-1061
E-mail: beckinn@swbell.net
Web: www.beckmanninn.com

Circa 1886. A wraparound porch with white wicker furniture warmly welcomes guests to the main house of this Victorian inn. Through the entrance and into the living room, guests stand on an intricately designed wood mosaic floor imported from Paris. Arch-shaped pocket doors with framed opaque glass open to the formal dining room, where breakfast is served. All the guest rooms feature 12- to 14-foot ceilings with fans; tall, ornately carved queen-size antique Victorian beds; colorful floral accessories; and antiques.

Historic Interest: Alamo, Spanish Governor's Place, Riverwalk, missions, King William Historic District.

Innkeeper(s): Betty Jo & Don Schwartz. $110-150. MC, VISA, AX, DC, DS, PC. 5 rooms with PB. Breakfast included in rates. Types of meals: Gourmet bkfst. Beds: Q. Cable TV, phone, ceiling fan, robes, hair dryers, irons/ironing boards and refrigerator in room. Air conditioning. Fax, copier and library on premises. Family reunions hosted. Amusement parks, antiquing, golf, Alamo, Riverwalk, missions, Mexican market, Spanish Governor's Palace, live the-ater, parks, shopping and sporting events nearby.

Publicity: *Texas Monthly, Country Folk Art, Country Inns, Dallas Morning News, Southern Living, Texas Highways, Vacations and Country.*

"The Beckmann Inn & Carriage House is truly a home away from home for all who stay there. Don and Betty Jo put their heart and soul into making every guest's stay a memorable experience."

A Victorian Lady Inn

421 Howard St
San Antonio, TX 78212-5531
(210)224-2524 (800)879-7116 Fax:(210)224-5123
E-mail: vli@swbell.net

Circa 1898. The innkeepers painstakingly restored this antebel-lum home back to its turn-of-the-century glory. The inn origi-nally was built for a cattle rancher and his wife. The rancher's family occupied the home for more than seven decades. Today, the Victorian Lady features 10 guest rooms, each boasting peri-od antiques, lacy curtains and Victorian decor. Full breakfasts are served daily in the grand dining room. An in-ground pool is secluded in a tropical setting with palms and banana trees.

Historic Interest: The Alamo, Monte Vista Historical District, Market Square, Riverwalk, LaVillita, San Antonio's Mission Trail and the King William Historic District are some of the nearby attractions.

Innkeeper(s): Joe & Kathleen Bowski. $89-150. MC, VISA, AX, DS. 10 rooms with PB, 3 with FP, 5 suites and 1 conference room. Breakfast included in rates. Types of meals: Full bkfst. Beds: KQD. TV, phone and ceiling fan in room. Air conditioning. Fax, swimming pool, Jacuzzi, wet bars and coffee makers on premises. Small meetings, family reunions and seminars hosted. Amusement parks, antiquing, fishing, golf, live theater, parks, shopping, sporting events and tennis nearby.

Publicity: *Fiesta, Today's Dallas Woman, Country Register and KENS-TV.*

"An oasis in the heart of San Antonio."

A Yellow Rose

229 Madison
San Antonio, TX 78204
(210)229-9903 (800)950-9903 Fax:(210)229-1691
E-mail: yellowrose@ddc.net

Circa 1878. This historic Victorian is located in the quiet and elegant King William Historic District, adjacent to San Antonio's downtown area. There are five distinctly decorated and spacious guest rooms to choose from, each with beautiful furnishings and decor, private entrance and porch. Turn-of-the-century antiques add a nostalgic ambiance. A two-block walk will take guests to the River Walk, and it's just a block to the trolley. Guests also can walk five blocks to the downtown area, convention center and many restaurants.

Historic Interest: Alamo (8 blocks), St. Francis Church (8 blocks), San Antonio Riverwalk (2 blocks), Mission Trail (one-half mile).

Innkeeper(s): Kit Walker & Deb Walker. $100-175. MC, VISA, DS, PC, TC. TAC10. 5 rooms with PB and 1 suite. Beds: Q. Cable TV, ceiling fan and robes in room. Air conditioning. VCR and library on premises. Amusement parks, antiquing, live theater, parks, shopping, sporting events and water sports nearby.

Publicity: *Aurum, Express News, Dallas Morning News, Fiesta Magazine, Patsy Swehnson's Cooking At Noon and The Today Show.*

"Recommendations will be forthcoming. Best Christmas gift we gave ourselves coming here! Thanks."

Adams House B&B

231 Adams St
San Antonio, TX 78210-1104
(210)224-4791 (800)666-4810 Fax:(210)223-5125
E-mail: adams@adams-house.com

Circa 1902. Southern tradition and hospitality abound at this bed & breakfast, decorated with sweeping verandas on both its first and second stories. The historic home has been painstakingly restored, including Oriental rugs, period antiques and handmade reproductions. Adams House is located in the King William Historic District. The River Walk is just two blocks away, and The Alamo is a 15-minute walk.

Innkeeper(s): Nora Peterson & Richard Green. $99-149. PC, TC. 4 rooms with PB. Cable TV, phone and ceiling fan in room. Air conditioning. VCR and spa on premises. Amusement parks, golf, Alamo, live theater, shopping and sporting events nearby.

Arbor House

540 N Saint Marys St
San Antonio, TX 78205-1706
(210)472-2005 (888)272-6700 Fax:(210)472-2007
E-mail: arborhaus@aol.com
Web: arborhouse.citysearch.com

Circa 1903. You'll remember far more than the Alamo when you stay in this Queen Anne Victorian compound in historic San Antonio. A Swiss cabinetmaker built the first part of the structure for his family in 1903. Recent renovations earned this home the coveted San Antonio Conservation Society Plaque. Four houses cluster around a beautiful garden

and each has three suites with high ceilings, pine floors and balconies. The inn has 19 guest bedrooms including eight bedrooms and 11 suites. The open-air "potting room" offers a cool, breezy spot for reading or just relaxing. After breakfast, guests may head out to tour the city. The inn is five minutes from the Henry B. Gonzales Convention Center, two minutes from The San Antonio River Walk and 10 minutes from the Alamo.

Innkeeper(s): Dale Schuette, Jeff Schuette, Reg Stark. $85-175. MC, VISA, AX, DS, PC, TC. TAC10. 19 rooms, 7 with PB and 11 suites. Breakfast included in rates. Types of meals: Cont. Beds: KQD. Cable TV, phone and ceiling fan in room. Central air. Fax and child care on premises. Weddings, small meetings, family reunions and seminars hosted. Amusement parks, antiquing, art galleries, golf, live theater, museums, parks, shopping, sporting events, tennis and wineries nearby.

Pets allowed: with pet carrier.

Beauregard House

215 Beauregard
San Antonio, TX 78204-1304
(210)222-1198 (888)667-0555 Fax:(210)222-9338
E-mail: info@beauregardhouse.com
Web: www.beauregardhouse.com

Circa 1900. This historic Victorian is located on a quiet street within San Antonio's King William Historic District. The Riverwalk is just a block away, and the home is near shops, restaurants and other attractions. Relaxation and comfort is the

theme at Beauregard House. Room amenities include cable TV, refrigerator and coffee service. Victorian period European furniture with old world charm decorates the bedchambers. Guests can relax on the front porch or play a game or watch movies in the home's living room. Homemade treats are served to guests upon arrival, and each morning brings with it the promise of a full gourmet breakfast. Fresh fruit dishes and homemade breads accompany entrees such as baked French toast.

Innkeeper(s): Al & Lisa Fittipaldi. $99-139. MC, VISA, PC, TC. TAC10. 5 rooms with PB, 1 with FP and 1 conference room. Breakfast included in rates. Types of meals: Gourmet bkfst, veg bkfst, early coffee/tea, picnic lunch and snacks/refreshments. Beds: KQT. Ceiling fan in room. Central air. Library on premises. Weddings, small meetings and family reunions hosted. Amusement parks, antiquing, art galleries, bicycling, fishing, golf, horseback riding, live theater, museums, parks, shopping, sporting events, tennis and water sports nearby.

Publicity: *Disney Channel, Discovery Channel, PAX TV, BBC World News and Oprah Winfrey Show.*

Bonner Garden

145 E Agarita Ave
San Antonio, TX 78212-2923
(210)733-4222 (800)396-4222 Fax:(210)733-6129
E-mail: noels@onr.com
Web: www.bonnergarden.com

Circa 1910. Mary Bonner was internationally renowned for her etchings and printmaking skills. Selected Bonner prints and works by other artists, including the Bonner House's owner, are displayed throughout the house. This Italian Renaissance inn has a rooftop patio and wet bar. The house made history when it was constructed by Atlee Ayres, who was one of the foremost architects of the era. The home was built of concrete, reinforced with

steel and cast iron, and clad in stucco. Exercise facilities include a 50-foot pool, Nordic Track exerciser and bicycles.

Innkeeper(s): Jan & Noel Stenoien. $85-125. MC, VISA, AX, DC, CB, DS, PC, TC. TAC10. 5 rooms with PB, 3 with FP. Breakfast included in rates. Types of meals: Full bkfst. Beds: KQ. Cable TV, phone, ceiling fan and VCR in room. Air conditioning. Fax, copier, swimming, bicycles, library, exercise room and rooftop spa on premises. Small meetings and family reunions hosted. Amusement parks, golf, live theater, parks, shopping, sporting events and tennis nearby.

"Second time was as great as the first."

Brackenridge House

230 Madison
San Antonio, TX 78204-1320
(210)271-3442 (800)221-1412 Fax:(210)226-3139
E-mail: benniesueb@aol.com
Web: www.brackenridgehouse.com

Circa 1901. Each of the guest rooms at Brackenridge House is individually decorated. Clawfoot tubs, iron beds and a private veranda are a few of the items that guests might discover. Several rooms include kitchenettes. Blansett Barn, often rented by families or those on an extended stay, includes two bedrooms, a bathroom, a full kitchen and living and dining areas. Many of San Antonio's interesting sites are nearby. The San Antonio Mission Trail begins just a block away, and trolleys will take you to the Alamo, the River Walk, convention center and more. Coffeehouses, restaurants and antique stores all are within walking distance. Small pets are welcome in Blansett Barn.

Innkeeper(s): Bennie & Sue Blansett. $99-200. MC, VISA, DC, DS, PC, TC. TAC10. 6 rooms with PB, 2 suites and 1 cottage. Breakfast included in rates. Types of meals: Gourmet bkfst and early coffee/tea. Beds: KQD. Cable TV, phone, ceiling fan, VCR, microwave, irons and ironing boards and hair dryers in room. Air conditioning. Fax, copier and spa on premises. Family reunions hosted. Amusement parks, antiquing, fishing, golf, live theater, parks, shopping, sporting events and tennis nearby.
Pets allowed: Small pets in carriage house.

"Innkeeper was very nice, very helpful."

Christmas House B&B

2307 McCullough
San Antonio, TX 78212
(210)737-2786 (800)268-4187 Fax:(210)734-5712
E-mail: christmashsb@earthlink.net

Circa 1908. Located in Monte Vista historic district, this two-story white inn has a natural wood balcony built over the front porch. The window trim is in red and green, starting the Christmas theme of the inn. (There's a Christmas tree decorated all year long.) Guest rooms open out to pecan-shaded balconies. The Victorian Bedroom offers pink and mauve touches mixed with the room's gold and black decor. The Blue & Silver Room is handicap accessible and is on the first floor. Antique furnishings in the inn are available for sale.

Historic Interest: Alamo (1.5 miles), Riverwalk (1.5 miles).

$85-125. MC, VISA, PC, TC. TAC10. 5 rooms with PB and 1 suite. Breakfast and snacks/refreshments included in rates. Types of meals: Full bkfst, veg bkfst and early coffee/tea. AP. Beds: KQ. Ceiling fan in room. Central air. Fax, library and ADA room on premises. Handicap access. Family reunions hosted. Amusement parks, antiquing, art galleries, bicycling, golf, live theater, museums, parks and shopping nearby.
Publicity: *Fort Worth Star Telegram.*

"What a treat to rise to the sweet smell of candied pecans and a tasty breakfast."

The Columns on Alamo

1037 S Alamo St
San Antonio, TX 78210-1109
(210)271-3245 (800)233-3364 Fax:(210)271-3245
E-mail: artlink@flash.net
Web: www.bbonline.com/tx/columns

Circa 1892. This bed & breakfast is located in an impressive Greek Revival home and a 1901 guest house in the King William Historic District. Victorian antiques and reproductions decorate the guest rooms, including pieces such as brass beds and fainting couches, four-poster beds, gas log fireplaces and several two-person Jacuzzis. The trolley stops a half block from the house, transporting guests to many of San Antonio's attractions. The River Walk and the Alamo are within walking distance, and the innkeepers recommend several restaurants that are right in the neighborhood.

Innkeeper(s): Ellenor & Arthur Link. $92-230. MC, VISA, AX, DC, CB, DS. TAC10. 13 rooms with PB, 5 with FP and 1 conference room. Breakfast included in rates. Types of meals: Full bkfst and early coffee/tea. Beds: KQ. Cable TV, phone, ceiling fan and clocks in room. Air conditioning. Fax, copier and library on premises. German spoken. Amusement parks, antiquing, riverwalk, Alamo, live theater, parks, shopping and sporting events nearby.

"The house has been an inspiration. Very friendly and helpful host and hostess."

Joske House

241 King William
San Antonio, TX 78204-1315
(210)271-0706

Circa 1900. Horse-drawn carriages set the stage in the King William Historic District, even before peeking through the inn's thick beveled-glass windows or walking through the 100-year-old solid oak door. Original parquet floors, stained glass, wood paneling and crystal chandeliers are elegantly enhanced by modern comforts such as air conditioning. Relax with a book in the parlor or on the wide verandas. Luxurious guest bedrooms feature comfortable antique tester and golden oak beds. Downstairs, the Library Room has its own porch. Linger over a generous breakfast in the formal dining room. Stroll to nearby Riverwalk, or the trolley to the Alamo is only two blocks away.

Innkeeper(s): Jessie Nora Margaret Simpson. $125-150. PC. 3 rooms with PB. Breakfast included in rates. Types of meals: Cont plus and early coffee/tea. Beds: KQ. Phone and ceiling fan in room. Central air. Bicycles and library on premises. Family reunions hosted. Amusement parks, antiquing, art galleries, live theater, museums, parks, shopping and sporting events nearby.
Publicity: *Heaven can Wait, Heaven & Hell and Dream Drives.*

Little Flower Inn

225 Madison
San Antonio, TX 78204-1321
(210)354-3116 Fax:(210)354-3116
E-mail: littleflower@satexas.com
Web: www.littleflowerinn.com

Circa 1907. The innkeepers of this elegant American Four Square house in historic King William District are dedicated to making every stay a memorable one. The inn is filled with early 1900s antiques, Oriental rugs, 14-foot floor-to-ceiling damask drapes, and rich wallcolors. The guest bedroom and suite boast private verandas. Read the paper with a cup of coffee on the front porch before indulging in fresh fruit, just-baked patisseries, and egg entrees seasoned with herbs from the garden. Eat breakfast in bed on a tray, in the formal dining room or poolside. Tea and delicacies are served every afternoon. A trolley goes to the Alamo and other sites, the Riverwalk is just two blocks away, and bikes can be rented to ride the Mission Trail.

Historic Interest: Alamo (less than 1 mile).

Innkeeper(s): Phil & Christine. $99. PC, TC. TAC10. 2 rooms, 1 with PB and 1 suite. Breakfast and afternoon tea included in rates. Types of meals: Gourmet bkfst, veg bkfst, cont plus, cont, early coffee/tea, picnic lunch and room service. AP. Beds: QT. Cable TV, phone, turndown service, ceiling fan, VCR, fireplace and swimming pool in room. Central air. Swimming and library on premises. Weddings hosted. Dutch and German spoken. Antiquing, art galleries, bicycling, hiking, live theater, museums, parks, shopping, tennis and wineries nearby.

Publicity: *Houston Chronicle.*

"What a peaceful vacation. We couldn't wait to get to Texas and do all of the fun stuff. When we arrived, the accommodations were so complete it was hard to venture out."

The Oge' House Inn on the River Walk

209 Washington
San Antonio, TX 78204-1336
(210)223-2353 (800)242-2770 Fax:(210)226-5812
E-mail: ogeinn@swbell.net
Web: www.ogeinn.com

Circa 1857. This impressive antebellum mansion is a Texas Historic Landmark. It rests on the banks of the beautiful San Antonio Riverwalk on an acre-and-a-half of gardens. Shaded by graceful oak and pecan trees, the inn has a gazebo and double-tiered veranda. There are nine fireplaces. Queen- and king-size beds are provided and all the rooms are distinguished with period antiques, handsomely upholstered sofas and chairs and Oriental carpets. The trolley, convention center and the Alamo are steps away.

Innkeeper(s): Sharrie & Patrick Magatagan. $110-325. MC, VISA, AX, DC, CB, DS, TC. 10 rooms with PB, 7 with FP and 1 conference room. Breakfast included in rates. Types of meals: Gourmet bkfst and early coffee/tea. Beds: KQ. Cable TV, phone, ceiling fan and VCR in room. Air conditioning. Fax and library on premises. Small meetings hosted. Amusement parks, antiquing, live theater, parks, shopping, sporting events and water sports nearby.

Publicity: *Victoria, McCalls, Texas Monthly, Texas Highways, London Times, New York Times, Glamour, Travel & Leisure and Southern Living.*

"Wonderfully relaxing weekend in an elegant home with pure Southern hospitality."

The Royal Swan B&B

236 Madison
San Antonio, TX 78204-1320
(210)223-3776 (800)368-3073 Fax:(210)271-0373
E-mail: theswan@onr.com
Web: www.royalswan.com

Circa 1892. This picture-perfect Victorian is filled with period furnishings that comfortably suit the handsome woodwork and polished floors. Crystal chandeliers, fireplaces and remarkable stained-glass windows add to the authentic atmosphere set by the foyer and a grand staircase, handsomely crafted out of pine. If you can't wait for the luscious peach or apple cobbler breakfast dessert, distract yourself with the quiche or crepes, bacon and fresh fruit, and the dessert will soon arrive. The Alamo, Riverwalk, restaurants and museums are all nearby.

Innkeeper(s): Sam & Renee Martinez. $100-130. MC, VISA, AX, DS, PC, TC. 5 rooms with PB, 1 with FP. Breakfast and snacks/refreshments included in rates. Types of meals: Gourmet bkfst and cont. Beds: Q. TV, phone and ceiling fan in room. Air conditioning. Fax and copier on premises. Antiquing, live theater and shopping nearby.

San Marcos F7

Crystal River Inn

326 W Hopkins St
San Marcos, TX 78666-4404
(512)396-3739 (888)396-3739 Fax:(512)396-6311
E-mail: info@crystalriverinn.com
Web: www.crystalriverinn.com

Circa 1883. This Greek Revival inn with its tall white columns has a fireside dining room with piano and wet bar. Innkeepers encourage a varied itinerary, including sleeping until noon and having breakfast in bed to participating in a hilarious murder mystery. Guests can rock the afternoon away on the veranda or curl up by the fireplace in their bedroom. Guest rooms include clawfoot tubs, four-poster and canopied beds. Texas' largest outlet mall, not too far away, features more than 200 designer stores.

Innkeeper(s): Mike, Cathy & Sarah Dillon. $85-150. MC, VISA, AX, DC, CB, DS, PC, TC. TAC10. 13 rooms with PB, 4 with FP, 3 suites, 1 cottage, 1 cabin and 1 conference room. Breakfast included in rates. Types of meals: Gourmet bkfst, cont plus, cont, early coffee/tea, lunch and dinner. Beds: KQDT. Cable TV, phone and ceiling fan in room. Air conditioning. Fax, copier, bicycles, child care, gardens, fish pond and veranda on premises. Handicap access. Weddings, small meetings, family reunions and seminars hosted. Amusement parks, antiquing, fishing, golf, live theater, parks, shopping, sporting events and water sports nearby.

Publicity: *Texas Monthly, USA Today, Country Inns, Southern Living, Dallas Morning News, Houston Chronicle, Boston Globe and Texas Highways.*

"Thanks for a smashing good time! We really can't remember having more fun anywhere, ever!"

Seabrook F9

Pelican House B&B Inn

1302 First St
Seabrook, TX 77586-3802
(281)474-5295 Fax:(281)474-7840
E-mail: pelicanhouse@usa.net

Circa 1902. An acre of lawns with live oak and pecan trees stretch to the banks of Old Seabrook's Back Bay from this cozy yellow country house. Just beyond a white picket fence, the inn's salmon shutters and inviting front porch welcome guests. Inside, there are two dining areas and a sitting room. Bed chambers feature queen-size beds and a nautical, whimsical decor. Baked eggs in pastry is a favorite morning entree. In April and September, great white pelicans assemble on the bay and fish for mullet. Ospreys and other shore birds are seen most of the year. Within walking distance are antique shops and restaurants. The Nasa Space Center is three miles away.

Innkeeper(s): Suzanne Silver. $90-100. MC, VISA, AX, DS, PC, TC. TAC10. 4 rooms with PB. Breakfast included in rates. Types of meals: Gourmet bkfst. Beds: Q. Ceiling fan in room. Air conditioning. VCR, fax and copier on premises. Small meetings hosted. Antiquing, fishing, golf, parks, shopping, tennis and water sports nearby.

Publicity: *Houston Life and Texas Highways.*

Smithville   F7

The Katy House Bed & Breakfast

201 Ramona St, PO Box 803
Smithville, TX 78957-0803
(512)237-4262 (800)843-5289 Fax:(512)237-2239
E-mail: thekatyh@onr.com
Web: www.katyhouse.com

Circa 1909. Shaded by tall trees, the Katy House's Italianate exterior is graced by an arched portico over the bay-windowed living room. Georgian columns reflect the inn's turn-of-the-century origin. Long leaf pine floors,
pocket doors and a graceful stairway
accent the completely refurbished
interior. The inn is decorated almost
exclusively in American antique oak
and railroad memorabilia. Historic
Main Street is one block away with a
fine collection of antique shops. Also

available are maps that outline walking or biking tours and point out scenic views such as that of the Colorado River from the city park. Guests usually come back from walking tours with pockets full of pecans found around town. Smithville was the hometown location for the movie "Hope Floats."

Innkeeper(s): Bruce & Sallie Blalock. $56-110. MC, VISA, AX, PC, TC. 5 rooms with PB, 1 suite and 2 cottages. Breakfast included in rates. Types of meals: Full bkfst and early coffee/tea. Beds: Q. TV, ceiling fan and VCR in room. Air conditioning. Fax and bicycles on premises. Family reunions hosted. Antiquing, fishing, parks and shopping nearby.
Pets allowed: With advance notice, in certain rooms.

Texarkana   C9

Mansion on Main B&B

802 Main St
Texarkana, TX 75501-5104
(903)792-1835 Fax:(903)793-0878
E-mail: mansiononmain@aol.com

Circa 1895. Spectacular two-story columns salvaged from the St. Louis World's Fair accent the exterior of this Neoclassical-style inn. Victorian nightgowns and sleepshirts are provided, and whether you are on a business trip or your honeymoon,

expect to be pampered. Five bedchambers, all furnished with antiques
and period appointments. Awake
to the aroma of dark roast cajun
coffee, and then enjoy a full
"gentleman's breakfast" in the
parquet dining room. The inn is
located in the downtown historic area. Enjoy a cup of rich coffee or a cool lemonade on the veranda. The inn offers plenty of amenities for the business traveler, including fax machine, desks and modem connections.

Historic Interest: Old Washington, a town frequented by the likes of Davy Crockett, Jim Bowie and Sam Houston, is 35 miles away. The historic Perot Theater, which was restored by native son Ross Perot, offers many productions throughout the year. The town also offers a living museum, the Ace of Clubs House.

Innkeeper(s): Laura Gentry. $74-109. MC, VISA, AX, PC, TC. TAC10. 5 rooms with PB. Breakfast included in rates. Types of meals: Full bkfst, early coffee/tea and afternoon tea. Beds: QD. Cable TV, phone, ceiling fan and Victorian sleepware in room. Air conditioning. Veranda, courtyard and gardens on premises. Weddings, small meetings, family reunions and seminars hosted. Antiquing, fishing, live theater and shopping nearby.
Publicity: *Arkansas Democrat, Texarkana Gazette and Dallas Morning News.*

Victoria   G8

Friendly Oaks B&B

210 E Juan Linn St
Victoria, TX 77901-8145
(361)575-0000 Fax:(361)575-0000
E-mail: innkpr@aol.com
Web: www.bbhost.com/friendlyoaks

Circa 1911. Listed in the National Register of Historic Places, this handsome home is embraced by a massive live oak, offering an enchanting adventure for first-time guests as well as repeats. Full of Texas country charm, there are several themed guest rooms including the Ranch, Thrifty Scot, the Preservation Room and the Boudoir, a favorite of couples celebrating anniversaries. Breakfasts, like everything else in Texas, are big. Guests start off with a variety of fruits, then might sample Texas-shaped scones and entrees such as pecan waffles or French toast. The grounds are covered with the namesake oak trees and the historic street known as the "Street of Ten Friends" is in the heart of historic downtown Victoria.

Innkeeper(s): Bill & CeeBee McLeod. $55-85. MC, VISA, AX, DS, PC, TC. TAC7. 4 rooms with PB and 1 conference room. Breakfast and afternoon tea included in rates. Types of meals: Gourmet bkfst and early coffee/tea. Beds: QD. Turndown service and ceiling fan in room. Air conditioning. VCR, fax and library on premises. Handicap access. Weddings, small meetings, family reunions and seminars hosted. Antiquing, fishing, golf, symphony, ballet, fine arts, live theater, parks, shopping, tennis and water sports nearby.
Publicity: *Country Extra and Lifestyle.*

"Thanks so much for the great food, the tour of the town and the step back in history."

Waco   E7

The Judge Baylor House

908 Speight Ave
Waco, TX 76706-2343
(254)756-0273 (888)522-9567 Fax:(254)756-0711
E-mail: jbaylor@iamerica.net

Circa 1940. This home was built by the head of the chemistry department at Baylor University, which is just one block away. There are five well-appointed guest rooms, each decorated with English antiques. Each room has something special. In one room, guests will discover French doors leading out to a patio. In another, there is a poster bed and hand-painted pedestal sink. Aside from the university and Elizabeth Barrett &
Robert Browning Library, the
home is near the Brazos
Riverwalk, Lake Waco, the Texas
Sports Hall of Fame, antique
shops, historic homes and more.

Innkeeper(s): Bruce & Dorothy Dyer. $72-105. MC, VISA, AX, PC, TC. TAC10. 5 rooms, 4 with PB and 1 suite. Breakfast and afternoon tea included in rates. Types of meals: Full bkfst, early coffee/tea and gourmet dinner. Beds: KQT. Ceiling fan in room. Air conditioning. VCR, fax, copier and library on premises. Weddings, small meetings, family reunions and seminars hosted. Antiquing, fishing, golf, live theater, parks, shopping, sporting events and tennis nearby.
Publicity: *Fort Worth Star-Telegram and Dallas Morning News.*

Utah

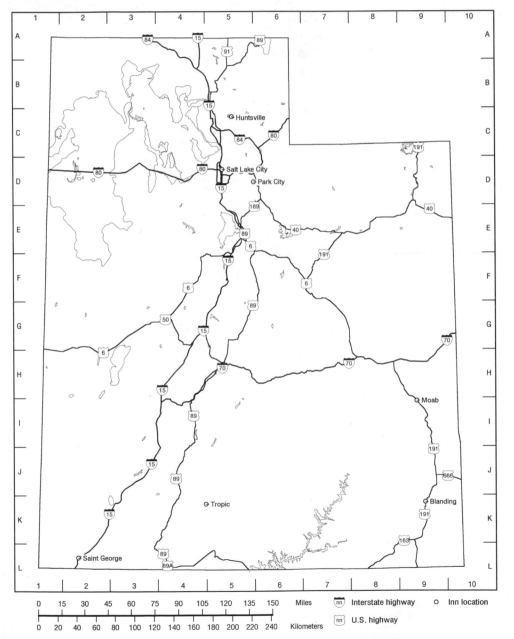

Blanding K9

The Grayson Country Inn B&B

118 E 300 S
Blanding, UT 84511-2908
(435)678-2388 (800)365-0868
E-mail: graysoninn@hotmail.com

Circa 1908. Over the years, The Grayson Country Inn has served a number of purposes, including a small hotel and boarding house. The inn is the perfect location to enjoy the many sites in the area, and is within walking distance from a pottery factory and gift shops. The area abounds with outdoor activities, as many national parks are nearby. Edge of the Cedars State Park is only a mile from the inn.

Historic Interest: Natural Bridges National Monument, Rainbow Bridge National Monument and viewing Anasazi ruins are among the day trips from the inn.

Innkeeper(s): Cliff & Diane Kerbs. $54-74. MC, VISA, AX. TAC5. 8 rooms with PB. Breakfast included in rates. Types of meals: Full bkfst. Beds: Q. Cable TV in room. Air conditioning. Small meetings and family reunions hosted. Fishing, hiking, parks and water sports nearby.

Publicity: *Salt Lake Tribune.*

Huntsville C5

Jackson Fork Inn LLC

7345 E 900 S
Huntsville, UT 84317-9778
(801)745-0051 (800)255-0672

Circa 1938. This former dairy barn was named after the hay fork that was used to transport hay into the loft of the barn. The inn has eight guest rooms, all in a two-story configuration with lofts and spiral staircases. Four rooms include two-person whirlpool tubs, and all are cozy and comfortable. A self-serve continental breakfast is prepared each day with muffins and fresh coffee. There's a restaurant on the first floor that offers fish, chicken and steak. The inn is ideal for skiers with its location near Powder Mountain, Nordic Valley and Snowbasin ski resorts.

Innkeeper(s): Vicki Petersen. $70-120. MC, VISA, AX, DS, PC, TC. 8 rooms with PB. Breakfast included in rates. Types of meals: Cont. Beds: Q. Ceiling fan in room. Air conditioning. Full breakfast on Sunday on premises. Weddings and small meetings hosted. Fishing, parks, shopping, downhill skiing, cross-country skiing and water sports nearby.

Pets allowed: With $20 fee - must be kept on leash.

Moab I9

Cali Cochitta

110 S 200 East
Moab, UT 84532
(435)259-4961 (888)429-8112 Fax:(435)259-4964

Circa 1800. This two-story sandstone brick Victorian is in Red Rock Country, which is known for its beautiful panoramas. Innkeeper Kim's beautiful garden has a fountain and is lit by torches at night. She grows both flowers and herbs. The inn is decorated with period Victorian pieces and is full of music and candlelight at night. It has five guest bedrooms including one suite and one cottage. Innkeeper David

Boger has 20 years in food management at country clubs and fine restaurants and has catered for international organizations and dignitaries including President George Bush. He cooks with fresh herbs from Kim's garden. Breakfasts include such gourmet fare as crab quiche, homemade blueberry muffins, banana bread, coffee cakes and fresh seasonal berries with the inn's secret Grand Marnier sauce. Other culinary requests, from picnic lunches to candlelight dinners, can be accommodated upon request. The inn is near Arches and Canyonlands National Park and not far from the town of Moab. Guests may enjoy antiquing, shopping touring museums and visiting wineries. Or they may go bicycling, canoeing, fishing, golfing, hiking or horseback riding. David and Kim suggest that guests get up early at least one morning during their stay, and sit on the front porch with a cup of coffee, tea or juice and soak in the magnificent Southern Utah sunrise.

Historic Interest: National Parks (Arches & Canyonlands).

Innkeeper(s): David & Kim Boger. $69-150. MC, VISA, AX, TC. 5 rooms with PB, 1 suite and 1 cottage. Breakfast and snacks/refreshments included in rates. Types of meals: Gourmet bkfst, lunch, picnic lunch and gourmet dinner. AP. Beds: QD. 100% cotton bathrobes in room. Central air. VCR, fax, copier and library on premises. Weddings, small meetings, family reunions and seminars hosted. Antiquing, art galleries, bicycling, canoeing/kayaking, fishing, golf, hiking, horseback riding, live theater, museums, parks, shopping, water sports and wineries nearby.

Sunflower Hill B&B

185 N 300 E
Moab, UT 84532-2421
(435)259-2974 (800)662-2786 Fax:(435)259-3065
E-mail: innkeeper@sunflowerhill.com

Circa 1895. Guests at Sunflower Hill stay either in a restored adobe farmhouse or a garden cottage. The one-and-a-half-acre grounds, dotted with gardens and wooded pathways, create a secluded environment, yet the home is only three blocks from downtown Moab. Guest rooms are decorated in country style with antiques and stenciled walls. A hearty breakfast buffet is served on an antique sideboard. Guests choose from a multitude of items, such as vegetable frittata, poached eggs with mushrooms and smoked turkey, lemon poppy seed scones, muffins, fresh fruit, honey-almond granola and more. There is an outdoor hot tub on the premises, as well as a laundry facility. Sunflower Hill is close to Arches and Canyonlands national parks.

Innkeeper(s): The Stucki Family. $90-195. MC, VISA, AX, DS, PC, TC. TAC10. 12 rooms with PB and 3 suites. Breakfast included in rates. Types of meals: Full bkfst, early coffee/tea, picnic lunch and snacks/refreshments. Beds: QD. Cable TV, ceiling fan and deluxe rooms have jet tubs and private balconies or patios in room. Air conditioning. VCR, fax, copier, spa and library on premises. Bicycling, fishing, golf, hiking, horseback riding, white water rafting, parks, shopping, cross-country skiing, tennis and water sports nearby.

Publicity: *Aspen Times, NBC Tonight Show with Jay Leno, Smart Money Magazine, Shape Magazine and Cowboys and Indians Magazine.*

"This place is awesome. We will be back."

Park City D6

The 1904 Imperial Hotel-A B&B

221 Main St, PO Box 1628
Park City, UT 84060-1628
(435)649-1904 (800)669-8824 Fax:(435)645-7421
E-mail: stay@1904imperial.com
Web: www.1904imperial.com

Circa 1904. The Imperial, a historic turn-of-the-century hotel, is decorated in a "Western" Victorian style. Several guest rooms include amenities like clawfoot or Roman tubs and sitting areas.

A few overlook Park City's historic Main Street. The inn's largest suite includes a bedroom and a spiral staircase leading up to a cozy loft area. There are ski lockers and a Jacuzzi on-site. Transportation to area ski lifts are located nearby.
Innkeeper(s): Nancy McLaughlin & Karen Hart. $80-245. MC, VISA, AX, DS, TC. TAC5. 10 rooms with PB and 2 suites. Breakfast included in rates. Types of meals: Full bkfst and snacks/refreshments. Beds: KQT. Cable TV and phone in room. Fax and copier on premises. Antiquing, fishing, live theater, parks, shopping, downhill skiing, cross-country skiing, sporting events and water sports nearby.

The Old Miners' Lodge - A B&B Inn

615 Woodside Ave, PO Box 2639
Park City, UT 84060-2639
(435)645-8068 (800)648-8068 Fax:(435)645-7420
E-mail: stay@oldminerslodge.com
Web: www.oldminerslodge.com

Circa 1889. This originally was established as a miners' boarding house by E. P. Ferry, owner of the Woodside-Norfolk silver mines. A two-story Victorian with Western flavor, the lodge is a significant structure in the Park City National Historic District.

Just on the edge of the woods is a deck and a steaming hot tub.
Historic Interest: Mining artifacts from the silver mining industry.
Innkeeper(s): Susan Wynne & Liza Simpson. $70-275. MC, VISA, AX, DC, CB, DS, PC, TC. TAC10. 12 rooms with PB, 3 suites and 3 conference rooms. Breakfast and snacks/refreshments included in rates. Types of meals: Full bkfst and early coffee/tea. Turndown service, ceiling fan, robes and clock in room. Fax, copier, spa and library on premises. Small meetings, family reunions and seminars hosted. Antiquing, fishing, live theater, parks, shopping, downhill skiing and cross-country skiing nearby.
Publicity: *Boston Herald, Los Angeles Times, Detroit Free Press, Washington Post, Ski, Bon Appetit. and ESPN.*

"This is the creme de la creme. The most wonderful place I have stayed at bar none, including ski country in the U.S. and Europe."

Washington School Inn

543 Park Ave, PO Box 536
Park City, UT 84060-0536
(435)649-3800 (800)824-1672 Fax:(435)649-3802
E-mail: washinn@xmission.com
Web: www.washingtonschoolinn.com

Circa 1889. Made of local limestone, this inn was the former schoolhouse for Park City children. With its classic belltower, the four-story building is listed in the National Register. Decorated in a European country-style, it is noted for its luxuriously appointed guest bedrooms and fireplace suites. Enjoy breakfast on an outdoor patio and garden area. Drinks and appetizers are served each afternoon in front of an inviting fire. A Jacuzzi and sauna are perfect places to relax. Concierge service is available. Ski storage is convenient, with ski lifts only one block away.
Innkeeper(s): Nancy Beaufait. $100-300. MC, VISA, AX, DC, DS, TC. TAC10. 12 rooms with PB, 2 with FP, 3 suites and 1 conference room. Breakfast, afternoon tea and snacks/refreshments included in rates. Types of meals: Full bkfst. Beds: KQT. Cable TV and phone in room. VCR, fax, spa and sauna on premises. Weddings, small meetings and family reunions hosted. Antiquing, fishing, live theater, parks, shopping, downhill skiing, cross-country skiing, sporting events and water sports nearby.
Publicity: *Bon Appetit, Sunset, Country Inns, San Diego Magazine, Arizona Daily Star and Salt Lake Tribune.*

"The end of the rainbow."

Saint George L2

Greene Gate Village Historic B&B Inn

76 W Tabernacle St
Saint George, UT 84770-3420
(435)628-6999 (800)350-6999 Fax:(435)628-6989
E-mail: stay@greenegate.com

Circa 1876. This is a cluster of nine restored pioneer homes all located within one block. The Bentley House has comfortable Victorian decor. The Orson Pratt House and the Tolley House are other choices, all carefully restored. The fifth house con-

tains three bedrooms each with private bath, a kitchen, living room and two fireplaces. Six of the bedrooms have large whirlpool tubs.
Historic Interest: First Mormon Temple in the West (1 mile), first Cotton Mill in the West (1 mile), Mormon Tabernacle.
Innkeeper(s): Mark & Barbara Greene. $75-139. MC, VISA, AX, DC, DS, PC, TC. TAC10. 15 rooms with PB, 8 with FP, 6 suites, 1 cottage and 1 conference room. Breakfast included in rates. Types of meals: Full bkfst, lunch, picnic lunch, snacks/refreshments and dinner. AP. Beds: KQDT. Cable TV, ceiling fan, courtyard and porches in room. Central air. VCR, fax, spa and swimming on premises. Handicap access. Weddings, small meetings, family reunions and seminars hosted. Antiquing, art galleries, bicycling, fishing, golf, hiking, horseback riding, live theater, museums, parks, shopping, tennis and water sports nearby.
Publicity: *Deseret News, Spectrum, Better Homes & Garden, Sunset and Country.*

"You not only provided me with rest, comfort and wonderful food, but you fed my soul."

Salt Lake City D5

The Anton Boxrud B&B

57 S 600 E
Salt Lake City, UT 84102-1006
(801)363-8035 (800)524-5511 Fax:(801)596-1316
E-mail: antonboxrud@earthlink.net
Web: www.netoriginals.com/antonboxrud/

Circa 1901. One of Salt Lake City's grand old homes, this Victorian home with eclectic style is on the register of the Salt Lake City Historical Society. The interior is furnished with antiques from around the country and Old World details. In the sitting and dining rooms, guests will find chairs with intricate carvings, a table with carved swans for support, embossed brass door knobs and stained and beveled glass. There is an out-door hot tub available to guests. The inn is locat-

ed just a half-block south of the Utah Governor's Mansion in the historic district. A full homemade breakfast and evening snack are provided.
Innkeeper(s): Jane Johnson. $69-140. MC, VISA, AX, DC, DS. 7 rooms, 5 with PB and 1 suite. Breakfast included in rates. Types of meals: Full bkfst, early coffee/tea, snacks/refreshments and gourmet dinner. Beds: KQT. Small meetings, family reunions and seminars hosted. Amusement parks, antiquing, fishing, live theater, shopping, downhill skiing, cross-country skiing, sporting events and water sports nearby.
Publicity: *Salt Lake Tribune.*

"Made us feel at home and well-fed. Can you adopt us?"

Armstrong Mansion Inn

667 E 100 S
Salt Lake City, UT 84102-1103
(801)531-1333 (800)708-1333 Fax:(801)531-0282
Web: www.Armstrong-BB.com

Circa 1893. A former Salt Lake City mayor built this Queen Anne-style home for his young bride. This beautiful mansion features the original carved-oak staircase and ornate wood-work.

Guest rooms are decorated with Victorian furnishings and walls feature stenciling that was designed after looking at old photographs of the home. Each room is decorated to reflect a different month of the year. The home is within walking distance to downtown shopping, businesses and other attractions. The area offers many outdoor activities, such as hiking and skiing.

Historic Interest: The home is located in Salt Lake's historic district.
Innkeeper(s): Judy & Dave Savage. $89-239. MC, VISA, AX, DS, TC. 13 rooms with PB. Breakfast included in rates. Types of meals: Full bkfst and gourmet dinner. Beds: KQD. Historic Temple Square, ski resorts and summer watersports, live theater and shopping nearby.

Ellerbeck Mansion B&B

140 North B St
Salt Lake City, UT 84103-2482
(801)355-2500 (800)966-8364 Fax:(801)530-0938
E-mail: kent_barrett@agfg.com
Web: www.ellerbeckbedandbreakfast.com

Circa 1892. Pleasantly located in the city's downtown historic district, this Victorian inn has been renovated for modern comfort and lovingly restored with original moldings, hardwood floors and stained glass. Impressive fireplaces can be found in the splendid main floor and upstairs galleries as well as in several of the six guest bedrooms. Different seasonal motifs adorn the bedrooms, so every day is a holiday in Christmas Wishes, complete with a sleigh bed. Autumn Winds and Spring Breeze can serve as an ideal suite for families. Enjoy a continental breakfast that is delivered to each room at an agreed-upon time. After exploring the local sites and nearby attractions, the turndown service, evening chocolates and complimentary soft drinks are welcome additions.

Historic Interest: Historic Temple Square, Old Desert Village, This is the Place Monument, Gardner's Historic Village, Historic Park City, Historic Homes Tour.
Innkeeper(s): Debbie Spencer. $115-135. MC, VISA, AX, DS, PC, TC. TAC10. 6 rooms with PB, 3 with FP. Breakfast and snacks/refreshments included in rates. Types of meals: Cont. Beds: KQ. Cable TV, phone, turndown service and fireplace in room. Central air. Fax on premises. Family reunions hosted. Antiquing, art galleries, bicycling, hiking, horseback riding, Historic Temple Square, live theater, museums, parks, shopping, downhill skiing and sporting events nearby.

Saltair B&B

164 S 900 E
Salt Lake City, UT 84102-4103
(801)533-8184 (800)733-8184 Fax:(801)595-0332
E-mail: saltair@saltlakebandb.com
Web: www.saltlakebandb.com

Circa 1903. The Saltair is the oldest continuously operating bed & breakfast in Utah and offers a prime location to enjoy Salt Lake City. The simply decorated rooms include light, airy

window dressings, charming furnishings and special touches. Breakfasts, especially the delicious Saltair Eggs Benedict topped with avocado, sour creme and salsa, are memorable. The inn is within walking distance to four historic districts and only one mile from Temple Square and the Governor's Mansion. Day trips include treks to several national and state parks and the Wasatch Front ski areas.

Innkeeper(s): Nancy Saxton & Jan Bartlett. $79-149. MC, VISA, AX, DS. TAC10. 7 rooms, 4 with PB. Breakfast and snacks/refreshments included in rates. Types of meals: Gourmet bkfst and early coffee/tea. Beds: QT. Fresh flowers in room. Air conditioning. VCR, fax and spa on premises. Seminars hosted. Antiquing, fishing, live theater, parks, shopping, downhill skiing, cross-country skiing, sporting events and water sports nearby.
Publicity: *Mobil, Logan Sun and Sunset.*

"Your swing and Saltair Muffins were fabulous."

Tropic   K4

Bryce Point B&B

61 N, 400 West
Tropic, UT 84776-0096
(435)679-8629 (888)200-4211 Fax:(435)679-8629
Web: www.brycepointlodging.com

Circa 1931. The innkeepers of this comfortable bed & breakfast have owned the home since 1951 and renovated it in the late '80s and soon after opened for guests. Each of the guests rooms is named for the innkeepers' children and their spouses, and each room feature comfortable furnishings and large picture windows. Relax on the wraparound porch or pick a movie from the innkeepers' library and snuggle up in your room to watch an old favorite. Six national parks surround the Tropic area, offering plenty of seasonal activities.

Historic Interest: Historic Bryce Canyon Lodge is nearby and offers hiking, horseback riding, hunting and fishing.
Innkeeper(s): Lamar & Ethel LeFevre. $60-120. MC, VISA, AX, DS. TAC10. 6 rooms, 5 with PB and 1 cottage. Breakfast included in rates. Types of meals: Gourmet bkfst. Beds: KQT. TV, phone, ceiling fan and VCR in room. Central air. Fax, spa and library on premises. Fishing, hiking, horseback riding, parks and cross-country skiing nearby.
Publicity: *The Toronto Sun, The Daily Spectrum, Country Hight and Atlanta Constitution (article by Clark Howard).*

"So many amenities abound: a comfortable, cheerful room, great sleeping, thoughtful touches, stargazing, scenery from your spacious deck, gracious hosts and so much more. We've been to many B&B's, Bryce Point is among the winners."

Vermont

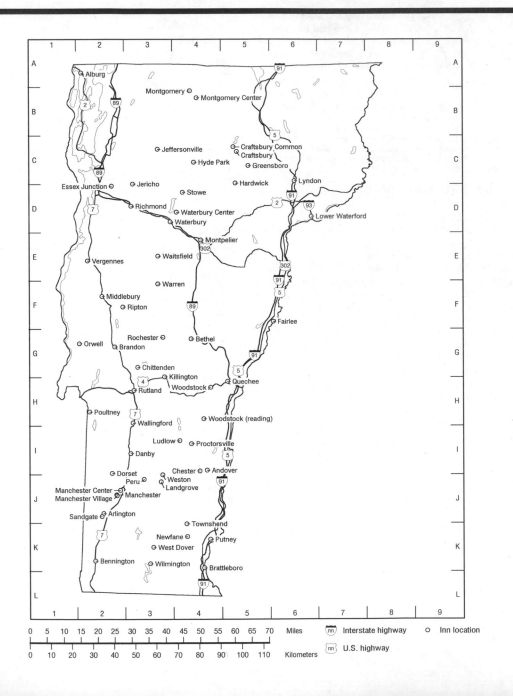

Miles 0 5 10 15 20 25 30 35 40 45 50 55 60 65 70

Kilometers 0 10 20 30 40 50 60 70 80 90 100 110

Interstate highway

U.S. highway

Inn location

Alburg A2

Ransom Bay Inn

47 Center Bay Rd
Alburg, VT 05440
(802)796-3399 (800)729-3393 Fax:(802)796-3399

Circa 1795. Once part of the Underground Railroad, this 1795 Federal-style stone home constructed of marble is in the Lake Champlain Islands, which are located between Montreal, Quebec and Burlington, Vermont. Just five miles from historic Fort Montgomery, the inn was originally built as an inn and tavern by Amos Ransom, and is now listed with the Vermont Register of Historic Places. The four guest bedrooms are decorated with antiques, and the living area has a huge stone fireplace. The inn has three fireplaces, an old-fashioned wood cook stove in the kitchen, and jelly cupboards filled with homemade jams. Breakfast includes such treats as homemade croissants, pancakes, two kinds of omelets, bacon, home fries and French toast made with croissants rolled in corn flakes and served with Vermont maple syrup. Guests will want to stroll through the charming village-like town of Alburg. They may also go biking, golfing, antiquing, boating, ice-skating, swimming and downhill or cross-country skiing. Watch the performances of the Royal Lipizzan Stallions in July and August.

Historic Interest: Fort Montgomery (5 miles).

Innkeeper(s): Richar & Loraine. $75. MC, VISA, PC, TC. 4 rooms with PB and 1 conference room. Breakfast included in rates. Types of meals: Country bkfst and veg bkfst. Beds: QD. Fans in room. Fax, copier and library on premises. Weddings, small meetings and family reunions hosted. French spoken. Amusement parks, antiquing, beaches, bicycling, canoeing/kayaking, fishing, golf, hiking, parks, shopping, cross-country skiing, water sports and wineries nearby.

Pets allowed: Small, stay in room.

Thomas Mott Homestead B&B

63 Blue Rock Rd on Lake Champlain
Alburg, VT 05440-4002
(802)796-4402 (800)348-0843
E-mail: tmott@together.net

Circa 1838. Each room in this restored farmhouse provides a special view of Lake Champlain. Most often it is enjoyed from the sitting room with a warm fire and complimentary Ben & Jerry's ice cream. Rustic yet refined with open beams, pine floors, stenciling, cotton linens and quilts, the English country cottage style blends comfortably throughout the home. Vistas of Mt. Mansfield and nearby Jay Peak are also eye-pleasing, and

Montreal Island is one hour away. There is a boat dock that extends 75 feet onto the lake. Ask about special quilting and mystery weekends.

Historic Interest: Saint Anne's Shrine, Hyde Cabin, two presidential birthplaces.

Innkeeper(s): Lee & Linda Mickey. $85-150. MC, VISA, PC. TAC10. 3 rooms with PB, 1 with FP and 1 suite. Breakfast included in rates. Types of meals: Full bkfst, early coffee/tea and snacks/refreshments. Beds: QD. Ceiling fan in room. Amusement parks, antiquing, fishing, live theater, parks, shopping, downhill skiing, cross-country skiing, sporting events and water sports nearby.

Publicity: *Los Angeles Times, St. Alban's Messenger, Yankee Traveler, Boston Globe, Elle, Outside, Prime Time* and *Vermont Life.*

Andover I4

The Inn at High View

753 East Hill Rd
Andover, VT 05143
(802)875-2724 Fax:(802)875-4021
E-mail: hiview@aol.com
Web: www.innathighview.com

Circa 1789. Relaxation is stressed at this spacious farmhouse inn in the Green Mountains. A fireplace, rock garden, swimming pool and gazebo add to guests' enjoyment. Cross-country ski trails are found on the grounds, hooking up with a series of others to provide up to 15 kilometers of uninterrupted skiing. The

inn offers advance-reservation dinner service for its guests on weekends and specializes in Italian fare.

Innkeeper(s): Gregory Bohan & Salvatore Massaro. $125-175. MC, VISA, DS, PC. TAC10. 8 rooms with PB, 2 suites and 1 conference room. Breakfast included in rates. Types of meals: Full bkfst, early coffee/tea, lunch and dinner. Beds: KQT. Sauna in room. VCR and cross-country skiing on premises. Weddings, small meetings, family reunions and seminars hosted. Italian, Spanish and English spoken. Antiquing, fishing, live theater, shopping and downhill skiing nearby.

Pets allowed: Special arrangements in suites only.

Arlington J2

Arlington Manor House B&B

Corner Buck Hill & Salter Hill Rd
Arlington, VT 05250-8648
(802)375-6784
E-mail: kitandal@arlingtonmanorhouse.com

Circa 1908. A view of Mt. Equinox is enjoyed from the spacious terrace of this Dutch Colonial inn in the Battenkill River Valley. The inn also sports its own tennis court and is within easy walking distance of the Battenkill River, where canoeing, fishing and river tubing are popular activities. A variety of accommodations is offered, and two of the inn's guest rooms have romantic fireplaces. A bikers' workshop and bench stand are on the premises.

Innkeeper(s): Al & Kit McAllister. $85-145. MC, VISA, AX, PC, TC. TAC10. 4 rooms with PB, 2 with FP, 1 suite and 2 conference rooms. Breakfast and afternoon tea included in rates. Types of meals: Full bkfst and early coffee/tea. Beds: KQD. TV and three with A/C in room. VCR, tennis, library, workbench and shops on premises. Weddings, small meetings, family reunions and seminars hosted. Antiquing, fishing, live theater, parks, shopping, downhill skiing, cross-country skiing and water sports nearby.

Arlington's West Mountain Inn

River Road, PO Box 40
Arlington, VT 05250-0481
(802)375-6516 Fax:(802)375-6553
E-mail: Info@WestMountainInn.com
Web: www.WestMountainInn.com

Circa 1850. Llamas graze the hillside of this sprawling New England farmhouse situated on 150 acres of meadows and woodland. The inn overlooks the Battenkill River. Each room

boasts amenities such as a lace canopied bed, a balcony or a fireplace. The Rockwell Kent Suite graced with a cathedral ceiling, features a fireplace and king-size bed. Back porches and decks are filled with Adirondack lawn chairs. The innkeepers include a former school principal and a Vermont state senator.

Innkeeper(s): The Carlson Family. $169-275. MC, VISA, AX, DS, PC, TC. 18 rooms, 9 with PB, 10 with FP, 9 suites and 2 conference rooms. Breakfast and dinner included in rates. Types of meals: Gourmet bkfst, veg bkfst, early coffee/tea and picnic lunch. MAP. Beds: KQT. Ceiling fan and fireplace in room. Air conditioning. VCR, fax, copier, swimming, library, child care and hiking trails on premises. Weddings, small meetings, family reunions and seminars hosted. Antiquing, art galleries, bicycling, canoeing/kayaking, fishing, golf, hiking, horseback riding, live theater, museums, parks, shopping, downhill skiing, cross-country skiing and tennis nearby.

Publicity: Family Circle, Schenectady Gazette, New York Post, Daily News, Vermont Life, New York Times, Yankee, National Geographic, Vermont Magazine, Boston Globe and Glamour.

"Excellent, warm, friendly, relaxing, absolutely the best!"

The Inn on Covered Bridge Green

3587 River Rd
Arlington, VT 05250-9723
(800)726-9480
E-mail: cbg@sover.net
Web: www.coveredbridgegreen.com

Circa 1792. A quaint red covered bridge over the Battenkill River leads to this colonial inn, home to Norman Rockwell for 12 years. The artist was inspired by Arlington's scenes and people, and the six guest rooms at the inn are named for the famous Rockwell paintings. The rooms are filled with comfortable chairs, old-fashioned dressers, antique armoires, desks and fireplaces, all in a Norman Rockwell style. A hearty New England breakfast reinforces your enjoyment of the countryside. The artist's actual two-bedroom studio may be rented as well as the one-bedroom art studio, both on the inn grounds.

Innkeeper(s): Clint & Julia Dickens. $125-280. 6 rooms with PB. Types of meals: Gourmet bkfst. Beds: Q. Fireplaces in room. Air conditioning.

Publicity: Vermont Life, The San Diego Union and The Boston Globe.

"We find it difficult to leave. Everything is perfect."

Ira Allen House

6311 VT Rte 7A
Arlington, VT 05250-9317
(802)362-2284 Fax:(802)362-0928
E-mail: stay@iraallenhouse.com
Web: www.iraallenhouse.com

Circa 1770. Built by Ethan Allen's brother, this Colonial Revival inn is a state historic site. Hand-blown glass panes, hand-hewn beams, handmade bricks and wide-board floors

provide evidence of the inn's longevity. Surrounded by farms and forest, the inn's setting is perfect for those searching for some peace and quiet. Plenty of recreational activities also are found nearby, including fine trout fishing, swimming and canoeing in the Battenkill River on the property.

Innkeeper(s): Sandy & Ray Walters. $75-100. 5 rooms and 2 suites. Breakfast included in rates. Types of meals: Full bkfst. Air conditioning. VCR on premises. Weddings and family reunions hosted. Antiquing, canoeing/kayaking, live theater, shopping, downhill skiing and cross-country skiing nearby.

Bennington   K2

Alexandra B&B

Rt 7A Orchard Rd
Bennington, VT 05201
(802)442-5619 (888)207-9386 Fax:(802)442-5592
E-mail: alexand@sover.net
Web: www.alexandrainn.com

Circa 1859. Located on two acres at the edge of town, Alexandra is a Colonial-style inn. There are king or queen beds in all the rooms, as well as fireplaces and views of Bennington Monument and the Green Mountains. Each bath offers water jets and showers. A full gourmet breakfast is served. Bennington College and the business district are five minutes from the inn.

Innkeeper(s): Alex Koks & Andra Erickson. $100-150. MC, VISA, AX, DS, TC. TAC10. 13 rooms with PB, 12 with FP, 7 suites and 1 conference room. Breakfast included in rates. Types of meals: Gourmet bkfst and early coffee/tea. Beds: KQ. Cable TV, phone and VCR in room. Air conditioning. Fax and copier on premises. Small meetings, family reunions and seminars hosted. French, Dutch, German and Latvian spoken. Antiquing, art galleries, bicycling, canoeing/kayaking, fishing, golf, hiking, horseback riding, live theater, museums, parks, shopping, downhill skiing, cross-country skiing, tennis, water sports and wineries nearby.

Pets allowed: Discuss.

Four Chimneys Inn & Restaurant

21 West Rd (route 9)
Bennington, VT 05201-6100
(802)447-3500 (800)649-3503 Fax:(802)447-3692
E-mail: innkeeper@fourchimneys.com
Web: www.fourchimneys.com

Circa 1783. Four distinctive chimneys rise from the roofline of this three-story Georgian Revival manor on 11 acres. Recently redecorated, most guest bedrooms offer fireplaces and jetted tubs; one features an enclosed porch. Accommodations also are available in the carriage house and ice house. Formal gardens with a fountain are often the setting for elegant weddings. Try the Lamb Rack at the well-known restaurant on site. Nearby activities include a museum, live theater, art center, historic sites and canoeing.

Innkeeper(s): Christine & Harold Cullison. $105-205. MC, VISA, AX, DC, CB, DS. 11 rooms with PB, 8 with FP. Breakfast included in rates. Types of meals: Cont plus and gourmet dinner. EP. Beds: KQ. Cable TV, phone, hair dryers, individual heat controls, most with ceiling fans and jetted tubs in room. Air conditioning. VCR, fax and copier on premises. Weddings, small meetings, family reunions and seminars hosted. Spanish spoken. Antiquing, canoeing/kayaking, fishing, golf, art center, historic sites, live theater, museums, parks, shopping, downhill skiing, cross-country skiing, tennis and water sports nearby.

South Shire Inn

124 Elm St
Bennington, VT 05201-2232
(802)447-3839 Fax:(802)442-3547
E-mail: relax@southshire.com
Web: www.southshire.com

Circa 1887. Built in the late 1800s, this inn boasts a mahogany-paneled library, soaring 10-foot ceilings, and three of the guest rooms include one of the home's original fireplaces.

Guest rooms feature antiques and Victorian décor. Rooms in the restored carriage house include both a fireplace and a whirlpool tub. Guests are pampered with both a full breakfast, as well as afternoon tea. Local attractions include the Bennington Museum, antique shops, craft stores, covered bridges and skiing.

Historic Interest: Bennington Museum and Monument-1 mile, Hildene (Lincoln Estate)-25 miles.

Innkeeper(s): George & Joyce Goeke. $110-185. MC, VISA, AX, PC, TC. TAC10. 9 rooms with PB, 7 with FP and 1 suite. Breakfast and afternoon tea included in rates. Types of meals: Full bkfst, veg bkfst and early coffee/tea. Beds: KQD. Cable TV, phone, ceiling fan, VCR and whirlpool tubs in room. Central air. Fax, copier, library and guest refrigerator on premises. Weddings, small meetings, family reunions and seminars hosted. Antiquing, art galleries, bicycling, canoeing/kayaking, fishing, golf, hiking, horseback riding, live theater, museums, shopping, downhill skiing and cross-country skiing nearby.

Bethel   G4

Greenhurst Inn

River St, Rd 2, Box 60
Bethel, VT 05032-9404
(802)234-9474 (800)510-2553
E-mail: info@greenhurstinn.com

Circa 1890. In the National Register of Historic Places, Greenhurst is a gracious Victorian mansion built for the Harringtons of Philadelphia. Overlooking the White River, the inn's opulent interiors include etched windows once featured on the cover of Vermont Life. There are eight masterpiece fireplaces and a north and south parlor.

Innkeeper(s): Lyle & Claire Wolf. $50-100. MC, VISA, DS, PC, TC. 13 rooms, 7 with PB, 4 with FP. Breakfast included in rates. Types of meals: Cont plus, cont and early coffee/tea. EP. Beds: QDT. VCR and library on premises. Weddings, small meetings, family reunions and seminars hosted. Spanish and French spoken. Antiquing, fishing, live theater, parks, shopping, downhill skiing, cross-country skiing and water sports nearby. Pets allowed: Dogs only.

Publicity: *Best Country Inns of New England, Victorian Homes, Washington Post, Boston Globe, Bride's Magazine, Los Angeles Times, Time, New York Times, Vermont Life and The Man Who Corrupted Hadleyburg.*

"The inn is magnificent! The hospitality unforgettable."

Brandon   G2

Churchill House Inn

3128 Forest Dale Rd, Rte 73 E
Brandon, VT 05733-9202
(802)247-3078 (877)297-2831
E-mail: innkeeper@churchillhouseinn.com
Web: www.churchillhouseinn.com

Circa 1871. Caleb Churchill and his son, Nathan, first built a three-story lumber mill, a grist mill and a distillery here, all water powered. Later, with their milled lumber, they constructed this 20-room house. Because of its location, it became a stagecoach stop and has served generations of travelers with comfortable accommodations. The inn is adjacent to Green Mountain National Forest, and excellent hiking, biking, skiing

and fishing are just steps away. The inn serves a four-course dinner and a full breakfast.

Historic Interest: Shelburn Museum, Billings Farm, Fort Ticonderoga (less than 1 hour away).

Innkeeper(s): Linda & Richard Daybell. $90-220. MC, VISA, AX, CB, DS, PC, TC. TAC10. 9 rooms with PB. Breakfast and dinner included in rates. Types of meals: Full bkfst and picnic lunch. MAP. Beds: QDT. Family reunions hosted. Antiquing, parks, shopping, downhill skiing, cross-country skiing and water sports nearby.

Publicity: *Country and Yankee.*

"We felt the warm, welcoming, down-home appeal as we entered the front hall. The food was uncommonly good — home cooking with a gourmet flair!"

The Gazebo Inn

On Rt 7 (25 Grove St)
Brandon, VT 05733
(802)247-3235 (888)858-3235
E-mail: gazebo@sover.net
Web: www.brandon.org/gazebo.htm

Circa 1865. Cozy elegance is found year-round at this classic New England clapboard home, which is listed in the National Register. Located in the foothills of the Green Mountain National Forest, the inn abounds with pastoral scenes and panoramic vistas. Furnished with Victorian antiques, common rooms include a library with TV/VCR, parlor, reading alcove and screened porch. Distinctive guest bedrooms offer air conditioning and featherbeds with down comforters. Mother-daughter hostesses Donna and Lindsay provide a four-course scrumptious breakfast and daily refreshments. There is much to enjoy with two acres of private landscaped grounds and a gazebo. Walk into town or swim or boat at Lake Dunmore, only 10 minutes away. During winter try cross-country skiing at Blueberry Hill.

Historic Interest: The entire village of Brandon, where the inn is located, is listed on the National Register of Historic Places. Stephen A. Douglas' birthplace is a few doors away.

Innkeeper(s): Donna & Lindsay Taylor. $80-115. MC, VISA, AX, DS, PC, TC. 4 rooms with PB. Breakfast and snacks/refreshments included in rates. Types of meals: Cont. Beds: QDT. Copier, bicycles and antique shop on premises. Spanish and Hebrew spoken. Antiquing, art galleries, bicycling, hiking, swimming, summer concerts, fine dining, downhill skiing, cross-country skiing and water sports nearby.

"Thank you for your hospitality. We had a wonderful time. We will try to make this an annual event."

Brattleboro   K4

1868 Crosby House

175 Western Ave
Brattleboro, VT 05301-3137
(802)257-4914 (800)528-1868
E-mail: lynn@crosbyhouse.com

Circa 1868. Guests of this elegantly restored Italianate Victorian home with Victorian gardens, gazebo and woodland trails, remember it for its attention to detail and a feeling of being pampered. The Victorian theme is represented throughout the inn's decor. Each of the three guest rooms boasts family heirlooms and collected antiques, fireplaces and private baths, as well as four-poster, canopy and paneled queen beds. There also are two self-catering apartment suites available for short or

longer stays. Bathrobes, specialty toiletries and luxurious bed and bath linens are provided. A full, gourmet breakfast is served in the oak-paneled dining room. The inn is a short walk from downtown. $100-145. MC, VISA, AX, DS, PC, TC. 3 rooms with PB, 3 with FP and 2 suites. Breakfast included in rates. Types of meals: Gourmet bkfst, early coffee/tea and room service. Beds: Q. Cable TV, phone, turndown service, ceiling fan, VCR and two-person whirlpool in room. Air conditioning. Fax and copier on premises. Weddings and small meetings hosted. Antiquing, fishing, golf, live theater, shopping, downhill skiing, cross-country skiing, tennis and water sports nearby.

40 Putney Road

192 Putney Rd
Brattleboro, VT 05301-2944
(802)254-6268 (800)941-2413 Fax:(802)258-2673
E-mail: frtyptny@sover.net

Circa 1931. Built to house the director of the Brattleboro Retreat and his family, this brick French Provincial estate overlooks the West River. A flagstone terrace leads to landscaped formal gardens with two fountains, specimen trees and plantings. It is a perfect site for small parties and weddings. The interior is comfortably elegant. Guest bedrooms are spacious, including a three-room suite, and some feature fireplaces. Enjoy a full gourmet breakfast to start the day. A private cottage includes a fully equipped kitchen, bath and living room with fireplace. An Internet pub onsite serves beer, wine and light fare. Play croquet or go lawn bowling on the newly surfaced grounds on the lower green. Hike the nature path for great photos.

Innkeeper(s): Mimi & Rob Hamlin. $100-230. MC, VISA, AX. 5 rooms with PB, 3 with FP, 1 suite, 1 cottage and 1 conference room. Breakfast included in rates. Types of meals: Full bkfst. Beds: QDT. Cable TV, phone, ceiling fan and fireplace in room. Air conditioning. Fax, copier and library on premises.

Chester 14

Chester House

266 Main St
Chester, VT 05143-9768
(802)875-2205 (888)875-2205
E-mail: innkeeper@chesterhouseinn.com
Web: www.chesterhouseinn.com

Circa 1780. This beautifully restored Federal-style clapboard home is listed in the National Register of Historic Places. It is situated on the village green in the quaint and historic village of Chester. The inn is tastefully furnished throughout with early American furniture and appointments. Some of the individually decorated rooms feature whirlpool baths or steam bath/showers.

Innkeeper(s): Paul Anderson. $95-169. MC, VISA, PC, TC. TAC10. 7 rooms with PB. Types of meals: Full bkfst and dinner. Beds: KQDT. Phone and some with gas fireplace and whirlpool bath in room. Air conditioning.

"The best hosts and the greatest of inns."

Hugging Bear Inn & Shoppe

244 Main St
Chester, VT 05143
(802)875-2412 (800)325-0519
E-mail: georgette@huggingbear.com

Circa 1850. Among the 9,000 teddy bear inhabitants of this white Victorian inn, several peek out from the third-story windows of the octagonal tower. There is a teddy bear shop on the premises and children and adults can borrow a bear to take to bed with them. Rooms are decorated with antiques and comfortable furniture. A bear puppet show is often staged during breakfast.

Innkeeper(s): Georgette Thomas. $65-145. MC, VISA, AX, DS, PC, TC. 6 rooms with PB. Breakfast included in rates. Types of meals: Gourmet bkfst and early coffee/tea. Beds: QDT. Teddy bear in room. Air conditioning. VCR and library on premises. Small meetings and family reunions hosted. Antiquing, fishing, golf, swimming, parks, shopping, downhill skiing and cross-country skiing nearby.

Publicity: *Rutland Daily Herald, Exxon Travel, Teddy Bear Review, Teddy Bear Scene and Boston Globe.*

Inn Victoria

On The Green, PO Box 788
Chester, VT 05143-0788
(802)875-4288 (800)732-4288 Fax:(802)875-2504
E-mail: innkeeper@innvictoria.com

Circa 1850. This elegant Victorian inn is located On the Green in the heart of Chester. Rooms are furnished with antiques and queen size beds. Guests enjoy the pleasures of fireside reading, soaking by candlelight in a warm Jacuzzi and strolls to nearby restaurants and shops. The Second Empire Victorian is among several historic houses and seven churches found in Chester's On the Green area. Many weekends include Victorian fairs and festivals. Overture to Christmas is a festive time for townspeople and visitors who dress in Victorian attire and go carolling door-to-door. Two summer theater groups are nearby.

Innkeeper(s): Jack & Janet Burns. $110-195. MC, VISA. TAC10. 7 rooms with PB, 3 with FP and 1 suite. Breakfast and afternoon tea included in rates. Types of meals: Gourmet bkfst and early coffee/tea. Beds: Q. Cable TV and fireplace in room. Air conditioning. Spa on premises. Weddings, small meetings, family reunions and seminars hosted. Antiquing, art galleries, canoeing/kayaking, fishing, golf, hiking, horseback riding, special town-wide events, shopping, downhill skiing, cross-country skiing and water sports nearby.

Stone Hearth Inn & Tavern

698 Rt 11 West
Chester, VT 05143
(802)875-2525 (888)617-3656 Fax:(802)875-1588
E-mail: innkeeper@thestonehearthinn.com
Web: www.thestonehearthinn.com

Circa 1810. Sheltered behind tall pines, this Federal-style farmhouse sits on six acres of tranquility. The historic inn was built with bricks made on-site in a kiln, and it features wide board pine floors and exposed beams from its Colonial days. Relax with a book from the library in front of the fire, enjoy a movie, play a game or soak in the hot tub. Several romantic guest bedrooms and suites feature fireplaces with candelabras. A hearty country breakfast overlooking the lawns and flower gardens may include Brent's blueberry buttermilk pancakes with locally made Vermont maple syrup and bacon or sausage. The Tavern menu is popular in the evenings.

Historic Interest: Chester Historical Society, Billings Farm & Museum.

Innkeeper(s): Chris Clay, Brent Anderson & The CAts. $59-139. MC, VISA, AX, DS, PC, TC. TAC10. 10 rooms with PB, 3 with FP, 1 suite and 1 conference room. Breakfast included in rates. Types of meals: Full bkfst, country bkfst, early coffee/tea and snacks/refreshments. Beds: KQDT. Some with A/C and fireplace in room. VCR, fax, spa, library and gift shop on premises. Weddings, small meetings and family reunions hosted. Antiquing, art galleries, bicycling, canoeing/kayaking, fishing, golf, hiking, horseback riding, live theater, museums, parks, shopping, downhill skiing, cross-country skiing, tennis and wineries nearby.

Pets allowed: Reservations must be made directly with the Inn, a pet policy applies.

Chittenden   G3

Fox Creek Inn

49 Chittenden Dam Rd
Chittenden, VT 05737
(802)483-6213 (800)707-0017
E-mail: ttinn@sover.net
Web: www.foxcreekinn.com

Circa 1830. Thomas Edison was a regular guest here when the house was the country home of William Barstow. The inn is surrounded by the Green Mountains on three sides with a stream flowing a few yards away. The guest rooms feature antiques and Vermont country decor. Most rooms offer Jacuzzis and some boast fireplaces. Guests enjoy both breakfast and dinner at the inn. Buttermilk pancakes topped with Vermont maple syrup are typical breakfast fare, and dinners include such items as medallions of pork topped with an  orange-apricot sauce and white chocolate cheesecake.

Innkeeper(s): Ann & Alex Volz. $179-400. MC, VISA, AX, PC, TC. TAC10. 9 rooms with PB. Breakfast and dinner included in rates. Types of meals: Full bkfst and early coffee/tea. MAP. Beds: KQ. Some with fireplaces and Jacuzzis in room. Library on premises. Weddings and small meetings hosted. Amusement parks, antiquing, fishing, live theater, parks, shopping, downhill skiing, cross-country skiing and water sports nearby.

Publicity: *New England Getaways.*

Craftsbury   C5

Craftsbury Inn

107 S Craftsbury Rd
Craftsbury, VT 05826-0036
(802)586-2848 (800)336-2848
E-mail: cburyinn@together.net

Circa 1850. Bird's-eye maple woodwork and embossed tin ceilings testify to the history of this mid-19th-century Greek Revival inn, which also features random-width floors with  square nails. The foundation and porch steps were made of bull's-eye granite, quarried in town. The living room fireplace once graced the first post office in Montpelier. Guest rooms sport country antiques and handmade quilts. The dining room is open to the public for dinner by advance reservation and features French inspired American cuisine.

Innkeeper(s): Bill & Kathy Maire. $80-175. MC, VISA, AX. 10 rooms, 6 with PB and 1 conference room. Breakfast included in rates. Types of meals: Full bkfst and gourmet dinner. MAP, AP. Beds: DT. VCR on premises. Weddings, small meetings, family reunions and seminars hosted. Antiquing, fishing, shopping, downhill skiing, cross-country skiing and water sports nearby.

Publicity: *Boston Globe and New York Times.*

"Very comfortable - the dining was a special treat!"

Craftsbury Common   C5

The Inn on The Common

PO Box 75
Craftsbury Common, VT 05827-0075
(802)586-9619 (800)521-2233 Fax:(802)586-2249
E-mail: info@innonthecommon.com
Web: www.innonthecommon.com

Circa 1795. The Inn on the Common, built by the Samuel French family, is an integral part of this picturesque classic Vermont village. With its white picket fence and graceful white clapboard exterior, the inn provides a quietly elegant retreat. Pastoral views are framed by the inn's famous perennial gardens. The inn also includes a notable wine cellar.

Historic Interest: Stonehouse Museum (20 miles), Saint Johnsbury-Atheneum museum, Fairbanks Museum (25 miles).

Innkeeper(s): Michael & Penny Schmitt. $250-300. MC, VISA, AX, PC, TC. TAC10. 16 rooms with PB, 2 suites and 1 conference room. Breakfast and dinner included in rates. Types of meals: Full bkfst. MAP. Beds: KQDT. Swimming and five-course gourmet dinner on premises. Fishing, golf, downhill skiing, cross-country skiing and water sports nearby.

Pets Allowed.

Publicity: *New York Times, Craftsbury Common, Harper's Hideaway Report and Discerning Travel.*

"The closest my wife and I came to fulfilling our fantasy of a country inn was at The Inn on the Common." — Paul Grimes

Danby   I3

Quail's Nest B&B

81 S Main Street
Danby, VT 05739
(802)293-5099 (800)599-6444 Fax:(802)293-6300
E-mail: quailsnest@quailsnestbandb.com

Circa 1835. Located in the village, this Greek Revival inn features six air-conditioned guest rooms with private baths and on each bed is found a handmade quilt. Full breakfasts are made to order by the innkeepers, and Nancy serves it in period clothing. Also provided is early morning coffee or tea, afternoon tea and snack. The Green Mountain National Forest is just to the east of the inn, providing many outstanding recreational opportunities. Outlet shopping is found just a few miles south in Manchester, and Alpine skiing is enjoyed at Bromley, Killington, Okemo, Pico Magic and Stratton ski areas, all within easy driving distance.

Historic Interest: 1835 Greek Revival house with original marble porches.

Innkeeper(s): Greg & Nancy Diaz. $60-120. MC, VISA, AX, DS, PC, TC. TAC10. 6 rooms with PB and 1 conference room. Breakfast and afternoon tea included in rates. Types of meals: Full bkfst and early coffee/tea. Beds: KQT. VCR on premises. Family reunions and seminars hosted. Antiquing, fishing, swimming, biking, hiking, live theater, shopping, downhill skiing, cross-country skiing, sporting events and water sports nearby.

Publicity: *Vermont.*

Dorset   I2

Cornucopia of Dorset

Rt 30 Box 307
Dorset, VT 05251
(802)867-5751
E-mail: innkeepers@cornucopiaofdorset.com
Web: www.cornucopiaofdorset.com

Circa 1880. Window boxes overflow with seasonal flowers inviting guests to this comely 19th-century colonial home. Shaded by tall trees, it is set on a peaceful lawn near the village green. All the guest rooms have poster or canopy beds and most have fireplaces. A handsome cottage tucked in the trees has its own kitchen and living room with a fireplace and cathedral ceiling. Dorset summer theater is within a five-minute walk.
Historic Interest: National Register.
Innkeeper(s): Donna Butman. $130-270. MC, VISA. 5 rooms with PB. Types of meals: Full bkfst. Beds: KQT. Phone in room.
Publicity: *West Hartford News, New York Times and Country Inn Magazine.*

Marble West Inn

PO Box 847, Dorset West Rd
Dorset, VT 05251-0847
(802)867-4155 (800)453-7629 Fax:(802)867-5731
E-mail: marwest@sover.net

Circa 1840. This historic Greek Revival inn boasts many elegant touches, including stenciling in its entrance hallways done by one of the nation's top craftspeople. Guests also will enjoy

Oriental rugs, handsome marble fireplaces and polished dark oak floors. Visitors delight at the many stunning views enjoyed at the inn, including Green Peak and Owl's Head mountains, flower-filled gardens and meadows and two trout-stocked ponds. Emerald Lake State Park is nearby.
Historic Interest: Dorset (2 miles), Old Bennington (30 miles), Norman Rockwell's West Arlington home (15 miles), Manchester Village (5 miles).
Innkeeper(s): Paul Quinn. $89-179. MC, VISA, AX, PC. 8 rooms with PB, 4 with FP and 1 suite. Breakfast and afternoon tea included in rates. Types of meals: Full bkfst. Beds: KQDT. Library on premises. Antiquing, fishing, designer outlet shopping, horseback riding, art galleries, biking, golf, tennis, fine dining, live theater, parks, shopping, downhill skiing, cross-country skiing and water sports nearby.

"A charming inn with wonderful hospitality. The room was comfortable, immaculate, and furnished with every imaginable need and comfort."

Essex Junction   D2

Allyn House B&B

57 Main Street
Essex Junction, VT 05452
(802)878-9408 Fax:(802)878-9408
E-mail: allynhouse@aol.com

Circa 1897. Built at the turn of the 20th century, the Allyn House features Queen Anne-style architecture. Rooms are decorated in Victorian style with antiques. Each room has a different theme. The Scottish Room includes an antique bed, as well as old photographs of the Highlands. The Russian Room

includes art from its namesake country. Other rooms evoke a French and Japanese ambiance. During the week, guests are served a continental breakfast with fresh fruit and baked goods. On the weekends, a full breakfast is served.
Historic Interest: Shelburne Museum (10 miles).
Innkeeper(s): AJ McDonald. $75-95. MC, VISA. 4 rooms, 3 with PB. Breakfast included in rates. Types of meals: Country bkfst and cont plus. Beds: QD. Air conditioning. VCR and library on premises. Small meetings and family reunions hosted. Antiquing, beaches, bicycling, canoeing/kayaking, golf, hiking, live theater, museums, shopping, sporting events, tennis and water sports nearby.

Fairlee   F6

Silver Maple Lodge & Cottages

520 US Rt 5 South
Fairlee, VT 05045
(802)333-4326 (800)666-1946
E-mail: scott@silvermaplelodge.com
Web: www.silvermaplelodge.com

Circa 1790. This old Cape farmhouse was expanded in the 1850s and became an inn in the '20s when Elmer & Della Batchelder opened their home to guests. It became so successful that several cottages, built from lumber on the property, were added. For 60 years, the Batchelder family continued the operation. They misnamed the lodge, however, mistaking silver poplar trees on the property for what they thought were silver maples. Guest rooms are decorated with many of the inn's original furnishings, and the new innkeepers have carefully restored the rooms and added several bathrooms. A screened-in porch surrounds two sides of the house. Three of the cottages include working fireplaces and one is handicap accessible.
Historic Interest: The Quechee Gorge, Maple Grove Maple Museum, Billings Farm & Museum and the Saint Gauden's National Historic Site are among the area's historic sites.
Innkeeper(s): Scott & Sharon Wright. $59-89. MC, VISA, AX, DS, PC, TC. TAC10. 16 rooms, 14 with PB, 3 with FP and 8 cottages. Breakfast included in rates. Types of meals: Cont. Beds: KQDT. TV in room. VCR, copier and bicycles on premises. Handicap access. Small meetings and family reunions hosted. Antiquing, fishing, live theater, parks, shopping, downhill skiing, cross-country skiing and water sports nearby.
Pets allowed: Cottage rooms only.
Publicity: *Boston Globe, Vermont Country Sampler, Travel Holiday, Travel America and New York Times.*

"Your gracious hospitality and attractive home all add up to a pleasant experience."

Gaysville   G4

Cobble House Inn

PO Box 49
Gaysville, VT 05746-0049
(802)234-5458

Circa 1864. One of the grandest homes in the area, this Victorian mansion commands a breathtaking view of the Green Mountains. The White River flows just below, enticing the more adventurous to spend the day tubing, canoeing or fishing for salmon and trout. Enjoy breakfast and afternoon treats. Grazing sheep and perennial gardens share the spacious grounds. Advance notice is needed for dinner, which can be served on the porch in a majestic setting or in the cozy dining room. **Historic Interest:** The Underground Railroad is rumored to have run through the area, and the surrounding area is full of history to discover.

Innkeeper(s): Karen & Tony Caparis. $115. MC, VISA, PC, TC. 4 rooms with PB. Breakfast included in rates. Types of meals: Gourmet bkfst. Beds: Q. Phone in room. Antiquing, fishing, live theater, downhill skiing, cross-country skiing and water sports nearby.

Publicity: *Vermont Country Sampler, Syracuse Alumni Magazine, Vermont Life, Women's Day and Vermont.*

"My favorite place!"

Greensboro C5

Highland Lodge

RR 1 Box 1290
Greensboro, VT 05841-9712
(802)533-2647 Fax:(802)533-7494
E-mail: hlodge@connriver.net

Circa 1865. With a private beach and 120 acres to enjoy, guests rarely have trouble finding a way to pass the time at this lodge. The lodge is located in a mid-19th-century farmhouse, and visitors either room here in country guest rooms or in a collection of cottages. The cottages have from one to three bedrooms, a living room, bathroom and a porch. All guests are welcome to use the lodge's common areas or simply relax on the porch, but there's sailing, swimming, fishing, boating and nature trails. In the winter, the lodge grooms 60 kilometers of cross-country ski trails and has a ski shop renting all the necessary gear. The breakfast choices might include French

toast, waffles, pancakes, eggs or muffins, and at dinner, guests choose from four entrees accompanied by salad, homemade bread and dessert.

Historic Interest: Greensboro Historical Society.

Innkeeper(s): Wilhelmina & David Smith. $199-255. MC, VISA, DS, PC, TC. TAC10. 11 cottages with PB. Breakfast and dinner included in rates. Types of meals: Full bkfst, early coffee/tea, lunch, picnic lunch and afternoon tea. MAP. Beds: QDT. Fax, copier, swimming, bicycles, tennis, library, child care, sailing, cross-country skiing and internet access on premises. Handicap access. Weddings, small meetings, family reunions and seminars hosted. Dutch spoken. Antiquing, golf, live theater and downhill skiing nearby.

Publicity: *New England Skiers Guide, Vermont Magazine, Hardwick Gazette, Rural New England Magazine, Better Homes & Gardens, Providence Sunday Journal, Yankee, Vermont Life and US Air Attache.*

"We had a great time last weekend and enjoyed everything we did—hiking, climbing, swimming, canoeing and eating."

Hardwick C5

Cynthia's Victorian Inn

79 Church St, PO Box 1087
Hardwick, VT 05843-1087
(802)472-6338
E-mail: cindysvictorian@aol.com
Web: www.cynthiasvictorianinn.com

Circa 1896. A cypress staircase, hardwood floors, crystal chandeliers and cherry woodwork lend a rich history to this Victorian home accented with antiques. Featherbeds grace each

of the guest bedrooms. The Garden Suite also features white wicker and a fireplace. Enjoy a candlelight breakfast with delights that may include Belgian waffles with cherry sauce, banana-walnut pancakes or homemade cinnamon rolls. In the evening, watch the sunset from one of the three porches. Inside, sip sherry by the fire. Caspian Lake Beach is a fun excursion nearby. When making reservations, ask about the inn's dinners.

Innkeeper(s): Cynthia & Cliff Morrow. $90-150. MC, VISA. 3 rooms. Breakfast included in rates. Types of meals: Full bkfst.

Hyde Park C4

Fitch Hill Inn

258 Fitch Hill Rd
Hyde Park, VT 05655-7363
(802)888-3834 (800)639-2903 Fax:(802)888-7789
E-mail: fitchinn@sover.net
Web: www.fitchhillinn.com

Circa 1797. This quiet Federalist-style home sits on 3 1/2 acres of hilltop land overlooking the picturesque Green Mountains. Surrounding the inn are numerous flower-filled gardens and guests enjoy strolling through the woods directly behind the inn. There is a three-level deck and two covered porches, one with a spectacular view. The five second-floor guest rooms share a period-furnished living room, TV room and movie library. Popular choices include the suite with a fireplace and Jacuzzi and the first-floor studio apartment with a whirlpool tub, fireplace, deck and kitchen. Breakfasts are served in the dining room.

Historic Interest: Chester A. Arthur birthplace/home (30 miles), Shelburne Museum (50 miles).

Innkeeper(s): Gary & Sharon Coquillette. $85-205. MC, VISA, AX, DS, PC, TC. TAC10. 6 rooms with PB, 2 with FP and 2 suites. Breakfast included in rates. Types of meals: Full bkfst, early coffee/tea and afternoon tea. Beds: QD. Cable TV, phone, ceiling fan, VCR and some with Jacuzzi in room. Air conditioning. Spa and library on premises. Weddings, small meetings, family reunions and seminars hosted. Amusement parks, antiquing, fishing, live theater, parks, downhill skiing, cross-country skiing and water sports nearby.

Publicity: *Stowe Reporter, Morrisville News Dispatch, Out & About, Eco-Traveller, Country Living, Bon Appetit and Yankee Magazine.*

Jeffersonville C3

Jefferson House

PO Box 288, Main St
Jeffersonville, VT 05464-0288
(802)644-2030 (800)253-9630
E-mail: jeffhouse@pwshift.com

Circa 1910. Three comfortable guest rooms, decorated in a country Victorian style, are the offerings at this turn-of-the-century home. As one might expect, pancakes topped with Vermont maple syrup are often a staple at the breakfast table, accompanied by savory items such as smoked bacon. There is an antique shop on the premises. Each season brings a new activity to this scenic area. In the winter,

it's just a few minutes to Smugglers' Notch ski area, and Stowe isn't far. Biking or hiking to the top of Mt. Mansfield are popular summer activities.

Innkeeper(s): Joan & Richard Walker. $60-80. MC, VISA, DS, PC, TC. 3 rooms with PB. Breakfast included in rates. Types of meals: Full bkfst. Beds: KQDT. Alarm clock in room. Air conditioning. VCR on premises. Antiquing, bicycling, fishing, hiking, canoeing, live theater, parks, shopping, downhill skiing, cross-country skiing, sporting events and water sports nearby.

Pets allowed: By prior arrangement.

Jericho   C3

Sinclair Inn B&B

389 Vermont Route 15
Jericho, VT 05465
(802)899-2234 (800)433-4658 Fax:(802)899-2007
E-mail: sinclairinn@aol.com
Web: www.sinclairinnbb.com

Circa 1890. Enjoy the ambiance of a bygone era in this fully restored Queen Anne Victorian inn. Built by Edward Sinclair to showcase his craftsmanship, the inn's stained glass, turrets, fretwork, wainscoting and woodwork retain the home's original splendor. Guests have been welcome since the late 1800s when it was first opened to travelers. Nancy and Jim continue that tradition, offering a complimentary beverage, homemade sweets and information on local events. Relax by a cozy fire in the living room before retiring to a guest bedroom with modern amenities, comfortable bed and sitting chairs. A generous four-course breakfast is  made from scratch. The grounds include surrounding trees, a river, extensive gardens and a pond with a waterfall. Gaze at the mountains from an Adirondack chair or wrought iron lawn furniture.

Historic Interest: Old Red Grist Mill in Jericho Village (3 miles), historical houses, barns, covered bridges (nearby).

Innkeeper(s): Nancy Ames & Jim Svendsen. $90-150. MC, VISA, AX, PC. 6 rooms with PB. Breakfast and snacks/refreshments included in rates. Types of meals: Full bkfst and early coffee/tea. Beds: KQT. One handicap equipped in room. Air conditioning. Fax and copier on premises. Handicap access. Antiquing, fishing, live theater, parks, shopping, downhill skiing, cross-country skiing, sporting events and water sports nearby.

Publicity: *Burlington Free Press and Champlain Valley Business News.*

Killington   G3

Mountain Meadows Lodge

285 Thundering Brook Rd
Killington, VT 05751
(802)775-1010 (800)370-4567 Fax:(802)773-4459
E-mail: havefun@mtmeadowslodge.com
Web: www.mtmeadowslodge.com

Circa 1850. Located in a pre-Civil War farmhouse, on 110-acre Kent Lake and the Appalachian Trail, Mountain Meadows Lodge is a family owned inn that offers a multitude of amenities and services for guests. The sweeping mountain views set the tone for relaxation and inspiration. Rooms range from cozy standard rooms to suites with fireplaces and rooms with balconies overlooking the lake. Guests enjoy a Vermont country breakfast with items such as the inn's signature mixed berry

griddlecakes served with warm Vermont maple syrup and hearty omelets. Boxed lunches are prepared for guests who want to enjoy a picnic next to a waterfall, on one of the lake's islands, or on Killington Mountain. Weekends are the time dinners are served in the post and beam dining room. Vermont smoked trout on toast points with caper cream cheese is a popular starter. Guests can choose from a number of main courses with everything from cheddar- and apple-stuffed chicken breasts to sirloin tips in puff pastry. Ask for the maplebread pudding for dessert. A variety of vegetarian choices also are available. Pub-style offerings are available midweek. The lodge's state-licensed children's center allows parents to leave children for an hour, half-day or all day. Activities at the center include farm animal feedings, cookouts and marshmallow roasts in summer and dog sled rides and cross-country skiing in winter.

Innkeeper(s): Mark & Michelle Werle. $85-140. MC, VISA, AX, TC. TAC10. 20 rooms with PB, 1 with FP, 1 suite and 1 conference room. Breakfast included in rates. Types of meals: Full bkfst, country bkfst, early coffee/tea, lunch, picnic lunch, afternoon tea, snacks/refreshments and dinner. MAP. Beds: QDT. Cable TV, phone and suite has hot tub/spa in room. VCR, fax, spa, swimming, sauna, library, child care, row boating, farm animals, canoeing/kayaking, fishing, hiking, Appalachian trail, cross-country skiing and water sports on premises. Weddings, small meetings and family reunions hosted. French, Spanish and German spoken. Amusement parks, antiquing, art galleries, beaches, bicycling, golf, waterfalls, live theater, museums, parks, shopping, downhill skiing, sporting events and tennis nearby.

The Vermont Inn

Rt 4
Killington, VT 05751
(802)775-0708 (800)541-7795 Fax:(802)773-9810
E-mail: relax@vermontinn.com
Web: www.vermontinn.com

Circa 1840. Surrounded by mountain views, this rambling red and white farmhouse has provided lodging and superb cuisine for many years. Exposed beams add to the atmosphere in the living and game room. The award-winning dining room provides candlelight tables beside a huge fieldstone fireplace.

Historic Interest: Calvin Coolidge birthplace and Bennington, V.T., Civil War exhibits.

Innkeeper(s): Megan & Greg Smith. $50-185. MC, VISA, AX, DC, DS, PC, TC. 18 rooms with PB, 5 with FP. Breakfast and afternoon tea included in rates. Types of meals: Full bkfst, early coffee/tea and gourmet dinner. MAP, EP. Beds: QDT. TV, ceiling fan and one with Jacuzzi tub in room. Air conditioning. VCR, fax, copier, spa, swimming, sauna, tennis, library and screened porch on premises. Handicap access. Weddings, small meetings, family reunions and seminars hosted. Antiquing, fishing, live theater, parks, shopping, downhill skiing, cross-country skiing & water sports nearby.

Publicity: *New York Daily News, New Jersey Star Leader, Rutland Business Journal, Bridgeport Post Telegram, New York Times, Boston, Vermont and Asbury Park Press.*

"We had a wonderful time. The inn is breathtaking. Hope to be back."

Landgrove   J3

Landgrove Inn

132 Landgrove Rd
Landgrove, VT 05148
(802)824-6673 (800)669-8466 Fax:(802)824-6790
E-mail: vtinn@sover.net
Web: www.landgroveinn.com

Circa 1820. This rambling inn is located along a country lane in the valley of Landgrove in the Green Mountain National Forest. The Rafter Room is a lounge and pub with a fireside sofa for 12. Breakfast and dinner are served in the newly renovated and stenciled dining room. Evening sleigh or hay rides are often arranged. Rooms vary in style and bedding arrangements, including some newly decorated

rooms with country decor, so inquire when making your reservation.

Historic Interest: Hildene, Robert Todd Lincoln's Georgian Revival mansion is nearby, as is the Norman Rockwell Museum.

Innkeeper(s): Kathy & Jay Snyder. $95-235. MC, VISA, AX, DS, TC. 18 rooms, 16 with PB and 1 conference room. Breakfast included in rates. Types of meals: Full bkfst, afternoon tea and dinner. Beds: KQD. Phone and some with fireplace and hot air massage tub in room. VCR, fax, copier, spa, tennis, heated pool, stocked fishing pond and hiking trails on premises. Weddings, small meetings, family reunions and seminars hosted. Antiquing, fishing, live theater, parks, shopping, downhill skiing and cross-country skiing nearby.

"A true country inn with great food — we'll be back."

Lower Waterford   D6

Rabbit Hill Inn

Lower Waterford Rd
Lower Waterford, VT 05848
(802)748-5168 (800)762-8669 Fax:(802)748-8342

Circa 1795. Above the Connecticut River overlooking the White Mountains, Samuel Hodby opened this tavern and provided a general store and inn to travelers. As many as 100 horse teams traveled by the inn each day. The ballroom, constructed in 1855, was supported by bent-wood construction giving the dance floor a spring effect.

The classic Greek Revival exterior features solid pine Doric columns. Romance abounds in every nook and cranny. Rooms are decorated to the hilt with beautiful furnishings and linens. The Loft room, which overlooks the garden,

includes cathedral ceilings and a hidden staircase. The Jonathan Commings Suite offers two fireplaces and a whirlpool with mountain view from its third-story private porch. Turndown service and afternoon tea are only a couple of the amenities. Glorious breakfasts and gourmet, five-course, candlelit dinners add to a memorable stay.

Historic Interest: There are several historic churches in the area. The Fairbanks Museum, Planetarium and Art Gallery is 10 minutes away, while the Robert Frost Museum is a 25-minute drive.

Innkeeper(s): Brian & Leslie Mulcahy. $260-410. MC, VISA, AX, PC. 20 rooms with PB, 15 with FP. Breakfast, afternoon tea and dinner included in rates. Types of meals: Full bkfst, early coffee/tea and picnic lunch. MAP. Beds: KQT. Nine rooms with whirlpool tubs for two in room. Fax, copier and five-course dinners available on premises. Antiquing, bicycling, canoeing/kayaking, fishing, golf, hiking, horseback riding, sleigh rides, massage services, parks, shopping, downhill skiing and cross-country skiing nearby.

Publicity: *New York Times, Los Angeles Herald Examiner, Today Show, Innsider, USA Today, Boston, Yankee, Bridal Guide, For the Bride, Country Living, Ski Magazine, National Geographic Traveler, NBC Today, Inn Country USA and Great Country Inns.*

"It is not often that one experiences one's vision of a tranquil, beautiful step back in time. This is such an experience. Everyone was so accommodating and gracious."

Ludlow   I4

The Combes Family Inn

953 E Lake Rd
Ludlow, VT
(802)228-8799 (800)822-8799 Fax:(802)228-8704
E-mail: billcfi@tds.net
Web: www.combesfamilyinn.com

Circa 1891. For many years this dairy farm supplied milk to the local communities, and maple syrup was produced from the sugar bushes. Now the 50 acres feature a renovated family-friendly farmhouse surrounded by meadows of wildflowers, apple trees, perennials and herb gardens. Furnished with turn-of-the-century oak, the lounge features barnboard paneling and a fireplace. Large, comfortable guest bedrooms and suites are decorated in early American country style. Okemo Mountain is seen from the bay window of the dining room, which features exposed beams. The rural setting and scenic beauty instills a return to carefree living. Children and the young at heart will enjoy games, videos and good food. Relax on the front porch, visit the neighbor's llamas or explore nearby lakes. Ask about special ski and seasonal packages.

Historic Interest: Calvin Coolidge birthplace and museum (5 miles), Weston (10 miles).

Innkeeper(s): Ruth & Bill Combes. $65-154. MC, VISA, AX, DS, PC, TC. TAC10. 11 rooms with PB and 3 suites. Breakfast included in rates. Types of meals: Full bkfst, country bkfst, veg bkfst, early coffee/tea, dinner and room service. MAP. Beds: QDT. Air conditioning. VCR, fax, copier and library on premises. Weddings, small meetings and family reunions hosted. French spoken. Antiquing, art galleries, bicycling, canoeing/kayaking, fishing, golf, hiking, horseback riding, live theater, museums, parks, shopping, downhill skiing, cross-country skiing, tennis and water sports nearby.

Pets allowed: In units attached to main house.

The Governor's Inn

86 Main St
Ludlow, VT 05149-1113
(802)228-8830 (800) GOVERNOR
E-mail: info@thegovernorsinn.com
Web: www.thegovernorsinn.com

Circa 1890. Governor Stickney built this house for his bride, Elizabeth Lincoln, and it retains the intimate feeling of an elegant country house furnished in Victorian fashion. Extraordinary details include slate fireplaces, polished woodwork and stained-glass windows that reside well with a tea cart and silver tea service, replica 1898 telephone, heirloom china, silver, crystal and oil lanterns on the dinner tables. Some of the antique-filled bed chambers boast Vermont Castings gas stoves, and all enhance the romantic ambiance. Enjoy a full hot breakfast with a coffee pot on each well-set table. Afternoon tea and turndown service add to the inn's gracious hospitality. Six-course gourmet dinners and picnics are

also offered. Discover Vermont from this delightful location.

Innkeeper(s): Cathy & Jim Kubec. $195-355. MC, VISA, AX, DS. TAC10. 8 rooms with PB, 3 with FP and 1 suite. Breakfast and afternoon tea included in rates. Types of meals: Gourmet bkfst, picnic lunch and gourmet dinner. MAP. Beds: KQDT. Culinary Magic Seminars on premises. Antiquing, bicycling, canoeing/kayaking, fishing, golf, hiking, horseback riding, historical sites, Priory, sleigh rides, snowmobiling, live theater, parks, shopping, downhill skiing and cross-country skiing nearby.

Lyndon
C6

Branch Brook B&B

PO Box 143
Lyndon, VT 05849-0143
(802)626-8316 (800)572-7712

Circa 1850. This Federal-style home is filled with charm. Exposed beams and homey rooms filled with antiques create a pleasant atmosphere. Meals are prepared at a unique English cookstove, which guests may try out. The honey and maple syrup on the breakfast table are prepared by the innkeepers and accompany items such as pancakes, French toast, bacon and eggs. Ski areas, lakes and rivers are close by, and there are antique shops, flea markets and auctions nearby.

Innkeeper(s): Ann Tolman. $72-94. MC, VISA. 5 rooms, 3 with PB. Breakfast included in rates. Types of meals: Full bkfst and early coffee/tea. Beds: KQ. Phone in room. VCR, copier and library on premises. Weddings, small meetings and family reunions hosted. Antiquing, fishing, covered bridges (5), golf, parks, shopping, downhill skiing, cross-country skiing and water sports nearby.

Manchester
J2

1811 House

Historic Rt 7A, Box 39
Manchester, VT 05254
(802)362-1811
E-mail: house1811@adelphia.net
Web: www.1811house.com

Circa 1775. Since 1811, the historic Lincoln Home has been operated as an inn, except for one time. It was the private residence of Mary Lincoln Isham, granddaughter of President Lincoln. It has been authentically restored to the Federal period with antiques and  canopy beds. The gardens look out over a golf course, and it's just a short walk to tennis or swimming.

Historic Interest: National Register.

Innkeeper(s): Bruce & Marnie Duff, Cathy & Jorge Veleta. $120-230. MC, VISA. TAC10. 14 rooms with PB. Types of meals: Full bkfst. Beds: KQ. Publicity: *New York.*

Manchester Highlands Inn

Highland Ave, Box 1754A
Manchester, VT 05255
(802)362-4565 (800)743-4565 Fax:(802)362-4028
E-mail: relax@highlandsinn.com
Web: www.highlandsinn.com

Circa 1898. This Queen Anne Victorian mansion sits proudly on the crest of a hill overlooking the village. From the three-story turret, guests can look out over Mt. Equinox, the Green Mountains and the valley below. Feather beds and down comforters adorn the beds in the guest rooms. Many with canopy beds and fireplaces. A game room with billiards and a stone fireplace are popular in winter, while summertime guests enjoy the outdoor pool, croquet lawn and veranda. Gourmet country breakfasts and home-baked afternoon snacks are served.

Historic Interest: Hildene, summer home of Robert Todd Lincoln (1 mile), Bennington Monument (20 miles), Southern Vermont Arts Center(1 mile).

Innkeeper(s): Patricia & Robert Eichorn. $110-165. MC, VISA, AX, PC, TC. TAC10. 15 rooms with PB. Breakfast and afternoon tea included in rates. Types of meals: Gourmet bkfst. Beds: QDT. TV and several with gas fireplaces

in room. Air conditioning. VCR, fax, swimming, library, game room and guest bar on premises. Weddings, small meetings, family reunions and seminars hosted. Limited French and German spoken. Antiquing, bicycling, canoeing/kayaking, fishing, golf, hiking, horseback riding, fly fishing, live theater, parks, shopping, downhill skiing and cross-country skiing nearby.

Publicity: *Bennington Banner, Gourmet, Toronto Sun, Vermont, Asbury Park Press, Vermont Weathervane, Yankee Traveler, Boston Globe and Cat Fanciers Magazine.*

"We couldn't believe such a place existed. Now we can't wait to come again."

The Inn at Manchester

PO Box 41, HR 7A
Manchester, VT 05254-0041
(802)362-1793 (800)273-1793 Fax:(802)362-3218
E-mail: stay@innatmanchester.com
Web: www.innatmanchester.com

Circa 1880. This restored Victorian became an inn in 1978, almost 100 years after it was originally built as a private home. Both the main building and Carriage House are in the National Register. Set on four lush acres with gardens and a meandering brook, enjoy pleasant guest bedrooms, comfortable common areas, a relaxing pool, porches and patio. Offering in-town convenience with a wonderful country atmosphere, it is a short walk to shops, restaurants and outdoor recreation.

Historic Interest: Robert Todd Lincoln's Estate and the Southern Vermont Art Center are within two miles of the inn. The Bennington Museum is 25 miles away.

Innkeeper(s): Ron & Mary Blake. $129-249. MC, VISA, AX, DS, PC, TC. TAC10. 14 rooms with PB and 4 suites. Breakfast and afternoon tea included in rates. Types of meals: Gourmet bkfst. Beds: KQDT. Clocks and some with fireplace in room. Air conditioning. Fax, copier and swimming on premises. Small meetings and family reunions hosted. Antiquing, fishing, golf, live theater, shopping, downhill skiing, cross-country skiing and tennis nearby.

Publicity: *New York Times, Boston Globe, Travel & Leisure, Gourmet & Newsday.*

"Come for peace, pancakes and pampering."

Manchester Center
J2

The Inn at Ormsby Hill

1842 Main St
Manchester Center, VT 05255-9518
(802)362-1163 (800)670-2841 Fax:(802)362-5176
E-mail: stay@ormsbyhill.com
Web: www.ormsbyhill.com

Circa 1764. During the Revolutionary War, hero Ethan Allen reportedly hid out in the smoke room at this Federal-style mansion. Robert Todd Lincoln and President Taft are among the other notable guests at this historic treasure. The town's first jail cell still exists in the inn's basement, complete with steel bars and the marble slab where prisoners slept. The inn offers beautiful views of the nearby Green Mountains. Inside, guests will marvel at the inn's conservatory, which was built to resemble a ship and looks out to the gardens and the mountains. Antique-filled rooms offer four-poster or canopy beds decked in fine linens. All rooms include fireplaces and  two-person whirlpool tubs. Innkeeper Chris Sprague's culinary talents, in addition to writing a cookbook, have been heralded in such publications as Food & Wine, Yankee and Colonial Homes. Vermont is bustling with activities, dozens of which are just a short drive from the inn.

Historic Interest: The adjoining estate to the inn, which itself is listed in the Vermont Register of Historic Places, was home to Robert Todd Lincoln, the son of Abraham Lincoln.

Innkeeper(s): Ted & Chris Sprague. $150-370. MC, VISA, DS. TAC10. 10 rooms with PB, 10 with FP. Breakfast and afternoon tea included in rates. Beds: KQ. Two-person whirlpool in room. Air conditioning. Fax and library on premises. Antiquing, fishing, hiking, live theater, downhill skiing and cross-country skiing nearby.

Publicity: *Gourmet, Getaways for Gourmets, Country Inns, Discerning Traveler, Colonial Homes, Yankee Traveler and Boston Globe.*

"After 17 years of visiting B&Bs in Vermont, we can truly say you are the best. On a scale of 1-10, you are a 12."

River Meadow Farm

PO Box 822
Manchester Center, VT 05255-0822
(802)362-1602

Circa 1797. The oldest portion of this New England farmhouse was built in the late 18th century, and in keeping with that era, Colonial-style furnishings decorate the interior. During one part of its history, the home served as Manchester Poor Farm. The living room with its grand piano and fireplace is an ideal place for those seeking relaxation. At breakfast, fresh fruit, coffee, teas and juice accompany traditional entrees such as eggs and bacon or pancakes topped with blueberries. There are 90 acres to explore at this farm, some of which border the Battenkill River.

Historic Interest: Hildene, the summer home of Robert Todd Lincoln, can be seen on a hill on the farm. The 1906 home is open for tours from May to October.

Innkeeper(s): Patricia J. Dupree. $70. PC, TC. 5 rooms. Breakfast included in rates. Types of meals: Full bkfst. MAP. Beds: DT. VCR and library on premises. Antiquing, fishing, live theater, parks, shopping, downhill skiing, cross-country skiing and water sports nearby.

"We really loved our stay and are planning to return as soon as possible."

Manchester Village   J2

The Reluctant Panther Inn & Restaurant

17-39 West Rd
Manchester Village, VT 05254
(802)362-2568 (800)822-2331 Fax:(802)362-2586
E-mail: stay@reluctantpanther.com
Web: www.reluctantpanther.com

Circa 1850. Elm trees line a street of manicured lawns and white clapboard estates. Suddenly, a muted purple clapboard house appears, the Reluctant Panther. The well-appointed guest rooms recently have been renovated and many include fireplaces, whirlpool tubs, cable TV and air conditioning. Guests will find a collection of gracious antique furnishings in their rooms. The inn offers suites with Jacuzzi tubs for two and many with a fireplace in the bathroom and a second fireplace in the bedroom. The Greenhouse is a beautiful setting in which to enjoy a romantic dinner on tables set with fine china, crystal and fresh flower baskets. Breakfasts are served in the inn's private dining room, a bright room warmed by a crackling fire.

Historic Interest: Hildene (1 mile), Norman Rockwell Museum (8 miles), Bennington Monument and battlefield (20 miles).

Innkeeper(s): Robert & Maye Bachofen. $109-425. MC, VISA, AX, DS, PC, TC. TAC10. 21 rooms with PB, 15 with FP and 11 suites. Breakfast included in rates. Types of meals: Gourmet bkfst, cont plus, cont and gourmet dinner. MAP,

AP, EP. Beds: KQT. Cable TV, phone, turndown service, Jacuzzi and hair dryers in room. Central air. Fax and copier on premises. Handicap access. Family reunions hosted. German, Spanish and French spoken. Antiquing, art galleries, bicycling, canoeing/kayaking, fishing, golf, hiking, horseback riding, live theater, museums, parks, shopping, downhill skiing, cross-country skiing and tennis nearby.

Publicity: *New York Times, Gourmet, Country Inns. and CNN.*

"We enjoyed our stay so much that now we want to make it our yearly romantic getaway."

Middlebury   F2

Linens & Lace

29 Seminary St
Middlebury, VT 05753-1216
(802)388-0832 (800)808-3897

Circa 1820. Located within easy walking distance of the historic village and Middlebury College, this quaint Victorian inn provides guests with a comfortable respite whether they're in town for the music festival, skiing, shopping or attending one of the many college functions. There are five guest rooms, all decorated in heirlooms and antiques. Linen and lace, thus the name, fresh flowers and sterling silver add to the inn's ambiance. Afternoon tea is  served on the porch overlooking the gardens, weather permitting, while a full breakfast of wild blueberry muffins, pancakes, bacon, orange juice and fresh fruit is offered in the dining room.

Innkeeper(s): Mary Botter. $89-129. PC, TC. 5 rooms, 3 with PB. Breakfast and afternoon tea included in rates. Types of meals: Full bkfst and early coffee/tea. Beds: QDT. Ceiling fan in room. Air conditioning. VCR on premises. Family reunions hosted. Antiquing, fishing, golf, hiking, bicycling, fine dining, parks, shopping, downhill skiing, cross-country skiing and tennis nearby.

Middlebury Inn

14 Courthouse Sq
Middlebury, VT 05753
(802)388-4961 (800)842-4666 Fax:(802)388-4563
E-mail: midinnvt@sover.net

Circa 1827. This red brick, white-shuttered inn that has hosted weary travelers for many generations, is celebrating its 174th-year anniversary this year. Guests can choose from several options when selecting a room. The grounds include three different prop- erties aside from the Middlebury Inn, which is an amazing structure to behold. The Porter Mansion boasts a porch with wicker furnishings, marble fireplaces and a curving staircase. At the Middlebury Inn, guests enjoy delectable afternoon teas on the veranda while viewing the Village Greens. The innkeepers include plenty of special touches such as stocking rooms with books, bath soaps and lotions. Complimentary continental breakfast and afternoon tea is served daily. The inn offers ski and bicycle storage and will help guests make arrangements for walking tours, a popular activity.

Historic Interest: The Middlebury Inn is a community landmark, listed in the National Register, and in the center of Middlebury's historic district, which offers 155 architectural gems within walking distance. Vermont State Craft Center, museums and a waterfall are nearby.

Innkeeper(s): Frank & Jane Emanuel. $88-395. MC, VISA, AX, DS, PC, TC. TAC10. 80 rooms with PB and 3 conference rooms. Breakfast and afternoon tea included in rates. Types of meals: Full bkfst, cont, early coffee/tea, lunch, picnic lunch and dinner. EP. Beds: KQDT. Cable TV, phone and hair dryers in

bathroom in room. Air conditioning. VCR, fax and copier on premises. Handicap access. Small meetings, family reunions and seminars hosted. Antiquing, fishing, parks, shopping, downhill skiing, cross-country skiing, sporting events and water sports nearby.
Pets allowed: Limited, fee charged.
Publicity: *Vermont, Country Inns, Chicago Tribune, Glamour, Burlington Free Press and New York Times.*

Montgomery   B4

Black Lantern Inn

Rt 118
Montgomery, VT 05470
(802)326-4507 (800)255-8661 Fax:(802)326-2024
E-mail: blantern@together.net
Web: www.blacklantern.com

Circa 1803. Originally this brick inn and restaurant served as a stagecoach stop. Carefully decorated throughout, the gracious inn's ambiance is enhanced by Vermont antiques. Some of the suites feature fireplaces and whirlpool tubs. The inn's restaurant offers entrees such as horseradish potato crusted salmon, roast duck and rack of lamb. A hot tub is popular on starry nights. A few minutes away, ride the tramway to the top of Jay Peak for novice and expert skiers. Montgomery Village is known for its seven covered bridges. Hike the Long Trail, fish or mountain bike.
Innkeeper(s): Deb & Bob Winders. $85-145. MC, VISA, AX, DS, PC, TC. TAC10. 8 rooms with PB and 7 suites. Breakfast included in rates. Types of meals: Full bkfst and gourmet dinner. MAP, EP. Beds: KQDT. TV, ceiling fan and VCR in room. Fax on premises. Weddings, small meetings, family reunions and seminars hosted. Antiquing, fishing, downhill skiing and cross-country skiing nearby.
Publicity: *Burlington Free Press, Los Angeles Times, Bon Appetit, Ottawa Citizen and Travel - CJCF Montreal.*

"...one of the four or five great meals of your life-Jay Stone, Ottawa Citizen."

Montgomery Center   B4

The Inn On Trout River

Main St, PO Box 76
Montgomery Center, VT 05471-0076
(802)326-4391 (800)338-7049
E-mail: info@troutinn.com
Web: www.troutinn.com

Circa 1895. Both a fine country inn and restaurant, The Inn on Trout River, offers an ideal location for enjoying Vermont's Jay Peak region and the historic district of Montgomery Center.

Antiques and comfortable furnishings decorate the inn. Feather pillows and down comforters top the queen-size beds. The innkeepers offer adventure packages and a "Teddy Bear Creation Weekend." New packages are added throughout the year. The inn's location provides close access to downhill and cross-country ski areas, snowmobiling, snowshoeing, hiking, biking, golf courses, swimming, fishing and hunting. Museums, shops, antique stores and auctions are other amusements. The area boasts seven covered bridges and endless acres of scenery perfect for shutterbugs and nature lovers alike.
Historic Interest: Covered bridges in Montgomery and within an hour circumference.
Innkeeper(s): Michael & Lee Forman. $58-125. MC, VISA, AX, DS. TAC10. 10 rooms with PB, 1 with FP and 1 suite. Breakfast included in rates. Types of meals: Full bkfst and gourmet dinner. MAP. Beds: KQT. Antiquing, bicycling, fishing, golf, hiking, snowmobiling, snowshoeing, snowboarding, museums, parks, downhill skiing, cross-country skiing and water sports nearby.

Publicity: *Caledonia-Record, Vermont Magazine, Cycle Canada Magazine and Yankee Magazine.*
"A superb place to stay."

Montpelier   E4

Betsy's B&B

74 E State St
Montpelier, VT 05602-3112
(802)229-0466 Fax:(802)229-5412
E-mail: betsysbnb@adelphia.net
Web: www.betsysbnb.com

Circa 1895. Within walking distance of downtown and located in the state's largest historic preservation district, this Queen Anne Victorian with romantic turret and carriage house features

lavish Victorian antiques throughout its interior. Bay windows, carved woodwork, high ceilings, lace curtains and wood floors add to the authenticity. The full breakfast varies in content but not quality, and guest favorites include orange pancakes.
Innkeeper(s): Jon & Betsy Anderson. $60-100. MC, VISA, AX, DS, PC, TC. TAC10. 12 rooms with PB. Breakfast included in rates. Types of meals: Full bkfst. Beds: QDT. Cable TV and phone in room. VCR, fax and laundry on premises. Small meetings and family reunions hosted. Some Spanish spoken. Antiquing, fishing, art & history museums, live theater, parks, shopping, downhill skiing, cross-country skiing and water sports nearby.

The Inn at Montpelier

147 Main St
Montpelier, VT 05602-2937
(802)223-2727
E-mail: mail2inn@aol.com
Web: www.innatmontpelier.com

Circa 1828. Two Federal-style homes comprise the Inn at Montpelier. Ten fireplaces, Greek Revival woodwork and glass-fronted china cupboards are original. A favorite guest room is number two with a lace-canopy bed. A block from the inn are restaurants, business districts and the 100-acre Hubbard Park. The inn holds a AAA three-diamond award.
Innkeeper(s): Rick & Rita Rizza. $90-177. MC, VISA, AX. 19 rooms with PB, 6 with FP and 1 conference room. Beds: K.
Publicity: *Glamour Magazine and The Times Argus.*
"My hunch that the Inn at Montpelier would be ideal was well-founded."

Newfane   K4

West River Lodge & Stables

117 Hill Rd
Newfane, VT 05345-9606
(802)365-7745 Fax:(802)365-4450
E-mail: capite@artacseel.com
Web: westriverlodge.com

Circa 1829. West River Lodge includes a picturesque white farmhouse next door to a big red barn, surrounded by meadows and hills. Flower gardens in view of the long front porch invite guests to linger. Many enjoy horseback riding nearby. Horse boarding is offered and lessons and a riding ring are available. The home was built in the early 19th century as part of a horse farm, and it has served as a horse farm for nearly two centuries. The cozy farmhouse offers comfortable guest rooms decorated with country antiques. A hearty breakfast with items such as blueberry pancakes, country sausage, eggs, homemade muffins and fresh fruit is included in the rates. Newfane offers everything from hiking to fishing, tubing, kayaking and canoeing, as well as antique shops and wonderful fall foliage. The West River is across the field from the lodge.

Innkeeper(s): Ellen & James Wightman. $85-100. MC, VISA, PC. 8 rooms, 4 with PB. Breakfast included in rates. Types of meals: Country bkfst. Beds: QDT. Fax, copier, swimming, stables & pet boarding on premises. Weddings, small meetings, family reunions & seminars hosted. Antiquing, art galleries, beaches, bicycling, canoeing/kayaking, fishing, golf, hiking, horseback riding, museums, parks, shopping, downhill skiing, cross-country skiing, tennis & water sports nearby.
Pets allowed: In some rooms.

Orwell   G2

Historic Brookside Farms Country Inn & Antique Shop

PO Box 36, Route 22A
Orwell, VT 05760
(802)948-2727 Fax:(802)948-2800
E-mail: hbfinnvt@aol.com
Web: brooksideinnvt.com

Circa 1789. More than 300 acres of lush meadows and scenic trails surround this estate comprised of a circa 1789 farmhouse and an 1843 National Register Neoclassical Greek Revival addition, designed by architect James Lamb. Nineteen stately Ionic columns grace the front of the mansion. The seven-room 1810 guesthouse also houses an antique shop with 18th- and early 19th-century furnishings  and accessories. A full country breakfast is served and by reservations guests can enjoy a candlelight gourmet dinner. Miles of trails invite cross-country skiing and hiking, while a 26-acre lake offers opportunities for boating and fishing. Lawn games are popular, as well. The farm is owned and operated by the Korda family.

Historic Interest: Mount Independence (2 miles), Fort Ticonderoga (15 minutes).
Innkeeper(s): The Korda Family. $95-175. PC, TC. 7 rooms, 3 with PB, 1 suite and 1 conference room. Breakfast and afternoon tea included in rates. Types of meals: Gourmet bkfst, early coffee/tea, lunch, picnic lunch, snacks/refreshments and dinner. MAP, AP. Beds: DT. Welcome tray with Vermont products in room. VCR, fax, copier, fishing, cross-country skiing and child care available with prior arrangement on premises. Handicap access. Weddings, small meetings, family reunions & seminars hosted. Golf, live theater, downhill skiing and tennis nearby.
Publicity: *New York Times, Burlington Free Press, Los Angeles Times, Preservation Magazine and and The Magazine Antiques.*

"Your home is a masterpiece in Americana antique country decor located in a setting that is exquisite."

Peru   J3

Wiley Inn

Rt 11 PO Box 37
Peru, VT 05152-0037
(802)824-6600 (888)843-6600 Fax:(802)824-4195
E-mail: historicinn@wileyinn.com
Web: www.wileyinn.com

Circa 1835. The innkeepers at Wiley Inn offer guests a choice of rooms, from romantic bedchambers with canopy beds and clawfoot tubs to family suites that can accommodate up to five people. For honeymooners or those celebrating a special occasion, there are two luxury rooms with a fireplace and double Jacuzzi. The nine-and-a-half acre grounds include a swimming pool and hot tub. The innkeepers offer winter ski packages.

Innkeeper(s): Judy & Jerry Goodman. $75-185. MC, VISA, AX, DS, PC, TC. 12

rooms with PB, 4 with FP, 2 suites and 1 conference room. Breakfast and afternoon tea included in rates. Types of meals: Full bkfst. EP. Beds: KQDT. VCR, fax, copier, spa, swimming, cybercafe and internet e- & e-mail on premises. Weddings, small meetings, family reunions and seminars hosted. Antiquing, fishing, golf, hiking, biking trails, family amusement area, canoeing, skating, snowmobiles, sleigh rides, shopping, downhill skiing, cross-country skiing and tennis nearby.

Poultney   H2

Bentley House B&B

399 Bentley Ave
Poultney, VT 05764
(802)287-4004 (800)894-4004
E-mail: towerhal@sover.net

Circa 1895. A three-story peaked turret lends the name to this Queen Anne inn located next to Green Mountain College. Stained glass, polished woodwork and original fireplace mantels add to the Victorian atmosphere, and the guest rooms are furnished with antiques of the period. A sitting room adjacent to the guest rooms has its own fireplace.

Innkeeper(s): Denise & Bob DiMaio. $55-85. 5 rooms with PB and 1 suite. Types of meals: Full bkfst. EP. AX room. Bicycles and guest kitchenette on premises. Small meetings hosted. Antiquing, fishing, parks, shopping, cross-country skiing and water sports nearby.
Publicity: *Rutland Herald and Rutland Business Journal.*

"Your beautiful home was delightful and just the best place to stay!"

Proctorsville   I4

Golden Stage Inn

399 Depot St, PO Box 218
Proctorsville, VT 05153
(802)226-7744 (800)253-8226 Fax:(802)226-7882
E-mail: goldenstageinn@tds.net
Web: www.goldenstageinn.com

Circa 1788. The Golden Stage Inn was a stagecoach stop built shortly before Vermont became a state. It served as a link in the Underground Railroad and was the home of Cornelia Otis Skinner. Cornelia's Room still offers its original polished wide-pine floors and view of Okemo Mountain, and now there's a four-poster cherry bed, farm animal border, wainscoting and a comforter filled with wool from the inn's sheep. Outside are gardens of wildflowers, a little pen with two sheep, a swimming pool and blueberries and raspberries for  the picking. Breakfast offerings include an often-requested recipe, Golden Stage Granola. Home-baked breakfast dishes are garnished with Johnny-jump-ups and nasturtiums from the garden. Guests can indulge anytime by reaching into the inn's bottomless cookie jar. Okemo Mountain Resort base lodge is less than four miles away and it's a 20 minute drive to Killington access.

Innkeeper(s): Sandy & Peter Gregg. $79-250. MC, VISA, AX, PC. TAC10. 10 rooms, 6 with PB and 1 suite. Breakfast included in rates. Types of meals: Full bkfst and dinner. MAP. Beds: KQDT. Central air. VCR, fax, copier, swimming, library and one room handicapped equipped on premises. Handicap access. Weddings, small meetings and family reunions hosted. Antiquing, fishing, golf, live theater, shopping, downhill skiing and cross-country skiing nearby.
Publicity: *Journal Inquirer, Gourmet and Los Angeles Times.*

"The essence of a country inn!"

Whitney Brook B&B

2423 Twenty Mile Stream Rd
Proctorsville, VT 05153-9703
(802)226-7460
E-mail: whitney_brook@yahoo.com
Web: www.wbrook.cjb.net

Circa 1870. Stone walls encompass the 200 acres that surround this historic farmhouse. The grounds include streams, meadows and woods. The guest rooms are decorated in country style. For example, the Newport room includes two poster beds topped with white and blue comforters. The walls are decorated with blue and white wallpaper and blue trim. The innkeepers keep books and games on hand, as well as information about local activities. The Vermont Country Store is a nearby attraction.
Innkeeper(s): Jim & Ellen Parrish. $55-95. MC, VISA, AX, DS, PC, TC. 4 rooms, 2 with PB. Breakfast included in rates. Types of meals: Full bkfst. Beds: QDT. Ceiling fan in room. VCR on premise. Antiquing, fishing, golf, live theater, shopping, downhill skiing, cross-country skiing and water sports nearby.
Publicity: *Philadelphia Enquirer, Newark Ledger Star and Boston Globe.*

Putney   K4

The Putney Inn

PO Box 181
Putney, VT 05346-0181
(802)387-5517 (800)653-5517 Fax:(802)387-5211
E-mail: putneyin@sover.net

Circa 1790. The property surrounding this New England farmhouse was deeded to an English Army Captain by King George in 1790. The grounds' first home burned in a fire, and this inn was constructed on the original foundation. Eventually it became a Catholic seminary, and then an elegant country inn. Rooms are located in a 1960s building, adjacent  to the main historic farmhouse. The rooms are decorated in a Colonial style with antiques. The inn's dining room, headed by renown chef Ann Cooper, features New England cuisine. The ingredients are fresh and locally produced, and might include appetizers such as smoked salmon on Johnnycakes with an apple cider vinaigrette. Entrees such as a mixed grill of local venison and game hen flavored by an apple-horseradish marinade follow. Craft and antique shops, hiking, skiing and biking are among the local activities.
Innkeeper(s): Randi Ziter. $78-158. MC, VISA, AX, DS, PC, TC. TAC10. 25 rooms and 4 conference rooms. Breakfast included in rates. Types of meals: Gourmet bkfst, cont plus, cont, early coffee/tea, gourmet lunch, picnic lunch, afternoon tea, snacks/refreshments and gourmet dinner. Beds: Q. Cable TV and phone in room. Air conditioning. VCR, fax, copier and full dining restaurant on premises. Handicap access. Weddings, small meetings, family reunions and seminars hosted. Amusement parks, antiquing, fishing, golf, national forest; nature hikes, biking, live theater, shopping, downhill skiing, cross-country skiing, tennis and water sports nearby.
Pets allowed: Smaller than a cow, not left alone in room.
Publicity: *Chicago Tribune, Boston Herald, Culinary Arts, US Air, Travel & Leisure, Vermont Life, Vermont Magazine. and Dine-Around.*

Quechee   H5

Parker House Inn

1792 Quechee Main St
Quechee, VT 05059
(802)295-6077 Fax:(802)296-6696
E-mail: parker-house_inn@valley.net

Circa 1857. State Sen. Joseph C. Parker built this riverside manor in 1857, and three of the guest rooms are named in

honor of his family. Mornings at the inn begin with a delicious country breakfast served in the Parker House Restaurant's cozy dining rooms. The chefs are justifiably proud of their "comfort food" cuisine. Guests can stroll next door to watch the art of glass blowing, or take a walk along the Ottaquechee River. The surroundings of this historic town provide hours of activity for nature-lovers and shutterbugs. Fall foliage, of course, is an autumnal delight.

Historic Interest: Calvin Coolidge's birthplace, the American Precision Museum and Dartmouth College are among the nearby historic attractions.
Innkeeper(s): Barbara & Walt Forrester. $115-155. MC, VISA, AX, PC. 7 rooms with PB. Breakfast included in rates. Types of meals: Country bkfst. AP. Beds: KQ. Ceiling fan in room. Air conditioning. VCR, fax and bicycles on premises. Antiquing, art galleries, bicycling, canoeing/kayaking, fishing, golf, hiking, horseback riding, golf, live theater, museums, parks, shopping, downhill skiing, cross-country skiing, sporting events, tennis, water sports and wineries nearby.
Publicity: *Vermont Magazine and Quechee Times.*

"The inn is lovely, the innkeepers are the greatest, excellent food and heavenly bed!"

Richmond   D3

The Richmond Victorian Inn

191 East Main St, PO Box 652
Richmond, VT 05477-0652
(802)434-4410 (888)242-3362 Fax:(802)434-4411
E-mail: gailclar@together.net
Web: www.richmondvictorianinn.com

Circa 1861. This Queen Anne Victorian, with a three-story tower, is accented with green shutters, a sunburst design, fish scale shingles and a gingerbread front porch. The Tower Room is filled with white wicker, delicate flowered wallpaper and an antique brass bed. The Rose Room offers two beds and white ruffled curtains,  while the Pansy Room features an antique bed, white walls and a stenciled pansy border. There are hardwood floors and leaded-glass windows throughout. From the tree-shaded porch, enjoy the inn's lawns and flower gardens after a full breakfast.
Innkeeper(s): Gail M. Clark. $85-125. MC, VISA, AX, PC, TC. 6 rooms with PB. Breakfast included in rates. Types of meals: Full bkfst and early coffee/tea. Beds: QD. VCR on premises. Small meetings, family reunions and seminars hosted. Antiquing, fishing, golf, parks, shopping, downhill skiing, cross-country skiing, sporting events and water sports nearby.

"Thank you for being such a fabulous host. We loved your Victorian home & enjoyed your warm hospitality. We will definitely spread the word for you in Canada."

Ripton   F2

Chipman Inn

Rt 125
Ripton, VT 05766
(802)388-2390 (800)890-2390
E-mail: smudge@together.net

Circa 1828. This was the home of Daniel Chipman, a prominent legislator and founder of Middlebury College. Chipman also managed the "Center Turnpike" (now Route 125) through the

Green Mountains. A replica of the tariff board stands near the inn. The inn's lounge/bar is in the original kitchen, with its old fireplace and bread oven. **Historic Interest:** Shelburne Museum (50 minutes), Fort Ticonderoga (1 hour). **Innkeeper(s):** Joyce Henderson & Bill Pierce. $85-135. MC, VISA, AX, DS, TC. 8 rooms with PB. Breakfast included in rates. Types of meals: Full bkfst. Beds: QDT. Air conditioning. Small meetings and family reunions hosted. Antiquing, fishing, parks, shopping, downhill skiing, cross-country skiing and water sports nearby. **Publicity:** *Gourmet, Food & Wine, NY Times & Addison County Independent.*

"Cozy, warm and friendly."

Rochester   G3

Liberty Hill Farm

511 Liberty Hill Rd
Rochester, VT 05767-9501
(802)767-3926
E-mail: beth@libertyhillfarm.com
Web: www.libertyhillfarm.com

Circa 1825. A working dairy farm with a herd of registered Holsteins, this farmhouse offers a country setting and easy access to recreational activities. The inn's location, between the White River and the Green Mountains, is ideal for outdoor enthusiasts and animal lovers. Stroll to the barn, feed the calves or climb up to the hayloft and read or play with the kittens. Fishing, hiking, skiing and swimming are popular pastimes of guests, who are treated to a family-style dinner and full breakfast, both featuring many delicious homemade specialties. **Historic Interest:** Calvin Coolidge birthplace (35 miles), Billmes Farm Museum, Rockefeller home (30 minutes), Shelburne Museum (50 minutes). **Innkeeper(s):** Robert & Beth Kennett. $140. PC, TC. 7 rooms. Breakfast & dinner included in rates. Types of meals: Full bkfst & early coffee/tea. MAP. Beds: QDT. VCR, swimming, library & child care on premises. Weddings, small meetings, family reunions & seminars hosted. Antiquing, fishing, live theater, parks, shopping, downhill skiing, cross-country skiing, sporting events & water sports nearby. **Publicity:** *New York Times, Boston Globe, Vermont Life, Family Circle, Family Fun, Woman's Day, Country Home, Boston Chronicle. & Good Morning America.*

"We had a wonderful time exploring your farm and the countryside. The food was great."

Rutland   H3

The Phelps House

19 North St
Rutland, VT 05701-3011
(802)775-4480 (800)775-4620

Circa 1912. This California ranch B&B is considered the state's first Frank Lloyd Wright house. Guests will be intrigued by the custom wall murals, hand-crafted dolls and parquet floors. Children of all ages will enjoy the basement, which features pingpong and pool. The B&B's location, next door to a city playground, also will please the recreation-minded. Guests play tennis on the inn's clay court, adjacent to a barn boasting an 80-foot mural painted by the innkeeper. **Innkeeper(s):** Betty Phelps. $75-85. PC, TC. 6 rooms, 1 suite and 1 cottage. Breakfast included in rates. Types of meals: Full bkfst. Beds: QDT. VCR, tennis and library on premises. Family reunions hosted. Downhill skiing and cross-country skiing nearby.

Sandgate   J2

Green River Inn

2480 Sandgate Rd
Sandgate, VT 05250
(802)375-2272 (888)648-2212 Fax:(802)375-2272
E-mail: stay@greenriverinn.com
Web: www.greenriverinn.com

Circa 1935. Since the 1930s, guests have visited this country inn, secluded on more than 400 acres. The inn affords views of the surrounding wilderness and mountains. Innkeepers Jim and Betsy Gunn offer 14 beautifully restored guest rooms, some with a fireplace or whirlpool tub. The rooms are decorated with antiques and hand-painted furnishings. Guests are treated to a full country breakfast, and the

inn dinners are gourmet prepared with an extensive wine list. Local attractions include hiking, nature trails, skiing, snowshoeing, canoeing and fishing area rivers, golfing, horseback riding or just enjoying the surrounding scenery. **Innkeeper(s):** Jim & Betsy Gunn. $70-170. MC, VISA, AX, DS, PC, TC. 14 rooms. Breakfast included in rates. Types of meals: Full bkfst, country bkfst and gourmet dinner. MAP. Beds: KQDT. Ceiling fan, whirlpools and fireplaces in room. VCR on premises. Handicap access. Weddings, small meetings, family reunions and seminars hosted. Antiquing, canoeing/kayaking, fishing, golf, hiking, horseback riding, live theater, parks, shopping, downhill skiing, cross-country skiing and tennis nearby.

Pets Allowed.

Stowe   D4

Brass Lantern Inn

717 Maple St
Stowe, VT 05672-4250
(802)253-2229 (800)729-2980 Fax:(802)253-7425
E-mail: brasslntrn@aol.com
Web: www.brasslanterninn.com

Circa 1810. This rambling farmhouse and carriage barn rests at the foot of Mt. Mansfield. A recent award-winning renovation has brought a new shine to the inn, from the gleaming plank floors to the polished woodwork and crackling fireplaces and soothing whirlpool tubs. Quilts and antiques fill the guest rooms, and some, like the Honeymoon Room, have their own fireplace, whirlpool tub and mountain view. A complimentary afternoon and evening tea is provided along with a full Vermont-style breakfast. A new two-bedroom cottage is now available, as well. The inn is a multi-time winner of the Golden Fork Award from the Gourmet Dinners Society of North America. **Innkeeper(s):** Andy Aldrich. $110-225. MC, VISA, AX. TAC10. 9 rooms with PB, 4 with FP. Breakfast and afternoon tea included in rates. Types of meals: Full bkfst and early coffee/tea. Beds: QDT. Six with whirlpool tubs and three with fireplace in room. Air conditioning. VCR, fax, copier, library, gardens and patio on premises. Weddings and small meetings hosted. Antiquing, fishing, tours, live theater, parks, shopping, downhill skiing, cross-country skiing, sporting events and water sports nearby. **Publicity:** *Vermont, Vermont Life, Innsider, Discerning Traveler and Ski.*

"The little things made us glad we stopped."

Foxfire Inn & Italian Restaurant

1606 Pucker S
Stowe, VT 05672
(802)253-4887 Fax:(802)253-7016
Web: www.foxfireinn.com

Circa 1850. This inn and 90-seat restaurant is in a restored farmhouse, bordered with colorful perennials. Shingles and many-paned windows add to the welcoming feeling. The inn is best known among Stowe visitors and locals as the best place for Italian food. Try the Chicken Ripieno stuffed with gorgonzola, pancetta and figs in a creamy Marsala sauce. For dessert you'll want to order the espresso/rum-soaked pound cake with chocolate mousse filling. Rated three diamonds by AAA, the guest rooms are furnished in a country decor with antiques.

Innkeeper(s): Robert Neilson. $65-90. MC, VISA, AX, DS, TC. 5 rooms with PB. Breakfast included in rates. Types of meals: Full bkfst and dinner. Beds: QDT. Air conditioning. Fax and copier on premises. Antiquing, fishing, golf, live theater, shopping, downhill skiing, cross-country skiing, sporting events and tennis nearby.

"A wonderful evening for the third straight year!"

The Gables Inn

1457 Mountain Rd
Stowe, VT 05672-4750
(802)253-7730 (800)422-5371 Fax:(802)253-8989
E-mail: inngables@aol.com
Web: www.gablesinn.com

Circa 1856. This inn originally served as a farmhouse, but opened as an inn in the 1930s. Guest rooms feature Colonial decor with canopy beds and comfortable furnishings. The front porch and several guest rooms afford a view of Mount Mansfield. Rooms with a fireplace or Jacuzzi tub are available. The two-and-a-half-acre grounds include a swimming pool, hot tub and a little bridge that leads to a pond. Guests can relax in the solarium, in front of a fire in the living room or they can play a game in the den. The inn's restaurant serves breakfast throughout the year, and guests can choose an entree from a menu that offers everything from pancakes with Vermont maple syrup to "Two on a Raft," an English muffin with tomato, sprouts, poached eggs and Vermont cheddar cheese. Dinners are available in winter, and a lunch menu is offered during the summer months. Skiing, snowshoeing, ice skating, hiking, golf and shopping are among the many local attractions.

Innkeeper(s): Annette Manachelli & Randy Stern. $78-240. MC, VISA, AX, DC, DS, PC, TC. TAC10. 18 rooms with PB, 7 with FP and 2 suites. Breakfast and afternoon tea included in rates. Types of meals: Gourmet bkfst and early coffee/tea. Beds: KQDT. Cable TV, phone and some with ceiling fan in room. Air conditioning. VCR, fax, swimming, bicycles and hot tubs on premises. Handicap access. Weddings, small meetings and family reunions hosted. Antiquing, fishing, golf, live theater, parks, shopping, downhill skiing, cross-country skiing, sporting events and tennis nearby.
Publicity: *Vermont Life Magazine.*

Green Mountain Inn

PO Box 60, 1 Main St
Stowe, VT 05672-0060
(802)253-7301 (800)253-7302 Fax:(802)253-5096
E-mail: info@gminn.com
Web: www.greenmountaininn.com

Circa 1833. This early 19th century inn is a member of the Historic Hotels of America. The main inn and adjacent depot building are listed in the National Register of Historic Places. Completely restored and decorated in early-American style with antiques and reproductions, the inn also boasts original Walton

Blodgett paintings. Guest bedrooms feature canopy beds, whirlpools and fireplaces. The health club offers a sauna, steam room and Jacuzzi. Enjoy the year-round outdoor pool and game room.

Historic Interest: The State House, Vermont's 114 covered bridges, Hubbardton Battlefield.

Innkeeper(s): Patricia Clark. $89-399. MC, VISA, AX, DS. 100 rooms with PB, 49 with FP and 1 conference room. Types of meals: Gourmet bkfst, cont plus, cont, early coffee/tea, gourmet lunch, afternoon tea, snacks/refreshments and dinner. EP. Beds: KQDT. Cable TV and phone in room. Air conditioning. VCR, fax, copier, sauna, game room, health club, Jacuzzi and year-round outdoor pool on premises. Handicap access. Weddings, small meetings, family reunions and seminars hosted. Antiquing, bicycling, fishing, hiking, live theater, shopping, downhill skiing, cross-country skiing and water sports nearby. Pets allowed: In annex rooms only.
Publicity: *Snow Country, Elle, National Geographic Traveler and Ski Magazine.*

Ski Inn

Rt 108
Stowe, VT 05672
(802)253-4050

Circa 1941. This traditional New England inn, on 27-tree-studded acres, was the first ski lodge in Stowe. The Heyer family have operated the inn since 1941. Rooms are large and colorful with comfortable furnishings. Guests gather around the fieldstone fireplace, the dinner table and the mountain-view windows to discuss skiing and the Vermont countryside.

Innkeeper(s): Harriet Heyer. $35-65. AX. 10 rooms, 5 with PB, 1 with FP and 1 conference room. Types of meals: Cont. Beds: DT. Phone in room.
Publicity: *The Stowe Reporter, New York Times and Ski.*

"Thanks again for a great time and providing a nice place to stay. The friendliness of hosts and guests make this the best inn we have ever stayed in."

Three Bears at The Fountain

1049 Pucker St Rt 100
Stowe, VT 05672-9802
(802)253-7671 (800)898-9634 Fax:(802)253-8804
E-mail: threebears@stowevt.net
Web: www.threebearsbandb.com

Circa 1820. A spring-fed fountain on the grounds and the innkeepers' Three Bears Restaurant inspired the name for this Vermont country inn. The historic home was built by the first couple married in the village of Stowe, and it is the oldest guest house in town, opening its doors for travelers in the 1920s. The main house dates to the 1820s, but an adjacent carriage house was built in 1796. Original fireplaces, restored wood floors and exposed beams add a historic ambiance. Guest rooms are decorated in country style with quilts and antiques. Vermont's highest peak, Mount Mansfield, is just six miles away and guests are afforded the wonderful views from the wraparound porch or while relaxing in the hot tub. The King Room includes a gas fireplace, cathedral ceilings and mountain views. The breakfast room is warmed by a fireplace; and the morning meal is served on country oak tables set with linen and fine china.

Innkeeper(s): Suzanne & Stephen Vazzano. $95-300. MC, VISA, AX, TC. TAC5. 6 rooms with PB, 4 with FP and 2 suites. Breakfast included in rates. Types of meals: Full bkfst. Beds: KQ. VCR, fax and copier on premises. Small meetings and family reunions hosted. Antiquing, fishing, golf, live theater, shopping, downhill skiing, cross-country skiing and tennis nearby.

Timberholm Inn

452 Cottage Club Rd
Stowe, VT 05672-4294
(802)253-7603 (800)753-7603 Fax:(802)253-8559
E-mail: info@timberholm.com
Web: www.timberholm.com

Circa 1949. Recently renovated, this four-acre farmhouse-style country inn has a rustic red cedar exterior with hunter green trim. Inside, the walls and floors are knotty pine. The sunny Great Room features a huge fieldstone fireplace, shelves of books, comfortable sitting areas and a glass wall leading to an outside deck with a fantastic view of the Worcester Mountain range. The downstairs game room provides darts, shuffleboard and videos. The guest bedrooms and suites are tastefully furnished with antiques and artwork. A self-serve country buffet includes delicious breakfast fare and regional treats. A soothing hot tub rounds off a fun day.

Innkeeper(s): Darrick Pitstick. $90-140. MC, VISA. TAC10. 10 rooms. Breakfast included in rates. Types of meals: Country bkfst and afternoon tea. Beds: QDT. Some with cable TV and refrigerator in room. Air conditioning. VCR, fax, library and hot tub on premises. Weddings, small meetings, family reunions and seminars hosted. Antiquing, art galleries, bicycling, canoeing/kayaking, fishing, golf, hiking, horseback riding, live theater, parks, shopping, downhill skiing, cross-country skiing, tennis and water sports nearby.

Winding Brook... A Classic Mountain Lodge

199 Edson Hill Rd
Stowe, VT 05672
(802)253-7354 (800)426-6697 Fax:(802)253-8429
E-mail: windbrklod@aol.com

Circa 1939. Set beside a mountain stream on five wooded acres, Winding Brook is Stowe's oldest existing ski lodge. After skiing, relax in the living room with its inviting fieldstone fireplace or enjoy a long soak in the outdoor hot tub. During warmer months, guests can enjoy a swim in the pool. Stowe is famous for its skiing and Mount Mansfield, Vermont's highest mountain. The resort village also offers many shops, galleries and restaurants.

Innkeeper(s): Patrick J DiDomenico. $65-195. MC, VISA, AX, PC, TC. TAC10. 15 rooms with PB. Breakfast included in rates. Types of meals: Full bkfst. Beds: KQT. Air conditioning. VCR, copier, swimming, library, game room and pool table on premises. Weddings, small meetings, family reunions and seminars hosted. Antiquing, fishing, golf, parks, shopping, downhill skiing, cross-country skiing, tennis and water sports nearby.
Publicity: *Stowe Reporter.*

Townshend   K4

Boardman House

PO Box 112
Townshend, VT 05353-0112
(802)365-4086

Circa 1840. This stately Greek Revival is located on the village green of Townshend in Southeast Vermont. Guests enjoy a full breakfast before beginning their day, which could include

antiquing, canoeing or kayaking in the West River or skiing at Bromley, or Stratton ski areas, all within easy driving distance. The inn boasts a large, lush lawn and gardens, a parlor with a library and a refreshing sauna. Early cof-

fee or tea is served and picnic lunches are available.

Innkeeper(s): Paul Weber & Sarah Messenger. $70-80. PC, TC. 6 rooms, 5 with PB and 1 suite. Breakfast included in rates. Types of meals: Gourmet bkfst. Beds: QT. Air conditioning. VCR, sauna and library on premises. Small meetings and family reunions hosted. Antiquing, fishing, golf, parks, shopping, downhill skiing, cross-country skiing, tennis and water sports nearby.
Publicity: *Boston Globe, Chronicle and Funny Farm.*

Vergennes   E2

Emerson Guest House

82 Main St
Vergennes, VT 05491-1155
(802)877-3293 Fax:(802)877-3293
E-mail: emersons@sover.net
Web: www.emersonhouse.com

Circa 1850. This historic 1850s Victorian home is situated on three-and-a-half acres near downtown Vergennes in the heart of Lake Champlain Valley. Choose from six spacious, airy guest rooms, filled with antiques and personal collections. Start the

day with a fresh breakfast of frittatas and homemade muffins, or French toast with apple praline topping. Then relax in the large backyard and flower gardens or walk to nearby antique shops and restau-

rants. The historic city of Vergennes is a welcome getaway, with activities such as swimming, boating or fishing in Lake Champlain and biking or hiking along mountain trails. At the end of the day relax on the large front porch and watch the sun set over the Adirondack Mountains.

Innkeeper(s): Suzanne Wyckoff. $65-125. MC, VISA, TC. TAC5. 6 rooms, 2 with PB, 1 suite and 1 conference room. Breakfast and snacks/refreshments included in rates. Types of meals: Gourmet bkfst, country bkfst and early coffee/tea. Beds: KQDT. Ceiling fan in room. Fax, copier, bicycles, library, croquet and trails on premises. Weddings and family reunions hosted. French spoken. Antiquing, art galleries, bicycling, canoeing/kayaking, fishing, golf, hiking, horseback riding, Lake Champlain, museums, parks, shopping, downhill skiing, cross-country skiing, sporting events, tennis, water sports and wineries nearby.

Strong House Inn

94 W Main St
Vergennes, VT 05491-9531
(802)877-3337
E-mail: inkeeper@stronghouseinn.com
Web: www.stronghouseinn.com

Circa 1834. This Federal-style home boasts views of the Green Mountains and the Adirondack range. Several rooms offer working fireplaces and all are richly appointed. Country breakfasts and afternoon refreshments are served, and on selected Sundays

don't miss the expansive afternoon tea, complete with pastries, tea sandwiches, and of course, a wide selection of teas. Nearby Lake Champlain offers boating and fishing. Golf, hiking, skiing and

some of the finest cycling in Vermont are all part of the area's myriad of outdoor activities. Innkeeper Mary Bargiel is an avid gardener and decorates the grounds with flowers and herb gardens. The innkeepers offer a selection of special weekends from a Valentine's Day to a quilter's weekend.

Historic Interest: The area has no shortage of antique shopping, and the inn itself is listed in the National Register of Historic Places.

Innkeeper(s): Mary Bargiel. $90-275. MC, VISA, AX. 14 rooms with PB, 6 with FP, 2 suites and 1 conference room. Breakfast included in rates. Types of meals: Gourmet bkfst, early coffee/tea and afternoon tea. Beds: KQT. Cable TV, phone, turndown service and VCR in room. Air conditioning. Weddings, small meetings, family reunions and seminars hosted. Antiquing, fishing, live theater, shopping, downhill skiing, cross-country skiing, sporting events and water sports nearby.

Publicity: *Vermont Magazine and Addison County Independent.*

"Blissful stay...Glorious breakfast!"

Waitsfield   E3

Featherbed Inn

Route 100, 5864 Main St
Waitsfield, VT 05673
(802)496-7151 Fax:(802)496-7933
E-mail: featherbedinn@madriver.com
Web: www.featherbedinn.com

Circa 1806. Surrounded by 25 acres of woods and meadows, this New England farmhouse has been renovated with extreme attention to preserving its historic integrity. Wide pine floors with square head nails, post and beam construction, mullion windows and Colonial decor retain the inn's quaint heritage. The common areas offer a formal living room with grand piano, an open, fieldstone fireplace in the lodge room (which has games and books), and a TV/VCR in the den. Spacious guest bedrooms and suites in the main house and cottage boast warm, comfy featherbeds. Breakfast begins in the sunny dining room with different items that may include cider-poached pears, strawberry bread, baked puff pancakes with orange-apricot sauce and featherbed eggs. Relax in the gazebo overlooking the pond, then explore the year-round activities of Mad River Valley.

Innkeeper(s): Tracey & Clive Coutts. $95-145. MC, VISA, AX, PC, TC. TAC10. 10 rooms with PB and 2 suites. Breakfast, afternoon tea and snacks/refreshments included in rates. Types of meals: Gourmet bkfst, veg bkfst and early coffee/tea. Beds: QDT. Air conditioning. VCR, fax and library on premises. Small meetings and family reunions hosted. Antiquing, art galleries, bicycling, canoeing/kayaking, fishing, golf, hiking, live theater, parks, shopping, downhill skiing, cross-country skiing and tennis nearby.

Publicity: *Ski Magazine, Montreal Gazette, Ski America and Boston Globe.*

Lareau Farm Country Inn

PO Box 563, Rt 100
Waitsfield, VT 05673-0563
(802)496-4949 (800)833-0766
E-mail: lareau@lareaufarminn.com
Web: www.lareaufarminn.com

Circa 1794. This Greek Revival house was built by Simeon Stoddard, the town's first physician. Old-fashioned roses, lilacs, delphiniums, iris and peonies fill the gardens. The inn sits in a wide meadow next to the crystal-clear Mad River. A canoe trip or a refreshing swim are possibilities here.

Innkeeper(s): Susan Easley. $80-135. MC, VISA, PC, TC. 13 rooms, 11 with PB, 1 suite and 1 conference room. Breakfast included in rates. Types of meals: Gourmet bkfst and early coffee/tea. Beds: QD. TV in room. Swimming and library on premises. Weddings, small meetings, family reunions and seminars hosted. Antiquing, fishing, live theater, shopping, downhill skiing and cross-country skiing nearby.

Publicity: *Pittsburgh Press, Philadelphia Inquirer and Los Angeles Times.*

"Hospitality is a gift. Thank you for sharing your gift so freely with us."

Mad River Inn

Tremblay Rd, PO Box 75
Waitsfield, VT 05673
(802)496-7900 (800)832-8278 Fax:(802)496-5390

Circa 1860. Surrounded by the Green Mountains, this Queen Anne Victorian sits on seven scenic acres along the Mad River. The charming inn boasts attractive woodwork throughout, highlighted by ash, bird's-eye maple and cherry. Guest rooms feature European featherbeds and include the Hayden Breeze Room, with a king brass bed, large windows and sea relics, and the Abner Doubleday Room, with a queen ash bed and mementos of baseball's glory days. The inn sports a billiard table, gazebo, organic gardens and a Jacuzzi overlooking the mountains. Guests can walk to a recreation path along the river.

Historic Interest: The Historic Round Barn and Shelbourne Farm & Museum are a short distance.

Innkeeper(s): Luc Maranda. $95-135. MC, VISA, AX. TAC10. 10 rooms with PB. Breakfast and afternoon tea included in rates. Types of meals: Gourmet bkfst. Beds: KQ. Turndown service and ceiling fan in room. VCR, fax and spa on premises. Weddings, small meetings and family reunions hosted. French spoken. Antiquing, fishing, live theater, shopping, downhill skiing, cross-country skiing, sporting events and water sports nearby.

Publicity: *Insider, Victorian Homes, Let's Live, Skiing, AAA Home & Away, Tea Time at the Inn and Travel & Leisure.*

"Your hospitality was appreciated, beautiful house and accommodations, great food & friendly people, just to name a few things. We plan to return and we recommend the Mad River Inn to friends & family."

Waitsfield Inn

5248 Main St
Waitsfield, VT 05673-0969
(802)496-3979 (800)758-3801 Fax:(802)496-3970
E-mail: waitsfieldinn@madriver.com
Web: www.waitsfieldinn.com

Circa 1825. This Federal-style inn once served as a parsonage and was home to several state senators of the Richardson family. The 1839 barn offers a Great Room with fireplace and wood-plank floors, or in winter you may enjoy sipping spiced Vermont apple cider and munching on fresh cookies in the sitting room. Guest quarters are furnished with period antiques, quilts or comforters and some rooms have exposed beams or hand stenciling. A full breakfast is served in the dining room, with fresh-baked breads, fruit, muffins and a main dish. As the inn is in the village of Waitsfield, the entire town's sites are nearby including a beautiful covered bridge. Visit Glen Moss Waterfall, fly fish, canoe, try a glider, golf or watch a polo match. Snowshoeing, skiing and visits to the New England Culinary Institute and Ben & Jerry's Ice Cream Factory are popular activities.

Historic Interest: Ethan Allen's estate is 35 miles from the inn and Montpelier is 20 miles away.

Innkeeper(s): Jim & Pat Masson. $105-150. MC, VISA, AX, DS, PC, TC. 14 rooms with PB. Breakfast included in rates. Types of meals: Full bkfst. Beds: QDT. Fax, copier, library and modem on premises. Small meetings, family reunions and seminars hosted. Antiquing, fishing, golf, canoeing, live theater, shopping, downhill skiing and cross-country skiing nearby.

Wallingford H3

I. B. Munson House

37 S Main St, PO Box 427
Wallingford, VT 05773-0427
(802)446-2860 (888)519-3771 Fax:(802)446-3336
E-mail: stay@ibmunsoninn.com
Web: www.ibmunsoninn.com

Circa 1856. An Italianate Victorian bed & breakfast, the inn was meticulously restored as the innkeepers preserved many original elements, such as the wood floors, ornately carved mantels and

woodwork. Period antiques and Waverly wallcoverings are featured in the guest rooms, three of which include a fireplace. All seven guest

rooms have private baths. Wallingford is a designated historic village, so there are many interesting old homes and buildings to see. Ski areas, shops and restaurants are within a couple of blocks.

Innkeeper(s): Tom & JoAnn Brem. $85-180. MC, VISA, AX, PC, TC. TAC10. 7 rooms with PB, 3 with FP and 2 suites. Breakfast included in rates. Types of meals: Full bkfst, early coffee/tea, afternoon tea and dinner. Beds: QDT. Turndown service and ceiling fan in room. VCR and fax on premises. Weddings, small meetings, family reunions and seminars hosted. Antiquing, fishing, parks, shopping, downhill skiing, cross-country skiing and water sports nearby.

Publicity: *The Rotarian and Mill River Area Current.*

"It was a pleasure to stay at your beautiful historic Bed and Breakfast. Wonderful hospitality! Delicious breakfast - a very special treat!! We will be back."

Warren F3

Pitcher Inn

Main St
Warren, VT 05674-0408
(802)496-6350 (888)867-4824 Fax:(802)496-6354
E-mail: pitcher@madriver.com

Circa 1890. Double verandas flank the entrance to this three-story Colonial inn, built after the previous building burned in 1993. Expect to experience luxury and a high standard of excellence combined with a comfortable ease. The decor, with antiques and original artwork, resonate Vermont history and

activities. A shuffleboard table and billiards provide entertainment in one of several common rooms, and a video library is well-stocked for all ages. Each

guest bedroom offers a nostalgic journey, local themes are showcased with hand-painted murals and coordinating furnishings. Balconies and private porches boast garden, brook and village views. Breakfast is a regionally inspired delight of contemporary American cuisine. A locker room with storage facilities, as well as glove and ski boot warmers, enhance Mad River Valley recreation.

Innkeeper(s): Heather & John Carino. $300-600. MC, VISA, AX, TC. 9 rooms with PB, 9 with FP and 2 suites. Breakfast and afternoon tea included in rates. Types of meals: Gourmet bkfst, early coffee/tea and gourmet dinner. Beds: KT. Cable TV, phone, turndown service, VCR and radiant heat in room. Air conditioning. Fax, copier, library and private dining in wine cellar on premises. Handicap access. Weddings, small meetings, family reunions & seminars hosted. Antiquing, bicycling, golf, snowshoeing, live theater, shopping and sporting events nearby.

West Hill House

1496 West Hill Rd
Warren, VT 05674-9620
(802)496-7162 (800)898-1427
E-mail: westhill@madriver.com
Web: www.westhillhouse.com

Circa 1850. This attractive inn boasts a great location, on a scenic country road, just a mile from the Sugarbush Ski Area and next to the Sugarbush Golf Course/Cross-Country Ski Center. The nine-acre grounds include three ponds, meadows, perennial gardens, a uniquely designed gazebo and winter mountain views.

All rooms offer a Jacuzzi and/or steam bath, and there are fireplaces in all of the bedchambers. Guests enjoy early coffee or tea before breakfast in one of the three spacious common areas, and later are served afternoon tea and bedtime snacks.

Candlelight dinners, served in the English antique dining room, are available for six or more guests by prior arrangement. Summer weddings here can accommodate up to 150 with a wedding tent, while indoor winter weddings are popular for smaller parties.

Innkeeper(s): Dotty Kyle & Eric Brattstrom. $105-160. MC, VISA, AX, DS. 7 rooms with PB, 6 with FP. Types of meals: Full bkfst, early coffee/tea, afternoon tea, snacks/refreshments and dinner. Beds: KQT. Cable TV, VCR and all with double Jacuzzi and/or steam bath in room. Three large common areas, front porch and back deck on premises. Weddings and family reunions hosted. Antiquing, bicycling, fishing, hiking, live theater, shopping, downhill skiing and cross-country skiing nearby.

Publicity: *Yankee Magazine, Innsider Magazine, Quilt Mania Magazine, UK Ski Magazine and Boston Globe.*

Waterbury D3

The Inn at Blush Hill

784 Blush Hill Rd
Waterbury, VT 05676
(802)244-7529 (800)736-7522 Fax:(802)244-7314
E-mail: inn@blushhill.com
Web: www.blushhill.com

Circa 1790. This shingled Cape-style house was once a stagecoach stop en route to Stowe and is the oldest inn in Waterbury. A 12-foot-long pine farmhand's table is set near the double fire-

place and the kitchen bay window, revealing views of the Worcester Mountains. A favorite summertime breakfast, served gardenside, is pancakes with

fresh blueberries, topped with ice cream and maple syrup.

Historic Interest: The inn has a 1760 fireplace with adjacent brick oven.

Innkeeper(s): Pam Gosselin. $79-150. MC, VISA, AX, DS, PC, TC. TAC10. 5 rooms with PB, 1 with FP. Breakfast, afternoon tea and snacks/refreshments included in rates. Types of meals: Gourmet bkfst and early coffee/tea. Beds: QT. TV, turndown service and ceiling fan in room. Air conditioning. Fax and library on premises. Antiquing, fishing, golf, Ben & Jerry's ice cream factory, live theater, parks, shopping, downhill skiing, cross-country skiing and water sports nearby.

Publicity: *Vermont, Charlotte Observer, Yankee, New York Times, Ski, New York Post. and WCAX Television.*

"Our room was wonderful — especially the fireplace. Everything was so cozy and warm."

Thatcher Brook Inn

PO Box 490, Rt 100 N
Waterbury, VT 05676-0490
(802)244-5911 (800)292-5911 Fax:(802)244-1294
E-mail: info@thatcherbrook.com
Web: www.thatcherbrook.com

Circa 1899. Listed in the Vermont Register of Historic Buildings, this restored Victorian mansion features a rambling porch with twin gazebos. A covered walkway leads to the historic Wheeler House. Guest rooms are decorated in classic country style. Four rooms have fireplaces, and six have whirlpool tubs. The inn's restaurant and tavern are located in the main inn. Guests can dine fireside by candlelight, or on the porch in summer.

Historic Interest: The inn is listed in the National Register.
Innkeeper(s): Lisa & John Fischer. $80-195. MC, VISA, AX, DC, DS, PC, TC. TAC10. 22 rooms with PB, 4 with FP, 1 suite and 1 conference room. Breakfast included in rates. Types of meals: Full bkfst and gourmet dinner. Beds: KQD. Phone, ceiling fan, most rooms have A/C and 6 have whirlpools in room. Fax, copier and internet access on premises. Handicap access. Weddings, small meetings, family reunions and seminars hosted. Antiquing, bicycling, fishing, hiking, horseback riding, live theater, parks, shopping, downhill skiing, cross-country skiing and water sports nearby.

"I'd have to put on a black tie in Long Island to find food as good as this and best of all it's in a relaxed country atmosphere. Meals are underpriced."

Waterbury Center   D4

The Black Locust Inn

5088 Waterbury-Steve Rd, Rt 100
Waterbury Center, VT 05677
(802)244-7490 (800)366-5592 Fax:(802)244-8473
E-mail: innkeeper@blacklocustinn.com
Web: www.blacklocustinn.com

Circa 1832. Set on a hill graced with tall black locust trees is this recently restored three-gabled farmhouse. The home once presided over a 90-acre dairy farm and looks out to the Green Mountain range and Camel's Hump. Guest rooms offer inviting beds with duvets, down comforters, and piles of pillows. Bathrobes, thick towels and hand-made soaps are among the amenities. Wooden rocking chairs line the porch and situated in scenic spots are gatherings of Vermont-made country furniture. A hammock swings between two locust trees. Afternoon appetizers and drinks are served, and in the morning a three-course candle-light breakfast might offer items such as freshly baked oat honey bread, poached pear served with Ben & Jerry's sorbet and Vermont summer vegetable quiche with maple-cured sausage.

Innkeeper(s): Len, Nancy & Valerie Vignola. $115-248. MC, VISA, AX, DS, PC, TC. 6 rooms w/ PB. Breakfast & snacks/refreshments included in rates. Beds: KQ. Publicity: *Hudson Dispatch, New York Times and Yankee.*

"We could not have asked to stay at a finer inn. Your hospitality was truly heartwarming. And the food!!! We are already planning our next visit."

West Dover   K3

Austin Hill Inn

Rt 100, Box 859
West Dover, VT 05356
(802)464-5281 (800)332-7352 Fax:(802)464-1229
E-mail: austinhi@sover.net

Circa 1930. This family-owned and operated inn is situated between Mt. Snow and Haystack Mountains just outside the

historic village of West Dover. Guest rooms feature country decor and furnishings. Romantic amenities include in-room fireplaces and votive candles at turndown. Guests are treated to a hearty New England breakfast, as well as afternoon wine and cheese or home-baked treats. In cool weather, guests enjoy the warm glow of the inn's fireplaces in the common rooms. The Austin Hill Inn is notable for its attention to detail and superior hospitality.

Innkeeper(s): John & Deborah Bailey. $115-195. MC, VISA, DS, PC, TC. 10 rooms with PB, 1 suite and 1 conference room. Breakfast and snacks/refreshments included in rates. Types of meals: Full bkfst and gourmet dinner. Beds: KQDT. Fax and copier on premises. Antiquing, bicycling, canoeing/kayaking, fishing, golf, hiking, chamber music, live theater, parks, downhill skiing and cross-country skiing nearby.
Publicity: *Country Inns, Getaways and Greenwich Magazine.*

West Dover Inn

Rt 100 Box 1208
West Dover, VT 05356
(802)464-5207 Fax:(802)464-2173
E-mail: wdvrinn@sover.net
Web: www.westdoverinn.com

Circa 1846. This inn, which served originally as a stagecoach stop and tavern, has been hosting guests for more than 150 years. It features a Greek Revival facade with wide columns and porches. Located in the heart of the tiny village of West Dover, the inn offers unpretentious charm. Two guest rooms and each of the four suites include a fireplace. The suites also have whirlpool tubs. Handmade quilts and period antiques add to the New England country appeal. A complimentary full country breakfast is included daily. Dinner at the inn's restaurant, Gregory's, is a treat. The New American menu includes starters such as a Thai-barbecue shrimp or perhaps pan-seared scallops and lobster cakes. These are followed by entree selections such as Black Angus sirloin with a Gorgonzola cream sauce, a grilled salmon filet or perhaps Caribbean-style pork.

Innkeeper(s): Greg Gramas & Monique Phelan. $100-200. MC, VISA, AX, DS, PC, TC. 12 rooms with PB, 6 with FP, 4 suites and 1 conference room. Breakfast included in rates. Types of meals: Full bkfst and gourmet dinner. Beds: QDT. Cable TV in room. VCR, fax and library on premises. Weddings, small meetings, family reunions and seminars hosted. Antiquing, fishing, golf, hiking, mountain biking, live theater, parks, shopping, downhill skiing, cross-country skiing, tennis and water sports nearby.

Publicity: *Springfield Sunday Republican, Deerfield Valley News, Glamour, Ski Magazine, Flair, Vermont Magazine and Country Accents.*

West Townshend   K4

Windham Hill Inn

RR 1 Box 44
West Townshend, VT 05359-9701
(802)874-4080 (800)944-4080 Fax:(802)874-4702
E-mail: windham@sover.net
Web: www.windhamhill.com

Circa 1825. Originally a working dairy farm with a three-story house, this peaceful Green Mountain home boasts upscale country decor with Oriental carpets, period antiques and fine locally made furnishings. The large music room was built with the help of Will Ackerman, founder of Windham Hill Records.

It features an 1888 restored Steinway piano, entertainment center and extensive CD collection. Wood-burning brick fireplaces add a warm ambiance to the two parlors. The main house and White Barn guest bedrooms and lofts all offer great views. Many feature fireplaces or Vermont Castings stoves, window seats, Jacuzzis or soaking tubs and private porches. Scrumptuously satisfying cuisine is served in the Frog Pond Dining Room. Play tennis on a native-clay court, and then enjoy a swim in the brick-terraced heated pool. Hike the four-mile network of trails through 160 acres of pine and maple forest. In the winter, the trails are groomed for cross-country skiing and snowshoeing, with ice skating on the pond.

Innkeeper(s): Grigs & Pat Markham. $160-230. MC, VISA, AX, DC, DS. 18 rooms with PB, 6 with FP. Breakfast and dinner included in rates. Types of meals: Full bkfst. MAP, AP. Beds: KQT. TV and phone in room. Handicap access. Antiquing, fishing, live theater, downhill skiing, cross-country skiing and water sports nearby.

Publicity: *Vermont Life, Country Decorating, Boston and New York.*

"...enhanced. That's how I felt after not very long at all at the end of this particular road. Enhanced by exquisite views, extraordinary food and amiable hosts." — James Tabor, Vermont Life

Weston   J3

The Darling Family Inn

815 Rt 100
Weston, VT 05161-5404
(802)824-3223
E-mail: dfi@vermontel.net

Circa 1830. This two-story inn also features two cottages. Located in the Green Mountains, just minutes from Bromley, Okemo, Magic and Stratton ski areas, the inn provides a taste of life from the early Colonial days. Guest rooms feature handmade quilts crafted locally. The cottages include kitchenettes, and pets are welcome in the cottages if prior arrangements are made.

Innkeeper(s): Chapin & Joan Darling. $85-145. PC, TC. 5 rooms with PB and 2 cottages. Breakfast included in rates. Types of meals: Full bkfst. Turndown service in room. VCR and swimming on premises. Small meetings and family reunions hosted. Antiquing, live theater, shopping, downhill skiing and cross-country skiing nearby.

Williston   D3

Catamount B&B

592 Governor Chittenden Rd
Williston, VT 05495
(802)878-2180 (888)680-1011 Fax:(802)879-6066
E-mail: lucy@catamountoutdoor.com
Web: www.catamountoutdoor.com

Circa 1796. This huge Federal Colonial Revival inn on 500 acres has been in the McCullough family since 1873. In its early years, the elegant homestead sponsored many grand balls, and today the home exudes a sense of rich family history. The inn is the oldest standing building in Williston, and it has been a Williston landmark for more than 200 years. It is located on the family farm where the family owns and operates a recreation center that includes many outdoor activities. The grounds

have one of the finest mountain bike facilities available. It has a professionally designed trail network that includes flat, rolling and steep trails that range from single-track to wide. And it has an acre of groomed ice for ice skating and a tree-free sledding hill. Guests who stay in the inn's three guest bedrooms (including one suite) enjoy a hearty continental breakfast each morning with courses such as homemade muffins, seasonal fruits, cereals, coffee and tea and sometimes waffles.

Innkeeper(s): Lucy & Jim McCullough. $75-105. MC, VISA, AX, DS, PC, TC. 3 rooms, 1 suite and 1 conference room. Breakfast included in rates. Types of meals: Veg bkfst, cont plus and early coffee/tea. Beds: D. VCR, fax, copier, bicycles, library, cross-country skiing, snowshoes, ice skating and 20 miles of trails on premises. Weddings, small meetings and seminars hosted. Amusement parks, antiquing, art galleries, beaches, bicycling, canoeing/kayaking, fishing, golf, hiking, horseback riding, Burlington, the cultural hub of Vermont., live theater, museums, parks, shopping, downhill skiing, cross-country skiing, sporting events, tennis, water sports and wineries nearby.

Wilmington   K3

Nutmeg Inn

Rt 9 W, Molly Stark Tr
Wilmington, VT 05363
(802)464-7400 (800)277-5402 Fax:(802)464-7331
E-mail: nutmeg@sover.net
Web: www.nutmeginn.com

Circa 1777. This red clapboard inn sits invitingly on a green lawn. Behind the inn, a forested hillside leads to a picturesque mountain brook. An extensive renovation has added to the charm of the inn. Quilts, four-poster and brass beds, rocking chairs and old-fashioned dressers maintain the Vermont country atmosphere. A hearty breakfast is provided in the dining room.

Historic Interest: Molly Stark Trail.

Innkeeper(s): Dave & Pat Cerchio. $89-299. MC, VISA, AX, DS. 10 rooms with PB, 10 with FP and 4 suites. Breakfast included in rates. Types of meals: Full bkfst, country bkfst and afternoon tea. Beds: KQ. Cable TV, phone, rooms have wood-burning fireplaces and suites have two-person whirlpools in room. Central air. German spoken. Antiquing, art galleries, bicycling, canoeing/kayaking, fishing, golf, hiking, horseback riding, sleigh rides, parks, shopping, downhill skiing, cross-country skiing, tennis and wineries nearby.

White House of Wilmington

178 Rt 9 East
Wilmington, VT 05363
(802)464-2135 (800)541-2135 Fax:(802)464-5295
E-mail: whitehse@sover.net
Web: www.whitehouseinn.com

Circa 1915. The White House was built as a summer home for a wealthy lumber baron, and he spared no expense. The inn has 14 fireplaces, rich woodwork and hand-crafted French doors. Nine of the guest rooms include fireplaces, and some have a balcony, terrace or whirlpool tub. Seven guest rooms are located in an adjacent guest house. There is an outdoor swimming pool, and the spa includes an indoor pool, whirlpool and sauna. Guests are treated to breakfast, and award-winning, gourmet dinners are available in the dining rooms.

Innkeeper(s): Bob Grinold. $118-195. MC, VISA, AX, DC, DS, PC, TC. TAC10. 23 rooms with PB, 9 with FP, 1 suite and 2 conference rooms. Breakfast included in rates. Types of meals: Full bkfst and gourmet dinner. MAP. Beds: KQDT. VCR, fax, copier, spa, swimming and sauna on premises. Handicap access. Weddings, small meetings, family reunions and seminars hosted. Antiquing, fishing, golf, live theater, parks, shopping, downhill skiing, cross-country skiing, tennis and water sports nearby.

Publicity: *New York Times, Boston Herald, Vermont Magazine, Yankee Travel Guide, PM Magazine and Good Morning America.*

Woodstock H4

Ardmore Inn

23 Pleasant St, PO Box 466
Woodstock, VT 05091
(802)457-3887 (800)497-9652 Fax:(802)457-9006
E-mail: ardmoreinn@aol.com

Circa 1850. This Greek Revival-style inn offers a gentle welcome with its pretty shutters and graceful entrance. Located on an acre in a village setting, it is furnished elegantly. For instance, the Tully Room has four eyebrow windows shedding sunlight on its four-poster queen bed, and there's a sitting area and marble bath. Enjoy breakfasts of Vermont flat bread served with truffle eggs, apple-smoked sausage and asparagus spears.
$110-175. MC, VISA, AX, PC, TC. TAC10. 5 suites, 1 with FP. Breakfast and afternoon tea included in rates. Types of meals: Gourmet bkfst. Beds: KQD. Air conditioning. Fax, copier and bicycles on premises. Weddings, small meetings and family reunions hosted. Spanish spoken. Antiquing, fishing, golf, mountain biking, fly fishing, live theater, parks, shopping, downhill skiing, cross-country skiing and tennis nearby.

Canterbury House

43 Pleasant St
Woodstock, VT 05091-1129
(802)457-3077 (800)390-3077
E-mail: innkeeper@thecanterburyhouse.com
Web: www.thecanterburyhouse.com

Circa 1880. National Geographic tabbed Woodstock as one of America's most beautiful villages, and this Victorian inn offers a lovely stopping place for those exploring the area. Visitors find

themselves within easy walking distance of antique stores, art galleries, museums, restaurants and shopping. Ski lifts at Killington, Pico and Okemo are only minutes away.
Historic Interest: The Dana Museum and Billings Farm Museum are some of the historic sites. Walking tours are available.
Innkeeper(s): Bob & Sue Frost. $100-175. MC, VISA, AX, PC. 8 rooms with PB, 1 with FP. Breakfast included in rates. Types of meals: Gourmet bkfst. Beds: KQDT. Air conditioning. VCR on premises. Weddings, small meetings and family reunions hosted. Antiquing, fishing, mountain bikes, live theater, parks, shopping, downhill skiing, cross-country skiing, sporting events and water sports nearby.
Publicity: *Boston Globe, Glamour Magazine and Travel & Leisure.*

Carriage House of Woodstock

455 Woodstock Road, Rt 4 W
Woodstock, VT 05091-1253
(802)457-4322 (800)791-8045 Fax:(802)457-4322
E-mail: stanglin@sover.net
Web: www.carriagehousewoodstock.com

Circa 1830. This century-old home has been generously refurbished and features rooms filled with period antiques and individual decor. Those in search of relaxation will find plenty of possibilities, from quiet music and conversation in the parlor to

relaxing on the wraparound porch overlooking the picturesque views. Antique shopping, galleries, the historic Billings Farm Museum and plenty of outdoor activities are found

in the Woodstock area. Fall and spring bring an explosion of color, and scenic drives will take you under covered bridges.
Innkeeper(s): Debbie & Mark Stanglin. $95-180. MC, VISA, AX, DS, PC, TC. 9 rooms with PB, 1 with FP. Breakfast and snacks/refreshments included in rates. Types of meals: Full bkfst. Beds: KQT. 1 with fireplace, 4 with cable TV, 3 with whirlpool tub and individual heat in room. Air conditioning. VCR, fax, refrigerator and microwave on premises. Weddings, small meetings, family reunions and seminars hosted. Antiquing, fishing, live theater, parks, shopping, downhill skiing, cross-country skiing, sporting events and water sports nearby.

Charleston House

21 Pleasant St
Woodstock, VT 05091-1131
(802)457-3843
E-mail: charleston@adelphia.com
Web: charlestonhouse.com

Circa 1835. This authentically restored brick Greek Revival town house, in the National Register, welcomes guests with shuttered many-paned windows and window boxes filled with pink blooms. Guest rooms are appointed with period antiques and reproductions, an art collection and Oriental rugs.
Some of the rooms boast four-poster beds, and some feature fireplaces and Jacuzzis. A hearty full breakfast starts off the day in the candle-lit dining room, and the innkeepers serve afternoon refreshments, as
well. Area offerings include winter sleigh rides, snow skiing, auctions, fly fishing, golfing and summer stock theater, to name a few.
Historic Interest: The Billings/Marsh National Historic Park and Calvin Coolidge Homestead are nearby attractions.
Innkeeper(s): Dieter & Willa Nohl. $110-205. MC, VISA, AX. 9 rooms with PB. Breakfast included in rates. Types of meals: Full bkfst. Beds: QT. TV in room. Jacuzzis and fireplaces on premises. Antiquing, fishing, golf, downhill skiing and cross-country skiing nearby.
Publicity: *Harbor News, Boston Business Journal, Weekend Getaway, Inn Spots and Special Places.*

The Jackson House Inn & Restaurant

114-3 Senior Ln (Rt 4)
Woodstock, VT 05091
(802)457-2065 (800)448-1890 Fax:(802)457-9290
E-mail: innkeepers@jacksonhouse.com
Web: www.jacksonhouse.com

Circa 1890. This beautifully restored late Victorian was built originally by Wales Johnson, a saw-mill owner and craftsman. The gleaming cherry and maple wood floors and moldings, exterior eaves and twin chimneys are a tribute to the original owner's attention to detail and workmanship. Although the inn passed hands a couple of times, the integrity of the interior and exterior designs has never been compromised. Fine antique furnishings, decorative arts and Oriental rugs are a few of the elegant and sophisticated features that have been maintained throughout the years.
French-cut crystal, a library of classics and a parlor with a welcoming fire add to the ambiance. Each guest room is inspired by a different style and period: French Empire, Brass and Bamboo inspired by Brighton Castle, and New England Country. A gourmet breakfast featuring house specialties such as Sante Fe omelets, fruit compote in champagne and poached eggs in puff pastry are offered daily. Listed in the National Register, the inn offers more than four lush acres of manicured gardens and pathways.

Innkeeper(s): Carl & LInda Delnegro. $195-380. MC, VISA, AX, PC. TAC10. 15 rooms, 6 with FP & 6 suites. Breakfast & snacks/refreshments included in rates. Types of meals: Gourmet bkfst and gourmet dinner. Beds: QT. Turndown service & ceiling fan in room. Air conditioning. VCR, fax, spa, swimming, library and steam room on premises. Weddings, small meetings, family reunions & seminars hosted. Spanish & French spoken. Antiquing, fishing, golf, live theater, parks, shopping, downhill skiing, cross-country skiing, tennis & water sports nearby.

Publicity: *Colonial Homes, Country Inns, Fitness Magazine, Travel & Leisure, New York Times and London Times.*

Kedron Valley Inn

Rt 106, Box 145
Woodstock, VT 05071
(802)457-1473 (800)836-1193 Fax:(802)457-4469
E-mail: kedroninn@aol.com

Circa 1828. Travelers have made this rustic, cozy inn a stopping point for 170 years. One of the guest buildings has a secret attic passageway and is rumored to have been a stop on the Underground Railway during the Civil War. A 60-piece quilt collection includes century-
old quilts created by the hostess'
great-grandmothers. Guests need
not leave the grounds to enjoy a
white-sand beach and swimming
lake. A stable with horses is nearby.
Seventeen of the rooms boast fire-
places, most rooms feature canopy
beds and four rooms have large Jacuzzis. After feasting on a delectable breakfast, spend the day searching for antiques, hiking or viewing historic estates. The gourmet dinners are a treat.

Historic Interest: Home of Augustine Saint Gaudens (25 miles), Billings Farm & Museum (5 miles), Calvin Coolidge Homestead (20 miles), Marsh-Billings National Park (5 miles).

Innkeeper(s): Max & Merrily Comins. $131-272. MC, VISA, AX, DS, PC. TAC10. 28 rooms with PB, 17 with FP, 5 suites and 1 conference room. Breakfast included in rates. Types of meals: Full bkfst and gourmet dinner. Beds: QDT. TV, ceiling fan and four rooms with Jacuzzi in room. Air conditioning. Fax, copier and swimming on premises. Weddings, small meetings, family reunions and seminars hosted. Antiquing, art galleries, fishing, hiking, trail, surrey rides, fitness, parks, shopping, downhill skiing and cross-country skiing nearby.

Publicity: *Good Housekeeping, Country Living, Country Home, Yankee, Gourmet, Ski, New York Times, London Times., Oprah Winfrey Show, Budweiser commercial and Country Inn Cooking with Gail Greco.*

"It's what you dream a Vermont country inn should be and the most impressive feature is the innkeepers ... outgoing, warm and friendly."

The Lincoln Inn at The Covered Bridge

530 Woodstock Rd, US Rt 4 W
Woodstock, VT 05091
(802)457-3312 Fax:(802)457-5808
E-mail: lincon2@aol.com
Web: www.lincolninn.com

Circa 1870. This admirable old farmhouse sits on six acres bordered by the Lincoln Covered Bridge and the Ottauquechee River. Lawns meander to a rise overlooking the water. A swing, park benches and a gazebo provide ample places from which to enjoy the view. Recent renovation has revealed hand-hewn beams in the library and a fireplace in the common room. The inn's world-class continental cuisine provides a memorable dinner.

Historic Interest: Lincoln Coverd Bridge, Rockefeller-Marsh-Billings National Park (3 miles).

Innkeeper(s): Kurt & Lori Hildbrand. $125-175. MC, VISA, AX, DS, PC, TC. 6 rooms with PB and 1 conference room. Types of meals: Gourmet bkfst, country bkfst, veg bkfst and gourmet dinner. Beds: KQD. Air conditioning. Fax, copier and library on premises. Weddings, small meetings and family reunions hosted. German, French and Spanish spoken. Antiquing, art galleries, bicycling, canoeing/kayaking, fishing, golf, hiking, horseback riding, live theater, museums, parks, shopping, downhill skiing, cross-country skiing, sporting events, tennis, water sports and wineries nearby.

Publicity: *Travelhost.*

"Feels like family!"

Woodstocker B&B

61 River St
Woodstock, VT 05091-1227
(802)457-3896 Fax:(802)457-3897
E-mail: woodstocker@valley.net

Circa 1830. This early 19th-century, Cape-style inn is located at the base of Mt. Tom at the edge of the village of Woodstock. Hand-hewn wood beams create a rustic effect. The seven guest rooms and two suites are individually appointed. Buffet-style, full
breakfasts get the day off to a great
start. Guests can take a short walk
across a covered bridge to reach
shops and restaurants. Hikers will
enjoy trails that wind up and around Mt. Tom. After a busy winter day, come back and enjoy a soak in the five-person whirlpool.

Historic Interest: Billings Farm and Museum, the Calvin Coolidge Homestead and Dana House Museum are some of the historic sites. Four of Woodstock's churches boast bells made by Paul Revere.

Innkeeper(s): Tom & Nancy Blackford. $85-175. MC, VISA, AX. 9 rooms with PB and 2 suites. Breakfast included in rates. Types of meals: Full bkfst and early coffee/tea. Beds: QD. Cable TV and ceiling fan in room. Air conditioning. VCR, fax and copier on premises. Weddings and family reunions hosted. Antiquing, fishing, live theater, shopping, downhill skiing, cross-country skiing, sporting events and water sports nearby.

"You have truly opened your home and heart to create a comfortable and memorable stay."

Woodstock (Reading) H3

Bailey's Mills B&B

1347 Bailey's Mills Rd
Woodstock (Reading), VT 05062
(802)484-7809 (800)639-3437
E-mail: goodfarm@vermontel.com
Web: bbonline.com/vt/baileysmills/

Circa 1820. This Federal-style inn features grand porches, 11 fireplaces, a "good-morning" staircase and a ballroom on the third floor. Four generations of Baileys lived in the home, as well as housing mill workers. There also was once a country store on the premises. Guests can learn much
about the home and history of
the people who lived here
through the innkeepers. Two of
the guest rooms include a fire-
place, and the suite has a private
solarium. There's plenty to do
here, from exploring the surrounding 48 acres to relaxing with a book on the porch swing or in a hammock. If you forgot your favorite novel, borrow a book from the inn's 2,200-volume library.

Historic Interest: Saint Gaudens National Historic Site (15 miles), Billings Farm Museum (11 miles), Calvin Coolidge Homestead (10 miles), American Precision Museum (10 miles).

Innkeeper(s): Barbara Thaeder & Don Whitaker. $90-140. MC, VISA, PC, TC. TAC10. 3 rooms with PB, 2 with FP and 1 suite. Breakfast included in rates. Types of meals: Cont plus and early coffee/tea. Beds: KQ. Fireplace (two rooms) in room. Swimming, library, pond, stream and graveyard on premises. Weddings and family reunions hosted. Antiquing, fishing, live theater, parks, shopping, downhill skiing and cross-country skiing nearby.

Pets allowed: Small, polite, innkeeper approval required.

Publicity: *Carnie Show.*

"If words could encapsulate what a wonderful weekend would be, it would have to be 'Bailey's Mills B&B.' Your home is beautiful. It is elegant yet homey."

Virginia

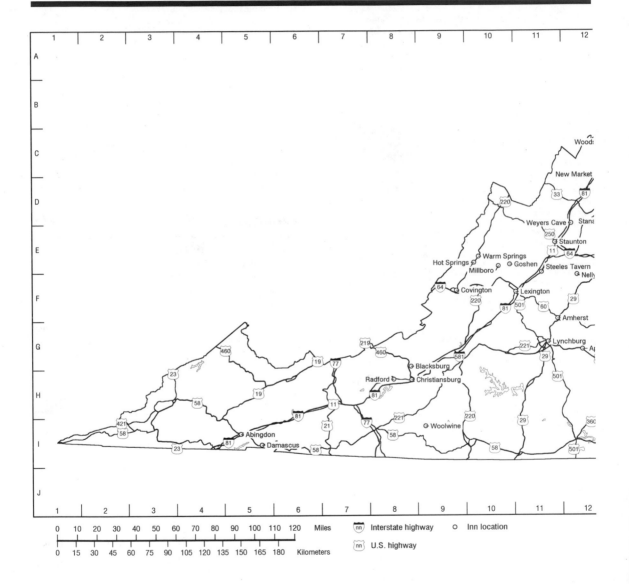

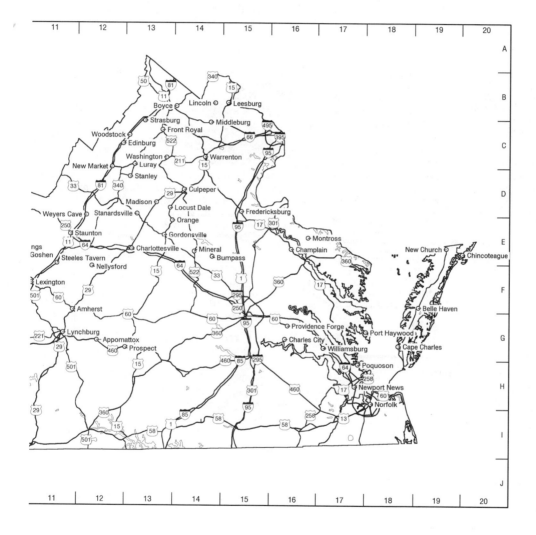

Abingdon 15

Victoria & Albert B&B

224 Oak Hill St NE
Abingdon, VA 24210-2824
(800)475-5494
E-mail: v&ainn@naxs.com
Web: www.abingdon-virginia.com

Circa 1892. Awarded AAA's coveted 4 Diamonds, this handsome green and white, three-story Victorian inn is situated on a quiet street within walking distance to Abingdon's celebrated theaters, museums, galleries and historic homes. Shaded porches, bay windows and tasteful decor are among the inn's special

features. Guest rooms offer ceiling fans and finely crafted traditional furnishings; all have gas fireplaces or whirlpool tubs. There are plenty of amenities such as hair dryers and CD players. In the late evening, desserts and wine are served, and the innkeepers pamper guests with evening turndown service. Full formal breakfasts are served in the dining room or guests can opt to enjoy the meal on the porches.

Historic Interest: The Victoria and Albert is located in Abingdon's historic district and within walking distance of shops and the Barter Theatre.

Innkeeper(s): Hazel Ramos-Cano & Richard Cano. $99-135. MC, VISA, DS, PC, TC. 5 rooms with PB. Breakfast included in rates. Types of meals: Full bkfst, early coffee/tea, snacks/refreshments and dinner. Beds: KQ. Cable TV, phone, turndown service, ceiling fan, VCR, robes, gas fireplace and hair dryers in room. Air conditioning. Library and gift shop on premises. Weddings, small meetings and family reunions hosted. Fishing, live theater and shopping nearby.

"With all of the luxuries that you provide for your guests, I truly felt like royalty! My hat off to you and what you have accomplished at the Victoria and Albert."

Amherst F11

Dulwich Manor B&B Inn

550 Richmond Hwy
Amherst, VA 24521-3962
(804)946-7207 (800)571-9011
E-mail: mfarmer@iwinet.com
Web: www.dulwichmanor.com

Circa 1912. This red Flemish brick and white columned English Manor sits on five secluded acres at the end of a country lane and in the midst of 97 acres of woodland and meadow. The Blue Ridge Parkway is minutes away. The entry features a

large center hall and a wide oak staircase. Walls are 14 inches thick. The 18 rooms include a 50-foot-long ballroom on the third floor. The inn is decorated with a creative mix of antiques, traditional furniture and collectibles.

Innkeeper(s): Mike & Georgie Farmer. $85-120. MC, VISA, PC, TC. TAC10. 6 rooms with PB, 3 with FP. Breakfast included in rates. Types of meals: Full bkfst and early coffee/tea. Beds: KQ. Phone, ceiling fan and two rooms with whirlpool tub in room. Air conditioning. Weddings, small meetings, family reunions and seminars hosted. Antiquing, fishing, hiking, historic sites,

Monticello, Appomattox Court House and Natural Bridge nearby, parks, shopping, downhill skiing, sporting events, water sports and wineries nearby.
Publicity: *Country Inn and Scene.*

Appomattox G12

The Babcock House

106 Oakleigh Ave, Rt 6 Box 1421
Appomattox, VA 24522
(434)352-7532 (800)689-6208 Fax:(434)352-9743

Circa 1884. This columned Greek Revival house occupies more than an acre in the center of the town's 19th-Century Homes Walking Tour. Dr. Havilah Babcock, English professor and noted hunting and fishing author, occupied the home with his family. Once operated as a boarding house, the home con-

tinues its tradition of hospitality and comfort, but now boasts cable television, private baths, ceiling fans and air conditioning. Guests still enjoy gathering at the end of the day on the front porch to share their adventures, which many times includes visiting

Appomattox Courthouse National Historic Park where General Robert E. Lee surrendered to General Grant. The innkeepers offer regional dining in their restaurant with a daily change of menu to reflect seasonal changes in ingredients.

Historic Interest: Boyhood home of Havilah Babcock-1884 classic example of turn of the century architecture, Appomattox Courthouse National Historic Park.

Innkeeper(s): Jerry & Sheila Palamar. $95-120. MC, VISA, AX, DS, PC, TC. TAC10. 6 rooms, 5 with PB, 1 with FP and 1 suite. Breakfast and snacks/refreshments included in rates. Beds: QT. Cable TV, phone and ceiling fan in room. Central air. VCR and full service restaurant and catering open for breakfast and lunch. dinner by reservation on premises. Handicap access. Weddings, family reunions and seminars hosted. Antiquing, bicycling, canoeing/kayaking, fishing and wineries nearby.

Spring Grove Farm Bed & Breakfast

Rt 4, Box 259
Appomattox, VA 24522
(804)993-3891 (877)409-1865 Fax:(804)352-7429
E-mail: springgrovefarm@msn.com
Web: www.springgrovefarm.com

Circa 1842. Experience epic-size pampering on this 200-acre, recently restored plantation with original woodwork, staircases, flooring and furnishings. Huge wing additions complement the Greek Revival architecture, adding an incredible expansiveness. Sixteen distinct fireplaces grace the many public areas such as the Parlor and Carriage House Great Room, each with a grand piano; casual Family Room; Media Room, for watching movies on the big screen satellite TV; and the brick-floored Pub Room, offering wine or beer. More fireplaces as well as whirlpool tubs or steam showers, are found in most of the spacious guest bedrooms and suites. A delicious breakfast using organic ingredients grown on-site is served in an intimate setting or with others in the green Breakfast Room, elegant Dining Room, cheery Sunroom or adjoining terrace. The Fitness Room enhances any workout level, or explore the idyllic countryside.

Historic Interest: Appomattox Courthouse National Park (7 miles), Jefferson's Poplar Forest (30 miles).

Innkeeper(s): Emily & Joe Sayers. $90-250. MC, VISA, AX, PC, TC. TAC10.

12 rooms with PB, 10 with FP, 3 suites and 4 conference rooms. Breakfast and snacks/refreshments included in rates. Types of meals: Full bkfst and early coffee/tea. Beds: KQT. Fireplace, robes and clocks in room. Central air. VCR, fax and library on premises. Handicap access. Weddings, small meetings, family reunions and seminars hosted. Antiquing, art galleries, bicycling, canoeing/kayaking, fishing, golf, hiking, horseback riding, live theater, museums, parks, tennis and wineries nearby.

Publicity: *The Burg.*

Belle Haven   F19

Bay View Waterfront B&B

35350 Copes Dr
Belle Haven, VA 23306-1952
(757)442-6963 (800)442-6966
E-mail: browning@shore.intercom.net

Circa 1800. This rambling inn stretches more than 100 feet across and has five roof levels. There are heart-pine floors, high ceilings and several fireplaces. The hillside location affords bay breezes and wide views of the Chesapeake, Occohannock

Creek and the inn's surrounding 140 acres. The innkeepers are descendants of several generations who have owned and operated Bay View. If you come by water to the inn's deep water dock, look behind Channel Marker 16. Guests can arrange to enjoy a boat tour along the Chesapeake Bay or Atlantic Ocean led by the innkeepers' daughter, U.S. Coast Guard-approved Capt. Mary.

Historic Interest: Kiptopeake State Park (30 miles), E.S. Historic Museum (12 miles), Chincoteague Ponies (40 miles).

Innkeeper(s): Wayne & Mary Will Browning. $95. PC, TC. TAC10. 3 rooms, 2 with PB, 1 with FP. Breakfast included in rates. Types of meals: Full bkfst. Beds: KDT. Phone in room. Air conditioning. VCR, swimming, bicycles and library on premises. Weddings, small meetings and family reunions hosted. Antiquing, fishing, golf, live theater, parks, shopping, tennis and water sports nearby.

Publicity: *Rural Living and City.*

"We loved staying in your home, and especially in the room with a beautiful view of the bay. You have a lovely home and a beautiful location. Thank you so much for your hospitality."

Blacksburg   G8

Clay Corner Inn

401 Clay St SW
Blacksburg, VA 24060
(540)953-2604 Fax:(540)951-0541
E-mail: claycorner@aol.com

Circa 1929. Clay Corner Inn is comprised of six houses on a corner one block from Virginia Tech and a couple blocks from downtown. There are 12 guest rooms, three of which are two-bedroom suites. Each room is decorated with a different theme, and all guest rooms have private baths, cable TV, telephones and queen or king beds. Two houses were built early in the century, two are a decade old and two others, circa 1940, are private residences. A full breakfast is served in the main house or covered deck outside. The inn also features an on-site heated swimming pool and a hot tub.

Historic Interest: Smithfield Plantation is one mile away, Blacksburg is 200+ years old.

Innkeeper(s): Joanne Anderson. $85-115. MC, VISA, AX. 12 rooms with PB. Breakfast included in rates. Types of meals: Full bkfst. Swimming on premises. Antiquing, golf, wineries, hiking and tennis nearby.

Boyce   B14

L'Auberge Provencale

13630 Lord Fairfax Highway
Boyce, VA 22620
(540)837-1375 (800)638-1702 Fax:(540)837-2004
E-mail: cborel@shentel.net
Web: www.laubergeprovencale.com

Circa 1753. This farmhouse was built with fieldstones gathered from the area. Hessian soldiers crafted the woodwork of the main house, Mt. Airy. As the name suggests, a French influence is prominent throughout the inn. Victorian and European antiques fill the elegant guest rooms, several of which include fireplaces. Innkeeper Alain Borel hails from a long line of master chefs, his expertise creates many happy culinary memories guests cherish. Many of the French-influenced items served at the inn's four-diamond restaurant, include ingredients from the inn's gardens, and Alain has been hailed by James Beard as a Great Country Inn Chef. The innkeepers also offer accommodations three miles away at Villa La Campagnette, an 1890 restored home. The home includes two suites and the Grand Master bedroom. Guests enjoy 18 acres with a swimming pool, hot tub and stables.

Historic Interest: Waterford, Luray Caverns, Holy Cross Abbey (Historic Long Branch).

Innkeeper(s): Alain & Celeste Borel. $145-275. MC, VISA, AX, DC, DS, PC, TC. TAC10. 14 rooms, 10 with PB, 6 with FP, 4 suites and 1 conference room. Breakfast included in rates. Types of meals: Gourmet bkfst, veg bkfst, early coffee/tea, gourmet lunch, gourmet dinner and room service. AP. Beds: KQD. Ceiling fan in room. Central air. Fax, copier, spa and swimming on premises. Weddings, small meetings, family reunions and seminars hosted. French and Spanish spoken. Antiquing, art galleries, bicycling, canoeing/kayaking, fishing, golf, hiking, horseback riding, live theater, museums, parks, shopping, tennis and wineries nearby.

Publicity: *Food & Wine, Romantic Homes, Bon Appetit, Glamour, Washington Dossier, Washington Post, Baltimore, Richmond Times, Southern Living, Travel & Leisure, Great Chefs of the East and Great Country Inns.*

"A magical place to spend a birthday. Wonderful food an ambiance. Very Romantic."

Bumpass   E14

Rockland Farm Retreat

3609 Lewiston Rd
Bumpass, VA 23024-9659
(540)895-5098
E-mail: roymxn@aol.com

Circa 1820. The 75 acres of Rockland Farm include pasture land, livestock, vineyard, crops and a farm pond for fishing. The grounds here are said to have spawned Alex Haley's "Roots." Guests can study documents and explore local cemeteries describing life under slavery in the area surrounding this historic home and 18th-century farmlands.

Historic Interest: Some of the oldest slave cemeteries are nearby.

Innkeeper(s): Roy E. Mixon. $79-89. MC, VISA, AX, DS, PC. TAC10. 4 rooms, 3 with PB, 1 suite and 2 conference rooms. Breakfast included in rates. Types of meals: Full bkfst, lunch and dinner. MAP. Beds: DT. Air condi-

tioning. VCR on premises. Weddings, small meetings, family reunions and seminars hosted. French and Spanish spoken. Amusement parks, antiquing, fishing, parks, shopping and water sports nearby.
Pets Allowed.
Publicity: Washington Post and Free Lance-Star.

Cape Charles   G18

Cape Charles House

645 Tazewell Ave
Cape Charles, VA 23310-3313
(757)331-4920 Fax:(757)331-4960
E-mail: stay@capecharleshouse.com
Web: capecharleshouse.com

Circa 1912. The Cape Charles House was the recipient of the 2000 Governor's Award for Virginia Hospitality. A Cape Charles attorney built this Colonial Revival home on the site of the town's first schoolhouse. Each room is named for someone important to Cape Charles history. The Julia Wilkins Room is especially picturesque. Rich blue walls and white woodwork are accented by blue and white pastoral print draperies, a private bath with whirlpool and a balcony. There is a seamstress dress form with an antique dress, rocking chair and chaise. Other rooms are decorated with the same skill and style, with fine window dress-

ings, artwork and carefully placed collectibles. Oriental rugs top the wood floors, and among the fine furnishings are family heirlooms. Breakfasts are gourmet and served in the formal dining room. Innkeeper Carol Evans prepares breakfast items such as chilled melon with a lime glaze and lemon yogurt topping, egg quesadillas, rosemary roasted potatoes and freshly baked muffins. From time to time, cooking classes and murder-mystery events are available. There are many attractions in the area, including sunset sails, historic walking tours of Cape Charles, antique shops, golfing, beach and The Nature Conservancy.
Innkeeper(s): Bruce & Carol Evans. $95-150. MC, VISA, AX, DS, PC, TC. TAC10. 5 rooms with PB. Breakfast, afternoon tea and snacks/refreshments included in rates. Types of meals: Gourmet bkfst and early coffee/tea. Beds: KQ. Ceiling fan and Jacuzzi (two rooms) in room. Air conditioning. VCR, fax, copier and bicycles on premises. Weddings, small meetings, family reunions and seminars hosted. Antiquing, fishing, golf, live theater, parks, shopping, tennis and water sports nearby.
Publicity: Southern Inns.

"Cape Charles House is first and foremost a home and we were made to feel 'at home.'"

Chesapeake Charm B&B

202 Madison Ave
Cape Charles, VA 23310
(757)331-2676 (800)546-9215 Fax:(757)331-3983
E-mail: info@chesapeakecharmbnb.com
Web: www.chesapeakecharmbnb.com

Circa 1921. Proudly situated in a large historic district on the banks of Chesapeake Bay, this American Revival inn maintains its original design construction. The hardwood floors, natural heart pine windows and architectural accents blend well with the period antiques and family furnishings that have been cherished since the house was first occupied. Families are welcome

here and easily accommodated. The guest bedrooms are comfortably elegant with gorgeous wallpapers and draperies. The private Bay Loft features a sitting area and whirlpool tub. Breakfast is always a treat, with a specialty gourmet entree, meat dish and homemade baked goods. Gather in one of the common rooms for afternoon refreshments and non-alcoholic beverages. Bikes are available for exploring the local sites.
Innkeeper(s): Phyllis S. Tyndall. $75-120. MC, VISA, AX. TAC10. 4 rooms with PB. Breakfast, afternoon tea and snacks/refreshments included in rates. Types of meals: Gourmet bkfst. Beds: QT. Cable TV, ceiling fan and VCR in room. Air conditioning. Fax, copier and bicycles on premises. Family reunions hosted. Antiquing, art galleries, beaches, fishing, golf, hiking, museums, parks, shopping, tennis and water sports nearby.

Champlain   E16

Linden House B&B & Plantation

PO Box 23
Champlain, VA 22438-0023
(804)443-1170 (800)622-1202
Web: www.lindenplantation.com

Circa 1750. This restored planters home is designated a state landmark and listed in the National Register. The lush grounds boast walking trails, a pond, an English garden, patio with fountain, gazebo, arbor and five porches. Each of the accommodations offers something special. The Carriage Suite features country decor, antiques, a private porch and a fireplace. The Robert E. Lee room has a high-poster bed, fireplace and private bath. The Jefferson Davis room has a luxurious bath with a Jacuzzi and steam room. The fourth-floor Linden

room affords a view of the countryside and features a queen-size bed and an alcove with a day bed adjoining the private bath. Other rooms also promise an enchanting experience. All rooms have their own television and refrigerator. With its new reception hall and verandas, the inn is popular for weddings, conferences and meetings.
Innkeeper(s): Ken & Sandra Pounsberry. $95-150. MC, VISA, AX, PC, TC. TAC10. 5 rooms with PB and 2 suites. Breakfast included in rates. Types of meals: Gourmet bkfst, early coffee/tea, snacks/refreshments and dinner. Beds: KQ. Some with ceiling fan in room. Central air. VCR, library and ballroom with large patio overlooking pond for catered receptions on premises. Handicap access. Weddings, small meetings, family reunions and seminars hosted. Amusement parks, antiquing, fishing, boarding school, live theater, parks, shopping and water sports nearby.
Publicity: Rappahannock-Journal, Richmond Times Dispatch and Cable TV.

Charles City   G16

North Bend Plantation

12200 Weyanoke Rd
Charles City, VA 23030-3632
(804)829-5176 Fax:(804)829-6828
Web: www.northbendplantation.com

Circa 1819. Civil war relics and southern hospitality await guests at this cultivated plantation located between Williamsburg and Richmond. Owned by the great, great grandson of Edwin Ruffin, the man who fired the first shot of the Civil War, the 1819 mansion has original mantels and stair carvings, as well as a number of Greek Revival features from the

1853 remodeling. The mansion is full of antiques, including the plantation desk used by General Sheridan when the Union Troops occupied the area in 1864. The desk still

has the labels Sheridan placed on pigeonholes, and the eastern edge of the property still has Civil War breastworks. The five guests rooms, each spacious and complemented with family antiques and collectibles, range from the quaint Maids Quarters to The Sheridan Room with a Queen tester bed circa 1810 and Sheridan's desk. After a full country breakfast including delights like homemade waffles, omelets, biscuits, bacon, sausage, fruit and juice, guests may venture out on the grounds to swim or play croquet, horseshoes or volleyball. A park with nature trails and a fishing pier is just three miles from the mansion and a public golf course is 20 minutes away.

Historic Interest: The inn is a designated Virginia Historic Landmark and listed in the National Register of Historic Places. Charles City County is the home of the historic James River Plantations.

Innkeeper(s): George & Ridgely Copland. $115-135. MC, VISA, PC, TC. TAC10. 4 rooms with PB, 2 with FP and 1 suite. Breakfast included in rates. Types of meals: Full bkfst, early coffee/tea and afternoon tea. Beds: QD. Cable TV, ceiling fan and refrigerator in room. Air conditioning. Fax, copier, swimming, bicycles, library, croquet, volleyball, horse shoes and hammocks on premises. Weddings, small meetings and family reunions hosted. Amusement parks, antiquing, golf, colonial Williamsburg, Jamestown, Yorktown, horse racing, parks and shopping nearby.

Publicity: *Daily Press, Richmond Times Dispatch, New York Times, Mid-Atlantic Country, Washington Post, Travel Talk, Southern Hospitality and Channel 12.*

"Your hospitality, friendship and history lessons were all priceless. Your love of life embraced us in a warmth I shall never forget."

Orange Hill B&B

18401 The Glebe Ln
Charles City, VA 23030
(804)829-6988 (888)501-8125
E-mail: orange-hill@juno.com
Web: www.orangehillbb.com

Circa 1898. Located on five acres between Richmond and Williamsburg, Orange Hill Bed & Breakfast is an 1898 white frame farmhouse. The three guest bedrooms are decorated in country Victorian, and as the rest of the house, are a showcase for the superior crafts-

manship of bygone eras. Enjoy a country breakfast including courses like pancakes, sausage, and Orange Julius, and then head out for historic sites such as Colonial Williamsburg, College of William and Mary, Civil War sites, Jamestown, Yorktown Battlefields, or The James River Plantations. Many guests choose to simply relax and look out for bluebirds, deer and wild turkey and wait for the sun to set over the 50 surrounding acres of working farmland.

Historic Interest: Colonial Williamsburg (18 miles), Jamestown Island (18 miles), Yorktown battlefields (32 miles), James River Plantations (12 miles).

Innkeeper(s): Mark & Kay Russo. $80-105. MC, VISA, DC, TC. 3 rooms, 2 with PB. Breakfast and afternoon tea included in rates. Types of meals: Country bkfst. Beds: QD. Central air. Library on premises. Weddings and small meetings hosted. Amusement parks, antiquing, beaches, bicycling, canoeing/kayaking, fishing, golf, horseback riding, civil war sites, historic homes, parks, shopping, sporting events and wineries nearby.

Charlottesville   E13

Chester

243 James River Rd
Charlottesville, VA 24590
(434)286-3960
E-mail: info@chesterbed.com
Web: www.chesterbed.com

Circa 1847. This historic Greek Revival house sits on seven acres of natural splendor. Beckoning from the front porch are traditional rocking chairs. Gracious Southern elegance is found throughout the inn. Visit the library or play the grand piano in the living room. The guest bedrooms and suite boast fireplaces, four-poster beds, Oriental rugs, down comforters, plush towels and fresh flowers. Enjoy breakfast served on china with fine linens. The grounds are an informal sanctuary for people and wildlife alike. A large holly tree, lily pond, fountains, English boxwoods and pondside patio reside impressively in extensive gardens.

Innkeeper(s): Jean & Craig Stratton. $165-225. MC, VISA, PC. 5 rooms with PB, 5 with FP. Breakfast included in rates. Types of meals: Gourmet bkfst and early coffee/tea. Beds: Q. Turndown service in room. Air conditioning. Fax, library and gourmet dinner available for groups of 6 or more on premises. Weddings, small meetings, family reunions and seminars hosted. Antiquing, fishing, live theater, parks, shopping, downhill skiing, cross-country skiing, sporting events and water sports nearby.

Clifton- The Country Inn & Estate

1296 Clifton Inn Dr
Charlottesville, VA 22911-3627
(804)971-1800 (888)971-1800 Fax:(804)971-7098
E-mail: reserve@cstone.net

Circa 1799. Thomas Mann Randolph, governor of the state of Virginia and son-in-law of Thomas Jefferson, built Clifton. One of the guest rooms boasts a winter view of Jefferson's estate, Monticello. Elegance and a careful attention to historical detail have enabled this historic country inn to garner national awards for its accommodations, cuisine and wine cellar. In addition to the main house, guests can choose Garden Rooms, Livery Suites or the two-level Carriage

House. Aside from the abundance of history, Clifton also offers a variety of recreational facilities, including a clay tennis court, swimming pool with waterfall, year-round heated whirlpool spa and private lake. Ask for a gardener-led tour of the inn's 40 acres of landscaped grounds. Breakfast at Clifton is a treat with continental breakfast buffet and full breakfast. Afternoon tea is also served. Clifton operates a gourmet, four-diamond restaurant featuring five- and six-course dinners prepared by Executive Chef Rachel Greenberg.

Historic Interest: Monticello is only four miles away. Montpelier is about 30 miles from the inn and the University of Virginia is only a 10-mile journey.

Innkeeper(s): Keith Halford. $165-415. MC, VISA, AX, DC, PC. TAC10. 14 rooms with PB, 14 with FP, 7 suites and 2 conference rooms. Breakfast and afternoon tea included in rates. Types of meals: Full bkfst, cont plus, early coffee/tea and gourmet dinner. Beds: QD. Turndown service in room. Air conditioning. Fax, copier, spa, swimming, tennis, library and child care on premises. Handicap access. Weddings, small meetings, family reunions and seminars hosted. Antiquing, fishing, wineries, live theater, parks, shopping, downhill skiing, cross-country skiing and sporting events nearby.

Publicity: *International Living, Country Inns, Washington Post, Baltimore Sun, Richmond Times Dispatch, Rural Retreats, New York Times and Travel & Leisure.*

Guesthouses B&B Reservations

PO Box 5737
Charlottesville, VA 22905-5737
(434)979-7264
E-mail: info@va-guesthouses.com
Web: www.va-guesthouses.com

Circa 1815. Guesthouses is thought to be America's first reservation service for bed & breakfast accommodations. It appropriately originated in an area with a centuries-old tradition of outstanding hospitality. Some of the homes are in the National Register. Other homes are located near the University of Virginia and throughout Albemarle County and have been inspected carefully to assure a pleasant stay. Most accommodations offer one or two  bedrooms in private homes or farms, but there is also a collection of private cottages including old renovated log houses. Mary Hill Caperton is the director.

Historic Interest: National Register.
Innkeeper(s): Mary Hill Caperton. $68-200. MC, VISA, AX.
Publicity: *Roanoke Times & World-News and Good Housekeeping.*

"The nicest B&B experience we had on our trip."

The Inn at Monticello

Rt 20 S, 1188 Scottsville Rd
Charlottesville, VA 22902
(804)979-3593
E-mail: stay@innatmonticello.com
Web: www.innatmonticello.com

Circa 1850. Thomas Jefferson built his own home, Monticello, just two miles from this gracious country home. The innkeepers have preserved the historic ambiance of the area. Rooms  boast such pieces as four-poster beds covered with fluffy, down comforters. Some of the guest quarters have private porches or fireplaces. Breakfast at the inn is a memorable gourmet-appointed affair. Aside from the usual homemade rolls, coffee cakes and muffins, guests enjoy such entrees as pancakes or French toast with seasonal fruit, egg dishes and a variety of quiche. The front porch is lined with chairs for those who wish to relax, and the grounds feature several gardens to enjoy.

Historic Interest: Aside from its close access to Monticello, the inn is five miles from James Monroe's home, Ashlawn Highland. The historic Michie Tavern is just one mile from the inn, and the University of Virginia, which was founded by Jefferson, is about seven miles away.
Innkeeper(s): Norman & Rebecca Lindvay. $110-160. MC, VISA, AX. TAC10. 5 rooms with PB, 2 with FP. Breakfast and afternoon tea included in rates. Types of meals: Gourmet bkfst and early coffee/tea. Beds: KQT. Air conditioning. Fax on premises. Small meetings and family reunions hosted. Antiquing, Blue Ridge Parkway Sky Line Drive, wineries, live theater, parks, shopping, downhill skiing and sporting events nearby.
Publicity: *Washington Post, Country Inns, Atlantic Country Magazine, Gourmet and Bon Appetit.*

"What a magnificent room at an extraordinary place. I can't wait to tell all my friends."

The Inn at the Crossroads

PO Box 6519
Charlottesville, VA 22906-6519
(804)979-6452
Web: www.crossroadsinn.com

Circa 1820. This four-story brick inn, which is listed in the National Register of Historic Places, was built as a tavern on the road from the Shenandoah Valley to the James River. It has been welcoming travelers since the early 1800s. The long front porch and straightforward, Federal-style architecture was common to ordinaries of that era. The four-acre grounds offer gardens of wild flowers and a swing hung under a grand oak tree, not to mention panoramic views of the foothills of the Blue Ridge  Mountains. Country breakfasts are served in the inn's keeping room. The inn is nine miles south of Charlottesville, and Monticello and the University of Virginia are close by.

Innkeeper(s): Maureen & John Deis. $85-125. MC, VISA, PC, TC. 6 rooms with PB, 6 with FP, 1 suite and 1 cottage. Breakfast and afternoon tea included in rates. Types of meals: Gourmet bkfst and early coffee/tea. Beds: KQD. Ceiling fan in room. Air conditioning. Weddings, small meetings and family reunions hosted. Antiquing, fishing, Monticello, Ash Lawn, Michie Tavern, live theater, parks, shopping, downhill skiing, cross-country skiing, sporting events, water sports and wineries nearby.

The Quarters

611 Preston Pl
Charlottesville, VA 22903
(434)979-7264 Fax:(434)293-7791
E-mail: info@va-guesthouses.com
Web: www.va-guesthouses.com

Circa 1815. This suite is in a cottage built to house slaves for John Kelly, who farmed about 500 acres. Thomas Jefferson wanted to buy the land, but built the University of Virginia on adjacent land instead. The suite is furnished with antiques, and there is a fireplace, TV and VCR in the sitting room. There are two bedrooms and one king bed, one single bed and a sleeper sofa. Monticello is five miles away. A sample breakfast menu is poached pears, cornbread, eggs, sausage, apple puffs and other hot breads. The innkeeper manages a reservation service and can offer a wide selection of B&B opportunities in the area.

Historic Interest: Jefferson designed University of Virginia (walking distance), Monticello (5 miles).
Innkeeper(s): Mary Hill Caperton. $125-175. MC, VISA, AX, DC, DS, PC, TC. TAC5. Breakfast and snacks/refreshments included in rates. Types of meals: Full bkfst and early coffee/tea. Beds: KT. Cable TV, phone and VCR in room. Air conditioning. Library and sleeper sofa on premises. Antiquing, art galleries, bicycling, fishing, golf, hiking, horseback riding, historic sites, live theater, parks, shopping, downhill skiing, sporting events, tennis and wineries nearby.

Pets Allowed.

Chincoteague
E20

The Watson House

4240 Main St
Chincoteague, VA 23336-2801
(757)336-1564 (800)336-6787 Fax:(757)336-5776

Circa 1898. Situated in town, this "painted lady" Victorian has a large front porch overlooking Main Street. The porch is a favorite spot of guests and often the location for afternoon tea and refreshments. Beach  towels, chairs and bicycles are complimentary, and there is an outdoor shower for cleaning up after sunning.
Innkeeper(s): Tom & Jacque Derrickson, David & Jo Anne Snead. $69-119. MC, VISA, PC, TC. TAC5. 6 rooms with PB and 2 cottages. Breakfast included in rates. Beds: QD. Ceiling fan and some with whirlpool tubs in room. Air conditioning. Fax and bicycles on premises. Antiquing, fishing, parks, shopping and water sports nearby.

Year Of The Horse Inn

3583 Main St
Chincoteague, VA 23336-1556
(757)336-3221 (800)680-0090
E-mail: richard@yearofthehorseinn.com
Web: www.yearofthehorseinn.com

Circa 1938. This inn overlooks Chincoteague Bay, and each room, except the two-bedroom apartment, has a picture window and sundeck from which to observe oyster catchers, sandpipers, cormorants or a rare great blue heron. Watching sunsets over the marshes is also a regular activity. A serve-yourself-breakfast offers fruit, oatmeal, granola and homemade muffins and breads. Chincoteague National Wildlife Refuge offers 16 miles of protected natural beach and Assateague's famous wild ponies, and it's only three miles from the inn.
Historic Interest: Chincoteague Lighthouse (3 miles).
Innkeeper(s): Richard Hebert. $69-150. MC, VISA, PC, TC. 5 rooms, 3 with PB. Breakfast included in rates. Types of meals: Veg bkfst and cont plus. Beds: KQDT. Cable TV in room. Central air. Library, outdoor grill, picnic decks and table for cookouts on premises. Weddings and family reunions hosted. French and Spanish spoken. Antiquing, art galleries, beaches, hiking, museums, parks, shopping and sporting events nearby.

Christiansburg
H8

River's Edge

6208 Little Camp Rd
Christiansburg, VA 24149
(540)381-4147 Fax:(540)381-1036
E-mail: innkeeper@river-edge.com
Web: www.river-edge.com

Circa 1913. The white and airy interiors of this spacious, 98-year-old farmhouse located near Virginia's Blue Ridge Mountains evoke an atmosphere of graciousness. The four guest rooms are individually decorated in shades of green and peach, green and rose or yellow and blue. The River room has a gas fireplace and the Garden room a king-size bed and large bath. Windows look out on an apple orchard, meadow or flower garden; all have views of the river. Rates at the inn include breakfast and dinner. Specialties include gingerbread

waffles, cheddar and chive eggs, and lime-baked French toast for breakfast and roast chicken with cornbread dressing and Southwestern cheese pie for dinner. Guests also have free use of the canoes and fishing poles. If you're lucky and catch something, the inn will either cook it for you or freeze it to take home.
Historic Interest: Smithfield Plantation (20 miles).
Innkeeper(s): Lee Britton. $150-165. MC, VISA, AX, DC, PC, TC. TAC10. 4 rooms with PB, 1 with FP. Breakfast and dinner included in rates. Types of meals: Full bkfst, veg bkfst, early coffee/tea, lunch, picnic lunch and snacks/refreshments. MAP. Beds: KQT. Central air. Fax and fishing poles on premises. Handicap access. Weddings, small meetings and family reunions hosted. French spoken. Antiquing, beaches, bicycling, canoeing/kayaking, fishing, golf, hiking, horseback riding, live theater, parks, shopping, sporting events, tennis, water sports and wineries nearby.
Pets allowed: Largest room.

Covington
F9

Milton Hall B&B Inn

207 Thorny Ln
Covington, VA 24426-5401
(540)965-0196
E-mail: milton_h@cfw.com
Web: www.milton-hall.com

Circa 1874. This regal manor house, fashioned from hand-made brick and boasting gothic details, is located in Virginia's western highlands. The historic 44-acre estate adjoins the George Washington National Forest, where guests can enjoy hiking, biking and fishing. The home was commissioned in 1874 by the Fitzwilliams, an English noble family. Guest rooms  are furnished with Victorian antiques and reproductions, creating an authentic Victorian ambiance. Each guest room includes a sitting area and fireplace. Guests are treated to both a gourmet breakfast and afternoon refreshments. The grounds include an English country garden. Guests can peruse through gifts and antiques at Lady Milton's Attic, a shop located in the carriage house.
Historic Interest: Humpback Bridge (2 miles), Falling Springs Waterfall (5 miles), Natural Bridge (45 miles), Lost World Caverns (25 miles), Greenbrier Resort (16 miles), VMI (48 miles).
Innkeeper(s): Suzanne & Eric Stratmann. $95-150. MC, VISA, TC. TAC10. 6 rooms with PB, 6 with FP. Types of meals: Full bkfst. Beds: KQD. Turndown service in room. VCR and fax on premises. Antiquing, fishing, live theater, parks and downhill skiing nearby.
Pets allowed: Must have prior approval and requires a $100 advance deposit.

"A lovely place, a relaxing atmosphere, delicious breakfasts, gracious hospitality. We thank you."

Culpeper
D14

Fountain Hall B&B

609 S East St
Culpeper, VA 22701-3222
(540)825-8200 (800)298-4748 Fax:(540)825-7716
E-mail: visit@fountainhall.com
Web: www.fountainhall.com

Circa 1859. Originally built as a country Victorian home, this inn was later reconstructed into the existing Colonial Revival mansion. Elegantly decorated and furnished, the spacious parlors are ideal for playing games, watching movies or selecting a book from the large library to read by the fire. The well-appointed, oversized guest bedrooms and suites offer comforts galore. Some feature a private porch, whirlpool tub, plush robes and sweeping views of the spectacular Blue Ridge Mountains. Enjoy a leisurely breakfast of just-baked flaky croissants with butter and jam, fresh fruits, yogurt, hot and cold cereals and beverages. The surrounding area is steeped in rich American history, and the meticulously landscaped grounds feature seasonal gardens and a lawn groomed for croquet and bocce ball.

Historic Interest: Brandy Station (5-10 miles), Chancellorsville, Wilderness (20 miles), Civil War battlefields.

Innkeeper(s): Steve & Kathi Walker. $95-150. MC, VISA, AX, DC, CB, DS, PC, TC. TAC10. 6 rooms, 4 with PB and 2 suites. Breakfast and snacks/refreshments included in rates. Types of meals: Cont plus and early coffee/tea. AP. Beds: QDT. Cable TV, phone, ceiling fan and VCR in room. Air conditioning. Fax on premises. Handicap access. Antiquing, art galleries, bicycling, canoeing/kayaking, fishing, golf, hiking, horseback riding, museums, parks, shopping and wineries nearby.

Publicity: *Culpeper Star Exponent, New York Times, Washington Post, Richmond Channel 8 and Local TV.*

"A great inn you run. We still look back on our stay at Fountain Hall as a standout."

Damascus   I5

Mountain Laurel Inn

22750 Jeb Stuart Hwy
Damascus, VA 24236
(540)475-5956 (888)684-6698 Fax:(540)475-3399
E-mail: natjim@naxs.net
Web: www.mountainlaurelinn.com

Circa 1901. A Swedish lumber baron built Mountain Laurel. The home served as post office and the owner as postmaster. The Victorian farmhouse's exterior features a wraparound veranda, and the home is surrounded by three acres of peaceful grounds. Each room has been decorated individually with American and European antiques. Florence's Room, named for the original owner's daughter, includes a fireplace. The Rambo Suite, named to honor the home's first family, includes a Jacuzzi tub and a living room. The home borders the Appalachian Trail, and the area offers plenty of activities, including South Holston Lake, two state parks, the Virginia Creeper Trail, Barter Theatre and the annual Virginia Highlands Festival.

Historic Interest: Barter Theatre (11 miles), Martha Washington Inn (11 miles).

Innkeeper(s): Nathalie & Jim Graham. $69-109. MC, VISA, PC. 6 rooms, 2 with PB, 2 with FP and 2 suites. Breakfast included in rates. Types of meals: Full bkfst, country bkfst, early coffee/tea, picnic lunch and dinner. Beds: QDT. Cable TV and ceiling fan in room. Central air. Fax, copier, croquet and volleyball on premises. Weddings, small meetings, family reunions and seminars hosted. Antiquing, art galleries, beaches, bicycling, fishing, golf, hiking, horseback riding, live theater, museums, parks, shopping, sporting events and wineries nearby.

Edinburg   C12

Dearbought Horse Center & B&B

1693 Swover Creek Rd
Edinburg, VA 22824
(540)984-4226 (800)335-8861 Fax:(540)335-8861

Circa 1752. What began as a German farmhouse on 54 rolling acres, remains a functional farm, now with a fenced barn and several outbuildings. Peaceful surroundings make a nice setting for B&B accommodations. A comfortable suite features a fireplace. A wholesome breakfast is made using vegetable and herbs fresh from the gardens. The grounds offer a meandering stream and colorful meadow against the contrast of the big, blue sky. Horse rentals for trail rides are available.

Innkeeper(s): Catherine Harvey. $60-80. TC. 4 rooms, 1 with PB, 1 with FP and 1 suite. Breakfast included in rates. Types of meals: Country bkfst, early coffee/tea, lunch, picnic lunch, afternoon tea, snacks/refreshments and dinner. VCR, stables, pet boarding and horse rentals on premises. Handicap access. Weddings, small meetings, family reunions and seminars hosted. Antiquing, beaches, canoeing/kayaking, fishing, golf, hiking, horseback riding, civil war area, live theater, museums, parks, shopping, downhill skiing, cross-country skiing and wineries nearby.

Pets Allowed.

Fredericksburg   D15

La Vista Plantation

4420 Guinea Station Rd
Fredericksburg, VA 22408-8850
(540)898-8444 (800)529-2823
E-mail: lavistabb@aol.com

Circa 1838. La Vista has a long and unusual past, rich in Civil War history. Both Confederate and Union armies camped here, and this is where the Ninth Cavalry was sworn in. It is no wonder then that the house is listed in the National Register of Historic Places. The house, a Classical Revival structure with high ceilings and wide pine floors, sits on 10 acres of pasture and woods. The grounds include a pond stocked with bass. Guest quarters include a spacious room with a king-size, four-poster bed, fireplace and Empire furniture or a two-bedroom apartment that can accommodate up to six guests and includes a fireplace. Breakfasts feature homemade egg dishes from hens raised on the property.

Innkeeper(s): Michele & Edward Schiesser. $115. MC, VISA, PC, TC. 3 rooms, 2 with PB. Breakfast included in rates. Types of meals: Full bkfst and early coffee/tea. Beds: KQDT. TV and phone in room. Air conditioning. Copier and library on premises. Amusement parks, antiquing, fishing, pond, rowboat and bird-watching, live theater, parks, shopping, sporting events and water sports nearby.

Publicity: *Mid-Atlantic Country, Free Lance Star and Richmond Times Dispatch.*

"Coming here was an excellent choice. La Vista is charming, quiet and restful, all qualities we were seeking. Breakfast was delicious."

On Keegan Pond Bed & Breakfast

11315 Gordon Rd
Fredericksburg, VA 22407-1725
(540)785-4662 (888)785-4662

Circa 1918. Bike to Civil War battlefields and visit historic Fredericksburg from this early 20th-century farm house located on five acres with a secluded spring-fed pond. The inn has three well-appointed guest rooms, one of which is a large suite. Start the day with a hearty breakfast before striking out on day trips to see historical sites like Montpelier, Strafford Hall, Mount Vernon, Manassas, Gunston Hall, and King's Dominion.

Historic Interest: Civil war battlefields and Salem Church (3 miles), Historic Fredericksburg (5 miles).

Innkeeper(s): Sandra Wallace. $65-110. PC, TC. 3 rooms, 2 with PB, 1 suite and 1 conference room. Breakfast and snacks/refreshments included in rates. Types of meals: Gourmet bkfst and veg bkfst. Beds: QT. TV, phone, ceiling fan and VCR in room. Central air. Library and stocked pond on premises. Weddings, small meetings, family reunions and seminars hosted. German spoken. Amusement parks, antiquing, art galleries, beaches, bicycling, canoeing/kayaking, fishing, golf, hiking, live theater, museums, parks, shopping and wineries nearby.

Publicity: *Freelance Star Webb Site.*

Front Royal C13

Chester House Inn

43 Chester St
Front Royal, VA 22630-3368
(540)635-3937 (800)621-0441 Fax:(540)636-8695
E-mail: mail@chesterhouse.com
Web: www.chesterhouse.com

Circa 1905. In the heart of the Historic District, this stately Italian Renaissance estate rests on two acres of terraced gardens, which include vast plantings of boxwood, wisteria arbors and a fountain fishpond. The main home features many original interior details, including an elaborately carved marble

mantel. Walk to downtown restaurants and shops, the Confederate Museum and the Civil War home of Belle Boyd. The inn is just minutes from Skyline Drive, wineries, caverns, golf and hiking, or canoeing on the Shenandoah River.

Innkeeper(s): Phillip Inge, Allen & Barbara Hamblin. $105-220. MC, VISA, AX, PC, TC. TAC10. 7 rooms, 6 with PB, 3 with FP, 1 suite and 1 cottage. Breakfast included in rates. Types of meals: Full bkfst and early coffee/tea. Beds: KQDT. TV and cottage with 2-person whirlpool bath in room. Air conditioning. VCR and fax on premises. Small meetings and seminars hosted. Antiquing, canoeing/kayaking, fishing, golf, hiking, live theater, parks, shopping and wineries nearby.

Publicity: *Washington Entertainment Magazine, Blue Ridge Country Magazine, Rural Living Magazine, Winchester Star, Northern Virginia Daily, Inns of the Blue Ridge, EPM Publications, Winchester Star, Northern Virginia Daily and Blue Ridge Country.*

"A home of greater charm would be hard to find."

Killahevlin B&B Inn

1401 N Royal Ave
Front Royal, VA 22630-3625
(540)636-7335 (800)847-6132 Fax:(540)636-8694
E-mail: kllhvln@shentel.net
Web: www.vairish.com

Circa 1905. This Edwardian Mansion is in the National Register due in part to its builder, William Carson, creator of Skyline Drive, Williamsburg, Jamestown and Yorktown. A Civil War encampment once was located on the property. Each guest room enjoys mountain views, handsome decor and a working fireplace with antique mantels. Five rooms offer whirlpool tubs. The innkeeper shares a common Irish heritage with Will Carson. Antiques, 19th-century Irish cottage furniture, wallpa-

pers and Killahevlin's private Irish Pub add to the atmosphere. In addition to views of the Blue Ridge Mountains, the inn's three acres include two restored gazebos and an ornamental fish pool with a waterfall.

Innkeeper(s): Susan O'Kelly. $135-235. MC, VISA, AX, DC, DS, PC, TC. TAC10. 6 rooms with PB, 6 with FP and 2 suites. Breakfast included in rates. Types of meals: Full bkfst and early

coffee/tea. Beds: Q. Phone, turndown service, ceiling fan, whirlpool baths and cable TV (suites) in room. Air conditioning. Library and Oriental fish pond on premises. Weddings, small meetings, family reunions and seminars hosted. Antiquing, canoeing/kayaking, fishing, golf, hiking, horseback riding, fine dining, live theater, parks, shopping, water sports and wineries nearby.

Publicity: *Washington Times, Boston Globe, Warren Sentinel, Winchester Star, Northern Virginia Daily, Ski Country and Washington Post.*

Gordonsville E13

Sleepy Hollow Farm B&B

16280 Blue Ridge Tpke
Gordonsville, VA 22942-8214
(540)832-5555 (800)215-4804 Fax:(540)832-2515
E-mail: sleepyhollowfarmbnb@ns.gemlink.com
Web: www.sleepyhollowfarmbnb.com

Circa 1785. Many generations have added to this brick farmhouse creating somewhat of an optical illusion, as the historic home appears much smaller from a distance. The pink and white room often was visited by a friendly ghost, believed to be a Red Cross nurse during the Civil War, according to local stories. She hasn't been seen since the house was blessed in 1959.

Accommodations also are available in Chestnut Cottage, which offers two suites with downstairs sitting areas and bedrooms and baths upstairs. One suite has a fireplace. The other suite includes a deck, full kitchen, whirlpool room and Franklin wood stove. The grounds include abundant wildlife, flower gardens, an herb garden, a gazebo and pond for swimming and fishing.

Historic Interest: Montpelier (5 miles), James Madison Museum (6 miles), Wilderness Battlefields (30 miles), Civil War Exchange Hotel (4 miles), Fredricksburg (30 miles).

Innkeeper(s): Beverley Allison & Dorsey Comer. $65-150. MC, VISA, PC, TC. TAC10. 6 rooms with PB, 2 with FP, 2 suites and 1 cottage. Breakfast included in rates. Types of meals: Full bkfst, early coffee/tea and snacks/refreshments. Beds: QDT. Cable TV, phone and VCR in room. Air conditioning. Fax, swimming, library, two rooms with whirlpools. In the main house cake and cookies available on sideboard on premises. Weddings, small meetings and family reunions hosted. Antiquing, art galleries, fishing, golf, hiking, steeplechase race, historic homes, live theater, museums, parks, shopping, downhill skiing, sporting events, tennis and wineries nearby.

Pets allowed: $10 first night, $5 each successive night. Cottage only.

Publicity: *Orange County Review, City Magazine, Town & County, Washington Post, New York Times and Country Inn Magazine.*

"This house is truly blessed."

Goshen E10

The Hummingbird Inn

PO Box 147, 30 Wood Ln
Goshen, VA 24439-0147
(540)997-9065 (800)397-3214 Fax:(540)997-0289
E-mail: hmgbird@hummingbirdinn.com
Web: www.hummingbirdinn.com

Circa 1853. This early Victorian villa is located in the Shenandoah Valley against the backdrop of the Allegheny Mountains. Both the first and second floors offer wraparound verandas. Furnished with antiques, the inn features a library and sitting room with fireplaces. The rustic den and one guest room comprise the oldest portions of the inn, built around 1780. Four-course dinners, which include wine, are available by advance reservation (Saturdays only). An old barn and babbling creek are on the grounds. Lexington, the Virginia Horse Center, Natural Bridge, the Blue Ridge Parkway and antiquing are all nearby.

Historic Interest: Historic Lexington, Stonewall Jackson House & Museum, Lee Chapel (23 minutes). Monticello (70 minutes).

Innkeeper(s): Diana & Jeremy Robinson. $110-155. MC, VISA, AX, DS, PC, TC. TAC10. 4 rooms with PB, 4 with FP. Breakfast included in rates. Types of meals: Full bkfst and early coffee/tea. Beds: Q. TV and ceiling fan in room. Air conditioning. VCR, fax, library and satellite TV on premises. Handicap access. Antiquing, fishing, live theater, shopping, downhill skiing and cross-country skiing nearby.

Pets allowed: Dogs with prior arrangements.

Publicity: *Blue Ridge Country and Inn Spots and Special Places.*

"We enjoyed our stay so much that we returned two weeks later on our way back for a delicious home-cooked dinner, comfortable attractive atmosphere, and familiar faces to welcome us after a long journey."

Hot Springs   E10

King's Victorian Inn

Rt 1, Box 622
Hot Springs, VA 24445-9614
(540)839-3134

Circa 1899. No matter the season, guests will feel welcome by the very sight of this charming gabled Victorian. In the spring and summer, trees shade the wraparound veranda. In the win-

ter months, warm lights glow in the windows, and during the Christmas season, a wreath is placed at each window. The healing powers of the hot springs brought Dr. Henry Pole to the town, and he built this house which features stained glass, pocket doors, high ceilings and a signature staircase. Guest rooms feature 18th-century reproductions and antiques. After a homemade country breakfast, meander down a walking trail to Hot Springs downtown area, where boutiques and antique shops await.

Innkeeper(s): Liz & Richard King. $89-150. PC, TC. 8 rooms, 4 with PB, 1 suite and 2 cottages. Breakfast included in rates. Types of meals: Full bkfst. Beds: KQD. Small meetings and family reunions hosted. Antiquing, fishing, golf, live theater, parks, shopping, downhill skiing, cross-country skiing and water sports nearby.

Publicity: *Roanoke Times, Richmond Times Dispatch and Country Magazine.*

Leesburg   B15

Leesburg Colonial Inn

19 S King St
Leesburg, VA 20175-2903
(703)777-5000 (800)392-1332 Fax:(703)777-7000

Circa 1830. In the historic district of Leesburg just 25 miles from Washington, D.C., stands this Colonial inn with polished wood floors, antique poster beds, Persian and Oriental rugs. It offers 10 guest bedrooms, some with fireplaces. A full gourmet breakfast with authentic 18th-century cuisine is served each

morning in the dining room at candle-lit tables. The inn is located in scenic Loudoun County, which is bordered by the Blue Ridge Mountains and Potomac River. Named for the Earl of Loudoun, John Campbell, who was both Governor of Virginia and the British commander in the early stages of the French and Indian War, the county and historic Leesburg are full of historic buildings and sites.

Innkeeper(s): Fabian Saeidi. $88-175. MC, VISA, AX, DC, CB, DS, PC, TC. TAC10. 10 rooms with PB, 4 with FP, 1 guest house and 1 conference room. Breakfast included in rates. Types of meals: Gourmet bkfst, veg bkfst, early coffee/tea, gourmet lunch, afternoon tea, snacks/refreshments, gourmet dinner and room service. Beds: QDT. Cable TV, phone and fireplace in room. Central air. Fax, copier, bicycles, cafe and restaurant on premises. Weddings, small meetings, family reunions and seminars hosted. Irish and French spoken. Antiquing, art galleries, bicycling, canoeing/kayaking, fishing, golf, hiking, horseback riding, live theater, museums, parks, shopping, sporting events, water sports and wineries nearby.

Pets allowed: 10 pounds with $50 deposit.

The Norris House Inn & Stone House Tea Room

108 Loudoun St SW
Leesburg, VA 20175
(703)777-1806 (800)644-1806 Fax:(703)771-8051
E-mail: inn@norrishouse.com
Web: norrishouse.com

Circa 1760. The Norris brothers, Northern Virginia's foremost architects and builders, purchased this building in 1850 and began extensive renovations several years later. They used the

finest wood and brick available, remodeling the exterior to an Eastlake style. Beautifully restored, the inn features built-in bookcases in the library and a cherry fireplace mantel. Evening libations are served.

Historic Interest: Harpers Ferry (18 miles), Antietam Battlefield (30 minutes), Manassas Battlefield (30 minutes), Washington, D.C. (32 miles), Gettysburg (50 miles).

Innkeeper(s): Pamela & Don McMurray. $85-150. MC, VISA, AX, DC, CB, DS, PC, TC. TAC10. 6 rooms, 3 with FP and 3 conference rooms. Breakfast included in rates. Types of meals: Full bkfst, early coffee/tea and afternoon tea. Beds: QD. Turndown service in room. Air conditioning. Fax and library on premises. Weddings, small meetings, family reunions and seminars hosted. Antiquing, fishing, hiking, biking, parks, shopping and water sports nearby.

Publicity: *New York Times, Better Homes & Gardens, Washingtonian and Country Home.*

"Thank you for your gracious hospitality. We enjoyed everything about your lovely home, especially the extra little touches that really make the difference."

Lexington   F11

The Inn at Union Run

Union Run Rd
Lexington, VA 24450
(540)463-9715 (800)528-6466 Fax:(540)463-3526
E-mail: unionrun@cfw.com

Circa 1883. This inn was named for the spring-fed creek that meanders in front of this restored farmhouse. Union troops, specifically the 2nd and 4th Michigan Calvary, camped on the grounds during the Civil War. The home is surrounded by 10 acres with a fishing pond and brook. The innkeepers have traveled extensively throughout Europe and have brought the influence into their inn. The furnishings, many of which were fashioned out of oak, are a mix of American and Victorian styles.

Innkeeper(s): Roger & Jeanette Serens. $95-120. MC, VISA, AX, TC. 8 rooms with PB, 4 with FP and 1 conference room. Breakfast and afternoon tea included in rates. Types of meals: Full bkfst, early coffee/tea, lunch, picnic lunch, snacks/refreshments, dinner and room service. MAP. Beds: Q. Phone, turndown service, ceiling fan and Jacuzzis (6 rooms) in room. Air conditioning. Handicap access. Weddings, small meetings, family reunions and seminars hosted. Antiquing, fishing, Civil War sites, live theater, museums, parks, shopping, cross-country skiing and water sports nearby.

Pets allowed: Call first.

Publicity: *News Gazette, Blue Ridge Country and Insider Guide of Virginia.*

Stoneridge Bed & Breakfast

PO Box 38
Lexington, VA 24450
(540)463-4090 (800)491-2930 Fax:(540)463-6078
E-mail: rollo_va@cfw.com
Web: www.webfeat-inc.com/stoneridge

Circa 1829. The Shenandoah Valley is the setting for this bed & breakfast, located on 36 secluded acres of woods, streams and rolling fields. The inn was built using bricks made on the property, and once served as a plantation home and possibly a stagecoach stop. The home still maintains original heart-of-pine

floors, ornate mantels and other period features. Guest rooms feature antiques, some are family heirlooms. Four guest rooms include fireplaces, and three offer double Jacuzzi tubs. Several rooms have a mountain view. A variety of reading material is available in the library. Stoneridge offers a large selection of Virginia wines to its guests for purchase. The gourmet country breakfasts might include blueberry buckle, stuffed French toast and baked eggs. The meal is served either in the candle-lit dining room or on the back patio.

Innkeeper(s): Norm & Barbara Rollenhagen. $95-160. MC, VISA, AX, DS, PC, TC. TAC10. 5 rooms with PB, 4 with FP and 1 suite. Breakfast included in rates. Types of meals: Full bkfst and afternoon tea. Beds: Q. Turndown service, ceiling fan and jacuzzi tubs for two in room. Air conditioning. VCR, fax and library on premises. Antiquing, fishing, live theater, parks, shopping and cross-country skiing nearby.

Publicity: *News-Gazette and Blue Ridge Country.*

Lincoln   B14

Creek Crossing Farm

37768 Chappell Hill Road
Lincoln, VA 20160
(540)338-7550 Fax:(540)338-4548

Circa 1773. Families and pets are welcome at this working farm. Organic blueberry fields, walking trails, barns and cattle encompass 25 acres. The library features an extensive collection of Civil War books and other available reading materials. The guest bedrooms and suite are comfortably furnished with period antiques. A custom breakfast is served in the conference room overlooking a fish pond and gardens. Afternoon tea is available upon request.

Historic Interest: A short drive from the farm takes guests to the historic sites of Leesburg, just 10 miles away. Washington, D.C., is about an hour from the farm.

Innkeeper(s): Barbara Baroody. $165-195. 4 rooms with PB and 1 suite. Breakfast and afternoon tea included in rates. Types of meals: Full bkfst and gourmet dinner. Beds: QDT. Antiquing, fishing, rafting, crafts, Civil War trails, fine dining and horse events nearby.

Pets Allowed.

"Thank you for sharing your fabulous home with us this past weekend. We enjoyed staying with you immensly."

Locust Dale   D13

The Inn at Meander Plantation

HC 5, Box 460A
Locust Dale, VA 22948-9701
(540)672-4912 (800)385-4936 Fax:(540)672-0405
E-mail: inn@meander.net
Web: www.meander.net

Circa 1766. This historic country estate was built by Henry Fry, close friend of Thomas Jefferson who often stopped here on his way to Monticello. The mansion is serenely decorated with elegant antiques and period

reproductions, including four-poster beds. Healthy gourmet breakfasts are prepared by Chef Suzie. Enjoy views of the Blue Ridge Mountains from the rockers on the back porches.

Ancient formal boxwood gardens, surrounding natural woodlands, meadows, pastures and Robinson River frontage are part of Meander Conservancy, offering educational programs and back-to-nature packages.

Historic Interest: Prehistoric Native American site on the property near the Robinson River. James and Dolley Madison's home (10 miles), Civil War battlefields: Cedar Mountain (4 miles), Brandy Station (15 miles), Manassas and Bull Run (50 miles).

Innkeeper(s): Suzie Blanchard, Suzanne Thomas. $120-200. MC, VISA, AX, PC, TC. TAC10. 8 rooms with PB, 5 with FP, 4 suites and 1 conference room. Breakfast included in rates. Types of meals: Full bkfst, early coffee/tea, lunch, picnic lunch, snacks/refreshments and gourmet dinner. Beds: KQD. Air conditioning. VCR, fax, stables, library, pet boarding and child care on premises. Weddings, small meetings, family reunions and seminars hosted. Antiquing, fishing, live theater, parks, shopping, downhill skiing, cross-country skiing and sporting events nearby.

Pets allowed: In dependencies only. Stabling for horses available.

"Staying at the Inn at Meander Plantation feels like being immersed in another century while having the luxuries and amenities available today."

Luray   C13

The Ruffner House

440 Ruffner House Rd
Luray, VA 22835-9704
(540)743-7855 (800)969-7855

Circa 1739. This 23-acre estate offers scenic pastures with grazing horses in the heart of the Shenandoah Valley. Peter Ruffner, the first settler of Page Valley and Luray, built the inn, a stately manor. Ruffner family members discovered a cavern opposite the entrance to the Luray Caverns, which were later discovered. In 1840 the house was sold and no Ruffners occupied it until this year when an 8th-generation Ruffner purchased it. The inn offers handsome antiques, two parlors and two enticing porches. Guest rooms feature a selection of amenities including some with fireplaces, Victorian tubs, ceiling fans and pastoral views. Afternoon tea is offered. A gourmet breakfast is served in the manor's elegant dining room and will provide sustenance for a full day of recreation. Visit wineries, battlefields, the Shenandoah National Park and Luray Caverns or enjoy horseback riding, canoeing, cycling, golfing or browsing the antique and boutique shops.

Innkeeper(s): Sonia Croucher. $98-150. MC, VISA, AX, DS, PC, TC. 6 rooms with PB, 3 with FP. Breakfast included in rates. Types of meals: Gourmet bkfst, early coffee/tea, picnic lunch, snacks/refreshments and gourmet dinner. Beds: QD. TV, ceiling fan and Victorian soaking tubs (two rooms) in room. Air conditioning. VCR and rocking chairs and swings on porches on premises. Weddings, small meetings, family reunions and seminars hosted. Antiquing, canoeing/kayaking, fishing, golf, hiking, horseback riding, parks, shopping, downhill skiing, cross-country skiing, sporting events and wineries nearby.

Publicity: *Page News & Courier and Washingtonian Magazine.*

"This is the loveliest inn we have ever stayed in. We were made to feel very welcome and at ease."

Shenandoah River Inn

201 Stagecoach Ln
Luray, VA 22835
(540)743-1144 (888)666-6760 Fax:(540)743-9101
Web: www.shenandoah-inn.com

Circa 1812. This gracious two-and-a-half-story white colonial inn, located on four landscaped acres along the Shenandoah River, was once a stagecoach stop. Graceful walnut trees and fruit trees dot the property's wide lawns. There are three

screened porches, all with water views. Guest rooms each have fireplaces, marble-floored baths and king or queen beds. Antiques, paintings, mirrors and a fireplace decorate the parlor. Gourmet candle-lit breakfasts may include Belgian waffles, fruit plate and breakfast meats. Seven-course dinners are available. Picnic by the river or try your hand at small-mouth-bass fishing. The innkeepers also offer a secluded cabin surrounded by national forest and on top of a mountain with 50-mile views.

Innkeeper(s): Paul Bramell & Ann Merrigan. $135-145. MC, VISA, AX, PC, TC. TAC10. 4 rooms with PB, 4 with FP and 6 cabins. Breakfast and afternoon tea included in rates. Types of meals: Gourmet bkfst, early coffee/tea, picnic lunch and gourmet dinner. Beds: KQ. Air conditioning. VCR, copier and swimming on premises. Handicap access. Weddings, small meetings, family reunions and seminars hosted. Antiquing, golf, horseback riding, parks, shopping, downhill skiing and water sports nearby.

Publicity: *Washingtonian.*

The Woodruff Collection of Victorian Inns

138 E Main St
Luray, VA 22835
(540)743-1494 Fax:(540)743-1722
E-mail: woodruffbnb@rica.net
Web: www.woodruffinns.com

Circa 1882. Prepare to be pampered. The Woodruffs entered the B&B business after years of experience in hotel management and restaurant businesses. They have not missed a detail, ensuring a perfect, relaxing visit. The Rooftop Skylight Fireside Jacuzzi Suite is often the room of choice because of its interesting shape and architecture, located where the attic was

before restoration. The suite boasts skylights, Jacuzzi tub for two and antique stained glass. Tasteful antiques and fresh bouquets of flowers framed by candlelight add a special ambiance. Besides the extra attention and comfortable accommodations, the Woodruffs include afternoon dessert tea, in-room coffee or tea and a full fireside gourmet breakfast in the rates. Candlelight sets the mood for the gourmet dinner, and none of the spectacular meals are to be missed. A romantic finish to each evening is a private dip in one of the garden hot tubs.

Historic Interest: New Market Battlefield (20 minutes), the famous underground Luray Caverns discovered in the late 1800s (minutes away).

Innkeeper(s): Lucas & Deborah Woodruff. $155-295. MC, VISA, DS, PC, TC. TAC10. 5 rooms with PB, 9 with FP, 4 suites and 1 conference room. Breakfast and afternoon included in rates. Types of meals: Gourmet bkfst and gourmet dinner. MAP. Beds: KQ. Coffeemaker in room. Air conditioning. Fax, spa, two outdoor gardens and Jacuzzi tubs for two on premises. Weddings, small meetings and family reunions hosted. Antiquing, fishing, caverns, Shenandoah River, Skyline Drive, parks, shopping, downhill skiing and water sports nearby.

Publicity: *Potomac Living, Cascapades Magazine, Blue Ridge Country Magazine, Cooperative Living, Virginia Wine Gazette and Food and Wine Magazine.*

Lynchburg   **G11**

Federal Crest Inn

1101 Federal St
Lynchburg, VA 24504-3018
(804)845-6155 (800)818-6155 Fax:(804)845-1445
E-mail: inn@federalcrest.com
Web: www.federalcrest.com

Circa 1909. The guest rooms at Federal Crest are named for the many varieties of trees and flowers native to Virginia. This handsome red brick home, a fine example of Georgian Revival architecture, features a commanding front entrance

flanked by columns that hold up the second-story veranda. A grand staircase, carved woodwork, polished floors topped with fine rugs and more columns create an aura of elegance. Each guest room offers something special and romantic, from a mountain view to a Jacuzzi tub. Breakfasts are served on fine china, and the first course is always a freshly baked muffin with a secret message inside.

Historic Interest: Appomattox Court House and Jefferson's Poplar Forest.

Innkeeper(s): Ann & Phil Ripley. $125-155. MC, VISA, AX, DS, PC, TC. TAC10. 5 rooms, 4 with PB, 3 with FP, 2 suites and 1 conference room. Breakfast, afternoon tea and snacks/refreshments included in rates. Types of meals: Full bkfst and early coffee/tea. Beds: Q. Cable TV, turndown service, portable telephone and portable VCR in room. Air conditioning. Fax, copier, library, conference theater with 60-inch TV (Ballroom) with stage and 50's cafe with antique jukebox on premises. Weddings, small meetings, family reunions and seminars hosted. Antiquing, fishing, golf, live theater, parks, shopping, sporting events and tennis nearby.

Publicity: *Washington Post, News & Advance, Scene and Local ABC.*

"What a wonderful place to celebrate our birthdays and enjoy our last romantic getaway before the birth of our first child."

Lynchburg Mansion Inn Bed & Breakfast

405 Madison St
Lynchburg, VA 24504-2455
(804)528-5400 (800)352-1199 Fax:(804)847-2545
E-mail: mansioninn@aol.com
Web: www.lynchburgmansioninn.com

Circa 1914. This regal, Georgian mansion, with its majestic Greek Revival columns, is located on a brick-paved street in the Garland Hill Historic District. The grand hall showcases an oak and cherry staircase that leads up to the solarium. Breakfasts are served in the formal dining room on antique china.

Romantic rooms feature inviting touches such as a four-poster beds, Laura Ashley and Ralph Lauren linens, Battenburg lace pillows and some include fireplaces. The Veranda Suite, as the name suggests, opens onto a romantic circular veranda and a treetop sunroom. The Garden  Suite, with its private garden entrance, includes an original clawfoot tub. There is a hot tub on the back porch, and the innkeepers have added gardens full of perennials, herbs, edible flowers and more, including a picturesque gazebo. Lynchburg offers many exciting activities, including the unique Community Market and plenty of galleries, antique shops and boutiques. Ski areas are about 45 minutes from the inn.

Historic Interest: Poplar Forest, Thomas Jefferson's retreat and Appomattox Court House are among dozens of historic attractions in the area. The Old City Cemetery serves as the resting place for more than 2,500 Confederate soldiers. The home of acclaimed poet and figure of the Harlem Renaissance, Anne Spencer is nearby, as are five historic districts.

Innkeeper(s): Mauranna and Bob Sherman. $109-144. MC, VISA, AX, DC. TAC10. 5 rooms with PB, 3 with FP, 2 suites and 1 conference room. Breakfast included in rates. Types of meals: Gourmet bkfst and early coffee/tea. Beds: KQ. Cable TV, phone and turndown service in room. Air conditioning. Period library on premises. Handicap access. Weddings, small meetings, family reunions and seminars hosted. Antiquing, live theater, shopping, downhill skiing and sporting events nearby.

Publicity: *News & Advance and Roanoker.*

"The Lynchburg Mansion Inn is the creme de la creme. You have earned all sorts of pats on the back for the restoration and hospitality you offer. It is truly elegant."

Norvell-Otey House B&B

1020 Federal St
Lynchburg, VA 24504
(434)528-1020 (877)320-1020 Fax:(434)528-8811
E-mail: norvelloteyhouse@aol.com
Web: www.norvelloteyhouse.com

Circa 1817. This 1817 Federal-style manor house near Charlottesville, Richmond and Roanoke has porches, gardens and a lovely patio as well as four guest rooms appointed with antiques. After a hearty breakfast, strike out for Monticello, National D-Day Memorial, Patrick Henry's home, Appomattox and other historical sites.

Innkeeper(s): Jenny West. $125-145. MC, VISA, AX, DC, DS, PC, TC. TAC10. 4 rooms, 3 with PB, 1 with FP and 2 conference rooms. Breakfast, afternoon tea and snacks/refreshments included in rates. Types of meals: Gourmet bkfst, veg bkfst, early coffee/tea, gourmet lunch, picnic lunch, gourmet dinner and

room service. Beds: QT. Cable TV and turndown service in room. Central air. VCR, fax, copier, spa, library, refrigerator, coffee, soft drinks, snacks, chocolates, card room, music room and newspaper on premises. Weddings, small meetings, family reunions and seminars hosted. Antiquing, art galleries, bicycling, canoeing/kayaking, fishing, golf, hiking, horseback riding, many historic sites, live theater, museums, parks, shopping, downhill skiing, cross-country skiing, sporting events, tennis, water sports and wineries nearby.

Publicity: *New York Times, Lynchburg News & Advance, Roanoke Times, Channel 13 and 7 10.*

Madison D13

Dulaney Hollow at Old Rag Mountain B&B Inn

HC 6 Box 215 - Scenic VA Byway, Rt 231
Madison, VA 22727
(540)923-4470 Fax:(540)923-4841
E-mail: oldragmtninn@nexet.net

Circa 1903. Period furnishings decorate this Victorian manor house on 15 acres of the Blue Ridge Mountains. There is also a cabin, cottage and hayloft suite available amid the shaded lawns and old farm buildings. Enjoy a delicious country breakfast. Take a bicycle jaunt or hike the hills around the Shenandoah River and National Park. Monticello, Charlottesville and Montpelier are within an hour's drive.

Innkeeper(s): Susan & Louis Cable. $85-135. PC, TC. TAC10. 6 rooms with PB, 1 suite and 2 cottages. Breakfast included in rates. Types of meals: Gourmet bkfst, early coffee/tea, gourmet lunch, picnic lunch, afternoon tea and gourmet dinner. Beds: QDT. Ceiling fan in room. Air conditioning. VCR, fax, copier, swimming, bicycles, pet boarding and Internet access on premises. Weddings, small meetings, family reunions and seminars hosted. Antiquing, fishing, golf, Civil War sites, historic sites and battlefields, Shenandoah National Park, wildlife preserve, live theater, parks, shopping, downhill skiing, cross-country skiing, sporting events, tennis, water sports and wineries nearby.

Pets allowed: for a fee.

Publicity: *Madison Eagle and Charlottesville Daily Progress.*

McGaheysville D12

Cave Hill Farm B&B

9875 Cave Hill Rd
McGaheysville, VA 22840
(540)289-7441 (888)798-3985 Fax:(540)289-7441
E-mail: info@cavehillfarmbandb.com

Circa 1830. Steeped in history, this English Manor house in the Shenandoah Valley has amazing stories to reveal. Recent restorations uncovered hidden letters written during and about Civil War battles. The basement housed the original kitchen and dining room. They now display an assortment of antique farm tools. The furnishings and decor exquisitely befit the ambiance and era of the home's heritage. Using fresh ingredients from the herb and vegetable garden, breakfast may include an Amaretto cream sauce fruit and nut appetizer, berry-stuffed French toast, quiche, garlic pepper parmesan potatoes and a regional meat selection. There are 400 acres of landscaped grounds, flower gardens, fields and hills on this farm.

Innkeeper(s): Jennifer Dowling. $139-159. MC, VISA, AX, DS, PC, TC. 5 rooms with PB, 5 with FP and 1 conference room. Breakfast included in rates. Types of meals: Gourmet bkfst, veg bkfst and early coffee/tea. Beds: Q. Cable TV, phone, turndown service and fireplace in room. Central air. VCR and fax on premises. Weddings, small meetings, family reunions and seminars hosted. Antiquing, bicycling, canoeing/kayaking, golf, hiking, horseback riding, Massanutten Resort, Shenandoah National Park, live theater, museums, parks, shopping, downhill skiing and wineries nearby.

Publicity: *Villager and Local Talk Radio.*

Middleburg **B14**

The Longbarn

37129 Adams Green Ln
Middleburg, VA 20118
(540)687-4137 Fax:(540)687-4044
E-mail: thlongbarn@aol.com
Web: www.members.aol.com/thlongbarn/

Circa 1889. Built in the late 1800s, this recently renovated barn offers private comfort amid eight acres of serene woodlands. Art lovers will appreciate the details of the Italian-European country décor inside, coupled with its picturesque surroundings. There is a large fireplace in the living room that guests can relax near. Take a walk through the European gardens to the gazebo for a picnic lunch and enjoy the pond. Rise each morning with fresh fruits, juice, omelets and grilled vegetables, homemade breads and breakfast meats. Nearby are many activities for the whole family, such as swimming, horseback riding, bicycling and golf.

Historic Interest: Leesburg, Manassas.

Innkeeper(s): Chiara Langley. $125. MC, VISA, PC. TAC10. 3 rooms with PB. Breakfast included in rates. Types of meals: Gourmet bkfst, veg bkfst, afternoon tea and dinner. Beds: KQT. Ceiling fan in room. Central air. Bicycles, library and exercise room on premises. Weddings and small meetings hosted. Italian, Spanish and some French spoken. Amusement parks, antiquing, art galleries, bicycling, golf, hiking, horseback riding, museums, parks, shopping, tennis and wineries nearby.

Red Fox Inn

2 E Washington St
Middleburg, VA 20117-0385
(540)687-6301 (800)223-1728 Fax:(540)687-6053
E-mail: innkeeper@redfox.com

Circa 1728. Originally Chinn's Ordinary, the inn was a popular stopping place for travelers between Winchester and Alexandria. During the Civil War, Colonel John Mosby and General Jeb Stuart met here. Guest rooms are furnished in 18th-century decor and most feature four-poster canopy beds.

Innkeeper(s): F. Turner Reuter, Jr. $150-325. MC, VISA, AX, DS, TC. 23 rooms with PB and 4 conference rooms. Breakfast included in rates. Types of meals: Cont, lunch and dinner. Beds: KQ. Cable TV and phone in room. Air conditioning. Fax and copier on premises. Handicap access. Weddings, small meetings, family reunions and seminars hosted. Antiquing nearby.

Publicity: *Washingtonian, Southern Living, Washington Bride and Virginia Wine Publications.*

Millboro **E10**

Fort Lewis Lodge

HCR 3 Box 21A
Millboro, VA 24460
(540)925-2314 Fax:(540)925-2352
E-mail: ftlewis@tds.net
Web: www.fortlewislodge.com

Circa 1840. Colonel Charles Lewis, under the command of George Washington, built one of the string of forts on this property to protect the southern pass of the Shenandoah Mountains from Indian raids. It is easy to revel in the natural beauty of this 3,000-acre mountain farm. Stay in quaint lodge rooms, including "sleeping in the round," a silo with spiral staircase. Two historic hand-hewn log cabins boast stone fire-

places. The newly restored Riverside House offers five spacious guest bedrooms. Enjoy Caryl's plentiful homemade meals served in the refurbished 19th-century grist mill. The local area features many opportunities to hike, hunt, bike and fish.

Historic Interest: A half-hour drive takes guests to Warm Springs, which includes soothing mineral baths designed by Thomas Jefferson. The famed Homestead Resort is five miles farther in Hot Springs.

Innkeeper(s): John & Caryl Cowden. $150-210. MC, VISA. 18 rooms with PB. Breakfast and dinner included in rates. Types of meals: Full bkfst and picnic lunch. Beds: KQT. Weddings, small meetings, family reunions and seminars hosted. Antiquing, fishing and water sports nearby.

Publicity: *Outside, AAA Today, Mid-Atlantic Country, Tasteful, Rural Living, Country, Washington Post and Washingtonian.*

"We have stayed at many inns in France, England and Germany, none have impressed me as much as yours. You have made the most of a beautiful piece of property and I feel privileged to share it with you."

Mineral **E14**

Littlepage Inn

15701 Monrovia Rd
Mineral, VA 23117
(540)854-9861 (800)248-1803 Fax:(540)854-7998
E-mail: littlepage@earthlink.net
Web: www.littlepage.com

Circa 1811. Two old fieldstone posts mark the country lane to this large plantation home, on the National Register. Heart pine floors and original glass window panes were preserved in a recent prize-winning restoration. The spacious rooms are filled with period furnishings, many original to the house. The inn's 125 acres offer gardens, fields, a wooded spring, a 19th-century smokehouse, ice house with Jacuzzi, barn and stable.

Innkeeper(s): Holly Currier. $99-215. 9 rooms with PB, 3 with FP and 1 cottage. Types of meals: Full bkfst, picnic lunch and dinner. Phone and central air & heat in room. Outdoor pool on premises. Weddings, small meetings, family reunions and seminars hosted. Antiquing, tours of American Historic sites and shopping nearby.

Montross **E16**

'Tween Rivers B&B

16006 Kings Hwy
Montross, VA 22520
E-mail: stay@tweenrivers.com
Web: www.tweenrivers.com

Circa 1921. Aptly named for the location of this Colonial Revival home midway between two of the rivers of the Northern Neck, this B&B is conveniently close to a variety of land and sea adventures. Boasting an elegant country ambiance, the first-floor parlor promotes fireside chats. The second-floor sitting room is great for listening to a CD or reading a book. The Chesapeake, Potomac and Rappahannock guest bedrooms offer four-poster beds and comfort-enhancing amenities. Breakfast specialties include baked pecan French toast, blueberry sour cream pancakes, ham and cheese frittata and scrambled eggs in puff pastry, served on vintage china. Oak rockers and wicker furniture beckon from the wraparound porch.

Call for rates.. Breakfast included in rates. Types of meals: Gourmet bkfst.

Nellysford F12

The Mark Addy

56 Rodes Farm Dr
Nellysford, VA 22958-9526
(434)361-1101 (800)278-2154
E-mail: johnmaddox11@msn.com
Web: www.mark-addy.com

Circa 1837. It's not hard to understand why Dr. John Everett, the son of Thomas Jefferson's physician, chose this picturesque, Blue Mountain setting for his home. Everett expanded the simple, four-room farmhouse already present into a gracious manor. The well-appointed guest rooms feature double whirlpool baths, double showers or a clawfoot tub. Beds are covered with vintage linens, feather pillows and cozy, down comforters. There are plenty of relaxing possibilities, including five porches and a hammock set among the trees.

Historic Interest: Dr. John Coleman Everett (son of Thomas Jefferson's physician) bought the estate in 1884.

Innkeeper(s): John Storck Maddox. $90-145. MC, VISA, PC, TC. TAC10. 9 rooms with PB and 1 suite. Types of meals: Gourmet bkfst, cont, early coffee/tea, gourmet lunch, picnic lunch and gourmet dinner. EP. Beds: KQDT. Ceiling fan and jacuzzi in room. Air conditioning. VCR and library on premises. Handicap access. Weddings, small meetings and family reunions hosted. German spoken. Antiquing, fishing, horseback riding, hiking, live theater, parks, shopping, downhill skiing and sporting events nearby.

Publicity: *Local paper.*

New Church E19

The Garden and The Sea Inn

4188 Nelson Rd, #275
New Church, VA 23415-0275
(757)824-0672 (800)824-0672
E-mail: innkeeper@gardenandseainn.com

Circa 1802. Gingerbread trim, a pair of brightly colored gables and two, adjacent verandas adorn the exterior of this Victorian. A warm, rich Victorian decor permeates the antique-filled guest rooms, an ideal setting for romance.

Several rooms include whirlpool tubs. The inn's dining room serves gourmet dinners by reservation. Pets are very welcome.

Innkeeper(s): Tom & Sara Baker. $75-185. MC, VISA, AX, DS, PC, TC. TAC10. 8 rooms with PB and 1 conference room. Breakfast included in rates. Types of meals: Full bkfst, snacks/refreshments and gourmet dinner. Beds: KQ. Ceiling fan in room. Air conditioning. VCR, fax, copier and library on premises. Handicap access. Antiquing, beaches, fishing, parks, shopping and water sports nearby.

Pets allowed: Quiet and leashed outside.

Publicity: *Washington Post and Modern Bride.*

New Market C12

Cross Roads Inn B&B

9222 John Sevier Rd
New Market, VA 22844-9649
(540)740-4157
E-mail: freisitz@shentel.net
Web: www.crossroadsinnva.com

Circa 1925. This Victorian is full of Southern hospitality and European charm. The innkeepers serve imported Austrian coffee along with their bountiful breakfasts, and homemade apple strudel is served as an afternoon refreshment. The home is decorated with English floral wallpapers, antiques and old family furnishings. Four-poster and canopy beds are topped with fluffy, down comforters. The historic downtown area is within walking distance.

Innkeeper(s): Mary Lloyd & Roland Freisitzer. $65-125. MC, VISA, TC. 6 rooms with PB and 1 conference room. Breakfast included in rates. Types of meals: Full bkfst, early coffee/tea, afternoon tea and snacks/refreshments. Beds: KQDT. Several with Jacuzzi or fireplace in room. Air conditioning. VCR, fax and copier on premises. Handicap access. Weddings, small meetings, family reunions and seminars hosted. Antiquing, fishing, musical summer festivals, live theater, parks, shopping, downhill skiing, sporting events and water sports nearby.

Newport News H17

Boxwood Inn

10 Elmhurst St
Newport News, VA 23603-1138
(757)888-8854 Fax:(757)557-3986
Web: www.boxwood-inn.com

Circa 1896. Formerly a Warwick County Hall of Records, a post office, a general store, and then home of the prominent Curtis family, this historic plantation-style inn has hosted many important political and social events. Antiques found in the sprawling attic are found in every room as part of the period decor. Local museums display the remaining cherished memorabilia. The guest bedrooms are eye-pleasing and hold stories of their own, housing soldiers and their families during both World War I and II. A savory breakfast is served in the Blue Willow Tea Room. Located in Historic Lee Hall Village, Colonial Williamsburg, as well as Revolutionary and Civil War battlefields are an easy drive.

Historic Interest: Lee Hall Mansion, Endview Plantation, Colonial Williamsburg (6 miles).

Innkeeper(s): Barbara & Bob Lucas. $75. MC, VISA, PC. TAC10. 4 rooms with PB. Breakfast included in rates. Types of meals: Gourmet bkfst, early coffee/tea and afternoon tea. Beds: Q. Ceiling fan and one with refrigerator in room. Air conditioning. Weddings, small meetings, family reunions and seminars hosted. Amusement parks, antiquing, beaches, hiking, museums, parks and wineries nearby.

Norfolk H18

Page House Inn

323 Fairfax Ave
Norfolk, VA 23507-2215
(757)625-5033 (800)599-7659 Fax:(757)623-9451
E-mail: innkeeper@pagehouseinn.com
Web: www.pagehouseinn.com

Circa 1899. This pristinely renovated Georgian Revival inn, in the National Register, is located in the Ghent Historic District. The parlor features polished wood floors, an Oriental carpet, period antiques, paintings and an elegant fireplace. Ask for the room with the king-size canopy bed, fireplace, sunken hot tub, bidet and steam shower for two. Amenities include luxury linens and robes, and turndown service is available by request. There are solid oak doors, insulated walls and floors, valet laundry and daily maid service. Breakfast options include candlelight breakfasts for suite guests by advance notice, continental breakfast served in your room or a formal breakfast in the dining room. Nearby is the Chrysler Museum of Art with original works by Andy Warhol and Edward Hopper. Antique shoppers will enjoy Virginia's largest concentration of antique shops.

Innkeeper(s): Carl Albero. $122-220. MC, VISA, AX, PC, TC. TAC10. 7 rooms with PB, 4 with FP and 3 suites. Breakfast, afternoon tea and snacks/refreshments included in rates. Types of meals: Full bkfst, early coffee/tea and room service. Beds: KQDT. Phone, turndown service, ceiling fan and VCR in room. Air conditioning. Fax and copier on premises. Small meetings hosted. Italian and some Spanish spoken. Amusement parks, antiquing, fishing, golf, opera, symphony, live theater, museums, parks, shopping, sporting events, tennis and water sports nearby.

Pets allowed: small dogs ($25/day fee).

Publicity: *Country Inns, Mid-Atlantic, Travel & Leisure and Southern Living.*

"What a treat this is to write a thank you note regarding 'quality,' which I define as giving someone more than they expect."

Orange   E13

The Holladay House

155 W Main St
Orange, VA 22960-1528
(540)672-4893 (800)358-4422 Fax:(540)672-3028
E-mail: jgearyhh@aol.com
Web: www.holladayhousebandb.com

Circa 1830. Each room in this Federal-style inn is furnished with family pieces and comes with its own sitting area. Rooms are decorated with freshly cut flowers. Breakfast may be served  to guests in their rooms. Specialties include apple muffins and puffs. Nearby attractions include wineries, antique shops, arts and crafts stores and President James Madison's home, Montpelier.

Innkeeper(s): Judy Geary. $95-205. MC, VISA, AX, DS, PC, TC. TAC10. 6 rooms, 4 with PB, 2 suites and 1 conference room. Breakfast, afternoon tea and snacks/refreshments included in rates. Types of meals: Gourmet bkfst and veg bkfst. Beds: QD. Cable TV, phone, ceiling fan, VCR, fireplace and two-person Jacuzzi in room. Air conditioning. Fax, copier and library on premises. Small meetings, family reunions and seminars hosted. Antiquing, art galleries, bicycling, fishing, golf, hiking, horseback riding, live theater, museums, shopping, sporting events and wineries nearby.

"Thank you so much for your wonderful hospitality (and apple puffs, apple puffs, apple puffs!!). We will definitely be back!"

Poquoson   H17

Martin-Wilson House

326 Wythe Creek Rd
Poquoson, VA 23662-1914
(757)868-7070 Fax:(757)868-9651
E-mail: mwilhouse@aol.com

Circa 1929. This historic home, ordered in the late 1920s from a Sears-Roebuck catalog, abounds with country Victorian appointments. Rooms are appointed with antique and floral wallcoverings. There is an antique shop on the premises, as well. There are more than two dozen shops and restaurants to enjoy in the historic village of Poquoson. Attractions at NASA and in Williamsburg aren't far away.

Innkeeper(s): Mary Holloway Barr. $70-110. MC, VISA, PC, TC. 3 rooms. Breakfast included in rates. Types of meals: Full bkfst. Beds: Q. Cable TV, phone and ceiling fan in room. Central air. Amusement parks, antiquing, art galleries, beaches, fishing, golf, museums, parks, shopping and wineries nearby.

Port Haywood   G18

Tabb's Creek Inn

PO Box 219 Rt 14 Mathews Co
Port Haywood, VA 23138-0219
(804)725-5136 Fax:(804)725-5136

Circa 1820. Surrounded by 30 acres of woods and located on the banks of Tabb's Creek, this post-Colonial farm features a detached guest cottage. There are maple, elm, magnolia trees and 150 rose bushes on the property. The suites and guest rooms feature fireplaces and antiques. Boats for rowing and canoeing, docks, a swimming pool, and private waterview porches make this an especially attractive getaway for those seeking a dose of seclusion.

Historic Interest: Williamsburg (45 miles), Norfolk (50 miles), Yorktown (25 miles).

Innkeeper(s): Cabell & Catherine Venable. $125. PC, TC. TAC10. 4 rooms with PB, 1 with FP and 2 suites. Breakfast included in rates. Types of meals: Full bkfst and early coffee/tea. Beds: KQD. Turndown service, ceiling fan and VCR in room. Air conditioning. Fax, copier, swimming, bicycles and library on premises. Weddings, small meetings and family reunions hosted. Antiquing, fishing and fine restaurants nearby.

Pets Allowed.

"A spot of tea with a bit of heaven. Truly exceptional hosts. The best B&Bs I've happened across!"

Prospect   G13

Brooklyn Plantation

897 Brooklyn Plantation Rd
Prospect, VA 23960
(434)574-6853

Circa 1813. An elegant 18th-century atmosphere is imparted at this faithfully restored Colonial home. Secluded on 84 acres of woods, fields and a formal garden, this B&B offers quiet luxury with period antiques throughout. All common rooms as well as one guest bedroom boast fireplaces. Breakfast recipes, often with an historical flavor, are made from scratch with some of the ingredients produced on the plantation. Walk to the pond or rest on benches on the lawn or porch. Visit the area's many historic sites.

Historic Interest: Lee's Retreat (8 miles), Sailor's Creek Battlefield (15 miles), Appomattox Court House National Historic Park (20 miles).

Innkeeper(s): Lynne & Phil Blaker. $70-90. PC, TC. TAC10. 3 rooms, 1 with PB, 1 with FP. Breakfast and snacks/refreshments included in rates. Types of meals: Gourmet bkfst, country bkfst and early coffee/tea. Beds: QDT. Phone and fireplace in room. Central air. Sauna and library on premises. Antiquing, fishing, golf, hiking, museums and parks nearby.

Providence Forge   G16

Jasmine Plantation B&B Inn

4500 N Courthouse Rd
Providence Forge, VA 23140-3428
(804)966-9836 (800)639-5368 Fax:(804)966-5679
E-mail: jasmineinn@aol.com

Circa 1750. Few travelers can boast that they have stayed at a mid-18th-century plantation. Jasmine Plantation is just such a place. Surrounded by more than 40 acres of Virginia countryside, it's not difficult to understand why the Morris family chose this spot for their home.
The property's first dwelling was built as early as the 1680s. Several guest rooms are named for members of the Morris Family, and all are decorated with antiques. The Rose Room features Victorian furnishings  and a whirlpool bath. The George Morris Room includes 19th-century pieces, king size bed, a fireplace and clawfoot tub. Memorabilia from multiple centuries add special charm to the place. The innkeepers have antique irons, old books and magazines, antique dolls and a sampling of vintage advertising signs for Philip Morris or Coca-Cola. Breakfasts are a true Southern treat.

Innkeeper(s): Howard & Joyce Vogt. $80-140. MC, VISA, AX, PC, TC. TAC10. 6 rooms, 5 with PB, 4 with FP. Breakfast and snacks/refreshments included in rates. Types of meals: Full bkfst and early coffee/tea. Beds: KQD. Ceiling fan in room. Air conditioning. VCR on premises. Weddings, small meetings, family reunions and seminars hosted. Amusement parks, antiquing, fishing, golf, sporting clays, horse racing, parks, shopping and water sports nearby.

Publicity: *Area newspapers and Area TV stations.*

"We were charmed by the plantation accommodations and the kindness of the beautiful host and hostess."

Radford   H8

Nesselrod On The New Gardens and Guesthouse

6221 Madison St
Radford, VA 24141-8896
(540)731-4970 Fax:(540)731-4864
E-mail: innkeeper@nesselrod.com
Web: www.nesselrod.com

Circa 1939. Noted architect Everette Fauber designed Nesselrod, a historic Colonial Revival home. The well-appointed grounds include gardens that have been in existence since the home's earliest days. Inside there are four guest rooms; each was given a special name to honor the home's gardens. The rooms include many luxurious amenities, from fine, European linens to specialty bath products to heated towel racks. Guests also are pampered with a lavish, three-course gourmet breakfast. A sample menu might begin with baked pears in custard, followed by Scottish oatmeal with Scotch whiskey, and topped off with baked eggs with locally prepared goat cheese or perhaps blueberry French toast.

Innkeeper(s): Eric Hanson, Moly Hosh, Jennifer Kemp. $105-250. MC, VISA, AX, PC, TC. 4 rooms with PB, 3 with FP, 2 suites and 1 conference room.

Breakfast included in rates. Types of meals: Gourmet bkfst, cont plus, early coffee/tea, afternoon tea and snacks/refreshments. Beds: QT. Cable TV, phone, turndown service and fireplace in room. Central air. VCR and fax on premises. Weddings, small meetings, family reunions and seminars hosted. Antiquing, bicycling, canoeing/kayaking, fishing, golf, hiking, horseback riding, Smithfield Plantation, Claytor Lake, Cascades, new river trail, museums, parks, shopping, sporting events, tennis and wineries nearby.

Publicity: *Roanoke Times and Blue Ridge Country Magazine.*

Stanardsville   D13

South River Cottage

3011 S River Rd
Stanardsville, VA 22973
(434)985-2901 (877)874-4473 Fax:(434)985-3833
E-mail: cbraun@sprintmail.com
Web: www.southrivercottage.com

Circa 1900. In the heart of South River Valley, this original Virginia-style farmhouse has been restored to provide modern comforts while retaining its authentic charm. The spectacular Blue Ridge Mountains are seen from each of the guest bedrooms, some of which feature Jacuzzi tubs for two. A wholesome country breakfast starts the day on this working farm. Hike, fish in one of the ponds or relax in a front porch swing, rocker or hammock. Shenandoah River activities are just a short drive away.

Historic Interest: Monticello (20 miles), Montpelier (15 miles).

Innkeeper(s): Judy & Cliff Braun. $75-179. MC, VISA, AX, DS, PC, TC. TAC10. 3 rooms with PB and 1 suite. Breakfast included in rates. Types of meals: Full bkfst, country bkfst, veg bkfst, early coffee/tea, lunch, picnic lunch and dinner. Beds: QDT. Cable TV and phone in room. Central air. Fax and bicycles on premises. Weddings, small meetings, family reunions and seminars hosted. Antiquing, art galleries, bicycling, canoeing/kayaking, fishing, golf, hiking, horseback riding, live theater, museums, parks, shopping, downhill skiing, sporting events and wineries nearby.

Stanley   D13

Jordan Hollow Farm Inn

326 Hawksbill Park Rd
Stanley, VA 22851-4506
(540)778-2285 (888)418-7000 Fax:(540)778-1759
E-mail: jhf@jordanhollow.com
Web: www.jordanhollow.com

Circa 1790. Nestled in the foothills of the Blue Ridge Mountains, this delightful 145-acre horse farm is ideal for those who love riding and country living. The colonial farm house is decorated with antiques and country artifacts. Horse boarding is available as is five miles of walking trails on the property.

Historic Interest: New Market Battlefield Museum, Luray Caverness, Skyline Drive.

Innkeeper(s): Gail Kyle & Betsy Maitland. $140-190. MC, VISA, DC, CB, DS, PC, TC. TAC10. 15 rooms with PB, 11 with FP and 1 conference room. Breakfast included in rates. Types of meals: Gourmet bkfst, picnic lunch and gourmet dinner. Beds: KQ. Cable TV, phone and whirlpool bath in some rooms in room. Central air. Fax, copier and spa on premises. Weddings, small meetings, family reunions and seminars hosted. Art galleries, canoeing/kayaking, fishing, golf, hiking, horseback riding, parks, shopping, downhill skiing, cross-country skiing, tennis, water sports and wineries nearby.

Publicity: *Country, Southern Living, Conde Nast, New York Times, Country Accents, Family Circle, Glamour, Vogue, Palm Beach and Washingtonian.*

"I keep thinking of my day at your lovely inn and keep dreaming of that wonderful lemon mousse cake!"

Staunton E11

Ashton Country House

1205 Middlebrook Ave
Staunton, VA 24401-4546
(540)885-7819 (800)296-7819 Fax:(540)885-6029
E-mail: ashtonhouse@aol.com
Web: www.bbhost.com/ashtonbnb

Circa 1860. This Greek Revival home is surrounded by 25 explorable acres where cows roam and birds frolic in the trees. A mix of traditional and Victorian antiques grace the interior. Four of the guest rooms include a fireplace, and each is

appointed individually. The inn's porches, where afternoon tea often is served, are lined with chairs for those who seek relaxation and the scenery of rolling hills. Woodrow Wilson's birthplace is among the town's notable attractions.

Innkeeper(s): Dorie & Vince Di Stefano. $70-140. MC, VISA, AX, DS, PC, TC. TAC10. 6 rooms with PB. Breakfast, afternoon tea and snacks/refreshments included in rates. Beds: KQ. Ceiling fan and fireplaces (four bedrooms) in room. Central air. VCR on premises. Handicap access. Small meetings and family reunions hosted. Antiquing, fishing, golf, New Shakespeare Playhouse, museums, parks, shopping and water sports nearby.

Pets allowed: with prior arrangement.

Belle Grae Inn

515 W Frederick St
Staunton, VA 24401-3333
(540)886-5151 (888)541-5151 Fax:(540)886-6641
E-mail: bellegrae@sprynet.com
Web: www.bellegrae.com

Circa 1870. Located in the Newton Historic District, this Victorian-Italianate inn offers 15 distinctive lodging rooms decorated with antiques and keepsakes. Guests can listen to the innkeeper relate the colorful history of the house as they sit and sip refreshments on the veranda and take in the view of nearby Betsy Bell and Mary Gray Mountains, from which the inn derives its name. The restaurant is an indoor/outdoor cafe serving dishes with a Southern flavor. Within walking distance of the inn are President Woodrow Wilson's birthplace, the Statler Brother's Museum and antique shops.

Innkeeper(s): Michael Organ. $99-299. MC, VISA, AX. TAC10. 17 rooms with PB, 14 with FP, 8 suites and 1 conference room. Breakfast and afternoon tea included in rates. Types of meals: Full bkfst. MAP, AP. Beds: KQDT. Cable TV, phone, turndown service, ceiling fan, Some rooms with wet bar and Jacuzzi and veranda in room. Air conditioning. VCR, fax, copier and bicycles on premises. Handicap access. Weddings, small meetings, family reunions and seminars hosted. Spanish spoken. Antiquing, art galleries, bicycling, fishing, golf, hiking, horseback riding, Civil War sites, live theater, museums, parks, shopping, downhill skiing, sporting events, tennis and wineries nearby.

Frederick House

28 N New St
Staunton, VA 24401-4306
(540)885-4220 (800)334-5575 Fax:(540)885-5180
E-mail: stay@frederickhouse.com
Web: www.frederickhouse.com

Circa 1810. Adjacent to Mary Baldwin College, this inn consists of six renovated town houses, the oldest of which is believed to be a copy of a home designed by Thomas Jefferson.

A full breakfast is served in Chumley's Tea Room. Guest rooms (some with fireplaces) are furnished with antiques and feature robes and ceiling fans. Original staircases and woodwork are highlighted throughout. Suites are available.

Historic Interest: Blue Ridge Parkway, Skyline Drive (12 miles), Woodrow Wilson birthplace (2 blocks), Museum of American Frontier Culture (2 miles), Shenadoah Shakespeare Black Friars Play House.

Innkeeper(s): Joe & Evy Harman. $85-170. MC, VISA, AX, DC, DS, PC, TC. TAC10. 23 rooms with PB, 6 with FP, 8 suites and 1 conference room. Breakfast included in rates. Types of meals: Gourmet bkfst and early coffee/tea. Beds: KQDT. Cable TV and phone in room. Air conditioning. Weddings, small meetings, family reunions and seminars hosted. Antiquing, fishing, Skyline Drive Blue Ridge Parkway, live theater, parks, shopping, downhill skiing, cross-country skiing, sporting events and water sports nearby.

Publicity: *Daily News Leader, Richmond Times-Dispatch, News Journal, Washington Post and Blue Ridge Country.*

"Thanks for making the room so squeaky-clean and comfortable! I enjoyed the Virginia hospitality. The furnishings and decor are beautiful."

The Sampson Eagon Inn

238 E Beverley St
Staunton, VA 24401-4325
(540)886-8200 (800)597-9722
E-mail: eagoninn@rica.net
Web: www.eagoninn.com

Circa 1840. The fall leaves provide a colorful backdrop for this pre-Civil War manor. Fresh fruits, homemade bread and specialties such as melt-in-your-mouth Grand Marnier souffle pancakes fill the wonderful breakfast menu and are served with an infor-

mal Southern style and hospitality. Antiques and reproductions from the innkeepers' personal collection decorate the home. Enjoy the charm of Staunton as you visit nearby attractions such as Woodrow Wilson's birthplace and museum (one block away). Monticello is a 35-minute drive through the beautiful countryside.

Historic Interest: The American Frontier Culture Museum is two miles away, and the Stonewall Jackson House & Lee's Tomb is 30 miles away.

Innkeeper(s): Laura & Frank Mattingly. $89-135. MC, VISA, AX. 5 rooms with PB and 2 suites. Breakfast and snacks/refreshments included in rates. Types of meals: Full bkfst and early coffee/tea. Beds: Q. Cable TV, phone and VCR in room. Air conditioning. Fax, copier, library, video library, snack bar and refrigerator on premises. Antiquing, fishing, cycling, hiking, live theater, parks, downhill skiing and sporting events nearby.

Publicity: *Country Inn, Gourmet, Southern Living, Washington Post, Baltimore Sun, Discerning Traveler and Travel & Leisure.*

"Everything was special and you are the most gracious and kind hosts."

Steeles Tavern E11

The Osceola Mill Country Inn

Steeles Tavern, VA 24476
(540)377-6455 (888)278-3462 Fax:(540)377-5148
E-mail: osceolamill@aol.com
Web: www.osceolamill.com

Circa 1849. Fourteen acres and three buildings comprise Osceola Mill Country Inn, once part of the McCormick Farm where Cyrus McCormick farmed. A 27-foot wheel, once driven by the waters of Marl Creek, serves as a constant reminder of the rich history of the area. The inn's open beams retain the rustic feel of the original mill. A 5,000-pound millstone serves as a coffee table. The honeymoon

cottage, formerly the mill store, boasts a great stone fireplace and whirlpool spa. The property provides a babbling brook, river, inviting paths and views of the Blue Ridge Mountains.
Innkeeper(s): Judith & Robert Wycoff. $100-169. MC, VISA, AX, CB, DS, PC. 12 rooms with PB, 1 with FP, 2 suites and 1 conference room. Types of meals: Full bkfst and gourmet dinner. Air conditioning. Fax on premises. Handicap access. Weddings, small meetings, family reunions and seminars hosted. Antiquing, fishing, hiking, biking, live theater, shopping, downhill skiing, cross-country skiing and sporting events nearby.
Publicity: *Richmond News Leader.*

Strasburg   B13

Hotel Strasburg

213 S Holliday St
Strasburg, VA 22657-2213
(540)465-9191 Fax:(540)465-4788
E-mail: thehotel@shentel.net
Web: www.hotelstrasburg.com

Circa 1902. Experience the romance of the Victorian era at this three-story hotel, situated on two acres, just one block from Main Street. Built in 1902 as a hospital, the building was converted into a hotel in 1915 after a doctor ran off with a nurse. Since then, it has been the social hub of Strasburg and offers luxurious accommodations and an exquisite dining area. Each room of the Victorian Clapboard inn holds the finest array of antique furnishings, all of which are for sale. Period pieces are continually brought into the inn from the innkeepers' travels. During their stay, guests enjoy hiking, canoeing, fishing and visiting nearby Civil War battlefields or taking an hour-long drive to Washington, D.C. Enjoy the elegance of Victorian gourmet dining in the hotel's dining room throughout the day.
Historic Interest: Belle Grove Plantation (3 miles), Cedar Creek battlefield (2 miles).
Innkeeper(s): Gary & Carol Rutherford. $79-175. MC, VISA, AX, DC, CB, DS, PC, TC. TAC10. 29 rooms with PB and 1 conference room. Types of meals: Full bkfst, cont plus, lunch, snacks/refreshments and gourmet dinner. Beds: KQDT. Cable TV, phone and some with hot tubs in room. Air conditioning. Fax and copier on premises. Weddings, small meetings, family reunions and seminars hosted. Antiquing, beaches, bicycling, canoeing/kayaking, fishing, golf, hiking, horseback riding, live theater, museums, parks, shopping, downhill skiing, tennis and wineries nearby.
Pets allowed: Call first.
Publicity: *Blue Ridge Country, Washington Post, Washingtonian, Country Victorian and BBC.*

Warm Springs   E10

The Inn at Gristmill Square

PO Box 359
Warm Springs, VA 24484-0359
(540)839-2231 Fax:(540)839-5770
E-mail: grist@va.tds.net

Circa 1800. The inn consists of five restored buildings. The old blacksmith shop and silo, the hardware store, the Steel House and the Miller House all contain guest rooms. (The old mill is now the Waterwheel Restaurant.) A few antiques and old prints appear in some rooms, while others are furnished in

a contemporary style. There are tennis courts and a swimming pool at the inn. A short walk over Warm Springs Mill Stream and down the road brings travelers to historic Warm Springs Pools.

Innkeeper(s): The McWilliams family. $80-100. MC, VISA, DS, TC. TAC10. 17 rooms with PB, 8 with FP, 5 suites and 1 conference room. Breakfast included in rates. Types of meals: Cont, picnic lunch, dinner and room service. MAP, EP. Beds: KQDT. Cable TV and phone in room. Air conditioning. VCR, fax, copier, swimming, sauna and tennis on premises. Weddings, small meetings, family reunions and seminars hosted. Fishing, golf, parks, shopping, downhill skiing, tennis and water sports nearby.
Publicity: *New York Times, Bon Appetit and Colonial Homes.*

"You have such a wonderful inn — such attention to detail and such a considerate staff."

Meadow Lane Lodge

HCR 01 Box 110
Warm Springs, VA 24484-9709
(540)839-5959 Fax:(540)839-2135
E-mail: meadowln@tds.net
Web: meadowlanelodge.com

Circa 1922. Meadow Lane Lodge boasts a colorful history. The lodge is located on a vast, 1,600-acre spread in the Allegheny Mountains, and its acreage was once part of a land grant made by King George III to Charles Lewis, a pioneer settler. The farm also is the site of Fort Dinwiddie, which was visited by George Washington on two occasions. Although the fort is no longer standing, a restored slave cabin still exists and is used as a reading room. An Indian village once rested on the property, and guests might discover an arrowhead while meandering the grounds. There are five guest rooms in the main lodge, decorated with a mix of comfortable furnishings and antiques. In addition to breakfast each day, Saturday night dinners are available by prior arrangement. Guests will find walking and biking trails on the grounds, a swimming hole and perhaps a beaver bog. Deer, fox and a variety of birds are other sights you're sure to see. Guests also can stay in nearby Warm Springs at a restored log house, which dates to 1820. A late 19th-century grain barn, located along the Jackson River, is another lodging option.
Innkeeper(s): Carter & Michelle Ancona. $105-260. MC, VISA, DS. 11 rooms with PB, 3 with FP and 1 conference room. Breakfast included in rates. Types of meals: Full bkfst, country bkfst and picnic lunch. Beds: KQDT. Some with cable TV, coffee maker, refrigerator and telephone in room. Air conditioning. Fax, swimming, stables, bicycles, tennis, library, fishing, hiking, massage, canoes, croquet and barn animals on premises. Weddings, small meetings, family reunions and seminars hosted. Antiquing, art galleries, canoeing/kayaking, fishing, golf, hiking, horseback riding, parks, shopping, downhill skiing, cross-country skiing and tennis nearby.

"This 1600-acre farm was very private and nice."

Warrenton   C14

The Black Horse Inn

8393 Meetze Rd
Warrenton, VA 20187
(540)349-4020 Fax:(540)349-4242
E-mail: blackhrs@citizen.infi.net
Web: www.blackhorseinn.com

Circa 1850. One can easily imagine the days when gracious Southerners gathered at this home to celebrate a successful hunt. Rich in history, the inn is named after an elite Confederate cavalry

unit. Only 45 minutes from Washington, D. C., the home rests on 20 acres of rolling Virginia countryside. A hunt country theme is evident in the inn's decor. Romantic guest rooms are appointed with four-poster canopy beds, fireplaces and Jacuzzi tubs. One guest room alone has inspired more than three dozen marriage proposals. Upon check-in, guests are treated to an afternoon "hunt-country" tea with a sampling of sherry and port wines. Gourmet breakfasts include items such as Inn at Little Washington French Toast, a rich entree stuffed with pecans and mascarpone cheese. Guests can spend the day hiking along the Appalachian Trail or enjoy winetasting, antiquing, cycling, paddling or horseback riding.

Historic Interest: Washington, D.C. (45 miles), Manassas battlefield (20 miles), Appalachian trail (30 miles).

Innkeeper(s): Lynn A. Pirozzoli. $125-295. MC, VISA, AX. TAC10. 8 rooms with PB, 4 with FP, 2 suites and 2 conference rooms. Breakfast and afternoon tea included in rates. Types of meals: Full bkfst, early coffee/tea, picnic lunch and snacks/refreshments. AP. Beds: Q. Turndown service and ceiling fan in room. Air conditioning. Fax, copier, stables, bicycles and library on premises. Weddings, small meetings and family reunions hosted. Antiquing, art galleries, bicycling, canoeing/kayaking, fishing, golf, hiking, horseback riding, health club, live theater, museums, parks, cross-country skiing, sporting events, tennis & wineries nearby. Pets allowed: Horse boarding only.

Publicity: *Washingtonian, Fauquier Magazine and Washington Post.*

Washington   C13

Caledonia Farm - 1812

47 Dearing Rd (Flint Hill)
Washington, VA 22627
(540)675-3693 (800)262-1812

Circa 1812. This gracious Federal-style stone house in the National Register is beautifully situated on 52 acres adjacent to Shenandoah National Park. It was built by a Revolutionary War officer, and his musket is displayed

over a mantel. The house, a Virginia Historic Landmark, has been restored with the original Colonial color scheme retained. All rooms have working fireplaces and provide views of Skyline Drive and the Blue Ridge Mountains. The innkeeper is a retired broadcaster.

Innkeeper(s): Phil Irwin. $140. MC, VISA, DS, PC, TC. TAC10. 2 suites, 3 with FP and 1 conference room. Breakfast and snacks/refreshments included in rates. Types of meals: Gourmet bkfst and early coffee/tea. Beds: D. Phone, turndown service, VCR and skyline Drive View in room. Air conditioning. Fax, copier, spa, bicycles, library, hayride and lawn games on premises. Small meetings, family reunions and seminars hosted. German and Spanish spoken. Antiquing, fishing, wineries, caves, stables, battlefields, live theater, parks, shopping, downhill skiing, cross-country skiing and water sports nearby.

Publicity: *Country, Country Almanac, Country Living, Blue Ridge Country, Discovery, Washington Post, Baltimore Sun. and Pen TV/Cable 15/PBS X3.*

"We've stayed at many, many B&Bs. This is by far the best!"

The Foster-Harris House

189 Main St
Washington, VA 22747
(540)675-3757 (800)666-0153
E-mail: foster-h@juno.com

Circa 1900. This Victorian farmhouse stands on a lot laid out by George Washington and is located at the edge of the village. The streets of the town are exactly as surveyed 225 years ago.

The village has galleries and craft shops as well as the Inn at Little Washington's five-star restaurant.

Historic Interest: Civil War battlefields & museums (less than an hour's drive).

Innkeeper(s): John & Libby Byam. $95-185. MC, VISA, DS. TAC10. 5 rooms with PB, 2 with FP and 1 suite. Breakfast and afternoon tea included in rates. Types of meals: Full bkfst. Beds: QD. Ceiling fan in room. Air conditioning. Small meetings hosted. Antiquing, fishing, live theater, shopping and cross-country skiing nearby.

Publicity: *Richmond Times-Dispatch, Southern Living and Washingtonian.*

Gay Street Inn

PO Box 237, 160 Gay St
Washington, VA 22747
(540)675-3288 Fax:(540)675-1070
E-mail: gaystinn@shentel.net
Web: www.gaystreetinn.com

Circa 1855. After a day of Skyline Drive, Shenandoah National Park and the caverns of Luray and Front Royal, come home to this stucco, gabled farmhouse. If you've booked the fireplace

room, a canopy bed will await you. Furnishings include period Shaker pieces. The innkeepers will be happy to steer you to the most interesting vineyards, organic "pick-your-own" fruit and vegetable farms and Made-In-Virginia food and craft shops. Breakfast and afternoon tea are served in the garden conservatory. Five-star dining is within walking distance at The Inn at Little Washington. The innkeepers can arrange for child care.

Historic Interest: Manassas Battlefield & Park and Chancellorsville are some of the area's many Civil War sites. The University of Virginia, historic Charlottesville and Monticello are other sites in the area, Mosby Country.

Innkeeper(s): Robin & Donna Kevis. $95-135. MC, VISA, AX, PC, TC. TAC10. 4 rooms with PB, 1 with FP and 1 suite. Breakfast and afternoon tea included in rates. Types of meals: Gourmet bkfst, cont plus and early coffee/tea. Beds: Q. Suite has TV in room. Air conditioning. Weddings, small meetings and family reunions hosted. Antiquing, fishing, golf, horseback riding, vineyards, live theater, parks, shopping and water sports nearby.

Pets allowed: Prior notice preferred.

Publicity: *Blue Ridge Country and Food Art.*

"Thank you for a wonderful visit. Your hospitality was superb."

Heritage House B&B

PO Box 427, 291 Main St
Washington, VA 22747
(540)675-3207 Fax:(540)675-1340
E-mail: hhbb@shentel.net
Web: heritagehousebb.com

Circa 1837. This two-story columned house is situated in the heart of the historic district of Washington, a town surveyed by George Washington in 1749. The inn is furnished with antiques and collectables. Guests are welcomed with refreshments and homemade cookies. Breakfasts also are a treat. Fresh fruit plate and homemade baked goods accompany the daily entree, perhaps a smoked salmon hash or Heritage eggs Florentine with artichokes. Wineries and farms are nearby, and guests can walk to craft and antique shops, art galleries, theaters and gourmet dining.

Innkeeper(s): Harry. $105-135. MC, VISA, PC, TC. TAC10. 5 rooms, 4 with PB and 1 suite. Breakfast and afternoon tea included in rates. Types of meals: Gourmet bkfst, lunch and snacks/refreshments. Beds: KQD. Air conditioning. Fax on premises. Weddings and family reunions hosted. Antiquing, fishing, golf, hiking, caverns, birding, world-class dining, live theater, parks,

shopping, tennis and water sports nearby.
Publicity: *Country Almanac* and *Washington Post.*

"Having been to a number of bed & breakfasts, yours is No. 1 in its setting, the wonderful food and your hospitality."

Weyers Cave D12

The Inn at Keezletown Rd B&B

1224 Keezletown Rd
Weyers Cave, VA 22486
(540)234-0644
E-mail: keezlinn@shentel.net
Web: www.keezlinn.com

Circa 1896. This lavender pink Victorian with gingerbread trim was the grandest of several homes built by a local doctor in this quaint Shenandoah Valley village. Rooms are furnished with Oriental rugs and antiques made in the valley. The inn  boasts views of the Blue Ridge Mountains; the grounds include herb and flower gardens and a goldfish pond. The full country breakfasts feature fresh eggs from the inn's chickens. The inn is close to Harrisonburg, Staunton, the airport, James Madison University and other colleges, hiking, auctions and antique shops.

Historic Interest: Civil War battlefields and Woodrow Wilson's birthplace are among the nearby historic attractions.

Innkeeper(s): Sandy & Alan Inabinet. $85-115. MC, VISA, PC, TC. TAC10. 4 rooms with PB. Breakfast included in rates. Types of meals: Full bkfst. Beds: KQT. Cable TV, phone and ceiling fan in room. Air conditioning. Small meetings hosted. Antiquing, fishing, golf, hiking, parks, shopping and downhill skiing nearby.
Publicity: *Daily News Record* and *Cooperative Living.*

"A paradise in microcosm, from your Chanticleer to your Botany. Where else could one breakfast to La Boheme? You provide much more than an inn; each hour here brings reflective joy."

Williamsburg G17

A Williamsburg White House

718 Jamestown Rd
Williamsburg, VA 23185
(757)229-8580 (866)229-8580
E-mail: info@awilliamsburgwhitehouse.com
Web: www.awilliamsburgwhitehouse.com

Circa 1904. One-half mile from historic downtown, this spacious Colonial graces a picturesque neighborhood. Decorated around an elegant and traditional presidential theme, the common rooms include the JFK library, where a fireside game of chess can be played while sipping sherry in a leather chair, and the diplomatic reception room, where afternoon tea and delicious treats are enjoyed. Guest bedrooms are considered presidential suites with four-poster and canopy featherbeds, robes, sitting areas and motif-matching memorabilia. Choose two hot entrees as part of a satisfying breakfast in the Reagan dining room, before a leisurely stroll through the rose garden.

Innkeeper(s): Debbie & John Keane. $125-185. 4 rooms, 1 with PB and 3 suites. Two with fireplaces in room.

Applewood Colonial B&B

605 Richmond Rd
Williamsburg, VA 23185-3539
(757)229-0205 (800)899-2753 Fax:(757)229-2873
E-mail: info@williamsburgbandb.com
Web: www.williamsburgbandb.com

Circa 1928. This stately home was built by the craftsman chosen to meticulously restore and reconstruct Colonial Williamsburg. Using the same high standards and hand-crafted architectural details, it is perfectly located along the Historic Corridor. The classic decor of the Colonial era is evident throughout the well-appointed rooms. Guest bedrooms and suites offer high four-poster canopy beds and boast modern conveniences. A magnificent candlelight breakfast is served on a pedestal table under a crystal chandelier in the dining room. Complimentary afternoon refreshments include fresh baked cookies, Virginia peanuts and beverages. In keeping with its name and extensive apple collection, delicious slices of apple pie are available every evening.

Innkeeper(s): Marty Jones. $100-175. MC, VISA, PC. TAC10. 4 rooms with PB, 1 with FP and 1 suite. Breakfast and snacks/refreshments included in rates. Types of meals: Full bkfst and early coffee/tea. Beds: Q. Cable TV, phone, VCR and hair dryer in room. Air conditioning. Weddings, small meetings, family reunions and seminars hosted. German spoken. Amusement parks, antiquing, fishing, Colonial Williamsburg, historic sites, live theater, parks, shopping, sporting events and water sports nearby.
Publicity: *Discerning Traveler.*

"Our accommodations were the best, and you were most kind."

Cedars

616 Jamestown Rd
Williamsburg, VA 23185-3945
(757)229-3591 (800)296-3591 Fax:(757)229-0756
E-mail: cedars@widomaker.com
Web: www.cedarsofwilliamsburg.com

Circa 1933. This three-story brick Georgian home is a short walk from Colonial Williamsburg and is located across from William and Mary College. Rooms are decorated with traditional antiques, Colonial reproductions, fireplaces and four-poster or canopy beds. The bountiful breakfasts include a hearty entree, fresh fruits, breads, muffins and cereals.

Innkeeper(s): Carol, Jim & Brona Malecha. $95-150. MC, VISA, PC, TC. TAC10. 8 rooms with PB, 2 with FP, 2 suites and 1 cottage. Breakfast included in rates. Types of meals: Full bkfst and early coffee/tea. Beds: KQT. TV and ceiling fan in room. Air conditioning. Library on premises. Family reunions hosted. Amusement parks, antiquing, historic sites, parks and shopping nearby.

Colonial Capital B&B

501 Richmond Rd
Williamsburg, VA 23185-3537
(757)229-0233 (800)776-0570 Fax:(757)253-7667
E-mail: ccbb@widomaker.com
Web: www.ccbb.com

Circa 1926. This three-story Colonial Revival house offers an excellent location three blocks from Colonial Williamsburg. An inviting plantation parlor welcomes guests on cool afternoons with its wood-burning fireplace. Canopied beds include an antique rope bed with turned posts in the York Room. A third-floor suite is comprised of two rooms for couples or families traveling together. Amenities include TVs, VCRs and

phones. Afternoon tea and wine are served in the parlor, porch, patio or deck. The inn has a mascot, a golden retriever. A gourmet breakfast is served.

Innkeeper(s): Barbara & Phil Craig. $76-135. MC, VISA, AX, DS, PC, TC. TAC10. 5 rooms with PB and 1 suite. Breakfast and afternoon tea included in rates. Types of meals: Gourmet bkfst and early coffee/tea. Beds: KQT. Phone, ceiling fan, VCR and hair dryer in room. Air conditioning. Fax, copier, bicycles and library on premises. Weddings, small meetings and family reunions hosted. Amusement parks, antiquing, fishing, biking, living museums, live theater, parks, shopping and water sports nearby.
Publicity: *Washington Post, Country Inns, Mid-Atlantic and The Romantic Southwest.*

"This stay will always be for me a wonderful 'souvenir' thanks to Barbara and Phil."

The Fife & Drum Inn

441 Prince George St
Williamsburg, VA 23185
(757)345-1776 (888)838-1783 Fax:(757)253-1675
E-mail: bscruggs@fifeanddruminn.com
Web: www.fifeanddruminn.com

Circa 1933. Having the distinction of being the only inn in the historic downtown area, the inn occupies the second floor of the Hitchens Building, which is noted for being instrumental in the restoration of Colonial Williamsburg. Furnished with the decor and ambiance of the 18th century with a modern streak, the common room includes a library of local interest publications, a relaxing sitting area and Colonial games to play by the fireplace. Beverages are available around the clock. Guest bedrooms and suites feature upscale amenities like fragrant imported bath products, cotton linens, fluffy duvets and plush robes. Folk art, signed originals, family heirlooms, maps, prints and local archaeological artifacts showcase attention to detail. Southern hospitality is generous, offering a breakfast buffet with a fresh fruit bowl, hot, flaky biscuits stuffed with thinly sliced Virginia ham and entrees ranging from an egg and cheese strata to blueberry French toast.

Historic Interest: Colonial Williamsburg (1 block).
Innkeeper(s): Sharon, Billy Scruggs. $145-165. MC, VISA, AX, DS. TAC10. 9 rooms, 7 with PB and 2 suites. Breakfast and snacks/refreshments included in rates. Types of meals: Full bkfst, country bkfst and early coffee/tea. Beds: KQT. Cable TV, phone, ceiling fan and VCR in room. Central air. Library on premises. Small meetings and family reunions hosted. Amusement parks, antiquing, art galleries, beaches, bicycling, fishing, golf, hiking, live theater, museums, parks, shopping, tennis, water sports and wineries nearby.
Publicity: *The Virginia Gazette.*

Liberty Rose B&B

1022 Jamestown Rd
Williamsburg, VA 23185-3434
(757)253-1260 (800)545-1825
Web: www.libertyrose.com

Circa 1922. This cozy retreat, located on the historic corridor, is tucked among tall trees only a mile from Colonial Williamsburg. The owner of Jamestown constructed this two-story clapboard home. The entry porch is marked with the millstone from one of Williamsburg's old mills. Antiques and collectibles abound in each of the rooms. The innkeepers have merged modern amenities with turn-of-the-century atmosphere. All rooms include telephones, TVs and VCRs with an excellent selection of movies. A gourmet country breakfast is served each morning. Each of the romantic guest rooms features something unique such as a lush canopy bed.

Honeymooners — the inn is often full of newlyweds — often return to celebrate their anniversaries.

Historic Interest: Colonial Williamsburg (1 mile), Jamestown 1607 (4 miles), Yorktown (12 miles), College of William & Mary (1/2 mile).
Innkeeper(s): Brad & Sandi Hirz. $155-225. MC, VISA, AX. 4 rooms with PB, 2 with FP and 3 suites. Breakfast included in rates. Types of meals: Full bkfst. Beds: Q. Cable TV, phone and VCR in room. Antiquing, live theater and water sports nearby.
Publicity: *Country Inns, Washington Post, Rural Living, Los Angeles Times, Glamour, Country Victoria, Bedrooms & Baths and Travel Magazine* (Romantic Weekends).

"More delightful than we could possibly have imagined. Charm & romance abounds when you walk into the house."

Newport House

710 S Henry St
Williamsburg, VA 23185-4113
(757)229-1775 Fax:(757)229-6408

Circa 1988. This neo-Palladian house is a 1756 design by Peter Harrison, architect of rebuilt Williamsburg State House. It features wooden rusticated siding. Colonial country dancing is

held in the inn's ballroom on Tuesday evenings. Guests are welcome to participate. There are English and American antiques, and reproductions include canopy beds in all the guest rooms. The host was a museum director and captain of a historic tall ship.

Historic Interest: Newport House is within walking distance of Colonial Williamsburg. Jamestown is six miles, Yorktown is a 12-mile drive from the inn. The historic James River Plantations are scattered throughout the area.
Innkeeper(s): John & Cathy Millar. $135-165. PC, TC. TAC10. 2 rooms with PB and 1 conference room. Breakfast included in rates. Types of meals: Full bkfst. Beds: QT. TV and VCR in room. Air conditioning. Fax and library on premises. Weddings, small meetings, family reunions and seminars hosted. French spoken. Amusement parks, antiquing, golf, historic buildings, parks, shopping, tennis and water sports nearby.
Publicity: *Innsider and Mid-Atlantic Country.*

"Host and hostess were charming and warm."

Piney Grove at Southall's Plantation-1790

PO Box 1359
Williamsburg, VA 23187-1359
(804)829-2480 Fax:(804)829-6888
E-mail: pineygrove@erols.com
Web: www.pineygrove.com

Circa 1790. Family heirlooms and antiques furnish the 1857 Ladysmith House, a modest Antebellum plantation home. Spacious guest bedrooms and suites offer modern amenities including coffee makers, refrigerators and hair dryers, which are appreciated as much as the historic artifacts and decor. After the farm bell rings, a hearty plantation breakfast is served by candlelight in the 1790 Log Room, a rare Tidewater log building listed in the National Register. Walk the nature trails, and then take a refreshing dip in the pool. Enjoy a barnyard of farm animals, a gazebo, gardens and lawn games. Relax with a mint julep on the front porch or a vintage selection from the Piney Grove wine cellar, enjoyed fireside.

Historic Interest: Colonial Williamsburg, the James River Plantations, and Civil War battlefields are some of the area's many historic attractions.
Innkeeper(s): Gordineer Family. $140-280. PC. TAC10. 5 rooms with PB, 5

with FP, 2 suites and 1 conference room. Types of meals: Full bkfst and snacks/refreshments. Beds: DT. TV and turndown service in room. Air conditioning. VCR, fax and swimming on premises. Limited German spoken. Amusement parks, antiquing, fishing, and plantation tours, live theater, parks, shopping, sporting events and water sports nearby.

Publicity: *New York Times, Richmond Times-Dispatch, Washington Post and Southern Living.*

"Thank you for your warm, gracious hospitality. We really enjoyed ourselves and look forward to returning."

Williamsburg Manor B&B

600 Richmond Rd
Williamsburg, VA 23185-3540
(757)220-8011 (800)422-8011 Fax:(757)220-0245
E-mail: thecateringoc@rcn.com

Circa 1927. Built during the reconstruction of Colonial Williamsburg, this Georgian brick Colonial is just three blocks from the historic village. A grand staircase, culinary library, Waverly fabrics, Oriental rugs and antiques are featured. Breakfasts begin with fresh fruits and home-baked breads, followed by a special daily entree. Gourmet regional Virginia dinners also are available.

Historic Interest: Historic Williamsburg (3 blocks), Jamestown (5 miles), Yorktown (20 miles), William & Mary College (1 block).

Innkeeper(s): Laura Reeves. $75-150. MC, VISA, PC. TAC10. 5 rooms, 4 with PB and 1 suite. Breakfast included in rates. Types of meals: Gourmet bkfst, cont plus, picnic lunch and gourmet dinner. Beds: QT. Cable TV and ceiling fan in room. Air conditioning. VCR and fax on premises. Weddings, small meetings, family reunions and seminars hosted. Amusement parks, antiquing, fishing, golf, live theater, parks, shopping, sporting events, tennis and water sports nearby.

Publicity: *Virginia Gazette, Williamsburg, Daily Press, Washington Post and San Francisco Examiner.*

"Lovely accommodations - scrumptious breakfast."

Woodstock   C13

The Inn at Narrow Passage

PO Box 608
Woodstock, VA 22664-0608
(540)459-8000 (800)459-8002 Fax:(540)459-8001
E-mail: innkeeper@innatnarrowpassage.com
Web: www.innatnarrowpassage.com

Circa 1740. This log inn has been welcoming travelers since the time settlers took refuge here against the Indians. Later, it served as a stagecoach inn on the old Valley Turnpike, and in 1862, it was Stonewall Jackson's headquarters. Most guest rooms feature working fireplaces and views of the Shenandoah River and Massanutten Mountains.

Historic Interest: Shenandoah County Courthouse (5 minutes), Cedar Creek Battlefield (15 minutes), New Market Battlefield (20 minutes).

Innkeeper(s): Ellen & Ed Markel. $95-145. MC, VISA. 12 rooms with PB. Breakfast included in rates. Types of meals: Full bkfst. Beds: Q. TV and phone in room. Antiquing, fishing, horseback riding, hiking, caverns nearby and water sports nearby.

Publicity: *Southern Living, Washington Post, Washington Times and Richmond Times-Dispatch.*

Woolwine   I9

The Mountain Rose B&B Inn

1787 Charity Hwy
Woolwine, VA 24185
(276)930-1057 Fax:(276)930-2165
E-mail: info@mountainrose-inn.com
Web: www.mountainrose-inn.com

Circa 1901. This historic Victorian inn, once the home of the Mountain Rose Distillery, sits on 100 acres of forested hills with plenty of hiking trails. A trout-stocked stream goes through the property and a swimming pool provides recreation. Each room has an antique mantled fireplace, which have been converted to gas logs. Guests can relax by the pool or in rocking chairs on one of the six porches. The innkeepers look forward to providing guests with casually elegant hospitality in the Blue Ridge Mountains. The Blue Ridge Parkway, Mabry Mill, The Reynolds Homestead, Laurel Hill J. EB Stuart Birthplace, Patrick County Courthouse and the Patrick County Historical Museum are located nearby. A three-course breakfast is offered every morning.

Innkeeper(s): Melodie Pogue & Reeves Simms. $99-119. MC, VISA, DS, PC, TC. TAC10. 5 rooms with PB, 5 with FP. Breakfast and afternoon tea included in rates. Types of meals: Gourmet bkfst and early coffee/tea. Beds: KQT. 5 working fireplaces in room. Air conditioning. VCR, fax, copier, swimming, bicycles and trout-stocked creek on premises. Weddings, small meetings, family reunions and seminars hosted. Antiquing, fishing, golf, hiking, Nascar racing, parks, shopping, tennis, water sports and wineries nearby.

Publicity: *Enterprise, Bill Mountain Bugle, New York Times, The Parkway Edition and "Best Romantic Getaway" City Magazine.*

Old Spring Farm Bed & Breakfast, Ltd.

7629 Charity Hwy
Woolwine, VA 24185
(540)930-3404
Web: www.oldspringfarm.com

Circa 1883. Country French decor complements period pieces and collectibles in this two-story farmhouse and separate retreat house. This mountain hideaway is located in Blue Ridge wine country with five wineries nearby. The Calamity Jane Room is perfect for a romantic occasion, offering a Jacuzzi and a private balcony that overlooks a pastoral setting featuring a pond. A hearty breakfast for the gourmand begins with farm produce and fresh breads with homemade jams, followed by a variety of delectable entrees. Ask Suzanne for a guided tour to view the Appaloosa horses raised here.

Innkeeper(s): Suzanne V. Pabst. $100-110. MC, VISA, PC, TC. 4 rooms, 2 with PB and 1 conference room. Types of meals: Gourmet bkfst, early coffee/tea, picnic lunch, snacks/refreshments and gourmet dinner. Beds: QDT. TV and ceiling fan in room. Central air. VCR on premises. Small meetings and family reunions hosted. Antiquing, art galleries, canoeing/kayaking, fishing, golf, hiking, horseback riding, swimming, Winston Cup Stock Car Race, museums, shopping, sporting events and wineries nearby.

Washington

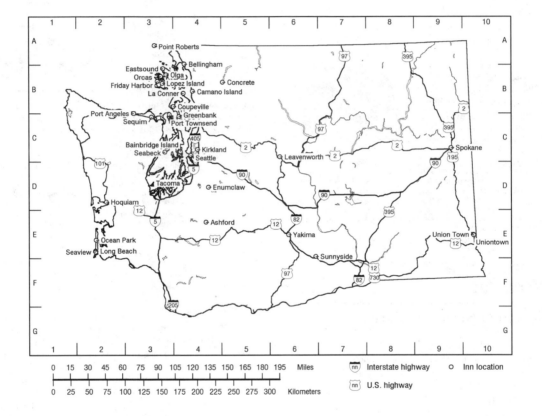

0 15 30 45 60 75 90 105 120 135 150 165 180 195   Miles

0 25 50 75 100 125 150 175 200 225 250 275 300   Kilometers

Interstate highway   Inn location

U.S. highway

Aberdeen/Cosmopolis   D2

Cooney Mansion B&B

PO Box 54, 1705 Fifth St
Aberdeen/Cosmopolis, WA 98537-0054
(360)533-0602 (800)977-7823
E-mail: cooney@cooneymansion.com
Web: www.cooneymansion.com

Circa 1908. This former lumber magnate's home, in a wooded setting, boasts 37 rooms. In the National Register, it was built with a ballroom in the daylight basement, nine bedrooms and eight bathrooms. There are soaking tubs in five of the rooms. The inn features original mission furnishings, and the Cooney suite has a fireplace, TV and VCR and original "rainfall" shower. Guests can enjoy the National Award Winning Lumber Baron's Breakfast.

Innkeeper(s): Judi & Jim Lohr. $65-185. MC, VISA, DC, CB, DS, TC. 8 rooms, 5 with PB, 1 with FP, 1 suite and 1 conference room. Breakfast and afternoon tea included in rates. Types of meals: Full bkfst, country bkfst, veg bkfst and early coffee/tea. Beds: KQDT. One with fireplace, VCR, refrigerator, coffee maker and most with TV in room. VCR, fax, spa, sauna, tennis, library and golf on premises. Weddings, small meetings, family reunions and seminars hosted. Antiquing, art galleries, beaches, canoeing/kayaking, fishing, golf, hiking, horseback riding, whale watching, rain forest, live theater, museums, parks, shopping, tennis and water sports nearby.

Publicity: *Sunset Magazine, Travel & Leisure, Country Inns, Northwest Travel, Seattle Times and Spokane Review.*

"A good B&B should offer the comforts of home, serenity, relaxation and good company. You gave us all we expected and more. Thanks for a romantic weekend."

Ashford   E4

Storm King B&B, Spa and Cabins

37311 SR 706
Ashford, WA 98304
(360)569-2964 Fax:(360)569-2339

Circa 1890. Guests at Storm King will appreciate the cozy, rustic setting of this 100-year-old mountain home located a mile from the Nisqually entrance to Mt. Rainier National Park on Highway 706. Guest rooms are large and feature comfortable furnishings, quilts and fresh flowers. A vegetarian mountain breakfast is served each morning. The breakfast is a great start to a day of hiking or cross-country skiing. The inn is an ideal location for park visitors and is four miles from the village of Ashford.

Innkeeper(s): Steve Brown & Deborah Sample. $70-110. MC, VISA, PC, TC. 3 rooms, 1 with PB. Types of meals: Veg bkfst. Spa, spa treatments and massage therapy and vegetarian cont-plus breakfast on premises. Cross-country skiing nearby.

Bainbridge Island   C4

Buchanan Inn

8494 NE Oddfellows Rd
Bainbridge Island, WA 98110
(206)780-9258 (800)598-3926 Fax:(206)842-9458
E-mail: jgibbs@buchananinn.com

Circa 1912. A short ferry ride will take you from Seattle's harbor to quaint Bainbridge Island and this New England-style barn house. The acre-and-a-half of grounds are dotted with gardens. Each of the guest rooms includes beds topped with luxurious Egyptian cotton linens, and two rooms include a fire-

place. Guests are pampered with a glass of wine in the evenings and a full breakfast each morning. The breakfasts are served on fine china and include gourmet coffee, fresh fruit, homemade baked goods and entrees such as Northwest Eggs Benedict or a ham and brie strata. Bainbridge Island offers many restaurants, shops and galleries. Guests can explore the island or head into Seattle. After a day in the city, return to the serenity of the island and inn, relaxing perhaps in the inn's hot tub, which is located in a little cedar cottage.

Innkeeper(s): Ron & Judy Gibbs. $119-169. MC, VISA, AX, DS, PC, TC. TAC10. 4 rooms with PB, 2 with FP and 2 suites. Breakfast and snacks/refreshments included in rates. Types of meals: Gourmet bkfst. Beds: KQ. Ceiling fan, hair dryers and robes in room. Fax, spa and library on premises. Weddings, small meetings and family reunions hosted. Antiquing, art galleries, beaches, bicycling, canoeing/kayaking, fishing, golf, hiking, live theater, museums, parks, shopping, cross-country skiing, tennis, water sports and wineries nearby.

"Would you adopt me so I can stay here."

Bellingham   B4

Schnauzer Crossing

4421 Lakeway Dr
Bellingham, WA 98226-5119
(360)734-2808 (800)562-2808
E-mail: schnauzerx@aol.com
Web: www.schnauzercrossing.com

Circa 1938. This contemporary Northwest house, nestled among tall evergreens and overlooking Lake Whatcom, is an outdoor lover's delight, with fishing, boating and swimming nearby. Maple, dogwood and birch trees abound, and fresh raspberries and blueberries can be picked from the garden. Guests enjoy lake or garden views from their comfortable rooms and the cottage. All rooms feature fresh flowers. The inn offers extensive gardens including a tea house, a wisteria covered pergola and a koi pond.

Innkeeper(s): Vermont & Donna McAllister. $125-215. MC, VISA, DS. 3 rooms with PB, 1 suite and 1 cottage. Types of meals: Full bkfst. Beds: KQ. Spa on premises.

Publicity: *Seattle Post-Intelligencer and Oregonian.*

"A lovely retreat. We'll be sure to return."

Camano Island   B4

Camano Island Inn

1054 S West Camano Dr
Camano Island, WA 98292
(360)387-0783 (888)718-0783 Fax:(360)387-4173
E-mail: rsvp@camanoislandinn.com
Web: camanoislandinn.com

Circa 1900. This waterfront Craftsman-style inn, located an
hour from Seattle or the Canadian border, was recently ranked
by Travel and Leisure Magazine as one of the top five B&Bs in
the country. All six guest rooms are waterfront, each with a private deck and view of Puget Sound and the Olympic
Mountains. Decorated in a romantic style, all rooms offer a luxurious bath and feature canopy featherbeds topped with down
comforters and plenty of pillows. Full breakfasts are served in
the dining room or delivered to rooms in baskets and include
homemade baked goods and fresh fruit, often from the inn's
own orchard. The innkeepers can arrange for massage services
or provide a kayak.

Innkeeper(s): Jon & Kari Soth. $120-195. MC, VISA, AX, DS, PC, TC.
TAC10. 6 rooms with PB and 1 conference room. Breakfast, afternoon tea
and snacks/refreshments included in rates. Types of meals: Full bkfst and
early coffee/tea. Beds: KQ. Cable TV, phone and VCR in room. Fax, copier,
spa, swimming, library, kayaks, massage and wine/beer/champagne on
premises. Handicap access. Weddings, small meetings, family reunions and
seminars hosted. Antiquing, art galleries, beaches, canoeing/kayaking, fishing, golf and hiking nearby.

Concrete   B5

Ovenell's Heritage Inn B&B

46276 Concrete Sauk Valley Rd
Concrete, WA 98237-9217
(360)853-8494 Fax:(360)853-8279
E-mail: breakfast@ovenells-inn.com
Web: www.ovenells-inn.com

Circa 1910. This historic farmhouse is part of a ranch that was
established in the late 19th century. The ranch includes more
than 500 acres boasting views of the Cascade Mountains. The
home itself was built in 1910 and is decorated in period style.
The accommodations include guest rooms in the main house,
which are decorated with antiques. A guesthouse includes two
suites with a common area with a living room and kitchen.
Several cabins, more rustic in style with exposed log walls and
country furnishings, also are available. In the mornings, a
gourmet breakfast is served with items such as fresh fruit,
homemade muffins and soufflés. The meal is served in a dining
room that looks out toward Mt. Baker.

Historic Interest: Town of Concrete (3 miles), Rockport (8 miles),
Marblemount (12 miles), Newhalem (32 miles).

Innkeeper(s): Eleanor, Norm, Cindy & Kris Ovenell. $75-115. MC, VISA, AX,
DS, PC. 9 rooms, 6 with PB, 3 with FP, 3 cabins and 1 guest house.
Breakfast and snacks/refreshments included in rates. Types of meals: Full
bkfst, country bkfst and early coffee/tea. Beds: QDT. Cable TV, phone, ceiling
fan, VCR and fireplace in room. Central air. Fax, copier and library on premises. Weddings, small meetings, family reunions and seminars hosted.
Antiquing, bicycling, canoeing/kayaking, fishing, hiking, horseback riding,
museums, parks, shopping and cross-country skiing nearby.

Coupeville   B4

Colonel Crockett Farm

1012 S Fort Casey Rd
Coupeville, WA 98239-9753
(360)678-3711 Fax:(360)678-3707
E-mail: email@crockettfarm.com
Web: www.crockettfarm.com

Circa 1855. In the National Register, this Victorian farmhouse
presides over 40 island acres of lawns, meadows and country
gardens. Sweeping views of Crockett Lake and Admiralty Inlet

may be enjoyed from the inn and
its grounds. The
Crockett Room, a
favorite of newlyweds,
has a blue chintz
canopied bed and a sit-
ting area with bay window. Danny DeVito, Michael Douglas
and Kathleen Turner stayed at the inn during the Coupeville
filming of War of the Roses.

Innkeeper(s): Bob & Beulah Whitlow. $75-105. MC, VISA. 5 rooms with PB.
Breakfast included in rates. Types of meals: Full bkfst. Beds: KQD. Small
meetings, family reunions and seminars hosted. Antiquing, live theater and
shopping nearby.

Publicity: *Peninsula, Portland Oregonian, Country Inns and Glamour.*

"Everyone felt quite at home...such a beautiful spot."

Inn at Penn Cove

702 N Main
Coupeville, WA 98239
(360)678-8000 (800)688-2683
E-mail: penncove@whidbey.net

Circa 1887. Two restored historic houses, one a fanciful white
and peach Italianate confection in the National Register, comprise the inn. Each house contains only three guest rooms
affording a variety of small parlors for guests to enjoy. The most
romantic accommodation is Desiree's Room with a fireplace, a
whirlpool tub for two and mesmerizing views of Puget Sound
and Mt. Baker.

Innkeeper(s): Gladys & Mitchell Howard. $60-125. MC, VISA, AX, DS, PC,
TC. TAC10. 6 rooms, 4 with PB, 3 with FP. Breakfast and afternoon tea
included in rates. Types of meals: Gourmet bkfst and veg bkfst. Beds: KQ.
Cable TV and ceiling fan in room. VCR, library, pump organ and music box
on premises. Small meetings and family reunions hosted. Antiquing, beaches,
bicycling, fishing, golf, hiking, horseback riding, live theater, museums, parks,
shopping and wineries nearby.

Publicity: *Whidbey News-Times, Country Inns and Glamour.*

*"Our hosts were warm and friendly, but also gave us plenty of space
and privacy - a good combination."*

Eastsound   B3

Turtleback Farm Inn

1981 Crow Valley Rd
Eastsound, WA 98245
(360)376-4914 (800)376-4914
E-mail: turtleback@interisland.net

Circa 1895. Guests will delight in the beautiful views afforded
from this farmhouse and the newly constructed Orchard
House, which overlooks 80 acres of forest and farmland, duck

ponds and Mt. Constitution to the east. Rooms feature antique furnishings and many boast views of the farm, orchard or sheep pasture.

Beds are covered with wool comforters made from sheep raised on the property. Bon Appetit highlighted some of the breakfast recipes served at Turtleback; a breakfast here is a memorable affair. Tables set with bone china, silver and fresh linens make way for a delightful mix of fruits, juice, award-winning granola, homemade breads and specialty entrees. Evening guests can settle down with a game or a book in the fire-lit parlor as they enjoy sherry, tea or hot chocolate.

Historic Interest: Orcas Island, once the apple capital of Washington, features many historic sites. The Orcas Island Historical Museum and Crow Valley School Museum are among several options.

Innkeeper(s): William & Susan C. Fletcher. $80-225. MC, VISA, DS, PC, TC. TAC10. 11 rooms with PB, 4 with FP. Breakfast included in rates. Types of meals: Full bkfst, early coffee/tea and picnic lunch. Beds: KQD. Library and refrigerator & self-serve beverage bar in dining room on premises. Handicap access. Weddings and family reunions hosted. Spanish and limited French spoken. Fishing, live theater, parks, shopping and water sports nearby.

Publicity: *Los Angeles Times, USA Today, Travel & Leisure, Contra Costa Sun, Seattle Times, Northwest Living, Sunset, Food & Wine, Gourmet, Northwest Travel, New York Times and Alaska Air.*

"A peaceful haven for soothing the soul."

Enumclaw   D4

White Rose Inn

1610 Griffin Ave
Enumclaw, WA 98022-2824
(360)825-7194 (800)404-7194 Fax:(360)802-2472
E-mail: innkeepr@whiteroseinnbb.com
Web: www.whiteroseinnbb.com

Circa 1920. Axel Hanson, owned the White River Lumber Company, built this 22-room, 8,500-square-foot Colonial man-

sion with Honduran mahogany and quarter-sawn oak. A large canopied four-poster cherry bed, crystal chandelier, and original fresco ceilings appropriately adorn the Paradise Room. There is a

rose garden, sunroom and formal dining room. Guests enjoy walking to town for dinner and shopping.

Innkeeper(s): Michael & Tami Dunn. $85-95. Breakfast included in rates. Types of meals: Full bkfst. Weddings, small meetings, family reunions and seminars hosted. Antiquing, hiking, biking, Mount Ranier, shopping, downhill skiing and cross-country skiing nearby.

Friday Harbor   B3

Panacea Bed & Breakfast

595 Park St
Friday Harbor, WA 98250
(360)378-3757 (800)639-2762 Fax:(360)378-8543
E-mail: stay@panacea-inn.com
Web: www.panacea-inn.com

Circa 1907. As the name promises, a getaway to this San Juan Island retreat should lift the spirits, relieve the stress of everyday life and inspire romance. Industrialist Peter Kirk,

who later founded the town of Kirkland, built this early 20th-century Craftsman as a vacation home. The Schutte family purchased and meticulously restored the home, maintaining the original woodwork and stained glass. Each of the four guest rooms has a private entrance. Two romantic rooms include a Jacuzzi tub and fireplace. Arts and Crafts furnishings and decor are a perfect complement to the Craftsman architecture. In the afternoons, refreshments are served on the veranda. After dinner, return to the bed & breakfast and you'll find chocolates and cordials set up on the sideboard. Breakfasts include the height of gourmet cuisine. One menu includes caviar, a summer fruit medley with pecan toffee and an entree such as eggs Florentine.

Innkeeper(s): Beverly & Bruce Schutte. $130-180. MC, VISA, DS, PC, TC. 4 rooms with PB, 1 with FP and 2 suites. Breakfast, afternoon tea and snacks/refreshments included in rates. Types of meals: Gourmet bkfst, early coffee/tea, picnic lunch and room service. Beds: KQ. Cable TV, turndown service and ceiling fan in room. Fax on premises. Small meetings hosted. Antiquing, fishing, golf, live theater, parks, shopping, tennis and water sports nearby.

San Juan Inn B&B

50 Spring St, Box 776
Friday Harbor, WA 98250-0776
(360)378-2070 (800)742-8210 Fax:(360)378-2027
E-mail: sanjuaninn@rockisland.com
Web: www.san-juan.net/sjinn

Circa 1873. In the National Register, this old European-style hotel is filled with stained glass, old photographs and flowers picked from the inn's garden. A Victorian settee is situated under a cherry tree within sniffing distance of the lilacs and roses. It's a half-block to the ferry landing.

Innkeeper(s): Linda Francis. $65-225. MC, VISA, AX, DS, PC, TC. TAC10. 10 rooms, 4 with PB and 2 suites. Breakfast included in rates. Types of meals: Cont plus. Beds: KQDT. Cable TV, ceiling fan and VCR in room. Fax and spa on premises. Small meetings and family reunions hosted. Spanish spoken. Fishing, live theater, parks, shopping and water sports nearby.

Greenbank   C4

Guest House Log Cottages

24371-SR 525, Whidbey Island
Greenbank, WA 98253
(360)678-3115
E-mail: guesthse@whidbey.net
Web: www.guesthouselogcottages.com

Circa 1925. These storybook cottages and log home are nestled within a peaceful forest on 25 acres. The log cabin features stained-glass and criss-cross paned windows that give it the feel of a gingerbread house. Four of the cottages are log construction. Ask for the Lodge and enjoy a private setting with a pond just beyond the deck. Inside are two Jacuzzi tubs, a stone fireplace, king bed, antiques and a luxurious atmosphere.

Innkeeper(s): Don & Mary Jane Creger. $165-325. MC, VISA, DS, PC, TC. 6 cottages. Breakfast included in rates. Types of meals: Full bkfst. Beds: KQ. Ceiling fan, VCR, kitchen and Jacuzzi in room. Air conditioning. Fax, copier, spa and swimming pool on premises. Antiquing, fishing, golf, parks, shopping and tennis nearby.

Publicity: *Los Angeles Times, Woman's Day, Sunset, Country Inns and Bride's.*

"The wonderful thing is to be by yourselves and rediscover what's important."

Hoquiam   D2

Hoquiam's Castle Bed & Breakfast

515 Chenault Ave
Hoquiam, WA 98550
(360)533-2005 (877)542-2785 Fax:(360)533-2005
E-mail: carpld@olynet.com

Circa 1897. This Victorian mansion is listed in the National Register. Recently restored to its original splendor, stained- and leaded-glass windows; wood columns and floors; and crystal chandeliers all enhance the antique furnishings. Soft music plays in the parlor, while the den provides videos, books, games and an afternoon and evening snack. The guest bedrooms are impeccably decorated, each a splendid showcase. They offer grand views of the harbor and the town, as does the turret, porch and garden. A generous gourmet breakfast is served in the privacy of the guest bedrooms, the tea room or dining room. Public tours of the Castle are available daily.

Innkeeper(s): Linda & David Carpenter. $75-140. MC, VISA, AX, PC, TC. TAC10. 5 rooms with PB and 2 suites. Breakfast, afternoon tea and snacks/refreshments included in rates. Types of meals: Gourmet bkfst and veg bkfst. AP. Beds: KQD. TV, phone, turndown service, VCR and fireplace in room. Copier and library on premises. Weddings, small meetings, family reunions and seminars hosted. Antiquing, beaches, bicycling, canoeing/kayaking, fishing, golf, hiking, horseback riding, live theater, museums, parks and shopping nearby.

Publicity: *Seattle P.I.*

Kirkland   C4

Shumway Mansion

11410 99th Pl NE
Kirkland, WA 98033
(425)823-2303 Fax:(425)822-0421
E-mail: info@shumwaymansion.com

Circa 1909. This resplendent 24-room, 10,000-square-foot mansion is situated on more than two acres overlooking Juanita Bay. With a large ballroom and veranda, few could guess that a short time ago, the building was hoisted on hydraulic lifts. It was then pulled three miles across town to its present site, near the beach.

Innkeeper(s): Richard & Salli Harris, Julie Blakemore. $85-120. MC, VISA, AX. TAC10. 7 rooms, 8 with PB and 1 suite. Breakfast included in rates. Types of meals: Full bkfst. Beds: Q. TV, phone and fans in room. Weddings, small meetings, family reunions and seminars hosted. Antiquing, fishing, live theater, shopping, sporting events and water sports nearby.

Publicity: *Northgate Journal, Journal American and Northwest Living.*

"Guests enjoy the mansion so much they don't want to leave — Northwest Living."

La Conner   B4

The White Swan Guest House

15872 Moore Rd
La Conner, WA 98273-7139
(360)445-6805

Circa 1898. Guests will marvel at innkeeper Peter Goldfarb's beautiful gardens as they wind up the driveway to reach this charming, yellow Victorian farmhouse. Inside, guests are greeted with luscious home-baked chocolate chip cookies in the bright, cheery kitchen and a vegetarian breakfast in the morning. Guest rooms are filled with comfortable, Victorian furnishings, and there's even a cozy Garden

Cottage to stay in, complete with its own kitchen and private sun deck. Each April, the area is host to the Skagit Valley Tulip festival. La Conner, a nearby fishing village, is full of shops and galleries to explore.

Historic Interest: The White Swan is only an hour from the historic sites of Seattle and about 90 miles from Vancouver. The new Museum of Northwest Art and the Skagit Historical Museum are both located in downtown La Conner.

Innkeeper(s): Peter Goldfarb. $75-160. MC, VISA, PC, TC. TAC10. 3 rooms and 1 cottage. Breakfast included in rates. Types of meals: Cont plus and early coffee/tea. Beds: KQD. Turndown service in room. Family reunions hosted. Antiquing, fishing, art museum and galleries, parks and shopping nearby.

Publicity: *Country Home, Bird & Blooms, Better Homes & Gardens and Ernst Commercial.*

"This has been a very pleasant interlude. What a beautiful, comfortable place you have here. We will be back."

Leavenworth   C6

Mrs. Andersons Lodging House

917 Commercial St
Leavenworth, WA 98826-1413
(509)548-6173 (800)253-8990 Fax:(509)548-9113
E-mail: info@quiltersheaven.com
Web: www.quiltersheaven.com

Circa 1895. This historic home is named for the widow that purchased the place just a few years after its 1895 construction. In order to support herself and two daughters, Mrs. Anderson transformed the place into a boarding house. Today, it still provides a cozy, relaxing haven for guests. Rooms feature whimsical names, such as the Double Wedding Ring, Grandmother's Flower Garden, Moon Over the Mountain and Leavenworth Nine Patch. As one might deduct, quilters are welcome here. In fact, quilting getaways are available and the home includes a shop filled with quilting supplies, quilting books, fabrics, stencils and other like items. Non-quilters can relax on the sun deck and enjoy the view. Leavenworth is known for its German heritage, and you'll find plenty of shops and boutiques, as well as many outdoor activities.

Innkeeper(s): Dee & Al Howie. $39-65. MC, VISA, DS. 10 rooms, 8 with PB and 1 conference room. Breakfast and afternoon tea included in rates. Types of meals: Cont plus and early coffee/tea. Beds: Q. Cable TV in room. Central air. Library on premises. Fishing, golf, hiking, horseback riding, live theater, museums, parks, shopping, downhill skiing and cross-country skiing nearby.

Long Beach   E2

Boreas Bed & Breakfast Inn

607 Ocean Beach Blvd, PO Box 1344
Long Beach, WA 98631-1344
(360)642-8069 (888)642-8069 Fax:(360)642-5353
E-mail: boreas@boreasinn.com
Web: www.boreasinn.com

Circa 1920. This oceanfront inn started as a beach house and was remodeled eclectically with decks and a massive stone fireplace. There are two living rooms that offer views of the dunes.

All of the five guest rooms feature ocean, garden or mountain views. Guests can enjoy private time in the hot tub in the enclosed gazebo, take the path that winds through the dunes to the surf or walk to the boardwalk, restaurants and shopping. There is also a three-bedroom cottage available. Breakfast and spa is not available at the cottage.

Innkeeper(s): Susie Goldsmith & Bill Verner. $130-140. MC, VISA, AX, DC, DS, PC, TC. TAC10. 5 suites and 1 cottage. Types of meals: Full bkfst. Beds: KQT. One with jetted tub in room. VCR, fax, spa and library on premises. Weddings, small meetings and family reunions hosted. Limited Spanish spoken. Antiquing, fishing, golf, hiking, horseback riding, birding, lighthouses, parks, shopping, tennis and water sports nearby.

Lopez Island   B3

MacKaye Harbor Inn

949 MacKaye Harbor Rd
Lopez Island, WA 98261
(360)468-2253 (888)314-6140 Fax:(360)468-2393
E-mail: mckay@pacificrim.net
Web: www.mackayeharborinn.com

Circa 1927. Launching a kayak from the inn's sandy beach is a favorite activity here, as well as watching otters, seals and eagles from the waterfront parlor. Four of the guest rooms boast views of the bay, and there are eight acres to explore, including a quarter mile of beach. The home was the first house on the island to have electric lights, as well as its first inn. In the evenings, guests are treated to chocolate truffles and an aperitif to enhance the sunset views. The innkeepers also take care of two luxurious carriage houses next door, popular for families with children and for couples seeking more seclusion. Complimentary mountain bikes are offered for cycling around the island.

Innkeeper(s): Robin & Mike. $89-175. MC, VISA, PC, TC. TAC5. 5 rooms, 3 with PB, 1 with FP, 1 suite and 1 conference room. Breakfast included in rates. Types of meals: Gourmet bkfst, early coffee/tea, picnic lunch and afternoon tea. Beds: KQDT. Turndown service in room. Fax, copier and BBQs on premises. Weddings, small meetings, family reunions and seminars hosted. Antiquing, bicycling, canoeing/kayaking, fishing, golf, parks and tennis nearby.

Publicity: *Los Angeles Times, Sunset, Northwest and Coastal Living.*

Mount Rainier National Park E4

National Park Inn

Mt Rainier Guest Services PO Box 108
Mount Rainier National Park, WA 98304
(360)569-2275 Fax:(360)569-2770
Web: www.guestservices.com/rainier

Circa 1920. Mt. Rainier National Park boasts a spectacular scenery of mountains and seemingly endless forests. For more than half a century, visitors from around the world have chosen National Park Inn for their park lodging. Old hickory and twig furnishings decorate the rustic, comfortable guest rooms. Breakfast, lunch and dinner service are available at the inn's dining room. From late October to May 1, rates include breakfast. Breakfast is not included during the high season, from May until about Oct. 28.

Innkeeper(s): James R. Sproatt. $72-101. MC, VISA, AX, DC, DS, PC, TC.

TAC5. 25 rooms, 18 with PB. Breakfast included in rates. Types of meals: Full bkfst, afternoon tea and dinner. AP. Beds: QDT. Coffee in room. Handicap access. Small meetings hosted. Hiking, mountain climbing and cross-country skiing nearby.

Ocean Park   E2

Whalebone House

2101 Bay Ave
Ocean Park, WA 98640
(360)665-5371 (888)298-3330
E-mail: whalebone@willapabay.org

Circa 1889. Proudly listed in the state's Historic Register, this restored Victorian farmhouse is an example of the area's early homes that blended the architectural styles of the Pacific Northwest and coastal Maine. Past the white picket fence and country gardens, the interior is furnished with a refreshing assortment of antiques, beach whimsies, primitives and family heirlooms. Guest bedrooms offer privacy and modern conveniences. Enjoy specialty dishes like Whalebone Hash (smoked salmon), a vegetable frittata and creme brulee French toast for sweet and savory breakfast treats. Relax on an enclosed sun porch or side deck.

Historic Interest: Noth Head Lighthouse (15 miles), Cape Disappointment Lighthouse (15 miles), Lewis and Clark Station Camp (30 miles).

Innkeeper(s): Jim & Jayne Nash. $105-115. MC, VISA, TC. TAC10. 4 rooms with PB. Breakfast, afternoon tea and snacks/refreshments included in rates. Types of meals: Gourmet bkfst, country bkfst, veg bkfst, early coffee/tea and picnic lunch. Beds: Q. Library and gift shop on premises. Small meetings, family reunions and seminars hosted. Antiquing, art galleries, beaches, bicycling, canoeing/kayaking, golf, hiking, horseback riding, Lewis & Clark historic sites, trails, landmarks, museums, parks and shopping nearby.

Publicity: *Pacific Press, Sunset and Chinook Observer.*

Olga   B3

Buck Bay Farm

716 Pt Lawrence Rd
Olga, WA 98279
(360)376-2908 (888)422-2825

Circa 1920. This farmhouse is secluded on five acres and is decorated in country style. Down pillows and comforters are a

few homey touches. Homemade breakfasts include items like freshly baked muffins, scones and biscuits still steaming from the oven.

Innkeeper(s): Rick & Janet Bronkey. $95-135. MC, VISA, AX, DS, PC, TC. TAC10. 5 rooms, 4 with PB and 1 suite. Breakfast included in rates. Types of meals: Full bkfst and early coffee/tea. Beds: Q. Spa on premises. Handicap access. Weddings, small meetings, family reunions and seminars hosted. Antiquing, canoeing/kayaking, fishing, hiking, whale watching, live theater, parks and shopping nearby.

Publicity: *Island's Sounder.*

Orcas B3

Orcas Hotel

PO Box 155
Orcas, WA 98280-0155
(360)376-4300 (888)672-2792 Fax:(360)376-4399
E-mail: orcas@orcashotel.com

Circa 1901. Listed in the National Register, this three-story Victorian inn across from the ferry landing has been a landmark to travelers and boaters since the early 1900s. The inn offers scenic views of terraced lawns and English gardens, as well as vistas of the water and harbor, making it an ideal site for business meetings, retreats, wedding receptions and family reunions. Breakfast, lunch and dinner are available in the hotel's bakery, cafe and restaurant.

Innkeeper(s): Laura & Doug Tidwell. $75-189. MC, VISA, AX. TAC10. 12 rooms, 5 with PB. Types of meals: Gourmet bkfst, veg bkfst, cont plus, early coffee/tea, lunch, picnic lunch, snacks/refreshments and gourmet dinner. AP. Beds: QT. Two rooms with hot tub/spa in room. Fax and copier on premises. Weddings, small meetings and seminars hosted.

Publicity: *Los Angeles Times, Seattle Times, New York Times, Coastal Living, Northwest Best Places to Kiss and Pilots Getaway.*

Orcas Island B3

Outlook Inn on Orcas Island

PO Box 210
Orcas Island, WA 98245-0210
(360)376-2200 (888)688-5665 Fax:(360)376-2256
E-mail: info@outlookinn.com
Web: www.outlookinn.com

Circa 1888. This inn was built as a homesteader's cabin and in the late 1800s was expanded to include a general store, barber shop and a jail. The ocean view is spectacular and the inn boasts its own private beach area. Rooms contain hand-carved beds and marble-topped dressers. A walk throughout the peaceful village is a relaxing way to spend the day. The ocean breezes and beautiful surroundings create the perfect atmosphere for weddings. The hospitality will make any bride feel pampered as she prepares for her wedding day.

Innkeeper(s): Mark Witt/Adam Farish. $49-275. MC, VISA, AX, TC. TAC10. 41 rooms, 11 with PB, 16 with FP and 16 suites. Types of meals: Full bkfst, lunch, dinner and room service. Beds: KQDT. Cable TV, phone and VCR in room. Fax, copier, spa and library on premises. Handicap access. Weddings, small meetings, family reunions and seminars hosted. Antiquing, fishing, golf, live theater, parks, shopping and tennis nearby.

"The ambiance was incredible and all due to your gracious hospitality."

Point Roberts A3

Maple Meadow B&B

101 Goodman Rd
Point Roberts, WA 98281
(360)945-5536 Fax:(360)945-2855
E-mail: mplmedbb@whidbey.com
Web: www.travel-wise.com/maple/index.html

Circa 1910. Maple trees, including one that's more than 200 years old, give the name to this 1910 farmhouse. Pastures, a creek, trees and horses cast a peaceful country atmosphere.

Separate from the main farmhouse is the Old Pumphouse Room, decorated in a blend of Victorian and 1940s furnishings. The Rosewood Room features a king-size rosewood bed and a clawfoot tub. Two of the other rooms share a bath and shower. The morning begins with the smell of hot cinnamon buns, followed by crab omelets (cooked with fresh local crab), strawberries and pan-fried potatoes. In the evening, you can enjoy an outdoor Jacuzzi while looking at the stars. Only a block away is Boundary Bay where you can observe bird and sea life and, if the weather is fine, see all the way from Mount Baker to the San Juan Islands. Located near the Canadian border, ferries to Victoria are only 15 minutes away, and downtown Vancouver can be reached by car in 40 minutes.

Innkeeper(s): Terrie & Keith LaPorte. $75-140. MC, VISA, PC, TC. 4 rooms, 2 with PB. Breakfast and snacks/refreshments included in rates. Types of meals: Gourmet bkfst, country bkfst, veg bkfst and early coffee/tea. Beds: KQT. Turndown service and ceiling fan in room. VCR, fax, spa, stables, bicycles and library on premises. Weddings and family reunions hosted. Antiquing, art galleries, beaches, bicycling, canoeing/kayaking, fishing, golf, hiking, parks, shopping and water sports nearby.

Publicity: *Calgary Herald, San Francisco Chronicle, Vancouver Sun and Seattle Post Intelligencer.*

Port Angeles C3

Domaine Madeleine B&B

146 Wildflower Ln
Port Angeles, WA 98362-8138
(360)457-4174 (888)811-8376 Fax:(360)457-3037
E-mail: romance@domainemadeleine.com
Web: www.domainemadeleine.com

Circa 1947. This unique inn blends French with Oriental decor and offers a romantic and very private setting on five acres with 168 feet of waterfront. The inviting landscape includes more than 100 rhododendrons and numerous wild and cultivated flowers. Huge Douglas firs, cedars, Japanese Maples and bamboo add to the garden's serenity and majesty. Deer often stroll by, whales can sometimes be seen off shore, and eagles can be spotted soaring above. The innkeepers take pride in helping guests plan their day's events so they can enjoy the area fully. There are maps, books and videos on hand for visiting the Olympic Peninsula hiking trails, waterfalls and exporations along the coast. Choosing a restaurant for dinner is made easier by browsing the inn's menu collection. Victoria, B.C., is a short hour and a half away by ferry.

Innkeeper(s): Jeri, Victor, Ann, Noi & Ryan. $145-225. MC, VISA, AX, DS, PC, TC. 5 rooms with PB, 5 with FP, 2 suites and 1 cottage. Breakfast included in rates. Types of meals: Gourmet bkfst and afternoon tea. Beds: KQ. Cable TV, phone, VCR and whirlpool in room. Air conditioning. Fax, copier and library on premises. Weddings and small meetings hosted. French, Spanish, German and Farsi spoken. Antiquing, bicycling, fishing, golf, hiking, live theater, parks, shopping, downhill skiing, cross-country skiing, tennis and water sports nearby.

Publicity: *Northwest Travel.*

"Nowhere have I found lodgings that compared to Domaine Madeleine. I consider four criteria in determining where to stay when I travel: accommodations, food, uniqueness and hospitality. Domaine Madeleine excels in all these categories."

Five SeaSuns B&B Inn

1005 S Lincoln St
Port Angeles, WA 98362-7826
(360)452-8248 (800)708-0777 Fax:(360)417-0465
E-mail: info@seasuns.com
Web: www.seasuns.com

Circa 1926. Five SeaSuns was built by a local attorney and later purchased by a prominent area family who hosted many social gatherings here. The restored home maintains much of

its historic ambiance with guest rooms decorated in 1920s style with period antiques. Guest rooms include amenities such as whirlpool or soaking tubs, balconies and water or mountain views. Picturesque gardens highlight the estate like

grounds. Artfully presented gourmet breakfasts are served with fine china, silver and candlelight.

Historic Interest: Federal building dedicated by Lincoln (1 mile), Port Angeles.
Innkeeper(s): Jan & Bob Harbick. $75-135. MC, VISA, AX, PC, TC. TAC10. 5 rooms with PB, 1 suite and 1 cottage. Breakfast, afternoon tea and snacks/refreshments included in rates. Types of meals: Full bkfst, veg bkfst, early coffee/tea and picnic lunch. Beds: QD. Turndown service in room. VCR and fax on premises. Weddings and family reunions hosted. Antiquing, art galleries, beaches, bicycling, canoeing/kayaking, fishing, hiking, live theater, museums, parks, shopping, cross-country skiing and wineries nearby.

Tudor Inn

1108 S Oak St
Port Angeles, WA 98362-7745
(360)452-3138
E-mail: info@tudorinn.com
Web: www.tudorinn.com

Circa 1910. This English Tudor inn has been tastefully restored to display its original woodwork and fir stairway. Guests enjoy stone fireplaces in the living room and study. A terraced flower garden with 100-foot oak trees graces the property.

Innkeeper(s): Jane Glass. $75-135. MC, VISA, AX, DS. TAC10. 5 rooms with PB, 1 with FP. Breakfast and afternoon tea included in rates. Types of meals: Full bkfst. Beds: KQ. VCR, library and English gardens on premises. Weddings hosted. Antiquing, fishing, scenic flights, live theater, parks, shopping, downhill skiing, cross-country skiing and water sports nearby.

Publicity: *Seattle Times, Oregonian, Los Angeles Times and Olympic Magazine.*

"Delicious company and delicious food. Best in hospitality and warmth. Beautiful gardens!"

Port Townsend   C3

Ann Starrett Mansion

744 Clay St
Port Townsend, WA 98368-5808
(888)385-3205
E-mail: edel@starrettmansion.com
Web: www.starrettmansion.com

Circa 1889. George Starrett came from Maine to Port Townsend and became the major residential builder. By 1889, he had constructed one house a week, totaling more than 350 houses. The Smithsonian believes the Ann Starrett's elaborate free-hung spiral staircase is the only one of its type in the United States. A frescoed dome atop the octagonal tower depicts four seasons and four virtues. On the first day of each season, the sun causes a ruby red light to point toward the appropriate painting. The mansion won a "Great American Home Award" from the National Trust for Historic Preservation.

Historic Interest: The inn is located in the Port Townsend National Historic District near Fort Worden and Fort Townsend state parks.
Innkeeper(s): Edel Sokol. $133-225. MC, VISA, AX, DS, PC, TC. TAC10. 11 rooms with PB, 2 with FP, 2 suites, 2 cottages and 2 conference rooms. Breakfast included in rates. Types of meals: Full bkfst and afternoon tea. Beds: KQDT. Cable TV and phone in room. VCR and fax on premises. German spoken. Antiquing, fishing, live theater, parks, shopping, cross-country skiing and water sports nearby.

Publicity: *Peninsula, New York Times, Vancouver Sun, San Francisco Examiner, London Times, Colonial Homes, Elle, Leader, Japanese Travel, National Geographic Traveler, Victorian, Historic American Trails, Sunset Magazine, Day Boy Night Girl and PBS.*

"Staying here was like a dream come true."

Bishop Victorian Hotel

714 Washington St
Port Townsend, WA 98368-5718
(360)385-6122 (800)824-4738
E-mail: swan@waypt.com

Circa 1890. Located in downtown Port Townsend's historic district, this Victorian originally served as the Owl Cigar Company. Today, it holds 16 guest suites, all include a fireplace. Each of the suites includes a sitting room with sleeper sofas and antiques. Although each suite also includes a kitchenette, a continental breakfast is delivered each morning. Guests have privileges at a fitness club one block away.

Innkeeper(s): Joe & Cindy Finnie. $89-199. MC, VISA, AX, DS, PC, TC. TAC10. 16 suites, 14 with FP and 2 conference rooms. Types of meals: Cont plus and cont. Beds: QD. Cable TV, phone and ceiling fan in room. VCR, fax, copier and health club access on premises. Weddings, small meetings, family reunions and seminars hosted. Antiquing, fishing, golf, live theater, parks, shopping, cross-country skiing, tennis and water sports nearby.

Captain John Quincy Adams House B&B Inn

1028 Tyler Street
Port Townsend, WA 98368
(360)379-8832 Fax:(360)379-8832
E-mail: owner@captnjqadams.com
Web: www.captnjqadams.com

Circa 1887. President John Quincy Adams' great-great grandson built this beautifully restored Queen Anne Victorian. The delightful exterior is painted a light shade of green with red and gray trim. A three-story turret is a highlight of the home's architecture. The name of each room and suite complements the room's décor. The half-canopy bed in the Victoria room actually came out of Queen Victoria's summer palace. The Armada affords a view of a bit of the Puget Sound and includes a claw-foot tub. The Presidential Suite is as opulent as would befit a president, encompassing five rooms and boasting a view of the water. The suite includes a master bedroom with a four-poster bed located in the home's turret, a spacious living area, a dressing room and a bathroom with a Jacuzzi tub. The sweet Lady Hamilton room is decorated with a French Baroque-era bedroom set dressed in flowery designer fabrics, and a bay window houses a sitting area with a sofa. In the evenings, homemade desserts are delivered to your rooms, and in the morning, the savory aroma of a full, gourmet breakfast ensures that no guest ever wakes up on the wrong side of the bed. Fresh fruit salad, homemade scones and entrees such as eggs and bacon with polenta and cheddar cheese are a typical menu. Port Townsend, a historic seaport town, offers a variety of shops, historic sites, restaurants, galleries and theater. With three state parks nearby, there are plenty of outdoor activities, as well.

Historic Interest: Fort Warden (1 mile).

Innkeeper(s): Marshall & Selena Raney. $135-250. MC, VISA, AX, PC, TC. TAC10. 4 rooms, 3 with PB, 4 with FP and 1 suite. Breakfast and snacks/refreshments included in rates. Types of meals: Gourmet bkfst and early coffee/tea. Beds: QDT. TV, ceiling fan and VCR in room. Hot tub on premises. Weddings hosted. Antiquing, art galleries, beaches, bicycling, canoeing/kayaking, fishing, golf, hiking, horseback riding, live theater, museums, parks, shopping, tennis, water sports and wineries nearby.

Chanticleer Inn

1208 Franklin St
Port Townsend, WA 98368-6611
(360)385-6239 (800)858-9421 Fax:(360)385-3377
E-mail: info@chanticleerinnbb.com
Web: www.chanticleerinnbb.com

Circa 1876. Located in the historic district, this is a Stick-style Victorian farmhouse, built Circa 1876. Guest rooms are in light colors and offer mountain and water views along with down comforters and cozy feather beds. Comfortable parlors and sitting rooms include traditional furnishings and Victorian antiques. The innkeepers create breakfasts of homemade granola and hot entrees such as blueberry-stuffed French toast, Mexican quiche or Mediterranean egg casserole with feta cheese, mushrooms and spinach. There are always home-baked breads, cinnamon rolls and muffins as well. Ask for advice on kayaking, sailing and river rafting opportunities or take a sunset cruise, go whale watching or visit Point Wilson Lighthouse.

Historic Interest: The entire town is historic.

Innkeeper(s): Pattye O'Connor & Shirley O'Connor. $99-160. MC, VISA, DC, PC, TC. 5 rooms with PB and 1 guest house. Breakfast and afternoon tea included in rates. Types of meals: Gourmet bkfst and veg bkfst. Beds: KQ. Ceiling fan, one room w/Jacuzzi bath, fully-equipped kitchen in guesthouse and some with TVs in room. Central air. VCR on premises. Weddings, small meetings, family reunions and seminars hosted. Antiquing, art galleries, beaches, bicycling, canoeing/kayaking, fishing, golf, hiking, horseback riding, live theater, museums, parks, shopping, downhill skiing, cross-country skiing, sporting events, tennis, water sports and wineries nearby.

Publicity: *Best Places to Kiss, Home and Garden Television (HGTV) and NPR Radio.*

The English Inn

718 F St
Port Townsend, WA 98368-5211
(360)385-5302 (800)254-5302
E-mail: macgillonie@english-inn.com

Circa 1885. A welcoming English atmosphere awaits at this Italianate Victorian inn. It was built by U.S. Customs Commissioner Henry Bush during the town's heyday serving the railroad and shipping industries. Overlooking the Olympic Mountains, guest bedrooms offer impressive views. Creative

breakfasts serve seasonal delights, offering raspberry strudel muffins, herbed poached eggs on crumpets, artichoke frittatas or broiled grapefruit with brandy sauce. From the gazebo in the fragrant English rose garden, enjoy gorgeous sunsets and scenic vistas.

Innkeeper(s): Martin & Jennifer MacGillonie. $95-105. MC, VISA, AX, PC, TC. 4 rooms with PB. Breakfast included in rates. Types of meals: Gourmet bkfst, early coffee/tea and afternoon tea. Beds: Q. Weddings, small meetings, family reunions and seminars hosted. Antiquing, fishing, mountain biking, live theater, parks, shopping and water sports nearby.

James House

1238 Washington St
Port Townsend, WA 98368-6714
(360)385-1238 (800)385-1238 Fax:(360)379-5551
E-mail: innkeeper@jameshouse.com

Circa 1889. This Queen Anne mansion built by Francis James overlooks Puget Sound with views of the Cascades and Olympic mountain ranges. The three-story staircase was constructed of solid wild cherry brought around Cape Horn from Virginia. Parquet floors are composed of oak, cherry, walnut and maple, providing a suitable setting for the inn's collection of antiques.

Historic Interest: Located within the historic district and one mile from the Fort Worden State Park.

Innkeeper(s): Carol McGough. $125-225. MC, VISA, AX. 12 rooms with PB, 4 with FP, 3 suites and 2 cottages. Breakfast included in rates. Types of meals: Full bkfst. Beds: QD. Phone in room. Antiquing, fishing, whale watching and live theater nearby.

Publicity: *Washington, Seattle Weekly, Northwest Best Places, Sunset, Victorian Homes, Coastal Living, Country Living, Pacific Northwest, Los Angeles Times, New York Times and Evening Magazine.*

"My dream house in a dream town."

Manresa Castle

PO Box 564, 7th & Sheridan
Port Townsend, WA 98368-0564
(360)385-5750 (800)732-1281 Fax:(360)385-5883

Circa 1892. When businessman Charles Eisenbeis built the largest private residence in Port Townsend, locals dubbed it "Eisenbeis Castle," because it resembled the castles in Eisenbeis' native Prussia. The home is truly a royal delight to behold, both inside and out. Luxurious European antiques and hand-painted wall coverings decorate the dining room and many of the castle's stately guest rooms. The turret suites are unique and many of the rooms have mountain and water views, but beware of the third floor. Rumors of ghosts in the upper floor have frightened some, but others seek out the "haunted" rooms for a spooky stay. Port Townsend offers a variety of galleries, gift shops and antiquing.

Historic Interest: Port Townsend and Manresa Castle are listed in the National Register. The town includes many examples of Victorian-style buildings and a historic district.

Innkeeper(s): Roger O'Connor. $70-175. MC, VISA, DS, TC. TAC10. 40

rooms with PB, 2 suites and 1 conference room. Breakfast included in rates. Types of meals: Gourmet dinner. Beds: KQD. Cable TV and phone in room. Fax, copier and library on premises. Weddings, small meetings, family reunions and seminars hosted. Antiquing, art galleries, beaches, bicycling, canoeing/kayaking, fishing, golf, hiking, live theater, museums, parks, shopping, tennis, water sports and wineries nearby.

Publicity: *Island Independent, Leader News, Province Showcase, Sunset Magazine, Oregonian, Northwest Palate Magazine, History Channel & Sightings.*

Palace Hotel

1004 Water St
Port Townsend, WA 98368-6706
(360)385-0773 (800)962-0741 Fax:(360)385-0780
E-mail: palace@olympus.net

Circa 1889. This old brick hotel has been restored and refurbished in a Victorian style. The Miss Rose Room has a Jacuzzi tub and is on the third floor. Some rooms have kitchenettes. Miss Kitty's Room, with its antique bed and wood-burning stove has great views of Puget Sound and downtown.

Innkeeper(s): Gary Schweitzer. $49-159. MC, VISA, AX, DS. TAC10. 17 rooms and 1 conference room. Breakfast included in rates. Types of meals: Cont plus. Beds: KQDT. TV in room.

Pets Allowed.

Seabeck   C3

Willcox House

2390 Tekiu Rd NW
Seabeck, WA 98380
(360)830-4492 (800)725-9477 Fax:(360)830-0506

Circa 1936. Colonel Julian Willcox selected Lionel Pries to build this home on a wooded bluff overlooking Hood Canal. Holding court thereafter, the family entertained fashionable Northwest personalities, including Clark Gable, Errol Flynn and Ernest Hemingway. The 10,000-square-foot mansion was angled to provide views of the shimmering waters, the Olympic mountains and forested hillsides. The inn has a library, game room, pub and movie theater. Watersports or just strolling along the seashore are among the outdoor activities.

Innkeeper(s): Cecilia & Phillip Hughes. $129-199. MC, VISA, DS. 5 rooms with PB, 1 with FP. Types of meals: Full bkfst, early coffee/tea, lunch, picnic lunch, snacks/refreshments and dinner. Beds: KQ. Fax, copier, private pier and small boats on premises. Weddings, small meetings, family reunions and seminars hosted. Antiquing, golf, museums, gardens and shopping nearby.

Publicity: *Country Inns, Seattle Times, The Olympian, Journal American, USA Today, London Times, Country Inns Magazine, "Great Country Inns," TV series and Shaping Seattle Architecture.*

"The natural beauty, coziness and hospitality have rekindled our romance of spirit."

Seattle   C4

Amaranth Inn

1451 S Main St
Seattle, WA 98144
(206)720-7161 (800)720-7161 Fax:(206)323-0772
E-mail: visitus@amaranthinn.com

Circa 1906. Explore all the city sites from this elegantly restored Grand Craftsman home built by a lumber baron. Spacious rooms feature high ceilings with crown moldings, Oriental carpets on hardwood floors, gentle wall colors graced with original Pacific Northwest artwork, and ell-placed antique furnishings. All but

one of the guest bedrooms or suites have fireplaces. Clean and comfortable, enjoy hand-pressed cotton bedding, handmade soaps, terry robes, jetted tubs and tiled baths. Made-to-order gourmet breakfasts are served on settings of crystal and china in the formal dining room. The sunroom and front porch are pleasant places for relaxing.

Historic Interest: Historic Pioneer Square (3/4 mile).

Innkeeper(s): Herman & Alea Foster. $75-165. MC, VISA, AX, DC, DS, TC. 8 rooms, 6 with PB, 7 with FP. Breakfast included in rates. Types of meals: Gourmet bkfst, veg bkfst and early coffee/tea. Beds: QT. Cable TV, phone, fireplace, down comforters, handmade soaps and terry robes in room. VCR, sun porch with fresh fruit available and reclining chairs on premises. Small meetings and family reunions hosted. Antiquing, art galleries, beaches, bicycling, canoeing/kayaking, fishing, golf, hiking, near train station, close to freeway access, live theater, museums, parks, shopping, sporting events, tennis, water sports and wineries nearby.

Gaslight Inn

1727 15th Ave
Seattle, WA 98122-2614
(206)325-3654 Fax:(206)328-4803
E-mail: innkeepr@gaslight-inn.com
Web: www.gaslight-inn.com

Circa 1906. Stay at this Four Square, large Arts and Crafts bungalow offering quality, comfort and a relaxed yet elegant atmosphere. Impeccably decorated with mission-style furniture, Turkish rugs, artwork and antique lamps, the interior has been restored in exacting detail with rich oak paneling, a wide staircase and an enormous entryway. Showcased in the living room is a big, oak fireplace. Another pleasant common room is the library. Guest bedrooms include refrigerators. Many feature gas fireplaces, and some have decks boasting wonderful views. A koi pond and perennial garden grace the grounds that also have a private, heated, in-ground pool surrounded by several decks and tropical foliage.

Innkeeper(s): Steve Bennett & Trevor Logan. $88-198. MC, VISA, AX, PC, TC. 16 rooms. Breakfast included in rates. Types of meals: Cont. Beds: QD. Cable TV, phone, ceiling fan and fireplace in room. Fax, copier and swimming on premises. Amusement parks, antiquing, art galleries, beaches, bicycling, canoeing/kayaking, fishing, golf, hiking, live theater, museums, parks, shopping, downhill skiing, cross-country skiing, sporting events, tennis, water sports and wineries nearby.

Green Gables Guesthouse

1503 2nd Ave W
Seattle, WA 98119-3007
(206)282-6863 (800)400-1503 Fax:(206)286-8525
E-mail: greengab@wolfenet.com
Web: greengablesseattle.com

Circa 1904. In the late Victorian Four Square style, this house is located on historic Queen Anne Hill. The Cherry Blossom Room offers a wraparound corner window, while Queen Anne's Lace provides a view of downtown Seattle and the Space Needle. Microbreweries, coffee houses, performing art and sport centers are easily accessed. The inn has private off-street parking and a large deck for entertaining or pleasant summer breakfast service. The innkeepers can accommodate business travelers.

Historic Interest: Ballard Mansion, Kerry Park Overlook.

Innkeeper(s): Mr Reonn Rabon. $79-169. MC, VISA, AX, DS, PC, TC. 8 rooms, 6 with PB, 2 suites, 2 guest houses and 1 conference room. Types of meals: Gourmet bkfst, country bkfst, early coffee/tea and snacks/refreshments. Beds: KQ. TV, phone and VCR in room. Fax and copier on premises. Small meetings and family reunions hosted. Antiquing, live theater, shopping and sporting events nearby.

Pioneer Square Hotel

77 Yesler Way
Seattle, WA 98104-3401
(206)340-1234 (800)800-5514 Fax:(206)467-0707
E-mail: sales@pioneersquare.com
Web: www.pioneersquare.com

Circa 1914. The estate of Seattle's founding father, Henry Yesler, built this historic waterfront hotel. The three-diamond hotel is well-appointed and elegant rooms feature coordinating prints. Business travelers will appreciate the direct dial telephones with data ports, and individual climate controls in each room. A generous continental breakfast is included in the hotel's rates. Restaurants and cafes are nearby, as is Historic Pioneer Square, Pike Place Market, ferries and shopping.
Innkeeper(s): Jo Thompson. $119-229. MC, VISA, AX, DC. 75 rooms with PB and 3 suites. Types of meals: Cont and room service. Beds: KQDT. Cable TV, phone and turndown service in room. Air conditioning. Fax, copier and library on premises. Handicap access. Weddings, small meetings, family reunions and seminars hosted. Live theater, parks, shopping, downhill skiing, cross-country skiing, sporting events and water sports nearby.

Tugboat Challenger

1001 Fairview Ave N
Seattle, WA 98109-4438
(206)340-1201 Fax:(206)621-9208
E-mail: ctugboat@uswest.net

Circa 1944. If you're a bit tired of the ordinary land-locked lodging, why not book a room and passage on this idyllic tugboat, docked in downtown Seattle's Chandler's Cove. The boat can sleep more than a dozen guests, in eight different cabins. The Admiral's Cabin is particularly suited to honeymooners, as it includes a four-poster bed, soaking tub and boasts city, lake and marina views. Not all rooms are as large and several main deck rooms include double or single bunks. The owners also have yachts available for renting, and each can accommodate four people. Tugboat guests enjoy a continental breakfast. The tug can be reserved for small parties and weddings.
Innkeeper(s): Jerry Brown. $55-185. MC, VISA, AX, DC, DS, PC, TC. TAC10. 10 rooms, 7 with PB and 3 suites. Breakfast included in rates. Types of meals: Cont plus. Beds: QD. Phone in room. VCR, fax, copier, video library and refrigerators on premises. Small meetings and family reunions hosted. Amusement parks, antiquing, fishing, live theater, parks, shopping, sporting events and water sports nearby.

"Our stay with you was the highlight of our accommodations. Your breakfast was terrific and the staff was even better."

Seaview   E2

Shelburne Inn

4415 Pacific Way, PO Box 250
Seaview, WA 98644
(360)642-2442 Fax:(360)642-8904
E-mail: innkeeper@theshelburneinn.com
Web: www.theshelburneinn.com

Circa 1896. The Shelburne is known as the oldest continuously operating hotel in the state of Washington, and it is listed in the National Register. The front desk at the hotel is a former church altar. Art nouveau stained-glass windows rescued from a church torn down in Morecambe, England, now shed light and color on the dining room. The guest rooms are appointed in antiques. Just a 10-minute walk from the ocean, the inn is situated on the

Long Beach Peninsula, a 28-mile stretch of seacoast that includes bird sanctuaries and lighthouses. The inn offers a full gourmet breakfast.

Innkeeper(s): David Campiche & Laurie Anderson. $119-249. MC, VISA, AX. 15 rooms with PB, 2 suites and 1 conference room. Breakfast included in rates. Types of meals: Gourmet bkfst, lunch, gourmet dinner and room service. Beds: QD. Fax and copier on premises. Handicap access. Antiquing and fishing nearby.
Publicity: *Better Homes & Gardens, Bon Appetit, Conde Nast Traveler, Esquire, Gourmet, Food & Wine and Travel & Leisure.*

"Fabulous food. Homey but elegant atmosphere. Hospitable service, like being a guest in an elegant home."

Sequim   C3

Glenna's Guthrie Cottage

10083 Old Olympic Hwy
Sequim, WA 98382
(360)681-4349 (800)930-4349
E-mail: glennas@olypen.com

Circa 1907. Once one of the largest working dairy farms on the Peninsula, this restored Craftsman home offers majestic views of the Olympic Mountains. Greeted with a small gift and tea service upon check-in, guests will find the spacious bedrooms continue to pamper with robes and comfortable furnishings in a country cottage decor. Suites have private entrances, one boasts a soaking tub and canopy bed. Enjoy a large-screen TV and karaoke in the common room. Breakfast is usually a five-course event highlighted by homemade jams, syrups, pastries and sorbets. Visit the gift shop and stargaze while in the hot tub.
Historic Interest: One of the oldest Dinosaur fields in the U.S.
Innkeeper(s): Glenna & Jack O'Neil. $69-135. MC, VISA, AX, DC, PC, TC. TAC5. 4 rooms, 2 with PB, 2 suites and 1 conference room. Breakfast and snacks/refreshments included in rates. Types of meals: Gourmet bkfst, country bkfst, veg bkfst and early coffee/tea. AP. Beds: KQD. Cable TV, turndown service, ceiling fan, VCR, hot tub, microwave, toasters, coffeepot (in suites), hair dryers and robes in room. Fax, spa, library, hot tub and gift shop on premises. Weddings, small meetings, family reunions and seminars hosted. Antiquing, art galleries, beaches, bicycling, canoeing/kayaking, fishing, golf, hiking, lavender & herb farm, boat tour, lighthouse, whale watching, bird watching, live theater, museums, parks, shopping, downhill skiing, cross-country skiing, tennis, water sports and wineries nearby.
Publicity: *Seattle Times.*

Spokane   C9

Angelica's Mansion

1321 W 9th Ave
Spokane, WA 99204-3211
(509)624-5598 (800)987-0053 Fax:(509)624-5598
E-mail: info@angelicasbb.com

Circa 1907. Built in 1907, this elegant brick mansion is a romantic getaway located on Spokane's South Hill, and listed in the National Register of Historic Places. A European Arts and Crafts influence is demonstrated throughout the home in warm woodwork, antique furnishings and diamond-paned, leaded-glass windows. Four guest rooms each have private baths and offer individual features such as canopy bed, wicker furniture or tiled fireplace. Enjoy a breakfast of broccoli and goat cheese quiche, and a croissant with a slice of country ham before heading out to explore the city. Just five minutes from downtown, it's easy to visit the Opera House, arena, museum or Riverfront Park. At the end of the day, savor a cup of coffee or afternoon snack in the Sunroom, or relax on the spacious veranda.

Innkeeper(s): Lynette & Ted Gustafson. $95-110. MC, VISA, AX, PC, TC. 4 rooms with PB, 1 with FP, 2 suites and 1 conference room. Breakfast and snacks/refreshments included in rates. Types of meals: Gourmet bkfst, veg bkfst, cont plus, cont, early coffee/tea, picnic lunch and afternoon tea. Beds: Q. Cable TV, phone and turndown service in room. Air conditioning. VCR, fax, copier and library on premises. Weddings, small meetings, family reunions and seminars hosted. Antiquing, art galleries, bicycling, fishing, golf, hiking, live theater, museums, parks, downhill skiing, cross-country skiing, sporting events, tennis, water sports and wineries nearby.

Publicity: *Romantic Decorating.*

Fotheringham House

2128 W 2nd Ave
Spokane, WA 99204-0916
(509)838-1891 Fax:(509)838-1807
E-mail: innkeeper@fotheringham.net

Circa 1891. A vintage Victorian in the National Register, this inn was built by the first mayor of Spokane, David Fotheringham. There are tin ceilings, a carved staircase, gabled porches and polished woodwork. Victorian furnishings and

stained-glass pieces are featured. Across the street is Coeur d'Alene Park and the Patsy Clark Mansion, a favorite Spokane restaurant. Walk two blocks to the Elk Public House.

Historic Interest: 1891 home of Spokane's first mayor.

Innkeeper(s): Irene & Paul Jensen. $95-115. MC, VISA, AX. 4 rooms. Breakfast included in rates. Types of meals: Full bkfst and early coffee/tea. Chocolates and amenities in room. Weddings, small meetings, family reunions and seminars hosted. Antiquing, live theater, museums, shopping and sporting events nearby.

Sunnyside   E7

Sunnyside Inn B&B

800 E Edison Ave
Sunnyside, WA 98944-2206
(509)839-5557 (800)221-4195
E-mail: sunnyside@sunnysideinn.com
Web: www.sunnysideinn.com

Circa 1919. This wine country inn offers spacious rooms, decorated in a comfortable, country style. Most of the rooms include baths with double Jacuzzi tubs. The one bedroom without a Jacuzzi, includes the home's original early 20th-century fixtures. Two rooms offer fireplaces. A full breakfast is served, as well as evening snacks.

Innkeeper(s): Karen & Don Vlieger. $69-109. MC, VISA, AX, DS, TC. 13 rooms with PB, 2 with FP. Breakfast and snacks/refreshments included in rates. Types of meals: Full bkfst. Beds: KQ. Cable TV, phone and ceiling fan in room. Air conditioning. Small meetings and family reunions hosted. Antiquing, fishing, golf, live theater, parks, shopping and cross-country skiing nearby.

Tacoma   D4

Branch Colonial House

2420 North 21st St
Tacoma, WA 98406
(253)752-3565 (877)752-3565
E-mail: reservations@colonialhousebnb.com
Web: www.colonialhousebnb.com

Circa 1904. Built in the early 20th century, this historic bed & breakfast looks out to the Puget Sound. The home, part of Tacoma's annual historic home tour, features Colonial Revival architecture. Several guest rooms afford a view of the Puget Sound, and the suites include a whirlpool tub. The Branch Quarters also has a fireplace. Tacoma is within easy driving distance of Seattle, and the town offers shops, museums, a zoo and an aquarium.

Innkeeper(s): Robin & Bennie Soto. $85-185. MC, VISA, AX, PC, TC. TAC10. 6 rooms with PB, 1 with FP, 3 suites and 1 conference room. Breakfast included in rates. Types of meals: Gourmet bkfst, veg bkfst, early coffee/tea and snacks/refreshments. Beds: KQ. Cable TV, phone and ceiling fan in room. VCR, fax, library and child care on premises. Small meetings hosted. Antiquing, art galleries, beaches, bicycling, canoeing/kayaking, fishing, golf, hiking, horseback riding, live theater, museums, parks, shopping, sporting events and water sports nearby.

Publicity: *Tacoma's New Tribune.*

Commencement Bay B&B

3312 N Union Ave
Tacoma, WA 98407-6055
(253)752-8175 Fax:(253)759-4025
E-mail: relax@great-views.com
Web: www.great-views.com

Circa 1937. Watch boats sail across the bay while enjoying breakfast served with gourmet coffee at this Colonial Revival inn. All guest rooms feature bay views and each is unique and individually decorated. The surrounding area includes historic sites, antique shops, waterfront restaurants, wooded nature trails and Pt. Defiance Zoo and Aquarium. Relax in a secluded hot tub and deck area or in the fireside room for reading and the romantic view. The innkeepers also offer an exercise room and video/book library. Business travelers will appreciate amenities such as an office work area and dataports, free e-mail and cable Internet access. The B&B is centrally located, 30 miles from both Seattle and Mt. Rainier park.

Historic Interest: Washington State Historical Museum (2 miles), Fort Nisqually first settlement in Washington, replica (2 miles), historic homes and buildings, driving tour (one-half mile) and Karples Manuscript Museum (1 mile).

Innkeeper(s): Sharon & Bill Kaufmann. $110-140. MC, VISA, AX, DS, PC, TC. TAC10. 3 rooms with PB. Breakfast, afternoon tea and snacks/refreshments included in rates. Types of meals: Full bkfst and early coffee/tea. AP. Beds: Q. Cable TV, phone, VCR, bay views, elegant decor and robes in room. Fax, spa, bicycles, computer data ports, exercise room, massages and exercise room on premises. Small meetings hosted. Antiquing, fishing, Washington State Historic Museum, botanical parks, the International Glass Museum, restaurants, live theater, parks, shopping, sporting events and water sports nearby.

Publicity: *Tacoma Weekly, News Tribune, Tacoma Reporter, Oregonian, NW Best Places.* and NBC *"Evening Magazine"*

"Perfect in every detail! The setting, breathtaking; the food, scrumptious and beautifully presented; the warmth and friendship here."

Dutch Embassy

1601 N 8th St
Tacoma, WA 98403-1013
(253)627-4192 Fax:(253)627-4192

Circa 1893. Named after entertaining a brother who was a diplomat from the Netherlands, this two-story Queen Anne is tastefully furnished in antiques and collectibles. Greeted in the entry hall with leaded- and stained-glass windows on the stair-

way landing, the parlor fireplace is a relaxing gathering spot. Guest bedrooms feature interesting curved footboard, half-canopy and four-poster beds. The Tower Suite with adjoining sitting room is in the finished attic and offers terry robes, as do all the other rooms. A satisfying breakfast is served in the dining room. Play badminton, basketball, pickle ball or paddle tennis on the outdoor court. It is an easy stroll to view the historic districts surrounding the inn.

Historic Interest: Mt. Ranier (50 miles), Historic Boeing Field (25 miles).

Innkeeper(s): Kenneth & Velda McDonald. $55-90. MC, VISA, PC, TC. 5 rooms, 1 with PB. Breakfast included in rates. Types of meals: Full bkfst. Beds: QDT. TV and VCR in room. Fax, copier, library and sport court on premises. Amusement parks, antiquing, beaches, bicycling, golf and museums nearby.

Publicity: *Tacoma Weekly.*

Uniontown   E10

Churchyard Inn

206 Saint Boniface St
Uniontown, WA 99179
(509)229-3200 Fax:(509)229-3213
E-mail: cyi@inlandnet.com
Web: www.pullman-wa.com/housing/chrchbb.htm

Circa 1905. Not surprisingly, this historic inn is located adjacent to a church. From 1913 until 1972, the home served as a convent. The three-story brick home is adorned with a second-story portico supported by two columns. The innkeepers restored the home to its turn-of-the-century grace and added a new wing. The inn's restored red fir woodwork is a highlight. The seven guest rooms include a spacious third-floor suite with a kitchen and fireplace. The home is listed in the National Register of Historic Places.

Innkeeper(s): Marvin J. & Linda J. Entel. $60-150. MC, VISA, DS. 7 rooms with PB, 1 with FP, 1 suite and 1 conference room. Breakfast included in rates. Types of meals: Full bkfst, cont and early coffee/tea. Beds: KQDT. Phone, ceiling fan and window fans in room. VCR and fax on premises. Handicap access. Weddings, small meetings, family reunions and seminars hosted. Antiquing, fishing, golf, parks, shopping, sporting events and water sports nearby.

Publicity: *Lewiston Tribune, Colfax Gazette, Moscow Daily News, Weekend Getaways, Best Places Northwest, KHQ Channel 6 Northwest Edition and Channel 10 PBS.*

"Beautiful property, location and setting. I would recommend this wonderful B&B to anyone coming to the area."

Yakima   E6

A Touch Of Europe™ B&B Inn Yakima

220 N 16th Ave
Yakima, WA 98902-2461
(509)454-9775 (888)438-7073

Circa 1889. A lumber baron built this Queen Anne Victorian as his residence, which still maintains period elements such as stained glass and rich woodwork. The home was purchased by the Williams family in 1904, and Mrs. Ina Philips Williams was the first woman member of the Washington State House of Representatives. Theodore Roosevelt, whose portrait is displayed among other historical photographs, was a guest of the Williams family. Elegant guest bedrooms feature period decor and classic Victorian furnishings. A signature, multi-course, candlelit breakfast is prepared by innkeeper, European chef and

cookbook author Erika Cenci, who also creates recipes and demonstrates them on local and international TV. This inn also offers fine dining, specializing in a variety of international cuisine. Private luncheons, traditional high teas or memorable multi-course dinners can be developed exclusively to fit almost any occasion or theme.

Innkeeper(s): Erika G. and James A. Cenci. $79-110. MC, VISA, AX, TC. TAC10. 3 rooms with PB, 1 with FP, 1 cottage and 1 conference room. Breakfast included in rates. Types of meals: Full bkfst. Beds: Q. Phone in room. Air conditioning. Library on premises. Small meetings hosted. German spoken. Antiquing, bicycling, golf, hiking, Convention Center, skiing, live theater, museums and wineries nearby.

Publicity: *KIMA-TV/Fisher Broadcasting.*

"Thank you for your warmth and friendliness and outstanding food! Your home is beautiful."

Birchfield Manor Country Inn

2018 Birchfield Rd
Yakima, WA 98901-9580
(509)452-1960 (800)375-3420 Fax:(509)452-2334

Circa 1910. Guests at this Prairie-style inn, once the centerpiece of a large sheep ranch, enjoy elegant decor and the tranquil scenery of seven rural acres. Four guest rooms have fireplaces, and some have double whirlpool tubs or a sauna shower. The innkeepers have won awards for their breakfasts, and for an additional charge, dinners are served on Thursday, Friday and Saturday nights.

Innkeeper(s): The Masset Family. $99-199. MC, VISA, AX, DC, PC, TC. TAC10. 11 rooms with PB, 4 with FP. Breakfast included in rates. Types of meals: Gourmet bkfst, early coffee/tea, gourmet dinner and room service. Beds: KQ. Phone, ceiling fan and VCR in room. Air conditioning. Swimming on premises. Handicap access. Weddings, small meetings, family reunions and seminars hosted. Antiquing, fishing, live theater, parks, downhill skiing and water sports nearby.

Washington, D.C.

Aaron Shipman House

PO Box 12011
Washington, DC 20005-0911
(202)328-3510 Fax:(202)332-3885
E-mail: bnbaccom@aol.com
Web: www.aaronshipmanhouse.com

Circa 1887. This three-story Victorian townhouse was built by Aaron Shipman, who owned one of the first construction companies in the city. The turn-of-the-century revitalization of Washington began in Logan Circle, considered to be the city's first truly residential area. During the house's restoration, flower gardens, terraces and fountains were added.

Victorian antiques, original wood paneling, stained glass, chandeliers, as well as practical amenities such as air conditioning and laundry facilities, make this a comfortable stay. There is a furnished apartment available, as well.

Innkeeper(s): Charles & Jackie Reed. $65-150. MC, VISA, AX, DS, TC. 6 rooms, 5 with PB, 3 with FP and 1 suite. Breakfast included in rates. Types of meals: Cont plus. Beds: QD. TV, phone and one with Jacuzzi in room. Air conditioning. Piano on premises. Weddings, small meetings and family reunions hosted. Antiquing, National monuments and Smithsonian, live theater, parks, shopping and sporting events nearby.

"This home was the highlight of our stay in Washington! This was a superb home and location. The Reeds treated us better than family."

Bull Moose B&B on Capitol Hill

101 5th Street NE
Washington, DC 20002
(202)547-1050 (800)261-2768 Fax:(202)548-9741
E-mail: reserve@bullmoose-b-and-b.com

Circa 1890. Just five blocks from the U.S. Capitol stands this 1890 Victorian, built when Theodore Roosevelt first served in Washington as a U.S. Civil Service Commissioner. Named for the Bull Moose Reform Party Roosevelt formed in 1912, the home has been a private residence and has also housed U.S. Senate pages whose names and comments are carved in the woodwork and upstairs desks. It has four guest rooms with private baths and two with shared baths. Continental breakfast is served each morning and includes courses like its signature hearty Bull Moose Granola, home-baked muffins, scones and fresh fruit. Enjoy the library, the turreted parlor and the dining room with its turn of the century British pub table. Then head out for a walking tour of the nation's capital. The inn is located near Congress, the Supreme Court, Georgetown University, the Smithsonian, the Vietnam War

Memorial and other national monuments. If you're in town on Saturday or Sunday be sure to visit the Eastern Market, one of our nation's oldest public markets.

Historic Interest: U.S. Capitol.

Innkeeper(s): Jim Pastore & JoAnne McInnes. $149-189. MC, VISA, AX, DS, TC. 10 rooms, 4 with PB. Breakfast included in rates. Types of meals: Cont. Beds: QDT. Air conditioning. Fax, daily newspapers and access to kitchen on premises. Small meetings hosted. Spanish, French and Russian spoken. Art galleries, National Mall, museums and parks nearby.

Doolittle Guest House

506 E Capitol St SE
Washington, DC 20003-1141
(202)546-6622 Fax:(202)546-5046
E-mail: doolittlehouse@yahoo.com
Web: www.doolittlehouse.com

Circa 1866. Experience a taste of elegance while staying at this Richardsonian Romanesque house in the residential Capitol Hill historic district. Federalist and Centennial decor is enhanced by stained-glass windows, period antiques, marble fireplaces, chestnut and walnut paneling. Well-appointed guest bedrooms and a suite offer pure cotton bed and bath linens and robes for personal comfort. A healthy breakfast is served in the sunny dining room. Keep abreast of current world events with major daily newspapers and various magazines in the foyer and library. The second-floor library offers a fully equipped business center. Washington's political, historic and cultural sites are all nearby.

Innkeeper(s): Bernadine & Raymond Prince. $115-175. MC, VISA, AX, DC, PC, TC. 3 rooms with PB, 1 suite and 1 conference room. Breakfast included in rates. Types of meals: Veg bkfst, cont plus and early coffee/tea. Beds: KQD. Phone, turndown service and ceiling fan in room. Central air. VCR, fax, copier and library on premises. Weddings, small meetings, family reunions and seminars hosted. Antiquing, art galleries, bicycling, canoeing/kayaking, golf, White House, U.S. Capitol, Washington Monument, Jefferson Memorial, Lincoln Memorial, Vietnam Memorial, Arlington National Cemetery, Holocaust Museum, live theater, museums, parks and shopping nearby.

Publicity: *Lonely Planet. Washington Traveler, Washington Print Club News and National Geographic and PBS documentaries.*

Dupont At The Circle

1604 19th St NW
Washington, DC 20009
(202)332-5251 (888)412-0100 Fax:(202)332-3244

Circa 1883. Completely restoring this Victorian townhouse infused this urban B&B inn with enhanced modern technology while retaining its historical flavor and integrity. Common areas include cozy parlors and a front patio. Antique furniture, fine ironed linens and upscale amenities offer luxurious comfort. Some guest bedrooms feature handcrafted reproduction stained-glass windows, four-poster canopy beds and whirlpool tubs. The Plum Suite spans an entire floor and boasts a living room with entertainment center, marble bath and whirlpool tub. The English Basement is a spacious studio apartment with a kitchenette and private entrance. Concierge services can arrange transportation, dinner reservations and access to a local health club.

Historic Interest: National Mall (1 mile).

Innkeeper(s): Anexora & Alan Skuirsky. $140-300. MC, VISA, AX, DC, CB, DS, PC, TC. TAC10. 8 rooms, 7 with PB, 1 suite and 1 conference room. Breakfast included in rates. Types of meals: Cont. Beds: QD. Phone, some with cable TV, CD player, refrigerator, stereo and VCR in room. Central air. VCR, fax and library on premises. Small meetings and seminars hosted. Spanish spoken. Antiquing, art galleries, bicycling, golf, live theater, museums, parks, shopping, sporting events and tennis nearby.

Publicity: *Travel & Leisure and Washington Times.*

The Embassy Inn

1627 16th St NW
Washington, DC 20009-3063
(202)234-7800 (800)423-9111 Fax:(202)234-3309

Circa 1910. This restored inn is furnished in a Federalist style. The comfortable lobby offers books and evening sherry. Conveniently located, the inn is seven blocks from the Adams Morgan area of ethnic restaurants. The Embassy's philosophy of innkeeping includes providing personal attention and cheerful hospitality. Concierge services are available. The inn does not have an elevator or parking on site.

Innkeeper(s): Susan Stiles. $79-150. MC, VISA, AX, DC, CB, TC. TAC10. 38 rooms with PB. Breakfast included in rates. Types of meals: Cont plus and snacks/refreshments. Beds: DT. Cable TV, phone and free HBO in room. Air conditioning. Fax, copier and Washington Post daily on premises. Antiquing, white House, live theater, museums and parks nearby.

Publicity: *Los Angeles Times, Inn Times, Business Review and N.Y. Times.*

"When I return to D.C., I'll be back at the Embassy."

Maison Orleans Bed'n Breakfast on the Hill

414 Fifth St, SE
Washington, DC 20003-2051
(202)544-3694
E-mail: maisonorln@aol.com

Circa 1902. Maison Orleans is located less than two blocks from Pennsylvania Avenue on historic Capitol Hill. The interior features family antiques from the 1930s and 1940s, as well as

antiques that once resided in other Capitol Hill homes. In the winter, guests in the Raspberry-Creole Room enjoy a view of the Washington Monument. Guests can walk the half-dozen blocks that lead to the Capitol building, Library of Congress and other important historic attractions.

Innkeeper(s): William Rouchell. $95-135. PC, TC. 3 rooms with PB, 1 with FP. Breakfast included in rates. Types of meals: Cont plus. Beds: KQT. TV, phone and ceiling fan in room. Central air. Family reunions hosted. Antiquing, art galleries, bicycling, Nation's Capitol, Whitehouse, live theater, museums, parks and shopping nearby.

Publicity: *Voice of the Hill.*

Swann House

1808 New Hampshire Ave NW
Washington, DC 20009-3206
(202)265-4414 Fax:(202)265-6755
E-mail: stay@swannhouse.com
Web: www.swannhouse.com

Circa 1883. Swann House is a splendid example of Richardson Romanesque architecture and all its glory. The gothic brick home includes a turret and an arched, covered front porch and a lavish, second-story balcony. The interior includes the original crown moldings, hardwood floors, a carved marble fireplace and original doors and paneling. The guest rooms and suites are decorated with an eclectic mix of antiques and contemporary furnishings. Several include a fireplace. Guests can take in the city

view from a rooftop deck or enjoy the backyard garden, which includes a fountain. The home is located in Dupont Circle, with Washington, D.C.'s, myriad of attractions all close by.

Historic Interest: White House, Arlington Cemetery, Mt. Vernon, National Mall.

Innkeeper(s): Mary & Richard Ross. $140-295. MC, VISA, AX, DC, DS, PC, TC. 9 rooms with PB, 6 with FP and 2 conference rooms. Breakfast and snacks/refreshments included in rates. Types of meals: Cont plus. Beds: KQ. Cable TV and phone in room. Central air. VCR, fax, copier, swimming, pool, roof deck, balconies and gardens on premises. Weddings, small meetings, family reunions and seminars hosted. Antiquing, art galleries, bicycling, Congress, memorials, historical attractions, live theater, museums, parks and shopping nearby.

The Windsor Inn

1842 16th St NW
Washington, DC 20009-3316
(202)667-0300 (800)423-9111 Fax:(202)667-4503

Circa 1910. Recently renovated and situated in a neighborhood of renovated townhouses, the Windsor Inn is the sister property to the Embassy Inn. It is larger and offers suites as well as a small meeting room. The refurbished lobby is in an Art Deco style and a private club atmosphere prevails. It is six blocks to the Metro station at Dupont Circle. There are no elevators or parking on site.

Historic Interest: White House (12 blocks), Arlington House (3 miles), Hillwood House (2 miles), Mount Vernon (14 miles).

Innkeeper(s): Susan Stiles. $89-199. MC, VISA, AX, DC, CB, TC. TAC10. 45 rooms with PB, 2 suites and 1 conference room. Breakfast included in rates. Types of meals: Cont plus and snacks/refreshments. Beds: QDT. TV, phone and some refrigerators in room. Air conditioning. Fax, copier and Washington Post daily on premises. Weddings, small meetings and family reunions hosted. French and Spanish spoken. Antiquing, live theater and parks nearby.

Publicity: *Los Angeles Times, Inn Times, Sunday Telegram, WCUA Press Release and New York Times.*

"Being here was like being home. Excellent service, would recommend."

West Virginia

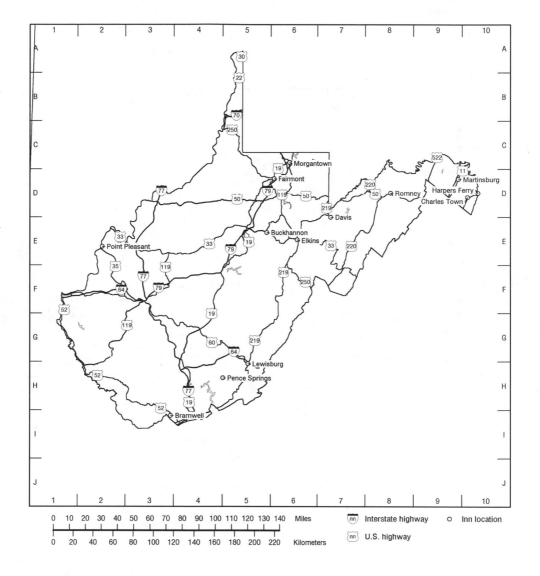

0 10 20 30 40 50 60 70 80 90 100 110 120 130 140 Miles

0 20 40 60 80 100 120 140 160 180 200 220 Kilometers

nn Interstate highway o Inn location

nn U.S. highway

Bramwell   I3

Perry House B&B

Main St, PO Box 188
Bramwell, WV 24715-0248
(304)248-8145 (800)328-0248
E-mail: perryhouse@netlinkcorp.com

Circa 1902. This brick Victorian was built by a bank cashier and remained in the family for 80 years. The rooms are decorated in period style with antiques. Although a small village, Bramwell once was home to more than a dozen millionaires, and some of these families' homes are located on the town walking tour. The inn is listed in the National Register.
Innkeeper(s): Joyce & Jim Bishop. $65. PC, TC. TAC10. 4 rooms, 1 with PB. Breakfast included in rates. Types of meals: Full bkfst. Beds: QDT. Air conditioning. Weddings and family reunions hosted. Antiquing, fishing, live theater, parks, shopping, downhill skiing and water sports nearby.

Buckhannon   E5

Post Mansion Inn Bed & Breakfast

8 Island Ave
Buckhannon, WV 26201-2822
(304)472-8959 (800)301-9309
E-mail: lham1945@aol.com

Circa 1860. This massive Neoclassical Revival mansion is constructed of brick and precision-cut stone. An attached three-story stone tower resembles a medieval castle. Located on six

acres, this National Register inn is bordered by the Buckhannon River on the front and back of the grounds. Victorian antiques furnish the inn.
Innkeeper(s): Lawrence & Suzanne Reger. $80. PC, TC. 3 rooms, 1 with PB and 1 conference room. Breakfast and snacks/refreshments included in rates. Types of meals: Full bkfst and early coffee/tea. Beds: KQ. Air conditioning. VCR on premises. Weddings, small meetings, family reunions and seminars hosted. Antiquing, golf, parks, downhill skiing and water sports nearby.
Publicity: *The Inter-Mountain and The Record Delta.*

"We were so pleased with everything and all the guests couldn't say enough about your beautiful home."

Charles Town   D10

Gilbert House B&B of Middleway

PO Box 1104
Charles Town, WV 25414-7104
(304)725-0637
E-mail: gilberthouse@hotmail.com

Circa 1760. A magnificent graystone of early Georgian design, the Gilbert House is located in one of the state's oldest European settlements. Elegant appointments include fine Oriental rugs, tasteful art and antique furnishings. During restoration, graffiti found on the upstairs bedroom walls included an 1832 drawing of the future President James Polk and a child's growth chart from the 1800s. The inn is located in the Colonial era mill village of Middleway, which contains one of the country's best collections of log houses. The village is a

mill site on the original settlers' trail into Shenandoah Valley ("Philadelphia Waggon Road" on Peter Jefferson's 1755 map of Virginia). Middleway was also the site of "wizard clip" hauntings during the last decade of the 1700s. The region was home to members of "Virginia Blues," commanded by Daniel Morgan during the Revolutionary War.
Historic Interest: Charles Town, Bunker Hill, Leetown (10 minutes), Antietam Battlefield (20 minutes), Winchester, Va. (25 minutes), Harpers Ferry (20 minutes).
Innkeeper(s): Bernie Heiler. $100-140. MC, VISA, AX, PC, TC. TAC10. 3 rooms with PB, 2 with FP and 1 suite. Breakfast included in rates. Types of meals: Gourmet bkfst. Beds: QT. Air conditioning. VCR and library on premises. German & Spanish spoken. Antiquing, sports car racing, slots, live theater, parks and shopping nearby.

"We have stayed at inns for fifteen years, and yours is at the top of the list as best ever!"

The Washington House Inn

216 S George St
Charles Town, WV 25414-1632
(304)725-7923 (800)297-6957 Fax:(304)728-5150
E-mail: emailus@washingtonhouseinnwv.com
Web: www.washingtonhouseinnwv.com

Circa 1899. This three-story brick Victorian was built by the descendants of President Washington's brothers, John Augustine and Samuel. Carved oak mantels, spacious guest rooms, antique furnishings and refreshments served on the wraparound veranda or gazebo make the inn memorable. For business travelers, dataports are available. Harpers Ferry National Historic Park, Antietam, and the Shenandoah and Potomac rivers are all within a 15-minute drive. Thoroughbred racing, slot machines and car racing are some of the popular area attractions.

Innkeeper(s): Mel & Nina Vogel. $99-150. MC, VISA, AX, DS, PC, TC. TAC10. 7 rooms with PB, 1 suite and 1 conference room. Breakfast and snacks/refreshments included in rates. Types of meals: Full bkfst, cont plus, cont and early coffee/tea. Beds: QT. Cable TV, phone and ceiling fan in room. Air conditioning. VCR, fax, copier, internet and antiques and collectibles for sale on premises. Small meetings, family reunions and seminars hosted. Antiquing, fishing, golf, history museums, horse racing, car racing, slots, live theater, parks, shopping and water sports nearby.

Davis   E7

Bright Morning Inn

William Ave, Rt 32
Davis, WV 26260
(304)259-5119 Fax:(304)259-5119
E-mail: brightmorninginn@yahoo.com
Web: www.brightmorninginn.com

Circa 1895. In the still of the night, you can almost hear the cork boots of the loggers who boarded in this rustic Old-West Frontier inn a century ago. The inn is still surrounded by nearly a million acres of forest, (the Monongahela National Forest). But today, the inn is a welcome respite for work-weary vacationers, who enjoy the picturesque town of Davis for its laid back attitude and its extraordinary altitude. Davis is located at the highest altitude of any town in West Virginia. Its seven guest bedrooms and one suite have charming elements such as antique sleigh beds, hand-made quilts and colorful rugs. A lush herb harden on site contributes to the gourmet country breakfasts that include such hot entrees as wild blueberry pancakes served with homemade blueberry conserve made from local berries. Lunches can be packed upon request. The side yard has picnic tables and a rope hammock. The inn is near the Canaan Valley and Timberline Ski Resorts and all manner of outdoor activities including hiking, biking, and white-water river activities. Cross-country ski packages are available, as well.

Historic Interest: Fairfax Stone Monument (10 miles), Coke Ovens in Thomas (5 miles), Harper's Country Store (230 miles), Seneca & Smoke Hole Caverns (30 miles).

Innkeeper(s): Susan Moore. $60-75. MC, VISA, PC. 8 rooms, 7 with PB, 1 suite and 1 conference room. Breakfast and snacks/refreshments included in rates. Types of meals: Country bkfst, cont and lunch. Beds: DT. Ceiling fan in room. Fax on premises. Handicap access. Weddings, small meetings and family reunions hosted. Antiquing, bicycling, canoeing/kayaking, fishing, golf, hiking, horseback riding, parks, shopping, downhill skiing and cross-country skiing nearby.

Pets allowed: Quiet, housebroken, must stay in room.

Elkins   E6

Tunnel Mountain B&B

Rt 1, Box 59-1
Elkins, WV 26241-9711
(304)636-1684 (888)211-9123

Circa 1939. Nestled on five acres of wooded land, this three-story Fieldstone home offers privacy in a peaceful setting. Rooms are tastefully decorated with antiques, collectibles and crafts. Each bedroom boasts a view of the surrounding mountains. The chestnut and knotty pine woodwork accentuate the decor. The fireplace in the large common room is a great place for warming up

after a day of touring or skiing. The area is home to a number of interesting events, including a Dulcimer festival and the state's largest festival, the Mountain State Forest Festival.

Historic Interest: Rich Mountain Battlefield (20 miles), Halliehurst Mansion (4 miles), Beverly Museum (10 miles), Historic Elkins Walking Tour (4 miles), Beverly Historic Cemetery (10 miles), Old Mill (20 miles).

Innkeeper(s): Anne & Paul Beardslee. $75-80. PC, TC. 3 rooms with PB. Breakfast included in rates. Types of meals: Full bkfst and country bkfst. Beds: QD. Cable TV in room. Air conditioning. One great room on premises. Antiquing, art galleries, beaches, bicycling, canoeing/kayaking, fishing, golf, hiking, horseback riding, rock climbing, mountain biking, live theater, museums, parks, shopping, downhill skiing, cross-country skiing, sporting events, tennis and water sports nearby.

Publicity: Blue Ridge Country, Washington Post. and WBOY.

The Warfield House B&B

318 Buffalo St
Elkins, WV 26241
(304)636-4555 (888)636-4555
E-mail: warfieldhouse@meer.net

Circa 1901. Restaurants, shops, boutiques, and theater are a five-minute stroll from the historic Warfield House, which is listed in the National Register. Guests can relax on the

wraparound porch, in front of a fire in the library or strum the ivories on the parlor's piano. The turn-of-the-20th-century home features five guest rooms, each decorated with antiques and quilts. Two include a whirlpool tub. The home faces a city park and is next to Davis and Elkins College. Elkins is the site of many annual festivals and events.

Innkeeper(s): Connie & Paul Garnett. $75-109. MC, VISA, PC, TC. 5 rooms with PB. Breakfast included in rates. Types of meals: Full bkfst. Beds: DT. Ceiling fan in room. Bicycles and library on premises. Small meetings, family reunions and seminars hosted. Antiquing, bicycling, fishing, golf, hiking, historic attractions, battlefields, rock climbing, live theater, parks, shopping, downhill skiing, cross-country skiing, tennis and water sports nearby.

Fairmont   D6

Acacia House

158 Locust Ave
Fairmont, WV 26554-1630
(304)367-1000 (888)269-9541 Fax:(304)367-1000
E-mail: acacia@acaciahousewv.com
Web: www.acaciahousewv.com

Circa 1917. Two maple trees frame this four-story brown brick home built in the American Four-Square style. As an antique dealer, innkeeper Kathy Sprowls has filled her home with a memorable assortment of collectibles, including butter pats, pill boxes and stone eggs from around the world. There's an antique store on the premises and some of the items found in the inn are also available for purchase. Guest rooms are handsomely furnished with antiques, of course. Kathy and her husband, George, serve a country breakfast in the dining room with stuffed French toast or puff pancakes, hot pepper bacon or West Virginia sausage and a fruit cup. As with most bed & breakfasts, smoking is not allowed.

Innkeeper(s): Kathy & George Sprowls. $45-70. MC, VISA, AX, DS, PC, TC. TAC10. 4 rooms, 2 with PB. Breakfast included in rates. Types of meals: Full bkfst, cont plus, cont and early coffee/tea. Beds: QDT. TV in room. Air conditioning. VCR, fax and library on premises. Small meetings and family reunions hosted. Antiquing, bicycling, fishing, golf, hiking, live theater, parks, shopping, sporting events and water sports nearby.

Harpers Ferry   D10

Fillmore Street B&B

PO Box 34
Harpers Ferry, WV 25425-0034
(304)535-2619

Circa 1890. This two-story clapboard Victorian was built on the foundation of a Civil War structure on land deeded by Jefferson Davis, Secretary of War. The surrounding acreage was an encampment for both the Union and Confederate soldiers (at different times). Within walking distance of the inn are the national park, museums, shopping and dining.

Historic Interest: Harpers Ferry National Historic Park (two blocks), Potomac and Shenandoah Rivers.

Innkeeper(s): Alden & James Addy. $80-85. PC, TC. 2 rooms with PB. Breakfast included in rates. Types of meals: Full bkfst, cont plus and early coffee/tea. Beds: Q. TV, turndown service and VCR in room. Air conditioning. Library on premises. Antiquing, bicycling, hiking, battlefields, historic exhibits, horse racing, gaming, parks, shopping and water sports nearby.

"Delightful! What superb hosts you two are. We enjoyed ourselves luxuriously."

Lewisburg H5

The General Lewis

301 E Washington St
Lewisburg, WV 24901-1425
(304)645-2600 (800)628-4454 Fax:(304)645-2600

Circa 1834. This gracious Federal-style inn boasts a columned veranda, flower gardens and long lawns. Patrick Henry and Thomas Jefferson registered at the inn's walnut desk, which was retrieved from an old hot springs resort in the area. A stagecoach that once delivered travelers to springs on the James River and Kanawha Turnpike, rests under an arbor. American antiques are featured through-out the inn, and Memory Hall displays household items and tools once used by local pioneers. Nearby are state parks, national forests, streams and rivers, as well as sites of the Revolutionary and Civil wars.

Historic Interest: Civil War Cemetery, Carnegie Hall, Pearl S. Buck's Birthplace.

Innkeeper(s): The Morgan Family. $99-120. MC, VISA, AX, DS. TAC10. 23 rooms with PB and 2 suites. Types of meals: Early coffee/tea. Beds: QD. Cable TV and phone in room. Air conditioning. Fax and copier on premises. Handicap access. Weddings hosted.

Publicity: *National Geographic Traveler, Colonial Homes and Travel & Leisure.*

"Personality, charm and gracious service."

Martinsburg D9

Boydville, The Inn at Martinsburg

601 S Queen St
Martinsburg, WV 25401-3103
(304)263-1448

Circa 1812. This Georgian estate was saved from burning by Union troops only by a specific proclamation from President Lincoln dated July 18, 1864. Tall maples line the long driveway leading up to the house. Guests can relax in rockers original to the inn on the spacious porch while gazing at 10 acres of lawns. The entry hall retains the original wallpaper brought from England in 1812 and hand-painted murals, fireplaces, and antiques adorn the spacious guest rooms. Sunlight filters through tree tops onto estate-sized lawns and gardens.

Historic Interest: Antietam Battlefield, Harpers Ferry, Berkeley Springs.

Innkeeper(s): LaRue Frye. $145. MC, VISA, PC. 7 rooms with PB and 1 conference room. Breakfast included in rates. Types of meals: Cont plus and early coffee/tea. Beds: QDT. Air conditioning. Library on premises. Weddings and family reunions hosted. Antiquing, Blue Ridge Outlet, golf, live theater, shopping and downhill skiing nearby.

Publicity: *Washington Post, Mid-Atlantic Country and Colonial Homes.*

"Your gracious home, hospitality and excellent amenities were enjoyed so much. Such a fine job of innkeeping."

Morgantown D6

Fieldcrest Manor B&B

1440 Stewartstown Rd
Morgantown, WV 26505
(304)599-2686 (866)599-2686 Fax:(304)599-2853
E-mail: innkeeper@fieldcrestmanor.com
Web: www.fieldcrestmanor.com

Circa 1920. A famous Italian stone mason built this English Country home, showcasing some of his finest work. The front veranda features stone with red and cream tiles. Surrounded by towering old maples and oaks, the inn's romantic ambiance is enhanced by five acres of manicured lawns and an English garden. Large windows provide a panoramic view of a valley and farmland beyond. Natural wood flooring adds character to the impeccable guest bedrooms, which contain computer/data jacks. Hospitality is lavished generously, and breakfast is a culinary creation that may include blueberry French toast or a vegetable frittata. Ask about a private candle-lit dinner for two. Enjoy visiting Pricketts Fort State Park, Coopers Rock State Forest and Cheat Lake.

Innkeeper(s): Sarah Lough. $80-90. MC, VISA, AX, PC, TC. 5 rooms with PB, 1 cottage and 1 conference room. Breakfast included in rates. Types of meals: Gourmet bkfst, country bkfst, veg bkfst, cont plus, cont and early coffee/tea. AP. Beds: QD. Cable TV, phone, turndown service and ceiling fan in room. Central air. Fax, copier and library on premises. Weddings, small meetings, family reunions and seminars hosted. Antiquing, bicycling, canoeing/kayaking, fishing, golf, hiking, live theater, parks, downhill skiing, cross-country skiing, sporting events, tennis, water sports and wineries nearby.

Pence Springs H5

Historic Pence Springs Grand Hotel

St Rts 3 & 12, PO Box 90
Pence Springs, WV 24962-0090
(304)445-2606 (800)826-1829 Fax:(304)445-2204
E-mail: pencehotel@newwave.net
Web: wvweb.com/www/Pence_Springs_Hotel

Circa 1918. Listed in the National Register, this plantation-style inn is known as one of the "historic springs of the Virginias." After local mineral waters captured a silver medal at the World's Fair, the waters' healing drinking properties drew many visitors. Prominent and wealthy guests flocked to this hotel in the 1920s. It later became a women's state prison. The inn is now fully restored with a decor reminiscent of the hotel's famous heyday. Open year-round, the inn's comfortable guest bedrooms and suites offer relaxation. Enjoy a full country breakfast served daily. During April through October a Sunday brunch also is enjoyed. The scenic surrounding area boasts many outdoor activities.

Historic Interest: The hotel is listed in the National Register and Pence Springs is designated as a National Historic District.

Innkeeper(s): John & Wendy Lincoln. $75-110. MC, VISA, AX, DS, PC, TC. TAC10. 15 rooms with PB, 3 suites and 3 conference rooms. Breakfast included in rates. Types of meals: Country bkfst, lunch, picnic lunch, gourmet dinner and room service. Beds: KDT. TV on request in room. Air conditioning. VCR, fax, copier, swimming, stables, bicycles, child care, antique shop, horseshoes, croquet, badminton, fishing and hiking on premises. Handicap access. Weddings, small meetings, family reunions and seminars hosted. Antiquing, fishing, golf, whitewater rafting, live theater, parks, shopping, downhill skiing and water sports nearby.

Pets allowed: Cannot be left in room; kennel space in basement, $15 fee (non-refundable).

Publicity: *Gourmet, Southern Living, Mid-Atlantic Country, West Virginia Quarterly, MIT Press Journal, Goldenseal and Travel Host.*

"As always, I left your place rejuvenated. The property grows even more beautiful year after year."

Point Pleasant — E2

Stone Manor

12 Main St
Point Pleasant, WV 25550-1026
(304)675-3442
E-mail: vancetj@zoomnet.net

Circa 1887. This stone Victorian sits on the banks of the Kanawha River with a front porch that faces the river. Point Pleasant Battle Monument Park, adjacent to the inn, was built to commemorate the location of the first battle of the Revolutionary War. In the National Register, the inn was once the home of a family who ran a ferry boat crossing for the Ohio and Kanawha rivers. Now restored, the house is decorated with Victorian antiques and offers a pleasant garden with a Victorian fish pond and fountain.

Innkeeper(s): Janice & Tom Vance. $50. PC. 3 rooms, 3 with FP. Breakfast included in rates. Types of meals: Full bkfst. Beds: QD. VCR in room. Air conditioning.

Romney — D8

Hampshire House 1884

165 N Grafton St
Romney, WV 26757-1616
(304)822-7171
E-mail: hhouse@raven-villages.net

Circa 1884. Located near the south branch of the Potomac River, the garden here has old boxwoods and walnut trees. The inn features ornate brickwork; tall, narrow windows; and fireplaces with handsome period mantels. A sitting room with a

well-stocked library, a cozy patio and a music room with an antique pump organ are favorite places. On-site massage available. One guest room has been renovated to allow full wheelchair accessibility.

Innkeeper(s): Jane & Scott Simmons. $75-95. MC, VISA, AX, DC, DS, PC, TC. TAC10. 5 rooms with PB, 3 with FP and 1 conference room. Breakfast included in rates. Types of meals: Full bkfst, early coffee/tea and snacks/refreshments. Beds: QDT. Cable TV, phone and VCR in room. Air conditioning. Bicycles and therapeutic massage on premises. Small meetings hosted. Antiquing, canoeing/kayaking, fishing, hiking, massage, Civil War museum, museums, shopping and water sports nearby.

Publicity: *Hampshire Review, Mid-Atlantic Country and Weekend Journal.*

"Your personal attention made us feel at home immediately."

Wisconsin

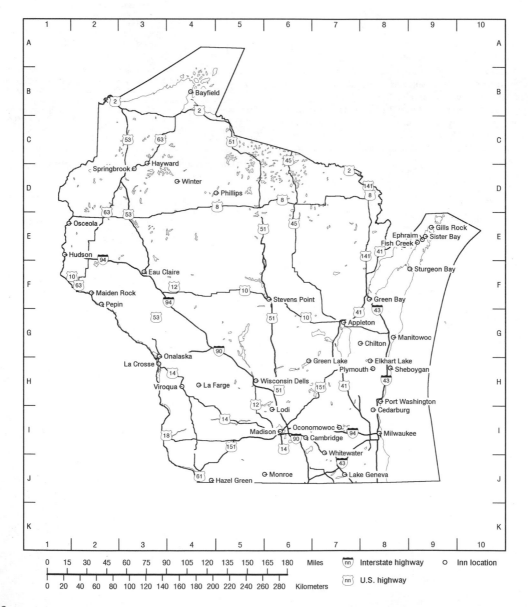

0   15   30   45   60   75   90   105 120 135 150 165 180   Miles

0   20   40   60   80   100 120 140 160 180 200 220 240 260 280   Kilometers

Interstate highway   ○ Inn location

U.S. highway

Appleton G7

The Queen Anne B&B

837 E College Ave
Appleton, WI 54911-5619
(920)831-9903 (888)241-0419 Fax:(920)739-1813

Circa 1895. This 1895 Queen Anne Victorian home on a tree-lined street in Appleton has polished oak, pine and maple floors and original stained-glass windows in the first-floor parlor and foyer. The inn is furnished with Victorian, Louis XV, Eastlake and Empire antiques. The four guest rooms include a bridal suite and a two bedroom suite. Coffee is served each morning in the guest room or the dining room 30 minutes before a full breakfast with homemade scones or muffins and a hot entrée. The Houdini Historical Center, the Green Bay Packer Hall of Fame and Lawrence University are all within walking distance or a short drive.

Innkeeper(s): Emilie & Tom Sabol. $85-150. 4 rooms, 2 with PB and 1 conference room. Types of meals: Full bkfst. Beds: Q. TV in room. VCR on premises. Museums nearby.

Publicity: *The Post Crescent and Valleysun.*

The Solie Home

914 E Hancock St
Appleton, WI 54911-5250
(920)733-0863

Circa 1905. Located in a quiet neighborhood this two-story stucco home is shaded by tall trees. Over the years, various collections have been organized in the built-in bookcases and on the walls. The turn-of-the-century home's sculptured plaster walls still remain. Guest rooms are comfortably appointed. Riley's Retreat offers an antique bird's-eye maple double bed. The innkeepers, who raised their four daughters here, offer a full breakfast every morning with homemade coffee cakes and freshly baked breads accompanying a hot entree.

Innkeeper(s): Riley & Carole Solie. $65-125. PC, TC. 3 rooms. Breakfast included in rates. Types of meals: Full bkfst and early coffee/tea. Beds: DT. Air conditioning. VCR on premises. Antiquing, fishing, golf, live theater, parks, shopping, cross-country skiing, sporting events and tennis nearby.

"Evening tea, fresh cookies and flowers were just what I needed."

Bayfield B4

Old Rittenhouse Inn

301 Rittenhouse Ave, PO Box 584
Bayfield, WI 54814-0584
(715)779-5111
E-mail: frontdsk@rittenhouseinn.com
Web: www.rittenhouseinn.com

Circa 1892. This rambling Queen Anne Victorian was built by Civil War General Allen Fuller, using cedar shingles and the local brownstone, for which Bayfield was famous. Antique furnishings abound throughout the inn, which has 22 working fireplaces. Underneath massive gables, a wraparound veranda is filled with geraniums, petunias and white wicker furnishings. There is a spectacular view of Lake Superior.

Innkeeper(s): Larry E. Cicero. $99-299. MC, VISA, PC, TC. 18 rooms with PB, 17 with FP and 3 suites. Breakfast included in rates. Types of meals: Gourmet bkfst, gourmet lunch, afternoon tea, gourmet dinner and room service. Beds: KQD. 9 luxury rooms/suites with whirlpool in room. Handicap access. Weddings, small meetings and family reunions hosted. Shopping nearby.

Publicity: *Wisconsin Trails and Midwest Living.*

"The whole decor, the room, the staff and the food were superb! Your personalities and talents give a great warmth to the inn."

Cambridge I6

Country Comforts B&B

2722 Highland Dr
Cambridge, WI 53523
(608)423-3097 (877)771-1277 Fax:(608)423-7743
E-mail: info@country-comforts.com
Web: www.country-comforts.com

Circa 1890. On the edge of town sits this Victorian farmhouse on four blissful acres of lawns and gardens. The inn is filled with family heirlooms and antique furnishings. Be entertained around the piano in the living room, curled up fireside, or in the Rainbow Room, an upstairs sitting room. Hospitality shows clearly in the generous amenities that include homemade cookies and fresh flowers. Wall hangings and leaded and stained glass accent the guest bedrooms and the Nightingale Suite, which also boasts a bay window, screened porch and sitting room with gas fireplace. A hearty breakfast changes with the bounty of the seasons, and may feature asparagus quiche and raspberry muffins served with scrambled eggs, herbed potatoes and fresh fruit. Linger over the paper on the front porch before wandering through Cam-Rock Park, biking Glacial Drumlin Trail or enjoying Lake Ripley.

Innkeeper(s): Mim Jacobson & Marian Korth. $99-149. MC, VISA, AX, DS, PC, TC. 4 rooms with PB, 1 with FP and 1 suite. Breakfast and snacks/refreshments included in rates. Types of meals: Full bkfst and early coffee/tea. Beds: Q. Cable TV, phone, ceiling fan, VCR and fireplace in room. Central air. Fax, copier, library and gift shop on premises. Handicap access. Small meetings, family reunions and seminars hosted. Antiquing, art galleries, beaches, bicycling, canoeing/kayaking, fishing, golf, hiking, horseback riding, swimming, bird watching, live theater, museums, parks, shopping, cross-country skiing, sporting events, tennis, water sports and wineries nearby.

Publicity: *Chicago Tribune, Wisconsin State Journal and Cambridge News.*

Cedarburg I8

The Washington House Inn

W 62 N 573 Washington Ave
Cedarburg, WI 53012-1941
(262)375-3550 (800)554-4717 Fax:(262)375-9422
E-mail: whinn@execpc.com
Web: www.washingtonhouseinn.com

Circa 1886. Completely renovated, this three-story cream city brick building is in the National Register. Rooms are appointed in a country Victorian style and feature antiques, whirlpool baths, vases of flowers and fireplaces. The original guest registry, more than 100 years old, is displayed proudly in the lobby, and a marble trimmed fireplace is often lit for the afternoon wine and cheese hour. Breakfast is continental and is available in the gathering room, often including recipes from a historic Cedarburg cookbook for items such as homemade muffins, cakes and breads.

Historic Interest: National Register.

Innkeeper(s): Wendy Porterfield. $85-215. MC, VISA, AX, DC, DS, TC. TAC10. 34 rooms with PB, 3 suites and 1 conference room. Breakfast included in rates. Types of meals: Cont plus and snacks/refreshments. MAP. Beds: KQD. Cable TV, phone, ceiling fan and VCR in room. Air conditioning. Fax, copier and sauna on premises. Weddings, small meetings, family reunions and seminars hosted. Antiquing, fishing, live theater, parks, shopping, cross-country skiing and sporting events nearby.

Publicity: *Country Home and Chicago Sun-Times.*

Chilton   G7

East Shore Inn

N3049 US Highway 151
Chilton, WI 53014-9445
(920)849-4230 Fax:(920)849-8521
Web: www.bbinternet.com/eastshore

Circa 1895. The Bub family purchased this working dairy farm in 1965 and offers guests a truly unique farm atmosphere. The guest cottage is rented out to one group or family at a time, insuring privacy. Guests are invited to join the Bubs as they work the farm. However, the work is optional, and relaxation is a priority. Quarters include a kitchen area and game room. Plenty of animals roam the grounds, and you're sure to see foxes, rabbits or deer. The surrounding area offers plenty of attractions, including cheese factories, boutiques, fruit farms and many outdoor activities.

Historic Interest: The inn is situated on what was a Native American reservation. Indian burial grounds are about five miles from the inn.

Innkeeper(s): Janice, Henry, Neil Bub. $75. PC, TC. 4 rooms. Beds: DT. TV, phone, ceiling fan and VCR in room. Central air. Library on premises. Antiquing, fishing, cross-country skiing and water sports nearby.

Pets Allowed.

Publicity: *Appleton Post Crescent, Chilton Times, Milwaukee Journal and Channel 11.*

"Our third trip. The kids love the kittens and feeding the calves. Beautiful sunset over the lake."

Eau Claire   F3

Otter Creek Inn

2536 Hwy 12. PO Box 3183
Eau Claire, WI 54702-3183
(715)832-2945 Fax:(715)832-4607
E-mail: info@ottercreekinn.net

Circa 1920. On a hillside overlooking a creek is this Tudor-style inn, surrounded by oaks and pines. Visitors immediately feel welcome as they make their way up the inn's curved pebblestone walk and step into a house with country Victorian decor. Each of the guest rooms includes a double whirlpool

tub, and many have a fireplace. The Rose Room, often the choice of honeymooners, features a cloverleaf-shaped whirlpool tub that overlooks the gardens and gazebo. The

spacious inn provides many spots for relaxation, including a gazebo, the great room with its inviting fireplace and a roomy patio surrounding the in-ground heated swimming pool.

Innkeeper(s): Shelley & Randy Hansen. $90-180. MC, VISA, AX, DC, CB, DS, TC. 6 rooms with PB, 4 with FP. Breakfast included in rates. Types of meals: Full bkfst, early coffee/tea and snacks/refreshments. Beds: KQ. Cable TV, phone, VCR and double whirlpools in room. Air conditioning. Swimming on premises. Antiquing, beaches, bicycling, canoeing/kayaking, fishing, golf, live theater, museums, parks, shopping, cross-country skiing, tennis and water sports nearby.

Publicity: *Country, Country Inns, Milwaukee Journal, St. Paul Pioneer Press, Country Gazette and Wisconsin West.*

"This is the perfect place to recharge your 'couple batteries'."

Elkhart Lake   H8

Boarding House B&B

121 S East, PO Box 746
Elkhart Lake, WI 53020
(920)876-3616

Circa 1923. Typical of the local architecture in the early 1900s, this house was built in the Four-Square style. It was named after its service of housing many of the surrounding area's

resort workers. Comfortable places to gather include the living room and game room, both furnished with antiques. Guest bedrooms feature terry robes and toiletry baskets. The main dining room showcases a full breakfast that offers dishes

like custard French toast with warm berries. The famous Road America racetrack is just two miles away.

Innkeeper(s): Bob & Cindy Roska. $85-130. MC, VISA, DS. 5 rooms. Breakfast included in rates. Types of meals: Country bkfst. Beds: KQDT. Cable TV and phone in room. Central air. Copier on premises. Antiquing, beaches, fishing, golf, hiking and sports car racing nearby.

Ephraim   E9

Eagle Harbor Inn

9914 Water St
Ephraim, WI 54211-0072
(920)854-2121 (800)324-5427 Fax:(920)854-2121
E-mail: nedd@eagleharbor.com

Circa 1946. The Eagle Harbor Inn is located in the Historic District and offers a variety of accommodations. Rooms in the inn are decorated with antiques. One and two-bedroom suites with six-foot whirlpool tubs and two-sided fireplaces, full kitchens and private decks. Breakfast (optional for guests in the suites) is home cooked and served in the garden in summertime. Afternoon refreshments are offered to all guests. There is an indoor current pool,

sauna and fitness room. A scenic sandy beach is a block away. Nearby are shops and galleries, and a half-hour drive leads guests to Rock Island, home of Wisconsin's first settlers. Door County Peninsula offers the largest selection of lighthouses in any U.S. county.

Innkeeper(s): Nedd & Natalie Neddersen. $69-224. MC, VISA, DS, PC, TC. 41 rooms, 9 with PB and 32 suites. Types of meals: Gourmet bkfst, early coffee/tea and afternoon tea. EP. Beds: Q. Cable TV, phone, ceiling fan, VCR, 9 B&B rooms have private baths, all suites have fireplaces, whirlpools and kitchens in room. Air conditioning. Fax, copier, spa, swimming, sauna, library, child care, gardens, croquette, playground and picnic areas with woods and stream on premises. Handicap access. Weddings, small meetings, family reunions and seminars hosted. Fishing, golf, antique shopping, historic walking tours, horse-drawn carriage rides, live theater, parks, shopping, cross-country skiing, tennis and water sports nearby.

Publicity: *Door County Advocate, Milwaukee Business Journal and Chicago Sun Times.*

"From the friendly greeting when we arrived, to the elegant room, to the wonderful four-poster bed, our stay has been everything we hoped."

Fish Creek   E9

Thorp House Inn & Cottages

4135 Bluff Ln, PO Box 490
Fish Creek, WI 54212
(920)868-2444
E-mail: innkeeper@thorphouseinn.com
Web: www.thorphouseinn.com

Circa 1902. Freeman Thorp picked the site for this home because of its view of Green Bay and the village. Before his house was finished, however, he perished in the bay when the Erie L. Hackley sank. His wife completed it as a guest house.

Each room is decorated with English or Victorian antiques. A stone fireplace is the focal point of the parlor, and four of the cottages on the property have fireplaces. Some cottages have whirlpools and all have kitchens, cable TVs and VCRs. Listed in the National Register of Historic Places, everything upon which the eye might rest in the inn must be "of the era." Breakfast is not available to cottage guests.

Historic Interest: The Asa Thorp Log Cabin and Noble House Museum are one block away. The Church of the Attonement is three blocks away, and the Peninsula Park Lighthouse is four miles from the inn.

Innkeeper(s): Christine & Sverre Falck-Pedersen. $95-195. PC, TC. 5 rooms with PB and 6 cottages. Types of meals: Cont plus and early coffee/tea. Beds: KQDT. Three with whirlpool, two with fireplace and central air in room. Bicycles on premises. Norwegian spoken. Antiquing, fishing, summer art school, music festival, live theater, parks, shopping, cross-country skiing and water sports nearby.

Publicity: *Green Bay Press-Gazette, Milwaukee Journal/Sentinel, McCall's, Minnesota Monthly. and Madison PM.*

"Amazing attention to detail from restoration to the furnishings. A very first-class experience."

Gills Rock   E9

Harbor House Inn

12666 Hwy 42
Gills Rock, WI 54210
(920)854-5196
Web: www.door-county-inn.com

Circa 1904. Built by the Weborgs almost 100 years ago, the inn has stayed in the family and been carefully restored. The main house features suites and guest bedrooms with classic Victorian and Scandinavian country decor. Danish Cottage

continues that theme, and Troll Cottage is a nautical cabin. The Lighthouse overlooks the quaint fishing village. A gazebo and private decks offer sunset and harbor views. A generous continental-plus breakfast is

served in the sitting room. Enjoy a Norwegian sauna and spa or take a short walk to the beach.

Historic Interest: Nautical Museum, many lighthouses.

Innkeeper(s): David & Else Weborg. $45-175. MC, VISA, AX, PC, TC. 15 rooms with PB, 2 with FP and 2 cottages. Breakfast included in rates. Types of meals: Cont plus and early coffee/tea. Beds: KQDT. Cable TV, ceiling fan, microwaves, kitchenettes and decks in room. Air conditioning. Fax, spa, sauna, bicycles, beach, gas grills, hot tub and bike rentals on premises. Handicap access. Danish spoken. Antiquing, art galleries, bicycling, fishing, golf, hiking, island ferry, sunset cruise, Nautical Museum, historical lighthouses, live theater, museums, parks, shopping and water sports nearby.

Pets allowed: Please inquire.

Publicity: *Wisconsin State Journal and Travel & Leisure.*

"Lovely inn. Thank you for your hospitality."

Green Bay   F8

The Astor House B&B

637 S Monroe Ave
Green Bay, WI 54301-3614
(920)432-3585 (888)303-6370
E-mail: astor@execpc.com
Web: www.astorhouse.com

Circa 1888. Located in the Astor Historic District, the Astor House is completely surrounded by Victorian homes. Guests have their choice of five rooms, each uniquely decorated for a range of ambiance, from the Vienna Balconies to the Marseilles Garden to the Hong Kong Retreat. The parlor, veranda and many suites feature a grand view of City Centre's lighted church towers. This home is also the first and only

B&B in Green Bay and received the Mayor's Award for Remodeling and Restoration. Business travelers should take notice of the private phone lines in each room, as well as the ability to hook up a modem.

Historic Interest: Green Bay City Centre (8 blocks), Lambeau Field, 1837 Hazelwood Historic Home museum.

Innkeeper(s): Greg & Barbara Robinson. $115-152. MC, VISA, AX, DS. TAC10. 5 rooms with PB, 4 with FP and 3 suites. Breakfast included in rates. Types of meals: Cont plus. Beds: KQDT. Cable TV, phone, VCR, gas fireplaces and double whirlpool tub (4 of 5 rooms) in room. Air conditioning. Amusement parks, antiquing, fishing, live theater, parks, shopping, cross-country skiing, sporting events and water sports nearby.

Publicity: *Chicago Sun-Times and Corporate Reports.*

Green Lake H6

McConnell Inn

497 S Lawson Dr
Green Lake, WI 54941-8700
(920)294-6430
E-mail: info@mcconnellinn.com
Web: www.mcconnellinn.com

Circa 1901. This stately home features many of its original features, including leaded windows, woodwork, leather wainscoting and parquet floors. Each of the guest rooms includes beds covered with handmade quilts and clawfoot tubs. The grand, master suite comprises the entire third floor and boasts 14-foot vaulted beam ceilings, Victorian walnut furnishings, a Jacuzzi and six-foot oak buffet now converted into a unique bathroom vanity. Innkeeper Mary Jo Johnson, a pastry chef, creates the wonderful pastries that accompany an expansive breakfast with fresh fruit, granola and delectable entrees.

Innkeeper(s): Mary Jo Johnson. $85-165. MC, VISA, DS. 5 rooms. Breakfast included in rates. Types of meals: Full bkfst.

Hayward C3

Lumberman's Mansion Inn

204 E Fourth St
Hayward, WI 54843-0885
(715)634-3012 Fax:(715)634-5724
E-mail: mansion@winbright.net

Circa 1887. This Queen Anne Victorian, once the home of a local lumber baron, sits on a hill overlooking the city, park and pond. An oak staircase, maple floors, tiled fireplaces, pocket doors and a carriage stoop are among the finely restored details. Antique furnishings blend with modern amenities such as whirlpool tubs and a video library. Wild rice pancakes, Wisconsin sausages and freshly squeezed cranberry juice  are some of the regional specialties featured for breakfast. The innkeepers host many seasonal events and evening lectures. Plays are sometimes performed on the front porch.

Historic Interest: Historic Company Store, museum, old growth forest, church.
Innkeeper(s): Jan Hinrichs Blaedel & Wendy Hinrichs Sanders. $70-100. MC, VISA, PC, TC. 5 rooms with PB, 2 suites and 1 conference room. Breakfast included in rates. Types of meals: Full bkfst, afternoon tea and gourmet dinner. Beds: Q. Spa and bicycles on premises. Antiquing, fishing, golf, biking, cross-country skiing and water sports nearby.
Publicity: *Sawyer County Record, Chicago Sun Times, Wisconsin Trails, Minneapolis Star Tribune and Wisconsin Country Life.*

"The food was excellent. And the extra personal touches (chocolate on the pillow, cookies & pie at night, muffins in the morning, etc.) were especially nice. This is definitely the best B&B we've ever been to."

Ross' Teal Lake Lodge & Teal Wing Golf Club

12425 N Ross Rd
Hayward, WI 54843
(715)462-3631
E-mail: amhisinn@teallake.com
Web: www.teallake.com

Circa 1908. Located on 250 acres bordering Teal Lake and Teal River, this is a great vacation spot for families, golfers and fishermen. Most of the Northwoods cabins here are of vertical log construction, and most feature fireplaces and kitchens. There are two beds in each room. Most rooms offer ceiling fans. Fishing guides and a fishing school for both children and adults offers fishing expertise and local folklore. (You'll learn how to catch the prized muskie, a fierce freshwater game fish.) An 18-hole golf course winds through the woods and has been recognized by Wisconsin Golf Magazine as one of the upper Midwest's best courses. Bicycles, tricycles and water bicycles are available to use. A family of eagles nest on the island, and you can watch them feed and learn to fly. Early springtime guests enjoy the otters that scramble around the inn's docks. Picnic and basket lunches are available. Breakfast and dinner are available in the lodge's dining room.

Innkeeper(s): Prudence & Tim Ross. $120-590. MC, VISA, PC, TC. TAC10. 24 rooms, 2 suites, 22 guest houses and 1 conference room. Types of meals: Full bkfst, cont, picnic lunch and dinner. MAP, AP, EP. Beds: KDT. Some with ceiling fans in room. Swimming, sauna, bicycles, tennis, library and golf on premises. Small meetings and family reunions hosted. Antiquing, fishing, golf, parks, shopping, cross-country skiing and water sports nearby.
Pets Allowed.

Hazel Green J4

Wisconsin House Stagecoach Inn

2105 Main, PO Box 71
Hazel Green, WI 53811-0071
(608)854-2233
E-mail: wishouse@mhtc.net
Web: www.wisconsinhouse.com

Circa 1846. Located in southwest Wisconsin's historic lead mining region, this one-time stagecoach stop will delight antique-lovers. The spacious two-story inn once hosted Ulysses S. Grant, whose home is just across the border in Illinois. One of the inn's guest rooms bears his name and features a walnut four-poster bed. Don't miss the chance to join the Dischs on a Saturday evening for their gourmet dinner, served by reservation only.

Innkeeper(s): Ken & Pat Disch. $65-120. MC, VISA, AX, DS, PC. TAC10. 8 rooms, 6 with PB and 2 suites. Breakfast included in rates. Types of meals: Gourmet bkfst, early coffee/tea and gourmet dinner. Beds: KQDT. Air conditioning. Copier, bicycles and library on premises. Weddings, small meetings, family reunions and seminars hosted. Antiquing, fishing, live theater, parks, downhill skiing and cross-country skiing nearby.
Publicity: *Travel & Leisure, Milwaukee Magazine, Chicago Magazine and Milwaukee Journal.*

Hudson E1

Jefferson-Day House

1109 Third St
Hudson, WI 54016-1220
(715)386-7111
E-mail: jeffersn@pressenter.com
Web: www.jeffersondayhouse.com

Circa 1857. Near the St. Croix River and 30 minutes from Mall of America, the Italianate Jefferson-Day House features five guest rooms with both double whirlpool tubs and gas fireplaces. Antique art and furnishings fill the rooms, and there is a formal dining room and living room. Ask for the Captain's Room and you'll be rewarded with a cedar-lined bathroom, over-sized shower, antique brass bed, and a gas fireplace visible from the whirlpool tub for two. A four-course breakfast is served fireside every morning, and complimentary spirits are offered.

Innkeeper(s): Tom & Sue Tyler. $99-179. MC, VISA, DS, PC, TC. 5 rooms with PB, 5 with FP. Breakfast and snacks/refreshments included in rates. Types of meals: Full bkfst. Beds: Q. 5 with double whirlpools in room. Weddings, small meetings and family reunions hosted. Amusement parks, antiquing, fishing, live theater, parks, shopping, downhill skiing, cross-country skiing, sporting events and water sports nearby.

Pets allowed: With advance notice; some restrictions apply.

"Absolute perfection! That's the only way to describe our stay in the wonderful St. Croix suite!"

The Phipps Inn

1005 3rd St
Hudson, WI 54016-1261
(715)386-0800 (888)865-9388
Web: www.phippsinn.com

Circa 1884. In the National Register of Historic Places, Phipps Inn is an outstandingly beautiful example of delicate Queen Anne Victorian architecture. The mansion offers wraparound porches, fluted pilasters, gabled dormers and an octagonal tower that rises three stories high. Located on a historic street in Wisconsin's St. Croix Valley, an appropriate Victorian decor compliments the interior's oak and maple woodwork. Guest rooms and suites offer romantic furnishings and  amenities such as brass, canopy or four-poster feather beds, and all feature large whirlpool tubs and fireplaces. There are a variety of rooms to wander into and enjoy, including the music room, billiards room and the inn's two parlors. Four-course breakfasts include a fresh fruit course, a pastry course, an entrée and a dessert. Antique shops, galleries, boutiques and a good selection of restaurants are nearby, as are parks and the St. Croix River. Octagon House, a museum in an 1855 house, is across the street from the inn.

Innkeeper(s): Rich & Mary Ellen Cox. $129-209. 6 rooms with PB. Types of meals: Gourmet bkfst and early coffee/tea. Beds: Q. Double whirlpool and fireplaces in room. Air conditioning. Bicycles on premises. Antiquing, art galleries, museums, parks, shopping and water sports nearby.

La Crosse   H3

Chateau La Crosse

410 Cass St
La Crosse, WI 54601-4508
(608)796-1090 (800)442-7969 Fax:(608)796-0700
E-mail: chateaulax@aol.com
Web: www.visitor-guide.com/chateaulacrosse

Circa 1854. Enter a personal fairy tale when you visit this inviting yet stately stone castle. A destination unto itself, it is the oldest stone house in the state that has been continuously occupied since it was built. In the National Register, the finely crafted interior offers elegant fireplaces, gleaming woodwork and elaborately detailed wood floors, renovated at a cost of more than $1 million. Relax in the elegant common rooms, which include a main parlor, drawing room, dining room, library and music room. If it's a special occasion, request the Master Bedroom to enjoy its masterful hand-painted mural ceiling and faux-painted marble walls complete with gold leaf trim.

There's a marble wood-burning fireplace, as well. The bath boasts marble floors and a tub of faux marble with a hand-painted mural of cherubs. The gardens offer a fountain, pond and variety of flowering trees such as a Japanese lilac tree. Red hibiscus, lilac, potted palms, elephant ears, hydrangeas and an arbor with roses completes the garden. A full champagne breakfast includes dishes such as quiche, cinnamon toast, French cashew waffles and usually a breakfast dessert such as cheesecake or peach pie. A gourmet restaurant on the premises offers six private dining rooms.

Innkeeper(s): JoAn Lambert Smith. $100-325. MC, VISA, AX, DC, DS, PC, TC. TAC10. 7 rooms with PB and 1 conference room. Breakfast and snacks/refreshments included in rates. Types of meals: Gourmet bkfst, country bkfst, veg bkfst, cont plus, early coffee/tea, gourmet lunch, picnic lunch, afternoon tea, gourmet dinner and room service. Beds: KQ. Cable TV, phone and ceiling fan in room. Air conditioning. VCR, fax, copier, spa and library on premises. Handicap access. Some German and Spanish spoken. Antiquing, art galleries, beaches, bicycling, canoeing/kayaking, fishing, golf, hiking, live theater, museums, parks, shopping, downhill skiing, cross-country skiing, sporting events and tennis nearby.

Publicity: *LaCrosse Tribune and Home & Garden.*

La Farge   H4

Trillium

RR 2 Box 121
La Farge, WI 54639-9802
(608)625-4492

Circa 1929. This little cottage once provided for Grandma when she came to live with her children on the farm. Stones from the banks of nearby Kickapoo River were used to construct the fireplace and the chimney for the old cookstove. Guests reserve the entire cottage, which sleeps six. In spring, a hammock sways beneath blossoming apple trees. A hearty country breakfast is served. Both children and adults enjoy watching deer, wild turkeys and owls or visiting the livestock.

Innkeeper(s): Rosanne Boyett. $100. Types of meals: Full bkfst. Beds: DT. Phone in room.

Publicity: *Milwaukee Journal.*

"It's a place to unwind, listen to the song birds, putter in the organic garden and orchard, stroll the long country lane, sit by the waterfall or relax in the hammock."

Lake Geneva   J7

Eleven Gables Inn on Lake Geneva

493 Wrigley Dr
Lake Geneva, WI 53147-2115
(262)248-8393
E-mail: egi@lkgeneva.com
Web: www.lkgeneva.com

Circa 1847. Built as a summer estate, this Carpenter Gothic inn does feature nearly a dozen of its namesake gables. Accommodations include rooms in the main house, as well as the restored coach house that is ideal for families or couples traveling together. The innkeeper has lived in the house since the 1950s and has decorated the historic home with what she describes as "Jackie O"-era furnishings. The innkeeper has been opening her home to guests since the 1960s. The homemade breakfasts include entrees such as a soufflé or perhaps eggs Benedict.

Historic Interest: Peterson House, Yerkes Observatory, Stone Manor.

Innkeeper(s): A.F. Milliette. $105-219. MC, VISA, AX, DC, CB, DS, TC. TAC10. 8 rooms with PB, 8 with FP, 2 suites, 2 cottages, 2 guest houses and 2 conference rooms. Breakfast included in rates. Types of meals: Full bkfst, veg bkfst and cont plus. Beds: KQ. Cable TV, ceiling fan, VCR, some with A/C and no smoking in room. Fax, copier and swimming in lake on premises. Handicap access. Weddings, small meetings and seminars hosted. Amusement parks, antiquing, beaches, bicycling, canoeing/kayaking, fishing, golf, hiking, horseback riding, parks, shopping, cross-country skiing, tennis and water sports nearby.

Pets allowed: In some rooms with prior approval.

Publicity: *Chicago Tribune and Lifestyles.*

General Boyd's B&B

W2915 County Trunk BB
Lake Geneva, WI 53147
(262)248-3543 Fax:(262)248-3362
Web: www.generalboydsbb.com

Circa 1843. Five acres with white oaks, old barns, perennial gardens and a meadow of wild flowers surround this Colonial Revival farmhouse. Notable for its fourth generation owner, Sue Morton, the great granddaughter to General Boyd, the home has always remained in the Boyd family. The collections of generations, including letters and handiwork, are available for guests to enjoy, and there are a number of antique furnishings original to the home. Guest rooms include the General's Room with a sitting area and views of the garden. Quiche, home-baked breads and fresh cobbler are menu items at breakfast, often featuring fruit and vegetables raised on the premises. It's a five-minute walk to the lake and Big Foot State Park, and restaurants are also within walking distance. The innkeepers will allow you to park your boat trailer on the property and are available to help arrange fishing guides.

Innkeeper(s): Bob & Sue Morton. $90-130. AX, DS, PC, TC. TAC10. 4 rooms with PB. Breakfast and afternoon tea included in rates. Types of meals: Gourmet bkfst, veg bkfst, early coffee/tea and snacks/refreshments. Beds: KQ. Cable TV, ceiling fan and VCR in room. Central air. Fax, copier and library on premises. Weddings, small meetings, family reunions and seminars hosted. Antiquing, art galleries, beaches, bicycling, fishing, golf, hiking, horseback riding, boating, snowmobiling, live theater, museums, parks, shopping, downhill skiing, cross-country skiing, tennis and water sports nearby.

Publicity: *The Week.*

Lazy Cloud Lodge B&B

N2025 N Lake Shore
Lake Geneva, WI 53125-1179
(262)275-3322 Fax:(262)275-8340
E-mail: lzcloud@genevaonline.com
Web: www.lazycloud.com

Circa 1920. Romance is the passion of the innkeepers at this secluded Cape Cod inn built in the 1920s as a polo lodge. The inn is set on three acres of gardens and lawns just a block and a half from Lake Geneva. From the gazebo in the English Country gardens to the hammocks slung among the trees, this setting is full of cozy sites to get reacquainted with your loved one. Author J. D. Salinger stayed here while writing Catcher in the Rye, and Paul Newman is another celebrity guest. The lodge has 10 guest suites, and three separate secluded cottages are also available. All suites and cottages have a double whirlpool in the sitting room or living room within view of the fireplace. Romantic décor includes lights with dimmer switches and plenty of candles throughout the inn and cottages. Breakfast is served on the cobblestone patio or in your room. Either way, you're sure to enjoy the inn's signature sticky pecan rolls, fresh fruit and homemade granola. An array of romantic

extras from flowers to books to chocolates may be arranged. You can even order the Enchanted Evening Picnic Basket and have dinner in your room in front of the fireplace.

Innkeeper(s): Keith & Carol Tiffany. $120-240. MC, VISA, AX, DC, DS, PC, TC. TAC10. 10 suites, 10 with FP and 3 cottages. Breakfast and snacks/refreshments included in rates. Types of meals: Cont plus and picnic lunch. Beds: Q. Whirlpool for two in room. Air conditioning. VCR, fax, copier and library on premises. Handicap access. Antiquing, fishing, golf, live theater, parks, shopping, downhill skiing, cross-country skiing, sporting events, tennis and water sports nearby.

Publicity: *Walworth Week, Press Publications and Channel 58 Milwaukee Evening News.*

"This room is by far a wonderful "cloud" in the heavens of the Lazy Cloud."

Roses A Bed & Breakfast

429 S Lake Shore Dr
Lake Geneva, WI 53147-2128
(262)248-4344 Fax:(262)248-57662
E-mail: markeljk@elknet.net
Web: www.rosesbnb.com

Circa 1926. A welcoming place to relax in casual comfort, this American Box-style home is only one block from the lake. The main level offers many common areas including a living and dining room. The cheerful guest bedrooms with modern conveniences are each named after the hosts' grandmothers. An English Country decor complements the oak or pine furnishings. Some feature fireplaces and a large balcony. More than just a meal, a two-course breakfast is served on the wraparound porch with wicker furniture. Often-asked-for recipes like peach-stuffed French toast with maple sausage, gingerbread pancakes with cinnamon apples, and Bananas Foster French toast, are found in the inn's Rise and Dine cookbook. Private parking, beach passes and bicycles ensure a stress-free stay.

Innkeeper(s): James & Kris Markel. $105-165. MC, VISA, DS, PC, TC. TAC5. 5 rooms with PB, 2 with FP. Breakfast included in rates. Types of meals: Gourmet bkfst, veg bkfst, early coffee/tea, picnic lunch, snacks/refreshments and dinner. Beds: Q. Cable TV, ceiling fan, VCR and fireplace in room. Air conditioning. Fax, bicycles and library on premises. Weddings, small meetings and family reunions hosted. Antiquing, art galleries, beaches, bicycling, canoeing/kayaking, fishing, golf, hiking, horseback riding, parks, shopping, downhill skiing, cross-country skiing, tennis and water sports nearby.

Pets allowed: One room only.

T.C. Smith Historic Inn B&B

865 W Main St
Lake Geneva, WI 53147-1804
(414)248-1097 (800)423-0233 Fax:(414)248-1672
E-mail: rr@tcsmithinn.com
Web: www.tcsmithinn.com

Circa 1845. Listed in the National Register of Historic Places, this High Victorian inn blends elements of Greek Revival and Italianate architecture. The inn has massive carved wooden doors, hand-painted moldings and woodwork, a high-ceilinged foyer, an original parquet floor, Oriental carpets, museum-quality period antiques and European oil paintings. Guests enjoy tea in the Grand Parlor by a marble fireplace, sipping morning coffee while taking in the view from the rooftop balcony and breakfasting on an open veranda overlooking Lake Geneva. The grounds are also impressive, boasting formal Victorian gardens, a spacious gazebo, a water garden and an exotic fish pool.

Historic Interest: Old World Wisconsin (45 minutes).

Innkeeper(s): The Marks Family. $135-375. MC, VISA, AX, DC, DS, PC, TC.

TAC5. 8 rooms with PB, 5 with FP, 2 suites and 2 conference rooms. Breakfast, afternoon tea and snacks/refreshments included in rates. Types of meals: Gourmet bkfst, early coffee/tea and room service. Beds: KQD. Cable TV, ceiling fan, VCR, fireplace and four with whirlpools in room. Air conditioning. Fax, copier and bicycles on premises. Weddings, small meetings, family reunions and seminars hosted. Antiquing, fishing, live theater, parks, downhill skiing, cross-country skiing and water sports nearby.

Pets allowed: In specific rooms only.

Publicity: *Keystone Country Peddler and Pioneer Press Publication.*

"As much as we wanted to be on the beach, we found it impossible to leave the house. It's so beautiful and relaxing."

Lodi I6

Victorian Treasure Inn

115 Prairie St
Lodi, WI 53555-1240
(608)592-5199 (800)859-5199 Fax:(608)592-7147
E-mail: innkeeper@victoriantreasure.com
Web: www.victoriantreasure.com

Circa 1897. Victorian Treasure features seven individually decorated guest rooms spread among two 19th-century Queen Anne Victorians. The interiors boast stained- and leaded-glass windows, pocket doors, rich restored woods and expansive

porches. Five suites include a whirlpool tub, fireplace, wet bar, TV/VCR and stereo. Guests are greeted with a wine and cheese reception. Full, gourmet breakfasts may include specialties such as eggs Florentine, herb vegetable quiche, or stuffed French toast topped with a seasonal fruit sauce. Guests enjoy hiking along the National Scenic Ice Age Trail which passes beside the inn.

Historic Interest: The Capitol Square in Madison (24 miles), Circus World Museum (20 miles), Wollersheim Winery (12 miles), Merrimac Car Ferry (5 miles).

Innkeeper(s): Todd & Kimberly Seidl. $109-199. MC, VISA, DS, PC, TC. TAC10. 7 rooms with PB, 5 with FP and 5 suites. Breakfast and snacks/refreshments included in rates. Types of meals: Gourmet bkfst, early coffee/tea and room service. Beds: Q. Phone and six with whirlpools in room. Air conditioning. Fax, copier and library on premises. Small meetings and family reunions hosted. Antiquing, bicycling, golf, hiking, bird watching, Taliesen, live theater, parks, shopping, downhill skiing, cross-country skiing, sporting events, tennis and water sports nearby.

Publicity: *Recommended Romantic Inns, Wisconsin State Journal, Chicago Sun-Times, Milwaukee Magazine, Wisconsin Trails, Victorian Homes and Country Inn Cooking with Gail Greco.*

"An elegant, romantic getaway that everyone wants to return to again and again."

Madison I6

Arbor House, An Environmental Inn

3402 Monroe St
Madison, WI 53711-1702
(608)238-2981
Web: www.arbor-house.com

Circa 1853. Nature-lovers not only will enjoy the inn's close access to a 1,280-acre nature preserve, they will appreciate the innkeepers' ecological theme. Organic sheets and towels are offered for guests as well as environmentally safe bath products. Arbor House is one of Madison's oldest existing homes and fea-

tures plenty of historic features, such as romantic reading chairs and antiques, mixed with modern amenities and unique touches. Five guest rooms include a whirlpool tub and three have fireplaces. The Annex guest rooms include private balconies. The innkeepers offer many amenities for business travelers, including value-added corporate rates. The award-winning inn has been recognized as a model of urban ecology. Lake Wingra is within walking distance as are biking and nature trails, bird watching and a host of other outdoor activities. Guests enjoy complimentary canoeing and use of mountain bikes.

Historic Interest: Frank Lloyd Wright designed many homes in Madison, and the Mansion Hill Historic District is nearby.

Innkeeper(s): John & Cathie Imes. $110-220. MC, VISA, AX, PC, TC. 8 rooms with PB, 3 with FP, 1 suite and 1 conference room. Breakfast included in rates. Types of meals: Full bkfst and cont plus. Beds: KQ. Cable TV, phone, ceiling fan and VCR in room. Air conditioning. Fax, copier and sauna on premises. Handicap access. Weddings, small meetings, family reunions and seminars hosted. Antiquing, fishing, parks, shopping, cross-country skiing, sporting events and water sports nearby.

Publicity: *Money Magazine, Coop America, E, New York Times, Natural Home and Offspring.*

"What a delightful treat in the middle of Madison. Absolutely, unquestionably, the best time I've spent in a hotel or otherwise. B&Bs are the only way to go! Thank you!"

Mansion Hill Inn

424 N Pinckney St
Madison, WI 53703-1472
(608)255-3999 (800)798-9070 Fax:(608)255-2217
Web: www.mansionhillinn.com

Circa 1858. The facade of this Romanesque Revival sandstone mansion boasts magnificent arched windows, Swedish railings, verandas and a belvedere. There are marble floors, ornate moldings and a magnificent mahogany and walnut staircase that winds up four stories. Lovingly restored and lavishly decorated, the inn easily rivals rooms at the Ritz for opulence. A special occasion warrants requesting the suite with the secret passageway behind a swinging bookcase.

Historic Interest: State Capitol (3 blocks).

Innkeeper(s): James Homann. $130-340. MC, VISA, AX, PC, TC. TAC10. 11 rooms with PB, 4 with FP and 2 suites. Breakfast and snacks/refreshments included in rates. Types of meals: Cont plus, early coffee/tea, picnic lunch and room service. Beds: KQ. Cable TV, phone, turndown service, VCR, whirlpool bath and some with desks in room. Central air. Fax, copier and library on premises. Weddings and small meetings hosted. Fishing, state Capitol, live theater, museums, parks, shopping and sporting events nearby.

Publicity: *Glamour, Country Inns, Chicago Sun-Times, Americana, Chicago Tribune, New York Times and Conde Nast Traveler.*

"The elegance, charm and superb services made it a delightful experience."

University Heights B&B

1812 Van Hise Ave
Madison, WI 53705
(608)233-3340 Fax:(608)233-3255
E-mail: simplybet@aol.com
Web: www.madison-lodging.com

Circa 1923. This Four-Square home offers a quiet residential neighborhood. Craftsman decor highlights the home's Frank Lloyd Wright influence. A large common area includes a fireplace and the two larger suites offer whirlpool tubs. Breakfast may include poached pears with raspberry Grand Marnier sauce, sorrel, leek and mushroom quiche and cherry almond scones.

Innkeeper(s): Betty Humphries. $85-155. MC, VISA, AX, DS, PC, TC. 4 rooms with PB, 2 suites and 1 conference room. Breakfast included in rates. Types of meals: Full bkfst and early coffee/tea. Beds: QD. Phone and ceiling fan in room. Air conditioning. VCR, fax, copier and bicycles on premises. Small meetings and family reunions hosted. Golf, capitol, UW Arboretun, Olbrich Botanical Gardens, live theater, museums, parks, shopping and sporting events nearby.

Maiden Rock   F2

Harrisburg Inn

W3334 Hwy 35
Maiden Rock, WI 54750
(715)448-4500 Fax:(715)448-3908
E-mail: ccbern@cannon.net
Web: www.harrisburginn.com

Circa 1892. A breathtaking view of Lake Pepin greets guests of this historic country house, which overlooks the Great Mississippi River Valley from its location high on the bluff. The Evening Primrose and Morning Glory Rooms boast private decks to further enjoy the lake view. Country-style breakfasts may be served on the porch. The inn is a pleasant drive from the Twin Cities. Nearby shops will delight those with an eye for the unique.

Historic Interest: Birthplace of Laura Ingalls Wilder (19 miles).

Innkeeper(s): Carol Crisp & Bern Paddock. $90-135. MC, VISA, AX, DS, PC, TC. 4 rooms with PB. Breakfast and snacks/refreshments included in rates. Types of meals: Full bkfst and early coffee/tea. Beds: Q. Ceiling fan, one with hot tub/spa and faux wood stoves (electric) in room. Central air. Fax, copier, library and faux wood stoves (electric) on premises. Antiquing, art galleries, beaches, bicycling, canoeing/kayaking, fishing, golf, hiking, live theater, museums, parks, shopping, downhill skiing and cross-country skiing nearby.

Publicity: *St. Paul Pioneer Press, Minneapolis Star Tribune, Red Wing Republican Eagle and Mississippi Valley Partners Travel Guide.*

"Thanks for your hospitality and good food!"

Manitowoc   G8

WestPort B&B

635 North Eighth St
Manitowoc, WI 54220
(920)686-0465 (888)686-0465

Circa 1879. This two-story Italianate-style bed and breakfast, built in 1879, was originally the home of a Civil War surgeon who had his practice in town. Renovated in 2001, four luxurious bedrooms provide ample private sitting space, fireplaces and double whirlpools to relax in. Start each morning with breakfast in bed or perhaps listening to birds chirping while sitting on the porch with a warm cup of coffee and a good book.

Take a ride on the ferry across Lake Michigan, or enjoy the beaches of Wisconsin in the summer. Catch a show at the theater, shop in town or see a live sporting event at nearby Green Bay. Hosts Keith and Kim Lazansky Philippi provide the comfort and local knowledge that guests need to thoroughly enjoy their stay in Manitowoc.

Historic Interest: Rahr-West art museum, Wisconsin Maritime museum (.5 miles), Pinecrest Historical Village.

Innkeeper(s): Kim Lazansky Philippi & Keith Philippi. $90-150. MC, VISA, AX, PC, TC. 4 rooms with PB, 2 with FP and 2 suites. Breakfast included in rates. Types of meals: Full bkfst, country bkfst, veg bkfst, cont plus, cont, early coffee/tea and room service. Beds: QT. Cable TV, ceiling fan, refrigerator, fireplaces and double whirlpool tubs in room. Air conditioning. Antiquing, art galleries, beaches, bicycling, fishing, golf, hiking, Lake Michigan car ferry, live theater, museums, parks, shopping, downhill skiing, cross-country skiing, sporting events, tennis and water sports nearby.

Publicity: *Herald Times, Wisconsin Trails and Great Lakes Cruiser.*

Milwaukee   I8

The Brumder Mansion

3046 W Wisconsin Ave
Milwaukee, WI 53208
(414)342-9767 (866)793-3676 Fax:(414)342-4772
E-mail: brumder@execpc.com
Web: www.brumdermansion.com

Circa 1910. Built in the English Arts & Crafts style, this majestic brick home with Victorian and Gothic elements is furnished with elegant antiques. Common rooms feature huge oak fireplaces and exquisite woodwork, like the foyer's massive Gothic oak stairway. The lavish parlor's comfortable chairs invite relaxation, and the library has a large selection of games, magazines and books. A friendly atmosphere is enhanced with complimentary wine or beverages and homemade snacks or chocolates. Spacious guest bedrooms offer romantic settings with decorative painting and fine linens. Three Suites include a double whirlpool, exquisite marble showers, CD player and TV/VCR. Enjoy the many flowers and view of the boulevard from the front porch.

Innkeeper(s): Carol & Bob Hirschi. $69-195. MC, VISA, AX, DS, TC. TAC10. 5 rooms, 2 with PB, 3 with FP, 3 suites and 1 conference room. Breakfast and snacks/refreshments included in rates. Types of meals: Veg bkfst, cont plus, cont and early coffee/tea. Beds: KQT. Cable TV, ceiling fan, VCR and fireplace in room. Central air. Fax, copier, spa and library on premises. Small meetings hosted. Antiquing, art galleries, beaches, live theater, museums, parks, shopping, sporting events, water sports and wineries nearby.

Pets allowed: Small dogs, but must be housed with owners dogs, not in guest room.

Publicity: *Milwaukee Magazine and HBO.*

Monroe   J6

Victorian Garden B&B

1720 16th St
Monroe, WI 53566-2643
(608)328-1720 (888)814-7909

Circa 1893. The original charm of this blue and white three-story Victorian home still remains today. Antiques and collectibles are found throughout the house, along with a vintage doll and teddy bear collection. Wraparound porches and flower

gardens are great for relaxing. Accommodations include the White Lace and Roses Suite featuring a clawfoot tub and shower for two. The Rosebud Room overlooks the hand-carved Italian fountain, and the Ivy Room is a quiet corner setting. A full breakfast is served in the formal dining room. Local attractions include the Monroe Depot and historic square. Come stay and visit with us, the pleasure is all ours.

Innkeeper(s): Judy & Ron Marsh. $80-90. MC, VISA, AX, PC. 3 rooms with PB. Breakfast included in rates. Types of meals: Full bkfst. Beds: QD. Air conditioning. Antiquing, bicycling, fishing, golf, hiking, parks, cross-country skiing and sporting events nearby.

Oconomowoc   I7

The Inn at Pine Terrace

351 E Lisbon Rd
Oconomowoc, WI 53066-2838
(262)567-7463 (888)526-0588
E-mail: innkeeper@innatpineterrace.com

Circa 1879. This inn's convenient location, two hours from Chicago, midway between Madison and Milwaukee and just north of the interstate that connects them, makes it equally appealing to business travelers and those seeking a romantic

retreat. The innkeeper bills the inn as a combination of a Victorian mansion and a small European hotel. Some rooms boast whirlpool tubs, and visitors are welcome to use the exercise room and the inn's in-ground swimming pool. A conference room is available for meetings, seminars and special occasions.

Innkeeper(s): Rich Borg. $65-170. MC, VISA, AX, DC, DS, PC, TC. 13 rooms with PB and 1 conference room. Breakfast included in rates. Types of meals: Cont plus. Beds: QT. Cable TV and phone in room. Air conditioning. Fax, copier, heated pool in summer, dining room and exercise room on premises. Weddings, small meetings, family reunions and seminars hosted. Antiquing, fishing, golf, excellent dining, nature trails, live theater, parks, shopping, downhill skiing, cross-country skiing, sporting events and water sports nearby.

Publicity: *Milwaukee Magazine.*

Onalaska   G3

Rainbow Ridge Farms B&B

N5732 Hauser Rd
Onalaska, WI 54650-8912
(608)783-8181
Web: www.rainbowridgefarms.com

Circa 1902. Horses, llamas, goats, sheep and ducks are the primary occupants of Rainbow Ridge's 35 acres. Pleasant pond-view guest rooms are offered in the old farmhouse. Woodland, meadow and surrounding wooded bluffs create a picturesque setting and explains why this was the site for one of Onalaska's original farms. Guests are offered the opportunity to enjoy the working farm with a hands-on experience by feeding the animals and collecting eggs. A hearty farm breakfast is offered on weekends and an expanded continental during the week. The farm is popular for family reunions and weddings.

Historic Interest: Hixon House-8 miles, Museum-8 miles, Norskedalen-25 miles, St Rose Convent Chapel-12 miles, Trempealeau Hotel-14 miles.

Innkeeper(s): Donna Murphy & Cindy Hoehne. $65-105. MC, VISA, PC, TC. TAC10. 4 rooms with PB. Breakfast and snacks/refreshments included in rates. Types of meals: Country bkfst, veg bkfst, cont plus and early coffee/tea. Beds: QDT. Central air. VCR, spa, bicycles, library, satellite dish, fire pit, refrigerator and grill on premises. Weddings and family reunions hosted. Antiquing, art galleries, beaches, bicycling, canoeing/kayaking, fishing, golf, hiking, horseback riding, live theater, museums, parks, shopping, downhill skiing, cross-country skiing, sporting events, tennis and water sports nearby.

Osceola   E1

St. Croix River Inn

305 River St, PO Box 356
Osceola, WI 54020-0356
(715)294-4248 (800)645-8820
E-mail: innkeeper@stcroixriverinn.com

Circa 1908. This stone house is poised on a bluff overlooking the St. Croix River. Bulls eye molding is an unusual feature, and guest rooms are filled with antiques with two- or four-poster beds and whirlpool baths. Some rooms offer fireplaces, floor-to-ceiling Palladian windows, private patios and river views. A full breakfast is brought to your room.

Innkeeper(s): Shelly Dixon & Vicki Labelle. $100-200. MC, VISA, DS. TAC10. 7 rooms with PB and 2 suites. Breakfast and snacks/refreshments included in rates. Types of meals: Full bkfst, early coffee/tea and room service. Beds: Q. Cable TV, phone and VCR in room. Central air. Deck on premises. Handicap access. Weddings, small meetings, family reunions and seminars hosted. Antiquing, beaches, bicycling, canoeing/kayaking, golf, hiking, snowmobile trails, scenic train ride, dinner cruises, dog sledding, spa services, casino, fine dining, live theater, parks, shopping, downhill skiing, cross-country skiing and water sports nearby.

Publicity: *Chicago Sun-Times, Skyway News* and *St. Paul Pioneer Press.*

Pepin   F2

Harbor Hill Inn Bed & Brunch

310 2nd St
Pepin, WI 54759
(715)442-2002
E-mail: stay@pepinsbest.com
Web: www.pepinsbest.com

Circa 1886. A third-story turret crowns the top of this Queen Anne Victorian surrounded by lush grounds with flower gardens, cherry trees and an apple orchard. Antiques decorate the interior. Guest rooms include antique beds dressed with posh Ralph Lauren linens and comforters. The Nob Hill Room includes the added amenity of a double whirlpool tub. Guests are treated to brunch each morning with a variety of dishes, from lemon souffle pancakes, apple and walnut soup, or perhaps rosemary chicken with steamed asparagus. After brunch, guests can explore the village of Pepin or perhaps relax and enjoy the view of Lake Pepin and the Mississippi River. Pepin is best known as the birthplace of author Laura Ingalls Wilder, and was the setting for "Little House in the Big Woods."

Historic Interest: Birth site of Laura Ingalls Wilder.

Innkeeper(s): Phil Fischer. $125-190. PC. 4 rooms with PB and 1 conference room. Types of meals: Gourmet bkfst. Beds: QD. Ceiling fan in room. Central air. Library and in season use of skating rink on premises. Small meetings and family reunions hosted. Antiquing, art galleries, beaches, bicycling, fishing, golf, hiking, live theater, museums, parks, shopping, downhill skiing and cross-country skiing nearby.

Publicity: *Minneapolis Star-Tribune, Rochester Post-Bulletin, New York Times and Travel & Leisure.*

Phillips   D5

East Highland School House B&B

West 4342, Hwy D
Phillips, WI 54555
(715)339-3492

Circa 1905. Guests are invited to ring the bell at this restored one-room schoolhouse. An addition to the building in 1920 features rooms with rustic exposed beams, brick walls and original light fixtures. Innkeepers Jeanne and Russ Kirchmeyer filled the home with family antiques and turn-of-the-century pieces. Lacy curtains, doilies and hand-hooked rugs lend to the romantic, country atmosphere. Two museums featuring a 1900s kit area, school area and old logging and farming tools have been added to the inn; one in the basement and one in the barn across the street. The kitchen, which once served as a stage for the school, is now where Jeanne prepares the expansive morning meals.

Innkeeper(s): Russ & Jeanne Kirchmeyer. $55-70. 4 rooms. Breakfast included in rates. Types of meals: Full bkfst.

Plymouth   H8

Yankee Hill Inn B&B

405 Collins St
Plymouth, WI 53073-2361
(920)892-2222
E-mail: yankee@excel.net

Circa 1870. Two outstanding examples of 19th-century architecture comprise this inn, one a striking Italianate Gothic listed in the National Register, and the other a Queen Anne Victorian

with many custom touches. Between the two impressive structures, visitors will choose from 12 spacious guest rooms, featuring antique furnishings and handmade quilts. Visitors can walk to downtown, where they will find an antique mall, shopping and fine dining.

Historic Interest: The Wade House, a state historical site, is five miles from the inn. Plymouth Historical Museum is within walking distance. Sheboygan County offers more than 200 locally landmarked buildings. The Historic Plymouth Walking Tour features 50 early Plymouth buildings.

Innkeeper(s): Peg Stahlman. $80-110. MC, VISA. TAC10. 12 rooms with PB. Breakfast included in rates. Types of meals: Full bkfst and early coffee/tea. Beds: QD. VCR on premises. Small meetings, family reunions and seminars hosted. Antiquing, fishing, bicycling, hiking, shopping and cross-country skiing nearby.

Publicity: *Wisconsin Country Life, Milwaukee Journal, Plymouth Review and Wisconsin Trails.*

"You have mastered the art of comfort. All the perfect little touches make this a dream come true. I only regret that we cannot stay forever."

Port Washington   H8

Port Washington Inn

308 W Washington St
Port Washington, WI 53074-1839
(262)284-5583 (877)794-1903 Fax:(262)284-5583
E-mail: info@port-washington-inn.com

Circa 1903. This three-story Victorian stands proudly on Sweetcake Hill, five blocks from Lake Michigan. Distinctive original woodwork, stained and leaded glass, gas and electric light fixtures, pocket doors, polished oak floors and lincrusta and

anaglypta wall coverings are among the historic features of this inn. There are four guestrooms, double parlors, and formal dining room with adjacent cozy library. Two gestrooms afford a bit of a lake view. Off-street parking is available. Walk to restaurants, shops and lake.

Historic Interest: Thrity minutes from Milwaukee.

Innkeeper(s): Rita, Dave & Aaron Nelson. $100-150. MC, VISA, AX. 4 rooms with PB and 1 suite. Breakfast and afternoon tea included in rates. Types of meals: Full bkfst, early coffee/tea and gourmet dinner. Beds: Q. Ceiling fan, VCR and soaps & shampoos in room. Air conditioning. Library on premises. Weddings, small meetings, family reunions and seminars hosted. Antiquing, fishing, hiking, biking, Mitchell Park Domes, live theater, shopping, downhill skiing, cross-country skiing, sporting events and water sports nearby.

Publicity: *Ozaukee Press and Suburban Life.*

"You have done an excellent job turning a charming old house into a warm and inviting B&B."

Sheboygan

Brownstone Inn

1227 No 7th Street
Sheboygan, WI 53081
(920)451-0644 Fax:(920)457-3426
E-mail: brwnstninn@aol.com
Web: www.brownstoneinn.com

Circa 1907. The descendants of the original owners of this handsome brownstone mansion have restored the property and added amenities for the pleasure of guests. A handsome polished and carved staircase, arched ceiling in the parlor and original chandeliers are some of the gracious appointments which remain. Each guest room offers a whirlpool tub and a shower, and some have beautifully carved fireplaces. There are porches, cozy reading areas and parlors. A billiards table is available. Walk to the lakefront, a sandy beach, marina, boardwalk or shops and restaurants. In summer plan to arrange for an excursion on the inn's sailboat.

Innkeeper(s): Frank A Ribich Jr. $150-250. MC, VISA, AX, DS, PC, TC. 7 rooms with PB and 1 conference room. Breakfast and snacks/refreshments included in rates. Types of meals: Veg bkfst, cont plus, cont, early coffee/tea and room service. AP. Beds: KQ. Cable TV, phone, turndown service and VCR in room. Central air. Billiards on premises. Weddings, small meetings and family reunions hosted. Amusement parks, antiquing, art galleries, beaches, bicycling, canoeing/kayaking, fishing, golf, hiking, horseback riding, live theater, parks, sporting events, tennis, water sports and wineries nearby.

Sister Bay E9

The Inn on Maple

414 Maple Dr
Sister Bay, WI 54234-9423
(920)854-5107
E-mail: innonmaple@dcwis.com

Circa 1902. Located on a quiet side street, a half block off Bay Shore Drive, this cozy inn is in the National Register of Historic Places because of its stovewood architecture. The inn is decorated with English antiques, ceiling fans and quilts. Full breakfasts are served on an enclosed front porch. Relax on the deck

or in front of the fireplace in the Gathering Room. Door County offers 250 miles of shoreline, and there are state parks, antique shops and art galleries near the inn.

Innkeeper(s): Bill & Louise Robbins. $85-105. MC, VISA, PC, TC. 6 rooms with PB. Breakfast included in rates. Types of meals: Full bkfst and early coffee/tea. Beds: QDT. Ceiling fan in room. Air conditioning. VCR, library, back yard deck, birdwatching and afternoon cookies and beverage on premises. Antiquing, art galleries, bicycling, fishing, golf, live theater, shopping, cross-country skiing, tennis and water sports nearby.

Springbrook D3

The Stout Trout B&B

W4244 Cty F
Springbrook, WI 54875-9801
(715)466-2790

Circa 1900. Located on 40 acres of rolling, wooded country-side, The Stout Trout overlooks a lily-ringed bay on Gull Lake. The lake can be viewed from the living room, dining areas and second-floor guest rooms. The inn features wood-plank floors, folk art, classic prints and country-style furniture. Homemade jams and maple syrup are served.

Innkeeper(s): Kathleen Fredricks. $75-80. 4 rooms with PB. Breakfast included in rates. Types of meals: Full bkfst. Beds: QD. Small meetings and family reunions hosted. Antiquing, fishing, shopping, cross-country skiing and sporting events nearby.

Publicity: *Chicago Tribune, Wisconsin West Magazine and Wisconsin State Journal.*

"Thank you again for the comfortable setting, great food and gracious hospitality!"

Stevens Point F6

A Victorian Swan on Water

1716 Water St
Stevens Point, WI 54481-3550
(715)345-0595 (800)454-9886
E-mail: victorian@g2a.net

Circa 1889. This Victorian is located a block and a half from the Wisconsin River. Black walnut inlays in the wood floors, crown moldings, walnut paneling and interior shutters are among the inn's architectural elements. The suite features a mural of a pastoral Mediterranean scene, a ceiling fan, whirlpool tub, fireplace and a balcony overlooking the garden. There are antique furnishings and lace curtains.

Breakfast items may include rum-baked fresh pineapple and "turtle" French toast stuffed with chocolate and pecans and served with caramel sauce.

Innkeeper(s): Joan Ouellette. $65-135. MC, VISA, AX, DS, PC, TC. TAC5. 4 rooms, 3 with PB, 1 with FP and 1 suite. Breakfast included in rates. Types of meals: Gourmet bkfst and early coffee/tea. Beds: KQDT. Ceiling fan and whirlpool and fireplace in suite in room. Air conditioning. VCR and library on premises. Weddings, small meetings, family reunions and seminars hosted. Antiquing, fishing, live theater, parks, shopping, downhill skiing, cross-country skiing, sporting events and water sports nearby.

"Thanks, you made a business trip away from home feel like a vacation. Your place is beautiful and inviting."

Dreams of Yesteryear B&B

1100 Brawley St
Stevens Point, WI 54481-3536
(715)341-4525 Fax:(715)341-4248
E-mail: bonnie@dreamsofyesteryear.com
Web: dreamsofyesteryear.com

Circa 1901. This elegant, three-story, 4,000-square-foot Queen Anne home is within walking distance of downtown, the Wisconsin River and the University of Wisconsin. The inn features golden oak woodwork, hardwood floors and leaded glass.

Each guest room offers exquisite decor; the third-floor Ballroom Suite boasts a whirlpool. Gourmet breakfasts are served in the inn's formal dining room. An excellent hiking trail is just a block from the inn.

Historic Interest: Historic downtown Stevens Point is nearby, and the inn is only a short trip from dozens of historical sites.

Innkeeper(s): Bonnie & Bill Maher. $62-149. MC, VISA, AX, DS, PC, TC. TAC5. 6 rooms, 4 with PB and 2 suites. Breakfast, afternoon tea and snacks/refreshments included in rates. Types of meals: Gourmet bkfst and early coffee/tea. Beds: KQDT. Cable TV and phone in room. Air conditioning. VCR, library, piano and victrolas on premises. Weddings, small meetings and family reunions hosted. Amusement parks, antiquing, fishing, historical attractions, hiking trails, live theater, parks, shopping, downhill skiing, cross-country skiing, sporting events and water sports nearby.

Publicity: *Victorian Homes, Reach, Stevens Point Journal. and News WAOW Channel 9.*

"Something from a Hans Christian Anderson fairy tale."

Sturgeon Bay F9

Chanticleer Guest House

4072 Cherry Rd (Hwy HH)
Sturgeon Bay, WI 54235
(920)746-0334 Fax:(920)746-1368
E-mail: chanticleer@itol.com
Web: www.chanticleerguesthouse.com

Circa 1916. Although Chanticleer is secluded on 70 acres boasting woods and fields of wildflowers, the home is just one mile from Sturgeon Bay. Each of the ten guest rooms, which consist of two cabins and eight bed and breakfast suites, has a fireplace and double whirlpool tub. Poster and sleigh beds are topped with country comforters. Delicate floral wallcoverings, exposed wood beams and paneled wood walls accentuate the elegant country decor. Breakfast is brought to your door, including such items as homemade muffins and fruit with fresh cream. Door County offers a multitude of attractions, including theater productions, musical festivals, watersports and hiking on trails in one of five state parks.

Innkeeper(s): Darrin Day & Bryon Groeschl. $120-210. MC, VISA, DS, PC, TC. 10 rooms, 10 with FP, 8 suites and 2 cottages. Breakfast and snacks/refreshments included in rates. Types of meals: Veg bkfst, cont plus and early coffee/tea. Beds: KQ. TV, ceiling fan, VCR and antiques in room. Central air. Fax, copier, swimming and sauna on premises. Handicap access. Antiquing, art galleries, beaches, bicycling, canoeing/kayaking, fishing, golf, hiking, horseback riding, live theater, museums, parks, shopping, downhill skiing, cross-country skiing, sporting events, tennis, water sports and wineries nearby.

Publicity: *New York Times Travel Section.*

Colonial Gardens B&B

344 N Third Ave
Sturgeon Bay, WI 54235
(920)746-9192 Fax:(920)746-9193
E-mail: colonialgardens@dcwis.com
Web: www.colgardensbb.com

Circa 1877. The original owner fought in the Battle of Bull Run during the Civil War and brought back some of the South's architectural ideas to build a hybrid Victorian and Southern Colonial with rosettes, ornate moldings, high ceilings and tall windows. This romantic inn offers private suites that all feature a double whirlpool in the sitting area with a fireplace. Choose from a water or garden view. A scrumptious full breakfast is delivered to each suite. Walk to historic downtown Sturgeon Bay.

Innkeeper(s): Joe & Debra Hertel. $100-175. MC, VISA, DS, PC, TC. 5 suites, 5 with FP. Breakfast and snacks/refreshments included in rates. Types of meals: Gourmet bkfst, veg bkfst, early coffee/tea, afternoon tea and room service. Beds: KQ. Cable TV, ceiling fan, VCR and fireplace in room. Central air. Fax and gift shop on premises. Antiquing, art galleries, beaches, bicycling, canoeing/kayaking, fishing, golf, hiking, horseback riding, live theater, museums, parks, shopping, downhill skiing, cross-country skiing, sporting events, tennis, water sports and wineries nearby.

Publicity: *Door County Advocate, Chilton Times Journal, Green Bay Press, MarketPlace Magazine and WLUK TV 11.*

Hearthside B&B Inn

2136 Taube Rd
Sturgeon Bay, WI 54235
(920)746-2136
E-mail: hearthside@itol.com
Web: www.hearthside-farm-bb.com

Circa 1880. Experience country comfort at this vintage farmhouse that boasts an impressive night view of a Lake Michigan lighthouse two miles away. The inn is decorated with quilts and cozy furnishings, and features a fireplace with a floor-to-ceiling mirrored mantel. The guest bedrooms and suite are suitable for singles, couples or families. After a hearty all-you-can-eat breakfast, lunch is seldom needed. Stroll the gardens, or venture out to explore the local sites. Weddings and reunions are welcome events.

Innkeeper(s): Don & Lu Klussendorf. $45-75. PC. 4 rooms with PB, 1 suite and 1 cottage. Breakfast included in rates. Types of meals: Gourmet bkfst. Beds: QDT. Cable TV and VCR in room. Air conditioning. Stables on premises. Weddings, small meetings, family reunions and seminars hosted. Antiquing, golf, Green Bay Packers, live theater, parks, shopping, cross-country skiing, sporting events and water sports nearby.

Publicity: *Green Bay Gazette.*

Inn at Cedar Crossing

336 Louisiana St
Sturgeon Bay, WI 54235-2422
(920)743-4200 Fax:(920)743-4422
E-mail: innkeeper@innatcedarcrossing.com
Web: www.innatcedarcrossing.com

Circa 1884. This historic hotel, in the National Register, is a downtown two-story brick building that once housed street-level shops with second-floor apartments for the tailors, shopkeepers and pharmacists who worked below. The upstairs, now guest rooms, is decorated with rich fabrics and wallpapers and fine antiques. The Anniversary Room has a mahogany bed, fireplace and double whirlpool tub. The Victorian-era dining room and pub, both with fireplaces, are on the lower level. The waterfront is three blocks away.

Historic Interest: Door County Historical and Maritime Museums.

Innkeeper(s): Terry Smith. $115-180.
MC, VISA, AX, DS, PC, TC. 9 rooms with PB, 6 with FP. Breakfast and snacks/refreshments included in rates. Types of meals: Gourmet bkfst, cont plus, early coffee/tea, lunch, picnic lunch, gourmet dinner and room service. Beds: KQ. Cable TV, phone, VCR, double whirlpool tubs and some fireplaces in room. Air conditioning. Fax, copier and library on premises. Small meetings hosted. Antiquing, fishing, art galleries, great biking, live theater, parks, shopping, downhill skiing, cross-country skiing and water sports nearby.

Publicity: *New Month, New York Times, Chicago Sun-Times, Country Inns, Bon Appetit, Gourmet, Green Bay Press Gazette, Midwest Living, Milwaukee Journal, Wisconsin Trails and New York Times.*

"The second-year stay at the inn was even better than the first. I couldn't have found a more romantic place."

The Reynolds House B&B

111 So 7th Ave
Sturgeon Bay, WI 54235
(920)746-9771 (877)269-7401 Fax:(920)746-9441
E-mail: jsekula@reynoldshousebandb.com

Circa 1900. A three-story, red-roofed Queen Anne Victorian house, the Reynolds House is painted in two shades of teal and yellow with white trim on its balustrades and brackets. Leaded-glass windows and a stone veranda that wraps around the front of the house are features. Rooms are cheerfully decorated and offer antique beds, attractive bed coverings and wallpapers.

 Tucked under the gable, the Winesap Suite includes a whirlpool, sitting room and fireplace. The innkeeper's kitchen garden furnishes fresh herbs to accent breakfast dishes, as well as flowers for the table.

Historic Interest: Door County lighthouses (30 miles), Sturgeon Bay.

Innkeeper(s): Stan & Jan Sekula. $70-155. MC, VISA, AX, DS. TAC10. 4 rooms with PB, 3 with FP and 1 suite. Breakfast and snacks/refreshments included in rates. Types of meals: Gourmet bkfst and early coffee/tea. Beds: Q. Cable TV and ceiling fan in room. Central air. VCR, fax, copier and library on premises. Weddings and family reunions hosted. Antiquing, art galleries, beaches, bicycling, fishing, golf, hiking, horseback riding, live theater, museums, parks, shopping, cross-country skiing, tennis and wineries nearby.

Publicity: *Door County Magazine and Midwest Living Magazine-Voted Best in the Midwest June 2001.*

"Sometimes the last minute things in life are the best!"

Scofield House B&B

908 Michigan St
Sturgeon Bay, WI 54235-1849
(920)743-7727 (888)463-0204 Fax:(920)743-7727
E-mail: scofldhs@doorpi.net
Web: www.scofieldhouse.com

Circa 1902. Mayor Herbert Scofield, prominent locally in the lumber and hardware business, built this late-Victorian house with a sturdy square tower and inlaid floors that feature intricate borders patterned in cherry, birch, maple, walnut, and red and white oak. Oak moldings throughout the house boast raised designs of bows, ribbons, swags and flowers. Equally lavish decor is featured in the guest rooms with fluffy flowered comforters and cabbage rose wallpapers highlighting romantic antique bedsteads. Baked apple-cinnamon French toast is a house specialty. Modern amenities include many suites with fireplaces and double whirlpools. "Room at the Top" is a sky-lit 900-square-foot suite occupying the whole third floor and furnished with Victorian antiques.

Historic Interest: Door County Lighthouses, Maritime Museum, Door County Museum (within walking distance).

Innkeeper(s): Mike & Carolyn Pietrek. $112-220. PC, TC. 6 rooms with PB, 5 with FP. Breakfast and afternoon tea included in rates. Types of meals: Gourmet bkfst. Beds: Q. Cable TV, ceiling fan, VCR and double whirlpools in room. Air conditioning. Fax, copier and movie library (free) on premises. Antiquing, fishing, live theater, parks, shopping, downhill skiing, cross-country skiing, sporting events and water sports nearby.

Publicity: *Insider, Glamour, Country, Wisconsin Trails, Green Bay Press Gazette, Chicago Tribune, Milwaukee Sentinel-Journal, Midwest Living, Victorian Decorating & Lifestyle, Country Inns and National Geographic Traveler.*

"You've introduced us to the fabulous world of B&Bs. I loved the porch swing and would have been content on it for the entire weekend."

White Lace Inn

16 N 5th Ave
Sturgeon Bay, WI 54235-1795
(920)743-1105 (877)948-5223
E-mail: romance@whitelaceinn.com
Web: www.WhiteLaceInn.com

Circa 1903. The romantic White Lace Inn is composed of four beautifully restored Victorian houses connected by meandering garden paths. Inviting rooms and suites offer fine antiques and ornate Victorian or canopy beds. The inn's suites include oversized whirlpool baths, fireplaces, white linens, down comforters and many other amenities. Often the site for romantic anniversary celebrations, a favorite suite has a two-sided fireplace, magnificent walnut Eastlake bed, English country fabrics and a whirlpool. Lemonade or hot chocolate and cookies are offered upon arrival. In the morning, the delectable offerings include items such as cherry apple crisp and creamy rice pudding. Year-round activities invite frequent visits - the Festival of Blossoms, the Lighthouse Walk, Cherry Festival and the Classic Wooden Boat event, for instance. Take museums and gallery strolls, and enjoy the area's great restaurants.

Innkeeper(s): Dennis & Bonnie Statz. $69-249. MC, VISA, AX, DS, PC, TC. 18 rooms with PB, 15 with FP and 5 suites. Breakfast included in rates.

Types of meals: Full bkfst. Beds: KQ. 12 with whirlpool tubs and 9 with fireplace and whirlpool in room. Handicap access. Antiquing, fishing, live theater, cross-country skiing and water sports nearby.

Publicity: *Milwaukee Sentinel, Brides, National Geographic Traveler, Wisconsin Trails, Milwaukee, Country Home and Midwest Living.*

"Each guest room is an overwhelming visual feast, a dazzling fusion of colors, textures and beautiful objects. It is one of these rare gems that established a tradition the day it opened - Wisconsin Trails."

Viroqua   H4

Viroqua Heritage Inn B&B's

217 & 220 E Jefferson St
Viroqua, WI 54665
(608)637-3306 (800)4HER-INN
E-mail: rhodsent@mwt.net
Web: www.herinn.com

Circa 1890. Formerly the Boyle House, named for its original owner, this Queen Anne Victorian is an architectural jewel showcasing a three-story turret, turned balusters and columns, leaded beveled glass and circle-top windows. Embellishments continue with hardwood floors, ornate oak fireplace mantles and staircase and brass and crystal chandeliers. The nostalgic ambiance is enhanced by antique furnishings and Oriental rugs. A parlor-music room features a victrola and baby grand piano. Enjoy a leisurely breakfast in the formal dining room, on the front porch or on the balcony overlooking the garden. Ask about the pampering products and services of Day Lily Spa.

Innkeeper(s): Nancy Rhodes. $60-120. MC, VISA, DS, PC, TC. TAC10. 9 rooms, 5 with PB, 1 with FP and 1 suite. Breakfast included in rates. Types of meals: Full bkfst and early coffee/tea. Beds: KQD. TV, phone, coffee pots and one with whirlpool bath in room. Air conditioning. VCR, bicycles, library, child care, refrigerator, exercise club, whirlpool tub, organic cooking and healing and nurturing spa on premises. Weddings, small meetings, family reunions and seminars hosted. Limited Spanish spoken. Antiquing, fishing, Amish shopping, community built city park, live theater, parks, shopping, downhill skiing, cross-country skiing and water sports nearby.

Publicity: *Smithsonian Magazine, Readers' Digest and Milwaukee Magazine.*

"Wonderful house, great hosts."

Whitewater   I7

Hamilton House Bed & Breakfast

328 W Main St
Whitewater, WI 53190-1958
(262)473-1900 Fax:(262)473-6436
E-mail: kathie@bandbhamiltonhouse.com
Web: www.bandbhamiltonhouse.com

Circa 1861. Local citizens saved Hamilton House, a fanciful Second Empire home, from the wrecking ball. The home is now listed in the National Register of Historic Places. The interior boasts original mantels, woodwork and stained glass. Most of the rooms include a fireplace, and some include a whirlpool tub. A full breakfast is served fireside on tables lit with candles. The Whitewater area offers four lakes and an abundance of outdoor activities, as well as shopping and theater.

Historic Interest: Indian Mounds (2 miles), Milton House.

Innkeeper(s): Jim & Kathleen Fleming. $90-150. MC, VISA, PC, TC. 8 rooms with PB, 7 with FP and 1 suite. Breakfast and snacks/refreshments included in rates. Types of meals: Full bkfst and early coffee/tea. Beds: KQD. Fireplace in room. Central air. Fax, copier, refrigerator, microwave and snack bar on premises. Small meetings and family reunions hosted. Antiquing, beaches, bicycling, fishing, golf, hiking, horseback riding, live theater, parks, shopping, cross-country skiing, sporting events and water sports nearby.

Victoria-On-Main B&B

622 W Main St
Whitewater, WI 53190-1855
(262)473-8400

Circa 1895. This graceful Queen Anne Victorian, shaded by a tall birch tree, is in the heart of Whitewater National Historic District, adjacent to the University of Wisconsin. It was built for Edward Engebretson, mayor of Whitewater. Yellow tulip and sunny daffodils fill the spring flower beds, while fuchsias and geraniums bloom in summertime behind a picket fence. The inn's gables, flower-filled veranda and three-story turret feature a handsome green tin roof. Each guest room is named for a Wisconsin hardwood. The Red Oak Room, Cherry Room and Bird's Eye Maple Room all offer  handsome antiques in their corresponding wood, Laura Ashley prints, antique sheets, pristine heirloom-laced pillowcases and down comforters. A hearty breakfast is sometimes served on the wraparound veranda, and there are kitchen facilities available for light meal preparation. Whitewater Lake and Kettle Moraine State Forest are five minutes away.

Innkeeper(s): Nancy Wendt. $75-85. MC, VISA. 3 rooms, 1 with PB, 1 with FP. Breakfast included in rates. Types of meals: Full bkfst and early coffee/tea. Beds: D. Ceiling fan in room. Air conditioning. Antiquing, fishing, live theater, parks, shopping, cross-country skiing and water sports nearby.

"We loved it. Wonderful hospitality."

Winter   D4

Chippewa River Inn Bed

N4836 County Road G
Winter, WI 54896-8000
(715)266-2662 (800)867-2447

Circa 1900. With 250 feet of river frontage and glorious river views, the Chippewa River inn sits under 200-year-old pines. There are flower gardens and guests may observe deer, otters and birds on the inn's two-acre grounds situated between Eau Claire, Wisc., and Duluth, Minn. Guests may linger over a hearty breakfast of juice, fruit, home-baked pastries and a hot entrée before heading out to go cross-country skiing or snowmobiling in the winter or fishing and canoeing the Chippewa River in the summer. Musky, Walleye and Sturgeon abound in numerous lakes nearby. Guests may wish to visit Al Capone's hideout, which is in Copper falls.

Innkeeper(s): Sue & Dean Hesselberg, Karen & Charles Nielsen. Call for rates. 4 rooms. Beds: QT. Ceiling fan in room.

Wisconsin Dells   H5

Terrace Hill B&B

922 River Rd
Wisconsin Dells, WI 53965-1423
(608)253-9363
E-mail: info@terracehillbb.com

Circa 1900. With a park bordering one edge and the Wisconsin River just across the street, Terrace Hill guests are treated to pleasant surroundings both inside and out. The interior is a cheerful mix of Victorian and country decor. The Park View suite includes a canopy bed and a clawfoot tub, other rooms offer views and cozy surroundings. There is a barbecue grill and picnic table available for guest use. The inn is just a block and a half from downtown Wisconsin Dells. Private parking in rear.

Innkeeper(s): Len, Cookie, Lenard & Lynn Novak. $85-140. PC, TC. 4 rooms with PB and 1 suite. Breakfast and afternoon tea included in rates. Types of meals: Full bkfst and early coffee/tea. Beds: Q. One with whirlpool tub and several with cable TV & VCR in room. Air conditioning. Eclectic library on premises. Small meetings, family reunions and seminars hosted. Amusement parks, antiquing, fishing, live theater, parks, shopping, downhill skiing, cross-country skiing and water sports nearby.

Wisconsin Dells Thunder Valley B&B Inn

W15344 Waubeek Rd
Wisconsin Dells, WI 53965-9005
(608)254-4145
E-mail: neldell@midplains.net

Circa 1870. The Wisconsin Dells area is full of both Scandinavian and Native American heritage, and the innkeeper of this country inn has tried to honor the traditions. The inn even features a Scandinavian gift shop. Chief Yellow Thunder, for whom this inn is named, often camped out on the grounds and surrounding area. The inn's restaurant is highly acclaimed. Everything is homemade, including the wheat the innkeepers grind for the morning pancakes and rolls. There is a good selection of Wisconsin beer and wine, as well. Guests can stay in the farmhouse, Guest Hus, or Wee Hus, all of which offer microwaves and refrigerators.

Historic Interest: Chief Yellow Thunder, a Winnebago Indian Chief, had a pow-wow behind the barn. He is buried nearby.

Innkeeper(s): Anita, Kari & Sigrid Nelson. $65-115. MC, VISA. 10 rooms with PB. Breakfast included in rates. Types of meals: Full bkfst. Beds: KQD. Air conditioning. Handicap access. Weddings, small meetings, family reunions and seminars hosted. Norwegian spoken. International Crane Foundation, Circus Museum, House on Rock, casino and farm animals and dairy nearby.

Publicity: *Wisconsin Trails Magazine, Country Inns, Midwest Living Magazine, Chicago Sun-Times, Milwaukee Journal-Sentinel* and *National Geographic Travel Magazine.*

"Thunder Valley is a favorite of Firstar Club members — delicious food served in a charming atmosphere with warm Scandinavian hospitality."

Wyoming

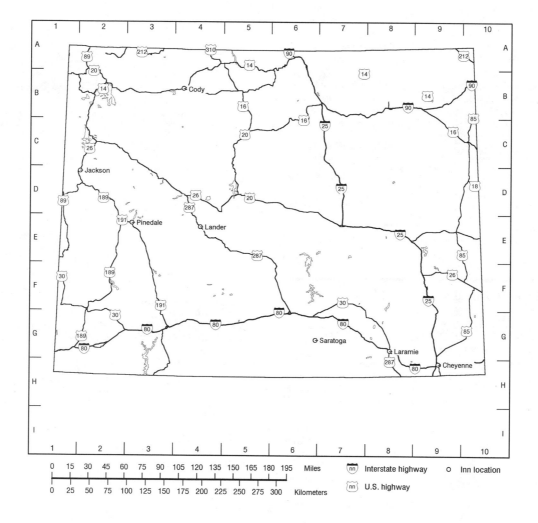

0	15	30	45	60	75	90	105	120	135	150	165	180	195	Miles

0   15   30   45   60   75   90   105 120 135 150 165 180 195   Miles

0   25   50   75   100 125 150 175 200 225 250 275 300   Kilometers

nn Interstate highway   o   Inn location

nn U.S. highway

Cheyenne H9

Nagle Warren Mansion B&B

222 E 17th St
Cheyenne, WY 82001
(307)637-3333 (800)811-2610 Fax:(307)638-6879
E-mail: josterfoss@aol.com
Web: www.naglewarrenmansion.com

Circa 1888. When this Victorian mansion was constructed, Cheyenne was the richest town in the world for its size. The home's brilliant architecture serves as a reminder of this grand time in the city's history. The home boasts meticulously restored woodwork, including a grand staircase adorned with an ornate gaslight. The cast bronze fireplaces are topped with mirrors that reach the ceilings. Bronze medallions were set in the front doors, and guests will find stained glass throughout the home. The home's parlor still includes two paintings commissioned by the home's first owner, Erasmus Nagle. Nagle made his fortune in both the grocery and cattle businesses. From 1915 until 1933, the home belonged to Senator F.E. Warren and his wife. The mansion is in the National Register as well as being listed in the Smithsonian Guide to Historic America.

$108-178. MC, VISA, AX, PC, TC. TAC10. 12 rooms with PB, 6 with FP, 1 suite and 3 conference rooms. Breakfast included in rates. Types of meals: Gourmet bkfst. Beds: KQD. Cable TV, phone and iron and ironing board in room. Air conditioning. Fax, copier, library, masseuse on call, hot tub gazebo and traditional English high tea is served Friday and Saturday on premises. Handicap access. Weddings, small meetings and family reunions hosted. Spanish and German spoken. Antiquing, golf, eight restaurants within walking distance, live theater, parks and shopping nearby.

"Thanks so much for your attention to the fine details of beauty in an old house. The food was great, the atmosphere was romantic."

Cody B4

Mayor's Inn Bed & Breakfast

1413 Rumsey Ave
Cody, WY 82414
(307)587-0887 (888)217-3001 Fax:(307)587-0890
E-mail: mayorsinn@vcn.com

Circa 1909. Considered the town's first mansion, this stylish two-story, turn-of-the-century home was built for Cody's first elected mayor. A romantic Victorian ambiance is achieved with  warm hospitality, antiques, soft lighting, chandeliers and splendid wall and ceiling papers. The parlor inspires nostalgia. The guest bedrooms feature a brass bed and clawfoot tub; a lodge pole pine bed, jetted tub and western art; or an open, sunny room with double shower. The suite boasts a fresh water hot tub and CD player. Offering private and open seating, breakfast is served in both of the dining rooms. The Carriage House is a cottage with fully equipped kitchen.

Historic Interest: Buffalo Bill Museum (7 blocks), Old Trail Town (4 miles), Irma Hotel (3 blocks).

Innkeeper(s): Bill & Daielee Delph. $70-205. MC, VISA, PC, TC. TAC10. 4 rooms with PB and 1 cottage. Breakfast and afternoon tea included in rates. Types of meals: Full bkfst and early coffee/tea. Beds: KQD. Cable TV, turndown service and hot tub in room. Central air. Fax on premises. Weddings, small meetings and family reunions hosted. Antiquing, art galleries, canoeing/kayaking, fishing, golf, hiking, horseback riding, museums, parks, shopping, cross-country skiing and water sports nearby.

Publicity: *Cody Enterprise and The Telegraph Travel.*

Parson's Pillow B&B

1202 14th St
Cody, WY 82414-3720
(307)587-2382 (800)377-2348 Fax:(307)587-2382
E-mail: ppbb@trib.com

Circa 1991. This historic building originally served as the Methodist-Episcopal Church, Cody's first church. Guests are free to practice a tune on the piano in the home's parlor, which also offers a TV and VCR. Guest rooms feature antiques and quilts. Clawfoot and oak-framed prairie tubs add to the nostalgia. The Buffalo Bill Historical Center and the Cody Historic Walking Tour are nearby.

Historic Interest: Buffalo Bill Historical Center, Old West Miniature Village & Museum, Cody Night Rodeo.

Innkeeper(s): Lee & Elly Larabee.
$75-95. MC, VISA, AX, DS, PC. TAC10. 4 rooms with PB. Breakfast included in rates. Types of meals: Gourmet bkfst and early coffee/tea. Beds: Q. Turndown service and ceiling fan in room. VCR, library and computer port on premises. Antiquing, fishing, golf, white water rafting, parks, shopping, downhill skiing, cross-country skiing, tennis and water sports nearby.

The Lockhart B&B Inn

109 W Yellowstone Ave
Cody, WY 82414-8723
(307)587-6074 (800)377-7255 Fax:(307)587-8644
E-mail: lockhart@fiberpipe.net

Circa 1890. Once the home of author and journalist Caroline Lockhart, this Victorian inn has beautiful mountain views from its veranda. The deck affords a view of the Shoshone River.  Rooms are decorated with antiques, old-fashioned beds and a clawfoot tub. Breakfast is served on fine china at your private table in the dining room. Making reservations for dining, river rafting, golfing, rodeo events and more, is offered.

Historic Interest: Teepee Rings, which feature petroglyphs, is two miles away. The town was founded by William "Buffalo Bill" Cody, and the inn is just minutes from the Buffalo Bill Historical Center, Old Trail Town and Cody Nite Rodeo.

Innkeeper(s): Don Kramer & Cindy Baldwin Kramer. $95-125. MC, VISA. TAC5. 7 rooms with PB. Breakfast included in rates. Types of meals: Full bkfst and picnic lunch. Beds: QD. Cable TV, phone and ceiling fan in room. Air conditioning. Piano on premises. Weddings, small meetings, family reunions and seminars hosted. Antiquing, fishing, live theater, shopping, downhill skiing, cross-country skiing, sporting events and water sports nearby.

Publicity: *Glamour, AAA Today, National Geographic Traveler, Windsurf, New York Times, Houston Post and Los Angeles Times.*

"Just like going to grandma's house, like coming home to family — home away from home."

Jackson D2

The Huff House Inn

240 E Deloney, PO Box 1189
Jackson, WY 83001-1189
(307)733-4164 (307)739-9091 Fax:(307)739-9091
E-mail: huffhousebnb@blissnet.com

Circa 1917. Originally built for the town's first medical doctor and town mayor, this Craftsman-style home served as both an office for seeing patients and a residence. The innkeepers have dedicated themselves to retaining the inn's historic character. Beveled-glass doors, chandeliers, antiques and brocade fabrics add to the inn's comfortable atmosphere. In addition to the five guest rooms in the main house, the inn features four separate cottages that boast hand-stenciled walls and Jacuzzi tubs. Breakfast is served  in the formal dining room or breakfast room. Baked apple French toast with a spicy applesauce topping is a house favorite. The inn is a block from the historic district, restaurants, shops and museums.

Innkeeper(s): Jackie & Weldon Richardson. $119-225. MC, VISA, DS, PC, TC. TAC10. 7 rooms, 3 with PB and 4 cottages. Breakfast included in rates. Types of meals: Gourmet bkfst and early coffee/tea. Beds: KQT. Cable TV, phone, VCR and cottages have fireplaces and whirlpool tubs in room. Air conditioning. Fax, copier, spa and library on premises. Small meetings and family reunions hosted. German/English spoken. Antiquing, fishing, golf, dog sledding, snowmobiling, horse back riding, hiking, live theater, parks, shopping, downhill skiing, cross-country skiing, tennis and water sports nearby.

Publicity: *Denver Post, Los Angeles Times and St. Louis Dispatch.*

"Our honeymoon could not have been nicer! The food was incredible and the cottage was perfect."

Lander E4

Blue Spruce Inn

677 S 3rd St
Lander, WY 82520-3707
(307)332-8253
E-mail: bluespruce@rmisp.com
Web: www.bluespruceinn.com

Circa 1920. Five blue spruce trees mark this large Arts and Crafts influenced home. Original chandeliers, stained glass, oak crown molding and woodwork add to the house's appeal. Mission-style furnishings are in keeping with the house's period. Ask for the Spotted Elk Room for a Native American-themed accommodation. There is a sun porch and front porch, and a block away is a  mountain trout stream. Lander is adjacent to the Wind River Indian Reservation, and it is on this reservation where the grave site of Sacajawea is located.

Historic Interest: In addition to small museums and cultural sites on the Wind River Indian Reservation, South Pass, a significant portion of the Oregon Trail is nearby. The Oregon/Mormon/California Trail is about 20 miles away. Historic South Pass City, a Wyoming State Historic Site, is 45 minutes away.

Innkeeper(s): Marvin & JoAnne Brown. $85. MC, VISA, AX, DS, PC, TC. 4 rooms with PB. Breakfast included in rates. Types of meals: Full bkfst and early coffee/tea. Beds: QT. Two rooms with phone and one with TV in room. VCR, bicycles and library on premises. Small meetings and family reunions hosted. Limited German spoken. Antiquing, fishing, Wind River Indian Reservation, museum, parks, shopping and cross-country skiing nearby.

Laramie G8

Vee Bar Guest Ranch

2091 State Hwy 130
Laramie, WY 82070-9734
(307)745-7036 (800)483-3227 Fax:(307)745-7433
E-mail: veebar@lariat.org

Circa 1896. Experience the Old West on this 800-acre guest ranch nestled on Little Laramie River at the base of the Snowy Range Mountains. Once the private residence of an English cattle baron, the main lodge was the home station for a stagecoach company. Today, the authentic western character of the lodge and its log cabins are preserved in the Ralph Lauren-style rustic furnishings, wood floors and stone fireplaces. A full country breakfast is included. The inn offers a variety of on-site recreational activities.

Innkeeper(s): Jim "Lefty" & Carla Cole. $100-150. MC, VISA, AX, DS, PC, TC. TAC10. 9 cabins and 1 conference room. Breakfast included in rates. Types of meals: Full bkfst. AP. Beds: KQDT. Fax, copier, spa and stables on premises. Handicap access. Small meetings, family reunions and seminars hosted. Fishing, snowmobiling, horseback riding, downhill skiing and cross-country skiing nearby.

Publicity: *Log Home Design Ideas Magazine and National Geographic Traveler.*

Pinedale E3

The Chambers House

PO Box 753, 111 W Magnolia St
Pinedale, WY 82941-0753
(307)367-2168 (800)567-2168
E-mail: anoble1227@aol.com

Circa 1933. This authentic log home once owned by one of the area's earliest pioneers was hand built during the Great Depression. It has been immaculately renovated and decorated with a mixture of period antiques and contemporary furnishings. With the Bridger Teton National Forest and Wind River Mountains just a short distance away, travelers can indulge in a variety of summer and winter sports. A gourmet breakfast is served in the dining room.

$55-120. MC, VISA, AX, PC, TC. TAC10. 5 rooms, 2 with PB, 2 with FP. Breakfast included in rates. Types of meals: Gourmet bkfst and early coffee/tea. Beds: QT. Cable TV, phone and VCR in room. Handicap access. Weddings, small meetings, family reunions and seminars hosted. Fishing, golf, parks, shopping, downhill skiing, cross-country skiing and water sports nearby.

Pets allowed: Dogs only.

Saratoga G6

Far Out West B&B

304 N Second St
Saratoga, WY 82331
(307)326-5869 Fax:(307)326-9864
E-mail: fowbnb@union-tel.com

Circa 1920. Located two blocks from downtown, this historic home maintains many original features, and there are two guest rooms located in the main house. As well, there is a unique room accessible only by a tiny, four-foot-high door. Inside, children will find toys, books  and other goodies. Out back, there are several accommodations with special names such as The Calamity Jane or The James Gang. The Hideout, located in a separate house, includes a kitchen, dining area and living room. Breakfast entrees, such as Gunfighter eggs, are accompanied by freshly baked biscuits, sausage, bacon and fresh fruit.

Innkeeper(s): Bill & BJ Farr. $100-130. MC, VISA, AX, DS, PC. TAC10. 5 rooms with PB and 1 cottage. Breakfast included in rates. Types of meals: Full bkfst and early coffee/tea. Beds: KDT. Cable TV, ceiling fan and robes in room. VCR, fax, copier and library on premises. Handicap access. Weddings, small meetings, family reunions and seminars hosted. Antiquing, fishing, golf, snowmobiling, natural hot springs, pet boarding, parks, shopping, cross-country skiing, tennis and water sports nearby.

Publicity: *Saratoga Sun.*

"An absolutely wonderful place for comfort, friendliness and food."

U.S. Territories

Puerto Rico

San Juan

El Canario Inn

1317 Ashford Ave
San Juan, PR 00907
(787)722-3861 (800)533-2649 Fax:(787)722-0391
E-mail: canariopr@aol.com
Web: www.canariohotels.com

Circa 1938. This three-story inn is only a block from San Juan's glorious white-sand beaches. Rooms are decorated in a tropical theme with rattan and wicker furnishings and Bermuda ceiling fans. Guests can relax on one of the patios. The inn is a charming escape from the multitude of high rise hotels along the coast. Casinos and discotheques are nearby, and sightseeing tours and boating trips can be arranged at the hotel.

Historic Interest: Old San Juan is only three miles away, and features forts, a museum, cathedrals and plenty of gracious Spanish architecture set among cobblestone streets.

Innkeeper(s): Jude & Keith Olson. $75-114. MC, VISA, AX, DC, DS. TAC10. 25 rooms with PB. Breakfast included in rates. Types of meals: Cont plus and early coffee/tea. Beds: DT. Cable TV, phone and ceiling fan in room. Air conditioning. Fax on premises. Fishing, parks, shopping and water sports nearby.

Publicity: *USA Today, Conde Naste Traveler and New York Times.*

Canada

Alberta

Calgary

Calgary Westways Guest House

216-25 Ave SW
Calgary, AB T2S 0L1
(403)229-1758 Fax:(403)228-6265
E-mail: calgary@westways.ab.ca
Web: www.westways.ab.ca

Circa 1912. Pampered luxury begins when leaving the airport in a Rolls Royce Silver Shadow Mark 1 to arrive at this Heritage house in the historic Mission district. It features Victorian details, hardwood floors, leaded-glass windows, box-beam ceilings and built-in cabinets. Specializing in romantic escapes, the guest bedrooms offer many relaxing amenities including robes, candles, jetted or soaker clawfoot tubs, entertainment centers and gas fireplaces. A satisfying breakfast is served in the dining room on bone china and cut crystal. Walk to the nearby city centre or visit Fort Calgary only one mile away.

Historic Interest: Fort Calgary (1 mile).

Innkeeper(s): Jonathon Lloyd. $70-130. MC, VISA, AX, TC. TAC10. 5 suites, 4 with FP. Breakfast included in rates. Types of meals: Gourmet bkfst and early coffee/tea. Beds: KQ. Cable TV, phone, ceiling fan, VCR and fireplace in room. Central air. Fax, bicycles, library, pet boarding, free internet access and video library on premises. Small meetings and family reunions hosted. Amusement parks, antiquing, art galleries, bicycling, canoeing/kayaking, fishing, golf, hiking, horseback riding, live theater, museums, parks, shopping, sporting events and tennis nearby.

Pets allowed: $5.00 per day.

Publicity: *Calgary Herald.*

British Columbia

Shawnigan Lake

Marifield Manor, an Edwardian B&B

2039 Merrifield Ln, RR 1
Shawnigan Lake, BC V0R 2W0
(250)743-9930 (800)506-2526
E-mail: mariman@pacificcoast.net
Web: www.marifieldmanor.com

Circa 1910. Overlooking Shawnigan Lake, this Edwardian mansion features wraparound verandahs. Guest rooms offer clawfoot tubs, antiques and fine, old linens. Most have views of the mountains and lake through the trees. Tea is served fireside or on the veranda, if weather permits. Tapestries and antiques are found throughout. The inn's artfully presented, gourmet breakfasts are served in the dining room or al fresco. The inn has become popular for meetings, workshops and retreats as well as receptions and family gatherings, recently hosting visitors on Heritage House Tour.

Innkeeper(s): Cathy Basskin. $75-200. TC. 6 rooms with PB, 2 suites and 1 conference room. Breakfast and afternoon tea included in rates. Types of meals: Gourmet bkfst, cont plus and early coffee/tea. Beds: QDT. Turndown service in room. Air conditioning. VCR, fax, copier, sauna, bicycles, library and e-mail on premises. Weddings, small meetings, family reunions and seminars hosted. French spoken. Antiquing, bicycling, canoeing/kayaking, golf, hiking, rowing, host of Shawnigan Lake Writers Village, boarding schools, Vancouver Island wineries and tours, live theater, parks, downhill skiing and water sports nearby.

Publicity: *North American, Country Inns and Western Living.*

Sooke

Ocean Wilderness Inn & Spa Retreat

109 W Coast Rd, RR 2
Sooke, BC V0S 1N0
(250)646-2116 (800)323-2116 Fax:(250)646-2317
E-mail: ocean@sookenet.com
Web: www.sookenet.com/ocean

Circa 1940. The hot tub spa of this log house inn is in a Japanese gazebo overlooking the ocean. Reserve your time for a private soak, terry bathrobes are supplied. Experience massage and mud treatments, ocean treatments and herbal wraps while meditation enhances your creative expression. The inn will arrange fishing charters, nature walks, wilderness treks and beachcombing. Coffee is delivered to your room each morning on a silver service. Guests are invited to enjoy breakfast in their room or in the dining lounge. Rooms include antiques, sitting areas and canopy beds. Two of the rooms have hot tubs for two with spectacular ocean and Olympic Mountain views.

Historic Interest: Botanical Beach and Hatley Castle are 15 miles from the inn, while Moss Cottage is only eight miles away. Butchart Gardens and the Royal B.C. Museum are within 35 miles.

Innkeeper(s): Marion J. Rolston. $85-175. MC, VISA, AX, TC. TAC10. 9 rooms with PB. Breakfast included in rates. Types of meals: Full bkfst and early coffee/tea. Beds: KQT. Fax and copier on premises. Handicap access. Weddings, small meetings, family reunions and seminars hosted. Antiquing, fishing, whale watching, live theater, parks and shopping nearby.

Pets allowed: By arrangement.

Publicity: *Puget Sound Business Journal, Getaways from Vancouver and Travel Holiday Magazine.*

"Thank you for the most wonderful hospitality and accommodations of our entire vacation."

Sooke Harbour House Inn

1528 Whiffen Spit Rd
Sooke, BC V0S 1N0
(250)642-3421 (800)889-9688 Fax:(250)642-6988
E-mail: shh@islandnet.com

Circa 1929. Extensive herb and flower gardens and the Olympic Mountains set off the spectacular ocean views from each of the guest bedrooms at this coastal retreat. Ask for the Victor Newman Longhouse room for a four-poster, king-size bed, skylight, wet bar, bathtub for two overlooking the water and a see-through fireplace. Each room boasts a private patio or balcony. The inn's evening cuisine, proclaimed by various travel and food writers as "one of the best in British Columbia," or the "best in Canada," features locally grown produce and fresh fish and seafood taken from local waters. There are Japanese and French influences in the offerings. Enjoy a revitalizing spa treatment, or visit the gift shop and gallery.

Innkeeper(s): Frederique & Sinclair Philip. $160-385. MC, VISA, DC, PC, TC. TAC10. 28 rooms with PB, 28 with FP. Breakfast included in rates. Types of meals: Full bkfst, cont, picnic lunch, gourmet dinner and room service. Beds: KQ. Phone and wet bar; VCR and cable on request in room. Fax, copier, child care, restaurant and spa treatments on premises. Handicap access. Weddings, small meetings, family reunions and seminars hosted. Antiquing, fishing, golf, parks, shopping and water sports nearby.

Pets allowed: $20.00 per day per pet.

Publicity: *Houston Chronicle, Gourmet, Harrowsmith, House Beautiful, New York Times, Wine Spectator Magazine., Sleeping With Strangers and Great Country Inns.*

Vancouver

Henley House B&B

1025 8th Ave, New Westminster
Vancouver, BC V3M 2R5
(604)526-3919 (866)526-3919 Fax:(604)526-3913
E-mail: henley@istar.ca

Circa 1925. Appreciate a warm welcome and an old-fashioned charm at this Craftsman-style home that is centrally located to access the best of the big city as well as rural environs. Relax by the fire in the living room or watch TV and videos in the upstairs lounge. Perfect for addressing postcards, a cozy writing room has its own balcony. Guest bedrooms offer robes and slippers, fresh flowers and evening chocolates. The decor and furnishings include antiques, a four-poster bed, old walnut, gumwood and maple pieces, quilts, chintz, original watercolors, candlesticks and a clawfoot tub. A traditional hot breakfast is served on china and crystal in the wainscoted dining room. Enjoy the sun on the spacious deck, soak in the hot tub or nap in the hammock.

Innkeeper(s): Anne O'Shaughnessy & Ross Hood. $70-85. MC, VISA, PC, TC. TAC10. 3 rooms, 1 with PB. Breakfast, afternoon tea and snacks/refreshments included in rates. Types of meals: Gourmet bkfst, veg bkfst, cont plus, cont and early coffee/tea. Beds: QD. Cable TV, phone, ceiling fan and VCR in room. Air conditioning. Fax, copier, spa and library on premises. Amusement parks, antiquing, art galleries, beaches, bicycling, canoeing/kayaking, fishing, golf, hiking, live theater, museums, parks, shopping, downhill skiing and tennis nearby.

Kenya Court Ocean Front Guest House

2230 Cornwall Ave
Vancouver, BC V6K 1B5
(604)738-7085
E-mail: h&dwilliams@telus.net

Circa 1927. Enjoy a piping hot cup of fresh, gourmet coffee as you gaze out over the ocean at this scenic bed & breakfast. Innkeeper Dorothy Williams not only provides a delectable spread of fresh breads, croissants, cereals and fruits, she serves it in a rooftop solarium. Williams, in charge of the piano department at Vancouver Academy, will serenade guests with piano concerts on some days. Roomy suites feature antiques, separate entrances and boast ocean views. The home is within walking distance to the Granville Market, the planetarium, city centres, 10 minutes from the University of British Columbia and 20 miles from the U.S. border. The athletically inclined will enjoy the use of tennis courts, walking and jogging trails and a heated outdoor saltwater pool across the street.

Historic Interest: A maritime museum is a five-minute walk from the bed & breakfast. An anthropology museum is 10 minutes by car.

Innkeeper(s): Dr. & Mrs. H. Williams. $95-110. PC, TC. 7 rooms with PB, 4 with FP and 5 suites. Breakfast included in rates. Types of meals: Gourmet bkfst and early coffee/tea. Beds: KQT. Cable TV and phone in room. VCR and library on premises. Weddings and family reunions hosted. Italian, French and German spoken. Antiquing, fishing, live theater, parks, shopping, downhill skiing, cross-country skiing, sporting events and water sports nearby.

Publicity: *Washington Times and Rocky Mountain News.*

"Beautiful home; we enjoyed the unsurpassed hospitality."

The Manor Guest House

345 W 13th Ave
Vancouver, BC V5Y 1W2
(604)876-8494 Fax:(604)876-5763
E-mail: info@manorguesthouse.com
Web: www.manorguesthouse.com

Circa 1902. This turn-of-the-century Edwardian still features many original elements, including carved banisters, polished wood floors and ornate wainscoting. The home is one of the city's oldest. The innkeeper has decorated it with a collection of English antiques. The penthouse suite, which includes a bedroom, loft, deck and kitchen, boasts a spectacular view of the city. Fresh fruits, home-baked breads and specialties such as a cheese and mushroom souffle or blueberry cobbler highlight the breakfast menu.

Innkeeper(s): Brenda Yablon. $65-125. MC, VISA, TC. TAC10. 10 rooms, 6 with PB, 1 with FP, 1 suite and 1 conference room. Types of meals: Gourmet bkfst. Beds: KQDT. Cable TV in room. VCR, fax, copier, free local calls, free internet access and free parking on premises. Weddings, small meetings, family reunions and seminars hosted. French and German spoken. Antiquing, live theater, parks, shopping, downhill skiing, sporting events and water sports nearby.

The West End Guest House

1362 Haro St
Vancouver, BC V6E 1G2
(604)681-2889 Fax:(604)688-8812
E-mail: wegh@idmail.com
Web: westendguesthouse.com

Circa 1906. Among the hustle and bustle of Vancouver sits this pink Victorian, which transports its guests out of the modern metropolis and back to the turn-of-the-century days. The

gracious home used to house a family of musicians and photographers. Innkeeper Evan Penner has preserved their past, placing lithographs and historical photos owned by the family throughout the house. Each of the rooms is individually decorated with glorious prints and beautiful antiques. The guest rooms are cozy and welcoming, the perfect place to snuggle down after a long day and sink into brass beds decked in fine linens and down comforters. Guests will enjoy relaxing on the second-story deck or strolling past the many plants and flowers in the back garden. A gourmet, country-style breakfast is served each morning, and homemade chocolates await guests as they arrive.

Historic Interest: The home is located in the heart of Vancouver, close to many historic sites, including Canada Place, the Canadian Pacific Railway Station and Gastown, a restored area full of interesting shops, restaurants and a unique steam-powered clock.

Innkeeper(s): Evan Penner. $118-250. MC, VISA, AX, DS, TC. TAC10. 8 rooms with PB, 2 with FP. Breakfast included in rates. Types of meals: Full bkfst and room service. Beds: KQDT. Cable TV, phone, turndown service and ceiling fan in room. Small meetings hosted. Limited French spoken. Amusement parks, antiquing, fishing, live theater, shopping, downhill skiing, cross-country skiing, sporting events and water sports nearby.

Publicity: *New York Times and Province News.*

"Quiet, comfort, convenience, homey, delicious food and good conversations with other guests. I will do nothing but sing the praises of B&Bs from now on, and I'm sure we will meet again."

Victoria

Abigail's Hotel

906 McClure St
Victoria, BC V8V 3E7
(250)388-5363 (800)561-6565 Fax:(250)388-7787
E-mail: innkeeper@abigailshotel.com
Web: www.abigailshotel.com

Circa 1930. Abigail's, a Tudor-style hotel, boasts three gabled stories, stained-glass windows, crystal chandeliers and tasteful decor. It holds a five-star rating as a heritage inn with Canada Select. Complimentary hors d'oeuvres and beverages are offered in the library, also a popular area for small weddings.

Rooms feature a variety of amenities such as canopied beds, fireplaces, Jacuzzi baths and antiques. The inn is located three blocks from Victoria's inner harbor, shops and restaurants. Rates are quoted in Canadian dollars.

Innkeeper(s): Daniel & Frauke Behune. $122-389. MC, VISA, AX, TC. TAC10. 22 rooms with PB, 14 with FP and 6 suites. Breakfast and snacks/refreshments included in rates. Types of meals: Gourmet bkfst and early coffee/tea. Beds: KQD. Phone in room. Fax, copier and library on premises. Weddings, small meetings, family reunions and seminars hosted. German spoken. Antiquing, fishing, live theater, parks, shopping and water sports nearby.

Publicity: *Seattle Magazine, Victoria Times Colonist and Country Inns.*

Amethyst Inn

1501 Fort Street
Victoria, BC V8S 1Z6
(250)595-2053 (888)265-6499 Fax:(250)595-2054
E-mail: innkeeper@amethyst-inn.com
Web: www.amethyst-inn.com

Circa 1885. Befitting its name, this Victorian mansion is a gorgeous gem. The inn is showcased in the prestigious heritage neighborhood of Rocklands, and it is the first home to be designated a heritage property in British Columbia. It has the original 13-foot ceilings, stained glass, wallpaper borders, and a freestanding double staircase in the wood-paneled foyer. The mansion was lovingly restored for comfort, elegance and romance, with great attention given to details like soundproofing. The decor, fixtures and furnishings authentically reflect the Victorian era. Impressive guest suites exude luxury and offer two-person clawfoot, soaker or hydrotherapy tubs. Most rooms feature Minton-tiled fireplaces. A full breakfast is prepared each morning by the chef and served in the dining room where tables are set with fine antique china and crystal.

$65-245. MC, VISA, TC. TAC10. 16 rooms with PB, 13 with FP, 1 suite and 1 conference room. Types of meals: Gourmet bkfst. Beds: QD. Ceiling fan, most with bar refrigerator and fireplace in room. Central air. Weddings hosted. Antiquing, art galleries, bicycling, canoeing/kayaking, fishing, golf, hiking, whale watching, live theater, museums, parks, shopping, tennis and wineries nearby.

Publicity: *Seattle Times and Readers Digest New Choices.*

Beaconsfield Inn

998 Humboldt St
Victoria, BC V8V 2Z8
(250)384-4044 Fax:(250)384-4052
E-mail: beaconsfield@islandnet.com
Web: www.beaconsfieldinn.com

Circa 1905. Beautiful grounds accentuate this turn-of-the-century English manor. Rooms are light and airy with antiques, original woodwork, Oriental carpets and stained-glass windows. Many of the rooms feature fireplaces and Jacuzzi tubs and all include cozy, down comforters. A luxurious gourmet breakfast is served in the dining room or conservatory and afternoon tea is sure to delight. Evening sherry is served in the library. There's plenty to do in this seaside town, and The Beaconsfield is only four blocks from downtown and the oceanfront.

Historic Interest: Butchart Gardens are 25 miles away, and Victoria has many historic buildings, homes and other sites. Old Town and several museums are close by.

Innkeeper(s): Emily & James Yungkans. $77-350. MC, VISA. TAC10. 5 rooms with PB and 4 suites. Breakfast and afternoon tea included in rates. Types of meals: Full bkfst and gourmet dinner. Beds: Q. Antiquing, fishing, live theater and water sports nearby.

Publicity: *Equity, Globe & Mail, New York Times, Country Inns, Seattle Times, Horizon Air, Dallas Morning News, Northwest Travel, Arkansas Democrat Gazette, Wichita Eagle, Look Travel, Vancouver Sun and Vancouver Province.*

"This place is about as close to heaven as one can get."

Dashwood Seaside Manor

One Cook St
Victoria, BC V8V 3W6
 (800)667-5517 Fax:(250)383-1760
E-mail: reservations@dashwoodmanor.com
Web: www.dashwoodmanor.com

Circa 1912. Dashwood Manor is a historic listed Edwardian Tudor Revival mansion with a rare oceanfront location. Choose between a first-floor suite with a fireplace, chandelier and beamed ceilings; a second-story "special occasion" suite; or a top-floor suite for spectacular balcony views of the ocean and the Olympic Mountains. Some suites include a Jacuzzi tub. To reach downtown Victoria, take a short walk through the park. The inn offers a self-catered full breakfast. Rates are quoted in Canadian dollars.

Innkeeper(s): Derek Dashwood Family & Staff. $75-345. MC, VISA, AX, DC. 14 suites, 3 with FP. Breakfast included in rates. Types of meals: Full bkfst. Beds: Q. Cable TV in room. Antiquing, fishing, live theater and shopping nearby.

Pets allowed: Small pets with kennel.

Publicity: *San Francisco Chronicle.*

"Enchanting, very soothing."

The Gatsby Mansion B&B

309 Belleville St
Victoria, BC V8V 1-X2
 (250)388-9191 (800)563-9656 Fax:(250)920-5651
E-mail: huntingdon@bctravel.com

Circa 1897. The Gatsby Mansion offers the luxury of two eras. The home's Queen Anne design captures one of the best remainders of the Victorian era, the architecture. One look inside and you'll know that Fitzgerald's Jay Gatsby would indeed be at home here. The antique-filled interior still maintains stained-glass windows, mahogany woodwork and frescoed ceilings. The veranda looks out to the harbors, and several rooms offer an ocean view. The mansion's restaurant serves a variety of West Coast-style specialties. Currency exchange is available at the inn, and it also houses a gift shop, art gallery and Artisans Lane featuring BC artists. It is less than two blocks from the legislative buildings, and guests can walk downtown. Several packages are offered, including whale adventure, golfing and romantic themes.

Innkeeper(s): Rita Roy-Wilson. $95-329. MC, VISA, AX, DC, DS, TC. TAC10. 20 rooms with PB. Breakfast included in rates. Types of meals: Full bkfst, cont, early coffee/tea, lunch, afternoon tea, snacks/refreshments, dinner and room service. Beds: KQDT. Cable TV, phone, in room movies and charges apply in room. Fax on premises. Weddings, small meetings, family reunions and seminars hosted. French and German spoken. Fishing, golf, live theater, parks, shopping and water sports nearby.

Gregory's Guest House

5373 Patricia Bay Hwy
Victoria, BC V8Y 2N9
 (250)658-8404 (888)658-8404 Fax:(250)658-4604
E-mail: gregorys@victoriabandb.com

Circa 1919. The two acres of this historic hobby farm are just across the street from Elk Lake, six miles from downtown Victoria and near Butchart Gardens. All the rooms are decorated in antiques and duvets, and they feature garden and lake views. The grounds include water gardens, a waterfall and a pond. A traditional, full Canadian breakfast is served, and after the meal, guests can enjoy the hobby farm and exotic birds or perhaps rent a boat at the lake.

Innkeeper(s): Paul & Elizabeth Gregory. $89-120. MC, VISA, PC, TC. TAC10. 3 rooms, 2 with PB. Breakfast included in rates. Types of meals: Full bkfst. Beds: QDT. Fax, library and parlor with fireplace on premises. Antiquing, fishing, Victoria Butchart Gardens, live theater, parks, sporting events and water sports nearby.

"Our family felt very welcome, loved the house and especially liked the super breakfasts."

Holland House Inn

595 Michigan St
Victoria, BC V8V 1S7
 (250)384-6644 (800)335-3466 Fax:(250)384-6117
E-mail: stay@hollandhouse.victoria.bc.ca
Web: hollandhouse.victoria.bc.ca

Circa 1915. Refurbished in a pristine English country style, the three-story Holland House Inn is accentuated with a white picket fence, pillared balconies and colorful flower boxes. Luxurious accommodations have been designed individually and include fireplaces, sitting areas, a balcony or patio, handsome antiques and unique pieces, matching wallpapers and draperies, goose down duvets and full baths (four with double soaking tubs). The Conservatory or patio is the site for the inn's lavish breakfast. Victoria's Inner Harbor, downtown and the Seattle and Port Angeles ferry terminals are within three blocks.

Innkeeper(s): Margaret & Harry Brock. $68-206. MC, VISA, AX. 17 rooms with PB. Breakfast included in rates. Types of meals: Full bkfst. Beds: KQT. Cable TV and phone in room. Weddings, small meetings and family reunions hosted. Antiquing, live theater and shopping nearby.

Publicity: *Northwest Special Places.*

Humboldt House Bed & Breakfast

867 Humboldt St
Victoria, BC V8V 2Z6
 (250)383-0152 (888)383-0327 Fax:(250)383-6402
E-mail: rooms@humboldthouse.com
Web: www.humboldthouse.com

Circa 1893. Just two blocks from the magnificent Empress Hotel and Victoria's Inner Harbor and one block from Beacon Hill Park with views of mountains and water sits this 5,000-square-foot 1893 Victorian inn. The bed & breakfast is owned and managed by a former restaurant owner and pastry chef. Its six guest bedrooms each have their own fireplace and Jacuzzi tub. Oft mentioned by enthusiastic travel reviewers is the gourmet champagne breakfast tucked into a basket and delivered to the privacy of the room each morning. It includes such courses as eggs Benedict, seafood crepes, French toast, fruit and home-baked croissants. In the afternoon, guests may enjoy a glass of wine and homemade delicacies in the common room.

Innkeeper(s): David & Vlasta Booth, Mila Werbik. $93-210. MC, VISA, TC. TAC10. 6 rooms with PB, 6 with FP. Breakfast and snacks/refreshments included in rates. Types of meals: Gourmet bkfst, early coffee/tea and picnic lunch. Beds: KQ. Turndown service in room. Library on premises. French, German, Czech and Japanese spoken. Antiquing, art galleries, beaches, bicycling, canoeing/kayaking, fishing, golf, hiking, horseback riding, live theater, museums, parks, shopping and tennis nearby.

Publicity: *Country Inns, Los Angeles Times and Western Living.*

Scholefield House B&B

731 Vancouver St
Victoria, BC V8V 3V4
(250)385-2025 (800)661-1623 Fax:(250)383-3036
E-mail: mail@scholefieldhouse.com
Web: scholefieldhouse.com

Circa 1892. Located on a quiet street downtown and three blocks from the Empress Hotel, this authentically restored Victorian B&B is shaded by tall trees that line the wide boulevards. A picket fence and gabled front entrance provide an inviting welcome to guests. Rooms are furnished with antiques

and period decor, and each has a private bath. The five-course champagne breakfast is served fireside in the Parlor and edible flowers decorate the abundant servings of eggs Florentine, French toast with Brie, smoked salmon and other entrees. Two favorite spots are the private library where guests may enjoy a glass of sherry or tea and coffee and outside, an English herb and rose garden. The innkeeper is an author, who enjoys the historic register home's connection to the original owner, who founded the library in the Legislature Building. Stroll to the Inner Harbour, restaurants, antique shops, and theater in Victoria's flower-filled environment sometimes called "more English than England."

Innkeeper(s): Tana Dineen. $100-150. MC, VISA, PC, TC. TAC10. 3 rooms with PB, 1 with FP and 1 suite. Breakfast included in rates. Types of meals: Gourmet bkfst. Beds: KQ. Turndown service and ceiling fan in room. VCR, fax and library on premises. Antiquing, canoeing/kayaking, fishing, golf, whale watching, salmon fishing, gardens, English high tea, live theater, museums and shopping nearby.

New Brunswick

Edmundston

Auberge-LeFief Inn

87 Rue De L'Eglise
Edmundston, NB E3V 1J6
(506)735-0400 Fax:(506)735-0402

Circa 1920. This red brick Victorian offers rooms decorated in a variety of cultural themes, reflecting the pioneer heritage of New Brunswick. There's Irish Mist, The Highland, The French Vineyard and The Malobiannah, to name a few. Among the inn's regional dishes is the local "ploye," a buckwheat type crepe occasionally offered at breakfast. The inn has a four-star rating from Mobile.

Historic Interest: King Landing (200 km).

Innkeeper(s): Sharon Belanger. $60-95. MC, VISA, TC. 8 rooms and 1 conference room. Breakfast, afternoon tea and snacks/refreshments included in rates. Types of meals: Early coffee/tea. Beds: KQD. Cable TV, phone, ceiling fan and VCR in room. Air conditioning. Fax, copier and library on premises. Weddings, small meetings, family reunions and seminars hosted. French spoken. Amusement parks, antiquing, art galleries, bicycling, canoeing/kayaking, golf, hiking, horseback riding, live theater, museums, parks, shopping, downhill skiing, cross-country skiing, sporting events, tennis and water sports nearby.

Shediac

Auberge Belcourt Inn

310 Main St
Shediac, NB E4P 2E3
(506)532-6098 Fax:(506)533-9398
E-mail: belcourt@nbnet.nb.ca
Web: www.sn2000.nb.ca/comp/auberge-belcourt

Circa 1910. Built in Victorian style, this early 20th-century home has been designated a local historical site. Original hardwood floors and stained-glass windows mingle with antique furnishings to create a warm, historic ambiance. Canopy and brass beds grace the guest rooms. Beach towels and sun umbrellas

are available for guests who wish to spend the day by the sea. With advanced notice and during the off-season, the innkeepers will prepare and serve a traditional Chinese dinner, either a five-course feast or a fondue where guests cook seafood, dumplings, beef, chicken, vermicelli and vegetables in savory broth. When its high season, spend some time looking over the innkeepers' collection of menus and choose a perfect place for your evening meal.

Innkeeper(s): Pauline & Christopher Pyke. $90-115. MC, VISA, AX, DC, TC. 7 rooms with PB, 1 with FP. Breakfast included in rates. Types of meals: Full bkfst. Beds: KQD. Fireplace in room. Central air. Fax and library on premises. Weddings and small meetings hosted. French and Cantonese spoken. Amusement parks, antiquing, beaches, bicycling, canoeing/kayaking, golf, hiking, horseback riding, parks, shopping and water sports nearby.

Newfoundland

Trinity

Campbell House Bed & Breakfast

High St
Trinity, NF A0C 2S0
(709)464-3377 (877)464-7700 Fax:(709)464-3377
E-mail: tgow@campbellhouse.nf.ca
Web: www.campbellhouse.nf.ca

Circa 1840. Combining the amenities of an upscale inn with the essence of a living museum this B&B was built with the full-studded construction typically used on the wood-rich Bonavista Peninsula. Situated in an historic coastal village, offering splendid views of the Atlantic Ocean, the heritage-designated restored buildings include two cottages that easily accommodate families. Romantic guest bedrooms instill a peaceful tranquility. After a delicious breakfast, relax on the waterfront decks and breathe deeply the sea air before exploring the town or strolling the hills and meadows of this four-acre retreat.

Historic Interest: Lester Garland Premises, Ryan Preasies Historic House (1 km), Bonavista Lighthouse, Kings Cove Lighhouse (45 minutes).

Innkeeper(s): Tinke Gow. $89-99. MC, VISA, AX, DC, CB, DS, TC. TAC10. 3 rooms with PB, 1 suite, 2 guest houses and 1 conference room. Breakfast included in rates. Types of meals: Gourmet bkfst, early coffee/tea, gourmet lunch, picnic lunch, afternoon tea and gourmet dinner. Beds: QDT. Cable TV, phone and VCR in room. Fax and library on premises. Weddings, small meetings, family reunions and seminars hosted. Dutch, French and English spoken. Art galleries, beaches, canoeing/kayaking, fishing, golf, hiking, live theater, museums, parks, shopping, downhill skiing and cross-country skiing nearby.

Nova Scotia
Canning

The Farmhouse Inn
9757 Main St
Canning, NS B0P 1H0
(902)582-7900 (800)928-4346 Fax:(902)582-7480
E-mail: farmhous@ns.sympatico.ca
Web: www.farmhouseinn.ns.ca

Circa 1840. Located 75 minutes from Halifax, this renovated farmhouse is accented with a welcoming front porch and colorful flower beds. All guest bedrooms and suites have TV/VCRs, phones and air conditioning; most have fireplaces. Some boast two-person whirlpool tubs sitting directly in front of the fireplace. A pressed-tin ceiling and pine floors add to the character of the dining room where a delicious breakfast menu changes daily. French toast, apple sausages, blueberry grunt, apple crisp, heavenly pears, eggs San Francisco, ham and cheese quiche, peach cobbler, and Canadian bacon are some of the dishes served. Afternoon tea includes fresh-baked goodies. Winter sleigh rides are available. Panoramic views of the valley and Minas Basin are found after an eight-minute drive up to the Look-Off. Other popular activities include cycling along Fundy Shore, watching the spectacularly fast tides at Kingsport Beach or visiting Blomidon Park's red cliffs. Rates are quoted in Canadian dollars. Inn has Canada Select four star rating.

Historic Interest: Grand Pré (15 miles), Fort Anne (60 miles).

Innkeeper(s): Doug & Ellen Bray. $69-139. MC, VISA, AX, TC. TAC10. 5 rooms with PB, 4 with FP and 4 suites. Breakfast and afternoon tea included in rates. Types of meals: Full bkfst and early coffee/tea. Beds: KQT. Cable TV, phone, ceiling fan and VCR in room. Air conditioning. Fax and copier on premises. Amusement parks, antiquing, art galleries, beaches, bicycling, golf, hiking, horseback riding, live theater, museums, parks, shopping, downhill skiing, cross-country skiing and wineries nearby.

Publicity: *Canadian Country Inns.*

Chester

Mecklenburgh Inn
78 Queen St
Chester, NS B0J 1J0
(902)275-4638
E-mail: meckinn@auracom.com

Circa 1903. Guests to this Edwardian Mission-style inn have plenty to see and do in the seaside village, which has catered to summer visitors for more than 150 years. Favorite activities include touring the historic streets, watching a yacht race, tennis, golf, and browsing the craft shops and boutiques. The living room is a popular place for sitting by the fireplace to talk and read from the selection of travel books and magazines. Local theater productions can be seen at the Chester Playhouse. Guests will be happy to know that the innkeeper is a Cordon Bleu chef. Rates are quoted in Canadian dollars.

Historic Interest: Oak Island (5 miles).

Innkeeper(s): Suzi Fraser. $65-85. VISA, AX. TAC10. 4 rooms. Breakfast

included in rates. Types of meals: Full bkfst and early coffee/tea. Beds: QDT. VCR on premises. Weddings and family reunions hosted. Antiquing, fishing, live theater, shopping, sporting events and water sports nearby.

Publicity: *Georgetown Times, Life Channel Network, Brides and Toronto Sun.*

"Lovely experience, great hospitality, yummy breakfast."

Clyde River

Clyde River Inn
10525 Highway 103
Clyde River, NS B0W 1R0
(902)637-3267 (877)262-0222 Fax:(902)637-1512

Circa 1874. This beautifully restored Victorian, once a stagecoach stop, features an inviting red exterior trimmed in a creamy shade of saffron. The interior is decorated with antiques in period, Victorian style. Guests are treated to an evening snack, as well as a full breakfast with items such as fresh fruit, homemade muffins and croissants, homemade preserves, yogurt and entrees such as blueberry pancakes. Golfing, fishing and beaches all are nearby.

Historic Interest: Black Loyalist Landing 1783 (8 miles), Old meeting house and woollen mill (10 miles).

Innkeeper(s): Michael & Pat Nickerson. $60-100. MC, VISA, TC. TAC10. 4 rooms with PB and 1 suite. Breakfast and snacks/refreshments included in rates. Types of meals: Full bkfst and early coffee/tea. Beds: QDT. Ceiling fan in room. VCR, fax and library on premises. Antiquing, beaches, bicycling, canoeing/kayaking, fishing, golf, museums, parks and shopping nearby.

Pets allowed: CAll ahead.

Peggys Cove

Peggy's Cove Bed & Breakfast
19 Church Rd
Peggys Cove, NS B0J 2N0
(902)423-1102 (800)725-8732 Fax:(902)423-8329
E-mail: dynamic.realty@ns.sympatico.ca

Circa 1940. Walk to the world famous Peggy's Cove lighthouse from this yellow farm house with wraparound veranda. Situated in the fishing village, it is on two acres of grounds. Enjoying the sunset views from a private balcony, sipping local wines and soaking in an outdoor hot tub are among the favorite experiences at the inn. A full stick-to-your-ribs breakfast is offered. Once owned by artist Bill de Garthe, the home was originally a fisherman's house. The art studio now features contemporary landscapes and marine art by local Nova Scotian artisans including the resident artist. Carvings and local crafts are also on exhibit.

Historic Interest: Swiss air flight monument (2 miles), Peggy's Cove Lighthouse(walking distance).

$75-125. MC, VISA, AX, PC, TC. TAC10. 5 rooms, 3 with PB. Breakfast and afternoon tea included in rates. Types of meals: Gourmet bkfst and early coffee/tea. Beds: QT. VCR, copier and spa on premises. Antiquing, art galleries, canoeing/kayaking, fishing, golf, hiking, horseback riding, museums, parks and shopping nearby.

Prospect

Prospect Bed & Breakfast

1758 Prospect Bay Rd
Prospect, NS B3T 2B3
(902)423-1102 (800)725-8732
E-mail: dynamic.realty@ns.sympatico.ca
Web: www.welcome.to/salt.sea

Circa 1854. Surrounded by ocean with magnificent views in all directions, this Victorian home is at the end of a point in the quaint fishing village of Prospect. Originally built as a summer home for the Premiere of Nova Scotia, the large, comfortable

rooms feature private baths and are furnished with antiques and original art. Kayak or canoe in the shelter of the bay, or explore one of the nearby, uninhabited islands with gull rookeries and secluded coves. Numerous nature trails on the cliffs along the coast provide opportunities for hik-

ing and bird or whale watching, accompanied by a stunning view of the sunset. Meals include gourmet breakfasts featuring home-baked goods and complimentary afternoon tea.

Historic Interest: Citadel Hill Halifax(15 miles), Peggy's cove (15 miles).

Innkeeper(s): Helena Prsala. $115-145. MC, VISA, AX, PC, TC. TAC10. 5 rooms with PB, 1 with FP. Breakfast and afternoon tea included in rates. Types of meals: Gourmet bkfst, country bkfst, cont and early coffee/tea. Beds: QT. Cable TV and VCR in room. Fax, copier, spa, library and canoe & kayaks on premises. Weddings and family reunions hosted. French and german czech spoken. Antiquing, art galleries, canoeing/kayaking, fishing, golf, hiking, horseback riding, live theater, museums, parks, shopping, sporting events and tennis nearby.

Publicity: *National Geographic and NS Tourism TV.*

Ontario

Gananoque

Manse Lane B&B

465 Stone St S
Gananoque, ON K7G 2A7
(613)382-8642 (888)565-6379

Circa 1860. Four comfortable guest rooms, two with a private bath, are available at this bed & breakfast. Breakfasts include items such as cereal, fruit, yogurt, cheeses, breads, bacon and eggs. Guests are within walking distance of local attractions.

Innkeeper(s): Jocelyn & George Bounds. $53-140. MC, VISA, AX, TC. TAC10. 4 rooms, 2 with PB. Breakfast included in rates. Types of meals: Full bkfst, early coffee/tea, afternoon tea and room service. MAP. Beds: QT. Air conditioning. Swimming on premises. Antiquing, fishing, golf, boat cruises, festivals, live theater, parks, cross-country skiing, tennis and water sports nearby.

"Thoroughly enjoyed the stay. It was great to see you again."

The Victoria Rose Inn

279 King St. West
Gananoque, ON K7G 2G7
(613)382-3368 (888)246-2893 Fax:(613)382-8803
E-mail: vr@victoriaroseinn.com

Circa 1872. Two acres of award-winning landscaped grounds surround this Victorian Italianate mansion situated in the historic region of the Thousand Islands. This elegant country home was originally built for the area's first mayor and now serves as a pleasurable retreat or romantic getaway. Curl up in front of the fire in the cozy parlor, play a game or put together a puzzle and converse with a companion. The deluxe guest bedrooms and suites offer privacy and tasteful period-style reproductions and antique furnishings. The Tower, Victoria and American Beauty suites each boast champagne, a double Jacuzzi and fireplace. Enjoy breakfast in the dining room or on the veranda. The English-style gardens have a waterfall leading to a lily pond and are terraced to an old stone wall.

Historic Interest: Fort Henry (15 miles).

$85-190. MC, VISA, AX, TC. 10 rooms, 4 with PB, 2 with FP, 6 suites and 2 conference rooms. Breakfast and snacks/refreshments included in rates. Types of meals: Gourmet bkfst, veg bkfst, lunch and gourmet dinner. EP. Beds: KQDT. Cable TV, fireplace and five with Jacuzzi baths in room. Central air. VCR, fax, copier and library on premises. Weddings, small meetings, family reunions and seminars hosted. Antiquing, art galleries, beaches, bicycling, canoeing/kayaking, fishing, golf, hiking, horseback riding, live theater, museums, parks, shopping, cross-country skiing, sporting events, tennis and water sports nearby.

Publicity: *Commercial for GM cars.*

Kingston

Painted Lady Inn

181 William St
Kingston, ON K7L 2E1
(613)545-0422

Circa 1872. Built as a church manse in 1872, this inn offers an inviting Victorian atmosphere with such original features as a romantic veranda, handsome parlor and elegant dining room. Rooms are decorated in Victorian style with Canadian antiques. Three luxury rooms feature double Jacuzzi tubs and fireplaces. Executive rooms offer private telephones for laptop computers and televisions. Freshly baked croissants, homemade waffles topped with fresh fruit, and omelets made with Canadian cheddar cheese are just a few of the breakfast possibilities. The inn is close to dozens of restaurants, pubs and shops. Kingston offers many other activities such as Thousand Islands boat cruises, Fort Henry and 17 historic museums.

Historic Interest: Thousand Island Boat Cruises (4 city blocks), Queen's University (4 blocks), Farmer's Market (4 blocks), Fort Henry (1 mile), Bellevue House (one-fourth mile), Kingston Prison Museum (one-fourth mile).

Innkeeper(s): Carol Franks. $75-140. MC, VISA, AX. 7 rooms with PB, 3 with FP. Breakfast included in rates. Types of meals: Full bkfst. Beds: QT. Hair dryers, shampoo/soap, new magazines, wine glasses/cork screw, two with cable TV and private telephone and three with double Jacuzzi tubs and fireplaces in room. Central air. Veranda, parking, balcony, Victorian parlor, breakfast dining room, snack nook for making tea and coffee, small refrigerator for storing beverages, iron and daily newspapers on premises. Antiquing, art galleries, beaches, bicycling, canoeing/kayaking, fishing, golf, hiking, horseback riding, open air summer market, live theater, museums, parks, shopping, cross-country skiing, tennis and water sports nearby.

Rosemount B&B Inn

46 Sydenham St S
Kingston, ON K7L 3H1
(613)531-8844 (888)871-8844 Fax:(613)544-4895
E-mail: rosemt@kingston.net
Web: www.rosemountinn.com

Circa 1850. Built in a Tuscan-villa style, Rosemount was designed by noted architect William Coverdale as the residence for a successful dry goods merchant. The two-story limestone house is distinguished by a three-story campanile, or bell tower, over the front door. High ceilings and chandeliers are found throughout the elegantly appointed living, dining and guest rooms. There is a private coach house retreat and a petit spa used for aromatherapy massage. Special touches include homemade chocolates, down duvets, and a gourmet breakfast with entrees such as crepes, Welsh toast, or Vidalia onion and apple frittatas.

Innkeeper(s): Holly Doughty & John Edwards. $119-250. 8 rooms with PB and 1 guest house. Types of meals: Full bkfst. Beds: QT. Phone, hair dryers and dual port telephones in room. Aromatherapy spa room on premises. Restaurants, farmers market, waterfront, museums and shopping nearby.

Publicity: *Whig-Standard, Toronto Star, Detroit Free Press and Readers Choice Award for North American Country Inns Magazine.*

"Four days in heaven! Thanks!"

Secret Garden Bed & Breakfast Inn

73 Sydenham St
Kingston, ON K7L 3H3
(613)531-9884 (877)723-1888 Fax:(613)531-9502
E-mail: baker@the-secret-garden.com

Circa 1888. The interior of this Queen Anne Victorian boasts many of the original features so prevalent in the grand homes of the 19th century. Stained-glass windows and elegant woodwork are found throughout the historic bed & breakfast, and the architecture includes a third-story turret. Three of the guest rooms include a fireplace, and all are furnished with antiques and reproductions. The elegantly appointed dining room is where guests enjoy the full, gourmet breakfast. The veranda is appointed with a swing and wicker furnishings, and there is a garden terrace with wrought iron tables and chairs where afternoon refreshments are served.

Innkeeper(s): John & Maryanne Baker. $95-145. MC, VISA, AX, DC, PC, TC. 6 rooms with PB, 3 with FP. Breakfast and snacks/refreshments included in rates. Types of meals: Gourmet bkfst. Beds: KQ. Ceiling fan and fireplace in room. Central air. Fax, copier and library on premises. Amusement parks, antiquing, art galleries, beaches, bicycling, canoeing/kayaking, fishing, golf, hiking, live theater, museums, parks, shopping, cross-country skiing, sporting events, tennis and water sports nearby.

Publicity: *Whig-Standard, Toronto Star and Watertown Daily Times.*

Kitchener

Snowshill B&B

518 Bridgeport Rd E
Kitchener, ON N2K 1N7
(519)578-1746
E-mail: klove60@hotmail.com

Circa 1910. Perfectly emulating an English manor house, this historic estate with ivy-covered walls is pleasantly situated in the secluded countryside. Each wing showcases an original Arts and Crafts-style staircase and multi-paned hinged windows.

Family heirlooms and period antiques abide well with Oriental carpets in a subtly traditional decor. The library is an appealing place to read by the fire. Exquisite oak and cherry beds scream luxury with Egyptian cotton sheets and goose down covers in the guest bedrooms. Seasonal breakfast favorites are made with fresh ingredients from the local farmer's market and are artistically garnished with herbs and edible flowers. Using Limoges china, Irish crystal and fine linens on an ornate walnut table, the dining room is a masterpiece. The breathtaking grounds are a melange of formal tiered English gardens, manicured lawns with classical stone benches and statuary, a woodland walk and steep, lush ravine.

Innkeeper(s): The Rummond Family: Geln & Kimberly. $85-105. MC, VISA. 3 rooms, 1 with PB. Breakfast included in rates. Types of meals: Gourmet bkfst, veg bkfst, early coffee/tea and afternoon tea. Beds: Q. VCR and library on premises. Weddings and family reunions hosted. Amusement parks, antiquing, art galleries, bicycling, canoeing/kayaking, fishing, golf, hiking, horseback riding, Micro-breweries, live theater, museums, parks, shopping, downhill skiing, cross-country skiing and tennis nearby.

New Hamburg

The Waterlot

17 Huron St
New Hamburg, ON N0B 2G0
(519)662-2020 Fax:(519)662-2114
E-mail: waterlot@sypmpatico.com

Circa 1844. Located beside a mill pond, this Victorian home boasts an imaginative architecture with gothic gables frosted with gingerbread trim and an unusual cupola. It houses the inn's most important asset, a French-country restaurant, Le Bistro, which seats 125 people. Overlooking the Nith River as it flows through the backyard, the restaurant has been well-known for more than two decades. Guest rooms are simple and housed beneath each of the inn's twin gables.

Innkeeper(s): Gord & Leslie Elkeer. $75-115. MC, VISA, AX, DC, PC, TC. 3 rooms, 1 suite and 2 conference rooms. Breakfast included in rates. Types of meals: Cont plus, lunch, picnic lunch and gourmet dinner. Beds: KQD. Fax and copier on premises. Weddings, small meetings, family reunions and seminars hosted. Amusement parks, antiquing, fishing, golf, live theater, parks, shopping, downhill skiing, cross-country skiing and tennis nearby.

Ottawa

Albert House Inn

478 Albert St
Ottawa, ON K1R 5B5
(613)236-4479 (800)267-1982 Fax:(613)237-9079
E-mail: contact@albertinn.com
Web: www.albertinn.com

Circa 1875. Albert House was built by Canadian architect Thomas Scott in 1875, and he lived there until 1895. Scott was appointed to the governmental post of Chief Architect and as such was responsible for the design, construction and maintenance of all federal buildings in Canada from 1871 to 1881. He designed part of the Parliament buildings and supervised the construction of the Library of Parliament. After Scott left Albert House, the structure was used by the

Victorian Order of Nurses and then it became Rosary Hall, a convent of The Sisters of Service. The inn is half a mile from the Parliament buildings and many other historic buildings in Ottawa. It has a cobblestone parking area. The inn is renowned for its large custom breakfast, which has an extensive menu, including fruits, cereals, and a choice of griddle and egg delights like French toast, blueberry pancakes, custom omelets, fried egg sandwiches, fried tomatoes, fried potatoes and numerous fresh breads.

Innkeeper(s): Catherine & John Delroy. $80-158. MC, VISA, AX, DC, TC. TAC10. 17 rooms with PB. Breakfast and snacks/refreshments included in rates. Types of meals: Full bkfst, early coffee/tea and room service. Beds: KQDT. Cable TV and phone in room. Air conditioning. Fax, copier and high speed internet access desk free to guests is on premises. Antiquing, art galleries, beaches, bicycling, canoeing/kayaking, fishing, golf, hiking, horseback riding, ten minutes from Rideau Canal, live theater, museums, parks, shopping, downhill skiing, cross-country skiing, sporting events and water sports nearby.

Auberge McGEE'S Inn

185 Daly Ave
Ottawa, ON K1N 6E8
(613)237-6089 (800)262-4337 Fax:(613)237-6201
E-mail: contact@mcgeesinn.com
Web: www.mcgeesinn.com

Circa 1886. The home was built for John McGee, Canada's first Clerk of Privy Council. The portico of this restored Victorian mansion is reminiscent of McGee's Irish roots featuring pillars that were common in Dublin architecture. Rooms are comfortable and decorated in soft, pleasing colors.

Amenities such as mounted hair dryers add a touch of modern convenience. The two Jacuzzi suites are decorated with a special theme in mind. One is named the Victorian Roses Suite, and the other is The Egyptian Room. For extended stays, the inn provides the use of laundry facilities and a guest kitchenette. The innkeepers celebrate 17 years of award-winning hospitality. Business travelers will appreciate items such as in-room Smart phones with data port and voice mail. There is no end to what guests can see and do in Ottawa. Visit the Byward Market, the many museums or the 230-store Rideau Center.

Historic Interest: Walking distance to Congress Centre, University of Ottawa, Parliament Hill, War Memorial at Confederation Square and Rideau Canal.
$98-198. MC, VISA, AX, TC. 14 rooms with PB, 3 with FP, 2 suites and 1 conference room. Breakfast included in rates. Types of meals: Full bkfst. Beds: KQDT. Cable TV, phone, some fireplaces and ceiling fans, hair dryers and refrigerator in room. Air conditioning. Free parking on premises. Family reunions hosted. French spoken. Antiquing, live theater, parks, shopping, downhill skiing, cross-country skiing, sporting events and water sports nearby.
Publicity: *Country Inns, Ottawa Citizen, LaPresse, Ottawa. and CBC.*

The Carmichael Inn & Spa

46 Cartier St
Ottawa, ON K2P 1-J3
(613)236-4667 Fax:(613)563-7529
E-mail: info@carmichaelinn.com
Web: www.carmichaelinn.com

Circa 1901. Carmichael Inn and Spa was built as the gracious residence of Supreme Court Justice Thibodeau Rinfret. Situated in a quiet residential area, the inn is conveniently

close to the Parliament buildings and the shops and restaurants of Elgin Street. Guest rooms are appointed in antiques such as mirrored armoires, mahogany desks, scrolled chairs and massive headboards. The inn also offers a range of spa services from soothing massages to herbal body wraps.

Innkeeper(s): Brian C. Fewster. $149. MC, VISA, AX. 10 rooms with PB and 1 conference room. Breakfast included in rates. Types of meals: Cont. Beds: Q. Phone in room. Fax, copier and spa on premises. Ice skating, museums, galleries and festivals nearby.

Gasthaus Switzerland Inn

89 Daly Ave
Ottawa, ON K1N 6E6
(613)237-0335 (888)663-0000 Fax:(613)594-3327
E-mail: switzinn@gasthausswitzerlandinn.com
Web: www.gasthausswitzerlandinn.com

Circa 1872. Constructed from limestone, this Vernacular Classical Revival home served

as a military rehabilitation facility during World War I. A welcoming inn since 1985, proud innkeepers Josef and Sabina provide splendid hospitality with a distinctively European flair. The well-appointed guest bedrooms and romantic suites are comfortably elegant. Some feature fireplaces, double jacuzzis, CD stereos, four-poster canopy beds and sparkling wine. A traditional Swiss, full breakfast is served buffet style, or delivered to the room. Parliament Hill is within an easy walk, as are interesting shops, museums and restaurants.

Innkeeper(s): Sabina & Josef Sauter. $88-228. MC, VISA, AX, DC, CB, TC. 22 rooms, 18 with PB, 4 with FP and 4 suites. Breakfast included in rates. Types of meals: Full bkfst. Beds: KQDT. Cable TV, phone and some with fireplace in room. Air conditioning. Fax and limited free parking on premises. Swiss, German and French spoken. Fishing, golf, cycling, parks, shopping, downhill skiing, cross-country skiing, sporting events, tennis and water sports nearby.

Peterborough

King Bethune Guest House

270 King St
Peterborough, ON K9J 2S2
(705)743-4101 (800)574-3664 Fax:(705)743-8446
E-mail: marlis@sympatico.ca

Circa 1893. This brick Victorian is downtown on a quiet tree-shaded street. Restored hardwood floors, original trim throughout, tall ceilings and handsome windows grace the interiors. Guest rooms are large with ensuite baths and offer antiques, as well as desks, data ports, TVs and VCRs. The Executive Suite has a king bed and private entrance as well as a private hot tub, sauna and steam bath. There's a restful walled garden with fireplace and patio, a favorite spot for breakfast.

Innkeeper(s): Marlis Lindsay. $104-180. MC, VISA, AX, PC, TC. TAC10. 3 rooms with PB. Breakfast included in rates. Types of meals: Gourmet bkfst, early coffee/tea, lunch, picnic lunch, afternoon tea, gourmet dinner and room service. Beds: KQ. Cable TV, phone, turndown service, ceiling fan, VCR, sauna and garden hot tub in room. Fax, spa, sauna, bicycles, library and English courtyard garden on premises. Small meetings and family reunions hosted. Amusement parks, antiquing, fishing, golf, live theater, parks, shopping, downhill skiing, cross-country skiing, sporting events, tennis and water sports nearby.

Pets allowed: owner supervised.

Publicity: *Canadian Country and Examiner.*

"We still have not found better accommodations anywhere."

Westport

Stepping Stone Inn

328 Centreville Rd, RR 2
Westport, ON K0G 1X0
(613)273-3806 Fax:(613)273-3331
E-mail: stepping@rideau.net
Web: www.steppingstoneinn.com

Circa 1840. Multi-colored limestone warms in the afternoon sun on this historic house located on more than 150 acres. Flower beds surround the wraparound veranda decorated in white gingerbread and fretwork. Rooms are furnished with antiques, and there is a solarium and dining room that overlook flower gardens, a picturesque swimming pond and waterfall. Guest rooms include luxury suites with Jacuzzis, fireplaces and private entrances. Plan ahead and the inn's chef will create a custom menu for you. Stepping Stone is popular for garden weddings and corporate meetings. The grounds offer a beaver pond, pastures and nature trails. The Rideau Canal System and many lakes are nearby.

Innkeeper(s): Madeleine Saunders. $75-150. MC, VISA, AX, TC. 10 rooms with PB, 3 with FP, 3 suites, 1 cabin and 1 conference room. Breakfast included in rates. Types of meals: Gourmet bkfst, early coffee/tea, picnic lunch, afternoon tea and gourmet dinner. Beds: QT. 5 with Jacuzzi's in room. Air conditioning. Fax and swimming on premises. Handicap access. Weddings, small meetings, family reunions and seminars hosted. French spoken. Antiquing, fishing, golf, hiking, skating, live theater, parks, shopping, cross-country skiing, tennis and water sports nearby.

Prince Edward Island

Charlottetown

Bagnall's Heritage Inn B&B

193 Prince St
Charlottetown, PE C1A 4R8
(902)368-1211 (888)418-7378 Fax:(902)569-5196
E-mail: bagnalls@attcanada.ca
Web: www.bagnallsheritageinn.pe.ca

Circa 1830. This 19th-century Colonial inn was used as a tailor shop starting in 1845. Its eight guest bedrooms are decorated in Victorian style with handmade quilts, and most rooms have Jacuzzi tubs. Full breakfasts are served each morning and include a choice of eggs, pancakes, French toast, bacon with homemade scones, biscuits and breads, homemade preserves, cereal and fruits. The inn is located within easy walking distance to theaters, shops, restaurants and the boardwalk. It is near Province House, "The Birthplace of Canada" and the Confederation Center of the Arts.

Historic Interest: Province House (1/4 mile), Confederation Center of the Arts (1/4 mile).

Innkeeper(s): Maryah MacDonald & Shaun Katz. $119-159. MC, VISA, AX, TC. 8 rooms with PB, 1 with FP. Breakfast included in rates. Types of meals: Full bkfst and early coffee/tea. Beds: KQDT. Cable TV, ceiling fan, one with fireplace, five with refrigerators, four with VCRs and five with hot tubs in room. Air conditioning. VCR and fax on premises. Amusement parks, antiquing, art galleries, beaches, bicycling, canoeing/kayaking, fishing, golf, hiking, horseback riding, live theater, museums, parks, shopping, downhill skiing, cross-country skiing, sporting events, tennis, water sports and wineries nearby.

Quebec

Ayer's Cliff

Ripplecove Inn

700 Rue Ripplecove, PO Box 246
Ayer's Cliff, QB J0B 1-C0
(819)838-4296 (800)668-4296 Fax:(819)838-5541
E-mail: info@ripplecove.com
Web: www.ripplecove.com

Circa 1945. This exquisite Victorian inn, located on the shores of Lake Massawippi, is one of only 10 establishments in Quebec to earn a Four-Diamond award from the American Automobile Association. Some of the well-appointed rooms offer whirlpool tubs, fireplaces and private balconies. The 12-acre grounds include a heated swimming pool and private beach, and guests can partake of skating, skiing and ice fishing without leaving the property. Meals at Ripplecove are a special treat, set on tables with sterling silver, fine linens, crystal and Royal Doulton china. Our Chef combines classical and nouvelle French artistry with local produce to create an array of mouth-watering specialties.

Innkeeper(s): Jeffrey & Debra Stafford. $280-450. MC, VISA, AX, TC. TAC10. 26 rooms with PB, 11 with FP, 5 suites, 1 cabin and 2 conference rooms. Breakfast and dinner included in rates. Types of meals: Full bkfst, lunch and room service. MAP. Beds: KQDT. Cable TV, phone and turndown service in room. Air conditioning. VCR, fax, copier, swimming, bicycles, tennis, library and child care on premises. Handicap access. Weddings, small meetings, family reunions and seminars hosted. French spoken. Antiquing, fishing, golf, live theater, parks, shopping, downhill skiing, cross-country skiing, tennis and water sports nearby.

Publicity: *Country Inns and Gazette.*

"We shall never forget Ripplecove Inn. Its elegant and intimate setting provided the perfect place to hold the kind of wedding we had dreamed of. The refined cuisine, the superb service and your own personal hospitality made our dream a reality."

Donnacona

Aux Trois Saules

1752 Rte 138
Donnacona, QB G0A 1T0
(418)285-2394 Fax:(418)285-5649
E-mail: auxtroissaules@videotron.com
Web: www.quebecweb.com/auxtroissaules

Circa 1870. An idyllic countryside near Quebec City is the perfect locale for this spacious inn. The Victorian/French Country decor creates a romantic setting with comfort and luxury. Relax in front of the fireplace and enjoy piano music, or play billiards in one of the inviting public rooms. The three guest bedrooms exude charm. A full gourmet breakfast is served, and coffee lovers may enjoy espresso or cappuccino.

Exercise equipment is available, or splash around in the swimming pool with a water slide. A walk along the small lake or hiking trails provides gorgeous views of the St. Lawrence River.

Innkeeper(s): Celine Breton. $65-125. MC, VISA, PC, TC. TAC5. 3 rooms, 1 with PB. Types of meals: Gourmet bkfst and early coffee/tea. Beds: QD. Cable TV, phone and VCR in room. Air conditioning. Fax, copier, swimming, bicycles and library on premises. Small meetings hosted. French and English spoken. Antiquing, art galleries, bicycling, canoeing/kayaking, fishing, golf, hiking, horseback riding, live theater, parks, shopping, downhill skiing, cross-country skiing, tennis and water sports nearby.

Montreal

Armor-Manoir Sherbrooke

157 Sherbrooke Est
Montreal, QB H2X 1-C7
(514)845-0915 (800)203-5485 Fax:(514)284-1126

Circa 1882. Montreal's bustling Latin Quarter is the location of this historic Victorian hotel. The elegant guest rooms and suites are individually decorated and boast fine woodwork and soaring ceilings with intricate designs. The three suites include a Jacuzzi. Guests can walk to many shops, restaurants and cafes. Old Montreal is a 15-minute walk from the hotel.

Innkeeper(s): Annick Morvan. $75-109. MC, VISA, TC. TAC10. 25 rooms, 16 with PB and 3 suites. Breakfast included in rates. Types of meals: Cont. Beds: QD. Cable TV, phone and jacuzzi in room. Air conditioning. Fax on premises. French and German spoken.

New Richmond

Auberge La Maison Stanley

371 Boul Perron O
New Richmond, QB G0C 2B0
(418)392-5560 Fax:(418)392-5592

Circa 1887. Lord Stanley, the Governor General of Canada, built this impressive Victorian home. Lord Stanley is known not only for his prominent political career, but also because he was the creator of the honorable Stanley Cup, which is now the coup de grace of the National Hockey League. Other Governor-Generals have lived in the maison, as well as an American senator. There are nearly a dozen guest rooms to choose from, some affording a view of the Baie des Chaleurs. A full, country breakfast is served each morning. New Richmond is located on Quebec's Gaspesian Peninsula with an entrance off the Grand Gascapedia River, and guests can enjoy some 1,500 feet of water frontage that is part of the grounds.

Innkeeper(s): Lucille & Edgar LeBlanc. $75-125. MC, VISA, AX. 11 rooms and 1 conference room. Breakfast included in rates. Types of meals: Full bkfst. Beds: QDT. Fax and library on premises. Small meetings and seminars hosted. English and French spoken. Art galleries, beaches, bicycling, canoeing/kayaking, fishing, golf, hiking, horseback riding, live theater, museums, parks, shopping and water sports nearby.

Publicity: *Ottawa Citizen and Montreal Gazette.*

Saint-Eugene, L'islet

Auberge des Glacis

46 Route Tortue
Saint-Eugene, L'islet, QB G0R 1X0
(418)247-7486 Fax:(418)247-7182
E-mail: aubergedesglacis@hotmail.com

Circa 1840. The stone walls of this graceful former flour mill add unusual character and warmth to the inviting rooms offered by Auberge des Glacis. Breakfast is served buffet style, or you can arrange for it to be delivered to your room. The inn's restaurant is notable for its gourmet French cuisine. Twelve acres of scenic grounds include a lake and landscaped lawns. Swimming, golfing, cycling, skiing, birdwatching and cruising are favored activities.

Innkeeper(s): Micheline et Pierre Watters. $57. MC, VISA, AX, DC, TC. TAC10. 10 rooms, 8 with PB and 2 suites. Breakfast and dinner included in rates. Types of meals: Gourmet bkfst. AP. Beds: QD. Air conditioning. Fax, swimming and bicycles on premises. Antiquing, art galleries, bicycling, canoeing/kayaking, golf, hiking, live theater, museums, parks and cross-country skiing nearby.

St. Sauveur des Monts

Le Petit Clocher

216 De L'Eglise
St. Sauveur des Monts, QB J0R 1R7
(450)227-7576 Fax:(450)227-6662
E-mail: lepetit.clocher@sympatico.ca
Web: www.bbcanada.com/lepetitclocher

Circa 1900. The exterior of Le Petit Clocher is of log construction and once served as a retreat house for priests. A cross remains, inspiring the name Le Petit Clocher (The Little Steeple). Inside, each fashionable guest chamber is different. The exposed log walls of the Rose Room add a rustic touch to this romantic retreat, which is furnished with a four-poster canopy bed topped with a floral comforter and piled high with pillows. The cozy Clocher Room, which affords an excellent view, includes a bed tucked away in an alcove where the ceiling slopes. Hand-painted stenciling graces the walls of the Muguet Des Bois, a spacious two-room suite. Guests can enjoy the views of the countryside and local ski areas from the living room that is warmed by the fireplace. Galleries, shops and restaurants are within walking distance. The inn holds a five-star rating by Hebergement Quebec.

Historic Interest: St. Sauveur Village (1/2 mile).

Innkeeper(s): Noelle Desruisseaux. $150-195. MC, VISA, AX, TC. TAC10. 5 rooms with PB and 1 conference room. Breakfast included in rates. Types of meals: Gourmet bkfst. Beds: Q. Cable TV and turndown service in room. VCR, fax, copier, bicycles, library and therapeutic massages on premises. Small meetings and family reunions hosted. French and English spoken. Antiquing, art galleries, bicycling, canoeing/kayaking, golf, hiking, horseback riding, water park, live theater, shopping, downhill skiing, cross-country skiing, tennis and water sports nearby.

Publicity: *Ma Maison.*

Inns of Interest

African-American History

Wingscorton Farm Inn
. . . . .East Sandwich, Mass.
Munro House B&B . . . . . .Jonesville, Mich.
Troutbeck . . . . .Amenia, N.Y.
Signal House . . . . .Ripley, Ohio
1790 House B&B Inn . . . . .Georgetown, S.C.
Golden Stage Inn . . . . .Proctorsville, Vt.
Kedron Valley Inn . . . .South Woodstock, Vt.
Rockland Farm Retreat . . . . . . .Bumpass, Va.
Sleepy Hollow Farm . . . . . .Gordonsville, Va.

Barns

Old Church House Inn . . . . . . .Mossville, Ill.
1794 Watchtide....by the Sea
. . . . .Searsport , Maine
Brannon-Bunker Inn . . . . . . .Walpole, Maine
BarnAgain B&B Inn . . . . .Ozark, Mo.
Kennedy's Red Barn Inn . . . . .Perry, Mo.
Candlelite Inn . . . . .Bradford, N.H.
Pine Barn Inn . . . . .Danville, Pa.
Cornerstone B&B Inn . . . . . .Landenberg, Pa.
Pace One Restaurant and Country Inn
. . . . .Thornton, Pa.
Jackson Fork Inn . . . . .Huntsville, Utah
Waitsfield Inn . . . . .Waitsfield, Vt.

Boats

Tugboat Challenger . . . . .Seattle, Wash.

Bordello (former, of course)

Cheyenne Canon Inn
. . . . .Colorado Springs, Colo.

Castles

Castle Marne-A Luxury Urban Inn
. . . . .Denver, Colo.
Castle Inn Riverside . . . . .Wichita, Kan.
Hoquiam Castle B&B . . . . .Hoquiam, Wash.
Manresa Castle . . . . . .Port Townsend, Wash.

Churches & Parsonages

The Parsonage . . . . .Nevada City, Calif.
The Parsonage . . . . . . .Santa Barbara, Calif.
Old Church House Inn . . . . . .Mossville, Ill.
Parsonage Inn . . . . .St. Michaels, Md.
The Beechcroft Inn . . . . .Brewster, Mass.
The Parsonage Inn . . . . .East Orleans, Mass.
The Parsonage on the Green . . . . .Lee, Mass.
Graycote Inn . . . . .Bar Harbor, Maine
The Wilmingtonian . . . . . .Wilmington, N.C.
The Abbey . . . . .Cape May, N.J.
Churchtown Inn . . . . .Churchtown, Pa.
Parson's Pillow . . . . .Cody, Wyo.

Civil War

Myrtledene . . . . .Lebanon, Ky.
Old Manse Inn . . . . .Brewster, Mass.
Anchuca . . . . .Vicksburg, Mass.
Cedar Grove Mansion Inn
. . . . .Vicksburg, Mass.
Munro House . . . . .Jonesville, Mich.
Red House Inn B&B . . . . . . .Brevard, N.C.
Churchtown Inn B&B . . . . .Churchtown, Pa.
La Vista Plantation . . . . . .Fredericksburg, Va.
Baladerry Inn at Gettysburg
. . . . .Gettysburg, Pa.
Brafferton Inn . . . . .Gettysburg, Pa.
The Doubleday Inn . . . . .Gettysburg, Pa.
James Getty Hotel . . . . .Gettysburg, Pa.
The Beechmont B&B Inn . . . . .Hanover, Pa.
Red Fox Inn . . . . .Middleburg, Va.
The Inn at Narrow Passage
. . . . .Woodstock, Va.
Fillmore Street B&B
. . . . .Harpers Ferry, W.Va.
Boydville, Inn at Martinsburg
. . . . .Martinsburg, W.Va.
Kedron Valley Inn . . . .South Woodstock, Vt.
Colonial Gardens B&B
. . . . .Sturgeon Bay, Wis.

Cookbooks Written By Innkeepers

Heartstone Inn & Cottages
.................Eureka Springs, Ark.
McCloud B&B Hotel ......McCloud, Calif.
The Old Yacht Club Inn
.................Santa Barbara, Calif.
Blue Spruce Inn ....Soquel, Calif.
One Centre Street Inn
.................Yarmouth Port, Mass.
Dockside Guest Quarters ......York, Maine
Garth Woodside Mansion
.................Hannibal, Mo.
Fearrington House ......Fearrington, N.C.
The Old Stone Inn ......Waynesville, N.C.
Mainstay Inn ....Cape May, N.J.
White Oak Inn ....Danville, Ohio
Whispering Pines B&B ......Delroy, Ohio
Grandview Lodge ......Waynesville, S.C.
MacKaye Harbor Inn
.................Lopez Island, Wash.
Roses B&B ....Lake Geneva, Wis.

Farms and Orchards

Scarlett's Country Inn ......Calistoga, Calif.
The Inn at Shallow Creek Farm
.................Orland, Calif.
Howard Creek Ranch ......Westport, Calif.
Homespun Farm B&B ....Jewett, Conn.
1810 West Inn ....Thomson, Ga.
Kingston 5 Ranch B&B ....Kingston, Idaho
Maple Hill Farm B&B Inn
.................Hallowell/Augusta, Maine
Baldwin Hill Farm B&B
.................Great Barrington, Mass.
Summer Hill Farm ....Lenox, Mass.
Gilbert's Tree Farm B&B
.................Rehoboth, Mass.
Wingscorton Farm Inn ....Sandwich, Mass.
Horse & Carriage B&B ....Jonesville, Mich.
Four Columns Inn ....Sherburn, Minn.
Caverly Farm & Orchard ....Bland, Mo.
Grandpa's Farm ....Lampe, Mo.
Rockhouse Mountain Farm Inn
.................Eaton Center, N.H.
Colby Hill Inn ....Henniker, N.H.
Take it for Granite ....Wilmot, N.H.
Agape Farm B&B ....Corinth, N.Y.

Fearrington House Inn ......Pittsboro, N.C.
The Mast Farm Inn ......Valle Crucis, N.C.
Volden Farm ....Lucerne, N.D.
Old Pioneer Garden Guest Ranch Unionville, Nev.
Wine Country Farm ....Dayton, Ore.
Springbrook Hazelnut Farm
.................Newberg, Ore.
Line Limousin Farmhouse B&B
.................Carlisle, Pa.
Ponda-Rowland B&B Inn ......Dallas, Pa.
Glen Isle Farm ....Downington, Pa.
Huntland Farm ....Greensburg, Pa.
Barley Sheaf Farm ....Holicong, Pa.
Cedar Hill Farm ....Mount Joy, Pa.
Cottage at Ross Mill Farm ....Rushland, Pa.
Field & Pine B&B ....Shippensburg, Pa.
B&B at Skogland Farm ....Canova, S.D.
Rockland Farm Retreat ......Bumpass, Va.
Dearbought Horse Center B&B
.................Edinburgh, Va.
Cave Hill Farm B&B
.................McGaheysville, Va.
Old Spring Farm B&B ....Woolwine, Va.
River Meadow Farm
.................Manchester Center, Vt.
West River Lodge & Stables
.................Newfane, Vt.
Historic Brookside Farms ....Orwell, Vt.
Liberty Hill Farm ....Rochester, Vt.
Colonel Crockett Farm
.................Coupeville, Wash.
Turtleback Farm ....Eastsound, Wash.

French and Indian War

Summer Hill Farm ....Lenox, Mass.

Gold Mines & Gold Panning

Julian Gold Rush Hotel ....Julian, Calif.
Dunbar House, 1880 ......Murphys, Calif.
Hotel Nipton ....Nipton, Calif.

Hot Springs

Rainbow Tarns B&B at Crowley Lake
........Mammoth/Crowley Lake, Calif.
Vichy Hot Springs Resort ......Ukiah, Calif.
Idaho Rocky Mountain Ranch
.................Stanley, Idaho

Boulder Hot Springs . . . . . . .Boulder, Mont.
Soldier Meadows Guest Ranch
. . . . .Gerlach, Nev.

Inns Built Prior to 1800

1600 Cottage at Ross Mill Farm
. . . . .Rushland, Pa.
1682 William Penn Guest House
. . . . .New Castle, Del.
1690 Penny House Inn . . . . . .Eastham, Mass.
1690 Brookside Manor . . . . . .Wakefield, R.I.
1691 The Great Valley House of
Valley Forge . . . . .Valley Forge, Pa.
1699 Ashley Manor Inn
. . . . .Barnstable, Cape Cod, Mass.
1700 Elias Child House B&B
. . . . .Woodstock, Conn.
1700 Casa Europa Inn & Gallery
. . . . .Taos, N.M.
1700 Evermay-On-The-Delaware
. . . . .Erwinna (Bucks County), Pa.
1704 Cornerstone B&B Inn
. . . . .Landenberg, Pa.
1705 Centre Bridge Inn . . . . .New Hope, Pa.
1709 The Woodbox Inn
. . . . .Nantucket, Mass.
1710 The Robert Morris Inn . . . .Oxford, Md.
1710 The Stockton Inn . . . . . .Stockton, N.J.
1711 La Hacienda Grande
. . . . .Bernalillo, N.M.
1712 Blue Gateways . . . . . . .Wellfleet, Mass.
1714 Pennsbury Inn . . . . . . .Chadds Ford, Pa.
1720 Butternut Farm . . . .Glastonbury, Conn.
1720 Old Babcock Tavern . . . .Tolland, Conn.
1721 Brimblecomb Hill
. . . . .Marblehead, Mass.
1722 AAA Jacob Hill Inn
. . . . .Providence, R.I.
1725 Cobblestone Inn . . . . .Nantucket, Mass.
1725 1725 Historic Witmer's Tavern
Inn & Museum . . . . .Lancaster, Pa.
1727 Logan Inn . . . . .New Hope, Pa.
1728 Red Fox Inn . . . . .Middleburg, Va.
1729 Harbor Light Inn
. . . . .Marblehead, Mass.
1730 Colonial House Inn
. . . . .Yarmouth Port, Mass.
1730 Tavern House . . . . .Vienna, Md.
1730 Glen Isle Farm . . . . .Downingtown, Pa.

1732 Armitage Inn . . . . . .New Castle, Del.
1732 General Lafayette Inn & Brewery
. . . . .Lafayette Hill, Pa.
1732 1732 Folke Stone Bed and Breakfast
. . . . .West Chester, Pa.
1732 The Kitchen House
. . . . .Charleston, S.C.
1734 The Village Inn of Bird-In-Hand
. . . . .Bird-In-Hand, Pa.
1735 Churchtown Inn B&B
. . . . .Churchtown, Pa.
1735 Antebellum B&B at The Thomas
Lamboll House . . . . .Charleston, S.C.
1736 Stone Mill Inn . . . . .Hallam, Pa.
1738 Brown's Historic Home B&B
. . . . .Salem, N.J.
1739 The Ruffner House . . . . .Luray, Va.
1740 Homespun Farm Bed and Breakfast
. . . . .Jewett City, Conn.
1740 Red Brook Inn . . . . .Old Mystic, Conn.
1740 Cape Cod's Lamb and Lion
. . . . .Barnstable, Mass.
1740 Ingate Farms B&B
. . . . .Belchertown, Mass.
1740 Sterling Orchards B&B
. . . . .Sterling, Mass.
1740 Barley Sheaf Farm . . . . . .Holicong, Pa.
1740 Pace One Restaurant and
Country Inn . . . . .Thornton, Pa.
1740 Willows of Newport - Romantic
Inn & Garden . . . . .Newport, R.I.
1740 Thirty Six Meeting Street
. . . . .Charleston, S.C.
1740 Du Pre House LLC
. . . . .Georgetown, S.C.
1740 The Inn at Narrow Passage
. . . . .Woodstock, Va.
1742 The Kelley House . . . .Edgartown, Mass.
1743 The Inn at Mitchell House
. . . . .Chestertown, Md.
1745 Black Walnut Inn . . . . .Amherst, Mass.
1745 Olde Rhinebeck Inn
. . . . .Rhinebeck, N.Y.
1745 General Warren Inne . . . . .Malvern, Pa.
1746 Deacon Timothy Pratt Bed &
Breakfast Inn . . . . . .Old Saybrook, Conn.
1747 Georgian House B&B
. . . . .Annapolis, Md.
1750 Candleberry Inn . . . . . .Brewster, Mass.

1750 Inn At Sandwich Center
. . . . .Sandwich, Mass.
1750 Waterloo Country Inn
. . . . .Princess Anne, Md.
1750 Isaac Hilliard House Bed,
Breakfast...and Beyond
. . . . .Pemberton Boro, N.J.
1750 Hickory Bridge Farm . . . .Gettysburg, Pa.
1750 Farm Fortune . . . .New Cumberland, Pa.
1750 Tattersall Inn . . . . . .Point Pleasant, Pa.
1750 The Melville House . . . . .Newport, R.I.
1750 Litchfield Plantation
. . . . .Pawleys Island, S.C.
1750 Linden House B&B & Plantation
. . . . .Champlain, Va.
1750 Jasmine Plantation B&B Inn
. . . . .Providence Forge, Va.
1752 The Olde Stage Coach B&B . . . .
Jennerstown, Pa.
1752 Dearbought Horse Center & B&B
. . . . .Edinburg, Va.
1753 L'Auberge Provencale . . . . .Boyce, Va.
1759 Chanceford Hall B&B
. . . . .Snow Hill, Md.
1760 Old Inn on The Green
. . . . .New Marlborough, Mass.
1760 Elk Forge Bed & Breakfast Inn, Spa,
and Retreat . . . . .Elk Mills, Md.
1760 Mountain Lake Inn . . . .Bradford, N.H.
1760 Francis Malbone House
. . . . .Newport, R.I.
1760 Charleston Governor's House
. . . . .Charleston, S.C.
1760 The Norris House Inn & Stone
House Tea Room . . . . .Leesburg, Va.
1760 Gilbert House B&B of Middleway
. . . . .Charles Town, W.V.
1761 The Bird & Bottle Inn
. . . . .Garrison, N.Y.
1762 The Annapolis Inn . . . .Annapolis, Md.
1763 Blackberry River Inn . . . .Norfolk, Conn.
1763 Causey Mansion Bed & Breakfast
. . . . .Milford, Del.
1763 Casa De Solana, B&B Inn
. . . . .Saint Augustine, Fla.
1763 Wingscorton Farm Inn
. . . . .East Sandwich, Mass.
1763 The Squire Tarbox Inn
. . . . .Wiscasset, Maine

1763 Smithton Inn . . . . .Ephrata, Pa.
1763 John Rutledge House Inn
. . . . .Charleston, S.C.
1764 Colonel Spencer Inn
. . . . .Campton, N.H.
1764 The Inn at Ormsby Hill
. . . . .Manchester Center, Vt.
1765 Bankhouse B&B . . . .West Chester, Pa.
1765 Harbor House . . . . . .Georgetown, S.C.
1766 Beekman Arms-Delamater Inn
. . . . .Rhinebeck, N.Y.
1766 1766 Osceola Mill House
. . . . .Gordonville (Intercourse), Pa.
1766 The Inn at Meander Plantation
. . . . .Locust Dale, Va.
1767 Birchwood Inn . . . . .Lenox, Mass.
1767 Lakeshore Inn Bed & Breakfast
. . . . .Rockland, Maine
1767 Highland Lake Inn B&B
. . . . .E. Andover, N.H.
1768 The Cedars Inn . . . . . .Beaufort, N.C.
1769 Thomas Bond House
. . . . .Philadelphia, Pa.
1770 The Parsonage Inn
. . . . .East Orleans, Mass.
1770 Sparrow Hawk Bed & Breakfast
. . . . .Stone Ridge, N.Y.
1770 Ira Allen House . . . . . . .Arlington, Vt.
1771 The Village Inn . . . . .Lenox, Mass.
1771 The Inn on Cove Hill
. . . . .Rockport, Mass.
1771 Publick House Historic Inn &
Country Lodge . . . . .Sturbridge, Mass.
1772 The Bagley House . . . . .Durham, Maine
1772 Jailhouse Inn . . . . .Newport, R.I.
1773 The Red Lion Inn
. . . . .Stockbridge, Mass.
1773 Isaac Merrill House Inn
. . . . .North Conway, N.H.
1773 Lodge Alley Inn . . . . . .Charleston, S.C.
1773 Creek Crossing Farm . . . . .Lincoln, Va.
1774 Gibson's Lodgings . . . . .Annapolis, Md.
1775 Pinecrest Cottage and Gardens-
A Bed and Breakfast . . . . . . .Louisville, Ky.
1775 Colonel Roger Brown House
. . . . .Concord, Mass.
1775 Inn At Richmond . . . .Richmond, Mass.
1775 Todd House . . . . .Eastport, Maine
1775 Kanaga House B&B Inn
. . . . .Carlisle (New Kingstown), Pa.

1775 1811 House . . . . .Manchester, Vt.
1776 Chase House B&B Inn
. . . . .Cornish, N.H.
1777 Doneckers, The Guesthouse, Inns
. . . . .Ephrata, Pa.
1777 Nutmeg Inn . . . . .Wilmington, Vt.
1778 The Inn at Chester . . . . .Chester, Conn.
1779 Old Talbott Tavern . . . . .Bardstown, Ky.
1780 Christine's Bed-Breakfast
. . . . .Housatonic, Mass.
1780 Garden Gables Inn . . . . . .Lenox, Mass.
1780 Birch Hill Bed & Breakfast
. . . . .Sheffield, Mass.
1780 Egremont Inn
. . . . .South Egremont, Mass.
1780 Catoctin Inn and Conference Center
. . . . .Buckeystown, Md.
1780 Mill Pond Inn
. . . . .Damariscotta Mills, Maine
1780 King's Hill Inn . . . . .South Paris, Maine
1780 Hacienda Antigua B&B
. . . . .Albuquerque, N.M.
1780 Chester House . . . . .Chester, Vt.
1783 The Towers B&B . . . . . . .Milford, Del.
1783 Overlook Farm B&B
. . . . .Center Sandwich, N.H.
1783 Four Chimneys Inn & Restaurant
. . . . .Bennington, Vt.
1784 The Old Mystic Inn
. . . . .Old Mystic, Conn.
1785 Weathervane Inn
. . . . .South Egremont, Mass.
1785 Oakland Plantation . . . . .Natchez, Miss.
1785 1785 Inn & Restaurant
. . . . .North Conway, N.H.
1785 Sleepy Hollow Farm B&B
. . . . .Gordonsville, Va.
1786 Windsor House . . . .Newburyport, Mass.
1786 Kenniston Hill Inn . . . .Boothbay, Maine
1786 The Brafferton Inn . . . . .Gettysburg, Pa.
1786 Limestone Inn B&B . . . . .Strasburg, Pa.
1787 Nereledge Inn . . . .North Conway, N.H.
1788 Golden Stage Inn . . . .Proctorsville, Vt.
1789 Stevens Farm B&B . . . . . . .Barre, Mass.
1789 Miles River Country Inn
. . . . .Hamilton, Mass.
1789 Longswamp B&B . . . . . .Mertztown, Pa.
1789 The Inn at High View . . . .Andover, Vt.

1789 Historic Brookside Farms Country
Inn & Antique Shop . . . . . . .Orwell, Vt.
1790 Riverwind . . . . .Deep River, Conn.
1790 Silvermine Tavern . . . .Norwalk, Conn.
1790 Tolland Inn . . . . .Tolland, Conn.
1790 Darley Manor Inn . . . .Wilmington, Del.
1790 Corner House . . . . .Nantucket, Mass.
1790 Tuck Inn B&B . . . . . .Rockport, Mass.
1790 Benjamin F. Packard House
. . . . .Bath, Maine
1790 Fairhaven Inn . . . . .Bath, Maine
1790 The Southern Hotel
. . . . .Sainte Genevieve, Mo.
1790 The Inn at Bingham School
. . . . .Chapel Hill, N.C.
1790 1812 on The Perquimans B&B Inn
. . . . .Hertford, N.C.
1790 Nestlenook Farm Resort
. . . . .Jackson, N.H.
1790 The Inn at Pleasant Lake
. . . . .New London, N.H.
1790 Stepping Stones B&B
. . . . .Wilton Center, N.H.
1790 Mill House Inn . . . .East Hampton, N.Y.
1790 The Altland House
. . . . .Abbottstown, Pa.
1790 Mill Creek Homestead B&B
. . . . .Bird-in-Hand, Pa.
1790 Jacobs Resting Place . . . . . .Carlisle, Pa.
1790 Pineapple Hill . . . . .New Hope, Pa.
1790 Field & Pine B&B
. . . . .Shippensburg, Pa.
1790 The Cuthbert House Inn B&B
. . . . .Beaufort, S.C.
1790 1790 House B&B Inn
. . . . .Georgetown, S.C.
1790 Jordan Hollow Farm Inn
. . . . .Stanley, Va.
1790 Piney Grove at Southall's
Plantation-1790 . . . . . . .Williamsburg, Va.
1790 Silver Maple Lodge & Cottages
. . . . .Fairlee, Vt.
1790 The Putney Inn . . . . .Putney, Vt.
1790 The Inn at Blush Hill
. . . . .Waterbury, Vt.
1791 St. Francis Inn
. . . . .Saint Augustine, Fla.
1792 King George IV Inn
. . . . .Charleston, S.C.

1792 The Inn on Covered Bridge Green
. . . . .Arlington, Vt.

1793 Bullard Farm B&B
. . . . .North New Salem, Mass.

1793 The Historic Temperance Tavern
. . . . .Gilmanton, N.H.

1794 Historic Merrell Inn
. . . . .Stockbridge, Mass.

1794 1794 Watchtide... by the Sea
. . . . . . .Searsport (Waldo County), Maine

1794 Governor Holmes House
. . . . .Natchez, Miss.

1794 Shaker Farm Bed & Breakfast
. . . . .Enfield, N.H.

1794 Lareau Farm Country Inn
. . . . .Waitsfield, Vt.

1795 Butler Greenwood Plantation
. . . . .Saint Francisville, La.

1795 The Swag Country Inn
. . . . .Waynesville, N.C.

1795 Acorn Inn . . . . .Canandaigua, N.Y.

1795 Bucksville House . . . . .Kintnersville, Pa.

1795 Historic Charleston B&B
   Reservation Service . . . .Charleston, S.C.

1795 Ransom Bay Inn . . . . .Alburg, Vt.

1795 The Inn on The Common
. . . . .Craftsbury Common, Vt.

1795 Rabbit Hill Inn
. . . . .Lower Waterford, Vt.

1796 Old Riverton Inn . . . . .Riverton, Conn.

1796 Summer Hill Farm . . . . . .Lenox, Mass.

1796 Whitewing Farm B&B
. . . . .West Chester, Pa.

1796 Catamount B&B . . . . . . .Williston, Vt.

1797 Sumner House . . . . .Shrewsbury, Mass.

1797 Williamsville Inn
. . . . .West Stockbridge, Mass.

1797 Colby Hill Inn . . . . .Henniker, N.H.

1797 Applebrook B&B . . . . . .Jefferson, N.H.

1797 The Post and Beam B&B
. . . . .Sullivan, N.H.

1797 Cashtown Inn . . . . .Cashtown, Pa.

1797 Peter Wolford House . . . . .Dillsburg, Pa.

1797 Fitch Hill Inn . . . . .Hyde Park, Vt.

1797 River Meadow Farm
. . . . .Manchester Center, Vt.

1798 The House on Bayou Road
. . . . .New Orleans, La.

1798 Edgartown Inn . . . . . .Edgartown, Mass.

1799 The Kennebunk Inn
. . . . .Kennebunk, Maine

1799 Dr. Jonathan Pitney House
. . . . .Absecon, N.J.

1799 Clifton- The Country Inn & Estate
. . . . .Charlottesville, Va.

Jail House

Jailer's Inn . . . . .Bardstown, Ky.

Inn at Ormsby Hill
. . . . .Manchester Center, Vt.

Lighthouse

Keeper's House . . . . .Isle Au Haut, Maine

Harbor House Inn . . . . .Gills Rock, Wis.

Literary Figures Associated With Inns

Louisa May Alcott
Hawthorne Inn . . . . .Concord, Mass.

Susan B. Anthony
The Park House . . . . .Saugatuck, Mich.

Henry Beston
Over Look Inn
. . . . .Eastham (Cape Cod), Mass.

Ralph Waldo Emerson
Island House . . . . .Southwest Harbor, Maine
Hawthorne Inn . . . . .Concord, Mass.
Emerson Inn By the Sea . . . .Rockport, Mass.

Frances Grey Patton
William Thomas House . . . . . . .Raleigh, N.C.

Nathaniel Hawthorne
Hawthorne Inn . . . . .Concord, Mass.
Island House . . . . .Southwest Harbor, Maine
Emerson Inn By the Sea . . . .Rockport, Mass.

D.H. Lawrence
Hacienda del Sol . . . . .Taos, N.M.

Jack London
Vichy Hot Springs Resort Inn
. . . . .Ukiah, Calif.

James A. Michene
Robert Morris Inn . . . . .Oxford, Md.

Becky Thatcher
Fifth Street Mansion B&B
. . . . .Hannibal, Mo.

Mark Twain/Samuel Clemnes
Vichy Hot Springs Resort Inn
. . . . .Ukiah, Calif.

Fifth Street Mansion B&B
. . . . .Hannibal, Mo.
Garth Woodside Mansion . . . .Hannibal, Mo.
Edith Wharton
The Gables Inn . . . . .Lenox, Mass.

Llama Ranches

Rockhouse Mountain Farm Inn
. . . . .Eaton Center, N.H.
1661 Inn & Hotel Manisses
. . . . .Block Island, R.I.
Rainbow Ridge . . . . .Onalaska, Wis.

Log Houses/Cabins

Ocean Wilderness Country Inn
. . . . .Sooke, B.C.
Anniversary Inn . . . . .Estes Park, Colo.
The Log House . . . . .Russellville, Ky.
Log Cabin An Island Inn
. . . . .Bailey Island, Maine
Lindgren's B&B . . . . .Lutsen, Minn.
Bad Rock Country B&B
. . . . .Columbia Falls, Mont.
The Swag Country Inn . . . .Waynesville, N.C.
Tall Timber Lodge . . . . .Pittsburg, N.H.
Trout House Village Resort . . . . .Hague, N.Y.
Pinehurst Inn at Jenny Creek
. . . . .Ashland, Ore.
The Inn at Evins Mill . . . . .Nashville, Tenn.
Old Hunter Rd Stagecoach Stop B&B
. . . . .New Braunfels, Texas
Heart of My Heart Ranch B&B
. . . . .Round Top, Texas
Piney Grove at Southall's Plantation
. . . . .Williamsburg, Va.
Arlington's West Mountain Inn
. . . . .Arlington, Vt.
Fort Lewis Lodge . . . . .Millboro, Va.
The Inn at Narrow Passage
. . . . .Woodstock, Va.

Movie Locations

Eden House . . . . .Key West, Fla.
"Criss Cross"
The Mason Place B&B . . . . .London, Tenn.
"Maverick"

Old Mills

Silvermine Tavern . . . . .Norwalk, Conn.
Arbor Rose B&B . . . . .Stockbridge, Mass.

Twin Gables Inn . . . . .Saugatuck, Mich.
Asa Ransom House . . . . .Clarence, N.Y.
1766 Osceola Mill House
. . . . .Gordonsville, Pa.
The Inn at Evins Mill . . . . .Nashville, Tenn.

Oldest Continuously Operated Inns

1859 Historic National Hotel, A Country Inn
. . . . .Jamestown, Calif.
Julian Gold Rush Hotel . . . . . . .Julian, Calif.
1857 Florida House Inn
. . . . .Amelia Island , FLa..
The Cranberry Inn at Chatham
. . . . .Chatham, Mass.
Emerson Inn By the Sea . . . .Rockport, Mass.
Candlelite Inn . . . . .Bradford, N.H.
Wakefield Inn . . . . .Wakefield, N.H.
Ebbie Guest House . . . . .Ocean City, N.J.
The Stockton Inn . . . . .Stockton, N.J.
The Bellevue House . . . . . .Block Island, R.I.
Kedron Valley Inn . . . . .Woodstock, Vt.

On the grounds of a U.S. National Monument

Cathedral House B&B . . . . . . .Rindge, N.H.

Plantations

Poipu Inn & Kauai Inn . . . . . .Koloa, Hawaii
Kuau Cove Plantation B&B
. . . . .Paia, Maui, Hawaii
Poipu Plantation . . . . .Koloa, Hawaii
Melhana, the Grand Plantation
. . . . .Thomasville, Ga.
Inglewood Plantation . . . . . . .Alexandria, La.
Madewood Plantation House
. . . . .Napoleonville, La.
The House on Bayou Road
. . . . .New Orleans, La.
Merry Sherwood Plantation . . . . .Berlin, Md.
La Maison Cappellari at Mostly Hall
. . . . .Falmouth, Mass.
Monmouth Plantation . . . . . . .Natchez, Miss.
Oakland Plantation . . . . .Natchez, Miss.
Six Runs Plantation . . . . . . .Rose Hill, N.C.
Mansfield Plantation B&B Country Inn
. . . . .Georgetown, S.C.
Laurel Hill Plantation
. . . . .McClellanville, S.C.

Rice Hope Plantation Inn
. . . . .Moncks Corner, S.C.
Spring Grove Farm Bed & Breakfast
. . . . .Appomattox, Va.
La Vista Plantation . . . . . .Fredericksburg, Va.
The Inn at Meander Plantation
. . . . .Locust Dale, Va.

Post Offices

The Goose & Turrets B&B
. . . . .Montara, Calif.
Boxwood Inn . . . . .Newport News, Va.

Ranches

Wit's End Guest Ranch . . . . .Bayfield, Colo.
Idaho Rocky Mountain Ranch
. . . . .Stanley, Idaho
Sixty Three Ranch . . . . . .Livingston, Mont.
Soldier Meadows Guest Ranch & Lodge
. . . . .Gerlach, Nev.
Pinehurst Inn at Jenny Creek
. . . . .Ashland, Ore.
Wine Country Farm . . . . .Dayton, Ore.
Hasse House and Ranch . . . . .Mason, Texas

Revolutionary War

Ashley Manor Inn
. . . . .Barnstable/Cape Cod, Mass.
Colonel Roger Brown House
. . . . .Concord, Mass.
Village Green Inn . . . . .Falmouth, Mass.
The Robert Morris House . . . . . .Oxford, Md.
Pace One Restaurant & Country Inn
. . . . .Thornton, Pa.
The Melville House . . . . .Newport, R.I.
The Kitchen House . . . . . . .Charleston, S.C.
John Rutledge House Inn
. . . . .Charleston, S.C.
Inn at Ormsby Hill
. . . . .Manchester Center, Vt.
Gilbert House B&B of Middleway
. . . . .Charles Town, W.Va.

Schoolhouses

Old Riverton Inn . . . . .Riverton, Conn.
The Roosevelt Inn . . . .Coeur d'Alene, Idaho
The Bagley House . . . . .Durham, Maine
Old Sea Pines Inn . . . . .Brewster, Mass.
School House B&B Inn . . . . .Rocheport, Mo.

The Inn at Bingham School
. . . . .Chapel Hill, N.C.
Bear Mountain Lodge . . . . .Silver City, N.M.
Washington School Inn . . . . .Park City, Utah
East Highland School House B&B
. . . . .Phillips, Wis.

Space Shuttle Launches

The Higgins House . . . . .Sanford, Fla.

Stagecoach Stops

The Dorrington Hotel & Restaurant
. . . . .Dorrington, Calif.
Simpson House Inn . . . .Santa Barbara, Calif.
Tidewater Inn . . . . .Madison, Conn.
Maple Hill Farm B&B Inn
. . . . .Hallowell, Maine
Historic Merrell Inn . . . . . .South Lee, Mass.
Egremont Inn . . . . . . .South Egremont, Mass.
The Mendon Country Inn . . .Mendon, Mich.
Alden Country Inn . . . . .Lyme, N.H.
Wakefield Inn . . . . .Wakefield, N.H.
Hacienda Antigua B&B
. . . . .Albuquerque, N.M.
Hacienda Vargas
. . . . .Algodones/Santa Fe, N.M.
The Inn at Bingham School
. . . . .Chapel Hill, N.C.
Penguin Crossing B&B . . . . .Circleville, Ohio
The Olde Stage Coach B&B
. . . . .Jennerstown, Pa.
Laurel Villa Country Inn . . . . . .Milford, Pa.
Old Hunter Rd Stagecoach Stop B&B
. . . . .New Braunfels, Texas
The Inn at Narrow Passage
. . . . .Woodstock, Va.
Churchill House Inn . . . . .Brandon, Vt.
Golden Stage Inn . . . . .Proctorsville, Vt.
West Dover Inn . . . . .West Dover, Vt.
The Inn at Blush Hill . . . . . .Waterbury, Vt.
Wisconsin House Stagecoach Inn
. . . . .Hazel Green, Wis.
The General Lewis . . . . . .Lewisburg, W.Va.

Still in the Family

Inglewood Plantation . . . . . . .Alexandria, La.
Oakland House Seaside Resort
. . . . .Brooksville, Maine
The Grey Havens . . . . . .Georgetown, Maine

Cedarcroft Farm/Cottage on the Knoll B&B
. . . . .Warrensburg, Mo.
The Sanders-Helena's Bed & Breakfast
. . . . .Helena, Mont.
Rockhouse Mountain Farm Inn
. . . . .Eaton Center, N.H.
The Chalfonte Hotel . . . . . . .Cape May, N.J.
Brae Loch Inn . . . . .Cazenovia, N.Y.
Northern Plantation B&B . . . . .Urbana, Ohio
Line Limousin Farmhouse B&B
. . . . .Carlisle, Pa.
Cedar Hill Farm . . . . .Mount Joy, Pa.
Castle Hill Inn & Resort . . . . .Newport, R.I.
Hasse House and Ranch . . . . . .Mason, Texas
Bay View Waterfront B&B
. . . . .Belle Haven, Va.
North Bend Plantation . . . .Charles City, Va.
Catamount B&B . . . . .Williston, Vt.
Harbor House Inn . . . . .Gills Rock, Wis.
The General Lewis . . . . . .Lewisburg, W.Va.

Taverns

Silvermine Tavern . . . . .Norwalk, Conn.
Red Brook Inn . . . . .Old Mystic, Conn.
Chapman Inn . . . . .Bethel, Maine
Birchwood Inn . . . . .Lenox, Mass.
The Historic Temperance Tavern
. . . . .Gilmanton, N.H.
Alden Country Inn . . . . .Lyme, N.H.
The Bird & Bottle Inn . . . . . . .Garrison, N.Y.
Giddings Garden Bed & Breakfast
. . . . .Syracuse, N.Y.
Rider's 1812 Inn . . . . .Painesville, Ohio
Smithton Inn . . . . .Ephrata, Pa.
James Getty Hotel . . . . .Gettysburg, Pa.
1725 Historic Witmer's Tavern Inn & Museum
. . . . .Lancaster, Pa.
The Inn at the Crossroads
. . . . .Charlottesville, Va.
Red Fox Inn . . . . .Middleburg, Va.
Rabbit Hill Inn . . . . . . .Lower Waterford, Vt.

Train Stations & Renovated Rail Cars

Inn at Depot Hill
. . . . .Capitola-by-the-Sea, Calif.
Trout City Berth & Breakfast
. . . . .Buena Vista, Colo.
Red House Inn B&B . . . . . . .Brevard, N.C.
Green Mountain Inn . . . . .Stowe, Vt.

Tunnels, Secret Passageways, Caves

Merry Sherwood Plantation
. . . . .Berlin, Maine
Ashley Manor Inn
. . . . .Barnstable/Cape Cod, Mass.
Wingscorton Farm Inn
. . . . .East Sandwich, Mass.
Munro House B&B . . . . . . .Jonesville, Mich.
Colonel Spencer Inn . . . . . . .Campton, N.H.
1725 Historic Witmer's Tavern Inn & Museum
. . . . .Lancaster, Pa.
Lynchburg Mansion Inn Bed & Breakfast
. . . . .Lynchburg, Va.
Kedron Valley Inn . . . .South Woodstock, Vt.
Mansion Hill Inn . . . . .Madison, Wis.

Underground Railroad

The Annapolis Inn . . . . .Annapolis, Md.
1732 Folke Stone Bed & Breakfast
. . . . .West Chester, Pa.

Unusual Architecture

Blue Belle Inn B&B . . . . .Saint Ansgar, Iowa

Unusual Sleeping Places

In a water tower
John Doughtery House . . . .Mendocino, Calif.
Above a gold mine
Chichester-McKee House B&B
. . . . .Placerville, Calif.
By waterfalls
Inn at Brandywine Falls
. . . . .Sagamore Hills, Calif.
In a bank
Landmark Inn at the Historic Bank of Oberlin
. . . . .Oberlin, Kan.
In a trading post
Hacienda Vargas . . . . .Santa Fe, N.M.
On or next to an archaeological dig site
The White Oak Inn . . . . .Danville, Ohio
In a tinsmith shop
Churchtown Inn . . . . .Churchtown, Pa.
Historic powerhouse
Abend Haus . . . . .Rapid City, S.C.

Waterfalls

Inn at Brandywine Falls
. . . . .Sagamore Hills, Ohio

Who Slept/Visited Here

John Adams
1725 Historic Witmer's Tavern
.........................Lancaster, Pa.

Ethan Allen
Inn at Ormsby Hill
...................Manchester Center, Vt.

Neil Armstrong
Beekman Arms ....Rhinebeck, N.Y.

John James Audubon
Weston House ....Eastport, Maine

Barrymore family
Evermay-on-the-Delaware
.............Erwinna/Bucks County, Pa.

Sarah Bernhardt
Abigail's "Elegant Victorian Mansion"
.......................Eureka, Calif.

Buffalo Bill Cody
The Pollard ....Red Lodge, Mont.

Calamity Jane
The Pollard ....Red Lodge, Mont.

Clara Bow
Hotel Nipton ....Nipton, Calif.

Aaron Burr
Beekman Arms ....Rhinebeck, N.Y.

Margaret Chase Smith
Peacock House ....Lubec, Maine

Salmon Chase
Chase House B&B Inn ....Cornish, N.H.

Henry Clay
Monmouth Plantation ....Natchez, Miss.

Samuel Clemens (Mark Twain)
Vichy Hot Springs Resort & Inn
.........................Ukiah, Calif.
Garth Woodside Mansion ....Hannibal, Mo.

Calvin Coolidge
Lehman House B&B ....St. Louis, Mo.
State Game Lodge ....Custer, S.D.

Jefferson Davis
Monmouth Plantation ....Natchez, Miss.
Anchuca ....Vicksburg, Miss.

Danny DeVito
Colonel Crockett Farm
.... Coupeville, Wash.

Michael Douglas
Colonel Crockett Farm
.... Coupeville, Wash.

Dwight D. Eisenhower
State Game Lodge ....Custer, S.D.

Clark Gable
Gold Mountain Manor Historic B&B
....................Big Bear, Calif.
Willows Historic Palms Springs Inn
...................Palm Springs, Calif.

Cary Grant
Mulburn Inn ....Bethlehem, N.H.

Ulysses S. Grant
Thayers Inn ....Littleton, N.H.
Misty River B&B ....Ripley, Ohio

Horace Greely
Beekman Arms-Delamater Inn
....................Rhinebeck, N.Y.

Alexander Hamilton
Bird & Bottle Inn ....Garrison, N.Y.

Mrs. Warren Harding
Watchtide, B&B By the Sea
................Searsport, Maine

Lillian Hellman
Barley Sheaf Farm ....Holicong, Pa.

Patrick Henry
General Lewis ....Lewisburg, Va.

Mrs. Herbert Hoover
Watchtide, B&B By the Sea
................Searsport, Maine

Howard Hughes
Colonial Inn of Martha's Vineyard
....................Edgartown, Mass.

Barbara Hutton
Mulburn Inn ....Bethlehem, N.H.

Andrew Jackson
Oakland Plantation ....Natchez, Miss.

General Stonewall Jackson
Inn at Narrow Passage ......Woodstock, Va.

Thomas Jefferson
1725 Historic Witmer's Tavern
.....................Lancaster, Pa.
Inn at Meander Plantation
....................Locust Dale, Va.
The General Lewis ....Lewisburg. W.Va.

William Jennings Bryan
The Pollard ....Red Lodge, Mont.
Beekman Arms ....Rhinebeck, N.Y.

General Lafayette
The Bird & Bottle Inn ....Garrison, N.Y.

Lillie Langtry
Abigail's "Elegant Victorian Mansion"
.....................Eureka, Calif.

D.H. Lawrence
Hacienda Del Sol ....Taos, N.M.

Robert E. Lee
The President's Quarters
· ·Savannah, Ga.
Abraham Lincoln
Patchwork Inn · · · · · · · · · · · · · ·Oregon, Ill.
Robert Todd Lincoln
Inn at Ormsby Hill
· · · · · · · · · · · · · · ·Manchester Center, Vt.
Carole Lombard
Gold Mountain Manor Historic B&B
· · · · · · · · · · · · · · · · · · · ·Big Bear, Calif.
Willows Historic Palms Springs Inn
· · · · · · · · · · · · · · · · · · ·Palm Springs, Calif.
Jack London
Vichy Hot Springs Resort & Inn
· ·Ukiah, Calif.
Marx brothers
Barley Sheaf Farm · · · · · · · · · ·Holicong, Pa.
Somerset Maugham
Colonial Inn of Martha's Vineyard
· · · · · · · · · · · · · · · · · ·Edgartown, Mass.
President William McKinley
Cheshire Cat Inn & Spa
· · · · · · · · · · · · · · · · · ·Santa Barbara, Calif.
Captain Cornelius J. Mey
Captain Mey's B&B Inn · · · · ·Cape May, N.J.
Edmund Muskey
Peacock House · · · · · · · · · · · ·Lubec, Maine
Georgia O'Keefe
Hacienda del Sol · · · · · · · · · · · · ·Taos, N.M.
S.J. Perlman
Barley Sheaf Farm · · · · · · · · · ·Holicong, Pa.
General Quitman
Monmouth Plantation · · · · · · ·Natchez, Miss.
Eleanor Roosevelt
Watchtide, B&B By the Sea
· · · · · · · · · · · · · · · · · ·Searsport, Maine
Franklin Roosevelt
Beekman Arms · · · · · · · · · ·Rhinebeck, N.Y.
Theodore Roosevelt
Vichy Hot Springs Resort & Inn
· ·Ukiah, Calif.
Lehman House B&B · · · · · · · ·St. Louis, Mo.
Troutbeck · · · · · · · · · · · · · · ·Amenia, N.Y.
A Touch of Europe B&B Inn
· · · · · · · · · · · · · · · · · · · ·Yakima, Wash.
John Rutledge
John Rutledge House Inn
· · · · · · · · · · · · · · · · · · · ·Charleston, S.C.
General W.T. Sherman

Cuthbert House Inn B&B · · · ·Beaufort, S.C.
William H. Taft
Inn at Ormsby Hill · · · ·Manchester Center, Vt.
Elizabeth Taylor
Beekman Arms · · · · · · · · · ·Rhinebeck, N.Y.
Kathleen Turner
Colonel Crockett Farm
· · · · · · · · · · · · · · · · · Coupeville, Wash.
Mark Twain (Samuel Clemens)
Vichy Hot Springs Resort & Inn
· ·Ukiah, Calif.
Martin Van Buren
1725 Historic Witmer's Tavern
· · · · · · · · · · · · · · · · · · · ·Lancaster, Pa.
George Washington
Bird & Bottle Inn · · · · · · · · · · ·Garrison, N.Y.
Jacob's Resting Place · · · · · · · · ·Carlisle, Pa.
Glen Isle Farm · · · · · · · · · ·Downington, Pa.
1725 Historic Witmer's Tavern
· · · · · · · · · · · · · · · · · · · ·Lancaster, Pa.
John Rutledge House Inn · · · ·Charleston, S.C.
Woolworth family
Mulburn Inn · · · · · · · · · ·Bethlehem, N.H.

World War II
Kilaeua Lodge · · · · · · · · · · ·Volcano, Hawaii

INN EVALUATION FORM

Please copy and complete this form for each stay and mail to the address shown. Since 1981 we have maintained files that include thousands of evaluations from inngoers who have sent this form to us. This information helps us evaluate and update the inns listed in this guide.

Name of Inn: _____

City and State: _____

Date of Stay: _____

Your Name: _____

Address: _____

City/State/Zip: _____

Phone: (__ __ __) __ __ __ – __ __ __ __

E-mail: _____

Please use the following rating scale for the next items.
1: Outstanding.   2: Good.   3: Average.   4: Fair.   5: Poor.

Location	1	2	3	4	5
Cleanliness	1	2	3	4	5
Food Service	1	2	3	4	5
Privacy	1	2	3	4	5
Beds	1	2	3	4	5
Bathrooms	1	2	3	4	5
Parking	1	2	3	4	5
Handling of reservations	1	2	3	4	5
Attitude of staff	1	2	3	4	5
Overall rating	1	2	3	4	5

Comments on Above: _____

_____

_____

_____

_____

MAIL THE COMPLETED FORM TO:
American Historic Inns, Inc.
PO Box 669
Dana Point, CA 92629-0669
(949) 499-8070
www.iLoveInns.com

INN EVALUATION FORM

Please copy and complete this form for each stay and mail to the address shown. Since 1981 we have maintained files that include thousands of evaluations from inngoers who have sent this form to us. This information helps us evaluate and update the inns listed in this guide.

Name of Inn: _____

City and State: _____

Date of Stay: _____

Your Name: _____

Address: _____

City/State/Zip: _____

Phone: (___ ___ ___) ___ ___ ___ – ___ ___ ___ ___

E-mail: _____

Please use the following rating scale for the next items.
1: Outstanding.   2: Good.   3: Average.   4: Fair.   5: Poor.

	1	2	3	4	5
Location	1	2	3	4	5
Cleanliness	1	2	3	4	5
Food Service	1	2	3	4	5
Privacy	1	2	3	4	5
Beds	1	2	3	4	5
Bathrooms	1	2	3	4	5
Parking	1	2	3	4	5
Handling of reservations	1	2	3	4	5
Attitude of staff	1	2	3	4	5
Overall rating	1	2	3	4	5

Comments on Above: _____

_____

_____

_____

_____

MAIL THE COMPLETED FORM TO:
American Historic Inns, Inc.
PO Box 669
Dana Point, CA 92629-0669
(949) 499-8070
www.iLoveInns.com

Publications From American Historic Inns

Bed & Breakfast and Country Inns, 13th Edition

By Deborah Edwards Sakach

Imagine the thrill of receiving this unique book with its FREE night certificate as a gift. Now you can let someone else experience the magic of America's country inns with this unmatched offer. *Bed & Breakfasts and Country Inns* is the most talked about guide among inngoers.

This fabulous guide features 1,500 inns from across the United States and Canada. Best of all, no other bookstore guide offers a FREE night certificate.* This certificate can be used at any one of the inns featured in the guide.

American Historic Inns, Inc. has been publishing books about bed & breakfasts since 1981. Its books and the FREE night offer have been recommended by many travel writers and editors, and featured in: *The New York Times, Washington Post, Los Angeles Times, Boston Globe, Chicago Sun Times, USA Today, Orange County Register, Baltimore Sun, McCalls, Martha Stewart, Good Housekeeping, Cosmopolitan, Consumer Reports* and more.

*With purchase of one night at the regular rate required. Subject to limitations.

416 pages, paperback, 500 illustrations   **Price $21.95**

The Official Guide to American Historic Inns
Completely Revised and Updated, Eighth Edition

By Deborah Sakach

Open the door to America's past with this fascinating guide to historic inns that reflect our colorful heritage. From Dutch Colonials to Queen Anne Victorians, these bed & breakfasts and country inns offer experiences of a lifetime.

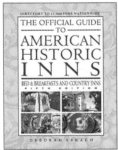

This special edition guide includes certified American Historic Inns that provide the utmost in hospitality, beauty, authentic restoration and preservation. Inns have been carefully selected so as to provide readers with the opportunity to visit genuine masterpieces.

With inns dating back to as early as 1600, this guide is filled with treasures waiting to be discovered. Full descriptions, illustrations, guest comments and recommendations all are included to let you know what's in store for you before choosing one of America's Historic Inns.

640 pages, paperback, 1,000 illustrations   **Price $16.95**

How To Start & Run Your Own Bed & Breakfast Inn
By Ripley Hotch & Carl Glassman

In this book you'll discover the secrets of the best inns. Learn how to decide whether owning or leasing an inn is right for you. Find out what business strategies characterize a successful inn and learn how to incorporate them in your own business.

If you've always dreamed of owning a bed & breakfast, this book is for you!

182 pages, paperback   **Price $15.95**

The Bed & Breakfast Encyclopedia
Completely Revised and Updated, Third Edition

By Deborah Edwards Sakach & Tiffany Crosswy

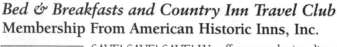

This massive guide is the most comprehensive guide on the market today. Packed with detailed listings to more than 2,600 bed & breakfasts and country inns, the Encyclopedia also includes an index to an additional 14,000 inns, detailed state maps and more than 1,200 illustrations. Recipes, helpful phone numbers, information about reservation services and informative articles about bed & breakfast hot spots, the best bed & breakfasts, inns of interest, how to start your own B&B and much, much more.

If you're planning a getaway, this all-inclusive guide is a must!

1,056 pages, paperback, 1,200 illustrations   **Price $18.95**

Bed & Breakfasts and Country Inn Travel Club
Membership From American Historic Inns, Inc.

SAVE! SAVE! SAVE! We offer an exclusive discount club that lets you enjoy the excitement of bed & breakfast and country inn travel again and again. As a member of this special club, you'll receive benefits that include savings of 25% to 50% off every night's stay!

Your membership card will entitle you to tremendous savings at some of the finest inns in America. <u>Members receive a guide with more than 1,000 participating bed & breakfasts and country inns to choose from.</u> Plan affordable getaways to inns nearby or visit an area of the country you've always wanted to experience.

The best part of being an American Historic Inns Travel Club Member is that the card can be used as many times as you like. The card is transferable and may be shared with friends and family.

In addition to your card, you will get a FREE night's stay certificate—truly a club membership that's hard to pass up!

All travel club members receive:
- Travel club card entitling holder to 25% to 50% off lodging.
- FREE night's stay certificate.
- Guide to more than 1,000 participating inns across America.

Membership is good for one year. Free night's stay with purchase of one night at the regular rate. Discount and certificate cannot be combined.

Introductory price with full benefits (Reg. $59.95)   **$49.95**

Golf Across America Club Membership

Introducing the best way to get free greens fees and other discounts at more than 700 courses nationwide! Golf Across America club discounts include:

- Free greens fees
- Buy-One-Get-One-Free greens fees
- 50% off greens fees.
- Plus More!

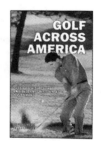

Your one-year Golf Across America membership card can be used as many times as you like. The average Golf Across America club member saves between $200-$400 each year. Get your one-year club membership and start saving today!

Introductory price with full benefits   **$39.95**

AMERICAN
HISTORIC
INNS
INCORPORATED

PO Box 669
Dana Point
California
92629-0669
(949) 499-8070
Fax (949) 499-4022
www.iLoveInns.com

Order Form

Date: __ __ / __ __ / __ __   Shipped: __ __ / __ __ / __ __

Name: _____

Street: _____

City/State/Zip: _____

Phone: (__ __ __) __ __ __ – __ __ __ __   E-mail: _____

QTY.	Prod. No.	Description	Amount	Total
_____	AHI13	Bed & Breakfasts and Country Inns	$21.95	_____
_____	AHIH8	The Official Guide to American Historic Inns	$16.95	_____
_____	AHIE3	Bed & Breakfast Encyclopedia	$18.95	_____
_____	AHIC2	Bed & Breakfast and Country Inn Travel Club	$49.95	_____
_____	CB03	How to Start Your Own B&B	$15.95	_____
_____	GOLF	Golf Across America Club Membership	$39.95	_____

Subtotal _____

California buyers add 7.5% sales tax _____

Shipping and Handling on Encyclopedia Book Orders
STANDARD (10-20 days): $3.50 for first book. Add $1 for each additional copy.
PRIORITY (3-5 days): $5.75. Add $2 each add'l copy. 2ND-DAY AIR: $10.75. Add $3.50 each add'l copy.

Shipping and Handling on Other Book and Travel Club Orders
STANDARD (10-20 days): $3 for first book. Add 75¢ for each additional copy.
PRIORITY (3-5 days): $4.50. Add $2 each add'l copy. 2ND-DAY AIR: $10.75. Add $3.50 each add'l copy _____

TOTAL _____

❑ Check/Money Order   ❑ Discover   ❑ Mastercard   ❑ Visa   ❑ American Express

Account Number __ __ __ __ __ __ __ __ __ __ __ __ __ __ __ __   Exp. Date __ __ / __ __

Name on card _____

Signature _____